P9-DKE-155

FOR REFERENCE

Not To Be Taken From This Room
Unless Given Permission

BELLEVUE
PUBLIC
LIBRARY

For Reference

Not to be taken from this room

C K   S E A   772342

• Antioch

• Damascus

Jerusalem •

Alexandria •

A N   S E A

E LOWENSTEIN

THE INTERPRETER'S BIBLE

THE INTERPRETER'S BIBLE

IN TWELVE VOLUMES

VOLUME VII

GENERAL ARTICLES ON THE
NEW TESTAMENT

THE GOSPEL ACCORDING TO
ST. MATTHEW

THE GOSPEL ACCORDING TO
ST. MARK

EDITORIAL BOARD

George Arthur Buttrick
Commentary Editor

Walter Russell Bowie
Associate Editor of Exposition

Paul Scherer
Associate Editor of Exposition

John Knox
Associate Editor of
New Testament Introduction
and Exegesis

Samuel Terrien
Associate Editor of
Old Testament Introduction
and Exegesis

Nolan B. Harmon
Editor, Abingdon Press

THE
INTERPRETER'S BIBLE

—

The Holy Scriptures

IN THE KING JAMES AND REVISED STANDARD VERSIONS

WITH GENERAL ARTICLES AND

INTRODUCTION, EXEGESIS, EXPOSITION

FOR EACH BOOK OF THE BIBLE

IN TWELVE VOLUMES

VOLUME
VII

Ἐν ἀρχῇ ἦν ὁ λόγος

NEW YORK *Abingdon Press* NASHVILLE

Copyright 1951 by Pierce and Smith in the United States of America. Copyright secured in all countries of the International Copyright Union. Published simultaneously in the United States, the Dominion of Canada, and Great Britain. All rights reserved. No part of the text may be reproduced in any form without written permission of the publishers, except brief quotations used in connection with reviews in magazines or newspapers.

Nashville, Tennessee 37203.

ISBN 0-687-19213-7

Library of Congress Catalog Card Number: 51-12276

The text of the Revised Standard Version of the Bible (RSV) and quotations therefrom are copyright 1946, 1952 by Division of Christian Education of the National Council of the Churches of Christ in the United States of America. Scripture quotations designated "ASV" are from the American Standard Version of the Revised Bible, copyright renewed 1929 by the International Council of Religious Education. Those designated "Moffatt" are from *The Bible, A New Translation*, by James Moffatt, copyright in the United States, 1935, by Harper & Brothers, New York; copyright in countries of the International Copyright Union by Hodder & Stoughton, Ltd., London. Those designated "Amer. Trans." or "Goodspeed" are from *The Complete Bible, An American Translation*, by J. M. Powis Smith and Edgar J. Goodspeed, copyright 1939 by the University of Chicago.

B-3

SET UP, PRINTED, AND BOUND BY THE
PARTHENON PRESS, AT NASHVILLE,
TENNESSEE, UNITED STATES OF AMERICA

ABBREVIATIONS AND EXPLANATIONS

ABBREVIATIONS

Canonical books and bibliographical terms are abbreviated according to common usage

Amer. Trans. — *The Bible, An American Translation,* Old Testament, ed. J. M. P. Smith
Apoc.—Apocrypha
Aq.—Aquila
ASV—American Standard Version (1901)
Barn.—Epistle of Barnabas
Clem.—Clement
C.T.—Consonantal Text
Did.—Didache
Ecclus.—Ecclesiasticus
ERV—English Revised Version (1881-85)

Exeg.—Exegesis
Expos.—Exposition
Goodspeed—*The Bible, An American Translation,* New Testament and Apocrypha, tr. Edgar J. Goodspeed
Herm. Vis., etc.—The Shepherd of Hermas: Visions, Mandates, Similitudes
Ign. Eph., etc.—Epistles of Ignatius to the Ephesians, Magnesians, Trallians, Romans, Philadelphians, Smyrnaeans, and Polycarp

KJV—King James Version (1611)
LXX—Septuagint
Macc.—Maccabees
Moffatt—*The Bible, A New Translation,* by James Moffatt
M.T.—Masoretic Text
N.T.—New Testament
O.T.—Old Testament
Polyc. Phil.—Epistle of Polycarp to the Philippians
Pseudep.—Pseudepigrapha
Pss. Sol.—Psalms of Solomon

RSV—Revised Standard Version (1946-52)
Samar.—Samaritan recension
Symm.—Symmachus
Targ.—Targum
Test. Reuben, etc.—Testament of Reuben, and others of the Twelve Patriarchs
Theod.—Theodotion
Tob.—Tobit
Vulg.—Vulgate
Weymouth—*The New Testament in Modern Speech,* by Richard Francis Weymouth
Wisd. Sol.—Wisdom of Solomon

QUOTATIONS AND REFERENCES

Boldface type in Exegesis and Exposition indicates a quotation from either the King James or the Revised Standard Version of the passage under discussion. The two versions are distinguished only when attention is called to a difference between them. Readings of other versions are not in boldface type and are regularly identified.

In scripture references a letter (*a, b,* etc.) appended to a verse number indicates a clause within the verse; an additional Greek letter indicates a subdivision within the clause. When no book is named, the book under discussion is understood.

Arabic numbers connected by colons, as in scripture references, indicate chapters and verses in deuterocanonical and noncanonical works. For other ancient writings roman numbers indicate major divisions, arabic numbers subdivisions, these being connected by periods. For modern works a roman number and an arabic number connected by a comma indicate volume and page. Bibliographical data on a contemporary work cited by a writer may be found by consulting the first reference to the work by that writer (or the bibliography, if the writer has included one).

GREEK TRANSLITERATIONS

$\alpha = a$	$\epsilon = e$	$\iota = i$	$\nu = n$	$\rho = r$	$\phi = ph$
$\beta = b$	$\zeta = z$	$\kappa = k$	$\xi = x$	$\sigma(\varsigma) = s$	$\chi = ch$
$\gamma = g$	$\eta = \bar{e}$	$\lambda = l$	$o = o$	$\tau = t$	$\psi = ps$
$\delta = d$	$\theta = th$	$\mu = m$	$\pi = p$	$\upsilon = u, y$	$\omega = \bar{o}$

HEBREW AND ARAMAIC TRANSLITERATIONS

I. HEBREW ALPHABET

א = '	ח = h	ט = ṭ	מ(ם) = m	פ(ף) = p, ph	שׂ = s, sh
ב = b, bh	ו = w	י = y	נ(ן) = n	צ(ץ) = ç	ת = t, th
ג = g, gh	ז = z	כ(ך) = k, kh	ס = ş	ק = q	
ד = d, dh	ח = ḥ	ל = l	ע = '	ר = r	

II. MASORETIC POINTING

Pure-long	Tone-long	Short	Composite *shᵉwa*
ָ = â	ַ = ā	_ = a	ֲ = ᵃ
.. = ê	.. = ē	ֶ = e	ֳ = ᵉ
or ֹ = î		ִ = i	ֱ = ᵉ
ֹ or ׳ = ô	׳ = ô	= o	= ᵒ
ֻ = û		= u	

NOTE: (*a*) The *páthaḥ* furtive is transliterated as a *ḥateph-páthaḥ.* (*b*) The simple *shᵉwa,* when vocal, is transliterated ᵉ. (*c*) The tonic accent, which is indicated only when it occurs on a syllable other than the last, is transliterated by an acute accent over the vowel.

vii

TABLE OF CONTENTS
VOLUME VII

GENERAL ARTICLES ON THE NEW TESTAMENT

THE GOSPEL ACCORDING TO ST. MATTHEW

THE GOSPEL ACCORDING TO ST. MARK

MAPS

GENERAL ARTICLES

on

THE NEW TESTAMENT

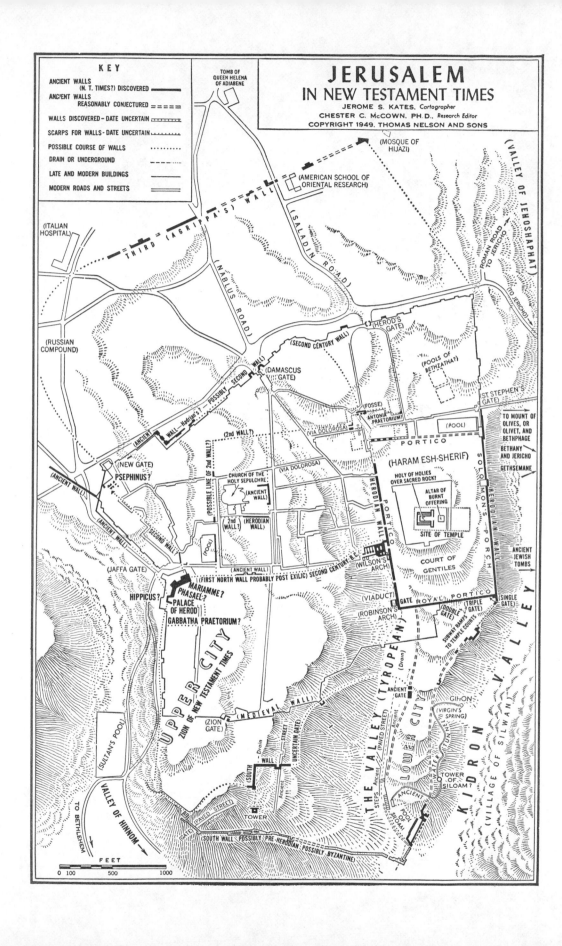

JERUSALEM
IN NEW TESTAMENT TIMES
JEROME S. KATES, *Cartographer*
CHESTER C. McCOWN, PH.D., *Research Editor*
COPYRIGHT 1949, THOMAS NELSON AND SONS

KEY

ANCIENT WALLS (N. T. TIMES?) DISCOVERED ──────

ANCIENT WALLS REASONABLY CONJECTURED ═════

WALLS DISCOVERED – DATE UNCERTAIN ········

SCARPS FOR WALLS – DATE UNCERTAIN ·······

POSSIBLE COURSE OF WALLS ············

DRAIN OR UNDERGROUND ─ ─ ─ ─

LATE AND MODERN BUILDINGS ──────

MODERN ROADS AND STREETS ══════

FEET
0 100   500   1000

THE GOSPEL
IN THE NEW TESTAMENT

by R. H. Strachan

In order to understand the term "the gospel" in the New Testament we must first turn to the Old Testament. The lineage of the word can be traced to the teaching of the prophets. In Deutero-Isaiah we have a series of prophetic utterances which center around the historic occasion of the nation's deliverance from captivity in Babylon. This deliverance is interpreted by the prophet in vivid imagery. In one passage the voice of a herald is heard suddenly announcing that God has intervened and is already on his way to liberate his chosen nation (Isa. 40:1-11). In another passage the messenger is seen speeding hotfoot to a beleaguered city with the good tidings of coming deliverance. The sentinels on the city walls lift up their voices in wonder and exultation at the sight (Isa. 52:7-8). These passages must very early have come to life in the mind of the Christian church as expressing the same sense of liberation and exultation which accompanied the proclamation of the apostolic gospel (Mark 1:3; Rom. 10:15). The noun *euangelion* is not found in the Old Testament—only the corresponding verb which may be literally translated "evangelize" if we follow the Septuagint version of the Hebrew word *bāsar*. The word, both in Greek and in Hebrew, actually demands three English words, "bring good tidings," if its full force is to be felt. "Evangelize" has become a rather lifeless term, whereas in both Hebrew and Greek the word has dynamic significance.

It denotes the announcement of one of God's mighty acts done on behalf of his chosen people. In that act, as in all their history which he shares with them (Isa. 63:9), he reveals his actual presence and care for them. "Say unto the cities of Judah, Behold your God!" (Isa. 40:9.) The revelation is made in a historical happening.

Before considering the way in which the gospel is stated in the more important parts of the New Testament we need to examine the history and meaning of the term itself.

I. The Gospel

The gospel—*euangelion*—is the term most often used in the New Testament to denote the Christian message. The word means "the good news." Sometimes it appears as "the gospel of God," meaning not merely good news about God but good news from God, who himself has taken the initiative in making it known to men. At other times the gospel is spoken of as "the gospel of Christ," which again means not only good news preached by Christ but good news whose content is Christ himself beginning with his human ministry.

The noun "the gospel" occurs only in the New Testament. The gospel in the New Testament also concerns a historical event. It is an event of supreme significance, the crowning divine event in the history of the nation and also the moment of its overwhelming tragedy,

It is the appearance of the divine Son who is both messenger and message. The chosen nation crucifies the messenger and despises his message (Mark 12:1-11). This is the main theme of the four Gospels. It is also the foundation of their gospel message. Even through the death of his Son on the Cross, God achieved a deliverance for the whole world by the "mighty act" of raising him from the dead. Thus the narrative of the Gospels is not a mere chronicle of events and sayings. The four evangelists present a historical portrait of Jesus who not only spoke but "wrought with human hands the creed of creeds." He was the "word made flesh." God spoke in the person and ministry of a "Son" (Heb. 1:1).

It is unfortunate that the term *kerygma*—"preaching"—has become in modern critical parlance a synonym for *euangelion* and tends to displace it. This fosters the idea that the "gospel" can be distinguished in thought from *didachē* or moral teaching. The Christian catechumen at baptism made confession of faith in the words "Jesus is Lord" (Rom. 10:9). In so doing he bound himself to put into practice the teaching of his Lord (Matt. 7:21-23; Luke 6:46). Both by confession and by manner of life the Christian disciple is an evangelist, "the salt of the earth," "the light of the world" (Matt. 5:13, 14).

In the New Testament it is assumed that no disciple of Christ can make adequate profession of his faith apart from membership in the Christian community, the new Israel. It exists not only to preach the gospel: the manner of its corporate life and its moral teaching are both needed to give reality to the gospel message. There are no solitary Christians in the pages of the New Testament. The forgiving love of God offered to the sinner is the central theme of the *euangelion*. Jesus makes it very plain that the proclamation and the acceptance of the Father's forgiveness must be accompanied by a forgiving spirit within the community itself. The sight of apparently irreconcilable personal antipathies overcome and broken relationships healed within the church of Christ gave a real and practical significance to the message of "peace" and "reconciliation" with God, and moved the pagan mind to apprehend what "salvation" meant. The corporate life of the community made its members feel that they were fellow workers with God in his own attitude toward the sinful. "Love your enemies . . . and you will be sons of the Most High" (Luke 6:35). "Be kind to one another, . . . forgiving one another, as God in Christ forgave you" (Eph. 4:32).

This vital relationship between the *kerygma* and the *didachē* as being together constituent elements in the Christian gospel is inherent in the teaching of Jesus, as the record in the Gospels clearly shows (see below in this article, pp. 10-11). The gospel comes to men from "beyond the flaming ramparts of the world" in the voice and in the person of the Son of man. It is heard as a tender and passionate invitation, "Come unto me," and promises "rest." It comes also as an inexorable moral demand, "Take up the cross, and follow me," even though that way may mean suffering, sacrifice, and violent death. The love of God is both uncompromising in its moral requirements and limitless in its compassion. In Pauline language the church in its corporate life is the "body of Christ," the hands and feet and voice of the living Lord, who is thus continually made both audible and visible to the world.

II. The Gospel in the Primitive Church

A. Speeches in the Acts of the Apostles.—It is now generally accepted that a more or less standardized outline of the message proclaimed by the first disciples is apparent in the sermons of Peter and Paul recorded in the earlier chapters of the book of Acts. One of these is represented as delivered by Peter to the multitude assembled on the day of Pentecost (Acts 2:14-36, 38-39); another after the healing of the lame man (Acts 3:12-26); a third to the Sanhedrin after the arrest of the apostles (Acts 4:8-12). A fourth speech is recorded in the story of Cornelius (Acts 10:34-43). A speech delivered by Paul at Antioch in Pisidia is also recorded (Acts 13:16-41). As these sources for an outline of the primitive evangel belong to the Lukan narrative it is necessary to deal with the question of authenticity.

Luke is the only writer who gives us any indication of the sources and the method he employed and of his motive in writing. In his prefaces to the Gospel and the Acts (Luke 1:1-4; Acts 1:1-4) he tells us that he has carefully selected his sources, and is concerned to guarantee the truth of his narrative. His general aim is to make an appeal to the Roman authorities through an important and friendly official named Theophilus, in the hope that he might induce them to adopt a more favorable attitude toward the Christians. For a detailed study of Luke's prefaces the reader must be referred elsewhere.[1] It may, however, be safely assumed that Luke follows the principles and method of the trained Greek historian. It is particularly important, therefore, for our pur-

[1] See H. J. Cadbury, "Commentary on the Preface of Luke," *The Beginnings of Christianity*, ed. F. J. Foakes Jackson and Kirsopp Lake (London: Macmillan & Co., 1922), II, 489-510. See also the Introduction to the Gospel of Luke in Vol. VIII of this Commentary.

pose to understand the Greek historian's attitude toward the recording of speeches delivered by the leading personalities who appear in the course of the history. That attitude is best described in the often quoted words of Thucydides in the preface to his history:

As regards the various speeches delivered before the outbreak of hostilities or while they lasted I have found it difficult to preserve verbal exactitude. This applies both to occasions where I was myself a listener or where other persons have given me reports from various sources. I therefore sought to give what seemed to me to be the most appropriate language for the speaker to use on each occasion, while preserving as faithfully as possible the general sense of what was actually said.

As to actual events that occurred during the war, I have thought it my duty to give them, not as conveyed by any chance informant nor as seemed to me probable. Where I was not myself present, I have investigated with the greatest possible accuracy every detail which came to me at second hand.

The startling statement is made by Cadbury [2] as an inference from Thucydides' words, that "from Thucydides downwards, speeches reported by the historians are confessedly pure imagination." This cannot be regarded as a just inference from the exposition of Thucydides of his own method, nor lead to a fair estimate of the historical value of Luke's records. Thucydides in repudiating verbal exactitude does so in the interests of true history. To have claimed verbal exactitude in an age when there were no shorthand reporters would have been, as Cadbury admits, an obvious falsehood. "Pure imagination," however, is a disquieting alternative to "verbal exactitude."

There is evidence in the speeches themselves that Luke has made use of trustworthy written traditions. In the speeches as he reports them there are signs of another style of writing than his own. There are important linguistic and grammatical indications that the Greek is a translation of earlier Aramaic sources. These Aramaic sources would originate in the Jerusalem community, and the translator betrays at various points that he knew Aramaic better than he knew Greek. Luke even maintains the translation-Greek with its stylistic peculiarities, as though he would refrain from altering such an original version of the primitive gospel. It is interesting to note that we are able to ascertain his more usual method in an instance where we actually have the source which he is using. If we compare Luke's version of Mark 13:3-37 (Luke 21:7-36), we find that it is written in a style characteristically his own. On the other hand the stylistic changes do not materially alter the substance of the Marcan thought.[3] We may assume, therefore, that in these apostolic utterances in the early chapters of Acts we have a reliable account of the primitive Christian gospel message.

We can discern in all the speeches recorded a recurring pattern of central themes which made up the Christian "gospel." In the following synopsis extensive use has been made of C. H. Dodd's analysis in his important work, *The Apostolic Preaching and Its Developments.*[4]

1. The dawn of the messianic age, and the fulfillment of the prophetic message of the Old Testament in the appearance of Jesus.
2. A brief account of the ministry, death, and resurrection of Jesus, in whose person and work, death and resurrection, the messianic age has been inaugurated in actual history.
3. The exaltation of the risen Christ at the right hand of God as head of the new Israel, the Christian church.
4. The Holy Spirit as the sign of Christ's active presence in the church and his continuous care for it.
5. The second advent of Christ as the final consummation of his rule (Acts 3:20-21; cf. 10:42).
6. An appeal for repentance and the offer of forgiveness in the name of Jesus.

In this primitive evangel Jesus Christ is both the subject and the object of faith. The gospel is also a creedal affirmation. It is most important to note that the history of the life and death and resurrection of Jesus interpreted as a divine event in history—"God was with him" (Acts 10:38)—becomes an integral factor of the whole gospel. There is not the slightest indication that these preachers were ever conscious of a distinction between the Christ of faith and the Jesus of history. Jesus, since his coming on earth, has already become for them the Jesus of all history, as he is for us today—"the same yesterday and today and forever." The influence of his personality upon them during his ministry, his own self-consciousness communicated to them, his teaching about his person and mission, his death and resurrection—all interpreted in the light of the resurrection experience and the illumination of the Spirit—have taken root and have begun to produce the fruit that is promised by Jesus (John 15:4-5). The creative personality of Jesus and his teaching brought into being the Christian gospel. The story of his life interpreted as a divine event appears as a brief creedal affirmation in

---

[2] *Ibid.,* II, 13; cf. V, 402-27.

[3] See H. J. Cadbury, *The Making of Luke-Acts* (New York: The Macmillan Co., 1927), 184-90; F. C. Burkitt, "The Use of Mark in the Essays According to Luke," *The Beginnings of Christianity,* II, 106 ff.

[4] London: Hodder & Stoughton, 1936, pp. 37-45.

the primitive gospel (Acts 2:22; 10:37-38) but is no by-product of Christian tradition. The other affirmations are vitally related to his own teaching and consciousness of his mission.

In considering further the message of the primitive church, I shall deal only with two of its aspects—the teaching about the Second Advent and the doctrine of the Holy Spirit. Other aspects such as the idea of the Christian church as the people of God or the new Israel, and the redemptive conception of the Cross may best be treated in connection with the Pauline thought and in the section on the Gospels.

B. The Second Advent.—It is commonly assumed that the primitive church lived in an atmosphere tense with the expectation that the advent or parousia of the exalted Christ was daily imminent, and that his return in power and glory would bring the present world to an end. An examination of the terms of the message proclaimed in the speeches of Peter in Acts does not corroborate this statement. Only twice in the speeches of Peter (Acts 3:19-20; 10:42) is the Second Advent mentioned. This paucity would be very remarkable if the expectation of it dominated the religious outlook of the community. The first passage (Acts 3:19-20) presents certain difficulties of translation. One is the meaning of the words translated "times of refreshing." Moffatt translates "a breathing-space," as though the final advent were delayed in order to give an opportunity for repentance to the Jewish nation. But this hardly suits the words that follow—strangely left untranslated by Moffatt: "from the presence of the Lord." A breathing space from the presence of Christ—assuming that "Lord" here means Christ—would be singularly inappropriate on the lips of one who speaks in the name of a church so deeply conscious of the Spirit as a token of the continual presence (προσώπου) of the exalted Jesus (Acts 2:33). It seems much better to translate, "that times of refreshing may come from the presence of the Lord" (RSV), and to understand a reference to the mission to the Jewish brethren. The tone is conciliatory (3:17). The words would then imply the hope of a response to the call for repentance, which if realized would make the church doubly conscious of the power and presence of the living Christ. The elect nation would have repented and at last accepted the Christ appointed for it in the eternal purpose of God. The prophecy in Deut. 18:15, 18-19 is quoted as foretelling the coming of another prophet "like unto Moses," to whom the people must listen. This prophet is identified with Jesus Christ. The consummation of the kingdom of God without the Jewish people is as unthink-

able to the speaker as it is to Paul when he writes Rom. 9–11.

It is sometimes stated that the alleged feverish expectation of the second advent of Christ represented a "primitive conception," largely a product of Jewish apocalyptic thought—a conception which had to be modified later inasmuch as the coming was delayed. At the basis of this assumption lies the outworn notion of an evolutionary process which always moves from the lower forms of life to the higher. We now know that the evolutionary process in biology is more correctly represented by the curves of a graph than by a straight line of continuous ascent. The same is true of the process of religious thought. It is now recognized, for example, that in the development of thought in the Old Testament, what appear to be primitive religious conceptions may still emerge and be active alongside of what we would call the more enlightened; that there is no absolutely continuous line of "progressive revelation." " 'Progressive revelation' has become for many a 'blessed word.' They seem to infer from it that when the revelation has progressed beyond any given point, what was previously revealed is now of little more than historical and antiquarian interest." [5] The mood in which the imminent return of Christ is expected occurs both in the earlier and in the late epistles of Paul. It emerges whenever the attitude of God's enemies appears most defiant, when the forces of evil seem to be massing themselves against the Christian cause. It is therefore most vividly present in one of the later books of the New Testament, the book of Revelation, written in a time of persecution. It implies despair of the present and the immediate intervention of God.

Of such a mood there is no trace in the Lukan story of the primitive church. A situation of general active persecution is not envisaged. There are attempts at repression by the ecclesiastical authorities, but they are unsuccessful. Christ has been slain by his enemies in vain. The boldness and fearless confidence of the apostles, and the healing power which they possess and exercise in the name of Jesus, silence opposition (Acts 4:13-14, 18-21). A triumphant joy has taken possession of the heart of the church, and it looks forward to the ultimate victory of God to be achieved through the valiant witness of the apostles. In spite of scourging and imprisonment they rejoice "that they were counted worthy to suffer dishonor for the name" (Acts 5:41). In Acts 4:23-31, which describes a scene reminiscent of Pentecost, the energy of faith is not absorbed in

[5] C. R. North, *The Old Testament Interpretation of History* (London: Epworth Press, 1946), p. 147.

picturing the future, but seeks to maintain a bold and enduring witness through word and life to the invincible sovereignty of God and the inviolability of his purpose, already manifest within the community by the presence of the Spirit. "Lord, look upon their threats, and grant to thy servants to speak thy word with all boldness, while thou stretchest out thy hand to heal, and signs and wonders are performed through the name of thy holy servant Jesus."

It would appear therefore that an early date for the second coming of Christ does not control the thinking of the apostles. "The time for the establishing of all things spoken by the prophets" is fixed by God and known only to him. The question "Will you at this time restore the kingdom to Israel?" is met with the reply, "It is not for you to know times or seasons which the Father has fixed by his own authority" (Acts 1:6-7; cf. Mark 13:32).

The second reference to the final advent of Christ in the primitive gospel occurs in Acts 10:42-43. There Christ is spoken of as "ordained by God to be judge of the living and the dead." There is every reason to think that in this passage the reference is not to the Parousia only; "the living" does not necessarily mean those who are alive at Christ's coming. He is already judge of men. The words that immediately follow confirm this interpretation: "To him all the prophets bear witness that every one who believes in him receives forgiveness of sins through his name" (Acts 10:43). In the primitive church the present is not given up in despair. Jesus taught his disciples to pray "Thy kingdom come," and then to say, "Thy will be done, on earth as it is in heaven." The quiet joyful confidence that breathes in the religious environment of the primitive church is not depressed by the thought of the judgment seat of Christ. Every day is a judgment day, and men's hearts are purged by it of mere emotional excitement and sustained at the holy height of conscience and moral endeavor which befits the Christian believer.

Another aspect of the thought of the primitive church which is hardly compatible with the expectation of a speedy advent of Christ was its consciousness of a mission to which it was called by the risen Christ himself, a mission to the world, of ever-widening scope (cf. Mark 13:10). Exaltation at the right hand of God constituted Jesus both Lord and Christ; he was the promised Messiah to the Jew, but also "Lord," that is, the Lord of all. The mission of the church is the continuation of the activity of the risen Christ (Acts 1:8; cf. Gal. 2:8), and therefore inherently universal. The primitive church in Luke's pages always appears as deeply conscious of this mission. A later gen-

eration, in times of distress, persecution, and "the breaking of nations," required to have its gaze turned from the future to a present of which it was tempted to despair. Such is the background of Mark 13: "The end is not yet." Believers needed to be reminded of their divine mission in this present world as it is, both as individuals and as members of the church of Christ. Therein lies the significance of the injunctions, "Be wakeful," "Be not dismayed"; and of such warnings as "The gospel must first be preached to all nations" and "He that endureth to the end shall be saved." But the Jerusalem church as yet needed no such warning. It was a witnessing church. It had powerful enemies—ecclesiastical authorities who loved things as they are—Caiaphas, Annas, and all the rest. These had already themselves been judged and the risen and exalted Christ had "put them under his feet" (cf. Heb. 2:8). The apostles were now sustained by the knowledge that their work and witness were carried on before the judgment seat of Christ. "We must obey God rather than men." Their "boldness" (Acts 4:13) and calm joyous confidence were based on the conviction that in life or in death they would share in Christ's final victory. They could have said with Paul, "He who began a good work in you will bring it to completion at the day of Jesus Christ" (Phil. 1:6).

C. Conception of the Spirit. 1. The Glossolalia.—Luke's version of the happenings at Pentecost is that the church received the miraculous gift which enabled it to preach the gospel in "the language of every nation under heaven." There are several indications in the story, and in the discourse that follows, that Luke has imposed his own interpretation upon a traditional version found in his sources. We are not concerned here with questions of pure historical criticism, but it is necessary to give an answer to certain questions that arise in the mind of the reader confronted with the Lukan version of Pentecost. The picture given in I Cor. 12, 14 of the phenomenon of glossolalia is irreconcilable with the Lukan idea of speech in foreign languages. In the Corinthian passages we are introduced to a newly founded Christian community which is met for worship. The "speaking with tongues" was evidently regarded as a regular feature of these gatherings and had been giving concern to some of the Corinthian leaders who had applied to Paul for advice on the matter. The phenomenon has often been associated with certain forms of religious revival. The "tongues" are outbursts of largely unintelligible speech under the influence of deep religious excitement.[6] Paul does not condemn the practice

6 See on Acts 2:5-12 and I Cor. 12:10 in the Exegesis, Vols. IX and X.

as mere uncontrolled emotion, but recognizes that the utterances are of the Spirit; they must, however, be made intelligible, so that the whole community may share in what he regards as a working of the divine Spirit. Of such elucidation the speaker may himself be quite incapable, but God has also included among his many spiritual gifts—*charismata*—to the church a capacity for sympathetic interpretation. This gift will enable some other Christian worshiper to translate into intelligible speech what the speaker with tongues is trying to say (I Cor. 12:10). If the utterance is so incoherent as to defy interpretation, the speaker is bidden to "keep silence in church and speak to himself and to God" (I Cor. 14:28).

Of the happenings at Pentecost Peter is the interpreter. He interprets the renewed gift of the Spirit as a sign of the dawn of the promised messianic age. There is no indication in his speech that what he is interpreting is anything but the glossolalia of which Paul speaks. In the opening words of his address he admits that the phenomenon might give the impression of drunkenness (Acts 2:15). Similarly Paul admits that the glossolalia in Corinth might, without an interpreter, give the pagan outsider the impression of insane raving (I Cor. 14:23). Peter, like Paul, does not meet the mocking accusation with a stern rebuke. He makes the commonplace statement that the idea of drunkenness is impossible as it is not yet 9 A.M.—the hour of morning prayer. Before that hour it was not permitted to Jews to eat or drink (Acts 2:15).

There is also a strange contradiction in Luke's account of the differing reactions in the mind of the spectators. In Acts 2:6 it is said that "the multitude gathered in bewilderment, for each heard them speak in his own language"; and in vs. 11, "We hear these men talking of the triumphs of God in our own languages!" On the other hand we are told immediately afterwards that all were "amazed and quite at a loss. 'What can it mean?' they said to one another. Some others sneered, 'They are brim-full of new wine!'" (vss. 12, 13, Moffatt). This latter would be a natural reaction on the part of the crowd to an outburst of glossolalia as described in I Corinthians.

These discrepancies are best explained by the hypothesis that Luke himself was unfamiliar with the phenomenon of glossolalia, and that he, knowing that Theophilus would be unable to understand it, has imposed his own interpretation on the traditional story. There can be no doubt that Luke means us to understand that the coming of the Spirit at Pentecost was a miraculous endowment of the church for its missionary task with the power of preaching the gospel in every known language. Luke's mind loves the miraculous. At the same time it is a tribute to his fidelity as a historian that he makes no attempt to alter the source from which he derived the material for Peter's speech at Pentecost by introducing into it the idea of a gift of foreign tongues.

2. The Spirit as the Source of Christian Character.—A serious misrepresentation of the meaning of the Holy Spirit in the life of the primitive church is involved in such a statement as that of Bernhard Weiss, "Nowhere does the Spirit appear as the principle of the new moral life." This is not the impression produced by careful examination of Luke's narrative.

The story of Pentecost, placed as it is at the very beginning of the account of the activities of the apostolic church, at once meets the eye. We must not, however, be misled into supposing that Luke, by the position which he gives it, regards Pentecost as the birthday of the Christian church. His narrative implies that the church is already in being. In 1:14 Luke already speaks of the "brethren." Also, in one tradition which he preserves and places earlier, the number of the twelve must be maintained, symbolic as it was of the "twelve tribes" and of the disciple band as the nucleus of the church, the new Israel (Acts 1:15-26). The community of believers is already the "new Israel," the church of God. It was not born at Pentecost. Rather was it endowed with "power from on high" for its world-wide mission (Acts 1:8).

Luke's version of the story is governed by the idea that the Spirit appears as a mysterious wonder-working power—*dynamis*—which enables the disciples to speak in foreign languages. Luke alone among the evangelists associates the idea of *dynamis* with the Spirit (Luke 1:17; 4:14). "You shall receive power when the Holy Spirit has come upon you" (Acts 1:8). In the birth stories (Luke 1:5–2:39) the Spirit appears as an intermittent power which endows with the gift of song or prophecy select individuals at special moments. Zechariah is said to be "filled with the Holy Spirit" when he utters his prophecy (Luke 1:67). Mary, under the influence of "the power of the Most High" which "will overshadow" her, is enabled to conceive the holy child (Luke 1:35). The Spirit "filled" Elizabeth and the "babe leaped in her womb" when she heard the greeting of Mary. She blesses Mary as "the mother of my Lord" (Luke 1:41, 43). To Simeon also the coming birth of Jesus has been announced by the Holy Spirit (Luke 2:25-26).

At the baptism in answer to the prayer of Jesus, the Spirit descends upon him "in bodily form, as a dove" (Luke 3:22). This is an external manifestation for the benefit of the by-standers, and may be compared with the audible sound as of "the rush of a mighty wind" at Pentecost and the visible phenomenon of the "tongues as of fire." Similarly at the gathering for worship in Acts 4:31, in response to fervent prayer the building was "shaken," and they were all "filled with the Holy Spirit." So also the laying on of the apostles' hands is the outward means of the reception of the Spirit by the Samaritan converts (Acts 8:17).

This thaumaturgic conception of the Spirit reveals an affinity with primitive Hebrew conceptions of the Spirit's operation. In the primitive Hebrew traditions the Spirit is conceived as a semimaterial or, perhaps more accurately, a subspiritual energy which can become actually effective in the physical world. The superhuman strength of Samson is due to an accession of "the Spirit of the LORD" (Judg. 14:6). The Spirit of the Lord fell upon Gideon as he sounded the trumpet to gather the clans, and the blast was irresistible (Judg. 6:34). The hot withering wind of the desert is identified in the poetic imagery of Deutero-Isaiah with the Spirit of God: "The grass withereth, the flower fadeth; because the spirit of the LORD bloweth upon it: surely the people is grass" (Isa. 40:7).

Even if Luke allows his primitive conception of the Spirit as a thaumaturgic power to obtrude itself at various points in his narrative, again we must not exaggerate its importance. He does not allow it to affect his version of the tradition generally. The picture he actually transmits of the early communal life gives another kind of impression. Taken by themselves, the appearances of Luke's thaumaturgic conception are responsible for the notion that the idea of the Spirit in the primitive community is nonethical, a spirit of power rather than of holiness. A closer scrutiny, however, of the life and conduct of the community reflected in his story shows that the Spirit is also the source and sanction of its ethical ideals as expressed in the normal channels of everyday life.

It is noteworthy that in Luke's narrative as it stands, in spite of his own conception of the Spirit as an intermittent supernatural power given to selected individuals at special moments, the Spirit is "democratized" (Acts 2:17-18). The Spirit is poured out "upon all flesh"—on "sons" and "daughters," on "menservants" and "maidservants" alike—in fulfillment of a prophetic utterance and therefore in accordance with the revealed will of God. Moreover in the same speech it is said that the Spirit is "poured out" by the exalted Jesus (Acts 2:33). The Spirit is therefore for all who are in need. It is a continuation of the power of the kingdom delegated to "this same Jesus" on earth, who,

in the power of the Spirit, came to "heal the broken-hearted" to "open the eyes of the blind" and to deliver "the captives" (Luke 4:18).

We are told that the church "continued steadfastly in the apostles' doctrine and fellowship" (Acts 2:42). "Fellowship" denotes the spirit that pervaded the community. It describes the quality of the relationships within the community itself which were created by the Spirit. The community of goods (Acts 2:44; 4:32) is the spirit of fellowship in action. It is simply the putting into practice again of the kind of community life which Jesus sought to create and to foster among his disciples during his ministry on earth, although it was so often marred by petty jealousies and personal ambitions. With all its imperfections, however, this earliest form of a Christian society could not have been impervious to the Cross as the supreme example of Christian living. It is an attractive hypothesis that in Phil. 2:6-11, Paul is adapting an early Christian hymn which he had "received" as he worshiped with his Christian friends. It was part of the rich Christian inheritance into which he came, and which belonged to "those that were in Christ before him." In a simple and childlike way these earliest disciples sought to put into immediate practice the teaching of Jesus. He uttered it with that kind of "revelational" spiritual authority which imposes itself and is not imposed from without. "Whosoever will be chief among you let him be your servant"; "Be not anxious for your life"; "Sell all that thou hast and give to the poor." Certain words of Johannes Weiss are here in place:

Every word of Jesus contained in the old collection of sayings is thus a witness to some ideal or conviction of the community. This applies with double force to the sayings which can only with some uncertainty, or perhaps cannot at all, be assigned to him. Such sayings record decisions made by the group in the spirit and guided by the will of Jesus, as they thought they understood him. . . . The fact that these words were preserved and collected is proof of the purpose that was dominant in the primitive community.[7]

Thus the primitive community may be assumed to have been the first gathering ground for the teachings of Jesus afterwards preserved in the Gospels.

The new communal life had its disillusionments and its failures. One of these is recorded by Luke. Beneath all the legendary accretions of the story of Ananias and Sapphira, it is apparent that it does not owe its preservation to the fact that it was the story of a miraculous

[7] History of Primitive Christianity, ed. F. C. Grant (New York: Wilson-Erickson, 1937), I, 77-78.

happening, however much Luke's choice of it may have been determined by that fact. The hypocrisy that was brought to light was a shock to the moral sense of the community, and Peter voices the community conscience when he condemns it as a sin against the Holy Spirit. The conception of the Spirit is based on the conviction that the Christian gospel makes an ethical demand, and that it searches out the secret motives of the human heart.

That the risen Jesus should be the giver of the Spirit thus meant great things for the primitive church. It was the announcement of a divine victory granted to the same Jesus whom wicked men had crucified, and of the divine acknowledgment that in obedience to the will of God he "died for our sins." Such is Paul's interpretation of the gospel he had "received" (I Cor. 15:3). If the forgiveness of sin is not explicitly connected in the primitive gospel with the death of Jesus, they were forgiven men who proclaimed it. In spite of all their past weakness, blindness, and cowardice, the risen Christ had sought them out in order to make them his "witnesses." The Spirit they received from the risen Christ was also the sign of victory for the kind of life he had lived and taught on earth. From what other source than the Spirit of Christ did these earliest believers derive their sudden courage, their willingness for self-sacrifice and also the bond that united them in their mission to the world?

III. The Gospel in the Gospels

The Fourth Gospel, owing to its distinctive character, will receive separate treatment in the closing section of this article. At the same time it will be cited occasionally as a record and interpretation of the teaching of Jesus. It is assumed that all four evangelists have essentially the same purpose in writing as is expressed by the Johannine author: "These [things] are written that you may believe that Jesus is the Christ, the Son of God, and that believing you may have life in his name" (John 20:31). The purpose of each evangelist is to deepen and strengthen the faith of the particular community for which he writes. None of them writes as though he were a biographer, giving an account of his subject for the benefit of readers who already knew little or nothing of Jesus. His readers were Christian. They had become familiar with Jesus of Nazareth, and most of the principal events in his life, as also very many of his sayings, were known to them through the voice of teacher or preacher. The disciples are introduced by name without any warning or such information about them as a biographer would naturally give. No account is given of the personal appearance of Jesus or

of his home and childhood save only one story in Luke's Gospel. Perhaps the most revealing fact of all is that proportionately so much space is given to the trial and death of Jesus. Remembering the place which the death of Jesus occupies in the apostolic gospel, we see that the main object of the writers was to promote faith. It was evangelical, "that believing you may have life in his name."

The church in Rome to which the Gospel of Mark is addressed had just passed through a sudden moment of fierce persecution at the hands of Nero in A.D. 64. In this persecution both Peter and Paul are generally believed to have laid down their lives. Temptation to deny the faith must have been present in the hearts of many Roman Christians. The common informer—*delator*—was busy even within the community. "Brother will deliver up brother to death" (Mark 13:12). Peter was a venerable and beloved figure in recent memory. That even he should have denied his Lord would have been both startling and encouraging to weak souls. Even the baser treachery of Judas did not retard the victory of Christ. This and all the trials of Jesus in the company of his disciples, along with his own self-confidence, transformed Mark's narrative into a gospel for fainting hearts.[8]

Mark opens his Gospel thus: "The beginning of the gospel of Jesus Christ [the Son of God]." Whether the divine title belongs to the original text or not, there is ample evidence that the author thinks of Jesus as a divine being, the "Son of God." In these descriptive words "the gospel" denotes the whole apostolic message. The "beginning" of the living gospel message was the appearance of Jesus Christ as the supreme divine event in history, the bearer of the kingdom of God. The word has the same significance as in Gen. 1:1; John 1:1. God created all things by his Word. A similar emphasis upon the historical basis and origin of the *euangelion* is apparent in Heb. 2:3. Mark's motive in writing his Gospel is to provide a surer historical basis and origin for the gospel message than was to be found in floating traditions on the lips of Christian preachers and teachers. The creative "word became flesh" (John 1:14).

Luke also claims that his Gospel is a record of "all that Jesus *began* to do and teach" (Acts 1:1). His evangelical motive already makes itself apparent in the nativity hymns of his opening chapter. These preludes of exultant song have the same joyful resonance as we hear in the prophetic message of Deutero-Isaiah spoken to the returning exiles. Luke is everywhere conscious that he is not merely writing

[8] Cf. A. E. J. Rawlinson, *The Gospel According to St. Mark*, pp. xvi-xvii, xxviii-xxix.

a narrative but proclaiming the gospel. His is the Gospel that records, in answer to the reproach on the lips of Christ's enemies, "This man receiveth sinners and eateth with them," three parables in succession which symbolize the divine joy in seeking out and finding "that which is lost." He alone preserves the saying, "the Son of man is come to seek and to save that which is lost" (Luke 19:10), and also the story of the penitent robber on his cross.

The prominence given to the teaching of Jesus is the chief characteristic of Matthew's Gospel. That prominence may have been meant to curb a condition of moral laxity in the church center—in all probability Antioch—for which the Gospel is written, "where the love of many is waxing cold." In this Gospel particularly the ethical teaching of Jesus is held to be of the essence of the *euangelion*. The two are never separated in thought as *kerygma* and *didachē*. The "mountain" on which the discourse known as the "Sermon on the Mount" is spoken can be found on no map. The long discourse itself is made up of isolated sayings and blocks of sayings of Jesus. Matthew's "mountain" is intended to suggest that the new law, the "law of Christ," was given with the same authority and accompanied by the same majesty as the promulgation of the law on Sinai. The evangelist's conception is in line with the primitive gospel. He sees in Jesus the prophet "like unto Moses," to whom men must listen (Deut. 18:15-16; Acts 3:22).

It is of interest to note the structure of Matthew's Gospel. The Sermon on the Mount is the first of five main discourses (5–7; 9:36–11:1; 13:1-53; 18:1–19:1; 24–25). A narrative, largely taken from Mark, precedes each discourse. Each section ends with practically the same formula, "It came to pass that Jesus, when he had ended all these sayings," etc. Did the author, as is suggested by several scholars, intend that these five discourses, with the narrative that precedes them, take an even higher and more authoritative place than the Pentateuch, the most sacred part of the Jewish Torah? [9]

The Sermon on the Mount is not, however, merely a rabbinical codification of moral precepts. In the other discourses of Matthew the note of the evangel is clearly heard (9:36; 13:16; 18:20; 24:14; cf. also 9:13). The same evangelical note is sounded at the very beginning of the sermon. The Beatitudes are messages of encouragement and forgiveness for all who take the penetrating and absolute moral demands

seriously and seek first the kingdom of God. The sermon teaches that Christ is the final judge of men (Matt. 7:22-23), but it is noteworthy that in the prophetic picture of the Last Judgment (Matt. 25:31-46) it is ultimately by the law of love and kindness to the needy and the suffering that men are judged. Love which expresses itself in this type of moral activity cannot be defined in words, but is an inward disposition. This inner disposition determines the outward action and also its moral value. Without it external obedience to moral precepts leads to self-righteousness, which is more occupied in protecting itself than in succoring others. He is no legalist who preserves a saying of Christ which allows that kindness is of eternal value even when it is not done by a Christian disciple (Matt. 25:37-40).

The character of the disciple of Christ is itself a concrete and visible gospel. "Ye are the salt of the earth"; "Ye are the light of the world"; "Let your light so shine before men, that they may see your good works, and give glory to your Father who is in heaven" (Matt. 5:13-16). It is the purpose of the heavenly Father that the disciple of Christ as the child of God should be given the power of reproducing the character of God in his own manner of life. "Be ye therefore merciful, as your Father also is merciful" (Luke 6:36). The Christian ethic is no categorical imperative nor lofty ideal, wherein if we fail,

> What I aspired to be
> And was not, comforts me,
> A brute I might have been, but would not sink i'
> the scale.[10]

"Love your enemies"; "Give, hoping for nothing again"—these precepts are the gospel of God for the world in which we live, preached in and through the characters of God's children.

What if we fail? Then we know that we are not merely baffled and frustrated idealists, but children of the Father who have sinned against his holy will and need forgiveness. The experience of forgiveness enriches the gospel of forgiveness which the child of God preaches or lives before men. It is also the most powerful stimulus to persistent goodness and love. The relation of sonship is deepened and strengthened. It is a far different thing from condonation which would make the offense seem as though it did not greatly matter. "We appreciate a great forgiveness only because we credit the forgiver with a true estimate of the gravity of the act he loves us well enough to forgive." [11] Only thus do the children of God

---

[9] This hypothesis of a Christian Pentateuch is as old as Papias (about A.D. 140). Compare F. W. Green, *The Gospel According to Saint Matthew* ("The Clarendon Bible"; Oxford: The Clarendon Press, 1945), pp. 4-7; see also, below, pp. 232, 235, etc.

[10] Robert Browning, "Rabbi Ben Ezra."

[11] A. E. Taylor, *The Faith of a Moralist* (London: Macmillan & Co., 1930), I, 188-89.

gain the courage and persistence to keep alive in themselves and in the world of men that tension between life as it is and life as it ought to be. "Blessed are those who hunger and thirst for righteousness."

A. *The Teaching of Jesus on the Fatherhood of God.*—Nowhere in the Bible is God regarded as an object of human speculation. Neither in the Old Testament nor in the New is there any metaphysical definition of God. Belief in the existence of a personal or "living" God was the essential factor in the religion of every Jew. "The nearest approach to a definition of God in the Old Testament is to be found in the words: 'I am the Lord thy God who brought thee out of the land of Egypt.' " [12] God is never thought of as abstracted from human life but as revealed within it. In bringing about the deliverance from Egypt, which decisively shaped the destiny of Israel as a nation, God revealed his character and purpose. So also in the deliverance from the Exile in Babylon (Isa. 40:9). As the God of Israel, he exercises providential care over the fortunes of his chosen people (Deut. 8:14-20). He shares all their vicissitudes: "In all their affliction he was afflicted, and the Angel of his presence saved them" (Isa. 63:9). God reveals himself to his people by his "mighty acts" on their behalf— his "lovingkindness," the "multitude of his mercies" in the course of their long history as the Father of his people, as their Shepherd (Isa. 40:11; Ezek. 34). In the prophetic teaching of the Old Testament God is always known for what he is by what he does. This is true not only in the history of the nation as a whole but in the experience of the individual. "The Lord is my Shepherd; I shall not want" (Ps. 23:1). "Like as a father pitieth his children, so the Lord pitieth them that fear him" (Ps. 103:13). In his message to the returning exiles Deutero-Isaiah proclaims the gospel of their mighty deliverance by the King of kings; he also speaks in the name of the same Lord words of great tenderness and compassion to the mothers and their children who will have to endure all the hardships of the weary trek homeward (Isa. 40:11). The Psalms are part of the liturgy of the priestly cult, but the prophetic conception of God and his personal relationship to men is still dominant. In the teaching of Jesus the sacrificial ritual is meaningless unless it is the expression of the inner life of the worshiper (Matt. 5:23). Jesus makes this prophetic doctrine his own. "I will have mercy and not sacrifice" (Hos. 6:6; Ps. 51:15-17; Matt. 9:13).

We do not enhance the value of the teaching of Jesus on the fatherhood of God by over-stating its novelty and emphasizing the uniqueness of his doctrine at the expense of the Jewish conception. The originality of Jesus is that he made the fatherhood of God the central doctrine of the Christian faith. He transformed the doctrine into a spiritual experience which gave new meaning and value to the whole of life. The transformation was not effected by explicit teaching or theological dissertation; it took place through the influence of his own religious life and personality. His inner life of prayer and faith so infected the hearts of the disciples that they hungered to possess it themselves—"Lord, teach us to pray"; "Lord, increase our faith." As they heard the word "Father" on the lips of Jesus in prayer, or heard him speak of "your heavenly Father," they felt themselves invited so to address God. The depth of the impression made upon them by the prayer life of Jesus is seen in the fact that the actual Aramaic word "Abba," which used to fall from the lips of Jesus, became in Christian worship, along with its Greek equivalent, a liturgical form of address in prayer. "When we cry, 'Abba, Father,' " says Paul, the Spirit of Christ is "bearing witness with our spirit that we are children of God" (Rom. 8:15-16).

It would be unwarrantable to say that the Pharisaic religion of his day, which Jesus so sternly rebukes, was completely representative of contemporary piety. We have the Lukan picture of the homes of Elizabeth and Mary, and the portraits of Zechariah and Simeon; also such figures as Nicodemus and Joseph of Arimathea and the fleeting appearance of the scribe who is "not far from the kingdom of God" (Mark 12:34). Yet we have ample proof that Pharisaism was the dominant type, and had little to give to "the common people." In this rabbinical type of piety the prophetic conception of God was relegated to the background. The great deliverances were past history. God was king chiefly in the sense that he was the divine legislator in faith and morals. The Bible of the Old Testament was the inspired book in which was laid down "what man is to believe concerning God and what duty God requires of man." In the mind of the scribe, the trained and sole authoritative interpreter, all the other sacred writings, including the prophetic, were but commentaries on the peculiarly sacred Mosaic law of the Pentateuch. The prophet "had ceased from Israel" and the Holy Spirit was given to the scribe, as the guarantor and purveyor of sound doctrine. The nation was put to school. The rabbi and the scribe were the schoolmasters. Rabbinical religion was a weary burden to the masses of the people. The gulf separating the rabbis from the masses is revealed in the words,

[12] H. Wheeler Robinson, *The Religious Ideas of the Old Testament* (London: Duckworth, 1934), p. 51.

"This crowd, who do not know the law, are accursed" (John 7:49).

It is to these that the mission of Jesus and his message of the fatherhood of God are directed. They are the "weary, and the heavy laden" to whom he promises "rest." This rest is primarily an inward experience, the knowledge that they are children in the family of God. It is his own experience of God that he seeks to give to them. It is "my yoke," one which he himself wears daily, his own yoke of perfect filial obedience to the Father. The writer to the Hebrews boldly says that Jesus "learned obedience through what he suffered" (Heb. 5:8). In Gethsemane he was still a learner. "Nevertheless, not as I will, but as thou wilt." The gospel message of Matt. 11:28 is preceded by the words which describe that unique knowledge of the Father which he alone possesses, but holds only in order to give it away to "whom the Son chooses to reveal" it. It is this same "rest," absolute trust in the heavenly Father, "my peace" (John 14:27), which Jesus describes in more detail in the message of Matt. 6:25-33, "Do not be anxious about your life, what you shall eat or what you shall drink, nor about your body, what you shall put on." "All things have been delivered to me by my Father" (Matt. 11:27) is not a claim to absolute sovereignty or complete autonomy, but means that he has nothing to give to men and nothing to teach them except what he himself has received and has learned of the Father, and also has put to the test in his own human experience. On the other hand all men are indebted to him for the knowledge that there is no region or experience of life which lies outside the domain of the fatherly love and care of God, or of his kingly power. "No man cometh unto the Father, but by me" (John 14:6).

The invitation is an invitation to "learn of me." The rest that he offers is not a spiritual sedative. The "yoke of the law" is a common rabbinical expression for the study of the Scriptures. "Take my yoke upon you." Jesus was a student of the Scriptures and he drew from them the nourishment of his own soul. In them he listened to the voice of his Father. The Fourth Evangelist preserves a saying which is an illuminating commentary in this connection. "You search the scriptures, because you think that in them you have eternal life; and it is they that bear witness to me; yet you refuse to come to me that you may have life" (John 5:39). The scribes searched the Scriptures but did not find therein the Christ of whom they spoke and whose coming they foretold. His is a lofty claim. He restores the prophetic writings to their rightful place in the Scriptures, and claims to be the embodiment in history of the eternal purpose of God which they revealed. The moral demand that God makes upon men in the sacred law is even intensified by his own deeper and more stringent interpretation of it. "But I say unto you." God seeks of men that they should reproduce his own character in themselves. "Be ye therefore perfect, even as your Father which is in heaven is perfect." Yet Jesus promises to his "learners" rest for their souls. That rest is not escape from life's burdens, but a sense of moral and spiritual competence to meet all the demands that human life, as thus interpreted by him, makes upon faith, courage, and love.

The "rest" of which Jesus speaks is no incidental theme but is the expression of the whole gospel which his coming made it possible to preach. It is the "gospel of the kingdom of God" (Mark 1:14). "Kingdom" means "kingship," the sway of God's sovereign power among men. The term is seldom found in the Old Testament save in the sense of an outward domain. On the lips of Christ the "kingdom of God" stands for the almighty sovereign purpose of God, who is the "King of kings," and has delivered his own people often from the hands of their enemies, and brought them to the present hour. The present hour is that "day of the Lord" foretold by the prophets, when his reign will be completed and realized on earth. "Thy kingdom come. Thy will be done, on earth as it is in heaven." "The time is fulfilled, and the kingdom of God is at hand; repent and believe in the gospel." This gospel of the kingdom is a visible gospel: "Blessed are your eyes, for they see, and your ears, for they hear. Truly, I say to you, many prophets and righteous men longed to see what you see, and did not see it, and to hear what you hear, and did not hear it" (Matt. 13:16-17; Luke 10:23-24). Thus did Jesus conceive the significance of his own presence and his whole ministry among men. Thus also is it conceived throughout by the evangelists, and it is in order to preserve and to proclaim this visible gospel that they write.

In that gospel the kingship and the fatherhood of God are revealed as one in purpose and in activity. The kingdom is "the kingdom of my Father." Jesus, to whom the power of the kingdom is delegated, heals sickness and cures the disordered mind. He grants the forgiveness of the Father to the penitent and seeks out the lost. He brings back the dead to life. All these are the activities of the divine "kingship" revealed in him. He is also the great teacher of those who are willing to learn of him. This reigning of the love of God on earth is also a day of judgment. Men judge themselves when they reject it; for the power of this kingdom is derived from the "finger of God" that wrote the sacred law (Luke 11:20; cf. Matt. 12:28). The kingdom is the Father's gift to men, and the manner of his reign is the revelation of himself. God reigns more for men than for himself, and believing this, men find rest and peace.[13]

We do not apprehend the full revelation which Jesus makes of the fatherly love of God toward the sinner if we give attention only to his words. The place of the Gospels in the Christian *euangelion* is that they represent it as something "seen." The gospel appeared in a form all too real and visible in the estimate of the Pharisee. "This man receiveth sinners, and eateth with them."

Rabbinical piety tended to think of God as Father only in the experience of the righteous doer of the law or of the repentant sinner. In the words of a distinguished Jewish scholar:

There was in the Pharisaism of all ages a real anxiety to make the return of the sinner easy. It was inclined to leave the initiative to the sinner, except that it always maintained *God's* readiness to take the first step. Jesus in his attitude towards sin and sinners was more inclined to take the initiative.[14]

But the attitude of Jesus was much more than an inclination. It was instinctive. The three great parables of Luke 15 do not describe "inclinations" but most powerful dominant human instincts to seek and to find again that which has been lost because it is of the greatest value to the finder.

It is the search for what is lost that gives the stories their significance. What is searched for until it is found must be of great personal value. In the Synoptic record Jesus uses very sparingly the language of love in describing his own relationship with men and theirs with him; but the "seeking" of sinners is the outward expression of "love to the uttermost," love that is inexorable. He is concerned not only to save men from a wrong way of life but to save them into a kind of life where his continual presence and friendship would give that life a quality which death and sin cannot destroy, "eternal life." A disciple of Christ by his own friendship and kindness may convey to the erring in word and deed the gospel of the divine

[13] It is of interest to note that this conception of the "rest" in Matt. 11:27 is confirmed by the outline of the primitive gospel in Acts 10:36-37: "You know the word which he sent to Israel, preaching good news of peace by Jesus Christ (he is Lord of all), the word which was proclaimed throughout all Judea." The whole passage might serve as an outline of the Gospel of Mark.

[14] Israel Abrahams, *Studies in Pharisaism and the Gospels*, 1st Ser. (Cambridge: University Press), p. 58.

forgiveness, but he needs personal faith in Christ and a personal sense of forgiveness to maintain that prayerful persistence, courage, and hope which convey to the heart of another the assurance of a love that will not let us go. Christ's own attitude to the sinner, even in the Synoptic record, gives the impression that he possesses, in order to give, what no one else has or can give, and that he is able to do for men what no one else can do. Men may undo themselves by rejection of what he has to give (Mark 8:36-37). Jesus sums up his whole mission and ministry in the words "The Son of man is come to seek and to save that which was lost." The initiative of the Son of man is the initiative of God the Father. Jesus will not have men think otherwise. "Why callest thou me good? there is none good but one, that is, God" (Mark 10:18).

B. Messianic Consciousness of Jesus.—In the Synoptic Gospels the baptism of Jesus represents the moment when he received his call to the messianic vocation. The story must have been told to the disciples by Jesus himself. The Gospel of Mark relates it in its simplest form. The accounts in Matthew and Luke show the marks of its transmission as a tradition of the church. Mark alone presents the vision of the dove and the voice from heaven as an inward experience of Jesus. In both the other accounts the voice is audible to the outward ear. In Luke the dove is externalized as an appearance "in bodily form."

The Baptist and his mission occupy a prominent place in the primitive gospel (Acts 10:37). It would, however, be generally admitted that the Baptist is there represented as holding a more outstanding position than he himself was conscious of possessing. He undoubtedly owes his place in the Christian tradition to the fact that the response which his preaching aroused in the hearts of the people had a profound significance in the mind of Jesus. His glowing words in Matt. 11:7-14 show how much he owed to the mission of the Baptist. The latter is "more than a prophet." He is the herald who prepares the way of the Lord, the "Elijah" of the popular messianic expectation who is to come before the great "day of the Lord." This estimate of the Baptist's mission had its origin in the mind of Jesus himself. The decisive factor in the traditional relationship between Jesus and the Baptist is not what John thought of Jesus but what Jesus thought of John. John by the results of his mission had prepared his way.

The effects of the Baptist's preaching on the community stirred the soul of Jesus most deeply. The awakened conscience of the nation and its mood of repentance had no doubt more in them of the fear of God's judgment than of joyful response to a message of good news from God. Therefore was Jesus moved with the same compassion that took possession of his heart as later he looked upon another multitude. These penitents are as "sheep without a shepherd." The Baptist, great prophetic personality as he was, could not supply their deepest need. "He who is least in the kingdom of heaven is greater than he" (Matt. 11:11; Luke 7:28). Their unsatisfied need was linked with the decisive call of the Father to inaugurate his messianic mission. Jesus began his messianic career not with preaching but with a characteristic act. He submitted himself for baptism. That he should be baptized with a "baptism for the remission of sins" created difficulty in the mind of the later church. This difficulty is reflected in Matt. 3:14-15. But what he did, he did instinctively. "It is not with angels that he is concerned. . . . Therefore he had to be made like his brethren in every respect" (Heb. 2:16-17). His action was motived by that loving sense of responsibility for sins not one's own, whose depth is always measured by the purity of the loving soul. That action is the symbol of his whole ministry on earth, and in essence the complete expression of the Father's love. He "was numbered with the transgressors" in order that he might offer them his friendship and his filial consciousness of the friendship of God and thus redeem them. The voice from heaven is the Father's recognition and approval of what he had done. The language of the voice is the language of the Word of God in Scripture. It is reminiscent of Ps. 2:7, a messianic psalm, and of Isa. 42:1, never formerly regarded as messianic. The latter describes "the servant" of the Lord as one in whom the Lord "delighteth." The servant is also one who "was numbered with transgressors; and he bare the sin of many" (Isa. 53:12). It is abundantly clear that Jesus interpreted his messianic vocation in the divine light of that which was foretold as the vocation of the servant of the Lord. The scriptural citations are a revelation of the inmost thoughts of the Christ as he read or recalled those places "in the volume of the book" where he could say "it is written of me" (cf. Luke 4:16 ff.).

Never in the Synoptic Gospels, and rarely in the Fourth, does Jesus designate himself "Son of God." He speaks of himself as "the Son." "Son of God" denotes in the Old Testament the reigning king as God's vicegerent on earth. His avoidance of the term "Son of God," and his use of the title "the Son," indicates that everywhere he interprets his messianic office through the channel of that unbroken and unique filial consciousness which was at all times open and obedient to the will of the Father. That the Messiah should be a free agent with the power to interpret his vocation, and to determine the use he is to make of his messianic power was startlingly new. That the Messiah should interpret his vocation as a call not only to submit to baptism but to end his career with a shameful death was revolutionary. The traditional Messiah was never conceived as a divine being. He receives divine power for the definite purpose of passing and carrying out judgment on the enemies of God's people and delivering them from their sway. Afterward he occupies no place of honor in the kingdom which he inaugurates. The traditional Messiah does not teach but judges.

Jesus at his baptism is by all the evangelists regarded as having been equipped with the power of the Spirit, and is free to interpret and apply it in the carrying out of his messianic work, controlled only by his filial consciousness of the will of the Father. It is this freedom that makes the Temptation possible. The Spirit "drove him out into the wilderness." He knew that the power of evil in the world is enormous and formidable, and can subtly make its appeal even to the best human instincts. His temptations are messianic, and are aimed at his vocation to make the kingdom of God a reality in the lives of men. To compromise with evil is at least to get a foothold from which to gain ascendancy over the minds of men. With unerring moral judgment he saw that to make terms with evil is to abdicate that messianic kingship conferred upon him through whom the reign of the Father on earth is to be realized. "He said to himself in this [the third] temptation what he afterwards said to all, What shall it profit a man if he gain the whole world and lose himself?" [15]

The sense of messianic kingship is apparent in many of the sayings of Jesus in the Synoptic Gospels. It appears as a consciousness that in all his ministry of deed and word he represents before men a cause which is infinitely greater than any other. In general this cause is described as "the kingdom of God." The sense of kingship is apparent in the words already quoted, where the kingdom which prophets and many good men in ages long past had yearned to see is said to be manifested in his person and ministry. That in one personality, and that personality himself, these "hopes of all the years" and the final purpose of God for the world should center, is a claim to transcendent greatness. As the Messiah carries on his beneficent work on earth, again and again we are made to feel that he stands for a cause toward

[15] James Denney, *Jesus and the Gospel* (New York: A. C. Armstrong & Sons, 1909), p. 212.

which there can be no neutrality. "He that is not with me is against me" (Matt. 12:30). Jesus claims to be the final judge of men.

In apparent contrast with these claims to transcendent greatness as the custodian and representative of a cause that lays greater responsibilities upon men, and in which greater issues are at stake than any other, we are also made aware that Jesus shows a studied reserve in his use of the messianic title. Much has been written on this subject and the reader must be referred to the commentaries on the various Gospels for its fuller treatment. To many people much the simplest and most convincing hypothesis, and also the most obvious, is that Jesus had to displace, in the minds of his more intimate disciples and of the populace, nationalistic and materialistic conceptions of the expected messianic kingdom, in order to make room for his own. As the Messiah he had not only to interpret himself to his disciples but at the same time to interpret the cause which he represented, the kingdom of God. By what title should the kingly Messiah of that kingdom be designated? Jesus chose the title "Son of man." It is never found on any other lips than his own.

There is no convincing evidence that in Jewish circles this title was ever widely applied to the Messiah. Its use as a messianic title in the Book of Enoch can have no possible bearing on its usage by Jesus. That portion of the book where the title occurs (The Similitudes of Enoch, chs. 37–71) may be post-Christian. In any case the conception there of the Son of man Messiah is so fantastic as to indicate that it was current in some obscure religious coterie and could have no affinity whatever with the mind of Jesus.[16] Any possible literary influence in his use of the title is to be found in the vision of Daniel (7:13-14). There the oppressed nation of Israel is symbolized by a human figure "like the Son of man," a frail human being in contrast with the four savage beasts armed with horn and claw, which represent the world powers to which it has been subjugated in past history. Israel appears in the likeness of a *man* "unarmed and inoffensive, incapable through any power of his own of making himself master of the world; he is only as a son of man. If ever he is to be master of the world, God must make him so."[17] In the vision God makes this nation, his own people so symbolized, master of the world. This humanlike figure in all its weakness is borne into

the presence of God "with the clouds of heaven." This expression, often so prosaically externalized, means really that the oppressed nation, the chosen instrument of the eternal divine purpose and with no power save that which it receives from God, is sponsored and chosen in heaven, in other words by God himself. It comes from above. The nations symbolized by the bestial figures come from below, the creations of ruthless imperial ambitions. Upon the nation of Israel thus divinely sponsored there is conferred "dominion, and glory, and a kingdom, that all people, nations, and languages, should serve him: his dominion is an everlasting dominion, which shall not pass away, and his kingdom . . . shall not be destroyed" (Dan. 7:14).

The whole conception is still nationalistic. It becomes transformed in the mind of Jesus into a conception of himself and his mission. What was thus prophetically spoken to the nation is realized in his own personality. With the coming of the Spirit upon him at the baptism, the divine power of a kingly Messiah is conferred upon him. His fitting title on earth is the Son of man. The name still denotes human weakness and also that nothing human is alien to him. "The Son of man came eating and drinking," and shared the common life of men. So true is this that from the parables and sayings of Jesus we are able to derive a picture of the everyday life of ordinary men and women in contemporary Palestine. Yet as he moves, a man among men, he speaks often in the tones of one who is conscious that to him "dominion and a kingdom" have been entrusted. "The Son of man hath power on earth to forgive sins." "The Son of man is lord even of the sabbath." Forgiveness of sins is a divine prerogative, and the sabbath, according to the law, is a divine institution. He speaks of his ministry of healing as a messianic war which he captains against the demonic powers, to whose sway, in the popular religion of the day, the lives of men had been given over in divine chastisement. These have been permitted to send upon them bodily illness, disorder of mind, and death. Satan is their chief, the tempter who assailed at the beginning of his ministry his messianic vocation (Matt. 12:25-29; Mark 3:27; Luke 11:17-22).

Meantime his kingly personality is unrecognized by the bulk of men. "The Son of man hath not where to lay his head." The home that is denied him is in the hearts of men. In these words there is revealed the consciousness that he is a monarch divested of his throne, a disinherited king. His own relatives, when they hear him so speak, say, "He is beside himself."

[16] See J. Y. Campbell, "The Origin and Meaning of the Term Son of Man," *Journal of Theological Studies,* XLVIII (1947), 145-48. But see also below, pp. 149-50.

[17] Gustaf Dalman, *The Words of Jesus,* tr. D. M. Kay (Edinburgh: T. & T. Clark, 1909), p. 242.

When he asks his disciples, "Whom say ye that I am?" he receives an answer full of personal loyalty and affection and an acknowledgment of his messiahship. Such affection and loyalty represent a personal relationship with the Messiah far different indeed from the traditional relationship between the Messiah and his people, but their loyalty stopped short of following him in his own thoughts as to how his throne can alone be won. So much were these thoughts at the very center of his vocational conception that he bade them keep silence.

At the same time he does not despise the imperfect response they had given. He had bound them to himself with cords of loyalty and love. His messiahship could not be described in words but discovered only by such as they who had become associated with him in such a spirit. This loyal affection gave him in the prospect that lay before him the only human hope to which he clung. Even at the very end, as he addressed them for the last time, this hope sustained him. "You are those who have continued with me in my trials." He casts them, as he casts himself, on the power and love of the Father and his eternal purpose. "As my Father appointed a kingdom for me, so do I appoint for you" (Luke 22:28-29).

The Son of man is represented in the Gospels as experiencing a deep sense of failure. We hear in Matt. 13:13-17 the cry of the defeated love of Jesus. In his consciousness it is also the cry of the defeated love of God. When Jesus interprets his own experience in the light of Isa. 6:9-10, he claims to share not merely the personal experience of the prophet but the very heart of God himself revealed to his mouthpiece the prophet. Here again there is implied a very lofty claim. This same divine sense of failure, mingled with a sense of royal greatness, reaches its climax in the lament over Jerusalem. He conceives himself as standing at the gate of the "city of the great King," the vicegerent of God on the day of her royal "visitation." What the city is about to do to him, it will do to Almighty God (Matt. 23:37-39=Luke 13:34-35). The cry is not uttered in the tones of stern judicial acquiescence. The agony of the cry is the knowledge that this great rejection is her doom. It is also filled with the sense of what he elsewhere calls "the mystery of the kingdom," the mystery hidden from the eyes of men. It is the mystery of the undiscouraged love of God hidden in his heart, soon to become an "open secret" for all the world in the Cross.

C. *The Messiah and the Cross.*—Mark devotes about half of his Gospel to the story of the last journey of Jesus to Jerusalem and the events of the trial and Crucifixion. This is a sign of the importance which the early tradition attached to the death of Jesus in its proclamation of the gospel message. The section Mark 8:27–10:45 is a narrative portrait of Jesus of which the dominant feature is his intense preoccupation in teaching his disciples that "the Son of man must suffer." The word "must" denotes not blind necessity, but the will of the Father which he has made his own. The section begins with the confession of his messiahship by Peter in the name of the others, and marks the transition from the public ministry to the story of the closing days which are spent mostly in the company of the twelve. In spite, however, of the fact that they had acknowledged him as Messiah, and as one who transcends in their minds all great and venerable personalities of the past, the disciples are enjoined to keep silence. They are as yet unfit to preach the gospel of a crucified Messiah who will reach his throne by the divinely appointed way of suffering and a shameful death (Mark 8:31; 9:31; 10:45). They are still men who think of the messianic kingdom in terms of earthly sovereignty and nationalistic aspirations. How startling and unfamiliar to their minds his teaching is appears in Peter's violent remonstrance. How great is the task of communicating to them such teaching looms before the eyes of Jesus as he utters his stern and devastating rebuke. He sees and hears the tempter, whom he had repelled in the wilderness, speaking again in the guise of a loyal and much loved disciple. The temptation is all the greater inasmuch as he is now not alone in the wilderness but is surrounded by his disciples. Are these men, with all their materialistic aims and selfish ambitions, the rock on which he seeks to found a church against which the gates of hell shall not prevail? Mark's narrative in this section is impressive as he sets before his readers all the time not only the magnitude but the apparent hopelessness of the task of teaching the way of the Cross. It is not without significance that Mark opens this section with a story of a blind man (8:22-26), and tells the story of another at its close (10:46-52). Jesus seeks to open their eyes but they remain blinded to the end. The transfiguration experience with its authenticating voice from heaven is an encouragement to himself. The voice is the voice of the Father proclaiming, as at the Baptism, that the way the Son is treading is the way of his own purpose. But nothing of this kind is conveyed to the minds of the disciples. When the experience is over, they see "Jesus only," the same Jesus as before, bent on his own destruction and the shattering of all their hopes (Mark 9:8). At one point in the journey there is inserted a vignette of the

Master walking, most unusually, ahead of his disciples, while they follow in fear and amazement. Even at the end of these days of teaching the earthly kingdom of the traditional Messiah still dominates their thinking (Mark 10:35-45). "There is no dead lift so heavy as that which is required to change an ideal. We do not wonder that at the moment it was too much for him as for them."[18]

The passion story in Mark's Gospel occupies 14:1–15:39. In its construction the story is of a pattern remarkably uniform in all the Gospels. The events follow one another in practically the same order and are carefully articulated—in strong contrast with the general structure of the Marcan narrative elsewhere. All this seems to indicate that Mark is making use of a narrative which is already fixed in the Christian tradition. There were strong reasons why it should be so. A carefully constructed and authoritative account of all the facts was demanded in the face of hostile versions of the story, in order to show how it was possible that a crucified messiah should be the subject of a message of salvation.[19]

The passion story, as it is related particularly in Mark's Gospel, is in itself what may be called a visible gospel in narrative form. Some such narrative may have been, in shorter form, part of a primitive liturgy for use in worship as an introduction to the celebration of the Lord's Supper. Paul recites the story of its institution as a narrative that he has "received," as similarly he tells that he had "received" the stories of the appearances after the Resurrection (I Cor. 11:23-26; 15:3 ff.). "As often as ye eat this bread, and drink this cup, ye proclaim [καταγγέλετε] the Lord's death until he come." In the passion story the treachery of Judas, the denial of Peter, the flight of the disciples, are not suppressed, much less excused. No comment of condemnation is pronounced upon the action of the enemies or the judges of Jesus. The sacrament is not the moment for the passing of human judgment on what had taken place. Both disciples and judges were guilty men. There is no calling attention to the sufferings of Jesus either during the trial or on the Cross.[20] He himself is silent during the trial and refuses to reply to the charges made against him. Hearers and readers are made to feel that this is not merely the result of self-command but the silence of one whose mind is living on a plane of thought which no insult can reach. It is the silence

under suffering of "the servant of the Lord," who was "conscious of the end God has in his pain, an end not to be served in any other way, and with all his heart he had given himself to it."[21]

Jesus was conscious of the end that God had in view for him. It was the purpose of his whole ministry on earth. He reveals his full consciousness of that purpose, and the assent of his own heart to it, when he says, "The Son of man also came not to be served but to serve, and to give his life as a ransom for many" (Mark 10:45). These words undoubtedly are meant to recall the prophecy of the suffering servant in Isa. 52:13–53:12. The "kingdom" conferred upon the "Son of man" in the vision of Daniel is for him a kingdom whose throne is to be won by a life of humble service crowned by the giving of himself in death "a ransom for many." "Ransom" simply means deliverance and is not to be pressed into the service of any theological theorizing on the efficacy of his death. That the vicarious suffering of the righteous has redemptive value for the community was no new idea in Jewish thought. It pervades the thought of Isa. 53. Indeed we may say that the idea is not even a dogmatic interpretation peculiar to Judaism but an experimental truth taught by the history of mankind. What is new is derived from the self-consciousness of Jesus. This distinguishes it from the martyr's death or one due to a miscarriage of justice. The door of his prison is locked from the inside. That he should die is the will of the Father which he freely and wholeheartedly accepts as his own (John 10:18). His is the mind of one who thought of his whole ministry as the coming of the kingdom of God, and the realization of the "day of the Lord," and the goal of history. All the great issues that were concentrated in the history of Israel converge in himself. His death is his final act of service for the "many," which on his lips means for all.

The new thing is that Jesus, "who had the keenest moral judgment ever known on earth," should regard himself as worthy to be and to offer a perfect and unblemished sacrifice which would secure redemption for all. In the prospect of death, when even his most faithful and devoted disciples review their lives and both give thanks for and seek the forgiveness of God, Jesus regards his sacrificial death as the final act of a life of unbroken fellowship with God and perfect moral obedience as his beloved Son. The sacrifice is offered as his life was lived

---

[18] Denney, *Jesus and the Gospel*, p. 35.

[19] See Vincent Taylor, *The Formation of the Gospel Tradition* (London: Macmillan & Co., 1933), pp. 44-62.

[20] Luke's narrative is a partial exception, and tends to represent Jesus' death as a martyr (23:37-41, 48).

[21] G. A. Smith, *The Book of Isaiah* (New York: A. C. Armstrong & Son, 1900), II, 376. In what has just been written and in what follows, I owe a deep debt to the memorable words of the same writer's *Jerusalem* (London: Hodder & Stoughton, 1908), II, 547-48.

—in the service of others. Without that sense of a life of perfect service, this final sacrifice would have been in vain.

The passion story, however, never allows us to forget that this life of perfect moral obedience and complete fellowship with the Father was not maintained without moments of intense spiritual struggle and deepest mental suffering. The agony in Gethsemane and the cry of dereliction on the Cross are salient instances. These have often been interpreted in an abstract theological fashion. The Gospels represent them as actual events, the human causes of which may be discovered. In Gethsemane, Mark tells us that Jesus began to be "full of terror and distress" (Weymouth; cf. Heb. 5:7-8). To his disciples he said, "My soul is very sorrowful, even to death; remain here, and watch." These men, however, were unaware that they themselves, their future and the future of the community of which they were the founders, were causing him the deepest concern. The anxiety of Jesus regarding his disciples, individually and collectively, is a marked feature of the closing days. There were other moments when, in a spirit of great trust, he could say of them, "Fear not, little flock, for it is your Father's good pleasure to give you the kingdom." But now they had failed entirely to apprehend the central meaning of the gospel of the kingdom. In the agony of Gethsemane the natural human shrinking of an exquisitely sensitive nature from the prospect of trial before judges who had already made up their minds, and from the certainty of a cruel and painful death, played their part. But an added bitterness was imparted by the utter imperceptibility of his most intimate disciples.

Only one human being, the woman who anointed him at Bethany, by her own generous action the symbol of an overflowing devotion, showed that she was with him in spirit and had entered at all into his own mind in face of the approaching tragedy. Her action he immortalized, giving her her place in the story of the gospel (Mark 14:9). The disciples had all deserted him in thought long before they deserted him in fact. In the garden itself he had again sought in vain their spiritual comradeship. He prayed the Father that the hour might pass when he would drink such a full cup of sorrow. "Nevertheless, not what I will, but what thou wilt."

As Jesus stands helpless and condemned before his judges, the victory of Gethsemane proclaims itself in the triumphant utterance which breaks the impressive silence he had hitherto maintained. "You will see the Son of man sitting at the right hand of Power, and coming with the clouds of heaven" (Mark 14:62). These words must surely be regarded as symbolical. We have already seen that the prophetic utterance which precedes the passion story in Mark (ch. 13 and its parallels in Matthew and Luke) is evidently intended to counter the influence of a literal and prosaic interpretation of "apocalyptic" sayings of Jesus such as this, or as those recorded in Mark 8:38–9:1. "The Power" is a reverential name for God, "the Almighty." As King and Lord of his church, he will come to men "borne on the clouds of heaven," as one sponsored from above and delegated with divine power needed for the mission of the church and its own strengthening. Thus do both Matthew and Luke understand the saying, as is apparent from their rendering, "from henceforth" or "from now on ye shall see." Thus also did the primitive community in Jerusalem interpret it in their own experience and in words chosen by themselves; "Being therefore exalted at the right hand of God, . . . he has poured out this which you see and hear" (Acts 2:33).

It is therefore very remarkable that in a short space after this triumphant utterance of Mark 14:62 there should also be recorded the cry of dereliction, "My God, my God, why hast thou forsaken me?" Was this cry also not the cry of one whose last thoughts were of his disciples and those for whom he had spent himself in service? He saw also what the people of God had become. Some spoken words of T. R. Glover are memorable:

> Strange to think that is the cry of the feeling of Jesus. One is almost tempted to say that there, as in a supreme instance, is measured the distance between feeling and fact. So he felt; and yet mankind has been of another mind that there, more than in all else that he was or did, there was God.[22]

There are moments in human experience when men, driven to look upon the world as other men have made it, or even upon their own lives and the world they have made for themselves, and unable to see the face of its Creator and Savior, utter a cry of despair. If mankind has been able to think otherwise and has been lifted out of the depths from which this cry has come, it is because we know that the love of God in Christ has been and still is where we are, as "a ransom for many."

Yea, once Immanuel's orphaned cry His universe hath shaken—
It went up single, echoless—"My God, I am forsaken!"

[22] Quoted by H. G. Wood in Arthur S. Peake, *A Commentary on the Bible* (London: Thomas Nelson & Sons, 1919), p. 699.

It went up from the Holy's lips amid His lost
creation,
That of the lost, no son should use these words of
desolation.[23]

Mark, along with the church that worshiped
the risen and victorious Christ, must have had
some such thought when he attached to the
closing scene the rubric: "The veil of the
temple," which hid the presence of God from
the spiritual gaze of the common worshiper,
"was rent in twain from the top to the bottom"
(cf. Heb. 10:19-22).

D. *Gospel of the Resurrection.*—When we
turn from the passion story in Mark's Gospel
to the narratives of the resurrection of our
Lord in the other three, we are met with a
complete contrast in literary structure. For
the moment we may leave aside the closing
chapter in the Fourth Gospel, which is clearly
an appendix and written by someone who
belonged to the Johannine circle. The resurrection narrative in Mark has been truncated,
and all that is left consists of a single incident
which ends very abruptly. In the other three
Gospels the narrative consists of more or less
isolated stories, loosely articulated as regards
time and place. Moreover they each follow
largely independent lines of tradition.

It does not lie within the scope of this article
to discuss the attempts made to establish the
historicity and factual consistency, or otherwise,
of the various resurrection stories. Efforts that
have been made in this direction, sometimes
with the help of psychical research or a search
for "clues" reminiscent of the detective romance, are not impressive. The discrepancies
and inconsistencies still obstinately remain.
This method of approach leaves the general
impression that questions are being asked of
these stories which they were never intended
to answer. Of course it was of the greatest
value that there should have been trustworthy
Christian personalities in the community who
were able to say that they had seen Jesus alive
after the Crucifixion and had spoken with him.
But such a testimony could not in itself be
"good tidings of great joy" to others who had
not seen him with their own eyes. Otherwise
it is incredible that the church should have
been content with such a loosely constructed
narrative of events, and should not have demanded and constructed a story as carefully
articulated and uniform in pattern as the passion story.

To approach the church's doctrine of the
Resurrection from the direction of the gospel
narratives of the appearances of Jesus to his
disciples, and the stories of the empty tomb,

[23] Elizabeth Barrett Browning, "Cowper's Grave."

is to make a false start. It is to ignore the central fact that the resurrection of Christ is like
a great river whose presence is felt wherever
believers speak of Jesus Christ in the New
Testament, and whose current continually sustains their faith and obedience, bearing them
on to share the day of his final victory over
sin and death. Every mention of the risen
Christ in the New Testament comes to us
charged with a moral and spiritual meaning
which the speaker or writer has discovered in
his own soul, either as the result of an "appearance" or as having experienced that "blessedness" which is promised to those "that have not
seen, and yet have believed." Without this deep
personal significance of the resurrection faith
firmly rooted in the worship of the church from
the first, as in the heart of the individual believer, not even a line of the Gospels could or
would have been written. Even confining ourselves for the moment to the appearances in
the gospel narratives, we must listen to Paul
when he speaks of these (I Cor. 15:4-11), and
at the end so movingly, of the appearance to
himself. Its whole significance for him was not
merely that Jesus was alive, but rather that
after such a death as men like himself had
inflicted upon him, he should now come in all
his "body of glory," still revealing that unwearied and undiscouraged love which was at
all times the supreme motive of his mission
on earth, "to seek and to save that which is
lost," even "enemies" like himself. In the
words "By the grace of God I am what I am,"
Paul expresses his own consciousness that this
appearance had been transformed into the
dominant passion of his own life, as it also
became translated into the central and basic
conception of his message to the world. Paul
saw in this vision on the Damascus road,
not a Christ "according to the flesh" *redivivus,*
but Jesus now "designated Son of God in
power . . . by his resurrection from the dead"
(Rom. 1:3-4).

There is a fundamental unity of thought in
all these stories, in spite of their discrepancies
and variations, which reveals that the Resurrection is the living core of the Gospel. They all
teach in narrative form that the risen Christ
still carries on the work which he began on
earth, "to seek and to save that which is lost."
He knows where to find his scattered disciples.
This knowledge is exquisitely depicted in the
Emmaus story, and in the appearance to Mary
in the garden. The form of the story of Jesus'
final meeting with the disciples which closes
the resurrection narrative in three of the Gospels (Matt. 28:19; Luke 24:46-49; John 20:19-
23) differs in each case, but it is everywhere
regarded as a meeting with the eleven disciples

THE GOSPEL IN THE NEW TESTAMENT

and others, who together are the nucleus of the Christian church. They are entrusted with the task of making "disciples of all nations" (Matt. 28:19); "that repentance and forgiveness of sins should be preached in his name to all nations" (Luke 24:47). The outlook is universalistic, and even in Matthew, whose preoccupation with the narrower apocalyptic conception is very evident elsewhere, the emphasis is upon a mission that opens up ever new possibilities for the world of men. The disciples receive their commission from a Christ to whom "all authority in heaven and on earth has been given." In the Johannine narrative the risen Christ "breathes upon" the disciples as though with the same creative power that made man "a living soul" (Gen. 2:7). The church becomes the "body of Christ," the living instrument of his gospel.

The existence of the church and the dynamic power of the gospel are the real proofs of the Resurrection. Both are based upon the conviction of a continuous partnership with the risen Christ in the church's missionary task. "Go therefore and make disciples of all nations, baptizing them in the name of the Father and of the Son and of the Holy Spirit, teaching them to observe all that I have commanded you; and lo, I am with you always, even to the close of the age" (Matt. 28:19-20). This partnership is a new covenant which Christ makes with his church, the new Israel. It is of the deepest interest and importance to note that in all the Gospels the final message of Jesus to his church is not couched in the language of Jewish apocalyptic. The "close of the age" is the final victory of God. It is not suggested that the days preceding the end will be few; rather does the saying imply that they will be many, often weary, barren, and dangerous. The Johannine writer describes this partnership with the living Christ as authority to forgive sins in his name; also, as in Matthew's Gospel, to proclaim the absolute sovereignty of his moral teaching as the judge of men, and to enable them to see their lives in the light of it. "Whosoever sins ye retain, they are retained." Even the risen Christ cannot point his disciples to any foreseeable event in the future which is to be identified with the final consummation (Matt. 24:36; Mark 13:22). The church is bidden to carry on its work come what may, knowing that Christ himself is present in its midst wherever it is sent.

IV. The Gospel in Paul

In true prophetic fashion Paul claims that his message was laid upon his lips by God. "I did not receive it from man, nor was I taught it, but it came through a revelation of Jesus Christ" (Gal. 1:12); that he was chosen by God to preach the gospel, and in particular to the Gentiles. Paul sums up the whole content of his gospel as "preaching Christ" (Gal. 1:16), or "the gospel of Christ."

What relation does the gospel of Paul bear to the primitive gospel? It is frequently said that Paul has overlaid a simpler message, complicating it with his own theological speculations. Paul's letters, however, do not represent his actual preaching of the gospel, but for the most part his defense of it against attacks from opponents within the church itself, or against the influx of pagan ideas, as at Colossae. The earlier part of his apostolic mission was marked by serious and persistent opposition from a section of Jewish Christians. Their emissaries dogged his steps, created in the young Christian communities serious situations of religious confusion, and stirred up revolt against himself and his teaching. There is no sign, however, that either the primitive church in Jerusalem or his opponents ever called his Christology in question. The opposition of these Jewish Christians was first aroused by Paul's refusal to impose upon his Gentile converts acceptance of the whole system of Judaism by submission to the rite of circumcision. To these "Judaizers" Christianity appeared as an extension of Judaism. The church had taken over the Old Testament as a Christian sacred book. These men no doubt regulated their attitude toward the Jewish moral and ceremonial law by the teaching and example of Jesus. He did "not come to destroy, but to fulfil." Some light on their teaching may be found in the catena of sayings embodied in Matt. 5:17-20, which has always presented a problem to the exegete. Utterances such as vss. 18-19 may represent genuine sayings of Jesus asserting the authority of the Torah or Word of God as "one revelation the essential core of which was of permanent validity." Paul himself defends the Torah as "holy and just and good" (Rom. 7:12). "In the course of time such utterances may have lost their original settings of time and place and have grown perhaps stronger and sharper in form, to become finally the watchwords of the conservative party in the church." [24] This Judaistic movement is important, inasmuch as the often fierce controversy it aroused, for example, in the Galatian church, is, as we shall see, largely responsible for Paul's so-called "technical" theological language.

Paul himself was profoundly concerned that his gospel should not be regarded as essentially

[24] B. Harvie Branscomb, *Jesus and the Law of Moses* (New York: Richard R. Smith, 1930), p. 216. I find myself in general agreement with his treatment on pp. 207-17, 224-26.

21

a divergence from the traditional Christian message. He evidently thinks of talks with Peter and others, whose knowledge of the human ministry and teaching of Jesus was so intimate, as an important part of his preparation for his apostolic mission (Gal. 1:18-19); but he is careful to assert that he carried away with him from these talks no mere "formula" of teaching to which he pledged adherence (Gal. 2:2). The doings and sayings of Jesus of Nazareth as recorded by his disciples—"a Christ according to the flesh"—were not the only source for the content of his gospel. In a moment of impatience when the example of Jesus in his attitude toward the law was quoted against him, he exclaims, "Even if my thoughts were once absorbed in the human Christ, I think of him so no longer" (II Cor. 5:16). Theological eccentricity alone can interpret these words to mean that Paul is not interested in the events of the life of Jesus between his birth and death. Yet his gospel was essentially "a revelation" of the risen Christ. As his letters abundantly testify, the story of the human life must have been told as an integral part of his gospel, as it was of the Jerusalem gospel. Paul's refusal to impose circumcision on his Gentile converts as a token of allegiance to the law of Moses does not imply failure on his part to instruct them in its moral teaching as interpreted, selected, and deepened by Jesus in the Sermon on the Mount and elsewhere. Sufficient proof is found in Rom. 12 alone, not to speak of the other ethical exhortations at the close of his letters.

The second visit to Jerusalem, recorded in Gal. 2:1-9, reveals Paul's anxiety regarding the attitude of the original apostles toward his gospel, and his profound relief when he and Barnabas "received the right hand of fellowship" and were sent on their way to continue their apostolic mission to the Gentiles. The importance he attached to this visit is evidenced further in the statement that the visit was made by "revelation"; in other words by the direct guidance of God, from whom he had received his gospel. It was Paul's fundamental conviction that the church, "the body of Christ" and his living instrument for the propagation of the gospel, should be united in its task. Christ is not divided (I Cor. 1:13). Otherwise Paul's own apostolic mission would be futile, a "running . . . in vain" (Gal. 2:2).

The gospel of the primitive church was, like Paul's, not "man-made." The speeches in the earlier chapters of Acts represent the distillation of a rich religious tradition which had its origin partly in the finest Judaism, but chiefly in the teaching of Jesus and the deep impression which his personality made on the disciples whom he had chosen "to be with him." When Paul entered the Christian church he inherited this tradition, made it his own, interpreting and applying it in the light of his own unique experience (cf. John 14:26).

The primitive church took over the Old Testament as the Christian Bible. Paul shares with the Jerusalem apostles the conviction that the messianic age foretold by the prophets had arrived with the coming of Jesus Christ. He found in that coming the fulfillment of what he called "the promises of God" to Israel (Rom. 3:2; 9:4). These do not denote merely individual utterances, but are a name for the whole divine messianic purpose which it was given to the prophets to discern in the history of the nation. "All the promises of God find their Yes in him" (II Cor. 1:20).

Paul also shared the rabbinical doctrine that the Scriptures, comprising practically the whole of our canonical Old Testament, were verbally inspired and represented the inviolable and only divine revelation of "what man is to believe concerning God, and what duty God requires of man," a belief unchanged in Christian days. As a Christian he acknowledged the teaching of Jesus as the paramount moral authority, and also his interpretation and use of the Old Testament as a channel of communion with the mind of the Father. By his conversion Paul was delivered not from "fundamentalism" but from religious legalism. In Christian days we find him still using legalistic rabbinical methods of interpreting scripture, as a way of escape from the tyranny of the letter, as in Gal. 3:16. Another notable example —this time of allegorical interpretation, which may show the influence of Hellenistic Judaism —is the use he makes of the unsavory story of Abraham and Hagar (Gal. 4:22-31). It is, however, striking to note that Paul's treatment of the faith of Abraham in Rom. 4 comes within hail of the conclusions reached by documentary criticism in uncovering the several sources of different dates that make up the Pentateuch (Rom. 4:10). "Which things are an allegory." To adapt Cromwell's words on religious tolerance by the state—"God, in seeking men to serve him, takes no notice of their opinions."

A. Conversion of Paul. 1. Silent Preparation. —Paul himself reveals that in his earlier life he experienced a religious crisis while he was a student of the law. He began his rabbinical training at an early age. This crisis and its result he describes in Rom. 7. The prophetic books were regarded as an authoritative part of the law, indeed as an inspired commentary upon the Pentateuch, the most sacred part. The prophets preached a gospel of pardon and repentance, but what did repentance mean even

22

to the greatest of them? "Let the wicked forsake his way [conduct], and the unrighteous man his thoughts [inner motives and purposes]: and let him return unto the LORD, and he will have mercy upon him" (Isa. 55:7). Paul's words, "He is a Jew who is one inwardly," may reflect the discovery which the Pentateuch, the most sacred part of the law, brought home to him in the commandment "Thou shalt not covet." Paul interprets covetousness in the deepest inward sense as passion and desire—the "thoughts" of "the unrighteous man." In the moving autobiographical fragment preserved in Rom. 7:7-11 he discovers that he cannot control inward desires. The temptations of adolescence, the attractions of the nobler elements in the pagan society around him, pride of birth and position, may all be present to his mind. The things stripped from his life, according to Phil. 3:5-8, which he had learned to regard as well lost for "the knowledge of Christ Jesus my Lord," tell us much of what he once most coveted. The prophet's injunction to "forsake" his evil thoughts brought him no inward peace. Neither did the rabbinical exhortation to those who sought to overcome the "evil impulse" (yēçer) that they should devote themselves to all-absorbing study of the law. Instead it provoked inward rebellion, which meant a sense of spiritual separation from God and of his condemnation. That condition Paul often describes as death in life. Yet even this earlier crisis was seen through Paul's regenerate eyes as a silent preparation. He must be speaking out of his own heart when he speaks of the law as permitted by God in order to deepen the sense of sinfulness (Rom. 5:20).

This earlier crisis in Paul's religious experience cannot be dismissed as an interesting psychological phenomenon, one of the many "varieties of religious experience." It is relevant to recall a famous passage from *The Pilgrim's Progress*, which describes a

Man clothed with rags with a Book in his hand, and a great burden upon his back. I looked, and saw him open the Book and read therein; and as he read, he wept and trembled; and not being able to contain, he broke out with a lamentable cry, saying, *"What shall I do?"*

Paul's "lamentable cry" is cognate in its origin. "Wretched man that I am! Who will deliver me from this body of death?" Neither Paul's experience nor Bunyan's is the only gateway into the kingdom of God. Yet both are lonely figures who represent not only themselves but the pulse throb of the mightiest movement in history. Puritanism is not the whole of Christianity, but Paul was a Jewish Puritan. God spoke to Bunyan through Paul. Of the former a

great English historian has said: "That man, multiplied, congregated, regimented was a force of tremendous potency, to make and to destroy."[25]

2. Influence of Paul's Conversion on His Message.—Most of the distinctive forms in Paul's theology have their origin in his catastrophic conversion experience. His own native and religious personality is vigorously present in all that he writes. The phenomena described in the three conversion narratives in Acts are not our concern in this article. No doubt his converts were made familiar with the facts. Paul never directly or indirectly refers to the experience except in terms of its religious significance. "It pleased God . . . to reveal his Son to Me" (Gal. 1:15-16). By no means at once was Paul able to clarify the full significance of his encounter with the risen Jesus. At first his mind must have been cast into utter confusion. A period of reflection was needed and sought: "I went into Arabia" (Gal. 1:17).

At the moment when he encountered the risen Jesus, Paul was on a mission as a champion of the God of his fathers, to destroy the church of Christ and remove a serious peril to his ancestral faith. He was suddenly unmasked as a rebel against the eternal redemptive purpose of God. This "crucified" Christ was clearly not a Jewish messiah. The Messiah expected by Judaism was to be God's vicegerent on earth and to be everywhere triumphant. This Christ, a condemned criminal and convicted of hostility to the law, could have been raised from such a death only by the power and will of God. It is noticeable that Paul rarely uses the name Christ as a title for the Messiah. The old title becomes part of the proper name, "Jesus Christ," and is submerged in new titles, "Lord" and "Son of God."

One dominating result of the conversion experience was a fundamental revolution in his religious thinking. He was compelled to become a Christian "theologian." He had to think out anew his conception of God of whom he speaks as the "God and Father of our Lord Jesus Christ." His former conception of the crucified Jesus was completely revolutionized. The new and overwhelming sense of the gracious love of God toward a fierce enemy brought a new content into the idea of the Spirit of God. The Spirit as God in action was no longer the source of abnormal manifestations; rather that Spirit enabled him, as a child in the family of God, to say when he prayed, "Abba, Father" (Rom. 8:15). It is remarkable that in one passage, where Paul uses an impressive word (*prosagōgē*, "access"), which might mean

[25] G. M. Trevelyan, *English Social History* (London: Longmans, Green & Co., 1942), p. 234.

"audience granted by a monarch," all three conceptions, Father, Son, and Holy Spirit are used: "Through him we both [Jew and Gentile] have access by one Spirit unto the Father" (Eph. 2:18).

B. The New Relationship with God.—This "access" of which Paul speaks he describes in varying terms which may now be briefly examined. These terms—"justification," "righteousness," "adoption"—are frequently regarded as technical and peculiar to the Pauline gospel. But Paul's so-called technical terms are all vitally related to his gospel which sprang from his conversion experience. In that context alone can this vital relationship be apprehended. When he makes use of them he is speaking in the language of doxology, not of abstract theology.

One prominent term is "justification by faith." Justification in Judaism has both a legal and a religious meaning. An accused person was "justified" when the judge acquitted him. Similarly a wronged person is "justified" or vindicated by the verdict of a righteous judge (Deut. 25:1). Now Paul is speaking of the divine forgiveness. Why does he use this technical term, which seems to enclose a compassionate conception in a hard theological shell? One chief reason was that controversy with Jewish opponents and argument to meet Jewish-Christian propaganda dictated its use. Paul was charged with encouraging antinomianism by his doctrine of the free and undeserved forgiveness of God, sinning "that grace may abound" (Rom. 3:8; 6:1). In Dostoevski's novel, The Brothers Karamozov,[26] the Grand Inquisitor says to Christ:

Thou didst desire man's free love, that he should follow Thee freely, enticed and taken captive by Thee. In place of the rigid ancient law, man must hereafter with free heart decide for himself what is good and what is evil, having only Thy image before him as his guide. But didst Thou not know that he would at last reject even Thy image and Thy truth, if he is weighed down with the fearful burden of free choice?

Thus speaks again, in the same tones as Paul once heard it, the old statutory religion from which Christ had set him free.

When Paul speaks of "justification by faith," he speaks in paradox. He tells his opponents that he had been acquitted without ecclesiastical scrutiny or trial. He was "justified for nothing" by the free grace which is God's "kindness toward us in Christ Jesus" (Eph. 2:7). The paradox is even more startling when he asserts that God justifies "the ungodly," the deliberate sinner for whom the law has no forgiveness (Ps. 73:12; Rom. 4:5). Such a free gift must be accepted by a free personal response of faith and trust in the Giver. "The freedom wherewith Christ has made us free" still leaves men with the personal choice to do wrong. On justification by faith the best commentary is the parable of the prodigal son.

Another word still more fully develops the idea of justification (dikaiōsis), namely, the word "righteousness" (dikaiosunē). It is not, as with us, primarily ethical in meaning, but is religious. Paul describes the gospel as "the righteousness of God . . . revealed from heaven" (Rom. 1:18). Righteousness is not in the first instance an attribute of God, but his character revealed in action. It is said to "go forth" (Isa. 51:5). Its result is the deliverance of the nation from the oppressor. Again in Paul's paradoxical use of the word, the righteousness of God revealed in the Christian gospel does not "justify" or vindicate one who is wronged but one who is in the wrong. He is offered "sonship" without conditions, save faith and "endeavor after new obedience."[27]

Another term which Paul employs to give expression to the new Christian relationship to God is huiothesia, "adoption" (Rom. 8:15; Gal. 4:5; Eph. 1:5). The tendency in modern English translations to render this word as "sonship" is unfortunate and misses Paul's intentional emphasis that the Christian is God's "son," not by nature, but by grace. So also immortality is not ours by nature. Eternal life, a corollary of sonship (Rom. 8:38-39), is the gift of God. The idea of adoption is closely bound up with Paul's doctrine of the Spirit: "You have received the Spirit of adoption, which enables us to cry, 'Abba, Father'" (Rom. 8:15). The Christian man is a "spiritual" man (pneumatikos), as distinct from the "natural" man (psychikos); compare I Cor. 2:14-15.

The ethical implications of justification, adoption, and righteousness are fully developed in Paul's use of the words "sanctification" and "saint." The saint is one who is holy and belongs to God. The justified or "righted" man, by virtue of the divine righteousness that has redeemed him, is committed to moral obedience. "Sonship" conferred is both a pledge and an inspiration of moral loyalty. Sanctification is the work of the Spirit in the believer enabling him to persevere in the building up of character by faith in the forgiving love of God and prayer for his succor (Rom. 8:26-27). The first thing to do with faith is to live by it (Gal. 2:20). Sanctification is the unwearied initiative of God

---

[26] Tr. Constance Garnett (London: William Heinemann, 1928), Bk. V, ch. 5, pp. 268-69.

[27] James Moffatt, Grace in the New Testament (New York: Ray Long & Richard R. Smith, 1932), pp. 209-16.

enabling us to become what we already are, "sons of God." It is implied in the words of Jesus, "Be ye therefore perfect, even as your Father which is in heaven is perfect."

Christian conduct is not the free enterprise of the individual Christian. There is no such figure as a solitary Christian in the New Testament. Often Paul recalls his readers to the thought that together they consitute the Christian church. "Saints" is always found in the plural. They represent the "body" of Christ and its members severally (Rom. 12:4-5). As regards the sacraments, while Paul does not minimize the ritual value of baptism and the Lord's Supper, his references to them are chiefly concerned with their inwardness.[28] They both witness before the world and also within the church itself to the spirit of mutual service in obedience to Christ who "took upon him the form of a servant" (Phil. 2:7; Rom. 6:3; I Cor. 10:17; 11:17-26). As the brain controls the limbs, so Christ is the "head" of the body, the church. Baptism presupposes faith and its public expression in the catechumen's vow, "Jesus is Lord" (I Cor. 12:3). It derives its meaning only from the gospel (I Cor. 1:17). In other words the sacraments are silent gospels. Paul's doctrine of the church will be treated fully elsewhere. The "ecumenical" or international character of the church is expressed in Paul's sense of mission to the Gentile world.

C. The Crucified Redeemer.—A religion based on the idea of a crucified Messiah, then proclaimed and worshiped as the Son of God, was in the later stages of Paul's Jewish career the deepest motive of his persecuting zeal. His whole being as Jewish patriot and worshiper of the God of his fathers shrank from the blasphemous doctrine. Then came the great and sudden change. What he once loathed as a "scandal" was transformed into an object of adoring wonder and love toward "Jesus Christ my Lord." It is therefore intelligible that this inward transformation which penetrated every fiber of Paul's personality should result in his setting the Cross in the very center of his message. It is possible that in the minds of the original apostles there were reasons for a certain reserve in speaking of the Crucifixion. All that happened must have made a deep impression upon them, but this included, as the passion story in all the Gospels shows, the treachery of Judas, Peter's denial, and the action of the rest who "all forsook him and fled." That story

was constructed most probably for use in worship and for the instruction of catechumens.[29] Paul and the primitive church, however, are one in preaching that "Christ died for our sins according to the scriptures" (I Cor. 15:3).

Paul has no systematic doctrine of the Cross, but certain central ideas emerge. He is convinced that Jesus died for sins not his own. The sinlessness of Jesus is with Paul, as with the earlier preachers, an axiom. The action of God in the Resurrection made any other supposition impossible. That mighty act of God— to Paul the mightiest of all his acts—was God's own final verdict upon the character and career of his Son. In Rom. 1:4 the "Spirit of holiness" was the integrating element in the personality of Jesus, and at the Resurrection he was "installed" as the Son of God "in power." The suffering and shameful death were vicarious. Paul, like the primitive apostles, evidently derives his thought from Isa. 53:6, "The LORD hath laid on him the iniquity of us all." That the sufferings of the righteous could atone for the sins of the nation was a conception present in contemporary Judaism (IV Macc. 17:22). The idea, however, like that of the atoning value of blood in sacrifice, is ultimately unanalyzed, and indeed unanalyzable.

Vicarious suffering freely endured is always substitutionary in character, but the concept of substitution must be rescued from the language of human jurisprudence. This accomplished, voluntary substitution becomes the motive of wonder and gratitude. Human suffering of this kind provides often a moving if fainter illustration. The innocent mother gifted by God with a pure and invincible love for her erring child does not cry out to God against a gift that makes her so sensitive to the wrongdoing. She feels it with a shame and poignancy which even the wrongdoer does not have, "bearing it out even to the edge of doom." She lovingly and instinctively accepts for herself the verdict to whose voice her child is deaf, but which, seen as voluntarily borne on her own heart, has redemptive power.[30] For Paul the sinless suffering love of Christ and the love of God are one (Rom. 5:8; 8:35-39).

The only utterance of Paul that might rightfully be interpreted as suggesting a penal view of the Atonement is to be found in Gal. 3:13: "Christ redeemed us from the curse of the law, having become a curse for us." This is one of Paul's obiter dicta which cannot be understood outside the limits of his own experience and his conception of the Scriptures as the verbally in-

---

[28] See H. A. A. Kennedy, *St. Paul and the Mystery Religions* (London: Hodder & Stoughton, n.d.), p. 270; *The Theology of the Epistles* (New York: Charles Scribner's Sons, 1920), pp. 147-52, where the suggested influence of the Hellenistic mystery religions on Paul's sacramental doctrine is discussed.

[29] Vincent Taylor, *Formation of the Gospel Tradition,* pp. 44-59.

[30] Compare R. C. Moberly, *Atonement and Personality* (New York: Longmans, Green & Co., 1902), pp. 81-82.

spired word of God. It is rabbinical in form. He reads in the law the curse pronounced upon the willful transgressor. Alongside it he puts another word of God which speaks of the curse that rests on the head of the criminal "hanged upon a tree," in which he sees a prophetic anticipation of the crucified Jesus. Does he also recall the cry of dereliction on the Cross?

Paul, in spite of the many-sided aspects of his doctrine of the Cross, may be said to have one governing idea—reconciliation. In that word the dominating motive of the divine redemptive activity is expressed. "God was [engaged] in Christ reconciling the world to himself" (II Cor. 5:19). Paul sees in the death and resurrection of Jesus the way in which God has appointed that we should "receive our reconciliation" (Rom. 5:10-11). Discussion as to whether God or only men need reconciliation is largely abstract. Estrangement from God must be much more than a tragic misunderstanding on the part of man. To limit the estrangement in such a way "leaves us in the dark as to how far it would really matter if this misunderstanding were not cleared up." [31]

In Paul's view the reaction in the heart of God toward blind and unrepentant humanity is described as "the wrath of God" (Rom. 1:18-32). The false impression that the term stands for an anthropopathic mood of resentment is fostered by the English translation "anger." But the idea that the wrath of God is equivalent to leaving the sinner to suffer the moral and spiritual consequences of flouting the moral and spiritual order does not meet the difficulty. Paul's own words spoken of the Gentile world, which has a "law written on its heart" by God himself—"God gave them up to dishonorable passions" (Rom. 1:26); "God gave them up to a base mind and to improper conduct" (Rom. 1:28)—raise the whole problem of the divine permission of evil. Pauline language and indeed biblical language ("the Lord hardened Pharaoh's heart") is the Jewish way of seeing the cause in the effect of willful separation from God. Underlying is the profound conviction that God is still in complete control of all that happens. Moral consequences are not automatically set in motion. Both the redemptive activity of God, the "gospel," and also the wrath of God, are said to be "revealed." In other words the latter too is a redemptive activity of God. The divine wrath is the symptom on earth of God's essential incapacity to let evil alone. [32]

Paul regards the Cross as a revelation of

[31] Emil Brunner, *The Mediator*, tr. Olive Wyon (London: Lutterworth Press, 1934), p. 489.
[32] See H. R. Mackintosh, *The Christian Experience of Forgiveness* (London: Nisbet & Co., 1927), p. 210.

God which, in Denney's words, makes redemption "not possible but credible." We "receive the reconciliation" (Rom. 5:11 ERV) at the cost of the sacrificial life and death of the Son of God. It is also the revelation of the sacrificial love of the Father (Rom. 5:8). His wrath and his love are alike the word that does "not return unto [him] void." If we pass from the stern words of Paul to the lament of Jesus over Jerusalem, we do not escape from the dark atmosphere of doom. His own rejection means judgment on the nation. The passionate love which breathes in the words of our Lord makes even the message of doom upon *his* lips "pure, sublime, and redemptive." It is still a message of invitation, "How often would I have gathered thy children together!"

D. The New Creation.—"If any one is in Christ, there is a new creation" (II Cor. 5:17). The idea of the "new creation" pervades Paul's message, and within it is contained the whole of Paul's "eschatology." This term has been so far as possible avoided in this article. It is an uncouth word and only with difficulty can be baptized into modern Christian usage. Eschatology is the doctrine of "the last things," of what happens on the day this world shall have an end. The lurid conceptions found in Jewish apocalyptic writings, even if some have passed over into a Christian writing such as the book of Revelation, are remarkably absent both from the teaching of Jesus and from Paul's writings. In Jewish apocalyptic writings the "day of the Lord" is often accompanied by the destruction of the present world and the creation of the new world. Paul's conception of the "end" is as little entangled with the thought of such physical catastrophe as Peter's is when, after Pentecost, he quotes the whole prophetic passage describing the "signs and wonders" of the closing days, applying it to the present world or "age." The "end" is essentially a religious conception. It stands above all for the fulfillment of the eternal purpose of God, as against any view of history as purposeless, whether it is the idea that things are so constructed that they will ultimately come right of themselves, or doctrines of despair that underlie many forms of Second Adventism. In the New Testament, and particularly in the Pauline thought, the central idea is the conviction that the "end" conceived as the ultimate and final victory of God over the world has already come with the "advent" of Jesus of Nazareth. The governing conception is that of the kingdom of God in the teaching of Jesus. Even the Johannine writer, with his conception of the person of Jesus as the "Word made flesh," the "bread of life," and the Son of God with a present power of executing judgment, retains his belief in a future final judgment by the "Son of man" (John 5:28-29).

Paul rarely uses the term "kingdom of God," probably because it would be largely unintelligible to Gentile readers. Other ways of expressing the conception can be found everywhere in his letters. "Eternal life" is the commonest. Among other equivalents I would place the expression "in Christ." A "man in Christ" is a Christian man, with a particular emphasis on his experience of the *present* action of the Spirit—the Spirit of "sonship"—in his heart. The man in Christ is the man who in his life here below ("in the flesh") really lives in a new world which God has created (II Cor. 5:17). He is already a "citizen of heaven" (Phil 3:20 ERV). We might best express this spiritual conception as living in and under a new "regime," where our ultimate allegiance is given to the risen and exalted Christ as "Lord."

It is in this context that we can most clearly discern the content of Paul's favorite title for the risen Christ as "Lord." Phil. 2:3-11, lyric in its tone, is not an abstract christological disquisition, but has as its central motif the completely self-effacing divine love manifested in the life and death of Jesus, as the ethical reference in vs. 3 shows. The whole passage, of course, assumes Paul's doctrine of the pre-existence of Christ, which is a deduction in his mind from the facts of his resurrection and exaltation, "the pendant and complement of the Resurrection," as A. B. Bruce says. In the meantime our purpose is to emphasize that this self-effacing of the eternal Son is owned by God as his own love in action. There is therefore conferred upon the risen Christ—*in the experience of men*—the divine name of "Lord." That "lordship" is exercised over both men and the universe, "all things." Of the latter I shall speak presently. Even Christ cannot attain lordship over human hearts just by stretching out his hand to "grasp" it (Phil. 2:6). Lordship is "equality" of sway with God in human experience and can be won only by a free human response. It could be achieved only by a divine being who "dispossessed himself," or to use Ronald Knox's translation, "humbled himself," became man, "took upon himself the form of a servant," endured a shameful death. This is a "revelation" in the personality of Jesus of the redeeming love of God. In the end it is God who acknowledged and conferred upon him his own name, "Lord" (*Kyrios*), used in the worship of Paul's ancestral religion, as he also created the new experience of men.[33]

"In Christ" is often regarded as an example of what is called Paul's "Christ-mysticism." If by the term is meant that ultimate sense of the presence of Christ in and with the individual soul, "*Jesu dulcis memoria*," so finely expressed by Bernard of Clairvaux and translated by Carswall in the hymn "Jesus, the very thought of thee"—if this is meant, Paul's own outbursts of adoration and praise are classical examples and the continual inspiration of the believer. It takes more than scholarship to understand them.[34] There is, however, no trace in Paul's language of the traditional "mystic" absorption of the personality in God or in Christ. "In Christ" is really equivalent to being "in the Spirit," or even in the church as a member of the body of Christ.

In the words quoted at the beginning of this section the "man in Christ" already lives in the environment of "a new creation," a new "universe." Paul's universe was conceived as a system of personal agencies, practically the demon world of the Gospels, a conception on which the Sadducee looked down as popular superstition. It is often felt to be a real problem that the human ministry and teaching of Jesus, and a great deal of the teaching of the New Testament, should assume this conception of the universe.

The modern scientist records objectively and in certain formulas the ways in which he sees nature behaving. But the modern man, like the ancient, keeps records in his heart of the ways in which he sees "nature" behaving toward himself and his fellow men. "Tribulation, or distress, or persecution, or famine, or nakedness, or peril, or sword" still reach him out of a mysterious region of existence where there seem to him to be no obvious signs of a supreme controlling and trustworthy power. The demon world with its incalculable and ineluctable agencies is still with us. At least such is the impression we receive as we hear men speak and overhear their thoughts about war, poverty, unemployment, sickness, or economic tryranny, as though these were inevitable and heedless natural forces.

Paul's conception of the risen Christ as "Lord" of the universe has its own deep relevance today. It is also an integral part of his message. Paul finds it impossible to have Jesus Christ as Lord of his own life, and at the same time leave him out of the universe. With an intellectual daring that has no parallel, he conceives the risen Christ as Lord, moving to victory over the "principalities and powers," the spiritual "rulers of this world," even those who inspired the hearts of men to crucify him (Phil. 2:9; I Cor. 2:8). In one passage Paul con-

[33] See the exposition of the passage by H. A. A. Kennedy, *The Expositor's Greek Testament* (New York: Dodd, Mead & Co., 1897), III, 432-39.

[34] See J. Weiss, *History of Primitive Christianity*, I, 40-43; II, 463-71.

ceives the Cross as a Homeric contest between Christ and these spiritual agencies, as a result of which Christ sets men free from their sway. Yet he thinks of Christ as still carrying on a work of reconciliation even among them (Col. 1:17-20; 2:15). Readers may like to be reminded of words that are set in the mouth of one of the characters in Arthur Quiller Couch's *Hetty Wesley:*

I see now that if God's love reaches up to every star and down to every poor soul on earth, it must be something vastly simple, so simple that all dwellers on earth may be assured of it, as all who have eyes may be assured of the planet yonder; and so vast that all bargaining is below it, and they may inherit it without considering their deserts.[35]

We should note that the faith that Christ is Lord of the universe is set side by side with the faith of the individual believer that he is also "our Lord," or as Paul characteristically sometimes says, "Christ Jesus my Lord." Paul does not promise his readers exemption from hardships, pain, sickness, or death, but he does assert that nothing can "separate us from the love of Christ." Also Paul's message of Christ in the universe as Lord, as he is "our Lord," means that the Christian man and the Christian church hold the key of the future fate of "civilization." In one remarkable passage he says, "The creation waits with eager longing for the revealing of the sons of God" (Rom. 8:19); "The whole creation has been groaning in travail together until now" (Rom. 8:22). Paul is able to express his whole "eschatological" hope, both in the present and in the future, in single words. One instance is his use of "now" (νῦν), in the passage just quoted, as marking the dawn of the "new creation." The other instance is that single word ἐγήγερται, translated "he [Christ] hath been raised." This single word is used seven times and sounds like the stroke of a bell throughout the whole of I Cor. 15:4-20. Paul uses what the grammarians call a "monumental perfect," denoting a fact, in this case an act of God, which is massive and permanent. The word proclaims that Christ is alive and reigns; "reigns," as Calvin once said, "more for us than for himself."

Paul's conception of Christ in the universe is profoundly religious, and is true apart from any scientific conceptions, ancient or modern. It has relevance for us at one point, at least, far beyond Paul's own horizon. The universe has been yielding up to men the secrets of its vast hidden forces. The faith that Jesus is Lord in the heart of man and also in the universe

that environs him means that all new discoveries must be used according to the will of God and the spirit and teaching of Jesus. These newly found secrets are not wrested from an unwilling God, and their discovery penalized as in the ancient myth of Prometheus and the stealing of the sacred fire. Paul has summed up in a single verse his whole philosophy of the "man in Christ" in relation to the cosmos in the words: "We know that in everything God works for good with those who love him, who are called according to his purpose" (Rom. 8:28).

V. The Gospel in the Johannine Writings

This article, within the limits set for it, cannot deal even summarily with all the contents of the New Testament. It was both appropriate and necessary that we should give largest attention to the most primitive period when the essential character of the gospel message and the essential lines of its development were being decisively determined. It would have been possible to discover the main outlines of the primitive gospel within the theological scheme of later books such as Hebrews, I Peter, Revelation, and the Pastoral epistles, and the particular occasions that first called them forth. It would also have been unnecessary, in view of the fact that readers of this work will find discussions of the theology of these books in subsequent volumes, where it will be apparent that the theology is rooted in the experience created by the preaching of the apostolic gospel.

We may, however, note that particularly in two of these books, Hebrews and I Peter, a remarkable prominence is given to the human life and teaching of Jesus of Nazareth and the significance of his personality. To these belong a revelational value as the historical origin of the Christian gospel. In the New Testament everywhere we hear a sound far clearer and more pervasive than "a whisper of his voice," and our eyes can penetrate farther than "the outskirts of his ways." [36] The writer to the Hebrews says that the gospel of "such a great salvation . . . was declared at first by the Lord" (Heb. 2:3). The sufferings and temptations of Jesus, of which he speaks so realistically (Heb. 2:18; 5:7; 12:2), qualify him for his office of eternal priesthood, a doctrine which is the center of his evangel (Heb. 4:14–5:10). I Peter is full of references to the teaching of Jesus. His bearing at his trial is at the heart of the message the writer seeks to convey to his readers called to pass through the "fiery ordeal" of persecution (I Pet. 2:21-23).

---

[35] *Hetty Wesley* (London: J. M. Dent & Sons, 1931), p. 260.

[36] R. H. Lightfoot, *History and Interpretation in the Gospels* (New York: Harper & Bros., 1935), p. 225.

Something, however, needs to be said about the gospel of the Johannine writer by way of supplement to our earlier section on "The Gospel in the Gospels." His theological interpretation of the person of Jesus is vitally related to the experience of the original disciples. "The Word became flesh and dwelt among us, full of grace and truth" (John 1:14). The testimony of the immediate disciples lies at the center of that "visible gospel" which the Johannine writer preaches in the name of the Christian church of which he is a mandatary (I John 1:1-4).

The Fourth Gospel is here assumed not to be the work of the apostle John. The anonymous writer is much more an original author than any of the other evangelists. These are for the most part editors of the traditional material available to them. In the Fourth Gospel the personality of the writer pervades the whole work. The diction and style are practically the same as those of the First Epistle of John, which is here assumed as the work of the same author. The utterances of the principal characters are cast in the same mold; Jesus, the Evangelist, and the Baptist all make use of the same Johannine idiom of thought and phraseology. It would be generally admitted that the long discourses of Jesus in the Gospel are interpretations of the mind of Jesus based on his recorded sayings. They represent his "word" rather than his words.

This personal note is due to profound religious reflection on the Christian tradition of the sayings and doings of Jesus. The author's reflections and interpretations are, however, not uncontrolled. The artistry of the story of the woman at the well, the dramatic power revealed in the Lazarus story which culminates in the strangely fantastic scene of the raising from the dead, and the pathos and beauty of the resurrection appearance to Mary in the garden are all spontaneous expressions of what he himself would regard as the work of the Spirit of truth in his own soul. The promise of Jesus is being fulfilled: "I have yet many things to say to you, but you cannot bear them now. When the Spirit of truth comes, he will guide you into all the truth; for he will not speak on his own authority, but whatever he hears he will speak, and he will declare to you the things that are to come. He will glorify me, for he will take what is mine and declare it to you" (John 16:12-14). Not only the words of Jesus but features of the narrative itself are found yielding up to his mind meanings other than factual, as, for example, the story of the spear thrust at the Cross, or the fact that the body of Jesus did not suffer the brutal *crucifragium* (John 19:33-37). The evangelist's governing conception is that both the traditional narrative and the traditional sayings of Jesus—his *ipsissima verba*—have a hidden symbolical meaning which is the meaning that God *intended* them to have. We have a striking example of this symbolical meaning in the interpretation given to the cynical words of Caiaphas, "It is expedient for you that one man should die for the people" (John 11:49-52). These words are transposed into an expression of the divine redemptive purpose in the death of Jesus. The spirit of prophecy falls even upon the sinister figure of Caiaphas, the high priest, who becomes, all unwittingly, the priest, speaking "not of himself," who presides at the sacrifice of "the Lamb of God, which taketh away the sin of the world." [37]

The Johannine writer gives us an estimate of his own work and a statement of his intention in writing: "These [things] are written that you may believe that Jesus is the Christ, the Son of God, and that believing you may have life in his name" (John 20:31). These are the words of a man who thinks of himself primarily as a preacher of the gospel, whose aim is to secure a response of faith or to deepen and strengthen a faith that already exists.

The evangelist's own summary of the gospel has become the classical statement of it: "God so loved the world that he gave his only Son, that whoever believes in him should not perish but have eternal life" (John 3:16). His central theme is the gospel of the Incarnation. For this evangelist the Incarnation is not a theological proposition which requires theological science in order to understand it; it is the love of God in action, a love to be measured not in abstract theological terms but by the observed—"which we have seen with our eyes" (I John 1:1)—and recorded fact of Jesus Christ. The magnitude of the divine love is estimated by the magnitude of the greatest divine *event* in history, the mightiest of all God's mighty acts of love and power, the complete revelation of himself: "He that hath seen me hath seen the Father" (John 14:9). The doctrine of the Incarnation is expressed in the untheological language of Christian experience. Those who heard Jesus speak and saw him at work have heard the Father's words and have seen God at work. This firsthand experience the evangelist had made his own: "The words that I say to you I do not speak on my own authority; but the Father who dwells in me does his works" (John 14:10). Both Jesus' words and his works are revelations of the love and power of God.

[37] See further, R. H. Strachan, *The Fourth Gospel*, 3rd ed. (London: Student Christian Movement Press, 1941), pp. 34 ff.; also the Exeg. of the Gospel of John, *ad loc.*, Vol. VIII of this work.

It is significant, however, that the Fourth Evangelist, in a narrative where most of the works of Jesus are miracles and which contains the stupendous miracle of the raising of Lazarus, does not describe these as "mighty deeds" (*dynameis*) as Mark does, but as "signs" (*sēmeia*), visible tokens of the active presence and power of God. This operative presence of God was akin to the "good news" proclaimed by the great prophet of the Exile: "Say unto the cities of Judah, Behold your God!" In the Fourth Gospel this good news is the gospel of the Incarnation, the "Word made flesh." In these terms the evangelist also proclaims, "Behold your God!" The speaker is both revealer and revelation. It is evident that in spite of all the heightening of effects in the Johannine miracles, the evangelist does not record them with the intention of enhancing the reputation or advertising the authority of Jesus. They are, as in the Synoptic Gospels, an integral part of the gospel of the kingdom of God which he proclaims.

It would be possible to indicate that the Johannine gospel conforms at every essential point to the pattern of the primitive gospel. We shall note, however, only certain modifications and interpretations of it which are peculiarly Johannine. The chief modifications of the original Gospel are to be found (*a*) in the Logos doctrine; (*b*) in the evangelist's insistence not only that the Christian gospel took its rise in the person, ministry, and teaching of Jesus Christ (Acts 10:36-38), but also, and more particularly, that the humanity of Jesus was real and true.

(*a*) The term Logos in this Gospel, on which so much has been written, is really a translation of the Hebrew *dābhār,* the "word" of God, which in the prophetic meaning bears within itself a power of fulfillment extending far beyond the range of the personality of the prophet himself. So far the Johannine Logos Christ is the fulfillment of the proclamation of the "day of the Lord" in the prophetic writings. The Johannine conception, however, assumes that the divine Word in Gen. 1, which brought order out of chaos and light out of darkness, is also a prophetic conception. In this view the writer is confirmed by modern scholarship. The conception of the Word in Genesis and of its activity is the same as that in the magnificent description of the creative power and sustaining providence of Yahweh in Isa. 40:12-27.

In the Johannine thought this semipersonified creative Word is actually personalized in the advent and ministry of the historical Jesus. It involves the theological doctrine of the preexistence of Christ, which is also an element in the Pauline thought. It is, however, not an integral element in the Johannine gospel. It occupies the same place and serves the same subordinate purpose as the doctrine of the Virgin Birth, which appears in Matthew and Luke, but is absent in Paul and in John. Both doctrines are pendants of the primitive gospel of the exalted Christ. They are theological interpretations deduced from the place which the exalted Jesus already has in the faith and worship of the church. The evangelist has no intention of associating the Logos with the functions ascribed to it in contemporary Hellenistic thought. He knows the name, but the content of the term is Hebraic.

This identification of Jesus with the eternal creative word of God has the same origin as the motive that compelled Paul to speak of the gospel that was born in his heart and laid on his lips when he encountered the risen Christ on the Damascus road, as the manifestation of the eternal creative power. In a less catastrophic fashion than Paul the Fourth Evangelist had also experienced Christ in such a way that in his own mind and soul light shone in darkness, and order took the place of chaos. Like Paul he could not have such a Christ in his heart and keep him out of the world in which he lived. His whole environment had to be rethought and brought into relationship with the overwhelming love which had sought and found him. "The Word became flesh and dwelt among us, full of grace and truth; . . . and from his fullness have we all received, grace upon grace" (John 1:14-16). Here we have a more restrained equivalent of Paul's lyric utterance in Rom. 8:31-39. The love or "grace" that both encountered was a divine love that humbled itself and "dwelt among us" as a man among men.

b) The Fourth Evangelist, in agreement with the primitive evangel, proclaims that the good news had its origin in a real human personality. "The Word became flesh." He makes a certain modification in the original gospel, stressing everywhere the humanity, inasmuch as he seeks, as it were, to bring it up to date. The doctrine of the truly human personality of Jesus was endangered by incipient Gnostic teaching within the church itself, which held that matter was essentially evil, and therefore that the body of Jesus could not have been a real human body of flesh and blood, subject to all the weakness and limitation of human existence. In the First Epistle of John a stern polemic is carried on against such teaching, which destroyed the historical basis and with it the whole fabric of the Christian faith, the truth and life conveyed by the gospel. The heretical doctrine is denounced as "Antichrist."

This evangelist allows certain human traits to appear in his portrait of Jesus. At the well of

Sychar he sits wearied and thirsty (John 4:6).
He wept at the grave of Lazarus (John 11:35).
These indications of true humanity, however,
are not so important for the author's purpose as
the emphasis which he continually lays on the
inward human dependence of Jesus upon God;
on what in theological language is called his
"subordination" to God the Father. We have already met this in his interpretation of the
miracles. "The Son can do nothing of himself, but what he seeth the Father do" (John
5:19). Again and again in this Gospel, always
on the lips of Jesus himself, this sense of
humble inward dependence on the will of the
Father is disclosed. This self-disclosure by Jesus
of a personal religious experience of his own,
in which his unique filial consciousness was
maintained and realized through human channels of faith and prayer, is the best commentary
upon such Synoptic sayings as "Why callest
thou me good? None is good, save one, that is,
God," or "I am meek and lowly in heart."
Jesus lays down his life voluntarily, but the
manner and the moment are controlled by the
Father who alone determines "the hour" (John
10:18; 13:1).

Thus the Fourth Evangelist presents the filial
consciousness of Jesus unique and unbroken as
it is, not as a theological doctrine, but so as to
make it an integral part of the Christian
gospel. The self-revelation of Jesus in the
Fourth Gospel is lifted out of the region of
abstract theological interpretation and becomes
the historical source of the message of good
news. This same human experience of God
speaks in the prayer that the disciples "may
have my joy fulfilled in themselves" (John
17:13), and in the words "My peace I give unto
you" (John 14:27). The "I am" sayings so
characteristic of this Gospel—"I am the bread of
life"; "I am the light of the world"; "I am the
door"; "I am the good shepherd"; "I am the
way, the truth, and the life"; "I am the resurrection and the life" [38]—cease to appear as
theological dogmas set on the lips of Jesus of
Nazareth; they are all divine answers to human
need and also gospel invitations born in the
soul of him of whom it is said in the primitive
gospel that "God was with him" (Acts 10:38).
They are indeed the "language of divinity" as
it is heard in the "Word" of the Old Testament
prophet; but they are also the language of one
in whom God humbled himself to share men's
needs and carry their sorrows. They appeal to
the hearts of all who know what it means to
hunger and thirst in their souls, to walk in the
dark, to be outside, wandering, and subject to
the fear of death. These utterances belong to
the *euangelion* of the church, and are securely
based on the life and mind of the historical
Jesus.

VI. Selected Bibliography

BRUNNER, EMIL. *The Divine Imperative,* tr. Olive
Wyon. New York: The Macmillan Co., 1937.
DENNEY, JAMES. *Jesus and the Gospel.* New York:
A. C. Armstrong & Sons, 1909.
DODD, C. H. *The Apostolic Preaching and Its Devel-
opments.* London: Hodder & Stoughton, 1936.
FEINE, PAUL. *Theologie des Neuen Testaments.* 4th
ed. Leipzig: J. C. Hinrichs, 1922.
HOWARD, WILBERT F. *Christianity According to St.
John.* London: Duckworth, 1943.
KENNEDY, H. A. A. *The Theology of the Epistles.*
New York: Charles Scribner's Sons, 1920.
LINDSAY, A. D. *The Moral Teaching of Jesus.* Lon-
don: Hodder & Stoughton, 1937.
MANSON, T. W. *The Teaching of Jesus.* Cambridge:
University Press, 1931.

[38] These sayings are not so purely Johannine as is
usually assumed. They have parallels in the Synoptic
Gospels. See W. F. Howard, *Christianity According to St.
John,* pp. 68-69, and the same author's commentary in
Vol. VIII of this work.

THE NEW TESTAMENT AND
EARLY CHRISTIAN LITERATURE

by Henry J. Cadbury

The New Testament is a collection of some twenty-seven early Christian writings. This collection has been separately treated since the third or fourth century, but in reality it is only a fragment of a larger and more varied amount of material that sundry Christians of the early days put in written form. Much of this other material has been lost. Some is preserved in later writings that made use of it as sources or quoted excerpts from it. Some is included in collections like the Apostolic Fathers or the Apologists. Other uncanonical Christian writings appear in the New Testament Apocrypha, in some cases having become available only through recent discovery. The New Testament writings, even when isolated for special study as in the present commentary, belong historically in the wider setting of the whole of early Christian writings and in the still more varied gamut of the writings of all sorts and conditions of men in the early Roman Empire. This setting needs to be kept in mind.

We have no way of knowing the full extent of writing in the early church. General considerations suggest that it was quite limited. The Jewish rabbis with whom Jesus had much in common depended on oral teaching. The books they knew and handled were not contemporary writings but the older Jewish Scriptures. The early Christian mission was also by word of mouth. Sermons were neither written in advance nor taken down in writing. There was little cultural ambition among the first believers that would impel them to aspire to produce literature in the sense of belles-lettres. This lack of ambition was not due to illiteracy,

however. In spite of the scorn of enemies (John 7:15; Acts 4:13), Jesus and his disciples could write as well as read (John 8:6, 8; Acts 15:23). Indeed it is quite probable that in the bilingual country of Palestine they could use two languages, Greek and Aramaic, just as could Paul, who wrote in the former language but could speak in either (Acts 21:37; 22:2).

No early Christian writings in Aramaic have come down to us and we have no certain evidence that any such existed. Papias declares that Matthew wrote the Lord's oracles (logia) in Hebrew and that they were subsequently translated, and that Mark had been the interpreter of Peter.[1] Perhaps in the case of Matthew he was thinking of a translation from classical Hebrew into Greek, and in the case of Mark from Aramaic into Latin, but he may have had in mind in both instances translations from Aramaic into Greek. It is almost certain that much of Jesus' teaching was delivered and first transmitted in Aramaic, and the hypothesis that behind whole sections of the New Testament Aramaic writings existed which have been simply translated into Greek is obviously one that cannot be dismissed as impossible, even though extended discussion has not commended it to a majority of competent scholars.[2]

However this may be, the fact remains that

[1] Eusebius *Church History* III. 39. 15, 16.
[2] On this hypothesis see the writings of Charles C. Torrey, *The Four Gospels,* 1933 (2nd ed., 1947); *Our Translated Gospels,* 1936; *Documents of the Primitive Church,* 1941; all published in New York by Harper & Bros.; and *The Composition and Date of Acts* (Cambridge: Harvard University Press, 1916). See also pp. 67-68 in this volume.

the extant Christian writings come to us first in Greek. Some were early translated into Latin, into Syriac (a Semitic language akin to Aramaic), and into the languages of Egypt. Original Christian writings in both Latin and Syriac date from as early as A.D. 200. This article is limited to the prior period and hence to Greek writings.

I. Motives for Writing

The motives for committing thoughts to writing must have been much the same inside Christianity as outside it. Most obvious is the motive of the letter—the desire of persons, so separated by space that they cannot converse, to communicate with one another by messenger. Travel in the eastern Mediterranean lands in the first century was comparatively simple and frequent. Special carriers could be sent to distant friends; or more often persons could be found who were planning to travel to the area where one wished to send a message. The letters of Paul and Ignatius and Polycarp were thus sent. Imprisonment, distance, or preoccupation elsewhere prevented the more natural and satisfactory alternative of conversation face to face.

Another service of the written form was its capacity for multiplication. It could be passed on from one reader or community to another and did not require that all for whom it was intended should be congregated at one place at one time. Such circulation of letters is contemplated in Acts 15:23 and Col. 4:16. Evidently it often took place with writings which originally had not been intended for circulation. The original autograph would be copied as well as forwarded. It may be doubted whether the authors of the New Testament writings provided in the first instance more than a single copy. Appreciative readers attended to the multiplication of copies.

Another motive for the use of writing was the preservation of record. Outside of Christianity this is well illustrated by the enormous use made of documents, as we now know from the papyri of Egypt, in government, law, and business. Receipts, certificates of birth or marriage, government orders, business contracts, and many other records supplied archival evidence to which appeal could be made in case of doubt or dispute. While the New Testament refers to such documents or implies their existence—now a bill of divorce (Mark 10:4), now a bond of indebtedness (Luke 16:6, 7; Col. 2:14), now a census list (Luke 2:1-3) or a roll of citizens (Acts 22:25-28; Rev. 13:8) — the motive for the production of its own books of record seems to lie primarily in what we should call an interest in history.

About half of the New Testament—the five books of the four evangelists—appears at least on the surface to belong to this category. Unfortunately few similar narrative Christian books are preserved outside the New Testament, and practically nothing of the sort dealing with the period after the close of Acts. The uncanonical gospels and acts are of the same narrative type as the canonical, but they add little information—at least little that can be trusted. None of these books in the New Testament is to be regarded as written quite with the purpose of sheer history, though for many centuries they have served that purpose to a grateful posterity. They were written for contemporary readers and for contemporary use. Much of the material that they contain had already been selected and shaped for the practical use of Christian preaching or edification. Certainly many of the first readers and writers fully expected the almost immediate return of the Lord, when records of his first appearance would be of little interest or value. These homely memoranda meanwhile were useful for reminder, for instruction, for defense against false insinuations. The work of Luke-Acts, though it has some external likeness to secular history, is both in the material that it uses and in the author's immediate intention some removes from a purely objective history. It and the other Gospels, even those which do not state their purpose as clearly as is done in Luke 1:1-4 and John 20:30-31, are to be understood as not dissimilar in aim from the works of missionaries and preachers that have come down to us from the same period. This is well illustrated by a comparison of the Gospel of John and the First Epistle of John.

Just as apparent history had a contemporary purpose, so did the writing of apparent prophecy. The Revelation of John is only one representative of books that were written in this vein. The written form not only facilitated circulation, it also made possible the claim of antiquity; and even where no such claim was advanced, as it was in the pseudonymous Jewish apocalypses, the command to write remains (Rev. 1:19). Other early Christian teachers, when they wished to claim for themselves another's authority, naturally put their own views in writing under the other's name. Examples of assumed names are admittedly found outside the New Testament, whatever one's opinion may be as to their possible occurrence within the canon.

II. Materials and Methods

The Christian writers shared the materials and methods of contemporary writers, and were somewhat influenced by extant forms. The almost universal writing material was papyrus, derived from the pith of a plant grown in Egypt. This pith was sliced thin, and strips running one way were pasted to strips running at right angles to form a mat or sheet. These sheets were glued to each other end to end to form a roll or scroll, and on this scroll the writing was done in successive columns. While the length of the scroll and the width of the columns varied, there were conventional or habitual limits. The amount of space for text usual in a single roll was hence an invitation to add extra pieces, if one work did not fill a scroll, and also it was a measure which a single work would not exceed without being divided into volumes. The two halves of Luke-Acts and the Gospel of Matthew are three books of almost identical length and may represent a standard maximum of the first century.

Quite early in Christian history, and earlier among Christian writings than with any non-Christian writings that we yet know of, another arrangement of papyrus leaves was used. This is the codex, which is one or more quires of sheets folded in the middle inside each other, much as in the modern printed book or copybook. Probably there was one column on each side of each leaf. This codex book could be made up in any size by the writer himself. Certainly it is a much more capacious unit than the usual scroll.

By the fourth century parchment was used in copying the early Christian writings. It was used in codex as well as in scroll forms. Its leaves were sometimes much larger because more durable and sumptuous than papyrus, but the columns continued to be narrow and hence there were sometimes two, three, or four to a page. This sort of book does not belong to the period of original production now under consideration, though the oldest complete copies of early Christian writings that have come down to us are of this description. This is true because parchment is much more durable than the original papyrus, which quickly perishes except under continuous dry conditions. For this reason old books on papyrus are found today only in Egypt. It is inferred that those which were once in other countries have disintegrated. This has doubtless been the fate of the actual autograph originals of the known early Christian books and of all early copies of lost works. Once copied on parchment, they had greater chance of survival almost anywhere. In the writing of books, whether on papyrus or parchment, pen and ink were used (II John 12; III John 13).

For very short memoranda one might inscribe broken fragments of pottery, called ostraca; if Paul carried any certificate of Roman citizenship, it was very probably of this kind.

Or one might use a wax tablet, cutting letters with a pointed stylus, afterwards melting the wax for new use. Such a tablet might well have been used by Zechariah in naming his son John (Luke 1:63). The only reference to Jesus' writing is in John 8:6, 8, where letters were formed with the finger or a pointed object on the sand. The lettering on stone or on clay was an ancient custom and was also practiced in New Testament times.

The writing was done in different scripts in different periods, and these differences become in turn a criterion of date. Many secular papyri exist from the times when the New Testament was being written and suggest the kind of running hand its writers probably employed. The capital or uncial letters of the great old parchment codices are not to be attributed to the earlier time. The letters and even the words were joined to each other; hence the reader spelled the text out as he went along, word by word or syllable by syllable (Herm.: Vis. II. 1. 4). Reading was very often done by one person reading aloud to a number of listeners (Rev. 1:3), but even when one read alone or for himself he did so aloud (Acts 8:30). Writing also was probably done aloud, certainly in cases where the writer like Paul dictated to an amanuensis (Rom. 16:22) and only added in his own hand a single sentence or paragraph by way of identification (I Cor. 16:21; Gal. 6:11; Col. 4:18; II Thess. 3:17). The oral character of both writing and reading means that communication was much more through the ear than through the eye. This explains the emphasis on rhetoric in contemporary literature and the occasional evidence of an oratorical, not necessarily artificial, element in the early Christian writings.

III. Forms of Composition

When one turns from the externals of early Christian writing to the actual content, one still finds much parallelism with then current forms of speech and composition. It is not necessary to remind the reader that the Greek language used was in the main ordinary Greek.[8] Here and there a Semitic idiom enters in, owing to the bilingual mind of the writer, to the Aramaic idiom in which the gospel story and teaching had previously circulated, or to the influence of the overliteral Hebraisms familiar from the Greek Old Testament with which most early Christians were acquainted. On the other hand extreme purisms and archaisms, affected by certain secular littérateurs of the period, are conspicuously absent from the New Testament. Its style is varied. Each of the

[8] See article "The Language of the New Testament," pp. 43-59.

authors has personal idiosyncrasies, and the several styles differ somewhat, though all within the range of a Greek that is neither excessively formal nor excessively uncultivated. Often where the idiom departs from the older standard, it merely coincides with what we know of the trends in current popular speech. The author of Revelation, alone of early Christian writers, seems in some details of grammar to be curiously *sui generis*. Other writers, like the authors of Luke-Acts and of Hebrews, use not only words but phrases that have a genuine Hellenic ring, or are at least clichés or proverbial expressions. In addition Luke-Acts has a regular preface (Luke 1:1-4) and the conventional secondary preface (Acts 1:1) employed by contemporary writers at the beginning of each subsequent volume. In his address in both these passages to a patron, Theophilus, Luke is following literary convention. The same is true of the later anonymous epistle (found usually with the Apostolic Fathers) addressed to "most excellent Diognetus."

The letters of Paul and of other Christians conform somewhat to the form of the personal letters of the time. These regularly began, "A to B greeting." A thanksgiving to the god or gods often followed, with a mention of prayer. Before the end salutations from and to named individuals other than the writer and addressee were given and the last word was "farewell" (Acts 15:29). The Christian word "grace" (χάρις), with all its expansions at the beginning and end of letters, is still a reminder of the parallel secular form, χαίρειν (Acts 15:23; 23:26).

These features of personal letter writing are taken from non-Christian letters. Yet it may be doubted whether any purely personal letters written by the earliest Christians have survived. There is an element of officialness even in Paul's letter to Philemon and in Ignatius' letter to Polycarp, and this is still more evident in the Pastoral epistles. Thus also in II John and III John a more than individual recipient seems to be in view. This application of letter form to a more general address extended even further. The pure essay or homily also tended to acquire an epistolary character. It has been suggested that the term "epistle" (as distinguished from "letter") properly designates such essays in letter form. Many of the writings that go under the name of epistle are really to be thought of as having had a somewhat different purpose. The letter features in Hebrews, in Rev. 2 and 3, and in several of the Catholic epistles and of the Apostolic Fathers show the popularity of a formalization toward letters. Even the typical preface to a book took on something of the character of a letter.

The epistles of Paul and also that of James have been influenced by another literary style, that of the diatribe. This name is applied to the popular philosophic or ethical discourse, written or oral, which was current in the Hellenistic world. It is marked by a kind of imaginary dialogue in which questions or objections are interposed and answered.

Perhaps other current forms affected uncanonical early Christian writings. The collections of Jesus' sayings are reminiscent of some rabbinical material like Pirke Aboth or are like the sentences (*apophthegmata*) of Greek philosophers. The Greek Christian apology was in effect a petition to a high official of government. Whether it was preceded by close Jewish models is not certainly known. Undoubtedly the book of Revelation had definite Jewish precedents, which in turn had been evolved out of Old Testament prophecy. In Revelation, we note, for example, animal symbolism, numerical cycles, gematria, the interpreting angel, sealing and unsealing of books, not to mention visions and auditions. All of these items represent features of Jewish apocalypses.

The Old Testament provided some models or forms for limited parts of the New. The very first words of two Gospels, Matthew and John, reflect opening formulas or phrases in Gen. 2:4 (LXX) and 1:1, respectively. The poetic passages in Luke-Acts (e.g., Luke 1:46-55, 68-79) are largely comprised of phrases from the Old Testament. Other early Christian poetry, like the Odes of Solomon, and early Christian prayers, show the same influence. There are, of course, many quotations by Christians from the earlier Scriptures, and the use of historical material, as for example in the genealogies of Jesus (Matt. 1:2-16; Luke 3:23-38) and in reviews of Hebrew history like Acts 7, Heb. 11, I Clement 4.

The literary influence of the Old Testament is much more extended than the definite quotations suggest. Thus the book of Revelation, while the author never indicates that he is about to cite the Old Testament, is so full of its language that it has affected the wording of fully half the verses in the book. As examples of Christian use in extended form of Old Testament themes, one may refer to the interpretation of Mosaic laws in the Epistle of Barnabas, of the Day of Atonement in Heb. 9, and of the exodus from Egypt in Melito's *Homily on the Passion*. Justin Martyr's *Dialogue with Trypho* is most prolific in the extended citation of Old Testament passages. It may well be that an early form of Christian composition was simply an ordered collection of Old Testament passages which could be used in the Christian propaganda. Such collections, later known as *testimonia,* may lie behind the formula of Matthew's citations and elsewhere.

It is possible that Christian writings themselves soon provided not only the impulse but the forms for later writings. Luke refers to earlier compositions like his own (Luke 1:1). The gospel form is in a sense a literary phenomenon developed in Christianity. It is not like the current biographies in any striking way. It is more like the memorabilia which non-Christian writers composed; so, at least, Justin Martyr in addressing non-Christians explains the term "gospels" (*First Apology* LXVI. 3). But the form once established in the Synoptic Gospels became influential in later gospels, whether relatively independent, like John and the apocryphal gospels, or whether, like the Gospel of Peter and several other gospels known only more fragmentarily, they seem to have drawn heavily on the canonical Gospels for contents as well as form.

Pseudonymous epistles and "acts" would conform to the classical examples that preceded them in Christian writing. They would endeavor to suggest verisimilitude by using the contents of the earlier literature for details. It is this tendency, of course, which makes it so difficult to distinguish what is genuine and early and what is imitative and late. The very practice of pseudonymity is to be noted as an example of recourse to a current pattern. The Jews of the period had long practiced it, and it was not unknown to the Gentiles. Any modern squeamishness about approving such a literary practice must not be allowed to color our judgment about the propriety, or the probability, of its use in antiquity. Not only were apostolic names conferred by posterity on anonymous writings, but Christians of the second and later generations deliberately and with good conscience composed books in the name of one or all of the apostles. The titles or opening words of the Didache (The Teaching of the Twelve Apostles) and of the Epistle of the Apostles can be cited as illustrations of a rather common practice.

IV. Traditional Groupings

The reader of the New Testament would undoubtedly be greatly helped if he could see it in some conspectus of literary arrangement. Several methods suggest themselves. One is arrangement according to date. It would seem natural that a collection of nearly thirty writings should be presented to the modern intelligent reader as are other source books of literature so that he could read them in the order in which they were written. The order conventional in our New Testament is due to other considerations, being accounted for partly by the chronology of subject matter (thus lives of Jesus precede the history and writings of apostles, and the latter are followed by the book which treats of "what must come to pass hereafter"); and partly by literary forms or content—Gospels together, epistles together, etc. Likewise, general ("catholic") letters are likely to be separated from those to churches, and these from letters to individuals; while, at the same time, letters by the same writer or to the same church or person tend naturally to fall into juxtaposition.

From the purely literary point of view the limits of the New Testament are quite arbitrary. The selection of its contents was a gradual and uncertain process. The books chosen are not different in aim or content from books outside the canon; and there is no criterion of date which justifies including II Peter in a collection that excludes, say, the Gospel of Peter or the much earlier I Clement. There is no point in finding fault with and no need to defend the limits of the New Testament. They were arrived at by a historical process culminating in later times and are not likely to be altered even if new discoveries should unearth writings of equal claim to accuracy, antiquity, inspiration, or apostolic authorship.

Other groupings of Christian books were made much later and have not the same persistent limits. The so-called Apostolic Fathers have come to include the Didache, discovered only in 1875. The Gospel of Peter, the Acts of Paul, the Epistle of the Apostles, and shorter fragments of other apocryphal works, discovered in recent decades, have been included with the older known, if not older, New Testament Apocrypha. Any modern collection of second-century Greek apologists would naturally include the recovered Apology of Aristides, at the same time excluding with equal propriety later and spurious treatises which former editors once accepted and included as the work of Justin Martyr. For the purposes of this essay, therefore, the traditional limits of early Christian collections cannot be regarded as satisfactory.

V. Date and Order

A chronological survey of early Christian literature would be desirable, and such surveys have been attempted. In other fields of literature they are frequently used, but in this field it is difficult to make one. Few of the pieces of writing that fall within the period can be closely dated. Not one bears an exact date, as did many ancient letters, or even the number of the year, as do most books of modern times. Sometimes the relative age of two or more writings is disclosed by their dependence one upon another, or acquaintance of one with another; but that does not tell us in just what year either was written. Chronological dates are frequently conjectured on the basis of the relation of the several writings to our knowledge of the development of Christian thought, but since that knowledge is derived exclusively from the same writings, we are always in danger of arguing in a circle. The occasional connections between the literature and external events supply the best criteria for dating documents; where these are lacking, the documents can be dated only approximately, on the ground of their apparent priority or posteriority to one another, or set somewhere in a sometimes long period between the earliest and the latest possible dates. Any more exact dating, either in this article or elsewhere, is usually more conjectural than the reader may suspect. Dating as regards the uncanonical documents is in most cases as precarious as for those of the canon.

For the purpose of giving some rough idea of order and date, one may conveniently divide the first century into three nearly equal parts. The period of the life of Christ would constitute one of the parts (4 B.C.—A.D. 30), and the apostolic age as described in Acts, a second third (A.D. 30-62); a subapostolic age from 62-96 would round out ninety-nine years. No extant and probably no lost Christian literature belongs in the first period. Neither Christ nor his disciples made any lasting record during his lifetime. The genuine letters of Paul are the only Christian writings belonging certainly to the second period, and they come from its last dozen years. In the third period the first three Gospels and Acts are usually thought to have been written, while to its very end an early tradition assigns the Revelation of John, and modern scholarship assigns I Clement. If we should add a fourth period of equal length (about 96-128), we should assign to it probably the letters of Ignatius and Polycarp, and perhaps the Gospel and Epistles of John; and either to it or to its predecessor the rest of the New Testament books, except II Peter. That belongs to the next half century (128-178), to which also all the rest of the writings here under review, including the Apostolic Fathers and the Greek apologists, probably belong. Any stopping place, like that just suggested, is of course arbitrary.

VI. The New Testament and Apocrypha

A. Gospels.—Mention has already been made of the fact that the Gospels come first in the New Testament because they deal with the earliest events, and not because they were the first to be written. Probably Paul's letters at least are older than most or all of them. In fact none of the New Testament is absolutely primitive; still less is it the foundation of the Christian movement. It is later than the early church and is the product of the church, not merely in its final canonization, but even in the composition of its several parts. This sequence it is important to remember. In so far as the Christian movement is the sequel to the earthly life of Jesus, it is dependent in the first instance, not on the Gospels, but on that which the evangelists belatedly record. Whether we begin with the Gospels as written or with the earliest epistles, we begin part way down in Christian history. To the evangelists their story was already an old story.

What was the history of its telling? At first it almost certainly circulated only orally and in fragments. The first writings, whether Greek or Aramaic, may well have been fragmentary also. Mark, if we may accept the common view that it is the earliest Gospel, lacks some later features of completeness. Only the narrative of the Passion and what preceded it seems to possess continuity and fullness. The teachings of Jesus are presented not very fully and that principally in three blocks in chs. 4, 9, and 13, of which the first consists of parables, the last of warnings about the future. These subjects and others were in time available in fuller collections of teaching, as our Gospels of Matthew and Luke show us. These Gospels are later than Mark, which they almost certainly used firsthand. A popular hypothesis, which, although not provable, is not disproved, is that they both used another earlier written Greek source, called by the scholars "Q," which differed from Mark in that it collected primarily sayings of Jesus. Such a specialized collection was as natural as would be a collection of his deeds, especially of his miracles, or a connected account of the circumstances of his death. In this context mention may be made of an example from a much later time, of which papyrus fragments from two different copies were happily discovered about the beginning of the twentieth century at Oxyrhynchus in Egypt.[4] In this collection sayings of Jesus are given, one after another, with a minimum of introduction, usually the words, "Jesus says . . . ."

In another sense the oldest written tradition of Jesus was incomplete. Mark's account of him begins with his ministry; Matthew and Luke both go farther back. Luke has an account of John's birth and a story of Jesus in Jerusalem at the age of twelve. Each of these Gospels also has an independent account of Jesus' birth and a chain genealogy of Joseph. These features

[4] Hugh G. Evelyn White, Sayings of Jesus from Oxyrhynchus (Cambridge: University Press, 1920).

may point to other written sources for these Gospels besides Mark or Q.

The Gospel of John, the last of the canonical Gospels, makes little and unequal use of its three predecessors, and may have had other written sources.

For fuller discussion of these questions, including suggestions of sources and dates, the reader is referred to the essay on "The Growth of the Gospels." [5] Here, however, we glance beyond the canon to other gospels of the second century. Some of these are known by name and by patristic quotation—the Gospel According to the Hebrews, the Gospel According to the Egyptians, the Nazarene Gospel. Others come down to us in fragments of text—the Gospel of Peter, and the "Unknown Gospel," a fragment of which was published by Bell and Skeat in 1935. [6] The last two can be dated as early as about A.D. 150. The others may be as old. Both groups have this in common, that they seem to depend upon the contents of our canonical Gospels quite a good deal. The Gospel of Peter and the "Unknown Gospel" combine what are practically quotations or at least data from both John and the Synoptic Gospels. A more thoroughgoing attempt to include the full content of all four Gospels in a single work belongs near the end of the period we are considering. It is the Diatessaron, compiled probably in Greek about A.D. 175 by Tatian, a Syrian, but it was soon translated into other languages and its influence extended into other lands and continued for many years. Of the Greek text only a small fragment has thus far been recorded, but the Diatessaron is known to us in translation throughout.

B. Acts.—Next after gospels should be mentioned the literary type of which the canonical example is the Acts of the Apostles. This book, as a matter of fact, was originally in the closest possible association with a gospel, for the Gospel of Luke and the book of Acts are really a single work by one author. Essentially a continuous narrative, it was divided into two parts for physical reasons, much as bulky modern books are sometimes published in two volumes. It is doubtful whether the volumes originally bore different titles, and in any case probably not the titles "Gospel" and "Acts." The existence of parallels to the first volume led to the attaching of it to these under the common title "the Gospel" (with four subdivisions, "According to Matthew," "According to Mark," etc.) rather than under the plural title "Gospels." Thus it was separated from the book of

Acts, with which it integrally belongs. Whether there were early parallels also to this latter work, we do not know; but none has survived. Possibly for this volume, as for the Gospel, the author had available written sources. The minor differences in character between Luke and Acts may be due partly to the different character of the sources. But they are also attributable to the difference in the historical situations dealt with in the two books. The Gospel is, of course, dominated by one central figure, a considerable body of whose teachings were remembered and preserved; in the Acts the movement which followed Jesus' resurrection was more scattered both in geography and personnel, and the speeches of the actors are much more the imaginative work of the writer. [7] On the whole the two works are quite similar. Besides having the same author, and being addressed to the same person, they are alike in style and show similar interests and methods of presentation, for example, in the miracles, in the emphasis upon travel, and in the biographical approach.

Thus only an accident of later development put the book of Acts into a seemingly separate literary genre. When, however, that had happened, a series of late narratives of individual apostles came into existence, so that we have apocryphal "Acts" of Peter, of Paul, of John, etc. Perhaps the Acts of Paul deserves particularly to be mentioned, as it was almost certainly compiled in the second century and has recently been recovered in part from manuscripts in Greek and Coptic. It is largely fictitious; the same may be said of the so-called Clementine literature, in which Peter is the hero.

C. Revelation.—The Revelation of John represents a distinctive literary form, common in later Judaism and early Christianity, known as the "apocalypse," that word being derived from the Greek word for our "revelation." The apocalypses were written successors to Jewish oral prophecy. Among their features are their strongly predictive character, their assurance that God will punish the wicked and avenge his saints, and their use of symbols—numbers, visions, interpreting angels, and the like. Daniel in the Old Testament, or at least part of it (chs. 7–12), is a good representative of this literary genre. Similar works, still partly preserved, bore the names of Enoch, Ezra, Baruch, Isaiah, etc. Pseudonymity, that is, the use of a borrowed name, was a common feature, as the books claimed to record what was revealed long ago to a chosen seer, and thus could include as evidence of foresight what was to the author and first readers actual history. This fiction of great antiquity is not shared by

[5] See below, pp. 60-74.

[6] *Fragments of an Unknown Gospel and Other Early Christian Papyri*, ed. H. I. Bell and T. C. Skeat (London: Trustees of the British Museum, 1935).

[7] See above, pp. 4-5.

the Revelation of John nor by the other known Christian apocalypses, such as the Revelation of Peter or the Shepherd of Hermas. For that reason pseudonymity cannot be regarded as an essential feature. Other less usual features found in the canonical book of Revelation are the symmetrical letters to the seven churches in chs. 2–3 and the lyrical or liturgical bits of song scattered through the book. The date and authorship of the book are singularly hard to determine, but are perhaps of less importance to the modern reader on account of the time-lessness of the message.

D. Epistles of Paul.—The genuine letters of Paul are for the historian a highly satisfactory body of material. No Christian writing, in the New Testament or out of it, has any certainty of date prior to the letters which Paul wrote probably in the fifties of the first century. These have all the earmarks of a distinctive person-ality, and give a remarkable impression of spontaneity.

The order of the letters as given in our Bibles is determined by length, in two groups: those to churches, of which Romans is the longest and II Thessalonians the shortest, and those to individuals. There is therefore no reason to assume that the letters were written in the order in which they appear. In fact the two Thessalonian letters at the end of the list are almost certainly among the earliest, and II Thessalonians may well be earlier than I Thessalonians. In spite of many unsolved prob-lems, which will be treated in detail elsewhere in this work, we have good reason to be certain that in the letters of Paul we possess a substan-tial, genuine, and early nucleus of our New Testament. This does not mean all of the letters sometimes ascribed to him. Hebrews ought never to have been associated with Paul's name. It is an early anonymous piece from a cultivated and able mind, no whit be-hind the work of the chiefest of the apostles. The two letters to Timothy and that to Titus (the so-called Pastoral epistles) belong together, but probably do not belong to Paul. They are "epistles," rather than natural letters. Of the rest, II Thessalonians and Ephesians have been most often denied Pauline origin. In each case is involved the relation to another epistle, namely, I Thessalonians and Colossians respec-tively. But these letters, whether Paul's or not, are much closer to Paul's thought than Hebrews or the Pastorals, and may provisionally remain listed with his other letters. There is no evi-dence of any early collection of his letters which did not contain them.

E. Catholic Epistles.—The Catholic epistles consist of the epistles of John (three), Peter (two), James, and Jude. These seven pieces entered the canon of the New Testament not as a group but individually, and their association is a by-product of their individual claims. The common name for them is only of quite recent origin and is intended to find for them a dis-tinction from the letters to persons or to named churches, for "catholic" in this title means "with a general address." It is not surprising that all of them were capable of being attrib-uted to some apostle, for otherwise they would not have been admitted to the canon, for which apostolicity was demanded. The letters of Peter clearly claim to be by that apostle; those of James and Jude had the advantage of names which appeared in the list of Jesus' four brothers as well as among his twelve disciples. Undoubtedly II John and III John, by an un-named elder, as well as the equally anonymous I John, secured their standing because of evi-dent connection in thought and style with the Fourth Gospel.

When one examines these letters apart from such doubtful and superficial criteria, they appear rather to be quite miscellaneous pieces. II John and III John, for example, are not addressed to a general audience and are there-fore not really "catholic" epistles: III John is sent to an individual and is concerned with specific problems; and II John, to a "lady" who, if not an individual, is at least a definite Chris-tian church. The five other Catholic epistles are warnings or advices, having at most limited or imitative or superimposed epistolary char-acter. This is evident in Jude and II Peter which, besides, have some definite literary con-nection with each other, the former probably supplying the substance of the middle chapter of the latter. I John is a somewhat discursive exhortation in the style of the Gospel attrib-uted to John; James, with even fewer marks of definite address, is a collection of advices on conduct in the quite different style of the con-temporary ethical "diatribe." I Peter alone has any indication of the readers' geographical location, and that includes the five Roman provinces occupying nearly all of Asia Minor. Of the seven "letters" in this group, I Peter, as regards definiteness and consistency of form and in the possibility of its genuineness, comes nearest to those of Paul.

F. Hebrews and Pastoral Epistles.—Before we leave the New Testament entirely, more should be said of four letters deferred for fuller mention when the letters of Paul were dis-cussed. The Epistle to the Hebrews is not only not by Paul—and modern Bibles, like ancient manuscripts, no longer include Paul in the title—but may perhaps be neither an "epistle" nor "to the Hebrews." Written in excellent Greek, it is rather a sustained and well-knit argument on the importance of Christian loyalty. It compares Christianity to Judaism in order to emphasize this importance. This reminder to second-generation Christians is equally appropriate for any group in the church, whether of Jews or Gentiles, and for any locality. For that reason the epistolary element, which appears in the last chapter and not at all in the beginning, may be an adaptation of what we should call rather a sermon or essay. As elsewhere in the New Testament and out of it, we need to be reminded that the letter form was frequently merely the form imposed or adopted for a less casual writing. The prestige of Paul and of his letters may have contributed much to this development.

Paul is certainly no unconscious influence upon the two letters to Timothy and that of Titus. The genuineness of these letters as they stand is difficult to maintain. They must therefore be the deliberate attempt of a later admirer of the apostle to convey his concern for the welfare of the churches and their leaders in terms of a little collection of Pauline pastoral letters. The difference between them and Paul's other letters—including Philemon, which also is addressed to an individual—is recognized by all, even by those who would like to count them genuine. Those features of style and point of view which differentiate them from Paul as he is known elsewhere at the same time link them closely to each other. From any angle they must be regarded as a separate division in the New Testament. The epistolary fiction, if fiction it is, has been carried through with unusual thoroughness, so that in certain places some have suspected that fragments of genuine letters have been embodied. But the total situation reflected in these writings remains improbable and is almost certainly quite imaginative. The writer has in mind the conditions of a post-Pauline period and the situation of the successors of Paul's intimate associates Timothy and Titus as officials of the local churches. He himself was the first of many writers concerned with regulations for the church.

VII. Apostolic Fathers

Second only to the New Testament in average antiquity is that collection of early Christian literature which for the last century or two has been known as the Apostolic Fathers. Its limits were not determined by any early ecclesiastical judgment, or even by widespread usage. These limits have in fact been altered by recent discovery and may be subject to future change. Some of the writings were early associated with the New Testament, as is shown by their inclusion in some early lists or manuscripts of that collection. Such is their overlapping in date and character with the books of the New Testament that any chronological or literary outline of early Christian writings would show some interweaving of the two collections. The titles and tentative dates may be given as follows:

I Clement	about 95
II Clement	about 150
Epistle of Barnabas	second century
Epistle of Polycarp	before 155
Epistles of Ignatius	about 115
Shepherd of Hermas	130-150
The Didache	second or third century
Epistle to Diognetus	third century

The earliest of these writings are genuine letters by representative leaders of the churches. An anonymous spokesman, long called Clement, writes on behalf of the church at Rome to the church of the Corinthians the document now known as I Clement. Ignatius, bishop of Antioch in Syria, writes letters in his own name while traveling to probable martyrdom at Rome. Seven of these are probably genuine, addressed to churches in Ephesus, Magnesia, Tralles, Rome, Philadelphia, and Smyrna, and to the bishop of Smyrna, named Polycarp. The same Polycarp wrote somewhat later his letter to the church at Philippi.

The Shepherd of Hermas also claims a certain amount of church connection, but it is less like an epistle, being rather a combination of (a) visions, like an apocalypse, (b) mandates of exhortation, and (c) parables or similitudes of very similar tendency.

The Didache is a newcomer in the collection, having been discovered in the latter part of the nineteenth century. It is a pseudonymous work whose full title in English would be "The Teaching of the Lord to the Gentiles through the Twelve Apostles." It also is a combination, the first part being a distinction between the ethics of two Ways, the last part, instructions about the use of the sacraments and about other church practices.

Closely connected with this, and perhaps a source for some of its contents, is the Epistle of Barnabas. It is a curious comparison of Jewish literal legalism and Christian ethical standards. Like I Clement, it is really anonymous and scarcely deserves its long standing attribution to the Barnabas who was a fellow missionary with Paul. II Clement, also anonymous, does not purport to be a letter at all; it is rather a sermon. The Epistle to Diognetus, on the other hand, would be better classed with apologies to be mentioned later. As happens elsewhere, the addressee's name, since it was included in the text, is preserved, whereas the author's has been lost.

This collection shows many of the same peculiarities as the older collection which we call the New Testament. It differs from the New Testament in that it contains no narrative books, unless we include, as is sometimes done, the Martyrdom of Polycarp, an early example of the "acts of martyrs," which later became a favorite form of Christian writing. But both collections have several anonymous writings under traditional names, and in both the form of letter is often used or assumed where it is scarcely an original reality. The lines of limitation for each collection follow no clear principle. Additions or omissions are conceivable or at least logically defensible in either group, though new discoveries have more chance of admission to the group of Apostolic Fathers because of its later development and its smaller prestige. Any arbitrariness in the classification of early Christian writings should not, however, lay suspicion on the sincerity, naturalness, and spontaneity of the writings themselves, even though their literary form is to us uncongenial.

VIII. Early Apologists

Many other written defenses of Christianity, besides the Epistle to Diognetus already mentioned, were produced in the second and third centuries and together form another collection, the early Christian Apologists. The writings longest and best known here are those by Justin Martyr, including his *Dialogue with Trypho*, which, though in dialogue form, is really a friendly presentation to a Jewish interlocutor of the Christian case against Jewish criticism. His "First" and "Second" Apology, and those of other writers, are addressed rather to Gentiles; often professedly to emperors or persons of rank. Some turn from defense to attack pagan religion, and it may be supected that they were of fully as much value in confirming believers as in convincing or even mollifying unbelievers. In their contents, quite as much as in their professed reading public, they represent Christianity moving out into touch with secular affairs. Omitting both the apologists whose works are not now available, and the works of apologists which are available but are not apologies, one may list the following:

Aristides of Athens: Apology reconstructed from a Syriac translation and from a form incorporated in a later Greek work

Justin Martyr: two Apologies and *Dialogue with Trypho*

Tatian: *Address to the Greeks*

Athenagoras: *Embassy on Behalf of the Christians*

Theophilus of Antioch: *To Autolycus* (three books)

IX. Other Arrangements

Before concluding this essay it may be well to remind the reader once more that its scope is incomplete and its manner of presentation in a sense arbitrary. While mention at least has been made of most of the substantial Christian writings before Irenaeus which have been preserved, the mention also of many others known to us by title, or by fragment, or not known to us at all, would have given a fuller and perhaps a quite different impression of early Christian literature. A strictly chronological arrangement would have been helpful to the reader if it were possible, but there is good reason for arranging the material by literary forms whether in the canon or not, as is done for example in the work of Martin Dibelius mentioned below. Sometimes an effort is made to arrange this literature according to the place of its origin, but obviously locality is not important when one is dealing with writers who traveled extensively; and not only Paul and Ignatius, but many others of the writers considered, either did not write from their fixed abode, or were transplanted in the course of their Christian career from one center to another. It is of course possible that Christianity developed differently in different Christian centers. Some have supposed that the four Gospels represent not merely four authors but also four localities of origin or influence. Unfortunately neither they nor many other early Christian books lend themselves to assured localization so that we can collect the literature under local "schools," as of Ephesus, Antioch, Alexandria, or Rome—to mention only four possible centers of Christian influence, as they were also four of the major cities of the Roman empire. Another classification might be attempted along lines of religious position, the distinction being made not so much between heretical and orthodox works, as between different kinds of religious temperament, the mystics, the ascetics, the moralists, and the like. Still another arrangement for some of the books could be on the basis of the simple succession of cause and effect, source and object of influence. Such a succession exists among the gospel writers; and perhaps the influence of Paul can be traced, as it fans out in more than one line.

The fact that these writings have been the object of sustained study, and that we must judge early Christianity almost entirely from them, should not be allowed to exaggerate our sense of their importance. None of the authors was merely an author, and Christianity was not mainly a movement of the written word. What the evangelists included was already a living and effective tradition before they wrote; what Paul said in letters was only supplementary to his major impact as a missionary. The Christian life, the Holy Spirit, the community of worship, the individual contact of person with person, played undoubtedly a larger part. Welcome as are the heterogeneous written remains of primitive Christianity, they must not be placed out of proportion to their own times or to ours. "The letter kills, the spirit gives life."

X. Selected Bibliography

The Ante-Nicene Fathers, ed. Alexander Roberts and James Donaldson. American reprint of Edinburgh edition. New York: Charles Scribner's Sons, 1899-1900.

The Apocryphal New Testament, tr. Montague R. James. Oxford: Clarendon Press, 1924.

The Apostolic Fathers, tr. Kirsopp Lake ("Loeb Classical Library"). London: William Heinemann, 1912.

BACON, BENJAMIN W. The Making of the New Testament. New York: Henry Holt & Co., 1912.

DIBELIUS, MARTIN. A Fresh Approach to the New Testament and Early Christian Literature. New York: Charles Scribner's Sons, 1936.

GRANT, ROBERT M. Second-Century Christianity: A Collection of Fragments. London: Society for Promoting Christian Knowledge, 1946.

KRÜGER, GUSTAV. History of Early Christian Literature in the First Three Centuries. New York: The Macmillan Co., 1897.

SCOTT, ERNEST F. The Literature of the New Testament. New York: Columbia University Press, 1932.

VON SODEN, HERMANN. The History of Early Christian Literature: The Writings of the New Testament, tr. J. R. Wilkinson. New York: G. P. Putnam's Sons, 1906.

THE LANGUAGE
OF THE NEW TESTAMENT

by BRUCE M. METZGER

Palestine stood at the crossroads of the Roman Empire. Merchants and soldiers, travelers and pilgrims from far and wide crowded into the Holy City (Acts 2:9-11). Amid their babel of tongues, three above all others could be detected. These three were those in which Pilate wrote the inscription fastened to the Cross: Hebrew, Latin, and Greek (John 19:20).

The nature of the language designated "Hebrew" requires some explanation. The native mother tongue of Palestinian Jews at that time was Aramaic. Though rabbis and learned scribes still had a fluent command of the classical Hebrew of the Old Testament, for the great majority of Jews this was a dead language. During the Exile they had begun to use Aramaic, a Semitic language related to Hebrew somewhat as Italian is related to Spanish. At the beginning of the Christian era, in the synagogues of Palestine as well as of Babylon, the text of the Pentateuch was regularly read not only in the original Hebrew but also in an Aramaic paraphrase—a Targum—for the benefit of those Jews in the congregation who knew little or no Hebrew. Perhaps because of false pride, but more probably because of simple indifference to scientific precision, the Aramaic language was popularly referred to as "Hebrew." Whether the inscription on the Cross was actually in Hebrew proper or in Aramaic—and the latter is far more probable—the common Semitic vernacular of Palestinian Judaism in the time of Jesus was Aramaic.

The second language of the inscription was Latin, the official language of the conquerors. It was used by the procurator Pontius Pilate, and by his minions down to the common soldiers of the Roman army of occupation. Very few Palestinian Jews knew more than the most common of everyday Latin words which had been, so to speak, naturalized wherever the Roman garrisons had been stationed. These were words such as "centurion," "colony," "denarius," "legion," "praetorium," and the like.

The Greek language, on the contrary, was widely understood in Palestine, particularly in "Galilee of the Gentiles," as it was called (Matt. 4:15). Here, more than in Judea to the south, Jews would rub elbows with Greek-speaking Gentiles; and, to be successful in the market place, bilingualism was an economic necessity. This bilingualism had its historical origin in the second century before Christ, when the Seleucidan emperors instituted the deliberate policy of Grecizing the Jewish population of Palestine. Though the Maccabean reaction had temporarily delayed the process of Hellenization, inevitably more and more of Greek culture and language permeated Palestine.

The three languages on the Cross symbolize the three streams of diverse cultures which met in what appears to be a divinely preordained confluence in the little land of Palestine during the first century of our era. Here were mingled the chief interests and contributions of three significant civilizations. One may say that the characteristic interest of the Hebrew was the *right;* of the Greek, the *ideal;* of the Roman, the *practical.* As regards chief contributions, Israel gave prophets and psalmists; Greece gave artists and philosophers; Rome gave statesmen and legislators. The favorite and indispensable words on the tongue of the Israelite were God, soul, sin, pardon, joy, holiness, glory, righteousness; of the Greek, man, reason, beauty, virtue, idea, wisdom, completeness, realization; of the Roman, authority, power, law, justice, order, dignity, duty, courage. The Jewish religion, the Hellenistic culture, and the Roman Empire each contributed its distinctive gift in "the fulness of the time [when] God sent forth his Son" (Gal. 4:4). The record of God's revelation of himself in and through his Son is enshrined in the twenty-seven books comprising the "New Covenant," and these are written in the Greek language.

I. Survey of the History of the Greek Language

In order to understand and evaluate the language of the New Testament it will be necessary first to survey the history of the Greek language, noting the place of the Greek of the New Testament in that history. A simplified outline of this history is as follows (the dates are, of course, intended to be convenient and not absolute termini): the classical period, from Homer, traditionally about 1000 B.C., to Aristotle, who died in 322 B.C.; the "koine" period, from Aristotle to A.D. 529, when the Christian Emperor Justinian closed the academy of Plato at Athens, confiscated its treasury, and prohibited the teaching of ancient Greek philosophy; the Byzantine period, from 529 to the capture of Constantinople by the Turks in 1453; the modern period, from 1453 down to the present.

A. Classical Greek.—Beginning perhaps at the end of the third millennium B.C. various tribes of Indo-European peoples wandered southward into the country and islands which later were to be called Greece. Since these regions abound in natural barriers, the newcomers were necessarily divided into small and scattered groups. Being thus deprived of close intercourse with each other, during succeeding centuries their language developed into a number of dialects. The most fruitful of these in a literary way were the Doric, Aeolic, Ionic, and Attic dialects. To mention only a few of the most famous Greek authors in each dialect we still have today the odes of Pindar in Doric

and fragments of Sappho's poems in Aeolic. Homer's immortal *Iliad* and *Odyssey* are in Old Ionic or Epic. Later Herodotus, the "Father of History," used Ionic proper for the first literary Greek prose. Because Attic, a modified form of Ionic, was used in the most important political and economic city-state, Athens, it became the most famous and important of the Greek dialects. In it were composed the tragedies of Aeschylus, Sophocles, and Euripides, the comedies of Aristophanes, the histories of Thucydides and Xenophon, the orations of Demosthenes, and the philosophical treatises of Plato.

B. Koine Greek.—The golden age of Greek literature came to an end with Aristotle (384-322 B.C.). At this time the military campaigns of Alexander the Great served to initiate a decided change in the Greek language. Into his armies were recruited men from north, east, south, and west—men who could understand each other's Greek dialect only with difficulty. The terse and sinewy speech of the Doric highlander and the poor and rude brogue of the Aeolic islander were heard side by side with the smooth and harmonious Ionic and Attic dialects. During prolonged campaigns tentfellows and messmates from all parts of Greece had no choice but to accommodate their mode of speech in its more individual characteristics to the average Greek which was being evolved among their comrades. In this process those features which were peculiar to a single dialect would have the smallest chance of surviving. Lest they be misunderstood or ridiculed, soldiers from the backwoods would try to conform their speech to that of the more sophisticated Attic standards. Thus from the chaos of the Hellenic dialects a new and nearly homogeneous world-speech was gradually created. The name given to this form of Greek is κοινή (koine), meaning "common [dialect]." It embodied elements of all the preceding, competing dialects, but Attic formed the base with borrowings chiefly from Ionic.

C. Spread of Koine Greek.—As the result of a vigorously pursued policy of disseminating Greek culture through the civilized world, begun by Alexander the Great and continued with more or less diligence by his successors, koine Greek had become, by the first century of our era, the lingua franca of the entire Roman Empire. Inscriptions in koine testify to its use over an area reaching from the Tagus in Spain to the Indus on the border of western India. Even in the capital of the Roman Empire, not Latin, but Greek was the favorite language among literary men, artists, and tradesmen. Paul, a Roman citizen, wrote his letter to the Romans in Greek. The early bishops and ecclesiastics of Rome were Greeks by descent or education, or both. The church at Rome, at the end of the first century, wrote in Greek an epistle, which is called I Clement, to the church at Corinth. Inscriptions in the oldest catacombs and the epitaphs of the popes down to the middle of the third century are in Greek.

If Greek had become so well known in Rome itself, it is not surprising that it was the common vernacular in Asia Minor, Egypt, Syria, and Cyprus—indeed wherever Paul and the earliest missionaries took the gospel. Side by side with Greek, the native vernaculars lived on—witness Paul's experience at Lystra with people who still spoke the Lycaonian speech of their fathers (Acts 14:11). But despite many divergent mother tongues, the almost universal knowledge of koine Greek served to solidify ancient culture and to provide a divinely ordained preparation for the propagation of the gospel.

D. Characteristics of the Koine.—Several characteristics of the koine distinguish it from classical Greek of the fifth and fourth centuries B.C. Perhaps the most comprehensive term describing these various features is the word "simplification." Shorter and simpler sentences supplanted the highly complex structure of classical syntax. Instead of the wealth of coordinating and subordinating conjunctions and particles—one of the "glories" of ancient Greek —a relatively few of the more commonplace connectives were forced to express all kinds of relationships. Most people, in conformity with the same tendency toward simplification, preferred direct discourse, with its less complicated syntax, to indirect discourse. Again, the special forms of verbs, nouns, and adjectives which had been employed when but two people or objects were referred to (the dual number) fell into disuse and were then forgotten. A similar fate was to be in store for the optative mood— which appears but sixty-seven times in the whole New Testament. In short, the subtle refinements of form and syntax of classical Greek failed to survive in the koine.

In addition to this tendency toward simplification there was also a constant striving for emphatic and vigorous expression, characteristic of every vernacular. It is by this proneness to emphatic expression that one accounts for the noticeable growth in the use of prepositions in composition with verbs as well as with their objects. The increased use of pronouns as subjects of verbs which do not require them, the preference for compound and even double-compound (sesquipedalian) words for simple words, the use of the vivid present tense instead of the future, the large number of words in the diminutive formation, the replacement by prepositional phrases of constructions originally involving merely the proper case—all of these are indications of striving after emphasis at the expense of precise and refined expression.

E. Varieties of the Koine.—On the whole the Greek which had spread throughout the Roman Empire was one language, without serious dialectal differences. But at the same time within the koine there were two varieties, the literary and the nonliterary type. Authors who pretended to be cultured tried with varying degrees of success to imitate Attic Greek of the classical period. The first author of prominence who wrote in the literary koine was the historian named Polybius, who died about 123 B.C. During the century before and following the birth of Christ some of the most notable non-Christian authors who used the literary koine were Diodorus, the historian (*fl. ca.* 40 B.C.); Strabo, the geographer (*ca.* 63 B.C.–after A.D. 21); two Jewish authors, Philo, the philosopher (*ca.* 20 B.C.–*ca.* A.D. 54), and Josephus, the historian and antiquarian (*ca.* A.D. 37–*ca.* 95); and Plutarch, the versatile essayist and biographer (*ca.* A.D. 46–*ca.* 120). The style of their Greek was something of a compromise between the older classical form and the contemporary vernacular.

Certain other authors of these centuries, such as Dionysius of Halicarnassus (*fl. ca.* 25 B.C.) and Dion Chrysostom (of the first century A.D.) disdained to write in the literary koine and consciously imitated the literary Attic. In attempting to revive Attic Greek the crusading spirit of more than one "purist"—such as Phrynichus and Moeris during the late second century—went to the extent of drawing up lists of Greek words which ought to be avoided by all who wished to speak or write elegantly. These misguided pedants were the greatest enemies of the common vernacular and placed a dead weight upon the growth of the living language. But despite this artificial Atticizing movement, the main stream of the koine was not to be dammed or diverted.

Side by side with the literary koine there flourished the nonliterary variety. It goes without saying that the speech of the street, the home, the market place, the farm, differed from that of the school and the lecture hall. The range of the varieties of the nonliterary koine extends from a crude and frequently ungrammatical form of Greek to the standard literary form. Our knowledge of this type of koine is derived chiefly from the large quantities of papyrus documents written by ordinary people and preserved in the dry climate of Egypt. The nature of these documents ranges from title deeds, business contracts, and tax receipts, to love notes, schoolboy letters, and magical incantations. Within the past generation both grammars and lexicons have been written utilizing this newly discovered fund of knowledge of the nonliterary koine.

F. *Byzantine and Modern Greek.*—The history of Byzantine and modern Greek can be dismissed in a few sentences. The process of simplification, so noticeable in the koine, advanced still further. From the beginning of the seventh century to the close of the eleventh, learning was at a very low ebb, and the Greek language lost much of its original character. Syntax underwent important changes, and hosts of new words were borrowed from other languages. Modern colloquial Greek, which begins to appear as early as the eleventh century, is the natural development of the koine in its spoken form. In present-day speech in the streets of a Greek village the ancient inflections have been greatly modified or eliminated. On the other hand the language of an educated Athenian today has been to a large extent deliberately assimilated to the ancient idiom. Although the *pronunciation* of modern Greek differs quite considerably from that in ancient Athens, it is likely that Demosthenes or Plato could have understood fairly well the Greek of many a book published in Athens in the twentieth century. The Greek language has thus had an unbroken literary history from Homer to the present day.

II. Individual Characteristics of New Testament Authors

How nearly similar to the cultured, literary koine on the one hand, or to the oftentimes crude and ungrammatical vernacular on the other, is the language of the New Testament? If one were to prepare a scale of literary excellence by which to measure the quality of koine Greek, where would the several documents of the New Testament fall? Obviously no hard-and-fast line can be drawn in making such an evaluation; only the general impression produced by the language of Paul, of Peter, of Mark, and the others, can be taken into account. Furthermore, it need scarcely be observed that in thus appraising the literary standard of their Greek, one does not pass judgment upon the amount of assistance the individual authors supply us in understanding the will of God.

Before such an evaluation can be attempted, however, it is necessary to refer to a circumstance which, above all others, must be taken into account in analyzing the language of the New Testament. The authors of almost all of the books of the New Testament were Jews. Though all of them wrote in Greek, their language as a whole was slightly further removed from the Greek used at Athens in her glory than was the koine of contemporary non-Jewish authors. To a greater or less extent the idiom of the New Testament manifests traces of Semitic coloring in vocabulary, syntax, and style. Part of this non-Greek influence was derived directly from the Hebrew of the Old Testament and from the contemporary Aramaic vernacular of Palestine. Most of the Semitic influence, however, was exerted indirectly through the Bible which all the authors of the New Testament used. During the third and second centuries B.C. a Greek translation of the Hebrew Old Testament was prepared—called the Septuagint, from the tradition that seventy (or seventy-two) translators worked upon it. Parts of the Septuagint follow so literalistically upon the Hebrew idiom that the Greek of these books would have been scarcely recognizable to an Athenian. To the extent that the authors of the New Testament (including Luke, who almost certainly was not a Jew[1]) had steeped themselves in the characteristic phraseology of the Septuagint, their Greek took on a Semitic cast. In this connection it is instructive to compare the influence which the King James Version has exerted upon the literary style of many an English author.

In the following analyses, therefore, it will be necessary not only to evaluate the extent to which an author uses a literary or a nonliterary type of koine, but also the degree to which a Semitic influence (Hebrew or Aramaic) has affected his idiom.

A. *The Epistle to the Hebrews.*—Starting with those books which are nearest in literary quality to the highest standard of koine Greek, we must undoubtedly give first place to the anonymous Epistle to the Hebrews. Curiously enough this author, although he addresses his epistle to "Hebrews," is the least Hebraistic writer in the New Testament. Except, of course, in quotations from the Old Testament—which are invariably from the Septuagint and never from the Hebrew—there is scarcely a trace of Semitic influence in his work. The author has a rich vocabulary at his command and uses it with great skill.

The style is even more characteristic of a practiced scholar than the vocabulary. In the first place the Greek text of the epistle is distinguished among the prose works of the primitive church by its rhythmical cadences, so much cultivated by "good" Greek authors. Again, the author likes to choose his words to produce alliteration. For example, in the first verse of

[1] Compare Col. 4:11 with vs. 14, where Paul seems to distinguish Luke from those who "are the only men of the circumcision among my fellow workers for the kingdom of God."

his treatise there are five words which begin with the syllable πολ-, παλ-, πατ-, or προ-; and in 9:27 out of five consecutive words four begin with α-. He also endeavors, as did careful classical authors, to avoid bringing two words together when the former ends in a vowel and the latter begins with a vowel (called hiatus).

Besides being acquainted with these tricks of the ancient rhetorician—and not only acquainted with them, but being able to use them—this unknown writer displays a most remarkable capacity for an architectonic style of composition. Unlike Paul, whose emotions occasionally run away with him, making havoc of syntax, this author knows at each moment precisely what his next sentence will be, and he follows meticulously an elaborate outline. In fact his treatise involves the longest sustained argument of any book of the New Testament. With delicate finesse he suggests an idea before he develops it at some subsequent point. For example, in 2:17 he mentions "high priest" and takes it up again at great length at 4:14 ff.; in 5:6 he mentions Melchizedek, but defers the full development of this typology to 6:20 ff. He deftly employs parentheses and asides, sometimes of considerable length (e.g., 3:7-11; 5:13-14; 8:5; 11:13-16). These and many similar features betray the hand of a careful and skillful author, whose work is easily recognized as coming closer to the definite literary style of a master of the Greek language than anything else in the New Testament.

B. The Epistle of James.—The brief Epistle of James shares many of the literary characteristics of the Epistle to the Hebrews. It too is written in excellent Greek and in a strikingly elevated and picturesque style resembling that of the Hebrew prophets. Though the tone is distinctly Jewish, there are very few Hebraisms in the epistle. The author observes certain niceties of grammatical distinctions (such as the correct usage of the two negatives in Greek, οὐ and μή) and maintains a high degree of precision in the idiomatic choice of moods and tenses. As to his vocabulary, he freely employs rare words and compounds, all of them correctly formed and some of them possibly formed by himself. He shows great rhetorical skill, making use of not a few figures of speech which were affected by the best koine authors. He exhibits a marked tendency to link together clauses and sentences by the repetition of the leading word or some of its cognates, a device known as paronomasia or assonance. He indulges in the gentle art of alliteration; for example, the three prominent words in 1:21 begin with δ. Frequently two or more words in close juxtaposition end with the same syllable or syllables, as in 1:7, 14; 2:16, 19; 5:5, 6. On the whole his sentence structure is terse, vivid, and rhythmical, being marked by a certain epigrammatic conciseness.

C. Luke and Acts.—Another author whose literary abilities were of a superior order was Luke, the physician (Col. 4:14). The Third Gospel and Acts reveal the hand of the most versatile of all the New Testament authors. The elaborately constructed preface to his Gospel (1:1-4) is a period of the purest Greek, one which may be compared, without too much disadvantage to Luke, with the prefaces to the histories of Herodotus and Thucydides. His breadth of culture is shown by his employing a good number of words and literary constructions unused or very rare in the rest of the New Testament. Thus his two books contain about 750 words not occurring elsewhere in the New Testament—more than 250 are in the Gospel and about 500 in Acts. He is familiar with nautical terms, which are correct without being strictly technical (Acts 27). Many scholars have supposed that it is possible to detect in Luke's books stylistic and verbal indications of his special knowledge of medicine, but almost all the examples generally adduced in proof of this supposition ought rather to be interpreted as showing merely that Luke was a cultured and cosmopolitan author of literary koine.

This does not mean, however, that his work lacks *all* indications which point to his profession. Given the knowledge supplied by Paul (Col. 4:14) that Luke was a physician, one may not unfairly interpret the choice of his language in several passages in his Gospel, when compared with parallel passages in Matthew and Mark, as reflecting a physician's point of view. Thus only he indicates that Peter's mother-in-law "was ill with a *high* fever" (4:38; cf. Matt. 8:14; Mark 1:30). Only he tells us that "there came a man *full* of leprosy" (5:12; cf. Matt. 8:2; Mark 1:40). Again, his professional pride prevented his repeating *in toto* (8:43) what he had read in Mark about the poor woman "who had suffered much under many physicians, and had spent all that she had, *and was no better but rather grew worse*" (Mark 5:26).

In characteristic details Luke commends himself as a capable littérateur. He uses the optative mood, which is totally lacking in Matthew, John, James, and Revelation, twenty-eight times. He makes frequent and generally idiomatic use of participles. Among Hellenistic authors who show certain affinities with Luke, so far as his vocabulary is concerned, are Polybius, Dioscorides, and Josephus. Cultivated Hellenistic authors disliked foreign and barbarous sounding words. Many passages which Luke derived from Mark show that he shared this repugnance. Thus he omits "Boanerges," the sobriquet of James and John (Mark 3:17; cf. Luke 6:14); "Bartimaeus, the son of Timaeus" (Mark 10:46; cf. Luke 18:35); "hosanna" (Mark 11:9; cf. Luke 19:38); "Gethsemane" (Mark 14:32; cf. Luke 22:39-40); "abba" (Mark 14:36; cf. Luke 22:42); "Golgotha" (Mark 15:22; cf. Luke 23:33); "Eloi, Eloi, lama sabachthani" (Mark 15:34; cf. Luke 23:44-45). In other cases Luke translates the foreign word into standard Greek. Thus, for example, the Jewish title of respect, "rabbi," which appears sixteen times in the other three Gospels, does not appear once in Luke; he alone prefers to use (six times) the classical Greek ἐπιστάτης meaning "commander, master." Again, the Semitic word of asseveration, ἀμήν, which appears in the other Gospels scores of times, can be found only six times in Luke's Gospel; in the remaining instances Luke omits it or replaces it with the classical ἀληθῶς meaning "truly."

On the other hand it must not be imagined that Luke completely rewrote the narratives which came to his hand. While smoothing certain details in accord with a native feeling for good Greek, he preserves unchanged many other features that reflect their original Palestinian background. Indeed so sensitive is he to matters of style that in the parts of his narrative which have their scene in Palestine, he prefers to retain a considerable amount of the Semitic idiom of his sources. Thus the syntax and language of the main body of his Gospel differ markedly from the carefully balanced sentence comprising the four introductory verses, and also, to a smaller extent, from the canticles in chs. 1–2, which consciously imitate the devotional phraseology of the Greek Old Testament. Strangely enough, Hebraisms have been found to be rather more abundant in Luke than in the other Gospels. Thus he is given to connect his narrative together by the more or less Hebraistic formulas, "It came to pass that . . . ," "In those days . . . ," "And behold! . . ." A particularly glaring Semitism is in 20:12, literally "he added to send." Likewise his second volume (Acts) is marked by two more or less clearly defined strata. In the first part, containing testimony from Palestinian witnesses, Luke retains proportionately more Semitic coloring than in the remaining chapters. In the latter, where Paul's missionary journeys into Gentile lands are described, the author appropriately clothes his account in more elegant Greek, which would have been quite out of character in the first part.

D. The First Epistle of Peter.—The language of I Peter is nearer to the standards of classical Greek than the vernacular koine. Although the author was deeply steeped in the Septuagint, he succeeds in impressing his own style upon what he borrows from that source. He employs the Greek definite article with a more elegant touch than does any other writer in the New Testament. For example, he affects the "envelope construction" at least eight times (1:17; 3:1, 3, 20; 4:14; 5:1 twice, 4). He observes, along with only the author of the Epistle to the Hebrews, a refined nicety in the use of ὡς (1:19; 2:16; 3:7). His vocabulary is marked by a certain dignity and elevation. Though the epistle embraces but five chapters, the range of words is wide. On the other hand very few connective particles, so dear to the heart of an Attic author, are used. The writer handles the language idiomatically and with a rather high degree of correctness, even though not in classical style. Since it is highly improbable that a Galilean fisherman, whose provincial Aramaic brogue betrayed his home (Matt. 26:73) and who, according to Acts 4:13, was "uneducated," was directly responsible for the diction of I Peter, the suggestion has frequently been made that the elegance of language is due to his secretary Silvanus (I Pet. 5:12).

If the writers mentioned above exhibit a vocabulary and style which more or less closely approximate the literary koine, other authors of the New Testament find themselves removed from such standards by a quite considerable distance. Conspicuous examples of the nonliterary koine are the Gospel According to Mark and the book of Revelation.

E. The Gospel of Mark.—The lack of polish in Mark's colloquial style is somewhat obscured when it is put in English dress. Even there, however, it is possible to observe with what monotonous frequency the simple connective "and" is used. In the King James Version, for example, of forty-five verses in the first chapter, thirty-five begin with "and"; and twelve of the sixteen chapters of the book begin with this same conjunction. This reflects faithfully what the reader of the Greek text can see, namely, that of eighty-eight sections and subsections into which the Second Gospel may be divided (Westcott and Hort's text), no fewer than eighty begin with καί. Mark's limited choice of connectives is matched by a rather small general vocabulary. He uses 1,270 words (besides 60 proper names) and of these only 80 are peculiar to him among the New Testament writers. In common with colloquial preference in every language, Mark has a predilection for diminutives and for accumulated negatives (see the Greek text of 1:44; 5:3; 16:8; etc.).

What Mark's style lacks in grace and polish it makes up in freshness and vigor. His language is characterized by homely simplicity and can on occasion be repetitious (as in 1:45; 4:8;

14:68), but more frequently it is marked by great brevity, particularly in reporting our Lord's teaching (cf. 8:29 with Matt. 16:15-20; 12:38-40 with Matt. 23).

Though Mark's Greek is the poorest of the evangelists', he is not to be considered illiterate. Doubtless more at home in Aramaic than in Greek—of the four Gospels Mark has the greatest variety of Aramaisms—he still has a sufficient command of popular, colloquial koine to convey truthfully, if not elegantly, the words and deeds of his Lord. In his own way, indeed, he was an artistic genius, for he invented a new type of literature. Nothing quite like a "gospel" as a piece of literature had existed in any language prior to Mark's work.

F. The Book of Revelation.—Along with Mark on the level of nonliterary koine must be placed the last book of the New Testament. As early as the middle of the third century Dionysius of Alexandria (according to Eusebius *Church History* VII. 25. 26) termed the Greek of the book of Revelation barbaric and ungrammatical. Since the time of this church father, who was acquainted with the standards of "good" Greek, every scholar working upon the Greek text of Revelation has been struck by its frequent violations of the rules of concord in Greek grammar and syntax. These have usually been explained by supposing that the author was far better acquainted with a Semitic tongue (Hebrew or Aramaic) than with Greek, and would therefore consciously or unconsciously lapse into non-Greek expressions. Thus, according to the usual Semitic idiom, he adds pleonastically the oblique forms of the personal pronoun to participles and relative pronouns; for example, "To him that overcometh, to him I will give . . ." (2:7) ; "I have set before thee a door opened, which no one can shut it" (3:8 literally translated). A linguistic eccentricity, so far as Greek grammar is concerned, which is nevertheless easily explicable on the basis of Hebrew grammar, is the co-ordination of a participle with a finite verb. Thus in 1:5-6 this author writes, "unto him that loves us . . . and he made us . . ."; in 2:20, "Jezebel, who calls herself a prophetess, and she teaches . . ." (where, in addition to the point under discussion, it may be mentioned that the Greek concord of cases is violated by the use of the nominative rather than accusative form of the participle) ; and in 7:14, "These are they that come out of the great tribulation and they have washed their robes."

Another linguistic peculiarity is the occasional disregard of genders (see the Greek text of 1:10; 4:1, 8; 11:4; 19:20; etc.). Since elsewhere the author is correct in his observance of gender, some of these examples are to be accounted for on the score of indifference or carelessness, and others as due to his thinking in a Semitic language while writing in Greek.

In spite of the presence of such bold disregard for the ordinary rules of Greek syntax, the book of Revelation is not lacking in literary power. Certain solemn and sonorous passages which are almost poetically rhythmical (4:11; 5:9-10; 7:15-17; 11:17-18; 15:3-4; 18:2-8, 19-24; etc.) have something of the Miltonic "organ-voice," discernible even in English translation.[2]

G. The Gospel of Matthew.—In characterizing the language of Matthew one may usefully compare it with Mark and Luke. Containing fewer marked mannerisms than either Mark or Luke, Matthew's style is less individualistic than theirs. It is smoother than Mark's and less varied (that is, more monotonous) than Luke's. As to vocabulary, Matthew's is about as much less rich than Luke's as it surpasses Mark's. According to one analysis, the characteristic words and expressions of Matthew number 95, as compared with 151 for Luke and 41 for Mark.[3] Matthew shows more care than Mark—but not so much as Luke—in avoiding words condemned as "barbarisms" by Atticizing purists. Thus he mends the Greek of Mark by substituting κλίνη (Matt. 9:2) for the vernacular κράβατος (Mark 2:4) ; he writes "they took counsel" (12:14) instead of Mark's "they were giving counsel" (Mark 3:6, literally translated; a variant reading in Mark is no better: "they were making counsel") ; and in many places he drops Mark's colloquial use of the historical present.

As regards composition, Matthew's penchant, in common with contemporary Jewish rabbis, was for arithmetical arrangements. He was particularly fond of grouping his material by three's. The following are some of the more obvious instances of this systematizing. There are three divisions in the genealogy of our Lord (1:1-17), three temptations (4:1-11), three illustrations of righteousness (6:1-18), three commands (7:7), three miracles of healing (8:1-15), three miracles of power (8:23–9:8), a threefold answer to the question regarding fasting (9:14-17), a threefold "fear not" (10:26, 28, 31), a threefold repetition of "he is not worthy of me" (10:37-38), three parables of sowing (13:1-32), three sayings concerning "the little ones" (18:6, 10, 14), three parables of warning (21:28–22:14), three questions by

[2] Only a poet can appreciate a poet. For this reason Christina G. Rossetti was able to detect and interpret certain nuances in Revelation which are lost upon more prosaic minds; see her book, *The Face of the Deep: A Devotional Commentary on the Apocalypse* (2nd ed.; London: Society for Promoting Christian Knowledge, 1893).

[3] John C. Hawkins, *Horae Synopticae* (2nd ed.; Oxford: Clarendon Press, 1909), p. 190.

his adversaries (22:15-40), three prayers in Gethsemane (26:39-44), three denials by Peter (26:69-75), and three questions by Pilate (27: 11-17). A sevenfold arrangement is represented, among other examples in Matthew, by the seven clauses in the Lord's prayer (6:9-13) — two more than in the Lukan version—seven demons (12:45), seven parables (ch. 13), seven loaves (15:34), seven baskets (15:37), forgiving not "seven times, but seventy times seven" (18:22), seven brothers (22:25), and seven "woes" (ch. 23).

On the whole the Greek vocabulary and style of the First Gospel lack any particularly distinctive traits. The language is neither very poor koine nor highly polished literary Greek.

There was a tradition in the early church that Matthew wrote his Gospel in "Hebrew" (Aramaic). In modern times several scholars have argued that one or more of the four Gospels were written originally in Aramaic and translated into Greek. None of the hypothetical Aramaic Gospels is extant. Most New Testament scholars believe that the internal evidence of all four Gospels indicates that they were composed in Greek, but embody Aramaic source material, some of which was oral and some of which perhaps was written.[4]

H. The Gospel and Epistles of John.—The language of the Gospel According to John has a simplicity and a grandeur which are unrivaled by any other book of the New Testament. Though John's vocabulary is far less extensive than that of the other three Gospels, he makes impressive, almost majestic, use of his fundamental words and phrases by the expedient of repetition. In comparison with the Synoptic Gospels, John has few compound verbs, few adjectives, few concrete nouns; he turns more to abstract nouns, although his use of these is restrained. Characteristic words which appear many times in both the Gospel and in one or more of the epistles are "truth," "love," "light," "to witness," "world," "sin," "judgment," and "life."

His syntactical construction is severely plain —almost childlike. Even where a particle of logical sequence might have been expected, John co-ordinates clauses and sentences, sometimes with a wooden "and" (parataxis), sometimes without any conjunction at all (asyndeton). Examples of parataxis where an adversative conjunction might have been expected include the following: "Search the Scriptures; for in them ye think ye have eternal life: and they are they which testify of me. *And* ye will not come to me" (5:39-40)—here the RSV

[4] For further discussion of the theory of Aramaic Gospels see article "The Growth of the Gospels," pp. 67-68 and Intro. to Matthew, p. 240.

clarifies the sense by using "yet" for the second "and"; "Did not Moses give you the law, *and* none of you keepeth the law?" (7:19 literally translated)—here the KJV, ASV, and RSV use "yet"; "Then they sought to take him: *and* no man laid hands on him (7:30)—the KJV and RSV substitute "but" for "and"; "Then Jesus said, Yet a little while am I with you, *and* I go to him that sent me" (7:33 literally translated)—where again the KJV and RSV attempt to improve the sense by reading "and then" (for other examples see 1:10; 3:19; 6:70; 8:20, 49; 10:25; 17:11). On the other hand sometimes the author dispenses with even the simple "and"; thus all the sentences in the first twenty verses of ch. 15 follow one another without any conjunction whatever. It is as though John remembered that someone had told him, "You must not always be saying 'and.'" From these instances of parataxis and asyndeton one gathers that the author frequently was not concerned to indicate the sequence of his reasoning, but left it to the sympathetic interpretation of the reader to determine the mutual relation of his sentences.

Another stylistic peculiarity of John is his fondness for combining positive and negative expressions of the same truth: as, "All things were made through him, and without him was not anything made" (1:3); "He confessed, and denied not" (1:20); "[Jesus] knew all men and needed no one to bear witness of man" (2:25); ". . . should not perish, but have everlasting life" (3:16; see also 3:36; 5:24, 30; 10:5; 18:20; I John 1:6; 2:4, 27; etc.).

John writes pure Greek as far as words and grammar are concerned, but more than once he puts his ideas into molds congenial to a typically Jewish point of view. Thus the phrase "the son of perdition" (17:12), which represents a relation between a spiritual principle and the person in whom it is incarnated; "to rejoice with joy" (χαρᾷ χαίρειν, 3:29); the use of the verb "to know" (as in 17:3 and elsewhere) to designate the most intimate spiritual union between God and man; the indicating of moral dependence upon another being by the expression "to be in" or "to abide in" (John 14:17; 15:4; I John 2:6; etc.)—all these are far more typical of Semitic idiom than of Greek. In common with koine Greek, as well as Semitic preference, John very seldom uses indirect discourse, even for the words and opinions of others (perhaps the only example of indirect discourse is the true text of 4:51; see RSV).

The reader of the Greek text soon discovers that John is particularly fond of the perfect tense. As compared with the Synoptic Gospels, John uses the perfect (and pluperfect) tense three times as often as Mark and Luke do, and five times as often as Matthew does; furthermore, I John uses it twice as often, proportionately to length, as does the Fourth Gospel. John's overworking of the perfect tense is probably to be explained by his wish to emphasize thereby the abiding consequences and eternal significance of the work and words of God's only Son.

Finally, two other marked peculiarities of John's literary style deserve mention. The Gospel is chiefly written in short, weighty sentences and phrases. Indeed it may almost be said that the shorter they are, the weightier! Typical examples are: "I am the light of the world" (8:12); "thy brother shall rise again" (11:23); "Jesus wept" (11:35); "and it was night" (13:30); "now Barabbas was a robber" (18:40); and see also 6:68; 7:19; 11:25; etc. The other notable characteristic of John's style is the circular or spiral motion of his reasoning (e.g., 8:38-44; 10:7-18; 14:10-12, 20-23; ch. 17; large sections of I John). The seemingly inane repetitions and the frequent retrogression to the preceding point before adding a new idea are devices which, though appearing tedious to the hasty reader, reveal how very solicitous John was that his readers should comprehend all the varied implications of what he wished faithfully to transmit to them.

J. The Epistles of Paul.—Of Saul of Tarsus we know more than of any other author of the New Testament. He was a Hellenized Jew and a Roman citizen. Probably he could make an address in Aramaic (such must be the meaning of Ἑβραΐδι, Acts 21:40) and in Greek equally well. Training at the feet of Gamaliel (Acts 22:3) would involve instruction in Hebrew (cf. Phil. 3:5). Though his birthplace Tarsus was a city second to few, if any, others as a seat of learning, it is difficult to be certain that he had studied rhetoric and philosophy there. Little or no evidence exists that his reading in Greek literature had gone very far. Not much can be inferred from his quotation of a line from *Thaïs* by the Greek comic dramatist, Menander (I Cor. 15:33). It was possibly a current quotation—like many a line from Shakespeare today. The same may be said of the verse from Aratus or Cleanthes which, according to Acts 17:28, Paul cited at Athens, as well as of the line of Epimenides embedded in Tit. 1:12. However these three references are estimated, the fact remains that classical Greek literature had done little to color Paul's style. A careful examination of his vocabulary shows that his words do not come from literary sources but from the common stock of ordinary spoken Greek. There is but one exception to this statement: though Paul shows so few signs of having been influenced by secular Greek literature, his ideas and language betray a strong influence from that piece of literature which he had studied more than any other, the Old Testament. Though he occasionally quotes from the Hebrew, it is the Septuagint which has exerted the most powerful influence upon his own use of Greek. Yet with the exception of the Epistle to the Ephesians, the Pauline correspondence contains remarkably few out-and-out Semitisms.

In analyzing Paul's literary style one observes that he frequently arranges his arguments in the form of a rhetorical dialogue of questions and answers. He allows his imaginary opponent to raise problems ("But someone will say . . . ," or "You will now say . . .") which he in turn often grants halfheartedly, only to counter with language so much the stronger in opposition. Frequently (twelve times) he expresses his abhorrence of an inference which he fears may be falsely drawn from his argument with a violent μὴ γένοιτο, rendered variously as "God forbid," "By no means!" or "Certainly not!" This species of literary causerie in pointed style has been explained as due to the influence of the Stoic diatribe on Paul, but it can also be accounted for largely in terms of contemporary rabbinical practice. It may also be mentioned that a few scholars have thought that Paul's language shows that he imitated the rhythmic *clausulae* so characteristic of certain Greek and Latin authors, but this opinion has not won wide assent.

Since it is likely that Paul customarily dictated his letters (see Rom. 16:22 especially in the RSV), it is not surprising that his style is more conversational than deliberately polished. The fact that Paul dictated his correspondence has other implications as well and may explain the occasional break in thought or style within a letter. After an interruption of an hour, a day, or a month, Paul would have resumed his dictation in quite a different mood. Again, it is difficult not to believe that different scribes were employed at various times; this also would account for variations in style. An inferior scribe would get down the main words correctly, but the little connecting links he may have filled in himself.

Borne along by his earnest and spirited emotions, Paul's colloquial Greek sometimes becomes elevated and dynamic. Indeed, according to the opinion of a famous modern critic of ancient literary style, in Rom. 8:31-39 and I Cor. 13 "the diction of the Apostle rises to the heights of Plato in the *Phaedrus*."[5] At other times the apostle's impetuosity would play

[5] Eduard Norden, *Die antike Kunstprosa, vom VI. Jahrhundert v. Chr. bis in die Zeit der Renaissance* (4th ed.; Leipzig and Berlin: B. G. Teubner, 1923), II, 509.

havoc with strict logical sequence. He starts a sentence in one way and ends it in another. Thus are to be explained, for example, the two breaks in grammar, called anacolutha, in Gal. 2:4, 6 (see especially the RSV). One of the most striking instances of anacoluthon in the New Testament is Rom. 5:12-13. In contrast to this exuberance, at other times Paul moves slowly and laboriously, struggling with periods of unwieldy length. In the first chapter of Ephesians, for example, his composition displays very little flexibility and ease.

The language of Paul, in short, is as varied as he was himself. Of scarcely anyone else is it more true, in de Buffon's memorable phrase, that *le style, c'est l'homme même* ("the style is the man himself"). To quote from a celebrated classical scholar: "Paul's Greek has nothing to do with any school or with any model, but streams awkwardly with precipitous bubbling right out of the heart; but it is real Greek."[6] It is a fact, however it is explained, that the style, diction, and vocabulary of the three Pastoral epistles (I and II Timothy and Titus) differ from the remainder of the epistles ascribed to Paul. Complete uniformity in these matters cannot, of course, be expected in any author, least of all in one who, like the apostle Paul, is so versatile and creative. But it is significant that not only is a change observable in the use of certain nouns and verbs, but also that the Pastorals lack certain Pauline particles, prepositions, enclitics, and pronouns.[7] The change in the subject matter (for the Pastorals deal largely with church government and conflict with heresy) would explain the difference in terminology required to express such concepts, but it is much more difficult to account for the change in the connective words. Furthermore the general tone of the Greek is perceptibly closer to the literary koine than are the other Pauline epistles. For the last century many scholars have held that these three epistles were written by one of his admirers a generation or so after the death of the apostle and were circulated under the name of Paul. On the other hand, though the Pastorals were not written with Paul's own pen, it may be supposed that in accord with the methods employed by ancients in writing letters, they were the work of a secretary writing at his order and under his constant supervision.[8]

[6] Ulrich von Wilamowitz-Moellendorff, *Die griechische Literatur und Sprache* (*Die Kultur der Gegenwart*, Teil I, Abteilung viii; 2nd ed.; Berlin and Leipzig: B. G. Teubner, 1905), p. 157.

[7] The most detailed treatment is by P. N. Harrison, *The Problem of the Pastoral Epistles* (London: Oxford University Press, 1921).

[8] Otto Roller, *Das Formular der paulinischen Briefe* (Stuttgart: W. Kohlhammer Verlag, 1933), pp. 4-22. See

K. The Second Epistle of Peter.—II Peter is perhaps the only book of the New Testament whose language, it seems, profits from being translated. Attracted by rare or unique words and occasionally using expressions which, so far as can be determined, appear to be contrary to correct usage, the author strikes many modern scholars as one who had learned his Greek chiefly from books. A noticeable idiosyncrasy is the writer's tendency to repeat a particularly solemn or sonorous Greek word; examples may be found in 1:3-4, 17-18; 2:1-3, 4-5, 12, 16-18; 3:3, 10-12. Though he strives rather artificially to produce a rhetorically elegant piece of literature, the few connective particles at his command, as well as his cumbersome and occasionally clumsy sentence construction, are clear indications of the poverty of his linguistic equipment.

The manifest divergence in style and language between I Peter and II Peter has often been observed. Jerome, and many after him, supposed that it was due to Peter's having employed different amanuenses. If this is true, Peter accorded great freedom to his secretaries, for there are about six times the number of disagreements between the vocabulary of each epistle as agreements. Calvin suggested that one of the disciples of Peter wrote at the apostle's command. Most scholars today, except Roman Catholics, regard II Peter as pseudepigraphic and dating from early in the second century when the artificial literary tastes of the Atticists reached their climax.

L. The Epistle of Jude.—Of the short Epistle of Jude, which is so similar to the second chapter of II Peter, little need be said. The author has a better command of Greek than does the author of II Peter. He selects his words with a certain amount of literary taste. As to style, he frequently groups words and phrases in triads (see vss. 2, 5-7, 8, 11, 12, 19, 22-23, 25). Within twenty-five verses the optative mood appears twice (vss. 2, 9). On the whole, Jude's little letter is a typical example of idiomatic koine written in a moderately good style.

M. The Language of Jesus.—In common with his Palestinian contemporaries Jesus undoubtedly spoke Aramaic as his mother tongue, but being a Galilean he very likely was able to use Greek as well. One would expect that most of his teaching to the common people of Palestine would be given in Aramaic. That this was the case is rendered practically certain by (*a*) the presence of four Aramaic words or phrases from the lips of Jesus preserved in the Greek

also the paragraph near the end of p. 51. [For other views as to the origin of these letters see above, pp. 39-40, and the treatment of I and II Timothy and Titus in Vol. XI.]

Gospels (*talitha cumi*, Mark 5:41; *ephphatha*, Mark 7:34; *abba*, Mark 14:36; and *Eloi, Eloi, lama sabachthani*, Mark 15:34; see also Matt. 27:46), and (*b*) the circumstance that several sayings of Jesus, when translated from Greek into Aramaic, involve plays on words or puns— a circumstance not likely to occur unless the puns were present in the original Aramaic. That the Hebrew people particularly enjoyed puns is shown by the presence of several plays on words in the Old Testament (see the Hebrew of Isa. 24:16-18; 27:7; Jer. 1:11-12; Amos 8:1-2). Jesus apparently shared this relish of his people for puns. Thus the typically Oriental hyperbole, "You blind guides, straining out a gnat and swallowing a camel!" (Matt. 23:24), must have involved a jingle of the Aramaic words for "gnat" and "camel"—*qalmā'* and *gamlā'*. Again, when Jesus said that "even the hairs of your head are all numbered" (Matt. 10:30), the Aramaic form of his statement may have embodied a play on the word for "hairs" (*menê*) and the root of the verb "to number" (*menā'*). In Aramaic the words for "commit" and "slave" are both regular forms of the triliteral root *'bd*, and in John 8:34 it seems as if one word has suggested the other: "Every one who *commits* sin is a *slave* to sin" (there is a similar play on the same root in Luke 7:8). According to Matt. 10:12-13, when Jesus sent out the twelve, he instructed them: "As you enter the house, salute it. And if the house is worthy, let your peace come upon it." Although in the Greek text the verb "salute" (ἀσπάζεσθε) has no verbal relation to the word "peace" (εἰρήνη), it is otherwise in Aramaic, where the usual verb of salutation means literally "to give peace" to someone.

Only rarely is the Greek able to reproduce an Aramaic assonance of words. Perhaps the only such example is in John 3:8, for the Greek word πνεῦμα means both "wind" and "spirit" just as does the Aramaic *rûhā'* which Jesus undoubtedly used in speaking with Nicodemus, a ruler of the Jews. Not quite so successful is Matthew's attempt to reproduce in Greek Jesus' famous saying to Simon Peter, "You are *kêphā'* and upon this *kêphā'* I will build my church" (Matt. 16:18). In Aramaic the apostle's name, or nickname, and the word for rock are identical, whereas in Greek one is a masculine form (Πέτρος) and the other feminine (πέτρα).

III. Interpretation of the Language of the New Testament

During the seventeenth and eighteenth centuries scholars disputed heatedly whether the language of the New Testament ought to be explained chiefly in terms of Hebrew syntax or of classical Greek. Since the New Testament agrees fully with neither, both the Hebraists and the Purists, as they were called, were forced to exaggerate the similarities and to explain away the divergencies from their respective standards by elaborate arbitrary assumptions. Thus under the name of enallage ("exchange") it was considered justifiable to take almost every tense, case, and particle for every other respectively. With the rise of scientific philology in the nineteenth century, this monstrous maltreatment of New Testament Greek was successfully discredited and finally abandoned. Grammarians, led by G. B. Winer in 1822, came to realize that the language of the New Testament must be interpreted in the light of what can be known of the historical development of the living Greek language.

Much assistance in the proper understanding of the vocabulary and syntax of the New Testament was made available at the close of the nineteenth century through the discoveries of great quantities of nonliterary Greek papyri preserved for two millenniums in the dry climate of Egypt. The first to observe the great significance of these papyri for the study of the language of the New Testament was a young German pastor at Marburg, Adolf Deissmann. One day while turning over in the library at Heidelberg University a volume of Greek papyri newly published at Berlin, he was suddenly struck by the similarity of what he was reading to the language of the New Testament. Further study revealed that many of the so-called peculiarities of biblical Greek are due simply to the fact that the writers of the New Testament for the most part made use of the ordinary colloquial Greek, the koine of their day. Deissmann's discovery met with enthusiastic response in other countries among such scholars as J. H. Moulton in England and A. T. Robertson in the United States. It is now a generally acknowledged fact that the books which set forth the One whom the common people heard gladly (Mark 12:37) were themselves written in their own speech.

Carried on by the exhilaration of having found a key that unlocks many lexical and syntactical puzzles in the New Testament, Deissmann and certain other scholars went to the extreme of neglecting to take into due account two other factors immensely important for a correct interpretation of the language of the New Testament, namely, the influence of the language of the Old Testament, and the creative vitality of the Christian faith. The pendulum has now begun to swing back to a more central position. The papyri are still recognized as indispensable to the understanding of much of the vocabulary and grammar of the New

Testament, but it is now perceived also that the most distinctive and the really important words in the New Testament are either borrowed from the Old Testament or are common, everyday words which the Spirit of God filled with new significance. The proper methodology in determining the meaning of any given word in the New Testament involves a threefold investigation: (a) Has the word acquired a different shade of meaning in the koine as compared with classical Greek? (b) How far has its use by Jews whose Bible was the Old Testament in Greek, the Septuagint, including the Apocrypha, colored its meaning? (c) Has the early church given it a new and distinctively Christian significance?[9] Several typical examples of changes in the meaning of certain Greek words will illustrate how much the interpreter of the New Testament can learn by pursuing each of these inquiries.

A. The Koine Element.—In translating Jesus' question "Which of you by being anxious can add one cubit to his ἡλικίαν?" (Matt. 6:27; Luke 12:25), Wycliffe, all the sixteenth-century translators, the King James translators, and the English Revisers (1881), having consulted dictionaries of classical Greek, chose the rendering "stature." But koine sources, not available to these translators, have taught modern scholars that the prevailing meaning of this word in common parlance in postclassical Greek was "span of life." With this knowledge, a warning of Jesus which seemed inane and unnecessary —for what normal individual worries because he is not half a yard taller?—becomes pointed and needful, particularly since worry shortens life!

According to the King James Version, Peter counsels his readers, "Desire the sincere milk of the word" (I Pet. 2:2). In the nonliterary papyri, as well as in modern Greek, the adjective here translated "sincere" is very frequently used to characterize food and drink as "pure" or "unadulterated."

Thousands of tax receipts discovered in the sands of Egypt employ the verb ἀπέχειν to signify that the debt was paid in full. When, therefore, our Lord uses this verb in referring to those who are ostentatious in their religious devotions (Matt. 6:2, 5, 16), we must understand him to mean that such persons have already received all the reward they can expect— the praise of men.

Since in many business documents ὑπόστασις refers to the possession of a piece of property, it is both legitimate and illuminating to render this word in Heb. 11:1, "Now faith is the *title deed* of things hoped for."

'Αρραβών is still another business term which, though also appearing in classical Greek, acquires fresh meaning from its frequent occurrence in papyrus agreements and contracts, where it refers to the "down payment" as a pledge that the remainder will be fully paid later. So when Paul writes of "the *earnest* of the Spirit in our hearts" (II Cor. 1:22; see also 5:5 and Eph. 1:14), he means that the gift of the Spirit is both a foretaste and a guarantee of our inheritance, which will be fully bestowed later.

All the major apostolic authors use the word παρουσία to describe the final coming of the glorified Christ. From papyrological sources it is now known that this term was widely employed from Ptolemaic times onward for the arrival or visit of the king or the emperor. Frequently the people of the city or district to be favored by such a visit were required to pay special taxes to defray expenses and to provide a costly crown for the ruler. Contrast "the crown of righteousness which the Lord . . . will award . . . to all who have loved his *appearing*" (II Tim. 4:8; cf. I Thess. 2:19). Occasionally the beginning of a new era in reckoning time was dated from the advent of the sovereign. According to the New Testament the final *parousia* of the Lord will inaugurate a new aeon (II Pet. 3:12-13), and in anticipation of this appearing his people should be blameless and pure (I Thess. 5:23; I John 2:28–3:3).

The papyri also reveal that during the centuries the meaning of more than one Greek word, which had originally been quite pointed and forceful, was worn down and weakened. Thus to insist upon the rendering "his own," "their own," etc., will frequently overtranslate ἴδιος in the New Testament (as in Acts 24:24 ASV mg.; I Cor. 7:37; Eph. 5:22 ASV; I Pet. 3:1, 5; etc.). Again, in the nonliterary koine the distinction between the prepositions εἰς and ἐν has become hazy and is often entirely obliterated, so that modern vernacular Greek has dispensed with ἐν altogether. In not a few passages the Greek of the New Testament reflects the mutual encroachment of each upon the functions of the other; see, for a particularly obvious example, the variant readings in the last part of Mark 4:8, where they have identical meanings.

The new sources also prove that certain other words, long designated "biblical" because they

---

[9] This in essence is the methodology followed by the contributors to Gerhard Kittel's monumental *Theologisches Wörterbuch zum Neuen Testament* (Stuttgart: W. Kohlhammer Verlag, 1933). A summary of the method may be read in English in Gerhard Kittel's *Lexicographia Sacra:* Two lectures on the making of the *Theologisches Wörterbuch zum Neuen Testament*, delivered October 20-21, 1937, in the Divinity School, Cambridge (London: Society for Promoting Christian Knowledge, 1938).

could not be found in any secular author, were very much at home in the common speech of the first century. Such a word is that which scholars had judged must be translated by "collection" (in I Cor. 16:1)—a translation now seen to be fully justified by its usage in papyri and inscriptions.

A few words in the New Testament still await further light from the papyri. A notable example is the word usually translated "daily" in the Lord's Prayer (Matt. 6:11; Luke 11:3). Since it does not appear (with one exception) in any Greek document outside the context of the Lord's Prayer, its exact import has been learnedly debated. A papyrus account book from the Fayyum in Egypt, dating from the fifth or sixth century, was found to contain the word in a fragmentary form, apparently referring to daily rations or provisions, but more light is required before its precise meaning can be ascertained.

B. The Semitic Element.—The meaning of many of the richest and most significant words in the New Testament cannot be found in the ordinary Greek dictionary. Instead of going to Athens for help, the interpreter must go to Jerusalem, for, in the pregnant phrase of Albrecht Ritschl, "the Old Testament is the lexicon of the New Testament." It is a fact that most of the religious terminology of the New Testament can be understood only as it is read against the background of the Hebrew Old Testament and its Greek translation, the Septuagint. Thus the Greek word for "law" (νόμος) shows a decided semantic shift in passing from a Hellenic to a Jewish environment. All classical Greek authors used the word for "law" very much as we understand it today, namely, as a "statute" or a "fixed rule." But since in the Septuagint this word translates the Hebrew word tôrāh, the Hellenized Jew regarded νόμος less as an abstract principle and more as the gracious revelation by a personal God of his will for his people This revelation is not expressed only by the indicative mood in a declarative statement, but more characteristically by the imperative in a sovereign call, to which the only proper response on the part of man is loving obedience (Matt. 22:36-40; Gal. 5:14).

The Greek words translated "to repent" or "repentance," which appear so often in the Gospels, occur comparatively infrequently in classical and koine Greek, and when they do appear there, their meaning involves a much more superficial change than that which the Judaeo-Christian tradition attaches to them. In extrabiblical Greek μετανοεῖν generally means to change one's mind or opinion, or to regret that some particular act was done or left un-

done, having thus to do with the details of behavior rather than with the disposition of the man himself. But prepared by the preaching of the Hebrew prophets, both John the Baptist and Jesus mean by their call to repentance a complete change in character and disposition, the abandoning completely of one attitude toward God and self and the acquisition of another. If a reason is sought why these words had taken on so much more strenuous and serious a note in the Judaeo-Christian literature, the answer is that it was in this same literature that the heinousness of sin was represented in a way seldom to be found among the more lighthearted Greeks.

Other Greek words are used in the New Testament in ways that must have seemed extremely strange if not nonsensical to a native Greek. Such common words as "church," "parable," and "the Christ," occur in certain contexts with meanings which were entirely foreign to classical and koine Greek.

Of the four chief meanings which the word "church" has in modern English—the church universal, a local congregation, a denomination, and an edifice—only the first two are found in the New Testament. Frequently assistance in understanding the Greek word is sought by pointing out that it was used originally by a public assembly of citizens *called out* (ἐκ and καλεῖν) from the whole population of a Greek city-state. But one who knows only this meaning in classical Greek is puzzled by the quite different way in which the authors of the New Testament use it. Contrary to its use in secular writings, where ἐκκλησία is never the title of a religious group, the biblical writers employ the definite article "*the* church." Still more peculiar from the point of view of the pagan was the phrase "the *ekklēsia* of God." Although this phrase would have been meaningless to an Athenian, to the Jew of the first century it was luminous with significance. He would recognize that *ekklēsia* appears frequently in the Septuagint as the translation of the Hebrew word qāhāl, and that the qāhāl of Yahweh is nothing more or less than "the people of the Lord."

At first this Hebrew phrase was used by Old Testament authors to designate an assembly of the Israelites, and then, after the Exile when Israel became more and more conscious of being a chosen race, to designate the congregation of Israelites as God's people, whether assembled or unassembled, distinct from everyone else. It is this usage that lies behind the Greek phrase taken over from the Septuagint into the New Testament. As a result of Jesus' teaching, his followers began at a very early date to designate themselves "the Israel of God," the "holy nation" (Gal. 6:16; I Pet. 2:9), as distinguished from the majority of Jews who had rejected the Messiah. Nothing was more natural than that they should also call themselves "the *ekklēsia* of God." A modification, indeed, takes place inasmuch as the Old Testament knew of but one *ekklēsia,* whereas the plural number frequently appears in the New Testament (e.g., I Cor. 7:17; 11:16; Gal. 1:2; Rev. 1:4; etc.). The New Testament usage is such as to suggest that the word primarily refers to the one church universal, but each separate and, it may be, scattered part of the body of Christ can also be truthfully called the *ekklēsia* because all belong organically to the whole. In each locality, therefore, where a number of Christians is found, whether that number is large or small, there *is* the church.

Another word in the New Testament which cannot be fully understood in terms of secular Greek of the preceding and contemporary centuries is παραβολή, "a parable." In harmony with Aristotle's definition of a parable,[10] we commonly understand a parable to be a lifelike but imaginary narrative designed to illustrate human relations. But not all the sayings of Jesus which are explicitly called parables can be subsumed under this definition. It seems very odd, for example, that the two sayings, "Physician, heal thyself" (Luke 4:23) and "There is nothing from without a man, that entering into him can defile him: but the things which come out of him, these are they that defile the man" (Mark 7:15; see vs. 17), should be designated parables (so the Greek and American Standard Version). The reason it seems so strange to call these sayings parables is that we try to define the parable by means of categories foreign to Semitic literary molds. The correct methodology is to see how παραβολή is used in the Septuagint, and what Hebrew word or words it translates. When such an investigation is made, the interpreter finds that this Greek word regularly renders the Hebrew noun *māshāl* and the verb *māshal.* Now in Hebrew literature the term *māshāl* is applied to a wide range of sayings, including not only what we call parables proper but also terse, pithy aphorisms and maxims or proverbs (see I Sam. 10:12; 24:13; Prov. 1:6; Ezek. 12:22-23; 18:2-3). Thus it is clear that certain sayings of Jesus can be called parables because they *are* parables—as defined by Semitic, and not Greek, categories.

The Greek word *christos* (χριστός) means literally "to be rubbed on" and was used in connection with ointments and salves. To give it as a title to a person was a usage of the word totally unknown to native Greeks. But when Jewish Christians called Jesus of Nazareth "the

Christ," they were deliberately using an honorific title which had its roots lying deep within Israel's history. Part of the inaugural ceremony in consecrating a king (e.g., I Kings 1:39) or a priest (e.g., Exod. 30:30) or a prophet (e.g., I Kings 19:16) involved the applying or pouring of sacred oil upon his head, thereby setting him apart for his official duties. Such a person became God's "anointed one" (Hebrew, *māshîaḥ;* English, Messiah). When Hebrew prophets began to look forward to a king who should uphold the throne and kingdom of David forever (Isa. 9:6-7) and who should become the great deliverer of his people (Jer. 23:5-6), the title of the Messiah, par excellence, naturally became attached to him (Dan. 9:25-26). The fact that Jesus of Nazareth came to be known among his followers as "the Messiah" (in Greek "the Christ") means that they recognized him to be the one "anointed"—that is, delegated and empowered by God's resident Spirit—to deliver his people and establish his kingdom (see Luke 4:17-21, especially vs. 18).

C. The Christian Element.—With the advent of Christianity there was let loose in the world a transforming energy which made itself felt in all domains, including that of language. Old, worn-out expressions were rejuvenated and given new luster. In a few cases, when nothing adequate seemed to be available, new words and phrases were coined. Words expressing servility, ignomiceny, and sin were washed clean, elevated, and baptized with new meaning. Others, standing in the bright light of the gospel, were revealed to be even more somber and wicked in their significance than had been previously realized. This mighty, transfiguring, creative force within Christianity is pervasive throughout the language of the entire New Testament and cannot be successfully set forth in isolated particulars. It would require far more space than can be allotted here to deal at all adequately with so expansive a subject; only a few of the particularly noteworthy monuments of the renovating and revolutionary power of the gospel can be mentioned.

Although the influence of Christianity upon the Greek language was chiefly lexical, a few characteristic grammatical constructions were also the products of new spiritual relationships. Thus the prepositional phrase ἐν Χριστῷ involves a special usage of the dative case which has no antecedents. No one had ever spoken of being *in* Plato or *in* Moses. But new wine requires new wineskins, and the only adequate explanation which Paul had for his spiritual life was that he was "in Christ." If a grammatical category is needed for this usage, perhaps "the mystical dative" is as good as any. Similar to this expression is the novel con-

[10] *Rhetoric* II. 20. 2-4.

struction of the verb "to believe" with a following preposition and a person. Used most frequently by John, πιστεύειν εἰς suggests more than mere belief; it is a deliberate, Christian formation [11] to signify a personal trust which brings the soul *into* that mystical union with Christ which Paul expresses by ἐν Χριστῷ. Again, perhaps John's fondness for the perfect tense, noticed above,[12] may be regarded as another example of a characteristic theological emphasis reflected in grammatical idiom.

The word "grace" (χάρις) was twice elevated in its journey from classical Greek to the New Testament, and once after it had arrived there. From Homer onward it means "gracefulness," "an act of kindness," and then "favor" and "good will," especially as shown by a superior to an inferior. The first elevation of the word is in the Old Testament expression "finding favor in the sight of God" (Exod. 33:12-13; II Sam. 15:25; etc.). In the New Testament, while retaining nearly all the classical usages, the word is lifted once again when used of God's "favor toward men contrary to their deserving." This meaning, which is especially characteristic of Paul, though not confined to him, is intensified when the word is brought into contrast with "debt" (Rom. 4:4) and with meritorious "works" (Rom. 11:6; Eph. 2:8-9). Though God exhibits his grace or favor or good will in all his gifts to mankind, it is in his only Son that the unmerited grace of God is displayed pre-eminently (John 1:17; Rom. 5:15; I Cor. 1:4; etc.). Jesus Christ shares the gracious attitude of God toward men (II Cor. 8:9; cf. Gal. 2:20-21), and has revealed it particularly in and through his death (Rom. 3:24-25; 5:8; Eph. 1:6-7).

But this is not the highest level which this word reaches; it is also used in a special connection with the *universality* of the divine favor. To the first Christians, all of them Jews by birth or proselytes to Judaism, the most surprising aspect of the mercy of God shown in Jesus Christ was that Gentiles were freely admitted to the privileges which had been Israel's heritage (see traces of this surprise in the context of Acts 11:17 with vs. 23; also Acts 15:7 with vs. 11). Though Paul refers to the Gentiles at Ephesus as having been "strangers to the covenants of promise, having no hope and without God in the world" (Eph. 2:12), he can also write that they "are fellow citizens with the saints and members of the household of God" (Eph. 2:19) because of "the stewardship of God's grace that was given to me for you" (Eph. 3:2).

[11] This expression occurs nowhere in any classical Greek author (so Stephanus) nor in the Septuagint.
[12] See pp. 50-51.

Another word which has undergone a considerable change is the word "peace." In classical Greek εἰρήνη means first of all freedom from or cessation of war or strife. But in the Old Testament it acquires a religious connotation by being used of the cessation of *God's* anger and the restoration of harmony between him and man (Pss. 29:11; 85:8, 10; Isa. 57:19, cf. vs. 21; Ezek. 34:25; Hag. 2:9). It is this higher and deeper peace of which the heavenly host sang at the birth of the Savior (Luke 2:14) and which the early church saw to be the result of Christ's work (Acts 10:36; Eph. 2:14-17). "Peace" in the New Testament means, therefore, the state of spiritual well-being into which the grace and mercy of God bring man by delivering him from sin. It involves a twofold aspect: objectively, the cessation of divine wrath against the sinner (peace *with* God: Rom. 5:1; see Col. 1:20), and subjectively, the tranquillity of soul which results from the assurance of being reconciled to God (peace *of* God: Phil. 4:7; Col. 3:15; see John 14:27; 16:33; Gal. 5:22). The history of the word reaches a climax in the statement "He is our peace" (Eph. 2:14). Christ does not bring us a new conception of "peace"; he *is* peace.

The early church soon learned to associate these two words, "grace" and "peace," in one phrase. All the epistles of Paul and Peter, as well as the book of Revelation (Rev. 1:4), open with this meaningful salutation. It is no doubt by design that the sequence invariably is "grace" and then "peace," intimating that God's gracious good will is the source of all real blessings, and that peace follows as its end or issue.

The word ταπεινοφροσύνη, meaning "lowliness of mind," "self-abasement," "humility," which appears seven times in the New Testament (Acts 20:19; Eph. 4:2; Phil. 2:3; Col. 2:18, 23; 3:12; I Pet. 5:5), has not been discovered either in the Septuagint or in previous secular authors. The defining element of the compound is the adjective ταπεινός, whose basic denotation is "low." This adjective is of frequent occurrence in classical authors, who almost always use the word in a bad sense, meaning "groveling," "abject," "servile," "base." By his own example our Lord (Matt. 11:29) raised lowliness to the level of a sovereign grace, and for the new virtue the apostolic church had to coin a new word.

An even greater transformation than that involved in any of the words thus far mentioned took place when the Greek word for "cross" (σταυρός), a shameful and ignominious instrument of torture and as suggestive of infamy as the electric chair is today, overcame the scandal involved in its associations (Gal.

5:11) and became a cause of rejoicing and thanksgiving (Gal. 6:14).

On the other hand, under the searching light of the new religion certain other words, more or less neutral in ethical implication, took on meanings and connotations decidedly pejorative. Two notable examples of this class of words are "world" and "flesh." For both Hebrew and Greek the world was good: for the Hebrew because God had made it and then pronounced it "very good" (Gen. 1:31), for the Greek because the word κόσμος also denoted "order" and "ornament." But in the New Testament this word comes to be used of mankind organized apart from and in opposition to God. When the early Christians meditated upon the incongruity that the best man whom they had ever known finally came to a violent death, they could not but regard the world which had treated him thus as being essentially and radically at enmity with him and his Father (John 1:10; 15:18; Jas. 4:4; I John 3:1, 13). The Christian, therefore, should have no love for "the present evil age" (Gal. 1:4) whose god is the devil (II Cor. 4:4; see also Eph. 6:11-12), for the world and all its pomps will pass away (I John 2:15-17).

In addition to its customary and everyday meanings in the New Testament the word "flesh" (σάρξ) acquires a distinctively evil connotation. Its usage in the Old Testament, though morally neutral, had begun to pave the downward path of this word. There it is frequently used of man in his weakness and frailty —referring to his creaturehood as over against God, the creator and sustainer (Deut. 5:26; Job 34:15; Ps. 78:39; Isa. 40:6-8; Zech. 2:13). Paul seizes upon this concept of man as over against God and deepens the gulf between by adding a moral and spiritual antithesis. In his epistles "flesh" is sometimes used to designate that element in man's nature which is hostile to God. From his own experience the apostle discovered that in his flesh there resided a tragic propensity to evil together with a pathetic helplessness to resist temptation (Rom. 7:13-25; 8:3-8). Yet Paul nowhere intends to identify the physical nature of man as such with sin; rather he includes in the term "flesh" everything in man—his will and mind (Rom. 8:7; Eph. 2:3; Col. 2:18; see I Cor. 3:1-3) as well as his body—which is not led by the Spirit of God (Rom. 8:9-14).

Though many other Greek words clamor for attention—such as "gospel," "life," "faith," "save," "saint," "meek," "expiation," "justification," "election," "the righteousness of God," "the will of God," "the kingdom of God"— space is left for but one more which is especially characteristic of the language and message of the New Testament, the word "love."

Classical Greek had four verbs meaning "to love": στέργειν, used of the mutual love of parents and children, or the love of a king for his people and their love to him; ἐρᾶν, used of the passionate love which craves the other for itself, especially sexual love; φιλεῖν, used of the solicitous love and warm affection which one has for friends; and ἀγαπᾶν, used of the loving admiration which one has for the object of one's esteem. Only the last two of these four verbs appear in the New Testament, and here ἀγαπᾶν, the more nondescript word of the two, takes the chief place. Furthermore, from the verb a noun ἀγάπη was formed, which is exceedingly rare outside the Scriptures. In the New Testament both verb and noun denote a love which possesses a character all its own, and of which the highest thought of antiquity was ignorant.

To attribute love of any kind to the deity seemed ridiculous to the Greek philosopher.[13] Although the doctrine of divine impassibility may have appeared correct in theory, the early followers of Jesus discovered by experience that the living and true God was active and had exhibited his love for mankind in and through his Son (John 3:16; I John 3:1). Even more astonishing than that God should love at all was the utterly astounding fact that he had condescended to bestow his love upon men who were sinners (Rom. 5:8; Eph. 2:4-5; I John 4:10). Jesus taught and revealed God's yearning for wayward humanity (Matt. 23:37; Mark 6:34; Gal. 2:20; Eph. 5:2; Rev. 1:5), descending to the lowest level of misery and wretchedness (see Phil. 2:5-8). This love is not dependent to the least degree upon the worth or actions of the loved one (see Matt. 5:45) but only upon the nature of God, who is *agapē* itself (I John 4:8, 16). Nothing, therefore, can "separate us from the love of God in Christ Jesus our Lord" (Rom. 8:39).

The New Testament employs these same two words (ἀγαπᾶν and ἀγάπη) to describe the proper response on man's part to God's love: "We love, because he first loved us" (I John 4:19). Those who appreciate the divine forgiveness the most will love the most (Luke 7:47; I John 4:10-11). This love is to be directed toward God (Matt. 22:37; I John 5:2-3), and also toward man (Matt. 22:38-39; John 15:12; Rom. 13:8-10; I John 4:20). The most difficult exercise of love is toward the unlovely, toward one's enemies (Matt. 5:44)—an attitude as amazing to the non-Christian world as God's unrequited love is to most men. It must be recog-

[13] See Aristotle *Eudemian Ethics* VII. 3. 4; 4. 5; and *Magna Moralia* II. 11. 6.

nized that this type of love is not an affair of the emotions but is an activity of the whole personality (cf. Mark 12:30), involving concern for another's genuine interests (John 15:13; Phil. 2:4). The fullest description of the character and actions of ἀγάπη is in Paul's inspired and inspiring "hymn of Christian love" (I Cor. 13). Even faith must work through love (Gal. 5:6), for faith apart from love is without avail (I Cor. 13:2). In short, "faith, hope, love abide, these three; but the greatest of these is love" (I Cor. 13:13).

IV. Selected Bibliography

In addition to the books mentioned in the footnotes the following will be found useful.

DEBRUNNER, ALBERT. Friedrich Blass's *Grammatik des neutestamentlichen Griechisch*. 7th ed. Göttingen: Vandenhoeck & Ruprecht, 1943.

DEISSMANN, ADOLF. *Light from the Ancient East*, tr. Lionel R. M. Strachan. New York: George H. Doran Co., 1927.

DODD, C. H. *The Bible and the Greeks*. London: Hodder & Stoughton, 1935.

MOULTON, JAMES H., and HOWARD, W. F. *A Grammar of New Testament Greek*. Vol. I, *Prolegomena*, 3rd ed. Edinburgh: T. & T. Clark, 1908. Vol. II, *Accidence and Word-Formation*. Edinburgh: T. & T. Clark, 1929.

MOULTON, JAMES H., and MILLIGAN, GEORGE. *The Vocabulary of the Greek Testament*. London: Hodder & Stoughton, 1930.

ROBERTSON, A. T. *A Grammar of the Greek New Testament in the Light of Historical Research*, 5th ed. New York: Richard R. Smith, 1931.

VERGOTE, J. "Grec biblique," *Dictionnaire de la Bible: Supplément*, ed. Louis Pirot. Paris: Librairie Letouzey et Ané, 1938. Vol. III, cols. 1320-69.

THE GROWTH OF THE GOSPELS

by Alfred M. Perry

It is nowhere recorded that Jesus himself ever wrote anything—save those enigmatic symbols on the sand before an adulterous woman. Indeed, in view of their imminent expectation of the new kingdom of God on earth, the making of books must have seemed, both to Jesus and to his disciples, the acme of futility. So it becomes clear that our treasured tradition of his words and deeds began simply in the things that his friends and followers remembered over the years.

I. The Historical Gap

A. Language of Jesus.—Jesus himself in all probability spoke almost always in the common language of the Galilean peasant, Aramaic. Where our evangelists have made an effort to preserve his very words (cf. Mark 5:41; 7:34; 14:36) they used that Semitic dialect; and though he, as a son of the synagogue, could recite the Scriptures in the Hebrew (cf. Luke 4:17), in his hour of agony the words of the psalmist which fell from his lips were in the more familiar Aramaic paraphrase (Mark 15:34). So while it is not impossible that in bilingual Galilee he had also a tradesman's knowledge of common Greek, it is today generally admitted that Jesus' own teachings, and most probably also the earliest oral reports of his deeds, were set forth in the common Aramaic speech of the Jews of Palestine.

B. Migration of the Tradition.—It is a far cry from Galilee to Ephesus or Rome. A generation or more has passed. In the interval the simple village and country life of Palestine has given way to the heat of the crowded industrialized cities. The Aramaic tongue of the Galilean peasant has been replaced by the Greek dialect common to most of the Mediterranean world. The tales and reminiscences passed from mouth to mouth by intimate friends have at last become written records, and finally books to be published to the world at large. The Christian message has passed from the hands of Jews to Gentiles whose past religious experience had been rooted in the innumerable faiths of the Hellenistic age. The informal group of intimate followers of Jesus has grown into a great family of churches in all the larger cities, strong enough to begin to attract the suspicious attention of the mighty empire. And the Jesus, who had once in Galilee seemed but a teacher and leader, is now proclaimed as Messiah and Lord and Son of God.

In short the tradition of Jesus has leaped every cultural barrier—of language, nationality, religion, theology, and way of life. The query is inevitable: By what channels was it thus transplanted? And a second question follows: How much was it transformed in the process?

C. Records of the Process.—The details of this process of transplanting are obscure, if not completely hidden. Only two fixed points stand out. The first is the fact that twenty-five years after the crucifixion of Jesus, Paul possesses at least two definite traditions about him, one connected with the sacrament of the Lord's Supper (I Cor. 11:23-25), the other with the witnesses to the Resurrection (I Cor. 15:3-8). These traditions, Paul says, he has "received," evidently in formal fashion; and he had them, or presents them, in the Greek language. The second fixed point is the fact that when our Gospels emerge, some forty to fifty years after the events they narrate, they give clear evidence of resting upon already written records. Luke's prefatory words (Luke 1:1) corroborate this in the statement that "many" had already "taken in hand" "to compile a narrative," and it implies at least that these were not themselves "eyewitnesses and ministers of the word."

Further evidence, from an unexpected quarter, has been sought in a few rabbinical sayings from the end of the first century, which convey warnings against the "Gospels [gilyônîm] and books of the heretics." [1]

The rest of the process lies in obscurity which only a careful scholarship can dispel. The ancient traditions regarding the origins of the Gospels are of doubtful value. The very titles of the books—"Matthew," "Mark," etc.—are an

[1] F. J. Foakes Jackson and Kirsopp Lake, *The Beginnings of Christianity* (London: Macmillan & Co., 1920), I, 318-20.

afterthought, as our oldest manuscripts show, appended when the four were first issued as a single collection, and we cannot tell on what earlier evidence or tradition they were based. The rest of the early tradition appears upon analysis to rest upon these titles and upon internal evidence from the writings themselves, such as modern scholars use. The ancient tradition of how the Gospels grew falls, then, into a secondary position, and must be accepted merely as one among all the lines of evidence which the scholar will pursue in seeking to bridge the gap between our Gospels and the historic Jesus.

II. The Synoptic Problem

A. Approach.—In modern times study of gospel origins has moved along two lines. On the one hand there has been a tendency to rely on the ancient traditions, variously interpreted —a tendency particularly marked in the study of the Fourth Gospel. On the other hand scholars have found themselves more and more compelled to depend on the internal evidence of the Gospels themselves, their agreements and differences, and other literary and historical features.

For more than a century the large amount of agreement among Matthew, Mark, and Luke has attracted attention; and these Gospels have been given the name "Synoptic" because their resemblances are so considerable that it is easy to set them in parallel columns in a "harmony" or "synopsis." As a corollary, the attempt to discover what forces produced their combination of agreements and differences has been named the "Synoptic problem."

B. Literary Processes.—The Synoptic problem, then, is a literary problem, and it is therefore important to bear constantly in mind the several literary processes through which the materials passed—oral transmission, translation, and written transmission.

It is natural for a writer or editor using written sources to reproduce them without material changes; for it is easier, in the short interval between reading and writing, to reproduce the original without much reflection. The order of the original, too, is likely to be followed with little change.

In oral tradition, on the other hand, though the material tends to become fixed in form (see below, pp. 68-72), it is likely to remain somewhat fluid as memory of details falters and inference or imagination seeks to fill the gaps. Oral tradition, too, is likely to lack continuity, unless there is a definite plot, and to shape its material more in unrelated anecdotes. Thus the use of written sources tends to produce agreement; that of oral traditions, differences.

Translation—for example, from Aramaic to Greek—is often betrayed by the appearance of idioms from the original tongue. But the quality of the translation is influenced by the nature of the original: translation of a *writing* may be literal in the extreme and show many characteristics of documentary transmission, while translation from *oral* tradition would have much of the freedom of this medium.

C. Critical Criteria.—The two criteria of dependence upon written sources are resemblance and continuity. Proof here does not rest upon casual similarity but upon the following rather definite similarities:

1. Resemblance of the contents: telling the same stories.
2. Resemblance in continuity: telling the stories in the same order.
3. Similar sentence and word order: telling the stories in the same way.
4. Extensive agreement (50 per cent to 60 per cent) in the words used.
5. Agreement in using unusual words or harsh constructions.

The concurrence of all these lines of evidence makes an impressive argument for dependence upon written sources, and agreements in wording (items 4 and 5) would rule out the likelihood of independent translations. But *where this concurrence is not consistent or close, it is not safe to consider documentary dependence proved.* To account for such lesser resemblances other possibilities must be explored.

D. Solution of the Problem.—Today the solution of the Synoptic problem is based solidly upon the internal data of the Gospels. It is worthy of note that these data represent the most objective evidence available to scholars; and excepting the slight evidence drawn from Paul, it is the earliest.

It may have been the great Christian scholar Augustine [2] who pointed the way to this critical study of resemblances and differences in the Gospels, though his own data were inadequate. In the nineteenth century it became the accepted approach. Every student, however, should heed the warning [3] that without a painstaking and detailed study of a Gospel "harmony" he has small right to opinions in this field.

E. The Accepted Solution.—The solution generally accepted by scholars today is, in outline, the following:

1. Mark was the first of our four Gospels. Some little time after its composition and publication, copies fell into the hands of Matthew and Luke, and they used Mark's narrative for

[2] *On the Harmony of the Gospels* I. 2. 4.
[3] F. C. Grant, *The Growth of the Gospels* (New York: Abingdon Press, 1933), p. 64 n.

the framework of their accounts. This fact explains the striking resemblance among the three Synoptics.

2. In addition to Mark the authors of Matthew and Luke had also another Greek document upon which they drew extensively for the words of Jesus. This document is frequently referred to by the symbol Q, which stands for the German word *Quelle*—"source." Thus we have what is known as the "two-document theory."

3. In addition to these sources, which can be pretty well identified by the agreements of Matthew and Luke, there remains a good deal of material in each of these Gospels which has no parallel, yet must have come from some good source. Indeed it is quite possible that some even of the parallel materials may have come from different "overlapping" sources. But there is not sufficient evidence in the Gospels to describe these sources as adequately as the other two.

We turn now to examine the evidence upon which this solution is based.

III. The Marcan Source

The three Synoptics to a very considerable degree tell the same story. To this "triple tradition" we must now apply the criteria already mentioned.

A. Similar Contents.—Mark is almost completely duplicated by either Matthew or Luke, if not by both together. The best text of Mark contains 661 verses, of which at least 610 are paralleled in either Matthew or Luke, and a large proportion in both. Mark contains about 88 separate paragraphs, of which only three (Mark 4:26-29; 7:32-37; 8:22-26) are absent from both the other Gospels.

B. Common Outline.—The order of the sections in Mark is always supported by at least one of the other Synoptics—chiefly by Luke in the earlier portion, by Matthew in the later—and the agreement between Matthew and Luke begins where Mark begins, and ends where Mark ends.

C. Word and Sentence Order.—A study of the harmony will reveal also that the three Synoptists tell the stories usually in much the same fashion. The details follow one another in nearly identical order, and even the order of words in the sentences is, more often than not, the same.

D. Identical Language.—The agreement extends to the exact words that are used in the Greek Gospels, insignificant words as well as key words. A count of parallel words in parallel verses of Mark and Luke reveals that 55 per cent of the language of Luke is in the words of Mark, and the proportion rises to 69 per cent in the quoted words of Jesus. In a similar test Matthew was found to repeat 59 per cent of Mark's words.

E. Unusual Language.—This agreement in language extends to rare words not likely to be used by writers in complete independence: "struck dumb" (Mark 1:22) for "astonished" (Mark 1:27); "rebuked" (Mark 8:30), which Luke in the parallel explains with "passed the word"; "an ass-mill round the neck" (Mark 9:42), which Matthew repeats but Luke softens to "millstone"; and "amputated the days" (Mark 13:20). These are all passages in which the roughness of the Greek is seldom reflected in the English translations.

Similar roughness appears also in constructions, as in Mark 2:10-11, where Jesus appears to begin a sentence addressing the scribes, breaks off, and concludes with the healing words addressed to the paralytic. The construction is extremely harsh; yet it appears in all three Synoptics, though it is difficult to believe that all three could independently have shaped it thus.

F. Mark, the Middle Term.—Besides this extensive agreement of Matthew and Luke with Mark, it is noteworthy that their agreements with each other are more limited. Though Luke's agreement with Mark is 55 per cent, his agreement with Matthew in the same sections is only 42 per cent, and his agreement with Matthew against Mark falls to less than 6 per cent. This makes it clear that Mark must be regarded as the middle term.

These facts—or rather the great mass of data exemplified by them—are deemed by most scholars sufficient to prove that (*a*) our first three Gospels have a close literary relationship; (*b*) this is based on written documents; (*c*) these documents must have been in Greek; and (*d*) the common source was a document either identical with or closely resembling Mark.

G. Mark More Primitive.—Augustine suggested that Mark might have reached this middle position by abbreviating Matthew; F. C. Baur regarded the Gospel as a compendium of the agreement between Matthew and Luke. But two considerations rule out such a secondary position for Mark. (*a*) The narrative in Mark is nearly always fuller, more detailed, and more picturesque than in the other Synoptists: in telling of the feeding of five thousand Mark (6:32-44) uses 194 words, Luke and Matthew 157 each, while the conversation in Mark 6:36-38 is much livelier. This is surely not "abbreviation" by Mark. (*b*) Mark's language is full of harsh expressions (often smoothed in the English translations) which Matthew and Luke either omit or improve: Mark (2:4) uses the military word "bunk," for which Luke has "cot" and Matthew "bedstead." Mark, despite his harsher language, is both more vivid and more accurate. Evidence such as this has compelled most scholars to conclude that Mark is not only the middle term, but the more primitive, and indeed, a source document for the other two Synoptists.

H. Minor Agreements Against Mark.—There are still some students who, though admitting that Mark is the middle term, maintain that not our present Mark but an earlier edition was the actual source. Proof of this they find partly in things omitted from Mark and partly in the instances where Matthew and Luke agree against Mark in narratives common to all three.

Omissions, however, provide merely negative evidence, and can have little weight when it is clear that both Matthew and Luke sought to condense Mark considerably. And a survey of the agreements reveals that though they amount to almost 6 per cent of the Gospel, the great majority of them are of no particular importance.

1. A large number of these agreements are accounted for by an accidental concurrence of Matthew and Luke in their effort to improve Mark's style: Mark has the historical present "he saith" about 150 times, and Matthew and Luke concur about twenty times in making the obvious change to the past "he said." It is worth noting that in this and similar cases the result is a more polished, not a more primitive, version of Mark.

2. A few of the agreements may be charged to textual corruption in the exemplar of our Marcan text. Thus in Mark 5:27 the woman is said to touch Jesus' "garment," but the other Synoptists write "the hem of his garment." Yet the latter phrase is also Marcan (cf. Mark 6:56) and may have been the original text here.

3. B. H. Streeter has pointed out that the text of the Gospels as printed is by no means final, and many of these agreements disappear in the light of other manuscript readings.[4]

4. Some also may be mere inferences from the narrative in Mark. It is fair to conclude, then, that the source used by Matthew and Luke did not differ in any material fashion from our present Mark.

IV. The Second Source

While Matthew and Luke rarely agree very closely against Mark, there is a considerable body of material consisting mainly of Jesus' sayings, and amounting to over two hundred verses, in which they agree quite closely although there is no parallel material in Mark.

[4] *The Four Gospels* (4th ed.; London: Macmillan & Co., 1930), ch. xi.

Here arguments of the same kind as proved their dependence upon Mark can again be advanced to demonstrate another common source.

A. Similar Contents.—Both Matthew and Luke tell in essentially the same way such stories as the temptation, and the cure of the centurion's boy, and report in similar language the preaching of John, the Sermon on the Mount, the Lord's Prayer, Jesus' warning against anxiety, and many other sayings.

B. Common Outline.—The student who will trace the order of these passages in Luke as far as 11:32 will find that their parallels stand in the same order in Matthew, except for Luke 7:18-35; 11:24-26. In Matthew, however, other materials paralleled in later chapters of Luke are interspersed. This accounts for about 118 verses, more than half the source.

C. Identical Language.—Similar order of sentences and words is found in these sections. Identity of wording is sometimes striking: of the seventy-two Greek words in the preaching of John, sixty-nine are identical. In general Luke's agreement with Matthew in these sections amounts to 60 per cent of the words; in his Marcan materials it is but 40 per cent, but the higher proportion of sayings here accounts for the difference.

D. Unusual Words.—Agreement in rare or rough words is not to be expected in any case since such words would naturally have been eliminated by the evangelists, yet there are a few remaining, such as the rare word for "daily" bread in the Lord's Prayer (Luke 11:3).

E. Existence of Q.—The evidence thus produced by this "double tradition" is of the same sort as that which proves the dependence of Matthew and Luke upon Mark, and is just as cogent. The conclusion is inevitable that there must be some close literary relation between Matthew and Luke here also; and the alternative explanations are either (a) that they are both dependent upon a common source, even though now lost, as they depend upon Mark; or (b) that one of them drew directly from the other Gospel.

This latter view, though held by a few scholars, is opposed by two chief considerations: first, that this dependence, of Luke upon Matthew or the reverse, seems improbable in view of their joint dependence upon Mark; and second, that neither of the evangelists shows a clear priority to the other. Matthew has generally been regarded as prior by those who have maintained this view; yet his versions of the Beatitudes and the Lord's Prayer, to cite only two examples, are clearly more developed than Luke's.

For such reasons scholars are nearly unani-mous in agreeing that Matthew and Luke drew not only upon Mark, but also upon a second source, though that document may have ceased to circulate soon after they incorporated it, and is now entirely lost.

F. Language of Q.—Under the influence of Schleiermacher this second source was identified with the "logia," which Papias, bishop of Hierapolis about A.D. 140, refers to in his famous statement: "Matthew composed the logia in the Hebrew [Aramaic] tongue." [5] But the evidence of the linguistic agreements is so strong that we must conclude that the immediate source for Matthew and Luke was a Greek document. Hence scholars in recent years have preferred the colorless designation "Q."

G. Contents of Q.—The double tradition provides all that we can know of Q with any certainty, and many scholars would prefer to limit the designation "Q" to this body of material. It consists of about 207 verses, mainly included in the sections: Luke 3:2–4:16; 6:20–7:35; 9:57–10:24; 11:2–12:59; 13:18-35; 17:20-37. A few scattered parallels are found outside these sections, and a few verses within them must be excluded.[6]

Is this all of Q? Many scholars believe that just as Matthew and Luke each omitted something from Mark, so they probably omitted from Q as well. Hence they have sought in the peculiar material of Matthew or Luke something of Q which may have been omitted by the opposite evangelist. There is little agreement, however, on the selection of this material.

Others have advanced the hypothesis that Q, in circulating through the churches, must have received many additions and revisions and so have appeared in different editions. By this theory of recensions they would explain the disagreements of Matthew and Luke in Q sections, and also account for much of the "single tradition," that is, material peculiar to Matthew or Luke. But again, agreement among scholars upon these points is slight.

H. Q and Mark.—The occasional resemblances between Mark and Q, particularly in brief striking sayings, together with the limited amount of discourse in Mark, have led many to believe that Mark was familiar with Q and wrote to supplement it with as little duplication as possible. Hence comes, they say, the abbreviated character of Mark's introductory paragraphs (Mark 1:4-13). But the contention rests on the unconscious assumption that any resemblance must imply dependence, and

---

[5] This statement of Papias is found only as a quotation in Eusebius *Church History* III. 39.

[6] For precise lists see A. Harnack, *The Sayings of Jesus*, tr. J. R. Wilkinson (New York: G. P. Putnam's Sons, 1908), pp. 127-46; or Streeter, *op. cit.*, p. 197.

ignores the spread of oral tradition; and a closer inspection reveals that Mark's story is quite differently conceived. In Mark 1:8, for example, John predicts a baptism with the Holy Spirit, in Q with the fire of the threshing floor; in Mark 1:13 Jesus seems to fight a supernatural duel with Satan; in Q he fasts and is spiritually tempted. It can hardly be alleged, then, that Q was in any real sense a source of Mark.

V. Additional Sources

Literary resemblance demonstrates the use of Mark and Q as sources, but for the remaining materials of Matthew and Luke the clue of parallels is wanting, and the identification of sources becomes both difficult and uncertain.

A. *Overlapping Sources.*—There are several instances, often called "doublets," where an evangelist repeats a certain saying, apparently from different sources. Thus the saying on bearing the Cross (Mark 8:34) is repeated exactly by Matthew and Luke in the same context (Matt. 16:24; Luke 9:23); but they also repeat, with rather less agreement, a similar saying (Matt. 10:38; Luke 14:27) apparently from Q, which has "whoever does not take" for Mark's "if anyone would come, let him take," and substitutes "come after" for "follow." There are about twenty of these "doublets" in the Synoptics; [7] and they seem to prove that many brief sayings were reported in more than one stream of tradition and so incorporated in different sources, their variations suggesting either independent translation or divergent oral traditions.

Overlapping of sources appears at other points. Thus Luke's account of the call of Simon (Luke 5:1-11) differs widely from Mark 1:16-20, and mere editorial rewriting is hardly a possible explanation. Indeed, overlapping may be suspected wherever two accounts vary considerably, as in the parable of the lost sheep, [8] or even the Beatitudes, where an extravagant amount of editorial revision must be postulated to derive either evangelist's version from the other's.

This overlapping of divergent traditions is a factor which has too often been overlooked, and the more recent studies of form criticism in the earlier oral tradition should give it new prominence.

B. *Luke's Passion Narrative.*—It is generally recognized [9] that in his narrative of the Passion (Luke 22:14–24:53; also 19:37-44; 21:10-38) Luke's relation to Mark is quite altered. In earlier chapters he holds quite closely to Mark's order and takes up Mark's material in large blocks; but in the passion story the reverse is true: (a) The Marcan order is reversed wherever the course of events permits—at least twelve times—as in placing the prediction of the betrayal after the supper (Luke 22:21-23); (b) there are several important additions woven into the story, not simply inserted in distinct blocks; (c) the verbal agreement with Mark is but half as great as in Luke as a whole, only 27 per cent. Thus the evidence which served to establish Luke's dependence upon Mark in general is strikingly lacking in this section. He does incorporate some details from Mark, and follows Mark's wording quite closely in so doing; but it seems hardly likely that he would have so varied the order of events had he not been following in the main a different written source.

Now it is the contention of the form critics that the passion narrative was the first portion of the gospel tradition to be formulated. Paul indeed was familiar with the main outlines of the story—Jesus' last supper, betrayal, death, burial, and resurrection—and he cites verbatim (I Cor. 11:23-25; 15:3-7) the beginning and the end of the cycle. If this was so early, it was the more likely to be circulated in versions agreeing on the essential points but differing in details; and it is not surprising that Luke should have possessed—and preferred—a different source from Mark's. The original form of this source we may only guess. It probably circulated independently at the beginning, first orally, then perhaps in written form; but it might later have been combined with other material in a longer document. [10]

C. *Luke's Private Materials.*—Aside from the infancy stories in Luke 1–2, there are about three hundred verses in Luke 3:1–19:28 which have no parallel. Concerning their source it is possible to do little more than hazard a guess. Still, because of Luke's general fidelity to his sources, his habit of using them in blocks, and the general homogeneity of the materials, many scholars believe that much of this material may have been drawn from a document, or documents, often referred to as "L." Some allowance, however, ought surely to be made for Luke's contact with the oral tradition, which Papias prized even half a century later, and which preserved such sayings as "It is more blessed to give than to receive" (Acts 20:35). Although it seems unlikely that a literary man, such as the author of this Gospel shows himself to be, would have had much recourse to oral tradition gathered in the very process of com-

---

[7] See V. H. Stanton, *The Gospels as Historical Documents* (Cambridge: University Press, 1909), II, 54-60.

[8] See Streeter, *op. cit.*, pp. 243-45.

[9] *Ibid.*, p. 203.

[10] On Luke's passion narrative see A. M. Perry, *The Sources of Luke's Passion Narrative* (Chicago: University of Chicago Press, 1920).

posing his Gospel, it is not impossible that the block of materials in Luke 14:1–17:37 was taken from the evangelist's notebook of oral traditions, gathered earlier.[11]

Some scholars would hold that these materials reached Luke already joined to Q, but it is better to accept his own statement (Luke 1:1) that he was familiar with a number of sources. His method of incorporating them in blocks suggests that they were for the most part in written form.

D. Matthew's Private Materials.—With the single tradition in Matthew the case is somewhat different because of his inclination to rearrange his materials in a topical order. His special materials, to which some scholars give the symbol "M," fall into several classes.

1. The student who will trouble to isolate the special materials in the Sermon on the Mount will find that they outline an elaborately constructed discourse (Matt. 5:17–6:18; 7:6) centering about three amendments to the law (ch. 5) and three acts of piety. In the latter particularly there is an elaborate strophic structure. This elaborate literary composition, probably written though possibly composed for memorizing, forms the framework of the sermon; the rest, including the Q sermon, is really interpolated.[12] But this source cannot be clearly identified elsewhere.

2. Matthew also includes a striking series of Old Testament citations introduced with the formula, "This was done that it might be fulfilled which was spoken by the prophet, saying, . . ." (Matt. 2:15, 17; etc.). These sayings may of course have been drawn directly from the Old Testament; but in view of the prevalence in early Christian circles of "testimonies"—collections of such proof texts already excerpted and applied to Jesus' career—it seems more likely that Matthew's source was one of these pamphlets. The large dependence upon the original Hebrew suggests it originated in Palestine.

3. Among the narratives peculiar to Matthew there are several with distinctly legendary flavor, such as the coin in the fish (17:24-27), Pilate's wife's dream (27:19), or the guard at the tomb (27:62-66; 28:4). In these the miraculous element is heightened, the theological interpretation enhanced, and the realism diminished. One may suppose that they were drawn directly from oral traditions such as proliferated into the "infancy gospels" of the next century.

Thus Matthew seems to have had a number of sources, written and oral; but they vary in character, and probably were not combined.

E. The Four-Document Hypothesis.—B. H. Streeter[13] advanced what he called a "four-document hypothesis": namely, that Matthew and Luke shared the two sources Mark and Q, and had each, in addition, his own private source, L or M. This is a clear and unmistakable statement of the facts, so long as Q and L and M are regarded as designating merely the bodies of material now discriminated by their location in the Gospels; and it has the advantage of simplicity.

But to assume that these bodies of material are coterminous with certain lost documents—Streeter is cautious about this—is taking a step not justified by the evidence. It might indeed be so; but it cannot be demonstrated. We do not know whether Q was one document, or perhaps several. We do not know but that some of L was actually part of the Q document but was omitted by Matthew: this seems not unlikely, especially as regards L passages in the midst of Q blocks. We do not know whether L was one continuous document, including the passion story, or a group of documents, as it came to Luke's hand; the infancy narratives, at least, seem independent. And the M material shows rather definitely the diversity of several lines of development. Though considerations of simplicity favor limitation of the number of common sources, the separate sources may have been numerous, and either written or oral.

F. Proto-Luke.—Streeter[14] contributed another hypothesis which has been much discussed, that of a first edition of Luke. He noted five sections—Luke 3:1–4:30; 6:12–8:3; 9:51–18:14; 19:1-27; 22:14–24:53—in which Luke is wholly or largely independent of Mark. They begin with a formal introduction (Luke 3:1-2) and end with a passion—and resurrection—narrative, thus forming practically a little gospel, comparable to Mark in length and scope, and consisting of alternating blocks of Q and L materials. Finally, since Luke uses but half as much material from Mark, Streeter concluded that this "Proto-Luke" was really Luke's first edition, later expanded by inserting narratives from Mark and prefixing the nativity stories. The theory has much to commend it, but scholarly opinion regarding it is widely divided.

G. Sources of Mark.—Thus far we have been treating Mark as a source of the other Synoptists, but the question of the sources of Mark's material also arises. Ecclesiastical tradition as-

[11] See A. M. Perry, "An Evangelist's Tabellae: Some Sections of Oral Tradition in Luke," *Journal of Biblical Literature*, XLVIII (1929), 206-32.

[12] See A. M. Perry, "The Framework of the Sermon on the Mount," *Journal of Biblical Literature*, LIV (1935), 103-15. [But see also, below, pp. 158-59.]

[13] *Four Gospels*, ch. ix.

[14] *Ibid.*, ch. viii.

serted that Mark received his material direct from Peter; but that account appears too simple to most modern scholars, though many would admit that Peter might have been the source of some of the narratives. Apart from the question of Mark's use of Q (see pp. 64-65, above), many stories hardly bear Peter's stamp, and it seems possible to trace a variety of styles in different sections. At several points, too, the individual anecdotes are grouped in small collections. Thus Mark 1:16-45 is a group of stories told rather baldly, for the sake of the miracles involved. But a different interest and a livelier style appear in Mark 2:1–3:6, which has a conclusion of its own. The same style recurs perhaps in Mark 4:35–5:43. Other groupings are discernible in Mark 6:30–7:37 (paralleled in 8:1-26), and in 11:15–12:40; and one naturally concludes that Mark was more dependent upon existing collections of material than upon the personal reminiscences of a single apostle. Some scholars have attempted to regroup these materials into as many as three definite sources; [15] but the data are few, and historical probability seems against the hypothesis.

H. Conclusion.—Study of the Synoptic problem for the past century has led to the following conclusions:

1. The earliest of our Gospels is Mark, which was probably composed on the basis of a number of written and oral sources, and may incorporate some of Peter's reminiscences. Mark became a primary source for both Matthew and Luke.

2. In addition Matthew and Luke shared a second written source (or sources) from which they drew the Q materials.

3. To these Matthew added material from other sources, oral and written—legends, "testimonies," the outline of the sermon, and a number of parables.

4. Luke also added, rather more extensively, nativity stories, the passion narrative, and a considerable body of teachings with a few narrative incidents. Some of these materials were written; some he may have collected from oral tradition.

5. There is some reason to suppose that most of Luke's non-Marcan materials were combined in a "Proto-Luke" before Mark was incorporated with them.

6. Nearly all these materials reached the evangelists in a Greek dress, probably largely in written form. Back of these sources, of course, lay a process of oral transmission and of translation. To uncover this development we need further techniques of investigation.

[15] A. T. Cadoux, *The Sources of the Second Gospel* (New York: The Macmillan Co., 1936).

VI. Behind the Sources

A. Aramaic Gospels.—The Talmud evidence for early Christian books bearing the name "gospel," with Papias' reference to Matthew's "logia in Hebrew," and Jerome's discovery of the Gospel of the Hebrews in Aramaic or Syriac, have led many scholars from the time of Lessing to look for the sources of the gospel tradition in an original Aramaic document or documents. A widely heralded attempt of this sort is that of Charles C. Torrey. [16]

According to Torrey, each of our four Gospels was originally composed in Aramaic, and later translated into Greek, and "with the former translations diligently compared and revised." The proof of this he finds, not only in the Semitic idioms of thought and expression which abound in the Gospels, as all would agree, but particularly in certain passages (about 250, nearly one to a page) which he believes are mistranslated, and whose obscurity he would remove by a "corrected" translation.

B. Objections to the Aramaic Theory.—1. The proposed "mistranslations" are hardly numerous enough to support the theory.

2. The scholars who accept the theory cannot agree where mistranslation exists, so that the line of argument appears very insecure.

3. Many of the passages, alleged to be obscure because "mistranslated," contain no real difficulty, or the difficulty can be better explained in other ways.

4. Aramaic idiom in the Gospels can be attributed to use of the common nonliterary Greek idiom, to the influence of the biblical Greek of the Septuagint, to the idiom of authors who thought more or less in a Semitic tongue, and to the undeniable fact that the tradition, and possibly some of the *sources*— not the complete Gospels—originated in Aramaic.

5. In order to account for the obvious Greek affinities of the Synoptics, Torrey has to resort to a very complicated theory of interrelated Aramaic gospels translated by interdependent workers who compared their work diligently with the Gospels already translated. Luke, for instance, would follow closely the Matthew version of Q sayings, but immediately turn to Mark for narratives; yet at the same time he could continue to introduce mistranslations. Not only is the theory unnatural, but it involves considerable conflict with the most assured results of Synoptic study.

6. Archaeological evidence, as well as Acts 6:1; 9:29, reveals the presence of Greek-speaking

[16] *The Four Gospels* (New York: Harper & Bros., 1933); *Our Translated Gospels* (New York: Harper & Bros., 1936).

Jews in Jerusalem; and it is quite as likely that the traditions were first written by some of them in the more literary language, Greek. Written records would be needed more for the missionary extension of the church, and it was primarily from these Hellenists that the Christian mission originated (cf. Acts 8:5; 11:19-20).

7. When gospels in the tongue of Palestine or Syria were later required, they were translated from our four.

Few scholars, therefore, would accept Torrey's theory. The "gospels" known to the rabbis might have been translations back into Aramaic, or smaller documents like the "logia" mentioned by Papias. But most scholars doubt that there ever were "original Aramaic gospels." Manuscripts which are represented as such are merely copies of the much later Syriac version, which was made from the Greek.

C. Paul's "Gospel."—Paul's missionary preaching is not at all completely reflected in his epistles. A careful reading of the Thessalonian letters, for instance, suggests that his first message there was essentially an eschatological warning of the end of the times, presenting Jesus as the coming Messiah (cf. I Thess. 1:10; 4:14-15; 5:1-2). And if in the more sophisticated Greek world he came to speak more of Jesus as a Savior-God, the message could still be summed up, as Luke reports it, "Believe on the Lord Jesus Christ, and thou shalt be saved" (Acts 16:31). But this primary challenge had immediately to be buttressed by definite information regarding this Jesus whom he named, and here Paul must make use of the tradition.[17]

D. Paul's Use of Tradition.—In some passages Paul states explicitly his dependence upon the tradition, using the technical terminology, "received," "delivered," "tradition" (cf. I Cor. 11:2; II Thess. 2:15). In I Cor. 11:23-26; 15:3-7, he quotes verbatim—the former passage has a liturgical sound, the latter a creedal. Again, he calls upon the authority of a "word of the Lord" (I Thess. 4:15; I Cor. 7:10) or acknowledges its absence (I Cor. 7:12, 25).

In many more passages he builds his appeal upon the common knowledge of the tradition about Jesus—e.g., "the law of Christ" (Gal. 6:2), "he became poor" (II Cor. 8:9)—and if the familiar passage on "the mind of Christ" (Phil. 2:5-11) is not original with Paul, it is the more positive evidence of his use of the common tradition.

In other passages, where Paul's direct dependence upon the tradition cannot be demonstrated, he nonetheless clearly writes as one who moves in the spirit and atmosphere of the

[17] See J. W. Bailey, "Light from Paul on Gospel Origins," *Anglican Theological Review*, XXVIII (1946), 217-26.

tradition of Jesus—e.g., in his citation of the law of love (Gal. 5:14; Rom. 13:8-10).

E. Source of Paul's Tradition.—Paul defended stoutly the independence of his "gospel"; but it is clear that he did not mean to imply his independence of the common tradition of the church. Indeed he insists that he shares the essential message with all (I Cor. 15:11; Gal. 2:7-9). He seems moreover to indicate the source of his acquaintance with it (Gal. 1:18) when, in describing his visit to Cephas shortly after his conversion, he refers to it with an unusual word, *historeō*, from which our word "history" is obviously derived —a word applied to acquiring knowledge of persons or events.

F. Form of Paul's Tradition.—1. It was quite surely an oral tradition; for he uses the same word for it that he applies to the Jewish scribal tradition (Gal. 1:14), and he nowhere gives any hint that he knew it in any written form.

2. It was in Greek as Paul brought it to his congregations; but this does not preclude the possibility that he himself was the translator— he was undoubtedly competent, as occasion demanded, to deliver in Greek the traditions he had memorized in Aramaic.

3. In wording, Paul's tradition differs enough from the Synoptic to have been an independent stream; yet the agreement is close enough to guarantee the substantial authenticity of both.

4. Paul insists that the tradition has the guarantee of the outstanding leaders of the church—Peter, James, and John (Gal. 2:7, 9).

Thus in Paul we find testimony to the tradition only a generation from its origins.

VII. Oral Tradition and Its Forms

The evidence of Paul brings us to a point near the beginning of the Gentile mission and hardly a score of years from the Resurrection. But what of these twenty years, clearly the most formative of all? For them no records are available; we must depend simply on the internal evidence in the traditions.

A. Setting of the Tradition.—The life of the primitive Christian church, so far as we can learn, seems to have centered in the communities in the crowded cities of the empire. We read of the church in Jerusalem, then of churches in Antioch, Ephesus, Corinth, Rome. But the atmosphere of the gospel tradition is remote from all this. It breathes the open air of the hills of Galilee, and the simple life of their little villages, of the flowers of the field, the grass burned in the oven, the fig tree, the vineyard, the seed falling on the narrow path, the mud roof dug through by earnest seekers, the house in the wadi washed away by the flood. The very atmosphere seems to authenticate the genuineness of the material; for it bears few traces of the surroundings and interests of the later Christian communities.

The same is true of the subjects which are discussed. We read of discussions about sabbath healing, sabbath observance, fasting, ritual purity, association with sinners, tribute to Rome. These were questions of vital interest in Palestine, but hardly among Gentile Christians. On the other hand there is little that deals with or applies to many of the questions which agitated Paul—the church, baptism and other such rites, speaking with tongues, the mission to Gentiles, circumcision, the Holy Spirit. It is natural to conclude, then, that this tradition took form mainly in the early church in Palestine, and was not essentially modified in its transmission in the Gentile churches.

B. Fragments of Tradition.—A casual examination of any one of the Synoptics will reveal that the account is largely made up of unrelated anecdotes and other bits of tradition. The evangelists, it is true, have attempted to weave these fragments together into a more or less connected narrative; but it is clear that each of them has recognized that the sections are quite independent, and has not hesitated to rearrange them at will. Almost any of these paragraphs can now be lifted from its context, and it will stand complete and self-explanatory. The gospel material, then, must be regarded as a collection of fragments. This fact lies right on the surface of the record; but the full realization of its significance we owe to the trend in scholarship which goes by the name of "form criticism."

C. Unwritten Records.—It is natural that traditions passed on orally should take on this fragmentary, unrelated character; for a short paragraph is the form most easily memorized. Written records tend more toward continuity. So we may well conclude that the gospel tradition was transmitted for a considerable period by means of memory and oral repetition. This conclusion is borne out, too, by the Palestinian atmosphere; for that seems to imply an Aramaic tradition, and there is no adequate evidence that the early church had many original Aramaic documents (cf. pp. 67-68, above). So we are justified in assuming that until Paul's time or later the gospel tradition was very largely oral in character.

D. Form Criticism.—For a tool to investigate this obscure period we have now the technique of form criticism. This is, in essence, an attempt to apply the conclusions reached by students of folklore to the tradition of early Christianity preserved in the Gospels. The names of two leaders stand out. In 1919 Martin Dibelius of Heidelberg set forth the principles of the technique in a volume translated under the title *From Tradition to Gospel;* and two years later Rudolf Bultmann of Marburg published a most exhaustive analysis of the gospel materials.[18]

Form criticism rests upon a few fundamental assumptions: (*a*) that in folk literature the material will assume certain more or less fixed "forms" (just as a limerick or conundrum has a well-defined form), and that these forms are transmitted with little change; (*b*) that these forms are shaped by, are in fact due to, the situation in which the tradition was fixed; (*c*) that therefore the history of the tradition itself (to be distinguished from the history it claims to convey) can be discovered from the form.

Each of the form critics, therefore, has sought to define the setting in which the tradition took shape. Dibelius, who has had the largest following, found it in the missionary preaching of the church. This preaching, it would seem, centered in the "kerygma," the proclamation of Jesus as the Savior and Messiah soon to return. This message, Dibelius believes, called immediately for further explanation of who Jesus was and what he had done.

But to Bultmann this description of the churches' activities seems all too meager; and he finds the origin of the forms more in the churches' controversies and in the need to give instruction in the Christian way of life to new converts. Thus there is no real agreement upon the setting for the forms, beyond the common affirmation of the rather obvious fact that they came out of the life of the Christian community.

E. Meaning of Form.—The word form as used by these critics can be somewhat misleading. While some of their classifications are indeed characterized by external features, others are distinguished more by their choice of subject, or the "style" in which the narrative is told. We shall understand the form better if we think of it as a "type" of paragraph.

F. Forms in the Tradition.—There is a considerable amount of agreement among the form critics regarding the description of the forms, though the nomenclature varies.

1. The first of the forms is that which Dibelius calls the *paradigm* and Bultmann the *apothegm.* The question about tribute to Caesar (Mark 12:14-17) is a good example of this form. It consists of a dialogue, often controversial, sometimes associated with a miracle, which leads up to a striking pronouncement by Jesus capable of general application. The interest of the pericope is centered in this saying, not in other

[18] *Die Geschichte der synoptischen Tradition* (Göttingen: Vandenhoeck & Ruprecht, 1921).

details or persons. For this reason Vincent Taylor [19] prefers the name "pronouncement stories." Dibelius and Bultmann agree in the main in the identification of these stories—Dibelius lists eighteen, Bultmann a few more—but there agreement ends. Dibelius classifies them with the narratives about Jesus, Bultmann with the sayings. Dibelius indeed hints that the "pronouncement" may have been added by the preacher who related them, to give general application to the story; Bultmann is often sure that the story was invented simply to give a setting for the saying.

2. The second of the forms is the *miracle story*, which is recognized fundamentally by its content, though Dibelius seeks to disguise this fact by calling it *novelle* ("tale"). Here the interest is in the display of power, and a regular pattern appears—description of the trouble, description of the method used, and report of the effect. A true miracle story is likely to be longer and more colorful than a paradigm, since the interest is in the event itself; but there is little in the style to distinguish it from a biographical anecdote.

3. A third classification is that of the *sayings*, to which Dibelius gives the name *paraenese* ("exhortations") because he believes these sayings were preserved for the instruction of new converts. This class really includes a number of forms—parable, poetic stanza, maxim, and so forth; Bultmann has offered a classification, but that too is based more on subject than on true form.

4. There remains a group of stories in which the practical interest is less apparent, and which the form critics therefore would dismiss as later and less authentic. Most of these are stories about associates of Jesus, from Peter to Zacchaeus, where a frank biographical interest appears. Finding an analogy in the tales of saints, Dibelius terms these *legende*. With them he would also include the nativity legends, which do in fact apologize for their late origin (cf. Luke 2:19, 51).

5. Finally, Dibelius adds a very small group of *myths*—much larger in Bultmann's view. He uses the term myth to describe pieces in which the action is clearly that of a divine, not a human, person. Such would be the story of the Transfiguration (Mark 9:2-8) and Dibelius would also include a few sayings, such as the familiar "Come unto me, . . . and I will give you rest" (Matt. 11:28), which convey a divine reassurance.

6. Besides agreeing on the forms of the independent pericopes most form critics agree that one section of the gospel tradition had a con-

[19] *The Formation of the Gospel Tradition* (London: Macmillan & Co., 1933), p. 30.

nected sequence almost from the beginning. This is the *passion story,* which gives a connected account from the inception of the final plot against Jesus (Mark 14:1) to his death on the Cross (Mark 15:39), though not including resurrection stories or some of the minor incidents now in the narrative. Such a story of how and why Jesus died was essential to the gospel preaching from the very beginning—to ground it in fact, and to remove the stigma of the Cross, justifying it as the will of God and the way of salvation. Further evidence of the fundamental position of the Passion in the tradition is that it appears in three separate versions, those of Mark, of Luke, and of John.

G. Forms in the Community.—Both Dibelius and Bultmann seem to regard the paradigms and the sayings as the oldest of the forms, and therefore the most authentic. Dibelius finds the origin of the paradigm in the need for concrete reference to Jesus in the missionary preaching. The sayings he refers to the moral instruction of the new converts by the "teachers" of the church. The use of the miracles, however, seems to him to be more secular and to border on mere entertainment, and he can identify no class of leaders in the church, otherwise known, from whom they may have sprung. Of the legends and myths he is frankly skeptical, but more on the ground of their content than of their form.

Dibelius thus finds grounds for believing that not only the passion story, but most of the material in the "sayings" and "miracles" as well, is early in form and firmly fixed in the life and needs of the church, and therefore authentic. Bultmann, however, is far more skeptical: he sees the origination of most of the material in the activities of the community (but cf. pp. 68-69, above), and so he allows as authentic only a small residue of the strikingly prophetic words of Jesus. Such wide diversity of opinion may well be regarded as an indication that the techniques of form criticism have not yet been developed to the point where it may be confidently used as a historical tool.

H. Significance of the Forms.—Form criticism has made an undoubted contribution to the study of the Gospels. It has emphasized the independence and completeness of the individual portions of tradition, which is a real service to interpretation. It has called attention to the vital relationship between the tradition and the life of the church.

Some at least of the forms are real literary types. The paradigm or apothegm is a distinct form. Among the sayings, the parable, poetic strophe, and other literary figures are real forms, and may well have been used by Jesus himself to add emphasis to his message. The myth, as a form in which divine action appears directly, is distinct, at least in its atmosphere and in its approach to its subject. This may be true in part of the legend also. But the distinguishing characteristics of the miracle story are simply the essential features of any such story, and the identification of this form therefore rests more on a subjective judgment regarding the subject matter.

There can be no question, however, of the existence of forms in the perpetuation of tradition. Any story frequently repeated is likely to be stripped down to the elements which are essential for its purpose, and we could hardly deny that this must have happened in the early transmission of the gospel material. Of the many reminiscences of Jesus cherished by his friends, some of them of little significance (cf. Mark 14:51-52), the most valuable were unconsciously selected by the Christian teachers and preachers, and in constant repetition were shaped into the most useful form. Note also that this form then acted as a conserving force; for the fixing of the form worked to prevent modification of the material, and the form presented the material in the shape most readily remembered. Thus in emphasizing the importance of form the school of Dibelius and Bultmann has made a notable contribution to the study of the Gospels.

J. Limitations of Form Criticism.—Like any new discipline, form criticism has not yet found its limitations. This is particularly true of its use as a historical tool. The attempt to combine literary and historical criticism in a single instrument has worked to impair even its literary value, for example, in the definition of legend or miracle story. Several considerations involving limitation of the method's usefulness may be noted:

1. Many pericopes actually have a mixed form, and the critic cannot identify many pure examples of any form. This fact brings into question one of the fundamental principles of the theory: that form is the decisive or predominant factor.

2. The assumption, tacit or open, that the form created the tradition is subject to doubt. Communities in general do not create; they shape and conserve. And the material of the gospel tradition bears marks of authenticity (see pp. 68-69, above) quite apart from the forms into which it has been shaped.

3. This failure to distinguish sharply between the history of the subject matter and the history of the form has introduced a subjective element into many of the critics' historical and literary judgments—of legends and miracles, for example.

4. The form critics have concentrated too narrowly on the forms in their construction of the history. Their picture of early church life is often one-sided and inadequate, ignoring the great variety which the records describe, and taking little account of the factors which would control the growth of tradition, other than the forms.

5. As a historical tool, then, we should limit form criticism to the history of the material and its use in the church; it will hardly provide us with primary evidence for the history of the church or the historical accuracy of the tradition.

K. Controls of the Tradition.—We may also note that tradition did not run wild in the church. There were several forces at work to control it and maintain its authenticity.

1. Actual memory of Jesus was always the historic basis of the faith; he was not a mere myth, like the redeemers of the mystery religions.

2. The leaders of the community, and many others, were themselves eyewitnesses of the events (cf. Luke 1:1), competent to correct errors in the tradition, and such eyewitness testimony was prized as late as the time of Papias (*ca.* 135).

3. There were eyewitnesses too among the opponents of Christianity, before whom it was necessary to justify the case for the gospel preaching.

4. The analogy of folklore is not entirely adequate, for there were educated people in the church from the outset. It is a mistake to assume that all unwritten "literature" is illiterate; the literature of Judaism offers striking confutations of such a supposition.

These were factors competent to control the subject matter of the tradition, if not its precise formulation; and its imperfect adaptation to the later needs of the community confirms the opinion that these communities did in the main effectively preserve the authentic tradition of Jesus. Yet since the essential character of the tradition is fragmentary, we cannot assume that they exercised the same control over the framework of the gospel narrative, on which indeed the evangelists themselves do not agree.

L. Conclusions.—The techniques of form criticism throw not a little light on the earliest development of the tradition. They reveal how, in the preaching, the passion story interpreted Jesus' death; the miracle stories confirmed the claims made for him; the apothegms and sayings invoked his authority for the control of the community life. Taken with the other internal evidence, these forms substantiate the essential authenticity and accuracy of the tradition, and give us reasonable confidence in our use of it.

In the final estimate, though its literary

canons have not yet greatly affected other fields of New Testament study, and though its historical deliverances need to be checked against other evidence, form criticism will be found a primary factor in a twofold reorientation of thought regarding the Gospels.

1. In the liberal direction the pregospel tradition can no longer be regarded as a static deposit, directly delivered by Peter or another, but as a living testimony organic to the experience of the church.

2. Yet in harmony with an older judgment, it again becomes apparent that the concern of this tradition is not with mere history, but with the salvation announced in the kerygma; it is oriented not to a memory from the past, but to a present experience, which we believe to have perpetual relevance.

VIII. Besides the Synoptics

Up to this point we have been discussing for the most part the tradition of the Synoptic Gospels, but we have noted that Paul made use of a cycle of tradition not altogether the same. There are indications of other streams of tradition too.

A. Independence of John.—It is clear to the casual reader that the Fourth Gospel differs extensively from the Synoptics. Aside from the passion story there are but four or five narratives which it shares with the previous Gospels. And although the passion story parallels the Synoptic version, even to the inclusion of minor features like the anointing of Jesus and Peter's denials, it contains much novel material, and differs at many points, even apparently as to the date of the Crucifixion.

It has usually been assumed that the resemblances are due to John's use of Mark and perhaps Luke. But adequate literary proof, like that of Synoptic interdependence, is wanting. The resemblances are not numerous, and suggest rather oral transmission. In telling of the feeding of five thousand, for example, John's verbal agreement is but 15 per cent over all, and in no places more than 33 per cent, while Luke's averages 42 per cent and rises to 83 per cent. The only significant words common to Mark and John are such key words as "five thousand," "two hundred denarii," "five loaves," "fragments," "twelve baskets"; but they are frequently differently placed, and John uses different words for "gather up" and "bless," describes the fish as "tidbits," the loaves as "barley," and tells the story in a different order throughout. The differences are those which naturally arise in oral traditions, and rightly raise the question whether John was in fact dependent upon any written Gospel, or upon oral traditions not unlike those incorporated in the Synoptics.

Proof of the latter hypothesis has been offered by P. Gardner-Smith,[20] who, by applying the linguistic tests familiar in the study of the Synoptic problem, reached the conclusion (a) that the few resemblances and many differences indicated the use of divergent oral traditions, rather than editorial revision of a written source, and (b) that there is not sufficient literary evidence to prove that John was dependent upon any of the Synoptics. This conclusion is important in the study of the tradition, and suggests one more independent stream, perhaps centered in a different church, and merging with the Synoptic stream at some points.

B. Forms in John.—The forms of which the Synoptic Gospels are composed are largely though not wholly wanting in John. The characteristic short pericopes give way to extended narratives and discourses. Indeed as Dibelius remarked, the whole Fourth Gospel is one long "epiphany," or revelation of a divine being, and falls into his class of "myths."

But there are occasional fragments of tradition of the Synoptic type, sometimes a narrative (e.g., John 2:1-10), sometimes a saying incorporated in the discourses (e.g., John 5:8; 12:25); and these are sufficient to indicate an original connection between John and the early tradition.

C. Johannine Tradition.—The conclusion to be drawn from these observations is that there was a stream of tradition drawn upon by the Fourth Gospel, which flowed originally from the early tradition of the church. This tradition, carried from Palestine to some point where it met the Alexandrian philosophy, was worked up by the evangelist into a literary product of a very different type from the Synoptic Gospels. But its original traditions, if we could isolate them, would have equal historical value.

D. "Outside" Tradition.—There were of course some elements of the tradition which were not incorporated in any of the Gospels. These naturally continued to circulate orally, and some of them, perhaps just as authentic as the gospel materials, have accidentally been recorded. Such are the story of the adulterous woman (John 7:53–8:11)—which surely was not an original element of the Fourth Gospel— and the fragment of paradigm about the man working on the sabbath, which is found in a few manuscripts of Luke 6:5. Discourse material is represented by the saying "It is more blessed to give than to receive" (Acts 20:35), or by the word from the Oxyrhynchus papyri, "Lift the stone and thou shalt find me, cleave the wood and there am I," and the interesting series of excerpts which Jerome made from the

[20] *St. John and the Synoptic Gospels* (Cambridge: The University Press, 1938).

Gospel of the Hebrews. Probably a considerable store of this material was preserved for a while in the earlier apocryphal gospels.

Along with more or less authentic material there was also a constant development of more mythical elements, which also found lodgment in apocryphal gospels; but such materials are more or less alien to this article. Like the authentic material of the Synoptic Gospels, however, each pericope of this material must be studied by itself to determine how authentic it may be: the place in which we now find it does not fully determine that.

IX. Growth of the Gospels

The ancient traditions which sought to bridge the gap between Jesus and the Gospels by describing the literary labors of apostles are themselves only guesses, and must be set aside. But other evidence has revealed to us some phases of the process. We may make a hypothetical reconstruction, as follows:

A. Oral Tradition, A.D. 30-50.—As soon as Jesus had departed there was a quickening of recollections of what he had done and had said, and an eager desire to know as much as possible of the manner of his death and to find a meaning in it. Wherever his followers met, these recollections would be exchanged and shared. The leaders of the group would stock their minds with such reminiscences, selecting of course those which seemed most important. Many anecdotes undoubtedly were lost in this fashion; but the significance of those retained was assured by this selection.

As the Christian mission grew, its preachers went farther abroad, proclaiming to Jews who feared the wrath to come and to Gentiles who recoiled from the futility and transience of life, "Believe on the Lord Jesus Christ, and thou shalt be saved." But the message demanded enlargement: Who was this Jesus, Messiah of Jews and Savior of Gentiles? How was it that he could save? The answer was given in apothegm and miracle story and passion narrative, describing how he had lived, how the power of God worked in him, and how his death and resurrection were ordained to be effective for the salvation of men. The Gospel of Mark, though later in date, still serves this interest in Jesus' life and death.

As the communities grew, particularly in Gentile lands, there emerged also a conflict between the Jewish ethical conception of religion and the Hellenistic mysticism which made few demands upon conduct. And teachers who saw that the genius of Christianity was rooted deeply in the old Jewish morality turned to the reports of Jesus' words for authority to control the vagaries of an unregulated mysticism (cf. I Cor. 7:10; 14:37; II Thess. 3:12). The Q source represents in a later form this side of the expanding life of the church.

The authenticity of these traditions was largely insured, too, not by the testimony of an individual eyewitness, as the early church fathers maintained, but by the authority of a community in which there were many "eyewitnesses and ministers of the word," as well as by the imperative need of the community to base its message upon historic facts; for Jesus was proclaimed as a historic person, not a legendary deity. Authenticity was still further maintained by the gradual shaping of the tradition into "forms" which aided the memory and helped to fix the wording.

This formulation of the tradition took place largely during the first twenty years of the Christian movement, and appears to have been largely accomplished before the time of Paul, who seems to regard the tradition as already fixed. Legend and myth, however, may be later developments. In this early period, too, the tradition passed over from the Palestinian environment of the original material, and the forms were fixed in a Greek dress. This translation very probably took place, not by any deliberate design, but in the minds of bilingual preachers like Paul, who, having first learned it in one tongue were faced with the necessity of delivering it in another.

B. Collections and Sources, A.D. 50-70.—Once the tradition was cast into these "forms," and began to circulate in the growing world of the Gentile churches, two things happened. First, a beginning was made toward bringing together the separate pericopes, and there emerged first such brief collections as we find in Mark, like the controversies of Mark 2:1–3:6, or the stanzas on good works in Matt. 6:1-18. These may have been partly formulated while the tradition was still oral, but eventually many of them were set down in writing.

Secondly, each of the great churches—Antioch, Ephesus, Rome, perhaps Jerusalem, Caesarea, and Alexandria—developed its own body of tradition, much of it shared with other churches, but changing as long as the tradition remained oral and fluid, and so developing in each center some distinctive shading and content of its own. These local bodies of tradition correspond to some extent to the different source documents of the Gospels, Mark embodying perhaps the tradition of Rome, Q that of Caesarea, M that of Antioch. Paul claims that his cycle was received at Jerusalem, and the Johannine was perpetuated in some circle where Alexandrian influence was strong. Thus at various centers the pericopes and collections which composed the local tradition were written down, and the source documents, Q L M and so forth were produced.

C. The Gospels, A.D. 70-100.—About A.D. 70, when the church found itself cut off from its Palestinian roots, when living witnesses were growing fewer, and the apocalyptic hope was waning, there came a demand for more adequate records. So the Gospel of Mark, perhaps taking up the Roman tradition, gathered various groups of material and separate pericopes, wove them together with a bit of narrative framework, and capped it all with the local version of the passion story.

Perhaps a bit earlier an evangelist in Caesarea (?) wove together Q and other materials, oral and written, and a slightly different story of the Passion, producing the semigospel Proto-Luke. Later the evangelist added to this a body of material from Mark, and legends of the birth of Jesus, to complete the Gospel of Luke.

About the same time the First Evangelist added Q to Mark and enriched both with the Judaistic and legendary materials of M. And last of all the Fourth Evangelist, in very different fashion, and without much dependence upon his predecessors, used the Johannine cycle of the tradition as the basis for his own mystical meditations. The cycle of tradition known to Paul may not have been preserved exactly in any of our Gospels.

D. Tradition and Apocrypha.—The writing of the tradition did not terminate its oral circulation. For a generation or so longer, men like Papias continued to prize the living voice whenever it spoke authentically. But unwritten authentic traditions were one by one forgotten, and fanciful and legendary tales multiplied. We find possibly authentic tradition attached to our Gospels occasionally, for example, the story of the man working on the sabbath, or the story of the adulterous woman. And in this period, early in the second century, both the Synoptic material and the growing fund of legend were being incorporated in apocryphal gospels of various types; but here the tradition passes beyond our immediate horizon.

E. Final Redaction, A.D. 125-50.—One further stage should be noted, the revision and editing which added the conclusion to Mark (16:9-20), the appendix (John 21) and perhaps a few other redactional touches to John, and which possibly contributed a few editorial alterations elsewhere in the Synoptics. This process also culminated in bringing the four Gospels together in one fourfold Gospel, and giving them their present titles. Here the growth of the Gospels ended, their development ceased, and they stood fixed, the "four pillars of immortality" for Irenaeus [21] and for the succeeding generations of the church.

X. Selected Bibliography

BULTMANN, RUDOLF. *Form Criticism: A New Method of New Testament Research*, tr. F. C. Grant. Chicago: Willett, Clark & Co., 1934.

DIBELIUS, M. *From Tradition to Gospel*, tr. Bertram Lee Woolf. New York: Charles Scribner's Sons, 1935. The fundamental treatment of form criticism, made by one of the originators of the method.

EASTON, B. S. *The Gospel Before the Gospels*. New York: Charles Scribner's Sons, 1928. The best critique of form criticism.

FILSON, FLOYD V. *Origins of the Gospels*. New York: Abingdon Press, 1939. A treatment of the whole subject with special attention to the minister's need.

GRANT, FREDERICK C. *The Growth of the Gospels*. New York: Abingdon Press, 1933. Provides an excellent and quite detailed survey.

STREETER, B. H. *The Four Gospels*, 4th ed. London: Macmillan & Co., 1930. The outstanding work on the Synoptic problem.

TAYLOR, VINCENT. *The Formation of the Gospel Tradition*. London: Macmillan & Co., 1933. An impartial study of form criticism.

[21] *Against Heresies* III. 11. 8.

NEW TESTAMENT TIMES
I. THE GRECO-ROMAN WORLD

by S. VERNON MCCASLAND

So far as ancient cultures are concerned, the Christian religion had two main sources: Hebrew and Greco-Roman. Yet each of these, like a tributary pouring into the river of Christianity, was fed in turn by earlier streams which had their own unique histories. The present essay lays emphasis on the history and culture of Greece and Rome in relation to the rise of Christianity, with brief glimpses of other pagan elements of that age. As Palestine receives full treatment in a subsequent section, it is given only enough consideration here to enable this study to fit into the general unity of the Commentary, and Judaism is presented only in its Hellenistic aspects.

I. The Hellenistic Age

The Hellenistic Age is specifically the period from the death of Alexander the Great to the founding of the Roman Empire by Augustus, 323-30 B.C. More generally, it is the four or five centuries during which the culture of Greece, which had attained a high state of maturity in its native land, was crossing Greek frontiers and blending with the other indigenous cultures of the Mediterranean world. Alexander's conquests only gave an impetus to the expansion of Greek influence which for a long time had been under way. Hellenic culture became a vogue. Every land traversed by Greek armies, penetrated by Greek colonists, or visited by the salesmen of Greek wines and objects of art or the representatives of Greek philosophies and religions, accepted the veneer if not the reality of Hellenic civilization. The most diverse peoples, from the Nile to the Indus, from the Black Sea to the Persian Gulf, swiftly came under the spell of the Greek spirit. Even Rome was a willing pupil of the Greek teachers, and the process of Hellenization came to its culmination only as the Roman Empire reached its maturity.

The culture of the period was characterized by syncretism, an interpenetration and amalgamation of arts, philosophies, and faiths. The influence of Greece was deeply felt by other peoples, but in the process of dissemination Greek culture itself experienced a modification which was no less profound.

The era was marked by the decline of the older states and cultures of antiquity—the civilizations of Mesopotamia and Egypt had long been in decadence, as were those of Palestine and Syria. Even the culture of Greece had passed its zenith. The Greek states were destined to undergo a period of dependence upon their conquerors and then to enter their long night of obscurity.

As the old political order perished, the world was held together by the rising power of Rome, which seized the fragments of the older nations and fused them into a new synthesis. The Roman Empire, the culmination of the political evolution of antiquity, was the strongest and most enlightened government of the ancient world. But there was decadence also in the heart of Rome. The autocracy of the empire crushed to death her democratic institutions, and faith in the old gods languished and failed.

The most striking characteristic of Hellenistic culture was its emphasis on the importance of individual persons. Men became concerned about their own eternal destinies. Both philosophy and religion attempted to satisfy this hunger in the human heart. At a time when wars of conquest flooded the slave markets so that human beings lost their commercial value, and when there were no limits to either exploitation or dissipation, man at last got a clear vision of the value of his own soul.

II. Geography and History

The Hellenistic world included all the countries around the Mediterranean and their hinterlands in so far as they were brought together by movements of commerce, social life, and culture. At different times biblical history involved all these lands.

A. Mesopotamia.—The story of the Hebrews began with the migration of Abraham from Mesopotamia—the region lying between the Tigris and Euphrates rivers, which supported in turn the empires of Sumer, Assyria, Babylonia, and Persia. Late in the fourth century B.C. this region was conquered by Alexander the Great, and was later held by Syria and by Parthia. In 64 B.C. Pompey seized the northern part of Mesopotamia and organized it into a Roman province, but the Parthians remained in firm control of the southern area until long after the time of Christ.

Only Egypt rivaled Mesopotamia in antiquity, unless perhaps India and China should be considered. At a very early period the inhabitants of Mesopotamia learned to divert water from the rivers to irrigate their farms, so that a stable economy based on agriculture was possible. Mesopotamia was important in Oriental commerce, its location making it the natural center for trade between the Mediterranean world and the Far East. This commerce brought the cultures of different peoples into contact with one another, and the customs and beliefs of the nations of Mesopotamia exercised a profound influence on the Hellenistic world, notably on the Hebrews, who during the days of their independence engaged in constant trade with Assyria, Babylonia, and Persia, and were finally made a subject part of each of these empires in succession. By the time of the rise of Christianity one of the strongest Jewish communities in the world had grown up in Mesopotamia.

B. Egypt.—Egypt, like Mesopotamia, drew its life from the fertility of a river valley. The mild climate and the dependability of its soil made possible the development of a notable civilization there before 4000 B.C. As early as 4241 B.C. Egyptian scientists devised a calendar year of 365 days, beginning on July 19, when Sirius first appears in the east at sunrise. That calendar was taken over by the Romans, and it has come down to us with some modifications.

About one hundred miles from the sea the Nile enters an area of alluvial soil, which the Greeks called the delta, because its triangular shape resembled the letter of the Greek alphabet by that name. This region has been the most densely populated and the best agricultural part of Egypt during all the historical period. Except for the delta, Egypt was limited almost entirely to the river valley, which is so narrow that at most places one can stand in the barren sand on one side and see clearly where the desert wastes begin on the other. The valley is usually about eight or ten miles wide. Its fertility depends entirely on the annual overflow of the river, supplemented by irrigation. Three crops are grown annually.

The Nile divides into two branches at the delta. The Damietta mouth on the east enters the Mediterranean about thirty-five miles from Port Said. A canal, making Egypt accessible by sea to all the countries of southern Asia, was cut from this branch to the Red Sea by Darius the Great about 500 B.C., and was reopened by Trajan about A.D. 100. Fifty miles west of Damietta the Rosetta mouth of the Nile flows into the sea. Alexander the Great built the city of Alexandria twenty-five miles southwestward on the coast from this point, his object being to facilitate commerce between Egypt and other Mediterranean countries. Cairo stands at the southern apex of the delta, on the eastern side of the Nile; just across, on the west side, is El Giza with its ancient pyramids, a spot which in prehistoric times apparently stood beside the sea.

There was a time when no deserts existed on either side of the Nile. Stone implements found in what is now the desert testify to prehistoric inhabitants, but as far back as our records go those regions have been desert, and of little significance, except as barriers isolating the Nile Valley from the rest of the world. Here and there, however, is an oasis able to sustain a small community. These oases were of some importance in the rise of early Christian monasticism, affording isolation and protection and, at the same time, a meager sustenance for the ascetics.

For centuries Egypt was the most powerful nation on the Mediterranean, but by the beginning of the Hellenistic period her power was gone. For a long time she had been only a province in the Persian Empire. Alexander found little resistance when he overran Egypt. Under the Ptolemies, who succeeded Alexander, Egypt experienced a considerable renewal of her former life. Greek culture was transplanted to Egypt by this dynasty; indeed, the transplantation was begun by Alexander himself. Alexandria, which he founded, soon became one of the great centers of Hellenistic life, noted for its schools, and especially for its library of more than 500,000 volumes. A large community of strongly Hellenized Jews lived at Alexandria. Christianity also obtained a foothold there at an early date, although we do not know just when or how. But by the middle of the second century Pantaenus had established a Christian school there, which produced Clement and Origen, the greatest scholars of the early church. This school, which was the first serious effort of Christianity to meet the challenge of Greek and Roman culture in a scholarly way, was the heir of a devotion to learning in Alexandria which was four hundred years old.

The Nile Valley produced much of the grain consumed by the Mediterranean peoples during the Hellenistic period. As the inhabitants of Rome came to depend more and more on the government to provide them with bread, the importance of Egypt in the economy and politics of the empire increased. Communication was not easy. The cereals were transported by sea, and the voyage was unsafe in winter. Even in summer, ships returning from Egypt had first to sail along the coast of Palestine and Syria, then across to Asia Minor, and from there to work their way home. It was probably on one of these ships that Paul embarked as he made his journey to Rome; the unwise captain, daring to cross as winter was beginning, lost both his cargo and his ship (Acts 27).

Scholarly developments in Egypt were facilitated by the art of making paper from the papyrus plant which grew along the Nile. Papyrus was used for both ordinary writing paper and books, the earliest Christian books probably being written upon it. Quantities of papyri have been found in recent times still well preserved—the material being practically indestructible in the dry climate of Egypt.

Egypt was made a Roman province by Augustus in 30 B.C., after he had defeated Antony and Cleopatra, the last of the Ptolemies, in the battle of Actium.

C. Greece.—When we think of ancient Greece, we usually mean the people and culture associated with Athens, where the Hellenic spirit achieved its most glorious expression. But we should not forget other important sites inhabited by Greeks from prehistoric times or colonized by them. The Greek mainland consisted of a group of city-states reaching from Thessaly on the north to Sparta on the south. Attica, of which Athens was the capital, was only a small part of this area. The Greek homeland was notable for its indented shoreline with numerous harbors, and for its rugged surface, the mountains dividing the country into many largely isolated segments. The climate was mild and well suited to agriculture, but the nearness of the sea drew the Greeks into a commercial life.

The earliest development of Greek culture may well have been on the island of Crete, but all the Aegean islands made their contributions, as did also the Ionian Greek cities of Asia Minor. There were ten of these Ionian cities, of which Miletus, where Paul said farewell to the Ephesian elders (Acts 20), was most vigorous and influential. The Greeks of Asia Minor came into contact with Oriental civilizations and mediated elements of those cultures to the Greek homeland. In a similar way Greece also acquired elements of Egyptian culture.

Corinth, which occupied a strategic site at the southern end of the isthmus connecting Attica and the Peloponnesus, was also outstanding not only in commerce but also in colonization, the great city of Syracuse on the island of Sicily being one of her colonies. The free population of Corinth included seamen, soldiers, merchants, and artisans. A good half of her residents were slaves. Strangers from many lands walked her streets, and her bazaars offered wines, foods, and products of both industry and art from all the ports of the Mediterranean and the Euxine.

The same thing could be said of many other Greek cities. The extent of Greek commerce is illustrated by the trade in wine carried on by the city of Rhodes. The island on which this city stood was famous for its wine, great quantities of which were shipped in tall, carrot-shaped amphorae. On one handle of the amphora was stamped the name of the priest of Helios for that year, presumably a device for giving the age of the wine. The other handle also carried a name, probably that of either the vintner or the potter. Large numbers of the handles with their picturesque stamps have been found in such widely separated places as Pergamum and Carthage, and thousands even in Palestine. There must have been an equally extensive trade in hundreds of other items.

The cult of Helios, the sun-god, was strong in Rhodes. The famed Colossus of Rhodes was a statue of Helios, constructed about 280 B.C. out of gratitude to the god for delivering the city from a siege. The natives had a myth that they were descendants of a marriage of Helios to Rhode, who had borne seven sons to the sun-god there. Many of the jar handles are ornamented with the head of Helios, from which the sun's rays are streaming; others have a beautiful rose, which perfectly symbolizes the island since its name is the Greek word for "rose."

With all their cultural achievements, the Greeks remained throughout most of their history divided into rival and hostile cities. They never succeeded in achieving enough political unity to enable them to withstand a powerful invader. They finally succeeded in driving out the Persians, but only after many of their cities, including Athens, had been ravaged. But wars between the Greek cities themselves were even more destructive. The Greeks were easily conquered by Philip of Macedon at Chaeronea in 338 B.C.—an event which brought enforced unity under Macedonian domination.

D. Alexander the Great.—The military achievements of Alexander were made possible by the extensive Greek colonization and commerce which had developed long before his time. A political and cultural map of the period shows that the Greeks had occupied Crete, most of Cyprus, all the islands of the Aegean, the shores of Asia Minor to a considerable depth, as well as large areas bordering the Euxine, the coasts of Libya and Cyrenaica in Africa, and that they had trading posts even at the mouth of the Nile. In the west they had penetrated southern Italy on a large scale and acquired substantial parts of Sicily, Sardinia, and Corsica, and had also established colonies in southern Gaul and Spain. Although this vast network of settlements was not a unified development in a political sense, since the colonies had been founded by rival Greek states, nevertheless there were strong cultural ties which bound them all together: they all spoke the Greek language, with only minor differences in dialect, and the classical literature, art, and learning of Greece were their common possession. In these widely separated communities Greek culture took new roots and flourished, in some cases rivaling if not surpassing that of the homeland.

Barbarians of Asia, Africa, and Europe, who came to the Greek centers to trade, learned the language, admired the architecture, sculpture, and painting, and in time absorbed much of the Greek spirit. Greek became the language of learning as well as of commerce throughout the Mediterranean world. This widespread use of Greek accounts for the almost incredible fact that when Paul wrote a letter to the church at Rome, shortly after the middle of the first century, he wrote it in Greek. All of our New Testament was written in Greek—even that which was produced in Latin-speaking Rome—and Latin did not make its way into Christian literature until well toward the end of the second century.

The world was also ready for Alexander in a military sense—the Persian Empire was decadent, and Rome had not risen to power. After making himself secure in the homeland, Alexander easily penetrated the Greek areas of Asia Minor and defeated Darius III at Issus, on the plains of Cilicia, in 333 B.C. He then moved southward into Syria and destroyed the city of Tyre, an ally of Persia, after building a causeway from the shore out to the rock in the sea on which the city was built. This ended the maritime career of the Phoenicians, who for centuries had been the merchants and seamen of the Near East and the only serious rivals of the Greeks. They had established powerful colonies in Cyprus, Sicily, Sardinia, Spain, and North Africa, where Carthage was the best known.

The Jewish priests at Jerusalem at first defied the conqueror, but when they saw how he dealt with Tyre, they quickly came to terms. Alexander accepted the allegiance of the city and left it essentially undisturbed. His next goal, Egypt, was conquered without a struggle; and the young hero was crowned Pharaoh by the Egyptians, who were glad to be liberated from the Persians. He then visited the historic shrine of Amon in the Libyan desert, where the oracle declared him to be the son of that god. Alexander reorganized the government of Egypt and established the city which bears his name near the Rosetta mouth of the Nile.

Alexander gave the final blow to the tottering Persian Empire at Arbela in northern Mesopotamia in 331 B.C., and after quickly subduing all its territories, he swept down through the Khyber Pass into India. There he established himself for a time, until he was defeated, not by an army, but by the climate. He returned to Babylon, where he died suddenly in 323 B.C. Alexander had begun his conquests at the age of twenty and was still less than thirty-three when he died. At the time of his death he was planning an expedition by sea around Arabia to Egypt, and no doubt had in mind eventually adding the western Mediterranean countries to his empire.

Although Alexander himself and ten thousand of his soldiers married Asiatic women, thus giving a symbol of the way in which the bars separating the East and the West were breaking down, still he provided no stable political bond to hold the world together. Alexander's kingdom was only a group of distantly related lands which he had united by conquest, and which fell apart the moment his strong hand was removed. But Alexander entrenched Greek culture by founding seventy cities and establishing Greeks in them. He believed in the intermingling of races and peoples on a basis of equality and was generous with the lands which he conquered, although he was convinced of the superiority of Greek civilization and did what he could to further its progress. The idea of universalism was basic in Alexander's philosophy, but he had a vision of a world united by the learning and spirit of Greece, and believed that it was his mission to bring this union about. This work of Alexander was a foundation on which Christianity was to build three centuries later. The universalism in the later Christian gospel, and in the doctrine that "in Christ" there can be neither Jew nor Greek, would have appealed to Alexander.

With Alexander the seat of world power shifted to Europe—for the first time Mesopotamia and Egypt were ruled from north of the Mediterranean. The end of Oriental supremacy had come. But Alexander's death left an unstable situation, with no political organization in existence which corresponded to the realities of the time. That political organization was to be the creation of Rome.

E. Rome.—When Alexander died, his generals entered upon a struggle for the territories which he had conquered. Antigonus I, to whom was first given the Greek peninsula, survived for only a short time. At his death rival Greek states contended for power until, in 196 B.C., Rome took a hand as the "protector" of the Greeks. When the Roman legions defeated the Macedonians at Cynoscephalae, the Greeks received them with enthusiasm. Fifty years later, however, in 146 B.C., when Corinth became insubordinate, the Romans destroyed the city without mercy and sold the inhabitants into slavery. The city lay in ruins for a century, but was rebuilt by Julius Caesar, who established a colony of his veterans there in 46 B.C. The new city prospered and soon regained its former importance as the commercial metropolis of Greece. By the time Paul founded his church there, Corinth had become one of the five great cities of the Mediterranean world, the others being Antioch, Ephesus, Alexandria, and Rome; but both political and cultural leadership had long since departed from the Greek mainland.

Ptolemy, who got possession of Egypt after Alexander's death, founded a vigorous Greek dynasty there, which came to its end when Cleopatra committed suicide after the battle of Actium in 30 B.C. Octavius, who had rejected the young queen's seductive approaches, then organized the nation as an imperial province.

Most of the eastern part of Alexander's empire fell to Seleucus I, who moved his capital from Babylon to Antioch in northern Syria. His successors never succeeded in creating a well-integrated and united nation out of the peoples occupying the regions from the Black Sea on the north and the Persian Gulf on the south to the borders of India on the east. Yet Seleucid rule survived at Antioch, although over territories which shifted radically from time to time, until Pompey the Great took over the country and annexed it to the Roman Empire in 64 B.C. Syria at once became a strategic imperial province.

The real heir of Alexander was Rome, but the Romans were late in coming to maturity, in spite of the fertile lands, favorable climate, and the good location of Italy for purposes of either commerce or war. The Romans were still leading a tribal life when the Greeks reached the height of their civilization. Indeed it was contact with the culture of Greece brought by traders and colonists to Italy that awoke the Romans to the possibilities in their grasp. Even in Alexander's time the Romans were still in their political adolescence; and they had apparently remained unaware of the cultures which had flourished in ancient Egypt and Babylonia, and were unconcerned about the great colonial and commercial developments of the Greeks and Phoenicians. Had Alexander lived a few years longer, he probably would have added all the western Mediterranean, including Italy, to his dominions; but his sudden death and the disintegration of his kingdom gave the Romans time to develop in their own way.

A primitive monarchy was overthrown at Rome about 500 B.C. and replaced by a sturdy republic which lasted until 30 B.C., when Augustus founded the empire. In Alexander's time the unification of Italy under the leadership of Rome was in process; by 264 B.C., when the first Carthaginian war began, it was complete. The rich Greek cities of southern Italy had given the conquering Romans a glimpse of the treasures which could be had for the taking. Sicily, filled with beautiful cities of the Greeks and Carthaginians, lay just off their southwestern coast; northward were the islands of Sardinia and Corsica. But across on the mainland of Africa stood the powerful city of Carthage, a Phoenician colony, which was older and richer than Rome itself. This industrious city had already filled the western Mediterranean with her ships, and through her numerous colonies she dominated the commerce from Sicily to Gibraltar. The struggle between Rome and Carthage was inevitable. In three terrible wars (264-241, 218-201, and 149-146 B.C.) Carthage was first stopped, then defeated, and finally destroyed. From 146 to 46 B.C. the city lay in ruins, but was rebuilt as a colony by Julius Caesar.

The destruction of Carthage left Rome supreme in the West, and she had already begun to take over the North and East. Substantial Alpine territory and all the Greek mainland, together with the eastern parts of Asia Minor, had been taken. Corinth was destroyed in the very year in which Carthage met her fate. Rome was now without a commercial or military rival closer than Egypt or Syria, and during the century that followed, these countries also were brought under her rule. Pompey conquered Pontus in 66 B.C. and Syria in 64 B.C. In the following year a civil war in Palestine between Hyrcanus and Aristobulus, last of the Maccabeans, gave him an opportunity to extend the power of Rome over the Jews. (See the article "New Testament Times: II. Palestine.") Pompey thus became Rome's most outstanding general—wealthy, popular, and ambitious for political power.

In 59 B.C. Julius Caesar, who was Pompey's only serious rival, began his conquest of Gaul, the thrilling story of which he put in writing for the people at home to read. In 49 B.C., with his legions behind him, he returned to Italy as the idol of the hour. Pompey hurried to the East to gather his forces, but one year later suffered a crushing defeat. At that time Caesar brought Egypt also into the Roman orbit by supporting Cleopatra, the seventeen-year-old queen who had been expelled from the throne by her guardians. The great Roman was now master of the world. Except in name he had become an absolute monarch when assassins struck him down in the senate chamber in March, 44 B.C.

The radicals who stabbed the dictator to death thought that in this violent way the republic could be saved, but they were soon to discover their error. They were ignoring forces in the nation which no threat of a dagger could hold in check. Caesar's will named as heir the eighteen-year-old Octavius who was the grandson of Caesar's sister. Mark Antony, who had been associated with Caesar in Gaul, attempted to disregard the will and seize power himself.

But Octavius was equal to the occasion. By a clever move he got the senate to appoint him general; then he brought his army into Rome and forced that body to make him consul.

His next step was to form a triumvirate with his rivals, Antony and Lepidus, whose aid he needed in crushing the republican army under Brutus and Cassius, the two leaders in Caesar's assassination. In the battle of Philippi in 42 B.C. the republican forces were defeated and Brutus and Cassius committed suicide. The triumvirs then divided the world between themselves. Antony received Gaul and the eastern provinces; Africa went to Lepidus; and Octavius got Italy and Spain. But Lepidus soon retired and gave Africa to Octavius. Shortly afterward Gaul fell into his hands. Antony in the meantime, spurning his wife, who was the sister of Octavius, had become infatuated with Cleopatra. When he demanded more troops for grandiose campaigns in the East, Octavius denied them. The rivals met at Actium in 31 B.C. Antony had the support of the great fleet of his beloved Egyptian queen, and Cleopatra led it into battle in person, but she fell out of line and fled as soon as the fighting started. Antony turned and followed her, leaving Octavius in triumph. He pursued the two lovers to Egypt, where Cleopatra caused Antony to commit suicide by sending him a false report that she was dying. Then after she had tried in vain to win the heart of Octavius, she took her own life. Octavius annexed Egypt and made it an imperial province.

The republic was now dead (30 B.C.), but Octavius did not assume a crown. He was consul (but for only four years at a time), tribune, general, *Pater Patriae, Augustus,* and *Princeps,* but was called neither king nor emperor. He was careful to preserve the form of democracy while he ruthlessly crushed its essence. His life was lived in simplicity, in good Roman tradition, not in the luxury of Oriental rulers. Augustus knew that the love of freedom was deeply entrenched in Roman hearts. When his long reign, marked by peace and prosperity, came to an end in A.D. 14, a new life had begun to surge through the empire. To those who could recall the bloody turbulence which had preceded it, this age seemed to be a divine gift to the world, and Augustus himself was credited with attributes of deity. The ceremony of deification which followed his death expressed the genuine gratitude and reverence in the hearts of his people.

III. Morality

The moral life of the pagan world was often referred to by early Christian writers whose view of the morality of the time was a stereotyped one inherited from their Jewish predecessors. Both Jewish and Christian authors agreed that the Gentiles were morally degenerate. The Old Testament story of Sodom and Gomorrah, on which the Lord had rained down fire and brimstone, represents the Hebrew attitude toward pagan wickedness, whether of Egyptians, Canaanites, Philistines, Assyrians, Babylonians, or Romans. Babylon, in particular, even to a greater extent than Sodom and Gomorrah, came to be a symbol of all evil. The Hebrews based their judgment first of all on the idolatry and other primitive religious rites of these peoples, and regarded low morality as an inevitable result of the crude religion.

In a notable passage Paul has painted, in colors commonly accepted as true, the picture of pagan morality which was current among the Jews and Christians of his time (Rom. 1:18-32). He first condemns the Gentiles for their gross failure to worship the true God as he is revealed in nature to everyone of understanding. The revelation in nature, he argues, leaves everyone without excuse. The savage who looks up into the sky at night, or observes the beauty of flowers, or any of the awe-inspiring wonders about him, should know God, and worship him as a spiritual being. But the pagans have worshiped God in every conceivable form of man, beast, bird, reptile, and insect. This statement is, of course, literally true. Anyone who has gone through a museum of ancient Egyptian culture, for example, has seen the images and mummies of a great variety of sacred birds, dogs, bulls, crocodiles, beetles, and the like. Indeed Paul may have had the Egyptians in mind. Yet the Egyptian picture is not essentially different from that of most other peoples of the time. With the possible exception of the Zoroastrians of Persia, it was a common practice for the pagan religions to use idols of one shape or another.

A. Sex Morality.—To this prevalent idol worship the apostle traces the immorality of the time. He is especially sensitive to sexual depravity. "God gave them up to dishonorable passions," he writes. "Their women exchanged natural relations for unnatural, and the men likewise gave up natural relations with women and were consumed with passion for one another, men committing shameless acts with men and receiving in their own persons the due penalty for their error."

But his catalogue of the immoralities of the age continues: "God gave them up to a base mind and to improper conduct. They were filled with all manner of wickedness, evil, covetousness, malice. Full of envy, murder, strife, deceit, malignity, they are gossips, slanderers, haters of God, insolent, haughty, boastful, inventors of evil, disobedient to parents, foolish, faithless, heartless, ruthless" (Rom. 1:26-31).

A similar picture is painted in lurid colors by the writer of Revelation. The Christian writers of the second century, like Ignatius, Justin, Irenaeus, Tertullian, Clement of Alexandria, and Origen, give testimony to the same effect. These men were in revolt against the evils of their society and felt an obligation as Christians to hold up to the world a pure theology and a high morality. They went about establishing little communities of Christians among the Greeks and Romans, like men lighting lamps on dark streets at night.

It is not difficult to document this picture of pagan morality from the Greek and Roman literature of the time. The practice of homosexuality, to which Paul referred with such a feeling of abhorrence, was called *paiderastia*. Plato in his *Symposium* and also in the *Phaedrus* shows that this practice was well known among the Greeks of his time. No dishonor was attached to this type of love. It was not regarded as in any sense inferior to the love of a man for a woman. Indeed Plato appears to idealize this love between men, especially brilliant young men. It is men of this type, he argues, who become the great leaders of the state. Yet Plato does not treat of sensual love. He distinguishes between the heavenly and the earthly Aphrodite (the goddess of love); only in the heavenly form is she to be worshiped by men of real insight. The love of a man for a woman or of a man for a man may be depraved, but in neither case *needs* to be. But Jews and Christians considered homosexuality to be against nature and the law of God, and regarded it as one of the most offensive expressions of decadent Hellenistic morality.

We do not know a great deal about the sex morality of the common people among the Greeks and Romans of Paul's time, but there is no lack of evidence concerning that of kings and nobles. Pausanias[1] says that the Macedonians of his day believed that Ptolemy Lagus, founder of the Egyptian dynasty, was not the son of Lagus at all, but of Philip of Macedon; that his mother was already pregnant before Philip gave her to Lagus. Then he tells how Ptolemy himself, although he was married to Berenice, took Eurydice, one of his wife's waiting ladies, as his mistress; and that she bore him a son, Ptolemy Philadelphus, who succeeded him on the throne. Julius Caesar, already married, took the young Cleopatra, who bore him a son; and after Caesar was dead, she became the mistress of Antony. The Gospel of Mark relates that Herod Antipas of Galilee set aside his own wife to take Herodias, the wife of his brother.

[1] *Descriptions of Greece* I. 6. 2, 8.

The letters of Paul throw some light on the sex morality of the common people of the time. A young man at Corinth had taken his father's wife, presumably a young stepmother (I Cor. 5:1-2). Although Paul in his emphatic way says that such immorality is unknown even among the heathen, it is clear from the discussion that the church is not much exercised over the matter. Such things must have been fairly common among them. This same general situation appears to be presupposed in Paul's other churches. He urges the Thessalonians to abstain from fornication and to keep themselves sexually pure (I Thess. 4:3-8). In a similar vein he writes to Colossae (Col. 3:5). An injunction of the same type is given to the Ephesians (5:3) and to the Galatians (5:19). We have already noted his discussion of the subject in his letter to the Romans. Whenever Paul draws up a catalogue of sins of the time, it is significant that sexual transgressions usually head the list. All Paul's letters, it is important to note in this connection, were written to Greek and Roman churches, that is, to persons who, with a few exceptions, had been converted from paganism to Christianity.

Further light is thrown on the morality of the time by the characters of the pagan gods themselves. Every conceivable type of immorality was attributed by the pagans to their deities.

Prostitution was a well-recognized institution in the Hellenistic world. Our word "fornication," which usually means intercourse with an unmarried woman, is derived from the Latin *fornix*, which meant "arch" or "vault." The brothels of Rome were conducted in underground vaults; hence to patronize a brothel was "to fornicate" (*fornicare*). Slave girls were the worst victims of this debauchery. The practice of exposing undesired infants was one of the most prolific sources from which prostitutes were derived, and it was evidently a custom to have both male and female prostitutes. Justin in his *First Apology* (ch. xxvii) upbraids the Roman world for this inhuman custom. He says that both boys and girls are exposed and that they are often seized by vicious persons and brought up as prostitutes. Some men, he says, even prostitute their own children and wives.

Prostitution was also rooted in religion—from very ancient times sexual rites were associated with the fertility of the fields, as well as of animals and human beings. Such rites, involving both male and female devotees, were well known among the ancient Canaanites. The cult took root even in Hebrew religion, and the prophets had great difficulty in eradicating it (cf. I Kings 14:23-24). These fertility rites were known in the Babylonian and Phoenician religions, and are still practiced by the Siva cult in the India of our own time. Strabo[2] relates that the temple of Aphrodite at Corinth had in ancient times a thousand sacred slaves, or temple prostitutes. He says that the slave girls had been dedicated to the goddess by both men and women. It was on account of these prostitutes, he writes, that the city was crowded and grew rich; ship captains in particular squandered their money with them. Whether this temple with its prostitutes existed in Paul's time we do not know.

B. Slavery.—One of the many cruel features of the culture of the Romans was the wholesale traffic in slavery. A common practice was to condemn prisoners of war to slavery; thus as many as 150,000 at a time might be enslaved. Human life was very cheap. Josephus[3] states that Titus collected 97,000 Jewish captives when he destroyed Jerusalem in A.D. 70. But there were also professional slave dealers. Cilicia and Crete were infested by corsairs who made a business of capturing inhabitants of Syria and the Greek islands and selling them into slavery. Slaves were often superior in intelligence and culture to their masters. There were notable cases where they were highly esteemed and permitted positions of great responsibility in the master's household. They were sometimes artists, teachers, and philosophers, the well-known Stoic philosopher Epictetus once having been a slave. He had the good fortune to belong to a man of character and insight, who recognized the young slave's ability, gave him an excellent education, and then set him free. But the position of the average slave was hard. The great building enterprises of the Romans, their systems of highways, and their vast commerce by land and sea, were made possible by slave labor. Roman slavery reached its most cruel stage about the time of the birth of Christ. The military campaigns which extended the empire more and more widely produced a steady supply for this traffic in human beings.

Slavery is reflected in the New Testament itself. Many of the sayings and parables of Jesus assume the presence of slaves as a regular feature of Jewish society at the time. Slavery was a part of Hebrew culture from the earliest times. The biblical laws were intended to improve the lot of slaves of Hebrew blood and, if possible, to set them free; but slavery was still practiced by the Jews in the time of Christ. The letters of Paul reflect the presence of numerous slaves in Christian households. Paul admonished them to obey their masters as their Christian duty; on the other hand he urged

[2] *Geography* VIII. 6. 20.
[3] *Jewish War* VI. 9. 3.

masters to be considerate of slaves, recognizing them as brothers in Christ. Paul states explicitly that in Christ "there is neither bond nor free" (Gal. 3:28); yet he does not repudiate slavery as an institution. The letter to Philemon shows Paul's attitude. Here he sends a runaway slave back to his master, but at the same time brings about a Christian reconciliation between them. There can be no doubt that Christian morality often eliminated many of the horrors of slavery; yet it has always been possible to engage in slavery and to cite New Testament precedents for doing so.

Various humane elements in Greek and Roman culture sought to improve the position of slaves, the Stoic teachers having taken a special interest in them. Epictetus [4] said that the master and his slave are brothers, both children of the same God, and that the master should always bear this fact in mind. Some eminent Romans, like Cicero and the younger Pliny, were noted for their humanity toward slaves. By the beginning of the second century the influence of Stoic teaching began to be reflected in Roman laws dealing with slaves. Domitian prohibited the commercial castration of slaves; Hadrian forbade a master to kill his slave unless the slave had been condemned by a magistrate; a first-century law prohibited the sending of slaves into the arena to fight with beasts without the assent of a court; but it was not until A.D. 428 that it became a crime for panderers to exploit their slaves by making prostitutes of them. To mention these limited expressions of a humane attitude toward slaves, however, is only to underscore the tragedy of their total lot.

The cross as a means of execution was characteristically Roman. During most of the period of the republic, crucifixion was used only for slaves, but in the imperial period it was extended to free men. Misconduct with the vestal virgins was punishable by crucifixion even under the republic. Tiberius crucified the priests of the temple of Isis in Rome, along with a female accomplice, for carrying out a plot which permitted Decius Mundus, a Roman knight, to violate the beautiful Paulina, wife of Saturninus.[5] The priests had permitted Mundus to impersonate the god Anubis. This method of execution was often used against political criminals. When Varus, the governor of Syria, had to march into Palestine shortly after the death of Herod in 4 B.C. to quell disorders there, he crucified two thousand men. During the siege of Jerusalem in the war of A.D. 66-70, Titus crucified as many as five hundred Jews daily outside the walls in plain view of the

city.[6] The execution of Jesus was on a political charge. Barabbas, who was released at the time, had been involved in an insurrection along with others (Mark 15:7). Crucifixion was used by the Romans until the time of Constantine, who abolished it for religious reasons.

Burning at the stake was also well known among the Romans. Tacitus [7] states that in the persecution under Nero in Rome, Christians were killed by dogs after they had been garbed in the skins of beasts, that some were crucified, and that others were burned, Nero offering his own garden for the spectacle. The letters of Ignatius, bishop of Antioch, were written about A.D. 115 while Ignatius was on his way to Rome, where he expected to be thrown to beasts. Polycarp, bishop of Smyrna, was burned at the stake about A.D. 155.

Another popular form of execution was to force the condemned to fight as gladiators in the arena for the amusement of the people. This type of sport, familiar in Rome, was also enjoyed by some communities of Palestine and Syria. Josephus [8] states that Titus exhibited shows at Caesarea Philippi in which great numbers of captives were thrown to wild beasts or made to fight with one another as if they were enemies. In similar spectacles, staged at Caesarea by Titus on Domitian's birthday, 2,500 captives were slain.[9] Exhibitions of this kind were first introduced to the Jews by Herod the Great,[10] who had built both a theater and an amphitheater. He celebrated great games every five years, to which people from neighboring lands were invited. Wrestling and other athletic events, musical contests, and chariot races were prominent, but there was also a collection of lions and other beasts, which fought with one another or with men who had been condemned to death.

C. A Brighter Side.—But a picture of the moral life of the Hellenistic world is distorted if it contains only the sensual and barbarous elements. Many of the sports and entertainments of the Greeks and Romans were highly artistic and cultural, notable examples being the great Greek games. Some of the finest creations of Greek art and literature were inspired by these contests. Nor should one forget the theater, in which no other culture has excelled the Greeks. Wherever Greek culture took roots the theater appears to have flourished—even as far from the Greek mainland as in the cities of Trans-Jordan. Ten cities in that region, settled by Greeks during the Hellenistic

---

[4] *Discourses* I. 13. 1-3.
[5] Josephus *Antiquities* XVIII. 3. 4.
[6] Josephus *Jewish War* II. 5. 2; V. 6. 5; V. 11. 1.
[7] *Annals* XV. 44.
[8] Josephus *Jewish War* VII. 2. 1.
[9] *Ibid.* VII. 3. 1.
[10] Josephus *Antiquities* XV. 8. 1.

period, were called the Decapolis. Gerasa, the modern Jerash, and Philadelphia, the modern Amman, built such excellent open-air theaters that they are still well preserved today.

One must not forget also the high attainments of both Greeks and Romans, not to mention Egyptians and Persians, in moral and ethical teaching. Men like Zoroaster and Socrates left a profound impression on the moral life of the ancient world. And in the Hellenistic period religious movements inspired by Persian influence and by popular philosophical systems like Stoicism had a similar effect. Some of the most noted men of that age were Stoics, of whom Epictetus and Marcus Aurelius are examples. Along with these may be mentioned men like Seneca and Pliny the Younger, in whose moral attainments any age might well take pride. These men illustrate the type of character which gave stability and permanence to the Roman Empire. No other nation of antiquity showed so much understanding of subject peoples and allowed so much freedom— especially at the time of the rise of Christianity. The all-pervasive influence of Rome gave the missionaries an assurance of safety on their travels among strange and inhospitable peoples. There were exceptions: a fanatic like Nero might occasionally come to power; but generally speaking, the Romans granted freedom to all religions in the empire.

These humane qualities in the Roman government reflected, as we have seen in the case of slavery, the influence of the Stoic philosophy. One of the most basic tenets of this school was the idea of universal brotherhood; that all men are children of the same God. The Bible teaches that all men are created in the image of God, but not that they are sons of God. In the Old Testament "son of God" is used in three senses: angels, the Hebrew king, and individual Hebrews; but it is never applied to all mankind. The Gospel of Luke, however, breaks slightly with this usage by tracing the genealogy of Christ back to Adam "the son of God," and Acts 17:28 allows Paul to quote the Stoic doctrine that men are the offspring of God. But these instances are exceptions. The general idea in the New Testament, especially in Paul, is that men become sons of God only by a moral and spiritual transformation; that only Christians are sons of God. The Stoic idea of universal brotherhood was later absorbed by Christian theology so completely that many persons assume as a matter of course that the belief comes from the Bible.

Early Christians were not entirely unaware of pagans who were outstanding examples of moral character. Paul, with penetrating insight, expresses his appreciation of such pagans in Rom. 2:12-16. The examples of morality among the Gentiles show, he says, that some men have the law of God written in their hearts although they have never heard the "law" as it is revealed in the Bible. Moreover, he states that God will take their good character into account in the Day of Judgment. Some later writers like Justin expressed the extraordinary view that demons had stolen some truth from the Hebrews and taught it to the Greeks in order to discredit the Christian faith.[11]

IV. Philosophy

It hardly needs to be stated that philosophy constituted an important aspect of Hellenistic culture. The philosophical approach to knowledge was the unique contribution of the Greeks to ancient civilization. Its essential feature is the emphasis on the primacy of reason in the attainment of truth. Religion has usually based its approach to truth on a belief in revelation. In the one case human reason is active, assuming a vigorous role, asserting its right to grapple with all the problems of the universe and confident that it can make substantial progress toward the goal of ultimate truth, even if it does not fully reach it. In the other case reason is more passive; it awaits a divine illumination. Religion gives an important place to feeling, ecstasy, and vision, stressing the realization of truth with the whole personality. These two approaches to reality have given the world the rationalistic philosopher and the inspired prophet. The prophet has not denied either the existence or the importance of reason, but he has refused to make it the supreme test of truth. The philosopher has sometimes, but certainly not always, denied the possibility of revelation, but he has refused to exempt truth, even that which purports to be revealed, from facing the criteria of reason. The religious approach to the problems of life was characteristically an Oriental attitude. All the great leaders of the Orient in antiquity were prophets rather than philosophers. This is illustrated in Moses and the other prophets of the Hebrews, as well as in Zoroaster and the Indian seers who wrote the Vedas. There was no philosopher among them—all of them based their work on inspiration and revelation.

The development of philosophy among the Greeks was therefore not only a new way of looking at life but the opening up of a new chapter in the story of civilization. It has a special importance for the student of the New Testament because Christianity originated as an Oriental religion, but before a half century had passed it had spread to all the important parts of the Greek and Roman world and had

[11] *First Apology* LIV.

begun to come to terms with all aspects of Hellenistic culture. Jesus and his disciples were Jews of the Orient. All of their experience was interpreted in the categories of inspiration and revelation. But in the second century leadership in the church passed to men who had been trained in the universities of Greece and Rome. They knew Greek philosophy. Some of the teachers even wore the traditional philosopher's mantle. When men who had studied in Greek schools became Christians, they did not forget their learning. The development of Christian theology bears the marks of the constant and profound influence which Greek philosophy exercised upon it.

A. Plato.—The philosophy of Plato (428-348 B.C.) continued to be of great importance during the Hellenistic period. The most distinctive and important feature of this philosophy was his theory of ideas. For every type or class of objects—such as man or horse or tree—there exists in the metaphysical realm a perfect "idea." This idea is an essence which has an objective, independent existence. It is the true reality. Individual objects of a given class are temporary and derive what degree of reality they have from the perfect idea or "form" in the metaphysical world. The invisible world therefore contains the true realities of all the objects which we perceive in our common experience. The universe is divided into the material and the spiritual realms, and only the spiritual is the ultimately real.

The meaning of knowledge for Plato is knowing the perfect ideas which constitute reality. It is characteristic of him that he relies solely on reason, believing that the human mind is able to attain absolute truth, and then to use it as the guide of life. True knowledge is not to be acquired by the senses or even by scientific study of the objects of the phenomenal world, but by a rational apprehension of the metaphysical realities.

Plato does not attempt to formulate a theology, but it is clear that he has discarded the anthropomorphic ideas of the old polytheism. In many ways he approaches—if he does not clearly express—a high, spiritual monotheism. In his hierarchy of values he places the Good at the top. This is a reality with an objective existence, not just a construct of the mind, and it has many qualities which might be regarded as attributes of God. The early Christians found a great deal of help in Plato in understanding their own religion. The author of the letter to the Hebrews (8:1-5; 12:22-23), with his belief that earthly things are only shadows or copies of those in heaven, has evidently made use of Platonic thought to express his Christian faith. This is only one of several instances of the appropriating of Plato's philosophy by Christian thinkers.

They made much of his belief in immortality. Plato's idea of immortality, however, involved only the soul. The physical body he regarded as an impediment, which he was glad to leave behind forever at death. The soul is in a sense limited and imprisoned by the body during life. Greek Christians with this background objected to the belief in the resurrection of the body, which had been taken over from Judaism. That was the situation which Paul faced in the church at Corinth. The Christians there believed in immortality, but they had no desire for a physical resurrection. Paul, on the other hand, held the Jewish view that personality included the body as well as the soul. Hence true immortality would require the resurrection of the body.

It is possible also that Plato's teaching about the body had some bearing on the Christian Gnostic ideas which emerged about the beginning of the second century. One of these was the view that Christ did not have a physical body during his earthly life. Gnostics either regarded the body of Jesus as having been a phantom, a mere appearance which could not suffer and die; or they said that the Christ was to be distinguished from the man Jesus—that the Christ came upon Jesus at his baptism, but departed from him before he died. This strange teaching was called "Docetism," from the Greek word "to appear." Many Gnostics also practiced an extreme asceticism, condemning all sexual relationships in particular. This was not a Platonic teaching, but one can see how Plato's disparagement of the body might be taken to support an ascetic position. Another point of contact between Plato and the Gnostics involved his idea of creation. He ascribed creation to a Demiurge, a sort of intermediate divine being, and in this way accounted for evil in the world. This belief in a Demiurge was taken up and exploited by Gnostics like Marcion, Valentinus, and Basilides. The physical world and the race of mankind, these men held, contain too much evil to have been created by the God whom Jesus Christ revealed. Marcion repudiated the Old Testament because it seemed to reveal a God who was less than good.

B. Aristotle.—Aristotle, the disciple and successor of Plato and tutor of Alexander the Great, distinguished himself in logic, metaphysics, and the sciences—in all these fields going beyond his master. In his thought the eternal ideas of which Plato made so much gave place to essence or substance. Every object is composed of substance and attributes. Substance is metaphysical and therefore beyond the reach of the senses. It has to be apprehended by reason. But substance achieves true reality only as it is embodied in material forms. This gives more importance to the phenomenal world and provides a solid basis for scientific investigation. Motion, Aristotle held, can be explained only by the assumption of a "prime mover" which is unlimited or unconditioned. This conclusion rested upon the observation that every result in our world has a finite cause which, in turn, was the result of another finite cause. But since no chain of finite causes can ever give a real explanation of motion, there must be an original cause or mover which is infinite. This prime mover or infinite cause is what religion calls God. Aristotle did not make a great impression on early Christian thinkers, but with the revival of classical learning in the twelfth and thirteenth centuries, he became the most important philosopher of antiquity. His idea of substance and attributes became the rational basis of the doctrine of transubstantiation. Thomas Aquinas said that the substance of the bread and wine is changed into the substance of the body and blood of Christ, although there is no change in the attributes. That is, no perceptible change takes place when the miracle of transubstantiation occurs. The idea of the prime mover also became basic in the rational argument for the existence of God.

C. Epicureanism.—The philosophy of Epicureanism, attempting to solve the metaphysical problem by denying its existence, had a considerable vogue during the Hellenistic period. It held that the material atom is the ultimate reality, and that pleasure is the highest good in life. The school was founded by Epicurus (341-270 B.C.) in Athens, and the Roman poet Lucretius (98-54 B.C.) was one of its best-known exponents. The purpose of its interest in atomic materialism was not to encourage science, but to undercut belief in all spiritual realities and so relieve men of fear and concern about the gods and the soul's eternal destiny. Contrary to popular belief, Epicurus did not encourage a sensual life. While he held that pleasure is the greatest good, he urged men to choose pleasures of the mind rather than those of the body. All the theology and rites of religion should be discarded as they are based on superstition and are the source of unnecessary anxiety. There is no soul, no immortality, no vengeance of the gods in a hereafter. Likewise the rigorous pursuit of learning and art is to be condemned. The simple fulfillment of natural desires, undisturbed by ambition or fear, is the ideal of Epicureanism.

That Epicureanism had come to be the philosophy of many sophisticated persons in the Hellenistic world goes without saying. Lucre-

tius must have had a market for his poems. Their preservation to the present day indicates how popular they were. This view of life has been congenial to many people all through the centuries, and in antiquity it was by no means confined to Greece. It was practically identical with the still older Lokayata philosophy of India; and the Hebrews in the late Persian or Greek period produced Ecclesiastes, the work of a thinker who had many points of affinity with Epicureanism.

D. Stoicism.—The most popular and influential of all schools of philosophy in the Hellenistic period was Stoicism. This school was founded by Zeno (340-265 B.C.) who, although a native of Cyprus, and probably a Semite, founded his school of philosophy at Athens, the intellectual center of the world. Seneca (A.D. 4-65), Epictetus (A.D. 60-110), and the Emperor Marcus Aurelius (A.D. 121-180) were able representatives of Stoicism in the early days of Christianity. Stoicism was a metaphysics on the one hand, and a system of ethics on the other. Its primary interest and emphasis were ethical. Like Plato, the Stoics believed that the ultimate principle of the universe is spiritual. This they called the Logos or Reason. They meant a universal reason, the organizing, integrating, and energizing principle of the universe. But unlike Plato, with his idea of perfect forms or ideas in the metaphysical realm, they emphasized the complete unity of universal reason. And unlike Plato again, the Stoics insisted that this spiritual ground of the universe achieved an existence only as it became incarnate in material objects. The universe is a perfect organism, uniting in itself the universal spirit, Reason or world-soul, and matter, which is its body. The Logos or Reason is divine. In its totality it is God, but an impersonal God. Owing to the presence of this all-pervading divine reality, the universe is itself divine, and everything that happens in it is an expression of the divine will. Intelligence in man is a fragment of the universal divine Reason. All men therefore are sons of the one God, and universal brotherhood is the basis of ethical living, as has been noted above (see p. 84).

The highest good according to Stoic teaching is the attainment of individual virtue; the ideal of the ethical life is to live in harmony with Reason. In his own conscience every man carries about with him the divine guide of life. To follow Reason means to subdue, if possible to eradicate, the emotions. The virtuous man should attain such an inner discipline over himself that he never gives way to mirth, sorrow, or anger. The emotions are an abnormal, diseased aberration of personality. The goal of Stoic discipline is to annihilate them. To the truly wise man there can be no evil in this world—only ignorance causes men to believe in evil. Everything that happens expresses the eternal will; hence it is good. But one must see all events under the guise of eternity. It is a mistake to judge anything from the limited point of view of one person; everything must be seen in the light of the whole. The individual must not overrate his own importance. Sickness, disappointments, and death come inevitably and naturally to all. Properly seen, these also are good.

Stoicism had many attractive features. Unquestionably it made a profound contribution to the moral character of the ancient world. In some ways it had prepared the way for Christianity. It was a philosophical expression of the spirit of universality which came in with Alexander the Great, and which achieved a permanent religious embodiment in the Christian religion. It was easy for people who were familiar with the ethics of Stoicism to understand a gospel which was intended for all nations. The emphasis on the religious basis of ethics was also a valuable preparation for the Christian faith. But Stoic discipline was too stern for common people; it was beyond the reach of the average man. Moreover, its denial of a legitimate place in life to the emotions indicates an unbalanced interpretation of personality. Christianity also required a severe ethical discipline, but it found a place for both joy and sorrow, and it filled the world with singing.

The Stoic idea of conscience informed by the divine Reason as the guide of life is not far removed from Christian teaching. Jeremiah (31:33) once spoke of a time when God's law would be written in men's hearts, and this idea was made use of by Paul, as has been noted, when he appraised the pagan morality of his time. This is apparently a divine inward monitor which all men by nature possess. But one of the most distinctive teachings of Paul was his idea of the Spirit of God which dwells in the hearts of Christians. This indwelling Spirit enables a Christian to recognize that he is a child of God (Rom. 8:14-17) and brings him into a constant divine fellowship. The good deeds of Christian morality are the normal expression of this Spirit-filled life (Gal. 5:16-24). Paul at other times identifies this Spirit with the indwelling Christ (Gal. 2:20).

The Stoic Logos also finds some counterpart in Christian teachings. As is noted in another connection, Philo, the Jewish philosopher of Alexandria, spoke often of the Logos as an intermediary of God in creation, and a somewhat similar concept appears in the Gospel of John (1:1-18). The evangelist begins his prologue with a reference to the Logos as the divine creator of the universe. The Logos was with God in the beginning and was divine. The Logos is an eternal light shining in darkness for the illumination of mankind, and for a time the Logos became flesh and blood and lived among men. In this way God revealed his glory for the redemption of mankind. The similarity of this concept of the Fourth Gospel to the Stoic Logos has often been pointed out. The author was probably familiar with the Stoic idea and certainly many of his Greek readers would be. He adopted a concept which all educated Greeks knew. Whether he intended to do it or not, he laid a bridge from Christian faith to Greek philosophy which was shortly to become a highway. Yet the thought of John is to be sharply differentiated from the Stoic idea. The Johannine concept retains a definitely Oriental character. Presented in story form as it is, it has the nature of a symbol or myth rather than the cold, abstract quality of philosophical analysis. Stoicism does indeed have the idea of incarnation, but it is only such incarnation as occurs in every human being. This is very different from the unique, supernatural incarnation of the Logos in Jesus Christ.

The Johannine concept of the Logos also moves within the pattern of a personal monotheism, a faith which was never achieved by Stoicism. Stoicism could be more accurately called a religious naturalism or a rationalistic pantheism. The universe itself is divine. The Logos or God is simply the indwelling reason or soul of the universe and has no existence apart from it. Stoicism knows only an immanent God. But the primitive Christian message laid the greater emphasis upon God's transcendence. Later Christian thinkers were to make a great deal of the immanence, but there is little of it in the Bible. In a limited sense the indwelling of the Spirit of God in the prophets and in Christians pointed in the direction of a doctrine of immanence, as did also the Incarnation. But biblical thought, whether in the Old Testament or the New, never tends toward pantheism. God is the creator of the world. He is above it and beyond it. He is never equated with it.

Another New Testament passage which shows affinity with Stoic thought is Heb. 4:12. The Logos of God, this writer states, is living and powerful, and sharper than any sword in penetrating every recess of personality and judging all the desires and thoughts of the human heart. This idea is certainly close to the omnipresent and omniscient Logos of Stoicism, yet it is not identical with it. The Logos here is the mind or intelligence of God, not God himself, as it would be in Stoicism. Again we have theism, not pantheism.

One might expect an influence of the Stoic belief in immortality on Christianity, yet there is little evidence that this occurred, at any rate not in the early centuries. The soul of man as a fragment of the infinite Logos, according to the Stoics, is by nature immortal. This applies to all men of every character. This conception has a resemblance to the biblical teaching that all men are created in the image of God. But the Stoics found no place for personal immortality. The soul was to be absorbed finally into the universal essence, like water returning to the sea. This is akin to the ideas of Hinduism and Buddhism, but very different from Jewish and Christian faith, which affirms a conscious, personal immortality.

V. Religion

When Paul appeared before the Stoic and Epicurean philosophers at Athens, he began his address by saying, "Men of Athens, I perceive that in every way you are very religious" (Acts 17:22). Thus he uncovered the religious paradox of Hellenism at the time of the rise of Christianity. That world was not irreligious, but it was in the process of losing its faith. The philosophers who heard Paul speak were interested in religion, and all the Greek philosophies, as has been noted, had a religious orientation. One of the main functions of philosophy has been to examine, criticize, and evaluate the ideas of religion, but the great tradition in philosophy has never been hostile to religion, and there is no way, even if it were desirable, to separate these two approaches to truth.

A. Paul on Mars' Hill.—The hill where the philosophers assembled to hear Paul, which was located on the west side of the Acropolis, and was the site where the highest Athenian court held its sessions, was named for Ares, the god of war. Ares—identified with Mars by Romans—a son of Zeus and Hera, was one of the great Olympians. The Greek word for virtue is ἀρετή, a noun derived from the word Ares, and reflecting the view that the basic quality of a virtuous man is bravery and skill in battle. Ares was the lover and the beloved of Aphrodite, goddess of love, an indication of the close association between love and war through the ages.

Paul's statement that the Athenians were a religious people can be fully documented from Pausanias, who wrote his *Description of Greece* about 125 years after the apostle was there. Pausanias begins his description with the Piraeus, the main seaport of Athens, where, he says, the most interesting thing to see was the precinct of Athena and Zeus, both with bronze images. By the sea was a sanctuary of Aphrodite. The Athenians also had two other harbors, he writes. One was Munychia, with a temple of Artemis. The other was Phaleron, which had shrines of Demeter, Athena, and Zeus, as well as many others, some of the altars being dedicated to gods called "Unknown." Paul perhaps stopped off at Phaleron on his way from Macedonia, as this harbor was reached by ships coming from the north some three miles before they arrived at the Piraeus. Paul and Pausanias may well have seen the same altars there. At any rate the apostle began his address in Athens with a reference to an altar to "an unknown god," which he had observed as he entered the city (Acts 17:23). Altars to unknown gods at Athens were also reported by Apollonius of Tyana,[12] who was a contemporary of Paul. The origin and exact meaning of these altars to unknown gods at Athens are obscure. It may be that the Athenians set them up at some time when good fortune had come to the city and they were uncertain to which of the gods to attribute it. Or it could be that the inscriptions were intended to express the philosophical insight of the Greeks that the veil which covers the divine world is never completely lifted before human eyes.

Pausanias went from the Piraeus to Athens, and he has given a detailed account of altars, graves of heroes, statues of gods and men, and the temples which he saw on the way. The great gods and goddesses of the Olympian pantheon —Zeus, Apollo, Ares, Hermes, Hephaestus, Poseidon, Aphrodite, Artemis, Athena, Demeter, Hera, and Hestia—appear most frequently, but a number of others not so well known are mentioned. There were even foreign gods, like the Egyptian Serapis. The religion of the Greeks in Paul's time was an elaborate polytheism, in which each god was supposed to have his particular function and not to trespass upon the domain or to interfere with the rights and privileges of other deities.

B. Zeus.—The chief of the pantheon was Zeus, who was believed to be the father of both gods and men. Greek theology gives a picturesque account of his origin and power. According to Homer, he was the son of Cronus, who had seized the government of the world from his father Uranus, and Rhea. Cronus was a vicious cannibal, even devouring his own children as soon as they were born. When Zeus was born, however, his mother saved him by giving the jealous father a stone, swaddled like a baby, to swallow. As soon as the infant grew to manhood he overthrew his vindictive father and became the all-powerful king of the world. This position was made secure by victories over all rivals, and he was never dislodged from the heavenly throne.

[12] *Life* VI. 3.

Zeus was said to be an amorous god with at least six wives, two of whom were his sisters, and is credited with being the father of about twenty children. He was a law unto himself in a moral sense, but this was true of the Greek gods generally. According to Greek belief, it was not unusual for a god or goddess to be in love with a human being. Achilles, famed hero of the Trojan War, was said to be the son of the man Peleus and his goddess wife Thetis. The idea of human beings having either a divine father or a divine mother was common among the Greeks.

Zeus, originally sole ruler of the universe, was said to have divided his dominion with his two brothers, Poseidon taking the sea and Hades the underworld, and he himself, as supreme governor, becoming in a special sense the god of the heavens. He was thus associated especially with storm and lightning, the thunderbolt being his favorite weapon and lightning an arrow which he shot from his bow. The earth was left after the division as the area to which all the gods had access.

C. Greek Polytheism.—The organization of the Greek gods was similar to that of feudalistic society. The capital of the divine realm was on top of Mount Olympus. This was the acropolis of the royal city of Zeus; its lofty top reached above the clouds and on its misty height the gods had their abode. Zeus could retire to it when he desired solitude, or he could summon the gods to an assembly there at his pleasure. These divine subjects of Zeus were strong willed. At times they became rebellious and could be kept in subjection only by the use of heroic measures on the part of the divine king. It was characteristic of Greek theology that it was exceedingly anthropomorphic. Generally speaking, the gods were like men. They had the same loves and hates, the same passions and desires. They surpassed men, not in moral character, but in the immortality which went with their divine nature and in greater physical strength, powers of movement, and intelligence.

There was a certain rationality about Greek polytheism. At one time Greek religion, like most religions of primitive peoples, had been a crude animism. The world had a vast spirit population, for every significant object or phenomenon of nature was believed to be the abode of a spirit. The heavenly bodies, winds, rivers, springs, mountains, forests, the sea, fields, fire, and the like, were believed to be the homes of these invisible inhabitants. As the lives of men depended on these spirits of nature, rituals or ceremonies were devised for the purpose of keeping them friendly to human life.

In a similar way the attributes of human personality acquired a spiritual interpretation. Different emotions and mental powers were ascribed to the action of appropriate supernatural beings. Ares represented the tendency of men to fight; Aphrodite caused human beings to love; Athena gave them wisdom. Stoic writers were inclined to interpret all the Greek polytheism in this way. Thus all the gods had a real existence as symbols of personal and natural attributes. As Greek culture matured, many elements of the old animism were cast away, and some progress was made toward a higher theology. Zeus at the head of the pantheon at least represented an approach to an idea of an orderly universe. It became easy for Greeks to ascribe all divine activity to Zeus or merely to God. This way of speaking was not unusual for a man like Plato. Yet the common people retained the polytheistic ideas and continued to patronize shrines of the deities who presided over the several activities or interests with which they were concerned at particular times.

While Paul waited at Athens for his assistants to come down from Thessalonica, he had time to observe the excessive idolatry (Acts 17:16). The keen eyes of Pausanias have given us the details. Strabo [13] was so overwhelmed by the sheer mass of holy places that he justified his omission of most of them by quoting the remark of an earlier writer, "Attica is a possession of the gods, who seized it as a sanctuary for themselves."

D. Athena and the Acropolis.—Both Strabo and Pausanias pay their tribute to the buildings which adorned the Acropolis of Athens, and Pausanias describes them with care. The Acropolis was the hill on which the original fortress of the city was built, and as the population increased and the bounds of the city were enlarged, the Acropolis came to be a symbol of the city's unity and strength. This made it an ideal site for its most sacred shrines. The chief deity of Athens was the virgin goddess Athena, and her principal temple, the Parthenon (from *parthenos,* virgin), crowned the hill. She was the protectress of the city in war, and her helmet, spear, and breastplate were popular symbols. Athena meant to the Athenians everything that made their city great. The Parthenon, whose beautiful columns stand to this day, was built about 440 B.C., in the age of Pericles, by Ictinus, who also constructed the temple of Demeter at Eleusis,[14] and its art work was done by Phidias.

E. Hades and the Underworld.—Although Hades, god of the underworld, was a brother of Zeus, he did not develop a strong cult in

[13] *Geography* IX. 1. **16.**
[14] *Ibid.* IX. 1. 12, 16.

Greece. Pausanias [15] found both a sacred enclosure and a temple to Hades at Elis, but he remarks that the Elians are the only people he knows who worship Hades. He says the temple is opened only once a year. Strabo [16] mentions a precinct sacred to Hades near Mount Minthe in Elis. He also states that the Elians held the temples of Hades in high honor, and attributes this reverence of the fearful god of the underworld to the contrariness of the soil in that region. He refers also to Elian temples to Demeter and Kore, the principal deities of agriculture and vegetation, and therefore the principal objects of Hades' hostility. One time, while Persephone (Kore) was picking flowers, Hades captured her and carried her off to the nether world to be his wife. Demeter went into mourning for her daughter, and all vegetation died. Finally Zeus intervened and Persephone was permitted to return to her mother. But because she had eaten a pomegranate while she was with Hades, she suffered the fate of having to spend one third of each year with him. He and she were the king and queen of the dead and the parents of the awful Furies. The Greeks shuddered at the thought of the dread spirits from the realm of shades. At death, according to the popular notion, the soul or "shade" was carried down into the underworld by Hermes. On reaching the river Styx, which surrounded the realm of Hades, the departing spirit was met by Charon, the boatman, who carried him across, but only after he had paid his fare. Once across the frontier there was no return, for the gate into Hades was guarded by Cerberus, a terrible three-headed dog with a serpent's tail. The Greeks had a custom of burying a corpse with a coin in its mouth, so that the shade would be able to pay the ghostly boatman.

F. The Eleusinian Mysteries.—Related to the cult of Hades in a negative sense, and vastly more influential, were the mysteries celebrated at Eleusis on the coast of southern Attica. The rituals of this cult were based on the cycle of the seasons, with emphasis upon the alternating death and birth of life witnessed in fall and spring. The deities around which the rituals centered were Demeter, who was the spirit of the fertile fields, Kore or Persephone, her daughter, the spirit of vegetation, and Hades or Pluto, the god of the dead, who in the autumn year by year brought death to all living things. The motif of the mystic drama enacted at Eleusis was the annual death and resurrection of the plant world. The Eleusinian mysteries were so influential that similar cults are said to have been celebrated in other Greek cities on the mainland and in the colonies.

Demeter, one of the great deities of the Olympian pantheon, had a vast number of shrines throughout the Greek world. These were important to the life of agriculture, on which Greeks mainly depended. But these sanctuaries must be distinguished from the Eleusis cult, which had a definitely personal meaning. Its important mysteries were revealed only to initiates. At first apparently only inhabitants of Eleusis could be initiated; then as Athens became dominant, the mysteries were opened to all Athenians; after that to all Greeks; and finally to persons of approved moral character throughout the world. Some Roman emperors like Augustus, Marcus Aurelius, and Commodus, were initiated, while Nero was apparently refused. Initiation was open to all classes, including women and slaves.

It is obvious that this was something more than a simple vegetation rite. As initiates were required to take an oath never to divulge the nature of what they saw, we do not know exactly what took place. But there is enough evidence left by the ancients to show that devotees of this cult were concerned, not primarily with the resurrection of plant life in the spring, but with their own eternal destiny. The idea that human souls are by nature immortal was accepted by Greeks generally, but a future life in the gloomy realm of Hades guarded by the dog-headed monster was all that most men looked forward to. It seems clear that the initiates at Eleusis believed that just as all nature is reborn in beauty in the springtime, so they also were being prepared for a more blessed future. They believed that Demeter was the mother of men as well as of nature, and that in the tragic Eleusinian passion drama the inexorable and remorseless Hades met his defeat.[17] The ceremonials of the mysteries thus became the Greek sacraments and festivals of immortality. In these mystic rites the emphasis in Greek religion passed from a desire for sensuous pleasure and material wealth in the present life to longing for the life eternal. The central element in the sacred myth was the story of a goddess who died and arose from the dead. The initiate believed that through identification with the divine conqueror of the underworld he too might break the enslaving chains of mortality.

G. The Cult of Dionysus.—On the southeastern side of the Acropolis at Athens Paul could see the great outdoor theater of Dionysus,[18] with seats for fourteen thousand spectators, where the Athenians had the privilege of seeing the finest drama that the ancient world pro-

[15] *Descriptions of Greece* VI. 25. 3.
[16] *Geography* VIII. 3. 14, 15.

[17] See H. R. Willoughby, *Pagan Regeneration* (Chicago: University of Chicago Press, 1929), pp. 36-67.
[18] *Ibid.*, pp. 68-113.

duced. The seats, which were built into an oval carved in the side of the Acropolis, with the open sky above, were first made of wood, but in the fourth century B.C. they were rebuilt of stone. From their elevated seats the audience had a clear view of the stage, which at first had only one actor but later as many as three, and of the orchestra before it, where a chorus of highly trained singers and dancers performed in honor of Dionysus. An altar of Dionysus stood in the center of the orchestra. This theater belonged to the state; the admission charge at first was one drachma, but Pericles reduced it to two obols, which was about six cents, and persons who had no money were admitted free. Here the Athenians saw the works of Sophocles, Euripides, Aristophanes, and other poets of Greece. A performance began at dawn and lasted until dusk, and the people brought their lunches with them.

The theater was a development of the cult of Dionysus, also called Bacchus, who, although he had other functions, was primarily the god of wine. Just as Demeter brought the nourishing grain from the soil, Dionysus was believed to bring the inspiring wine. The two great festivals of this god were celebrated in winter and spring. Dionysus, like Persephone, was a vegetation spirit who died and arose again. The festivals reflected this cycle in nature. Throughout the Greek states devotees of Dionysus celebrated his festivals. He was also god of animals, with which he was closely identified. His worshipers believed that in eating the raw flesh of animals sacred to him they shared in his divine life; and that in drinking the new wine or engaging in his ecstatic dances they became filled with his spirit.

Comedy and tragedy, the two dramatic forms which we know, arose from the contrasting moods which characterized the people during the festivals of winter and spring. "Comedy" appears to be derived from two Greek words meaning a village song feast. It was a humorous production intended to cheer the people during the dreary winter days. "Tragedy," derived from "goat song," came from the solemn rite of eating the flesh of the goat in communion with the god. It belonged to the spring festival and expressed the deepest fears and hopes, all the pathos, of Greek life. Tragedy in particular was thus one of the profoundest expressions of Greek religious experience. The cult of Dionysus, in spite of all its barbarity, greatly enriched the culture of mankind in its inspiration of the dance, of music, and of the drama, arts which, each in its own way, give expression to the entire range of human experience.

H. Olympian and Other Games.—Another side of Greek religion is reflected in the games which were celebrated in honor of the gods. Among these the Panathenaea, celebrated annually at Athens in honor of Athena, was typical of the festivals honoring individual deities in different Greek states. All the people of Attica joined in this great religious festivity. Processions from all over the state converged on Athens, where the ceremony reached its climax in the Parthenon. But the most significant of these popular festivals were those which brought Greeks from all the states together. There were four of these, of which the best known was the Olympian games, celebrated every four years at Olympia in Elis in honor of Zeus. Others less noted were the Nemean games, held in honor of Zeus at Nemea in Argolis every two years; the Isthmian games held on the isthmus under the patronage of Corinth every other spring in honor of Poseidon; and the Pythian games held every fourth year at Delphi in honor of Apollo. These popular festivals gave clear expression to many of the ideals of Greek culture. Great contests in athletics, poetry, and music—to which only persons of unblemished moral character were admitted—in honor of the gods the Greeks worshiped, were expressive of the natural quality and the wholesome love of life which belonged to the genius of Greek religion.

J. Apollo and the Delphic Oracle.—The cult of Apollo, a son of Zeus, exercised a very strong influence in Greek culture, possibly greater than that of any other god.[19] He was the god who punished. It was his arrows which brought death to men; hence he was represented with a bow and arrow. But he was also the helper of mankind; he was the father of medicine, and one of his most important functions was the inspiration of poets, seers, and prophets. There were numerous oracles of Apollo, the most important being at Delphi at the foot of Mount Parnassus in Phocis. Both private persons and state officials came from all over the Greek world to consult Apollo at Delphi. The great temple was constructed over a cavern from which arose vapors believed to be the breath of the god. As the priestess who sat on a tripod over the cavern inhaled the vapors, she went into a trance and muttered words which were written down and interpreted by attending priests. This shrine was important in Greek politics. Although the oracles were at times ambiguous, the wisdom of the Delphic priests contributed to the unity and stability of Greek culture.

In former times Delphi had been called Pytho. Hence the name Pythian Apollo came to be associated with the shrine. The spirit

[19] See Martin P. Nilsson, *A History of Greek Religion*, tr. F. J. Fielden (Oxford: Clarendon Press, 1925), pp. 188-210.

which inspired the priestess was also called simply the Python. When Paul arrived at Philippi on his second missionary journey, he encountered a slave girl who, according to Acts 16:16, was possessed by the Python. Luke reports that when Paul drove the spirit out of the girl, her masters, who were exploiting her as a fortuneteller, had him cast into prison. The mentally ill girl was being represented as nothing less than a walking oracle of Apollo, and no doubt was so received by many.

K. Asclepius, the Divine Physician.—It was only natural that Apollo should be regarded as the father of Asclepius, who was the most important god of healing among the Greeks.[20] Asclepius himself had two sons, physicians in the Greek army of the Homeric period, and a daughter, Hygeia, the goddess of health. Pausanias[21] observed a sanctuary of Asclepius at Athens, situated between the theater and the Acropolis, and another at Cenchreae,[22] both of which must have been seen by Paul. The shrines of Asclepius were numerous throughout the Greek world and they spread to many parts of the Roman Empire. Pausanias[23] mentions shrines of Asclepius in Epidaurus, Smyrna, Pergamum, and even in such faraway places as Cyrene in North Africa and Lebene on the island of Crete. The sanctuaries of Asclepius were to that world what hospitals and sanitariums are to ours. But the healings which occurred in them were always given a religious interpretation and were attributed to the divine physician.

The most important of the temples of Asclepius was at Epidaurus in Argolis. Most of the others appear to have been derived from it. Pausanias says that the sanctuary of Asclepius at Epidaurus stood in a sacred grove which was surrounded by mountains, and that within the enclosure no death or birth was permitted to occur. The image of Asclepius was of ivory and gold and was half the size of that of Olympian Zeus at Athens. The god sat on a throne, grasping a staff in one hand and holding the other over the head of a serpent. A dog crouched at his side. To this day the classical symbol of the physician's art is the staff of Asclepius with a serpent entwined about it. Near the temple was a dormitory in which patients slept. The god was believed to reveal remedies to them in dreams. Pausanias found six tablets set up within the enclosure which gave the names of men and women who had been healed, the

remedies, and the diseases from which they had been cured. In recent times archaeologists have recovered some of these inscriptions, as well as some from the temple of Asclepius at Rome. They were like the testimonial letters which patent medicine manufacturers today publish to advertise their wares. Pausanias relates that two varieties of serpents were used in the Asclepian temple at Epidaurus and that they could be found nowhere except in Epidauria. These snakes were carried wherever new shrines were to be established.

The cult of Asclepius made its way even into Palestine. Just south of the city of Tiberias on the Sea of Galilee a hot spring flows from a hillside and runs into the sea. The natives of Palestine to this day believe that spirits inhabit springs. They say that hot springs are the abode of jinn, who heat the water. The hot springs at Tiberias were a healing resort in ancient times. In the first century A.D. the cult of Asclepius had taken root there. A bronze coin was struck for the city of Tiberias in A.D. 99 which shows Hygeia, the daughter of the Greek god of healing, seated on a rock holding a serpent, while the fountain gushes forth at her feet. Hygeia was evidently believed to be the nymph which inhabited the hot spring. The coin was restruck in A.D. 108 and again in A.D. 189. Asclepius was also well known in Phoenicia, several writers referring to his sacred grove near Sidon. His cult merged with that of the god Eshmun throughout the Phoenician colonies.

L. The Great Mother Cult.[24]—Up to this point emphasis has been placed on the religious cults which originated on the mainland of Greece. But it would be a grave error to assume that all the religions of that period came out of Greece. Egypt, Mesopotamia, Palestine, Syria, Asia Minor, and Italy each had its own religion long before these countries came into contact with Greece. Even after the dominant Greek influence caused their faiths to be overlaid with the veneer of Hellenism, many essential features of the old cults survived. This survival of the old along with the new not only meant an increase in the number of cults, but also led to the merging of elements from different faiths. It was popular to be a devotee of several cults at the same time. While the Hellenistic religions were in many cases rivals of one another, intolerance appears to have been rare.

Syncretism is illustrated in the mystery religions. The Greeks had their own mystery cult at Eleusis, as we have seen. Asia Minor had a very similar cult which centered about Cybele, the earth-mother, and Attis, her lover, the vegetation spirit who died annually in the autumn and rose from the dead in the spring.

[20] See S. V. McCasland, "Religious Healing in First-Century Palestine," *Environmental Factors in Christian History* (ed. McNeill, Spinka, and Willoughby; Chicago: University of Chicago Press, 1939), pp. 18-34.

[21] *Descriptions of Greece* I. 21. 7.

[22] *Ibid.* II. 2. 3.

[23] *Ibid.* II. 26. 1-10; 28. 1.

[24] See Willoughby, *Pagan Regeneration*, pp. 114-42.

In the barbaric rites of this cult the priests slashed out their genitals and cast them upon the altar of Cybele as they whirled in a frenzied dance. Characteristic also was the bloody taurobolium, in which a bull was sacrificed upon a grating while a devotee lay beneath to be drenched by the sacred blood. It was believed that in this way one's sins were purged away and one was reborn for eternity. This orgiastic faith had a considerable vogue. It was introduced into Rome in 204 B.C., when the city was desperately seeking deliverance from the armies of Hannibal.

M. Mithra, God of Soldiers.—The worship of Mithra [25] was one of the most picturesque of the mysteries. This god was worshiped first by the ancient Aryans, who carried him to India and also to Persia. Thence his cult spread into Asia Minor. In 67 B.C., when Pompey conquered the pirates on the coast of Cilicia on the southern shore of Asia Minor, he carried with him to Rome some prisoners who were devotees of Mithra. From them the worship spread to Roman soldiers, with whom it became exceedingly popular. Only men were allowed to be initiated into the mysteries of Mithra. From earliest times Mithra was associated with the bright sky, and in the Roman world he was identified with the sun-god. He was called *Sol invictus Mithra,* the unconquered Sun Mithra. He was also the guardian of covenants, of loyalty. His worship was carried on in underground chapels, each of which appears to have had by its altar a relief of Mithra Tauroctonus, the bull-slayer. It shows Mithra, or his priest, in the act of slaying a bull with his dagger, while a dog, a serpent, and possibly other animals and birds stand by to drink its blood, and a scorpion clutches its genitals. The rite of the taurobolium associated with the Cybele-Attis religion is also thought to have been practiced by the Mithra worshipers. Shrines of Mithra have been found all the way from the Near East to Britain, wherever Roman armies were stationed. There was a time in the third century of our era when Mithraism was the strongest rival of Christianity for the allegiance of the Roman world. The winter solstice was interpreted by Mithraists as the time of the rebirth of Mithra. Throughout the late summer and autumn the hours of sunlight had decreased day by day, but on or about December 21 the sun appeared to recover its vigor. The Romans celebrated this victory of the sun in the Saturnalia. The Mithraists observed the birthday of Mithra on December 25. As Christianity gained the ascendancy over its rival, it became a custom to use the old festival day for the celebration of the birth of Christ. In this way the church undertook to Christianize a celebration deeply rooted in Roman culture.

N. Isis and Immortality.—The Isis cult was a development of Egyptian religion.[26] From its stronghold in Egypt it spread widely over the Mediterranean world. As in all the mystery religions, its initiates took a vow of secrecy about the rites and teachings of the cult; but it is clear that the theology of the Isis cult, like that of the other mysteries, was related to the cycle of the seasons. Isis was the earth-mother, and Osiris, her brother-husband, was the vegetation spirit. Isis and her son, Horus, were the original Madonna and child of the Hellenistic world. Osiris had a brother, Set, who was evil. He murdered Osiris and concealed his body. As Isis wept for her dead husband, she was aided by other deities in finding his body and restoring it to life. So the story deals with the death and resurrection of a divine being. At first it was obviously an interpretation of Egyptian agriculture and intended to insure the fertility of the soil and the regularity of the harvest; but in time it also developed into a religion of personal redemption. Those who were initiated into its secret rites were assured that, like Osiris, they could triumph over death. This cult had the magnificent old culture of Egypt as a background, which gave it a rich treasury of ethical and theological teachings. It freely appropriated magical practices, and its rituals were elaborate and ornate. The Ptolemies, a Greek dynasty who ruled Egypt after the time of Alexander, appear to have been responsible for the spread of the Isis cult in the Mediterranean world. Under their influence Alexandria was made the center of the cult. Osiris receded into the background in favor of Serapis (a word formed from Osiris-Apis), a more Hellenistic deity. Isis was associated with other mother-goddesses, such as Demeter and Aphrodite; and Serapis, with their consorts. In this guise the cult spread to the Mediterranean islands, to the Greek mainland including Athens, to Italy—where the opposition of the senate could not keep it out—and evidently it had some vogue even in Palestine. An inscription to Serapis may still be seen cut in the east pier of the Zion gate in the south wall of Jerusalem. It was put there by a standard-bearer of the third legion of Cyrene about A.D. 115. From the second century on, numerous coins with the image of Serapis were struck by the Romans for Jerusalem, Caesarea, and Neapolis.

O. Roman Religion.—The old state religion of the Romans [27] was in many ways parallel to

---

[25] *Ibid.,* pp. 143-68.

[26] *Ibid.,* pp. 169-95.

[27] See Franz Altheim, *A History of Roman Religion,* tr. Harold Mattingly (London: Methuen & Co., 1938), esp. pp. 286-472.

the classical polytheism of the Greeks. During the Hellenistic period it was customary to use the names of many Greek and Roman deities interchangeably. Zeus and Jupiter, Aphrodite and Venus, Poseidon and Neptune, Hephaestus and Vulcan, Demeter and Ceres, and so forth, were identified. Yet the Roman religion had many unique features. These appear especially in its priesthoods, of which the Pontifex Maximus was the head, and in its annual calendar of festivals. Toward the end of the Hellenistic period the old cults had lost much of their appeal among the Romans. The mystery religions, which were largely international and universalistic in character and offered personal redemption to the individual himself, were attracting larger and larger numbers and were rapidly spreading.

Roman rulers were disturbed by this decline of the state religion. It seemed to indicate a loss of patriotism. But the decline continued, in spite of the interest which the emperors took in repairing old temples and building impressive new ones. Augustus attempted to preserve the religious character of patriotism by his institution of the imperial cult. He elevated Julius Caesar to a divine status and decreed that the genius of the emperor should be worshiped even during the emperor's lifetime. In the strict sense Augustus did not claim divine honors for himself while he lived; but the genius of the emperor could not be separated completely from the living emperor. He accepted sacrifices to himself in the provincial cults away from Rome. When an emperor died, he was deified in a ceremony of apotheosis. Worship of the genius of the living emperor or of the dead emperors as divine became the test of patriotism throughout the empire. Such unbalanced emperors as Nero and Domitian demanded worship of themselves while they lived. In their reigns Christians suffered persecution—they were willing to be loyal subjects of the Roman government, but held that worship belonged only to God. Generally speaking, however, the Roman government was tolerant of both Jews and Christians, and it understood that their theology was not hostile to good citizenship.

This was certainly true of the Christians in the earliest period. Whenever missionaries, such as Paul at Lystra, Ephesus, or Jerusalem, came into conflict with local prejudices which endangered their lives, they knew that the presence of Roman soldiers on the spot, or the power of Rome in the background, was their best assurance of protection. (For fuller discussions of the relationship of the Christian church to the Roman state see Introductions to Revelation and I Peter.)

VI. Hellenistic Judaism

Palestine itself was powerfully affected by the cultural transformation of the Hellenistic period. We often speak of the Palestinian environment of Christianity in contrast with its Hellenistic background. Properly qualified, such a distinction is accurate, but Palestine also felt the impact of Hellenization and could not maintain the isolation which had been attempted in former times. The Hebrew state had been crushed, and the religion of the Hebrews, like other state religions of antiquity, had to struggle for its life. With no state to serve, it became on the one hand an underground nationalism; on the other it took on new forms as it followed the Jewish communities "dispersed" and now well established in many parts of the world. The following essay will deal with Palestinian Judaism; we are here more concerned with the Dispersion.

A. Universalism and Nationalism.—Judaism is in some respects a good example of Hellenistic religion. There were tendencies away from nationalism and toward universalism which, though they received fullest expression in Christianity, were operative within Judaism also. Old Testament writers like Second Isaiah and the author of Jonah made attempts to dissociate the worship of God from Hebrew nationalism. They believed that all nations stood on an equal basis before God; that he was just as surely concerned about Assyria and Ethiopia as he was about the Hebrews; and that it was an error to limit the worship of God to any nation. This liberal view was aided by the tragedies of history, which dispersed the Hebrews from the Nile to the Tigris, and then throughout the Roman Empire. Even Rome had a large Jewish community, created mainly from captives carried there by Pompey in 63 B.C., Titus in A.D. 70, and Hadrian in A.D. 136.

Commercial interests also drew the Jews away from their homeland or kept them away after wars had transplanted them. The great centers of Jewish culture outside Palestine were Babylonia, Egypt, and Rome, but there were important communities in other cities, such as Antioch of Syria and Damascus. Small cities like Antioch, Iconium, and Derbe in Asia Minor had Jewish elements. Paul himself had grown up in the Jewish community of Tarsus, and began his missionary preaching in Jewish synagogues. The Acts of the Apostles reflects the wide dispersion of the Jews, Acts 2:5 stating that there were devout Jews from every part of the world in Jerusalem for a Pentecost festival. The author quotes these Jews as saying: "Are not all these who are speaking Galileans? And how is it that we hear, each of us in his own native language? Parthians and Medes and Elamites and residents of Mesopotamia, Judea and Cappadocia, Pontus and Asia, Phrygia and Pamphylia, Egypt and the parts of Libya belonging to Cyrene, and visitors from Rome, both Jews and proselytes, Cretans and Arabians, we hear them telling in our own tongues the mighty works of God" (Acts 2:7-11). This not only indicates the different lands from which Jews and proselytes had come to the festival at Jerusalem, but also that they had been away so long that they were foreigners even in Palestine. They no longer understood the language of Galilee. Their parents or grandparents had migrated or been carried away, and they themselves had grown up speaking the vernaculars of the places where they lived.

B. Revolt Against Jerusalem.—Even during the Persian period the Jewish population of Egypt became so strong and self-confident that the people were able to defy the religious authorities at Jerusalem. Although it had been held since the publication of Deuteronomy and the reformation of Josiah in 621 B.C. that no sacrifices could be offered outside Jerusalem, the Jews of Egypt built themselves a temple on the island of Elephantine, whose ceremonials were similar to those of the temple at Jerusalem. This temple was destroyed by enemies of the Jews shortly before 400 B.C. The evidence of these events is derived from papyrus records found in 1903.[28] Egyptian Jews built at Leontopolis in the reign of Ptolemy Philometor (181-146 B.C.) another temple for the reproducing of the rituals of the temple at Jerusalem.[29]

A third Hebrew temple, which became a strong rival of the temple at Jerusalem, was built by the Samaritans at Shechem, at the time when the emphasis of Nehemiah and Ezra on racial purity excluded the mixed population of Samaria from the temple rites at Jerusalem. This Samaritan temple flourished until the Maccabean period, and was destroyed by John Hyrcanus in 129 B.C.[30] The hostility of the Maccabeans toward the Samaritans was a heritage from the early period of Hebrew history, when David wrested the kingship from the house of Saul and conquered the northern tribes. After Solomon died, Israel revolted from Judah, and the breach never healed. Yet the Samaritans traced their ancestry back to the patriarchs and kept their own interpretation of the Law of Moses. But they intermarried readily with the colony of Assyrian soldiers

stationed there after the fall of Samaria in 721 B.C., and were less devoted to the traditions of the fathers and more open to assimilation than were the Jews at Jerusalem. When Antiochus Epiphanes undertook to exterminate the Jewish religion about 167 B.C., the Samaritans boldly disclaimed their Hebrew origin and said they were Sidonians.[31] They even asked permission to name their temple on Mount Gerezim for Zeus, indicating the extent of Hellenization in Samaria. They freely accepted the Greek rites with which the Syrian king was attempting to regiment the native religions of his synthetic kingdom. Hellenization is only another name for assimilation, which the Samaritans were more willing to accept than the Jews. This accounts for their all but complete disappearance. Only two or three hundred of them still survive today. They live at the little village of Nablus in Palestine, maintaining their own version of the Hebrew faith.

C. Jerusalem a Symbol of Unity.—The Jewish temples in Egypt and Samaria in competition with the temple at Jerusalem indicate that Judaism was torn by inner struggles during the centuries of the Exile. But the temple at Jerusalem, owing to the prestige of its tradition and the military security of its location, survived the others, and in the end gained the undivided devotion of all Jews throughout the world except the Samaritans.

It was the Syrian Antiochus Epiphanes (175-164 B.C.) who, quite contrary to his own intentions, brought the temple in Jerusalem back to the center of Jewish life. His effort at regimentation was just what was needed to rekindle to vigorous life the smoldering flame of Jewish religion. The Maccabean movement was one of the most brilliant underground movements in history. Its success turned the eyes of Jews throughout the world toward Jerusalem again, and the temple became the symbol of the new unity. It was this intensified loyalty which caused Herod the Great to rebuild the temple on a plan whose magnificence exceeded that of the original structure of Solomon. Its impressive masonry and rituals provided the ceremonial integration of Jewish life during the days of Jesus, and for more than half of the first century, until the agitation of radical zealots provoked the war with Rome in A.D. 66-70, in which the temple was destroyed.

In the history of both Judaism and Christianity A.D. 70 was a decisive date. It marked the end of animal sacrifices, in which Jews and many Christians had continued to participate. Even Paul, in spite of his argument for salvation by faith, and freedom from the ceremonial law, went up to Jerusalem for the temple

---

[28] See Jack Finegan, *Light from the Ancient Past* (Princeton: The University Press, 1946), pp. 200-1.

[29] Josephus *Antiquities* XIII. 3. 1-3; *War* I. 1. 1; VII. 10. 3.

[30] *Ibid.* XIII. 9. 1; XIII. 10. 2.

[31] *Ibid.* XII. 5. 5; II Macc. 6:2.

ceremonials whenever it was possible. The destruction of the temple settled this issue once for all. There was no longer a place where animals might be sacrificed according to the Deuteronomic law and synagogues have never had animal sacrifices. Jewish Christians, and all other Jews, had to readjust themselves to the realities of a new situation. They faced the world without a temple. Orthodox Jews still pray for a restoration of the temple and expect it when the Messiah comes. Their priests are trained and ready to resume the temple rituals instantly, whenever that event occurs. Nevertheless, for almost two thousand years Jewish piety has been nurtured by a worship which is similar to that of a Christian church. Jews chant the psalms, pray, read the Scriptures, sing hymns, and listen to a sermon. Indeed Christians learned how to worship from the Jews.

D. The Synagogue and Its Rabbi.—The break in Jewish religion when the temple was destroyed was therefore more superficial than real. Even at that time Jewish life of necessity centered more in the synagogue than in the temple—the synagogue was a place of worship, a school, and a social center. Every Jewish community throughout the world had its synagogue, whose rabbi controlled its religious life. The city of Jerusalem had its synagogues in the time of Jesus, as did every village of any size in Palestine. Although Jesus went up to the temple at times, he grew up in the piety of the synagogue. During his ministry he continued to attend the synagogue, where he would read the Scriptures and interpret them to the people (Luke 4:16). This practice was followed also by Paul and other early Christian missionaries out in the Greek world (Acts 13:15, 44; 14:1; 17:1; 18:4; 28:17). All of this is evidence of the universality of the synagogue and of its importance in Jewish life. The synagogue, which was probably at first intended to be only a temporary expedient, became the main support of Jewish faith. Judaism owes its survival to the synagogue rather than to the temple; to the rabbi rather than to the priest; to its universal element rather than to its nationalism. Yet the paradox remains that through the centuries Judaism has carried in its heart the dream of becoming a nation again.

The loyalty of the Jews to the temple during the Hellenistic period, regardless of the country in which they lived, was manifested by the half-shekel tax for the support of the temple, which every devout Jewish man sent to Jerusalem each year. The tax began apparently when Ezra issued a decree that one third of a shekel should be paid annually (Neh. 10:32-34). The levy was necessary to keep the temple going, for after the fall of Jerusalem in 586 B.C., the subsidy from the royal treasury was no longer available. The tax was increased to a half shekel in the period after Nehemiah and became a part of the law of the Pentateuch (Exod. 30:11-16). All males twenty years of age and above were required to make the payment. By the time of Christ the tax appears to have been accepted as a matter of course by Jews everywhere. Josephus writes of the collection of this tax by Babylonian Jews and of the precautions they took to get the money safely transported to Jerusalem.[32] The payment of the tax in Palestine itself is reflected in the story about Jesus, who sent Peter to get money from the mouth of a fish (Matt. 17:24-27). Payment had been demanded by officials of the temple who were no doubt sent into Galilee for that purpose. The evangelist relates that Jesus told Peter he would find a shekel in the fish's mouth, with which he could pay the tax for both of them. We may assume that such collectors of the temple tax visited every community of Jews throughout the world, beginning in Palestine.

When the temple was destroyed in A.D. 70, there was no longer a reason for this tax from the Jewish point of view, but Vespasian promptly decreed that Jews should pay two drachmas annually (a shekel was four drachmas) to the temple of Jupiter Capitolinus in Rome.[33] Possibly this was a naïve effort of the emperor to develop loyalty to Rome in Jewish hearts, but it produced only bitter resentment. A coin from the reign of Nerva about A.D. 97 indicates that the ignominy of devoting the money to support pagan worship had been removed, but that the tax was still being levied.[34]

The synagogue was Judaism's greatest adaptation as it underwent the transformation from a typical state religion of antiquity to one of the most powerful and widespread of the Hellenistic religions. The genius of the religion of the synagogue was its concern for the individual, more than for a state which no longer existed. The Hellenistic period witnessed the rise of eschatology in the Jewish faith, with its emphasis on a hereafter and the immortality of the soul, matters which were of little concern in the religion of ancient Israel. The prominence which Judaism gave to Satan, demons, angels, and their influence on the destiny of men, was also a development of the late period. It shared many of these beliefs with other religions of the age, in particular with those derived from Persia and Babylonia.

[32] *Antiquities* XVIII. 9. 1.
[33] Josephus *Jewish War* VII. 6. 6.
[34] Emil Schürer, *A History of the Jewish People in the Time of Jesus Christ*, tr. Taylor and Christe (New York: Charles Scribner's Sons, n.d.), Div. II, Vol. II, p. 267.

E. The Greek Bible.—Not even the Hebrew Bible was to escape the influence of Hellenization. Before the time of Christ it had been translated into Greek, and a number of books, constituting what we know as the Old Testament Apocrypha, had been added to the canon. The late books, however, were never accepted in Palestine. The Greek translation of the Old Testament was called the Septuagint from the legendary tradition about its origin. Ptolemy Philadelphus of Egypt (285-246 B.C.) had the translation made, it was said, as a part of his vast project of collecting all the books of the world into a library at Alexandria. In order to gain the co-operation of the Jewish authorities of Jerusalem in translating their Scriptures into an alien tongue, a thing which had never been done before, he redeemed the 120,000 Jews held as slaves in Egypt and set them free. He sent fifty talents of gold, with a collection of precious stones, to be made into vessels for the temple, and one hundred talents in money for the sacrifices. He was then in a position to ask Eleazar the high priest for good copies of the Scriptures and for six competent scholars out of every tribe to assist in the undertaking. Eleazar rewarded this generosity with his consent and assistance. The seventy-two scribes arrived in Alexandria with manuscripts written in letters of gold, were received with great honor, and finished the translation in seventy-two days.

Although the essentials of this story are true, most of the details are legends. Certainly the Hebrew Scriptures were translated into Greek, but that the work was done at the insistence of the king of Egypt, by six scholars out of each of the twelve tribes, and in exactly seventy-two days, is pious fiction. The true reason for the translation is that Jews living in Egypt, as well as in other parts of the Roman Empire, no longer were able to read Hebrew well; on the other hand they spoke Greek as their mother tongue. They needed a Greek Bible. This literary development was carried farther in the apocryphal books, some of which were composed outright in Greek, and all of which were associated intimately with the Greek Old Testament.

The Greek Bible was the only sacred Scripture with which the Christian church began. It was indeed the only Scripture possessed by the apostles and the churches they founded until well into the second century, when the process of canonizing the New Testament writings began. Some of the first Jewish Christians of Palestine could no doubt read the Hebrew Scriptures, but it is generally agreed that the writers of the New Testament quoted the Old Testament from the Greek translation. The Greek version was ideally suited for the missionary work of Paul and other early Christians who spread the new religion through Asia Minor, Greece, and Italy. The majority of these new Christians, although they had some previous knowledge of Judaism and the synagogue, knew no Hebrew. The Greek Old Testament had made it possible for every person with an elementary knowledge of Greek to read the Jewish Scriptures in his own tongue. When the missionaries came, it was only necessary to build on the foundation already laid, by telling the story of Jesus and interpreting the Scriptures in the light which that story provided.

F. Inroads of Greek Thought.—Hellenism left its mark also on Jewish thought. This is manifested first in the Old Testament, particularly in the wisdom literature. Job, Proverbs, and Ecclesiastes, in the Old Testament, and the Wisdom of Sirach and the Wisdom of Solomon, from the Apocrypha, are the best examples of this form of writing. These books in many points reflect the insights of Greek philosophy.

The clearest instance of the impact of Hellenistic philosophy on Jewish thought may be observed in Philo,[35] the Jewish philosophical writer who flourished in Alexandria about the middle of the first century A.D. He had been profoundly influenced by the Greek philosophies; yet he held firmly to the essence of his Hebrew faith. Plato's theory of ideas as the invisible patterns of all earthly realities is basic in Philo's thought. God in creating the world, he says, first formed the idea or plan of the world, like an architect's blueprint. Then he made the world according to the plan. At the same time the divine Logos or Reason, an emanation of God, is the agency through which God created the world.[36]

Philo was an eclectic in philosophy, selecting from the various schools elements which appealed to him, and utilizing them in writing interpretations of the Scriptures. Most of his writings are comments on the law of Moses. His favorite method is allegory; the real truth of a story is to be found, not in its literal meaning, but in a concealed allegorical sense. Thus the Scriptures have an esoteric character and are always in need of interpretation by one who has the allegorical key. The modern reader is surprised to find, for example, that when Genesis states that heaven and earth were created, it means mind and sense-perception.[37] The spring which, according to Gen. 2:6, sprang up and watered all the face of the earth is the mind, and the face of the earth, in turn, means

[35] Erwin R. Goodenough, *An Introduction to Philo Judaeus* (New Haven: Yale University Press, 1940).
[36] Philo *On the Creation* 16-25.
[37] Philo *The Allegories of the Sacred Law* I. 1-2.

the sense perceptions. Abraham is the higher metaphysics; Sarah, particular and specific virtues; and Hagar, the lower secular culture.[38]

Greek thought was mediated to Christianity also by Philo, especially in Egypt. The famous Christian school there, led by such outstanding men as Pantaenus, Clement, and Origen, continued to apply the allegorical method, which it had inherited from Philo, to the interpretation of the Scriptures. The Jewish philosopher was often quoted with approval by Christians, one of whom remarked that Philo's mind was naturally Christian.

G. Influence of Greek Art.

—The influence of Hellenism on Jewish culture was also felt in the realm of art. During the ancient period Hebrew culture had developed no sculpture or painting except as a few bold spirits defied the dominant ban on these arts. It was generally held that the prohibition of images in the Decalogue must be taken in this literal and radical sense. There must have been some artistic progress in connection with the golden bulls used in the shrines of the northern kingdom, but this practice was not accepted in Judah. The temple remained to the end without images. No image of a conqueror was tolerated in Jerusalem—not even an image on the coins. The Hebrews produced nothing to compare with the sculpture, painting, and architecture of the Greeks. Yet during the Hellenistic period a considerable modification of their point of view took place. The evidence of this has come to light in the synagogues constructed during that time and excavated in recent years.[39] One of the most interesting was uncovered at Dura, on the Euphrates, and in its restored form now stands in Damascus. The walls of this building were decorated with well-executed paintings illustrating episodes from biblical stories. Similar decorations on the walls and mosaics in the floor have also been found in other synagogues. Those so far brought to light are probably from the third century A.D. and belong to the area of Syria and Palestine. How much further this artistic devlopment had gone it is impossible to say, but it is clear that the rabbis had found a way to interpret their law that permitted some use of the decorative arts.

But in spite of these and other evidences that Jews were influenced by successive waves of Hellenism, their deepest instinct was to resist. They held tenaciously to their belief in a covenant with God which guaranteed them a national as well as a religious future. Unlike most other conquered peoples of antiquity, the Jews insisted on maintaining their own racial and cultural identity and continuity. They surrounded themselves with an impenetrable wall of law and custom within which they attempted to live in cultural isolation. On the whole they succeeded. In this way on the one hand they guarded themselves against the debasing influence of certain elements in alien cultures; on the other they retained in considerable measure the values of their own.

H. Anti-Semitism.

—But this refusal of the Jews to be assimilated brought upon them the suspicion and at times the hatred of their neighbors. Anti-Semitism has a very long history. It appears as the motivation of the Exodus from Egypt in the time of Moses. The story of Esther reflects the presence of bitter anti-Semitism among the Persians. The Maccabean movement was provoked by the unwise effort of the Syrian king to break down the Jewish resistance to assimilation by force. The Romans in turn found it impossible to get the Jews to accommodate themselves to Roman domination. There were violent outbreaks which led at last to the destruction of the Jewish nation in two devastating wars.

The Jews in Egypt were subjected to bitter persecution during the reign of Gaius about A.D. 40, while Flaccus was governor of that country. They sent an embassy to the emperor, of which the eminent philosopher Philo was the head, but Gaius rebuffed it. Philo has left vivid accounts of these matters in his *Flaccus* and the *Embassy to Gaius*. He also wrote a work called the *Hypothetica* in which he sought to overcome anti-Semitism. A similar effort was made by Josephus, a contemporary of Philo. He was a well-educated priest of Jerusalem who was appointed commander of the Jewish forces facing Vespasian in Galilee in A.D. 66. After a feeble resistance he was captured by the Romans. He ingratiated himself with Vespasian and was kept as a trusted adviser on Jewish affairs until the war was over. Then Vespasian brought him to Rome, provided him with a house and a pension, while he wrote his *Jewish War*, his *Antiquities of the Jews*, his *Life*, and *Against Apion*. In all these works Josephus was trying to overcome the hostility of the Roman world toward the Jews; *Against Apion* deals with this subject specifically. Apion was one of the leaders of the pogrom in Egypt in which Philo was involved.

This hostility toward the Jews was manifested also in early Christian writings. The Jewish authorities at Jerusalem had sought to stamp out the Christian movement at its inception. And there was the almost inevitable continuing opposition whenever the two communities came into close contact with each other. The Christians based their religion on an interpretation

[38] Philo *On the Cherubim* 4-6.

[39] Finegan, *Light from the Ancient Past*, pp. 226-27, 404-5.

of the Old Testament which the Jews held to be false. Naturally Jews repudiated the Christian belief in the deity of Jesus. It is not surprising therefore to find the Gospel of John grouping all the Jews together as a malign enemy determined to destroy the Christ. By the time that Gospel was written the breach between Christians and. Jews had become wide. A popular Christian pamphlet like *The Martyrdom of Polycarp* was calculated to increase the hostility by its inflammatory style. On the other hand writers like Justin and Origen attempted to meet the Jews on an intellectual plane.

Christianity was greatly indebted to Judaism for its heritage; yet it had to face the Roman world at first under the handicap of anti-Semitism. It was well known that Christianity began as a Jewish sect—Christians were therefore regarded as Jews and subjected to the same disabilities. That is one of the reasons why the church had to break with the synagogue and assert its own independence in the eyes of the Roman Empire.

VII. *Epilogue*

The genius of Christianity is its universality and its sole concern is the redemption of individual men. The central theme in the teaching of Jesus is the love of God for every human being. Christianity repudiated the nationalism from which Judaism has never been able to escape; from the beginning it has also been an interracial gospel; and it has regarded the whole world as its field. Multitudes of Greeks and Romans heard this good news with joy because in Christ they found the abiding substance for which they had searched their paganism in vain. The culture of the Hellenistic age itself is the best documentation of Paul's observation that Christ was born in "the fulness of the time." As it brought faith and hope to peoples whose religions had come to be regarded by many as worn-out superstitions, the Christian religion gave a new moral and spiritual fiber to the life of the ancient world.

VIII. *Selected Bibliography*

ANGUS, SAMUEL. *The Environment of Early Christianity*. New York: Charles Scribner's Sons, 1920.
————. *The Religious Quests of the Graeco-Roman World*. London: J. Murray, 1929.
CASE, SHIRLEY JACKSON. *The Evolution of Early Christianity*. Chicago: University of Chicago Press, 1941.
————. *Experience with the Supernatural in Early Christian Times*. New York: The Century Co., 1929.
DILL, SAMUEL. *Roman Society from Nero to Marcus Aurelius*. London: Macmillan & Co., 1920.
GLOVER, T. R. *The World of the New Testament*. Cambridge: The University Press, 1931.
————. *The Conflict of Religions in the Early Roman Empire,* 12th ed. London: Methuen & Co., 1932.
MACCHIORO, VITTORIO. *From Orpheus to Paul*. New York: Henry Holt & Co., 1930.
SCOTT, ERNEST FINDLAY. *The Gospel and Its Tributaries*. Edinburgh: T. & T. Clark, 1928.

NEW TESTAMENT TIMES
II. PALESTINE

by MORTON S. ENSLIN

"In the fifteenth year of Tiberius," when the ministry of Jesus began, Palestine was firmly held by the possessive hand of Rome. The little land, like all Gaul, was divided into three distinct parts: Samaria, Judea, and Idumaea constituted the province of Judea, governed by a Roman official resident in the land with headquarters at Caesarea; Galilee and a strip of land east of the Jordan known as the Perea constituted the tetrarchy of Antipas, a son of Herod the Great, who, under Rome, had governed the whole of Palestine a generation before; the districts to the north and east of the Sea of Galilee were in the hands of another of Herod's sons, Philip the Tetrarch. The form of Roman control thus differed in the three sections of the land, with considerable latitude and with marked deference to local customs; nonetheless, whether in Jerusalem or in the nominally independent tetrarchies of Antipas or Philip, Rome was mistress. The days of Jewish independence were long since past.

I. From Alexander to Pompey

Centuries before, for a time—a very short time—Palestine had had a semi-independent existence, and in consequence Jewry looked back through lenses of a high degree of magnification to the golden days of independence and prowess under David and Solomon. But from the days of the divided kingdoms she had rapidly waned, and one alien culture after another held sway. The spectacular conquest of the East by Alexander had brought to an end the two centuries of Persian domination, during which many Jews had drunk deep draughts from wells which they had not dug. At Alexander's death his kingdom had split overnight. New kingdoms, Greek in essence and outlook, were established, and little Palestine lay between two of the most powerful of them, Ptolemaic Egypt and Seleucid Syria. Both of these powers were committed to the policy of achieving a fictitious unity through the eradication of local cultures, and Israel became a victim of this policy. Finally the break came. The Seleucid Antiochus IV (styled Epiphanes, and the object of loathing in Jewish eyes), in a vain attempt to re-establish his weary and tottering kingdom, overplayed his hand and rashly attempted to "exterminate those who kept alive the Jewish superstitions." The result of this act of folly was the Maccabean revolt and the resultant spectacular but ephemeral period of a restored and independent kingdom which sought to become a tiny empire.

The three sons—Judas, Jonathan, and Simon—of the old Hasmonean priest who had touched off the fire of revolt were able through a combination of amazing military prowess, shrewd political maneuvering, and great good luck, to force first religious tolerance and next essential political independence from the Seleucids, then so weakened by internal strife and external conquest as to be powerless to prevent it.

And no sooner was the new Hasmonean dynasty of high-priest-kings in control than it sought to re-establish the fabled days of "Jewish" supremacy under David and Solomon. John Hyrcanus (ruled 135-105 B.C.), Aristobulus (ruled 105-104 B.C.), and Alexander Jannaeus (ruled 104-78 B.C.), one after the other devoted themselves to increasing the boundaries of the little would-be Jewish empire with Jerusalem as its capital. And on paper the results look impressive. Before the death of the last of these three priestly rulers, Jerusalem held sway from the foothills of the Lebanons to the Egyptian frontier, and had overrun and held all (save Ascalon) of the seacoast cities south of Carmel, and broadly speaking, most of the territory east of the Jordan to the Arabian desert. But the "empire" was fragile in the extreme. All this territory had been superficially "Judaized"—regularly the conquered had been forced to be circumcised. But lasting unity was not to be achieved by such rough-and-ready methods. Much of the territory was definitely non-Jewish. One of the earliest acts of Judas Maccabaeus had been to centralize all the Jews in the environs of Jerusalem. Naturally this had left large sections of territory, especially in Galilee and the Perea, where few if any Jews were to be found. All the seacoast towns were Greek—or at least alien to Judaism—with a non-Jewish, non-Hebrew, tradition of many centuries standing.

Nor was all quiet among the Jews themselves. The excesses of Antiochus in his attempt to blot out all things religious had led to a momentary all-out policy of outraged opposition. But once religious toleration had been accomplished, many had lost interest. The growing dreams of the leaders for political independence were far from being widely shared. To many the continued spectacle of their high priest crusading at the head of mercenary armies was disquieting. No longer was Israel's faith in danger. David, because he was a man of war, had not been permitted even to build a temple. Yet here were men—Hyrcanus, Aristobulus, Alexander Jannaeus—officiating as God's anointed high priests, with their arms red to the elbows.

Thus arose a gradual but deep-seated opposition to the royal house. It had probably started during the years of Hyrcanus; it became very vocal during the years of his two successors, especially of the bloodthirsty Alexander Jannaeus. At one time, when the latter had suffered a particularly humiliating defeat, a civil war broke out which for five years drenched Jerusalem and its environs with blood. Actually, for the instant some of the rebels toyed with the idea of asking foreign aid against their king. The rebellion was brutally crushed; and to the end of Alexander Jannaeus' reign the land was numb. But the opposition was not dead, as his widow soon discovered. By great shrewdness and good sense this doughty woman, Alexandra, averted the storm that must otherwise have broken. She strengthened her precarious position by permitting to a greater degree the voices of her nonimperialistic subjects, by giving the local Jerusalem council vastly more authority than it had formerly enjoyed, and by introducing into this council, in addition to the nobles and priests, a new group, the scribes, who had already displaced in the popular eye the less highly educated priests as the real religious leaders of Israel. But though she rode out the storm and her nine-year reign (78-69 B.C.) was looked back upon during the days of the far more absolute Herod as truly halcyon days, it was only a temporary lull.

Alexandra's death was the signal for violence once more, and her two sons, called by the good Hasmonean names Aristobulus and Hyrcanus, were at each other's throats. The ambitious Aristobulus was a true son of his war-loving father, and behind the reluctant and incompetent Hyrcanus stood the wily Antipater, former chief adviser of Alexander Jannaeus and destined to be for many years the dominant figure in local affairs.

II. Under Rome

It was at this moment, when Hyrcanus with a motley force abetted by Nabataean Arabs was besieging his brother in Jerusalem, that Rome intervened and assumed control. Rome had already created the strong province of Syria out of the remains of the old Seleucid kingdom, and what autonomy and authority Jerusalem possessed had for a long time been held only by Roman sufferance. But when Pompey, the Roman general, entered the city in 63 B.C., even the semblance of Jewish independence was destroyed. All the extra-Judean territory (save Idumaea), which had been gained at such terrible cost, was stripped off. The Greek cities of the seacoast and across the Jordan were set free from the hated Jewish yoke. Samaria and Galilee were appended to the newly constituted province of Syria.

Nor was this policy of dispossessing local tyrants aimed only at the Jews. Many usurpers who had got control of cities or districts of the decaying Seleucid empire were unceremoniously ousted and executed. Others, like Hyrcanus in Jerusalem and Tigranes in Armenia, who could show reasonable claim or were ready to make amends and keep the peace, were left in possession. Thus the coming of Rome, although it spelled disaster to many ambitious hopes, was hailed by many as the day of liberation and freedom. Of course the "freedom" required recognition of Roman supremacy, but to the non-Jewish territories which had been under Jewish sway it was a blessed relief. Josephus lists many such liberated cities: Gaza, Azotus, Jamnia, Joppa, Strato's Tower, and

Dora, on the seacoast; Samaria, Scythopolis, Hippos, Gadara, Pella, and Dion, inland. But there must have been many others. Nine cities across the Jordan joined with Scythopolis in a trade alliance, the "ten-city alliance," or as it was popularly known, the Decapolis. Thus to many it might well have seemed that once more the wheel had turned and that the little Jewish state stood precisely where it had been one hundred years before, at the time of the Maccabean revolt, stripped of lands and independence, subject to a foreign power. But the experiences of these years—hopes, dreams, successes, awful disillusionment—these had not been lost but were to bear bitter fruit. And besides, Rome was a vastly different mistress from the moribund Syria.

This difference consisted not only in the enormously greater strength and vitality of the Roman Empire, but also in the greater wisdom of her policies in governing conquered territories. Indeed although it was hard for the Jews to see it so, the coming of Rome to the East was in reality a blessing in disguise, for it meant orderly and responsible government in the place of irresponsible tyranny and confusion. It was essential to Rome's now far-spread possessions and interests that the irresponsible boundary jumping by ambitious and reckless local chiefs and petty kings, which had followed the collapse of the older kingdoms, of which the empire of the Seleucids was one, be stopped. And stopped it was. Rome's genius for government and her dearly bought experience in managing restive and unruly districts resulted in a stable government with an amazing tolerance to local customs, especially religious folkways. Her policy in provincial administration—at least in the East—was definitely *laissez faire*. She made no attempt to Romanize; rather she continued the practice inaugurated nearly three centuries earlier by Alexander of Hellenizing the East. When it became necessary to establish cities in rural areas for more effective civil control, they were essentially Greek, not Roman, cities. Greek remained the language of culture and government. The governors Rome sent never dreamed of imposing the Latin tongue; rather they translated into Greek their decrees and regulations.

Nor did Pompey or his successors upset the forms of local government. The towns continued to manage their own affairs. The native courts continued to settle difficulties quite without reference to Roman law. The governor saw that the laws prevailed, that order was kept, that the frontiers were quiet, that travel and communication were safe, that the taxes and tithes were properly and promptly paid, and that any Roman citizen who chanced to be in his territory might have ready access to Roman law. Whenever it was possible, local officials who knew and understood the peculiarities of the various districts were preferred in positions of responsibility. It was in line with this sensible preference for local rulers that, as we have seen, Pompey allowed Hyrcanus II to serve as nominal head, the ethnarch, of Jerusalem.

Although many of the liberated cities in Palestine had hailed the advent of Pompey as the dawn of their independence, and many of the Pharisees and their followers had rejoiced in the collapse of the hated Hasmonean line, Jews generally did not share this enthusiasm. Much as they honored the scribes, they prized their freedom more. And as they watched the signs and felt the force of their new subjugation, the abuses and tyranny under which they had suffered retreated into the background. The result was that party strife was for the moment forgotten and Rome was seen as a common foe.

Following a brief time of numbed quiet came a five-year period of rebellion and unrest, in consequence of which the little seeming independence that Pompey had extended was lost. Judea was no longer even an ethnarchy; Hyrcanus was stripped of his small political power, and the little city-state was made a part of the province of Syria.

A. The House of Herod.—But this was soon to change. During these ten years (63-53 B.C.) Antipater, the former chief adviser of Alexander Jannaeus and later the champion of Jannaeus' easily controlled elder son Hyrcanus, had played his cards well. Remaining always out of sight, he had come to be the trusted friend and lieutenant of the Roman officers. As a result of his effective aid Hyrcanus was eventually reappointed ethnarch; but by then the real power lay in Antipater's own hands, as the deferential and unobtrusive minister of the ethnarch.

Then came the terrible years of civil war in Rome, beginning with Caesar's crossing of the Rubicon and ending with the victory of Octavian (later Augustus) at Actium. Every event of those years of unrest and confusion (49-31 B.C.) was mirrored in little Palestine. Through it all Antipater and, after his death, his son Herod, whom he had contrived to have appointed governor of Galilee, managed to stay on the side of the victors. Thus they weathered one storm after another by their nimble transfer of allegiance: after Pharsalia, loyalty was transferred from Pompey to Caesar; after Philippi, to Antony; after Actium, to Octavian.

And for all this they had been rewarded, for they never made the mistake of approaching the victor with empty hands. Caesar, in gratitude for Antipater's effective aid, had removed many of the earlier restrictions. The galling division of the little Jewish territory into five mutually independent petty districts had been abolished. Hyrcanus had been confirmed ethnarch of a reunited Judea and granted senatorial rank; Antipater had received the prized Roman citizenship and had been authorized as Hyrcanus' prime minister; the dangerous claims of Antigonus, the son of Aristobulus, had been contemptuously disallowed; Jerusalem, once more the nominal capital of the little Jewish state, had had its walls rebuilt and had been granted an outlet to the sea through the return of the seaport city, Joppa; perhaps best of all—at least it so proved in the long run—Jews were exempted from service in the Roman legions, and thus their scruples against violating the sanctity of the sabbath were safeguarded. Rome rarely made the mistake, which had cost the Seleucids so dearly, of allowing religious convictions to become of political moment.

But more was still to come. Herod, the able son of the wily Antipater, had already proved himself a valuable ally to Roman officers in the East. Shortly after Herod's appointment to Galilee, the Roman governor of Syria had made him military governor of the whole southern frontier (Coele-Syria) of that province. The death of Antipater had enabled Herod to succeed to virtual control of Jerusalem and the little Jewish state. Local opposition to him was vigorous but powerless. The nationalists and the supporters of the Hasmonean line, with dreams of a restored throne free from Roman domination, rightly saw in Herod, the Idumaean, their greatest obstacle and menace. Actually their opposition and plotting were their own undoing. When one of them, the discredited Hasmonean claimant, Antigonus, sought and gained the help of Parthia, which Rome rightly feared as the one great menace to the security of her eastern frontier—when this occurred, Rome recognized that Palestine could easily become a danger spot, and seeing in Herod the ideal opponent to these claims, she bestowed on him in the year 40 B.C. the title "king of the Jews." Despite the lack of assistance which at first seemed to make the title an empty one, Herod had proceeded in able fashion to make it a reality. And he was successful. After three years of labor and disappointment, Jerusalem was his, and the Hasmonean aspirant, Antigonus, was executed.

Once more the Jews had a king, and one worthy of the name. Despite his unpopularity —he was hated as the tool of Rome, as the one responsible for the fall of the royal house, as an Idumaean, not a Jew—he proved to be Israel's greatest king. For nearly forty years he governed the little land so efficiently that section after section was added to his domain by Rome. Never did he make the mistake of failing to recognize what was involved in the title *rex socius*. He wore the diadem, but he wore it because Rome so desired.

With the triumph of Octavian over Antony and Cleopatra came an era of peace and prosperity, welcomed alike by Rome and by her widespread provinces and dependencies, exhausted by the years of unrest and civil war.

B. Augustan Reforms.—By a series of masterly moves Augustus had obtained complete authority over the Roman state; yet through his deference to the senate, especially in matters of small concern, he had achieved this position in such a way as to avoid the onus of seeming either a tyrant or dictator. All the provinces and other dependencies which needed military supervision because they lay on open frontiers, or because local conditions might cause them to be danger spots, he kept in his own hands. Governors responsible to him were appointed for indefinite terms of service, determined solely by their effectiveness and success. The remaining provinces, as for example Asia and Achaia, where no legions were necessary, he returned with a flourish to the oversight of the senate. To these latter were appointed officers with the title "proconsul," for a single year of service. This distinction between the "provinces of the people" and the "provinces of Caesar" was one of the most important elements in the plan of government set up by Augustus, who had learned much from the discomfiture of his uncle, Julius Caesar.

In so important a province as Syria the governor was a Roman with the title "propraetor"; in such districts as Palestine, Augustus preferred a native prince, provided a dependable man could be found. Herod was such a man in Augustus' eyes. During the years of corruption and mismanagement in the East, brought about in no small degree through the weakness of Antony in Egypt, Herod had acquitted himself well in an impossible situation. Thus when Antony and Cleopatra had fallen, and Augustus was in sole command, the latter sensed that Herod, who had remained Antony's loyal supporter to the end, would be a most valuable ally. Accordingly he gladly confirmed him "king of Judea." Nor was the shrewd Roman mistaken; while never popular, despite his best efforts to become so, Herod had the knack of rule. During the many years of his reign, when a serious misstep would have meant his immediate removal, he kept the peace and solidified his little state. So able did he prove that, in the course of the years, district after district was added to his domain. At the end he had control of a territory as large as that which his predecessor Alexander Jannaeus had seized; but as administered, it was far more stable and on the whole was admirably managed.

C. The Rebuilding of Palestine.—The Augustan age was a time of opulence and splendor. Augustus found Rome in brick and left it in marble; the same can be said of Herod in Jerusalem and throughout his domain. Temples, gymnasiums, cloisters, amphitheaters, aqueducts—all these evidences of prosperity and culture appeared in the little Jewish state. Cities were built and ruins rebuilt. Thus Samaria, long a ruin, was rebuilt and named Sebaste in honor of the emperor. To provide a harbor on the inhospitable coast the magnificent city of Caesarea Stratonis was erected on the site of Strato's Tower. This city soon became the leading city of Palestine, and years later, when Roman procurators had succeeded to Herod's power, Caesarea was their official residence and capital. Other cities too appeared, many of them named after Herod's relations and friends: Antipatris, Phasaëlis, Agrippium, to mention but a few. Citadels, strategically set, encircled his domain and discouraged any hope of successful revolt. And far outside his now sizable kingdom evidences of his munificence as an eager if not especially understanding patron of culture were to be found.

But the temple in Jerusalem was his chief triumph. Built of white marble and overlaid with gold and jewels, gleaming high on the summit of Zion, a spectacular sight to pilgrims as they toiled over the top of Olivet on the Jericho road, it gave rise to the byword: "Whoever has not seen the temple of Herod, has seen nothing beautiful." Ever careful to guard against offense, Herod is said to have seen to it that the workmen on the temple were priests especially taught the trades of mason and carpenter, so that no unconsecrated foot need defile holy ground. And Herod himself appears never to have entered the shrine which he made possible. The actual work of building the temple proper took eighteen months; eight years more were required on the surrounding courts and porticoes. And the last detail was not complete (cf. John 2:20) until the days of Albinus, less than a decade before it was turned to ashes by the conqueror's torch.

But not only in building and as a patron of culture did Herod prove a miniature Augustus; he was effective also in other ways. After years of conquest and exploitation the land was at peace; banditry had been put down, and with a firm hand. To some Herod's efficient secret police and rigidly enforced curfew legislation may well have seemed irksome, but they not only made the government secure but checked the looting of orderly citizens. Undoubtedly taxes were high—such building and munificence required money, and plenty of it—but this was no new experience for Palestine, and actually at least twice drastic reduction in taxes took place: 33 per cent in 20 B.C., 25 per cent six years later. Free grain was provided in times of famine, the clothing of whole villages in times of distress—yet despite all this, Herod was never popular, and his death in 4 B.C. was eagerly hailed.

Against the lurid stories of intrigue and bloodshed in his own palace and family, gladly told in full detail by the later Josephus, and against the legend of the slaughter of the Bethlehem babes, stands the unassailable fact that for nearly forty years Herod held together—and without the use of armies—a land which was singularly tough-bitted and restive. Indeed he did this so effectively that Augustus, whose oversight of his provinces was very exacting, had added section after section, in confidence that they would be well governed. It may also be remarked that while within Judea proper popular resentment toward this Idumaean tool of Rome may well have been always present, outside Judea, where religious prejudices were less intense, Herod seems to have been a popular ruler, and again and again his subjects, both Jews and Gentiles, found that his hand, though heavy, was just.

D. The Division of Palestine.—His death, some three decades before Jesus seems to have made his public appearance, led to drastic and far-reaching changes. Herod's kingdom was split into three parts, administered by three of his several sons: Archelaus, Antipas, and Philip. Galilee and the Perea fell to Antipas, and the districts to the north and east of Galilee were given to Philip. Both of these men had long "reigns," remaining in office until well after the crucifixion of Jesus. Thus while Jesus stayed in Galilee or traveled south in the land beyond the Jordan, he was in the domain of Antipas, who, while never popular with Augustus, for years basked in the favor of Augustus' successor, Tiberius; if he made the trip recorded in the Gospels of Mark and Matthew to Caesarea Philippi, he entered the territory and capital city of Philip. This ruler remained in control —and apparently well liked by his subjects— until his death in A.D. 34. Antipas remained five years longer in Galilee; then through the clever maneuvering of his nephew Agrippa he fell into disfavor with the new emperor, Gaius, and was banished.

Archelaus, who had received the southern section of his father's kingdom—Judea, Samaria, and Idumaea—did not fare so well. The death of Herod the Great, and the departure of his sons to Rome to await Augustus' decision, had been the signal for riots and insurrection in this part of Palestine. These were promptly and severely punished by Varus, the propraetor of Syria, who in the interim felt responsibility for the domain to the south. Finally Augustus decided to accept Herod's will and to confirm his appointees, with the qualification that Archelaus was denied the title king. His term as ethnarch was far shorter than were those of his brothers. In A.D. 6 he was accused of gross mismanagement and was promptly summoned to Rome by Augustus. He could not defend himself and was speedily removed from office and banished. Augustus determined to turn this ethnarchy into a province under direct rule from Rome in the person of a procurator, as the governors of the lesser imperial provinces were called. This was speedily done, and Coponius was sent as first procurator. These governors, like the propraetors in the more important imperial provinces, were responsible solely to the emperor and remained in office so long as their administration was approved.

The installation of Coponius and the setting up of the necessary machinery for enrolling the citizens as provincials and for assessing the taxes were conducted by Quirinius, then governor of Syria. The resulting census, an echo of which is to be found in Luke 2:1-5, though apparently in error—it is dated a decade too early—resulted in fresh unrest and bloodshed. The real ground for the resulting insurrection, in the course of which Judas of Galilee (cf. Acts 5:37) was slain, was opposition to what seemed a still further loss of independence.[1] Galilee, the home of Judas, was of course not directly involved; but the dismemberment of Herod's kingdom had not destroyed the feeling of Jewish solidarity.

E. Early Opposition to Rome.—Though the rebellion was a mere flash in the pan and was promptly squelched, it deserves a further word. Writers often speak of this revolt as the start of the Zealot party, which in its intense opposition to Rome was subsequently ever eager to force the issue and drive the nation into war with Rome. But actually this party had had its beginning long before, although that name was used only later. From the time of Pompey's enactments there had been a movement—whether organized or not is of little consequence—fired

[1] Josephus refers to this Judas as a Gaulonite of "a city whose name was Gamala" (Antiquities XVIII. 1. 1.), who apparently, although this has been denied, had also been involved in the abortive outbreak of violence ten years before.

by such hostility to the intruder and by such eagerness to restore independence as to fear no violence. Its later slogan was "The sword and not sparingly; no king but Yahweh." Josephus records that after Herod had first been sent to Galilee by his father, Antipater, he had come into contact with a band of brigands led by a Hezekiah. Herod had crushed them and executed the ringleader. The resulting indignation in Jerusalem over these stern repressive measures makes it highly probable that Hezekiah and his followers considered themselves patriots of the first water and that their activities were really directed against Rome and her hirelings, of whom Herod was the local representative.

It must be remembered that Josephus, writing in Rome at the end of the first century, supported by Roman grants and in reasonably good favor with his Roman patrons, was in a difficult situation. Years before had occurred that terrible and disastrous rebellion which for seven years (A.D. 66-73) had drenched the land in blood and had ended the visible evidence of Jewish solidarity—the temple and its daily service. And worst of all, Josephus himself had been, more or less reluctantly, a conspicuous if not especially gallant figure in the rebellion. To be sure, he had been speedily eliminated as a leading rebel, and by clever strategy had neatly extricated himself and had become of real service to Vespasian and Titus in their relentless campaign against the rebels. Throughout his writings, especially in the later ones, there is a manifest desire to minimize and soft-pedal the hatred of Jews toward Rome. The fact of the rebellion could not be hidden. It could, however, be explained and extenuated; and Josephus sought valiantly so to do. Thus regularly he depreciates the importance of the group which he dubs "the fourth philosophy"—a colorless term to distinguish the revolutionaries from the other three "philosophies," namely, the Pharisees, Sadducees, and Essenes, which he lists as influential in Jewish life. Jews as a whole, he constantly implies, were not unfriendly to Rome and would never have rebelled; a few hotheads there were, but until a succession of incompetent and cruel Roman governors—each worse than the preceding—gave provocation, these agitators had been powerless. It would appear that this interpretation of history, while not unnatural under the circumstances, shows signs of bias.

Thus, far from "starting" in the act of Judas in A.D. 6, the movement had been long under way. The acts of Hezekiah, the acts of insurrectionists at the time of Herod's death, and at the time of the census ten years later—all were part of the activity of what for want of better name may be styled the "home rule group," implacably opposed to subservience to the hated overlords and eager to foment strife, confident that, as in the days of Joshua and Gideon, if the nation would strike the first blow, God would rally to their side and give them victory, despite the enormous odds against them.

For years the revolutionaries were not able to arouse the nation. To the Pharisees, who for the most part had no interest in civil power but were content to remain the spiritual mentors of Israel, they were fanatics to be dismissed contemptuously. Of course the presence of Rome was an outrage, but it was largely God's scourge to punish Israel for her sins; when he saw fit to intervene, he would do it speedily and effectively without the aid of this absurd crew. To the Sadducees, who by this time, while no longer numerous, were possessed of great wealth and considerable influence, and who by tradition and interest were conservative guardians of the *status quo*, and to others in positions of wealth and leadership, these enthusiasts were an unmitigated outrage and danger. These conservatives realized how easy it would be to upset the already heavily loaded ship of state and thus destroy not only their privileges but the nation's existence.

So long as life continued tolerable, and so long as no overt acts by the Romans outraged Jewish religious sensibilities, these superpatriots were unable to achieve their end. But they were constantly present, eager to detect abuses and to goad their easygoing brethren into action. Naturally occasional overt acts occurred —for example, Gaius' (A.D. 37-41) repressive gestures and his widely heralded determination to set up his own statue in the holy of holies— and each of these gave the restless nationalists a talking point. Thus gradually the constant dripping was wearing down the stone. As unrest grew, naturally the governors found it necessary to be more severe. This in turn but added to the unrest. Palestine was fast becoming a powder chest, ready to be set off at the first spark; and the explosion which came entirely justified the earlier hostility of the more cautious solid citizens toward the growing revolutionary movement.

But let us return to the act of Judas in the days of Coponius and Quirinius. As has been said, this was definitely not the start of the home rule party but only one additional step in the opposition to Rome which had first blazed out years before against Antipater and his son, and which was destined to continue as a constant menace until it had achieved its end. It is probable, although impossible to prove, that not a few of the sayings in the Gospels deprecating violence and warning of the peril to those who would take the sword—sayings often regarded as independent pronouncements against war as such—were originally spoken against this background and these claims. Nor is it hard to imagine the response of members of this belligerent group who may have heard Jesus' reply to the query as to the justifiability of paying tribute to Caesar.

There is no apparent justification for applying the term "Zealot" to this group. Josephus never employs it of them. The first use by him of the term is of one group of disgruntled patriots, headed by the doughty John of Gischala, years later in A.D. 66. Nor is it proper to style the revolt of Judas "messianic." The first leader of such a revolt in Jewish history was Bar Cocheba, who, in the days of Hadrian, about A.D. 132, led the second and even more disastrous revolt against Rome. The use of technical terms in a loose and inexact sense, and the tendency to read back to earlier groups titles which subsequent generations evolved, while popular, are to be deplored.

F. Judea Under the Procurators.—The popular picture of Judea being ground down by harsh and rapacious governors is greatly overdrawn. As has been suggested, Rome was a remarkably astute mistress, avoiding many of the pitfalls of the earlier empire builders. Local customs were rarely interfered with, even those which seemed most distasteful to the Roman. Governors were instructed to allow their domains as much freedom as possible. Thus in the province of Judea most of the actual control was vested in the Sanhedrin.[2] Popular fancy saw this council as the genetic descendant of the seventy elders who had aided Moses in his deliberations (Num. 11:16). Actually it is impossible to trace the origin of this senate farther back than the beginning of the Greek period; the first express mention of it under the title "Sanhedrin" is by Josephus, who refers to its hostility to Herod because of the latter's treatment of Hezekiah in Galilee. But at any rate in the days of the early procurators it was regarded with great respect. It was comprised apparently of some seventy members, presided over by the high priest, and largely dominated by the priestly and moneyed aristocracy, although there can be but little question that it also contained representatives from the more popular faction, the Pharisees. How vacancies were filled, for how long the members held office, and the exact form of procedure—all this we do not know. Herod had stripped this council of most of its power. But under the procurators it became once more the real gov-

---

[2] Not to be confused with the *Bet Din*, or Court of Justice, said to be at Jamnia after the fall of Jerusalem, and described in the tract Sanhedrin in the Mishnah.

erning agency of the province. Its actual authority was limited to the eleven toparchies into which Judea was divided; its influence, however, upon Jewish life and practice may well have been far more extensive. The procurator allowed it almost complete power, both legislative and judicial. Apparently—although this is not certain and has been frequently denied—the sentence of death could not be imposed by this body, or at least it had to be ratified by the governor. Otherwise it was supreme. Not all cases would come before it, for each of the eleven toparchies had its own local court, comprised of twenty-one members. But when invoked, its sentence was final and not open to review.

Nor did Judea suffer from the financial rapacity of its governors. The earlier abuses under which the provinces had suffered had long since been corrected. The governors received fixed salaries; taxes were no longer farmed out but were collected by salaried officials whose books were under careful audit. A large part of the revenue was expended in bettering the province. The one weakness in an otherwise admirable system was the matter of the internal revenue or customs. These were still farmed out to the highest bidder and were thus liable to abuse. The publican (tax farmer) and his underlings were cordially hated as the most visible and immediate agent of Rome with whom the ordinary man came into contact. Were they not engaged in daily theft of what properly belonged to Yahweh, the true lord of the land? Small wonder that in the Gospels they are regularly associated with harlots and sinners, a byword of reproach.

Thus the actual government was in the hands of the native aristocracy at whose head stood the high priest. At the death of Herod, and again ten years later, when Archelaus had become involved in difficulties, Jews had requested that the territory be appended to Syria. The reason for the request is clear. It was prompted by the hope of getting rid of domination by the house of Herod; it seemed a good way to achieve a measure of independence although under the aegis of Rome. Though this request had not been granted, and a local governor was now in the province, it must have become increasingly evident to the more dispassionate realists that things had turned out far better than they might have expected. For the most part the governor remained in Caesarea, coming to Jerusalem usually only at times of feasts, to make certain that the festival throngs did not become overboisterous. Thus those in positions of influence, while they might look on Rome with inherited disfavor, accepted the new order with resignation if not enthusiasm;

and they were forced willy-nilly into the position of being constantly vigilant lest some ill-advised action—by the fanatically minded home rule enthusiasts or by an occasional wilderness preacher with a dangerous message of a new day, with axes laid at the roots of trees—endanger the *status quo*. The hostility to a John the Baptist or to his greater successor is not hard to explain.

The first four procurators came and went. To us they are scarcely more than names. The fifth, Pontius Pilate, is of special interest because of his part in the tragedy on Calvary. The popular picture painted of him is unfavorable; that he had occasional clashes with his provincials is clear. Against this is the fact that for ten years he was held in office by Tiberius, who kept a very close watch on his provinces and accepted no excuses for mismanagement or unrest. Thus when Pilate intervened in Samaria, in a situation which might well have seemed to him dangerous in the extreme, he was at once removed from office. The fact that for ten years Tiberius found no serious fault in Pilate's administration should be remembered when one attempts to tally up the score of this luckless governor who appears to have sought zealously and honestly to maintain order and to better his province, and who may well be excused for having found it a perplexing, even baffling, task to keep clear of the shoals and quicksands.

G. Agrippa and the Last of the Procurators. —Five years after the removal of Pilate came a real if only temporary change in Judean politics. Tiberius died in A.D. 37. He was succeeded by his young grandnephew Gaius (Caligula), who soon proved a terrible disappointment to many Romans who had found the late emperor's hand unduly heavy. Two acts of Gaius had especial consequence in Palestine. The first was the appointment of his boon companion, Agrippa, grandson of the late Herod, to the territory which had comprised the tetrarchy of Philip. At the death of the latter in A.D. 34 it had been appended to Syria. Then, somewhat increased in area, it was made the kingdom of Agrippa. Five years later it was again enlarged by the addition of the tetrarchy of Antipas, who had incurred Roman suspicions as a consequence of the deft if unprincipled acts of the ambitious and ungrateful Agrippa. Then came the death of Gaius and the accession of Claudius in A.D. 41.

Agrippa had become increasingly popular in Jewish eyes through his opposition to his patron Gaius' rash and pettish intention to set up in the temple in Jerusalem his own statue. This ill-advised act had convulsed the southern province. It had been averted by the wise caution of the Syrian governor; but to Agrippa had gone the credit in Jewish eyes. Claudius, partly out of a desire to repay an earlier obligation to Agrippa, determined to revert to the earlier practice of Augustus. Thus the province of Judea was added to the kingdom of the ambitious Agrippa. For three years a Jewish king again sat in the seat of David and ruled a united Palestine. And Agrippa, unlike Herod, had Jewish blood in his veins. His grandmother had been the Hasmonean princess Mariamne, the ill-starred favorite of the passionate Herod. Agrippa was as popular as his grandfather was hated; during his brief reign (A.D. 41-44) he apparently even toyed with the idea of making his little kingdom actually independent. Though his plans miscarried, they may well have added to his popularity—and made the task of his successors the more difficult. A sudden illness brought his reign to a close (Acts 12:21-23), and with it the kingdom of the Jews.

But the subsequent procurators, of whom Cuspius Fadus was first, were governors of a far larger territory than Pilate and his predecessors had held. Palestine had been temporarily reunited under Agrippa; consequently the new province had the same extent, no longer restricted to Judea, Samaria, and Idumaea. Thus Galilee, the Perea, and the districts to the north and east were now under direct Roman rule from Caesarea. As has been suggested, during the subsequent twenty years tension increased. It may well be that the temporary interlude under King Agrippa, when there was a semblance—though only a semblance—of independence, had served to encourage the revolutionists. However that may be, during the next two decades, while the early Christian missionaries were at work within Palestine and without, tensions were increasing, and the disaster, which those who were politically weather-wise must long before have discerned, drew ever closer.

H. The Revolts Against Rome.—Finally the storm broke. As is usually the case, an act in itself of little consequence proved the spark that set fire to the accumulated pile. In A.D. 66 the long-threatened rebellion started, which resulted four years later in the fall of Jerusalem, the burning of the temple, the cessation of sacrifice, and the end of the Sanhedrin as an active and effective agent of government. For a hundred years Rome's iron hand had controlled the little Jewish land; but the hand had worn the proverbial velvet glove. As far as possible the affairs of state had been administered through local officials. Now this was past. To Rome the rebellion was an evidence that as far as Palestine was concerned, her latitude and tolerance had been ill-advised; she would not suffer from the same mistake again.

The consequences of the fall of Jerusalem and the destruction of the temple—that outward symbol of Jewish pride and exclusiveness—were far-reaching. It can scarcely be doubted that they had their effect in the growing separation between synagogue and church. The fact that Jewish Christians had fled from Jerusalem to Pella in the dark hours of certain defeat was never forgotten or forgiven by their non-Christian neighbors. On the other hand the fall of the temple and the destruction of the city that had doomed their Lord seemed to the Christians an answer of God—certain, if long delayed. Literally not one stone was left upon another of those great buildings. The dreadful cries: "His blood be on us, and on our children" and "We have no king but Caesar," whatever their origin, still evidence the early conviction that "though the mills of God grind slowly, yet they grind exceeding small."

Of the years following the fatal rebellion we have little direct information. Did the very fact that once again the tyrant's heel was on the nation's neck prove a spur to hope? The destruction of the temple may well have been construed as a direct attack upon religion, and such attacks always reminded the Jew of Yahweh's power. However that may be, it is surely within the realm of sober certainty that many a Jew, whatever his outward action might have been, became more and more convinced that the dreadful events he had suffered could not be the end of the drama, but only the prelude to a greater climax. Eventually in God's own good time another Gideon would arise, the trumpets would be blown, the lights beneath the pitchers would be revealed, and victory would come. Against that day the lamps must be kept trimmed and burning.

And sixty years later, in the days of Hadrian, the pitchers were smashed. In line with his dreams of rebuilding the East the emperor had decided—at least such seems to have been the rumor in Jerusalem—that on the site of the ancient Jerusalem, now scarcely more than a ruin, should be built a new and stately city. This may well have proved a call to arms. So long as Jerusalem remained a ruin it was the promise of a restored Zion. A heathen city meant the end of such dreams. A new temple of Capitoline Zeus on the site of God's house! It is not hard to imagine how the reports were bandied about. To make things worse Rome had banned circumcision. Once again, as in the days of the Maccabees, the fatal hour had struck.

Actually Rome's policy was not directed against the Jews; Hadrian had not picked out that little people as the object of his wrath. Neither of the acts which had so infuriated

Jewry as attempts to root true religion from the earth was so regarded by the Roman. Jerusalem was but one of many ruins to be restored in the bigger and better Roman world. The ban of circumcision was only a corollary to the imperial edict against bodily mutilation, aimed especially at castration, a practice in several of the Eastern cults making large inroads on Roman soil and long an object of loathing to the average Roman.

But the Jews were in no mood to view these matters dispassionately. They were always nervously self-conscious of being the especial target of the adversary's displeasure since they were alone the object of Yahweh's love and trust. And speedily the rebellion grew. We have little knowledge of the details; one point is, however, highly significant. Now for the first time —at least we have no clear evidence of an earlier claimant—a Jewish patriot made definite claim to be God's long expected champion, the Messiah. This hardy soul was the obscure Bar Cocheba. And even more significant is the change of temper in the more staid and sober circles of Jewry. Whereas a century before, the leaders—religious as well as political—had looked askance at the antics of those who would involve the nation in an ill-advised and suicidal revolt, now all was changed. No less a figure than the scholarly Rabbi Akiba sponsored Bar Cocheba's claims, and like the later Peter the Hermit in Europe, toured Palestine as his champion and gave most effective aid in rallying men to his banners. Nor is this change of temper surprising. Once again religion seemed to be menaced. Just as the Hasideans (the "pious") had three centuries before supported Judas the Maccabee so long as the latter was fighting for freedom to worship by the rites of their fathers, so now. The affairs of God were at stake.

Of course the rebellion was abortive. Had we a detailed account, as we have of the earlier rebellion in the pages of Josephus, the story would probably be even more dreadful. Jerusalem was rebuilt as the Roman city, Aelia Capitolina, and Jews were forbidden, on pain of instant death, to enter its gates. Years later a slight concession was made; once a year Jews might enter to wail for their lost glories and to dream dreams of a better time. Once again they realized they had been precipitate. God had not been ready; the hour of their deliverance had not been at hand. But though the temple was gone, the priesthood stripped of its power, Zion trodden and ruled by uncircumcised Gentiles who aspired to the glories of the throne of David; not yet had the final assize been held or judgment pronounced. God still reigned; he had promised, and his promises could never fail.

III. The Law and Its Interpreters

Judaism took itself very seriously as a religion of revelation. Failure to recognize this basic fact cannot fail to lead to a total misunderstanding of this people whose ability through the years to undergo disaster and survive destruction has proved a constant marvel.

A. The Nature of the Law.—God stood at the center of the Jews' life and thought. From before the creation of the world he had formed his purposes and laid his plans. Through the fathers, and especially through Moses, God had revealed a religion which was destined to become the universal religion of all mankind. This revelation of God was complete and all-embracing: everything that men were to do and be he had revealed to them. Not alone the way in which they were to regard him and the forms their worship was to take, but all their attitudes of mind and will, their conduct toward him, their brethren, and the outside world—in a word God's entire and unchanging will—this he had revealed. It was man's for the knowing. The law—the Jew called it Torah—was accordingly God's greatest gift to men.

Keeping the law stood as man's paramount obligation. But it was no hardship for the Jew. He did it with no ulterior end in view; he did it because he loved God and wished to do God's will. It was God, not venial and self-seeking men, who had framed the law. His motives were entirely pure and beneficent. Failure to obey God's revealed will, heedless or deliberate violation—these spelled disaster. Thus for the Jew, unlike the Greek taught by such as Socrates, sin was not an error of judgment, unwitting missing of the mark—it was a deliberate and willful act of filial defiance to a gracious and loving father. The father said, "Son, go work to day in my vineyard." The son replied, "I will not." In such a situation but one course of action was possible. The son must repent of the folly of his disobedience, must turn about-face and enter the vineyard; the prodigal must return in rags from the far country and implore the father's forgiveness. For centuries the ancient adage had stood: "Cease to do evil; learn to do well" (Isa. 1:16-17). Man could repent if he would. Even before the creation of the world, while yet God's all-inclusive law was still only in the mind of God, he had realized that slips were bound to occur and had conceived this sole means of return to his favor—repentance.

As God had revealed the law, so in turn the law revealed God—his justice, his insistence upon moral purity, his accessibility to man, his understanding heart, and his plans for the future. Thus the true Jew sought as the supreme object of life to be as much like God as possible; nor was this goal altogether beyond reach. Had not God created man in his own likeness? One Jew gave it worthy expression: "My good men, the best of all prayers, and the end, and proper object of happiness, is to attain to a likeness of God." [3] Nor is it too much to say that by and large this was the well-nigh universal attitude of orthodox Jewry.

This complete law of God was contained in the revelation he had made, the Scripture. But it was implicit, not always explicit. The Scripture is not always intelligible; parts might seem to be in conflict with each other. But for every problem or situation which in subsequent ages could ever arise, the answer was to be found here. Thus there could be no such thing as a "developing revelation." Things might seem new; they were not. They were but discoveries —often rediscoveries—of what God had from the beginning planned and ordained and announced. To illustrate by one example: The eighth-century prophets might seem to their opponents—and to us—to be sounding a new and revolutionary note. But such a view would have scandalized them. Rather they believed that they were calling men back to the original paths from which they had strayed.

And this confidence that *all* had been revealed led of necessity to constant poring over the law to discover its hidden truths. Since God manifestly never changes, whatever now is under his blessing must always have been his will and purpose. Thus as the years went by, new procedures, new developments, were not regarded as new but as rediscoveries—often discerned by ingenious allegorical exegesis— implicit in the ageless revelation. Once a temple, a visible house for God among his people, had been built, it seemed inconceivable that they could ever have been without one. But in this particular case the origin of the temple was an event too clearly ingrained in men's memories to be disregarded. In consequence arose the notion of the tabernacle, that earlier mobile temple, in which God had formerly dwelt with his people—and which all subsequent architects have found so extraordinarily difficult to reconstruct from the seemingly explicit specifications. Or again, once the office of high priest had emerged, in consequence of the downfall of the kingdom and the resultant transfer to the priesthood of what little authority had survived the end of the monarchy, this office was read farther and farther back, until Aaron was seen clad with that dread authority, and in the appropriate vestments.

A final example—and in many ways the most significant one—of this tendency in Judaism to read back present-day observances and institutions into the distant past is to be seen in the synagogue, which in the days of Jesus had eclipsed the temple as the actual center of Jewish life. The centralization of worship and the prohibition of sacrifice outside of Jerusalem, in the days of Josiah and the so-called Deuteronomic reform, may well have corrected many earlier abuses and have aided the emergence of a more orderly and unified cultus. It could, however, easily have spelled the downfall of Judaism, for with the destruction of Jerusalem, and the resultant dispersion of the leading Jews in the days of Nebuchadrezzar, opportunity for sacrifice was past. It was in this situation that the institution later to be known as the synagogue would seem to have arisen, as a sort of surrogate for the temple. To be sure, sacrifice could not be offered there, but those portions of the Torah dealing with this all-important rite could be read and expounded. From this beginning the institution steadily grew.

When later another temple was possible, these places of popular assembly remained unaffected. Few Jews outside Jerusalem could attend with any degree of regularity the temple services; many living at a distance—in Alexandria, Rome, or even within the bounds of Palestine itself—would be fortunate if once in their lifetime they were privileged to make the pilgrimage to Zion. The temple remained a glamorous symbol, a loadstone rock which exerted a romantic pull on the emotions of its sons and daughters wherever their lot might be cast, a visual proof of the nearness of God, and a promise of the coming time of reunion; but it had ceased to be the real center of Jewish life. Synagogues, on the other hand, were to be found in every city and hamlet of far-flung Jewry. Here twice a week, in addition to three times every sabbath and four times on the Day of Atonement, Jews met for the study of the law and for prayer.

In these services selections from the Pentateuch and the prophets were read aloud in Hebrew, the reader stopping frequently to permit a paraphrase into Aramaic.[4] (These oral translations were eventually reduced to writing and came to be known as Targums.) The read-

[3] Philo *Concerning the Ten Commandments* XV.

[4] Hebrew, the language of Jewish scholarship, had not been spoken for centuries, having been supplanted by Aramaic. Greek was spoken in such cities as Caesarea, Sebaste, and those of the Decapolis, and may well have been understood by many in Jerusalem; yet Palestine was not, and never became, bilingual. In Alexandria, on the other hand, Greek was not only the language of culture but of business. At an early date Jews residing there had found a translation of their Scriptures into vernacular Greek essential. This translation, known as the Septuagint, was widely used by Greek-speaking Jewry until Gentile Christians appropriated it as their own. But Palestinian Jews knew only the Hebrew Bible.

ing and translating were followed by a sermon. There was no fixed ministry; any qualified man (cf. Luke 4:16; Acts 13:15) might be asked to read or translate or speak. In the gradual growth of the synagogue to central importance is surely to be seen one very important reason for the gradual transfer of allegiance from the priests to the scribes, teachers of the law, as the real religious leaders of Israel. By the time of Jesus all memory of the actual origin of the synagogue had been forgotten. It seemed inconceivable that there could ever have been a time when men had not so met for the study of God's revelation. Thus it was in popular practice read back to Moses, and its prayers to the worthies who were said to have succeeded Ezra and were referred to with reverence as the "men of the Great Synagogue."

B. The Oral Law and the Rabbinical Literature.—Here in essence is the explanation of the so-called "oral law" or tradition, which was the pride of orthodox Judaism. This tradition or oral law was simply the consequence of the ingrained confidence that all of God's revelation was contained in the written law. It was there, but it was often so compressed, so terse or so hidden, that it was intelligible only to the closest and most reverent study. And this the scribes, who were the scholars and teachers of Israel, sought to provide. Thus through the years—as new occasions taught new duties and historical changes brought new problems and their solutions—the mass of oral law grew and became the actual source of orderly life in the Jewish world. In theory the Constitution is the source of law and order in the United States; but it is the Constitution as interpreted and applied by the legislatures and the court decisions that governs American life. So it was in Palestine. The oral law was not regarded as an addition to the Scripture but the legitimate interpretation of what the Scriptures contained. Thus year by year the material increased and was passed on by teacher to student.

Eventually in the second century of our era this tradition came to be reduced to written form. We call the results the rabbinical literature. This huge mass of interpretation of the Scripture, the fruit of the devoted efforts of hundreds of different scholars, was gradually ordered and codified in two forms: (*a*) Cast in the form of running commentaries on the written law, called Midrashim or Midrashes; (*b*) systematically classified on the basis of a list of subjects, called "orders"—this came to be known as Mishnah. As the years went by, several Mishnahs—all containing the same six orders of material—arose. Gradually one of them, popularly ascribed to Judah the Patriarch, gained pre-eminent, almost canonical,

rank. It then came to be the basis for further study and interpretation. The results of this process were the Talmuds, which sought to interpret and explain the Mishnah. Of the two Talmuds, the one called the Babylonian and completed in the sixth century eventually gained priority. It consists of the whole of the Mishnah, quoted literally section by section in the original Hebrew, each section being followed by the new interpretative material. This material, written in Aramaic after the editing of the Mishnah, is known as the "Gemara."

While the reduction of all this material to writing took place after Christianity had begun, the process of creation was going on much earlier. It was the consequence of the fundamental conviction that God had revealed in the Torah his whole will. Given this assumption of an unchanging law in a changing society, only two courses of action were possible. One was to retreat from the new society, to retire to the wilderness and to refuse to have anything to do with the newfangled ways. In essence that is what the so-called ascetic sects, like the Essenes and Therapeutae, and more particularly the Covenanters of Damascus, sought to do. In their camps and communities they sought to relive the days of the wilderness experience of Israel. It may also be remarked that in the course of this fancied "reliving" they introduced many ascetic notions quite alien to the genius of Judaism. But by and large these groups exerted little influence. The other and important answer to this problem of a static law in a dynamic society was given by the Pharisees.

C. Pharisees and Sadducees.—This Pharisaic answer was to adapt and modify the law to make it workable, to fit it to new conditions and experiences. Of course they did not think of themselves as innovators; indeed they could have been—and often were—scandalized by the charge. Yet it was because of this willingness to "modernize" the law that the Pharisees became the religious leaders of Israel. They were, to quote Josephus, himself a Pharisee, a "sect of the Jews who appear more religious than others, and seem to interpret the laws more accurately." [5] Or as he elsewhere explains:

What I would now explain is this, that the Pharisees have delivered to the people a great many observances by succession from their fathers, which are not written in the law of Moses; and for that reason it is that the Sadducees reject them, and say that we are to esteem those observances to be obligatory which are in the written word, but are not to observe what are derived from the traditions of our forefathers. [6]

[5] *Jewish War* I. 5. 2.
[6] *Antiquities* XIII. 10. 6.

111

The Sadducees, aristocratic and stand-pat supporters of the *status quo* in both religion and politics, simply refused to see the need for change. They closed their eyes in the fashion of fundamentalists of every age, and the problem conveniently vanished. When their temple crashed about their ears in A.D. 70, they never emerged from the wreckage.

The Pharisees honestly sought to adopt the old law to new ways, or as they would have phrased it, sought to find the answers to the new problems in the old law. Much that is adverse has been written about their casuistry and hairsplitting (cf. Matt. 15:1-9). There may well have been many Pharisees of harsh and unlovely disposition, perhaps even such as the sorry specimen in Luke 18:9-14, just as today there are many pious Christians who can make the ways of God seem very harsh and repellent. But this was not the genius of Pharisaism any more than the unfortunate attitude of their modern descendants is representative of Christianity. The aim of the Pharisee was to simplify the meaning of the will of God, not to complicate it. "Remember the sabbath day to keep it holy" is easily said. How did that apply in contemporary Jerusalem? What was work? Finespun distinctions as to what was, what was not, to be counted within the permitted maximum of two thousand cubits for a sabbath day's journey; the seeming fussiness about the ceremonial washing of hands—all this and the hundreds of other niceties which to many modern men seem so absurd and burdensome, were prompted solely by the desire to preserve God's law intact and to make its observance possible.

Thus in the case of the rule "Abide ye every man in his place, let no man go out of his place on the seventh day" (Exod. 16:29)—by interpreting the word "place" as meaning "city," not a particular house, the scribes were able to permit a man to cross the whole of Jerusalem and to continue nearly a mile beyond its border without incurring the onus of being a lawbreaker. The emphasis upon the washing of hands, against which thoughtless criticism has so often been raised, was an attempt to remove the hardship entailed in the older law which demanded not merely the bathing of the whole body but the lapse of time until sunset before the man would again be Levitically clean. These few examples are representative of the whole. The Pharisees' aim, at times of course not attained, was not to devise new and hampering restrictions in addition to those already present in the old law, but to make that law apply in circumstances far different from those which had existed in the hoary past of its origin.

IV. The Jewish Hope

Few maxims—and Judaism has evolved many of them—are more revelatory of the genius of this sturdy religion than the word of the wise man: "Whom the Lord loveth he chasteneth, and scourgeth every son whom he receiveth" (Heb. 12:6; cf. Prov. 3:12). That was a lesson which, it seemed, the whole history of the nation had taught. Through the fires of adversity God was perfecting his chosen people, was burning away their dross, was subjecting them to constant and bitter punishment, but with the purpose of fitting them for their glorious destiny.

Through sin they had fallen far short—hence slavery to one heathen overlord after another; hence also the misfortune of being scattered over the face of the earth, far from the Promised Land. Of the 4,000,000 to 4,500,000 Jews, perhaps 7 per cent of the total population of the Roman world at the time of the ministry of Jesus, scarcely 700,000 dwelt in Palestine. There were far more Jews in Alexandria than in Jerusalem; many more in Syria than in the whole of Palestine. And many who dwelt within the borders of nominally Jewish territory were a minority among their Gentile neighbors. The herds of swine mentioned in the famous story of the Gerasene demoniac (Mark 5:1-20) would scarcely have been found on Jewish soil.

In the future, when the time of testing and trial was over, when Israel had truly repented of her many sins, and as obedient sons and daughters performed the Father's will, once again the age of gold would dawn. In all phases of Jewish thought there was an amazing latitude for individual judgment; in none is this more clearly seen than in their dreams of the future. It is probably scarcely an exaggeration to say that every pious Jew was confident that good times were in store, that an era of peace and blessing, which would not prove transient and fleeting like similar periods in their now romantic and idyllic past, would in God's own good time come to pass. But while this was the common denominator of all Jewish thought, it was viewed in many different ways.

For some it was seen in terms of a restored monarchy, with a Jewish king once more established on the throne of David. For others the still vivid and bitter memories of Alexander Jannaeus [7] and, to a measure, of Herod had robbed this particular view of much of its charm, but in some circles, especially in days of

---

[7] The Hasmoneans were the tribe of Levi, rather than of Judah; it was not this fact which discredited them, however, but rather the excesses of the later kings.

adversity, it still undoubtedly had appeal. For others the dream was of a theocracy, with God himself, and not his agent, holding the actual reins. Many details were probably very vague. Of course in that day God would be worshiped by all, and in the right way; but whether this would be a result of the gradual conversion of the heathen, of their destruction by the fiat of God, or in some other way—about those details there was no agreement or certainty.

Over against this type of thinking, which may be styled "Jewish," was a totally different set of views, not Jewish or even Hebrew in origin, but gradually adopted by many Jews during their years of domination by Persia. According to this type of thought a great cataclysmic change was in store. The age would come to an abrupt close as the direct consequence of the final clash between the forces of good and evil. The world would be consumed by fire. The righteous would rise to take their places on a new earth. A final judgment would be held, presided over by an angelic figure especially sent by God for this function, and the fates of men would be settled. By the time of the beginnings of Christianity these conceptions, in no small part due to the popularity they had gained in the book of Daniel, were widely held; and the colorless phrase "son of man," which in Semitic idiom was precisely the equivalent of the Latin *homo* (man) and which chanced to be used in that apocalypse, had come to be employed of this expected supernatural final judge who would inaugurate the "age to come."

This type of thought was, of course, very different from what has been described as purely Jewish. In the "Jewish" outlook there was no place for a final judgment or a final judge. On this earth, not on a new earth arising from the ashes of the final conflagration which would bring "this age" to a close, Israel would reign and prosper. For some who saw the coming good time in terms of a restored monarchy there was often involved the picture of an anointed king. But his function was not to preside over a final judgment, nor would he be a supernatural figure; instead he would be a human being of good Jewish stock and would reign as a king. In a word the two notions—Messiah (that is, a king anointed to rule) and Son of man (an angelic visitant sent to inaugurate and preside over a final assize)—were totally distinct and mutually exclusive.

It may well be that elements of these two conflicting sets of ideas came to be confused and eventually identified. It is always hard to keep parallel notions in watertight compartments. Actually we know that years later Christians did precisely this when they came to identify their Lord as both Son of man and Messiah, and thus came to regard and use the two titles as essentially synonymous. But while it is intrinsically possible that years earlier in orthodox Jewish circles a similar confusion may have existed in some circles, there is no clear evidence that such was actually the case.

It is always unwise to seek an impression of ordered simplicity when actually matters are obscure and vague. Thus the attempt to weave all these various strands together into one common pattern and to style it "the messianic hope" is misguided. There was no one view which could by any stretch of imagination be styled "the hope"; and in many circles there was a conspicuous absence of emphasis upon the "coming one." In short the expectation was of the *age* or *era* of bliss, not of the person who was to bring it in or mark its advent. But such differences of conception must not obscure the fact that in the blood of the Jew, whether his lot was cast on a Galilean hillside or within the walls of fabled Zion, whither the tribes went up, was the steadying confidence that he was not alone but was a part of a people guarded and guided by the Lord God of hosts; that it was this God who was directing the affairs of men; and that the last chapter in the perplexing book of life—and a supremely glorious one—was yet to be written.

V. Selected Bibliography

CHARLES, R. H. *The Apocrypha and Pseudepigrapha of the Old Testament*. Oxford: Clarendon Press, 1913.

ENSLIN, MORTON SCOTT. *Christian Beginnings*. New York: Harper & Bros., 1939, pp. 1-143.

FAIRWEATHER, WILLIAM. *Jesus and the Greeks*. Edinburgh: T. & T. Clark, 1924.

GUIGNEBERT, CHARLES. *The Jewish World in the Time of Jesus*, tr. S. H. Hooke; New York: E. P. Dutton & Co., 1939.

JACKSON, F. J. FOAKES and LAKE, KIRSOPP, eds. *The Beginnings of Christianity*. London: Macmillan & Co., 1920, Vol. I.

JOSEPHUS. *The Jewish War* and *The Antiquities*, tr. H. St.J. Thackeray and Ralph Marcus; London: William Heinemann, 1926-43.

JUSTER, JEAN. *Les Juifs dans l'empire romain*. Paris: Paul Geuthner, 1914.

MOORE, GEORGE FOOT. *Judaism in the First Centuries of the Christian Era*. Cambridge: Harvard University Press, 1927.

SCHÜRER, EMIL. *A History of the Jewish People in the Time of Jesus*. New York: Charles Scribner's Sons, 1896-97.

WOLFSON, HARRY A. *Philo*. Cambridge: Harvard University Press, 1947.

THE LIFE AND MINISTRY
OF JESUS

by VINCENT TAYLOR

By reason of the greatness of Jesus and the limitations of our knowledge any attempt to describe in outline the story of his life and ministry is a perilous and presumptuous undertaking. Nevertheless the attempt is necessary if we are to form any just appreciation of his person and the effects he has produced in history and religious experience. In part the difficulty is due to the character of our historical sources. Apart from isolated notices in Josephus, Tacitus, and Suetonius, and late traditions in the Talmud, the available evidence is limited to the four Gospels and the epistles. The testimony of the Gospels is fragmentary and varied, ranging from excellent historical traditions based on the testimony of eyewitnesses to secondary narratives which are colored by later Christian belief, and in consequence it is necessary to apply to their use the accepted principles of literary and historical criticism. The nature of the sources is not, however, the main difficulty which confronts us, for there are many great figures in antiquity for the study of whose lives and teachings we have much less and much inferior evidence. The greater problem is

to do justice to the place of Jesus on the field of human history and his creative influence upon the faith, devotion, and worship of the church throughout the centuries.

The sketch which follows is based on Streeter's four-document hypothesis.[1] I shall take the Marcan outline as a framework, using material from all our sources, including valuable historical traditions embodied in the Gospel of John. In using these sources selection is unavoidable and a scientific use of imagination is necessary. It must be left to the reader to distinguish personal opinions from well-based historical inferences. Many things in the story of Jesus are mysterious and some problems are insoluble. The tests to be applied to honest

[1] B. H. Streeter, *The Four Gospels* (London: Macmillan & Co., 1924). According to this hypothesis the primary sources are Mark, the sayings-source Q, used independently by Matthew and Luke, the sayings-source M, used by Matthew, and the source L (which I believe to be a layer of tradition connected with Caesarea) combined with Q (Proto-Luke) in Luke's Gospel. Two smaller cycles of tradition complete the Synoptic sources: the narratives peculiar to Matthew and the birth stories of Luke. See also the article "The Growth of the Gospels," pp. 60-74, above.

attempts to tell that story are fidelity to the sources and a full appreciation of the wonder and greatness of Jesus.

I. The Period Before the Galilean Ministry

A. Birth and Childhood of Jesus.—Jesus was born in the closing years of Herod the Great, perhaps as early as 8 B.C., and according to early tradition in Bethlehem of Judea. If we had only the Gospel of Mark at our disposal, like its first readers we should suppose that he had been born at Nazareth (cf. Mark 1:9; 6:1), and if our only Gospel were that of John, we should not know where he was born. These considerations are enough to show that the question is not one of first importance. In view of the nature of the exquisite birth stories of Luke, and the picturesque narratives of Matthew, we shall not use their contents for a purpose for which they are not suited, except to say that with great art Luke admirably depicts the piety of the circles in which Jesus was born, and in his story of the visit of the boy Jesus to Jerusalem at the age of twelve he truly reflects the spirit of the boyhood of Jesus. "How is it that you sought me? Did you not know that I must be in my Father's house?" (Luke 2:49) tells us more than any ambitious reconstructions of his childhood could convey.

Our story begins at the point where Joseph and Mary are found settled in Galilee. To them subsequently were born four other sons, James, Joses, Judas, and Simon, and daughters whose number and names are not known (cf. Mark 6:3). Nazareth is not mentioned in the Old Testament, nor by the historian Josephus, nor in the Jewish Talmud. In itself a town of no importance, its situation among the hills of Galilee gave it a character well suited to the boyhood of Jesus. There he grew in wisdom and in years "and in favor with God and man" (Luke 2:52). From the hills above the town he could command a view of the historic plain of Esdraelon, associated with great events in the history of Israel, and crossed by caravan routes traversed by merchants and soldiers. There he gained that familiarity with nature, with birds and trees and flowers, which afterwards enriched his sayings and parables. But the incomparable gift of Nazareth was home life under the roof of Joseph and Mary. In that home, as the eldest member of a family, he came to know the meaning of comradeship and responsibility, especially if, as seems probable, Joseph died at an early age. Serving as a carpenter, making plows and yokes, he knew what life meant in its joys, its strains, and its conflicts. Little time can have been left for study, although doubtless he was taught by his parents the history and traditions of his people,

and at the school of the local synagogue he came to read and to value the law and the prophets. From his teaching we can infer that he enjoyed a close communion with his Father in prayer and meditation. Even in the early years he must have thought long and earnestly of his people and the mission he was to fulfill.

With his dreams and hopes there may have been little sympathy in the village home, for later his family went out to apprehend him in the belief that he was mad (Mark 3:20-21), and addressing his disciples, he said: "Here are my mother and my brother! Whoever does the will of God is my brother, and sister, and mother" (Mark 3:34-35). About thirty years were spent in this little Galilean town, until tidings of the ministry of John and the moving of the Spirit led him south to the river Jordan.

B. John the Baptist.—In John the Baptist, who preached and baptized in the Jordan, men heard again the long silent voice of prophecy. By his clothing and manner of life, but most of all by his uncompromising message, John showed himself to be in the succession of Elijah. The day of the Lord, he declared, of which the prophets had spoken, was at hand. "You brood of vipers!" he said to his hearers. "Who warned you to flee from the wrath to come?" (Luke 3:7.) Let them bear fruits that befit righteousness, he counseled, and not say, "We have Abraham as our father," for of the stones God was able to raise up children to Abraham. Already the ax was laid to the root of the trees, and every tree not bringing forth good fruit would be cut down and thrown into the fire. The multitudes were bidden to share their food and clothing, the taxgatherers to collect no more than their dues, and the soldiers to accuse no one falsely and to be content with their rations. In ringing tones he announced the coming of one mightier than himself, the latchet of whose shoes he was unworthy to unloose. "His winnowing fork," he said "is in his hand, to clear his threshing floor, and to gather the wheat into his granary, but the chaff he will burn with unquenchable fire" (Luke 3:17).

This stern message was made the basis of an appeal to men to repent and to signalize their repentance by submitting to the rite of baptism. Such teaching made a deep impression and evoked an astonishing response. Crowds streamed from Galilee and Judea to hear the prophet of the "end time," and confessing their sins, they were baptized by him in the Jordan (Mark 1:4-5).

Later John was arrested (see below, pp. 126-27). When from his prison at Machaerus he displayed a dawning hope that Jesus might be the Messiah, by the question: "Are you he who is to come?" Jesus said of him when the messengers had gone: "What did you go out into the wilderness to behold? A reed shaken by the wind? What then did you go out to see? A man clothed in soft raiment? Behold, those who are gorgeously appareled and live in luxury are in kings' courts. What then did you go out to see? A prophet? Yes, I tell you, and more than a prophet. This is he of whom it is written,

'Behold, I send my messenger before thy face who shall prepare thy way before thee.'

I tell you, among those born of women none is greater than John; yet," he added, "he who is least in the kingdom of God is greater than he" (Luke 7:24-28).

C. The Baptism and Temptation.—The fact that Jesus was baptized by John is one of the most certain facts of the earliest tradition. Later tradition explained that John hesitated to baptize him (Matt. 3:14-15), and the Fourth Gospel alludes to his baptism without describing it (John 1:32-33). Apparently Christians of the second and third generations found the story an embarrassment. Why had Jesus come to John and what did his baptism signify? The Gospel of Mark shows that the incident was regarded as a foreshadowing of Christian baptism: "I have baptized you with water; but he will baptize you with the Holy Spirit" (Mark 1:8). What John actually said was that whereas his baptism was a water-baptism, the Messiah would baptize men "with fire" (cf. Matt. 3:11; Luke 3:16).

The original facts are at once simpler and more obscure. Unnoticed and unknown, Jesus came with others from Galilee and was baptized in the waters of the Jordan. It is improbable that John saw anything unusual in his coming. The motives which led Jesus to undergo baptism can only be conjectured. Neither on this occasion nor on any other does he betray any consciousness of sin; it is therefore impossible to suppose that for him it was "a baptism of repentance for the forgiveness of sins." It may be that his action was one of self-dedication. He turned from the quiet life which hitherto had been his and accepted a mission which it was given to him to fulfill. It is possible also that there was a deeper motive. Not infrequently in studying the sayings of Jesus we receive the impression that like psalmists and prophets before him, his consciousness was communal as well as personal. We are reminded of the pronoun "I" in the Psalms, which may represent both the speaker and the community, and of "the servant of the Lord," who can be the nation, the righteous element in the people, or an individual in whom the ideal is embodied. Was Jesus conscious of a sense of oneness with sinful and unworthy men? Did he identify himself with

others? In the story itself there is reason to think this; and if so, the Matthaean narrative mentioned above is not without insight when in it Jesus says: "Let it be so now; for thus it is fitting for us to fulfill all righteousness" (Matt. 3:15).[2]

The story tells what happened in the soul of Jesus. The rending of the heavens and the voice of God were seen and heard by none save by him. How far the experience was visual and auditory we do not know, but that Jesus gained the certainty that he was God's Son and servant is clear. "Thou art my beloved Son; with thee I am well pleased." The words are significant, for they combine the messianic language of Ps. 2 and the servant idea of Isa. 42. It is commonly said that at his baptism Jesus gained the assurance that he was the Messiah. The Messiah he was, in his own acceptance of the term, for at the confession of Peter he tacitly accepted the title and before the priests endorsed it. But it was a name with which he was never happy because of the nationalism which endeared it to the people. He thought of himself rather as God's Son; and it is the authenticating of his filial consciousness which is the essence of the baptismal experience. "Thou art my beloved Son." The conviction was permanent. He was the Son of God in a sense to which there is no parallel among men.

The experience at the Jordan led inevitably to a season of trial. Mark suggests this when he says that straightway the Spirit drove him out into the wilderness (1:13). There in the wild uncultivated country he was "tempted by the devil" (Luke 4:2). As modern men, we would like to believe that Jesus did not accept popular beliefs in the existence of a personal head of the kingdom of evil, but sayings like Mark 3:27 and Luke 10:18 suggest the contrary. More important, however, is the experience itself. The temptations are commonly explained as three: the temptation to prove his sonship by a work of power, to reveal it by a dramatic sign, and to endorse accepted ideas of messiahship. It may be, however, that this explanation interprets the traditional threefold form of the narrative too literally, and that only one course of action is involved—the temptation to break the power of Rome and lead Israel to fulfill her divine destiny. The objection that secondary ideals can never have presented themselves to the mind of Jesus fails to do justice to the reality of his humanity. It also ignores the fact that temptation presents itself not as evil, but

[2] See John W. Bowman, *The Intention of Jesus* (Philadelphia: The Westminster Press, 1943), pp. 22-40. See also H. D. Major, T. W. Manson, C. J. Wright, *The Mission and Message of Jesus* (New York: E. P. Dutton & Co., 1938), pp. 333, 442.

as good; only by spiritual illumination is evil seen for what it is. Thus it was that Jesus cried: "Begone, Satan! for it is written,

'You shall worship the Lord your God,
and him only shall you serve'" (Matt. 4:10). The temptation tested the quality of his sonship and challenged the implications of his task as the servant of the Lord. His use of the Old Testament is significant and shows how deeply he had reflected on its teaching. The victory was decisive; but Luke shows insight when he says that the devil "departed from him until an opportune time" (4:13). Echoes of conflict persist through the story of Jesus, not only here, but also during the withdrawal to the borders of Tyre (Mark 7:24) and perhaps also in the retirement to Perea (John 10:40); they can be heard in the saying: "I have a baptism to be baptized with; and how I am constrained until it is accomplished!" (Luke 12:50), and most of all in the prayer of Gethsemane: "Abba, Father, all things are possible to thee; remove this cup from me; yet not what I will, but what thou wilt" (Mark 14:36).

D. Interval Before the Galilean Ministry.— From the Synoptic Gospels we learn nothing of what happened between the Temptation and the opening of the Galilean ministry, but the Fourth Gospel describes what has been called a preliminary Judean ministry during which Jesus met some of the disciples of John, including Andrew and an unnamed disciple (John 1:40-41). Andrew, it is recorded, brought his brother Simon to Jesus, and later Philip and Nathanael were added to the company (John 1:43-51). It has been conjectured that for a while Jesus worked together with the Baptist, but that after a disagreement concerning purifying (cf. John 3:25) they separated and carried on their ministries independently. This reconstruction is highly speculative and rests on a very slender basis. It is not even certain that Jesus taught at all during this period, or did more than converse with individuals, but it is not at all unlikely that at this time he met some of those who afterward became his disciples. That the cleansing of the temple took place at this time (cf. John 2:13-22) is doubtful, its place in the Fourth Gospel being guided by dramatic rather than historical interests. In the main the period seems to have been one of quiet preparation; it was broken by the tidings that John the Baptist had been arrested and cast into prison by Herod Antipas (Mark 1:14).

II. The Galilean Ministry

From the wealth of material which belongs to the Galilean ministry, selection is inevitable. Only a few themes indicating its character can be treated.

A. Opening of the Galilean Mission.—On hearing that John had been arrested Jesus came into Galilee and immediately began to proclaim "the gospel of God," that is, good news about God. God's time, he declared, was completed and his rule was near. Men were therefore bidden to repent and believe the good news (Mark 1:15). All this is very summarily stated by the evangelist, and much more must have been preached at this time. Indeed it is certain that many of the parables of the kingdom, scattered in various contexts in the Gospels, must have been told first during this period. Meantime Mark relates the calling of the first disciples in a story told from the standpoint of the fishermen by the lake. As he passed by, Jesus summoned them to follow him. "Come ye after me," he said, "and I will make you to become fishers of men." And without hesitation, we are told, they left their nets, and in the case of James and John, their father Zebedee with the hired servants, and went after him (Mark 1:16-20). Even if we allow for the possibility of an earlier meeting with Jesus, the dramatic character of their response is striking; and it reveals the magnetic influence which the personality of Jesus exerted upon them.

B. Message of the Kingdom.—What was this message of the kingdom which Jesus proclaimed?[3] Without some knowledge of this teaching his work remains an enigma.

The word "kingdom" in the phrase "kingdom of God" is misleading because it suggests, as the primary idea, a realm or order of society which God would establish. Undoubtedly something like this is the ultimate meaning of the kingdom, a domain in which God's will is truly done; but the primary idea in Jesus' teaching is that of the rule or reign of God. The sovereignty of God in the individual heart and in the lives of men is what Jesus meant by the kingdom. When that rule was a reality, then the kingdom would have come. Jesus began his ministry in the belief that this time was near. The kingdom of God, he said, was at hand. Several modern scholars have maintained that his distinctive message was that the kingdom had already come in himself and in his mission. In a sense this is true. When he said to the scribes, "If it is by the finger of God that I cast out demons, then the kingdom of God has come upon you" (Luke 11:20), he was undoubtedly speaking of things visible to their eyes and was claiming that his mighty works were a sign of the presence of the kingdom. But it is difficult to bring all his sayings and parables under this conception. His opening announcement, for example, was: "The king-

[3] See also article "The Teaching of Jesus: I. The Proclamation of the Kingdom," pp. 145-54.

dom of God is near," rather than "has come." In this respect he shared the conviction of John the Baptist; but a whole world of difference separated his view of the kingdom from that of John; for whereas the Baptist announced it as a prophet of doom, Jesus spoke of it as God's good gift, as the most precious of things which a man might possess. John spoke of a threshing floor and a fan and of an ax ready to strike, but Jesus pictured the joy of finding hidden treasure (Matt. 13:44) or of lighting upon a pearl of great price (Matt. 13:45-46). The kingdom had the explosive force of leaven (Matt. 13:33) and all the potency of growth found in a tiny mustard seed (Matt. 13:31-32), and it was essentially the work of God himself, for while a man might sow his seed, the blade, ear, and full corn followed beyond his knowledge, his task being to put in his sickle because the harvest was come.

These parables and many others lie strewn throughout the pages of our Gospels, for they were undated and the evangelists did not know when and in what circumstances they were first spoken; but we need not doubt that many of them were told in the first days of the Galilean ministry, for otherwise from the summary character of the announcement in Mark 1:15 and the first accounts of the synagogue preaching of Jesus, we are at a loss to know why his hearers said, "What is this? A new teaching!" (Mark 1:27), and why the report of him went out far and wide (Mark 1:28). Jesus believed that great things were happening and were about to happen. Either now or later he said to his disciples: "Blessed are the eyes which see what you see! For I tell you that many prophets and kings desired to see what you see, and did not see it, and to hear what you hear, and did not hear it" (Luke 10:23-24).

C. *Coming of the Son of Man.*—In announcing the advent of the kingdom of God did Jesus also speak of the elect community of the Son of man? [4] Usually the teaching about the Son of man is said to belong to the later ministry, and so far as the personal use of this name and its connection with suffering are concerned, this claim is valid. Only after the confession of Peter near Caesarea Philippi does Jesus begin to teach that "the Son of man must suffer" (Mark 8:31). But this usage does not exclude the possibility that he used the term earlier and in a communal sense. Jesus derived the idea from Dan. 7:13, and here it is undoubtedly communal: the one like unto "a son of man" represents "the saints of the Most High" to

[4] See T. W. Manson, *The Teaching of Jesus* (Cambridge: University Press, 1931), pp. 211-36; C. J. Cadoux, *The Historic Mission of Jesus* (New York: Harper & Bros., 1941), pp. 90-103.

whom a kingdom is given by God, "the Ancient of days" (Dan 7:27). Jesus, therefore, can have used the term to describe a community, "the little flock" to whom it was the Father's good pleasure to give the kingdom (Luke 12:32). The distribution of the relevant sayings does not preclude this possibility. Many of the sayings which speak of the coming of the Son of man are isolated sayings, or are loosely attached to parables, or again are found in eschatological discourses artificially compiled in expectation of the second coming of Christ. In principle, therefore, there can be no valid objection to placing some of them early in the story of Jesus. [5] Certainly the two ideas, the kingdom of God and the elect community, are complementary: there is no rule of God apart from those over whom it is exercised, and there is no elect community save where God reigns. Jesus could scarcely announce the one without mentioning or implying the other. It is probable, therefore, that there was a period in his preaching when Jesus spoke of the Son of man in a communal sense.

This conclusion does not exclude the possibility that later Jesus used the name in a personal sense, with respect both to his suffering and his return in glory. Unfortunately the character of the sayings tradition is such that it is difficult and perhaps impossible to decide which of the sayings are personal and which are communal, or to determine their date. In this matter much depends on whether there was a development in the thought of Jesus and whether periods can be distinguished which mark stages in this development. Much depends also on our interpretation of the mission of the twelve when Jesus sent forth his disciples, two by two, to announce that the kingdom of God was near. On general grounds such a development seems probable. At the beginning Jesus proclaims that the kingdom is near, and in a sense is present in his person and work. But he still teaches his disciples to pray that the kingdom may come. The saying "Truly, I say to you, there are some standing here who will not taste death before they see the kingdom of God come with power" (Mark 9:1) implies that the kingdom will be seen shortly, but leaves the impression that the expectation is less immediate than in the first preaching. Later, either with reference to the kingdom or the coming of the Son of man, Jesus says, "Of that day or that hour no one knows, not even the angels in heaven, nor the Son, but only the Father" (Mark 13:32). Here the day is not relegated to the distant future; it may be near;

[5] See Vincent Taylor, "The 'Son of Man' Sayings Relating to the Parousia," *Expository Times* LVIII (1946), 12-15.

but the sense of immediacy is much less pronounced, and everything is left to the Father's good pleasure.[6] The development is organic. The movement is wrongly conceived if it is pictured as the substitution of one idea for another entirely different in kind. Like the theme in a fugue, a uniting idea runs through the teaching of Jesus and all his conceptions of his mission. Phrased, harmonized, and introduced continually, it persists to the end. This idea is the rule of God. That the rule is near is the constant theme. What changes is the emphasis on the conditions on which it depends, the grasp of the means by which it comes into being.

D. Political, Social, Religious, and Economic Background.—Before considering further the Galilean ministry of Jesus, it is necessary to glance at the external conditions which provide the background against which it must be set and interpreted.[7] From 4 B.C. Galilee and Perea had been ruled over by the tetrarch Herod Antipas, "that fox," as Jesus called him (Luke 13:32), and the Transjordanian regions of Trachonitis, Gaulonitis, Batanea, and Panias by Herod Philip, who has been called "the best of the Herods." Both were the sons of Herod the Great: they ruled, not as independent monarchs, but as suzerains of the Roman Empire, and displayed marked Greco-Roman sympathies which found expression in the love of architecture, in the founding and naming of Tiberias by Antipas, and of Bethsaida Julias and Caesarea Philippi by Philip. The eldest son of Herod, Archelaus, ruled Judea until A.D. 6, but was deposed in that year after bitter complaints from his subjects to the emperor, and was replaced by successive Roman procurators who governed under the imperial *legatus* of Syria. From A.D. 26 to 36 the procurator was Pontius Pilate, a man of cruel and rapacious tendencies, swayed by political expediency and vacillating in character.

Among the Jews the principal sects were those of the Pharisees and the Sadducees. The Pharisees or "separatists" were the spiritual descendants of the Hasidim, or "pious ones," who had successfully resisted the Hellenizing policy of Antiochus Epiphanes. Many of them were also scribes, or teachers of the law, renowned for their zeal for the law and the oral traditions of their fathers and reverenced as the religious elite of the nation. Entirely different in spirit were the Sadducees, belonging mainly to the high priestly families of Jerusalem, who adhered to the teaching of the Penta-

teuch, rejected later teaching concerning angels, spirits, and the resurrection, and were anxious to maintain the political *status quo* and so to avoid conflict with the imperial power. Allied to the Pharisees, but much more extreme in their nationalistic sympathies, were those who subsequently were known as Zealots, to whose excesses the horrors of the siege of Jerusalem in A.D. 68-70 were largely due. The mass of the people, "the people of the land," as the Pharisees contemptuously called them (cf. John 7:49), sat loosely to the demands of the law, but nonetheless revered the Pharisees and despised the tax collectors who gathered the imperial dues for superiors to whom the taxes were farmed. No allusion is made in the Gospels to the Essenes, a sect of religious purists who dressed in white, lived in lonely places, submitted to frequent lustrations, rejected animal sacrifices, and turned their faces in worship to the rising sun. To these it has been suggested John the Baptist belonged, but there is no evidence for this, nor again of any contact of Jesus with them. His spiritual antecedents are to be found rather among the "quiet ones" described by Luke in the birth stories, who gave themselves to worship and prayer and looked for the coming of God's salvation (cf. Luke 1:6; 2:25, 37).

In the Gospels we see Jesus in constant contact with the scribes, Pharisees, Sadducees, and above all, the people of the land. His not infrequent allusions to the destruction of Jerusalem show that he was alive to the perils of the political situation and warned his hearers against them (cf. Mark 13:1-2; Luke 13:34-35; 21:20-21). A Zealot, Simon the Cananaean (Mark 3:18), found a place among the twelve. The relationships of Jesus with the scribes and Pharisees were not always hostile (cf. Mark 12:34; Luke 7:36; 11:37), but for the most part he lived and worked among "the great throng" who "heard him gladly" (Mark 12:37) and repeatedly crowded to hear him (Mark 1:33, 45; 2:2, 13; 3:7-12; 4:1; etc.). In most cases poor, and engaged mainly in agriculture and fishing, they accorded him a ready hearing in the towns and villages of Galilee and by the Lake of Gennesaret. They were arrested by his prophetic declaration that the kingdom of God was at hand, by the freshness and originality of his teaching, but still more by the magnetism of his personality. They were attracted by his "gracious words" (Luke 4:22), and were spellbound by the note of authority in his teaching (Mark 1:22).

E. Character of the Ministry.—It was a sound instinct which led Mark to describe a period of twenty-four hours in Jesus' ministry (Mark 1:21-39). Here more than in any part of his

---

[6] For the question of the distinction between the earlier and later views of Jesus regarding the future see Cadoux, *Historic Mission of Jesus*, pp. 183-207.

[7] See also article "New Testament Times: II. Palestine," pp. 100-13, above.

Gospel, except perhaps in the passion narrative, we have reason to rely on the tradition of "the elder" mentioned by Papias (A.D. 140) in the well-known words from his *Expositions of the Lord's Oracles:* "Mark, having become the interpreter of Peter, wrote down accurately all that he remembered of the things done and said by Christ, but not however in order." [8]

In Mark 1:21 the scene is laid at Capernaum in the synagogue on the sabbath day when Jesus taught the people. Their astonishment is mentioned at the contrast between his teaching and that of the scribes, but the subject of his teaching is not recorded. Instead the evangelist's interest is concentrated upon the interruption of "a man with an unclean spirit," who has an uncanny knowledge of something superhuman in the personality of Jesus, and asks: "What have we to do with thee, thou Jesus of Nazareth?" and defiantly adds: "Art thou come to destroy us?" (1:24.) Here at the beginning of the gospel story we are brought face to face with the contemporary view, shared by educated and uneducated alike in the ancient world, and held apparently by Jesus himself, which ascribed many ailments, and epilepsy in particular, to demon possession. Jesus treated the man on this assumption. "Be silent," he cried, "and come out of him." The word of authority prevailed. With a paroxysm and loud cries the unclean spirit came out of the man, so that all were amazed and questioned among themselves: "What is this? A new teaching! With authority he commands even the unclean spirits, and they obey him." It is not surprising that at this point Mark outstrips his narrative and records that the report of Jesus went out at once everywhere throughout Galilee.

From the synagogue Jesus went into the house of Simon and Andrew, with James and John, and when tentatively they told him of Simon's wife's mother, who was sick of a fever, he took her by the hand and raised her up. With the almost breathless note which characterizes these primitive narratives, Mark adds that the fever left her and she served them. Evening came, "when the sun did set," and the sick and demon-possessed were brought to Jesus, so that, with hyperbole Mark declares that "all the city was gathered together at the door." Many of the sick were healed and many demons cast out, and a charge to secrecy was laid upon the latter, "because," says Mark, "they knew him."

In these artless stories we are confronted with two problems which still provoke debate: the healing power of Jesus and the injunctions to secrecy which, according to Mark, he frequently

[8] Quoted, Eusebius *Church History* III. 39. 15, 16.

imposed upon the sick and their friends. In a day when the triumphs of psychotherapy are matters of common knowledge, few New Testament scholars dispute the historical character of the healing works of Jesus, but it is recognized that his methods were spiritual rather than scientific, dependent upon the secret of his personality and his unbroken fellowship with God in faith and prayer. It was "by the finger of God" (Luke 11:20), or "by the Spirit of God," as Matthew puts it (12:28), that Jesus expelled demons, and there is no better explanation of his works of healing. The commands to keep silence are for the most part historical, but in some cases may be literary in origin. In its extreme form the theory of Wrede, that these commands are a literary device on the part of Mark to account for the fact that the messiahship of Jesus was not recognized until after the Resurrection, must be rejected in the light of such stories as the confession of Peter, the Transfiguration, and the Triumphal Entry, not to speak of the reply of Jesus to Caiaphas (Mark 14:62) and the title set upon the Cross. It is true that Mark overworks the idea that Jesus concealed his messiahship, but there can be little doubt that the Master found the effects of his cures an embarrassment. Nowhere is this fact so clear as in the story which closes the group in Mark 1:21-39. Very early in the morning, a great while before it was day, Jesus slipped away from Capernaum into the wilderness for prayer. Later Simon and his friends tracked him down with the half-reproachful tidings, "Every one is searching for you"; but to them he gave the discouraging reply, "Let us go on to the next towns, that I may preach there also; for that is why I came out" (Mark 1:38). Not so easily, however, could the appeal of suffering be denied, as the story of the leper shows (Mark 1:40-45). Afflicted with a skin disease, not to be confused with modern leprosy, the man was confident that Jesus could make him clean. For reasons which can only be conjectured Jesus was angry. Nevertheless he stretched out his hand and touched him, with the authoritative word, "I will; be thou clean." Then moved with deep emotion, he bade the man keep silence and show himself to the priest with the required offering. The result was that Jesus was compelled to avoid towns. Nevertheless people came to him from every quarter.

F. Conflicts and Misunderstandings.—After an interval of some days Jesus returned to Capernaum and resumed his ministry there. From this point it is not possible to tell his story in detail, for, as compared with Mark 1:21-39, Mark 2:1-3:6 is a pre-gospel compilation arranged topically, the object being to show how inevitably Jesus came into mortal conflict with the rabbis, so that in the end the Pharisees and the Herodians conspired together to destroy him (Mark 3:6). Among the things which caused offense were his claim to pronounce the remission of sins (2:6-10), his association with taxgatherers and sinners (2:16-17), the neglect of fasting by his disciples (2:18-20), their breach of the laws of the sabbath (2:23-26), and his own action in healing on the sabbath day (3:1-5). Incidents such as these, which happened at various times and can no longer be precisely dated, are strung together in Mark 2:1–3:6 in order to answer a question which puzzled the first Christians: "How was it that Jesus, who went about doing good and proclaiming the advent of the kingdom of God, came to a shameful death at the hands of his enemies?" A similar topical collection in Mark 11:27–12:37 shows how his adversaries sought to entrap him on such issues as the exercise of his authority (11:27-33), the payment of tribute money to Caesar (12:13-17), and the question of the resurrection (12:18-27). Through the medium of such stories we can see how the opposition to Jesus steadily mounted, although Mark 2:1–3:6 mentions too early the death plot of the Pharisees and the Herodians.

We can see also the reactions which the ministry of Jesus provoked. His relatives thought him mad (Mark 3:21), and the scribes attributed his mighty works to Beelzebul and even to collusion with Satan. The reply of Jesus to this charge illustrates his power in controversy as well as the ideas he held concerning himself and his ministry. Thus he asked, "How can Satan cast out Satan?" "If a kingdom," he said, "is divided against itself, that kingdom cannot stand. And if a house is divided against itself, that house will not be able to stand. And if Satan has risen up against himself and is divided, he cannot stand, but is coming to an end" (Mark 3:23-26). If it was by Beelzebul, he countered, that he cast out devils, by whom did their sons cast them out; but if by the finger of God, then indeed had the kingdom of God come upon them. The spoiling of Satan's goods meant that he had been bound. "When a strong man, fully armed, guards his own palace, his goods are in peace; but when one stronger than he assails him and overcomes him, he takes away his armor in which he trusted, and divides his spoil" (Luke 11:21-22). It is not clear from this saying whether Jesus thought of himself or of God as the binder of the "strong man," but it is manifest that he attributed human ills to the ravages of a beaten foe and that he looked with confidence for the speedy coming of the rule of God.

In Mark 7:1-23 a further group of stories and sayings reveals the breach with the scribes. The section is arranged topically, and must have been compiled before the Gospel was written for the instruction of Christians in Rome. It is impossible now to fit its parts into the story of Jesus, for we do not know when and where the incidents happened. It is mentioned here because its contents imply a pronounced state of conflict on more fundamental issues. The scribes noticed the carelessness of the disciples about ceremonial washings, and they made it a ground of attack. "Why do your disciples not live according to the tradition of the elders, but eat with hands defiled?" (Mark 7:5.) Jesus took up the challenge. He recalled the words of Isa. 29:13: "This people honors me with their lips, but their heart is far from me." "Well did Isaiah prophesy of you hypocrites," he said with biting irony. "You leave the commandment of God, and hold fast the tradition of men" (Mark 7:8).

Either then or on another occasion he reminded them of a current scribal opinion, that if a son declared on oath that the provision he might otherwise have made for his parents was Corban, that is, devoted to God, his oath was binding. Thus, he claimed, by their tradition they made void the word of God. Subsequently Mark mentions one of the most revolutionary of the sayings of Jesus: "Hear me, all of you, and understand: there is nothing outside a man which by going into him can defile him; but the things which come out of a man are what defile him" (Mark 7:14-15). Mark comments on the saying. "Thus," he writes, "he declared all foods clean" (Mark 7:19). The comment goes beyond the immediate intention of Jesus, for otherwise the vision of Peter on the housetop at Joppa (Acts 10:9-16) and the sharp dispute at Antioch (Gal. 2:11-14) would never have happened. But Mark correctly caught the drift of Jesus' teaching and shows how inevitable the ultimate break with Judaism was.

G. Choice and Appointment of the Twelve.—The Galilean ministry had not long been in progress when Jesus took a decisive step in the choice and appointment of the twelve.

Mark 3:13 records that Jesus went up "into a mountain" and called to himself those whom he desired. The number twelve corresponds, and apparently was meant to correspond, to the twelve tribes of Israel, and indicates that Jesus meant the chosen disciples to play a part in his mission to Israel. Among the purposes of the appointment Mark mentions two: the twelve were to be in daily association with Jesus, and to receive a commission to preach and to cast out demons. It is natural to suppose that the preaching was the proclamation of the coming of the kingdom, as indeed is indicated in the narrative of the mission of the twelve (Mark 6:7-13). Authority to cast out demons meant that they were leagued with Jesus in his fight against the powers of evil (Mark 3:22-27). If, further, we are justified in relating to the twelve a saying apparently isolated in the tradition, and variously placed by Matthew and Luke, it was also his intention that the twelve should exercise functions of government in the future messianic community. In its Matthaean form (Matt. 19:28) this saying is eschatological. It is perhaps better preserved in Luke 22:29-30: "As my Father appointed a kingdom for me, so do I appoint for you that you may eat and drink at my table in my kingdom, and sit on thrones judging the twelve tribes of Israel." [9]

As Mark records them, the names of the twelve are Simon (Peter), James and John, the sons of Zebedee, Andrew, Philip, Bartholomew, Matthew, Thomas, James, the son of Alphaeus, Thaddaeus, Simon the Cananaean, and Judas Iscariot (Mark 3:16-19). Several of these are merely names to us—there is no record of any part which they played in the life of the primitive church. Moreover the later lists given by Matthew (Matt. 10:2-4) and Luke (Luke 6:14-16; Acts 1:13), while in substantial agreement with Mark's list, do not agree with it exactly, and we cannot solve the identity of Thaddaeus, Lebbaeus (mentioned by some manuscripts in Matt. 10:3), and Judas, son of James (mentioned in the Lukan lists). More important still, outside the Gospels the twelve are expressly mentioned only in Acts 6:2; I Cor. 15:5, and (in the phrase "the twelve apostles of the Lamb") in Rev. 21:14. Instead of "the twelve," we read of "the apostles," a larger body which includes not only Peter, James, and John, but others who were not of the twelve, James the Lord's brother, Paul, Barnabas, Timothy and Silas (I Thess. 2:6), Andronicus and Junias (Rom. 16:7), and others again whose names we do not know. Missionaries and witnesses of the Resurrection, these men go forth to Syria, Cyprus, Antioch, Macedonia, Achaia, and Rome, establishing new communities and laying the foundations of the church. Such are the facts. What is the explanation?

To deny the historical character of the institution of the twelve is unwarranted, so deeply is the tradition concerning them rooted in the Gospels. Apparently they were chosen for a special purpose connected with the Galilean mission, afterwards fulfilled in the mission of the twelve when, as with a fiery cross, they went out, "with no purse or bag or sandals" (Luke 22:35), to proclaim the advent of the kingdom of God. Before and after this event they seem to have been merged in the larger group of "the disciples," from whom they are distinguished in such a phrase as "those who were about him with the twelve" (Mark 4:10), and pointedly in the case of Judas Iscariot, "one of the twelve" (Mark 14:10, 20, 43).

The conclusion to be drawn is clear. The appointment of "the twelve" was of the things that pass, because its purpose was fulfilled; in the expansion of Christianity the future lay with "the apostles."

H. The Great Sermon.—After the choice of the twelve, either upon the mountain itself or more probably on a level place below (Luke 6:17), Jesus gave to his disciples a manifesto or address which has come to be known as the Sermon on the Mount.[10] Matthew has combined two different accounts (from Q and M) of the sermon, while Luke gives the Q version, but both evangelists have not unnaturally included in it isolated sayings kindred in character which could not be located exactly in the story of Jesus. It is impossible, therefore, to reconstruct the sermon in its entirety, but it is clear that it contained a number of beatitudes, in which Jesus described the mind and spirit of those who submit themselves to the rule of God and the principles which should guide their mutual relationships; probably also a group of antitheses (Matt. 5:21-48), in which notable injunctions of the law are set in contrast with new and more spiritual interpretations which with his majestic "I say unto you" he announced to his hearers; and various sayings regarding judging, almsgiving, fasting, and prayer, the Golden Rule, the practical tests of good fruits in life, and the necessity of doing the will of God. Apparently the sermon concluded with the parable of the house built upon a rock. It may well be also that the teaching about anxious care, with the counsel: "Do not be anxious about tomorrow, for tomorrow will be anxious for itself" (Matt. 6:25-34), belongs to the sermon, although Luke places it in another context (Luke 12:22-31), for it accords well with that spirit of perfect trust in God which was to be the mark of the new community.

J. Lakeside Ministry.—Although the story of daily teaching by the Sea of Galilee cannot be told in detail, we are given a living picture of its character in the summary statement of Mark 3:7-12: "Jesus withdrew with his disciples to the sea, and a great multitude from Galilee followed; also from Judea and Jerusalem and Idumaea and from beyond the Jordan and from

---

[9] See R. N. Flew, *Jesus and His Church* (New York: Abingdon Press, 1938), pp. 39-40, 105-6.

[10] See article "The Teaching of Jesus: II. The Sermon on the Mount," pp. 155-64, below.

about Tyre and Sidon a great multitude, hearing all that he did, came to him. And he told his disciples to have a boat ready for him because of the crowd, lest they should crush him; for he had healed many, so that all who had diseases pressed upon him to touch him. And whenever the unclean spirits beheld him, they fell down before him and cried out, 'You are the Son of God.' And he strictly ordered them not to make him known."

In this spirited description there is a touch of hyperbole in the list of places mentioned and in the phrasing of the confession of the demoniacs, but the uncanny insight of these demented men is rightly stressed, as well as the amazing popularity of Jesus at this stage in his ministry, illustrated by the reference to the thronging crowds and the necessity of teaching them from a boat moored near the shore.

One such day in particular is described in Mark 4:1-9, when Jesus told the parable of the sower. It may be that in his allusions to the wayside, the shallow ground, and the soil choked with thorns, Jesus was thinking of his own experiences as a teacher; but the main emphasis of the parable lies upon the amazing harvest, thirtyfold, sixtyfold, a hundredfold, which follows the sowing of the seed upon the good ground. The parable expresses his belief that despite unresponsive hearers, the field was white unto harvest (John 4:35).[11] Notable indeed is the emphasis he laid upon the need for attentive hearing: "He who has ears to hear, let him hear" (Mark 4:9). Jesus meant men not to miss the signs of the times, and above all, the proofs of God's redemptive work.

Similitudes, parables, and illustrative stories played a great part in the teaching. Apparently Mark has misconceived their purpose. Influenced by the difficulties of interpretation encountered by the church, and his own view that the true nature of Jesus was hidden during his ministry, Mark speaks of parables as if they were meant to conceal the truth. Thus he represents Jesus as saying to his disciples: "To you has been given the secret of the kingdom of God, but for those outside everything is in parables; so that they may indeed see but not perceive, and may indeed hear but not understand; lest they should turn again, and be forgiven" (Mark 4:11-12; cf. Isa. 6:9-10). At a later stage in his ministry Jesus may well have applied to his situation these words,[12] in which Isaiah describes his call from the standpoint of

his actual experiences as a prophet; but they have no bearing upon the use of parables. Parables were used to reveal the truth to attentive hearers, and Mark gives a truer estimate of their importance in the words: "With many such parables he spoke the word to them, *as they were able to hear it;* he did not speak to them without a parable, but privately to his own disciples he explained everything" (Mark 4:33-34). The real intention of Jesus is indicated in the sayings which Mark has inserted in the chapter. The place of a lamp, he taught, is on the stand, in order to give light; and if anything is hidden, it is only that in the end it should be made known (Mark 4:21-22). Everything goes to show that in various ways, by parable and pointed sayings alike, Jesus sought to convince the Galilean multitudes that the rule of God was at hand.

K. Mighty Works.—In the late afternoon of the day when Jesus told the parable of the sower, the disciples took him, just as he was, in the boat to the other side of the lake (Mark 4:35-36). One of those sudden storms of wind for which the lake is famous sprang up, and in Mark's graphic words, "the waves beat into the boat, so that the boat was already filling." In the meantime Jesus was asleep, using the wooden seat as a headrest, and in their extremity the disciples awoke him, addressing him curtly: "Master, do you not care if we perish?" Jesus awoke and rebuked the wind and said to the sea, "Peace! Be still!" And a great calm followed. "Why are you afraid? Have you no faith?" he asked his disciples. Their reply was a muttered comment among them, "Who then is this, that even wind and sea obey him?"

Such is the story, and it is told fully because it raises in an acute form the question whether Jesus wrought miracles on nature. There is probably not the slightest need to question anything recorded in the narrative. The suggestion that actually Jesus rebuked, not the wind, but the disciples, is an unsupported guess. A more naïve attitude to nature (cf. Mark 11:23), as natural to him as it is strange to the modern man, may have led him to address the elements directly in implicit dependence upon his Father's will. It is much less certain that he stilled the storm, although the comment in the boat is most natural and can have been made on the spot. The question is not settled by the argument that nature is not a closed system and that miracles are not impossible, but by the historical and doctrinal issue whether, within the limitations of his true humanity, it is likely that Jesus wrought such miracles, and whether it is not more likely that the original events have been given a miraculous interpre-

---

[11] See C. H. Dodd, *The Parables of the Kingdom* (New York: Charles Scribner's Sons, 1936), pp. 180-83.

[12] But not the closing words "and be forgiven," which agree neither with the Hebrew nor the Septuagint, but are given by Mark in a form found also in the later Jewish Targum.

tation. In the stilling of the storm it is reasonable to conclude that what happened was "a miracle of divine providence"; and if so, it is just to allow for possible secondary miraculous coloring in other narratives of the kind.

The application of this principle is valid in the two incidents which follow, the Gerasene demoniac and the raising of Jairus' daughter. Each narrative is full of vivid detail, but it is not skepticism to ask what in each case really happened.

Landing probably at Kersa, or Kursa, on the eastern shore of the lake, Jesus was met by a man afflicted with the tortures of a "disassociated personality," whom Mark (5:5) vividly describes as dwelling in the tombs, "crying, and cutting himself with stones." The details are taken from life and there is no valid reason, with Martin Dibelius,[13] to suppose that a story originally told of a Jewish exorcist has been erroneously ascribed to Jesus. The one element which as modern men we are at liberty to interpret differently is the destruction of the swine; and for this no better explanation has been offered than that the panic was occasioned by the paroxysm of the cure.

The raising of the daughter of Jairus belongs to the subsequent return of Jesus and his disciples to Galilee. Exactly where it happened we do not know, but Capernaum and Bethsaida have been conjectured. Again the narrative is full of artless details which leave upon the mind a strong impression of originality, in this case strengthened by the manner in which the story is intercalated with that of the woman with the issue of blood. In the latter narrative Mark offers the explanation that Jesus was conscious that "power had gone forth from him" at the woman's touch, but so far from ascribing a supernatural knowledge to him, he represents him as asking, "Who touched my garments?" (Mark 5:30.) What happened at the house of Jairus is one of those questions which the reader of today must settle for himself. The recalling of a living spirit from death stands in a different category from the cursing of a fig tree or the multiplying of loaves, and there is not a little in the Marcan story to encourage the opinion of those who agree with Luke when he says that "her spirit returned" (Luke 8:55). The astonishing thing about the Marcan account is that another opinion is also possible. It is probable that Mark himself interpreted the event as one of resurrection. The messengers reported that the girl was dead, the family lamented her death, and the chosen witnesses in the bed chamber were "lost in utter amazement" (Mark

5:42 Moffatt). On the other hand Jesus ignored the tidings of death and bade Jairus fear nothing; to the weeping family he said, "The child is not dead but sleeping"; and in the chamber he commanded "Talitha cumi. . . . Little girl, . . . arise." The narrative is ambiguous; one who concludes that the incident of the young man in Nain (Luke 7:11-17) was a case of premature burial, and that the facts behind the didactic drama of the raising of Lazarus (John 11:1-46) cannot be recovered, will take the view that the girl was roused from a state of coma.[14] We know too little about the moments preceding and following "death" to dogmatize on the subject.

It is not to be supposed that the four incidents treated in succession by Mark are the only events which happened during this period. After Mark 5:13, 20, 21, there are gaps during which incidents unrecorded in that Gospel can have happened. The evangelist writes on the basis of a tradition which preserved fragmentary knowledge of the movements of Jesus from one side of the lake to the other, and he has recorded in historical succession "mighty works" which stood out in the recollections of an eyewitness. Other events also, including visits to the lakeside and inland towns of Galilee, must have followed the Jairus incident, when, in the open air and in synagogues, Jesus announced the coming of the kingdom, spoke of the Son of man, and uttered his incomparable sayings and parables.

L. End of Synagogue Preaching.—From whence Jesus came to Nazareth we cannot say, for Mark's "from there" (6:1) is indeterminate. In saying that he came into "his own country" Mark anticipates the significance of the event. On the sabbath he began to teach in the synagogue. His fame had preceded him, for in their astonishment many asked, "Whence hath this man these things?" and "What is the wisdom given to him?" The meaning of his "mighty works," of which report told, was also a matter of speculation to them. No small part of their perplexity arose because they had known him in childhood and youth and knew the members of his family. "Is not this the carpenter, the son of Mary and brother of James and Joses and Judas and Simon, and are not his sisters here with us?" (Mark 6:3; cf. Luke 4:22). If Luke has recorded the same incident, the attention of the hearers is still more vividly depicted; the eyes of all were fixed upon him and all wondered at the words of grace which came from his mouth (Luke 4:20,

[13] *From Tradition to Gospel*, tr. Bertram Lee Woolf (New York: Charles Scribner's Sons, 1935), p. 89.

[14] See C. H. Turner, "The Gospel According to St. Mark," *A New Commentary on Holy Scripture*, ed. C. Gore, H. L. Goudge, and A. Guillaume (New York: The Macmillan Co., 1946), Part III, p. 69.

22). The Marcan statement that all took offense at him appears very abruptly, and implies either that accounts of different visits have been telescoped or that a provocative sermon was preached, like that which Luke describes. Jesus replied in words which then as now were proverbial: "A prophet is not without honor, except in his own country, and among his own kin, and in his own house." Luke records that the scene ended in attempted violence (Luke 4:29-30), but Mark makes the more significant statement that beyond laying his hands upon a few sick people, he was unable to do any "mighty work" and that he marveled because of their unbelief (Mark 6:5-6). This objective statement is one of the most remarkable observations which the Gospels contain, revealing as it does the reality of the humanity of Jesus, the intense emphasis which he placed upon faith, and the rising tide of criticism to which, despite the enthusiastic interest of many, he was exposed. Nowhere again is he said to have taught in a synagogue. That phase of his public activity was over. Mark 6:6 records that "he went round about the villages, teaching." We may surmise that there he received a more ready response to his message than in the larger towns and in more pronounced religious circles. It is at this point in his story that he launched the mission of the twelve, an event closely bound up with his conception of his ministry and destined to exercise a decisive influence upon it.

M. Mission of the Twelve.—At some point subsequent to the rejection at Nazareth Jesus sent forth the twelve, two by two, to announce the imminent coming of the kingdom of God.[15] Like Jesus himself (Mark 1:15), they were to go to "the lost sheep of the house of Israel" (Matt. 10:6) with the message: "The kingdom of God is come near unto you" (Luke 9:2; 10:9; Matt. 10:7), to summon men to repent, to cast out devils (Mark 6:13), and to heal the sick. The instructions given to the disciples reveal the epoch-making character of this mission.[16] Their equipment was to be reduced to the barest essentials. They were to take no bread, no wallet, no money. According to Mark, they were permitted to take a staff and sandals, but in Q even the staff and shoes are prohibited and only a single shirt is allowed (Matt. 10:10). Like Gehazi of old (II Kings 4:29), and con-trary to the immemorial custom of the East, they were to salute no man by the way. They were to accept the first hospitality that offered; to pay no attention to the kind of food provided; to bespeak peace on the house that received them; to shake off the dust under their feet against the place that would not hear them. The time was one of harvest, but the laborers were few, and they were to pray the Lord of the harvest that he would send forth laborers into his harvest (Matt. 9:37-38). They were the representatives of Jesus, so that to receive them was to receive him, and to receive Jesus was to receive him that sent him (Matt. 10:40).

Everything goes to show that the twelve were sent out under an overwhelming sense of urgency. A crisis was imminent; it was the eve of expected events. Nothing could be more mistaken than to think of their mission as a simple evangelistic tour in which, so to speak, they were "tried out" as healers and preachers. The instructions show that they were to be "like an invading army, and live on the country."[17] They were heralds of the advent of the kingdom of God. The general rejection of the "thoroughgoing eschatology" of Albert Schweitzer has tended to obscure the emphasis he rightly laid upon the crucial importance of the mission and its significance for Jesus himself. Schweitzer is fully justified in insisting that "the whole history of 'Christianity' down to the present day . . . is based on the delay of the Parousia."[18] He is mistaken in supposing that Jesus looked for the end of history in the coming of a supernatural Son of man from heaven, but not in holding that for Jesus the inbreaking of the kingdom was near. What Jesus expected, and what he sent the twelve to announce, was the speedy coming of the rule of God and the setting up of the messianic community of the Son of man. It was in this expectation that he assured his disciples that they would not have gone through the cities of Israel before the Son of man would come (Matt. 10:23).[19]

Some indication of the mind of Jesus at this time is afforded by a saying which Luke records in his account of the return of the seventy. When the disciples returned exulting that even the demons were subject unto them in his name, he replied: "I saw Satan fall like lightning from heaven" (Luke 10:18). "Rejoice not," he continued, "that the spirits are subject unto you; but rather rejoice, because your

[15] Whether Jesus also dispatched the seventy on a similar tour need not be discussed here, since this problem leaves untouched the epoch-making character of the earliest mission.

[16] Mark 6:8-11. For Q see Luke 10:2-3, 8-12, 13-16 (with parallels in Matthew); for M, Matt. 10:5-8, 9-16, 23-25; 10:40—11:1; for L, Luke 10:1, 4-7, 17-20. See Major, Manson, Wright, *Mission and Message of Jesus,* pp. 366, 471-76, 548-51.

[17] *Ibid.,* p. 473.

[18] *The Quest of the Historical Jesus,* tr. W. Montgomery (London: A. & C. Black, 1911), p. 358.

[19] The preservation of these words was due to the controversy regarding the Gentile mission, as modern criticism holds; it should be insisted, however, that they were not invented for this purpose, but reinterpreted.

names are written in heaven." These words show that during the disciples' absence Jesus had seen in vision the downfall of Satan, an idea traditionally associated with the victory of God, and that he thought of the disciples as already members of the elect community.

Was, then, the mission a failure? In a sense it was. "The disciples returned to Him; and the appearing of the Son of Man had not taken place." [20] Nevertheless Jesus did not renounce, and never renounced, his conviction that the rule of God was near, as the story of the sacramental meal in the wilderness clearly shows. Through the failure of the mission, the fate of the Baptist, and his own profound meditation upon the servant teaching in Isa. 53, Jesus was led to seek a fuller and deeper interpretation of the doctrine of the Son of man; and it is to the birth and elucidation of the conviction that the Son of man "must suffer" that we must trace his withdrawal from public teaching, and even from association with the twelve, during the period when he retired to the borders of Tyre (Mark 7:24), thence to emerge in renewed consort with his disciples in the villages of Caesarea Philippi (Mark 8:27), and finally to take the road to suffering and death at Jerusalem.

N. After the Mission of the Twelve.—What befell immediately after the mission of the twelve is one of many insoluble problems in the story of Jesus. Renewed visits to towns on or near the lake are implied by sayings like Luke 10:13-15, which speak of "mighty works" wrought in Bethsaida, Chorazin, and Capernaum. Many writers of "lives" of Christ have spoken of a waning of the favor of Jesus with the masses at this time, in consequence of which he devoted himself exclusively to the training and instruction of his disciples; but of this declining popularity the documents give no sign. On the contrary Herod is concerned at the "success" of Jesus (Mark 6:14-17); and when Jesus seeks to retire with his disciples across the lake, crowds follow from the adjacent towns and precede the boat at the point of landing (Mark 6:30-34). Even at the descent from the mount of transfiguration a great multitude surrounds the disciples (Mark 9:14-15); and, later still, when he comes into "the region of Judea and beyond the Jordan . . . crowds gathered to him again" (Mark 10:1). It is not a waning popularity which compels Jesus to regard his Galilean mission as a failure and drives him into seclusion; it is the popularity itself, and above all, its character. The people do not repent, and along with this they do not believe that the kingdom of God is at hand.

[20] Schweitzer, op. cit., p. 357.

It is in this sense that we must interpret the "woes on the Galilean towns" mentioned above: "Woe to you, Chorazin! woe to you, Bethsaida! For if the mighty works done in you had been done in Tyre and Sidon, they would have repented long ago, sitting in sackcloth and ashes. But it shall be more tolerable in the judgment for Tyre and Sidon than for you. And you, Capernaum, will you be exalted to heaven? You shall be brought down to Hades." (Luke 10:13-15.) These words, incorporated by Luke in the mission charge to the seventy, clearly belong to a time subsequent to the mission, where indeed they are placed by Matthew (11:21-24), and they bespeak a feeling of the most intense disappointment. To this same period, or to a somewhat earlier time, belongs also the saying, undated in Q: "To what then shall I compare the men of this generation, and what are they like? They are like children sitting in the market place and calling to one another,

'We piped to you, and you did not dance;
we wailed, and you did not weep.'

For John the Baptist has come eating no bread and drinking no wine; and you say 'He has a demon.' The Son of man has come eating and drinking; and you say, 'Behold, a glutton and a drunkard, a friend of tax collectors and sinners!' Yet wisdom is justified by all her children" (Luke 7:31-35). The unreceptiveness of his generation appears to have astonished Jesus, just as at Nazareth he marveled at their unbelief. Here undoubtedly is a factor of great importance in the further course of his story.

O. Herod Antipas and the Fate of John the Baptist.—What effect did the hostility of Herod Antipas and the murder of John the Baptist exert upon the mind of Jesus at this time? Some modern interpreters, notably Maurice Goguel, think that Herod's threats had not a little to do with the withdrawal of Jesus from public activity and his subsequent wanderings outside Galilean territory—his action was one of prudent flight.

When Herod first began to take a political interest in the work of Jesus we do not know, but Mark has appropriately placed the story of Herod's fears (6:14-16) immediately after the mission of the twelve. It was not, however, on the mission that Herod speculated, but on the activity of Jesus himself. People were saying that he was John the Baptist risen from the dead, others that he was Elijah returned to earth, others that he was a prophet like one of the ancient prophets. According to Mark, Herod took the first of these views, but when he said, "John, whom I beheaded, has been raised," he really meant, "It is John the Baptist all over again." Luke brings this out when he represents Herod as saying, "John I beheaded; but who is this about whom I hear such things?" (Luke 9:9.) Luke adds significantly, "And he sought to see him," and it is not at all necessary to amend this grim word to "sought to kill him," as some critics have conjectured, in order to perceive his mordant interest. Jesus was a marked man, a danger to the state.

Mark underlines this interest by relating the story of the murder of John which had happened some time before. He tells a story which, as A. E. J. Rawlinson[21] has suggested, was whispered darkly in the bazaars of Palestine: how that, stimulated by wine and wrought upon by the malice of Herodias, his brother's wife, who was angry because of John's prophetic denunciation of their adultery, Herod murdered John at the request of a dancing girl. Josephus, the historian, gives a different explanation:

Herod, who feared lest the great influence John had over the people might put it into his power and inclination to raise a rebellion (for they seemed to do anything he should advise), thought it best, by putting him to death, to prevent any mischief he might cause, and not bring himself into difficulties, by sparing a man who might make him repent of it when it should be too late.[22]

There is no need to regard the two accounts as alternatives. Herod is not the only tyrant who has combined political expediency with profligate folly. This much, however, is clear. Had it been the intention of Mark to describe the withdrawal of Jesus as "a flight from Herod," he would have stressed the political hostility of Antipas rather than his profligacy; and as a matter of fact, it is Matthew who says that "when Jesus heard [of the death of John], he withdrew from there in a boat to a lonely place apart" (Matt. 14:13). Nowhere does Mark say anything of the kind; and this is significant since he associates the Herodians with the scribes in their hostility to Jesus (Mark 3:6; 12:13).

The true attitude of Jesus to the threats of Herod comes out in Luke's story about certain Pharisees who bade him depart because Herod desired to kill him. "Go and tell that fox," he replied, " 'Behold, I cast out demons and perform cures today and tomorrow, and the third day I finish my course. Nevertheless I must go on my way today and tomorrow and the day following; for it cannot be that a prophet should perish away from Jerusalem'" (Luke 13:32-33). These are not the words of one who was likely to take to the hills as a fugitive for

his own security. In one respect only is it probable that Herod's hostility affected the plans of Jesus: it may account for Jesus' perception that messianic excitement might provoke his followers to armed revolt against Rome. Cadoux[23] has made a valuable contribution to our knowledge of the life of Jesus in warning against undervaluing his teaching upon the folly of revolution. So far as we can place this teaching, it belongs to the closing stages of his ministry; but the danger of rebellion may well have occupied his thoughts even at this earlier period, and may have been a factor in leading to his withdrawal from Galilee. The fate of John was a warning that could not be ignored. We are right to take account of every consideration which may bear upon an undeniable change in the methods and plans of Jesus; but we shall go astray unless we place first in importance the failure of the Galilean people to respond to the message of the kingdom as Jesus preached it. Why did the kingdom tarry? That question is the key to the obscure period in the ministry of Jesus to which we have now come.

P. Fellowship Meal in the Wilderness.— Where Jesus was and what he did during the mission of the twelve we are not told. All that Mark says is that the missionaries gathered themselves together and reported what they had done and taught, and that Jesus invited them to come apart to a wilderness place for rest (Mark 6:30-31). The attempt was frustrated by the people who saw them departing and met them at the place of landing. Unable to resist the silent appeal of the multitude, whom he saw as sheep not having a shepherd, Jesus began to teach the people and continued until late in the afternoon. The disciples were alarmed about the hunger of the multitude, and when Jesus bade them feed the crowd, they said somewhat sarcastically, "Shall we go and buy two hundred denarii worth of bread, and gave it them to eat?" Jesus inquired what food was available, and when the people at his command had seated themselves in companies of fifty upon the green grass, he took the loaves and fishes and gave thanks and broke them, bidding the disciples distribute them to all.

Such is the story. At an early period the incident was interpreted as a miracle, although it is curious that the only indication of this in the narrative is the statement "And they all ate, and were satisfied." It is clear also from the statement regarding the breaking and distribution of the bread that the story was thought of as in some sense an anticipation of the Last Supper (cf. Mark 6:41; 14:22). This opinion is probably connected with the original signifi-

21 *The Gospel According to St. Mark* (3rd ed.; London: Methuen & Co., 1931), p. 82.

22 *Antiquities* XVIII. 5. 2.

23 *Historic Mission of Jesus*, pp. 163-74, 266-79.

cance of the event. Schweitzer calls it "an eschatological sacrament." Jesus probably intended the fellowship meal in the wilderness to be an anticipation and a pledge of the messianic feast, which in Jewish thought was closely connected with the kingdom of God. This feast is mentioned in Isa. 25:6: "And in this mountain shall the LORD of hosts make unto all peoples a feast of fat things." There is an allusion to it in the comment of a guest who on one occasion sat at meat with Jesus, "Blessed is he who shall eat bread in the kingdom of God" (Luke 14:15); and to it Jesus himself referred at the Last Supper when he said, "Truly I say to you, I shall not drink again of the fruit of the vine, until that day when I drink it new in the kingdom of God" (Mark 14:25). The supper was literally a "Last Supper," with a new significance because it was celebrated on the eve of the Crucifixion, and apparently it had been preceded by other, and perhaps by many, meals of the same kind, when Jesus with his disciples looked forward to the perfecting of God's rule. If we may consider the feeding of the five thousand as a meal ending in an act of this sacramental character, it is clear that despite delay, Jesus had not renounced his belief in the imminence of the kingdom. It would come, and of it the meal was the pledge and seal.

Confirmation of this view is afforded by the immediate sequel to the meal. John, who also tells the story, says that Jesus perceived that the people were about to come and "take him by force, to make him a king" (John 6:15). Although Mark does not make this statement, his narrative shows that Jesus was at pains to separate his disciples from the crowd, to dismiss the people, and to retire to the mountain to pray: "Immediately he made his disciples get into the boat and go before him to the other side, to Bethsaida, while he dismissed the crowd. And after he had taken leave of them, he went into the hills to pray" (Mark 6:45-46).

From this passage it is safe to infer that Jesus was conscious of a dangerous undercurrent of messianic excitement among his disciples, stimulated against his will by his teaching and the fellowship meal in the wilderness. Hopes had been kindled that might well issue in armed revolt, against which first Antipas and then the Romans would be compelled to take action. Instead of the rule of God would come the confusion of men; instead of the elect community, red ruin. It was necessary to take his disciples aside and teach them the way of messianic suffering.

The account of what happened at Gennesaret is in complete harmony with this tragic situation. When the disciples were driven back from Bethsaida, Jesus rejoined them. Wading through the surf, he came upon them suddenly, so that at first they thought his form was that of a ghost and they cried out in fear. The wind fell and they reached the western shore from which they had started earlier in a vain quest for rest. Intense excitement greeted their return. The people "ran about the whole neighborhood and began to bring sick people on their pallets to any place where they heard he was" (Mark 6:55). The sick were laid in the market places, and sufferers sought to touch even the fringe of his garment. Nothing is said of a preaching tour and it is not certain that Jesus, as he passed through villages and towns, was accompanied by his disciples. Johannes Weiss[24] suggested that perhaps Matthew more truly follows the original source in implying that Jesus remained at the landing place to which the people came with their sick; but it is more probable that Mark records what really happened. Jesus went from place to place to see for himself. With approval M.-J. Lagrange[25] quotes Loisy's opinion that Jesus had supposed he would not be recognized, and meant at the first opportunity to continue his journey to a place where he and his disciples would be in peace and security. He feared to attract the attention of Herod in exciting the enthusiasm of the people in a region so near to Tiberias. All this is possible; but it is more probable that it was the enthusiasm itself which drove him from Gennesaret. He turned his back on a facile popularity, which to him was failure, and on a demand for signs, which he roughly rejected (Mark 8:11-13), and withdrew beyond the borders of Galilee. There, in communion with God, he sought a new orientation of his mission.

III. The Withdrawal from Galilee

With the fellowship meal in the wilderness the Galilean ministry reached its close, and we must now consider a difficult and somewhat confused period which separates it from the ministry in Jerusalem.

A. Withdrawal to the Region of Tyre.—In the light of Mark's explicit statements there can, I think, be no doubt that at this period Jesus retired for a while to the region of Tyre. The withdrawal itself is of the utmost importance for our understanding of his work and ministry, but before this question can be usefully considered it is necessary to discuss a confusion in Mark 7:24—8:26. The relevant passages concerning the withdrawal are two: "And

[24] Das älteste Evangelium (Göttingen: Vandenhoeck & Ruprecht, 1903), p. 208.

[25] Évangile selon Saint Marc (Paris: Librairie Lecoffre, J. Gabalda & Fils, 1929), p. 178.

from there he arose and went away to the region of Tyre," [26] (Mark 7:24), and "Soon after this he returned from the region of Tyre, and went through Sidon to the sea of Galilee, through the region of the Decapolis" (Mark 7:31). Between these two passages is the story of the Syrophoenician woman (Mark 7:24b-30), and after the second, the account of the cure of the deaf mute (Mark 7:32-37), and the stories of Mark 8:1-26, that is, the account of the feeding of the four thousand and its sequel.

It has long been observed that between 6:30–7:23 and 8:1-13 there is a curious parallelism: in each case a fellowship meal is followed by the crossing of the lake and a controversy with the Pharisees. This relationship may be indicated as follows:

A	B
1. 6:30-44: The feeding of the five thousand	1. 8:1-9: The feeding of the four thousand
2. 6:45-53: The crossing to Gennesaret	2. 8:10: The crossing to Dalmanutha [27]
3. 7:1-23: A controversy with the Pharisees	3. 8:11-13: A controversy with the Pharisees

The subject of the two controversies is different, but the account of the feeding of the four thousand and the subsequent crossing (B, 1 and 2) is widely believed to be a duplicate of the story of the feeding of the five thousand and the crossing to Gennesaret (A, 1 and 2). One notable gain of this critical hypothesis is that the series—a meal, a crossing, and a controversy—is doubly attested in Mark and must represent a well-remembered historical succession of events. Of the two controversy stories the first, as indicated earlier,[28] is a topical collection of stories and sayings, the contents of which might belong to almost any period in the Galilean mission. It follows, therefore, that the original series of events is A 1, A 2, B 3, that is, 6:30-53 + 8:11-13.

Where in this series are we to place the withdrawal to Tyre, 7:24-31? The opening phrase "and from there," is vague, and we can place it between 6:30-53 and 8:11-13 or after 8:11-13. Of these alternatives the second is, on the whole, better, for 8:14-19 describes a recrossing of the lake which ends at Bethsaida (8:22). If this

reconstruction is accepted, a clear account of the movements of Jesus can be given. Leaving Gennesaret after the refusal to grant the desire of the Pharisees for a sign (8:11-13), Jesus crosses to Bethsaida and from there withdraws into the region of Tyre. From this retirement, after the incident of the Syrophoenician woman, he returns to Bethsaida, and somewhere in the locality he heals the deaf mute (7:32-37) and the blind man (8:22-26) before going into the villages of Caesarea Philippi, where Peter makes his confession (8:27-33). Perhaps this reconstruction of events should not be called certain, but it seems to give the best account of an obscure period in the life of Jesus.[29]

B. Significance of the Withdrawal.—What happened during the withdrawal to the borders of Tyre? If progress in a historical inquiry consists in asking the right questions, there can be few questions more important than this. Before the withdrawal there is no evidence that Jesus associated the mission of the Son of man with suffering. Immediately afterwards in the villages of Caesarea Philippi he began to teach that "the Son of man must suffer" (Mark 8:31). There cannot be any reasonable doubt that if the idea did not come to him at that time, it was then that it fructified and became the dominating conception which determined all his future activities. This, and nothing less, is the significance of his sojourn beyond the border. It is true that Mark does not tell us of this, but for his silence there are good reasons: Mark's information concerning this period of the life of Jesus is very limited, and he makes no attempt to describe Jesus' inner thoughts; on the contrary, as already indicated, he is preoccupied by his desire to show that at this time Jesus ministered to Gentiles. Nevertheless what he does relate is in harmony with the suggestion that it was a season of spiritual illumination and discovery; and the sequel shows that such it was.

How far Jesus went into the region of Tyre is not said; he may not have gone far beyond the border. Apparently he was alone, for the disciples are not mentioned. "He entered a house, and would not have any one know it" (Mark 7:24). A desire for retirement is clearly evident and a need for reflection, just as clearly as when he departed to the wilderness after his baptism. It is not idle speculation to suggest

[26] RSV, but omitting "and Sidon" with some ancient authorities. In 7:31 Wellhausen conjectures that "through Sidon" is a misrendering of the original Aramaic for "through Bethsaida." If this conjecture can be accepted, there is no need to allow for a long and apparently purposeless journey northward across the hills and down the Jordan Valley.

[27] The exact location of Dalmanutha is not known, but it is generally believed to have been on the west shore of the lake in the neighborhood of the plain of Gennesaret.

[28] P. 121. On this same "parallelism" see also p. 758, below.

[29] The most baffling phrase in Mark's geographical statements is "through the region of the Decapolis" (Mark 7:31). Probably this phrase was added because Mark thought the feeding of the four thousand (8:1-9) took place in Gentile territory, for his desire in 7:24–8:26 is to suggest a ministry of Jesus to Gentiles, a representation which, if it could have been carried through, would have been of the greatest interest and importance to his Roman readers.

that his thoughts turned to the Galilean mission and the preaching of the kingdom, the mission of the twelve, the attitude of the people, and the delay in the coming of the elect community. Some indication of his reflections is afforded by his words to the Syrophoenician woman, "Let the children first be fed: for it is not right to take the children's bread, and throw it to the dogs" (Mark 7:27), and still more when he said, "I was sent only to the lost sheep of the house of Israel" (Matt. 15:24). Jesus was preoccupied with the thought of his mission to the Jews, and it is to this tension that the apparent harshness of his words is due; he was speaking to himself as well as to the Gentile woman. The woman herself was quick to perceive this and dared to carry his thought further. Emboldened by his reference to household dogs and his use of the word "first," she continued, "Yes, Lord; yet the dogs under the table eat the children's crumbs." Jesus was delighted by her wit. "For this saying go thy way," he said, "the devil is gone out of thy daughter"—a confident assurance rather than a miracle wrought at a distance. Mark has no other story to tell, and his silence is not surprising if Jesus was alone at the time.

In the light of what follows we may conclude that it was with tension relieved and a solution reached that he returned to his disciples. Soon after this he returned from the region of Tyre, and went through Sidon [30] to the sea of Galilee, through the region of the Decapolis" (Mark 7:31). He knew that it was not enough to summon men to repent, not enough to await God's good pleasure in the giving of the kingdom (Luke 12:32). As the prophet had long ago seen, the servant of the Lord must suffer (Isa. 53), and if the servant, then the Son of man, since the two were one. No more original or far-reaching inference has been drawn in the history of religion, and it is far more reasonable to believe that it was made by Jesus himself rather than at a later date by the Christian community, a convenient phrase which tells us nothing. We do not need to decide whether the idea was communal or personal in its reference, since probably it was both. The elect community of God was a suffering and a saving remnant, and it was his mission as head of that community, the Son of man indeed, to "suffer many things, and be set at nought" (Mark 9:12b). So, and so only, could the rule of God come. With such thoughts he left Tyrian country to rejoin his disciples. He had great things to tell them. It may not be entirely fanciful to suppose that when later he said to the deaf mute, "Ephphatha" ("Be opened"), and to the blind man,

[30] Perhaps "through Bethsaida." See footnote 26 above.

"Do you see anything?" he thought of his disciples—perhaps even of himself.

C. Confession of Peter and the Transfiguration.—Shortly after his return from Tyre, Jesus went forth with his disciples into the villages of Caesarea Philippi. As they journeyed he asked them first, "Who do men say that I am?" and then, "But who do you say that I am?" (Mark 8:27, 29.) The first question led to the second, but it may have been asked for information, since Jesus had been in retirement. It is surprising that among the answers given—John the Baptist, Elijah, one of the prophets—none indicates that he had been recognized as the Messiah. Manifestly messianic excitement ran as an undercurrent among the disciples and the immediate hearers of Jesus rather than among the mass of the people. Yet Jesus had seen the danger of the situation. At Gennesaret there was tinder which at a flash might leap into flame. It was essential, therefore, that his disciples should learn a new conception of messiahship. Thus it was that pointedly he asked: "But who do you say that I am?" Characteristically Peter answered for the rest, "You are the Christ" (Mark 8:29). Matthew records that Peter was pronounced blessed in that he had received so great a revelation (Matt. 16:18-19). Mark says nothing of this, but records that after laying upon them a ban of silence, intelligible enough in the circumstances, "he began to teach them that the Son of man must suffer many things, and be rejected by the elders and the chief priests and the scribes, and be killed, and after three days rise again" (Mark 8:31). Granting that the terms of this prediction, repeated in 9:31 and 10:33-34, have been amplified by the knowledge of subsequent events, we need not doubt that Jesus gave this teaching. Far from being a product of dogma, the belief that the Son of man "must suffer" is the keynote of his career. This view is strongly supported by the story of Peter's rebuke. "God forbid, Lord!" Peter said, "This shall never happen to you" (Matt. 16:22). It is clear that the foresight of Jesus was amply justified. His disciples did expect him to be the Davidic Messiah, a leader of revolt against the power of Rome. Seeing the rest of the disciples, Jesus turned and rebuked Peter. "Get thee behind me, Satan: for thou mindest not the things of God, but the things of men" (Mark 8:33 ERV).

With literary and historical appropriateness Mark inserts at this point sayings on cross-bearing, sacrifice, and the peril of forfeiting the soul (Mark 8:34-37). The sayings on loyalty (Mark 8:38) and the coming of the kingdom within the lifetime of some who stood by (Mark 9:1) were probably spoken earlier. Perhaps Mark felt the latter to be a fitting prelude to the story of the Transfiguration, when, six days after the confession, Jesus brought Peter, James, and John into a high mountain apart (Mark 9:2-8).

The story of the Transfiguration is difficult to interpret. Some commentators treat it as a symbolic narrative; others explain it as a post-resurrection story read back into the life of Jesus; others again, with greater probability, as a visionary experience with a historical basis. Mark's statement that "he was transformed" and Luke's words, "the appearance of his countenance was altered," are ancient explanations of phenomena which to this day are strange and mysterious. In modern speech we should prefer to say that in rapt communion with his Father, and in a situation tense as Gethsemane itself, the face of Jesus shone with heavenly light. But such language is interpretation also. To go further and to say that his "essential form" (Phil. 2:6) was disclosed is a speculation which goes beyond our knowledge. Enough to say that in an unforgettable experience the personality of Jesus was revealed in prayer in a manner only to be expressed in symbolism. At length, "heavy with sleep" (Luke 9:32), the disciples slumbered. What followed was a vision, perhaps that of Peter only, such as mystics the world over have known and attested. For such an experience all the religious and psychological antecedents were present. The vision of Moses and Elijah, the representatives of the law and the prophets, confirmed Peter's bold confession, "You are the Messiah." In accordance with Old Testament analogies the cloud was the dwelling place of God, the heavenly vehicle whence came the words: "This is my Son, my Beloved; listen to him." When the disciples awoke, they saw Jesus only. Descending from the mountain they were sure that he was God's Son and that what he said was true, but new questions were prompted, and they disputed what was meant by rising again and how the scribal view that Elijah must come first was to be interpreted. Jesus indicated that Elijah had indeed come in the person of John, and with the patience of a teacher drew their attention to the far more important question: "How is it written of the Son of man, that he should suffer many things and be treated with contempt?" (Mark 9:12b.) Not unnaturally, as in the case of Peter's confession, a charge to maintain silence was laid on the three; indeed this was imperative in view of misapprehensions all too easily aroused. Below were the nine, vainly engaged in the attempt to restore an epileptic lad who foamed at the mouth, ground his teeth, and pined away. Few more dramatic contrasts can be imagined!

D. Journey to Jerusalem.—Not long after the confession of Peter and the Transfigura-tion, Jesus with his disciples began the journey to Jerusalem which was to end with his death. It appears to have been made with many halts and interruptions. Mark indicates it in several ways but in two passages in particular: in 9:30, presumably with reference to the neighborhood of Caesarea Philippi, when he says, "They went on from there, and passed through Galilee"; and, more clearly, in 10:1: "He left there [apparently Capernaum] and went into the region of Judaea and beyond Jordan"; and, incidentally, Mark alludes to the journey in 10:17 ("into the way") and 10:32 ("they were in the way going up to Jerusalem"). Finally Jesus and his disciples passed through Jericho (Mark 10:46) and approached Jerusalem by way of Bethphage and Bethany (Mark 11:1). The memory of this journey appears to have left a deep mark on the gospel tradition. Luke makes it a turning point in the story when he writes: "When the days drew near for him to be received up, he set his face to go to Jerusalem. And he sent messengers ahead of him" (Luke 9:51); and Luke has further references to it in 13:22; 17:11; 19:11.

The purpose of the journey has been variously understood. It has been described by some as "a journey to death," and by others as a journey undertaken to begin a teaching ministry in Jerusalem. Evidence can be found for both these views, and in the circumstances it is mistaken to accept either to the exclusion of the other. Jesus knew that his ministry in Jerusalem would end in suffering and death, as his saying, "It cannot be that a prophet perish out of Jerusalem" (Luke 13:33), shows, but evidence abounds that nonetheless he still carried on a teaching ministry and engaged in controversy with the scribes and Pharisees.

The first part of the journey was made in secrecy: when he passed through Galilee, "he would not that any man should know it" (Mark 9:30); and the reason given by Mark is that again he sought to teach his disciples the secret of messianic suffering (Mark 9:31). It has been held that the three predictions of the Passion in Mark 8:31; 9:31; 10:33-34, are variants of the same tradition. If so, the tradition is triply attested; but it is just as probable that this teaching, so strange to Jewish ears, was repeated, and the statement that "they understood not the saying, and were afraid to ask him" (Mark 9:32) gives individuality to the scene. At Capernaum, Jesus gave his disciples a much-needed lesson in humility. He had observed them disputing in the way who was the greatest, and sitting down he said to them: "If any one would be first, he must be last of all and servant of all" (Mark 9:35). In the statement that he took a little child and set him in the midst of them, the use of the phrase "taking him in his arms" suggests some confusion with the story of the blessing of the children (Mark 10: 13-16) ; but similar incidents are not necessarily the same, and the use of a child as an example is distinctive of the present story. If this is so, the saying recorded only by Matthew may have been spoken on this occasion: "Truly, I say to you, unless you turn and become like children, you will never enter the kingdom of heaven. Whoever humbles himself like this child, he is the greatest in the kingdom of heaven" (Matt. 18:3-4).

The Marcan saying (9:37) on receiving little children in Christ's name may have been derived from a collection of sayings arranged by mnemonic links ("in my name," etc.) to assist catechetical instruction (Mark 9:37-50). To this collection apparently the story of the strange exorcist belonged (Mark 9:38-41; cf. "in your name" in vs. 38). Mark's use of this material shows that he lacked detailed information regarding the incidents of the journey.

From Galilee Jesus came into Samaria. Luke tells how Samaritan villagers refused him hospitality (Luke 9:51-56). James and John wanted to call down fire from heaven to consume them, but Jesus rebuked his disciples and they went to another village. Luke has included many incidents and sayings in his long account of the journey, but manifestly he had no detailed knowledge of its course. Some of the incidents he relates probably belonged to the Galilean ministry; the parables he knew were unconnected with time or place; the sayings and discourses were derived from Q. It is necessary, therefore, to return to Mark.

Omitting Samaritan incidents, Mark tells us that Jesus came "into the region of Judaea beyond Jordan" (Mark 10:1). What does this strange expression mean? Some manuscripts insert "and" before "beyond Jordan," thus distinguishing two separate localities; others read "through." Probably the latter reading is a scribal gloss, but it may show what Mark meant: Jesus came to Judea, but by way of Perea on the east side of the Jordan. F. C. Burkitt [31] conjectured that Jesus, with James and John, journeyed south through Samaria, while Peter and the rest went through Perea; but this inference is not really necessary. If it is objected that a detour through Perea would have brought Jesus into a region ruled by Herod, it may be replied that he had already gone through Galilee, and that to describe his movements as "a flight from Herod" is a dubious hypothesis.

[31] *The Gospel History and Its Transmission* (Edinburgh: T. & T. Clark, 1906), pp. 96-97.

Apart from the opening statement, Mark had little information about this part of the journey. He therefore followed the plan adopted elsewhere (Mark 2:1–3:6; 3:19b-35; 7:1-23) of assembling pronouncement stories and sayings without connecting links other than phrases like "multitudes came together again" (10:1) and "as he was going forth into the way" (10:17). First comes the question about divorce (10:2-9), to which allied sayings are added, then the blessing of the children (10:13-16), the question about eternal life (10:17-22), the discourse on riches (10:23-27), and the story concerning rewards (10:28-31). None of these narratives is strictly relevant to the circumstances of the journey, except perhaps the first, which may reflect knowledge of the adultery of Herod and Herodias, but the amount of detail is more than we should expect in purely popular stories, and it may indicate tradition derived ultimately from Peter. At what point Jesus first crossed and then recrossed the Jordan we do not know. He was following what has been called "the pilgrim way" and must have crossed the river at one of the fords which led to the road to Jericho.

E. Approach to Jerusalem.—A striking passage in Mark compensates for want of detail in his account of the approach of Jesus to Jerusalem. "And they were on the road, going up to Jerusalem, and Jesus was walking ahead of them; and they were amazed, and those who followed were afraid" (Mark 10:32). Mark's intention is to represent Jesus pressing ahead in a manner which filled his companions with a sense of awe. Elsewhere the evangelist describes the emotions of Jesus—his anger, his indignation, and his sighing—but nowhere to a degree comparable with the present passage except the statement that he began to be "greatly amazed, and sore troubled" in the story of Gethsemane. The passage is even more striking if we accept the conjecture of C. H. Turner and read the singular "he was amazed," for then the fear of the disciples is inspired by the bearing of Jesus. It is in favor of this conjecture that the accepted text compels us to distinguish two groups of people, the disciples and "they that followed." In short the conjecture brings out more pointedly what Mark appears to mean.

The words introduce the third prediction of the Passion (Mark 10:33-34). More than Mark 8:31 and 9:31, this prophecy has been adapted to the circumstances detailed in the passion narrative—the handing over to the Sanhedrin, the condemnation of Jesus, his being delivered to the Romans, the mocking, scourging, death and Resurrection. But while in its detail the passage is a "prophecy after the event," the picture of Jesus deeply moved by the shadows of impending events is lifelike in its realism.

The incident of the ambitious request of James and John (Mark 10:35-45) may have been current as an isolated story, but it is introduced with great art at this point. As a story which does them no credit, the narrative cannot be traced to pious imagination; on the contrary it rests on the best tradition. The question, "Can ye drink of the cup that I drink of? and be baptized with the baptism that I am baptized with?" (Mark 10:38), reveals the thoughts of Jesus at this time.

The death which draws nearer daily is for him more than martyrdom; it belongs to his mission to drink the cup of messianic suffering. That Jesus promises to James and John a share in his cup and baptism agrees with the communal and personal sense in which he interpreted the task of the Son of man, for it is idle to dismiss his words as foreshadowing their joint martyrdom. In particular the martyrdom of John finds most dubious support in the alleged quotation from Papias that "John the divine and James his brother were killed by the Jews." [32] The indignation of the ten and Jesus' reply are effectively related by Mark (10: 42-45) : "You know that those who are supposed to rule over the Gentiles lord it over them, and their great men exercise authority over them. But it shall not be so among you; but whoever would be great among you must be your servant, and whoever would be first among you must be slave of all. For the Son of man also came not to be served but to serve, and to give his life as a ransom for many."

These words cannot be dismissed on the ground that they are Pauline, for neither the thought nor the vocabulary is distinctively Pauline, and in any case "Paulinism" is rooted in primitive Christianity. It is wise to remember that the reference to a "ransom" is metaphorical, but equally wise not to forget that as such it is meant to convey an arresting thought. How much meaning Jesus put into the metaphor we may not be able to say, but we shall certainly be mistaken if we think that it expresses no more than the spirit of self-sacrifice. Jesus speaks as the Son of man, the head and lord of a redemptive community whose mission is to suffer and to serve, but he speaks more particularly of himself. He believes that he will suffer on behalf of and in the name of men. Fear of unethical and obsolete theories of the Atonement must not be allowed to hide from us this deep conviction of his. Such suffering is his cup and his baptism. With these thoughts he pressed on toward Jerusalem.

At Jericho, some fifteen miles from the city, incidents happened which illustrate his deep concern for the needs of men. He could not resist the appeal of suffering, and when the son of Timaeus hailed him as the "Son of David," undeterred by a cry that had unwelcome messianic associations, he healed him with the words, "Go your way; your faith has made you well" (Mark 10:52). This emphasis upon faith at this point in the story forbids us to think that when he spoke of his self-giving as a "ransom," he was speaking of a transaction in which the human response plays no part. The story of Zacchaeus (Luke 19:1-10) points more clearly in this direction, for here is a despised man in need of spiritual aid. "I must stay at your house today," said Jesus. His acceptance of a destiny of messianic suffering had only deepened that compassion for social outcasts which led the Pharisees to despise him as "a friend of tax collectors and sinners" (Luke 7: 34). In Zacchaeus Jesus saw "a son of Abraham," and to seek and restore such a man he deemed to be the heart of his mission as the Son of man (Luke 19:10).

IV. In Judea

A. *Ministry in Jerusalem.*—With the arrival of Jesus at Jerusalem we reach a point at which it is impossible to tell the story of his mission if we follow exclusively any one of the Gospels. The Gospel of Mark suggests that the sequel followed with great rapidity: a week saw the life of Jesus end in the ignominy of the Cross. There are reasons for this representation. Mark uses a very early sketch of the passion story which originally was drawn up to meet the needs of worship, instruction, and faith. Thus the story is divided into days and moves swiftly to its tragic climax. Nevertheless even in Mark there are indications of a longer ministry in Jerusalem. Jesus has friends there (11:2-6; 14:13-14) and teaches "day after day" in the temple (14:49). In Luke this impression is deepened (19:47; 21:37-38); in John it is confirmed by a series of passages in chs. 7–12, which show that the evangelist had access to a valuable source (7:10, 14, 32, 37; 8:20; 10:22, 40-42; 11:54; 12:1).

The relationships between the Synoptic and the Johannine accounts are discussed with great learning and insight by Maurice Goguel.[33] He is successful in showing that Jesus left Galilee with his disciples shortly before the feast of Tabernacles (John 7:2) in September or October, that he continued to teach in Jerusalem until the feast of the Dedication (John

[32] See Vincent Taylor, *The Gospels: A Short Introduction* (5th ed.; London: Epworth Press, 1946), pp. 101-2.

[33] *The Life of Jesus*, tr. Olive Wyon (New York: The Macmillan Co., 1933). See also the Introduction to the Gospel of John in Vol. VIII of this work.

10:22) in December, and that soon afterward he retired across the Jordan to Perea (John 10:40; 11:54), returning to the capital "six days before the Passover" for the final entry which led quickly to his arrest and death (John 12:1; Mark 11:1).[34] Within this framework we are justified in setting some of the five controversy stories in Mark 11:27-33 and 12:13-37, for like Mark 2:1–3:6, this group was compiled earlier than the Gospel itself to illustrate the conflict of Jesus with the rabbis. An artificial compilation, these historical incidents are used in Mark to describe a very crowded day, and the story gains in realism by redistribution. With considerable justification Goguel[35] conjectures that the story of the cleansing of the temple (Mark 11:15-17) belongs to this period. Its place varies in Mark, Matthew, and John, and nothing is lost by detaching it from its present connection with the legend of the withered fig tree (Mark 11:12-14, 20-23). Goguel attaches great importance to the saying regarding the destruction of the temple (Mark 14:58; 15:29; John 2:19) and argues that it was in consequence of this utterance that Jesus was compelled to withdraw to Perea and finally was condemned to death.

There can be no doubt that during this period Jesus was frequently engaged in discussion with the scribes, who sought to entrap him by their dialectical skill. Allowing for the fact that the Fourth Evangelist's deepest interests are doctrinal, and that he dramatizes the scenes he describes, we are bound to recognize how truly he pictures the ferment of opinion created by the Galilean prophet and his teaching. It is natural that messiahship was a primary issue. Some of the descriptive passages are very lifelike: "Is not this the man whom they seek to kill? And here he is, speaking openly, and they say nothing to him! Can it be that the authorities really know that this is the Christ? Yet we know where this man comes from; and when the Christ appears, no one will know where he comes from" (John 7:25-27). "Is the Christ to come from Galilee? Has not the scripture said that the Christ is descended from David, and comes from Bethlehem, the village where David was?" (John 7:41-42.) "How long will you keep us in suspense? If you are the Christ, tell us plainly" (John 10:24).

We are in the same situation in the five Marcan controversy stories mentioned above, when the scribes and elders come to Jesus in the temple and ask, "By what authority are you doing these things, or who gave you this authority to do them?" (Mark 11:28); when the Sadducees question him about the resurrection (Mark 12:18); and when Jesus turns the tables by asking, "How can the scribes say that the Christ is the son of David?" (Mark 12:35). Mark tells us that in the end no one dared to ask him a question (Mark 12:34).

From skillful argument Jesus turned to attack. Mark gives us a brief extract which shows how he arraigned the scribes in the presence of the people: "Beware of the scribes, who like to go about in long robes, and to have salutations in the market places and the best seats in the synagogues and the places of honor at feasts, who devour widows' houses and for a pretense make long prayers. They will receive the greater condemnation" (Mark 12:38-40). Using a fuller account of this polemic in the M source, Matthew shows how Jesus condemned them for their love of titles, their teaching on oaths, their scrupulosity about tithes to the neglect of justice, mercy, and faith, their concern for the outside of the cup and the plate—in a word their play acting (Matt 23:1-36; cf. Luke 11:39-52). It has been claimed that the hostility of Jesus to the scribes is overstated in the Gospels, especially by Matthew.[36] There is, it is true, another side. Mark, for example, tells of a scribe to whom Jesus said, "You are not far from the kingdom of God" (Mark 12:34), and Luke shows that sometimes Jesus was invited to dine in the houses of Pharisees (Luke 7:36; 11:37; 14:1). Pharisees indeed warned him of the murderous intentions of Herod (Luke 13:31). But a desire to be fair must not blind us to the fact that, believing sins of the spirit to be more heinous than sins of the flesh and that the observance of rules is no substitute for piety, Jesus rebuked the teachers of the law in terms of great severity.

The result was inevitable. John tells us how the Pharisees sent officers to arrest him (John 7:32), and speaks of occasions when "the Jews," presumably the rulers, took up stones to stone him (John 8:59; 10:31). In the closing scenes the bitter hostility of the hierarchy was due, not only to the belief that Jesus was a blasphemer, but also to the memory of occasions when in the presence of the people they had been worsted in the cut and thrust of argument. Meantime plots to destroy him were thwarted by his marked popularity with the masses. All the Gospels bear witness to this fact (Matt 21:46; Mark 12:12, 37; Luke 19:48; 21:38; John 7:43-49). It can have been only with popular approval that, in opposition to the vested interests of the priests, he was able to

[34] Ibid., pp. 238-50, 400-28.
[35] Ibid., pp. 412-19.

[36] See James William Parkes, Jesus, Paul and the Jews (London: Student Christian Movement Press, 1936); C. G. Montefiore, The Synoptic Gospels (2nd ed.: London: Macmillan & Co., 1927).

protest effectively against the profanation of the temple by money-changers and those who sold pigeons in its courts. "Is it not written," he cried, " 'My house shall be called a house of prayer for all the nations'? But you have made it a den of robbers" (Mark 11:17). No wonder that, baffled for the moment, they waited for an opportunity to destroy him!

B. Teaching in Jerusalem.—What form did the teaching of Jesus take in Jerusalem, and what were its principal themes? We have seen that frequently he was involved in disputes about messiahship, although the demand that he should speak plainly (John 10:24) shows that he maintained his earlier attitude of reserve. Messiahship was not the subject of his teaching but an issue arising out of it. His sayings on the night of the Last Supper (Mark 14:25; Luke 22:30) show that the kingdom of God was in his thoughts until the end. It was a sure instinct which led Matthew to include parables of the kingdom in the later chapters of his Gospel. Many of these parables have clearly been reinterpreted under the influence of the apocalyptic hopes of early Christianity, but not to such a degree that we can no longer trace their original form.[37] It is tempting to follow Matthew's lead and assign to the Jerusalem ministry parables which enjoin watchfulness (Matt. 24:45-50; 25:1-13) and fidelity (Matt. 25:14-30), but to locate such parables is mainly guesswork. We are on safer ground if we follow Mark, who connects the parable of the wicked husbandmen (Mark 12:1-11) with Jerusalem.

The parable relates that a landlord sent his slaves in turn to receive the amount due from the produce of a vineyard. In the end he sent his beloved son, but the husbandmen took and killed him. What will the owner of the vineyard do? The objection that the parable reflects the theology of the early church is not convincing.[38] It is true that in it Jesus alludes to himself, but in the circumstances this allusion is natural. The story was a pointed commentary on the situation in which he found himself. Mark says that the priests and elders sought to arrest him, "for they perceived that he had told the parable against them" (Mark 12:12). Dodd queries the originality of the reply in Mark 12:9: "He will come and destroy the tenants, and give the vineyard to others"; but it may be argued that it was just this remark which aroused the anger of the priests, and it is certainly in line with an interest in the religious and political situation of Jerusalem on the part of Jesus which marks these closing days.

This concern for the fate of the city is illustrated in a detached story which Mark has used to introduce the apocalyptic discourse in ch. 13. As Jesus came out of the temple, one of his disciples said to him, "Look, Teacher, what wonderful stones and what wonderful buildings!" Jesus replied: "Do you see these great buildings? There will not be left here one stone upon another, that will not be thrown down" (Mark 13:2). Goguel [39] thinks that Jesus was speaking of some natural catastrophe like an earthquake, but there is nothing in the story to suggest this; it is much more probable that Jesus foresaw the calamities which were to end in the fall of Jerusalem. Such sayings are probably more numerous than has been commonly supposed and there is no need to regard them as *vaticinia post eventum*.[40] Luke 17:31-37 pictures the urgent need for flight amid the horrors of warfare: "On that day, let him who is on the housetop, with his goods in the house, not come down to take them away; and likewise let him who is in the field not turn back. Remember Lot's wife. . . . I tell you, in that night there will be two men in one bed; one will be taken and the other left. There will be two women grinding together; one will be taken and the other left. And they said unto him, 'Where, Lord?' He said to them, 'Where the body is, there the eagles will be gathered together.' "

Warnings of this kind have been fused together with apocalyptic material in the discourse of Mark 13. This chapter is the despair of commentators. There can be little doubt that its basis is an apocalyptic forecast of the Parousia eagerly expected by the first Christians, a forecast which includes genuine sayings of Jesus, but by its emphasis upon premonitory signs (Mark 13:8, 14, 24) after the manner of a Jewish apocalypse, gives a wrong impression of the eschatological teaching of Jesus.[41] We are nearer to his mind in the parts of Luke 21:20-36, which are independent of Mark (Luke 21:20, 21b, 22, 23b-26a, 28, 34-36). Here Jesus speaks of "men fainting with fear and with foreboding of what is coming on the world." He bids his disciples raise their heads because their redemption would be drawing nigh, to watch at all times, and to pray that they may have strength to escape the things which

---

[37] See especially C. H. Dodd, *The Parables of the Kingdom* (New York: Charles Scribner's Sons, 1936).

[38] *Ibid.*, pp. 124-32.

[39] *Life of Jesus*, pp. 402, 419.

[40] See Cadoux, *Historic Mission of Jesus*, pp. 266-79.

[41] See R. Bultmann, *Jesus and the Word*, tr. Louise Pettibone Smith and Erminie Huntress from the author's 2nd ed., 1934 (New York: Charles Scribner's Sons, 1934), p. 39: "Jesus thus *rejects the whole content of apocalyptic speculation*, as he rejects also the calculation of the time and the watching for signs." See also T. W. Manson, *The Teaching of Jesus* (Cambridge: University Press, 1931), pp. 260-61.

would happen, and to stand before the Son of man. They themselves would be fitted for all that they would have to endure. "Settle it therefore in your minds," he said, "not to meditate beforehand how to answer." They would be given "a mouth and wisdom" which all their adversaries would not be able to withstand or contradict. And they would suffer no real harm: "But not a hair of your head will perish. By your endurance you will gain your lives" (Luke 21:18-19). Thus the Jerusalem teaching had a note of finality. Jesus feared for his generation, but was confident of the ripening purposes of God. Jerusalem would be destroyed, but the kingdom would come.[42]

Did Jesus at this time speak to his disciples of his return as the Son of man? That he did so is in every way probable. As we shall see, at his trial before Caiaphas he declared that the prophecy of Dan. 7:13 would be fulfilled: "You will see the Son of man sitting at the right hand of Power, and coming with the clouds of heaven" (Mark 14:62). If Jesus was speaking of himself, as most New Testament scholars think, the question is answered, unless the saying is rejected as unauthentic; but even if he was speaking of the messianic community, the same conclusion follows, for there can be no coming of the community which is not also accompanied by the coming of its Lord and head. Moreover we account best for the radiant expectation of the Parousia which marked the church from its birth (Acts 3:17-21; I Thess. 4:13-18; II Thess. 1:7-8; 2:1-2; etc.) if we recognize that he himself had said that he would return in glory. We also explain the confusion of the apocalyptic discourse in Mark 13, in which prophecies of political upheavals and Parousia sayings are almost inextricably mingled. In what form Jesus spoke of his return it is more difficult to say, but while the sayings are colored by Christian expectations, it is also probable that he used Old Testament imagery to describe an event for which prosaic speech fails. Doubtless also he expected that the interval would be short. And if, in fact, his return has proved to be a return in the power of his Spirit, in the life of the church, and in the believer's experience, even this, as a true fulfillment of his prophecies, does not foreclose a final consummation impossible to picture, irreverent to forecast.

But we throw out of perspective an account of the last days at Jerusalem if we suppose that the mind of Jesus was preoccupied with thoughts

about "the last things." A more immediate situation confronted him—the prospect of messianic suffering and death. All the inevitability of this destiny, upon which he had reflected at the close of the Galilean ministry, was underlined by his experience in Jerusalem; and he met this situation, as he had faced it before, by withdrawing from public teaching and controversy. The noise of Jerusalem gave place to the peace of Perea.

C. Withdrawal to Perea.—Just as Jesus was driven into the wilderness after his baptism, and just as he withdrew to the borders of Tyre at the close of the Galilean ministry, so now, after his three months' Jerusalem ministry, "he went away again across the Jordan to the place where John at first baptized" (John 10:40). There he remained and later went to the country near the wilderness, "to a town called Ephraim," where he stayed for another period of three months with his disciples (John 11:54). It cannot be accidental or unimportant that at each of three turning points in his ministry he went into retreat.

Of this sojourn our records supply no clear information, for it is impossible to recover the original facts which lie behind the dramatic and didactic account which John gives of the raising of Lazarus (John 11:1-44). The account of the meeting of the chief priests in the Sanhedrin, when Caiaphas gave his counsel that it was expedient that Jesus should be put to death, is also dramatically pictured, but it delineates with a great artist's brush the situation as the Jewish ecclesiastics saw it (John 11:45-53).

What was the significance of this withdrawal to Perea for Jesus? In the absence of explicit testimony two considerations afford ground for historical inferences. The first of these is Jesus' popularity and the embarrassment it caused him. We know sufficiently, although not completely, the issue of the Jerusalem ministry, and in greater detail what happened when Jesus returned to the city for the final entry. The Jerusalem ministry saw Jesus triumphant over his opponents and in favor with the people. It can only have been because of his great popularity with the citizens that the priests refrained from putting him under arrest; and this is exactly what our records attest (Mark 12:12; Luke 19:47-48; John 7:44; 8:20). Nevertheless Jesus can have interpreted this success only as failure; it repeated again what had already happened in Galilee. It meant that what he really taught about the kingdom of God was either not accepted or rejected as foolishness. The people of Jerusalem, no less than those of Galilee, wanted a Messiah after their own hearts. "How long will you keep us in

---

[42] For the critical problems of Luke 21 see A. M. Perry, *The Sources of Luke's Passion Narrative* (Chicago: University of Chicago Press, 1920), p. 38. See also the detailed discussion in Vincent Taylor, *Behind the Third Gospel* (Oxford: Clarendon Press, 1926), pp. 101-25.

suspense? If you are the Christ, tell us plainly" (John 10:24). The question told Jesus that he had failed. It was this perception which drove him across the Jordan, defeated by success.

Goguel has powerfully suggested the theory that it was Jesus' claim that he would destroy the temple and rebuild it in three days which drove him from the city. The words meant a rupture with Judaism, a claim that Judaism had had its day.[43] Then it was that he cried, "O Jerusalem, Jerusalem, killing the prophets and stoning those who are sent to you!" (Matt. 23:37-39; Luke 13:34-35), and promised: "You will not see me again, until you say, 'Blessed be he who comes in the name of the Lord.'" He hoped, Goguel argues, that on his return the masses would come out boldly for him and that thus he would be able to brave the opposition of the priests.

It may be that we have done less than justice to this revolutionary saying, and that its cruciality is hidden from us because Mark attributes it to false witnesses (Mark 14:56-59), but it is improbable that it gives the clue to his departure from the city. If he could look to the support of the masses later, he could look to their support then. He never lost their favor till on his return he destroyed it by his own act. Moreover, no more than in the case of the departure from Galilee, is it likely that he went to Perea for refuge. He fled, not from his foes, but from his friends.

The second consideration is the sequel to the entry. As we shall see, after that event there is no more teaching. The last appeal has failed and there was nothing left to him but to die. The view that he went to Jerusalem to die does not cover the full course of his story from the departure from Galilee, for though death lay before him, he had work still to do; but it applies precisely to the final visit. He came then to crown his ministry in death.

If these two considerations are valid, the significance of the withdrawal to Perea is manifest. He went there to ponder the secret of messianic suffering and death.

We have been too much afraid of reading doctrine into the story of Jesus, too anxious to be liberal and detached. Yet forty years ago Schweitzer showed us that there is such a thing as "dogmatic history," that is, "history as moulded by theological beliefs."[44] We shall not be tempted to read back into the thought of Jesus the scholarly theories of later times, the "ransom theory" of the early church, the "satisfaction theory" of Anselm, the "moral influence" views of Abelard, the "forensic" interpretation of the Reformation period. But we must cease to cherish the delusion that Jesus went to death without the shadow of an idea of why he must die and what ends his death would serve. His calm and confident bearing throughout all the final scenes is that of one who knows his destiny and moves on steadily to his appointed goal. Though much is still hidden from him, so that in the garden he prays that the cup may pass from him, he is convinced that all is of the Father's appointing and that his mission is summed up in one decisive act.

The unknown town of Ephraim was the crucible of his thinking. Thoughts which had long been clarifying gained the decisiveness of inevitable purpose and action. Jesus had his own "doctrine," and he shaped it among the stones of the wilderness.

V. The Passion and Resurrection

For this final part of the story we are dependent mainly upon Mark and a special passion narrative from the L tradition incorporated into Luke. With later additions Matthew follows Mark closely, and John stands nearer to the Synoptic outline than in any other part of his Gospel. The first Christians thought of the passion story in the light of the Old Testament, and in all the narratives there are details which reflect that interest and in some cases are colored by it. The note of wonder pervades the story. It is striking how rarely Jesus speaks. The first narrators rightly felt that it was enough to tell the story without pausing to comment upon it, and without making Jesus the mouthpiece of their views, as in the later apocryphal gospels.

A. Final Entry.—A few days before the Passover Jesus made a significant entry into Jerusalem. The incident is often described as the triumphal entry, but this name is misleading. The idea of a messianic demonstration finds most support in Matt. 21:1-17. Here Jesus is hailed as "the Son of David." The whole city is stirred. The blind and the lame are healed in the temple; the children cry, "Hosanna to the Son of David"; and Jesus answers the protests of the priests by saying, "Yes; have you never read,

'Out of the mouths of babes and sucklings thou hast brought perfect praise'?"

In Mark the sequel is quite different. Jesus enters the temple, looks around like any other pilgrim, and sets out for Bethany (Mark 11:11). It is clear that Matthew has embellished his source; and some indication of this is given by the reply of the crowd when the people of Jerusalem ask, "Who is this?" "This," answers the crowd, "is the prophet Jesus from Nazareth

[43] *Life of Jesus*, p. 423.
[44] *Quest of the Historical Jesus*, p. 349.

of Galilee." Manifestly the reply is not in line with the rest of the Matthaean story.

Although all the records have much in common, we gain a truer understanding of the event from Mark and Luke. In one important point Matthew and John agree in adding a reference to Zech. 9:9, a prophecy which describes the coming of a king, not as a warrior on horseback, but as one speaking peace to the nations, lowly, and riding upon an ass. Neither evangelist has fully understood the reference, for John depicts a regal figure greeted with branches of palm and hailed as "the King of Israel"; and Matthew, following a misreading of the Hebrew "an ass, even the colt of an ass," mentions two animals.

The incident appears to have been intended to forestall a messianic acclamation. Inspired by the prophecy of Zechariah, Jesus determined to enter Jerusalem in a manner which in itself would dramatize his spiritual conception of messiahship. Perhaps by previous arrangement with the owner, he dispatched two of his disciples for the colt which they found tied at the door in the open street at Bethany. Bringing it to Jesus, the disciples threw their clothes on it, and set him thereon. Many spread their clothes on the road; and others, leafy sprays which they had gathered from the fields. There is a curious restraint in the acclamation which stops just short of a messianic ovation: "Hosanna! Blessed be he who comes in the name of the Lord! Blessed be the kingdom of our father David that is coming! Hosanna in the highest!" (Mark 11:9-10.) Already the situation was growing dangerous. Luke says that some of the Pharisees urged Jesus to rebuke his disciples, but for once at least he agreed with them. "I tell you, if these were silent, the very stones would cry out" (Luke 19:40). It is common to interpret this reply as a defense of the disciples. But what if it is a cry of anguish! Jesus feels that nothing he can say, and nothing he can do, is of any effect to dispel the atmosphere of political messianism. The very stones are impregnated with it! It is in harmony with this interpretation that when the white pinnacles of the city came in sight, he wept over the city. "If thou hadst known in this day, even thou, the things which belong unto peace! but now they are hid from thine eyes!" (Luke 19:42 ERV.) The incident breaks off and passes almost unnoticed. No reference is made to it in the trial by the authorities, as would have been the case if it had been a triumphal entry. Jesus looks at the temple courts and departs. His last appeal had failed. Perhaps he had known that it would fail, but had felt that no effort must be spared to wean his followers from futile hopes. It failed, and it sealed his fate. A chill

must have fallen upon the hearts of all his friends. They remained with him for a while, hoping against hope. There was nothing else they could do. But one of the twelve, Judas, more intelligent than the rest, knew that the farce, as it seemed to him, was ended. Jesus had no intention of being a Messiah! What must he do?

Meantime Jesus retired to Bethany, or bivouacked upon the Mount of Olives (Luke 21:37). With prophetic insight he said of the woman who broke the alabaster jar of ointment upon his head, "She has done what she could; she has anointed my body beforehand for burying" (Mark 14:8).

B. The Betrayal.—The betrayal of Jesus by a chosen disciple has the pathos of a Greek tragedy. The first Christians were stunned by it. "One of the twelve," reiterates Mark (14:10, 20, 43). Matthew says that his price was thirty pieces of silver (Matt. 26:15); John charges him with habitual theft (John 12:6); we are told of his frightful end (Matt. 27:3-10; Acts 1:18-19). Attempts to excuse his dark deed are vain; yet it is not beyond understanding. A vain hope that Jesus might be forced to assert himself has been charitably suggested as a motive for the crime, but it is more likely that the act was one of disillusionment and despair. He read the secret of Jesus better than anyone else, and missed its glory completely, blinded by sight. Luke says that Satan entered into him (Luke 22:3). John says the same (John 13:27), and, in describing the supper, writes with dramatic irony: "So, after receiving the morsel, he immediately went out; and it was night" (John 13:30). Thus from the beginning men have speculated about one who has given his name to all traitors: "a Judas!"

With the insight of perfect goodness Jesus knew Judas better than anyone else. At the supper he said: "Woe to that man by whom the Son of man is betrayed! It would have been better for that man if he had not been born" (Mark 14:21). At the arrest, as a last appeal to a darkened heart, he gave him the old familiar greeting, "Friend, why are you here?" (Matt. 26:50.) [45] If, as Matthew tells, Judas cast the silver in the temple, and cried, "I have sinned in betraying innocent blood" (Matt. 27:4), it was the love of Jesus that convicted and slew him.

What was it that Judas betrayed? The well-known answer of Schweitzer,[46] that it was the messianic secret of Jesus, is not lightly to be rejected. The priests had long wanted to arrest

[45] See A. Deissmann, *Light from the Ancient East,* tr. Lionel R. M. Strachan (New York: George H. Doran Co., 1937), pp. 125-31.

[46] *Quest of the Historical Jesus,* p. 394.

him as a messianic pretender dangerous to peace, but they lacked evidence, as the incriminating question at the trial shows. There can be little doubt that they would have welcomed Judas as a witness for the prosecution. But this explanation does not exclude the older answer, that Judas betrayed the secret of the place where Jesus might be found. It is true that spies might have secured this information, but it was a great advantage to the priests that they had no need to take any steps of the kind. In the greatest secrecy, guided by a disciple, they could arrest Jesus. And this they did.

C. The Last Supper.—Like the final entry, the Last Supper has all the signs of deliberation and intention. As at Bethany, so in Jerusalem Jesus had made arrangements with a householder. "Go into the city," he said to two of his disciples, "and a man carrying a jar of water will meet you; follow him, and wherever he enters, say to the householder, 'The Teacher says, Where is my guest room, where I am to eat the passover with my disciples?' And he will show you a large upper room furnished and ready; there prepare for us" (Mark 14:13-15). From this descriptive passage it is clear that the meal which Jesus hoped to celebrate with his disciples was the feast of the Passover, and since Mark immediately goes on to describe the meal, we must infer that he identified it with the Passover, in the belief that the intention of Jesus was fulfilled. Several features in Mark are inconsistent with this view. No lamb is mentioned and there is no reference to bitter herbs. Moreover, later in the evening some of the disciples and the men who effected the arrest were carrying arms. More important still, according to the Fourth Gospel, at the time of the trial before Pilate the feast of the Passover had not yet been celebrated. The Jews "did not enter the praetorium, so that they might not be defiled, but might eat the passover" (John 18:28; cf. 19:14). There is thus a difference between Mark and John as regards the date of the Last Supper. Attempts to reconcile the two are not convincing, and accordingly we must choose between them. There can be little doubt, I think, that the Fourth Gospel is correct, supported as it is by indirect evidence supplied by Mark. But if this is so, it follows that Jesus, owing to the swift march of events, was compelled to celebrate the final meal twenty-four hours earlier than he had intended. This fact alone shows how much importance he attached to it.

The supper was no ordinary meal. Irresistibly it reminds us of the fellowship meal in the wilderness. The same verbs are used: "he *took* bread, and *blessed*, and *broke* it, and *gave* it to them" (Mark 14:22; cf. 6:41); and with reference to the wine he said, "Truly, I say to you, I shall not drink again of the fruit of the vine until that day when I drink it new in the kingdom of God" (Mark 14:25; cf. Luke 22:16). The supper, then, looked forward; it anticipated the coming of the kingdom of God. But that is not all: the eating of the bread and the sharing of the cup were more than symbolic actions; they were effective symbols pledging the disciples a share in the life of the kingdom. But even this is not all, for thus far the supper does not differ in substance from the earlier fellowship meal, or meals, in Galilee. The Last Supper is literally the last, and it has a distinctive character imposed upon it, and intentionally imposed, by Jesus himself in the light of his impending death. Taking the bread, he broke it and said: "Take; this is my body." By these words he did not intend to identify the bread with himself, in the sense that he changed its substance, but he did give to it a totally new significance—a change, in fact, of values. In virtue of his command the act of eating was to be, not merely physical, but spiritual, a means by which they might share in the power of his approaching sacrifice.

This significance is made even more explicit in the words spoken by Jesus at the giving of the cup. "This," he said, "is my blood of the covenant, which is poured out for many" (Mark 14:24; cf. I Cor. 11:25). "They all drank of it," Mark writes. Their action was meant to be the pledge of sharing in the new covenant just as surely as the Israelites were given a share in the covenant of Sinai, when Moses took blood and sprinkled it upon them (Exod. 24:8).[47] It is not to be supposed that the twelve understood at the time all that Jesus meant. It is indeed characteristic of him that he did not always aim at being immediately understood. Nor, if we believe that Jesus is likely to have been more creative than his followers, is it plausible that the story owes its origin to Greek ideas and practices. The Old Testament and the genius of Jesus himself supply all that we need to account for the narrative.

Important as the story is in its bearing upon the supreme rite of Christian worship, it is even more significant to the historian in that it is a window through which can be seen something of the mind of Jesus as he faced rejection and death.

As he approached his death, Jesus did not think of it primarily as a judicial murder or a physical tragedy, but as the means whereby a

[47] See Rudolf Otto, *The Kingdom of God and the Son of Man*, tr. Floyd V. Filson and Bertram Lee Woolf (London: Lutterworth Press, 1943), pp. 265-311. Also Vincent Taylor, *Jesus and His Sacrifice* (London: Macmillan & Co., 1937), pp. 114-42.

new covenant would be established between God and men. He would suffer as the Son of man, as the representative of the new messianic community which it was his Father's will to establish. His life, like that of the servant of God, would be poured out for many, and by his stripes they would be healed.

In this confidence he conversed with his disciples after the supper in words preserved in fragments by Luke in 22:24-38, by Mark in his account of the journey to the garden (Mark 14:26-31), and spiritually interpreted in the sublime meditation of John 14–17. With clear eyes he saw the approaching defection of Peter; and when puzzled and impetuous hearts cried, "Look, Lord, here are two swords," he answered enigmatically, "It is enough" (Luke 22:38). So at length they sang a hymn, perhaps the second part of the "Hallel," Pss. 115–118, and "went out to the Mount of Olives" (Mark 14:26).

D. Gethsemane and the Arrest.—"And they went to a place which was called Gethsemane; and he said to his disciples, 'Sit here, while I pray'" (Mark 14:32). In what simpler and more poignant words could the story be introduced?

In a phrase difficult to translate Mark says that he "began to be greatly distressed and troubled." The calm of the upper room was gone. Peter, James, and John were with him, but otherwise he was alone. It is part of the realism of the Gospels that they do not attempt to explain the agony, and in truth no one can explain it fully. We can be sure at least that his anguish was not fear of death or of punishment imposed upon him for the sins of men. For my part I do not think that we are reading the story through the spectacles of dogma if we describe his suffering as "sin-bearing," since in smaller ways that is the lot of all who love their fellows greatly. Was it possible for Jesus to see the hypocrisy of the scribes, the pride of the priests, the rapacity of the elders, the materialism of the masses, the treachery of Judas, the debauchery of Antipas, and view these things with the detachment of a philosopher? Jeremiah had said: "For the hurt of the daughter of my people am I hurt" (Jer. 8:21); and of the servant it was written "He bare the sin of many" (Isa. 53:12). As the Son of man and servant of God, he must have felt the sins of Israel as a burden he could not escape, which rather it was his mission to carry. We have no saying to this effect; the nearest is his allusion to Isa. 53 in Luke 22:37, "I tell you that this scripture must be fulfilled in me, 'And he was reckoned with transgressors'"—which is relevant if we may read the Greek which follows, "for my life draws to its end." Yet although he does not expressly speak of sin-bearing, in what other sense can we explain "the cup" which he asks to be taken away from him, but which nonetheless he is ready to drink? (Mark 14:36.) The Old Testament use of the symbol of the cup (Ps. 75:8; Isa. 51:17-23; Jer. 49:12; Lam. 4:21; Ezek. 23:31-34) makes it relevant as a description of intense suffering.

The agony was all the greater because it was unshared. The chosen three were asleep. What sorrow speaks in the words: "Simon, are you asleep? Could you not watch one hour? Watch and pray that you may not enter into temptation; the spirit indeed is willing, but the flesh is weak" (Mark 14:37-38). It is possible that the words spoken the third time should be rendered: "Still asleep? Still resting? The end is far away? The hour has come!" [48]

The arrest was made by a company, armed with swords and clubs, sent by the chief priests and led by Judas (Mark 14:43). John says that a cohort of Roman soldiers was present (John 18:12); and if there was collusion with Pilate,[49] the presence of a detachment is probable. At this point Mark records that "they all forsook him, and fled" (14:50).

E. Trial Scenes Before the Priests and Pilate.—The trial scenes are not trials in the strict sense of the term, since it is clear that the chief priests had already determined upon their course of action and wished only to give it a show of legality. In Mark the trial before the priests takes place at night and is followed by a short session the following morning. With greater probability Luke places it in the morning, and represents Jesus in custody during the night at the high priest's house, where he is roughly handled by the temple police who had effected his arrest (Luke 22:54-65). Veiling his eyes, they struck him, saying, "Prophesy! Who is it that struck you?" Meantime, within sight of his Master, Peter denied that he was a disciple or a Galilean: "Man," he said, "I do not know what you are saying." With a sense of the dramatic, Luke writes: "And the Lord turned and looked at Peter. And Peter remembered the word of the Lord" (Luke 22:61). He had indeed denied Jesus before cockcrow. Mark says that "he broke down and wept" (14:72). With this representation John is in substantial agreement. The house to which his captors led Jesus was that of Annas, who after a preliminary examination sent Jesus bound to his son-in-law Caiaphas, the high priest (John 18:13, 19, 24).

At the trial which followed, every effort was made to press the accusation that Jesus had said, "I will destroy this temple that is made

---

[48] Vincent Taylor, *Jesus and His Sacrifice*, p. 155.
[49] See Goguel, *Life of Jesus*, p. 468.

with hands, and in three days I will build another, not made with hands" (Mark 14:58). Mark thinks that the charge was false, and says that the witnesses did not agree (14:57, 59), but later he records that the same taunt was made while Jesus hung upon the Cross: "Aha! You who would destroy the temple and build it in three days, save yourself, and come down from the cross" (Mark 15:29). In any case Jesus refused to reply to the accusation. Then it was that Caiaphas put the direct challenge: "Are you the Christ, the Son of the Blessed?" (Mark 14:61.) In Matthew and in Luke, Jesus answers this question with a certain reservation, but in Mark with a direct affirmative: "I am." According to Matt. 26:64, he answers, "You have said so"; according to Luke 22:70, "You say that I am." Important manuscripts in Mark give the reply in the form: "Thou saidst that I am," and it is probable that this is the answer he gave. It was not an evasion, not even a hesitating reply, but it threw the onus on Caiaphas, as much as to say: "Yes, but the word is yours." No answer could show more clearly how much Jesus disliked the title "Messiah," not because he rejected the office, but because his interpretation of it and that of the priests were poles apart.

Jesus then went on to speak of the session of the Son of man on high and his coming with the clouds of heaven: "You will see the Son of man sitting at the right hand of Power, and coming with the clouds of heaven" (Mark 14:62). "Power," or rather "the Power," means God. The reference is to Ps. 110:1, and the phrase about the clouds is an allusion to Dan. 7:13. Matthew says that the session on high will be seen "hereafter" by the priests (Matt. 26:64). Luke describes it as a state which will obtain "from now" and omits the reference to the clouds of heaven (Luke 22:69). Probably Mark's version is more original, and in view of Mark 8:38 and 13:26, we may infer that the evangelist understood the words to refer to a spectacular return of Christ to earth. It is less certain that this was Jesus' meaning. He may have meant that the priests and their generation would live to see the messianic prophecies of Ps. 110:1: "The LORD said unto my Lord, Sit thou at my right hand," and of Dan. 7:13: "One like a son of man came with the clouds of heaven," fulfilled in history. He himself would be acknowledged as the Son of his Father, and the elect community would be established in the earth. The advantage of this interpretation is that, if it is valid, we see at once why the high priest tore his mantle and cried, "Blasphemy!" It was not blasphemy to claim to be the Messiah, but to speak calmly of sharing the throne of God and of bringing Daniel's

vision to pass, that was blasphemy indeed. No wonder Caiaphas cried: "Why do we still need witnesses? You have heard his blasphemy. What is your decision?" and that Mark writes: "And they all condemned him as deserving death" (Mark 14:63-65).

It is still a disputed question whether at this time the Sanhedrin had lost the power to pass capital sentences. The implication of the gospel narratives is that this right belonged to the Roman procurator, and in essentials the historian Mommsen says that Mark is accurate.[50] The nature of the accusation of the priests is best indicated in Luke's special source: "We found this man perverting our nation, and forbidding us to give tribute to Caesar, and saying that he himself is Christ a king" (Luke 23:2). Such a charge Pilate could not have dismissed lightly, even if he had wished to do so. It is a question for historians to debate whether he had already determined to destroy Jesus on grounds of public policy, and whether his repeated declarations in the gospel narratives that he found no crime in him, and his offer to chastise him and let him go (e.g., Luke 23:4, 16, 22), are imputed to him by later writers with an apologetic motive. In favor of this view is the character of the man, described by Agrippa I as "inflexible, merciless, and obstinate,"[51] and illustrated by the reference in Luke 13:1 to the Galileans whose blood he had mingled with their sacrifices; but in favor of the view that he hesitated to condemn Jesus is the fact that all our sources describe his vacillation, though some of them to the point of overemphasis (Matt. 27:24-26; John 19:12). The custom of releasing a prisoner at the time of the Passover (Mark 15:6; Luke 23:18-19; John 18:39) is not attested outside the Gospels, but it may nonetheless have existed; and Mark in fact accounts for the presence of the crowd by saying that they "came up and began to ask Pilate to do as he was wont to do for them" (Mark 15:8). The choice, dramatically depicted by John in the cry "Not this man, but Barabbas!" (John 18:40), has left a deep impression on the earliest tradition. It is doubly dramatic if, by the irony of history, as the Caesarean text of Matt. 27:16-17 attests, the rebel's name was "Jesus Barabbas."

The astonishing change in the crowd, from hanging upon the words of Jesus (Luke 19:48) to crying "Crucify him," is due only in part to the traditional fickleness of crowds. As Mark tells us, they were incited by the priests (Mark 15:11), and perhaps enraged at the fear of

[50] *Ibid.*, pp. 471-74.
[51] In a letter to Caligula mentioned by Philo, *On the Legation to Gaius*, 38. Cf. also Josephus *Antiquities, passim; Jewish War* II. 9:2, 3, 4.

being robbed of the release of Barabbas, but most of all disappointed at the passivity and silence of Jesus. Like Judas, they had perceived that he had no intention of being a national leader. There is no rage like that of a crowd deceived in its dearest expectations, no idol that it will not throw down when worship gives way to contempt. Only one thing must be done. "Away with him." "Crucify him."

In this amazing story, in which drama colors every page, the action of Pilate is described with deadly restraint, perhaps most of all by Luke, who records his threefold attempt to let Jesus go. "And their voices prevailed. . . . He released the man who had been thrown into prison for insurrection and murder, . . . but Jesus he delivered up to their will" (Luke 23: 23-25).

If ever a preacher thinks he lacks a sermon let him simply tell the story of the trial. It will speak for itself.

F. The Crucifixion.—The outstanding characteristic of the crucifixion narratives is their restrained realism. The dreadful facts are faithfully reported, but no attempt is made to dwell upon the details of what Cicero described as "the most cruel and hideous of punishments." [52] The scourging with loaded whips is mentioned by Mark in a single word (Mark 15:15). The mocking by the soldiers which followed is told more fully. Jesus was clothed in a purple cloak and crowned with a chaplet of thorns, while the soldiers saluted him with the words "Hail, King of the Jews," struck his head with a reed, spat upon him, and knelt down in mock homage before him (Mark 15:16-20). A similar story is told by Luke of Herod's soldiers (Luke 23:11-12) which many scholars believe to be a variant of the Marcan story, though Streeter gives good reasons for accepting it as genuine. [53]

It was the custom for a condemned man to carry the crossbeam (*patibulum*) of his own cross, and John states that Jesus did this (John 19:17), but it is probable that he was physically unable to carry it, and Mark relates that the soldiers forced a passer-by, Simon of Cyrene, to bear it for him. A genuine reminiscence is implied by this statement, for Mark mentions in passing that Simon was "coming in from the country" and was "the father of Alexander and Rufus," people who must have been known to Mark's readers (Mark 15:21; cf. Rom. 16:13). It is a welcome relief to the sheer tragedy of the story that some had compassion on Jesus. Luke tells of a great multitude of the people and of women who bewailed and lamented him, to whom Jesus said, "Daughters of Jerusalem, do not weep for me, but weep for yourselves and for your children" (Luke 23:28). Jesus was still thinking of the fate of the city. Enigmatically he said, "If they do this when the wood is green, what will happen when it is dry?" (Luke 23:31.)

The place of execution was called in Aramaic "Golgotha," from its resemblance to a skull (Mark 15:22; Luke 23:33). "And they crucified him"! The fact is recorded as barely as that. Before crucifixion, in accordance with a merciful custom, they offered Jesus a draught of drugged wine, but he refused to drink it. In the later account of Matt. 27:34 the statement that the wine was mingled with gall shows the influence of Ps. 69:21: "They gave me also gall for my meat; and in my thirst they gave me vinegar to drink." The fact that the soldiers divided his garments among them, casting lots to decide which each should take (Mark 15:24), reminded the first narrators of Ps. 22:18: "They part my garments among them, and cast lots upon my vesture." (John 19:24 cites the Septuagint verbatim.) But the action is so natural that there is no reason to suppose that this detail was suggested by the psalm. Mark expressly notes that it was the third hour, that is, about nine o'clock, when Jesus was crucified (Mark 15:25). C. H. Turner [54] prefers the Western reading, "and they watched him" (cf. Matt. 27:36; Luke 23:35), but the repetition "and they crucified him" may be deliberate. The inscription, placed according to custom on the crossbeam, "The King of the Jews," is contemptuous in its brevity, and was probably meant by Pilate to satirize the Jews rather than Jesus. John says that the chief priests wished it to be altered, but Pilate showed unexpected firmness.

Throughout the accounts the question arises how far the details reflect the interest of the first Christians in the fulfillment of Scripture, and of Ps. 22 in particular. The fact that Jesus quoted this psalm in his undoubtedly authentic cry, "My God, my God, why hast thou forsaken me?" (Mark 15:34; cf. Ps. 22:1) must have drawn their attention to this psalm, and have led them to ponder the significance of other Old Testament passages. On this question sweeping judgments are to be deprecated. Facts will have suggested allusions and in some cases allusions will have colored details. In general the signs of the influence of the Old Testament are most evident in the later Gospels of Mat-

---

[52] *The Verrine Orations* V. 64.

[53] See B. H. Streeter, "On the Trial of Our Lord Before Herod: a Suggestion," *Oxford Studies in the Synoptic Problem*, ed. W. Sanday (Oxford: Clarendon Press, 1911), pp. 229-31.

[54] "The Gospel According to St. Mark," *A New Commentary on Holy Scripture*, ed. C. Gore, H. L. Goudge, and A. Guillaume (New York: The Macmillan Co., 1946), Part III, p. 116.

thew and John. In Mark and Luke the question is most relevant in connection with the reference to the malefactors, where scribes added (in Mark 15:28 [omitted by recent versions]), "And the scripture was fulfilled which says, 'He was reckoned among the transgressors,'" and in connection with the accounts of the taunts of the chief priests and the soldiers. The taunts of the chief priests closely follow Ps. 22:7-8: "All they that see me laugh me to scorn: they shoot out the lip, they shake the head, saying, 'Commit thyself unto the LORD; let him deliver him: let him deliver him, seeing he delighteth in him'" (ERV). Here at least dramatization seems probable, especially since it is doubtful if members of the hierarchy would be present. The reference of unknown spectators to the saying about destroying the temple, and the jeers of the soldiers, are credible.

A much more important historical question concerns the seven sayings from the Cross. The Johannine sayings, "Woman, behold your son"; "Behold your mother"; "I thirst"; "It is finished" (John 19:26, 27, 28, 30) must be judged from the standpoint of the interpretative purpose which governs that Gospel. *Tetelestai,* "It is finished," is the magnificent climax of the Johannine narrative, which ends with the words, "And he bowed his head and gave up his spirit" (John 19:30). In this narrative Jesus dominates the scene to the very end. Of the three Lukan sayings: "Father, forgive them; for they know not what they do"; "Truly, I say to you, today you will be with me in Paradise"; "Father, into thy hands I commit my spirit" (Luke 23:34, 43, 46), the first is the most important, and though ill-attested, the most genuine. Textual critics are sharply divided on the question whether it is an original part of the Lukan text, but it is highly significant that Hort, who judged it to be a later addition, wrote: "Few verses of the Gospels bear in themselves a surer witness to the truth of what they record than this first of the Words from the Cross."[55] More recently Streeter has maintained that the authenticity of the saying deserves serious consideration, and he quotes with approval the suggestion of J. Rendel Harris that the passage was deleted because some Christian in the second century found it hard to believe that God could or ought to forgive the Jews.[56]

The most challenging and the most difficult of the sayings is the solitary example given by Mark, who records that after the darkness, which lasted from midday until three o'clock in the afternoon, Jesus cried with a loud voice, "Eloi, Eloi, lama sabachthani?" which means, "My God, my God, why hast thou forsaken me?" (Mark 15:34.) Nowhere are attempts to explain a saying of Jesus as a "community product" so thin and unconvincing. A saying recognized as genuine by P. W. Schmiedel, Arno Neumann, and Joseph Klausner, is not likely to be an invention. The implications of the saying are another matter. The view that Jesus was abandoned by the Father, and endured the pains of the lost, no longer merits discussion. The opposite interpretation, widely received in modern times, that, as the opening verse of a psalm which breathes the spirit of trust, the saying expresses faith rather than despair, is a reaction against older and obsolete views. On this exegesis D. F. Strauss made a pertinent comment when he observed that if the cry is a declaration of faith, it is singular that Jesus should quote the verse least adapted to his purpose.[57] The only alternative is to recognize that the saying expresses a feeling of utter desolation, a sense of abandonment and despair. T. R. Glover has finely observed that there "never was an utterance that reveals more amazingly the distance between feeling and fact."[58] This statement is true only so far as the sense of abandonment is concerned and may do less than justice to the experience of one who feels the full weight of human misery and sin as only perfect goodness can feel it.

Mark relates that some of the bystanders thought Jesus was calling for Elijah and that one ran, and putting a sponge full of vinegar on a reed, gave him to drink. But mercifully the end had come. "Jesus uttered a loud cry, and breathed his last" (Mark 15:37). The statement that the veil of the temple was torn from top to bottom is probably doctrinal in origin. Mark attached great importance to the saying of the centurion. He may have said, "Truly this man was a son of God" (Mark 15:39), but Mark reads into his words the deepest secret of the person of Christ.

So the narrative ends. At a distance looking on stood Mary Magdalene, Mary the mother of James and Salome, together with other women who had come up with Jesus to Jerusalem. At the request of Joseph of Arimathea, a member of the Sanhedrin, Pilate gave permission for burial: "And he bought a linen shroud,

[55] B. F. Westcott & F. J. A. Hort, *The New Testament in the Original Greek* (London: Macmillan & Co., 1882), Appendix, p. 68.

[56] *Four Gospels,* p. 138. For the other side see B. S. Easton, *The Gospel According to St. Luke* (Edinburgh: T. & T. Clark, 1926), p. 348; J. M. Creed, *The Gospel According to St. Luke* (London: Macmillan & Co., 1930), p. 286.

[57] *The Life of Jesus,* tr. George Eliot (5th ed.; London: Swan, Sonnenschein & Co., 1906), p. 688.

[58] *The Jesus of History* (London: Student Christian Movement Press, 1917), p. 192.

and taking him down, wrapped him in the linen shroud, and laid him in a tomb which had been hewn out of the rock; and he rolled a stone against the door of the tomb" (Mark 15:46).

G. The Resurrection.—In the most marked contrast with the continuous story of the Passion stand the fragmentary narratives of the Resurrection.[59] While from the first it was necessary to tell the passion story as a whole, in order to make it intelligible, the immediate need in the case of the Resurrection was "assurance about a new and astounding fact," namely, that Jesus had risen and had appeared to his disciples. When the time came to coordinate the original facts, the evangelists could do no more than supply the local traditions of the churches for which they wrote, traditions which vary in value and cannot in all points be reconciled. Some of the stories contain legendary details, as for example, when the risen Christ is said to have eaten a piece of broiled fish (Luke 24:42). Others are products of conscious art, as in the story of the journey to Emmaus (Luke 24:13-35), and the Johannine stories of Mary Magdalene in the garden (John 20:11-18), of Thomas (John 20:19-29), and the appearance by the Sea of Tiberias (John 21:1-14). The Marcan story of the visit of the women to the tomb (Mark 16:1-8) is a story told at Rome at a time when interest in the empty tomb had awakened.

These are imperishable narratives which will always quicken Christian interest and focus Christian belief; but they are not the primary foundations of primitive testimony. The true basis for belief in the risen Christ is the earliest Christian preaching disclosed in the Acts of the Apostles (cf. 2:24, 32; 3:15; 4:10; 10:40; etc.), the testimony of Paul (I Cor. 15:8; Rom. 1:4; etc.), and the very existence of the Christian church. What would we not give for the close of the Gospel of Mark, after the words "for they were afraid" in 16:8! Perhaps the

[59] For an explanation of this fact see Vincent Taylor, *The Formation of the Gospel Tradition* (2nd ed.; London: Macmillan & Co., 1935), pp. 59-62.

end has been lost by the accidents of time; perhaps death or imprisonment prevented Mark from supplying it; perhaps it might not have contained a tradition comparable to the best elements in that Gospel—passages in which Peter stands, as it were, only a little from us. In any case, and to our greater enrichment, we have a list of appearances, supplied by Paul with complete confidence only twenty-five years after the original events: "For I delivered to you as of first importance what I also received, that Christ died for our sins in accordance with the scriptures, that he was buried, that he was raised on the third day in accordance with the scriptures, and that he appeared to Cephas, then to the twelve. Then he appeared to more than five hundred brethren at one time, most of whom are still alive, though some have fallen asleep. Then he appeared to James, then to all the apostles. Last of all, as to one untimely born, he appeared also to me" (I Cor. 15:3-8). We have also the searching question of Paul, underlined by subsequent centuries of faith and experience, "Why is it thought incredible by any of you that God raises the dead?" (Acts 26:8.)

Not incredible as the climax of the life of Jesus, for it was not possible for death to hold him.

VI. Selected Bibliography

BOWMAN, J. W. *The Intention of Jesus.* Philadelphia: The Westminster Press, 1943.

BURKITT, F. C. *The Earliest Sources for the Life of Jesus,* 2nd ed.; London: Constable & Co., 1922.

CADOUX, C. J. *The Historic Mission of Jesus.* New York: Harper & Bros., 1943.

CASE, S. J. *Jesus.* Chicago: University of Chicago Press, 1928.

GOGUEL, MAURICE. *The Life of Jesus,* tr. Olive Wyon. London: George Allen & Unwin, 1933.

GRANT, F. C. *The Gospel of the Kingdom.* New York: The Macmillan Co., 1940.

KNOX, JOHN. *The Man Christ Jesus.* Chicago: Willett, Clark & Co., 1941.

———. *Christ the Lord.* Chicago: Willett, Clark & Co., 1945.

MACKINNON, JAMES. *The Historic Jesus.* London: Longmans, Green & Co., 1931.

THE TEACHING OF JESUS

I. THE PROCLAMATION
OF THE KINGDOM

by CLARENCE TUCKER CRAIG

According to our earliest Gospel, Jesus began his ministry with the proclamation, "The time is fulfilled, and the kingdom of God is at hand; repent, and believe in the gospel" (Mark 1:15). Though this announcement of the kingdom disappears almost completely in the Gospel of John, there can be no doubt that it was central in the teaching of Jesus. The correct understanding of what he meant by it is the key to an appreciation of the career of Jesus.

I. Background in Judaism

The idea of the kingdom of God roots in the Old Testament, although that exact phrase is not found. The term almost never appears in the Jewish Talmud, which uses instead "the coming age," "Gan Eden," or "life." It is to be found, however, in the Jewish prayers of the tannaic period, and also in the Targums (Aramaic translations of the Old Testament). The "kingdom of God" means the kingly rule or dominion of the God who is believed to be the sole God of the universe. The emphasis is upon his sovereignty rather than upon the place where that sovereignty is exercised. Still the local significance cannot be excluded.

Since all titles applied to God are derived from social analogies, it is natural that "king" was not used before the time of the actual kingdom in Israel. Jewish ideas concerning the kingship of God passed through various stages of development. We are concerned here not with a detailed reconstruction of those ideas, but with the resultant conceptions at the beginning of the Christian era. Three different aspects of the kingship of God may be isolated: (*a*) it was an eternal fact; (*b*) it was a present manifestation in the lives of men; (*c*) it was a consummation still to come in the future.

(*a*) God, the creator of heaven and earth, was king in the world which he had made. In Daniel we read, "His kingdom is an everlasting kingdom, and his dominion is from generation to generation" (4:3). The book of Enoch records the liturgical expression, "Praised be thou, O Lord and King, great and mighty in thy greatness; Lord of the whole creation of the heaven; King of Kings and God of the whole world" (84:2). This conception also manifestly underlies such words of the psalmist as "The LORD hath prepared his throne in the heavens; and his kingdom ruleth over all" (Ps. 103:19).

(*b*) But the perfect rule of God was no longer found on earth. Men had rejected him since the Flood and his full reign was confined to the heavens above. His sovereignty was reestablished on earth when Yahweh became the king of Israel. But as a result of Israel's sin, the kingdom was taken away from her and she was subjected to heathen nations. Yet the sovereignty of God did not entirely disappear, even from the earth. Where men give loyalty, trust, and obedience to God, there his rule is to be found. The later rabbis believed that whenever a pious Jew recited the Shema, or fulfilled the Torah (law), he was "taking upon himself the yoke of the kingdom."

(*c*) But so long as sin and suffering were rife, so long as God's people suffered under the heel of heathen powers, the actual rule of God was incomplete. An increasing dualism had come into the later Jewish thought. There were fallen angels as well as sinful men; countless demons peopled the world. A kingdom of evil stood in the way of any completed reign of God. But the devout looked forward to its completed consummation when "the LORD shall be King

145

over all the earth" (Zech. 14:9). This was the expectation of the later apocalyptists: "And the kingdom and dominion, and the greatness of the kingdom under the whole heaven, shall be given to the people of the saints of the Most High, whose kingdom is an everlasting kingdom" (Dan. 7:27). "Then will his government appear over all his creatures; then will the devil have an end and sorrow be done away" (Assumption of Moses 10:1).

The future consummation of the reign of God was closely related to the so-called "messianic hope" of the Jews. This was not primarily the hope of a coming messiah or anointed one. It was the restoration of the rule of God and his people. The number of passages in the Old Testament where the rule is delegated to a king of the house of David is relatively small. Though there was wide variety in the later Jewish hopes, certain main lines of development are clear. According to the earlier prophetic hope, Jews looked for a restoration in Palestine, or at least on earth, of a kingdom in which they would be compensated for their former miseries. The book of Daniel may be said to be the first writing in which a sharp separation is made between this age and the age to come, because we find there, for the first time clearly expressed, the hope of a resurrection of the dead. Participation in the coming reign would not be a prerogative of the last generation alone; many would be raised up to join in it. Since Jesus certainly believed in the resurrection of the dead, his hope cannot be identified with that of the earlier prophets who shared no such expectation. Acceptance of this expectation had in the two centuries before Christ led to the adoption of various otherworldly conceptions of God's kingly rule. In some of the apocalyptic literature the hope is of Paradise, or a heavenly Jerusalem, or some other form of transcendental salvation. In others it is of a transformed earth.

No words about the Messiah or the messianic age are preserved from rabbis who belonged to the period before the national catastrophe in A.D. 70. The teaching preserved from the later rabbis corresponds with that in II Esdras and II Baruch in presenting a double form of hope. Between this age and the age to come, which are separated by the resurrection and the judgment, fall the "days of the Messiah." These days have sometimes been characterized as "the Jewish good time." This form of hope provided a compromise between national dreams of glory and power, and the more developed religious conceptions of salvation as a condition not bounded by earthly limitations. Christian developments of this belief in two periods of future bliss are to be found in Paul (I Cor.

15:23-28) and in the Revelation of John (20:2-7), where the duration of this intermediate period is put at one thousand years.

When Jesus used the phrase "the kingdom of God" in the eschatological sense, did he refer to "the days of the Messiah" or to "the age to come"? There is only one passage in the Synoptic Gospels which would suggest two periods. In Mark 10:29-30 those who have suffered for the sake of the gospel are promised a reward "in this time"; in the age to come they will obtain eternal life. "This time" probably refers to the period of the church in Mark's own day, when persecutions were being suffered. The preaching of Jesus dealt with the age to come rather than with the days of the Messiah.

Most Jews were in agreement that the kingship of God must come through the act of God himself; the consummation of his rule would come through his saving power. Only the adherents of the "fourth philosophy" (later called "Zealots") believed that they could force the hand of God by active revolt. But there were also Pharisees who taught that if Israel would keep two sabbaths perfectly, God would send his kingdom. The kingdom presented a social hope in that a new society would come among men. It was not social, however, in the sense of involving a program of social reconstruction through the agency of men. The kingdom was not a human project, but God's salvation.

II. Usage in the Synoptic Gospels

Many different terms are used for this concept in the first three Gospels. Only Matthew employs the "kingdom of heaven." This does not mean a kingdom *in* heaven; the expression is to be considered simply as an effort to avoid the use of the divine name. Sometimes the kingdom is the "kingdom of the Son of man" or "the kingdom of Christ" (Matt. 13:41; 16:28; Luke 23:42). Sometimes it is the "kingdom of the Father" (Matt. 13:43; Luke 12:32). Often it is simply "the kingdom," without further designation (Matt. 4:23; 9:35; 13:19; 24:14). All of these phrases refer to the same expectation.

Six times the word "kingdom" is put on the lips of others than Jesus (Matt. 3:2; 20:21; Mark 11:10; Luke 14:15; 23:42, 51). While these represent usages familiar to the evangelists, they would not necessarily agree with the conceptions ascribed to Jesus. Also, some of the words attributed to Jesus by the evangelists probably represent later developments rather than actual words of the historic Jesus. Stress upon the delay of the kingdom (Luke 19:11) and upon apocalyptic signs of the end (Luke 21:31) reflect a later time; the same may be true of the most explicit words of repudiation of the Jews (Matt. 21:43).

There is no uniformity among the evangelists as to the occasions where the word "kingdom" is used. Only Matthew in 3:2 ascribes its use to John the Baptist. Luke has the saying contrasting those who "do" and those who say "Lord, Lord," but he does not relate it, as Matthew does, to the kingdom (Luke 6:46). Matthew in 18:9 speaks of "entering into life" rather than "into the kingdom," as his Marcan source read. On the other hand he changes "glory" (Mark 10:37) to "kingdom" (Matt. 20:21). It is clear from this variety of usage that no purely linguistic study can isolate the teaching of Jesus about the kingdom.

The most characteristic form of Jesus' teaching was the parable. Eleven times parables are introduced by some such phrase as "the kingdom of heaven is like." Two are in Mark (4:26, 30); one of these and an additional parable are in passages usually assigned to Q (Matt. 13:31, 33); the other eight are peculiar to Matthew (13:24, 44, 45, 47; 18:23; 20:1; 22:2; 25:1). Particularly for Matthew does this appear to be a stock formula. He uses it not only to introduce the parables which he adds in ch. 13 to the collection in Mark, but likewise in his parables of grace and judgment. In the similar parables in Luke the phrase is never used. If the central message of Jesus concerned the kingdom of God, Matthew apparently thought that any part of it might be described as a teaching concerning the kingdom, whether that was a parable of forgiveness as the indication of true repentance, a story showing that salvation was a gift of grace, or an illustration of the rapid spread of the message. We must make certain in our interpretation of any of these parables just how it is related to that kingdom.

III. What Was New in the Message of Jesus?

The kingdom of God was in no sense a new theme to an audience of first-century Jews. Nowhere in the Gospels does Jesus define the phrase. There was common agreement, not only as to the existence of the kingdom, but also as to its threefold character. The burden of Jesus' message was that this kingdom was near (Mark 1:15). This was to be the proclamation of the disciples when they were sent out (Luke 9:2); they were to pray for the coming of that kingdom (Matt. 6:10; Luke 18:7). It is not said that if men would repent, they could then work in co-operation with God for the coming of a new order. That new order was coming whether they repented or not. The only question was whether they would enter.

This eschatological foundation of the teaching of Jesus is clearly indicated by our earliest traditions. There were those standing in Jesus' presence who would not taste of death until it came with power (Mark 9:1; 13:30); that was certainly also Paul's understanding (I Cor. 15:51; I Thess. 4:15). The kingdom was symbolized by a meal at which some of his hearers would recline with Abraham and Isaac and Jacob (Matt. 8:11). On his last night Jesus said to his disciples that he would not drink of the fruit of the vine until he drank it with them new in the kingdom of God (Mark 14:25; Luke 22:16, 18). Its coming would bring the judgment, when men would either enter into the kingdom prepared from the foundation of the world (Matt. 25:34) or be cast into outer darkness. The later charting of apocalyptic signs indicates a weakening of this hope and a postponement of the consummation. But for Jesus himself the kingdom was at hand.

In some ways Luke is the least eschatological of the Synoptic evangelists, but he assembled a whole series of words which enforce the eschatological message. Jesus had come to cast fire upon earth (Luke 12:49) and bring a sharp division among men (Luke 12:51-53). The people of that generation could not read the signs of the times (Luke 12:54-56); otherwise they would get right with their neighbors. Soon they would face the Judge and it would be too late (Luke 12:57-59). Jesus' hearers should not think that they were more righteous than the eighteen upon whom the tower of Siloam fell (Luke 13:1-5). In the coming judgment they would all perish unless they repented. They had one more chance, just a little time of respite (Luke 13:6-9). They should strive to enter the narrow gate, for soon the door would be shut (Luke 13:23-25).

Therefore Jesus weeps over the city of Jerusalem which had continually rejected the prophets sent to her (Luke 13:34-35) and soon was to be left desolate. Woes are as much a part of his message as beatitudes (Luke 6:24-26), but they are not curses so much as prophetic pronouncements of judgment. They rest on classes of people like the rich or the Pharisees (Luke 11:39-52), and on cities like Chorazin or Bethsaida (Luke 10:13-15). It would be more tolerable in the coming judgment for the wicked Gentile cities than for them. That judgment would come as unexpectedly as the crisis in the days of Noah and Lot (Luke 17:26-30). Hence those who do repent must be alert and faithful. They must be like servants awaiting the return of their master, or like the householder who cannot anticipate when a thief may try to break into his house but must always be ready (Luke 12:35-40).

In view of these indications that Jesus shared the current eschatological view, what shall we regard as the new aspects in Jesus' teaching about the kingdom? A popular answer has been that he replaced the idea of an imminent catastrophe with the conception of the slow evolutionary development of the kingdom. This meaning has been found in the parables of growth. Such an answer, however, reflects modern wishful thinking. Neither yeast nor a seed of grain (Matt. 13:31-33) provides an appropriate comparison with a long process of development. Moreover this way of interpreting the parables of growth slights the importance in them of the harvest, a standing figure for the judgment. At the most these comparisons suggest a brief process of growth. But most modern interpreters believe that the point of these parables lies in the contrast between the small beginnings and great endings.[1]

A second answer to the question about Jesus' originality has been the assertion that Jesus had in mind an inner spiritual kingdom instead of an outward manifestation of divine sovereignty. Since the days of Origen it has been popular to find this conception in Luke 17:21 by adopting the translation, "the kingdom of God is within you." But this rendering fits neither the situation nor the context. Jesus is speaking not to "the poor," but to Pharisees. It may be added that if this inwardness of the kingdom is the great contribution of Jesus, he must have been a very unsuccessful teacher, because this conception is preserved only in a doubtful translation of one verse preserved in a single Gospel. Such a complete transformation of Jewish ideas would have required constant reiteration. Of course Jesus believed that entrance to the kingdom of God called for inner spiritual change; but that was not what was meant by the coming of the sovereignty of God. The Greek phrase ἐντὸς ὑμῶν, sometimes rendered "within you," is rather to be translated "among you" or "in your midst." Jesus' reference may be to the preliminary signs of the new age to be found in his ministry, or as the context would indicate, to the sudden coming of the kingdom in their midst. Decision between these cannot be made on the basis of the tense of the Greek verb, for there would have been no verb at all in the underlying Aramaic used by Jesus.

If neither of these modernizing expedients is defensible, what was the new element in Jesus' teaching about the kingdom? The answer is threefold: (a) he promised entrance to the kingdom to an entirely different group of people than most expected; (b) he affirmed a preliminary realization of the sovereignty of God

in his own ministry; (c) he took the kingdom hope of his people with a new seriousness in his ethical appeal to his contemporaries.

(a) Who comprised the "little flock" to whom the gift of the kingdom was promised through the Father's grace (Luke 12:32)? Jesus' answer was a revolutionary overturning of most contemporary expectations. It was not for the rich but for the poor (Luke 6:20); wealth was no preparation for entrance to the kingdom of God but a supreme handicap (Mark 10:23). Not the wise scribes, but the little children and the childlike had the qualifications necessary for entrance (Mark 10:14-15). The tax collectors and sinners would enter before the Pharisees, who prided themselves on their righteousness (Matt. 21:31). Entrance was not a prerogative for the Jews alone; many would come from the East and the West and the North and the South (Matt. 8:11-12). A special mark of those who would enter was the suffering of persecution (Matt. 5:10). Such experiences were part of the messianic woes before the coming glory. Some interpreters have been misled into thinking that this language presupposed that the kingdom was already present. But it has been conclusively shown that "enter the kingdom of God" was an eschatological expression among Jews.[2] Jesus promised entrance to a radically different group of people.

(b) Yet Jesus did believe in a certain presence of the kingdom in his ministry. As the red glow is in the eastern sky before the sun rises, so signs of the kingdom were already manifest in his ministry. The demon exorcisms, which held such a prominent place in the work of Jesus, were a sign of the realized presence of the kingdom (Matt. 12:28). Satan is bound already if his kingdom is being despoiled (Mark 3:27). Jesus beheld him fall like lightning from heaven (Luke 10:18). Hence God's reign had in a sense already begun. So Jesus could say to those who responded to his message, "Blessed are the eyes which see what you see!" adding that the men of old had not seen this day though they had looked forward to it (Luke 10:23-24). When messengers came from John the Baptist, Jesus is said to have referred them to the great deeds accompanying his ministry. The fulfillment of the messianic prophecies was to be seen in his healing ministry (Matt. 11:2-6). There is no other explanation for the space which Mark gives to the healing ministry. It is the merit of the modern school of "realized eschatology" that it emphasizes this element in Jesus. But when it denies to Jesus belief in a future eschatological consum-

---

[1] See B. T. D. Smith, *The Parables of the Synoptic Gospels* (Cambridge: University Press, 1937), esp. ch. vii.

[2] H. Windisch, "Die Sprüche vom Eingehen in das Reich Gottes," *Zeitschrift für die Neutestamentliche Wissenschaft*, XXVII (1928), 163-92.

mation it betrays an unwarranted skepticism concerning the records and gives a distorted picture of early Christian history.

(c) Finally, Jesus took the kingdom hope of his people with a new seriousness. For many others it was a speculative theory or a wishful dream. For Jesus it was a profound conviction that the righteous God of history was about to assert his full sovereignty. That gave searching directness and stirring urgency to every deed and utterance. Entrance to the kingdom should be the supreme objective of man's striving (Matt. 6:33). It was better to sacrifice an eye or a hand and enter the kingdom than to go with all one's members into the Gehenna of fire (Mark 9:47). Fine words without obedience would be of no avail (Matt. 7:21), for the righteousness of those who enter the kingdom must exceed that of the Pharisees (Matt. 5:20). Once discipleship was undertaken, there was no turning back (Luke 9:62). Just as a pearl merchant would make any sacrifice to obtain a fine specimen, and anyone would sell all that he had to buy a field in which a great treasure lay hidden, so entrance into the kingdom of God was worth any conceivable sacrifice (Matt. 13:44-45).

IV. Jesus and the Kingdom

We have seen that Jesus announced the nearness of the kingdom of God. After his resurrection his disciples proclaimed that he was the anointed king or Christ. Now that they knew the identity of the king, they did not announce the coming of the kingdom but the return of the king. Although they may have prayed, "Thy kingdom come" (Matt. 6:10), their earnest petition was "Maranatha, our Lord, come!" (I Cor. 16:22.) They were already experiencing the outpouring of the Spirit promised by the prophet Joel for the last times (Acts 16:16-33). Paul could say of the Lord Jesus Christ that he had delivered them from the present evil age (Gal. 1:4).

But did Jesus himself teach his own messiahship in any form? That is still a very controversial question among New Testament scholars, even among those who are in complete agreement concerning the other aspects of his message about the kingdom.[3]

The reader who confines his attention to the Gospel of John is not aware of any problem. There Jesus' belief in his messiahship is expressed at the very opening of his ministry. The debates with the Jews involve his claims concerning his own person. Jesus speaks continually of his own saving significance. But in the other three Gospels the situation is entirely different. In Mark, which forms the basis for the other two, there is no public proclamation of messiahship. When Peter expresses for the disciples their belief about him, Jesus charges him to tell no one (Mark 8:30). Though Mark seems to present the entry into Jerusalem as a messianic announcement, the subsequent events do not substantiate that impression. Jesus never defends his authority by messianic claims (Mark 11:27-33). In the hearing before the high priest there are not even "false witnesses" to assert that he claimed to be Messiah. That question is introduced only by the direct cross-examination of Jesus (Mark 14:56-61). As at Caesarea Philippi, the specific reply of Jesus was about the Son of man. All the Gospels agree that the inscription above the Cross contained a messianic charge.

The interpretation of this evidence is complicated by the fact that "Messiah" was not a concept with a single definite meaning within Judaism. The word meant simply "anointed," and could be applied to any figure through whom God might assert his divine sovereignty. Many forms of Jewish hope did not involve a messiah at all. God himself would be king in the new age. It is clear from the career of Jesus that he rejected any idea of being a political leader to raise the standard against Rome. The popular hopes for a scion of David who would restore the kingdom were far from his mind. It is often said that Jesus was reticent about announcing his messiahship because it was necessary to educate the disciples to his own "spiritual" conception. But what was this conception? Many theologians have believed that Jesus found the key to his mission in the figure of the suffering servant of Isa. 53. But it is clear that this chapter was not given a messianic interpretation in first-century Judaism.[4] Furthermore Jesus never called himself "the servant of the Lord," nor did he quote from the chapter in any genuine passage.[5] Allusions to other passages in Isaiah which modern criticism includes among the "servant songs" cannot be adduced to substantiate the claim that Jesus had Isa. 53 in mind.

[3] See Clarence T. Craig, "The Problem of the Messiahship of Jesus," in New Testament Studies, ed. E. P. Booth (Nashville and New York: Abingdon-Cokesbury Press, 1942), pp. 95-114.

[4] The attempt to prove a merging of the figure with that of Messiah in pre-Christian Judaism must be rejected as unsuccessful. See William Manson, Jesus, the Messiah (Philadelphia: The Westminster Press, 1946). Of course that could have been the original insight of Jesus, as many have contended, including John W. Bowman, The Intention of Jesus (Philadelphia: The Westminster Press, 1943). But evidence for that is quite lacking. For other views here see above, pp. 14-17, 130, 140.

[5] Clarence T. Craig, "The Identification of Jesus with the Suffering Servant," Journal of Religion, XXIV (1944), 240-45.

In all the gospel passages the suffering is affirmed of one who is called "the Son of man." That is the term which Jesus constantly uses in our records. The term appears in a first-century B.C. Jewish work, the Similitudes of Enoch, as the title of a heavenly being who in the last days will be God's agent of judgment and salvation. Jesus clearly applies this term to himself. If we restrict the term "messiah" to an earthly son of David, then we must admit that Jesus made no claim that he was such a figure. But if we admit the wider connotation of "the one through whom God would consummate his rule," then we must include the figure of the Son of man coming on the clouds of heaven, as portrayed in the Similitudes of Enoch (46:1; 62:5; 69:29; etc.). It is certain that the Gospels ascribe that conception to Jesus. The term Son of man does not refer to the lowly humanity of Jesus. He is the one who must suffer before he comes into his glory and the one who is decisive in the coming judgment.[6]

Since the Son of man was to come on the clouds of heaven, many interpreters believe that it was impossible for Jesus to have described himself thus. That identification must have come from the church which was awaiting his return. I do not see why this conclusion is necessary. How can we affirm what was possible for a first-century prophet who was announcing the final divine denouement? Particularly is this the case if we share the Christian faith about him. The most adequate explanation of the development of early Christian faith is that Jesus did identify himself with the Son of man. Rudolf Otto [7] suggests that the book of Enoch opened the way to such an identification by asserting that a preacher of judgment could be exalted to heaven and proclaimed "Son of man" (Enoch 71:1). But such speculation is hazardous.

As to how the idea of suffering became associated with Jesus' conception of the Son of man, several possibilities are open. Perhaps this association had already taken place in Jewish thought. Perhaps it was made by Jesus himself under the pressure of the situation which lay before him. Or it may be that it was first the early church which thus read back the later experience of Jesus into the record of his

[6] It is true that the term "Son of man" is not used directly in connection with the kingdom. But the two terms are inseparably joined through their connection with the judgment. The consummation of the kingdom brings the judgment; the coming of the Son of man brings the judgment; therefore these two expectations cannot be separate.

[7] *The Kingdom of God and the Son of Man*, tr. F. V. Filson & Bertram Lee Woolf (London: Lutterworth Press, 1943).

understanding of himself; it is striking that no passage assigned to Q speaks of the suffering of the Son of man. But whatever judgment is accepted on this particular point, it was as Son of man that Jesus connected his own person with the kingdom of God. There seems to be no good reason why the testimony of the Gospels should be rejected. Some time before his death Jesus came to see in that inescapable experience his supreme service for men (Mark 10:45; 14:22-24).

Was the messiahship of Jesus present or future? The answer is to be found in his message concerning the kingdom of God. Since the consummation of that kingdom was still to come, his own rule as God's representative was future. That explains why there is no public announcement and why Jesus never presented himself as the ruler. But the kingdom was in a sense already present in their midst. This was indicated by the mighty works which inaugurated the overthrow of the kingdom of Satan. So likewise there was a hidden messiahship perceived only by those who had eyes to see and understand. "Blessed is he who takes no offense at me" (Matt. 11:6). Regarding both the kingdom and messiahship there is the same tension between present and future.

How may we summarize the conclusions on this complicated and difficult question? Jesus never came forward with claims to messiahship. It was not a matter of human ambition but of divine choice. The full exercise of rule under God must wait for the time of God's intervention. The mission of Jesus was to call men to repentance and to serve their needs. But whenever the question of messiahship was directly raised, it was impossible for Jesus to deny his connection with the heavenly Son of man. Because of this he could make no denial before the Council or before Pilate (Mark 14:62; 15:2). The story says that Jesus told the high priest that he would see the Son of man coming on the clouds of heaven.

That official never experienced a direct fulfillment of the prediction. But something greater happened. The central position of Jesus in the kingship of God was vindicated when God raised him from the dead. From that time on, the message of the kingdom became the message about Jesus and what God had done for men through him. The believer who sings "Jesus is king" is not setting forth the result of a long historical investigation. He is expressing his central conviction about the place of Jesus in God's saving act. The kingdom of God is not a human task but God's salvation. Since Jesus is central in mediating that salvation, his messiahship is the seed from which all later expressions of faith grow.

V. The Kingdom and the Church

All the words of Jesus which we possess come to us through the tradition of the early Christians. The development of their experience inevitably influenced the wording of the Gospels at many points. Particularly in Matthew do we see development in two directions. One is toward an emphasis upon the church which had come, the growing body of believers replacing the Judaism which had rejected its Messiah. The other is toward apocalyptic speculation, particularly regarding the punishment of the wicked. In the form in which it stands in Matthew, the parable of the weeds concerns the actual church of the time of the evangelist; it looks forward to the judgment which will bring division between worthy and unworthy members (Matt. 13:24-30, 36-43). The parable of the dragnet is given a similar apocalyptic conclusion, though the story may have originally referred to the diversified audience to which Jesus brought his message of the kingdom (Matt. 13:47-50).

Uncertainty surrounds the interpretation of many passages in this Gospel. When the question is asked about the greatest in the kingdom (Matt. 18:1, 4), is reference being made to the existing church or to the future consummation? In which—church or future kingdom—is the one who breaks the least commandment given the lowest place (Matt. 5:19)? From which is John the Baptist excluded (Matt. 11:11)? To which does Peter hold the keys (Matt. 16:19)? From which are the scribes shutting men out (Matt. 23:13)? From which is that scribe not far away who assents to the two great commandments as the sum of the law (Mark 12:34)?

Probably the proper reply in each case is "both." Even Matthew does not think in terms of an institutionalized church which should continue down the centuries. The body of believers, who necessarily had a certain amount of organization for discipline and instruction, was the remnant of the true Israel which should inherit the kingdom of God. With his moralistic interest, Matthew knows a judgment upon the church as well as upon the world. But there was direct continuity between the developing community and the perfected reign of God beyond the judgment, whose imminence Matthew was so eager to stress.

The answer in substance has already been given to the question whether Jesus intended to found a church. His message dealt with the coming kingdom of God and the preparation of men and women for entrance into that kingdom. Those who responded to his summons were not organized into separate worshiping communities. Jesus continued to attend synagogue and temple worship to the very end of his life. His work was dedicated to the gathering of a faithful, repentant remnant, which might have included all Israel, but which in fact embraced only a small part.

In only two passages does the word "church" (ecclēsia) occur in the Gospels. Matt. 18:17 clearly has in mind a later separate Christian community with machinery for the discipline of its members. Matt. 16:18, however, might be understood as the body of believers waiting for the new age. The gates of Hades cannot prevail against the church of Christ, for it will not perish in the judgment; it is the nucleus for the new age. It is highly probable, however, that this verse contains later Antiochian tradition supporting the primacy of Peter as opposed to James. But it should be recognized that there is no reason why Jesus may not have used some Aramaic equivalent of ecclēsia, for the idea is implicit in his reported utterances. That would not mean a legal and cult institution, such as we understand by the word "church," but the faithful remnant waiting for God to establish his complete reign.

A very different trend is to be found in the Gospel of John. There the word kingdom appears in only two passages. To Nicodemus, Jesus says that one must be born anew of water and the Spirit if one is to enter the kingdom of God (John 3:3, 5). Before Pilate, Jesus insists that his kingship is not from the world (John 18:36). That does not mean an otherworldly kingdom; it is to come from heaven into this world. Elsewhere in the Gospel the gift which is bestowed through Christ is eternal life. Harmonistic interpreters have often insisted that this is simply John's equivalent for the kingdom. It is truer to say that it is his substitute, for the conception of salvation in this Gospel is quite different from that in the other Gospels. In Mark 10:17 eternal life is clearly the life of the age to come. But throughout the Gospel of John life is the present possession of those who believe on God's only Son. Jesus is the messenger from the heavenly world who alone is able to bestow life and light and truth on humanity. The language of resurrection at the last day is occasionally found. But this no longer has vital significance. Eschatological urgency is replaced by a present crisis of faith. He who believes has eternal life and has passed from death to life (John 5:24).

This Johannine reinterpretation has been of tremendous significance in the life of the church. It has provided a most attractive solution for the problem of the delay of the Parousia. Some interpreters have sought to show that this was in fact the real position of the historic Jesus. But such a solution is purchased at too great cost. It would mean that the entire first generation of Christians was quite mistaken concerning what Jesus had taught and that the creative forces of the earliest period were really derived from some other source than Jesus. It would mean that the great mass of the tradition about Jesus which was circulated in the early church was entirely unreliable. Such skepticism is really fatal to any belief that we can know the content of the historic message of Jesus.

VI. Reinterpretations in Christian History

When the Christian church was compelled to abandon its original eschatological expectations, it was natural that the kingdom of God in Jesus' teaching should be interpreted in new and different ways. Archibald Robertson [8] classifies the three leading interpretations in the following way: (a) the perfect reign of God in heaven after the Judgment; (b) the visible reign of Christ on earth between the Second Coming and the Last Judgment; (c) the visible church on earth between the First and the Second Coming. These might be described as the otherworldly, the millenarian, and the ecclesiastical interpretations.

In the modern world what might be called a fourth interpretation became widely prevalent through the influence of rationalism and the liberal movement. For Kant the kingdom of God was "the ethical state." Albrecht Ritschl described it as "the *summum bonum* which God realises in men; and at the same time it is their common task, for it is only through the rendering of obedience on man's part that God's sovereignty possesses continuous existence." [9] Walter Rauschenbusch did much to popularize this conception: "The Kingdom of God is humanity organized according to the will of God. . . . It is the Christian transfiguration of the social order." [10] It is significant that in 1934 the faculty of the institution where Rauschenbusch had taught honored his contribution to Christian social thinking with a special publication; but in it they disavowed the exegetical basis for his teaching and affirmed the eschatological character of the teaching of Jesus. [11]

The credit for establishing that character in a way no modern interpretation can succeed in ignoring goes to Johannes Weiss in a monograph on *The Preaching of Jesus on the Kingdom of God.* [12] It is usual to associate this

achievement with the name of Albert Schweitzer, who did much to popularize it in his brilliant writings—but the credit belongs to Weiss. Schweitzer's original contribution lay at a quite different point. He went beyond the position that the message of Jesus was eschatologically oriented to the claim that all of the activity of Jesus was controlled by eschatological dogma. He taught that Jesus at first expected the kingdom to come before his disciples returned from their tour of Galilee (Matt. 10:23). When it failed to come, he revised his strategy and went up to Jerusalem with the deliberate intention of being killed in order to bring in the kingdom (Mark 8:31; 9:31; 10:33). While the eschatological character of Jesus' thinking about the kingdom of God is widely accepted today, Schweitzer's reconstruction is followed by very few. Because it posits a sharp division between two periods in the career of Jesus, it is to be rejected together with other modern theories which divide the teaching of Jesus into two periods. Our gospel tradition was not preserved in a way which permits any such discrimination.

Yet resistance to the eschatological way of interpreting Jesus' teaching has continued and is still probably the dominant attitude among Christians generally. This ascription of eschatological expectations to Jesus has been obnoxious to the liberal, who desires to make Jesus immediately useful without reference to the apostolic message about him, and also to the devout, who is unwilling to ascribe to Jesus unfulfilled expectations. Hence there have been many attempts to ascribe the apocalyptic eschatology of the Gospels to the early church. [13]

It is often contended that what Jesus anticipated was the fall of Jerusalem at the hands of Rome, a political judgment, and that it was the later church which turned this into a cosmic event accompanying the coming of the Son of man. It seems likely—and here is the crucial issue—that the transformation of the tradition took exactly the opposite direction. The message of Jesus did not deal with political prognostication, but with the coming of God's salvation. When the events which Jesus predicted did not take place, it was natural for the church to point instead to the fall of Jerusalem which *had* occurred. But even for the later evangelists this disaster was only one of the signs which should precede the end. Such speculation belonged to the later tendency to postpone the coming of the great day. In the original teach-

[8] *Regnum Dei* (New York: The Macmillan Co., 1901).

[9] *The Christian Doctrine of Justification and Reconciliation,* tr. H. R. Mackintosh (Edinburgh: T. & T. Clark, 1902), p. 30.

[10] *A Theology for the Social Gospel* (New York: The Macmillan Co., 1917), pp. 142, 145.

[11] *Colgate-Rochester Seminary Bulletin,* March, 1934.

[12] *Die Predigt Jesu vom Reiche Gottes* (Göttingen: Vandenhoeck & Ruprecht, 1892).

[13] Among these is that found in the works of H. B. Sharman, notably *Son of Man and Kingdom of God* (New York: Harper & Bros., 1943); also F. C. Grant, *The Gospel of the Kingdom* (New York: The Macmillan Co., 1940).

ing of Jesus the kingdom was near and would come without warning. Apocalyptic teaching shows a *weakening* of eschatology rather than an enhancement.

Notice should also be taken of the "realized eschatology" position which C. H. Dodd [14] has advocated and which to some has seemed to be a means of bringing greater unity into the New Testament message. Dodd holds that the message of Jesus was strictly "eschatological," but that its "eschatology" was completely realized in the ministry of Jesus. Jesus taught that the kingdom *had come*. All words about a future coming represent an alien importation from the beliefs of the disciples. The only future consummation for Jesus lay in the eternal world, and Jesus did not teach that that was near in point of time. The exegetical argument for this interpretation has been amply refuted.[15] Like the other nonfuturistic interpretations, this conception fails to face a crucial question: Where is the source of the vivid eschatological hope which inspired the disciples? Until that source is discovered elsewhere, it is a much sounder historical position to accept the truthfulness of our earliest tradition in finding the source of this inspiration in Jesus himself.

VII. Value and Significance of Jesus' Teaching

The delineation of what Jesus taught about the kingdom of God is a strictly historical task. We should never come to the Gospels with preliminary assumptions about what we are willing to accept. We must sit down patiently before the evidence and let Jesus speak to us from the historical record. But that is never the end of the matter for a Christian believer. He must go on and ask the theological question: What is the significance of this for me and for faith?

It is clear at the outset that the form in which Jesus presented his message of the kingdom cannot be held by us today in the same way. Nineteen centuries have passed and no such catastrophic event as he seems to have predicted has taken place. We have no biblical authority to transfer that imminence to our own time. When the New Testament writers said "soon," they meant "soon" in relation to their own time. If "with the Lord one day is as a thousand years" (II Pet. 3:8), then civilizations may continue through two million years as well as two thousand. When a modern premillennialist predicts the coming of the Lord in our time, that is his own reinterpretation of the biblical teach-

[14] *The Parables of the Kingdom* (New York: Charles Scribner's Sons, 1936).

[15] James Y. Campbell, "Contributions and Comments," *The Expository Times*, XLVIII (1936-37), 91-94; Clarence T. Craig, "Realized Eschatology," *The Journal of Biblical Literature*, LVI (1937), 17-26; Kenneth W. Clark, "Realized Eschatology," *ibid.*, LIX (1940), 367-83.

ing, just as truly as any other modern eschatology represents such an adaptation.

The devotee of the "liberal Jesus" likewise faces embarrassment. The message of Jesus cannot be related directly to our concern for social and economic reconstruction. That type of "Jesus-ology" cannot be substituted for the historic faith of the church without violence to the records. The message of the kingdom does not deal with our social task but with God's saving act. This fact should never be made an excuse for quietism. If Jesus saw in his healing ministry "signs" of the coming of the kingdom, we may interpret signal victories of social and economic justice in similar fashion. Though the perfected rule of God never comes completely into time, it is still always possible to attain a more Christian social order. The resistance of man's radical sinfulness should never plunge us into defeatism and despair. Though our faith is not *in* man, we must retain hope *for* man. It is possible to taste here and now something of the powers of the age to come (Heb. 6:5). But Jesus will first become fully meaningful to us when we realize the different orientation of his own ministry and the eschatological background of his ethical teaching.

The stumbling block for conservative and liberal alike has been that the acceptance of the eschatological reading of the Gospels seems to mean that Jesus was mistaken at an important point. But the man of Christian faith should not be troubled that Jesus saw the finality of God's redemption in foreshortened perspective. That fact affords but one more illustration that the Incarnation was real. Jesus' belief in demon possession is another illustration. If Jesus did not share in the beliefs of his time, then the Incarnation was not real and we are in the realm of Docetic fantasy. A genuine incarnation involves limitations of human knowledge. Otherwise we would simply have a deity masquerading in human flesh. With Jesus those limitations were those of the first-century Jewish horizon rather than of the twentieth-century American, but from any absolute point of view the latter would involve just as much restriction as the former.

What positive values are to be found in this eschatological conditioning of the teaching of Jesus? First it provided the historic situation in which the radical, ultimate ethic of Jesus was proclaimed. Another article is being devoted to the ethical teachings of Jesus, and these cannot even be summarized here. It is a mistake to interpret the ethics of Jesus as "interim ethic." He never gave advice "because of the shortness of the time." What he did was to call for absolute obedience to the will of God in the light of the coming of God's perfect rule. We should not go so far as to say that the ethical teaching of Jesus could not have been the same except for his belief in the imminence of the kingdom; but the fact is that the two did go together. The revolutionary ethic came from the God who was about to make all things new.

In the second place the kingdom hope of Jesus finds in God the basis of confidence rather than in man. Individuals are not helpless; they may truly repent. But our assurance does not rest upon the precarious foundation of their cleverness or goodness. It rests upon the nature of the ultimate power, God himself. The man of Christian faith can never despair, even in the darkest hour. His faith rests not upon the seen but the unseen, the God who sends his kingdom. We do not believe that this God is completely divorced from man and his world; nevertheless it is God upon whom we must depend. No human contriving is a substitute for his saving power. His activity is ever near, and men of faith may be used as channels even now.

Finally, the eschatological framework of the teaching of Jesus is of permanent significance because it provides a symbol of the truth that history finds its consummation in him. We do not know how many civilizations will rise and fall before the end of the historic process on this planet. Atomic bombs may blot out our own, but new civilizations will follow. But this we believe: that history has its meaning in the rule of the God and Father of our Lord Jesus Christ. God judges the world through him. He is the center of history and not simply one of the successive waves on the stream of time. No matter how rebellious the sons of men remain, the victory of God is assured by his free act. He who created in the beginning will determine the consummation, for all life is in his hands. Hence we must take these long polysyllables out of the vocabulary of biblical specialists and let a true "Hallelujah Chorus" ring out in our own time: "The kingdom of the world has become the kingdom of our Lord and of his Christ, and he shall reign for ever and ever" (Rev. 11:15).

VIII. Selected Bibliography

CADOUX, C. J. *The Historic Mission of Jesus.* New York: Harper & Bros., 1943.

HÉRING, JEAN. *Le royaume de Dieu et sa venue.* Paris: Librairie Félix Alcan, 1937.

KITTEL, G. *Theologisches Wörterbuch zum Neuen-testament,* article on *Basileus.*

KÜMMEL, W. R. *Verheissung und Erfüllung.* Basel: Heinrich Majer, 1945.

MANSON, T. W. *The Teaching of Jesus.* Cambridge: University Press, 1931.

OTTO, RUDOLF. *The Kingdom of God and the Son of Man,* tr. F. V. Filson and Bertram Lee Woolf. London: Lutterworth Press, 1943.

SCHWEITZER, ALBERT. *The Quest of the Historical Jesus.* London: A. & C. Black, 1910.

SCOTT, E. F. *The Kingdom of God in the New Testament.* New York: The Macmillan Co., 1931.

WOOD, H. G., and others. *The Kingdom of God and History.* Official Oxford Conference Books, Vol. III. Chicago: Willett, Clark & Co., 1939.

THE TEACHING OF JESUS

II. THE SERMON ON THE MOUNT

by AMOS N. WILDER

In the fifth, sixth, and seventh chapters of the first book of the New Testament appears a discourse of Jesus to which throughout the centuries an incomparable significance has been attached. Shorter portions of the Bible such as the Ten Commandments, the Lord's Prayer, the Golden Rule, and certain of the parables have been similarly fixed upon by the common sentiment of Christians for exceptional attention and familiarity, but none to this extent and scope. For hosts of men this section of the New Testament has well-nigh taken on the character of a shorter canon within the canon, and has been counted the touchstone of Christianity. Men have been inclined to find in it both the most characteristic compendium of the teaching of Jesus of Nazareth and the perfect portrait of the Christian life. Such unofficial canonization has no doubt had a large justification. Christians, moreover, will not demur greatly when men—like Gandhi—of other faiths seize upon this portion of Scripture as uniquely representative of the faith.

If we were to attempt to account for the incalculable sway exercised by this discourse over the hearts of men of many generations and many races, we would no doubt be led finally to those elements that make up the greatness of Jesus, especially in his role of teacher. It is true that the sermon comes to us enshrined in the Gospel of Matthew and that the words carry with them there the authority of the Christ, the Son of God, and have been transmitted through the years in the canon of the church. But the survival power of these words has not lain chiefly in the book in which they were later inscribed, or in the manuscripts in which they were copied, or even in the office of him who first pronounced them. These words were winged words and contain their own immortality. The earliest recorded comment occasioned by the teaching of Jesus and applied by Matthew to this discourse states the true nature of the case: "The crowds were astonished at his teaching, for he taught them as one who had authority" (Matt. 7:28-29).

The intrinsic quality and force of the sayings of Jesus point us to many considerations, but what especially concerns us here is his moral teaching. The Sermon on the Mount has generally been accounted the most searching and powerful utterance we possess on what concerns the moral life. It awakens men to an immense seriousness and responsibility, and quickens the conscience to unsuspected ranges of obligation. It discovers man's moral nature to him. It plants a seed of permanent dissatisfaction in the soul, even in the case of the individual who professes not to understand or acknowledge the obligations indicated. It is like a ray of light playing in the recesses of a cave. Our most hidden motives and equivocations are brought into the light. Woe to him, indeed, who once hears or reads these words! For they are so formulated and proclaimed that the obligation they impose is self-evident, and one can never thereafter free oneself of their burden. In this sense the sermon creates conscience where it did not before exist. The sayings compel us to confront and do homage, not to what the natural man but to what the Spirit demands. And this makes for pain, for inner division, and for fateful consequences. For Jesus strikes at the root of worldliness, and disputes with the great tyrannies over the soul: the lust of the flesh, the lust of the eyes, and the pride of life.

Though the import and authority of the sermon have been variously misunderstood and sometimes fiercely repudiated, no one can possibly estimate its total impact upon the life of the world, when we think of the compounding of its influence upon countless individuals throughout Christian history.

Yet the problem of interpretation and application of the discourse has always been a pressing and difficult one. The Christian conscience continually seeks clarification, especially where new knowledge affects our understanding of it or where new conditions in the church and the world create moral dilemmas. Enemies have attacked the teachings of the sermon; defenders of it have sometimes added to the confusion. There has been a tendency to water down and emasculate the teachings or, on the other hand, to count them irrelevant and impracticable. Difficulties arise not only because of "man's unchristened heart" but also because of honest perplexities, whether of the scholar facing a complex literary problem or of the Christian layman confronted with the conundrums of ethical behavior today. We must first understand as far as possible the origin of the sermon and its original meaning, and then inquire into its modern relevance.

I. Literary and Historical Analysis

A. Setting of the Discourse in Matthew and Its Occasion.—Apart from his preamble (chs. 1–2) and epilogue (chs. 26–28) Matthew appears to have constructed his work in five parts, each one of which includes a discourse of Jesus of some length. Each discourse, moreover, is preceded by material, largely narrative, which is chosen to illuminate it or prepare for it. Each discourse and therefore each part of the Gospel ends with a characteristic transitional formula leading to the next part, similar in form to that found at the close of the sermon, "And when Jesus finished these sayings . . ." (Matt. 7:28; cf. 11:1; 13:53; 19:1a; 26:1).

It is important for our realization of the relative scope of the subject matter of the Sermon on the Mount, which is the first of these discourses, that we should have in mind the themes of the other four. All five with their limits may be defined as follows: [1]

1. Concerning discipleship, Matt. 5–7
2. Concerning apostleship, Matt. 9:36–10:42
3. Concerning the hiding of the revelation, Matt. 13:1-53
4. Concerning church administration, Matt. 17:22–18:35
5. Concerning the judgment, Matt. 23–25

[1] See B. W. Bacon, Studies in Matthew (New York: Henry Holt & Co., 1930), pp. xxii, 82, 269-325. See also below, p. 235.

It should be noted, therefore, that in the view of Matthew, Jesus dealt at large with themes other than those chiefly treated in the Sermon on the Mount, and that we should not expect to find the whole of his thought in that one utterance. It is, however, true that it receives a special prominence both because of its position at the beginning of the series and the occasion to which it is assigned. It is also true that it includes some mention of themes found in the other discourses.

It should be further observed that Matthew's five discourses appear to be made up of materials gathered together in topical arrangement from diverse sayings or groups of sayings found isolated or in other connections in the other Synoptic Gospels. The evangelist appears to work on this principle in the ordering of his Gospel, for the same policy guides him in narrative sequences as well. This procedure creates a presumption, therefore, that to some degree the sermon represents a planned arrangement by the evangelist of diverse elements rather than a single unit of teaching received by him in that form. [2]

The narrative matter which introduces the Sermon on the Mount in Matthew's first part begins at 3:1. It includes a summary of the work of John the Baptist, the baptism and temptation of Jesus, the beginning of his announcement of the kingdom, the call of four disciples, and a summary of a period of teaching, preaching, and healing throughout Galilee, together with a reference to his fame and the concluding statement that "great crowds followed him from Galilee and the Decapolis and Jerusalem and Judea and from beyond the Jordan" (Matt. 4:25). Thus the author, utilizing the indications of his tradition in Mark, sets the stage for his first discourse. He prepares the way promptly for Jesus' first great utterance, but makes it clear that a period of preaching the kingdom and of calling disciples has preceded it. In Luke, the sermon—as reported in ch. 6—follows expressly and naturally upon the appointment of the twelve. This detail is not found in Matthew, who, as a matter of fact, first lists the twelve in connection with his second discourse (Matt. 10:1-4).

If we observe closely the way in which Matthew uses his Marcan source in the early part of his work, we can note the precise point at which he introduces his first great discourse into the story of the Galilean ministry. He takes

[2] For a presentation of varying views regarding the unity or composite character of the sermon see Clyde W. Votaw, "The Sermon on the Mount," in James Hastings, A Dictionary of the Bible: Extra Volume (New York: Charles Scribner's Sons, 1904), pp. 1-45. We shall speak of the evangelist as Matthew without prejudging the question of his identity.

the situation described in Mark 3:7, 8, 10, 13 as the appropriate occasion, as we can see from Matt. 4:24, 25; 5:1, which parallel these verses. In Mark we have the great multitude from many regions, the healings, and the ascent to the higher ground above the lake, all following upon a period of work which Matthew has abbreviated, and upon incidents which he postpones for later use. The content of the sermon also makes it clear that Jesus had been long enough at work so that his followers were now a distinct group exposed to obloquy if not persecution. The time had come to make clear the meaning of discipleship and to define the teacher's message over against the teachings of the synagogue. Luke (6:12-19) has assigned his version of the sermon to a similar stage of Jesus' work, though here Jesus descends from the high land to deliver it.

Both evangelists think of the sermon as intended first of all for the disciples, though they also understand that Jesus spoke in the hearing of the multitudes. This view probably goes back to the common source they had. When Matthew writes that Jesus "opened his mouth and taught them" (Matt. 5:2), he is referring to the "disciples" spoken of in the preceding verse. Similarly Luke begins his version of the sermon with the words: "And he lifted up his eyes on his disciples, and said . . ." (Luke 6:20). The reference in either case is not confined to the twelve (cf. Luke 6:13, 17).

B. Outline and Contents.—

THE RIGHTEOUSNESS OF THE KINGDOM OF HEAVEN
I. Characteristics of members of the kingdom (Matt. 5:3-16)
  A. Test and rewards: The Beatitudes (Matt. 5:3-12)
  B. Influence (Matt. 5:13-16)
II. Relation of this righteousness to that of the scribes and Pharisees (Matt. 5:17–6:18)
  A. Summary (Matt. 5:17-20)
  B. With regard to the current teachings: six topics (Matt. 5:21-48)
  C. With regard to the current piety (Matt. 6:1-18)
    1. Alms (Matt. 6:2-4)
    2. Prayer (including the Lord's Prayer) (Matt. 6:5-15)
    3. Fasting (Matt. 6:16-18)
III. Singlehearted devotion to God (Matt. 6:19-34)
  A. With regard to possessions (Matt. 6:19-24)
  B. With regard to anxiety (Matt. 6:25-32)
  C. Conclusion (Matt. 6:33, 34)
IV. Various injunctions (Matt. 7:1-23)
  A. Judge not, yet discriminate (Matt. 7:1-6)
  B. Encouragement to prayer: God's bounty and our consequent obligation: The Golden Rule (Matt. 7:7-12)
  C. The narrow gate (Matt. 7:13-14)
  D. False prophets and false disciples (Matt. 7:15-23)
V. The concluding parable (Matt. 7:24-27)

Any careful attempt to outline the sermon and to identify the relationships of the parts will suggest the following observations:

1. One cannot but be moved to admiration at the artistry and design of the whole. Even to so brief a composition we can apply words spoken of Milton's *Paradise Lost*, "For what is greatly planned we keep our astonishment." The sublime opening with the Beatitudes, the powerful closing parable, the cumulative contrasts, the transitions from covering injunction to concrete illustration, the way in which the thought of one saying plays upon the sayings which precede or follow, the reinforcement of the imperatives now by a call to the imitation of God, now by appeal to consequences, and now by the authority of the teacher; all these combined with the rhetorical features of the particular sayings — parallelism, numerical grouping, chiasmus, stanza, aphorism—make for an incomparably great utterance.

2. Matthew's section 6:19–7:23 gives more difficulty to those who have sought to outline the sermon than the earlier parts. Some commentators are satisfied to group the sayings, Matt. 6:19–7:6, as a series of prohibitions, and Matt. 7:7-23 as a series of commandments. In any case it should be noted that the general theme of anxiety versus trust, Matt. 6:25-34, is resumed in Matt. 7:7-12. The section on judging, Matt. 7:1-6, is related to Matt. 5:38-48, and in Luke's sermon follows it (Luke 6:36, 37). A key to the connection of much of Matthew's seventh chapter is found if we recall that Matthew is much concerned with "false brethren" and "false prophets." This bears immediately upon Matt. 7:6, 15-20, 21-23, but also upon the rest of the chapter.

3. It remains true nevertheless that we are aware of the abruptness of many of the transitions. Thus Martin Dibelius, bearing in mind the character of the other four discourses of Matthew in the light of their source analysis, is led to say:

That the Sermon on the Mount is not a real discourse the nature of its elements clearly demonstrates. They are mostly individual sayings, *e.g.*, the beatitudes, the new commandments and the parables of the builders. Each group is complete in itself and has no visible connection with the other groups. Indeed, it is necessary to suppose that the different groups were addressed to *different hearers* and, consequently, were spoken at *different occasions.*[3]

Apart from the abruptness of the transitions, many readers have felt that the close-packed and dense character of the discourse suggests

[3] *The Sermon on the Mount* (New York: Charles Scribner's Sons, 1940), p. 15. By permission.

that we have a summary of the texts or cores of numerous discourses, on any of which the Galilean teacher may well have expatiated and commented at greater length. The sermon would then represent the result of a sifting and selecting process: ore twice and thrice refined. To such conclusions we are pointed by immediate observation, and the study of the literary relationships of the material, to which we now turn, tends to confirm these impressions.

C. Literary Relationships and Source Analysis.—Once the student of the Sermon on the Mount has familiarized himself with its character, he will wish to go behind it and to inquire into its literary relationships with the material in the other Gospels, and into the sources or tradition out of which it is composed. Only so can he visualize the steps by which it assumed its present form and be in a position to picture to himself the underlying earliest reports of Jesus' teaching. Study of this section of Matthew in a harmony of the Synoptic Gospels immediately calls atttention to those extensive portions which appear, often in very similar form and order, in Luke. These portions scholars commonly assign to a hypothetical source often designated as Q. The following table of the material in Matthew's sermon, classified under four heads, will make the matter clearer.[4]

(1) Discourse common to Matthew and Luke:

Matthew	Luke		Matthew	Luke
(a) 5:3	6:20	(c)	7:1, 2	6:37, 38b
4, 6*	21b, 21a		3-5	41, 42
5	....		12*	31
11, 12	22, 23	(d)	16-20	43, 44
(b) 38-42	29, 30		21	46
43-48*	27, 28, 32-36		24-27	47-49

* Change of order.

(2) Scattered passages collected by Matthew and paralleled in Luke:

5:13	14:34-35 (Mark 9:50)		6:19-21	12:33-34
15	11:33 (8:16; Mark 4: 21)		22, 23	11:34-36
			24	16:13
18	16:17		25-33	12:22-31
25, 26	12:58, 59		7:7-11	11:9-13
32	16:18		13, 14	13:24
6:9-13	11:2-4		22, 23	13:26, 27

(3) Passages peculiar to Matthew:
5:7-10, 14, 16, 19, 23, 24, 31; 6:7, 8, 14, 15, 34; 7:6, 15.

(4) Discourse peculiar to Matthew:
Thesis: 5:17 (18-19), 20
(a) The righteousness of the scribes, 5:21-37, 38-48: murder (vss. 21, 22), adultery (vss. 27-30), false oaths (vss. 33-37).

[4] This table is taken from Alan Hugh McNeile, *The Gospel According to St. Matthew* (London: Macmillan & Co., 1915), pp. 99, 100; in a slightly modified form it is found in Bacon, *Studies in Matthew*, p. 172. Bacon's modifications are introduced into the table.

(b) The righteousness of the Pharisees, 6:1-6, 16-18: the general principle (vs. 1), alms (vss. 2-4), prayer (vss. 5, 6), fasting (vss. 16-18).

This table exhibits a number of striking features. (a) Note first how much overlapping there is between Matthew and Luke, as evidenced in secs. (1) and (2). On the other hand, as a harmony shows, Matthew's material here has very little relation to Mark. It is clear that Matthew and Luke have drawn upon a common stock, for it is unlikely that Luke was acquainted with Matthew directly, or vice versa. But what is particularly striking in this connection is the fact, which appears under sec. (1), that the contents of Luke's sermon on the plain, Luke 6:20-49, appear almost *in toto* in Matthew and, with minor exceptions, in the same order, though Matthew includes other sayings at certain points which now, as it were, interrupt Luke's sequence. It would appear therefore that a previously existing source containing a discourse of Jesus underlies the sermon as reported by Matthew and Luke. This discourse began with the Beatitudes, urged the love of enemies and nonresistance, warned against judging, and concluded with the saying concerning the tree and its fruits and the final parable of the builders. Such a source may have come to the two evangelists in somewhat different "editions," or one or both may have been responsible for the present divergencies through omission, supplementation, or alteration.

(b) There is moreover, as sec. (2) shows, a great deal more material, about a fourth of Matthew's sermon, also shared with Luke but not found in the sermon in Luke 6. This includes the passage Luke 12:22-34, for example, corresponding to Matt. 6:25-33 and 6:19-21. Close examination of all this common material shows that the various sayings ordinarily have a more natural setting in the various connections assigned them by Luke. We are thus led to the conclusion that Matthew or his sources have gathered them into the present sermon context, where they did not presumably belong originally. Yet the form in which all this common tradition appears in the two Gospels is so similar that most scholars agree that they were using a common written source, or sources, for the greater part of it.[5] Variations can most often be put down to the respective evangelists who have their own special interests and style, and who show in their use of Mark how much freedom they allowed themselves in handling their sources.

(c) The material common to Matthew and Luke, including both secs. (1) and (2), makes

[5] See Horace Marriott, *The Sermon on the Mount* (London: Macmillan & Co., 1925), pp. 3-8.

up a little less than half of the total content of the sermon. When we turn to an examination of the remainder, following the table, another striking feature appears—namely, the discourse sequences peculiar to Matthew under sec. (4). Except for certain intrusions, we find here two rather fully elaborated sections for which there is little or no parallel in the third Gospel. The first sequence, Matt. 5:17-48, is made up of six contrasts between Jesus' teaching and that of the current interpreters of the law. The second, Matt. 6:1-18, consists of three contrasts in what concerns practice. Presumably this evangelist in both sequences is using written sources—the formal characteristics so suggest—which Luke either did not know or did not choose to employ. Some scholars believe that these were all part of the common sayings source used in both Gospels, or at least were part of the original sermon.[6] It seems more likely that this material, in view of its particular concern with the relation of the law to the gospel, came to Matthew independently. This would be probable for Matt. 6:1-6, 16-18 at least. In 5:17-48 Matthew has used some source characterized by a series of contrasts between old and new, but has elaborated it by extending the formula "You have heard that it was said" upon material from Q. (So 5:31, 32, 38-42, 43-48.)[7]

The picture of the composition of the great discourse is then the following: Matthew has taken the sermon source represented in Luke 6 as his framework, finding in it his beginning (the Beatitudes) and ending (the parable of the builders). In this framework he has incorporated his two sequences (roughly, Matt. 5:17-37 and 6:1-18) and other lesser units of various provenance, no doubt himself supplying a certain number of the connecting transitions.

D. *Special Features of the Material and Composition.*—At this point our analysis passes beyond the identification of sources, and we are led to inquire into the effect upon the form of the sermon of the life situations out of which the various parts of the discourse come and concerning the stamp placed upon the sermon

[6] So Marriott, *op. cit.;* B. W. Bacon, *The Sermon on the Mount* (New York: The Macmillan Co., 1902).

[7] B. H. Streeter, *The Four Gospels: A Study of Origins* (New York: The Macmillan Co., 1925); A. M. Perry, "The Framework of the Sermon on the Mount," *Journal of Biblical Literature,* LIV (1935), 103-115, and others have urged a different view of the composition of the discourse, according to which a continuous M source underlies the larger part of the sermon, including the Beatitudes, and determines its outline. I subscribe to Bacon's criticism of this view as held by Streeter and in an earlier form by Burton. I would also, however, question Bacon's derivation of the essential parts of Matt. 5:17–6:18 from the source underlying Q. See Bacon, *Studies in Matthew,* ch. 12 and appended note viii. See also pp. 235-39.

in its present form by the evangelists themselves.

1. So far as the common material of Matthew and Luke is concerned, it is probable, as we have seen, that Matthew is responsible for many of the divergencies. Thus for the direct address of the Beatitudes in Luke's form, "Blessed are you poor" (Luke 6:20), Matthew substitutes the third person. Matthew sees Jesus as speaking generally to the Christians of the evangelist's own time, whereas Jesus originally addressed directly his little flock in the second person. A similar alteration of viewpoint is the best explanation for the differences between Luke 6:46 and Matt. 7:21, 22. In the latter passage the role of Christ as judge in the last day, a prominent feature in the first Gospel, displaces Luke's very simple parallel. To return to the Beatitudes, Matthew paraphrases Luke's "poor" with "poor in spirit" to give the term its true connotation, and combines further beatitudes with the four given in his source. In keeping with Matthew's tendency, this section has a more moralistic cast than the corresponding passage in Luke, but the original congratulatory character and the "good news" setting are not lost. Again, the form of the Lord's Prayer shows some elaboration, growing no doubt out of church use. Such liturgical modification of the prayer had a later development in the concluding formula (Matt. 6:13b) absent from the primitive text.

Matthew's special concern with persecution, with numerical arrangement, his addiction to certain terms like "righteousness" (see Matt. 5:6, 10, 20; 6:1; etc.) and "our Father in heaven" are manifest here as elsewhere. A good example of Matthew's editorial work is found in 5:25, 26. In Luke's context (Luke 12:58, 59) this counsel of reconciliation is a parable of warning to a generation confronting the judgment, and the hearers are called upon to repent in time. Matthew brings it into his section on anger and contempt toward men, and subjoins it to the injunction to reconcile oneself to one's brother (Matt. 5:23, 24), altering the opening words to fit the context. Yet throughout, Luke also has left his stamp on the common material as he presents it, and no doubt we sometimes find the older form of the teaching in Matthew.

2. In much of the section 5:17–6:18 Matthew is using sources with a special interest in the relation of the gospel to the law or the tradition. The text for this material appears in Matt. 5:17, "Think not that I have come to abolish the law and the prophets, . . . but to fulfill them." That they are not to be abolished is further stressed in vss. 18, 19 (cf. 23:2, 3). That they are to be fulfilled appears in 5:20 and in the several contrasts that follow. The

two themes are not easy to reconcile if we take 5:18, 19 and 23:2, 3 at their face value. Moreover, Jesus' prohibition of divorce and remarriage (in Matthew with the one exception), not to mention his apparent prohibition of all oaths, appears to represent a real revision of the Mosaic law. Discussion of the issues raised would carry us far beyond the Sermon on the Mount. It is enough to say here that scholars recognize a strain in some of Matthew's tradition of a very conservative Jewish-Christian point of view, which, so far as it goes back to Jesus, may or may not have been correctly transmitted. That the evangelist can place in close juxtaposition sayings of such diverse import suggests that he did not read the legalistic sayings in a strictly legalistic way. It is worth noting that Matt. 5:17 and 5:20 both appear to come from the evangelist himself; in any case the theme of fulfillment is determinative for him. Our conclusion must take account of the fact that Jesus himself made no open break with the law of Moses, and that he was not always unsympathetic with the oral tradition. The Sermon on the Mount reflects the varied impulses within the early church as it sought to come to terms with the problem of its relationship to the Jewish law. The evangelist, while including evidence of this fluctuation, in the final impression he leaves has not misrepresented the attitude of Jesus in this particular, especially if we compare his treatment with that of Mark.

3. When we survey the whole character of the sermon in the light of its sources, we can characterize more precisely the stamp placed upon it by the evangelist. Matthew has more or less consciously set Jesus over against Moses as a new lawgiver. The new law for the church is set over against the old law of God's people, not as abolishing but fulfilling it. Corroboration for this view is found in the study of Matthew's Gospel as a whole. It follows that Matthew conceives of this teaching as having a rather concretely legislative character. The authority of Christ is stressed not only in what precedes the sermon but in the discourse itself. Emphasis moreover is laid on obedience, performance, good works. Much of this no doubt is original with the older tradition of Jesus' teaching, but Matthew in systematizing the various sayings and in construing them against the background of the church of his day has modified their character appreciably. Here "the substance of the teaching of Jesus has been capitalized or funded, so to speak, so as to bear interest of itself as an objective summation of the Christian doctrine of righteousness." [8]

4. When we look behind the Sermon on the Mount as it appears in Matthew and Luke, we can recognize an earlier compendium, or earlier compendiums, of Jesus' teachings already formed by the church in earlier days. These have the priceless merit of suggesting to us "what the first Christians regarded as the most characteristic features of his message," [9] at least in certain areas. And with new tools, scholarship is able to establish probabilities regarding the actual sayings of Jesus and the history of their transmission. The chief transmutations to which they were subject can be identified, and thus the way is opened to a more exact understanding of their original import. The task of the interpreter is in this way illumined, and he is better able to appreciate both the teaching of Jesus and the guidance of the Holy Spirit as he led the first Christians to renew and apply it.

II. Interpretation and Relevance

A. History.—The student of the Sermon on the Mount should make a serious effort to distinguish between its original meaning and its modern application. Interpreters have not always kept this distinction in mind, and they have often lacked the necessary resources and aids for making it. We can benefit from the teaching, not by reading our own ideas into it, but by letting it speak for itself. Historical interpretation should precede homiletical interpretation.

Our task will be illuminated if we review some of the chief conceptions that have been held concerning the meaning and intention of the discourse. Matthew's own special understanding of it has been sufficiently set forth. In the early centuries this view of it as a Christian code tended to increase. Later, however, its requirements came to be viewed as a counsel of perfection, and were felt to be obligatory only for members of the monastic orders living outside the world. At the Reformation this double standard was abandoned for Protestants. The commands were looked upon as the uncompromising expression of the divine righteousness, directed to all. Where, however, men fell short of obedience, they could look to the great principle of justification by faith for a solution of the difficulty. Where we cannot attain to righteousness by performance, we can attain it through the grace of God laid hold of in the Cross, by faith. Indeed Lutherans saw the danger of a new kind of legalism or works-righteousness in any overemphasis on the Sermon on the Mount viewed as the norm of the gospel. This was the reproach later leveled at those pietists or evangelicals who proposed to take the commandments at face value for the whole con-

[8] William Manson, *Jesus the Messiah* (Philadelphia: The Westminster Press, 1946), p. 114.

[9] Dibelius, *Sermon on the Mount*, p. 29.

duct of life and who aimed at the perfection called for by the teacher. It has been widely held by orthodox Protestants that the absolute standards of the Sermon on the Mount are calculated to drive men to a sense of failure and despair and so to prepare them for the message of salvation in the Cross alone.

In the later nineteenth century another view became widespread and dominates much thinking today. According to this view, Christ was not laying down rules either for the church or the world. He was inculcating principles, prescribing attitudes and a fundamental, inward disposition. It was his expectation that his hearers would thus be led to renew their inner life, and so give effect to the teaching in the various circumstances that life offers. The last thing that Jesus intended, so it was held, was to put a new yoke on his followers, only just emancipated from the yoke of the Jewish law. He was concerned with spiritual freedom and knew that moral power and the development of moral personality come with freedom. His teachings bear therefore upon what we should *be* rather than on what we should *do*. This means also that we should make ample allowance for his use of figurative language and paradox. It is evident that following this line of interpretation it was quite easy for men to accommodate the teaching of Jesus to their own standards. Schweitzer was justified in his protest that men had nullified the great imperious demands of the gospel so that they became, to use his figure, like shells from which the fuses had been removed.

It was the work of Schweitzer himself, among others, that led to another view, at least among scholars. Jesus meant the requirements very explicitly, he showed, but the radical formulation of the requirements is to be explained by the imminence of the kingdom of God. The judgment was immediately at hand and an extraordinary ethic was proper for an extraordinary emergency. We have then, in Schweitzer's term, "interim-ethics," immediately relevant only to Jesus' disciples in the brief period before the end. That some relevance in the sayings for later Christians can be found was not denied, but such preoccupation was absent from Jesus' own outlook. While the view of Schweitzer, in the precise form in which he stated it, has been increasingly abandoned by scholars, his insight that the teaching is significantly governed by the drawing near of the new age is today generally accepted.

One influential form of this view is that of Dibelius, to whose volume on the sermon reference has been made. As he sees it, Jesus gives utterance to the perfect and pure will of God, irrespective of the difficulties so raised for those who are still living in the world, in the old age. The commandments cannot be carried out fully in this age, but they are signs of the eternal kingdom and its total claim, and they constantly urge us on toward the divine likeness. Dibelius does not accept the view that Jesus intended by the very impossibility of the teaching to drive his disciples in despair to the Cross. This is to read back later theology into the mind of Jesus. For all their difficulty, he offered his sayings as words to be obeyed. Nor is their rigor to be minimized by supposing that he spoke as a poet. Nor again, is the sermon to be understood as an "ideal way of life." Jesus was not voicing an ideal but a demand, the proper demand of the new world that was breaking in. It should be said that Dibelius is first of all thinking of the original teaching of Jesus which underlies Matthew's sermon. The latter also assumes actual obedience on the part of the disciple, but here as church law.

B. Approach of the Interpreter.—There are a number of important considerations which our better historical knowledge requires us to keep in mind in the task of interpretation.

1. For one thing we must not oversimplify the character of the sermon. It includes a diversity of teaching: generalized counsels ("be ye therefore perfect" and the Golden Rule), specific imperatives ("swear not at all"), illustrations of the desired conduct (the turning of the other cheek), hyperbolic illustrations ("if thy right eye causeth thee to stumble, pluck it out"), and at least one rule, namely, on divorce, which, however, owes its character to the way in which Matthew construes it. Another way of identifying the variety is to note that Jesus' sayings are sometimes most closely related to the tradition of the wisdom teachers of Israel, sometimes to that of the prophets, and sometimes to that of the rabbis. Moreover from the prophetic tradition and from Deuteronomy comes the practice of calling for perfect obedience and making a total demand. In this connection also we are to bear in mind at how many points the Jewish literature of this period offers parallels to the sayings.

2. Attentive study also shows that, contrary to frequent assumptions, we cannot easily characterize Jesus' ethics as directed to disposition rather than action, to inwardness as against outward performance. This is convincingly shown in the work of Hans Windisch.[10] It is true that Jesus warns against ostentation and any parade of piety, and that he assigns sin to intention as well as to act. But his prohibitions refer to acts —the lustful look or the word of contempt— and his counsels refer to positive conduct and

[10] *Der Sinn der Bergpredigt* (Leipzig: J. C. Hinrichs, 1929).

deeds. Even in the saying concerning the tree and its fruits, all we can say is that being and doing are for him inseparable. The modern Christian has the right to formulate the distinction between intention and act, between disposition and its expression, but Jesus did not couch his moral teaching in these terms.

3. The imperatives of Jesus are presented in a religious context and a very particular one, belief in the imminent new age, the kingdom of God which was "at hand." This meant good news and moral power. The ethics were the ethics of the kingdom and were addressed to members of the kingdom. The sanctions of the commandments are religious sanctions: rewards and penalties, gratitude to God, the imitation of God, the glory of God. Jesus could also appeal to men's native discernment, but this appeal was made to men trained in the whole Jewish outlook. We must also recognize the religious sanction implicit in the authority of the teacher himself, unformulated in the original teaching, though everywhere present, and made very explicit in the setting assigned to the sermon by Matthew.

4. Here, as in the rest of Jesus' teaching, there is little evidence of concern with questions involving civic and political life and responsibility. Jesus did not occupy the office of a scribe (lawyer) or legislator, and he repudiated the role of judge or arbitrator in this world's litigation. He was, moreover, speaking to a group that had no considerable responsibility for the conduct of the world's business, and Matthew elaborates the sermon for a church similarly situated. The teaching, again, comes out of a "small world," a rural and small-town society of a comparatively simple kind, in a semitropical climate. Some account also needs to be taken of the figurative and picturesque element in the teaching, though this element should not be exaggerated.

5. Attention should be given here also to the absence in the sermon of certain themes which appear elsewhere in the Gospels. We have to look outside it to find the double great commandment as the summary of the law and the prophets, and for specific formulation of Jesus' great principle of service. In the discourse we have corollaries and applications rather than the principles themselves. Neither does Jesus speak of his death and its significance, nor directly of justification and the Holy Spirit, nor of the church, the new covenant, baptism, and the Lord's Supper. We have only to look at the other discourses in Matthew, and at numerous notable parables in Luke, for example, to be reminded of other teachings only briefly alluded to, if at all, in the sermon. The teacher thus makes here but one specific mention of his

unique office (Matt. 7:22-23), and that in connection with his future role as judge. Comparison with the parallel passage in Luke 13:25-27 indicates that Matthew is here responsible for this one exception.

With these cautions and distinctions in mind the interpreter is in a position to find a sounder basis for his task. He has a clearer conception of the original sense of the sayings. When it becomes necessary to apply them, he is aware not only of the difficulty of the operation but also of the freedom that must be exercised.

C. The Modern Dilemma.—Otto Riethmueller has written:

Like a magnetic mountain, [the Sermon on the Mount] has continually attracted towards itself the greatest spirits (not only Christendom!) with undiminished force through all the centuries. For that reason also, it has had to put up with more opposition, distortion, dilution and emasculation than any other writing in the literature of the world.[11]

A few of the negative reactions to the sermon can be briefly mentioned. Nietzsche includes it in his charge of "a slave morality" directed against the gospel ethics. Paulsen misses in it any note of the chivalrous defense of the weak or any summons to the concrete redressing of wrong. The Marxists see here an encouragement to the acceptance of the *status quo* with compensatory dreams of otherworldly satisfactions. Many public-spirited moderns find it irrelevant and charge that it does not convey any clear summons for Christians today on crying needs or on pressing issues such as public order, political freedom, and social strife.

Dibelius has put it well:

The great mass of our contemporaries confronted with the Sermon on the Mount will merely shrug their shoulders. Most of them, even those who are radical opponents of the Christian Church and of Christianity, have the impression that the preacher on the Mount was a righteous and benevolent man, perhaps a Saint, but that his sermon is not applicable, not suited to the modern struggle for existence —in the field of economics as well as of politics. It seems to testify to the olden times, to a patriarchal ideal which no longer concerns us.[12]

The difficulty of the sermon for modern men can be illustrated by four of its imperatives. "Do not swear at all" (Matt. 5:34) has troubled many Christians. In the last of the Thirty-Nine Articles, "Of a Christian Man's Oath," one body of Christians is assured "that Christian Religion doth not prohibit, but that a man may

[11] "The City on the Mount," *The Student World*, XXX (1937), 203.
[12] *Sermon on the Mount* (New York: Charles Scribner's Sons, 1940), p. 127. By permission.

swear when the Magistrate requireth, in a cause of faith and charity, so it be done according to the Prophet's teaching, in justice, judgment, and truth." Perhaps the most harassing of the issues raised by the sermon has been in connection with the words "Do not resist one who is evil" (Matt. 5:39). Note further, "Give to him who begs from you" (Matt. 5:42). After sad experience Luther construed this to mean: "Give to him who begs of you, but not what he asks for." Finally, the saying "Judge not" (Matt. 7:1) has appeared to many to strike at the foundation of social order.

When, however, we turn from the individual commands, we find that the supreme difficulty of the teaching lies in the fact that Jesus sets up God as the model: "You, therefore, must be perfect, as your heavenly Father is perfect" (Matt. 5:48), and ". . . that you may be sons of your Father who is in heaven" (Matt. 5:45). The rigor lies, moreover, in Jesus' insistence that there must be *no* anger, *no* desire to retaliate, *no* hatred; that the heart must be wholly pure.

D. Meaning of the Imperatives.—We have seen that in their original intention, and in Matthew's formulation particularly, the requirements of Jesus called for concrete obedience. There were indeed several broad principles and several illustrative sayings among them, but in general Jesus formulated these demands in terms of action. Yet they were not, in Jesus' intention, rules or laws, for Jesus was evidently not a lawmaker for his people; the rabbis and the Sanhedrin carried out this function. Neither was he drawing up canon law for the church; this lay beyond his horizon. The larger part of Jesus' ethical teaching falls in the category of prophetic injunction. With this is combined a considerable amount of observation and of appeal to the wisdom tradition. While Matthew's arrangement has somewhat changed its character, Jesus himself spoke as prophet and teacher. The prophets always went deeper and asked more than the letter of the statutes. Like Jesus, they asked for act as well as intention. And, like Jesus, they demanded complete obedience and an entire devotion. Like Jesus, again, they set up God as the model: "Ye shall be holy; for I am holy." The rigor of Jesus' demands is explained partly, then, by the tradition to which he belonged.

Yet Jesus deepened the requirements, whether of prophets or wise men. It is not so much that he had a different conception of God as that he was more conscious of God's action and reality. For the kingdom was drawing nigh. Indeed Jesus was more than prophet—he was the prophet and bearer of the kingdom of God, its voice and agent. His ethics is that of the new age and the new covenant. The Sermon on the Mount is directed to those who have already begun to enter into the new age and who have begun to share its new powers. It should never be forgotten that both its ethical teachings and its confidence in God are spoken in a context of salvation. The Beatitudes make that clear at the beginning. The standards set are otherwise both impracticable and implausible—and the trust in God naïve.

If the Sermon on the Mount were only an ethical code, there would be none more impossible. One does not love by command. And the very nature of the passions is just that we are unable to master them. Covetousness, desire, hatred arise from the depths of our being which are beyond our conscious self.[13]

But the preaching of the moral demands is accompanied by the transforming work of God in the preacher and in the gospel.

E. Modern Relevance and Application.—We are left, however, with the question of the meaning of these moral demands for us. This is finally a matter of every Christian's individual conscience, guided by the Holy Spirit and the experience and brotherly counsel of other Christians. Yet our historical study of the sermon has shown that Jesus' words were conditioned by special circumstances and a special outlook. We therefore face a task of reinterpretation. His utterances did not constitute a set of laws, and even where they represented express commands we are under obligation to appropriate them in a free and responsible way, applying them to our own situation. For all Christians they should be a matter of constant earnest struggle and wrestling, lest we evade their force either by legalizing them or watering them down.

Windisch has well demonstrated that Jesus in his own situation proclaimed these demands as mandatory. His disciples did not then take them solely as a guide to the proper disposition or spirit. *But this is often precisely our task.*

It is we who do not regard Jesus' sayings as rules and regulations that require literal fulfilment. It is we who interpret them as general principles and as illustrations of the way these principles work themselves out in concrete historical situations. It is we who hold that as illustrations they are not mandatory upon us. It is we who, from suggestions in individual sayings, have put together the portrait of a child of God, of a disciple of Jesus, of a man who longs for God's kingdom and his righteousness, sins, and still remains the object of God's grace. It is we who see in the Sermon on the Mount an

[13] Suzanne de Dietrich, "Righteousness of Men and Righteousness of God," *The Student World*, XXX (1937), 214-15.

ethos that is never static and that cannot possibly be defined as the sum of separate commandments.[14]

This would mean, then, that in any given moral dilemma the Christian looking to Jesus of Nazareth for direction will be guided, not by any one saying, but by his whole utterance and example, bearing in mind the disparity between his situation and ours. The disciple today will ask: What were the supreme insights and concerns that found expression in Jesus' sayings and conduct? He will then be in a position to deal with specific choices today. He will be further counseled by the experience of the church and by the Holy Spirit. Individual Christians will differ in the conclusions reached on particular issues. Here too the mystery of vocation will be a factor. Some are called to bear costly witness in the moral sphere at points where their fellows have not as yet been obligated.

It is evident, in any case, that the sermon taken seriously sets up a conflict with the current codes of the common life. Even where the Christian is not led to break with the patterns and institutions in which he is involved, and in which the church is involved, he will be constantly testifying against them in word and deed. The gospel and the church represent an invasion of the world by the power and grace of God. There cannot but be collision and costly witness here. Thus those who seek to live by the insights and directives of the Sermon on the Mount will constitute a continual ferment in society, breaking out here and there in open defiance and non-co-operation. This is the meaning of the figures of the salt, the light, and the leaven.

Particular difficulty in the modern world inheres in those reassurances offered to disciples by Jesus in connection with his sayings on anxiety and providence. The divine provision for the fowl of the air and the lilies of the field seems no sufficient warrant to the insecure of any time, and men and women find it a hard saying that they should cast off all anxiety about their temporal needs. The example of those saints or faithful ones who have cultivated a prayerful improvidence, and who have been cared for, does not reassure burdened parents caught in the jeopardies of modern society—with its depressions, droughts, famines, and the devastations of war. Interpretation of these passages in the sermon is aided if we note that Jesus' main preoccupation here, as the context indicates, is with true and false treasure, with

the service of God and the service of mammon. In what is said about providence and prayer the realism of Jesus should also be borne in mind. He knew that prophets perish, that there were those who devoured widows' houses, and he reassured his disciples concerning those who might destroy the body. Prayer and piety are no guarantee of safety and temporal well-being. This needs to be stressed when there are so many who are inclined to turn this aspect of the faith in the direction of magic. Yet when all is said, Christian experience has recognized an inexhaustible meaning in Jesus' teaching on prayer and trust, and the prayer for daily bread properly belongs in the Lord's Prayer. Those who fulfill the obligations of the sermon are the ones best qualified to speak of its promises.

The question of the practicability of the Sermon on the Mount is relieved of certain difficulties by the considerations that have been adduced. This question is most acute only for those who take its specific injunctions at face value as letter and as law. On the other hand, even with the interpretation here proposed, the question of practicability is still with us. But here it refers rather to the moral resources of the disciple than to the compatibility of the sermon with existing society. In speaking of the narrow gate Jesus envisaged this aspect of the question. We have been too prompt often to cry down the practicability of the mandates on love, forgiveness, purity, and nonretaliation because we have failed to take account of the redemptive action of the gospel. There are levels of Christian attainment and endowment paid for at a great price, all too rarely exhibited. In some lives the generosities of God and the charities of Christ overflow in such measure that what can only be called moral miracles result, and man's ancient foes are decisively worsted.

III. Selected Bibliography

BACON, B. W. *The Sermon on the Mount: Its Literary Structure and Didactic Purpose.* New York: The Macmillan Co., 1902.

DIBELIUS, MARTIN. *The Sermon on the Mount.* New York: Charles Scribner's Sons, 1940.

GORE, CHARLES. *The Sermon on the Mount.* London: V. Murray, 1900.

LINDSAY, A. D. *The Moral Teaching of Jesus: An Examination of the Sermon on the Mount.* New York: Harper & Bros., 1937.

VOTAW, CLYDE W. "The Sermon on the Mount," *A Dictionary of the Bible: Extra Volume,* ed. James Hastings. New York: Charles Scribner's Sons, 1904, pp. 1-45.

WINDISCH, HANS. *Der Sinn der Bergpredigt.* Leipzig: J. C. Hinrichs, 1929; 2nd ed., 1937.

---

[14] *Der Sinn der Bergpredigt,* pp. 170-71; cited by S. MacLean Gilmour, "Interpreting the Sermon on the Mount," *Crozer Quarterly,* XXIV (1947), 56.

THE TEACHING OF JESUS

III. THE PARABLES

by WALTER RUSSELL BOWIE

The teachings of Jesus, as they have come down to us in the four Gospels, include brief words spoken here and there in the midst of action, longer and more deliberate instruction to the people at large or to the disciples, and—according to the Gospel of John—meditations on great mystical themes. In that varied record, every element has its priceless value; and certainly, to multitudes of Christians, high up in the scale will stand the parables.

For the parables have an arresting quality which has etched them deep in memory. They are based on things seen, and they awake immediate and vivid images which are seen again in the mind. As John Bunyan knew, the citadel of Man-Soul is stormed more easily through eye-gate than through ear-gate; and it is because they enter through the visual imagination that the parables have penetrated so surely into the thought and conscience of innumerable folk. Into the thought and also into the *conscience*, be it noted, for the parables provoke far more than curiosity. They not only arrest attention; they arouse something deep within. It was said of Jesus that the common people heard him gladly; and no wonder, for the extraordinary quality of his teachings, and especially of his parables, was that they said what ordinary men and women could take hold of. When Jesus spoke, it was not as though some unfamiliar idea were coming from outside, but rather as though an instinctive recognition were being awakened in the listeners' own selves. "That is the way life really works," they felt. "That is how truth is." The parables did not bring alien information; rather they focused and called into action what people already half knew was so, and now suddenly could fully see.

It would be a fascinating study to search through history and biography and write a record of the influence of the parables on human life. A missionary to Japan, whose work was among the lowest and neediest of the population, translated the story of a Japanese condemned murderer, Tokichi Ishii, who read the New Testament when he was in prison and was converted and transformed. The story was contained in scraps of the man's own writing and in notes by prison officials. On one of the pages of his diary he wrote concerning the new inspiration which had come to him: "I cared nothing about these things when I was out in the world, and for that reason was but a demon in human form. I was, however, born a human being, and . . . I want to die knowing at least what I can about the teachings of God, and the true path of man." [1] And one of the passages which he records is the climax of Jesus' parable of the lost sheep: "I say unto you, that likewise joy shall be in heaven over one sinner that repenteth, more than over ninety and nine just persons, which need no repentance" (Luke 15:7).

During World War II there appeared a remarkable little book, *The Raft*. It is the story of three men in an American navy scouting plane who, when the plane crash-landed in the Pacific Ocean and sank, were left with nothing but an inflated rubber raft, eight feet by four feet, on which to keep afloat for thirty-four days until they drifted a thousand miles to shore. The leader of the three, bomber pilot Harold Dixon, remembered some of the things he had been taught from the New Testament in Sunday school. "So each evening I told one story. . . . One of my hazy parables would snap us out of our depression and start a flood of dis-

[1] *A Gentleman in Prison, with the Confessions of Tokichi Ishii*, tr. Caroline Macdonald (New York: George H. Doran Co., 1922), p. 126.

cussion in which our dismal outlook was forgotten." [2]

In what numberless other ways and times, one wonders, have the parables come to men in "dismal outlook" with their message of God's mercy and their summons to human trust and fidelity and mutual help? Often the dismal outlook has been changed by the spirit of the parables into something different. What else than a re-enacted parable in our own generation has been the work of Sir Wilfred Grenfell and of Albert Schweitzer—an old parable re-enacted by men who heard again the question "Who is my neighbor?" and went out in the spirit of Jesus to find the needy neighbor on the bleak shores of Labrador or in the forests of equatorial Africa.

I. Parables in the Synoptic Gospels

In the Gospels of Matthew, Mark, and Luke there are fifty-three passages which may be classed as parables. Listed according to the places of their occurrence, they are as follows.

PARABLES RECORDED IN MATTHEW, MARK, AND LUKE

	Matt.	Mark	Luke
New patches on old garments	9:16	2:21	5:36
New wine in old wineskins	9:17	2:22	5:37-38
The sower (or the soil)	13:3-23	4:2-20	8:4-15
The mustard seed	13:31-32	4:30-32	13:18-19
The wicked tenants of the vineyard	21:33-45	12:1-12	20:9-19
The budding fig tree	24:32-33	13:28-29	21:29-31

PARABLES RECORDED IN MATTHEW AND LUKE

	Matt.	Luke
The house on the rock and the house on the sand	7:24-27	6:47-49
The leaven	13:33	13:20-21
The lost sheep	18:12-14	15:3-7
The wise steward	24:45-51	12:42-48

PARABLES RECORDED IN ONLY ONE GOSPEL

In Matthew

The tares	13:24-30
The hidden treasure	13:44
The precious pearl	13:45-46
The dragnet	13:47-50
The unmerciful servant	18:23-35
The laborers in the vineyard	20:1-16
The two sons	21:28-32
The marriage of the king's son	22:1-14
The wise and foolish virgins	25:1-13
The ten talents	25:14-30
The sheep and the goats	25:31-46

In Mark

The seed growing silently	4:26-29
The porter on watch	13:34-37

[2] Robert Trumbull, *The Raft* (New York: Henry Holt & Co., 1942), p. 84.

In Luke

The good Samaritan	10:25-37
The friend at midnight	11:5-10
The rich fool	12:16-21
The watchful servants	12:35-38
The barren fig tree	13:6-9
The guests who made excuses	14:16-24
The lost coin	15:8-10
The prodigal son	15:11-32
The dishonest steward	16:1-9
The rich man and Lazarus, the beggar	16:19-31
The master and the servants	17:7-10
The persistent widow	18:1-8
The Pharisee and the publican	18:9-14
The pounds	19:11-27

It would be possible to make the foregoing list still longer if every figurative expression of Jesus were included. Among the passages which here have been classed as parables some are exceedingly brief: two or three vivid phrases, the flash of a signal that blazes only for an instant sufficient to show the direction in which thought can follow. Some of them are longer, like the immortal story of the prodigal son, or the unforgettable picture of the good Samaritan.

II. Definition and Nature of a Parable

Technically some of these passages might be called by another name than that of parables. The *Century Dictionary* has a comparison of several terms that might be applicable.

"[A] simile is a statement of . . . likeness in literal terms." So when Jesus said, "The kingdom of heaven is like unto leaven, which a woman took, and hid in three measures of meal" (Matt. 13:33), it might be held that he has given us a simile and no more.

"[A metaphor is a figure of speech that] taxes the imagination by saying that the first object is the second, or by speaking as though it were." Not in the first three Gospels, but in the fourth, there are many passages which thus are metaphors, such as "I am the door" (John 10:7), "I am the living bread" (John 6:51), "I am the good shepherd" (John 10:11), "I am the way" (John 14:6).

"[An] allegory personifies abstract things." Furthermore the representation of abstract truth in an allegory is thoroughgoing and precise. Not only one central feature but every detail of the description or the story has some parallel meaning. Therefore it is sometimes considered that the so-called parable of the sower, with its description not only of the seed sown but of the different kinds of soil in which the seed fell, has the nature of an allegory.

"A parable is a story that is or may be true and is used generally to teach some moral or religious truth." A simile is a hint to the imagination of a story that might be told; an allegory is a story in which the meaning may be intricate and only suggestively revealed; but a parable is a story or a suggestion concentrated on one point so plain that he who runs may read it.

The parables of Jesus which are most characteristic of his teaching are those in which the story element is so direct and simple that the interest of the hearer is caught immediately and swept along its swift and vivid stream. And this is true, even though we have, as we must remember, only a partial echo of Jesus' words. Nobody wrote down what he said when he was speaking. Many years later when the Gospels came to be compiled, nobody could recall all the sentences he had used; but the central current of his thought flows through as unmistakably as the fresh waters of the Amazon flood out where sailors can drink from them far at sea. There is a quality in the parables which time and distance cannot dilute or destroy. "Never man spake like this man," the temple police are said to have reported to the chief priests and Pharisees (John 7:46). Is that record only the unrestrained exaggeration of tradition? Ordinarily a phrase like that would be called so. But the curious fact is that nobody else has put truths so imperishable into forms so indestructible as Jesus did when he told his parables. Many other teachers have told stories that were lively; but he created life. The shepherd going after the lost sheep, the good Samaritan on the Jericho road, the publican praying God's forgiveness in the temple, are more alive to modern consciousness than the flesh-and-blood people who supposed themselves to be important in Jesus' day, and more vital than most of the living persons who crowd our contemporary streets.

III. Old Testament Parables and the Parables of Jesus

Thus the parables represent an unmatched achievement. But they did not represent an unheard-of idea. Other teachers besides Jesus, and some of them before Jesus, put what they had to say in the form of parables. When the prophet Nathan determined to confront David with a message of God's judgment for his murder of Uriah and his theft of Uriah's wife, he did so by the parable of the rich man's flocks and the poor man's one loved lamb (II Sam. 12:1-14). An unnamed "certain man of the sons of the prophets" confronted King Ahab with a grim parable that was partly spoken and partly acted out (I Kings 20:35-42). One of the great passages in the prophecy of Isaiah is the comparison of Israel with a vineyard planted by the hand of God and tended with patience and devotion that it should bring forth grapes but bringing forth at last nothing but wild grapes (Isa. 5:1-7); and in this we may see the unmistakable precursor of another parable of the vineyard which Jesus told in his own way. The famous story which Jotham told to the men of Shechem in order to make their choice of Abimelech seem contemptible—the story of the trees that wanted a king and when they were rebuffed by the olive tree, the fig tree, and the vine, could get no one finally for king except a bramble (Judg. 9:7-20)—is a fable rather than a parable, since it is built upon a fantasy rather than upon a parallel with actual life; but it too is illustrative of that pictorial way of presenting truth which is at the heart of the parables of Jesus, the agelong desire for which gives the parables their sure appeal. Always it has been and is true that when abstract propositions knock in vain at the doors of attention, the

> . . . truth embodied in a tale
> Shall enter in at lowly doors.[3]

When Jesus, therefore, spoke his message, which he intended to be unmistakable, he was too wise to invent some pattern that might be unique; he used instead the pattern that answered to an instinct that is universal. He knew that people understand best not bare truths but thoughts put into pictures. They want to see truth, and he therefore presented it so that it could be seen and not forgotten.

We are touching here something obviously deeper than a question of expression. It is a question rather of the way in which reality is approached. It may be approached abstractly. The mind may try to capture it by verbal formulas; but then what is possessed turns out not to be reality itself but only a thin specter of it. On the other hand reality may be conceived concretely. In that case it will be looked for not in a disembodied notion but in truth which can be seen embodied in some fact of our familiar world, a truth so *substantial* that it feeds imagination and does not merely outline an idea. It was that way of conceiving reality which was always characteristic of the Hebrew mind—that Hebrew mind which was the human heritage of Jesus. The men of the Old Testament did not put into a creedal formula, for instance, their faith in the providence of God; they said, "The Lord is my shepherd; I shall not want" (Ps. 23:1). They did not expatiate as a philosopher might upon the thesis that there is a religious impulse in the nature of man; they said, "As the hart panteth after the water brooks, so panteth my soul after

[3] Alfred Tennyson, *In Memoriam*, st. xxxvi.

thee, O God" (Ps. 42:1). They did not discourse upon heredity; they said, "The fathers have eaten sour grapes, and the children's teeth are set on edge" (Ezek. 18:2). Like the psalmists and the prophets whose way of thinking echoed again in him, Jesus also felt truth thus intuitively and put it into the vivid symbols which all men would understand.

IV. Interpreting the Parables

The recognition of this fact should shut the gate against one interpretation of the parables which is sometimes possible but which, when all is said and done, would be a misinterpretation—the kind of interpretation which turns a parable into a mystery instead of a means of light.

Now it must be granted that arguments can be marshaled to support the thought that a parable may be a sort of mystery. We may be pointed to such words as those of Mark 4:11-12, in which Jesus is recorded to have said to the disciples after he had told the parable of the sower: "Unto you it is given to know the mystery of the kingdom of God: but unto them that are without, all these things are done in parables: that seeing they may see, and not perceive; and hearing they may hear, and not understand; lest at any time they should be converted, and their sins should be forgiven them." Here indeed it would look as though a parable were meant to wrap up truth rather than to reveal it. It must be remembered too that in the Old Testament the word "parable" is sometimes used with a suggestion similar to that. The Hebrew *māshal* has as its root meaning "to be like," and is applied most simply to popular sayings which convey comparisons universally recognized as true; but *māshal* can also have the meaning of an oracle or of a riddle or of a saying so dark that it will not be understood. "I will open my mouth in a parable," said one of the psalmists, "I will utter dark sayings of old" (Ps. 78:2). With that background of Old Testament example it is possible to maintain that Jesus intended in his parables to give a message that only the initiated could grasp, while to the crowd it would be no more than a bewilderment and rebuff. This would seem to be exactly what Mark meant to say.

The interpretation and purpose of this parable of the sower are expressed in Matthew and Luke in words somewhat different from those of Mark. The detailed comparison of the three Gospels at this point will be found in the parallel exegesis of the three books. But the important positive points to be noted now are two.

First there is the fact that all three Gospels are here reflecting a passage from Isaiah. In the temple the prophet has seen a vision of God "sitting upon a throne, high and lifted up," surrounded by the glory of the seraphim; he has heard the call of God and his lips have been touched with the burning coal of consecration. Then at the climax comes the voice of God: "Go, and tell this people, Hear ye indeed, but understand not; and see ye indeed, but perceive not. Make the heart of this people fat, and make their ears heavy, and shut their eyes; lest they see with their eyes, and hear with their ears, and understand with their heart, and convert, and be healed" (Isa. 6:9-10). Read literally that sounds as though the prophet's mission was directly ordained and meant from the beginning not to heal but to harden, not to persuade but to perplex and to antagonize. But that, on the face of it, is incredible. Apparently these verses represent Isaiah's conclusions in later years when he looked back upon his call through the long and often bitter perspective of Israel's opposition. Since in spite of his utmost efforts the people had rejected the Word of God, it seemed to him that this had been foreordained; and with the Hebrew's conception of the transcendent and awful sovereignty of God, he regarded the disobedience of the people as having only one possible explanation: namely, that God had willed that too. Much the same thought may have been in the mind of Mark when he took the tradition of the words of Jesus that had come down to him and saw it colored by the actual course of Jesus' life and by the Crucifixion. It is not strange that it should have seemed to him that the rejection of Jesus was foreordained, and that his teachings, which the mass of the nation despised, must have been something which they were not fit to appreciate, and therefore were never from the beginning expected to understand.

The second fact to remember is that what the evangelists thought in retrospect does not necessarily mean what Jesus originally thought. Later, as the ring of misunderstanding and hostility hardened round him, he too, like Isaiah, may have felt so deep a fatefulness in the people's alienation that it seemed finally of no use to try to make his teachings plain. But at the outset, and through all his ministry so far as he could keep it what he wanted it to be, surely the last thing he would have chosen was to let his words seem riddling or obscure. "That He desired not to be understood by the people in general, and therefore clothed His teaching in unintelligible forms," wrote C. H. Dodd, "cannot be made credible on any reasonable reading of the Gospels."[3] He taught in

[3] *The Parables of the Kingdom* (New York: Charles Scribner's Sons, 1936), p. 15.

parables because parables conveyed ideas and feelings that every plain man could appropriate. He taught in parables because through them the truth would most vividly appear. As W. O. E. Oesterley has put it, with the emphasis of italic type, "Whatever other uses a 'parable' served, its prime purpose was to *teach*. . . . In the large variety of what are called parables in the Old Testament, . . . the great majority are easily understood, and are intended to be so." [4] As this was true of the parables in the Old Testament, so it was equally true of the parables of Jesus in the New. It is certainly desirable that it should be more nearly true of the preaching and teaching put forth by his interpreters.

J. Middleton Murry, English man of letters, has given to one of his books the title *Jesus, Man of Genius*. That would be inadequate as a description, but as a partial suggestion it is true. In his human fascination, and in his power to express what flamed in his own mind and heart, Jesus was a genius, as the great artists and poets are. The parables as we have them now are printed words upon a page, but the parables as the people of Galilee heard them were realities visualized before them as they listened to the voice of Jesus and read his face and followed the movement of his hands. Only by lift of the imagination can we hear all that they heard then.

V. What the Parables Reveal About Jesus

The parables throw light on many subjects, but the first subject on which they throw their light is the teller of the parables himself.

One sometimes reflects wistfully upon what it would have meant to us if some contemporary could have recorded the words of Jesus as fully as Boswell recorded those of Samuel Johnson. No such a one existed. But the parables give us clues about some of the things in which Jesus was interested, and the area in which his mind was moving. Some of them may point to those associations which were earliest and deepest in his consciousness.

Psychology and its study of personality have brought a new realization of the fact that rarely if ever does a child grow up into a maturity that is assured and strong unless in its earliest years it feels itself secure. Unless it knows love it will be afraid; for only love can create the outgoing confidence which meets the world with fearlessness—as the man Jesus met his world. Through the years in Nazareth, Jesus grew up in the shelter of a human home, and in a home

[4] *The Gospel Parables in the Light of Their Jewish Background* (New York: The Macmillan Co., 1936), pp. 4-5.

endowed with all the rich inheritance of Judaism which Joseph and Mary could transmit to him. As Winifred Kirkland, with fine insight, has written:

Twenty centuries ago, Judaism dared to have convictions and educated its children in accordance with them, and thereby obtained results in energy, spiritualized energy. It is high tribute to the child-training which he received as a Hebrew boy, that from the first moment you meet him you can discover no deviation in the life purpose of Jesus. You cannot split his character into compartments, assuming, Here we will study his acts, here his words, here his thoughts, for Jesus is a personality perfectly fused. In the education of Jesus, from babyhood to manhood, there was never any severance between the beautiful and the ethical, between the material and the spiritual, between the secular and the sacred. One result of this education may be seen in a character which is at the same time profoundly integrated and profoundly energized. [5]

And if it should seem that words like those equate the development of Jesus too closely with the way we see other lives unfold, it should be remembered that the very meaning of the Incarnation is that he who was to be the Savior did enter fully into our human lot. Certainly Jesus was not sent down abruptly out of the sky full grown and independently mature. He came as a baby laid in a woman's arms. He grew as a little boy who followed a woman's footsteps, looked up into a woman's eyes, and reached for a woman's hand. So it may be that memories of his mother are reflected in some of the most clear-cut parables which long afterwards Jesus framed. As a tiny child he may have watched with fascinated eyes the bubbling of the leaven as his mother's fingers kneaded it into the meal. He had seen her mend the all too precious clothes which could so easily wear out, and he knew that there came a time when no more new patches could be put on old cloth. He had gone with her to the village well, and he knew the gratefulness of a cup of cold water taken from her hands. He may have been thinking of her when he told the parable of the woman who lost a coin and, when she had swept her house until she had found it, called in all her neighbors to rejoice. He still may have been remembering her or remembering the too often forgotten figure of Joseph, the strength of whose affection must have been the background of his boyhood years, when he said to a crowd in which there were mothers and fathers, "If ye then . . . know how to give good gifts unto your children, how much more shall your Father which is in heaven give good things to them that ask him?" (Matt. 7:11.)

In his parables one sees the reflection of other things on which his attention had lingered as

[5] *Portrait of a Carpenter* (New York: Charles Scribner's Sons, 1931), pp. 59-60. By permission.

he went about the little town of Nazareth and off to the hills and fields around it—the simple, homely things that might mean nothing, and yet could mean so much. Recall the images that flashed into his mind and illuminated his teaching: the scarlet anemones spreading like flame across the Galilean meadows after the rain, of which he said that Solomon in all his glory was not arrayed like one of these (Matt. 6:29); a hen gathering her chickens under her wing (Matt. 23:37); birds finding room for their nests in a bush that had grown from a tiny mustard seed (Matt. 13:31-32); a man sowing in the springtime and the reapers sifting out the wheat from the tares (Matt. 13:24-30); children playing in the market place (Matt. 11:16-17); a shepherd going out to look for his lost lamb (Luke 15:4-6). One of the biographers of Wordsworth wrote of him:

Wordsworth saw things that other people do not see, and he saw with quite unique clearness and frequency things which they see at most rarely and dimly. This is his originality. . . . Wordsworth sets out always from impressions common to himself and to you and me. He so sees objects as in the act of contemplating them to release them from the tie of custom, from their commonness, their familiarity. The old becomes new.[6]

What is suggested in those words was supremely true of Jesus. For him the ordinary things of earth had an illimitable interest because he saw this as his Father's world, and beheld the heavenly meaning breaking through to make— as with Moses in the wilderness—a common bush aflame with God.

Nor was his observation limited to the world of things. The pageant of human life arrested him. He marked its lights and shadows, its nobility and pathos, its struggles and confusions, and its victories and defeats. He knew what was in man because he knew actual men —knew them, and knew the life they lived through sharing it in a sure companionship. It tells us something about Jesus to know that fishermen were his friends, and it tells us something more about him to consider that apparently there was no constraint or awkwardness when Matthew arranged a dinner and "tax collectors and sinners came and sat down with Jesus" (Matt. 9:10). All life drew him with a great instinctive sympathy, and it was because he had such human understanding that his divine judgments could be so unerring in their praise or condemnation. Through his parables we see again the sort of people he saw, and we see them with the meaning of what they were and what they did made unmistakable: the

devotion of the humble widow in the temple (Luke 21:2-4); the penitence of the publican (Luke 18:13); the greathearted mercy of the man from despised Samaria who put a Levite and a priest to shame (Luke 10:30-37); the shepherd's faithfulness (Luke 15:4); the single-mindedness of the man whose passion was to find the perfect pearl (Matt. 13:45-46); the father's love which no rebellion of his son could kill (Luke 15:11-32); the patient integrity of the man who built his house on a rock (Matt. 7:24-25); and, on the other hand, the pompousness of men who push their way to seats of honor (Matt. 23:5-7); the pride of the rich fool who thought his crowded barns were more important than his soul (Luke 12:16-21); the servant indifferent to his trust (Matt. 25:25); the men who sent back their glib excuses for not coming to the wedding feast where they were supposed to be (Luke 14:18-20); the silly bridesmaids whose lamps had no oil to keep them burning at the one great hour (Matt. 25:1-13). These and other figures belonged to the first century, but they live now in every century and in every place.

Thus the parables bear witness to the intensity of interest with which Jesus looked upon his world. But they reveal something else about him which is deeper and more important. They show, as already we have begun to see, that when he looked at life, he saw in it not only its vivid human fascination and its moral lessons; he saw in it at its best the immediate meaning of God. As Charles A. Dinsmore wrote:

The prophetic spirit of Israel was not unmindful of nature as a revelation of the Most High; the heavens declared the glory of God, the clouds were his chariot, and the flames of fire his ministers, but when it most earnestly sought the face of God, it turned not outwardly to nature, but inwardly upon itself. Not in the earthquake, wind, or fire, but by a still, small voice Jehovah spoke. It interpreted God, not predominantly through natural symbols, but through man's own moral and spiritual nature. To the loftiest consciousness of Israel God was intensely personal, he was a Spirit. . . . Recognizing the inner compulsion as divine, they conceived of the Eternal in the terms of their own highest being. . . . Man was the chosen and habitual avenue through which the spiritual genius of Israel sought to know God.[7]

To some those sentences of Dinsmore will seem misleading. It will be thought that they exalt the worth of man too much. The mighty and majestic reality of God is not enclosed within the obvious appearances of human life, nor can it be contracted into hasty inferences

---

[6] H. W. Garrod, *Wordsworth: Lectures and Essays* (Oxford: Clarendon Press, 1923), pp. 95, 104.

[7] *The English Bible as Literature* (Boston: Houghton Mifflin Co.; London: George Allen & Unwin, 1931), p. 48. By permission.

drawn from these. Certainly when Jesus looked at the world of men and things he did not do so with a kind of miscellaneous pantheism that found God equally in everything he saw. Steeped as he was in the august conceptions of the law and the prophets, his mind and soul were filled with a sense of the transcendent holiness of God. That is true, and it needs to be remembered; but in the theological thinking of the first quarter of the twentieth century there arose the danger that this truth might be turned into a dark exaggeration. Karl Barth in *The Word of God and the Word of Man* speaks of God as the *"Wholly Other"*;[8] and Emil Brunner has this to say:

A God who is identical with the depths of the world or the soul is not really God. . . . He reveals himself as the unheard-of, unrecognized, mysterious person, who cannot be discovered anywhere in the world. His revelation is a communication, through his personal word, of what no one knows and no one has.[9]

To say that God is not "identical" with what we see even in the deepest and highest aspects of human life is true enough; but to go on beyond that to the stark insistence that God "cannot be discovered anywhere in the world" is to establish a kind of theological masochism and to shroud in grim denial the bright encouragement which the most beautiful of Jesus' parables in the Synoptic Gospels bring. The God whom Jesus told of was no *"Wholly Other,"* but the Father whose will and purpose are at least partially reflected in the best that is in his children's lives.

VI. Parables in the Several Gospels

As we have noted, the parables appear unevenly in the Synoptic Gospels. Six appear in all three—Matthew, Mark, and Luke. Three appear in Matthew and in Luke. Of parables which appear in one Gospel only, there are eleven in Matthew, fourteen in Luke, and only two in Mark. The teaching of Jesus seems to have been secondary in Mark's interest; what concerned him most was the story of what Jesus did and of what others did for him or against him, and so his Gospel lingers only briefly for any record of what Jesus said and hurries on instead in a terse narrative of events from the Baptism to the Resurrection. It is possible that the reason why Mark includes so few parables is that these were all he knew; but since the parables, by their pictorial quality, were so likely to be remembered and so easy to

transmit, it may be that Mark was familiar with some at least of the parables included only in the later Gospels but simply did not use them. It is now an almost unquestioned tenet of New Testament scholarship that both Matthew and Luke were familiar with Mark's Gospel and incorporated most of it into their own longer accounts. Many scholars also believe that Matthew and Luke had in addition another written document, technically known as Q, which was partly a record of events but which included further memories of Jesus' teaching. Then there are parables which have been transmitted only by Matthew or only by Luke, parables more numerous than all the rest, and among them some of the most beautiful and most precious.

How is it that parables, such as those of the laborers in the vineyard and the wise and foolish virgins in Matthew, and the good Samaritan and the prodigal son in Luke, should have come down to us through only one channel of transmission, and but for that single channel might have been lost entirely? No sure answer to that question can be given, but in the midst of uncertain details stands the important central fact which Ernest F. Scott has pointed out as follows:

Our knowledge of Jesus' teaching has . . . come to us along a variety of channels and it cannot be contended that all of them are equally trustworthy. One of the chief services of criticism has been that it has enabled us to sift our evidences, and so to obtain a clearer vision of Jesus as he actually lived and taught. But taken as a whole the record may be accepted as essentially true to fact; and for this conclusion we are not wholly dependent on methods of literary analysis. It is significant that all our accounts of Jesus' ethical teaching are in perfect harmony. They have come from many quarters, and do not borrow from each other, but they all carry the same stamp. If we take as our touchstone sayings which may be indubitably ascribed to Jesus we find in them just the same elements as mark the teaching generally. We have not to do with a miscellaneous collection of pious maxims, but with a consistent body of thought, which everywhere displays the same spirit and the same attitude to life. As to the authenticity of this particular utterance or that, there will always be difference of opinion, but no one can seriously doubt that the main principles of the message of Jesus have been faithfully preserved in our Gospels.[10]

And as to the special material in the Gospel of Luke, Scott has written:

The very fact that this source makes so little of the distinctive Christian message is a proof of genuineness. As time went on the thought of the

---

[8] Tr. Douglas Horton (Boston: The Pilgrim Press, 1928), p. 74.

[9] *The Theology of Crisis* (New York: Charles Scribner's Sons, 1929), pp. 29, 33.

[10] *The Ethical Teaching of Jesus* (New York: The Macmillan Co., 1924), pp. 10-11. By permission.

church became more and more concentrated on Jesus' claim to Messiahship, and all his teaching was viewed in relation to it. Luke's special source cannot be the product of this later period. It can only be accounted for on the ground that it goes back to reminiscences which had not yet been touched by theological reflection. Wherever it came from it is valuable in the highest degree. More than anything else in the Gospel record it takes us into the mind of Jesus, and helps us to understand the attraction he exercised as a teacher.[11]

Taking the parables as they actually appear in Matthew, Mark, and Luke, one might ask whether there is any general character discernible in the parables of one Gospel as distinguished from those of another, and whether, therefore, the difference between the Gospels in the parables included may mean, in part at least, just that the evangelists had different interests, and not necessarily that their knowledge was as segregated as it seems. The question may fairly be answered "yes." Mark, for example, would seem to have had one dominant conception sounding in all his thought, the same that he expressed in the first words with which he brings Jesus into view. "Jesus came into Galilee, preaching the gospel of the kingdom of God, and saying, The time is fulfilled, and the kingdom of God is at hand" (Mark 1:14-15). The coming of the kingdom, its immediate presence among men through the person of Jesus, the imperious call for entrance into it, the judgment upon those who rejected it—this was the message by which Mark was possessed. The parables which he repeats, therefore, have to do with that one overwhelming theme. Others which might touch a wider range of human life and character do not come within the scope of his intense concern.

Matthew is like Mark in his essential emphasis, but the emphasis is sounded upon a wider scale. His parables, like Mark's, are such as stress the critical immediacy of the kingdom and of men's relation to it; and he deepens the message of Mark with notes of judgment more profound and more prolonged. Mark has the somber parable of the wicked tenants of the vineyard; Matthew repeats that and he adds to it, like the sound of iron bells of doom, such parables as those of the talents (Matt. 25:14-30), of the wedding guest cast into outer darkness (Matt. 22:13), of the bridesmaids whose lamps went out (Matt. 25:1-13), and of the last day when men shall be separated, as sheep are separated from goats, the righteous to go into everlasting joy and the condemned to "depart . . . into everlasting fire" (Matt. 25:41).

In the Gospel of Luke the mood is different. It is as though one were listening to a sym-

[11] *Ibid.*, pp. 9-10.

phony played by other instruments, keyed to a gentler and more wooing music. The great chords of moral responsibility still are there, as in the other Gospels; but these blend into the greater theme of the love and compassion of God. It was this echo of the message of Jesus which had registered with Luke.

Thus the Synoptic Gospels bring their different contributions to our knowledge of what Jesus taught in his parables. What now is the impression made by that teaching as a whole?

We observe first that there is a change from the earlier parables to the later ones. Granted that it is not possible to assume any sure chronological accuracy in the order of the parables, nevertheless it remains true that there are natural references and connections which show a general time sequence which the Gospels have reflected rightly. They put parables such as those of the mustard seed (Matt. 13:31-32; Mark 4:30-32; Luke 13:18-19) and of the leaven (Matt. 13:33; Luke 13:20-21) relatively early in their record of Jesus' ministry, and such a parable as that of the wicked tenants of the vineyard near the end (Matt. 21:33-45; Mark 12:1-12; Luke 20:9-19). When Jesus first began to preach and teach in Galilee, the atmosphere was one of expectation. The leaven of God's Spirit might spread transformingly through human life; the tiny seed might grow into the spreading shelter for many far-winging hopes. But as time passed and the dark shadow of antagonism to Jesus deepened, the freshness of the morning turned to afternoon and to signs of approaching night. Jesus saw that his people would not respond to his call for a new spirit that would fit them for the kingdom, and that at the end of his own road might be what the world would call disaster. So it appears that into his parables—as into all his teaching—there entered increasingly a tragic note. Here is the point of justification for what A. B. Bruce has written, provided that his interpretation were applied to the closing days of Jesus' ministry, and not to all that went before.

There is . . . a parabolic mood, which leads a man . . . to present his thoughts in this form. It is the mood of one whose heart is chilled and whose spirit is saddened by a sense of loneliness, and who, retiring within himself, by a process of reflection frames for his thoughts forms which half conceal, half reveal them—reveal them more perfectly to those who understand, hide them from those who do not: forms beautiful, but also melancholy, as the hues of the forest in late autumn.[12]

So, near the end there doubtless was an infinite sadness in the parables of Jesus, but this impres-

[12] *The Parabolic Teaching of Christ* (New York: A. C. Armstrong & Son, 1892), p. 20.

sion should not be carried back to cloud our picture of the beginning. For his ministry there had been a springtime, with the dew of the morning on it; it was not all autumn, with winter coming on.

It is important for us to remember this, for otherwise we fall into the mistake of conceiving the kingdom of God, and Jesus' preaching of it, too much in catastrophic terms. The kingdom of God was proclaimed first as a gospel of joy. Although its ultimate fulfillment rested in the hidden hands of God, the foregleams of it could already appear within the fellowship of those whose way of life was being changed and made new by Jesus. Men and nations might have to pass through tragic crises before God's purpose for human history should be accomplished, but already among responsive and obedient souls his reign on earth could manifest its beginning. Much would have to wait for the last days, the *eschaton;* but in the immediate present there could be what one New Testament scholar has called a "realized eschatology." [13] Here and now men could learn what it means to live "in the power of an endless life."

Therefore as the parables of Jesus portray the infinite worth and wonder of the kingdom, so they proclaim the qualities of mind and soul that must be present in those who would possess it. In this respect one of the most suggestive classifications of the parables is that which has been given by George A. Buttrick in *The Parables of Jesus.*[14] He lists first the "Parables of the Early Ministry," as expressing the one great note of "The Good News of the Kingdom of God." Last come "Parables of the Passion Week," marked now by another emphasis— the tragic emphasis of "The Kingdom of God as a Judgment." But between these, and expressive of the life which human souls must strive for if they are to enter the kingdom, there are listed the parables which express "The Conditions of Discipleship"; "The Marks of Discipleship"—humility, the spirit of forgiveness, the recognition of duty, sympathy, and true neighborliness—and finally "The Love of God."

In those last four words we touch most nearly the heart of the message which comes through all of Jesus' teaching, and especially through his parables. It is the message which Sir Wilfred Grenfell echoed in one of the final paragraphs of *What Life Means to Me:*

That is what life means to me—a place where a Father above deals differently with his different children, but with all in love; a place where true joys do not hang on material pegs, and where all the while the fact that God *our* Father is on his throne lines every cloud with gold. It means a chance for every one to be helping lame dogs over stiles, a chance to be cheering and helping to bear the burdens of others, a field for the translation of unfailing faith in the love of God above into deeds that shall please his children below, and therefore please him also—filling this poor life with satisfaction, otherwise unattainable.[15]

VII. Principles of Interpretation

One matter for consideration remains. What are the principles that are to be followed in interpreting the parables?

First and most important is the realization that most of the parables have each of them one main point and only one. The whole comparison focuses on that point, and everything else in the description of the story is subordinate to that. To be distracted from the main point and possessed instead by a passion of clever speculation about details is to lose the essential meaning of the parable.

Always there has been the temptation thus to treat the parables with an enthusiastic fancifulness so unrestrained that it ends in an intricate unreality. Not only ordinary and unlearned people, but some of the great and learned doctors of the church—and all the more elaborately because of their learning—have been sinners in this respect. The parable of the good Samaritan, for example, has a purpose which is single and emphatic. It is to show who is the true neighbor: not necessarily the man who lives next door, nor the man supposed to be of the right race and the right religion, but the man whose heart is big enough to make him go to the help of another man who needs a neighbor. That truth is what is important in this parable, and all the details of the picture are incidental to that. But even the great Augustine could not let the shining simplicity of the parable stand alone. He had to garnish it with all sorts of overwrought ideas which his fertile mind invented. In Augustine's treatment the swift parable of Jesus is turned into an amazing allegory. The "certain man" who went down from Jerusalem to Jericho is Adam. Jerusalem is the city of Peace from which Adam fell. Jericho is our human mortality toward which he goes. The flesh and blood thieves of the parable who fall upon the real man on the Jericho road become now the devil and his angels, who strip Adam of his immortality, beat him into sinfulness, and thus leave him stripped of his communion with God and so half dead The priest and Levite represent the priesthood and ministry of the Old Testament from which Adam could expect nothing. The Samaritan is

---

[13] Dodd, *Parables of the Kingdom,* p. 51.
[14] New York: Harper & Bros., 1928.
[15] Boston: The Pilgrim Press, 1910, p. 13.

Christ himself. The binding up of the wounds is restraint of sin, oil is the comfort of the hope, and wine is the encouragement of a new spirit. The beast is the flesh in which Christ deigned to come to earth, and the wounded Adam set upon the beast means that humanity is now carried by belief in the Incarnation. The inn is the church, the innkeeper is Paul, and the two-pence given to the innkeeper are either the two commandments of love or the double promise of this life and the life that is to come.[16]

Such was the astonishing manner in which Augustine interpreted this particular parable; and if he is perhaps the most conspicuous, he is certainly not the only example of the length to which pious ingenuity could go. Tertullian, when he wrote on the parable of the prodigal son, though he does not commit himself flatly to a particular interpretation, reflects various interpretations which were current. The father in the parable is God; perhaps the oldest son represents the Jew and the younger son the Christian, though Tertullian points out objections to that idea. He seems content, however, with the interpretation that the father's property which he shared with his son is the knowledge of God one has by birthright. The citizen to whom the prodigal hires himself out is the devil, the robe which the father puts on him when he returns is the sonship from which Adam fell, and the feast is the Lord's Supper.[17] A much more modern commentator deals in the same inventive fashion with so simple a parable as that of the leaven. Why three measures of meal? It was not enough to assume that this was simply the ordinary amount of meal that women used when they made bread. Instead, the three measures of meal become either the sanctification of body, mind, and spirit, or the three branches of the human race descending from Shem, Ham, and Japheth, sons of Noah.[18]

The trouble with these eager and too fanciful interpretations of the parables is that the commentator begins with the assumption that a parable is the same as an allegory. But the typical parable is not. In an allegory every detail of the story has some parallel significance, the great example being *Pilgrim's Progress*. Some of the parables of Jesus do have some partial likeness to an allegory, since the spiritual parallels may be more numerous and complex than in most of his parables. That is true, for example, in the parables of the sower and of the wicked husbandmen. But as George Henry Hubbard says, the typical parable of Jesus

is the embodiment of one central thought to which all details are subordinate. It is not a string of pearls, or a connected series of truths. It is a single gem with such setting or background as shall display it to the best advantage. The parable is like a lens, which gathers many of the sun's rays and brings them to a focus upon a single point. It is like a circle with many radii of detail meeting at the center, and this center it is which the expositor is concerned to find.[19]

This fact leads to a recognition of the second principle which should be borne in mind in the interpretation of the parables. It is the fact that the parables were spoken mostly to simple people. Because they were cast in the form of a comparison, they were devised to make people think, but—as we have noted before—they certainly were not devised to bewilder their thinking. Ideas which would have had no meaning whatever to the listeners in Galilee or Judea cannot be the heart of Jesus' message. He was not devising cryptograms to be spelled out by clever commentators centuries afterward. He was speaking straight home to the minds and hearts of living men and women to whom he wanted to bring the immediate message of God. The interpreter of the parables may well make it his desire to do with them what the Book of Common Prayer bids men pray that they shall do with the Scriptures as a whole: namely, "hear them, read, mark, learn, and inwardly digest them." Especially this last. The parables must be so presented that ordinary folk can absorb their meaning, and for that to happen the parables must not be cluttered up with intricate paraphernalia of elaborate notions put forward as though they were as important as the parables themselves. A man can digest food, but should not be asked to digest the dish.

Finally, for the right interpretation of the parables there is needed an informed mind plus a disciplined imagination.

An informed mind means a knowledge of the setting of the parables and of the circumstances of first-century life in Palestine which they reflect. To read a book like *The Parables, Their Background and Local Setting*, by N. Levison, himself by birth a Jew and brought up in Galilee within sight of Nazareth, or *The Gospel Parables in the Light of Their Jewish Background*, by W. O. E. Oesterley, is to have a new perception of the actual scenes which Jesus used for his comparisons and so to be anchored closer to fact instead of being led off into irresponsible fancy.

[16] *Quaestiones Evangeliorum*, II, 19 (summarized by C. H. Dodd in *The Parables of the Kingdom* [New York: Charles Scribner's Sons, 1936], p. 12).

[17] Harold Smith, *Ante-Nicene Exegesis of the Gospels* (London: Society for Promoting Christian Knowledge, 1928), IV, 132.

[18] R. C. Trench, *Notes on the Parables of Our Lord* (London: Macmillan & Co., 1874), p. 118.

[19] *The Teachings of Jesus in Parables* (Boston: The Pilgrim Press, 1907), p. xvi.

But information is not enough. Over and above everything else must be imagination—an imagination disciplined by knowledge, but imagination still. Without that no one can reflect the swift and spontaneous thoughts of Jesus with their instinctive sense of the wideness and wonder of God's world. To interpret his parables truly one must understand his way of apprehending truth, not as dogma, but as the poetry of God's meaning revealed through the life and scenes of every day. To know that is not only to be the better able to teach the recorded parables; it is also to have the eyes unsealed to perceive those parables of God which in every generation are again enacted wherever human life goes by.

VIII. Selected Bibliography

ABRAHAMS, ISRAEL. *Studies in Pharisaism and the Gospels*, 1st Series. Cambridge: University Press, 1917.

BARNETT, A. E. *Understanding the Parables of Our Lord*. Nashville: Cokesbury Press, 1940.

BRUCE, A. B. *The Parabolic Teaching of Christ*. New York: A. C. Armstrong & Son, 1892.

BUTTRICK, GEORGE A. *The Parables of Jesus*. New York: Harper & Bros., 1928.

DODD, C. H. *The Parables of the Kingdom*. New York: Charles Scribner's Sons, 1936.

HUBBARD, GEORGE HENRY. *The Teachings of Jesus in Parables*. Boston: The Pilgrim Press, 1907.

JÜLICHER, ADOLF. *Die Gleichnisreden Jesu*. Leipzig: J. C. B. Mohr, 1899.

LEVISON, N. *The Parables, Their Background and Local Setting*. Edinburgh, T. & T. Clark, 1926.

LUCCOCK, HALFORD E. *Studies in the Parables of Jesus*. New York: The Abingdon Press, 1920.

MARTIN, HUGH. *The Parables of the Gospels*. New York: The Abingdon Press, 1937.

OESTERLEY, W. O. E. *The Gospel Parables in the Light of Their Jewish Background*. New York: The Macmillan Co., 1936.

TRENCH, RICHARD C. *Notes on the Parables of Our Lord*. London: Macmillan & Co., 1874.

THE HISTORY
OF THE EARLY CHURCH
I. THE BEGINNINGS

by ERNEST F. SCOTT

It has sometimes been maintained that the idea of the church was entirely foreign to the mind of Jesus. He had promised, it is urged, the kingdom of God, the new order of things in which a willing obedience to the higher law would take the place of all outward institutions; and by their creation of an organized society the followers of Jesus obscured the whole purpose of his message. But while it may be granted that he did not foresee the historical church, with its rules and ceremonies, its systems of doctrine and government, there can be no real question that he was its founder. He made demands of a social nature which could be carried out only in a community. He gathered around him a group of disciples, the twelve who were constantly with him and a much larger number who accepted him as Master. It was out of this fellowship which he had himself called into being that the church arose by a natural process of growth.

I. The Meaning of "the Church"

We must not think therefore of Jesus' followers as deciding after his death that they would form a society for carrying on his work. The church had no definite beginning. While Jesus was still with them the disciples had been accustomed to pray together and to close the day with a common meal. They had looked for the coming of the kingdom of God. They had called themselves brethren. After his departure they continued to live as he had taught them. New believers were drawn from time to time into their company and the numbers went on increasing until there was a large society.

It could not hold together without some kind of organization, and various rules and practices were adopted as the need arose. The church thus formed itself gradually and unconsciously in the effort to perpetuate what Jesus had himself begun.

This Christian society was known, apparently from the first, by a Hebrew or Aramaic name which was translated into Greek as the "ecclesia." The original word has unfortunately been lost, but there is no reason to doubt that it was rendered literally by the Greek one, which means an assembly. In the Greek translation of the Old Testament this word is sometimes used to denote Israel, assembled at a stated festival as the people of God, and from this it has been inferred that the church took over and applied to itself the Old Testament idea. In ancient times God had chosen a nation to worship him, and the holy nation was now represented by the church. At the outset, however, the disciples could not have made this claim. They were anxious to maintain their place within the Jewish community, and would not have assumed a name which implied a challenge and a condemnation. A time was to come when the church declared itself the true Israel, but this could not have been in those early days when the name ecclesia was first used. To begin with it probably meant nothing more than "the meeting." Day by day the little company met together to worship in the name of Christ. The nature of their calling was still uncertain and they could only describe themselves by indefinite names. Individually they were the "disciples," the "believers," "those who called on the Lord." As a group they were the ecclesia, the association.

This sense of a union among those who believed in him had begun in Jesus' lifetime, and although he formed no sect or party, he had sought in every way to confirm it. He had impressed on his followers that they were brethren. He had united them in ardent devotion to himself. He had called on them to throw in their lot with the coming kingdom, and in doing so they could not but feel that they stood together, apart from the mass of men whose interest was still in this passing world. His death on the Cross had broken up the fellowship. He had himself been the bond of union, and now he was gone. His promise of the kingdom had apparently proved vain. The disciples had come up with him to Jerusalem, expecting a signal triumph for his cause, and the great disaster had plunged them in despair. They fled from the city and made their way back, one by one, to Galilee, with no intention but to lapse again into their old way of living. So the company which had gathered around Jesus seemed to be utterly dissolved. How did it come to be reestablished?

II. The Resurrection of Christ

We are here faced with the most baffling of all historical problems, and no final solution of it will ever be possible. One thing is certain, that the conviction was borne in on the disciples that their Master who had been crucified was risen from the dead. Behind this conviction there must have been a real experience, but what it was we cannot now determine, for the accounts of it are all different, and at many points they contradict each other. In the Gospels the main stress is laid on the testimony of certain women of Jesus' company, who returned when the sabbath was over to anoint his body, and found the sepulcher empty. Paul, in his brief but careful statement in I Cor. 15:3-8, says nothing of the empty tomb, and speaks only of six occasions on which followers of Jesus had an actual vision of him after his death. This account of Paul must be regarded as primary. It was written at least twenty years earlier than any of the others by one who was acquainted with the eyewitnesses, and who solemnly asserted that they were all agreed on this testimony (I Cor. 15:11). It is confirmed too by accidental references which are found elsewhere. Luke indicates that the Lord first appeared, as Paul says, to Peter (Luke 24:34). He declares in the book of Acts (1:3; 13:31) that the appearances continued over a lengthened period, and Paul takes this for granted when he includes among them his own vision on the way to Damascus. In like manner Mark thinks of Jesus as manifesting himself to the disciples in Galilee, and at least two of the appearances mentioned by Paul (to James and to five hundred brethren at once) must have been in that locality.

The accounts in the Gospels can be allowed only a secondary value. It may well have been that after their own marvelous experiences, the disciples met the women and learned how they had found the tomb empty; but this can have served only to confirm their testimony. Taken by itself, the evidence of the tomb would have little weight. In the dim light of dawn the women might have mistaken the tomb, or as Jewish unbelievers asserted, the body might have been secretly removed. Matthew and John feel it necessary to supplement the story of the tomb with the episode of how Jesus himself appeared to the women. Without a positive testimony of this kind there could be no assurance that the Lord had risen, and it was upon the appearances to a number of witnesses at different times that the church rested its faith. Paul confines himself wholly to the actual visions, and he seems also to assume that what the disciples saw was not merely the body which had been laid in the grave. The chief purpose of the argument in I Cor. 15 is to prove that in the future life the earthly body will give place to a spiritual body, immaterial and incorruptible. Christ had risen, not only from the grave, but into a new state of being to which his people also are destined. So it was no mere physical body which Paul saw on the way to Damascus but a radiant form in the sky—the body of glory that Jesus had assumed. He regarded this vision of his own as similar in character to those of the earlier disciples.

However we seek to explain it, the Resurrection must always be a mystery, and this not so much because of any obscurity in the records as because of our ignorance of the world beyond. If the facts had all been laid before us in the fullest and exactest detail, our difficulties would be just as great as they are now. We know life only under earthly conditions, and we have no means of guessing how one who had entered into the other life could make contact with those who were still on earth. Too much attention has been fixed on the mere circumstances of the Resurrection. In what form did Jesus appear? Did he manifest himself to the bodily eyes, or to some inner sense which can apprehend that which is invisible? Such questions, even if they could be answered, only affect the outward side of the mystery. Whatever may have been the mode in which their experience came to them, it served to convince the disciples that the Lord had risen from the dead. This is the vital fact of the resurrection story, and all the rest may be left to speculation. In a manner which we cannot now explain, and which they themselves could not explain, the followers of Jesus were made aware that he was still with them as a living presence, and on this certainty they built their faith.

III. The Primitive Jerusalem Church

The disciples' fellowship had been broken, but in consequence of the visions they drew together and made a momentous decision. Assured that Jesus was living and that he was indeed the promised Messiah, they abandoned all former interests and connections and migrated to Jerusalem. From this time onward Galilee, where Jesus himself had worked, disappears from the history. It cannot be that he was utterly forgotten in the towns and villages which had responded so eagerly to his message, or that all who believed in him departed in a body from Galilee and never thought of it again. If the little province has no further place in the record, the reason can be only that it had lost its importance. Christianity had come out into the open. Its future clearly lay in a larger world, and the humble scene of its origin fell out of sight.

Nothing is told us of the motive which caused the migration to Jerusalem. It cannot have been that already the disciples were bent on a great mission which could be carried out more effectually in the capital than in an outlying district. As yet they had no plans for the future, and their action can be explained only from the ecstatic hopes awakened in them by their visions. Jesus had risen. He was the true Messiah, and would presently return in his messianic character to bring in the kingdom of God. His followers must be at hand to meet him when he returned, and there could be only one place where they might expect him. It had been foretold in Scripture that "the Lord, whom ye seek, shall suddenly come to his temple" (Mal. 3:1). All the hopes of Israel centered on the holy city, and it would surely be there that the Messiah would appear. As we find them in the opening chapters of Acts, the disciples were "continuing daily . . . in the temple." They had come to Jerusalem for this purpose—to wait in the neighborhood of the temple so that they might welcome the Lord at his glorious coming.

A. The Gift of the Spirit.—The mood of the first believers—and this must never be forgotten —was one of rapturous hope. Attempts have often been made to discover some recondite purpose in everything they did. It is assumed that they were always planning for the future, and never took a step without anxious consideration of everything it might involve. But the truth is that the men who made the church were unconscious of what they were doing. They acted from no design but were swept on by movements of the Spirit which they never tried to understand. They lived in a spiritual world which was more real to them than the material one, and it was in this period of ecstasy that the church took shape. The initial fervor wore off, and the effort was then made to define the Christian beliefs, regulate the customs, and devise plans and methods for the mission. In this task the church has been engaged ever since. But at the outset all was done by the Spirit, and this first period was decisive for all the later history. While it was still a little group of visionaries, waiting from hour to hour for the Lord's coming, the church assumed its essential character. All that came afterward in the growth of Christian ideas and institutions was only the development of what was given spontaneously in those earliest days.

Our knowledge of this brief but all-important period is derived almost wholly from the opening chapters of Acts, in which history and legend can hardly be distinguished. This itself is evidence of the exalted mood in which the first believers were living. As they looked back at a later time on those weeks at the beginning, they could remember nothing clearly. They could not tell what was fact and what was vision, for even common events had worn a halo of the supernatural. So the record in Acts, with its mixture of realism and miracle, gives a more faithful picture of that time than if it had all been a sober chronicle. Some of the memories, however, can be taken literally. The original company consisted of about a hundred and twenty persons (Acts 1:15), from which it may be gathered that only the most ardent of the Galilean believers had settled in Jerusalem, joining themselves with other followers of Jesus who were there already. They were constantly together, either in the courts of the temple or in private houses, where they engaged in prayer and shared in a common meal and listened to the apostles' teaching (Acts 2:42). They had no official leaders, but Peter was the moving spirit. He had been closer to Jesus in his lifetime than any other, and had been the first to see the risen Lord. Moreover he was a man of passionate nature, capable of inspiring others with his faith and loyalty. Such a man was the indispensable leader in the first critical days, when the one thing necessary was unquestioning devotion to the cause. At a later time the church required leaders of a different type, men who could plan and reflect and organize, and Peter fell gradually into the background. But his initial service was of inestimable value, and fully entitles him to his name of Prince of the Apostles. Without Peter, so far as we can see, the church could never have secured its footing and survived.

It first emerged from its mysterious beginnings on the day of Pentecost, seven weeks after the Passover at which Jesus had died. The believers were met together according to their custom when they suddenly became aware of a power which had taken possession of them and enabled them to speak with strange tongues. In the strength of this new faculty they appeared before the multitude and began to proclaim their message. In his account of this episode there can be little question that Luke has misunderstood the nature of the speaking with tongues. Paul, who himself possessed the gift in a high degree (I Cor. 14:18), discusses it at length (I Cor. 12–14), and shows unmistakably that it consisted in the expression of thoughts and feelings by means of arbitrary sounds, which were varied like articulate speech. This "glossolalia" has appeared at different times in religious history, and is still practiced in the worship of some emotional sects. Sometimes the resemblance to a language has been so close that even trained philologists have been in doubt. Luke appears to hold the theory that the unintelligible "tongues," to which he must often have listened at the church meetings, were foreign modes of speech which would be understood by those who used them. On this theory he bases his story of Pentecost. He describes a gathering in which all nations were represented, so that there were some at least who heard the gospel proclaimed to them in their own native tongues.

Much in the narrative is open to question, but it preserves the record of a day uniquely memorable in the history of the church. On that day the believers first became conscious of a supernatural power working in them. Joel, the prophet, had foretold that when the new age was at hand God would pour out his Spirit on all flesh. This Spirit had now descended on those who believed in Christ. It had manifested itself in the speaking with tongues, and along with this marvelous gift it would bestow new capacities of every kind on those who possessed it. They would work miracles, understand mysteries, face every danger with unflinching courage. Luke dates the beginning of the church from the day of Pentecost, and in one sense he is right. The church already existed, but only as a child exists before it is born. It entered on its conscious life only when it received the Spirit, the divine power which was henceforth to direct and sustain it. In the strength of this power, according to Luke, the disciples were moved to announce their message to the outside world. As yet they had sought only to support and encourage one another, but then the task was laid on them of bringing all men into their fellowship. Of themselves they could never have ventured on this enterprise, but the assurance was given them that God would aid them with his Spirit. The book of Acts is written throughout in this belief that the apostles were only the instruments, and that the real power was that of the Spirit, working through their agency for the conversion of the world.

B. Organization, Beliefs, Worship.—This conception of the Spirit must always be borne in mind if we would understand the early history of the church. We must not think of it as an ordinary society, gradually establishing and expanding itself by well-devised measures. Its aim was to entrust itself wholly to the control of the Spirit and to dispense, as far as possible, with all methods of human prudence. It had no official leadership or organization. It refused to make plans for the future, and was content to move forward, step by step, as the Spirit might lead. Its members were brethren, all on an equal footing, and in their meetings each one spoke freely as the Spirit prompted him. When a decision was necessary, they sat in a company and waited silently until the Spirit, by some inward monition, declared its will. The primitive church has in all ages been regarded as a pattern, and each ecclesiastical system has claimed to model itself on this original type. But it resembled no later system, for the very idea of system was foreign to it. The believers looked for the kingdom of God, and sought to conduct their lives as if they belonged already to the future kingdom. They were not subject, as in an earthly society, to any set rules and forms of government. In their action as a community, and also as individuals, they threw themselves wholly on the guidance of the Spirit.

In like manner we must understand the beliefs of the primitive church. It has often been assumed that from the outset the apostles drew up some kind of definite creed, to which all who joined their company were bound to conform. Attempts are made to recover, from indications in the New Testament, the exact terms in which this original creed was formulated. But in a brotherhood which owned no authority but that of the Spirit there can have been no fixed statement of belief. There were indeed certain primary convictions on which all followers of Jesus were agreed, and it was this common faith which held them together. They acknowledged Jesus as the Messiah; they accepted his teaching as their rule of life; they were assured that he had risen from the dead and would shortly return to bring in the kingdom; they saw in his death the appointed means by which the kingdom was made possible. But these convictions were not defined in any rigid terms. Each believer was left free to interpret them in his own way as the Spirit might direct him, and from the first there was a wide variety of opinion. Paul could declare at a later day, "With the heart man believeth unto righteousness" (Rom. 10:10), and this well describes the position of the early church. All that was required was the heartfelt response to Christ and his message, and no restraint was laid on the faculties of reason, which might present the same truth in different ways to different men.

In so far as there was anything which could be called a creed, it was summed up in the confession "Jesus is Lord." We can infer from Paul's use of it in three solemn connections (Rom. 10:9; I Cor. 12:3; Phil. 2:11) that this was the pronouncement made by every convert at his baptism. The confession, however, was not so much a statement of belief as an oath of allegiance. Each new disciple affirmed that he took Jesus for his Master, whom he bound himself from that time onward to obey. The later creeds all grew out of this baptismal confession, and aimed at defining in theological language what was implied in calling Jesus the Lord. The early disciples did not feel the need of such definition. They simply surrendered themselves to Jesus as to one who had redeemed them, and whom therefore they must serve. From all that we learn of Christian teaching in the primitive time its whole purpose was to ensure a full confidence in Jesus. Several speeches are attributed to Peter in the opening chapters of Acts, and there is no reason to doubt that they preserve an outline of Christian preaching in its earliest phase. They all turn on the right of Jesus to be accepted as Lord. He had impressed men while he lived with his power and goodness. He had given fulfillment to the scripture promises of the Messiah. He had offered salvation to those who obeyed him, and though he had been put to death he had risen from the dead, proving triumphantly that he had come from God.

From the outset the new community observed the two ordinances of baptism and the Lord's Supper. Jesus himself had instituted the supper and, according to Paul, had commanded his disciples to keep repeating it as a memorial feast. Whether this was his conscious intention has been questioned, but it was natural that those who had supped with him on that sacred occasion should commemorate the rite by which he had bidden them farewell. Apparently they closed each of their daily meals together by repeating what he had then said and done, reminding themselves in this manner that they were still in fellowship with him. The practice of baptism is more difficult to account for.

Jesus had received men into his company without any outward rite, and this was one of the marked differences between his ministry and that of John the Baptist. Why was it that after Jesus' death the church fell back on the example of John? No answer to this riddle is offered us in the New Testament, where it is simply assumed that all converts from the very first were admitted by baptism. It may be that the original disciples, like Jesus himself, had undergone the baptism of John, and took for granted that this rite was necessary for those who desired to enter the kingdom. Or perhaps the custom of baptism sprang of its own accord out of the belief in the Spirit. Faith in Christ was supposed to bring with it the gift of the Spirit, and baptism served as a visible token that the Spirit has been bestowed. Wherever the rite is mentioned in the New Testament and in later times, it is associated with the Spirit, and had been apparently from the outset. But however it originated, it was the acknowledged sign that the believer now gave himself to Jesus and thereby entered on a new life. He was baptized "in the name of Jesus." This name, it would appear, was solemnly pronounced over him to indicate that he was made over to Jesus as one of his people. He uttered the confession "Jesus is Lord," thus declaring that Jesus and no other was his Master. And as the servant of Jesus he was adopted into the society which looked for the kingdom of God, and was controlled in all its action by the Spirit.

In theory the church has always been the spiritual community, representing here and now that higher order of things which will prevail when God's will is sovereign on earth. This is still the underlying idea which gives meaning to the church, but in the first days it could be accepted literally and in some degree put into action. The disciples were few in number and were all inspired by the same enthusiasm. They were able to dispense with rules and officers such as were necessary in all other societies. They could also do away with individual property. All possessions were thrown into a common stock, and no one called anything his own. This has sometimes been described as a socialistic order, but the use of such a modern term is quite misleading. These first believers had no thought of an economic system. All that they did was done spontaneously on the impulse of the Spirit, and this was as true of their ordinary living as of their faith and worship. As brethren in the service of Christ they could not but share with one another. They did so the more freely, as earthly possessions meant little to them. They believed that in a short time, perhaps in only a few days or weeks, the whole order would come to an end, and material wealth had no value, except to tide over the brief interval of waiting.

C. Separation from Judaism.—It was only in that first period, however, that the church could commit itself wholly to the leading of the Spirit. As the Lord's coming was delayed, and the community grew in numbers and was faced with rising opposition, some kind of system had to be devised. This was the more necessary as the church was not merely a religious society. It made itself responsible for the whole life of its members, and the common fund could not be properly administered unless books were kept by competent officers. However impartially they carried out their work, complaints and jealousies were sure to arise. The one purpose in the sharing of possessions was to bind the community together in a perfect brotherhood; but the effect in practice was sometimes just the contrary. The first of all the dissensions in Christian history grew out of that noble resolve to have all things in common.

Behind the immediate cause, however, lay a deeper one. The original disciples were all native Jews, and while they believed in Jesus and followed his way of life, they never doubted that they had still to observe the law and confine their mission to the chosen people of Israel. But at an early time, perhaps on the very day of Pentecost, a new element found its way into the community. Jewish colonies had established themselves in all the great cities of the Roman Empire, and the foreign-born Jews, commonly known as the Hellenists, since Greek was their language, maintained their connection with Palestine and the temple. Many of them had returned to settle in Jerusalem and their motive in doing so was doubtless a religious one. It was the holy city, and there alone they could serve God truly under the shadow of his immediate presence. It is not surprising that these devout Jews from abroad were strongly attracted to the Christian message. They had come to Jerusalem to practice their religion in its purity and many of them must have been bitterly disillusioned. Their life in the progressive Gentile world had given them a wider outlook, and in the neighborhood of the temple they found too little besides local rivalries and petty disputes about details of the ritual and the law. The new teaching was manifestly on a higher plane than the current Judaism. It preserved all that was most valuable in the ancient religion and added much more. In a short time the Hellenists formed a large proportion of the church in Jerusalem, and the accession of those foreign converts was to have momentous consequences.

D. Beginnings of Persecution.—Its first effect was to bring the Christian movement under suspicion. The apostles hitherto had carried on their work unmolested, although they taught openly in the very courts of the temple. This may appear strange when we consider that Jesus had shortly before been crucified, and that the very men who had been responsible for his death were still in power. But it must be remembered that Judaism was a ceremonial religion. Nothing was required of the orthodox Jew but to conform to the ordinances of the law, and in matters of opinion he was left free. A large number of sects had sprung up under various leaders, and the liberty they enjoyed could not be forbidden to the followers of Jesus. Whatever might be their beliefs, they were faithful in their observance of the law, and the religious authorities could take no measures against them. No doubt they were opposed and disliked, and more than once their teachers were brought up before the council; but on each occasion they were dismissed with an admonition. Their views might be erroneous but it was clear that in religious practice they did nothing contrary to the law.

The position was changed when the Hellenists in growing numbers attached themselves to the church. These converts had been drawn to the new teaching because they were dissatisfied with Judaism as they saw it in Jerusalem. They perceived, as the native believers had not yet done, that Jesus had placed little value on outward ceremonies, and it was from this point of view that they welcomed his message. The religious authorities took alarm. They could recognize in the Christian movement a possible menace to the whole ritual system of which they were the guardians. The native Christians also had come to regard the Hellenists with misgiving. They could not but feel that these new disciples, who spoke an alien language and had adopted many foreign customs, were different from themselves. A quarrel finally broke out because the Hellenists alleged that they were unfairly treated in the distribution of the common fund, and we can well believe Luke's testimony that a dispute of this kind brought matters to a head. Outsiders are always touchy, and are apt to discover slights and injuries where none have been intended. But it seems evident that the cleavage between the two sections of the church had a more serious origin. The native Christians wished still to remain faithful Jews; the Hellenists had begun to realize that the new faith was no mere addition to Judaism but was rooted in a different principle and involved a break with ancient practices which had up to that time been deemed essential.

To avoid an open break, which would have been disastrous to the young community, it was agreed that the two parties should work separately. The Hellenists were to have teachers of their own, who would present the gospel as they understood it, while the older apostles would minister to the Palestinian Jews. Seven men were chosen, whose names, it is significant, are all Greek, and it is unlikely that they could have been appointed merely to act as "deacons," assisting the regular apostles in temporal affairs. Stephen at once came forward as the leading Christian teacher; Philip became known pre-eminently as the "evangelist." It is evident that these seven men were elected as full colleagues of the apostles, with the one difference that they pursued their mission among the Greek-speaking Jews.

The most gifted of the Hellenistic teachers was undoubtedly Stephen. His period of activity was limited to a few weeks or months, but he was the most remarkable man who had yet appeared in the church, and in the brief period allotted to him he gave a new direction to the whole history of the new religion. The speech of Stephen, which occupies the longest chapter in the book of Acts, can hardly be the one he delivered at his trial, for in such a connection it would have been quite out of place; but there is no reason to doubt that it preserves a general outline of his type of teaching. He held that Israel as a nation had been unfaithful to its trust, and that the true Israel was represented by the church, which had accepted the promised Messiah. Along with the nation he condemned the ritual worship with which its religion was now identified. He cannot have rejected the law itself, as Paul was to do after long hesitation many years later; but he openly attacked the claims made for the temple, and when the temple was assailed, the law itself was clearly in danger.

Stephen was brought to trial before the council on a charge of blasphemy. There is no record of his condemnation, and it may be gathered from Luke's account that while the trial was still in process he was dragged out by an angry mob and stoned to death. On every ground it is quite unlikely that Paul was responsible for his martyrdom. As a young man lately arrived in the city, Paul cannot have taken more than a subordinate part in the accusation, and if Stephen was the victim of a street riot, no one man could be singled out as his murderer. Several times in his epistles Paul magnifies his guilt as a persecutor but never once alludes to the death of Stephen, which would have lain more heavily on his conscience than anything else if he had been the prime agent. He may have joined in the complaints against Stephen's teaching, and when the heretic was removed he certainly raised no protest.

"Saul," we are told, "was consenting to his death" (Acts 8:1). This, however, was very different from causing him to die.

E. Expulsion of the Hellenists.—The authorities, fully awakened to the danger of the new movement, still held back from a general persecution. The apostles, with their Palestinian followers, were allowed to remain in the city, while the Hellenists were expelled. They returned for the most part to their former homes, and in this manner became the pioneers of the Gentile mission. A Christian community arose at Antioch and another at Damascus. In all probability the church at Rome was founded at this time, for when Paul wrote to it not much more than twenty years afterward, it was already large and flourishing. The Hellenists were Jews, and their missionary activity in foreign cities was mainly confined to their own countrymen. All Jewish communities looked for guidance to Jerusalem, and the council sent emissaries to the synagogues abroad, warning them against the new beliefs and calling for the punishment of those who held them. Among those who offered themselves to do this errand for the council was the young man Saul, as yet an ardent Pharisee. His task was not one of active persecution, for the council had no civil authority outside Palestine. All that he could demand was the infliction of some ecclesiastical penalty, and even this might be refused. Every foreign synagogue was free to act on its own judgment, although a recommendation from Jerusalem was always treated with respect. It was while he was approaching Damascus on this commission that Saul saw the vision which changed his life.

The followers of Stephen, driven out of Palestine, thus carried the gospel to the West, but the original disciples were also active in the missionary cause. According to later tradition, they were the founders of churches which arose here and there in Eastern countries, as far distant as Mesopotamia and India. Of this there is no real evidence, and it is much more likely that they purposely confined their work to Palestine. Some hint of this may be discerned in the saying ascribed to Jesus, "Ye shall not have gone over the cities of Israel, till the Son of man be come" (Matt. 10:23). Clinging to the belief that the end was close at hand, the disciples resolved to employ the short remaining interval in the service of their own people. In so far as they contemplated a wider mission, they felt that it could be best promoted through a converted Israel. A Christian nation should be established and become the nucleus, as the prophets had anticipated, of a world-wide kingdom of God. When a division was made of the missionary field at the council of Jerusalem,

Paul and his companions were permitted to go to the Gentiles while the older apostles undertook to work among the Jews (Gal. 2:9). They come before us in the book of Acts as stationed in Jerusalem, but constantly visiting the daughter communities which had sprung up over the country, in Judea and Samaria and in towns along the coast. If they seem to have accomplished little, it must be remembered that Palestine was already in a disturbed condition, and that all other interests were submerged, before many years had passed, in the war with Rome.

F. Leaders and Issues.—The chronology of the early period is uncertain, but it cannot be far wrong to place the death of Stephen and the conversion of Paul in A.D. 32, two years after the Crucifixion. During the next ten years the community at Jerusalem was steadily growing and sending offshoots into the various regions of Palestine. The first date that can be definitely fixed is A.D. 42, when an event took place which had far-reaching consequences. In one of their many attempts to conciliate Judea the Romans restored it to the status of a kingdom under Herod Agrippa, grandson of Herod the Great. To win favor with the Jewish people, who regarded him as an alien, he professed much zeal for their religion, and set himself, among other measures, to destroy the church. From this we may infer that while the church had been tolerated, Jewish opinion was strongly against it. We can infer too that it must have made notable progress, or the attempt to suppress it would not have been worth the trouble. By order of the king several of the leading Christians were put to death, among them James, the brother of John. Peter was thrown into prison, with the same fate in prospect, but made his escape in a manner which gave rise to a miraculous story. The persecution lasted only a short time and Herod presently died, but the church at Jerusalem had for the moment been shattered. When its members were able to unite again, it had become in great measure a different church.

Its leader up to that time had been Peter, but he had gradually been yielding his place to James, the Lord's brother. During Jesus' ministry James had held aloof, and on one memorable occasion had joined with the family in an effort to withdraw him from his work. After the Crucifixion, James had attached himself to the disciples and had been among the first to receive the vision of the risen Lord. He had come up with the others to Jerusalem, and from the outset had held an honored position owing to his personal relationship to Jesus. It is evident, however, that he had other claims to precedence. From all that we know of him he was a man of strong character with a natural gift for leadership. He had also a practical capacity which was lacking in Peter, and when the church had once found its footing, it relied not so much on the enthusiast as on the man who could rule and organize. When the community at Jerusalem took shape again after Herod's persecution, James took the leadership, apparently as a matter of course. He continued for twenty years to be the acknowledged head of the Palestinian church, with a body of elders under him. He has sometimes been described not unaptly as the first bishop in Christian history.

James was identified with the Jewish section of the church, and it might appear from some later traditions that he was more Jew than Christian. This is certainly a wrong conception of him. He was devoted to the Christian cause, and ended his life by martyrdom. Up to a point he was broad-minded. Although he took an opposite side to Paul, he admired his sincerity and tried to do him justice. He gave him the right hand of fellowship when he set out on his Gentile mission, and cordially welcomed him when he returned on his final visit, doubtful of his reception. Paul speaks bitterly of the Judaists who sought to break up his churches, but he plainly indicates that they acted for themselves without any sanction from James. But while he was generous to those who differed from him, James was firm in his own position. He was convinced that the law was a necessary element in Christianity. He was scrupulous in his personal observance of the law, so much so that among the Jews themselves he earned the surname of "the Just"—the model of legal righteousness. His death by violence was popularly regarded as one of the crimes which God had punished by permitting the destruction of the temple. This reverence for its leader was doubtless one of the safeguards of the church when the tide of Jewish sentiment had turned decisively against it.

Nevertheless the long predominance of James was a misfortune, alike for the wider mission and for the Christian cause in Palestine. Peter had been in sympathy with the movement toward a free Christianity, and when he visited Antioch he had made no scruple about eating with Gentiles until "certain men came from James" and dissuaded him (Gal. 2:12). If Peter had continued to be the guiding influence in Palestine, the rupture of Jewish and Gentile Christianity might have been averted, and Paul might have gone forward with the full confidence that the mother church was behind him. As it was, his work was continually thwarted. His own churches were divided, since it was known that the chief Christian authority was opposed to his gospel. And the church in Palestine was itself the greatest sufferer. Under the auspices of James it was committed to a type of religion which could not possibly be accepted by the world at large. Refusing to advance, it became more and more reactionary, and was finally disowned by the great movement which it ought to have led.

Some years after Herod's persecution, probably in A.D. 49, the church was called on to make its decision on the vexed question of the law. Paul had returned to Antioch after his first missionary journey, and he was assailed by Jewish Christians who held that apart from the law faith in Christ was ineffectual. He determined to have the matter settled once for all and went up to Jerusalem with Barnabas to obtain the judgment of the church. Two accounts of the momentous council have come down to us (Acts 15; Gal. 2), and at some points they are in conflict, so much so that in the view of some scholars they deal with two different councils. This is highly improbable, and in spite of discrepancies the main facts are sufficiently clear. Paul defended his position before a full assembly of the church and also conferred privately with James, Peter, and John. A strong party was against him, and he was urged even by his friends to make concessions, but he refused to give way. An agreement was finally reached which appeared satisfactory to both sides. Paul and Barnabas were to have entire freedom in their work among the Gentiles, while the other apostles were to preach their own gospel to the Jews. At the best this was a compromise, and as the sequel soon proved, it was impracticable. The fundamental issue whether Christianity was still tied up with Judaism was left doubtful. Instead of arriving at a settlement the church was broken definitely into two camps, which for years to come were in controversy with each other.

At this point the main interest in Christian history shifts from Palestine to the great Gentile world. Now and then we are allowed a glimpse of the community at Jerusalem, but only when its action in some way affected the larger enterprise. We can gather, however, that it still remained vigorous and that its work kept expanding, although only within the narrow borders of Palestine. Faith in Christ was combined with observance of the law, but was not on that account less real, for in the Jewish homeland the law was accepted as a matter of course, and the whole emphasis was laid by Christians on their new beliefs. The church in Palestine had its saints and martyrs no less than the churches in Ephesus and Rome. In some respects it had a harder struggle, for Jewish hostility was more bitter than that of pagans, whose attitude in religious matters was mostly one of indifference. It suffered, moreover, from a chronic poverty, due chiefly, it may be assumed, to the disabilities laid on Christians by the synagogues, which controlled the social and commercial as well as the religious life of the country. One of the duties which Paul took on himself in the later period of his mission was that of collecting money from the richer Gentile churches for the relief of Christians in Palestine.

All the difficulties came to a head when the little country, long seething with discontent, broke into open rebellion against the power of Rome. From the outset the Christians were opposed to this desperate venture. Their attitude has sometimes been condemned as unpatriotic, and it so appeared to their countrymen at the time; but as Christians they could adopt no other. Their hope was for the kingdom of God, and the aim of the rebels was to set up an earthly kingdom, accomplishing by violence what the Lord himself was to do when he returned as Messiah. It was apparently because of his effort to restrain the war fever that James met his death. When Jerusalem itself was threatened with siege, the Christians moved out in a body to Pella beyond the Jordan, and there remained until the tragedy was over. They came back to the ruined city and reconstituted the church, but it lacked its former significance. It had represented the Jewish nation, which existed no longer. It had been associated with the holy city; and the temple, which had made the city holy, had disappeared. Above all, the Gentile church had taken root and was spreading out its branches ever more widely. It was manifest to everyone that Christianity was henceforth to find its home in the Gentile world. The church in Palestine still lingered on, and may perhaps be identified with the obscure sect of the Ebionites, which was condemned in the second and third centuries as heretical. Such was the melancholy ending of this community which had given the new religion to mankind.

G. Significance of the Palestinian Church.— The brief career of the church in Palestine has commonly been treated as a mere prelude to the real history which opened with the work of Paul. He has been called "the second founder of Christianity," with the suggestion that before him the religion had not properly come into existence. Such a view is totally wrong. That initial period of which we know so little was not only the first but the most important in all Christian history. It was followed by centuries of great events enacted on a far wider stage, but the later imperial church owed almost everything to that small community which grew up in Palestine and withered away after little more than a single generation.

For one thing it was that primitive church that saved Christianity. With the death of Jesus his cause, to all appearance, had gone down in disaster, but a handful of believers maintained it in being. That is their chief claim to our lasting gratitude. They did more, however, than preserve Christianity and so ensure its mighty future. They formed a society of a unique character, one which existed under earthly conditions and yet stood for that higher order which would finally be established. This has always been the essential idea of the church, and it was first realized by that little company of believers who waited for the Lord's return. Not only did they inaugurate the church but they gave it the institutions which ever since have been vital to its well-being. They bequeathed to it the rites of baptism and the Lord's Supper. They took the form of worship which was practiced in the synagogue and adapted it to Christian use. They identified the Christian calling with the care of the sick and poor, with the sense of human brotherhood. It may truly be said too that the fundamental Christian beliefs were laid down in those early days and have never substantially changed. We think of Paul as the father of Christian doctrine, but again and again he acknowledges his debt to the church before him. Of almost all his primary conceptions he might have said, "I delivered unto you . . . that which I also received." His one purpose was to reaffirm the accepted beliefs, while probing them more deeply and working them out to their further issues. In this task a long succession of thinkers have since been engaged, but the beliefs themselves are still those of the primitive church.

It is sometimes assumed that while its earlier work had been invaluable, the church in Palestine fell wholly into the background after the advent of Paul. Henceforth it had nothing to contribute, and was little more than a drag on the great forward movement. But although it remained secluded within its own borders and made no visible mark on the church's general history, it still performed many necessary functions. For one thing it provided a base for the larger work then in process. Luke tells in his Gospel how the message would be preached "among all nations, beginning at Jerusalem"; and with this idea in his mind he constructs the book of Acts. He thinks of each missionary expedition as setting out from Jerusalem and returning to it. The mother community is regarded as the center from which the work spreads out in ever-expanding circles until it covers the most distant lands. This conception may be imaginative, but in a broad sense it corresponds with the facts. The Gentile churches were widely separated and were in constant danger of falling apart, but they were all aware that they originated from the one church which had its seat in Jerusalem. Their relation to it might be only one of sentiment, but it supplied the visible bond which held them together. By its mere existence the church in Palestine preserved the feeling of Christian unity.

In virtue of this reverence which was paid to it by all other churches it exercised a very real authority, even while it seemed to stand aloof. Paul's chief anxiety all through his mission was to secure the approval of the mother church. The worst trouble he ever encountered was from the interference of teachers who professed to speak in its name. They held no regular commission and in themselves were insignificant, but the mere fact that they came from Jerusalem made them formidable. In the eyes of Gentile converts they represented the Christian faith in its genuine and authoritative form. All through the early period the church in Palestine, although it seemed to have been superseded, was a powerful influence. In some respects this was unfortunate. The fall of Jerusalem was a blessing inasmuch as it freed Christianity of a restraint which hindered its natural development. Yet in the main the restraining influence was salutary. Paul himself had to contend in his later days not so much with Jewish conservatism as with false teaching which came in from the pagan side. For a century after his death the church was involved in a desperate struggle with the Gnostic heresy, and would probably have succumbed if the foundations laid in the previous age had been less stable. For this stability it had largely to thank the community in Palestine, which had refused to go the whole length with Paul. In the critical years of transition, when Christianity was becoming a Gentile religion, the older church had put a check on a too hasty progress. It had ensured that the change was made gradually, and that the new religion was safely anchored to those abiding principles in which it was at one with Judaism.

In a more definite way the older church made a contribution of priceless value after it seemed to have outlived its usefulness. It brought together and preserved for all later times those records of the life and teaching of Jesus which were ultimately embodied in the Gospels. The formation of the Gospels is a vast and intricate subject which does not here concern us, but there can be no doubt that the works of Mark, Matthew, and Luke—and to some extent of John—were compiled from earlier documents, and that these were based on reminiscences of Jesus which were collected in the Palestinian church. The mind of this church was conservative, and by clinging to institutions which had served their day it missed its share in the great missionary enterprise. But with this reverence for the past it cherished the memory of Jesus as he had actually been. Paul refused to know Christ after the flesh, and the Gentile church, like its grand apostle, was devoted to the living Lord, risen and glorified. In Palestine the believers still looked back to the earthly Master. They recalled the things he had done on earth; they gathered up his sayings and recited them in their meetings for worship. Pious Jews had their memories trained to store up the utterances of famous teachers, and to hand them down from one generation to another. This faculty was now employed for Christian purposes, and the records which were first transmitted orally were later put into writing and finally woven together in literary form. The Gospels as we now have them were produced in the Gentile church, but their material was all derived from the church in Palestine, and the original language can still be traced beneath the Greek translation. Without these records of the life of Jesus our religion would be incalculably poorer, and they come to us out of that period when the Palestinian church appeared to be so inactive that it is hardly mentioned in history.

It was the misfortune of this church that it left us no documents of its own similar to the book of Acts and the letters of Paul. The epistles ascribed to Peter and James and Jude are almost certainly of later date and have no light to throw on Christianity in Palestine. If one of those Judaistic teachers whom Paul denounces had put his own case into writing, we might have formed an impartial judgment on the controversy, but all our evidence is contained in Paul's letters and in some brief notices in Acts dealing only with outward events. The impression is thus left that while the great work went forward, the church in Palestine stood still, or wasted its energies in futile discussions about the law. But while it left no formal records, the primitive community speaks for itself indirectly in the Synoptic Gospels. It was attracted to those aspects of the life of Jesus which were most in keeping with its own Christian ideals. It selected the sayings which appeared to bear directly on its present needs and difficulties. From these records therefore we can learn not only what Jesus himself taught, but what those Jewish Christians believed, and in what manner they were seeking to fulfill their calling.

So it is from the Synoptic Gospels that we derive our best knowledge of the church in Palestine. When we consider only the other evidence we are apt to think of it as fettered to old traditions and never more than half awakened to the real purpose of the Christian message. This view, however, is manifestly unjust. The church which treasured the memory of Jesus, and lovingly collected his sayings and parables, and required of its members that they should live by his teaching, was in the fullest sense a Christian one. Its hope was fixed on the kingdom of God which Jesus had promised, and for which he had died. While holding to the law it looked first to the weightier matters, justice and mercy and truth. If it took little part in the wider enterprise, it guarded the message and gave the church those records of Jesus on which its faith has rested ever since. Paul himself was never forgetful of how much he owed to the community in Palestine, and indignantly denied that he taught another gospel. However he might differ from the earlier apostles—and there were undoubtedly some differences—he could truly say, "Whether it were I or they, so we preach, and so ye believed" (I Cor. 15:11).

IV. Selected Bibliography

BACON, B. W. *The Founding of the Church*. Boston: Houghton Mifflin Co., 1909.

HORT, F. J. A. *Judaistic Christianity*. Cambridge: Macmillan & Co., 1894.

JACKSON, F. J. FOAKES, and LAKE, KIRSOPP, eds. *The Beginnings of Christianity*. London: Macmillan & Co., 1920-33.

LIETZMANN, HANS. *The Beginnings of the Christian Church*, tr. Bertram Lee Woolf. New York: Charles Scribner's Sons, 1937.

McGIFFERT, A. C. *A History of Christianity in the Apostolic Age*. Rev. ed.; New York: Charles Scribner's Sons, 1920.

MEYER, EDUARD. *Ursprung und Anfänge des Christentums*. Stuttgart: J. G. Cotta, 1921.

ROPES, J. R. *The Apostolic Age in the Light of Modern Criticism*. New York: Charles Scribner's Sons, 1906.

WEISS, JOHANNES. *History of Primitive Christianity*, tr. F. C. Grant, *et al.* New York: Wilson-Erickson, 1937.

WEIZSÄCKER, K. H. *The Apostolic Age of the Christian Church*, tr. from 2nd ed. by James Millar. London: Williams & Norgate, 1894-95.

WERNLE, PAUL. *The Beginnings of Christianity*, tr. G. A. Bienemann. New York: G. P. Putnam's Sons, 1903-04.

THE HISTORY
OF THE EARLY CHURCH

II. THE LIFE OF PAUL

by WILLIAM H. P. HATCH

The role of the apostle Paul in the establishment of Christianity in the Greco-Roman world and in the development of Christian theology was second to that of no other figure in the history of our religion. He was primarily a preacher of the gospel and a missionary, and he was convinced that God had called him and set him apart to do this work (Rom. 1:1; Gal. 1:15-24). But Paul was more than a preacher and missionary. He was also a religious thinker of the first order, and it was inevitable that he should apply his mind to the many perplexing problems raised by the new religion. What about God's dealings with men—Gentiles as well as Jews? What about the person and work of Christ? What about the manifestations of the Spirit in the lives of believers? These and many other questions demanded an answer; and to answer them was to lay the foundations of Christian theology.

This article presupposes the preceding one on Palestinian Christianity and also the essay on the Hellenistic world (above, pp. 75-99), and therefore aims only to give an account of the life and work of the Apostle to the Gentiles, and of the founding of churches in certain parts of the Roman Empire during his lifetime. The period covered begins with the future apostle's conversion to Christianity on the road to Damascus and ends with his martyrdom in Rome. It is likely that his conversion took place in A.D. 32, and his death in 64 or 65. Thus about thirty-two or thirty-three years are in-cluded in the period of his active career as an apostle. The year 32 cannot be taken as the starting point for the discussion, however, since some attention must be paid to Paul's spiritual heritage and family background as well as to his education and early environment. Moreover the gospel had been preached and converts had been made outside the confines of Palestine before Paul was converted. These earlier developments cannot be ignored.

I. Sources

Apart from our knowledge of the apostle and his career, we know very little about the history and development of Christianity in the Roman Empire during his period. Our only trustworthy sources are the epistles ascribed to Paul in Christian tradition and the canonical book of Acts. The Apostle to the Gentiles is not mentioned elsewhere in the New Testament, with the exception of the incidental reference to "our beloved brother Paul" in II Pet. 3:15. Of the Pauline epistles most scholars at the present time think that only nine were composed by the apostle—Romans, I and II Corinthians, Galatians, Philippians, Colossians, I and II Thessalonians, and Philemon. Ephesians, I and II Timothy, and Titus are Pauline only in a secondary sense. Ephesians is best understood as the work of a Paulinist, and the Pastoral epistles contain genuine Pauline elements in varying degrees. Of the latter, II Timothy is the most valuable as a source for the life and work of Paul. The historical value of the Acts depends upon the trustworthiness of the sources upon which the book is based. Several sources seem to have been used, and they are not all of equal value. In the second half of the work the author had before him a diary kept by a traveling companion of the apostle. Some scholars think that the writer of the diary and the author of the Acts were the same person.

The apocryphal Acts of Paul, a work written in the second half of the second century, recounts certain travels of the apostle and incidents in his life that are not found in the canonical book of Acts; but these are wholly legendary. Similarly, little or nothing can be learned from statements preserved in the writings of the church fathers, because these are in part inferences drawn from the Pauline epistles or the book of Acts and in part mere legends. Furthermore secular works contribute only indirectly to our knowledge of the history and development of Christianity in the Roman Empire. The Christian communities were for the most part made up of people of the plainer sort. Very few of them were wealthy or prominent, and their lives and activities were ignored by historical writers (I Cor. 1:26-29). In other words Christianity had not yet become sufficiently important in the eyes of pagans to be mentioned in literary works. Hence for the study of the life and work of Paul and the growth of Christianity in the Greco-Roman world during his lifetime, the only sources that we need to take seriously into account are the epistles which bear the apostle's name and the canonical book of Acts.

II. The Gospel in Palestine and on Gentile Soil

Immediately after the death and resurrection of Jesus, the disciples began to preach and make converts in Jerusalem. Their message was that their Master, despite his ignominious death on the Cross, was in truth the Messiah whose coming the ancient Hebrew prophets had foretold. The new movement gained adherents rapidly among the Jews, and quite naturally it also aroused much opposition. This opposition soon developed into bitter hostility, which culminated in the stoning of Stephen outside the wall of Jerusalem (Acts 7:58-60). He was the first person to suffer death for believing that Jesus was the Messiah. It is interesting to recall at this point that a certain young man whose name was Saul—or Paul—was present at Stephen's death, and that he approved of the cruel deed. This event seems to have occurred in the year A.D. 31 or 32. According to the account in the Acts a great persecution of the disciples took place in connection with the martyrdom of Stephen, and most of them fled from Jerusalem, only the leaders remaining in the city. But in the providence of God much good came from this unhappy incident, for wherever the fugitives went they took the gospel with them. In this way the good tidings were published in Judea and Samaria.

Some of the brethren traveled still farther afield, making their way to Phoenicia, Cyprus, and Antioch. These, according to the author of the Acts, preached the gospel only to Jews (Acts 11:19). But according to the same authority, there were among them some Cypriotes and Cyrenians who journeyed on to Antioch and there proclaimed the good news also to the Gentiles. The names of these early missionaries are unknown to us, but we read that "the hand of the Lord was with them," and that many believed and "turned to the Lord" (Acts 11:21). No record of any evangelistic work done by the disciples as they went northward through Phoenicia is preserved in the Acts; but the preachers may well have stopped for a short time and delivered their message in Ptolemais, Tyre, or Sidon, which were important cities on the Phoenician coast. Paul visited Tyre and Ptolemais some twenty-five years later, and in both places he found Christian communities (Acts 21:3-7). In Tyre he was received in a very friendly and hospitable manner. It is not unreasonable to suppose that these communities were founded by the brethren who fled from Jerusalem at the time of Stephen's death. On his journey to Rome as a prisoner the apostle was permitted by the centurion to go to his friends in Sidon and be cared for by them (Acts 27:3). These friends were undoubtedly Christians, and their church may have owed its origin to the efforts of these early missionaries. Those who went to Cyprus doubtless sailed from some Phoenician port to the east coast of the island, landing perhaps at Salamis or Citium; and there can be no doubt that they preached the gospel wherever they had an opportunity to do so. In this way Christianity secured a foothold in Cyprus. Although Barnabas was a Cypriote, he was converted to the new religion at an earlier date, probably in Jerusalem; and he seems to have been a prominent member of the church in that city (Acts 4:36-37).

We have already seen that some of the disciples who left Jerusalem at the time of Stephen's martyrdom journeyed on to Antioch in northern Syria. There they proclaimed the Christian message, made converts, and established a strong and influential church. The Christian community in Antioch was made up of Gentiles as well as Jews. In planting Christianity in this strategic place the emissaries of the gospel showed great wisdom. Antioch, which was situated on the river Orontes at the eastern end of the Mediterranean Sea, was the capital and principal city of Syria, with a large and mixed population of Syrians, Greeks, and Jews; and among the cities of the empire it ranked next in importance after Rome and Alexandria. Its public buildings were noted for their beauty; it was outstanding as a commercial center; and it was the leading seat of Hellenistic culture on the continent of Asia. Luxury and immorality abounded there. Such a cosmopolitan city offered a great challenge and opportunity to the preachers of the gospel, and it proved to be a fertile field for their work. It was in Antioch that the disciples of Jesus were first called Christians, that is, adherents of the Messiah (Acts 11:26). A thriving church existed in this city some years before Paul came.

The gospel had also been established in Rome; but when or how it found its way to the capital of the empire is wholly unknown. According to the book of Acts, some Jews from Rome were in Jerusalem at Pentecost in the year of Jesus' death and resurrection (Acts 2:5-11); and some scholars think that they carried the disciples' message back to Rome with them, and that in this way Christianity obtained a foothold in the metropolis. This is of course quite possible. Since travel was common in the empire during the first century of our era and many people went to the capital on business or for pleasure, it is possible that some of these travelers, converted to Christianity somewhere in the East, carried the new religion with them to the Imperial City. But however the new faith may have arrived on the banks of the Tiber, there can be no doubt that there was a flourishing Christian community in the Imperial City before either Paul or Peter set foot on Italian soil. When Paul reached Rome, this community was composed of both Jews and Gentiles, and it may well have been a church of mixed membership from the beginning. (See also Intro. to Epistle to the Romans in Vol. IX.)

Rome was the capital of the empire and the chief center of culture in the West. The population of the city has been estimated at a million and a half persons, including representatives of various nations and races, among whom its many Jews formed a distinctive bloc. It was inevitable that a church located in Rome should play a leading part in the history of Christianity.

Thus Christianity spread at an early date from Jerusalem to Cyprus, Antioch, and Rome; and in Antioch and in Rome, which were both strategic centers, permanent Christian communities were established. Of course the gospel may have been preached and churches may have been founded elsewhere in the Greco-Roman world before the Apostle to the Gentiles began his missionary work, but our sources tell us nothing about any such evangelistic activity.

III. Paul's Life Before His Conversion

Before we take up the main subject of this section, a preliminary matter of considerable interest must be discussed briefly—the apostle's name. In all his extant letters he refers to himself as Paul, and this is the name by which he is universally known. However, he was named Saul by his parents, probably after King Saul, who also belonged to the tribe of Benjamin. In the apostle's time many Jews had two names, of which one was Semitic and the other frequently either Greek or Latin. So Paul was known by the Latin cognomen "Paulus," which means "little," as well as by his Hebrew or Aramaic name, Saul. His Latin cognomen may have been given to him in infancy or childhood on account of his smallness. It is not unlikely that to his parents he was "the little fellow." In any case we may be sure that the name Paul was not assumed arbitrarily by the apostle, as some have supposed, after the conversion of the Roman proconsul Sergius Paulus at Paphos (Acts 13:6-12). Since Paul's father was a Roman citizen, a Latin cognomen was not inappropriate for him. He may indeed have had a full Roman name; but if he did, his praenomen and nomen are not known.

The apostle was born in Tarsus in Cilicia, which was at that time incorporated in the province of Syria. Tarsus is described as "no mean city" in one of the speeches attributed to Paul in the book of Acts (21:39). This, however, is an understatement; for Tarsus was an ancient and well-known city, and its role in history was not insignificant. It was situated in a fertile plain astride the river Cydnus, and it was the chief city of Cilicia. Since it had access to an excellent harbor via the Cydnus, and since it lay at the southern end of the great trade route over Mount Taurus to Cappadocia and Lycaonia, Tarsus early became an important commercial center; and in the first century after Christ it had a large and mixed population, including many Jews. It bore the title of metropolis and enjoyed the status of an *urbs libera* or "free city." Moreover Tarsus was also a renowned seat of learning. In this respect it was comparable with Athens and Alexandria. It is important to remember this fact in view of the influence which the apostle's birthplace must have had on him as he was growing up. No keen and intelligent youth could have been unaffected by the intellectual life of a city like Tarsus. The date of Paul's birth is not known. We are told, however, that as a young man he was present at the stoning of Stephen. Since this event probably occurred in A.D. 32 or shortly before, it is not unreasonable to suppose that the apostle was born in the first decade of the first century after Christ. Paul was thus a younger contemporary of Jesus, but there is no evidence that he ever saw the Prophet of Nazareth during the latter's lifetime.

The apostle's parents were Jews, and they belonged to the sect of the Pharisees (Acts 23:6) ; but their names are unknown. The father at least was a member of the tribe of Benjamin. Nothing is known about his occupation or station in life, nor do we know whether he was living when his son became a disciple of Jesus. We are also uninformed about the size of the family in which Paul was reared. According to the book of Acts, he had a sister living in Jerusalem when he was a prisoner in that city (Acts 23:16). No brothers are mentioned. With such an ancestry, the apostle could proudly declare many years after his conversion to Christianity that he was a Hebrew of Hebrews (that is, a man of pure Hebrew stock, without any admixture of alien blood), an Israelite, of the seed of Abraham, and of the tribe of Benjamin (Rom. 11:1; II Cor. 11:22; Phil. 3:5). Moreover he was circumcised on the eighth day after his birth in accordance with the prescription of the Mosaic law; and he doubtless had the normal upbringing of a Jewish boy. Since his parents were Pharisees, Paul was naturally reared in the tradition of Pharisaism; and as long as he adhered to Judaism he continued to be a Pharisee.

Many young men of the apostle's race, even the sons of well-to-do parents, learned a trade; and the youthful Paul was no exception to this rule. He became a tentmaker, probably at Tarsus (Acts 18:3), and in later years he supported himself at times by working at his trade. But he was not interested solely or even primarily in his handicraft. His chief interest lay in the fields of religion and ethics, which to him, as to all Jews of his time, were very closely related. To achieve the ideal of righteousness was to do the will of God, and the will of God was made known in the Mosaic law. Hence it was only natural that Paul should go up to Jerusalem in his youth and become a pupil of Rabban Gamaliel the Elder, who at that time enjoyed a great reputation as a liberal teacher of the law. Having grown up in a pagan environment and having been subjected to its influence for a considerable time, Paul may have desired to live for a while in Jerusalem, the spiritual capital of the Jewish nation, and to learn from an authoritative source the facts connected with his ancestral religion.

Apparently even from his youth his heart was set on righteousness; and he tried scrupulously to order his life according to the precepts of the Mosaic legislation, which he naturally regarded as the divinely appointed means of attaining righteousness. The apostle himself declares that before he was converted he had advanced in Judaism beyond many of his Jewish contemporaries, being more zealous than they for their common ancestral traditions (Gal. 1:14) ; and also that according to the righteousness prescribed by the law, he was blameless (Phil. 3:6). By this claim Paul meant merely that he had tried conscientiously to keep the law of his fathers, that on the whole he had succeeded in doing so, and that therefore he could not justly be blamed or censured.

He had attended regularly the services of the synagogue, where he heard the Law and the Prophets read and expounded. It is probable that he himself sometimes read Old Testament passages aloud in the synagogue and explained them in homiletical discourses. In these synagogical addresses the Scriptures were often interpreted allegorically, and it was apparently from the services of the synagogue that Paul derived his allegorical method of interpreting the Old Testament. His conversion to Christianity did not change his view of the Scriptures. He still regarded them as divinely inspired and infallible; and as certain passages in his letters show, he continued to understand them allegorically (I Cor. 10:1-11; Gal. 4:22-31). Such were some of the dominating influences in the life of the future apostle before his conversion; and they made him in his pre-Christian period a true Israelite, loyal to his ancestral religion and strict in the performance of the many obligations which it laid upon him.

On the other hand it must be remembered that he was born and brought up in the city of Tarsus. There, during his most impressionable years, he came into daily contact with various phases of paganism. He must have learned something about pagan philosophy and pagan religion. He may have listened to the Stoic and Cynic philosophers as they preached on the street corners and in the market places, expounding their views to everyone who would give them a hearing. Moreover the temples and statues of the heathen gods and goddesses were to be seen on every side, and the youthful Paul must have looked upon them with the abhorrence and loathing which a devout Jew naturally felt for the symbols of idolatry. He may also have found out in some way whatever a person who had not been initiated into one of the mystery religions could know about them, but it is obvious that he could have had no esoteric knowledge of these cults. The sacramental ideas and worship of these soteriological religions, which were wholly unlike anything to be found in orthodox Judaism, would certainly have seemed to him strange and exotic. Furthermore the apostle must have seen with his own eyes much of the good and much of the evil in the lives of his Gentile fellow citizens; and although the evil shocked and pained him deeply, he was not without appreciation of the good. If the apostle had been brought up in a purely Jewish community, his knowledge of men and the world would have been much more limited. His outlook also would have been narrower and less cosmopolitan, and he himself would have been less well equipped for his work as a missionary to the Gentiles.

Looking back in later years upon his life before his conversion to Christianity, Paul says that he "persecuted the church of God exceedingly and made havoc of it" (Gal. 1:13). Being a man of strong conviction and great force, he tried as hard as he could to destroy what he regarded as a new and dangerous heresy, and at that time he seems to have had no conscientious scruples about the rightness of his course. In view of the apostle's intellectual and spiritual background and his ardent temperament, it is easy to understand why he acted as he did toward those who accepted Jesus of Nazareth as the Messiah. The same zeal that made Paul the Pharisee a relentless persecutor of the disciples of the Nazarene Prophet later made him an indefatigable missionary of the gospel. Such miracles happen when the power of God working in and through Christ enters a man's life.

IV. Conversion of Paul

We come now to the most momentous event in the life of Paul. While he was actively engaged in persecuting the followers of Jesus wherever he could find them, "breathing out threatenings and slaughter against the disciples of the Lord" (Acts 9:1), something occurred which completely revolutionized his thinking and radically changed his life. He himself became a member of the sect which he had been trying to exterminate. We do not know what thoughts may have been revolving in his mind when he became convinced that the risen Lord had spoken to him, nor do we know how long he may have been pondering over the question of Jesus' messiahship. However, the denouement came suddenly, and the future apostle's decision was definite and permanent.

According to Acts (9:3-19; 22:6-21; 26:12-18), the circumstances were as follows: Paul had obtained letters from the high priest and the council of elders in Jerusalem which authorized him to arrest as many disciples of Jesus as he could find in Damascus and to bring them to Jerusalem as prisoners, in order that they might be punished. Probably without delay the persecutor set out for the Syrian city with a few companions; but as he and his company drew near to Damascus, suddenly about midday an exceedingly bright light shone around about him from heaven. Having fallen down to the ground, he heard a voice saying to him, "Saul, Saul, why persecutest thou me?" When he asked, "Who art thou, Lord?" the voice replied, "I am Jesus, whom thou persecutest." He was also bidden by the voice to arise and go into the city, where he would be told what he should do. When the future apostle rose up from the ground, he was unable to see on account of the brightness of the light which had shone around about him; and he had to be led into Damascus by his companions. There a disciple named Ananias initiated him into the Christian fellowship and conveyed to him God's call to apostleship. These are the essential facts connected with the conversion of the Apostle to the Gentiles according to the book of Acts. The event is related three times in this work—once where the author thought it belonged in the history of the expanding church (Acts 9:1-19) and twice in speeches attributed to Paul (Acts 22:1-21 and 26:2-23). There is so much similarity of wording in the three accounts that they cannot be regarded as independent of each other. The one given in the speech delivered before the procurator Festus and King Herod Agrippa II is the simplest, and the other two may well be based upon it.

The apostle himself rarely refers to his conversion in his letters. In I Cor. 15:3-8 he mentions it in connection with the appearances of the risen Jesus after his resurrection from the dead: "For I delivered to you as of first importance what I also received, that Christ died for our sins in accordance with the scriptures, that he was buried, that he was raised on the third day in accordance with the scriptures, and that he appeared to Cephas, then to the twelve. Then he appeared to more than five hundred brethren at one time, most of whom are still alive, though some have fallen asleep. Then he appeared to James, then to all the apostles. Last of all, as to one untimely born, he appeared also to me." It is clear from these words that Paul regarded his own experience of Christ on the road near Damascus as being essentially like that of Cephas and James and the others to whom the risen Lord had appeared. He also recognized it as a free and gracious act of God (Gal. 1:15-16). It was in no way dependent upon his own merit, for he had been and was at that moment actively engaged in persecuting the followers of Jesus.

The apostle's experience on the way to Damascus revolutionized his thinking and radically changed the course of his career. It made him forthwith and for the remainder of his life a stanch believer in Jesus of Nazareth and a devoted preacher of the gospel. The date of this momentous event must be determined from certain events which are not immediately connected with what occurred on the road to Damascus. The problem is complicated and cannot be discussed here. But it seems likely that the conversion occurred not long after the stoning of Stephen, which the hostile Pharisee witnessed with approval; and therefore it can hardly be dated earlier or much later than A.D. 32. At that time the future apostle would have been close to thirty years old.

V. After the Conversion

Immediately after his experience on the road to Damascus, Paul spent "some days" with the disciples of the Lord in that city. During this time he preached in the synagogues of Damascus that Jesus of Nazareth was the Son of God, that is, the Messiah, whose coming the Hebrew prophets had foretold. We do not know how successful he may have been in his efforts to win converts among the Damascene Jews; but we read in the book of Acts that those who heard him were amazed at his teaching and pointed out the stark inconsistency between his preaching of Jesus' messiahship in Damascus and his former conduct as a persecutor of those who believed in the Prophet of Nazareth (Acts 9:19-21).

At this time the apostle felt, like many another who has passed through a trying experience, that he needed retirement and seclusion, in order to think out in a leisurely way the many pressing problems which his conversion had raised. Therefore, as he himself says, he withdrew into Arabia (Gal. 1:17). Some scholars think that this region was the Hauran, a fertile basin which lay some fifty miles south of Damascus and directly east of the southern part of the Sea of Galilee; others believe that the country of the Nabataeans and the Sinaitic peninsula are meant. The former was much nearer to Damascus and more accessible, but the latter had religious associations of a unique sort, which would have made it a congenial place for meditation. On the whole, however, it seems more probable that the term "Arabia" is used to denote the barren country which extends eastward and southeastward from Damascus and is known as the Syrian Desert. We do not know how long the apostle remained in this region, but he probably did not tarry there very long. He had much work to do, and he was doubtless eager to begin it.

From Arabia, Paul returned to Damascus and resumed his preaching. His message was the same as it had been before he went into retirement in Arabia, but now he "increased the more in strength, and confounded the Jews who dwelt in Damascus, proving that this is the Messiah" (Acts 9:22). The apostle had doubtless by this time thought out at least the main outlines of his position in regard to Christ, and he was ready to declare it positively and forcefully. His work in the Syrian city continued for three years.

Paul's zeal inevitably aroused hostility among those whom he was trying to convert, and they undertook to stop the subversive preaching by forming a plot to kill the missionary. However, the apostle heard of the scheme before it could be carried out, and he escaped from Damascus with the help of his Christian friends (II Cor. 11:32-33; Acts 9:25), and went up directly to Jerusalem (Gal. 1:18). This was the apostle's first visit to the Holy City since his experience on the road to Damascus; and if the date of his conversion given above is accepted as correct, this first visit to Jerusalem must have occurred in the year 35. Paul says that his purpose was to visit Cephas, and that he remained with this leader of the Jerusalem church fifteen days.

When this first visit to Jerusalem was concluded, the apostle says that he went into the regions of Syria and Cilicia (Gal. 1:21). He undoubtedly traveled northward by land to Syria; and then, passing through the eastern part of Cilicia, he seems to have arrived in Tarsus. Here he apparently settled down and remained for some time. Unfortunately he does not tell us why he went to Syria and Cilicia, or what he did in these regions. He may have journeyed along in a leisurely way, stopping off here and there to make converts; but in any case we may be sure that he was engaged in the work of the gospel. Paul, as we have seen, was born and brought up in Tarsus. So far as we know, the gospel had not yet been preached either in the city itself or in its neighborhood; and the apostle must have welcomed a chance to proclaim it in his birthplace. However, we know little about this period of his life—how successful he may have been in his work, or just how long his labors may have continued. But there can be no doubt that Paul did not neglect an opportunity to preach the Christian message and to make as many converts as possible, and that he did not lack either zeal or courage in prosecuting the work of the gospel. As to the duration of his labors in and about Tarsus, we have to rely largely on conjecture, and naturally scholars are divided. However, it seems not unreasonable to suppose that the apostle's work in Cilicia occupied about eight years.

In the meantime, as we have seen, Christianity had become established in Antioch through the efforts of certain missionaries who came thither from the mother church in Jerusalem. While the Apostle to the Gentiles was preaching the gospel in Tarsus, Barnabas was taking a leading part in the life of the church in the Syrian capital. He is described in the book of Acts as "a good man, full of the Holy Spirit and of faith" (Acts 11:24). Since a helper was needed in the Christian community at Antioch, Barnabas went to Tarsus and persuaded Paul to go back with him and assist in the work there. It was while he was working with Barnabas in the Syrian capital that a great famine threatened the residents of Judea. The Christians of Antioch, naturally desiring to do what they could to relieve the sufferings of their Judean brethren, took up a collection for them; and according to the book of Acts, the two apostles were sent to Jerusalem with the gift (Acts 11:28-30). It should be remarked, however, that the mention of a journey to Jerusalem at this time by the author of the Acts is hard to reconcile with what the apostle himself says about his visits to the capital in the Epistle to the Galatians (Gal. 1:18; 2:1). If the journey in company with Barnabas is accepted as historical, Paul must have momentarily forgotten it when he was writing to the Galatians. But it hardly seems possible that this visit to the Holy City, however brief it may have been, could have been thus forgotten. An alternative explanation of this discrepancy is that Paul and Barnabas were both in Antioch when contributions were collected for the Judean sufferers, and that the author of the Acts thought the two apostles took the offering up to Jerusalem; whereas in fact Barnabas alone made this journey. In any case the famine seems to have occurred in A.D. 44 or 45, and it is entirely in keeping with the chronological scheme followed in this article to suppose that Paul was working in the Syrian capital at that time.

VI. First Missionary Journey

It was after laboring a year in Antioch that the apostle entered upon the most interesting and significant stage of his career. This was the period in which he preached the gospel and established churches in widely separated areas of the Roman Empire. The author of the Acts relates that during a religious service in the Syrian capital, the Holy Spirit bade certain prophets and teachers set apart Paul and Barnabas for a special preaching mission in territories which lay to the west (Acts 13:2–14:28).

The two apostles accordingly went down to Seleucia, which was the port of Antioch on the Mediterranean Sea, taking with them John Mark, a cousin of Barnabas, as a helper on the expedition. At Seleucia the three missionaries boarded a ship bound for Cyprus, the birthplace of Barnabas; in due time they arrived at Paphos, which was the capital of Cyprus. Here Paul converted the Roman proconsul, whose name was Sergius Paulus. The Christian message, as we have seen, had been proclaimed in Cyprus several years before Paul and Barnabas visited the island; but it had been preached only to Jews. The apostles, however, brought the good news to Gentiles as well as to Jews.

From Paphos the three missionaries set out for the mainland of Asia Minor, taking a ship for Perga, the capital of Pamphylia. At Perga, for some unknown reason, John Mark withdrew from the expedition and returned to his home in Jerusalem. Perhaps the plans of the party had changed, and Mark was unwilling to enter upon a long and hazardous journey and to remain away from home for an indefinite period. At any rate Paul seems to have resented the young man's departure as an act of desertion, and later he would not consent to have his former helper accompany him on a missionary tour (Acts 15:38). Paul and Barnabas soon departed from Perga and traveled northward to Antioch in the northern part of Pisidia, which was an inland district. Here the evangelization of Asia Minor really began. This whole peninsula, with the exception of Cilicia in the southeastern corner, was virgin soil for the preachers of the gospel. In Pisidian Antioch the two apostles delivered their message in the synagogue on the sabbath, and they were warmly welcomed both by the Jews and by the proselytes. On the following sabbath, however, the Jews became jealous and turned violently against the strangers, so that the latter were obliged to leave the city.

The two apostles made their way in a southeasterly direction into the neighboring region of Lycaonia. They went first to Iconium, an important commercial city in the western part of this territory; and here the missionaries conducted a highly successful mission for a considerable time. The gospel was preached in the local synagogue, and many converts were made. However, the unbelieving Jews incited and embittered the Gentiles against the Christians; and the inhabitants of the city were divided, some siding with the Jews and some with Paul and Barnabas. Finally, when the latter became aware of the bitter hostility that prevailed against them in Iconium, they fled southeastward to Lystra and Derbe. These two cities, neither of which was of first-rate importance, were in the eastern part of Lycaonia. In Lystra a man who was lame from his birth was healed of his deformity; and the pagan population of the city, thinking that two Greek gods had come down to the earth in human form, called Barnabas "Zeus" and Paul "Hermes." Moreover the local priest of Zeus, joining with the crowds, prepared to offer sacrifice; and the apostles had some difficulty in preventing this from being done.

While the missionaries were in Lystra, some Jews from Pisidian Antioch and Iconium stirred up the crowds and instigated a violent personal attack upon Paul; but he was rescued from this peril by his disciples. Nevertheless on the following day Paul and Barnabas left Lystra and journeyed on to Derbe. In this city the preachers proclaimed the message of salvation and made a considerable number of converts. The apostles now decided not to proceed farther east, but to retrace their steps and visit the brethren whom they had converted. Accordingly they returned to Lystra, Iconium, and Pisidian Antioch. Wherever they went they strengthened the disciples and exhorted them to be steadfast in faith; and in the various churches which had been established by their efforts Paul and Barnabas appointed presbyters. Finally they arrived in Perga, where they delivered their message; and then they went down to Attalia, which was an important seaport and the metropolis of Pamphylia. Here the missionaries boarded a ship for Antioch in Syria, which they had left two years before. During this time they had visited Cyprus, Pamphylia, Pisidia, and Lycaonia; and in all these places the gospel had been preached and converts had been made.

VII. The Apostolic Council

About a year and a half after Paul and Barnabas returned to Antioch, certain Jewish Christians came down from Judea and caused much trouble in the Antiochian church by their teaching that a person must be circumcised in order to be saved. According to them, Gentiles could enter the church only through the gate of Judaism. Naturally dissension arose among the disciples, and the question was warmly debated. Therefore it was decided that Paul and Barnabas should go up to Jerusalem and consult the apostles and presbyters about the matter (Acts 15:1-2). According to his own account, this was the second visit of Paul to the capital after his conversion, and it took place fourteen years after his first journey to Jerusalem and seventeen years after his experience on the road to Damascus (Gal. 2:1). If the apostle was converted in A.D. 32, this second visit to the Holy City must have occurred in A.D. 49. When the apostles and presbyters of the mother church assembled to consider the question which had been raised at Antioch, Paul set forth to them the gospel preached by him among the Gentiles.

According to the book of Acts, he and Barnabas related the evidences of God's favor which they had seen on their missionary tour in Cyprus and southern Galatia; and Peter spoke with some feeling against requiring Gentile converts to undergo circumcision and keep the Mosaic law. Finally James, who presided at the conference, also took the liberal view in regard to the admission of Gentiles into the church. When the discussion was over, it was resolved that no other obligation should be laid upon the Gentiles than that they should abstain from these four things, namely, meats offered to idols, blood, things strangled, and fornication (Acts 15:6-21). In other words the apostolic council decreed that Gentiles should be permitted to enter the Christian fold without being required to undergo circumcision or to keep the law of Moses. The provisions of this decree were strictly in accord with the practice which Paul and Barnabas had followed in their missionary work, and they were thus fully justified. This conference of the apostles and presbyters in Jerusalem was apparently held in A.D. 49.

The apostle says in the Epistle to the Galatians that James and Cephas and John, having given the right hand of fellowship to Barnabas and himself, agreed that the latter should preach the gospel among the Gentiles and that they themselves should work among the Jews (Gal. 2:9). However, as is clear from what the author of the Acts relates, this division of labor according to race did not preclude Paul from proclaiming the message of salvation in Jewish synagogues.

An unfortunate incident occurred in Antioch soon after the apostolic council adjourned. Peter, who had ignored the fact that he was a Jew, and had even eaten with his Gentile brethren of the Antiochian church, "drew back and separated himself" when certain Judaizing disciples came from Jerusalem. He acted in this way because he feared the Jews, and even Barnabas was "carried away" by the insincerity of Peter and the Jews who joined with him. Paul was much incensed by Peter's conduct, and he rebuked him sharply for it in the presence of all the brethren (Gal. 2:11-14). Peter's behavior belied his principles, and he was untrue to the agreement made at the conference in Jerusalem.

VIII. Second Missionary Journey

Not long after this unhappy incident Paul proposed to Barnabas that they should go and see how the brethren were getting along in every city in which they had preached the gospel. (For this journey see Acts 15:36—18:22.) Barnabas wished to take Mark with them again; but Paul, recalling that the young man had withdrawn somewhat abruptly on the earlier journey, was opposed to this plan. The disagreement of the two friends resulted in a rupture; and Barnabas and Mark sailed off to Cyprus, leaving Paul to undertake the present expedition without either of his former companions. But the apostle was resolute and equal to the emergency; and he chose Silas, one of the leading members of the church in Jerusalem, to be his fellow worker. After passing through Syria and Cilicia, the two missionaries journeyed on to Derbe and Lystra in Lycaonia. In Lystra there was a highly esteemed disciple named Timothy, whom Paul wished to take on the expedition as an assistant; but being the offspring of a mixed marriage, he had not been circumcised. So Paul circumcised him in order to placate the Jews who lived in Lystra and its neighborhood. Some scholars, however, think that the apostle could not have done this in view of the fact that he had recently rebuked Peter sternly at Antioch for Judaizing; and furthermore because his former companion Titus, who was also a Gentile, was not required to undergo circumcision (Gal. 2:3). However, the case of Timothy was different from that of Titus; and we cannot be sure whether the latter was circumcised or not. In any case Paul set out from Lystra with Silas and Timothy, and the three passed through the various cities of the region.

Unfortunately the preachers' journey from this point until they arrived in Troas is very briefly related in the book of Acts. We read that they went through "the Phrygian and Galatian region," and then we are told that they continued on their journey and finally came down to Troas. Scholars, however, are divided as to the meaning of the phrase just quoted. Some think that Phrygia and northern Galatia are meant, and they assume that the apostle and his friends traveled west as far as Synnada in Phrygia and north as far as Ancyra in northern Galatia. The book of Acts, however, contains no mention of a visit to any of these places. From Ancyra they are supposed to have journeyed westward through Mysia to Troas on the Aegean Sea. On the other hand many scholars believe that "the Phrygian and Galatian region" of Acts 16:6 is the Phrygo-Galatian territory which extends from Iconium to Pisidian Antioch. From this region the missionaries made their way in a northwesterly direction to Troas in Mysia. They were divinely restrained from preaching the gospel in the Roman province of Asia and from going into Bithynia; and there is no evidence that any missionary work was done as they moved on toward Troas, an important city on the west coast of Mysia. Here Paul saw a vision which caused the party to cross over the northeastern corner of the Aegean Sea to Macedonia. They landed at Neapolis, which was the port of Philippi; and thence they proceeded without delay to Philippi itself.

Philippi, a Roman *colonia,* was situated in the southeastern part of Macedonia. Here the gospel was first preached in Europe, and some converts were made. However, before very long Paul and Silas were accused of disturbing the city and proclaiming anti-Roman customs; and they were beaten and thrown into prison. But when the magistrates heard that these men were Romans, they became fearful and asked the missionaries to depart from Philippi. With this request the latter readily complied. Although the preachers spent only a short time in this city, a Christian community was founded there which always continued to be loyal to Paul, and which he regarded with great affection as long as he lived.

When the three missionaries left Philippi, they moved on along the Via Egnatia in a southwesterly direction, passed through Amphipolis and Apollonia, and came to Thessalonica on the Thermaic Gulf, the most important place in Macedonia and the capital of one of the four districts into which the province was divided. It had a large population, which was partly Jewish. The gospel was preached there, and some Jews and many proselytes were converted. These became the nucleus of a strong, generous, and influential church. After a time, however, the Jews grew jealous and incited the crowd and the magistrates of the city against the apostle and his two friends; and consequently the brethren sent the latter away by night to Berea, which was a populous inland city of Macedonia, lying to the southwest of Thessalonica. Here many Jews and not a few Gentiles, including some people of prominence, were converted by the preachers. But when the Jews of Thessalonica learned of the missionaries' success in Berea, some of them came down and stirred up the crowds against the believers. Thereupon Paul departed and went by ship to Athens. Silas and Timothy, however, remained in Berea; but they were charged by the apostle to come to Athens as soon as possible.

Athens was the most famous city in the province of Achaia and the chief literary and intellectual center of the Hellenic world. Paul must have welcomed an opportunity to preach the gospel in such a place. He was profoundly shocked, however, by the many evidences of idolatry which he saw in Athens; for he believed, like the Hebrew prophets, that idolatry was the source of many of the world's worst evils. He tried to reach as many people as possible, discoursing not only in the synagogue but also in the market place. He also disputed with certain Epicurean and Stoic philosophers. The latter, thinking that Paul was trying to introduce strange divinities and wishing to learn more about his teaching, took him to Areopagus, in order that he might expound his religious views to a larger number of people. There he spoke at some length, and an Athenian of prominence named Dionysius and some others were converted. The apostle's work in Athens was apparently not very successful. Nevertheless, although no great church was founded there at this time, the Christian message was proclaimed in this ancient center of Greek culture.

After a brief sojourn in Athens, Paul journeyed on westward to Corinth, which was the capital as well as the leading commercial city of Achaia. Much of the trade between the Orient and the Occident passed through Corinth, and naturally the population of the place was made up of many peoples and races. Among these there were many Jews. Although Corinth enjoyed some reputation as a center for the study of rhetoric and philosophy, the city was notorious for its luxury and immorality. In Corinth the apostle preached the gospel to his own people and also to the Gentiles, and his work was highly successful. Here, as in Thessalonica, a strong and influential church was established.

Silas and Timothy came down from Macedonia and rejoined Paul in Corinth. Timothy reported from Thessalonica that certain erroneous views concerning the return of Christ were rife among the disciples there, and that idleness and immorality were all too common among them (I Thess. 4:3-8, 11; 5:14). The apostle was much disturbed, and without delay he addressed a letter to the church in Thessalonica to set matters right. This is I Thessalonians, and most scholars think that it is the earliest extant letter of Paul. It was almost certainly written in the spring of the year 50.

However, some of the brethren in Thessalonica, still believing that the Lord would return very soon, were neglecting their ordinary occupations (II Thess. 3:6-12) and, probably within a few weeks after writing the first letter, the apostle sent his second epistle to the disciples in Thessalonica. Both letters were composed soon after the author arrived in Corinth. Some scholars think that the Epistle to the Galatians also was written during this sojourn of Paul in the Achaian capital. If so, it is certainly later than the letters to the Thessalonians. After the apostle and his friends had worked a little more than a year and a half in Corinth, the Jews accused Paul of persuading men to worship God in a manner contrary to that prescribed by the law of Moses. The charge was brought before Gallio, who had recently become proconsul of Achaia; but he declined to take cognizance of questions concerning the Jewish law. Soon after this incident the apostle sailed off for Syria. On the way Paul stopped at Ephesus in the western part of Asia Minor, and here he preached the gospel to the Jews. Probably the name of Christ had not been heard previously in Ephesus. The apostle, however, was eager to reach Antioch; and he soon boarded a ship for Caesarea in Palestine. After arriving at this seaport he may have gone up to Jerusalem ("he went up and greeted the church"—Acts 18:22), and after a brief sojourn in the Holy City he may have proceeded thence to the Syrian capital. However, Jerusalem is not mentioned by name, and consequently many scholars think that Paul went directly from Caesarea to Antioch by land.

With Paul's return to Antioch the second missionary journey ended. It apparently occupied somewhat more than two years; and if the chronological scheme followed in this article is correct, the second missionary journey must have extended from A.D. 49 to 51. According to the book of Acts, the apostle spent "some time" in Antioch—how much we do not know. He may have needed to recuperate after his long and arduous journey, and certainly there were many things to relate to the brethren of the Antiochian church. Some scholars think that Galatians was written soon after Paul's arrival in the Syrian capital.

IX. Third Missionary Journey

It was not long before the apostle was ready to set out on his third missionary tour (Acts 18:23–21:15). Traveling at first northward and then in a westerly and northwesterly direction, he passed through the Galatian region and Phrygia. He visited the cities in southern Galatia in which he and Barnabas had preached the gospel on the first missionary journey. However, the scholars who believe that Paul worked in northern Galatia on his second missionary journey hold that he went thither at this time. But the other view is more probable. After visiting the Christian communities in southern Galatia, the apostle set forth from Pisidian Antioch for Ephesus. The route chosen lay in a westerly direction through the upland districts of the province of Asia, probably traversing the Cayster Valley. So far as we know, Paul did not stop along the way to preach the gospel.

Ephesus, situated near the mouth of the river Cayster, was the capital and metropolis of the province of Asia and one of the leading commercial centers of Asia Minor. The city ranked with Antioch and Alexandria in importance, and it was renowned for its temple of

Artemis and its spacious theater. In Ephesus the apostle preached at first to the Jews in the synagogue, but after a short time he turned to the Gentiles and discoursed daily in the school of a certain Ephesian named Tyrannus. This work continued over a period of two years; and many people in the province of Asia, both Jews and Gentiles, heard the message of salvation. Thus the gospel was proclaimed not only in the capital, but also in other parts of the province. During this time Paul made many friends in Ephesus, as is evident from the brief note of commendation given to Phoebe when she was about to visit the capital of the province of Asia (Rom. 16:1-23). On the other hand he also made enemies; for he himself says that he fought with wild beasts there, meaning probably with savage adversaries (I Cor. 15:32). It is possible, however, that the apostle refers to an actual combat with wild beasts in the arena. If so, he must have been arrested and condemned to this cruel ordeal, and he must have escaped almost certain death. But the author of the Acts says nothing about anything of this sort. We are told, however, that near the end of Paul's two-year stay he incurred the enmity of a certain Demetrius and of others who were engaged in making images and other objects connected with the worship of Artemis. Paul's preaching against idolatry interfered with their business. The agitation against him led to a riot in the temple, and Paul was forced to hasten his departure from the city. This happened in or near the year 55.

Meantime difficulties of various kinds had arisen at Corinth. Paul, greatly disturbed by these, had already dispatched several letters to that church and had sent Timothy as his personal representative, besides making at least one visit himself. Then he set out for Corinth again, going by way of Macedonia. Arriving in Philippi, he journeyed westward through Amphipolis and Apollonia to Thessalonica. Most scholars think that from Thessalonica the apostle traveled on westward along the Via Egnatia, at least as far as the eastern boundary of Illyricum, which was a mountainous province situated between Macedonia and the Adriatic Sea (Rom. 15:19). The gospel had not been heard previously in this region. Apparently after a short time Paul retraced his steps eastward toward Thessalonica and came finally to Corinth. Here he remained three months—the three winter months of the year 55-56. According to some scholars, Galatians was composed either while the writer was en route from Macedonia to Achaia or during his sojourn in Corinth. Romans was written soon after Galatians and in the period of the apostle's stay in the Achaian capital.

Paul wanted to go to Jerusalem at this time with a contribution which had been made by his churches for the brethren in the Holy City. At first he planned to sail directly to Syria, but on account of a plot formed against him by the Jews, he decided to proceed by land through Macedonia. There the apostle and the friends who accompanied him boarded a ship soon after Passover and sailed along the western coast of Asia Minor. They put in for short periods at several points, including Miletus, the port of Ephesus, when Paul said what proved to be a final farewell to the elders of that church. Eventually they landed at Tyre on the Syrian coast. Despite the disciples' warnings not to go up to Jerusalem, Paul and his party continued on to Ptolemais and from this point went by land to Caesarea. Although the apostle was again warned of the danger that awaited him in the Holy City, he could not be dissuaded from carrying out his purpose; and so he and his companions journeyed on from Caesarea to Jerusalem, where they were well received by the brethren.

When Paul arrived in Jerusalem at Pentecost, probably in A.D. 56, his third missionary journey was ended. Since he set out from Antioch on this expedition he had preached the gospel in the regions around the Aegean Sea, he had revisited most of the places in which he had previously worked, and he had labored in Ephesus and its neighborhood for three years.

X. Paul's Arrest in Jerusalem and His Journey to Rome

Serious trouble, however, was now in the offing (Acts 21:27–28:16). Both in Jerusalem and elsewhere the apostle had the reputation of not observing the Mosaic law himself and of teaching others to disregard it. Consequently when some Jews from the province of Asia saw him in the temple soon after his arrival in the city, they stirred up the crowd and made an attack upon him. Thereupon an uproar ensued, and the Roman authorities arrested Paul on the charge of disturbing the peace. The apostle spoke at length on the temple steps, recounting how he had formerly persecuted the disciples and relating what had happened on the road to Damascus. Finally he was taken to the barracks to be examined by scourging; but when the military tribune learned that Paul was a Roman citizen, he ordered that the prisoner be unbound and allowed to confront his accusers. But so much clamor and dissension arose as the apostle was speaking that the tribune had him conducted back to the barracks to ensure his safety. While Paul was being held there, the tribune learned that a considerable number of Jews had conspired to kill him; accordingly the prisoner was sent with an armed escort to Caesarea, the residence of the Roman procurator Felix. The latter promised to hear the case fully when the accusers should appear, and ordered the apostle to be kept under guard in Herod's palace. An attempt to prosecute Paul before Felix failed, and the prisoner was held in *libera custodia*—that is, he was kept under guard, but he lived in his own quarters and enjoyed many privileges—at Caesarea for two years. Some scholars think that the epistles to the Colossians and to the Ephesians as well as the personal letter to Philemon were written during the apostle's imprisonment in Caesarea, but a later date for these letters is more probable.

After two years there was a change of administration in Palestine. Felix, an unsuccessful administrator, was recalled; and Porcius Festus, a man of much better character, succeeded him. According to the chronological scheme followed in this article, Festus became procurator in A.D. 58. When the new procurator refused to hear Paul's case in Jerusalem, certain Jews came down from that city to Caesarea and brought grave charges against the apostle. The latter, however, denied categorically that he had committed any offense either against the Jewish law or temple or against Caesar. When Festus asked Paul if he wished to have his case tried in Jerusalem, the apostle appealed to Caesar; and after a brief consultation with his advisors, the procurator allowed the appeal. As a Roman citizen the apostle had the right to appeal to the emperor, and he availed himself of this right undoubtedly because he thought that he would be more likely to get a fair trial in Rome than in Jerusalem or Caesarea. After appealing to Caesar and before departing for Rome, Paul spoke at length before King Agrippa II and his sister Bernice, who had come to Caesarea for a visit. Again, as on the temple steps in Jerusalem, he gave an account of his life as a Pharisee and recounted his experience on the road near Damascus. According to the book of Acts, this speech made a favorable impression upon all those who heard it.

When the time came for the apostle to go to Rome, he and some other prisoners were delivered to a centurion, who put them aboard a ship and took them first to Sidon and then to Myra in the southwestern part of Asia Minor. Here the centurion transferred his charges to an Alexandrian vessel bound for Italy, and the party put to sea. It was autumn, and storms were likely to make navigation difficult and dangerous. Still no very serious trouble was encountered at first; but when the ship was off the southern coast of Crete, a terrific northeast wind caught her and drove her on past the little island of Cauda and out into the open sea. The storm raged violently fourteen days, the vessel was buffeted by the waves, and the passengers and crew were in imminent danger of death. After suffering many hardships and being carried a long distance westward, the party came at last to Melita, that is, Malta, which is directly south of Sicily; and the 276 persons aboard the ship were all landed safely.

After a sojourn of three months in Malta, Paul and the others set out for Syracuse; and in due time they arrived without any further misadventure. From Syracuse they sailed on northward to Rhegium and Puteoli, where the sea voyage ended. From this point the centurion and his prisoners passed along the Via Appia in a northwesterly direction to Rome. The apostle was now at last in the political and intellectual capital of the West. He had long since desired to visit Rome and proclaim the message of salvation there, but up to this time he had been prevented (Rom. 1:10-13). Even then he did not enter the Imperial City as a free man. The apostle probably arrived in Rome early in the year 59.

XI. Paul's Imprisonment in Rome

During his imprisonment in Rome (Acts 28:16-31), Paul was not treated like a criminal or an ordinary prisoner. He was a Roman citizen who had appealed his case to Caesar, and he enjoyed what has already been described as *libera custodia*. The apostle was able to explain to the leading Jews of the city what he had done, and why he was held in custody; and it was also possible for him to preach the gospel to any who would come to his house, and to send letters to distant places. He was required merely to live in Rome under the supervision of the authorities, in order that he might be on hand when the government should be ready to hear his case. It is probable that at least three of the extant Pauline epistles were written during this period—Colossians, Philemon, and Philippians.

The book of Acts ends abruptly, as if the author had left his work unfinished, or as if he had intended to continue his history in a later volume. The narrative apparently closes in the early part of the year 61, and at that time the apostle had been a prisoner in Rome for two whole years. It hardly seems likely that the authorities would have kept him in suspense much longer than this before granting him a hearing, and in two years his accusers would have had ample time to collect evidence and to prepare their case against him. Nothing, however, is said about Paul's trial or its outcome, and it is quite possible that his case never came before the emperor. There are three possibilities: (*a*) He may have been brought to trial, condemned, and executed; (b) he may have been tried and acquitted; (c) it may have been impossible to obtain enough evidence against the prisoner to justify bringing him to trial. Some scholars think that the apostle lost his case and was put to death, and others believe that he was tried and found not guilty. However, at least four considerations can be urged in support of the third possibility just mentioned: (a) It would have been necessary to bring Paul's accusers and the witnesses in the case from Jerusalem to Rome; (b) the offenses charged against the apostle were allegedly committed several years earlier; (c) these alleged offenses were mostly infractions of the Mosaic law, with which the Roman authorities did not concern themselves; (d) according to the author of the Acts, the Jews in Rome knew of no evil that Paul had done, and they were not hostile to him. Thus it is possible that after the apostle had been a prisoner in Rome for two years, the case against him was either dropped or dismissed. He may well have been released early in the year 61, when the narrative of the Acts closes.

XII. Paul's Second Imprisonment and Death in Rome

If this release occurred—and it must be remembered that we are on very uncertain ground in affirming it—our knowledge of Paul's life in the period which followed is derived from certain incidental references in the Pastoral epistles and in some other early Christian writings. From these sources it would appear that the apostle traveled about and carried on his missionary work for some time after his release.[1] He may have gone to Spain in this period (Rom. 15:24; I Clem. 5:7), as he had long hoped to do; and he seems to have revisited the Aegean area—Crete (Tit. 1:5), the province of Asia (II Tim. 4:13, 20), Macedonia (I Tim. 1:3), and Achaia (II Tim. 4:20). We do not know how much time these journeys occupied. Few scholars think that the Pastoral epistles in their present form were composed by Paul. However, they contain many genuine

[1] Eusebius *Church History*, II. 22, 2.

Pauline elements which clearly date from the last period of the apostle's life. In other words they were written after his release from his first imprisonment in Rome.

Paul was arrested again and imprisoned a second time in Rome, but we are wholly ignorant of the time or place or cause of his arrest. However, Nero's hatred of the Christians burst out into a violent persecution in the year 64; and it is reasonable to suppose that the apostle was taken into custody by the emperor's agents and committed to prison along with many others. He must have been brought to trial and condemned to death; but we do not know what charge was made against him, and we have no information concerning the conduct of his trial. In any case Paul suffered martyrdom at Rome, probably in A.D. 64 or 65. According to tradition he was beheaded. So ended the career of perhaps the greatest and most influential figure in the history of Christianity.

XIII. Selected Bibliography

BACON, B. W. *The Story of St. Paul*. New York: The Century Co., 1927.

DEISSMANN, G. ADOLF. *Paul: A Study in Social and Religious History*, tr. William E. Wilson. New York: George H. Doran, 1926.

FINDLAY, G. G. "Paul the Apostle" in James Hastings, ed. *A Dictionary of the Bible*, Vol. III. New York: Charles Scribner's Sons, 1900.

GLOVER, T. R. *Paul of Tarsus*. New York: Richard R. Smith, 1930.

KNOX, W. L. *St. Paul and the Church of Jerusalem*. Cambridge: University Press, 1925.

MCNEILE, ALAN HUGH. *St. Paul, His Life, Letters, and Christian Doctrine*. Cambridge: University Press, 1920.

NOCK, ARTHUR D. *St. Paul*. New York: Harper & Bros., 1938.

RAMSAY, W. M. *St. Paul the Traveller and the Roman Citizen*. New York: G. P. Putnam's Sons, 1896.

ROBINSON, B. W. *The Life of Paul*. Chicago: University of Chicago Press, 1918.

WEINEL, HEINRICH. *St. Paul, the Man and His Work*, tr. G. A. Bienemann. New York: G. P. Putnam's Sons, 1906.

WREDE, WILHELM. *Paulus*. Tübingen: J. C. B. Mohr, 1906.

THE HISTORY OF THE EARLY CHURCH

III. PAUL THE APOSTLE

by PAUL S. MINEAR

Any discussion of Paul's apostleship, if it is to be fruitful, sooner or later turns into a conversation with Paul. And any conversation with him makes progress only on the basis of his personal correspondence with those who knew him and his work. We meet him, if we meet him at all, in his letters, where he opens his heart and reveals his inmost desires and loyalties. This means that we strike up a dialogue with him, not at the beginning of his career and not at the end, but in the very midst of his strenuous activity. His Lord had sent him to live on the frontier where the gospel elicited the strongest resistance from the world. For that reason a conversation with him about his vocation takes us to that front-line post, where the most strategic battles were being waged and where his own fortunes were fused with the wider strategies of his Master. There we find him vigorously engaged in conflict, directing his strongest and sharpest thrusts perchance from a prison cell.

Christian readers who are content to deal with Paul, not in this original context, but from a position nineteen centuries later, may unwittingly avoid this more intimate and exciting dialogue. We are so aware of the intricate threads of influence that link the life of this man to every generation of Christian history that we take quite for granted both our debt to him and his own greatness. His letters have a secure place in our Scripture and his authority is seldom challenged, at least within the church. Opening his letters, however, we immediately discover that such acceptance was not at first so readily granted. In them we catch vivid glimpses of a career that was far from a triumphal procession of a recognized genius. Rather we detect echoes of a story of suffering not unlike that passion story of Paul's Lord. Like his Master, Paul was "despised and rejected of men; a man of sorrows, and acquainted with grief" (Isa. 53:3). Nor was Paul unaware of this analogy. To him the path of every Christian was patterned after the way of this Lord, and the career of an apostle resembled at many points the race that Jesus ran. It was in running this race that Paul became implicated in every major controversy between the gospel and the world, whether this conflict appeared within the church itself or between the church and its external foes. To renew an acquaintance with this man on his own terms, as he was before the so-called verdict of history could be rendered, we may well scan his letters to discern the character of his work and the reasons for these antagonisms.

I. Man of Conflict

We should not, of course, overlook the evidences of hearty support which Paul was often accorded by men of his own day. In Galatia men received him "as an angel of God, as Christ Jesus" and were willing to sacrifice their own eyes for him (Gal. 4:14, 15). In Philippi there were yokefellows who eagerly lent their shoulders to every burden he carried, however great the risk. When he was embroiled in riots, they stood beside him. When he left them for work in other cities, they dispatched supplies and helpers to him. When he was jailed, they sent a loyal emissary with food and encouragement (Phil. 2:25-30). Nor were the Philippians the only friends with sufficient devotion to risk their lives in his behalf. Among his companions in danger one might mention Prisca, Aquila, Andronicus, Junias, Aristarchus, Mark, Justus, Timothy, Titus, Epaphras, Luke, and Demas (Rom. 16:3-7; Col. 4:10-14). Here is sufficient proof that his message and example had extraordinary power to constrain men and women to renounce every security and to abandon every fear. If we had access to the separate stories of these people, with all the episodes in their dealings with Paul, they would surely provide an impressive tribute to his leadership.

Even this evidence, however, is not unequivocal. As Paul learned to his dismay, his supporters could quickly repudiate his authority and distort his message. The Galatians who had received him so warmly were readily "bewitched" by another gospel (Gal. 3:1). The disciples at Philippi who had sent him help were not immune to the invasion of evil-working "dogs" (Phil. 3:2). Among the brothers at Corinth there were partisans whose support he repudiated because their party cry "in the name of Paul" betrayed a serious misunderstanding of Christ (I Cor. 1:10-17) There were those who, when he was near by, loudly affirmed their allegiance to him; but they were quite willing, when he had gone farther away, to join in scorning his authority (Gal. 5:2-12). He learned from such fickle friends that he must be wary of their undiscerning enthusiasm.

There were many, to be sure, who patiently endured the greatest affliction in loyalty to Christ Jesus. Paul was comforted and strengthened by their fidelity (II Cor. 1:3-11; I Thess. 2:13-16). He rejoiced over every such indication of God's power. Nevertheless these examples of courage did not lighten the burden that he carried, because such loyalty brought upon his friends a full measure of the world's hatred, and Paul was more concerned about their sufferings than he was about his own. The more his friends participated in his mission, the clearer became the cleavage between that mission and its adversaries. The existence of such friends and such adversaries merely widened the circle of conflict through which he moved.

It is customary to chart the course of Paul's career by tracing his several journeys as a missionary, as has been done in the preceding article. One may just as easily trace the same course by charting the controversies which that career precipitated: in Damascus immediately following his first confession, on each of the trips to Jerusalem, in Antioch, and in Cilicia,

Galatia, Macedonia, Achaia, Asia, and Rome. For each visit to a province in the line of duty there remains an echo of bitter animosity during or following that visit. Paul himself described his path as a sequence of "afflictions, hardships, calamities, beatings, imprisonments, tumults, labors, watching, hunger." He spoke of himself as one who had been treated as an impostor, "as unknown, . . . dying, . . . punished, . . . sorrowful, . . . poor, . . . having nothing" (II Cor. 6:4-10).

What colorful annals we would have if Paul had opened fully his store of memories! Who were these adversaries that were responsible for the unremitting pressure of hostility? Why did they hound him so relentlessly? Paul was not of the sort to brood over his wounds, and consequently we cannot recover the whole story. But behind his remarks we can glimpse the shadows of his enemies and the occasions for their enmity.

There were instances of collision with political authorities—police officers, local wardens and magistrates, provincial agents of the empire. The many arrests, floggings, court hearings, and prison sentences clearly indicate this. Nor can we fail to note the calculating hatred of priests and retainers of pagan cults, who found their gods and their livelihood threatened by this intrepid courier of the one true God. Businessmen in many trades took fright wherever the news of Christ freed their customers from prevailing habits and thus reduced the market for their wares (Acts 16:19; 19:23-41).

Even less relenting, however, was the hatred from his own kinsmen, "Israelites according to the flesh" as he called them. And in the forefront of these kinsmen appeared the Pharisees, those popular leaders of the synagogues who had a burning "zeal for God" (Rom. 10:2). It was at their instigation presumably that he was stoned. It was to them that he was indebted for the five occasions when his back had been laid open by the thirty-nine lashes (II Cor. 11:24). In their eyes he had more than merited such penalties. Had he not blasphemed the God of Israel? Had he not committed treason against his own people by encouraging the desecration of the temple and the profanation of the law?

But among all his adversaries those within the church most deeply wounded him—leaders who not only opposed his policies but also followed him from city to city, fomenting suspicion among his own converts. It was this "danger from false brethren" that he feared the most, not because of what they could do to him but because of what they were doing to his churches in Galatia and Philippi and Corinth. We need not tarry to identify all these antagonists. On certain matters Paul was forced to oppose even

Cephas, whom he recognized as the first apostle to be called (Gal. 2:11-21). He was placed in the position where he had to contend with James, the Lord's own brother, and with delegates who claimed to come from James. There were times of bitterness between Paul and such revered associates as Barnabas and Mark (Gal. 2:11-13; Acts 15:36-40). No longer can we draw with certainty all the lines of dispute that divided these men. In most cases it may well have been the unauthorized followers of Cephas or James or the "pillars" of the Jerusalem church who stirred up the dissension. But whoever the prime antagonists were, they "commended themselves" as apostles of Christ, endowed by Christ and by the "chief apostles" with prestige superior to that of Paul. They were Hebrews of recognized "orthodoxy," seeking to preserve the divinely granted prerogatives of Israel. Some of them had known Jesus before his death. Most of them had become apostles before Paul's commissioning, and unlike him had retained a large measure of support from the churches in Judea. On the one hand their credentials seemed less debatable than his; on the other their work as apostles had brought them fewer scars than he had suffered. Yet notwithstanding all this, Paul branded them as "deceitful workmen, disguising themselves as apostles of Christ" (II Cor. 11:13).

As far as his own personal safety was concerned, Paul had perhaps more to fear from the pagans and the Pharisees. But as far as the success of his mission was concerned, he had much more to fear from these "false brethren." It is therefore one mark of selfless devotion to his mission that he concentrated his attention on this latter group, defending his personal integrity only where such defense coincided with the defense of the gospel, only where the faith of his Christian friends was jeopardized by the insidious arguments of his adversaries. Paul limited his apostolic labors to areas not yet reached by the preaching of others (II Cor. 10:14-16; Rom. 15:20). But the competing apostles recognized no such limits, being concerned to spy upon Paul, to visit his churches in an effort to counteract the results of his work, and even to stir up resentment among the unconverted populace. Why were they so hostile? What was there in Paul's message that aroused such antipathies? The answer may be found only in the letters of Paul himself, a number of which were prompted by this very conflict. And although the evidence comes from only one side of the debate, it is trustworthy because Paul realized that a rebuttal of their charges would be successful only if prefaced by an honest statement and a perceptive understanding of

them. He was not a boxer who could afford to strike often at the empty air; rather he must make every blow reach the precise spot where it would accomplish the maximum good (I Cor. 9:26). What, then, were the major charges leveled against Paul's vocation?

Basically these "superfine apostles" feared the effects of Paul's message upon his converts and through them upon the institutions of Israel. They did not deny his right to preach to the Gentiles and to enlist them as servants of Christ (Gal. 1:9). They were alarmed, however, by what he encouraged these converts to do. He did not ask them to be circumcised or to accept the obligation to fulfill the requirements of the law. He talked as if the law had been completely abrogated by the work of Christ. He used faith to overthrow the law, seeming to teach that the law itself is sinful (Rom. 3:31; 7:7). His gospel, his enemies claimed, implied that justification by grace was in effect a justification of sin and lawlessness. Let us "continue in sin that grace may abound" (Rom. 6:1). Let us "sin because we are not under law but under grace" (Rom. 6:15). "Why not do evil that good may come?" (Rom. 3:8.) Paul's adversaries feared that his teaching would induce men to impugn God's justice and to deny that God will judge all men's deeds according to his law. "If our wickedness serves to show the justice of God [is he not] unjust to inflict wrath on us?" (Rom. 3:5.) According to Paul's message, any man by faith alone could become a true son of Abraham and an heir of all the promises made to Israel. This would mean that the Jew no longer had any advantage. If "all things are lawful" and if Gentiles inherit God's grace without any obligation to the law, the covenants would lose their validity.

The line of action for these apostles was clear and definite. They must follow Paul and seek to undo the damage he had done. His converts must be persuaded to accept the duties defined by the law, being brought within the family of Israel by circumcision. They must be taught to live like Jews, to consider themselves as unforgiven sinners until they had fulfilled the righteousness of the law, observing the sabbath and the holy festivals (Gal. 2:3-5, 14; 3:1-20; 4:10, 21; 5:2-8).

In weaning Paul's children from dependence upon him, these "superfine apostles" were forced to challenge his motives as well as his methods. Why had he so completely abandoned the authority of the law? Because he wanted to make salvation easy for Gentiles, who would accept the gospel more readily on these minimal terms. Why did Paul do this? Because he was at heart seeking men's favor by this means of appeasing them (Gal. 1:10). Why? So that he could lord it over his easily won followers. From the outset he had been really commending himself and preaching himself. He had acted through worldly motives, tampering with God's word for the sake of quick popularity and personal power (II Cor. 1:24; 3:1-5; 4:1-5; 10:3-9; Gal. 5:1-3; I Thess. 2:3-6). Only thus could his enemies explain why he had endorsed such radical liberties, why he had proclaimed as salvation the freedom to live as they pleased.

When these seeds of distrust had been planted in Paul's field, it did not take long for them to produce a large crop of accusations. "He was crafty and got the better of us by guile." "He was very meek when he was among us, but grows very bold when he gets to a safe distance." "His public speaking is quite inferior to that of these orators." "He doesn't act like an accredited ambassador, but debases himself by earning his food like a common tradesman, whereas a true delegate from Christ would insist upon the dignity and privileges of his rank." "On these important issues he seems to waver to meet popular pressures; in some cases he circumcises his converts, but in other cases he does not." "What authority does he have, after all, for acting like a judge in our personal affairs?" "Where is the proof that, as he used to say, it is Christ who is speaking in him?" "If he is a true apostle, why should he be repudiated not only by Rome and Israel, but also by these men from the 'mother church' who assure us that he has no standing there?" (For the substance of such charges see II Cor. 1:17, 24; 3:1-5; 10:1-12; 11:5-10; 12:11-19; 13:1-3.)

Thus the charges ricocheted from one Christian community to another, posing questions which Paul could not evade without denying his apostleship. As a Christian he was embarrassed by any need for self-defense, yet he was impelled to overcome his reticence because his behavior as a missionary implicated the truth of his gospel. It was not his personal stake in the battle that alarmed him. If it was true that he was proclaiming a false gospel, he wanted to be accursed (Gal. 1:8). But if it was truly a message from Christ, then he must defend it at whatever cost to himself. It was this situation that required of him a spirited defense of his vocation, even though to defend himself he must speak "as a fool" (II Cor. 11:16-23). These superior apostles called themselves Jews and denounced him as a renegade. He reversed both the claim and the charge, for he was a true son of Israel and they were faithless to the covenants. They exalted the law and branded him with profaning it. He reversed this, defining the purpose and character of the law as Christ had disclosed them. They asserted their loyalty to God's will and accused him of blaspheming God's name among the Gentiles. He turned their words back against themselves (II Cor. 12:11-13).

Step by step the struggle grew in intensity, and at every stage the debate pivoted on the integrity of Paul's apostleship and the authenticity of his message. Time and again he was compelled to restate the origin of his call by Christ, and the specifications of the mission on which Christ had sent him. He did this not for his own sake, but for the sake of disciples for whose welfare he knew himself to be responsible. Let us follow him, then, into the origins of that mission and the mandate which he considered so binding.

II. Slave of Christ

Paul frequently spoke of himself as Christ's "slave," a term often translated "servant" to minimize its harshness to modern ears. Paul used so strong a designation because he knew that he had been bought with a price and therefore belonged to a new owner. In speaking of himself thus, Paul was not asserting any superiority over other slaves of the same Master. Everyone who is called in the Lord becomes such a slave (I Cor. 3:23; 7:22-23). His new Master has an exclusive right to command and to constrain every wish, thought, and act; the slave is no longer at liberty to please himself or to seek the favor of men. It is from the Lord that he derives his power, and to the Lord that he must render an account. Only the Lord's judgment, not his own or that of other men, can determine his own faithfulness. So far, therefore, as Paul exerted authority, that authority belonged not to himself but to Christ.

The same thing holds true for freedom. A slave's freedom is not his own possession, used for his own ends; it is a gift of Christ that must be utilized to accomplish the purposes of Christ. It is never the servant's own mind that discerns the difference between truth and falsehood; only Christ's mind at work within him rightly discerns what is the true will of God. Every slave, so far as he is a faithful slave, has access to this mind (Phil. 2:1-18). The living Christ is present in the church, his body, directing all its activities in accordance with the disclosed design of God. Christ's love pours into the heart of the slave and passes through the latter's loving service into the hearts of others. Every slave has a share in the ministry of reconciliation. It is because one slave participates with all others in this common life that they can appeal to one another "by the meekness and gentleness of Christ" (II Cor. 10:1); "by the mercies of God" (Rom. 12:1); "by the grace given to me" (Rom. 12:3); and "by the name of our Lord Jesus Christ" (I Cor. 1:10).

These slaves receive together the highest gift of God, the gift of Jesus Christ himself. Each brother is in Christ, and Christ is in him. Each has access to the same grace, the same forgiveness, the same suffering, the same freedom, the same triumph. Because each has received the highest gift, no slave may count himself as better than another, as meriting any favor that places him on a higher footing in the eyes of the Lord. None may boast in his own self-importance or self-accomplished work. All may boast in whatever work Christ accomplishes through them by his word and deed (I Cor. 3:18–4:7; Rom. 15:17). And in such a work— whether effected through Cephas, Apollos, or Paul, whether through false motives or pure— all servants of the Lord may boast. Paul gloried over what Christ was doing through his own personal adversaries, and he felt that they should take equal joy in what Christ was doing through him. All were engaged in the same mission, a process by which God was redeeming the world through his Son (Phil. 1:15-30).

Although the most important gift was this life in Christ which all had in common, it was yet true that Christ bestows special gifts upon particular servants so that they may execute distinctive assignments in the building up of the church (I Cor. 12:4-30). Paul was among those who had been called for such a special function. How did he estimate this task? In the first place he had been set apart to proclaim the good news. His was the commission of an ambassador, received not from men but from Christ himself, who had appeared to him for this very purpose. He summoned Paul to give his witness to the unconverted, in order that they might accept the invitation to share in God's kingdom. More narrowly, Paul's mandate was "to bring about obedience to the faith . . . among all the Gentiles" (Rom. 1:5; cf. Rom. 15:16; Gal. 1:1-6; I Cor. 9:1-2). The seal of this apostleship he found in the people who, in response to his message, "turned to God from idols, to serve a living and true God, and to wait for his Son from heaven" (I Thess. 1:2-10). His witness was so compelling that they chose to die with Christ, being crucified to the world, in order that they might live with Christ.

The work of an apostle, however, was not completed when he had brought a man into "obedience to the faith." The apostle was accountable for the growth of the "babe," and this meant a continuing concern for every temptation that beset the convert. Paul spoke of himself as a father who not only shared the travail of childbirth but who thereafter had primary responsibility for the discipline of his children (Gal. 4:19). They might have many guides, but they could have but one father in Christ (I Cor. 4:15; I Thess. 2:11). He compared himself to a nurse, gently caring for the infants, adjusting their diet to their needs (I Cor. 3:1-3; I Thess. 2:7). In another context he confessed a divine jealousy for the church in Corinth because "I betrothed you to Christ to present you as a pure bride to her one husband" (II Cor. 11:2-3). Or changing the analogy again, he spoke of that church as God's field in which he had planted the seed, leaving others to water the growing shoots. Or he thought of it as God's building for which he had been instructed to lay the foundation, with others assigned to the masonry (I Cor. 3:6-15). Whatever the metaphor he used, it is clear that he looked upon his converts as his particular "work" in the Lord, which he must protect at whatever cost to himself (Phil. 2:12-18; I Thess. 2:19-20). Their welfare was of first importance to him because his mission would not be complete until they fulfilled theirs, the mission to which he as apostle had called them. The apostle was so closely related to his children that he suffered in their afflictions and was comforted by their strength. They in turn could rejoice in his joy because they sorrowed over his adversities (II Cor. 1:3-7).

The terms of his commission constrained him to make the gospel free of charge, so that none of his converts would feel indebted to him rather than to Christ. He must preach the gospel from inner necessity, and not from the desire for any earthly compensation. He must humble himself, becoming all things to all men, becoming as weak as the weakest, as poor as the poorest, for this was the only way that he and his children would truly share in the blessings of the gospel and advance its conquest of the world. He insisted that an apostle who does not do everything out of love, utter love of God and man, is disqualified from the very race to which he has called others (I Cor. 9:16-27).

Because of this understanding of the apostolic vocation, it is not surprising that in listing the specialized gifts of the Spirit, Paul placed apostleship in first place. Next in order he ranked the gift of prophecy (I Cor. 12:28). What assignment does Christ give to his prophets? The prophet must edify the church by speaking to men "for their upbuilding and encouragement and consolation" (I Cor. 14:3). He is enabled by the Spirit to uncover the secrets of men's hearts (I Cor. 14:25). He acts as a judge among his brothers, issuing orders in the Spirit for the settling of community disputes (I Cor. 5:1-5). To him also the Spirit discloses the secret wisdom of God, enabling him to utter this wisdom for the illumination of the brotherhood. This secret wisdom may convey a specific command addressed to a single emergency in the life of the church, or it may deal with the more inclusive mystery of the divine design. When one prophet speaks, other prophets should weigh what is being said so that the spirits of the prophets remain subject to the prophets.

Paul was acquainted with all these functions of prophecy, because he himself had on occasion been empowered by the Spirit to exercise them. He issued commands from the Lord which he expected other prophets in the church at Corinth to verify and support (I Cor. 14:37). Though absent in body, he was authorized to pronounce judgment upon a man guilty of incest, just as if he were prophesying in the meeting where that man was present (I Cor. 5:3-5). He was impelled at times to exercise the rod of power (I Cor. 4:19-21). At other times he imparted to believers the mystery of how all Christians "at the last trumpet" would be transformed (I Cor. 15:51-57). The Spirit enabled him to discern the signs of the times, and to distinguish between human wisdom and divine wisdom. It probed the deep things of God, giving to men spiritual words as the vehicle for spiritual truths. The spiritual man is thus qualified to judge all things, and to be judged by no man, because Christ himself is the "speaker" (I Cor. 1:18–2:15). Paul received this gift and learned at first hand both its power and the hazards of abusing it. He used it in adjudicating very complex problems in the church at Corinth, but he took great pains not to confuse his own opinions with the demands which the Lord had imposed (I Cor. 7). In the Spirit he spoke with authority, subject only to the Spirit who was also speaking to other prophets in the church. But he well knew the temptation of absolutizing his own prejudices by claiming for them the sanction of the Spirit. He resisted this temptation, not because he feared the adverse verdict of a human tribunal, but because he was strictly accountable to the Lord for his stewardship of the mysteries that had been entrusted to him (I Cor. 4:1-5; Eph. 3:1-13; 6:18-20).

But Christ gave other gifts to Paul than these two, apostleship and prophecy. On occasion he spoke in tongues as volubly as any other (I Cor. 14:18). On occasion he baptized and instructed catechumens like other teachers (I Cor. 1:14-17). His faith was strong enough, if not to move mountains, at least to perform amazing demonstrations of power (I Cor. 2:4; II Cor. 12:12). Yet he did not capitalize on these spectacular endowments, but rather depreciated them by comparing them to the primary gifts, and by evaluating their efficacy in terms of the spiritual health of the community as a whole. All gifts are deceptive and futile apart from

love. Love is the ultimate mark of every slave of Christ, for love is precisely that power which knits all Christians into the body of him who is the supreme Gift, so that any boasting over special attainments is ruled out, and all Christians profit from every genuine gift. Considering all the special gifts bestowed on him, Paul yet said, "If I . . . have not love, I am nothing" (I Cor. 13:1-3). It was this love, God's love "poured into our hearts through the Holy Spirit" (Rom. 5:5), that remained the source of Paul's highest vocation. It was this love that made him a slave of Christ, an apostle of Christ, a prophet, and a steward of the mysteries of Christ.

Yet we need again to remind ourselves that it was his fidelity to this love that aroused the sharpest conflicts. Before the love of Christ captured him, he had, to be sure, pursued a path of violence; but then he had been the aggressor. Since that capture, he became the one who received the blows. And the blows that were hardest for Paul to accept were those struck by other leaders within the church. Moreover it is clear that their animosity was not directed against all Gentile Christians, nor against all Jewish Christians who chose to scorn the ancestral law. The antagonism centered upon this particular apostle just because of his conception of his mission, because of the authority he claimed for that mission, and because of the vigor with which he prosecuted it. The more loyally he obeyed what to him were the mandates of his Lord, the more bitter the enmity of other men who claimed to be servants, yes, and more faithful servants, of the same Lord. If we are to grasp the dimensions of this conflict, we must therefore go further than merely to define his apostleship. We must explore the conditions under which he received his commission, noting if we can the origins of the conflict in the initial terms of that commission.

III. Apostle to the Gentiles

Paul traced his commission as an apostle to a single decisive event when Jesus was revealed to him as Lord, and when he was crucified with Christ and was raised to a new life as God's son. In this event God humbled Paul so radically that he never again could wholly yield himself to self-righteousness. At the same time God exalted him so decisively that he never again could wholly yield to despair. Henceforth he was an apostle, but he was "the least of the apostles, unfit to be called an apostle, because I persecuted the church of God" (I Cor. 15:9). Why had he persecuted the church? The answer may be summed up in three sentences: (a) This church accepted as Savior a crucified person who, it asserted, had been raised from the dead as God's Son, empowered to establish the kingdom of God. (*b*) Certain spokesmen for this Messiah were announcing openly that God had thus abrogated the requirements of circumcision, righteousness through the law, and sacrifice in the temple. (*c*) As a Pharisee, Paul had developed a driving zeal for righteousness, which demanded that he defend the race, the law, and the temple against this new blasphemy. A word must be said about each of these three.

This son of Benjamin was too shrewd a warrior not to know why he was trying to destroy the church (Gal. 1:13). That reason was the stanch allegiance of the disciples of Jesus to him as the Messiah. Paul knew that the scribes and elders had rejected this man because of his teaching concerning the law and his behavior in associating with publicans and sinners. This teaching and behavior would not have been so obnoxious had Jesus not announced that through his work God was offering a place in his kingdom to the lawbreakers and outcasts, passing by the deserving defenders of the covenants. He had appealed to the authority of heaven as the justification for setting aside as unnecessary the most sacred institutions which God had himself ordained, offering final blessedness to men who deserved it least of all. Jesus' execution had been the merited punishment of such blasphemy; it had proved for all time that he was nothing more than an impotent impostor. Paul, the stanch Pharisee, could not, by any flight of fancy, accept such a man as the expected Messiah. Yet in spite of its absurdity, the followers of this man had begun heralding him as none other than the Messiah, who had been exalted from his depth of infamy to the highest place in creation, at God's right hand. His death had been the supreme mark, not of degradation and sin, but of his faithfulness to God and of his enemies' perfidy. In his exaltation the day of God's deliverance had dawned, and only those who now accepted Jesus as the Christ would be included in this deliverance.

If this had been the worst, Paul might not have carried his campaign to the point of violent resistance. For many disciples of the Crucified lived quietly and piously, without openly flaunting the traditions of Israel. The more judicious Pharisees were confident that this temporary excitement would soon fade, and that these deluded enthusiasts would soon return to the sober wisdom of their fathers. Any threat to the life of God's people would wither under the dry winds of reality. But to his alarm Paul learned that instead of withering, the movement flourished. It was developing into a numerous, bold, and powerful sect. The most popular aspects of its message were precisely the most

dangerous. Its most effective leaders were those on its extreme left wing, who appealed persuasively to sinners and Gentiles on the fringes of the Jewish community. Such men as Stephen shouted boldly in the very temple that Jesus was the true descendant of Abraham, Moses, and David, and that his opponents were descendants of the faithless rebels in Israel. These bold preachers charged the enemies of Jesus with reliance on outward circumcision to conceal an inward uncircumcision, an apparent loyalty to the law and the temple to cover up a sinful apostasy (Acts 7). In defiance of them God had opened his kingdom freely to Gentiles who need not burden themselves with the yoke of the law or the support of the temple. Thus were the privileges of Israel, which had been preserved through centuries only by the greatest sacrifices, being offered to men who did not merit them, to men whose inclusion meant the profanation of those privileges. And hundreds of them were rushing forward to accept the offer. It is small wonder that the elders and scribes bitterly attacked the messengers who spoke "words against this holy place and the law," who indeed were bold enough to proclaim that Jesus "will destroy this place and will change the customs which Moses delivered to us" (Acts 6:13, 14).

It was because of his ardor for the traditions of his fathers that Paul volunteered to help fight this evil. He was a Hebrew born of Hebrews, of a lineage as noble as that of any of his fellows. "Circumcised on the eighth day," he was confident of his place in the chosen race. He had been trained to live by the standards of the strictest sect in Israel, the Pharisees, who exalted, defended, and applied the law as rigorously as was humanly possible. By those standards he, like the rich young ruler, had become blameless "as to righteousness under the law." His vocation as a Pharisee—nothing could be higher—was to attain "a righteousness of my own, based on law" (Phil. 3:4-9). Viewing the new movement from the standpoint of such a vocation, there seemed to be no other course than to eradicate its menace. He was carrying forward the work of God; Jesus' followers must be doing the work of the devil.

At the peak of his campaign as a defender of Israel, Paul experienced the revelation from God which made clear the true state of affairs. According to a later narrator, the Lord himself appeared to him and said "I am Jesus of Nazareth whom you are persecuting" (Acts 22:8). No longer could Paul judge Jesus according to the previous standards; no longer could he view any one from a human point of view. He was a new man, and for him "the old has passed away, behold the new has come." And the whole transformation was a work of God (II Cor. 5:16-18).

What now of the death of Jesus, which had earlier been so offensive? Jesus had died for him, as an expression of God's love. "We are convinced that one has died for all; therefore all have died. And he died for all, that those who live might live no longer for themselves but for him who for their sake died and was raised" (II Cor. 5:14, 15). It was the Cross that proved Jesus' innocence and faithfulness as God's servant, a reversal not without precedent in Israel's history. In what men had supposed to be weakness God had chosen to display his power; in what they had taken to be folly he had manifested his wisdom; in what they had thought was sin he had revealed the true righteousness. This Cross was the index not of futility but of the future. Through this deed God had intended to underscore the sin of Paul and of all who in blindness opposed his way. But in demonstrating their sin, God had also offered them a free forgiveness, whether they were under or outside the law. God had thus taken the stone rejected by the builders and had made it the true cornerstone of his new temple, which was now being built among those same men.

What of the messengers of Jesus whom Paul had harried from place to place? They were now seen to be the true ambassadors from God, to whose witness Paul was completely indebted. What they had said and done—about circumcision, the law, the temple, the rebellion of Israel—had all been true. Those whom he had hated most bitterly had been the genuine slaves of Christ, who had enabled them to endure death with his own forgiveness and power in their hearts. Their ministry had been the means of reconciling their chief persecutor to God (II Cor. 5:18—6:2). Far from being a blasphemous threat to the hopes of Israel, they had actually been fulfilling the destiny of Israel as "a light to the Gentiles." And in opposing their royal commission, the scribes had been the worst sinners, not worthy to be counted as sons of Abraham or David.

What then of Paul himself, an exemplar of Pharisaic zeal? What did all this signify regarding God's purposes for him? He was a man who had opposed most ruthlessly the disciples of the Messiah. What sin could be worse? Especially when he considered it in the light of the fact that God had chosen him at the very peak of his career as persecutor. "While we were yet helpless," "while we were yet sinners," "while we were enemies," Christ died for us and we were reconciled to God by this death (Rom. 5:6-11). And if God had done this amazing thing for Paul, the chief of his enemies, all others must be included in the same condemnation of sin and in the same gift of forgiveness. None could be more hopelessly estranged from God than he himself had been. His desire for righteousness had been a mark of his blindness, a blindness that infected all others who trusted in the law, whether the law of Israel or of the various religious and moral systems in the Gentile world. Their blindness had made them slaves to the law, of which slavery the unintended fruit had been death. God in his exhaustless mercy, however, had terminated the most deeply rooted slavery, buying their freedom at tremendous cost. Since their emancipation had required the suffering of the Messiah, the price of freedom was that they should become slaves who belonged to him. Called into his service, they must carry on his mission of reconciliation to the world, as the sign of their gratitude. For Christ's sake they must carry the same Cross as the way to inherit his power and his joy.

Knowing God's purpose in the Cross, Paul could now grasp the hidden meaning of his earlier life. On the one hand he could do no other than count his former privileges and attainments as worthless, relinquishing any pride in a "righteousness under the law" or a righteousness of his own (Phil. 3:1-9). On the other hand he could now discern that God had been using his activity as a Pharisee to bring him to his knees before the crucified Lord. God had in fact been preparing him from his birth—by his loyalties to family, race, and religion—for this very mission (Gal. 1:15). God needed an honest interpreter who had experienced the maximum success as a "righteous man," and could now be trusted with the truth of the maximum futility of that success. God needed Paul's previous experience to make him apprehend the mystery of the divine love so that he could disclose that mystery to others. Paul could not therefore repudiate the whole of his earlier allegiances, because God had used them to prepare him for understanding the full scope and freedom of the redemption offered in Christ (Rom. 3:1-9; 7:1-14; 9:1-18; Gal. 3:1-29).

This same Cross served to make Paul see what would be his path into the future. First of all it marked that path as one of total abandonment to the service of Jesus Christ. He must no longer consider Jesus or any other man from a human point of view, or in any of the perspectives provided by human scales of power or goodness. He must live as one who dies daily with Christ, and in the dying receives Christ's life and strength. He must live as one who is dead to that which once held him captive —the law, the flesh, sin, and death itself (Rom.

7:4-6). He must rely wholly on the love of Christ, making all decisions according to the mind of Christ. This element in his mandate is discussed below.

In making him a slave of Christ, God also called Paul as a spokesman to spread the truth about Christ. He was assigned to proclaim "Christ crucified, a stumbling-block to Jews and folly to Gentiles, but to those who are called, both Jews and Greeks, Christ the power of God and the wisdom of God" (I Cor. 1:23, 24). Because of his own history, Paul could testify how the Cross exerted the power to reveal the wrath of God against men "who by their wickedness suppressed the truth," and "the righteousness of God through faith in Jesus Christ for all who believe" (Rom. 1:16-18; 3:21-26).

Only in fulfilling this mandate could he honor his debt to those servants of Christ whom he had been hounding to death. Had they never uttered their message, had they not taken the gospel to Gentile sinners, had they not accepted with peace their suffering, he would never have known Christ. He was therefore under obligation to carry on their mission. He must announce, as they had, the obsolescence of all human institutions as necessary means of salvation, at the same time joyously testifying to the freedom to which Christ called men. He must go to the Gentiles, not as one who condescends from a position of greater righteousness, trying to bring them under the law, but as one who shares their poverty of status and is indeed a greater sinner than they. "To those outside the law I became as one outside the law . . . that I might win those outside the law" (I Cor. 9:21). How has the Pharisee fallen! To be sent by God to Gentiles *as* a Gentile! What could be greater evidence of the disruptive power of the new mandate? Only a call coming from God and not from men could produce such complete renunciation of former advantages and prejudices.

It was due to his loyalty to this mandate— and Paul had already proved the tough fiber of his loyalties—that he became at once the chief target of those from whose ranks he had been drawn. Not only did they persecute him through the same motives that had led him to harass the followers of Jesus; they hated him doubly because he, their leader, had now become traitor to their cause and the most dangerous of enemies.

Paul clearly saw, however, that this "danger from the Jews" was an inescapable part of his service of Christ. He was debtor to the Pharisees, for they had unconsciously prepared him for his new work. Nor could he renounce his love for his own kinsmen. He confessed great sorrow and unceasing anguish for them, desiring their salvation so deeply that he wrote, "I could wish that I myself were accursed and cut off from Christ for the sake of my brethren" (Rom. 9:3). But how could he bridge the chasm that separated them from him, a chasm even wider than that which had yawned between him and Stephen? The answer was obvious. By doing what Stephen and the others had done. By proclaiming the lordship of the Crucified, by defending the freedom of Gentiles in Christ, by accepting in love and joy the buffeting from his adversaries. The only message which could save them was one that would initially provoke their wrath. "I magnify my ministry in order to make my fellow Jews jealous [as I was jealous], and thus save some of them [as I was saved]" (Rom. 11:13). It was through its rejection by the Jews that salvation had come to the Gentiles. It will be through the ministry to the Gentiles, with all its hazards, that God will ultimately accomplish the inclusion of Israel as "life from the dead" (Rom. 11:11-16). God had thus intended Paul's mission to the Gentiles as a step toward the ultimate deliverance of Israel from its blindness. His sufferings in the line of duty had been intended as a means toward the reconciliation of his kinsmen. Every affliction incident upon his ministry became a weapon of righteousness so long as it was accepted as an occasion for "genuine love, truthful speech, and the power of God" (II Cor. 6:4-7).

This, then, is the mandate which Paul received from God: to be a faithful slave of Christ, obeying him in everything, imitating his example, and thus extending his work among men; to be an ambassador for Christ, "God making his appeal through us," and "entrusting to us the message of reconciliation" (II Cor. 5:20, 19); to go to the Gentiles as a Gentile, in order to save them; to accept with joyful gratitude the hatred of his kinsmen as God's means for their judgment and conversion; to endure every trial in patience, understanding it as a manifestation of God's power to bring life from the dead, and to perfect his strength in human weakness.

The reader of Paul's letters cannot fail to note the urgency with which Paul executed his task. He worked as a servant awaiting the return of his lord. This Lord had already given his estate to his servants, with a particular job for each. Their task placed them on the boundary where the old age was being transfigured by the new. The time for fulfilling their mission was short. They must redeem every moment of that time for their own sakes and the sake of all the sons of God. Soon the Master would return to his field in his full glory. He would hold a reckoning of their service, fulfilling the work which he had begun. Should they delay that work, they would be guilty of a final and fatal treason (Mark 13:32-37).

This exposition may suffice to suggest the dynamics of Paul's apostleship, the dimensions of his mission, the source of the energies which coursed through his frail body. But now the questions arise: How faithfully did he carry out his assignment? How truly did he serve his Master? How effective was he as an apostle and steward of the mysteries? How greatly was the church "edified" by his efforts? All these questions involve an appraisal of his contribution to Christ's church.

IV. Builder of the Church

Such an appraisal is unavoidably affected by our later perspective. We cannot ignore the cumulative influence of this man upon centuries of historical developments. Our estimate cannot be precisely the same as that of his contemporaries, nor could theirs be identical with ours. Even when we take into account these unavoidable differences, however, we are brought back to the realization that the range of possible estimates remains much the same, from the greatest antipathy to the greatest appreciation. All these estimates, from right to left, will betray some misunderstanding of the man's work; but it may also be said that all of them will rest to some degree upon understanding, for from his day to ours his enemies have often understood his message better than some of his friends. There *is* reason for offense as well as reason for approval, and those reasons are very deeply imbedded in the gospel to which Paul surrendered his life.

His letters and example indicate that we should not take any of the estimates as ultimate or final verdicts. In the first place, from his day to ours antagonism to Paul has often proved to be the prelude to conversion by him, has proved to be the initial sign that his word has actually been heard. His enemies have at times discovered that their enmity has been a stage in the preparation for reconciliation to Paul's God. On being thus reconciled they have become deeply indebted to this intrepid if obnoxious messenger. Their very hostility has become the measure of their debt. In the second place there are many who consider themselves Paulinists, in the front rank of his friends, whom he has repudiated as betraying his teaching because it has been turned into a new legalism, a new dogmatism, or a new libertarianism. Here is a figure whose stature is manifested through this power to play havoc with the external alignments of friends and foes. In the third place we must listen to Paul's own appraisal of such appraisals. Of all men he knew best what lack

of understanding is hidden in the effort to compare ourselves one with another. "It is not the man who commends himself that is accepted, but the man whom the Lord commends" (II Cor. 10:18). One who takes Paul at his word is thus inhibited from taking any human appraisal of Paul as overly important.

Having said this, however, we must also note that to Paul it was a matter of soberest concern how faithfully he fulfilled his assigned duties. If we do not forget what his vocation was and what were his standards of measurement, we may legitimately discuss how Christ as head of the body used this member to serve the entire body. And we may express the conviction that while Paul worked among men of his own generation, his vocation was not limited to that generation. The fellowship of Christ's body spans the centuries, and the service of the body in one generation is a service of the whole church. His influence upon the communion of saints in every generation can therefore be assessed in terms of his special mission to those of his own generation. We shall therefore consider that influence in terms of the two major aspects of his call: "A *slave* of Jesus Christ, called to be an *apostle*" (Rom. 1:1).

It has been pointed out that the basic vocation of Paul, a call which he shares with every Christian, was to live as a slave of Jesus Christ. This meant the bringing of all relationships to men under the one rule of subjection to Christ. Whether a disciple lives or dies, he lives and dies unto the Lord (Rom. 14:7-9). In everything he does he must bring every thought and impulse and act into captivity to Christ, so that every work is a work done in the Lord. The slave of Christ actually lives as a free son of God, born anew through God's grace. He is an heir of God and a fellow heir with Christ. He is filled with the fullness of God, the Spirit providing the power by which he can live and pray and work (Rom. 8:12-17). The true definition of sonship is provided by the Son of God.

Life as a son is the continuing enactment of the prayer "Not my will, but thine be done." This prayer, when genuine, is tantamount to the putting off of the old nature and the putting on of the Lord Jesus Christ (Rom. 13:14). This can be described as a repeated repentance from dead works, or as a daily dying to self, or as a putting to death of the deeds of the body. To pray without ceasing means that one's hopes and fears are no longer oriented around the center of self-will, but around God's will. The one who thus lives forgets what lies behind and presses on toward the goal (Phil. 3:12-16).

The abandonment of the "mind of the flesh" means that one's mind constantly is being renewed, torn loose from its conformity to the world, and transformed into conformity to the mind of Christ. Such a transformation opens the way to peace with all men. The slave with the mind of Christ humbles himself beneath his antagonist, counting the other better than himself. He considers the enemy's needs, renounces all vengeance, forgives him, and tries to bear his burden. The prohibition of conceit in any form enables the slave to identify himself fully with those who rejoice as well as with those who weep. All suffer when any suffers, all rejoice when any rejoices, because each seeks not to please himself but rather to serve his neighbor for his neighbor's own good (Rom. 12:9-21; 15:1-2).

It is thus that the victory of the new mind eliminates self-concern and nourishes the love that "bears all things, believes all things, hopes all things, endures all things" (I Cor. 13:7). The follower of Christ learns from both his prosperity and his adversity to be thankful, to be patient, to be joyful in the hope that does not fail (Rom. 5:1-5). No set of circumstances, however dreadful or pleasant according to the mind of this world, can separate him from Christ's love. Rather he knows that all situations are shaped to produce good for those who love God. He knows how to be abased and how to abound, how to face plenty and hunger, because of the strength that operates through his weakness (Phil. 4:11-13). Whatever the future holds, it belongs to him so long as he belongs to Christ. And Christ has supreme power to protect his own possessions (I Cor. 3:22, 23).

This blessedness, however, is always accompanied by a blunt requirement—to love as Christ loved. Men owe nothing to one another except to love one another as Christ loves them. Love is the end of the law, the sum and substance of the law, the fulfillment of the law, because it is the law of him who is the final judge and savior. It is his command that induces his servants to subject themselves to human authorities, not through fear of them or the desire to flatter them, but through God's intention to save them. Love is the core of all one's duties to those above and below, whether to husband or wife, parent or child, owner or slave, emperor or commoner. Love provides an adequate guide to follow in every situation where human wills clash. It enables a person to observe the rules and customs of earthly institutions without being imprisoned by them, thus creating a spiritual freedom that is motivated throughout by love. It is this love that silently and pervasively knits together the sinews and ligaments of Christ's body (Eph. 4:16).

This, then, is what being a slave of Christ meant to Paul. If we ask whether this is a true reading of the mind of Christ, the answer is not difficult. Paul's accent comes directly from the teachings of Jesus as recorded in the Gospels. Repentance, forgiveness, obedience, trust, joy, gratitude, hope, love—each of these is reduplicated in Paul's letters. To be sure, the apostle seldom quotes verbatim a saying of Jesus to assure a literal proof. But the substance of the demands of Jesus is faithfully preserved in Paul's message.

More significant than this, the teaching of Paul is strikingly faithful to the example of Jesus. On many occasions Paul appealed directly to the behavior of the Master as the chief norm for the disciple (Eph. 5; Phil. 2; Col. 3). And even when this appeal is not explicit, it is undeniably present. Behind the words of Paul looms the clear figure of the one in imitation of whom Paul lived his life. The apostle went far beyond lip service in his loyalty to the mind of Christ. Without flinching he accepted the condition of discipleship: "If any man would come after me, let him deny himself and take up his cross and follow me" (Mark 8:34). Like his Master, he sought the company of the sick, the sinful, and the ostracized. When he was reviled, "he opened not his mouth." When he knew that danger awaited him in Jerusalem, he set his face to go to that city because he had a duty to fulfill among his adversaries there (Rom. 15:30-32).

There are, of course, those who deny the above assertions. Did not Paul at times speak angrily at his enemies, cursing them in a way forbidden by Jesus? Did he not too dogmatically insist that the church follow his edicts? Was his stricture against the immoral Christians in Corinth as gentle and generous as Jesus' attitude toward the harlots? Were his rules on marriage consistent with the principles of freedom and love? Did his practice of becoming all things to all men trick him into impossible equivocations? Was he not trying to please everyone by granting men a right to eat anything they pleased, only to curtail this liberty lest the prudish be offended?

Of many of these accusations Paul was aware. Against some of them he defended himself vigorously. Against some he appealed to the highest tribunal with confidence in his vindication there. But he made no claim to perfect righteousness and no assertions of personal superiority. He knew how much he had to forget and how many temptations he had to overcome. He knew how subtly temptations took advantage of the best intentions. He had a temper hard to control, a pride that tried on every cloak, a desire for self-vindication that occasionally made him talk like a fool, a concern for his children that made him impatient of their foibles. But it was this manifest power of his "old nature" that made him marvel continually at the power of Christ, that made him always grateful for the grace of God.

The validation of Paul's vocation lies in the genuineness of this struggle to be worthy of his call. The persistence of the struggle indicates at once his refusal to tone down the majestic glory of the Christian life, the tenacity of the forces that resist the divine love, and the sterling honesty with which he confessed both the grandeur of the goal and his own deficiencies. He could ask others to imitate him only because he was seeking so earnestly to imitate Christ, only because he knew this quest as a radically humbling process that keeps removing any ground for complacency. One mark of his integrity was his admission that when he caused pain to his children, it had been intended for their good and had caused more grief to himself than to them (II Cor. 2:1-4; 7:3-12). A more convincing mark is his confession that he would rather be discredited himself and have them hold fast to the gospel than to be proved right at the cost of their damnation. "Not that we may appear to have met the test, but that you may do what is right, though we may seem to have failed (II Cor. 13:7).

Was Paul, then, faithful to his call as a slave of Jesus? One need not defend him more ardently than he defended himself in order to give an affirmative answer. Who can number the followers of Christ who from that day to this have found in his letters a true word from Christ and a true reflection of the image of Christ? Who can count the saints who have been encouraged by Paul's appeal and example to renew their minds according to the pattern in Christ? It is a constant witness on the part of those who have most selflessly trod the disciples' trail that Paul has gone ahead of them up the trail, and that the imitation of Paul has been in fact an imitation of the Lord. In full confidence Paul submitted his understanding of Christ to the judgment of the church, and the church has given a favorable verdict. Those who hesitate to accept Paul's example without reservation must admit that it was Paul's enunciation of the law of love that places his own behavior under such severe scrutiny. And this enunciation, expressed in such rigorous yet gracious language, provokes perennially an uneasiness within the church's conscience concerning its own faithfulness to its Lord. And this very self-examination by the Christian and the church affords an indirect testimony to the clarity with which Paul saw and stated the eternal demands made by the Lord of the church upon his servants.

And now to the final question: What has the church decided concerning the fidelity of Paul to his call as an apostle to the Gentiles? About the effectiveness of his work in that first generation there can be little dispute. It was through his efforts that nucleuses of Christian fellowship came into existence in many provinces, drawn mainly from pagan circles. And these small churches, clusters of meek and lowly folk in a hostile world, exhibited extraordinary powers of survival and growth. Here and there a church died. Here and there a church repudiated its founder. But the very preservation of the apostle's letters points to the fact that many of his churches persevered in their difficult tasks and in their allegiance to his gospel. That these informal and occasional writings were cherished to such an extent that they were ultimately accepted as Scripture is a measure of the church's judgment on Paul's apostleship.

To treat such evidence rightly we must recognize that Paul's vocation as an apostle did not cease with his death or with the death of those to whom he wrote. Wherever the Christian mission has gone, his letters have been listened to as God's word. And this word has not been void of power. Ever and again it has called the church to accept its missionary mandate. And wherever the church has followed that mandate, it has discovered that in one way or another it has been continuing Paul's work. Each rediscovery of Paul has stimulated a surge forward in evangelistic enterprise, and the keynote of that enterprise has been the gospel that Paul preached, the motives that constrained him, and the method he endorsed.

Let us consider this matter of method for a moment. According to this exemplar of preaching where the gospel has not been heard, the apostle must first identify himself with the people to whom he goes, humbly accepting their heritage, conventions, and outlook as his own. Then he must recount the story of Jesus in its entirety as the story of God's saving power. He must show how the Cross places all men under a final judgment, revealing the slavery which men have tacitly accepted—the tyranny of custom, law, race, and religious institutions. In the same message he must give his testimony to the new freedom which the Cross assures for men, through its announcement of God's forgiveness and love. To those who respond in repentance and faith he must make plain the purpose of their new freedom. He must depict the way of the Cross as a way which they must follow, so that the Gentile convert will again "become as a Gentile" in order that he may win other Gentiles. Only thus does the love of Christ continue its course of triumph over the world.

As Paul's successors extend his mission into new areas, they come to understand why men in all generations resist his gospel. The forces of entrenched worldly wisdom and power resent this exposure of their impotence and folly. The defenders of prevailing systems of law and temple, jealous of the standing which they have achieved through established institutions, are impelled by their own "righteousness" to oppose the apostle. The age of persecution is never far distant so long as a missionary proclaims with authority the freedom which Christ won for men through his death on the Cross, and so long as men for the sake of this freedom are emboldened to die to the law and to put to death the hope for righteousness under the law. For this reason Paul still stands on the frontier between the church and "Israel according to the flesh," between the church and all Gentile idolatries. The vigorous offense which his message provokes is a major seal of his continuing apostleship, as is the power of that message to break down the barricades and to transform persecutors into friends. When controversy over Paul's gospel ceases, that will be the sign that his vocation as an apostle nears an end.

No, Paul's work as an ambassador of the good news is not yet completed; neither is his work as father, as nurse, or as builder of the church. We have noted that when new sons enter the family of God they give to the apostle new responsibilities. Their diet and their discipline must be guided. The new faith elicits new temptations, and this spiritual struggle is decisive for their development. The apostle must counsel them on what weapons to use and how to handle these weapons (Eph. 6:10-20).

How successful was Paul in accomplishing this part of his vocation? During that first generation much evidence was at hand to support both a positive and a negative verdict. Individuals and churches alike rejected his advice, choosing other weapons than those which he counseled. Some among the more cautious dreaded the results of freedom and reverted to a narrower faith. Others insisted on a faith less fettered by concern for the brotherhood. Converts accepted either the security of inherited patterns of behavior or the enticement of unrestrained license. Those at one extreme blamed Paul for encouraging the errors of those at the other extreme. Yet there is ample evidence that this blame was unjustified. In more churches than one he successfully defeated the inroads of both "the circumcision party" and the "freedom party." He was enabled to reconcile Jews and Greeks, slave and free, male and female, political conservatives and radicals, in a fellowship that transcended all human distinctions. His handling of very delicate problems of social intercourse led to constructive solutions of those problems. And he could do this only by keeping clear in men's minds the true dimensions of a faith that works through love. In churches torn by dissension he recognized with joy the "work of faith and labor of love and steadfastness of hope in our Lord Jesus Christ" (I Thess. 1:3). Even in such a troublesome community as Corinth he testified that the humble believers were themselves a sufficient "letter of recommendation, written on your hearts, to be known and read by all men . . . ; a letter from Christ delivered by us, written . . . with the Spirit of the living God" (II Cor. 3:2-3). Later Christians have in the main accepted this letter of recommendation as perhaps the most impressive credential that Paul could submit.

One reason, of course, for such acceptance has been the enduring ability of the apostle to produce such letters. His words have manifested their agelong authority by repeatedly transforming men into slaves of Christ. And these babes have found in Paul's counsel a diet adjusted to the various stages of their growth. They have sensed in him both the nurse's tenderness and the rod of parental authority. Listening to his prophet's voice, they have found it sharp enough to penetrate the secrets of their hearts, laying bare sins that had escaped detection. Christian leaders, entangled in organizational problems and jurisdictional disputes, have often discerned in his attitudes toward leadership a humbling correction of their own pride and anxiety (I Cor. 1–4). When the exercise of spiritual gifts has led to disorder, a return to Paul's evaluation of such gifts has often brought peace. Heretics on the right and left alike have claimed his support, only to find him an honest critic of their own half-truths and defensive motives. In the midst of all the complex difficulties of church life his wisdom has been consulted. And when his teaching has been interpreted by faith and by the Spirit, in full accord with his example, it has helped to focus the issues, to restate the goals, and to nurture the mind of Christ in the disciples, so that the difficulty has become a means of grace. Wherever believers have engaged in the struggles appertaining to faith, they have continued to receive unmeasured aid from this "man of conflict" who appeals to them still "by the meekness and gentleness of Christ" (II Cor. 10:1). Wherever the church is actually Christ's body, whether men approve or disapprove of this apostle, he continues to commend himself as a slave of Jesus Christ and an apostle to the Gentiles, "through great endurance, in afflictions, hardships, . . . labors, . . . by purity, knowledge, forbearance, kindness, the Holy Spirit, genuine love, truthful speech, and the power of God" (II Cor. 6:4-7).

V. Selected Bibliography

DEISSMANN, G. ADOLF. *Paul: A Study in Social and Religious History,* tr. William E. Wilson. New York: George H. Doran, 1926.

DODD, C. H. *The Meaning of Paul for Today.* New York: George H. Doran, 1920.

JACKSON, F. J. FOAKES. *The Life of Saint Paul.* New York: Boni & Liveright, 1926.

NOCK, ARTHUR D. *St. Paul.* New York: Harper & Bros., 1938.

PORTER, FRANK C. *The Mind of Christ in Paul.* New York: Charles Scribner's Sons, 1930.

SABATIER, AUGUSTE. *The Apostle Paul,* tr. George G. Findlay. New York: James Pott & Co., 1891.

SCHWEITZER, ALBERT. *Paul and His Interpreters,* tr. W. Montgomery. London: A. & C. Black, 1912.

SCOTT, C. A. A. *St. Paul, the Man and the Teacher.* Cambridge: University Press, 1936.

STEWART, JAMES S. *A Man in Christ.* New York: Harper & Bros., 1935.

WEINEL, HEINRICH. *St. Paul, the Man and His Work.* New York: G. P. Putnam's Sons, 1906.

WEISS, JOHANNES. *The History of Primitive Christianity,* tr. F. C. Grant, *et al.* New York: Wilson-Erickson, 1937. Bks. II, III.

THE HISTORY OF
THE EARLY CHURCH

IV. THE POST-APOSTOLIC AGE

by MASSEY H. SHEPHERD, JR.

In A.D. 62 James, the brother of the Lord and the head of the church in Jerusalem, was stoned.[1] Shortly afterward the church over which he had presided as vicegerent of the Messiah removed, in obedience to a "revelation," to the Gentile city of Pella across Jordan, in order not to become embroiled in the growing spirit of rebellion among the Jews against Roman domination.[2] The unsuccessful war waged by the Jews for their liberation (A.D. 66) ended, as Jesus had foreseen and prophesied, with the destruction of Jerusalem and the demolition of the temple.[3] With these events the outward ties binding Christianity to its parental roots were forever cut.

Outside of Judea the scattered mission churches planted and nurtured by apostolic zeal had already been expelled from the synagogues of Jewry, and had initiated their separate, independent organization and life. Roman authorities were slow in recognizing this emergence of a new religion in their midst. Twenty years after Jesus' death the proconsul Gallio at Corinth saw nothing in the disputes issuing from the apostolic preaching but a wrangle among Jews "about words and names and the law" (Acts 18:15). Not until Nero's savage cruelty, vented upon the Christians on the occasion of the fire of Rome in July of A.D. 64,[4] is there any clear indication that the government had come to distinguish the new "superstition"

as separate from and more "detestable" than the old. The authenticity of early tradition that Peter and Paul gave their lives for the faith during Nero's reign has not been successfully challenged by modern research, though the precise time and manner of their ordeals are not certainly known.

Only untrustworthy legends remain regarding the fate of other apostles who had seen the Lord. In particular the tradition about John, son of Zebedee, is dubious—that he lived to a ripe age toward the close of the first century and fathered the literature ascribed to him. More probably he won a martyr's crown also, in Palestine, before the outbreak of the Jewish revolt against Rome.[5]

The crisis for the church created by these events of the decade 60-70 was so momentous that for more than a century it was uncertain whether Christianity would survive in any form recognizable as organically continuous with the form of faith and order given it by its original apostles. As it turned out, the severest pressure upon the church was not the external one of persecution. Although this was a constant concern of the Christian communities, it proved to be too intermittent and unorganized in execution to be at any single time a formidable menace to the growth, much less to the existence, of the new faith. Far more serious was the internal problem arising from the removal of those who "from the beginning were eyewitnesses and ministers of the word" (Luke

---

[1] Josephus *Antiquities* XX. 9. 1; Hegesippus in Eusebius *Church History* II. 23. 4-18.

[2] Eusebius *Church History* III. 5. 2-3.

[3] Matt. 24:2 ff.; Mark 13:2 ff.; Luke 19:43-44; John 2:18-20.

[4] Tacitus *Annals* XV. 44; cf. Suetonius *Nero* 16.

[5] See the discussion of the tradition in B. W. Bacon, *The Gospel of the Hellenists* (New York: Henry Holt & Co., 1933), pp. 7-51.

1:2), and the emergence of "false" apostles, prophets, and teachers.

The increasingly preponderant Gentile element in the church's ranks, gathered out of the multiform and variegated syncretisms of Hellenistic paganism, afforded fertile soil for the cultivation of all sorts of hybrid systems designed to accommodate the Christian faith and cultus to the dominant religious motifs of the age. Similar efforts to absorb Judaism into broader religious syntheses had not been without success in some quarters in the first century. Gentile Christianity was far more vulnerable to such attacks. Already freed from the insulating restrictions which the Jewish law had provided, it possessed as yet no comparable institutional standards by which to control innovation. It possessed only the living voice of oral tradition. That the post-apostolic church did succeed in formulating and securing objective safeguards for its deposit of faith with an investment of apostolic authority, and at the same time kept its tradition sufficiently flexible to allow for development in interpretation, is its most signal achievement.

It is unfortunate for the historian that the detailed steps of the process by which "the catholic church" [6] emerged from the struggle, secure from disintegration, cannot be recovered. The extant sources of the post-apostolic age are slender, and many are tantalizingly fragmentary. Later generations were unconcerned to transmit to posterity what became stigmatized as heretical or what proved to be inadequate to its own needs. And earlier, more primitive generations had their gaze so riveted upon the age to come that they had little inclination to become antiquarian, unless it served some immediate purpose of apologetic.

It is often assumed that the early Christians, being drawn for the most part from the lower classes, were not interested in literary production. But such a claim can be made only of the very earliest days of the Christian mission, when the expectation of the near end of the world and the return of the Lord was uppermost in the church's mind. Men of whatever social and economic status, with a message of salvation, soon learn to utilize every possible means of communicating their faith to others, and there is every reason to believe the church early developed a literary interest. (On this matter see pp. 32-34, above.) In this case, however, the historian is confronted not only with the loss of much that would be material of primary significance, but he often cannot date and place with any precision sources which he does have. Many documents appeared under pseudonyms; and in not a few cases the false claim was suc-

cessful. Modern criticism has not yet arrived at settled conclusions regarding questions of authenticity, occasion of composition, or literary interdependence. Any account of the post-apostolic age, therefore, must be but a tentative reconstruction, ever subject, with advances in historical science, to modification in more than its details. There is also the added possibility of new discoveries of lost sources.

I. Palestine

The Jewish Christians of Palestine continued for some time after the death of James to be led and guided by members of the family of Jesus. We know little of their fortunes, however, and there are indications that during the second century disintegrating forces were at work to split them among various sects and heresies. Our best picture of their tradition and life in the years immediately following the fall of Jerusalem in A.D. 70 can be gleaned from the material which is peculiar to the Gospel of Matthew. They are poor, humble folk, who viewed themselves as "the salt of the earth" and as "the light of the world." Bitterly hostile to the Pharisaic leaders of Jewry, these Jewish Christians were no less zealous for the permanently binding character of the law, even to the "least commandments." They took no interest in any mission to Samaritans or Gentiles, since they considered that the Messiah was "sent only to the lost sheep of the house of Israel." Jerusalem in all her misery and ruin remained for them "the Holy City." The prophet was still the honored disciple to be welcomed on his itinerant visits; but there are indications of trouble from "false prophets, who come . . . in sheep's clothing but inwardly are ravenous wolves." There are signs also of more tragic divisions within family circles—the foes of one's own household (Matt. 10:36). Vivid expectations of imminent, sudden judgment at the coming of the Lord continued to be central in their message, as these are preserved to us in the parables of the tares, the wise and foolish virgins, and the separation of the sheep from the goats.

Though all of them kept the law according to their lights and interpretations, they continued to be divided, as in apostolic times, over the question of the binding yoke of the law upon Gentile converts.[7] Many accepted the position taken by Peter and James at the apostolic conference in Jerusalem.[8] These are probably to be identified with the Jewish Christians who came to be known as the Nazareans, whom we find as late as the fourth century flourishing in the neighborhood of Beroea. Their gospel

---

[6] The term is first used about 110 in Ign. Smyr. 8:2.

[7] See Justin Martyr *Dialogue with Trypho* 47.

[8] Acts 15; Gal. 2.

was an Aramaic Targum of Matthew, sometimes cited by the early Fathers as the Gospel According to the Hebrews. The less liberal-minded wing of Jewish Christianity in the second century are generally known as the Ebionites ("the poor"). They seem to have been more vulnerable to unorthodox views and practices, and many of them found their way into syncretistic baptist, ascetic, or Gnostic sects. It is difficult to gain a clear view of their beliefs and activities, since orthodox writers upon whom we depend for our information were either ill-disposed or indifferent toward them. They produced their own heretical Gospel According to the Ebionites, though it is possible that some used the Gospel of Matthew or the Nazarene Gospel According to the Hebrews.[9]

In some cities, such as Caesarea or Pella, the Jewish-Christian churches were not altogether isolated from the main currents of Gentile Christianity or even from Greek culture, and in outward appearance they were closely akin to the Greek-speaking synagogues of the Jewish Dispersion. The author of the Epistle of James —the letter form is purely artificial—has collected some brief homiletic expositions and exhortations on keeping the law and the necessity of good works and certain prophetic denunciations against the rich and worldly. His themes are developed in typically rabbinical fashion from sayings of Jesus which have come down to him either through oral tradition, or possibly through direct acquaintance with the Gospel of Matthew, but they are presented in the style of the Hellenistic diatribe. Significantly he addresses his short sermons to the "twelve tribes in the Dispersion." [10] About A.D. 140 a Jewish Christian of the church in Pella, named Aristo, published an apology for his faith in the form of a dialogue, a common Greek literary type, between a Christian named Jason and a Jew named Papiscus. This work is now unfortunately lost, but it had a wide reading among both Christians and non-Christians at the time of its appearance.[11]

[9] See Irenaeus *Against Heresies* I. 26. 2; Origen *Against Celsus* V. 61.

[10] It is, of course, impossible to date and place with certainty the Epistle of James. It could have been produced in any church of the Roman world which had a strong Jewish tradition. It is certainly later than the publication of the collection of Paul's letters and of I Peter. Thus it can hardly be earlier than the last years of the first century. See the discussion of it by W. L. Knox, "The Epistle of St. James," *Journal of Theological Studies*, XLVI (1945), 10-17; see also the introduction and commentary by Burton Scott Easton in Vol. XII of this work.

[11] It is first quoted by the pagan opponent of Christianity, Celsus, whose *True Discourse* against the Christians was published about A.D. 150. See Origen *Against Celsus* IV. 52. Aristo's work most probably influenced the form of Justin Martyr's *Dialogue with Trypho*, and

There are extant in the *Church History* of Eusebius some extracts from the voluminous memoirs of one Hegesippus (Joseph), a Christian of Jewish birth, from Palestine or Syria, which were published in the third quarter of the second century. Hegesippus traveled widely among the churches of the Roman world collecting data of an antiquarian sort regarding their early leaders and their teaching. We do not know whether Hegesippus was a product of the Jewish-Christian communities, or whether he belonged to a Gentile church. He was, however, thoroughly conversant with the traditions and writings of Judaism and Jewish Christianity.[12] The Ebionites numbered among their members for a time one Symmachus, a translator of the Old Testament into Greek, and a writer of commentaries on the Scriptures. He belonged to that group of the Ebionites which strongly opposed the Gospel of Matthew.[13]

II. Syria

The predominant position held by the church of Jerusalem in the earliest days of Christianity was inherited, even before the end of the apostolic age, by the church of Antioch and its missionary offshoots in Syria. There the tensions of orthodox and Hellenizing Jews, of Gentile proselyte to Judaism and Gentile Christian, of Semitic and Greco-Roman religious world-view and culture, involved groups more evenly balanced; and the time required for assimilation or reconciliation was more prolonged. It was there that Gnostic heresy, which was to threaten the entire church in the second century, had its cradle. It was there too, most probably, that episcopal authority, succeeding to the position of the apostles, first emerged, though it was to have its most significant successes elsewhere. Yet we know all too little of the history of this important church in that crucial period. Between Ignatius the martyr in the early part of the second century, reputedly the second bishop of Antioch, and Theophilus the apologist in the latter part of the same century, who is counted as the sixth bishop, we have almost a complete blackout of assured information about the fortunes of Christianity in Syria. It may well have come near to being overwhelmed in the flood tide of heretical movements. Probably also it was the church in Antioch which first felt the shock of state opposition, for the word "Christian" was first used to describe the disciples of the new "Way" in Antioch, and this word is of Latin derivation.[14] At any rate Syrian

possibly also the *Octavius* of Minucius Felix. See Eusebius *Church History* IV. 6.

[12] Eusebius *Church History* IV. 22.

[13] *Ibid.*, VI. 17. This information is undoubtedly derived from Origen.

[14] Acts 11:26.

Christianity produced in Ignatius the first known martyr of distinction after the apostles, and the first literature of Christian apologetics of which there is any record, the so-called Preaching of Peter. It may be objected that the two-volume work addressed to an official named Theophilus, which we know as Luke-Acts, should be considered the first Christian "Apology" for the faith. But even so there are cogent reasons for assigning the place of origin of this work also to Antioch.[15]

Through a slighting reference of the apostle Paul (Gal. 2:11 ff.) we know that Peter was for a time domiciled at Antioch. How long Peter stayed there is unknown, but he left behind him an impression as great as Paul's if not greater. When all the apostolic leaders had been removed from the scene of Syrian Christianity, it was Peter who was remembered as having had the pre-eminence. By the middle of the decade A.D. 70-80 two documents concerning the life and teaching of the Lord Jesus were circulating in Syria. One was a Gospel by a Roman disciple and interpreter of Peter, named Mark, who had recorded after Peter's death what he could remember of the apostle's preaching about Jesus. The other was a collection of teaching material, for the most part, "sayings of Jesus," which in form was much like an Old Testament prophetic book.[16] Two Syrian Christians, independently one of the other, combined these two works into new Gospels, adding to them other stories and sayings circulating in oral tradition or perhaps recorded in other documents. Thus they sought to provide the

church with authoritative guides to apostolic traditions about Jesus, now that the church was bereft of the living voice of the apostles themselves. Both of these new Gospels, the one "According to Matthew," the other "According to Luke," appeared sometime between A.D. 80 and 90. The latter was in fact more than a gospel. It was a "church history," for its second volume contained an account of the church's mission and expansion in the apostolic age.

In Matthew, Peter is the rock upon which the church is built, and to him the "keys of the kingdom" are entrusted (Matt. 16:17-19). In Luke-Acts Peter's pre-eminence in the founding of the church is unmistakably in evidence. He is the first witness of the resurrected Lord (Luke 24:34), and he fulfills the Lord's prophecy and prayer that he would turn and strengthen his brethren despite his temporary failure in faith and his ignominious denial in the crisis of his Lord's arrest and trial (Luke 22:31-32). In Acts, Peter appears as the accepted spokesman of the church in its earliest days, whether in its decisions regarding inner organization and life or in its preaching of the good news to the world outside. Peter is the first to suffer persecution "for the name"; and in the opinion of the author of Acts he is the first to initiate, in obedience to revelation, the mission to the Gentiles.

Second-century writers in the Syrian church continued to appeal to Peter's authority for their traditions and doctrines, however unorthodox they might be. We need not put any credence in the claim of the Gnostic heretic Basilides, who in the early years of the Emperor Hadrian seems to have removed his base of operation from Syria to Egypt, that he received his peculiar teachings from one Glaucias, an interpreter of Peter.[17] Basilides wrote twenty-four books of commentaries or, as he called them, "exegetics" on the Gospels, from the extant fragments of which we know that he used Matthew and Luke.[18] We cannot, moreover, trace with any certainty the development of a body of legendary lore recounting the conflicts of Peter with the Samaritan magician Simon Magus, reputed father of all the heresies of this period. Syria was the incubator of these romantic tales, beginning with the altercation of Peter and Simon recorded in Acts 8:18-24. The stories are perhaps best understood as popular legends reflecting the struggle of ecclesiastical authority to preserve its identity with apostolic

[15] The tradition that "Luke" was an Antiochian is very ancient. The second-century "anti-Marcionite" prologues of the Gospels state this: from these Eusebius probably derived his information, *Church History* III. 4. 6. See R. M. Grant, "The Oldest Gospel Prologues," *Anglican Theological Review*, XXIII (1941), 231-45. The Western text of Acts 11:28, which doubtless goes back to the second century also, even though it may not be original, is a "we-passage," and hence associates the author of Luke-Acts with the church in Antioch. It is not necessary to assume that the writing of Luke-Acts was actually done in Antioch. But the author certainly leaned heavily upon Antiochian traditions and sources, and his knowledge of the missionary activity of Paul is confined to those journeys which had their point of departure in Antioch.

[16] This collection of "sayings" is a more extensive document than the hypothetical Q, a symbol used by scholars to denote the material common to Matthew and Luke. The nature of this "gospel" from which both the First and Third Evangelists drew much of their information has been best described by B. H. Streeter as a work comparable to an Old Testament prophecy; see his essay in *Studies in the Synoptic Problem*, ed. W. Sanday (Oxford: Clarendon Press, 1911), pp. 141-64. (See also above, pp. 63-65 and below, pp. 235-39, as well as the Introduction to Luke in Vol. VIII of this work. Some disagreement on these matters of gospel origins and relationships is to be expected among the scholars.)

[17] Clement of Alexandria *Miscellanies* VII. 17.

[18] These fragments are conveniently collected in English translation in R. M. Grant, *Second-Century Christianity* (London: Society for Promoting Christian Knowledge, 1946), pp. 18-21.

tradition against inspired innovators who were not incapable of charlatanry.[19] A sizable fragment is extant of a Gospel of Peter, which had considerable vogue in the second century, and which is probably of Syrian provenance. Its historical contents were distinctly "second-hand," but its theological bent made it acceptable in heretical circles. Yet it was not so highly colored with doctrinal novelty as to be immediately suspect among the orthodox. As late as the last decade of the second century we find this gospel being read in the liturgical worship of the church at Rhossus, a city not far to the northwest of Antioch. When Bishop Sarapion of Antioch visited the parish, he was asked for an opinion about the book from certain parties who were concerned about its heterodox tendencies. After a cursory examination, the bishop gave it an imprimatur, but upon later inquiry into its contents after his return home, he changed his mind and advised the church in Rhossus accordingly.[20]

Another Syrian production which circulated early in the second century under the name of Peter gave occasion to a series of apologies or defenses of Christianity designed for the general public. It is known as The Preaching of Peter. Its inspiration is doubtless the speeches of the book of Acts, but its actual contents, so far as can be recovered from the citations in later writers, show a large indebtedness to current apologies for Judaism. The work aims at a simple exposition of the chief doctrines which distinguish Christianity from both pagan and Jewish religions, and propounds the view that Christianity is a new or "third type," fulfilling the older forms of worship among the Jews and Greeks in a synthesis of both "Law and Word [Logos]." Not only this threefold classification of religion was taken up by later apologists, but the other basic ideas of The Preaching of Peter were to become the stock in trade of succeeding defenders of the faith. Among these were: the utterly spiritual nature of the Creator-God, who needs no material offerings from the things he has made; the Logos, or Son of God, who was the Father's agent in creation; the ignorance and folly both of idolatrous polytheism and Jewish ceremonialism with its service of angels and months and moons; the fulfillment of Old Testament prophecy in Christ; the moral superiority of Christianity; and the call to repentance and faith as prerequisites for salvation. The Preaching of Peter has also this similarity to later Apologies: it is "orthodox" and devoid of the heretical speculations of the age.

Before the close of the first century, heretical tendencies were manifesting themselves and agitating the Christian communities both in Syria and Asia Minor. The earlier phase, known as Docetism, was more devotional than speculative in character. Sharing the pessimistic outlook of much contemporary pagan sentiment respecting the evil inherent in material existence, Docetist teachers posited in Christ a heaven-sent Redeemer from the world of matter, a divine Savior manifest in the appearance, but not the reality of human flesh—hence the term "Docetism," from the Greek word meaning "to seem." They denied that he had been born of a human mother as other babes, that he had really suffered death upon the Cross—for how inconceivable it was that a god should suffer pain and death!—and that he was raised in the body of flesh. Needless to say, such doctrines not only undercut the foundations of the church's inherited witness from the apostles, but it dissolved the ancestral ties with Jewish faith in a Creator-God and his revelation in the scriptures of the Old Testament. Christian revelation was no longer rooted in and continuous with history; it was instead a novel though simple mythology. And the accepted, if as yet unformulated, sources of the church's authority were sharply challenged.

The Docetist Christology was soon elaborated by minds of a more daring speculative temper into systems of cosmology and theodicy, with bizarre mixtures of pagan, Jewish, and Christian terminology. Each system claimed to be the saving *gnōsis* or "knowledge" (whence comes the name Gnosticism to describe the movement as a whole) revealed by Christ for the redemption of the spiritually elect from their entanglement in an evil material world, fashioned by an inferior demiurge or creator as a result of some precosmic disturbance or mischance in the heavenly realm of light and spirit. Many of the earliest Gnostic teachers were active in Antioch, from whence they wandered to Asia Minor, Egypt, or Rome—Menander, reputed disciple of Simon Magus, Saturninus, Cerdo, and above all, Basilides and his son Isidore. In the hands of Basilides, Gnostic speculation produced a comprehensive theology which wrestled valiantly with the high themes of the origin of evil, the nature of sin, the ethics of forgiveness and punishment, and the problems of predestination and transmigration of souls.[21]

[19] The romance is developed in the Acts of Peter, a later second-century document, not necessarily of Syrian origin, and in the "Clementine" *Recognitions* and *Homilies* of the early fourth century, which are most probably productions of Syrian Christianity.

[20] Eusebius *Church History* VI. 12.

[21] The teachings of these early Gnostics are known only through the polemical references of later orthodox writers. The relevant fragments are conveniently collected in Grant, *Second-Century Christianity*. There is as yet no comprehensive work on the Gnostic movement in

A redoubtable opponent of the Gnostic development was found in the martyr-bishop of Antioch, Ignatius, who was thrown to the wild beasts in the amphitheater at Rome sometime in the reign of Trajan (98-117).[22] During the course of his dolorous journey as a prisoner from Antioch to Rome, he had the opportunity of visiting several of the churches in Asia and meeting a number of their leaders, notably Polycarp, young bishop of Smyrna. The brief corpus of his extant writings, containing letters to these churches (specifically those to Ephesus, Magnesia, Tralles, Philadelphia, and Smyrna), a personal letter addressed to Polycarp, and a letter of anticipation sent to the church in Rome, is an imperishable record of the outer and inner conflicts of the church at this period, as they become vividly personalized in a highly sensitive and mystical, if overwrought, temperament.

Ignatius' primary concern was to strengthen the authority of the bishops in the several churches, as safeguards against the insidious dangers of Docetic teaching, both to the tradition of apostolic faith and the sacramental cultus of the church. In passionate affirmations of the reality of Christ's birth, sufferings and death, and resurrection in the flesh, no more a mere "semblance" than his own endurance of martyrdom in the flesh, Ignatius appealed to his Christian friends in Asia to resort only to those assemblies for instruction and worship presided over by the bishop or his authorized deputy, for only in them could they find that true and secure communion in "one bread, which is the medicine of immortality, the antidote that we should not die but live forever in Jesus Christ." [23]

The letters of Ignatius give us the first clear indication of the emergence of the "monarchical episcopate," that is, the rule of a single bishop over a Christian community, in government, doctrine, and worship, with the counsel of a college of presbyters and the assistance of deacons in pastoral and liturgical duties. The "spirits" of prophets and teachers, with other lesser charismatic gifts, which enjoyed so preeminent a place in the life of the churches in apostolic times, were becoming progressively suspect unless subject to the directive control of the bishop. The crisis produced by Docetism, not to mention the growing menace of perse-

cution, called for a stronger administrative hand, permanently settled in the local communities, which could protect the faithful from disintegrating forces and speak with the authority of apostolic tradition, the assurance of a regular, continuous commission. "See that all of you follow the bishop, just as Jesus Christ follows the Father," wrote Ignatius, "and the presbytery as if it were the apostles; and reverence the deacons as the command of God. Let no one do any of the things pertaining to the church without the bishop." [24]

The lead taken by the urban Christian communities in strengthening the authority of the local ministries established by the apostles, as against the vagaries of wandering "inspired" leaders, was gradually extended to the outlying country villages. We have a glimpse of this process in the hinterland of Syria about the middle of the second century in a little manual known as the Didache or Teaching of the Twelve Apostles. The tract opens with a model catechetical instruction, to be used in preparation for baptism, utilizing an older Jewish-Christian treatise on the "two ways" of life and of death, but enriching it with gospel material, chiefly from Matthew. To this ethical material were added regulations regarding the administration of the sacraments and rules of private devotion in fasting and prayer, model forms for the thanksgivings said at the churches' common meal, and detailed directions for testing "inspired" visitors in order to distinguish true prophets from false. The problem created by these charismatics, however, does not seem to have been so much one of heretical infiltration as of "bogus" prophecy—Christian charlatans of the type so mordantly satirized by the pagan Lucian of Samosata in his *On the Death of Peregrinus*. The need resulting from the decline of true inspiration in prophetic leadership of the communities was to be met by the appointment of bishops and deacons, whose offices of liturgical ministration were equally honorable, said the Didachist, with those of prophets and teachers.

III. Asia Minor

Confronted with many of the same problems of the churches in Syria, with whom they were in close touch, were the flourishing Christian communities of Asia Minor. Many and diverse cultural and religious strands freely intermingled in the rich cities of the Hermus and Meander valleys, through which the apostolic preaching had spread from Ephesus up into the mountainous interior. Philosophies, pseudo-

---

English, other than the summary chapters in the standard histories of the early church (such as Gwatkin, Duchesne, Lietzmann, etc.). Adolf von Harnack's famous interpretation of Gnosticism as "an acute secularizing of Christianity" (*History of Dogma*, tr. Neil Buchanan [Boston: Roberts Bros., 1895], I, 265 ff.) has been severely criticized, but his study is fundamental, and important.

[22] Eusebius *Church History* III. 36.

[23] Ign. Eph. 20:2.

[24] Ign. Smyr. 8:1. See M. H. Shepherd, "Smyrna in the Ignatian Letters, A Study in Church Order," *Journal of Religion*, XX (1940), 141-59.

philosophies, superstitions, and mere quackeries, all had their devotees. Judaism, whether in orthodox form or in numerous agnostic and syncretistic varieties, was strongly represented. Above all, the cultus of the imperial state worship of Rome was enthusiastically received by the Asiatics in return for the peace and prosperity which Roman rule had restored to the region. This cultus was a potent factor in the menace of persecution with which the Christians of Asia Minor were constantly faced.

The diversity and fluidity of its religious environment were reflected in the sharp divisions and contrasts which marked the inner life of the church, or better, the individual churches. For it is impossible to generalize. Each Christian community had its own variety of tension and conflict, as one may gather from reading between the lines of Ignatius' letters or the letters to the seven churches which preface the Revelation of John. In some instances the diversity stemmed from rival apostolic traditions, whether Pauline or Palestinian; in others it developed from contrasting attitudes toward the Roman state; in still others it was the result of conflict between ecclesiastical authority and prophecy, or between Jewish and Gnostic interpretation in doctrine and cult practice. In the same community one could find mystic and millenarian, martyr and conformist, legalist and libertarian. The vitality of Christianity in Asia Minor in the sub-apostolic age was matched only by its disunity. In no area was the achievement of ecclesiasical order more difficult or the process more prolonged.

The Pauline tradition was revivified about A.D. 90, when an enthusiastic disciple of the apostle collected a corpus of his letters and published them in Ephesus under coverage of an introductory, general epistle—our canonical Ephesians—redolent with Pauline phrases and ideas.[25] This collection not only assured that the basic Pauline emphases would exert a continuing force in the doctrinal development of the church, but it fostered the use of the epistolary form as a means of interchange of ideas, whether hortatory or polemical. The seven letters of the book of Revelation were doubtless suggested by the Pauline corpus, as was also the collection of the letters of Ignatius, with which Polycarp busied himself.[26] Other examples of its influence, to cite only collections made in Asia Minor, are the Johannine letters and the Pastorals.

The Jewish revolt against Rome in A.D. 66-70

was the occasion for an exodus of many leaders of the church in Palestine to Asia Minor. Among them were Philip, one of the Seven (Acts 6:5), and his four daughters, virgin-prophetesses, who settled in Hierapolis. Two "disciples of the Lord" also appear among these refugees, one Aristion and a presbyter named John. Their deeds and sayings, their traditions about Jesus and the earliest apostles, were avidly collected by Papias, bishop of Hierapolis in the first half of the second century, in a verbose, five-volume work entitled Interpretation of the Lord's Oracles.[27] Only a few quotations from this treatise in the writings of Irenaeus and Eusebius are extant. They reveal two characteristics which seem to stem from Palestinian Christian tradition: a strong preference for oral, as against written, tradition concerning the Lord's teachings, and a vigorous millenarian, apocalyptic outlook. It is quite probable that the "seer of Patmos" (Rev. 1:9) himself belonged either to this group of Palestinian emigrés or worked upon Jewish-Christian apocalyptic material brought by them.

The two strands in Asian Christianity of Pauline mysticism and sacramentalism on the one hand, and of Palestinian Jewish Christianity on the other, entered into a creative work of genius, written about the turn of the second century, probably in Ephesus—the Gospel According to John. We do not know the name of the author of this Gospel (and of the epistles generally associated with it [28]) or the specific sources, whether firsthand or secondhand, which he used. The interminable debates of modern critics about these questions move only in circles; we need not be detained by them here. It is important to remember, however, that it is not a biography or theological treatise but a *gospel,* whole and entire, intended neither to correct nor to supplement others in circulation which the author may or may not have known, but designed to present the revelation of the eternal Word of God in the historical Jesus in such wise that men may be won to him in faith and service, and united in that historic fellowship of the apostolic church which he founded.

[25] Edgar J. Goodspeed, *The Meaning of Ephesians* (Chicago: University of Chicago Press, 1933).

[26] Polyc. Phil. 13:2. This single extant letter of Polycarp is itself modeled on Paul, of whose letters Polycarp makes frequent use.

[27] Eusebius *Church History* III. 39.

[28] C. H. Dodd has reopened once more the question of the unity of authorship of the Gospel and the First Epistle of John: "The First Epistle of John and the Fourth Gospel," *Bulletin of the John Rylands Library,* XXI (1937), 129-56, and in his commentary on the Johannine epistles in the "Moffatt New Testament Commentary," *The Johannine Epistles* (New York: Harper & Bros., 1946). The inclusion of the brief epistles of "the Elder" (II and III John) among the works of the same author is another problem in itself. Only the most conservative critics maintain that the same "John" wrote also Revelation, a position considered untenable by reputable critics of the second and third centuries.

There are in the Fourth Gospel such paradoxical contrasts and syntheses, however, as to put it in a position all its own. Hebraic in style, frequently rabbinical in argument, it is at the same time vigorously anti-Semitic in sentiment and Hellenistic in its basic philosophical outlook. Although it is sometimes more accurate concerning its facts than the Synoptic Gospels, as for example its dating of the passion, it treats history symbolically. Full of Gnostic terminology, proponent of salvation by "knowledge" (gnōsis), it is an archfoe of all forms of Docetic Christology and insistent upon the reality of the Incarnation. Its sacramentalism is as realistic as Paul's, and as spiritual. The first Epistle vividly expects the imminent final end with the appearance (in current heresy) of the Antichrist; the Gospel conceives of the judgment as already accomplished and the new age as realized. There is strong mystical fervor in the Johannine meditations upon "light" and "life" and "truth," yet without mysticism; and universalism is found together with a definite conception of predestination and election.

Theologically the Fourth Gospel stands nearest to Ignatius, and seems to have been nourished by the same or similar sources of tradition. Yet neither Ignatius nor Polycarp reveals any knowledge of the work, though it must have been produced in their time, and, according to late second-century tradition, Polycarp was on intimate terms with its reputed author, the apostle John! For a generation it appears to have been more in favor with the Gnostics than with the orthodox.

The Docetism attacked by the Fourth Evangelist was not the only heresy which troubled the peace of the churches in Asia Minor in this period. In some cases visionary speculations were combined with the practice of Jewish ceremonial and custom. The seer of Patmos attacked these groups in the churches at Smyrna and Philadelphia, and Ignatius gave warnings of them also to Philadelphia and to Magnesia. It is possible that the "Nicolaitans" of Ephesus and Pergamos were of this type.[29] A notorious teacher was Cerinthus. It was related by Polycarp that once, upon entering the baths at Ephesus, the disciple John saw Cerinthus and immediately left, saying, "Let us fly lest the baths fall in, since Cerinthus, the enemy of the truth, is within.[30] Other sectaries, rejecting all legalistic regulations, made of Christian liberty a cloak for licentiousness. Such was the prophetess "Jezebel" at Thyatira and the teachers of the "doctrine of Balaam" at Pergamos (Rev. 2:14, 20).

By far the most serious heretic spawned by Asia Minor was Marcion, the son of a bishop in Sinope in Pontus. We know little of his activity before his arrival in Rome in the reign of Antoninus Pius; but he appears to have troubled the already disturbed waters of Asian Christianity on his way westward.[31] In the year 144 he was expelled from the church in Rome. A thoroughgoing dualist and Docetist—though devoid of interest in the speculative theology of advanced Gnosticism, for he was an exegete rather than a philosopher—his views were the result of a close study of the Scriptures, and particularly of the letters of Paul. The Pauline antitheses of law and faith, justice and grace made such a profound impression upon him that he exaggerated the difference between Judaism and Christianity, with the result that he eliminated the Old Testament entirely from his religion as being the revelation of an inferior, vindictive, and jealous Creator-God of the evil world of matter, in opposition to the loving God and Father of Jesus Christ. These views he set forth in a book of exegesis which he entitled, appropriately enough, Antitheses. Unable to retain the Old Testament, Marcion conceived the idea of a New Testament canon of Scripture in its place, for which he selected the letters of Paul and the Gospel of Luke, Paul's companion. But in both cases he bowdlerized the texts by eliminating all passages which either clearly identified the God of Judaism with the God of Jesus, or spoke plainly of the reality of Christ's human life, such passages being considered by Marcion as interpolations. His pessimistic doctrine of matter led Marcion to foster an ethic of strict asceticism. His followers are known to have furnished many martyrs to their Christian faith.

The story of the orthodox church's polemic against Marcion and his movement goes beyond the period of this article. In Asia Minor specifically it left its literary mark in a new corpus of Pauline letters, the Pastorals, fragments of genuine personal letters of the apostle worked into ecclesiastical "church orders," in which Paul is depicted as a legislator of a safe and sound church polity and discipline, vigilant against "perverse disputings of men of corrupt minds, destitute of the truth," "profane and

---

[29] The attempt of both Irenaeus and Clement of Alexandria to father the Nicolaitan heresy upon the deacon Nicolaus of Acts 6:5 is gratuitous.

[30] Irenaeus Against Heresies III. 3. 4; cf. Eusebius Church History IV. 14. 6.

[31] Polycarp's encounter with Marcion, in which he denounced him as "the first-born of Satan," probably belongs to the time of Polycarp's visit to Rome, about 154. Irenaeus Against Heresies III. 3. 4, reproduced in Eusebius Church History IV. 14. 6-7. The anti-Marcionite prologue to the Fourth Gospel recounts also a brush between Papias and Marcion. See note 15 above.

vain babblings," and "itching ears." [32] More important was the impetus given to the catholic church in the formation of an authoritative canon of the New Testament adopted by all the churches, in which Marcion's apostolic canon of Paul, without Marcion's "higher criticism," was enlarged to include other gospels and letters which could reasonably claim authorship by apostles or their immediate associates. Similarly the orthodox churches drew up confessions or creeds of the faith, for use in prebaptismal instruction and apologetic, designed to exclude the dualist and Docetist aberrations from apostolic tradition. Of these creeds that of the church in Rome, the so-called Apostles' Creed, is still in use.

Not only heresy but also prophecy distressed the church in Asia Minor. Vividly expectant in its millennial hopes, utterly uncompromising in its hostility to the Roman state, the beastly "Babylon," prophecy was a provocative agent in an area intensely loyal to the Roman imperium and its ruler-worship. In the sharp clashes which ensued between the government and the church the prophets were unsparing in their criticism of Christian behavior, especially of the "lukewarm" sort. The contrast in attitude is well exemplified in two documents emanating from the Domitianic terror, about 95-96—I Peter and Revelation. Warning of the imminent danger was sounded in I Peter, a letter addressed from Rome to the Christians in Asia Minor, exhorting the faithful to steady, calm, sober watchfulness and patient endurance under affliction, as following the example of Christ. But there must be no provocation, no cessation of well-doing to the enemy and slanderer without, but a ready and humble submission to the "king" and his governors in the fear of God. In marked opposition to I Peter's tone of reasonable, responsible, ecclesiastical authority stands the impassioned, vitriolic symphony of war and triumph against the satanic foe in the Revelation of John the seer.

Emphasis upon the speedy return of Christ and the descent of the New Jerusalem marked the rigoristic, uncompromising prophetism which led to the Montanist schism. This heresy, the "Phrygian frenzy," broke out in the village of Ardabau, not far from Philadelphia, about the middle of the century. In the ecstatic utterances and trances of one Montanus (who was, according to some accounts, a former priest of the orgiastic cult of Cybele, the Earth-Mother Goddess of Phrygia) and his two women disciples, the prophetesses Prisca and Maximilla, the Paraclete was supposedly heard announcing the imminent inauguration of the New Jerusalem in the little town of Pepuza. With great labor church leaders sought to contain the infection, but with only partial success. In north Phrygia, in the Tembris Valley, it remained strongly entrenched throughout the third century. [33]

The conflict between church and state in Asia Minor contributed materially to the shaping of Roman juridical procedure against Christianity. There is no evidence for the existence at this time, even after the government was aware of the distinction between Christianity and Judaism, of any edict proscribing Christianity as such. Like other Oriental religions, it stood under the vague threat of action against unauthorized religions and illicit associations, but as a matter of fact individual cases against Christians appear to have been dealt with *ad hoc*. Nero availed himself of an imputed charge of arson; the basis of Domitian's action is obscure. And it was just such ambiguity of legal precedent which induced the judicious Pliny, while governor of Bithynia in 112, to seek advice from Trajan. [34] The advances of Christianity in the province were marked, for there had been noticeable decline in the devotion shown at the temples, and preliminary trials of Christians, despite numerous apostasies, showed a widespread attachment to the faith. Pliny had used the offering of sacrifice to the image of the emperor as a convenient test in exposing true Christian believers, and considered their obdurate refusal to comply in this devotion as sufficient ground for punishment—for their "obstinacy," if for nothing else. But he was uneasy. Trajan's reply by no means clarified the issue, that is, whether Christians should be punished solely for profession of the name itself, or for the crimes which were alleged to be associated with it. He simply commended Pliny's method of handling the situation, adding a strong warning against the acceptance of anonymous accusations. It is little wonder, therefore, that Christian apologists of the second century complained that the church was persecuted for the mere name of "Christian" without any endeavor on the part of the state, in the teeth of its whole tradition of justice, to prove the charges of crime which the name was suspected of concealing.

The government, however, was unwilling to

---

[32] One's view of the date of the Pastorals depends in large part upon whether one sees in I Tim. 6:20 a specific reference to Marcion's *Antitheses*. If so, there remains the problem of their provenance, whether Asia Minor or Rome. For a pre-Marcion dating, about the year 100, see B. S. Easton, *The Pastoral Epistles* (New York: Charles Scribner's Sons, 1947).

[33] For discussion of the origins of Montanism see W. M. Calder, "Philadelphia and Montanism," *Bulletin of the John Rylands Library*, VII (1922-23), 309-54.

[34] Pliny the Younger *Letters* 96, 97.

take the initiative in bringing Christians to book, and accusations were left to private enterprise or public clamor. Conscientious magistrates were not always prone to give in to popular outcries. In 124 Hadrian sent a reply to the proconsul of Asia, Minicius Fundanus, reaffirming the principles laid down by Trajan. Accusations must be proved in open court, the punishment must fit the crime; blackmailers were to be severely dealt with.[35] What popular fury was capable of doing, in the way of forcing the hand of civil magistrates, may be read in the moving account sent by the church in Smyrna to its sister church in Philomelium—the *Martyrdom of Polycarp*. The companion of those who had "seen the Lord," the leader of the church in Asia Minor through a troubled generation, was sacrificed to the flames, after eighty-six years of service to his King, February 22, 156.[36]

IV. Greece

Across the Aegean the churches in Greece struggled similarly, if less conspicuously than their fellows in Asia Minor, with heresy, persecution, and problems of church order. Hegesippus, who visited Corinth about the middle of the second century, related that the church there was free of heresy until the bishopric of Primus, but we do not know the date of Primus' hegemony.[37] About the year 95, however, the Corinthian church was involved in a notorious factional dispute—a thing endemic at Corinth? (cf. I Cor. 1:10 ff.)—when certain parties of the younger brethren succeeded in removing from office the leaders of the church and appointing new bishops and deacons. Possibly the disgruntled groups were affected with a novel form of *gnosis,* not necessarily of the speculative variety, but of the boastful "being in the know" sort of liberty in behavior, offensive, as it had been there in Paul's time, to weaker brethren. The Roman church sent a forceful letter of rebuke—the epistle known as I Clement—admonishing the church to humility,

Christian charity and peace, and reminding the Corinthians of the sacrosanct order of church polity established by the apostles. But the letter reveals to us more of the mind and spirit of the church in Rome than of the details of the situation in Corinth.

Apparently the intervention of the Roman church was successful, for we find its letter regularly read in the liturgical assemblies at Corinth. Bishop Dionysius of Corinth spoke of this custom in a communication sent to Soter, bishop of Rome, about 166-74, thanking him for some generous material aid sent to Corinth by the Roman church. He also spoke of having read at the Sunday Eucharist the letter of Soter, sent with the gift. Many scholars believe that this letter of Soter is the homily which has been preserved under the title of II Clement. Eusebius had in his library other letters of Dionysius, some to churches in Greece and Crete, others to churches in Asia Minor, from which he made brief extracts in his *Church History.*[38] Marcionism was a special worry of church leaders in Greece. Polycarp, a generation before Dionysius, had warned the Philippians of the "first-born of Satan," [39] referring probably to Marcion; and one of Dionysius' correspondents, Philip, bishop of Gortyna in Crete, wrote a treatise (not extant) against Marcion.[40]

The church in Athens contributed two apologists for the Christian faith against paganism—appropriately enough, for the address to the Areopagus there, which the author of Acts attributed to Paul, is the germinal seed of all later Christian apologetic to the heathen. After the martyrdom of their bishop, Publius, the Athenian church wavered in its steadfastness to the faith, but it was restored to the truth by a philosopher-bishop named Quadratus. When the emperor Hadrian visited Athens in the year 125, Quadratus addressed to him an apology for Christianity, a brief extract of which is preserved by Eusebius.[41] A modern critic has plausibly argued that this extract is taken from the classic little treatise which has come down to us, incomplete and anonymous, as the Epistle to Diognetus.[42] True or not, the artful rhetoric of this "epistle" is well worthy of an Athenian origin. Its compact, paradoxically phrased description of Christians as "in the world, but not of it," is one of the most famous passages in Christian literature.

[35] The authenticity of this rescript of Hadrian has frequently been questioned. The original Latin version which Justin Martyr appended to his first *Apology* 68 has been lost, and in its place is the Greek translation of Eusebius *Church History* IV. 9.

[36] Or according to some authorities, February 23, 155. This is the oldest account of a "martyrdom" which has come down to us, and the first testimony to the observance in the local churches of the anniversaries of their martyrs with liturgical celebration. A party of Philadelphian brethren suffered with Polycarp. Also a "Phrygian," with characteristic zeal, freely offered himself for the ordeal, but failed to bear up under the test. Calder, *op. cit.,* p. 334, points out the anti-Montanist implication here: "Better, like Polycarp, withdraw and try to avoid arrest; if it is the will of God that arrest cannot be avoided, then a good Catholic can die as bravely as any Phrygian fanatic of them all."

[37] Eusebius *Church History* IV. 22. 2.

[38] IV. 23.

[39] Polyc. Phil. 7:1.

[40] Eusebius *Church History* IV. 25.

[41] *Ibid.* IV. 3; cf. IV. 23. 2-3.

[42] Andriesson, "The Authorship of the Epistula ad Diognetum," *Vigiliae Christianae,* I (1947), 129-36. According to Andriesson, the Eusebian extract belongs to the lacuna of VII. 6-7. "Diognetus," the tutor of Marcus Aurelius, is Hadrian.

They dwell in their own fatherlands, but as if sojourners; they share all things as citizens, and suffer all things as strangers. Every foreign country is their fatherland, and every fatherland a foreign country. . . . They live upon earth, but their citizenship is in heaven. . . . In short, what the soul is to the body, that the Christians are in the world.

The other Athenian apologist was Aristides, whose work was addressed to Antoninus Pius sometime between 138 and 147. Less original than Diognetus it follows closely the pattern of ideas in The Preaching of Peter, with particular emphasis upon Christians as a "third race."

V. Egypt

The story of the origins and development of Christianity in Egypt down to the last two decades of the second century is wrapped in obscurity. No credence can be given to the legend, first recorded by Eusebius,[43] that Mark the Evangelist, disciple of Peter, first brought the gospel to Egypt and founded churches in Alexandria. The Western text of Acts 18:25 states that Apollos was not only a native of Alexandria, but had been instructed in the Christian faith in his native land. There is nothing inherently impossible about this tradition. It would have been strange indeed if Christian missionaries had not been early attracted to mission work among the large and influential Jewish population in Egypt, and had not won some converts there in circles of Jewish scholars "mighty in the Scriptures." The typological and allegorical exegesis of the Old Testament which characterized the Jewish schools in Alexandria, and which was promoted with such vigor and ingenuity in the Christian catechetical school there in the time of Clement and Origen, has given occasion to many modern scholars to associate with the Christian community in Alexandria two documents of the sub-apostolic period—the Epistle to the Hebrews and the so-called Epistle of Barnabas.

The literary associations of Hebrews, whether it was written to or from Alexandria, link it more definitely to the history of the church in Rome. In the case of the Epistle of Barnabas there is actually no precise indication of its place of origin. Until the fourth century, however, the epistle was highly esteemed in Egypt and generally accepted as authentic and canonical. The epistle consists of two sections, one of *gnosis* or theological exegesis, the other of *didachē* or ethics. The former is a highly polemical, anti-Jewish tract which seeks to establish the notion, by means of tortuous and fanciful

allegories, that the Old Testament cannot be understood literally, as the Jews imagined, but only as a prefiguring of Christianity. The latter section (chs. 18–20) contains the teaching of the "two ways," found also in the Syrian Didache, though in a much less systematic arrangement. It seems to have been a later addition to the epistle, derived from the same source used by the compiler of the Didache.[44] The date of the Epistle of Barnabas is problematical. Many scholars assign it to the year 130-31 because of the allusion in ch. 16 to the rebuilding of the temple in Jerusalem by the Gentiles. But the author refers not to the temple of Jupiter which Hadrian contemplated erecting on Mount Zion, but to the Jewish temple; and there is no evidence that the Romans ever had any such project in mind. A better indication of date is afforded by the apocalyptic passage in ch. 4, based upon Dan. 7:7-8 (cf. Rev. 13:1). The reference to the "ten horns," succeeded by a "little horn" which plucks up the preceding three horns, makes a date in the reign of Nerva (96-98) or in the early years of Trajan more probable.

The attitude of the author of Barnabas with respect to the Old Testament gives the epistle certain affinities with nascent Gnosticism. We know that many of the early Gnostic teachers found their way to Alexandria, notably Basilides and his son Isidore. Egypt also produced the greatest of all the Gnostic theologians, Valentinus, although it is not certain whether Valentinus had developed his system before he left Alexandria for Rome. All the evidence which we possess respecting the history of Christianity in Egypt before the end of the second century, fragmentary though it is, indicates the pervasive influence of Gnostic ideas, particularly those of an ascetic and docetic tendency. Some critics have with reason maintained that Egyptian Christianity was predominantly Gnostic until the time of Bishop Demetrius, about 189-232, who succeeded, with the support of the Roman church, in steering the church in Alexandria into a more orthodox course. If such a judgment is correct, it would explain in large part the loss of so much of early Egyptian Christian sources, inasmuch as later generations would have no interest in preserving heretical literature. Even the great catechetical school, whose history first emerges under the leadership of Pantaenus, about 180, and his successor Clement, was not entirely free of Gnostic speculation. The thinly veiled Docetism of Clement's

[43] *Church History* II. 16. See H. I. Bell, "Evidences of Christianity in Egypt During the Roman Period," *Harvard Theological Review*, XXXVII (1944), 185-204.

[44] Edgar J. Goodspeed, *A History of Early Christian Literature* (Chicago: University of Chicago Press, 1942), pp. 31-33, 168-70; and his article "The Didache, Barnabas and the Doctrina," *Anglican Theological Review*, XXVII (1945), 228-47.

Christology, his fondness for the term "Gnostic" to describe the advanced Christian, whose knowledge placed him on a higher spiritual plane than that of the simple believer, his conception of God as the philosophical Absolute—these and other of his doctrines came very near the edge of heresy. Indeed his most important theological work, the *Hypotyposes*, seems to have fallen beyond the bounds of orthodoxy. From the animadversions of later writers upon this work one may easily surmise the reason why it is no longer extant. After Clement's retirement from Alexandria, owing to the sharp persecution which broke out in Egypt in 202, Bishop Demetrius took the initiative in reconstituting the school under closer episcopal supervision, and appointed the youthful Origen as catechist. But even Origen, bitter foe as he was of Gnosticism, proved too daring a thinker and too insubordinate a protégé for his patron. Origen was dismissed in 231.

By the middle of the second century there were circulating in Egypt two gospels at least, other than the four canonical Gospels—the Gospel According to the Hebrews (not to be confused with the Nazarene gospel mentioned above) and the Gospel According to the Egyptians, both in Greek. The latter seems to have been the primary "gospel" in Egypt until it was supplanted by the canonical Gospels in the last quarter of the second century. It has been conjectured that the "Hebrews' Gospel" was the one used by the Jewish Christians in Egypt, the "Egyptians' Gospel," by the Gentile Christians. It is impossible to say, because of the meagerness of extant fragments, what literary relationship they had, if any, with the canonical Gospels. Clement quotes both of them with great respect. The Gospel According to the Egyptians was particularly ascetic in tendency, and Clement speaks of its use by the ascetic sect of the Encratites. There is evidence of its use in Gnostic and other unorthodox circles down to the fourth century.

Other collections of gospel tradition circulated freely in Egypt in the early third century. The "Sayings of Jesus" found among the Oxyrhynchus papyri in 1897 are perhaps the most famous. Whether they were culled from written gospels, including the canonical four, cannot be definitely determined. In 1935 the British Museum trustees published a sizable fragment of a hitherto unknown written gospel, which has been dated as prior to 150.[45] Analysis

proves that the compiler used the Gospel of John, but his use of the canonical Synoptic Gospels is debatable. Confirmation of the circulation of the Fourth Gospel in Egypt by the second quarter of the second century was adduced the same year by the discovery among the papyri of the John Rylands Library of a fragment of the Fourth Gospel itself, of slightly earlier date than the British Museum fragment.[46] These finds attest to a vigorous and varied dissemination of Christianity at least a half century before the great literary productions of the Alexandrian school. The Gospel of John was particularly favored by the Gnostic schools, especially that of Valentinus. Clement of Alexandria considered it the "spiritual" Gospel, to be preferred above all the others.

VI. Rome and the West

Outside of Rome we have no information about Christian communities of the earliest period in the western, Latin part of the empire. In the capital itself the church was predominantly eastern and Greek-speaking in membership, gathered from the heavy Jewish and foreign settlements, particularly in the regions of the Aventine, Trastevere, and the Subura.[47] Yet we know from archaeological evidence that by the middle of the second century, if not earlier, the Roman church counted certain influential protectors and members among the Roman aristocracy, notably the Flavian and Acilian families. The church was noted for wealth and generosity.

Despite abundant documentary material, some of which we have already had occasion to note—such as Hebrews, I Peter, I Clement, etc. —it is impossible to trace the development of the inner organization of the Roman church after the death of Peter and Paul. Lists of its early bishops, gathered by Hegesippus and Irenaeus, are sufficiently authentic regarding the names, but are utterly devoid of chronological data. We do not know whether the Roman church was "monarchically" governed from the first, or whether it passed through a period of a "collegiate episcopate." Ignatius, when writing to the church in Rome, made no reference to its leaders or government, since he knew nothing of it. It is probable, as La Piana has suggested, that the Christians in Rome formed at first separate communities or *ecclesiolae*, according to their varying native backgrounds, trades, or points of view, after the

---

[45] H. I. Bell and T. C. Skeat, eds., *Fragments of an Unknown Gospel and Other Early Christian Papyri* (London: Trustees of the British Museum, 1935), and *The New Gospel Fragments* (London: Trustees of the British Museum, 1935). See also C. H. Dodd, "A New Gospel," *Bulletin of the John Rylands Library*, XX (1936), 56-92.

[46] C. H. Roberts, "An Unpublished Fragment of the Fourth Gospel in the John Rylands Library," *Bulletin of the John Rylands Library*, XX (1936), 45-55.
[47] G. La Piana, "Foreign Groups in Rome During the First Centuries of the Empire," *Harvard Theological Review*, XX (1927), 183-403 (a fundamental study for the background of Christianity in Rome)

manner of the religious associations of non-Christian immigrants. By the latter part of the second century these had been gradually welded into a strong, unified organization.

Only when this process of unification was well under way did the Roman church find itself confronted with heretical tendencies brought thither by Marcion and other Gnostics. Roman Christian literature down to the time of Justin Martyr, about 150, reveals little interest in or worry about theological speculation. Its concerns were ethical and practical. It is characteristic of this church that its written Gospel, Mark, portrayed Jesus primarily within the sphere of action rather than of discourse. In its ethos the Roman church was continuous with the spirit of the Hellenistic Jewish synagogue. The law of the Old Testament, idealized and universalized, stripped of its particularistic elements, transfused with Christian virtues of humility and love, remained as an authoritative pattern of precept and example. In I Peter and I Clement one senses this continuity of ethics between the moral law of the old covenant and the commandments of the gospel, between the heroes of faith and fortitude before and after Christ. Even in the more theologically oriented Epistle to the Hebrews the continuity is there—between the foreshadowing types of atonement and the high priestly offering of Christ, between the examples of patient faith among the "elders" and "cloud of witnesses" and Jesus "the author and finisher of faith." The liturgical prayer of I Clement could have been recited with slight alteration in the synagogue.

The one controversy which marred the orderly peace of inner development at Rome concerned the discipline of penitents. Generally speaking the primitive church was severe with grievous sinners. The author of Hebrews sided with the rigorists: "It is impossible to restore again to repentance those who have once been enlightened . . . if they then commit apostasy" (Heb. 6:4-6). But there were voices of moderation, advocates of the second chance. Among them was a minor prophet of the church named Hermas, a brother of bishop Pius (about 140). In the collection of his visions, commandments, and similitudes, called The Shepherd—materials which he was permitted to deliver from time to time in the church's assemblies—we find the first formulations of a doctrine and discipline of Catholic penance. When the issue was settled in the third century in favor of the moderates, the Roman church added to its creed the clause "I believe . . . in the forgiveness of sins."

In the work of Justin Martyr the church in Rome entered fully and decisively into the main stream of theological development. We find in Justin a broad approach to Christian truth at once scriptural and philosophical. He was squarely loyal to traditional faith and morality, yet free in appropriating the truer insights of contemporary non-Christian speculation to the service of the church. A native of Samaria, Justin early became a peripatetic seeker for truth amidst the various philosophical schools, until one day a chance meeting with a Christian at Ephesus brought him to the end of his quest. About the year 150 he established himself at Rome as a lay professor of Christianity, a kind of philosopher-catechist. About 165 he was martyred, a victim of the revenge of a Cynic philosopher Crescens, whom Justin had worsted in a public discussion. The simple but eloquent account of Justin's martyrdom together with a few of his companions and pupils has come down to us. In his resolute and valiant defense of the faith before the prefect Rusticus, Justin said, among other things:

I have endeavoured to learn all doctrines, but I have acquiesced at last in the true doctrines, those namely of the Christians, even though they do not please those who hold false opinions. . . . Through prayer we can be saved on account of our Lord Jesus Christ, even when we have been punished, because this shall become to us salvation and confidence at the more fearful and universal judgment-seat of our Lord and Saviour.[48]

Of Justin's voluminous writings, among them treatises against Marcion and other heretics, only two survive: an *Apology*, with a later appendix commonly called the *Second Apology*, addressed to Antoninus, and a lengthy apology against Judaism called *Dialogue with Trypho*.[49] Both works were written at Rome within the decade 150-160. The key to Justin's theology is his doctrine of the Logos or Word of God. With Stoic and Platonic terms he developed the idea adumbrated in the prologue of the Fourth Gospel. The Logos as divine or "second God" is the mediator between God and the world, the agent of creation, the inspirer of prophets and wise men of old, both Jewish and pagan, incarnate in Jesus, and the assistant of every rational creature in its warfare against evil demons of error and sin. In his exegesis of Scripture Justin laid great emphasis upon the fulfillment of Old Testament prophecy in Christ, an argument which had much to do with his own conversion, and one which served him in debate with Jew and Gnostic alike. He also took great pains to answer the popular calumnies against the church's cultic practices,

48 See B. J. Kidd, *Documents Illustrative of the History of the Church* (London: Society for Promoting Christian Knowledge, 1920), I, 84-86, for an English translation of the *Acta Justini*.
49 See note 11.

and in so doing argued persuasively for the nobility of Christian ethics and the rationality of Christian worship.

The defects of Justin on the critical side are sufficiently obvious to rob him of a place among the world's great thinkers, or even the church's most eminent theologians. Yet it is fair to say that no Christian writer has exerted a more far-reaching influence, if only for the reason that no succeeding generation of Christian apologists and theologians has been able to ignore the signposts along the way toward truth which he marked out. In the generation which immediately followed Justin all the titans of Catholic faith—Irenaeus, Tertullian, Hippolytus, and Origen—were conscious disciples and developers of Justin's doctrine.

VII. Selected Bibliography

BARDY, G. *The Church at the End of the First Century*, tr. P. W. Singleton. London: Sands & Co., 1938.

GOODSPEED, E. J. *A History of Early Christian Literature*. Chicago: University of Chicago Press, 1942.

GRANT, R. M. *Second-Century Christianity*. London: Society for Promoting Christian Knowledge, 1946.

HARNACK, ADOLF VON. *History of Dogma*, tr. Neil Buchanan. Boston: Roberts Bros., 1895-1903.

KLEIST, J. A. *Ancient Christian Writers*, Nos. 1 and 6. Westminster, Md.: The Newman Bookshop, 1946, 1948.

LEBRETON, J., and ZEILLER, J. *The History of the Primitive Church*, tr. E. C. Messenger. London: Burns, Oates & Washbourne, 1942-46, Vols. I-III.

LIETZMANN, HANS. *The Beginnings of the Christian Church*, tr. Bertram Lee Woolf. New York: Charles Scribner's Sons, 1938.

————. *The Founding of the Church Universal*, tr. Bertram Lee Woolf. New York: Charles Scribner's Sons, 1938.

LIGHTFOOT, J. B. *The Apostolic Fathers*, rev. ed. London: Macmillan & Co., 1889, 1890, Vols. I-V.

WEISS, J. *The History of Primitive Christianity*, ed. F. C. Grant. New York: Wilson-Erickson, 1937, especially II, 707-866.

The Gospel According to

ST. MATTHEW

Introduction and Exegesis by SHERMAN E. JOHNSON
Exposition by GEORGE A. BUTTRICK

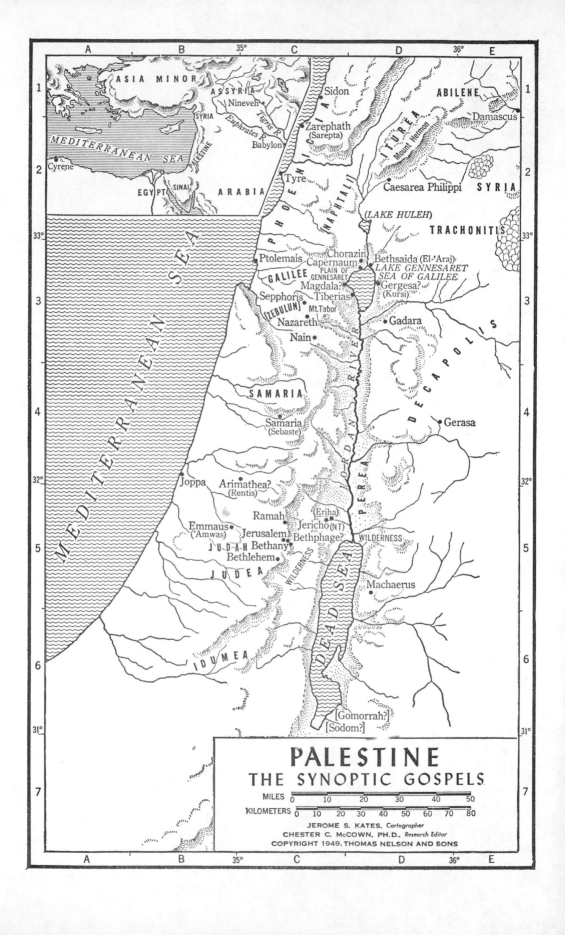

PALESTINE
THE SYNOPTIC GOSPELS

MILES 0   10   20   30   40   50
KILOMETERS 0   10   20   30   40   50   60   70   80

JEROME S. KATES, *Cartographer*
CHESTER C. McCOWN, PH.D., *Research Editor*
COPYRIGHT 1949, THOMAS NELSON AND SONS

MATTHEW

INTRODUCTION

When a convert to Christianity in the late first century or early second century read the Gospel According to Matthew for the first time, he read it as a manual of membership rather than as a part of his Bible. It was one of the recent "best sellers" of Christian literature. A present-day reader who is adequately "introduced" to this most influential of all Christian books should be led to look at it, not as one who has had some acquaintance with it all his life, but as an ancient Christian into whose hands it has just come. This is a difficult feat of historical imagination, but it is worth attempting.

I. Place in the Christian Church

Sometime in the second century the "Gospel" emerged as a fourfold collection, the components of which bore the titles "According to Matthew," "According to Mark," "According to Luke," and "According to John." [1] Matthew headed this collection, and one reason among many for this pre-eminence is the fact that nearly every second-century Christian writer quotes the book more frequently than any other Gospel; for example, the citations from Matthew in Bks. III and IV of Irenaeus *Against Heresies* are more numerous than those from all other Gospels combined.

Matthew has never lost this popularity. As the gospel manuscripts were copied and corruptions crept in, it was Matthew's wording which most often affected the text of the other Gospels, rather than the reverse. Church lectionaries, of course, attempt to use the Gospels equally—the Sunday Gospels of the Roman Mass are evenly divided between Matthew, Luke, and John, with Mark a poor fourth—yet in the 1929 revision of the American Book of Common Prayer Matthew is favored over Luke

with thirty-seven to thirty-three pericopes, John being used twenty-seven times and Mark six times. Matthew's account of the Passion, read on Palm Sunday, is the best known of the four. Groups as radically different from each other as Roman Catholics and Christian Scientists appeal to Matthew for the support of their particular doctrines—the former because of the honor paid to the apostle Peter, the latter because this Gospel sets the miracles forth in a form most likely to inspire confidence. It is not hard to understand why Roman Catholics and many conservative Protestants attach the greatest weight to the tradition that one of Jesus' twelve disciples wrote the Gospel. The layman frequently says that John, or perhaps Luke, is his favorite of the four; yet it is probable that he will make actual use more often of Matthew, either for defense and controversy or for the upbuilding of his moral and spiritual life. Even if there were no other reasons, its presence at the beginning of the printed New Testament—and its inclusion of the Sermon on the Mount—would ensure this.

Matthew came into its prominent position in the second-century church almost certainly because it had been the first of all the Gospels to be accepted by some great center of Christendom. This center was probably Antioch.[2] Books were not originally called "gospels": there was but one gospel, the good news of salvation through Jesus Christ. This document, the "Gospel" of Matthew, contained the gospel as it was thought Matthew had understood it; it was believed to be "according to" Matthew's teaching or point of view. Soon the book was carried to other parts of the empire where similar writings already existed. It is likely that in Rome the dominant authority was the book we know as the "Gospel According to Mark."

[1] See article "The Canon of the New Testament," Vol. I.

[2] B. H. Streeter, *The Four Gospels* (4th ed.; London: Macmillan & Co., 1930), pp. 500-23.

Matthew, being fuller and more evidently useful, nearly crowded it out, and it is only by a kind of happy miracle that Mark was preserved at all. The document known later as "According to Luke," though it was somewhat discredited by the backing of the heretic Marcion, must have been firmly established in the regions whence Marcion came, and elsewhere, and its intrinsic excellence demanded its preservation. Latest of all, the hauntingly beautiful and mysterious Gospel of John found a secure place in the sacred quadrangle. Thus Matthew, which had been most widely popular, and which for many must have been *the* Gospel, came to be the first among equals—in Renan's crisp Gallic phrase, the "most important book in the world."

II. Character

But why did laymen and leaders in the house-churches of the Greco-Roman world read Matthew so avidly? Partly because of its completeness. Not only did it contain practically all the narrative material of Mark; to this it added accounts of Jesus' infancy and resurrection appearances, and the fullest collection of his ethical teaching then available. Whatever form the Sermon on the Mount had when it was first written down, Matthew must have expanded it by the addition of material from other sources, particularly in ch. 6; and as it left the evangelist's hand it gave an arresting picture of Christian morality as contrasted with earlier and easier ethical systems. The convert who knew something of Greek philosophy or Judaism and read Matthew could never forget. "Ye have heard that it was said to them of old time . . . : but I say unto you . . ."

Whether by conscious design or not, Matthew in every way met the needs of church life. This was the principal reason for its popularity. The book was conveniently arranged and could easily be separated into sections for reading in public worship or elsewhere; and its style was smooth, pithy, and quotable. Matthew quietly eliminated questions and doubts which Mark's Gospel had too easily raised in the reader's mind. Jesus' baptism could not be interpreted as a sign of personal repentance; Peter was praised for hailing the Master as Messiah; the miracles took place instantaneously; the body of Jesus was not stolen from the tomb, and such a story arose only because the guards had been bribed. Matthew had but a limited space for composition—perhaps he originally wrote on a papyrus roll thirty feet or less in length—hence he told only such stories as were useful for preaching and teaching. Mark's interest in the story for its own sake disappeared, and accounts of miracles were boiled down to their essential elements.

Members of the Jewish synagogue lived according to the law, which had an answer for every problem of life. It was notorious that the apostle Paul and some of his followers had repudiated the Jewish law, at least as the rabbis understood it. Were Christians then "without law"? No one who read Matthew could be in any doubt. Jesus' teaching was itself a new law, which did not so much abrogate the old as "fill" it with the meaning God had intended it to have. It was important that a Christian should learn and understand this law, after the pattern of the earliest disciples, who were scribes trained for the kingdom of heaven (13:52). The Sermon on the Mount, simple though it seemed to be, was a formal code which Jesus intended his disciples to observe. The evangelist never failed to remind his readers that they would be judged on the basis of their performance (12:37; 16:27), and the great day might come soon. When the Son of man sits on the throne of his glory, men will be rewarded for their deeds of mercy, even if they do not realize that to help men in misery is to help Christ himself (25:37-40).

Christianity was the perfect morality; hence its laws regarding retaliation, oaths, and sexual relationships. But the evangelist knew that there were hard cases; and even if "hard cases make bad law," the law nevertheless takes account of them. Hence we find in his book, as we do also in the Pauline letters (I Cor. 7:12-15), the beginnings of ecclesiastical law: there is *one* situation in which divorce is permissible (5:31-32; 19:9). Christians are free from the temple tax, which bound only the Jews; but they should pay it in order to avoid giving offense (17:24-27). There is also a kind of penitential system. Every Christian should know from the Sermon on the Mount how to behave toward brothers in the community, but what could the congregation do if one member wronged another and was recalcitrant? Hence the Gospel ruled that if both personal entreaty and the judgment of the group were unavailing, the offender must be treated as a "heathen" and a "tax collector," that is, excommunicated (18:15-17). Presbyterian church law follows this provision at the present day. A modern—especially if he has never experienced a warm and intimate church life—might raise the uncomfortable question, "Just how *did* Jesus treat heathen and tax collectors?" But the evangelist never doubted that the judgment of the group was ratified in heaven, for where the church is, Christ is present (18:18-20).

Over against the lofty standard of the sermon and the rule of excommunication stands the emphasis on forgiveness and the boundless mercy of Christ. The evangelist was not only a large-hearted man; he had caught the spirit of the original Christian message. The penitent brother must be welcomed back, not seven but seventy-seven times (18:21-35). The conclusion of this piece of church law is the magnificent parable of the unforgiving slave. Matthew would certainly be slow to invoke stern discipline; he bids Christians to let the weeds grow along with the wheat, for God himself in his good time will make the separation (13:37-43). Here he is very different from those Christians of the first two centuries who wished to keep the church pure at all costs, and refused to reinstate the excommunicated more than once, if at all.

Such liberality had its dangers. If the Christian church was to be a society of education, discipline, and mercy for the weak and sinful, what was to become of the ideal standard which stood in the forefront of Jesus' teaching? Matthew seemed to answer that perfection was still possible for a few rare spirits. It might, for example, be better not to marry; but not everyone can accept this advice (19:10-12). The rich young man, though unwilling to sacrifice his personal property, had nevertheless kept the commandments which were binding on all men; he failed only to be numbered among the "perfect" (19:21). This is only a slight and subtle difference from Mark's story, but it is important: the distinction between ordinary Christians and the "perfect" has had momentous consequences for Christian ethics. Matthew, who was writing for the church, had to deal somehow with the needs of the many and at the same time to recognize the uncompromising character of Jesus' teaching. The problem is still with us.

Christ's teaching on the devotional life, as Matthew has edited it, reflects the self-consciousness of the church as separate from Judaism. The new way is contrasted with that of the Gentiles and the hypocrites, who for Matthew must represent the orthodox Jews of his time. The evangelist is especially interested in promoting prayer, fasting, and almsgiving, and whenever possible he emphasizes the power of faith and prayer. His version of the Lord's Prayer is fuller and more liturgical than Luke's.

Many other passages reflect the same churchly interests. Mark, Q, and the apostle Paul had all tried to explain why Israel had rejected Jesus, though his mission was to the chosen people. Although Paul laid part of the blame on the Jews' willfulness (Rom. 10:18-21), he sometimes spoke as though they could not altogether help their own blindness (II Cor. 3:12-16; 4:3-4). Mark believed that the stumbling of the Jews was part of the divine plan and that Jesus had taught in parables in order to conceal the message (Mark 4:10-12, 33-34). Matthew develops this idea further. For example, Jesus originally spoke the parable of the great supper (22:1-5, 8-10) against the Pharisees who criticized him for inviting to the marriage feast (that is, into the kingdom) not suitable guests, but any who could be found in the streets. But Matthew—or perhaps his source—inserted vss. 6 and 7: because the Jews slighted the invitation and slew Christ's messengers, God has sent his armies, destroyed those murderers, and burned their city. Thus Jesus himself was made to predict Israel's rejection of the gospel and its punishment (cf. also 23:29-36). According to Matthew this was also foreshadowed in the cornerstone saying of Ps. 118: the kingdom of God will be taken away from the Jews and given to a nation producing the fruits of it (21:42-43). This nation is the church, which is composed of Jews and Gentiles alike. Matthew, more than any other evangelist, seeks to prove that Jesus is the true Messiah of the Jews. At the very beginning of his book stands a genealogy showing his royal descent from Abraham and David to Joseph (1:16-17). Micah and other prophets foretold the birth and ministry of Jesus and the signs which accompanied them (2:6, 15, 18; 4:15-16; 12:18-21; etc.). But Israel "after the flesh" had repudiated him, and now he belonged to the new community.

The Old Testament was in fact a Christian book. Jesus, like his contemporaries, quoted it as a Jewish book, even though he often insisted on its spirit rather than its literal meaning, and sometimes cited one passage in opposition to another (Mark 10:5-9); even in the severest controversies it was still "our" book, "our" common presupposition. But Matthew and most early Christians read it in the light of the gospel and expected to find every significant event of Christ's life foreshadowed there. The evangelist's use of quotations often seems strange to us—especially those which are prefixed by the formula "that it might be fulfilled which was spoken by the prophet"—but it can be laid to his twofold doctrine: what Jesus did must have been part of the divine plan; and every prediction of the prophets must come to pass, especially in the age ushered in by the Messiah.

First-century Judaism was a missionary religion. The impulse to propagate it was not precisely that which sent Christians to the end of the earth, namely, the desire to save souls in danger of damnation, for according to many Jewish teachers righteous Gentiles would be saved. Rather it was the Jews' horror of the pagan way of life, with its moral and ritual defilement, and their desire to bring to others the rich spiritual benefits of life according to the law, and to add to the glory of the God of Israel and his people. Whatever the original motive, rabbis like Hillel took it as axiomatic that proselytes should be encouraged. There was another significant difference: to become a Jew meant joining a new national group. Jewish proselyting was sporadic—it was often opposed by political forces, and it could not often be promoted on a large scale—nevertheless, Matthew knew of those who crossed land and sea to make a single proselyte (23:15). The Christian community which Matthew represented was even more aggressively missionary. Its Lord's parting commission, according to Matthew, had been to make disciples of all nations, to baptize them, and to teach them all of Jesus' commandments; he himself would be with the missionaries till the end of the age (28:18-20). The good news had to be proclaimed to all nations before the end could come (24:14). This may help to explain why the evangelist includes the parable of the laborers in the vineyard (20:1-16), for God will reward those who go to work for him even at the last hour.

Many kinds of believers are caught up in a movement which develops in such urgent haste. An enemy sows poisonous weeds among the wheat (13:25, 38-39), and the dragnet gathers fish of every kind (13:47-49). Not only does the church contain loose-living members, but on the fringe of it are eccentric groups which someday will be called heretical. Many are caused to stumble, and they hate and destroy each other (24:10); many false prophets have arisen, and the love of many Christians has grown cold because of the increase of lawlessness (24:11-12). Perhaps Matthew is thinking of the doctrine that believers need not be subject to any law at all. In this connection we are to understand his hope that in the great tribulation Christians will not have to flee on the sabbath (24:20) for a good Christian, like a Jew, keeps the sabbath law. His only solution for the problem of antinomianism, however, it to leave the erring to the judgment of God at the end of the age.

Apparently Matthew came close to equating this very mixed community, which we call the church, with the kingdom of God. It is "out of his kingdom" that the Son of man will purge "all causes of sin and all evil-doers" (13:41); and the kingdom of heaven is like the net which draws all kinds of fish (13:47). On the other hand "the field is the world" (13:38), and perhaps his thought is that the message of the kingdom attracts these people, rather than that the church is the kingdom. Yet the close connection remains, and for all practical purposes those who enter the kingdom also enter this world-wide church, to which the commission has been given, and at whose congregational meetings the risen Christ is present (18:20). Its teachers or rabbis have the power to bind and loose, that is, to permit or forbid certain courses of action, and their decisions are ratified in heaven (18:18). Among the disciples Peter has a certain pre-eminence, even though his occasional lack of faith is just as much emphasized as in the Gospel of Mark (Matt. 14:31); the reason is that to him God first revealed the full secret of Jesus' messiahship (16:17). Though he had been a waverer, Jesus made a rock of him; a man of such gifts and character provides a firm foundation for the church (16:18). Of the four evangelists only Matthew uses the word "church" (16:18; 18:17; in the latter passage it refers to the local congregation). Peter is for Matthew the ideal Christian rabbi; if he had named his own book he might well have called it "The Good News According to Peter." Perhaps he is consciously opposing those who claim for James and other earthly relatives of Jesus the supreme leadership of the Christian community. Traditionally James was the first bishop of Jerusalem; whether this is strictly accurate or not, he was succeeded by other men who were his kinsmen, and as late as the reign of Domitian the grandsons of Jude held a special position in the Palestinian church. It is a fair guess that in the first Gospel the church of Syria is meaning to claim for its hero Peter (not Paul or James or any other) the truest understanding of the original Christian message.

The message of Matthew, as we have seen, is not merely the good news of salvation; it involves also the new law and the new church. Hence Matthew's great emphasis on Christian leadership. True disciples are missionaries (28:19), scribes or rabbis instructed for the kingdom of heaven, who bring out of their storehouses things new and old (13:52), prophets and wise men (23:34), and workers of miracles who show the "signs of an apostle" by healing the sick and casting out demons (10:1, 8; these commands come at the conclusion of a series of Jesus' miracles).[3]

Matthew is a catholic or ecumenical Gospel in more than one sense of the word. It could serve the needs of a world church because its material represented more than one point of view. Many of its stories and sayings received their form in the early days of the Christian movement when most Christians kept the law, though with a difference, and perforce became involved in rabbinical controversies; it is from one point of view the most Jewish of the Gospels. In other ways it is anti-Jewish and pre-

[3] B. W. Bacon, *Studies in Matthew* (New York: Henry Holt & Co., 1930), p. 187.

supposes the Gentile mission. Side by side we find the law and Christian freedom; one can quote Matthew either for or against Pharisaic authority (23:2; 15:12-14), for or against fasting and the sabbath regulations. One reason for this may be that Matthew recognized that Jewish and Gentile Christianity alike had merits, which he wished to preserve; another is that he was an honest compiler. He had sources of various kinds, and for the most part reproduced them faithfully.

III. Framework and Method of Composition

Discussion of the date and authorship of the Gospel has been postponed because a judgment on these questions depends partly on the character of the book and what we can learn about its relation to the other Gospels and to early Christianity generally. It may be considered settled, with as great certainty as one can ever achieve in literary criticism, that Mark is the principal source used by Matthew and Luke.[4] Therefore it is well to compare Matthew's Gospel with the others in order to discover the author's methods.

Mark attempts to tell his story in chronological order. We can discover no traces of any long, connected narrative in the other Synoptic sources, and when Matthew and Luke attempt a different order, they probably have no independent tradition of the sequence of events on which they can rely. Even Mark has to arrange his materials in his rough framework as best he can. Throughout his Gospel we find quick, abrupt transitions from one incident to another, and verbose editorial summaries. Matthew and Luke adopt much of Mark's framework and most of his materials. But unlike Matthew, Luke groups his Marcan stories and sayings in large blocks and in between them puts other blocks of non-Marcan material. For example, Luke 5:12–6:19 is largely a rewriting of Mark 1:40–3:19, and this is followed by 6:20–8:3, a section made up of material from a source usually called Q (largely paralleled in Matt. 5; 7; 8; 11) plus pericopes not found in the other Gospels. Luke at 8:4 again begins to copy Mark. The special character of Luke's Gospel is owing to his use of peculiar sources and to the relative smoothness with which all the parts are edited. Luke did not organize his book topically. He put his sections into what he took to be the best chronological order, roughly that of Mark; where he lacked this basis for a chronological judgment, he was governed either by artistic considerations or by the order in his other sources.

A glance at the outline (pp. 246-49) will show that Matthew put his Gospel together very differently, but with the greatest artistry and care. His framework is a marvelous combination of the chronological and the topical. He preserved the main lines of Mark's order but treated its details freely; for example, ch. 9 is largely made up of stories from Mark 2:1-22; 5:21-43; and 10:46-52, all of which came under the topic of miracles. As Bacon and others have discovered, the story of Jesus' life in Matthew is interrupted by five great discourses (5:1–7:29; 9:35–11:1; 13:1-58; 18:1–19:1; 24:1–26:2), most of which conclude with a special formula (e.g., 7:28-29, 11:1).[5] Some such fivefold arrangement may have existed in Q, but in the discourses and elsewhere Matthew weaves Q in with Mark and other sources. A good place to observe this in detail is in 9:35–10:40 or in ch. 13 (especially the parable of the mustard seed, 13:31-32). The reader who carefully studies these sections can see why investigators insist on the priority of Mark and the hypothesis of Q. It is easier to suppose that Matthew has used Mark and Q than that Mark has done the abbreviating (with expansions in some places); and it is easier to suppose that Luke has used Q than that he has followed Matthew, carefully separating non-Marcan material and putting it in Mark-free areas.

Perhaps it was for purposes of easy memorization that Matthew often grouped his materials in threes, fives, sevens, and other numerical schemes. For example, the miracles in chs. 8 and 9 are in groups of three, and there are seven parables in ch. 13. The genealogy is in three fourteens.

IV. Use of Sources

By comparing his Gospel with Mark, one can learn much about how Matthew deals with his sources. Many of his changes are dictated by doctrinal motives. He is, for example, eager to safeguard Jesus' divine power and his perfect goodness against any possible denial or detraction. The changes in the story of the Baptism and at a few other points have already been mentioned. Matthew's omissions are significant; for example, Mark 1:43 (Jesus' apparent harshness toward the leper); Mark 3:5; 10:14 (his anger); Mark 1:24; 3:11 (the theory that the demons recognized him, no doubt omitted because Jesus had been charged with commerce with Beelzebul); Mark 3:21 (the charge of insanity); Mark 6:48 ("he wished to pass them by"); Mark 2:7b ("Who can forgive sins, except one, namely God?"). In Mark 10:17-18 Jesus is called "Good teacher," and answers that no one

---

[4] See article "The Growth of the Gospels," pp. 60-74 of this volume.

[5] Bacon, op. cit., pp. xv-xvii.

is good but God; in Matt. 19:16-17 he says, "Why do you ask me concerning what is good?" The addition of Matt. 12:5-7 justifies Jesus' sabbath teaching as being in accordance with the Jewish law; contrast also 26:61 with Mark 14:58. Finally, Jesus is no longer the carpenter (Mark 6:3) but the carpenter's son (Matt. 13:55).

Matthew also defends the honor of the twelve. More clearly than Mark he pictures them as Jesus' special disciples, comparable to the students of a rabbi. They, not the crowd, are his true family (12:49=Mark 3:34), and unlike the crowd they have spiritual perception (13:16-17; contrast Mark 4:13). Even before Caesarea Philippi they hail him as Son of God (14:33). References to their ignorance and bewilderment are deleted (Mark 9:6, 10, 32) or toned down (cf. Matt. 16:9-12 with Mark 8:17-21). It is not the sons of Zebedee, but their mother, who asks special honor for them in the kingdom (Matt. 20:20=Mark 10:35). Matthew once calls them apostles (10:2); as in Luke, they are coming to be identified with the traveling missionaries of the early period.

Matthew edits the teaching materials in such a way as to make them more precise and more applicable to life in the Christian community. Not only is the exception clause put into the divorce section (19:1-9=Mark 10:1-12; cf. Matt. 5:31-32) but the entire pericope is rearranged (cf. 15:1-11 for Matthew's rearrangement of Mark 7:1-15), and the disciples' question is sharpened—"Is divorce permissible *for every cause?*"—for this was one point at issue between Hillel and Shammai, the heads of two contemporary schools of rabbinical teaching. In Matt. 9:28 the miracle depends upon belief in Christ's ability to perform it. Mark's story of the strange exorcist (Mark 9:38-41) is omitted, apparently because of its conflict with Matt. 12:30 (=Luke 11:23). The section 18:1-5 (=Mark 9:33-37) is expanded by the addition of the substance of Mark 10:15. In this way Matthew explains two Marcan passages and teaches that humility is the childlike quality which fits one for the kingdom. Frequently he adds moralizing passages which teach the necessity of good works, e.g., 21:41*b*, 43; 16:27*b*; cf. 21:28-32. The phrase "on these two commandments hang the whole law and the prophets" (22:40) is in thorough accord with rabbinical teaching. The typology which was dear to the early church sometimes crops out in Matthew. Many readers must have found Jesus' saying about the sign of Jonah obscure. Matthew connected it with the prophet's sojourn in the whale's belly and interpreted this as a foreshadowing of the death and resurrection of Christ. His Gospel has a dogmatic program of church history. Jesus' earthly mission had been to Israel (15:21-28), and the Gentile mission began only after the Resurrection. This is perhaps a variation of Mark's theory of the messianic secret (see Matt. 12:15-21).

Many changes have no particular theological significance. Matthew rearranges the story of Jesus' last days in Jerusalem so that the cleansing of the temple takes place on the day of the triumphal entry. The characters in a scene are sometimes doubled (two blind men in 9:27-31, two demoniacs in 8:28-34), and numbers are increased (14:21, five thousand men *besides women and children;* 26:44, Jesus in Gethsemane says the prayer a third time). Mark's editorial summaries are occasionally expanded (e.g., 4:23-25). The evangelist often augments biblical quotations or adds new citations or allusions, sometimes with curious results (e.g., gall substituted for myrrh, 27:34; the ass *and* the colt, 21:7; the thirty pieces of silver, 27:3-10). The name Levi (Mark 2:14) is changed to that of Matthew (9:9). Joseph of Arimathea is now regarded as a disciple (27:57), and the young man at the tomb becomes an angel (28:2; cf. Mark 16:5).

A comparison of the two later evangelists in their rewriting of the Marcan source shows that Matthew makes fewer changes in the wording that he copies, but compresses the narratives drastically; Luke, on the other hand, omits a greater portion of Mark and keeps more of the details in the sections he reproduces, but at the same time rewrites more thoroughly. Luke seldom deserts the order of Mark, but Matthew in his first twelve chapters makes a number of rearrangements.

Scholars have sometimes supposed that the copy of Mark which Matthew had before him was in some ways different from the Gospel known to us; this is one form of the "Urmarcus" or proto-Mark hypotheses.[6] One reason why this has been suggested is that at first glance there appear to be fifty-five verses of Mark (according to Streeter's count) which Matthew does not reproduce. Were these in the original draft of Mark? By way of answer it may be said that Luke has copied twenty-four of these fifty-five, and so they were present in the form of Mark which he knew. There are grounds for thinking that Matthew knew at least five of these twenty-four (Mark 4:21-24; 6:30; cf. Matt. 5:15; 7:2; 10:26; 13:12; 14:12). Doctrinal reasons will explain why he omitted most of the other nineteen. There remain thirty-one verses of Mark which neither Matthew nor Luke copied, yet most of them must have been in the gospel that Matthew used. The parable of the seed growing secretly (Mark 4:26-29) is perhaps rewritten into the parable of the tares; at least some of

6 See article "The Growth of the Gospels," p. 63.

Mark's words (καθεύδω, βλαστάνω, χόρτος, καρπόν) reappear there; and two of the miracles (Mark 7:32-37; 8:22-26) suffer a sea change; cf. also Mark 13:33-37 with Matt. 25:13b; 24:42. Dogmatic considerations explain the omission of Mark 3:20-21; obscurity, the excision of Mark 9:48-49; and Mark 1:1 and 14:51-52 were no doubt left out (as were the names of Alexander and Rufus in Mark 15:21=Matt. 27:32) because they served no useful purpose. This leaves only Mark 2:27; 7:3-4; and 9:29. Matthew replaces 9:29 with a substitute from Q (17:20), and it is at least possible that he inserted what we have as Matt. 12:8 in place of Mark 2:27, and that the former crept into Mark's text as vs. 28. We now have good manuscript evidence (Codex 2427) for the omission of Mark 7:3-4.[7] If one considers the likelihood that the quotation from Malachi in Mark 1:2, which both Matthew and Luke omit, is an early interpolation into Mark, it is probable that Matthew's copy of Mark differed from our own text, though only in a few minor details.

The second principal source of Matthew is the lost document Q. Its existence is postulated because Matthew and Luke possess extensive materials not found in Mark.[8] For present purposes it is sufficient to note the following points:

1. There is some evidence of a definite order in Q, for example:

MATTHEW	LUKE
5:1-3, 6. 11-12	6:20-23
5:46-48	6:32-33, 36
7:1-5	6:37-38, 41-42
7:16-18	6:43-44
7:21, 24-27	6:46-49
8:5-10	7:1-9
8:13	7:10

The order is slightly disturbed in

5:39-41	6:29-30
5:44	6:27-28
5:45	6:35

Luke probably follows the order of Q more faithfully than Matthew.

2. How much Q contained is much debated. Bacon believed that the second source (which he called S, reserving the symbol Q for actual Matthew-Luke parallels) was a complete gospel, including a passion narrative.[9] Burton and Goodspeed divided the non-Marcan sources of the two Gospels differently, distinguishing a "Galilean" source in Luke 6:20—8:3 and a "Perean" source in Luke 9:51—18:14 and 19:1-28.[10] These sections, of course, include many passages found only in Luke, which are often assigned to an L document. At the present time most scholars suppose that Q was primarily a collection of Jesus' sayings, perhaps beginning with the preaching of John the Baptist (Matt. 3:7-10=Luke 3:7-9) and concluding with the parable of the talents or pounds (Matt. 25:14-30=Luke 19:12-26).[11]

3. It is possible that Mark and other sources contained some of the materials found in Q, though in a different form. For example, cf. Mark 4:30-32 with Luke 13:18-19 (=Matt. 13:31-32); Mark 9:50 with Matt. 5:13-14 (=Luke 14:34-35); Mark 10:11-12 with Luke 16:18 (=Matt. 5:32). The question then arises whether Mark may not have known Q; perhaps he had heard it read on a few occasions and remembered sayings from it.[12]

4. One can distinguish the source by using a harmony of the Gospels and underlining in black all words and phrases in Matthew and Luke which agree with Mark, and in red all words and phrases possessed in common by Matthew and Luke but not found in Mark. But not all the words marked in red necessarily belong to Q. Certainly Matthew and Luke, independently of each other, frequently change Mark's rough phraseology into a more acceptable form (for example, by substituting εἶπεν for the historic present λέγει). Furthermore some of the parallel sections are very different in wording, for example, the parables of the lost sheep (Matt. 18:12-14=Luke 15:4-7); the great supper (Matt. 22:1-10=Luke 14:15-24) and the talents or pounds. It is a nice question whether Streeter is right in assigning Matthew's form of these stories to the special source M.[13] More probably the two evangelists have independently edited Q; for example, 18:14 looks like Matthew's own work, while in the parable of the pounds Luke weaves together two stories which originally had no connection. Yet other questions remain. Q's usual designation for Jesus is "Son of man." Frederick C. Grant has suggested that sections such as the story of the temptation (Matt. 4:3-10=Luke 4:3-12) and Jesus' solemn self-revelation (Matt. 11:25-27=Luke 10:21-22), with their Son of God Christology, belong to a separate source. Such an assumption might also help to explain the relationships in Mark 1:7-13 and parallels, where Mark appears to be abbreviating a longer source. Finally, should Q be thought of as a complete and unchanging document? There is at least one place where differences between Matthew and Luke may be ac-

---

[7] E. C. Colwell, "An Ancient Text of the Gospel of Mark," *Emory University Quarterly*, I (1945), 73.

[8] See article "The Growth of the Gospels," pp. 63-65.

[9] *Studies in Matthew*, pp. viii-xiii, 91-104.

[10] See especially E. D. Burton, *Some Principles of Literary Criticism and Their Application to the Synoptic Problem* (Chicago: University of Chicago Press, 1904).

[11] F. C. Grant, *The Growth of the Gospels* (New York: Abingdon Press, 1933), pp. 74-81.

[12] *Ibid.*, p. 137.

[13] *Four Gospels*, pp. 242-46.

counted for by variant translations from the Aramaic (Luke 11:41, δότε ἐλεημοσύνην, Aram. *zakki*; Matt. 23:26, καθάρισον, Aram. *dakki*).[14] If our present Gospels were treated freely by copyists, it is even more likely that Q was expanded and changed in the course of time; and if parts of it were originally written in Aramaic, they may have been translated more than once.

Since we can tell how Matthew used Mark, we may reasonably infer that he treated his other sources similarly. He would not have compressed the sayings of Jesus as much as he did Mark's narratives, but in other respects his methods should be the same throughout. A partial control can be established by studying Luke's methods in editing Mark, noting the same editorial peculiarities in Luke's form of the Q sections and allowing for them, and then comparing the Q parallels in Matthew to observe the latter's procedure. In such a way one can often approximate the wording of Q; the reconstruction of Matthew's special sources is more conjectural.

Indeed when we now turn to the special sources, it may seem like the croquet game in *Alice in Wonderland*, where flamingos were used for mallets and hedgehogs for balls. The material peculiar to Matthew [15] may be classified as follows: (*a*) brief additions to the Marcan source in the body of the Gospel (3:3*a*, 14-15; 10:5-6, 8, 16*b*, 23; 12:5-7, 36-37; 14:28-31; 15:12-14*a*, 23-24; 16:17-19; 18:10; 19:10-12; 21:15-16, 28-32; 24:10-12, 14) ; (*b*) in the passion narrative (26:52*b*-54; 27:3-10, 19, 24-25, 51*b*-53) ; and (*c*) in the resurrection story (27:62-66; 28:2-4, 9-20) ; (*d*) chs. 1 and 2; (*e*) the peculiar passages in the Sermon on the Mount (5:4-5, 7-10, 14, 16, 17-20, 21-24, 27-28, 33-37 [38-39*a*?], 41; 6:1-8, 16-18; 7:6, 13-14, 15) ; (*f*) passages which may belong to Q or to a special source (5:3-12, 31-32, 38-41, 43-45; 6:19-20; 7:21-23; 10:25-26, 41-42; 11:23*b*, 24, 28-30; 18:12-14; 22:1-14; 23:4, 13, 27-28; 25:14-30); (*g*) other special pericopes throughout the Gospel (13:24-30, 36-43, 44-52; 17:24-27; 18:17-20, 23-35; 20:1-16; 23:1-3, 5, 8-10, 12, 15, 16-22, 24; 25:1-13, 31-46) ; (*h*) the Old Testament quotations prefaced by Matthew's peculiar formula (1:22-23; 2:15, 17-18, 23; 4:14-16; 8:17; 12:17-21; 13:35; 21:4-5; 27:9-10; cf. 13:14-15; 26:56) ; and (*i*) the summaries at the end of the discourses (7:28-29; 11:1; 13:53; 19:1; 26:1) .

A careful study of the vocabulary of these sections yields no positive evidence of the use of separate literary sources. All one can say is that the well-known characteristics of Matthew's style, which one observes in his rewriting of

Mark, are more abundant in some places than in others. For example, the brief additions to Mark, wherever found, practically always betray Matthew's hand, and if any of them are based on tradition, the tradition was probably not in written form. The same is true of the first two chapters, which are composed in a smooth, homogeneous style, somewhat reminiscent of the Septuagint but obviously not a translation. Here, if anywhere, we can find the evangelist's own style. His peculiar information must have come to him from oral tradition, and the only written source was probably the genealogical list. The Old Testament quotations introduced by a special formula appear to be translated directly from the Hebrew, though occasionally they remind one of already existing Greek translations. The formula, which has parallels in Jewish writings, is a mark of Matthew's style (cf. Matt. 3:3 and Mark 1:2) . The summaries at the end of the discourses are also his composition. It has been suggested that the model was in Q (7:28-29=Luke 7:1) , but the Greek wording is different at every point. If there was ever any contact between the two, it was in an Aramaic source.

Streeter assigned most of the remaining material to an M source, namely, the peculiar portions of the Sermon on the Mount, the sections only doubtfully traceable to Q, and other special pericopes. He correctly recognized that much of the Jewish Christian, anti-Gentile character of the Gospel was owing to these portions. His follower Redlich produced a reconstruction of M containing about 260 verses, so complete that one would suppose the evangelist had used, for the most part, a scissors-and-paste method, even to the point of snipping out half verses of M and inserting them here and there.[16]

The M hypothesis stands up well in the Sermon on the Mount.[17] Chs. 5–7 were probably made up out of two sermons, one from Q (well represented by Luke 6:20-49) , and one from M, plus other sections from Q. To the M source one may assign the introductory section, 5:17-20; the three examples of the law, 5:21-24, 27-28, 33-37; the three examples of piety, 6:1-4, 5-7, 16-18. Also 7:15 is M; perhaps the Beatitudes, 5:4-5, 7-10, and some of the sections that overlap Q, especially 7:13-14. But how much of the remaining material belongs to the same source? The sections which fit best with the Jewish Christian tendency are (*a*) 10:5-6, 23, 25, 41; 13:52; and 15:24, which deal with Christ's mission and that

---

[14] Julius Wellhausen, *Das Evangelium Lucae* (Berlin: Georg Reimer, 1904), p. 61.

[15] According to a count made by Charles H. Buck, Jr., this consists of 436 verses or parts of verses.

[16] E. B. Redlich, *The Student's Introduction to the Synoptic Gospels* (London: Longmans, Green & Co., 1936), pp. 203-18.

[17] A. M. Perry believes that M furnished the actual structure of the sermon; see article "The Growth of the Gospels," p. 66. But see also article "The Sermon on the Mount," pp. 46-59.

of the disciples; (b) the legal and ethical sections 12:5-7; 16:19; 18:19-20; and 25:31-46, perhaps also 18:21-35; and (c) the sayings directed against the Pharisees, 23:2-3, 5, 8-10, 15-22, 24; perhaps also 21:28-32. Of the parables which have parallels in Luke, 22:1-10 and 25:14-30 harmonize best with M's point of view. Most of these sections teach the necessity of positive moral action, and Matthew himself has underscored this teaching by his editorial additions in various parts of the Gospel.

But there is no special reason why the parables of the hid treasure, the pearl of great price, and the seine (13:44-48) should belong to M; indeed the last named is too liberal in its outlook. The passage 19:10-12 is probably a Gentile section, and the parable of the laborers in the vineyard (20:1-16) overturns the doctrine of reward. The parable of the ten young girls (25:1-13) reminds one of the eschatological parts of Q. There are other sections, for example, the stater in the fish's mouth (17:24-27), which even Redlich does not credit to M. In so brief a Gospel as Mark there are indications of earlier sources (for example, groups of parables and controversies), and it is probable that Matthew's special material comes from at least two or three written documents, as well as from oral tradition. Finally, one may consider the possibility that Matthew occasionally composes a pericope. He might have rewritten Mark 4:26-29 into the parable of the tares (13:24-30) in order to provide a twin parable for 13:47-48. The interpretations appended to both (13:36-43, 49-50) are even more clearly the work of the evangelist.

After the Gospel has been analyzed into sources, the historian must try to isolate the separate units of oral tradition, to discover, if possible, their original form, and to decide where the interests and needs of the church have influenced the tradition, and where one can be reasonably sure of the actual words and deeds of Jesus. This process, which is usually called "form criticism," is the most delicate and important part of the task, and the place where the critic finds it most difficult to be objective.[18] Some incidents and sayings are most simply and naturally explained as historical occurrences in the ministry of Jesus. Others appear to reflect the life of the church. In between these groups is a large mass of material more difficult to assess. The methods by which a judgment is attempted can be observed in the commentary.

V. Language

The New Testament was written in koine or common Greek, the dialect which spread over the eastern Mediterranean region after the

conquests of Alexander the Great, and which in the first century was spoken and written in nearly every place where the earliest Christian missionaries went. Probably it was descended from the everyday speech of Athens; at any rate it was basically a simplified Attic, with elements from the Ionic and other dialects. There was a "literary" koine, to be found in Polybius, Josephus, and other writers, but the thousands of nonliterary papyri discovered in Egypt in the past sixty years prove that the New Testament was not written for connoisseurs of literature, or in a special "biblical" or Semitized Greek. Instead its language was that of the common people, even simpler than that of Epictetus, whose classroom lectures have been preserved by Arrian. (See article "The Language of the New Testament," pp. 44-46.)

Of the New Testament writings, Hebrews, James, and parts of Luke-Acts (e.g., Luke 1:1-4; Acts 26:1-23) approximate most closely the literary standards of the day. Revelation, with its numerous Semitisms, is at the other end of the scale. The Gospels lie in between. Mark and John have many traits of the spoken language, and Mark is especially rough and colloquial. Matthew's language can best be observed in chs. 1, 2, and 28. His prose differs from that of Plato to approximately the extent that the English in the news columns of a well-written metropolitan daily differs from that of Shakespeare and the King James Version. The Greek of the Gospel is fluent and clear, easily read by simple people but generally without offensive colloquialisms. The evangelist continually improves on Mark's crabbed style. He often changes a historic present or an imperfect to an aorist, omits καὶ εὐθύς, πάλιν, and also ὅτι before direct quotations; substitutes δέ for καί and often uses μέν with δέ; changes ἤρξατο with the infinitive to another construction; and generally avoids repetition and redundancy. Occasionally one finds artistic turns of speech, e.g., 24:30, καὶ κόψονται . . . καὶ ὄψονται. Yet Matthew is not so pedantic as to exchange κράββατος (the poor man's bed of 9:2, 6) for another word, as Luke always does.

Matthew's favorite expressions are easily recognizable throughout the Gospel: lawlessness (ἀνομία); kingdom of the heavens; in that place shall be the weeping and the gnashing of teeth; at that time; behold (ἰδού); that it might be fulfilled which was spoken by the Lord through the prophet, saying; λεγόμενος; disciples (μαθηταί); of little faith (ὀλιγόπιστος); ὅπως; παρουσία; the Father who is in the heavens; your Father; my Father; προσέρχομαι with the dative; Sadducees; end of the age; what do you think (τί σοι δοκεῖ); τότε; hypocrite; φημί; was likened (ὡμοιώθη). The "weeping and gnashing of teeth" may have been found in Q (8:12= Luke 13:28). It is characteristic of Matthew to adopt an expression from one of his sources and to use it constantly.

Was the Gospel originally written in Greek? Papias of Hierapolis, who flourished in Phrygia about A.D. 130-140, wrote a book called *Exposition of the Oracles of the Lord,* now lost to us save for a few tantalizing fragments. One of these reads: "Matthew composed the oracles [τὰ λόγια, the sayings] in the Hebrew language, but everyone interpreted them as he was able." "Hebrew" was the usual designation for Aramaic. "The oracles" might be the sayings of Jesus in such a document as Q, but Papias was more probably referring to the Gospel of Matthew. Similar statements are made by Irenaeus (*Against Heresies* III. 1. 2), Origen (in Eusebius *Church History* VI. 25. 4), Eusebius (*Church History* III. 24. 6), and Jerome (*Commentary on Matthew* Prooem. §5); but most of these writers add no information of importance and they are probably dependent on Papias for their tradition. Jerome had indeed consulted an Aramaic gospel, current among the "Nazarenes" of Beroea in Coele-Syria, which seems to have been a form of Matthew containing a number of Targumic additions. The Nazarene gospel was in all probability a free translation of the Greek Matthew. Could Papias have mistaken such a document for the original Gospel?

A few modern critics, indeed, hold that Matthew was originally written in Aramaic.[19] But most of these, like Torrey, believe that the same is true of the other three Gospels. Apart from the relative paucity of Aramaic literature in the first century,[20] and the natural koine language of all four Gospels, the principal difficulty is that Matthew (like Luke and John) so obviously uses Greek sources. Torrey therefore finds it necessary to suppose that the author of Aramaic Matthew used Aramaic Mark, and that the translator of Matthew used the Greek translation of Mark in making his rendering.[21] This is a multiplication of hypotheses for which there is no objective evidence. All the facts are accounted for if we suppose that Matthew originally wrote in Greek, using Mark as a source, and that he had enough knowledge of Hebrew and Aramaic to make direct quotations from the Hebrew Bible and to use written and oral Aramaic sources. There can be little doubt

that Aramaic ultimately underlies much of the Synoptic tradition. The Semitic coloring shines through many of the sayings of Jesus and the old stories. It is most noticeable in the central parts of pericopes (Matt. 5:22; Luke 12:20; 16:4; Mark 4:8 [according to DW]) which the evangelists disturb least; one seldom sees it in the editorial sutures.

VI. Date and Location

The date of Matthew depends partly on that of Mark, since Mark is one of the sources. But just here we are in an area where it is difficult to be precise. The letters of Paul can be dated to within a few years, thanks to the Gallio inscription and other evidence, but the Gospels can be dated only relatively. Mark cannot be earlier than A.D. 40, for Caligula's attempt to profane the temple is reflected in ch. 13; John, the latest of the Gospels, cannot be dated long after the year 100, for a papyrus fragment of it, found in upper Egypt, has been assigned to the second century by competent papyrologists.[22] Matthew is mentioned by Papias, and it was in all probability known to Ignatius, who was martyred about the year 115. The question then arises: How much can the gap of seventy-five years, from 40 to 115, be narrowed?

It would not be completely impossible to date Mark shortly after the year 40, but a date in the neighborhood of 70 is far more likely. As Bacon has shown, the whole tendency of Mark is to suppress the apocalyptic excitement which arose in 40, again about the year 50, and once more in 66-70 (see especially Mark 13:32-37).[23] Furthermore Mark gives the impression of having been written after the bitter experiences of the Neronian persecution, and according to the tradition of Irenaeus and most of the ancient writers, it was composed after the deaths of Peter and Paul.

On this view Matthew and Luke would be still later. Luke certainly seems to have been written after Jerusalem has already fallen (Luke 21:20; "When you see Jerusalem surrounded by armies, then know that its desolation has come near"; cf. also Luke 19:43-44; 21:24). Matthew gives the same impression. The reference to the king who sent his armies and burned the city (22:7) would not be decisive by itself. More impressive is the way in which Mark 13 is rewritten. Matthew believes that the first sign of the end of the age will be a world-wide persecution (24:9), followed by dissension in the church (24:10), false prophets (24:11), and the "love of the many" growing cold

[19] See article "The Growth of the Gospels," pp. 67-68. See also Matthew Black, *An Aramaic Approach to the Gospels and Acts* (Oxford: Clarendon Press, 1946).

[20] See A. T. Olmstead, "Could an Aramaic Gospel Be Written?" *Journal of Near Eastern Studies,* I (1942), 41-75, and E. J. Goodspeed's rejoinder, "The Possible Aramaic Gospel," *ibid.,* pp. 315-40.

[21] C. C. Torrey, *The Four Gospels* (New York: Harper & Bros., 1933), p. 279.

[22] W. H. P. Hatch, *The Principal Uncial Manuscripts of the New Testament* (Chicago: University of Chicago Press, 1939), Plate I.

[23] *Studies in Matthew, op. cit.,* pp. 67-68.

(24:12); yet before the end can come, the good news must be proclaimed to all the Gentiles (24:14). Previous predictions of the return of the Son of man have apparently failed, and it is one of Matthew's principal interests to revive apocalyptic fervor by assuring Christians that Christ will nevertheless come; hence his addition of 24:37-51; 25:1-12, and especially his own addition of 25:13. Note also his rewriting of Mark 13:14. The "abomination of desolation" is the one spoken of by Daniel (Matt. 24:15; Dan. 12:11), and it will stand in a holy place—perhaps a Jewish or Christian synagogue or the site of the now-ruined temple. We can account for these changes if we suppose that the following developments had meanwhile occurred: after the Neronian persecution and the destruction of the temple, Christians settled down to an easier and more peaceful life; a second generation grew up without the fervor of their fathers; a few became relatively prosperous; and because the earlier missionaries had died, it was easy for false prophets like Menander and El-Kesi to deceive the people. It is even possible that revolutionary activity had revived among the Jews (hence the warning in 26:52). Finally, in the reign of Domitian (81-96) the danger of persecution arose once more, not only in Rome but also in Asia Minor. The situation of Matthew would thus be similar to that which is presupposed in Hebrews and Revelation and perhaps I Peter.

Now it is perfectly true that there is relatively little direct evidence for a general persecution under Domitian.[24] Our evidence consists of many bits of information which, taken together, are best explained by such a persecution. One of the most important of these is the observable fact that the book of Revelation as a whole fits best into the reign of Domitian.[25]

We must also recall all that has been said of Matthew's interest in church order. The Gospel belongs to a time when the church is being consolidated as a separate organization and has developed its own worship, theology, ethics, procedure, and leadership in the face of internal laxity and dissension and external competition and persecution. This is the situation of I Clement, Hermas, the Ignatian letters, the Pastoral epistles, and the Gospel of John. In the very same generation, moreover, a parallel movement was going on in orthodox Judaism. After the Jewish War the great rabbinical school of Jamnia was established by Johanan ben Zakkai, and his followers began the process of preserving and codifying the oral law.[26] Matthew seems to follow the rabbinical method of protecting and preserving his religion; he codified the Christian law and adjusted it so as to make it a practical guide for life. It therefore seems appropriate to date Matthew not far from the year 100.

There are, of course, those who would date Mark about the year 40, and Matthew and Luke in the sixties, while preserving the traditional date of John (95-100). It still remains true that the New Testament books, and the corresponding development of the Christian church, must be kept in the same *relative* order. Several questions then arise. Can this whole development of heresy, dissension, theology, and organization be telescoped into the thirty years after the Crucifixion? Can the later books of the New Testament, especially the Pastoral epistles, have been written almost immediately after the death of Paul? If there was such a rapid development in the first thirty years, why was development so slow in the next two generations? The church of Ignatius' time exhibits very little development beyond Matthew, except in the one matter of episcopal organization. To date Matthew in the sixties would mean that we have no evidence of its wide use for sixty or seventy years after its composition.

Streeter believes that Matthew was written in Antioch. But there is no evidence to justify locating it so precisely, and there is the difficulty that Ignatius, bishop of Antioch, while he seems to know the Gospel, has a very different theological outlook. Furthermore it is possible—though not necessary—to assign the Fourth Gospel to the same region, and of all the Gospels John is the most unlike Matthew. But a great deal can be said for Syria. In northern Palestine there seems to have been much apocalyptic expectation of the sort we find in Matthew. Syria is near enough to Palestine that Jews and Christians would be in daily contact. Old Palestinian traditions could be preserved there and yet be expanded and changed without much control. Syrians might very easily make "Targumic" and legendary additions to the Gospel of Mark. In Antioch and Damascus, and perhaps elsewhere in Syria, the stater equalled two didrachmas (Matt. 17:24-27). Bacon suggests that the Gospel may have been written in a city of eastern Syria, such as Edessa or Apamea, where star worship was popular among the heathen. Here men would tell with intense interest the story of those astrologers who saw the star and followed it to Bethlehem.[27]

[24] E. T. Merrill, *Essays in Early Christian History* (London: Macmillan & Co., 1924), pp. 148-73.

[25] See S. J. Case, *The Revelation of John* (Chicago: University of Chicago Press, 1919), pp. 42-54; also Intro., Revelation, Vol. XII of this Commentary.

[26] A vivid imaginative portrait of Johanan is given by the novelist Lion Feuchtwanger in *Josephus* (New York: The Viking Press, 1932), pp. 246-53, 446-47.

[27] *Studies in Matthew*, p. 36.

VII. Authorship

According to ecclesiastical tradition, the author was Matthew, one of the twelve, whose name appears eighth in the Matthaean list with the designation "the tax collector" (10:3), seventh in the lists of Mark (3:18) and Luke (6:15), and eighth in that of Acts (1:13). "The tax collector" of 10:3 is somehow connected with 9:9, where "Matthew" replaces the "Levi" of Mark 2:14 (=Luke 5:27). Bacon points out that several Western and Caesarean manuscripts read "James the son of Alphaeus" in Mark 2:14. He suggests that because of this, "the tax collector" was added to the margin of an early manuscript of Matthew, opposite "James the son of Alphaeus" in 10:3, that it crept into the text after the name Matthew instead of that of James, and that finally 9:9 was changed to correspond to 10:3.[28] This ingenious hypothesis tells us nothing about the authorship of the Gospel, but it may explain the peculiarity of 9:9 and cast further doubt on the theory, sometimes advanced, that the evangelist had two names, Matthew and Levi. As a matter of fact, while a first-century Jew might be known by a title ("Judah the Prince"), a patronymic ("James the son of Alphaeus"), a place name ("Simon of Cyrene"), or his occupation ("Simon the tanner"), and might have both a Jewish and a Greek name ("Saul" and "Paul"), it would be exceptional for him to have two Jewish given names.

The tradition rests on Irenaeus (*Against Heresies* III. 1. 1), who seems to assume that the author was an apostle, and on Origen (in Eusebius, *Church History* VI. 25. 4), Eusebius (*Church History* III. 24. 5-6), and Jerome (*Concerning Famous Men* §3; *Preface to the Fourth Gospel*; *Commentary on Matthew*, Prologue §5). Papias, in the extract quoted above, says nothing of Matthew being one of the twelve, but probably assumed that he was. The κατά ("according to") in the title of the Gospel does not affirm authorship in the strict sense. As Plummer says, it need mean nothing more than "drawn up according to the teaching of," but Papias probably assumed that Matthew was author of an Aramaic book from which our Gospel was translated.[29] The original author could, of course, have been a later Christian who bore this common Jewish name, but when the name became attached to the Gospel, it must have been generally assumed that "Matthew" was the apostle.

The principal difficulty with the tradition is

not its attestation or its intrinsic character. To be sure, the tendency of tradition is always to attach an apostolic name to a book, and "the burden of proof is on those who would assert the traditional authorship of Matthew and John and on those who would deny it in the case of Mark and Luke."[30] But Matthew is one of the more obscure of the twelve names, and one wonders why the name of Peter or Andrew was not chosen if the purpose was to gain prestige for the book. The difficulty is rather the character of the Gospel itself—a Greek Gospel, using Greek sources, written for a predominantly Gentile church, at a time when the tradition had become mixed with legend, and when the ethical teaching of Jesus was being reinterpreted to apply to new situations and codified into a new law. A careful reading of Matthew, especially when it is compared with Mark, shows that the book cannot have been written by an eyewitness. It is a compendium of church tradition, artistically edited, not the personal observations of a participant.

Unless the tradition is an ancient piece of higher criticism deduced from the peculiarity of 9:9, the disciple Matthew may have had something to do with collecting the sayings of Jesus. It has often been suggested that the Q document, or the earliest Aramaic nucleus of it, was his work. In such a case the later book is still in a real sense a Gospel according to Matthew.

VIII. Place in the History of Primitive Christianity

During the first half century the Christian churches developed almost entirely without central control. There were at first no creed, no liturgy or canonical writings distinct from those of Judaism, no external organization. The resources of the new way were the message of salvation through Christ, the personalities of the missionaries and their memories of Jesus' words and deeds, the Old Testament Scriptures, and a certain amount of Jewish tradition. Within a generation the communities in various parts of the empire had begun to develop distinctive interpretations of the message. The church in Antioch seems to have been formed by liberals who sat loosely to the requirements of the Old Testament law; the Roman church—or at least an important part of it—was more conservative. The disciples in Jerusalem remained even more strictly faithful to the law than Jesus had been; at least they acknowledged only such modifications as the Messiah had explicitly made. The church nearly split into two separate movements in the late forties over the question of admission of uncircumcised Gentiles; and even when Paul won on this point, some strict Christian Jews

[28] *Ibid.*, pp. 39-40.

[29] *An Exegetical Commentary on the Gospel According to S. Matthew* (London: Robert Scott, 1909), p. vii; cited in Bacon, *Studies in Matthew*, pp. 28-29.

[30] Streeter, *Four Gospels*, p. 562.

refused to eat at Gentile tables and sought to enforce some minimum food laws among the converts. The Jerusalem leaders were able to exercise some control over the churches of Syria and Cilicia, and Paul could make his influence felt in the communities which he himself had founded. But each congregation, no doubt claiming the presence of the heavenly Lord (18:20; I Cor. 5:3-5), was the final authority in its own affairs. At least there was no way of coercing it except by such spiritual means as Paul used in his letters; and in dealing with a non-Pauline church, such as that in Rome, the apostle had to be extremely tactful.

When the missionaries and founding fathers died, difficult situations must often have arisen. We know, for example, of trouble in Corinth about the year 95. The congregation, or a group in it, had deposed some of its bishops; we do not know whether the issues were doctrinal or nontheological or both. The church in Rome undertook to restore order by dispatching a letter which we call I Clement. The author argued that the apostles had arranged for their places to be taken by other approved men (ch. 44). But as a secure basis for church unity, Clement had no New Testament to which he could appeal; he drew some of his arguments from the letters of Paul, but mainly relied on the Old Testament. Twenty years later Ignatius was trying to unify the churches of Asia Minor and stamp out a heresy which taught that Jesus only seemed to have a human body, and his method was to urge the churches to obey their local bishops; but although he held up before them the example of Paul, he made no appeal to the Old Testament and said nothing about these bishops having received authority from the apostles. There was no generally accepted basis of unity, and Ignatius had to rely on his own prestige as bishop, prophet, and martyr.

The church's earliest controversies had been concerned with the ceremonial law. When, after the year 70, strife arose over the authority of the Old Testament, the reconciliation of penitent sinners, and the interpretation of Christ's person—especially his genuine humanity—a concrete authority was sorely needed. Probably some churches read and valued the Old Testament and others did not; some had the letters of Paul; some had very full traditions of the life and teaching of Jesus, while others may have known only the barest outlines of the message. The appearance of Mark's Gospel made unified religious education possible. Even so, Mark contained relatively little of Jesus' teaching, and it was a still more important event when two men, who seem to have worked independently, saw the usefulness of Mark and combined it with Q and other sources to pro-

duce the Gospels of Matthew and Luke. This was done at a time when the church was actually in danger of falling apart. The two authors met the situation by saying in effect: "The message *about* Jesus as Son of God, Son of man, and Messiah, born of a virgin, crucified, and risen, is fundamental, and so is the story of his human life as an Israelite; so also are the teaching *of* Jesus, and the Old Testament, which confirms the whole story; furthermore, this story is guaranteed to us by the twelve, who were the church's original apostles." In the forties and fifties the church had many apostles (that is, missionaries)—Paul, Barnabas, Silvanus, Timothy, Andronicus, and Junias are a few of the names. Matthew (10:2, 40) and Luke (6:13, "twelve, whom he named apostles") explicitly trace this institution back to the twelve. Thus these writers were able to say to churches founded by Paul and other apostles, "Here is the original apostolic message." This was especially necessary because there is reason to believe that some of Paul's followers, like Marcion later on, distrusted the religion which stemmed from Jerusalem and the twelve. Like Marcion again, they may have exaggerated some features of Paul's teaching in such a way as to cause controversy and schism.

Clement sought, by means of a formal church letter, to unify Christians under a leadership which claimed to be apostolic. The author of Ephesians, who probably collected the Pauline letters, appealed for unity on the foundation of the Christian "apostles and prophets" (Eph. 2:19-22). Matthew and Luke set forth written Gospels as embodiments of the apostolic message. All these books, which were produced within a few years of one another, must have done much to bring Christians together. And so arose the concept of "apostolicity," which has had the most momentous consequences for Christianity.[31]

IX. Historical and Religious Interpretation

The historian of Jesus' life and teaching must make some allowances for Matthew's special interests. No matter how honest he was, no matter how good his sources—and he was an honest man who had some good sources—he was an evangelist, not a historian, and he was influenced by his theology and the needs of his church. For example, he has pictured Jesus as more anti-Pharisaic than he probably was; in heightening the miracles he has made him appear absolutely omnipotent; and he leaves the reader with the impression that Jesus was very

[31] See S. E. Johnson, "The Emergence of the Christian Church in the Pre-Catholic Period," in H. R. Willoughby, ed., *The Study of the Bible Today and Tomorrow* (Chicago: University of Chicago Press, 1947), pp. 345-65.

much concerned to predict the future and to lay plans for a Christian church. Matthew is as ready to accept late traditions as early; he is not affected by the fact that Mark says nothing about the Virgin Birth, and perhaps even does not know that Paul is likewise silent. The story is current in his church, and it is useful as showing when and how Jesus became the Son of God. Since he is an ancient, not a rationalistic modern, it seems perfectly appropriate to him that Joseph, the magi, and Pilate's wife, should be warned by dreams. But though allowances are to be made, the historian may be thankful that Matthew is as faithful as he is in reproducing his sources. Our most secure knowledge of Jesus' life and teaching is gained from the incidental references to be found in the letters of Paul, together with those Synoptic sources in whose preservation Matthew had so large a part.

Christianity is, like Hebraism and Judaism, a historical religion. It is not so much a system of ideas as a faith and life based on the double story of God's dealings with man and man's response and aspiration. Therefore the entire story, as it unfolds, is relevant. Of course it is true that the Gospels, read simply and uncritically, will make one "wise unto salvation" and give a reasonably clear picture of the character of Jesus and his teaching. What the critical and historical study of the Gospels *can* do, in addition, is to bring the picture of Jesus into sharper focus, and to remove distracting elements which blur it at some points; to exhibit the earliest forms of the good news of salvation and the earliest interpretations of Jesus' significance, as distinct from the later; and to outline many of the stages by which Christianity developed from a Jewish movement which had universal possibilities into an institutionalized Gentile church.

Such a study throws a fresh light on many theological problems. Not the least of these is the question, inescapable in a historical religion, of event versus tradition. All Christians would agree that in some way the life and teaching of Jesus is normative. It does not destroy the significance of the Old Covenant, nor does it reduce the meaning of Hebrew religion to a "preparation for the gospel" and nothing else; yet it sums it up and provides a standard by which the several stages in the development of that religion can be tested and evaluated. On the other hand although Jesus Christ is for Christians the unique truth, it was inevitable that there should be a continual change in the interpretation of the good news and its application to life. In other words there was a tradition which was perforce embodied in a living community of worshiping people. Since this is essential for the preservation and spread of the

gospel, it is in some way divinely willed; but the Christian conscience has from time to time rightly insisted that institution and tradition must stand under the scrutiny and judgment of the original facts and faith. The modern study of the Gospels shows that in the New Testament period itself the reinterpretation was already going on, and that this process should be studied reverently but critically. Matthew and John are the two Gospels which have the clearest and most consciously worked out theological points of view; hence they insistently and searchingly raise the problem of event versus tradition, and illuminate it in different ways. One who studies the Gospels historically and genetically has the instruments to restate this and many other theological problems, and to find a solution—if not an absolute, permanent solution, at least one which comes as close to the truth as our age can reach.

X. Text

Matthew's text has fundamentally the same characteristics as those of the other Gospels, since all four were regularly copied and bound together. Since there exist more than fourteen hundred Greek manuscripts of the Gospels, ranging in date from the third century down to modern times, not to mention lectionaries, large numbers of manuscripts of versions, and many quotations in the church fathers, the text is extremely well attested. Although there is a rich wealth of variants, owing to both accidental and deliberate changes, the text is in good condition, and the true reading can often be established without difficulty. Frequently the choice of a reading has some bearing on interpretation; yet it is probably true that no fundamental question of Christian faith and morals hinges on a disputed text. The chief practical value of textual study is that it sharpens our understanding of the writer's own message and therefore of the life and thought of the early Christians.

The King James Version was made from a type of Greek text, usually known as the Byzantine, Koine, or K (that is, Kappa) text, which grew up from the fourth century on. One of the characteristics of this text—also found in other text types—is its fullness. If, in a given verse, two or more earlier groups of manuscripts had more than one reading, the tendency of later scribes was to combine them into a longer reading. For example, in 5:44 some of the best authorities read, "But I say unto you, Love your enemies and pray for them which persecute you." Others, however, add from Luke 6:28, "bless them that curse you"; still others add from Luke 6:27, "do good to them that hate you"; and another group expands the last clause to read, "them which despitefully use you, and persecute you." The text of the King James Version represents the final combination of all readings (cf. 10:3 for another example). Another feature of the K text is that it makes corrections with a view to producing a better sense, as in 6:1, where "righteousness" is changed to "alms" to conform to 6:2, or in 15:39, where the unfamiliar "Magadan" becomes the well-known "Magdala." Other types of variant seen in the K and other text types will be discussed below.

Westcott and Hort believed that the K text developed from the weaving together of several local text types which were in existence from the second century on. This judgment is no longer generally accepted, but there are manifestly various text types which we can roughly distinguish.[32] The most important of these is the Alexandrian, which Westcott and Hort named "Neutral" because they believed it to represent the purest form. Its best example is the great Codex Vaticanus (B). Sinaiticus (א), 33, and the Bohairic Coptic version also belong to this type of text. Three other important texts are the Western (represented by D or Bezae, and the Old Latin version and several early fathers), the Caesarean (Koridethi [Θ], parts of the Freer Codex [W], two families of minuscules headed by Codices 1 and 13 respectively, etc.), and the Old Syriac (consisting of two manuscripts, the Sinaitic and the Curetonian). Ideally the textual student would like to construct a stemma or genealogical table showing the descent of our manuscripts, but this is impossible. The most that can be done is to isolate the several texts, and the clans and families of manuscripts which represent them, on the basis of their peculiar readings, because so much cross-fertilization has occurred in the transmission of the text that the genealogical lines are tangled beyond straightening out. Indeed, no existing manuscript has an unmixed text, and the critics have not yet established the make-up of texts and families on a completely scientific basis. Vaticanus (B), which is perhaps our best single manuscript, clearly has an Alexandrian text in the Gospels; but that is not to say that all its readings are Alexandrian or that it is at all points the best, or even a very good, representative of that text.

Westcott and Hort followed the general principle that the Alexandrian reading had the best claim to represent what the author originally

wrote. Where the Western text (in which they included the Caesarean and other non-Alexandrian types) had a shorter reading and the "Neutral" semed to be interpolated, they frequently followed the Western. Most textual critics now believe that this principle must be modified. Future editors, one may hope, will have more information on the exact characteristics of the several texts and families, and will use an eclectic method. That is to say, one hopes that while showing respect for the massive claims of the Alexandrian text, they will give due weight to superior readings found in other texts.

In order to give a rough illustration of this principle a list was made of twenty-eight of the most important and interesting passages in Matthew where variants occur, and where one can make a plausible guess at the true reading. It was then noted which of the texts attested each of the readings, with the following result:

	ATTESTED THE BEST READING	ATTESTED A POORER READING	REPRESENTATIVES DIVIDED IN ATTESTATION, OR EVIDENCE NOT CLEAR
Alexandrian	19	3	6
Western	9	11	8
Caesarean	11	12	5
Old Syriac	7	10	11

One must insist that these results are at best a very rough approximation, for only a few of the variants in Matthew were studied, and the four texts were in most cases represented by only a few authorities. Yet this will serve to show that the best text type is not infallible and that a poorer text may contain excellent readings. It may be added, incidentally, that the K text in the great majority of cases represented the poorer reading.

Textual critics, of course, cannot work mechanically. They must also take into consideration various rules of textual criticism; for example: "The more difficult reading is usually to be preferred"; and "That reading is the oldest which can best explain the production of the other readings." One important point to remember is that the text of one of the Synoptic Gospels tends always to influence the other two; and since each of the evangelists has his own style, that reading which is in harmony with the author's habits has a special claim to consideration. A clear case of this is found in 17:20, where most late manuscripts read ἀπιστίαν, while representatives of four early texts read ὀλιγοπιστίαν, a characteristic Matthaean word.

A number of variant readings are studied in

[32] See the important criticism of the Westcott-Hort theory by E. C. Colwell, "Genealogical Method: Its Achievements and Its Limitations," *Journal of Biblical Literature*, LXVI (1947), 109-33; also Colwell's article, "The Text and Ancient Versions of the New Testament," in Vol. I of this Commentary.

the Exegesis. We may, however, illustrate several types of textual change.

1. Growth of tradition.—Details are often added to stories as they are told orally, and these sometimes affect the biblical text. Thus one Old Latin codex adds to 3:16 the words "and when he was baptized a great light shone about from the water, so that all who had come were afraid," and another has the gloss in similar form; cf. 8:13, where a number of manuscripts, including Sinaiticus (‭א‬) add, "and when the centurion returned to his house, at that very hour he found the servant well"; 26:15, where some Western manuscripts substitute "staters" for "pieces of silver"; and 27:38, where an Old Latin codex gives the names Zoatham and Camma to the two thieves.

2. Changes dictated by reverence and doctrinal interest.—In 5:11 the word ψευδόμενοι is added by practically all authorities except D (Bezae) and the Old Latin: what is said against the disciples is said falsely. The teaching of 5:22 is weakened by the usual reading εἰκῇ ("without a cause"); but the word is omitted by ‭א‬ B, two minuscules, the Vulgate, and some fathers. Compare 6:4, 6, 18, where "openly" has been added. Some good authorities ascribe the quotation in 13:35 to the prophet Isaiah; either the name was mistakenly added, or it stood in Matthew's text and was deleted by a corrector; cf. 27:9, where some manuscripts and versions omit "Jeremiah." According to the earliest Christian doctrine, Jesus was "raised up," and Matthew undoubtedly used forms of the verb ἐγείρω in 17:9, 23; 20:19; but later copyists substituted forms of the verb ἀνίστημι ("to rise up"). Liturgical influence is no doubt responsible for the addition of the doxology to the Lord's Prayer (6:13).

3. Influence of other biblical passages.—One who has read widely in the Bible and attempts to quote it from memory or to copy out a passage may easily weave together passages from two or more books. In such ways the text of one book may affect another. This has happened especially in the Synoptic Gospels, which already so much resemble one another. Thus the influence of the Gospel of Luke may account for the presence of Matt. 9:34 (omitted by D, two Old Latin manuscripts and the Sinaitic Syriac); the addition to 10:12 of the words "saying, Peace be to this house" (‭א‬ D Θ etc. but not the King James); the word "children" instead of "deeds" in 11:19; and the addition of 16:2b-3; 18:11; 23:14 and perhaps 21:44. From Mark 9:29 (in its later form) comes Matt. 17:21. Matthew's own text is responsible for the addition of "among the people" in 9:35 (cf. 4:23). At the end of 20:33 one Old Latin codex has an interpolation which

duplicates 9:28. Matt. 27:35b is an addition based on John 19:24 (=Ps. 22:18) and is introduced by Matthew's favorite formula for biblical quotations. There are several variants in 27:46, one of which substitutes for σαβαχθανεί the word ζαφθανεί, which represents the original Hebrew of Ps. 22:1.

It is frequently difficult to decide which is the original reading, especially where doctrinal and historical questions are involved. The important variants to be studied in the Commentary include those found in 1:16 (the paternity of Jesus); 5:32 and 19:9 (sayings on marrying a divorced woman); 21:29-31a (the two sons); 11:27 ("no one knows the Son except the Father"); 5:4-5 (the original order of the Beatitudes); 25:1 (the bridegroom *and the bride*); 27:16-17 (Jesus Barabbas). These illustrate the difficulty and the fascination of textual study.

XI. Outline of the Gospel

I. Beginning of the narrative (1:1–4:25)
  A. The genealogy of Jesus (1:1-17)
  B. Birth and childhood (1:18–2:23)
    1. The birth of Jesus (1:18-25)
    2. The visit of the magi (2:1-12)
    3. The flight into Egypt (2:13-15)
    4. The slaughter of the children (2:16-18)
    5. Removal from Egypt to Nazareth (2:19-23)
  C. The ministry of John the Baptist (3:1-12)
  D. The beginning of Jesus' ministry (3:13–4:25)
    1. The baptism (3:13-17)
    2. The temptation (4:1-11)
    3. Jesus' preaching in Galilee (4:12-25)
      a) The prophetic setting (4:12-16)
      b) Jesus' proclamation (4:17)
      c) Calling of the first disciples (4:18-22)
      d) Summary of his first activity (4:23-25)
II. First discourse: addressed to the disciples. The new law, designed for the community whose members will inherit the kingdom (5:1–7:29)
  A. Introduction (5:1-2)
  B. The discourse (5:3–7:27)
    1. Nine beatitudes, contrasting future joys with present sufferings and duties (5:3-12)
    2. The relation of the disciples to the world (5:13-16)
    3. The new law is the completion of the old, not its destruction (5:17-20)
    4. Contrasts between the old interpretation of the law and the new (5:21-48)
      a) Murder and anger (5:21-26)
      b) Adultery and lust (5:27-30)
      c) Divorce (5:31-32)
      d) Oaths (5:33-37)
      e) Retaliation (5:38-42)
      f) Hatred and love (5:43-47)
      g) Summary (5:48)

k) Seventh woe: their hypocritical honor of the prophets (23:29-33)

l) Concluding threat and lament (23: 34-39)

X. Fifth discourse: addressed to the disciples. The end of the age (24:1—26:2)
   A. Detailed prophecy of the end (24:1-36)
      1. The disciples' question (24:1-3)
      2. First signs of the end (24:4-8)
      3. Persecution and apostasy (24:9-14)
      4. Events in Judea (24:15-22)
      5. Warning against a false Parousia (24:23-28)
      6. Signs of the Parousia (24:29-31)
      7. Example of the fig tree (24:32-33)
      8. The exact time is unpredictable (24:34-36)
   B. On being prepared (24:37—25:13)
      1. Most humans will be taken unawares (24:37-41)
      2. "Be you ready" (24:42-44)
      3. Good slaves and bad (24:45-51)
      4. A parable on preparedness (25:1-13)
   C. A parable on the use of capabilities (25:14-30)
   D. A parable on the basis of the Last Judgment (25:31-46)
   E. Summary and prophecy of arrest (26:1-2)
XI. Resumption of the narrative: Jesus' death and the events leading up to it (26:3—27:66)
   A. Preliminary events (26:3—27:26)
      1. The plot (26:3-5)
      2. Jesus' anointing (26:6-13)
      3. Judas agrees to betray him (26:14-16)
      4. The Last Supper (26:17-30)
      5. Jesus' prophecy and Peter's promise (26:31-35)
      6. Gethsemane (26:36-46)
      7. The arrest (26:47-56)
      8. Hearing before Caiaphas (26:57-68)
      9. Peter's denial (26:69-75)
      10. Hearing before Pilate (27:1-26)
         a) Jesus is led before Pilate (27:1-2)
         b) Judas' suicide (27:3-10)
         c) The hearing and condemnation (27:11-26)
   B. The Crucifixion (27:27-56)
      1. Jesus is mistreated by the soldiers (27:27-31)
      2. The journey to the Cross (27:32)
      3. Jesus on the Cross (27:33-44)
      4. Jesus' death (27:45-56)
   C. The burial of Jesus (27:57-66)
      1. The burial (27:57-61)
      2. The watch on the tomb (27:62-66)
XII. The Resurrection (28:1-20)
   A. The angel and the women (28:1-8)
   B. Jesus' appearance to the women (28:9-10)
   C. The false witness of the guards (28:11-15)
   D. Final appearance to the eleven (28:16-20)

XII. *Selected Bibliography*

COMMENTARIES

A few of the most useful commentaries are included. Commentaries on Mark and Luke, some of which are listed in the bibliographies to those Gospels, are frequently indispensable for the study of Matthew.

ALLEN, W. C. *A Critical and Exegetical Commentary on the Gospel According to S. Matthew* ("The International Critical Commentary"). New York: Charles Scribner's Sons, 1907. One of the most complete and generally satisfactory commentaries in English.

GREEN, F. W. *The Gospel According to St. Matthew* ("The Clarendon Bible"). 2nd ed. Oxford: Clarendon Press, 1945. On the English Revised Version; brief and up to date.

KLOSTERMANN, ERICH. *Das Matthäusevangelium* ("Handbuch zum Neuen Testament," Vol. IV). 2nd ed. Tübingen: J. C. B. Mohr, 1927. Perhaps the best brief commentary in any language. Klostermann's commentary on Mark, in the same series, must frequently be used with it.

McNEILE, A. H. *The Gospel According to St. Matthew*. London: Macmillan & Co., 1915. One of the most adequate commentaries in English.

MONTEFIORE, C. G. *The Synoptic Gospels*. 2 vols. 2nd ed. London: Macmillan & Co., 1927. From a liberal Jewish point of view; contains much rabbinical material.

ROBINSON, T. H. *The Gospel of Matthew* ("The Moffatt New Testament Commentary"). New York: Doubleday, Doran & Co., 1928.

STRACK, H. L. and BILLERBECK, PAUL. *Kommentar zum Neuen Testament aus Talmud und Midrasch.* 4 vols. Munich: C. H. Beck, 1922-28. An indispensable work for the careful student.

OTHER WORKS

BACON, B. W. *Studies in Matthew*. New York: Henry Holt & Co., 1930. The most complete treatise on the problems of Matthew; difficult but rewarding.

KILPATRICK, G. D. *The Origins of the Gospel According to St. Matthew*. Oxford: Clarendon Press, 1946. A useful and reliable treatment of introductory problems.

MOORE, G. F. *Judaism*. 3 vols. Cambridge: Harvard University Press, 1927-30. The best single treatment of the Jewish background.

ANCIENT WRITINGS

The Gospel of Matthew, both in form and content, is closely related on the one hand to the Jewish literature of the centuries immediately before and after Christ, and on the other hand to the Christian literature of the second century. The commentator has attempted to provide enough references to place the reader in touch with this rich illustrative material, but has at the same time largely confined these to a few books which are available in any good theological library. Books of the Apocrypha and Pseudepigrapha, the various tractates of the Mishnah (e.g., Aboth, Kilaim), the Apostolic Fathers, and the writings of the Apocryphal New Testament are cited by chapter and verse, as in the Bible. The historical works of Josephus and Eusebius are cited by book, chapter, and section (e.g., II. 15. 6). When quoting from the Mishnah, the commentator has attempted his own translation or paraphrase. References are only occasionally made to other rabbinical writings.

The following are the principal ancient sources cited in the Commentary.

CHARLES, R. H. *Apocrypha and Pseudepigrapha of the Old Testament*. 2 vols. Oxford: Clarendon Press, 1913. Vol. II of this work contains such books as Jubilees, Enoch, and the Testaments of the Twelve Patriarchs.

DANBY, HERBERT. *The Mishnah*. Oxford: Clarendon Press, 1933.

JAMES, M. R. *The Apocryphal New Testament*. Oxford: Clarendon Press, 1924.

LAKE, KIRSOPP. *The Apostolic Fathers*. 2 vols. London: William Heinemann, 1912-13.

LAWLOR, H. J. and OULTON, J. E. L. *The Ecclesiastical History and the Martyrs of Palestine*. Vol. I. London: Society for Promoting Christian Knowledge, 1927. Also available in the "Ante-Nicene Fathers" series.

MATTHEW

TEXT, EXEGESIS, AND EXPOSITION

I. BEGINNING OF THE NARRATIVE (1:1–4:25)

A. THE GENEALOGY OF JESUS (1:1-17)

Matthew begins his book with a genealogy. His purpose is to prove that Jesus is the rightful Messiah according to Jewish law by showing his descent from Abraham, from David and the kings of Judah, and from Zerubbabel, head of the Jewish community in the postexilic period (Hag. 2:23; Zech. 3:8; 4:6-14). The list of ancestors may originally have been compiled by a Jewish Christian who believed that Jesus was "son of David" through Joseph and who perhaps regarded James the Lord's brother and others of Jesus' family as the appropriate leaders of the church after the Resurrection.

Many Jewish families possessed genealogies which were accurate for a number of generations. Such lists were necessary for a number of purposes—for example, to establish priestly descent. This genealogy, however, with its scheme of fourteens, shows signs of being artificially constructed. The fourteens may originally have been accidental; but appearing in the list are errors which a careful compiler would not have made, or which, if present in his source, he could easily have corrected from the Bible. Luke's genealogy (3:23-38) by contrast appears more genuine and more true to the facts. It contains forty-two names after David's, instead of Matthew's twenty-seven, and traces the descent, not through kings, but through David's son Nathan (II Sam. 5:14) and many obscure people, though Shealtiel and Zerubbabel also appear.

Matthew's list, down through Zerubbabel, probably is based on the LXX text of

---

The Gospel: the Good News.—Good news concerns an act or an event: "The most wonderful thing has happened!" Thus the gospel is never merely man's interpretation or even man's deepest conviction, but the Act and Event without which there could be no conviction or interpretation. *The* Act: "Very God of very God; . . . who for us men and for our salvation came down . . . and was made man" (Nicene Creed). The preacher is the herald of that Act, the teacher is its interpreter. "God so loved the world" (John 3:16) is a glowing summary of the Act and the Event. Food vendors in the streets of Damascus cry "Ya Karîm, Ya Karîm—the gift of the bountiful One." So this author cries, of a better gift than food or water. In that Act is the self-revealing of God, the meaning of history,

and the unfolding of personal destiny. For illustration see the nine closing lines of Browning's "Karshish, the Arab Physician."

According to St. Matthew.—Good news requires messengers, else it may be lost. The teller of the Event becomes instinct with its joy and converting power. Each teller finds new accents of wonder in the Good News. *The* gospel thus is "*my* gospel" (II Tim. 2:8). Notice the distinctive accents which Matthew hears: God's love for Israel and the fulfillment in Christ of Israel's highest promise; the royal authority of Jesus as Teacher and as Savior-King; the fruit of the gospel in the *ecclēsia*, the liturgy, polity, and function of "the beloved community"; a profound sense of redemption and judgment. (See Intro., pp. 232-35.) These insights make his

1 The book of the generation of Jesus Christ, the son of David, the son of Abraham.

2 Abraham begat Isaac; and Isaac begat Jacob; and Jacob begat Judas and his brethren;

3 And Judas begat Phares and Zara of Thamar; and Phares begat Esrom; and Esrom begat Aram;

4 And Aram begat Aminadab; and Aminadab begat Naasson; and Naasson begat Salmon;

1 The book of the genealogy of Jesus Christ, the son of David, the son of Abraham.

2 Abraham was the father of Isaac, and Isaac the father of Jacob, and Jacob the father of Judah and his brothers, 3 and Judah the father of Per'ez and Ze'rah by Ta'mar, and Per'ez the father of Hez'ron, and Hez'ron the father of Ram,*a* 4 and Ram*a* the father of Am-min'a-dab, and Am-min'a-dab the father of Nah'shon, and

a Greek *Aram.*

I Chr. 1–3. We can best understand the omission of Joash, Amaziah, and Azariah if the compiler took 'Οζείας (vss. 8-9) to refer to Azariah instead of Ahaziah. We do not know the source of vss. 13-16.

Matthew probably obtained his list from a source instead of compiling it himself. If he himself had "searched the scriptures," it is likely he would have done so more carefully. The genealogy does not harmonize well with his doctrine of the Virgin Birth. No doubt he was able to use it as further evidence of Jesus' messiahship only by interpreting it as a legal, not a physical, genealogy.

1:1. Book of the genealogy: "List" might be better. Matthew aims to give the flavor of biblical style, and his phrase may be patterned after Gen. 5:1 LXX, "This is the book of the origin [genesis] of men," or he may have Neh. 7:5 in mind. **Christ** is an English form of Χριστός, which represents the Hebrew *māshîaḥ,* "anointed." In Jewish literature the term came to be a title for the king who would bring salvation in the final age, and probably it derives from such passages as Pss. 2:2; 18:50; I Sam. 2:10; etc. In the Psalms of Solomon and other pre-Christian writings the form is usually "the anointed of the Lord" (Pss. Sol. 17:36; cf. Luke 2:26); later it is simply "the Messiah," as in II Esdras 7:28-29; II Baruch 29:3, and rabbinical literature. The rabbis often refer to the future age as the "days of the Messiah." First-century Christians believed that Messiah had already come; throughout the N.T. the term is used to refer to Jesus, only occasionally as a title. The Gospels usually refer to the central figure as "Jesus," and the formula **Jesus Christ** is infrequent. Here, as often in the epistles, "Christ" is practically a surname.

The son of David, the son of Abraham: Jesus, as heir of David, is Messiah (Pss. Sol. 17:23[21]; Acts 2:29-36; but contrast Mark 12:35-37, where this argument is repudiated). Jews did not universally hold that Messiah was son of David, but from 63 B.C. on, this was the prevalent opinion. It was standard Jewish doctrine that "to Abraham and his seed were the promises made" (Gal. 3:16; Gen. 22:18). The rabbis would have regarded Abraham and David as the high points in the genealogy.

3. The father of Perez and Zerah by Tamar: Women were not usually mentioned in Jewish genealogies, but Rahab, Ruth, and Bath-sheba are included here, as well as Tamar. Jewish legends celebrated Tamar and Ruth as ancestors of Messiah, vindicated Bath-sheba as far as possible, and praised Rahab. Yet Ruth was a foreigner and scandals were attached to the other names. The thought behind this was that the God of Israel, in his infinite power and love, could make great kings out of the descendants of even these women. Matthew wholeheartedly adopts this idea, and adds the supreme miracle,

---

Gospel in true sense the "first Gospel." The fact that we do not surely know the name of the author can be gladness rather than dismay: God has more prophets than we knew, and the gospel more messengers.

1:1-17. The Genealogy.—This is not barren ground. It yields bright flowers for those who search. In vs. 1 all history is gathered up in Christ. The sovereignty of Christ is stressed throughout, for there is utmost care to trace his descent through Israel's royal line. Yet name after name in the list (e.g., vs. 5) spells our human frailty; he was "found in fashion as a man" (Phil. 2:8). How many names are ordinary: God has not despised our obscure life! The number of women mentioned is an inter-

5 And Salmon begat Booz of Rachab; and Booz begat Obed of Ruth; and Obed begat Jesse;

6 And Jesse begat David the king; and David the king begat Solomon of her *that had been the wife* of Urias;

7 And Solomon begat Roboam; and Roboam begat Abia; and Abia begat Asa;

8 And Asa begat Josaphat; and Josaphat begat Joram; and Joram begat Ozias;

9 And Ozias begat Joatham; and Joatham begat Achaz; and Achaz begat Ezekias;

10 And Ezekias begat Manasses; and Manasses begat Amon; and Amon begat Josias;

11 And Josias begat Jechonias and his brethren, about the time they were carried away to Babylon:

12 And after they were brought to Babylon, Jechonias begat Salathiel; and Salathiel begat Zorobabel;

13 And Zorobabel begat Abiud; and Abiud begat Eliakim; and Eliakim begat Azor;

14 And Azor begat Sadoc; and Sadoc begat Achim; and Achim begat Eliud;

15 And Eliud begat Eleazar; and Eleazar begat Matthan; and Matthan begat Jacob;

16 And Jacob begat Joseph the husband

Nah'shon the father of Sal'mon, 5 and Sal'mon the father of Bo'az by Ra'hab, and Bo'az the father of O'bed by Ruth, and O'bed the father of Jesse, 6 and Jesse the father of David the king.

And David was the father of Solomon by the wife of U-ri'ah, 7 and Solomon the father of Re-ho-bo'am, and Re-ho-bo'am the father of A-bi'jah, and A-bi'jah the father of Asa,[b] 8 and Asa[b] the father of Je-hosh'a-phat, and Je-hosh'a-phat the father of Jo'ram, and Jo'ram the father of Uz-zi'ah, 9 and Uz-zi'ah the father of Jo'tham, and Jo'tham the father of A'haz, and A'haz the father of Hez-e-ki'ah, 10 and Hez-e-ki'ah the father of Ma-nas'seh, and Ma-nas'seh the father of Amos,[c] and Amos[c] the father of Jo-si'ah, 11 and Jo-si'ah the father of Jech-o-ni'ah and his brothers, at the time of the deportation to Babylon.

12 And after the deportation to Babylon: Jech-o-ni'ah was the father of She-al'ti-el,[d] and She-al'ti-el[d] the father of Ze-rub'ba-bel, 13 and Ze-rub'ba-bel the father of A-bi'ud, and A-bi'ud the father of E-li'a-kim, and E-li'a-kim the father of A'zor, 14 and A'zor the father of Za'dok, and Za'dok the father of A'chim, and A'chim the father of E-li'ud, 15 and E-li'ud the father of E-le-a'zar, and E-le-a'zar the father of Matthan, and Matthan the father of Jacob, 16 and Jacob the father of Joseph

[b] Greek *Asaph.*
[c] Some authorities read *Amon.*
[d] Greek *Salathiel.*

although of course in this case there was no suggestion of scandal; Jesus was not physically the son of Joseph, and yet God ordained him as the heir of the theocratic monarchy.

5. Salmon the father of Boaz by Rahab: But Rahab belonged to the much earlier times of Joshua, who, according to Jewish tradition, was her husband.

9. Uzziah the father of Jotham: Uzziah (**Ozias,** KJV) is Ahaziah. The names of Joash, Amaziah, and Azariah are missing.

11. Josiah the father of Jechoniah: The name of Jehoiakim is missing.

12. Shealtiel the father of Zerubbabel: So Hag. 1:1, etc., and some LXX MSS of I Chr. 3:19; but according to the Hebrew of this verse, Zerubbabel is son of Jechoniah's other son Pedaiah.

16. There are three main textual forms in which this verse is transmitted: (*a*) **Jacob the father of Joseph the husband of Mary, of whom Jesus was born, who is called**

esting item, especially **Rahab** and **Bath-sheba** (**the wife of Uriah**) in their mixed good and evil and **Ruth** as representing blood other than that of Jewish exclusiveness. The proclamation in vs. 16 is climactic—no human birth, however royal, can account for Jesus; he came

by the direct and creative act of God. There is a mystery in Christ which human factors alone cannot possibly explain. Thus the genealogy unfolds the treasure of the Good News.

16, 21, 23, 25. *The Name of Jesus.*—With us a name is often hardly more than an identifica-

of Mary, of whom was born Jesus, who is called Christ.

17 So all the generations from Abraham to David *are* fourteen generations; and from David until the carrying away into Babylon *are* fourteen generations; and from the carrying away into Babylon unto Christ *are* fourteen generations.

the husband of Mary, of whom Jesus was born, who is called Christ.

17 So all the generations from Abraham to David were fourteen generations, and from David to the deportation to Babylon fourteen generations, and from the deportation to Babylon to the Christ fourteen generations.

Christ. This is the reading of the Alexandrian and Byzantine texts. (*b*) "Jacob begot Joseph, to whom [the] virgin Mary, having been betrothed to him, bore Jesus who is called Christ." So Koridethi (Θ), the Ferrar group, and (with variations) some O.L. MSS and the Curetonian Syriac. (*c*) "Jacob begot Joseph. And Joseph, to whom was betrothed [the] virgin Mary, begot Jesus who is called Christ." So the Sinaitic Syriac. Reading *c* fits better with the original purpose of the genealogy. On the other hand, Matthew is a strong proponent of the virgin birth doctrine, and reading *a* looks like his own attempt to make the genealogy conform to this doctrine. This was not difficult because, according to the Mishnah, if a man acknowledged his son's paternity, there was no further question about it (Baba Bathra 8:6). Possibly Matthew's source contained some such reading as *c*. If that source continued to be extant for some time, the reading may have crept into some MSS of Matthew. Reading *b* may be an attempt to combine the other two. **Mary** is a form of the O.T. name Miriam.

17. There are fourteen names in each of the first two groups, but only thirteen in the third. If Jehoiakim were restored to the second group, there would be forty-two names, but the count would be fourteen, fifteen, thirteen; and there is the further difficulty of the other three missing names (see on vss. 9, 11). We can only speculate on the original form of the list. Since the Hebrew letter daleth (ד) has the value of four, and waw (ו) of six, fourteen may be a symbol for David (דוד).

---

tion tag. Rarely is its meaning a major item. It is chosen rather for its associations, as when a child is named after a relative or friend; or for its sound, as when we "like the name." But the Hebrews chose a name for its meaning in God— to acknowledge his gift, or to express hope or destiny in him—as a study of the original purport of Hebrew names (see any good dictionary) will show. "John" and "Elizabeth" are instances. Names then meant nature. This chapter gives three names for Jesus.

The name **Jesus** is both a human tenderness and a prophecy of a work which a mere man could never do. Jesus was a fairly common name in Israel, and has a strong yet winning sound. But it means "The Lord is salvation": **for he shall save his people from their sins.** You and I can, and should, forgive injury done to us; but we cannot forgive sins, for sins are ultimately not against ourselves or our neighbors but against the Creator. A liar breaks faith, not only with his fellow men, but with living Truth; and therefore only Truth can forgive him. Only *incarnate* Truth can forgive him, for only so can he know himself forgiven. This prime office of Jesus is made the more difficult because deliverance from sin is oftentimes the last need we consider or desire. Amiel rightly

insisted that "the cardinal question is that of sin." [1] Thus Jesus is the name for the Son of man who is also the Son of God. For illustration see the story by J. Colwell in connection with this verse in *The Great Texts of the Bible.*[2]

Emmanuel is another name for Jesus: **God with us.** The word "dwelt" in John 1:14 could be translated "tabernacled," and echoes that far-off time when the ark of the covenant was the center of the huddled tents of Israel by night and the vanguard of the march by day. There is similar meaning in the word **Emmanuel.** Through the incarnation, God has made common cause with man to share and bear our sorrow, to rejoice in our joys, and to carry the burden of our sins. "The Beloved Captain" portrayed by Donald Hankey,[3] a man who voluntarily became partner of every experience of the men in the ranks, and who at last died for them, gives only a pale hint of the voluntary comradeship of God with men.

Christ is the other name for Jesus. It is, of course, the Greek form of the Hebrew title

[1] *Amiel's Journal,* tr. Mrs. Humphry Ward (New York: Brentano's, 1928), p. 14.

[2] Ed. James Hastings (New York: Charles Scribner's Sons, 1914), *St. Matthew,* pp. 9-10.

[3] *A Student in Arms* (New York: E. P. Dutton & Co., 1917), ch. iv.

18 ¶ Now the birth of Jesus Christ was on this wise: When as his mother Mary was espoused to Joseph, before they came together, she was found with child of the Holy Ghost.

19 Then Joseph her husband, being a just *man,* and not willing to make her a

18 Now the birth of Jesus Christ[e] took place in this way. When his mother Mary had been betrothed to Joseph, before they came together she was found to be with child of the Holy Spirit; 19 and her husband

[e] Some ancient authorities read *of the Christ.*

B. BIRTH AND CHILDHOOD (1:18–2:23)
1. THE BIRTH OF JESUS (1:18-25)

18. Some MSS omit **Jesus.** Matthew probably wrote: "Now the birth of the Messiah was thus." **When his mother Mary had been betrothed to Joseph, before they came together:** A Jewish betrothal could be dissolved only by the man's giving the woman a writ of divorce, and a betrothed virgin was considered a widow if her fiancé died. Note the phrase **Mary thy wife** (vs. 20). Yet betrothal was distinguished theoretically and actually from marriage, which took place only when the bridegroom took the bride to his home and the marriage was consummated.

With child of the Holy Spirit: Here, as in the O.T., the phrase suggests the all-creative power of God. A similarly simple concept of the Spirit is found in Mark 1:12; Acts 8:39. The O.T. knew of many births which took place only through divine intervention (e.g., Gen. 18:11-14; 25:21; I Sam. 1:4-20), but this story differs in that Jesus had no human father. Luke's account (1:26-38; 2:1-7) could have been originally a story of a miraculous birth of the more traditional kind, which was developed into a virgin birth story, perhaps by the addition of Luke 1:34-37 and the words "his betrothed" in Luke 2:5. (Mary was legally Joseph's wife if she traveled with him.) But Matthew's account presupposes the Virgin Birth throughout. Pagan mythology had many tales of children born from intercourse between a god and a woman or a goddess and a man—indeed most "heroes" were thought to have been so born—but Jesus' story is of a very different sort. We do not have data which enable us to pronounce on the historical value of Matthew's account. We can only point out that: (*a*) Matthew and Luke alone mention the Virgin Birth. Other writers, such as Mark, the Fourth Evangelist, and Paul teach a high Christology without reference to it. (*b*) Matthew and Luke have knowledge of such a story from separate and independent sources. (*c*) The story first appears in Christian circles which are in close touch with Jewish tradition. If it arises out of pious speculation, it is nevertheless based on faith in the unlimited power of the one God, not on pagan mythology (see, e.g., W. L. Knox, *Some Hellenistic Elements in Primitive Christianity* [London: British Academy, 1944], pp. 22-25; Morton S. Enslin, "The Christian Stories of the Nativity," *Journal of Biblical Literature,* LIX [1940], 317-38).

19. **A just man** is one who observes the Jewish law. According to the law, two courses were permissible in such a situation as Joseph saw confronting him: he might expose Mary by bringing her before the court—the Greek word does not necessarily mean **make her a public example** as in KJV—or he might divorce her privately by handing

---

"Messiah." This "first" Gospel is sure that Jesus is the fulfillment of Jewish hope and prophecy. He is Judge and Savior and King. But he gave to these titles a new, deep meaning: the savior-hood was no mere deliverance of the nation from bondage to the oppressor, but a re-creation of human nature; and the kingship was rooted in divine compassion. The deliverance from sin which Christ brought was not by violence or by Mosaic threatenings, but by catharsis through his suffering love. These names are the index of Christ's nature. Bernardino of Siena recommended that the holy name should be

inscribed on the walls of homes and public buildings, and he himself is said to have carried about with him a piece of parchment with the monogram IHS.[4]

18-20. *The Character of Joseph.*—Too little attention has been given to Joseph's part in the gospel story. Reading these lines and between the lines we can see the manner of the man. He was just, a word which in Matthew

[4] See F. R. Weber, *Church Symbolism* (Cleveland: S. H. Jansen, 1938), ch. vii; Paul Thureau-Dangin, *Saint Bernardine* (New York: E. P. Dutton & Co., 1906), pp. 66-67, 73, 77, 81.

public example, was minded to put her away privily.

20 But while he thought on these things, behold, the angel of the Lord appeared unto him in a dream, saying, Joseph, thou son of David, fear not to take unto thee Mary thy wife: for that which is conceived in her is of the Holy Ghost.

21 And she shall bring forth a son, and thou shalt call his name JESUS: for he shall save his people from their sins.

22 Now all this was done, that it might be fulfilled which was spoken of the Lord by the prophet, saying,

23 Behold, a virgin shall be with child, and shall bring forth a son, and they shall call his name Emmanuel, which being interpreted is, God with us.

24 Then Joseph being raised from sleep did as the angel of the Lord had bidden him, and took unto him his wife:

25 And knew her not till she had brought forth her firstborn son: and he called his name JESUS.

Joseph, being a just man and unwilling to put her to shame, resolved to divorce her quietly. 20 But as he considered this, behold, an angel of the Lord appeared to him in a dream, saying, "Joseph, son of David, do not fear to take Mary your wife, for that which is conceived in her is of the Holy Spirit; 21 she will bear a son, and you shall call his name Jesus, for he will save his people from their sins." 22 All this took place to fulfill what the Lord had spoken by the prophet:

23 "Behold, a virgin shall conceive
  and bear a son,
  and his name shall be called
    Em-man'u-el"

(which means, God with us). 24 When Joseph woke from sleep, he did as the angel of the Lord commanded him; he took his wife, 25 but knew her not until she had borne a son; and he called his name Jesus.

---

her a writ in the presence of two witnesses. The Greek of **and unwilling** might mean "and *yet* not willing"; or the meaning may be: Just *because* of his righteousness he was unwilling.

20. Matthew, like the E writer in the Pentateuch, frequently tells of revelation through dreams. Vss. 20-21 appear to be in the form of Hebrew poetry.

21. **Jesus: for he shall save:** The play on words (Yēshûa', Jesus; yôshîa', shall save) is possible in Hebrew but not in Aramaic. The name Joshua or Jesus means "Yahweh is salvation." **His people** is the honorific title of Israel. **From their sins:** In Jewish thought salvation from sin is not an essential part of Messiah's vocation, but on the other hand, one of the characteristics of the days of the Messiah was that sin would disappear. Messiah was to judge and destroy sinners and demons, and God would pour out his Spirit, which brings holiness (Test. Judah 24).

22. On the formula **this took place to fulfill** see Intro., p. 233. Similar formulas are known in rabbinical writings.

23. The word παρθένος (here taken from Isa. 7:14 LXX) normally means **virgin,** and the word in the Hebrew, 'almāh, means "young woman." Occasionally the LXX translator uses παρθένος to refer to a girl who is no longer a virgin (e.g., Gen. 34:3). Even if ideas of a miraculous birth originally lay behind Isa. 7:14, they had been forgotten by the first century; but Matthew seized on this text as further confirmation of his story. It was especially appropriate because of the name **Emmanuel,** which he correctly translated **God with us.** Isaiah's thought was: "The deliverance will be so striking that a mother will give her child this name."

25. **But knew her not until she had borne a son:** The phrase does not support the theory of Mary's perpetual virginity, and it is presupposed in 13:55-56=Mark 6:3 that

---

implies both religious scruple and obedience to the will of God. Here the word may also mean sympathy and kindness. He was sensitive to divine visitation—as in his dream—and quick to heed the call of the luminous moment. There

is cause to assume that he was devoted to Mary and the children of his household. The word "Father" as an ascription for God had been used in the O.T. (Pss. 68:5; 103:13), but the word was fairly infrequent, and it implied na-

2 Now when Jesus was born in Bethle-hem of Judea in the days of Herod the king, behold, there came wise men from the east to Jerusalem,

2 Now when Jesus was born in Bethle-hem of Judea in the days of Herod the king, behold, wise men from the East came

---

Jesus had brothers and sisters. However, two ancient MSS read only: "And she bore a son."

2. The Visit of the Magi (2:1-12)

The adoration of the magi, like the other narratives in this chapter, has no parallel in any other first-century Christian writing. There is thus no way to ascertain whether it has been embellished, or indeed, whether it "happened" at all as a matter of literal fact. The value and importance of the narrative do not depend on its accuracy; the story is rather to be thought of as a work of art which the evangelist presents to the Christ child as his offering. Christians who hear it read during the Christmas or Epiphany season instinctively recognize its value, regardless of the question of fact. It expresses the truth that men have been brought from far and by many ways to worship Christ. It also breathes the sense of wonder and thanksgiving that through the birth of this Child, and his subsequent life, death, and resurrection, the world has been redeemed. Matthew and his contemporaries felt that even nature itself could not be unmoved in the presence of such a stupendous event.

2:1. Bethlehem is five miles south of Jerusalem, and a church there marks the traditional site of Jesus' birth. If this story had originally been connected with the foregoing, the note of time, **in the days of Herod the king,** would not have appeared at this point, but earlier. **Herod** the Great was made king of the Jews by the Roman Senate

---

tional perhaps more than individual relationship. But Jesus used it in ways most intimate, and taught us in the Lord's Prayer so to use it. That fact is partially, though not ultimately, a tribute to Joseph's care for his household—all the tribute one man need desire. It is fair to assume that Joseph was the human channel through which Jesus drew some of his incomparable wisdom.

2:1. Bethlehem.—The name is made dear by Phillips Brooks's hymn, "O little town of Bethlehem." It means "house of bread," that is to say, the village in the grainfields; and the meaning is driven deeper by Christ, who is the bread of life. To Matthew the name Bethlehem signified the sovereignty of Christ; for Bethlehem, rich in tradition, was the wellspring of a royal stream (see vss. 5-6). To us Bethlehem means lowliness, smallness: "O little town of Bethlehem" (see original, Mic. 5:2). So it was a fit birthplace for a meek King, for he was thus identified with all the seeming pettiness of our common days. He has made it both a "well of Bethlehem" (II Sam. 23:15) and a "house of bread."

1, 3, 7, 16, 19. Herod.—Matthew portrays the old king in his cunning and cruelty as a man alarmed by the coming of the new King seemingly weak but actually divine. This is the clash that shakes all our history. Herod had magnificence; Christ was born in a manger. Herod had energy; Christ was a helpless babe.

Herod had power and used it to cruel ends; Christ had compassion and a different power. Herod was crafty; Christ guileless. Herod had **all Jerusalem with him,** and Jesus seemed almost unbefriended. Notice how the story stresses these contrasts. The enigma of history is this: How does goodness survive when badness has both conspiracy and the sword? The answer is in a governance of history above and beyond the wit of wicked men. That governance is here traced. Right may be on the scaffold and wrong on the throne, but "standeth God within the shadow, keeping watch above his own." [5]

1-10. The Star in the East.—The fact that this story may be after the fashion of the Midrash Haggada [6] does not impair its inner Christian truth. The issue here is not astronomical fact but lofty business of the soul. Christ does not need these stories to enthrone him; he enthrones them.

So we may notice here the beckonings of God. He set the sign, far above man's reach, in the mystery and majesty of the sky, and in man's longing, for our prime need is not for the grocer or even for the doctor, but for the Savior. This yearning is wider than any one man or one land; astrology in its searching of the sky is but confession of the need, which can be met only from beyond our earth. Thomas Hardy, despite

[5] James Russell Lowell, "The Present Crisis."
[6] See Asher Feldman, *The Parables and Similes of the Rabbis* (Cambridge: University Press, 1924), pp. 2 ff.

2 Saying, Where is he that is born King of the Jews? for we have seen his star in the east, and are come to worship him.

3 When Herod the king had heard *these things,* he was troubled, and all Jerusalem with him.

to Jerusalem, saying, 2 "Where is he who has been born king of the Jews? For we have seen his star in the East, and have come to worship him." 3 When Herod the king heard this, he was troubled, and all

---

in 40 B.C. and gained control of his realm a few years later. He died in 4 B.C. **Wise men** is a translation of μάγοι. The magi seem originally to have been a Median tribe of priests; later the word refers to the Zoroastrian priestly caste. An embassy of Parthian magi paid homage to Nero at Naples in A.D. 66 and returned home by another route. "Magi" also denotes astrologers and magicians generally. The N.T. and the rabbis usually employ it in an evil sense ("magicians"), but Matthew probably thinks of Babylonian astrologers.

2. Magi believed that a **star** could be the fravashi (counterpart or angel) of a great man. Jews often identified the star out of Jacob (Num. 24:17) with the Messiah. Closer parallels are found in pagan antiquity and in the late Jewish stories that stars announced the births of Isaac and Moses. The story meant to Ignatius that all magic had been overthrown by the birth of Christ (Ign. Eph. 19:3). Matthew may draw this contrast: the Gentiles worship him; Herod seeks to kill him. We cannot identify the star, though attempts to do so have been made. Jupiter and Saturn were in close conjunction three times in 7 B.C.; Halley's comet passed over the perihelion on October 8, 12 B.C. The words **in the east** might be translated "at its heliacal rising," i.e., its first appearance in the east at the time of sunrise. **Worship** may mean to Matthew divine worship, or the homage paid an Oriental king.

---

his almost impervious skepticism, found in a thrush's song "such ecstatic sound" that he guessed "there trembled through" it

Some blessed Hope, whereof he knew
And I was unaware.[7]

God leaves no man without sign of himself.

Yet this story is also a token of man's seeking. There is purpose in the journey itself; that is why Christ was not born in the town where the wise men lived. God safeguards our freedom; he gives the sign, but we may stay or journey. The journey provides also that hazard which every true man covets. The journey always seems to be against common sense; the "practical people" condemn it, and later live by borrowing its courage. The journey is always blocked both by nature's barriers and by the Herod-systems of the world. But it leads to life for all who venture. Some do not venture, and share the sad lot of Babouscka of Russian folklore.[8]

Thus the story tells of home at journey's end. The wise men found God—and themselves—when they worshiped. Marco Polo tells of a Persian village from which, so the villagers claimed, the wise men started. The young king found, so they said, a young Christ; the king of

middle years found a Savior of his own age; and the old king found in Christ an old Companion (Bk. I, chs. 13–14). For each man finds his true life in Christ, and every nation finds in him "the desire of all nations." The stars seen from beneath seem cold, even though the sky is jeweled; but seen from above they are the sign and sacrament of God. Perhaps this story is the answer to all earth's seeming imperturbabilities! A queen once stopped her carriage to help a lost child, and thus became a poor parable of all that God has done in Christ. The storms of history and its wildernesses seem to mock the star, but not if we follow—**and lo, the star which they had seen . . . went before them.**

1-12. *The Wise Men.*—See Exeg. for instances of just such journeys taken by astrologers. Certain items about the magi are significant for Christian truth. They saw the star when busy at their own task; daily fidelity gives men a quicker awareness of the truth. The Connecticut senators, on the famous "dark day" in New England's history, were wise to remain at the day's task rather than to leave it for frantic prayer.[9] The magi were foreigners—a fact that the church has celebrated in the feast of the Epiphany, Christianity being a world-wide faith. The statue of Christ on the ridge of the Andean mountains between Chile and Argen-

---

[7] "The Darkling Thrush," *Poems of the Past and the Present* (New York: Harper & Bros., 1902).

[8] Carolyn S. Bailey and Clara M. Lewis, *For the Children's Hour* (New York: Milton Bradley Co., 1922), p. 235.

[9] See Edwin Markham, "A Judgment Hour," *The Gates of Paradise and Other Poems* (Garden City: Doubleday, Page & Co., 1920), p. 36.

4 And when he had gathered all the chief priests and scribes of the people together, he demanded of them where Christ should be born.

5 And they said unto him, In Bethlehem of Judea: for thus it is written by the prophet,

6 And thou Bethlehem, *in* the land of Juda, art not the least among the princes of Juda: for out of thee shall come a Governor, that shall rule my people Israel.

7 Then Herod, when he had privily called the wise men, inquired of them diligently what time the star appeared.

8 And he sent them to Bethlehem, and said, Go and search diligently for the young child; and when ye have found *him,* bring me word again, that I may come and worship him also.

Jerusalem with him; 4 and assembling all the chief priests and scribes of the people, he inquired of them where the Christ was to be born. 5 They told him, "In Bethlehem of Judea; for so it is written by the prophet:

6 'And you, O Bethlehem, in the
land of Judah,
are by no means least among
the rulers of Judah;
for from you shall come a ruler
who will govern my people Israel.'"

7 Then Herod summoned the wise men secretly and ascertained from them what time the star appeared; 8 and he sent them to Bethlehem, saying, "Go and search diligently for the child, and when you have found him bring me word, that I too may

---

4. The chief priests were probably members of the families from which the high priests were at that time appointed. The **scribes** were experts in the religious law. The term "scribe" may include both those scholars who were members of the Sanhedrin and their pupils. A scribe was ordained, probably by his teacher, with the laying on of hands. About this time the honorific title "rabbi" ("my great one") began to be given to scribes. A scribe could act as a judge in criminal cases and decide civil cases as they arose. The Sanhedrin of Jerusalem—which was the religious and also the civil and criminal supreme court—seems to have been made up of the "chief priests," scribes, and perhaps also the "elders" or heads of influential families (Luke 22:66). Herod would not have convened this entire assembly to inquire where the Messiah **was to be born.** He might have consulted a few of its members.

5. Bethlehem of Judea was the birthplace of David, king of Judah.

6. The Targum paraphrases Mic. 5:2 thus: "Out of thee shall go before me the Messiah, to exercise lordship over Israel, whose name is known to me since the beginning." Matthew's quotation is not from the LXX; apparently it is a fresh translation from the Hebrew, and the wording is changed: Bethlehem once was, but is no longer, **least among the rulers of Judah** (Goodspeed: "leading places of Judah"). Some scholars believe that O.T. prophecy is the sole source of the tradition that Jesus was born there.

7. What time the star appeared would be important for astrology, and also would enable Herod to determine the age of the child.

8. Klostermann remarks that the actual Herod, when **he sent them to Bethlehem,** would have sent murderers along with them.

---

tina points us to the only source of world peace. The magi acted with abandon. The knowledge of Chinese, which our modern world would endorse as very necessary knowledge, began with the "folly" of Morrison's attempt to break the Great Wall. Later he was honored by scholars and philological societies for his original research in the Chinese language.[1] But he did not go to China to study language or to blaze a trail for trade; he went to tell the good news. The course of life is too often this: we do at

last from shabby and selfish motives what we should have done at first in a fine rapture of the soul. But the magi journeyed in a noble abandon. There is a further fact about the wise men which proves them wise: they were **come to worship him.** Thus John Ruskin in *Fors Clavigera:* "These men, for their own part, came—I beg you very earnestly again to note this—not to see, nor talk—but to do reverence. They are neither curious nor talkative, but submissive."[2] Thus we are confronted again with the question: Why are we born? All penultimate an-

[1] See W. J. Townsend, *Robert Morrison* (New York: Fleming H. Revell Co., 1888), pp. 87-88, 110, 112 ff., 123.

[2] Letter xii, 23d December, 1871.

9 When they had heard the king, they departed; and, lo, the star, which they saw in the east, went before them, till it came and stood over where the young child was.

10 When they saw the star, they rejoiced with exceeding great joy.

11 ¶ And when they were come into the house, they saw the young child with Mary his mother, and fell down, and worshipped him: and when they had opened their treasures, they presented unto him gifts; gold, and frankincense, and myrrh.

12 And being warned of God in a dream that they should not return to Herod, they departed into their own country another way.

13 And when they were departed, behold, the angel of the Lord appeareth to

come and worship him." 9 When they had heard the king they went their way; and lo, the star which they had seen in the East went before them, till it came to rest over the place where the child was. 10 When they saw the star, they rejoiced exceedingly with great joy; 11 and going into the house they saw the child with Mary his mother, and they fell down and worshiped him. Then, opening their treasures, they offered him gifts, gold and frankincense and myrrh. 12 And being warned in a dream not to return to Herod, they departed to their own country by another way.

13 Now when they had departed, be-

---

9. It is not certain how Matthew visualized this sign.

11. **Their treasures,** i.e., the containers. Matthew no doubt thinks of Isa. 60:6, where "they from Sheba," i.e., south Arabia, bring gold and incense. In Ps. 72:10, "the kings of Sheba and Seba bring gifts." No symbolism is intended. Gold and fragrant resins, used in worship, perfume, medicine, embalming, would be appropriate gifts for a monarch.

12. **Warned:** The Greek word means "instructed by an oracle."

3. The Flight into Egypt (2:13-15)

13. **Egypt** included the Sinaitic peninsula, and its nearest part was not far from Bethlehem. As early as the beginning of the second century A.D. there was a Jewish story

---

swers yield at last to the real answer: "To glorify God, and fully to enjoy Him forever." [3]

11. *The Gifts of the Magi.*—The hymn "We three kings of Orient are" gives the details with which legend has adorned the well-loved story. Gold, brought by Caspar, can represent our gifts of substance. Livelihood usurps the place of life unless life is rigorously made dedicate to God revealed in Christ. How much of our strife is caused by clutching at things! Abraham Lincoln once said of his two quarreling sons that they were a symbol of the whole world: "I have three English walnuts and each boy wants two." Trade is now so interlocked—examine a linen collar for proof, with its attendant machinery, materials, finance, export—that it becomes a fratricide unless it is first a worship.

Melchior brought frankincense which, because it is a fragrance, can represent our inner treasure of thought and influence. The wise men were the scientists of their time. Is science safe unless it becomes worship? The music that most enthralls us is essentially religious, and our greatest architecture is a prayer in stone. So scientific knowledge must be dedicate. Our keenest thought, even that concerned only for

"the truth," easily becomes a pride or threat; and influence, even that which for popularity is willing to be kind, easily becomes miasmic rather than a fragrance. Thought is worthy only when it is marked by reverence.

Balthazzar brought myrrh. We must be careful not to read our interpretation into the story, for the original intends only that myrrh was precious and therefore a gift fit for the King. But it is almost inevitable and fitting that myrrh, because of its use in embalming, should stand in this instance for our sorrow and suffering. This bitter gift is, however strangely, the hardest for us to give to Christ: we prefer to keep it for its luxury of bitter protest. The reason why sorrow hardens one man and melts another is just that the one man keeps his sorrow selfishly and the other offers it in oblation. Harriet Martineau tells of a joy which only the disappointed can know—the joy of "agreeing with God silently when nobody knows what is in their hearts." It is worth noting that all three kings brought their best. George Frederick Watts had inscribed on his seal, "The Utmost for the Highest." This could be the motto written across the matchless story of the magi.

13. *Into Egypt.*—See Exeg. for comment on the parallel between this story and the Pharaoh-

[3] *The Larger Catechism of the Presbyterian Church in the United States of America,* Question 1.

Joseph in a dream, saying, Arise, and take the young child and his mother, and flee into Egypt, and be thou there until I bring thee word: for Herod will seek the young child to destroy him.

14 When he arose, he took the young child and his mother by night, and departed into Egypt:

15 And was there until the death of Herod: that it might be fulfilled which was spoken of the Lord by the prophet, saying, Out of Egypt have I called my son.

16 ¶ Then Herod, when he saw that he was mocked of the wise men, was exceeding wroth, and sent forth, and slew all the children that were in Bethlehem, and in all the

hold, an angel of the Lord appeared to Joseph in a dream and said, "Rise, take the child and his mother, and flee to Egypt, and remain there till I tell you; for Herod is about to search for the child, to destroy him." **14** And he rose and took the child and his mother by night, and departed to Egypt, **15** and remained there until the death of Herod. This was to fulfill what the Lord had spoken by the prophet, "Out of Egypt have I called my son."

16 Then Herod, when he saw that he had been tricked by the wise men, was in a furious rage, and he sent and killed all

---

that Jesus learned magic in Egypt. Such tales, some of which date his visit in the reign of Jannaeus (104-78 B.C.), are probably based on Matthew, and are not independent evidence for the flight into Egypt.

15. The story may be built up out of the quotation from the Hebrew text of Hos. 11:1. Early Christians often thought of the Exodus with its miracles as a type of Christian redemption (e.g., I Cor. 10:1-5; John 6:49-51); the rabbis likewise believed that it foreshadowed the messianic age, when all its miracles would be re-enacted.

4. The Slaughter of the Children (2:16-18)

16. The account fits the character of Herod, who for political reasons murdered many people, including his son and other relatives. Augustus is said to have remarked that he would rather be Herod's pig ($\tilde{\upsilon}\varsigma$) than his son ($\upsilon\dot{\iota}\acute{o}\varsigma$). Josephus, our principal authority for Herod's life, does not know Matthew's story. According to the Talmud, Pharaoh slew the Israelite children because of a prophecy that the redeemer of Israel would be

---

Moses story. Remember also the assertion, which early became current among the foes of Christianity, that Jesus toiled as a laborer in Egypt (where large numbers of Jews then lived) and there learned Egyptian magic by which later he wrought his miracles. Was Matthew intent to refute this lie? Is this part of the reason for the recital of the Egyptian episode? For us the very word Egypt implies mystery. We recall Elizabeth Barrett Browning's poem on the death of a child:

> She has seen the mystery hid
> Under Egypt's pyramid:
> By those eyelids pale and close
> Now she knows what Rhamses knows.[4]

We recall also the Luc Olivier Merson picture, "Repose in Egypt," which shows Mary and the Babe asleep in the hollow between the body and the right paw of the Sphinx, the halo light from the Child's head lighting the face of the Sphinx. The enigma of life remains—it is well typified by the Sphinx and by the cruelty of Herod. Our human caravan goes its way before the face of a vast question-mark—"the burthen of the

[4] "Little Mattie."

mystery . . . of all this unintelligible world."[5] The Sphinx symbolizes also the contradictions in ourselves, for our nature sometimes seems a mixture of serpent, winged bird, lion, and man! But if the Sphinx remains, the Christ child is born and sleeps peacefully between the lion's paws! Christ abides, the answer to our yearning, the pardon for our sins, the promise written across our death. He awaits only the venture of our faith to prove himself the answer to the mystery.

16, 18. *The Slaughter of the Innocents.—*Here is the problem of pain in its stark and terrible maximum. **Ramah** is our world, and the cry heard in Ramah has often been the voice of the world's weeping. It is no comfort, but only doubled sorrow, to say that others suffer loss. It is poor comfort to say that many children are spared; that fact sharpens the sense of inequality. It is not enough comfort to plead that sorrow refines life; for sorrow, in itself and unredeemed, is not purification, but death. There is no logic to explain the slaughter by Herod or such a tragedy as that of the Children's Crusade.

[5] Wordsworth, "Lines Composed a Few Miles Above Tintern Abbey."

coasts thereof, from two years old and under, according to the time which he had diligently inquired of the wise men.

17 Then was fulfilled that which was spoken by Jeremy the prophet, saying,

18 In Rama was there a voice heard, lamentation, and weeping, and great mourning, Rachel weeping *for* her children, and would not be comforted, because they are not.

19 ¶ But when Herod was dead, behold, an angel of the Lord appeareth in a dream to Joseph in Egypt,

20 Saying, Arise, and take the young child and his mother, and go into the land of Israel: for they are dead which sought the young child's life.

21 And he arose, and took the young child and his mother, and came into the land of Israel.

22 But when he heard that Archelaus did reign in Judea in the room of his father Herod, he was afraid to go thither: notwithstanding, being warned of God in a dream, he turned aside into the parts of Galilee:

23 And he came and dwelt in a city called

the male children in Bethlehem and in all that region who were two years old or under, according to the time which he had ascertained from the wise men. 17 Then was fulfilled what was spoken by the prophet Jeremiah:

18 "A voice was heard in Ra'mah,
 wailing and loud lamentation,
 Rachel weeping for her children;
 she refused to be consoled,
 because they were no more."

19 But when Herod died, behold, an angel of the Lord appeared in a dream to Joseph in Egypt, saying, 20 "Rise, take the child and his mother, and go to the land of Israel, for those who sought the child's life are dead." 21 And he rose and took the child and his mother, and went to the land of Israel. 22 But when he heard that Ar-che-la'us reigned over Judea in place of his father Herod, he was afraid to go there, and being warned in a dream he withdrew to the district of Galilee. 23 And he went and dwelt in a city called Nazareth,

---

born. Similar stories are told of the infancy of Heracles, Sargon I, Cyrus, Romulus and Remus, and especially of Cypsalus, son of Aetion (Herodotus *History* V. 92). **From two years old and under** indicates that the astrologers first saw the star two years before.

18. Rachel was ancestress of Benjamin and Ephraim. Her traditional tomb is at Ramath Rachel, halfway between Jerusalem and Bethlehem. **Ramah** was an Ephraimite town eight miles north of Jerusalem. Jer. 31:15 has in mind the Ephraimites going into exile in Babylon.

5. Removal from Egypt to Nazareth (2:19-23)

20. Sought the child's life is a Semitic expression derived from the story of Moses (Exod. 4:19).

22. Herod willed Judea, Samaria, and Idumaea to **Archelaus** with the title of king, but Augustus granted him only the rank of ethnarch. Many Jews opposed his accession. His brutality soon manifested itself (Josephus *Antiquities* XVII. 13. 2; *Jewish War* II. 6. 2) and he was removed in A.D. 6 and banished. Thenceforth Palestine was a small imperial province ruled by a procurator except in the time of King Herod Agrippa I (A.D. 41-44); see Acts 12:1-4, 20-23. See also article, "New Testament Times: II. Palestine," above, pp. 100-13.

23. He shall be called a Nazarene (or "Nazorean"): The allusion may be to Judg. 13:5, "The boy shall be a Nazarite," or perhaps to Isa. 11:1. Matthew apparently plays on

---

By such attempted logic **Rachel . . . would not be comforted.** The one way of resolvement is in the fact that God is, and that his abiding is a surer truth even than the verity of pain. To this fact Paul clings: "Who shall separate us?" (Rom. 8:35, 39). He says that though pain strikes like a sharp sword on the bond between the soul and God, it cannot break the bond for

those who trust and pray. Matthew's Gospel here hints that great truth. Christ was not slain: he abides, the earnest of a heaven here and hereafter which no Herod can destroy.

23. *A City Called Nazareth.*—The names Nazareth and Nazarene are not without point. Nazareth stands as a symbol of our common life; it was a town without much pride of his-

Nazareth: that it might be fulfilled which was spoken by the prophets, He shall be called a Nazarene.

3 In those days came John the Baptist, preaching in the wilderness of Judea,

that what was spoken by the prophets might be fulfilled, "He shall be called a Nazarene."

3 In those days came John the Baptist, preaching in the wilderness of Judea,

---

words as the rabbis loved to do, and his point is: "The Scripture should be understood as saying *noçrî* [Nazarene], not *nâzîr* [Nazarite] or *nēçer* [sprout]." One may compare the rabbinical saying about the law: "Read not *ḥārûth* [engraved] but *ḥērûth* [freedom]" (Aboth 6:2).

The village of Nazareth is not mentioned in any ancient records. For this and other reasons it has been occasionally doubted whether "Nazorean" means "man from Nazareth," but this is still the most likely explanation. The village en-Naṣira is traditionally identified with Nazareth, no doubt correctly. See G. F. Moore, "Nazarene and Nazareth," in F. J. Foakes Jackson and Kirsopp Lake, *The Beginnings of Christianity*, Part I, Vol. I (London: Macmillan & Co., 1920), 426-32; and W. F. Albright, "The Names 'Nazareth' and 'Nazorean,'" *Journal of Biblical Literature*, LXV (1946), 397-401.

C. The Ministry of John the Baptist (3:1-12)

3:1. Early Christians thought **John** so important that he figured in the fundamental proclamation of salvation through Christ (e.g., Acts 10:37). The earliest authoritative account of Jesus' life, the Gospel of Mark, begins by mentioning John, calling him "the one who baptizes" (Mark 1:4). In Matthew he is given the formal title **the Baptist. The wilderness of Judea** is the mountainous region west of the Dead Sea; here it must include the Jordan valley.

---

tory—a typical town! But it was not remote. Important caravan routes passed near it, and it echoed with news of the world. Jesus shared the commonalty, and lived at the friction points of life. There are further facts of interest: **Nazarene** may have been originally "Nazorean," which means "preserver." Matthew may have been intent to show that in Jesus and his followers Israel found the true remnant by which life is bequeathed to our world. **Nazarene** seems to have been a slur: "Can there any good thing come out of Nazareth?" (John 1:46). If the word **Nazarene** was thus used, the slur becomes a kingliness, as the Cross—a curse at the first— becomes a salvation. The author of this Gospel seems to have lived in a region (Syria?) where the Christians were first known as Nazarenes— or Nazoreans. Perhaps this verse is the signature of his homeland. Either word is an honorable name, even though it was soon to be superseded by the name "Christian" (Acts 24:5).

3:1. *John the Baptist.*—Here was a truly great man, as Jesus categorically told us (11:11), and we may learn from him the marks of greatness. He was dedicated, probably first by his parents (Luke 1:11 ff.), but later by his own resolve born of brooding and prayer. Life to him was more than body or the unthinking acceptance of what the days might bring; it was God-given for a God-ordained task. He disciplined his life to this holy end. He chose a desert. He was ascetic in dress. He was ascetic in food, eating no more than tree honey and locusts. He dwelt in solitude, and heard in the desert wind the accents of the Eternal. We, realizing that such asceticism may easily become a self-flagellation, sometimes try thus to excuse ourselves from any discipline. John can teach us that if we wish to go east, we must of necessity cut off all chance of other journeyings.

He was a stern realist concerning right and wrong. We argue about shades of guilt; the complexities of our time confuse the issue. But John saw first that there is a "great divide," and insisted that men must live on the right side of that stern ridge. We debate relativities; he looked long on the fact of a moral law, and would tell us that it is better to err on the side of scruple than on the side of laxity. Aware of judgment, he saw the need for confession. Without that confession the dead tree is cut down and burned, and no mere appearance of good can save it. On the day of Atonement there was some general confession of national sins, and on occasion there were those who confessed individual transgressions. But John insisted on public confession forthright and complete. The crowds thus confessing must have been a stirring sight. John was a surgeon requiring that the boil must be lanced lest the poison should spread unto death.

He required integrity in daily life. We rightly speak of his sense of social righteousness, though he had in mind the deeper fact of

2 And saying, Repent ye: for the kingdom of heaven is at hand.

3 For this is he that was spoken of by the prophet Esaias, saying, The voice of one crying in the wilderness, Prepare ye the way of the Lord, make his paths straight.

4 And the same John had his raiment of camel's hair, and a leathern girdle about his loins; and his meat was locusts and wild honey.

2 "Repent, for the kingdom of heaven is at hand." 3 For this is he who was spoken of by the prophet Isaiah when he said,
"The voice of one crying in the
    wilderness:
Prepare the way of the Lord,
    make his paths straight."
4 Now John wore a garment of camel's hair, and a leather girdle around his waist; and his food was locusts and wild honey.

---

2. It was Jesus who announced that **the kingdom of heaven** (or "of God") **is at hand** (Mark 1:15). Matthew is probably mistaken in attributing this teaching to John, whose message was doom. (See on 4:17.)

3. In Isa. 40:3, which is quoted here, **the Lord** is Yahweh; Matthew no doubt thought of Jesus.

4. The Gospels often compare John to Elijah (11:14). Like Elijah he wore **a leather girdle around his waist.** But the **garment** roughly woven **of camel's hair** is not part of the description of Elijah in II Kings 1:8. Several species of **locusts** are still eaten by Arabs and are permitted by the Jewish food laws.

---

divine judgment. Luke 3:10 ff. gives his counsel. A man must do right, be neighborly in kindness, avoid the bane of wealth and rank. He must bear "fruit" of integrity in his daily dealing. John, if living now, would be a flail to our inequalities among men and nations. But John was yet lowly. What could be more moving than his acknowledgment that he was only the slave (see vs. 11 on sandals) of the coming Messiah? Only a truly great man could thus face and accept his menial place. He fails by contrast with Christ; he falls short of Christian grace. He is O.T., and only the forerunner of the N.T. Yet what was great in him is always great.

2. On Repentance.—The word "repent" implies a radical change of mind. It looks to the past in honesty and remorse, and then in a rightabout-face it looks to the future in resolve on a new way of life. Thus someone has rightly said that repentance is a Janus word.[6] Honest remorse is not easy. We evade the contemplation of our own sins by the condemnation of other people's sins. Thus the government or the institution—of marriage or property—becomes our scapegoat. Another of our favorite evasions is to label our neighbor's sins in realism ("He is a skinflint") and then to euphemize our own sins ("I am only being careful and thrifty"). Perhaps our sins so blind us that we cannot repent except by God's gift. This seems to be N.T. doctrine (see Acts 5:31; 11:18; Rom. 2:4; II Tim. 2:25). That gift came through the flame of judgment in the voice and countenance of John the Baptist. The other item in repentance,

the new resolve, is equally hard. We claim that our will is weak, as indeed it is; but we rarely use what will we have to "screw [our] courage to the sticking-place." In truth it can be said of us, "Ye have not yet resisted unto blood, striving against sin" (Heb. 12:4). Any true exposition of repentance should notice the difference between John's doctrine and Christ's; Christ said, "Repent, and believe this good news" (Mark 1:15 Goodspeed). That last phrase, which only Christ could incarnate and fulfill, gave his doctrine of repentance a new power and a new hope.

3. Preparing the Royal Road.—Matthew seems to have seen in John the Baptist not merely a man like Elijah, but Elijah come to life. There was more than the wilderness to suggest the likeness; the two men were one in spirit and office, for both were sent to prepare **the way of the Lord.** In every age this work is required. How can it be done? As John the Baptist has shown. By changing the conditions that make difficult the entrance of Christ—by lifting the valleys (the poverty that embitters and gnaws) and lowering the hills (the wealth that leaves men in blind pride), by smoothing the rough road (the desolate hardships that canker the soul)—by fulfilling all the magnificent program sketched in Isa. 40:4. This crusade of social righteousness will not save men, but it can make them more susceptible to the coming of Christ; hungry and embittered folk do not readily listen to the preacher. The work can be done also by personal example. In this, too, John was a true forerunner. He had renounced in his own life the insincerity of the temple religion and the current "itch for

[6] For details of the Janus myth see Charles Mills Gayley, *Classic Myths* (Boston and New York: Ginn & Co., 1911), pp. 60-61.

5 Then went out to him Jerusalem, and all Judea, and all the region round about Jordan,

6 And were baptized of him in Jordan, confessing their sins.

7 ¶ But when he saw many of the Pharisees and Sadducees come to his baptism, he said unto them, O generation of vipers, who hath warned you to flee from the wrath to come?

5 Then went out to him Jerusalem and all Judea and all the region about the Jordan, 6 and they were baptized by him in the river Jordan, confessing their sins.

7 But when he saw many of the Pharisees and Sad'du-cees coming for baptism, he said to them, "You brood of vipers! Who warned you to flee from the wrath to

5. Went out to him: The Greek imperfect suggests a repeated occurrence.

6-7. Were baptized by him, or perhaps "immersed themselves under his direction." Mark 1:4 describes this as a "baptism of repentance for the forgiveness of sins"—i.e., a baptism presupposing repentance. Some have thought of John's baptism as modeled on proselyte baptism, which the school of Hillel regarded as the decisive ceremony of conversion to Judaism; if so, John says in effect, "You are no better than heathen, and must begin all over again." The only difficulty is that proselyte baptism was a Levitical purification, not necessarily involving moral regeneration; hence some suppose that the basis of John's ceremony is Ezek. 36:25 or 9:4; another possibility is Isa. 1:16-18. Josephus' explanation (*Antiquities* XVIII. 5. 2) sounds too rationalistic: John "commanded the Jews to exercise virtue, both as to righteousness towards one another, and piety towards God, and so to come to baptism . . . not in order to the putting away of some sins, but for the purification of the body; supposing that the soul was thoroughly purified by righteousness." Most ancients did not draw this sharp distinction between the moral and ceremonial. And John was not merely a baptist hermit like Bannus, whom Josephus mentions in his *Life* (ch. 2) ; he was a prophet, and no doubt believed that his rite was ordained by God and necessary if men were to be saved from **the wrath to come.** Finally, like the rabbis, Paul believed that the Israelites had been baptized in the Red Sea before entering the Promised Land (I Cor. 10:2) .

Matthew adds **Pharisees and Sadducees** to his source (which may be Q; cf. Intro., pp. 237-38) . In Luke 3:7 all the hearers were a "brood of vipers" who fled like snakes from a field being harvested or on fire.

The name "Pharisees" is not known before the time of the high priest John Hyrcanus, *ca.* 120 B.C. It is usually taken to mean "those who are separated"— probably from defilement and irreligion. On one occasion Peter was accused of breaking the law by eating with Gentiles, whereupon he "separated himself" from them (Gal. 2:12) —which illustrates the principles of "separatism." The Pharisees were perhaps the successors of those *ḥaṣîdhîm* who in the second century B.C. resisted the tendency to adopt pagan culture. They apparently banded themselves into brotherhoods for the purpose of keeping the law more strictly and of promoting their interpretation of the O.T. For examples of their rulings see Mark 7:3-4; Josephus *Antiquities* XIII. 10. 6; Aboth 3:14; Sanhedrin 11:3. The Pharisees opposed the despotism and Sadducean tendencies of John Hyrcanus, Aristobulus, and Alexander Jannaeus, and passively resisted Herod (*Antiquities* XV. 10. 4; XVII. 2. 4) and the Romans when religious issues were at stake. The first-century revolutionists were principally from the Pharisaic party (*Antiquities* XVIII. 1. 1) , though most Pharisees were pacifists. (See Acts 22:3; 26:5; Phil. 3:5;

things," and so heralded the coming of the King. It was as if he said, in language better than words alone, "My life shows the kingdom that is at hand." The work is done also by proclamation; words have their power, especially when linked with congruous life. The words of John shook the land. Words driven by God are mightier than all swords or bombs. John cried,

as every true prophet must cry, "One cometh after me whose sandals I, his slave, am not worthy to carry." The social change, the example, and the proclamation are all born in faithful prayer. God has so ordained life that Christ does not come without the preparation we can make. Yet we are not the King; only he himself can give new life.

8 Bring forth therefore fruits meet for repentance:

9 And think not to say within yourselves, We have Abraham to *our* father: for I say unto you, that God is able of these stones to raise up children unto Abraham.

10 And now also the axe is laid unto the root of the trees: therefore every tree which bringeth not forth good fruit is hewn down, and cast into the fire.

11 I indeed baptize you with water unto repentance: but he that cometh after me is mightier than I, whose shoes I am not

come? **8** Bear fruit that befits repentance, **9** and do not presume to say to yourselves, 'We have Abraham as our father'; for I tell you, God is able from these stones to raise up children to Abraham. **10** Even now the ax is laid to the root of the trees; every tree therefore that does not bear good fruit is cut down and thrown into the fire.

11 "I baptize you with water for repentance, but he who is coming after me

---

Josephus *Life* 38; *Antiquities* XVIII. 1. 3; and Louis Finkelstein, *The Pharisees: The Sociological Background of Their Faith* [Philadelphia: Jewish Publication Society of America, 1938], 2 vols.; G. F. Moore, *Judaism* [Cambridge: Harvard University Press, 1927], especially I, 56-121; also article, "New Testament Times: II. Palestine," above, pp. 100-13.)

Less is known about the Sadducees, who are described in *Antiquities* XVIII. 1. 4, and all our information comes from their enemies. They may have taken their name from Zadok, Solomon's priest (I Kings 1:38-39), and have claimed to be his spiritual descendants. They were conservatives in religion, rejecting the Pharisees' development of the oral law and doctrine of resurrection. They were also political conservatives, many of them wealthy landowners who lived in Jerusalem and were friendly to the Roman government. Most of the first-century high priests and their friends were Sadducees, and it is this group which, more than any other Jewish group, instigated the crucifixion of Jesus.

9. Many Jews, though not all, believed that with **Abraham** as their **father** they had special protection. Yet the warning that from **these stones** (*'ebhānîm*) God can **raise up children** (*bānîm*) to Abraham is in the O.T. spirit and reflects the Jewish doctrine of God's omnipotence.

10. Is cut down: The present tense, because the prophecy's fulfillment is immediate and certain. **The fire** of Gehenna: "Fire" in Jewish apocalypses often describes the final judgment (cf. Philo *On Dreams* II. 61-64).

11. He who is coming after me is Matthew's play on words which reflects later events: it means both "my disciple," for the student literally dogged the rabbi's steps, and "my

---

9. False Assurances.—**Think not to say within yourselves:** "Because of this-and-this everything will be all right." Yet that is precisely our false strategy. The Pharisees trusted to their descent: **We have Abraham as our father.** We give that plea a reverse twist: "I had too much religion when I was young"—which means either "I had too much irreligion masquerading as religion" or "I did not have too much, but I grew tired and the world beguiled me." Whatever the meaning, we make the assumption, "God understands, and he's a good fellow." The Pharisees trusted to outward observance, and that also is our danger. Respectability is not religion. It can be fear or selfishness or even self-righteousness. Going to church can be merely custom or "fire insurance" or even an attempt to bribe God. The Pharisees trusted that they would be saved because others seemed more wicked; they

were not as wicked as the cruel and pagan Romans or as the mob that forgot to worship. This also is our false assurance. We are especially prone to it in time of war: "We are not as the aggressor." We preen ourselves that we are "not as other men" (Luke 18:11). The Pharisees doubtless trusted also to a vague tomorrow, and said—as we say—"There is time." Yet no false assurance saves us from the flame of judgment. When that fire starts, we also are a "generation of vipers" (vs. 7)—we scurry away before the heat, but find no refuge. There is no substitute for "truth in the inward parts" (Ps. 51:6). There is no home except in God.

11. The Two Baptisms.—We must guard against reading our interpretation into John's mind. It is not clear that he thought of the baptism that Christ would give as being essentially different from his own practice. He probably

worthy to bear: he shall baptize you with the Holy Ghost, and *with* fire:

12 Whose fan *is* in his hand, and he will thoroughly purge his floor, and gather his wheat into the garner; but he will burn up the chaff with unquenchable fire.

13 ¶ Then cometh Jesus from Galilee to Jordan unto John, to be baptized of him.

is mightier than I, whose sandals I am not worthy to carry; he will baptize you with the Holy Spirit and with fire. 12 His winnowing fork is in his hand, and he will clear his threshing floor and gather his wheat into the granary, but the chaff he will burn with unquenchable fire."

13 Then Jesus came from Galilee to the Jordan to John, to be baptized by him.

---

successor." There is a rabbinical saying, "Every work which a slave performs for his lord, a disciple must do for his teacher, except loosing his shoe." John's disciples continued as a separate group long after his death. Jesus was at one time reckoned his disciple; and the evangelists do all that they can to minimize this, as one can see especially in John 1:26-30. Luke 3:16 and Matthew add the words **and with fire** to Mark's phrase "with the Holy Spirit." Was the baptism with the Holy Spirit mentioned in Matthew's second source as well as in Mark? The question opens up two possibilities: (*a*) Either John was only a prophet of doom, like Amos (Amos 5:18-20), and prophesied that the messianic judge would punish with fire, or (*b*) he believed the repentant would receive the outpouring of the Spirit mentioned in Joel 2:28 (cf. Acts 2:17), while the sinners would be consumed.

12. The **winnowing fork** or shovel was used to toss wheat into the air. The wind took the chaff away.

D. The Beginning of Jesus' Ministry (3:13–4:25)

The Synoptic Gospels picture a definite and formal beginning for Jesus' ministry at the time of the Baptism and Temptation (cf. Mark 1:1-15; Luke 3:21-22; 4:1-30). It seems certain that Jesus was baptized by John and shortly afterward entered for the first time upon his public activity, preaching repentance, as John had done, but adding to this his own distinctive good news. The chief questions debated by historians concern the temptations and the revelation of his sonship to Jesus, at the time of the Baptism.

Our oldest Gospel, Mark, depicts the vision, and perhaps the voice also, as coming

---

conceived of Christ's act as being only **mightier** —a baptism in a deeper river, by mightier wind, and by more consuming fire. Apparently John did not contrast the two baptisms, as we must do; he perhaps thought of his own as preparation and of Christ's as confirmation. But inevitably we establish the contrast. Baptism in Christ is more searching because he is Christ, "the fulness of the Godhead bodily" (Col. 2:9). The fire does not destroy (as perhaps John believed) but refines. The ancient refiner watched the silver in the crucible, and kept the flame burning until the base metal had all come to the top and been skimmed off, until all agitation had ceased, and until he could see his face in the silver as in a mirror. That is a parable of the refining fire of baptism in Christ. Baptism in Christ grants access of new life. **The Holy Ghost** has that gracious truth for us, whatever the words meant to John the Baptist. Through Christ there is poured down upon us the spirit of God. We have not only a purging of the old nature, but the gift of uncreated life. There is the story of a Crusader ship preparing for de-

parture from the port of Marseilles in France. There was no wind to fill the sails. In those days to be becalmed meant, for long voyages, to be thwarted. At the urging of the captain, the Crusaders began to sing, *"Veni Creator Spiritus,"* and even as they sang "a breeze of wind" came upon them from the west to carry them on their venture.[7] By that prayer we have our baptism in Christ:

> Come, Holy Ghost, our souls inspire,
> And lighten with celestial fire.

So there are two baptisms—one the baptism of righteous fear, the other the baptism of redeeming love.

13-15. *Why Was Jesus Baptized?*—Scholars have debated the question and found no single answer. To an expositor, even if he is not a scholar, it seems that the three main answers given are not antagonistic: far from excluding one another, they may add up to the real

[7] Lord John de Joinville, *Chronicles of the Crusades: The Crusade of Saint Louis* (London: Henry G. Bohn, 1848), p. 383.

14 But John forbade him, saying, I have need to be baptized of thee, and comest thou to me?

15 And Jesus answering said unto him, Suffer *it to be so* now: for thus it becometh us to fulfil all righteousness. Then he suffered him.

14 John would have prevented him, saying, "I need to be baptized by you, and do you come to me?" 15 But Jesus answered him, "Let it be so now; for thus it is fitting for us to fulfill all righteousness." Then he

to Jesus, not to the crowd. Matthew reproduces this exactly. The story therefore rests on what must have purported to be Jesus' account of his own experiences, or else on a divine revelation to the author of the source. The difficulty often raised is that elsewhere Jesus gives little direct teaching about his own mission and person; and this story is very formal and stylized and much like other epiphany stories known to us. It would be very natural for early Christians to assume that Jesus' ministry must have begun with such a revelation of the divine favor, whether he himself told the story or not. Furthermore, the Son of God Christology is almost lacking in the Synoptic material except in the Baptism, the Temptation, and in 11:25-30. On the other hand, it may well be that the *form* of the story was given it by Christian reflection, while the essential kernel goes back to Jesus. If so, he told his disciples that at the Baptism he received the divine commission to begin his work.

What word describes this vocation? "Messiah," "Son of God," "Son of man," "prophet"? Not Messiah, as the term was then understood, for Jesus resisted the use of this title; perhaps Messiah in *our* sense, but Christians have transformed the meaning of the word. Perhaps Son of God, but this term, like the others, calls for more definition. Certainly prophet, at the very least. But it is better to suppose that Jesus did not try to find a name or title describing himself and the work he had to do; he simply followed the will of God as it was revealed to him. The question is further discussed in the general notes on 16:13-20 and 21:1–23:39.

1. The Baptism (3:13-17)

13. Unlike Mark, Matthew states that Jesus' purpose in leaving Galilee was **to be baptized.**

14-15. Would have prevented him is the imperfect of attempted action. The Christians of Matthew's time wondered why Jesus, whom they believed to be sinless, had submitted to a baptism which presupposed repentance. The Gospel According to the Ebionites

reason. John the Baptist's rite of baptism was not merely a copy of that baptism by which proselytes became Jews. It is not even certain that the baptism of proselytes was then practiced. (See Exeg.) John regarded his ritual as being almost like a mark on the forehead: it sealed a man against the day of imminent judgment. Then why did Christ, being Christ, seek and submit to that baptism from one who by admission was only his forerunner? Three reasons have been proposed, and each has truth. First: Jesus was renouncing, not any guiltiness, but the dear and sheltered life of home, that he might be consecrate to the dangerous mission to which he felt called. Thus at his baptism Christ took up that cross which he carried all his life and on which at the last he died. He forewent his home to become a homeless Man who had "not where to lay his head" (8:20). Second, and perhaps centrally: Jesus at baptism took upon himself the common sin. Thus it became

him to fulfill all righteousness. John and Jesus may or may not have met until this climactic moment, for John apparently had lived in Judea while Jesus lived in Galilee. If they had met, it was perhaps at the feast days in the temple courts. But John recognized instinctively the holiness of Christ: I have need to be baptized of thee. Yet sinlessness does not either parade itself as sinless or hold itself aloof from the world's sin. That aloofness would be token that sinlessness had fallen into sin. Sinlessness can never be a negative scruple: it must be a holy and outgoing love. Righteousness without love ceases to be righteous. Thus John Galsworthy's novel, *The White Monkey*, makes a returned soldier say of an employer who (on plea of strict justice) refuses to re-engage an employee who was dishonest but has now reformed: "The old blighter's too just"! Jesus at his baptism took the sin of mankind unto himself, assuredly not to become party to the sin,

16 And Jesus, when he was baptized, went up straightway out of the water: and, lo, the heavens were opened unto him, and he saw the Spirit of God descending like a dove, and lighting upon him:

17 And lo a voice from heaven, saying, This is my beloved Son, in whom I am well pleased.

consented. 16 And when Jesus was baptized, he went up immediately from the water, and behold, the heavens were opened *f* and he saw the Spirit of God descending like a dove and alighting on him; 17 and lo, a voice from heaven, saying, "This is my beloved Son,*g* with whom I am well pleased."

f Some ancient authorities add *to him.*
g Or *my Son, my* (or *the*) *Beloved.*

quotes John, after the voice has spoken from heaven, as asking Jesus to baptize him. The Gospel According to the Nazarenes reads: "Behold, the Lord's mother and his brothers said to him: 'John the Baptist baptizes for the remission of sins; let us go and be baptized by him.' But he said to them: 'In what have I sinned, that I should go and be baptized by him? Unless perhaps this very word which I have just spoken is [a sin of ?] ignorance.'" Matthew's addition to the story is also a conjecture, but a happier one: "It is fitting for us to perform every righteous act." Ign. Smyrn. 1:2 makes a similar statement. None of the gospel material suggests that Jesus had any consciousness of personal sin; but Israel as a whole needed to repent, and Jesus no doubt assumed that any right-minded man would associate himself with John's movement.

16. Some MSS and patristic quotations of this passage tell of miraculous signs accompanying the Baptism, and Luke 3:22 pictures the Spirit in visible form. Matthew merely says that **the heavens were opened,** Mark that Jesus "saw the heavens splitting open." This, like the descent of the **Spirit of God,** was observed by Jesus, not by the bystanders. Through the impartation of the Spirit, God turns the repentance-baptism into an ordination of Jesus for his ministry, for the Messiah must be "anointed" before he enters on his work. Justin Martyr (*Dialogue with Trypho* 8:4) quotes Trypho, the Jew, as saying: "Messiah, even supposing he has been born and exists anywhere, is unknown. He does not even recognize his own identity and he has no power at all until Elijah comes to anoint him and make him manifest to all." The **dove** is the usual rabbinical symbol for the people of Israel, and only occasionally is it identified with the Spirit.

17. The rabbis told many stories of hearing **a voice from heaven.** They called it *bath qôl,* "daughter [perhaps meaning echo] of the voice [of God]." Often, as here, the voice speaks in words of Scripture. **This is my . . . son** is a quotation from Ps. 2:7. Mark 1:11 has it in more exact form, but Matthew directs it to the bystanders. "**The beloved**" is a

but to share the shame and pain; and, by absorbing the sin into the whiteness of his own love, to redeem sinners. He repented *with* men as man, to redeem men—in God. Third: Jesus sought baptism because, in a deepening sense of destiny, he knew that God had some commission to lay upon him; and because he believed that the voice of God might come pleadingly, piercingly, and with divine endowment through the ministry of his brave cousin who was disciplined in righteousness. So it befell: God uses just such men as his channels.

16-17. *The Commissioning of Christ at Baptism.*—It is not irreverent to assume a slow clarifying of Christ's mind, a deepening awareness during his years at Nazareth that God had for him a destined and destiny-making task. That psychological movement is no false or sacrilegious assumption: it is rather the reverent

acknowledgment of Christ's accepted humanness. We can but guess the inward stirring, the flash and flame, by which he slowly knew that he must walk a path awful and alone in human history. Perhaps he was finally sure, as he went to be baptized, that the soul-shaking moment was at hand. Thus his experience at baptism is in one sense the issue of his brooding: "My Son, my beloved," was a composite from well-loved and long-pondered scripture (Ps. 2:7; Isa. 42:1). But the voice at the baptism was also and creatively a divine invasion, as the very words imply: **This is my beloved Son, in whom I am well pleased.** Even if the experience is described as "subjective" (a word that can never imply that any soul is utterly separate from the universe or eternity!), the fact of God's poignant arrival is here the supreme fact. The manner of God's coming is such as to melt the soul. **Like**

4 Then was Jesus led up of the Spirit into the wilderness to be tempted of the devil.

4 Then Jesus was led up by the Spirit into the wilderness to be tempted by the

---

messianic title (Eph. 1:6; Assumption of Moses). **With whom I am well pleased** is no doubt a reminiscence of Isa. 42:1, which deals with the Servant of Yahweh, and which the Targum applies to Messiah. It can be paraphrased "This is my Chosen One," and in Enoch "Chosen One" means "Messiah."

2. The Temptation (4:1-11)

The temptation story is "double tradition" (i.e., it is found also in Luke, but not in Mark), and therefore it is usually supposed to be from Q. But its theology is not identical with that of other Q material, and some form of the incident is known to Mark (see Intro., p. 237). Similar stories are told of the testing of founders of religions and prophets, e.g., Zoroaster (H. P. Houghton, "On the Temptation of Christ and Zarathustra," *Anglican Theological Review*, XXVI [1944], 166-75; Mary E. Andrews, *"Peirasmos,* a Study in Form Criticism," *ibid.,* XXIV [1942], 229-44). This highly stylized anecdote, in which each temptation is answered by a quotation from the LXX, could easily be derived from Christian preaching. It would seem appropriate that Jesus should have his vocation tested, and that his ministry should begin with a struggle between God's kingdom and Satan's, in which both God and his Son are vindicated. One can, however, suppose that Jesus set forth his inner experiences in some dramatic form such as this for the edification of his disciples. Certainly the three temptations—to work miracles for the satisfaction of immediate need, to give a convincing sign, and to exercise political power —continually recurred in the course of his ministry.

4:1. Mark 1:12 gives a more lively picture of the Spirit's activity; and the Gospel According to the Hebrews reads, "Just now my mother the Holy Spirit took me by one

---

a dove—in swift yet gentle movement, in power like that which brooded over primeval chaos to bring order and light (Gen. 1:2). **And lo a voice**—mysterious yet personal. "This is my Son, the beloved"—thus the seal is set. This is a far different commission from that which John the Baptist had predicted. How else can prisoners of the world's transgression be released except One come from beyond? How else can they be led into light except by One who knows that land? Yet the One must take human form, and share the dark hopelessness of the dungeon. This is the task, utter and alone, a traffic between heaven and earth—with attendant pains to rend the spirit—to which Christ at that moment was ordained, by the laying on of God's own hands.

4:1, 11. *Temptation.*—There is no contradiction between **led up of the Spirit** and **tempted of the devil.** God's ordaining had been laid on Jesus, and he must think through this mission. How could it best be fulfilled? The exaltation was inevitably followed by a reaction. The vision faded "into the light of common day." The Spirit led him into this searching of heart, yes, and into the accompanying testing. Yet the testing and the period of letdown were the devil's chance. Notice the O.T. doctrine of the devil. He is personal. Are not the seductions that beset us personal persuasions, and not

merely of ourselves? He is chief of testers. Is not the world's evil, as in Hitlerism, organized into hierarchies of wickedness? He is ultimately under God's control and sovereignty.

Thus we see here the nature of temptation. It is a fork in the road, the leading of the Spirit and the opportunity of the devil, and we must choose. It is a chance to rise as much as it is a chance to fall.

> When the fight begins within himself,
> A man's worth something,[8]

for men and steel are alike uncertain until they are tested.

We see here the overcoming of temptation by the power of God. Power sought only in the onset may not be enough, for then a man may not be sufficiently open to receive it. The power should be sought both in crisis and beforehand in habitual prayer. When Dwight L. Moody was upbraided because he failed to attend a prayer meeting in the midst of threatened shipwreck, he replied: "I'm prayed up." Jesus had his Bible at his command, and he had prayed much, and now Bible and prayer were carried into resolve.

We see here the issue of temptation. **Angels came and ministered unto him.** The Red Indians have a legend that the strength of the

[8] Browning, "Bishop Blougram's Apology."

2 And when he had fasted forty days and | devil. 2 And he fasted forty days and forty
forty nights, he was afterward ahungered. | nights, and afterward he was hungry. 3 And
3 And when the tempter came to him, he |

of my hairs and brought me up to the great mount Tabor" (in Hebrew and Aramaic the
word for "spirit" is feminine). (See M. R. James, *The Apocryphal New Testament*
[Oxford: Clarendon Press, 1924], p. 2.) **The devil** (ὁ διάβολος, the slanderer) is the term
usually found in the later N.T. books. Paul and the earlier gospel pericopes call him
"Satan" (the "adversary" or "accuser"; Zech. 3:1-2; Job 1:6-9, etc.; Rev. 12:9-10). The
rabbis taught that Satan stirs up the *yēçer hārā'* or evil impulse in man, seduces him
into sin, denounces him before God, and then punishes him with death.

2. Forty is a round number. Moses fasted "forty days and forty nights" when he was
in the mountain with Yahweh (Exod. 34:28) and the Israelites were tested forty years
in the wilderness. **He was hungry** might be translated as an inceptive aorist: "he got
hungry."

3. The O.T. and Jewish literature apply the term **Son of God** to angels or divine
beings (Gen. 6:2; Job 38:7), to the Israelite nation (Hos. 11:1), and occasionally to an
anointed king (Ps. 2:7). In Semitic idiom it should mean "godlike" or "specially related
to God." When used by the O.T. to refer to an individual or to the nation, it usually
calls attention to the moral relationship of love and filial obedience which should exist
between a father and his son. In Judaism it never became a standard messianic title,
and it is applied to the Messiah in only a few apocalyptic books (Enoch 105:2; II Esdras
7:28-29; 13:32, 37, 52) and occasionally in a late rabbinical source. Christians used it very
early to refer to Jesus. The term is found frequently in the letters of Paul (e.g., Rom.

slain foe enters into the victor. Better, the
strength of God comes upon the victor in temptation. It comes as trust, as sympathy for tested
folk, and as strong confidence.

1-11. *The Temptation of Jesus.* —His struggle, as one commissioned to a task alone and
eternal, was so intense that he forgot food for
an indefinite time. Characteristically his first act
after the celestial voice ("This is my Son") was
to pray. How to fulfill God's will? How to accomplish the task? He must now go out, more
than Abraham, "not knowing whither he went"
(Heb. 11:8). The story is obviously his own
account. The fact that it is highly dramatic in
form is testimony, not solely or mainly to the
poetry and vigor of his mind, but to the fierceness of the struggle. Again the word "subjective"
confronts us: the epochal strife was within him,
yet his soul was a battleground of ultimate antagonisms between which he must choose. The
battle was not a sham encounter, despite an assumption that dies hard. It was not mere shad-
owboxing. It was real because it followed (humanly) on his ecstasy. It was real because of his
physical hunger. It was real because of its setting of wilderness and wild beasts, that is to say,
in its accentuated loneliness: there was no touch
of elbow-to-elbow in the ranks, no bugle blown:
temptation is always lonely business. It was real
in that Jesus might have failed. It was dramatic,
but not play acting: the devil was there as if
with audible voice. Thus the story does not
mock our human straits, but is our strength.

Tremendous issues hung on that encounter, and
because Jesus overcame we can sing:

> In the hour of trial,
> Jesus, plead for me.

Clearly the temptation is linked with the revealings of the baptism: How should Jesus act
as Son? The struggle was the more fierce because
Jesus was so utterly intent on God's will. Some
exegetes have suggested that the three temptations correspond to the methods of the three
dominant parties—Sadducees, Pharisees, and
Herodians. The Bible quotations Jesus used all
come from Deuteronomy. Is that because Jesus
must now lead the way of the new Israel? Certainly contemporary views of messiahship entered into the battle.

3-4. *The First Temptation.* —Notice the approach of temptation: **If thou be the Son of
God.** Had doubt begun? Suppose the intimations received on Nazareth hills were false, and
the Voice at baptism only a trick of the imagination. That is always the devil's central plea—
that conscience is a figment, that prayer is a
projection, and that God (unproved) is only a
defense mechanism. Notice the proposals of
temptation: **Command that these stones be
made bread.** Many elements entered to
strengthen the false plea. Christ's physical hunger at that moment was a factor. Should he presume on the power, which by fair inference the
commission of God had given him, to satisfy his
own craving and to defeat the barrenness of the

said, If thou be the Son of God, command that these stones be made bread.

4 But he answered and said, It is written, Man shall not live by bread alone, but by every word that proceedeth out of the mouth of God.

5 Then the devil taketh him up into the holy city, and setteth him on a pinnacle of the temple,

6 And saith unto him, If thou be the Son of God, cast thyself down: for it is written, He shall give his angels charge concerning thee: and in *their* hands they shall bear thee up, lest at any time thou dash thy foot against a stone.

the tempter came and said to him, "If you are the Son of God, command these stones to become loaves of bread." 4 But he answered, "It is written,

'Man shall not live by bread alone,
  but by every word that proceeds from
    the mouth of God.'"

5 Then the devil took him to the holy city, and set him on the pinnacle of the temple, 6 and said to him, "If you are the Son of God, throw yourself down; for it is written,

'He will give his angels charge of
    you,'

and

'On their hands they will bear you
    up,
  lest you strike your foot against a
    stone.'"

1:3-4) and the Gospel of Mark; and in John 1:1-18 it denotes the metaphysical relationship between God and his incarnate Logos. When Gentile converts first heard it used, they would naturally think of Jesus as a savior and healer like Asclepius, who had both human and divine traits, though they would understand that there was and could be only one Son of God (see Ludwig Bieler, ΘΕΙΟΣ ΑΝΗΡ [Vienna: O. Höfels, 1935-36], 2 vols.). In this passage "Son of God" calls attention to Jesus' unique relation to God and his superhuman powers, and Matthew connects this sonship with the Virgin Birth.

4. God, being omnipotent, can sustain life without bread, for he once gave manna (Exod. 16). The contrast between stone and bread is found also in 7:9.

5. The holy city is Jerusalem. Maccabean coins bear the inscription "Jerusalem the Holy," and the Arabic name is El-Quds, "the holy." The pinnacle of the temple may be an eminence on the royal cloister on the south side of the temple enclosure, which consisted of four rows of Corinthian columns. Josephus says there was a steep precipice there (*Antiquities* XV. 11. 5).

6-7. Jesus is tempted to put God's promise of protection (Ps. 91:11-12) to the test; but this would really be "unfaith clamoring to be coined to faith by proof." It would

desert? The need of men was a factor. Jesus had seen how Roman taxes ground down the poor, and man's pathetic struggle for livelihood touched his heart. His sonship was perhaps the main factor. Surely it is righteous and merciful to overturn social injustice; surely by that path the kingdom shall come. A subtle temptation! Yet it leaves unanswered the profounder questions. From what motive? By what power? Toward what end? Evident injustice and Christ's compassion give this temptation a terrific force. Notice the answer to temptation. Jesus would not forsake the comradeship, or ever use for himself powers given only for use in love. Jesus would not center his mission in an economic crusade. He would not live merely for time, or forsake a Cross for a bakeshop. Man does live by bread, and economic righteousness is Christian concern; but man does not **live by bread alone.** The famished Bedouin, finding treasure

in the desert, cried, "Alas, it is only diamonds." Man in his deepest hunger always cries, "Alas, it is only bread." He lives by bread, but not mainly by bread. The bread is the means, not the end. He lives in God, and the circumference of life cannot be rightly drawn until the Center is set. Carlyle said that not all the "Finance Ministers and Upholsterers and Confectioners of modern Europe . . . ," in joint stock company," could "make one shoeblack happy . . . above an hour or two." [9] We live by forgiveness, the Presence, and eternal life; and only from these can any true economy grow and live.

5-7. *The Second Temptation.*—Again there is the subtle insinuation of a doubt: If thou be. . . . The **pinnacle** is perhaps a tower (used by Roman guards?) on which a man could be seen by crowds in Jerusalem. Maybe the Messiah was expected thus to appear. The ninety-first

[9] *Sartor Resartus,* Bk. II, ch. ix.

7 Jesus said unto him, It is written again, Thou shalt not tempt the Lord thy God.

8 Again, the devil taketh him up into an exceeding high mountain, and showeth him all the kingdoms of the world, and the glory of them;

9 And saith unto him, All these things will I give thee, if thou wilt fall down and worship me.

10 Then saith Jesus unto him, Get thee hence, Satan: for it is written, Thou shalt worship the Lord thy God, and him only shalt thou serve.

7 Jesus said to him, "Again it is written, 'You shall not tempt the Lord your God.'"
8 Again, the devil took him to a very high mountain, and showed him all the kingdoms of the world and the glory of them; 9 and he said to him, "All these I will give you, if you will fall down and worship me." 10 Then Jesus said to him, "Begone, Satan! for it is written,

'You shall worship the Lord your God,
and him only shall you serve.'"

---

contravene Deut. 6:16, and this kind of test is forbidden by Ecclus. 3:26 and rabbinical literature. What is the motive of the temptation? One suggestion is that Jesus would thereby convince the doubtful. A rabbinical tradition reads, "When the King Messiah reveals himself, then he comes and stands on the roof of the Holy Place." That Jesus refused to perform signs to prove his authority is well known (12:38-42; Luke 16:19-31). It has also been suggested that he was tempted to reassure himself, rather than others, that his vocation was genuine. Matthew's third temptation (vss. 8-10) is a more obvious climax, but this second one might well be the most subtle and dangerous to one who was spiritually sensitive. It is interesting that in Luke 4:9-11 it stands in third place.

8. The "taking up" may be in a vision or in the imagination.

9. The story assumes, as Luke 4:6 says, that the devil actually possesses **all these things.** This is the only temptation which may be called "messianic." If Jesus could obtain this secular power, he might be able to enforce his reforms; but he must acknowledge the devil's kingship to get the power.

10. Matthew adds to the source **Begone, Satan!** In 16:23 (=Mark 8:33), Peter is addressed as Satan because he tempts Jesus.

---

psalm was at that time given a messianic interpretation. The temptation again has both a personal and a social impact. As for its personal force, if Jesus should cast himself headlong in some utter risk, he could prove both his own trust and God's power. As for its social force, he might startle a shallow generation out of its indifference into sudden belief. Noble spirits are tempted to the sensational for the sake of God. Jesus felt the temptation, and was ready to court instant death for the cause of the kingdom. He could imagine the crowd watching: "Surely he is not going to jump! Look, he has jumped! He is safe! Is this the Messiah?" Again the suggestion is probed. Would the multitude thus find God, and follow him? Perhaps men live by portents even less than they live by bread. "Neither will they be persuaded, though one rose from the dead" (Luke 16:31). Conviction goes deeper than the eyes. God is not proved by sleight of hand: the soul has its own testimony, and God is his own interpreter. But this scrutiny was not the main rebuttal to the devil's proposal. The answer came through the ancient truth, newly given, that man has no right to force God's hand. How often we try,

not only to dictate the way of Providence, but to play our own providence! That sin disfigured the old Israel in the desert (Deut. 6:13-14). Jesus realized that it must not disfigure the new covenant. He would not choose his own way: he would live his life and fulfill his ministry waiting upon God and trusting in him.

8-10. *The Third Temptation.*—Could Jesus in his physical weakness endure further assault? There was yet another and a worse temptation. Mark its nature. The devil drops the "if thou be the Son of God," but brings now his keenest weapon: He showeth [Jesus] **all the kingdoms of the world.** The appeal was to political leadership, a dream that had long haunted Jewry. They had visioned the day when "all nations" should honor Israel and Israel's God. The ambition had been provoked: Israel had been a buffer state, often trampled in the midst of mightier powers. At that moment the Romans had a garrison in every sizable town, by which they levied crushing taxes and ruthlessly suppressed any attempt at revolt. There were six million Jews scattered through that ancient world. If the right leader came to make them a confederacy, perhaps in alliance with the Par-

11 Then the devil leaveth him, and, behold, angels came and ministered unto him.

12 ¶ Now when Jesus had heard that John was cast into prison, he departed into Galilee;

13 And leaving Nazareth, he came and dwelt in Capernaum, which is upon the seacoast, in the borders of Zabulon and Nephthalim:

14 That it might be fulfilled which was spoken by Esaias the prophet, saying,

11 Then the devil left him, and behold, angels came and ministered to him.

12 Now when he heard that John had been arrested, he withdrew into Galilee;

13 and leaving Nazareth he went and dwelt in Ca-per'na-um by the sea, in the territory of Zeb'u-lun and Naph'ta-li, 14 that what was spoken by the prophet Isaiah might be fulfilled:

---

11. The **angels** serve him, in accordance with the promise of Ps. 91:11-14. Matthew now begins again to copy Mark (cf. Mark 1:13).

3. Jesus' Preaching in Galilee (4:12-25)

a) The Prophetic Setting (4:12-16)

12. Now when he heard that John had been arrested: The story is told in 14:3-12. Luke, for artistic reasons, mentions this before the baptism of Jesus (Luke 3:19-20). The Fourth Gospel assigns Jesus an extensive ministry before John's arrest (see, e.g., John 3:22-30).

13. Matthew anticipates Mark 1:21 and states that Jesus actually **dwelt in Capernaum,** which is probably the modern Tell Ḥum. He defines this as in **the territory of Zebulun and Naphtali** in order to prepare for the quotation which follows.

---

thians . . . ! That was the temptation. Its danger gave it appeal, and the commission at baptism guaranteed "right leadership." How he hungered for those **kingdoms**—both for his people's peace and for the glory of God! But the temptation was temptation. The bane of political leadership is its expediency and compromise: "The end justifies the means." Actually means and ends are joined, like a river flowing into a lake. If there is poison in the means, we arrive at a poisoned lake. The devil was so sure of his last appeal (**All these things will I give thee**) that he made no attempt to hide the price: **If thou wilt fall down and worship me.** He knew how Jesus chafed at narrow limits—for God's sake. But Jesus had stronger defense than the devil's attack. Meditation on the Bible until the mind glowed, and constant prayer, now stood Jesus in good stead. He summoned every resource of will: **It is written, Thou shalt worship the Lord thy God, and him only shalt thou serve.** He would follow God's leading day by day, in wide or narrow limits, known or unknown, without any self-will. Temptation did not end for Jesus in that wilderness. It often recurred. It came again with terrific power when the Cross neared, and in Gethsemane. But he had made answer in the wilderness, and chosen his path: "Not my will, but thine, be done" (Luke 22:42).

12-16. *Galilee of the Gentiles.*—The divine leading to which Jesus was now pledged becomes clear. The arrest of John the Baptist was the sign for Jesus to lift the banner of the kingdom. When one ministry ended, another and better ministry began: the promise of dawn gave place to the daybreak. Perhaps Jesus left Nazareth because he had already met opposition there. If so, the providence of God worked through that seeming failure, as well as through the arrest of John, to send Jesus to Capernaum. Strange providence! Capernaum was a vantage point for the new gospel. It was a busy commercial town in the midst of a thriving region. It was less under the constraint of the priests than Judea and more tolerant. It was a land of mixed races near the trade route between Damascus and Egypt (see vs. 15: **Galilee of the Gentiles**). Matthew is interested in Capernaum, not because it is a vantage point, but because he sees in these events the fulfillment of prophecy. The story from which he quotes refers to the overrunning of northern Palestine by the Assyrians in 730 B.C. Perhaps he has this event in mind, or perhaps he is thinking of the arrest of John the Baptist. In either case he sees in the coming of Christ a compensation for sorrow. Those who **sat in the region** [very home] **and shadow of death** (such is the graphic phrase) now receive "beauty for ashes, . . . the garment of praise for the spirit of heaviness" (Isa. 61:3). What God takes away with the left hand he restores in double measure with the right hand.

15 The land of Zabulon, and the land of Nephthalim, *by* the way of the sea, beyond Jordan, Galilee of the Gentiles;	15 "The land of Zeb'u-lun and the land of Naph'ta-li,
	toward the sea, across the Jordan,
	Galilee of the Gentiles—
16 The people which sat in darkness saw great light; and to them which sat in the region and shadow of death light is sprung up.	16 the people who sat in darkness have seen a great light,
	and for those who sat in the region and shadow of death
17 ¶ From that time Jesus began to preach, and to say, Repent: for the kingdom of heaven is at hand.	light has dawned."
	17 From that time Jesus began to preach, saying, "Repent, for the kingdom of heaven is at hand."

15-16. The original point of the prophecy (Isa. 9:1-2) was that even these regions would share in the coming bliss. Matthew uses it to explain why Jesus worked in despised Galilee, rather than Judea. The quotation differs from the LXX, and it may come from an independent Greek version or an oral Targum. (Cf. S. E. Johnson, "The Biblical Quotations in Matthew," *Harvard Theological Review*, XXXVI [1943], 138-39.) **The way of the sea** in Isaiah may have referred to the Mediterranean; here it denotes the region of the Sea of Galilee. **Across the Jordan** is Trans-Jordan, which, like Galilee, was under the tetrarch Herod Antipas. "Galilee" means "circle" or "region"; and **Galilee of the Gentiles** originally meant "region of non-Jews." Many of its residents were forcibly converted to Judaism in the Maccabean period.

b) JESUS' PROCLAMATION (4:17)

17. The Greek word translated **repent** basically denotes "change of mind," but in the LXX it often stands for a Hebrew word meaning "to grieve for one's sins." Repentance is one of the most important of all Jewish doctrines. It involves profound sorrow for sin, restitution so far as possible, and a steadfast resolution not to commit that particular sin again. Such repentance unfailingly brings divine forgiveness without the need of any mediation or ritual act. A man can never be certain, however, that his repentance is perfect unless he sucessfully resists a second temptation to commit the sin. There is a famous saying of R. Aḥa (*ca.* A.D. 320): "If the Israelites would repent for one day, the Messiah Son of David would come immediately." Jesus' teaching on repentance builds on the foundation of the O.T. and Judaism.

The terms **kingdom of heaven** and **kingdom of God** are used interchangeably in the Synoptic Gospels. The former translates literally the rabbinical phrase *malkûth shāmáyîm;* "heaven" is used partly to avoid mentioning the divine name. The O.T. does not contain the exact phrase, but the idea is there (e.g., Ps. 145:11-13). Its basic meaning is the "reign" or "sovereignty" of God. The O.T. thinks of this sovereignty as eternal because God created the world; his reign is present already in so far as he is king of Israel, and it will be manifested perfectly in the future age. Rabbinical thought develops this concept. Man rejected God's kingship in the days of Noah, and thenceforth God was

17. *Repentance and the Kingdom of Heaven.* —Jesus began to preach. Words, backed by deeds and carried on the influence of a consecrated soul, were his chosen method. Words: the immediate contact of man with man. Words: that instrument so various, so flexible, so instant, so piercing, so freighted with personality that there is no substitute. Let the preacher and teacher take courage. Christ's first word was the word John the Baptist had used: **Repent.** We must face its implications. There is something wrong with us, and hope lies in our honesty,

even though it lies more deeply in God's grace. Thus the first requirement is confession, and the second is a new resolve. Without that honesty neither creed nor ritual can save us. "I have sinned against heaven, and in thy sight" (Luke 15:21). For any prodigal that is the road home—that and setting foot upon the road. George Eliot's *Adam Bede* has described our failure with pointed fidelity: "It's like a bit o' bad workmanship—you never see th' end o' the mischief it'll do." So we must confess, and then resolve after the manner of the soldier

18 ¶ And Jesus, walking by the sea of Galilee, saw two brethren, Simon called Peter, and Andrew his brother, casting a net into the sea: for they were fishers.	18 As he walked by the sea of Galilee, he saw two brothers, Simon who is called Peter and Andrew his brother, casting a net into the sea; for they were fishermen.

king only in heaven until Abraham, Moses, and the children of Israel accepted his sovereignty. Because Israel disobeyed him, lordship over the world passed to the heathen. Nevertheless, the reign of God is realized whenever a man consciously submits himself to God's will, and an individual takes the "yoke of the kingdom" upon himself by reciting the Shema (Deut. 6:4-9; 11:13-21; Num. 15:37-41). God's reign will extend to all men in the world to come and will be openly visible to all. Some of the earliest synagogue prayers, e.g., the Eighteen Benedictions and the Kaddish (Simeon Singer, *Authorised Daily Prayer Book* [London: Eyre & Spottiswoode, 1929], pp. 37-39, 44-54), contain petitions for the coming of the kingdom.

The kingdom is central in Jesus' teaching. He generally emphasizes its future and miraculous aspect; furthermore, it is **at hand** (literally "has drawn near"), and the faithful have not long to wait. But he gives the doctrine certain particular emphases: (*a*) Man must, of course, prepare for the kingdom by moral effort, but it is pre-eminently God's gift (Luke 12:32); after the seed is once sown, God will bring the harvest (Mark 4:1-9=Matt. 13:1-9; Mark 4:26-29; Matt. 13:31-33). (*b*) The kingdom is the sum of all gifts and as such is indescribable except through poetry (13:44-46). (*c*) Though it will come in its complete glory only in the future, it is already beginning to manifest itself in the events connected with Jesus' ministry (12:28=Luke 11:20; 11:12-13=Luke 16:16; 13:16-17=Luke 10:23-24), and it is in the disciples' midst (Luke 17:20-21). In the Lord's Prayer (6:9-13=Luke 11:2-4) the sanctification of God's name is closely connected with the coming of the kingdom, and 6:10 equates the kingdom with the doing of God's will on earth as it is in heaven. This sense of the dawning of the kingdom, the appearance of its first fruits, the combination of thanksgiving for present bliss with the most poignant expectation of glory in the near future—these features run through the whole N.T. and account for the special quality of its eschatology. (See F. C. Grant, *The Gospel of the Kingdom* [New York: The Macmillan Co., 1940], especially pp. 145-46.) (*d*) Indeed, men can enter the kingdom now (5:20; 18:3; 20:1-16), and the Beatitudes (5:3-11) are intended to describe the character of its members. Conditions of entrance are no longer national or racial, but purely moral and religious. There is a close relation between the kingdom and the group of disciples, and it is not surprising that Matthew tends to equate it with the church (13:47, 52; 16:18-19). (*e*) Jesus is the herald of the kingdom and he is intimately involved in its present manifestations. Critics are not agreed as to whether he himself expected to be its bringer in the age to come. There is no necessary logical connection between the kingdom of God and the Messiah or Son of man, but the two types of expectation are combined in the Gospels, as in some Jewish writings. (See also article on Jesus' teaching about the kingdom, above, pp. 145-54.)

c) CALLING OF THE FIRST DISCIPLES (4:18-22)

18. Simon is a Greek name used in place of the Hebrew "Simeon." **Peter** (Πέτρος) is his nickname (πέτρα, rock; see on 16:18). Many Jews in all parts of Palestine had

who said, "Jesus Christ said to me, 'Rightabout-face.' And I heard him and obeyed him in my heart." But Christ's word is yet as different from John's as heaven from earth: **The kingdom of heaven is at hand.** Who has not known the futility of human resolves? Sin leaves us with powers too weak to refashion life in our own resource. But our resolve is met, yea, beckoned and prompted, by God's resolve in our behalf. **At** midmost and deepest of the dark river of

confessed failure a Hand grips our hand, and we reach the other shore of faith and hope. Only Jesus could speak that word, for the Word was incarnate in him.

18-22. *The Calling of the Disciples.*—The call and the answer may not have been as sudden as the story seems to show. John 1:35 ff. may give us the prelude to this incident. What kind of men did Jesus summon to his kingdom-cause? They were not impoverished: they were busy

19 And he saith unto them, Follow me, and I will make you fishers of men.	19 And he said to them, "Follow me, and I will make you fishers of men." 20 Im-mediately they left their nets and followed
20 And they straightway left *their* nets, and followed him.	him. 21 And going on from there he saw two other brothers, James the son of Zeb'e-
21 And going on from thence, he saw other two brethren, James *the son* of Zeb-edee, and John his brother, in a ship with Zebedee their father, mending their nets; and he called them.	dee and John his brother, in the boat with Zeb'e-dee their father, mending their nets,

Greek names, and **Andrew** is an example. **Casting a net,** probably a circular net with weights and a draw rope around its edge. Fishing was an important industry in the Sea of Galilee.

19. Follow me here means "be my disciple." Rabbinical discipleship demanded intimate daily contact with the teacher; one formed one's character and learned the law by example as well as precept. Aboth 6:5 is worth reading as an example of the rabbinical ideal of discipleship. In rabbinical and Greek literature "to catch men" usually has an evil sense, as in Jer. 16:16. Jesus turns the idea around; his disciples become **fishers of men** in order to save them. Like the rabbis, he had special disciples, and much of his teaching is addressed directly to them. But, unlike the rabbis, he gave a brief training in a few simple principles; and their vocation was not to be scholars but heralds of the kingdom, actively seeking out and saving those who were most in need.

20. The story is told dramatically, as in the call of Elisha (I Kings 19:19-21) . Perhaps Jesus had previously known the brothers, but it would not be exceptional in the Near East for men to follow such a summons without further ado.

21. James and Jacob are variant English forms of the same Hebrew name.

fishermen, these four. They were *average* men. The Sanhedrin could ask with confidence, "Have any of the rulers or of the Pharisees believed on him?" (John 7:48.) These four came from "Main Street." They had petty ambitions even when they had been with Jesus for many months. They quarreled. They were not out-standingly brave: at the Crucifixion they all forsook him and fled. It seems clear that Jesus could find many like them in our town. They were *individual* men, not twelve copies. They were representative. Peter was headstrong, Andrew was homespun and loyal, James and John were "sons of thunder" (Mark 3:17). Each after his own kind was needed to enrich the kingdom-witness. Jesus did not obliterate their distinctiveness: he gathered their several gifts into an orchestra of praise. They were friendly, honest, *enthusiastic* men. They were capable of leaving home and their accustomed life for a new cause. They kindled to a leader and a venture. Better still, they glowed to the purpose of God: they were *reverent* men. These Jesus chose in deliberate prayer, and counted them of such worth that he gave them the best of his time and thought. He set on them an ultimate trust. They were the "light of the world" (5:14) and the "salt of the earth" (5:13). He challenged them to risk all for God's kingdom in him. His words were, "Here, after

me!" in manly and divine appeal. We speak with some despair about the multiplication of the ordinary man. Jesus chose such to be his heralds and the builders of the new world. Now our best art and architecture honor them. But only because of Jesus.

19. Fishers of Men.—It is a genial and dra-matic metaphor. Augustine says rightly, "Fisher-man Peter did not lay aside his nets but changed them." Jesus appealed to their discon-tent. They were "unlearned and ignorant men" only in the sense that they had not been trained in any sacred school. But fishing nets could not satisfy them: livelihood is not life. They craved wider seas. So with us: we can claim no genius or "success"; but we, like other men, are

. . . homesick in their homes,
And strangers under the sun.[1]

We rush feverishly, but can never escape our discontent.

Jesus satisfied their longings: "Here, after me!" There was such authority in him that these men, used to wrestling with storms in darkness, found in him a worthier manhood. His eagerness caught their youth, his certitude their loyalty, his tenderness their love; and

[1] G. K. Chesterton, "The House of Christmas." Used by permission of Dodd, Mead & Co.; Burns, Oates & Washbourne; and the executrix of the late Mr. G. K. Chesterton.

22 And they immediately left the ship and their father, and followed him.

23 ¶ And Jesus went about all Galilee, teaching in their synagogues, and preaching the gospel of the kingdom, and healing all manner of sickness and all manner of disease among the people.

24 And his fame went throughout all Syria: and they brought unto him all sick people that were taken with divers diseases and torments, and those which were possessed with devils, and those which were lunatic, and those that had the palsy; and he healed them.

and he called them. 22 Immediately they left the boat and their father, and followed him.

23 And he went about all Galilee, teaching in their synagogues and preaching the gospel of the kingdom and healing every disease and every infirmity among the people. 24 So his fame spread throughout all Syria, and they brought him all the sick, those afflicted with various diseases and pains, demoniacs, epileptics, and paralytics,

---

d) SUMMARY OF HIS FIRST ACTIVITY (4:23-25)

Matthew omits Mark 1:21, 23-28, 35-38, and postpones 1:22, 29-34. He now constructs an editorial summary out of Mark 1:39; 3:7-8, 10. (See Benjamin W. Bacon, *Studies in Matthew* [New York: Henry Holt & Co., 1930], p. 169.)

23. Teaching in their synagogues was an activity open to any layman competent to carry it on. It is mentioned, e.g., in Mark 1:21; Luke 4:16-30. **Every disease and every infirmity** is a favorite phrase of Matthew (see 9:35; 10:1).

24. All Syria probably denotes the region north of Galilee. If Matthew wrote in Syria, this place reference would especially interest his readers. In the first century "Syria" is sometimes used to include Palestine. **Those which were lunatic** (i.e., moon-struck) is a literal rendering of the Greek. In 17:15, and according to RSV here, this rare word

---

some divine solitude in him called to the deeps of their soul. They left home and livelihood for a Life that had movements out beyond time and place. For at long last we must believe; and we can believe, not in a philosophy or a creed, but only in a Person; for only a Person can draw love, and principles without the Person are a land of ice. Jesus linked their longing to a Cause.

Their livelihood, even when they returned to it, was only a net with which to catch men. Always Jesus burned with a passion for the human. If people spoke of harvest, he spoke of the human harvest (John 4:35). If they mentioned fishing nets, he proposed that they be fishers of men. If they talked of a well, he talked of "living water" (John 4:10). Where others saw buildings, governments, battles, or laws, he saw —his brethren. To win his brethren to their true home is every man's real task. Is there any other canceling of discontent than Christ, and any other satisfying work than that we be fishers of men for his sake?

23. *Jesus and the Synagogue.*—There was a synagogue for every hamlet—wherever there were ten adult men, according to the accepted rule. The synagogue was at once school, local council, and "church." The priest had less power than we have assumed: he pronounced the blessings. The synagogue was governed by

elders. The ruler of the synagogue was the chief elder: he conducted worship, and chose from the laity the man who should preach. Next in rank was the teacher, who had charge of the building and conducted the weekday school. He also carried out the judicial decisions of the elders who governed the community both in civil and religious affairs. They could excommunicate and even scourge (Luke 6:22; Matt. 10:17). Sometimes a synagogue would have also an interpreter who changed the ancient Hebrew into the colloquial Aramaic. Thus Jesus could preach in the synagogue if chosen by the ruler for that work, or he could be expelled from the synagogue. Trace the influence of the synagogue on his training. Mark his regard for it and his loyalty (Luke 4:16). See how his mind was stored with great words from the law and the prophets. Notice how widely he used the synagogue in his early ministry. Ask why the synagogue failed him. Was it because of worship of the letter, "patriotic" prejudice, self-righteousness, loss of concern for the common man and his burdens? The answer is not without point for present-day churches.

23-25. *Teaching, Preaching, Healing.*—Note these three cardinal words and methods. The Christian church has emulated Jesus in the preaching, though with what ill preparation and poor fervor! As for the teaching, that has

25 And there followed him great multitudes of people from Galilee, and *from* Decapolis, and *from* Jerusalem, and *from* Judea, and *from* beyond Jordan.

5 And seeing the multitudes, he went up into a mountain: and when he was set, his disciples came unto him:

and he healed them. 25 And great crowds followed him from Galilee and the Decap'o-lis and Jerusalem and Judea and from beyond the Jordan.

5 Seeing the crowds, he went up on the mountain, and when he sat down his

---

is applied to **epileptics.** Modern English, however, uses "lunatics" to mean insane people; these are the **demoniacs** of the Gospel. First-century Palestinians attributed many diseases, but especially insanity, to demons (see on 8:28-34). **Paralytics** is the correct translation at the end of the verse. What we now call **palsy** is only one form of paralysis; the Greek word is more inclusive.

25. The **Decapolis** ("ten cities") was a league of Greek-speaking (and largely pagan) city-states. All the towns which Pliny mentions as forming the group were east of the Jordan except Scythopolis (Bethshan). Some of the best known were Damascus, Gadara, Pella, Gerasa, and Philadelphia (modern Amman). Here the term may include the territory surrounding them. (See map of Palestine on p. 230 of this volume and G. E. Wright and F. V. Filson, *The Westminster Historical Atlas to the Bible* [Philadelphia: Westminster Press, 1945], pp. 83-84; also Jack Finegan, *Light from the Ancient Past* [Princeton, N. J.: Princeton University Press, 1946], pp. 230-32.)

II. First Discourse, Addressed to the Disciples. The New Law, Designed for the Community Whose Members Will Inherit the Kingdom (5:1–7:29)

Matthew now introduces the most striking and characteristic feature of his entire Gospel. He has sometimes been called "ecclesiastical," "legalistic," or "Judaistic," but actually his greatest interest is in the moral life of the Christian community. This discourse, which is put at the forefront of his Gospel, deals with the righteousness which exceeds that of the scribes and Pharisees (5:20), and is appropriate for those who pray for the kingdom of heaven and will inherit it. This righteousness is prophetic rather than rabbinical (as Bacon remarks, *Studies in Matthew,* p. 165), and it is worth noting that the last of the five discourses (see Intro., p. 235) concludes on the same exalted note of transcendent righteousness (25:31-46). Some of Matthew's special material, which is often assigned to an M source, has an inverted rabbinical interest; i.e., it is directed against the law as understood by the Pharisees. But the passages which are drawn from the sermon as it is found also in Luke 6:20-49, and also from other parts of Q, deal with right action in the widest sense of the word. The Sermon on the Mount is a whole new Torah or teaching tradition and not merely a new halakah or lawbook.

---

largely gone except for the halfheartedness of the Sunday school. For Jesus the synagogue was the school: all secular knowledge was thus gathered into a noble faith, not into a thin worship of "facts." Our teaching has gone into the hands of secular authorities. As for healing, that function has been almost entirely surrendered to medicine and psychiatry, despite the fact that both these fine endeavors are largely robbed of meaning unless they have the right spirit, and are directed to the true end of life. Some healing cults may be wrong both in philosophy and method, but they are right in their intention, and they are within the original

mandate of Christ. (For the nature of the sicknesses described in vs. 24 see Exeg.) Christ was concerned for the health of both body and soul. To him pain was not in itself a blessing, even though it could be turned to noble ends. Body and soul were "fitly joined together and compacted" (Eph. 4:16), and he came to give abundant life. Note **all Galilee** and vs. 25: they show the vigor and zeal of the early ministry.

5:1-12. *The Beatitudes.*—If the Beatitudes are seven in number, seven is a holy number. If they are eight, as most of us assume, they form the octave of kingdom-music. If they **are**

2 And he opened his mouth, and taught them, saying,

disciples came to him. 2 And he opened his mouth and taught them, saying:

Jesus would not have given all this teaching on a single occasion. The sermon is made up of aphorisms, maxims, and illustrations which were remembered and treasured out of many discourses.

Up to this point in the story Jesus has called only four special disciples, and apparently the discourse is addressed to them; but Matthew actually has in mind the crowds, and the sermon is intended to apply to all Christians.

It is a curious fact that both Matthew (4:24-25) and Luke (6:17-19) begin their sermons after a summary of healings, and in each case the summary is based on Mark 3:7-12. Possibly Q introduced the sermon in a similar fashion. In any event, the sermon, like the preaching of John the Baptist in 3:1-12, is addressed to a group of people who have come away from their homes to hear the word. (See the articles, "The Growth of the Gospels" and "The Sermon on the Mount" [above, pp. 60-74, 155-64]; also Martin Dibelius, *The Sermon on the Mount* [New York: Charles Scribner's Sons, 1940]; Hans Windisch, *Der Sinn der Bergpredigt* [2nd ed.; Leipzig: J. C. Hinrichs, 1937].)

A. INTRODUCTION (5:1-2)

5:1. The preceding section prepares for the mention of **the crowds. He went up on the mountain** as he did when he was transfigured (17:1) and when he gave his parting commandment (28:16), and as Moses did to receive the law (Exod. 19). Here and in 28:16 Matthew may have a particular mountain in mind. The mountain (or "hills") is mentioned also in Luke 6:12; Mark 3:13. **He sat down:** This was the appropriate posture for a Jewish teacher, and especially fitting for so important a discourse.

---

ten, as some scholars have suggested was Matthew's intention, they are the New Decalogue. In any event they are of signal importance. **Mountain** hints a loftiness of teaching, a new Sinai. **He opened his mouth** implies the utterance of solemn truth. **Sat** and **taught** indicate a pondered verity. Jesus here traces the living law of the new kingdom. He writes the charter of the Christian life.

It is revolutionary teaching. Jesus had watched and searched the type of righteousness called righteous in his day, and now joined issue with it. The Beatitudes, far from being passive or mild, are a gauntlet flung down before the world's accepted standards. Thus they become clearer when set against their opposites. The opposite of **poor in spirit** are the proud in spirit. The opposite of those who **mourn** are the light-headed, always bent on pleasure. The opposite of the **meek** are the aggressors. The opposite of the **persecuted** are the men who always "play it safe," and compromise. The account in Luke (6:20 ff.) shows even more sharply this break with the world. In the Beatitudes Jesus said in effect what he later said explicitly: "Those who are supposed to rule over the Gentiles" do thus and so, "but it shall not be so among you" (Mark 10:42, 43; cf. Luke 22:25, 26). Not only did the Beatitudes cut across the ethic of that time (and our time); they cut across the sacred law of Moses

(see vs. 22). They are not "principles," but jets of light and love kindled against the darkness of the age.

They reveal the secret of happiness. Carlyle insists that blessedness is the better word, lest happiness be confused with a mere hedonism at which men grasp, and, grasping, miss: "Blessedness! . . . which God-inspired Doctrine art thou also honoured to be taught; O Heavens! and broken with manifold merciful Afflictions, even till thou become contrite and learn it!" [2] A magazine-sponsored round-table discussion, held to discover or recognize the kind of people who are really happy, concluded that a craftsman busy at his task, a mother bathing her babe, and a surgeon called at midnight to perform a critical operation might serve as instances. A saint engaged in his philanthropies and prayers should have been included. They all fulfill the teaching of the Beatitudes—an item that the discussion did not mention. Happiness is within —a by-product of a way of life and of worship. But happiness does not dwell within unless it is shared, and unless an attempt is made to embody it in our social modes. John Bright, speaking of the death of his friend Richard Cobden, said: "We have put Holy Writ into an Act of Parliament." We need not be in doubt about the meaning of the Beatitudes: Christ fulfilled them.

[2] *Sartor Resartus*, Bk. II, ch. ix.

| 3 Blessed *are* the poor in spirit: for theirs is the kingdom of heaven. | 3 "Blessed are the poor in spirit, for theirs is the kingdom of heaven. |

B. THE DISCOURSE (5:3–7:27)

1. NINE BEATITUDES, CONTRASTING FUTURE JOYS WITH PRESENT SUFFERINGS AND DUTIES (5:3-12)

The Beatitudes are all promises of the kingdom of God, for to be in the kingdom is to **be comforted**, to **inherit the earth** or the promised land, to **be satisfied**, to **obtain mercy, to see God,** and to be called his **sons.** They are also descriptions of those who receive the promises. Such people cleave to God in simple trust, are single-minded in their love for him, and, although they are oppressed by the world, are merciful to others, and, wherever they go, are the bringers and founders of peace. Jesus clearly expects his teaching to be put into practice. It is not a formless ethical ideal; and, although Paul and John are able to sum it up in the word "love," the Sermon on the Mount is concrete and specific. Yet the Beatitudes show that for Jesus righteousness is more than the sum of his commandments; it is a total attitude of mind, a particular kind of character. Those who are praised in the Gospel are men and women of humility, love, trust, fidelity, and courage. They are not yet perfect, but they are converted. Their interests and desires are turned in the direction of the kingdom of God.

Matthew apparently has nine beatitudes, though the eighth and ninth may constitute but one; and if vs. 5 is removed there may be only seven. Luke 6:20-23 contains four beatitudes, all of which have parallels here. Q probably had these, and in the third person rather than the second, as in Luke; Matthew, however, added such phrases as **in spirit** (vs. 3) and **righteousness** (vs. 6). Were there also beatitudes in L and M? If so Luke's four woes (6:24-26) may be from L, and at least some of Matthew's beatitudes may come from M.

As they stand, Matthew's beatitudes are no mere patchwork. When such glosses as **in spirit** are removed, they are in poetic form; C. F. Burney believes that the underlying Aramaic had both rhythm and rhyme (*The Poetry of Our Lord* [Oxford: Clarendon Press, 1925], pp. 165-68). The eighth beatitude artistically repeats the phrase "kingdom of the heavens." Even the long ninth beatitude may be in accordance with the conventional forms of Jewish poetry.

3. The Greek word rendered **blessed** is used in pagan literature to denote the highest stage of happiness and well-being, such as the gods enjoy. Here it stands for the

---

3. *The First Beatitude.*—Some scholars believe that this beatitude is the root from which the others grow, and that in a proper printing of the Beatitudes it should be a centered headline. Certainly it summarizes them all, and strikes the key of the kingdom-music. It is not a blessing on the poor-spirited or the craven-hearted. There is nothing cringing in the man here described. Then who are the poor in spirit? No single, clearly demarked group. The word covers many groups in its benediction. We cannot evade Luke's short description, "poor." We cannot dismiss it as due merely to his righteous and characteristic protest against social inequalities. His form of the Beatitudes may be the original form. Riches easily become pride: the "successful" man soon forgets that he is the mendicant of God. The poor by contrast easily keep compassion: they remember their dependence, and so are blessed. But Matthew's addition (or the later gloss), **in spirit,**

is needed, for poverty of itself is not blessed: it can become carking care or a worse bitterness. Thus the word **poor** covers also all who would learn, who come like children to the great book of life; and who, like Newton, know at last that all their knowledge is but a handful of pebbles on an illimitable shore. It covers those who are content with simplicity, who flee from the world's blatant advertising, and who could say with Thoreau: "I went to the woods because I wished to live deliberately, to front only the essential facts of life, and see if I could not learn what it had to teach. . . . An honest man has hardly need to count more than his ten fingers. . . . Simplicity, simplicity, simplicity!" [3] It covers all the lineal descendants of those who in the time of Jesus were the peasants of Galilee, whom the religionists in Judea despised, and whom they called "folk of the soil"! Jesus pronounced blessing on lowly, unspoiled folk

[3] Henry David Thoreau, *Walden.*

| 4 Blessed *are* they that mourn: for they shall be comforted. | 4 "Blessed are those who mourn, for they shall be comforted. |

Hebrew *'ashrê,* "how happy!" as in Pss. 1:1; 32:1; 112:1. It is often used as a congratulatory salutation as in Luke 1:42; 11:27-28. The Beatitudes state who are happy in God's sight. **The poor,** οἱ πτωχοί, Hebrew *'aniyyim,* primarily denotes their state of poverty, but they are the despised, oppressed, and pious poor of Pss. 9:18; 10:9; 12:5; 34:6; Jas. 1:9; 2:5-6, who look to God for their vindication and for whom God cares. They are not merely miserable in body; they are afflicted **in spirit** (cf. Isa. 61:1) and "feel their spiritual need" (Goodspeed). The phrase **in spirit,** added by Matthew, is an accurate and happy gloss. **Theirs is the kingdom:** The **is** should not be emphasized; in Aramaic there would be no copula. Jesus may be thinking of the age to come, but in prophecy present and future are never clearly distinguished.

4. They **mourn,** perhaps for their own sins and those of Israel, but also because the wickedness of the world oppresses their spirits. **They shall be comforted** by God. In Isa. 61:2 and Luke 2:25 the "consolation of Israel" means the coming age of bliss. Some rabbis gave the name "Comforter" to the Messiah.

whose prayers are the more real because un-pretended and undisplayed.

Indeed the deepest meaning of the word is in this realm of prayer and faith. The "poor and needy" mentioned in the O.T. (e.g., Pss. 10:2; 40:17) were those who, when oppressed by the wicked, still kept a godly conviction and a godly course. Even when not oppressed they were like Isaiah in the temple: they saw the King high and lifted up, and therefore knew their sin and pleaded for pardon. Perhaps the best commentary, outside the Bible, is the account, in *The Divine Comedy,* of Virgil and Dante meeting the Angel of Humility. The angel struck Dante's forehead with his wings, and thus erased the pride-mark, while angel choirs sang, *Beati pauperes spiritu.* Then Dante walked with light step because when the pride-mark is erased all the other sins become a smaller burden.[4] Pride is the root of sin: poverty of spirit is the root of the virtues. The blessed bow to Providence. Asking no gain or fame, they worship the Will.

The benediction was perhaps at first the same in each beatitude. We cannot know, but perhaps Jesus by very reiteration makes it clear beyond cavil that only men of such-and-such soul find a home in the new kingdom. We cannot stress the apparent present tense (see Exeg.) but the way to heaven is through heaven. To be poor in spirit is reward in itself—and in God. Already these "have passed from death unto life" (I John 3:14). Compare this radiance with the darkness of the rabbinical parallel: "Ever be more and more lowly in spirit, since the expectancy of men is to become the food of worms."[5] The poor in spirit are like the artist George Frederick Watts, of whom it was

written that he had "always in his work a window left open to the infinite." The light streams in upon them: their lowliness is its own joy—or God's joy in his Son, who "took upon him the form of a servant" (Phil. 2:7). This is "the glorious gospel of the blessed God" (I Tim. 1:11).

4. *The Second Beatitude.*—It is a startling paradox: "Blessed are the mourners" (Goodspeed). The world says, "Enjoy!" Christ says, "Grieve!"—a sharp denial of the world's standards. This is the transvaluation of all values. Yet Jesus knew full well that grief in itself is not blessed. Its effect can be seen on any face of sorrow: it disfigures and slays. Certainly it is not "happy." Yet the beatitude stands, and in Luke's version it is even more unqualified: "Blessed are ye that weep now" (Luke 6:21). Then what kind of mourning brings this blessing? **Blessed are they that** accept their own sorrow with resolve to learn, and to make the sorrow an oblation. Our instinct is to rebel against pain, or to try to evade it, or to "forget it" in work or pleasure. But some people bare their body to the spear. So inevitable a fact, they surmise, has meaning: the spear may be tipped with life instead of with poison. They cannot conceive that life is given only for their comfort. Darkness may reveal stars, worlds on worlds, which the garish sun can only hide. So they confront the fact of death, and they creatively accept pain, offering hospitality to a strange guest. Thus they entertain "angels unawares" (Heb. 13:2). **Blessed are they that** voluntarily share their neighbors' pain. They could sidestep it: "It is not my business; I have enough troubles of my own." They could even pretend that sorrow does not exist. But they expose themselves to the world's misery. Like Arnold von Winkelried, Swiss hero of the battle of Sempach, they stand in the pass and gather

4 "Purgatory," Canto xii.
5 In J. R. Dummelow, *A Commentary on the Holy Bible* (New York: The Macmillan Co., 1946), p. 639.

5 Blessed *are* the meek: for they shall inherit the earth.

5 "Blessed are the meek, for they shall inherit the earth.

---

5. Some early MSS transpose vss. 4 and 5, perhaps in order to bring the **poor** and **meek** together; however, vs. 5 may be an early gloss based on Ps. 37:11, in which case its place in the text might vary. Πραεῖς here means **meek** or humble-minded rather than gentle. It represents "the meek" of Ps. 37:11, who are "the poor" looked at from a different point of view. They will **inherit** the (promised) land or perhaps the restored **earth** of the messianic age. The English word "meek" now has unfortunate associations, but that was not always true: Moses was "very meek, above all men" (Num. 12:3) .

---

all the spears into their own breast. They visit the home where death has come. They enter into the hidden tumult of the criminal in jail. They agonize over slums, and become leaders in civic righteousness. None is bound except they also are bound. They are the compassionate of the earth, and their reward is to grow in compassion.

The word has even deeper meanings. **Blessed are they that** mourn for their sins. Others are content with an unexamined life: sin is to them a trivial affair. But the "mourners" see God grieving in holy love. Their conscience is quick: "God be merciful to me a sinner" (Luke 18:13) . They can say with the sensitiveness of the psalmist: "My sin is ever before me" (Ps. 51:3) . So God is ever before them, and they dwell in the Presence; for the reverse side of remorse is supernal Light. **Blessed are they that** mourn for their neighbors' sins. Such mourners are few in number: most men are not greatly troubled by the shame of the streets, the greed of the market place, and the violence of nations. But elect souls mourn; yes, and count themselves guilty in the common guilt. Like Moses of old they say, "Blot me . . . out of thy book . . . yet . . . forgive their sin" (Exod. 32:32) . They are the conscience of their age, not as acid reformers, but as heart of love.

Such sorrow finds comfort. The Greek word apparently means "to call to the side of." This mourning summons the aid of God because it is akin to his nature. Our English word in its original Latin meaning properly conveys the idea of strength: *con-fortis*. This comfort is no mere soothing: it is tenderness and reinforcement. Fiona Macleod (William Sharp) has a story which tells of

a grey pool, the weeping of all the world, fed everlastingly by the myriad eyes that every moment are somewhere wet with sorrow, or agony, or vain regret, or vain desire. And those who go there stoop, and touch their eyelids with that grey water . . . and their songs thereafter are the sweetest that are sung in the ways of Pharais.[6]

[6] *Pharais and the Mountain Lovers* (New York: Duffield & Co., 1909), pp. 168-69.

It is a parable. Only such have joy and song: only they are in tune. Joy is not the opposite of pain, or in respite of pain, or despite pain: it is because of pain, and through pain. Joy is sorrow accepted in contrite love. The mourners thus enter life's secret; others are barred at the door.

5. *The Third Beatitude.*—**Blessed are the meek.** This is a direct quotation from Ps. 37:11. Our English word **meek** obscures the meaning. We link the words "meek" and "little"—"A meek little man" is a title which, rightly, no one covets. But true meekness is not weakness. In their versions of the N.T. the French use *débonnaire*—a word that at least cancels out the false sadness we have linked to "meek," and hints a man who is so gladdened and overcome by God's greatness that he counts his own life as nothing, but gaily gives it for love's sake. The Greek word means good will toward man and reverent obedience toward God. It has sinew: it is not sad resignation.

Who are **the meek**? This beatitude is akin to the first beatitude, but it is not a repetition. If "poor in spirit" is the opposite of proud in spirit, "meek" is the opposite (both in nature and in act) of aggressive. They are not harsh, not self-assertive, not covetous, not trampling in brute force: they are humble in the strength of reverence. Others claim their rights, but the meek are concerned about their duties. Others are clamant and advertise, but the meek walk in a quiet godliness. Others seek revenge, but the meek "give place unto wrath" (Rom. 12:19) . How the word must have cut across the fashion of Christ's own time! The Jews asserted their pride of race, the Romans their pride of power, the Greeks their pride of knowledge, even as modern nations insist on their "place in the sun"; but the meek are content to walk in the shadow where God keeps watch over his own. In a world where our knowledge and control of the forces of nature may well at any time, because of some absurd and tragic impasse, threaten the very extinction of human life, genuine meekness becomes man's one hope.

This meekness has an astonishing reward: it inherits the earth. Notice the word **inherit.** The

| 6 Blessed *are* they which do hunger and thirst after righteousness: for they shall be filled. | 6 "Blessed are those who hunger and thirst for righteousness, for they shall be satisfied. |

6. Q probably read: "Blessed are those who hunger, because they shall be filled." With the word **righteousness** added, the meaning may be: (*a*) they desire righteousness in the sense of "vindication" (Isa. 62:2; cf. Luke 18:7); (*b*) they strive to be upright (Prov. 21:21); (*c*) they depend, not upon their own power to achieve righteousness, but upon God. The third interpretation cannot be reconciled with rabbinical Judaism; the closest Synoptic parallel is Luke 18:10-14. But taking the sermon as a whole, we are probably right in choosing this third meaning: one can only **hunger and thirst** for the righteousness required; its demands cannot be met by a frontal attack or sheer will power. **Shall be filled** need not necessarily refer to physical eating; in the Greek text of Ps. 16 (17) :15 and in Tob. 12:9 the expression is used figuratively.

reward comes as gift and legacy: it comes thus because the meek would never seize it. An heir is the true child of the real possessor! The promise, however seemingly incredible, is true, and gathers evidence. The mammoth creatures that once terrorized the planet are gone. They blundered to destruction, victims of their own too great strength; but the sheep still graze on the hills. Men of sterling conscience, not meeting persecution with persecution, inherited America—the Kansas Mennonites being for witness. Immanuel Kant tells of the forbearance of his father when his father's interests were affected by a quarrel between the rival guilds of the harness makers and of the saddlers: the father gained his son's love, a better reward than added profits. Kant says: "Even in the conversation of the family the quarrel was mentioned with such forbearance and love toward the opponents . . . that the thought of it, though I was only a boy then, will never leave me." [7] Jesus was meek, and inherits the earth—which our aggressions can only destroy. [8] We can see why the inheritance comes. The aggressor is at odds with himself: there is something in his nature which his own cruelty affronts. So, being divided within himself, his judgment becomes blind, and he stumbles to his doom. But the man of reverent lowliness is organized in personality round a noble concern—he is intent on God. Thus he is strong: self-control for God's sake is fortitude indeed, not weakness. God made the earth, and his sovereignty is never usurped. It is his will so to turn history as to put down the "mighty from their seats" and to exalt "them of low degree" (Luke 1:52). He bequeaths the earth to the sons of his own spirit, and to his Son. Jesus, "when he was reviled, reviled not again; when he suffered, he threatened not; but committed himself to

him that judgeth righteously" (I Pet. 2:23). By that judgment **the meek . . . inherit the earth,** not merely in some distant heaven, but now in spirit, and continuingly in very fact.

6. *The Fourth Beatitude.*—The word **hunger** is a strong word meaning intense desire. **Thirst** is perhaps a stronger word: only people in desert lands can properly understand pangs of thirst. In the time of Jesus water cisterns were a matter of life and death. The words have gracious meanings. Who among us can claim righteousness? Our history is failure. But the requirement in this beatitude is not righteousness, but **hunger and thirst after righteousness.** Here Jesus takes the intention for the deed: "Whereas it was in thine heart to build a house unto my name, thou didst well that it was in thine heart" (I Kings 8:18). The **hunger,** it should be noted, is for **righteousness** both within the man and within his world. Righteousness means equity and humanity, the realm of the Christ-spirit. Our life is dominant hunger, "the urge to completeness." Everyone is vexed by discontent. Jesus saw (and sees) people hungering, but not for righteousness, and especially not for his righteousness, which is justice held in love. Mark the restless craving in every face. For what? There are times, however, when we do hunger, not after the spotlight or gold or flesh, but after Christ. And do we not assume that every hunger, bad or good, has its food? There are bread and water for the hunger of the mouth, and there is light for the hunger of the eyes. Why should it be hard for us to believe that there is fulfillment for the thirst of the soul?

Consider hungers and their fulfillment. Some hungers are not filled (e.g., the hunger that an amputated leg may grow again), and if they find no compensation, how often death comes, for life is hope! Some hungers, when fulfilled, are only mocked. "They have their reward" (6:16): they longed for adulation, they now have it—and they find it empty. Life has be-

[7] J. H. W. Stuckenberg, *The Life of Immanuel Kant* (London: Macmillan & Co., 1882), pp. 9-10.

[8] See Charles Rann Kennedy's play, *The Terrible Meek* (New York: Harper & Bros., 1912).

7 Blessed *are* the merciful: for they shall obtain mercy.

7 "Blessed are the merciful, for they shall obtain mercy.

7. The merciful are those who behave toward the unfortunate with sympathetic lovingkindness, as witness the Samaritan of Luke 10:37 and the *Kyrie eleison* of Matt. 17:15. See also 6:14-15; 7:1-2; I Clem. 13:2.

come a one-way street, and they can now only stand and die. Some hungers, when fulfilled, lead only to satiation. Roman epicures would use an emetic that they might return to the table with an appetite. Theirs is not the only craving which, when granted, ends in self-disgust. But there are other hungers which, once granted, are renewed in higher hunger; and are again fulfilled through further enhancement to eternal life. Such is the hunger for beauty, the hunger for music, the hunger for highest truth. See Browning's "A Grammarian's Funeral," the stanza beginning, "That low man seeks a little thing to do." Recall Robert Louis Stevenson's comment that "to travel hopefully is a better thing than to arrive." Those who hunger after Christ both travel hopefully and arrive. They are "changed into the same image from glory to glory" (II Cor. 3:18). "Happy are they that. . . ." Other hungers find only a passing pleasure for their answer, but the man who thirsts after Christ finds joy. His is a positive passion. No longer are his eyes on his sins, either to cherish them or unduly to bemoan them. His eyes are on Christ, and Christ draws him: "As for me, I will behold thy face in righteousness: I shall be satisfied, when I awake, with thy likeness" (Ps. 17:15). Was there not a king in a legend who opened up for his people a triple fountain that gave water, milk, and wine? [9] Jesus gives a better joy: water of righteousness for the cleansing of sin, milk of righteousness for the sustaining of inner motive, wine of righteousness—the zest and joy of eternal life.

7. The Fifth Beatitude.—**Blessed are the merciful.** This beatitude hardly seems as revolutionary as the others, and is therefore easier for us to accept. But when it was spoken, it was as drastic as the others in its overturning of accepted standards. The Romans despised pity. The Stoics might offer succor, but they looked askance at compassion. The Pharisees were harsh in their self-righteousness: they showed little mercy (see 23:23). Besides, the commonly accepted explanation of suffering saw in it only the deserved punishment for sin. So Jesus here took sharp issue with his world. In the carillon of the Beatitudes this bell could ill be spared. For what is mercy? The question brings the

Red Cross to mind. Rightly, for mercy is the Red Cross spirit in the world. Mercy lays claim on us whenever and wherever there is suffering. It pities and succors every creature, not man alone. It refrains from cruel sport as well as from cruel speech. It abjures cruelty even in cases of deserved punishment. It has mitigated the harshness of our penal systems and must still further transform them. It lays hands, this "quality of mercy," on the injustices of trade and on the vast cruelty of war, and resolves to erase them. But mercy has deeper movements than those usually assigned to the Red Cross, for it is no true mercy to restore a man's body and neglect his spirit. Thus resolute prayer is part of mercy. See, for an instance, the conversation in Tennyson's "In the Children's Hospital," between a doctor and a nurse. Thus sacrificial love is part of mercy. What of the morally crippled? What of those poor in honor, however they may be rich in money? What of those diseased by greed? What of the wicked in the world? We are to "give for alms those things which are within" (Luke 11:41)—and that is costly business, requiring our tiny calvary within his Calvary.

The practice of mercy thus becomes clear. It *is* practice, not mere feeling or sentiment. To Aristotle pity was a troublesome emotion, and drama provided perhaps its best outlet. But this proxy pity is not enough: if untranslated into deeds it becomes septic. Jesus required deeds of mercy held within prayers of mercy, and prayers of mercy held within the sacrificial pangs of the heart. If no deed is possible, words have power. Thus the beggar to whom the Russian poet and reformer said, "Do not be angry with me brother; I have nothing with me!" answered, "But you called me brother—that was a great gift." If no words are possible, tears have saving grace.

As for the benediction promised to the merciful, Shakespeare's lines have caught its truth:

The quality of mercy is not strain'd,
It droppeth as the gentle rain from heaven
Upon the place beneath: it is twice blest;
It blesseth him that gives and him that takes:
'Tis mightiest in the mightiest: it becomes
The throned monarch better than his crown.[1]

"Twice blest"! The merciful are too aware of their own sins to deal with others in sharp condemnation. So they draw down on themselves

[9] Alexander Maclaren, *The Wearied Christ* (London: Alexander & Shepheard, 1893), pp. 120-21 has one version of the story.

[1] *The Merchant of Venice*, Act IV, scene 1.

8 Blessed *are* the pure in heart: for they shall see God.

8 "Blessed are the pure in heart, for they shall see God.

---

8. The pure in heart need not be thought of as the morally perfect; and there is no special reference to sexual purity. "Heart" in Semitic speech includes the mind as well as the emotions. The purehearted man of Ps. 24:4 "has had no desire for falsehood, and has not sworn to a lie" (Amer. Trans.). A rabbinical commentary interprets "such as are of a clean heart" (Ps. 73:1) as meaning those "whose heart is strong through fulfilling the law." The phrase almost means "those who are right with God," "those who with singleness of mind [Col. 3:22] try to do God's will" (cf. also Jas. 4:8).

Such people will **see God,** not merely in the metaphorical sense of worshiping in his house (Ps. 42:2), nor in a purely mystical sense, but rather in the sense that God will reward them by permitting them to see him face to face in the age to come (Rev. 22:4). This beatitude of Jesus is distinctive and we know of no rabbinical saying like it.

---

in penitence the mercies of God. Being merciful they arouse no harsh feelings among their neighbors, and are not likely to awaken enmities: they receive as they give. Even when bitterness is visited on them, as it sometimes is visited even on the merciful (Christ and his Cross being for witness), God deals with them as they deal with their neighbors. They **obtain mercy,** and need fear no day of judgment.

8. The Sixth Beatitude.—Blessed are the pure in heart. It would be ungrateful to pick and choose among the Beatitudes, but probably for most people this sixth beatitude is the "bright particular star" in the constellation. It seems also the most inaccessible. We hardly know which is more beyond us, the condition or the promise—purity of heart or seeing God. But Christ has not mocked our hopes. What is purity of heart? "Heart" in the Bible usually means the whole personality. It involves mind and will, not only the emotions. The word "pure" occurs twenty-eight times in the N.T., and ten times it is translated "clean." Used of linen, it means white linen; of gold, unalloyed gold; of glass, clear glass. Two meanings are perhaps dominant—rightness of mind and singleness of motive. As for the rightness of mind, whatever our revolt against a false "puritanism," impuritanism will not save us. Matthew Arnold said that chastity and charity were the marks of early Christianity, and that chastity was perhaps as winning a virtue as the charity because it gave a pagan world release from a more consuming bondage.[2] As for singleness of motive, that meaning is more central: Jesus said that "harlots" given to lust would go into the kingdom before the Pharisees—who were double-minded (21:31). Yet how hard it is to have a "single eye"! How few swing like a compass to the will of God, and are thus without prejudice in their dealings with their neighbors! In politics or trade how few men are thus "clear" in their intention, and in inner desire how few are even reasonably free from duplicity!

What is meant by seeing God? The beatific vision has been the agelong goal both of philosopher and saint, but this beatitude promises more than mere vision. Perhaps our deepest wish, if we could analyze our longing, is to see God. Tennyson left instruction that his "Crossing the Bar" was always to be placed at the end of his published works. It closes:

> I hope to see my Pilot face to face
> When I have crost the bar.

In the Medo-Persian Empire there were seven intimate counselors and friends "which saw the king's face" (Esth. 1:14). Perhaps this custom of the time was in the mind of Christ when he gave this promise. More likely he meant that the pure in heart see God in the world about them when others are blind; that the pure in heart are aware of the movements of the Divine Will in their lives even in the midst of pain, when others are rebellious or despairing; that the pure in heart have by intuition the leading of God's spirit when others feel bereft; that the pure in heart have times of vision when earth and flesh fall away—"the flight of the Alone to the Alone"—and that at last they shall veritably see God in the consummation of the kingdom. Galahad saw the Holy Grail, though others failed, because his heart was pure. The promise is fulfilled. The poet Shelley insisted that this beatitude is only "a metaphorical repetition" of our commonly expressed conviction that "virtue is its own reward."[3] But to Christ, God is not abstract virtue. He is Fact and Life. The saints have traced his ways and felt his presence. James Reid says that to the impure man life is like a stained-glass window seen from the outside, but that the pure man

---

[2] See his essay "A Comment on Christmas," in *St. Paul and Protestantism with Other Essays* (London: Smith, Elder & Co., 1892), p 154.

[3] *Shelley Memorials,* ed. Lady Shelley (London: Smith, Elder & Co., 1859), pp. 258-60.

| 9 Blessed *are* the peacemakers: for they shall be called the children of God. | 9 "Blessed are the peacemakers, for they shall be called sons of God. |

9. The **peacemakers** are those who "seek peace, and pursue it" (Ps. 34:14). "Peace" in the O.T. means more than just the absence of strife; it is personal and social well-being in the widest sense of the word. Jesus' disciples will bring into all their relationships a quality which makes for harmony and blessing. Monarchs like Augustus were praised as "peacemakers"; but the peace known to the Bible springs from trust, love, and obedience toward God. The rabbis put the same high valuation on peacemakers. Hillel, Jesus' contemporary, said, "Be of the disciples of Aaron, loving peace and pursuing peace" (Aboth 1:2). Such persons will **be called sons of God.** In the O.T. the phrase "sons of God" occasionally refers to angels or divine beings (Job 38:7), but it most often means the Hebrews, whom God created (Deut. 32:6), who are the objects of God's love and care and are under obligation to obey him. For example, Hos. 1:10 promises that the repentant Israelites, who have not been God's people, will be called "sons of the living God" (see on 4:3). Vss. 44-45 furnish the best possible comment on this verse. Those who seek peace by loving their enemies are doing as God himself does, and are his true sons in every way.

sees it from the inside—from a true and single motive.[4] This beatitude does not mock us. God can cleanse the heart on the instant of penitent prayer. Then shall a man say with Saul Kane:

> Out of the mist into the light,
> O blessèd gift of inner sight![5]

9. The Seventh Beatitude.—Blessed are the peacemakers. The emphasis on peace and peacemaking is frequent in the teachings of Jesus: it was fitting that the angels who hailed his birth sang of "peace on earth." He said, "Love your enemies, . . . do good to them that hate you, and pray for them which despitefully use you" (vs. 44). John's Gospel tells us that his last bequest was peace: "My peace I give unto you" (John 14:27). Rightly, therefore, the word "peace" is now a cardinal Christian word. It occurs repeatedly in the N.T., its central meaning being reconciliation with God. Jesus Christ is the Prince of peace, peace in the soul and peace among men. His age was torn by animosities. The exclusiveness of many Jews was proverbial. Their contempt for the Samaritans is an instance. In all ages nations are at odds, trade and home are torn by strife, and the individual soul is alienated from God. From that deepest alienation, the separation from God, all other conflicts spring.

Peacemakers are peace*makers*—makers of peace, and they are few: it is easier to fan the ashes of ancient feuds than to allay warfare. The appeal to angered prejudice is the stock in trade of some politicians, while the plea for understanding is often a lonely cry. The peace-makers, who seem cowardly, and are certainly not popular, may really be a heroic company. Those who assume that peace "just comes," or even that preparation for war is the best preparation for peace, are simply peace-hopers or peace-eulogizers. They cumber the earth. Jesus *made* peace: he fashioned it from very life and sacrifice. So his peace is peace indeed (Eph. 2:14-16); whereas what we call peace is not peace, but only smoldering grudges and exhausted hatreds.

What is this work of peace? It is the task of reconciliation between groups and men at odds. It keeps centrally in view the holy love of God. It knows that there can be no real peace until men are reconciled with him. It abstains from provocation, moves with gentleness, and pleads in love. Augustine says of his mother, Monica, that "she shewed herself such a peacemaker, that hearing on both sides most bitter things, . . . she never would disclose aught of the one unto the other, but what might tend to their reconcilement."[6] Monica lived after this fashion, not in some superficial mood of "anything to keep the peace," but because by prayer and the commitment of her will she lived within the holy love of God.

Peacemaking is also a preventive task. If poverty embitters the masses of men and thus tends to war, the peacemaker enlists to banish unmerited poverty. If insecurity or maladjustment in toil makes a man fractious in his home, the peacemaker strikes at that root of the problem. At times he thus seems to be a troublemaker. Actually he is curing the disease instead of merely salving the symptoms. His fundamental work is always to reconcile men with God. For as long as men are at odds with God, they are at odds with themselves and with their

[4] *The Key to the Kingdom* (New York: George H. Doran Co., 1928), p. 159.

[5] *The Everlasting Mercy.* Copyright, 1911, by John Masefield. Used by permission of The Macmillan Company, The Society of Authors, and Dr. Masefield.

[6] Confessions, IX. 21.

10 Blessed *are* they which are persecuted for righteousness' sake: for theirs is the kingdom of heaven.

11 Blessed are ye, when *men* shall revile you, and persecute *you,* and shall say all manner of evil against you falsely, for my sake.

10 "Blessed are those who are persecuted for righteousness' sake, for theirs is the kingdom of heaven.

11 "Blessed are you when men revile you and persecute you and utter all kinds of evil against you falsely on my account.

10-11. For righteousness' sake appears to be more primitive than **on my account** or "on account of the Son of man" (Luke 6:22 RSV), and it fits well with vss. 3-4. Codex Bezae (D) and some O.L. MSS read "righteousness" in vs. 11 also. **On my account** raises the whole question whether Jesus demanded that his disciples confess him before men (10:32-33); but whether he did or not, it was still true that faithful adherence to Jesus' understanding of the law might bring scorn and persecution, and in a sense this would be on his "account." The Bible almost everywhere assumes that God's servants must remain true even at the risk of their lives. The rabbis later ruled that a man might, if his life were in danger, break any commandments except those against idolatry, unchastity, and murder. Yet they also taught that martyrs were rewarded in the world to come. **Falsely** is probably an unnecessary gloss; some Western authorities and the Sinaitic Syriac omit it, as does Luke.

neighbors. Therefore the true evangelist is the best peacemaker: he pleads that men shall turn to Christ, who himself breaks down "the middle wall of partition" (Eph. 2:14), thus making peace. So the most important work of the peacemaker is the practice of the presence of God. Through that communion the peacemaker can give peace from the overflow of his own peace-filled heart.

The reward of the peacemaker is that God acknowledges him as very child. The world cannot always see in him this essential family likeness, but God sees it; **the peacemakers** are one in spirit with the Father, and therefore recognize all men as their brothers. The world sometimes calls them "sentimentalists" or "cowards," but God calls them his children; and the names God gives them are the names that finally stand. When it was suggested to Richard Cobden that he might attain such fame as to be buried in Westminster Abbey, he replied that he hoped not: "My spirit could not rest in peace among these men of war." It is a tragic fact that the world has usually reserved its highest honors for the warmakers. But only God's honors endure. They are kept, in family joy and warmth of home, for the peacemakers.

10-12. The Eighth Beatitude.—**Blessed are those . . . persecuted.** This beatitude is not out of place in our time. It is not the echo of "battles long ago." Persecutions recur unto blood, and the followers of Christ are ever and again chained "in prisons dark." Perhaps they should be; possibly our alleged Christianity is condemned when it is so tepid that the wicked do not persecute it but simply ignore it. Could there be a more startling paradox than this saying? Other leaders, such as Garibaldi, fore-

seeing much trouble, bade their followers anticipate it and confront it. But Jesus bade his followers to be glad in hardship, and to "leap for joy" when persecution came. He offered as reason that the prophets were so persecuted. That fact seems to us a cause only for grief: the blindness and cruelty of ages gone still disfigure our world. But Jesus plays havoc with that mood. He bids us rejoice. He implies that the prophets are a joyous company, welcoming their successors into a radiant fellowship (cf. I Pet. 1:6-12).

Not every persecution is here pronounced blessed. The motive must be right: **for righteousness' sake, . . . for my sake** (see Exeg.). Some persecutions do not fulfill that requirement. There are some that we unworthily invite by our intolerance. But when every qualification has been made and heeded, it is clear that Jesus expected his followers to be persecuted. His warnings to that effect are repeated. They culminate in the word "cross," the strange guerdon which he offered to his disciples—the nails driven, the beam lifted. But persecution should never be allowed to become a martyr complex or a morbid self-pity, for persecution for his sake is great gladness. Thus persecution awaits the honest politician, the tradesman who will not compromise for profits, the teacher who cleaves to truth. Bitter persecution may await the man who is foresworn to Jesus: "The disciple is not above his master" (Luke 6:40). While sin remains, it is that kind of world; and an unpersecuted Christianity may in some instances be an effete faith.

The reasons and rewards which Jesus offered are as startling as the way of life proposed. **For great is your reward in heaven** is the promised benediction. We despise the doctrine of re-

12 Rejoice, and be exceeding glad: for great *is* your reward in heaven: for so persecuted they the prophets which were before you.

13 ¶ Ye are the salt of the earth: but if the salt have lost his savor, wherewith shall it be salted? it is thenceforth good for nothing, but to be cast out, and to be trodden under foot of men.

12 Rejoice and be glad, for your reward is great in heaven, for so men persecuted the prophets who were before you.

13 "You are the salt of the earth; but if salt has lost its taste, how shall its saltness be restored? It is no longer good for anything except to be thrown out and trodden under foot by men.

---

12. Your reward is great in heaven: This does not necessarily mean that reward is confined to heaven. It is enjoyed in heaven as well as on earth, and it is laid up for man in heaven (6:20) and thus guaranteed by a faithful God. The rabbis recognized that to do a good deed "for its own sake" or "for love" was to do it with a higher motive than that of reward; but neither Jesus nor the rabbis hesitated to speak of reward, since God had promised it. Highly organized religious systems often succumb to the temptation to make reward in heaven a matter of bookkeeping, but Jesus avoids this danger because he teaches: (*a*) that God's reward cannot be measured, for it consists of salvation in the age to come, and it is identical for all (20:1-16; 25:21, 23); (*b*) that it is out of all proportion to the service rendered (19:29; 25:21, 23); and (*c*) that, in the last analysis, it is a gracious gift, for "when you have done all that is prescribed for you, say, 'We are mere slaves; we have only done what we ought'" (Luke 17:10). The differences between Jesus' teaching on reward and that of the rabbis are discussed in the notes on 20:13-14. The O.T. tells how **prophets** like Amos and Jeremiah were **persecuted**. In the first century it was also believed that Isaiah had been martyred by being sawed in two. (See Heb. 11:37; Ascension of Isaiah 5; C. C. Torrey, *The Lives of the Prophets* [Philadelphia: Society of Biblical Literature, 1946], pp. 34-35.)

2. THE RELATION OF THE DISCIPLES TO THE WORLD (5:13-16)

13. The saying about tasteless salt may once have circulated separately, and its meaning must necessarily depend on its context. The context of Luke 14:34-35 has to do with discipleship, and Matthew explicitly says the disciples are **the salt of the earth**, i.e., that which keeps the world from spoiling or being tasteless. The second-century

---

wards. We may be right, or we may show small discernment. Some reward there must be, or life is robbed of meaning. We would hardly ask that the return for Christian living should be misery and wickedness, or that a different life should have no different result. Our protest is really against a doctrine of earthy, selfish, and godless rewards. It is a proper protest: to the true follower of Christ such rewards would be punishment. The beatitude tells us that the outcome of Christ's way of life is written by God on a man's soul, and that it is at last an eternal at-homeness with God. **For so persecuted they the prophets which were before you** may be mainly a simple statement of fact, but it nevertheless implies blessings. The persecuted have the stamp of courage on their faces and in their hearts. They have joined a noble company —Elijah, Amos, Isaiah, Jeremiah. That company lives, not merely in memory, but in agelong venture and in eternal life. Leo Tolstoy tells the story of Ivan the Fool, a czar who kept open house, requiring only one condition of

any would-be guest: the man's hands must be horny with toil. The persecuted share the hardships of the prophets, thus joining the prophetic company; and the heaven they reach is one into which the prophets of old shall welcome them. Perhaps a deeper blessing is hinted: the followers of Christ, members of an agelong company foresworn to God, see others redeemed through their sacrifice and so fulfill their vocation.

13. The Salt of the Earth.—Salt was greatly valued in the time of Christ. In the climate of Palestine it was indispensable for the preservation of food. A bag of salt was reckoned as precious as a man's life. Thus **salt of the earth** is no mean title. We stand amazed that Jesus should thus exalt his disciples. Consider what is implied. Salt gives zest to food. This is one item in the parable. Christian folk ought to add joy to the common day because they are Christian—the zest of serenity, trust, and worship. Salt is a preservative: food spoils without it. That is a second item in the parable, and was probably even more in Jesus' thoughts.

14 Ye are the light of the world. A city that is set on a hill cannot be hid.	14 "You are the light of the world. A

Epistle to Diognetus (chs. 5–6) eloquently develops the theme that the world would come to destruction if the Christians were not present in it. The O.T. and ancient secular writers employ the metaphor of salt to refer to what is most useful. Salt is also that which stimulates the appetite. A talmudic proverb says that "the salt of money is [its] scarcity (חסר), but the salt of money is [also] charity (חסד)." Salt which has lost its taste no longer has any reason for existence. As Chaucer says, with reference to the morals of the clergy, "If gold ruste, what shuld iren doo?" Pure sodium chloride does not deteriorate. Jesus may have in mind, not deterioration, but adulteration; or perhaps he means that it should be as unthinkable for the disciples to lose their character as for salt to become saltless. The "salt" of the parallel saying in Mark 9:50 refers to a quality of peaceableness which the disciples must have within themselves.

14. The rabbis frequently call God, Israel, the Torah, etc., the light of the world. David is the lamp of Israel (II Sam. 21:17), and his descendants are called lights in

Society easily becomes corrupt. Greed, lust, and indifference lead to decay. These are the forces of death, and they are not stayed unless some folk are salt. Thus Jesus, with amazing confidence, told these twelve whom he had chosen from the villages of the lake, Ye are the salt of the earth.

Ponder the method. There is no despair because the group is small: a pinch of salt is effective out of all proportion to its amount. There is no hermit strategy: the disciples are to stay in the world, touching even its unworthy life, if they would redeem it. There is no call to a sensational witness: salt is inconspicuous, ordinary, and admixed with common things. The proposal is for a day-by-day witness for Jesus; the implied promise is that again the city shall be saved by ten righteous men (Gen. 18:32).

Ponder the warning. In William M. Thomson's *The Land and the Book* there is an account of a merchant in Sidon who bought quantities of salt from the marshes of Cyprus, and hid them in houses on a remote mountain to avoid payment of the tax. But the floor of the houses was common earth, and soon the salt by that contact lost its saltness. It was then used to make the hard surface on the road. The Christian either redeems the world, or the world robs him of his Christianity. Dwight L. Moody once wrote in a man's Bible: "This Book will keep you from your sins, or your sins will keep you from this Book."[7] The warning is solemn: Jesus told his followers that they might lose the gift and grace which he had given, and that then they would be no better than a roadway for the casual traffic of the world. They would need to pray and discipline themselves if his word was to find fulfillment: "Have salt in yourselves, and have peace one with another" (Mark 9:50).

[7] The Bible was once shown to me, but I do not know whether Moody composed the epigram or quoted it.

14-15. The Light of the World.—Perhaps Jesus had just pondered the mystery and benediction of the dawn. In the night the fields drowse, the wheels of toil are still, the streets are empty except for prowling wickedness, and the windows of home are blind. Then the sun rises. It is a parable of Jesus' light in the world; and also of the light of his followers, for he has power to shine in them (cf. II Cor. 4:6). They in him are the light of the world.

They are to reveal God, saying to all men in word and life, as Jesus said to them, "Your Father which is in heaven." God had been obscured in Jesus' time by the darkness of the pagan cults and by those religionists who had turned a noble faith into a mere form. If no true light shone, the world would perish in darkness. He, Jesus, had come to shed light, that men might see God through him; and they, his followers, were to shine for his sake. Thus God would appear, not as a frowning deity, but as a holy Father with whom men may be at home in the spirit of Jesus.

The disciples, now as in the days of Jesus' flesh, are to reveal the true nature of man. Margaret Gordon wrote to Thomas Carlyle, "Let your light shine before men, and think them not unworthy the trouble." Is man by nature worthy or unworthy? Man can make darkness and try to live in it; but darkness slays him, because darkness is not his true nature. His eyes and soul alike are made for light. But there is a cleavage within us. One alternative is so base that, if we choose it, it leads us to the darkness of the "far country." But the true choice takes us home: "When he came to himself, . . . he arose, and came to his father" (Luke 15:17, 20). This paradox in man, and this bright destiny, the disciples of Jesus were and are called to reveal. Ye are the light of the world. They are to show man as he is in the vocation of God.

15 Neither do men light a candle, and put it under a bushel, but on a candlestick; and it giveth light unto all that are in the house.

16 Let your light so shine before men, that they may see your good works, and glorify your Father which is in heaven.

city set on a hill cannot be hid. 15 Nor do men light a lamp and put it under a bushel, but on a stand, and it gives light to all in the house. 16 Let your light so shine before men, that they may see your good works and give glory to your Father who is in heaven.

I Kings 11:36; Ps. 132:17; Luke 2:32. Test. Levi 14:3 applies the term to the Jews: "Be ye, the lights of Israel, purer than all the Gentiles. . . . What will all the Gentiles do if you are darkened by transgressions?" The saying about the **city** may, like vs. 13, originally have been a secular proverb; its meaning depends on its context. Here the thought is: "Light is certain to be noticed."

15. Light, like salt, must be useful. The clay lamp of Palestine lights the entire one-room house. A **bushel** (μόδιος) is more nearly a "peck-measure" (Goodspeed).

16. The application shifts from the character of the disciples to their good works, which result from that character. The verse may be Matthew's comment. For **your Father who is in heaven** see on 6:9.

Thus they are to shed the light of hope for all the tomorrows. "Out, out, brief candle!" cried Macbeth; and declared that man, after his tiny fret on earth, "is heard no more." But Jesus implies that man is meant to be in himself the bearer of the eternal light. The sun warms by radiation. So the Christian, gathering and reflecting light from Christ, can be radiant in the true sense of the word; and the light in him confers its own immortality—the better immortality of eternal life. This, age on age, is the Christian calling. This is a man's true work in field or home. This is the prime task of the Christian fellowship—to be as a lighted city set on a hill. Only so can the darkness of the world give place to dawn.

14-16. *Let Your Light So Shine.*—To this vocation Jesus called men from their daily toil, for this is man's essential labor. These verses give instruction about the way in which the light is to be shed. Where shall the light be placed? This whole passage hints at widening circles of illumination. Thus, vs. 15 speaks of a **house.** A disciple who forgets his faith there, who is gracious to the stranger in the street but keeps only an ill-humor for his own home, denies his faith and darkens his light. There is mention of a **city** in vs. 14. In olden times the watchman would move through city streets at nightfall, crying, "Hang out your lights!" We talk to neighbors, we work at common tasks, we inevitably play our part in the life of the community; and, for Christ's sake, we should do all in shining faith. To what horizons? The same verse declares that the **world** is the sphere of the light. Present problems are all world problems; and every man has some measure of world influence, if only by that mystery of influence which binds mankind in one life. The Christian is the light-bearer of a world faith.

How is the light to shine? Freely, without hindrance. Just as there is danger that salt shall lose its saltness, so there is danger that light may be lost in darkness if not tended and given chance to shine. In one sense the Christian should be inconspicuous; in another sense he cannot remain hidden if he would remain Christian. His faith should be evident. It is so different from the world's darkness that men cannot help but notice it. So it must not be darkened on any pretext—such as, "It is wisdom to work slowly"—or from any fear. It must not be covered by any flour bin of greed, or by any smoke of human pride. It must shine, at whatever honorable risk to the light-bearer, lest it become only part of the world's tragic blackout.

By what motive, for what purpose, should the light shine? That men may be blessed by "good works" and that God may be glorified. The term "works" in the N.T. covers both practical helpfulness and stanch character. Leo Tolstoy complained that the "Christians" of his day in Russia left him unmoved and unconvinced because "only actions, proving their conception of life to have destroyed the fear of poverty, illness, and death, so strong in myself, could have convinced me." [8] Origen and others have testified that the lives lived by the early Christians were their invincible witness; for men might have argued against a creed, but could not gainsay a creed that issued in courage, love, and joy. But there is a deeper purpose than any service to others: the light is to shine as an act of the worship of God. All light comes from the sun. George Stephenson was fond of expounding the theory that his famous engine was driven by fuel and steam indeed, but only because these derived their light and power from the central

[8] *My Confession, My Religion, the Gospel in Brief* (New York: Thomas Y. Crowell & Co., 1899), p. 48.

| 17 ¶ Think not that I am come to destroy the law, or the prophets: I am not come to destroy, but to fulfil. | 17 "Think not that I have come to abolish the law and the prophets; I have come not to abolish them but to fulfill |

3. THE NEW LAW IS THE COMPLETION OF THE OLD, NOT ITS DESTRUCTION (5:17-20)

These sayings, like 23:1-3, seem to teach a complete acceptance of the old religion, while in other passages the new and the old are sharply contrasted; see, e.g., 11:12-13 (=Luke 16:16); 15:11 (=Mark 7:15); Luke 13:10-17; Mark 3:1-6. The same apparent contradiction is found even in the sermon, for Jesus sweeps aside the law of oaths (vss. 33-37). Could Jesus have spoken vss. 18-19 if he made radical changes in the sabbath and purity laws? Scholars are not agreed regarding his attitude to the written and oral Torah. The position of B. H. Branscomb seems essentially correct (*Jesus and the Law of Moses* [New York: Richard R. Smith, 1930], especially pp. 262-71). Jesus accepted the O.T. law in principle and assumed that it was the permanently binding revelation of God; but he made the ritual commandments subordinate to moral duties, opposed the development of purity laws, and went further than the Pharisees in relaxing the sabbath laws to meet human needs. In fact, his emphasis on the spirit of the law, and his occasional quoting of one passage against another, necessarily involved a new view of Torah. Was he fully conscious of the implications of this? His opponents, at least, realized that his teaching endangered their position. (See on 15:1-20.) When his movement finally impinged on the Gentile world, his teaching was carried to its logical conclusion by Stephen, the Hellenists, and Paul.

17. This may well express Jesus' purpose. The Gospels contain several sayings which begin with the words "I am come." Harnack and some other scholars are inclined to doubt their genuineness because they deal with the nature of Jesus' mission, which was of such vital interest to the church. But Jesus could have made such a statement as this in controversy. **To fulfill** means simply "to fill"; i.e., "to enforce" or "to express it in its full significance." Thus the saying serves as an introduction to vss. 21-48. Jews, in their second-century controversies with Christians, quoted it thus: "I, the gospel, am not come to take away the Torah of Moses, but to add to it."

---

sun.[9] The lamp is not important; the light is everything. The light, coming from God, belongs to God, and should shine for his glory. If it should shine only for man it might be a pride-filled exhibitionism; shining for God it is true piety. In any event God's glory is man's best joy. Thus group responsibility is involved as well as individual responsibility: **your light . . . your good works . . . your Father.** It is as serious a task, as fraught with the issues of life and death, as keeping alive the light of a lighthouse. It is not an advertising light: it is an altar flame. It must be fed if it would burn; so prayer is essential. And sacrificial devotion: if necessity arise, the wick must burn out for Christ.

17-19. Jesus and the Law.—Not . . . to destroy, but to fulfil. The interpreter should read with especial care the exegesis of these difficult verses. Whether they are directly authentic or are a partial redaction, the best commentary on their meaning is found in the whole teaching and life of Jesus. Doubtless he aroused worthy Jewish

fears. His recognition of that fact is found in the words **think not.** He seemed to threaten both the Mosaic law and the temple. Every new prophet confronts such misgiving. Jesus met it in double measure. Every age, our own included, wonders if the prophet intends to tear it from its proven moorings and to cast it helplessly adrift. Thus these verses have prime importance.

In certain ways Jesus came to conserve. Robespierre in the French Revolution tried to substitute a ten-day week for the accustomed division, and changed even the names of the days and of the months. If these verses are a transcript of Christ's words, it is interesting to note that he proposed to change no essential verity. His own faith was fed from the O.T. It was in his blood and bone. He could not and would not disown it. He was no iconoclast; he was the Redeemer. He was no revolutionist, and saw no hope in shattering bombs; he was Friend and Savior of mankind. A faith cannot renounce its roots, yet it cannot live without the growth of new branches and leaves. Every law, our common law as well as the law of

---

[9] Samuel Smiles, *The Life of George Stephenson* (Boston: Ticknor & Fields, 1858), p. 425.

18 For verily I say unto you, Till heaven and earth pass, one jot or one tittle shall in no wise pass from the law, till all be fulfilled.

19 Whosoever therefore shall break one of these least commandments, and shall teach men so, he shall be called the least in the kingdom of heaven: but whosoever shall do and teach *them,* the same shall be called great in the kingdom of heaven.

them. 18 For truly, I say to you, till heaven and earth pass away, not an iota, not a dot, will pass from the law until all is accomplished. 19 Whoever then relaxes one of the least of these commandments and teaches men so, shall be called least in the kingdom of heaven; but he who does them and teaches them shall be called

18. **Truly** (RSV) and **Verily** (KJV) are the nearest English equivalents of *'āmēn,* a Hebrew word which the Greek Gospels leave untranslated. "Amen I say to you" is one of Jesus' characteristic phrases, and marks a solemn assertion of divine truth (cf. on vs. 22). Vss. 17-20 must have been useful to conservative Jewish Christians in their disputes with liberals. These verses perhaps received their present form between A.D. 30 and 50. Even though they are in the language of Oriental hyperbole, they apparently validate the entire ceremonial law. The law in question is the written O.T. **Not an iota**—iota is the smallest Greek letter and corresponds to *yôdh* (ʼ), the smallest character of the Hebrew alphabet—**not a dot,** or perhaps a corner or stroke of a letter, **will pass** away from this law. Almost identical rabbinical sayings can be found.

19. **Whoever . . . relaxes:** The Greek verb is translated "loose" in 18:18, a verse which refers to the rabbinical prerogative of declaring certain actions permitted or forbidden. **One of the least of these commandments:** The rabbis drew distinctions between "light" and "heavy" precepts, sometimes contrasting easier commands with those which are more difficult, sometimes referring to those whose infraction was a more or less serious matter. But, in general, they held that all were law and were to be observed. The Mishnah says, "Be as circumspect about a light commandment as about a heavy." (Aboth

Moses, withers when it is torn from its past; yet it cannot live without constant reinterpretation and enlargement. Jesus knew that any law is originally God's gift, who himself writes it on the tablets of man's heart. So Jesus was intent to keep and strengthen the hidden root of the law.

Yet he came to pioneer. Unmistakably he told us so: vss. 20-22 sharpen the truth. He fulfilled the law, but in such sudden growth that he seemed to have changed even its inmost nature. This he himself admitted, and taught that we could not put new wine into old wineskins. Yet the new wine came from an age-old vine. How did Jesus creatively fulfill the law? He pioneered by carrying its disciplines into deeper disciplines. It is a mark of the revolutionary, in contrast to the pioneer, that he is at least in part a nihilist: he destroys, and counts himself free from all conventions. But it is the mark of the pioneer that he accepts for himself and lays on his followers a deeper restraint. All this is evident in the six instances of the law which follow these verses. Christ pioneered in that he enlarged the law. He changed its negative into positive: the old "thou shalt not" became in his lips and life "blessed are they that. . . ." He changed its narrowness into wide horizons. The love shown by the old law toward friends is

shown in the new law also toward foes, and the loyalty formerly given to one nation is now to be given to all mankind. He changed its shallowness into depth: the constraint that beforetime rested on the act now rested on the motive. Six instances of these changes are given in vss. 21-47. He pioneered in that he redeemed the law. Laws soon set the teeth on edge, not only by their coercion, but by the despair that follows man's impossible attempt to fulfill them. Christ brought forgiveness for failure, and new power to indwell the new resolve. He redeemed the old Sabbath in the new Lord's day, the old Passover in his new table of the Sacrament, the old law of sacrifice in his Cross.

So these difficult verses are pertinent for our time. Each age has its iconoclasts—men who try to exorcise devils by Beelzebub. The warning given in vs. 19 is addressed, in deeper interpretation, to the church in every age. The followers of Christ are to conserve the old root, and to fulfill the new branches and the new fruit. Honoring old seed, they are yet by courageous vision to bring forth new harvests for new times by new labor; and they are ever to bear in mind that there is only one fulfillment: "Love [for God in Christ] worketh no ill to his neighbor: therefore love is the fulfilling of the law" (Rom. 13:10).

20 For I say unto you, That except your righteousness shall exceed *the righteousness* of the scribes and Pharisees, ye shall in no case enter into the kingdom of heaven.

great in the kingdom of heaven. 20 For I tell you, unless your righteousness exceeds that of the scribes and Pharisees, you will never enter the kingdom of heaven.

2:1; cf. also Jas. 2:10-11; Gal. 5:3.) To **teach men so** is, if possible, worse than breaking the law oneself; Jeroboam, the son of Nebat, was proverbially wicked because he not only sinned but made Israel to sin (I Kings 14:16). The saying could easily have been used against Paul. For the phrase **called least in the kingdom of heaven,** cf. on 11:11. According to 20:25-27, greatness in the kingdom is based on lowly service.

20. This verse fits reasonably well with vs. 17 but not with vs. 19. **Scribes and Pharisees** are overlapping but not identical groups. Among the scribes or experts in the law were to be found both Pharisees and Sadducees, and only a small proportion of the Pharisaic party was composed of scribes. There was no finer standard of righteousness in the ancient world than the Pharisaic, with its emphasis on personal holiness and social

---

20. *Adventurous Righteousness.*—**Except your righteousness shall exceed. . . .** (See the comment in Exeg. on Pharisees.) Here Jesus is pioneer in very truth. He takes issue with the religious leaders of his time. He hints that they may be barred from the gate of heaven, and says plainly that his followers shall not enter unless they show a better righteousness. How this upstart from Galilee must have staggered his hearers! Even we, after centuries of the study of Christ, find this doctrine strong meat. Who were the scribes and Pharisees? The scribes interpreted and expounded the law, and as jurists administered it. Granted their undue concern, as it might seem to us, for ablutions and ceremonies, they were held in honor. Children learning from them were expected to esteem them even above their own parents. In the days of Ezra scribes had died courageously to protect the books of the law. The Pharisees were "separated"—meticulous in religious observances and disciplined in conduct. They were in public favor—patriotic, opposed to the worldliness of the Sadducees, intent to bring religion to the people, in many instances generous to the needy, and (at least in a narrow sense) "good men." Yet Jesus here uses them as warning, as types of the "not enough"; and elsewhere he speaks of them in condemnation. Why?

Their righteousness was not *long* enough. It had no reach. A man not keeping the outward observances was to them an outcast: they would not buy food from him. They would have few dealings with a foreigner. They drew their robes tightly about them to avoid contamination. Compare the creed of the Pendyce family in John Galsworthy's *The Country House:* "I believe in my father, and his father, and his father's father, the makers and keepers of my estate, and I believe in . . . my son and my son's son. And I believe that we have made the country. . . . And I believe . . . in things as

they are, for ever and ever. Amen." [1] How much of our righteousness similarly falls short! Compare the compassion of Christ! Their righteousness was not *broad* enough. Too often their religion narrowed itself down to prohibitions. During World War I, a questionnaire widely answered by British men in arms made it clear that they believed the teaching of the church to be almost exclusively: "Thou shalt not smoke. Thou shalt not swear. Thou shalt not lust." Obviously disciplines have their inevitable place in any true religion. We are "separated" from unworthy habits, but only because we are first "separated unto Christ." Besides, a merely external and negative religion will soon ask how many liberties it can take: the Pharisees made "long prayers" and "devoured widows' houses" (23:14). Their righteousness was not *deep* enough. They judged men in censure. They judged by heredity. How, then, would Lincoln or Keats have stood? They judged by the deed of failure, asking about neither inward longing nor secret resistance. They judged by the standard of the law. They would not have understood the pure-minded wife who said to a defaulting husband: "Since you and I have done this thing, we must share its consequence." They had no deep-probing eyes of love, and no grace of vicarious suffering. Their righteousness was not *high* enough. It was satisfied: it had no "beyond" to beckon it, no risks, no aspiration, no abandon of worship. It was a low-vaulted and formal righteousness. They yearned to no vision of a worthier world, and could see in Christ no hidden grace. They killed him at last, and thought they did God service. The righteousness of Christ has length beyond all walls, breadth beyond all mere prohibitions, depth unto love's sacrifice, and mountain height toward God's own intention.

20. *The New Sinai.*—**For I say unto you. . . .** Imagine the consternation. This Artisan from

[1] New York: G. P. Putnam's Sons, 1907, p. 180.

| 21 ¶ Ye have heard that it was said by them of old time, Thou shalt not kill; and whosoever shall kill shall be in danger of the judgment: | 21 "You have heard that it was said to the men of old, 'You shall not kill; and whoever kills shall be liable to judgment.' |

responsibility. But, like most systems of ethics, it was adjusted to the capabilities of mankind, and it made allowances for the weakness of human nature and the demands made on man by his environment. Thus the Mishnah teaches (Aboth 3:16) that at the final judgment a man will be judged on the basis of the majority of his deeds. Jesus, on the contrary, would have men aspire, not to what is socially expedient, but to that righteousness which will be perfectly manifest in the kingdom of God. His disciples are, so far as possible, to live in this age as though they were already living in the age to come.

4. Contrasts Between the Old Interpretation of the Law and the New (5:21-48)

Contrasts a), b), and d) (vss. 21-26, 27-30, 33-37) are alike in that Jesus takes an O.T. maxim and surpasses it by forbidding not only the overt crime but the disposition behind it. But contrasts c), e), and f) (vss. 31-32, 38-42, 43-47) are annulments of the existing code as it was popularly understood. Some of the latter sayings may not originally have begun with a formula. Vs. 31 contains the formula but the parallel verse, Luke 16:18, does not.

a) Murder and Anger (5:21-26)

21. The hearers presumably are unlearned. Instead of reading the Bible they **have heard that it was said to** (not **by,** as in KJV) **the men of old;** or, perhaps: "this is the

Galilee weighed the sacred law in his balances, and found it wanting. If two Jews of that day quarreled, and one could claim, "But the law says . . . ," the argument was ended. The burden of our familiarity with Scripture is that it breeds, if not contempt, then an impervious mind. Joseph Parker titles a sermon on this passage, "Things No Man Could Say." [2]

There was a new age when Christ came. Sinai was given "to the ancients," but at the birth of Christ, God drew a climactic line across history. Sinai was the flush in the eastern sky that faded. It was what the Eskimos call a "false dawn." It betokened coming day, but was not itself the day. The sun rose in Christ. He is sovereign over history: heaven and earth may pass, but his word shall not be removed. No king or brilliant culture can long take issue with his light.

There was a new law when Christ came. It was no requirement of mere abstinence: it imposed positive obligations of spirit and deed: and gave men forgiveness and power to obey. It searched the heart. The old law was inscribed on tablets of stone; the new law was written on the inmost heart. The old law came from a mountain; the new law came from the soul of a Man. We make our treaties and institute our laws: they can stand only as they move obediently toward Christ. When Mrs. Humphry Ward argued with Walter Pater that "ortho-

doxy could not possibly maintain itself long against its assailants . . . and that we should live to see it break down," Pater answered, "I don't think so. . . . Take that saying, 'Come unto me, all ye that are weary and heavy-laden,'" and added his comment: "There is a mystery in it." [3]

There was a new disclosure of God when Jesus came. For the old law, which Jesus claimed to supersede, was not the word of man alone: it was the utterance of God. In deepest sense man received it, and God gave it. Now God uttered a new word, not in edict but in a life. Can there be any revelation more ultimate than God in a life? Who, then, is "this Jesus"? He is not "beside himself" (Mark 3:21). He alone is sound of mind. We could well classify our planet as lunatic, with its mania for wholesale war, and the classification would be by contrast with his serene wholeness. He is no brazen impostor: others deceive, but he has the ring of lowly truth. Thus his **for I say unto you** is a great divide. We doubt and deny; or we face fact, and follow in faith where fact leads us. If we follow, we become children of the new age, the new law, the new life in God.

21-26. First Instance: The New Law on Murder.—Jesus proceeds to give six instances of the way in which the law of his kingdom fulfills, and therefore supersedes, the Mosaic law. The first instance concerns murder, strife, and

[2] The City Temple Pulpit (London: Hodder & Stoughton, 1900), III, 13.

[3] Mrs. Humphry Ward, A Writer's Recollections (New York: Harper & Bros., 1918), I, 163.

22 But I say unto you, That whosoever is angry with his brother without a cause shall be in danger of the judgment: and whosoever shall say to his brother, Raca, shall be in danger of the council: but whosoever shall say, Thou fool, shall be in danger of hell fire.

22 But I say to you that every one who is angry with his brother[h] shall be liable to judgment; whoever insults[i] his brother shall be liable to the council, and whoever says, 'You fool!' shall be liable to the hell[j]

[h] Many ancient authorities insert *without cause*.
[i] Greek *says Raca to* (an obscure term of abuse).
[j] Greek *Gehenna*.

tradition you have received." **You shall not kill** is the command of Exod. 20:13; Deut. 5:17; etc. The next phrase sums up the O.T. law: **Whoever kills shall be liable to judgment,** i.e., conviction and punishment by properly constituted authority (presumably the local sanhedrin composed of twenty-three members).

22. But I say to you: A rabbi cited authorities, and a prophet said, "Thus says Yahweh" or "oracle of Yahweh." Jesus, perhaps deliberately, dispenses with such locutions, either because of a sense of divine inspiration or because the truth of his assertion should be transparently clear. He certainly spoke as one having authority (7:29). **Without a cause** is not found in some of the best MSS and earliest fathers. It is a gloss which seriously weakens Jesus' teaching. Under Jewish law, how could an angry man **be liable to judgment;** and can Jesus mean that the courts should punish anger? It seems better to suppose that he thinks of the divine judgment.

The essential meaning of the verse is clear. Murder is a result of anger; and Jesus would prevent crimes of violence by rooting out the elements in man's character which make him kill. A first-century rabbi is quoted as saying, "He who hates his neighbor, behold he is one who belongs to the shedders of blood." The difference is that Jesus proposes to take vigorous action against anger.

But the details of the saying are difficult. (*a*) Are the sins arranged in ascending order: anger, the insult **Raca,** and the worse insult **fool?** But the consequences of the three sins are not in this order, unless the **judgment** is an earthly one. A talmudic passage, however, reads: "He who says 'slave' to his neighbor shall be excommunicated; he who says 'bastard' to him shall receive the forty [lashes]; he who says 'godless' to him, it is a matter of his life." (*b*) Perhaps **shall be liable to the council** is an interpolation. In this case **Raca** and **fool** are coupled together as putting one in danger of Gehenna, and all three members of vs. 22 stand in contrast to vs. 21. (*c*) Or perhaps: "The ancients have been told, whoever says 'Raca' to his brother shall be liable to the sanhedrin, but I say to you that whoever says 'fool' [a similar insult] shall be liable to the Gehenna of fire."

Raca has often been identified with the rabbinical *rēqa'*, "good-for-nothing" or "wretch," which would mean about the same as "fool." But a Greek insult ραχᾶς, of which *racha* is probably a vocative, has been discovered in a papyrus (see E. J. Goodspeed, *Problems of New Testament Translation* [Chicago: University of Chicago Press, 1945], pp. 20-23, and Morton Smith's review of this book in *Journal of Biblical Literature,* LXIV [1945], 501-14). Its exact meaning is unknown. Forms of the Greek *moros* (**fool**) are known in rabbinical literature as loan words, and there is a Hebrew word *môreh,* "stubborn," "insubordinate."

contempt. The strong feeling burning in his words shows the sharpness of the issue. Jesus says that whereas under the old law only murder and other "extreme" offenses are reckoned guilty of death, under his law angry temper is similarly judged. Indeed the contempt that exclaims "Stupid!" or "Scoundrel!" is worthy of penalty by the court or of burning in Hinnom (the valley where refuse was burned). Mark the words **brother** and **every one.** His law has uni-

versal sway, and every man is a brother man under God's fatherhood. We may call this warning rhetorical, but we must not dilute its astringent passion.

Notice the inwardness of the new law. Anger (if it is not righteous indignation) and contempt are incipient murder. Killing is not done by knives alone, but by contemptuous sneers and by the casual indifference that regards men as less than men. Our law courts address them-

23 Therefore if thou bring thy gift to the altar, and there rememberest that thy brother hath aught against thee;

24 Leave there thy gift before the altar, and go thy way; first be reconciled to thy brother, and then come and offer thy gift.

25 Agree with thine adversary quickly, while thou art in the way with him; lest at any time the adversary deliver thee to the judge, and the judge deliver thee to the officer, and thou be cast into prison.

26 Verily I say unto thee, Thou shalt by no means come out thence, till thou hast paid the uttermost farthing.

of fire. 23 So if you are offering your gift at the altar, and there remember that your brother has something against you, 24 leave your gift there before the altar and go; first be reconciled to your brother, and then come and offer your gift. 25 Make friends quickly with your accuser, while you are going with him to court, lest your accuser hand you over to the judge, and the judge to the guard, and you be put in prison; 26 truly, I say to you, you will never get out till you have paid the last penny.

By the first century A.D. many Jews believed in **the hell** (Gehenna) **of fire** as a place where sinners were tormented, either after the final judgment or in the intermediate period before the judgment. The name is derived from the *gê Hinnôm* or valley of Hinnom (Josh. 15:8), southwest of Jerusalem, where human sacrifices had been offered and refuse was still burned. When this allusion was combined with the ideas of Isa. 31:9; 66:24, the conception of a fiery hell resulted (Enoch 54:1-2; 56:3-4; II Baruch 59:10; 85:13). The older idea had been that good and bad alike went to Sheol, where there was no punishment and no joy.

23. The **gift** is probably a special sacrifice (as in 23:18-19). The original hearers would interpret **brother** as "fellow Jew," but Jesus probably did not so restrict it (Luke 10:29-37).

24. It is idle for a man to try to maintain right relations with God through worship if he is not at peace with his neighbor. As the Mishnah says, "The day of Atonement atones for offenses of man against God, but it does not atone for offenses against man's neighbor, till he reconciles his neighbor" (Yoma 8:9). It is better to leave the church at the most sacred moment of worship than to delay a reconciliation.

25-26. Matthew's context for the saying is artificial. To him it means: "Tomorrow it may be too late to be reconciled, and you will be in danger of Gehenna." Luke

selves to the act, the end of the process; Christ is concerned with the motive and thought, the beginning of the process. Who among us can escape this judgment? George Gissing asks rightly: "What proportion of the letters delivered any morning would be found to be written in displeasure, in petulance, in wrath? The postbag shrieks insults or bursts with suppressed malice." Only occasionally do we admit the secret guilt: "There go I but for the grace of God." Human courts perforce deal only with the act, but God's court is not crippled in knowledge or reach or power.

Notice the humaneness of the new law. Christ could not thus have spoken if contempt had not cut him to the quick. He had pity for every "stupid" man, and deep pity for every "scoundrel." This pity rested, not merely on his knowledge of our secret motives and secret resistances, but on the deeper fact that every man, however wayward and however vicious (Jesus realistically confronted the fact of the demonic in human nature), is yet potentially the child of God. It

was a custom to place a large gold coin beneath the mainmast of old sailing vessels. So even a wreck had value to those who knew. Jesus knew; and whatever was done in anger and injury was done to his universal and sensitive heart.

Notice the Godwardness of the new law. This is throughout implied. Men are brothers because they are first children of God. The court is God's court, and is therefore not fettered either with "unsolved crimes" or for lack of power. Quarreling is wrong because it is alien from his nature. The proposal that a man with a grudge should quit his worship, even to leaving his **gift before the altar,** is not any depreciation of worship: it is rather the exaltation of worship. For God sees the inmost motive, and must be worshiped in truth—worship being the crowning act of life; and a heart harried by grudges cannot offer any wholeness of adoration. It is our shallow custom to treat the Sermon on the Mount as if it were dominantly an ethic. But any reading that goes below the surface will find in it religion that requires an

27 ¶ Ye have heard that it was said by them of old time, Thou shalt not commit adultery:

28 But I say unto you, That whosoever looketh on a woman to lust after her hath committed adultery with her already in his heart.

27 "You have heard that it was said, 'You shall not commit adultery.' 28 But I say to you that every one who looks at a woman lustfully has already committed adultery

12:57-59, the parallel passage, is in a context dealing with the end of the age, where it fits better. The thought is: "If you were on your way to the trial, you would try to settle the case out of court. Likewise, the time to get right with God is now." One should not attempt to find allegorical meanings for the accuser, judge, and guard, which are simply details of the figure, though Aboth 4:22 says that God is judge, witness, and plaintiff.

b) ADULTERY AND LUST (5:27-30)

27. Jewish law restricted the term adultery to sexual intercourse with the wife or the betrothed of a Jew. But in vs. 28 the term apparently denotes illicit intercourse with any woman. As in vs. 32, the man is thought of as the one directly responsible for the sin.

28. There are close parallels in Epictetus (Discourses II. 18. 15) and in rabbinical literature, e.g., "Everyone who looks at a woman [lustfully] is as though he had lain with her." Coveting a neighbor's wife was forbidden by the tenth commandment (Exod. 20:17; Deut. 5:21). Jesus simply emphasizes this. He considers that the desire is as culpable as the act, and, as in the previous section, would prevent the act by reforming man's desires (cf. also 7:16-18 and parallels). The rabbis, however, held generally that a man's good intentions are reckoned to him as good deeds, while his evil intentions are counted only if he succumbs to them.

ethic—an ethic so searching that even the inmost thought must be offered on an altar. Thus a man is not safe from murder and anger, from contempt and indifference, until his daily life is such that on his knees he may cry with joy: "My Lord and my God!" "Who is sufficient for these things?" (II Cor. 2:16.) No one. This so-called "ethic" carries us far beyond the span of mortal years, and leaves us helpless so far as our own power can avail. That is its glory: it proclaims us children of eternity, and seals us as those who must live in yoked service with the sufficient power and presence of God. The ethic of Christ thus drives us into the deepest places of prayer.

27-30. Second Instance: The New Law on Adultery.—This recalls the sixth beatitude, and re-emphasizes purity as a cardinal Christian virtue. The converse of Christ's concern for Christian chastity is his awareness of the ruin that awaits unchastity. We should remember in this regard the teachings and practices of the pagan cults: Christ here sharply contradicts his age. Sholem Asch in The Apostle (see description of the worship of Diana) traces this cleavage. Someone has said that fleshliness is "a recurring decimal." So strong is Christ's insistence on the virtue of purity as passport to his kingdom that he carries impurity back beyond the

lustful act to the first touch of the hand and the first look of the eye, and back beyond these to the first inception of desire. Nowhere is the inwardness of his teaching more evident. So Christ advocates and requires stringent discipline. We are careful nowadays to indicate that no literal fulfillment of cutting off the hand or plucking out the eye is expected (and, plainly, if that self-violence were done, the remaining members, not to mention the secret desire, could still offend), but we use the carefulness as escape and as excuse for indifference. The sharpness of the language shows the stringency of the required discipline. We dramatize our temptations, and go to meet them, instead of thrusting them from us. Even if the hand should not be amputated, the lustful book should—and the amusement, and the friendship. Even though these be as dear as the right hand (the right being more useful and more precious than the left) and the right eye, they should go. A Christian surrenders what is "lawful" for the sake of a dedicated soul. The fact that Christ speaks in dramatic figure is poor reason for trying to dilute or evade his stern truth. His essential verity remains in sovereign demand.

Yet the demand is not repression but fulfillment. Elsewhere (18:8-9) the discipline is levied with the key phrase, "it is better for you to

29 And if thy right eye offend thee, pluck it out, and cast *it* from thee: for it is profitable for thee that one of thy members should perish, and not *that* thy whole body should be cast into hell.

30 And if thy right hand offend thee, cut it off, and cast *it* from thee: for it is profitable for thee that one of thy members should perish, and not *that* thy whole body should be cast into hell.

31 It hath been said, Whosoever shall put away his wife, let him give her a writing of divorcement:

with her in his heart. **29** If your right eye causes you to sin, pluck it out and throw it away; it is better that you lose one of your members than that your whole body be thrown into hell.*j* **30** And if your right hand causes you to sin, cut it off and throw it away; it is better that you lose one of your members than that your whole body go into hell.*j*

31 "It was also said, 'Whoever divorces his wife, let him give her a certificate of

j Greek *Gehenna.*

29-30. A similar saying in 18:8-9 occurs in a context dealing with stumbling blocks. Here the connection is more artificial, for the emphasis tends to be put on one kind of sin only. Jesus mentions the **right eye** because he will speak next of the **right hand,** which is ordinarily more useful than the left. Note, however, that Bezae (D) and the Sinaitic Syriac omit vs. 30. The eye can provoke to sin; there are parallels in Job 31:1, in the rabbis, and in pagan writers (Propertius II. 15. 12: *oculi sunt in amore duces*). **Causes you to sin** correctly explains the familiar Jewish metaphor of the stumbling block, which is discussed in the note on 11:6. The idea that the moral life is a walk or journey also lies behind the terms "halakah" (the way to walk) and "transgression," and such sayings as 7:13-14. This saying, like Mark 10:25, is Oriental hyperbole and teaches that one must, at all cost, remove from one's life anything which will lead to sin.

c) DIVORCE (5:31-32)

A similar saying is found in Luke 16:18. Both may come from Q (see S. E. Johnson, "Jesus' Teaching on Divorce," in *Five Essays on Marriage* [Louisville, Ky.: The Cloister Press, 1946], pp. 48-60); or, vss. 31-32 may be from M, as Grant thinks ("The Mind of Christ on Marriage," *ibid.*, pp. 34-38). Other evidence on Jesus' attitude to divorce is found in 19:3-9 (=Mark 10:2-12) and in I Cor. 7:10-11. The Marcan section, like this passage, contrasts the O.T. law with Jesus' ruling.

31. The **certificate of divorce,** prescribed in Deut. 24:1, had the effect of clarifying the woman's status; the husband had no further claim on her. The tannaitic rabbis put the emphasis on the rights of the more helpless party, and took every precaution to

---

enter life maimed"—than to miss the gate. The purpose of the discipline is abundant life. The body, in Christ's teaching, is not evil. His prohibitions are always means to enrichment. In these instances of the new law his central concern is still the joy of the kingdom. The long hours of musical training are for the ultimate joy of the Bach chorales. The pruning is for the sake of fruit. In this instance the promised joy is not merely the joy of a pure earthly home, but the better joy of God's home.

31-32. *The Third Instance: The New Law on Marriage and Divorce.*—The Exeg. should be read with care, especially regarding the meaning of the word **fornication** and regarding the authenticity of the qualifying phrase **saving for,** etc. By any exegesis the stringency of the demand is evident, and also its courage and humaneness. We must remember that Christ is here speaking against the background of a de-

bate among the rabbis. The sterner school of Shammai insisted that divorce was permissible only on grounds of adultery; the more liberal school of Hillel allowed it on many, even relatively trivial, grounds. All schools were too much busied with the minutiae of the legal pronouncement, pretending that only so could they defend the rights of the woman. Christ goes beyond even the school of Shammai to trace the terms and spirit of Christian marriage. With great courage he truly defends women, and thus also the wholeness of mind and happiness of children. Between the lines we read his solicitude for the home and his high appraisal of its strategic value in the Christian life. His warning against remarriage may indicate also his longing that wide room should be left for chance of repentance. It is possible that Mal. 2:14-16 is lingering in his memory, and also the moving story of Hosea. Certainly he is

32 But I say unto you, That whosoever shall put away his wife, saving for the cause of fornication, causeth her to commit adultery: and whosoever shall marry her that is divorced committeth adultery.

33 ¶ Again, ye have heard that it hath been said by them of old time, Thou shalt not forswear thyself, but shalt perform unto the Lord thine oaths:

divorce.' **32** But I say to you that every one who divorces his wife, except on the ground of unchastity, makes her an adulteress; and whoever marries a divorced woman commits adultery.

33 "Again you have heard that it was said to the men of old, 'You shall not swear falsely, but shall perform to the Lord

insure that if she was divorced she should receive a writ which was valid in every respect and could not be retracted by a whimsical husband. While the woman could not divorce her husband, she could go before the court and compel him to divorce her if he had certain diseases, if he was engaged in certain obnoxious trades, made vows to her detriment, or forced her to make such vows. According to the school of Hillel the husband could, theoretically, divorce his wife "for any cause" (19:3), though the rabbis bitterly condemned divorce for frivolous reasons. The school of Shammai regarded unchastity and perhaps immodesty as the only allowable causes for divorce.

32. The phrase **except on the ground of unchastity** is regarded by most modern critics as Matthew's (or perhaps M's) addition to the original tradition. Jesus originally made no exceptions, but the church, as here and in I Cor. 7:12-15, had to legislate for hard cases. Matthew believed (18:18) that Jesus had given the church this power. Whether the church was justified in taking this stand is a question of theology, not of scientific exegesis. The word translated "unchastity" is πορνεία. It may refer to premarital unchastity, or it may also include adultery (μοιχεία). Hermas (Mandates IV. 1. 5) uses the two words indiscriminately to refer to the wife's sin. **Makes her an adulteress:** The assumption is that she would probably marry again. This may be Matthew's rewriting of Mark 10:12, rather than a word of Jesus. **Whoever marries a divorced woman:** The emphasis is on the sin of the man, whose offense is partly against the first husband. The woman does not "marry"; she is "given in marriage."

d) OATHS (5:33-37)

33. This is not an exact citation of any O.T. passage, but a summary of the teaching of Lev. 19:12; Exod. 20:7; Deut. 5:11; Num. 30:3; Deut. 23:22.

here concerned, not with the statute books of the state, but with Christian marriage; and the Christian marriage service that we use reflects his mind: "Until death do us part."

Much is here implied. Jesus teaches Christians to renounce utterly any entering into marriage with the back door left open: "We can always get out of it if it doesn't work." That cheapness any worthy man, Christian or unchristian, will despise. Marriage is more even than a life adventure, and more even than a solemn mutual commitment before the eyes of God. It is a sacramental act shadowing forth the love between God and mankind. Certainly Christ would approve the training of youth in regard to Christian marriage: such training is not merely a preventive of divorce, but a cultivation of the creative life. Biologically marriage is for the ongoing of the race. More deeply it is for the sake of the family, that Christian souls may enter into life by means of the comforts and responsibilities of the home. Most

deeply, it is a road into the kingdom. For that cause it is given of God, by that cause it is judged, to that cause it must be dedicate. Many vexed and thorny problems remain, but Christ's injunction, here stated, is clear beyond cavil. In Christian marriage the bride and groom should give themselves to a preparation of the soul, far, far more deeply than in our "wedding rehearsals."

33-37. *The Fourth Instance: The New Law on Oaths and Truthfulness in Speech.*—This also is a brave comment by Christ on a controversy of his time. The rabbis engaged in endless hairsplittings on the meaning of the third and ninth commandments. If a man prefixed a statement with "I swear," what he said (so the rabbis contended) constituted an oath. Perhaps the repetition of the word "yes" or "no" similarly committed the speaker, as did the word "God." Oaths by **heaven** or **earth** or **Jerusalem** were not binding. Mark 7:11 gives an instance of the slippery ways by which the rabbis per-

34 But I say unto you, Swear not at all; neither by heaven; for it is God's throne:

35 Nor by the earth; for it is his footstool: neither by Jerusalem; for it is the city of the great King.

36 Neither shalt thou swear by thy head, because thou canst not make one hair white or black.

37 But let your communication be, Yea, yea; Nay, nay: for whatsoever is more than these cometh of evil.

what you have sworn.' 34 But I say to you, Do not swear at all, either by heaven, for it is the throne of God, 35 or by the earth, for it is his footstool, or by Jerusalem, for it is the city of the great King. 36 And do not swear by your head, for you cannot make one hair white or black. 37 Let what you say be simply 'Yes' or 'No'; anything more than this comes from evil.*

ᵏ Or the evil one.

34-35. Instead of inculcating greater fidelity to oaths, Jesus sweeps away the whole mechanics of swearing. The very taking of oaths presumes that men frequently lie and will not tell the truth unless they are compelled to do so. (See also Dibelius, *Sermon on the Mount,* p. 60.) But Jesus' followers must be completely truthful. Their simple assertion should be sufficient. If the divorce saying is taken as a law, it is difficult to escape the conclusion that this, and vss. 38-42, are also laws. Jesus' Jewish hearers would have understood the saying in this way, since all types of oaths and vows were in the same legal classification. Properly speaking, an oath was by the name of Yahweh, but the rabbis regarded various other names of God as equally binding. Swearing by **heaven** or **earth** was not, however, binding. Jesus thus prohibits idle and meaningless swearing along with the religious oath. He alludes to Isa. 66:1 in giving his reason: to swear by God's creations is to swear by the creator; cf. on 23:16-22. Vows by **Jerusalem,** though not oaths, are known in rabbinical literature (Nedarim 1:3). The principle is the same: it is the city of God, who is its **great King** (Ps. 48:2; Tob. 13:15).

36. Sanhedrin 3:2 holds that the adjuration "Swear to me by the life of thy head" is binding, though R. Me'ir ruled otherwise. Jesus says that such an oath is by **God,** who alone has power over the color of one's hair.

37. A simpler (and possibly more nearly original) form of the saying is found in Jas. 5:12. The doubled affirmative and negative (ignored in RSV) are merely for emphasis. Oaths result from the **evil** which is present in the world or perhaps from "the Evil One" (cf. 6:13; 13:38). In the latter case, Matthew has probably added the phrase.

mitted men to escape the force of a given promise. Jesus cuts through this equivocation. He says that oaths are token of the loss of truthfulness. If lying had not become a habit, there would be no need for oaths. Therefore the remedy is simple truth, not only in the word, but "in the inward parts." Some of the early fathers, and more recently the Society of Friends, have understood this word of Christ to outlaw all oaths, even in a court of law. Certainly they have caught the spirit of Christ, and may demonstrate a value even in practical application. The best commentary is perhaps Jas. 5:12: "Let your yea be yea; and your nay, nay; lest ye fall into condemnation."

There is implied here an acknowledgment of the power of words. They are deeds—the deeds of the lips. They are fraught with power. Gamaliel Bradford's *Damaged Souls* says of certain discredited figures in American history that almost without exception they achieved their ends by skillful but unworthy words. Consider the mendacious adjectives in our advertising,

and our eagerness to be "brilliant conversationalists." Compare this with Jesus' insistence that society cannot stand and God cannot be honored except by truth on the lips and truth in the heart. Law courts, strongboxes, and state control are at long last no safeguard: the only guarantee is that a man's word shall be his bond. **Yea** and **nay** commended by Christ come from prayer's silence, and then from speech sober and reverent.

Notice also Christ's acknowledgment of the sovereignty of God. The references to **heaven** and **earth,** to **Jerusalem** and **thy head,** all indicate oaths then popular. But in Christ's mind they are each instantly carried back to God. The sky is God's throne, the earth is God's footstool, Jerusalem is God's city (**the city of the great King**); and a man's head is safeguarded only by God's providence. The black hair of youth and the white hair of age are both by his ordaining. Oaths cannot change them: only God is King. So the new law regarding oaths holds in every eventuality—the law that rests

38 ¶ Ye have heard that it hath been said, An eye for an eye, and a tooth for a tooth:

39 But I say unto you, That ye resist not evil: but whosoever shall smite thee on thy right cheek, turn to him the other also.

40 And if any man will sue thee at the law, and take away thy coat, let him have *thy* cloak also.

38 "You have heard that it was said, 'An eye for an eye and a tooth for a tooth.' **39** But I say to you, Do not resist one who is evil. But if any one strikes you on the right cheek, turn to him the other also; **40** and if any one would sue you and take your coat, let him have your cloak as well;

---

e) Retaliation (5:38-42)

38. The principle of retaliation is expressed in Exod. 21:24; Deut. 19:21; Lev. 24:20. It is as old as the Code of Hammurabi and can be paralleled in the Roman Law of the XII Tables and Aeschylus (*Choephoroi* 308-9). It is possible, though not certain, that in Jesus' time some rabbis permitted a monetary payment in lieu of this punishment. But such a consideration is irrelevant, since the legal principle theoretically still held good.

39. Do not resist through violent means of self-defense. **One who is evil** (RSV) is the correct translation; not **evil** in the abstract (KJV). The saying is an illustration of how **a** right-minded man will act, not a rule to be interpreted legally. Canon Green is mistaken in saying that Jesus enjoins this "as a positive principle of action with the definite purpose of . . . reconciliation of an enemy." Such is the idea of Rom. 12:21 and Prov. 25:21-22, but Jesus' saying has no prudential motive of any kind. His point is that the mere fact that wrong has been done a man does not give him license to do wrong. Jesus' followers must not retaliate and they must suffer the same injury again, simply because it is God's will that their attitude and conduct should be of this kind. (See H. J. Cadbury, *The Peril of Modernizing Jesus* [New York: The Macmillan Co., 1937], pp. 108-14.) The servant of God in Isa. 50:6 suffered similar ignominy (cf. also Lam. 3:30). Jesus has in mind the personal relationships of individuals. How far the principle can be applied to groups, and especially to political life, is constantly debated.

40. The **coat** (χιτών: Hebrew *kuttôneth*, Aramaic *kittûnā'*) is the long undergarment made with sleeves; the **cloak** (ἱμάτιον) was worn over it, and the poor used it as **a** coverlet at night (Exod. 22:26-27).

---

on a man when he stands before God "naked soul to naked soul."

38-42. *Fifth Instance: The New Law on Revenge.*—The world of Jesus' day was under the law of retaliation. The Mosaic law, the Code of Hammurabi, and the Roman law all required that the wrongdoer should "get as good as he gave." In Jesus' time the equivalent in money was exacted by the courts as recompense for injury, and that practice may have represented some advance: it placed restraints on private retaliation or clan vengeance. But the principle remained, and the law of the kingdom took direct issue with it: Jesus here proposes a gentle revolution. Consider his instances. A blow in the right cheek was an insult—with the back of the hand, so that the palm of the hand could return with a blow on the left cheek. To sue for a tunic was the procedure of a man taking court action to protect his rights; and to yield the outer garment—the cloak—was to go to the limit of real suffering, for the cloak was bed covering by night as well as garment

by day. To be compelled to go a mile perhaps refers to the Roman soldier's custom of obliging the people of a conquered nation to carry his impedimenta. We use the phrase "second mile" to mean working harder than necessary, or being kinder than is expected; but it is much sterner doctrine. We can see in it a legionary saying to a Jew (to Jesus, at the end of a hard day?), "Here! Get this on your back and come along!" The borrower in the fourth instance is perhaps a beggar turned bully. In each case Christ insists that his followers must not resist the evildoer.

What does such teaching mean? Our imagination recoils before it, and our everyday morality (our speedy recourse to law, for instance, and our ultimate dependence on force) flatly contradicts it. Christ has in mind the injured man. Such a man's concern for justice is never pure: it is subtly entangled with vindictiveness. Christ warns him against that revenge. Revenge is not sweet, despite the proverb: it is poison, strife breeding strife in endless circle. Has Christ in

41 And whosoever shall compel thee to go a mile, go with him twain.

42 Give to him that asketh thee, and from him that would borrow of thee turn not thou away.

43 ¶ Ye have heard that it hath been said, Thou shalt love thy neighbor, and hate thine enemy.

41 and if any one forces you to go one mile, go with him two miles. 42 Give to him who begs from you, and do not refuse him who would borrow from you.

43 "You have heard that it was said, 'You shall love your neighbor and hate

41. The Greek word translated **forces** originally had to do with the Persian royal mail; and the English legal term "angary" is derived from it. Couriers could impress men or their property into service to carry the king's messages. Here the word refers to any kind of forced labor, whether required by the government or by private persons. The Roman **mile** was a little shorter than the English mile.

42. This does not fit well here, since it has nothing to do with force or retaliation. Matthew apparently includes it because it stood here in the Q sermon, as its position in Luke 6:29-30 shows. Jewish literature is full of counsels to be generous. Jesus does not raise any question as to whether indiscriminate almsgiving is wise (contrast Did. 1:5-6), or whether one has duties toward one's own family, etc.: the point simply is that a religious person will have generous impulses and will act upon them.

f) Hatred and Love (5:43-47)

43. Lev. 19:16-18, which is quoted here, speaks of **neighbor** in the sense of "fellow Israelite." Jewish commentators correctly point out that the law never commanded the Jew to **hate** his **enemy;** but the O.T. represents many different stages of religious development, and alongside the friendliness toward aliens inculcated by books like Ruth there are many passages which permit, and even encourage, hostility and retaliation. In Semitic idiom, however, **hate** may mean no more than "love less" or "not to love."

mind also the man guilty of inflicting injury? Do our law courts and jails really "satisfy" the oppressed, or reclaim the oppressor? How often they confirm the oppressor in guilt, leave the injured unrequited, and thus hurt everyone! The wrongdoer must be brought to truer manhood, and that change is not wrought by retaliation. Above all, Christ has God's will in mind: he intends that the world shall be a home in which children dwell in mutual love. He is not pleading for any cowardly yielding, and the phrase "passive resistance" is almost a parody of his teaching. The children of the kingdom must show good will, with no other strategy and no ulterior motive. We should not try to escape this teaching by our customary evasion: "The Oriental mind is full of paradox." The dramatic and figurative language of Jesus is full of truth. Consider the story of Calvary: he obeyed literally his own precepts. George Fox obeyed them literally, as did also James Gilmour in Mongolia. A literal obedience raises problems in our ambiguous world, but is better far than the evasion which says, "This is figurative language."

Notice Christ's implication that this is a strategy of true victory. By this method the injured man does not lower his standards to those of his oppressor: he keeps a banner lifted above the accepted "standards" of the world. By this method the oppressor's mind may be changed, if not at once, then by sight of suffering. See, in George Bernard Shaw's *Saint Joan,* the comment of de Stogumber after he had witnessed the martyrdom of the maid.[4] By this method both oppressed and oppressor are thrown back on God. "Vengeance is mine; I will repay, saith the Lord" (Rom. 12:19). Only in God's hand is justice safe and sure, for in him it is held in an eternity of holy love.

43-47. *Sixth Instance: The New Law of Love.* —Love your enemies. This is an unequivocal and startling demand. It might startle us more if we could fully understand how sharply it cut across the ethic of Christ's day; or if, with eyes suddenly opened, we could see it in contrast with the "little churchinesses" that often pass with us as Christianity. Examine three words in these verses: let them be windows into the newness of this law and life.

One word is **neighbor.** Leviticus had enjoined love for a neighbor. The O.T. nowhere expressly enjoins hatred of enemies. Occasionally it looks with no disfavor on that emotion; occasionally it hints a larger compassion than

4 New York: Brentano's, 1924, p. 154.

44 But I say unto you, Love your enemies, bless them that curse you, do good to them that hate you, and pray for them which despitefully use you, and persecute you;

45 That ye may be the children of your Father which is in heaven: for he maketh his sun to rise on the evil and on the good, and sendeth rain on the just and on the unjust.

46 For if ye love them which love you, what reward have ye? do not even the publicans the same?

your enemy.' 44 But I say to you, Love your enemies and pray for those who persecute you, 45 so that you may be sons of your Father who is in heaven; for he makes his sun rise on the evil and on the good, and sends rain on the just and on the unjust. 46 For if you love those who love you, what reward have you? Do not even the tax col-

---

44. The word translated **love** originally meant "to welcome, entertain, be well pleased, contented," and in the LXX it has as wide a reference as the English word "love." In the N.T., however, it denotes the love of God for man and of man for God (I John 3–5) and the benevolent lovingkindness which seeks the material and spiritual good of others (I Cor. 13). When Jesus commands love of enemies, he thinks primarily of personal relationships and perhaps also of the relationships of small groups. Such love is the supreme test of the religious man's character. Jesus never deals with the responsibilities of free citizens in a democratic state. His teaching of course has political implications, but how it should be applied is one of the most difficult problems of Christian social ethics.

45. This love is to be extended to enemies and persecutors, for such is God's way of dealing with those who neglect him, insult him, and do wrong to his other children. Exod. 23:4-5 and numerous rabbinical sayings look in this direction, but the idea is never made a general maxim for conduct in Judaism. God is better than the highest that man knows, and those who imitate God become, or show themselves to be, his **sons** in the ethical sense (cf. on 5:9). Jesus assumes that God is completely omnipotent and cares directly and personally for all that he has made. Though Jesus is fully conscious of the misfortunes in the world, he raises no question whether rain and sunshine are not sometimes destructive. It is God's lovingkindness which stands out and claims his full attention.

46. The **tax collectors** of the Gospels are probably the Jewish employees of chief collectors. Poll taxes and land taxes levied in Judea must have been collected by government officials under the procurator, for Judea was part of the empire. Export and import

---

love only for neighbors. In the time of Christ enemies were usually hated, and the hatred was not deemed alien from true religion. That ancient world was chasmed by hatreds. Thus the story of the good Samaritan must have seemed subversive folly to those who first heard it. Jesus would have no fences around the word neighbor. Despite the farmer in Robert Frost's poem "Mending Wall," "good fences" do not necessarily "make good neighbors."[5] Jesus quietly insists that the man who curses us is a neighbor, and the man who persecutes us for our religion, and the man who hates or **despitefully** uses us. To the Christian the word neighbor is as wide as mankind.

Another word is **love.** In N.T. times there were three words which we translate "love."

[5] *Collected Poems* (New York: Henry Holt & Co., 1939), p. 47.

One indicated physical and aesthetic love, another was used of the love that binds family and friends, and the third—used here—betokened the glow and persistence of good will in Christ. So the demand of Christ is not that we "resolve to like everybody," but rather that we act in good will from God toward those we like and those we do not like. The taxgatherer is used as instance (see Exeg.). Because he served the Roman conqueror, and because he was likely to be guilty of extortion, he was generally disliked; yet he showed kindly feeling toward his friends. There is nothing new in that sentiment. The worldling has it, even toward the poor whom he does not know, sometimes in measure that puts alleged Christianity to shame. John Wesley, overcome by the conditions of the sick in Marshalsea Prison, remarked that even in a pagan country such scenes could not be found:

47 And if ye salute your brethren only, what do ye more *than others?* do not even the publicans so?

48 Be ye therefore perfect, even as your Father which is in heaven is perfect.

lectors do the same? 47 And if you salute only your brethren, what more are you doing than others? Do not even the Gentiles do the same? 48 You, therefore, must be perfect, as your heavenly Father is perfect.

---

duties were, however, farmed out to a *publicanus* who contracted to furnish a fixed sum every year. In the empire as a whole such a contractor was often a Roman citizen of equestrian rank, though we are not certain that this was so in Judea; his employees, the τελῶναι or **tax collectors** of the Gospels, were probably Jews. In Galilee and Trans-Jordan the duties were collected for the tetrarch's treasury, and even the *publicanus* may have been a Jew. The system made for inequality and oppression, and the Gospels usually couple tax collectors and sinners. Rabbinical writings pass the same unfavorable judgment, and the second-century satirist Lucian classes tax collectors with adulterers and brothel keepers.

47. The usual Jewish greeting was "Peace (*shālôm*) be to you"; in 10:12-13 the disciples use a similar salutation. Since *shālôm* includes not only peace but prosperity, and refers to every kind of material and spiritual well-being, the greeting was actually a prayer. The rabbis taught, by precept and example, that a pious man should greet everyone and be the first to make the salutation; but probably not everyone was so well-disposed. The verse is omitted by the O.L. codex *k*, the Sinaitic Syriac, and Tatian.

g) SUMMARY (5:48)

48. The word rendered **perfect** is frequently used in Greek to refer to the gods. It has much the same scope as the English word "perfect," and in addition can refer to a "full-grown" man (Eph. 4:13) or to the member of a Gnostic sect. When Jesus says that his followers must be perfect, he probably does not expect that they will be absolutely

---

even the Indians of Georgia succored one another in sickness. He exclaimed, "O who will convert the English into honest Heathens!" [6] But there is something new in a love whereby a man oppressed by a traitorous taxgatherer acts with generous good will toward his oppressor. To that love Christ calls his followers: they are to **bless** those who upbraid them, and to **pray** for those who persecute them for their faith. For illustration (not perfect because it involves bloodshed) see Kipling's poem "Cold Iron."

The third word is **Father**. It occurs seventeen times in the Sermon on the Mount—sufficient evidence that Christ is concerned with much more than an ethic. God's love is universal: he lavishes sunlight on the niggardly and the generous, and sends rain on the just and the unjust. The interpreter should notice this reading of nature: it is not naturalistic or pantheistic, but providential. So God gives us example of love. We are his children: *Noblesse oblige!* God gives us example in our own lives: we have received in nature and supremely in Christ a love we do not deserve, and we must try to treat all men in that same heavenborn love.

[6] *The Journal of Rev. John Wesley,* ed. Nehemiah Curnock (New York: Eaton & Mains, 1909), IV, 52; his diary for February 8, 1753.

God gives us power thus to love. This good will, which can never be derived from any whipping up of our "resolve to like everybody," is possible by his gift and grace, as the story of Stephen shows. Thus *agapē* (the new love of the new kingdom) is a divine reinforcement at the core of our new nature. The six instances in this chapter are only instances. "If any man be in Christ, he is a new creature" (II Cor. 5:17).

48. *The Perfect Life.*—The verb is future, and the saying is perhaps a promise as well as a command. "Ye shall be perfect . . ." ("The Clarendon Bible"). But it still seems irony. Are we, frail dust, to be **perfect**—we, beset by such perversity that we burn our fingers a hundred times in the same fire; we, tormented by a guilty past? It seems like demanding higher mathematics from a child who has not yet mastered the "two-times" table. But the saying is in the spirit of this whole passage, and Jesus does not mock us. The word does not require celestial purity (see Exeg.), but we should not try to discount its meaning. Luke translates it "merciful," and its antecedents in this chapter show that mercy is a prime ingredient. Yet the whole sermon traces perfection. The Greek word used by Matthew means "that which is at the end."

6 Take heed that ye do not your alms before men, to be seen of them: otherwise ye have no reward of your Father which is in heaven.	6 "Beware of practicing your piety before men in order to be seen by them; for then you will have no reward from your Father who is in heaven.

flawless. "Straight" or "square" would be more accurate, and the sense is given by Gen. 6:9; Job 1:1; Jas. 1:4; and especially Deut. 18:13, on which F. C. Grant remarks: "You must be honest with him [Yahweh], upright and sincere, having wholeness and integrity, not double-dealing" (*The Earliest Gospel* [New York and Nashville: Abingdon-Cokesbury Press, 1943], p. 221). In other words, the religious man's attitude toward other men must be like that of God: candid, sincere, constant, not turned aside toward vengefulness no matter how great the provocation. The parallel, Luke 6:36, "be merciful," which in turn has a parallel in the Jerusalem Targum on Lev. 22:28, does not cover so broad a field.

5. Contrasts Between the Old Practice of Religion and the New
(6:1-18)

a) Introduction: Against Ostentation (6:1)

6:1. Jesus takes it for granted that his followers will do religious acts, but they must be performed with a pure motive and without ostentation. There is very little in this section which is foreign to the best thought of Judaism. Jesus was not so much interested in remodeling institutions as in transforming the minds and attitudes of those who used the institutions. His primary concern was that men should share his vivid consciousness of the reality, power, and omnipresence of God. Worship is simply meaningless unless it is performed solely for his sake and the sake of his kingdom. At the same time, a profound acceptance of this principle inevitably leads men to criticize and reform the institutions themselves.

Plainly Jesus is bidding us press on into God's light.

A man's reach should exceed his grasp,
Or what's a heaven for? [7]

And his journey should exceed his reach. Thus in Christ there must be no limit to friendship, and kindness should never be fractional. It is all or nothing. Life is not a problem to be solved, and much less a respectability to be conventionally fulfilled: it is an adventure in good will eagerly taken, with vistas and far leagues to beckon us. Just as plainly Jesus here speaks his faith in our human nature. He was realistic: no one saw with such clear eyes the devilishness in man. "Out of the heart proceed evil thoughts, murders, adulteries . . ." (15:19). But no one believed more stanchly in that seed in us which, given into God's care and power, can grow into eternal life. Plato's *Republic*, Augustine's *City of God*, More's *Utopia*, and any man's best yearnings are proof of the incipient heaven in man's heart.

But—how to remove the apparent mockery of this promise or demand? The memory of sin remains. The wings on which we would mount are still caught fast in ignorant clay. Dreaming of eternity, we are yet prisoners of time. We cannot flog our souls into heaven. If we try, we shall fail; and we may end by flogging other folk in censure. How is this contradiction to be resolved? Lynn Harold Hough tells a story of a young girl who was quite sure she could climb a mountain. She danced ahead, confident of her strength. But soon the road became a trail, and soon the trail became frowning rocks. She dragged along now, and after a time sank from exhaustion. Then—her father: with his arm to guide and steady her she reached the summit. **Be ye . . . perfect:** we were never meant to climb that mountain in our own strength. Failure comes to teach us that life is an affair, not of man alone or of man with man, but of man with God and God with man. The word **Father** is key to the Sermon on the Mount. There the ethic breaks into faith and comradeship. There we find forgiveness and new power —and life's secret meaning. Thus **as your Father which is in heaven is perfect** sums up the new law and the new life.

6:1-4. Christianity and Almsgiving.—Notice that the RSV treats vs. 1 as an introductory statement: Christ proposes to trace the distinction between his faith and the then current religion. The latter was manward-turning in pride, but his faith was Godward-turning in gratitude and dependent lowliness. This contrast he illustrates through three instances—almsgiving,

[7] Browning, "Andrea del Sarto."

2 Therefore when thou doest *thine* alms, do not sound a trumpet before thee, as the hypocrites do in the synagogues and in the streets, that they may have glory of men. Verily I say unto you, They have their reward.

2 "Thus, when you give alms, sound no trumpet before you, as the hypocrites do in the synagogues and in the streets, that they may be praised by men. Truly, I say

---

b) ALMSGIVING (6:2-4)

2. Alms was an exceedingly important feature of Jewish piety. Tob. 12:8-9 says: "Good is prayer with fasting and alms and righteousness, . . . for alms rescues from death and it will cleanse from all sin." **Sound no trumpet** is probably a metaphor, like our colloquial "Don't blow your own horn." Matthew may have in mind an actual Jewish custom, whether Jesus did or not. The community's poor were supported by a graduated tax, which was supplemented by freewill offerings collected in synagogues and schools. Trumpets were sounded during public fasts in times of drought and there were prayers in the streets. (Cf. Adolf Büchler, "St. Matthew 6:1-6 and Other Allied Passages," *Journal of Theological Studies,* X [1909], 266-70.) It may well be that collections for the poor were made at these public fasts. The trumpet helped to call attention to acts of generosity. The **hypocrites** (Aramaic *ḥanêfā'*) of the Gospel no doubt include those who pretend to be more pious than they are, but the sayings of Jesus which contain the word usually "seem to point . . . to the incongruity of behavior, straining out the gnat and swallowing the camel, concerned for the mote and ignoring the beam," in other words inconsistency and discrepancy (H. J. Cadbury, *Jesus: What Manner of Man* [New York: The Macmillan Co., 1947], p. 83). The classical meaning of the Greek word is "actor in a play." The corresponding Aramaic word means "a profane person." A second-century rabbi remarked acidly that "there are ten portions of hypocrisy in the world, and nine of them are in Jerusalem." **They have** already received **their reward**—namely the praise of men—and God is quits with them. The verb ἀπέχω is used in papyrus receipts as a formula: "Received of. . . ." Jewish theology often assumed that one who

---

prayer, and fasting. Almsgiving was so stressed in Pharisaic religion that the word was sometimes synonymous with "righteousness." Charities brought extra merit because they were not specifically required under Jewish religious law. Collections for the poor were frequent, and there was plenty of chance for ostentatious giving. Notice the insincerity of pride that so easily besets piety. The word **hypocrite** originally meant actor. The **trumpet** is probably a figurative expression, even though trumpets were used to call the community to fasting in time of drought. The hyperbole is instance of Christ's humor—and also of his deep repugnance in regard to pride: "By that sin fell the angels." [8] The *Expositor's Greek Testament* has a pithy phrase to show that the "secrecy" here commended by Christ is not at odds with his "let your light so shine" (5:16): it says the rule for the Christian is: "Show when tempted to *hide,* hide when tempted to *show.*" [9]

Notice the deep disclosures concerning reward. The word as first used—**They have their**

[8] Shakespeare, *King Henry VIII*, Act III, scene 2.
[9] Ed. W. Robertson Nicoll (Grand Rapids: Wm. B. Eerdmans Publishing Co., n.d.), I. 116.

reward—means a receipt paid in full. Thus it is one of the most terrible condemnations in the N.T.: they "got what they wanted"—and found it empty. Meanwhile they cut off their future: there was no joy beyond, but only a repetition of joy turned sour. Life was for them a blind alley: they could only stand and die. The Stoics gave alms in secret, but still only for their own satisfaction. Their generosity too was cankered by the same pride, only more refined, that marked the Pharisees. In the temple at Jerusalem there was a "treasury of silence" where gifts were made for poor children. We may safely guess that Jesus used it as means for his gifts, and rejoiced in it. Carlyle says: "Observe too, . . . how the insignificant, the empty, is usually the loud; and, after the manner of a drum, is loud even because of its emptiness." [10] The other word used for reward—**your Father . . . shall reward**—could perhaps better be translated "render": it carries the whole issue back to God, the only safe place for it. There is a commerce in the universe by which true compassion receives its own, not in any "receipt" but in the gladness of a Presence who is all compassion. The Presence moves in lowly ways, and prefers

[10] "Essay on Characteristics."

3 But when thou doest alms, let not thy left hand know what thy right hand doeth:

4 That thine alms may be in secret: and thy Father which seeth in secret himself shall reward thee openly.

5 ¶ And when thou prayest, thou shalt not be as the hypocrites *are:* for they love to pray standing in the synagogues and in the corners of the streets, that they may be seen of men. Verily I say unto you, They have their reward.

6 But thou, when thou prayest, enter into thy closet, and when thou hast shut thy door, pray to thy Father which is in secret; and thy Father which seeth in secret shall reward thee openly.

to you, they have their reward. 3 But when you give alms, do not let your left hand know what your right hand is doing, 4 so that your alms may be in secret; and your Father who sees in secret will reward you.

5 "And when you pray, you must not be like the hypocrites; for they love to stand and pray in the synagogues and at the street corners, that they may be seen by men. Truly, I say to you, they have their reward. 6 But when you pray, go into your room and shut the door and pray to your Father who is in secret; and your Father who sees in secret will reward you.

receives his reward now will not be rewarded in the age to come. There are parallels in rabbinical writings and in Epictetus. Glory was more frankly and openly sought in the ancient world, whereas Christians at least pay lip service to modesty and humility.

3. Even your most intimate friend must not know of your generosity.

4. Your Father who sees in secret is an idea found in Epictetus *Discourses* I. 14. 14. **Openly,** as in vss. 6 and 18, is an early gloss, found in Koridethi (Θ) and the Sinaitic Syriac. The Mishnah teaches that he who profanes the name of God in secret will be punished openly (Aboth 4:4); but he who studies the Torah in secret will be proclaimed to the people.

c) Prayer (6:5-15)

(1) Sayings on Prayer (6:5-8)

5. Standing was the most usual posture for prayer in Jewish, Christian, and pagan antiquity. At the time of the daily *tāmîdh* offering there were public prayers in the temple (Tamid 5:1; Acts 3:1; Luke 18:10), and people would join in prayer no matter where they happened to be, as Moslems do at the prayer hours or Catholics at the Angelus.

6. For parallels see Test. Joseph 3:3; Epictetus *Discourses* I. 14. 14. Jesus does not condemn public worship (5:24; Luke 18:9-14); but one who engages in common prayer must be as free of self-consciousness as if he had gone into his room and shut the door. Prayer is a direct personal relationship with a **Father** God, and an attitude of play-acting destroys its spirit. This attitude is similar to that of the rabbis. (See C. G. Montefiore and Herbert Loewe, *A Rabbinic Anthology* [London: Macmillan & Co., 1938], pp. 342-81.)

to see in secret. The reward comes in secret: that word **openly** is a clumsy gloss. For illustration see Lloyd C. Douglas' *The Magnificent Obsession*, in which the hero, Dr. Hudson, builds his life on the counsel **Let not thy left hand know what thy right hand doeth,** and thus lives in a secret companionship.

5-8. *Christianity and the Way of Private Prayer.*—It is important that we see in mind's eye the background of religion against which Jesus spoke. Too many "men of prayer" in his day were hypocrites—actors—and they went where they could find an audience. In the synagogue they would loudly recite their own prayers instead of being content to share in the accustomed congregational prayers. They "made

broad their phylacteries" (see Exeg. on 23:5). At the three times of daily prayer—when the pious workman would quit his work, and the teacher his teaching, to turn toward Jerusalem in acknowledgment of God—the professionally pious would so arrange life as to be caught at a crowded corner; and then they would sometimes stand for three hours in their devotions. Thus the comment of Jesus: nowhere is his hatred of form and cant more clear. He gives by implication certain rules for private prayer. It is essential—the burning center of life. Public or corporate prayer is also essential, for prayer inevitably has its social expression. Jesus enjoined public prayer in both word and act. But corporate prayer will lack sincerity and

7 But when ye pray, use not vain repetitions, as the heathen *do:* for they think that they shall be heard for their much speaking. 8 Be not ye therefore like unto them: for your Father knoweth what things ye have need of, before ye ask him. 9 After this manner therefore pray ye: Our Father which art in heaven, Hallowed be thy name.	7 "And in praying do not heap up empty phrases as the Gentiles do; for they think that they will be heard for their many words. 8 Do not be like them, for your Father knows what you need before you ask him. 9 Pray then like this: Our Father who art in heaven, Hallowed be thy name.

Vss. 7-15 are parenthetical, a kind of footnote to vss. 5-6. They are largely drawn from Q or at least run parallel to it. They were not found in either M's or Q's sermon.

7. Do not heap up empty phrases: The Greek verb means "to babble." Though Jewish prayer was often filled with honorific phrases, as in the Kaddish, and was often long (II Chr. 6:14-42; Dan. 9:4-19), there are rabbinical sayings which counsel brief prayer. Jesus condemns the theory that if fifteen minutes of prayer is good, a half-hour is twice as good; it reminds one of heathenism, with its magical texts. A good example can be seen in these nonsense syllables from "Charm for Securing an Attendant Spirit" (E. J. Goodspeed and E. C. Colwell, *A Greek Papyrus Reader* [Chicago: University of Chicago Press, 1935], p. 78): *"auōi ptaucharēbi aōuosōbiau ptabaïn aaaaaa aeēiouōuōoiēea chachach chachach charcharachach. . . ."* Seneca referred to those who "tire out the gods" (*Epistles* XXXI. 5).

8. God does not need to be informed, as though he were unconscious of man's needs, nor does one have to wheedle him into action, as heathen worshipers attempted to do. On the other hand, Jesus teaches confident, loving persistence in prayer, as in 7:11 and especially Luke 18:1-7.

(2) THE LORD'S PRAYER AS AN EXAMPLE (6:9-13)

It is not certain whether Matthew's form of the prayer comes from Q, as Luke 11:2-4 probably does, or from M. The form in Luke is nearer the original; and, as Dibelius shows

depth without private prayer—as witness the aridity of much public worship. The soul must be gathered in, not to itself (for there is peril in introspection), but to God. This is the wellspring of life, this is the food of the spirit, without which the soul of man dies.

Prayer must be sincere, as thoroughly sincere as our wavering will can offer. The door must be shut against the distractions of the world, lest we bring to God a divided mind. The church bell can be heard in stillness, but not amid the roar of traffic. What is even more important, a man must be where he cannot pose or pretend: **Thy closet, . . . thy door, . . . thy Father**—he, the person, stands before God stripped of every disguise, and the dissemblings of life drop. He makes his confession freely and fully, offers gratitude for mercies he has never merited, and draws strength for a destiny newly understood.

The prayer must be childlike in simplicity; RSV says **not . . . empty phrases.** (See Exeg. for meaning of the word.) Compare the repetitions used in Baal worship, as by the "priests of Baal" on Mount Carmel, in contest with Elijah (I Kings 18:22-40); or in the pagan cults (Acts

19:34). We should not construe Jesus to mean that repetition is always **vain:** he himself used repetition under stress of great emotion in Gethsemane. But compare that repetition with the prayer wheel of Tibet. Jesus' plea is for such simplicity as a man must use when, stripped of every disguise, he stands alone before the Alone. Implied also is the intimacy of complete trust. That God knows our need before we ask does not argue against our asking. But it does argue against the ever-encroaching folly of trying to turn God's holy purpose, and against the attempt to use God for our own ends. Petition is inevitable in our humanness, and is indeed the part of honesty. But true petition remembers that God is our all-knowing and all-loving Father. It is made in childlike trust: "Thy will be done." Such prayer is the missing "main contact." Our works and ways all fail in that lack: we, like Samson, meet the Philistines, and discover only then that our strength has gone. For strength is gathered in the secret place.

9-13. *The Lord's Prayer: A General Comment.*— (See Exeg.) **Pray then like this. . . .** An artist attempting to portray Niagara Falls flung down his brush in despair. There are

(*Sermon on the Mount*, p. 75), it consists basically of three petitions: for the coming of the kingdom, for daily bread—i.e., all that is needed for earthly existence—and for forgiveness of sins in the past and the future. These sum up all the needs of those who, as in the Beatitudes, await the coming of the kingdom. Matthew's prayer may have been developed out of this into a sevenfold form designed for public worship; the first three petitions (vss. 9-10) are centered in God, the other four (vss. 11-13) in our needs. Did. 8:2 contains Matthew's version with slight variations and with the doxology (vs. 13*b*) appended, and commands Christians to say it three times a day. Jesus' disciples no doubt employed the prayer in their common worship from the beginning, but Jesus' primary purpose was to furnish an example of what true prayer is like (vs. 9). The prayer is thoroughly Jewish and nearly every phrase is paralleled in the Kaddish and the Eighteen Benedictions; thus it is Jesus' inspired and original summary of his own people's piety at its best.

9. Luke's prayer begins, "Father." The simple "Abba" must have been Jesus' usual address to God (Mark 14:36; Rom. 8:15; Gal. 4:6), but it can also be translated **our Father,** which is a frequent address to God in Jewish prayer. The phrase **who art in**

---

thunders and powers and a spectrum mist in this prayer: it defies our wit, and yet is our salvation. It is *brief:* the eighteen petitions offered three times daily in the prayers of pious Jewry were ten times as long; this prayer by its terseness cuts into the mind and is easily remembered. It is *childlike* in simplicity: statesman and man in the street, philosopher and rustic, bishop and the youngest catechumen are one here: **Our Father;** and no prayer could more unqualifiedly set forth God's sovereign love and man's dependence. It is *daring* in its freedom. Imagine this Craftsman teaching his disciples a prayer that they shall use more centrally than the agelong Jewish prescribed prayers! Yet it is not novelty: in it there are phrases found in the best Jewish prayers of that time. Not novel, yet new—in its order, its insight, and in the spirit of him who taught it. It *sets first things first:* its first three petitions (do they correspond to the traditional "Holy, holy, holy"?) are adoration: they concern God's nature, God's kingdom, God's will; while the next (and secondary) four petitions concern man's need—our daily temporal needs, our need of forgiveness, our defense against the onset of temptation, our deliverance from evil. This is the due order and proportion of prayer. It *is example* and form of prayer, but is yet a creative focus. Form criticism may show that the Matthew version was used at the Eucharist, and that the Luke version (probably the original) was used in informal group settings and in baptism. Apparently Jesus intended his followers to use the prayer regularly, but not to recite it slavishly; and, because this is what has measurably come to pass, the prayer is a treasure both of public worship and of private devotion, and also a seed plot for new prayers age on age. It is a *universal* prayer. **Our:** it speaks the common longing and deepest aspiration of

the heart of man across every class and race. The suggestion has been made that this might be the creed of all religion. Above all, it is the *prayer of Christ.* It is not an excursion into theology: it is rather an adoration from the soul. Yet in its awareness of human need it is his gift, and could be his alone, who is the Son of man; and in its authority and disclosure of God it is his gift, and could be his alone, who is the Son of God. This is the charter of prayer.

9. Our Father.—The word occurs in the O.T. —not in prayer—but is used to describe God's dealings primarily with the nation rather than with the man. Rabbinical prayers had begun to use it in Jesus' time, but Jesus made it his best name for God—the hallmark of his truth, an imprint which he has set forever on our world. The phrase **which art in heaven** saves the word from our humanness; and the petition **hallowed be thy name** enthrones it in awe. Thus the critic cannot use the jibe "anthropomorphic"; and, if he should, he himself blunders worse by speaking about the "laws of the universe": for it is a worse anthropomorphism to compare sovereign Power with a lawbook than with a father. The only words we have are human words; we are not angels. Jesus taught us to compare God with our best, and then to acknowledge a Mystery beyond the best which no words can hint.

The word speaks holy authority, even though the authority is one of love. God made the world, and is above it even while in it, and he rules it. "Smart politics" is at last folly, and "enlightened self-interest" is at last benighted nonsense, because he is **Father.** There is no indulgence in the name. The optimism in the *Rubáiyát of Omar Khayyám* is false optimism: "He's a Good Fellow, and 'twill all be well." Crime, hard to conceal from man, is impossible to conceal from God; and inevitably it "finds

heaven is sometimes added in synagogue prayers (Singer, *Authorised Daily Prayer Book*, p. 9), but it is found more frequently in rabbinical teachings than in prayers. God is frequently referred to (Deut. 32:6; Jubilees 1:24-25, 28; III Macc. 5:7; etc.) or addressed (Isa. 63:16; Ecclus. 23:1, 4) as father of Israel or of an individual Israelite (Jubilees 19:29; Wisd. Sol. 2:16; Ecclus. 51:10), and the term is used once in a pre-Christian writing as a substitute for the name of God (Test. Judah 24:2). Only occasionally does a Jew address God as "my Father" (Ecclus. 23:1, 4; Wisd. Sol. 2:16) and the rabbis regarded this as appropriate only on the lips of a saint. Other religions often speak of the deity as father. The meaning of such a symbolic word depends on the total religious and cultural context in which it is spoken. It is difficult to define exactly how Jesus' use of it differs from that of the best of his contemporaries. Perhaps the difference is that when he speaks of God as Father, he uses the word with profound and loving intimacy. He consistently thinks of religious relationships in terms of family life.

Hallowed be thy name means approximately the same as "Father, glorify thy name" (John 12:28), but here the passive form is used, as in the Kaddish, to avoid a direct

---

out" the wrongdoer, because God is holy Father. The universe cannot keep a secret—because its heart is open and honest, and because God rules. Yet the name is Love: he gathers man into a tender care and so ennobles our common life. Man, the creature of an hour and stained by selfishness, may speak to God, who summons the stars from the void and before whom angels veil their faces, as—**Father**. The authority remains and is not usurped, but it intimately lives with us for our utmost good. The love shows in the order of the world and in daily providence, whatever the paradox of pain. It shows also in home, the discipline of toil, and the pangs of remorse. It shows, heaven-sent, in Christ. Thus we are children of his grace: "Herein is love, not that we loved God, but that he loved us, and sent his Son to be the propitiation for our sins" (I John 4:10). That fact gives the prayer its centrally Christian impact. It justified Marc Antoine Muret in his famous answer. The surgeons thought him as ignorant as he was poor: *"Faciamus experimentum in anima vili"* ("Let us experiment upon this worthless fellow"). He replied in Latin as good as theirs: *"Vilem animam appellas pro qua Christus non dedignatus est mori"* ("You call one worthless for whom Christ did not refuse to die").[1] The proof of this Love is in the faith and venture of the prayer—with fact enough in experience and in the experience of Christ to warrant the venture.

The name is a commonalty: **Our Father.** The whole church is in that pronoun, and the whole family of nations and men. A man cannot be complete without this "beloved community," and the community is bereft without the man. Prayer, even when private, is still a social expression. Here all the barriers are down—the race barriers, the political blocs, the fences between classes and nations. The ancient mariner,

in the Coleridge poem, was becalmed and his vessel held in a deathlike trance until he prayed in compassion for all God's creatures. See the stanza: "He prayeth best who loveth best."[2] Thus the name gives both meaning and power. "Pray devoutly, hammer stoutly" is a good motto. The prayer gives direction to the deed and empowers it. Here is a theophany and a theology. Here is childlike trust. Here is freedom and reinforcement. Here is forgiveness and the promise of eternal life: **Our Father which art in heaven.**

9. *First Petition.*—**Hallowed be thy name.** We ask, "What's in a name?" There is something in it, or people would not choose one name rather than another, or wish to change their name. But there is not much in our names: they are a code-sign, a tag for the convenience of the mailman. But names were important in the time of Jesus (see the meaning in Hebrew names); they were promise and hope in God. There is everything good in God's name, for name here means essential nature. God's name is the "quality" of the eternal Spirit, God's disclosure of himself. For the Christian, God's name is the soul of Christ. Thus the prayer means: Our Father, cause thine eternal nature, revealed in Christ, to be hallowed by us and by all men. This is properly the first petition. We pray it before we pray for the coming of the kingdom, inasmuch as that coming is for the honor of God's nature; and before we pray for daily bread, for we misuse daily bread if God is not glorified; and even before we pray for pardon, for the pardon must be understood as the gift of holy love. We pray this petition first, because God must come first with us if we would live.

God's name must be sanctified in our thought of him. If we think of him as on the side of big battalions, we make him mere tyrant. If we

[1] Charles Dejob, *Marc Antoine Muret* (Paris: Ernest Thorin, 1881), p. 60.

[2] *The Rime of the Ancient Mariner*, part 7, st. xxiii.

| 10 Thy kingdom come. Thy will be done in earth, as *it is* in heaven. | 10 Thy kingdom come, Thy will be done, On earth as it is in heaven. |

imperative. God is asked to sanctify his name and to cause men to sanctify it. The sanctification of the name is a rich and many-sided concept in Jewish thought. God sanctifies his name by condemning and opposing sin, by separating Israel from the world and giving it his commandments and his love and grace. It is also Israel's task to sanctify God's name by sanctifying itself, in keeping his commandments and doing all other things which redound to his glory. God's name will be fully sanctified in the age to come, when everything that opposes his will has been removed and punishment is no longer necessary.

10. **Thy kingdom come:** As in the Kaddish and the Alenu, this petition follows the prayer for sanctification of the name. See on 4:17 for a discussion of the kingdom of God. As this concept is two-sided, so is the prayer; God is asked to exercise his kingship

imagine that we can avoid the penalty of greed, we slander his holy sovereignty. If we say, "I am too insignificant for his notice," we brand him as one who judges only by physical size. If we say, "I'll turn to him when I need him," we scorn him as mere ambulance. How do we think about God? It is a crucial question.

God must be hallowed in our words. The Roman Catholics have a Holy Name Society. It is needed, even though blasphemy of speech can perhaps be conquered best, not by frontal attack, but by cultivation of the root of reverence. The Jews of old almost shrank from speaking or writing the name of God, but our modern fashion is to use it far too freely—for a curse or an embellishment of unworthy language. Our speech has a thrust into our neighbor's life, and a sharp reaction into our own—and can be a grief to God.

God's name should be hallowed in our daily conduct. The Mohammedan turns to his minaret five times daily and prays: "God is great." We have no such custom, though if we were wise we would punctuate our day with periods of prayer. A sterner demand rests on the Christian: his work and play must kneel in reverence. Advertising, business practice, politics, friendships must all honor the name. That road is hard—like the road to Palm Springs Canyon, but, like that road, it ends in verdure.

God's name should be hallowed in worship. It might seem that such a demand could be taken for granted, but perhaps irreverence has made its worst inroads where reverence should most deeply live. Worship can be made a compensation for unruly life—after the manner, though not to the measure, of brigands who say their Pater Nosters and then proceed to their brigandage. Even the Lord's Supper can subtly be turned into an aesthetic selfishness. Protestant worship has sometimes become cheap—prefaced and ended in casual conversation, interrupted by a casual "announcement period," and disfigured by hymns that are poor jingles and by preachments that are a "noisy gong." This is the first prayer. Jesus lived the prayer he offered: "Father, glorify thy name" (John 12:28). In thought and speech, in deed and worship, he reverenced the nature of God, who is all and in all.

10. *The Second and Third Petitions.*—**Thy kingdom come, thy will be done.** (For more detailed exposition of **thy will be done,** see comment on last phrase of 26:39.) Perhaps the first three petitions grow out of one another: God's nature cannot be honored until his kingdom comes, and his kingdom cannot come until man does his will. Perhaps **the thy** is emphatic —**thy name** rather than the powerless names of the Pantheon; **thy kingdom** rather than "earth's tragic empires"; **thy will** rather than our selfish purposes. Almost certainly the phrase "as in heaven, so on earth" (see "The Clarendon Bible") attaches to all three petitions. The word **kingdom** is suspect in our modern world: therefore it is important to remember the second word of the prayer: "May thy Fatherly realm come, may thy Fatherly will be done, as in heaven so on earth." Yet all authority derives from the invincible sovereignty of God.

The kingdom already is, or it could not come. It exists in the precision and majesty of the stars; in higher orders of life perchance—

Thousands at his bidding speed,
And post o'er Land and Ocean without rest;[3]

in man's physical constitution; and in the laws of social life, flouting which we bring strikes and wars upon ourselves. There is a deeper sense in which the kingdom has come: Christ has come, and can say to us (in far better truth than the bishop said to Jean Valjean), "You no longer

[3] Milton, "On His Blindness."

11 Give us this day our daily bread. | 11 Give us this day our daily bread,[1]

    [1] Or *our bread for the morrow.*

---

and to cause men to take the yoke of the kingdom upon themselves (11:29). Rabbinical writings usually refer to the "revealing" or "appearance" of God's kingdom instead of its "coming." **Thy will be done,** not found in Luke, is an early and accurate gloss; where God's will is done, there his sovereignty is acknowledged and effective.

11. The word translated **daily** is not found in Greek writings independent of Christian literature, except for one occurrence in a single papyrus, and its meaning and derivation have never been satisfactorily explained. Various suggestions have been made: (*a*) "necessary [for life]," so Chrysostom, Cyril of Jerusalem, and the Syriac Peshitta and Arabic versions; (*b*) "steadfast, faithful," so the Sinaitic Syriac (of Luke) and the

belong to evil, but to good. It is your soul that I have bought; . . . I offer it to God." [4] But because the kingdom is a Father's kingdom and we are but unruly children, it has not yet come. Nevertheless it must come—through the free will with which he has endowed his children. The kingdom presses in on us like light, but we can close our eyes—to our own misery and the hurt of others. It comes only through our welcome. So this prayer acknowledges a personal and social obligation: Make **thy kingdom come** through me. Our discussions of what is wrong with our country or world easily become psychological transfers, and thus an evasion. We express in political denunciation the truth we should express in daily life. Yet the word "me" is not hermetically sealed. We carry it with us into the street and into business: we cannot imprison it. So J. E. Roberts has said, "The coming of the kingdom would mean the death of flunkeyism . . . in the personal life, the death of mammon in the social life, and the death of jingoism in the national life." It is a major operation. "One World" indeed, but only in a kingdom and a Will.

The kingdom is a realm of joy. Why do we regard it as threat and shadow? Is it because of our cherished sins? We have turned **thy will be done** into sad resignation—an inscription on a tombstone. There indeed it belongs, but as a promise of dawn. "An act of God" in our legal term is almost synonymous with catastrophe. A fetid swamp was in old days "an act of God," and it was not to be drained; while the amazingly recuperative powers of the body that could still live in fetidness, and man's power to drain a swamp, were apparently not acts of God! "The kingdom of God is . . . righteousness, and peace, and joy in the Holy Ghost" (Rom. 14:17). It is such righteousness and peace and joy as are found in Jesus, and constantly it knocks on our door. Thus great insights are hidden in this prayer. It reminds us that the world is not ours, and that we do not rule it. Our political plans must fail unless they

    [4] Victor Hugo, *Les Misérables.*

are consonant with the Will. The only "progress" is in the movement of the kingdom. It reminds us that the prayer itself is power, such power as is the tragic lack of every age. Our cultures are like perfect buildings left dark because we have electricity but no main contact, or like a man with strong physique who dies because he will not drink from the wellspring at his door. It reminds us of life's prime purpose: **Thy kingdom come, thy will be done.** It is a blowing of trumpets and an unfurling of banners. The doctor is not just a doctor: he is a consul of the kingdom. The businessman is not "in business for himself": he is a regent of the Will. One who cut the words **"thy will be done"** into his weather vane, when asked by a flippant neighbor if God's love was thus unpredictable, answered, "No, I mean that from whatever quarter the wind may happen to blow, God is still love." "The will you are asked to obey," says J. D. Jones, who told the story, "is your Father's will." [5]

11. *The Fourth Petition.*—**Our daily bread.** See Exeg. for word translated **daily.** By any translation the prayer is concerned with day-by-day needs, and neither temporal nor spiritual interpretations are excluded. Bread is the stuff of drama. "Bread and the circus" echoed the social tensions and conflicts within the Roman Empire, and the Ukraine with its wheat fields was a factor in World War II. The saint even in his prayers is still dependent on bread. So this prayer is a confession of need. No man has "independent means": he cannot eat dollar bills for breakfast. His tractors could not help him if life should fail within the seed, or fertility should fail within the soil. Witness the "dust bowl"! Why talk of the "laws" of nature? They are marvelously adapted to our daily need, and therefore are more than laws.

This prayer is a plea that we may be faithful, for daily bread requires each man's co-operation with God's constant labor. Yet the faithfulness and co-operation are also gifts. A man must not

    [5] *The Model Prayer* (New York: George H. Doran Co., 1899), p. 92.

12 And forgive us our debts, as we forgive our debtors.

12 And forgive us our debts,
As we also have forgiven our debtors;

Curetonian Syriac; (c) "daily" or "for the day in question," from ἐπὶ τὴν οὖσαν (ἡμέραν), so the O.L.; (d) "for the morrow" or "for the future," perhaps from ἡ ἐπ-ιοῦσα or τὸ ἔπιον, so the Gospel According to the Hebrews (mâḥâr), the Bohairic Coptic, and Cyril of Alexandria. The third and fourth are the most likely possibilities. The papyrus, where the word is found, may be from the fifth century A.D.; it was published by Sayce in W. M. Flinders Petrie, *Hawara, Biahmu and Arsinoe* (London: Field & Tuer, 1889), pp. 33-35. It is a leaf from a cook's household account book, and the word occurs as the first of the items for the fifteenth day. Here the most natural translation is "for the day's expenses [not otherwise tabulated]" or "for various everyday items." The teaching of 6:34 also speaks in favor of "daily." Probably the term was not understood by Matthew's and Luke's readers; hence the evangelists feel the need of adding an explanatory phrase: **this day,** in the case of Matthew, and "each day" in the case of Luke.

12. Debts is a Jewish figure for "sins," well illustrated by 18:23-35. He who sins is under special obligation to make amends and is not free until he has fulfilled that obligation. Those who use this prayer do not presume to ask forgiveness save in so far as they have forgiven others (cf. Ecclus. 28:2).

---

be a parasite either on God or on his fellow men. To shirk, or to indulge in sharp practice, or to engage in work that adds nothing to the world's health is parasitic: "Give us to be faithful in daily toil, and thus to be worthy of thy daily gift." The prayer implies that we should live in simplicity. The petition is for bread, not for luxuries. It is a plea for day-by-day provision, not for a lifetime security. In any event bread does not keep. We are to live soberly in daily dependence on God's sufficient grace.

This is a prayer of the human comradeship: **our** daily bread. Here is a reminder that mankind is a family. Do we need reminder? We are interdependent. The coffee supply failed when World War II came, because ships were sunk off Brazil. New York was threatened with hunger when the tugboatmen went on strike. Social righteousness is really a matter of table manners: we ought not to glut ourselves while others hunger. "Pass the bread, please." In a modern play, *Panic,* by Archibald MacLeish, a woman, watching a news bulletin which told of forthcoming depression and unemployment, cried out, "Forgive us our daily bread"—and she made no mistake. The eyes of the disciples of the Emmaus Road were opened when Jesus took bread and broke it and gave to them. This prayer asks Christ to preside at the world-table.

But this is a prayer for more than bread. A mourner pushes away the plate: "I cannot eat anything." In short, food is neither joy nor sustenance unless we have also food for the spirit. This prayer is offered, not to a celestial flour merchant, but to the Father of our spirits. Emerson has said, "Man does not live by bread alone, but by faith, by admiration, by sympathy." He should have added, as one taught by

Jesus, "and 'by every word that proceedeth out of the mouth of God' " (4:4). An Irish manuscript of the eleventh century reads, *"Panem verbum Dei celestem da nobis hodie:* Give us today for bread the Word of God from heaven." [6] If conscience is only a foolish scruple, love only a trick of the nerves, and Jesus only a sad blunder—if there is no joyous reality in God—bread is ashes. Thus the deeper prayer. Here also we live "one day at a time." No generation can live solely on the consecration shown by the fathers. Manna from heaven spoils unless daily gathered. Give us day by day thy secret bread! This is an answered prayer. We may not always be aware of answer. A man is not instantly aware of the healing from an infrared lamp. When we seek the mind of Christ, and pray in sincerity the prayer he taught, a change is wrought—bread for the body, bread for the family of mankind, bread for the soul. "Lord, evermore give us this bread" (John 6:34).

12. The Fifth Petition.—Forgive us our debts. The expositor should carefully note the locale and meaning of each of the three words: debt, sin, trespass. (See Expos. on vss. 14-15.) By any translation Jesus here refers to failure in duty. There is no escape from the basic fact of obligation or from awareness of our shortcomings. The word "bravery" implies the possibility of cowardice, and the word "dishonest" implies the possibility and obligation of honesty. There are personal sins—each man's greed and deceit. There are social sins—class pride, racial prejudice, national selfishness. Man cannot solve the problem of sin. George Bernard Shaw makes Cusins in *Major Barbara* say that "for-

[6] *The Expositor,* Ser. 8, X (1915), 423.

13 And lead us not into temptation, but deliver us from evil: For thine is the kingdom, and the power, and the glory, for ever. Amen.

13 And lead us not into temptation,
    But deliver us from evil.[m]

[m] Or *the evil one.* Many authorities, some ancient, add, in some form, *For thine is the kingdom and the power and the glory, forever. Amen.*

13. The word rendered **temptation** might mean "trial" or "persecution," but the petition is usually taken as a request that God will remove occasions of sin or the evil impulse which prompts sin. God's omnipotence and providence are, as always, assumed; but there is no reflection on the question raised by Jas. 1:13-14, "Does God tempt man?"

giveness is a beggar's refuge. . . . We must pay our debts." But he does not tell us how. If a man is honorable today, he has not canceled yesterday's dishonor, which meanwhile has run out into life like ink in water. Who can cleanse history? Who can cleanse memory? No man has power even to return to the past, let alone to redeem it.

There is no easy forgiveness. Forgiveness can be defined as laying aside revenge and claim for requital, but a dictionary definition cannot plumb the depths that true forgiveness must sound. A mother forgiving a wayward son has no thought of revenge or requital. Jesus washing the feet of Judas is not concerned with claims and equities. Forgiveness is possible only by one morally sensitive and therefore grieved, who is willing to give all and bear all that the wrongdoer may be won back into life. Only God can do this work for man. The Cross is the thrust of God's pardon—the incarnation of his pain and self-giving. But for the Incarnation how could we have seen the work of pardon, or accepted it? The gift of pardon is sheer bounty. "Give us our bread," and **forgive us our debts:** just as the earth brings forth food in multiplied harvests, so the love of God brings forth forgiveness. It is not purchased by *our* "good works": to imagine that would be to add the sin of self-righteousness. The hymn is right:

> Nothing in my hand I bring,
> Simply to thy cross I cling.

Does the penalty remain? The consequence remains. The mark of sin may be on a man's body and mind, and distrust may be in his neighbor's mind. But in God's pardon the consequence becomes discipline, and may be turned to strange gain. The Russian bell, "Tsar Kolokol," that fell before ever it was rung, so that a gap was torn in its side, became a tiny shrine; and the gap provided the door by which people entered to pray.[7] Thus Paul's earlier brokenness became sympathy for men, lowliness, and trust in God. Then it might pay a man to sin? "God forbid!" That would be devil's work, and lead to a devil's destiny.

[7] Gordon Hurlbutt, *Windows and Wings* (Louisville: The Standard Press, 1928), p. 215.

What of the other phrase—**as we forgive our debtors?** It is not a business transaction: God does not keep office ledgers. He is "our Father." It means that the two forgivenesses go together. If a man should say, "I'll never forgive you!" he can hardly be forgiven: he is not in the mood. He is not penitently aware of his sins, but only vengefully aware of another man's sins. He is not thinking about God: he is intent rather on his prideful self. This truth must be underscored because Jesus underscored it in what Matthew presents as a kind of codicil to the prayer. An unforgiving spirit in us shuts the door in God's face, even though his compassions still surround the house. He is ready to forgive, but we are not ready to be forgiven. The parable of the unforgiving debtor (18:23-35) is also for witness. How little forgiveness there is in our world! Our law courts are sufficient proof. When General Oglethorpe said to John Wesley, "I never forgive," Wesley properly answered, "Then I hope, sir, you never sin." "Be ye kind one to another, tender-hearted, forgiving one another, even as God for Christ's sake hath forgiven you" (Eph. 4:32). This prayer breaks the circle of hate breeding hate, as Stephen's prayer of forgiveness changed Saul (Acts 7:60). This prayer is the world's spring of hope. In one of the da Vinci legends, the artist is said to have painted his enemy's face on the shoulders of Judas, and, the story goes, he could not then conjure up the face of Christ. But when he forgave his enemy and painted out the insult, he saw Christ's face in a dream that night. **Forgive us . . . as we forgive.**

13. *The Sixth Petition.*—**Lead us not into temptation.** The word **temptation** is hard. If it means seduction, the prayer would seem unnecessary: does God seduce? If the word means testing, the prayer seems unworthy: we ought not to shrink from due testing. Probably the word includes both meanings; and probably the prayer is best explained as the plea of conscious weakness—not as an exercise in logic, but as a cry of the soul. We need testing, as the prayer tacitly admits. Psychologists know the man who avoids testing: "I have always been needed at home." He is no joy either to himself or to his neighbor; he lives in excuses and

The clause **but deliver us from evil,** not found in Luke, may be Matthew's gloss, which stands in poetic parallelism to the previous petition; if so, it probably does not mean "from the Evil One," which is another possible translation. **For thine is the kingdom, . . . Amen** is a doxology added in the later MSS to round the prayer out liturgically. Except for the words **the kingdom and** it is found in the Didache version. The source of the doxology may be I Chr. 29:11. A briefer formula is found in II Tim. 4:18.

---

therefore in inner conflict. Unless a ship can ride a storm, what use is it? Perhaps we can go further and guess that we ought to be tested morally. Jesus was tested the more sharply because the allurements seemed to be quicker ways of bringing God's kingdom. But we should never invite the temptation, or try to play our own providence.

It is no sin to be tempted when life honorably brings the temptation: it is sin only to fall, for we have as our avail a Strength beyond our own strength. But we should never be sure of ourselves. Yet how sure we are! We court temptation, and when anyone warns us we dub him a prude. We take moral chances, as a man going over Niagara Falls in a barrel takes physical chances, not in bravery but in foolhardiness. Our plea that "we need the experience" is a confession of spiritual irresponsibility. This skating on thin ice comes because we have no deep love for God, and therefore no deep fear or hatred of evil. "This is your hour, and the power of darkness," said Jesus (Luke 22:53); but to us evil is no midnight and no desperate threat. We pray, "Deliver us from sickness, fear, poverty, unpopularity"; but cannot understand why we should pray, **Deliver us from evil.** The wrong in the world is not merely economic or psychological maladjustment, though these factors may be present: it is wickedness. So this prayer has deep meaning. It admits our weakness, pleads for hatred of evil, and therefore breathes our love for God. The temptation comes subtly, suddenly, camouflaged, with weapons appropriate for each walk and decade of our life. Before the two world wars we had the planet well under control, so we thought, but actually we were drowsing by the fire while a lion crept on us from the thicket. The prayer **lead us not into temptation, but deliver us from evil,** has not been outmoded or outgrown.

The prayer confesses also that only God's power can save us. Only he can deliver. He enters the struggle—in the grace of Jesus Christ. Thus we know him, our holy Ally. The myths foreshadow the encounter. Circe, for an instance, turned men into beasts after enticing them to her palace with sweet music. They were not quite beasts: they had human memory and discontent. But they were no longer men: they turned foul faces to the foul earth. How were **they** delivered? Mercury, sent from heaven, gave Ulysses "a sprig of the plant Moly," that was proof against the enchantment, and Ulysses set free the captives. Christ heaven-sent: the interpreter may point that moral! In many ways God delivers us: through this prayer, by turn of event, by sudden insight, by access of strength, by our resolve not to fail those who trust us, by work, and by worship. But the focus of deliverance is in Christ. Thus this prayer, seeming to plunge the soul into darkness, lifts us into light. There is deliverance, or Christ would not have taught us to pray for it. He is answer to the prayer. We need not despair either of ourselves or of our world. The deliverance is not complete on earth? It saves earth from disconsolate doom, and is complete in its promise and assurance.

13. The Ascription to the Lord's Prayer.— The phrase was almost certainly not in the original prayer. (See Exeg. for how and when the addition was made.) It corresponds with the doxology used at the temple services: "Blessed be the name of the glory of his kingdom for ever" (e.g., Ps. 72:19). But we may be glad for the addition; it is a final peal of trumpets. Christ prompted this doxology. Why should a small and persecuted church add such a climax of praise to a prayer taught them by One from Galilee? It is like David's praise at the bringing of gifts for the new temple (I Chr. 29:11). Christ had died—on a Cross. Was this "deliverance from evil"? This the coming of the "kingdom"? Surely his followers must then have been tempted to say at Calvary what Africans said to Livingstone about the Zambezi River, that it "by sand is covered." But Christ rose: the river disappearing into the sand came back again into the sun. So the doxology of the Lord's Prayer is the church's praise for his risen power. His prayer became a nobler temple: God's redeeming presence. Therefore the early church said, **For thine is the kingdom. . . .**

The doxology and prayer interpret the word "kingdom." History traces the rise and fall of empires:

Age after age their tragic empires rise,
Built while they dream, and in that dreaming weep:
Would man but wake from out his haunted sleep,
Earth might be fair and all men glad and wise.[8]

---

[8] Clifford Bax, "Turn back, O man, forswear thy foolish ways." Used by permission of A. D. Peters, literary agent.

14 For if ye forgive men their trespasses, your heavenly Father will also forgive you:

15 But if ye forgive not men their trespasses, neither will your Father forgive your trespasses.

14 For if you forgive men their trespasses, your heavenly Father also will forgive you;

15 but if you do not forgive men their trespasses, neither will your Father forgive your trespasses.

(3) A Comment on Forgiveness (6:14-15)

14-15. Similar teachings are given in Mark 11:25-26 and especially Matt. 18:23-35 (see notes on that section) ; also Ecclus. 28:1-2; Test. Gad 6:3-7; I Clem. 13:2.

Man thinks he can play a lone and powerful hand. If he would wake, he would know that already he is held in an invisible kingdom. Kingdoms break that are built on selfish force and selfish fear, but one Kingdom does not break. It comes even through a Cross—like some invincible springtime. The doxology and prayer interpret the word **power**, for "power" means such power as pulses in the prayer. What kind of power? Power in what motive? Power for what end? Lord Acton said, "Power tends to corrupt, and absolute power corrupts absolutely." He meant man's pride in power. What of the power that surrenders power in love? This doxology is the praise of the early church in the contemplation of God's power through Calvary and Easter. The doxology and the prayer interpret the word **glory**. Gray's "Elegy" says, "The paths of glory lead but to the grave." When a new pope is crowned, the words are intoned: *"Sic transit gloria mundi"* ("Thus passes away the glory of this world") . But the glory of God led Christ through a grave into sovereign light. Compare the story of Moses: "I beseech thee, show me thy glory"; and God's answer, "I will make all my goodness pass before thee" (Exod. 33:18, 19) . We too see God only when he has "passed by"—in the merciful ongoing of his ways, in his redeeming goodness.

Christ through this doxology can remake our world. We can live for "the world," or we can live for "the Father"; and we must choose. If we do not worship God in constant doxology, we shall end in a grotesque and ruinous self-worship. If we do not follow Christ, we shall make a state-idol or some equally futile and debasing surrender. The earth finds no light except from above the earth, and only God is worthy of worship. His is the kingdom and the power and the glory. The only enduring center of the "City of Mansoul" [9] is an altar, and science and trade are alike suicidal unless they are consecrate. The early church even in persecution cried, "For thine is the glory," and so had power. The word **amen** is a massive word fallen on evil days. It is the word Jesus used when he said, in our version, "verily." It is man's resolve: "So let it be!" It is, more deeply,

trust and assurance that God can bring great things to pass: "So let it be!" By right instinct the church added a doxology and an **amen** to the Lord's Prayer.

14-15. *Further Word about Trespasses.*—The word ὀφειλήματα (vs. 12) is perhaps best translated by our word "debts." The word παραπτώματα (vss. 14, 15), translated in both KJV and RSV as **trespasses**, carries the idea of "missing the mark." The word ἁμαρτίας in Luke's version of the Lord's Prayer (Luke 11:4) can best be rendered by our word "sins." The teacher should note the three pictures of human life here reflected. First, life is an obligation to be met. Duty often seems irksome, and we rebel against its impossible demands. But this imperious "ought" is really our best crown: it proclaims us children of an ultimate right. It is not enough to be 50 per cent kind or 75 per cent pure: we are born for an unseen perfection. To break the obligation is to be in debt, and we cannot pay the debt; for if on any day we were 100 per cent compassionate or true, we would have no "works of supererogation" by which to overtake yesterday's indebtedness. Only God can cancel moral debt. Second, life is an aiming at the mark, a pilgrim's progress toward a wicket gate of heaven. "I press toward the mark" (Phil. 3:14). To choose a lower mark, or to miss the mark, is failure. "We needs must [ought to] love the highest when we see it." [1] G. F. Watts had as his motto: "The Utmost for the Highest." How many of us are satisfied with proximate goals! Third, life is devotion to goodness. The story of the mother is true of all men: "A white bird, she told [Marius] once, looking at him gravely, a bird which he must carry in his bosom across a crowded public place—his soul was like that!" [2] What stains are on our purity! Only God can give cleansing. As these verses imply, we daily need a canceling of debts, a clarifying of aim and rededication to it, and a cleansing of the whole purpose and practice of our life. Notice the reiteration of the truth that a man unwilling to forgive bars the door against the proffer of God's pardon:

[9] See Bunyan, *The Holy War.*

[1] Tennyson, "Guinevere," *Idylls of the King.*
[2] Walter Pater, *Marius the Epicurean* (New York: The Macmillan Co., 1891), pp. 15-16.

16 ¶ Moreover when ye fast, be not, as the hypocrites, of a sad countenance: for they disfigure their faces, that they may appear unto men to fast. Verily I say unto you, They have their reward.

17 But thou, when thou fastest, anoint thine head, and wash thy face;

18 That thou appear not unto men to fast, but unto thy Father which is in secret: and thy Father which seeth in secret shall reward thee openly.

19 ¶ Lay not up for yourselves treasures upon earth, where moth and rust doth cor-

16 "And when you fast, do not look dismal, like the hypocrites, for they disfigure their faces that their fasting may be seen by men. Truly, I say to you, they have their reward. 17 But when you fast, anoint your head and wash your face, 18 that your fasting may not be seen by men but by your Father who is in secret; and your Father who sees in secret will reward you.

19 "Do not lay up for yourselves treas-

---

d) FASTING (6:16-18)

According to 9:14-15 (=Mark 2:18-20) and 11:18-19 (=Luke 7:33-34), Jesus and his disciples were conspicuous because they fasted seldom, if at all. This passage, even though it presupposes fasting, collides directly with Jewish custom. Anointing was a symbol of joy, and therefore forbidden on the day of Atonement and other days of fasting and mourning. Jesus would have his disciples, even at the risk of criticism, avoid the conventional display of humility.

16. **They disfigure their faces,** probably by leaving them unwashed. Cf. Test. Joseph 3:4, "Those who fast for God's sake receive beauty of face."

6. OTHER TEACHINGS ON THE RELIGIOUS LIFE (6:19–7:12)

a) THE RIGHT USE OF PROPERTY (6:19-24)

Vss. 19-21 are apparently in poetic form—two strophes of three members each and a strophe of two members—and constitute a kind of proverb. Luke 12:33 erects the saying into a general command to the disciples to sell their property and give alms, probably in view of the end of the age (cf. Acts 2:45; 4:34-37).

19. **Rust** translates the Greek βρῶσις. Since this word means "eating," it is often taken to mean "the worm" (RSV mg.), i.e., "the eater." The word is also used by Galen

---

he is in no mood to be forgiven. When Queen Caroline died, someone said: "An unforgiving, unforgiven dies." The two words are linked. Conversely the man ready to forgive opens the door to God who always waits ready to pardon.

16-18. *Christian Fasting.*—The chapter here returns to the discussion of the three main forms of piety as expressed in the new kingdom. There were only five or six fasts annually in Jewish practice. But many Pharisees kept two fasts each week, on Thursday and Monday, the days when Moses respectively ascended and descended Mount Sinai. This ritual they observed with faces unwashed, drawn looks, bare feet, and ashes on the head. The whole question of Christian discipline is here raised. Perhaps Jesus assumes that his followers will fast, though of that fact we cannot be sure. Is any fine devotion—music, home, medical research, or any other—possible without some discipline (7:13-14)? The requirement of self-restraint is written in our constitution and in the constitution of the world. There are dangers involved: the ascetic practice may be so stringent as to warp

character, or it may become an end in itself and thus a self-mutilation, or it may become a parade of self-righteousness. But the dangers must be risked, for an undisciplined Christianity soon becomes unworthy. The gains from this discipline far outweigh the dangers. It helps us to master the flesh, it fits the mind for devotion, and it sets an example of simplicity of life. Jesus covets this gain for his followers. He counsels a measure of asceticism. Our self-indulgent age should note. But he still takes issue with the religious practice of his time. Fasting should be occasional, secret, and joyous —as with gifts of charity. It must flee every inducement to spiritual pride. An explorer is disciplined for the zest of the venture, and a violinist for the rapture of music. So the Christian is disciplined in glad fealty to Christ and in ultimate love for God. The pruning is for the purpose of "much fruit" for Christ's sake. So Christian discipline is positive and radiant in aim, lowly in spirit, and instinct with joy.

19-21. *Treasure in Heaven.*—These three verses may be connected with the next three,

rupt, and where thieves break through and steal:

20 But lay up for yourselves treasures in heaven, where neither moth nor rust doth corrupt, and where thieves do not break through nor steal:

21 For where your treasure is, there will your heart be also.

22 The light of the body is the eye: if therefore thine eye be single, thy whole body shall be full of light.

ures on earth, where moth and rust[n] consume and where thieves break in and steal, **20** but lay up for yourselves treasures in heaven, where neither moth nor rust[n] consumes and where thieves do not break in and steal. **21** For where your treasure is, there will your heart be also.

22 "The eye is the lamp of the body. So, if your eye is sound, your whole body

[n] Or *worm.*

---

in the sense of "rotting, putrefaction"; cf. Epistle of Jeremy 12 (ἰοῦ καὶ βρωμάτων) and Hos. 5:12, where moth and rottenness are coupled. In either case, βρῶσις, like the moth, attacks wealth in the form of rugs or expensive garments. If we translate "rust," we should think of tools of iron. Thieves **break through** by digging through the mud or plaster wall of a Palestinian house; Aristophanes *Plutus* 565 uses the verb in a similar connection.

20. Parallels are found in Tob. 4:9; Pss. Sol. 9:9 (5), "He who does righteousness lays up life for himself with the Lord"; Test. Levi 13:5, "Do righteousness, my sons, on earth, that you may have treasure in heaven."

21. This may originally have been a piece of secular wisdom, "A man's real interests are where his investments are"; "If you want to get a man interested in something, get him to put his money into it." Here it may mean: "If you act in this way, your whole inner disposition will increasingly be turned in the right direction."

22. The eye is the lamp of the body: As in 5:15, the figure is that of the one-room Palestinian house. Philo expresses the thought that the eye is to the body that which

---

and thus with the rest of the chapter. They are here so interpreted. Life is like the gathering of wealth, says this embryo parable, and a choice confronts us: treasure on earth or treasure in heaven. Treasure on earth is beset by risks, and it ends inevitably in total loss. Wealth in Christ's day was partly in fabrics—in rugs, garments, and hangings. Vermin threatened the stored treasure, and thieves could easily break through the mud walls. In any event death soon would overtake the owner. Today Jesus might speak of inflations, depressions, and the uncertainty of fluctuating stocks. He would remind us that "you can't take it with you," and declare again that the mind set on earthly treasure soon becomes overanxious or hard. But there is another kind of wealth: it is of man's spirit, and of an invisible kingdom. He can store truth and love and faith. Vermin and thieves cannot touch this treasure, and death is only a door to its closer possession. Christ gives counsel on how to become wealthy. One meaning suggested for the word "single" is "generous." There is good evidence that the meaning of "evil" is "niggardly" (see Exeg.; see also Expos. vss. 22-23). Dickens' *Christmas Carol* has an interesting parallel: the dog pulls his blind master down an alley when Scrooge approaches, because Scrooge has an "evil eye." Henry van Dyke's story, *The Mansion,* may also be an ac-

curate commentary on our verses. The rich man had his mansion on earth and only a tiny hut when he reached heaven, but the poorer doctor found to his surprise that he had a mansion in heaven: he had forwarded all the necessary materials. The generous eye stores up heavenly love; the evil or niggardly eye, cankered within itself, turns the world dark until its only dwelling is darkness. The issue cannot be straddled or evaded: "Ye cannot serve God and mammon" (vs. 24). Earthly wealth or heavenly wealth? This choice, worthily made, does not necessarily preclude a home or sufficient money income, but it does require that a man should "sit loose" to the world. For some it may mean a vow of poverty such as Francis of Assisi took; for others acceptance of a vocation that will always spell partial poverty; and for all who would follow Christ that the heart should be set on him. The world passes away, but a heart at leisure from the world and bent on God is undismayed: there is real treasure in heaven.

22-23. *The Optic Nerve of the Soul.*—These verses, though probably a middle link as shown above, call for separate comment. Shakespeare's lines come to focus in them:

> The fault, dear Brutus, is not in our stars,
> But in ourselves; [3]

[3] *Julius Caesar,* Act I, scene 2.

23 But if thine eye be evil, thy whole body shall be full of darkness. If therefore the light that is in thee be darkness, how great *is* that darkness!

24 ¶ No man can serve two masters: for either he will hate the one, and love the other; or else he will hold to the one, and despise the other. Ye cannot serve God and mammon.

will be full of light; **23** but if your eye is not sound, your whole body will be full of darkness. If then the light in you is darkness, how great is the darkness!

24 "No one can serve two masters; for either he will hate the one and love the other, or he will be devoted to the one and despise the other. You cannot serve God and mammon.

---

reason is to the soul (e.g., *On the Creation* § 17). **Sound** (RSV) is better than the more literal **single** (KJV), for ἁπλοῦς probably stands for the Hebrew םת, or its Aramaic equivalent, and means much the same as "perfect" in 5:48. Test. Issachar 3:1–5:2 describes the man who walks with "singleness of eye," never coveting or meddling in his neighbor's affairs, but doing good in simplicity of spirit. The "eye" is thus the spirit of man, his moral and religious faculty.

23. The **evil eye,** in Jewish speech, denotes a grudging, selfish character (cf. 20:15); hence Cadbury (*Peril of Modernizing Jesus,* p. 54) would paraphrase: "The door to the body is the hand; he whose charity is open-handed . . . but when the hand is closed, etc." This is the most natural interpretation of the proverb in the present context. Thus the final clause would mean, "If the spirit which guides your actions is selfish, how selfish your total personality must be!" But if vss. 22-23 were detached, their reference would be wider: "You think your moral faculties are a guide to life, but if they are actually darkness, how completely dark you are!"

24. The verse has three parts. **No one can serve two masters,** even though a slave might legally be the property of two owners. Perhaps this is originally a secular proverb like the Oriental saying, "No one can carry two melons in one hand"; and there are

---

and another truth, namely, that the fault in ourselves is not as complicated as often appears, since life can be brought at last to one issue. Life is made for mastery; and fealty is given either to God or to some form, crude or refined, of worldliness. That fealty is the optic nerve of the soul. The eye given to God is generous; the eye given to the world is niggardly. The eye turned Godward is sound (that may be the meaning of the hard word "single"); the eye turned earthward is diseased, as if by tumors or cataracts. The one eye is single, the other "sees double." The one eye is loving; the other "envious" (the word used in Mark 7:22). As the eye, so the world. By dimness of sight the bright colors of the world can be dimmed. By distortion of sight the true proportions of earth are falsified. The last end of that encroaching evil is darkness. Then the glory of the world is but an unlighted midnight. **If then the light in you is darkness, how great is the darkness!** But if the inner eye is cleansed and cured, a wonder breaks like that known by Saul Kane:

> O glory of the lighted mind.
> How dead I'd been, how dumb, how blind.
> The station brook, to my new eyes,
> Was babbling out of Paradise.[4]

[4] *The Everlasting Mercy.* Copyright, 1911, by John Masefield. Used by permission of The Macmillan Company, The Society of Authors, and Dr. Masefield.

Thus the trenchant appeal, clearly implied though not spoken, is, "Take heed to thyself." The world cannot be new until our inner eyes are new. "Out of [the heart] are the issues of life" (Prov. 4:23). In crucial sense we are doctors of the optic nerve; or, rather, we must come to Christ for that surgery. For the whole visible world depends for us on our eyes. "Open thou mine eyes, that I may behold wondrous things out of thy law" (Ps. 119:18). "Lord, that I might receive my sight" (Mark 10:51).

24. *God or Mammon.*—**No man can serve two masters.** This is not a threat, but a comment on life in a parable that speaks its own truth. A master in those days had a life-and-death control. Personality is made for homage, and is such that the homage cannot be divided. Life must find its mastery. This is true even in work, if work is to be well done: e.g., an auto mechanic or rug merchant. It is true in art, which in any great artist becomes a passion. It is true in philanthropy—a man becomes the bondslave of a cause. All these smaller loyalties must likewise find their allegiance—the supreme fealty of life. We can choose: that fact is implied by Christ. However strong the forces of heredity and circumstance, a rational man still has a central shrine of liberty. He may forge an apparently unbreakable chain of logic to prove he is not free, but the next moment he

| 25 Therefore I say unto you, Take no thought for your life, what ye shall eat, or what ye shall drink; nor yet for your body, what ye shall put on. Is not the life more than meat, and the body than raiment? | 25 "Therefore I tell you, do not be anxious about your life, what you shall eat or what you shall drink, nor about your body, what you shall put on. Is not life more than food, and the body more |

many other parallels in Plato, Philo, etc. The conclusion of this first part is the third, **You cannot serve God and mammon.** "Mammon" is simply the word for property and is not always used in an evil sense. It is found in the Hebrew text of Ecclus. 31:8, the Targums, and Aboth 2:12 ("Let the property of your associate be dear to you as your own"). The middle clause is explanatory, and deals with a situation in which one tries to do the impossible. The "either-or" contrast is probably to be explained thus: "Either he will hate A and love B, or he will be devoted to A and despise B."

b) ANXIETY AND TRUST (6:25-34)

A man who wishes to store up treasure in heaven (vs. 20), to have the guiding principle of his life straight (vs. 22), and to serve God rather than property (vs. 24), must get free of worry.

25. Do not be anxious (RSV) is more accurate than **Take no thought** (KJV), for there are times when Jesus counsels prudence (Luke 14:28-32), but "anxious" is still not strong enough. The idea is: "You must not be distracted by cares." It is remarked in Mark 4:19 that "the cares of the world . . . choke the word." Here Jesus uses the argument "from the light to the heavy," which is so often employed in Jewish teaching. If God has given **life,** which is so much **more than food,** will he not give the lesser gift of sustenance? See the discussion of Cadbury (*Peril of Modernizing Jesus*, pp. 58-59). At first glance this saying appears to be nothing more than a word of comfort and encouragement; but this is a superficial impression. As almost any pastor can testify, anxiety over daily bread can be

will assume the very freedom he has denied. Every invitation, every warning, every condemnation, every regret, every approval assumes this limited but unimpeachable power of choice.

The choice narrows to an alternative, here termed God and mammon. The question finally concerns, not a hundred possible masters, but two, as Christ repeatedly taught. Sheep or goats, figs or thistles, right or wrong, the "world" or the "Father," the broad road or the narrow road, time or eternity—the alternative has many names, but remains the one immemorial human choice. This fact does not mean that man's character is black or white, for obviously character runs through many intermediate grays. But it does mean that the choice finally narrows, and that any man at any moment has a dominant direction: he is for God with whatever lapses, or for mammon with whatever compunctions. God and mammon are good names for the alternative; for the word God is ultimate, and the word mammon well betokens the many facets of worldliness (money, success, pride of possession, or subtler pride of mind) by which every man is tempted.

We must choose. This our nature itself requires: it must come to unity. This the nature of the universe requires: Ruskin's "If you read this, you cannot read that" is truth. A man who is selfish cannot at the same time be kind: no

man can travel in two directions at one time. A choice allowed to go by default is still a choice: to defer a duty is to end in irresponsibility. The *Divine Comedy* tells of a special region of hell reserved for people who are neither hot nor cold in their allegiances.[5] Personality is an organism, a unity, and if it is cut it bleeds. Anatole France tells of one Serenus, hero of a philosophical tale by Jules Lemaitre, who suggested that in difficult decisions we should enter in one column all reasons for a choice, and in another all reasons against it; but who himself never followed his own advice, because he realized that he would use all the reeds of the Nile and his own stylus before he exhausted all the subtleties. The account concludes, "Is it necessary then to act?" and replies, "Beyond question it is!"[6] So, "Choose ye this day." In matters of judgment second thoughts may be wise, but in matters of sound conscience and moral choice first thoughts are best, and second thoughts are a ruinous parleying with the foe. "Our wills are ours, to make them thine."[7]

25-32. Anxiety and Trust.—Do not be anxious about your life. This whole passage, so hard for a modern man to accept and follow, is plainly

[5] Dante, "Inferno," Canto III.
[6] *On Life and Letters, The Works of Anatole France*, tr. A. W. Evans (New York: John Lane Co., 1911), p. 12.
[7] Tennyson, *In Memoriam*, Intro., st. iv.

26 Behold the fowls of the air: for they sow not, neither do they reap, nor gather into barns; yet your heavenly Father feedeth them. Are ye not much better than they?

than clothing? 26 Look at the birds of the air: they neither sow nor reap nor gather into barns, and yet your heavenly Father feeds them. Are you not of more value than

---

paralyzing in its effect on the religious life. It is imperative for the Christian to come to terms with his creaturely existence if he is to know how to pray. He must face the hard fact that his standard of living and his health cannot be made absolutely secure, and learn to trust humbly that God will give him all that is needful. The saying is therefore a commandment, and perhaps the most difficult of all to obey. The fourth-century pagan philosopher Themistius said, "For the soul is far superior to the body and the body to possessions." The difference is that Jesus does not share the Greek philosophical idea that the body is unimportant and only the life of the mind significant.

Dibelius remarks (*Sermon on the Mount,* p. 52), that this section is crucial for the understanding of Jesus' teaching. It is the pure will of God that his children should be free from anxiety, but they can obey the commandment perfectly only in the kingdom of God: "The passage is to be taken *in an absolute sense because it is eschatological.*" Dibelius is no doubt correct in saying that we cannot divest ourselves of anxiety altogether, but, with the help of God's grace, it is possible to make some progress in this direction. The Christian is free to imagine that Jesus, at the very moment when he gave this commandment, looked forward to the possibility of his own earthly failure and death.

26. Cadbury remarks: "The religion of Jesus was not centered about a specifically religious experience. It was rather the religious interpretation of unspecifically religious experience." (*Peril of Modernizing Jesus,* p. 190; cf. also p. 162.) As in Job (especially chs. 38–41), man is bidden to look at nature to find an answer to his questions and problems. The Mishnah has a parallel saying: "Have you ever seen a wild animal or a bird practicing a trade? Yet they have their sustenance without care." (Kiddushin 4:14.) A similar idea is found in Epictetus *Discourses* I. 16. 3.

---

linked (quite apart from the "therefore") with what precedes it. It is a continued warning against the lure of mammon. If men's minds were set on God they would not lack the needful things of this earth. Anxiety or calculated care in regard to such items as food and clothing is egocentricity. The reasons against anxiety are not enumerated, but they are given and are not hard to find. First, a man's calculations must always err, for man does not own or rule the world. Its intricacies and inviolabilities always defeat his best plans: **Which of you** [by calculated care] **can add one cubit to his span of life?** Second, it is a fair assumption that God, having given the great gift of life, will not fail to provide its temporal needs: **Is not life more than food?** If God cares for birds, and even for grass which is used for fuel, we may take for granted his care for man. The word **life** thus implies that man's spirit is a precious mystery linked with the Eternal. Third, there is ample evidence of this kindly providence. The birds are fed, the flowers are clothed, and even the grass is sustained in its proper life. These "creatures" all fulfill their nature, and God provides for them. If man fulfills his na-

ture (not idleness, but trustful work) God does not fail him, even though death may come. The interpreter should notice the Franciscan quality of the passage, or rather the Christ-quality which Francis of Assisi learned: birds and flowers are here treated almost as friends. Fourth, calculated concern about garments and clothing, a mind focused on this world, is a pagan attitude: **For the Gentiles seek all these things.** Life is not food; food is but the means. The Gentiles, being unduly exercised about the means, forget the end. Thus they miss "life." If they were truly men they would "live" by trust in God's all-knowing love: **Your heavenly Father knows that you need them all.**

This teaching is a stumbling block for the modern man. If he is a pagan, the whole passage is alien doctrine. If he is compassionate, he asks, "Shall I speak thus to a man out of work, whose children are hungry?" The honest interpreter must face a "hard saying." Certain considerations are reasonably clear. This Jesus is not disparaging work or the need to work. He did not despise a carpenter's shop. We must work if we would eat, and earn our livelihood in a universe that is a "friendly enemy." Both the

27 Which of you by taking thought can add one cubit unto his stature?

28 And why take ye thought for raiment? Consider the lilies of the field, how they grow; they toil not, neither do they spin:

29 And yet I say unto you, That even Solomon in all his glory was not arrayed like one of these.

30 Wherefore, if God so clothe the grass of the field, which to-day is, and to-morrow is cast into the oven, *shall he* not much more *clothe* you, O ye of little faith?

31 Therefore take no thought, saying, What shall we eat? or, What shall we drink? or, Wherewithal shall we be clothed?

they? 27 And which of you by being anxious can add one cubit to his span of life?[o] 28 And why are you anxious about clothing? Consider the lilies of the field, how they grow; they neither toil nor spin; 29 yet I tell you, even Solomon in all his glory was not arrayed like one of these. 30 But if God so clothes the grass of the field, which today is alive and tomorrow is thrown into the oven, will he not much more clothe you, O men of little faith? 31 Therefore do not be anxious, saying, 'What shall we eat?' or 'What shall we drink?' or 'What shall we

[o] Or *to his stature.*

---

27. This may be an independent saying, connected to the context by the phrase **by being anxious. One cubit** is the length of the forearm, i.e., about a foot and a half. The translation **unto his stature** (KJV) is a vivid paradox, but few people would desire such an addition to height. A man might want a longer **span of life** (RSV), but worry will not add even the length of time in which one can walk another cubit; cf. Ps. 39:5, "Behold, thou hast made my days a few handbreadths."

28-29. The **lilies of the field** cannot be identified, since the word is used of all kinds of wild flowers, but it has been suggested that here the scarlet anemone is compared to the royal robes of **Solomon,** whose lavishness was proverbial. **How they grow,** πῶς αὐξάνουσιν, T. C. Skeat ("The Lilies of the Field," *Zeitschrift für die neutestamentliche Wissenschaft,* XXXVII [1938], 211-14) would emend to πῶς οὐ ξαίνουσιν, "how they card not."

30. Which today is, and tomorrow is [not] is a common rabbinical phrase. Bread was baked in a preheated **oven**; dry flowers, grass, and other fuel were tossed in and burned, after which the coals were raked out.

---

world and our best nature require such labor. This also: Jesus does not condemn wise planning, even if the passage originally had an eschatological stress (see Exeg.). It is hard to believe that the Red Cross, insurance, and old-age pension plans would not have his approval. But it is harder to believe that modern obsession with business would win his blessing. **Meat** has victimized "life" in our civilization; livelihood has usurped the art of living; work threatens worship. The cult of advertising and the all-absorbing fever of trade—how do they stand—or fall—by the test of this teaching? This also: there is no argument here against compassion. That we should trust God does not imply that we should fail in neighborly feeling or neighborly "works." God's providence is not in baskets lowered from the sky, but through the hands and hearts of those who love him. The lad without food and without shoes made the proper answer to the cruel-minded woman who asked, "But if God loved you wouldn't he send you food and shoes?" The boy replied, "God told someone, but he forgot." A neighborly scheme of toil would be far different from "free

enterprise" or Soviet "five-year plans": it would exemplify God's abundant providence in its whole purpose and movement.

But when every qualification has been made, this passage requires a joyous abandon of trust in God. "Take no anxious thought" is five times repeated. It is cardinal teaching. Jesus did not think in proximate terms, such as our "laws of nature." He knew that life is an intimate relationship—a friendship between man and God. God watches man and bird: his gracious eye is always on each of us. He will keep a man on earth until the man's word is spoken and his work is done. Jesus would undoubtedly say to a preacher: "Do not 'trim your sails.' Speak the truth in love. If you lose your job, that loss is no loss. If you are concerned first and last to fulfill God's purpose, and if you work faithfully, he will provide for you. Living or dying, you are in his kind and all-competent hands." Jesus himself lived in that sort of trust. How did he manage as to livelihood, and how were his disciples (married men?) supported, when he made the great venture of leaving Nazareth to proclaim the kingdom? There is a Franciscan

32 (For after all these things do the Gentiles seek:) for your heavenly Father knoweth that ye have need of all these things.

33 But seek ye first the kingdom of God, and his righteousness; and all these things shall be added unto you.

wear?' 32 For the Gentiles seek all these things; and your heavenly Father knows that you need them all. 33 But seek first his kingdom and his righteousness, and all these things shall be yours as well.

32. Green quotes a statement of Cicero as illustrating the attitude of **the Gentiles** toward prayer: "We do not pray to Jupiter to make us good but to give us material benefits. . . . We must pray to God for the gifts of *fortune,* but wisdom we must acquire for ourselves." But, as Dibelius points out (*Sermon on the Mount,* pp. 75-76), other Hellenistic theologians consider thanksgiving the only appropriate prayer to God, while Jesus quite frankly bids his disciples pray for daily bread. The true contrast is between the confident reliance on God exemplified in 6:11; 7:7-11, and the anxious ambition of worldlings.

33. **His righteousness:** The saying may originally have read, "its [i.e., the kingdom's] righteousness" (W. H. P. Hatch, "A Note on Matthew 6:33," *Harvard Theological Review,* XXXVIII [1945], 270-72). Cf. Kiddushin 4:14, "A man enjoys the reward [of the law] in this world and its whole worth remains for the world to come." Origen *De Oratore* II. 2; XIV. 1, transmits an alleged saying of Jesus: "Seek the great things and the little things will be added to you, and seek the heavenly things and the earthly things will be added to you."

element in all true Christianity. Most of us who call ourselves Christians fail sadly in this joyous trust in God.

33. The Priority of the Kingdom.—Seek ye first. . . . The novelist Alexander Black was fond of asking, "If you were to receive a million dollars tomorrow, what would you do with it?" It was his way of finding out what came first in a person's desires. What does come first? It is a leading question. A man must think about food and clothing, but he should not think about them first: thus Jesus sums up the teaching of vss. 19-34. Psychologists distinguish between the focal and marginal in our attention. A man intent upon a book may still be marginally aware of the temperature of the room and the ticking of the clock, but the book meanwhile dims other impressions. What is center for us? Life should be a solar system—Christ the sun, as personal focus of the kingdom, and all else revolving round him. Perhaps our fault is not that we are "bad," but that we live for the "good" instead of the best.

Yet how can a man live for a "kingdom"? The word is forbidding, and the idea kindles no excitement. George Bernard Shaw in the preface to *Saint Joan* has written about our "evolutionary appetite"—a drabber title than "kingdom"! —and rightly insists that "the selfish pursuit of personal power does not nerve men" as do unselfish pursuits such as even the crusade to extend man's power over nature. In short, even a fairly good man is more excited over building a hospital, which he may not live to see com-

pleted, than over a larger bank account. Call this passion what we may, it is passion and it is life. Besides, for the Christian its focus is Christ: thus a man lives, not for some vague ideal, but in a personal fealty.

This truth should be brought to cases. When business thinks of profits first and people second, depressions plague us. When it thinks of people first and the intent of God second, pride betrays us. Economics rests back on conscience, not conscience on economics. Another instance? Suppose the church in the nineteenth century had taken seriously the demand of Christ that the gospel should be carried through the world; would wars then have been so likely to desolate our earth? We place the kingdom second, and so spend more money for jails and hospitals than we would have spent on decent homes and city planning. Henry Drummond used to say to his theological students: "Don't be an amphibian, half in one world, half in another"; and again, "Do not touch Christianity unless you are willing to seek the kingdom of heaven first. I promise you a miserable existence if you seek it second." [8] That is likewise political and economic wisdom. This verse remains also a personal demand. We can determine what comes first if we ask, "For to me to live is . . ." (Phil. 1:21)? We seek pleasure first, and find nausea. We seek safety first, and find a cowardly and defenseless mind. We seek profits first, and

[8] George Adam Smith, *The Life of Henry Drummond* (New York: Doubleday & McClure Co., 1898), pp. 517; 451-52.

34 Take therefore no thought for the morrow: for the morrow shall take thought for the things of itself. Sufficient unto the day *is* the evil thereof.

7 Judge not, that ye be not judged. 2 For with what judgment ye judge, ye shall be judged: and with what measure ye mete, it shall be measured to you again.

34 "Therefore do not be anxious about tomorrow, for tomorrow will be anxious for itself. Let the day's own trouble be sufficient for the day.

7 "Judge not, that you be not judged. 2 For with the judgment you pronounce you will be judged, and the measure you

---

34. How can tomorrow . . . be anxious for itself? Perhaps it is playful humor; or "Tomorrow will take care of itself." The final sentence has rabbinical parallels, and both sayings may originally have been secular proverbs.

c) THE CENSORIOUS SPIRIT (7:1-5)

7:1. Judge not, that you be not judged, i.e., by God. The principle is found in the Mishnah: "Do not judge your fellow until you are in his position" (Aboth 2:5) ; "When you judge any man weight the scales in his favor" (Aboth 1:6). In Luke 6:37 and I Clem. 13:2 this saying is combined with commands to be merciful and generous. It is a warning against self-righteous severity, not a command to be neutral toward moral issues.

2. For with the judgment you pronounce you will be judged is found in the I Clement parallel but not in that of Luke. The principle is contained in the Mishnah:

---

find fratricide. It is hard for a man to hammer nails upwards: he is going against the law of things. It is wise to live in the movement of the kingdom. Martin Luther once wrote, "My conscience has become free, and that is the most complete freedom. Therefore, I am a monk, and yet not a monk; a new creature, not the pope's, but Christ's." [9]

34. *One Day at a Time.*—Do not be anxious about tomorrow. Hard counsel! But Jesus obeyed it, though he lived in a conquered land and had "not where to lay his head" (8:20). This is a warning against borrowing trouble from the future, not a veto against wise planning. It is homey and humorous: "Tomorrow will have enough troubles of its own." How did Jesus keep this wisdom? Life was a hierarchy, with God on the throne. Thomas Goodwin, famous London preacher of the seventeenth century, once said, "If a man should go to London to get a pardon . . . and should . . . spend his time . . . seeing the lions at the Tower, the tombs in Westminster Abbey, . . . or in visiting friends, would he not be a fool?" [1] Why did the man go to London? Why did we arrive on earth? Not to be a squirrel hoarding nuts, or to be a walking clotheshorse! Emerson said, "If a man owns land, the land owns him." [2] So Jesus conquered worry by keeping his eye and mind on life's main business. That business is sometimes best done through adversity.

[9] Arthur Cushman McGiffert, *Martin Luther, the Man and His Work* (New York: Century Co., 1911), p. 230.

[1] Quoted by Joseph Parker, *The People's Bible* (New York: Funk & Wagnalls Co., 1881), XVIII, 203.

[2] Essay "Wealth."

In this faith many troubles can be met and mastered. Sickness can be turned to sympathy, and sorrow to insight. Sir Francis Younghusband said, "The doom of Everest is sealed, for the simple . . . reason that Man grows in wisdom and stature, but the span of mountains is fixed." But the mastery is almost impossible if we borrow trouble, for by that folly we drain away strength from today to waste it on tomorrow in fears that may never be fulfilled. God had a purpose when he divided our life into days, and brought down on each day the curtain of night. Perhaps much fear of the future comes of wrongdoing. Christ was committed to God, and thus lived free from fear. "White ants pick a carcass cleaner than a lion": little things worry us (more than great crises) because by our chaotic conduct we bring on ourselves an anxiety neurosis. To kneel before God in confession and surrender is the best worry cure. Then small besetments and great crises are alike held in a warm devotion. Christ says in homey cheer, "Don't worry about tomorrow." It is his promise that "as thy days, so shall thy strength be" (Deut. 33:25).

7:1-2a. *On Judgments.*—Judge not, that ye be not judged. We cannot help judging. Gossip is a mass of verdicts on our neighbor's conduct, and everybody talks about his neighbors. Politics, national or international, is considerably concerned with judgments. These are inevitable: appraisals are a stock in trade of the mind. Ethical verdicts gather into worthy tradition. Who can rightly remain silent in face of flagrant wrong? So we must be clear about the

"With what measure a man metes it shall be measured to him again" (Sotah 1:7; also Aboth 2:5; Rom. 2:1). Here, as in 6:14-15, it is applied to forgiveness.

meaning of this word: Jesus here speaks of censorious judgment and too quick condemnation. He draws a line between ethical appraisal and sharp-tongued criticism, and bids us keep on the right side of the line. He says that critical censure is a boomerang.

The censure may be wrong, and thus recoil upon us. During World War II a captain and three sailors escaped from a sunken submarine. The captain was under a shadow: he seemed to have broken a noble rule of the sea by deserting his men. Later it was found that he was not the captain of the vessel, but an observer for the construction company, and that he had volunteered to go by the safety-outlet when he knew the ship was fifteen miles from land. Almost certainly he would be drowned, but he took the risk in hope of attracting attention from some passing ship. His seeming cowardice was actually finest heroism. Even when a man has done wrong, our judgment should be slow, for

> What's done we partly may compute,
> But know not what's resisted.[3]

Burns wrote the lines, and they may have had their truth in his own case. The mast of the vessel is broken, and the decks in chaos—but is it through neglect or from a storm? Thus ignorance may blind judgment.

Besides, in every censure we reveal ourselves. If we call someone lazy, we confess that we know what laziness means. How? Presumably by being lazy. Thus our censure is often directed to the fault in others that is first in us. By "transfer" we blame a neighbor in order to escape the realities of self-blame (see vs. 3). The liar is always on guard lest others should lie to him. This is an issue to ponder. F. D. Maurice thus pondered it: "Looking [in other people] for the faults, which I had a secret consciousness were in myself, . . . has more hindered my progress in love and gentleness . . . than all things else."[4] See in Masefield's, *The Widow in the Bye Street*, the section beginning: "O God, Thou knowest I'm as blind as he."[5] Easily we make other nations and other men a convenient scapegoat. We shall do well to trace the line between righteous indignation and censorious blame, and to live on the right side of the line. Compare Christ's **judge not** with his "Father, forgive them; for they know not

what they do" (Luke 23:34). The two bear comparison.

2b. Measure for Measure.—For with what measure ye mete: The other reason against quick censure is that life gives back what we pour into it. If we frown at life, it frowns at us. If we pour poisonous criticism into it, it brings poison back upon us. When did a shrew draw an instant and joyous love? Thomas Hood has a poem, "The Dream of Eugene Aram, the Murderer," in which a gentle schoolmaster dreams he murders "a feeble man and old." He had cast the corpse into a deep pool, but the next day

> saw the Dead in the river bed,
> For the faithless stream was dry.

Once more he tried to hide the murdered man under a heap of leaves in a lonesome wood, but

> a mighty wind had swept the leaves,
> And still the corse was bare![6]

Does not revenge breed revenge, and condemnation bring condemnation?

The truth has its radiant side. "If ye forgive men their trespasses, your heavenly Father will also forgive you" (6:14). Luke's version of the saying promises far more than an equal return for any good we show: the measure we give comes back to us multiplied—"good measure, pressed down, and shaken together, and running over, shall men give into your bosom" (Luke 6:38). The universe is just: if we greet life with good will, a harvest of good will is ours, even though through pain and after long delay. See e.g., John Burroughs' poem, "Waiting." Seed cast on the flood finally roots, and there is bread "after many days" (Eccl. 11:1). This teaching, verified in experience, has its implied theology. God is on the throne. He deals out better than an even-handed justice. Censure brings censure, just as love brings love. Yet "God sent not his Son . . . to condemn the world; but that the world through him might be saved" (John 3:17).

> There is no place where earth's sorrows
> Are more felt than up in heaven;
> There is no place where earth's failings
> Have such kindly judgment given—[7]

even when the judgment is most severe. The plea of Christ is that we judge one another in mercy, for thus mercy abounds in the earth, even as God's mercy abounds toward us.

---

[3] Robert Burns, "Address to the Unco Guid."
[4] *The Life of Frederick Denison Maurice*, ed. Frederick Maurice (New York: Charles Scribner's Sons, 1884), I, 129-30.
[5] Part VI, st. vii.
[6] Sts. xxviii, xxx.
[7] Frederick W. Faber, hymn "There's a wideness in God's mercy."

3 And why beholdest thou the mote that is in thy brother's eye, but considerest not the beam that is in thine own eye?

4 Or how wilt thou say to thy brother, Let me pull out the mote out of thine eye; and, behold, a beam *is* in thine own eye?

5 Thou hypocrite, first cast out the beam out of thine own eye; and then shalt thou see clearly to cast out the mote out of thy brother's eye.

6 ¶ Give not that which is holy unto the dogs, neither cast ye your pearls before swine, lest they trample them under their feet, and turn again and rend you.

give will be the measure you get. 3 Why do you see the speck that is in your brother's eye, but do not notice the log that is in your own eye? 4 Or how can you say to your brother, 'Let me take the speck out of your eye,' when there is the log in your own eye? 5 You hypocrite, first take the log out of your own eye, and then you will see clearly to take the speck out of your brother's eye.

6 "Do not give dogs what is holy; and do not throw your pearls before swine, lest they trample them underfoot and turn to attack you.

3-5. The word rendered **speck** may be a splinter of wood. **Log** (RSV) is better than **beam** (KJV), which to the uninstructed often suggests a beam of light. A δοκός is a timber used in building. The figure is purposely grotesque, like the camel and the needle's eye (19:24) and Kipling's story of the elephant's child. Nothing is more absurd than for a man to try to improve others when he does not improve himself. Such a man is a **hypocrite.** He may deliberately cover up his own sins by being a reformer, or his helpfulness may have behind it an unconscious defensive desire to criticize (see on 6:2).

d) Pearls Before Swine (7:6)

6. It is hard to see why the verse is in this context. Perhaps in Matthew's special source it immediately followed 6:1-8, 16-18. In that case the connection was: "Just as religious acts are not done for self-advertising, so religious teaching is appropriate only in the presence of those who are ready to appreciate it." The Midrash on Song of S. 1:2 compares

---

3-5. *The Splinter and the Log.*—The interpreter should not miss the broad humor: **beam** is the log beam of a house, and **mote** is a speck or splinter. The hyperbole underscores the truth. This is perhaps a Jewish proverb which Jesus made new. In the jargon of our time Jesus might be interpreted as saying here that acid criticisms (see above) are a "transfer": a man looking at his neighbor's faults can thus avoid looking at his own more serious failures. "For wherein thou judgest another, thou condemnest thyself; for thou that judgest doest the same things" (Rom. 2:1). In sour mind the man enjoys correcting his neighbor: the exercise gives him feelings of virtue to compensate for the failure in himself that he will not face. Instances? It seems unlikely, despite some commentators, that Jesus had in mind his first followers in their comments on pagan practice; but so-called Christians have not been free from this vice. The Pharisees certainly provided instance: they carped at "lesser breeds" who failed in some splinter of the religious law while they themselves were guilty meanwhile of a girder-fault of pride and inhumanity. Nations can be disfigured by this sin: Cobden remarked on England's disposition to "regulate the affairs" of other nations while blind to the giant evils

which Cobden, Bright, and others strove to eradicate. Have we not known also of rapacious corporations whose officials would instantly dismiss a man for petty theft? The word "hypocrite" means apparently that the critic thus disguises his own evil, posing as a friend: "I am saying this for your own good." The common man has looked askance at the reformer, but has instinctively loved the saint. Perhaps he has been right: the reformer is intent on the sins of his neighbors, the saint is concerned about his own sins; and so the saint can see clearly the need of mankind. The beam which is in the eye of most of us is lack of love. Other men's faults by comparison may be but a splinter.

6. *Guarding the Holy.*—This saying also has earlier Jewish parallels. Perhaps, though not certainly, there is a striking picture in it, for **holy** is a word repeatedly used of the flesh prepared for altar sacrifice. The priest takes a piece of a spotless lamb from the altar, and flings it to a scavenger dog. **Pearl** is the word Jesus used to describe the pricelessness of the kingdom; **dogs** and **swine** were to the Jews shameless and filthy. This saying may be a redaction. Possibly it reflects the attitude of the early church, which was careful to exclude the unbaptized from the Eucharist, and which did **not**

| 7 ¶ Ask, and it shall be given you; seek, and ye shall find; knock, and it shall be opened unto you:

 8 For every one that asketh receiveth; and he that seeketh findeth; and to him that knocketh it shall be opened. | 7 "Ask, and it will be given you; seek, and you will find; knock, and it will be opened to you. 8 For every one who asks receives, and he who seeks finds, and to |

the words of Torah to a treasure which is to be revealed only to the pious. Another parallel is found in Plato *Timaeus* 28C, "To find the maker and father of this universe is a difficult task; and when you have found him, you cannot speak of him before all people." But Jesus did not teach esoteric doctrines; and if he said these words, it was to warn his disciples to turn away from opponents toward those who were receptive, as in 10:13-14; 22:8-10. Jewish Christians no doubt found the saying comforting in times of controversy. Did. 9:5 applies it to the Eucharist, but this is "modernization." It is probably the **swine** that **trample the pearls underfoot** and the **dogs** that **turn to attack.** Both were unclean animals abhorred by the Jews, and Palestinian scavenger dogs were vicious.

e) CONFIDENCE IN PRAYER (7:7-11)

Even Matthew probably did not think of these verses as connected with 7:6. Luke has them where they belong (Luke 11:9-13), at the end of a section on prayer.

7-8. The emphasis is on **ask**; prayer is essential for the religious person. Petition is a natural expression of the family relationship, and it is enough for one to be humble and to trust. This section does not raise any of those theological questions which we find it difficult to avoid. Jesus does not teach that every wish will be granted (26:39), and such sayings as 21:21-22 are hyperbolical.

teach catechumens the creed until just before baptism, lest enemies should learn it, use it for persecutions, and thus **turn . . . and rend the faithful.** But the saying is true to certain reticences in the mind of Christ, and binding on any Christian age. In a blatant time we should the more remember that there is a mood of reserve in the gospel. Any worthy spirit dedicate to Christ lives within restraints and sanctities. Zeal becoming headlong may bring the gospel into mockery and disrepute. Road signs about the "blood of Christ" are perhaps an instance. How easy it is for a casual sexuality to profane the temple of the body—flinging a sacrament to the worldling! How easy to surrender the silent adoration of worship for cheapness—in hope of attracting the ungodly! How easy to lay bare the soul's passion for Christ before the shallow-minded—in the vain hope that thus the world will heed the kingdom! For those who understand there is no contradiction between this saying and vss. 1-5. Christ has interpreted this truth. When Herod tried to make mockery of his teaching, to provide a circus for his court, Jesus "answered him nothing" (Luke 23:9). Before Pilate's cynical worldliness Jesus was likewise silent. His cause is best served, not by exposing it to the raucous, but by living it—until a sated world comes to find the secret of life.

7-10. *Ask, . . . Seek, . . . Knock.*—Ask, and it shall be given you. The context in Luke (11:9-13) seems better: it is there set after the Lord's Prayer and the parable of the friend at midnight. We need not limit the truth of this passage to a way of prayer, but its main application is doubtless in that realm. George Meredith wrote despondently:

> Ah, what a dusty answer gets the soul
> When hot for certainties in this our life! [8]

But Christ assures us that life responds to our best longing, not deceiving or thwarting us, but opening in answer to the soul's quest. Here, then, is Christ's reassurance to our misgivings about "this unintelligible world." He says that the world is not unintelligible, but proves at last a Father's love if a man will be but patient and urgent in the quest. But why does God require the beseeching and the search? That question we can only partly answer. Some facts guide us: God's gifts are not in gold, but in ore to be mined and refined; or they are music to which we must listen long before its wonder is truly known. Thus God schools us in patience and in work. Beyond doubt the waiting and the labor purify our desires and shape our souls.

[8] *Modern Love* (Boston: Roberts Bros., 1892), Sonnet 50.

9 Or what man is there of you, whom if his son ask bread, will he give him a stone?

10 Or if he ask a fish, will he give him a serpent?

11 If ye then, being evil, know how to give good gifts unto your children, how much more shall your Father which is in heaven give good things to them that ask him?

him who knocks it will be opened. 9 Or what man of you, if his son asks him for a loaf, will give him a stone? 10 Or if he asks for a fish, will give him a serpent? 11 If you then, who are evil, know how to give good gifts to your children, how much more will your Father who is in heaven give good things to those who ask

---

9-10. A loaf is shaped somewhat like **a stone,** and **a fish** like **a serpent.**

11. This is not a reflection on man's depravity, but a recognition that in comparison to God all men are sinful (Mark 10:18; Luke 17:10; Ps. 14:2-3). The same type of argument is found in Luke 11:5-8; 18:1-8. If persistence in petition will move a surly Palestinian peasant and an unjust judge, how much more will it avail with a loving Father!

Notice the progression: **Ask, seek, knock** are not merely different metaphors for one truth, but seem rather to indicate a journey. Sometimes we are children in helplessness, and can only **ask**—"with no language but a cry"; [9] and this dependence is upon us to our journey's end. Sometimes we become pioneers and **seek.** That is right: we must not be panhandlers, merely asking, for idleness is no blessing. Knowledge is through long study, gold is hidden in the earth, and music requires a discipline. We must enter deeply into the life of the world, fling away the lower self, and carry the sorrow and hope of mankind. But sometimes, whatever our pioneering hardihood, we come upon a closed door in a mountain fastness. Then we must **knock,** perhaps with bleeding knuckles at midnight. Who can open the door of pardon for an evil past? Or the door of life beyond death? Only God, in answer to man's knocking. But life opens to a faithful pilgrim. Why? Because God is our Father. He does not mock us with any counterfeit good. He does not thwart the soul's desire (vss. 9, 10). We may not receive just what we ask, or find just what we seek, or discover on the other side of the closed door just what we hoped. We seek lesser goods, and find—the best. We seek escape from sorrow and death and find—life eternal. For we could not seek if God had not already found us: he is the secret guide of the pilgrimage.

11. *The Ladder of Confidence.*—An epitaph quoted by George MacDonald in his novel, *David Elginbrod,* reads:

Here lie I, Martin Elginbrodde;
Hae mercy o' my soul, Lord God;
As I wad do, were I Lord God,
An' ye were Martin Elginbrodde.

That is not irreverent: it has the sturdiness of a fine faith. Notice the faith: **Your Father.** We

[9] Tennyson, *In Memoriam,* LIV, st. v.

call God by the name Power, but cannot deny that the Power gleams with purpose and brought forth love. We call him by the name Law, but cannot deny that the Law is providentially matched to our need. We use the name Mystery, but the Mystery still whispers in each man's ear in conscience and compassion. How can we reach a true idea of God? Jesus replies: "Take the finest earth can give, read that into God, and then exclaim 'How much more!' until it fills earth and sky." Earth's best is not mere power or law or mystery, but the love that girds a true home. That is the core of our common life, not self-expression or the class struggle. **If ye then, being evil.** . . . Jesus had no romantic view of human nature. It is evil. Yet it knows how to treat children with some measure of worthiness. Only someone inhuman would taunt and deceive a child. Then **how much more!** By that three-runged ladder we can climb from earth to heaven.

This is not anthropomorphism, or if it is, there is no escape. Our thought of God is necessarily through our own nature. We think as men; we cannot assume the mind of angels. Perhaps the proper answer to the old gibe, "An ox would regard God as a larger ox," is, "Of course. How else?" The scientist who describes the world as "matter," "law," or a "machine" is himself locked in anthropomorphism of a baser kind than the Christian word "Father." Actually Christ safeguards us from anthropomorphism by his **how much more.** Human parents are blind, **evil,** and limited, but God is not a larger man: he is God. He can create and destroy: man can only refashion. There are deeps on deeps of mystery in God, yet his goodness is like our best goodness. But **how much more!** If we take our best as clue to God's nature, we can partly understand life's worst; whereas if we were to take the worst as clue, life's best

12 Therefore all things whatsoever ye would that men should do to you, do ye even so to them: for this is the law and the prophets.

him? 12 So whatever you wish that men would do to you, do so to them; for this is the law and the prophets.

f) A General Rule for Behavior (7:12)

12. The negative form of the Golden Rule is widely attested in Judaism. One formulation of it is ascribed to Hillel, the greatest of first-century rabbis: "What is hateful to you, do not do to your neighbor; this is the whole Torah, all else is interpretation." The Letter of Aristeas (207) gives the negative Golden Rule and adds, "for God draws all men by forbearance." Did. 1:2 combines it with the "summary of the law" (22:37-40) and perhaps draws both from a Jewish source. Other forms of the maxim are found in Tob. 4:15; Test. Naphtali 1 (Hebrew text); Philo in Eusebius *Preparation for the Gospel* VIII. 7. 6. Similar maxims (usually negative) are found elsewhere. See L. J. Philippides, *Die "Goldene Regel" religionsgeschichtlich untersucht* (Leipzig: Adolf Klein, 1929) .

Jesus' form of the Golden Rule is positive. He taught that the essence of righteousness is the constructive doing of good, not the negative avoidance of sin. This point can be exaggerated, but it is nevertheless important. The parables of the last judgment (25:31-46) and the good Samaritan (Luke 10:25-37) are good examples of his emphasis on activity. It is possible to ask, as Israel Abrahams does, whether the negative rule is not

---

would be an enigma. A wise parent says "No" to some askings of his children, and does not spare his child from hardship or sorrow. Thus we may partly understand pain and sadness. But a low explanation of God leaves Christ and our yearning for him forever unexplained.

If only this word regulated Christian theology! It would have cured us of the notion both of the vindictiveness of hell and the sugariness of heaven. It would have fostered faith in eternal life, for no earthly parent would willingly snuff out his children as if they were candles. It would have guarded us from ideas of "the sweet presence of a good diffused," [1] the destruction of individuality in an ocean of being, for a parent should honor the personality of his child. This verse is also an implied doctrine of prayer: we are to pray in faithful toil, in daily love for God's other children, in submission to a Father whose wisdom is far greater than ours, yet in great confidence and trust. We have here the crowning instance of William James's "ladder of faith." He marked off the rungs as follows: (a) there is nothing absurd in a certain high view of the world; (b) it might be true under certain conditions; (c) it may be true even now; (d) it is fit to be true; (e) it ought to be true; (f) it must be true; (g) it shall be true, at any rate for me.[2] Christ has here given us the real "ladder of faith."

12. *The Golden Rule.*—Twenty years before Christ the Rabbis Shammai and Hillel were asked mockingly by a Gentile to teach him the

whole law while he stood on one foot. Shammai in great wrath bade him begone; Hillel replied: "Do not unto others what you would not have others do to you." Hillel thus taught and practiced the law, and the man became his disciple. This is not a new rule. Lao-tzu, Confucius, Plato, and the O.T. all taught it in positive or negative form. It tells us how to live with our neighbors. That wisdom we need because we excel in mechanics, but bungle human relationships. A survey of 4,400 people who had lost their jobs showed that the main lack was not in skill but in comradeship. Thus this rule: it is brief, portable, rememberable—especially in its colloquial form: "Do as you would be done by." But it is not a sinecure in the sense of being easy to apply. Editorials offer it as panacea, almost hinting that if a man has this rule he hardly needs religion. Luncheon clubs and politicians bandy it about, unaware that it has deeps on deeps. It does not mean: "Whatever you would like men to do to you. . . ." For by that interpretation it could mean fleshliness, or indulgent escape from sins, or even trading among drug addicts.

So let us try to sound its meaning. First: **Whatsoever** you ought to wish that men should do to you. Thus the rule demands a more alert conscience than any man can claim. It requires a light found only in God. It rests back on purest religion. Second: **Whatsover ye would that men should do to you** if you were in their place. Such is the clear implication. If you were a clerk in a department store, or a Negro, or a man in jail, how would you wish to be treated? So the rule, having first required purest conscience, now requires ultimate love. It asks

[1] George Eliot, "O May I Join the Choir Invisible."
[2] *The Will to Believe* (New York: Longmans, Green & Co., 1897), pp. 96-97.

13 ¶ Enter ye in at the strait gate: for wide *is* the gate, and broad *is* the way, that leadeth to destruction, and many there be which go in thereat:

14 Because strait *is* the gate, and narrow *is* the way, which leadeth unto life, and few there be that find it.

13 "Enter by the narrow gate; for the gate is wide and the way is easy,[p] that leads to destruction, and those who enter by it are many. 14 For the gate is narrow and the way is hard, that leads to life, and those who find it are few.

[p] Some ancient authorities read *for the way is wide and easy.*

---

more realistic and practicable, in view of the immense amount of evil in the world and our limited powers of doing good. But the only thing that matters to Jesus is what God wills. He never permits the "native hue of resolution" to be "sicklied o'er" with such misgivings. It is enough for a true child of God to try to do his Father's bidding, no matter what others may do, or what the condition of the world may be.

If the Golden Rule is lifted out of its context, it becomes little more than a piece of prudential secular wisdom. It has often been remarked that to do as you would be done by is good for your business and your social relationships, and usually this is true. But Jesus gives the rule for an entirely different reason. This is God's world, and his children must, in simple faith, exhibit the same outgoing lovingkindness which their heavenly Father shows toward them. It is noteworthy that in the Q sermon (Luke 6:31) the Golden Rule stood as an introduction to sayings which command the disciples to love their enemies (Luke 6:32-36). Here it is more than ordinary wisdom; it is a demand for heroic love which requires divine help for its performance.

7. WARNINGS (7:13-23)

Matthew may insert vss. 13-14 here because he reflects that few follow the Golden Rule. These warnings are, however, attached to the sermon as a whole rather than to any one part of it.

a) THE WAY IS FOR FEW (7:13-14)

14. Luke's form (13:24) is nearer the original, but his introduction (13:23) is artificial. The original point was: "How hard it is to enter the kingdom of God!" (Mark 10:24). Matthew rewrites the saying to harmonize it with the familiar teaching that there are two ways—of life and death (Deut. 11:26; Jer. 21:8; Did. 1:1; Barn. 18:1). **Life** here is "eternal life," as in Pss. Sol. 9:9; 14:7, a term frequently used for the "world to come."

---

complete understanding and sympathy: "If you were in his place." Third, the meaning is: **Whatsoever ye would that men should do to you** in your need. All our human need is here implied, for if there were no need there would be no need for the rule. We need more than food, though that need remains. We need strength in temptation, comfort in sorrow, forgiveness in our sins. We need to be treated as if there were something in us that is beyond price despite our brokenness. Ultimately we need God. So this "ethical rule" is so far beyond ethics that it carries us into the presence of the pardoning Father. There may thus be a better version: "Now the end of the commandment is charity out of a pure heart [in their place], and of a good conscience [ought to wish], and of faith unfeigned [as only God can meet our need]" (I Tim. 1:5). The trouble with our glib use of the Golden Rule is that we leave out the Man who spoke it. An Indian chief said of it:

"It is impossible. It cannot be done. If the Great Spirit that made man would give him a new heart, he could do as you say, but not else."[8] Thus the need for the Incarnation. The Emperor Severus inscribed the rule on his palace walls, and perhaps doomed his palace thus, had he understood. We should inscribe it on our hearts. We cannot at once fulfill it, but we can try; and, trying, find that it marks us for eternity by laying on us an eternal task and by driving us in our need to the strength of God.

13-14. The Narrow Gate.—Note in the Exeg. the Lukan parallel and its simplicity. In Luke the simile is a door; here it is a gate, presumably to a city or street. A discipline is required of anyone who would enter the kingdom. Dummelow's commentary gives interesting parallels, one from Cébès (a disciple of Socrates) as fol-

[8] Told of Tedynscung, chief of Delaware Indians of North America, *ca.* 1780. *The Dictionary of Illustrations* (London: R. D. Dickinson, 1872), pp. 322-23, no. 2652.

15 ¶ Beware of false prophets, which come to you in sheep's clothing, but inwardly they are ravening wolves.	15 "Beware of false prophets, who come to you in sheep's clothing but inwardly are

b) FALSE PROPHETS AND THEIR RECOGNITION (7:15-20)

15. The **false prophets** are not Pharisees or Sadducees, for the rabbis did not claim to prophesy. These are teachers who belong to eccentric schools of thought on the fringe of the Christian church. The verse reflects the problems of Matthew's own time. It is predicted in 24:5, 11, 24 that these prophets will come in the last days. Did. 11–12 tells how to detect impostors. **Sheep's clothing** suggests that they creep into the sheepfold, i.e., the church. God's people are compared to sheep in Pss. 78:52; 80:1; 100:3, and the metaphor of **wolves** is also frequently found in the Bible (e.g., Zeph. 3:3; Matt. 10:16; John 10:12; Acts 20:29).

lows: "Seest thou not a certain small door, and a pathway before the door, in no way crowded, for only a very few travel that way, since it seems to lead through a pathless, rugged, and stony tract? That is the way that leadeth to true discipline." [4] Every worthiness has a narrow entrance. Even football demands arduous practice and a "training table." Surgery asks six or eight years of preparation and a lifelong fidelity. It is strange that people are unwilling to pay for Christlikeness even part of the price they pay to become athletes or scientists. Renunciation is the rule of worthy life: we are so constituted that we must forego many roads in order to walk one narrow road. To surrender worthiness is easy: that way is wide, and it is so well filled that we never lack neighbors to bolster our fictitious self-respect. But the true way is **strait** (cf. 6:16-18).

The nature of the renunciation is not far to seek: it is dictated by the nature of the kingdom. If a man would enter into Christlikeness, he must surrender un-Christlikeness. The Pharisees gave up bodily comfort (standing long at street corners to pray, so as to build a reputation for piety) for the sake of pride; the Christian must forego pride itself for the sake of Christ and his cause. Israelites should have understood: their history was a required discipline that they might be God's instrument. George Matheson says shrewdly that the baggage which the would-be Christian must "lose" to enter the narrow door is a large mirror. The renunciation is not a mutilation. It is hard, but the **gate** leads to a city of light. Only the entrance is **narrow**: beyond it is wide room for joy. As illustration: Alice Meynell's sonnet, "Renouncement," [5] telling of stern self-discipline, which led nevertheless to rare usefulness and whiteness of soul. Strange indeed that we pay a high price for a fictitious joy which proves to be **destruction,** and refuse the discipline that brings true **life.** This parable is not a pessimism,

[4] *A Commentary on the Holy Bible,* p. 650.
[5] *Poems* (London: Oxford University Press, 1941), p. 69.

but it is a realism. The plain fact is that **those who find it are few:** there are not many people who are willing to pay the price of surrendered pride and a vigil of prayer. Few give themselves to the adoration of the Will; few practice any spiritual discipline. Most drift with the crowd on the broad and easy way. The parable, however, is not an eschatology. See the context of Luke's version. If that context can be trusted, Christ rebukes the curiosity that would ask, "Are there few that be saved?" (Luke 13:23). His requirement of discipline gives us no license to estimate the population of heaven and hell. But the realism underscores the demand: "Strive to enter by the narrow door" (Luke 13:24).

15-16. *Prophets False and True.*—The interpreter should link these verses with the whole passage through vs. 23. The Exeg. on **prophets** and **Lord, Lord** is particularly important. There is little doubt that the **prophets** here described were not Pharisees or even spurious imitators of John the Baptist, but false leaders in the early Christian church. Perhaps we can gather cheer from that fact to the extent of not despairing so easily of our present Christianity. But there is more warning than cheer: our Christianity also is easily infected with falsity. The whole passage is momentous for Christian leadership. The marks of a false prophet are here given, and they convict us. **False prophets** are outwardly true: their manner—**sheep's clothing**—appears to certify them as members of the flock of Christ. But they are **ravening** in their influence: they leave the church stripped of funds, chaotic in emotion rather than serene, and drained of homespun virtue and staying power. They are correct in theology and ardently punctilious in their phraseology: **Lord, Lord.** They even win a measure of success: they drive out demons and work cures, and crowds gather to their message. Sound elements in the early church called them "Christ-merchants." The reader should notice the truth of this description when applied to a mercenary class of evangelists. The

16 Ye shall know them by their fruits. Do men gather grapes of thorns, or figs of thistles?

17 Even so every good tree bringeth forth good fruit; but a corrupt tree bringeth forth evil fruit.

18 A good tree cannot bring forth evil fruit, neither *can* a corrupt tree bring forth good fruit.

19 Every tree that bringeth not forth good fruit is hewn down, and cast into the fire.

20 Wherefore by their fruits ye shall know them.

ravenous wolves. 16 You will know them by their fruits. Are grapes gathered from thorns, or figs from thistles? 17 So, every sound tree bears good fruit, but the bad tree bears evil fruit. 18 A sound tree cannot bear evil fruit, nor can a bad tree bear good fruit. 19 Every tree that does not bear good fruit is cut down and thrown into the fire. 20 Thus you will know them by their fruits.

16-20. These verses are paralleled by 12:33-35=Luke 6:43-45. Are they from M, or are they Matthew's rewriting of Q? (Cf. Bacon, *Studies in Matthew*, p. 185.) As they stand, they are poorly arranged, and perhaps the original order was vss. 16*b*, 18, 20 (=Luke 6:44*b*, 43-44*a*). Vs. 16*a* is a topic sentence, and vs. 17 a positive statement from another source. Matthew brings vs. 19 in from the teaching of John the Baptist (3:10=Luke 3:9) because of the word "tree" and his interest in the Last Judgment. Vergil says that in the coming age "blushing grapes shall hang on the rude brambles" (Eclogue IV. 29).

---

falsity is the more tragic because the church cannot live without true evangelists: the gospel is the Evangel.

The marks of a true prophet are also given. The Didache (ch. 11) supplements, as with a bill of particulars, Christ's word, **Ye shall know them by their fruits.** It says that if a prophet imposes on the hospitality of a lowly Christian by staying in his house more than two days, or if he asks on leaving for more food than is necessary for one day's journey, or if in a trance he sees a table lavishly spread and indicates that such a table is obviously required for him by God's revelation, the prophet is no prophet but a fake. **Fruits** means more than outward act: it means inner motive relentlessly showing itself in the course of time by word and conduct. Fruit grows slowly, but it unimpugnably proclaims the tree. Thus the test is one of inner and outer Christlikeness proved by time —the eyes of Christ being the judgment. Illustrations are not needed: let the interpreter cite them, meanwhile looking rigorously to his own life. The sovereignty of Christ is here portrayed. History comes to its climactic in him: "in that day"! He rules, dividing the sheep from the goats, goats that in the dimness of our sight look like sheep. He pronounces judgment on the false prophet. "I never knew you," as if to say, "I never gave your falsity any ordination in the spirit." He welcomes the true prophet who outwardly may have won no spectacular success: "Come, ye blessed of my Father" (25:34). There is a difference between a "Christ-merchant" and a Christian.

16-18. Trees Sound and Unsound.—See Luke 6:44-45, especially the words "out of the good treasure of his heart." Jesus apparently was fond of this simile to describe both the Christian man and the Christian society (cf. Ps. 1:3 and Luke 12:33-35). The simile hints certain evidences and necessary energies of the really Christian life. Christian life is rooted in the faith and power of God made known in Jesus Christ. Christian life is cultivated by discipline of worship and work in Christ, lest it become degenerate, as an apple tree becomes a "wild" tree with bitter fruit if neglected. Christian life grows slowly, as fruit slowly comes to harvest. Granted this root and cultivation, it need not be "shaped"; it grows by nature—by its new nature. **Good** as applied to tree and **good** as applied to fruit are not one word, but two, in the original. The RSV rightly has two words. The first **good** means sound; and the second, though it should be translated by our word good, has also some measure of the meaning "beautiful." Ps. 1 says, "His leaf also shall not wither": the Christian man fills the world with healing shade and with loveliness, as well as with sustaining food. This tree is not only planted, but transplanted. It is taken from "the world" and rooted alongside the river of Christ. It is secretly fed from vital springs, and brings forth fruit which it could never have borne in the barren soil of the merely human. The novel *Embezzled Heaven*, by Franz Werfel, is apparently intent to show that even a poor variety of Christian life (as represented in Teta) is more fruitful than the most urbane,

21 ¶ Not every one that saith unto me, Lord, Lord, shall enter into the kingdom of heaven; but he that doeth the will of my Father which is in heaven.	21 "Not every one who says to me, 'Lord, Lord,' shall enter the kingdom of heaven, but he who does the will of my Father who is in heaven. 22 On that day many will say to me, 'Lord, Lord, did we not prophesy in your name, and cast out demons in your name, and do many mighty
22 Many will say to me in that day, Lord, Lord, have we not prophesied in thy name? and in thy name have cast out devils? and in thy name done many wonderful works?	

c) Lip Service (7:21-23)

21. Luke 6:46, which parallels both halves of this verse, may be more nearly what Jesus said. His point was: "It is absurd to address a man as 'my teacher' if you pay no attention to his teaching." The disciples had probably come to address him as **Lord** (κύριος), and this word may translate the word *rabbi*, "my great one," i.e., "my teacher" (23:7-8; 26:25, 49; Mark 9:5; John 1:38), a term of respect then coming into use, or perhaps the Aramaic *mār* (I Cor. 16:22). The Greek word κύριος actually could mean anything from "sir" to the divine "lord" of a cult or the Yahweh of the O.T., but by the middle of the first century it had special overtones, particularly for Gentile Christians. When they heard Jesus spoken of as "Lord," they thought of him as lord of heaven and earth. When Jesus insisted that it is absolutely essential to do **the will of my Father who is in heaven,** his words would have sounded familiar to his hearers. The tractate Aboth in the Mishnah says: "Do his will as if it were your will" (2:4); "Be strong as the leopard and swift as the eagle, fleet as the gazelle and brave as the lion to do the will of your father who is in heaven" (5:20).

22. In that day is almost a technical term for the messianic age or the world to come (Isa. 2:11, 17; Zech. 14:6). Matthew has added the phrase and has also connected this teaching with the work of Christian prophets, exorcists, and miracle workers. All such ministers act *in the name,* and therefore with the power, of Jesus. (See, e.g., Mark 9:38; Acts 19:13; I Cor. 5:3-5; Matt. 18:20.) In Luke 13:26 the Palestinians appeal to the messianic judge on the ground that they have been his table companions and he has taught in their streets.

intelligent, and honorable worldly culture. So it is: a vital Christianity can bring forth both strength and solace, loveliness and life.

21-23. *Profession and Life.*—Not every one that saith unto me, Lord, Lord. This passage implies no disparagement of worship. We ought to say **Lord, Lord,** both in private devotion and in corporate worship. But there were those in the early church who used the name as a magic formula. By incantation they brought a mere temporary peace to slaves victimized by their masters and harried by belief in demons. They cast out devils, but granted no new life. They turned worship into a racket, temporarily appealing but ultimately condemned. The warning is that worship may become a substitute for worth, even though worship (by meaning of the word) is "worthship"—ascribing worth to God, and from him drawing worth into dependent souls. Christianity can become a stock in trade both to the preacher and the layman. The preacher develops a stained-glass voice and his religion becomes a profession, that is, something merely professed. The worshiper can

turn even the sacrament into an emotional substitute for works. Thus the emphasis of Jesus on **he that doeth the will.** It is a stanch and forthright demand. The phrase was current in the time of Christ, but he gave it new depth. The will of God is not always clear, especially with regard to the intricacies of daily conduct in our baffling world. But often the will is clear, and its main directions are always clear. A man ought not to expect light on God's will in life's intricacies of conduct if he is unwilling to follow a clear will in life's simplicities. Thus when a jaunty skeptic admitted his grave doubts about the Trinity, a man of simple faith rightly answered, "But aren't you weak also on the Ten Commandments?" Mere profession of a Christian life does more harm perhaps than undisguised wickedness. "There goes the leader of our local atheist society," was spoken of a church elder who always professed (but did not live) his love for Christ.

The temporary success of professionalism in Christianity need not deceive us. Men who used **Lord, Lord** as an incantation in the early

23 And then will I profess unto them, I never knew you: depart from me, ye that work iniquity.

24 ¶ Therefore whosoever heareth these sayings of mine, and doeth them, I will liken him unto a wise man, which built his house upon a rock:

25 And the rain descended, and the floods came, and the winds blew, and beat upon that house; and it fell not: for it was founded upon a rock.

works in your name?' 23 And then will I declare to them, 'I never knew you; depart from me, you evil-doers.'

24 "Every one then who hears these words of mine and does them will be like a wise man who built his house upon the rock; 25 and the rain fell, and the floods came, and the winds blew and beat upon that house, but it did not fall, because

---

23. The quotation is from Ps. 6:8. **Iniquity** (ἀνομία, lawlessness) is a favorite word of Matthew's, but it was also in Q. Here it refers to sin in general; there is no necessary reference to Gentile Christians' freedom from the law, though at one time Jewish Christians may have understood the saying thus.

8. Concluding Parable (7:24-27)

24-27. Some of the ancient law codes (Lev. 26:3-45; Deut. 28:3-6, 16-19) concluded with a blessing and a curse. This is not, however, a direct statement that God will reward or punish, and it can be applied either to the coming judgment or to the crises of life. Similar ideas are found in Ps. 1:1; Jer. 17:5-8. A rabbinical parable found in the Aboth R. Nathan reads: "A man who has works and has learnt much Torah, to what may he be likened? To a man who builds below with stones and above with adobe; and when much water comes and surrounds it, the stones are not moved from their place. But a man who has no good works and learns Torah, to what may he be likened? To a man who builds first with adobe and then with stones, and when even small streams come, they are immediately toppled over."

---

church won, in some instances, a striking success. But their harvest had no root and soon withered. "Successful churches" should analyze and verify their success. The early church rated "voices" and exorcisms as poorer evidence of Christian grace than the difficult work of Christian good will (e.g., Mark 9:38; Acts 19:13-19; I Cor. 14:1-19). Only real Christianity survives. This whole passage (vss. 15-23) throws a vivid light on the early church. It was mixed good and evil, like our churches. How has the church survived? We can see manifold reasons why it should not survive, and every age has writers of worldly wisdom who prophesy the imminent death of the church. But it survives. Why? That is the question to which the magazine articles should be addressed. Christ, the Incarnate Word, is regnant in the church. He purges it of mere profession—"I never knew you"—and he brings to fruitfulness even after many days the discipleship which is true. Genuine Christianity may seem to fail, but it enshrines Christ's eternity and finally comes to harvest.

24-27. *Wise and Foolish Builders.*—The expositor should notice significant differences in the Lukan account, such as "whosoever cometh to me" (Luke 6:47), and he "digged deep" (Luke 6:48). Two builders each built on a

dry watercourse, the one without foundation, the other upon the deep-hidden rock. **Floods** means "stream": in winter the watercourse became a spate. The metaphor is apt: a man's character is like a house. Such a comparison must have been doubly appealing to Christ. He may have been a builder; as a carpenter he certainly worked on houses. Every thought is like a piece of timber in our house of life, every habit like a beam, every imagination like a window, well or badly placed; and they all gather into some kind of unity, seemly or grotesque. Of the two builders one is a thoughtful man who deliberately plans his house with an eye to the future; the other is not a bad man, but he is thoughtless, and casually begins to build in the easiest way. The one is earnest; the other is content with a careless and unexamined life.

Notice the claim and authority of Christ. He is the architect: **Whosoever heareth these sayings of mine, and doeth them.** Only on his truth can the life of men or nations stand. We discuss our psychological methods, or our systems of national defense and world government, and we do not take seriously this claim of Christ; but history's logic falsifies us, and confirms him. The house cannot be built except on his vertical,

26 And every one that heareth these sayings of mine, and doeth them not, shall be likened unto a foolish man, which built his house upon the sand:

27 And the rain descended, and the floods came, and the winds blew, and beat upon that house; and it fell: and great was the fall of it.

28 And it came to pass, when Jesus had ended these sayings, the people were astonished at his doctrine:

it had been founded on the rock. 26 And every one who hears these words of mine and does not do them will be like a foolish man who built his house upon the sand; 27 and the rain fell, and the floods came, and the winds blew and beat against that house, and it fell; and great was the fall of it."

28 And when Jesus finished these sayings, the crowds were astonished at his

---

Matthew's form is in most respects more primitive than Luke's (6:47-49). Its two characters are Palestinian. The wise one builds on a rock, but the foolish one builds a house of mud bricks in a wadi or dry torrent bed, which is smooth and inviting, like our Southwestern arroyos. When spring and fall rains come, such watercourses may quickly become raging rivers. Luke thinks of the wise man as digging deep to build foundations. This is perhaps more natural in a Greco-Roman city.

C. Summary (7:28-29)

28-29. Matthew, upon arriving at 4:22, departed from Mark 1:20, which he had been copying. He now artistically weaves Mark 1:22 into the first of his five summary colo-

---

the line between God and man which he has traced; and on his horizontal, the dealings of man with man which his truth requires. Those two lines are in his cross, one the grace of God toward man and man's answering obedience, the other a crossbeam running through every man's life in love. Likewise Christ is the foundation (cf. I Cor. 3:11). Beneath all the surface wisdom of the world he is rock. The thoughtful man digs into his truth until on that foundation life rests. The foundation is not seen: perhaps the foolish man's house appears more substantial, and almost certainly it appears more handsome, than the thoughtful man's house. The fool lives for appearances; the sage searches for a secret strength. Likewise Christ is the builder: **He that heareth . . . and doeth.** Ever the wise man listens to Christ, ever he tries in consecrated will and in dependent prayer to fulfill the truth received. Thus truth is inwrought in him: day by day the house is built. There is a story of a rich man who engaged a builder to build "the finest house you have ever dreamed of building." No expense was spared, and the builder was well pleased with his work until the rich man said, "The house is yours, but you must live in it." Then the botches stared at him, and he realized how much better he could have built. A man must live in what he builds.

Every house is tested. Such is the frank realism of the story. Summer does not stay. Providence has different seasons. No man escapes temptation, testing, sorrow, or the claims of responsibility. Often "flash storms" come. Whose house

stands the test? There is drama in the story. Notice the repeated **and.** Notice the inversion of the phrases: "Down came the rain, down swept the spate, heavily beat the wind." Could any preacher but Christ dare to end a sermon thus: **Great was the fall of it?** This is Christ's comment on people who "live any old way" or build on surface values. But the wise folk provide for themselves and for other men a refuge in the time of storm. Their house stands.

28-29. *The Authority of Christ.*—**As one having authority.** The common people were astonished. He was not a scribe. He had no religious credentials. Yet he spoke like a king. His sayings were a new Sinai. The scribes quoted authorities; he spoke with authority. They loved tradition, and no rabbi won a hearing unless he could prove that his word was based on past wisdom; so the scribes drew stale water from closed cisterns. But the words of Jesus were like a spring, clear, fresh, with power to slake the soul's thirst. Besides, he laid men under obligation as one who had right to command. What was the secret of his sovereignty?

He had authority of silence. The scribes babbled what others had said, but Jesus prayed and pondered. He did not cut himself off from the best wisdom of the past, but he meditated on it in silence until it became his own, in very spirit, not merely in its letter. When a poet boasted to an old Quakeress that every hour of his day was filled with this energy or that study, she replied, "When dost thou do thy thinking?" People listened to Jesus, and then said: "That is what I have always known deep down, even

29 For he taught them as *one* having authority, and not as the scribes.

8 When he was come down from the mountain, great multitudes followed him.

2 And, behold, there came a leper and

teaching, 29 for he taught them as one who had authority, and not as their scribes.

8 When he came down from the mountain, great crowds followed him; 2 and

---

phons. (See Intro., p. 235.) Jesus **taught them as one who had authority:** Cf. on 5:22. **Scribes,** however, cited the authority of previous sages whenever possible, e.g., Aboth 3:9: "R. Dosethai b. Yannai said in the name of R. Meʿir . . ." The Jewish idea of a continuing tradition is well expressed in the famous passage, Aboth 1:1-12.

III. Resumption of the Narrative: A Ministry of Mighty Works
(8:1–9:34)

This part of the Gospel consists of three groups of miracles, separated from each other by two teaching sections which inculcate absolute loyalty to Christ and draw a sharp distinction between the new dispensation and the old. Matthew's purpose is to exhibit Jesus as the pattern for the Christian missionary (cf. Bacon, *Studies in Matthew*, p. 187), who is expected to show the signs of an apostle (II Cor. 12:12; cf. Acts 3:1-12; 4:8-10), although the mere performance of miracles is not sufficient without Christian behavior (7:22). This narrative section leads up to the second great discourse (9:35–11:1), which sums up the lessons taught by the narrative (cf. especially 9:37-38; 10:1, 7-8; 11:5). The miracles are ten in number, corresponding to the tradition in the Mishnah: "Ten wonders were wrought for our fathers in Egypt and ten at the sea. . . . Ten wonders were wrought for our fathers in the temple" (Aboth 5:4-5). The climax of the section is 9:26 and Matthew may have added the last two miracles to complete this traditional number.

---

though I have no words to say it." He dwelt in the silence of God, and therefore spoke from sound intuition.

He had authority of love. **Not as the scribes:** they drew their robes about them lest they should be contaminated by touching some sinner "who knoweth not the law" (John 7:49). But Jesus spoke from a deep fund of compassion. He healed the sick, he played with children, he had a "great heart." Judge political speeches by this test, judge sermons by it: some are clever, some are specious, some fulminate and provoke strife, but how many are instinct with love for the common man?

He had authority of life. "Not as the scribes": in them the beauty of the psalms they taught and the flaming truth of the prophets they expounded were mocked by drabness or deformity of conduct. J. D. Jones tells the secret of a minister whose sermons carried power even though he lacked the extrinsic gifts of a great preacher: people said of him, "There are twenty years of holy life behind every sermon." [6] The face of Jesus was an interpretation of his words; his deeds were of one piece with his commands. His hearers knew there were reserves of soul in him which his teaching had not tapped.

[6] *The Gospel of Grace* (London: James Clarke & Co., 1907), p. 63.

He had authority from God. The springs of truth in him came from a far deeper source than any human probing could find. "Not as the world giveth, give I unto you" (John 14:27). As people listened, they caught the accent of another world above and beyond and around our world. The eternity in them quickened. Deep called to deep. They knew then that they were prisoners on an island of time, and longed for the homeland of the soul. That was and is his best authority: the mystery of God's will is in his word. "Never man spake like this man" (John 7:46). Yet the authority was denied. The sermon failed. People knew, dimly or clearly, that his teaching was touched with soul: but they preferred sense to soul; and the teaching, though it was pricked with heaven's own light, was lost on them, until he died and rose. For instance, there was a day when he spoke in his home synagogue, and people "wondered at the gracious words" (Luke 4:22); but because his truth cut across their selfish prejudice, they hurried him to a precipice to kill him. Because men are thus free, Christ must die; and by his death overcome their failure, and lead them to heed his truth.

8:1-4. The Leper.—The interpreter should read with care the discussion of Jesus' mighty works (see pp. 123-24). He should note that the present chapter marks a new departure in this

The evangelist draws on Q for two of the miracles (8:5-13; 9:32-33) and one of the teaching groups (8:19-22) —otherwise Mark is the sole source. Matthew has taken all the available material in Mark down to Mark 2:22, except 1:23-28, which he omits, partly because he wishes to compress two healings of demoniacs into one (8:28-34). To this he adds miracles from Mark 4:35-41 and 5:1-43, and develops the story of the two blind men from Mark 8:22-26 and 10:46-52, with a few touches from Mark 1:43-45. He freely rearranges Mark's framework to achieve a smooth narrative; e.g., 9:1 replaces Mark 2:1 because Jesus has been on the other side of the sea.

A. DESCENT FROM THE MOUNTAIN AND THREE HEALINGS (8:1-17)

The transition made by vs. 1 is necessary because of 4:25; 5:1.

Jesus' healing powers are attested by numerous traditions in Christian and non-Christian writings. Both Christians and their competitors accepted it as a fact that Jesus worked miracles. The difference was that his enemies ascribed this to magic (12:24). A Talmudic tradition, in fact, says that Jesus was hanged on the eve of Passover because he practiced sorcery and led Israel astray. Well-attested healing stories have been told of Jewish rabbis and Hellenistic teachers, and of Christian saints and healers down to the present day. (For ancient parallels see L. J. McGinley, *Form-Criticism of the Synoptic Healing Narratives* [Woodstock, Md.: Woodstock College Press, 1944], which contains a full bibliography on pp. 155-62.) The Emperor Vespasian was said to have healed a blind man by the use of saliva (Tacitus *Histories* IV. 81) as Jesus did according to Mark 8:23; compare the old English custom of the king's "touching" people for scrofula and other diseases. Thus the historian is able to compare the stories of Jesus' miracles with similar narratives and to observe that such accounts often undergo some development in the course of time (cf. Matt. 9:18 with Mark 5:23; and see Martin Dibelius, *From Tradition to Gospel* [London: Ivor Nicholson & Watson, 1934], p. 166).

No scientist or historian has in his hands the data by which he might decide categorically, at this late date, just what powers Jesus exercised, or exactly what event lies behind this or that story. And although the believer must insist that the full understanding of Jesus' activity can be had only through faith, it is yet fair to say that many of his healings are partially understandable in terms of present-day medical science. He cured some diseases which involve psychological—and, we may add, spiritual—factors, and it comes as no surprise to the scientist that Jesus had this ability. Where the scientist's work ends, the theologian's begins. A "miracle" may be defined as an event which evokes wonder and religious awe and leads the beholders to give praise and thanks to God. It may, or may not, be explicable in terms of ordinary ideas of cause and effect (Bacon, *Studies in Matthew*, pp. 369-74). Ancient Christians, of course, drew no distinctions between nature miracles and healing miracles, or between different types of healings. Far from raising questions in the minds of readers, these stories were for them actual evidence of Jesus' power and divinity, and the Fourth Gospel frankly uses them as such. No doubt some of the narratives were used to reinforce various ideas, e.g., that Christ's power was always available and that he would always stand by his people (see on 8:23-27); but they were accepted literally and not as mere symbols.

Gospel. He should understand the Gospelist's purpose in the three miracles here and in the sequence of ten miracles (see Exeg.). It is worth remembering that chaulmoogra oil is now being injected, apparently with some measure of success, into the veins of lepers in Christian mission hospitals. The Exeg. has a paragraph on the healing miracles and it should be carefully read. Here we are concerned primarily with the moral and spiritual implications of the story. Leprosy, or the skin diseases

thus named in the N.T., may be regarded as a parable of man's spiritual malady. There is the comparable feeling of being unclean, as any sensitive conscience knows. There is a comparable loneliness: the leper was required to keep his distance, and to cry, "Unclean, unclean" at the approach of any healthy man. He was a pariah and accursed—type of that sense of estrangement from God and man which sin lays upon us. There is the comparable pitiableness, and the comparable fact that there are

worshipped him, saying, Lord, if thou wilt, | behold, a leper came to him and knelt
thou canst make me clean. | before him, saying, "Lord, if you will, you

---

Ancient Jews and Christians sometimes explained sickness as God's punishment for man's sin, and sometimes ascribed it to the activity of demons. The two ideas were not mutually exclusive, for the demons might lead men to wickedness for which they would be punished. The world was regarded as full of evil spirits (4:8-9; I John 5:19; I Cor. 5:5; John 12:31; Eph. 2:2; etc.), and these demons frequently smote human beings or entered into them. There is some reason to think that in the earliest form of the gospel tradition all types of sickness were ascribed to demons (9:32-33; Acts 10:38; Luke 13:11; Mark 9:25), and the distinction sometimes drawn between demoniacs and other sufferers may belong to a later stage of development. (See Friedrich Fenner, *Die Krankheit im Neuen Testament* [Leipzig: J. C. Hinrichs, 1930], pp. 21-26.) Jesus himself seems to have regarded his healings as a sign that God's kingdom was at last overcoming the kingdom of Satan (12:28=Luke 11:20; cf. also the notes on 11:4-5).

1. THE HEALING OF A LEPER (8:2-4)

A recently discovered gospel fragment contains a story based on Matthew, Mark, and Luke, which begins: "And behold there comes to him a leper and says, 'Teacher Jesus, journeying with lepers and eating with them in the inn I myself got leprosy'" (H. I. Bell and T. C. Skeat, *Fragments of an Unknown Gospel and Other Early Christian Papyri* [London: British Museum, 1935]). Some scholars conjecture that in the original story behind Mark 1:40-45 the healing was not instantaneous but was expected to occur while the leper was on his way to the priest. Thus it would resemble the stories of Naaman (II Kings 5:1-14) and of the ten lepers (Luke 17:12-14).

8:2. The biblical law concerning **a leper** is found in Lev. 13–14; Deut. 24:8. The affliction was common enough in Palestine for the entire tractate Negaim in the Mishnah to be devoted to it. The rabbis usually regarded it as a direct punishment for various sins, and though the law presupposes that it was curable, they said that its healing was as difficult as the raising of the dead. Lepers were not shunned merely for fear of contagion; contact with them rendered the holy people of Israel unclean (Lev. 13:45-46). Biblical leprosy (Greek λέπρα; Hebrew *çārā'ath*) includes several skin diseases variously identified as contagious ringworm, psoriasis, leucoderma, and vitiligo (see Lev. 13:30 Amer. Trans. and Moffatt). Since it was thought also to attack clothing and the walls of buildings (Lev. 13:47; 14:34), "leprosy" may often have been due to a fungus. The disease now called leprosy, Hansen's disease, or *Elephantiasis Graecorum* was perhaps known in ancient Egypt, but is not referred to here. (See "Leprosy, Leper," *Encyclopedia Biblica* [ed. T. K. Cheyne; New York: The Macmillan Co. 1899-1903], III, cols. 2763-68; "Leprosy," *The Universal Jewish Encyclopedia,* ed. Isaac Landman [New York: The Universal Jewish Encyclopedia, 1942], VI, 610-11, and literature cited there; Friedrich Fenner, *op. cit.,* pp. 67-68.) If the leper **came** to Jesus, it was probably outdoors, for the mere entrance of a leper into a house polluted everything in it (Kelim 1:1, 4). The words **if you will** do not necessarily imply that the leper thought Jesus unwilling to heal. He speaks to Jesus as if he were a wonder-worker whom he wishes to please with compliments (Epictetus *Discourses* III. 10. 14-15 uses a similar expression: "Why then do you flatter the physician? Why do you say, 'If you are willing, sir, I shall get well'?").

---

so few to pity. To that basic ailment Christ comes—with power.

The story bears witness to the *love* of Christ. The leper did not doubt Christ's power: **Lord, if thou wilt, thou canst** . . . , and perhaps he did not doubt the will of compassion. Instantly Christ **touched him.** Christ could have spoken the cure. Or could he? Perhaps love required

that touch, at risk. Christ bridged the six-foot distance which regulations imposed. He crossed the chasm. Love cannot live at arm's length. Social service has found that a card index is a nonconductor, and that there is no substitute for the actual sharing of life. The settlement movement was based on that very conviction: the settlement worker must live on the **same**

3 And Jesus put forth *his* hand, and touched him, saying, I will; be thou clean. And immediately his leprosy was cleansed.

4 And Jesus saith unto him, See thou tell no man; but go thy way, show thyself to the priest, and offer the gift that Moses commanded, for a testimony unto them.

5 ¶ And when Jesus was entered into Capernaum, there came unto him a centurion, beseeching him,

can make me clean." 3 And he stretched out his hand and touched him, saying, "I will; be clean." And immediately his leprosy was cleansed. 4 And Jesus said to him, "See that you say nothing to any one; but go, show yourself to the priest, and offer the gift that Moses commanded, for a proof to the people."*q*

5 As he entered Ca-per'na-um, a centurion came forward to him, beseeching

q Greek *to them.*

3. Stretching out the hand and touching were familiar gestures of healing (II Kings 5:11; Mark 8:22-23). Touching the leper would have made Jesus unclean, according to the law (Negaim 3:1). Immediate cleansing of leprosy, even in its milder forms, would be supernatural (Exod. 4:6-7; Num. 12:9-14).

4. **See that you say nothing to any one:** Mark, from whom these words come, probably thought that Christ's messiahship must remain secret. If Jesus gave this order, it was because he did not wish to be surrounded by a curious crowd looking for displays of miraculous power. Jesus respected the functions of the priests; and the man could not be restored to normal social relationships until he was publicly declared clean, hence the command **show yourself to the priest,** i.e., the one officiating. The purification ceremony could be performed only in Jerusalem. **The gift that Moses commanded** consisted of two birds, one of which was slain and the other released as part of the disinfection ceremony (Lev. 14:4-7). **Unto them:** We should expect "to him" instead of "to them." Who are those spoken of in the plural? Perhaps Jesus' critics, though the story has not mentioned them; the RSV translators conjecture that **the people** generally are meant.

2. The Healing of a Centurion's Servant (8:5-13)

Matthew and Luke (7:1-10) describe the sickness and the circumstances of this cure somewhat differently, but give the conversation in almost identical words. Luke's account is introduced by the mention of friendly Jewish elders. Matthew lacks this touch and instead includes a saying about the rejection of the Jews (vss. 11-12). The emphasis is not on Jesus' healing powers, but on how a Gentile came to believe in Jesus and was praised for it.

5. At Tell Ḥum, probably the ancient **Capernaum** (cf. 4:13), a splendid second-century synagogue has been excavated. This probably took the place of the one which,

street, hand to hand, heart to heart. Sinai thunders the command; Calvary stretches forth the hand. The story tells the *power* of Christ. His words are abrupt, assured, forthright in glad confidence: **I will: be clean.** The command to the man to fulfill the Jewish ritual has the same terse sovereignty. In the realm of the spirit's malady Christ has power: "The Son of man hath power on earth to forgive sins" (9:6). He is conscious of divine commission. He is the revealing of God; he is the channel of God's renewal. The story tells the *wisdom* of Christ. If the man did not report to the priests, and make the sacrifices required by the law, he would still be an outcast. Besides, public hygiene was safeguarded by these ordinances. If the man delayed, he might never go—to his **own** loss, and at the cost of misgivings in the

public mind. His love and power and wisdom are one flame. In the impasse of evil the presence of Christ gives practical wisdom, and sets our feet on the right path. We shall have cause in this chapter to trace in greater detail the necessity of faith. But let it here at least be noticed. The leper's faith was perhaps only a partial faith. Yet it was an act, like the tiny act of touching a switch, without which light and power might not have been released. There are interesting queries that arise. Did the man follow? If not, was the healing any real blessing?

5-13. The Centurion.—(See also Expos., vss. 10-12.) This picture hardly needs an interpreter. Once brought into a clear light and contemplated, it speaks its own word. The centurion was a minor Roman officer exposed to all the temptations of military office. He

6 And saying, Lord, my servant lieth at home sick of the palsy, grievously tormented.

7 And Jesus saith unto him, I will come and heal him.

8 The centurion answered and said, Lord, I am not worthy that thou shouldest come under my roof: but speak the word only, and my servant shall be healed.

9 For I am a man under authority, having soldiers under me: and I say to this *man,* Go, and he goeth; and to another, Come, and he cometh; and to my servant, Do this, and he doeth *it.*

him 6 and saying, "Lord, my servant is lying paralyzed at home, in terrible distress." 7 And he said to him, "I will come and heal him." 8 But the centurion answered him, "Lord, I am not worthy to have you come under my roof; but only say the word, and my servant will be healed. 9 For I am a man under authority, with soldiers under me; and I say to one, 'Go,' and he goes, and to another, 'Come,' and he comes, and to my slave, 'Do this,'

---

according to Luke 7:5, was built by the **centurion.** In the Roman army a centurion commanded one hundred men and his rank was comparable to that of a modern noncommissioned officer. This man was probably in charge of troops used for police purposes by Herod Antipas, tetrarch of Galilee and son of Herod the Great. Antipas did not have the right to maintain an army.

6. The word translated **Lord** (κύριε) need not mean more than "sir" in this context. The word rendered **servant** is an intimate term which also means "boy." We do not know in what way he was **paralyzed;** perhaps through gout or arthritis, though Fenner (*Krankheit im N.T.,* p. 59) suggests a type of hysteria.

7. Jesus' answer, with its emphatic **I** in the Greek, might be read as a question: "Shall I come . . . ?"

8-9. The centurion is not merely polite; he may fear that Jesus has scruples against entering a Gentile house. Furthermore, he has confidence in the sufficiency of Jesus' **word** alone; since he knows both how to receive and to give commands, he assumes that when the command is given the result will follow.

---

could have despised the conquered Jews, but he built them a synagogue and loved their nation (see Luke 7:5). He could have been brutal to his servants—Caesar once apologized for feeling pity for a slave—but instead he sought the help of Christ for a favorite servant. He could have trampled on the prejudices of the Jews, but instead, he understood and acknowledged them: **I am not worthy** may mean that he knew that a Jew believed himself to be defiled by entering a Gentile home, and that he regarded the prejudice at least with understanding. He could have trusted only in brute force, but he was a man of faith and aware of a spiritual world. He had learned to cross lines of class, nation, and creed. Not strangely Jesus rejoiced in him.

The emphasis of the story is on the centurion's faith. He may not have believed that the universe is kind, but he was ready to believe in the power of Jesus. If he used the word "God" in any sense as Jewish religion used it, he believed that God is good, and that he intends abundant life for his children. Perhaps he had learned from Jewish friends to look for the Messiah, and found in Jesus that awaited

deliverer. Certainly his heart went out in trust to Jesus. So fully did he trust that he was ready to stake all his hope on Jesus' power. As a centurion commanded soldiers, so Jesus could command the forces of good to the expulsion of the alien evil and disease. This faith was a far cry from Roman pride and the worship in pagan temples.

The response of Jesus was instant. His kindness was shown even to the partial faith of the centurion: **I will come and heal him.** To Jesus there was no defilement in entering a Gentile home. He confronted need; and to his compassion need was a command. The joy of Jesus is like a daybreak. **He marveled.** What gives us sudden joy? Evidence of faith brought that surprise to Christ. This man believed in God, and to some measure in goodness, and was therefore "open": the power of Jesus found entrance. Thus the healing by the word of Jesus. Whatever interpretation may be set on the miracles, we need have little doubt that there was healing in Jesus for both body and mind. His kindness was effective and empowered kindness. The body ultimately died, but through the body the grace had entered to print its saving

10 When Jesus heard *it,* he marveled, and said to them that followed, Verily I say unto you, I have not found so great faith, no, not in Israel.

11 And I say unto you, That many shall come from the east and west, and shall sit down with Abraham, and Isaac, and Jacob, in the kingdom of heaven:

12 But the children of the kingdom shall be cast out into outer darkness: there shall be weeping and gnashing of teeth.

13 And Jesus said unto the centurion, Go thy way; and as thou hast believed, *so* be it done unto thee. And his servant was healed in the selfsame hour.

and he does it." 10 When Jesus heard him, he marveled, and said to those who followed him, "Truly, I say to you, not even*r* in Israel have I found such faith. 11 I tell you, many will come from east and west and sit at table with Abraham, Isaac, and Jacob in the kingdom of heaven, 12 while the sons of the kingdom will be thrown into the outer darkness; there men will weep and gnash their teeth." 13 And to the centurion Jesus said, "Go; be it done for you as you have believed." And the servant was healed at that very moment.

r Some ancient authorities read *with no one.*

10. This **faith** may be at present no more than confidence in Jesus' power, but on this foundation a more important trust can be built.

11-12. These verses are found in a different context in Luke 13:28-29. The metaphor is that of the great banquet in the days of the Messiah, alluded to in 26:29 (=Mark 14:25); Luke 22:29-30; Enoch 62:13-16; II Baruch 29:3-8; II Esdras 6:49-52. The idea that **many** Gentiles will be accepted is found in Isa. 45:6; 49:12; Mal. 1:11. The **sons of the kingdom** are Jews, who are its natural heirs. John the Baptist made a similar statement (3:9). This attitude to Gentiles follows logically from Jesus' other teachings. The **outer darkness** and the **weeping and gnashing of teeth** were thought of earlier in Jewish history as characteristics of Sheol; by Jesus' time they were part of the usual description of Gehenna.

13. The servant was healed **at that very moment.** A striking parallel to this is found in a rabbinical story of the first century A.D., according to which the son of Rabban Gamaliel was healed at a distance at the moment when another rabbi prayed for him. (See Paul Fiebig, *Jüdische Wundergeschichten* [Tübingen: J. C. B. Mohr (Paul Siebeck), 1911], p. 19.)

mark on the soul. The would-be interpreter needs little guidance beyond the story: in the character of the suppliant and in the response of Christ it lays its saving truth on life in every age.

10-12. *The Cruciality of Faith.*—Form criticism has helped us to understand that the story of the centurion may be a frame for the pronouncement-saying in these verses. Such an interpretation does not dispute the historicity of the story, but it does serve to make clear the importance of this logion on faith. What is faith? A native expectancy quickened in the course of man's experience by the promptings of God. F. W. H. Myers said that the leading question is "Is the universe friendly?" We are born with that hope, and the hope is rooted in "the numinous"—in our awareness of God. We expect well of life: we believe that even tragedy has its secret blessing, and that death is at last swallowed up in life. At basis this confidence is the response of the whole life to God, even though a man may live long without recognizing its nature. God sends his signs to cheer

those who believe. Christ is God's focal prompting—his self-disclosure. The centurion believed, and Jesus rejoiced in his faith.

Why is faith necessary? Jesus constantly stressed the essentiality of faith. Why? Because this confidence is the main "drive" of our nature. It is more central than reason, for the journeys of reason are all by the impulsions of faith. The research doctor first believes that the disease can be cured, and then applies his reason. If he ceased to believe, his reason would be drained of its lifeblood. Thus the misanthrope is an affront on human nature. He has denied himself, and barred the door to God's visitations. Doubt at its best is the necessary odds of faith, but at its worst it always involves a certain measure of stubborn perversity. Jesus can enter if a man should say, "This may be God's word"; but is barred if the man should say, "God is not, and if he were, he has no word for my life."

The reward of faith is written in the story: the joyous friendship of Jesus was a deeper blessing even then and there than the healing

14 ¶ And when Jesus was come into Peter's house, he saw his wife's mother laid, and sick of a fever.	14 And when Jesus entered Peter's house, he saw his mother-in-law lying sick with a fever; 15 he touched her hand, and the
15 And he touched her hand, and the fever left her: and she arose, and ministered unto them.	fever left her, and she rose and served him. 16 That evening they brought to him many who were possessed with demons; and he
16 ¶ When the even was come, they brought unto him many that were possessed with devils: and he cast out the spirits with *his* word, and healed all that were sick:	cast out the spirits with a word, and healed all who were sick. 17 This was to fulfill what was spoken by the prophet Isaiah, "He took our infirmities and bore our
17 That it might be fulfilled which was spoken by Esaias the prophet, saying, Himself took our infirmities, and bare *our* sicknesses.	diseases."

3. The Healing of Peter's Mother-in-law and Others (8:14-17)

14. Peter's wife is mentioned in I Cor. 9:5. Some commentators believe this to be a story told by Peter himself. The **fever** has sometimes been identified as malaria or thought of as due to a psychological disturbance.

15. According to Mark 1:31, Jesus took her by the hand and raised her up, a gesture of healing well known in ancient stories. At a later time the rabbis forbade women to serve at table, but probably Galilean peasants had no such scruples.

16. An abbreviation of Mark's summary (Mark 1:32-34).

17. The quotation is a translation of Isa. 53:4 independent of the LXX. Isaiah had referred to the servant of God who **took our infirmities** by suffering them himself, but Matthew thinks merely of Jesus' healing power. Early Christians loved to identify their Messiah with the suffering servant. It is not certain that the rabbis interpreted Isa. 53 as referring to the Messiah earlier than the third century A.D., since the Aramaic Targum of the prophets may be that late. See, however, C. C. Torrey, "The Messiah Son of Ephraim," *Journal of Biblical Literature*, LXVI (1947), 253-77.

of the servant. The reward is categorically stated in the logion: **Many will come . . . and sit at table.** The ushering in of the kingdom was frequently represented as a feast. Faith makes this Gentile the soul-compatriot of the patriarchs; lack of faith bars even the Jew, despite his heritage, from the final joy. A startling truth! How did his hearers receive it? Faith is ultimately heaven; lack of faith is **darkness** (as though a man had lost his eyes) and **gnashing of teeth** (life issuing only in bitter disappointment). This pronouncement-saying has deep meaning for our day. What of our refusal to believe anything that our senses do not confirm? We have made a merit of skepticism, and deny the very axioms of our nature. Thus we easily despair both of ourselves and of our world. The promise written in us is a better trust than "man's wisdom." The leap of the spirit toward Christ is our best clue, if we would but follow.

14-17. The Great Physician.—Of the three miracles this is interesting as coming from the apostle-circle. The home of Peter is the scene. He has his Christ-given name, Peter, not his original Simon. The person healed is Peter's wife's mother. Thus the story seems well at-

tested. The sickness is a fever, possibly of the sudden kind that is prevalent in tropical lands. The story tells that Christ wrought the cure with a touch of his hand. The cure was so complete that the fever left no aftermath of weakness: the woman rose and attended her guests at table. Fever is an appropriate word for deeper ills. May we not rightly say that pursuit of money and pleasure is a fever? Our whole civilization tosses restlessly from its secret infections. How this sickness cries for cure! At Capernaum, when news traveled of the cure in Peter's home, many sick were brought—at evening time, when the end of the Sabbath permitted the labor. Capernaum thus became the whole city of our human need.

Christ the physician is sovereign over the sickness. **He . . . healed all that were sick.** He himself used the title of physician concerning himself (e.g., Mark 2:17). It is a physician's task to live where sickness is: "The Son of man is come to save that which was lost" (18:11). He knew the truth of *mens sana in corpore sano:* sickness in the body afflicts the whole man. Thus a hospital and especially medical missions are consonant with his gospel. **Pain can**

18 ¶ Now when Jesus saw great multitudes about him, he gave commandment to depart unto the other side.	18 Now when Jesus saw great crowds around him, he gave orders to go over to the other side. 19 And a scribe came up and said to him, "Teacher, I will follow you wherever you go." 20 And Jesus said to him, "Foxes have holes, and birds of the air have nests; but the Son of man
19 And a certain scribe came, and said unto him, Master, I will follow thee whithersoever thou goest.	
20 And Jesus saith unto him, The foxes have holes, and the birds of the air *have* nests; but the Son of man hath not where to lay *his* head.	

B. INTERLUDE: TEACHING ABOUT DISCIPLESHIP (8:18-22)

Luke has this section in a better context (Luke 9:57-60), at the close of the Galilean ministry, when Jesus is preparing to go to Jerusalem. At this point in Matthew, Jesus still has a home in Capernaum, and vs. 20 is not very appropriate. Those who speak to him are not necessarily candidates for special discipleship, but they wish to accompany him on his journey and hear him teach.

19. Luke 9:57 does not call the man a **scribe.**

20. Son of man can mean "a man," "a human being" (as in Ezek. 2:1; etc.), perhaps "I myself, being a man"; or it can mean the celestial figure who comes on the clouds at the end of the age to establish the final order (Enoch 46:1-4; 48:2; Mark 13:26; 14:62; Luke 17:22-37). One of the antecedents of the idea is found in Dan. 7:9-14, but this passage may do no more than contrast the humane Israelite empire of the future ("one like the Son of man") with the beast empires of the past. What connection it may have with speculations about the "primal man" created by God at the beginning of the world is much debated (see I Cor. 15:21-22, 45-49 and C. H. Kraeling, *Anthropos and Son of Man* [New York: Columbia University Press, 1927]). Some first-century Jews may

be turned to gain, but in itself it lacerates: it is not indigenous in the kingdom; "neither shall there be any more pain" (Rev. 21:4). The story is a parable: the body is not the essential man. The lesion in the soul, the infection in the will, is the real malady. If that is not healed, life ebbs more tragically than when the flesh is cut. Therefore the flash of truth in Matthew's apt quotation: **He took our infirmities and bore our diseases.** We must not read too much into Matthew's mind: he possibly was thinking primarily of the physical boon. Perhaps that passage from Isaiah was not given a messianic import by the rabbis until a date much later than this Gospel; there is disagreement on that score. Yet for ourselves, as for all the Christian centuries, we can hardly forego the deeper interpretation. The worst sickness is in the soul. Man cannot cure it, for it is sin against God. God cannot cure it save at cost: this redemption is not by "turn of eye, wave of hand." [1] A physician must come himself into the very place and presence of disease. Must not God so come in incarnate Love? **He took our infirmities.** Here is perennial truth. Our fever is our bane. The redemption is given. All we need is—need, and the wisdom to turn believingly to Christ. He is obedient to our

need because of his love, and he is sovereign in his power. "Behold the Lamb of God, which taketh away the sin of the world!" (John 1:29).

18-20. The Impulsive Disciple.—This scribe, a lawyer and an interpreter of Israel's religious tradition, was perhaps the first influential man who had offered to become a disciple (but see Exeg.). He was a key man, a member of a group not easily impressed. But Jesus virtually repelled him. That was an act of courage, and a fact of significance for the church. The man came with deference: he called Jesus "rabbi." He came with admiring enthusiasm: **I will follow you wherever you go.** Yet Jesus rebuffed the apparent zeal. The answer of Jesus is noteworthy, whatever the meaning of Jesus' assumed title, **Son of man** (see Exeg.)—whether it was an enigmatic claim to messiahship, or an avowal of his universality as representative man, or a declaration of manhood *simpliciter,* for each of these interpretations gives implications to the answer. Jesus' confession of homelessness had no trace of self-pity: he was thinking, not of himself, but of the scribe and the kingdom. The homelessness was a literal fact, and was accentuated as he neared the Cross. To a fisherman, working all night in an open boat, homelessness was partly tolerable; but to a scribe, accustomed to his scrolls and his home, homeless-

[1] Browning, "Saul," st. xvii.

21 And another of his disciples said unto him, Lord, suffer me first to go and bury my father.	has nowhere to lay his head." 21 Another of the disciples said to him, "Lord, let me first go and bury my father." 22 But Jesus
22 But Jesus said unto him, Follow me; and let the dead bury their dead.	said to him, "Follow me, and leave the dead to bury their own dead."

have identified the Messiah and the Son of man, but this was not the prevalent doctrine. Early Christians certainly made the identification, and Mark (but not the Q document) teaches that "the Son of man must suffer" (Mark 8:31). Jesus must have referred to himself as Son of man, for in the Gospels the term is never used except in words attributed to him (though see Acts 7:56), but it is much debated whether the teaching that he would return in apocalyptic glory actually goes back to him. Matthew and Luke no doubt thought of this verse as a sharp paradox: "The heavenly Son of man is homeless." Yet the words may be merely a sad observation that those who follow Jesus do not have as much of a home as the wild animals. (See on 16:21.)

21-22. The duty to **bury** one's **father** was so sacred that it dispensed one from the duty of reciting the Shema (Berakoth 3:1). Tobit (4:3; 6:14) also teaches the importance of this pious act. Even a priest, who ordinarily must avoid the defiling contact with the dead, was permitted to bury his father (Lev. 21:2-3). Elijah permitted Elisha to say good-by to his mother and father (I Kings 19:20; cf. Luke 9:61-62), but Jesus does not allow the fulfillment of this sacred obligation! Various explanations have been given: a weakness in the character of this prospective disciple, the fact that for seven days he would be unclean and so unable to follow Jesus to Jerusalem or to carry on religious work, etc. But whatever the circumstances, the principle is quite simple: the claims of the kingdom of God, as laid upon men by Jesus, take precedence even over family obligations (12:48-49; 19:29). Those who do not accept these claims are spiritually **dead;** let them **bury their own dead.**

ness was a stern demand. Jesus doubtless had in mind a deeper homelessness: the scribe was "safe" in his traditions, but Jesus must venture on a new path at the call of God. Foxes and birds need make no choice. They have a home: they are not troubled by conscience or vocation. But a man must forsake his "low-vaulted past." [2] He is plagued by unrest. He is aware of transience. Here he has no abiding city: he must leave his Ur and seek another City. This loneliness was doubly required of Christ, and of any who would follow him.	4:10). The disciple-sayings of Jesus are frequently hard. They nobly sift men "as wheat," separating the chaff from the grain (cf. Luke 22:31). Jesus offered wounds and death, and valiant souls accepted the challenge. Perhaps the church must relearn this strategy and truth. We have made discipleship so easy that it is not worth persecuting, for it has no cutting edge. But true discipleship is at cost of disciplines and hardships.
The intention of this word is clear. Despite some commentators, Jesus did not repel the man because of the group from which he came: Jesus honored each personality. He had read the man. He knew he was impulsive. So he asked him to count the cost. There must be no gilding of the sharp flint, no softening of the shadows. If the man followed from emotion only and then faltered, he would hurt the cause of God: compare the story behind Browning's poem beginning, "Just for a handful of silver he left us." [3] He would hurt himself, and perhaps be a worse man than if he had waited until there were mind and will within the feeling: perhaps Demas became a worse man than if he had never followed and faltered (II Tim.	**21-22.** *The Reluctant Disciple.*—Another means not merely "additional" but "of another kind." Jesus does not judge men in the mass. Personality is a treasure. So: another man, another method. Perhaps this man was already a disciple. If not, he was ready to make his commitment—with reservations and delays. The demand seems almost ruthlessly hard. If **bury** means that the father was already dead, the funeral rites and the consequent settlements would spell several weeks of delay; but this task was considered so binding that the law excused such a sorrower even from the requirement of the daily prayers. If **bury** means that the father was aged, there might be a much longer delay in discipleship. But have the aged no claims? **Let the dead** evidently means, "Let the spiritually dead, who have not caught the zeal and passion of the kingdom, perform the routine tasks, even if these spell honor and loyalty to

[2] Oliver Wendell Holmes, "The Chambered Nautilus."
[3] "The Lost Leader."

23 ¶ And when he was entered into a ship, his disciples followed him.

24 And, behold, there arose a great tempest in the sea, insomuch that the ship was covered with the waves: but he was asleep.

25 And his disciples came to *him,* and awoke him, saying, Lord, save us: we perish.

23 And when he got into the boat, his disciples followed him. 24 And behold, there arose a great storm on the sea, so that the boat was being swamped by the waves; but he was asleep. 25 And they went and woke him, saying, "Save, Lord; we are

---

C. Other Miracles (8:23–9:8)

This second group embraces three deeds of superhuman authority: power over nature, exorcism, and the new power of declaring, on God's behalf, the forgiveness of sins. Matthew believes that the man of God, who does Jesus' work, must exercise the same authority and with the same faith.

1. Power over Natural Forces (8:23-27)

This is abbreviated from Mark 4:36-41, the preceding verse in Mark, 4:35, already having been copied in vs. 18, above. Test. Naphtali 6 tells the story of how Jacob and his sons are shipwrecked and scattered, but the ship is miraculously restored and makes port (as in John 6:21; Ps. 107:28-30) after Levi prays to the Lord. This parable, which promises the restoration of the dispersion to the Jewish homeland, the Jonah story, and other elements of Jewish sermonic tradition, may influence the way the evangelists relate the narrative before us. To ancient Christians it no doubt meant that Jesus could deliver his people out of any storm, literal or figurative (Pss. 65:7; 69:1-2; 18:16-17; 42:7) .

---

home; but you, whom the kingdom has seized, must follow." It is an irony that the man's family, if he obeyed Christ, probably treated him as dead. Families in India have sometimes carried a casket in public procession as sign that they now regard as dead one who has embraced Christianity.

Consider the meaning. It was perhaps inevitable that some, like Ernest Renan, should argue that Christ is here trampling on human love and on the sanctities of home; and that "he had forgotten the joy of life, of love, of sight, of feeling." [4] But they have little argument. They lack even pretext. He cared for his own mother, even when he was on the Cross. It is a fair assumption that there were others in the home of this would-be disciple who could discharge the home duties. Home can be a bondage. Perhaps Jesus had lost men of promise by their overemphasis on home ties. Why otherwise the sudden passion and burning conviction in Christ's answer? Ultimately home has no safeguard except in Christ and by the grace of those who follow Christ. Thus this sifting word, more stringent than a Gideon test. We see here, not only the revolutionary newness of the gospel, but the sovereignty of Christ. He brooks no rival, not even dearest human loyalty. The past, even a man's home, can be a dead weight on the kingdom. Old areas of cities, however

[4] *Life of Jesus* (Boston: Little, Brown, & Co., 1910), pp. 310-11.

honored, must be torn down for needed roads. Political forms and cherished traditions must not be barriers to Christ. In Galsworthy's play *Loyalties* a sardonic observer, seeing a wife defend an unworthy husband because of the marriage bond, and a father for love's sake hiding his daughter's shame, and other people fettered by similar secondary loyalties, says caustically: "Criss-cross—we all cut each other's throats from the best of motives." She should have said, "From the second-best of motives." If Christ had been sovereign, the drama would have taken a very different turn, and all the human loyalties involved would have been redeemed. Life is lord over the past, and Christ is Lord of life. The demand of Christ is imperious, but history and the soul are its sufficient logic.

23-27. *Master of the Storm.*—The Rembrandt picture of this scene has every line of the picture converging on Christ. There is a shaft of light from a rift in the clouds, token that help is from God. All else is in tumult and shadow, token of the frantic helplessness of the disciples. The picture is a true commentary. The storm was just such a tempest as was frequent on that little lake. Its waters were six hundred feet below sea level, and the surrounding mountains were so set that their deep valleys acted like funnels. The word **tempest** here means earthquake—a word eloquent of sudden fury. The Jews were never fully at home on water: heaven to them was "no more sea." Thus the Sea of

26 And he saith unto them, Why are ye fearful, O ye of little faith? Then he arose, and rebuked the winds and the sea; and there was a great calm.

27 But the men marveled, saying, What manner of man is this, that even the winds and the sea obey him!

28 ¶ And when he was come to the other side into the country of the Gergesenes,

perishing." 26 And he said to them, "Why are you afraid, O men of little faith?" Then he rose and rebuked the winds and the sea; and there was a great calm. 27 And the men marveled, saying, "What sort of man is this, that even winds and sea obey him?"

28 And when he came to the other side,

Yet they also took it as an actual occurrence. Such sudden storms are not unknown on the Sea of Galilee.

26. Here the faith is trust in God (Rom. 4:20). Matthew omits Mark's words of rebuke, "Silence! be muzzled!" perhaps because they seem like the binding of a spell. E. C. Hoskyns and Noel Davey (*The Riddle of the New Testament* [2nd ed.; London: Faber & Faber, 1936], pp. 86-89) note that the **great calm** after the storm corresponds to the healing of the demoniac in the next story.

2. Power over Demons (8:28-34)

Jews did not keep swine, and it has been argued that therefore this story could have been current only among Gentiles. Yet Jewish Christians may have told it with some

Galilee is a fit symbol of our life, with its alternate shine and cloud. How suddenly the storms come—in sickness, treachery within and without, wars, and death! They are as unpredictable, as fear-quickening, and as menacing as this tempest.

Thus our human helplessness is here depicted. The disciples were in panic, and panic multiplied the threat. Their language (see the Greek original) was disjointed and distraught. Perhaps the function of crisis is to remind us of our essential helplessness. In a speech at Bristol in 1780 Burke exclaimed, quoting a Mr. Coombe who had suddenly died, "What shadows we are, and what shadows we pursue!" In the sunshine we can trust our own powers and imagine ourselves self-sufficient: then our science and skill seem an ample defense. But when a "Titanic" strikes an iceberg, or a hidden microbe lays waste our boasted strength, or death impends, we relearn the truth that man is neither able nor intended by creation to live in his own resource. Then we ask the ultimate question, "To whom shall we go?" (John 6:68).

The disciples found in Christ a deliverer. He would have slept through the storm. Wearied by intense effort, he slept when and where he could—at peace with men, and in trust toward God. When they woke him (compare the accounts in the Synoptics) he was immediately master of the storm. Even a naturalistic explanation of the miracle has the problem of explaining the "coincidence": the word "coincidence" hides a mystery and a miracle. He broke through their fears, and convinced them of the power and presence of God; and that is

the essence of miracle. Augustine has a fine comment:

Lo! what is the cause, stouthearted man, that thy heart is disturbed? That ship in which Christ is asleep is the heart in which faith is asleep. . . . So then the tempest beats furiously against thine heart; beware of shipwreck, awake up Christ. . . . Christ dwelleth in thee by faith. Present faith, is Christ present; waking faith, is Christ awake; slumbering faith, is Christ asleep. Arise and bestir thyself; say, "Lord, we perish." . . . Let thy faith awake, and Christ begins to speak to thee.[5]

The expositor should notice the words **what manner of man . . . ?** The phrase almost means "from what land and birth?" We see here, in these miracles as in the three miracles of healing already studied, the accenting of two facts—Christ's authority and the essentiality of faith in him. This issue is always drawn: shall we trust our poor wisdom and skill—or Christ? Man is a vain thing for any real "safety." But Christ abides. Mark's account (4:35-41) hints that he saved, not only the boat in which the disciples journeyed, but the other boats. Christian faith blesses the unbeliever also, even though he does not know whence his salvation comes.

28-33. *The Gadarene Demoniacs.*—This is a difficult passage. The location of the incident is uncertain. The divergences in the three Synoptic accounts are not easy to reconcile. There is danger that we may read too much into the

[5] *Sermons on Selected Lessons of the New Testament, A Library of Fathers of the Holy Catholic Church* (Oxford, John Henry Parker, 1844), Sermon XXXI, sec. 8, pp. 251-52.

there met him two possessed with devils, coming out of the tombs, exceeding fierce, so that no man might pass by that way.

29 And, behold, they cried out, saying, What have we to do with thee, Jesus, thou Son of God? art thou come hither to torment us before the time?

to the country of the Gad-a-renes',[s] two demoniacs met him, coming out of the tombs, so fierce that no one could pass that way. **29** And behold, they cried out, "What have you to do with us, O Son of God? Have you come here to torment us

[s] Many ancient authorities read *Gergesenes;* some, *Gerasenes.*

---

amusement, since it recounts the destruction of the unclean animals. The narrative embodies one of Mark's favorite ideas, viz., that the demons, being spirits, recognized Jesus as Son of God even when human beings did not. One finds it hard to believe that Jesus would bargain with the demons and permit them to possess the swine, and perhaps these details have been added to the story. Matthew omits the most edifying part of the narrative, the picture of the exorcised man clothed and in his right mind, yet it remains a dramatic portrayal of Jesus delivering men from the powers of evil. The locale must be in the Gentile territory of the Decapolis.

28. Manuscript evidence shows that Matthew must have written **Gadarenes,** not **Gergesenes;** Gadara was the city he knew best. But Gadara is several miles away from the lake, and Gerasa or Jerash is still farther (though some of the best MSS of Mark read "Gerasenes"). Mark's original reading, like Luke's, is no doubt "Gergesenes"; and ruined towns named Kersa and Gerge are to be found on the eastern shore of the Sea of Galilee.

Matthew makes this a story of **two** men: either to take the place of the omitted Mark 1:23-26, or perhaps for no conscious reason at all. See 9:27; 20:30 for other examples of this editorial habit.

29. Some of the demons, it is assumed, will plague mankind until the day of judgment, when their power will be broken (Enoch 16:1; Test. Levi 18:12; Jubilees 10:8-9); Jesus is therefore acting **before the** expected **time.**

---

title **Son of God.** The story of the swine has become controversial ground. Gladstone defended the story against Huxley's contention that Jesus had wantonly destroyed an innocent man's property, and the vain contention has continued since that day.[6] One critic has even suggested (let us hope he had his tongue in his cheek) that the owner of the herd could have escaped loss by cutting up the drowned swine, salting some pieces, and making smoke-dried hams of others![7] (On all these items, and on how the swine story may have become attached to the story of the miracle, see Exeg.) There are some significant touches. The incident occurred in Gentile territory: there are no national or racial fences around the compassion of Christ. Furthermore, he showed pity on the insane, whom all feared and few pitied. **Before the time** is pathetic: it was believed in those days that a maniac was at death plunged into hell, and/or that humanity must be vexed by demons until Judgment Day. Our treatment of insanity leaves much room for improvement, but Christ's pity has left its mark on our asylums. The courage of Jesus is here evident:

maniacs fierce in nature and issuing from tombs did not dismay him. He is always sovereign Lord.

The issue of demonology is a striking item. There Christianity wrought a great deliverance, for until Christ drove out the demons from men's belief, the whole age lived under blight and threat. The space between earth and heaven was filled with demons who were ruled by "the prince of the power of the air" (Eph. 2:2; 6:12), and who might at any time enter life to bring sickness and evil. Demons had certain traits: they were unclean, they hated to be dispossessed when once they had made their home in a man (see Christ's parable of the empty house [12:43-45; Luke 11:24-26]), and they were almost invincible until their name was known. (See Mark's account on the name "Legion.") T. R. Glover in his *Jesus in the Experience of Men* has a chapter describing how a pall was lifted from the world when Christ drove out fear of the demons.[8]

This story is a parable as well as miracle. Today we might describe the sickness as delusionary insanity. That is a fit symbol for our soul sickness. We are divided against ourselves (our name is "Legion"); we are gloomy thereby as

[6] W. E. Gladstone, *Later Gleanings* (New York: Charles Scribner's Sons, 1897), pp. 248-49.

[7] *Expositor's Greek Testament,* I, 146.

[8] New York: George H. Doran Co., 1921, ch. i.

30 And there was a good way off from them a herd of many swine feeding.

31 So the devils besought him, saying, If thou cast us out, suffer us to go away into the herd of swine.

32 And he said unto them, Go. And when they were come out, they went into the herd of swine: and, behold, the whole herd of swine ran violently down a steep place into the sea, and perished in the waters.

33 And they that kept them fled, and went their ways into the city, and told every thing, and what was befallen to the possessed of the devils.

34 And, behold, the whole city came out to meet Jesus: and when they saw him, they besought *him* that he would depart out of their coasts.

before the time?" 30 Now a herd of many swine was feeding at some distance from them. 31 And the demons begged him, "If you cast us out, send us away into the herd of swine." 32 And he said to them, "Go." So they came out and went into the swine; and behold, the whole herd rushed down the steep bank into the sea, and perished in the waters. 33 The herdsmen fled, and going into the city they told everything, and what had happened to the demoniacs. 34 And behold, all the city came out to meet Jesus; and when they saw him, they begged him to leave their neighborhood.

---

31. A story in the Talmud tells of a similar request on the part of a demon.

32. The Jews believed that demons liked to dwell in unclean places, such as tombs, and—unlike Tam o' Shanter's Scottish devil—in bodies of water.

---

if living among tombs; we sadly identify ourselves with our lower nature, as these men identified themselves with the demon; and we are helpless until Christ comes as revelation of God to quicken our faith. His healing rends us: the lower life must go. But the issue is fulfillment and peace. Mark's account (5:18-19) says that when the healed man wished to follow Christ, the desire was denied; and that Christ told him to preach the good news to his family and friends. That instruction also has its application.

34. *The Unwanted Christ.*—**They begged him to leave their neighborhood.** Surely this is one of the most haunting phrases of the gospel story. They held Jesus in regard, perhaps in awe. The phrase **they besought him** implies respect. Certainly they used no violence. He had wrought a marvelous cure. Nevertheless, they wished to be rid of him. Why? Mostly from inertia and a poor self-content. His presence and power disrupted the customary round, and they did not wish to be disturbed. It is an old story. Sometimes we pretend that we wish, and sometimes we actually do wish, that Christ were once more with us in the flesh. But secretly we are aware that he would be both challenge and unrest. Sometimes we invite him; more often we beg him to leave our neighborhood.

Why is Christ unwanted? When he is near we are under sense of awe. We are convinced of God, and our life is no longer our own: it **takes** on vast horizons, and we are ill at ease in any neighborhood, even a neighborhood as wide as earth and mortal life. When Christ is near, we can no longer treat our neighbors as mere "customers" or "workmen" or "Negroes" or "enemies": they are our brothers because we are all children of one Father. Even a maniac has claims upon us: we can no longer consign him to hell and forget him. He has claim upon our pity, at cost. When Christ is near, our whole way of life is under challenge. If we may safely link the story of the swine with the act of healing, his presence had meant monetary loss. That happens in every age. When his eyes are upon us, we are compelled to rethink our whole way of livelihood—our trade practice, our advertising, our tariffs, our munitions making: he is a very disturbing and costly neighbor. When Christ is near, boundaries of race and nation are down, and we must surrender our dearest prejudices. The people in the story were Gentiles, and he was from the land of the Jews. We are more comfortable when we can keep our fences of nation and race. When Christ is near, we are obliged to ponder the whole future. Even the maniacs besought him not to **torment us before the time,** meaning perhaps "before death brings condemnation." Always he lays on men the sense of judgment. We feel safer in the dugout of our present world. Yet when we beg him to leave our neighborhood, we banish our salvation. He went (see 9:1). He can work no wonders where he is unwanted. Ever he returns, but we must open the door. The mysterious freedom of our will remains: he covets us as

9 And he entered into a ship, and passed over, and came into his own city.

2 And, behold, they brought to him a man sick of the palsy, lying on a bed: and Jesus seeing their faith said unto the sick of the palsy; Son, be of good cheer; thy sins be forgiven thee.

9 And getting into a boat he crossed over and came to his own city. 2 And behold, they brought to him a paralytic, lying on his bed; and when Jesus saw their faith he said to the paralytic, "Take heart,

3. Power to Forgive Sins, Now Available to Men (9:1-8)

Matthew uses this story as an example of the new powers of Christians. In Mark its function is slightly different; it is the first of a series of controversy stories, of which Matthew includes two in vss. 10-15. Most form critics assume that the original kernel is a simple story of how Jesus saw the faith of the men and said "Arise, take up your bed," etc. On this theory the controversy over forgiveness of sins was added to the tradition, perhaps before Mark received the narrative. Yet one can argue, with Fenner (*Krankheit im N.T.*, pp. 55-57), that the controversy is part of the original story, and that the man was healed of a functional paralysis.

9:1. His own city, i.e., Capernaum.

2. The man's **bed** was probably a rug or light pallet. Matthew omits the digging through the mud roof, which shows the Palestinian origin of the story. **Your sins are forgiven,** i.e., by God. Jewish speakers often use the impersonal passive form to avoid pronouncing the divine name.

friends, not as slaves. If we were wise, we would face the disruption. His coming then would be like the opening of a prison door, or like springtime upon winter fields. What of our age? Are we like that **whole city** that, **when they saw him, . . . begged him to leave their neighborhood?**

9:1-8. *The Cure of Paralysis.* — (See also Expos., vs. 2 and vss. 3-6.) This story may be a frame for the important dictum, **That you may know that the Son of man has authority on earth to forgive sins.** Yet this account (of the third miracle in Matthew's second series of three) has rich meaning in its own right. The paralysis, judging from the comment of Jesus, may have come from the man's transgression. Psychologically, therefore, a sense of hopelessness was probably added to his helplessness. He deserved the affliction, and it was fixed more firmly than the albatross about the neck of the ancient mariner.[9] Others could carry him, but they could not cure him. Yet they could bring him to Jesus; and, as events proved, their faith atoned for the lack of faith there may have been in him. The portrait of Jesus is here particularly detailed. We see his intuition. He needed no testimony about this man, but read the sufferer's history and unhappiness at a glance. He knew the cause of the sickness; he knew the secret despair. We see his appreciation of friendship: instantly he honored the neighborliness that went to such lengths. We see his kindness and contagious strength: **Take heart, my son.** The phrase might be translated, "Courage, child!"

[9] "The Rime of the Ancient Mariner," Part II, st. xiv.

The expositor might well trace this word through the Gospels and the epistles. It was a favorite word with Jesus, and the apostles learned it well from his lips. What resourceful and homespun kindliness: **My son!** What contagious strength: "**Courage**"!

Well roars the storm to those that hear
A deeper voice across the storm.[10]

We see his authority and power. Both the sickness and the sin were subject to him: "Who forgiveth all thine iniquities; who healeth all thy diseases" (Ps. 103:3). The man was so thoroughly healed that he not only walked, but carried his pallet. So the story brings tidings of hope. Men suffer from inward paralysis. There seems to be no escape. But no failure need be doom; no paralysis is beyond Christ's power. It faith is lacking in the victim, the vicarious faith of others may still avail to draw the healing of Christ. To that issue we now turn.

2. *Vicarious Faith.* — **Jesus seeing their faith saith unto the sick** man. It has been made clear in all these miracle stories that faith in man opens the door to the power of Christ. His authority working through human faith—that is the recurring motif. But in this story the factor of faith takes a new form: **seeing their faith.** Perhaps the man had very little faith of his own account. The vicarious faith of his neighbors provided Christ with the necessary opening. Faith for others is often seen in the Gospels. The Capernaum centurion believed in

[10] Tennyson, *In Memoriam, op. cit.,* CXXVII, st. i.

3 And, behold, certain of the scribes said within themselves, This *man* blasphemeth.

4 And Jesus knowing their thoughts said, Wherefore think ye evil in your hearts?

5 For whether is easier, to say, *Thy* sins be forgiven thee; or to say, Arise, and walk?

my son; your sins are forgiven." 3 And behold, some of the scribes said to themselves, "This man is blaspheming." 4 But Jesus, knowing[t] their thoughts, said, "Why do you think evil in your hearts? 5 For which is easier, to say, 'Your sins are for-

[t] Many ancient authorities read *seeing*.

---

3. Since sickness was due to sin, healing was made possible by repentance and forgiveness. Jesus does not insist on an expression of repentance, and the **scribes** may have thought that he did not regard sin seriously enough. Yet the blasphemy is not this; it is rather that Jesus presumes to pronounce the forgiveness of sins. The scribes of course believed that God was gracious and unfailingly forgave the repentant; but it was presumptuous for a human being to announce that this had actually taken place in any concrete instance. No rabbi would utter such a "declaration of absolution," and not even Messiah had this prerogative. Jesus could not be charged with blasphemy in the strict rabbinical sense, which is cursing God in the name of God. The word is apparently used more loosely here.

5. The argument is that if Jesus can free the man from his ailment, God must have forgiven him; therefore Jesus is justified in declaring the forgiveness. The word **easier** is perhaps used because the scribes would think: "It is an easy thing to say he is forgiven, because no one can really tell."

Christ's power on behalf of his servant (8:5-13), and the ruler believed on behalf of his daughter (9:18 ff.). We see this believing compassion at work in our own world. It is a prime mark of love. Every man has known those who trusted for him when he himself could not trust; e.g., Baron von Hügel and his niece.[1] Every evangelist, whether for some physical healing or for the saviorhood of Christ, shows this vicariousness. **They brought to him:** it was an anonymous ministry. The word **they** recurs in the N.T. We are blessed by unknown hands and unknown faith. Jesus liked these neighbors the more for their willingness to be unknown, for he himself was like that fabled Greek goddess whom no one saw: people were aware of her only because a stream flowed where yesterday there was but a stagnant pool, and a tree blossomed where yesterday there was only a lightning-blasted stump.[2] The marks of this vicariousness are plain to tell. It is a symbol of the true bond that binds man with man. It carries contagion through the neighborly life, both by word and by radiance. It finds issue in deeds, as resolute as the moving of a roof. It is fed by prayer, as consecrated as that of the contemplative orders whose members are dedicated for life to an apostolate of intercession.[3] Here is a

prime task of the church. The world does not believe in Christ. It believes in itself, even though that latter "faith" is put to shame. Therefore mankind becomes hopeless: despair is a first fruit of transgression. So the church must believe in Christ for the world's sake, and in that faith must thus believe in the world. Only so can the church keep her own life; only so can she be God's instrument to save the world.

3-6. *Blasphemy and Forgiveness.*—**The Son of man has authority on earth to forgive sins.** Form criticism has taught us that this saying may be the pronouncement for which the story provides a framework. The scribes believed that only God can forgive sins. They were right. Sin is against God. Even when, according to our sight, it injures only the sinner or some neighbor, it is still sin against the Creator and his handiwork. The proper picture of sin is the rebellious baron aiming his spear against the sky. For that reason only God can forgive, and for a further reason: only God has power over the inexorable past to turn it to the gain of the unknown future, and only he can mend his creation. So the scribes shrank even from the pronouncement of forgiveness. But Jesus did not shrink: he claimed to know when forgiveness was effective, and he became its channel. Therefore the scribes charged him with blasphemy: he had assumed authority that belonged to God alone (Mark 2:7). Nor could they be blamed, unless there is in Jesus the aloneness of the eternal Word. Thus the whole question of the nature of Christ is here raised.

[1] *Letters from Baron Friedrich von Hügel to a Niece,* ed. Gwendolen Greene (London: J. M. Dent & Sons, 1929).

[2] Quoted, *Great Texts of the Bible,* ed. James Hastings, vol. *Job to Psalm XXIII,* p. 309.

[3] E. Herman, *Creative Prayer* (New York: George H. Doran & Co., 1921), pp. 15 ff.

6 But that ye may know that the Son of man hath power on earth to forgive sins, (then saith he to the sick of the palsy,) Arise, take up thy bed, and go unto thine house.

7 And he arose, and departed to his house.

8 But when the multitudes saw *it*, they marveled, and glorified God, which had given such power unto men.

9 ¶ And as Jesus passed forth from thence, he saw a man, named Matthew, sit-

given,' or to say, 'Rise and walk'? **6** But that you may know that the Son of man has authority on earth to forgive sins" — he then said to the paralytic — "Rise, take up your bed and go home." **7** And he rose and went home. **8** When the crowds saw it, they were afraid, and they glorified God, who had given such authority to men.

9 As Jesus passed on from there, he saw

---

6. Mark (and perhaps Matthew) understood **Son of man** to mean the Messiah. If this is an exact quotation of Jesus' words, he may have meant that humans have the right to make this declaration. Certainly Matthew believes that, through this incident and saying, Jesus reveals that the Christian congregation now has this power (vs. 8). See on 18:15-20. The right to forgive or to withhold forgiveness was claimed by Paul (I Cor. 5:5; II Cor. 2:10) and the church for which the Fourth Evangelist wrote (John 20:23). Many Roman Catholic and Protestant service books contain forms of absolution; this is not characteristic of Jewish worship.

D. The Difference Between Jesus' Disciples and Others (9:9-17)

By a happy coincidence, these sections, which follow at this point in Mark, are useful for Matthew's purposes, for they include the typical calling of a disciple and teachings on discipleship.

1. Calling of a Tax Collector (9:9)

9. Another story of the calling of disciples is found in 4:18-22. Mark 2:14 and Luke 5:27 give the name as "Levi." **Matthew** may have been substituted here by a very early

---

The answer of Christ first meets their doubt of his ability. **Which is easier?**: anyone could say, "Thy sins be forgiven," and no one could clearly prove or disprove the effectiveness of the absolution. But if a man should say, "Rise up and walk," the issue either vindicated him or put him to shame. So Jesus first healed the man. That victory answered also the charge of authority: the man's sickness was the bitter fruit of his sin, and the power to heal was the sign of God's authority resting on Christ. That word **easier** has depths on depths, as has the phrase **on earth**. It is not easy to forgive. Forgiveness is much more than laying aside claim to requital or revenge: it is love bearing the pain and shame with strong will to redeem. In the play *The Green Pastures* a voice off stage says of Christ bearing his Cross that it is "a terrible burden for one man to carry!" [4] There is in this story more than a hint that Jesus here delegates power to forgive. Part of the hint may be in the title **Son of man**: Jesus acted as man, not only as God's incarnate Son. The other part

of the hint is in vs. 8: "had given such power unto men." Paul claimed the power (see II Cor. 2:10). But the claim was never exercised in the early church except in the name of Christ. There is the striking fact: as the scribes pronounced forgiveness in the name of God, the church pronounced it in the name of Christ; and the church, together with the common man (see vs. 8), rejoiced that God had thus visited his people **on earth** with such redemption.

9. *Matthew the Taxgatherer.*—Matthew is hardly more than a name. Consult Intro. and Exeg. for the difficulties raised by Mark's apparent identification of Matthew with Levi, the son of Alphaeus. But that Christ called toll-gatherers to his discipleship there is no doubt. Therefore the story has rich meanings, despite the obscurity which surrounds the identity of Matthew. The scene is not hard to reconstruct. The toll office was possibly at Capernaum or on the caravan route, just north of the Sea of Galilee, from Damascus to the Mediterranean. Prominent Romans bought the right to collect taxes in a given area, and then engaged local men (such as Matthew) to do the work. Matthew may have been an agent of Herod Antipas.

[4] Marcus Cook Connelly, Part II, scene 8. See *Twenty Best Plays of the Modern American Theatre*, edited by John Gassner.

| ting at the receipt of custom: and he saith unto him, Follow me. And he arose, and followed him. | a man called Matthew sitting at the tax office; and he said to him, "Follow me." And he rose and followed him. |

copyist (see Intro., p. 242). **Tax office** (RSV) or "tollhouse" (Goodspeed) is clearer than **receipt of custom** (KJV). From Matthew or Mark we might suppose that this was at Capernaum, which was near the border of Galilee, but other places in the neighborhood would be equally possible locations.

The Greek word here used seems to imply that the taxes were on exports, such products as salt and fish. Jesus probably had often seen Matthew in Capernaum, and had shown friendship. Matthew was an unlikely man for discipleship. As tollgatherer he was despised by the Jews, both because of his unpatriotic conduct and because his trade easily lent itself to graft and extortion. A tollgatherer's money was not accepted as alms; his evidence was not accepted in the law court; he was an outcast. John Masefield, working as "mistake-finder" in a carpet mill, bought a copy of Chaucer, then of Keats, read long and late, and "knew then that . . . my law was to follow poetry, even if I died of it." [5] Jesus saw a child of God and a herald of the kingdom in the unlikely man—before the man himself awoke to his destiny. Jesus woke him by sharp challenge. The call was sudden, however long the friendship. Charles Kingsley once wrote, "I have been for the last hour on the sea-shore. . . . Before the sleeping earth and the sleepless sea and stars I have devoted myself to God; a vow never (if He gives me the faith I pray for) to be recalled." [6] Jesus required just such a renunciation. Matthew's way of life was not condoned, but Matthew was not ostracized. Rather, Jesus trusted him: **Follow me.** Matthew followed. He followed for need's sake: he longed for the cleansing and the venture which Jesus could give. He followed for love's sake: here was One to whom his whole soul could be given. He was blessed, and the history of man was blessed through him: his sword of extortion was reforged into a plowshare of the evangel.

9. Follow Me.—Rightly these words have been used again and again as a simple summary of Christian discipleship. The command implies that Christianity is a personal loyalty, as shown in Whittier's lines:

> Our Friend, our Brother, and our Lord,
>   What may thy service be?—
> Nor name, nor form, nor ritual word,
>   But simply following thee. [7]

Ritual is necessary, but only as support and expression of a personal love. Theology is inevitable, but only as an attempt required by our mind to set forth in due order the implications of the Christ to whom we are committed. We live by faith, and faith is in essence personal trust.

This loyalty fulfills our soul's need. We are not intended to walk alone: our wisdom is both short and blind. Carlyle asserted rightly that not all the "Finance Ministers and Upholsterers and Confectioners of modern Europe . . . , in joint stock company," can "make one shoeblack happy." [8] We need a Redeemer, lest our sins should cripple us by inward chaos and outward strife. We need a Guide, for the way is hard and hidden. We need a Captain, for our nature cries out for the dangerous quest and for the bread of courage. We need One to worship, for we find life only in an ultimate homage. **Follow me!**

The command is an implied promise. It means surely, "I will not mislead you, and I will not fail you either in monotony or crisis." Other leaders must perforce say, "Follow this rule," or "Obey my ethic." Every other leader fails within himself, and fails also to provide the cleansing and power by which his commands can be obeyed. Only Christ is above our lies and hankering, our bloodletting and our blundering. The church may fail in its obedience, but the Leader meets all the tests. Sir Ernest Shackleton, pressing on with two companions through the well-nigh impenetrable mountains of the antarctic wilderness, felt that "a fourth comrade" was with them, but said nothing. Afterwards Worsley, one of the other two, said, "Boss, I had a curious feeling on the march that there was another person with us." [9] This is life's real decision. It is basic, and undergirds all other choices such as that of vocation or of a life partner. Any worthy man, when challenged, would admit that he must live for "kindness," or "truth." He could enumerate thus a list of principles. But principles are but misty guidance until they take face and form. Only then can they enlist our love and life. **Follow me!**

[5] *In the Mill* (New York: The Macmillan Co., 1941), pp. 94-97.
[6] *Charles Kingsley, His Letters and Memories of His Life,* ed. by his wife (New York: Scribner, Armstrong & Co., 1877), p. 49.
[7] "Our Master."

[8] *Sartor Resartus,* Bk. II, ch. ix.
[9] Ernest Henry Shackleton, *South* (London: William Heinemann, 1919), p. 209.

10 ¶ And it came to pass, as Jesus sat at meat in the house, behold, many publicans and sinners came and sat down with him and his disciples.	10 And as he sat at table*u* in the house, behold, many tax collectors and sinners came and sat down with Jesus and his disciples. 11 And when the Pharisees saw this, they said to his disciples, "Why does your teacher eat with tax collectors and sinners?" 12 But when he heard it, he said, "Those who are well have no need of a
11 And when the Pharisees saw *it,* they said unto his disciples, Why eateth your master with publicans and sinners?	
12 But when Jesus heard *that,* he said unto them, They that be whole need not a physician, but they that are sick.	*u* Greek *reclined.*

2. Jesus Associates with Sinners (9:10-13)

This is another "controversy story" or "paradigm," the point of which is contained in the saying of vs. 12.

10. Sat at table, literally "reclined," for this was the Greco-Roman custom, followed also at formal Jewish banquets; but it is not necessary to suppose that this was always true of Jewish meals, especially in Galilee. Mark says "in his house," presumably Jesus' home in Capernaum. This fits with **I came not to call** or "invite" in vs. 13. **Many tax collectors and sinners:** Cf. on 5:46. The **sinners** may include those who were careless about the minutiae of the law and also those guilty of serious moral lapses.

11. The Mishnah taught the duty of hospitality, "Let your house be open wide and let the poor be members of your household" (Aboth 1:5) ; but the rabbis had in mind hospitality to the pious poor, and taught, "Keep far from an evil neighbor and do not associate with the wicked" (Aboth 1:7). At one time Peter adhered to the Pharisaic principle of exclusiveness and separated himself from the Gentiles (Gal. 2:11-12) ; on another occasion he laid himself open to criticism by eating with them (Acts 11:3).

12. The famous Cynic Diogenes said, "Neither does a physician who is capable of giving health practice his profession among those who are well" (Stobaeus *Florilegium* III. 462. 14). C. G. Montefiore (*The Synoptic Gospels* [2nd ed.: London: Macmillan & Co., 1927], I, 55) points out that the rabbis would not have criticized Jesus merely because he cared for the outcast, the poor, and the sinner. "They too welcomed the *repentant* sinner." What is new is that Jesus *sought out* the sinner. "To deny the greatness and originality of Jesus in this connection, to deny that he opened a new chapter in men's attitude toward sin and sinners, is, I think, to beat the head against the wall." This principle of Jesus is set forth in 18:12-14; Luke 15:3-6, 8-9.

10-13. *Christ Feasting with Sinners.*—Beyond much doubt the words of Jesus interpreting this scene are the important item. The call of Matthew is related because it provides the setting and occasion. The scene is dramatic and easy to imagine. A dinner, possibly in an expansive courtyard; tollgatherers, their cronies, and others who neglected the religious law are the guests. Jesus is chief guest, with his disciples. To many it was a scandalous affair; and the Pharisees, entering the courtyard, as the custom of the time allowed, lifted shocked hands. They asked the disciples, "**Why does your teacher eat with tax collectors and sinners?**" The reason was made clear by Jesus himself. It was a bold act, not calculated to win him public favor (see Exeg.) Today most Christians would probably say that a comparable act "would be impolitic." Why this program? Love dictated it: **Those who are well have no need of a physician,** but those who are sick. Jesus had the cure for the malady of wickedness. So he went where sin was most evident, for he dared not refuse the healing gift. Besides, he was convinced that ostracism was both wrong and foolish. To treat a man as a pariah would not cure him of his perversity, but rather tend to confirm him in it. How do our moral quarantines and our penal systems stand by Christ's tests? Who in our society corresponds to these **sinners?** Besides, God required that he live with sinners, for God had said to Hosea of old: "I desired mercy, and not sacrifice" (Hos. 6:6). Ritual as sign of a worshiping heart is acceptable to God, but ritual as a substitute for compassion is an offense. These reasons Jesus gave. If the church today does not honor them, the church is convicted by its Lord.

So we see the Savior in the midst of sinners. Some of the sinners were plainly unrighteous;

13 But go ye and learn what *that* meaneth, I will have mercy, and not sacrifice: for I am not come to call the righteous, but sinners to repentance.

14 ¶ Then came to him the disciples of John, saying, Why do we and the Pharisees fast oft, but thy disciples fast not?

15 And Jesus said unto them, Can the children of the bridechamber mourn, as long as the bridegroom is with them? but the days will come, when the bridegroom shall be taken from them, and then shall they fast.

physician, but those who are sick. 13 Go and learn what this means, 'I desire mercy, and not sacrifice.' For I came not to call the righteous, but sinners."

14 Then the disciples of John came to him, saying, "Why do we and the Pharisees fast,[v] but your disciples do not fast?"

15 And Jesus said to them, "Can the wedding guests mourn as long as the bridegroom is with them? The days will come, when the bridegroom is taken away from

[v] Many ancient authorities add *much* or *often*.

---

13. The quotation from Hos. 6:6 does not fit well here, though it expresses a principle which Jesus followed. The remainder of the verse, together with vs. 12b, probably constitutes a poetic couplet. Jesus no doubt calls his hearers to the kingdom of God, as the householder does in the parable of the great banquet (Luke 14:21). **To repentance is** not found in most of the best MSS.

3. His Disciples Do Not Fast (9:14-15)

14. Fasting was obligatory only on the day of Atonement—Yom Kippur—and publicly proclaimed fast days. The reference is to private, voluntary fasting, which was not characteristic of Jesus' followers.

15. **Wedding guests** (RSV) is the proper explanation of the Semitic "sons of the bridechamber." The **bridegroom** is not necessarily Jesus. He reminds his hearers that no one fasts as long as a marriage feast is going on; at such a time the guests were dispensed from certain religious duties, and even rabbis were expected to forsake the study of the law. But this is not all. Jewish teaching often described the "days of the Messiah" with the figure of a wedding feast; and Jesus and his disciples in their life together already enjoy a foretaste of that messianic bliss. Fasting is not appropriate if the kingdom is being manifested in Jesus' mighty deeds. The second half of the verse, which does identify Jesus with the bridegroom, belongs to a later stage of the tradition and is used to justify the later Christian custom of fasting.

---

they broke the law of the synagogue, were guilty of graft and extortion, and Jesus did not condone them. Some of the sinners were **righteous,** namely, those who at that moment criticized Christ for seeking the company of unrepentant sinners. There is immense irony in the phrases **those who are well** and **the righteous.** In truth Christ's call to the **righteous** must be in vain until they know their unrighteousness. Pride and lovelessness are perchance a greater affront than the extortion of the tollgatherers. "The tax collectors and the harlots go into the kingdom of God before you" (21:31), Christ afterward told them. Christ would have given health and home to the **righteous** sinners, as well as to the unrighteous, had they come in felt need.

14-15. *The Joy of the Christian Faith.*—Who asked the question about fasting? The Gospels appear to disagree: Matthew says John the Baptist's followers, Mark says they and the Pharisees, Luke says "they"—the anonymous

inquirers pointing to the example of John's followers and the Pharisees. Probably many people asked many times. (On fasting see Expos., 6:16-18.) The Pharisees multiplied fasts; John's followers, an important group in the first days of the faith, were presumably fasting both because of their leader's teaching and because of his arrest and imprisonment. Jesus and his followers seem to have kept few fasts, and were thus at sharp variance with the contemporary religious practice. The answer of Christ was in true sense diplomatic: he honored John, and would not hurt John's cause. He honored the best in Judaism, from which his own soul had been fed. John has already called Jesus the bridegroom, if we may assign John 3:29 to an earlier date than this incident. Jesus used the word to avoid cleavage between his followers on the one hand, and the followers of John and the best elements in Judaism on the other.

16 No man putteth a piece of new cloth unto an old garment; for that which is put in to fill it up taketh from the garment, and the rent is made worse.

17 Neither do men put new wine into old bottles: else the bottles break, and the wine runneth out, and the bottles perish: but they put new wine into new bottles, and both are preserved.

them, and then they will fast. 16 And no one puts a piece of unshrunk cloth on an old garment, for the patch tears away from the garment, and a worse tear is made. 17 Neither is new wine put into old wineskins; if it is, the skins burst, and the wine is spilled, and the skins are destroyed; but new wine is put into fresh wineskins, and so both are preserved."

4. THE OLD AND THE NEW CANNOT BE COMBINED (9:16-17)

These sayings were not originally connected with those in vs. 15, but they fit better with the first half of that verse than with the second. Their interpretation depends entirely on their application; by themselves they teach only the danger of the new. If you want to preserve **old wineskins** do not put **new wine** in! Jesus may have used these proverbs to convey that his teaching could not and need not be reconciled with that of the conservatives, or that the dawning kingdom of God bursts the framework of the old order (11:12-13=Luke 16:16). The metaphors of wine and the new mantle are often used to refer to the new world which God will create (Heb. 1:10-12; Acts 10:11; 11:5).

16-17. The **unshrunk cloth** will shrink the next time the garment is washed, thus putting a disastrous strain on the old fibers. No one would bottle new wine while it was in its first fermentation; but even after the bottling some fermentation is bound to occur, and only elastic new skins can stand the pressure.

Is joy a lost note in our Christian faith? Jesus is **the bridegroom** (though vs. 15 does not necessarily state that fact), his disciples are friends of the bridegroom, and their companionship is like the gladness of a wedding feast! Why not? God is Father, not a taskmaster to be satisfied with many fasts. God intends his children to know the gladness of abundant life. Sins are pardoned for all who come to God trustingly, and with resolve to live by the trust. Life's pilgrimage is in the comradeship of an unseen Friend, and death is a door into fuller joy. Undoubtedly the great appeal of early Christianity was its joy, even amidst persecutions, in a world sated by its pleasures and saddened by its fears. The proper language of Christianity is praise. How does a modern church congregation fare by that test? Christianity is not always clear shining: **then shall they fast.** Perhaps this is a hidden reference to the days when Christians in the time of Matthew were suffering as grievously as John the Baptist. The evil sadness of the world does what it can to darken the gladness of Christian faith. In any event, as well as for that reason,

> Man was made for joy and woe;
> And when this we rightly know,
> Thro' the world we safely go.[10]

If the dark day turns us to the secret resources waiting those who trust God, gladness is renewed, and the fast brings in its turn a deeper joy.

16-17. *Old Forms and New Faith.*—The question of fasting is now enlarged into the question of the relationship between the new faith of Christ and the old Judaism, the latter being represented at its best by John the Baptist and at its worst by a narrow Pharisaism. There was real danger of schism, not only between the followers of Christ and the followers of John, but also within Christ's new order of discipleship. The deep wisdom of Christ is here manifest. The parable of the patch of undressed cloth on an old robe is perhaps partly a deference to Judaism. The **patch** is new, uncarded and uncombed: it would shrink and so tear the old robe. There is a lot of comfort in old clothes. They fit. It is foolish to destroy them before their time. Yet they wear out, and someday must be thrown away: "Time makes ancient good uncouth."[1] Besides, Christianity is not a patch: it is a new robe altogether. The parable of the new wine is a striking statement of the revolutionary character, the creative fermentation, of the new faith. If unwise people try to keep it within Judaism, like **new wine** in **old wineskins,** both the wineskin (Judaism) will be broken and the new wine (the new order of the kingdom) will be spilled. Thus both will be destroyed in the attempted compromise. The whole question of the new and the old is thus raised and met. The joy of the kingdom does

[10] William Blake, "Auguries of Innocence."

[1] James Russell Lowell, "The Present Crisis."

| 18 ¶ While he spake these things unto them, behold, there came a certain ruler, and worshipped him, saying, My daughter is even now dead: but come and lay thy hand upon her, and she shall live.

19 And Jesus arose, and followed him, and *so did* his disciples. | 18 While he was thus speaking to them, behold, a ruler came in and knelt before him, saying, "My daughter has just died; but come and lay your hand on her, and she will live." 19 And Jesus rose and fol- |

E. Other Miracles (9:18-34)

The first two stories emphasize the absolute necessity of faith. Note how Matthew has changed Mark's wording in vs. 18 (=Mark 5:23) and vs. 28 (=Mark 10:47-52). The note of faith was present in Mark's corresponding stories, with the exception of Mark 8:22-26. If the narratives are detached from their context, Dibelius may appear to be right when he says the "faith" is no more than confidence in Jesus' power to heal. But Jesus did more than heal. He always called men back to the one God. His presence and teaching must have awakened religious faith in those to whom he ministered so that they actually put their trust in God, whose power flowed through him.

1. Power over Chronic Illness and Death (9:18-26)

It has often been suggested that Mark, or some earlier narrator, has combined the two miracle stories artistically so as to indicate the passage of some time between the coming of the synagogue official and Jesus' entrance into the house; but it is not difficult to assume that the incidents occurred just as Mark tells them. The narrative of the ruler's daughter may be compared with the stories told about Elijah (I Kings 17:17-24), Elisha (II Kings 4:17-37), and Peter (Acts 9:36-42); and there are also Jewish and pagan parallels.

18. The word rendered **ruler** is *archōn,* which in Greek is applied to various kinds of officials. Here it may mean the same as Mark's "ruler of the synagogue," perhaps the *rō'sh-hakkeneṣeth,* who was no doubt chosen by the elders from among their number to

not go well with fasting. There must be congruity between faith and form. The new faith must make its own new forms. This requirement, we might add, rests on every age. Christianity does not change in content: the gift of God in Christ is given once for all. But its forms must change. The seed must ever be newly sown, and ever newly harvested; but the gospel is the same "yesterday and today and forever" (Heb. 13:8).

18, 19, 23-26. *Jesus in the Home of Jairus.*—(See Expos., vss. 20-22.) Mark's Gospel and Luke's both tell us that the ruler's name was Jairus. He was probably a man of character, or he would not have been chosen ruler of the synagogue. The story shows that he was perhaps a man of wealth. The synagogue authorities were dubious about Jesus. So Jairus' coming was a mark of confidence. How should we interpret the miracle? Many scholars say that Jesus here raised the dead, and they have evidence, e.g., the words **they laughed him to scorn.** Others, equally consecrate to the saviorhood of Christ, believe that we must take his words at their face value: **The girl is not dead but sleeping.** The account in Matthew obviously intends the reader to believe that the girl

was dead. Mark 5:23 says that the girl was not yet dead. The medicine of that day knew cases of suspended animation. Long before Christ, the Greek physician-god Asclepius is said to have saved one such man from burial;[2] perhaps Jesus in this instance effected such a rescue. Clearly no one can dogmatize. In any event the girl later died, and there are meanings in the story whichever interpretation we may accept.

Here is a new occasion of Christ's power-in-love. His touch was a quickening touch in heartbreaking tenderness: "Little girl, get up!" (Mark 5:41). That was probably just what her mother had said to her morning by morning. Thus the ridicule of the crowd (ridicule is an earthy weapon: "Mockery is the fume of little hearts"[3]) was put to shame. Instantly Christ obeyed the call of human need; instantly he met the need; and the motive was all love. Most expositors have missed the significance of Christ's attitude to the trappings of funeral services. The flute players and the wailers were

[2] See George Grote, *A History of Greece* (London: John Murray, 1846), I, 246-51; Charles M. Gayley, *The Classic Myths,* pp. 38, 104, 260.
[3] Tennyson, *Idylls of the King,* "Guinevere," 1. 628.

20 ¶ And, behold, a woman, which was diseased with an issue of blood twelve years, came behind *him,* and touched the hem of his garment:

21 For she said within herself, If I may but touch his garment, I shall be whole.

22 But Jesus turned him about, and when he saw her, he said, Daughter, be of good comfort; thy faith hath made thee whole. And the woman was made whole from that hour.

23 And when Jesus came into the ruler's house, and saw the minstrels and the people making a noise,

lowed him, with his disciples. 20 And behold, a woman who had suffered from a hemorrhage for twelve years came up behind him and touched the fringe of his garment; 21 for she said to herself, "If I only touch his garment, I shall be made well." 22 Jesus turned, and seeing her he said, "Take heart, daughter; your faith has made you well." And instantly the woman was made well. 23 And when Jesus came to the ruler's house, and saw the flute players, and the crowd making a tumult,

---

preside over the services and business of the synagogue; but *archōn* may simply mean the head of the local community or one of the elders. Luke uses the word frequently. **My daughter has just died:** In Mark 5:23 the father says, "My little daughter is at the point of death." Here the father manifests very great faith, since no raising of the dead has previously been reported in this Gospel.

20. A woman who had suffered from a hemorrhage would be unclean, and perhaps this is why she **came up behind him.** Her condition could have had a psychological basis. She may have **touched the hem** (KJV), seam, or corner of his outer garment, or **the fringe** (RSV), probably the tassel or *çîçîth* which every Jew wore (Num. 15:38-41; Deut. 22:12).

22. Her **faith** is praised, but it is not necessary to suppose that Jesus means, "Faith, rather than touching me, has healed you." The evangelists probably assume that God's healing power was always present in Jesus (Luke 8:46); but it is made available only when faith is present. Certainly the Gospels never despise physical means such as touching.

23. For a funeral "even the poorest in Israel should hire not less than two flutes and one wailing woman" (Ketuboth 4:4).

---

reckoned necessary; they were part of the "custom." Mark's version tells us that he dismissed the crowd. It is perhaps a fair assumption that their curiosity, their hope to share in the feasting that marked a funeral, the morbidity, and the professional mourners were all distasteful to him—not alone because of the insincerities involved, but because they were all alien from the joy of the kingdom. (But see Exeg.) God is our Father, and for those who trust God death is the "shade of His hand, outstretched caressingly." [4] Not strangely the followers of Jesus believed that he had power over death: life was in him.

20-22. *The Hem of His Garment: Faith and Great Deliverance.*—It has been written that those who met Jesus are like ships sailing from darkness into the track of his light, and then back into darkness. The saying is only partly true: they do not go back into darkness. They are transfixed on history; and in some way, rich or poor, they share his immortality. This woman is such a one: the episode is of the stuff of drama. Her weary-long ailment, her uncleanness in the eyes of the religious law, her hopes in

doctors often raised and as often dashed, and now her resolve to steal the blessing of Christ— the story is indelibly etched. She would touch the holy tassel on his robe, and instantly be healed—and who need know? Psychology could describe, though not explain, the cure. The "power of autosuggestion" and "the tenseness of the plot," and "the crowd-emotion" would be the phrases, all of them probably true enough, yet touching only the mystery's edge.

Her faith may have been spiritually poor. Perhaps it was hardly higher than a belief in magic that saw in the tassel of his robe a holy charm. Maybe she had only a dim understanding of his spirit. But Jesus honored the faith, even though she beheld him afar off. Henry Martyn, the missionary, saw an old crone kissing the feet of a stone image, and wondered if his more intellectual faith had as much to commend it. Beyond doubt Christ wishes us to believe great things of God, and to expect great things from God; that trust, however poor in form, counts more with him than the intellectual pride that easily robs life of holy wonder.

Once more we see the compassion of Christ. He was not "too busy," despite the crowd. He

[4] Francis Thompson, "The Hound of Heaven."

24 He said unto them, Give place: for the maid is not dead, but sleepeth. And they laughed him to scorn.

25 But when the people were put forth, he went in, and took her by the hand, and the maid arose.

26 And the fame hereof went abroad into all that land.

27 ¶ And when Jesus departed thence, two blind men followed him, crying, and saying, *Thou* Son of David, have mercy on us.

28 And when he was come into the house, the blind men came to him: and Jesus saith unto them, Believe ye that I am able to do this? They said unto him, Yea, Lord.

24 he said, "Depart; for the girl is not dead but sleeping." And they laughed at him. 25 But when the crowd had been put outside, he went in and took her by the hand, and the girl arose. 26 And the report of this went through all that district.

27 And as Jesus passed on from there, two blind men followed him, crying aloud, "Have mercy on us, Son of David." 28 When he entered the house, the blind men came to him; and Jesus said to them, "Do you believe that I am able to do this?"

---

24. Sleep is a common euphemism for death among Jews as well as Christians, but here the thought is that this death is only temporary. The same play on the idea is found in John 11:11-15.

25. The crowd are put outside as in the stories of Elijah, Elisha, and Peter and Tabitha. Similar procedure in pagan parallels is usually taken to mean that unbelievers must not be allowed to see the miracle. The rabbis held that raising the dead was God's prerogative, and that it could take place through the instrumentality of righteous men. To all appearance the girl was dead; on the other hand, medicine knows of cataleptic states which can be mistaken for death. Since we have no way of investigating the event, we shall do well to avoid overconfident theorizing.

2. POWER OVER BLINDNESS (9:27-31)

See the general note on 8:1–9:34, above. The mention of **two blind men** makes the plural in the Greek of 11:5 more appropriate.

27. The **blind men** appeal to him as Son of David, as in 20:30 (=Mark 10:47). This is one of the regular titles of the Messiah (e.g., Pss. Sol. 17:23[21]), and Jesus is so addressed because of the belief that the Messiah could work miracles (John 7:31).

28. As in 15:23, Jesus gives no answer at first. Then he insists that they must believe in his power; this emphasizes the teaching of vss. 18 and 22.

---

was on his way to the house of Jairus, the story tells us, yet he paused in love. Mark Guy Pearse has said splendidly that this woman began as Nobody, became Somebody ("Somebody hath touched me"), and in the mercy of Christ ended as Everybody;[5] for Jesus dealt with her as if she were the only one. He deals so with each of us, and deals with all of us as if we were all one. "Courage, daughter!" That word courage is thus almost a refrain in this chapter. However poor our faith, and however poor our contact with Christ, he honors our first movement toward him. Thus the words "Who touched my garments?" (Mark 5:30) opened the way for the woman's confession. So he leads our faith on and out—from desire for healing to a longing

for purity of heart, from the tassel of his robe to the claims and joys of his eternal kingdom.

27-31. The Healing of the Blind.— (See Exeg. for an account of Matthew's use here of Mark, and also regarding the connection with 20:29-34.) Presumably the Gospelist wishes to direct attention mainly to the words which the story enshrines. Blindness is a vivid parable. "The Blind Ploughman" acknowledged the mystifying providence of

> God, who took away my eyes,
> That my *soul* might see![6]

Physical blindness was common in Palestine. It is a grievous fetter: the eagerness with which people hurry to help a blind man is eloquent

---

[5] *The Gentleness of Jesus* (New York: Thomas Y. Crowell & Co., 1898), ch. v.

[6] Marguerite Radclyffe-Hall, *Songs of Three Counties and Other Poems* (London: Chapman and Hall, 1913).

29 Then touched he their eyes, saying, According to your faith be it unto you.

30 And their eyes were opened; and Jesus straitly charged them, saying, See *that* no man know *it*.

31 But they, when they were departed, spread abroad his fame in all that country.

32 ¶ As they went out, behold, they brought to him a dumb man possessed with a devil.

They said to him, "Yes, Lord." 29 Then he touched their eyes, saying, "According to your faith be it done to you." 30 And their eyes were opened. And Jesus sternly charged them, "See that no one knows it." 31 But they went away and spread his fame through all that district.

32 As they were going away, behold, a dumb demoniac was brought to him.

30-31. See that no one knows it is a stern command drawn from Mark 1:43-44. Mark believed that Jesus wished to keep secret not only the healings and the truth about his messiahship, but also the significance of his parables. Such an extreme theory cannot be correct; but it is possible that Jesus did not wish to be known as a miracle worker. This kind of **fame** would attract many curious people who cared nothing about his message.

3. Power over Dumbness (9:32-33 [34?])

This incident seems to be drawn from Q. It corresponds to Luke 11:14 more closely than does the doublet Matt. 12:22. There are also contacts with the story of the deaf man with a speech impediment in Mark 7:32-37. Blindness, deafness, and dumbness due to psychological causes (usually hysteria) are well known to medicine (Fenner, *Krankheit im N.T.*, pp. 70, 72-73).

32. The word translated **dumb** (κωφός) can also mean "deaf," as in 11:5=Luke 7:22; Mark 7:32. The corresponding Hebrew word is used in rabbinical writings to refer to deaf-mutes. Here the context gives the sense.

---

testimony to that fact. But what of inner blindness? It is a far more pitiable handicap. We are blind to the meaning of life, blind to the deepest nature of our neighbors, blind to the ongoings of God in our world:

Here, thro' the feeble twilight of this world
Groping . . .[7]

The blind men in this story thus offer the universal prayer: **Have mercy on us.**

The requirement of faith is never more clearly written. Jesus asked pointedly, **Do you believe that I am able to do this?** A surgeon would not thus address a patient. If the patient should say, "I have no confidence in you," he might be referred to another surgeon; but in the realm of merely physical cure faith does not seem to be the prime essential. It is essential in the dealings of Christ with men. Jesus rested salvation on it. For faith is not something we stubbornly resolve to believe against the evidence: that is make-believe. Faith is something which God sets in us as native gift, and which constantly quickens, if we will receive the quickening. It is primal trust. How can the mutuality necessary in spiritual healing ever be established without the trust? Do we believe

that Christ can bring peace on earth? If not, why should we trouble to pursue that road? And to what purpose, then, the sacrificial work of Christ? His question to the blind men was not a cruel probing: it was a girding of the gift of God in them. Faith has a much deeper seat in us than doubt, but most men choose to believe their doubts against their faith rather than their faith against their doubts; or they are content with a seesaw of faith and doubt. It is a prime requirement of life to cleave to faith.

The stern charge of Christ to these men not to "broadcast" the cure (the word translated **sternly** in RSV is used in the Greek of the snorting of horses and the fury of men) may mean by fair presumption that Jesus was afraid of having his mission victimized by a popular demand that he work wonders (see Exeg.). He risked unpopularity, as when he feasted with tax collectors; but he feared popularity. Our age should mark! The two men disobeyed him: they thought more of the physical cure than of the spiritual kingdom. It is easy to "use" Christ for our comfort, and meanwhile to disobey him.

32-34. The Healing of the Dumb.— (See Exeg. for strange echoes here of 12:22 ff.) Once again we must assume that the author is intent on a literary plan, and on the words

[7] Tennyson, *Idylls of the King*, "Geraint and Enid," 1. 5.

33 And when the devil was cast out, the dumb spake: and the multitudes marveled, saying, It was never so seen in Israel.	33 And when the demon had been cast out, the dumb man spoke; and the crowds marveled, saying, "Never was anything like this seen in Israel." 34 But the Pharisees said, "He casts out demons by the prince of demons."
34 But the Pharisees said, He casteth out devils through the prince of the devils.	
35 And Jesus went about all the cities and villages, teaching in their synagogues,	35 And Jesus went about all the cities

34. This verse is omitted by Bezae (D), two O.L. MSS, and the Sinaitic Syriac. It has probably been added to the text from Luke 11:15. Here it is out of place, since it introduces the controversy over the casting out of demons, which is not dealt with fully until ch. 12.

IV. Second Discourse. The Work and Behavior of Special Disciples (9:35–11:1)

Matthew has just finished telling stories of Jesus' healings which serve as a pattern for the Christian minister. He now pictures the formal commissioning of the earliest disciples for their task, and does it so skillfully that at first glance his discourse appears to be entirely appropriate on Jesus' lips. But it is woven out of earlier sources and provides us with a good example of how Matthew uses his materials.

The evangelist actually has in mind more than the original disciples and their work. The saying in 10:23 is addressed to the whole early Christian community, which expects its Lord to return before it has finished its preaching mission through the cities of Palestine. The section 10:5-6, which may have been written when conservative Jerusalem Christians disapproved of work among Samaritans, does not fit well with 10:16, for there the disciples are not going to the lost sheep of the house of Israel but into the midst of avowed enemies. In 10:17-20 the disciples are to bear witness before Jewish sanhedrins

which the story enshrines—in this instance the word of the crowd and the conflicting word of the Pharisees. The story hints the constant pressures on Jesus. As they (the blind men) were going away a dumb man vexed with insanity confronted him. Do we think our life is hard? Do we rebel because "so much time is wasted with worthless people"? Jesus met incessant demands from "problem cases," therein proving the peace and power of God. Dumbness is a parable, as we must be quick to see.

What if Earth
Be but the Shadow of Heav'n? [8]

To be blind to that divine sign is tragic, but to be incapable of speaking what the eyes see may be a worse affliction. If the sight is itself deranged, the prison is within a prison. In newspapers we sometimes read of a city visited by flood or storm: "Communications with the outside world are broken." Such a city is indeed under threat. Perhaps the man was dumb through melancholia. Psychiatry today knows just such cases. If that was the affliction, the cure is made more vivid. The man was set free from the darkness of demonic perversity: the joy of the love in Christ pierced the black cloud.

[8] Milton, Paradise Lost, Bk. V, l. 574.

Notice the mixed reception of the cure. The people, unspoiled in simplicity of motive however negligent in fulfillment of religious ritual, marveled; but the Pharisees, cankered by self-righteous pride, insisted that Jesus knew too much about demons, and that he had power over them only because he was in league with "the prince of the power of the air." Jesus had answered that charge: a bad tree cannot grow good fruit (7:18). Later he would answer it again: A house divided against itself shall not stand (12:25). Did the Pharisees believe their own charge? It is likely that they did believe it, because they wished to believe it, because in their self-concern they had fallen into the habit of playing fast and loose with the mind's integrity.

35-36. The Compassion of Christ.—How does a crowd affect us? It can arouse a vague excitement. It can feed our pride—as in some parades. It can make us combative. It can quicken blood lust or some other frenzy. But does it fill us with compassion? That was its effect on Jesus. The word translated compassion is actually a much stronger word: it implies pain of love. He saw the people of his land as shepherdless people. They were as if wolves had harried them and left them bleeding, because they had none to lead and protect them. What a com-

and preaching the gospel of the kingdom, and healing every sickness and every disease among the people.	and villages, teaching in their synagogues and preaching the gospel of the kingdom, and healing every disease and every in-

and synagogues and kings like Herod Agrippa I, and—Matthew adds—before the Gentiles. Vss. 21-22 suggest the persecutions which overtook Christians in the years 40-70. Matthew writes for the church of his own day. By now it is conscious of its mission to the entire world (28:19), though there was once a time when this was not so (Acts 11:1-3, 19-20). Therefore, the evangelist takes the old traditions of Jesus' sayings and recasts them in a form suited to the new situation, even though he retains passages like 10:5-6, 23, which do not fit well with his purpose. Since the sending (10:5) is purely formal, there is no account of the disciples' success and return (contrast Luke 10:17).

The sources are easy to distinguish. Matthew uses Mark 6:6b as an introduction, and weaves Mark's calling of the twelve (Mark 3:14-19) in with two mission discourses: (a) A charge from Q, which has been preserved in a somewhat purer form in Luke 10:1-16. (b) Another from Mark 6:7-11, which represents a later stage of tradition. He includes also: (c) sayings which forbid the disciples to leave Palestine (10:5-6, 23), perhaps from the M source (cf. Intro., p. 238); and also (d) sayings on persecution and discipleship drawn from Mark 9:41; 13:9-13, and from various parts of Mark and Q.

Matthew regards the twelve as the undisputed heads of the church, though in the apostolic age there had been controversies over the personnel and power of the apostolate (e.g., II Cor. 10-12; Gal. 1-2). Jesus did not make plans for an organized church. He sent his disciples out to herald the kingdom, and his principal purpose was to insure that the poor had the good news preached to them (11:5). Men who did this work made short trips and needed no luggage (10:9-10a); they were entertained by receptive friends (Luke 10:7) and could not waste their time in places where the word was not accepted (10:14).

A. INTRODUCTION (9:35–10:4)

1. TEACHING AND HEALING (9:35)

35. This is a fair summary of the manifold activity of Jesus. Here and in the following verses the thought is that the twelve are to do precisely the same work. There is no suggestion, such as we find in Luke 10:17, that the disciples later discovered powers that they did not know they possessed, for in 10:1 they are expressly bidden to exorcise.

mentary on the state of a nation! What an indictment of Roman power and of Jewish religion! The latter, when it should have been both solace and strength, imposed a spiritual tax to compare with the Roman money tax. Jesus **had compassion**. He loved the common man because he knew him to be uncommon. Socrates and Plato both held the common man in mild scorn; and they kept their schools, not for the *hoi polloi*, but for gentlemen's sons. We have asked how we respond to a crowd. We might have asked how a crowd responds: the lovelessness of modern life has made the crowd a threat. The "common" man, resenting that adjective, mills about in a vague iconoclasm or tries to find greatness in the false cry of demagogue or tyrant.

How to describe the compassion of Christ? It is so vast and deep that we are almost driven to use negatives. Thus the compassion of Jesus is not patronizing. Men are brother men, not "cases," or "unfortunates," or even "disadvantaged." His compassion is not a devious movement through organized channels, though these are necessary, but direct—man to man, and heart to heart. The word charity is down at the heel: it has come to mean giving a small coin to a beggar. But to Jesus charity was life shared in love. The compassion of Jesus was not shallow or sentimental. He did not ignore the perversity in men. He never pretended that wages and hours alone can solve man's dilemma. He cared for the body, and knew that a starving man is ill-prepared to receive the news of God's love; but he knew also that a full stomach is no guarantee of heaven's grace. Thus his compassion met man's need from finger tip to inmost motive. The compassion of Jesus was not a mere palliative. For compassion is more than "feeling with": if it were only that it might easily add to the woe. For to feel the pangs of suffering, and meanwhile to have no

36 ¶ But when he saw the multitudes, he was moved with compassion on them, because they fainted, and were scattered abroad, as sheep having no shepherd.

37 Then saith he unto his disciples, The harvest truly *is* plenteous, but the laborers *are* few;

38 Pray ye therefore the Lord of the harvest, that he will send forth laborers into his harvest.

firmity. 36 When he saw the crowds, he had compassion for them, because they were harassed and helpless, like sheep without a shepherd. 37 Then he said to his disciples, "The harvest is plentiful, but the laborers are few; 38 pray therefore the Lord of the harvest to send out laborers into his harvest."

2. The Need for Special Disciples (9:36-38)

The work of the ministry is like gathering a scattered flock and like harvesting grain. The lost are brought back and new converts are added. Sayings from different contexts may have been brought together, for vss. 37-38 do not fit perfectly either here or in Luke 10:2.

36. The metaphor of **sheep without a shepherd** is drawn from I Kings 22:17.

37. The word translated **laborers** often means "farm workers," as in 20:1. **Harvest** is often a symbol for the age to come.

38. Perhaps Jesus gave this command on some other occasion. Does Matthew think of the words as addressed to a larger crowd of Galileans? In that case Jesus answers the prayer by giving the twelve authority. Or does he think of this as a general prayer for the increase of the ministry? In John 4:35-38 later disciples share in the ministry of their predecessors.

cure, might add frenzy to the pain. Jesus felt the pain, and yet could lift a banner above it. The compassion of Jesus was not costless. When was any real love without its price? The man who brings fire from heaven, as the myth of Prometheus shows, is chained to a rock with eagles pecking at his vitals.[9] The compassion of Jesus, because it was grounded in holy love, took him to a Cross. Beautifully these verses imply that Jesus is the true Shepherd of the human flock. He lays down his life for the sheep. But he is not defeated by time and death: he has power to lay down his life, and power to take it again. Only in his shielding strength and wise leading is the flock safely fed.

37-38. White Harvest.—Jesus thus gives a second picture of mankind. The first is sad: the multitude is like a ravaged flock. But this is glad: the multitude is like a harvest field waiting for the reaper. There are two natures in man, divided by a cleft in the very will. Man is perverse, but he can still say with truth (as Peter said with truth despite his failures): "Lord, thou knowest all things; thou knowest that I love thee" (John 21:17). Thus Jesus saw men ready to respond to the gospel. Granted enough reapers, that is, men of Christian speech and Christian heart, many of the multitude could be won for God, as they should be, for men are God's field, made for life

[9] For details of the Prometheus myth see Charles M. Gayley, *Classic Myths*, p. 11.

with him, since he is **Lord of the harvest.** But (so urgent is the task) without reapers the harvest may be lost. So Jesus yearned for more men of his mind to help him. He knew that he must delegate the work. We see in these verses the beginnings of an ordained ministry—and of an unordained ministry. What kind of ministry? Men who see life as God's field; men who work with abounding hope, because the **harvest truly is plenteous;** men who live only for their fellow men and God in self-forgetting love; men who labor to gather other men home to the **Lord of the harvest;** men who really labor, since reaping is hard, hard work.

These verses hint at the cruciality of prayer: **Pray ye therefore. . . .** The prayer is not to be a substitute for the labor: the disciples were to be reapers as well as praying men. But the work will not be done without prayer. Intercession has mighty power: it is the channel chosen by God for raising up leaders in the Christian cause. This saying of Christ has wide implications. For example: the world needs fewer men to invent things and manipulate things, and far more men to cultivate the field of mankind and reap the harvest of the soul. This necessary change of emphasis has profound meaning for economics and education, as well as for mission field and church. Oliver Goldsmith dedicated his poem "The Traveller" to his preacher-brother, Henry, and in the dedication complimented his brother on entering a real harvest

10 And when he had called unto *him* his twelve disciples, he gave them power *against* unclean spirits, to cast them out, and to heal all manner of sickness and all manner of disease.

2 Now the names of the twelve apostles are these; The first, Simon, who is called Peter, and Andrew his brother; James *the son* of Zebedee, and John his brother;

10 And he called to him his twelve disciples and gave them authority over unclean spirits, to cast them out, and to heal every disease and every infirmity. 2 The names of the twelve apostles are these: first, Simon, who is called Peter, and Andrew his brother; James the son

3. Authority Is Conferred on the Twelve (10:1)

10:1. Matthew has previously spoken of Jesus' **disciples** in a general way, without distinguishing clearly between general adherents and "special disciples," though 4:19 must refer to the latter. Now he mentions the **twelve** for the first time. The inner group was approximately of this number, though its personnel may have fluctuated somewhat. An old Jewish tradition said that Jesus had five disciples named Mattai, Naqai, Neçer, Buni, and Toda. To cast out **unclean spirits** is the work of the high-priestly Messiah in Test. Levi 18:12. Mark 6:7 (=Luke 9:1) pictures Jesus as giving this power, but Q does not (Luke 10:9).

4. List of the Twelve (10:2-4)

Similar lists are given in Mark 3:16-19, Luke 6:14-16, and Acts 1:13; the second-century Epistle of the Apostles has a very different list (ch. 2). The Fourth Gospel gives no list of twelve, and its most prominent disciples are not those of the Synoptics.

2. Only here does Matthew use the word **apostles.** In the N.T. the term is applied not only to the twelve but to various others—Paul and Barnabas (Gal. 1:1; Acts 14:14), Matthias (Acts 1:26), James and the other brothers of the Lord (I Cor. 9:5; Gal. 1:19), Andronicus and Junias (Rom. 16:7). It designates those who are "sent with a commission" (the meaning of ἀποστέλλω) to proclaim salvation through Christ. It is sometimes argued that all apostles had seen the risen Lord (I Cor. 9:1; 15:7; Acts 1:22). The corresponding Hebrew word *shāliaḥ* denotes one who is commissioned as an agent in legal matters by an individual or by a court, or who is entrusted with offering prayer. At a later time the Jewish patriarch or *nāsî* often sent an apostle to collect funds or to root out heresy, and perhaps Paul's work was analogous to this, both before and after his conversion. Matthew elsewhere prefers to speak of the twelve as disciples, since he thinks of the ideal Christian leader as a rabbi (cf. on 13:52; 16:19), but here he exhibits the view of late first-century Christianity, which is that the twelve were the first apostles. Such an idea dominates Luke-Acts, but is absent from Mark. **Simon** or Simeon is almost always thought of as **first** in rank among the twelve. His surname **Peter** (Πέτρος) translates his Aramaic nickname *Kêphā'* (rock, πέτρα), which we find in Gal. 1:18; I Cor. 1:12; John 1:42, and elsewhere. Cf. 4:18-22.

field: "You have left the field of ambition, where the labourers are many, and the harvest not worth carrying away." [1]

10:1-5. *These Twelve.*—The lives of the apostles are largely unknown. Some of them (see Exeg. on Matthew and Thaddeus, for instance) are uncertain even in name. Others are hardly more than names, and the stories told of them are legend rather than history. The fact that the records leave us in this ignorance may be further evidence that they were ordinary men

[1] *Miscellaneous Works,* ed. Washington Irving (Philadelphia: J. Crissy & Thomas Coperthwait & Co., 1840), p. 147.

when judged by human standards. They found their greatness through Christ. Certain items about them are clear. They were diverse in temperament and gift. Some led, others followed. All needed encouragement and the correction of individual bias—a need which led Christ to send them out two by two (Mark 6:7). In Matthew's list, we should note, the names occur in pairs. In every list Peter is named first. He was apparently the acknowledged spokesman. James and John also stood out. Their intense and forthright nature is reflected in the incident reported in Luke 9:54. They earned the nickname "sons of thunder" (Mark 3:17).

3 Philip, and Bartholomew; Thomas, and Matthew the publican; James *the son* of Alpheus, and Lebbeus, whose surname was Thaddeus;

4 Simon the Canaanite, and Judas Iscariot, who also betrayed him.

5 These twelve Jesus sent forth, and commanded them, saying, Go not into the way of the Gentiles, and into *any* city of the Samaritans enter ye not:

of Zeb'e-dee, and John his brother; 3 Philip and Bartholomew; Thomas and Matthew the tax collector; James the son of Alphaeus, and Thaddaeus;[w] 4 Simon the Cananaean, and Judas Iscariot, who betrayed him.

5 These twelve Jesus sent out, charging them, "Go nowhere among the Gentiles,

[w] Some ancient authorities read *Lebbaeus* or *Lebbaeus called Thaddaeus.*

---

3. Philip, like Andrew, is a Greek name. The *bar* in **Bartholomew** ought to mean "son of," but the derivation of the rest of the name is uncertain. John 11:16; 20:24 translates **Thomas** as δίδυμος, "twin," and the name may be a Hellenized form of the Aramaic word for twin. **Matthew** appears in all lists of the twelve and is substituted for Levi in 9:9. **Alphaeus** is a Greek name, but attempts have been made to find Aramaic equivalents such as Clopas (John 19:25). **Thaddaeus** is the reading of Vaticanus, Sinaiticus, and a few other good MSS and is adopted by RSV; while Codex Bezae (D) reads "Lebbaeus" here and in Mark 3:19. The text of KJV combines the two. Ecclesiastical tradition has identified this disciple with Judas son of James (Luke 6:16; Acts 1:13). This variety has led some scholars to ask whether the number of the disciples was always exactly twelve.

4. Simon the Cananaean (RSV) was probably not a **Canaanite** (KJV). The word may be an Aramaic equivalent of the "Zealot" of Luke 6:15. Perhaps before his conversion Simon had been one of a band of anti-Roman revolutionaries (Josephus *Jewish War* IV. 3. 9, etc.), but there is no other evidence for this. He may simply have been zealous for the law (cf. Sanhedrin 9:6). The meaning of **Iscariot** is a famous problem, and the usual explanation is "man of Kerioth," i.e., a certain village. C. C. Torrey ("The Name 'Iscariot,'" *Harvard Theological Review,* XXXVI [1943], 51-62) derives it from the Aramaic *'ishkaryā* "the false." The phrase **who betrayed him** would thus mean almost the same thing. Cf. on 26:47-50.

B. The Discourse (10:5-42)

1. The Disciples' First Mission Is to Israel Alone (10:5-6)

Jesus generally worked in Jewish territory, though Mark 7:24-31; 8:27–9:1 tell of his travels on Gentile soil and, according to Luke, he was once in the neighborhood of Samaria. Would it have been necessary for Jesus to give this command? The presence of this saying in the tradition helps to explain why a Gentile mission developed so late. There is a tradition in the second-century Preaching of Peter that Jesus told the disciples to wait twelve years before going to the Gentiles (James, *Apocryphal N.T.,* p. 17).

5. A way of the Gentiles is probably a road leading to a Gentile city, such as one of the cities of the Decapolis. Jews were forbidden to go on such a road at the time of a

---

Andrew was homespun and loyal, like Sir Bedivere in "Morte D'Arthur." Thomas was apparently a doubter, and was yet (or therefore?) chosen to be an apostle. If "Iscariot" means "son of Kerioth," as seems not unlikely, he may have been fanatically Judean, out of place among these Galileans, and resolved that Jesus should prove himself a nationalistic Messiah. The company of the apostles is thus like an orchestra, requiring a variety of men and instruments. Each man's distinctiveness is needed in the symphony of the kingdom.

Yet they were apostles. The office exalted

them and turned their average manhood to genuine greatness. Certain qualities were doubtless required in them. They were capable of sincerity, of being stanch in loyalty. They were adventurous in spiritual-mindedness, ready to forsake all for the cause of God. Even so, they would not have come to holy power without Christ. He chose them as apostles. The word means much more than messenger: it means ambassadors and personal representatives of him by whom they were sent. It was as if Christ went in them, as indeed he did. Just as there were twelve patriarchs of the old covenant,

6 But go rather to the lost sheep of the house of Israel.

7 And as ye go, preach, saying, The kingdom of heaven is at hand.

and enter no town of the Samaritans, **6** but go rather to the lost sheep of the house of Israel. **7** And preach as you go, saying,

pagan festival if the road led only to the Gentile city (Abodah Zarah 1:4). Intermarriage with Samaritans was forbidden; and the Mishnah says, "He who eats the bread of the Samaritans is like one who eats pork" (Shebiith 8:10).

6. Jesus did much work among the **lost sheep of the house of Israel.** These may have been the Amhaarez, "people of the land" or country people, careless of the details of the law, whom the Pharisees regarded with contempt. Hillel, one of the greatest of all rabbis, said that "no '*am hā'āreç* is religious" (Aboth 2:6), and in John 7:49 the Pharisees say, "This crowd, who do not know the law, are accursed." But Jesus' attitude is seen in 22:8-10; Luke 15:3-10; etc.

2. THE NATURE OF THEIR WORK (10:7-8)

7. This is Jesus' message in Mark 1:15, and Q may have contained such a command (Luke 9:2).

these men were the twelve apostles of the new covenant, commissioned under the sovereign authority of Christ. They were Christ's solemn choice. Luke's Gospel tells us that the choice was exercised only after long prayer. Mark hints that these twelve were drawn from a much wider group of followers. We must learn that in the Christian community there are those who lead and those who follow. Which is harder? Both must surrender human pride: only lowliness of spirit can learn to follow, and no man can lead in the Christian cause unless he is first led of Christ.

5-10. *The Kingdom Mission: Method and Message.*—Notice the paragraph division in RSV at vs. 16. To that point we have instructions for the mission. See Exeg., general introduction to this whole section of the Gospel (9:35 ff.). Vss. 16-23 bear the marks of a much later utterance (see Exeg.).

The message is clearly summarized: **The kingdom of heaven is at hand.** The new apostles could not yet teach the profundities of the kingdom-truth, but they could tell about Jesus in whom the kingdom was incarnate. The first preaching was doubtless a personal testimony: "This he has said." "This he has done for me and for other men." Such preaching, and only such, has real power. Their ministry was not to stop at the lips (see vs. 8). These words are possibly, though not probably, a gloss. But, in any event, we know from all Jesus said and did that the word of the gospel is an energy of the whole life: the messenger, by his healing kindness, is himself the message, of which the word of his lips is the joyous overflow.

The locale of the message is traced (vss. 5-6) in words hard to construe. How shall we interpret this command to go to the Jews only?

As a word spoken later, on the eve of the Crucifixion for instance, and to be linked with vs. 23 as a policy for that hour only? Or as an echo of division in the early church, the author of this strand taking a Jewish standpoint? Or as a concession to the inexperience of the apostles, and therefore as only a temporary strategy? (See Exeg.) One fact is clear: Jesus' own actions (in the healing in the Decapolis, for instance [Mark 7:31]) and his own words (as in the parable of the good Samaritan [Luke 10]) do not accord with this command. The adjective **lost** is a poignant word. Its interpretation is in Luke 15. **Lost** is the word, not "wicked," though the lostness often comes of transgression. Mankind is lost through folly or helplessness like a sheep, lost through carelessness like a coin from a headpiece, lost through willfulness like the prodigal son. Mankind is lost to social usefulness, lost to true joy, lost to God. The message is urgent: it is carried to a lost world.

The method of the mission is also clearly traced. It is at first a house mission. The apostles are not to travel as if bent on business or pleasure. They are not to carry a beggar's bag (see Exeg. on **scrip**). They are to provide only the simple necessities of travel and livelihood, and must not accept even "copper" (let alone silver or gold) for any help they give. They are entitled to enough in food and clothing by which to live in frugal joy, but should neither ask nor take more than enough. Their business is the kingdom mission. Therefore they may have the simplicities of food and clothing, lack of which might cripple their evangelism; but they are not to have more than simplicities, lest an encroaching worldliness should be a worse fetter than penury. That rule still holds for those who would fulfill the kingdom ministry.

8 Heal the sick, cleanse the lepers, raise the dead, cast out devils: freely ye have received, freely give.

9 Provide neither gold, nor silver, nor brass in your purses;

10 Nor scrip for *your* journey, neither two coats, neither shoes, nor yet staves: for the workman is worthy of his meat.

11 And into whatsoever city or town ye shall enter, inquire who in it is worthy; and there abide till ye go thence.

'The kingdom of heaven is at hand.' 8 Heal the sick, raise the dead, cleanse lepers, cast out demons. You received without pay, give without pay. 9 Take no gold, nor silver, nor copper in your belts, 10 no bag for your journey, nor two tunics, nor sandals, nor a staff; for the laborer deserves his food. 11 And whatever town or village you enter, find out who is worthy in it, and stay with

---

8. Chs. 8 and 9 have given examples of this activity on the part of Jesus. The Jews believed that several great rabbis had the power to **raise the dead.** Their finest teachers also acted on the principle **You received without pay, give without pay;** cf. Aboth 4:5, "He who makes profit out of words of the law removes his life from the world."

3. Behavior While Traveling (10:9-15)

9. Mark 6:8 mentions only χαλκός or **copper;** Jesus' disciples seldom had **gold** and **silver.** Coins were often carried in **belts.**

10. The **bag** might be for food. Even a change of undergarments was unnecessary. Mark, writing for Gentiles, permits a **staff** and **sandals,** but Q did not. Of course, most of the journeys were short; but T. E. Lawrence went through his Arabian campaigns barefoot. **The laborer deserves his food** is a Jewish principle; cf. I Cor. 9:3-14; Did. 11:6, 12; Aboth 4:5.

11-13. Luke 10:5-6 preserves a more primitive saying. The missionary, on entering, must say, "Peace be to this house," and if a "son of peace" (i.e., one who will receive the

---

8. *The Kingdom Mission: Blessing and Obligation.*—Freely ye have received, freely give. This word of Christ claims a separate comment. It is a favorite instruction in the church service in regard to the money offering. That use is valid. But its original meaning and proper fulfillment have a much wider range. What had they received? Jesus Christ! It was some worth in them that they had welcomed him, but they could never have provided that gift. They had received, by God's outright grace, Jesus himself. "All this and heaven too," for with Jesus had come the truth about God for man's living and dying, for man's sinning and hoping, for man's sorrowing and believing. "Of his fulness have all we received, and grace for grace (John 1:16). God gives the universe to the eyes, but has a larger gift for the soul—"his only begotten Son" (John 3:16). Circumstances alone cannot conspire to bring him, and history does not fashion him: he is God's "unspeakable gift" (II Cor. 9:15). If we really tried to measure this blessing, we could not afterward rightfully complain about any hardship.

This blessing is itself a debt. We do not own the gift: we are only its trustees. The kingdom remains ours only as we share it. In this it is like a field, or like great music, but with a deeper import. We hold in benediction only as

we share. The apostle is a human reservoir: the water of life does not stay pure in him, and cannot quench any neighbor's thirst, unless it flows through him by this channel and that channel in daily word and deed. In many a Christian the "good news" has ceased to be good news because he has ceased to share it in word and life. For Christ is the breath of life. If a man were able to hold his breath he would die. Constantly he receives strength of body and soul, constantly he must expend it. There is a systole and diastole of the gospel. The "saints" who hug their salvation are soon cankered by a repellent kind of selfishness. There are wide meanings here, for commerce also must become an evangel. So must any true education. That collection plate over which the preacher says, **Freely ye have received, freely give,** is wider even than mortal life: its rim circles eternity.

11-15. *The Kingdom Mission: Welcome and Rebuff.*—The plan was detailed. The apostles were to inquire, on entering a village, for people of like mind. Finding such a home, they were to ask hospitality; and, if welcomed, they were to **abide** there, and not to move from home to home. They were to tell the good news, finding through that home contact with others who might welcome the gospel. Such were the beginnings of the Christian mission.

12 And when ye come into a house, salute it.

13 And if the house be worthy, let your peace come upon it: but if it be not worthy, let your peace return to you.

14 And whosoever shall not receive you, nor hear your words, when ye depart out of that house or city, shake off the dust of your feet.

15 Verily I say unto you, It shall be more tolerable for the land of Sodom and Gomorrah in the day of judgment, than for that city.

16 ¶ Behold, I send you forth as sheep in the midst of wolves: be ye therefore wise as serpents, and harmless as doves.

him until you depart. **12** As you enter the house, salute it. **13** And if the house is worthy, let your peace come upon it; but if it is not worthy, let your peace return to you. **14** And if any one will not receive you or listen to your words, shake off the dust from your feet as you leave that house or town. **15** Truly, I say to you, it shall be more tolerable on the day of judgment for the land of Sodom and Go-mor'rah than for that town.

16 "Behold, I send you out as sheep in the midst of wolves; so be wise as serpents and

---

blessing and respond to it in like manner) is present, the blessing will take effect; if not, the blessing returns to the missionary and will be bestowed on others (cf. on 5:9, 47). Matthew's use of the word **worthy** introduces a moralistic note which was almost certainly not originally present.

14. Jews who had been in pagan territory shook **the dust from** [their] **feet** so that they might not make the holy land unclean. An unfriendly **house or town** is to be treated as heathen; similar gestures are found in Neh. 5:13; Acts 18:6. This verse may contemplate conditions of later missionary work but the basic idea comes from Jesus: when you are not accepted, do not waste time but go elsewhere (22:8-9).

15. Sodom was proverbially the wicked city (as in 11:23-24; Ezek. 16:48-50; Luke 17:29). It abused its guests (Gen. 19:4-9), though this is not said of the equally wicked **Gomorrah.** The rabbis debated whether the people of Sodom would be resurrected and judged on **the day of judgment** (Sanhedrin 10:3).

4. Opposition (10:16-39)

This section is primarily addressed to the Christian church rather than to the original disciples. The distinction between leaders and people largely disappears, for

---

They cause us to ask if the Christian crusade has not been choked, rather than helped, by its too intricate organization. The disciples would be welcomed by **worthy** folk. The adjective means worthy in spirit and worthy to receive messengers of the gospel. They were perhaps not wealthy in goods, but were worthy in good —"waiting for the consolation of Israel." There the apostles were to pronounce **peace** (such as is in Christ); the benediction would bring peace.

Elsewhere they might be rebuffed. Why? People of "scribal" mind might fear heresy. People of stingy mind might begrudge hospitality. People bent on fame might deem it unwise to associate "with one of these new movements." People of iconoclastic mind might despise religion and plead for recourse by sword. In such instances the apostles were to **shake off the dust** from their feet. This was what the Pharisees did when leaving "heathen" territory. But the apostles were not to do it in Pharisaic mood. John Oman has called this act "the Sacrament

of Failure." [2] Perhaps we need such a "sacrament": often the Christian appeal meets denial and abuse. So the disciples were to perform the simple ritual, not in anger, not in pride, not in wounded irritation; in love rather, as those who, reaching the end of human wit and power, are content to leave all issues to the judgment of God. That judgment is sternly uttered in vss. 15. Some commentators think the logion is a gloss, or that it belongs in some darker context. Its basic truth remains. Sodom could at least plead some measure of ignorance. But Jewry had been prepared through centuries for the revealing of God. Privilege always spells responsibility. The applications of that truth are legion, but they rest most heavily on the church.

16-18, 23. *How to Meet Persecution: (a) By Compassionate Shrewdness.*— (See Expos., vss. 19-22.) The next section (vss. 16-31) does not accord with the instructions given to the apos-

[2] *Vision and Authority,* rev. ed. (New York: Harper & Bros., 1929), ch. ix.

17 But beware of men: for they will deliver you up to the councils, and they will scourge you in their synagogues;

18 And ye shall be brought before governors and kings for my sake, for a testimony against them and the Gentiles.

19 But when they deliver you up, take

innocent as doves. 17 Beware of men; for they will deliver you up to councils, and flog you in their synagogues, 18 and you will be dragged before governors and kings for my sake, to bear testimony before them and the Gentiles. 19 When they deliver you

---

anyone might undergo these dangers. It is not surprising that Matthew includes this teaching, for although ministers had special functions they did not constitute a professional class and the same moral and religious qualities were expected of all Christians.

a) How to Meet Persecution (10:16-22)

16. Jesus may have spoken these two poetic proverbs at a time when his teaching had begun to arouse criticism. The similes have parallels in Jewish writings and elsewhere. The verses that follow are used as a comment on the proverbs, and are such a close reproduction of Mark 13:9-13 that the evangelist does not use that material again in ch. 24, when he rewrites Mark 13.

17. The **councils** are presumably the local sanhedrins, composed of twenty-three members each, which functioned in Jewish cities other than Jerusalem (Sanhedrin 1:6). They probably met in the **synagogues**. Deut. 25:1-3 provides for the scourging, which was usually administered by the *ḥazzān* or synagogue attendant; but according to Acts 22:19 Paul himself had beaten Christians. Rabbinical law restricted the strokes to thirty-nine, and Paul underwent this punishment five times (II Cor. 11:24).

18. The **governors** may be Roman officials like Pilate, and **kings** can include tetrarchs like Herod Antipas as well as such local kings as Herod Agrippa I (Acts 12:1). A good example of such **testimony** is found in the *Acts of the Scilitan Martyrs*. These martyrs suffered in north Africa in 180 (see J. C. Ayer, *A Source Book for Ancient Church History* [New York: Charles Scribner's Sons, 1913], pp. 66-68).

19-20. Carefully worked out defenses will not necessarily protect Jesus' followers.

---

tles for the kingdom mission. In mood and substance it seems to be a later utterance, perhaps spoken at the Last Supper. Perhaps it echoes the stern persecutions suffered under Nero, and perhaps those as late as Trajan, by the early church. Notice the realism of Christ. Winston Churchill, early in World War II, warned his people to expect "blood, toil, tears, and sweat."[3] Christ issued a darker warning. The new faith would bring his disciples before synagogue courts, local rulers, and even kings. Besides, it would divide homes, so that in bitterness brother would persecute brother, and parents their children. The warning was tragically fulfilled. Christians were flogged by synagogue courts (Acts 22:19; II Cor. 11:24); they were hailed before governors and kings, and the new faith did divide families. This whole section is counsel on how to meet persecution. If it seems outdated, that may be an indictment of our Christianity. It was pertinent enough in Europe during the Nazi regime. Jesus says that a shrewdness-in-love is an asset. His followers are to be wise as serpents, but yet as harmless as

[3] Speech delivered to the House of Commons, May 13, 1940.

doves. The rabbis said that Jews should be like doves to those of Israel, but like serpents to the Gentiles; but that is not Christ's meaning. His disciples are not to court martyrdom. They are not to provoke the ungodly to violence. It may be wise for them when persecuted in one city to flee to a kindlier locale. They are not to cast life away without due occasion. So Jesus met his opponents: see, for instance, his question to his critics (21:25). So Paul used his wits, as when he pleaded his Roman citizenship to thwart his Jewish persecutors (Acts 22:25). The Christians who lowered Paul over the city wall in a basket (Acts 9:25) fulfilled the injunction of Christ. There have been occasions when the "children of light" have been quicker witted than the "children of darkness." But their action has been in love; otherwise it has been alien from Christ's mind. Besides, this shrewdness is not always in place. There are other ways of meeting persecution.

19-22. How to Meet Persecution: (b) By Trust at the Time of Crisis.—Sometimes the persecution could not be escaped. What then? The synagogue was a court. It could administer floggings (see Exeg. on vs. 17). There were higher

no thought how or what ye shall speak: for it shall be given you in that same hour what ye shall speak.

20 For it is not ye that speak, but the Spirit of your Father which speaketh in you.

21 And the brother shall deliver up the brother to death, and the father the child: and the children shall rise up against *their* parents, and cause them to be put to death.

22 And ye shall be hated of all *men* for my name's sake: but he that endureth to the end shall be saved.

23 But when they persecute you in this city, flee ye into another: for verily I say unto you, Ye shall not have gone over the cities of Israel, till the Son of man be come.

up, do not be anxious how you are to speak or what you are to say; for what you are to say will be given to you in that hour; **20** for it is not you who speak, but the Spirit of your Father speaking through you. **21** Brother will deliver up brother to death, and the father his child, and children will rise against parents and have them put to death; **22** and you will be hated by all for my name's sake. But he who endures to the end will be saved. **23** When they persecute you in one town, flee to the next; for truly, I say to you, you will not have gone through all the towns of Israel, before the Son of man comes.

It is far better for them to speak the prophetic word of God and to leave their fate in his hands. **Your father** is characteristic of Matthew's style.

21-22. The details of these verses suggest the first great persecution of Christians under Nero in the year 64 (see Tacitus *Annals* XV. 44; Ayer, *op. cit.*, pp. 6-7). Since they were charged with "hatred of the human race," they no doubt felt they were **hated by all** and suffered for the sake of Jesus' name (cf. I Pet. 4:12-16). Later persecutions were, in fact, because of the "name" alone (see Pliny *Epistles* 96, 97; Ayer, *op. cit.*, pp. 20-22). **He who endures to the end will be saved.** This saying in Mark 13:13 referred to the great tribulation at the end of the age; here it means that one who endures persecution heroically will save his soul.

b) Counsel to Flight (10:23)

23. No doubt because this tradition was in circulation, the Jewish Christians of Jerusalem for the most part remained there until the very outbreak of the Jewish War of 66-70. Eusebius (*Church History* III. 5. 3) says that at that time, in obedience to a divine revelation, they moved to Pella in Trans-Jordan. This saying was formulated by Christians who thought of Christ primarily as the heavenly **Son of man.** Cf. general note on 9:35–11:1, above.

courts, such as those of the provincial governors; and courts still higher in rank, such as that of Felix, before which Paul appeared. In the persecutions under Nero and Trajan the name "Christian" was sufficient warrant for death "for my sake." What if courage should fail? What if tongue should fail, and Christ be put to shame? These are the questions that hagride any honorable follower of Christ. Christ here answers the questions. He gives three assurances. First, that God will supply both words and courage to those who trust him. They need not rehearse any speech. They need not worry about the manner or the matter of their reply to the charges of persecutors. God will speak through them, and both valor and testimony shall be given **in that [very] hour.** Second, their testimony shall mightily proclaim the kingdom (see **vs. 18**) **against them (the enemy) and the**

Gentiles (the whole world of men). That assurance has found multiplied fulfillment. There is the instance of Polycarp: He waved his hand toward the throng of lawless heathen in the arena and said, "Eighty and six years have I been His servant, and He hath done me no wrong. How then can I blaspheme my King who saved me?" [4] Such testimonies, in words so simple in their complete trust that they needed no rehearsing, have been the noblest and most effective weapon of the kingdom. Third, this trust will save those who thus bear their witness (see vs. 22). It hints that persecutions are not interminable. God gives enough respite to his own. There are seasons of clear shining after storm. Death itself is a haven for the faithful.

[4] Lucius Waterman, *The Post-Apostolic Age* in *Ten Epochs of Church History*, ed. John Fulton (New York: Charles Scribner's Sons, 1898), II, 138.

24 The disciple is not above *his* master, nor the servant above his lord.

25 It is enough for the disciple that he be as his master, and the servant as his lord. If they have called the master of the house Beelzebub, how much more *shall they call* them of his household?

26 Fear them not therefore: for there is nothing covered, that shall not be revealed; and hid, that shall not be known.

24 "A disciple is not above his **teacher,** nor a servant[y] above his master; 25 it is enough for the disciple to be like his teacher, and the servant[y] like his master. If they have called the master of the house Be-el'ze-bul, how much more will they malign those of his household.

26 "So have no fear of them; for nothing is covered that will not be revealed,

[y] Or *slave.*

---

c) Persecution Is to Be Expected (10:24-25)

24-25. Luke 6:40 has a different form of the saying, which probably means: "Even when the disciple is completely educated, he is no greater than his teacher." Here the thought is that the Christian may not expect to be treated better than his Master was. The principle is valid even in times of relative peace, for courageous following of Christ may at any time result in opposition, and the missionary has no right to demand success. Jesus is elsewhere accused of being in league with **Beelzebub**; cf. on 12:24. **Master of the house** may be a play on the form **Beelzebul,** which can mean "lord of the house."

d) Counsels to Speak the Word Bravely, with a Promise of Reward (10:26-39)

These sayings stood in Q, the first group of them (vss. 26-33) containing a threefold refrain (vss. 26, 28, 31). Matthew has inserted the refrain at the beginning of vs. 26.

26. This seems to assume that Jesus' teaching was not widely known until after the

---

Meanwhile those who testify for Christ are **saved**—saved from cankering cowardice, saved from the inward chaos that besets those who deny the truth, saved from trust in themselves to proven trust in God.

24-25. *How to Meet Persecution: (c) By Remembrance of Christ.*—A disciple is not above his teacher. Notice the double picture: Jesus is Teacher, and the followers are pupils in the school of life; Jesus is Master, and his followers are bondmen in the house of life. Certain implications are plain, and they continue age on age. Teacher and scholar are closely bound. That comradeship is fatal when teachers are blind: they "both [teachers and scholars] fall into the ditch." When the teacher is lowly, that same lowliness is required of the pupil, as is beautifully illustrated in John 13:13-14. If the teacher suffers persecution, that same lot awaits the pupil. The teacher and pupil find a closer bond through suffering for the truth. This is not explicitly said in these lines, but it is said between the lines; and the truth is scored deep in history. Is there not record of a missionary who was struck by stones during the Boxer uprising, and who, suddenly feeling the warm blood streaming from a wound in his head, exclaimed, "Now I am a Christian!"? He meant more than that he had met the test for Christ's sake: he meant that Christ was never more near

and dear, for the bond had been made strong through shared suffering. The pupil grows more like the teacher in the experience of persecution. The Christians under the persecutions of the second century were called "haters of mankind," but their sufferings proved their love. They were called "atheists," but their courage under testing became an irrefutable argument for God. The crisis released in them a power dormant in quieter days, and men "took knowledge of them, that they had been with Jesus" (Acts 4:13). Persecution would refine them until they became like their "Master." The persecution would reveal Christ's presence. This also is not written in the lines, but it is implied. The symbol of Christianity is not an hourglass or a tomb: it is an empty Cross and a conquered grave. The remembrance of Jesus thus quickens into a Presence. Stephen in his martyrdom was not alone. He became like his "Master," even to praying for those who slew him. His face was like that of an angel as he died, because he was not alone (Acts 7:54-60). The remembrance became a Voice saying, "I am with thee." A Friend, who had first suffered a deeper tribulation, was by his side.

26-31. *How to Meet Persecution: (d) By a Good Courage.*—Fear not (see Expos., vss. 29-31). The words occur three times in this passage. Often when persecution comes the fol-

27 What I tell you in darkness, *that* speak ye in light: and what ye hear in the ear, *that* preach ye upon the housetops.

28 And fear not them which kill the body, but are not able to kill the soul: but rather fear him which is able to destroy both soul and body in hell.

29 Are not two sparrows sold for a farthing? and one of them shall not fall on the ground without your Father.

or hidden that will not be known. 27 What I tell you in the dark, utter in the light; and what you hear whispered, proclaim upon the housetops. 28 And do not fear those who kill the body but cannot kill the soul; rather fear him who can destroy both soul and body in hell.*a* 29 Are not two sparrows sold for a penny? And not one of them will fall to the ground without

a Greek *Gehenna.*

Crucifixion. He may originally have meant: "The message now seems to reach only a few, but God will see to it that it has great effect" (cf. on 13:3*b*-9).

27. Rabbis often **whispered** to their disciples certain secret doctrines such as the interpretation of Ezek. 1; but Jesus' teaching is not esoteric. Therefore the meaning must be: "That which is now taught in small groups must be proclaimed widely." This is the idea of Luke 12:3.

28. The one **who can destroy both soul and body in hell,** i.e., in Gehenna, is probably God. Although it was believed that evil men and Satan could tempt one and so lead one to destruction, only God could pronounce the sentence to Gehenna; cf. Wisd. Sol. 16:13-15; IV Macc. 13:14-15; Jas. 4:12. The saying merely teaches that God is omnipotent, and no special emphasis on the severity of his judgment need be intended. This and the following sayings have martyrdom in mind.

29. Diocletian in the early fourth century fixed a price for sparrows which was not much higher (cf. Adolf Deissmann, *Light from the Ancient East,* tr. L. R. M. Strachan

---

lower of Christ cannot honorably flee to another city, but must proclaim his faith in boldness. The rabbi, according to the custom of the time, would whisper his teaching into the ear of an interpreter, who then would translate it in clear tones into the colloquial speech. Public announcements, and the proclamation that the sabbath was at hand, were made from "the roof"—the flat roof of temple or house. Thus the metaphor which Christ here employs. The truth he has given his disciples in obscurity or private conversation they are to publish to the world, at whatever cost (see Exeg., vs. 27). The follower of Christ should not fear, because cruelty of persecution cannot touch the soul. Flames and spears cannot reach the essential man: their power stops at the wall of the flesh, and the man is always more than flesh. The word here translated **soul** has three meanings in the N.T. Sometimes it means the life principle, sometimes the reason, but here spirit-in-flesh, the very self that is bound by the kingdom truth to the living God. We cater to the body even in our beneficence: a parent fears disease for his child more than he fears racial prejudice. Browning in "An Epistle" speaks of these two concerns, the concern for the body and the concern for the soul. See the lines beginning, "Discourse to him of prodigious armaments." [5] The eyes of Christ were on the real man. Persecution could not touch essential man, but treachery to

the truth could kill both soul and body. Gethsemane was not primarily a test of the flesh and nerves: "My soul is exceeding sorrowful" (26:38). So Jesus bade his followers not to fear men whose threat is against the flesh. They need not fear, for God is watching over them. He marks every turn of event. He sees even a sparrow's fall. He counts the hairs of a man's head. His children are precious in his sight (see Expos. vss. 29-31). The body may perish, but not the man. God will keep the man on earth until his kingdom-word is spoken and his kingdom-work is done, and will gather him home at death. There is profound psychology in this plea of **fear not.** Jesus here requires his followers to face the fear, even at its possible worst. Then he gives them a faith to overcome the fear, namely, that the spirit of man is beyond earthly threat, and that God is mighty to save. Two events only could befall his followers—life and death; and both are in the hand of God. **Fear not:** the Christian life is the ultimate valor.

29-31. *The Worth of Human Life.*—Have we lost the sense of personal worth? War is the symptom of that loss. Perhaps men go to war partly to compensate for the loss: they try to restore their ego by identification with the "glorious banners" of their country. Our forefathers apparently did not unduly suffer from an inferiority complex: that is a modern malady. It cannot be blamed on the new astron-

[5] Line 146.

30 But the very hairs of your head are all numbered.

31 Fear ye not therefore, ye are of more value than many sparrows.

32 Whosoever therefore shall confess me before men, him will I confess also before my Father which is in heaven.

your Father's will. 30 But even the hairs of your head are all numbered. 31 Fear not, therefore; you are of more value than many sparrows. 32 So every one who acknowledges me before men, I also will acknowledge before my Father who is in heaven;

[New York: George H. Doran, 1927], pp. 272-74). In this context the verse refers to the death of a sparrow. W. H. P. Hatch has suggested that the Aramaic saying may have been still stronger, "Not a sparrow alights on the ground," etc.

30. Like several of Jesus' sayings, this is hyperbolical. It emphasizes God's constant and personal care for all his creation. The expression **hairs of your head** may come from I Sam. 14:45.

31. The same reasoning is found in 6:30.

32-33. In Luke 12:8-9, which is probably the Q form of the saying, it is the Son of man who will acknowledge or repudiate men in the divine judgment, and Jesus does

---

omy. The physical magnitudes of the universe can enlarge the soul, rather than dwarf it; and we secretly know that life should not be judged by weight and measure. This denial of the worth of life comes from "man's inhumanity to man," [6] and from his denial of God. Pride of financial power has made multitudes regard themselves as failures: most men are (and perhaps must be) failures if money is the accepted standard of success. Pride of impersonal cities has dwarfed the individual until he seems to have no value. It is truth in paradox that the more man becomes proud, the more he minimizes his own worth. The antidote? To gaze, not on man, but on God and on God's providence: **Are not two sparrows sold for a penny?** There is no mass production in God's world. Everything is his handicraft. Even the dust on a moth's wing, when it is seen under a microscope, is a cluster of waving plumes, each strand of each plume with its own distinctiveness. That individuality is doubly marked in man. Beauty whispers each man in the ear, so that one man becomes artist in sound and another man artist in stone. So Duty speaks: Edith Cavell becomes a nurse, and Jacob Riis a builder of settlement houses. Thus each man holds day by day a private conversation with God. Our denials are all in vain. We may say, "Mankind is dust," but it is strange dust that declares itself to be dust. Inevitably we worship and pray.

Then how can the sense of personal worth be recovered? First, by confession, for we "feel small" when we fail. "Guilt consciousness" is not merely a morbid or nervous condition, but what the name implies. We ourselves cannot cancel the bane of guilt. Only God who made us can remake us. So confession and plea for mercy is the first step. Next, we recover the sense of worth by obedience, for we "feel small"

when we break the bond between ourselves and God. In all other regards we are small: our body is pygmy as compared with the fixed stars. We derive greatness from his greatness—by worship, by prayer, by obedience to his will. Thus the decline of worship has been a much more fertile cause of the cheapening of human life than the new science. *The Song of Bernadette*, by Franz Werfel, tells of a girl, from an unpromising home and apparently marked for "inferiority," who became great and turned her city into a shrine, by obedience to God. The other way to overcome "inferiority" is by the practice of good will, for we "feel small" whenever we try to make others "feel small." John Woolman traveled steerage lest, by paying to conform "to this world," he should make other people feel poor.[7] A man exalts himself whenever he humbles himself in love for God or man. A legend of Adam says that he dreamed he was a seraph, and believed the dream. He woke to find an angel at his side, who told him that he was still a man: "But within thee dwells a seraph. Yet he soareth only as thou dost learn to bend the knee." The recovery of the sense of man's worth is in the reverence that first acknowledges God and then honors the treasure in a neighbor's life. "Blessed are the meek, for they shall inherit the earth" (5:5).

32-33. How to Meet Persecution: (e) By Awareness of the Advocacy of Christ.—These verses continue the discussion of persecution and how to meet it. They speak of a double confession of faith. When a man confesses Christ on earth, Christ confesses his belief in that man before the throne of God. Public profession is required: **before men.** In the days of the early church that was dangerous, as it was in Nazi days in Europe. Everywhere it is

[6] Robert Burns, "Man Was Made to Mourn," st. vii.

[7] *The Journal of John Woolman* (Boston: Houghton Mifflin Co., The Riverside Press, 1871), pp. 238-41.

33 But whosoever shall deny me before men, him will I also deny before my Father which is in heaven.

34 Think not that I am come to send peace on earth: I came not to send peace, but a sword.

35 For I am come to set a man at variance against his father, and the daughter against her mother, and the daughter-in-law against her mother-in-law.

36 And a man's foes *shall be* they of his own household.

33 but whoever denies me before men, I also will deny before my Father who is in heaven.

34 "Do not think that I have come to bring peace on earth; I have not come to bring peace, but a sword. 35 For I have come to set a man against his father, and a daughter against her mother, and a daughter-in-law against her mother-in-law; 36 and a man's foes will be those of his own house-

not explicitly identify himself with that figure. But there, as well as here, what is important is witnessing to Jesus. This introduces a new idea, for in vss. 1, 7-8 the disciples are to heal and to proclaim the kingdom of God rather than the Messiah. Matthew and John often quote Jesus as speaking of God as **my Father;** Luke only infrequently.

34-36. The basic ideas are the same as in the parallel Luke 12:51-53, though the wording is different. Jesus regarded the truth as more important than temporary harmony in the family or the community, and never regarded the family or the social order as an end in itself. Only the kingdom of God was ultimate (6:33). The rabbis and apocalyptic writers believed that the days of the Messiah would be ushered in by wars and family strife. The Jewish **daughter-in-law** was expected to obey the **mother-in-law.** The saying is based on Mic. 7:6. (See also Cadbury, *Peril of Modernizing Jesus,* pp. 135-38, 143-44.) Arnold J. Toynbee uses these verses as an illustration of the almost intolerable tension which arises in society when a creative genius comes forward. Ordinary men and women must either oppose him or—at great cost to themselves—accept his new order (*A Study of History,* Abridgement of Vols. I-VI by D. C. Somervell [New York: Oxford University Press, 1947], p. 213).

difficult. We say, "I do not profess to be a Christian, but. . . ." The "but" either cites some Christian virtue which the speaker does profess, or criticizes some neighbor for not being a Christian. So when the phrase is analyzed it means, "I admire Christ's ethic, but prefer a half confession plus a half worldliness to any forthright allegiance." Most men have that preference, and think they can exercise it. But it is not possible very long to be half pagan and half Christian. Nor is it logical to say that "all religions are true in their setting." For they could not be: they hold contradictory views of life, and truth cannot contradict itself. So the Christian is required to burn his bridges: For weal or woe I believe that Christ "is what God means by 'Man.' He is what man means by 'God.' " [8] The danger is in half profession, or in a formalism that chokes the faith. This public profession is the stuff of judgment. The world of Spirit is the real world. There is "joy . . . in heaven over one sinner that repenteth" (Luke 15:7). Likewise there is confidence in heaven over one man who makes his brave confession. The man says on earth, "I believe in Christ," and Christ thereupon says in heaven, "I believe

in that man." Our doctrine of "one world at a time" is impossible in man's nature, and it is false by the facts as Christ taught them. Heaven is watching our every move, and we have an Advocate before the throne whence

. . . Thousands at his bidding speed
And post o'er Land and Ocean without rest [9]

to strengthen those who make their brave confession. Do we remember that whenever we confess Christ, by word against the world's fashion or by deed for Christ's sake, the event is seen in another world and is there spoken of with gladness? Our life is not drab: it is the drama of two worlds.

34-36. Not Peace, but a Sword.—The main import of these words is not literal. The confession of Christ has brought in actuality the sword of persecution; and there has been behind our wars a conflict of life views, one being more Christian than the other. But there is no justification here for the war method—not while the Sermon on the Mount remains. Luke's version gives us the meaning of the word **sword:** "Suppose ye that I am come to give peace on earth? I tell you, Nay; but rather division"

[8] J. S. Whale, *Christian Doctrine* (New York: The Macmillan Co., 1941), p. 104.

[9] Milton, "On His Blindness."

37 He that loveth father or mother more than me is not worthy of me: and he that loveth son or daughter more than me is not worthy of me.

hold. 37 He who loves father or mother more than me is not worthy of me; and he who loves son or daughter more than

37. Luke 14:26 expresses the principle in more extreme language; cf. also Matt. 12:46-50. According to the Mishnah, a man must honor God and the law more than his teacher, and his teacher more than his father (Baba Mezia 2:11).

(Luke 12:51). The saying holds of any new idea. There are ancient Babylonian inscriptions which endorse it. The idea of an eight-hour day in industry split business and politics into two camps. So did the idea of "one world," and the movement against slavery. Any step toward public housing projects divides men into "for" and "against," not without strife. But Christ is more than an outstanding instance of this division: he is the instance, for our interpretation of heaven and earth and our whole manner of life turn on him. Revelation (1:16) tells us of him, "Out of his mouth went a sharp two-edged sword." His doctrine is either true or untrue, his Cross is either a pathetic and ironic tragedy or a very redemption. Neutrality is not possible: we are either for him or against him, and between the two camps there is inevitable clash.

Why should not the gospel come peaceably? Because darkness in the ethical and spiritual realm hates the light, because antichrist is always intent to defeat Christ. If we press the question further back, and ask why man and the world are so made, we confront a mystery. We ourselves would not value an easy faith:

. . . when the fight begins within himself,
A man's worth something.[1]

We can but believe that God's method, the truth which at first makes strife, and then turns strife into peace, is the best way for us to realize our sonship with him. Notice that in the description of the strife (vs. 35) the young are ranged against the old. This rule is not without exception, for we sometimes see a brave veteran of the faith ranged against a young worldling. But there is hint here that Christianity is a venture for those young in soul. It is springtime tidings. It is forever impatient with the old stubborn bloodstained ways of earth, and forever intent on the new age. In both young and old in years Christ's kingdom is always a new daybreak. Notice also that the saying has an autobiographical force: Jesus met bitterness in his home, and was at odds with his mother and brethren (12:50). His gift is assuredly peace, as he said; but it is not peace by compromise or evasion. It is peace by strife (strife between the

[1] Browning, "Bishop Blougram's Apology," l. 693.

good and evil in us and in our world), and peace by the resolving of strife in the regnancy of his spirit.

37. Christ First.—Compare Luke 14:26: "If any man come to me, and hate not his father, and mother. . . . " Did Matthew tone down that harsh word? Or were Matthew and Luke using different reports of one saying? The Syrian mind was not afraid of hyperbole or striking metaphor. The meaning of the saying is clear. Christ does no violence to natural affection. Rather he honors it. But he requires, in peremptory demand, that he shall come first, with no rivals, in the allegiance of his followers. The history of Christian faith illustrates his meaning. The rich father may angrily oppose the son who chooses social service instead of business success. The worldly mother may disown the daughter who proposes "to waste" her life on the mission field. And what of the Moslem or Brahman who forsakes the ancestral faith for Christ? He runs into enough trouble at home, and must make his choice between natural affection and the claims of Christ.

The reason for the demand is not hard to seek. If Christ is first in truth, if he is the disclosure of God and the true life of man, he should come first in our life. If our nature so needs him—for guidance, for pardon, for challenge—that we cannot live the creative life without him, he should come first. Milton risked (and lost) his failing eyesight in writing his Defence of the English People. But he knew that his conscience would be violated and his nature thrown into chaos if he loved "his own life" more than truth. If the world so needs Christ that without him trade becomes a fratricide and home life a selfishness, Christ should come first. Behind the demand is precisely that claim—that he is first, and that he is the true life of men and society. The interpreter should note that the word "love" means in the original our "natural affections." Jesus here kept his own precept. As man he did not love his own life, but gave it upon a Cross for God's sake and the world's. Likewise he turned his back on home ties for the call of the kingdom. The rule is this: if natural affection wars against Christ, it must be sacrificed for his sake. Yet, by paradox, only by that surrender is natural affection saved from its own decay.

38 And he that taketh not his cross, and followeth after me, is not worthy of me.

39 He that findeth his life shall lose it: and he that loseth his life for my sake shall find it.

me is not worthy of me; **38** and he who does not take his cross and follow me is not worthy of me. **39** He who finds his life will lose it, and he who loses his life for my sake will find it.

---

38. A condemned man had to **take his cross** and carry it (cf. 27:32; John 19:17) — not the entire cross, but the crossbeam which would later be fixed to the stake. If Jesus and his followers were to be taken for revolutionaries and arrested by the Romans, this kind of death was possible, and they made their last journey to Jerusalem in the consciousness of this danger. However, the words "and let him take up his cross" are omitted from the parallel passage, Mark 8:34, in the newly discovered Codex 2427, which is related to Vaticanus and other Alexandrian MSS.

39. He who risks his life and hands it over to God will share in the life of the world to come, whether martyrdom is his lot or not; but cowardice is certain death for the soul. Luke 17:33 does not contain the words **for my sake.**

---

38. *Taking up the Cross.*—This saying recurs in this Gospel (16:24), a fact that may show its centrality. The teaching cannot be diluted: the Cross is no mere inconvenience. The context makes clear that Jesus was speaking of martyrdom. His disciples had seen condemned men carrying their cross to some near-by golgotha. That is the picture, whether or not Christ was hinting of the manner of his own death. W. M. Clow has drawn a distinction between burden, thorn, and cross. He says that a burden is the inevitable load which life lays on every man; that a thorn is the sharp affliction which most people must bear in some form, as Paul bore his "thorn in the flesh" (II Cor. 12:7); and that the cross is our voluntary self-denial for Christ's sake.[2] These distinctions cannot be made arbitrary, but Clow is right to differentiate between the burdens we are conscripted to carry and the cross for which we volunteer. A man "takes up" his cross for Christ's sake, and cannot worthily avoid it. Grenfell need not have gone to Labrador, even as Paul need not have hazarded his life in his mission to the Gentiles. The cross is a self-denial which "comfortable people" choose to evade. The exposition of the next saying below is closely bound with this comment. The motive is a main issue. Jesus nowhere proposed an asceticism for its own sake. The "martyr complex" is quite alien from his gospel. Simeon Stylites is not the best instance of Christian sainthood. "For my sake" is the motive, and vss. 40-42 trace the manner of fulfillment.

Thus the words **and followeth after me** are pivotal. To take up the cross is hard enough, but to carry it day by day to the place of crucifixion is harder. Luke 9:23—"take up his cross daily"—has caught the meaning. John Henry Newman once described this demand as "the continual practice of small duties distasteful to us."[3] But that is hardly accurate: it is not so much duty as an abandon of the soul which suffers the loss of all things for Christ's sake, and which thereafter proves the voluntary surrender in issues both great and small. The words of Christ are in some copies of the N.T. rightly printed in red. J. H. Jowett used to say that the Christian life is like the alpine rope which has "a red worsted strand running through it from end to end. . . . The sealed followers of the Lord are known by their red strand, . . . the red endless line of sacrifice."[4] What is the result of cross-carrying? It leads to life: see vs. 39. It is like wheat sown: it brings its joyous harvest (John 12:24). Ruskin once said that the Christian church has turned the cross from a gallows into a raft,[5] and the stricture is worth heeding; but the fact remains that carrying a cross does open life to Christ's salvation. Phillips Brooks has reminded us in this connection that the sacrifices of O.T. days were made to the accompaniment of trumpets.[6]

39. *Finding Our Life.*—A man would never be lost if his life were where his body is, but—! Do we not say of some neighbor, "He has never found himself"? Most people are in that predicament. By any interpretation this saying implies a cleft in our nature, even allowing for an eschatological stress. **He who finds his [lower] life will lose** his higher life. Both lower and higher life in this saying may perhaps be roughly identified with the self. But Christ taught often that the higher self is our true nature. When the prodigal "came to himself"

[3] Quoted, *Expositor's Dictionary of Texts,* I, 855.

[4] *Sharing His Sufferings* (London: James Clarke & Co., 1911), p. 104.

[5] Quoted, *Great Texts of the Bible,* vol. on *St. Matthew,* p. 326.

[6] "The Joy of Self-Sacrifice," in *The Candle of the Lord* (New York: E. P. Dutton & Co., 1896), especially pp. 27, 37.

[2] *The Cross in Christian Experience* (New York: George H. Doran Co., 1908), p. 232.

40 ¶ He that receiveth you receiveth me; and he that receiveth me receiveth him that sent me.	40 "He who receives you receives me, and he who receives me receives him who

5. Rewards for Aiding Jesus' Followers (10:40-42)

40. This saying concluded the discourse in Q (cf. Luke 10:16; Mark 9:37). It is one of a number of sayings in which Jesus speaks definitely of his mission and purpose and uses such phrases as "I am come." These are relatively infrequent in the old dialogues and sayings groups of the Synoptic Gospels but appear everywhere in John; and specialists are not agreed as to how many of them are historical. Early Christians believed, of course, that Jesus had been **sent** with full authority, and the Jewish rule applied that "a man's emissary is like the man himself" (Berakoth 5:5). The noun "apostle" is derived from the Greek verb used here. Parallels to this verse can be found in John 13:20; Did. 11:1; 12:1.

(Luke 15:17), he returned home—to God. There seem to be a million roads down which a man can seek life, but in fact there are only two. We may describe the choice as that between body and soul: Jesus confronted his followers with just that decision, for he is here discussing the likelihood of their martyrdom. We can describe the choice as that between earth and heaven, and Jesus had that alternative in mind: a faithful confession on earth would win his advocacy before the throne of God. The alternative can be labeled thus: flesh or spirit. But by whatever name, there are only two roads. We cannot travel both: if we travel one we necessarily lose the other, despite the fact that many people try to travel east and west at the same time. Again the question of motive is stressed. People can be "righteous" through low-hankering, because it is "safer," or because it "pays," or because they can thus enjoy a "good reputation." The motive here implied is the motive of the Christian faith, the flinging away of low ambition for the sake of that Christ who is the disclosure of eternity.

This is truth on any level. If money is hoarded, it is soon lost. If health is hoarded, it becomes hypochondria. If life is clutched, it is lost; but if it is nobly lost, it is found. As instance of the tragic losing Peer Gynt will serve: his past life in its selfishness was stripped away as he pondered it, like the skins of an onion, until the center, when reached, was—nothing.[7] As instance of the noble finding, recall Galahad as portrayed in the Edwin A. Abbey mural in the Boston Public Library. The perilous seat to which he moved bore a scroll of letters in a tongue no man could read. Of it Merlin, in "The Holy Grail" said, "For there no man could sit but he should lose himself." Galahad answered, "If I lose myself, I save myself," and thereupon took the vows of the knights of the Round Table, while the knights made the sign of the cross with the uplifted

hilt of their swords.[8] The realism of the saying should be noted. It is not good advice merely, but eternal verity more sure than the stars. Every kind of life involves surgery because there is a cleft—and a basic choice—in our nature. If we choose the lower, we cut away the higher and become disconsolate. If we choose the higher, as it is seen incarnate in Christ, we cut away the lower by slow or swift means. To choose the lower is gratuitous pain; to choose the higher is the pruning which leads to life.

40-41. *The Exaltation of the Obscure.*—This is J. W. Shepard's title.[9] These verses are linked with vss. 5-14, and continue the instruction given to the apostles as they set forth on the kingdom mission. Notice with care the Exeg. on **sent** and **prophet.** Christ here sees in his mind's eye the lowly folk, as well as apostles and proven followers, who will welcome his ambassadors. Chrysostom in his *Homilies* says, "Seest thou what mighty persuasions He used, and how He opened to them the houses of the whole world."[1] This promise is a sublime ending to the "instructions." Indeed it is like radium—not striking in appearance, but filled with light and healing. It should never have become "a neglected saying." Once again motive is the crux. To receive a traveler from good nature or in hope "to receive again" is one thing; to receive him because he is the emissary of Christ is another thing. Apparently Christ had in mind the sad likelihood of false prophets. Thus the phrase repeats with **righteous man** substituted for **prophet.** The righteousness instanced is Christ's righteousness—the way of the kingdom, and the welcome instanced is the welcome given to a man because he is bent on kingdom business.

There is more here than tender regard for

[7] Henrik Ibsen, *Peer Gynt*, Act V, scene 5.

[8] Tennyson, *Idylls of the King:* "The Holy Grail," 1. 173.

[9] In *Light and Life*, quoted, *Expositor's Dictionary of Texts*, I, 855.

[1] *The Homilies of Saint John Chrysostom on the Gospel of St. Matthew*, Homily xxxv. 4.

41 He that receiveth a prophet in the name of a prophet shall receive a prophet's reward; and he that receiveth a righteous man in the name of a righteous man shall receive a righteous man's reward.

42 And whosoever shall give to drink unto one of these little ones a cup of cold *water* only in the name of a disciple, verily I say unto you, he shall in no wise lose his reward.

sent me. **41** He who receives a prophet because he is a prophet shall receive a prophet's reward, and he who receives a righteous man because he is a righteous man shall receive a righteous man's reward. **42** And whoever gives to one of these little ones even a cup of cold water because he is a disciple, truly, I say to you, he shall not lose his reward."

41-42. Three groups seem to be distinguished: prophets, righteous men (who perhaps are tested and honored Christians), and little ones or ordinary disciples. The Christian **prophet** is frequently mentioned, and his powers and functions are similar to those of an apostle (e.g., Acts 11:27; 13:1-3; I Cor. 12:28; Did. 11:3-12). But there is no distinction as regards the **reward**, which, as Chrysostom said, is eternal life. **A cup of cold water** is a proverbial expression for a minor service. As in the parable of the last judgment (25:31-46), Matthew concludes an important doctrinal section by emphasizing the need for practical lovingkindness. This is the final result and test of discipleship.

---

the obscure, though that tenderness does clearly shine. Christ's heart went out always to the lowly saint, and conversely he had warning for the glamour of great talent. But there is more than that deep feeling. Christ is saying that all talents are small when compared with supernal light; or rather, that all Christ-dedicated talents are great, and that the man who gives bed and board to a prophet is himself numbered among the prophets. The lowly host reveals himself in his hospitable act. He is not himself a prophet, but he thereby tells God what he would like to be; and God takes the intention for the deed. It is "not what man Does which exalts him, but what man Would do!" [2] Notice, therefore, the broad equivalence of reward. It is a rightful equivalence. Talents, few or many, are given; and a man has no more occasion to be proud of many talents or to despair of few than he has occasion for pride or despair because he was born at three in the morning. The test is what we do with the gifts that God gives. The man who has talent only to be host to a kingdom messenger, and is true to the best use of the gift, is as noble as any man could prove himself; and God takes his pale gleam of dawn for the splendor of full day.

> All I could never be,
> All, men ignored in me,
> This, I was worth to God, whose wheel the
> pitcher shaped.[3]

A prophet's reward is to be a better prophet, and to journey on into the bright vistas of the kingdom.

42. *A Cup of Cold Water Only.*—This is a boldness in very truth. All the sayings recorded

[2] Browning, "Saul," st. xviii.
[3] Browning, "Rabbi Ben Ezra," st. xxv.

in vss. 38-42 were apparently spoken with great emotion, that fact being attested by a striking absence of participles in the Greek original. Even the noun **water** is omitted: the reading is, "a cup of cool." The **little ones** are Christ's disciples, setting forth on their hazardous mission. To interpret **little ones** as primarily children or the indigent does violence to the mood of the promise. Christ foresaw the persecution of his followers: they were like lambs in the midst of wolves. He foresaw also that some would minister to their need—at risk of unpopularity and perhaps of bitter loss. There were some who would "receive a prophet." To them is this promise given.

Thus the gift is not mere charity, for it is motivated by the fact that the **little ones** are messengers of Christ. To act from **pity** is a worthiness, but it is not so fine as the desire to prosper the cause of the kingdom. Nor is the gift very small. There is some danger that this saying may be made a pack horse for stinginess. Many a man has given a cup of water for the cause of Christ, and counted it righteousness, when he should have given his house and land. The word "cool" is in contrast with the fierceness of thirst in that sun-struck land, and with the merciless swords of the sun. A cup of cold water meant more than a trip to an underground cistern, though that might involve a small journey, for cistern water was not likely to be very cold. It meant a trip to the well—no small sacrifice. So the promise is to those who receive the prophet as if receiving the prophet's Lord, those ready to suffer more than inconvenience for that high—but unpopular—cause.

The promise has found its way into many a lovely story, and deserves that immortality. James Russell Lowell's "The Vision of Sir

11 And it came to pass, when Jesus had made an end of commanding his twelve disciples, he departed thence to teach and to preach in their cities.

2 Now when John had heard in the prison the works of Christ, he sent two of his disciples,

11 And when Jesus had finished instructing his twelve disciples, he went on from there to teach and preach in their cities.

2 Now when John heard in prison about the deeds of the Christ, he sent word by

C. Summary (11:1)

11:1. This verse, like 7:28-29, marks the conclusion of one of the major sections of the Gospel. One would expect that at this point the disciples would go out and preach, but Matthew perhaps believed that the disciples did not begin their mission until after the Resurrection (28:19-20). At any rate, he makes no mention of their experiences as evangelists or of their return from the mission.

V. Resumption of the Narrative: Jesus' Rejection (11:2–12:50)

Early Christians were vividly conscious that they were living in the final age of history and were seeing what many prophets and righteous men had longed in vain to see (13:17). They were citizens of heaven (Phil. 3:20), endowed with the first fruits of the Spirit (Rom. 8:23), and had already tasted the powers of the age to come (Heb. 6:5). Secure in this possession, they were able to triumph over all the miseries of the present time. They therefore found it almost impossible to understand how anyone who heard the message of salvation through Christ could reject it. Yet it was ignored or despised, and not merely by the Gentiles. The ancient chosen people of God, who were rightly God's sons, and to whom belonged his presence, the covenants, the law, the temple worship, the promises, the patriarchs, and the Messiah (Rom. 9:4-5), had very largely rejected Jesus. God must therefore have permitted this. In Rom. 9–11 Paul wrestles with the problem. He concludes that Israel's "hardening" is only temporary, for after the Gentiles have been converted, all Israel will be saved (Rom. 11:26). Mark and the Q source also dealt with the difficulty, and in this part of the Gospel Matthew undertakes to explain the mystery by combining parts of these earlier books which dealt with the theme. He first shows that, although John the Baptist and his disciples do not belong to Jesus' movement, John's work was a prophetic preparation for the Messiah and the great prophet did not actually reject him. The full revelation of Jesus' nature (11:25-30) is, however, not made until after the departure of John's emissaries. Concrete examples of acceptance and rejection follow, and these lead up to the discourse on the kingdom of heaven (ch. 13). Though Jesus proclaims the kingdom publicly, Matthew (like Mark) believes that only a few are ready to accept his teaching. The revelation is at one and the same time hidden and disclosed. But whereas Mark emphasizes the stupidity of the disciples, Matthew insists on their receptiveness and insight (13:16).

Launfal" is a bright instance. The hero purposed to ride far in search of the Holy Grail, but realized in a dream that the leper at his gate was the concern of Christ and his means of serving Christ: "Inasmuch as ye have done it unto one of these least. . . ." Thereupon the cup of water he gave to the leper was turned on the sudden into the Holy Grail. But most such stories still miss the tender and tragic meaning of these little ones.

What is the reward? Not the crass rewards of earth. The saint does not wish to "rest in a golden grove, or to bask in a summer sky." He covets "the wages of going on."[4] It seems certain

4 Tennyson, "Wages."

that Christ had heaven in mind—the heaven of the soul here, and very heaven when this life is done. The reward is that God will quench the soul's thirst in the donor, even as the donor has been willing at risk to minister to the lowly ambassador of Christ.

11:2-6. *Art Thou the Coming One?*—This chapter begins what might be called "the third book of Matthew," the second book beginning at chapter eight. If book two is the evangel, this book is the apologia. It describes deepening enmity to Christ, and pleads his claims. So it raises at once the cardinal question: Is Christ the true Deliverer? The question is asked pointedly by the followers of John the Baptist. Per-

3 And said unto him, Art thou he that should come, or do we look for another?	his disciples 3 and said to him, "Are you he who is to come, or shall we look for

A. The Relation of John the Baptist to the New Order (11:2-19)

Matthew does not work out a completely clear explanation of how the old religion is related to the new. He insists that Jesus is the true Messiah of Israel, who was prophesied in the O.T., and that the law, as Christ reformulated it, is absolutely valid; but at the same time "the law and the prophets were until John," though in 11:12-13 (=Luke 16:16) he blunts the edge of the Q saying. His uncertainty arises partly because he wishes to include as much of his source material as possible.

John the Baptist actually belonged to the old order. His rite was a "baptism of repentance for the remission of sins" in preparation for the final judgment and the dawn of the new age. Josephus (*Antiquities* XVIII. 5. 2) in no way connects him with Jesus. The Q source here pictures him as uncertain about Jesus' significance. Disciples of John are mentioned several times in the N.T. (e.g., Luke 11:1; John 1:35; 3:25), and Acts (18:25; 19:1-4) knows of those who had received only the baptism of John. There is some evidence that after John's death his disciples continued as a separate Jewish party or sect outside the Christian church, and this may explain why the Fourth Gospel insists in every possible way that John was nothing more than Jesus' forerunner. Further information can be found in C. R. Bowen, *Studies in the New Testament* (Chicago: University of Chicago Press, 1936), pp. 30-76; M. Goguel, *Au Seuil de l'Évangile: Jean-Baptiste* (Paris: Payot, 1928).

How closely was Jesus' work, in the beginning, connected with that of his predecessor? This passage indicates that though his mission was different, it was in some sense a continuation of John's. He speaks of John in terms of the greatest praise, and on another occasion he couples his own authority with that of John (21:23-27). A rite of baptism became a permanent feature of Christianity. Jesus must have begun by co-operating with the Baptist, but striking new elements were soon exhibited in his teaching and activities.

1. A Delegation of John's Followers Visits Jesus (11:2-6)

2. The parallel Luke 7:18 does not say that this occurred when John was **in prison.**

3. **He who is to come,** ὁ ἐρχόμενος, may be a technical term for the expected redeemer (cf. 3:11; Dan. 7:13; Heb. 10:37; Rev. 1:4). It is also found in the liturgies of the Mandaeans, a Gnostic sect which regarded John the Baptist as a messiah.

haps the inquiry sprang from dawning faith, but it seems likelier that they, or he, or both, had their doubts. Why? Partly because John was in prison, in the fortress of Machaerus. The eagle was caged. The waiting fretted his soul. Perhaps the doubt came in part because John's followers were jealous of the growing cause of Jesus: the two groups may have seemed to each other to be rivals. But doubt grew chiefly on the fact that Christ did not fulfill either the hope of the Messiah as nationalistically interpreted, or the picture that John himself had drawn. As for the latter portrayal, where was the "axe at the root of the tree," and where the consuming "fire"? (see 3:10, 12). John's doubt is perchance our doubt. Is this the Christ? If not, we also must look for **another,** for it is not in our own power to work our own salvation. Christ's answer, though it seems at first blush all too mild, was actually as much of an affirmative as

his honoring of our freedom could allow. He refers clearly to Isa. 35:5; 61:1-3. Both these scriptures were deemed messianic. Preaching to the poor was an accepted sign of the new age. **Go and show John:** it was an invitation to the imprisoned prophet to reconsider his description of the kingdom. The Messiah might come through love rather than through violent judgment. Apparently Christ still shrank from open announcement. The time was not ripe, and in any event he would not force the issue: he must leave room for the soul's brave confession.

What do we nobly wish in God's true Messiah? Perhaps we also are impatient, and perhaps our expectations are mistaken (see Expos., 16:20-21). We properly wish in the "Coming One" manhood like our own: he must share our life. We wish light, not flickering shore lights, but a sun and star. We wish love, homey, universal, holy, not indulgent, redeeming. We wish

4 Jesus answered and said unto them, Go and show John again those things which ye do hear and see:

5 The blind receive their sight, and the lame walk, the lepers are cleansed, and the deaf hear, the dead are raised up, and the poor have the gospel preached to them.

6 And blessed is *he,* whosoever shall not be offended in me.

7 ¶ And as they departed, Jesus began to say unto the multitudes concerning John, What went ye out into the wilderness to see? A reed shaken with the wind?

another?" 4 And Jesus answered them, "Go and tell John what you hear and see: 5 the blind receive their sight and the lame walk, lepers are cleansed and the deaf hear, and the dead are raised up, and the poor have good news preached to them. 6 And blessed is he who takes no offense at me."

7 As they went away, Jesus began to speak to the crowds concerning John: "What did you go out into the wilderness to behold? A reed shaken by the wind?

4-5. What you hear and see are the wonders which Jesus performed in chs. 8–9, and which the disciples were commanded to do also. Jewish writers believed that in the messianic age all sickness would be healed (e.g., Jubilees 23:26-30; Enoch 5:8-9). The Q writer probably regarded these miracles as the fulfillment of the prophecies of Isa. 35:5-6; 61:1-2. The latter passage begins by promising that the good news will be announced to the lowly, and in these verses the good news is the climax. Jesus interpreted his great works as a sign that the new age was dawning, but most important of all was the good news to the poor.

6. He who takes no offense at me is literally "anyone who is not scandalized" or "caused to stumble" by me. The word σκανδαλίζω usually means "to lead into sin" or "to cause someone to lose his faith." The metaphor is that of a trap or snare or anything which causes one to stumble and fall (Mal. 2:8; Rom. 9:32-33; I Cor. 8:13), and thus to be turned aside from the straight way of righteousness. Jewish moral teachers thought of life as a journey, and gave the name "halakah," i.e., the way to walk, to directions for conduct. In this context the saying must mean: "It is not necessary for John to understand and acknowledge the full meaning of these events; I shall be content if he does not join my opponents in condemning my ministry. Anyone who looks on this work with friendly eyes is blessed."

What can have been the sequel to this scene? Did John acknowledge Jesus as the "Coming One"? And, if so, did his disciples ignore such testimony?

2. Jesus Praises Him and Identifies Him as the Forerunner
(11:7-15)

The kernel of this section is found in vss. 7-9, 11; and vss. 12-14 are based on a separate saying about John, which is also found in Luke 16:16.

7. Manuscripts of the N.T. were originally written without punctuation. Editors, when they punctuate, are dependent on ancient commentators and their own reasoning.

---

life, above our transience and tears. Yet we do not wish such a blinding revelation that our faith would be seared and coerced. If the true Messenger were to come with cleaving sword, we might be compelled to believe. Such belief is not belief, but compulsion and the embezzlement of our manhood. The disclosure must still be veiled in flesh: only so can we make our venture. Thus we also are confronted by the very answer that Jesus gave to John the Baptist. What kind of Christ do we wish when we are at our best? Does Jesus fulfill that wish? Belief is at basis a personal trust in response to God's sign and gift. God comes in Jesus; we must

make the venture both in faith and life. The comment of Jesus holds poignantly of our time, for our lower wishes—nationalistic, proud, comfort-loving—easily gain precedence over the soul's sincere desire: **Blessed is he who takes no offense at me.**

7-11. *Jesus' Tribute to John the Baptist.*—Who would dare appraise contemporary leaders? We all try, but we are well aware that history may falsify our judgments. Yet Christ appraised the ministry of John the Baptist. John's followers were there, with the crowd that believed John to be a prophet. John's enemies were there, who regarded him as an adventurer

8 But what went ye out for to see? A man clothed in soft raiment? behold, they that wear soft *clothing* are in kings' houses.

9 But what went ye out for to see? A prophet? yea, I say unto you, and more than a prophet.

10 For this is *he,* of whom it is written, Behold, I send my messenger before thy face, which shall prepare thy way before thee.

11 Verily I say unto you, Among them that are born of women there hath not

8 Why then did you go out? To see a man[b] clothed in soft raiment? Behold, those who wear soft raiment are in kings' houses.

9 Why then did you go out? To see a prophet?[c] Yes, I tell you, and more than a prophet. **10** This is he of whom it is written,

'Behold, I send my messenger before thy face,
who shall prepare thy way before
thee.'

11 Truly, I say to you, among those born

[b] Or *What then did you go out to see? A man.*
[c] Many ancient authorities read *What then did you go out to see? A prophet?*

If the question marks are placed differently, the Greek reads: "Why did you go out into the wilderness? To gaze at a reed shaken by the wind?" This makes good sense, and fits better with the punctuation and translation adopted by RSV in vss. 8-9. Just as the crowds did not make the journey into the Jordan Valley merely to look at reeds blowing in the wind, which can always be seen there, so they were not led there by a man of weak and wavering character. The evangelists no doubt take this to mean also that John, despite his question in vs. 3, cannot really doubt Jesus.

8. No one could imagine that John was the sort of man who was accustomed to live luxuriously. The crowds went out, not to see an aristocrat or a pretender to the kingship, but one like an O.T. prophet in character and appearance. If they had the perception and moral earnestness to accept John, they should accept the greater events that are now taking place.

9-10. The crowds took John to be **a prophet,** but he was **more than a prophet.** Vs. 10, which is probably a very early addition to the tradition, explains that he was, in fact, the messenger of the covenant (cf. vs. 14). The quotation from Mal. 3:1 seems to be translated directly from the Hebrew. It has been Christianized by substituting **thy** for "my" to make it refer directly to Jesus.

11. Those born of women is simply another way of saying "human beings." Nowhere else in the tradition does Jesus call him **John the Baptist.** An earlier title was "the

rather than a prophet. Yet Jesus, though in a ticklish spot, sprang to John's defense, and delineated John's ministry in lines sure as light. He deliberately measured the man and his cause. History has not falsified the judgment. Jesus esteemed John with a soul's loyalty. His spirit quickened to the courage that did not flinch from dungeon and death. The appraisal is couched in dramatic questions. **What did you go out into the wilderness to behold?** Not a **reed:** the Jordan valley was filled with ordinary reeds, and John was no ordinary man. **A reed shaken with the wind?** No, John was not swayed by winds of favor, nor did he ever trim his truth to the popular whim. **Why then did you go out?** Not to see a **man clothed in soft raiment:** John was no sycophant or comfort-seeker. He was in a king's palace now, but in a dungeon—for his brave word of truth. **Why then did you go out? To see a prophet?** More than a prophet; for John, as forerunner of the Messiah, ended and crowned the line of the O.T. prophets. More, he was God's fit man for

God's apt deed. So Jesus, filled with love and longing for one whose voice had cried in a desert and would soon be silenced in a dungeon, boldly told the crowd that John was greater than their prophets.

Then, with perhaps greater boldness, Christ traced the limits of John's character and cause. John had a better eye for the flames of judgment than for the quiet dawn of good will. To him God was Judge rather than Father. So when Christ did not meet his expectations, John began to doubt. Therefore there was a deep sense in which the lowliest follower of Christ was **greater,** in privilege and insight if not in character, than John (see next Expos.). How did John's followers and the crowd accept the delineation? We are not told. This pro and con of appraisal is filled with meaning for our time. There is still a conflict between the followers of John and the followers of Jesus. What kind of kingdom do we wish, and by what method? Are our doubts rooted in a false expectation which has met disappointment? Three facts

risen a greater than John the Baptist: not-withstanding, he that is least in the king-dom of heaven is greater than he.

12 And from the days of John the Bap-tist until now the kingdom of heaven suf-fereth violence, and the violent take it by force.

13 For all the prophets and the law prophesied until John.

of women there has risen no one greater than John the Baptist; yet he who is least in the kingdom of heaven is greater than he. 12 From the days of John the Baptist until now the kingdom of heaven has suf-fered violence,*d* and men of violence take it by force. 13 For all the prophets and the

d Or has been coming violently.

---

baptizer" (Mark 1:4). **He who is least in the kingdom of heaven** cannot refer to those who will be in the kingdom when it is manifested completely. In that case John and all the prophets would be excluded, and Jesus never doubts that they will share in the world to come. Therefore the saying refers to Jesus' disciples, who are experiencing the "first fruits" of the kingdom. They are **greater,** not in their moral character or achievements, but in their privileges. This is one of the most important of those sayings which indicate that the kingdom is already present.

12-13. Matthew's form of this saying may mean: (*a*) "From John's time till now, the kingdom [i.e., the Christian movement, or God's people] has been oppressed, and the oppressors are still ravaging it. The law and the prophets were until John, but with the fulfillment of their prophecy came persecution also." In this case Matthew interprets

---

stand out in bold relief—the **more than a prophet's** grandeur in John, Christ's bold de-lineation of a man to whom his soul went out in quickening love, and the sunrise wonder of the new kingdom.

11, 13. *Yet He Who Is Least.*— (See Expos., vs. 12.) These words are hard to interpret; or if they are to be taken at face value, hard to believe. We hug the past: "There were giants . . . in those days." We are slow to believe that God draws climactic lines across history, and that expectant souls in the new era have "greater" verity than the bravest seers of the past. But Jesus boldly proclaimed a new age. History has seasons and eras. Indeed, it has "contingencies" and crises: to the Christian it is the writing of a mysterious Providence. Jesus marveled at men who, while they could read the sky to prophesy rain or fine weather, could not read "the signs of the times" (16:3). Is the era of nationalism now ending? The era of machine dominance? The era of Protestant divisions? It is a Christian's obligation to ask when and where God draws his lines across history. But Jesus is concerned in this saying with the line of the kingdom, the "great divide" made by his coming into the world. When he said, **yet he who is least,** he had no poor thought about John, but rather great thoughts about the kingdom. Do we understand that this is the climactic line? That blank page between the N.T. and the O.T. is a mountain ridge that divides time. It is a great act of God, a new creation. People who live on one side, even though they are as noble as John, even though they foretell the new age as did John, are not

as "great" in favor and understanding as the lowliest who, trusting Christ, have entered the new land.

The marks of the new age are not hard to trace. The dominant claim when Christ comes is not rights or even duties, but love. A man no longer says, "I'm better than you," or even, "I'm as good as you"; but, "You and I will love and serve because we are both children of God through Jesus Christ." The least in the new realm is greater than the noblest in the other country. Is there not the story of a mother who nailed her photograph on the wall of each cheap rooming house in town (thus seeking her wayward daughter), with a scribbled mes-sage on the picture: "Come home—Mother." Shall we say reverently that Jesus is that picture of God? George Matheson once said that Jesus is God's picture of us—a picture that he hangs on heaven's wall to keep himself from despair.[5] Jesus "makes all the difference," not only be-tween two ages of history, but between life and death. That line traced in the words "The New Testament"—on which side do we live? The least on Christ's side of that line are greater—not by merit, but by grace—than the noblest in the old dispensation.

12. *The Kingdom of Heaven Has Suffered Violence.*—This word is hard to construe. We cannot be sure of its meaning. If the context were certain, interpretation would be easier; but, as the Exeg. repeatedly shows us, this Gospel groups sayings with scant regard for the original setting. We can bring three meanings

[5] *Searchings in the Silence* (London: Cassell & Co., 1894), pp. 108-9.

14 And if ye will receive *it*, this is Elias, which was for to come.

law prophesied until John; 14 and if you are willing to accept it, he is Elijah who

the saying as referring to events of his own time. The oppressors may be earthly rulers or demonic powers. Or the passage may mean: (*b*) "From John's time until now, zealots or revolutionists have sought to seize God's kingdom [i.e., they have tried to establish his sovereignty by forceful means] and by so doing they are only ravaging it." This does not fit well with the present form of vs. 13, but otherwise has much to commend it. The stories of revolts in first-century Palestine can be read in Josephus (*Antiquities* XVIII. 1. 6; XX. 5; XX. 8. 5-7, 10; *Jewish War* II. 8. 1; II. 12. 4; II. 13. 2-7). Or: (*c*) "From John's time until now, the kingdom is exercising its own spiritual force, and men of spiritual force are able to lay hold of it, for the law and the prophets were until John, but now the new age has come." This is the idea of Rudolf Otto (*The Kingdom of God and the Son of Man*, tr. F. V. Filson and Bertram Lee Woolf [London: Lutterworth Press, 1943], pp. 108-12). Here the verb βιάζεται is taken as a middle, not a passive. Though this interpretation is daring, it brings out the contrast between the old and the new.

The saying in Q may have read: "The law and the prophets were until John; since then the kingdom of God βιάζεται" ("suffers violence" or "exercises its power"). All we can be sure of is that the saying contrasted the previous age with the new and spoke of violent power in connection with the kingdom.

14. The messenger of the covenant, alluded to in vs. 10, is now explicitly identified with Elijah. According to Mal. 4:5, Elijah would return before the day of the Lord. Some first-century Jews believed that Elijah had been hidden by God until the time of his

(among many) into focus. Read carefully the exegetical note. Each could be true. Therefore each has point for the interpreter. Meanwhile it is worth remembering that the very contention as to the meaning is a tribute to Christ: treasure makes the contention. Perhaps the saying is a description of John's ministry. He stormed heaven with vehement zeal, as soldiers storm a town. What a breach he made when he declared that Abrahamic descent was no passport to God's favor! (3:9.) The old standards and methods were overturned when the common people streamed out into the desert to hear tidings of God. The new age came like an invasion—with both bane and gain. By this interpretation the saying is closely linked with the preceding words. But perhaps the saying means that the kingdom in its coming is marked by violence wrought upon it by its foes, or by revolutionists who believed in open revolt. If this is the meaning, Jesus may have been making oblique reference here to the imprisonment and impending death of John the Baptist and to the fate in store for many of his followers. Or the words may echo the persecutions which befell Christians in Matthew's own time. The words then would be a variant of Jesus' warning that he came to bring not peace, but a sword; and would underscore his challenge to would-be disciples to gird themselves for suffering and death.

There is another interpretation: the saying may be a description of the zeal which must attend the good news. If the word is out of its

original context, this interpretation might well hold. The kingdom bursts ancient bounds—like the headiness of new wine. Harlots and toll-gatherers enter it, when the "righteous" delay. Christ commands "Follow me!" and old habits of life are stormed and captured. Men discover when Christ calls that there is a Samson-strength in them, and they go forth to spiritual battle. No one can dogmatize about the meaning of the word. But that such zeal is needed who can doubt? We become semimaniacs about football or salesmanship, but remain tepid or judicial about the gospel—as though the kingdom could come by Talleyrand's motto, *Point de zèle, Monsieur* (No zeal, sir).[6] The kingdom is flaming zeal, and it turns the world upside down.

> What man can live denying his own soul?
> Hast thou not learned that noble uncontrol
> Is virtue's right, the breath by which she lives?
> Oh, sure if any angel ever grieves
> 'Tis when the living soul hath learned to chide
> Its passionate indignations and to hide
> The sudden flow of rapture, the quick birth
> Of overwhelming loves.[7]

The kingdom comes by overwhelming love for Christ, and by a zeal that storms the strongholds of ancient wrong.

[6] Henry Lytton Bulwer, *Historical Characters* (London: Richard Bentler, 1868), I, 153.
[7] John Philip Varley, "To One Who Having a Talent for Music Would by Persuasion Have Hid It in the Earth," *Sylvian and Poems* (New York: Brentano Bros., 1885).

15 He that hath ears to hear, let him hear.

16 ¶ But whereunto shall I liken this generation? It is like unto children sitting in the markets, and calling unto their fellows,

17 And saying, We have piped unto you, and ye have not danced; we have mourned unto you, and ye have not lamented.

is to come. 15 He who has ears to hear,[e] let him hear.

16 "But to what shall I compare this generation? It is like children sitting in the market places and calling to their playmates,

17 'We piped to you, and you did not dance;

we wailed, and you did not mourn.'

[e] Some ancient authorities omit to hear.

---

return (Josephus *Antiquities* IX. 2. 2); and Justin Martyr speaks of a Jewish belief that Elijah would announce the Messiah (cf. note on 3:16). Here and elsewhere Matthew expresses the Christian doctrine that John is Elijah (cf. 17:12-13). He does not necessarily mean that he is identical with the earlier prophet; he simply exercises his functions and fulfills the prophecies regarding him.

15. Matthew has inserted this saying at this point. It is commented on at 13:9.

3. John and Jesus Are Alike Rejected (11:16-19)

In Q this section was no doubt connected with vss. 7-11 but was probably separate from it in the oral tradition. It has been changed little, if at all, in transmission. Luke's introduction (Luke 7:31) is much like that of a rabbinical parable, and there is, in fact, a rabbinical story with a similar point: Jeremiah complains to God that people mocked at Elijah for his long hair and then said to Elisha, "Go up, thou baldhead; go up, thou baldhead" (cf. B. T. D. Smith, *The Parables of the Synoptic Gospels* [Cambridge: University Press, 1937], pp. 174-76).

16-17. The parable pictures two groups of children. One group wishes to play with the other group and proposes the game of "Weddings." When this offer is petulantly refused, the game of "Funerals" is proposed, but with no better results. The criticism could not apply to all the people of **this generation**, but no doubt many criticized both John and Jesus (cf. 21:23-27). The Aramaic words for **dance** and **mourn** may have rhymed with one another.

---

15. *Ears to Hear.*—For these words see Expos. under 13:9, 43.

16-19. *Playing at Religion: Children in the Market Place.*—We have noticed that this chapter gives an account of developing opposition to Jesus, and that it defends his claims. John the Baptist's doubt is the first instance of adverse forces. Now the antagonism of contemporary religion, especially as represented in the Pharisees, is described—in Christ's own words. The change in temper toward Jesus was undoubtedly wider than the Pharisaic party, as we shall note (see Expos., vss. 20-24), and this parable seems to have in mind both official leaders and average listener. Jesus drew the parable either from his own childhood or from watching children as they played in the market place. He describes John the Baptist's ministry and his own in vivid and contrasting metaphors. John's, he said, is like a funeral—gloomy, sincere, stern. His own? Like a wedding. It is a figure which he frequently used as token of the joy of the good news. But the representa-

tives of Jewish religion had no use for John: they said he was possessed by a demon. They had less use for Jesus: they called him a glutton and a tippler because of his "humanness" and sociability.

Actually they condemned themselves: they were playing at religion, as children played at weddings and funerals in the market place. They may not have known they were playing, but in fact they were—using outward semblance for inward verity. They had less sincerity than children, for children live in their play while it lasts; but the Pharisees used their acting to deceive both their neighbors and themselves. So they resisted every earnestness, whether of John or Jesus, with confused and stubborn mind. Children rate the imitation above the reality. So the Pharisees rated the formalisms of their faith above its deep commitments. Epictetus described such people: "I would have you observe that you will be turning back like children. . . . You too are now an athlete, now a gladiator, then a philosopher, after that a

18 For John came neither eating nor drinking, and they say, He hath a devil.

19 The Son of man came eating and drinking, and they say, Behold a man gluttonous, and a winebibber, a friend of publicans and sinners. But wisdom is justified of her children.

18 For John came neither eating nor drinking, and they say, 'He has a demon'; 19 the Son of man came eating and drinking, and they say, 'Behold, a glutton and a drunkard, a friend of tax collectors and sinners!' Yet wisdom is justified by her deeds.'ƒ

ƒ Many ancient authorities read *children* (Luke 7. 35).

18. Neither eating nor drinking means that his prevailing habits were ascetic. If Jesus was accused of being in league with Beelzebul, it is not strange that John, whose ways were extraordinary, was said to have a **demon**.

19. The Son of man, i.e., "I myself." Jesus could not have feasted often, but he felt no embarrassment in the wholehearted enjoyment of life; and common life with him was like a wedding feast (9:14-15). He went where he was most needed, not waiting for **tax collectors and sinners** to repent beforehand, and the obvious remark was made: "A man is known by the company he keeps." Nevertheless the **wisdom** of Jesus' course of action was **justified** by its results. A similar argument is used in John 5:36. Luke's reading, "her children" (Luke 7:35), may be that of Q; in that case, "wisdom is justified as against her children," i.e., against the Pharisees, who consider themselves heirs of wisdom. The Q writer may even think of the divine Wisdom, with which Jesus is identified (I Cor. 1:24); she is justified by her **true children**, who accept the message.

rhetorician, yet with your whole soul nothing." [8] Many of the Pharisees were in truth not as good as that description. For they were like peevish and irritable children, refusing to play any game but the one they could play best. Was there ever sharper or more damning indictment of hollowness in religion? Thus truth confronts us. There is warning truth: it is easy to make religion a game, and meanwhile to imagine that the reproduction is the reality. There is positive and saving truth: the joy of the good news. Jesus is one with us: he is at home in our homes. That fact shines clear behind the sneer of the Pharisees. The parable he used only underscores the fact. He had watched with a smile while children wailed with the flute players at a "funeral," and danced to the music at a "wedding." He shared their life. He shares our life, to redeem it from its pretenses and outright wrongs, if we will; and to fill it with his own pure joy.

19. Wisdom and History.—The gnomic saying with which the parable (see foregoing) concludes occurs in a different form in Luke. Matthew says, **Wisdom is justified by her deeds**; Luke (7:35) says, "Wisdom is justified of all her children." Probably Luke's version is the original form (see Exeg.). Luke certainly is in closer echo of Prov. 8:32, which clearly refers to wisdom's children. Wisdom may be the divine Wisdom. In that case wisdom is more than power to see life as God sees it. It is the emanation, almost the personification, of Truth in God—the light to which John owed his inspiration, and which Jesus embodied in his own

mind and life. If the saying is a comment of the evangelist, it is an unconscious tribute to the early church. The lowly in Jesus had both joy and power: the Pharisees, growing harder in pride, had clung to ways that were doomed. We today could make the comment in surer retrospect. Formalisms vanish, empires rise and fall, "Caesar is dust"—but the church of the lowly and faithful abides to fructify the life of mankind. If the saying come from Christ's own lips—and why not?—it is a boldly predictive and meditative word. He may even be quoting a taunt of the Pharisees and turning it against them. Pharisaic religion was buttressed by the temple with its power of system and tradition, while the new tidings had but a handful of seemingly insignificant "disciples." But Jesus was content to rest the verdict with history; or rather, with the God of history. Some tire manufacturer, using a clever pun, has claimed that his tires are "best in the long run." There is wear and tear also on systems and faiths. The Roman Empire, apparently impregnable, slowly decayed. It grew weaker behind an imposing façade, and then the façade collapsed; while the church it first despised, and then tried to kill by persecution, lives on in a strange and secret strength. The strength is the strength of a Presence—Christ's presence who hailed the future because he revealed the eternal God. It was said of Lincoln, "Now he belongs to the ages." [9] Perhaps every man and system must make the choice which Christ made—to belong to an age or to belong to eternity. **Wisdom is justified of her children.**

[8] *Discourses* III. 15.

[9] Edwin M. Stanton, at Lincoln's deathbed.

20 ¶ Then began he to upbraid the cities wherein most of his mighty works were done, because they repented not:

21 Woe unto thee, Chorazin! woe unto thee, Bethsaida! for if the mighty works, which were done in you, had been done in Tyre and Sidon, they would have repented long ago in sackcloth and ashes.

22 But I say unto you, It shall be more tolerable for Tyre and Sidon at the day of judgment, than for you.

23 And thou, Capernaum, which art exalted unto heaven, shalt be brought down to hell: for if the mighty works, which have been done in thee, had been done in Sodom, it would have remained until this day.

20 Then he began to upbraid the cities where most of his mighty works had been done, because they did not repent. 21 "Woe to you, Cho-ra'zin! woe to you, Beth-sa'i-da! for if the mighty works done in you had been done in Tyre and Sidon, they would have repented long ago in sackcloth and ashes. 22 But I tell you, it shall be more tolerable on the day of judgment for Tyre and Sidon than for you. 23 And you, Caper'na-um, will you be exalted to heaven? You shall be brought down to Hades. For if the mighty works done in you had been done in Sodom, it would have remained

B. Contrast Between Those Who Accept and Those Who Reject (11:20-30)

The babes of vs. 25, or the least in the kingdom (vs. 11), are now contrasted with the Galileans who reject Jesus.

1. Woes on the Galilean Cities (11:20-24)

20. This is Matthew's editorial introduction.

21. Chorazin may be the ruin Kerâze, northwest of Tell Ḥum or Capernaum. There is no record of Jesus' **mighty works** in **Bethsaida**, except that Mark places here the healing of a blind man (Mark 8:22-26). **Tyre and Sidon** were heathen cities. The book of Jonah has the similar idea that Nineveh, an exceptionally brutal and wicked city, repented immediately at Jonah's preaching. **Sackcloth** appears to have been a coarse haircloth. Originally slaves wore a loincloth of this material, and it came to be a mark of suppliants, penitents, and mourners (I Kings 20:31-32; Rev. 6:12). Strewing **ashes** on oneself or sitting in ashes was likewise a gesture of mourning and penitence, well known in the O.T. and in Homer.

23. The saying is based on Isa. 14:13, 15 (Hebrew, not LXX). There "Lucifer, son of the dawn," i.e., the king of Babylon, says, "The heavens will I scale," and is told, "But down to Sheol are you brought, to the recesses of the Pit" (Amer. Trans.). We do not know what exhibition of pride or presumption led Jesus to say this. Mark 2:1-2 gives the impression that he was very successful in **Capernaum.** One may conjecture that Jesus, hearing a self-satisfied remark about the wickedness of Tyre, Sidon, and other heathen cities, reminded his hearers that even Capernaum was far from penitent. RSV follows the older MSS and versions in reading this as a question. Jesus does not say directly that Capernaum **is**, or claims to be, **exalted to heaven**; he asks if its residents think they will be.

20-24. The Doom of Prosperous Cities.— Doubt on the part of John the Baptist, peevishly cruel opposition on the part of the Pharisees, and now the growing indifference of men in cities—such is the record of opposition written in this chapter. We must assume a lapse of time between the sending out of the apostles (see Luke's different context for this pronouncement of doom) and the attitude toward Christ here described. These cities are in two instances hardly more than names. **Chorazin** is only a name, and we know of only one **mighty work** being wrought in **Bethsaida.** The fact is striking indication of the fragmentariness of the gospel portrait. If only we knew more of what Jesus said and did! Capernaum was the working center of the kingdom crusade, and should therefore have reckoned herself doubly blessed. Why were these cities singled out for condemnation? They were at once prosperous and indifferent to Christ, and the prosperity was a main reason for the indifference. At first

24 But I say unto you, That it shall be more tolerable for the land of Sodom in the day of judgment, than for thee.

25 ¶ At that time Jesus answered and said, I thank thee, O Father, Lord of

until this day. 24 But I tell you that it shall be more tolerable on the day of judgment for the land of Sodom than for you."

25 At that time Jesus declared, "I thank

---

2. A Solemn Self-Revelation (11:25-30)

The section is in three parts: (a) vss. 25-26; (b) vs. 27; (c) vss. 28-30. The first two are paralleled in Luke 10:21-22; the third is found only in Matthew. It is a piece of solemn rhythmic prose, similar in style and tone to many parts of the Fourth Gospel, and is often called "the Johannine passage." Few sections of the Synoptics have been so thoroughly debated. If these are the exact words of Jesus, many parts of John have an equal claim to be considered as such. But nowhere else in the Synoptic Gospels is Jesus represented so explicitly as claiming unique sonship to God. The most serious difficulty is in the statement that no one knows the Father but the Son (vs. 27), for almost everywhere Jesus presupposes that his hearers know God and his character from the O.T. revelation and from God's constant fatherly care for the world. Eduard Norden (*Agnostos Theos* [2nd ed.; Berlin: B. G. Teubner, 1923], pp. 277-308) notes that the three parts of the passage are: (a) a thanksgiving for the revelation received, addressed to the Father; (b) a statement of what the revelation is; and (c) an appeal to the hearers to accept the revelation and its benefits. He discovers a similar scheme, though not in the identical order, in Ecclus. 51, in the conclusion of the first tractate of the Hermetic writings (the so-called *Poimandres*), and elsewhere. It is therefore a regular form used in early Gnostic mystical and theosophical writings. W. L. Knox (*Some Hellenistic Elements in Primitive Christianity*, pp. 6-7) agrees with Norden in the main but insists on the thoroughly Semitic character of the form and ideas. The O.T. also contains the idea that man knows God because God first knows him (cf. Gal. 4:8-9; I Cor. 13:12 with Jer. 1:5; Amos 3:2). Other important discussions can be found in B. W. Bacon, *The Gospel of Mark* (New Haven: Yale University Press, 1925), pp. 250-51; B. S. Easton, *The Gospel According to St. Luke* (New York: Charles Scribner's Sons, 1926), p. 167; Martin Rist, "Is Matt. 11:25-30 a Primitive Baptismal Hymn?" *Journal of Religion*, XV (1935), 63-77; T. Arvedson, *Das Mysterium Christi* (Upsala: A.-B. Lundequistska, 1937).

The passage is unquestionably old, and probably all of it stood in the document or documents which we call Q. Some of the phrases may reflect ideas and sayings of Jesus;

---

the cities had been stirred from spiritual lethargy by the fiery denunciations of John the Baptist, and then had been excited by the healing gladness of the good news brought by Christ. But they soon sank back into the accustomed round of "getting and spending."[1] Christ was only a nine days' wonder. Wordsworth was right: a pagan faith—"Proteus rising from the sea" or Triton blowing "his wreathèd horn"[2]— is better than the no-faith of money and body comfort. Lewis Mumford's book *The Culture of Cities* is a commentary on this passage in Matthew's Gospel.

Such cities are doomed, as Tyre, Sidon, and Sodom were doomed before them; and for the same cause. In cities men easily imagine that they can live on one another by their wits. They forget man's elementary dependence on field and sky; and worse, they forget man's ultimate

dependence on God. They lose sight of the Givenness in which all men live, and end by ignoring and despising the Giver. Soon, therefore, they are inwardly at odds (the starved soul crying out against the braggart body), and outwardly they are soon in social chaos. Indeed the three cities near the Sea of Galilee would suffer a darker fate than Tyre, Sidon, and Sodom. The woe pronounced by Christ prophesied a deeper shame than that foretold by Amos 1:9 or Isa. 23 or Ezek. 26, for Christ had visited Galilee; and the greater privilege spelled greater obligation, and therefore (in breach of obligation) a sterner judgment. Heaven and Hades are not theological constructs, but that fact does not weaken the words. This is a tremendous reprehension. None but the blind could miss its pertinence for our urban "civilization."

25-27. *The Ecstasy of Jesus.*—This is Canon F. W. Green's appropriate title for the whole

---

[1] Wordsworth, "The World Is Too Much With Us."
[2] *Ibid.*

heaven and earth, because thou hast hid these things from the wise and prudent, and hast revealed them unto babes.

26 Even so, Father; for so it seemed good in thy sight.

thee, Father, Lord of heaven and earth, that thou hast hidden these things from the wise and understanding and revealed them to babes; 26 yea, Father, for such

---

but the verses as they stand are best understood as an utterance of a Christian prophet who spoke in the Spirit. Prophetic revelations on behalf of Christ were probably frequent in the churches founded by Paul (I Cor. 14:26), and are known as late as the *Homily on the Passion,* delivered by Melito of Sardis late in the second century. Other examples are found in Rev. 1:10-20; Ign. Phila. 7:1, "When I was among you I cried out, I spoke with a great voice, God's voice." A few Synoptic passages may have originated in this way (e.g., 23:8-10; Luke 11:49-51). The Synoptists for the most part tried to distinguish between words spoken before the Crucifixion and utterances of the risen Christ, but the distinction was sometimes obscured. The earliest Christians did not doubt that sayings of both kinds were authoritative.

a) THANKSGIVING TO GOD (11:25-26)

25. The words ἐξομολογοῦμαί σοι can mean **I thank thee** or "I confess to thee." They are found also in Ecclus. 51:1 and are the normal language of Jewish piety. The **wise and understanding** are probably the scribes. Stoic philosophers thought that only the wise man could be pious, and Jewish teachers sometimes made similar remarks (Aboth 2:6), though they also spoke of fools and children prophesying the truth. **These things** are either the recognition that the kingdom is present, or the teachings of Jesus in general. The **babes** or unlearned readily accept them (similar ideas are found in 5:3; I Cor. 1:21). The saying is a very natural one for Jesus to utter.

---

section, vss. 25-30.[3] M. J. Lagrange describes it as "Matthew's Pearl of Great Price."[4] It is a climactic utterance, sublime in meaning and poignant in love. The interpreter should realize that the passage is a unity, with vs. 27 as its core. It is here in three expositions only for practicality, and because of its immense treasure. It is a burst of praise—**I thank thee, Father**—in striking contrast with the pronouncement of doom on the indifferent cities. The occasion of Christ's joy is that some received the good news. They were not the **wise and understanding** in religion or in the ways of the selfish world. But "these little ones"—**babes** in scribal wisdom—believed the gospel. They were the workers of the world, the untutored folk of the villages. They were the common people. By implication Christ warns of spiritual pride and intellectual self-sufficiency. Science and philosophy and self-confidence are slow to find God, because each enlists only a fragment of the man (they fail in soul-commitment and personal trust), and for deeper reasons: they do not know their own helplessness and need. Perhaps it has always been true of essential Christianity that "not many wise . . . not many mighty" are called (see I Cor. 1:17-30).

[3] See *Gospel According to Saint Matthew,* "The Clarendon Bible," p. 177.
[4] *Ibid.*

But there is a deeper root of joy, namely, Christ's consciousness of oneness with God. The interpreter should read the Exeg. with utmost care, noting the close parallelism of this whole passage with Ecclus. 51 and similar sources. The parallelism is due probably to some Johannine influence, with its stress on Christ as the incarnation of the eternal Wisdom; though we must not rule out the possibility that the saying is a bold appropriation of earlier writings by Jesus himself. In either event its truth remains. The first chapter of John's Gospel is no clearer or profounder in its central affirmation of the Christian faith. The passage has the authentic ring of deep knowledge and conviction. It comes apparently from a sure and early source. (Contrast Mark 13:32.) Harnack's testimony stands even if this verse is not a transcript from the lips of Jesus, and Dummelow properly quotes it in his comment: "Jesus is convinced that he knows God in a way in which no one ever knew Him before. . . ."[5] But even Harnack's comment does no full justice to essential Christian faith, for that faith has been driven by the Resurrection to avow a pretemporal mystery in Christ, a oneness with God in very nature, and therefore a revelation of God once for all in our human history. As wisdom was given (described by Ecclus. 51) to the lowly nationhood

[5] *Commentary on the Holy Bible,* p. 666.

27 All things are delivered unto me of my Father: and no man knoweth the Son, but the Father; neither knoweth any man the Father, save the Son, and *he* to whomsoever the Son will reveal *him*.

28 ¶ Come unto me, all *ye* that labor and are heavy laden, and I will give you rest.

was thy gracious will.*g* **27** All things have been delivered to me by my Father; and no one knows the Son except the Father, and no one knows the Father except the Son and any one to whom the Son chooses to reveal him. **28** Come to me, all who labor and are heavy-laden, and I will give you

g Or *so it was well-pleasing before thee.*

---

b) Jesus the Son of God (11:27)

27. The word **delivered** is often used technically to refer to the delivery of the Jewish tradition (Mark 7:4; I Cor. 15:3) ; and Norden argues that it can also refer to an esoteric knowledge of God. Here the thought is that all of Jesus' tradition comes directly from his **Father. Father** and **Son** are used similarly in Mark 13:32. An early variant reading, found in Marcion, Justin, and elsewhere, is as follows: "No one has known the Father except the Son, nor has [anyone] known the Son except the Father and those to whom the Son reveals [himself]." But this is probably not the original reading. Easton takes **Son** to mean "the Messiah," but the word is more inclusive. It probably means "revealer and redeemer" and approximates the idea of John 1:1-18.

c) An Appeal to Mankind (11:28-30)

Interesting parallels are found in Ecclus. 51:23, 26-27.

28. Jesus addresses those who **labor** to do the works of the law and are **heavy laden** with the burdens which the scribes put on them. The same figure is used in Mark 7:2-5, 8; Acts 15:10. In the next chapter Matthew gives examples of the weight of the law. Jews who had grown up in the legal tradition, particularly from the second century on, would not admit the justice of this criticism; for them, as for the psalmist (Ps. 119:24, 35, 97) , the law was a delight and a protection against evil. But at this time the rules of priestly purity are being extended to laymen, and in some ways the Pharisaic law may have been more burdensome than it was later on (cf. on 15:3-6) .

---

of the old-time Jews, so Christ is given to these "little ones." He is Way, Truth, and Life.

Thus the joy became tranquillity. The fact that the **wise** and mighty did not receive him had its own mysterious purpose. The proximate cause of that refusal was man's pride and the abuse of human freedom; the ultimate cause was hidden in the eternal will. The fact that **babes** did receive him was also ordained. From one group God in sovereign providence **hid** the truth; to the other he **revealed** it. Meanwhile even the proud and obtuse depended on Christ through whom all wisdom comes. There is a basic contrast between "natural" and "revealed" religion: the lowly who receive Christ are aware that they cannot even know heaven, much less reach it, unless heaven stoops to earth. Jesus "stooped to bless." There, at least in part, lay the secret of tranquillity, whatever befell: **Yea, Father, for such was thy gracious will.**

28. *The Great Invitation.*—What other title? Surely these must be the words that inspired the Thorvaldsen statue of Christ.*6* In their very

6 In the Church of Notre Dame in Copenhagen. For a description see Eugène Plon, *Thorvaldsen* (Paris: Henri Plow, 1867), pp. 202 ff.

sound they are a benediction, the cathedral bell of man's pilgrimage. To whom is the invitation given? **All** those who are burdened in toil. The reference is to the "works of the law" (Rom. 9:32) but indirectly to all the workers of the world, with a profounder reading of the soul than communism has even glimpsed. The burden immediately in mind is that of Pharisaic and scribal religion: the contrast between that heavy yoke and the genuine disciple-joy of Christ is implied in this whole passage. But we cannot limit the application. The priests took what Roman taxes left; but the real burden, in every land and time, is a burden of anxious fear, and the worse burden of a broken conscience. Christ set no limits around that blessed **all.** The sad in heart are included, and all who bend beneath time's load. It is a staggering claim. Richard H. Hutton is right: these are words which "no mere man could ever have uttered without jarring every chord in the human conscience."*7* If the words were testimony to Christ, they would still outrage every sensibility if spoken of any other in human history.

7 *The Incarnation and Principles of Evidence* (New York: Pott & Amery, 1871), p. 59.

29 Take my yoke upon you, and learn of me; for I am meek and lowly in heart: and ye shall find rest unto your souls.

30 For my yoke *is* easy, and my burden is light.

rest. 29 Take my yoke upon you, and learn from me; for I am gentle and lowly in heart, and you will find rest for your souls. 30 For my yoke is easy, and my burden is light."

29-30. Rabbis often spoke of the **yoke** of the law (Aboth 3:5) or of the commandments (Berakoth 2:2), but always in terms of praise. To accept this yoke, they said, is to put off the yoke of earthly monarchies and worldly care. Jesus' yoke was a simple following of the O.T. law, as interpreted by him in a prophetic and nontechnical spirit, and the emphasis was on justice, mercy, and the love of God (23:23=Luke 11:42). He and his followers felt the same joy and freedom of which the rabbis spoke. It is true that Jesus does not draw Paul's distinction between law and grace (Gal. 5:4), law and freedom (Gal. 4:21-26), law and faith (Gal. 3:23-26). Yet he dealt so freely with the law that Paul's teaching is more a restatement of Jesus' attitude than something entirely new. His yoke demands the most earnest effort, but when men have been converted and their lives are given to God, its actual prescriptions are **easy** and **light** and it gives **rest** to their **souls.**

The invitation is pendant to vs. 27. Jesus had right to remove the yoke of the law because he had higher authority than the law. Imagine these words on the lips of a contemporary statesman, or even of the finest poet, or even of the (still needy) saints. He only has right and power and welcome-of-soul to speak them— the incarnate God.

How does Christ give rest? He offers a transfer of yokes (see Expos., vss. 29-30). For the burden of the law, with its endless proscriptions and ritualistic claims, he offered his law of worship and love: a man need only love God made known in Jesus, and in that power strive to love his fellows. For the yoke of selfish pride, such as rested on officials of a false religion and on the greedy in trade, Jesus offered his meek obedience and his lowliness of heart. For the load of "uncharted freedom," which soon chafes and tires, Jesus offered his freedom—the freedom of dutiful sons of God the Father. For the burden of sin Jesus offered the joy of sins forgiven and the power of "an endless life." For the heavy weight of taxes and time Christ offered, not escape, but the perfect faith that frees a man from both fear and hatred, and enables him to find "honey in the rock" (Deut. 32:13). The result is rest. The word can be better translated "refreshment." With each turning toward Christ the "weary" find cheer of soul. This refreshment is not idleness, not slackness of either hands or spirit, not exemption from toil or any honorable demand, but— peace, the deep calming of man's heart. Was it not Augustine who said that he found no such invitation in Cicero or Plato? How could he? "No one knows the Father except the Son" (vs. 27). He has peace and bestows it. His invitation is man's blessed Angelus.

29-30. *The Yoke of Jesus.*—The people to whom Jesus spoke were already wearing a yoke, the yoke of the law. Jesus here proposes an exchange of yokes. The rabbis themselves referred to their religion as the yoke of the law. Jesus boldly appropriates their figure, and makes it more vivid. We should remember that as a carpenter he probably made yokes for oxen. His is a voluntary yoke: **take.** We need a bondage, provided it is a beneficent bondage. The carefree life is not free from care, the reason being that our nature is made for homage. The soul of man is always given in fealty, for it is incomplete in itself; and the yoke galls and chafes when life is given to a low fealty instead of to God. Jesus pleads that life should be given in homage to God. That word **easy** means "kindly" when it is used of people, and "good of its kind" when used of things.

How shall we describe the yoke? It is the yoke of faith. For though faith is implanted in us by God, and though he quickens it by frequent signs, it is also our act: "This I do believe, and thus will I live." It is the yoke of conscience, both the faith and the conscience being illumined by Christ: we strive to do what is right in his sight. It is the yoke of love, at cost— like that of the man who abjured marriage and was counted a misanthrope, but who was found on death to have saved all his money to give his drought-cursed village a water conduit from the hills. It is, in short, the yoke of personal allegiance to Christ. Thus it is a meek servitude. For Christ is meek (with hidden fires of righteous wrath), not in spite of the prodigious claims in vs. 27, but because of them. For God is meek in constant love; and the proud man, whether in religion or in commerce, cannot know him. This is the yoke of meek obedience

12 At that time Jesus went on the sabbath day through the corn; and his disciples were ahungered, and began to pluck the ears of corn, and to eat.

2 But when the Pharisees saw *it*, they said unto him, Behold, thy disciples do that which is not lawful to do upon the sabbath day.

12 At that time Jesus went through the grainfields on the sabbath; his disciples were hungry, and they began to pluck ears of grain and to eat. **2** But when the Pharisees saw it, they said to him, "Look, your disciples are doing what is

---

C. EXAMPLES OF OPPOSITION AND REJECTION (12:1-50)
1. CONTROVERSY OVER PLUCKING OF GRAIN ON THE SABBATH (12:1-8)

This little story is an excellent example of a type of gospel narrative which has been given the name "paradigm." It is a brief account of a conversation which culminates in a pithy saying of Jesus and is useful as a paradigm, or example, in a sermon. It can also be classed as a "controversy story," of which the Gospels contain several. The tone and setting are Palestinian, and the anecdote must have received a fixed form in the oral tradition at a very early time. From it we gain an excellent picture of how Jesus taught. He did not make abstract statements about ethics or set down theoretical principles for interpretation of the law. Like the rabbis, he made rulings in concrete situations, and we must deduce his principles from stories like this.

12:1-2. To pluck ears of grain was technically to reap; **to eat** involved threshing, as Luke 6:1 remarks. These are two of the thirty-nine principal classes of work that were **not lawful . . . on the sabbath** (Exod. 34:21; Shabbath 7:2) . The Mishnah says that "[he is guilty] who takes . . . ears of grain equal to a lamb's mouthful" (Shabbath 7:4) . The incident might occur in the spring when the grain was ready for harvesting. A passer-by was permitted to help himself to grain in this manner (Deut. 23:25) .

---

to the meek God made known in the meek Christ. Such lowliness does not chafe. But pride and selfishness go contrary to our deepest nature, and therefore tear us.

The outcome is refreshment. It is such peace as Dante craved. He knocked at the gates of the Franciscan monastery at Lunigiana, and was asked by the friar who opened the door, "What do you wish?" Dante answered in one word, "Peace." [8] Christ sets the monastery within: it is his own presence. The initiate **learns** of him —not merely of his teaching, but of his very life and self. Matthew Henry says the yoke is easy because it is "lined with love." [9] Bernard of Clairvaux exclaims with truth: "O blessed burden that makes all burdens light! O blessed yoke that bears the bearer up!" [1] There is a legend that the birds at first had no wings, and that they rebelled when wings were given because the wings seemed to be a burden; but when they accepted, the burden lifted them to the sky.[2] The weight of Christ's yoke is wings to the soul. Christ himself wore a yoke. The words that could have been inscribed on it were—*Deus vult*. Vs. 27 is the key to this whole

passage. In God alone, revealed in Christ, can men find rest.

12:1-8. *Controversy Regarding the Sabbath.*— (See Expos., vs. 8.) Matthew here returns to the growing hostility to Jesus. Enemies were watching both him and his disciples. Perhaps there is a hint in these verses that the disciples were "people of the land," i.e., careless of the religious law. Faith must expect attacks from both ignorance and wickedness. The gentle writer of Ps. 23, and Christ also, met "enemies." In this instance the charge was not that the disciples stole grain (the law permitted them their handful) , but that they broke the sabbath law. To **pluck** was technically to "reap," and to rub away the husk was technically to "thresh." Thus the disciples broke two of the thirty-nine sabbath proscriptions, and consequently the fourth commandment.

The defense offered by Jesus has striking features. He answered the questioner as well as the question. He met the Pharisees with their own arguments. Thus he strove for their friendship, or at least avoided inciting them to worse hate. David was their hero: had he not "broken" the sabbath at the claim of human hunger? The temple was the focus of their faith and the dwelling place of God: did not the priests in the temple on due occasion "break" the sabbath, since they must work? (Note Exeg. on the

[8] John T. Slattery, *Dante* (New York: P. J. Kenedy & Sons, 1922), p. 20.
[9] Quoted, *Great Texts of the Bible*, vol. on *St. Matthew*, p. 276.
[1] *Ibid.*
[2] *Ibid.*, vol. on *Acts and Romans I-VIII*, p. 474.

3 But he said unto them, Have ye not read what David did, when he was ahungered, and they that were with him;

4 How he entered into the house of God, and did eat the showbread, which was not lawful for him to eat, neither for them which were with him, but only for the priests?

5 Or have ye not read in the law, how that on the sabbath days the priests in the temple profane the sabbath, and are blameless?

6 But I say unto you, That in this place is *one* greater than the temple.

7 But if ye had known what *this* meaneth, I will have mercy, and not sacrifice, ye would not have condemned the guiltless.

not lawful to do on the sabbath." 3 He said to them, "Have you not read what David did, when he was hungry, and those who were with him: 4 how he entered the house of God and ate the bread of the Presence, which it was not lawful for him to eat nor for those who were with him, but only for the priests? 5 Or have you not read in the law how on the sabbath the priests in the temple profane the sabbath, and are guiltless? 6 I tell you, something greater than the temple is here. 7 And if you had known what this means, 'I desire mercy, and not sacrifice,' you would not

3-4. The incident is told in I Sam. 21:1-6 and the **house of God** referred to was at Nob. **The bread of the Presence,** i.e., the loaves placed in the presence of God, is prescribed in Exod. 25:30; 35:13; 39:36. According to Josephus (*Antiquities* III. 10. 7) this was baked on Friday and brought and laid on the holy table early on the sabbath. It remained there until the next sabbath, when it might be eaten by **the priests** (Menahoth 11). The later rabbis saw a difficulty here and tried in various ways to justify David's action. Jesus reasons that if David, whose righteousness was taken for granted, could take the holy bread from the temple because he and his men were hungry, his disciples are all the more justified in doing the trivial act of plucking grain to obtain food. The rabbis could not accept this reasoning, or that of vs. 5. They would have said that if one's life were in danger for want of food, the plucking of grain was permitted (Yoma 8:6). But there is nothing to show that this was the case. Jesus, however, held that minor acts of labor to meet human need and comfort did not violate the spirit and intent of the sabbath law.

5. Vss. 5-7 may well be Matthew's additions. **Vs.** 5 reflects his knowledge of Jewish law. Technically **the priests in the temple profane the sabbath.** The Mishnah uses this same expression (Shabbath 18:3), but finds them **guiltless,** for Num. 28:9-10 prescribes sabbath sacrifices. From the second century on, the rabbinical rule was that obligations of the Torah which cannot possibly be discharged on the sabbath eve "override the sabbath," i.e., take precedence over the sabbath law.

6. Jesus' authority is **greater than the temple** (cf. vs. 8 and 9:6). The verse is based on his saying in vss. 41-42.

7. **I desire mercy, and not sacrifice** is from Hos. 6:6, where it means "Mercy is more important than sacrifice," not "I forbid sacrifice." As in 5:23-24, this is also Jesus' principle. But the verse does not fit well here.

authenticity of the record of this second argument.) Jewish law and sacred history showed that there are higher claims than the claims of law. A preacher may learn from the reply of Christ to answer men with their arguments rather than with his own—and with the better argument of a life of righteous love.

Jesus thus raises and meets the whole issue of law versus life. It is a frequent dilemma for any follower of Christ. John Galsworthy has discussed it in two plays, *Justice* and *Escape*. There is threat as well as protection in all law. It

may set rules in the place of holy reflection, and thus encourage irresponsibility. It may cabin righteousness ("I have done what the law requires"), and thus lower conscience to mere respectability. "Except your righteousness shall exceed the righteousness of the scribes, . . ." (5:20). Always it is an irritant, always a judgment, and it may subtly induce the view of God which sees in him only a lawmaker and a judge. Human destiny in God is higher than law. (Note Exeg. which suggests that the Marcan version of vs. 8 is more authentic. Yet

8 For the Son of man is Lord even of the sabbath day.

9 And when he was departed thence, he went into their synagogue:

8 For the Son of man is lord of the sabbath."

9 And he went on from there, and en-

---

8. A. E. J. Rawlinson remarks, "Our Lord would not have been likely to say that 'man' was 'lord of the Sabbath,' which had been instituted by God. On the other hand it is almost equally unlikely that He would have emphasized His personal lordship of the Sabbath" (*St. Mark* [3rd ed.; London: Methuen & Co., 1931], p. 34). Mark 2:28 contains the substance of this verse, but prefaces it with vs. 27, which says that "the sabbath was made for man, not man for the sabbath"—a statement that has Jewish parallels. This would be a better conclusion for the argument of vss. 3-4 (=Mark 2:25-26). The newly discovered Codex 2427 actually omits Mark 2:28. Thus Mark 2:27, which Matthew omits, may have been the original conclusion.

2. Controversy over Healing on the Sabbath (12:9-14)

The story is based on Mark 3:1-6, but Matthew omits vss. 4b-5a because the mention of "doing evil" and "killing" aroused needless questions and controversies, and in vs. 11 he introduces the instance of the sheep in the pit, which he draws from Q (cf. Luke 14:5).

The problem is similar to that of the previous story. The rabbis permitted healing on the sabbath when a man's life was in danger; but this healing, which could have been performed on the following day, would seem to them a needless defiance of God's revealed will. For the implications of this issue, see Gregory Vlastos, *Christian Faith and Democracy* (New York: Association Press, 1939), pp. 32-40.

Matthew had a true instinct.) Jesus, the revelation of man's destiny by grant of pardon and power, is **lord of** [law and] **the sabbath.**

8. *The Christian Sabbath.*—Form criticism would say that the story is told to provide a frame for the dicta in vss. 7-8. B. Harvie Branscomb indicates that there is general agreement among scholars that **Son of man** in this instance means "man." [3] This judgment supports our exegete's opinion that Mark 2:27 gives the original form of Christ's pronouncement.

The claim of man in his basic need is here championed against the claims of the sabbath law. But the human claim is not absolute: a man has no right to do whatever he will with the sabbath. In our time license has replaced sabbath stringency. But Christ deals with sabbath license more sternly than with the coercion that turns the sabbath into the galling fetter. The sabbath is "made": it is a gift from God to be used as befits the Giver. It is to be used, not abused or neglected. Man's claim on the sabbath against a too stringent law is the claim of basic need, not the claim of selfish whim.

So the claim of God is still supreme. He made man. He made the sabbath for man. It is God's gift to the weary that they may find his rest for body and soul, God's gift to the seeking that they may realize anew his nearness, God's

[3] *The Gospel of Mark*, "The Moffatt New Testament Commentary" (London: Hodder & Stoughton, 1937), p. 58.

gift to the sinful that they may hear the good news and find both forgiveness and strength. This is "the Lord's day" (Rev. 1:10). Even tools keep a sharper edge if they have one day's rest in seven. During World War I, it was discovered that factory workers accomplished less in seven days of unremitted labor than in six days with one day's respite. What is true of body is more deeply true of soul: "The world is too much with us." [4] No man can safely ignore appointed times and seasons. No man can sit loose to a habit of worship. Sunday well kept is not loss: it is clear gain—both in worthy business, and in business of the soul.

The claim of Jesus remains. Whatever the source of vs. 8, its essential truth is sure. He kept the sabbath in rigorous joy (Luke 4:16). Worship was the breathing of his soul. It must have hurt him to the quick to be charged with irreligion. He shows elsewhere how the sabbath should be kept: primarily for worship and prayer, and after that for "doing good" (Mark 3:4) and for the hallowing of family ties. He came, not to destroy the sabbath, but to fulfill it. By his resurrection he gave a new sabbath, and filled it with his risen power. The sabbath is made for man, but only as man finds life in Christ.

9-14. *The Value of Human Life.*—This is another instance of the controversy between Jesus and his foes. Healing a man is the issue

[4] Wordsworth, "The World Is Too Much With Us."

10 ¶ And, behold, there was a man which had *his* hand withered. And they asked him, saying, Is it lawful to heal on the sabbath days? that they might accuse him.

11 And he said unto them, What man shall there be among you, that shall have one sheep, and if it fall into a pit on the sabbath day, will he not lay hold on it, and lift *it* out?

12 How much then is a man better than a sheep? Wherefore it is lawful to do well on the sabbath days.

13 Then saith he to the man, Stretch forth thine hand. And he stretched *it* forth; and it was restored whole, like as the other.

tered their synagogue. 10 And behold, there was a man with a withered hand. And they asked him, "Is it lawful to heal on the sabbath?" so that they might accuse him. 11 He said to them, "What man of you, if he has one sheep and it falls into a pit on the sabbath, will not lay hold of it and lift it out? 12 Of how much more value is a man than a sheep! So it is lawful to do good on the sabbath." 13 Then he said to the man, "Stretch out your hand." And the man stretched it out, and it was re-

10. The **man** probably had an atrophied **hand** or arm. We can only speculate as to whether psychological factors were involved.

11. Strack and Billerbeck believe that on this question there were two opinions, the rigoristic and the lenient. In Galilee at this time the answer to Jesus' question may have been "Yes." Of course, here the animal's life was in danger; the man's life probably was not.

12. **It is lawful to do good on the sabbath** is an affirmative statement, whereas in Mark 3:4 Jesus asks a question; but there can be no doubt that the statement represents his point of view. The school of Hillel held that on the sabbath one might comfort a mourner and visit a sick man and pray for him, and that this was "to do good." Jesus goes further: to do an act of mercy by releasing a man from sickness is not "labor" in the sense of something which violates God's intention for the sabbath.

now, not plucking grain; but the sabbath law is still the prime question. The apocryphal Gospel According to the Hebrews says that the man was a stonemason, and that he appealed to Jesus to heal him that he might be saved from living as a beggar. If so, the drama is heightened. There was probably a difference of opinion among the rabbis about the law's requirements concerning sabbath healings. Shammai and his followers may have adopted a rigorous view (e.g., that not even a fracture could be set until after the sabbath), while the school of Hillel proposed a more lenient interpretation. The question asked by Jesus seems to indicate that the lenient view was generally adopted in his time. But the paralytic's life was not in danger. So Jesus was "guilty," even under a fairly lenient interpretation of the law.

How much then is a man better than a sheep? is the dictum that validates true democracy. We do not yet honor the dictum. The retort "It all depends on the price of wool" is unfortunately more than a cheap witticism; for we give more care in some instances to animals than to children. Democracy is deeper fact than political form: it is spiritual faith. When it ceases to be a spiritual faith, it fails as a political form. Despite something demonic in man—a

perversity well illustrated by the Pharisees in this picture—there are in him the tokens of divine life, by which alone he knows the demonic and responds to God's plea to rise above it. Man is infinitely precious because he can be host to the indwelling of God. This is the fact that gives man worth. The ground of his true dignity is found in God's redemption. And that worth, that dignity, is the bastion of democracy. In token of it modern man, whatever his failures, does recognize the primary value of human life; for if a child were caught in a landslide, he would forsake his getting and spending to attempt the rescue. No trade is large enough to justify the loss of a child. So we should be careful to note that true democracy is not a mere rule of the people, for that has again and again elected demagogues and sometimes made war. True democracy is the rule of the people according to the true nature of the people. It is at long last a theocracy. Here is the deepest implication of this dictum of Christ.

With imperious truth Jesus thus cut through the red tape and sophistries of scribal law. Mark the courage of his act. Mark the compassion of it: he saw people, dear to God, where others saw only rule and custom. How easily we become

14 ¶ Then the Pharisees went out, and held a council against him, how they might destroy him. 15 But when Jesus knew *it,* he withdrew himself from thence: and great multitudes followed him, and he healed them all; 16 And charged them that they should not make him known: 17 That it might be fulfilled which was spoken by Esaias the prophet, saying,	stored, whole like the other. 14 But the Pharisees went out and took counsel against him, how to destroy him. 15 Jesus, aware of this, withdrew from there. And many followed him, and he healed them all, 16 and ordered them not to make him known. 17 This was to fulfill what was spoken by the prophet Isaiah:

14. Some **Pharisees** apparently wished to **destroy him,** and Mark 3:6 implies that they informed against him to Herod Antipas' men. But there are indications that Jesus had friends among the Pharisees (Mark 12:28, 32-33), and it would be wrong to suppose that the entire party was aligned against him.

3. Interlude: The Revelation Must Be Hidden from Israel
(12:15-21)

15-16. This passage is a brief summary of the editorial section Mark 3:7-12, on which the evangelist drew in 4:24. Up to this point Matthew has avoided repeating himself, but from now on he seems to be less careful, and several "doublets" occur in the course of the Gospel (cf. 19:9 with 5:32 and 20:26-27 with 18:4 and 23:11). After vs. 16, he appends a quotation from Isa. 42:1-4, introduced with his usual formula. The wording does not follow either the Hebrew or the LXX closely. Mark believed that Jesus, in accordance with God's plan, deliberately veiled the secret of his messiahship from Israel (cf. on 13:10-15). Matthew accepts the idea in part, but here he ascribes Jesus' reticence to his modesty and humility and introduces the scripture quotation with the purpose of proving it.

blind! The Pharisees, at the very moment of charging Jesus with a breach of the sabbath, were themselves using it to trap him and to plot his death. Perhaps Jesus' recognition of that fact is the tragic undertone of Mark 3:4. Yet God has strange ways: some commentators teach that the opposition of the Pharisees drove Jesus out of the synagogue into the open air, where he was nearer to the people, and prompted him to teach by the "open secret" of unforgettable parables.

The sovereign power of Jesus strikes through the story. He is Lord over sickness: the healing miracles are strongly attested, and are assuredly not less wonderful if psychologically interpreted. Someone has made the comment, "To understand the methods God uses is not ourselves to be God." He is Lord over his enemies: they could not stop his mercy, for his Cross gave only a profounder cure. He is Lord over the conscience of mankind: his appeal here is an appeal beyond the rules to an ultimate awareness of right and wrong. He is Lord over our loyalty and will: who can but love him as he challenges his foes and brings power to the helpless?

15-21. *The Hidden Revelation.*—Why did Jesus hide himself? The act is alien from our modern mood of "publicity," and seems to run counter to the requirement of Christian witness. The N.T., in accord with O.T. teaching (cf. Isa. 6:9-12), sometimes affirms that this is the fulfillment of the divine plan. **The Gentiles** (vss. 18, 21) thus received the Word, and Israel's mission was fulfilled. Or must we say that Matthew, following Mark, is trying to explain the slowness in growth of the early Christian movement? The story itself gives the human reason and occasion: the opposition of the Pharisees drove Jesus into semiretirement; the perversity of man temporarily limits divine grace. Further reason is found in the lowly wisdom of Jesus. He shall not **cry aloud:** notoriety is a hindrance to the gospel; and the humility of Jesus leads him to serve men like that goddess of Greek fable who was not seen, but whose presence men knew because a fountain gushed where beforetime there had been a stagnant pool.[5] Perhaps we may find still another reason in our own need: the revelation is veiled so as to leave room for our venture of faith; God's disclosure in Christ is clear enough to inspire faith, but not so clear as to spare us the venture.

[5] Quoted, *Great Texts of the Bible,* vol. on *Job to Psalm XXIII,* p. 309.

18 Behold my servant, whom I have chosen; my beloved, in whom my soul is well pleased: I will put my Spirit upon him, and he shall show judgment to the Gentiles.

19 He shall not strive, nor cry; neither shall any man hear his voice in the streets.

20 A bruised reed shall he not break, and smoking flax shall he not quench, till he send forth judgment unto victory.

21 And in his name shall the Gentiles trust.

22 ¶ Then was brought unto him one possessed with a devil, blind, and dumb:

---

18 "Behold, my servant whom I
     have chosen,
my beloved with whom my
     soul is well pleased.
I will put my Spirit upon him,
     and he shall proclaim justice
     to the Gentiles.
19 He will not wrangle or cry
     aloud,
nor will any one hear his
     voice in the streets;
20 he will not break a bruised
     reed
or quench a smoldering wick,
till he brings justice to victory;
21 and in his name will the
     Gentiles hope."
22 Then a blind and dumb demoniac

18-21. It is only late in Jewish history that the Targums identify the **servant** with the Messiah, but early Christians delighted in the figure of the "suffering servant" and took the passages as referring to Jesus. Examples can be found in Rom. 4:25; I Pet. 2:24-25; Acts 8:32-33. To Matthew the passage meant that, although the Pharisees **now** rejected Jesus, he would be accepted by **the Gentiles** (cf. 21:42-43; 28:19).

4. Healing of a Blind and Dumb Man, Which Results in a Charge of Magic and a Controversy (12:22-32)

The evangelist uses Mark 3:22-29 in making up this section, but he omits Mark 3:20-21, perhaps because it might appear that his associates or family thought Jesus mad (but see notes on that passage). He relies principally, however, on Q material, which is

18-21. The Gentleness and Might of the Messiah.—The Exeg. dates the beginning of the interpretation that identifies Jesus with the suffering Servant portrayed in Isa. 53. That sublime picture is so true to the revelation in Christ, the likeness so inevitable, that Christians have rightly found in their Lord the suffering Servant for man's salvation.

Nature apparently shows small concern for "hopeless cases." The "survival of the fittest" is a truth that must be carefully construed, for the meek do inherit the earth; but a certain "ruthlessness" in nature can hardly be denied. Human nature also has been impatient with weaklings. Even today we have our unimpressive doctrines of "inferior peoples."

But Christ's method is one of patient tenderness. A reed, whether to be used for a flute or understood as simply another reed among the multitudinous rank growth of the river bed, seems to have no value, especially when bruised. Someone has said that every reed has a blemish. Likewise a hard wick in a lamp is a smoky offense rather than a source of light. Why should it be treasured? The **reed** and the **wick** are types of humanity—the reed bowed before

the storms of life, and the wick offering but faint promise.

Christ brings hope. The **bruised reed** he binds, and it brings forth the music of God, as in Zacchaeus. The **smoking wick** he carefully tends until it gives light, as in Peter. Is there not a legend that Nicodemus, after Christ's death and resurrection, tried to carve a crucifix and made only a clumsy failure; but that while Nicodemus slept Christ took the clumsy carving, and shaped it into loveliness and awe?

Nor shall Christ fail. It is strange that the Gospelist omits the phrase in Isaiah, "He shall not fail nor be discouraged" (Isa. 42:4), but that truth is implied. Those who trust Christ find that he has the resources of divine power. Do we seem hopeless, to others and to ourselves? That sense of inferiority is behind much of the blatancy and cruelty of our time. Does our world, blundering into recurrent wars, seem doomed? Can we offer, even at best, only a poor intention of good? These verses ring with hope and life.

22-30. By Power of Beelzebub or of God?— Christ's age believed in demons: the middle air was filled with malign spirits. When a man was

and he healed him, insomuch that the blind and dumb both spake and saw.

23 And all the people were amazed, and said, Is not this the Son of David?

24 But when the Pharisees heard *it*, they said, This *fellow* doth not cast out devils, but by Beelzebub the prince of the devils.

was brought to him, and he healed him, so that the dumb man spoke and saw.

23 And all the people were amazed, and said, "Can this be the Son of David?"

24 But when the Pharisees heard it they said, "It is only by Be-el′ze-bul, the prince of demons, that this man casts out demons."

---

also preserved in Luke 11:14-23; 12:10. The little story (vss. 22-23) may originally have stood alone, as in 9:32-33, where it is found in almost identical form, but in Q it was used as a setting for the controversy over the casting out of demons.

22. Matthew, by saying that this demoniac is also **blind**, indicates that this is not the same story as 9:32-33. The phraseology is similar to 9:27-31; Luke 11:14.

23. The Messiah or **Son of David** would have power to work miracles.

24. The true reading, found in practically all Greek MSS, is **Beelzebul.** This is the Aramaic form of *ba'al zebhûl* (בעל זבול), which in the first century may have been understood as "lord of the high house" or "of the temple." It is a very ancient divine name. The Ras Shamra texts (about 1400 B.C.) describe the Canaanite god Aleyan Baal as "Zebul, baal of the earth," and here *zebhûl* means "exalted one." The god of Ekron mentioned in II Kings 1:2 must have been called Baal-zebul, but the biblical writers call him Baalzebub ("lord of flies") to show their contempt for him. Jerome adopted the form **Beelzebub** for the Vulg. N.T., from which it has come into the English versions. The Jews, as this passage shows, regarded Beelzebul as **the prince of demons** and not a god. The charge that Jesus practiced magic is found in the Talmud and also in Justin (*Dialogue with Trypho* 69; Origen *Against Celsus* I. 28).

---

afflicted with ill health or apostasy, the malady was attributed to the incoming of a demon. These evil spirits were ruled by "the prince of the power of the air" (Eph. 2:2). His name in this story is Beelzebub (see Exeg.), the ruler of the house of the demons. The story is a tribute to Christ's healing power, without which it makes no sense. His enemies charged that this miraculous gift was of the devil. Later enemies said Christ learned his tricks from an Egyptian juggler, a charge that Celsus adopted and embellished. He pictured an orthodox Jew addressing Christ scornfully: "You cured diseases . . . ; you restored dead bodies to life; you fed multitudes with a few loaves. These are the common tricks of the Egyptian wizards, which you may see performed every day in our markets for a few half pence." [6]

Christ makes an unanswerable reply in a threefold argument. First, to cast out demons by the power of demons would imply a rift in the house of the demons, and Satan is too astute thus to defeat himself (see Expos., vss. 25, 30). Second, certain followers of the scribes and Pharisees claimed power of exorcism: were they also inspired by Beelzebub? Third, Christ's healings were manifestly good: how, then, were

they possible unless Jesus had bound the power of Beelzebub, and stolen his enthralled (human) **goods** (vs. 29)? In rapier thrust of mind the enemies of Jesus were no match for him. But his play of mind was always used in lowly service of the Spirit. There was no rancor in the retort, only a patient and persistent pleading. (See below on "the unpardonable sin.")

What moved the Pharisees to the blasphemy that confused Jesus and Satan? Basically it was pride—"by that sin fell the angels." [7] They were proud of their righteousness, their religious standing in the community, their interpretation of the law. They were correspondingly malicious towards anyone who offended their pride. Blinded thus, they could see neither the pathos of the man stricken by sightlessness and loss of speech, nor the wonder of Jesus' mighty love. The danger of pride besets every age. The Renaissance was perhaps not primarily a flowering of the human spirit; it was more a withering: man became absorbed in himself and in his world. There is no joy except in God, no sight except as the eye is turned to him.

How easy it is to evade the challenge of Christ! Thus he wrought; thus he lived. Thus he died; thus he rose. What do these facts mean? To dismiss them as "hypnotism" or a trading on human "illusion" brings us into the

[6] James Anthony Froude, *Short Studies on Great Subjects,* 4th ser. (New York: Charles Scribner's Sons, 1883), pp. 254-57.

[7] Shakespeare, *King Henry VIII,* Act III, scene 2.

25 And Jesus knew their thoughts, and said unto them, Every kingdom divided against itself is brought to desolation; and every city or house divided against itself shall not stand:

26 And if Satan cast out Satan, he is divided against himself; how shall then his kingdom stand?

27 And if I by Beelzebub cast out devils, by whom do your children cast *them* out? therefore they shall be your judges.

28 But if I cast out devils by the Spirit of God, then the kingdom of God is come unto you.

25 Knowing their thoughts, he said to them, "Every kingdom divided against itself is laid waste, and no city or house divided against itself will stand; 26 and if Satan casts out Satan, he is divided against himself; how then will his kingdom stand? 27 And if I cast out demons by Be-el'ze-bul, by whom do your sons cast them out? Therefore they shall be your judges. 28 But if it is by the Spirit of God that I cast out demons, then the kingdom of God has

---

25-26. It would be natural to use Beelzebul as a name for **Satan,** though this is not done in Jewish literature. Mark uses both names, but the Q section which mentions Satan perhaps belonged originally to a separate but similar tradition. Vs. 27 could easily follow vs. 24, while vss. 26 and 29 naturally belong together. Satan's kingdom or sovereignty is opposed to that of God and consists of the human beings whom he is able to capture. If he, or one of his demons, casts out demons, his **house is divided against itself** and civil war will bring it to an end. A philosopher might argue that evil cannot remain united and must at last defeat itself. But Jesus does not consider this possibility. He certainly does not suppose that it is unnecessary to fight Satan, nor does he underestimate Satan's power to do damage.

27. Your sons are probably exorcists who belong to the Pharisees. The rabbis believed that evil spirits had gained control when men served other gods, but there were always some righteous men like Solomon who could exorcise the demons and control them (see Tob. 6:7, 16-17; 8:2-3; Josephus *Antiquities* VIII. 2. 5). If the Pharisees' works are valid, certainly those of Jesus are! To condemn him is to condemn all who are liberating the oppressed.

28. But if neither Jesus nor the other exorcists have their power from Beelzebul, they act **by the Spirit of God.** And this is a sign that in some sense the **kingdom of God has** already **come,** for the power of demons will be broken in the messianic age. Indeed, according to Test. Levi 18, it is the messianic high priest who will do this great deed. Thus the decisive act of history has occurred, and it is only a question of time until the kingdom will be fully manifest. Jesus and the others work toward the same end; but Jesus' healings are so numerous and striking that it is evident that God has intervened actively.

---

near neighborhood of the Pharisees who charged that he "has a devil." To confront his truth is the first demand, whatever happens to our pride. Besides, the fact of evil is too mighty to be overcome in our own strength. Whence this dark perversity? Who organizes it into a kingdom of darkness? How can the malignities of our time be vanquished? We need Christ through the Holy Spirit that he may **bind the strong man,** and deliver those enslaved to evil.

25, 30. *A House Divided Against Itself.*—The Gospelist is interested, not primarily in the healing miracle, but in the truth taught by Jesus as he replied to his foes, and in the calm certainty of Jesus that God's power through him could and would overcome evil. Probably

the phrase a **house divided against itself** was proverbial in that day. Christ makes all things new; the proverb here receives fresh impact.

By God's ordaining, unity is strength. When the brain's wholeness is impaired, the limbs suffer from locomotor ataxia: the scattered thought and the physical energies in conflict are incapable of meeting life. Behind Christ's first retort to the Pharisees is the implied saying, "Satan is too astute to permit a division of counsels within his house." In that regard "the children of this world are . . . wiser than the children of light" (Luke 16:8). The striking statement in vs. 28, "the kingdom of God is come unto you," means that God has come in incarnate power; and that henceforth there

29 Or else, how can one enter into a strong man's house, and spoil his goods, except he first bind the strong man? and then he will spoil his house.

30 He that is not with me is against me; and he that gathereth not with me scattereth abroad.

31 ¶ Wherefore I say unto you, All manner of sin and blasphemy shall be forgiven unto men: but the blasphemy *against* the *Holy* Ghost shall not be forgiven unto men.

come upon you. **29** Or how can one enter a strong man's house and plunder his goods, unless he first binds the strong man? Then indeed he may plunder his house. **30** He who is not with me is against me, and he who does not gather with me scatters. **31** Therefore I tell you, every sin and blasphemy will be forgiven men, but the blasphemy against the Spirit will not be

---

29. A saying on the same theme, but with a different metaphor, which all three evangelists introduce here. It connects well with vs. 26, **how then . . . or how . . . ?** The **one** who enters into the **house** may be God, acting through Jesus; the **strong man** is Satan, and his **goods** the humans whom he has captured. The point is: "Satan will not cast out Satan; it is necessary for someone else to bind him"—a "stronger one," as Luke 11:22 says. Is the **house** a reference to Beelzebul as "lord of the house"? Parallels are found in Enoch 10:4-5; 21:1-2. (Cf. also R. Otto, *Kingdom of God and Son of Man*, p. 97.)

30. An apparently contradictory saying is found in Mark 9:40, where Jesus remarks that one who also casts out demons is not likely to be an enemy of Jesus. Here: "One who will not help in this all-important work of rescue **is against me.** He who will not help me to **gather** God's people into his kingdom from the four corners of the earth actually **scatters** the flock." The metaphor of gathering is found in Did. 9:4 and in Jewish prayers; e.g., Singer, *Authorised Daily Prayer Book*, p. 48.

31-32. This "hard saying" also occurred in Q (Luke 12:10). The Mishnah says that those who deny the resurrection, those who deny that the law is from God, and

---

would be an irrepressible conflict between Christ's kingdom and Satan's realm, and that men must choose.

Our planet must find a true focus. It can no longer endure the divisions made by national sovereignties. Lowell's lines, "Once to . . . every nation,"[8] thus find a new and more urgent occasion. The church likewise must find real unity. There are times when the Protestant must bear witness to the original simplicities of Christian faith, and when (within the Protestant witness) a Wesley must leave the sheltered sanctuary and carry the gospel to the people. But that time passes, and a new age cries out for new unity. Otherwise the enemies of the faith will win by the old strategy, *divide et impera.* Each man also must find integrity in the fine literal meaning of that word. He cannot remain neutral, or for long keep competing loyalties in uneasy balance. Jean Ingelow has a poem called "Divided": two friends, following "a tiny bright beck," could for a time hold hands across it, but soon it became too wide; and, if friendship was to be kept, they had to decide to walk on one side or the other.[9] The maladjustment of our time is due to the malady of a divided self. "Unite my heart to fear thy name" (Ps. 86:11).

Anarchy is weakness and finally collapses. Only true unity endures in power.

Thus Jesus declared that the lines are drawn. Once and for all, men must choose between him and Beelzebub. Kierkegaard's "either/or" is a profound insight.[1] Notice the unqualified demand for unqualified choice recorded in vs. 30, and the force of the words **gathereth** and **scattereth.** Christian faith has its necessary theology; but faith is more than the assent of the mind, as when a man says, "This doctrine seems to me to have firmer intellectual rivets." Likewise Christian faith has its emotional rapture, but it penetrates deeper than feeling. At long last it is a choice and a commitment of the will— an "either/or." The divided life soon ceases to live.

How is the true unity achieved? By God's initiative: he sent Christ to be the propitiation for our sins. Then, by our response in clear-cut decision. Then, by his indwelling power: for no man in mere human strength can keep the demons at their distance. God answers the prayer: "Unite my heart to fear thy name" (Ps. 86:11).

31-32. *The Unpardonable Sin.*—Almost every minister is called upon to help people who fear

---

[8] James Russell Lowell, "The Present Crisis," st. v.
[9] *Poems* (Boston: Roberts Brothers, 1863).

[1] *A Kierkegaard Anthology,* ed. Robert Bretall (Princeton: Princeton University Press, 1946), pp. 97-108.

32 And whosoever speaketh a word against the Son of man, it shall be forgiven him: but whosoever speaketh against the Holy Ghost, it shall not be forgiven him, neither in this world, neither in the *world* to come.	forgiven. 32 And whoever says a word against the Son of man will be forgiven; but whoever speaks against the Holy Spirit will not be forgiven, either in this age or in the age to come.

"Epicureans," will have no share in the world to come (Sanhedrin 10:1; Aboth 3:12). As B. H. Branscomb remarks on Mark 3:28-30, the words are a warning against presumption and not a limitation of God's grace. Perhaps the thought is: "To ascribe the Spirit's work to Satan is to overturn all moral values. He who takes such an attitude shuts himself out from forgiveness by his very stubbornness and impenitence. Words against Jesus are not as serious as those spoken against the Spirit, for they may arise out of misunderstanding" (cf. 11:6). The extreme statement, either in this age or in the age to come, is not found in Luke 12:10, and may have been added to the tradition.

---

they have committed the unpardonable sin. There is a pathetic instance in George Borrow's *Lavengro*.[2] In some cases the fear may become a monomania. Of course people who fear they are thus guilty could not be guilty, as we shall see, for conscience is alert in them. But for everyone these stern verses bring a chill.

We should not overlook the pledged mercy: All manner of sin and blasphemy shall be forgiven unto men. The self-effacement of Jesus also is like a daybreak: Whosoever speaketh a word against the Son of man, it shall be forgiven him. Gladstone and Lincoln were both silent under calumny, but they only hint the patience of Christ. But this gentleness throws into blacker relief the dread warning. What is the unpardonable sin?

Perhaps Matthew deliberately linked these verses with the controversy about Beelzebub. The paragraphing in RSV implies that connection. The term Holy Spirit is not here linked with the (later in date) doctrine of the Trinity. Its general meaning is perhaps the light that comes from God. Jesus says that some sins are due to ignorance or to failure under sudden temptation. Thus men can deny his claims and question his teaching, and still find pardon. But there is another kind of sin—willful blindness. In obdurate pride men can call the light darkness, or Jesus' works of mercy the black magic of Beelzebub. Thus they gouge out their own eyes. This is moral suicide. C. G. Holt, preaching on this theme, said, "I do not think there is one so depraved as to say that . . . the beauty, and the fragrance of these flowers are the work of the devil," thus indicating the nature of unpardonable sin.[3] But there *are* people so depraved: the enemies of Jesus insisted that a work of mercy was the sign of a devil.

Modern propaganda may approach this

iniquity. It sometimes hints that truth is a lie, and offers a lie as the truth. When a man declares there is no difference between his left foot and his right, how can he walk? The Spirit convinces "the world of sin, and of righteousness, and of judgment" (John 16:8), but what hope for a man who not only denies this axiomatic light but calls it midnight? What of those who say with the witches in *Macbeth*, "Fair is foul, and foul is fair"?[4] The sad declension is, "Grieve the Spirit," "Resist the Spirit," "Quench the Spirit" (cf. Eph. 4:30; Acts 6:10; I Thess. 5:19). At long last there is no pardon, because there is no desire for pardon—or even recognition of it. Whittier describes that doom:

What if thine eye refuse to see,
　Thine ear of Heaven's free welcome fail,
And thou a willing captive be,
　Thyself thine own dark jail?[5]

An interpreter of these verses must not try to drive them beyond their appointed truth. It is dangerous to build on them an elaborate system of "venial" sins and "mortal" sins. We easily enter a realm of conjecture if we draw the deduction, "Then some sins, though not others, are forgiven in the next world." Note the suggestion (see Exeg.) that the closing phrase of vs. 32 may be a later addition. Furthermore, the central meaning of αἰώνιος ("eternal") is not everlasting duration. We shall be wise to cleave to the stern warning: a man who deliberately tampers with the light God gives may rob himself of the power even to see pardon, let alone receive it. There is a threefold word written of Pharaoh—that (by way of proximate cause) he hardened his heart (Exod. 8:15), that (by way of ultimate cause) God hardened his heart (Exod. 7:13), and that (by way of inexorable result) his heart was hardened (Exod. 8:19).

[2] New York: G. P. Putnam, 1851, pp. 403-4.
[3] Quoted, *Great Texts of the Bible*, vol. on *St. Mark*, p. 119.

[4] Shakespeare, *Macbeth*, Act I, scene 1.
[5] "The Answer," st. xv.

33 Either make the tree good, and his fruit good; or else make the tree corrupt, and his fruit corrupt: for the tree is known by *his* fruit.

34 O generation of vipers, how can ye, being evil, speak good things? for out of the abundance of the heart the mouth speaketh.

35 A good man out of the good treasure of the heart bringeth forth good things: and an evil man out of the evil treasure bringeth forth evil things.

33 "Either make the tree good, and its fruit good; or make the tree bad, and its fruit bad; for the tree is known by its fruit. 34 You brood of vipers! how can you speak good, when you are evil? For out of the abundance of the heart the mouth speaks. 35 The good man out of his good treasure brings forth good, and the evil man out of his evil treasure brings forth

5. Interlude: Sayings About Good and Bad Men (12:33-37)

33. Parallels are found in 7:16-20 and Luke 6:43-44. The explanation of the curious form **either make . . . or make** is that Matthew forces the saying into a context where it does not belong and connects it with vss. 27-28. His idea is: "You must declare that the exorcist and his results are good, or that they are both bad."

34. This leads Matthew to explain that, just as exorcism is the fruit of the good tree, so Jesus' accusers make their charge because they are **evil. Brood of vipers** is borrowed from 3:7. **For out of the abundance,** etc., may be a little secular proverb which here is given a specific application.

35. One can see by general observation that this principle is true. Jesus does not state it in precise, dogmatic terms, and there is no reflection on the point that even good people have some evil in them.

Thus the issue of divine law and man's stubborn disobedience! But if we hear these words of Christ and heed them, we need not fear: we shall be saved.

33-35. Radical Religion.—Christ goes to the radix—to the root. This the Gospelist has already made clear (see Expos., 7:16-20). Notice also the link with all that has preceded in ch. 12. The trouble with the Pharisees was not superficial, but at the root of motive.

The simile varies. In vs. 33, fruit from a tree; in vs. 34, stream from a fountain; in vs. 35, gift from a treasure; in vs. 36, words as the issue of the heart. But these are the images of one truth. What is this fruit? A man's conduct—in expressions of the face, in every manner of deed. He is to be judged, not by profession, not by his promises, not by a reputation sedulously cultivated (as in the case of some Pharisees), but by acts. Outwardly he may dissemble for a time, but not for long: he must soon unmask and reveal himself: **An evil man . . . bringeth forth evil things.** What people finally see in a man is the fruit of unseen motive.

What is the root of a man's life? Not "character" in our glib use of that word. Too often we mean by character that which a man himself can fashion. True goodness is not of mere human making, for what man makes is soon cankered by pride. Both Epictetus [6] and Kant [7]

declared that there is nothing in the whole world good except a good will. But even that word has unplumbed depths: the springs of the will are ultimately in the Creator, and a man is good only as he dwells in God: "There is none good but one, that is, God" (19:17; Mark 10:18; cf. Luke 18:19).

Note in Exeg. the explanation of **make** in vs. 33. But wittingly or unwittingly, that is the proper word. For the ultimate problem is how to make human nature good. Politicians ignore the question. But no national defense will avail, and no law offer hope, except as human nature becomes good in the will. Man cannot make his own life. The reply of the physician to Macbeth, when asked what can "pluck from the memory a rooted sorrow," was an unintentional mockery: "Therein the patient must minister to himself." [8] That is precisely the point of the patient's impotence. He is too baffled by his own nature, and too infirm in his own will, to work his own cure. Manners will not save him: he needs regeneration. Ethical teaching will only set his teeth on edge: he needs a power of love from beyond his life to cut away the evil and reinforce the good. Behold the Man! God in Jesus Christ had wrought healing; those to whom he spoke had seen it. He makes the tree good.

[6] *Discourses* II. 16.

[7] *The Philosophy of Kant,* selected and tr. John Watson, "The Metaphysic of Morality," iv. 241, sec. 1 (Glasgow: James Maclehose & Sons, 1908), p. 225.

[8] Shakespeare, *Macbeth,* Act V, scene 3.

36 But I say unto you, That every idle word that men shall speak, they shall give account thereof in the day of judgment.

37 For by thy words thou shalt be justified, and by thy words thou shalt be condemned.

38 ¶ Then certain of the scribes and of the Pharisees answered, saying, Master, we would see a sign from thee.

evil. 36 I tell you, on the day of judgment men will render account for every careless word they utter; 37 for by your words you will be justified, and by your words you will be condemned."

38 Then some of the scribes and Pharisees said to him, "Teacher, we wish to see

36. The rabbis frequently make such a statement, and Matthew inserts it here with vs. 24 in mind.

37. The word translated **justified,** i.e., acquitted or declared righteous at the Day of Judgment, is explained in notes on Rom. 3:21-31. Teachers like Paul would say that it is not quite so simple a matter as this, but Matthew accepts the dominant Jewish idea that performance is what counts in the end. Similar statements are found in 7:24-27; 21:28-32.

6. The Demand for Signs (12:38-42)

Parallels are found in Luke 11:29-32. This passage stood in Q in the same general context as the sayings in vss. 22-30. It comes in strangely just after Jesus has pointed to the casting out of demons as a sign of the kingdom's presence. But early Christians would have seen no contradiction, because: (*a*) the healings were not for the purpose of authenticating Jesus' words, but were the manifestation of something still greater; (*b*) Jesus was not interested in his own honor but in doing his work as bringer of the kingdom; and (*c*) his words do not require any external attestation. Their truth should be obvious to candid readers of the O.T.

38. A Jewish **teacher** was often asked for a **sign** that his teaching was true.

36-37. *Words . . . and Destiny.*—These verses have links with the foregoing. The wicked words of the Pharisees and the answering words of Christ provide contrasting illustration of fruit springing from the deep root of motive. But here is truth worthy of separate study, with depths to defy our sounding lines. Christian faith has great concern with words.

Words have almost terrifying power, even when they are **idle** or insipid words. Perhaps there is a deliberate difference between ῥῆμα in vs. 36—repeated words, slogans, trite sayings—and λόγων in vs. 37—conscious and considered words. Words can rob a man both of substance and good name; words can murder, and drive to murder. Gamaliel Bradford's *Damaged Souls* gives instance after instance of how evil men become adept at inflaming speech. On the contrary, words can heal and bless. The "Gettysburg Address" continues to nerve a nation; and Dante's "In His will is our peace" [9] is benediction. Contracts that govern business and statecraft are but written words.

The connection with vss. 33-35 is right, for **words** are conduct. They are deeds of the lips, as veritably as performing a surgical operation or carving a statue is a deed of the hands. Of all deeds, words are perhaps the most revealing,

[9] *The Divine Comedy,* "Paradiso," canto iii.

the most flexible to use, the most instantly available, the most freighted with personal influence. It is not strange that much of the world's traffic is conducted along rivers of words. The church has done too little justice to Christ's frequent dicta on this issue.

The trouble with "idle speech" is not on the tongue, but in the heart. How many **idle words** are spoken, words that do not work, not least from the pulpit! But the remedy is not in classrooms that teach "effective speech," despite the advertisements. There a channel may be cut for the stream, but such teachers (unless they are more than teachers of speech) have no power to give strength and purity to the spring. Nor is it always true that "Speech is silvern, Silence is golden": [1] sometimes silence is cowardice. The salvation of speech is that it shall issue from a silence where God cleanses the penitent heart and sets his own message on the lips. Thus the preacher should preach as a sinful man to sinful men—after he has made confession, and prayed in adoration of divine grace, and received the divine word.

38-42. *Signs False and True.*—Why should the Pharisees ask a sign when they had just

[1] Thomas Carlyle, *Sartor Resartus,* translating the Swiss inscription *Sprechen ist silbern, Schweigen ist golden,* Bk. III, ch. iii.

39 But he answered and said unto them, An evil and adulterous generation seeketh after a sign; and there shall no sign be given to it, but the sign of the prophet Jonas:

40 For as Jonas was three days and three nights in the whale's belly; so shall the Son of man be three days and three nights in the heart of the earth.

41 The men of Nineveh shall rise in judgment with this generation, and shall condemn it: because they repented at the preaching of Jonas; and, behold, a greater than Jonas is here.

42 The queen of the south shall rise up in the judgment with this generation, and

a sign from you." 39 But he answered them, "An evil and adulterous generation seeks for a sign; but no sign shall be given to it except the sign of the prophet Jonah. 40 For as Jonah was three days and three nights in the belly of the whale, so will the Son of man be three days and three nights in the heart of the earth. 41 The men of Nin'e-veh will arise at the judgment with this generation and condemn it; for they repented at the preaching of Jonah, and behold, something greater than Jonah is here. 42 The queen of the South will arise at the judgment with this generation and

---

39-40. That this **generation** is **evil and adulterous** is shown by the fact that it does not recognize the truth. According to Psalms of Solomon (8:9-11) and the Mishnah (Soṭa 9:9), it was literally adulterous; but here the adultery is probably apostasy from the true God, as in Isa. 57:3-4. Luke 11:30 does not have this typology of the Resurrection. Matthew has rewritten the verse; he is like many other Christians who, when they think of **Jonah,** can remember only **the whale.** He may presuppose the Christian doctrine of the descent into Hades, found also in I Pet. 3:18-20. The **sign** of Jonah to which Jesus alluded must be the preaching of repentance, as Luke's saying indicates. Jonah offered no other sign to the Ninevites, and they accepted his word without any other proof. In other words, as Mark 8:12 says, "No sign shall be given to this generation." Luke 16:19-31 shows that Jesus insisted very strongly on this point. Not even the resurrection of Christ will necessarily convince the stubborn!

41-42. The Ninevites and the queen of Sheba (i.e., south Arabia, I Kings 10:1-13), though heathens, will be appropriate witnesses against Israel in the Last Judgment,

---

witnessed a remarkable work of healing? Because they had called that the sign of the prince of devils; and because by **sign** they meant a prodigy like a light streaming from heaven at midnight, or like the dividing of the River Jordan, as the impostor Theudas promised,[2] or like the plucking of a star from the sky. Perhaps the Pharisees feigned the eagerness. Certainly they were intent to discount him. Perhaps they were so calloused in mind as to believe that truth is not truth unless accompanied by sensational portents: Jesus must leap from the pinnacle of the temple.

Christ repudiated the demand. They were "adulterous"—that is, apostate. How, then, could any sign help them? If a miracle had been wrought to their order, they might still have ascribed it to the devil's power. Or they might have said that their eyes and ears deceived them. Or, as each miracle was wrought, they might have called it commonplace, and demanded a more prodigious wonder. It is true of sleight of hand, and of cheap sensational preaching, that the dose of marvel must ever be increased to

satisfy the itch for "signs." Christ's critics did not desire truth. In their pride they hated the light. What good would any proof have done them until they were ready to repent as Nineveh repented under Jonah?

The **sign of the prophet Jonah** is probably just such a sign, the sign of preaching that wrought repentance. Jonah had arrived at Nineveh without credentials, except for the credential of God's truth making its impact on guilty hearts to bring repentance. The sign of Solomon was a wisdom that instantly found the soul. At any rate the Queen of Sheba (I Kings 10) was so eager for wisdom that she travelled far in her deep longing. Yes, there would be a sign, our Gospelist (or some later believer) adds: a Resurrection more wonderful than the deliverance of Jonah from the whale. But that Resurrection would be stern judgment. It would not convince the enemies of Christ, for, as he himself said, "neither will they be persuaded, though one rose from the dead" (Luke 16:31).

This refusal of Christ is not to be construed as a denial of the healing miracles. He had such power; the whole controversy between him

---

[2] Josephus *Antiquities* XX. 5. 2. (May be the same Theudas mentioned in Acts 5:36.)

shall condemn it: for she came from the uttermost parts of the earth to hear the wisdom of Solomon; and, behold, a greater than Solomon *is* here.

43 When the unclean spirit is gone out of a man, he walketh through dry places, seeking rest, and findeth none.

44 Then he saith, I will return into my house from whence I came out; and when he is come, he findeth *it* empty, swept, and garnished.

condemn it; for she came from the **ends** of the earth to hear the wisdom of Solomon, and behold, something greater than Solomon is here.

43 "When the unclean spirit has gone out of a man, he passes through waterless places seeking rest, but he finds none. 44 Then he says, 'I will return to my house from which I came.' And when he comes he finds it empty, swept, and put

---

because they were receptive (cf. 11:20-24). Josephus (*Antiquities* VIII. 6. 5-6) gives Jewish traditions about this queen. The Greek word rendered **something greater** is neuter. It is possible to interpret the verse as meaning that Jesus is a greater figure than Jonah, or that his age brings an infinitely more important event.

7. Interlude: A Saying About Demon Possession (12:43-45)

These verses are found here in Matthew and Luke because they deal with the general subject of exorcism.

43. An **unclean spirit** which has been driven out flees far away (Tob. 8:1-3). He will not find rest in **waterless places,** perhaps because, according to Jewish folklore, demons like water. But in Isa. 13:21; 34:14 evil spirits dwell in deserted places, and the saying may refer merely to the homelessness and restlessness of the demon.

44. The **house** may be **swept, and put in order,** but it is nevertheless **empty** and therefore ready for the demon. If the demon is not to return, the empty space must be

---

and the Pharisees assumes the healings. The faithful will find **a sign** in such works of mercy, and a greater "sign" in Jesus Christ himself. But Christ wrought healing only when and as it was given him of God, and only under impulse of compassion (not to "prove" his own power) ; and there is evidence of his constant fear that by healings he might win men's eyes, but lose their souls.

How *is* truth attested? What *is* the "proof"? Truth is proved as light is proved: a man cannot prove light except as he uses light. The impact of light is its own evidence. The Pharisees were convicted by the light of Christ, but they scurried away into the darkness of their own pride, and then said: "Prove that it is light!" The word **greater** is neutral: **A greater** [thing] **than Jonah is here.** Thus the word can hardly be interpreted as a messianic claim. But it refers, directly or indirectly, to the dawn—the breaking on the world of new light; and Christ was the incarnation of the light. He is his own evidence. We "prove" him by our response to his claims, by commitment of mind and deed of hand. His truth cleanses, commissions, and empowers in valid Christian experience. What better "proof"? "O taste and see that the Lord is good" (Ps. 34:8) .

43-45. *The Story of the Empty House.*—A story to chill the blood. The demon, expelled

from a man's house of life, wanders in a wilderness. Then, homeless, returns to look from far at **my house.** Finding it swept and set in order, but empty, he summons seven other devils each worse than himself; and they, in alliance too strong for the man, come to possess him. His **last state is** [thus] **worse than the first.** Empty houses never remain empty. Dust gathers in the corners, rats gnaw at the floorboards, and a ghost slams the door. Devils laugh in glee at the sight of an empty house.

There is a terrible persistence in wickedness: it returns, and the soul not indwelt by the rightful Tenant is always beleaguered. Reformation is never enough, not even though it be as thorough as the cleansing of the Augean stables: [3] at best it is only prelude to a new loyalty. Nature and human nature both abhor a vacuum: no faith is almost worse than a bad faith, for no faith invites a swarm of bad faiths. Hitler enters when men cease to believe in God, for no life remains empty of worship. These truths Jesus did not labor. Instead he enshrined them unforgettably in a story.

There is need for a positive faith—in Christ. Psychology may cast out the demon self-deception or fear or inferiority complex; but if psychology has no new love or higher loyalty to offer, the last state of the patient . . . ! There is

[3] See Gayley, *Classic Myths*, p. 218,

45 Then goeth he, and taketh with himself seven other spirits more wicked than himself, and they enter in and dwell there: and the last *state* of that man is worse than the first. Even so shall it be also unto this wicked generation.

46 ¶ While he yet talked to the people, behold, *his* mother and his brethren stood without, desiring to speak with him.

47 Then one said unto him, Behold, thy mother and thy brethren stand without, desiring to speak with thee.

in order. **45** Then he goes and brings with him seven other spirits more evil than himself, and they enter and dwell there; and the last state of that man becomes worse than the first. So shall it be also with this evil generation."

46 While he was still speaking to the people, behold, his mother and his brothers stood outside, asking to speak to him.[i]

[i] Some ancient authorities insert verse 47: *Some one told him, "Your mother and your brothers are standing outside, asking to speak to you."*

filled—with a right spirit, prayer, good deeds, the love of God. In I Cor. 3:16 Paul speaks of human beings as God's temple in which the Holy Spirit dwells (cf. II Cor. 6:16).

45. This is a vivid picture of a relapse. It refers primarily to insanity and other illnesses, but applies very well to moral backsliding. Matthew adds the last sentence: the Jewish nation, now being healed, is in danger of falling into the clutches of demonic powers.

8. Concluding Example: Jesus' True Family (12:46-50)

The story is told simply to point the moral of vs. 50. (Similar teaching is found in Luke 11:27-28.) It is not meant to imply that Jesus paid no attention to family ties. His earthly family, however, played a very small role in the traditions preserved in Mark and Q, and the infancy stories represent a special interest in the Messiah's early life which is not noticeable in the gospel tradition generally.

47. This verse is redundant and was interpolated from Mark 3:32 into the "Western text." It is found in Bezae (D) and some O.L. MSS. It is properly omitted in RSV.

no lack of evidence. A confident selfishness is a poor salvation from an inferiority complex. Good citizenship committees may stop the wicked, cleaning out organized vice; but their energy will be wasted unless they start the true. The world drove out Kaiserism, and left the house empty; so Hitlerism arrived with seven other devils—anti-Semitism, the scientific contempt for life, and all the evil brood. It does not greatly help a man to know what he does *not* believe, unless he knows also what he does believe. Too often the astringent mind intent on truth is only empty. A church edifice having been deserted as the congregation moved uptown, became successively a night club, a junk shop, and an auction room; and therein is a parable.

The Pharisees who questioned Jesus had cast out the gross sins, but they left life empty of any loyalty beyond themselves. So seven other devils arrived, such as money-greed, self-righteousness, and contempt for "lesser breeds without the Law."[4] But the followers of Christ had invited him to live in a house which, when he first came, was not even swept or garnished. Yet soon their table was spread, for he was their

[4] Kipling, "Recessional."

Bread of life; and they feared no darkness, for he was their Light; and death held no terror, for he was their Resurrection and Life.

After every war the world begins to fear the next. The demons expelled once more look in through the window at an empty house. When shall we learn that our personality is made for a divine indwelling? When shall we learn to say, "Him I do believe and love"? Our world needs that passionate and positive commitment. Otherwise our emptiness invites a worse fate. When Christ comes to live in us, the devils keep their distance.

46-50. Spiritual Kinship.—The friends of Jesus, and perhaps his family, thought him deranged: "He is beside himself" (Mark 3:21). According to the Fourth Gospel, his mother and brothers did not understand him. Mark, the earliest gospel record, gives little stress to the human relationships of Jesus. Yet we may be sure that Jesus was devoted to his home, and held his kindred and friends in dear regard. The Fourth Gospel, while it portrays Mary's failure to comprehend Jesus, shows him tenderly caring for her even amid the agonies of the Cross. Perhaps there is intense longing for his home behind such a saying as, "The Son of

48 But he answered and said unto him that told him, Who is my mother? and who are my brethren?

49 And he stretched forth his hand toward his disciples, and said, Behold my mother and my brethren!

50 For whosoever shall do the will of my Father which is in heaven, the same is my brother, and sister, and mother.

48 But he replied to the man who told him, "Who is my mother, and who are my brothers?" 49 And stretching out his hand toward his disciples, he said, "Here are my mother and my brothers! 50 For whoever does the will of my Father in heaven is my brother, and sister, and mother."

---

48. The Synoptists do not attempt to present Jesus' **mother** as an important personage, omitting to mention even her presence at the Crucifixion; that tradition is found in John 19:25-27. John pictures the mother as faithful but not completely understanding her son (John 2:4-5). Acts 1:14 associates her with the disciples after the Crucifixion. If Jesus was Mary's first-born son (1:25), the **brothers** were younger than Jesus. This is the most natural way to understand the gospel story. Many Christians of the third and fourth centuries chose to believe in the perpetual virginity of Mary and therefore assumed either (a) that the brothers were sons of Joseph by a former marriage—the theory of Epiphanius and others—or (b) that they were cousins, the sons of another Mary (27:56)—the theory of Jerome. Such theories are derived from pure speculation, and the gospel record gives no support to them. According to John, the **brothers** did not believe in Jesus (John 7:5), but we know from other sources that they were active in the affairs of the early church (I Cor. 9:5).

49. Matthew regards the **disciples,** perhaps the twelve, as Jesus' true family; in Mark 3:34 it is all those who are seated there with him.

---

man hath not where to lay his head" (8:20; Luke 9:58).

So these verses should not be construed as any denial of the strong claims of human love. Renan charged Jesus with "trampling upon the flesh . . . and warring against the most legitimate cravings of the heart,"[5] but there is no real evidence to support the charge. That Jesus should have chosen the word **Father** as his best name for God testifies to his feeling for home, and his awareness that the family is basic in our common life. **He stretched forth his hand** means perhaps a gesture wrung from him by the renunciation which he was about to utter.

For Jesus knew, and would have us know, that God's claims are sovereign over even the dearest human claims; and that the spiritual bond between disciples of the kingdom is paramount over even blood bonds. Sometimes it is required that a man shall appear to "hate" his parents in order to obey God's command (Luke 14:26). This theme recurs (see Expos., 8:21; 10:21; 10:35, 36). Almost inevitably Jesus was misunderstood. Mrs. Poyser, in *Adam Bede,* could account for Dinah Morris' leaving home to preach the gospel only by declaring that "there's a bigger maggot than usual in your head."[6] Yet it remains true that human loyalties

themselves fester and fail unless they are subject to an all-embracing loyalty to God.

There is a joy beneath the pain in this confession by Christ. Here was the family of the "twice-born" through the grace of the incarnate Son. Here was a love more sure and tender than any human love: the love of the Father for his children, and their penitent and adoring love toward him. Here was a spiritual bond stronger than any bond of flesh, an eternal bond far surer than the death-broken bonds of time. Here was a devotion fashioned in the dangerous business of doing God's will (Mark 3:35), a loyalty held in God's own hands. If these verses seem stern teaching, we should remember the comfort they brought to those who then were disowned by their families because of the new faith. Jerome's letter to Heliodorus, written in A.D. 396, reveals both the sternness and the deeper joy of a Christian kinship.[7] Meanwhile it should be remembered that Christian faith proves soon that it is not the breach, but the safeguard and salvation, of human love.

Is church membership a family, and Christian discipleship a home? It should be so. Within the church the lowly should find understanding, security, mutual love, and the challenge of the

[5] *Life of Jesus,* pp. 310-11.

[6] Bk. I, ch. vi.

[7] "A Letter of Consolation for the Death of Nepotianus," *Select Letters of St. Jerome,* tr. F. A. Wright (New York: G. P. Putnam's Sons, 1933), Letter LX, pp. 265 ff.

13 The same day went Jesus out of the house, and sat by the sea side.

2 And great multitudes were gathered together unto him, so that he went into a ship, and sat; and the whole multitude stood on the shore.

3 And he spake many things unto them in parables, saying, Behold, a sower went forth to sow;

13 That same day Jesus went out of the house and sat beside the sea. 2 And great crowds gathered about him, so that he got into a boat and sat there; and the whole crowd stood on the beach. 3 And he told them many things in parables, say-

VI. Third Discourse, Addressed to the Crowds. The Kingdom of Heaven (13:1-58)

This chapter illustrates Matthew's attempt to combine the chronological and the topical methods. He follows Mark's framework as far as he can, but Mark and his other sources are not arranged according to a consistent plan. At this point in Mark comes an important collection of parables, which Matthew adopts and expands, using it as a general discourse on the kingdom of heaven, its acceptance and rejection. The two previous chapters have led up to this. Despite the varied character of the material, the result is amazingly appropriate. The evangelist thinks of most of this discourse as addressed to the crowds, but there are asides to the disciples.

A. Introduction (13:1-3a)

13:1-3a. Jesus certainly said **many things in parables,** and Matthew has already used teaching which can be so classified (e.g., 7:24-27; 11:16-17). The term parable covers a variety of forms. It includes (a) stories drawn from life, or fictitious stories, to illustrate one and only one point—the "true parable" (e.g., 20:1-16; Luke 16:1-8a); (b) example stories (e.g., Luke 10:29-37); (c) brief metaphorical sayings or similes (e.g., 7:16); and (d) an occasional allegory (e.g., Mark 12:1-12). (See general article "The Teaching of Jesus: III. The Parables" above, pp. 165-75.)

B. A Parable on Reception of the Message (13:3b-23)

Jesus' actual teaching is to be looked for in vss. 3b-9, and in vss. 11a, 12, 16-17, which come out of a different context; perhaps also vs. 13. The interpretation in vss. 18-23 is the work of Mark or some other early Christian.

1. Parable of the Sower (13:3b-9)

This is a "true parable," told to illustrate only one point, and drawn from observation of everyday life. Jesus pictures a man who broadcasts seed. It falls in all sorts of places, and much of it is lost, but enough strikes fertile ground so that the sowing is more than worth while and one need not worry about what is lost. So it is with the work of Jesus and the disciples, who herald the kingdom and do deeds which manifest it. God will bless it abundantly, and they need not be discouraged. (See especially B. W. Bacon, *The Story of Jesus* [New York: The Century Co., 1927], pp. 211-14.) A similar idea is found in Heb. 6:10. II Esdras 8:41 uses the metaphor of sown seed to illustrate a different point.

3b. The vivid description of A. M. Rihbany (*The Syrian Christ* [Boston: Houghton Mifflin Co., 1916], pp. 286-87) illustrates how **a sower went out to sow.** In Palestine seed

---

kingdom. For the followers of Christ are a family "around the feet of God."

13:3, 10-15, 34. Teaching by Parables.—This was Christ's characteristic method. The rabbis also asked, "Unto what may this be likened?" [8]

[8] Asher Feldman, *Parables and Similes of the Rabbis,* pp. 49, 50, 94, 96, 97.

but could not approach his incomparable skill. The difference was in more than skill: they lacked his love and consecration. They lacked the gift of God in him. As a storyteller he was unrivaled, and it is not surprising that **a whole multitude** heard him. People "like" what is "like." Similes and metaphors are a joy. Even

4 And when he sowed, some *seeds* fell by the wayside, and the fowls came and devoured them up:

5 Some fell upon stony places, where they had not much earth: and forthwith

ing: "A sower went out to sow. 4 And as he sowed, some seeds fell along the path, and the birds came and devoured them. 5 Other

---

is sown *before* the plowing, and thus some of it falls on ground which only later is seen to be unsuitable.

4. Along the path may mean "by the path" (Goodspeed) or actually on it, where the **birds** could see it.

5. Rocky ground could mean "ground full of rocks" (Thayer) ; but, more probably, soil which thinly covers a rock ledge. The seed sprouts **immediately** because the soil is warmed by the rock.

---

our scientific and philosophical thinking is by analogy: do we not speak of "waves" of sound and a "field" of force? Those who heard Jesus looked around them at the sower, a woman baking bread, a torn garment, a lost sheep; and, under his divine touch, saw everywhere "an earthly story with a heavenly meaning."

Why this method? Not that Jesus might deliberately blind and baffle men, despite vss. 14-15. Jesus chose to teach in parables because, eager to make known the "good tidings," he must in valid ways win the interest of the hearers. Thus he could quicken in them some measure of that awareness of God which was his own daily bread. If only the preacher would remember that dullness is failure, and perhaps a breach in love and therefore sin! Jesus taught thus because the truth must be made clear even to simple minds; and because, when exhortation and argument fail,

> . . . truth embodied in a tale
> Shall enter in at lowly doors.[9]

If only preachers would remember that when they win an argument from the pulpit they are likely to have lost the congregation, since no one likes to be worsted in an argument! Jesus taught in parables because a parable disarms, and wins, when an argument might alienate; and because a story lingers in the mind like music, and may bring salvation after many days; and because a story is a seed plot ever yielding new and deeper truth. But what brooding goes into a good story, and what vigil of prayer into a Jesus-parable! It is far easier to argue and fulminate!

The full reason why Jesus chose to speak in parables is that he loved both God and man. He could not have deliberately confused any man. The Isaiah quotation (vss. 14-15) may have been bitterly ironical in its origin; certainly it should not be interpreted as conveying any shadowed theory of election. The verses in

this setting have at least this meaning: God is not taken unawares by apostasy, and Jesus chose parables lest he should harden the already hard heart by a more frontal attack. He loved people, and loved them more because they were eager to hear a story; and in responding eagerness, as they crowded round him, he said, "Unto what shall I liken it?" He loved God, and saw everywhere the celestial sign. Every bush was aflame with the divine fire.

> What if Earth
> Be but the shadow of Heav'n, and things therein
> Each to other like, more than on earth is thought?[1]

To Jesus earth was "but the shadow of Heav'n." He pointed to the "shadow"—a shepherd, a woman searching for a lost coin, or a fisherman hauling in his nets—and said: "This dimly shows the worth and wonder of the real world." So, for love of man in the love of God, he told these incomparable stories. They will long outlast all our science and skill.

3-8. The Parable of the Soils.—The first parable: **Behold, a sower.** The man was perhaps there before their eyes. Were the disciples and even Christ himself perplexed because these stories, glowing and thrilling in their truth, still failed to win men? That is also our bafflement. Why does the gospel apparently fail in our time, why does it fail in any time, despite its manifest joy, despite the tragedy that besets alien ways? Perhaps Jesus himself hoped for swifter success. Perhaps there is a touch of autobiography in this story. He was not dazzled by the "multitude." He knew human nature: he could not coerce, and some men would not respond. But the parable is a parable, not an allegory. That is, it has a central truth; and the central truth is apparently vs. 8. So this story is a wellspring of hope.

The soil, not the **sower,** is closely described. The teller of good news is not the main concern: this parable portrays the congregation.

[9] Tennyson, "In Memoriam," XXXVI, st. ii.

[1] Milton, *Paradise Lost,* Bk. V, l. 574.

they sprung up, because they had no deepness of earth:

6 And when the sun was up, they were scorched; and because they had no root, they withered away.

7 And some fell among thorns; and the thorns sprung up, and choked them:

8 But other fell into good ground, and brought forth fruit, some a hundredfold, some sixtyfold, some thirtyfold.

9 Who hath ears to hear, let him hear.

seeds fell on rocky ground, where they had not much soil, and immediately they sprang up, since they had no depth of soil, 6 but when the sun rose they were scorched; and since they had no root they withered away. 7 Other seeds fell upon thorns, and the thorns grew up and choked them. 8 Other seeds fell on good soil and brought forth grain, some a hundredfold, some sixty, some thirty. 9 He who has ears,*j* let him hear."

j Some ancient authorities add here and in verse 43 "to hear."

---

8. Josephus speaks of the unusual fertility of the plain of Gennesaret (*Jewish War* III. 10. 8). Mark's "thirtyfold and sixtyfold and a hundredfold" gives a better emphasis, but Matthew reverses the order. In the United States, where the average yield of wheat for the country is fifteen to twenty bushels per acre, twentyfold to thirtyfold would be average, and a good crop might return forty times the sowing or more. Higher yields could be expected in a warm climate where soil is exceptionally fertile, but in any case a hundredfold is a large figure which Jesus chooses for the purpose of emphasis.

9. To hear is omitted by some of the best Alexandrian and O.L. MSS and the Sinaitic Syriac. Matthew left it out for the sake of smoothness, but it was added again

---

They are in four main groups. Some are dull, indifferent, calloused. Perhaps circumstances have hardened them, perhaps they are self-hardened. In either event the soil of their life is like a pathway through a field. Everything goes over it, weddings, trade, pleasure; and the seed cannot even find lodgment. Only the plowshare of tragedy, their own or some tragedy of another's loss, can break up the stubborn soil. Therein is one "reason" for failure. Others in the congregation are shallow in nature. They are good soil, but lack depth: there is a flat ledge of rock an inch below the surface. They have sentimental fervor and an instant response: the wheat "springs up." But zeal soon flags. How can shallow people become profound? "Sitting down they watched him there" (27:36), even at the Cross. Only the long-patient suffering of God can give them depth. Others live a divided life. Farmers would call them "dirty soil": the rich earth is cluttered with thorns. They could be splendidly Christian; they have potential gift and potential zeal. But they crave the world, and will not surrender it, even while they are drawn to Christ. Lancelot, in *Idylls of the King,* is a type. His sin was strangely mixed with consecration, and worldliness finally stifled his true life, until tragedy cleansed him.

But the parable is not a half despair. It is very hope. For some seed falls on ground so clear and good that it multiplies thirtyfold, sixtyfold, a hundredfold. This is not hyperbole, but sure promise. "For God is not unrighteous to forget your work and labor of love, which ye have showed toward his name" (Heb. 6:10). Here is the answer to any age of disillusion. "What's the use?" Such use that any word for Christ, any love shown for his sake, will in some men find welcome and nurture, and become a hundred gospels and a hundred deeds of love.

Beyond doubt this is the central "drive" of the story. The gospel seems as small as a seed falling on an alien world. What chance does it have with shallowness, worldliness, and cruel "isms"? But it has a secret life and will not fail. The sower must sow, even if some seed falls on stone or thorns. He must leave the issue in God's hands, and still labor; for his seed is the very bread of the soul. The Millet picture, "The Sower," [2] portrays the true herald of God's grace: he is sometimes weary and often lonely, and the field is wide. The world seems to mock his labor. Nay, the mockery is no seeming, but a stark fact. But some soil brings forth a hundredfold, and men are fed. The plowshare of tragedy may break up the soil and be the means by which God prepares a great harvest. In every age there are some who wait for his coming. But what responsibility rests with free human soil. The next exposition deals with needed verity.

9, 43. *Ears and No Ears.*—The seed was good seed, and the sower a faithful man, but the soil still determined his success or failure. Perhaps the saying was proverbial, but Jesus gave

[2] See Julia Cartwright, *Jean François Millet* (New York: The Macmillan Co., 1896), pp. 110-12.

10 And the disciples came, and said unto him, Why speakest thou unto them in parables?

11 He answered and said unto them, Because it is given unto you to know the mysteries of the kingdom of heaven, but to them it is not given.

10 Then the disciples came and said to him, "Why do you speak to them in parables?" 11 And he answered them, "To you it has been given to know the secrets of the kingdom of heaven, but to them it

from Mark 4:9. There it may represent a Semitic idiom; hence Goodspeed translates, "Let him who has ears listen!"

2. Prophetic Explanation: Understanding Is Given Only to the Disciples (13:10-17)

Matthew apparently derives vss. 10-13 from Mark and vss. 16-17 from Q. There are also contacts between vss. 10-11 and Luke 8:9-10. Did these verses stand in Q or has Matthew's text influenced that of Luke? In vs. 2 Jesus was teaching from the boat; Matthew here ignores this.

11. This cannot have been the original reason for speaking in parables, for a parable is designed to illustrate the truth and make it clear. But Mark and the other evangelists frequently found it hard to understand Jesus' figures because the context was lost, and they were also baffled by the fact that Jesus had been rejected; hence Mark adopted the theory that the parables were esoteric teachings.

it urgent meaning; and it seems to have been often on his lips. It is sharp kindness.

We have marked Christ's comment on the responsibility of speaking (12:36-37)—a plea we often ignore. Now we must mark his even less heeded plea about the responsibility of hearing.

We listen—and what does it matter? We hear great music—and why should it be our burden? We give ear to the prophet, and admit his prophetic truth—but that is all we give. Sometimes we blame the prophet because he does not speak a better truth, and what we hear "goes in at one ear and out at the other." Strength is a responsibility under God, as we sometimes admit: they "that are strong ought to bear the infirmities of the weak" (Rom. 15:1). Money is a responsibility under God: "Whoso hath this world's good, and seeth his brother have need, and shutteth up his . . . compassion . . ." (I John 3:17). But power to hear, we think, is not a responsibility. Then Christ tells the story of the soils. The hearer has power to thwart the gospel or to bring it to fulfillment.

Hearing is an act: the herald is under obligation to catch and hold our attention, but we are required to heed in an energy of response. "Friends, Romans, countrymen, lend me your ears." [3] Hearing is a prayer; for everyone about to hear music or the music of the good news must ask God to teach him the wise husbandry of the heart. Hearing is a welcome, and a nurture, and a subsequent venture of conduct. Unless hearing is translated into deeds, it can be

[3] Shakespeare, *Julius Caesar*, Act III, scene 2.

as wicked as a cure discovered but never made known. Ears are a very responsible wealth.

Jesus is not suggesting that some people are not capable of listening. He who has ears implies that every man has some power to receive. A few have acute hearing—sensitive ears, like those of a musician, to catch undertones and overtones of truth: such people have a sterner obligation. 'For unto whomsoever much is given, of him shall be much required" (Luke 12:48). The seed is partly in the power of the soil. The gospel is partly in the power of the pew.

10-15. *The Secret of the Kingdom.*—Here we must be doubly careful to be true to the Exeg. Jesus did not speak in parables to darken counsel and baffle men's minds. Not even commentators of severely literal mind dare give these verses a literal turn. The early church could not understand the apparent failure of Christ. They lacked his realism. So they proposed this dark doctrine of election, finding seeming warrant for it in the Isaiah quotation. Furthermore, they borrowed from the mystery cults the idea of a secret which would give them standing in their time, and which, according to the cults, must not be divulged. [4]

But it is still true that Christians have a secret. Notice Paul's use of the word "mystery." There is an open secret, hidden from "the wise and prudent" but revealed unto "babes" (11:25). The lowly, reverent, and expectant folk, like Simeon, receive Christ and find in him

[4] B. Harvie Branscomb, *The Gospel of Mark*, comment on Mark 4:10-12, pp. 78-79.

12 For whosoever hath, to him shall be given, and he shall have more abundance: but whosoever hath not, from him shall be taken away even that he hath.

13 Therefore speak I to them in parables: because they seeing see not; and hearing they hear not, neither do they understand.

14 And in them is fulfilled the prophecy of Esaias, which saith, By hearing ye shall hear, and shall not understand; and seeing ye shall see, and shall not perceive:

15 For this people's heart is waxed gross, and *their* ears are dull of hearing, and their eyes they have closed; lest at any time they should see with *their* eyes, and hear with *their* ears, and should understand with *their* heart, and should be converted, and I should heal them.

has not been given. 12 For to him who has will more be given, and he will have abundance; but from him who has not, even what he has will be taken away.

13 This is why I speak to them in parables, because seeing they do not see, and hearing they do not hear, nor do they understand. 14 With them indeed is fulfilled the prophecy of Isaiah which says:

'You shall indeed hear but never understand,
and you shall indeed see but never perceive.

15 For this people's heart has grown dull,
and their ears are heavy of hearing,
and their eyes they have closed,
lest they should perceive with their eyes,
and hear with their ears,
and understand with their heart,
and turn for me to heal them.'

12. The verse is in a different context in Mark 4:25, but the context of both evangelists shows that they took it to have the meaning of Prov. 9:7-9: the spiritually receptive will get more and more, while others will become more stupid. The saying may originally have been a secular proverb: "The rich get richer and the poor get poorer." If Jesus used it in connection with the saying in Mark 4:24b (=Luke 6:38b), he may have meant: "The more generous you are [in almsgiving or in teaching], the more you will ultimately possess."

13. As Matthew makes clear in vss. 14-15, the verse refers to Isa. 6:9-10. Isaiah does not necessarily think it is God's will that the people should be unreceptive. His bitterly ironical words are for the purpose of shocking his hearers into understanding. But the gospel writers took this as an expression of God's purpose, and John 12:37-41 also quotes the passage. Paul has a similar thought in Rom. 9:6-33. Rudolf Otto (*Kingdom of God and Son of Man*, pp. 91-92, 143-44) thinks that in Mark 4:11 Jesus' original saying has been misunderstood; he intended to say, "To them [the outsiders] everything becomes riddles."

14-15. The quotation is almost verbatim from the standard LXX text of Isa. 6:9-10 and therefore is not a part of Jesus' original words. It is discussed by C. C. Torrey (*Documents of the Primitive Church* [New York: Harper & Bros., 1941], pp. 66-68).

the very revealing of God. Other men, who are "wise in [their] own conceits" (Rom. 12:16) or absorbed in the world, see little in Christ "that they should desire him."

I give you the end of a golden string;
Only wind it into a ball,
It will lead you in at Heaven's gate,
Built in Jerusalem's wall.[5]

The lowly, trusting in God, follow the clue: the worldly-minded despise it. But the lowly

lose the secret unless they share it. For it is an "open secret": "God so loved the world . . . that whosoever . . ." (John 3:16).

Behind these verses is the harsh fact that Jesus came into an alien age. His teaching, to men of earthly motives, was a riddle. What could awaken them? Only his death! Noble tragedy is catharsis to those who will receive it, and man's sin is purged only by a divine sorrow. De Stogumber, the chaplain in George Bernard Shaw's play, *Saint Joan*, believed that he was rendering God a service by the martyrdom of Joan of Arc—until he actually saw

[5] William Blake, *Jerusalem*, Preface to ch. iv, "To the Christians."

16 But blessed *are* your eyes, for they see: and your ears, for they hear.

17 For verily I say unto you, That many prophets and righteous *men* have desired to see *those things* which ye see, and have not seen *them;* and to hear *those things* which ye hear, and have not heard *them.*

18 ¶ Hear ye therefore the parable of the sower.

16 But blessed are your eyes, for they see, and your ears, for they hear. 17 Truly, I say to you, many prophets and righteous men longed to see what you see, and did not see it, and to hear what you hear, and did not hear it.

18 "Hear then the parable of the sower.

16-17. Matthew adds the word **but** to connect these verses with the foregoing. Luke 10:23-24, which is probably closer to Q, praises the disciples, not because they see, but because of what they have been vouchsafed to see, i.e., the first manifestations of the coming age. Matthew delights in mentioning **righteous men** (as in 10:41; 23:29) and here substitutes the word for Luke's "kings." The saying is another indication that Jesus believed the kingdom to be present (cf. 12:28; Pss. Sol. 18:7).

3. Interpretation of the Parable (13:18-23)

Allegory was a Greek method of interpreting sacred texts. Philo, the Alexandrian Jewish philosopher, employed it, and so did many teachers of the later Christian church.

---

her die. Then truth came.[6] The ultimate truth pierces us from the Cross.

The secret of the kingdom grows in those who hold it in prayer and life (vs. 12). The "rich grow richer"—in money, in used talents, in the saving knowledge of Christ. There is nothing arbitrary in this providence. A man who exercises his strength increases it: such is his due reward. A man who neglects his muscles loses them: such is his proper penalty. We ourselves would not deeply wish it otherwise. The universe, meaning the very rule of God, is not a moral topsy-turvydom, but a rectitude in love. What joy to know that the secret of Christ is like a seed: there is the multiplied joy of harvest! **To you** (vs. 11) means, not only to the apostles, but to all seeking souls—to you!

16-17. The Privileges of Disciples.—A college diploma entitles a man "to all the rights and privileges" of a graduate and alumnus. They are not always used or even claimed. Often they are but a name. Are the privileges of the Christian, the "blessedness" here pledged, claimed and used? Perhaps we stress too much the renunciations which Christian faith assuredly requires. What of the renunciations which worldliness demands? Judas and the rich young ruler renounced the chance to write a fifth gospel. Sin sacrifices both a quiet conscience and the light of the Presence. Christian faith is essentially a joy. The best witness of early Christians was their peace and gladness and strength. "These things have I spoken unto you, that my joy might remain in you, and that your joy might be full" (John 15:11).

The privilege is defined. What did the

prophets desire to see? What vision did **righteous men** (note Matthew's change from Luke's "kings") strain to catch? They longed to see God, and the coming of God's kingdom, and the redemption of the earth. This joy the disciple does see—in Christ. What word did the greathearts of old desire to hear? Some clear word of pardon, spoken from lips dowered with purity beyond this life; some tracing of the mystery of pain and sorrow. This very word the disciples did hear: "The Word became flesh and dwelt among us" (John 1:14). History was a partly closed book to other ages. But the Christian age sees the pierced hands of Christ open the book, and hears him reading its promises of life. This is joy deeper than any joy.

It is still true that the Christian faith demands renunciations. Whatever life a man may live, that obligation remains. It is not possible to go east and west at the same time: to go east is to renounce the west. The worldling sometimes tries to keep real religion and clutch the flesh. But this is impossible: "Ye cannot serve God and mammon" (6:24). What gratuitous renunciations, what a sterile sacrifice, besets the man who lives only for the eyes and the moment! But the abnegation required of the Christian is never arbitrary and never a frustration. It is a true pruning—for the sake of the joy of the harvest. It is a discipline that brings new power. "They got what they wanted"—and it proved only a shadow. But other men receive Christ, renouncing the world, and find themselves **blessed**. **Blessed** *are:* notice the present tense: these benefits are not delayed!

18-23. The Interpretation of the Parable of the Soils.—Expositors are largely agreed that

[6] Scene 6.

19 When any one heareth the word of the kingdom, and understandeth *it* not, then cometh the wicked one, and catcheth away that which was sown in his heart. This is he which received seed by the wayside.

20 But he that received the seed into stony places, the same is he that heareth the word, and anon with joy receiveth it;

21 Yet hath he not root in himself, but dureth for a while: for when tribulation or persecution ariseth because of the word, by and by he is offended.

22 He also that received seed among the thorns is he that heareth the word; and the care of this world, and the deceitfulness of riches, choke the word, and he becometh unfruitful.

23 But he that received seed into the good ground is he that heareth the word, and understandeth *it;* which also beareth fruit, and bringeth forth, some a hundredfold, some sixty, some thirty.

19 When any one hears the word of the kingdom and does not understand it, the evil one comes and snatches away what is sown in his heart; this is what was sown along the path. **20** As for what was sown on rocky ground, this is he who hears the word and immediately receives it with joy; **21** yet he has no root in himself, but endures for a while, and when tribulation or persecution arises on account of the word, immediately he falls away.[k] **22** As for what was sown among thorns, this is he who hears the word, but the cares of the world and the delight in riches choke the word, and it proves unfruitful. **23** As for what was sown on good soil, this is he who hears the word and understands it; he indeed bears fruit, and yields, in one case a hundredfold, in another sixty, and in another thirty."

[k] Or *stumbles.*

But rabbis used it sparingly, and almost never to interpret a parable. This interpretation contains a number of technical terms—such as **the word,** meaning "the Christian message"—which are not found elsewhere in the Synoptic Gospels; it also changes the parable into an allegory of different kinds of soil. The curious language shows that the writer is forcing the interpretation; for example, in vs. 23, **what was sown on good soil** should be **the word** (vs. 8), but it is here identified strangely with the one **who hears the word.** Some interesting sayings on different types of disciple are found in Aboth 5:12, 14-15.

21-22. Mark and Matthew lived at a time **when tribulation or persecution** had arisen **on account of the word** (i.e., the Christian gospel) and when many Christians were immersed in **the cares of the world and the delight in riches.** The combination of these two elements fits the period after A.D. 70. Similar comparisons are found in Ecclus. 23:25; Wisd. Sol. 4:3.

the interpretation is a later addition to the original record. Few believe that it is the very word of Jesus. The parable is simple and crystal-clear; the interpretation is somewhat devious, and would not help hearers of the parable to understand it. The interpretation confuses the soil with the seed, makes birds the symbol of the devil (an idea surely alien from Christ's mind), and turns the parable into an allegory.

Yet the interpretation not only has value for believers, but carries its own real truth. It reflects a time, perhaps very late in the first century, when persecution was thinning the ranks of the church (vs. 21), and when worldliness was an even worse threat (vs. 22). Perhaps it was not persecution that was dominantly in the mind of Jesus when he spoke of seed falling on the pathway. Yet persecution does steal away

good seed. There is no physical torture of Christians nowadays except in a few tyrannous lands, but the hazard still remains—in a hundred subtle ostracisms not easy to endure. On the other hand, worldliness probably *was* in Christ's mind when he spoke of thorny soil. Certainly the years proved that truth to the early church. During a "boom" period, a Wall Street paper admitted that more men can brave battle trenches than can resist the lure of quick money. Thus history revealed new truths in the parable of the sower. Has not our history, personal and in the world, revealed new facets in Christ's eternal verity?

So this interpretation, though it may not have come from Christ's lips, has truth in its own right. How is truth known from age to age? What of the words that Christ did not speak because men could not "bear them now"

24 ¶ Another parable put he forth unto them, saying, The kingdom of heaven is likened unto a man which sowed good seed in his field:

25 But while men slept, his enemy came and sowed tares among the wheat, and went his way.

26 But when the blade was sprung up, and brought forth fruit, then appeared the tares also.

24 Another parable he put before them, saying, "The kingdom of heaven may be compared to a man who sowed good seed in his field; 25 but while men were sleeping, his enemy came and sowed weeds among the wheat, and went away. 26 So when the plants came up and bore grain, then the

C. A Group of Parables Dealing with the Future (13:24-43)

Matthew probably thinks of all three parables as referring to the future coming of the kingdom, since he puts his interpretation of the tares at the end of them. The mustard seed and the leaven actually do not indicate whether the kingdom is present or future.

1. The Tares (13:24-30)

The mustard seed and the leaven (vss. 31-33) are twin parables, and so are the hidden treasure and the costly pearl (vss. 44-46). The story of the tares has some similarity in wording to Mark 4:26-29, a parable not found in any other Gospel. It has been suggested (see Intro., p. 239) that Matthew rewrote Mark's parable into the parable of the tares in order to provide a twin for the parable of the seine (vss. 47-48), and then furnished both with explanations. Mark 4:26-29 was intended to teach that men can only sow the seed, while God gives the increase (I Cor. 3:6), but it was a very obscure parable, and we can easily understand how the later evangelist thought that it needed the explanation which he gave.

25. Slept is a word from Mark 4:27. The **enemy** is needed for the story only if the parable is an allegory which refers to the devil (vs. 39), for any field might have a certain proportion of **weeds**. One can, however, imagine a personal enemy doing this mischief to the Palestinian farmer. The weed is the poisonous bearded darnel (*lolium temulentum*), which grows to about the same height as wheat and was regarded by the rabbis as a perverted kind of wheat (Kilaim 1:1).

(John 16:12), the unrecorded words that he spoke to his disciples in the Syrian dusk or to Simon on the Via Dolorosa, the words that he would speak to us were he here in the flesh? History reveals them, if we pray and seek the guidance of the Holy Spirit, and if we venture in faith and valorous deed. Truth did come in such fashion to the unknown disciple who wrote for his own age a new interpretation of the parable of the soils.

24-30. The Parable of the Tares.—Admittedly this story is hard to expound. There are two main interpretations. One, held by only a few scholars, accepts the parable at its face value as an original utterance of Jesus. The other, more and more held by men of unquestionable reverence, regards it as a rewriting of a story once told by Jesus—perhaps that of Mark 4:26-29, perhaps of some parable lost to us. The Exeg. clearly inclines to the second main interpretation. How hard the story is to construe is

shown by agelong disputes about its meaning.[7] The interpretation of the word **world** (vs. 38) alone has occasioned endless debate.

But by whatever exegesis, the story has a salient and perennial truth. It confronts the mystery of wickedness. Why is there evil in our world, in our hearts, and even in the church? The mystery is not explained by this story, but it is not evaded or ignored: **An enemy hath done this.** Wickedness is wicked, not an "illusion": it is false wheat in the field of human life. Wickedness is wicked, not a "greenness" or "immaturity": it is alien, a demonism beyond mere human control and power, that corrupts the will. Christ draws the line of an irrepressible conflict.

How should we fight this battle? Our instinct is to pluck up the tares instanter. We propose to eradicate the wickedness, and perhaps

[7] See George Arthur Buttrick, *The Parables of Jesus* (New York: Harper & Bros., 1931), pp. 61, 62.

27 So the servants of the householder came and said unto him, Sir, didst not thou sow good seed in thy field? from whence then hath it tares?

28 He said unto them, An enemy hath done this. The servants said unto him, Wilt thou then that we go and gather them up?

29 But he said, Nay; lest while ye gather up the tares, ye root up also the wheat with them.

30 Let both grow together until the harvest: and in the time of harvest I will say to the reapers, Gather ye together first the tares, and bind them in bundles to burn them: but gather the wheat into my barn.

weeds appeared also. **27** And the servants[1] of the householder came and said to him, 'Sir, did you not sow good seed in your field? How then has it weeds?' **28** He said to them, 'An enemy has done this.' The servants[1] said to him, 'Then do you want us to go and gather them?' **29** But he said, 'No; lest in gathering the weeds you root up the wheat along with them. **30** Let both grow together until the harvest; and at harvest time I will tell the reapers, Gather the weeds first and bind them in bundles to be burned, but gather the wheat into my barn.' "

[1] Or *slaves.*

---

28. Slaves would not ordinarily ask permission to do this, though peasants today sometimes cut off the heads of grain above the weeds (B. T. D. Smith, *Parables of the Synoptic Gospels,* pp. 196-98). These **servants** are of course disciples of Jesus who wish to purge the church of unfaithful members; and the purpose of the question is to bring out the point of vs. 30.

30. Let both grow together: This is not emphasized in the interpretation (vss. 36-43), but it is the point of the parable. It is disastrous to try to achieve a "pure" church in which there are no sinners. This wise principle was followed by Paul (I Cor. 4:5), though he occasionally had to excommunicate a gross offender. The church discipline of the late first and second centuries was, however, generally more rigorous (see, e.g., Heb. 6:4-8; 12:15-17; I John 5:16-17; and Hermas *passim*), but in the third century, under the influence of Bishop Callistus of Rome, Matthew's policy became dominant. To gather the **weeds first** and bind them **in bundles** is not the usual practice of farmers. Furthermore, the **reapers** do not seem to be the same people as the slaves of vs. 27. Both these touches indicate that this is an allegory of the Last Judgment.

---

even the wicked. Indeed *The Abingdon Bible Commentary* hints that the story reflects the timidity of the early church in dealing with evils that had revealed themselves in its midst.[8] But why should we quickly assume that the patience recommended in the story is unwise? If the parable concerns discipline in the early church (see above), or if it concerns Christ's own problem with Judas, as A. T. Cadoux argues,[9] patience has proved itself. Had Jesus summarily dismissed Judas, he might by that act have lost others of the twelve. Besides, are we always sure that apparent heresy is real heresy? Darnel and wheat are hard to distinguish until both are in the ear: and the "heretic" has sometimes become the pioneer of truth. Excommunication has sometimes done more harm than good; and persecution by the church, far from being a cleansing, has become a worse blot.

There is another item which we strangely

miss. Would we ourselves like to be "purged" from the church and from the fellowship of Christ? We are tares: only by a self-righteous pride could we claim to be a weedless field. "There go I, but for the grace of God."[10] Perhaps the more accurate word might be, "There I ought to go, for my despising of the grace of God." Surely "all have sinned." We should be ruthless with the evil in ourselves, but cautious in our dealings with evil in others—since our eyes and understanding are both short; and we should be grateful to God's patience that he does not "liquidate" us.

Meanwhile we should trust God. The mystery of evil is not mystery to him, nor is his sovereignty usurped. There is a coming Judgment. **In bundles to be burned** cannot be hardened into a theology, but its truth cannot be blinked. God does not elect some men for the fire, but he does not endlessly tolerate unholiness. God rules, now and in the coming days, on earth and in heaven.

[8] New York and Nashville: Abingdon-Cokesbury Press, 1929, p. 977.

[9] *The Parables of Jesus* (New York: The Macmillan Co., 1931), pp. 157-59.

[10] Variously attributed to John Bradford, Philip Neri, Richard Baxter, and others. See John Bartlett, *Familiar Quotations,* p. 18.

31 ¶ Another parable put he forth unto them, saying, The kingdom of heaven is like to a grain of mustard seed, which a man took, and sowed in his field:

32 Which indeed is the least of all seeds: but when it is grown, it is the greatest among herbs, and becometh a tree, so that the birds of the air come and lodge in the branches thereof.

31 Another parable he put before them, saying, "The kingdom of heaven is like a grain of mustard seed which a man took and sowed in his field; 32 it is the smallest of all seeds, but when it has grown it is the greatest of shrubs and becomes a tree, so that the birds of the air come and make nests in its branches."

2. Twin Parables: The Mustard Seed and the Leaven (13:31-33)

The parable of the mustard seed occurs in two different forms: Luke 13:18-19, which may represent Q, and Mark 4:30-32. Matthew has apparently woven these two sources together.

31. The kingdom of heaven is like: The longer introductions in Mark and Luke resemble more closely the rabbinical formula: "A parable. To what is the matter like? It is like," etc. **Mustard** was cultivated in Jesus' time for its **seed** and also as a vegetable. The rabbis regarded it as a **field** crop and forbade its planting in a garden (Kilaim 3:2; contrast Luke 13:19).

32. It may grow to a height of ten feet or more. **Birds** do not, however, ordinarily **make nests in its branches.** This is a reference to Dan. 4:20-21, where Nebuchadrezzar's kingdom is likened to a great tree in which the birds of the air roost. The Babylonian king's sovereignty was destined to come to an end, but God's kingdom will increase. Its future greatness is out of all proportion to its seemingly insignificant beginnings in a group of Jesus' disciples. Like the sower, this and the leaven are parables of encouragement.

31-32. *The Parable of the Mustard Seed.*— Some critics tell us that a mustard seed is not the **smallest,** and that the birds do not "nest" in its branches. But that seed was proverbially used as symbol of the tiny (see 17:20), and birds did settle on its branches. Besides, the phrase about "nesting" had dear and striking associations with Jewish hope, as we shall note. We must not bring a literal mind to the interpretation of the parables of Jesus.

Plainly this is a parable of hope: there shall be mighty growth from small beginnings. How small was the seed! A Babe born into a harsh world, a Teacher on a hillside, a condemned Man slain on a shameful Cross, an empty grave, and eleven men believing in him: what a tiny seed in a vast and alien field! How could such a seed ever come to harvest? The story rebukes our cult of bigness. Our pride in huge cities and mighty explosions has little to do with Jesus, or even with any human good. Actually our human life is small—a series of breaths, a sequence of footsteps, a frail chain of words. It is worth noticing that Jesus preferred a cult of smallness, for he stressed "a cup of cold water only" (10:42) and faithfulness "in that which is least" (Luke 16:10). Science is teaching us the infinite in the tiny; but Jesus taught it long ago, both as to the worth of man and as to the significance of the seemingly small kingdom.

There has indeed been great growth. The faint and far beginning in Galilee has become our planet's finest architecture and art and music. Paganism is not yet subdued, but Christ has won a world-wide homage. The soil, seemingly alien and certainly vast, has provided homage for the seed. There has been mysterious adaptation of soil and seed, and a vitalism in the seed, which no merely human theory can explain. Martyrdoms have come, but "the blood of the martyrs is the seed of the church." [1] As for the phrase about the birds nesting, it echoes Dan. 4:12. That may have been the reason why Jesus used it: there is apocalyptic power in the seed. "The tree grew, and was strong, and the height thereof reached unto heaven, and the sight thereof to the end of all the earth" (Dan. 4:11).

The parable is thus reassurance and promise and abounding hope. The disciples needed this cheer: they were seeds cast upon the vast world. What could they do against the seduction and wealth of pagan cults, and against the frowning power of military empires? They could do little, but God through them could do all things. The Christian should live in a great expectancy. In our time also, swept by "world forces" and "economic revolutions," we need this heartenment. God's seeds can cover the earth with harvest.

[1] Tertullian *Apologeticus.* 50.

33 ¶ Another parable spake he unto them; The kingdom of heaven is like unto leaven, which a woman took, and hid in three measures of meal, till the whole was leavened.

34 All these things spake Jesus unto the multitude in parables; and without a parable spake he not unto them:

35 That it might be fulfilled which was spoken by the prophet, saying, I will open my mouth in parables; I will utter things which have been kept secret from the foundation of the world.

33 He told them another parable. "The kingdom of heaven is like leaven which a woman took and hid in three measures of meal, till it was all leavened."

34 All this Jesus said to the crowds in parables; indeed he said nothing to them without a parable. 35 This was to fulfill what was spoken by the prophet:*m*

"I will open my mouth in parables,
    I will utter what has been hidden
        since the foundation of the
        world."

m Some ancient authorities read *the prophet Isaiah.*

33. N. C. Wyeth's paintings have caught remarkably the Palestinian flavor of this and other parables. This story contrasts the small amount of yeast with the large mass of leavened dough, and also hints at the miraculous, apocalyptic character of the growth. Although Paul (I Cor. 5:6-8) and the rabbinical writers always use **leaven** as a symbol of evil influence and teaching (as the Gospels do also in 16:6, 12=Mark 8:15), Jesus does not hesitate to employ it to describe the kingdom; and perhaps the parable was especially startling to the original readers for just this reason. The woman **hid** the yeast by dissolving "starter" from the previous baking in water and mixing it with dough. The **three measures** are three seahs, a very large amount (Goodspeed, "a bushel"). This perhaps calls attention to the vastness of the world, which the kingdom must transform, secretly and irresistibly.

3. Second Prophetic Explanation of the Hiding of the Revelation (13:34-35)

34-35. At this point Mark rounded off the parables with a brief editorial section. Matthew abbreviates this and adds a quotation from Ps. 78:2 to show that Jesus' way of teaching had long ago been foreshadowed or foretold. It may have been almost literally true that **he said nothing to them without a parable.** The quotation is apparently from the Hebrew.

33. *The Parable of the Leaven.*—This parable is twin with that of the mustard seed. It is just as homey. We should not destroy its simplicity by any attempt to allegorize the **three measures.** If the amount of dough was large, as the Exeg. suggests, that fact would give added force to the story; if perhaps the three measures were the amount of a customary baking, that fact would make vivid the comparison with daily life; but the **three** is not a word to be placed in any theological strait jacket.

The kingdom of Christ is silent and imperceptible, like yeast. If the twin parable rebukes our cult of bigness, this story rebukes our cult of noise. Advertising does not help the church, unless it is as reverent as the gospel; and sensationalism can easily be a curse. The big booming forces soon pass: seed and leaven remain. The majestic power of the stars is silent, and the stars themselves are lowly as candles. Perhaps we need a "noise-abatement" movement in the church. Any true sound is born in silence.

But the kingdom, though silent, is yet dynamic. It is a yeasty ferment. It is a quiet revolution. No area of earth is left untouched by the redemptive trouble of its coming. The Epistle to Philemon is gentle enough and makes no noise, but it shows the yeast of the gospel subduing the stubborn dough of ancient slavery. In your heart and mine, and in the customs and institutions of our time, the leaven is at work. We should not fear the gentle agitation or the persistent change. The spirit of Christ is yeast in our world.

Took and **hid** are significant words. The gospel is not our gospel, for it came from God; but we must appropriate his power for his ends. Furthermore the **leaven** does not work if held aloof; the Christian faith has no monastic heart, even though at times it may need to follow a "separatist" path. The Christian must identify himself with the world and its stubborn life, and there work by contagion even though his life may apparently be lost. Thus Robert Morrison went to China, and Robert Raikes into the streets of Bristol, and John Wesley carried

36 Then Jesus sent the multitude away, and went into the house: and his disciples came unto him, saying, Declare unto us the parable of the tares of the field.

37 He answered and said unto them, He that soweth the good seed is the Son of man;

38 The field is the world; the good seed are the children of the kingdom; but the tares are the children of the wicked one;

39 The enemy that sowed them is the devil; the harvest is the end of the world; and the reapers are the angels.

40 As therefore the tares are gathered and burned in the fire; so shall it be in the end of this world.

41 The Son of man shall send forth his angels, and they shall gather out of his kingdom all things that offend, and them which do iniquity;

36 Then he left the crowds and went into the house. And his disciples came to him, saying, "Explain to us the parable of the weeds of the field." 37 He answered, "He who sows the good seed is the Son of man; 38 the field is the world, and the good seed means the sons of the kingdom; the weeds are the sons of the evil one, 39 and the enemy who sowed them is the devil; the harvest is the close of the age, and the reapers are angels. 40 Just as the weeds are gathered and burned with fire, so will it be at the close of the age. 41 The Son of man will send his angels, and they will gather out of his kingdom all causes

---

4. INTERPRETATION OF THE PARABLE OF THE TARES (13:36-43)

36. Then he left the crowds: The interpretation is addressed to **his disciples;** so are the parables which follow.

37. Son of man in the apocalyptic sense.

38. For Matthew and his church the missionary **field** is the entire **world** (as in 28: 19). A few Jewish parables compare the world to a garden. **Sons of the evil one** is the harsh judgment passed on the Jews in John 8:41, 44. Does Matthew perhaps believe that some people are inherently evil?

39. Συντέλεια αἰῶνος (or τοῦ αἰῶνος) is a favorite phrase of Matthew's; in fact these are the last words in the Gospel (28:20). The Hebrew word 'ôlām (עוֹלָם) can mean **world** or **age.** Its **end** or consummation is the beginning of the age or world to come. Similar expressions are found in Dan. 12:4, 13; Test. Levi 10:2; II Baruch 13:3; 27:15; etc.

41. A distinction is drawn between the **kingdom** of the **Son of man,** i.e., the church, and the Father's kingdom (vs. 43). Here the **angels** accompany the Son of man, as they accompany God when he comes to judgment in Enoch 1:3-9. Jesus therefore is given the prerogatives of the Father. Men are spoken of as "scandals" or **causes of sin,** as in 16:23, where RSV translates the word as "hindrance" (cf. on 11:6). **Evil-doers,** literally

---

the gospel to the village green. The kingdom works by contagion in day-by-day friendship. No handclasp is in vain; no word of witness fails of its purpose. Not always can the revolution be seen, but it moves on its course. It is irresistible. It gives lightness and wholeness to the world—**till the whole [is] leavened.**

36-43. The Interpretation of the Parable of the Tares.—These verses confront the expositor with an even harder task than that posed by the interpretation of the parable of the sower. For the latter story has all the marks of genuineness, even though its accompanying interpretation may be of later authorship; whereas both the parable of the tares and its accompanying interpretation show signs of redaction. These verses now before us ignore the main point of the

parable—the problem of what to do when false wheat and true wheat grow close together over all the field, but by that very ignoring we see revealed the problems of the early church. The conclusion is largely apocalyptic in nature. We are almost obliged to regard it, not as the word of Jesus, but as the product of the church in the last years of the first century.

Yet as such it has its truth. The definition of sin in vs. 41 ("doers of lawlessness") has rigor and verity. Crime is a breach of the public law; sin is a breach of God's law. Many crimes are never brought to justice, but no sin evades the justice of God; for the divine recompense is written both in the man and in his world. The definition hints at libertinism in the early church. If so, the warning has a sharp edge

42 And shall cast them into a furnace of fire: there shall be wailing and gnashing of teeth.

43 Then shall the righteous shine forth as the sun in the kingdom of their Father. Who hath ears to hear, let him hear.

44 ¶ Again, the kingdom of heaven is like unto treasure hid in a field; the which when a man hath found, he hideth, and for joy thereof goeth and selleth all that he hath, and buyeth that field.

of sin and all evil-doers, 42 and throw them into the furnace of fire; there men will weep and gnash their teeth. 43 Then the righteous will shine like the sun in the kingdom of their Father. He who has ears, let him hear.

44 "The kingdom of heaven is like treasure hidden in a field, which a man found and covered up; then in his joy he goes and sells all that he has and buys that field.

"those who do lawlessness." The evangelist thinks of sin in terms of breaking the law (I John 3:4). He may, indeed, have in mind Christians who claim to be emancipated from any legal restrictions whatever.

42. The **furnace of fire** is an apocalyptic figure found in II Esdras 7:36. **Gnashing of teeth;** cf. on 8:12.

43. **Then the righteous will shine** is an allusion to Dan. 12:3.

D. Another Group of Three Parables (13:44-50)

These parables, as we have observed, are addressed to Jesus' disciples, because Matthew believes they describe, not ordinary adherents, but convinced disciples who are ready to sacrifice everything.

1. Twin Parables on the Joy of the Kingdom: The Treasure Trove and the Pearl of Great Price (13:44-46)

44. **Treasure hid in a field** always captures the imagination; witness the popularity of all stories of pirate gold. B. T. D. Smith (*Parables of the Synoptic Gospels*, pp. 143-45) gives examples of similar narratives. Peasants in the Near East still occasionally find hoards of coins. It may be poor ethics to conceal the value of such a field, but, as in the

---

Christians are not free from God's law, but free in it and through it. He is Father, yet righteous Father.

There are other values in the interpretation. For instance, there is splendid missionary passion: *the field is the world.* Empires have a false world hunger; God in Christ has a true world hunger, for "God so loved the world, that he gave his only begotten Son . . ." (John 3:16). Christ yearned to "draw all men" (John 12:32), and his followers must share the ache and longing of his heart: "Go ye therefore, and teach all nations" (28:19). Thus the imperative commission of evangelism. Thus the inescapability of the world missionary enterprise.

No careful reader of these verses could overlook their testimony to the sovereignty of Christ. In vs. 41 he is represented as in command of **angels**—a prerogative of God. His kingdom on earth is pictured as vestibule to "the Father's" eternal kingdom. He is mighty to prevail, however wickedness may seem to flourish. At long last he is Lord of Judgment (as in 25:31). Those who deny him **gnash their teeth** (in the famine and cold of outer dark-

ness and in anger at their now-manifest folly), but **the righteous . . . shine like the sun** coming suddenly from behind a cloud. So did the early church keep faith and hope in an evil time.

44. *The Parable of Treasure-Trove.*—Stories of treasure-trove are a delight to young and old. Who has not thrilled to the tale of Long John Silver?[2] Beyond doubt the treasure is the bright focus of the parable. The finder showed a doubtful ethic when he purchased the field while still keeping the owner in ignorance of its real worth, but the ethic is not the issue: it hardly touches the reason why the story was told. Cadoux's contention[3] that **hidden** is the story's outstanding feature leaves us unconvinced. Every word in the tiny but exciting parable points in the direction of **treasure.** In Palestine, long subject to invasion, such discoveries were not unknown. Somebody buried the money at a time of threat, was killed or exiled; and then, perhaps years later, the blade of some poor plowman unearthed it.

[2] Robert Louis Stevenson, *Treasure Island.*
[3] *Op. cit.* p. 143.

45 ¶ Again, the kingdom of heaven is like unto a merchantman, seeking goodly pearls:

46 Who, when he had found one pearl of great price, went and sold all that he had, and bought it.

45 "Again, the kingdom of heaven is like a merchant in search of fine pearls, **46** who, on finding one pearl of great value, went and sold all that he had and bought it.

---

parable of the unjust steward (Luke 16:1-8), the man's character has nothing to do with the point of the parable. The kingdom of God is so desirable that out of sheer joy a man will sell all his worldly possessions to have it and count that he has made no sacrifice whatever (cf. 19:29 and R. Otto, *Kingdom of God and Son of Man*, pp. 128-30).

45-46. The companion piece, the parable of the pearl of great price, has exactly the same point. Here, however, the pearl is found only after long search. And, whereas one might spend part of the treasure, all that the merchant has is the pearl. Nevertheless he is satisfied. **A merchant in search of fine pearls** might travel as far as the Persian Gulf or India. Pearls were an article of commerce at this time (Rev. 18:12).

It is fair to assume that the finder was poor. Are we not all poor? Earthy hopes disappoint us, we make wreck of faith and a good conscience, and in rags of unrighteousness we long for pardon. Apparently the man was not looking for the treasure. He did not expect to find it, but was taken by surprise. In the verisimilitude of the parable some other man years before had lost the treasure; but in the facts of the gospel, God sets it there for men to find. Life seems drab, the sky closes in on us, and past blundering robs tomorrow of its promise. Then God in great goodness gives us a new start in the grace of Christ. "I was found of them that sought me not" (Rom. 10:20). We trudge through life, expecting little and deserving less, when suddenly—heaven! Is there not the story of a Klondike prospector, who, making the long trek homeward without any gold, the rain adding to his misery, found in the road a nugget that the storm had dislodged? Thus the plowman found the treasure—in his dull and weary field.

Treasure! The gospel is treasure, and Christ is supreme joy. His secret transforms our life. Of course the man gave all he had to buy that heaven-blessed field, and of course a man must give "all for all" when he finds Christ. But the point of the parable is precisely that the man hurried to give all. He did not speak of "sacrifice": perhaps if we understood the joy of Christ we would have less use for that word. "What things were gain to me, those I counted loss" [worthless] "for Christ. For to me to live is Christ, and to die is gain" [of Christ] (Phil. 3:7 and 1:21). **Goes, . . . sells, . . . buys:** the present tense shows the man's eagerness and joy. He had found Christ and the kingdom.

45-46. *The Parable of the Precious Pearl.*— This story is twin with that of the treasure-trove. But it has significant differences. The "hero" of the other parable was presumably a

poor man: the merchant in this story was presumably rich, and perhaps a connoisseur of pearls. He may have traveled to the Persian Gulf or even to India in search of gems. The plowman did not expect to find, but the merchant was on the *qui vive* for a surpassing jewel. Yet the focused truth of the story is the same: the kingdom is the supreme good.

Are we not all seekers? Do we not always yearn for a fairer pearl? Money is good, but not without friendship; friendship is good, but not outside a higher devotion; devotion to art and music is good, but not without a clear conscience; a clear conscience is good, but impossible without forgiveness. So the thoughtful man is ever dissatisfied with moderate joys and shortened goals. Earth-bound prizes, even in the noble court of King Arthur, could not hold Lancelot or Galahad: they sought the Holy Grail. Haunting all human eyes is this longing; driving all human steps is this quest. We travel farther than the Persian Gulf, over mountains, through fetid swamps, across deserts.

The finding of the pearl was no accident. In the providence of God it waits hidden for those who seek. "Eye hath not seen, nor ear heard, neither have entered into the heart of man, the things which God hath prepared for them that love him" (I Cor. 2:9). If there is thirst, it is a proper assumption that there is water; if we have eyes, we may hope for light; if we seek, the pearl of great price awaits us. For God does not mock our quest. Nay, the finding is better than our dream. For the merchant was almost as much taken by surprise as the plowman: he could not believe that any pearl could be as perfect as this pearl. Always until that day he had said, "I have seen pearls almost as fair." But that day he rushed to sell every pearl he owned that he might possess the one supreme jewel.

The story does not stress the "sacrifice," be-

47 ¶ Again, the kingdom of heaven is like unto a net, that was cast into the sea, and gathered of every kind:	47 "Again, the kingdom of heaven is like a net which was thrown into the sea and gathered fish of every kind; 48 when it was
48 Which, when it was full, they drew to shore, and sat down, and gathered the good into vessels, but cast the bad away.	full, men drew it ashore and sat down and sorted the good into vessels but threw away the bad. 49 So it will be at the close of the
49 So shall it be at the end of the world: the angels shall come forth, and sever the wicked from among the just,	age. The angels will come out and separate the evil from the righteous, 50 and throw them into the furnace of fire; there
50 And shall cast them into the furnace of fire: there shall be wailing and gnashing of teeth.	men will weep and gnash their teeth.

2. PARABLE OF THE SEINE (13:47-50)

47. This **net** is the σαγήνη or seine, not the ἀμφίβληστρον of 4:18. One end can be fastened to shore and the other to a boat, or two boats may work it. One who has seen such a net come to shore will observe that it gathers **fish of every kind.** This is probably the point of the parable. The kingdom draws into itself people of very different motives, attitudes, cultures, and moral attainments, and those who spread its net dare not draw too many distinctions (cf. vs. 30). Jesus, unlike the Pharisees of his time, had no interest in forming a pure church composed only of the perfect. God, in his good time, will judge; it is the prerogative of Jesus and his followers to offer salvation and forgiveness.

48. The **bad** are fish that do not have scales or fins (Lev. 11:9-12), and so are prohibited to Jews.

49-50. The interpretation of the parable of the seine is very similar to vss. 41-42. Vs. 50 is a kind of refrain.

---

cause the man did not stress it. He could have said with Augustine, "What I feared to be parted from, was now a joy to part with. For Thou didst cast them forth from me. . . . Thou castedst them forth, and for them enteredst in Thyself, sweeter than all pleasure." [4] Cadoux would have us believe that the man entered into the transaction because it was profitable.[5] It was profitable indeed, but this was no mere business: the pearl was not the means to an end, but the end itself, even eternal life. The sacrifice he made was no sacrifice, for true Christian faith is not a weary duty or a sad return, but very joy: "Bring forth the best robe, and put it on him" (Luke 15:22).

There is perhaps an individual application in these two parables, and perhaps a proportionate social stress in those recorded earlier in the chapter. But all of them apply both to man and to his world. Here we are told that Christ is the *summum bonum,* for whom life and time are well lost. A friend has said that if he were to try to write a religious tract, better than the somewhat dreary tracts commonly offered, he would entitle it: "Are You Satisfied?" and that he would then preach Christ as the only answer to the discontent, secret or admitted, that afflicts our modern world. These

[4] *Confessions,* IX. 1.
[5] *Op. cit.,* p. 146.

parables are that tract—written as only Christ can write it.

47-50. *The Parable of the Dragnet.*—The disciples must have been fascinated by this story. They themselves had drawn the weighted net. They themselves had brought the squirming catch to the beach, and themselves had sorted it. The fish without scales and fins, which the Levitical law forbade as food, they had thrown away; the edible fish they had kept to sell. Little had they known, until Jesus spoke, that the exciting scene was so apt a parable of the event of the kingdom.

Day by day the net is being drawn, for the kingdom is an event. By sorrow and joy, by work and play, by testing and pondering, and by the thrust into the world of Christ himself, God draws the net. No man can escape: life is not in our control. Every breath brings us nearer to the shore, every sickness and recovery, every decision made or evaded. Foolishly we imagine that we can slip through the meshes, but life is not our ordaining: "It is he that hath made us, and not we ourselves" (Ps. 100:3).

It should not surprise us that the net gathers "many kinds." Men good and bad are caught by the net of the kingdom. The church holds both the pride of Bishop Ugolino and the lowliness of Francis of Assisi, the saint trying to keep the simplicity of his order while the ecclesi-

51 Jesus saith unto them, Have ye understood all these things? They say unto him, Yea, Lord.

52 Then said he unto them, Therefore every scribe *which is* instructed unto the kingdom of heaven, is like unto a man *that is* a householder, which bringeth forth out of his treasure *things* new and old.

51 "Have you understood all this?" They said to him, "Yes." 52 And he said to them, "Therefore every scribe who has been trained for the kingdom of heaven is like a householder who brings out of his treasure what is new and what is old."

E. The Scribe Instructed for the Kingdom of Heaven (13:51-52)

51. Matthew insists that, although the disciples have asked for the interpretation of the parables (vs. 36), they have **understood all this.**

52. This is Matthew's ideal for the Christian disciple. He should be a rabbi, but one **trained for the kingdom of heaven.** Bacon remarks finely (*Studies in Matthew*, p. 131) that here the evangelist furnishes an unconscious portrait of himself. **What is new** is perhaps Jesus' new law; **what is old,** the riches of the O.T. and the rabbinical tradition, in which Matthew is expert. A famous rabbinical saying describes two disciples thus: "R. Eliezer ben Hyrcanus is a plastered cistern which loses not a drop. . . . R. Eliezer ben Arak is a welling spring" (Aboth 2:8).

---

astic tries to make it serve the ends of ecclesiastical prestige.[6] From many motives men follow Christ, and in none are the motives unmixed. Many ideas occur to those who espouse the Christian cause, and not all ideas are worthy, as the history of theology has shown. Many methods are tried by the followers of Christ—persecutions, sensationalisms, and pondered ways that seem false at first but are later found true. Some thoughts and motives are worthy; some are not food for the soul, and are condemned by a deeper law than that written in Leviticus.

How can we know which is worthy and which is worthless? We cannot always know at once, and we can never fully know on earth. We should "judge nothing before the time" (I Cor. 4:5). But the kingdom, which casts a net and draws men, makes also the sure sifting. Note the words **sat down:** the division is quiet, deliberate, and with no chance of error. There are Eyes that see at once the worth of the soul. Some men are intent on light, whatever their lapses into darkness; and some love darkness, whatever their compunctions concerning light. The sorting continues, while the net is again drawn. History, and each man's secret history, itself is a judgment. Beyond history also there is a Judgment. Though vss. 49-50 almost repeat vss. 41-42, and though we must admit that the language fits burning tares rather than a fisherman's catch, the central truth is not impaired. We need assume no fatalism concerning our life: no parable can do justice to all the facts. Men have freedom, and can live for him who draws the net.

[6] Ernest Raymond, *In the Steps of St. Francis* (New York: H. C. Kinsey & Co., 1939), see Index under "Ugolino."

51-52. The Parable of the Kingdom-Scribe.— Note the Exeg.; it suggests, following Bacon, that this little parable is perhaps a portrait of the gospel's author. Certainly he must have rejoiced in it, and obeyed its truth. What true reverence he shows for the old covenant, and what devotion to the Lord of the new kingdom! Like Jesus, this Gospel of Matthew comes not "to destroy, but to fulfill" (5:17).

There is always a struggle between the **new** and the **old** until some cause is found that is sovereign over time. We see the struggle between the young man and the old man: the young think the old are fossilized, and the old think the young are brash and reckless. The old say, "I used to think that when I was your age"; the young retort, "I shall probably think that when I am your age." We see the struggle in politics: the "leftists" are the accelerator, the "rightists" are the brake, and the voters determine which pedal the times demand. Plainly the same struggle rages in social and economic theory. Life will not let us stop, yet it penalizes us for rash advance. By what wisdom can we settle the issue between the old and the new?

The kingdom-scribe has wisdom. He is "trained": there is no virtue in ignorance. But his training is in the fact and friendship of Jesus, and is therefore more than training. He is not ashamed of old truth, any more than a farmer is ashamed of seed from last year's harvest; but he is not afraid of new truth, any more than a farmer should be afraid to cast the seed into land newly plowed. He is not a brash revolutionary, neither is he a hidebound conservative. He is neither a cistern nor an erratic geyser (see Exeg.) but a wellspring. For he knows the gift of God in Christ, and responds

53 ¶ And it came to pass, *that* when Jesus had finished these parables, he departed thence.

54 And when he was come into his own country, he taught them in their synagogue, insomuch that they were astonished, and said, Whence hath this *man* this wisdom, and *these* mighty works?

53 And when Jesus had finished these parables, he went away from there, 54 and coming to his own country he taught them in their synagogue, so that they were astonished, and said, "Where did this man get this wisdom and these mighty works?

F. Another Concluding Example (13:53-58; cf. 12:46-50)

Bacon believed that Matthew's "third book" concludes with vs. 53, which contains the usual formula (*Studies in Matthew,* p. 296); but that verse is closely connected with this story and the entire section can be regarded as a conclusion. It deals with Jesus' rejection, one of the main themes of chs. 11–13, and it runs parallel to 12:46-50, an incident which closes the narrative section. A similar story, but more highly elaborated by tradition, is told in Luke 4:16-30.

R. H. Lightfoot (*History and Interpretation in the Gospels* [New York: Harper & Bros., 1935], pp. 182-208) considers the story in Matthew and Mark to be a "paradigm" symbolizing Jesus' lack of success in Galilee or perhaps all Israel. This is shown by the place assigned to it by the evangelists in their framework. Certainly the early church loved to develop the theme that Jesus "was despised and rejected of men," but there is no reason to doubt that this story is historical.

54. His own country is not further specified, but it most naturally refers to Nazareth or the surrounding region. The word πατρίς is used only in these Synoptic stories of the rejection, in John 4:44, and in Heb. 11:14, where it refers to heaven. Mark may choose it in order to point out that "he came to his own home, and his own people received him not" (John 1:11). Anyone who was competent was allowed to teach in the **synagogue.** The preacher or *darshān* (דרש) would ordinarily paraphrase the scripture lesson and emphasize its warnings and promises with scripture quotations or illustrate it with parables. The Mishnah contains an example of such a sermon in Sotah 8. Matthew perhaps thought of the miracles of chs. 8–9 as **these mighty works,** but the words might refer to any miracles of which the people had heard.

---

to the movement of the Eternal within our human time. By prayer, by faithful contemplation of history and experience, by venture in the Spirit, he brings forth **things new and old.** The obvious application of the parable is to the O.T. and N.T. But there are wider instances: from both the N.T. and O.T. God has "new light" to "break forth from his word." Every interpreter must be like the householder, and bring forth the new insights of recent scholarship within the old evangel. Men are not fed except by old seed cast into new plowing to bring a new harvest.

53-56. Wisdom and the Carpenter.—These verses seem to have elements of artless and unconscious biography. As such they have double value. They enable us, as we read between the lines, to visualize the early life of Jesus. He lived in Nazareth, and from nearby hills looked out over the fertile plain. Surely he must have journeyed as a boy to the nearby caravan route from Damascus, and talked with the traders from far lands. He had several brothers and sisters. His schooling was no more than the home and synagogue school could provide. He worked as a carpenter or builder; and, if Joseph died when Jesus was still young, he was perhaps for a time the main breadwinner of the family. When he returned to Nazareth, his wonder-workings widely known, and proved his wisdom as he spoke in the synagogue, his own village spurned him.

"Is not this the carpenter?" (Mark 6:3). Yes —as a momentary answer. He shared our toil. He shared its necessity: if there were a world-wide strike mankind would be but a few weeks from starvation, and neither money nor cities would save us. He shared its anxieties and poverties. He shared its bestowals; honest week-day labor leads by nature to Sunday worship, but slipshod weekday work alienates us from God and threatens the sabbath. In Jesus work and worship were woven into one fair texture. He shared our manual toil and our mental toil. He shared our home, and the besetments of the home. He shared the joys and griefs of kinship and friendship. Thus he set the mark of heaven on our nature. For though there is but one In-

55 Is not this the carpenter's son? is not his mother called Mary? and his brethren, James, and Joses, and Simon, and Judas?

56 And his sisters, are they not all with us? Whence then hath this *man* all these things?

57 And they were offended in him. But Jesus said unto them, A prophet is not without honor, save in his own country, and in his own house.

55 Is not this the carpenter's son? Is not his mother called Mary? And are not his brothers James and Joseph and Simon and Judas? 56 And are not all his sisters with us? Where then did this man get all this?" 57 And they took offense at him. But Jesus said to them, "A prophet is not without honor except in his own country and in

---

55. It would be natural in the Semitic world for a man to be called the **carpenter's son.** Matthew would not feel any conflict between this and the idea of the Virgin Birth (see on 1:16). He may indeed prefer this to Mark's statement that Jesus was "the son of Mary," which might be considered a slur on his legitimacy. Some Caesarean, Alexandrian, and Western authorities read in Mark 6:3, "Is not this the son of the carpenter and of Mary?" F. C. Grant ("Studies in the Text of St. Mark," *Anglican Theological Review,* XX [1938], 116) conjectures that Mark originally read, "Is not this the son of the carpenter and brother of James . . . ?" Τέκτων can mean one who builds with stone or wood. For traditions about the lives of Jesus' **brothers** see Johannes Weiss, *History of Primitive Christianity,* ed. F. C. Grant (New York: Wilson-Erickson, 1937), II, 709-12, 716-22.

57. And they took offense at him: Montefiore (*Synoptic Gospels,* I, 118-19) remarks that the villagers are half inclined to believe, but do not wish to; it hurts their

---

carnation, Jesus has shown us that our manhood can be host to the Eternal.

"Is not this the carpenter?" (Mark 6:3). No—as an ultimate answer. By acknowledgment of his neighbors there was a wisdom in him that no schooling (or lack of it) could explain, authority deeper far than the "authorities" of the scribes, and a power like only the thrust of God. Always we try to account for an "effect" by its "cause." We assume that if Jesus cannot be explained by family or training or environment—he is an impostor! Always we try thus to exile God—at least to the distance of some remote "First Cause," and always God puts our theories to confusion.

The dilemma remains. The world must choose: it must either try to dwarf Christ to its own thinking and so reject him, or it must confess in him the mystery of God. **Whence then hath this man** this universality of spirit so that he is at home in every land, this power to win our basic homage, this right and might to forgive sins (the prerogative of God alone), this strange abidingness so that always he is present with us? We answer; and either we are skeptics in some modern Nazareth, or followers who say: "My Lord and my God" (John 20:28). "Is not this the carpenter?" Yes, but he is also the Son of God.

57-58. Rejected Prophet.—If only we could hear Jesus preach in church! But the people of Nazareth where Jesus grew up had that chance; and, by Luke's account, instead of being converted, they were so incensed that they tried to

kill him. This is not incredible: it is an oft-told story with its sequel in our time.

> Seven cities warr'd for Homer being dead,
> Who living, had no roofe to shroud his head.[7]

The rejection at Nazareth evidenced so oft-repeated a perversity in men that Jesus said sadly: **A prophet is not without honor, save in his own country.**

Why were his neighbors so blind? They judged by wrong tests. Jesus, a carpenter, had not sat at the feet of famous rabbis and philosophers; therefore he could have no wisdom—"never having learned." That crass folly remains in our time. Jesus was lowly born, of a family so poor that they could provide only the humblest sacrifice prescribed by the law when he was presented as a babe in the temple (Luke 2:24); therefore he, not being born with a silver spoon in his mouth, could never claim greatness. Does not that blindness also remain? Besides, they knew his family: by what right did he presume to rise above his station? We still judge men by race, by upbringing, by social standing, by schooling; and so God's gift of light, which shines where God may choose, comes in vain.

Why was Nazareth deaf to his plea and blind to his glory? Modern psychology might say that the villagers suffered from a sense of inferiority. Perhaps they were not mainly to blame. An inferiority complex comes when people are

[7] Thomas Heywood, *The Hierarchie of the Blessed Angells.*

58 And he did not many mighty works there because of their unbelief.

his own house." **58** And he did not do many mighty works there, because of their unbelief.

---

pride that one who grew up among them has done wonderful things that they cannot imitate. The first of the Oxyrhynchus papyri gives Jesus' saying as follows:

> A prophet is not acceptable in his own country,
> Nor does a physician cure those who know him.

Martin Dibelius (*The Message of Jesus Christ*, tr. F. C. Grant [New York: Charles Scribner's Sons, 1939], pp. 14, 139) regards this as the original form.

58. As in 9:22, belief is a necessary condition for the miracle.

---

bruised, and they were a conquered folk despised alike by the Romans and by their own city-people in Jerusalem. Perhaps they were mainly to blame, for people feel inferior when they bruise others; and perhaps Nazareth had long been guilty of cruel prejudice. "Inferiority" is a reverse form of human pride. Henry Crabb Robinson reports in his diary that, when visiting Wordsworth in 1816, a neighbor asked him, "Is it true—as I have heard reported—that Mr. Wordsworth ever wrote verses?"[8] There is ignorance, if not insult, in the word "verses."

But we have not yet probed to the deepest cause of Nazareth-blindness. "Familiarity breeds contempt," but familiarity is a result rather than a cause. It comes ultimately from a low view of God. He has made a drab world, the "familiar" mind avows, and nothing can ever change its drabness. God has no thunders and lightnings, no secret ways of glory, no vast goodness in store for his children. A newspaper cartoon, printed some years ago on Lincoln's birthday, showed a hunter remarking to a neighboring farmer: "Any news down t'th' village, Ezra?"—and the reply, "Nuthin' a tall, nuthin' a tall, 'cept fer a new baby down t' Tom Lincoln's. Nuthin' ever happens out here." To dull minds, flowers and stars, saints—and Jesus—do not belong to God's world because God (to dull minds)) is dull. Contrast the expectancy of Martin Luther's schoolmaster who used to remove his biretta whenever he met his class of small boys—for who might not be there? There might be "a future mayor, or chancellor, or learned doctor!"[9]

Mark (6:6) tells us that Jesus was astonished at their unbelief. They recognized his **wisdom**, they acknowledged his **mighty works**; but their motives were set against him, and they lived in clay-shuttered houses. He was astonished, grieved, and stricken in soul. They knew not

[8] *Diary, Reminiscences and Correspondence of Henry Crabb Robinson*, ed. Thomas Sadler (Boston: Fields, Osgood & Co., 1869), I, 343.

[9] Julius Köstlin, *Life of Luther*, tr. from the German (New York: Charles Scribner's Sons, 1883), p. 16.

God, or they would have known that God would not leave his people desolate. Perhaps Jesus realized that only a Cross would make them see.

58. *Thwarted by Unbelief.*—This is the result of Nazareth-blindness. Mark has a significant comment: Jesus, he says, could heal only "a few" slightly ailing "folk," but could do no wondrous works. There was no lack of power in Jesus and no lack of love's desire, but there was no faith or longing in such people. His power was short-circuited by their woodenness.

We touch here the mystery of human freedom. If we are not free, we cannot become God's children, for a forced goodness would be only coercion. If we are free, there is danger in the universe, for we can thwart even the power of Christ. He repeatedly said that human faith is necessary for the effectiveness of his grace. At Nazareth there was no faith, at least not in the majority of those who heard him in the synagogue; thus he could not help them. The seed was vital, but the soil gave no welcome.

The unbelief had bitter fruit. The unresponsive in Nazareth hurt themselves: they cheated themselves of the life that might have been theirs in Christ. They hurt their neighbors: it is tragic to remember that the afflicted in Nazareth who might have been healed were not healed, all because the people who were up and about showed a lack of faith. They hurt Christ: he yearned to bless, but could not, and went to his home that night thwarted at the point of his compassion. It is impossible even to hint the poignancy of that pain. Often we think of skepticism as being our private affair: we can believe or not believe, according to our choice. Little do we realize that skepticism is a desperate hurt both to our neighbor and to Christ: it short-circuits heaven's power.

We see in this story the cause of the apparent failure of Christianity in our time. The lack is not in Christ. We are like men coming to a great symphony and saying, "It will scarcely meet our tests. We know the composer, and he is an ordinary man. He was never trained in music, and

14 At that time Herod the tetrarch heard of the fame of Jesus,

2 And said unto his servants, This is John the Baptist; he is risen from the dead; and therefore mighty works do show forth themselves in him.

14 At that time Herod the tetrarch heard about the fame of Jesus; 2 and he said to his servants, "This is John the Baptist, he has been raised from the dead; that is why these powers are at work in

VII. Resumption of the Narrative: Founding of the Universal Church (14:1–17:27)

The entire framework for this section and nearly all the material is drawn from Mark 6:14–9:32. Matthew at times abbreviates his source and adds small sections not found in other Gospels, but he does not desert Mark's order.

These chapters tell how Jesus' messiahship was revealed to the disciples as never before, how the church was founded after Peter's expression of faith, how the disciples were decisively freed from the Pharisaic interpretation of the law, how the Lord's Supper was foreshadowed in miraculous feedings, and how Jesus predicted his crucifixion. This section, like the corresponding part of Mark, is therefore the watershed of the gospel story. By contrast, we may note that Luke-Acts dates the foundation of the Christian community from Pentecost, while in the Fourth Gospel the church is given its charter at the time of the Last Supper (John 13–17). But in Matthew the great moment is Peter's confession at Caesarea Philippi. The narrative leads up to an important discourse (18:1–19:1), which lays down methods of discipline in the new community. For a full treatment of Matthew's methods in composing this section, see Bacon, *Studies in Matthew,* pp. 397-403.

A. The Menace of Herod Antipas (14:1-12)

14:1. Herod Antipas was **tetrarch** or prince of Galilee and Perea (Trans-Jordan) from 4 B.C. to A.D. 39. He was son of Herod the Great (2:1) by his Samaritan wife Malthace, and thus full brother of Archelaus (2:22).

2. Perhaps Herod thought of John as literally **risen from the dead;** more probably he meant that one in whom **these powers are at work** is "John all over again."

his family (no better than the neighbors) lives down our street. The music is likely to be an affront to right-thinking folk." It would not be surprising if the music did not find us, and had no quickening power. Skepticism is sometimes a fundamental honesty, but sometimes it is a dull and calamitous prejudice.

Was Christ finally thwarted? No, the plowshare of tragedy can still break the stubborn soil. The tragedy, national and personal, visited Nazareth. Robert Hichens has the story of a great sea painter searching for a boy in whose face he might find (to portray) the wonder of the sea. He chose, not a boy from the seacoast, for to that boy the sea was an ordinary and accustomed affair, but a boy from London slums who had never seen the ocean.[1] Sometimes only deprivation can teach us the wonder of Christ. It is double tragedy that the tragedy must also strike Christ—that by his Cross the soul may be shocked from lethargy, taught its guilt, and cleansed by his dying love. Only so is unbelief

[1] *Tongues of Conscience* (New York: Frederick A. Stokes Co., 1900), pp. 23-29.

broken, and the power of Christ released in the world. Perhaps the tragedy of our times may become the prelude to his new power.

14:1-2. *Herod.*—Note Exeg. on the difficulty of reconciling the gospel's account of John's death with that given in Josephus.[2] If Josephus is right—and there are phrases in the Gospels that confirm him—this story raced through the bazaars in Palestine and lost nothing in the telling. If the Gospels are right, we must assume that Josephus shrank from the stark realism with which the Gospels portray man's wickedness. By any interpretation, the character of Herod the worldling is here accurately limned.

Herod appears three times in the record. The first is this present instance; the second, when certain Pharisees gave Jesus warning that Herod might kill him; the third, at the trial of Jesus, when Herod and Pilate were made "friends." Herod was worldly. He built palaces and was given to display. In love of luxury he aped the Greek practice of celebrating birthdays with lavish feasts and with dancing shows after the

[2] *Antiquities* XVIII. 5. 2.

3 ¶ For Herod had laid hold on John, and bound him, and put *him* in prison for Herodias' sake, his brother Philip's wife.

4 For John said unto him, It is not lawful for thee to have her.

5 And when he would have put him to death, he feared the multitude, because they counted him as a prophet.

him." 3 For Herod had seized John and bound him and put him in prison, for the sake of He-ro'di-as, his brother Philip's wife;[n] because John said to him, 4 "It is not lawful for you to have her." 5 And though he wanted to put him to death, he feared the people, because they held him

[n] A few ancient authorities read *his brother's wife.*

---

3. Josephus tells a different story of John's death (*Antiquities* XVIII. 5. 1-2). Antipas had married the daughter of Aretas, king of Nabataean Arabia (9 B.C.–A.D. 40), but fell in love with **Herodias,** who was wife of his half brother Herod. Josephus does not call this brother "Philip." The tetrarch Philip, mentioned in Luke 3:1, married his half niece Salome, the daughter of Herodias. Aretas' daughter, discovering Antipas' plan to marry Herodias, fled to her father, who made war on Antipas. Such a marriage was forbidden by Lev. 20:21, but a glance at the Herodian family tree will show that the Herods paid no attention to the degrees of relationship within which marriage was prohibited.

4. Josephus says nothing about John's denunciation of the marriage, and merely remarks that "Herod, fearing lest his great influence over the people might lead to some revolt—for they seemed to do anything he counseled—thought it much better to execute him first, before any revolutionary movement should arise because of him, than to get himself into difficulties and regret, after it was too late, that he had not acted." This attitude is not surprising, since Galilee was the scene of more than one revolt in the first century. Accordingly, says Josephus, John was sent to Machaerus, a fortress near the Dead Sea, and put to death there. When, at a later time, Herod's army was destroyed by Aretas, the people considered this a just punishment sent by God for what he had done to the Baptist. The story in the Gospels is no doubt the version told in the villages. It is difficult to reconcile it with Josephus.

---

meal (vs. 6). To worldliness he added fleshliness: he coveted his brother's wife and married her, with contempt for all the decencies; and when, flushed with wine, he was pleased by a dancing girl, he recklessly pledged her whatever she might wish. To fleshliness he added cunning cruelty. John might rouse the people to revolt, so he slew John secretly in the lonely fortress of Machaerus. Jesus stigmatized him forever as "that fox" (Luke 13:32). To cunning cruelty he added large ambition. Josephus tells us that he coveted the title of king, and journeyed to Rome to beg the favor;[3] and the friendship with Pilate at the time of the Crucifixion hints a man eager to make "good connections." Herod had streaks of conscience in him—Mark reports that he held conversations with John the Baptist and "heard him gladly" (Mark 6:20)—but he was the worldling. There is no better portrait—ostentatious, fleshly, cunning, and ambitious.

He stands also as prototype of the worldling's fate. He was victimized by his evil associates and by his own pride. When his vanity was pierced by John's rebuke, Herodias and her daughter had their chance. He was at odds with himself. He was drawn this way by fear of the people,

[3] *Jewish War* II. 9. 6.

and that way by his ambition; another way by his acknowledgment of some authority in John, and still another way by his fleshly cravings. He was troubled in conscience, which in his weakness took the form of superstitious terror; for he believed that even a wicked oath must be kept, and that Jesus was John **risen from the dead.** The worldling always carries retribution within himself. Herod's subsequent history shows that events also, in the overruling of God, became his nemesis. His first wife's father made war upon him and defeated him; and when he went to Rome to plead for the title of king, charges of misrule were brought against him, and he was exiled to Spain. Herod was the man to whom Jesus at his trial "answered . . . nothing" (Luke 23:9). Was that silence Christ's anger at Herod's flippancy, or his rebuke to the man who had killed John the Baptist; or was Herod by that time so impervious to any noble plea that words even from Christ would have availed nothing?

1-12. *The Death of John the Baptist.*—Could there be a sharper contrast between two men than between Herod and John? Herod was sensual; John had disciplined his appetites and lived the ascetic life. Herod was ambitious; John had renounced the world. Herod was sly;

6 But when Herod's birthday was kept, the daughter of Herodias danced before them, and pleased Herod.

7 Whereupon he promised with an oath to give her whatsoever she would ask.

8 And she, being before instructed of her mother, said, Give me here John Baptist's head in a charger.

9 And the king was sorry: nevertheless for the oath's sake, and them which sat with him at meat, he commanded it to be given her.

10 And he sent, and beheaded John in the prison.

11 And his head was brought in a charger, and given to the damsel: and she brought it to her mother.

12 And his disciples came, and took up the body, and buried it, and went and told Jesus.

to be a prophet. 6 But when Herod's birthday came, the daughter of He·ro′di·as danced before the company, and pleased Herod, 7 so that he promised with an oath to give her whatever she might ask. 8 Prompted by her mother, she said, "Give me the head of John the Baptist here on a platter." 9 And the king was sorry; but because of his oaths and his guests he commanded it to be given; 10 he sent and had John beheaded in the prison, 11 and his head was brought on a platter and given to the girl, and she brought it to her mother. 12 And his disciples came and took the body and buried it; and they went and told Jesus.

6. The only **daughter of Herodias** known to history is Salome, who married Philip and later her cousin Aristobulus. Oriental parties were usually for men only. While the Herods were lax in their morals, it would have been exceptional for a princess to dance before such a company. At the time when this occurred, she may already have been married to Philip.

8. Mark tells a much more detailed and lively story. The **platter** is a gruesome detail that the girl thought up without her mother's prompting.

12. Mark 6:29 recounts the burial by John's disciples. Mark 6:30 tells how the apostles returned from their mission and reported to Jesus. Matthew combines the two verses. He considers it appropriate that John's **disciples** should now report to the great successor of their master, and this furnishes an added reason for Jesus to leave the place where he was (vs. 13).

John was straight and clear as light. These two men make incarnate the moral choice.

In John we see true courage. It is more than the bravery of nerves and muscle. The man who has such natural hardihood that he "knows no fear" can know no real valor. John was brave "for righteousness' sake." John was brave in his loneliness; there were no bands playing for him in the fortress of Machaerus, and no one touched elbows with him on the march. He was brave in the face of specific and powerful evil. It is comparatively easy to condemn wickedness in the weak, or to indulge in general denunciations of wrongdoing. But John said bluntly to Herod, well knowing Herod's cruel power, **It is not lawful for thee to have her.** Christ, in understatement that was therefore a more splendid tribute, said of John that he was no "reed shaken with the wind" (11:7). John's courage was for the right—with lonely trust in God.

Of course John suffered for his moral courage. There can be no truce between a Herod and a

prophet like John; and Herod, being armed with swords, has temporary victory over a saint armed only with the sword of the Spirit. John suffered more than loneliness and death. Doubts came upon him. Perhaps that was psychologically almost inevitable: he was an eagle-soul caught in a stone cage, and he bruised his wings against the walls. It would seem that he doubted Jesus whom he had once hailed as the Messiah (see Expos., 11:3). God understood that doubt, and was "not ashamed to be called [his] God" (Heb. 11:16). John suffered exile and death. No record remains of his closing moments, but we may be sure that he did not flinch. If Herod is prototype of worldliness, John is living symbol of brave rectitude.

Was his death in vain? So it seems: "Truth forever on the scaffold, Wrong forever on the throne." But the "scaffold sways the future." [4] These verses bear evidence to the fact that the crowd honored John—more in death than in life. Nor did John cease to speak, even to

[4] James Russell Lowell, "The Present Crisis," st. 8.

13 ¶ When Jesus heard *of it*, he departed thence by ship into a desert place apart: and when the people had heard *thereof*, they followed him on foot out of the cities.

14 And Jesus went forth, and saw a great multitude, and was moved with compassion toward them, and he healed their sick.

13 Now when Jesus heard this, he withdrew from there in a boat to a lonely place apart. But when the crowds heard it, they followed him on foot from the towns. 14 As he went ashore he saw a great throng; and he had compassion on them, and

B. Miraculous Episodes (14:13-36)

1. Feeding of the Five Thousand (14:13-21)

There are three versions of the story: (*a*) the one found here and in Mark 6:35-44 and Luke 9:12-17; (*b*) 15:32-39=Mark 8:1-10; and (*c*) John 6:1-14. All appear to be variant forms of the same tradition. John's story draws on both the feedings of the five thousand and the four thousand and has a few touches which suggest Matthew as well as Mark. His "barley loaves" (John 6:9) is reminiscent of Elisha's miracle in II Kings 4:42-44, which, together with I Kings 17:9-16, may be a model for the stories in the Gospels. Christians believed that what Elijah and Elisha did, Jesus could also do, and stories of miraculous plenty are current in Syria to this day. The Acts of John, a second-century book by a writer who believed that Jesus was only apparently human, attempts to explain that the Lord could feed people miraculously by giving each of them a very small morsel (ch. 93; James, *Apocryphal N.T.*, pp. 252-53). The Talmud contains a Jewish miracle story of a similar nature.

The Synoptic Gospels frequently speak of eating and drinking in connection with the satisfaction of spiritual need, and more than once they portray the kingdom of God in terms of a banquet (e.g., 22:1-14; Luke 14:16-24). The story of the miraculous feeding

Herod: **This is John . . . risen from the dead.** People call their sons by the name John. Who would call his son by the name Herod? In the mystery of God such a death as John's is seminal: it brings forth harvests after many days. Besides, strength is given to those who dare for God: John had his own joy and his own secret power. No man should pity him.

12. *They Told Jesus.*—We must be true, here as everywhere, to the facts of the Exeg. The author of this Gospel has (unwittingly?) transferred a phrase relating to Christ's disciples—a phrase which he found in the Marcan document—and attributed it to John's disciples. Thus we have a clear instance of the Synoptic problem. If the phrase **went and told Jesus** is true of John's disciples after the death of their prophet (and, frankly, that application seems doubtful), they were wise. Matthew's transfer of the phrase can in any event teach us wisdom. When a prophet like John is worsted and done to death, when the tyrant comes to power and the universe seems awry, what are we to do? Tell it to Jesus! He has comfort, the true comfort that comes "with strength" (*con-fortis*) from the place of prayer. He has reinforcement, and bids us persist though all the swords are with the tyrant and all the martyrdoms are with the righteous. He has interpretations: "Ought not Christ to have suffered these things,

and to enter into his glory?" (Luke 24:26). This unintelligible world may well overwhelm us except for the disclosures of God's truth and power which only Christ can give.

But Mark's use of the phrase, they "told him all things" (Mark 6:30), is clearly more natural and convincing. Christ's disciples came to report on their preaching and healing. Perhaps they had failed: if so, they needed his reassurance. Perhaps they had succeeded: if so, they needed his defense against their success, since success is a greater threat than failure. He took them into "a lonely place" that they might "rest" (Mark 6:31). An artist is said to have purchased a number of jewels which he could ill-afford—ruby, amethyst, emerald, sapphire, pearl. Why? That he might gaze on them when his sense of color became jaded. They went **and told Jesus**: that is life's central strategy. We need his insight into the meaning of tragedy, his kindly correction and pardon in our failure, his warning in our success. Above all, we need to be with him in "a lonely place" night and morning. Only so can we keep the things that belong to our peace, and live the eternal life in the midst of time.

13-14. *The Compassion of Christ.*—(See Expos., 9:36.) On that occasion he was **moved with compassion** because the people were like sheep, shepherdless and harried by wolves,

15 ¶ And when it was evening, his disciples came to him, saying, This is a desert
place, and the time is now past; send the
multitude away, that they may go into the
villages, and buy themselves victuals.

16 But Jesus said unto them, They need
not depart; give ye them to eat.

17 And they say unto him, We have here
but five loaves, and two fishes.

healed their sick. 15 When it was evening,
the disciples came to him and said, "This
is a lonely place, and the day is now over;
send the crowds away to go into the villages and buy food for themselves." 16 Jesus
said, "They need not go away; you give
them something to eat." 17 They said to
him, "We have only five loaves here and

suggests the messianic banquet in more ways than one. Without attempting to pronounce
on the question of miracle, one may remark that the story seems to point to an occasion
when Jesus and a large gathering of his followers in Galilee broke bread together. The
Lord's Supper of Christians is probably derived not merely from the last meal with the
twelve, but also from many common meals which had a strikingly religious character
and were thought of as foretastes of the great banquet in the kingdom of God.

17. The **five loaves** may have been baked from wheat flour, but barley bread was
the more common food of poor people, and is mentioned in John 6:9. Smoked or pickled
fish were a delicacy often eaten as a relish for the bread. The rabbis said that in the
messianic age the great sea monster Leviathan would be salted and given to the people
as food (as in Ps. 74:14). Early Christian art often uses bread and fish as symbols of the

ravaged by false religious leaders and by Roman might. In this instance the sicknesses of
the people wrung his heart. Notice the repetition of **compassion,** both to describe Jesus and
as a word used by him in his parables. It is a
strong word. It indicates poignant sympathy.
But sympathy, however poignant, is not enough
to save harried sheep or to heal disease. When
compassion is used of Jesus, it means also power
to save. In that sense Jesus alone, sent of God,
has true compassion. (On the healing power of
Jesus see Expos., 14:34-36.)

15-21. Feeding the Multitude.—Thorny problems beset this story. Some readers can accept
the miracle at its face value. They are in some
senses fortunate. No man has sufficient ground
to meet them with flat contradiction, or has
any right dogmatically to deny the miraculous
power of Christ. But other readers cannot
ignore sharp questions, and their neighbors of
less troubled faith have no right to traduce
them. The problems are these: (1) The story
nowhere, in any of the six accounts in the
Gospels, asserts that Jesus multiplied the food;
and there are such obvious parallels to the
Elisha story (II Kings 4:42-44) that even so
conservative a scholar as William Sanday admits
that a present-day observer of the scene might
give it a different description.[5] (2) Eucharistic
parallels are even clearer, and these seem to
constitute the major interest of the recorders,
as the Exeg. shows. (3) There are likewise hints
of the messianic banquet to which all pious
Jews looked in hope. One must deal faithfully
with these matters. But they need not become a

bone crosswise in the throat of any man. Indeed,
they can suggest the outline of an exposition.

Notice the miraculous multiplication of our
human resource. Take the miracle at its face
value, and that fact is startlingly clear. **Five
loaves, and two fishes** are the parable of our
penury, but they become Christ's abundance.
Take the story as an echo of the Eucharist-meal,
and the miracle is perchance a greater miracle:
the symbols of bread and wine are the means of
Christ's presence, and are multiplied in love
both human and divine. So let neither "conservative" nor "liberal" take issue: by any interpretation the people could not have been fed
without the wonder-working of the grace of
Jesus Christ. Mary Andrus, wife of Dr. Laffin,
went as missionary to central Africa, and after
little more than a year died. That brief time
was all she could offer. But a plaque in the
parish house of the Park Central Presbyterian
Church, Syracuse, New York, commemorates
her; and through the years the Spirit of Christ
has multiplied her consecration so that multitudes have been fed. The human little is
needed (see Expos., vss. 17-18, 20-21), but it
remains helpless without a higher grace.

Notice the sacramental gift. This is a major
feature. Whatever the origin of the story, there
can be no doubt that the early church found in
it the type and instance of the blessings that
come through the Lord's Supper. The eyes lifted
in prayer, the bread broken and blessed, the disciples acting as did the elders and deacons in
the early church when the bread was distributed to the orderly company—these all bespeak
the Sacrament. Earthly bread would turn to

[5] Hastings, *Dictionary of the Bible,* II, 628.

18 He said, Bring them hither to me.

19 And he commanded the multitude to sit down on the grass, and took the five loaves, and the two fishes, and looking up to heaven, he blessed, and brake, and gave the loaves to *his* disciples, and the disciples to the multitude.

20 And they did all eat, and were filled: and they took up of the fragments that remained twelve baskets full.

21 And they that had eaten were about five thousand men, beside women and children.

two fish." **18** And he said, "Bring them here to me." **19** Then he ordered the crowds to sit down on the grass; and taking the five loaves and the two fish he looked up to heaven, and blessed, and broke and gave the loaves to the disciples, and the disciples gave them to the crowds. **20** And they all ate and were satisfied. And they took up twelve baskets full of the broken pieces left over. **21** And those who ate were about five thousand men, besides women and children.

Eucharist, as, for example, in the magnificent mosaics of eṭ-Ṭabgha on the Sea of Galilee; see A. M. Schneider, *The Church of the Multiplying of the Loaves and Fishes* (London: Alexander Ouseley, 1937).

19-20. Mark says that the **grass** was green, and this suggests the spring of the year. Jesus **looked up to heaven**—this is a suitable gesture still prescribed in the Roman Mass at the beginning of the prayer of consecration—and **blessed**, i.e., spoke a prayer of praise and thanksgiving, as at the Last Supper (26:26). The usual prayer at the beginning of a Jewish meal is: "Blessed art thou, O Lord our God, king of the world, who hast brought forth bread from the earth." The prayers at the end of the meal were longer. It was customary for the father of the family or the host to break the bread. The **disciples**, like the deacons in the early Christian Eucharist, gave the bread to the **crowds** and collected the **broken pieces** afterward. This was also the custom at banquets given by religious Jews. The word translated **baskets** (κόφινοι) is used by Juvenal (*Satires* III. 14) to refer to the little food baskets which Jews carried so that they might eat only food prepared according to the food laws. The number **twelve** suggests that each of the special disciples had such a basket.

21. Matthew adds **besides women and children**, thus increasing the total number.

ashes without the sacramental Bread. Strength of body is only a threat without the cleansing of the soul. The writer of the Gospel sees in Christ the giver of the bread of life.

Notice in this meal the foretaste of the banquet of God's kingdom. (See 22:1-14 and Luke 14:16-24; together with Luke 22:30 they provide the parallels.) One of our hymns gives the Jewish hope in Christian terms:

> There is the throne of David;
> And there, from care released,
> The song of them that triumph,
> The shout of them that feast.[6]

The early Christians believed that their captivity would one day become victory, and their penury a banquet. The disciples remembered a meal with their Lord; and, with kindled and grateful hearts, saw in it the pledge of kingdom-gladness. So do we. What other pledge than Christ? But he is pledge, promise, and fulfillment.

17-18, 20-21. *Man's Little and God's Abundance.*—When the story is taken as parable its

[6] "Jerusalem the golden."

truths overflow, as expositors of every school have seen. **Five loaves, and two fishes** betoken our human helplessness. The problems that beset mankind have always, not simply in our time, seemed beyond human power. The seeming is more than seeming. It is fact. Human troubles are too great for human strength. Let the reader ask himself "How much can I do?" and he will be appalled by his helplessness, unless he is a man of faith in God. **Bring them hither to me** betokens the power and mastery of Christ. The bounty of the earth is witness. If only men knew how to distribute it! The spiritual bounty given through prophets, martyrs, and saints is deeper evidence. If only men knew how to draw upon it! **Bring them hither to me:** our physical bounty will not be distributed aright, nor our spiritual bounty properly invested, unless they are brought to him.

Christ did not feed the multitude without the human instrument. The bread did not come as manna from the sky, but through the work and kindness of some human hand. The little we can do, even though it be but a word of cheer or some neighborly act, even though it

22 ¶ And straightway Jesus constrained his disciples to get into a ship, and to go before him unto the other side, while he sent the multitudes away.

23 And when he had sent the multitudes away, he went up into a mountain apart to pray: and when the evening was come, he was there alone.

22 Then he made the disciples get into the boat and go before him to the other side, while he dismissed the crowds. 23 And after he had dismissed the crowds, he went up into the hills by himself to pray. When

---

2. Jesus Walks on the Water (14:22-27)

Both Mark and John connect this incident with the miraculous feeding, and do it in such a way as to suggest that one who can multiply the loaves is not subject to the usual conditions of earthly existence (cf. Mark 6:52; John 6:22-26). Rawlinson (*St. Mark*, p. 88) speaks of the encouragement this story would have given to the Christians in Rome in the sixties and seventies. After the martyrdom of Peter, the disciples were alone and the wind would seem "contrary" to them, but no matter how severe the tribulation, the Savior would certainly come to their aid. The narrative in 8:23-27 has a similar effect. It has been suggested that the story was originally told as an appearance of Jesus after his resurrection, or as the vision of an early Christian, or that Jesus was walking *by*, not on (ἐπί), the lake; but such speculations are fruitless.

22. The other side, according to Mark 6:45, is in the direction of Bethsaida. This suggests that the feeding took place on the western side, perhaps near the plain of Gennesaret (vs. 34).

---

may seem useless against the vast need, we must do. We must bring our tiny field to God's sky, our filament of wire to his electric power. Thus the scientist brings his labored search, and God gives the flash that leads to new discovery. Thus the dramatist brings his pen and seeming poverty of thought, and—suddenly the inspiration. Thus the saint brings Francis-consecration, and there is a new climate in the world.

Vs. 20 has many meanings. It implies, of course, that God can and does give "exceeding abundantly above all that we ask or think" (Eph. 3:20). But there are other meanings. The practice of gathering what remained was carefully observed after the Sacrament: men must not presume on the divine bounty or ever fail in reverence. When plenty comes, it is easy to forget God, and to preen ourselves. Furthermore, there was a belief in those days that if food was not gathered after the meal, a demon would possess the negligent men. Perhaps that belief is here reflected. Demons do come when God's gifts are not measured and soberly used.

But the main truth, next to the deep sacramental meanings suggested in Expos., vss. 15-21, is that of alliance between man's little and God's abundance. Let reminder be given for our cheer that, if we do what we can in trust and consecration, God will give the increase.

22-23. Mountain-Prayer.—Notice the word **constrained.** RSV says, **He made the disciples get into the boat,** as if to tell us that they were reluctant, and he urgently aware that they must go. It is not unlikely that John 6:15 provides

the setting. The crowd wished to make him king. He knew the crowd view of messiahship: he was to be a flag of revolt against Rome, while Jewish hearts and Roman hearts remained unaltered. He knew the futility of outward change when motives are unchanged. He feared eyes that were turned manward instead of Godward. So he knew that he must go. He knew that the disciples must go. Many scholars believe that the act drew a climactic line across his ministry: he would henceforth devote himself to his disciples, and break with the Jewish law (see 15:1-20). Thus the withdrawal to pray.

Jesus in his prayers was not independent of outward aids. It was **evening:** the fading light brought tenderness and awareness of ebbing strength, and set both the day and the lifetime in retrospect. The **mountain** gave a sense of strength and carried the eyes to the sky. **By himself** gave needed loneliness: it is necessary to meet God face to face. But these aids were only aids. To speak to God was the real concern, and to listen while God spoke. That waiting was Jesus' chief work. So he waited as the parched ground waits while the rain falls; as a Son waits for the love and light of the Father. He waited until the fourth watch (vs. 25), that is, until three o'clock in the morning; and he was hardly aware of the turning of the vast wheel of stars. That place of flame and silence, of the Presence and the Power, is the place that we think we do not need!

Jesus recovered perspective. Pasteur wrote to Père Didon, who had been banished to

24 But the ship was now in the midst of the sea, tossed with waves: for the wind was contrary.

25 And in the fourth watch of the night Jesus went unto them, walking on the sea.

26 And when the disciples saw him walking on the sea, they were troubled, saying, It is a spirit; and they cried out for fear.

27 But straightway Jesus spake unto them, saying, Be of good cheer; it is I; be not afraid.

evening came, he was there alone, 24 but the boat by this time was many furlongs distant from the land,⁰ beaten by the waves; for the wind was against them. 25 And in the fourth watch of the night he came to them, walking on the sea. 26 But when the disciples saw him walking on the sea, they were terrified, saying, "It is a ghost!" And they cried out for fear. 27 But immediately he spoke to them, saying, "Take heart, it is I; have no fear."

⁰ Some ancient authorities read *was out on the sea.*

---

25. The fourth watch of the night implies the Roman division of the night into four watches, as in Mark 13:35. This would be some time between 3 and 6 A.M. The Jews reckoned the night as having three watches.

27. It is I translates ἐγώ εἰμι, which can also mean "I am." These words are often used to mark a self-revelation of God, as in Exod. 3:14; John 6:35; 8:12, 58; 9:5; 10:9, 11; 11:25; 15:1.

Corsica: "You will come back with your soul still loftier, your thought more firm, more disengaged from earthly things."[7] Jesus came back in the singleness of a heart intent only on God's will and made new in God's power. He was again the sure Master of men and circumstance: our story shows him in that fourth watch ruling the storm. His eyes were cleansed of the world's veil. The will that repelled the **tempter in the** wilderness was now strong to endure. In the mad rush and distraction of our life he bids us "come apart and rest." In that word "rest" is the promise of true renewal. The mountain could not too long claim him. Rest is not stagnation. True living is the alternation between rest and work, between prayer and the daily task.

24-27, 32, 33. *Walking on the Lake.*—Some commentators accept the story without question;[8] others say flatly that it is a "pious legend";[9] others see in it the account of a resurrection appearance to Peter, and cite the fact that its language belongs to resurrection days—such language as προσεκύνησαν in vs. 33, as compared with the language in the Marcan account (6:52); and still others would translate **on the** sea as "by the sea." The interpreter, whatever his choice, will find scholarly and reverent authority. (See Exeg.) The story has the tang of actuality. The third possibility is perhaps preferable.

The story is eloquent of human distress. The torture of the spirit of men is here ascribed to the boat. That is real art. But the boat could

not feel. The storm came, not when the disciples had embarked on some foolish enterprise of their own choice, but "in the line of duty": they were obeying Christ's injunction. Storms come to the righteous, as well as to the wicked. The lake, at the place suggested by the story, was perhaps only four or five miles wide; but the expanse was vast compared with the size of the boat. "Our boat is little, but the sea is wide." What storms beset the early church in the time of Nero! What storms beset all men, not least the man of faith! In the mystery of human life we are helpless without help from Beyond. Thus do we find Christ. Perhaps that is one reason why storms come.

What is a miracle? Not the arbitrary rending of "natural law," but rather any event so ordered that it pierces our dullness or despair to convince us of the presence and power of God. This miracle blessed the disciples, and our world, in Christ. He came in crisis, when the limits of human resource had been reached and passed. He came beyond their hope, for they did not expect him: they thought he was an "apparition" to fear rather than a Savior to bless. He did what men cannot do: the Egyptians represented the impossible by a man walking on water. He proved his lordship. The words, **It is I** (ἐγώ εἰμι), are those used for the self-disclosure of God (see Exeg.), and their response (προσεκύνησαν) was properly one of worship.

All commentators are agreed that this story brought comfort and strength to the Christians in days of persecution and martyrdom. The critic may answer, "But did it save them from death?" No, for no man is finally saved from the body's death. The disciples died, even

---

[7] Quoted, John Edgar McFayden, *The City with Foundations* (New York: A. C. Armstrong & Son, 1909), p. 233.

[8] Dummelow, *Commentary on the Holy Bible,* p. 676.

[9] Branscomb, *The Gospel of Mark,* p. 117.

28 And Peter answered him and said, Lord, if it be thou, bid me come unto thee on the water.

29 And he said, Come. And when Peter was come down out of the ship, he walked on the water, to go to Jesus.

30 But when he saw the wind boisterous, he was afraid; and beginning to sink, he cried, saying, Lord, save me.

28 And Peter answered him, "Lord, if it is you, bid me come to you on the water." 29 He said, "Come." So Peter got out of the boat and walked on the water and came to Jesus; 30 but when he saw the wind,[p] he was afraid, and beginning to sink

[p] Many ancient authorities read strong wind.

3. Peter Is Taught to Have Faith (14:28-33)

Bacon regards this as one of the little "targumic" stories added to Mark's tradition in Syria, where Peter was held in the highest esteem (*Studies in Matthew*, pp. 298-99). Peter's resolution to come to Jesus required great courage, and although his faith wavered, Christ strengthened him before it was too late. This passage therefore foreshadows Peter's denial of Jesus and his restoration after the Crucifixion (cf. Luke 5:1-11; 22:32, "when you have turned again, strengthen your brethren"; John 21:15-22). Matthew thinks of Peter as the prototype of the Christian disciple and principal guarantor of the tradition in his Gospel, whose teaching can be followed with confidence. He includes the present section to exhibit Peter in this light. For the same reason he inserts 16:17-19 to show that Peter recognized Jesus as Messiah because of a divine revelation vouchsafed him, and 17:24-27 to teach that Peter had been given the power to make decisions regarding the law of Christ.

though Christ delivered them in many a storm. But the early church found that Christ stayed the oncoming of death in ways of surprising rescue, and they found that he saved men and women *in* death—in a still more surprising redemption. In death their eyes were opened, and Christ appeared; and death was not death, but life.

28-31. Faith Lost and Found.—Exegetes generally agree that the Peter episodes peculiar to this Gospel are expressly intended by its author to validate the leadership of Peter in the first-century church. The Exeg. above quotes the word "targumic" to describe the story. *The Abingdon Bible Commentary* employs the word *midrash*. The interpreter may find here a story, singularly true not alone to what we know of the character of Peter, but true as well of every man's faith at the point of its failure and of its redemption.

Peter is characteristically impulsive: always he leaps before he looks, which is still better wisdom than that of the man who looks for so long that he never leaps. Peter is mixed in motive: he genuinely wishes to be with Jesus, but he wishes also to prove that he can do what Jesus did; love and pride in him—as in us—are strangely intertwined. The church in the time of the Crusades preached the Holy War in a genuine passion, and then bought the lands of the responding nobles at a quick-sale bargain! Peter is both courageous and cowardly: he begins well, but when he sees the storm, he is overcome with terror. Peter is helpless at last, as

every man is without God; for our human nature and our world are so made that man, caught in crisis, must make contact with Power beyond himself if he would be saved. Therefore Jesus came, and comes, to plead for and offer that "main contact" by which life is lifted to eternal life.

Why did Peter's faith fail? Because, when his venture began, he had his eyes partly on Peter, and partly on Christ; and because, as the venture continued, he began to look at the storm rather than at Christ. **When he saw the wind, he was afraid,** even though Christ had said **come.** In the days of the sailing vessels, when a new hand climbed the narrow rope ladder to the crow's-nest, the old hands would cry, "Look up! Look up!" If the lad looked down, he might become dizzy and fall. Faith is strong when its motive is pure, and when its eyes are fixed on Christ. Peter's motives were mixed, and his eyes wavered: **O man of little faith, why did you doubt?** But Christ never fails even a half faith: **Jesus immediately reached out his hand and caught him.** Trust in Christ is never misplaced trust: in him the impossible tasks can be done, and the impossible challenges met and overcome.

Galahad's strength was "as the strength of ten," because his "heart" was "pure": [1] that purity of motive, as much as in us lies, is the beginning of faith's power. Its continuance is in eyes fixed on Christ—"looking unto Jesus" (Heb. 12:2). Its end is Christ himself in rescue

[1] Tennyson, "Sir Galahad," st. i.

31 And immediately Jesus stretched forth *his* hand, and caught him, and said unto him, O thou of little faith, wherefore didst thou doubt?

32 And when they were come into the ship, the wind ceased.

33 Then they that were in the ship came and worshipped him, saying, Of a truth thou art the Son of God.

34 ¶ And when they were gone over, they came into the land of Gennesaret.

35 And when the men of that place had knowledge of him, they sent out into all that country round about, and brought unto him all that were diseased;

36 And besought him that they might only touch the hem of his garment: and as many as touched were made perfectly whole.

he cried out, "Lord, save me." 31 Jesus immediately reached out his hand and caught him, saying to him, "O man of little faith, why did you doubt?" 32 And when they got into the boat, the wind ceased. 33 And those in the boat worshiped him, saying, "Truly you are the Son of God."

34 And when they had crossed over, they came to land at Gen-nes'a-ret. 35 And when the men of that place recognized him, they sent round to all that region and brought to him all that were sick, 36 and besought him that they might only touch the fringe of his garment; and as many as touched it were made well.

31. **O man of little faith** translates a word which Bacon paraphrases aptly as "Thou half-believer." The Christian whose faith is not quite mature is a familiar figure in the Fourth Gospel (John 3:10; 6:26; 7:5; 11:16, 21-22; 14:8-9; 20:25).

33. The disciples give Jesus full Christian worship. In the parallel passage, Mark 6:52, their hearts are still hardened.

4. SUMMARY OF VARIOUS HEALINGS (14:34-36)

34. **Gennesaret** was a wonderfully fertile plain on the northwest side of the Sea of Galilee. It is described by Sir George Adam Smith in *The Historical Geography of the Holy Land* (25th ed.; London: Hodder & Stoughton, 1931), pp. 439-63.

36. **The fringe of his garment** marked Jesus as a devout Jew, as in 9:20.

when faith fails and in redemptive comradeship. This story is the epitome of Peter's career: "Thou shalt deny me" (26:34). "And when you have turned again, strengthen your brethren" (Luke 22:32).

34-36. *Healer of Mankind.*—The name Gennesaret has significance for the interpreter. It was an unusually fruitful plain (see Exeg.). The rabbis called it "paradise" and "the garden of princes." But even there misery was rife. That physical plenty can bring peace of body and mind is indeed a vain hope. **All that were diseased.** Roman nobles spoke of "the profane rabble." What would they have said of a crowd of afflicted folk? Jesus not only did not shrink from them, but loved them, and saw in them the reason for his coming to earth. Christ surrounded by a crowd of diseased: it is a picture to kindle the poet and artist, and to melt any but the hardest heart.

He healed them in body. The distinction between "this-worldly" and "otherworldly" religion is false. Christianity is both: men cannot be saved except where they are, and they cannot be saved except from Beyond. The fact that

Christ healed men's bodies is the sign and seal of his immediate concern with medicine, psychiatry, economics, housing, and all forms of social welfare. Perhaps Cobden was right in refusing the plea of his rector to subscribe for the erection of ten new churches in Manchester until the poor were fed.[2]

Christ healed them in soul. **Made well** has the implication of complete cure. So perhaps Cobden was not right. To feed and heal a man, if the man is intent on murder, is not necessarily a blessing. Carlyle wrote to James Hutchinson Stirling, when the latter, then a twenty-year-old medical student, was wondering if he should continue to follow medicine as a career, that "he that can abolish pain, relieve his fellow mortal from sickness, he is the indisputably usefullest of all men."[3] But with all honor to Carlyle and a noble profession, is he? He is if the word "sickness" is made wide enough. Otherwise healing (mere physical healing) is not

[2] John Morley, *Life of Richard Cobden*, p. 156; and a similar idea, p. 126.

[3] David Alec Wilson, *Carlyle on Cromwell and Others* (New York: E. P. Dutton & Co., 1925), p. 116.

15 Then came to Jesus scribes and
Pharisees, which were of Jerusalem,
saying,
2 Why do thy disciples transgress the
tradition of the elders? for they wash not
their hands when they eat bread.

15 Then Pharisees and scribes came to
Jesus from Jerusalem and said,
2 "Why do your disciples transgress the tradition of the elders? For they do not wash

C. Controversy over Ritual Cleanliness (15:1-20)

The law is here rejected in a much more sweeping fashion than in the Sermon on
the Mount (cf. on 5:17-20; 11:13). The passage is drawn from Mark 7:1-23, a section
which includes some genuine sayings of Jesus but has been given its present form as a
result of controversies between Christians and Jews. We can find a sound historical basis
for interpreting Jesus' teaching on the law by considering the great controversy over the
admission of uncircumcised Gentiles which took place about A.D. 46 (Gal. 2:1-14; Acts
15:1-5). No dispute could have arisen between Paul and the Jerusalem leaders if the
conservatives had not been able to say that Jesus lived a life faithful to the law, though
they would have conceded that he modified its details. Nor, on the other hand, would
there have been disagreement unless Paul and the Christians of Antioch could appeal to
sayings and deeds of Jesus which, when carried to their logical conclusion, abolished
the law's distinctions. If Paul had nothing but "visions and relevations of the Lord" on
which to rely, would the Jerusalem leaders have accepted his gospel as genuine? It is
noteworthy, too, that Peter, who was respected by all parties, is regarded as a mediating
influence (Gal. 2:12; Acts 15:7-11). He must have recognized that there was some justice
on each side. Vs. 11 (=Mark 7:15) is probably a genuine teaching of Jesus. It actually
destroys the distinction between Jew and Gentile by saying that ceremonial cleanliness
is irrelevant; but its logical effect may not at first have been recognized. At the same time,
one must remember that Jesus accepts in principle the validity of the O.T. revelation
(vss. 3-6=Mark 7:9-13).

1. The Question Is Raised (15:1-2)

15:1. Pharisees and scribes . . . from Jerusalem would be looked upon as learned
authorities.

2. It frequently happens in the gospel stories that it is the **disciples,** and not Jesus,
who are criticized. This probably indicates that there were serious controversies over the
religious law between Christians and their fellow Jews in Palestine. **The tradition of the
elders** is the traditional interpretation of the law, which in the first century was always
passed from rabbi to pupil in oral form. Some of its rulings were very ancient, but as
new situations arose it was continually expanded. The Sadducees had some oral tradition

man's deepest need, and its cure is not man's
noblest service. Better a man should die in
compassion than live in cruelty. A true doctor
is more than a doctor. To Jesus the afflictions
of the body were the type, and sometimes the
issue, of afflictions of the soul; and he was intent
upon the wholeness of the will set on God.

The "diseased" in Gennesaret seemed to have
known in some dim way their deepest need.
For they touched the **fringe** of his garment (see
Num. 15:38), the tassel that marked him as a
pious Jew. That Jesus was careful to observe
the law in that regard has its meaning. So has
the fact that they touched him at the insignia of
his faith. **As many as touched** him there **were
made well.** All they could do was to reach a
hand—to the sign of God in him. What they

could do, they must do. But it was enough, however little, for Christ had come.

15:1-9. Jesus Breaks with the Tradition.—
This was a crux in his career. This was a
determinative and irrevocable act. We must understand it: it marked, and still marks, a path
for Christian faith. The controversy in the early
church concerning the admission of Gentiles
may be reflected; certainly direction and truth
in such a controversy are given. Controversies
in our time may also find in this episode their
solving word. Matthew underscores the importance of the issue. The critics of Jesus came with
the authority of **Jerusalem.** Their attack was
frontal and sharp (vss. 1-2). The reply of Jesus
was both categorical and condemning (vss. 3,
7).

3 But he answered and said unto them, Why do ye also transgress the commandment of God by your tradition?

4 For God commanded, saying, Honor thy father and mother: and, He that curseth father or mother, let him die the death.

their hands when they eat." **3** He answered them, "And why do you transgress the commandment of God for the sake of your tradition? **4** For God commanded, 'Honor your father and your mother,' and, 'He who speaks evil of father or mother, let

to supplement the Bible—temple worship could not otherwise have been carried on—but it was principally the Pharisees who developed the tradition and put it on an equal footing with the written law. The Mishnah expresses their theory in Aboth 1:1: "Moses received the [oral] Torah from Sinai and transmitted it to the prophets, and the prophets transmitted it to the men of the Great Synagogue. They said three things: Be deliberate in judgment, raise up many disciples, and make a hedge about the Torah," i.e., expand the law in such a way that a man cannot even come near to transgression. This tradition was afterward codified, and the first and most important deposit of this process was the Mishnah, which was written down in the early third century. (For a summary of the history of this process, see above, p. 111.)

The Pharisaic brotherhoods apparently adopted at some time in the first century A.D. the practice of ceremonial washing of **hands** before and after eating. This was part of the "hedge about the Torah." Priests were required to make a ceremonial ablution before eating sacrifices offered in the temple (Lev. 22:1-16). The Pharisaic rule may be a partial enforcement on laymen of a priestly law, on the theory that if it is good for a priest to be "holy," it is also appropriate for a member of the holy people. But the exact origin of the custom is not certain. The tractate Yadaim in the Mishnah contains many of the later regulations. Even though the washing of hands was not yet universally regarded as binding on all laymen, it is likely that enthusiastic individuals among the Pharisees looked with disfavor on those who did not follow their custom.

2. Jesus' Answer: The Corban Ruling Is Wrong (15:3-9)

3. In Mark's tradition this saying was not originally connected with the Corban controversy. Mark 7:8 is at the close of a self-contained section, and there the point is simply that the Pharisees often forsake "the commandment of God, and hold fast the tradition of men." But Mark, like Matthew, also used it to introduce what follows. It is not a very suitable introduction, because the decalogue and the law enforcing oaths were part of the written law, and if the Pharisees at this time enforced a vow which wrought cruel hardship, they were not following their **tradition** but what purported to be the **commandment of God.**

4. The quotations are probably based on the Greek text of Exod. 20:12; 21:17.

What was the quarrel? There were scribal interpretations of the law of Moses. They grew with the years, and were designed "to make a hedge"—a phrase used by the Pharisees to indicate a safeguarding stringency which would set Israel apart as a "holy nation." The particular issue which the Pharisees raised here was the requirement of hand-washing before meals. This originally had been an obligation only of the priests, but latterly had been levied on laymen: a pious Jew, the Pharisees said, must use not less than a certain minimum of water in such and such a way on the wrists before he ate. The deeper issue was ritual versus righteousness.

Why the anger of Jesus? The Pharisees were ignoring a primal goodness to exalt a rule.

Thus, according to them, if a man said of his disposition of his property, "It is an oath," he could claim exemption from caring for his parents. Jesus indignantly appealed from the rules of men to what a man intuitively knows to be right and kind. The Pharisees were corrupting people with their hypocrisies: in the instance given they were destroying the home. Furthermore, they were estranging the common folk whom Jesus yearned to win for God: they were branding them lawless, and further alienating them by a parody of religion. It would be hard to find an exact modern parallel, for history does not quite repeat itself. But . . . someone, visiting a mining town in the bad old days, when the company store had the town in debt bondage, when the mines had few protections

5 But ye say, Whosoever shall say to *his* father or *his* mother, *It is* a gift, by whatsoever thou mightest be profited by me;

6 And honor not his father or his mother, *he shall be free.* Thus have ye made the commandment of God of none effect by your tradition.

7 *Ye* hypocrites, well did Esaias prophesy of you, saying,

8 This people draweth nigh unto me with their mouth, and honoreth me with *their* lips; but their heart is far from me.

9 But in vain they do worship me, teaching *for* doctrines the commandments of men.

10 ¶ And he called the multitude, and said unto them, Hear, and understand:

him surely die.' 5 But you say, 'If any one tells his father or his mother, What you would have gained from me is given to God,q he need not honor his father.' 6 So, for the sake of your tradition, you have made void the wordr of God. 7 You hypocrites! Well did Isaiah prophesy of you, when he said:

8 'This people honors me with
their lips,
but their heart is far from me;
9 in vain do they worship me,
teaching as doctrines the precepts of men.' "

10 And he called the people to him and

q Or *an offering.*
r Many ancient authorities read *law.*

5-6. Matthew omits the word "Corban" (Mark 7:11), which originally meant "gift," but is frequently used as the formula for a vow or oath. The Corban and other vows are discussed by Saul Lieberman, *Greek in Jewish Palestine* (New York: Jewish Theological Seminary of America, 1942), pp. 115-43. The hypothetical case referred to is not clear to us. The man might have sworn to give **to God** the property needed for support of **his father or his mother,** or he may merely have sworn not to support them. By the end of the first century, the rabbis ruled that a man need not keep a vow if it interfered with his duty to father or mother (Nedarim 9:1); and the general rule of the Jewish law is that the commandment of Exod. 20:12 takes precedence over a number of other commandments, such as the sabbath law. The criticism attributed to Jesus has force only if in his time there were those who took a rigorous attitude to vows; but see Samuel Belkin, "Dissolution of Vows and the Problem of Anti-Social Oaths in the Gospels," *Journal of Biblical Literature,* LV (1936), 227-34. In any case, vss. 3 and 9 are beside the point. Jesus seems to hold that it is the spirit of the law, or God's purpose in giving it, that counts, and not its literal interpretation. But instead of using legal methods to resolve a conflict of laws, he appeals to the average layman's conscience, which is capable of discerning right and wrong (Luke 12:57).

8-9. The quotation is drawn from Mark 7:6. Since it is not dependent on the LXX, it belongs to a very early stage of Christian tradition.

3. A General Statement on Clean and Unclean (15:10-11)

10. This introductory verse (based on Mark 7:14) indicates that the saying in vs. 11 was originally a floating saying which has now been combined with other teachings of Jesus.

against ever-threatening death, and the miners were ill-paid, heard a sermon against sabbath-breaking (most of the miners being absent from the service), while company officials nodded assent from the pews. What would Jesus have done in that town? Gone to church to worship God, and condemned the deeper iniquity—at cost.

He himself kept the law. We may remember the "fringe" on his robe (see Expos., 14:34-36). The law as he construed it, the basic law of God written on the fleshly tablets of the heart, provided no laxity, let alone a libertinism. But

he held righteousness above ritual. It is easy in any age to succumb to externalism in religion. It is easy to forget that codes must change under the prompting of an ever-living Law. Motives—the set of a man's will under the secret scrutiny of God—are more important than trappings and observances. Jesus evidently felt that the Pharisees, in the main body of their opinion, could not be changed except through an irrepressible conflict—and the Cross. From this day of his brave and compassionate challenge the shadow darkened on him (see below).

11 Not tnat which goeth into the mouth defileth a man; but that which cometh out of the mouth, this defileth a man.

12 Then came his disciples, and said unto him, Knowest thou that the Pharisees were offended, after they heard this saying?

said to them, "Hear and understand: 11 not what goes into the mouth defiles a man, but what comes out of the mouth, this defiles a man." 12 Then the disciples came and said to him, "Do you know that the Pharisees were offended when they heard

11. It has been suggested that this is a statement like "I desire mercy and not sacrifice" (cf. on 12:7) and therefore means only: "Wrong thoughts and sayings are more defiling than forbidden food." Yet since Jesus ruled as he did on the sabbath laws, he more probably meant that the rules of cleanliness must give way if they stand in the way of real need or moral obligation. To this the rabbis might have answered in the words of R. Johanan ben Zakkai, who lived a generation later: "It is not that a dead body defiles or that water makes clean, but it is a commandment of the King of Kings," i.e., the rule is valid simply because it is God's revealed will. C. G. Montefiore remarks (*Rabbinic Literature and Gospel Teachings* [London: Macmillan & Co., 1930], p. 255) that Jesus may not have realized the implications of his saying, but the rabbis "could see whither the principle led, and they could not do other than reject a principle which had such revolutionary and heretical implication."

11, 15-20. *Inner Defilement.*—See Expos., vss. 12-14.) Jesus knew how many questions throng when the break is made with the "tradition." Perhaps vs. 10 means that he deliberately carried the issue to the people, and that he was resolved to throw in his lot henceforward with them—the "people of the land," the "lesser breeds without the Law." [4] Perhaps vs. 12 means that the disciples themselves had doubts about so iconoclastic a course. Do we not all say—of a change in the moral code, for instance, or a new interpretation of the letter of Scripture— "If we allow this liberty, where will it end?" So Jesus gave a fuller explanation of his mind.

He clearly believed that there is a spring of light in human nature, simply because God has endowed us with the power to distinguish between right and wrong. In the intricacies of conduct the way may not always be clear, but a rational man knows that the bogus oath of a bogus religion must not be used to exempt him from caring for his needy parents. So Jesus would say, "Yea, and why even of yourselves judge ye not what is right?" (Luke 12:57). He constantly appealed to this primal awareness in order to refute outmoded rules. At the same time he knew that a black stream flows from the fount of the human will. To the naïve sentimentalism that asks, "Human nature is essentially kind, so why not trust it?" Jesus gives realistic answer in vs. 19. When he said to his disciples, in response to their angry plea that he call down fire on an inhospitable village, "Ye know not what manner of spirit ye are of" (Luke 9:55), he possibly had in mind their primal sense of right as well as the demonisms that lurk at the place of man's volition.

With these facts before us, look at Jesus'

[4] Kipling, "Recessional."

doctrine: "Nothing from without a man . . . can defile him" (Mark 7:15). Nothing? Not any scurrilous sight or covetous sign? No, nothing, unless it finds a welcome indoors. "To eat with unwashen hands" (ritually unclean hands) does not defile, but gluttony defiles. To "eat with publicans and sinners" (Mark 2:16) does not defile, but self-righteousness defiles. "*Dilege et quod vis fac*": "Love [God] and do what thou wilt." [5] But that teaching is no license to build or permit a world of external abominations. The heart-will is determinative, but its proneness to evil cannot safely ignore the outward fashion of things. The print of the Gospels is a better environment than a collection of ribald stories or the sight of money in the bank. Yet it remains true that the originative fount of wickedness is in the will.

We must go further: man cannot in his own strength solve the dilemma of his will. Shall the primal light prevail, or shall he be overcome by the demonisms? He needs the incarnate God as pardoner and ally. Until the will is set on God, schemes of human betterment are in vain. A magazine cartoon showed a questioner at a public meeting asking the speaker, "Just how are we going to have this brave new world with all the same old people in it?" The circumference of the circle, the economics and statecraft, must be changed; but the government is from the center. Only when God visits that center can there be a reverse movement from the circumference to the center. Again let it be said, there is no least justification for any undue "liberty." Jesus spoke these words because he feared defilement (see below).

12-14. *The Appeal from Man to God.*—Jesus seemed to be the proclaimer of a perilous law-

[5] Augustine *On the Epistles of John* VII. 8.

439

13 But he answered and said, Every plant, which my heavenly Father hath not planted, shall be rooted up.

14 Let them alone: they be blind leaders of the blind. And if the blind lead the blind, both shall fall into the ditch.

15 Then answered Peter and said unto him, Declare unto us this parable.

16 And Jesus said, Are ye also yet without understanding?

17 Do not ye yet understand, that whatsoever entereth in at the mouth goeth into the belly, and is cast out into the draught?

this saying?" 13 He answered, "Every plant which my heavenly Father has not planted will be rooted up. 14 Let them alone; they are blind guides. And if a blind man leads a blind man, both will fall into a pit." 15 But Peter said to him, "Explain the parable to us." 16 And he said, "Are you also still without understanding? 17 Do you not see that whatever goes into the mouth passes into the stomach, and so passes on?[s]

[s] Or is evacuated.

---

4. Pharisaic Authority Rejected (15:12-14)

13. The nation of Israel is often referred to as a **plant** which God has planted (Ps. 80:8; Jubilees 1:16; 16:26). The "traditions of men" were **not planted** by God. The saying, which is found here only, may come out of later controversies.

14. In the context of Luke 6:39 this saying teaches that one who would teach must first be instructed. Matthew applies it to the unreceptiveness of the Pharisees. Paul points out that the Jew, with his admittedly superior revelation, is sure that he is a guide to the blind (Rom. 2:19); and this must have been the claim of those who tried to convert Gentiles to the Jewish religion. Educators of the blind remark that it is often best for the physically **blind** to instruct and **lead the blind;** but moral blindness is quite another matter. The order of words in Greek (τυφλὸς δὲ τυφλὸν ἐὰν ὁδηγῇ) is very striking and dramatic.

5. Further Explanation, with a Catalogue of Defiling Vices (15:15-20)

15-16. These verses are another example of Mark's point of view. As in Mark 4:10, 34, even the disciples cannot understand Jesus without special instruction. Matthew makes **Peter** the interlocutor because of the belief that it is he who transmitted to the church these important decisions.

---

lessness. It was physically dangerous for him, as the disciples evidently saw (vs. 12). It carried deeper dangers for all men. If one breach in the law is made, will not the enemy then come like a river flood through one hole in the dyke? What safeguards remain? God's sovereign working and control! God had planted. Some things are ordained from the foundation of the world. That word **planted** was dear to Israel (see Exeg.). What God plants man cannot completely uproot; what God has not planted is not long suffered to remain. This was the appeal of Cromwell to Parliament:

If it be of God, He will bear it up. If it be of man, it will tumble; as everything that hath been of man since the world began hath done. And what are all our Histories, and other Tradition of Actions in former times, but God manifesting Himself, that He hath shaken, and tumbled down and trampled upon, everything that He had not planned?[6]

[6] Thomas Carlyle, *Oliver Cromwell's Letters and Speeches*, Speech 4.

Perhaps Cromwell was too sure that he was ordained as God's trampler, but his truth remains.

God's sovereignty is such that he works through a man's wickedness, despite the man: the blind lead the blind into the ditch! The slave trade raises problems (of which the dark legacy remains) that destroy it. The tyrant becomes blind in judgment or cankered in worldliness, and his realm falls into chaos. Worldly shrewdness is soon folly, and the "devil is an ass." Thus Jesus rested his cause and his soul on the surety of God. There are ages when systems must be broken, and then recast in a kindlier mold. In such times we must take the venture with Christ in that same trust which he has given. But we must be clear in much Christian prayer that the time has come, and that our hands are "clean," and—that "the heart" is set on God in Christ. In that confidence we can trust our **heavenly Father.**

15-20. See Expos., vss. 11, 15-20.

18 But those things which proceed out of the mouth come forth from the heart; and they defile the man.

19 For out of the heart proceed evil thoughts, murders, adulteries, fornications, thefts, false witness, blasphemies:

20 These are *the things* which defile a man: but to eat with unwashen hands defileth not a man.

21 ¶ Then Jesus went thence, and departed into the coasts of Tyre and Sidon.

22 And, behold, a woman of Canaan came out of the same coasts, and cried unto him, saying, Have mercy on me, O Lord, *thou* Son of David; my daughter is grievously vexed with a devil.

18 But what comes out of the mouth proceeds from the heart, and this defiles a man. 19 For out of the heart come evil thoughts, murder, adultery, fornication, theft, false witness, slander. 20 These are what defile a man; but to eat with unwashed hands does not defile a man."

21 And Jesus went away from there and withdrew to the district of Tyre and Sidon. 22 And behold, a Canaanite woman from that region came out and cried, "Have mercy on me, O Lord, Son of David; my daughter is severely possessed by a demon."

---

19. Thirteen vices are contained in the list of Mark 7:21-22, while Matthew has but seven. Matthew adds **false witness,** perhaps because he is thinking of the Ten Commandments. Lists of vices and virtues, such as we find in Rom. 1:29-31 and Gal. 5:19-23, are more characteristic of Greco-Roman popular philosophy than of Judaism.

D. The Principle of Jewish Separatism Having Been Rejected, Jesus Benefits the Gentiles (15:21-39)

The evangelists now represent Jesus as spending some time in Gentile territory. This is shown even more clearly in Mark than in Matthew. It is not difficult to imagine that, after the controversy over the clean and the unclean, he was forced to withdraw from his homeland for a time. Caesarea Philippi, where the great confession of Peter took place, is actually on heathen soil. Like Mark, Matthew brings together in this section incidents which indicate a ministry among Gentiles.

1. Healing of the Canaanite Girl (15:21-28)

The story is very different in details from the parallel in Mark 7:24-30, though many of the words of the conversation are the same. Has Matthew rewritten it freely or does he have it from a separate source? The saying in vs. 24, at any rate, may come from M.

21. Matthew adds **and Sidon** from Mark 7:31.

22. Mark calls the **woman a Greek**—because she speaks that language—of Syrophoenician descent. Here she is a **Canaanite.** Perhaps Matthew regards Syrophoenicians

---

21-28. *The Syrophoenician Woman.*— (See Expos., vs. 23.) Jesus had left his own land. He was now in the Gentile world. This was a new occasion, fraught with meaning and possibility. Did he seek rest? Was he driven into semiexile by Herod and the hate of the Pharisees? May we guess that he was intent to "think through" his course, now that he had made the momentous break with "the tradition"? Perhaps he was impelled by all these reasons. If so, the incident here recorded has the more striking significance.

The character of the woman is clear, as is also the prejudice which Jews felt toward her. Matthew says **Canaanite,** thus indicating that she was from a people of "reproach" (see Exeg.) . She had a mother's love, ready to follow

any clue that might bring healing to her daughter. She had persistence and quick wit. Jesus was master of retort, but she crossed rapiers with him; and she won him, not by the wit mainly, but by a quickness that was born of love and faith. She was not presumptuous, but lowly; and she believed. Matthew would tell us that faith, an eager belief in God's power, was her dominant motive. It brought joy to Christ in a trying time, and it gave opening to his grace. (See the exclamation in vs. 28, and contrast it with 13:58.)

How are we to interpret the story? The Exeg. gives us some suggested explanations. Expositors find the story hard to construe. It seems clear that Jesus did believe that his mission was first and centrally to his own people.

23 But he answered her not a word. And his disciples came and besought him, saying, Send her away; for she crieth after us.

24 But he answered and said, I am not sent but unto the lost sheep of the house of Israel.

25 Then came she and worshipped him, saying, Lord, help me.

26 But he answered and said, It is not meet to take the children's bread, and to cast *it* to dogs.

23 But he did not answer her a word. And his disciples came and begged him, saying, "Send her away, for she is crying after us." 24 He answered, "I was sent only to the lost sheep of the house of Israel." 25 But she came and knelt before him, saying, "Lord, help me." 26 And he answered, "It is not fair to take the children's bread and throw it

---

as descendants of the Canaanites, who in the O.T. are often spoken of with reproach (Gen. 24:3; Ezra 9:1; Zech. 14:21; see also Gen. 9:18, 22, 25; 28:1). **Son of David** is a messianic title, as in 9:27.

24. This saying heightens the pathos of the woman's appeal. Cf. on 10:6, and see B. S. Easton, *What Jesus Taught* (New York: Abingdon Press, 1938), p. 120.

26. There are rabbinical sayings which designate godless people and heathen **as dogs.** One must, of course, remember that this is not the invariable attitude of the ancient Jews and that there are in rabbinical literature many sayings and anecdotes exhibiting friendliness to Gentiles. Few passages in the Gospels have so insistently troubled the minds of Christian readers as this. Various attempts have been made to explain its difficulties: (*a*) It is suggested that Jesus playfully used the diminutive word for dogs (κυνάρια, "doggies" or "puppies"), thus indicating that he did not really despise foreigners, as many other Jews did. But late Greek uses diminutives carelessly, and we do not know what Semitic word Jesus might have employed. (*b*) Or he is saying, in effect, "My disciples regard Gentiles as dogs; what have you and I to say to that?" In other words, he is trying to teach his followers a lesson. But there is no evidence for this in the story, and it seems strange that, when the woman was deeply distressed over her daughter's illness, he should needlessly keep her in suspense. (*c*) Or he is simply testing

---

The minor reason for this belief was a wise reluctance not to "spread" his energy, but to give it rightful channel; a major reason was that he intensely shared the Jewish faith that God had chosen that nation as his instrument for saving the world. Now he had broken with the "tradition." We can imagine Jesus' agony. Was there no "opening" through Israel? When a Canaanite woman showed more faith than the chosen people, did God intend him to fulfill his purpose through the Gentiles? Perhaps his silence when the woman first made her plea, and his sharp argument with her, are the outward sign of this inward bafflement and struggle. If the words here attributed to Jesus are verbatim, that tension of spirit provides the explanation of their seeming harshness.

His language to her is harsh—harsher than Jesus, so it seems, could use. The other explanation would come through the admission that there has been a rewriting on Matthew's part: compare his version with his source in Mark 7:24-30. Matthew exalts the Petrine authority in the early church. Perhaps in his writing of this story he is eager to steer a middle course between the conservatism of James and

the outright liberty of Paul, and perhaps this purpose has moved him to give some comfort to both camps. This supposition and/or the tension of soul in Jesus provide a sounder basis for interpretation, it would seem, than the assumption that Jesus is eager to teach his disciples a lesson by temporarily expressing their prejudice, or that he is humorous in the use of the diminutive word **dogs.** He did believe that God intended him to work through Israel. He did respond to Gentile faith. He could not be cruel to a mother's pain. He did heal the girl. These are the salient facts. The story gives warrant for the magnificent venture of the early church into the Gentile world. We should mark the emphasis on faith. The expectancy that hopes great things of God is passport to the kingdom. Only in that welcome can Christ work the wondrous works of his love.

23. *The Silence of Jesus.*—This topic is too vital to ignore. Jesus was silent, according to Matthew, when approached by the Syrophoenician woman. He was silent before Herod (Luke 23:9). He was silent before Pilate (27:14). There are other silences, not written in the lines, but clearly to be traced between the

27 And she said, Truth, Lord: yet the dogs eat of the crumbs which fall from their masters' table.

28 Then Jesus answered and said unto her, O woman, great *is* thy faith: be it unto thee even as thou wilt. And her daughter was made whole from that very hour.

29 And Jesus departed from thence, and came nigh unto the sea of Galilee; and went up into a mountain, and sat down there.

to the dogs." 27 She said, "Yes, Lord, yet even the dogs eat the crumbs that fall from their masters' table." 28 Then Jesus answered her, "O woman, great is your faith! Be it done for you as you desire." And her daughter was healed instantly.

29 And Jesus went on from there and passed along the sea of Galilee. And he went up into the hills, and sat down there.

the sincerity of her humility and faith. (d) Or, as Klostermann and Branscomb suggest, Jesus is asked to give foreigners that which he is prevented from bestowing on his own people, and this is his first immediate response. On this theory the story represents a new stage in Jesus' view of his own mission. The situation with which he is faced leads him to act on the principle "that God shows no partiality" (Acts 10:34). (e) Finally, it is just barely possible that vss. 26-27 are from some old anecdote which was not originally connected with Jesus at all, and have crept into the gospel tradition. In any case, it must be remembered that Jesus healed the girl.

27. The woman answers with wit and spirit. She is willing to receive help, whatever Jesus' attitude toward foreigners may be.

28. Here the woman is thought of as an example of faith (cf. 9:22). Mark may have thought of her humility, receptiveness, or persistence in prayer. Matthew concludes the story with a phrase similar to 8:13, emphasizing the instantaneous character of the healing.

2. Various Healings (15:29-31)

29-31. In place of the story of the healing of the deaf mute (Mark 7:31-37), which he may have rejected because physical means were used, Matthew inserts a general account of healings. What was done among Jews (9:1-8, 27-33) is now repeated among Gentiles, who glorify the God of Israel.

lines—as when he "looked" on the rich young ruler. There were many occasions when he thus "looked"—on the crowd when his brothers tried to dissuade him from his mission, on his disciples, on men casting their gifts into the treasury, on Peter after the denial, on the sky as he prayed. A concordance gives the seeking interpreter these interesting references.

In silence Jesus searches our hearts, and the silence is then more potent than speech. In silence he searches his own heart: it may be that this was the reason why he did not at once answer the Syrophoenician woman. In silence he watches our world, as once he watched men casting gifts into the treasury—among them a woman bringing "two mites" (Mark 12:42); and his eyes are always upon us. In silence he forgives: the silent look of Jesus broke Peter's heart, and brought redemption. In silence he despairs: what could he say to Herod and Pilate, when the flippancy of one and the brutal power-lust of the other had so corroded them that there was no true metal left on which his words could ring? In silence, as he looked upon the crowd,

his flashing eye gave token of the great urgency of what he would next say. With which silence does Jesus look on us?

In silence he prayed. Mark tells us that before one healing he "sighed" (Mark 7:34). The silence and the speech became a sigh wrung from him. All his words were born in silence: they came from those mountain prayers in which he met with God face to face. All his power came from silence: "Be still, and know that I am God" (Ps. 46:10). In him were

Persuasive speech, and more persuasive sighs,
Silence that spoke, and eloquence of eyes.[7]

The words of Carlyle were even more fulfilled in him: "Silence is as deep as eternity." [8] His speech therefore has eternal power.

29-31. *Healing the Multitude.*—This topic has been discussed in connection with 14:34-36. Here there are interesting items of difference. Apparently these healings were wrought be-

[7] Homer, *The Iliad*, Bk. XIV, 1. 251.
[8] "Essay on Sir Walter Scott."

30 And great multitudes came unto him, having with them *those that were* lame, blind, dumb, maimed, and many others, and cast them down at Jesus' feet; and he healed them:

31 Insomuch that the multitude wondered, when they saw the dumb to speak, the maimed to be whole, the lame to walk, and the blind to see: and they glorified the God of Israel.

32 ¶ Then Jesus called his disciples *unto him,* and said, I have compassion on the multitude, because they continue with me now three days, and have nothing to eat: and I will not send them away fasting, lest they faint in the way.

33 And his disciples say unto him, Whence should we have so much bread in the wilderness, as to fill so great a multitude?

34 And Jesus saith unto them, How many loaves have ye? And they said, Seven, and a few little fishes.

35 And he commanded the multitude to sit down on the ground.

36 And he took the seven loaves and the fishes, and gave thanks, and brake *them,* and gave to his disciples, and the disciples to the multitude.

37 And they did all eat, and were filled: and they took up of the broken *meat* that was left seven baskets full.

38 And they that did eat were four thousand men, beside women and children.

30 And great crowds came to him, bringing with them the lame, the maimed, the blind, the dumb, and many others, and they put them at his feet, and he healed them, 31 so that the throng wondered, when they saw the dumb speaking, the maimed whole, the lame walking, and the blind seeing; and they glorified the God of Israel.

32 Then Jesus called his disciples to him and said, "I have compassion on the crowd, because they have been with me now three days, and have nothing to eat; and I am unwilling to send them away hungry, lest they faint on the way." 33 And the disciples said to him, "Where are we to get bread enough in the desert to feed so great a crowd?" 34 And Jesus said to them, "How many loaves have you?" They said, "Seven, and a few small fish." 35 And commanding the crowd to sit down on the ground, 36 he took the seven loaves and the fish, and having given thanks he broke them and gave them to the disciples, and the disciples gave them to the crowds. 37 And they all ate and were satisfied; and they took up seven baskets full of the broken pieces left over. 38 Those who ate were four thousand men, besides women

3. Feeding of the Four Thousand (15:32-39)

The story is drawn from Mark 8:1-10. There, as well as here, it is probably intended as a miracle done among the Gentiles to parallel the feeding of the five thousand, which was for the Jews. But it was originally only a separate tradition of the other feeding (cf. on 14:13-21). It differs only in details, such as the numbers and the word for "basket" (σπυρίς, a fisherman's basket made of rushes).

38. Matthew again adds **besides women and children,** as in 14:21.

yond the bounds of Galilee: thus Jesus blessed the stranger as he had blessed his own people. The crowd craved the lesser good. What would they do with the health he bestowed? It was better perhaps that the dumb remain dumb than that they use their new-found speech to curse God. But Jesus' compassion was "helpless" and potent before their need. There is in vs. 30 a graphic picture of the sicknesses that infest an Oriental city. Mark's parallel passage is of interest: the healing of the deaf and dumb man (Mark 7:31-37) shows remarkably the psychological method in the healing, besides

bearing testimony to the agony which such a healing exacted of Jesus. The phrase **God of Israel,** in vs. 31, is significant. The healings showed them the weakness of their Gentile gods, and they now turned to the God of Israel; not, however, to the God of Pharisaic ritual, but to the God of Israel newly revealed in the compassion of Jesus.

32-39. *Feeding the Multitude.*—Most scholars, and their number grows, believe that this is one of several "doublets" in Matthew's Gospel. That is, it is a variant of the story that appears in 14:15-21 (see Expos. on those verses). Perhaps

39 And he sent away the multitude, and took ship, and came into the coasts of Magdala.

16 The Pharisees also with the Sadducees came, and tempting desired him that he would show them a sign from heaven.

2 He answered and said unto them, When it is evening, ye say, *It will be* fair weather: for the sky is red.

3 And in the morning, *It will be* foul weather to-day: for the sky is red and lowering. O *ye* hypocrites, ye can discern the face of the sky; but can ye not *discern* the signs of the times?

4 A wicked and adulterous generation seeketh after a sign; and there shall no sign be given unto it, but the sign of the prophet Jonas. And he left them, and departed.

and children. 39 And sending away the crowds, he got into the boat and went to the region of Mag′a-dan.

16 And the Pharisees and Sad′du-cees came, and to test him they asked him to show them a sign from heaven. 2 He answered them,*t* "When it is evening, you say, 'It will be fair weather; for the sky is red.' 3 And in the morning, 'It will be stormy today, for the sky is red and threatening.' You know how to interpret the appearance of the sky, but you cannot interpret the signs of the times. 4 An evil and adulterous generation seeks for a sign, but no sign shall be given to it except the sign of Jonah." So he left them and departed.

t Many ancient authorities omit the following words to the end of verse 3.

39. According to Mark 8:10, Jesus crossed to Dalmanutha, a place which cannot now be identified. The ancients were puzzled by this. Matthew seems to have substituted **Magadan,** though the late MSS read "Magdala," which was on the west side of the lake. The name "Magadan" or "Mageda" suggests Megiddo, which is more than twenty miles from the lake. It has been suggested that "Dalmanutha" is a corruption, and that "Magdala" was Mark's original reading; cf. J. Jeremias, "Zum Problem des Ur-Markus," *Zeitschrift für die neutestamentliche Wissenschaft,* XXXV (1936), 280-82. Finegan (*Light from the Ancient Past,* p. 225) points out that the names Magadan and Dalmanutha might be traced to Magdal Nuna or Nunaita ("Magdal of fish").

E. Both Pharisees and Sadducees Are Now Rejected (16:1-12)

1. Their Demand for a Sign (16:1-4)

Vss. 1 and 4 are drawn from Mark 8:11-13, and in addition vs. 4 derives from the Q saying found also in 12:39=Luke 11:29. Vss. 2b-3 are omitted by Sinaiticus (‭א‬) and Vaticanus (B), some other Greek MSS, the Old Syriac, etc.; they are a rewriting of Luke 12:54-56 and were probably added to the text at a later time. They do not fit the rest of the verses, since they teach that there *are* signs for men to see.

16:1. Matthew adds **and Sadducees,** as in 3:7; 16:11-12; etc.

2-3. The weather signs in Luke 12:54-56 are Palestinian—a west wind brings rain; a southeast wind, the sirocco. Jesus' hearers should be able to observe the wickedness in Israel and realize that there is little time left for repentance, since doom and judgment are coming. This is the teaching of Luke 13:1-9.

4. Mark 8:12 says, "No sign shall be given this generation." Cf. on 12:39.

Matthew was intent here to show that the miracle belonged also to the Gentiles.

16:2, 3. *Signs of the Times.*—Notice in Exeg. that these verses are not in the basic MSS. Yet they have an authentic ring, and are certainly consonant with the main teaching of Jesus. Most men are not trained weather prophets, but almost any man can learn from experience —in regard to weather. A red sunset betokens a fine tomorrow; a lowering sunrise threatens

storm. Few men are able to forecast the issues of the complicated economic and political affairs of any generation. But that is not the demand. The demand is that in affairs of life a man shall not ignore the clear signs. Does pride, individual and national, go before a fall? Does merely formal religion collapse under test? Is goodness an ultimate resource? The Pharisees and Sadducees, according to the setting given in this Gospel, had asked for a sign. There were

5 And when his disciples were come to the other side, they had forgotten to take bread.

6 ¶ Then Jesus said unto them, Take heed and beware of the leaven of the Pharisees and of the Sadducees.

7 And they reasoned among themselves, saying, *It is* because we have taken no bread.

5 When the disciples reached the other side, they had forgotten to bring any bread. 6 Jesus said to them, "Take heed and beware of the leaven of the Pharisees and Sad'du-cees." 7 And they discussed it among themselves, saying, "We brought

2. WARNING AGAINST THEIR TEACHING (16:5-12)

This section (from Mark 8:14-21) belongs to a late stage of the gospel tradition. Vs. 6 may embody a saying of Jesus, but it is mainly the product of Christian preaching and can be compared with John 6:26-27.

5. They had forgotten to bring any bread: This provides a setting for the rest of the discussion.

6. Leaven is used here in the usual sense of "false teaching" or "evil influence," as in I Cor. 5:6-8. Matthew refers it to the *teaching* of the religious parties (vs. 12; cf. 15:13-14), but Mark couples Pharisees and adherents of Herod, and must be thinking of their evil influence.

7. They suppose that since they **brought no bread** Jesus is warning them against eating the food of their opponents.

signs galore, but they could not read them, though they were as clear to read as a stormy sky.

Frederick William Robertson, writing of people in France on the eve of the revolution, has this:

They (the Jews of old) were very weather-wise, but could not read "the signs of the times." . . . Parisian ladies were equally astonished when, having spent such enormous sums on their *coiffures* and ribbons, they one day found their head dress arraigned for them at the national expense, à la guillotine.[9]

Are we wiser than they? Whither has trust in military might always led? What happens to a nation when work-morality declines, when wealth falls into the hands of the few, or when many people buy on credit? Every war takes most people by surprise. Every depression in business is an "unbelievable calamity." Is a machine age threat instead of promise unless men learn a new measure of comradeship? There are questions with an even deeper thrust: what happens when men trust their own wisdom and skill, and forget God?

We are here told that there is no *non sequitur* in the ethical and spiritual realm. There is realism in the question in vs. 3, and there is robust religion. Some signs are repeated in human history and in personal experience. More surely than a red sunset they portend a

fair tomorrow; or more certainly than a red sunrise they threaten calamity. Jesus stood before his generation as a sign—and they asked that he work some portent to prove himself. For us his life has been lived, his cross raised, and he has overcome death. What clearer sign could we ask? (For fuller discussion of the demand for a sign see Expos., 12:38-42.)

6-12. *The Leaven of the Pharisees and Sadducees.*—See the Exeg., to the point that much of this passage may be of late origin, but that vs. 6 has the force of a word of Christ. **Leaven** could have three meanings: (*a*) It was sometimes used for bread: hence the dullness of the disciples was perhaps not as dull as our verses seem to imply. (*b*) It sometimes meant teaching, and could have that meaning in the present context. (*c*) Often it meant evil influence: the Exeg. guides us to believe, on the strength of the Marcan parallel, that this is its meaning in the present instance.

What is the leaven of the Pharisees and of the Sadducees? Leaven works subtly and in secret: evil influence causes the fermentation of a false life before men are aware. The Pharisees were formalists in religion. They substituted ritual for life, and then used the false standard to condemn the "unrighteousness" of their neighbors. They were "hypocrites" (the word means "actors") and thought they were truly righteous. That substitution is easy: it works subtly, and we should be on guard.

The Sadducees were in one sense even more rigorous for rules than the Pharisees, for they believed that the "five books of Moses" were

[9] *Life and Letters of Frederick W. Robertson*, ed. Stopford A. Brooke (London: Kegan Paul, Trench, & Co., 1883), II, 143-44.

8 *Which* when Jesus perceived, he said unto them, O ye of little faith, why reason ye among yourselves, because ye have brought no bread?

9 Do ye not yet understand, neither remember the five loaves of the five thousand, and how many baskets ye took up?

10 Neither the seven loaves of the four thousand, and how many baskets ye took up?

11 How is it that ye do not understand that I spake *it* not to you concerning bread, that ye should beware of the leaven of the Pharisees and of the Sadducees?

12 Then understood they how that he bade *them* not beware of the leaven of bread, but of the doctrine of the Pharisees and of the Sadducees.

13 ¶ When Jesus came into the coasts of Caesarea Philippi, he asked his disciples,

no bread." **8** But Jesus, aware of this, said, "O men of little faith, why do you discuss among yourselves the fact that you have no bread? **9** Do you not yet perceive? Do you not remember the five loaves of the five thousand, and how many baskets you gathered? **10** Or the seven loaves of the four thousand, and how many baskets you gathered? **11** How is it that you fail to perceive that I did not speak about bread? Beware of the leaven of the Pharisees and Sad'du-cees." **12** Then they understood that he did not tell them to beware of the leaven of bread, but of the teaching of the Pharisees and Sad'du-cees.

13 Now when Jesus came into the dis-

8-10. If these verses are detached from the context of vss. 6, 11-12, they ought to mean: "Why should you worry about bread, since I have shown that I can always provide it?" But here the thought is: "The miraculous feedings are symbols of my teaching, which will always be sufficient for you. You do not need the teaching of these false leaders, and you must beware of it."

F. Jesus' Second Self-revelation (16:13–17:13)
1. Peter's Confession at Caesarea Philippi (16:13-20)

The primary source is Mark 8:27-33. In that place, after Peter's statement of faith, "You are the Messiah," Jesus instructs the disciples to say nothing about it, and teaches that the Son of man must suffer. But when Peter objects to this, he is rebuked and called "Satan." The story had been modified in the oral tradition and perhaps Mark himself made changes. The dialogue in Mark 8:27-29 is highly compressed, for much more would have been said on this occasion. Furthermore, Mark 8:31 contains the idea of the suffering Son of man, which is not found in Q or in any old source except Mark. Yet the story probably preserves the memory of an actual conversation, in which Peter and perhaps other disciples hailed Jesus as Messiah and begged him to exercise the kingship over Israel. There is a tradition in John 6:15 that after the feeding of the five thousand some people tried to force Jesus to become a king. He was acclaimed as Son of David on at least one occasion (Mark 10:47-48); the Triumphal Entry (21:7-8=Mark

the whole law, and that no man could add to them or subtract from them. In that sense they were purists. But in practice they believed in a compromise with the conquering Romans and with the conquering culture of the Greeks. Thus, though they were in control of the temple—faithful in its ritual and unyielding in the letter of the Mosaic law—they were proud in their education and secular in their adoption of the fashions of their time. They were "high society." They were in collusion with the traders whom Jesus drove from the temple, and "enlightened" in certain skepticisms, for example, about angels and the resurrection of the dead.

Leaven in very truth, and not unknown in our time! How can we be on guard? Only as the disciples were on guard: by Christ's power. They continued in his teaching, they let the leaven of the kingdom work in them, and they prayed as he taught. So they were defended.

13-15. But Who Do You Say that I Am?— Christ may ask, Who do men say that the Son of man is? but soon he brings the question to a sharply personal challenge: Who do you say ...? The world has many opinions: Christ is myth, or teacher, or highest prophet after the order of Isaiah or Jeremiah. But Christ is so searching a fact that soon or late each man

11:7-10) and the anointing at Bethany (26:6-7=Mark 14:3) can best be understood as messianic demonstrations; and Jesus was certainly crucified on the charge of being a pretender to the Jewish throne. It is clear that, on this occasion, he rejected the title of Messiah. If he had permitted it to be attached to himself, the crowds would have understood only one thing by it: that he intended to establish an earthly, theocratic monarchy and exercise political force. And this meant revolution and war. The word "messiah," moreover, did not fully describe the work that he intended to do. His purpose, so far as we can discern it, was to go to Jerusalem, and there to appeal to the nation to follow his teaching and religious leadership. He intended to call upon the people to accept the yoke of the kingdom of God as he understood that yoke, and so to make themselves ready for the kingdom when it should please God to reveal it. The attempt must be made, though it might issue in failure, suffering, and death. And when Peter protested that God's Chosen One must not and could not suffer, Jesus' answer was that Peter was speaking Satan's language and tempting him to turn back from his duty.

Yet the idea of political kingship did not die so quickly. Jesus continued now and then to be addressed as Son of David, and this, together with some of his deeds in Jerusalem, led to his crucifixion. At his trial he refused to make a clear statement as to whether or not he was Messiah (26:64; 27:11). After the Resurrection the term "messiah" was given a new content by Jesus' followers. It came to express the faith that he would return and exercise a universal kingship in the age to come, and it gathered into itself all that they believed about his relationship to God and man.

At this point the reader may perhaps ask, "What, then, becomes of our Christian faith if Jesus did not speak clearly about his messiahship?" The answer is that the gospel tradition shows that he was conscious of a unique vocation, so great and transcendent that none of the religious terms then in use was capable of expressing it. He knew that he was commissioned, with an authority greater than that of any prophet or king, to teach and lead the people of God. He expected his disciples to obey and follow him, no matter what the cost, not so much for his own sake as for the sake of God and his kingdom. We observe this in the attitudes of Jesus and the disciples more than in any single thing that he said. Furthermore, he regarded his own death as a sacrifice which would avail for the salvation of his people, and at the Last Supper he symbolized this by a solemn ceremony. If Jesus had come making explicit claims and definitions of his nature and authority, the result would have been to restrict man's faith, for no language could express fully how he was related to God and to mankind. As it was, the N.T. writers used a great variety of terms, each of which pointed to one aspect of Jesus' person and work, and each of these words in turn took on the coloration of his unique personality. We must also remember—though it is difficult for us to do so—that the question did not have the same interest for Jesus that it has for us. *We* wish to clothe with appropriate language our faith in God in Christ. *He* was far more concerned to do the will of God and to lead men to God than to be praised and worshiped. Even the Fourth Evangelist recognized that Jesus did not seek glory for himself (John 7:16-18; 8:50, 54) ; and this in itself is the hallmark of his character. See general note on 21:1–23:39 and notes on 21:25; 26:26-28, 64; 27:11.

Matthew could not be content with a story which left Jesus' messiahship ambiguous. Therefore he inserted a saying (vss. 17-18) praising Peter for his faith and declaring him the "Rock Man" on whom the new church was to be founded. This tradition was no doubt current in Syria, where Peter had been the principal leader and was looked upon as the church's truest teacher. To this was added also the saying in vs. 19, another Syrian tradition which had not necessarily been connected with the rest of the story. Finally, Matthew rewrote Mark 8:30 so as to make it perfectly clear that Jesus had merely commanded secrecy about his messiahship.

It is very unlikely that vss. 17-19, and the similar saying in 18:18, were spoken by Jesus. They do not fit with the picture of his teaching which the earliest sources give us, and are quite exceptional in the N.T. Jesus apparently never contemplated the

saying, Whom do men say that I, the Son of man, am?

14 And they said, Some *say that thou art* John the Baptist; some, Elias; and others, Jeremias, or one of the prophets.

15 He saith unto them, But whom say ye that I am?

16 And Simon Peter answered and said, Thou art the Christ, the Son of the living God.

trict of Caes-a-re'a Philippi, he asked his disciples, "Who do men say that the Son of man is?" 14 And they said, "Some say John the Baptist, others say Elijah, and others Jeremiah or one of the prophets." 15 He said to them, "But who do you say that I am?" 16 Simon Peter replied, "You are the Christ, the Son of the living God."

---

formation of a new church separate from Judaism (cf. on 15:1-20), and he did not even repudiate the ceremonies of the temple. Elsewhere in the Synoptic tradition the commission to make Gentile converts comes only in the postresurrection appearances (28:19-20; Luke 24:46-49). This unusual emphasis on the future church and on Peter's place in it is to be explained by churchly—and perhaps even partisan—interests.

13. The tetrarch Philip refounded the ancient Paneas (modern Bânyâs) and named it Caesarea in honor of Augustus. It came to be called **Caesarea Philippi** to distinguish it from the many other cities which bore this name. Paneas was at one of the sources of the Jordan. It was named from the grotto of the Greek god Pan, and remains of temples are still to be seen there. The Gospels do not say that Jesus entered the city itself, but Christians have often meditated on the contrast between the pagan worship which was then going on and Peter's worship of the true Son of God. Matthew adds **Son of man** here in order to make it clear that Jesus is both celestial Son of man and the Messiah, and therefore omits the phrase in vs. 21 (=Mark 8:31).

14. There are no Jewish traditions which make **Jeremiah** an important figure in the messianic age. Matthew names him because he is one of the greatest **of the prophets**.

16. **The Christ,** i.e., the Messiah (cf. on 1:1). Matthew adds **Son of the living God** because he and the other evangelists regard Jesus as much more than the Messiah of

---

must make his own decision. The decision cannot go by default, for that is tantamount to saying either "Christ doesn't matter," or "I will make the decision in conduct, and by my silence pretend that I have not made it." So default is likely to be denial.

Jesus' teaching persists. It may be found in near parallel, here a phrase, there a phrase, in earlier Scriptures; but it becomes new on his lips. The Golden Rule is a different affair when his eyes look through it. Disobedience should long ago have killed his words; but they do not "pass away," however systems and customs change. Is his teaching ultimate? What do *you* think?

Jesus Christ himself persists. He is amazingly a linking of opposites—sovereign yet neighborly, eager in zeal yet tranquil, austere yet compassionate, rigorous in demand yet forgiving. He is at home in every land: Tolstoy, Schweitzer, Livingstone, Pascal, Kierkegaard, Kagawa—each is sharply national in type and outlook, but each is committed to Christ. "A face like all men's faces."[1] Is he the Son of man? What do *you* think?

[1] Ivan S. Turgenev, quoted by J. S. Whale, *Christian Doctrine*, p. 101.

There is a root of mystery in him. He quickens man's awe. He forgave sins, and that is the function of God alone. Meanwhile we need forgiveness—come near, that we may see and understand and consent! So does his Cross persist, though our world has been cluttered with crosses, and though there were two other crosses close to his when he died: his cross persists in a certain deep vitality. Is it the "sorrow of God" by which our world finds cleansing?

A man must live by some faith. That he cannot help. Some men live by a merely inherited faith, which is therefore custom rather than faith. Most men echo the vague faith or unfaith of the society in which they find themselves. But choice is given us, and we cannot avoid choice. Manhood grows from root choices. Jesus still stands over against our world, and in it, asking, **But who do you say that I am?** The answer cannot finally be evaded. It determines man's life and his world. The answer is destiny. Who do you say . . . ?

16-19. *Explanatory Note: The Troubles of an Expositor.*—How can these verses be expounded? They are a storm center, not only of exegetical controversy, but of long strife between Protestants and Roman Catholics. How

Jewish expectation. Matthew thinks of this sonship as established by the Virgin Birth; cf. also on 4:1-11; 11:25-30.

can one unravel many threads of interpretation, and find the one thread that leads to truth? Yet the effort must be made. Here is an unraveling in honest attempt.

Suppose the verses literally true, as the Latin Church dogmatically claims. Does **this rock** refer to Peter or to Peter's faith? Rather plainly it refers to Peter. The attempt of some scholars to capitalize on the feminine gender of the Greek word for rock (see RSV footnote) is perhaps ill-advised; for Cephas, the Aramaic name which Jesus used, was plainly Peter's nickname, and in Aramaic there is no distinction of gender (see Exeg.). Then does **rock** mean Peter as a man of faith or Peter chosen as first in a line of monarchical bishops? Surely, as a man of faith. Ambrose so taught.[2] Even Cyprian (*ca.* 246) argues that Peter was chosen only to manifest the unity of the church.[3]

But *are* these verses literally **true**? Theories, not captious but cogent, throng to confuse us. Rudolf Bultmann argues that the words appear to stem from the utterance of a primitive Christian community.[4] C. H. Turner and others suggest that they come from a resurrection vision and logion.[5] The word **church** is a puzzle. Does it mean the N.T. church? If so, that church was not in existence when Christ is purported to have spoken these words, and his language could only have baffled Peter. Or does **church** mean "the synagogue of the last days," and does **the powers of death** refer likewise to the end of the age; and has the whole passage thus an eschatological stress? Does **rock** mean that Peter was to be the rock of the new covenant, only as Abraham was the rock of the old covenant? Does **keys** mean keys of administration, or authority to decide on the interpretation of Christ's words, or is it used of the power to forgive sins? Did Jesus, in any event, claim the Jewish title of Messiah? (See Exeg.) Why are vss. 16-18 carefully poetic in structure? Would Christ and Peter in the passion of the moment speak in measured poetry? Thus the questions throng.

How much has Matthew contributed to these verses? That is perhaps the crucial question. We must remember carefully both the late first-century date of this Gospel, and the church nexus from which it came. It was written in circles where the primacy of Peter was of major concern. Would James, brother of Jesus and

leader of the church in Jerusalem, have agreed that vs. 18 was the mind of Christ? Would Paul, who looked with deference on the leadership of James (Gal. 2:9), have agreed? Would the Johannine circle have agreed? They portray the Beloved Disciple as a more trustworthy leader than Peter (who denied his Lord), and carefully tell us that Jesus on the Cross committed his mother to the care of John. Matthew's emphasis on the primacy of Peter is not confirmed in the N.T. Even Matthew seems to contradict himself (see 18:18). Mark, also Petrine in its emphases, in the very passage from which Matthew has plainly drawn (Mark 8:27-30), makes no mention of the appointment of Peter as rock (or head) of the church. The rebuking of Peter is mentioned, but not this investiture. The epistles, written earlier than Matthew, insist that only Christ is the rock: "Other foundation can no man lay than that is laid, which is Jesus Christ" (I Cor. 3:11). When "apostles and prophets" are mentioned, Christ is still "the chief corner stone" (Eph. 2:20). Thus the teaching of these verses is countered, rather than supported, in the other books of the N.T.

In this maze of fact and theory the expositor must choose a path of exposition. May it not well be that Peter confessed the messiahship of Jesus, and that there was a long conversation of which we have in Mark a compressed but authentic and revealing account? May not vs. 18 have its nucleus in some (lost) word of Jesus, with a possible origin in Mark 3:16? It is more than likely that the present form of the sentence, and much of the whole passage, has been changed and colored by the author of the Gospel in his understandable and not unworthy purpose to exalt the leadership of Peter. Surely what we have at present does not accord with either the totality of Christ's teaching or with the centralities of N.T. truth. Vs. 19 does not ring like a word of Christ: it seems more like a description of the monarchical bishops who came to power in the church in Syria in the time of this Gospel. Always Matthew presents Peter as *via media* between the conservatism of James and the apparently too venturesome liberalism of Paul. That purpose is here strongly reflected. No comment need be made on the brash literalism and credulous grasping with which the Roman Church makes these verses the validation for its temporal power and totalitarian ecclesiasticism. Anyone who honestly faces the exegetical problems must be appalled at such temerity. The church is built on Christ alone, who can use weak men like Peter

[2] Quoted F. W. Green, *Gospel According to Saint Matthew*, "The Clarendon Bible," p. 207.

[3] Lucius Waterman, *Post-Apostolic Age*, p. 388.

[4] *Form Criticism*, tr. Frederick C. Grant (Chicago: Willett, Clark & Co., 1934), pp. 144-47.

[5] *Catholic and Apostolic* (Milwaukee: Morehouse Publishing Co., 1931), ch. v, especially pp. 193-94.

17 And Jesus answered and said unto him, Blessed art thou, Simon Bar-jona: for flesh and blood hath not revealed *it* unto thee, but my Father which is in heaven.

18 And I say also unto thee, That thou art Peter, and upon this rock I will build my church; and the gates of hell shall not prevail against it.

17 And Jesus answered him, "Blessed are you, Simon Bar-Jona! For flesh and blood has not revealed this to you, but my Father who is in heaven. 18 And I tell you, you are Peter,[u] and on this rock[v] I will build my church, and the powers of death[w] shall not

[u] Greek *Petros*.
[v] Greek *petra*.
[w] Greek *the gates of Hades*.

17. **Bar-Jona** means "son of Jonah." **Flesh and blood** is often used in Jewish writings to mean "humanity" as contrasted with divinity. Paul says that when God "was pleased to reveal his Son to me, . . . I did not confer with flesh and blood, nor did I go up to Jerusalem to those who were apostles before me (Gal. 1:16-17); i.e., he did not receive his gospel from Peter or James or any other man. Here, no doubt, the church of Syria answers that its apostle Peter also received his gospel and apostleship, not "through flesh and blood," but by direct divine revelation. Do vss. 17-19 represent a vision which Peter saw after the Resurrection?

18. **Peter** is the English form of Πέτρος, i.e., "Rock Man," **rock** being the translation of πέτρα. In Aramaic there would be no separate form to indicate the masculine gender: "You are *Kêphā'*, and on this *kêphā'* I will build," etc. Cf. on 10:2. The N.T. often portrays Peter as hesitating and wavering (14:28-31; 26:69-75; Gal. 2:11-14; Acts 10:13-15), and the suggestion is frequently made that Jesus gave him the name Rock to teach him that he must be firm. The word rendered **church** (ἐκκλησία) occurs many times in

(or John or Paul) as stones in his temple, when they confess that he is **the Son of the living God** and trust in his power.

16. *The Finality of Christ.*—Whatever the origin of this verse (see Expos., vss. 16-19), the confession ascribed to Peter is the central faith of the church. Christ is the song, the music, and the vibration that makes the music. "I believe . . . in Jesus Christ, His only Son our Lord." [6] "Believe" there means, not merely an intellectual affirmation, but a soul-trust for time and eternity. Christ is the center, the storm center and power center: Christ is *Christ*ianity.

This is a soul-arresting affair. He was a carpenter in a village not rich in heroic names. He had neither learning nor money wealth. The leaders of his day did not believe in him. He left his teachings (but no writing) to the precarious memory of his friends. He framed no statecraft, propounded no philosophy, led no army, wrote no music. The historians of his time thought him unworthy of mention. His cradle was a borrowed manger, his deathbed a felon's cross. Now, whatever men believe about him, his name is the inescapable name. His critics cancel one another. To some he is "fanatic," to others indulgently mild. To some he lacks "artistic genius," to others he proposes "impossibly beautiful dreams." To some he is too feminine, to others too rigorous in demand. Wise men do not enter that debate: they pair off the critics and leave them to their strife. The

[6] The Apostles' Creed.

criticisms testify to his amazing poise: the orbit is complete.

We stand before him. What did he say of himself? Little in direct claim. But what of the indirect claim? What of his quiet assumption to speak the final word?—"But I say unto you" (5:22, 28, 32, 34, 39, 44). What of his reiterated demand on man's complete loyalty?—"He that loveth father or mother [or "his own life"] more than me" (10:37) "cannot be my disciple" (Luke 14:26). What did those who walked with him think about him? That answer is in the N.T.: they hailed him as risen Lord. Then what do *we* think? His constraint is laid also on us. There is enough of the disclosure of the very God in him to warrant our venture. but never enough to spare us the venture. If we follow, as the disciples learned to follow, at risk and cost, we also shall find the power in Christ. He will hold us too, living and dying, and give us now the pledge of eternal life. **Thou art the Christ, the Son of the living God.**

18. *My Church.*—The honest exegete knows the questions that beleaguer these words, yet he hears in them the echo of an authentic word of Christ (see Expos., vs. 16). So an interpreter treats them, not in the bondage of the letter, but in the liberty of the spirit and in the whole context of the teaching of Jesus. In the mosaic of the Master's truth there are stones which, to our dim sight, seem brighter or duller, but true meanings are found only as we are faithful to the whole design.

Acts, the epistles, and the book of Revelation. There it denotes the universal fellowship of Christians, or the local congregation, which is thought of as a manifestation of that fellowship. But it is not found in the four Gospels except here and in 18:17. (For a discussion of the evidence, see George Johnston, *The Doctrine of the Church in the New Testament* [Cambridge: University Press, 1943], pp. 35-45.) Jesus cannot have spoken often of the church, if he did so at all. If this verse reflects any genuine saying of his, he may have thought of "the new, reformed Israel" or his new and true "way" within Judaism. This church can be founded on a man of Peter's character. Several parallels are to be found in Jewish literature. According to one midrash quoted by Strack and Billerbeck, *ad loc.*, a certain king (i.e., God) desired to erect a building, but as he dug down he found only morasses; at last he found a rock (i.e., Abraham), and on this he was able to lay his foundations. **The powers of death** is a correct paraphrase, for the Greek word is not "Gehenna" but "Hades," which usually stands for the Hebrew *She'ôl*, or place of the dead. The phrase "gates of Sheol" is found in Isa. 38:10. Death itself will not be able to destroy this church. On the whole passage, see the literature cited by Olof Linton, *Das Problem der Urkirche in der neueren Forschung* (Uppsala: A.-B. Lundquistska, 1932).

Here we see the foundation and central verity of the church: "Thou art the Christ, the Son of the living God" (vs. 16). The lights of earth could not reveal San Francisco Bay on a dark night, but a flash of lightning could: a man on the hills behind Berkeley could then see it, see the Golden Gate, and the edge of ocean. So "flesh and blood" (vs. 17), the learning and traditions of men, could not of themselves discover the verity in Christ: the flash from God himself is needed, and an answering flash in a man's soul. Christ is the heartbeat of the eternal Spirit, God's thrust into our world and life. A lightning flash of truth revealed the little bay of our mortality, and Christ as the Gate, and the mysterious Ocean. A farmer says, "Of this seed I will win my harvest." A builder says, "Of this stone I will build my house." Christ says, "Of this faith I will raise my church." What faith? The faith that what is highest in spirit, namely, the spirit of Jesus Christ, is deepest in the universe.

Here we see an ecclesia, a separate and new society, of which Christ is the Head. The forthright Peter is in that group, the mystic-minded John, and the faithful Andrew. The strength of the church is in Christ, as he empowers men who say, in "the soul's invincible surmise," [7] "Thou art the Christ, the Son of the living God" (vs. 16). G. K. Chesterton has written:

All the empires and kingdoms have failed, because of this inherent and continual weakness, that they were founded by strong men. . . . But this one thing, the historic Christian Church, was founded on a weak man, and for that reason it is indestructible. For no chain is stronger than its weakest link. [8]

[7] George Santayana, *Poems* (New York: Charles Scribner's Sons, 1923), Sonnet iii.

[8] *Heretics* (New York: John Lane Co., 1905), p. 67.

No, not for that reason; but because the weak man has now acknowledged Christ, and because Christ makes him strong. But Chesterton has a partial truth: Christ chooses to build his church on weak men who confess him, and who thus discover in him power beyond that of men. To this society each man brings his gift, and they become one life—the Agape, the Love.

Here we see an invincible city: **The powers of death shall not prevail against it. Death** (Sheol) seems to be the right translation, and **gates** means the point at which hosts issue to attack. Or perhaps the church moves to the assault. **Death!** All the corrosion of the years, all the mortality of mortal men, all the wages of sin, all the unknown powers of the underworld shall not be able to overthrow the fellowship that is held in the power of Christ. The site from which Voltaire hurled skeptic thunderbolts is later occupied by the headquarters of a Bible society. Kingdoms topple, ideologies rise and pass away, wars sink into exhaustion and disillusionment, cities crumble, armies move into limbo—but the church strangely endures. The Greeks had a statue of "Wingless Victory" —wingless because victory would never leave the Acropolis. But both time and the iron heel of the conqueror have overcome Athens. The Cross of Christ is the only wingless victory, because it is the victory in defeat, the triumph of the sacrificial love of God. The church is on the earth, and of the earth; yet

> . . . she on earth hath union
> With God the Three in One. [9]

So **the powers of death** do not prevail. Do we see the flash? Do we trust its truth? Do we confess the Deity in Christ? In us also, in our

[9] "The church's one foundation."

19 And I will give unto thee the keys of the kingdom of heaven: and whatsoever thou shalt bind on earth shall be bound in heaven; and whatsoever thou shalt loose on earth shall be loosed in heaven.

20 Then charged he his disciples that they should tell no man that he was Jesus the Christ.

21 ¶ From that time forth began Jesus to show unto his disciples, how that he must go unto Jerusalem, and suffer many things of the elders and chief priests and scribes, and be killed, and be raised again the third day.

prevail against it. 19 I will give you the keys of the kingdom of heaven, and whatever you bind on earth shall be bound in heaven, and whatever you loose on earth shall be loosed in heaven." 20 Then he strictly charged the disciples to tell no one that he was the Christ.

21 From that time Jesus began to show his disciples that he must go to Jerusalem and suffer many things from the elders and chief priests and scribes, and be killed, and

---

19. The keys of the kingdom would be committed to the chief steward in the royal household and with them goes plenary authority. In Isa. 22:22 the key of the house of David is promised to Eliakim. According to Paul, Jesus is the only foundation (I Cor. 3:11), and in Rev. 1:18; 3:7, Jesus possesses the key of David and the keys of death and Hades. But in this passage Peter is made the foundation (cf. Eph. 2:20, where the Christian apostles and prophets are the foundation and Christ is the cornerstone) and holds the keys. Post-Apostolic Christianity is now beginning to ascribe to the apostles the prerogatives of Jesus (cf. 10:40). In rabbinical language to **bind** and to **loose** is to declare certain actions forbidden or permitted; e.g., Terumoth 5:4: "If one seah of unclean Heave-offering falls into a hundred seahs of clean, the School of Shammai bind [forbid] the entire lot, but the School of Hillel loose [permit] it." Thus Peter's decisions regarding the O.T. law (e.g., in Acts 10:44-48) will be ratified in heaven. Later Christian tradition extended this principle to include the power to forgive or retain sins (18:18; John 20:23), but this was not its original meaning.

2. JESUS' PREDICTION OF HIS SUFFERING AND FUTURE GLORY (16:21-28)

21. Matthew omits the statement that the Son of man must suffer, which is one of the most striking touches of Mark 8:31. Mark's idea is that, though Jesus is unrecognized on earth, he is the celestial Son of man who, like the servant in Isa. 53, will suffer, but will afterward return in glory to judge the world. In the Q materials Jesus frequently speaks of himself as "Son of man," but not in connection with his future glory; when he mentions the Son of man as future judge, he does not explicitly identify himself with that figure; and Q never says that the Son of man must suffer. Hence many scholars do not think that Jesus claimed to be the "Man from heaven." On the other hand, the evangelists do not employ the term "Son of man" except in words attributed to Jesus. For discussions, see on 8:20, and also B. Harvie Branscomb, *The Gospel of Mark* (New York: Harper & Bros.), pp. 146-49; F. J. Foakes Jackson and Kirsopp Lake, *The*

---

weakness, Christ makes perfect his strength, and builds his church.

19. See Expos., vss. 16-19.

20-21. *Dark Prophecy.*—We should carefully note the Exeg. The power of detailed prediction is implied in these verses. Does it accord with Jesus' sharing of our humility, or with the admission of Jesus that no man knows the hour and day? If the prediction had been so sharp, why were the disciples so crushed by the Crucifixion? But, though this passage may show signs of a rewriting of Jesus' words in the light of Calvary and Easter Day, we have here doubtless

a core of Christ's teaching. He feared current concepts of messiahship, and feared lest men in their blindness should regard him as an earthy Messiah. Already he foresaw that suffering might await him. Therefore this warning. We assume that apocalyptic views of messiahship, the coming of one who by military might would confound national foes, are a dead concept. But are they? What do we ourselves wish in a Messiah? The canceling of our psychological frustrations and fears, the confusion of our national enemies, and an era of material plenty? Perhaps these desires are not alien

22 Then Peter took him, and began to rebuke him, saying, Be it far from thee, Lord: this shall not be unto thee.

23 But he turned, and said unto Peter, Get thee behind me, Satan: thou art an offense unto me: for thou savorest not the things that be of God, but those that be of men.

24 ¶ Then said Jesus unto his disciples, If any *man* will come after me, let him deny

on the third day be raised. **22** And Peter took him and began to rebuke him, saying, "God forbid, Lord! This shall never happen to you." **23** But he turned and said to Peter, "Get behind me, Satan! You are a hindrance[x] to me; for you are not on the side of God, but of men."

24 Then Jesus told his disciples, "If any

x Greek *stumbling-block.*

Beginnings of Christianity, Part I, Vol. I (London: Macmillan & Co., 1920), pp. 368-84; H. B. Sharman, *Son of Man and Kingdom of God* (New York: Harper & Bros., 1943); R. Otto, *Kingdom of God and Son of Man;* C. T. Craig, "The Problem of the Messiahship of Jesus," in E. P. Booth, ed., *New Testament Studies* (New York and Nashville: Abingdon-Cokesbury Press, 1942).

If Jesus predicted his suffering, death, and resurrection in such explicit terms, it is difficult to see why in the Gospels the disciples are portrayed as crushed by the Crucifixion and surprised by the Resurrection. Perhaps the simplest assumption is that Jesus now said that his visit to Jerusalem would lead to his rejection and death. It has, of course, been pointed out that here he predicts his resurrection but does not say that he will be *seen.*

Elders and chief priests and scribes made up the great Sanhedrin in Jerusalem. **The third day,** counting Friday as the first of the three, expresses the usual idea of the Gospels. But "after three days," in Mark, ought to refer to Monday at the earliest.

23. Get behind me, Satan! may mean "Get out of my sight!" (Satan is similarly addressed in 4:10), or "It is time for you to follow loyally behind me, and not oppose me." **You are not on the side of God,** literally, "You are not thinking God's thoughts."

24. The rebuke is immediately followed by some very striking sayings on discipleship. Jesus' willingness to lay down his own life is a concrete expression of his conviction that

---

from the earthy and vindictive ideas of messiahship that were current in the time of Christ.

Mark saw in Christ (see Exeg.) the fulfillment of the "suffering Servant" of Isaiah's prophecy, that is a very different concept from the view held by Jewish nationalism. God has strange ways. Men try to establish the kingdom through material plenty and "victory": God chooses the way through suffering and death. Have we really come to terms with these facts? The early church learned them through its suffering.

22-23. *You Are Not Thinking God's Thoughts.*—Peter had confessed Jesus to be the Christ, the Messiah. The words "Son of the living God" (16:16) imply a Messiah far worthier in method and nature than the Messiah of ordinary Jewish hope. But here Peter voices the current nationalistic longing. The Roman Church chooses the Peter of vs. 16, but blandly ignores the Peter of vs. 22. Peter is not here the "rock"; he is the tempter. Perhaps the rebuke is not so violent in language as earlier translations indicate, but the phrase is still the same as that used by Jesus to refute the devil in the wilderness temptation (4:10).

Can a man "think God's thoughts"? No and yes. Man is man, and must think man's

thoughts. But there is a cleft and paradox in human nature: our very sense of time implies a sense of eternity. We can think as people who are carried on the transitory stream, and we can also think as people contemplating the flow. We can be worldly-minded, and often are; but we can also see ourselves as worldly-minded, and often do. Always two ways of thinking compete for our will. Life comes as choice. How often we "think as a man"! We echo the common prejudice, clutch at the sensate, and adopt the crowd's standards of success. Then God's flash comes: we see that the worldly is temporal and unworthy. But often we still keep an earthy mind. This cleft in our nature we ourselves cannot heal, nor can we in our own power rise above our lower self. Christ came, as Resource from beyond men, that we might learn to think God's thoughts. Often we say to him, **God forbid, Lord!** But it is we who try to forbid; it is not God. Thus we become tempters. What pains are inflicted on Christ by those who think they are his friends! "For my thoughts are not your thoughts, . . . saith the Lord" (Isa. 55:8). Whose thoughts do we think—man's or God's?

24. *Condition of Discipleship.*—Every leader has made clear the terms of discipleship. Jesus

himself, and take up his cross, and follow me.

25 For whosoever will save his life shall lose it: and whosoever will lose his life for my sake shall find it.

man would come after me, let him deny himself and take up his cross and follow me. 25 For whoever would save his life will lose it, and whoever loses his life for my sake

self-sacrifice is the true way to serve God and his kingdom. He could easily have said that a follower must **take up his cross** if he considered the possibility that the Romans would execute him as a revolutionist. Crucifixion was only too well known in first-century Palestine. But the newly found MS of Mark, Codex 2427, omits **and take up his cross** in Mark 8:34, and the words may not originally have been in the text of that Gospel.

25. A man who protects and hoards his life may **lose it** anyhow. Perhaps to protect it is to lose it in the most real sense of the word, for cowardice means spiritual death.

never hid the sharp demand. Our Gospel here states it in words that echo the Crucifixion. Jesus does not mean that every follower shall die a violent death: Francis of Assisi died in his bed. But every follower must meet the conditions of discipleship. W. M. Clow [1] has drawn a distinction between a burden and a cross (see Expos., 10:38). We are conscripted to carry a burden: burdens are the "thousand natural shocks that flesh is heir to." [2] But we volunteer to carry a cross, as seems to be implied in **take up**, for a cross is somebody else's burden or the suffering which we choose to endure for Christ's truth. This is real self-denial. The word "denial" is from the same root as that of the word used when Peter is described as "denying" Christ. The unworthy self disputes the claims of Christ. A. J. Cronin's novel *The Citadel* shows one doctor following the easy course of coddling wealthy hypochondriacs, and another devoting himself, with but little recompense in cash, to the needs of a Welsh mining town. Christ-love called one way, and self-love the other. Besides, the Welsh doctor had to plead for new sanitation, and so found himself in conflict with political-economic conservatism and greed. Following Christ is not easy.

There is danger that we may sentimentalize the Cross. Christ's cross is different from ours: only he can atone for human sin. Yet in one sense it is the token of ours; and it is stern, even though we fashion it in flowers on Easter Day, or wear it as an ornament. To carry a cross to a place of execution was no sentimentalism. But we must as clearly understand that a cross is no self-mutilation. The higher self cannot live unless the lower self is nailed down to die. The Cross is the plucking off of poor buds that one fine bud may come to flower; it is the pruning of the tree that there may be an abundant harvest. "Who for the joy that was set before him endured the cross" (Heb. 12:2). The joy goes far beyond the individual experi-

ence of the cross-bearer: he bequeaths joy to the world, and quickens joy in a watching heaven. So his joy is double joy. **Come** *after me:* Christ has blazed this trail which only he could pioneer. **Deny** *himself:* better than denying Christ. *Take up* **his cross:** a voluntary act, each man having his destined self-surrender. *Follow:* into liberation, light, and the coming of the kingdom.

25. *Losing to Find.*—(See Expos., 10:39.) These words are not merely good advice to be taken or ignored. They are unbreakable truth. They could not be more true if Jesus had said instead, "Day follows night." Notice that they are recorded six times in the Gospels, and that they occur (with variants) in all four Gospels. Do we not say of a neighbor, "If only he could find himself"? Jesus here points the way to that discovery. At first blush his pronouncement seems a juggling with words. But if we insert two adjectives, the saying is clear: "Whosoever will save his [lower] life shall lose his [higher] life." There seem to be a thousand roads to travel. Actually there are but two: for when we say a man is kind, we imply that he could have been cruel; and when we say of Lincoln that "he belongs to the ages," we infer that he could have lived for the moment. Name any road and it is still one of two roads. That is why the adjective "selfish" is so elusive. A saint is selfish in the sense that he is doing what he pleases, yet he has willed to seek his pleasure by the high road. Thus we rightly keep the word "selfish" to describe the low road: it is the road of self rather than of God. The high road is the road of **my sake** rather than of self.

This choice, this fork in the road, is the sign and occasion of our freedom. If there were no choice, we would not be free; if there were a million equally good choices, we would not be free. Isaac Newton's dog "Diamond" has been accused (perhaps apocryphally) of knocking over the candle which set fire to scientific papers on which Newton had lavished years of labor; [3]

[1] *The Cross in Christian Experience*, pp. 232 ff.
[2] Shakespeare, *Hamlet*, Act III, scene 1.

[3] David Brewster, *Memoirs of the Life, Writings and Discoveries of Sir Isaac Newton*, II, 138.

26 For what is a man profited, if he shall gain the whole world, and lose his own soul? or what shall a man give in exchange for his soul?

will find it. 26 For what will it profit a man, if he gains the whole world and forfeits his life? Or what shall a man give in return for

---

26. The first question may embody an observation of life in general: a man may win material success only to die before he can enjoy it, and in that case it is all for nothing (cf. Luke 12:15-20, the story of the rich fool). Neither Greek nor the Semitic languages draw a distinction between **soul** (KJV) and **life** (RSV); ψυχή, like its Semitic

---

but the dog in any event was not blameworthy: it was not confronted by any moral choice. The choice is our danger: we can lose the higher life. The choice is our blessedness: we can gain the higher life. It is profitless to try to deny the choice, for we shall reassume the necessity of choice before the denial is complete. Omar in one breath says, "We are . . . but helpless Pieces of the Game He plays," and in another, "Come, fill the Cup"[4] How can we "come" if we are "helpless" pieces? The disillusion of any man or generation derives from commitment to a cause deemed high and found to be low, or from refusal to choose a high cause. We are made for fealty, and real life eludes us until we live in homage.

This truth is cosmic truth. It is true of health: health fussily safeguarded becomes hypochondria, but health expended in energy may grow. It is true of harvest: the seed must die to live. It is true of friendship: a man enjoys no friends until he becomes a friend. It is true of a nation: its good is found only as it forgets its good to serve the world. It is true of a church: it dies if it seeks its own power, and lives if it proclaims the gospel. This is not pious advice, still less a pulpit platitude: it is axiom of the soul and the will of God from the "foundation of the world" (25:34). There is surgery—either way. If we cut off the higher, remorse is the bleeding of a wound that does not heal. If we cut off the lower, the wound heals and the surgery spells health. Christ made the sacrifice joyously, as with the sound of trumpets. We live when we make the choice for his sake.

26. *Poor Exchange.*—The Emperor Charlemagne was buried, not as if sleeping in his shroud, but seated on a throne in robes of state, with an open Bible on his knee, and one finger pointing to words that spoke when he could no longer speak: **For what is a man profited, if he shall gain the whole world, and lose his own soul?** The Exeg. tells us that vs. 26*a* may refer to a man's life in the certain prospect soon or late of death, and vs. 26*b* to his self or life in the approach of the judgment. The soul is not something hidden away inside us, to be saved by Sunday worship and labeled

[4] *Rubáiyát of Omar Khayyám,* sts. lxviii, lxix, vii.

for heaven, while all the rest of us remains earthy. The soul is the self. What profit if a man gain $100,000 in the bank and lose his health? The minister says over his grave, "Forasmuch as it hath pleased Almighty God of his great mercy to take unto himself . . ."[5] but we can be reasonably sure that in one sense it did not please God. What profit if a man gain political preferment and salutations in the clubs, and lose his option in the enjoyment of nature or in the joy of great books or in genuine friendship? Poor exchange!

But there is a deeper self, and there is a judgment. As to that twin fact the Bible only confirms what we already inwardly know. This self is not our body or even the measure of our intellectual acumen. A man is not judged in heaven by his physical stature or his intelligence quotient. No botanist by dissection can find the flower; no surgeon's knife can lay bare the self. The real self says of political graft and economic ugliness, as well as of private shuffling, "That is not I." The real self says of all that is found in Christ, "That is I, if I could become myself." What profit is it to gain the whole world, and lose that real self? When that real self is lost, what can a man give to recover himself? He has nothing to give: he has traded all that is worth giving and has received only a bauble.

Thoreau discussed this text. He graduated from a famous university, but thought the diploma too expensive at five dollars; and he lived in a house which cost less than the one-year cost of his undergraduate room. He said of the N.T. that most people favored it outwardly, defended it with bigotry—and hardly ever read it:

There are, indeed, severe things in it which no man should read aloud more than once: "For what is a man profited, if he shall gain the whole world, and lose his own soul?" Think of this, Yankees! . . . Think of repeating these things to a New England audience! . . . Who, without cant, can read them aloud? Who, without cant, can hear them? . . . They never were read. They never were heard.[6]

[5] Church of Scotland, *Book of Common Prayer.*
[6] *A Week on the Concord and Merrimack Rivers,* diary for Sunday.

27 For the Son of man shall come in the glory of his Father with his angels; and then he shall reward every man according to his works.

28 Verily I say unto you, There be some standing here, which shall not taste of death, till they see the Son of man coming in his kingdom.

his life? 27 For the Son of man is to come with his angels in the glory of his Father, and then he will repay every man for what he has done. 28 Truly, I say to you, there are some standing here who will not taste death before they see the Son of man coming in his kingdom."

---

equivalents, denotes the animate element in man and animals. The second question, in this context, may be paraphrased: "There is nothing that you can offer with which to buy back your life at the Judgment if you have forfeited it."

27. Mark 8:38 speaks of the necessity of fearlessly acknowledging the Son of man, i.e., Jesus. Matthew recasts the saying to make it a general prediction of the Last Judgment. The same moralizing note is found in 12:36-37; 21:41b, 43.

28. Mark's saying (9:1) had nothing to do with the idea of the **Son of man** and probably is not from the same source as the foregoing. The prediction was not fulfilled, and later Christians found it necessary to explain that it was metaphorical and had been fulfilled at Pentecost. John 21:22-23 deals with a similar promise that the "beloved disciple" would not die, and tries to explain it as a misunderstanding. It would not be strange if Jesus believed that within a generation the kingdom would be manifested in full glory, for certainly most early Christians and many Jews thought so. The thought-forms of the day were what we call "eschatological"; God had created the world as we know it, and he would bring it to an end. Yet we possess equally well-attested sayings of Jesus which warn against calculating "times and seasons" (e.g., Luke 17:20-22). We cannot decide with certainty exactly what Jesus thought would happen in the future, and it is not important that we should. What is important is that he called men away from idle speculation about signs of the kingdom (12:38-39; 16:1-4; Luke 13:1-9) and insisted that they must at all times behave like men prepared for it (25:1-13; Luke 12:35-46). The question is discussed further in the general note on 24:1–26:2. (See also discussions, setting forth a number of different views, of Jesus' teaching about the end of the age in articles by R. H. Strachan and C. T. Craig, above, pp. 12-20 and 145-54. Comments on parallel passages in other gospels should also be consulted.)

The question Jesus asked is not a question. It is a verdict. If the verdict goes against us, there is nothing to do but cast ourselves on his mercy. He can restore the bartered self, and teach us how to keep it—by losing it for him.

27. Coming Glory.—The Exeg. should be read with care, and Matthew's changes in the Marcan original duly noted. The interpreter must ask when and why the changes were made. Whatever the origin of these words—whether they are the early church's rewriting of a remembered logion of Jesus, or the transcript of his very speech—their wonder abides. Men had come to know, by his cross and resurrection, that Christ is the judgment both in this world and the next. He was no longer the Galilean Carpenter, no longer merely a Friend warning them of sufferings to come: he was throned in power—**in the glory of his Father with his angels.**

According to his works is not the underscoring of man's accomplishments, as if he of himself could shape his character. **Works** is a wide word. It gathers in both motives and deeds. Its reference is both to a man's basic loyalty and to its issue in conduct. **Works** thus includes "for my sake." Yet it requires of us more than pious intentions and constantly remorseful prayers. **He shall reward every man:** he is the criterion of judgment and himself the Judge, and every man must stand before him. **Every** means that the race is judged, and that every individual in the race must give individual account. In that day the sufferings of the faithful are ended, and evil men who imposed the sufferings are seen in true light. They were "great" on earth, but are unmasked in heaven. The N.T. frequently describes the panoply and pomp of judgment: that is tribute to the resurrection sovereignty of Christ. But the essence of judgment is Christ himself, and that quietly spoken question that G. A. Studdert-Kennedy predicts will be asked by Christ concerning our mortal days—"Well?" [7]

[7] See his poem "Well?" in *The Sorrows of God and Other Poems* (New York: George H. Doran Co., 1924).

17 And after six days Jesus taketh Peter, James, and John his brother, and bringeth them up into a high mountain apart,

17 And after six days Jesus took with him Peter and James and John his brother, and led them up a high mountain

3. Divine Confirmation in the Transfiguration (17:1-8)

Various theories have been advanced to account for the origin of this story. (a) It is often explained as a resurrection appearance which has been transferred back into Jesus' earthly ministry. For example, M. S. Enslin, "The Data of Peter's Confession," in *Quantulacumque*, ed. R. P. Casey, Silva Lake, and A. K. Lake (London: Christophers, 1937) regards this vision as the source of Peter's confession of Jesus as Messiah. (b) It has sometimes been considered an epiphany story which had no origin other than the imagination of early Christians and was told to express the doctrine of Jesus' divinity; see, e.g., Dibelius, *From Tradition to Gospel*, pp. 275-76. (c) Many commentators regard it as historical in the strict sense. It is not difficult to suppose that behind the story lies a striking religious experience in which the three disciples participated.

The story, as we now possess it, is rich in allusions to Jewish and Christian religious ideas and stories. Peter and the others would have tried to interpret what they saw, and in any case Christian tradition and preaching have influenced the details. The narrative can be divided into two parts, a theophanic vision (vss. 2-3) and a voice from heaven like the *bath qôl* of Jewish tradition (vs. 5), with Peter's remark in between. It is not, however, necessary to suppose that the two elements were originally separate. Vss. 6-8 are mainly editorial.

Recent investigators have been more concerned with the meaning, purpose, and background of the story than with its historical origins, for it has much to tell us about early Christian thought. Thus Harald Riesenfeld traces all the ancient motifs and allusions in his *Jésus Transfiguré* (Copenhagen: Ejnar Munksgaard, 1947), which contains a full bibliography. According to Riesenfeld, the story is fundamentally "historical" and relates a vision of the enthronement of Jesus as Messiah and High Priest, which Peter and the others behold. G. H. Boobyer, "St. Mark and the Transfiguration Story," *Journal of Theological Studies*, XLI (1940), 119-40, denies that it has any connection with the Resurrection. The Transfiguration is, instead, a foreshadowing of the Parousia, or second coming, of Christ in glory, as in II Pet. 1:13-18 and the Apocalypse of Peter.

Toynbee remarks that the Transfiguration furnishes the supreme example of the "withdrawal-and-return" motif, which dominates the entire gospel story (*Study of History*, pp. 222-23).

17:1. After six days is reminiscent of Exod. 24:9-18. There Moses first goes up into the mountain with Aaron, Nadab, and Abihu (three men, as here), together with seventy elders, and they see God. Later he goes up alone. For six days the cloud covers the mountain, and on the seventh day the Lord calls to Moses. James and John are the sons of Zebedee (4:21). The evangelists regard Peter and these two disciples as the most important of the twelve (cf. 20:20). A high mountain is a suitable place for revelation, as in 4:8; 5:1; 28:16. A much later tradition identifies the mountain as Tabor, but Hermon (9,100 ft.) is nearer Caesarea Philippi.

17:1-7. *The Transfiguration.*—The transfiguration story was precious to the early church, and it has enriched all ages of the faith. Each of the three Synoptic accounts is brilliant in the simplicity of its writing and passing rich in allusion; the story itself is such a sudden light that—we are gladly constrained to believe—it must have come from awe-filled actuality. The main fact is—theophany. Every line of the picture portrays God's visitation. Every allusion underscores the fact of the divine glory. Six days is an echo of the experience of Moses on Mount Sinai. Transfigured in this company of revelation words can mean only transformation into a higher nature. Shone (again notice the echo of the Mount Sinai story) implies the divine light. White garments are the high priestly robes of the Messiah. The bright cloud is the Shekinah

2 And was transfigured before them: and his face did shine as the sun, and his raiment was white as the light.

3 And, behold, there appeared unto them Moses and Elias talking with him.

apart. 2 And he was transfigured before them, and his face shone like the sun, and his garments became white as light. 3 And behold, there appeared to them Moses and

---

2. The word translated **transfigured** (μετεμορφώθη) is found also in Rom. 12:2; II Cor. 3:18. Paul uses a related noun in Phil. 2:6-7, when he says that Jesus, who originally existed in the nature or form (μορφή) of God, took upon himself the nature of a slave. Moses' face also **shone** after he had conversed with God (Exod. 34:29-35). Philo (*Moses* II. 51, 288) explained Moses' vision as a preparation for immortality: God changed his body into a mind-substance like the radiance of the sun. Thus on the mountain Jesus was transformed or glorified, or at least his true nature was disclosed and a promise of his future glory was given. The idea is further developed in II Cor. 3:18, where those who behold the glorified Christ are metamorphosed into the same glory. Perhaps the same thought is suggested here: the three disciples, having seen Christ, are ultimately to be transformed, and will exchange their earthly **booths or tents,** i.e., their mortal bodies, for heavenly vesture (II Cor. 4:16–5:5). Jesus' **white** clothing suggests the priestly garments which proclaim the Messiah as high priest.

3. Moses is an appropriate figure because of the story's connections with Exod. 24:9-18. It was sometimes thought that he, like **Elijah,** had not died. Thus the two prophetic visitants from heaven are fitting companions for Jesus, who will also ascend to heaven. Boobyer thinks of them as examples of those who will accompany Christ at his second coming (I Cor. 15:22-23; I Thess. 4:14-17). Riesenfeld calls them the prototypes, precursors, and attendants of the messianic King.

---

or cloud of God's glory, whence came the divine **voice.** Even **booths** may have its apocalyptic undertone (see Exeg.): did the three disciples believe, in that burning light, that God had come to "dwell with men" (Rev. 21:3), and that they must therefore provide a new tabernacle? **Moses and Elijah,** according to Jewish faith, had not tasted death, but were to be forerunners of the "great day" of the final age. There has been a rewriting of the story. That we must assume—if only because the writing is consummate literary art. There are eschatological features (see vs. 11) appropriate to that age, and perhaps not inappropriate in any age. But the central and overpowering truth, which no interpreter should miss, is the truth of God in Christ. The Transfiguration is not merely the divine seal on the ministry of Jesus: it records the fact that God has broken into our world through him.

The experience was thus God's signature on the choice and commitment that Christ had made. Surely the Gospels have the right chronology and/or the true understanding: this incident occurred after Christ's realization that suffering awaited him. The story itself shows that his mind was much occupied with thoughts of sacrifice and death. Was rejection the way? Could the kingdom come through apparent failure? Was the path of lowly dependence, which he had chosen in the wilderness temptation, the right path? Perhaps Jesus asked these questions in the prayer which, according to Luke, gave rise to the Transfiguration. In the midst of the struggle and doubt there came the Shekinah, and the very **voice** which had commissioned him at the Baptism. So Jesus knew that eternal life is round about well-chosen death, that apparent failure can be truest gain, and that the Father was **pleased** in the commitment of the Son. Soon the vision faded, and he was left alone (vs. 8), but he had received light and power with which to meet encroaching darkness.

The Transfiguration is thus confirmation for our faith. The story nerved the early church: we can almost feel the new strength that entered Peter as, according to the author of one of the general epistles, he remembered the time when three men were "eyewitnesses of his majesty" (II Peter 1:16). The story is our reminder that Jesus is Christ and Lord: God has entered our world in him. Our nature therefore may be transfigured, after our own kind, in Christ, a fact which Paul splendidly proclaims: For "we . . . are changed"—it is the very word "transfigured"—as we gaze on Christ, "into the same image from glory to glory" (II Cor. 3:18). Prayer is the occasion—prayer and following Christ in his obedience to the strange ways of God. Our transfiguration as a profound emotion of course has its dangers (see Expos., vs. 4), but when rightly used it is still the sign and seal of God,

4 Then answered Peter, and said unto Jesus, Lord, it is good for us to be here: if thou wilt, let us make here three tabernacles; one for thee, and one for Moses, and one for Elias.

5 While he yet spake, behold, a bright cloud overshadowed them: and behold a voice out of the cloud, which said, This is my beloved Son, in whom I am well pleased; hear ye him.

6 And when the disciples heard it, they fell on their face, and were sore afraid.

7 And Jesus came and touched them, and said, Arise, and be not afraid.

Elijah, talking with him. 4 And Peter said to Jesus, "Lord, it is well that we are here; if you wish, I will make three booths here, one for you and one for Moses and one for Elijah." 5 He was still speaking, when lo, a bright cloud overshadowed them, and a voice from the cloud said, "This is my beloved Son,ⁱ with whom I am well pleased; listen to him." 6 When the disciples heard this, they fell on their faces, and were filled with awe. 7 But Jesus came and touched them, saying, "Rise, and have no fear."

ⁱ Or my Son, my (or the) Beloved.

4. The **booths** or tents suggest the tent in the wilderness where God's worship was carried on (Acts 7:44) and also the feast of Tabernacles. There is some reason to believe that in this period that festival was marked by enthusiasm over the coming triumph of Israel. Zech. 14:16-19 prophesies that all nations will come up to Jerusalem to worship at the feast of Tabernacles. Peter may think that the final age is come, the great festival will be celebrated, and Moses and Elijah will remain there permanently. He therefore wishes to build abodes which will be suitable for the new age, when God and Christ will dwell with men (Rev. 21:3-4). But, as the evangelists realize, the disciples misunderstand the dimensions of this revelation. It is not yet time for the Second Coming. Or, as II Cor. 5:1 says, the Christian who has left his earthly tent has "a house not made with hands, eternal in the heavens." He who sees Jesus in his true nature will be transformed into his likeness and has no need of an earthly dwelling.

5. The **bright cloud,** from which God speaks, reminds one of Exod. 24:15-18, and also of the cloud out of which the returning Christ will be revealed (26:64; Acts 1:9-11; I Thess. 4:17). When Yahweh spoke to Moses, he gave commands for building the tent of meeting; here his message concerns his **beloved Son.** Matthew adds **with whom I am well pleased** from 3:17; cf. note on that verse.

6-7. These verses are Matthew's editorial work. Similar motifs are found in 28:4-5; Mark 16:5-6; Rev. 1:16-17.

4. *Escape from Life.*—The Exeg. suggests that Peter, James, and John thought that the final age had arrived, and that they could forever dwell in its light. They mistook "the dimensions" of the revelation: the "great day" had not yet come, even though they had received its assurance and foretaste. How often men have been caught in that misunderstanding! How often they have forsaken the common task for a vain hope, forgetting that when God comes he would rather find us fulfilling life's appointed round—praying if it is time to pray, working if it is time to work.

We try many ways of escape from life: "Oh that I had wings like a dove!" (Ps. 55:6). We try fantasy; but that, unless used in moderation, ends in mental sickness and a cleft personality. We try travel, but that is vain; for we take ourselves on our travels. We try "the world, the flesh, and the devil"; but that is at best an intoxicant and at worst an enslavement. We try work, for that can be an escape from

the real business of living; but the challenge looks over our shoulder while we work. We try religious emotion, for it is a painful fact that a selfish mysticism can be a substitute for genuine faith, all the way from the cult of "tongues" to a religious aestheticism; but the vision fades and the valley-need beckons us. An airplane can fly above the rain clouds, moving through a realm of clear light and even rainbows, but soon it must come down to earth. So the three disciples and Jesus returned from the Mount of Transfiguration to the pitiable and urgent need of the valley. There is work to be done—the sometimes humdrum work of livelihood, the more urgent work of neighborliness, and the central work of God's kingdom without which livelihood and even neighborliness lack meaning and worth. While mortality remains the vision fades "into the light of common day."[8] If we were wise, we would not covet any different life on earth.

[8] Wordsworth, "Ode on Intimations of Immortality."

8 And when they had lifted up their eyes, they saw no man, save Jesus only.

9 And as they came down from the mountain, Jesus charged them, saying, Tell the vision to no man, until the Son of man be risen again from the dead.

8 And when they lifted up their eyes, they saw no one but Jesus only.

9 And as they were coming down the mountain, Jesus commanded them, "Tell no one the vision, until the Son of man is

4. Second Statement of Jesus' Relation to the Baptist (17:9-13)

Matthew has rewritten Mark 9:9-13 in such a way as to avoid some of the difficulties of that passage. Thus he eliminates Mark 9:10, which indicates that the disciples did not understand about the Resurrection. The saying about the Son of man, which breaks the context in Mark 9:12b, is transferred to the end of Matt. 17:12 and rewritten. In both Gospels the context is artificial and obscure. Why would the command of vs. 9 lead to the question of vs. 10, and how could the question arise at all, since Elijah has just come and announced the Messiah? Mark's tradition apparently contained a little dialogue on the subject of John the Baptist and Elijah. The most appropriate place to insert it seemed to be just after the Transfiguration; and so Mark placed it there, together with a warning that nothing should be said about the vision until after the Resurrection. This was in accord with his theory of the messianic secret.

9. **Is raised** (ἐγερθῇ), the reading of Vaticanus (B) and Bezae (D), is probably correct. The earliest Christian doctrine was that Jesus was "raised up" by God (Acts 2:24), not that he "arose."

But the "high hour" of vision is much more than respite. It is the confirmation of our faith: we know again that Jesus is Lord, and that the seal of God is in him. It is the renewal of our strength: God "breaks through" once more, and we are empowered. It is promise of a world beyond our world: not always shall we dwell in this alternation of shadows and surety. The gates of the city toward which we move "shall not be shut at all by day: for there shall be no night there" (Rev. 21:25).

8. *Jesus Only.*—The phrase must not be wrenched from its context: it means that they saw Jesus again in his familiar aspect, and that Moses and Elijah (see vs. 4) and the "cloud of glory" had disappeared. But the words are so vibrant in their own right that inevitably and rightly they have quickened many a Christian plea.

In the temptation to escape from life the three found Jesus only, and he was sufficient guidance and friendship; for he did not ask that he might dwell on the mount, but made his way through the valley-need to Jerusalem and death. In their fears (vs. 7) they saw Jesus only; and that was right, for man's dim sight cannot bear the supernal light, but needs "the gates of saving flesh and bone." [9] No man can see God and live, "but we see Jesus" (Heb. 2:9). In their sins they learned to see Jesus only: only he, sent from God, can understand our waywardness, and keep us in the realism that sees the sinfulness of sin, and still forgive us in the depth of divine love. In the approach of death

[9] Rudyard Kipling, "The Prayer of Miriam Cohen."

they learned to see Jesus only: he has "the words of eternal life" (John 6:68).

The phrase suggests man's need for a central faith. There is a basic homage and trust in us. It is personal, and can be given at long last only to a Person. It is fealty and love: it is the joy and danger of a complete commitment. No "ism" or "ology" can finally content us: "Not what, but *Whom,* I do believe." [1] Yet no human love can ever satisfy that deepest longing, for the One we believe must be above our lies, hankerings, and transience. Jesus only.

The words also bespeak his loneliness. His heavenly companions had gone. The mountain now was hard rock, for by God's gift and his own brave acceptance he had taken "the form of a servant" and was "found in fashion as a man" (Phil. 2:7, 8). He was alone, yet not alone. He turned from the Transfiguration to go down to the valley. The more reason therefore that for us he should be all in all: Jesus only!

9-13. *Elijah, John the Baptist, and Jesus.*—This passage should be compared with the Marcan source. Branscomb holds even of the Marcan passage that it is a later reflection on the ministry of Jesus and on some problems which it raised, rather than a transcript of the dramatic actuality. [2] The Jews believed that Elijah would return as forerunner of the messianic age (Mal. 4:5; Luke 1:17). There was a debate in the early church around the question:

[1] John Oxenham, "Credo," *Bees in Amber* (London: Methuen & Co., 1913).

[2] *Gospel of Mark,* pp. 163-64.

10 And his disciples asked him, saying, Why then say the scribes that Elias must first come?

11 And Jesus answered and said unto them, Elias truly shall first come, and restore all things.

12 But I say unto you, That Elias is come already, and they knew him not, but have done unto him whatsoever they listed. Likewise shall also the Son of man suffer of them.

13 Then the disciples understood that he spake unto them of John the Baptist.

14 ¶ And when they were come to the multitude, there came to him a *certain* man, kneeling down to him, and saying,

15 Lord, have mercy on my son; for he

raised from the dead." 10 And the disciples asked him, "Then why do the scribes say that first Elijah must come?" 11 He replied, "Elijah does come, and he is to restore all things; 12 but I tell you that Elijah has already come, and they did not know him, but did to him whatever they pleased. So also the Son of man will suffer at their hands." 13 Then the disciples understood that he was speaking to them of John the Baptist.

14 And when they came to the crowd, a man came up to him and kneeling before him said, 15 "Lord, have mercy on my son,

---

11. Mal. 4:5-6 taught that Elijah would come before the day of the Lord, to reconcile sons and fathers; cf. on 11:14.

12. **Elijah has already come** in the person of John the Baptist; but he was not recognized. Mark 9:13 adds that his sufferings were predicted by Scripture, but there is no evidence of a Jewish belief that Elijah would suffer. Mark's text is confused and that evangelist may have meant to say that they have done to the **Son of man** what they wished. At any rate, Matthew understood it so. It is possible that Jesus connected John the Baptist with the suffering servant of Isa. 53, but there is no other evidence for this.

G. An Example for the Disciples: Healing of the Epileptic Boy
(17:14-20)

The context for this story is carefully chosen. As in the preceding scene, the disciples are unable to understand the revelation or to do works of faith appropriate to it. Their helpless confusion is reminiscent of Exod. 32:1-6, where Moses comes down from the mountain only to discover that Aaron and the Israelites have fallen into idolatry. Moses angrily punished his people; but Jesus' first act on descending from the mountain is a deed of mercy.

15. **He is an epileptic** is the correct translation; cf. on 4:24. Mark (9:17-18, 20) gives other details which lead many commentators to regard the illness as epilepsy; but Fenner

---

If Jesus is the Messiah why has Elijah not come? These verses echo that strife. Jesus is here represented as saying that Elijah has come, not in reincarnation, but in striking likeness of the flesh and in verity of the spirit. John, dressed like Elijah, lived in the desert as Elijah had lived, and defied Herod and Herodias as Elijah had defied Ahab and Jezebel (cf. 11:14). Granted that John came as Elijah, a further question remained: Why did Elijah not **restore all things** according to promise? Why had the golden age not come?

The controversy about Elijah seems ancient to us, but the question why the golden age comes on leaden feet is always new. The answer Jesus is purported to have given has its truth for us: men did not see in John the prophet of God, and in heedlessness they slew

him. Mankind has a certain freedom, and darkly abuses it. The golden age cannot be forced upon them, for then it would not be gold, but only a gilded coercion. The golden age comes only through golden souls. So the Messiah must die on a Cross. Thus Elijah awakens and Christ renews, Elijah arouses penitence and Christ forgives—if men will see and believe. But they will not see. So Christ must die that they may be cleansed of sin and sorrow by that ultimate tragedy. These are deep issues that become clear only when Christ is raised from the dead.

14-18. *Mountain Vision and Valley Need.*— Most commentators have realized that the Raphael canvas is a better commentary here than any words. He was right, as the Gospels are right: the Mount of Transfiguration and the pain-filled valley ought to be shown in one

is lunatic, and sore vexed: for ofttimes he falleth into the fire, and oft into the water.

16 And I brought him to thy disciples, and they could not cure him.

17 Then Jesus answered and said, O faithless and perverse generation, how long shall I be with you? how long shall I suffer you? bring him hither to me.

18 And Jesus rebuked the devil; and he departed out of him: and the child was cured from that very hour.

19 Then came the disciples to Jesus apart, and said, Why could not we cast him out?

for he is an epileptic and he suffers terribly; for often he falls into the fire, and often into the water. 16 And I brought him to your disciples, and they could not heal him." 17 And Jesus answered, "O faithless and perverse generation, how long am I to be with you? How long am I to bear with you? Bring him here to me." 18 And Jesus rebuked him, and the demon came out of him, and the boy was cured instantly. 19 Then the disciples came to Jesus privately and said, "Why could we not cast it

---

(*Krankheit im N.T.*, pp. 42-44) argues that it is a type of hysteria. A similar description is found in Lucian (*Philopseudes* 16).

16. The **disciples**, like Gehazi in II Kings 4:31, **could not heal him.** This differs from most of the miracle stories in that the power of Jesus is contrasted with the helplessness of the disciples, who still have much to learn.

17. O faithless and perverse generation, a reminiscence of Deut. 32:5 (cf. Phil. 2:15).

18. The illness is ascribed to **the demon;** cf. general note on 8:2-17.

19-20. The evangelists include the story in order to teach that **faith** is the indispensable condition for healing (cf. on 9:22). As in 19:24, Jesus purposely uses hyperbole to bring out his point. Faith does not move physical mountains by magic, but its own proper triumphs are more marvelous than large-scale engineering. Steam shovels can

---

picture.[3] This particular case of pain is pathetic: the lad was epileptic, as all the symptoms show, and the father was torn between faith and doubt (see Mark 9:23-24). Could any contrast be sharper than this between the rapt theophany of the mountain and the woebegone suffering of the valley?

Here is life's true alternation. The vision fades and does not return unless the power and insight there gained are used for God's sake and man's sake in works of love. The story of the monk has agelong truth: he feared to leave his prayers lest he should miss the divine visitation, but could not deny the claims of the hungry to whom at that hour he was wont to give bread. So he fed the hungry, and returned to his cell to find Christ waiting—and to hear Christ say, "Hadst thou stayed, I must have fled."[4] The Transfiguration is an "end in itself," yet it is also given as goal and strength for life's compassionate energy. But the truth moves also in reverse direction: unless a man seeks the mount of prayer and is there renewed, his daily

labor will lack sense—and become nonsense. It will have no high occasion, no direction, no power; soon it will be the work of a blind man on a treadmill. It would be hard to know which is worse—a cause without work, thus becoming a selfish sentimentalism; or work without a cause, thus becoming a drudgery and bitterness. Our world is filled with both tragedies.

Would the healing have been a true gain unless it had carried the spirit of Christ? Would that wellspring of the spirit have continued to flow if Christ had denied the tragic human plea? The denunciation in vs. 17 may have come from some other setting, but we cannot doubt that Christ did feel that kind of grief. How much suffering comes from "man's inhumanity to man"![5] How much vision has never been geared to its human task! How much healing is fictitious healing because it carries no divine love and light! The Raphael canvas is the portrayal of Christ's work in its due proportion. It is guidance also for our true life in Christ.

19-22. *The Mighty Power of Faith.*—This passage is so important that it may even be the reason why the Gospelists relate the story of the epileptic. The teaching is cardinal, and never more strikingly uttered than in this setting and this language. What is faith? An ex-

[3] J. D. Passavant, *Raphael of Urbino* (New York: The Macmillan Co., 1872), pp. 282-83. Beneath the hill are depicted a father and his demoniac boy. The disciples, unable to heal, point upward to the Master. Also see Cynthia Pearl Maus, *Christ and the Fine Arts* (New York: Harper & Bros., 1938), p. 251.

[4] Henry Wadsworth Longfellow, *Tales of a Wayside Inn:* "The Theologian's Tale."

[5] Robert Burns, "Man Was Made to Mourn," st. vii.

20 And Jesus said unto them, Because of your unbelief: for verily I say unto you, If ye have faith as a grain of mustard seed, ye shall say unto this mountain, Remove hence to yonder place; and it shall remove: and nothing shall be impossible unto you.

21 Howbeit this kind goeth not out but by prayer and fasting.

22 ¶ And while they abode in Galilee, Jesus said unto them, The Son of man shall be betrayed into the hands of men:

out?" 20 He said to them, "Because of your little faith. For truly, I say to you, if you have faith as a grain of mustard seed, you will say to this mountain, 'Move hence to yonder place,' and it will move; and nothing will be impossible to you."*z*

22 As they were gathering*a* in Galilee, Jesus said to them, "The Son of man is to

z Some ancient authorities insert verse 21, "*But this kind never comes out except by prayer and fasting.*"
a Some ancient authorities read *abode.*

move mountains, but they cannot do the works of faith. Matthew has inserted the saying from Q (it is found also in Luke 17:6); but there is a similar saying in Mark 11:22-23 (=Matt. 21:21). The reading of the Alexandrian and Caesarean MSS, **little faith** (RSV), is what Matthew wrote, not **unbelief** (KJV).

21. This verse, which is omitted by Sinaiticus (א), Vaticanus (B), 33, and some of the older versions, was not originally part of the text. It furnishes an interesting example of the growth of tradition. The original reading of Mark 9:29 was: "And he said to them, 'This kind cannot be driven out by anything but prayer.'" We may, however, ask whether Mark originally contained this verse, since Matthew and Luke do not reproduce it, and since it introduces an alien note, the moral of the story being faith rather than prayer. The later MSS of Mark add the words "and fasting," because early Christians believed that this practice brought many spiritual benefits (cf. Did. 7:4). It was this later form of the Marcan verse which was added to Matthew.

H. Second Prediction of Suffering (17:22-23)

22-23. The three predictions of the Passion (this passage, 16:21, and 20:17-19) come in like solemn strokes of a great bell, warning of the impending doom. The second and

pectancy of the soul, a thrust into the future, an innate trust in God. Faith is mixed with our human clay, and is thus our birthright. It is quickened constantly by God's signs—in the surprise and the steadiness of nature, in the friendship of fellow human beings, in secret experience, and supremely in Jesus Christ. Much happens to provide odds for faith, but more happens to encourage it. Yet we ourselves must nurture faith: it lives, not despite us, but by the alliance of our will. Just as reverence can be cherished like a flowering plant, so faith can be encouraged within us or killed. Cynicism is the sign of faith done to death. Cynicism, not doubt, is faith's opposite. Doubt is inverted faith, but cynicism is the decay of slain faith.

Jesus tells us that even a small faith (notice that **mustard seed** is once more the symbol of the small) has mighty power. **This mountain** is not to be taken literally (see Exeg.). Faith capriciously moving land and sea and stars would not be faith: it would be wantonness and chaos. Yet the mountains that faith can move are higher and harder to move than The Himalaya. Faith *has* removed mountains—mighty empires, pagan cults, entrenched wickedness. Faith would today remove how many mountains of

greed, how much of the blood-soaked habit of war, if we would expect great things of God and venture on the expectation! Faith is a gift, quickened by God and nourished by man, validated in the incarnation of Jesus, and proved in the venture.

Faith is not given for evil works: by them it would bring its own ruin. Its proper habitat is good works, as in this story. Farming is by faith in the seasons. A better illustration, since farming depends upon long-proved fidelities in nature, is a rightful business venture or some healing quest in modern medicine. The redemption of the world is by our deeper expectancy, our trust in God. Notice that vs. 21 is not found in the earliest manuscripts. But it is interesting, as a later addition to the record, because it discloses the mind and experience of the early church. The need for faith is the central teaching of this passage. But the followers of Christ had found that prayer is the food of faith, and that the discipline of fasting—rightly used—gives vigor to the soul.

22-23. *The Second Prediction of the Passion.* —There are three such predictions. They break in like "the solemn strokes of a great bell." (See Exeg.) Doubtless Jesus frequently re-

23 And they shall kill him, and the third day he shall be raised again. And they were exceeding sorry.

24 ¶ And when they were come to Capernaum, they that received tribute *money* came to Peter, and said, Doth not your master pay tribute?

be delivered into the hands of men, 23 and they will kill him, and he will be raised on the third day." And they were greatly distressed.

24 When they came to Ca-per'na-um, the collectors of the half-shekel tax went up to Peter and said, "Does not your teacher

---

third sayings are probably rewritings of the first. Matthew omits the statement that the disciples did not understand (Mark 9:32).

J. An Example of Christian Freedom: The Temple Tax (17:24-27)

A poll tax of a half shekel for each Israelite is imposed by Exod. 30:11-16 for the support of worship (but in Neh. 10:32-33 the Jerusalemites agreed to make an annual offering of a third of a shekel apiece). According to the Mishnah, notice was given on the first of Adar, six weeks before Passover, that the half-shekel dues must be paid (Shekalim 1:1). On the fifteenth the tables of money-changers were set up in outlying districts, and on the twenty-fifth in the temple itself (Shekalim 1:3). The money was due from all free male Jews who had attained twenty years of age, with the possible exception of priests. After the fall of Jerusalem, the Romans continued to collect the tax for the support of the temple of Jupiter Capitolinus which they erected on the temple mount (Josephus *Jewish War* VII. 6. 6).

Since Jesus accepted the temple worship without question, he and his followers would scarcely have doubted their obligation to pay the tax. But at a later time, particularly when many Christians considered themselves free from the Jewish law, the question would arise. The story probably had its origin in Palestine or Syria. It claims to be a tradition going back to Peter, who has the power to make decisions (16:19), but it differs from most of Matthew's special material. The moral theology is that of Paul: the Christian, being a child of God (Rom. 8:14-17) is free from the law (Gal. 4:1-7, 21-31), but he must so use his freedom that he does not cause others to stumble (I Cor. 8:9–9:23). Such liberal ideas were no doubt current even among Christians of Jewish descent.

Johannes Weiss believed that the controversy had concerned payment of the tax to the temple of Jupiter. Klostermann points out that the story must have arisen before A.D. 70, when the tax was thought of as paid to God by his children, and not to the kings of the earth.

At the time when Matthew wrote, the story was still relevant for Christians. Since God is the true king of the earth, his children might easily think themselves free from any external authority, but it was necessary to remind them that they must give free and willing obedience to the state. Or perhaps, as Bacon says (*Studies in Matthew*, p. 229), the teaching is that Jewish Christians must remember that they are still subject to taxes imposed by the Romans on their nation.

24. The introductory phrase **when they came to Capernaum** is drawn from Mark 9:33. Taxes were probably collected there (9:9). The word translated **half-shekel tax**

---

peated the warning, and the Gospel repeats it (if we can trust the vague chronology) with artistic fitness. There is an item of difference here as compared with the first prediction: the disciples do not at this time take issue with Jesus, but they are greatly distressed (see Expos., 16:20-21).

24-27. Christian Freedom and the Temple Tax.—The story raises problems. The rule about the tax was clear (see Exeg.). We have

no reason to believe that Jesus refused to pay it. He held the temple in dear regard. His indignation in the cleansing of the temple is sufficient proof of that fact. When Peter, according to this record, was asked if Jesus paid the tax, the answer was simple and clear: "Yes." Then why is the issue raised? Apparently it dates from the early church. When Christians were driven out of the synagogue, their enemies would wonder if they could any longer be classified as

25 He saith, Yes. And when he was come into the house, Jesus prevented him, saying, What thinkest thou, Simon? of whom do the kings of the earth take custom or tribute? of their own children, or of strangers?

26 Peter saith unto him, Of strangers. Jesus saith unto him, Then are the children free.

27 Notwithstanding, lest we should offend them, go thou to the sea, and cast a hook, and take up the fish that first cometh up; and when thou hast opened his mouth, thou shalt find a piece of money: that take, and give unto them for me and thee.

pay the tax?" 25 He said, "Yes." And when he came home, Jesus spoke to him first, saying, "What do you think, Simon? From whom do kings of the earth take toll or tribute? From their sons or from others?" 26 And when he said, "From others," Jesus said to him, "Then the sons are free. 27 However, not to give offense to them, go to the sea and cast a hook, and take the first fish that comes up, and when you open its mouth you will find a shekel; take that and give it to them for me and for yourself."

and **tax** is δίδραχμα. The LXX equates the half shekel with the drachma, but Josephus (*Antiquities* III. 8. 2) reckons the shekel at four Attic drachmas; hence the tax is sometimes called the didrachma, as here (*Antiquities* XVIII. 9. 1). The drachma had the same value as the denarius (20:2). (For information about this tax, its origins and history, see article, "New Testament Times: I. The Greco-Roman World," above, p. 96.)

25. The answer is **yes**, probably because it was well known that Jesus had not disobeyed such laws.

26. That **the sons are free** is taught in Gal. 3:23-26; 4:1-7.

27. As we know from 18:5-7, Jesus taught that his disciples must not **give offense** (cf. on 11:6). A Christian must even forego his privileges as a free man rather than cause others to fall (I Cor. 8:9-13). Strack and Billerbeck quote a rabbinical parable as follows: "It is like a king of flesh and blood who came to a toll house. He said to his servants, 'Give toll to the collectors.' They answered him, 'Does not all the toll belong to you?' He said to them, 'All who pass by shall learn from me that they may not be exempt from the toll.'"

Some commentators have suggested that Jesus does not promise a miracle, but merely tells Peter to catch a fish and sell it to pay the tax. A single fish would hardly sell for such an amount, though a large catch might. The **piece of money** is a stater. In Antioch and Damascus this coin equaled four drachmas or a **shekel**; cf. B. H. Streeter, *The Four Gospels* (4th ed., London: Macmillan & Co., 1930), p. 504. (See G. A. Barrois's study of coins in Vol. I.)

loyal Jews, and therefore if they could be taxed; and the Christians themselves, knowing that in Christ they had a temple far holier than that built on the rock in Jerusalem, would also be loath to support temple worship. This story probably has echoes of that problem.

Notice that no miracle is alleged concerning the finding of the coin. Even so conservative a commentator as Dummelow admits the wide doubt.[6] *The Pulpit Commentary* hopefully tells of a watch found in a codfish![7] But nearly every modern commentator agrees that the writer of the story was not interested in any miracle or portent. The Gospel is manifestly concerned with the primacy of Peter and with

[6] *Commentary on the Holy Bible,* p. 685.
[7] Ed. H. D. M. Spence and Joseph S. Exell, *St. Matthew* (London: Kegan Paul, Trench, Trübner & Co., 1898), II, 181.

an answer to a knotty problem. Perhaps Jesus told Peter to work as a fisherman, and that he would then find the necessary coin; and the story was later embellished. The answer to the problem is in strikingly Christian spirit. Jesus and his followers are verily "sons" of the Father, and therefore could claim to be free from the tax. But if they did not pay it, their action would be misconstrued. They might even be accused of irreligion. Thus they might fail in love, and bring the kingdom into disrepute. So they should surrender their rights in order to fulfill their obligations of love. Let them pay the tax. This is the plea of the epistles in similar issues. When ought we to stand for a right, and when to surrender it? It is hard to know. But the Holy Spirit guided the early church. The guidance is splendidly reflected in this story.

18 At the same time came the disciples unto Jesus, saying, Who is the greatest in the kingdom of heaven?

18 At that time the disciples came to Jesus, saying, "Who is the greatest in

---

VIII. Fourth Discourse, Addressed to the Disciples. Community Problems (18:1–19:2)

The preceding narrative section (14:1–17:27) is Matthew's picture of the founding of the church and its liberation from the Pharisaic law. But it was not enough for Christians to have their liberty, for freedom could too easily degenerate into license and anarchy. The Christian was "not . . . without law toward God but under the law of Christ" (I Cor. 9:21). The problem was to keep unity and coherence in a community which contained Jews who were loyal to the O.T. and also an increasing number of Gentiles. The author of Luke-Acts believed that the most satisfactory basis of union was the "apostolic decree," which required Gentiles to observe certain food laws (Acts 15:23-29). On the contrary, his hero Paul had insisted on complete freedom from the law, though he did much to avoid unnecessary offense to his Jewish brothers. As Bacon points out (*Studies in Matthew*, pp. 407-11), the viewpoint of Mark and Matthew was very similar to that of Paul. Matthew, instead of declaring that Jesus had absolutely abolished the distinction of clean and unclean (as Mark did in 7:19), records his conviction that Peter had the power to make decisions on such matters. If disputes should arise in the church, he teaches that every effort should be made to conciliate the "weak" and keep them from sinning or deserting the fellowship (18:5-7), but the church has the right to make final decisions (18:15-20) and it should exercise this power in the spirit of Christ (18:21-35).

This explains why Matthew incorporates into his book a section dealing with the treatment of little ones. These little ones are not merely children but the "weaker brethren" who did not understand the implications of their faith and therefore might easily fall into sin on the one side or into self-righteous exclusiveness on the other. Actual children are not his primary interest, and he deals with them only in passing. In making up the section the evangelist draws on Mark 9:33-37, 42-48, and adds other materials from his sources and his own free composition. He omits Mark 9:38-41, the story of the strange exorcist, perhaps because it can be misunderstood as suggesting that membership in the Christian community is not very important. Mark 9:49 was obscure and the teaching of Mark 9:50*a* had already been given in Matt. 5:13. The principle of Mark 9:50*b* runs through the rest of his chapter.

A. The Importance of "Little Ones" (18:1-14)

1. The Childlike Spirit (18:1-4)

The source, Mark 9:33-37, is a composite section. Mark 9:33-35 teaches that lowly service is what makes one "first" in the kingdom; Mark 9:36-37 that to minister to a child, or indeed to any "little one," is to serve Christ himself. Matthew attempts to smooth this out and to combine it with the mysterious saying in Mark 10:15.

18:1. According to 5:19, **the greatest in the kingdom of heaven is one** who observes and teaches the least of the commandments; cf. also 11:11.

18:1-4. *The Child in the Midst.*—Notice from the Exeg. that "little ones" (vs. 6) has a wider meaning than children. The disciples discussed ambitiously who of them would be greatest in the kingdom of heaven. Chrysostom comments that we are worse: We covet the chief places in the kingdom of earth.[8] If you were asked who are the greatest people in

[8] *The Homilies of Saint John Chrysostom on the Gospel of St. Matthew*, pp. 788-90.

your town, to what kind of men and women would your mind turn? Money, prestige, learning, military conquest—in these realms men seek or acknowledge "greatness." We hardly dare even to contemplate, let alone follow, the dictum of Christ that childlikeness is the only greatness.

A child's personality is not a *tabula rasa*—a mere blank. Some children are fractious and selfish. Grade-school politics have often made

2 And Jesus called a little child unto him, and set him in the midst of them,

3 And said, Verily I say unto you, Except ye be converted, and become as little children, ye shall not enter into the kingdom of heaven.

4 Whosoever therefore shall humble himself as this little child, the same is greatest in the kingdom of heaven.

5 And whoso shall receive one such little child in my name receiveth me.

the kingdom of heaven?" 2 And calling to him a child, he put him in the midst of them, 3 and said, "Truly, I say to you, unless you turn and become like children, you will never enter the kingdom of heaven. 4 Whoever humbles himself like this child, he is the greatest in the kingdom of heaven.

5 "Whoever receives one such child in

---

3. The disciples must **turn**, i.e., change their dispositions and habits. The corresponding Hebrew verb (שׁוּב) is often used in the O.T. to denote thoroughgoing repentance. Rabbinical literature often uses children as examples of purity, and in John 3:3 Nicodemus is told that he must be born again (or "from above").

4. But Matthew thinks of humility as the characteristic note of childhood, probably because Mark 9:35 had spoken of humble service. The original saying (Mark 10:15) may, however, have referred to the wonder, receptiveness, and unsophistication of children.

2. RESPONSIBILITY FOR CHILDREN (18:5-6)

5. This saying may originally have taught that it is important to help little children. The rabbis likewise praised kindness to orphans and waifs. But the pagan world did not necessarily put the same valuation on children. An affectionate papyrus letter from an Egyptian laborer named Hilarion to his wife Alis, written at the beginning of the Christian era, advises her that when their child is born, she should rear it if it is a boy,

---

a Sebastian [9] (with more numerous arrows) of the boy who is "odd." That brand of childishness we are to outgrow: "When I became a man, I gave up childish ways" (I Cor. 13:11). Nevertheless what Jesus meant is still clear. A child is dependent and trusting—at least until adult unworthiness breaks the trust. A child is friendly and unconscious of rank or race: a king's child will play with the ragman's child, until adult prejudice spoils the friendship. A child is candid, as witness the Hans Christian Andersen story of the emperor's new clothes: the adults admired them, fulfilling the "conventions," until a little child said, "But he has nothing on!" [1] A child lives in a constant wonder, makes toys out of trash, and finds life a high romance. This Francis Thompson has penetratingly and beautifully said in his famous essay on Shelley: see section beginning, "Know you what it is to be a child?" Thus a child expects great things of life, and finds them. The faith that Jesus prized is instinct in a child.

But Jesus may also have had in mind a child's innocence. The selfishness above mentioned is not yet selfish, for conscience is not yet born.

[9] See Jacobus de Voragine, *The Golden Legend* (New York: Longmans, Green & Co., 1941), pp. 104 ff.

[1] "The Emperor's New Clothes."

How we long to return to that first purity! And how impossible it is, conscience now being broken, for us to return! The businessman going to the "old swimming hole" of his boyhood is intent on more than quickened memories: he longs for an innocence that he cannot recover. Yet there is a new innocence—on the far side of our sinning. Unless you turn means a rightabout-face and a conversion. The pardon of God can do what we cannot do of ourselves. We can once more become childlike. Then we are trusting. As sinful men who have received forgiveness, we depend now, not on our proved weakness, but on God's strength. Then we are candid and sincere: the world's struttings and evasions no longer claim us. Then we are expectant: have we not received a new beginning by God's grace? This childlikeness is greatest in the kingdom of heaven. There is no other greatness.

5-6. *Responsibility for Children.*—Dostoevski makes one of his characters in *The Idiot* say that if she were painting a picture of Christ, she would show Jesus musing—one hand resting on a child's bright head, his eyes gazing out with a far-off expression, "thought, great as the whole world, dwells in His eyes. His face is sorrowful." The child would be gazing up at him as only children gaze, "pondering as little chil-

6 But whoso shall offend one of these little ones which believe in me, it were better for him that a millstone were hanged about his neck, and *that* he were drowned in the depth of the sea.

7 ¶ Woe unto the world because of offenses! for it must needs be that offenses come; but woe to that man by whom the offense cometh!

my name receives me; **6** but whoever causes one of these little ones who believe in me to sin,[b] it would be better for him to have a great millstone fastened round his neck and to be drowned in the depth of the sea.

7 "Woe to the world for temptations to sin![c] For it is necessary that temptations come, but woe to the man by whom the

[b] Greek *causes . . . to stumble.*
[c] Greek *stumbling-blocks.*

but if it is a girl, she should allow it to die. Jesus' concern for children as persons and objects of God's love communicated itself to the early church, and has made a permanent difference in the attitudes of Christians. Here, as in 10:40-42 and 25:31-46, the saying is applied also to the least of Jesus' followers. To help them is to help him. **In my name** means "at my command" or "for my sake."

6. Montefiore (*Synoptic Gospels,* I, 222) points out that the rabbis regarded Jeroboam the son of Nebat as the greatest of sinners because he not only sinned himself but caused Israel to sin (I Kings 14:16). It is far better to suffer physical death than to cause spiritual harm to others. In this context the saying may refer to actions which, while harmless in themselves, cause disunity in the church. I Clem. 46:8 applies the saying in a similar way. The **great millstone** is the μύλος ὀνικός, one so large that an ass was employed to turn it.

3. Occasions of Sin Which May Harm "Little Ones" (18:7-9)

7. This verse is drawn from Q (cf. Luke 17:1). Jesus never explains why **it is necessary that temptations come.** He simply takes it for granted that, as the world is now constituted, they will occur (cf. on 6:13). Since he is too practical to speculate about the problem, he tells his followers that they must be sure that *they* do not lead others into temptation; cf. Cadbury, *Peril of Modernizing Jesus,* pp. 102-3. The word rendered **temptations** or **offenses** is σκάνδαλα, stumbling blocks; cf. on 11:6.

dren sometimes ponder." The picture is easy to imagine, so true is it to Christ. But suppose someone should hurt the child. What would Christ say? These verses tell what he would say. The ancient world, by and large, had little sense of responsibility toward children (see Exeg. and the reference to the letter of Hilarion). Though such teaching as this was not unknown in his time, Jesus gave it a new horizon and depth. He meant by the words **receives . . . in my name** much more than natural kindness. Children are God's children, and they are candidates for the new kingdom.

But Jesus intended also by **child** and **little ones** all those who are children in faith. This fact is clearly shown in **who believe in me.** Notice the suggestion in the Exeg. that this whole chapter is "edited" with an eye to possible schism and apostasy in the early church. The Pharisees by their self-righteous pride "caused" the ordinary folk "to stumble." Those Jews in the first century church who too easily discarded ancient religious practices caused their more cautious brethren to look askance at the new faith. Scandals of controversy or scan-

dals in conduct always tend to breed despair in recent converts to Christ.

The sin of causing others to sin: how little we face that heinousness! To many it hardly seems heinous. But Jesus said that such a sinner deserved to have a huge millstone (not the millstone turned by hand, but one so large that a horse or ass must be hitched to it to turn it) hung about his neck, and to be drowned in the depths of the sea— so that the body could never come to the surface to receive burial. The exclamation is the measure of Jesus' horror of the sin of causing weak neighbors to sin. He pursues the theme:

7-9. *The Sin of Causing Others to Sin.*—What depth of pity is in Jesus' woe to the world! A seismograph registers distant earth tremors, but is a poor parable of the love in Jesus which registers every temptation to sin and the accompanying woe. He does not speculate on the problem "Why are temptations allowed in God's world?" They necessarily come. Does Jesus mean that a forced goodness would not be good? That a man who automatically ticked out virtue would be, not virtuous, but only a

8 Wherefore if thy hand or thy foot offend thee, cut them off, and cast *them* from thee: it is better for thee to enter into life halt or maimed, rather than having two hands or two feet to be cast into everlasting fire.

9 And if thine eye offend thee, pluck it out, and cast *it* from thee: it is better for thee to enter into life with one eye, rather than having two eyes to be cast into hell fire.

10 Take heed that ye despise not one of these little ones; for I say unto you, That in heaven their angels do always behold the face of my Father which is in heaven.

temptation comes! 8 And if your hand or your foot causes you to sin, cut it off and throw it from you; it is better for you to enter life maimed or lame than with two hands or two feet to be thrown into the eternal fire. 9 And if your eye causes you to sin, pluck it out and throw it from you; it is better for you to enter life with one eye than with two eyes to be thrown into the hell[d] of fire.

10 "See that you do not despise one of these little ones; for I tell you that in heaven their angels always behold the face

[d] Greek *Gehenna*.

8-9. These verses do not deal with what scandalizes others, but with temptations to sin in one's own life. This is another place where Matthew repeats himself; cf. on 5:29-30, where a similar form of the saying is found.

4. God's Care for Little Ones (18:10)

10. **These little ones** are probably children, as in vs. 5. **Their angels** may be guardian angels; in Dan. 10:13, each nation has its angel; in Rev. 1:20, the seven churches are addressed through their seven angels; and in Acts 12:15, the disciples think that Rhoda has seen, not Peter, but his angel. Rabbinical Judaism also knows of guardian angels who have the form of those whom they protect. Back of this may lie the Iranian concept of fravashis or angelic counterparts who **always behold the face of** Ormazd **in heaven;** cf. Otto, *op. cit.,* pp. 180-81. The saying emphasizes the supreme value which God places on each of the little ones.

mechanism? That comradeship involves the risk of evil incitement? He gives no direct answer. (Note the Lord's Prayer: "Lead us not into temptation.") But he deals realistically with the temptation. **Temptations to sin** may be direct, through cynical scoffings at honesty, or persuasion to evil-doing, or flaunted fleshliness. On the other hand, the seduction may be indirect— by the living of a life, or the perpetuation of a twisted social order, that speaks for the devil more loudly than any words. Is there not a story that some youth pointed one day to a man and said, "There goes the leader of our local atheists' society." "But I thought he was an elder of the church," came the rejoinder. "He is!" The hypocrisy wrought more harm than avowed skepticism.

To enter life is why we are born into this adventure of earth. Often an amputation is performed to save a life. It is better to lose a leg than a life. Christ gives that wisdom a deeper turn. Would it not be better to lose an eye, hand, or foot rather than to lose the spirit's life, the very self? Actually it is not the eye that offends, but the desire and will behind the eye. "So the counsel is not literal?" someone asks. Perhaps not, but the discipline required

is therefore deeper and more sharp. Better the most cruel self-denial, even to the point of seeming mutilation, than the loss of true life. Better any loss than the loss of soul through the sin of causing others to sin (see Expos., 5:27-30).

10. *The Sin of Contempt.*—This verse reiterates the teaching of vs. 5, but with such new loveliness of phrase and thought that it claims separate exposition. Probably the main reference is to children, but the truth holds of all who are weak in social standing, in mental acumen, or in Christian development. **These little ones** is a phrase Jesus often used of his lowly and unpromising disciples. We need not shy away from the angelology of the verse. In Jesus' time people believed that each nation had its patron angel. In the Revelation of John each of the "seven churches" had its angel (Rev. 2:1, 8). Job had an angel (Job 33:23). So did Peter (Acts 12:15). Sometimes this doctrine insisted that the angel was the pure counterpart of the guarded man on earth. Jesus speaks in the language of this prevalent belief of his day. Why should the belief be false? It would be egregious conceit on our part to suppose that God can have no orders of personal life better

11 For the Son of man is come to save that which was lost.

12 How think ye? if a man have a hundred sheep, and one of them be gone astray, doth he not leave the ninety and nine, and goeth into the mountains, and seeketh that which is gone astray?

of my Father who is in heaven.*e* 12 What do you think? If a man has a hundred sheep, and one of them has gone astray, does he not leave the ninety-nine on the hills and go in search of the one that went astray?

e Other ancient authorities add verse 11, *For the Son of man came to save the lost.*

---

5. Parable of the Lost Sheep (18:11-14)

Q is no doubt the source of the parable. Streeter (*Four Gospels,* pp. 243-45) is wrong in assigning it to M, for all the peculiar features in it can be accounted for by Matthew's usual editorial methods; cf. G. D. Kilpatrick, *The Origins of the Gospel According to St. Matthew* (Oxford: Clarendon Press, 1946), pp. 28-29.

Jesus may have spoken the parable to encourage outcasts who needed penitence and forgiveness, or more likely to explain why he forsook the "righteous" in order to minister to those who needed him most. The setting given in Luke 15:1-2 is significant. The same explanation fits the other parables in Luke 15 and also 22:1-14 (cf. notes on that passage). The original conclusion is probably Luke 15:7 and not Matt. 18:14. Although Judaism put more emphasis on the salvation of the nation than of the individual, the rabbis showed this same concern for the individual soul, and there is a beautiful story of how Moses brought back an erring individual (B. T. D. Smith, *Parables of the Synoptic Gospels,* pp. 187-91; cf. also on 9:12). The difference at this point between Jesus and the choicest spirits of Judaism lies in Jesus' emphasis upon God's active initiative in saving men.

Although Matthew finds it necessary to provide for excommunication, it is very significant that he hedges that harsh teaching about with this parable and with vss. 21-35. One is reminded of the remark of Hillel in Aboth 1:12, "Be of the disciples of Aaron, loving peace and pursuing peace, loving human beings and bringing them near the law."

11. This verse is not found in the best ancient MSS. It appears, however, in D Θ, and in certain MSS of the O.L. and Syriac.

---

than our blundering humanity. Surely Milton was right:

> Thousands at his bidding speed,
> And post o'er Land and Ocean without rest;
> They also serve who only stand and wait.[2]

No words could more strongly convey the Christian truth regarding the preciousness of personality. Every child, every seemingly drab neighbor, has his angel—bright counterpart of the soul which is closed in by a "muddy vesture of decay." [3] The angel is an "angel of the Presence," a confidant given constant access to the face of the King. The King is Father, and each little one is born in the wonder of his eternal life. These facts we recognize in crisis: in case of an accident a city's traffic would be stopped to save one child. But all too rarely do we remember in the routine day. For then children "get in the way," or they are the "nuisance" that limits adult pleasures. Then we despise them by neglect, by failing them in Christian nurture, and by a civilization cruel

and cankered in its adult pride. If only we knew, the child could save us. Why then despise him? "Of such is the kingdom." Dannecker, the German sculptor, trusted a child's verdict. When the child said of his statue of Christ, "He was a great man," he changed the statue until the child said, "That was the Christ who said, 'Suffer the little children to come unto me.' " [4] He loves us, his grown children, and can save us from this sin of contempt.

12-14. *Parable of the Lost Sheep.*—It seems likely that the story had a context such as Luke 15:3-7 gives it. But Matthew's context has striking features. He is concerned about church discipline, and feels obliged to show the occasional need for excommunication (see vss. 15-20). But the discussion of excommunication has, on the one side, this tender story of the Shepherd's love; and, on the other side, the parable of the unforgiving servant. Thus the rigorism is held in deep compassion—a fact characteristic of this Gospel.

Notice the portrait of the man gone astray. Perhaps the guilty seductions of the world have

[2] "On His Blindness."
[3] Shakespeare, *Merchant of Venice,* Act V, scene 1.

[4] Quoted, *Great Texts of the Bible,* Vol. on *Mark,* p. 235.

13 And if so be that he find it, verily I say unto you, he rejoiceth more of that *sheep,* than of the ninety and nine which went not astray.

14 Even so it is not the will of your Father which is in heaven, that one of these little ones should perish.

15 ¶ Moreover if thy brother shall trespass against thee, go and tell him his fault between thee and him alone: if he shall hear thee, thou hast gained thy brother.

13 And if he finds it, truly, I say to you, he rejoices over it more than over the ninety-nine that never went astray. 14 So it is not the will of my*f* Father who is in heaven that one of these little ones should perish.

15 "If your brother sins against you, go and tell him his fault, between you and him alone. If he listens to you, you have

f Some ancient authorities read *your.*

---

13. Easton remarks: "The shepherd might feel normal contentment in the possession of his flock and he naturally would have been better satisfied if none of the sheep had wandered, but he could experience *joy* only through such an event as this" (*The Gospel According to St. Luke* [New York: Charles Scribner's Sons, 1926], p. 234).

B. Procedure When a "Little One" Sins (18:15-35)

This entire section is Matthew's expansion of the short Q saying found in Luke 17:3-4.

1. A Rule for Church Discipline (18:15-17)

15. If your brother sins against you makes excellent sense here, in view of vss. 21-35, but the words "against you" are omitted by Sinaiticus (א), Vaticanus (B), and a few other good authorities. The church for which Matthew wrote must have applied the principle also to sins against God and the community. This rule is not unknown in rabbinical Judaism, but from the second century on, as Strack and Billerbeck show, Jews were not inclined to rebuke their brothers personally because they were afraid of transgressing the principle which Jesus formulates in 7:1-5 ("mote and beam").

---

enticed him. Perhaps he himself is wayward or headstrong. He has left the flock: his life has no bond with his fellow men in love and high purpose. He has left the Shepherd: his life has no bond with God. A man's life loses both nurture and meaning when it is thus lost, but the man himself is still precious in Christ's eyes. A soul is earth's ultimate worth. No journey or pain is too great if it promises to restore such a one to the flock. The interpretation which suggests that humanity is the lost sheep, and that the angels are the ninety and nine, has its own poignant truth; but it misses the main verity, namely, that every individual sinful man is dear to the Shepherd's love. Here we are told, not only that "God so loved the world" (John 3:16) but that God so loved each erring child of man.

Notice the portrait of the Shepherd. The lines are few, as in a Japanese picture, but every line is eloquent. The Shepherd is not careless of **the ninety and nine,** for he leaves them **on the hills,** where clouds and dew keep the grass thick and green. But he yearns over the lost sheep, and is careless of himself. What unfulfilled longings pain him! **If so be that he find it** means that he may be thwarted by hu-

man perversity. What pains he endures! He may be overcome at last—on Calvary!—by those who ravage the flock. That God in Christ does thus seek us needs no argument. Conscience is not a word shouted to a mass, but a whisper spoken to the individual **gone astray.** Compassion is not a general plea, but a Friend pleading with a friend. The challenge of Christ is not indiscriminate: he seeks out you and me. When we are "found" again, the Shepherd asks our help in the quest: notice the change from **my Father** in vs. 10 to **your Father** in vs. 14. The word "joy" is like a sunstart. **Heaven** watches each of us. The major concern is whether we are fulfilling our life of love in the flock, and whether we remain in the Shepherd's wisdom. **Heaven** knows when we stray, and grieves. **Heaven** knows when we are found, and rejoices; for then the journey is not in vain, the pain is forgotten, the lost is restored. Surely the Gospel would be incomplete without this story.

15-18. *Discipline in the Church.*—Did Jesus speak thus of the church, the local Christian congregation, while as yet there was no church? Would he, could he have said, **Let him be to you as a Gentile and a tax collector?** Such words certainly do not accord with his other

16 But if he will not hear *thee, then* take with thee one or two more, that in the mouth of two or three witnesses every word may be established.

17 And if he shall neglect to hear them, tell *it* unto the church: but if he neglect to hear the church, let him be unto thee as a heathen man and a publican.

18 Verily I say unto you, Whatsoever ye shall bind on earth shall be bound in heaven; and whatsoever ye shall loose on earth shall be loosed in heaven.

gained your brother. 16 But if he does not listen, take one or two others along with you, that every word may be confirmed by the evidence of two or three witnesses. 17 If he refuses to listen to them, tell it to the church; and if he refuses to listen even to the church, let him be to you as a Gentile and a tax collector. 18 Truly, I say to you, whatever you bind on earth shall be bound in heaven, and whatever you loose on earth

16. The rule of **two or three witnesses** is quoted from Deut. 19:15. A rabbinical application of it can be seen in the Mishnah (Sotah 1:1-2).

17. Paul had already employed the principle of excommunication on the basis of such testimony (I Cor. 5:3-5, 9-13; II Cor. 13:1-3), and by now it must have been a regular rule in many Christian churches, as the story of Ananias and Sapphira indicates (Acts 5:1-11). This is one of the two passages in the Gospels where the word **church** is used, and here it denotes the local congregation (cf. on 16:18). The expelled member is to be regarded **as a Gentile and a tax collector:** this is a clear indication that the maxim owes its origin to the later church, and not to Jesus; one has only to ask how he treated such people (8:11-12; 21:31-32) to see that this is true. It is also clear that as yet in the average congregation there is no official who wields full disciplinary power.

2. THE CHURCH'S SPIRITUAL POWER (18:18-20)

Matthew now reinforces the teaching just given by bringing in two bits of tradition to prove that the church has Christ's power. The first (vs. 18), which is found in a variant form in 16:19, seeks to show that Jesus committed to the congregations the general power of judgment. The second (vss. 19-20) must originally have had to do with prayer, but is now used to indicate that Christ is spiritually present at congregational meetings and ratifies their decisions.

18. Cf. on 16:19. The promise is now made, not to Peter alone, but to Christians assembled together. The figures **bind** and **loose** originally referred to decisions as to what is "forbidden" and "permitted," but Matthew here connects them with absolution and condemnation. The author of the Fourth Gospel believed that the risen Christ had given the disciples such power when he committed the Holy Spirit to them (John 20:23). Certainly by the end of the first century the church exercised this prerogative; cf. also 9:8.

teaching or with his own acts: he healed Gentiles, and went to the home of Zacchaeus the tax collector. Rather than attempt impossible "reconciliations," it is better to assume that these verses—however they may in many ways reflect Christ's teaching—are not a transcript of his very words, but a reflection of the thought and practice of the early church. Nevertheless they hold Christian meaning for our time. Robert Louis Stevenson has written of our quarrels, "With a little more patience and a little less temper, a gentler and wiser method might be found in almost every case." [5] Here Christian patience is described in gentleness and wisdom. A friend is to go to the offender,

[5] *Across the Plains with Other Memories and Essays* (New York: Charles Scribner's Sons, 1892), p. 314.

thus making the first advance. He is to point out the fault, but privately and in lowly friendship. His purpose is not to humiliate or condemn, but to gain a **brother**—to gain him for friendship and for the church of Christ. Even if the private plea fails, the culprit is not to be branded publicly; but two or three men, chosen for Christian grace, are to be told of the failure, in order that their urgings may be added. Only if they fail is the whole congregation to know, and even then they must not thrust the sinner from their comradeship except in his continued obduracy. We gain thus a glimpse into the problems of the early church. There were, even then, careless and wayward members; and sometimes there was open scandal. The epistles confirm this picture: there was gluttony at the very

19 Again I say unto you, That if two of you shall agree on earth as touching any thing that they shall ask, it shall be done for them of my Father which is in heaven.

20 For where two or three are gathered together in my name, there am I in the midst of them.

shall be loosed in heaven. 19 Again I say to you, if two of you agree on earth about anything they ask, it will be done for them by my Father in heaven. 20 For where two or three are gathered in my name, there am I in the midst of them."

---

19. John 14:13-14 makes a similar promise; but John (15:7) is careful to show that if the promise is to be effective, the disciples must be spiritually united with Jesus and must keep his words.

20. The Mishnah (Aboth 3:2) contains a similar saying: "If two sit together and there are no words of the Torah between them, this is the seat of the scornful, as it is written, 'Nor sitteth in the seat of the scornful' [Ps. 1:1]; but if two sit together and there are words of the Torah between them, the Shekinah [i.e., the presence of God] rests between them, as it is written, 'Those who feared the Lord spoke with one another' [Mal. 3:16]." Thus we see that an ancient Jewish teaching about the presence of God is recast to refer to the presence of Christ. In I Cor. 5:4, Paul claims that Jesus' power has been present with him when he excommunicated the sinner, and Acts 15:28 can be translated "resolved by the Holy Spirit and ourselves"; see Kirsopp Lake and H. J. Cadbury, *The Beginnings of Christianity*, Part I, Vol. IV (London: Macmillan & Co., 1933), p. 180. A still later development of the idea is found in *Oxyrhynchus Papyri* 1. 10, in M. R. James, *Apocryphal N.T.* p. 27.

---

sacrament of the Lord's Supper (I Cor. 11:21-22). Christ then, as now, could use a weak and unworthy instrument. The promise of vs. 18 has been fulfilled; the church has sometimes been able to determine wisely what interpretations and practices should be forbidden (**bound**) and what should be sanctioned (**loosed**). But the early church was not always as gentle in discipline as our Gospel here proposes. It sometimes acted with cruel rigor. The church in later generations has repeated the blunder. In some ages there have been wholesale excommunications. The curse and penalty discussed in I Cor. 5:5 are no gentleness, and they have carried far beyond Paul's time. But Matthew has combined in his injunction a Christian patience and a great yearning for the unity of the church.

19-20. Christ in the Midst.—Did vs. 20 come originally from a setting of prayer? Or is it a claim, and an experience, that the present Christ ratifies the decisions and authority of the church? The claim is undoubtedly made in the N.T., as witness Acts 15:28, where the decision of the Jerusalem council is apparently identified as the work of the Holy Spirit. In our time vs. 20 is more regarded as a true and well-loved expression of a prime spiritual fact: that the real presence of Christ dwells with and empowers faithful corporate prayer and love. This passage casts no shadow on the need and the radiance of private prayer. Our life comes to individual focus, and secret prayer (with the "door shut") is an inalienable requirement

and resource. But our nature is also inescapably social, so that private prayer without corporate prayer would wither like a leaf without its tree. Christ came to create, not a plurality of anchorites, but "The Beloved Community." Ultimately we can no more pray alone all the time than we can live alone; and besides, corporate prayer has peculiar light and joy.

The conditions that invite Christ are clear. **In my name**—in my nature, for my sake—shows the required sincerity of motive. **Gathered together** points to the necessary accord. Perhaps vs. 19 indicates the dominance of intercession, for some exegetes believe that it is a reference to the prayer of penance and absolution that was practiced in the early church. If there is a link between vss. 18-20 and vss. 15-17, we must draw the deduction that Christ is in the midst when the church intercedes in prayer for the offender. The Mishnah said that the Shekinah, the glory of God's presence, is found when two agree in meditation on the sacred law (see Exeg.). Thus the Christians gave new form to an ancient truth, for they had found God in Jesus Christ. **Two or three** is a general phrase, not necessarily limited to describe a handful of disciples: the words mean "more than one." Yet the tiny congregations in the midst of a pagan world in the first century must have found great cheer in the phrase. The church does not depend on numbers. **Two or three,** met with Christ, are not merely *added:* they multiply each other's faith, and are multiplied in power by him who is **in the midst.**

21 ¶ Then came Peter to him, and said, Lord, how oft shall my brother sin against me, and I forgive him? till seven times?

22 Jesus saith unto him, I say not unto thee, Until seven times: but, Until seventy times seven.

21 Then Peter came up and said to him, "Lord, how often shall my brother sin against me, and I forgive him? As many as seven times?" 22 Jesus said to him, "I do not say to you seven times, but seventy times seven.ᵍ

ᵍ Or *seventy-seven times.*

---

3. The Principle for the Exercise of the Church's Power
(18:21-35)
a) Patient, Repeated Forgiveness (18:21-22)

21-22. Luke 17:4 may be closer to the Q form of the saying. Matthew uses it to introduce his great parable and probably rewrites it, using Peter as the interlocutor, to indicate that the greatest of the apostles guarantees the teaching. Because the "seven times" of Q might be understood as a limitation on forgiveness, he increases the number to an indefinitely large one, so that the church may clearly understand that the backslider must be forgiven as often as necessary. On the other hand, the more extravagant phrasing is undoubtedly true to Jesus' mind, and may well be authentic. Goodspeed argues that the Greek numeral must be translated "seventy-seven times"; cf. his *Problems of New Testament Translation* (Chicago: University of Chicago Press, 1945), pp. 29-31. But RSV, like the earlier English versions, renders it **seventy times seven.** The meaning of the saying is in any case the same.

21-22. *The Limits of Forgiveness.*—Note that the Exeg. links these verses with those that precede. **Seventy times seven** is four hundred and ninety: we can "do it in our heads." But this is celestial arithmetic: we must "do it in our hearts." Jesus meant "seventy times seven times seven times seven"—to infinity. It is a problem in conduct rather than in arithmetic. Trivial offenses we quickly forgive: "Oh, don't mention it," words that could not imply any real forgiveness. But what of malicious slander? Or treachery where friendship was pledged? The rabbis said that three pardons were enough. Peter proposed magnanimity, and so suggested seven. How satisfying to use a stick on the offender after the seventh offense! But Jesus insisted that there must be no limits to forgiveness. The dictionary says that forgiveness means "to give up resentment or claim to requital." But *is* this true pardon? To forgive but not forget usually means not to forgive. Only to forgo resentment is a poor half forgiveness. Luke 17:5 tells us that when the disciples heard this requirement of Jesus for unlimited forgiveness, they exclaimed, "Increase our faith"! "Yes, but. . . ." How the "buts" gather! "Yes, but can we forgive if our enemy does not repent?" Jesus might answer, "Can your enemy repent unless you or someone is willing to forgive?" While Joan of Arc fought, the English chaplain did not repent; but when she forgave and suffered martyrdom, he was brought to repentance.[6] The Scottish clan feuds were from generation to generation, until someone was willing to break the vicious circle. Jesus on his cross prayed that his enemies might be forgiven, and forgave them while they were still intent on his death. "Yes, but is there not need to uphold the law?" What law? The law of Moses with its tit for tat? To apprehend a man under the law may be a necessary step, but it does not absolve society (and especially Christian society) from the duty of forgiveness.

> Though justice be thy plea, consider this,
> That in the course of justice, none of us
> Should see salvation: we do pray for mercy;
> And that same prayer doth teach us all to render
> The deeds of mercy.[7]

"Yes, but would it work?" That question implies that we ourselves are blameless, and we are not. The pragmatic test is dangerous: it is foreshortened in time, depends too much on human appraisals, is too materialistically construed. But—would we like forgiveness to work *for us?* Has any other rule worked? Has anger, or the rule of reprisal and revenge, worked? Revenge is not sweet, despite the proverb. It is worse than a futility: it is black poison.

But Jesus' way has "worked," though at cost of a Cross. When Thomas Arnold was headmaster of Rugby School in England, the boys used to say that it was "a shame to tell him a lie—he always believes one." [8] Why do we think

[6] George Bernard Shaw, *Saint Joan*, scene 6.

[7] Shakespeare, *Merchant of Venice*, Act IV, scene 1.
[8] *Arnold of Rugby*, ed. J. J. Findlay (Cambridge: University Press, 1897), p. 59.

23 ¶ Therefore is the kingdom of heaven likened unto a certain king, which would take account of his servants.

24 And when he had begun to reckon, one was brought unto him, which owed him ten thousand talents.

25 But forasmuch as he had not to pay, his lord commanded him to be sold, and his wife, and children, and all that he had, and payment to be made.

26 The servant therefore fell down, and worshipped him, saying, Lord, have patience with me, and I will pay thee all.

23 "Therefore the kingdom of heaven may be compared to a king who wished to settle accounts with his servants. 24 When he began the reckoning, one was brought to him who owed him ten thousand talents;[h] 25 and as he could not pay, his lord ordered him to be sold, with his wife and children and all that he had, and payment to be made. 26 So the servant fell on his knees, imploring him, 'Lord, have patience with me, and I will pay you everything.'

[h] This talent was probably worth about a thousand dollars.

b) Parable of the Unforgiving Slave (18:23-35)

The parable illustrates the principle of the Lord's Prayer (6:12, 14-15), and enshrines one of the most important of all Christ's teachings. It is a very striking story and entirely accords with what we know of his attitude. God freely forgives men, even the outcasts and sinners, and man can have no more important privilege than to mediate to others the forgiveness which he himself experiences. The mighty power vouchsafed to man to forgive sins in God's name (see on 9:2-8) must be exercised. He who forgives is dealt with on the basis of mercy, but he who fails to forgive has no right to expect anything more than strict judgment on his own sins.

The special source M may have contained the parable; see Intro., p. 239, and Kilpatrick, *Origins of Matthew*, p. 35. Matthew perhaps edited it here and there, for vss. 23 and 35 show marks of his style—e.g., "my heavenly Father." For Matthew's use of the parable in this context, see general note on 18:1–19:2.

23. A king is frequently the chief protagonist in rabbinical parables, and he usually stands as a symbol for God. These servants (literally "slaves") must be great satraps, since the debt is so huge: cf. B. T. D. Smith, *Parables of the Synoptic Gospels*, pp. 217-20.

24. The value of ten thousand talents has been variously estimated. The margin of RSV reckons a talent at about a thousand dollars, and this is sufficiently precise. The purchasing power of ten million dollars was much greater in antiquity than now.

25. The O.T. sometimes speaks of selling people into slavery to pay a debt, e.g., Amos 2:6; 8:6; Neh. 5:4-5.

the way of Jesus is weak, when other ways than his are so weak that they bring only disaster? Is a nation strong when it instantly springs to arms to "defend national honor"? A man thus touchy would be laughed out of court, and dueling is comic in its theatrical conceit. Forgiveness is not supine, but a beneficent invasion. It is alert and patient and creative. Nor should we forget what forgiveness accomplishes in the life of the forgiver. In the teaching of Jesus the pardon of God is always linked with man's willingness to pardon. "If ye forgive, . . . your heavenly Father will also forgive you" (6:14). John Morley, commenting on Gladstone's amazingly constructive handling of an extortioner, and on his readiness to forgive, wrote: "There was no worldly wisdom in it, we all know. But then what are people Christians for?"[9] What

[9] *The Life of William Ewart Gladstone* (London: Macmillan & Co., 1904), III, 419.

are people Christians for? That they may learn from Christ to forgive until seventy times seven.

23-35. *The Parable of the Unforgiving Slave.* —This story summarizes unforgettably the teachings that, in this Gospel, have preceded it. The author has "placed" it with consummate skill and artistry, born of the spirit of Christ. The debtor is the kind of man "by whom temptation comes." He despises "one of these little ones" (vs. 6). He has no concern for a sheep gone astray. He is himself forgiven "until seventy times seven" (vs. 22), but himself fails to forgive even once. Thus a whole range of teaching comes to succinct and dramatic verity. Only Luke has given us the parables of the good Samaritan and of the prodigal. Only Matthew has given us this parable. In its simplicity, its sharply etched truth, and its pleading of compassion, it is unsurpassed.

A parable has a central impact. It is not an

27 Then the lord of that servant was moved with compassion, and loosed him, and forgave him the debt.

28 But the same servant went out, and found one of his fellow servants, which owed him a hundred pence: and he laid hands on him, and took *him* by the throat, saying, Pay me that thou owest.

29 And his fellow servant fell down at his feet, and besought him, saying, Have patience with me, and I will pay thee all.

30 And he would not: but went and cast him into prison, till he should pay the debt.

31 So when his fellow servants saw what was done, they were very sorry, and came and told unto their lord all that was done.

32 Then his lord, after that he had called him, said unto him, O thou wicked servant, I forgave thee all that debt, because thou desiredst me:

33 Shouldest not thou also have had compassion on thy fellow servant, even as I had pity on thee?

27 And out of pity for him the lord of that servant released him and forgave him the debt. 28 But that same servant, as he went out, came upon one of his fellow servants who owed him a hundred denarii;[i] and seizing him by the throat he said, 'Pay what you owe.' 29 So his fellow servant fell down and besought him, 'Have patience with me, and I will pay you.' 30 He refused and went and put him in prison till he should pay the debt. 31 When his fellow servants saw what had taken place, they were greatly distressed, and they went and reported to their lord all that had taken place. 32 Then his lord summoned him and said to him, 'You wicked servant! I forgave you all that debt because you besought me; 33 and should not you have had mercy on your fellow servant, as I had mercy on you?'

[i] The denarius was worth about twenty cents.

27. **The debt,** literally "the loan." Apparently the king had lent him the money; the situation was not simply that the slave had failed to turn over the royal revenues. This does not, however, affect the point of the parable; there is no reference to any particular kind of sin or obligation to God.

28. **A hundred denarii** or twenty dollars would perhaps have purchased five or ten times as much in the ancient world as it does now. Jesus suggests that the offense which one man commits against another is trivial in comparison with the crime against God which God forgives so freely.

30. Adolf Deissmann (*Light from the Ancient East* [2nd ed.; New York: Doubleday, Doran & Co., 1927], p. 270) gives papyrus examples of men who put others in **prison** for **debt.**

allegory: no parable need be pressed in each detail. We need not seek the symbolism of **ten thousand** or **jailers.** The spear thrust of the story is in vs. 35. Who can escape that thrust? Consider the contrast between the **king** and the high-ranking **servant.** The satrap owed his king a huge sum.[1] The lowly slave owed the satrap only one six-hundred-thousandth part of the amount which the satrap owed the king. That is one contrast. The other contrast is more sharp: the king forgave the vast debt, though his debtor had asked only for time in which to pay; but the satrap, allowing no chance for repayment, promptly flung his debtor into jail. Has this contrast, like midday and midnight, any real verity as between God and us? Or is it deliberately overdrawn? It is not over-

drawn. We pray, "Forgive us our debts" (6:12). How many such debts have we incurred? How many in a single day? How far has our evil influence carried, in the lies we tell and the shuffling example we set? Surely the hymn has strict truth:

> Could my zeal no respite know,
> Could my tears forever flow,
> All for sin could not atone.[2]

The injuries we receive, the debt that others owe us, is one six-hundred-thousandth part of what we owe to God. Signally we fail to realize our own failure. Could we be unforgiving if we tried to calculate our own indebtedness?

There is no escape from the story's insistence that God's forgiveness and man's are linked. We

[1] For comparisons that show the enormity of the debt see Buttrick, *Parables of Jesus*, pp. 99-100.

[2] "Rock of Ages, cleft for me."

34 And his lord was wroth, and delivered him to the tormentors, till he should pay all that was due unto him.

35 So likewise shall my heavenly Father do also unto you, if ye from your hearts forgive not every one his brother their trespasses.

19 And it came to pass, *that* when Jesus had finished these sayings, he departed from Galilee, and came into the coasts of Judea beyond Jordan;

2 And great multitudes followed him; and he healed them there.

34 And in anger his lord delivered him to the jailers,*j* till he should pay all his debt. 35 So also my heavenly Father will do to every one of you, if you do not forgive your brother from your heart."

19 Now when Jesus had finished these sayings, he went away from Galilee and entered the region of Judea beyond the Jordan; 2 and large crowds followed him, and he healed them there.

j Greek *torturers.*

---

34. Parables are not allegories, and the **jailers** are not to be identified; they are simply characters in the story. The point is only that God's forgiveness is withheld until one forgives others. The severe penalties remind one of 24:50-51=Luke 12:46.

35. Kilpatrick (*Origins of Matthew,* p. 29) suggests that Matthew has built this verse out of Mark 11:25.

C. Summary (19:1-2)

This is the fourth of the summaries (cf. 7:28-29; 11:1; 13:53; 26:1) with which Matthew marks the conclusion of a major portion of his book. The usual formula is woven into his rewriting of Mark 10:1, which he now resumes.

19:1. The region of Judea beyond the Jordan might include Perea, which in Jesus' time was part of Antipas' tetrarchy, and some of the territory of the Decapolis. Mark 10:1 carefully distinguishes Judea and Perea, but Matthew uses the former term loosely, perhaps in accordance with geographical usage in his own time.

2. The evangelist wishes to indicate that Jesus' ministry was always the same: he not only taught the crowds, as in Mark 10:1, but also **healed them** (cf. 9:35).

---

have preached the divine mercy, but overlooked the human condition. God is always ready to forgive, but he cannot enter an unforgiving heart: the door is barred against him. God is not arbitrary: he does not demand a *quid pro quo.* It would perhaps be more accurate to say that he is helpless in love: he cannot forgive an unforgiving man, because to be unforgiving closes life against God. The Lord's Prayer makes clear that fact: "Forgive us our debts, as we forgive our debtors" (see Expos., 6:12). The harshness of the story's ending must not be hardened into a theology, but has its inescapable realism and truth. The anger of the king, the arrival of the jailers, the flinging of the satrap into prison, are indeed the righteousness of God; for God is Father, not indulgent Father. But these items of the story, seen from another angle, are the debtor's own dark folly whereby he jails himself. Shakespeare has written his exposition on this story:

> Earthly power doth then show likest God's
> When mercy seasons justice.[8]

[8] *Merchant of Venice,* Act IV, scene 1.

Many people complain that they cannot feel or do not know God's mercy. Do they themselves forgive?

19:1-9. *The Question of Divorce.*—Scholars agree that Matthew's story here gathers urgency as with quickened pace it moves toward the climax of Calvary. We come now to the "chapter" and period of judgment. In this more intense mood Matthew presents the teaching of Jesus on certain great issues—divorce, celibacy, children, money, and the rewards of discipleship. That age favored easy divorce. So does our own. Hence it is doubly important to know the mind of Christ.

The Pharisees tempted him. Herod, in whose realm Jesus was journeying, had divorced his wife to marry Herodias. Besides, Jewish opinion on the subject of divorce was sharply divided. The Essenes advocated and practiced celibacy. The school of Hillel believed that a man could divorce his wife if she found "disfavor" in his eyes. The more stringent thinking of Shammai and his followers interpreted "disfavor" to mean only the disfavor caused by her "adultery." All groups agreed that the male was dominant. The common practice allowed a man to give his

3 ¶ The Pharisees also came unto him, tempting him, and saying unto him, Is it lawful for a man to put away his wife for every cause?

4 And he answered and said unto them, Have ye not read, that he which made

3 And Pharisees came up to him and tested him by asking, "Is it lawful to divorce one's wife for any cause?" 4 He answered,

---

IX. Resumption of the Narrative: Jesus Goes to Jerusalem
(19:3–23:39)

Bacon (*Studies in Matthew,* pp. 308-25) gives the title "Concerning the Judgment" to this narrative section and the accompanying discourse (24:1–26:1). It is no doubt true that Matthew, like the other evangelists, sees Jesus as "coming to judgment" in Jerusalem (John 9:39; 12:35-50); and these chapters lead up to a powerful climax. At the same time, the framework of the narrative is furnished by Mark, and some of the sections have nothing particularly to do with God's judgment or that of Jesus (e.g., 19:13-15).

A. Demands on Jesus' Followers and Their Reward (19:3–20:28)

Discipleship—its requirements and its reward—is the common theme running through this part of the book. Teachings on this subject have already appeared in 8:19-22 and 10:5-42. But here discipleship is especially emphasized, and the reason is to be found in the structure of Mark. Nearly everything in that Gospel from Mark 8:27 on has to do with Jesus' journey to Jerusalem and the duty of following him in the way of the Cross. But why is discipleship treated in just this way, and why particularly is the blessing of children included?

The explanation may possibly be connected with the teaching methods of the early church. Several of the N.T. epistles contain catechetical sections on the duties of various groups of church members. Thus Col. 3:18–4:1 treats successively of wives, husbands, children, fathers, slaves, and masters; and I Timothy has instructions for men, women, bishops, deacons, and deacons' wives (I Tim. 2:8–3:13), older and younger men and women, widows, presbyters, and slaves (I Tim. 5:1–6:2). Other examples can be found in Eph. 5:22–6:9; Tit. 1:5-9; 2:2-10; I Pet. 2:13-18; 3:1-7; 5:1-5. By the time Mark was written a simple catechism, based on Jesus' sayings, may already have existed. This would have dealt with married people (Mark 10:1-12=Matt. 19:1-9), children (Mark 10:13-16=Matt. 19:13-15), rich men (Mark 10:17-27=Matt. 19:16-26) and church leaders (Mark 10:28-30, 35-45=Matt. 19:27-29; 20:20-28).

1. Marriage (19:3-12)

a) The Divorce Rule (19:3-9)

Matthew has already discussed divorce in 5:31-32; cf. notes on that passage. He draws this section from Mark 10:2-12, which consists of two parts: (*a*) Mark 10:2-9, a little "paradigm" or "pronouncement story," which culminates in the saying, "Therefore what God has yoked together, let not man separate"; and (*b*) Mark 10:11-12, a sayings group from a separate source, which resembles the Q logion in Luke 16:18. Mark links the two together with vs. 10. Matthew, wishing to construct a smoother story, transposes the substance of Mark 10:3-5 to follow Mark 10:9, and makes other changes to accord with his own point of view.

3. Matthew writes for Christians who probably know that the rabbinical schools of Hillel and Shammai debate the legal grounds for divorce (cf. on 5:31); hence he adds the phrase **for any cause.**

4-6. Almost the same argument is given in the "Fragments of a Zadokite Work" 7:1-3: "The builders of the wall [the Pharisees?] are caught by fornication in taking two wives during their lifetime. But the fundamental principle of the creation is 'Male and

them at the beginning made them male and female,

5 And said, For this cause shall a man leave father and mother, and shall cleave to his wife: and they twain shall be one flesh?

6 Wherefore they are no more twain, but one flesh. What therefore God hath joined together, let not man put asunder.

7 They say unto him, Why did Moses then command to give a writing of divorcement, and to put her away?

8 He saith unto them, Moses because of the hardness of your hearts suffered you to put away your wives: but from the beginning it was not so.

"Have you not read that he who made them from the beginning made them male and female, 5 and said, 'For this reason a man shall leave his father and mother and be joined to his wife, and the two shall become one'?[k] 6 So they are no longer two but one.[k] What therefore God has joined together, let not man put asunder." 7 They said to him, "Why then did Moses command one to give a certificate of divorce, and to put her away?" 8 He said to them, "For your hardness of heart Moses allowed you to divorce your wives, but from the

[k] Greek *one flesh.*

Female created He them.' And they who went into the Ark, 'Two and two went into the Ark.' " (R. H. Charles, *Apocrypha and Pseudepigrapha of the Old Testament* [Oxford: Clarendon Press, 1913], II, 810.) Like the principle in Luke 16:18, this teaching, if taken by itself, would seem to rule out divorce entirely. In any case, Jesus goes beyond the Pharisees in emphasizing the permanence of marriage. God's purpose is a stable family life, and divorce is no part of that purpose.

7-8. By postponing the mention of **Moses** to this point, Matthew softens the contrast between Moses' teaching and that of Jesus. The **command** referred to is Deut. 24:1. The contrast between the law of Moses and that of God is not as sharp as in ch. 5, for it is standard Jewish teaching that God frequently adjusts a high principle of law to human weakness. E. P. Gould explains the **hardness of heart** as "the rude nature which belongs to a primitive civilization" (*A Critical and Exegetical Commentary on the Gospel According to St. Mark,* "International Critical Commentary" [New York: Charles Scribner's Sons, 1905], p. 184). But this temporary and practical concession gives way now that the law is "fulfilled" or enforced in full.

---

wife **a writing of divorcement,** and so to be rid of her. If Christ took stringent ground, he would offend Herod and the Hillelites; if he took lenient ground, he would be at odds with the followers of Shammai, and would be accused of laxity in his views. Thus they "tested" him.

His answer took mountain ground above the whole debate. He said in effect that God instituted marriage at the creation, for human blessedness. God made man and woman complementary in nature. They were intended to become "one flesh"—the word means "personality" as well as "flesh." This unity made by God cannot rightly be unmade by man: they are no longer two, but one. The exception **except for unchastity** was probably not part of Jesus' own utterance. It is not found in the Marcan account, which is obviously Matthew's source. That qualifying phrase probably reflects the ethic on which the Christian church had settled when and where Matthew wrote. Jesus did not discuss exceptions and permissibilities. He said simply that God had made marriage a sacred unity which must not be broken. Of

course the critics of Jesus promptly asked him why Moses had "commanded" the custom whereby a man could use the **writing of divorcement.** Jesus replied, by plain implication, that Moses had not commanded it and ought not to be regarded as patron of the practice: Moses had only **suffered** it, as an unwilling concession, because people were too hard of heart to obey God's law and intent.

Is there guidance in this for our time? There is an ideal here—a man and woman, in a lifelong and holy bond of marriage, fulfilling in family love the intention of God when he made a new and wondrous unity. There is a righteous cause here—Jesus rallied to the defense of women in an age when they were almost defenseless. There is a sob here and a realism—some things have to be **suffered** until men and women are no longer stiff-necked toward the will of God. But there is no yielding here—Jesus refused to accommodate his teaching to any civil law, still less to any human craving for pleasure or comfort. Man and woman are complementary: they form a unity of self more

9 And I say unto you, Whosoever shall put away his wife, except *it be* for fornication, and shall marry another, committeth adultery: and whoso marrieth her which is put away doth commit adultery.

10 ¶ His disciples say unto him, If the case of the man be so with *his* wife, it is not good to marry.

beginning it was not so. 9 And I say to you: whoever divorces his wife, except for unchastity,[l] and marries another, commits adultery."[m]

10 The disciples said to him, "If such is the case of a man with his wife, it is not

[l] Some ancient authorities, after *unchastity*, read *makes her commit adultery*.
[m] Some ancient authorities insert *and he who marries a divorced woman commits adultery*.

9. Mark 10:12 applies to a situation which might arise in Gentile society—the Roman wife could divorce her husband. Matthew, who is thinking of the Jewish background, omits this, and also introduces the clause **except for unchastity**. This exception does not go back to Jesus (cf. on 5:32). F. L. Cirlot (*Christ and Divorce* [Lexington, Ky.: Trafton Publishing Co., 1945], p. 10) argues that the original text, after the word "unchastity," contained the words **makes her commit adultery**, as in 5:32. If that judgment is correct, this passage does not permit the husband to contract a second marriage, though 5:32 might. But early Christians, like Jews, probably assumed that a divorce implies the right to contract a new marriage. If Matthew relaxed vss. 5-6 only to the point of a "divorce from bed and board," would he have taken such pains to introduce his exception clause twice?

b) A SAYING ON EUNUCHS (19:10-12)

The origin of the saying is unknown. It probably does not come from Q or M, since its spirit is entirely Gentile. The main stream of Judaism looked on celibacy as an abnormal state, and marriage was not merely permitted but commanded by God (Yebamoth 6:6; Gen. 1:28). The eunuch was one of the most pitied of human beings and needed special consolation (Isa. 56:3-5). The O.T. forbade eunuchs to act as priests (Lev. 21:20). Religious celibacy was known only among minority groups such as the Essenes. Sayings on celibacy attributed to Jesus in noncanonical writings can be found in James (*Apocryphal N.T.*, pp. 10-11); and these verses may represent an attempt to put Jesus' authority behind this practice. It was well known that no tradition of any kind existed which implied that Jesus had ever married; and sayings were current which praised those who left their families for the sake of the gospel (19:29=Mark 10:29-30). Paul had also praised celibacy (I Cor. 7:26-35). Though this saying is startling, it is simply another extension of Jesus' principle that the kingdom of God takes precedence over all lesser loyalties (cf. 8:21-22; 13:44-46).

10. The **disciples** object that if a man can never escape from an unhappy marriage—save on one condition—he is much happier if he never marries. Many of Matthew's original readers no doubt shared this feeling. This leads Matthew to consider the whole question of celibacy as a condition of discipleship in certain special cases.

marvelous than the separate unity of either man or woman, and from that unity there come the joy and duty of a home. The unit in our society is not the individual, but the family. To break the unity created by God through marriage and the home is to do hurt like that done in schizophrenia. To keep the unity is to find life's true fulfillment. Marriage is more than human joy, more than a biological purpose and means: it is the outworking of God's creative act, and should therefore be a consecration.

10-12. *The Question of Celibacy.*—The loftiness of the ideal of Christ's teaching on marriage

is reflected in the question in vs. 10. Christ had called them to a rigorous consecration. He now distinguishes between three groups of celibates. Some are disabled by birth or by disinclination; some, such as the male guardians of harems, are cruelly made eunuchs by the act of rulers; and some choose a life of continence for the sake of the kingdom of God. These last mortify the flesh by self-discipline. But there is no comfort here for those who, like Origen, practice a physical self-multilation for righteousness' sake.[4] The teaching is clear. Some disciples, because

[4] Lucius Waterman, *Post-Apostolic Age*, p. 337.

481

11 But he said unto them, All *men* cannot receive this saying, save *they* to whom it is given.

12 For there are some eunuchs, which were so born from *their* mother's womb: and there are some eunuchs, which were made eunuchs of men: and there be eunuchs, which have made themselves eunuchs for the kingdom of heaven's sake. He that is able to receive *it*, let him receive *it*.

13 ¶ Then were there brought unto him little children, that he should put *his* hands on them, and pray: and the disciples rebuked them.

expedient to marry." 11 But he said to them, "Not all men can receive this precept, but only those to whom it is given. 12 For there are eunuchs who have been so from birth, and there are eunuchs who have been made eunuchs by men, and there are eunuchs who have made themselves eunuchs for the sake of the kingdom of heaven. He who is able to receive this, let him receive it."

13 Then children were brought to him that he might lay his hands on them and pray. The disciples rebuked the people;

11. **Precept** (RSV) is not a happy translation unless it refers to vs. 9. If it describes vs. 12, it is simply a **saying** (KJV) or counsel. Roman Catholic ascetic theology traditionally draws a distinction between "precepts" or laws binding on all Christians, and "counsels"; and it appeals to Matthew for the three "evangelical counsels" of chastity (vs. 12), poverty (vss. 16-22), and obedience (vss. 27-30). The counsel **is given** only to those able to receive it (vs. 12).

12. **Eunuchs who have been so from birth** is a rabbinical phrase. **Eunuchs who have made themselves eunuchs for the sake of the kingdom of heaven** is metaphorical. Such people, to be sure, make a sacrifice; but others have had to undergo the same loss without their own consent.

2. INTERLUDE: THE BLESSING OF CHILDREN (19:13-15)

See general note on 19:3–20:28. This section furnishes a kind of charter for Christian education and the ministry to children.

13. The Jewish people placed a high valuation on family life, and rabbinical writings contain tender passages on the subject of children, especially school children. Examples are given by Joseph Klausner (*Jesus of Nazareth* [New York: The Macmillan Co., 1925], p. 306). It was the custom of children to ask their parents to **pray** for them and bless them, and of disciples to make the same request of rabbis. The one who granted the request would often **lay his hands on them** in blessing. **The disciples** may have thought that Jesus was too busy to be disturbed.

they fear the distractions of the flesh and the world, or because they do not wish to involve wife and children in persecutions that they themselves are ready to face—because, in short, they would be fully consecrated to the kingdom of God—choose this life of self-denial. They are of the elect: they know that God's will must be paramount. Yet they must guard against spiritual pride, and must recognize that their rule, if applied to any large number of men, would defeat God's creation of "male and female." **He that is able to receive it** is a warning against forced interpretations of the teaching. It is an appeal to spiritual intelligence, as if Jesus had said, "Be careful not to misconceive the meaning." Plainly these verses do not command the celibacy of a sacerdotal order or encourage the elaborate system of monasticism.

13-15. Jesus Blessing Children.—The discussions of marriage and celibacy give added drama to this picture. Marriage is a God-created unity, and children are therefore dear in God's sight. Celibacy may be the rigorous choice of a few men, and they may therefore be approved of God; but the life of a family is the normal life, and is central in the divine purpose (see 18:1-4, 10-14). **To such belongs the kingdom of heaven** does not mean that childishness and immaturity have any merit. Mark's account tells us that Jesus was "indignant" because his disciples tried to spare him the intrusion of the mothers and children, and that Jesus took each child in his arms. The Marcan account also stresses the phrase "receive the kingdom of God like a child" (Mark 10:15). That receptiveness is the mark of the kingdom. A child looks on the

14 But Jesus said, Suffer little children, and forbid them not, to come unto me; for of such is the kingdom of heaven.

15 And he laid *his* hands on them, and departed thence.

16 ¶ And, behold, one came and said unto him, Good Master, what good thing shall I do, that I may have eternal life?

14 but Jesus said, "Let the children come to me, and do not hinder them; for to such belongs the kingdom of heaven." 15 And he laid his hands on them and went away.

16 And behold, one came up to him, saying, "Teacher, what good deed must I do,

14. To the early church this would have meant that **children,** no matter how young, could receive benefits from participation in Christian worship and rites. There are rabbinical sayings to the effect that the children even of godless pagans will have a share in the world to come. Matthew omits Mark 10:15 (cf. on 18:4); this is unfortunate, since that verse is the high point of the story.

3. A Rich Young Man (19:16-26)

a) The Story (19:16-22)

Mark's narrative (10:17-22) caused the early church much perplexity and searching of heart, and Clement of Alexandria found it necessary to write a tract on the subject "What Rich Man Is Saved?" Matthew was one of the first to be disturbed by its problems. He changed Jesus' startling question "Why do you call me good?" (Mark 10:18) and altered the heroic demand of absolute self-surrender so as to make it appear that, while the precepts of the Ten Commandments were binding on all men, the counsel to poverty was only for the **perfect** (vs. 21).

world with wondering and expectant eyes, and lives in glad trust. So Christ's followers must live—not in childishness, but in childlike faith, dependent on the strong mercy of God.

These verses are the charter of religious education. Shallow folk sometimes ask if it is right "to force the mind of children into a mold." The phrase is false. A wise parent does not allow a child to choose his own food or his own books. In these matters the wisdom of parents is not only permitted: it is required if truth and compassion are to be honored. Why not also in the high matters of religion? The choice of a faith cannot be delayed until the child is of age, though unthinking parents sometimes make that strange assumption. A child's mind will be shaped by the street corner gang, or by any passer-by, if it is not shaped by godly parents. So these verses underscore the need of religious education, and require the welcoming of children into the family of the church.

The method of religious education is also indicated. The mothers wished their children to hear the words of Jesus. The story of his life and death and resurrection, and the teaching of his words, are central in Christian nurture. The mothers wished their children to feel the contagion of his presence. The influence of people who know him is an indispensable need. The mothers came hoping he would **pray:** religious education rests upon that act. Our world is a selfish, adult world. Cities are built for adults.

Treaties are drawn in adult ambition and fear: if children were remembered, treaties would take a different form. Even the church has failed to give children central place: the Christian nurture of children has often been treated as a side issue. Nevertheless **to such belongs the kingdom of heaven.**

16-22. The Rich Young Ruler.—It is doubtful if the man was young: the words **from my youth** indicate a man in younger middle life. Luke (18:18) says that he was a ruler—a member of some council. All accounts agree that he was rich. There was an engaging eagerness about him: he "ran up and knelt before him" (Mark 10:17). Perhaps we may assume that he was dissatisfied with conventional Jewish religion. But he betrays a certain shallowness of mind. That is implied in the sharp answer of Jesus: **Why callest thou me good?** The man was genial, but not profound: he had not probed deeply into the meaning of goodness, for goodness belongs only to God. Jesus need not be construed as repudiating the application of the adjective to himself, except as he himself was wholly committed to God in utter lowliness. The force of Jesus' reply is probably a rebuke to the easy and unexamined use of ultimate words. Yet the ruler was not altogether shallow. He knew that truth is ethical more than ritualistic: **What good deed must I do . . . ?** He was drawn to Jesus, and Jesus was drawn to him. Perhaps Jesus saw in him unusual material for dis-

17 And he said unto him, Why callest thou me good? *there is* none good but one, *that is,* God: but if thou wilt enter into life, keep the commandments.	to have eternal life?" 17 And he said to him, "Why do you ask me about what is good? One there is who is good. If you would enter life, keep the commandments."

The Gospel According to the Nazarenes goes at the problem in a different way: "And the Lord said to him, 'How can you say, "I have kept the law and the prophets"? for it is written in the law, "You must love your neighbor as yourself"; and see, there are many of your brothers, sons of Abraham, clothed in filthy garments, dying of hunger, and your house is full of many good things, and nothing whatever goes out from it to them.' " (James, *Apocryphal N.T.,* p. 6.) But, as Cadbury points out (*op. cit.,* pp. 106-7), the story in the canonical Gospels is not directed toward the needs of the poor but toward the rich man, who needs to sacrifice his possessions if he is to have "treasure in heaven."

17. **Why do you ask me about what is good?** This is apparently the reading of the Alexandrian, Western, Caesarean, and Old Syriac texts; KJV represents the later Byzantine reading. Περὶ τοῦ ἀγαθοῦ almost suggests a philosophical discussion of "the good," but it is used here merely to avoid suggesting that Jesus is not as good as God. In this context the next sentence must mean: "God alone is unconditionally good; to ask what good thing you should do means to ask about his commandments, and these must be kept." In Mark the commandments are simply given as one step in the discussion. Here eternal life depends directly on them.

cipleship, if the self-righteousness of the law had not spoiled him.

The man must have been disappointed by Jesus' reply. He hoped for some new command, a brilliant fresh departure in religion; and all that Jesus told him was what he already knew by heart, the commandments of the Decalogue. Apparently Jesus singled out the "social" commandments—those that concern a man's duty to his neighbors. A mechanic tried to confound Bishop Wilberforce by asking suddenly the way to heaven. "Turn to the right, and go, my friend, straight on," said the bishop.[5] This was the substance of what Jesus said to his questioner. "All these have I observed" (Mark 10:20), said the man. Had he? Jewish self-righteousness sometimes made that claim. Moses, Aaron, and Samuel were said to have kept the whole law. But what man ever keeps the whole law? Having done all, "we are unprofitable servants" (Luke 17:10). Then came the sharp thrust. The man had looked for some new and startling word, and now he heard it. Mark's Gospel probably has the true account. **If you would be perfect:** Matthew's interpretation seems to shy away from the stern demand that was actually made. **Go, sell what you possess and give it to the poor . . . ; and come, follow me.**

The man was not mercenary, or Jesus would not have "loved" him (Mark 10:21). Yet he was not willing to burn his bridges. He lacked the touch of "divine madness." There was no abandon of the soul that would have taken

Christ at his word. Francis of Assisi obeyed the same command from the Lord, and changed the face of Italy. Perhaps this "ruler" was a Francis, who remained as he was—in Assisi, an honored citizen, lacking only the courage of a glorious surrender, It is true that Jesus was not issuing a universal rule when he said, **sell what you possess;** but that fact does not change the truth that he demands of us the surrender of money, comfort, ambition—anything that hinders us from commitment to God. Christ spoke to the man's will: **sell what you possess.** He spoke to his compassionate conscience: **give it to the poor.** He spoke to his fealty: **follow me.** The Gospels are not interested in "what happened afterward." The sequel to the story is hidden, and guesses will not profit us. The man went away **sorrowful.** Perhaps he could have written a Fifth Gospel, had he followed!

17. *The Commandments and Life.*—Commandments set the teeth on edge. We rebel against them. We can at least understand Shelley's revolt against what he called "the accursed book of God,"[6] for every man craves "freedom." Yet we crave commandments too, even though at other times we rebel; for we are contradictory creatures. A high-school boy idolizes the football coach, and delights to obey him. It is somewhere written of Alexander Pope that he "resembled one of the inferior bodies of the solar system."[7] So do we all: our nature is made to move in some orbit of homage and obedience.

[6] "Queen Mab," note on Sec. 5, 1. 189.
[7] Quoted, *Historical Lights,* ed. Charles E. Little (New York: Funk & Wagnalls Co., 1886), item 2238, p. 265.

[5] G. W. Daniell, *Bishop Wilberforce* (Boston & New York: Houghton Mifflin Co., 1891), p. 215.

18 He saith unto him, Which? Jesus said, Thou shalt do no murder, Thou shalt not commit adultery, Thou shalt not steal, Thou shalt not bear false witness,

19 Honor thy father and *thy* mother: and, Thou shalt love thy neighbor as thyself.

20 The young man saith unto him, All these things have I kept from my youth up: what lack I yet?

21 Jesus said unto him, If thou wilt be perfect, go *and* sell that thou hast, and give to the poor, and thou shalt have treasure in heaven: and come *and* follow me.

22 But when the young man heard that saying, he went away sorrowful: for he had great possessions.

23 ¶ Then said Jesus unto his disciples, Verily I say unto you, That a rich man

18 He said to him, "Which?" And Jesus said, "You shall not kill, You shall not commit adultery, You shall not steal, You shall not bear false witness, 19 Honor your father and mother, and, You shall love your neighbor as yourself." 20 The young man said to him, "All these I have observed; what do I still lack?" 21 Jesus said to him, "If you would be perfect, go, sell what you possess and give to the poor, and you will have treasure in heaven; and come, follow me." 22 When the young man heard this he went away sorrowful; for he had great possessions.

23 And Jesus said to his disciples,

18-19. The commandments are taken from Mark 10:19, but "do not defraud," which is not in the O.T., is omitted. Their wording is changed in the direction of the Hebrew text of Exod. 20:12-16, which Matthew knows by heart. Jesus includes only the "moral" commandments, probably because he regards them as "heavier" or more important than the others. He adds to them the saying from Lev. 19:18, which is also part of the "summary of the law" in 22:37-39.

20. Matthew adds that the man was a **young man,** and Luke 18:18 describes him as a "ruler," perhaps a synagogue official. If he was young, the words **from my youth up** (KJV) are not appropriate; the later MSS, however, borrow them from Mark and insert them.

21. According to this passage, only certain Christians are **perfect.** But in 5:48, perfection in the O.T. sense is demanded of all Jesus' followers (cf. note on that passage). Bacon (*Studies in Matthew,* p. 240) remarks that this represents the neolegalism of the later church. Jesus would not have separated his followers into two classes. It is possible that he regarded riches as the special spiritual danger of this particular man, and one must cut off one's hand or foot—or one's property—if it is a temptation to sin or if it keeps one from the kingdom (5:30; 18:8). Or, as Easton suggests, he may have invited the man to be one of the inner group of disciples, in which case his riches would be a burden (*What Jesus Taught,* pp. 84, 108).

22. The gospel tradition is never concerned with the sequel of a story. The evangelists probably assumed that the man rejected Jesus' invitation and did not get another opportunity to accept it.

Fundamentally we are creatures subject to a Will. So we cannot escape commands. The earth commands us to work if we would eat. The springtime commands us to sow seed at once, if we would reap harvest. "Take heed that ye do not your alms before men" (6:1) is just as inviolable a rule, if we would escape the death that waits on pride. "Enter by the narrow gate" (7:13): there is no alternative to that discipline. If you would enter life, keep the commandments. True commandments are friendship and life: "Ye are my friends, if ye do whatsoever I command you" (John 15:14).

But can we obey God's commands? No. We try, and we fail. But the failure flings us back on the mercy of God. Then we can obey the one central command: Christ's "Come." That is both command and pardon. We can come; we can learn to live by his pardon and in his power. Thus, loving him and our fellow men in him, we enter into life.

23-24. *The Burden of the Rich.*—It is rather worse than foolish to try to soften vss. 23-24. **Eye of a needle** does not mean the wicket gate in a large door, and **camel** is not a miswriting of the Greek word for rope. The Babylonian Talmud

shall hardly enter into the kingdom of heaven.

24 And again I say unto you, It is easier for a camel to go through the eye of a needle, than for a rich man to enter into the kingdom of God.

"Truly, I say to you, it will be hard for a rich man to enter the kingdom of heaven. 24 Again I tell you, it is easier for a camel to go through the eye of a needle than for a rich man to enter the kingdom of God."

b) DISCUSSION OF RICHES (19:23-26)

24. This verse is the kernel of the section; vs. 23 is a less colorful variant of it. Attempts have often been made to blunt its sharpness. For example, it has been suggested that the original word was not **camel** (κάμηλος) but "rope" (κάμιλος) or that the "Needle's Eye" was a gate through which a camel might barely squeeze. And the later MSS of Mark 10:24 read, "how hard it is *for those who trust in riches . . .*" But Jesus deliberately utters a "hard saying"—it is impossible for a rich man to get into the kingdom of God—which is rightly interpreted in vs. 26.

This distrust of riches is often to be observed in the Jewish and early Christian tradition. Several of the canonical psalms contrast the pious poor and their rich oppressors (Pss. 9:18; 10:9; 12:5; 34:6); the Epistle of James contains tirades against the rich (Jas. 2:1-7; 5:1-6); the Magnificat praises God because "he has filled the hungry with good things, and the rich he has sent empty away" (Luke 1:53); and in the book of Revelation the rich merchants wail over the destruction of Babylon (Rev. 18:11-20). By contrast, numerous passages in the O.T. tell how pious men were rewarded with wealth (e.g., Job 42:10); and Jeshua ben Sira includes among the saints "rich men furnished with ability, living peaceably in their habitations" (Ecclus. 44:6). Rabbinical Judaism strikes a balance between these two attitudes. On the whole, the rabbis believed that riches were a blessing, and that when used properly they were an ornament to a righteous man. God might give a man poverty as punishment for a particular sin or as a test of his fidelity. But Judaism also taught that there were dangers and temptations in riches, and that a poor man might have inner freedom and spiritual possessions.

Jesus took his stand with those biblical writers who feared riches and power, as we can see from his teaching in 6:19-21, 24; Luke 12:13-21. We must remember that he does not define how much property a man must have in order to be considered rich. There might be considerable difference of opinion on this point—a man can be "rich" in one social group and "poor" in another. The Zacchaeus story (Luke 19:1-10) indicates that a penitent rich man can be saved—the saying is therefore not to be taken as an absolute statement, but as the most serious warning possible of the spiritual danger of riches. Jesus had no doubt observed how wealth, or the desire for it, corrupts men's morals, protects them against facing the issues of life, and keeps them from actively serving God and fellow man.

twice speaks of an elephant passing through a needle's eye.[8] Christ often spoke in flashing hyperbole, especially when, as here, he wished to give emphasis to unpopular truth.

The O.T. sometimes condemns the rich (see Exeg.). The prophets in particular castigate those who "sold . . . the poor for a pair of shoes" (Amos 2:6). But there are many passages in the O.T. which play the other tune, and regard material prosperity as a sign of divine favor (Ps. 112:3). The disciples apparently held this doctrine (see vs. 25). Jesus takes a clear stand in the debate. The rich may meet less temptation in one way than a hungry man,

[8] See Branscomb, *Gospel of Mark*, "Moffatt New Testament Commentary," p. 183.

and may have more opportunity to do good; but, by and large, they are under such threat of soul that their state should be feared. The hyperbole of vs. 24 testifies to the urgency with which he spoke.

Wherein is the threat? Money-making is an absorbing pursuit, and easily leads a man to forget God. Weak men are corrupted by money, like Dives, and become sensualists; men of stronger will are hardened by money, and become avaricious and proud. They are under temptation to imagine that their own skill and strength can fashion life. They forget the brotherhood on which they are dependent. They forget the God who loved them into life. They forget that they must die, and try to live in

25 When his disciples heard *it,* they were exceedingly amazed, saying, Who then can be saved?

26 But Jesus beheld *them,* and said unto them, With men this is impossible; but with God all things are possible.

27 ¶ Then answered Peter and said unto him, Behold, we have forsaken all, and followed thee; what shall we have therefore?

25 When the disciples heard this, they were greatly astonished, saying, "Who then can be saved?" 26 But Jesus looked at them and said to them, "With men this is impossible, but with God all things are possible." 27 Then Peter said in reply, "Lo, we have left everything and followed you. What

---

25. The disciples, as they are pictured here, regard riches as a mark of piety. If a man whom God has signally rewarded cannot get into the kingdom, who then can be saved?

26. The Bible everywhere holds that **with God all things are possible,** and Jesus might have uttered this saying in a different context. In itself it could refer to anything which **is impossible** for men.

4. Rewards for Disciples (19:27–20:28)

After the sections on marriage, children, and rich men come several pericopes dealing with church leaders (cf. general note on 19:3–20:28). Matthew makes these over into a section on the general subject of reward by inserting the parable 20:1-15. His purpose is to show that those who have been meagerly rewarded in this age will be compensated in the age to come, but the actual effect is to indicate that God deals with all men more generously than they deserve.

---

time instead of in eternity. John Webster in his play, *The White Devil,* makes Flamineo exclaim

Prosperity doth bewitch men, seeming clear;
As seas do laugh, show white, when rocks are near.[9]

Jesus did not sweepingly condemn all rich men. Zacchaeus was a rich man, Nicodemus and Joseph of Arimathea were both rich. So, we may guess, was the man who provided the "upper room." But Jesus insisted that in these cases riches still made insuperable odds, and that only the grace of God gave the victory. It is characteristic of our age to try to soften the sternness of these verses. But the words stand.

25-26. The Impossible Made Possible.—How final and how far-reaching! It applies to more than man's inability to overcome the temptation of riches. A man cannot save himself from fear: self-assurance easily evaporates in a time of panic. A man cannot save himself from sin: how would he begin? The will he must use is precisely the locale of his disease. He cannot reach a hand into the past to erase the black marks of his transgression, nor can he track down all the issues of his evil influence to cancel the spreading hurt. A man cannot save himself from death. **With men this is impossible.**

But God can do what man cannot do. Thus

the Christian ethic can speak of a "possible impossibility." God can still the storms of the world which he has made. He can cleanse the past, and make it subserve the future gain: is he not the ruler of time? He who ordained death can draw the sting of death. Did not Jesus in these words give hint that in him God had come to earth to make common cause with man—to perfect his strength in man's helplessness, and so to bind man to him forever? Faith is the act whereby man goes down into the river which in his own power he cannot cross. By faith he finds, at midmost of the stream, when it seems that footing must be lost, a Hand stretched out to grip and steady him. As for the money temptation, Archbishop Trench says that God solves that problem by taking the money from the man, or by taking the man from his money: "All other [riches] either leave him or he leaves them."[1] **With God all things are possible.**

27-29. The Rewards of Discipleship.—Perhaps Peter's question was naïve and tinctured with worldly ambition. Perhaps it was wrung from him—or from those for whom he is here made spokesman—by the persecutions and apparent inequalities of life. Is right always to be "on the scaffold," and wrong always to be "on the

---

[9] Act V, scene 6.

[1] Richard Chenevix Trench, *Sermons Preached in Westminster Abbey* (New York: W. J. Middleton, 1860), p. 355.

28 And Jesus said unto them, Verily I say unto you, That ye which have followed me, in the regeneration when the Son of man shall sit in the throne of his glory, ye also shall sit upon twelve thrones, judging the twelve tribes of Israel.

29 And every one that hath forsaken houses, or brethren, or sisters, or father, or mother, or wife, or children, or lands, for my name's sake, shall receive a hundredfold, and shall inherit everlasting life.

then shall we have?" 28 Jesus said to them, "Truly, I say to you, in the new world, when the Son of man shall sit on his glorious throne, you who have followed me will also sit on twelve thrones, judging the twelve tribes of Israel. 29 And every one who has left houses or brothers or sisters or father or mother or children or lands, for my name's sake, will receive a hundred-

---

a) Jesus' Promise (19:27-30)

The parallel passage, Mark 10:28-30, is general enough to refer to any Christian who follows Christ at great cost to himself, though it may have a special application to church leaders. Matthew inserts vs. 28b from Q (cf. Luke 22:28-30), thus making it refer directly to the twelve.

27. Peter speaks for the inner group of disciples: "The rich man has chosen not to follow Jesus, but **we have.** Surely there must be some reward for us."

28. The promise has to do with **the new world.** This is a happy rendering of παλινγενεσία, literally **regeneration** or "rebirth." The idea is that in the age to come there will be a new heaven and a new earth (Isa. 65:17; 66:22; Rev. 21:1-5), a new or renewed creation (Gal. 6:15; Rom. 8:18-22; II Baruch 32:6; II Esdras 7:75). Josephus (*Antiquities* XI. 3. 9) uses the word to refer to the rebirth of the land of Israel. **When the Son of man shall sit on his glorious throne** may be Matthew's addition to the source (it is found also in 25:31). The heavenly Son of man is judge of the world, and his followers assist him in **judging** (and therefore ruling) **the twelve tribes of Israel.** Matthew adds that the **thrones** are **twelve** in number, thus connecting the saying with the apostles. The original saying referred to Jesus' followers generally (cf. I Cor. 6:2, "Do you not know that the saints will judge the world?").

29. Many a Christian had left **brothers or sisters,** etc., to follow Jesus. Luke (18:29) adds "wife," perhaps because he values celibacy, and the word "wife" has crept into late MSS of Matthew and thus appears in KJV. Matthew merely states that all these will have **a hundredfold** reward; Mark 10:30 promises new relationships in the family of God, together with persecutions.

---

throne"?[2] Beyond much doubt these verses reflect the hardships of the early church. As such they bring sense of pathos and a nerving of our soul. Many *had* left brother and sister, father and mother; or rather, they had been thrust from home as blasphemers and heretics; for, we must remember, the doctrine of the lordship of Christ was anathema to the "Judaizers." Christians were in many instances excluded from the synagogue, denied leadership in civic affairs, and ostracized in the markets. How costly is *our* faith?

Yet there is reward, even though hankering for the reward may relegate the "first" to "last" (vs. 30). There is reward in the present time (Luke 18:30). This fact also is written across the early church. The Christian found in the *agapē* new brothers and sisters. Paul said that the mother of Rufus was also his "mother"

(Rom. 16:13). The joy of the new fellowship was a **hundredfold** more than the joy foregone. There is reward in the world to come. **Regeneration** or **new world** may be eschatological, a reference to Jewish hope that this present world will be restored to pristine perfection; or it may be also hope of what we call heaven. The language breaks into light and music. There are **thrones** and **glory.** The followers of Christ, often hailed before synagogue courts and judged, shall now judge (cf. I Cor. 6:2-3). They shall **inherit eternal life.** Whence this faith of the early church? They could see judgment at work in this present world. So can any man who has eyes to see: the proud inherit alienation even here, and the lowly in righteousness win human love. But the hope of the Christian community was focused in Christ. He was the disclosure of God. He was the living sign of the verdicts of eternity.

[2] James Russell Lowell, "The Present Crisis," st. viii.

30 But many *that are* first shall be last; and the last *shall be* first.

20 For the kingdom of heaven is like unto a man *that is* a householder, which went out early in the morning to hire laborers into his vineyard.

fold,[n] and inherit eternal life. 30 But many that are first will be last, and the last first.

20 "For the kingdom of heaven is like a householder who went out early in the morning to hire laborers for his vine-

[n] Some ancient authorities read *manifold.*

---

30. In the age to come conditions will be reversed, as in Luke 1:52-53; 13:28-30; the disciples, who are now **last,** will be **first.** A similar idea is found in rabbinical writings. See also Toynbee, *Study of History,* pp. 308-9. Matthew repeats this saying in 20:16, thus giving the parable as an example of the principle; but this is not the original point of the parable.

b) Equality of Rewards: Parable of the Workers in the Vineyard (20:1-16)

Jesus did much of his work among country people who were out of touch with the main stream of Judaism. Some of these may have belonged to that group whom the Pharisaic leaders called Amhaarez (cf. notes on 9:10-13; 10:6). Such people were regarded as irreligious—"the Pharisees" in John 7:49 express a common judgment: "This crowd, who do not know the law, are accursed." The "people of the land" in turn often expressed their hatred of the Pharisees.

---

30. Reversals in Judgment.—Who has not dimly seen that earth is a broken reflection of the real world? Who has not said, "If we could know this in its true light, our verdicts would be changed"? So Jesus spoke, apparently more than once (see Matt. 20:16; Luke 13:30). These words are warning. Those who are **first** in time may be **last** when the race is run. Success has its sharp temptations. Judas, who had walked with his Lord day by day, became the "child of loss"; but the penitent thief on the cross was instantly welcomed into paradise. Those who are first in gifts may be last in consecration. The young ruler, attractive in person and upright in life, with the world at his feet, made the great refusal; but loyal Andrew, homespun and seeking no prominence, won a name that is held in honor. The judgment of heaven puts little store by size or glitter; it is not swayed by the appraisals of men. Even "success" in Christian work is no guarantee of heaven's favor. Were there not those who claimed to have "done many wonderful works" (7:22) in Christ's name, who yet were disowned by him? The judgments of heaven are concerned with motives, and they search the heart.

These words are equally encouragement. The beggar Lazarus came to his own. Some on that last great day cannot even remember their good deeds done for Christ's sake: "When saw we thee ahungered?" (25:37). But Christ remembers, and his lowly ones inherit the kingdom prepared for them "from the foundation of the world" (13:35). There is the story of a

king who built a great temple, and hoped to receive honor for the gift. When the temple was built, he was aghast and angry to find on it the name of an unknown woman. She was identified; she lived near the temple. But she had not inscribed her own name on the temple, and had no ambitions to fame. Actually she had done nothing even to help the building, except that one day she took pity on the oxen, and for Christ's sake fed them wisps of hay.[3] How many obscure heroes will be discovered at the Judgment! There are overturnings of human verdicts even in this world. Here and now the meek enter again and again into their inheritance. Hereafter all the seeming inequalities of earth will be redeemed. Christ is the disclosure of God and the rule of judgment. He is holy love. **Many that are first will be last, and the last first.**

20:1-16. The Parable of the Laborers and the Hours.—Interpreters of the Gospels have found it hard to expound this story. Calvin said that it is a rebuke of Peter's question in 19:27.[4] Irenaeus proposed that the men who worked longer hours represent the patriarchs and prophets of the O.T., while the eleventh-hour servant represents the disciples of Christ.[5] Many commentators ancient and recent—Gregory is

[3] Quoted, *Great Texts of the Bible,* Vol. on *St. Matthew,* p. 246.
[4] *Commentary on a Harmony of the Evangelists,* tr. William Pringle (Edinburgh: The Calvin Translation Society, 1845), II, 409.
[5] Quoted, Richard Chenevix Trench, *Notes on the Parables of Our Lord* (London: Kegan Paul, Trench, & Co., 1886), p. 170 n.

2 And when he had agreed with the laborers for a penny a day, he sent them into his vineyard.

3 And he went out about the third hour, and saw others standing idle in the market place,

4 And said unto them; Go ye also into the vineyard, and whatsoever is right I will give you. And they went their way.

5 Again he went out about the sixth and ninth hour, and did likewise.

yard. 2 After agreeing with the laborers for a denarius[o] a day, he sent them into his vineyard. 3 And going out about the third hour he saw others standing idle in the market place; 4 and to them he said, 'You go into the vineyard too, and whatever is right I will give you.' So they went. 5 Going out again about the sixth hour and the

[o] See note on 18. 28.

Jesus went to the "unchurched" because they needed him most (9:12), while on the other hand the Pharisees and "religious people" often rejected what he had to offer (22:2-5, 8-10). In this parable he justified his own practice, and answered the objection that he was offering the joys of the world to come in equal measure to the evil and the good alike. The point is found in vs. 15, not in vs. 16. Kilpatrick (*Origins of Matthew*, p. 35) assigns the parable to M. This may be correct, but it does not necessarily have the characteristics of that source; cf. Intro., p. 239.

20:1. The story may originally have begun, "A parable. To what is the matter like? It is like a householder" or owner of an estate. Matthew makes it clear that it has to do with man's relationship to **the kingdom of heaven.**

2. The working day was reckoned from the rising of the sun to the appearing of the stars. **A denarius** or drachma, about twenty cents in silver, was apparently the usual daily wage (Tob. 5:14), though Klostermann thinks it generous for that time and place (cf. on 18:28). Such a verbal agreement for wages was binding in law.

3. The daylight part of the day extended from sunrise to sundown and was divided into twelve hours; **the third hour** might roughly be 8-9 A.M. Those who could not find work or did not wish to work would naturally congregate **in the market place.**

4. The employer promises **whatever is right** and no figure is set.

5. He goes out again about noon and 3 P.M.

---

typical of the ancient, A. T. Cadoux[6] of the recent—believe that the many-hour workers are the Jews, and the "fortunate" worker is the Gentile church; and Gregory even divided Jewish history into periods to correspond with **third hour, sixth hour,** and the rest.[7] The Exeg. submits this theory: the Pharisees are the long-term servants of God, while "the people of the land" (those who failed to "keep the law" and were despised by the Pharisees, and who in turn hated the Pharisees) are the eleventh-hour servant. This interpretation has the advantage of bringing the story to bear on a crucial issue which Jesus then faced, and it establishes the proper parallel with the story of the prodigal son. The whole debate has been perhaps too much concerned with the application, and the central truth may have been overlooked. That truth may be in vs. 15 (see Exeg.).

How clear and sharp are the lines of Jesus' parables! A problem which we often face is not merely hinted: it is etched. The men who

[6] *Parables of Jesus,* p. 102.
[7] Quoted, *Pulpit Commentary,* ed. Spence and Exell, Vol. *St. Matthew,* II, 279.

worked most of the day were not defrauded: they received a generous wage in fulfillment of a just promise. But when the men who had worked only one hour received as much as they, they **murmured:** if the master could be thus generous, they deserved a bonus. Perhaps few commentators have sufficiently stressed the need of the eleventh-hour recruit. He needed work and money, or he would not have waited all day in the market place. Apparently he was willing and able to work. Yet would not such an "eccentric" master have given the man his chance at the eleventh hour even if the man had been profligate and lazy? Yes, as he received home the prodigal. But in that instance also the man's need would have been a prime factor. What, then, is the central truth? Let us strike it off in forthright phrase.

The rewards of God are not according to what men think is their merit. In the vineyard of the kingdom of heaven (vs. 1) how much merit can any man claim? Yet we make the claim, though we have all grievously sinned. The Roman Church has its appalling doctrine of "works of supererogation"—extra and unre-

6 And about the eleventh hour he went out, and found others standing idle, and saith unto them, Why stand ye here all the day idle?

7 They say unto him, Because no man hath hired us. He saith unto them, Go ye also into the vineyard; and whatsoever is right, *that* shall ye receive.

8 So when even was come, the lord of the vineyard saith unto his steward, Call the laborers, and give them *their* hire, beginning from the last unto the first.

9 And when they came that *were hired* about the eleventh hour, they received every man a penny.

10 But when the first came, they supposed that they should have received more; and they likewise received every man a penny.

ninth hour, he did the same. **6** And about the eleventh hour he went out and found others standing; and he said to them, 'Why do you stand here idle all day?' **7** They said to him, 'Because no one has hired us.' He said to them, 'You go into the vineyard too.' **8** And when evening came, the owner of the vineyard said to his steward, 'Call the laborers and pay them their wages, beginning with the last, up to the first.' **9** And when those hired about the eleventh hour came, each of them received a denarius. **10** Now when the first came, they thought they would receive more; but each

---

8. The O.T. provided (Lev. 19:13; Deut. 24:15) that the worker must be paid each day's wages that very day. This was not always followed in practice, though the worker had the right to demand immediate payment if he chose. The rule would presumably be observed here because this was casual labor and there was no assurance of more than one day's work. **Beginning with the last** might better be translated "including the last." The phrase has no special significance; it is simply a touch which prepares for the climax of the story in vss. 10-12.

9. The employer is thinking of the workmen's need. If they go home with wages for only a single hour, their families cannot be fed (Joachim Jeremias, *Die Gleichnisse Jesu* [Zürich: Zwingli-Verlag, 1947], pp. 18-19).

10-12. They supposed that an employer who was so generous with late-comers would give a bonus to those who had **borne the burden of the day and the scorching heat** of the sirocco off the desert. Their attitude is like that of the elder brother in Luke 15:29, "Lo, these many years I have served you, and I never disobeyed your command; yet you never gave me a kid, that I might make merry with my friends. But when this son of yours came . . . !" On the face of it the objection appears reasonable; why should "the tax collectors and the harlots go into the kingdom of God before" those whose lifelong performance was unquestionably greater? (21:31.)

---

quired goodness! The Protestant Church also is not free from the drab rubric of "works." On the face of the problem the "murmuring" was right; at the loving heart of the problem it was wrong. The rabbinical parallel to this story quoted in the Exeg. is significant. It tells of a rabbinical religion that still persists. "Merit" is not a meaningless term, but

> . . . merit lives from man to man,
> And not from man, O Lord, to thee.[8]

The rewards of God are not arbitrary. They are built on tests that are higher than ours, as the sky is above the earth. **Am I not allowed to do what I choose with what belongs to me?**

[8] Tennyson, *In Memoriam*, Intro., st. ix.

does not mean that God is a God of capricious whim and fiat mind. It means that he has his own criteria which we, in mortal sight and selfish aim, cannot comprehend. Dimly we see the criteria: they are the demands on God of his own love, not the dreariness of man's legal *quid pro quo*. Thus the rewards of God ought to enlist our glad assent, not our murmuring. Why did the earlier workers not rejoice that the man who had waited long in the market place was now at peace, with money to take home to his family? Why did not the elder brother rejoice that the prodigal was now restored, set free from the rags and hunger of a far country? If only we had but a tincture of God's love would we not be glad, as heaven is glad, that the lost sheep is safe in the fold, de-

11 And when they had received *it,* they murmured against the goodman of the house,

12 Saying, These last have wrought *but* one hour, and thou hast made them equal unto us, which have borne the burden and heat of the day.

13 But he answered one of them, and said, Friend, I do thee no wrong: didst not thou agree with me for a penny?

14 Take *that* thine *is,* and go thy way: I will give unto this last, even as unto thee.

15 Is it not lawful for me to do what I will with mine own? Is thine eye evil, because I am good?

of them also received a denarius. 11 And on receiving it they grumbled at the householder, 12 saying, 'These last worked only one hour, and you have made them equal to us who have borne the burden of the day and the scorching heat.' 13 But he replied to one of them, 'Friend, I am doing you no wrong; did you not agree with me for a denarius? 14 Take what belongs to you, and go; I choose to give to this last as I give to you. 15 Am I not allowed to do what I choose with what belongs to me?

13-14. The first answer is that God's justice cannot be impugned; the contract was made and has been kept. As Paul says, when one works for God on a contract basis, "his wages are not reckoned as a gift but as his due" (Rom. 4:4). Perhaps these men can justly claim their reward; if so, they have it and they are quits.

The rabbis told a similar parable, but with a significantly different point. A king had many laborers, but one was an unusually good worker. The king permitted him to work for two hours and then let him off, and when he gave him the same pay as the others, his answer to the objectors was: "This man has done more in two hours than you have done in the entire day" (B. T. D. Smith, *Parables of the Synoptic Gospels,* pp. 71-72). This illustrates the *general drift* of Jewish teaching, which can be summarized thus: (a) Righteous action is required of all; "If you have done much in the Torah do not claim merit for yourself, because for this purpose you were created." (Aboth 2:8.) But (b) "the reward is in proportion to the toil." (Aboth 5:23.) It is important to be fair to the rabbis. In many ways they modified and spiritualized this teaching, and as far as possible guarded against "externalism." They realized that God by his grace made up for man's deficiencies and that God's goodness was out of proportion to man's merit. They held, too, that the motive and spirit of righteous action were important; to do a deed for the love of God was better than to do it for reward. "Do not be like slaves who serve the master for the sake of reward, but be like slaves who serve the master not for the sake of reward, and let the fear of heaven be upon you." (Aboth 1:3.) "The reward of a duty accomplished is another duty to be performed." (Aboth 4:2.) One may also compare Aboth 2:14-16 and the many passages cited by C. G. Montefiore and Herbert Loewe (*A Rabbinic Anthology* [London: Macmillan & Co., 1938], pp. 202-17). Yet the Pharisees always held to the general principle that reward is in proportion to performance.

Jesus, like the rabbis, taught that no man was exempt from moral obligation, and that mere obedience entitles no man to special privilege (Luke 17:9). And he did not hesitate to appeal to the motive of reward (5:12). The principal difference is that for him the ultimate reward was the kingdom of God or the life of the world to come, and that this was given alike to all who served God. In the light of this, all other rewards were trivial, and all attempts to make comparisons between one man's reward and another's were out of place and did less than justice to God. Rabbinical teaching no doubt comes very close to that of Jesus at this point; but the basic doctrine was that both toil and reward were quantitative. The other doctrines of the rabbis are merely modifications of this basic conviction.

15. Jesus of course does not mean to teach that an earthly employer can do anything that he chooses with his own property, any more than he teaches that all employees must receive equal wages. Indeed, an employer who behaved in this fashion might get into serious difficulties. But *God* can deal in this way, because he alone is the ultimate owner of all things and can do what he chooses with what belongs to him, or "on his own

16 So the last shall be first, and the first last: for many be called, but few chosen.

17 ¶ And Jesus going up to Jerusalem took the twelve disciples apart in the way, and said unto them,

18 Behold, we go up to Jerusalem; and the Son of man shall be betrayed unto the chief priests and unto the scribes, and they shall condemn him to death,

19 And shall deliver him to the Gentiles to mock, and to scourge, and to crucify *him:* and the third day he shall rise again.

Or do you begrudge my generosity*?*?' **16** So the last will be first, and the first last."

17 And as Jesus was going up to Jerusalem, he took the twelve disciples aside, and on the way he said to them, **18** "Behold, we are going up to Jerusalem; and the Son of man will be delivered to the chief priests and scribes, and they will condemn him to death, **19** and deliver him to the Gentiles to be mocked and scourged and crucified, and he will be raised on the third day."

ᵖ Or is your eye evil because I am good?

---

premises" (W. H. P. Hatch, "A Note on Matthew 20:15," *Anglican Theological Review,* XXVI [1944], 250-53). The logical result of this teaching is that schemes of merit are wiped out. Man is expected to give himself over unreservedly to God's will, and God on his part lavishes grace on man to a degree that cannot be merited. **Do you begrudge my generosity?** is a good paraphrase of the "evil eye" and "good eye" metaphors, which are found also in Prov. 22:9; 23:6; 28:22; Aboth 2:9.

16. See on 19:30. Matthew puts the saying here because of the language of vs. 8. The words **for many be called, but few chosen** (KJV) have even less to do with the parable. They have crept in from 22:14 and are properly omitted by RSV on the authority of Sinaiticus (ℵ), Vaticanus (B), and the Coptic versions.

c) INTERLUDE: THIRD PREDICTION OF SUFFERING (20:17-19)

17-19. Mark 10:32-34 is the source; cf. on 17:22-23. This third prediction serves to indicate that Jesus is now on the way to Jerusalem for the last time.

---

livered from briars and wolves? "Do you begrudge my generosity?" God asks. Wordsworth is right:

Give all thou canst; high Heaven rejects the lore
Of nicely-calculated less or more.⁹

The lovelessness of the long-term workers is here set in contrast with the love of God.

How hard the doctrine of merit dies! How proud we are of our "works"! How blindly we offer our legalities in protest against God's free grace! How loveless we are toward the sinner! This story is the gospel warrant for a great word of Paul: "For by grace are ye saved through faith; and that not of yourselves: it is the gift of God: not of works, lest any man should boast" (Eph. 2:8-9).

17-19. *Third Prophecy of Death.*— (See Expos., 16:21 and 17:12.) This is the third tolling of the bell. The story quickens toward its crisis and climax. There seem to be subtle differences of stress in this prophecy. The word **Jerusalem** is a sob. Jerusalem was the city of God, and the temple kindled a sacred rapture; but Jesus knew that there he must die. The manner of death is for the first time clearly spoken: **mocked and scourged and crucified.**

⁹ *Ecclesiastical Sonnets,* Sonnet XLIII.

Contrast those words with **Jerusalem:** you have the contrast between the holy and loving intention of God on the one hand, and on the other hand the perversity of man. The Marcan account (10:32-34) is fuller and gives poignant details. There we are told that the disciples were "in dismay" and "afraid": the sight of that face "set like flinty stone" to go to Jerusalem struck awe and fear. Courage was in it: the high courage of lonely consecration. Obedience was in it: he would do the Father's will and drink the bitter cup. Redemptive love was in it: he would die in utter love for God and man. Between the lines we can read the voluntariness of the act. He could have gone to Galilee instead of to Jerusalem. He could have chosen safety, with long years of settled teaching, instead of death; and that safe choice could have been plausibly justified. He stood at the fork of the road, and chose the dangerous right instead of the plausible wrong. He cast the vote of his life for an abandon to God's will, instead of following man's apparently wise "wisdom." His enemies killed him, and his blood was on their hands. But they were only small-part actors in the drama of redemption: "The good shepherd giveth his life for the sheep. . . . No man taketh it from me, but I lay it down of myself" (John 10:11, 18).

| 20 ¶ Then came to him the mother of Zebedee's children with her sons, worshipping *him,* and desiring a certain thing of him. | 20 Then the mother of the sons of Zeb'e-dee came up to him, with her sons, and kneeling before him she asked him for something. 21 And he said to her, "What do you want?" She said to him, "Command that these two sons of mine may sit, one at your right hand and one at your left, in |
| 21 And he said unto her, What wilt thou? She saith unto him, Grant that these my two sons may sit, the one on thy right hand, and the other on the left, in thy kingdom. | |

d) Greatness Is Based on Service (20:20-28)

The section consists of two parts: (*a*) a little anecdote, vss. 20-23, which finds its point in vs. 23; and (*b*) a sayings group, vss. 25-28. The two are linked together by vs. 24, which is editorial. The two parts teach different lessons: (*a*) God himself chooses those who are given special honor, and (*b*) among Jesus' disciples, greatness is based solely on service.

20. Matthew puts the onus for making this request on **the mother of the sons of Zebedee** because, unlike Mark, he is concerned for the honor of **her sons.**

21. In your kingdom and "in your glory" (Mark 10:37) no doubt mean the same. The evangelists think of the age to come, but James and John may have hoped that Jesus would go to Jerusalem as Messiah, drive out the Romans, and reign in glory. They wish to sit at his **right hand** and **left** as chief cabinet officers in the new monarchy. This, together with 20:31 and 21:8, is another indication of the political excitement aroused by Jesus' activity.

20-23. *Thrones Are for the Christlike.*—Note in Exeg. that these verses are perhaps separated from those that follow (by the editorial vs. 24), and therefore are separately expounded. Probably Mark is right in his report that James and John themselves asked the favor: Matthew's change may be due to his desire to defend apostolic worthiness and authority. But Salome may have reinforced the request of her sons, and (if she was a sister of Mary, the mother of Jesus) may have pleaded the family relationship (cf. 27:56, Mark 15:40, John 19:25). We see in this forthright ambition why the two men were called "the sons of thunder" (Mark 3:17). The incident has the tang of actuality. It lets us look behind the scenes. We understand better how the disciples thought of their Master. They believed in him: they were sure he had power to establish the messianic kingdom. But their conception of the kingdom was earthy: he would triumph over his foes, domestic and foreign, and would establish an empire with ranks and thrones. One man would sit on his right as next in power, and another on his left as third in power. We need not despise the disciples for their littleness. Are we purged of hankering for "the chief places"? As their idea of the kingdom was earthy, so their appraisal of human nature was cankered with undue optimism and false pride. Their **we are able** is the very stuff of blindness, pathos, and tragedy.

We have done poor justice to Christ's answer. He says in effect: "I have nothing to do with conferring honors in God's kingdom." This accords well with his lowliness, and, perhaps we should add, with that limitation of human nature and knowledge which the Incarnation implies. The answer has implications which we may well heed. God's ordainings are not by "pull" or money or comeliness. To us they may seem arbitrary, because our minds are finite. Why are some men given ten talents, and some two? Why are some men great artists, by birthright and due occasion? Why have some a true magnetism of person so that naturally they come to leadership? These questions are beyond our full answer. Yet God's ordainings are not arbitrary: they are **prepared.** They are not by whim or any sudden thought, but part of a pondered and unstayed creation. They are "from the foundation of the world" (13:35)—a magnificent word in which the Galilean Carpenter lays his hands in worship on the bastions of the righteous universe. Furthermore, the ordainings of God are not by rule of empire: they are by rule of a home, for they are the will of Christ's **Father.** Some are called to leadership—but in a home, not in a hierarchy. We are driven to the inference that in this whole issue the choices of God bring staggering surprise. In God's realm Don Quixote's sorry nag may be worthy of the name Rosinante, and his ill-

22 But Jesus answered and said, Ye know not what ye ask. Are ye able to drink of the cup that I shall drink of, and to be baptized with the baptism that I am baptized with? They say unto him, We are able.

your kingdom." 22 But Jesus answered, "You do not know what you are asking. Are you able to drink the cup that I am to drink?" They said to him, "We are

---

22. The cup is not the cup of joy and success (Pss. 23:5; 116:13) but the cup of suffering (26:39; Pss. 11:6; 75:8; Isa. 51:17). The words found in KJV, **and to be baptized with the baptism that I am baptized with,** are not in the old MSS and have been added from Mark 10:38. They can be paraphrased, "Can you pass through the dark waters of suffering through which I must pass?" The same metaphor is found in Ps. 42:7; Isa. 43:2.

---

favored wife may really be Dulcinea! [10] We know dimly the manner of God's choosing: vss. 25-27 are separate, and yet not unlinked with these high issues. God's kingdom breaks through into our world. The destiny of souls is in his hands, but all his dealings are according to the love of Christ. In the kingdom only those who "serve" are great. The Pasteurs inherit the thrones; the Napoleons find exile.

22a. Ignorant Prayer.—Branscomb suggests that this verse may be a later addition to the record.[1] However that may be, it has value for Christian faith. Must Christ not say of many of our prayers, **You do not know what you are asking?** Sometimes our prayers are glib, thoughtless, by rote. If we really pondered the petitions of the Lord's Prayer as we say them, could we pray in such casual mind? The bare attempt to fulfill that prayer would revolutionize our world. Sometimes we sincerely desire heaven's boon, but do not count the cost. For instance, we pray for humility and genuinely desire a lowly heart; but we forget that humility comes often by the mortification of our pride and the reproach of men. "Make me a true follower of Christ" is a prayer that might spell both loss and danger. Sometimes we crave leadership, like James and John, but overlook the fact that all leadership carries proportionate responsibility and anxiety. We aspire to the throne, but have no wish to live "in that fierce light which beats upon a throne." [2] Stephen prayed to be Christian, as we pray, but he died on forsaken land, stoned to death as a martyr (Acts 7:58-60), and few knew that he had died. Sometimes, nay always, we pray forgetting that God's thrones are already **prepared** for those for whom he has ordained them; and that the ordination may or may not rest on us; and that "his ways," though beneficent, are "past finding out" (Rom. 11:33).

Our main prayer must always be for clearer vision of God's purpose and for readiness to

obey. It would help us to pray out loud: the hearing of our own words would bring a new reality to our praying. It would help us to pray slowly, thinking of each word as we speak it. Even the prayer for faithfulness in reading God's word is not an easy prayer: Charles Lamb in his India House days wrote, "Few but laugh at me for reading my Testament." [3] Always we must add the saving word to our prayers "Thy will be done" (6:10). But even for our blundering Christ has only kindness. He deals with us in firm friendship, as with James and John. If we pray in the sight of Christ, he will teach us obedience to the mystery—and bring us to see that the mystery is personal Love.

22b. Rash Confidence.—They said to him, **"We are able."** There is evidence (see Exeg., as also Branscomb, *op. cit.*) that Mark 10:38, 39, from which Matthew's record is drawn, is a later addition written when the persecution of the early church was a clear fact. Vs. 21 anticipates thrones and gladness; but this conversational sequence has echoes of martyrdom. It is therefore just as true to Christian experience. **We are able:** the words are almost the motto of man's pride since the Renaissance. **We are able** to overcome physical sickness and perhaps even death: we forget the matter of our nerves, and that God has his own ordainings. **We are able** to cancel our psychological frustrations (new name for sin!): we forget that psychology must recognize a guilt complex, and that no human power can cleanse history. **We are able** to lay the ancient scourge of war: we forget man's dark perversities, and so we drive war into atomic war with its wholesale cruelty and threatened annihilation of man. Always we are tempted to exaggerate our powers. We forget the human paradox: we are strong only when we know our weakness and trust to God's strength.

The false confidence is worse because it does not pause to contemplate God's strange ways.

[10] Miguel de Cervantes, *The Adventures of Don Quixote.*

[1] *Gospel of Mark*, p. 188.

[2] Tennyson, *Idylls of the King*, Dedication.

[3] *The Complete Works and Letters of Charles Lamb* (New York: The Modern Library, Random House, 1935), p. 608.

23 And he saith unto them, Ye shall drink indeed of my cup, and be baptized with the baptism that I am baptized with: but to sit on my right hand, and on my left, is not mine to give, but *it shall be given to them* for whom it is prepared of my Father.

24 And when the ten heard *it,* they were moved with indignation against the two brethren.

25 But Jesus called them *unto him,* and said, Ye know that the princes of the Gentiles exercise dominion over them, and they that are great exercise authority upon them.

able." 23 He said to them, "You will drink my cup, but to sit at my right hand and at my left is not mine to grant, but it is for those for whom it has been prepared by my Father." 24 And when the ten heard it, they were indignant at the two brothers. 25 But Jesus called them to him and said, "You know that the rulers of the Gentiles lord it over them, and their great men

23. We know that James the son of Zebedee was martyred (Acts 12:1-3); and there is a tradition, ascribed to the second-century writer Papias, that his brother suffered a similar fate. The first half of this verse is sometimes thought to be a hint that this happened. It is the second half of the verse, however, that is essential. Jesus disclaims knowledge of the details of the future, or the power to choose the greatest in the kingdom. All this is in the hands of God.

25. It was taken for granted in antiquity—and usually is today, except where Christianity has modified men's view of what is fitting—that **the rulers,** and indeed all who are in authority, will **lord it over** their subordinates and show them who is master. The worldling asks, "What advantage is there, otherwise, in being 'top dog'?"

The "thrones" are reached by the drinking of a bitter cup and by the baptism of dark waters. Strange road to a throne! Besides, if God has **prepared** the position of trust for others, we ought not to be **able:** the task is not for us. James was martyred (see Acts 12:1-3 which may suggest that he perished in the Neronian persecutions). John's fate is not known, but is surrounded by stories of hardship and exile. In deeper sense they **were able,** because they later learned to trust the hidden ways and invincible power of a risen Lord.

24-27. *The Greatness of the Slave.*—Notice that the word for **minister** is διάκονος, and remember the function of the deacon in the early church. Notice that the Greek word for **servant** is δοῦλος, bond servant or slave. We have here a picture of the pagan world. Jesus had watched the Roman governor pass in procession through the ranks of a servile population. He had seen the centurion exercising a life-and-death control. He had seen folk fawn on the grandee: "Benefactor! Benefactor!" The poor served the rich, and the weak served the strong. Can we say that our world is radically different? An old history book has a picture of King Canute (the same man who expected the tide to obey him) being rowed down the River Dee by six tributary kings. That dramatic representation of "greatness" perhaps remained imprinted for years on the pupils' minds. Imagine the great-

ness of a king who could **lord it** over six kings! Someday the history books will be rewritten: they will have little to say about fictitious "power," and more to say of the growth of the mind of Christ among men. When Cardinal Wolsey bade "Farewell! a long farewell, to all my greatness!"[4] he was actually leaving his *littleness* and becoming great. Who are the truly **great** in any land? Probably not those whose names quickly occur to us, but perchance some mother in a hard-pressed home or some teacher in a village school.

Christ's is an insurgent gospel. It flatly contradicts the accepted order. It is a challenge flung in the teeth of standards that men take for granted: **It shall not be so among you.** The world's idea of greatness is like a pyramid—with the great man standing at the peak, and most people scrambling to reach the next higher level where there are fewer equals and more subordinates. But Christ's idea of greatness is like an inverted pyramid: the nearer to the peak, the greater the burden, and the more people are carried in love. The steps in Christ's lowliness are written eloquently in Phil. 2:6-8. On the Cross he reached the point of love's inverted pyramid, and there bore the sins of the world. Among Christian folk the pagan questions, "How much salary does he have? What is his social standing?" must go. We must

[4] Shakespeare, *King Henry VIII,* Act III, scene 2.

26 But it shall not be so among you: but whosoever will be great among you, let him be your minister;

27 And whosoever will be chief among you, let him be your servant:

28 Even as the Son of man came not to be ministered unto, but to minister, and to give his life a ransom for many.

exercise authority over them. **26** It shall not be so among you; but whoever would be great among you must be your servant, **27** and whoever would be first among you must be your slave; **28** even as the Son of man came not to be served but to serve, and to give his life as a ransom for many."

26-27. The word translated **minister** or **servant** is διάκονος, from which the ecclesiastical term "deacon" is directly derived. Every minister, and indeed every Christian, is a "deacon" who is under obligation to serve others, and there is no higher office in the kingdom of God than this. The parallel word **slave** often denotes a worshiper of God (Ps. 34:22), or one who is called by God to a special service (Josh. 1:1; Jer. 7:25; Rom. 1:1). Here "the true servant of God will be slave to the brethren." The most distinguished title of the bishops of Rome is "Servus Servorum Dei," adopted by Gregory the Great.

28. If Jesus used these precise words, **the Son of man** need mean no more than "I myself"; to the evangelists it had a more profound significance. The idea that he did not come **to be served but to serve** is found also in Luke 22:27, which is either a separate tradition or a rewriting of the Marcan passage. In Luke 12:37 the Lord, when he returns, will reward the faithful slaves by waiting on them. This statement certainly expresses Jesus' way of dealing with other people. **To give his life as a ransom for many** introduces a new idea as a climax to the section. It is true that Jesus' primary interest was not in interpreting his own vocation (cf. Cadbury, *Peril of Modernizing Jesus*, pp. 135-45). On the other hand, he probably went to Jerusalem prepared to give his life, if it should prove necessary, for the sake of the kingdom of God. Such a sacrifice would be on behalf of **many.** Jesus' action at the Last Supper, when he broke the bread as a sign that his body would be broken, and distributed the fragments to be eaten (26:26), shows that this saying is in harmony with the rest of the gospel tradition. The idea is not derived from the mystery religions or any other Hellenistic source, but is in accord with Jewish thought (II Macc. 7:37-38; IV Macc. 6:28; 17:21-22). Montefiore and Loewe give examples of the rabbinical doctrine that the death of the righteous atones for others (*Rabbinic Anthology*, pp. 225-32). The words of the passage must not be pressed too far. 'Αντί probably does not mean "in place of"; it simply affirms that the benefits of this death are for others. **Ransom** is the usual translation of λύτρον, that which looses or redeems. There is no necessary implication that the ransom is paid to someone (God or the devil, for example); the thought is only that it costs greatly to rescue men from their enslavement.

Some MSS of the Western text, and the Curetonian Syriac, add an abbreviated form of Luke 14:7-10 at this point. This furnishes an interesting illustration of how, in a traditional book, materials dealing with a certain theme tend to be collected together.

---

ask the new questions, "Does he forget himself? Is he sensitive to the sufferings of the poor, the criminal, the sad? Is he quite ready to be last, if thereby he can honor Christ?" The Napoleon standard has been too long with us: we all have fifty lowly neighbors who are far greater than Napoleon. This truth must be applied as fearlessly to nations and churches and businesses: we must ask, "Is it like a slave in lowly service?" Mark carefully: Jesus covets greatness for his followers, but only a true greatness. He consigns none of us to littleness or nonentity. But the conditions of real greatness are nevertheless fixed from the foundation of the world. There

is no dearth of titles in Christ's kingdom. But there the aristocracy is one of lowly love.

28. *A Ransom for Many.*—We must be careful not to read too much, or too little, in these words. They have rightly become focal and dear in Christian faith. For (άντί) does not necessarily mean "in place of": the word can hardly bear the weight of substitutionary theories of the Atonement. But these theories are valid on other grounds. Similarly, the word **ransom** cannot be turned into a dogmatism, for the word has many meanings. Yet the meanings themselves are an illumination of Christ's saving sacrifice: **Ransom** meant (a) the money ransom

| 29 And as they departed from Jericho, a great multitude followed him. | 29 And as they went out of Jericho, a |

B. HEALING OF TWO BLIND MEN (20:29-34)

Mark 10:46-52 narrates the healing of Bartimaeus, and Matthew rewrites this as the healing of **two blind men,** perhaps because he has omitted Mark 8:22-26. Mark's story can be classified as a "paradigm" or sermonic illustration. The emphasis is not on the miracle but on the man's persistence, and the story is told for the sake of Jesus' saying, "Your faith has saved you" (Mark 10:52). Matthew omits these details and adds in vs. 34 that he **touched their eyes** (ὄμματα, as in Mark 8:23), thus making it into a more conventional miracle story.

The tradition possibly located this story at Jericho, just before the entry into Jerusalem. Mark, and perhaps Matthew also, may have seen some theological symbolism in this. Mark's other story of the healing of a blind man came just before Peter's confession and the Transfiguration, in which Peter's eyes were opened. This narrative involves a confession of messiahship (as in the healing story of John 9) and it comes just before the great events—triumphal entry into Jerusalem, cleansing of the temple, crucifixion and resurrection—which opened the eyes of all Jesus' followers to the significance of his work. (See also the article by Vincent Taylor, "The Life and Ministry of Jesus," above, pp. 132-44.)

29. Jericho is about 15 miles northeast of Jerusalem. Being 3,300 feet lower in altitude, it is in striking contrast with the Holy City. Herod the Great had done much building there, and in Jesus' time it was a flourishing locality. Jesus had probably traveled

---

that freed a man from slavery; (b) the payment that freed a man from crime, as when one whose ox had gored a neighbor gave money in atonement of the wrong; (c) the price a father paid in lieu of his failure to offer his first born to the life of the priesthood. There were other meanings, but these are enough to show that dogmatisms, such as those which suggest that God paid a price to the devil, are not in place.

But we see here the shadows of great facts. One is the fact of human enslavement, and of human failure to live the priestly (consecrated) life. Beyond doubt Christ grieved more over inner bondage than over outward servitude: he said little about the Roman occupation, but again and again said by implication as well as plain word that "every one who commits sin is a slave to sin" (John 8:34). Perhaps Jesus would tell us that it is of little use to be "free" from military conquest or economic domination if we remain unconcerned about secret bondage. That latter slavery is a far worse yoke upon the will.

Another great fact is that we ourselves cannot pay the price of our redemption. How would we follow a lie to wash out its stain? How would we cancel the treachery of which we were guilty ten years ago? How, with only a weak will for our weapon, can we will our wholeness? In warfare a general is worth more in ransom than a private. In ancient warfare a comely woman was worth more in ransom than a drab slave. Who is worth enough in divine power and love to set

free **many**—or to atone for the common guilt in which every man in history is involved? Thus:

The great fact is the cross of Christ. Perhaps the word of later theology has been flung back into this verse, or perhaps later theology learned the word **ransom** from the lips of Christ. In either event the truth remains. Only one sent from God can cleanse history.

> Nothing in my hand I bring,
> Simply to thy cross I cling.[5]

A physician lives by the rule of **ransom:** he must be willing to catch disease and die for his patient. But there is a worse than mortal sickness here: there is a sickness from which man suffers to his eternal destiny. Only the Great Physician can pay that price for every human physician and every patient.

29-34. Blind Eyes Opened.—A blind man wins our sympathy. He does not lack for unknown friends to help him cross the street. These men could not see Jericho, "City of Roses," or the blue of the sky, or the face of loved ones in their homes. But why do we withhold sympathy from a worse blindness? Men cannot see when disaster impends, as witness World War II. Men are blind to the nobility in George Washington Carver. Men miss the joy of good will and the deeper joy of prayer. The artist Turner said of his work, "I know that no man now living in Europe cares to understand

[5] "Rock of Ages."

30 ¶ And, behold, two blind men sitting by the wayside, when they heard that Jesus passed by, cried out, saying, Have mercy on us, O Lord, *thou* Son of David.

31 And the multitude rebuked them, because they should hold their peace: but they cried the more, saying, Have mercy on us, O Lord, *thou* Son of David.

32 And Jesus stood still, and called them, and said, What will ye that I shall do unto you?

33 They say unto him, Lord, that our eyes may be opened.

34 So Jesus had compassion *on them,* and touched their eyes: and immediately their eyes received sight, and they followed him.

great crowd followed him. **30** And behold, two blind men sitting by the roadside, when they heard that Jesus was passing by, cried out,*q* "Have mercy on us, Son of David!" **31** The crowd rebuked them, telling them to be silent; but they cried out the more, "Lord, have mercy on us, Son of David!" **32** And Jesus stopped and called them, saying, "What do you want me to do for you?" **33** They said to him, "Lord, let our eyes be opened." **34** And Jesus in pity touched their eyes, and immediately they received their sight and followed him.

q Many ancient authorities insert *Lord.*

---

on the east side of the Jordan and crossed the fords near Jericho. The town was the last stage of his journey.

30. They hail Jesus as **Son of David,** i.e., Messiah (cf. on 9:27).

31. They were told to **be silent** possibly because an open proclamation of messiahship endangered Jesus' safety. Even though he did not desire political power, there were those who wished to bestow it on him (cf. general note on 16:13-20).

34. They **followed him** as disciples.

---

it; and the better I do it, the less he will see the meaning of it." [6] Jesus could have spoken thus of his work with more poignant truth.

Blindness, except when psychological blindness, is almost beyond human cure. What of the worse blindness? Our fellow men cannot there help us: they also are blind. The Emperor Hadrian accidentally stabbed a servant in the eye with his stylus, and promised the man any boon; but all the man could say was, "I wish I had my eye." All any man can say is, **Lord, let our eyes be opened.** But we are not utterly helpless. The **blind men** could hear. They could sense the excitement as Jesus came. They could catch tag ends of conversation as some people wondered out loud if Jesus could be the Messiah. They could plead when Jesus came alongside, and continue to plead. Has a rumor reached us that there is a cure for blindness of soul? Have we heard footsteps coming near in mercy?

Then why are we not healed? Have others blocked our path, as the crowd **rebuked the blind men** in this story? There is a fable of a blind man who carried a lantern. What good would it do him? "So others will not stumble over me," he said. Or is our pride too great, so that we are unwilling to admit our sightlessness? Or is our faith too small? Modern scholars are sure this story is a paradigm: the interest is not only in the miracle, but in the persistence of the

blind men and in the words spoken by Jesus. **Son of David!** they cried. It was a messianic title. They believed God would come in great deliverance, and their faith saved them. **They heard that Jesus was passing by:** the moment had come and they must seize it, or it might forever pass. Such moments do come, and they must be taken.

Jesus stopped and called them. The cry of need stopped him. It stops all heaven. **What do you want me to do?** Leading question! If these men were relieved of begging, they would have to work. Did they wish honest livelihood and pure motive? Sholem Asch, in his novel *The Nazarene,* imagines a blind man, whom Jesus could have cured, mocking the Master and his way of life; and he shows Jesus saying, "What shall it avail if thou art made seeing with thy eyes and thy heart remaineth blind?" [7] Why do we wish to see? The men **followed** Jesus. That is, they became then and there disciples. That was proof of the sincerity of their prayer. Scholars agree also that Jesus was now on his way to suffering and death. Let us hope that the men still followed. All we need is faith and sincerity to seize that moment when the **Son of David** draws near. Then our eyes are opened; for our needs stop and hold heaven's energies. **Jesus in pity touched their eyes, and immediately they received their sight and followed him.**

[6] John Ruskin, *Modern Painters,* V, 436.

[7] New York: G. P. Putnam's Sons, p. 276.

21 And when they drew nigh unto Jerusalem, and were come to Bethphage, unto the mount of Olives, then sent Jesus two disciples,

21 And when they drew near to Jerusalem and came to Beth'pha-ge, to the Mount of Olives, then Jesus sent two

C. Events in Jerusalem (21:1–23:39)

This section has a twofold purpose. It contains a series of brief narratives which show how the opposition to Jesus developed in Jerusalem and led to the Crucifixion, and it also includes the last collection of his teaching—except for the great discourse on the end of the age, which follows immediately. Its dramatic effect is striking. Mark is still the principal source. Q is drawn on for the main substance of 22:1-10; 23:4, 13, 23-39. Special sources may have contributed 21:28-32; 23:2-3, 5, 8-10, 15-22, 24. The brief additions to these materials are Matthew's own work, and his interests can be clearly recognized in them.

It is always worth remembering that the units of the gospel tradition at one time circulated independently of one another. The church did not often recall when and where a given saying was first spoken. Yet it is possible that some of the teachings recorded here were spoken in Jerusalem. The framework of the Synoptic Gospels is based on Mark, and Mark knew of only one visit to the Holy City. On the other hand, John tells of at least four visits to Jerusalem; and a priori it seems likely that Jesus had been there more than once during his public ministry, especially since Mark contains indications that he was well known there (Mark 11:2-3=Matt. 21:2-3).

One can only speculate as to the purpose of this last visit. The evangelists seldom try to assess Jesus' motives. They refrain from this attempt, partly because of their conviction that his thoughts, like God's, are not those of men; partly because they view his purpose theologically—he goes in order to redeem mankind by his cross and resurrection; and partly because the tradition itself was objective—it contained only accounts of Jesus' deeds and words, not speculation as to what he meant by them. To the evangelists he was mysterious and holy, and his presence evoked awe and wonder. Analysis was out of place.

Nevertheless the modern reader cannot avoid asking why Jesus went to Jerusalem. Perhaps he wished to appeal to the nation, solemnly gathered for the festival, to follow his way, and so make possible the establishment of the kingdom of God on earth. Perhaps he wished to confront the leaders of the nation with the claims of that kingdom, so that they would either repent and follow its righteousness, or exhibit themselves as disobedient. Or it may be that he was simply carrying on his work as he had always done, and had no object different from that which had been his concern in Galilee. At any rate, according to the sources, he realized that it was dangerous to make the journey, and he was willing to risk death rather than be untrue to his task. Indeed, he may have known that death was practically certain for one who had so often been recognized as Messiah, and so he prepared to die, assured that even in and through his death his cause would triumph. Reverent reserve is appropriate for the commentator as it was for the evangelists. We can say only that the events turned out to the glory of God, and Jesus himself would have asked no more than that.

1. The Triumphal Entry (21:1-11)

21:1. Matthew has **Bethphage** in place of "Bethany," which is the reading of the Western text of Mark. Other MSS of Mark mention both places. "Bethphage" apparently

---

21:1-6. A Meek King.—We now move in a certain inevitableness toward the climax of Calvary. The description is objective, yet terse and tense with urgency. We do not know what motives impelled Jesus to go to Jerusalem at this time. Perhaps he had resolved on a last

plea to the people and rulers to enter the "new way." It seems clear that he knew it might be just that, a last plea. There is much debate among students of the Gospels about the Triumphal Entry (see Expos., vss. 8-11). But, by any interpretation, Jesus was at pains to

2 Saying unto them, Go into the village over against you, and straightway ye shall find an ass tied, and a colt with her: loose *them,* and bring *them* unto me.

3 And if any *man* say aught unto you, ye shall say, The Lord hath need of them; and straightway he will send them.

4 All this was done, that it might be fulfilled which was spoken by the prophet, saying,

5 Tell ye the daughter of Sion, Behold, thy King cometh unto thee, meek, and sitting upon an ass, and a colt the foal of an ass.

6 And the disciples went, and did as Jesus commanded them,

7 And brought the ass, and the colt, and put on them their clothes, and they set *him* thereon.

disciples, 2 saying to them, "Go into the village opposite you, and immediately you will find an ass tied, and a colt with her; untie them and bring them to me. 3 If any one says anything to you, you shall say, 'The Lord has need of them,' and he will send them immediately." 4 This took place to fulfill what was spoken by the prophet, saying,

5 "Tell the daughter of Zion,
    Behold, your king is coming
      to you,
    humble, and mounted on an ass,
    and on a colt, the foal of an
      ass."

6 The disciples went and did as Jesus had directed them; 7 they brought the ass and the colt, and put their garments on them,

means "house of figs." It is known to the Mishnah, which reckons it as an outlying part of Jerusalem (Menahoth 11:2). It must have been near **the Mount of Olives,** which is in full view of the city, and at which, according to popular belief, the Messiah would appear (Josephus *Jewish War* II. 13. 5; *Antiquities* XX. 8. 6). Medieval tradition places it about halfway between Bethany and Jerusalem.

2. **The village opposite you** must be Bethphage. Matthew pictures Jesus as ordering both the **ass** and the **colt** to be brought, and riding on them both (vs. 7) because he believed that Zech. 9:9 must indeed be fulfilled literally and in every detail. Justin Martyr saw in this incident also a reminiscence of the blessing of Judah (Gen. 49:11).

3. **The Lord** may be Jesus, but the evangelists seldom use this designation and Jesus does not use it of himself. Zahn suggested that the owner of the ass was one of the disciples, who had put the animal at Jesus' disposal. This would indicate that he had friends in Jerusalem.

4-5. Matthew, realizing that Jesus' action suggested the prophecy of Zech. 9:9, introduces the passage here. The quotation agrees in part with the LXX, but is probably drawn directly from the Hebrew. If Jesus had any special purpose in riding into the city, it was to make it clear to all beholders that he came for peace and had no intention of exercising force. The king of Zech. 9:9-10 is a man of peace. Jesus took no part in the fanatical nationalism which in the years 66-70 led to the destruction of Jerusalem.

7. The translation **he sat thereon** avoids the literal meaning "on them."

show that he led no movement of fanatical nationalism or armed revolt: he had chosen another way. So much at least Matthew understood: the quotation from Zech. 9:9, which is found only in this Gospel, is sheer insight.

Christ was a new kind of king. King Saul towered in physical strength and military prowess; King Solomon in wealth and wisdom. The throne of Byzantium was set with jewels, the throne of the Moguls with priceless peacocks' feathers (token of pride), and many a Napoleon has waded through blood to dominance. But Christ was meek. He needed the lowly ass, the service of the unknown friend to whom the disciples were sent, and the friend-

ship of his followers. He rode on an animal that was symbol of quietness, not on a war horse; palm branches, not spears, were his escort; the songs of children, not the shout of soldiers, were his welcome. When he died, a reed was his scepter. But he was kingly. There is command in every move recorded in these verses. The root meaning of the word king is "the one who is able." Christ is able to lift life above its low estate to an eternal verity. He is able to redeem its dross and make it kingly gold. He rules the world as light rules—with beauty and bounty. Rudyard Kipling's poem "Cold Iron" has caught the paradox of meekness and majesty in Christ. His crown was a crown of thorns. That

8 And a very great multitude spread their garments in the way; others cut down branches from the trees, and strewed *them* in the way.

9 And the multitudes that went before, and that followed, cried, saying, Hosanna to the Son of David: Blessed *is* he that cometh in the name of the Lord; Hosanna in the highest.

and he sat thereon. 8 Most of the crowd spread their garments on the road, and others cut branches from the trees and spread them on the road. 9 And the crowds that went before him and that followed him shouted, "Hosanna to the Son of David! Blessed be he who comes in the name of

---

8-9. Though Jesus wished to show that he had no intention of being king, some of his enthusiastic followers thwarted him. They **spread their garments on the road,** as Jehu's followers placed their garments on the stair when he was proclaimed king (II Kings 9:13). The **branches** may be myrtle and willow, with a spray of palm leaf. This was the lulab, which, with the ethrog or citron, was carried in procession at the time of Tabernacles. The shouts of **hosanna** belong to the regular ritual of the feasts of Tabernacles and Hanukkah (Rededication); cf. Moore, *Judaism,* II, 43-48, 50. At these two feasts the Hallel (Pss. 113–118) was recited, and this passage (Ps. 118:26) is quoted. Matthew does not consult the Hebrew or the LXX but copies Mark 11:9-10 with some changes. **Hosanna** means "Save now!" In adding **to the Son of David,** does Matthew mean "Save us, Son of David" or does he forget the meaning of "hosanna" and think of it as a shout of praise? "Save now **in the highest**" does not make sense, unless it means "Up with your hosannas," i.e., your wands, or "Save us now, O thou who dwellest in heaven"; but Mark may have thought of Ps. 148:1, "Praise him in the heights." **Blessed be he who comes in the name of the Lord** was understood as a blessing on all pilgrims who came to the feast of Tabernacles, but Matthew thinks of it as addressed to Jesus. Mark's striking phrase—which Matthew omits—"Blessed be the coming kingdom of our father David," indicates that the crowd turned a festival pilgrimage into a messianic demonstration.

---

is why the ages sing, "Crown him with many crowns, the Lamb upon his throne."

8-11. *The First Palm Sunday.*—There are three main interpretations of the account of the Triumphal Entry. One holds that Jesus intended it as a messianic proclamation: at first he had hid his messiahship, then pledged his disciples to secrecy concerning it, but now he allowed his initiates to honor it, and soon before Pilate he would straightly avow it. A second view holds that his followers, despite Jesus, proclaimed his messiahship—in a mingling of spiritual and earthy hopes. A third view holds that the procession may have come at the feast of Tabernacles, and that the followers of Jesus, in the jubilation of the time, honored him as a prophet who might usher in the expected reign of God. We lack sufficient evidence to settle dogmatically on any one of these views. All three could be right. But it is clear that the procession did not represent a mass movement. Jerusalem was largely indifferent. Men still talked of the price of wheat and of the Roman occupation. They knew not "the time of [God's] visitation" (Luke 19:44). Some hoped Christ might be an earthly Messiah; others hankered to see him perform a miracle. Perhaps a few caught

the wonder of his soul, and perhaps these were the ones who spread their garments before him, as once people had welcomed King Jehu (II Kings 9:13). Probably most people in that crowd gave little thought to the meaning of **Hosanna!** It meant, "Help, we pray!" Perhaps its meaning had broadened to mean, "Help Israel, O God." If only they had understood their deep need, and had really prayed the prayer! But soon the crowd, instigated by shouters planted by the enemies of Jesus, would cry "Crucify him" (Luke 23:21). He had reason to weep over Jerusalem.

The church through the ages has celebrated Palm Sunday in right mood. It is not a joyous festival, but token of the blindness and fickleness of human "loyalties." It is the proper prelude to the Cross. John Kelman in his *Thoughts on Things Eternal* has well said that the Triumphal Entry is a pageant of "Royalty and Death," and that "royalty and death are in the heart of Christ, and we are called upon to reckon with that dread purpose of His, each of us for ourselves." [8] Perhaps any modern city would today treat Christ in the same way—a few hailing him, and only a few of them under-

[8] (London: Hodder & Stoughton, 1917), pp. 84, 88.

10 And when he was come into Jerusalem, all the city was moved, saying, Who is this?

11 And the multitude said, This is Jesus the prophet of Nazareth of Galilee.

12 ¶ And Jesus went into the temple of God, and cast out all them that sold and

the Lord! Hosanna in the highest!" 10 And when he entered Jerusalem, all the city was stirred, saying, "Who is this?" 11 And the crowds said, "This is the prophet Jesus from Nazareth of Galilee."

12 And Jesus entered the temple of

Burkitt believed that this incident occurred, not at the time of Passover, but of Rededication (in December), and that Jesus after his triumphal entry cleansed the temple and "dedicated" it (see his *Jesus Christ: An Historical Outline* [London and Glasgow: Blackie & Son, 1932], pp. 42-43). Branscomb (*Mark,* pp. 199-200) prefers Tabernacles, and points out that the half-shekel dues, which made money-changing necessary, had to be collected nearly two weeks before Passover. Thus, if Jesus entered the city only a week before Passover, the money-changers of vs. 12 would already have finished their work. Jesus' last visit to Jerusalem may therefore have occupied a longer time than the Synoptic Gospels indicate. If this incident occurred in the spring, it must have been two or three weeks before Passover. In that case it would be necessary to suppose that ceremonies like those of Tabernacles were carried on also in the weeks preceding Passover. There is no other evidence that this was true.

11. The crowds would naturally consider Jesus a **prophet**—his riding into the city, and his cleansing of the temple, suggested this role. Matthew emphasizes this in order to indicate that the demonstration was not political.

2. Cleansing of the Temple (21:12-17)

Matthew dates this incident on Jesus' first day in Jerusalem; but according to Mark 11:11 Jesus on that day merely entered the temple enclosure, looked around, and

---

standing his real majesty; most living in indifference, and crying "Crucify!" when he disappointed their hatred and greed. The hymn has taught both the divine royalty and the divine passion:

> Ride on! ride on in majesty!
> In lowly pomp ride on to die.

10-11. Who Is This?—The bafflement of serious minds concerning Jesus is reflected in the original setting. This Gospel in vss. 5 and 9 proclaims Christ's messiahship, a deep messiahship of the soul, not an earthly messiahship of swords. But here it says that the crowd regarded Jesus as a **prophet** who had come to foretell the reign of God, but only as a prophet. Thus the debate continues through the years.

Some believed that he was, or should be, an armed Messiah. They would be "free," they thought, if only someone would throw off the Roman yoke. In every war men have looked for victory to bring that miracle, and victory has always failed them. Some believed him an impostor and a trouble breeder. That view persists: there are leaders in state and industry who, whatever the lip service they pay to Christ, would think it worse than unfortunate if many people should take him too seriously. Some be-

lieved him a prophet. That view has always been popular: Jesus is a good man and a great teacher, perhaps even the best and greatest; but he is not Savior, for a man must trust to his own wisdom and skill. Some paid no attention to him. Some saw in him the flash of the mystery of Godhead. In the crowd on the first Palm Sunday were represented all the half-beliefs about Christ that mark our own day.

Scholars nowadays agree that the gospel writers incorporated in their record the afterthoughts which came only through the light of Christ's resurrection. That interpretation has gospel warrant: John strikingly tells us, regarding the Triumphal Entry, "These things understood not his disciples at the first: but when Jesus was glorified, then remembered they that these things were written of him, and that they had done these things unto him" (John 12:16). **Who is this?** *We* have the verdicts of Christian history to help us, more especially the great exaltation that followed Calvary. But we shall still not reach truth until we lay aside our presuppositions and make our venture. Only then shall we be able to say adoringly, "My Lord and my God!" (John 20:28).

12-16. The Cleansing of the Temple.—Matthew's account is astonishingly meager. Apparently our author did not fully realize that this

bought in the temple, and overthrew the tables of the money changers, and the seats of them that sold doves,

God[r] and drove out all who sold and bought in the temple, and he overturned the tables of the money-changers and the

[r] Some ancient authorities omit of God.

---

returned to Bethany to spend the night. John 2:13-22 puts the cleansing of the temple at the beginning of Jesus' ministry, but this is most unlikely. This highhanded action could not have been ignored by the authorities. At the very least it was a prophetic act which condemned them, and this helps to explain why they denounced Jesus to Pilate as a revolutionary.

Sellers of wine and sacrificial animals had booths in the Court of the Gentiles, surrounding the inner courts on three sides. The money-changers also set up their tables there from Adar 25 to Nisan 1, so that Jews might exchange other coins for the half-shekel pieces in which the annual tax had to be paid (Shekalim 1:1-3). There is no evidence that the Jewish people protested against any irregularities in connection with the money-changing. On the contrary, it was a convenience which enabled them to comply with the law. The sale of sacrificial animals may have been a different matter. The Talmud contains curses on the Sadducean priesthood for its greed (Strack and Billerbeck, I, 851, 853; II, 570). Shortly before the fall of Jerusalem, a rabbi relaxed the rules for purification sacrifices because there had been profiteering in doves. About the same time, according to Josephus (*Antiquities* XX. 8. 8; 9. 2), the "chief priests" seized the tithes with the result that poorer priests starved. The Pharisees, whose sympathies were with the common people, hated the family of Annas, which controlled the temple during much of the first century and which owned markets for the sale of sacrificial animals. In driving out the sellers of doves Jesus may have been protesting against extortion. It was not, however, a protest against sacrifice nor against the sale of animals for sacrifice. In the general confusion the benches of the money-changers were overturned.

What did Jesus hope to accomplish by this deed? He could hardly have wished for a popular uprising which would drive out the high priest and his friends, though Mark's account shows that the authorities were afraid to touch Jesus because the crowd supported him. In some sense he actually controlled the temple precincts for the time being (Mark 11:16, 18-19). The cleansing of the temple was probably an act of prophetic symbolism, such as those performed when Isaiah went naked and barefoot (Isa. 20:1-6), when Jeremiah buried his loincloth (Jer. 13:1-11), and when Agabus bound his feet and hands with Paul's belt (Acts 21:11-12). The O.T. contains numerous prophecies against the temple. Jer. 7:1-16 is such a denunciation, and a phrase from that passage is quoted here in vs. 13. In Malachi, which is directed against the priesthood, the messenger of the covenant will come to purify the sons of Levi (Mal. 3:3), and Yahweh himself will come and sit in judgment (Mal. 3:5). Jesus was not acting against the temple or its worship, but against current abuses. Mark 11:16 tells us that he did not permit anyone to carry a vessel through the temple enclosure and so use it as a short cut between different parts of the city. God's house must be treated with proper reverence. The action may therefore mean: "As I have this day executed judgment against the priesthood, so, unless you repent, God himself will come to judge more severely."

12. The word translated **money-changers** (κολλυβιστῶν) denotes those who received the *qôlbôn* or fee for changing other currencies into the coinage of Tyre, in which the

---

incident was probably the immediate cause of Christ's death. Important phrases, such as "for all nations" in Christ's dictum about the temple, are omitted. Why? Matthew, as we have seen, was a mediator between the Jewish and Gentile Christians. So, of course, he had no anti-Gentile bias. Perhaps we must assume that because the

temple had been destroyed when Matthew wrote, the cruciality of Christ's cleansing of the temple was partly lost on him. The other accounts (Mark 11:15-19; Luke 19:45-48; John 2:13-22) should be carefully read. (See Exeg. for a description of the money changing, the sale of sacrificial animals in the Court of the

13 And said unto them, It is written, My house shall be called the house of prayer; but ye have made it a den of thieves.

seats of those who sold pigeons. 13 He said to them, "It is written, 'My house shall be called a house of prayer'; but you make it a den of robbers."

---

half-shekel tax had to be paid. For further information, see on 17:24-27 and Israel Abrahams, *Studies in Pharisaism and the Gospels,* 1st ser. (Cambridge: University Press, 1917), pp. 82-89.

13. The saying is quoted from Isa. 56:7 and Jer. 7:11, LXX. Matthew borrows it from Mark, omitting "for all the nations," perhaps because he thinks of the temple as a house of prayer for Israel only.

Gentiles, and the vested interests of "the sons of Annas.")

Jesus' protest was not against the system of sacrifices or against the half-shekel tax. Doubtless the words of Isaiah (1:13-17) were the very fiber of his conscience; but the temple was dear to him nevertheless, and he rejoiced in its ordinances when they were kept in sincerity. His protest was against extortion and graft, not only because they were an injustice to men, but because they were an offense to God in God's own house. In prophetic and symbolic act, not in armed might, Christ attacked outright the vested interests of the Sadducees and the family of the high priest. In every age that attack is the dangerous heresy. Preachers are bidden by wealthy men to "stick to the gospel." If preachers obeyed the behest, what tumults would ensue! The cleansing of the temple is in the very texture of the gospel.

Perhaps we have failed to see that the protest was also against a selfish nationalism. Those who controlled the temple believed in "Jerusalem for the Jews," a slogan that has found nationalistic echo in every land. Yet the Jews had been given tidings of the holy God, not that they might bask in the sunshine of the revelation, but that they might proclaim it to all nations. That historic mission had been forgotten. Jesus here recalled Israel to her rightful task: "My house shall be called a house of prayer *for all the nations*" (Mark 11:17). The indignation of Jesus was stirred for the Gentiles: *their* court was being desecrated. Where scribes and rabbis were wont to teach in the portico—where the tidings of the one God should have been made known—there was marketing and a greedy rabble. The high priest gathered the graft.

The protest was for a primal reverence. Mark 11:16 is significant: God's house must not be turned into a thoroughfare. Jesus was contending for an attitude: all man's thought and work must be Godward. If men had been thinking of God, there could have been no graft or selfish nationalism, especially in the temple. The temple was a house of prayer. The

disclosure of God in Jesus here shines with burning light. He was angry: true Christianity is known by its indignations as well as by its gentleness, by its foes as well as by its friends. He was clothed with authority: he was master of that frenzied and unseemly mob. They scurried from him like vermin from the light. He was clothed with power, and the proper word to describe him is: "The Lord . . . shall suddenly come to his temple. . . . But who may abide the day of his coming?" (Mal. 3:1, 2). And for this—he died.

13. *A House of Prayer. But Ye Have Made It. . . .*—By God's creative intent it was **a house of prayer** for all nations, by man's making it was a grafting market place. Man has a terrible freedom, and within his own measure a creatorship. But if man's making be wrenched away from God's intent, it becomes first a disfigurement and then a tragedy. An enemy destroyed the temple? Yes, but the Jews themselves had already destroyed it; and, in the strange outworkings of history, the enemy was a scourge in the hand of God.

A true temple is the radiating center of a mission. For the Jews before Jesus' time that mission was the tidings of the one God; for a Christian church today, the proclamation of the gospel. The temple in the time of Christ was trying to live on and for itself, and so died. A true temple is the home of a brotherhood. Jesus was concerned for the rights-in-love of the Gentiles. Their court in the temple had been outraged. Doubtless the inscription placed between that court and the inner court grieved him: "No stranger is to enter within the balustrade. . . . Whoever is caught will be answerable for his death, which will ensue." [9] No man was a "stranger" to Jesus. Are there balustrades of racial and class prejudices within our churches? No fences exist within the mercy of God, or even within our common need and hope.

A true temple is a home of worship and prayer. Marketing is right, if it obeys God. When it usurps the place of God it is a raucous

[9] Hastings, *Dictionary of the Bible,* IV, 713-14. Also see Josephus *Jewish War* V. 5. 2; and *Antiquities* XV. 11. 5.

14 And the blind and the lame came to him in the temple; and he healed them.

15 And when the chief priests and scribes saw the wonderful things that he did, and the children crying in the temple, and saying, Hosanna to the Son of David; they were sore displeased,

16 And said unto him, Hearest thou what these say? And Jesus saith unto them, Yea; have ye never read, Out of the mouth of babes and sucklings thou hast perfected praise?

17 ¶ And he left them, and went out of the city into Bethany; and he lodged there.

18 Now in the morning, as he returned into the city, he hungered.

14 And the blind and the lame came to him in the temple, and he healed them.

15 But when the chief priests and the scribes saw the wonderful things that he did, and the children crying out in the temple, "Hosanna to the Son of David!" they were indignant; 16 and they said to him, "Do you hear what these are saying?" And Jesus said to them, "Yes; have you never read,

'Out of the mouth of babes and
　　sucklings
thou hast brought perfect praise'?"

17 And leaving them, he went out of the city to Bethany and lodged there.

18 In the morning, as he was returning

---

14. See on 19:1-2.

15-16. These verses are in Matthew's style and probably do not come from a written source. The picture of **children crying . . . Hosanna** was probably suggested to him by meditation on the line from Ps. 8:3, LXX. An incident full of political tension and danger is given a different tone by the devoted and innocent praise of children.

17. This statement is drawn from Mark 11:19. **Bethany** was probably near the village of el-Azarîyeh, nearly two miles southeast of the temple area. Jesus may have **lodged there** frequently in these last days.

3. Cursing of the Fig Tree (21:18-22)

The story has raised many questions in the minds of readers. Quite apart from the issue of nature miracles, was it like Jesus to curse the fig tree, particularly if, as Mark 11:13 says, "it was not the season for figs"? We must, of course, realize that the

---

greed that invites the judgment. If a man should say, "I can worship God anywhere and at any time," he is pitiably ignorant of the finitude of our human nature. We need seasons and places. We need both private and corporate worship. No man has right to limit that word **prayer**. It is no small punctilio, no private enclosure, permitting a man to do as he will with the rest of his life—as witness the cleansing of the temple! Yet prayer is the burning focus. We need God—Father, Son, and Holy Spirit—not as a coward needs a refuge, but as a hero needs a challenge. We need him as the body needs bread, and as the soul needs pardon and an eternal home. We could wish that the words quoted by Christ were somewhere inscribed on every church as reminder and as goal.

14-16. *Innocence and Greed.*—These verses are peculiar to Matthew, and characteristic in style. Vs. 14 may originally have been found in another setting. Yet there is a providence, with or without the awareness of the author, in the locale of this picture. For we have here truth through contrast. On the one hand are the priests and traders in greedy collusion; on the other hand, a strange confraternity of suffering

folk and children. On the one hand is an act of sacrilege which Jesus purged; and on the other, his healing mercy. The blind and the halt knew their need of God, and were therefore more fortunate than the hale, rich traders. The children sang in innocence: God was in the primal springs of their lives. So they **perfected praise** where rapacious men had silenced it. The indignation of the chief priests was probably not entirely a pose. They were in character: such men would be outraged by children singing hosannas to the Messiah. They thought it childish blasphemy, and were blind to the real blasphemy of their own lives. Vss. 15-16 deserve a place alongside 19:13-15. For they confirm that charter which gives children a central place in the church. Children instinctively worship Jesus. What better testimony to him? He loved them and found strength in their love.

17-18. *Out of the City.*—Perhaps we can rightly read between these lines the rhythm of the life of Jesus. We know that he practiced an alternate prayer and work, so that his prayers were a loving labor of the soul, and his work itself a prayer. Perhaps we may find here an-

19 And when he saw a fig tree in the way, he came to it, and found nothing thereon, but leaves only, and said unto it, Let no fruit grow on thee henceforward for ever. And presently the fig tree withered away.

20 And when the disciples saw *it,* they marveled, saying, How soon is the fig tree withered away!

21 Jesus answered and said unto them, Verily I say unto you, If ye have faith, and doubt not, ye shall not only do this *which is done* to the fig tree, but also if ye shall say unto this mountain, Be thou removed, and be thou cast into the sea; it shall be done.

22 And all things, whatsoever ye shall ask in prayer, believing, ye shall receive.

to the city, he was hungry. 19 And seeing a fig tree by the wayside he went to it, and found nothing on it but leaves only. And he said to it, "May no fruit ever come from you again!" And the fig tree withered at once. 20 When the disciples saw it they marveled, saying, "How did the fig tree wither at once?" 21 And Jesus answered them, "Truly, I say to you, if you have faith and never doubt, you will not only do what has been done to the fig tree, but even if you say to this mountain, 'Be taken up and cast into the sea,' it will be done. 22 And whatever you ask in prayer, you will receive, if you have faith."

ancients told such stories to bring lessons home to their hearers, never asking themselves whether their tales were lifelike. The rabbis believed that any curse might be effective, especially that of a sage or righteous man (Aboth 2:10), and this incident would illustrate such a point. The most natural supposition, however, is that this is a dramatized form of Jesus' parable in Luke 13:6-9. God comes seeking from Israel (the fig tree) the fruits of repentance; the nation has but one more year, and if it does not repent it will be destroyed. In Mark's story a day intervenes between the cursing and the withering of the leaves; this suggests that some time elapses after the prophecy is made before it is fulfilled.

21-22. These verses are made up of independent sayings which the evangelists have applied to point a different moral. As G. K. Chesterton remarked, Jesus' style is sometimes "gigantesque," with camels leaping through needles and mountains hurled into the sea (*Orthodoxy* [New York: John Lane Co., 1909], p. 272). This is just the way in which a genuine Semitic teacher would impress on his hearers the importance of faith. One may compare the stories of Elijah at Mount Carmel (I Kings 18:20-39) and Elisha and the chariots of fire (II Kings 6:8-23). The Fourth Evangelist, in dealing with this theme, adds the necessary warning that **prayer** must be in accordance with the spirit of Jesus and the will of God (John 15:7).

other alternation, namely, private friendship and public mission. We know some of the friends of Jesus—his disciples, the members of Mary's family, and the Bethany group of Mary and Martha and Lazarus. Others we know only by indirection—the man who loaned the ass for the Triumphal Entry, and the other unknown friend who owned the house with the "upper room." Perhaps Jesus went often to visit these friends, and found in them, not only respite and solace, but reinforcement for his life's task. After the crowded day, the quiet evening in Bethany. But he did not immure himself in Bethany. **In the morning** he moved again among the fickle crowd in Jerusalem, and came to grips once more with unworthy foes. **Bethany was a rock, but the purpose of the rock was to enable him to enter again the swirling waters**

of our human need. **Out of the city** to the quiet Bethany of human love, and of prayer which apprehended God's love: **returning to the city** to fulfill his commissioned task. That is the alternate weaving of any worthy life.

19-22. *Faith and a Fig Tree.*—The difficulties of the story should be frankly faced. To propose that Jesus saw the tree was already diseased, and said so, does no justice to the undeniable curse in vs. 19. It also overlooks the fact that men then believed that a righteous man's curse had power. To propose that Christ would blast a tree, but not a human life, is similarly unconvincing. Would Christ deal thus even with a tree, especially if—as Mark's Gospel says—it was not the season for fruit? It is better to assume that this is a rewriting of the parable of the Jewish nation recorded in Luke 13:6-9. It is

23 ¶ And when he was come into the temple, the chief priests and the elders of the people came unto him as he was teaching, and said, By what authority doest thou these things? and who gave thee this authority?

23 And when he entered the temple, the chief priests and the elders of the people came up to him as he was teaching, and said, "By what authority are you doing these things, and who gave you this au-

4. Discussions and Controversies (21:23–22:46)

One of the most striking features of the Gospel of Mark is a series of little controversy dialogues which appear in Mark 1–3; 7; 10–12. Mark 11:27–12:37 is almost entirely made up of such stories. The evangelist may have found some of them in a written source, but it is more likely that they existed in a somewhat fixed oral form and were written down by Mark; see F. C. Grant, *The Growth of the Gospels* (New York: Abingdon Press, 1933), p. 136, and Grant's work on Mark in this volume. Matthew simply retains Mark's framework and inserts other material from his sources. It is not necessary to suppose that all of these discussions took place during the final visit to Jerusalem.

a) Controversy over Jesus' Authority (21:23-27)

23. This incident must be the direct consequence of the cleansing of the temple. **The chief priests and the elders of the people** are presumably representatives of the Sanhedrin, whose authority Jesus had defied. **These things** are not the cursing of the fig tree but the driving out of the traders. According to rabbinical ideas, the **authority** to teach and make binding decisions was conferred by the *semikhāh,* or laying on of hands, by which a man was ordained a rabbi. The question implies that Jesus does not belong to the rabbis or accredited teachers.

significant that Luke does not record this story except as a parable.

A tree, standing alone where all men could see it, having promise of fruit but no fruit—a fitting symbol of Jewry in the time of Christ. The Gentile nations were also barren, yet not as guilty; for they had not been cultivated for a special mission as had the Jews. They had no luxuriant law and ritual to deceive men's hope. It is trenchant teaching: our religion may be no better than a tree "gone to leaf." We must ask ourselves certain sharp questions. What of my practice as compared with my profession? How much real kindliness have I shown for Christ's sake? How much have I been willing to suffer for his truth? The fact of judgment cannot be blinked: the Jewish tree did wither. In the soul's country there is no indulgence for a fruitless tree.

The sayings about faith and prayer doubtless come from another setting. But there is value in their being linked with this parable. The real mountain is our unregenerate nature. That can be cast into the sea if we have faith, and if the faith lives in prayer. The vividness of Jesus' language should arouse our gratitude: it makes his dicta forever memorable. He did not teach in drab phrase or tepid imagination. A true faith (one that expects great things of the Christlike God) and true prayer (that asks

greatly for blessings that are in the nature of Christ) can move mountains—higher and harder mountains than any made of rock. Faith and prayer can move even the mountain of human self-will that offers God profession instead of practice.

23-27. *By What Authority?*—This incident is crucial. **The chief priests and the elders of the people** means that the Sanhedrin now directly challenged him. **By what authority** implies that he had no rabbinical ordaining, no imprimatur from the temple. **These things** refers doubtless to his cleansing of the temple. There was now an open conflict between Christ and the temple leaders. Perhaps they hoped he would claim kingship, for they knew that Rome would deal with that claim. Perhaps they hoped he would claim messiahship: this they could denounce as blasphemy, with some likelihood of support from the crowd that apparently regarded him only as a prophet. His answer was much more than verbal sparring. Rabbis were accustomed to teach their truth by posing a question in answer to a question, and Jesus here followed that method. Jesus was intent, not on a debate, much less in escape for himself: he was proclaiming truth. When he inquired concerning the authority of John, he both refrained from a claim and made a claim. He refrained from the claim of messiahship, though he may have

24 And Jesus answered and said unto them, I also will ask you one thing, which if ye tell me, I in like wise will tell you by what authority I do these things.

25 The baptism of John, whence was it? from heaven, or of men? And they reasoned with themselves, saying, If we shall say, From heaven; he will say unto us, Why did ye not then believe him?

26 But if we shall say, Of men; we fear the people; for all hold John as a prophet.

27 And they answered Jesus, and said, We cannot tell. And he said unto them, Neither tell I you by what authority I do these things.

thority?" 24 Jesus answered them, "I also will ask you a question; and if you tell me the answer, then I also will tell you by what authority I do these things. 25 The baptism of John, whence was it? From heaven or from men?" And they argued with one another, "If we say, 'From heaven,' he will say to us, 'Why then did you not believe him?' 26 But if we say, 'From men,' we are afraid of the multitude; for all hold that John was a prophet." 27 So they answered Jesus, "We do not know." And he said to them, "Neither will I tell you by what authority I do these things.

24. Jesus' behavior in the temple had been that of a prophet, and his logical answer would have been that God had called him to prophesy. Analogies to this might be found in Amos' answer to the priest of Bethel (Amos 7:14-15) and Paul's statement that he was an apostle "not from men nor sent by any man" (Gal. 1:1 Goodspeed). But, as was often the custom in Jewish discussions, he answered the question by asking another.

25. **The baptism of John** rested on his authority as a prophet, which had been received directly **from heaven,** i.e., from God; and Jesus' authority to teach and do prophetic signs was the same. Christians should remember that the office of prophet was the highest of which Jews could conceive, with the sole exception of messiahship; and Messiah was, among other things, a prophet. When Jesus made this claim, he implied that his words and deeds were the words and deeds of God. He was not evading the issue when he asked the question, though it presented his opponents with a practical dilemma; the issue was whether the new revelation of John and Jesus was true, or whether the only legitimate truth of God came through the recognized teachers.

26-27. The opponents were not willing to accept the challenge. They might have denied **that John was a prophet,** or have argued that Jesus' teaching was not the same as John's. But they did not wish to have a public discussion of John's authority. Jesus therefore refused to deal with them further. In effect, this was to reject their authority to examine him.

hinted that John was his forerunner; but he claimed God's ordination. The implication of his reply is that he needed no rabbinical or temple credentials: he had God's direct word.

There are here striking meanings. Jesus said in effect that when truth is spoken, it rings on the conscience as a true coin rings on stone. Like light, it needs no validation: light is its own evidence. If we tried to prove light by anything beyond itself, we would have to use light for the proof. Thus, every man has the primal gift to recognize truth. There are perversities and an evil bias in his nature, but the Holy Spirit working in him yet convicts him "of sin, and of righteousness, and of judgment" (John 16:8). Pride, especially the pride of rank and greed, tempts us to evasions. **We cannot tell,** said the delegation from the Sanhedrin. If they had not feared the people, to whom John was a hero, they would have answered Jesus with a lie. They had been convicted by John's truth, and more deeply by Christ's truth, but their prestige and comfort were more important than truth. And we? The N.T. is a transcript of our age. The words of Jesus, whether in the Bible or on the lips of some lonely prophet of our time, convict us. If our pattern of industrialism is impeached someone promptly asks: "By what authority? What does he know about business?" If our racial prejudice is shown in true light the question is leveled, "What does he know about the facts?" If our scientism is put to shame by some praying soul we demand, "What proof has he? By what authority?" Thus we sin against light, which is always its own evidence. If only we would face the light! If only the Sanhedrin had admitted: "This is truth, and we are convicted." But, instead, they sent Jesus to his death—and themselves and their nation to a miserable doom.

28 ¶ But what think ye? A *certain* man had two sons; and he came to the first, and said, Son, go work to-day in my vineyard.

29 He answered and said, I will not; but afterward he repented, and went.

30 And he came to the second, and said likewise. And he answered and said, I *go,* sir; and went not.

31 Whether of them twain did the will of *his* father? They say unto him, The first. Jesus saith unto them, Verily I say unto you, That the publicans and the harlots go into the kingdom of God before you.

32 For John came unto you in the way of righteousness, and ye believed him not; but the publicans and the harlots believed him: and ye, when ye had seen *it,* repented not afterward, that ye might believe him.

28 "What do you think? A man had two sons; and he went to the first and said, 'Son, go and work in the vineyard today.' **29** And he answered, 'I will not'; but afterward he repented and went. **30** And he went to the second and said the same; and he 'answered, 'I go, sir,' but did not go. **31** Which of the two did the will of his father?" They said, "The first." Jesus said to them, "Truly, I say to you, the tax collectors and the harlots go into the kingdom of God before you. **32** For John came to you in the way of righteousness, and you did not believe him, but the tax collectors and the harlots believed him; and even when you saw it, you did not afterward repent and believe him.

b) Parable of the Two Sons (21:28-32)

The original parable is found in vss. 28-31 and perhaps comes from M, since its point is that repentance and actual obedience, not lip service, are what avail with God. Matthew adds vs. 32 to make a special application connecting this story with the foregoing.

The parable occurs in three textual forms. KJV and RSV are based on the reading of Sinaiticus (א), Ephraemi (C), etc., which is probably the correct one. Vaticanus (B), Koridethi (Θ) and others transpose the two brothers, but it is still said that the son who refused to go, but later went, is the one who did the father's will. But Bezae (D), some O.L. MSS, and the Sinaitic Syriac read as follows: "He answered, 'I will not go'; afterward he repented and went. . . . The latter said, 'I will, sir,' and did not go. . . . They say, 'The latter.' " If this reading was original, the opponents of Jesus adopted a position curiously like that of an old Jewish parable quoted by Strack and Billerbeck, I, 865. In this story God offered a field (his Torah) to all the nations, but only Israel was willing to take responsibility for cultivating it. And even though Israel let the field lie fallow, it belonged to the Israelites because they were willing to undertake the task. Thus the opponents seem to argue that it is better to make resolutions and to *try* to do God's will than never to commit oneself at all.

Jesus' teaching is in any case clear. What counts with God is actual righteous conduct; and even those who do not know they are working for God will be rewarded (7:21; 25:31-46). He may have spoken the parable to justify his ministry to the tax collectors and the harlots; cf. on 20:1-16. The second half of vs. 31 is a hard saying, but the idea is found also in Luke 18:10-14. The irreligious can often be awakened to a realization of their spiritual need, while those who are actually more righteous are sometimes impervious to the gospel and make no progress beyond the formal morality which they already possess.

28-32. Two Sons.—The story is crystal-clear. It is a direct challenge to the Pharisees in their formalism and to the Sadducees in their pretended devotion to the temple. But, because of that very fact, there is danger that we may try to lock the story in the past. In vs. 32, which may have been a later addition to the record, there is one plain application of the truth. But we must not make scapegoats of the enemies of

Christ: the story has applications in our time. The second son is token of a low religion. He was not insincere: he probably intended to obey. That is our case. Christianity appeals to our reason, especially now when we see the tragic issues of an unchristian way of life. Christianity appeals to our emotions: we are drawn to Jesus as he dies pierced in lonely love. Worship kindles our dormant souls. So we vow obedience.

33 ¶ Hear another parable: There was a certain householder, which planted a vineyard, and hedged it round about, and digged a winepress in it, and built a tower, and let it out to husbandmen, and went into a far country:

33 "Hear another parable. There was a householder who planted a vineyard, and set a hedge around it, and dug a wine press in it, and built a tower, and let it out to tenants, and went into another country.

---

c) PARABLE OF THE WICKED FARMERS (21:33-43)

This parable illustrates the difficulty and delicacy of the historical study of the Gospels. There are readers who, having worked through the Gospel up to this point, still find little difficulty in holding that Jesus taught unambiguously that he was Messiah and unique Son of God. Such students will no doubt judge that this entire parable is the teaching of Jesus. Others will have noted that Jesus, while claiming the fullest prerogatives of a prophet, does not express himself clearly and completely on the subject of his own mission and person. To these readers the following difficulties will have much force: (a) The parable as it now stands is an allegory, a form which Jesus uses seldom, if ever. Thus the owner of the vineyard is God, the tenant farmers are the Jewish people or perhaps the scribes, the fruit is righteousness, the slaves sent to collect are the prophets, and Jesus is the heir. (b) Jesus not only predicts his excommunication and death, but clearly states his authority as Son of God, and this he had just refused to do. One might, of course, conjecture that the parable was spoken privately to his disciples. But did he actually give a body of esoteric teaching about his own person? (c) Finally, if we take the story as it is found in Luke 20:9-18, omitting such interpretative touches as the casting of the son out of the vineyard and the two verses at the end (Luke 20:17-18), we have a consistent parable which reflects conditions in Galilee in the first century. Here there was such resentment against absentee ownership that this incident might actually have occurred. The owner sends a slave, then another, then a third (three being a favorite number in folk stories), and at last his son. "Only if the owner lives in a foreign country can the farmers entertain the stupid hope that after the murder of the heir they will be able to enjoy the possession of the property" (Jeremias, *Gleichnisse Jesu,* pp. 47-48). But at last the owner comes and executes judgment personally. Some scholars object further that the sending of the son is an allegorical touch, but this is not necessary. Jesus may use an actual incident to illustrate Israel's rejection of the last and most decisive offer of salvation. Matthew has no other source than Mark 12:1-12. Such additions as vs. 43 are his own interpretation.

33-34. The **householder** cared for his **vineyard** as Yahweh did in Isa. 5:1-7. The parable therefore clearly refers to Israel and the fruits of righteousness. It was customary

---

But **today** is too soon, and the discipline of trying to live our faith is too hard. So, though we have pledged our response to Christ, we do not **go.** The first son points us to a high religion. He had been curt and rebellious, and chosen his own will. Who among us has not? But he **repented.** That fact means that he had meditated on life and faced the facts of conscience. It means also that he had laid aside his pride. Why is it that we are not greatly ashamed to sin, but are greatly ashamed to confess our sin? Pride dies hard, but this son admitted his wrong without any attempt at excuse. Then he **went.** Perhaps his work was not impressive, perhaps his former insolence had impaired both his skill and his staying power. But he did his best, and God reckoned the attempt for the deed.

What of our sickbed promises? **I go, sir.** What

of the vows we have made when God has not dealt with us after our sins, or when unhoped-for joys have come? **I go, sir.** But we have not gone. There is some evidence that the disciples of Jesus may have been drawn from "the people of the land"—those multitudes who kept not the law. Yet they obeyed, and became the heralds of God's new kingdom. But the custodians of the temple, ever promising obedience (if only by their ritual) but never obeying, were judged and convicted. The story holds promise: we need not be slaves to an insolent past. It holds warning: even while professing **Christ** we may become castaways.

33-41. *The Wicked Vinedressers.*—The difficulties of this allegory should be frankly faced. They are involved in the question: Did Jesus proclaim his messiahship? To those who are

34 And when the time of the fruit drew near, he sent his servants to the husbandmen, that they might receive the fruits of it.

35 And the husbandmen took his servants, and beat one, and killed another, and stoned another.

36 Again, he sent other servants more than the first: and they did unto them likewise.

37 But last of all he sent unto them his son, saying, They will reverence my son.

38 But when the husbandmen saw the son, they said among themselves, This is the heir; come, let us kill him, and let us seize on his inheritance.

39 And they caught him, and cast *him* out of the vineyard, and slew *him*.

40 When the lord therefore of the vineyard cometh, what will he do unto those husbandmen?

41 They say unto him, He will miserably destroy those wicked men, and will let out *his* vineyard unto other husbandmen, which shall render him the fruits in their seasons.

34 When the season of fruit drew near, he sent his servants to the tenants, to get his fruit; **35** and the tenants took his servants and beat one, killed another, and stoned another. **36** Again he sent other servants, more than the first; and they did the same to them. **37** Afterward he sent his son to them, saying, 'They will respect my son.' **38** But when the tenants saw the son, they said to themselves, 'This is the heir; come, let us kill him and have his inheritance.' **39** And they took him and cast him out of the vineyard, and killed him. **40** When therefore the owner of the vineyard comes, what will he do to those tenants?" **41** They said to him, "He will put those wretches to a miserable death, and let out the vineyard to other tenants who will give him the fruits in their seasons."

---

for large landowners to **let** properties **out to tenants,** usually on a sharecropping system. The farmer paid his own expenses and returned to the landlord from one quarter to one half of the crop.

35. Galilee had been in a state of intermittent unrest since the revolt of Judas the Galilean, shortly after A.D. 6, and such incidents may well have occurred.

41. Matthew adds that the **other tenants . . . will give him the fruits.** He may refer to the leaders of the Christian church, or he may think of Christians generally.

---

sure he did, this story has no problems, and they may be right. To those who hold that Jesus did not claim messiahship because he feared the earthy connotations that had gathered round that title, the passage bristles with problems. These latter argue that here is an allegory, so detailed that the **hedge** is the law and the **tower** is the temple; and that therefore it is probably not an original word of Jesus, for the reason that he spoke in parables rather than allegories. They argue further that if vss. 37-39 are omitted, as being the addition made by the Christian community, the story gathers convincingness; and that vss. 42, 44 would have been merely baffling if Jesus had spoken them, and that they savor strongly of the preaching of the early church. There is as yet no final answer in this discussion. In any event the abiding truth of the story is not impaired. But we must at least confront the problems, and admit grounds for two opinions.

The parable, a fine rewriting of Isa. 5:1-5, is

a symphony richer in memorable themes than any by Beethoven or Tchaikovsky. There is the theme of God's kindly providence: in what a gracious vineyard our life is set! There is the theme of man's freedom: it is a limited liberty, but permits us to refuse God's overtures or to welcome them. There is the theme of our responsibility under God: our life is ours, but ours only that its fruits may be dedicate to him. There is the theme of "greatness passing by": [1] he sends his messengers, high light on their faces and his word on their lips, and they become at once our heaven or our judgment. There is the theme of God's grief as he watches life on this turbulent planet. The immediate application of the story was to Israel. But this symphony should stir any age.

Concerning the claim of messiahship: **My son . . . the heir.** Jesus may have spoken it: in any event he spoke it in life and death and resur-

[1] John Drinkwater, *Abraham Lincoln* (Boston: Houghton Mifflin Co., 1919), p. 72.

42 Jesus saith unto them, Did ye never read in the Scriptures, The stone which the builders rejected, the same is become the head of the corner: this is the Lord's doing, and it is marvelous in our eyes?

42 Jesus said to them, "Have you never read in the scriptures:

'The very stone which the builders rejected
has become the head of the corner;
this was the Lord's doing,
and it is marvelous in our eyes'?

---

42. The quotation is from the LXX of Ps. 118:22-23 and is taken over from Mark. In Mark the rejected **stone** must be Jesus, but Matthew, by adding vss. 41*b*, 43, makes it refer to Christians. It is appropriate that this psalm should be quoted here, because it also played a role in the story of the Triumphal Entry. The passage seems to have been a commonplace of early Christian preaching, since it is also found in Peter's speech in Acts 4:11 and in I Pet. 2:7. Perhaps Mark added it to the parable.

---

rection. The church may have added it to the "original deposit" of the story. Does it matter? In the latter case Jesus still spoke it to and through the church. We may be grateful that it is here, for he has become to us the major motif of the symphony of history and life. His power to pardon, the inevitability of his teaching, the inescapable constraint of his death, and his abidingness in the conquest of death all reveal him as God's Son and the heir of the ages. Therefore our failure may be worse even than that painted here in such dark colors. "A nation producing the fruits" may, in the mind of the author of the Gospel, have been the Christian fellowship. But have we honored "greatness passing by"? Have we reverenced the Son? The Christian fellowship also must live under fear of judgment. Suppose judgment should begin with the church! The very awareness of Israel's failure may blind us to our own rebellious defection.

42. Rejected Cornerstone.— (See Exeg.) This verse was a favorite theme in the preaching of the early church. A cornerstone in those days had to be sound, and strong enough to serve as binder for the two walls. The temple had cornerstones as long as nineteen feet, and seven feet thick. When a building collapsed, a builder might recognize a discarded stone as the very stone that might have prevented disaster. Thus Christ "comes back." We forget him or deny him, but in the consequent disaster we say, "If only we had built on him!" "The return of the Exile." We covet the title of builder: "builders of the state." But what we build without Christ buckles under the strain of poverty and war. Even of the church men ask, "Can it stand?" The world often discovers that it has built on poor wooden props. It is not hard to see a lonely Figure, and to hear the old words, **The stone which the builders rejected. . . .** We built in one world war to "make the world safe for democracy," and succeeded twenty-five years later in making it tolerably safe for dictatorships. Did we forget the true binding stone, the keystone of the arch?

Christ has strange returnings. Science builds on deductive truth, but finds that without truth-in-the-soul science itself and all else are under threat of extinction. Government builds on organization, only to find that each man is a stone, and that humanity needs some binding loyalty and some binding pardon. Katherine Mansfield in 1916, facing sickness and the great unknown of death, writes, "I have read the Bible for hours on end. . . . But I feel so bitterly I should have known facts like this: they ought to be part of my breathing." [2] Aldous Huxley forgets the cynicism of his *Antic Hay* or *Point Counter Point,* and begins to write about the Christian mystics.[3] When disaster impends, the builders see the discarded stone and say, "If only we had built on him!" How can we build unless we use a binding stone that will join classes and nations and races? What binding stone except the universal and forgiving Christ, and our response of love toward him? In the *Odyssey* there is a picture truer of Christ than of any Odysseus. The wanderer returned to find his homestead held by the enemy. Only a mere handful of his followers remained, and they were in despair. No one knew him. "And the dark evening came on . . . and the maids of Odysseus, of the hardy heart, held up the lights in turn." Their leader, still unrecognized, sends them to sleep: "I will minister light to all these that are here. For even if they are minded to wait the throned Dawn, they shall not outstay me, so long enduring am I." [4] The return of the Exile! In every night Christ trims the lamp, and, still unrecognized, waits the dawn. He is

[2] *Journal of Katherine Mansfield,* ed. J. Middleton Murry (New York: Alfred A. Knopf, 1929), p. 56.
[3] *Grey Eminence:* A Study in Religion and Politics (New York: Harper & Bros., 1941) and *The Perennial Philosophy* (New York: Harper & Bros., 1945).
[4] Bk. XVIII, ll. 307 ff.

43 Therefore say I unto you, The kingdom of God shall be taken from you, and given to a nation bringing forth the fruits thereof.

44 And whosoever shall fall on this stone shall be broken: but on whomsoever it shall fall, it will grind him to powder.

45 And when the chief priests and Pharisees had heard his parables, they perceived that he spake of them.

46 But when they sought to lay hands on him, they feared the multitude, because they took him for a prophet.

22 And Jesus answered and spake unto them again by parables, and said,

2 The kingdom of heaven is like unto a certain king, which made a marriage for his son,

43 Therefore I tell you, the kingdom of God will be taken away from you and given to a nation producing the fruits of it."[s]

45 When the chief priests and the Pharisees heard his parables, they perceived that he was speaking about them. 46 But when they tried to arrest him, they feared the multitudes, because they held him to be a prophet.

22 And again Jesus spoke to them in parables, saying, 2 "The kingdom of heaven may be compared to a king who

[s] Some ancient authorities add verse 44, *"And he who falls on this stone will be broken to pieces; but when it falls on any one, it will crush him."*

---

43. The **nation** is the Christian church, composed of both Gentiles and Jews. The rabbis also taught that in previous ages **the kingdom** had been taken away from Israel because of its unfaithfulness. As in 22:7, Matthew may have the Jewish War in mind.

Vs. 44, which is omitted by Western authorities and the Old Syriac, is not part of the original text. It is a reminiscence of Isa. 8:14-15 and was borrowed from Luke 20:18. Early Christians loved to weave together texts on the **stone** and apply them to Christ.

d) The Plot Against Jesus (21:45-46)

45-46. The evangelists believed that Jesus had spoken the parable pointedly and publicly. There were, however, other sufficient reasons for his opponents' desire **to arrest him.** Matthew adds that the reason for their fear of **the multitudes** was that the latter **held him to be a prophet.** Moreover, Jesus, like many of the Pharisees, was the champion of the common people against the corrupt high priestly group.

e) Parable of the Rejected Invitation (22:1-14)

When this section is compared with Luke 14:16-24, it is easy to see that both evangelists have made additions to the original parable. The story which they found in Q included the substance of 22:2-5, 8-10=Luke 14:16-21. One cannot be sure whether it had to do with a "king" or "a certain man," though rabbinical parables frequently speak of God as a king. Matthew is probably responsible for making it a marriage feast for the king's son, for he wished to add vss. 11-14. Jesus used the parable to give still another

---

not like Odysseus: he does not slay his foes, but waits and suffers in love—until the day dawns.

22:1-10. *The Parable of the Wedding Feast.* — (See also Expos., vs. 5.) A comparison of Matthew's version and Luke's version of this parable (Luke 14:15-24) provides an interesting study of how the Gospels were written. "A certain man" in Luke becomes **a certain king** in Matthew. Luke's "great supper" becomes in Matthew **a marriage feast for his son.** Luke hints that the truth intended in the story is that we should show kindness, not only to those who can return the favor (Luke 14:12-14), but rather to the halt and maimed; whereas Mat-

thew offers the story as added reason why Jesus went to the irreligious with his "good news." As to the teaching and occasion, Matthew is probably right.

A marriage feast with sumptuous fare is the token of joy. Is that how we think of the Christian faith? Perhaps we stress its disciplines too much: it is the secret and unstayed fount of gladness. Probably the early Christians won favor by their spirit of praise. The forced gaiety of the ancient world hid a bitter sorrow, but the self-denial of the Christians was the sign and means of joy. Why did the guests refuse the summons to such a feast? Not because of

3 And sent forth his servants to call them that were bidden to the wedding: and they would not come.

4 Again, he sent forth other servants, saying, Tell them which are bidden, Behold, I have prepared my dinner: my oxen and *my* fatlings *are* killed, and all things *are* ready: come unto the marriage.

5 But they made light of *it,* and went their ways, one to his farm, another to his merchandise:

6 And the remnant took his servants, and entreated *them* spitefully, and slew *them.*

gave a marriage feast for his son, 3 and sent his servants to call those who were invited to the marriage feast; but they would not come. 4 Again he sent other servants, saying, 'Tell those who are invited, Behold, I have made ready my dinner, my oxen and my fat calves are killed, and everything is ready; come to the marriage feast.' 5 But they made light of it and went off, one to his farm, another to his business, 6 while the rest seized his servants, treated them shamefully, and

explanation of why he went to sinners and irreligious people. God had first invited to his messianic banquet the righteous, who would naturally be included in such an invitation. But, although they were moral people, they had no time for Jesus and no interest in the joyful news of the kingdom of God. They were content with their ordinary business and their conventional religious pursuits. Therefore God, who was calling them by means of Jesus' ministry, turned to those who were more receptive, and these will have a share in the great banquet of the age to come (cf. on 8:11-12; 11:16-19; 14:13-21; 20:1-16).

Luke has expanded the parable by adding a second invitation. After all the receptive Jews have entered there is still room, so God sends into the highways and hedges and invites the Gentiles also (Luke 14:22-24). Matthew speaks only of the Jewish mission but turns the parable into an allegory. The invited guests are Jews who insult and kill the messengers (as in the previous section, 21:33-43), and the king is God who punishes these Jews by sending the Romans at the time of the Jewish War (vss. 6-7). Matthew also places here the parable of the wedding garment, to indicate that something more is needed than merely to accept the invitation; one must be clothed with righteousness.

22:3. It was probably the custom to call those who were invited just before the feast.

5-6. To scorn a king's invitation would in itself be a serious insult. The servants whom Matthew has in mind are perhaps the apostles and martyrs like Stephen (Acts

outright wickedness, but because of absorption in home and business. The affairs of the day were more important than the call of Christ. Listen to the conversations on a railroad train or in the street: they are concerned with automobiles, prices, furniture, and sports. A man who discusses human destiny or the claims of Christ is "odd": the others in the company shuffle in discomfort. When sickness comes or the shadow of death darkens, we are tongue-tied, for we are accustomed only to trivial topics. When the crisis has passed we return with relief to our casual speech.

There is a judgment on this drab worldliness. That Matthew speaks of troops (vs. 7), as well as the fact that the whole story is heavily allegorized, points to its late origin. Jerusalem was destroyed in A.D. 70 by the armies of Titus and Vespasian. To Matthew this was not an accident of history, but the scourge of God's wrath. Has not selfishness in home and business always brought war? The conventional religion of the

Pharisees and the conventional worldliness of the Sadducees are not harmless. The man who always converses on material things is not a "nice enough man": that way of life invites dark tragedy. The story insists that God's plans are not defeated. The banquet is held—for those who want to learn ways of true joy. The heritage of the Jews was given to the Gentile church.

5. *The Bane of the Frivolous.*—They made light of it. For them the invitation of God was not where the weight of life rested. The message of Christ did not matter. "Five yoke of oxen" (Luke 14:19) are important: they are almost "big business." Marriage is important (Luke 14:20), so important that a man would be justified in losing two weeks' profits for a honeymoon. A farm is important. Merchandise is important. Here is the very stuff of livelihood, and livelihood has usurped the throne of life. But Christ is not important. "I do not pretend to be religious," says the modern man, for to him religion is a side issue. So we give our at-

7 But when the king heard *thereof,* he was wroth: and he sent forth his armies, and destroyed those murderers, and burned up their city.

8 Then saith he to his servants, The wedding is ready, but they which were bidden were not worthy.

9 Go ye therefore into the highways, and as many as ye shall find, bid to the marriage.

10 So those servants went out into the highways, and gathered together all as many as they found, both bad and good: and the wedding was furnished with guests.

11 ¶ And when the king came in to see the guests, he saw there a man which had not on a wedding garment:

killed them. 7 The king was angry, and he sent his troops and destroyed those murderers and burned their city. 8 Then he said to his servants, 'The wedding is ready, but those invited were not worthy. 9 Go therefore to the thoroughfares, and invite to the marriage feast as many as you find.' 10 And those servants went out into the streets and gathered all whom they found, both bad and good; so the wedding hall was filled with guests.

11 "But when the king came in to look at the guests, he saw there a man who had

7:57–8:1), James the son of Zebedee (Acts 12:2), and James the brother of the Lord (Josephus *Antiquities* XX. 9. 1).

7. Matthew is almost certainly thinking here of the climax of the Jewish War in A.D. 70, when the temple itself was burned. It is curious that Matthew should think of the Roman army as God's **troops;** yet he probably believed that God had used them to execute this judgment.

8. **Worthy** is Matthew's word to denote those whom God accepts, as in 10:11, 13.

10. The evangelist believes that the church on earth must contain **both bad and good,** and this idea dominates 13:24-30, 36-43, 47-50. But, as the following verses show, God in his own good time will separate and destroy the bad.

11. Those who went to a Jewish banquet were expected to wear suitable and clean attire. We have no evidence that special garments were furnished to wedding guests, and

tention to the scaffolding, and forget the building. Livelihood and the accompanying pride of property are made a poor substitute for life.

This way of existence is a repression. A normal man must ask, "Why am I?" When his children are born, the question comes, "Why am I entrusted with the ongoing of the mystery of life?" When death threatens—the threat is fulfilled for every man—he wonders, "Why and whither?" In short, the real questions do not concern a farm: they concern a soul and a destiny. If these questions are repressed, they emerge deviously—in a poor galvanized activism, in fleshliness, in loss of certitude, in mutual criticism which in the large is war. Thus vs. 7 is but Matthew's true account of an inevitable tragedy. World wars are the truth about a civilization that forgets ends because of its absorption in means. Darwin's confession—"My mind seems to have become a kind of machine for grinding general laws out of a large collection of facts. . . . The loss . . . is a loss of happiness, and may possibly be injurious to the intellect and more probably to the moral character"[5]

—is typical of the contrition to which our age must come.

Jesus is concerned with life. In him livelihood has goal and proportion. He is concerned with ends, without which means may be only nonsense. Our excuses—"I have been too busy," "I had too much religion as a boy," etc.—are hardly as convincing as those offered in the story. Life never accepts them. Neither does Christ. He is concerned with us, not with our trivial affairs. His "good news" governs a man's destiny. Vachel Lindsay has a striking poem about General Booth's arrival in heaven.[6] Vixens and drabs and "unwashed legions with the ways of death" crowd joyously into the banquet hall. Where are the "religious," the successful, the go-getters? Not there! The poet has only modernized what Matthew wrote: "And those servants went out into the streets and gathered all whom they found, both bad and good; so the wedding hall was filled with guests" (vs. 10).

11-14. *The Parable of the Wedding Garment.* —This is a different story. It concerns a wedding, so Matthew naturally joins it with the

[5] *The Life and Letters of Charles Darwin,* ed. Francis Darwin (New York: D. Appleton & Co., 1887), I, 81-82.

[6] *General William Booth Enters into Heaven and Other Poems* (New York: The Macmillan Co., 1916).

12 And he saith unto him, Friend, how camest thou in hither not having a wedding garment? And he was speechless.

13 Then said the king to the servants, Bind him hand and foot, and take him away, and cast *him* into outer darkness; there shall be weeping and gnashing of teeth.

14 For many are called, but few *are* chosen.

15 ¶ Then went the Pharisees, and took counsel how they might entangle him in *his* talk.

no wedding garment; 12 and he said to him, 'Friend, how did you get in here without a wedding garment?' And he was speechless. 13 Then the king said to the attendants, 'Bind him hand and foot, and cast him into the outer darkness; there men will weep and gnash their teeth.' 14 For many are called, but few are chosen."

15 Then the Pharisees went and took counsel how to entangle him in his talk.

---

this detail may be allegorical. The **wedding garment,** like the fine linen of the saints in Rev. 19:8, would thus symbolize righteousness or, as in rabbinical teaching, repentance. It is possible for everyone who comes into the church to be so clothed, and if anyone is not, it is his own fault.

12. **He was speechless.** When God confronts a sinner, his mouth is stopped (Rom. 3:19).

13. In Enoch 10:4, the Lord commands Raphael to bind the rebellious angel Azazel "hand and foot and cast him into the darkness." Just so, the human sinner is to be punished in Gehenna (cf. on 8:12).

14. This may be an independent saying which Matthew uses as a climax to the story. Some rabbis taught a similar doctrine.

f) Controversy over the Poll Tax (22:15-22)

This is a "paradigm" or "pronouncement story." It must be interpreted in the light of the all-important kernel saying, vs. 21, for the sake of which the story is told. Few

---

parable of the wedding feast. But it offers a different, even if related, truth. God's invitation is one of free grace. Christ feasted "with tax collectors and sinners" (9:11). But no man can abuse grace: the gift requires in him the true response. "Bad and good" (vs. 10) enter the banquet hall. But they are under scrutiny: **The king came in to look at the guests.** In a Spanish mission, built in the early days in Texas, there is a room (apparently used by the monks for self-examination) which has a large eye painted on the center of the ceiling. It is a poor, though needed, parable of the all-seeing eye of God. **Friend,** said the king—in kindliness, but in searching of heart—**how did you get in here?**

There is no need to join the debate as to what is meant by the **wedding garment.** We need only ask what a man must show as passport to God's offered mercy. He does not require prior righteousness: he can come in filthy rags of sin, and may be the more welcome. But he must be sincere, and he must cast himself in trust on the divine grace. If he should make confession in order that he may more comfortably return to his sins, or if he should come with a sidelong glance at his "humility," or if his purpose is to win and deceive the confidence of his

neighbors, or if he seeks a "religious thrill," he is there without the proper garment. If we seek pardon and a new life, we are welcome to the feast, and God himself will provide the new garment of penitence. If we have a lower motive, the king will say, **Friend, how did you get in here?** Such "friends" do not come in through the door, but through the window.

And he was speechless. The moment comes, in this life or the next, when truth strikes. Then a man is unmasked: the masquerade of his life is ended. He has nothing to say. What can a man say when the X ray of God's truth shines right through him? Of course he is in **outer darkness** after that, where **there shall be weeping and gnashing of teeth.** We have seen falsity reaching its hell in this world. Why should we affront both our intelligence and our moral instinct by supposing there is no hell in the judgment of death? **Many are called** is not an undue pessimism. It is realism: few Jews did respond to Christ, and Matthew lived at a time when the church was persecuted. Perhaps the realism holds also for our age.

15-21. *Tribute to Caesar?*—What tribute of another kind they paid to Jesus! They had to admit, however unwillingly, that he was candid,

16 And they sent out unto him their disciples with the Herodians, saying, Master, we know that thou art true, and teachest the way of God in truth, neither carest thou for any *man:* for thou regardest not the person of men.

16 And they sent their disciples to him, along with the He-ro′di-ans, saying, "Teacher, we know that you are true, and teach the way of God truthfully, and care for no man; for you do not regard the position

sayings of Jesus have been more tragically misunderstood. According to some commentators Jesus assigned a whole area of man's life to Caesar or the government. The political order, they say, is autonomous within this sphere, while God and the church have to do only with "spiritual" matters. But Jesus, like the greatest spirits of the O.T. and of later Judaism, held the strictest possible view of God's monarchy. God was directly concerned with everything in human life, and whatever opposed him was sinful and must some day be brought to nought. Jesus' saying can best be understood against the background of Pharisaic teaching. In general the rabbis held that the existing government must be obeyed (as Paul did, Rom. 13:1-2). They were usually pacifists and did not wish to be involved in politics. "But," as Israel Abrahams says, "though thus prepared to obey Rome and abide by all its lawful regulations, there was to be no compromise when Caesar infringed the sphere which appertained to God" (*Studies in Pharisaism and the Gospels,* 1st ser., p. 64). It was difficult in practice to work out the relation between this subsidiary loyalty to the state and the ultimate loyalty to God, as both Pharisees and Christians discovered, and there were times when one group of Pharisees was inclined to revolt and another group to remain patient. But there was never any doubt that God was supreme even in the realm which Caesar was permitted to have. Such was the position of Jesus; because of his doctrine of the kingdom of God, he could have had no other conviction.

15. The story may indicate that Jesus' political views were not well known. Here was one who had given no political teaching and yet was hailed by enthusiastic followers as "Son of David." If some **Pharisees** wished **to entangle him in his talk,** they probably suspected that he was a revolutionary. When the dialogue was ended, however, they discovered that he and they were in agreement!

16. **The Herodians** were not a religious party but simply partisans of Herod Antipas or the Herodian family. Jesus' answer may have been aimed partly at them, for they did not always render to God what was God's. Those who visited Jesus appealed to his candor and courage. We need not suppose that they spoke hypocritically. It is not Mark, but Matthew, who calls them **hypocrites** (vs. 18).

faithful in speaking God's truth, and fearless before **any man,** whether a mob or a king (vs. 16). Therefore, they thought, he was the easier to trap. Should they in Jewry, which Jews regarded as a theocracy, pay the Roman capitation tax? The issue was, of course, surcharged with popular resentment. If he said yes, the people would call him traitor; if he said no, the Roman rulers would promptly deal with him. By either alternative the Pharisees and Herodians reckoned that they could break his power. Christ's answer has been seriously misunderstood. Dummelow, for instance, says that Christ here sympathized with imperialism, with a "great and beneficent empire," so that "submission and loyalty to civil power is a duty binding on the conscience." [7] What, always? Let us answer plainly that Jesus, in his whole teaching, taught the sovereignty of God in all things.

God has made us; the heaven is his throne, and the earth his footstool. Christ cannot ever be construed as dividing the world into secular and sacred, or as allowing that any ruler has a realm or power independent of the Creator.

Then what did Christ mean in vs. 21? That word is obviously the reason why the Gospels relate the incident. Where is the line drawn? What things are Caesar's and what things God's? If only we could have heard the tone of voice and seen the expression of the face! Clearly he said that the tax should be paid; let us cleave to facts. But he was not giving us a rule of thumb or a scientific formula by which to determine for all time the relationship of church and state. It is doubtful if Jesus ever enunciated what the pulpit has fatuously called "principles," though assuredly principles can be and should be deduced from his teaching. Instead of offering abstract truth, he brought

[7] *Commentary on the Holy Bible,* p. 697.

17 Tell us therefore, What thinkest thou? Is it lawful to give tribute unto Caesar, or not?

18 But Jesus perceived their wickedness, and said, Why tempt ye me, *ye* hypocrites?

19 Show me the tribute money. And they brought unto him a penny.

20 And he saith unto them, Whose *is* this image and superscription?

of men. 17 Tell us, then, what you think. Is it lawful to pay taxes to Caesar, or not?" 18 But Jesus, aware of their malice, said, "Why put me to the test, you hypocrites? 19 Show me the money for the tax." And they brought him a coin.ᵗ 20 And Jesus said to them, "Whose likeness and inscrip-

ᵗ Greek *a denarius.*

---

17. The **taxes** mentioned here (κῆνσος) probably were the poll tax or *tributum capitis,* levied on those who were under direct Roman rule. In Jesus' time this would apply in Judea but not in Galilee, which was ruled by Antipas. It was this levy which Judas of Galilee resisted (Josephus *Antiquities* XVIII. 1. 1; *Jewish War* II. 8. 1). The question may be paraphrased: "Can a Jew conscientiously pay the imperial tax in the holy land, or must he fight for independence on the ground that God alone is King of Israel?"

19-20. It has often been remarked that Jesus did not have a denarius in his possession. He asks them to **show** him one so that he may call attention to the **likeness** of Tiberius, or possibly Augustus, and the **inscription** which gave his name and titles.

---

heaven's light to bear day by day on earth's actual complexities, and left us to trace the implications for our time under the guidance of the Holy Spirit. Thus he directly answered the Pharisees, who, despite their patriotism, had in certain ways invited the Romans after the wicked reign of Archelaus: "You brought him, and must pay for him." Thus he spoke specifically to the actual situation of the Herodians, who had notoriously compromised with Rome, even to giving their half-consent to pagan temples: "Render unto God his due." He was speaking, not in abstractions, but to the issue that then confronted men: "It is his coinage. He has brought you some benefits. Revolution will only deepen darkness. Pay the tax. God has his own ways of working deliverance." Thoreau has a nice comment: he says that Christ left them "no wiser than before as to which was which; for they did not wish to know." ⁸ Incidentally, it could be argued that the chaos of the Jewish wars in the first century came because Jews did not take Christ's counsel.

There are undertones of meaning. Suppose they had asked him, "Shall we worship Caesar?" There would have been a vastly different answer. It is clear also that Jesus had no sympathy with a fanatical nationalism. Suppose the Romans had gone, and the Jews had been ruled by the house of Annas, would Jewry have profited by the exchange? It is clear likewise that he would not have his gospel identified with the bloodshed of "the revolution." There are still deeper implications: apparently his views on the Roman question were not widely known. Why? Not because he ever avoided the

⁸ "Essay on Civil Disobedience."

sharp thrust of current issues, or ever preached a gospel remote from the realities of instant life. No, but because his attack was from higher ground. In that supreme task he was so absorbed that even the Roman yoke was among the trivia. From what vantage point do we make the main attack on the wickedness of the world? Flanking movements and subsidiary sallies may be added: but whence the main attack? "Seek ye first the kingdom of God, and his righteousness; and all these things shall be added unto you" (6:33). Let men deal with the inner bondage (in Jewry in his time that bondage was plain to see): God has his own way with empires. If the vertical line to God is established, the horizontal line of human relations can then be fastened on it. In any building, in affairs of state and home, the plumb line is the thing. Rome collapsed because Rome had no vertical allegiance, and therefore no power "coming down from God."

20. *Whose Image and Superscription?*—Christ asked for a denarius. Apparently he did not carry money. He pointed to the picture and inscription on the coin: **Whose likeness and inscription?** There on the coin was the imperious, somber face of the current edition of the Caesars. Each individual life is like a coin, separately minted in God's creation. **Whose likeness?** The likeness and image of God, for he made us. In this realm also, as in political realms in the time of Jesus, the issue of coinage is token of sovereignty. The pristine impacts of conscience, the troublings of compassion, and our response—however unwilling—to the life and cross of Christ, are God's inscription on us: "All souls are mine" (Ezek. 18:4).

21 They say unto him, Caesar's. Then saith he unto them, Render therefore unto Caesar the things which are Caesar's; and unto God the things that are God's.
22 When they had heard *these words,* they marveled, and left him, and went their way.
23 ¶ The same day came to him the Sadducees, which say that there is no resurrection, and asked him,

tion is this?" 21 They said, "Caesar's." Then he said to them, "Render therefore to Caesar the things that are Caesar's, and to God the things that are God's." 22 When they heard it, they marveled; and they left him and went away.
23 The same day Sad′du-cees came to him, who say that there is no resurrection;

---

21. If **Caesar's** coin is generally recognized as legal tender in Judea, he is the regularly constituted authority. It is **therefore** not sinful to **render . . . to Caesar** what is his. Jesus sets himself against fanatical nationalism. Though he claimed the leadership of Israel, he did disclaim a kingship which was concerned with political power. But the supreme and all-inclusive duty is to render **to God the things that are God's.** In a state like the Roman Empire, where the subject had no political freedom, this may often be compatible with mere civil obedience. For a citizen in a free republic it involves intelligent and conscientious participation in politics so that God's will may be done as fully as possible.

g) Controversy over the Resurrection (22:23-33)

23. The **Sadducees,** though not often mentioned in the Gospels, must have been Jesus' most dangerous enemies (cf. on 3:7). The high priest and his friends, who denounced him to Pilate, belonged to this party. The Sadducees were political and social conservatives and biblical literalists, and they said **that there is no resurrection** because they did not find that it was explicitly taught in the O.T. Dan 12:2-3 does indeed teach the doctrine, but we do not know what they thought about this passage, if they took note of it. The Pharisees, on the other hand, were stanch defenders of the resurrection doctrine and said that those who denied it had no share in the world to come (Sanhedrin 10:1).

Why, then, is the image worn smooth? Why are coins defaced? A Babylonian brick recently unearthed shows the print of a dog's foot over the original royal stamp![9] Human coins are more than coins: there is in us a mystery of freedom, a proneness to evil, and the tragic possibility of making wreck of God's creation. If the image is defaced or gone, what can we do? God sent his Son to remint our poor, broken coinage. God may temporarily suffer the Caesars of the world, but his **image and superscription** are rightly stamped on all life. In what fires Christ remints the souls of men! Ambrosius, the monk in Tennyson's *Idylls of the King,* says concerning the knights of the Round Table,

> For good ye are and bad, and like to coins,
> Some true, some light, but every one of you
> Stamp'd with the image of the King.[1]

This should be true of Christians: other people should be able to detect Christ's image and

superscription in his followers. Can they? Not unless we have given ourselves into his hands. This coinage is the only true currency. It is genuine metal, not the poor alloy of the world, and all men can understand and use it. So it wins honor and becomes standard.

23-29. *Concerning the Resurrection.*— (See also Expos., vss. 24, 30 and 31-33.) The Sadducees, though not mentioned in the Gospels as often as the Pharisees, were probably more dangerous foes of Christ. They were purists regarding the law, accepting only the Pentateuch. As a result they did not believe in the resurrection. In matters of religion and state they were standpatters, and favored co-operation with Rome. They lived on the emoluments of the temple. They prided themselves in being the intelligentsia. These were the men who came to Jesus, not with an honest question, but with a "poser" which, so they believed, would reduce his teaching to absurdity (see Exeg. on the levirate law). Apparently the Pharisees believed in the resurrection: the old conception of Sheol, a shadowy realm of half life, had slowly yielded to some measure of faith in personal identity after

[9] Edward Chiéra, *They Wrote on Clay,* ed. George G. Cameron (Chicago: University of Chicago Press, 1938), p. 94.
[1] "The Holy Grail," ll. 25-27.

24 Saying, Master, Moses said, If a man die, having no children, his brother shall marry his wife, and raise up seed unto his brother.

25 Now there were with us seven brethren: and the first, when he had married a wife, deceased, and, having no issue, left his wife unto his brother:

26 Likewise the second also, and the third, unto the seventh.

27 And last of all the woman died also.

28 Therefore in the resurrection, whose wife shall she be of the seven? for they all had her.

and they asked him a question, 24 saying, "Teacher, Moses said, 'If a man dies, having no children, his brother must marry the widow, and raise up children for his brother.' 25 Now there were seven brothers among us; the first married, and died, and having no children left his wife to his brother. 26 So too the second and third, down to the seventh. 27 After them all, the woman died. 28 In the resurrection, therefore, to which of the seven will she be wife? For they all had her."

24. The quotation is perhaps a paraphrase of the LXX version of Deut. 25:5-6. This is the so-called "law of levirate marriage," which is presupposed in Gen. 38:8, and its purpose was to make sure that the deceased should have a son to succeed him. Millar Burrows ("The Marriage of Boaz and Ruth," *Journal of Biblical Literature,* LIX [1940], 23-33, 445-54) discusses its origin. Deut. 25:7-10 and Ruth 3:9–4:12 show that the law was modified at an early time, and the tractate Yebamoth in the Mishnah deals with its later development.

25-28. The Sadducees, in order to show that the resurrection doctrine is absurd, cite a purely hypothetical case which could scarcely have arisen in later Judaism. If there is a **resurrection,** levirate marriage, which God has ordained, will surely make for domestic difficulties!

death. The Pharisees were perhaps in two groups: one group trusted to a reanimation of this present body (in conjunction with the revival of national glories), and the other group held more "spiritual" theories.

Jesus in his reply endorses this second school of Pharisaic thought, as against the Sadducees. But he goes far beyond the faith held by the Pharisees. Branscomb is right in his comment that Jesus here offers strikingly new conceptions that flash with divine light.[2] What is Jesus' argument? First, that the Sadducees did not know the scriptures. Perhaps Jesus referred to such passages as Dan. 12:2-3. More likely he meant that the whole faith and implication of the O.T. lead to a belief in the resurrection. So it does: what else can be implied in such a word as, "The Lord is my shepherd" (Ps. 23:1) or "In all their affliction he was afflicted" (Isa. 63:9)? Second, the Sadducees did not know **the power of God.** If they had known, they would have understood that God was not at his wit's end when he fashioned mortal life. This earth is but the poor charcoal sketch: hereafter God will reveal the glowing canvas. The implication is that the power of God is far greater than our best longing, and that his greatness is one with his goodness.

"You do not know" implies on the lips of Jesus, "I do know." His appeal was at the core

an appeal to his own experience and knowledge of God. He gave no comfort to those who hoped for a (mercenary) revival of national glories. Heaven is a different and more wonderful place than earth. **The resurrection** is not a "natural immortality": it is the gift of God and the deed of his power. This whole issue is so important that two following expositions are offered. Meanwhile we may note that death, according to Jesus, is God's chance—at the last limit of human power: to man death is tragic finality, but to God it is an opening for his resurrection grace. The resurrection is no poor replica of earth: it is angels and heaven.

24, 30. *Marriage in Heaven.*—These verses have been so strangely and tragically misunderstood that an interpreter must try to clarify them. Three facts are clear:

(a) This view of immortality rebukes by its purity the crude views that obtained in the time of Christ and still persist. Men then believed that the Jewish state would be restored to an earthly glory, and that other nations would be destroyed. Ideas of personal immortality were hardly less crude: there was a widespread hope that the bodies of faithful Jews would be carried by underground channels to Jerusalem, and there reanimated in the final judgment. Christ definitely turned from these notions (and from similar notions in our time), and spoke of the bright mystery of selfhood and its ongoing in

[2] *The Gospel of Mark,* p. 218, see on 12:18-27.

29 Jesus answered and said unto them, Ye do err, not knowing the Scriptures, nor the power of God.

30 For in the resurrection they neither marry, nor are given in marriage, but are as the angels of God in heaven.

31 But as touching the resurrection of the dead, have ye not read that which was spoken unto you by God, saying,

32 I am the God of Abraham, and the God of Isaac, and the God of Jacob? God is not the God of the dead, but of the living.

29 But Jesus answered them, "You are wrong, because you know neither the scriptures nor the power of God. 30 For in the resurrection they neither marry nor are given in marriage, but are like angels[u] in heaven. 31 And as for the resurrection of the dead, have you not read what was said to you by God, 32 'I am the God of Abraham, and the God of Isaac, and the God of Jacob'? He is not God of the dead,

[u] Many ancient authorities add *of God*.

---

29. Jesus might conceivably have answered, on the same scholastic premises, that she was really the wife of the first brother and the others were only "rearing a family for their brother." But he discusses the resurrection doctrine on its merits. The Sadducees do not **know . . . the scriptures.** We do not know to what passages he referred. Perhaps the thought is that one who knows the Bible thoroughly will understand **the power of God.** A famous rabbinical story teaches that if God can form man out of human seed, he can certainly make him out of the dust of the earth.

30. Furthermore, conditions in the age to come cannot be compared with our present life. A third-century rabbi said, "In the coming world there is no eating and drinking, no begetting and procreation, no trade and traffic, no envy, enmity or controversy, but the righteous sit with crowns on their heads and bask in the light of the glory of God."

31-32. This is a separate saying which became attached to the foregoing story. In itself the argument seems to be a verbal one: in Exod. 3:6 **God** speaks of **Abraham, Isaac** and **Jacob** as though he is still their God and they are living; therefore they must be alive, or at least will be raised up. It is worth remarking that when the phrase "God of

---

the reach and range of God's marvelous creation. His promise was not merely of immortality, but of resurrection to new life in the gospel: I Cor. 2:9 is true to the horizon radiance of this verse.

(*b*) But this truth is not an affront to human love in our present world. It is not a denial that love will persist in the hereafter. Charles Kingsley wrote of this verse: "All I can say is, if I do not love my wife, body and soul, as well there as I do here, then there is neither resurrection of my body nor of my soul."[3] He misunderstood. Here Christ does not break the bonds of human love: he strengthens them. He says that hereafter the bonds shall be of finer texture, and that love shall have truer and holier instrumentalities.

> . . . all lost things are in the angel's keeping, Love;
> No past is dead for us. . . .[4]

We shall know our loved ones—with eyes not filmed by flesh, and with surer faith.

(*c*) This is an avowal of God's goodness. There shall be recompense in heaven for seem-

ingly futile tears. Noblest hopes shall find fulfillment. There shall be work there without the poisons of fatigue:

> . . . the heavy and the weary weight
> Of all this unintelligible world [5]

shall become a rapture—momentary dissonance in the eternal music. The worthy shall have the "wages of going on"[6] from strength to strength and from grace to grace. There human love shall be transfigured—not lost, but redeemed in the resurrection promised in the gospel.

31-33. God of the Living.—The literal argument used in the Gospels—God said **I am the God of Abraham,** therefore Abraham still lives—hardly appeals to our more skeptical age. Every age has its own validations. The arguments of our time may seem shabby to succeeding years. Of course Christ is making far more than a literal plea. He is saying that God is faithful. That is what the phrase meant: **The God of Abraham, . . . Isaac, and . . . Jacob** (notice the repetition of the word **God**) implies that God is sure, generation after generation, and all generations are held in him. Jesus

[3] Charles Kingsley, *His Letters and Memories of His Life*, p. 267.

[4] Helen Hunt Jackson (H. H.), "At Last," *Poems* (Boston: Roberts Bros., 1892).

[5] Wordsworth, "Lines Composed a Few Miles Above Tintern Abbey," l. 39.

[6] Tennyson, "Wages."

33 And when the multitude heard *this,* they were astonished at his doctrine.

34 ¶ But when the Pharisees had heard that he had put the Sadducees to silence, they were gathered together.

35 Then one of them, *which was* a lawyer, asked *him a question,* tempting him, and saying,

but of the living." 33 And when the crowd heard it, they were astonished at his teaching.

34 But when the Pharisees heard that he had silenced the Sad'du-cees, they came together. 35 And one of them, a lawyer, asked him a question, to test him.

Abraham, Isaac and Jacob" is used, it nearly always is for the purpose of emphasizing God's faithfulness to his promises. He who stood by the patriarchs is the God **of the living** and will give his servants a share in the world to come.

33. The phraseology is reminiscent of 7:28-29.

h) The Greatest Commandment (22:34-40)

The "summary of the law" is a combination of two verses of Scripture, Deut. 6:5 and Lev. 19:18; and it exemplifies a favorite Jewish method of teaching. The rabbis loved to make aphorisms summing up the heart of religion, as in Aboth 1:1-2; 2:9; and there was much discussion as to which were the "weightiest" commandments. One rabbi told how Moses gave 613 commandments, but David reduced them to eleven (Ps. 15:2-5), Isaiah to six (Isa. 33:15), Micah to three (Mic. 6:8), Amos to two (Amos 5:4), and Habakkuk to one (Hab. 2:4). The Golden Rule is another excellent example of such a summary (cf. on 7:12), and Jas. 1:27 is another. Rabbi Akiba, who was martyred about A.D. 135, said that Lev. 19:18 was the great principle of the law.

Matthew derives this section from Mark 12:28-34 and from Q, which is represented by Luke 10:25-28. In the Q passage it is an unknown **lawyer** who utters the saying, and Jesus praises him for it; in Mark it is Jesus' summary, and a scribe responds with warm and sincere appreciation. Jesus is therefore not the first to have summed up the law in this manner; at this point he and the Pharisees stand on common ground. The difference is that Jesus deals freely with the positive prescriptions of the oral and written law. They must be so interpreted as to come up to the spirit of God's word, as set forth here.

34. This is Matthew's editorial introduction. Luke has the anecdote in a very different setting.

35. Lawyer (νομικός) is probably a synonym for the word usually translated "scribe." It means "rabbi," "one learned in the religious law."

---

is saying also that the sovereignty of God is true sovereignty. He is no small monarch reigning over a graveyard. If he were, death would be the real king, and God would be a local deity ruling by sufferance. He **is not the God of the dead, but of the living.** The very word **God** implies sovereignty over life and death.

Jesus is saying, furthermore, that the love of God for men is real love. Even in human love the proper language is "forever." To stop loving is not to love; it is the defect and absence of love. An ice-bar once silenced the majestic music of Niagara Falls; but, as Jesus here tells us, death has no ice-bar that can still the ever-flowing love of God toward man. A pledge once given by God is given once for all. He does not at death extinguish the light of the soul in his human friends. How could such Hitlerism ever be Godlike? The name "Father," which Jesus taught us in prayer, is not merely an anthropomorphism; but neither is it a cruel mockery

that would slay man and all his hopes. What Jesus means is that God is really Godlike, and that therefore he is the God of the living.

The appeal of Jesus, then, is not to the letter of an ancient scripture, but to an experience of God in every age, and especially to his incarnate Word. When he said to the Sadducees, "You do not know," he implied, "I *do* know." He knew, by direct tidings of God's indwelling, that men do not live and die like linnets in a cage. How shall *we* know? Not primarily by argument of human logic or human science, but by faith in Christ whose Resurrection is seal upon his promises; and by the practice of the presence of God in prayer and obedient love. Then we shall "know whom [we] have believed" (II Tim. 1:12). We shall more and more be sure that he is **God . . . of the living.**

35-40. *The Great Commandment: Love to God.*—Here are four expositions on "the royal law." They could be four hundred: this is an

36 Master, which *is* the great commandment in the law?	36 "Teacher, which is the great commandment in the law?" 37 And he said to him,
37 Jesus said unto him, Thou shalt love the Lord thy God with all thy heart, and with all thy soul, and with all thy mind.	"You shall love the Lord your God with all your heart, and with all your soul,

37-39. The quotations are found in different forms in Mark and Q, and Matthew weaves the two forms together; cf. S. E. Johnson, "The Biblical Quotations in Matthew," *Harvard Theological Review,* XXXVI (1943), 146-48.

unplumbed sea. There was need in Jesus' day that the 613 commandments, 365 negative and 248 positive, of the Jewish law should be reduced to some central simplicity. We also, amid the complexities of our life, need some vivid and memorable summary of Christian duty—truth in a nutshell. There was a debate in Christ's time about this epitome. Luke's version of the incident is probably correct: the scribe himself recited the compendium—from Deut. 6:5 and Lev. 19:18—and Christ endorsed it. Judaism at its best had fine ethical and religious insight. Notice the verb ἀγαπήσεις. The love is not ἔρος, fleshly love; nor φιλία, affection for family and friends; but ἀγάπη, which here means the outgoing of the whole nature in reverent devotion. But can love, especially such love, ever be commanded? Yes. The majesty of stars, the bounty of daily providence, the pleading of conscience and compassion, the basic awe in us, all command us to love God; and we intuitively recognize the rightfulness of the command. But our strange freedom remains—we can disobey. Obedience is freedom and joy, but many people learn only through slow pain.

This is the **first commandment**. Just as mariners take their bearings by the sky and find their harbor only as they journey, our relationships with our neighbors become chaos except we first love God. Our neighbors have no final wisdom: we cannot travel safely by the lights of other ships or by flickering shore lights. Our neighbors are creatures like ourselves. Our deepest bond is with the Creator. Only in him can we learn the purpose of life, or find power to fulfill it. The vertical line of life is *the* line: only when we have rightly established a relationship with God can we hope for stable and shining friendships with our fellow men.

How is this love nurtured? The true nurture of human love provides a dim parable. We seek the company of earthly friends: they cannot become friends if we only raise our hat to them on occasion as they pass on the other side of the street. We consult their worthy interests and aspirations, forgetting ourselves. We share with them our inmost heart. We try to serve them in a deep good will, and gratefully receive gifts at their hands. So the parable: we seek

God's company, we try to trace his mind, we tell him of our deep desire, we serve him in a daily faithfulness. Best of all, we find him through the open door of Christ. Then God himself nurtures the love: he

> Disdains not his own thirst to slake
> At the poorest love was ever offered:
> With true love trembling at the brim,
> He suffers me to follow him
> For ever! [7]

The Great Commandment is possible only in God's love: "We love him, because he first loved us" (I John 4:19). It is a simple commandment—as simple as the Atlantic Ocean seen through the Narrows of New York harbor, and far more vast. No life is long enough for obedience: the commandment itself hides the promise of eternity. No man succeeds in keeping this law: we need the pardon which God gives in Christ. Yet this law is life eternal.

35-40. *The Great Commandment: Love to Our Neighbor.*—Stephen Vincent Benét's *John Brown's Body* shows a captain of a slave ship, faithful in his prayers, yet having no sense of the unrighteousness of his traffic.[8] But no wedge can thus be driven between love for God and love for our neighbor, for each dies without the other. The second law is **like** the first: the word means almost "the same as." If a man despises God's other children, how can he love the Father? (see I John 4:20). "Who is my neighbor?" Perhaps Luke (10:29-37) has given us the right sequel to the lawyer's inquiry about the Great Commandment. Christ recognizes no fences around the word neighbor. No unworthiness, no racial or national heritage, no barriers of class or culture, can make a man other than a neighbor. The inescapable implication of the story of the good Samaritan is that a neighbor is anybody to whom I can be a neighbor. Christ did not discover the law: but he made it new in a new picture of God and a new defining of **neighbor**.

How shall I love my neighbor? Walt Whitman said nobly, "Whoever walks a furlong with-

[7] Browning, "Christmas-Eve and Easter-Day," "Christmas-Eve," st. ix.

[8] New York: Doubleday, Doran & Co., 1928, pp. 11-17.

38 This is the first and great commandment.

39 And the second *is* like unto it, Thou shalt love thy neighbor as thyself.

40 On these two commandments hang all the law and the prophets.

and with all your mind. **38** This is the great and first commandment. **39** And a second is like it, You shall love your neighbor as yourself. **40** On these two commandments depend all the law and the prophets."

---

out sympathy walks to his own funeral drest in his shroud." [9] But that comment still needs a definition of "sympathy." Is it mere fellow feeling? Such a world might still perish of frenzy or despair. Is it the "low road" of kindness such as the worldly hospitality offered by any "hail fellow well met"? That way of loving neighbors might lead to the decay of all life. Or is it the "high road" that Jesus took? Kant said that true neighborliness means treating every man, not as a means, but as an end.[1] Yet no man can be an end-in-himself, for he is a creature. We must love our neighbor as we first love God. We must love our neighbor in God, who "so loved the world, that he gave his only begotten Son" (John 3:16). This kind of love rescues social service from materialism, for those served or serving are not mere "cunning casts in clay," [2] but children of God. It rescues such service from transience, for those involved are not creatures of an hour; and from despair, for it gives both goal and power. Human love stands against the background of what God has done for us in Christ, and can never therefore be exempt from any needful ministry: the world that shapes a neighbor's soul must itself be shaped. With all thy heart is a commitment required in love for our neighbor, as well as in love for God. One law is like the other: they cannot be separated.

35-40. *The Whole Man for God.*—The Shema was offered daily in the prayers of every pious Jew. The word means "Hear." It is so named from the first word of the Great Commandment: "Hear, O Israel: The Lord our God is one Lord: And thou shalt love the Lord thy God with all thine heart. . . . " (Deut. 6:4-5.) We need not ask just what is meant by **heart, mind, soul,** and strength, in the various versions of the law. The words plainly mean that we are to love God with all our powers.

We are made to love and worship. Our life is not a lake without outlet, but a river flowing to the sea. If we become locked within ourselves, we stagnate and die. So there is a command in our very nature—the same command that Jesus underscored. We are made to love with the whole self. A partial devotion leaves us with a divided life. The psychologist tells us

that a cleavage in personality is tragic, and that mental health is under threat unless the cleft is healed. Some people worship God with the emotions, but not with their thoughts: they dare not confront their doubts; they will give no time and effort to deep ponderings on God's mystery. Some love God on Sunday, but forget him during the workday week. Some love him in their home, but ignore him in their business. They all suffer from schizophrenia. Faraday, in his boyhood, while he was delivering newspapers in Edinburgh, thrust hands and arms through an iron railing to clasp a fence. Being even then something of a philosopher and scientist, he mused over the situation: If his head was on one side, his heart and body on the other, on which side was he? [3] The poor "I" in such a dilemma is no longer one but two, and must be restored to unity.

It goes without saying that this cleft in a man's life is grievous to God. If there is "joy in heaven" (Luke 15:7) over a repentant sinner, there is grief over a life stricken with schism. God saddens at the sight of a man destroying his own wholeness. The division is as plainly a threat against our neighbor. To cite only one hurt, is there any more fertile cause of skepticism than the sight of a man loving God in church and despising him in business? Only Paul's motto is large enough: "This one thing I do" (Phil. 3:13). By that devotion a man's life flows like a river to the sea of divine destiny. For such a river there is no eddy of despair and no stagnation of death. The deep draws him: he is moved by love for God and man.

35-40. *The Great Commandment: Self-love, New Version.*—As **thyself** seems to enjoin self-love. By a paradox of our nature we contemplate our life, and yet are immersed in it. What use shall we make of this power to contemplate and shape the self? We are under obligation to develop under God what God has given. The word self-respect acknowledges this duty. How shall we love ourselves? Always we are two selves. Life is thus an affair of choice. By the choice our selfhood grows or withers. False self-love, better called selfishness, chooses the low road; true self-love, better called unselfishness or sainthood, chooses the high road. The saint "does as he likes," but he is yet saintly;

[9] "Song of Myself."
[1] "The Metaphysic of Morality," sec. 2.
[2] Tennyson, "In Memoriam," part cxx.

[3] Bence Jones, *The Life and Letters of Faraday* (London: Longmans, Green & Co., 1870), I, 10.

| 41 ¶ While the Pharisees were gathered together, Jesus asked them, | 41 Now while the Pharisees were gathered together, Jesus asked them a question, |

j) Controversy over the Son of David (22:41-46)

This is the climax of the series of controversy stories. It is often argued that this discussion did not arise in Jesus' time but only after the church began to speculate on the significance of its Lord's mission. All early Christians understood that Jesus was a descendant of David (Acts 2:25-36; Rom. 1:3); but he did not derive his authority from his physical descent, and the Messiah must be thought of, not as a national monarch but as the Lord of all, exalted far above David. If Jesus himself spoke the words, his point was much the same: Messiah is no mere earthly king who will drive out the Romans and restore Israel's freedom, and David cannot be compared to him. This would be one more indication that Jesus rejected the title "Messiah, son of David." Cf. Mark 12:35-37.

for he has consistently denied the self of flesh and sense in so far as these would lower him, and has chosen the high road until it has become both habit and joy. In a slapdash altruism we propose to "give ourselves" to our times. But what kind of self? Only through a true self-love can we love our neighbor.

"Be yourself!" is our slang phrase. But which self? There are two selves with conflicting claims. They must become one self in devotion to God. "Act your age!" we say. Perhaps we could better say, "Act your eternity!" for our true self is in God. When Shakespeare wrote,

> This above all: to thine own self be true,
> And it must follow, as the night the day,
> Thou canst not then be false to any man,[4]

either we have to make him mean that we should be true to our highest self which is self in God, or we have to acknowledge that the words have no worthy meaning. How would we like our neighbors to love *us?* Merely as bundles of flesh, or as fleshly bundles of infinity? As we would deeply wish our neighbors to love us, so we must try to love ourselves. As God has loved us in Christ, so we must honor our own life. In him we know that we are dear to God. In that awareness we must love ourselves, and our neighbor as ourself.

41-46. Greater Than David.—See also Expos., vs. 42.) This passage has echoes of an early Christian debate. The Jewish hope believed that Jesus would be the **Son of David**. (See Rev. 22:16: "I am the root and the offspring of David.") But the early church found in Jesus far more than the Jewish hope. Preaching in that day rejoiced in Ps. 110 as a garden of proof texts to validate Jesus as both **Son of David** and Son of God. The N.T. is sprinkled with these quotations: e.g., I Cor. 15:25; Eph. 1:20, 21; Heb. 1:13; 10:13. And Ps. 110 was regarded as both Davidic and messianic. In its first verse the Messiah is described, not only as

Son of David, but as at the right hand of God. Some scholars, such as Middleton Murry, believe that these verses are the very saying of Jesus; and Murry strangely deduces that Jesus thus denied the story of his birth at Bethlehem.[5] For that deduction there is little warrant. Besides, this passage does not contradict the hope that the Messiah shall be **Son of David,** but rightly claims that he must have more than human lineage. Other scholars believe that we have here rather an instance of early Christian preaching. In any event the verses are consonant with the mind of Christ. He constantly rebuked the mere humanness, the materialism, and the nationalism of the then current conceptions of the Messiah.

Of our lineage and of the line of David: such a Messiah would but partly meet our need. The deliverer assuredly must share our life. The president of the United States must be an American born. Behind the requirement is the conviction that a leader must fully share the life of those whom he would lead. How can the Messiah save us unless he knows our need—from within? How could we honor him except he shares our tears and joys? A visiting seraph might be an affront to our tragedy of sin and sorrow. Yet is it not true that a deliverer fully sharing our life would still come far short of all our need and longing? To be the true Messiah must he not have light and power from above our earth? He must come from God's right hand. The scholars who think this passage is of later origin see in it the joy of the Resurrection. "The right hand of God," echoing Ps. 110:1, is a phrase dear to the Christian creeds. It proclaims the fact of the exaltation of Christ. The Protestant cross is an empty cross: Christ is now the regnant Christ. It is in this sense that Peter quotes the same verse from the same psalm (see Acts 2:25). The joy of the Resurrection must have glowed in Matthew's mind also as he transcribed the words.

[4] *Hamlet,* Act I, scene 3, l. 78.

[5] *Jesus Man of Genius* (New York: Harper & Bros., 1926), pp. 3, 4.

42 Saying, What think ye of Christ? whose son is he? They say unto him, *The son* of David.

43 He saith unto them, How then doth David in spirit call him Lord, saying,

44 The LORD said unto my Lord, Sit thou on my right hand, till I make thine enemies thy footstool?

45 If David then call him Lord, how is he his son?

46 And no man was able to answer him a word, neither durst any *man* from that day forth ask him any more *questions.*

23 Then spake Jesus to the multitude, and to his disciples,

2 Saying, The scribes and the Pharisees sit in Moses' seat:

42 saying, "What do you think of the Christ? Whose son is he?" They said to him, "The son of David." 43 He said to them, "How is it then that David, inspired by the Spirit,[v] calls him Lord, saying,

44 'The Lord said to my Lord,
    Sit at my right hand,
    till I put thy enemies under thy
        feet'?

45 If David thus calls him Lord, how is he his son?" 46 And no one was able to answer him a word, nor from that day did any one dare to ask him any more questions.

23 Then said Jesus to the crowds and to his disciples, 2 "The scribes and

[v] Or *David, in the Spirit.*

---

43. David was traditionally considered the author of the Psalms, and both the M.T. and the LXX call Ps. 110 a "psalm of David."

44. The psalm was originally addressed to a divinely appointed king, and some Jewish teachers identified this king as the Messiah. It contained other verses which Christians interpreted as prophecies of Christ, e.g., Ps. 110:4 (Heb. 5:6). Here Ps. 110:1 is quoted, perhaps from the LXX. Acts 2:34-35 in a similar way contrasts David and Jesus.

45. This is not an absolute statement that Messiah cannot be David's son; the point is that he cannot be thought of *merely* in these terms.

5. SOLEMN DENUNCIATION OF SCRIBES AND PHARISEES (23:1-39)

The chapter begins with a general criticism of the "scribes and Pharisees" (vss. 1-12). This is followed by seven "woes" (vss. 13-33), which remind one of the Ash Wednesday

---

42. What Think Ye of Christ?—Notice the wording of the question. Matthew represents Jesus as asking, not what the Pharisees thought about him (Jesus), but what conception they had of the office and person of the Messiah. It is a leading question now as then: how *do we* conceive deliverance and lordship? Many of the Pharisees hoped for a Messiah who would overthrow the Roman conqueror and inaugurate a prosperous Jewish state. That was partly why they were blind to the light of Christ. That shabby dream persists. We also covet victory over our foes and an era of material plenty: "A chicken in every pot, and a car in every garage." Victory has often come for an armed nation, but with how much genuine peace? Individuals, and in some eras nations also (e.g., the United States during the "boom" of 1925), have been rich in *goods,* but not in real *good.*

When we probe to the depth of our desire, we find there a longing for genuine renewal. We crave a Messiah who will walk the road with us as companion, and yet carry a lantern

that is far better than our human lamps. We crave a Messiah who will not shrink from the shame of our sins, but who yet in his purity can cleanse us of our sins. We crave a Messiah who can grant us power to rise above our dead selves to very life. We crave a deliverer who is willing to taste death, and who yet conquers death to give assurance of eternity. In the depth of our desire the Messiah is—Christ:

> Thou, O Christ, art all I want;
> More than all in thee I find.[6]

What do you think of the Christ? Until that question is answered in the honesty and depth of our human need, it is doubtful if Jesus has much chance with us. So he comes as of old, "What kind of a Messiah do you want?" What kind of Messiah do we eternally need?

23:1-7. The Condemnation of Pharisaism.— This chapter, apart from two brief interludes (vss. 8-12, 37-39), is a series of denunciations.

[6] "Jesus, Lover of my soul."

service in the English Prayer Book with its litany of curses. A threat and lament (vss. 34-39) round off the chapter.

Some commentators count this as the fifth of Matthew's great discourses and chs. 24–25 as the sixth, but there are only five "colophons" or summary sections, and 26:1-2 is the last of these. It is therefore probable that Matthew divided his Gospel into only five books, the fifth being on the subject of the Last Judgment. Ch. 23 might be looked upon as a transition section between the controversies and the apocalyptic discourse. Here Jesus, who has come into the world for judgment (John 9:39), pronounces condemnation on the religious leaders, while in chs. 24–25 he deals with God's final judgment on all mankind at the end of the world.

The chapter comes in at this point because Mark's brief condemnation of the scribes (Mark 12:38-40) followed the controversy over the Son of David, and also because Matthew found this an appropriate place to put the curses. He used part of Mark 12:38-39, omitting vss. 40-44. The bulk of his material was drawn from Q. Vss. 4, 13, 23, 25-27, 29-36 are paralleled in Luke 11:46, 52, 39-42, 44, 47-51, and vss. 37-39 in Luke 13:34-35. Luke probably follows the order of Q. From his special source M, Matthew draws vss. 2-3, 5, 8-10, 15-22, 24 (cf. Kilpatrick, *Origins of Matthew*, p. 35), and vs. 11 is from Mark 10:43-44 (cf. Matt. 20:26-27). The evangelist has freely rewritten this material and worked it together. He expands the "woe to you" phrase of Q into the solemn "woe to you, scribes and Pharisees, hypocrites," and uses that formula even where the sources did not (vss. 15, 16, 25), just as he did with the contrasts between the old and the new in the Sermon on the Mount (cf. general note on 5:21-48).

The interpreter who asks what Jesus actually taught must steer between two fixed points. (a) Jesus certainly criticized some of the nation's religious leaders and aroused opposition so bitter that it led to his death. (b) But the Gospels have exaggerated his denunciations of the Pharisees. As we have seen, sometimes he was in complete agreement with the Pharisees on individual issues (22:15-33); and not all of his criticisms apply to them. Sometimes he may have denounced individual Pharisees, but not the whole party. On the other hand, the later church collided directly with the Pharisees, who were the only important religious influence in Judaism after A.D. 70. The gospel tradition has probably applied against the Pharisees denunciations which were originally directed toward others, and has added other "woes" which reflect the struggle between the two religions. These are the fixed points, and one who ignores either of them will be drowned in Charybdis or snatched away by Scylla. The reader can see at once that such a warning is necessary, for vss. 2-3 say that the teaching of the Pharisees is entirely trustworthy, but vss. 4, 16-22, 25-26 are direct criticisms of that teaching.

a) Their Authority and Principles Are Commended but Their Deeds Are Condemned (23:1-3)

23:1. Matthew directs the teaching **to the crowds** and to the special **disciples. All** Christians must therefore heed it.

2. The scribes and the Pharisees are overlapping groups. Not all rabbis were Pharisees, nor were all Pharisees rabbis (cf. on 5:20). **Moses' seat** was probably the name given to the chair in the synagogue where the authoritative teacher of the law sat (E. L. Sukenik, *Ancient Synagogues in Palestine and Greece* [London: British Academy, 1934],

---

The interpreter must beware of them. Denunciations are a dangerous indulgence that grows with use. Condemnation of others is a much favored way of evading responsibility and excusing wrongdoing. Jesus had right to judge, but it is doubtful if this chapter is an exact transcript of his words. The Pharisees were not all of them bad. Scribal interpretations of the O.T. often had great insight (see vs. 3). So

Jesus could not have indulged in any absolutely sweeping castigation of the Pharisees and scribes. Perhaps this chapter partly reflects the strife between the leaders of Judaism and the early church toward the end of the first century. Perhaps the denunciations have gathered virulence in transmission.

Yet the sins here described did mark some scribes and Pharisees; and, because the sins

3 All therefore whatsoever they bid you observe, *that* observe and do; but do not ye after their works: for they say, and do not.

4 For they bind heavy burdens and grievous to be borne, and lay *them* on men's shoulders; but they *themselves* will not move them with one of their fingers.

the Pharisees sit on Moses' seat; 3 so practice and observe whatever they tell you, but not what they do; for they preach, but do not practice. 4 They bind heavy burdens, hard to bear,ʷ and lay them on men's shoulders; but they themselves will not

ʷ Some ancient authorities omit *hard to bear*.

---

pp. 57-61). The scribe or rabbi in practice exercised the authority of Moses, and the main lines of the oral law were believed to go back to him (Aboth 1:1). Jesus did not acknowledge this authority as legitimate (5:33-37; 15:1-11; 21:27), and Matthew believed that the true authority had passed to Christian leaders (16:19; 18:18). But this saying criticizes the rabbis only because **they preach, but do not practice.** It may have circulated among Jewish Christians in Jerusalem who were very zealous for the O.T. law (Acts 15:5; Gal. 2:4, 12-14). Even so, could the one who first spoke the words have had *all* Pharisees in mind? There were hypocrites among the Pharisees, as in every religious group since the beginning of time, and no one knew it better than the rabbis; but all the evidence shows that hypocrisy was not the primary characteristic of the Pharisees; see Israel Abrahams, *Studies in Pharisaism and the Gospels,* 2nd ser. (Cambridge: University Press, 1924), pp. 29-32. Jesus may have taught something like this: "The scribes are actually in a position of authority, and in so far as they teach what God intends, they are to be obeyed. But their actual rulings on cases, and therefore their practices, are not always the true law."

b) THEIR HEARTLESSNESS (23:4)

4. They bind may be a technical term, as in 16:19. **Hard to bear** is redundant and probably not part of the original text; it is omitted by various good MSS and versions. **Lay them on men's shoulders** suggests the figure of the "yoke of the law" (cf. on 11:30). Jesus' controversy with the Pharisees at this point involves questions of fact and judgments of value. Certainly the Pharisees built a "fence" about the law (Aboth 1:1), and this meant that the average person who became a Pharisee had to know and keep many more rules than before. It is also possible that some of the first-century teachers made the law more strict than did the later Pharisees. On the other hand, we know that many Jews welcomed the Pharisees' teaching. The "fence" kept them far from transgression, for if they observed it, there was no chance of infringement in doubtful cases. Pharisaism appealed to those who wanted a "safe" way of salvation and would have feared Jesus' nontechnical, adventurous, and prophetic approach to religion. Those who accepted the oral law willingly found a positive delight in it. Furthermore, the Pharisees did **move** many burdens with more than **their finger;** they relaxed numerous rules of the written law which were almost impossible for the ordinary person to keep. But they did not take away the **heavy burdens** of ceremonial law which Jesus wished removed. Instead they often increased them. Jesus believed in fewer rules and a larger area of individual judgment and responsibility, while the Pharisees wished to have all doubtful questions answered by the constituted authority.

---

placed "stumbling blocks" before Christ's "little ones," his condemnation came with righteous anger. But we should mark that the burning indignation was always rooted in a prior love. What were the sins? Three are here cited. (*a*) The cleft between teaching and deed (vs. 3). In that issue every man fails. But those who **sit in Moses' seat**—i.e., in the chair of the teacher of religion—are under all the greater

obligation to practice their own precepts. (*b*) The heartlessness (vs. 4) that imposed a heavy burden of "laws" on weak men, yet gave no help in the carrying of the load. We are reminded of "My yoke is easy, and my burden is light" (11:30). A man who overloads a horse is nowadays chargeable before the law. What of a man who loaded 613 commandments on "the people of the land" who had no religious train-

5 But all their works they do for to be seen of men: they make broad their phylacteries, and enlarge the borders of their garments,

6 And love the uppermost rooms at feasts, and the chief seats in the synagogues,

7 And greetings in the markets, and to be called of men, Rabbi, Rabbi.

8 But be not ye called Rabbi: for one is your Master, *even* Christ; and all ye are brethren.

move them with their finger. 5 They do all their deeds to be seen by men; for they make their phylacteries broad and their fringes long, 6 and they love the place of honor at feasts and the best seats in the synagogues, 7 and salutations in the market places, and being called rabbi by men. 8 But you are not to be called rabbi, for you have one teacher, and you are all

---

c) THEIR OSTENTATION (23:5-12)

5. Matthew believed that they did **all their deeds to be seen by men**; cf. on 6:1-18. Such a criticism could apply only to some of the scribes. The Palestinian Talmud speaks of "shoulder-Pharisees who carry all their performance of commandments on their shoulders." The **phylacteries** or amulets were the *tephillin* which pious Jews wore in order to obey literally the commands of Exod. 13:16; Deut. 6:8; 11:18. These were leather cases containing strips of vellum on which were written the words of Exod. 13:1-10, 11-16; Deut. 6:4-9; 11:13-21. Since the oral tradition did not prescribe the size of these, it is possible that some enthusiasts made them ostentatiously **broad**. The **fringes** are the *çiçiyyôth* of 9:20.

6. Branscomb remarks that this criticism might apply better to the high-priestly group. Of course it is human nature to **love the place of honor at feasts and the best seats in the synagogues,** as one can observe in secular society and even among Christians (Jas. 2:1-4). The rabbis generally deplored ostentation and praised humility, but it is not surprising if there were some to whom this criticism applied. We do not know from any contemporary source whether in Jesus' time there was a fixed custom of seating in the synagogues.

7. Salutations in the market places are often ceremonious in the Near East (cf. on 10:11-13). **Rabbi** means "my great one" or "my Lord." This honorific title for scholars was just coming into use in the first century, and some individuals must have taken special pride in it.

8-10. These are words of a Christian prophet or teacher. The title **rabbi,** by which Jesus was sometimes addressed, is reserved for that **teacher** (i.e., **Christ**) alone. Though

---

ing; and then, having done nothing to help them, condemned them as godless? (c) Ostentation (vss. 5-7) in prayers at street corners, in extra wide phylacteries, in extra large blue tassels of holiness on the robe, in seeking the chief seats in the synagogues, and in conceited delight when folk said "My great one" in the market place. This description is withering: was there ever a more complete exposure of human pride?

Yet only Christ can judge. If we judge, the judgment is worthy only as we judge in him. Otherwise we are judged with our own judgment, for our judgment reveals that we know and harbor the sins we judge. We must guard against the psychological "transfer" that besets human judgments. Thus we shall be wise to give this passage a positive turn. What grace does Christ covet in his followers? The opposite of the sins here condemned: some homespun at-

tempt to do the truth we know, the neighborliness that helps all our fellow men in the faith, and a lowly heart. Christ is both our pattern and our power.

8, 10. *Bond of Brotherhood: Christ Is Master.* —(See also Expos., vs. 9.) Any war, strike, or local quarrel is the sign of broken brotherhood. We all know that men should brothers be, for brotherhood is written both as fact and as necessity in our human nature. Literally we are of "one blood." We are joined in one pilgrimage of life, and at the end of days we travel through one valley of the shadow. Our joys and fears, our sins and sorrows, differ only in form: we are brothers under the skin. We cannot live without the common life, yet brotherhood is not an acknowledged fact honored in the deed. That is why our world is torn asunder. Every man goes as Cain in Pierre Prudon's famous canvas—with winged Vengeance above him car-

9 And call no *man* your father upon the earth: for one is your Father, which is in heaven.

10 Neither be ye called masters: for one is your Master, *even* Christ.

brethren. 9 And call no man your father on earth, for you have one Father, who is in heaven. 10 Neither be called masters,

---

there must be teachers in the church (16:19; 18:18), **you are all brethren** and there can be no external distinction of rank. Elisha addressed Elijah as **father** (II Kings 2:12; cf. also II Kings 6:21). In N.T. times the term usually referred to the patriarchs (e.g., Rom. 9:5). It may also have been applied to distinguished scribes of the past, for one tractate of the Mishnah is called Aboth ("The Fathers"). This would have been very natural. The word "abbot" is derived from the Aramaic *'abbā'*, "father," and in the last century it has become customary in English-speaking lands to address not only monks but all priests

---

rying scales and a torch, and Justice carrying a sword![7]

How can brotherhood be made real? Not by the windy speeches of politicians, for men cannot be flogged into love either by whips or words. Not by fear, for fear of strife will not keep us from it even in the atomic age: anger forgets all fear and sanity. When President William Howard Taft referred to the Filipinos as "our little brown brothers," his political enemies turned a jingle to try to defeat him:

He may be a brother of William H. Taft,
But he ain't no brother of mine.[8]

There can be no brotherhood until that perverse selfishness is purged from our nature. How can this be done?

By someone who is above us, who can draw forth in every man the deep awe that is the core of our nature, and who can redeem us from our sins. These steel-filings fall into a pattern of brotherhood only as such a Magnet moves above them. We are led into brotherhood by Someone who, with wisdom become deeper wisdom in love, lives out his brotherliness on our earth; by Someone dying for that faith—for we are saved not by love, but by the cleansing that comes when love dies rather than surrender love. How little we have understood the road and the cost of brotherhood! How glib our speeches and how shallow our minds! Certain east African tribes have a custom, the *sáre* or brother oath, whereby two men make an incision in each other's breast, and each rubs his blood into the other man's wound;[9] as if each said of his brother's need, "It is I myself who am now in trouble." But the mingling of our human blood is hardly enough: it is still embit-

tered blood. Do we understand the Cross and the Sacrament: "This is my blood . . . which is shed for many" (26:28) —"the new covenant in my blood" (I Cor. 11:25)? **One is your Master, even Christ.** This is the bond of brotherhood. The Incarnation has given us One above us— in wisdom, in love, in love unto death. Can he win mankind? He can, he has, if we will.

9. *Bond of Brotherhood: God Is Father.*— How many secular minds use and approve the word brotherhood, yet never pause to reflect that there cannot be brotherhood without Fatherhood! The politician tries to equate brotherhood with democracy. But they are not equal: brotherhood implies a family, and only in that sense a democracy. The rallying cry of the French Revolution was *Liberté, Égalité, Fraternité*. The important word came last, and too late. The only true liberty is in the family love of God, and the only equality that is not fictitious is in his home. When shall we realize that the word brotherhood is empty without high religion? We are sons, but what if we are prodigal sons? It is no supposition. By misuse of "liberty" and a vain clutching at "equality" we have broken "fraternity." In the attempt to be our own god, to live apart from the family and the Father's care, we have become orphans. That problem besets every attempt at human brotherhood. There is no answer except "God so loved the world, that he gave his only begotten son" (John 3:16) —to redeem us as our elder Brother.

There is but **one Father.** This dictum reveals the deep concern of the early church lest any human leader should pose as special favorite of God or try to set himself up as intermediary between God and his fellow men. The rule is— God is the one Father, Christ is the one Master, and all men are brethren both in station and in need. The patriarchs were sometimes called "father" (Rom. 9:5, 10). Perhaps the name was sometimes given also to leading scribes. It were better that the name were kept for God. But we should be on even sharper guard against

---

[7] "La Justice et la Vengeance divine." The original is in the Louvre.

[8] Francis McHale, *President and Chief Justice, The Life and Public Services of William H. Taft* (Philadelphia: Dorrance & Co., 1931), p. 71.

[9] Richard F. Burton, *The Lake Regions of Central Africa* (New York: Harper & Bros., 1860) pp. 92-93.

| 11 But he that is greatest among you shall be your servant. | for you have one master, the Christ. **11** He who is greatest among you shall be your servant; **12** whoever exalts himself will be humbled, and whoever humbles himself will be exalted. |
| 12 And whosoever shall exalt himself shall be abased; and he that shall humble himself shall be exalted. | |

as "father." Matthew deplores all insignia of rank; only God is Father and only **Christ** is **master,** i.e., "teacher" or "professor." If one takes this command literally, the titles "doctor" and "professor," as well as "rabbi" and "father," are forbidden to Christians in addressing their leaders.

11. The Christian leader can ask nothing greater than to be the **servant** of his brothers. "Serving man" is the literal translation of the Greek διάκονος and the Latin *minister,* which the Vulg. uses here.

12. This saying is also found in Luke 14:11; 18:14 and may be echoed in Matt. 18:4. Perhaps it is a familiar secular proverb which Jesus used to point the religious lesson of humility.

the national pride, the racial arrogance, and the social ambition which make mock of brotherhood and sadden the Father's heart. The name **Father** is no warrant for waywardness. He is not indulgent Father. His love is holy love. "Hallowed be thy name" (6:9): May thy nature as Father ever be revered! By creation (for we are born in him), by daily providential care, by the sending of his Son, God is our Father. There can be no other basis of human brotherhood.

11-12. *Christian Lowliness.*—An oft-repeated plea—we have already seen it in 18:4 and 20:26. Luke (14:11 and 18:14) has it in almost these very words. The Exeg. suggests that Christ may have appropriated an accepted proverb. That seems likely; but Christ glorified everything he touched, and gave the proverb his own grace. **Humbles himself** before whom? Humility is not obsequiousness. No fellow man is worthy of worship. No fellow man deserves even honor except as he honors or might yet honor God. Meekness is never human cringing or fawning: that is weakness or cowardice. Meekness is never a pose that seeks ultimate gain: that is shrewdness and greed. The only true humility is humility before God—not because of power alone, but because his power is in love, and because he himself is lowly and stoops to our human need.

We are slow to believe this precept. It is certainly forgotten in the social "climbing" and the business aggressiveness, to say nothing of the imperialisms, that mark our time. Yet we all understand why the proud man fails. For one thing, he is content with himself, and so cuts himself off from fuller growth and joy. There is a story of an artist who was asked, "Don't you think this is your best work?" and who answered, "I am afraid I do." Well might he fear: he was in a blind alley. For another thing, the proud

man likewise shuts himself off from his fellows. He imposes and coerces, and men resent him. The soul is not made to be driven. So the proud man is held to the common life by only tenuous bonds, and his strength fails. For the worst thing, the proud man shuts himself off from God. God is lowly, and therefore beholds the proud "afar off." God's face is turned from no man; but when a man turns his face from God he lives in shadow. Of course it is true that he who **exalts himself will be humbled.**

But we are still slow to learn. In 1831, Rajah Rammohun Roy, at the home of Dr. Thomas Raffles of Liverpool, was discussing brotherhood:

You say that you are all one in Christ, all brethren, and equal in Him. . . . Go to the Cathedral at Calcutta; there you see a grand chair of crimson velvet and gold—that is for the Governor-General. . . . Then there are other chairs of crimson and gold—they are for the members of council; and then there are seats lined with crimson—they are for the merchants, . . . then there are bare benches for the common people and the poor. . . . If [the poor man] goes and sits in the chair of the Governor-General, they will break his head! Yet you are **all** one in Christ! [1]

The Brahman perhaps did not see that his Brahmanism also was thus indicted. Slowly we learn—that humility before God made known in Christ gives range on range of life, ever stronger bonds with our neighbor, and ever stronger bonds with God. The Christian minister is minister (servingman), pastor (undershepherd), steward (caretaker), preacher (herald who goes before his Lord). Every Christian should wear these titles in lowliness.

[1] Thomas Stamford Raffles, *Memoirs of the Life and Ministry of the Rev. Thomas Raffles, D.D., LL.D.* (London: Jackson, Walford & Hodder, 1864), p. 292.

13 ¶ But woe unto you, scribes and Pharisees, hypocrites! for ye shut up the kingdom of heaven against men: for ye neither go in *yourselves,* neither suffer ye them that are entering to go in.

14 Woe unto you, scribes and Pharisees, hypocrites! for ye devour widows' houses, and for a pretense make long prayer: therefore ye shall receive the greater damnation.

15 Woe unto you, scribes and Pharisees, hypocrites! for ye compass sea and land to

13 "But woe to you, scribes and Pharisees, hypocrites! because you shut the kingdom of heaven against men; for you neither enter yourselves, nor allow those who would enter to go in.*x* 15 Woe to you, scribes and Pharisees, hypocrites! for you traverse sea

x Some authorities add here (or after verse 12) verse 14, *Woe to you, scribes and Pharisees, hypocrites! for you devour widows' houses, and for a pretence you make long prayers; therefore you will receive the greater condemnation.*

d) First Woe: They Lock up the Kingdom (23:13)

13. In Luke 11:52 this "woe" is the climax: the lawyers have taken away the key of knowledge. Presumably they have made knowledge of the law so difficult and abstruse that neither they nor others are able to come to God. Matthew has them lock up **the kingdom of heaven;** one may contrast 11:12, where "men of violence take it by force," and 16:19, where the authority of the keys has passed from the rabbis to Peter. The Pharisees certainly wished to "bring men near to the law" (Aboth 1:12), not to shut them off from it. But in order to do this they formed brotherhoods in which the law was strictly kept, and—like some Jewish Christians, according to Gal. 4:17—they excluded from these brotherhoods those who did not conform to the law. Christians who practice "close Communion" and "fence the table" proceed on a similar principle. The gospel saying points to the danger inherent in this exclusiveness.

Vs. 14 is not in the Alexandrian and Caesarean texts or in the Sinaitic Syriac. It is borrowed from Mark 12:40. The criticisms which it contains could have applied only to degenerate religious teachers.

e) Second Woe: The Character of Their Proselytes (23:15)

15. Judaism, in the first century, was a missionary religion. The initiation of a convert involved baptism, circumcision (for men), and an offering in the temple. One who

13. Seven Woes: 1. To Those Who Block the Door of the Kingdom.—The Lukan form, "For you have taken away the key of knowledge" (Luke 11:52) may be the earlier version. It is more vivid, and serves thus to sharpen truth. **Against men** indicates that many were eager to enter. Among both Jews and Gentiles there were those who were stricken by a discontent. The world had deceived their hopes, they were secretly aware of their own failure and wrongdoing, and they were ready to knock at the door of any man who appeared to have the word of true peace. Does **kingdom of heaven** stand here for the early church? In any event it stands for the life that is very life. In that pagan world men craved life and could not find it. Could any sin be worse than the sin against that eager quest? Yet the scribes and Pharisees took away "the key" of the Scriptures, by exalting the letter and forgetting the spirit. The Scriptures reveal God's quest for man and man's quest for God, but a false Judaism had turned them into a burden of rules too heavy to be borne. False leaders had taken away not only the Scriptures but the key to life. A Gentile

became a Jew only by baptism, circumcision, and a gift to the temple: the stress was on the external act rather than on a change of heart. So they blocked the door to the kingdom. We would be blind indeed if we could not find here a warning against falsities in our own alleged Christianity.

Ye neither go in yourselves: They could not! To be sure, they had brotherhoods in which the law was strictly kept; but they ignored those on the outside, and thus ended by regarding all others with contempt and condemnation. Eager to avoid heresy of form, they committed the worse heresy of spirit. More and more they became capsuled—and died. Vs. 14 is a gloss, but it shows how egregiously conduct can become separate from creed—a man foreclosing on a widow's too-heavy mortgage, and meanwhile sanctimoniously saying his prayers! The **woe** comes in very truth to such lives, for God is not mocked and not weakly indulgent of evil.

15. Seven Woes: 2. To False Proselyters.—The word **proselyte** means an alien or stranger. Apparently there were leaders of Judaism, both in Jerusalem and among the Diaspora, who had

make one proselyte; and when he is made, ye make him twofold more the child of hell than yourselves.

16 Woe unto you, *ye* blind guides, which say, Whosoever shall swear by the temple, it is nothing; but whosoever shall swear by the gold of the temple, he is a debtor!

17 *Ye* fools and blind: for whether is greater, the gold, or the temple that sanctifieth the gold?

18 And, Whosoever shall swear by the altar, it is nothing; but whosoever sweareth by the gift that is upon it, he is guilty.

and land to make a single proselyte, and when he becomes a proselyte, you make him twice as much a child of hell^y as yourselves.

16 "Woe to you, blind guides, who say, 'If any one swears by the temple, it is nothing; but if any one swears by the gold of the temple, he is bound by his oath.' **17** You blind fools! For which is greater, the gold or the temple that has made the gold sacred? **18** And you say, 'If any one swears by the altar, it is nothing; but if any one swears by the gift that is on the altar, he

^y Greek *Gehenna*.

---

thus became a Jew had all the privileges and obligations of a native Jew; see Moore, *Judaism*, I, 323-53, and F. M. Derwacter, *Preparing the Way for Paul* (New York: The Macmillan Co., 1930). The school of Hillel welcomed converts, and no doubt there were those who traversed **sea and land** in their zeal **to make a single proselyte**. The rabbis knew that not all conversions were sincere, and some distrusted the proselyte. Jesus' point, however, is that an enthusiastic convert often becomes more bigoted and narrow than those who converted him, and is so concerned with minutiae that he misses the heart of religion. This may be in Paul's mind as he opposes the conversion of the Galatians to Judaism (Gal. 5:2-6; cf. Col. 2:16-23).

f) Third Woe: Their Rulings on Oaths (23:16-22)

16-22. The teachers of Jesus' time probably ruled as vs. 16 indicates; see Lieberman, *Greek in Jewish Palestine*, pp. 115-43. The rabbis tried to prevent people from making any oaths or vows whatever, since oaths should be taken advisedly and observed religiously, but they sought to preserve the sanctity of oaths made in proper form. Since

---

immense zeal to win converts to their faith. **Compass sea and land** was a proverbial phrase for such fanaticism. This **woe** prompts us to ask what is the difference between proselyting and a true missionary passion. We cannot help bearing testimony to our faith and joy. To forbear would be as difficult as to keep trying to hold our breath, and as ruinous to our world as the loss of friendship. But proselyting, we all see, is a hateful endeavor. Wherein is it different from the work of a missionary? Proselyting has these characteristics: (*a*) It is concerned with a cult or a form, rather than with the large horizons of new life; (*b*) it is conducted by men well satisfied with themselves, and thus is marked by self-righteousness; (*c*) it is subtly intent, not on God, nor even on the good of the convert, but on the access of prestige that will come to the cult and the zealot. William E. Gladstone defined it thus: "A morbid appetite for effecting conversions, founded too often upon an overweening self-confidence and self-love." [3]

Compare the Christian mission. It is eager for God in Christ, not for a cult. It is conducted by sinners who have found very peace and

power, and who wish to share the boon. It does not coerce, but is concerned reverently for the personality of those to whom it goes, and is content to rely on the contagion of life if words seem a duress. Its best weapon is the light of a discovered joy. The Gentile convert to Judaism was often worse off than before: **twice as much a child of** Gehenna (see Exeg. on Paul's concern for such neophytes). The ties of natural affection were broken, with only a poor rubric as compensation; and the convert, as often happens, became more bigoted than his guide. It is a striking fact that Christianity found its likeliest opportunity among such proselytes: a narrow Judaism was no answer, but the Christians gave evidence in life of the longed-for joy.

Need it be said that we must forever be on guard in the Christian venture lest the angularities of proselyting should disfigure a true missionary zeal?

16-22. *Seven Woes: 3. To False Swearers and Casuists in Oaths.*—We have here a picture of an age in which people, and perhaps especially the masses of people, were addicted to oaths. What kind of society is thus revealed? With what deep regard for truth? It is hard to imagine the casuistry which this verse describes. But

[3] *Later Gleanings*, p. 292.

19 *Ye* fools and blind: for whether *is* greater, the gift, or the altar that sanctifieth the gift?

20 Whoso therefore shall swear by the altar, sweareth by it, and by all things thereon.

21 And whoso shall swear by the temple, sweareth by it, and by him that dwelleth therein.

22 And he that shall swear by heaven, sweareth by the throne of God, and by him that sitteth thereon.

23 Woe unto you, scribes and Pharisees, hypocrites! for ye pay tithe of mint and anise and cummin, and have omitted the weightier *matters* of the law, judgment, mercy, and faith: these ought ye to have done, and not to leave the other undone.

is bound by his oath.' **19** You blind men! For which is greater, the gift or the altar that makes the gift sacred? **20** So he who swears by the altar, swears by it and by everything on it; **21** and he who swears by the temple, swears by it and by him who dwells in it; **22** and he who swears by heaven, swears by the throne of God and by him who sits upon it.

23 "Woe to you, scribes and Pharisees, hypocrites! for you tithe mint and dill and cummin, and have neglected the weightier matters of the law, justice and mercy and faith; these you ought to have done, with-

---

the common people were incurably addicted to all sorts of oaths, the rabbis were gradually forced to make terms with popular custom, and therefore they drew these distinctions. Jesus, however, swept aside all distinctions, holding that all oaths bear some relation to God, the creator of all things. His solution of the problem is to defy popular custom and forbid swearing altogether (5:33-37). He uses the a fortiori argument, as in 6:25; if to swear **by the gold of the temple** is binding, how much greater **are the temple** to which the gold has been given and God **who dwells in it!**

g) Fourth Woe: Their Rulings About Trifles (23:23-24)

Vss. 23-33 faithfully represent Jesus' teaching. Here his denunciations are directed not merely against scribes and Pharisees but against deep-seated tendencies in human nature. The most that can be said is that certain Pharisees, Sadducees, and "people of the land" also, furnish examples of these vices; but the worst example is the "bad Pharisee," since his party is the most earnest about religious practice.

23. Deut. 14:22-23 prescribed tithes of grain, wine, and oil. The rabbis, in building a fence about the law, included vegetables, fruits, and nuts in the command. The tithing of **dill and cummin** is expressly provided for in the Mishnah (Maaseroth 4:5; Demai 2:1).

---

apparently an oath was regarded as gathering strength in proportion to its particularity: an oath by the gold of the temple was stronger than an oath by the temple. The scribes could release a man from his oath by asking if it was general or specific. They turned religion into the practice of a "slick" lawyer.

This **woe** cuts through the casuistry with a sharp knife. An oath by the sacrifice is an oath by the altar, and therefore by the temple—and therefore by the God who made heaven and earth. False swearers cannot mock him, and they are in his hands. The fashion in oaths changes, but the foolish practice does not die. We can see the danger. An oath not kept makes a liar of the man who thus falsely swears. It substitutes language for life. It weakens all resolve, and finally cankers character. We have seen that **Jesus** enjoined his followers to have done with

oaths altogether (5:33-37); he proposed the end of the whole custom. But is there not some value in an oath? Yes, if it registers a true intent; and if, aware of human weakness, it has learned to rely on God's strength. But in that instance the oath has already become a prayer, and a prayer is far better than an oath.

23-24. *Seven Woes: 4. To Those Who Honor the Niceties of Form and Forget the Great Truth in Life.*—The punctilios of the Pharisees seem so remote that we may easily assume that this **woe** has no meaning for us. But it is not a picture imprisoned on an ancient page: it is a thrust of truth into our modern world. It concerns tithes (see Exeg.). Religious men in those days turned religion into scrupulosity. See them at their scales weighing out the mint (even the stalks) and the cuminseed! They must be sure to give God his tenth! But they forgot **weightier**

24 *Ye* blind guides, which strain at a gnat, and swallow a camel.

25 Woe unto you, scribes and Pharisees, hypocrites! for ye make clean the outside of the cup and of the platter, but within they are full of extortion and excess.

26 *Thou* blind Pharisee, cleanse first that *which is* within the cup and platter, that the outside of them may be clean also.

out neglecting the others. 24 You blind guides, straining out a gnat and swallowing a camel!

25 "Woe to you, scribes and Pharisees, hypocrites! for you cleanse the outside of the cup and of the plate, but inside they are full of extortion and rapacity. 26 You blind Pharisee! first cleanse the inside of the cup and of the plate, that the outside also may be clean.

This verse is perhaps the earliest example in literature of the Jewish distinction between **weightier** and lighter commandments. The rabbis might have added that they too strove for **justice and mercy and faith,** but Jesus thinks it absurd to spend time on the tithing of trifles; one who does so may shift the center of religion and distort it so that the most important things are forgotten. The phrase **these you ought to have done, without neglecting the others** spoils the point of the saying and may have been added by Matthew; in Luke 11:42 it is omitted by Codex Bezae (D) and Marcion. Jesus would certainly say that the tithe law of Deuteronomy must be kept, but not these Pharisaic elaborations.

24. A separate saying, with a similar point. Like 7:3-5 and 19:24, it is in the grotesquely humorous style that Jesus sometimes adopted. Both **gnat** and **camel** were unclean animals; in their eagerness to avoid a tiny defilement the Pharisees are polluted by a huge one. **Strain at** is a typographical error for "strain out." The English printers, not the King James translators, are to blame for **it.**

h) FIFTH WOE: THEIR RULINGS ON CLEANLINESS (23:25-26)

25-26. In Jesus' time the laws of ceremonial purity were undergoing development, and it was customary to keep a supply of water on hand to purify men's bodies and the vessels they used (Mark 7:2-4; John 2:6). Rules respecting cleanliness of **the cup** and

things. In the marvelous phrase of Jesus, they "strain out the [wine-]gnat and swallow the camel." The **weightier matters** are described in language that almost echoes Mic. 6:8. Judgment is a deep concern for **justice** in the earth, **mercy** is a love of compassion toward the weakest and the worst, and **faith** is fidelity to righteousness and mercy in daily life. The very list is our indictment. Are there no modern parallels to this disproportion in Pharisaic religion? What of the woman deeply concerned for temperance in the matter of strong drink, but most intemperate in her prejudices and condemnations? What of the businessman who is meticulously polite and most regular in church attendance, yet champions glaring inequalities in the social structure and drives a hard bargain in trade? The chief priests would not put Judas' blood money into the treasury because it was unclean (27:6), but they paid it that Christ might be betrayed!

These ought ye to have done is probably a gloss: it would be hard to imagine Jesus endorsing those weighing-scales. Yet it would be easy to imagine him endorsing the desire and obligation of a man to give to the temple the

right share of his income—as token that all of it must be consecrated. We must be careful not to discard worship in our plea for right daily conduct. Prayer and work are "both-and," not "either-or." They are proper alternation of our days, like the systole and diastole of the heart. We must remember the **woe:** it is visited on Pharisaism in every age. How is the disproportion cured? By the lancet of this scripture to let out the poison, and by the healing that comes from our confession of sin and from our trust in Christ.

25-26. *Seven Woes: 5. To Those Who Neglect Heart Purity for External Correctness.*—The **inside of the cup:** the very phrase has become proverbial. The American author, Winston Churchill, has a novel by that title. Charlotte Brontë's *Jane Eyre* deals with the same theme. The rules of ceremonial cleanness in Jesus' day required, of course, that both sides of the cup should be cleansed. Perhaps the reference is to the food in the cup: that, in the case of the temple leaders, was purchased by **extortion and rapacity.** Why should men place such emphasis on ritual? The underscoring is the work of human pride. Obedience purchases a reputation

27 Woe unto you, scribes and Pharisees, hypocrites! for ye are like unto whited sepulchres, which indeed appear beautiful outward, but are within full of dead *men's* bones, and of all uncleanness.

28 Even so ye also outwardly appear righteous unto men, but within ye are full of hypocrisy and iniquity.

27 "Woe to you, scribes and Pharisees, hypocrites! for you are like whitewashed tombs, which outwardly appear beautiful, but within they are full of dead men's bones and all uncleanness. 28 So you also outwardly appear righteous to men, but within you are full of hypocrisy and iniquity.

---

the plate and the method of cleansing them can be found in the tractate Kelim of the Mishnah. Of course the rabbis were even more concerned for the **inside** than for **the outside** of a vessel. Jesus is contrasting the external cleanliness of vessels with the internal uncleanness of men's hearts and minds. Indeed, the original saying may not have referred to vessels but to cleanliness of the body (Easton, *St. Luke,* pp. 189, 193). But any kind of ceremonial purification is bootless if **extortion and rapacity** are part of man's character. The issue between Jesus and the Pharisees is the same as in vs. 23. He believes that the holiness rules are not an aid to righteousness, but the reverse. Many a man is willing to compromise with religion by keeping only the outward conventions. Greed and oppression were more characteristic of the Sadducean priesthood than of the Pharisees.

j) Sixth Woe: Their External Righteousness (23:27-28)

27. This saying has much the same point as the previous one. The illustration is a strange one. The **tombs** were **whitewashed,** not in order that they might **appear beautiful,** but that men would not "walk over them" and contract defilement unwittingly (Luke 11:44). Such chalking of graves was done on Adar 15 to insure purity during the Passover festival (Shekalim 1:1). Of course the actual result was that the tombs presented a better appearance, and a Jew might contrast this with the contents which he abhorred.

28. Certainly in any religious culture many who **outwardly appear righteous** . . . are **full of hypocrisy and iniquity.** But Jesus goes further. His standard was not man's outward behavior—even in ethical matters—but the inner disposition of his mind (5:22, 28, 44-45). By his test even the saint is in some degree a sinner.

---

for character. Men say, "There is a good man." Perhaps the Pharisee half consciously believed that he could deceive God also, for it is part of human blindness to ask, "Doth God see?" Besides, ceremonial religion has another advantage in the eyes of respectable sinners: it seems to permit the coveted pleasures. Canon Green states that **excess** translates a famous Greek word meaning "pleasure." [3] Jesus was obviously impatient with the minutiae of Pharisaism. Tombs whitened lest men should step on them and become "defiled" may be a case in point (see Expos., vss. 27-28). An outward law, however necessary, may tend to distract men from the necessity of true motive. God looks at the heart. How can one **cleanse the inside of the cup?** By confession, a slaying of human pride. By conversion, a turning from evil ways. By trust in the mercy of God made clear in Christ.

27-28. *Seven Woes: 6. To Those Who Are Like Whited Tombs.*—Perhaps this denunciation has echoes of Jesus' boyhood. He had seen

the landscape dotted with whitened tombs. They were so marked lest pilgrims to the Passover, inadvertently touching them, should be made "unclean," and thus be barred from the festival. His boyhood imagination shuddered perhaps at the contrast between the outer cleanness and the inner hidden death. Was hypocrisy ever pilloried in a more stinging simile? **Like whitewashed tombs:** the sins of respectability! Even the Christian church is slow to realize that the sins we most condemn, Jesus would less strongly condemn; and that the sins we condone as defective uprightness, he would call heinous. He never condoned sins of passion, but he had sharper warning for sins of pride and greed. He said plainly that a "harlot" would enter heaven more easily than a "righteous" man greedy for reputation but indifferent to the injustices of his age (21:31). Yet we visit ostracisms on the "gross sins," and regard a money-shrewd but "respectable" man as a reputable citizen. **Dead men's bones:** we should give the words their proper force. Respectable sinners, uncharitable and self-righteous and always looking for the

29 Woe unto you, scribes and Pharisees, hypocrites! because ye build the tombs of the prophets, and garnish the sepulchres of the righteous,

30 And say, If we had been in the days of our fathers, we would not have been partakers with them in the blood of the prophets.

31 Wherefore ye be witnesses unto yourselves, that ye are the children of them which killed the prophets.

29 "Woe to you, scribes and Pharisees, hypocrites! for you build the tombs of the prophets and adorn the monuments of the righteous, 30 saying, 'If we had lived in the days of our fathers, we would not have taken part with them in shedding the blood of the prophets.' 31 Thus you witness against yourselves, that you are sons of those who

k) Seventh Woe: Their Hypocritical Honor of the Prophets
(23:29-33)

29. Many an Independence Day orator who eulogizes Lincoln or Washington would have been a bitter opponent of these men if he had lived in their days. It is much more convenient to honor dead **prophets** than to heed living ones. Official traditions about the **righteous** usually contain only their miracles or their noncontroversial teachings. Yet these observations do not completely explain Jesus' remark. The religion of the rabbis was a wonderful synthesis of the legal, prophetic, and wisdom elements of the O.T.; but just because this was true, the sharpness of the prophets' teaching was blunted. The rabbis, to be sure, recognized that the prophets had been critics of their own age and had spoken direct words of God; but all that they had said had been in agreement with Moses, and—according to Pharisaic belief—they had transmitted the tradition of the oral law to the "men of the great synagogue" (Aboth 1:1). Jesus, whose approach was prophetic rather than legal, could not square the dominant teaching of his time with the religion of the prophets.

30-31. Although they think they **would not have taken part with** their fathers **in shedding . . . blood,** it is still "like father, like son." Semitic wisdom assumed that true **sons** would pattern themselves after their **fathers,** and Jesus plays on this idea with bitter irony.

"main chance," are really dead. Jesus used the word **dead** for spiritual death, not for the physical event that we call death. The Pharisee goes through the antics and gestures of life, but in spirit he is entombed. Rudyard Kipling's "The Old Men" is a fitting commentary.

There is danger again that we may try to imprison this **woe** in the past, and so draw its sting. Perhaps our whole civilization is like **whitewashed tombs.** We have marvelous machines, towering buildings, and a thousand signs of what we call "progress"; but **within** we have unstayed restlessness, strife between men and nations, the unrelieved burden of the poor, and the **dead men's bones** of wholesale wars. Still we try to safeguard ourselves by calcimining the tomb. Still we trust to porcelain bathrooms and business efficiency to protect us from defilement. The Lukan form of this **woe** is striking: it reads "unsuspected tombs" (Luke 11:44, Moffatt). The people stumbled on the Pharisees, not knowing that they had touched death, and were thus "defiled." If only respectable sinners held their poison **within** themselves! But the **within** of life has either a corrupting or a benef-

icent infection. This **woe** is not ancient history; it is an always contemporary warning.

29-35. Seven Woes: 7. To Those Who Honor the Prophets of Yesterday and Slay Those of Today.—The Exeg. cites Lincoln as instance, and asks how we would treat Lincoln in our time. It is a probing instance, for Lincoln's home town newspaper, commenting on the Gettysburg speech, accused him of "falsifying history"; another journal wrote of "the President's silly little speech," and still another criticized him for using soldiers' "graves as a stump for political oratory." [4] When Thomas Jefferson spoke of "entangling alliances" he was manifestly pleading for a new and adventurous course, a break with old habits; in more recent years conservative minds, by twisting his words from their purpose, have tried to make him the apostle of reaction. When a prophet is dead, he can no longer disturb our selfish comfort. We can praise him then, and make the praise a substitute for courageous righteousness in our time. Or by clever distortion in orotund speeches we can claim to be sons of "the found-

[4] Barton, *Life of Abraham Lincoln,* II, 220.

32 Fill ye up then the measure of your fathers.

33 *Ye* serpents, *ye* generation of vipers, how can ye escape the damnation of hell?

34 ¶ Wherefore, behold, I send unto you prophets, and wise men, and scribes: and *some* of them ye shall kill and crucify; and *some* of them shall ye scourge in your synagogues, and persecute *them* from city to city:

murdered the prophets. **32** Fill up, then, the measure of your fathers. **33** You serpents, you brood of vipers, how are you to escape being sentenced to hell?*ʸ* **34** Therefore I send you prophets and wise men and scribes, some of whom you will kill and crucify, and some you will scourge in your synagogues and persecute from

ʸ Greek *Gehenna.*

---

32. This comment may be from Matthew or the author of Q. Men like Stephen and James have been martyred (Acts 7:54–8:1; 12:2). As in I Thess. 2:16, there are Jews who fill to the brim **the measure** of guilt which their **fathers** began to fill.

33. Matthew's editorial comment is based on 3:7.

l) Concluding Threat and Lament (23:34-39)

Vss. 34-36 are paralleled in Luke 11:49-51, which represents better the wording of Q. There the words are spoken by "the Wisdom of God," which probably means the risen Christ (I Cor. 1:24) speaking through a Christian prophet. This oracle in its earliest form was probably delivered some time between A.D. 42 and 50, and is reflected in Paul's bitter words in I Thess. 2:16; see S. E. Johnson, "Notes and Comments," *Anglican Theological Review,* XXIII (1941), 173-76, and literature cited there. Its background is the martyrdom of James and the flight of Peter and other apostles. Vss. 37-39 are perhaps another piece of prophetic preaching. Like the passage 11:25-30 in its present form, these verses can be thought of as "the divine spirit of redeeming Wisdom yearning for the restoration of the wayward and disobedient people" (Bacon, *Studies in Matthew,* p. 248).

34. Luke 11:49 couples "apostles" with the **prophets.** These are therefore Christian prophets, as in I Cor. 12:28; Eph. 2:20; 4:11. The **wise men and scribes** are also Christians (as in 13:52). There is no evidence that Jews crucified anyone; this was a Roman method of execution. **Scourge . . . and persecute from town to town;** cf. on 10:17, 23.

---

ing fathers." The Pharisees made that claim: "We be sons of the fathers." With caustic indignation Jesus countered the claim: **You are sons of those who murdered the prophets.**

Why do we garland the graves of ancient worthies, but persecute their contemporary successors? Because of lethargy: new truth is disturbing and compels us to "rethink our world." Partly from outright selfishness: our prestige or our pocketbook is threatened. Thus the seer is a "radical" or a "troublemaker" while he lives, and a hero after—sufficiently long after—his death. Yet each in his own day has his own fierce joy. He is alive in deepest sense, and carries a secret peace amid the outward turbulence. So Jesus taught us in the eighth beatitude. Manifestly there are echoes of Christian history in vs. 34. The phrases **kill and crucify, scourge in your synagogues,** and **persecute from town to town,** describe what happened to the leaders of the Christian cause in the first century. The Christian is adventurous in righteousness, or should be: he is the true successor of Isaiah and

Jeremiah and Hosea. If the world is now so little exercised about "Christians" that it no longer persecutes them, perhaps Christianity so-called in our time has lost its savor of courage.

Is it meet and just that **all the righteous blood** should be visited on one generation? Perhaps Jesus meant that his age would be the age of judgment. The Jewish wars were a judgment in very truth. But the warning has other facets that we should not blink. There is a solidarity in history. Besides, the **sons** have the benefit of seeing their **fathers'** sins in the clearer light of the years, and so are under worse condemnation if they repeat those sins. Suppose Jesus were to return in the flesh. Many think they would like to see him. But would they? Suppose he should speak as in these woes. Our newspapers pay him lip service, but what would Jesus say about some aspects of the newspaper trade? Would the newspapers still pay him lip service? How would our superpatriots regard him? Every one of us must ask himself, "Were you there when they crucified my Lord?"

35 That upon you may come all the righteous blood shed upon the earth, from the blood of righteous Abel unto the blood of Zacharias son of Barachias, whom ye slew between the temple and the altar.

36 Verily I say unto you, All these things shall come upon this generation.

37 O Jerusalem, Jerusalem, *thou* that killest the prophets, and stonest them which are sent unto thee, how often would I have gathered thy children together, even as a hen gathereth her chickens under *her* wings, and ye would not!

town to town, 35 that upon you may come all the righteous blood shed on earth, from the blood of innocent Abel to the blood of Zech-a-ri'ah the son of Bar-a-chi'ah, whom you murdered between the sanctuary and the altar. 36 Truly, I say to you, all this will come upon this generation.

37 "O Jerusalem, Jerusalem, killing the prophets and stoning those who are sent to you! How often would I have gathered your children together as a hen gathers her brood under her wings, and you would

---

35-36. Zechariah the son of Barachiah is the O.T. prophet Zechariah. According to a tradition in the Lives of the Prophets, which may be early, this man died a natural death. The murder of Zechariah the son of Jehoiada in the court of the temple is the last murder recounted by the chronicler (II Chr. 24:21), but this was centuries before Jesus' time. Josephus (*Jewish War* IV. 5. 4) tells how a Zechariah the son of Baris was slain in the middle of the temple during the last days before the siege of Jerusalem. If the saying refers to this, it has been rewritten after the Jewish War. Certainly it was at the time of this war that **all this** did come **upon this generation.**

37-38. Jesus wished to gather the Jewish people together into the kingdom of God as a bird (ὄρνις, not necessarily a **hen**) **gathers her brood.** But the words are spoken from the point of view of later Christians, who saw the **house,** i.e., God's temple in Jerusalem, **forsaken and desolate.** According to Josephus (*Jewish War* VI. 5. 3), at the time of Pentecost, just before the temple's fall, the priests heard a portentous voice say, "We are departing hence." It must have been generally believed that God's presence had forsaken his house.

36-39. *The Lament over Jerusalem.*—Rarely have words been so filled with mingled beauty and pathos. The repetition **Jerusalem, Jerusalem** deepens the sadness. Did not David cry, "Absalom, Absalom"? (II Sam. 18:33.) No expositor, not even great artist or musician, could more than hint this heartbreak of love. That some exegetes believe these words to have come originally from a Christian wisdom literature does not weaken them (see Luke 11:49). In that event we can say that Jesus is to our Gospelist the incarnation of the Wisdom of the Eternal, and that this lament is rightly set on his lips. Christ loved Jerusalem—for its delight to the eye, for its history wherein Isaiah and Jeremiah had walked its streets, for its association with the scriptures that he loved, and because God had chosen it as his voice and hand. Here is patriotism at its best: Jesus loved Jerusalem, and could not see its temple even from a distance without a stirring of soul.

As a hen gathers her brood under her wings. There are echoes here of Pss. 17:8 and 57:1. The city could have lived "beneath the shadow of his wings." Different wings from those of the Roman eagle! The pleading and the pardon had been again and again renewed. Every

restoration after national disaster, every reminder of a noble history, every prophet voice had been the overture of God—**how often!** Yet the city, "beautiful for situation" (Ps. 48:2) and doubly beautiful in gift of truth, had only killed the prophets. **Desolate:** this word gathers all the pathos into one cry (notice the Exeg.: "We are departing hence"). Ichabod! (I Sam. 4:21.) **Your house** means the city, the homes in the city—and the temple, which should have been an ark of the covenant to the huddled dwellings of men. Is there anything more desolate than a desolate home, unless it be a desolate temple? The account in Josephus of the Jewish wars which laid waste Jerusalem makes as terrible reading as any war has ever provided.

We can see Jesus looking down on Jerusalem. We can almost overhear the lament. Yet this is more than a Bible picture. He could have saved Jerusalem: beneath his sadness there is a mighty confidence. If Jerusalem had "turned," even then, there would have been a different history. Events are his logic: after disaster men realize that in him there could have been joy, and they cry too late, **Blessed is he that cometh in the name of the Lord.** But our freedom remains. We can be like Jerusalem in our obsti-

38 Behold, your house is left unto you desolate.

39 For I say unto you, Ye shall not see me henceforth, till ye shall say, Blessed *is* he that cometh in the name of the Lord.

24 And Jesus went out, and departed from the temple: and his disciples came to *him* for to show him the buildings of the temple.

not! **38** Behold, your house is forsaken and desolate.ᶻ **39** For I tell you, you will not see me again, until you say, 'Blessed be he who comes in the name of the Lord.' "

24 Jesus left the temple and was going away, when his disciples came to point out to him the buildings of the tem-

ᶻ Some ancient authorities omit *and desolate.*

---

39. Luke 13:35 puts this saying long before the Triumphal Entry and so makes it a prophecy of that event, but in Matthew, Jesus has already been hailed in this fashion (21:9). Here the saying is an immediate introduction to the prophecy of doom, and to Matthew it must mean: "You will not see me again until I return in glory" (24:30-31).

X. Fifth Discourse, Addressed to the Disciples. The End of the Age
(24:1—26:2)

Matthew, in constructing this discourse, has a twofold purpose. (*a*) He wishes to awaken in his readers a vivid expectation that Jesus will come again in glory, even though his advent has been delayed. It is true that the Parousia or return of Christ was expected at the time of the Jewish War. But this had been a mistake, for there must first come a period of apostasy (24:10-12) followed by a mission to all the nations; only then can the end come (24:14). (*b*) The evangelist also wants to make it plain that the Christian must do more than reckon the times and seasons. No one can tell *exactly* when the Lord will come (24:42). Jesus expects his followers to be ready at every moment (24:43-44), prepared in every way (25:4), making use of their talents (25:14-30), and actively engaged in works of mercy (25:31-46).

The largest part of the discourse (24:1-36) is a rewriting of the powerful thirteenth chapter of Mark, which deals with the doom of Jerusalem and the return of the Son of man. Only one Q passage (vss. 26-28) is inserted; other changes which the author makes are probably not due to written sources. In place of Mark's conclusion (13:33-37), which dealt with the need for watchfulness, Matthew constructs his own treatment of the same theme. Part of this, 24:37-51, is drawn from Q discourses on the end of the age, which are also found in Luke 17:26-27, 34-35; 12:39-40, 42-46. The last part of the conclusion is the parable of the ten young girls, which echoes a Q saying (Luke 13:25) and reminds one more of Q than of M. The discourse ends with two other parables of the Judgment. One of these (25:14-30) teaches that the Christian will be judged on his use of what has been committed to him; the other (25:31-46) that he will be judged by whether he has helped Christ's brothers who are in need. The two principles are complementary, not contradictory. A good treatment of the critical problems can be found in Bacon, *Studies in Matthew,* pp. 67-68, 244-46, 427-28.

The sayings of Jesus quoted in these chapters teach that the world, as now constituted, will come to a catastrophic end, perhaps within a short time after the writing of

---

nate rejection of God's love. If freedom were destroyed, we should be no longer men; and not even God can save us by destroying us. We were poor in imagination indeed if we could not see Christ gazing thus on our world: "How often would I have gathered thee, as a bird her brood beneath her wings, but ye would not."

24:1-2. *Buildings Are No Surety.*—Through this chapter and the next we find different strands of writing, not all of them attributable

to Jesus (see Exeg. and also Expos., vss. 3-5). It is probable, however, that vs. 2 is Christ's own word. At his trial his enemies accused him of planning to destroy the temple, and there are many indications of his sad conviction that disaster might soon come on his nation. Mark (13:1) reports the disciples' exclamation: "What manner of stones and what buildings!" The stones in some instances were almost forty feet long. They were of green-white color, and apthe Gospel. Most twentieth-century readers have been trained to think of history as a long and unbroken process, and share the prevailing view that men have been living on the earth for many millenniums. Such readers cannot help asking what Jesus taught about the end of the age, particularly since the sayings which the evangelists attribute to him are sometimes hard to reconcile with one another. One may answer somewhat as follows: The best place to study Jesus' eschatological teaching is in old stories and sayings where the eschatology is incidental and therefore the bearers of tradition are not tempted to make additions, e.g., 22:1-5, 8-10; 20:1-15; 24:43, 45-51; Luke 13:6-9; Mark 4:26-32. We then discover that a similar point of view is found in certain "eschatological" passages, such as Luke 12:54-56; 17:20-30, 34-35 (=Matt. 24:26-28, 37-41), and from all this we draw the following conclusions. (a) Jesus shared the view of history which nearly all Jews accepted and which we call "eschatological." That is, God is the sovereign of the world; he created the world as it now is, man has defaced it, and in his own good time God will bring history to an end. This age will be superseded by a permanent order of righteousness and bliss, the kingdom of God. This will come about, not as a result of evolutionary processes, but by God's direct action. There are, indeed, signs that God's kingdom is dawning, and salvation is not merely a future hope but a present experience. Jesus never discusses or debates these assumptions: they are taken for granted and are the glass through which he looks at human life. See on 4:17; 14:13-21; 16:13-20. (b) Jesus disclaims any special knowledge of the exact scheme of events which will precede the end. He points out that previous disasters have taken mankind unawares (24:37-39), and it is therefore incumbent upon God's servants to be ready to meet him at all times (24:43-44). This, and not the detailed predictions of 24:4-25, 29-31, seems to be his genuine teaching. Thus he accepts the eschatological world view but uses it only as a stimulus to moral effort. It is not important for men to have their questions answered; it is important only that they should do God's will even at the cost of their lives. (c) Common sense and intelligent reflection should, however, teach men that the world is hastening to crisis and disaster (24:32-33; Luke 12:54-56; 13:6-9), and even Jerusalem and the temple will not escape (24:2; cf. 26:61; 21:12-13 and notes on that passage). If the nation as a whole repents, perhaps the judgment can be averted; but even if the nation does not repent, the individual must (Luke 13:5). We cannot be certain whether or not Jesus directly connects the judgment on the nation with the end of the world. He was probably not interested in answering a theoretical question of this sort.

A. DETAILED PROPHECY OF THE END (24:1-36)

Vss. 5-8, 15-22, 29-31 (=Mark 13:6-8, 14-20, 24-27) are sometimes called a "little apocalypse." They are such only in the sense that they give certain detailed signs of the end. They are not, however, an "apocalypse" like Daniel or Revelation, in which the secret knowledge purports to be mediated by dreams, visions, or auditions. Some of these verses may come from a prophecy delivered in A.D. 40, when Jews and Christians alike feared that Caligula would profane the temple by setting up his statue there.

---

peared from the distance like the surface of a shimmering ocean. The front of the temple was sheathed in plates of gold. The immense portals were almost as high as the building.

It is a fair assumption that Jesus reckoned the zealots' ultranationalism as folly: it would—and did—precipitate the fierce and overwhelming vengeance of Rome. There is a pessimism here that cannot be evaded. Jesus hoped even yet that there might be a mass penitence in his land, but he was a realist and could not deny the stubborn signs. He saw a dark day coming, and he could not hide the truth. What if he were thus pessimistic about our land? Would

his patriotism be called in question? Have we not a fatuous slogan about "throw away your hammer and buy a horn"? He loved the temple. It was right in his eyes that men should dedicate their skill and wealth to God's house, and worship the Lord "in the beauty of holiness" (Pss. 29:2; 96:9). Yet he knew that there is a subtle danger in all the works of men's hands. Great buildings, even temples, cater to men's pride. Baedeker's guidebooks list them—as if masonry were more important than men. Thus a tower soon becomes a tower of Babel. Besides, massive stones, especially in banks, beckon men to a false security. The bank could not stand with-

2 And Jesus said unto them, See ye not all these things? verily I say unto you, There shall not be left here one stone upon another, that shall not be thrown down.

3 ¶ And as he sat upon the mount of Olives, the disciples came unto him privately, saying, Tell us, when shall these things be? and what *shall be* the sign of thy coming, and of the end of the world?

4 And Jesus answered and said unto them, Take heed that no man deceive you.

ple. 2 But he answered them, "You see all these, do you not? Truly, I say to you, there will not be left here one stone upon another, that will not be thrown down."

3 As he sat on the Mount of Olives, the disciples came to him privately, saying, "Tell us, when will this be, and what will be the sign of your coming and of the close of the age?" 4 And Jesus answered them, "Take heed that no one leads you

1. The Disciples' Question (24:1-3)

24:2. A setting for this saying, which was no doubt spoken by Jesus, is provided by vs. 1. Palestine in the first century suffered from heavy taxation and bad government, and the response of many Jews was unrest and revolt. But Jesus regarded fanatical nationalism as disastrous. In the coming war even the temple would be **thrown down,** as one of the greatest rabbis predicted about the same time. Far from regarding this catastrophe with satisfaction, Jesus contemplates it with sorrow. (See Grant, *Gospel of the Kingdom,* pp. 101-10, 141-42.)

3. Matthew makes the question more explicit (contrast Mark 13:4). **Coming** is by now a technical term for the Second Advent. The Greek word παρουσία, which is thus translated, was sometimes used to refer to the visit of a monarch. **The close of the age** is one of the evangelist's favorite expressions; cf. on 13:39.

2. First Signs of the End (24:4-8)

4. At the time when the Gospels were written it was very important **that no one** should lead the Christians **astray,** for they desired eagerly "to see one of the days of the Son of man" (Luke 17:22), and might be led to follow a prophet like Simon, who pretended to be Messiah or the great power of God (Acts 8:9-11).

out God's gifts in earth and sea, still less without man's acknowledgment of God. But we forget, and then imagine that we can live on our own skill. "Mind over matter"—but what kind of mind? Mind is not long over matter unless it be "this mind . . . which was also in Christ Jesus" (Phil. 2:5). Jesus could see strife among men bringing chaos, because men had forgotten God; but his hope was not in eclipse. The world was still in God's hand, and the divine sovereignty was not usurped. Some would witness faithfully in the earth. Then buildings would have a real foundation, not in rock alone, but in man's commitment to the eternal Will.

3-5. *Signs of the End of the Age: 1. False Messiahs.*—The introduction to chs. 24–25 should be read with utmost care (see above). There are at least three strands in this weaving: first, a Christian "Little Apocalypse" written in the middle of the first century, and used both by Mark (13:4 ff.) and by Paul (I Thess. 4:15; II Thess. 2:1-10); second, Matthew's additions to and changes in that text; and, third, elements drawn directly from Christ's own words. The advice "flee to the mountains" (vs. 16) was not

followed by the Christians at the sack of Jerusalem: they fled to Pella in the Jordan Valley. So we judge that that sentence in the Little Apocalypse was written earlier than the siege of the city. But "many will fall away" (vs. 10) refers apparently to the Neronian persecutions, and may therefore be judged to be Matthew's writing toward the end of the first century. The sayings in vss. 2 and 36, and others seem to be the authentic word of Christ. Even conservative commentaries [5] acknowledge that these two chapters are a mixed harvest. The Little Apocalypse has the traditional language and trappings of that form of literature. Yet Jesus shared the outlook of his age, though with the sharp corrections shown in the Exeg.

Individual life, it is worth noting, is apocalyptic. Death comes. Shears cut the thread, whatever "development" may seem to take place across the years. Why should we be sure that history is "evolutionary"? What if evolution is also apocalyptic in nature? What may be regarded as signs of steady ascent seem often interwoven with indications of reversion to type. In an atomic age the words "the heavens

[5] *Expositor's Greek Testament,* I, 287 ff.

5 For many shall come in my name, saying, I am Christ; and shall deceive many.

6 And ye shall hear of wars and rumors of wars: see that ye be not troubled: for all *these things* must come to pass, but the end is not yet.

7 For nation shall rise against nation, and kingdom against kingdom: and there shall be famines, and pestilences, and earthquakes, in divers places.

8 All these *are* the beginning of sorrows.

astray. 5 For many will come in my name, saying, 'I am the Christ,' and they will lead many astray. 6 And you will hear of wars and rumors of wars; see that you are not alarmed; for this must take place, but the end is not yet. 7 For nation will rise against nation, and kingdom against kingdom, and there will be famines and earthquakes in various places: 8 all this is but the beginning of the sufferings.

5. The words **the Christ** are added by the evangelist. **I am** is reminiscent of Exod. 3:6, 14. It is a formula often used in sayings of Jesus and was employed by prophets and religious teachers, Christian and non-Christian. One who spoke in such prophetic style might **lead many astray.**

6. The evangelists insist that, no matter how dreadful the Jewish War had been, Jesus had predicted that **the end is not yet. The end** is the end of this age and the beginning of the age to come, as in Dan. 12:4. Paul, in II Thess. 2:1-2, similarly warned the Thessalonians that the day of the Lord had not yet come.

8. **The sufferings,** literally "childbirth pains," are probably the "birth pangs of the Messiah," of which the rabbis spoke. Such woes, it was believed, had to take place before Messiah could appear (Isa. 26:16-19; Mic. 4:9-10; Rev. 12:1-5), and all that the Christians had experienced was only **the beginning of** these.

shall pass away with a great noise, and the elements shall melt with fervent heat" (II Pet. 3:10) can hardly be dismissed as an "outmoded apocalyptic viewpoint."

The danger of a time of turbulence is that we may surrender to hysteria and to a morbid curiosity about "last things." These banes tempt us in turn to slack hands and even to a forsaking of high standards. Thus calamity-mongering is fertile ground for the false messiah. Three such false messiahs find mention in the book of Acts—Theudas (5:36), Judas of Galilee (5:37), and "the Egyptian" (21:38). Have we not known them in our own age? Hitlerism was precisely a depraved messianism. The warnings in these verses are not ancient history. Many a movement, feeding on the ego of its leader, the prideful hankerings of the people, and the mass hysteria of a turbulent time, has tried to steal the Christian name. But it cannot steal purity, nor bring forth the fruits of purity. Nor can it justify itself in the hour when men pray for the guidance of the Holy Spirit. Matthew's clarion challenge is that we have cool heads and a brave heart—and a steadfast loyalty to the Savior of men. He warns that false messiahs are not the sign of the age's end: they are only "the beginning of the sufferings" (vs. 8).

6-8. *Signs of the End of the Age: 2. The Four Horsemen.*—There were wars and rumors of wars. Nations were at odds. There were famines and earthquakes. Matthew writes of the

convulsions which shook that era. Many Jews had believed that the destruction of Jerusalem was the sign of the end. But time did not "have a stop." Hence the warning in vs. 8. *The Abingdon Bible Commentary* gives instances of these tumults.[6] **The sufferings** probably means "the birthpangs of the Messiah"—a phrase used by Jewish writers to describe the sorrows which, as they believed, would usher in the golden age.[7] (See Isa. 26:16-17.) How did such a belief arise? Why should men see in widespread pain the harbinger of spring? Is it because pain reveals truth, as darkness discloses the stars? Or because pain throws a man or a generation back on God, so that he comes in surprise of mercy when men are at their wits' end? Mark the persistence of human hope. Why do sailors set sail with such eagerness, though every vessel goes at last to the junk yard or an ocean grave, and though every sailor must die? Why do poets write or artists paint when they know that every book and canvas must crumble into dust? How does human hope endure? Emerson has said that man "is like a ship in a river; he runs against obstructions on every side but one, on that side all obstruction is taken away, and he sweeps serenely over a deepening channel into an infinite sea." [8] So these verses look beyond convulsions to the

---

[6] Pp. 702-3.

[7] Quoted, Green, *Gospel According to Saint Matthew,* "The Clarendon Bible," p. 235.

[8] Essay on "Spiritual Laws."

9 Then shall they deliver you up to be afflicted, and shall kill you: and ye shall be hated of all nations for my name's sake.	9 "Then they will deliver you up to tribulation, and put you to death; and you will be hated by all nations for my name's sake. 10 And then many will fall away,*a* and betray one another, and hate one another. 11 And many false prophets will arise and lead many astray. 12 And because wickedness is multiplied, most men's love will grow cold. 13 But he who endures
10 And then shall many be offended, and shall betray one another, and shall hate one another.	
11 And many false prophets shall rise, and shall deceive many.	
12 And because iniquity shall abound, the love of many shall wax cold.	*a* Or *stumble.*
13 But he that shall endure unto the end, the same shall be saved.	

3. Persecution and Apostasy (24:9-14)

9. This is the merest summary of Mark 13:9-13, most of which Matthew has incorporated into 10:17-21. Christians now think of themselves as **hated by all nations.** Tacitus (*Annals* XV. 44) speaks of them as "a class hated for their abominations"; cf. on 10:21-22.

10-12. Matthew inserts these verses because he wishes to show that before Christ's return **many will fall away** in a widespread desertion of the Christian cause. This is also the teaching of II Thess. 2:3. The Epistle to the Hebrews is written to prevent such apostasies; the book of Revelation speaks of those who have "abandoned the love [they] had at first" (Rev. 2:4; cf. Rev. 3:1-4, 15-17); and the Shepherd of Hermas promises only one more period of repentance for apostates. The phrase **hate one another** suggests schism, and there is evidence for this in Eph. 4:14; I John 2:18-22; and in the Pastoral epistles, the letters of Ignatius, and the Ascension of Isaiah. The **false prophets** may be men like Menander and El-Kesi; cf. Weiss, *History of Primitive Christianity*, II, 756-66; Bacon, *Studies in Matthew*, pp. 73-74. The Didache (ch. 11) deals with the testing of prophets.

13-14. Those Christians **will be saved** who can endure the trying period in which Matthew lives, when despite the apostasy **the gospel** must **be preached throughout the**

redeeming act of God. **For this must take place:** his hand is still on the helm, and there is haven beyond the storm. So the plea becomes, not a catering to hysteria or to morbid curiosity, but a summons to fidelity in Christ.

9-14. *Signs of the End of the Age: 3. Persecution and Endurance in Discipleship.*— (See also Expos., vs. 13.) This is almost certainly a picture of the troubles of the church in the time of Matthew. It shocks us by its black shadows, and wins us by its light. Christians were **hated** in every land, and charged with all manner of infamies. Some did **fall away.** Under the threshings of persecution, some proved to be chaff rather than wheat. When they were seized and imprisoned, they even gave information against fellow Christians, and tried thus to save their own skins. There was a period of apostasy. The stream did not fertilize the desert: the desert seemed rather to swallow the stream. Are there no warnings here for our own time? Specious "isms," poor earthly faiths, win men's fanatic loyalty. Meanwhile Christianity seems "too slow"—as though a timepiece were the evidence of truth! Or it seems too dangerous if

rigorously followed. We also live in an age of defection. But some endured to the end. The very persistence of this Gospel is a heart of hope. We know now that the Christian faith has abiding value, and can ride the fiercest storm. We know now the difference between treachery and fidelity. Truth concerning God and Christ came to sharper focus in that suffering. Dependence on God became a fact rather than a phrase. Brotherhood became real, for it was a brotherhood of danger unto death. Meanwhile, as the saints were driven forth in the earth, they became as scattered seed; and harvests sprang from strange fields. The Christian witness became brighter against the dark backdrop of the times. These are the unsuspected gains of endurance to the end.

13. *But He Who Endures.*—For the follower of Christ the world is an alien world, and experience is a "friendly enemy." He should not expect comfort. Indeed, human nature is such that comfort enervates and bores. However slow we may be to learn, the fact remains that we need the test of endurance and danger. Thus there is a sense in which the faith is always a

14 And this gospel of the kingdom shall be preached in all the world for a witness unto all nations; and then shall the end come.

15 When ye therefore shall see the abomination of desolation, spoken of by Daniel the prophet, stand in the holy place, (whoso readeth, let him understand,)

to the end will be saved. 14 And this gospel of the kingdom will be preached throughout the whole world, as a testimony to all nations; and then the end will come.

15 "So when you see the desolating sacrilege spoken of by the prophet Daniel, standing in the holy place (let the reader

---

whole world. The **end** cannot come until this process is complete. One may compare the idea of Paul that the gospel must be preached everywhere (Rom. 10:12-15), after which the "full number of the Gentiles" will come to faith and "all Israel will be saved" (Rom. 11:25-26). (Oscar Cullmann, *Christus und die Zeit* [Zürich: Evangelischer Verlag, 1946], pp. 143-47.)

4. Events in Judea (24:15-22)

15. The word **so** (οὖν) indicates that vss. 15-28 are a further explanation of what is meant by the foregoing (Bacon, *Studies in Matthew*, pp. 68-69, 77-79). The events predicted in these verses do not come after those which are mentioned in vss. 9-14, but

---

minority faith—on trial for its life. At times there is little that a Christian can do except to pray and to stand fast. He cannot advance then: "Having done all" he can only "stand" (Eph. 6:13). At times the sky is so black that he seems to have nothing left except the half-blind faith that God is Christlike—and the dogged will to endure. Sometimes he has apparently only "the half of a broken hope for a pillow," only the "shade of a word" for comfort.[9] But it is Christ's word, and the Christian knows that if he betrays Christ his soul will shrink and the world be thrown into blacker night. At times the kingdom tarries. But the Christian does not live by "times." The clock is not the symbol of his faith. If the advocate of some earthy "ism" suggests that Christianity is "too slow," the disciple asks him when speed became the test of truth. The times and seasons are in God's hands: it is required of a disciple that he serve his Lord. In that endurance the disciple "wins" his soul. Notice how in Luke's Gospel RSV changes "possess" to "gain" (Luke 21:19). Our life is God's gift, but we receive the gift by our endurance. We are not mere clay: we can help God, by our holding on, in his bestowal of grace. Deep breathing strengthens the lungs. The hard problem gives sinew to the mind. Endurance under hardship for Christ's sake wins the soul. Do we not say of someone, "He is a brick"? The soft clay has been burned in the fire, and now can be used for building a kingdom.

14. A Testimony to the Nations.—By what faith did Matthew say that **the end** of the age could not come until Christ's gospel had been proclaimed to all nations? This is a far remove from Jewish exclusiveness. We see at last that

[9] Robert Louis Stevenson, "If This Were Faith."

all problems are world problems. Our planet has shrunk to a neighborhood. Brazil is in the coffee on our breakfast table, Indonesia in the rubber sheathing of the electric wires in our walls. One test of any truth nowadays is: Can it become a world truth, and does it unite mankind? But this was not clear in Matthew's age of persecution. The **nations** were a harsh and alien world. Why must **this gospel . . . be preached throughout the whole world?** For man's sake: **the gospel** is his destiny and his abundant life, and every man must be given chance to receive it. For God's sake: he had sent his Son to redeem and glorify his world.

These words are eloquent of Matthew's joy. He had found a life which no persecution could darken. He knew a joy that he must share. He was no mere propagandist. If a man is ready to distribute bread in a famine, we do not call him a propagandist: he is a bringer of life. If a man has a gospel to proclaim, good news in a world of hates and strifes and secret conviction of sin, he is no propagandist: he is the herald of God. Strange world in which it is wisdom to export automobiles and guns, but only "forcing religion on people" to export a joy that conquers both sin and death! These other exports will destroy the common life if there is no gospel to unite mankind. Matthew, in an age when he and his fellow Christians were persecuted in every land, was moved by a strange passion. He was sure that history could not terminate until all men had heard the gospel. He had learned well the love of his Lord.

15-22. Signs of the End of the Age: 4. The Desolating Sacrilege.—We can be sure of the historical reference in vs. 15. Matthew gives it. He has in mind the building by Antiochus

16 Then let them which be in Judea flee into the mountains:

17 Let him which is on the housetop not come down to take any thing out of his house:

18 Neither let him which is in the field return back to take his clothes.

19 And woe unto them that are with child, and to them that give suck in those days!

20 But pray ye that your flight be not in the winter, neither on the sabbath day:

21 For then shall be great tribulation, such as was not since the beginning of the world to this time, no, nor ever shall be.

22 And except those days should be shortened, there should no flesh be saved: but for the elect's sake those days shall be shortened.

understand), 16 then let those who are in Judea flee to the mountains; 17 let him who is on the housetop not go down to take what is in his house; 18 and let him who is in the field not turn back to take his mantle. 19 And alas for those who are with child and for those who give suck in those days! 20 Pray that your flight may not be in winter or on a sabbath. 21 For then there will be great tribulation, such as has not been from the beginning of the world until now, no, and never will be. 22 And if those days had not been shortened, no human being would be saved; but for the sake of the elect those days will

---

before them. **The desolating sacrilege spoken of by the prophet Daniel** (Dan. 11:31) was the statue of Zeus set up in the temple by Antiochus IV, king of Syria, in 168 B.C. The story is told in I Macc. 1:54-64; Josephus *Antiquities* XII. 5. 4. The original Little Apocalypse of A.D. 40 reinterpreted this prophecy of Daniel to refer to Caligula's plans, and Mark gave it still another interpretation connected with the Jewish War. Matthew either looks back to that war or supposes that still another desecration will occur in "a holy place," not necessarily **the holy place.** The Jewish War, in fact, began with the profanation of a synagogue in Caesarea (Josephus *Jewish War* II. 14. 5). On the other hand, a pagan shrine was later erected on the site of the temple. **Let the reader understand** is a warning that the verse contains a hidden meaning which Christians should be able to discern.

16-18. The desecration will result in war, and Christians are not to remain in Jerusalem but **flee to the mountains** for their lives. One who is on **the housetop** must come down the outside stairway and not even go into **his house** for his possessions.

19-20. An expression of pity. Flight **on a sabbath** involves a breach of the law in addition to all the miseries. The church for which Matthew writes still keeps the Jewish sabbath.

21. Anyone who reads Josephus' *Jewish War* can understand the evangelists' feeling that no **tribulation** ever had been, or could be, worse than this.

22. The idea is that God had set a definite length of time for the tribulation, but in his mercy had afterward **shortened** it. A similar thought is found in Barn. 4:3; II Baruch 20:1-2; 83:1.

Epiphanes in 168 B.C. of a pagan altar (with the sacrifice of pigs!) on the site of the Jewish altar (see I Macc. 1:37-59). We cannot be sure of the identity of the new profaner-tyrant. The Exeg. suggests that for the writer of the Little Apocalypse he may have been Caligula. Luke identifies him with the Roman army in the Jewish wars (Luke 21:20). Branscomb [1] and others are sure that Antichrist is meant: Mark certainly gives that impression (Mark 13:14: note masculine pronoun). Behind the apocalyptic imagery there is a profound conviction of

[1] *Gospel of Mark,* p. 237, note on Mark 13:14-23.

an evil power in our world. The power may strike so suddenly that a man descending by the outer steps from the flat roof of his Palestinian home had better not enter his door for any possessions: he had better escape. And he had better pray that the onslaught come not on the sabbath, when the duty of his religious devotions would prevent flight and expose him to death. Have we ourselves not seen the suddenness and dark treachery of demonic power? We wonder, appalled, how Hitlerism could "come from nowhere" and so deceive and enthrall men. There are historical and economic ex-

23 Then if any man shall say unto you, Lo, here *is* Christ, or there; believe *it* not.

24 For there shall arise false Christs, and false prophets, and shall show great signs and wonders; insomuch that, if *it were* possible, they shall deceive the very elect.

25 Behold, I have told you before.

26 Wherefore if they shall say unto you, Behold, he is in the desert; go not forth: behold, *he is* in the secret chambers; believe *it* not.

27 For as the lightning cometh out of the east, and shineth even unto the west; so shall also the coming of the Son of man be.

be shortened. 23 Then if any one says to you, 'Lo, here is the Christ!' or 'There he is!' do not believe it. 24 For false Christs and false prophets will arise and show great signs and wonders, so as to lead astray, if possible, even the elect. 25 Lo, I have told you beforehand. 26 So, if they say to you, 'Lo, he is in the wilderness,' do not go out; if they say, 'Lo, he is in the inner rooms,' do not believe it. 27 For as the lightning comes from the east and shines as far as the west, so will be the coming

---

5. Warning Against a False Parousia (24:23-28)

23-24. These verses (from Mark 13:21-22) appear to be a variant form of the Q saying in vss. 26-27 (cf. Luke 17:23-24).

24. Signs and wonders were supposed to have been done by Simon Magus (Acts 8:9); cf. also II Thess. 2:9-12, which refers to the Antichrist, and Rev. 13:13; Did. 16:4.

26. It was **in the wilderness** that Moses had seen God, and Jews and early Christians looked back with nostalgia to the great days of the Exodus. Josephus tells of rebels who led people into the wilderness or the neighborhood of the Jordan, promising them deliverance (*Antiquities* XX. 8. 6, 10; *Jewish War* II. 13. 5; Acts 21:37-38). **In the inner rooms** suggests the Oriental doctrine of the hidden Messiah or redeemer (John 7:27; cf. on Matt. 3:16).

27. The coming of the Son of man will not be in secret but as public as **the lightning** which flashes from horizon to horizon. Jesus may well have said that when the Son of man comes there will be no mistaking him. It is not necessary to have hidden knowledge to recognize the advent of the kingdom of God.

---

planations, but they all leave unexplained the satanism of the onslaught. Yet God's sovereignty remains. Note the phrase **and if those days had not been shortened.** The word **shortened** means almost "amputated." God cuts away the evil thing before it destroys his creation. Through all the black chaos and persecution of his age Matthew was sure that God reigns. His Gospel is ours to strengthen our faith.

23-28. *Signs of the End of the Age: 5. False Dawns.*— (See also Expos., vss. 27 and 28.) Toward the end of the arctic winter there are false dawns: light glimmers with promise of the day, and then fades. But soon the real day breaks. One of the false dawns before the Golden Day, says Matthew, will be the appearance of false prophets. Thus he returns to the theme of vs. 5 (see Expos.). Here we need only add that every crisis breeds counterfeit leaders who for their own gain exploit humanity's widespread fear. Moreover each age has crises: we should be on guard. There are leaders who may propose to devastate the world with atomic power and rule a wilderness. Some play on hatred and prejudice, and yet claim to be a "Christian Front." Some would persuade us to quit our wonted

tasks because—so they insist—the millennium has come. These verses, by implication, are a breath-taking testimony to Jesus. Those who had believed had his word. They had seen his life. The wonder of his cross had broken on them. They knew his resurrection-power. They could not understand the tumult of events, but they were sure that his control could not be shaken. God had exalted him, and he was Lord both of stillness and of tumult, both of souls in heaven and of souls on earth.

27. *As the Lightning.*—We must be true to the context: the writer believed that Christ would return in some immense cosmic flash to confound false messiahs and to convince the whole race of men with instant truth. But when the terms of honest interpretation have been met, it is justifiable to find here a true token of Christ in every age. He is like lightning. How strikingly visible his truth! It is of its own kind, and cannot be hid. How universal! It is seen **from the east and shines as far as the west,** and we find certitude in the fact that Christ is light wherever he is proclaimed. How revealing is his verity! Just as a lightning flash lays bare a whole landscape in an instant, so the path of

28 For wheresoever the carcass is, there will the eagles be gathered together.

29 ¶ Immediately after the tribulation of those days shall the sun be darkened, and the moon shall not give her light, and the stars shall fall from heaven, and the powers of the heavens shall be shaken:

30 And then shall appear the sign of the Son of man in heaven: and then shall all the tribes of the earth mourn, and they shall see the Son of man coming in the clouds of heaven with power and great glory.

of the Son of man. 28 Wherever the body is, there the eagles[b] will be gathered together.

29 "Immediately after the tribulation of those days the sun will be darkened, and the moon will not give its light, and the stars will fall from heaven, and the powers of the heavens will be shaken; 30 then will appear the sign of the Son of man in heaven, and then all the tribes of the earth will mourn, and they will see the Son of man coming on the clouds of heaven with

·b Or vultures.

28. This may be a secular proverb to which Jesus gave a new application. It fits better in Luke 17:37, and in that context it means: "Wherever there is reason for judgment, the judgment will take place." **Vultures** (RSV mg.) are more likely to be found around a carcass than **eagles.**

6. Signs of the Parousia (24:29-31)

29. The advent of the Son of man will be ushered in by cosmic disasters more miraculous than the events of vss. 6-7, 15-22. This is usual in apocalyptic; and good examples can be found in Rev. 8; 9; 16.

30. Matthew adds that the Parousia will be preceded by a mysterious **sign of the Son of man in heaven.** Christians a few decades later seem to have understood this to be the

human pilgrimage is revealed by him in sudden clarity. How his truth clears the air! After sultry days comes a thunderstorm, and folk say, "This will clear the air, and we shall have coolness." So Christ brings health to save us from sticky and heated "isms." When Matthew wrote, lightning was a mysterious power. It was taken to be a visitation of God. Franklin had not yet proposed his theory of an electric storm—only to be accused by some preachers of being himself a demon![2] Accepted explanations, however, do not change the fact that in Christ *are* mysteries—the visitation of dynamic power and love from above our world. **As the lightning!**

28. *There the Vultures.*—In the history of the exegesis of the Gospels there have been astonishing interpretations of these words. The **body** has been Christ, and the "vultures" (Moffatt) his enemies; or the **body** has been Christ, and the "vultures" have been Christian saints feeding on him; or the **body** has been antichrist, and the "vultures" have been the avenging saints. Probably this is an Oriental proverb which Christ adapted to his own use, and which now carries the force that only he can give.[3] The Greeks believed in Nemesis, the daughter of Night, the avenging goddess. They believed also in the Furies, who leaped from the head of the

mutilated Uranus with hair that writhed with serpents, and they tracked down the wrongdoer with unerring knowledge and terrible penalty.[4] But this proverb is more vivid than any Greek myth. The godless life has in it corruption and death, and brings down judgment—for God is holy—more surely than a carcass brings vultures. The vulture has a keen and voracious eye, and leaves nothing more than bones picked clean. God is love, but (or therefore?) he does not deny his own nature or surrender his world to any usurpation of evil.

Perhaps the proverb was applied to Jewry, though it is not certain that the Roman eagles are here intended. The Pharisaic way of life and the bloodthirsty hatred of the zealots were corruption that led to death. Then the enemy came—God's vultures. Such a proverb appearing anywhere but in the Christian scriptures would leave us in chill terror. But he who spoke it offered mercy. He came into our world, not only to utter God's verdict against corruption and death, but to instill new life. Even while he spoke, his hearers could have found the grant of joy in him: "The wages of sin is death; but the gift of God is eternal life through Jesus Christ our Lord" (Rom. 6:23) .

29-31. *Signs of the End of the Age: 6. The True Advent.*—After the "birthpangs" the Messiah would come. His advent would write finis to the world drama. The prophecy has not been

[2] Bernard Faÿ, *Franklin, the Apostle of Modern Times* (Boston: Little, Brown & Co., 1929), ch. viii.
[3] See Rudolf Bultmann, *Form Criticism* (Chicago: Willett, Clark & Co., 1934), pp. 52-55.

[4] Gayley, *Classic Myths*, pp. 38, 54.

31 And he shall send his angels with a great sound of a trumpet, and they shall gather together his elect from the four winds, from one end of heaven to the other.

32 Now learn a parable of the fig tree; When his branch is yet tender, and putteth forth leaves, ye know that summer *is* nigh:

33 So likewise ye, when ye shall see all these things, know that it is near, *even* at the doors.

power and great glory; 31 and he will send out his angels with a loud trumpet call, and they will gather his elect from the four winds, from one end of heaven to the other.

32 "From the fig tree learn its lesson: as soon as its branch becomes tender and puts forth its leaves, you know that summer is near. 33 So also, when you see all these things, you know that he is near, at

---

appearance of the Son of man on the cross with outstretched hands (Did. 16:6; Barn. 12:2-5; Epistle of the Apostles 16). Zech. 12:10-14 predicts the mourning of the **tribes,** and **the Son of man** comes **on the clouds of heaven** as in Dan. 7:13-14. The two scripture allusions are also combined in Rev. 1:7, where the tribes presumably mourn because they have caused the death of Messiah.

31. In Isa. 27:13 the **trumpet** gathers the dispersed Israelites; in I Thess. 4:16 and Sibylline Oracles IV. 174 it announces the resurrection of the dead. God will **gather his elect,** according to Enoch 61:1, 5; Test. Naphtali 6; Did. 9:4; 10:5. The Eighteen Benedictions of the synagogue service contain the petition: "Sound the great horn for our freedom; lift up the banner to gather our exiles, and gather us from the four corners of the earth" (Singer, *Authorised Daily Prayer Book,* p. 48).

7. EXAMPLE OF THE FIG TREE (24:32-33)

32. The **fig tree** is one of the commonest trees of Palestine, and its budding is a **sure** sign of spring.

33. Anyone can see by **all these things . . . that he is near** and there can be no mistake; the point is the same as in Luke 12:54-56. The Greek (ἐγγύς ἐστιν) does not make it clear whether "he" or "it" is near. The original saying may have referred to the end of the age or the doom of Jerusalem. In this context **these things** are the signs previously mentioned.

---

fulfilled as Matthew believed. Perhaps we would not vision last things in the imagery and hope of Matthew's age. But there is hardly a detail in this tremendous picture that lacks value for our time. There would be signs in the sky. It is a favorite idea with our Gospelist, and indeed throughout the N.T., that nature accents the history of mankind—with sunshine when Christ is honored, and face dark with storm when Christ is denied (27:50-51). The drama of man's soul as he meets Christ is the real drama of history: nature, despite the vastness of powers in earth and sky, is but the stage setting. There would be, says Matthew, the dominant sign of **the Son of man.** This sign has been variously interpreted—as Christ himself, as a star like that which greeted his birth, as a blinding light, and as his cross. This last interpretation appears as early as the Didache, and has been underscored by the conversion vision of Augustine,[5] and by the flaming cross of Constantine whose motto became *in hoc signo vinces.* Actually we have no means of knowing what is meant by the sign that would bring loud

[5] *Confessions* VIII. 12.

lamentations on earth. But John 19:37 and Rev. 1:7 provide a commentary true in essence and dear to the Christian faith.

Clouds and (angelic) **power and glory** all indicate that Christ is exalted in heaven and is vindicated by heaven's might. The figures in which the reign of Christ is described may change, but the faith in his regnancy remains age on age. The **trumpet** is that which summons the faithful from death. The wicked are not mentioned: their temporary control and the powers of death are all swallowed up in the life of the elect in Christ. This passage is apocalyptic: the form is characteristic of the period in which Matthew wrote. But the core of truth remains, with deep meaning for our world and its own apocalyptic happenings. Christ will be vindicated; God rules the drama of history. Therefore—to use the grand words of the Lukan version—"When these things begin to take place, look up and raise your heads, because your redemption is drawing near" (Luke 21:28).

32-34. *From the Fig Tree Learn Its Lesson.—* We have a proverb, "Coming events cast their

34 Verily I say unto you, This generation shall not pass, till all these things be fulfilled.

35 Heaven and earth shall pass away, but my words shall not pass away.

the very gates. 34 Truly, I say to you, this generation will not pass away till all these things take place. 35 Heaven and earth will pass away, but my words will not pass away.

8. The Exact Time Is Unpredictable (24:34-36)

34. Matthew cannot have thought of **this generation** as lasting only thirty or forty years after the Crucifixion. He probably believed, however, that the end would come before *all* of Jesus' hearers had died (cf. 16:28). The saying may be essentially genuine but its exact force is uncertain (cf. general note on 24:1–26:2).

shadows before." [6] It is so true that it has become a household word. Christ said that leaves on a fig tree are the sure sign of summer's nearness. He added, in a striking contrast, that hatreds and wars among men, with distress on earth, are the sure sign of his advent or of the close of an era. The fig tree in Palestine was the commonest of trees. Yet men could read the seasons in it. Why can we not read the meaning of our commonplace experience? Wickedness always brings strife, and strife carried to the point of desperation brings the end of an age. We see it in the realm of man's toil. Greed brought unions and the strike weapon. These in turn brought widespread public suffering, and the realization that the realm of toil could not endure as an armed camp. Now there are socializations and other experiments in almost every land. Economic systems are in flux, and beyond doubt some new order is being born. But how many understand the signs, though they are so clear that "he that runs may read"? [7] Christ bids us look with open eyes on a world that is God's page. There are penalties for those who are stubbornly blind to his writing. But the figure Christ chose was not tragic. He chose the sign of spring. "If Winter comes, can Spring be far behind?" [8] Surely Christ did not choose the instance of a springtime tree without intent to bring us hope. The very penalties of life, the distresses and the tears, are still harbingers of summer for those who trust his grace and follow his steps.

35. His Deathless Words.—To casual minds Christ seems naïve. He is "back there" in the childhood of the race, offering impossible dreams; while we are "here" in a real and complex world. "Try to imagine Jesus in a telephone booth," someone said. For that matter, try to imagine him in the control room of a modern liner. "Can anyone tell us whether Christ would have approved of the pattern of our present civilization at all, and if not, how are we to escape from it?" asks W. Macneile

Dixon. He adds that no one could tell us "unequivocally" what Christ thinks of our education or commerce or of our legal system; and he hints some sympathy with those who maintain that Christianity has shot its bolt. [9]

But is life so different now? Its trappings are, but not its essence. Misrepresenting an automobile in the twentieth century is not essentially different from lying about the age of a camel in the first century. "What would Jesus do in conquered Poland?" someone has asked. But he lived in a conquered Poland—conquered Palestine. He knew poverty so poor that "two sparrows sold for a farthing" (10:29). He knew about sharp dealing in trade—the guilt of men who "devour widows' houses" (23:14; Mark 12:40; Luke 20:47). He knew national hatreds such as those between Jews and Samaritans; and the sword of the tyrant, even the slaughter that mingled the "blood" of men with "their sacrifices" (Luke 13:1). He did not live in some Arcadia. He lived in our very world.

Sharper question: *Is he remote?* A novel is published called *Christ in Concrete*. A play is produced entitled *Family Portrait*—the portrait of his home. A poem is written about Woolworth's store: "I did not think to find You there:" [1] His sayings are hardly antediluvian: they are the stab of truth. Far from his being "back there," he is always "on ahead." Though we cannot say "unequivocally" what would be his mind about this or that problem of our time, his light breaks on our world like the re-creating wonder of the dawn. We do know if he would approve the pattern of our present civilization. We know he would not; we know it so well that we try to evade the lancet of that knowledge.

Another question: Do we wish from Jesus at every turn of our journey some unequivocal word? What would happen to us if at every juncture Christ were to tap us on the shoulder

[6] Thomas Campbell, "Lochiel's Warning."
[7] Tennyson, "The Flower."
[8] Shelley, "Ode to the West Wind."

[9] *The Human Situation* (New York: Longmans, Green & Co., 1937), pp. 36 ff.
[1] Teresa Hooley, "Christ in Woolworth's," in Thomas C. Clark, *The Master of Men* (New York: Richard R. Smith, 1930), p. 160.

| 36 ¶ But of that day and hour knoweth no *man*, no, not the angels of heaven, but my Father only. 37 But as the days of Noe *were*, so shall also the coming of the Son of man be. | 36 "But of that day and hour no one knows, not even the angels of heaven, nor the Son, but the Father only. 37 As were the days of Noah, so will be the coming of |

36. Nor the Son is found in the best representatives of the Alexandrian, Western, and Caesarean text types; KJV omits it with the Byzantine MSS. "Son" is used here in the sense of "Son of God" (cf. on 4:3). Thus the saying is expressed in terms of later Christian thought, but the idea may go back to Jesus.

B. On Being Prepared (24:37–25:13)

1. Most Humans Will Be Taken Unawares (24:37-41)

37. It was believed that events of Moses' time, such as the manna miracle, would be repeated in the messianic age, and that the age to come would be like the Garden of Eden; hence it was natural that the judgment should be thought of as striking as in the days of Noah.

and say, "Do this" or "Say that"? Such a Christ would be no Savior but only a dictator. Even a grade-school boy can and should learn to do his own homework when once a friend has given him a start. It is part of life to wait for Christ's will, to search for it, and to try to do it: an "unequivocal word" would soon be a dungeon. But there is an unequivocal Presence. There are words that are seminal, ever bringing forth fresh harvests. There is a spirit playing through the words, so that they strike fire on every new occasion. There is a human heart age on age that rings in answer to what he said —and to the eternal Word of his life and death and resurrection.

36. *Last Things: Only God Knows.*—We must honestly admit the discrepancy between vss. 34 and 36. One expositor has rightly said that Christ's "whole manner of speaking concerning the second advent seems to have two faces." [2] So the student is left at a loss. The Exeg. offers a wise solution: vs. 34 is Matthew's belief, and vs. 36 has authentic marks of Christ's own utterance. Paul W. Schmiedel has argued rather convincingly that when words ascribed to Jesus run counter to the native hopes of the disciples, we may doubly trust their authenticity. Thus Schmiedel takes this particular saying as a "foundation-pillar." [3] Notice that the phrase **nor the Son**, though it is omitted from some MSS, has strong warrant. Theological problems are thus raised which need not here concern us. The "self-emptying" of Jesus, as set forth in Phil. 2:7, comes to mind. The Incarnation, by the very meaning of the word, spells limitation; but probably we would be wise not to use this saying to try to trace dividing lines in the area

[2] *Expositor's Greek Testament*, I, 297, see on vss. 32-36.
[3] *Jesus in Modern Criticism* (London: Adam & Charles Black, 1907), pp. 16-17, 33.

of Christ's knowledge. The weight of stress here is not negative so much as positive: God knows, and is sovereign over both the half wisdom of the good man and the schemings of the evil.

We must be faithful to our human ignorance about all things, and especially about "last things." How little we know! Our political and economic wisdom is again and again confounded by events. We misjudge even our own human nature. We cannot predict what one day may bring. Why, then, should we imagine that we can read with accuracy the scroll of history, or be sure when it will be sealed? It is a mercy that we do not know. If tomorrow were as clear now as it will be tomorrow night—if we live through tomorrow—we would probably presume on its joys or be distracted by its sorrows. Assuredly we would lose the zest of living, and be robbed of the courage that comes only through faith. Our life is so constituted that we must live by venture—the venture does not lack either God's beckonings or inner certitudes— and by a better Light than man's wisdom. God knows: that fact is paramount. God has his own calendar, his **hour** and day. Jesus plainly believed that history has an apocalyptic character: it is not an interminable squirrel cage, or a meaningless running down of the clock, or an inevitable ascent, for God is always at work in our world and in man's strange freedom. God has his "little advents" day by day, and a climactic advent in each man's death, and at the last that advent in which he writes finis to the story of this planet. Therefore a man should always be ready. To that truth this Gospel now turns.

37-41. *Noah's Day and Ours.*—The play *The Green Pastures* showed Noah busily at work on the ark while his neighbors laughed at his folly.

38 For as in the days that were before the flood they were eating and drinking, marrying and giving in marriage, until the day that Noe entered into the ark,

39 And knew not until the flood came, and took them all away; so shall also the coming of the Son of man be.

40 Then shall two be in the field; the one shall be taken, and the other left.

41 Two *women shall be* grinding at the mill; the one shall be taken, and the other left.

42 ¶ Watch therefore; for ye know not what hour your Lord doth come.

the Son of man. 38 For as in those days before the flood they were eating and drinking, marrying and giving in marriage, until the day when Noah entered the ark, 39 and they did not know until the flood came and swept them all away, so will be the coming of the Son of man. 40 Then two men will be in the field; one is taken and one is left. 41 Two women will be grinding at the mill; one is taken and one is left. 42 Watch therefore, for you do not know on what

---

38-39. There was nothing wrong in their **eating and drinking** and their other lawful pursuits. What was wrong was that they were heedless and entirely immersed in ordinary occupations. **The flood** is pictured as a sudden rush of waters (contrast Gen. 7:11-12, 17-19).

40. But though this is sudden, it is not an indiscriminate destruction. **One is taken,** i.e., accepted and preserved, **and one is left** to his doom.

2. "BE YOU READY" (24:42-44)

42. This summary of Mark 13:35 points the moral of vss. 37-41 and introduces the saying which follows.

They paused on their way to fling half-pitying jests at a man crazy enough to believe in **the flood.** Most of us on the eve of world calamity, or on the threshold of any joy or sorrow, are numbered with those neighbors. We would be wrong to construe **eating** as gluttony, or **marriage** as license. The point of vs. 38 is precisely that Noah's neighbors were busy with the routine of life. They were absorbed in this world. They were heedless of God. History was a river down which their boat would move in steady progress. There were no waterfalls, no shrines at which they should pray, no dark chasms, no rapids. If God had anything to do with it, he had finished his work when he set the boat moving on its journey. They were not concerned to know if there was any port of debarkation. They were careless of any deep meaning in human life.

William Morris has a striking comment on our "progress":

I used really to despair once because I thought what the idiots of our day call progress would go on perfecting itself: happily I now know that all that will have a sudden check—sudden in appearance, I mean—"as it was in the days of Noë." [4]

The prediction has certainly been fulfilled. Climactic lines are drawn across history, and

across each man's personal history; for history is not the steady movement of a man-guided boat down a river, but a commerce and conversation between man and God. There is striking truth in vss. 40-41. A flood is no respecter of persons. In that regard it is not a good metaphor for God's advents, for he divides man from man unerringly: he can read the heart. Thus two men working in the same furrow are divided, or two women working at the same hand mill: one is **taken** and the other is **left. Taken** and **left** are words with vast though untraced horizons—the one of joy and the other of doom. In a world of change and death, of tears and sudden gladness, of events apocalyptic in their sweeping change, how can any man be heedless or absorbed in what he thinks is a world of even tenor?

42-44. *Watch Therefore!*—The householder seems to have been a man in ordinary circumstances. He lived in a house with baked clay walls through which a thief could dig. This story might be called the parable of the householder and the thief. A thief's strategy is to strike when a man is absent, asleep, or so absorbed that he is off guard. Who could have imagined that the thief would come when we forgot to lock the door "just that once"? "Confidence men" succeed—why? Because the victim is asleep. Yes, but more because he is greedy, intent upon quick cash more than upon

[4] J. W. Mackail, *The Life of William Morris* (New York: Longmans, Green & Co., 1899), pp. 144-45.

43 But know this, that if the goodman of the house had known in what watch the thief would come, he would have watched, and would not have suffered his house to be broken up.

44 Therefore be ye also ready: for in such an hour as ye think not the Son of man cometh.

45 Who then is a faithful and wise servant, whom his lord hath made ruler over his household, to give them meat in due season?

day your Lord is coming. 43 But know this, that if the householder had known in what part of the night the thief was coming, he would have watched and would not have let his house be broken into. 44 Therefore you also must be ready; for the Son of man is coming at an hour you do not expect.

45 "Who then is the faithful and wise servant, whom his master has set over his household, to give them their food at the

---

43. Note the past tense. Jesus may be speaking of a recent occurrence that the whole village would have known about. An American proverb speaks of "locking the barn after the horse is stolen."

44. An ancient rabbinical saying goes, "Three things come unexpectedly, Messiah, the discovery of a treasure, and a scorpion." Elsewhere in the N.T. the metaphor of the thief refers to condemnation (I Thess. 5:4; Rev. 3:3). The original saying of Jesus probably was concerned with the catastrophe of vs. 39, and not with the joyful coming of the Son of man.

3. Good Slaves and Bad (24:45-51)

It is characteristic of Matthew that he concludes this section, not with an apocalyptic scheme, but with an emphasis on the moral quality of God's judgment. The parables of ch. 25 are a coda on the same theme.

45. Who then is . . . faithful and wise . . . ? In folk stories this is a favorite way of expressing a moral (cf. 21:31; Luke 10:36). The evangelists may think of the servant or slave as a Christian minister (cf. 20:25-28), but Jesus probably spoke the parable against the high-priestly group or other Jewish leaders. Or perhaps the only point is that

---

true worth of character. That fact is a central issue in this story. Watch. It is an oft-repeated word on the lips of Jesus. A man must live with open eyes. It is easy to become absorbed in livelihood, and thus to forget life. It is easy to miss God's writing on earth and sky. A man must "Stop, Look, Listen" for more than railroad trains!

The practice of prayer is therefore crucial. It is far more than a clamoring for what we think would be blessing. A wise man prays, "Lord, open my eyes that I may see thy comings and goings in the earth. Lord, open my ears that I may not miss thy whisper. Lord, the enemy may take me unawares: keep me sensitive to thy touch of warning and help." To watch does not mean that a man should forsake his daily task, or ever become distraught in it. If a man is always scanning the sky for signs, he will not reap. If always he exclaims, "Tomorrow may be the day," he will not be whole either in home or heart. How does a man plow? So let him watch. One minute his eyes are fixed on the furrow, for by the terms of life God requires that he should plow; but the next minute his eyes are set on the distant mark that

the furrow may be straight. Ever and again the plowman pauses to greet his neighbor—and pray to God. Watch therefore!

45-51. The Ready and the Unready: Reward and Doom.—It is characteristic of this Gospel that this "apocalyptic" section should come to a pause, not in any satisfying of a morbid curiosity, but in an ethical and spiritual plea. If the previous story could be called the parable of the householder and the thief, this might be named the parable of the ready and unready servants. Its homeyness is a dominant feature: the faithful servant gets the meals ready at the proper time. To whom is the plea addressed? Perhaps to the religious community in Christ's land and time. Perhaps Matthew has turned it toward the Christian herald, in which event **food** is the bread of the gospel. Perhaps it is intended for every man. Certainly the **food** is life—mediated through livelihood. If we do not minister to our neighbor in more than garden produce and shelter, we tragically fail him; he has sky in his nature more centrally than he has earth.

Mark the qualities of a good servant. He is **faithful** and **wise** and alert for the coming of

46 Blessed *is* that servant, whom his lord when he cometh shall find so doing.

47 Verily I say unto you, That he shall make him ruler over all his goods.

48 But and if that evil servant shall say in his heart, My lord delayeth his coming;

49 And shall begin to smite *his* fellow servants, and to eat and drink with the drunken;

50 The lord of that servant shall come in a day when he looketh not for *him,* and in an hour that he is not aware of,

51 And shall cut him asunder, and appoint *him* his portion with the hypocrites: there shall be weeping and gnashing of teeth.

25 Then shall the kingdom of heaven be likened unto ten virgins, which took their lamps, and went forth to meet the bridegroom.

proper time? **46** Blessed is that servant whom his master when he comes will find so doing. **47** Truly, I say to you, he will set him over all his possessions. **48** But if that wicked servant says to himself, 'My master is delayed,' **49** and begins to beat his fellow servants, and eats and drinks with the drunken, **50** the master of that servant will come on a day when he does not expect him and at an hour he does not know, **51** and will punish*c* him, and put him with the hypocrites; there men will weep and gnash their teeth.

25 "Then the kingdom of heaven shall be compared to ten maidens who took their lamps and went to meet the

c Or *cut him in pieces.*

whoever is entrusted with duties must perform them faithfully and be ready to render an account at all times. It is incumbent on all Christians to see that other members of the master's **household** have **their food at the proper time.**

47. He who does the will of God will be a **ruler** in the age to come (as in **I Cor.** 6:2-3).

51. If διχοτομήσει is to be taken literally (**cut him in pieces** RSV mg.), the parable has been changed into an allegory of the Last Judgment. B. T. D. Smith (*Parables of the Synoptic Gospels,* p. 63) notes that in the old story of Ahikar, Nadan, who had flogged his uncle's servants, swelled up and burst asunder; and this may have influenced the parable. Matthew has added his customary **weeping and gnashing of teeth** and has changed the "unfaithful" of Luke 12:46 to **hypocrites.** Jesus may have used an Aramaic word which means "rascals."

4. A Parable on Preparedness (25:1-13)

25:1. A wedding party was one of the greatest of all festivities in a Palestinian village. The bride, groom, and guests were dispensed from certain religious duties, such as sleeping in booths at the feast of Tabernacles. Scholars forsook the study of the Torah, because attending a wedding was a more important duty and privilege. The neighbor

his Lord. **Faithful** means that the man has staying power, and will not be diverted from the Christian confession he has made. **Wise** means sound in both judgment and foresight—in trust in the better Wisdom. **Ready** means that he is not pessimistic if the kingdom tarries, is not beguiled by delay, but is on the alert for Christ's return. The servant thus fulfills the appointed task, with eyes ever and again lifted to the door, in hope that he may come. Why does Christ seem to depart? Why is there a rhythm in the Christian life—seasons when the Lord leaves us, and seasons of his bright return? Because love grows in the very longing, with chance to prove stanchness during the times of delay; and because absence proves that Christ,

though unseen, is not absent. The man who assumes that Christ has "gone for good," and therefore proceeds to follow his own will or whim, is "cut in pieces" in very truth. Have not the movements of history proved it? Yet God is passing kind: the prepared servant is set . . . over all his possessions.

25:1-13. *Parable of the Maidens at the Wedding.*— (See also Expos., vss. 5-6 and 9.) It is not surprising that this story was dear to the early church. In their expectation of the second coming of Jesus in the flesh, the **bridegroom,** so it seemed, **was delayed.** The parable here recorded was their comfort. One can readily understand why in later years it became a favorite theme in mystery plays, for it is unforget-

2 And five of them were wise, and five *were* foolish.

3 They that *were* foolish took their lamps, and took no oil with them:

4 But the wise took oil in their vessels with their lamps.

bridegroom.*d* 2 Five of them were foolish, and five were wise. 3 For when the foolish took their lamps, they took no oil with them; 4 but the wise took flasks of oil with

d Some ancient authorities add *and the bride.*

---

maidens, like all girls, would be eager to be present. **The bridegroom and the bride** (RSV mg.) is the reading attested by Bezae (D), some Caesarean MSS, the Latin versions, and the Sinaitic Syriac, and is probably correct. The high point of the wedding came when the bridegroom took the bride from her father's house to her new home, usually in a litter, and his attendants and guests escorted her there. The words "and the bride" are missing in some MSS probably because the "bridegroom" was understood as an allegorical reference to Christ, and the copyists could see no way of fitting the bride into the allegory.

2. No symbolic meaning should be sought in the number **five** or in other details of the story.

3. A medieval Jewish commentator speaks of the **lamps** or torches, about ten in number, which were carried at a wedding.

---

table alike for its loveliness, its pathos, and its drama (see Exeg. on the probable ending at vs. 10). The story needs no other moral than its own simplicity of truth.

Everybody loves a wedding. Jesus said in effect that the joy of a wedding is the proper sign of the kingdom of God. In Jewry a wedding absolved bride and groom even from certain religious duties, and gave warrant for the scribe to forsake for a time his holy books. Thus the gladness of Christ overwhelms even the "dear delights" of customary religion. Why should worldly pleasures, that go no deeper than the senses and may be bitter in the aftermath, have a monopoly on the phrase "a good time"? Jesus gave as motto of his way of life, "Happy are they that. . . ." He overcame the stern demands of the law—"Thou shalt not . . ."—with the gladness of new life.

What is this coming of Christ? There is little doubt that to the early church it meant his second advent. Chs. 24–25 are centrally apocalyptic. The parable still has that meaning. That is why the expositions of ch. 24 have stressed the apocalyptic and eschatological character both of personal experience and of the history of mankind. But the second advent has not occurred in the fashion Matthew expected. Has the story therefore no meaning for us? Jesus comes again and again in the twin adventure of life and death, and there is no day when this parable lacks pertinence. The theme is preparedness, not for the worst—that readiness we hold comparatively well in mind—but for the best. Preparedness is the crux of the story. What preparedness? What is represented by the oil which some maidens had bought and some lacked? We need not turn the parable into an

allegory: call the oil faith in Christ—a faith fed by prayer and confirmed in obedient life. All the maidens welcomed the bridegroom; all were Christian in outlook. But with some the faith had become perfunctory, while with others it was eager and alert. These latter had gone to the dealers: they had tapped the resources of God's power, and in faithful life had trimmed the wick. They lived, not merely for the moment, but against tomorrow's emergency of joy. This preparedness each maiden made, or failed to make, for herself. There is an individuality of response to Christ which no bestowal of the whole church can ever cancel. The wise ones in their foresight were not deceived by apparent delay or by the routine march of days. They knew that life has apocalyptic gladness. Again and again they renewed their trust in God made known in Christ.

"There is a tide in the affairs of men." It is taken or (so far as that tide is concerned) forever lost. There may be other tides, but that tide does not return. Such is Shakespeare's[5] version of **the door was shut.** Tennyson has his version, based on this very story, in a poem of haunting loveliness and pathos: "Late, late, so late!"[6] The poem is doubly pathetic when the history of Guinevere is borne in mind. What is represented by oilless lamps? W. L. Watkinson suggests that it is ecclesiasticism without righteousness, morality without godliness, and enthusiasm without perseverance.[7] That list will serve. Have we the faith, fed by prayer, made clear in obedient life, that will brighten the midnight when the King comes in joy?

[5] *Julius Caesar*, Act IV, scene 3.
[6] *Idylls of the King*, "Guinevere," 1. 166.
[7] *The Christian World Pulpit*, January 18, 1905.

5 While the bridegroom tarried, they all slumbered and slept.

6 And at midnight there was a cry made, Behold, the bridegroom cometh; go ye out to meet him.

7 Then all those virgins arose, and trimmed their lamps.

8 And the foolish said unto the wise, Give us of your oil; for our lamps are gone out.

9 But the wise answered, saying, *Not so;* lest there be not enough for us and you: but go ye rather to them that sell, and buy for yourselves.

their lamps. 5 As the bridegroom was delayed, they all slumbered and slept. 6 But at midnight there was a cry, 'Behold, the bridegroom! Come out to meet him.' 7 Then all those maidens rose and trimmed their lamps. 8 And the foolish said to the wise, 'Give us some of your oil, for our lamps are going out.' 9 But the wise replied, 'Perhaps there will not be enough for us and for you; go rather to the dealers

---

5. Matthew probably thinks of Christ as the **bridegroom** who **was delayed;** to him this is a reference to the Parousia, which had long been expected. But in the original parable the delay was only an incidental part of the story.

9. It would be unusual for shops to be open at midnight, although if the whole village was awake the girls might have been able to **buy.**

5-6. *At Midnight There Was a Cry.*—The delays of Christ's kingdom are hard to explain. Their full meaning and purpose are hidden from us. We can partly understand. How else except through delay could we learn the grace of endurance, and how else savor the joy of haven after the long buffetings of the sea? But these "reasons" are poor comfort when the blessing for which we have ardently prayed still tarries, or when the peace for which nations yearn comes on leaden feet. **They nodded and slept,** and there was no crime in the slumber. But the foolish just fell asleep, while the wise slept only after they had made due preparation. So the wise were awake at once, and as quickly *en rapport* with the event. **At midnight:** precisely at the darkest hour, when least expected, Christ came. Man is not left to slumber and die.

Joy at midnight! It seems almost a contradiction in terms. When slumber was deepest, when strength was spent, Christ came. Always we prepare for the worst: why do we not prepare for the Lord? Nations prepare for war, but peace and the opportunity to confirm peace find them napping. A man buys insurance against fire, but makes no preparation in mind or spirit for married joy. Even "Christianity" of a kind makes the mistake of being ready only for death, meanwhile being unready for life here and hereafter. The midnights of life are not the sign of doom: they are the hour when heaven comes to offer heaven's joy for man's weariness. But when the cry sounds, there is no time for preparation. The torches then make patterns of joy on tree and hillside, and the procession moves on toward the house of banqueting; and those without lamps are left in darkness. When they finally reach the hall, the door is shut. In the daytime wise and unwise seem alike: midnight is the test and the judgment—and the offered gladness. "Therefore you also must be ready" (24:44).

9. *The Individuality of Response.*—**Perhaps there will not be enough for us and for you** is a sentence that seems rather worse than unchristian: it seems heartless in its selfishness. We must be careful not to allegorize a parable. A parable has one central beam of light. In this instance it is the wisdom of readiness. The details of a parable serve mainly to add verisimilitude, and to make the story vivid in the memory. So we should not impose theological meanings on this particular verse. Yet the fact remains that spiritual preparedness cannot instantly be shared. If we consult experience, we shall not find it strange that the wise maidens could not give of their oil. But someone may ask, "The grace of Christ is free: why, then, was the door shut against the unwise?" Of a truth his grace is free, offered "without money and without price" (Isa. 55:1). But it is not a gift to man without any response on man's part. Each man must receive and appropriate it. Christ cannot forgive, for instance, without our acceptance and trust, or without willingness on our part to forgive our neighbors. This response cannot be shared or borrowed, at least not in full.

Why? We are individuals. Our faith in Christ is inevitably in some measure an individual faith. Can a man trained in Christian courage give it on demand to a neighbor who all his life has lived in cowardly comfort? Can a saint who has gathered insight from long years of prayer

10 And while they went to buy, the bridegroom came; and they that were ready went in with him to the marriage: and the door was shut.

11 Afterward came also the other virgins, saying, Lord, Lord, open to us.

12 But he answered and said, Verily I say unto you, I know you not.

13 Watch therefore; for ye know neither the day nor the hour wherein the Son of man cometh.

14 ¶ For *the kingdom of heaven is* as a man traveling into a far country, *who* called his own servants, and delivered unto them his goods.

and buy for yourselves.' 10 And while they went to buy, the bridegroom came, and those who were ready went in with him to the marriage feast; and the door was shut. 11 Afterward the other maidens came also, saying, 'Lord, Lord, open to us.' 12 But he replied, 'Truly, I say to you, I do not know you.' 13 Watch therefore, for you know neither the day nor the hour.

14 "For it will be as when a man going on a journey called his servants and en-

---

10. The parable may originally have ended here. In that case, with all the noise going on, no one noticed that the girls were outside, and it is not necessary to suppose that the groom deliberately kept **the door . . . shut.** The point of the parable is: If you do not make preparation in time, you will be **too late** for the kingdom of God, as the girls were too late for the party.

11-12. Matthew has worked a Q saying in at this point (cf. 7:21-23; Luke 13:25-27), with the effect of allegorizing the story somewhat. The bridegroom is now the heavenly Judge. He does not acknowledge those who have not made preparation while there was yet time. The idea that someday it may be too late to repent is also found in Heb. 12:17 and Herm. Vis. III. 5. 5; III. 8. 8-9.

13. The command to **watch,** i.e., keep awake, is put in by Matthew to link the parable with 24:42. But it is not appropriate here. Both the wise and foolish girls slept (vs. 5), and there was no harm in that; what was wrong was that some had not provided themselves with oil before they went to sleep.

C. A Parable on the Use of Capabilities (25:14-30)

The wording of the story in Matthew differs considerably from Luke's parable of the minae or pounds (Luke 19:12-27), and attempts have been made to assign the former to the M source. But it seems better to assume that Q contained some form of the parable. Matthew perhaps changed "minae" to **talents** to make it more impressive,

---

give that insight on request to someone who has always been careless of God? It does not profit a greedy self-seeker to say, "My father was a man of prayer, and my next-door neighbor lives in Christian charity." That fact may deepen the greedy man's guilt. Preparedness is only partly transferable. The bridegroom would have gone unwelcomed, and the midnight would still have been midnight, if the wise had tarried the belatedness of the unwise. **Buy for yourselves:** that rule remains while there is any meaning in individuality. We need no money with which to buy: we need bring only our pathetic lack and longing. But nobody can go for us. We may take another man's name, but we cannot assume his nature. That fact abides, and with it the tragedy of the closed door.

14-30. The Parable of the Talents.— (See Expos., vss. 18, 21, 29.) This story in the

KJV has given a key word to our language— talents. A doctrinaire assumption that there is complete equality among men, or a demand for such equality, is folly. Jesus knew and clearly taught that men differ in talents. There are diversities of gifts. Some men draw plans for a cathedral, some compose music for its organ, some carve the stone, and some build the road to the door. But every man is talented. No man is without some gift essential to the building.

All men, whatever their endowments, are bond servants. Perhaps we should not envy greater capacity: it spells greater responsibility. The Jews, with their deeper truth concerning God—the parable may have been addressed particularly to them—were under heavier burden of accountability. The architect of the cathedral is not a prince among men: equally with the hod carrier he is the bond servant of God. That

15 And unto one he gave five talents, to another two, and to another one; to every man according to his several ability; and straightway took his journey.

16 Then he that had received the five talents went and traded with the same, and made *them* other five talents.

17 And likewise he that *had received* two, he also gained other two.

18 But he that had received one went and digged in the earth, and hid his lord's money.

19 After a long time the lord of those servants cometh, and reckoneth with them.

trusted to them his property; 15 to one he gave five talents,*e* to another two, to another one, to each according to his ability. Then he went away. 16 He who had received the five talents went at once and traded with them; and he made five talents more. 17 So too, he who had the two talents made two talents more. 18 But he who had received the one talent, went and dug in the ground and hid his master's money. 19 Now after a long time the master of those servants came and settled accounts

e See note on 18. 24.

and added allegorical touches such as vs. 30 and "share your master's joy" in vss. 21 and 23. On the other hand, Luke has altered the original by giving all the slaves the same endowment and weaving in a second story which obscures the point (Luke 19:12b, 14-15a, 27). The parable of the great supper similarly underwent divergent changes at the hands of the two evangelists (cf. on 22:1-14).

15. In English we commonly say that people have received **talents** of music, business acumen, leadership, and the like. That use of the word is derived from this parable. A talent was originally a measure of weight. Later the word came to denote a fixed amount of silver or gold, roughly equivalent to $1,000 (as in Goodspeed's translation). The owner, like the king in 18:23-35, is pictured as very rich. **He went away** like the master in Luke 12:35-40, 42-48; Mark 13:33-37.

18. In antiquity money was often hidden for safekeeping (cf. 13:44). The ancient coins now to be seen in museums come from such hoards.

kind of equality is not doctrinaire. Neither is the equality of opportunity. Why does God seem to desert us for **a long time?** He has not deserted us: he thus gives us chance to prove our stewardship. Always there is sufficient space for the human work and the human will. We are only tenant farmers, but we have liberty to decide on the rotation of crops and how we shall spend our time. For a long period we have both a measure of initiative and some control of our hours and labor.

But there is a day for settling our account. The Lord returns to receive his own possessions. Far more is involved than money, for this is a parable of the kingdom. Money waste may be small compared with other squanderings. What use do we make of the talent of friendliness or of prayer? How have we sowed and harvested our yearnings for justice among men? God expects the increase. That is the story's central thrust. Talents are not museum pieces, still less the occasion for human pride. Our environment is so constituted in the wisdom of God that it is like soil and weather to our kingdom seed. But not unless we sow. A man must venture for Christ at risk. He must not be content with "things as they are." He must break new soil. We miss the point of the story

if we fail to see that Christ requires of his followers the hazard of the untried road.

So there are equalities. Not in gifts, for these differ; but in opportunity, and in responsibility proportionate to the gift. Furthermore, there is equality in the love of God, for the man with five talents and the man with two entered equally **into the joy of** their lord. Some exegetes suggest that **joy** could be translated "feast." It is God's **well done**, a gladness so radiant that it compensates overflowingly for all the delay and all the irksomeness of labor. So to each man his gift and his place in the kingdom. There should be no envy and no pride: all are bond servants, and responsibility rests on all. Besides, they are equally blessed in God's love and joy.

18. The One-Talent Man.—It is hard to escape the conviction that the story was told mainly for this man. He stands center stage in the drama. There are more one-talent men and two-talent men in the world than five-talent men. Only a few are poets like Keats, inventors like Edison, statesmen like Lincoln, or preachers like Chrysostom. Peculiar dangers beset the one-talent man. He is tempted to say, "With my poor equipment nothing will be expected of me: what can I do?" That is a devilish whisper in a man's ear: "What can I do?" The one-

20 And so he that had received five talents came and brought other five talents, saying, Lord, thou deliveredst unto me five talents: behold, I have gained beside them five talents more.

21 His lord said unto him, Well done, *thou* good and faithful servant: thou hast been faithful over a few things, I will make thee ruler over many things: enter thou into the joy of thy lord.

22 He also that had received two talents came and said, Lord, thou deliveredst unto me two talents: behold, I have gained two other talents beside them.

23 His lord said unto him, Well done, good and faithful servant; thou hast been faithful over a few things, I will make thee ruler over many things: enter thou into the joy of thy lord.

with them. 20 And he who had received the five talents came forward, bringing five talents more, saying, 'Master, you delivered to me five talents; here I have made five talents more.' 21 His master said to him, 'Well done, good and faithful servant; you have been faithful over a little, I will set you over much; enter into the joy of your master.' 22 And he also who had the two talents came forward, saying, 'Master, you delivered to me two talents; here I have made two talents more.' 23 His master said to him, 'Well done, good and faithful servant; you have been faithful over a little, I will set you over much; enter into the

---

21. Enter into must mean "share" (Goodspeed). Matthew thinks of heaven or "eternal life," into which one enters (19:17). The master's remark is paralleled in Luke 16:10.

---

talent man is also prone to resentment. He may hold a grudge against life and envy against his fellow men because he is poorly gifted as compared with brilliant neighbors. The picture of his complaint in the parable is incisive in its psychological truth. He blamed God: "I knew you to be a hard man" (vs. 24). He even accused God of reaping where he had not sowed. Criticism of God and man is the escape of people who feel and resent mediocrity.

But the real reason for his failure was his fear: "I was afraid" (vs. 25). He dared no venture. He lacked faith in life and God. He was churlish and poor-spirited—words that well express "wicked and slothful" (vs. 26). Milton said that he could not praise "a fugitive and cloistered virtue." [8] Therein Milton was true to the mind of Jesus. Charlotte Brontë wrote in even sharper phrase, "Better to try all things and find all empty, than to try nothing and leave your life a blank." [9] The one-talent man in his failure is content with power diplomacy, with the old greedy patterns in trade, and with routine in the Christian church. If he lives in Hitler's Germany, he is silent when he should speak. By his default, not by his outright crime, he is an encouragement to hold wickedness. He is a digit in a supine mass. To him can be traced much of the deadly lethargy of our world. He fails to see how much he is needed. He does not realize that while a man may not

have Shakespeare's gift, Shakespeare cannot become current coin without the printer and the bookbinder. The one-talent man is one note on the piano; but his failure can play havoc, as one sour or silent note can play havoc on a keyboard. The one-talent man can speak, vote, work, and pray. In reality he is many-talented, and the ongoing of the kingdom depends on him. Had he been true, in the story Jesus told, he also would have entered into the joy of his lord.

21. Good and Faithful Servant.—What gladness in the greeting! **Well done**—"Excellent!" God is that kind of God, not a policeman who almost hopes to catch men in wrongdoing. The world is that kind of world: it finally rewards the venture of faith. That fact cannot be overstressed, for the clear implication of the story is that life is like a fertile field to the man who courageously sows the seed. The new world awaits Columbus: he does not sail on an empty or deceitful sea, however long the voyage. Of what nature were these men who won their lord's approval? They were prompt. they "went at once" (vs. 16). They indulged no daydreams and entertained no fears, but set to work. They were **good**, a word that seems here to mean devoted. Christ was their central concern, whether he seemed near or distant. They were **faithful**: full of faith, persistent, and nobly venturous. They asked little respite. They believed labor to be good for them; they gave leisure no more than its strict place in life, lest it should become laziness and defeat.

[8] *Areopagitica.*
[9] *Shirley* (New York: E. P. Dutton & Co., 1940), ch. xxiii.

24 Then he which had received the one talent came and said, Lord, I knew thee that thou art a hard man, reaping where thou hast not sown, and gathering where thou hast not strewed:

25 And I was afraid, and went and hid thy talent in the earth: lo, *there* thou hast *that is* thine.

26 His lord answered and said unto him, *Thou* wicked and slothful servant, thou knewest that I reap where I sowed not, and gather where I have not strewed:

27 Thou oughtest therefore to have put my money to the exchangers, and *then* at my coming I should have received mine own with usury.

28 Take therefore the talent from him, and give *it* unto him which hath ten talents.

29 For unto every one that hath shall be given, and he shall have abundance: but

joy of your master.' 24 He also who had received the one talent came forward, saying, 'Master, I knew you to be a hard man, reaping where you did not sow, and gathering where you did not winnow; 25 so I was afraid, and I went and hid your talent in the ground. Here you have what is yours.' 26 But his master answered him, 'You wicked and slothful servant! You knew that I reap where I have not sowed, and gather where I have not winnowed? 27 Then you ought to have invested my money with the bankers, and at my coming I should have received what was my own with interest. 28 So take the talent from him, and give it to him who has the ten talents. 29 For to every one who has will

24. Jesus does not mean to suggest that God is like the **hard man** any more than he is like the unjust judge of Luke 18:1-8; nevertheless, one who is entrusted with talents cannot presume on his good nature.

25. The slave supposes that if he returns the deposit intact he has at least done his duty. This is the point of those touching rabbinical parables which refer to the death of a beloved son as a rendering back to God of that which has been entrusted; cf. B. T. D. Smith, *Parables of the Synoptic Gospels*, pp. 160-69; Montefiore and Loewe, *Rabbinic Anthology*, p. 552.

26-27. Ancient rates of **interest** were high. If the master could not make 100 per cent profit (as in the other cases), he could at least gain a substantial sum for having the money lent out.

28. The severity of this judgment disturbed the ancients, as it does modern readers. It is therefore not surprising that the Gospel According to the Hebrews contained a "moralized" form of the parable, in which one slave made money with what was entrusted to him, a second hid his talent, and the other spent it with harlots and flute girls. The first was accepted, the second rebuked, and the third punished (James, *Apocryphal N.T.*, p. 3).

29. But Jesus' point is that talents are given to be used. Not to employ an opportunity means to lose it (cf. Luke 12:48b and Aboth 1:13, "He who does not increase decreases").

What was their reward? Three jewels of joy set in their lord's joy. They received the jewel of joy in one another, for we should assume that there was comradeship between the five-talent man and the two-talent man—like the comradeship between Livingstone and the little Negro servant Chuma, who accompanied his master's body back to England.[1] They received the jewel of increased gifts: "To him that hath shall be given." They received also the jewel of increased responsibility, for they did not covet idleness: Kipling's "L'Envoi" is a fine expression of their enhanced powers and new exhila-

rating tasks. All these jewels were set in the joy of their lord. The glad greeting, **Well done!** from the lips of Christ is earth's only true guerdon. Any man may gain it, for every man is talented. If he ventures, Christ is for ally, and for the reward of joy.

29. *The Kingdom Law of Increase.*—For to every one who has will more be given. That dictum seems harsh. We wonder why the richer should always become richer. But from him who has not, even what he has will be taken away. That seems even harsher. We wonder why the poor should sink into worse poverty. But we must not make these words the whim of a tyrant. They are to be understood in the

[1] James I. Macnair, *Livingstone the Liberator* (London & Glasgow: Collins Clear-Type Press, 1940), p. 360.

from him that hath not shall be taken away even that which he hath.

30 And cast ye the unprofitable servant into outer darkness: there shall be weeping and gnashing of teeth.

31 ¶ When the Son of man shall come in his glory, and all the holy angels with him, then shall he sit upon the throne of his glory:

more be given, and he will have abundance; but from him who has not, even what he has will be taken away. 30 And cast the worthless servant into the outer darkness; there men will weep and gnash their teeth.'

31 "When the Son of man comes in his glory, and all the angels with him, then

---

Jesus may, indeed, intend for his hearers to draw a more specific moral. The Jews—or perhaps their religious teachers—have been entrusted with the Law and the Prophets and innumerable gifts of God's grace. If they can do no more than guard the "deposit of the faith," they will surely lose their special privileges (cf. 21:43; Luke 13:6-9) .

30. At least part of this conclusion is added by Matthew (cf. on 8:12) .

D. A Parable on the Basis of the Last Judgment (25:31-46)

No other piece of Jesus' recorded teaching expresses so eloquently and beautifully the ethical spirit of the O.T. and Judaism. At this point he and the finest of his contemporaries were in perfect accord. The parable may well have been preserved by those Jewish Christians who compiled the M source, for it expressed the heart of religion as they understood it. With it we may compare such passages as Jas. 1:27; 2:14-16; Luke 10:30-37, and the saying from the Nazarene gospel quoted in the note on 19:16-22.

It would be superficial to say that for Jesus religion means this kind of outgoing love and nothing else. The righteousness of the kingdom of God is many-sided and it is based on a particular relation of trust, receptiveness, and fidelity toward God. But this love is the end product or fruit of genuine religion; and by this fruit one's true relation to God is known (7:20-21) . The most striking note of the parable is that on Judgment Day some men will discover that, although they have not known it, they have been on God's side all the time (vss. 37-39) . One of the characteristics of the true saint is that he forgets himself in service of God and man.

31. This is the glorified **Son of man,** who comes as judge at the close of the age. Jesus is not represented here as identifying himself with that figure (cf. on 16:21) . Since

---

setting of the story. To the five-talent man and the two-talent man more was given. As for the one-talent man, his talent was taken from him. The parable, in its account of faithfulness and unfaithfulness, is our medium of interpretation. "Money makes money" if money is ventured: it is sure that money not ventured will make nothing, but at last crumble into dust. An arm or an eye used will gain strength, at least as long as years climb to their zenith; but an arm not used will atrophy, and an eye always protected from hazard will become blind. The central thrust of the story is a plea that we live in courageous faith. Friendship ventured will not fail, even though it may find a cross; while a friendship withheld in fear or suspicion will turn to hate. But this law of increase must not be lifted from its setting to justify a man who chooses money instead of friendship, for such a man is never justified. There is a proverb which says, "The dice of God are always loaded." It means, when applied to this verse, that the promptness and **devotion and faith that marked two of the**

men in the story do not ultimately fail, for they are guarded by the faithfulness of a holy and loving God. Such is the wonder of this kingdom law. If we fail to sow the Christian seed, we shall lose it, like any other seed that is merely kept in a bin. But if we trust it to the hazard of the weather and the wide fields of the world, it may "lose its life" but it will find its harvest. Then it will provide both multiplied seed and bread for the hunger of mankind. This law is not an arbitrariness: it is a promise of rich grace from the eternal God.

31-46. *The Parable of the Judgment.*— (See also vss. 34, 38, 40, 44, 45.) This is haggada as much as parable, and has elements of magnificent Hebrew poetry. There is no finer writing in the Gospel, and no finer truth. The writer's skillful hand is involved, but without doubt the central teaching and phrasing go back to remembered words of Jesus. Here Jesus is not only **King,** but **Son of God** in his glory. The angelic hosts in all their powers are his retinue and friends. **All the nations are gath-**

32 And before him shall be gathered all nations: and he shall separate them one from another, as a shepherd divideth *his* sheep from the goats:

33 And he shall set the sheep on his right hand, but the goats on the left.

he will sit on his glorious throne. **32** Before him will be gathered all the nations, and he will separate them one from another as a shepherd separates the sheep from the goats, **33** and he will place the sheep at his right hand, but the goats at

---

Son of man occurs in this parable only in this one verse, and "King" is used elsewhere (vss. 34, 40), it is likely that the original parable referred to the King Messiah. Jesus could easily have spoken of the future Messiah—especially in a parable—without affirming or denying any particular messianic doctrine.

32. The **sheep** of Palestine are usually white and the **goats** black, and **a shepherd** could easily **separate them.**

33. The **right hand** is, as usual, the side of honor and blessing.

---

ered before his judgment throne. Some scholars [2] have argued that **all the nations** means the Gentiles, who, because they do not yet know Christ, are judged, not by his proclaimed truth, but by "common humanity." Others, such as Dummelow,[3] hold that the people under judgment are the Jews, because the parable assumes that those before the throne do know Jesus, even though they do not recognize his identity with the poor and oppressed. It is perhaps well to accept both opinions, and to take **all the nations** at its face value. To Matthew, Jesus was King of the whole world.

The test was unerring. **The sheep** were gathered to the **right hand** of approval and honor, the **goats** to the **left** hand of condemnation. Syrian sheep were white; Syrian goats were black. They could be told apart even in the dusk. In the Judgment Day there was no shadow of doubt. Not so in *The Revolution in Tanner's Lane.* There Zachariah Coleman says, "I never, hardly, see a pure breed, either of goat or sheep." [4] And we all incline to agree with that verdict. We have a jingle:

There is so much good in the worst of us,
And so much bad in the best of us,
That it hardly becomes any of us
To talk about the rest of us.[5]

But we are not asked to judge, for judgment is not our human right. Christ is judge, and he sees unerringly the main set of the soul. No man can face in two directions: Jesus knows our dominant motive.

The criterion of judgment is a daybreak and an astonishment. From the sea of faces each man is singled out in turn. He is asked, not about his creed or his worship or his standing

in the community, but "What have you done for that Negro family on the other side of town? Ever make any visits to the local jail?" The hungry, the thirsty, the homeless, the naked, the physically afflicted, and the prisoner are here made the test. What we have done for them, or failed to do, is judgment on us for weal or woe. Notice well that list. Such people require of us sympathy, both in the imagination and in the deed. They demand real self-denial, for none of the unfortunates mentioned can quickly make any recompense. They ask obedience to God's quickening within us, for "love is of God" (I John 4:7).

As we ponder this criterion the questions throng. Is the whole of the Christian life mere charity, the giving of a dollar to a beggar? No, but such charity, springing from the love made known in Christ, is an essential act without which faith languishes and dies. Is individual charity enough? No, we must lay hands on iniquitous systems, so that they may no longer maim our fellow men; but this wider sense of justice is of small account without instant and personal kindness. Then is prayer of no concern? Prayer is an inescapable factor, for only by prayer can the grace of love in us be truly fed. Is integrity of conduct no prime consequence? It is indispensable, for "charity" from an impure heart is a miasma and a mockery. Then does it matter nothing what a man believes? It matters everything; for love springs from faith—the faith that men are worth loving, and the faith that God loves and bids us love. Besides, Christ is on the throne. Judgment and love are both clearly understood only in him.

So the questions can be answered. But the test remains. William Hale White (Mark Rutherford), in *Miriam's Schooling,* tells of Mrs. Joll, who was unkempt, quarrelsome, not delicate either in speech or in manners, but who instantly came to the help of a stranger in his illness. The novelist says that she had

[2] See *Expositor's Greek Testament,* p. 305.
[3] *Commentary on the Holy Bible,* p. 707.
[4] William Hale White (Mark Rutherford), ed. Reuben Shapcott (New York: Dodd, Mead & Co., 1899), p. 330.
[5] Author unknown.

34 Then shall the King say unto them on his right hand, Come, ye blessed of my Father, inherit the kingdom prepared for you from the foundation of the world:

35 For I was ahungered, and ye gave me meat: I was thirsty, and ye gave me drink: I was a stranger, and ye took me in:

36 Naked, and ye clothed me: I was sick, and ye visited me: I was in prison, and ye came unto me.

37 Then shall the righteous answer him, saying, Lord, when saw we thee ahungered, and fed *thee?* or thirsty, and gave *thee* drink?

the left. 34 Then the King will say to those at his right hand, 'Come, O blessed of my Father, inherit the kingdom prepared for you from the foundation of the world; 35 for I was hungry and you gave me food, I was thirsty and you gave me drink, I was a stranger and you welcomed me, 36 I was naked and you clothed me, I was sick and you visited me, I was in prison and you came to me.' 37 Then the righteous will answer him, 'Lord, when did we see thee hungry and feed thee, or thirsty and give

---

34. My Father is a mark of Matthew's style. Reward in the age to come is described more than once as an inheritance (5:5; 19:29; cf. Gal. 4:1-7, 21-31). To **inherit the kingdom** means to be recognized as a true child of God. It is standard Jewish doctrine that the kingdom is **prepared . . . from the foundation of the world.** Matthew may believe that some are predestined for it (cf. 20:23); but this is not certain.

35-36. Note how concrete and physical the ministrations are. A similar concreteness is found, for example, in Job 31:13-32.

37-38. The surprise of **the righteous** is perhaps the most poignant touch of the whole parable.

"the one thing needful"; and he adds incisively, "the one thing which, if ever there is to be a Judgment Day, will put her on the right hand; when all sorts of scientific people, religious people, students of poetry, people with exquisite emotions, will go to the left and be damned everlastingly." [6] The comment is true to the central light of this story. That "damned everlastingly" is perhaps too dogmatic, for vs. 46 is conventional in language, and may have been added by the Gospelist (see Exeg.). In any event the words do not necessarily imply a finality. Κόλασιν may have the meaning of remedial, although severe, pruning rather than of arbitrary and vindictive torment (the God and Father of Jesus is neither arbitrary nor vindictive); and αἰώνιον means agelong in the sense of spirit and quality rather than of unending duration. But the shadows, however we might try to soften them, are still deep. We must not make a theology from details of a parable, but by the same token we must be honest with the darkness of the punishment. **Depart** is a terrible word; **come** has all heaven's light and love.

34. *From the Foundation of the World.*— Perhaps these words come from Matthew's belief in some fixed and fiat election of souls. But it seems likelier that they come directly from Jesus. We have noted (in 20:23) his phrase, "for whom it has been prepared by my

Father." John 17:24 and Eph. 1:4 offer an interesting commentary. Nothing in God's universe is by sudden whim; nothing is by cold tyranny. The throbbing heart of the creation is the love of God for his world—the love made known in Jesus Christ. His yearning is that his children shall live in that same love. What picture do you have of God? Is he policeman, judge, first cause, "the Power not ourselves that makes for righteousness"? [7] Jesus gave us another picture: **my Father.** The love of God for man that through man feeds the hungry and visits the prisoner is—the foundation of the world. The world may not always wear that appearance. If it did, love might be tempted to become only a shrewd wisdom looking for reward. But whatever the appearance of the world, hatred must fail; for hatred is not built on the only lasting foundation. Love, contrariwise, will always stand; for "other foundation can no man lay than that is laid, which is Jesus Christ" (I Cor. 3:11). Men can burn much that is on our planet, but they cannot burn God's eternal order. Wickedness can destroy man's body and bring his soul to judgment, but it cannot destroy the divine purpose. The life of love endures **from the foundation of the world** (cf. I Cor. 13:13).

So we need not despair. Selfish politics and trade cannot shake the pillars of the universe.

[6] Ed. Reuben Shapcott (London: T. F. Unwin, 1893), p. 107.

[7] Matthew Arnold. Quoted, Edgar Sheffield Brightman, *The Problem of God* (New York: Abingdon Press, 1930), p. 90.

38 When saw we thee a stranger, and took *thee* in? or naked, and clothed *thee?*

39 Or when saw we thee sick, or in prison, and came unto thee?

40 And the King shall answer and say unto them, Verily I say unto you, Inasmuch as ye have done *it* unto one of the least of these my brethren, ye have done *it* unto me.

41 Then shall he say also unto them on the left hand, Depart from me, ye cursed, into everlasting fire, prepared for the devil and his angels:

thee drink? 38 And when did we see thee a stranger and welcome thee, or naked and clothe thee? 39 And when did we see thee sick or in prison and visit thee?' 40 And the King will answer them, 'Truly, I say to you, as you did it to one of the least of these my brethren, you did it to me.' 41 Then he will say to those at his left hand, 'Depart from me, you cursed, into the eternal fire prepared for the devil and

---

40. The Messiah identifies himself completely with the interests and needs of **the least of these my brethren.** Jesus teaches that the one who holds in his hands the fate of all men, living and dead, cares just this much about the hungry, the sick, the naked, the strangers, and the prisoners. Whether or not he intends to speak of himself at this point, the saying discloses his own interests and his character as do few passages in the Gospels. Such is the Messiah whom Christians acknowledge.

41. **Eternal fire is prepared for the devil and his angels** as in Rev. 20:10, 15; Enoch 10:13; cf. Jude 6-7.

They never move its foundation. Lincoln told how men feared, on a night that was filled with "falling stars," that the end of the world had come. But, he said, the grand old constellations, fixed in their places, still stood back of the meteors.[8] If we build in love, we can build in hope; for we then build on what God has built from eternity. Perhaps "love" etymologically comes from "leave"—by leave of. We would like to think that it is the past tense of "live." But whatever the etymology, a man who has loved has lived—enduringly in God.

38, 44. *The Surprises of the Judgment.*—If vs. 38 is "the most poignant touch" in the whole story (see Exeg.), by the same token vs. 44 gives deepest dismay. The loving folk were so lowly that it did not occur to them that their daily kindnesses could ever have been a personal service to the King, or that they had done anything worthy of reward. The unloving were so callous, their religion so perfunctory, that they never thought of Jesus as being linked with men in love, or as asking from anyone any forthright deed of compassion. The unloving were not ignorant concerning Jesus. Apparently they knew him to whom they spoke. But they had been so long unloving that their faith was now not a faith, but only a ritual observance and a correct creed. They had separated Jesus from the doings of daily life. At length they had come to believe that he had no concern with their failure in compassion, but was indeed the remote patron of their lovelessness. No word could more sharply underscore the callousness

that afflicts the loveless man, and his resultant blindness, than the question addressed to Jesus, **When did we see thee hungry?**

But the true saint forgets himself in love. So it does not occur to him that there is any splendor in him. When Elizabeth Fry[9] reached heaven she was doubtless surprised to see the mighty, acclaimed among men, waved aside, and doubly surprised when Jesus said to her, "Come, . . . blessed of my Father" (25:34). Doubtless she replied, "I often visited the prisoners in Newgate, but when did I see You there?" For even the saint, despite his insight, does not realize the closeness of that mysterious bond by which everyone, especially the needy, is bound to Christ. Even the saint finds it hard to believe that love, seen in Jesus, is the central test of life in earth and heaven. There was a man who was a saint. He pressed clothes for a living, and would not charge more than his bare necessity for the work. He went each Sunday to visit at the local jail. He did not "preach" to the prisoners; neither did he condone. He used to say, "They must be lonely." Often he would speak admiringly of leaders in the community, and of "how much good they are able to do." It is sure that he was surprised at Christ's "Come," and that he answered, "Lord, when did I see thee a stranger?" In very truth "the most poignant touch of the whole parable."

40, 45. *The Oneness of Christ with Men.*—Inasmuch: the word is now proverbial, and a good leaven in our common life. Christ is **King,** and the fate of all men is in his hands. But, like

[8] Cited, *The Complete Prose Works of Walt Whitman* (New York: G. P. Putnam's Sons, 1902), II, 296-97.

[9] *Memoir of the Life of Elizabeth Fry,* ed. by two of her daughters (London: Charles Gilpin, 1847).

42 For I was ahungered, and ye gave me no meat: I was thirsty, and ye gave me no drink:

43 I was a stranger, and ye took me not in: naked, and ye clothed me not: sick, and in prison, and ye visited me not.

44 Then shall they also answer him, saying, Lord, when saw we thee ahungered, or athirst, or a stranger, or naked, or sick, or in prison, and did not minister unto thee?

45 Then shall he answer them, saying, Verily I say unto you, Inasmuch as ye did *it* not to one of the least of these, ye did *it* not to me.

46 And these shall go away into everlasting punishment: but the righteous into life eternal.

26 And it came to pass, when Jesus had finished all these sayings, he said unto his disciples,

his angels; 42 for I was hungry and you gave me no food, I was thirsty and you gave me no drink, 43 I was a stranger and you did not welcome me, naked and you did not clothe me, sick and in prison and you did not visit me.' 44 Then they also will answer, 'Lord, when did we see thee hungry or thirsty or a stranger or naked or sick or in prison, and did not minister to thee?' 45 Then he will answer them, 'Truly, I say to you, as you did it not to one of the least of these, you did it not to me.' 46 And they will go away into eternal punishment, but the righteous into eternal life."

26 When Jesus had finished all these sayings, he said to his disciples,

---

46. Here and in vs. 41 the picture of Gehenna is entirely conventional. This verse may be added by the evangelist.

E. SUMMARY AND PROPHECY OF ARREST (26:1-2)

26:1. The wording is like that of other summary colophons, e.g., 7:28; 11:1. These verses mark the end of Matthew's "fifth book."

---

some fabled king, he walks in beggar's disguise through the streets of his kingdom. Here is the N.T. fulfillment of Isa. 53:4: "Surely he hath borne our griefs," and of Isa. 63:9: "In all their affliction he was afflicted." Saul, as he journeyed to Damascus to persecute the Christian church, heard Christ say, "Why persecutest thou me?" (Acts 22:7). Christ is lowly: he goes incognito in the poor and the imprisoned. He is happiest to dwell with these least. The intensity of this oneness of Christ with mankind no words can tell. Parent and child are so closely bound that the misfortune of one becomes the equal misfortune of the other, but the bond between Christ and men is closer than any human tie. He is the Son of man in more intimate meaning than that title at first hinted. There is between him and mankind a bond of the eternal Spirit. Our gladness or woe not only affects him: it is in him more poignantly than in us. He is troubled by our sorrow, not merely as a seismograph is shaken from a distance, but in very heart; for the bond between him and men is not mere nearness, but love's identity.

In such love our human lines of cleavage disappear. The question is not centrally one of formal belief or wealth or race or class. Rather is it, "What is his need as a brother man indwelt by Christ?" Alice Meynell's poem, with

its prayer, "O Christ in this man's life," [1] has caught the truth: the stranger in her pew, as she took the Sacrament, was also paten and cup—the shrine of the Real Presence. **Inasmuch** is almost the burning heart of the parable. If that word had not been spoken, the kindness described might still have been a mockery—antic of ingenious dust toward the fictitious need of ingenious dust. For if that word had not been spoken, the kindness might still have moved in low motive—the saving of ourselves from the down-pull of the disinherited, or some clutching at social boons. Nay, if that word had not been spoken, the kindness might have been vitiated by human pride—each man of us assuming that he himself is not poor, but can stoop condescendingly to the needy. But the word is forever spoken. Christ has come to us in our prison. Therefore we live in love, because of grateful love for him; and we are able to love all men, even the unlovely, because he loves them and us in the intense love of a very indwelling.

26:1-5. The Shadow of the Cross.—We have noticed the threefold prediction of the death of Jesus: 16:21; 17:12; 20:17-19. These verses now before us are not a fourth prediction; they are the beginning of the dramatic account of how

[1] "The Unknown God."

2 Ye know that after two days is *the feast of* the passover, and the Son of man is betrayed to be crucified.	**2** "You know that after two days the Passover is coming, and the Son of man will be delivered up to be crucified."
3 Then assembled together the chief priests, and the scribes, and the elders of the people, unto the palace of the high priest, who was called Caiaphas,	**3** Then the chief priests and the elders of the people gathered in the palace of the high priest, who was called Ca′ia-phas,

2. The Passover was eaten on the fifteenth of the Jewish month Nisan (March-April), i.e., at any time after sundown on the fourteenth. According to all the Gospels, Jesus was crucified on a Friday. **After two days** indicates that the following events were thought to have occurred on Wednesday, Nisan 13; cf. on vs. 17.

XI. Resumption of the Narrative: Jesus' Death and the Events
Leading up to It (26:3–27:66)

Most of the stories and sayings of the gospel tradition at one time circulated separately as small independent units and only later were brought into a chronological framework. Such, at least, is the prevailing opinion. But with the story of Jesus' passion it was different. No other element of the tradition evoked more wonder and interest. The story must ordinarily have been told at some length, and it constituted a missionary sermon or proclamation in itself. Paul speaks of "the word of the cross" as "the power of God" (I Cor. 1:18). In all likelihood the passion narrative was the first part of the gospel to be stereotyped into a fixed form, and its original elements therefore constitute the historical bedrock of the gospel. But since it was the kind of story that stirred the imagination and aroused reflection, additions were inevitably made. Part of these were no doubt actual reminiscences of events, while others arose out of religious imagination or out of the conviction that Christ's death fulfilled the prophecies of the O.T.

Mark's Gospel is the oldest witness to the passion story. Luke may indeed have had independent narratives which he wove in; cf. A. M. Perry, *The Sources of Luke's Passion-Narrative* (Chicago: University of Chicago Press, 1920); Grant, *Growth of the Gospels,* pp. 170-71. But Matthew had no passion narrative except that which he drew from Mark, and his additions come either from bits of floating tradition (26:52*b*; 27:3-10, 19, 24-25, 51*b*-53, 62-66) or are due to his reflection on the O.T. (26:54; 27:34, 43).

Form critics have sought to go back of Mark's passion story and recover its original form, and also to distinguish additions made to it before it came into Mark's hand. See, e.g., Frederick C. Grant, *Earliest Gospel,* pp. 175-83. According to this proposed reconstruction, Matthew contains the following passages from the original narrative: 26:2*a*, 3*a*, 14-16, 20, 26-28*a*, 29, 30-35, 47*a*, 48-51, 55, 56*b*, 57*a*; 27:1-2, 12-18, 20-23, 26, 31*b*-33, 35*a*, 37-39*a*, 44-51*a*, 54*a, c*. The following are passages added to the story before Mark received it: Matt. 26:17*a*, 21-23, 28*b*, 47*b*, 56*a*, 58, 69-75; 27:11*b*, 34. Other parts of Mark's account were added by that evangelist from various sources.

A. Preliminary Events (26:3–27:26)
1. The Plot (26:3-5)

3. Mark's "chief priests and the scribes" is vague and may refer only to a few persons. Matthew thinks of a meeting of the whole Sanhedrin (2:4; 16:21), or at least of a number of its members. **Caiaphas** was **high priest** from *ca.* A.D. 18 to 36.

---

the three predictions were fulfilled. The crucifixion story is probably the original nucleus of the Gospels. It early took vivid form, for use with catechumens and in the observance of the Eucharist. The most wonderful story ever told! The space given to it may seem to the casual reader to be disproportionately large, but the eye of devotion will understand: Calvary is God's redeeming act of grace. **The chief priests and the elders** and **Caiaphas** give us the clue to the real enemies of Jesus. They gathered in the courtyard of the high priest. They were the

4 And consulted that they might take Jesus by subtilty, and kill *him*.

5 But they said, Not on the feast *day*, lest there be an uproar among the people.

6 ¶ Now when Jesus was in Bethany, in the house of Simon the leper,

4 and took counsel together in order to arrest Jesus by stealth and kill him. 5 But they said, "Not during the feast, lest there be a tumult among the people."

6 Now when Jesus was at Bethany in

4-5. Jesus' popularity with the people (21:8-9, 26) accounts for the precautions. The word rendered **tumult** (θόρυβος) is used by Josephus to denote the bloody insurrections that occurred in Palestine in the first century (*Jewish War* II. 12. 1-2). The leaders do not wish **to arrest Jesus . . . and kill him . . . during the feast** of Unleavened Bread (which begins with the Passover). This is an argument in favor of the tradition in John 19:14, according to which Jesus was not only arrested but also executed before Passover. See on vs. 17.

2. Jesus' Anointing (26:6-13)

The gist of this story is that an unknown woman anointed Jesus as Messiah (cf. Bacon, *Story of Jesus*, pp. 239-41). Like the spreading out of garments at the entry into Jerusalem (21:8) and the other acclamations (16:16; 20:30-31), it indicates that many of the common people wished Jesus to take over political control of the nation. The woman may even have hoped to force Jesus' hand. The anointing was in private, as in the case of Saul (I Sam. 10:1), Solomon (I Kings 1:38-39), and Jehu (II Kings 9:4-10); and this suggests the hope of a revolt or *coup d'état*. Jesus, however, does not accept the acclamation and says, somewhat wryly, that it is an anointing for burial, not kingship. The evangelists did not understand the story. Mark, or the tradition behind him, expanded it by praising the woman for her great love and devotion. In Luke 7:36-50 the woman becomes a great sinner who is thankful for the forgiveness of her sins, and in John 12:1-8 she is identified with Mary, the sister of Martha and Lazarus.

6. The incident could have occurred elsewhere, but it comes appropriately after the Triumphal Entry; and **Bethany,** where Jesus spent his nights outside the city (21:17), is a natural location. **Simon** perhaps had been healed of leprosy. If Jesus had entered the house of an uncleansed **leper,** many people would have avoided contact with him.

Sadducees and temple leaders. Jesus was apparently popular with the people. Though they were blind to the deeper meanings of his life, they still regarded him as a "prophet." So the temple leaders were loath to oppose Jesus in public: the crowd might revolt under him as national prophet, and the futile insurrection might cause rivers of blood from Roman swords. The **elders** had no love for Rome, but they had even less wish to risk their own lofty station. They resented the rebuke implied in Jesus' cleansing of the temple. They feared the loss of their emoluments and rank. They were a vested interest filled with pride. That in part was what crucified Jesus. It is an old story—and as modern as today. We should notice the careful way in which Matthew connects the death of Jesus with the date of the Passover. Calvary was another passover: the angel of God again visited his people. There was another blood sprinkled on the doorposts of our earth. There was another paschal Lamb, another Life given for the remission of sins. "Christ our passover is sacrificed for us" (I Cor. 5:7). Thus there is

a great faith and a great gratitude behind the careful indication of dates in vs. 2.

6-13. *The Anointing of Jesus.*— (See Expos., vss. 8 and 12.) **A woman:** who was she? We do not know her name. Luke tells us that she was a sinner. John says that she was Mary of Bethany, the sister of Martha and Lazarus. Mark's account, obviously the earliest, unless Luke has reported another and similar occasion, gives no name. There are items in the story which throw doubt on John's surmise. We cannot identify her. Why did she anoint Jesus? If only we knew! Kings were anointed at their coronation, and it is not unlikely that she anointed Jesus, in a zeal that had more abandon than insight, as King of the Jews. If that was her intention, the Gospelists have misunderstood the incident. On their own admission they often misunderstood. Thus Luke—unless he reports a different incident—has explained the act as that of a forgiven sinner; while John, attributing the anointing to Mary of Bethany, has interpreted it as a deed of penetrating love. We do not know. But if the gift was the over-

7 There came unto him a woman having an alabaster box of very precious ointment, and poured it on his head, as he sat at meat.

8 But when his disciples saw *it*, they had indignation, saying, To what purpose *is* this waste?

9 For this ointment might have been sold for much, and given to the poor.

10 When Jesus understood *it*, he said unto them, Why trouble ye the woman? for she hath wrought a good work upon me.

11 For ye have the poor always with you; but me ye have not always.

the house of Simon the leper, **7** a woman came up to him with an alabaster jar of very expensive ointment, and she poured it on his head, as he sat at table. **8** But when the disciples saw it, they were indignant, saying, "Why this waste? **9** For this ointment might have been sold for a large sum, and given to the poor." **10** But Jesus, aware of this, said to them, "Why do you trouble the woman? For she has done a beautiful thing to me. **11** For you always have the poor with you, but you will

---

7. Presumably Jesus and the others are sitting cross-legged on the floor eating out of a common bowl, so that it is easy for the woman to pour the **ointment . . . on his head.** Contrast Luke 7:38, where they recline at table, and his feet are nearest to the woman; cf. C. C. McCown, "Luke's Translation of Semitic into Hellenistic Custom," *Journal of Biblical Literature,* LVIII (1939), 217-20.

9-11. Mark gives the value as more than three hundred denarii, a year's wages. Such an amount of unguent might have lasted many years. But if the disciples understood the messianic character of the act, even the waste of wealth would not surprise them. These verses belong to a later stage of the tradition. Jesus is usually much more interested in **the poor** than in this kind of devotion, however sincere and touching it may be. The remark is "out of character," though it seemed appropriate to the evangelists as they looked back on the events.

---

enthusiastic act of someone trying to force Jesus' hand and to make him a nationalistic Messiah, his answer is all the more poignant both in its gentleness toward her and in its own pathos. He knew that his coronation would be—the Cross. But he accepted the deed as if it came from a higher motive: **For she has done a beautiful thing.**

Why this waste? is a question demanding separate exposition, for it raises a thousand other questions (see on vs. 8). **For you always have the poor with you** may be Jesus' own word, or, as form criticism perhaps leads us to believe, it may be a commentary on the incident by the early Christian community. But in any event it cannot be twisted into a justification for selfishness. It is hard to be patient with the comfortable folk who say, "Christ told us that poverty is a fixed and presumably necessary institution in human affairs." Christ told us no such thing, and there are few blasphemies worse than that which makes him the apostle of selfish indifference. Maxim Gorky is much nearer truth: "A beggar . . . is Christ's brother, he is the bell of the Lord, and rings in life for the purpose of awakening our conscience." [2] We must strive always to banish unmerited poverty: God has given our race enough and to spare, if we work and have compassion. But there are

times when feeding the poor must give place to other acts, or the poor, because of spreading greed, will not be fed.

But you will not always have me. There are crises when the cause of Christ is threatened by eclipse. Then a sign must be lifted for him, despite any plenty or any hunger. If he should be forgotten among men, plenty would become a worse hunger. The anointing was just such a symbol—a dramatic sign to anoint him for burial, and thus for a higher coronation. There are moments when Christianity cannot take a routine course: the vase of life must then be broken in an abandon of love. Thus the missionary and the martyr give their lives. The shattered alabaster spreads its fragrance, and changes the climate of our world. This woman helped Christ, perhaps in deeper ways than she intended; and she helped the poor, and she preached the gospel.

8. *Why This Waste?*—How the questions throng! The reproof spoken by Judas and the other disciples was not in pure motive. Such purity belongs to no human judgment. The disciples may have resented the intrusion of a woman. They may have been brought up among "the people of the land," and thus may have despised the rich folks' cult of perfumes. But their question, from whatever the mixture of motive, has force. The vase and its contents were worth more than a man's wage for a

[2] *Foma Gordeev,* tr. Isabel F. Hapgood (New York: Charles Scribner's Sons, 1901), p. 149.

12 For in that she hath poured this ointment on my body, she did *it* for my burial.

13 Verily I say unto you, Wheresoever this gospel shall be preached in the whole world, *there* shall also this, that this woman hath done, be told for a memorial of her.

not always have me. **12** In pouring **this** ointment on my body she has done it to prepare me for burial. **13** Truly, I say to you, wherever this gospel is preached in the whole world, what she has done will be told in memory of her."

12. Jesus perhaps means that "to be anointed king over Israel in these days is almost certain death."

13. Gospel (εὐαγγέλιον) is used by Mark eight times. Luke and John never employ it. Matthew uses it in three other passages, all of them editorial. This verse is almost certainly Mark's comment on the incident.

whole year. The gift could have canceled someone's pitiable poverty. There is the problem! But there is an answer. The poor arc more than mouths to be fed. The poor have needs which money cannot meet. Thus the censure brought by the disciples was an oblique insult to the poor. God made harvest fields beautiful in waving grain, as well as bountiful; and he has transfigured the dust of the ground on which we walk and the air our lungs must breathe into the rapture of sunrise and sunset. Why has God sprinkled fields with flowers and the sky with stars? The utilitarians cannot explain our world, and they cannot meet the deepest hunger of man's heart.

"She has done a beautiful thing" (vs. 10). "A thing of beauty is a joy forever."[3] It is food for the poor, because the poor hunger for more than bread. The woman's deed was not only beautiful: it was symbolic—of Christ's death. We need symbols: they vivify the unseen mercy of God, and they unite mankind; for though men may quarrel over the phrasing of a creed, they cannot quarrel over the bond of a symbol. The woman's deed was not only symbolic: it was sacramental, the outward and visible sign of an inward and invisible truth. Our dust is worse than dust unless we see in dust the sacrament of a spirit. When Christ dies on a cross let no man ask, **Why this waste?** Then when shall we feed the poor with bread, and when with the bread of the soul? There is no rule of thumb, for the good reason that every thumb has a different thumbprint. Times and seasons give us the clue: a man does not discuss art in a home where children are starving, but neither will he be long content that children should live in ugly houses on ugly streets. Stirrings of the soul give us the clue: some temptations a man must repudiate, even though he may starve. Talents also point the road: Beethoven must not forsake his music, except in direst emergencies, to run a soup kitchen. Crises also bring their message: when Christ is about to be

crucified, or when God in some luminous moment has called us to "Madness and Exultation,"[4] we should forget baker's bread that God through us may bring the bread of life. Our too-scientific age has much to learn. If Judas asked this question, we should notice that John's Gospel reports Jesus as saying of Judas, "None of them is lost but the son of"—waste (John 17:12). There are squanderings far worse than the waste of cash.

12. For My Burial.—Whatever the origin of the word (see Exeg. and Branscomb's comment on the parallel passage in Mark[5]), its truth and pathos remain. The woman may have intended to anoint him as nationalistic Messiah. He knew that his kind of messiahship could bring only death. This was not anointing for coronation: it was anointing for a burial. Yet there are people who argue that Christ is sentimental rather than a realist! Carlyle had truth: Christ is "a fact—the most indubitable of facts."[6] Always he lived in sight of facts and in sight of God. Maybe these words echo the remorse of the disciples. Jesus' body was perhaps not anointed (see Mark 16:1). They not only forsook him and fled, but failed him even in the last sad offices shown to the dead. It was a comfort to them later to see in the woman's act an anticipatory anointing. She had done to the living Jesus what they had failed to do even in his death. The strange workings of remorse!

The anointing *was* for a coronation. The crown was a crown of thorns, and the throne was a cross; but they were royal in very truth. He came to his kingdom because, in God's universe, the love of the just for the unjust is the kingly sign. God "gave his only begotten Son" (John 3:16) as seal that God is holy love. Thus the woman's deed was not lost. God being holy love, "There shall never be one lost

[3] Keats, "Endymion."

[4] *Redemption, An Anthology of the Cross*, ed. George Stewart (New York: George H. Doran & Co., 1927), quoting Franz von Liszt, p. xxiv.
[5] *Gospel of Mark*, pp. 244-46, on Mark 14:3-9.
[6] *Latter Day Pamphlets*, "Jesuitism."

14 ¶ Then one of the twelve, called Judas Iscariot, went unto the chief priests,

15 And said *unto them,* What will ye give me, and I will deliver him unto you? And they covenanted with him for thirty pieces of silver.

16 And from that time he sought opportunity to betray him.

14 Then one of the twelve, who was called Judas Iscariot, went to the chief priests 15 and said, "What will you give me if I deliver him to you?" And they paid him thirty pieces of silver. 16 And from that moment he sought an opportunity to betray him.

---

3. Judas Agrees to Betray Him (26:14-16)

14-16. Judas Iscariot (cf. on 10:4) was undoubtedly responsible for Jesus' arrest. What he betrayed to the authorities was probably the place where his master could be found (vss. 47-49). Why he did it is not so certain. Mark's tradition (Mark 14:11), which is very ancient, says that **the chief priests** agreed to give him money; but could this be a sufficient motive for an intimate disciple **to betray** Jesus? Was Judas disappointed because Jesus refused to be king of Israel and lead a revolt against the Romans? Did he think that in this way he could force Jesus to defend himself and assert his kingship? Or did he hope to protect him from assassination by putting him under arrest? No one can say. If Judas received money, it was probably because the authorities wished to bind the bargain by such means. Matthew adds that **they paid him** (literally "weighed him out") **thirty pieces of silver.** This touch comes from Zech. 11:12; cf. notes on 27:3-10.

---

good!" [7] Browning's Abt Vogler was right: every fugitive strain of music, and every deed of the soul's abandon—"The passion that left the ground to lose itself in the sky"—abide. "Enough that he heard it once: we shall hear it by-and-by." [8] "Wherever this gospel is preached" (vs. 13): the words have been fulfilled. Chrysostom has rightly said, "For lo! what He said is come to pass, and to whatever part of the earth thou mayest go, thou wilt see her celebrated. . . . The world shall know that which has been done in a house, and in secret." [9] Those who come into the light of Christ do not go again into darkness, like ships which come from the dark and move across a track of light only to be lost again in the dark; they are immortalized with his eternity. Truly there is not "one lost good."

14-16. *Judas.*—Matthew tells us that Jesus said of Judas a terrible thing: "It would have been better for that man if he had not been born" (vs. 24). Judas and Pilate stand together in the execration of mankind, and most people judge Judas the guiltier. "Like the base Júdean," writes Shakespeare, who "threw a pearl away richer than all his tribe." [1] Eleven disciples are called saints, but no one says "St. Judas." He sold Jesus for the price of a slave. We watch in a fascination of horror and pity, horror for the deed and pity for the man. Why did he betray? Matthew is apparently not in-terested in motives, but only in the fact that prophecy was fulfilled (27:9). Was Judas the only Judean in the group? If "Iscariot" means "from Kerioth," that theory may hold. He may have been gloomy and fiercely fanatical, and lonely in the group of Galileans. The motive of greed advanced by John's Gospel is not convincing. It does not accord with utter remorse and sudden self-loathing. It may have been an element—Judas may have hoped for lofty and lucrative position in the kingdom of an earthly messiah—but in itself it seems a poor clue. Then had Judas gone over to the Sadducean attitude? Had he resented the cleansing of the temple? Did he fear that Jesus, wittingly or unwittingly, would lead his nation to a futile and bloody insurrection? Perhaps that was the motive. Or to propose the opposite reason, was he disappointed that Jesus was not a nationalistic messiah? And did he betray him, not to kill him, but to force his hand to display his messianic might? To many scholars nowadays that seems the most tenable theory. But we cannot tell. The motive may have had as main ingredient a sudden fear of death when the temple powers turned against Jesus: Judas may have been intent to save his own skin. Novels multiply about Judas, assuming to know the man. But apparently the Gospels do not know, and we do not know.

One explanation, that of Luke, is true beyond a doubt: Satan entered into him (Luke 22:3). There are volcanic fires in human nature. They have their sudden and unpredictable eruptions, and then a fair countryside is blackened and laid waste. There was greed in

[7] Browning, "Abt Vogler."
[8] *Ibid.,* st. x.
[9] *Homilies of Saint John Chrysostom on the Gospel of St. Matthew,* Homily LXXX.
[1] *Othello,* Act V, scene 2, l. 347.

17 ¶ Now the first *day* of the *feast of* unleavened bread the disciples came to Jesus, saying unto him, Where wilt thou that we prepare for thee to eat the passover?

17 Now on the first day of Unleavened Bread the disciples came to Jesus, saying, "Where will you have us prepare for you to

---

4. THE LAST SUPPER (26:17-30)

17. The first day of Unleavened Bread ought strictly to mean the fifteenth of Nisan, which begins at sundown on the fourteenth. Jews would **prepare . . . to eat the passover** on the fourteenth. The meal began toward evening on that day and continued into the night, so that it was concluded on the fifteenth. Matthew, in accordance with ordinary Jewish usage, draws no sharp distinction between the two feasts, and so refers to events on the fourteenth.

This dating, which is also that of Mark 14:12 and Luke 22:7, conflicts with John 18:28; 19:14, 31. According to John, Jesus was crucified on the day of preparation, the fourteenth of Nisan, and the Last Supper was on the evening of the thirteenth-fourteenth. All evangelists, of course, agree that he suffered on a Friday. According to the Fourth Gospel, Jesus' crucifixion took place at the very time when the paschal lambs were being slain. Most scholars now hold that John's dating is correct, even though the fact that it fits so well with the theological idea that "Christ our passover was sacrificed for us" (I Cor. 5:7) is bound to raise a question. Some of the arguments against the Synoptic dating are as follows: (*a*) the authorities did not wish trouble during the feast (26:5); (*b*) it is strange—though not quite impossible—that members of the Sanhedrin and Jesus and his followers should engage in so much activity on this holy night; (*c*) the Talmud contains a tradition that Jesus suffered on the eve of Passover; (*d*) most of the special features of the Passover are not mentioned in the Synoptic account. If the Last Supper was not a Passover, the most probable theory is that it was a solemn banquet of the kind celebrated by a *ḥabhûrāh* or religious brotherhood; see F. L. Cirlot, *The Early Eucharist* (London: Society for Promoting Christian Knowledge, 1939), pp. 1-16. It has also been explained as a special kiddush meal; but there is not sufficient evidence to prove that Jews held such a meal on the night before Passover. Several scholars have attempted to reconcile the evidence of Mark (and Matthew) with that of John by assuming that the Pharisees and Sadducees celebrated the Passover on different days or differed as to the reckoning of the calendar; the arguments are given by August Arnold (*Der Ursprung des christlichen Abendmahls* [Freiburg im Breisgau: Herder & Co., 1937], pp. 70-73). Julian Morgenstern has argued that Jesus and the Galilean Jews, in strict conformity with the procedure set forth in Exod. 12:1-14, began the observance of the Passover festival with the slaying of the paschal lamb and the eating of the Passover meal on the eve of the fourteenth of Nisan, while the Jerusalemites followed what was then, and has continued ever since to be, the established procedure of normative Judaism, and sacrificed the paschal lambs and began the celebration of the festival with the eating of the Passover meal on the fifteenth of Nisan.

A. T. Olmstead identified the day of Jesus' crucifixion as Friday, April 7, A.D. 30—probably correctly if the Jerusalem Jews followed the Babylonian calendar in reckoning Passover; see his *Jesus in the Light of History* (New York: Charles Scribner's Sons, 1942), pp. 279-80.

Judas, and jealousy, and proud ambition—a demonic spirit. No man can be indifferent to Christ. At long last we love him with however blundering a love, or—we betray him. If only Judas had been true, and written his Gospel! If only, his dark deed being done, he had repented sooner and died with Jesus! If only he had sought out Jesus after the trial and made full confession! But Judas in his self-planned execution is still a nobler figure than Pilate. Imagine Judas living on respectably, as a trader with false weights in Kerioth, or as a Pharisee making long prayers at street corners! His fierce death was better than that hypocrisy. It is possible for us to know Christ well, and yet betray him. There are demonic forces of greed, jealousy, and pride in us. We also may renounce the methods of Jesus. He holds no man by

18 And he said, Go into the city to such a man, and say unto him, The Master saith, My time is at hand; I will keep the passover at thy house with my disciples.

19 And the disciples did as Jesus had appointed them; and they made ready the passover.

20 Now when the even was come, he sat down with the twelve.

21 And as they did eat, he said, Verily I say unto you, that one of you shall betray me.

eat the passover?" 18 He said, "Go into the city to such a one, and say to him, 'The Teacher says, My time is at hand; I will keep the passover at your house with my disciples.'" 19 And the disciples did as Jesus had directed them, and they prepared the passover.

20 When it was evening, he sat at table with the twelve disciples;ᶠ 21 and as they were eating, he said, "Truly, I say to you,

ᶠ Many authorities omit *disciples*.

The tractate Pesahim in the Mishnah contains ancient laws bearing on the Passover, many of which must have been observed in Jesus' time. Many translations of the modern Passover service have been published, e.g., David and Tamar de Sola Pool, eds., *The Haggadah of Passover* (New York: National Jewish Welfare Board, 1944). See also Moore, *Judaism*, II, 40-43, and articles on "Passover" in *Jewish Encyclopaedia*, ed. Joseph Jacobs (New York: Funk & Wagnalls, 1906) and *Universal Jewish Encyclopaedia*.

18-19. Mark 14:13-16, from which these verses are abridged, presupposes that Jesus had friends in the city and had arranged to eat the Passover in the house of one of them. Matthew adds **my time is at hand** as a prophecy of the crucifixion (cf. vs. 29 and John 12:23).

21. Jesus may have heard a report that **one of** his disciples would **betray** him, or perhaps Judas' facial expression suggested it to him. The evangelists think of supernatural knowledge. Vss. 21-25 may not be part of the original passion narrative.

force. Is that why Christianity fails—that there are so many Judases among us?

18. The Unknown Friends of Jesus.—The incident is interesting on many counts. It hints an earlier ministry in Jerusalem not described in the Synoptics, and it therefore underscores the elements of historicity in John's Gospel. It leads us to believe that Jesus was staying at Bethany, was intent to keep his movements a secret from his foes, and that perhaps he planned a final appeal to the Passover throng. Certainly he left nothing to chance. He was not waiting on events, but was deeply master of them. The "goodman of the house" (24:43) was an unknown friend. Contrast him with Judas. This man provided a secret meeting place for Jesus and his disciples: Judas betrayed the meeting place and the movements of his Lord. We have only a few facts from which to sketch this man's portrait. He was rich: he had a large upper room, and he had slaves (see Luke's parallel account with its reference to a slave bearing a pitcher of water). He was unassuming, content to be host without being included in the inner group. He was brave: the man who entertained Jesus might well bring on himself the vengeance of Jesus' foes. Was the slave also a secret friend of Jesus? It is good to remember that at the moment of betrayal Jesus had the loyalty of such as "the goodman of the house." He and the slave were perhaps one—

talent men. They were not apostles or martyrs. Their names are on no Christian shrine. But they were Jesus' friends. Was the "goodman" the father of John Mark? Did the disciples flee to that same house after the Crucifixion? Was that upper room the scene of Pentecost? In any event the "goodman" had his reward. What of us in what seems to us our lowly post? Are we faithful and brave and modest? The kingdom is not a drab collection of equal digits, but a symphony. The music is poor if any man's instrument is silent or out of tune.

21-22. Is It I, Lord?—A common meal, especially the Passover, implied a pledge and obligation of love. "Com-panion": the man who eats with us. No wonder the disciples were sad when they were told that one of them was a traitor. They **began to say.** Does that mean after an aghast silence? Who could read the motive behind, **Is it I, Lord?** Phillips Brooks argued that it was a mark of nobility that each man read his own heart instead of accusing his neighbor.² But perhaps each man meant "It could not be I," and thus obliquely accused his neighbor. Perhaps they sensed the gathering storm and feared for their lives, and thus spoke in a hidden frenzy. Perhaps they trembled lest they might betray. If so, they proved their wisdom, especially in carrying the question to the

² *Sermons* (New York: E. P. Dutton & Co., 1878), ch. xiv.

22 And they were exceeding sorrowful, and began every one of them to say unto him, Lord, is it I?

23 And he answered and said, He that dippeth *his* hand with me in the dish, the same shall betray me.

24 The Son of man goeth as it is written of him: but woe unto that man by whom the Son of man is betrayed! it had been good for that man if he had not been born.

25 Then Judas, which betrayed him, answered and said, Master, is it I? He said unto him, Thou hast said.

26 ¶ And as they were eating, Jesus took bread, and blessed *it,* and brake *it,* and gave *it* to the disciples, and said, Take, eat; this is my body.

one of you will betray me." 22 And they were very sorrowful, and began to say to him one after another, "Is it I, Lord?" 23 He answered, "He who has dipped his hand in the dish with me, will betray me. 24 The Son of man goes as it is written of him, but woe to that man by whom the Son of man is betrayed! It would have been better for that man if he had not been born." 25 Judas, who betrayed him, said, "Is it I, Master?"ᵍ He said to him, "You have said so."

26 Now as they were eating, Jesus took bread, and blessed, and broke it, and gave it to the disciples and said, "Take, eat; this

ᵍ Or *Rabbi.*

---

23. Mark 14:20 means only: "One of you who dip in the dish with me"; but Matthew rewrites it in such a way as to suggest a particular individual. At any meal the group would dip into a common **dish.** If this was the Passover, the reference is to the *ḥarôṣeth* sauce into which the bitter herbs were dipped.

24. A saying found also in Q (18:7=Luke 17:1; cf. I Clem. 46:8) has been used here to heighten the solemn tragedy of the occasion.

25. Matthew adds this verse, in order to make it clear that Jesus foresaw the course of events (cf. John 13:26-27). **You have said so** is a literal rendering of σὺ εἶπας, which must mean "Yes," since Matthew uses the same words in vs. 64 as a substitute for the affirmative answer of Jesus in Mark 14:62 (cf. Goodspeed, *Problems of N.T. Translation,* pp. 64-68).

26-28. These verses closely follow Mark 14:22-24, in which the bread is first broken and then the cup is passed. This is also the order in I Cor. 11:23-25 and Justin *Apology* LXVI. 3. But in the corresponding passage in Luke, Codex Bezae (D) and some O.L. MSS omit Luke 22:19*b*-20, so that there is but one mention of the cup and this precedes the bread, as in the present-day Jewish kiddush prayers. Whatever may be the true explanation of this, Mark's tradition is very old and can be reconciled with both Passover and

---

strength of Christ. Perhaps they were curious to know the name of the traitor. Perhaps all these motives were in them: the heart of man is a mixed and multitudinous heart.

Matthew reports Jesus as singling out the man. But the Marcan account (14:18), which is plainly Matthew's source, leaves the charge in general terms: "one of you." Jesus may have had information from his friends concerning the movements of Judas. Doubtless he read the face of the traitor. It seems probable that he spared Judas' feeling: "one of you"—as several hands moved toward the dish. We must not shrink from the present truth of this heart-breaking drama. We also can go from the Sacrament to betray Christ. We do not know the mixed good and evil in us, and may well ask, **Lord, is it I?** If we are faithful in small matters, we shall be less likely to be treacherous in the crisis. If we guard our thoughts in habitual prayer, we shall be less prone to perfidy in the

open or secret deed. But our main safeguard is to keep bringing the question back to him, in trust upon his strength: **Is it I, Lord?**

26-29. *The Sacrament.*—These expositions are not primarily concerned with certain perplexities that beset the study of the Sacrament. What was the date of the Last Supper? Was it a Passover meal? What of the obvious discrepancies in the Lukan account as compared with John and Mark? The Exeg. has provided wise guidance through a labyrinth of questions. There are similarly helpful discussions in Branscomb ³ and in Green.⁴ An expositor is at a loss to know how to do even scantiest justice to the "depth of the riches" in these verses and in the Sacrament thus instituted. Let certain names given to the Sacrament be our guide.

The Lord's Supper: It is his table. He instituted the feast. He offered the priceless gifts.

³ *Gospel of Mark,* pp. 259-64.
⁴ *Gospel According to Saint Matthew,* pp. 246-48.

27 And he took the cup, and gave thanks, and gave *it* to them, saying, Drink ye all of it;

28 For this is my blood of the new testament, which is shed for many for the remission of sins.

is my body." 27 And he took a cup, and when he had given thanks he gave it to them, saying, "Drink of it, all of you; 28 for this is my blood of the[h] covenant, which is poured out for many for the forgiveness of

[h] Many ancient authorities insert *new*.

ḥabhûrāh customs. **Jesus took bread,** as the father or host did at any Jewish meal, **and blessed, and broke it.** The words he used were no doubt the usual formula of blessing or thanksgiving, "Blessed art thou, O Lord our God, king of the world, who dost bring forth bread from the earth." The added words, **this is my body,** suggest two things: (*a*) As the bread is broken, so Jesus' body will be—perhaps by stoning, at the hands of an angry mob, as in the case of Stephen (Acts 7:57-58). (*b*) As they eat the bread and are nourished by it, so Jesus' death will be, not a tragic loss, but for their benefit. The idea that a martyr's death avails for the salvation of Israel was not a new one (cf. on 20:28). The ancient tradition that Jesus spoke these words is our best evidence that he thought of his coming death as sacrificial. It is sometimes thought that the phrase **this is my blood** was added to the tradition for the sake of symmetry. But it is not necessary to draw that conclusion, particularly if we consider the variant form of the saying in Luke 22:20. This verse may be paraphrased: "This cup represents the new covenant that will be sealed by my blood, which is to be poured out for you." Jesus may well have made such a remark in connection with the "cup of blessing" which came later in the meal. **The blood of the covenant** is an allusion to Exod. 24:8. There the sacrificial blood was dashed on the altar, the book of the covenant, and the people, to confirm the solemn agreement which the people had made to observe God's law. Here it is **for the welfare of many,** as in 20:28. The early Christians believed that Jesus' blood availed **for the forgiveness of sins** (Rom. 3:25; Eph. 2:13; I John 1:7); and it was natural for Matthew to add this phrase.

This fact is understood by some to have implications for church architecture and for the way the feast should be celebrated. An altar against a wall has its subtle dangers, namely, that a priest, as a member of a sacerdotal order, shall preside over a "mystery" of which the people are only spectators. A table also has subtle dangers—of too great familiarity. Originally Jesus presided as host, and his disciples gathered about the table as his guests. This is "the table of believers," and the ministers are his servants—as their name implies—distributing his gifts of bread and wine. Who is invited? Anyone whom Jesus would invite. Who should be excluded? Those whom, in reverent love, he would exclude: he would never make a casualness, let alone a mockery, of that high feast. It is his table because he alone can give the gifts of redemption. Only the incarnate Lord can identify himself with all our human need. Only he can forgive, for forgiveness is of God. Only he can offer the perfect sacrifice. All we can do, at least in initial instance, is to take. It is his table: we receive at his pierced hands the gifts of grace.

The Sacrament: A sacrament is an outward and visible sign of an inward and invisible grace. We live by signs. A frown or a smile is index to the unseen mind and mood. A wedding ring is token of a pledged troth. Earth and sky are the hieroglyphs of a Presence. The man who pretends that he needs no symbols is trying to live as a disembodied spirit. Reduce religion to its ultimate simplicities, and it has still its signs: the silence, the handshake, the kiss of peace, the vocabulary. This symbol, the Sacrament, is without compare. Consider its lowliness: here is no monument in stone, no massive shrine (though such shrines have their place), but—bread and wine. Consider its commonalty: it links Jesus with every home. Consider its aptness, even to a stab of the heart: bread comes of seed that died to live, and wine is wrung from the wine press. People may quarrel over creeds, but who could easily quarrel over this bread and wine? They are a door by which Christ comes, and any penitent man may enter the banquet hall of the Redeemer.

The Eucharist: The word means "the thanksgiving." Notice from the Exeg. that Jesus himself, when he blessed the bread, probably said, "Blessed art Thou, O Lord our God, King of the world, Who dost bring forth bread from the earth." Surely it is not strange that the Sacrament has been a mighty praise. The Didache, in its instructions for the celebration of the

29 But I say unto you, I will not drink henceforth of this fruit of the vine, until that day when I drink it new with you in my Father's kingdom.

30 And when they had sung a hymn, they went out into the mount of Olives.

sins. 29 I tell you I shall not drink again of this fruit of the vine until that day when I drink it new with you in my Father's kingdom."

30 And when they had sung a hymn, they went out to the Mount of Olives.

29. This verse belongs to the oldest part of the tradition. The supper is not only a farewell but a pledge that the **kingdom** will be established and all God's people reunited in the messianic banquet; cf. on 14:13-21. Matthew changes "kingdom of God" to **my Father's kingdom.**

30. If the supper was a Passover, the **hymn** was probably the second half of the Hallel, i.e., Pss. 115–118. Leaving the house was forbidden by Exod. 12:22, but is not contrary to the ordinary Passover practice of later Judaism.

Eucharist, provides a litany that is praise in every line. The thanksgiving should range across life and the world, for the whole creation is sacramental, but it should focus in Jesus Christ. It should praise God for Jesus' word, his walk among men, his saving cross, his resurrection, and his gracious Presence. Truly a man should come confessing his sins. But the confession should be swallowed up in praise, for Christ at his own table offers pardon: **Take, eat; this is my body** "which is broken for you" (I Cor. 11:24).

The Commemoration: This heart of worship is for "remembrance" of him. He wished to be remembered: love and forgetting are almost a contradiction. But that was not the central reason for his command: "this do in remembrance of me" (Luke 22:19). Suppose the world should forget him! Toil then would be a treadmill, trade a dusty death, sin a final obscenity, and sorrow a blank despair. Once a speaker castigated the missionaries in acid terms, and then added: "But I am not willing that Christ should be forgotten"! The tokens of the Sacrament, and those who partake of them, "show forth Christ." They are a sign and witness to him among men. How can Christ be remembered unless some folk speak of him, and worship in his name? But the Sacrament is more than commemoration. The symbol of the Christian faith is not an hourglass or a grave, but an empty cross and an empty grave— and bread from living seed, with wine from living vines. Perhaps we should say that Christianity has no fixed or absolute symbols: it has a Presence. Age on age the church has found that when he is remembered in the vivid symbols of the Lord's Table, he uses the very act as highway of his presence, and he is in the midst to grant pardon and power.

The Covenant: This name came obviously from Jesus' own description of the cup as my **blood of the covenant.** The reference is to Exod. 24:8, and perhaps to Isa. 42:6, and al-

most certainly to Jer. 31:31. This was a covenant of pardon through Christ's shed blood, a covenant of wider fellowship—if Isa. 42:6 was in mind—a covenant that God's blessing shall attend the new Israel of the church, and a covenant of future glory. That last is clear in vs. 29: the Sacrament is Christ's pledge to his own of the messianic banquet.

The Offering: This name has been much used in some branches of the church. Rightly, for a covenant has two parties. All grace is of Christ, yet the covenant is not ratified unless we give our pledge of gratitude and loyalty. It is his table, yet we must **take.** The gift of pardon is his, but we must receive it in thankful love. We must offer ourselves to serve him in love, and to live in comradeship with all his children. Properly the Sacrament from earliest times has been the occasion of gifts to the poor. Is not that inevitable among those who offer themselves to Christ?

The Communion: It is a blood bond of a new and higher kind. Through the Sacrament sinful men are brought again, as forgiven men, into the fellowship of God. Therefore they are in new relation also with one another: they become members of the brotherhood of the church. They regard men beyond the church as men dear to Christ—for whom Christ dies. Thus they yearn for the redemption of mankind, and are in communion with all men. So the name *the Communion* is right in very truth. Art and architecture have gathered to this lofty theme. Music has brought its homage. The Holy Grail has moved through the Christian year "shattering all evil customs everywhere." [5] This vast river of blessing flows because once, on a tragic night before death came, he said: **Take, eat.**

30. *When They Had Sung a Hymn.*—We have too often imagined Jesus going to his cross as a man haggard with woe. Here we are told

[5] Tennyson, *Idylls of the King,* "The Holy Grail," l. 477.

31 Then saith Jesus unto them, All ye shall be offended because of me this night: for it is written, I will smite the shepherd, and the sheep of the flock shall be scattered abroad.

32 But after I am risen again, I will go before you into Galilee.

33 Peter answered and said unto him, Though all *men* shall be offended because of thee, *yet* will I never be offended.

31 Then Jesus said to them, "You will all fall away because of me this night; for it is written, 'I will strike the shepherd, and the sheep of the flock will be scattered.' 32 But after I am raised up, I will go before you to Galilee." 33 Peter declared to him, "Though they all fall away because of

5. Jesus' Prophecy and Peter's Promise (26:31-35)

31. If Jesus anticipated his arrest, it is not surprising that he should predict that the disciples would **fall away because of** him. Did he wish to have them remain with him, and bear their witness, to the end? If he intended that they should carry on his work, there is nothing culpable in their flight, which is recounted in vs. 56. But there was danger that they might give up their work altogether. The quotation from Zech. 13:7 suggests Christian reflection on the event. This O.T. book must have been used considerably by Christian preachers (cf. 24:31; 26:15). Matthew derives his form of the quotation from the Hebrew text as well as from Mark.

32. This verse breaks the context and looks forward to 28:7 (cf. Mark 14:28; 16:7). Grant (*Earliest Gospel,* p. 177) suggests that the parallel verse in Mark is a gloss. Weiss translates it: "I will lead you into Galilee" (*History of Primitive Christianity,* I, 18). This would presuppose a tradition that the first resurrection appearances were in Jerusalem.

33-35. The point of these verses may be that Peter was all the more guilty because he had promised what he could not perform. To early Christians they would serve as a

that he went singing—with a heart utterly dedicate, and therefore with a strange joy. Pss. 113–114 were sung before the meal of the Passover (supposing the Last Supper to have been that meal), and Pss. 115–118 after it. Look at that last psalm: "The Lord is on my side; I will not fear: what can man do unto me? . . . Bind the sacrifice with cords, even unto the horns of the altar. . . . O give thanks unto the Lord; for he is good: for his mercy endureth for ever." It was a song of courage—a greater courage than that of Margaret Wilson who, in the days of the Covenanters, sang in martyrdom, bound to a stake in the waters of the Solway until the tide should drown her;[6] for Margaret Wilson drew her courage from Christ. The psalm sung at the Last Supper was one of trust in God and love for men. Christ was indeed "a man of sorrows" (Isa. 53:3). But there was a joy deeper than sorrow. He sang on the way to the Cross. Hymns around the Table of the Lord come of the brave and joyous faith with which we are taught to meet life and death, and they are empowered by the Presence given through the Sacrament.

31-32. *Shepherd of the Fear-stricken Flock.*—It is possible that Matthew, following Mark, quoted Zechariah to answer the question in the

early church, "Why did the disciples desert Jesus?" That prophecy might be fulfilled. Yet vss. 33-35 show that our Gospelist did not use the excuse to condone all human failing. We see here the intimacy of the relationship between Christ and his followers. The shepherd calls his sheep by name. We see his confidence in them: one of them was false, and the others were weak, yet they must carry on his work. We see therefore his suffering: suppose they should utterly fail? Love, anxiety, apprehension for the future are all in this warning. When the wolf comes down on the flock, the shepherd stands as defense: "The good shepherd lays down his life for the sheep" (John 10:11). Our human helplessness remains, and our folly in failing to realize our weakness. But the Shepherd stands sure:

Souls of men, why will ye scatter
Like a crowd of frightened sheep?
Foolish hearts, why will ye wander
From a love so true and deep?[7]

33-35. *Rash Confidence.*—The emphasis in these verses is not on the apparent power of Jesus to make accurate prediction. **Before the cock crows** was the proverbial phrase for early

[6] Thomas B. Macaulay, *The History of England* (London: Longmans, Green & Co., 1889), I, 245.

[7] Frederick W. Faber, hymn "God Our Father." Most hymnals omit this stanza and start with the one beginning "There's a wideness in God's mercy."

| 34 Jesus said unto him, Verily I say unto thee, That this night, before the cock crow, thou shalt deny me thrice.

35 Peter said unto him, Though I should die with thee, yet will I not deny thee. Likewise also said all the disciples.

36 ¶ Then cometh Jesus with them unto a place called Gethsemane, and saith unto the disciples, Sit ye here, while I go and pray yonder. | you, I will never fall away." 34 Jesus said to him, "Truly, I say to you, this very night, before the cock crows, you will deny me three times." 35 Peter said to him, "Even if I must die with you, I will not deny you." And so said all the disciples.

36 Then Jesus went with them to a place called Geth-sem'a-ne, and he said to his disciples, "Sit here, while I go yonder and |

warning to "count the cost" of discipleship (cf. 8:18-22; Luke 14:25-33). **Before the cock crows** seems to be a regular way of saying "before early in the morning." By Roman time reckoning "cockcrow" was the third watch of the night, roughly from midnight to 3 A.M.; cf. on 14:25.

6. Gethsemane (26:36-46)

The Gethsemane story was not an indispensable part of the passion narrative, and it may have come from a separate tradition. It has sometimes been regarded as a dramatization of the phrase "lead us not into temptation" in the Lord's Prayer, or of the idea expressed in Heb. 5:7-8. Many commentators have asked how the disciples could have known what went on in Gethsemane if they were not with Jesus (vss. 36, 38, 40, 42). It has been argued that early Christians would describe Jesus as acting in a fashion appropriate to his human nature, and that this passage and Heb. 5:7-8 need be nothing more than the product of theological reflection. On the other hand, the Gospels most often show the opposite tendency and remove or reduce elements which suggest Jesus' finitude or weakness. The simplest explanation is that the disciples actually recalled that, as the time of his arrest drew near, Jesus suffered acutely. The original tradition need not have contained much more than the substance of vss. 38-39.

36. The Aramaic name **Gethsemane** means "oil press." The olive grove east of the Kidron valley has been identified ever since the fourth century as the site.

in the morning," and **three times** means "repeatedly." The stress is on the fact that the treachery will come soon and often, despite Peter's protestations. Peter thought he knew better than his Lord, and so do we. We trust our own "sagacity": no man can walk down the street or be one hour at his work without finding instances of human "wisdom" that flatly contradict what Jesus has taught. Peter set himself above his fellow men in virtue—**though they all fall away**—and so do we; for there are races of men and individual neighbors whom we regard almost with despising for their weakness. Peter overestimated his powers of will in the struggles of the soul, and so do we; for we dramatize the temptation in imagination, so sure are we that we can resist, and we even go "across lots" looking for seduction in the confidence that we can examine evil without yielding to it. The Lukan parallel has interesting variants (Luke 22:31-34): "sift you like wheat" is a dramatic phrase; "when you have turned again" is full of promise. The stumblings of our weakness, when we are forgiven, can be turned to gain. We can become, in a new lowliness,

warning to our neighbors. It seems almost certain that the report of this episode is from Peter himself. If so, we are the more sure of his greatness, for he had learned to say: "Look at me. I thought I was strong. But I denied Jesus. I was as weak as a child. No man is strong except in the power of Christ."

36-46. *Gethsemane.*— (See also vss. 39, 41.) There is an enclosed spot at the foot of the Mount of Olives called **Gethsemane** to this day. Its eight olive trees are believed, despite all evidence, to have been part of the original grove. Beggars infest the road. With the wisdom of their craft they importune visitors only on their return from the Garden, for then hearts are melted! The place is the world's shrine, because Jesus there prayed, **Thy will be done**. He left eight disciples near the entrance to the grove, and took with him into the shadow the three who saw his transfiguration. One of the twelve had already gone to sell him to his foes. He himself went in loneliness **a little farther**— the distance of a whole eternity. There he flung himself prostrate in an agony of prayer. And the three slept! Luke 22:45 tells us that they

37 And he took with him Peter and the two sons of Zebedee, and began to be sorrowful and very heavy.

38 Then saith he unto them, My soul is exceeding sorrowful, even unto death: tarry ye here, and watch with me.

pray." 37 And taking with him Peter and the two sons of Zeb′e-dee, he began to be sorrowful and troubled. 38 Then he said to them, "My soul is very sorrowful, even to death; remain here, and watch[i] with

[i] Or keep awake.

37. Peter and the two sons of Zebedee are the principal disciples and the witnesses of the Transfiguration (17:1). This story claims to be a personal tradition transmitted by them. **Sorrowful** replaces Mark's stronger word ἐκθαμβεῖσθαι, "distressed" or "terrified." The word translated **troubled** is also a strong word. Moffatt translates Mark's phrase as "appalled and agitated"; Goodspeed, "began to feel distress and dread." The evangelists do not often try to describe Jesus' emotions. Here they wish to suggest that he faces terrors hitherto unknown. We may imagine that these strong feelings were evoked, not merely by the prospect of torture and death, but by the realization that his own people had rejected him. By all human standards his mission had failed.

38. Very sorrowful, even to death, i.e., "I am almost at the point of dying from sorrow." The word rendered **watch** can mean **keep awake** (RSV mg.). The evangelists so far as possible use the story to point a moral—all Christians should be ready to "watch" with Christ. The disciples especially should have been able to share their master's suffering and give him human companionship in his hour of trial.

slept "for sorrow," spent by the foreboding and inner tumult of the crucial time. Mark does not gloss that sleep, but tells us that Jesus spoke in gentle remonstrance to Peter, the man who had protested his loyalty: "Simon, are you asleep? Could you not watch one hour?" (Mark 14:37). All their failure in loyalty and all Christ's loneliness of anguish are in that word.

We cannot fully know the dread ingredients of his **cup**. The word holds memories: "Are you able to drink the cup . . . ?" (20:22); "And he took a cup . . . for this is my blood of the covenant" (vss. 27, 28). We cannot enter into his depth of sorrow. Thus one artist has rightly shown him in the garden with his face in shadow, and the prostrate form made central.[8] It was not the cup of fear, despite the jibes of Celsus:[9] the martyrs learned their valor from him who refused an opiate on the Cross that he might meet death with open eyes. It was not a cup of physical pain alone. This was a soul agony: **My soul is very sorrowful.** We can reverently surmise that it was a cup of rejection: in that dread moment all his word and work seemed eclipsed in failure, and soon even his closest friends would desert him. It was a cup of lonely grief for sin: the whole race of men had chosen a way like that of Judas, and were rushing headlong to destruction,

Mad from life's history,
Glad to death's mystery;[1]

[8] Giovanni Bellini, "Christ at Gethsemane," National Gallery, London.
[9] James Anthony Froude, "Origen and Celsus," Short Studies on Great Subjects, pp. 254 ff.
[1] Thomas Hood, "The Bridge of Sighs."

and there was no one to understand, let alone to share, his poignancy of grief. But not even this anguish is the "appalling" sorrow of the cup. In Gethsemane he saw the black wave of wickedness coming upon him. With what a baptism he was baptized! And only he, by the indwelling Word, could meet and cleanse that black flood. He was asked to drink God's cup, God now being the mysterious host who shared the cup: "God was in Christ, reconciling the world unto himself" (II Cor. 5:19). His agony was **unto death.** There is no human parallel: God "made him to be sin for us, who knew no sin" (II Cor. 5:21). Like a passionate lover of fields immured in a city slum? No, the picture is all too thin and earthy: there are no parallels for his pure pain.

Watch and pray: that warning can stand in its own right (see on vs. 41). **Not as I will:** those words also are scored forever into our human story (see on vs. 39). The "great divide" of our world is not in any philosophy or statecraft, not in any conflict of human wills: "Over the brook Cedron" (John 18:1) is the line between God's will and man's will, and that is the great divide. The city of Jerusalem, Judas, the approaching armed guard, the temple leaders, were all on one side of the brook. The disciples were on the other, but had not yet made the great surrender. Jesus alone prayed the prayer: **Not as I will, but as thou wilt.** This is the crux of life: "Our wills are ours, to make them thine."[2] Ruskin has reminded us that an olive press gives strength (athletes rub their bodies with that oil), light for lamps, and holiness—as

[2] Tennyson, In Memoriam, Intro., st. iv.

39 And he went a little further, and fell on his face, and prayed, saying, O my Father, if it be possible, let this cup pass from me: nevertheless, not as I will, but as thou *wilt*.

40 And he cometh unto the disciples, and findeth them asleep, and saith unto Peter, What, could ye not watch with me one hour?

me." 39 And going a little farther he fell on his face and prayed, "My Father, if it be possible, let this cup pass from me; nevertheless, not as I will, but as thou wilt." 40 And he came to the disciples and found them sleeping; and he said to Peter, "So, could you not watch[i] with me one

[i] Or *keep awake.*

---

39. Matthew removes the Aramaic word "Abba," which Jesus must often have used in prayer (cf. on 6:9), and keeps the translation **my Father.** The **cup** is the cup of suffering, as in 20:22. **Not as I will, but as thou wilt** expresses Jesus' authentic spirit (6:10, 32; 7:11). Only such prayer is appropriate in a religion in which God is recognized as being as one, just, and loving. A prayer made in this spirit is preserved from magic and presumption.

40-41. It is difficult to understand how the disciples could have fallen asleep at a time like this, unless they were exhausted by the emotional strain through which they had passed. **Peter,** as in the story of the denial, is an example of the disciple who has not

---

in the temple anointings.[3] It is a parable. What strength and light and anointing Jesus was given through that prayer! **Let us be going:** it is almost the word of an explorer to his followers as he moves into the unknown. He met disaster; he did not wait for it to overtake him. He met it, and mastered it: He "was lord of his event."[4]

39. *Not My Will, but Thine.*—If mankind were granted only one prayer, what other could we choose? For this prayer is all prayer in one prayer. Some captious mind may ask, "Then why pray at all, if God knows what is best, and if his will must always be done?" The question is its own condemnation: prayer is not a beggar's mat with only money as its hankering. Prayer is friendship with the great Companion. Other questions arise, and they are pardonable, for our human sight is dim. This question, for example: "But can we help praying in petition?" No, we cannot. The root meaning of the word prayer seems to indicate an asking. We are dependent and blind: we cry out on God for succor, and we cannot help planning for our own desires. Nor are we unduly guilty: if a musician knows his gift, he cannot bear the thought that he may die with all his music in him, but must pray in specific entreaty: "Lord, that I may go to music school!" These beseechings are not necessarily against God's will. Answers to prayers according to man's asking have been too frequent in man's history, and have come with too sharp an impact of conviction ever to be dismissed as "coincidence." God is gentle and deals with us as we with children:

he sometimes guides through our expressed desires.

But we are selfish, and easily ascribe to God the ambitions which spring from our own pride. We are earthy: too little and too late we covet the best gifts. We are blind, and often ask for "boons" which if we had them would work us harm; and, if God were a devil, perhaps the most devilish torment he could plan for us would be to give us our own wish. We are perverse: wittingly and unwittingly we try to bend God to our own desires, and thus become our own god. In this selfishness, earthiness, blindness and perversity, there is but one safeguard: **Thy will be done.** Why should we be slow to pray the prayer? God is the "God and Father of our Lord Jesus Christ" (Eph. 1:3, 17), and therefore his thoughts toward us are always for good. Harriet Martineau has a story in which a mother says to her son, "They soon had a new and delicious pleasure, which none but the bitterly disappointed can feel—the pleasure of rousing their souls to bear pain, and of agreeing with God silently, when nobody knows what is in their hearts."[5] The rapture of prayer lives in that pain—the pain of "agreeing with God silently." **Thy will be done.**

41. *Watch and Pray.*—The loneliness of Jesus, and his craving for human loyalty, are in these words. But the main urgency is the warning. The soldier must not sleep on sentry duty. The priests in the temple were counted guilty of sin if they failed to keep watch through the night hours. But the disciple is under more serious discipline: he must keep integrity of soul and fidelity to the comradeship; or the foe may at any moment take him unawares. The

[3] *The Queen of the Air.*
[4] John Drinkwater, *Abraham Lincoln*, p. 3; a recurrent theme through the play.

[5] Quoted, *Expositor's Dictionary of Texts*, II, 159.

41 Watch and pray, that ye enter not into temptation: the spirit indeed *is* willing, but the flesh *is* weak.

42 He went away again the second time, and prayed, saying, O my Father, if this cup may not pass away from me, except I drink it, thy will be done.

43 And he came and found them asleep again: for their eyes were heavy.

44 And he left them, and went away again, and prayed the third time, saying the same words.

45 Then cometh he to his disciples, and saith unto them, Sleep on now, and take *your* rest: behold, the hour is at hand, and the Son of man is betrayed into the hands of sinners.

46 Rise, let us be going: behold, he is at hand that doth betray me.

hour? 41 Watch[i] and pray that you may not enter into temptation; the spirit indeed is willing, but the flesh is weak." 42 Again, for the second time, he went away and prayed, "My Father, if this cannot pass unless I drink it, thy will be done." 43 And again he came and found them sleeping, for their eyes were heavy. 44 So, leaving them again, he went away and prayed for the third time, saying the same words. 45 Then he came to the disciples and said to them, "Are you still sleeping and taking your rest? Behold, the hour is at hand, and the Son of man is betrayed into the hands of sinners. 46 Rise, let us be going; see, my betrayer is at hand."

[i] Or *keep awake.*

yet gained the strength to stand up to an emergency. He must **watch and pray that he may not enter into temptation** (cf. the Lord's Prayer [6:13]). **The spirit indeed is willing, but the flesh is weak,** appears to be a Christian reflection on the difficulties of the spiritual life. The saying is artistically constructed, with the particles μέν and δέ pointing that contrast between **spirit** and **flesh** which is so common in the Pauline letters (e.g., Gal. 5:16).

42. Matthew supplies a wording for the **second** prayer; Mark 14:39 says merely that he spoke the same words.

45. RSV follows Moffatt, Goodspeed, and most modern commentators in taking the words not as an ironical statement but as a question: **Are you still sleeping . . . ? The hour** of Jesus' crucifixion **is at hand,** as in 26:18; John 12:23; 17:1. The evangelists contemplate this hour with awe (see vs. 53), for it means that the heavenly **Son of man,** who will come again with power and great glory (24:30), **is** now **betrayed into the hands of sinners.**

46. Jesus either sees Judas or foresees him.

terrible undertone of the Gethsemane story is Jesus' sense of the evil's appalling threat. "Sorrowful" (vs. 37) is a midnight word, but it still does no justice to the word in Mark's (original?) account. "Appalled and shaken unto death" would hardly be too strong a translation. This hideous demonism assaults human souls. It comes stealthily, like a lion crouching for the spring upon a man sleeping by a dying campfire. It comes whence we least expect, and breaks us, as a wind coming from an unwonted quarter will break a tree that has stood many storms. It comes with sinister intent, and sears the spirit, as fire blackens a green forest into charred stumps and grotesque death. We fear contagion of physical disease. Why do we not fear the threat to the soul?

Watch and pray!—"Keep awake and seek the power of God!" Without that wisdom men are blind to the hour, as the sleeping disciples were blind to Christ's hour. Without that alertness

men are disloyal to Christ, and lead him to some new Calvary. Without that guard set men are without defense: the spirit may be willing, but the flesh is weak. Yet there is a resource. Our alertness in itself would not be enough; and by the same token, prayer of itself would fail us. God is our resource. The saving strategy is trust in God renewed and again renewed in earnest prayer, plus the act of our own will. It will do us little good to pray if, having prayed, we parley with the foe. Diabolus asked only that he might set one foot in the City of Mansoul. That was all he needed for victory.[6] Yet our own will, even though to utmost resolve, is a weak reed without prayer and God's power. **Watch and pray.** There are those who have been obedient to Christ's warning. Through them the dark flood of evil is stayed. They are the real bulwark of the race.

[6] Bunyan, *The Holy War.*

47 ¶ And while he yet spake, lo, Judas, one of the twelve, came, and with him a great multitude with swords and staves, from the chief priests and elders of the people.

48 Now he that betrayed him gave them a sign, saying, Whomsoever I shall kiss, that same is he; hold him fast.

49 And forthwith he came to Jesus, and said, Hail, Master; and kissed him.

50 And Jesus said unto him, Friend, wherefore art thou come? Then came they, and laid hands on Jesus, and took him.

47 While he was still speaking, Judas came, one of the twelve, and with him a great crowd with swords and clubs, from the chief priests and the elders of the people. 48 Now the betrayer had given them a sign, saying, "The one I shall kiss is the man; seize him." 49 And he came up to Jesus at once and said, "Hail, Master!"ʲ And he kissed him. 50 Jesus said to him, "Friend, why are you here?"ᵏ Then they came up and laid hands on Jesus and seized

ʲ Or *Rabbi.*

ᵏ Or *do that for which you have come.*

7. The Arrest (26:47-56)

47. The **great crowd** which comes **from the chief priests and elders of the people** is probably composed of the high priest's servants and perhaps some of the temple guards. Matthew has no thought that Roman soldiers were present (contrast John 18:3). They come at night **with swords and clubs** because they regard Jesus as a revolutionist who may offer resistance.

48. Jesus might have been recognized without **a sign,** but his captors wish to take no chances because mistakes can easily be made at night, particularly if a struggle occurs.

49. He **kissed** Jesus because this was the natural way for a disciple to greet his **Master** (literally **Rabbi,** RSV mg.).

50. This question is found only in Matthew. Like the different question in Luke 22:48, it may be intended as a rebuke. Matthew is the only N.T. writer to use the word rendered **Friend** (11:16; 20:13; 22:12).

47-50. *The Arrest and Betrayal of Jesus.*—We would not name a child, or even a dog, Judas. Yet it is a good name. If it comes from Judah, it means worthy-to-be-praised. But now it is a loathing, because of a night when Judas betrayed his Master with a kiss. We cannot tell his motives. This incident would seem to hint that he feared that the followers of Jesus would lead an insurrection, and had therefore thrown in his lot with the caution and compromise of the Sadducees. But perhaps he wished Jesus to stage a nationalistic revolt, and had resolved on an act that would commit Jesus to use his "messianic" power. We do not know. Certainly there was a mixture of motives: ambition, lonely jealousy, greed. For no man's heart is single, even in evil. The kiss was the customary greeting given by a pupil to a rabbi; but even though Judas' act was not unusual, it was betrayal. It may not have been utterly insincere, for the base and the noble in us are strangely intertwined.

There is a story that Benedict Arnold once asked, "What will be my fate if I am taken prisoner?" The man questioned is said to have answered, "Why, sir, they will cut off that shortened leg of yours wounded at Quebec and Saratoga, and bury it with all the honors of war; and then hang the rest of you on a gibbet."[7] If only our treacheries could be confined to one part of us! Surgery then might be our salvation. But as it is, we are not saved except by an abandon of loyalty in which we can forget ourselves, and that abandon is not fully given except to Christ—through the Cross.

So much for the traitor. What of the victim? He was no victim. There was a certain voluntariness about his arrest. Some man, stricken in the lungs when he attempted a rescue in a fume-filled mine, was asked by an embittered miner, "So they took your health too?" "No," said the rescuer, "I gave it." Jesus gave his life: no man took it. He gave it for others. Between the lines of this story we see him standing forth to be arrested, perhaps to make more sure that his disciples might be spared. John's Gospel states it specifically: "I have told you that I am he: . . . let these go their way" (John 18:8). A Bruckner symphony is wrung from a soul struggle. So, more deeply, is the salvation of mankind. From the wine press that night there came the cup of a new covenant.

What of ourselves? Perhaps we are weak precisely at the point of Judas' treachery. We have brains to devise the astonishing mechanisms of our world. We have skill to organize,

[7] Malcolm Decker, *Benedict Arnold* (Tarrytown: William Abbatt, 1932), pp. 417-18.

51 And, behold, one of them which were with Jesus stretched out *his* hand, and drew his sword, and struck a servant of the high priest, and smote off his ear.

52 Then said Jesus unto him, Put up again thy sword into his place: for all they that take the sword shall perish with the sword.

53 Thinkest thou that I cannot now pray to my Father, and he shall presently give me more than twelve legions of angels?

54 But how then shall the Scriptures be fulfilled, that thus it must be?

him. 51 And behold, one of those who were with Jesus stretched out his hand and drew his sword, and struck the slave of the high priest, and cut off his ear. 52 Then Jesus said to him, "Put your sword back into its place; for all who take the sword will perish by the sword. 53 Do you think that I cannot appeal to my Father, and he will at once send me more than twelve legions of angels? 54 But how then should the scrip-

51. At least one of Jesus' companions had a **sword** and used it. The precautions against resistance were not altogether unjustified.

52. Matthew alone transmits this verse, which may embody a genuine saying of Jesus spoken on this or some other occasion.

53. The phrase **my Father** suggests that this is Matthew's reflection. Like the Fourth Evangelist, he cannot imagine Jesus as "crucified through weakness" (II Cor. 13:4); the Lord could have escaped, had he so desired. The **twelve legions of angels** are contrasted with the helpless twelve disciples and suggest the fiery chariots of II Kings 6:17.

and a certain generosity in friendship. But what of our loyalty to Christ at cost? It could hardly be denied that we lack that stern sinew. Therefore we also betray, and hurry him to his cross. There could have been, and should have been, another ending to the story. Judas betrayed himself. A legend has him wandering through the night in a blank frenzy, and coming upon a group of workmen fashioning a cross. Then he understood what he had done, and straightway chose another gallows.[8] There is a sense in which God cannot be betrayed: every betrayal is man's betrayal of himself, for God abides. Judas hanging himself is still a nobler figure than Judas would have been if he had invested his thirty pieces of silver and become rich and respectable. But if only Judas in betrayal had copied Peter in denial: if only he had flung himself in confession on the grace of Jesus! For us there can be another ending to our betrayals.

51-54. *They That Take the Sword.*—Those who arrested Jesus were probably emissaries of the high priest and members of the temple guard. John tells us there were also Roman soldiers. That seems not unlikely: there is evidence of collusion between Pilate and the temple. Clearly the enemies of Jesus feared armed insurrection. Perhaps the fear was not unfounded: one or more of Christ's followers

[8] For the Judas legends see H. A. Guerber, *Legends of the Virgin and Christ* (New York: Dodd, Mead & Co., 1896), pp. 150-59; Anna Jameson, *Sacred and Legendary Art* (London: Longman, Brown, Green & Longmans, 1848), I, 234-40.

had a sword. We cannot build a dogmatism on these words ascribed to our Lord. No man can quote them as final argument either for the Christian use of arms or for a Christian pacifism. "Christian" as an adjective is always dangerous; that ultimate Name should be a noun. The meaning of these words is not clear beyond cavil. They could be the comment of the early church rather than the very words of Christ: the Jewish War was evidence of the folly of taking the sword. Or they could mean a warning against defiance of magisterial powers. Or the stress could be on the word **take**. This is not a proof text.

Yet no man could deny its fundamental truth. A threat breeds a threat, for there is a certain self-respect in human nature that will not be coerced; and generals who plead that "we should be strong enough to defeat any foe" should realize that generals in other lands offer the same counsel with the same right—or the same folly. Likewise revenge breeds revenge, as the bitter feuds of all the years have shown. Besides, the use of force looses man's worst passions; and by the time a "war for justice" has brought victory, the passion for justice has been changed to bitterness, disgust, and a weary soul; and by the time our "fierce love" has overcome the foe, the love is turned—with the help of lying propaganda—into a bedraggled hate. War never accomplishes its avowed end of peace. How could it? The bodies of men may be compelled for a time, but swords cannot change man's spirit. Jesus' comment about **legions of angels** may be actually an addition

55 In that same hour said Jesus to the multitudes, Are ye come out as against a thief with swords and staves for to take me? I sat daily with you teaching in the temple, and ye laid no hold on me.

56 But all this was done, that the Scriptures of the prophets might be fulfilled. Then all the disciples forsook him, and fled.

tures be fulfilled, that it must be so?" 55 At that hour Jesus said to the crowds, "Have you come out as against a robber, with swords and clubs to capture me? Day after day I sat in the temple teaching, and you did not seize me. 56 But all this has taken place, that the scriptures of the prophets might be fulfilled." Then all the disciples forsook him and fled.

---

55. The word translated **robber** is used by Josephus to describe those revolutionists who combined banditry and violent nationalism (e.g., *Antiquities* XX. 8. 5). Jesus is not one of these; he has taught in public and could have been apprehended peaceably at any time.

56. What parts of **the scriptures** are referred to here and in vs. 54? Perhaps this is a general reference to such passages as Isa. 53 and Pss. 22 and 69, which early Christians regarded as prophecies of the Crucifixion. Although **all the disciples forsook him and fled,** they probably remained in the vicinity of Jerusalem, and were present at some of the events that followed or heard of them from eyewitnesses.

---

of the early church to show that he did not die in helplessness, or it may be his word. In either event not even angel swords, one legion for each of the twelve disciples, could change wicked men into good men.

The whole question of means and ends is here involved. Because it is a question of ends it always goes beyond our human wisdom. But we need not continue to be blind to the fact that means and ends are not separate: if there is poison in the means the poison flows down the river-of-means into the lake-of-ends, so that when we reach the lake it also is poisoned. Yet how speciously we use ends to justify means. The Jamaican planters justified slavery on the ground that it gave men a chance to preach the gospel! The word has been tragically true: **they that take the sword shall perish with the sword.** The Christian church must come to terms with that truth.

55. *As . . . a Thief?*—Some commentators think this passage is an early Christian commentary. Yet surely it is consonant with Jesus' whole teaching. Besides, a bitter ingredient of his bitter cup was the failure of those closest to him to understand his method and truth. That trial of soul is again and again revealed: "How long am I to bear with you?" (17:17). There are disavowals here, both spoken and implied. Jesus was not a robber, preying on mankind. There may have been sharp irony in the retort: Green confidently advances the theory that the temple authorities were in collusion with the robbers of the Jordan Valley.[9] The word **robber** means thief and violent rebel against the Roman conqueror. Jesus was not a man of violence

or a mere nationalist. He was not given to slinking away to caves: he was not a coward fearing arrest.

These disavowals, though dramatic indeed, are not as striking as the avowals. Here is the claim that Jesus was both a man of candor and a man of peace. A true Christian faith is "not done in a corner" (Acts 26:26). When did Jesus shrink from opposing wrong? The cleansing of the temple was a deed for all men to see. When did Jesus ever deceive any man about the hardships and joys of his discipleship? He did not hide the sharp flint or gild the shadows. When did he pretend to knowledge that was not his? "Of that day and hour no one knows, . . . nor the Son" (24:36). Our modern propaganda is ostensibly a desire for truth, but secretly a shrewd plan for the gain of a partisan group. But the Christian faith is in the open: it is both candor and peace. We may well mark the fact. Our "peace" is too often peace at the price of truth; and our "candor" is too often proud or self-seeking censure. The triumph of the Christian faith, a triumph through apparent defeat, is won by its openness of truth combined with its peaceable love for all men.

56. *They Forsook Him and Fled.*—They all fled, even Peter who had protested that he would die rather than desert, even the faithful Andrew, even the deep-seeing John. The prophecy reported in the Fourth Gospel was fulfilled: "Behold, the hour cometh, yea, is now come, that ye shall be scattered, every man to his own, and shall leave me alone" (John 16:32). Why did they flee? How could they desert such a Lord? We swear that we would not have done it. But fear comes suddenly to start our feet. Perhaps if we could stand for one instant, we

[9] *Gospel According to Saint Matthew*, p. 249, note on Matt. 26:55.

57 ¶ And they that had laid hold on Jesus led *him* away to Caiaphas the high priest, where the scribes and the elders were assembled.

57 Then those who had seized Jesus led him to Ca'ia-phas the high priest, where the scribes and the elders had gathered.

---

8. Hearing Before Caiaphas (26:57-68)

The story in vss. 59-68 raises several difficulties. (*a*) It pictures a meeting of the entire council (vs. 59). Even if this was not the night of Passover, would a full meeting of the Sanhedrin have been held? The rule of the Mishnah, which of course may be later, is that "in capital cases they hold the trial in the daytime and the verdict must also be reached in the daytime. . . . In capital cases an acquittal verdict may be reached on the same day, but a conviction verdict not until the following day. Therefore trials may not be held on the eve of a Sabbath or the eve of a festival" (Sanhedrin 4:1). This "trial" in fact violates the rules of Jewish judicial procedure in almost every possible way. (*b*) According to Pharisaic rules, the only blasphemy punishable by death was one in which the divine name was used blasphemously. The claim to be Messiah or to sit on the right hand of the power of God could scarcely be a capital offense. (*c*) Scholars are not agreed as to whether the Sanhedrin at this time had the power to pronounce and carry out the death sentence for violations of the Jewish law. The Palestinian Talmud held that this right of the Sanhedrin had ceased to exist in A.D. 30, but the evidence of Josephus can be cited on the other side (*Antiquities* XIV. 9. 3; *Jewish War* VI. 2. 4; see also the arguments of Branscomb, *Gospel of Mark,* pp. 271-77). It is not important to decide this point, since in any case Jesus was not put to death on the charge of blasphemy. He was not stoned to death by the Jews but was condemned by Pilate on the charge of high treason, and the Romans executed him by the Roman method of crucifixion. (*d*) Vss. 59-68 (=Mark 14:55-65) interrupt what is otherwise a continuous story, and 27:1 (=Mark 15:1) tells of a morning meeting of the Sanhedrin as though no previous meeting had taken place. Commentators also frequently object

---

would not desert; but we run, and the running increases fear. Why were they cowards? The cause seemed hopeless, for the enemies of Jesus now had overwhelmed him. The cause often seems hopeless, unless we have eyes to see the hills filled with spiritual powers. Why did they flee? Because the dark power had seized them: "This is your hour, and the power of darkness" (Luke 22:53). There are malignities in us and about us with which no man can cope in his own poor strength.

"Yet I am not alone," Jesus is reported to have said (John 16:32). We must give our answer to the question: Are there powers beyond our human eyes? What would you have given for the chances of Gilmour's gospel after he had worked in China for years without one convert? "I have not, as far as I am aware, seen anyone who even *wanted* to be a Christian." [1] Or for the chances of the church under the persecutions of Nero? Voltaire boasted that he would destroy the Christian faith, and the boast had much to support it so far as eyes could judge. Then why and how was his printing press later used to print Bibles? There *are* other powers and other ways! But we may yet fear

men and flee, unless by watching and prayer we have learned to fear God in holy love.

57. The Character of Caiaphas.—Perhaps he was more guilty than Pilate or even Judas. Beyond much doubt he was the prime mover in the murder of Jesus. Yet he could not have entered the priesthood without some elements of genuine religion. It is a safe guess that he loved the temple. Probably he had real affection for his family: his wife was the daughter of Annas, the predecessor of Caiaphas in office, and between the lines of the story we can read the family bond. W. M. Clow has said that Caiaphas was dominantly "the ecclesiastic" in all that is good and bad in that kind of man. [2] Caiaphas was concerned for the institutions of religion, so concerned that any proposal of change seemed to him a traitorous heresy. Do we not all know men to whom change in our institutions is "subversive activity," who assume that God has no better thing in store for mankind? They are "good" men after their kind, and yet they share with the anarchical mind the responsibility for bloody revolution. Caiaphas was much concerned for theological rectitude: it was blasphemy to use the divine

[1] Quoted, J. H. Jowett, *Sharing His Sufferings,* pp. 55-56.

[2] *The Day of the Cross* (New York: George H. Doran Co., 1909), pp. 15 ff.

that the disciples could not have known the details of the trial if none of them was present. This objection, however, can be answered. (*e*) On the other hand, some elements of the story appear to be likely. There is evidence that Jesus at some time prophesied the destruction of the temple (24:2; 27:40; Acts 6:14). Furthermore, it is easier to understand why he was executed by Pilate if he declared that he was Messiah— or at least refused to deny it (vs. 64).

The simplest way to understand the story is to suppose that Caiaphas and some of his friends assembled at night in the hope of gathering evidence against Jesus. They were unable to find witnesses whose testimony agreed on any point that would make a conviction possible. It was a cardinal doctrine of the Pharisees that witnesses must be cross-examined separately and they would have taken every precaution to protect any man accused of a capital offense. Thus it would have been quite impossible to convict Jesus in a Jewish court. Accordingly the Sadducean priests tried to get Jesus to say that he was the Messiah, in order to accuse him to Pilate as a pretender to the Jewish throne. Jesus may actually have answered that he was the Messiah. At least this was the report which came out of the meeting. The disciples of course were not present at the proceedings, and we cannot be sure that the wording of vs. 64 is exactly that of Jesus; in fact it suggests the dominant theology of Mark.

57. The traditional house of **Caiaphas the high priest** is south of Zion Gate, just outside the present walls and near the southwest corner of the Old City, a considerable distance away from the Mount of Olives.

name in certain ways, and Christ must be stoned if guilty of blasphemy. Do we not all know men who instantly condemn any deviation from the letter of the creed, but who harbor the pride and greed which are worse heresies of the spirit? The "church" and the creed thus become cover for the crucifixion of Jesus.

Caiaphas was imperious. "You know nothing at all" (John 11:49), he could say to his fellow members on the Sanhedrin. He was born master of the minds and moods of weaker men. He was an actor, and he was interesting (he had "personality," and "put on a good show"): notice the histrionic gift as he laid Jesus under oath (vs. 63), and rent his high priest's robes, and asked, "Why do we still need witnesses?" (vs. 65). He was a shrewd politician and manipulated events with sure skill: he knew how the crowd could be kept in order, and how the hand of Pilate could be forced, and why Jesus must be killed. Caiaphas at last was utterly unscrupulous: truth meant nothing, and the life of an innocent man was a bagatelle. Perhaps he deceived even himself: perhaps he really believed he was concerned for God and the temple when in actuality he was concerned only for Caiaphas in high office. What chance has Jesus against such a man? Age on age that question repeats, and the answer comes: "Not by might," nor by shrewd diplomacy, "but by my spirit, saith the LORD" (Zech. 4:6). Zona Gale has the story of two tadpoles.[3] One believed there was a world vaster than their little puddle, but the other mocked: it was folly to believe in

[3] Quoted, *We Believe in Prayer*, ed. Sidney Strong (New York: Coward-McCann, Inc., 1930), p. 68.

a world of men who could change or destroy that eternal pool! John's Gospel has an interesting comment on Caiaphas (John 11:51-52): he did not know that God would use Jesus to gather his people! Caiaphas was soon deposed by Rome. God was using Caiaphas in holy love, far more surely than Caiaphas was using Jesus in selfish pride.

57-68. *Jesus Before Caiaphas.*—The interpreter must be honest with the exegetical problems which are raised by this passage, and should read with care the Exeg. By Mark's and Matthew's account all Sanhedrin rules were broken. The meeting was not held at the stated place, nor in the daytime, nor was the verdict of condemnation postponed a day, nor was the charge of blasphemy sustained by the evidence; and we must remember that Caiaphas and his friends were meticulously careful about the rules, even if about nothing else. We must assume either that Luke has correctly reported the time of the meeting (Luke 22:66) or that Caiaphas called to his home a few members whom he could trust, "to see what they could get on the man." Perhaps the conspirators resolved, before they slept, that it would be safer to let Rome do the killing rather than risk some action by the people who still considered Jesus a prophet.

Most exegetes agree that the "charges" brought against Jesus have a core of historicity. He was accused of threatening to destroy the temple. This charge was probably a garbled account of his prophecy that events under God would bring about the destruction both of Jerusalem and of the temple. We can imagine

58 But Peter followed him afar off unto the high priest's palace, and went in, and sat with the servants, to see the end.

59 Now the chief priests, and elders, and all the council, sought false witness against Jesus, to put him to death;

60 But found none: yea, though many false witnesses came, *yet* found they none. At the last came two false witnesses,

61 And said, This *fellow* said, I am able to destroy the temple of God, and to build it in three days.

62 And the high priest arose, and said unto him, Answerest thou nothing? What *is it which* these witness against thee?

63 But Jesus held his peace. And the high priest answered and said unto him, I adjure thee by the living God, that thou tell us whether thou be the Christ, the Son of God.

64 Jesus saith unto him, Thou hast said: nevertheless I say unto you, Hereafter shall ye see the Son of man sitting on the right hand of power, and coming in the clouds of heaven.

58 But Peter followed him at a distance, as far as the courtyard of the high priest, and going inside he sat with the guards to see the end. 59 Now the chief priests and the whole council sought false testimony against Jesus that they might put him to death, 60 but they found none, though many false witnesses came forward. At last two came forward 61 and said, "This fellow said, 'I am able to destroy the temple of God, and to build it in three days.' " 62 And the high priest stood up and said, "Have you no answer to make? What is it that these men testify against you?" 63 But Jesus was silent. And the high priest said to him, "I adjure you by the living God, tell us if you are the Christ, the Son of God." 64 Jesus said to him, "You have said so. But I tell you, hereafter you will see the Son of man seated at the right hand of **Power, and**

60. **Two** witnesses were needed to sustain any charge (Deut. 17:6; 19:15). Many of the rules in the tractate Sanhedrin of the Mishnah for examining witnesses were probably in force at this time. By the first century B.C. the Pharisees succeeded in enforcing the rule that witnesses must be cross-examined separately, and the story of Susanna celebrates this victory.

61. Some early Christians may also have claimed that Jesus would destroy the temple and rebuild it (Acts 6:14). But Jesus may well have said: "If Israel does not repent, the temple will be destroyed; but **in three days** the true worship of God can nevertheless be restored." This was the actual experience of the Jewish people. The loss of the temple was a deeply mourned tragedy, but the development of Judaism was advanced rather than arrested by it.

63. **I adjure you** means "I demand that you testify on oath." **The Christ, the Son of God** is a combination of titles used more by Christians than by Jews (cf. on 4:3). The high priest would have been more likely to say "Messiah, son of David."

64. Matthew understood the saying thus: "I am Messiah, but that is not all. I shall return as Son of man, seated at the place of honor beside God." **You have said so** (σὺ εἶπας) is Matthew's substitute for the affirmative "I am" in Mark 14:62 and must mean

the hatred that such a prophecy would breed in those whose emoluments and pride were supported by the temple, and the anger with which they remembered how he had cleansed the temple courts. Jesus was accused also of claiming messiahship. Most commentators now agree that he was slow to make the claim, not least because the title carried earthy and nationalistic connotations among the Jews. But granted the historicity of the incident (and it has authentic marks), Jesus here would not forswear himself, but confessed that he was

the anointed of God. Thus the very charges become tribute to him and to his truth.

Could there be a more striking contrast of soul than that between Caiaphas and Jesus? Caiaphas dominant, Jesus strong in the strength of submission to God's will; Caiaphas shrewd and a clever actor, Jesus guiltless in candor; Caiaphas the champion of entrenched systems, Jesus asking no haven but the wide sky of God's verity; Caiaphas unscrupulous, Jesus patiently trusting the unseen might of holy love. Jesus here stands as a beam of light among the en-

65 Then the high priest rent his clothes, saying, He hath spoken blasphemy; what further need have we of witnesses? behold, now ye have heard his blasphemy.

66 What think ye? They answered and said, He is guilty of death.

67 Then did they spit in his face, and buffeted him; and others smote *him* with the palms of their hands,

68 Saying, Prophesy unto us, thou Christ, Who is he that smote thee?

coming on the clouds of heaven." 65 Then the high priest tore his robes, and said, "He has uttered blasphemy. Why do we still need witnesses? You have now heard his blasphemy. 66 What is your judgment?" They answered, "He deserves death." 67 Then they spat in his face, and struck him; and some slapped him, 68 saying, "Prophesy to us, you Christ! Who is it that struck you?"

"Yes." The word rendered **but** (πλήν) means "furthermore" here; see Goodspeed, *Problems of N.T. Translation*, pp. 64-68. **Power** probably represents the Aramaic *gebhûrtā'*, "omnipotence," a word used to avoid mentioning the divine name. The **Son of man** will come on the clouds of heaven, as in 24:30. Jesus did not willingly choose the title "Messiah," because it immediately suggested armed revolt (cf. notes on 16:13-20; 21:4-9; 26:6-13), but he could not deny that he was in a real sense the anointed leader of his people. The **Son of man** saying could conceivably mean, "I am the Messiah, but the Son of man is yet to come." The evangelists carefully preserved this ambiguity, because there was no tradition that Jesus clearly identified himself with the heavenly Son of man.

65. Though **the high priest** was not allowed to tear **his robes** in mourning for the dead (Lev. 10:6; 21:10), this was the proper behavior when one heard **blasphemy**. Here the blasphemy does not consist in the claim to messiahship but in the prediction that Jesus would be at God's right hand. This was not punishable by death because the ineffable name of Yahweh was not used. The word blasphemy is used in a looser sense (cf. on 9:3).

66. The high priest and his associates judge that Jesus **deserves death**, but this is not a legal verdict reached in accordance with law, and they do not dare to carry out the sentence.

---

croaching powers of darkness. We ask again: What chance has Christ in such a world? Always the swords and the money are in the hands of evil men, and always the saints seem defenseless. How the kingdom of God endures is the agelong miracle. Anatole France somewhere shows a philosopher, Lamia, and Pilate meeting after many years, and Lamia asking the other casually, "Pontius, do you remember anything about the man?" and Pilate replying, "Jesus—of Nazareth? I cannot call him to mind." [4] The ruler had forgotten, so little did Jesus matter in his world! But God does not forget. Caiaphas would have gone into oblivion but for Jesus. "Standeth God within the shadow, keeping watch above his own!" [5]

67-68. *The Mocking of Christ.*—We can scarcely bear to read the lines. To spit in a man's face is always and everywhere a mark of utter contempt. To slap a helpless man's face is sadism. To mock Christ—"Prophesy who struck thee!" (was a cover over his face because he had been condemned to death?) —is demon-

ism become incarnate in a deed. Crowd psychology was at work. A crowd can have a good effect, as when people gather to watch a worthy historical pageant or to hear great music. In such instances the good in individual men is enhanced. But a crowd can also quicken a blood lust, as at a lynching. Perhaps we should all ask ourselves before joining any crowd, "For what purpose do they gather?" For a crowd may sweep us beyond ourselves for good or ill. The servants who mocked Jesus probably would have been ashamed to act that way had each man been alone. How is the blood lust of a crowd overcome? By our refusal to join it except for a noble purpose. And by the sacrifice of the victim! The monk Telemachus began the overthrow of the blood lust of the Roman "holiday" when he rushed into the arena and was "overwhelmed under a shower of stones." [6] God was not idle when Jesus was mocked. How did the mockers feel when they finally took their rest that night? There is a Spirit who convicts men of sin. There is a sovereign Will,

[4] *Golden Tales of Anatole France* (New York: Dodd, Mead & Co., 1926), p. 25.

[5] James Russell Lowell, "The Present Crisis," st. viii.

[6] Edward Gibbon, *Decline and Fall of the Roman Empire* (Philadelphia: J. P. Lippincott & Co., 1875), III, 210.

69 ¶ Now Peter sat without in the palace: and a damsel came unto him, saying, Thou also wast with Jesus of Galilee.	69 Now Peter was sitting outside in the courtyard. And a maid came up to him, and said, "You also were with Jesus the Galilean." **70** But he denied it before them all, saying, "I do not know what you mean." **71** And when he went out to the porch, another maid saw him, and she said to the bystanders, "This man was with Jesus of Nazareth." **72** And again he denied it with an oath, "I do not know the man." **73** After a little while the bystanders came up and said to Peter, "Certainly you are also one of them, for your accent betrays you." **74** Then he began to invoke a curse on himself and to swear, "I do not know the man." And immediately the cock crowed. **75** And Peter remembered the saying of Jesus, "Before the cock crows, you will deny me three times." And he went out and wept bitterly.
70 But he denied before *them* all, saying, I know not what thou sayest.	
71 And when he was gone out into the porch, another *maid* saw him, and said unto them that were there, This *fellow* was also with Jesus of Nazareth.	
72 And again he denied with an oath, I do not know the man.	
73 And after a while came unto *him* they that stood by, and said to Peter, Surely thou also art *one* of them; for thy speech bewrayeth thee.	
74 Then began he to curse and to swear, *saying,* I know not the man. And immediately the cock crew.	
75 And Peter remembered the word of Jesus, which said unto him, Before the cock crow, thou shalt deny me thrice. And he went out, and wept bitterly.	

9. PETER'S DENIAL (26:69-75)

Peter is often thought to have been the original narrator of the passion story, or at least of the scenes at which he was present. It is sometimes argued that he alone would be likely to tell the shameful story of how he denied his Lord, and this point has some weight. At the same time the real moral of the story is the richness of God's grace. The disciple who showed himself so craven was nevertheless the first witness of the Resurrection (I Cor. 15:5; Luke 24:34) and became the rock-apostle and a pillar of the church (Gal. 2:9). This section resumes the story begun in vss. 57-58.

69. Peter was in the **courtyard** or atrium rather than the **palace**. The **maid** was probably one of the household servants.

73. Peter's **accent** was Galilean. The Aramaic of Galilee, like the Arabic spoken there today, had dialectical peculiarities.

74. Jesus had condemned such curses and oaths (5:33-37), and this story illustrates one reason for his ruling: an oath is no guarantee of the truth of a statement. The evangelists think of the actual crowing of a cock, though "cockcrow" is a fixed time of the night and a bugle may have sounded in the Roman garrison at that hour.

and therefore Christ is exalted. Could the mockers ever have dreamed that their victim would be worshiped in every land, and they remain only as a warning and an execration?

69-75. The Denial of Peter.—While Jesus was being tried before Caiaphas, Peter also was being tried as in a furnace. Jesus, mocked by earthy men, suffered a more cruel mockery in the faithlessness of a friend. Jesus had taught Peter to deny himself, but Peter denied his Lord. Maurice Goguel [7] and others have argued that the story cannot be authentic because, had it been true, Peter could never have come to leadership in the church. But such a theory

[7] *The Life of Jesus* (New York: The Macmillan Co., 1933), pp. 490-92.

raises far more questions than it settles: if the story were not true, would Peter and his friends ever have allowed it to become fixed and central in the Christian scriptures? Peter himself must have told the story, and that fact does him honor. The honesty, and his Lord's redeeming trust in him, are the very reasons why Peter rose to acknowledged apostleship.

Peter was caught unawares by the servant girl's question. He was not without excuse. He was physically tired, and his guard was down. The cause of Jesus seemed in eclipse, and he was tempted to despair. Besides, he did follow Jesus to the courtyard of Caiaphas, and that action did not lack courage. If he could have been forewarned of the test, he probably would

27 When the morning was come, all the chief priests and elders of the people took counsel against Jesus to put him to death:

2 And when they had bound him, they led *him* away, and delivered him to Pontius Pilate the governor.

27 When morning came, all the chief priests and the elders of the people took counsel against Jesus to put him to death; 2 and they bound him and led him away and delivered him to Pilate the governor.

---

10. Hearing Before Pilate (27:1-26)

a) Jesus Is Led Before Pilate (27:1-2)

27:1. A meeting of the Sanhedrin in the **morning** was more in accord with law than the night meeting (cf. on 26:57-68). Here it is said only that they **took counsel against Jesus.** They presumably relinquished jurisdiction over their prisoner in order to accuse him in the Roman court.

2. Tacitus and Josephus know **Pontius Pilate** by these two names (the "gentile" name and cognomen). His praenomen is unknown. From *ca.* A.D. 26 to 36 he was governor or procurator of Judea. A procurator was an official of the equestrian class who was set over one of the smaller imperial provinces and held office at the pleasure of the emperor. The procurator of Judea lived at Caesarea but must have spent much time in Jerusalem. It is not certain whether Pilate was subject to the legate of Syria or directly responsible to the emperor. Pilate's administration must have been satisfactory to Tiberius, who kept close watch over his provinces; otherwise he would not have kept him in office for so

---

have kept faith. But temptation comes, as Jesus often told his followers, "like a thief in the night" (I Thess. 5:2). How shall we forfend against the sudden test? By instant recoil, not without much prayer. One lie led to another, and would have led to chaos if the deepening curse had not been stayed by Christ. Aristotle said that the penalty of telling a lie is that the liar is not believed when he tells the truth.[8] That is to say, all confidence is broken, and soon there is no bond between men. Perhaps Matthew's description (there are discrepancies in the four accounts) is psychologically sound: first a denial, then a denial with an oath, then a denial with curses.

Always something betrays us in our perfidy. There is no "perfect crime." Peter was betrayed by his Galilean accent. He was betrayed, or convicted, by the crowing of a cock. Is there not the story of a murderer, seen in his deed only by a heron, shouting out years later when he saw a flight of herons, "The avengers of Ibycus!"—and so confessing his guilt?[9] All nature conspires against the sinner. Peter was betrayed, like every sinner, by an inner torment. He was caught at last by one look from Jesus (see Luke 22:61). That look was his undoing, and he burst into tears. "All things betray thee, who betrayest Me."[1] The quick penitence of Peter became him. This story is told, not to pillory Peter, but to point to the grace by which he

[8] *Diogenes Laertius* XI.
[9] Gayley, *Classic Myths*, pp. 196-97.
[1] Francis Thompson, "The Hound of Heaven."

was restored. He was wiser than Judas: he wept, made confession, and found peace. "Go, tell his disciples and Peter" (Mark 16:7). Thus the truth of the Resurrection was especially granted to the man who had denied. He became a "rock" in very fact; for he who had quailed before the question from a servant girl faced a mob unafraid after Pentecost. That is why the story is told: that we may know that our denials need not be the last word, because Christ is pardon and power.

27:1-2. Pilate.—He was appointed procurator of Judea in A.D. 26, and held office for ten years. In the emperor's circle in Rome the appointment was doubtless regarded as "a small job." It was made at the pleasure of the emperor, presumably at the instance of friends. Pilate's palace was at Caesarea, and perhaps he was in Jerusalem at this time because the Passover crowds might cause trouble. Judea was a fractious little province, and the procuratorship was therefore no sinecure. Pilate was probably the kind of man who would seek that kind of appointment:

> . . . Man, proud man,
> Drest in a little brief authority,
> Most ignorant of what he's most assured.[2]

Commentators have found signs of compunction in him, and have argued that he was impressed by the spiritual power of Jesus; but the assumption has little to support it either in the Scriptures or in other historical records.

[2] Shakespeare, *Measure for Measure*, Act II, scene 2.

3 ¶ Then Judas, which had betrayed him, when he saw that he was condemned, repented himself, and brought again the thirty pieces of silver to the chief priests and elders,

4 Saying, I have sinned in that I have betrayed the innocent blood. And they said, What *is that* to us? see thou *to that.*

3 When Judas, his betrayer, saw that he was condemned, he repented and brought back the thirty pieces of silver to the chief priests and the elders, 4 saying, "I have sinned in betraying innocent blood." They said, "What is that to us? See to it yourself."

long. But from time to time Pilate had difficulties with his subjects—once because he brought troops into Jerusalem without removing from their insignia the medallions which bore the emperor's picture, and once because he seized temple funds to construct an aqueduct. His brutality in putting down a small uprising in Samaria led to his downfall (Josephus *Antiquities* XVIII. 3. 1-2; 4. 1-2).

b) Judas' Suicide (27:3-10)

This story of Judas' death probably comes to Matthew from oral tradition. The brief account in Acts 1:18-19 says that Judas used the money to buy a farm which came to be known as "the field of blood," and died a horrible death but not necessarily by his own hand. Behind both narratives may be a simple and primitive tradition that land was purchased with the money and that the betrayer came to a bad end. The details of Matthew's story are influenced by the scripture quotations in vss. 9-10.

3. The remorse of **Judas** is understandable in any case, but especially so if he did not intend that Jesus should be **condemned** (cf. on 26:14-16).

In point of fact he seems to have been devoid of principle; and, what is more, of real religion. His question "What is truth?" (John 18:38) was probably not an inquiry, but a sneer. Truth and God were a chimera; real men preferred to live in a real world where money, rank, and swords are the only valid currency. He stole the money of the temple tax to build an aqueduct. He despised the Jews, not least for their fanatic concern with religion: "Am I a Jew?" (John 18:35). The trial of Jesus shows this contempt: he tried expedient after expedient (Herod, Barabbas, scourging) to release Jesus, not because he had any pity for Jesus, but because he was resolved to outwit leaders whom he despised. He was ruthless. He knew no arbiter but the sword. Once he equipped his soldiers with medallions of the emperor, though this was a violation of the Pax Romana which made it a policy not to offend the religious scruples of the conquered peoples. He was finally deposed because of his brutality in suppressing a Samaritan revolt which actually was less a revolt than a demonstration of religious zeal.

At only one point was Pilate vulnerable: his pride in office. The Emperor Tiberius, though stern with treason, was equally stern with any ruler who dealt unjustly with conquered people. Pilate dared not risk being deposed, and that fact was his downfall. We have slim ground indeed for assuming any religious compunctions in such a man, and less ground for believing

that he was softened by the spiritual nobility of Jesus. His religion was probably a perfunctory emperor worship, and Jesus was to him a dreamer and a fool. Jesus in the hands of two men like Caiaphas and Pilate! In the aftermath of history was there ever a more striking instance of the weakness of the world's "power"? Yet we still trust in "power." Why? The trust is folly. Pilate now is a "horrible example"—a name in the Creed to prove that Jesus Christ was very man (though more indeed!) living in an actual world. Jesus would probably have died a violent death at the hands of Caiaphas, secretly or by public stoning, in any event; but he would not have been crucified except for Pontius Pilate.

3-10. The Death of Judas.— (See also Expos., vss. 6-7.) We must honestly face the discrepancies in the two accounts, that is, in this story as compared with Acts 1:18-19. Here we are told that Judas hanged himself; in Acts we are left to assume that he met some other violent end. There are other difficulties: Matthew has obviously been at some pains to explain the name of a cemetery, and somewhere along the line the mistake has been made of ascribing to Jeremiah a quotation that comes from Zechariah. The Exeg. has given us wise guidance, without any attempt at strained and unconvincing "reconciliations" of stories that can hardly be reconciled. The Jews thought of suicide as murder. We think of it with pity in those instances which show a mind driven beyond

5 And he cast down the pieces of silver in the temple, and departed, and went and hanged himself.	5 And throwing down the pieces of silver in the temple, he departed; and he went and hanged himself. 6 But the chief priests, taking the pieces of silver, said, "It is not lawful to put them into the treasury, since they are blood money." 7 So they took counsel, and bought with them the potter's field,
6 And the chief priests took the silver pieces, and said, It is not lawful for to put them into the treasury, because it is the price of blood.	
7 And they took counsel, and bought with them the potter's field, to bury strangers in.	

5-7. The remaining verses are an interesting example of Jewish Christian reasoning. Some teacher must have woven together the scripture passages in vss. 9-10 and used them as a sermon on Judas. It was assumed that all O.T. prophecies must be fulfilled in the days of the Messiah, and so nothing was more natural than to take these verses which referred to money and use them to piece out the fragmentary account of Judas' death. The **throwing down** of **the pieces of silver in the temple** is derived from Zech. 11:13, "So I took the thirty shekels of silver, and cast it into the treasury in the house of the LORD" (Amer. Trans.). "Treasury" (*ha'ôçār*) is probably the original reading of Zechariah, but the word has been changed in the M.T. to the similar (*hayyôçēr*), "the potter." Matthew (or his source) takes the word both ways and supposes that the prophecy is doubly fulfilled: the money was cast into the treasury and also given to the potter to buy the field. From this passage we derive the term **potter's field** to denote a cemetery for paupers. To the Jews suicide was murder, and they regarded it with horror.

rationality, and with recoil in those instances which seem deliberate. Suicide may strangely imply a kind of hope: the known world has failed the unhappy man, and the unknown cannot be a worse fate. But no man has right to play providence to his own life: he is neither wise enough nor pure enough to be his own god. If Judas killed himself, he is further proof that men and nations which are morally and spiritually dead proceed then to be their own hangmen in physical death.

Whatever the origin of this story, it is the sign of remorse. **When Judas . . . saw that he was condemned:** perhaps he did not intend to kill Jesus. Wickedness always brings more tragedy than it proposes or expects: "I did not mean to. . . ." **Repented** here is not a profound word: it seems to indicate a change of feeling rather than a change of will. What a pity that Judas made his confession to his fellow conspirators! The story would have had a still somber but perhaps a noble ending if Judas had confessed to his fellow disciples (they thus standing as representatives of the moral judgment of mankind) and to God. The early church was sure that Judas came to a "bad end." That faith is unshakable in mankind: God is not mocked. Sin finds us out, even if it is not found out: our excessive busyness and our poor excuses betray the inward chaos. It is unfortunate that we call a paupers' cemetery a "potter's field." Our age is condemned, and its standards are revealed as mercenary, when it regards all

poverty as a Judas state. Francis of Assisi married poverty before an altar which by that act was made doubly an altar. If Judas knew that he had **sinned in betraying innocent blood,** that is to his credit. He did not hide his wickedness. He is nobler in his death than Caiaphas and Pilate in their respectable loftiness. And if we feel pity, we may be sure that God's heart is not unmoved.

6-7. Conscience Twisted and Stained.—The callousness of the priests and elders leaves us almost afraid. Is human nature capable of such hardening? The story, from whatever source, provides illustration, from which we may well shrink back in revulsion, of the human mind trying to salve its wickedness. They had not done the actual betraying, so they were not guilty: "See to it yourself." That is an old, and very modern, evasion. Some years ago, in the heyday of a corrupt political machine, a cartoon appeared showing how the blame could be fixed. A number of men were grouped as if walking around and around in a circle, editor and politician and businessman and John Doe the voter, each with his thumb pointing accusingly over his shoulder at the man behind him. One of the acute problems of an age of huge organizations—in business, politics, war, and the church—is that conscience is spread so thin it disappears. Every one of us must constantly ask, "How much am I an accessory before the fact?" The "elders" had another trick of self-condonation: they observed all the proprieties of

8 Wherefore that field was called, The field of blood, unto this day.

9 Then was fulfilled that which was spoken by Jeremy the prophet, saying, And they took the thirty pieces of silver, the price of him that was valued, whom they of the children of Israel did value;

10 And gave them for the potter's field, as the Lord appointed me.

11 And Jesus stood before the governor: and the governor asked him, saying, Art thou the King of the Jews? And Jesus said unto him, Thou sayest.

12 And when he was accused of the chief priests and elders, he answered nothing.

to bury strangers in. 8 Therefore that field has been called the Field of Blood to this day. 9 Then was fulfilled what had been spoken by the prophet Jeremiah, saying, "And they took the thirty pieces of silver, the price of him on whom a price had been set by some of the sons of Israel, 10 and they gave them for the potter's field, as the Lord directed me."

11 Now Jesus stood before the governor; and the governor asked him, "Are you the King of the Jews?" Jesus said to him, "You have said so." 12 But when he was accused by the chief priests and elders, he made no

---

8. The field of blood is the name found also in Acts 1:19, where it is given as a translation of "Akeldama." It has been suggested that this Semitic word should mean "field of sleeping," i.e., cemetery, but this is by no means certain.

9. Then was fulfilled what had been spoken by the prophet. This is the formula which Matthew uses for a few special quotations (e.g., in 1:22). The passage is not from **Jeremiah**, but is a free paraphrase of Zech. 11:13, with some slight reminiscence of Jer. 18:2-3; 32:6-15.

c) The Hearing and Condemnation (27:11-26)

11. You have said so (σὺ λέγεις), like the similar phrase in 26:64, might be taken to mean "Yes." But it can also be regarded as a question, "Do *you* say so?" And it must be noted that Jesus refuses to answer the charges against him (vs. 14). This suggests that the accusers have twisted the evidence. Jesus is innocent of any revolutionary act, and knows that anyone who has heard his public teaching can testify to this. He certainly would not have said that he was **the King of the Jews** in the sense of claimant to the throne of the Maccabees and Herod, and nothing in his present behavior suggests such a claim. At the same time, he has been acclaimed as Messiah and he cannot deny that he has been anointed by God as the religious leader of the people to restore the true observance of the law (5:17).

---

religion. It was right to take money from the treasury to pay Judas, but it was not right to restore the money when he returned it and when the foul thing had been done! Deut. 23:18 was probably their historical authority: they had kept the letter of the law, and their conscience therefore was clean! We may well be afraid of the subterfuges by which we deceive ourselves and our neighbors, and by which we half hope to deceive God. It is possible in any age to use the forms of religion as substitute for the actual faith. "What doth the Lord require of thee, but to do justly, and to love mercy, and to walk humbly with thy God?" (Mic. 6:8). Those "elders" now seem guiltier than Judas. No religious form could cleanse their hand and heart. God is not mocked.

11-14. *Beginning of the Trial Before Pilate.* —Notice the charge that had been brought. It **was** no longer a charge of blasphemy against

God and the Jewish faith, but of treason against the Roman Empire. The real "crime" was actually neither blasphemy nor treason: it was the "crime" of a true soul taking issue with the vested interests of the temple leaders, and thereby threatening some vague trouble against the Roman state. Apparently Pilate knew the charge was false. He had no sympathy for Jesus —only a fool would spend himself in zeal for "truth" and "the gods"—but the procurator was worldling enough to see at once that the temple leaders had their own reasons for wishing to get rid of "the Man." So he asked Jesus, You, . . . **King of the Jews?** That sorry figure could not be king of anything by Pilate's tests. What did Jesus answer him? It is hard to tell. The phrase **thou sayest** is not clear. Moffatt translates it "certainly." But Branscomb [3] and others believe that Jesus made the reply purposely vague:

[3] *Gospel of Mark,* pp. 285-88.

13 Then said Pilate unto him, Hearest thou not how many things they witness against thee?

14 And he answered him to never a word; insomuch that the governor marveled greatly.

15 Now at *that* feast the governor was wont to release unto the people a prisoner, whom they would.

16 And they had then a notable prisoner, called Barabbas.

17 Therefore when they were gathered together, Pilate said unto them, Whom will ye that I release unto you? Barabbas, or Jesus which is called Christ?

answer. 13 Then Pilate said to him, "Do you not hear how many things they testify against you?" 14 But he gave him no answer, not even to a single charge; so that the governor wondered greatly.

15 Now at the feast the governor was accustomed to release for the crowd any one prisoner whom they wanted. 16 And they had then a notorious prisoner, called Bar-ab′bas.[l] 17 So when they had gathered, Pilate said to them, "Whom do you want me to release for you, Bar-ab′bas[l] or Jesus

[l] Some ancient authorities read *Jesus Barabbas*.

14. The word translated **wondered** is sometimes used to express awe in the presence of the supernatural (9:33), but **the governor wondered greatly** because most men, whether innocent or guilty, loudly protest their innocence.

15. The custom of amnesties at festival times is known the world over. It used to be said that there was no evidence for such a proceeding in Palestine at this time, but there is a Talmudical rule that a paschal lamb may be slaughtered for one who has been promised release from prison; see the article by C. B. Chavel, "The Releasing of a Prisoner on the Eve of Passover in Ancient Jerusalem," *Journal of Biblical Literature*, LX (1941), 273-78.

16-17. The Sinaitic Syriac and some Caesarean MSS read **Jesus Barabbas** (RSV mg.) in these two verses, and this is probably correct. The tendency would be to drop the name Jesus out of reverence for the Messiah. Mark 15:7 describes Barabbas as a rebel "who had committed murder in the insurrection." Perhaps the trouble over the aqueduct had occurred only recently (Josephus *Antiquities* XVIII. 3. 2) and Barabbas had been involved in it. Pilate would prefer to release the other **Jesus who is called Christ** because he was not politically dangerous.

"That is your statement." He was not **King of the Jews** as Pilate understood those words, and he was not **King of the Jews** as Jewish religionists or revolutionaries understood kingship. Would he then have said "Yes," and left himself open to a low interpretation of the answer? If he did make reply, he claimed to be God's anointed. But perhaps we would be wise to see in vs. 14 the central fact.

We cannot greatly stress the words **wondered greatly**. It is easy to ascribe to Pilate some measure of the homage which all right-minded men now feel in the presence of Jesus. But Pilate was of the earth, unprincipled and ruthless; and the only appeal that could be made to him, as the sequel shows, was through his self-interest. His "wonder" was probably only at sight of a man of the conquered race who did not noisily protest his innocence. Jesus before Pilate: it is no surprise that artists have been fascinated by the scene. Every expositor should study the Mihály von Munkácsy canvas.[4] It is

[4] *The Bible in Art*, ed. Clifton Harby (New York: Garden City Publishing Co., 1936), p. 232.

an amazing transcript of human emotions as they are revealed on the faces of the temple leaders, Pilate, the crowd, and Jesus. Easter throngs in Philadelphia, intent on Easter finery, are brought to reverent silence as they gaze on it from the busy aisles of a great department store. Who was doing the shuffling—Jesus or Pilate? Who was on the throne as leader of men? Who was being judged? Therein is the fascination and judgment of the picture: man displays his "power," but is still in other Hands. The Other, he with whom we have to do, was even then overturning all man's plans, and bringing to nought all man's wickedness and pride.

15-17, 21. *Jesus or Barabbas?*—Jesus was a common name at that time. It seems likely that certain early MSS are right in calling Barabbas by the name of Jesus Barabbas. The early church would tend to hide the name so far as Barabbas was concerned. Mark's awkward phrase omitting the man's own name, giving only the surname—"There was one named Barabbas" (Mark 15:7)—may thus be ex-

18 For he knew that for envy they had delivered him. | who is called Christ?" 18 For he knew that it was out of envy that they had delivered

---

18. **Envy** does not fully describe the motive of the Jewish authorities. They were offended by his cleansing of the temple and feared the power of a prophetic movement which endangered their prestige.

---

plained; and also the strange emphasis in Pilate's inquiry, **Jesus who is called Christ.** Branscomb has argued that the Barabbas incident has been "read back" into the story,[5] but Deissmann offers the shrewd comment that the elimination of the name of Jesus from Barabbas is evidence of the trustworthiness of the record.[6] We need not assume that all the members of the crowd called for the insurrectionist to be released: criers scattered through the mob by the high priest probably "touched off" enough enthusiasm for the "robber" to start a general tumult. We know little about the man. He was apparently a zealot, a patriot so intent on his country's liberation that he would resort to any violence. Perhaps he added brigandage to the zeal: Mark 15:7 tells us that he had "committed murder." His name means "son of a father," an ambiguity which may mean "son of a teacher." More than these facts we do not know. But we can understand how such a man might make an appeal to the patriotism of the crowd at the Passover.

Two men by the name of Jesus—and the choice still confronts mankind. On the surface it is the choice between noise and quietness. Barabbas appeals to the eye and the ear; Jesus to the conscience and the heart. One man works by bombast and the sword; the other by persuasion and proven love. More deeply it is a choice between coercion of the body and the winning of the soul. Suppose Barabbas had led his zealots to military victory over Rome: they must still keep the enemy at bay, having made him more obdurate by desire for revenge. The strategy of Jesus aims to make the enemy a friend of God, and therefore a friend of men. Robespierre was a revolutionary, like Barabbas, and was resolved on a new week of ten days, and new names for the days of the week, and new names for the months;[7] but revolutions only revolve unless men's wills are changed. So most deeply the choice is between God and man. Barabbas is intent upon a man-made scheme, with whatever show and play of emotion he may worship God; Jesus is intent upon God's will, and therefore brings heaven to earth. Every item in the Calvary story seems to be a

testing stone to separate dross from gold. Every generation must answer Pilate's question, **Barabbas or Jesus who is called Christ?** We blame the crowd that once gathered in Jerusalem, but can we claim that our generation has thus far made a better choice?

18. *For Envy?*—That is strange reason to offer. Does it mean envy of Jesus' popularity with the people, who clearly regarded him as a prophet, or envy of his miraculous power to heal, or envy of his very character and being? Pilate was worldly-wise enough to read earthy motives. We are told that he saw through the schemes of the temple leaders, and knew that they were moved by—envy! Many deeds and words of Jesus had aroused the anger of the high priest and his friends, and many motives impelled them to seek the prisoner's death. If one action of Jesus can be singled out as the prime occasion of their wrath, it would doubtless be his cleansing of the temple. That action may have made him something of a hero—for the crowd had no excessive love for the temple graft; he certainly threatened both the prestige and the profits of the Sadducean leaders. But if one motive were singled out in them, would it be envy?

Perhaps it would. The Italian painter Giotto has a picture of Envy—a being set on malicious gossip, eager to hear anything bad about a worthier neighbor; and so he is portrayed as having large, distended ears. He is greedy; and therefore he clutches a bag of gold with one hand, and reaches out with the other, his fingers sharpened to claws. He is poisonous in cunning; and so a serpent springs from his mouth; and, since slander always defames the slanderer, the fangs of the serpent fasten on Envy's own brow. He lives in self-torture and despair; so flames start about his feet, and burn both him and his world.[8] Pilate had reason to recognize envy when he saw it: it lived within his own breast. Darkness hates the light, and, while hating, wishes it were not darkness. Perhaps the venom of the world against a pure soul is a perverted yearning which slays that which it despairingly loves. Why should we envy Christ? His own love is given us, if we will receive it.

---

[5] *Op. cit.*, pp. 288-90.

[6] Quoted, Green, *Gospel According to Saint Matthew*, pp. 251-52.

[7] Lodge, *Student's Modern Europe*, p. 545.

[8] One of the Vices in the frescoes of "The Seven Virtues and Seven Vices" in the Arena chapel, Padua. For a description see Basil de Selincourt, *Giotto* (New York: Charles Scribner's Sons, 1905), p. 161.

19 ¶ When he was set down on the judgment seat, his wife sent unto him, saying, Have thou nothing to do with that just man: for I have suffered many things this day in a dream because of him.

20 But the chief priests and elders persuaded the multitude that they should ask Barabbas, and destroy Jesus.

21 The governor answered and said unto them, Whether of the twain will ye that I release unto you? They said, Barabbas.

22 Pilate saith unto them, What shall I do then with Jesus which is called Christ? *They* all say unto him, Let him be crucified.

him up. 19 Besides, while he was sitting on the judgment seat, his wife sent word to him, "Have nothing to do with that righteous man, for I have suffered much over him today in a dream." 20 Now the chief priests and the elders persuaded the people to ask for Bar-ab'bas and destroy Jesus. 21 The governor again said to them, "Which of the two do you want me to release for you?" And they said, "Bar-ab'bas." 22 Pilate said to them, "Then what shall I do with Jesus who is called Christ?" They all said, "Let him be crucified."

---

19. Matthew tells of revelations **in a dream** in 1:20; 2:12, 13, 19. Caesar's wife Calpurnia tried to keep him from going to the Forum on the day of his death because she had been warned by a dream (Appian *Civil Wars* II. 480).

20. One need not suppose that all **the people** were **persuaded . . . to ask for Barabbas and destroy Jesus.** The noisier members of the crowd needed little urging; and if any of Jesus' true friends were present they were helpless.

---

19. *Pilate's Wife.*—This striking incident is recorded only in Matthew. We wish we knew more about the "heroine." Legend tells us that her name was Claudia Procla, that she showed interest in the Judaistic faith of the people whom her husband ruled as conqueror, and that finally she became a Christian. The Greek church has therefore canonized her. But there is only conjecture for such an act. Her plea to her husband is not incredible: the Exeg. above reminds us that Calpurnia had a similar dream regarding Caesar, and made a similar plea. We know that the Roman senate permitted the wife of a procurator to accompany her husband if he went to a fairly peaceable land. It is easy to imagine that rumors of Jesus and his works had reached the palace, and not too difficult to believe that she may have seen and heard Jesus in the streets of Jerusalem. Perhaps she had been moved by his nobility and compassion. Add her knowledge of Tiberius' anger against any procurator who coerced the innocent, and we have ground enough for her dream. Perhaps she feared for her husband's continuance in office. Often a dream provides grotesque or distorted outlet for a suppressed hope or fear.

But we are still indulging in conjecture as we make the guess. It is better to be faithful to our ignorance. Perhaps Clow is right in his surmise that Pilate's wife had the insight of a true-hearted woman, and that she was trying to stay her husband's headlong callousness.[9] But we might be as near the mark if we said that she was a superstitious woman frightened by a dream. We do not know. There are meanings in

dreams, as modern psychology has taught us, and there is some value in reading them. God can use that medium for his secret message. But it is on any count a second-rate religion that recommends an action because of what has been **suffered . . . in a dream.** Our waking conscience under the impact of Christ is a better mentor than our dreams. God is more likely to speak to us clearly through our conscious prayers than through the subconscious release of our repressions.

22. *Then What Shall I Do with Jesus?*—Who could have guessed that the question would have come hurtling down the years? Every man is here Pilate. He puts the query to his world—and to himself. In every life the throne is set, the clamor raised, and the question asked. Every political party must decide: **What shall I do with Jesus?** Every chamber of commerce and every labor union must meet that challenge. Every church also: for whenever the church confronts the racial issue, or a building program, or a problem of church unity, Christ himself stands behind the issue; and always the real crux is what shall be done with him. He is in truth the inescapable Christ. The novelists cannot long forget him, as books like Lew Wallace's *Ben Hur* or Antonio Fogazzaro's *The Saint* well show. Drama cannot exile him, but must produce plays like *The Servant in the House*, *The Passing of the Third Floor Back*, and *Family Portrait*. Whenever a marriage is planned, the question must be asked, "Shall the service be in his name?" Whenever we see a beggar on the street, we overhear a Voice saying, "Inasmuch as ye have done it unto one of

---

[9] *Day of the Cross*, ch. vii, especially pp. 103-5.

23 And the governor said, Why, what evil hath he done? But they cried out the more, saying, Let him be crucified.	23 And he said, "Why, what evil has he done?" But they shouted all the more, "Let him be crucified."

23. Why, what evil has he done? The Gospels give the impression that Pilate either vacillated somewhat weakly and then gave in to pressure from the crowd, or had decided at the start to crucify Jesus and was playing a heartless game. One must remember, however, that the Emperor Tiberius was very severe with governors who mistreated his provincial subjects—indeed it was because of brutality that Pilate lost his position—and therefore the procurator hesitated to condemn an innocent and harmless man. On the other hand, Tiberius was merciless toward anyone suspected of treason. This trait of Tiberius' character made it easier for Jesus' enemies to persuade Pilate to do their will. Like Herod Antipas, who executed John the Baptist, he preferred to take no chances of an insurrection. John 19:12 gives an accurate picture of the political situation.

the least of these. . . ." (25:40). Christmas comes, and he is with us. Easter arrives, and we cannot escape the sign of his cross. We date a letter—from his birthday. Wherever two people meet, Jesus is the shadowy Third.

Pilate was confronted with alternatives when he asked what he should do with Jesus. So is every man. We can be content to admire Christ, and offer him—like the newspapers—an occasional editorial obeisance. That is a safe choice which permits us for the rest of the year to fill the columns with sports, business, political comment, wars, advertising, society news, and motion-picture programs. Or we can ignore Jesus, or try to ignore him, and forget meanwhile that indifference is a still more cruel slur than any outright opposition. Studdert-Kennedy has a poem which represents Christ as crouching against a city wall, not because he is being shuffled off to some new crucifixion, but because nobody gives him even passing notice.[1] Or we can reject Jesus, as did Pilate. We can crucify him. That is still the favorite course. Many church people, who pay him lip service, would condemn him were he to reappear in the flesh and speak as once in Palestine. Whatever we do, he reappears—just when we think we are rid of him; and then the question must be asked again, **What shall I do with Jesus?**

Within the Christian church, despite all its defections, there has always been a heart of loyalty which has enthroned Jesus as "Prophet, Priest, and King." He is the Prophet of adventurous truth. He is Priest who, being Son of man and Son of God, has made atonement for the sins of the world. He is King, and by right claims man's utter fealty. Therefore Reims Cathedral is erected in his name, and Handel's *Messiah* is dedicated to him, and the art of Raphael's "Sistine Madonna" is offered to him in homage of the soul. The main question is not primarily one of theology or philosophy or or-

ganization (through whatever "ism") but one of personal response to Jesus Christ. Pilate little dreamed that he was asking the question which is the crux of life and death. **What shall I do with Jesus?** Perhaps the whole reason for our human pilgrimage is that we may give answer.

23. What Evil Has He Done?—Pilate intended no acknowledgment of purity in Christ. On the contrary he was sparring for time, vacillating as to his own course. In his fear of Tiberius he could neither condone treason nor punish the innocent. In his hatred for the temple leaders he had no wish to do their desire, but he had still to consult his own interests. He hoped that the crowd might plead for the release of Jesus. Therefore his question. But every question Pilate asked has become an unwitting tribute to Jesus, and Pilate himself is now the dark foil for Jesus' radiance. According to Luke, Pilate twice declared that he could find "no fault" (Luke 23:4, 14) in Jesus; according to John, the protestation was made three times (John 18:38; 19:4, 6). The Christian church has found in the words an unintended confession of the sinlessness of Christ. "He . . . who knew no sin," says Paul to the Corinthian church (II Cor. 5: 21). "In all points tempted like as we are, yet without sin," says the author of Hebrews (Heb. 4:15). There can be no logical proof in detailed fact. Who are we to determine sinlessness? Blind men do not judge the light. All we know is that the critics of Christ cancel each other (those who declare him too sentimental answer those who think him too stern); and that we ourselves, with the scrutiny of the years as our asset, can "find no fault in this man" (Luke 23:4). J. Middleton Murry, positing some sense of sin in Jesus, was yet obliged to add that probably we would not have counted it sin [2]—an academic and unreal argument in very truth!

"Sinlessness" is a poor word. It is negative,

[1] "Indifference."

[2] *Jesus Man of Genius*, pp. 8-9.

24 ¶ When Pilate saw that he could prevail nothing, but *that* rather a tumult was made, he took water, and washed *his* hands before the multitude, saying, I am innocent of the blood of this just person: see ye *to it.*

25 Then answered all the people, and said, His blood *be* on us, and on our children.

24 So when Pilate saw that he was gaining nothing, but rather that a riot was beginning, he took water and washed his hands before the crowd, saying, "I am innocent of this man's blood;[m] see to it yourselves." 25 And all the people answered, "His blood be on us and on our children!"

[m] Some authorities read *this righteous blood* or *this righteous man's blood.*

24-25. At the time when the Gospels were written, relations between the Christian church and the Jewish community were far from happy. The Jewish authorities were now excommunicating Christians (John 9:34; 16:2) and about this time a curse on heretics was added to the synagogue service. Christian Jews who were thus excluded no longer had the privileges which as Jews they had always enjoyed in the empire. Their assemblies were unlicensed and illegal, and they were liable to persecution. It is not strange that they tried to emphasize their loyalty to the emperor and to prove that their Messiah had been unjustly condemned because of the machinations of Jewish leaders. The story contained in these verses arose because of this tragic situation. It is hard to imagine that Pilate would make this dramatic gesture of handwashing. It would be an act of weakness in the presence of "colonials," and furthermore would put Pilate in an impossible position with respect to the emperor. If he actually held Jesus to be innocent, he might be asked why he had executed him; if, on the other hand, he was guilty, the governor must so proclaim. Certainly **the people** of Israel (ὁ λαός) would not cry, **His blood be on us and on our children;** i.e., "We accept the responsibility and guilt." This represents the anti-Judaism of later Christians who regard the Jewish War as a punishment for the crucifixion of Jesus. The apocryphal Gospel of Peter develops the tradition still further. None of the Jews washes his hands at the time of the condemnation, and after Jesus is buried the leaders and people cry out, "Woe for our sins! The judgment and the end of Jerusalem have drawn near" (James, *Apocryphal N.T.,* pp. 90, 92).

and the passion of Jesus' purity is always a positive passion of holy love. Pilate consulted his own pride; Jesus obeyed his Father's will. Pilate followed the standards of earth (and that was why he asked, **What evil has he done?**); Jesus walked in the light of God. We can find in Jesus no deviation from this ardor of good will toward God and man. Therefore he died, for "every one that doeth evil hateth the light" (John 3:20). Therefore he could die for us, "the just for the unjust" (I Pet. 3:18). When doctors give a transfusion of blood, they are careful that the blood shall be free from disease and shall be of the proper type. Our blood is weak and impure. Where shall one be found whose blood is true, yet comes from veins like our veins? It is a poor parable, but it may give some insight into a profound truth: "For our sake he made him to be sin who knew no sin, so that in him we might become the righteousness of God" (II Cor. 5:21).

24-25. *The Hand Washing.*—We must be true to the Exeg. It is quite improbable Pilate would insist that he was not guilty of an innocent man's death: that act would have exposed him to the instant reprimand of Tiberius. It is

even more improbable that the temple leaders and the people would assume a blood guilt. It seems likely that this story has been "read back" into the record as a reflection of the animus of the early church against the Jewish leaders. In one sense the church cannot be too greatly blamed for the animus: the early followers of Jesus were in many instances excommunicated from the synagogue, robbed of certain privileges under the empire because they were "heretics," and ostracized in the markets. Behind this story we can see the tragic consequence of synagogue coercion: it has had its evil fruit in anti-Semitism through all the succeeding years. How blessed the synagogue might have been if it had made a welcome for the "heretics"! Likewise we can see the baleful results of the animus in the early church: not always have Christians shown the meekness of their Lord.

Who *did* kill Jesus? In the first instance the vested interests of the temple. Christ's opposition to money greed and pride of privilege was a worse "crime" than any alleged blasphemy. That fact should be noted: the real "heresy" is opposition to man's comfort and pride. In the

26 ¶ Then released he Barabbas unto them: and when he had scourged Jesus, he delivered *him* to be crucified.

27 Then the soldiers of the governor took Jesus into the common hall, and gathered unto him the whole band *of soldiers*.

26 Then he released for them Bar-ab'bas, and having scourged Jesus, delivered him to be crucified.

27 Then the soldiers of the governor took Jesus into the praetorium, and they gath-

---

Where, then, does the guilt lie? Certainly not on the Jewish people as a whole, or on any considerable number of them. The high-priestly group, who were largely Sadducean politicians concerned mainly for their own privileges, must bear some of the responsibility. But the person most to blame is Pilate, who if he had been just and morally courageous, would never have given such a sentence. Jesus' condemnation is in fact a dramatic manifestation of the general sin of mankind. Human beings continually acquiesce in slaying the innocent in order to protect their own privileges, or to maintain what they think is the right social order, or because the forthrightness of prophets offends their self-righteousness.

26. We know from Josephus (*Jewish War* II. 14. 9) that it was a Roman custom to scourge condemned men before crucifying them. A leather whip, with pieces of bone and metal set in it, was used. Jesus was **delivered** over to the soldiers.

B. The Crucifixion (27:27-56)

1. Jesus Is Mistreated by the Soldiers (27:27-31)

27. The **soldiers** were probably a detachment of the Second Italian Cohort, which was stationed in Palestine at the time. It is unlikely that **the whole battalion** or cohort of six hundred men was present.

The **praetorium** was the government house or seat of the procurator during his visits to Jerusalem; his permanent headquarters were at Caesarea. A tradition which is not older than the Middle Ages identifies the praetorium with the Castle of Antonia, which was undoubtedly located at the northwest corner of the temple enclosure (see Hugues Vincent, "L'Antonia et le Prétoire," *Revue Biblique*, XLII [1933], p. 83). But Pilate's

second instance Pilate was to blame, despite the attempt of the early church to gloss over his cowardice. He could have saved Jesus, and he should have saved him: but there seemed to be less risk to Pilate in Jesus' dying than in his living, and so Jesus died. **All the people** were not apostate as Matthew's record implies, but Jewry was faithless and cannot be acquitted of blame. The disciples also, by denial and treachery and fear, added to their Master's pain. The plain fact is that everyone had some share, greater or less, in the deep guilt of the Crucifixion. We must lay that to our own charge. No hand washing could have availed. How easily we think we can transfer our culpability! How easily we devise expedients to excuse ourselves! A man cannot be redeemed unless he makes some real attempt at honesty. We think almost inevitably of Lady Macbeth: she could not cleanse her hands with water—nor her heart.[3] Cleansing comes through his sacrifice whom we send to a cross.

27-30. *The Second Mocking of Jesus.*—The devilishness of the horseplay of the soldiers almost sears the page, as indeed it sears our mind

in the reading. The soldier's life is beset by temptations. He may begin as a crusader. But in our time at least, hatred is whipped up by propaganda; and in the fear and violence of battle elementary passions are loosed. Some soldiers are like Donald Hankey,[4] but some become like the group which mocked and tortured a helpless Jesus, and all too many become calloused. We defend our bodies—at dire risk to our souls. Every item in the mockery has become the insignia of Jesus' nobility. The scarlet robe was probably a soldier's red cloak, but it is now the crimson of royalty. The crown was probably a laurel wreath such as victors wore, and Jesus has made it a victor's wreath in very truth. The reed has become a scepter, a better scepter than any made in pride of wealth or rank, for a meek scepter well becomes the meek Savior. The mock homage of the soldiers, an echo of the "Hail, victor!" with which the Roman populace greeted an emperor returning victorious from the wars, is now the homage of all the reverent world. This is a miracle of God's spirit: everything was done to Jesus to ensure his eclipse in shame, but the black clouds have

---

[3] Shakespeare, *Macbeth*, Act V, scene 1.

[4] *A Student in Arms* (E. P. Dutton & Co., 1917).

28 And they stripped him, and put on him a scarlet robe.

29 ¶ And when they had platted a crown of thorns, they put it upon his head, and a reed in his right hand: and they bowed the knee before him, and mocked him, saying, Hail, King of the Jews!

30 And they spit upon him, and took the reed, and smote him on the head.

31 And after that they had mocked him, they took the robe off from him, and put his own raiment on him, and led him away to crucify him.

32 And as they came out, they found a man of Cyrene, Simon by name: him they compelled to bear his cross.

ered the whole battalion before him. 28 And they stripped him and put a scarlet robe upon him, 29 and plaiting a crown of thorns they put it on his head, and put a reed in his right hand. And kneeling before him they mocked him, saying, "Hail, King of the Jews!" 30 And they spat upon him, and took the reed and struck him on the head. 31 And when they had mocked him, they stripped him of the robe, and put his own clothes on him, and led him away to crucify him.

32 As they were marching out, they came upon a man of Cy-re′ne, Simon by name; this man they compelled to carry

---

headquarters were much more probably at the palace of Herod, located at the present Citadel, at the western wall of the Old City, for later procurators lived there (Josephus *Jewish War* II. 14. 8; 15. 5; V. 4. 4; see also Gustaf Dalman, *Jerusalem und sein Gelände* [Gütersloh: Bertelsmann, 1930], p. 86).

28. The **scarlet robe** is often thought to have been the sagum or Roman soldier's scarlet cloak. The soldiers **put it upon him** as a mock-royal vestment because they are about to hail him as king.

29. The **crown of thorns** corresponds to a royal diadem, and the **reed** (a touch added by Matthew) to a scepter. **Hail, King of the Jews!** reminds one of the salutation to the emperor: *"Ave, Caesar, victor, imperator!"* (cf. on vs. 37).

2. THE JOURNEY TO THE CROSS (27:32)

From the time of the Punic wars the Romans had employed crucifixion as a punishment for rebels, slaves, and criminals of the lowest classes. Josephus tells how, at the time of the siege of Jerusalem, the Romans crucified so many Jews who escaped from the city "that there was not enough room for the crosses or enough crosses for the bodies" (*Jewish War* V. 11. 1). Crucifixion was death by torture. At the place of execution upright poles had been driven into the ground. The condemned man was scourged and then forced to carry, not the entire cross, but the *patibulum* or crossbeam. Upon arrival at the place he was stripped, his hands were nailed or tied to the crossbeam, his body was supported on the pole by a block, his legs were lashed out in an unnatural position, and his feet were fixed to the upright stake so that they were just off the ground. Thirst,

---

only enhanced the brightness of his light. He has returned triumphant from a nobler warfare. There is always danger that the N.T. story may become a faraway page—a picture on which we may or may not gaze. So let us say to ourselves again that this mocking may be on the near side of our eyes, and even within our central heart. Perhaps a merely perfunctory loyalty or an indifference is harder for Christ to bear than outright hostility. **They spat upon him, and . . . struck him.** But to treat him as if he did not matter or did not exist is not any milder insult or any gentler blow.

32. *The Man Who Carried the Cross.*—Simon evidently came from the populous Jewish colony in Cyrene. The tradition that he was a Negro,

though we could wish it true, can gather almost no evidence. It is far likelier that he was a faithful Jew visiting Jerusalem for the Passover. His two sons, Rufus and Alexander, may have been well known in the Christian church (Mark 15:21; Rom. 16:13). How little Simon could have guessed, when he left Cyrene, what would befall him in Jerusalem! Jesus sank under the weight of the crossbeam: he was weak from scourging and from anguish of soul. Those thongs, loaded with jagged pieces of bone, were the proper symbol of the treachery and violence of men. The Roman soldiers, who would never carry that shameful gallows, impressed Simon for the task. We do not know if Simon's face had shown pity or if he resented the odious

33 And when they were come unto a place called Golgotha, that is to say, a place of a skull,

his cross. **33** And when they came to a place called Gol'go-tha (which means the place of

---

exposure, and the cutting off of circulation added to the torture. Men sometimes suffered on the cross for long periods before death released them. Jesus seems to have been unable to carry the crossbeam, and **a man of Cyrene** in North Africa, **Simon by name**, was impressed into service. He was probably a member of the large Jewish community in Cyrene (cf. Acts 11:20; 13:1), and he must have become a Christian, since his sons Alexander and Rufus were well known to members of the church (Mark 15:21).

The traditional Stations of the Cross begin in the Via Dolorosa, one of the principal east-west streets of ancient Jerusalem, at the barracks near the present Chapel of the Flagellation and the Convent of the Sisters of Zion. An ancient pavement, sometimes thought to be the "Gabbatha" of John 19:13, has been discovered at the Antonia, the site of which lies between the chapel and convent and may be partly occupied by both. The stations continue west and south from this point to the Church of the Holy Sepulchre (see Hugues Vincent and F.-M. Abel, *Jérusalem* [Paris: Gabalda, 1914-1922], II, 3, pp. 562-86, and map on p. 627). But if, as seems probable, the praetorium was not at the Antonia but at Herod's palace (see note on vs. 27), the original Way of the Cross began on the other side of the city, and its further course is unknown.

3. JESUS ON THE CROSS (27:33-44)

33. The Aramaic word *galgaltā'* means **skull** or head. The usual assumption is that the place was a hill whose form resembled a skull. The traditional location of **Golgotha** is within the precincts of the Church of the Holy Sepulchre. Although this is far inside

---

burden. One moment he was spectator, the next moment he was moving in that strange procession. The two thieves were presumably robbers, men of violence. But who was the third? He did not look like a man of violence. Soon Simon was carrying that man's cross, a gallows reserved for rebels against the empire and for lowest criminals. Often life compels us to some irksome task, and we find—life in the burden. Often we ourselves must choose whether we shall be spectators of the woe of the world or sharers of it.

What did Jesus say to Simon as they trudged toward Calvary? Jesus spoke to the weeping women (Luke 23:27-31): it is hard to imagine that he was silent to Simon. Perhaps Simon then and there became a follower of Christ. Perhaps the word which Jesus spoke and the blessing he gave were so God-laden that Simon became a new man. We would like to think that Simon sought out Jesus' disciples, and that he was with them in the joy of the Resurrection. We do not know. But we can be forgiven for imagining that when Simon reached his home in Cyrene, he called his boys and wife, and began to tell them: "Hear what a strange thing happened to me in Jerusalem!" Alexander and Rufus became Christians: that we know.

A Grecian philosopher, who called himself "the friend of wisdom," when asked why he attended the Olympian games, answered: "Some are attracted with the desire of obtaining crowns and honours, others come to expose their different commodities to sale, while curiosity draws a third class." Pythagoras adds, not without some self-satisfaction, that while many struggle for "the glory of a name" or "the advantages of fortune," a few are "gratified to be spectators of the wonders, the hurry, and the magnificence of the scene."[5] Many people share his notion that a philosophic spectator plays a noble role—like an angel or God. But it is not given to anyone merely to look on: we are born under obligation. Least of all is it given to God and angels. Angels rejoice to do God's bidding, and God incarnate in his Son carries a heavy crossbeam—to Calvary. At long last there may be only two courses open to us—to help crucify him, or to help carry his cross.

33. Golgotha.—A favorite hymn of the Passiontide begins:

> Beneath the cross of Jesus
> I fain would take my stand.[6]

But there are recoils by which a man with any shred of honor would rather stand anywhere than there, for nowhere else is there such damning indictment of our human wickedness. Yet perhaps that is why we should take our stand to

[5] J. Lempriere, *A Classical Dictionary* (London: Thomas & Joseph Allman, 1827), p. 581.
[6] Elizabeth C. Clephane.

34 ¶ They gave him vinegar to drink mingled with gall: and when he had tasted *thereof,* he would not drink.	a skull) [34] they offered him wine to drink, mingled with gall; but when he tasted it,

the walls of the present Old City, it may have been outside the second wall of Jerusalem, which was standing in the first century—according to Heb. 13:12, Jesus suffered outside the gate. Unfortunately the exact location of the second wall has never been settled. It is possible that the traditional Calvary was once a rocky eminence, which was largely cut away in subsequent years, for the Holy Sepulchre is a rock-cut tomb, and west of the rotunda which encloses it is a rock fourteen feet high in which are the so-called tombs of Joseph of Arimathaea and Nicodemus. The tradition cannot be traced further back than the fourth century, but this is the only site for Golgotha and the sepulchre which has any archaeological basis. The so-called "Garden Tomb" or "Gordon's Calvary," north of Herod's Gate, is, however, more helpful to the pilgrim who wishes to picture to himself what Golgotha looked like.

34. It was a pious Jewish custom to give a condemned man unmixed wine or wine with an opiate in it to make him unconscious. Mark 15:23 speaks of "myrrhed wine,"

---

watch Jesus die: we had better face the whole truth. In these next nine expositions we shall see what happened in death to the purest soul earth has ever known. How can we ever again trust human nature except as human nature is flung back on the mercy and power of God?

Jesus was first scourged with thongs loaded with metal or pieces of bone. That was a cruelty which, for cruelty's sake, Rome dealt to a man condemned to be crucified. So Jesus trudged to Calvary with open wounds and streaming blood. He was compelled to carry the crossbeam of his gallows, and we are left to infer that he sank beneath the load. The Exeg. has given us a moving description of the Cross itself. The victim suffered from exposure to heat and a swarm of flies, and from a worse exposure of flesh and mind to the insults of sadistic men; for the Cross lifted him not far from the ground. Jesus would not wish us to stress his physical sufferings, for these were not the worst of his pain, but truth requires that we confront them. The unnatural position of the arms and legs, the drawing down of the blood, the accompanying thirst, were all a torture that devils might have devised. Sometimes a man would hang there through days of slow death. Jesus was so spent in body and soul that he died after a few hours.

> There is a method in man's wickedness;
> It grows up by degrees.[7]

When human pride—such as Caiaphas' coveting of gold and rank, or Pilate's lust for empire—is full grown, it crucifies the Christ of God. "Beneath the cross of Jesus" we see, as nowhere else, the sinfulness of sin; and we should not shrink from the sight, however deeply we ourselves may be condemned. But if that were all we could see, it might almost be best for us to seek a Judas end. Blessedly it is not all, for, as we take our stand, we are stricken too by the sight of divine love. Perhaps this conviction was given its force through the Resurrection; perhaps Jesus' followers then learned to say, "He is God's anointed. Therefore his words shall endure. Therefore his death is the new Passover. Therefore his power avails now to save us from the sin that sent him to a cross." However the conviction came, it abides; and the Cross now means God's love more than it means human sin. Therefore it is a call to us to follow, as forgiven men—"the high calling of God in Christ Jesus" (Phil. 3:14).

Apparently the hill was shaped like a skull. Jesus died on a hill, not in a cave: his death was as open as his life. Tennyson has a description of Death as a warrior—a skeleton "high on a night-black horse," issuing forth at midnight. But when Gareth's sword cut through the skull, there was in it

> . . . the bright face of a blooming boy
> Fresh as a flower new-born.[8]

It is a poor illustration. The expositor's despair is that there are no parallels for the work of Christ. But the skull of that hill is now broken by the courage and compassion of God in Christ, so that there is in it the birth of a new life for all the world.

34. *To Meet Death with Open Eyes.*—We must notice discrepancies in the three accounts of this incident. Matthew says that Jesus tasted wine mixed with gall, and then refused it; Mark says the wine was an opiate, and that Jesus would not drink it (Mark 15:23); and John

[7] Francis Beaumont and John Fletcher, *A King and No King*, Act V, scene 4.

[8] *Idylls of the King*, "Gareth and Lynette, l. 1373.

35 And they crucified him, and parted his garments, casting lots: that it might be fulfilled which was spoken by the prophet, They parted my garments among them, and upon my vesture did they cast lots.

he would not drink it. **35** And when they had crucified him, they divided his gar-

---

but Matthew changes this to **gall.** His thought is that the prophecy of Ps. 69:21 has been fulfilled. The **vinegar** of KJV, which means "sour wine," may also be derived from that psalm verse.

35. Perhaps the **garments** of a condemned man were the perquisites of his executioners. One may suppose either that the detail is supplied from Ps. 22:18 or that the actual course of events suggested to Christians that the prophecy had been fulfilled. The quotation added by KJV has Matthew's usual formula and is attested by three uncials, some O.L. MSS, and other authorities; but it is in the exact wording of the LXX and is probably a later addition to the text.

---

says that Jesus "received" the vinegar (John 19:30). Almost certainly Mark gives the trustworthy story. **They gave him:** who were **they?** Our Gospel seems to assume that they were Roman soldiers, but it is likelier that they were the women of Jerusalem who made it a practice thus to temper Roman cruelty. If the deed was compassion, Jesus, we may be sure, found comfort in it even while refusing it. Anesthetics are now rightly regarded as a boon. Pain in itself is no blessing: it is only a laceration. But pain nevertheless has its own revealings to those who bear it in true spirit. Why did Jesus refuse the opiate? Perhaps in the courage of a stanch soul. The Browning words come to mind:

> . . . so—one fight more
> The best and the last!
> I would hate that death bandaged my eyes and forebore,
> And bade me creep past.[9]

But perhaps there were deeper reasons: perhaps Jesus was resolved to be "tempted like as we are" (Heb. 4:15), carrying to the final moment of his life the full sharing of our human journey.

All this being true, we may not yet have probed to the deepest ground of Jesus' refusal of the stupefying draught. He had prayed that "this cup" might pass (26:39), but that in any event he might do God's will. The cup remained—in what bitterness! He was resolved to carry obedience to the last moment of life, even though God's purpose might be hid in mystery. So he met the pain that he could have escaped. He greeted death with open eyes. Suppose we had not had "the words from the Cross." Think through those seven words: they are a sevenfold altar-light in our darkened world. This treasure is ours because Jesus, whatever pain might come, would not drug his mind in the onset of death. John's Gospel gives us words of Jesus that anticipate the divine courage of the Cross:

[9] "Prospice."

"The cup which my Father hath given me, shall I not drink it?" (John 18:11). Therefore he refused the other cup, even on a cross.

35. *They Cast Lots.*—They gambled beneath the Cross. Notice how the Gospel, following Mark's account, hurries over the phrase **and they crucified him:** that was a perfidy on which we hardly dare to dwell. The underclothing of a man thus killed was apparently divided among the soldiers, who then threw dice for the tunic. In this instance the tunic, according to John (19:23-24), had especial value. If John is right, the gambling may have been in tense excitement. Gambling is not wrong in itself, for life obliges us to take risks at almost every turn of the road. The parable of the talents blames the one-talent man for not taking risks. But gambling in which we play our own providence with risks that we arrange, for which we use gifts that God has given, for earthly and greedy rewards—that is another item. Here we see the end result of what the world calls gambling: casting lots for the clothes of a Christ we have crucified. It is a sorry business.

Caiaphas and Pilate and their respective followers also gambled that day, perhaps without knowing it. They said, "I will take a risk that man can control his world and that God does not care." They cast lots for their pride against conscience, for their plans against God's plans. They had a "sure thing": their violence and hate were to have the last word. They gambled —to their eternal loss. When Japan marched into China to seize Chinese land, a New York columnist wrote his article on the theme: "It will come back!" God sometimes seems to be only an absentee God, and often his ways seem slow, but a man is a fool to gamble against God.

Shall we say in deep reverence that Jesus also took his risks that day? "I, if I be lifted up from the earth, will draw all men unto me" (John 12:32). How could he tell? That venture, judged by the sight of the eyes, was doomed to

36 And sitting down they watched him there;	ments among them by casting lots; **36** then they sat down and kept watch over him
37 And set up over his head his accusation written, THIS IS JESUS THE KING OF THE JEWS.	there. **37** And over his head they put the charge against him, which read, "This is

36. They kept watch over him, perhaps to keep his friends from rescuing him. Matthew adds this as a preparation for vss. 62-66.

37. It was Roman custom to put a titulus around the neck of a criminal stating the crime for which he was condemned. **The charge** in this case can be identified as *crimen laesae majestatis* or high treason. It is expressed in these words in order to give the Jewish provincials an unmistakable reminder: "This is what we Romans will do to any 'King of the Jews.' " This titulus was very offensive to Jewish sensibilities (John 19:21-22) and is absolute proof that Jesus' case was disposed of in the Roman court.

fail. "Father, into thy hands I commend my spirit" (Luke 23:46). But would God ever bring to harvest the seeds that he had cast into the cruel soil of his day? It seemed a poor risk. See the men gambling for his garments: see him daring a gallows and a soul against the worst that men and history might do. There is the contrast of dark and bright in very truth. The Christians were sometimes called "riskers" in the early days of the church. They buried the dead in times of plague, when others would not risk life in such a task. Paul says of the loyalty of Epaphroditus that "he nearly died for the work of Christ, risking his life to complete your service to me" (Phil. 2:30). "Risking" is there the exact translation, and it throws a sudden light on the KJV. The Christian must take risks, for his faith is not a timid respectability: he must take the risks to which Christ has pointed him by the venture of the Cross.

36. They Watched Him There.—That word watched does not mean that they looked at him, but that they guarded him. They still believed that he might be an insurrectionist, and that his followers might try to rescue him. Besides, crucified men were sometimes taken from the cross in what seemed their death throes only to be revived. Death came with slow agony on the cross, and the soldiers on guard duty were therefore allowed to sit. Always the world assumes that gentler folk may be ready to use the world's own violence. So Jesus may be an insurrectionist, and men must be on guard. So George Fox, the Quaker, suffered imprisonment eight times because the world thought him a dangerous character![1] So the enemies of Jesus misread his motives, and in the blunder they revealed their own. Of course they also watched him in the sense that they gazed, with curiosity of blood desire, upon his agony. A story of a Christian youth induced to attend a fight in the Roman arena tells us that at first he refused to watch, and covered his eyes with his hands, but

later opened his eyes with a cry of dark desire.[2] There are black perversities in us that we gratify at our peril, and at the peril of all that is good in our world. They thought they were guarding Jesus. It is always the blindness of empire to imagine that it can imprison a soul. "John Brown's Body," though often sung unthinkingly, has its primal truth. The truth gathers unearthly light and power in the soul of Jesus. Even then he was escaping them. Even then God was planning a broken tomb. It was he who was guarding them against every onslaught of evil, if they had only known.

37. King of the Jews.—Again we are confronted by different accounts in the different Gospels. Mark's title is simplest: "The King of the Jews" (Mark 15:26). Matthew prefixes the name Jesus. John has a longer prefix, "Jesus of Nazareth" (John 19:19); while Luke tells us that the inscription read, "This is the King of the Jews" (Luke 23:38). John adds the information that the title was written in Latin, Greek, and Hebrew. Mark's account has prior claim. Our present knowledge does not go far beyond that comment. The Romans were accustomed to announce, in gypsum letters on a rough board, the crime for which a man was executed. This titulus was hung round the culprit's neck, and apparently was later fastened above his cross. So Jesus was killed for treason. The Roman power is chargeable with the actual deed. The accusation, of course, was false. Jesus, far from being an insurrectionist, pleaded with his nation not to indulge the folly of rebellion; and it would not be difficult to argue that his whole method was one of nonviolence. But Jesus always seems treasonous to empire: sacrificial love on the one hand, and pride of power buttressed by physical coercions on the other, have little in common. Even in a democratic state the faithful preaching of the gospel will create a tension; and the tension, if we confront

[1] See his *Journal* or John Selby Watson, *The Life of George Fox* (London: Saunders, Otley & Co., 1860).

[2] Told originally by Augustine and found in Ludwig Friedländer, *Roman Life and Manners Under the Early Empire* (New York: E. P. Dutton & Co., 1908), II, 79-80.

38 Then were there two thieves crucified with him; one on the right hand, and another on the left.

Jesus the King of the Jews." **38** Then two robbers were crucified with him, one on the

---

38. The **robbers**—"bandits" is a better translation—may have been revolutionaries. Later tradition gives them such names as Zoatham and Camma—in this verse in an O.L. codex—Dysmas and Gestas, etc.

---

the demands of truth, will then lead to a higher fashion of democracy. Mark the charge of treason.

That titulus was plainly a warning to the Jews. It said, in letters of blood as well as of gypsum, "This is what will happen to you if you try to defy the empire." Perhaps John's Gospel in its record of this incident has outright historicity: perhaps Pilate wished also to insult the temple leaders who had forced his hand: "Behold your King!" (John 19:14). But notice how the title has changed from an insult and a warning to an unintended tribute. Branscomb has an interesting theory.[3] He says that at first the Cross was an offense even to the church. Crucifixion was a curse in Jewish eyes. Besides, how were the early Christians to answer the charge that their Lord was hung as a rebel? But they discovered, as they tested their faith in the hazard of life, that Christ was sufficient for every need, and that he ruled both sin and death. Then they found deep truth in the titulus: God had proclaimed the royalty of Christ through an unwitting Pilate. Then the "offense" of the Cross became their joy, and the "stumbling block" became a step toward heaven. So John adds his comment to the story, and tells us that the titulus was written in three languages for all the world to read. Certainly the theory, proved or unproved, keeps step with early Christian experience. That fact is a proper cue for the interpreter. In Latin: the language of government and power. In Greek: the language which bound the ancient world in one life, and through which men have learned culture and the joy of beauty. In Hebrew: the language through which God made known the tidings of himself. In all these realms Christ is King. "Crown him with many crowns." Except he rule, organization is brute coercion, culture a decay, and religion a blindness. In every language Christ is King. It is right that we should stand for the singing of the "Hallelujah Chorus":[4] Christ *is* "King of Kings and Lord of Lords."

[3] *Gospel of Mark,* p. 294, on Mark 15:24.
[4] From Handel's *Messiah.* It is said that at its first performance in 1742, the audience was "so transported that they all together with the King [George II of England] . . . started up and remained standing till the chorus ended." See R. A. Streatfield, *Handel* (2nd ed.; London: Methuen & Co., 1910), p. 177.

38. *Two Robbers.*—The men were probably revolutionaries, and may have been arrested with Barabbas. It is not unlikely that they were also robbers. Rebels against the injustices of government often turn to banditry. There are two ways of breaking man's law—from above it and from below it. Jesus did not break the Roman law, and if he broke the Jewish religious law the breach was in the letter and not in the spirit. But his light and life judge every law that men had made: he broke the law from above it. The rebels broke the law from below it: angry with the domination of Rome, they were intent only on the earthly domination of Jewry. So Jesus and two robbers were crucified on the same hill; because the world does not inquire concerning a breach of the law, whether it is from above or from below. Yet it fitted Christ's saviorhood that he should be crucified between two thieves. In his life he had eaten "with tax collectors and sinners" (9:11). In his death he was "numbered with the transgressors" (Isa. 53:12). The Crucifixion threw into black contrast all manner of human sin. So he died as he lived, seeking and saving those who are lost to joy and lost to God.

Luke's version (23:39-43) tells us that one thief confessed, implored pardon of Jesus, and at once received at his lips the assurance of "paradise." Thus life sprang from his death—like a phoenix from the ashes.[5] Often we are unseeing and unmoved until tragedy strikes upon our helplessness. Perhaps that is why tragedy comes, a plowshare to cut through stubborn ground. The penitent thief was saved as the Pope, in Browning's *Ring and the Book,* said that Guido might be saved, as suddenly as a lightning flash brings sight.[6] The other thief, Luke's account reports, still railed at Christ. Matthew says that both had joined in the crowd's reviling. Perhaps we should not blame: the almost unbearable pain broke in a torrent of bitterness. They were not utterly bad men: they loved their land, but chose the wrong way to serve it. How hard it is to keep both loftiness of soul and genuine love for mankind! Perhaps no man ever succeeds: the loftiness becomes pride, or the love becomes compromise. But

[5] For this legend see Thomas Bulfinch, *The Age of Fable* (New York: E. P. Dutton & Co., 1915), p. 315.
[6] "The Pope," last paragraph.

39 ¶ And they that passed by reviled him, wagging their heads,

40 And saying, Thou that destroyest the temple, and buildest *it* in three days, save thyself. If thou be the Son of God, come down from the cross.

41 Likewise also the chief priests mocking *him,* with the scribes and elders, said,

42 He saved others; himself he cannot save. If he be the King of Israel, let him now come down from the cross, and we will believe him.

right and one on the left. 39 And those who passed by derided him, wagging their heads 40 and saying, "You who would destroy the temple and build it in three days, save yourself! If you are the Son of God, come down from the cross." 41 So also the chief priests, with the scribes and elders, mocked him, saying, 42 "He saved others; he cannot save himself. He is the King of Israel; let him come down now from the cross, and we

---

39. The **wagging** of **heads** is an Oriental gesture of scorn, known also from Ps. 22:7; Isa. 37:22; Jer. 18:16. One need not suppose that Ps. 22 has affected the tradition at this point. Such gloating over the unfortunate was all too usual in the ancient Orient.

40. Cf. on 26:61. **The Son of God** is a touch added by Matthew here and in vs. 43 because of the wording of 26:63.

41. Would members of the Sanhedrin have joined in the mockery? If so, they probably belonged to the Sadducean priestly group.

42. **He saved,** i.e., healed and rescued, **others. The King of Israel** or Messiah should be able to show a sign to make people **believe;** cf. on 12:38-42; 16:1-4.

Jesus kept obedience to God without any lowering of his spirit from God's royal claim, and without any failure in his tender love for our wayward humanity. Never was that truth more clear than in his death.

39-44. *The Third Mocking.*—(See also Expos., vs. 42.) The servants of the high priest mocked him before he was condemned. The soldiers mocked him after he had been sentenced to die. Now the crowd mocked him in his agony of death. The account of the third mocking may have been heightened in the telling by Christian preaching in the first century which rightly saw in Jesus the deep fulfillment of Ps. 22 and Isa. 53; but it was a cruel age, and we have little reason to doubt that Jesus was vilified on the Cross. **Those who passed by:** the Cross was near a public roadway. Men who were intent on business or pleasure turned aside for a moment, some perhaps in morbid curiosity, others to join the blood lust and to jeer. The indifference of hosts of godless men is here impaled in one phrase: **those who passed by.** Business and pleasure were important, but God did not matter. So they paused for a moment, and had their ribald fun. They said "Another fool being crucified!" and went their way.

Did the Sadducees join in the mockery? Perhaps the hatred of the early church for the Jewish leaders has colored that item. But it is not impossible, and scarcely improbable. The charge of destroying the temple recurs: they hated Jesus for destroying *their* temple—their money and their worldly pride. Their demand for a sign recurs (vs. 42) ; for to them the proof

of messiahship was some fabulous portent—turning the moon to blood, or a miraculous escape from the nails and cords of the Cross. They paid him an unconscious homage, but they intended only hate. Thus they rubbed salt into Jesus' wounds. All through the months of his teaching he had been misunderstood, and the dark misconstruing of his words followed him to the end. Day by day he had yearned that men would "believe" the good news, and almost the last word he heard was that word **believe** flung as a bitter jibe. Always he had pleaded with men to trust God, and now his own trust was vilified. Men still looked for a merely external salvation, and still resisted the essential change of will. That mockery was hardest to bear. Psychology has taught us much about mockery. The proper question to ask ourselves when we loose a sarcastic tongue and a bitter spirit, is "Why do I hate myself?" There is room in a Christian's life for flaming indignation, but no room for acid scorn. The mocking which Jesus endured is a fearful revelation of the inner life of the mockers: what a swarm of evil things in them squirmed under his light! That he could endure the mockery in silence is proof that in him was "no darkness at all" (I John 1:5) .

42. *He Saved Others.*—God rules even our mocking words. For his own purpose he turns our jeers into the coronet of Christ. Who could have dreamed that God, from the venom of the foes of Jesus, would distill a fragrance? Christ could have saved himself, in our poor sense of the word "save." While Napoleon vainly sought

43 He trusted in God; let him deliver him now, if he will have him: for he said, I am the Son of God.

44 The thieves also, which were crucified with him, cast the same in his teeth.

45 Now from the sixth hour there was darkness over all the land unto the ninth hour.

46 And about the ninth hour Jesus cried with a loud voice, saying, Eli, Eli, lama sabachthani? that is to say, My God, my God, why hast thou forsaken me?

will believe in him. 43 He trusts in God; let God deliver him now, if he desires him; for he said, 'I am the Son of God.' " 44 And the robbers who were crucified with him also reviled him in the same way.

45 Now from the sixth hour there was darkness over all the land[n] until the ninth hour. 46 And about the ninth hour Jesus cried with a loud voice, "Eli, Eli, la'ma sa-bach-tha'ni?" that is, "My God, my God,

[n] Or earth.

43. The first part of the verse is an independent translation of the Hebrew of Ps. 22:8. The second part has a striking parallel in Wisd. Sol. 2:18, "For if the righteous man is God's son, he will uphold him, and he will deliver him out of the hand of his adversaries." The evangelists may have the entire passage Wisd. Sol. 2:12-20 in their minds as they write.

44. Mark and Matthew do not seem to know the tradition of the "good thief" of Luke 23:40-43.

4. Jesus' Death (27:45-56)

45. Matthew omits the statement of Mark 15:25 that Jesus was crucified at the third hour (i.e., 9 A.M.), but appears to presuppose it. **The sixth hour** is noon and **the ninth hour** about 3 P.M. The Gospel of Peter 5:15 reads, "It was noon and darkness gripped all Judea." We therefore probably should translate **all the land,** not "all the earth." Luke 23:45 explains the phenomenon as an eclipse. An eclipse is astronomically impossible during paschal full moon, but the evangelists think of a mighty miracle.

46. The words of Jesus in Mark 15:34 are an Aramaic translation of Ps. 22:1, but in Matthew the "Eloi" has been changed back to the Hebrew form **Eli,** which is also found in the Aramaic Targum on this verse. The simplest explanation of this cry is that

to rally his men at Waterloo, the cry ran over the lost field, "We are betrayed! Save himself who can!" [7] In that low meaning of the word Christ could have saved himself. His obedience to God was not automatic: it was a considered choice which spurned a low safety.

Notice the tribute which Jesus drew even from his foes. They were obliged to admit that he had healed and rescued others. Thus from their mouths we have the picture of one who "went about doing good." In deeper sense than they intended Christ **saved others** by his life and death. Jowett once used an illustration of the red worsted strand running through an Alpine rope: "The blood sign, the red endless line of sacrifice." [8] Throughout the journey his blood was given. What the foes of Jesus did not understand was that, in the ordering of God's providence, it is not possible for any man—let alone for the Christ—to save the higher life of his neighbors while preserving his own lower life. If they had known the truth, they would

have said in reverence: "He saved others: therefore he could not save himself." The fable of the princess who cast herself into an open grave, and was thus buried, to save her land from drought is true to the essentials of the soul; and it is a flash of insight in the story which insists that then a river of water flowed from her grave.[9] A teacher, a doctor, every man confronts that choice: himself or others. Jesus confronted the choice in agonies of spirit which we cannot more than glimpse. The enemies of Jesus were right in saying that he could not save himself. But God could save him. His abandon of love and obedience was not in vain. "Wherefore God also hath highly exalted him, and given him a name which is above every name: that at the name of Jesus every knee should bow" (Phil. 2:9).

46-49. *Cry of Dereliction.*—These verses raise many questions. The "cry" has so touched the heart of mankind that discussion of linguistic and exegetical problems seems like geologizing on holy ground. But exposition is hardly possible unless the problems are faced and some an-

[7] Thomas E. Watson, *Napoleon I, Emperor of the French* (New York: The Macmillan Co., 1902), p. 665.

[8] *Sharing His Sufferings,* p. 104.

[9] *Great Texts of the Bible,* Vol. *Mark,* p. 5.

47 Some of them that stood there, when they heard *that*, said, This *man* calleth for Elias.

48 And straightway one of them ran, and took a sponge, and filled *it* with vinegar, and put *it* on a reed, and gave him to drink.

49 The rest said, Let be, let us see whether Elias will come to save him.

why hast thou forsaken me?" 47 And some of the bystanders hearing it said, "This man is calling Elijah." 48 And one of them at once ran and took a sponge, filled it with vinegar, and put it on a reed, and gave it to him to drink. 49 But the others said, "Wait, let us see whether Elijah will

---

Jesus was repeating various verses of the Psalms, and perhaps meditating on them, as he hung on the cross. The circumstances would naturally suggest Ps. 22 to his mind. No one can say with dogmatic assurance what he meant when he quoted this psalm. The psalm itself is a prayer of complaint which ends on a note of triumph (vss. 23-31). We know that pious Jews used it in times of adversity and gained encouragement from it, and certainly it does not suggest a loss of faith in God. Jesus may employ it as a prayer for deliverance, an expression of faith, or an ejaculation which expresses his sense of loneliness and loss.

47. The Jews believed that **Elijah** was the rescuer of the pious in their time of need. It has been objected that the Jewish **bystanders** would not confuse *'elāhî* ("my God") and *'ēliyyāhû* ("Elijah"), but if Jesus was in great pain his words may not have been distinct.

48. The drink that is now offered on the **sponge** and **reed** is not the drugged wine of vs. 34 but **vinegar.** This is sometimes identified with the posca, a drink made of water, sour wine, and egg, which Roman soldiers drank. If this is correct, the soldiers do a deed of mercy. But the evangelists may think of it as another kind of mistreatment—"When I was thirsty, they gave me vinegar to drink" (Ps. 69:21).

49. Wait (RSV) and **Let be** (KJV) make good sense in this context, but ἄφες should not be translated at all. It is probably only an auxiliary for the subjunctive ἴδωμεν, and the two Greek words together mean **let us see.**

---

swer found. It is possible that the "cry" is the reverent comment of the early church: we must give honest consideration to the fact that the description of the death of Jesus closely parallels Ps. 22. If we regard vs. 46 as an authentic word of Christ—and most exegetes do—the questions still throng. Mark's version gives the cry in Aramaic; Matthew changes the Aramaic "Eloi" to the Hebrew "Eli." In which language did Jesus speak? No Jew could mistake "Eli" for the name of Elijah: the taunt, if properly reported, must have been a deliberate play on words. The main question still remains: was Jesus in the depth of despair, or was he meditating on the words of Ps. 22 in its confidence in God's victory? To that we can make no dogmatic answer, for plainly we do not know.

The church has called the words "the cry of dereliction." It is a terrible name: a derelict ship is deserted by both rats and men, and is driven helplessly before the gale. "Dereliction" is probably too strong a word. But Jesus, sharing our human nature, shared also our grief— and perhaps our bafflement and doubt. The Temptation shows him weighing alternatives **in a struggle of mind and soul.** The Agony

shows him praying that the bitter cup might pass, even though the prayer was instantly caught up into a resolute submission. He knew tension and periods of darkness: the straits of dark baptism. Did he share also our human sense of being forsaken of God? Did he, like ourselves, fling his agonized "why" against what seems an uncomprehending sky? The Gospelists speak of a great darkness covering the land, as if nature matched the incalculable midnight through which Jesus passed. The taunt about Elijah, whom the Jews regarded as stanch ally of the righteous in their trials, added human bitterness to nature's travail. James Stalker spoke of this cry as "a cry out of the lowest depths of despair. Indeed it is the most appalling sound that ever pierced the atmosphere of this earth. . . . It cannot be heard even at this day without causing a cold shudder of terror." [1] But we cannot say: it may have been confident meditation on the psalm. What we do know is that Jesus shared our human struggle, both throughout his life and on his cross.

Luke speaks of an eclipse of the sun. That

[1] *The Trial and Death of Jesus Christ* (London: Hodder & Stoughton, 1894), pp. 218-19.

50 ¶ Jesus, when he had cried again with a loud voice, yielded up the ghost.

51 And, behold, the veil of the temple was rent in twain from the top to the bot-

come to save him."*o* 50 And Jesus cried again with a loud voice and yielded up his spirit.

51 And behold, the curtain of the tem-

o Many ancient authorities insert And another took a spear and pierced his side, and out came water and blood.

---

50. Matthew substitutes **yielded up his spirit** for Mark's "breathed his last," perhaps with the thought that Jesus acted voluntarily. The same belief is found in John 19:30. It was remarkable that Jesus should die after so brief a time (Mark 15:44).

51-53. The tearing **in two of the curtain of the temple** symbolizes either the uninterrupted access to God made possible by Jesus' sacrifice (Heb. 9:11-12; 10:19-22) or divine

---

was hardly possible at the time of the paschal full moon. Perhaps the early church, in writings at some distance of time from the event of Calvary, could not imagine the death of Jesus without a cosmic midnight—terrible token of the divine judgment. In any event, even if the surmise is true that Jesus knew the darkest depths of doubt, the faith of Jesus was not in eclipse. He still cried **my God, my God!** Always some measure of faith remains even for us, and assuredly for him.

The other interpretation of the words may be true. That is, he may have recited for the strengthening of his soul the noble words of Ps. 22. By that interpretation onlookers caught only the opening lines, but he spoke other great words to his own heart and to God: "They cried unto thee, and were delivered," "Be thou not far from me, O Lord," "All the ends of the earth shall remember and turn unto the Lord." Thus both interpretations could be true: if choice must be made, each expositor must make his own under the guidance of the church—as he and the church pray, and thus understand Christ by the guidance of the Holy Spirit. God heard the prayer. Though all others had forsaken Christ, God was with him, never closer than in the obedience of his holy sacrifice. Nay, God was so close that "God was in Christ, reconciling the world unto himself" (II Cor. 5:19).

50-53. The End.— (See also Expos., vs. 51.) It came quickly. In some instances a crucified man would languish for days. The time of the Crucifixion and of its various accompanying events as recorded in the various Gospels is hard to construe. Most exegetes believe that the Crucifixion began at nine in the morning, and that Jesus died at three in the afternoon. Thus death came with merciful speed. Jesus, we judge, was physically strong: the portrait in the Gospels has the marks of virile manhood. The quickness of death may have been due in part to the severity of the flogging dealt by the Roman soldiers, but probably was due mainly **to the throes of a pure heart**—to his mighty

grappling in love with the grief and sin of men. Matthew makes a significant change in Mark's, "Jesus . . . breathed his last" (Mark 15:37). Our Gospelist's **Jesus . . . yielded up his spirit** is clearly intended to tell us that his very death was a voluntary act. Thus also Luke's "Father, into thy hands I commit my spirit!" (Luke 23: 46). John's "It is finished" has the same triumphant meaning: "It is accomplished." The last act of the earthly life of Jesus was like the last grand chord of a symphony—the completion of the music of perfect love toward God and men. Wicked men took his life. But they were only small-part actors who did not understand the depths of the drama: Jesus gave his life. He yielded his spirit in death, in that same filial love in which he had lived out his life.

What are we to make of the rending of the temple veil, the earthquake, and the **opened graves?** The Gospels give different accounts of these portents: only Matthew speaks of **opened graves.** To the ancient world these "signs" were the natural accompaniment of tragedy, and the Gospelists could hardly tell of Calvary without assuming that God would write the lines of his judgment on mountain and sky. But this story cannot be dismissed as mere "legendary accretions." For the very description of the portents implies a great faith in the early church. This faith: God watched his Son on the Cross; God wrote in darkened sky and torn mountains his judgment on our wickedness, and his love for Christ; and God proved himself then and there the Lord of death and life. The portent of the **opened** graves has special meaning. Christ became "the firstfruits of them that slept" (I Cor. 15:20). Notice the safeguarding clause **after his resurrection.** That event was to the early church the vindication of God upon the truth and life of his Son, and the promise of eternal life to those who follow Christ in sincerity of faith and venture of deed.

51. The Rending of the Temple Curtain.— There were two veils or curtains in the temple, one between the outer court and the holy place,

tom; and the earth did quake, and the rocks rent;

52 And the graves were opened; and many bodies of the saints which slept arose,

53 And came out of the graves after his resurrection, and went into the holy city, and appeared unto many.

54 Now when the centurion, and they that were with him, watching Jesus, saw the earthquake, and those things that were done, they feared greatly, saying, Truly this was the Son of God.

ple was torn in two, from top to bottom; and the earth shook, and the rocks were split; 52 the tombs also were opened, and many bodies of the saints who had fallen asleep were raised, 53 and coming out of the tombs after his resurrection they went into the holy city and appeared to many. 54 When the centurion and those who were with him, keeping watch over Jesus, saw the earthquake and what took place, they were filled with awe, and said, "Truly this was a son of God!"

---

judgment on the Jewish people. Josephus and the Talmud both tell of portents which preceded the fall of Jerusalem, and there is even a tradition that some of these occurred forty years before the event, i.e., about the year of the Crucifixion. Matthew adds some miraculous touches not found in other sources. The raising of **many bodies of the saints** is more than a portent. It suggests that Jesus' **resurrection** is the first fruits of the general resurrection (I Cor. 15:20) and that at his second coming, when all the dead are raised, he will be accompanied by the departed saints (I Thess. 4:16). Ign. Mag. 9:2 contains what may be an allusion to this story.

54. In Mark 15:39 **the centurion** is impressed by the manner of Jesus' death. Here he **and those who were with him** are **filled with awe** by all the events. **Truly this was a son of God!** is probably intended as dramatic irony. The beholders think of him as a Greco-Roman demigod; but the evangelists and their readers know that he is the unique son of the only God.

---

and the other between the holy place and the holy of holies. Josephus tells us that they were sixty feet high, and woven with lavish richness.[2] One of the apocryphal scriptures tells us that the lintel on which the curtain was hung shattered of itself on the day when Jesus died.[3] We cannot say what thought was dominant in the mind of Matthew as he recorded these marvels. Certainly the rent curtain meant the judgment of God. The temple leaders had been false to the covenant, and their place now was left desolate. Nothing could more dramatically show the displeasure of God than that the holy of holies, with its supernal secret of the Presence, should now be exposed to public view.

But perhaps Matthew had in mind the new and open way into "the secret place of the Most High" (Ps. 91:1), which Christ by his life and death gave to all men. That certainly is the thought in Heb. 10:19-20): "Boldness to enter into the holiest by the blood of Jesus, by a new and living way, which he hath consecrated for us, through the veil, that is to say, his flesh." The old covenant had been disobeyed and thus broken. Besides, its law and ordinances were in their rigor a condemnation and a despair; they only deepened in man the sense of sin. But Jesus by his sacrifice overcame sin, and

by his resurrection "brought . . . immortality to light" (II Tim. 1:10). So every man through him has open access to the Father. How many dividing curtains Christ tore from top to bottom by his death! The division between priest and worshiper now is gone: the church is the priesthood of believers. The division between Jew and Gentile now is gone: the Gentile now can go beyond the outer court into the holy place, yes, and into "the holiest." The barrier between bond and free now is broken, for all are bond servants of Christ and therefore have perfect freedom. **The curtain of the temple was torn in two.**

54. *The Centurion.*—The centurions mentioned in the N.T. are represented as worthy men. The centurion at Capernaum (8:5) and Cornelius (Acts 10:1) occur to mind. These officers of lower rank are thus in striking contrast with their ruthless or dissolute lords, such as Pilate and Herod. We do not know the name of the centurion in charge of the Crucifixion. Tradition has given him many names—Longinus, Petronius—and has woven many stories around him. Whoever he was, he could have told us, perhaps better than any man, the history of the last hours of Christ. The three accounts of the centurion's words are interesting in their differences. Mark (15:39) says, in the correct translation of RSV, "Truly this was a

[2] *Jewish War* V. 5.
[3] *The Gospel According to the Hebrews.*

55 And many women were there beholding afar off, which followed Jesus from Galilee, ministering unto him:	55 There were also many women there, looking on from afar, who had followed Jesus from Galilee, ministering to him;
56 Among which was Mary Magdalene, and Mary the mother of James and Joses, and the mother of Zebedee's children.	56 among whom were Mary Mag'da-lene, and Mary the mother of James and Joseph, and the mother of the sons of Zeb'e-dee.

55-56. Matthew may believe that the **women** are guarantors of the tradition. They **had followed Jesus from Galilee, ministering to him,** as did the women of Luke 8:1-3. **Mary Magdalene** appears in that list as well as here. **Mary the mother of James and Joseph** is probably the same as "Mary the mother of James the younger and of Joses" in Mark 15:40; the later MSS change **Joseph** to **Joses** here. Matthew identifies Zebedee's wife with the "Salome" of Mark because he has pictured her (20:20) as journeying with the disciples.

son of God." Luke (23:47 RSV) records the comment: "Certainly this man was innocent!" Mark's version is first in point of time. We would have to know the man's tone of voice before we could tell what his words implied. The Exeg. suggests that it could have been a sarcasm, spoken when he saw the "king" die in helplessness, and compared him with Roman might.

But the words could be a tribute, as Charles Rann Kennedy's play has depicted.[4] **A son of God** probably meant to the Roman officer a superhuman person worthy to be numbered among the Roman gods. If Luke is right, the centurion contrasted the calm fortitude of Jesus with the railing of the thieves, and saw that the charge of treason was manifestly false. That much he might have seen from the start. Was he justified, then, in blindly obeying orders to kill Jesus? There is a question! Supposing his words sincere, they express only a pagan faith: he had not yet come to the knowledge of the true God. He felt only a vague "awe": he knew no better heaven than a gallery of gods. There is no doubt that the Gospelists found in his exclamation a confession of faith in their Lord and Master: the man who killed Jesus was his first follower after death, and the first to avow himself a follower of the incarnate Son of God. But whatever happened to the centurion, we can be sure of what happened to the men who wrote the N.T. They found in the cross of Jesus Christ the apocalypse of divine love: "Behold, the Lamb of God, who takes away the sin of the world!" (John 1:29).

55-56. *The Women Who Watched.*—Though some scholars have doubted the authenticity of these verses, there is good reason for trusting them. A legendary addition to the gospel record would have been tempted to place the women nearer to the Cross, for that account would have been more appealing in its drama. Moreover, the women here described set the

disciples in a cowardly light, and the story might therefore have been suppressed rather than written, had it not been true. The sparseness of the record adds to its poignancy. Who were the women? **Mary Magdalene** we know. Incidentally, the tradition that identifies her with a notorious woman is unjustified: there is nothing in the Gospels to prove it. Jesus had freed her from "seven devils"—perhaps from what we might call an acute melancholia, or some similar affliction of body and mind. The other Mary mentioned cannot be identified with positiveness (see Exeg.). The third woman, whom Mark names Salome, may have been correctly described by Matthew: there is little reason to doubt his account. Note, however, that these were only three of the company: there were **many women.**

Their motive in following Jesus to the Cross was a blend of gratitude, courage, and love. The gratitude came because of the blessings he had bestowed on them. The courage is shown in the fact that they followed, though the disciples fled: they followed afar because of the brutality of the Roman soldiers, but they followed. The love was the source of the courage: their intuition concerning Jesus was surer truth than any that came of man's reasoning, and they had given him a pure devotion. Could he see them in the distance as he died? If so, they tempered his pain and lightened his darkness. They could do little other than watch, but their seeming helplessness proved to be power. Perhaps they gave us the story of the Crucifixion! Many a commentator has remarked on the fact that the Calvary account is written with austerity, as if the drama were being seen from some distance. Perhaps these women were the guarantors and transmitters of the great and ongoing tradition of the gospel. That is what Matthew's mention of them clearly implies. So their helpless watching was not helpless: indeed it was the very transmission of the faith.

[4] *The Terrible Meek.*

57 When the even was come, there came a rich man of Arimathea, named Joseph, who also himself was Jesus' disciple:

58 He went to Pilate, and begged the body of Jesus. Then Pilate commanded the body to be delivered.

57 When it was evening, there came a rich man from Ar-i-ma-the′a, named Joseph, who also was a disciple of Jesus. 58 He went to Pilate and asked for the body of Jesus. Then Pilate ordered it to be given to him.

C. THE BURIAL OF JESUS (27:57-66)
1. THE BURIAL (27:57-61)

57. Joseph is called **rich** because Matthew so interprets εὐσχήμων in Mark 15:43. That Greek word often represents the Latin *honestus* and can be taken to mean honorable, respected, or rich. Mark described him as a "member of the council," perhaps of a sanhedrin in his own city. **Arimathea** is often identified with Ramathaim-zophim (I Sam. 1:1), about fifteen miles east of Joppa. Matthew and John (19:38) call him **a disciple of Jesus,** but Mark 15:43 indicates only that he was a pious Jew who hoped for the kingdom of God and therefore might be sympathetic to Jesus' teaching.

58-60. To bury the dead was an act of piety which might be expected of such a man (Tob. 1:16-18; 2:1-8). It was usual to bury people on the day of death, and the body of an executed man was not allowed to remain gibbeted overnight (Deut. 21:23) because

---

57-61. *The Burial of Jesus: Joseph of Arimathea.*—Dostoevski shows us two men standing before a picture of the descent from the Cross. One man tells later of the "strange uneasiness" it produced. "The people surrounding the dead man . . . must have experienced the most terrible consternation . . . which had crushed all their hopes, and almost their convictions."[5] He meant that death is a wedge driven into life and love, and that Jesus' death is a wedge driven by sinful men into purest life and holiest love; and that therefore such a picture was a symbol of grotesque injustice. But "the descent from the Cross" has not been an occasion of doubt. From the first it bred courage, and the story is stranger than fiction. We would have expected that Mary, the mother of Jesus, or Peter would come to perform the last sad offices for the body of Jesus. But no: they were either overborne by grief or hiding in fear.

Who did come? Joseph of Arimathea. Matthew says that he was **rich**—a translation of Mark's "honorable," perhaps under the influence of Isa. 53:9. He must have had some means, or he could not have performed this act of piety. He was a "councilor," a word which may mean either a member of the Sanhedrin, or perhaps more likely, a member of some local council. Luke tells us that "he was looking for the kingdom of God" (Luke 23:51), a phrase which means that he cherished the hope of Israel's deliverance through the Messiah. John (19:38) tells us, perhaps in an elaboration of the story, that Joseph was "a disciple of Jesus" but kept the loyalty secret, fearing the temple leaders. This man gave Jesus honorable burial. Suppose him a man of noble Jewish faith.

He believed "Moses and the prophets," and therefore his sincerity led him into the circle of Jesus. There is more goodness among men than our pessimism grants. Suppose him a member of the highest Sanhedrin and a secret follower of Jesus. The secrecy was tragic. It was tragic for Joseph: there was a lesion in his soul. As he heard Jesus in the colonnade of the temple his soul leaped to meet the truth; as he met with the Sanhedrin he nodded sage assent to the fears expressed about "this upstart from Galilee." No man can live creatively with such a civil war in his life. The secrecy was tragic for Jesus. A French king rode into apparently hopeless battle crying, "Let him who loves me follow me."[6] So Jesus fought a fiercer battle with no sword except the sword of the Spirit—and Joseph did not follow. Instead he watched Jesus overborne by his foes. If only some "follower" had dared to follow to Golgotha! But if Joseph was a secret follower, he was no worse than we, for we are all more Christian in secret conviction than in our shuffling deeds. We are sometimes aghast at man's denial of Christ through racial prejudice, economic greed, or political chicanery; but—do we say it and take our stand?

Rome might have left the body of Jesus on the Cross, as a prey for carrion birds. The Jewish authorities would probably have given him some sort of burial (see Deut. 21:23). Jewish law provided that a condemned man should not be buried in the tomb of his fathers. So the fact that Jesus was laid in a new tomb does not imply an honor, but only that he was condemned. If John's account is authentic, Nicodemus, another member of the council, came to help Joseph; and brought far more spices

[5] *The Idiot,* tr. Constance Garnett, pp. 388-89.

[6] Francis I of France at the battle of Marignano, 1515.

59 And when Joseph had taken the body, he wrapped it in a clean linen cloth,

60 And laid it in his own new tomb, which he had hewn out in the rock: and he rolled a great stone to the door of the sepulchre, and departed.

61 And there was Mary Magdalene, and the other Mary, sitting over against the sepulchre.

62 ¶ Now the next day, that followed the day of the preparation, the chief priests and Pharisees came together unto Pilate,

59 And Joseph took the body, and wrapped it in a clean linen shroud, **60** and laid it in his own new tomb, which he had hewn in the rock; and he rolled a great stone to the door of the tomb, and departed. **61** Mary Mag'da-lene and the other Mary were there, sitting opposite the sepulchre.

62 Next day, that is, after the day of Preparation, the chief priests and the Phari-

---

it polluted the holy land. The **clean linen shroud** agrees with rabbinical custom. Joseph may have intended the **new tomb** for the use of his family, but he probably would not have used it again because the rabbis forbade one to bury one's fathers in the tomb where an executed man was laid. Family tombs were outside the city walls and usually in the form of a chamber with recesses on either side into which bodies were put. They might be natural caves or **hewn in the rock,** as here. The **great stone** which was **rolled . . . to the door of the tomb** might have been a rectangular door on stone hinges, or, more probably, a disk-shaped stone that could be rolled back and forth across the opening. Good examples of this type of tomb are still to be seen in Jerusalem, e.g., the so-called "Garden Tomb" and the "Tombs of the Kings."

61. Friends or relatives often watched at the tomb in case the apparently dead person should revive. Mark says only that the two women saw where he was buried.

2. THE WATCH ON THE TOMB (27:62-66)

This story and 28:11-15 are two parts of a legend which is found in a more developed form in the Gospel of Peter 8:29–11:49 (James, *Apocryphal N.T.,* pp. 92-93). Mark 16:1-8 must have given rise to a controversy, the Christians maintaining that the empty tomb was a proof of the Resurrection, and their Jewish opponents answering that the body had been stolen by the disciples. Matthew gives the rebuttal: the tomb was watched, but the "custodians" were bribed to say that the body was stolen. He probably received the story from oral tradition.

62. Next day was the sabbath and probably also the first day of Unleavened Bread.

---

than were needed for the embalming, to save his own sad conscience from decay! The story is stranger than fiction. Was Joseph barred from the feast—supposing the Crucifixion to have been close in date to the Passover—because he had touched the body of a condemned man? To bury the unknown dead was reckoned a mark of great piety. Did that act bring Joseph into the Christian group? We do not know. The legends have multiplied.[7] One says that Joseph used the cup of the Last Supper to catch the blood of Jesus on Calvary, and that the cup thus became the Holy Grail. Another says that Joseph preached the gospel in Britain, and that he sank down one day, spent by his labors, exclaiming, "We be weary all!"—and that thus he gave the name to Wirral Hill. Another tells us that Joseph struck his staff into the ground, and it blossomed in snow-white

hawthorne at Christmastide.[8] These legends have truth: he who courageously buried the body of Jesus, thinking him dead forever, became the bearer of the gospel. There are many occasions when Jesus seems doomed; but if we are true, our loyalty lights a new torch of faith.

62-65. *The Watch at the Tomb.*—Even conservative commentators are obliged to admit that these verses are probably legend. Thus *The Expositor's Greek Testament* says that this story is "among the less certain elements of the Passion history."[9] The same story is written in fuller detail in the apocryphal Gospel of Peter.[1] We have here the echo of a great controversy between the synagogue and the early church. The strife raged through several generations.

[8] Anne Thaxter Eaton, *The Animals' Christmas* (New York: Viking Press, 1944), p. 21.

[9] I, 334, note on vss. 62-66.

[1] J. Rendel Harris, *The Newly-Recovered Gospel of St. Peter* (New York: James Pott & Co., 1893), pp. 36-37.

[7] See Guerber, *Legends of the Virgin and Christ,* pp. 165-66, 168-71, 206-16.

63 Saying, Sir, we remember that that deceiver said, while he was yet alive, After three days I will rise again.

64 Command therefore that the sepulchre be made sure until the third day, lest his disciples come by night, and steal him away, and say unto the people, He is risen from the dead: so the last error shall be worse than the first.

65 Pilate said unto them, Ye have a watch: go your way, make *it* as sure as ye can.

66 So they went, and made the sepulchre sure, sealing the stone, and setting a watch.

sees gathered before Pilate **63** and said, "Sir, we remember how that impostor said, while he was still alive, 'After three days I will rise again.' **64** Therefore order the sepulchre to be made secure until the third day, lest his disciples go and steal him away, and tell the people, 'He has risen from the dead,' and the last fraud will be worse than the first." **65** Pilate said to them, "You have a guard[p] of soldiers; go, make it as secure as you can."[q] **66** So they went and made the sepulchre secure by sealing the stone and setting a guard.

[p] Or *Take a guard.*
[q] Greek *know.*

63. The charge was often made by Jewish and pagan writers in the second and third centuries that Jesus was an **impostor** and magician who deceived the people (cf. on 2:13). This verse presupposes that the predictions of suffering and resurrection which Jesus made privately to his disciples (16:21; 17:23; 20:19) were known to the general public.

65. The **guard of soldiers** might be Jewish, but is probably Roman, as in the Gospel of Peter, where a centurion named Petronius commands them. In that case the imperative **take a guard** (RSV mg.) is a natural translation.

The synagogue said that Jesus was an impostor and his resurrection an invention. They alleged that the disciples stole the body to give credit to the story of an empty tomb. The church replied that there could have been no such theft: Pilate and the temple leaders set a guard over the grave. The synagogue returned to the attack, arguing that in such an event the soldiers must have seen the resurrection miracle. To that the church answered, "They did see it, but they were bribed to keep the miracle a secret." The word **impostor** is striking. It meant at first "wanderer" or "vagabond," then "deceiver," then "impostor." It is worth remembering that Jesus—of all people—has suffered that accusation. The controversy was futile on both sides, like many another controversy. The proofs cited by the church in this instance were not convincing. There were far better proofs. Acts 1:3 and I Cor. 15:3-8 give us the core of the resurrection faith. That appearing struck light into the mind, for the disciples suddenly saw and understood where before they had been blind; and it gave power to the will—they sprang with courage upon a ruthless world to spread everywhere the tidings of a risen Savior. Light and power are sure proof of an overmastering experience. Behind this legend we see, not only what a commotion Jesus made beyond his death, but a mighty faith. The faith indeed wrote the legend.

66. *So They Made the Sepulchre Secure.*— This is the final comment of our Gospelist on the earthly life of Jesus, for his next chapter deals

straightway with the daybreak of the Resurrection. His enemies did all that human power can do to destroy Jesus and all his works. Their last act was to try to make the tomb forever his prison. Their false hope is the symbol of man's agelong folly. Do we not all try to imprison Christ in a tomb? We try to lock him in a prison of force: the relentless persecution visited on his prophets, generation after generation, is for witness. But Nero is still helpless after all his cruelty, for Christ still lives. We try to lock Christ in a prison of things: we store up wealth and beguile ourselves by the scientism of our age. But we cannot forget him: the lilt of an old hymn brings him back to mind, and his words now are so interwoven with our words that he is always just around the corner of our conversation. We try to lock him in a prison of busyness: we flog the spirit into activism, and resolve so to escape him. But the flesh tires and the nerves rebel, and then some picture of him seen in a store window quickens the old longings of the soul. So they **made the sepulchre secure.** Not very secure! The seal was firm and the stone was large, but soon "an angel . . . rolled back the stone, and sat upon it" (28:2)—making a park bench of those strong barriers that man had raised against his neighbors and against God. The sum of the Calvary story is this: men did their worst in wickedness, but it was not enough to defeat the power of God's love. They thought they had guaranteed the eclipse of Jesus in hatred and in shame. They killed Jesus and made the tomb secure. But it

28 In the end of the sabbath, as it began to dawn toward the first *day* of the week, came Mary Magdalene and the other Mary to see the sepulchre.

28 Now after the sabbath, toward the dawn of the first day of the week, Mary Mag′da-lene and the other Mary went

---

XII. The Resurrection (28:1-20)

The resurrection of Jesus Christ is historically the foundation of the Christian church. It is presupposed in every part of the N.T. and is appealed to as a most certain fact which can confirm other truths (I Cor. 15:12-20, 29-32). The nature of the resurrection appearances and their ultimate validity is an issue beyond the scope of scientific and historical investigation and belongs in the realm of faith and theology. But it is an established historical fact that Peter and numerous other Christians were certain that they had seen the risen Lord. The tradition in the Gospels has undergone some development and one can detect discrepancies in details, but it is essentially harmonious with the oldest narrative, I Cor. 15:3-8, and with the accounts in Acts of the apostolic preaching (e.g., Acts 10:37-43).

Matthew's principal written source is Mark 16:1-8. Unless 16:8 is the original ending of Mark (as many scholars hold), it is quite possible that Matt. 28:16-20 is a rewritten form of the lost conclusion of that Gospel; cf. E. J. Goodspeed, *New Solutions of New Testament Problems* (Chicago: University of Chicago Press, 1927), pp. 116-22. In any case these verses contain an old and important tradition. Vss. 4, 11-15 belong to the legend of the guardsmen, and vss. 2-3 may be the evangelist's free composition. Vss. 9-10 recount an actual appearance of Jesus, but their language is mainly derived from vs. 7.

It is curious that the old tradition contained so little description of the actual resurrection appearances. The best example of such a story is the Emmaus episode of Luke 24:13-35, which Luke has probably filled out and expanded. The earliest Christians seemingly thought it sufficient to proclaim the great fact of their Lord's resurrection and were little concerned with the details. See general article, "The History of the Early Church: I. The Beginnings," in this volume, pp. 177-78.

A. The Angel and the Women (28:1-8)

28:1. After the sabbath is the correct translation: cf. Goodspeed, *Problems of N.T. Translation*, pp. 43-45. The women come just before **dawn** on Sunday morning. Matthew omits Mark's statement that they intended to anoint the body, presumably because the

---

was not enough. He is the incarnate God, and it was not possible that death should hold him. "Thanks be to God, who gives us the victory through our Lord Jesus Christ" (I Cor. 15:57).

28:1. The Easter Dawn.—No book ever had a climax of such triumph as that recorded in the Gospels. No other book could tell that joy, except in echo of the Gospels, for there is only one Christ and only one Easter. Compare the last sentence of the last chapter with this first sentence. **Toward the dawn:** it was not yet light. There was darkness rather, with all the threats of darkness, and a world sunk in uneasy sleep. But there was a vague promise of light, as if Someone had kindled a fire far below the eastern horizon. Perhaps that tomb, sealed and guarded by armed might, was not the last word. **Toward the dawn!**

After the sabbath. That holy day had run from (what we would call) sunset on Friday until sunset on Saturday, and the time was

now about three o'clock on (what we would call) Sunday morning. Notice that interpolation—"what we would call." Easter was so climactic that it changed the Jewish sabbath, which was bastioned deep in Jewish history and in centuries of worshipful tradition, into the Christian Sunday. It is in such facts, accessory to the main issue, that we may perhaps best measure the tremendous impact of the resurrection event. The Jewish Pentecost soon would be transformed into a new Pentecost; the old covenant would be superseded by a new covenant; and the sabbath would become a new day, the day on which Jesus rose from the dead. Nothing but a great **dawn**, a new daybreak in our human story, could thus change the agelong institutions men have made.

They went to see the sepulchre. They did not expect God's miracle of resurrection grace. Every account of Easter confirms the fact that the followers of Jesus were surprised and over-

2 And, behold, there was a great earthquake: for the angel of the Lord descended from heaven, and came and rolled back the stone from the door, and sat upon it.

3 His countenance was like lightning, and his raiment white as snow:

4 And for fear of him the keepers did shake, and became as dead *men.*

5 And the angel answered and said unto the women, Fear not ye: for I know that ye seek Jesus, which was crucified.

to see the sepulchre. 2 And behold, there was a great earthquake; for an angel of the Lord descended from heaven and came and rolled back the stone, and sat upon it. 3 His appearance was like lightning, and his raiment white as snow. 4 And for fear of him the guards trembled and became like dead men. 5 But the angel said to the women, "Do not be afraid; for I know

---

watchers at the tomb would have prevented this. **Mary Magdalene** is not mentioned in the list in I Cor. 15. She is an important figure in the gospel accounts because the story of the empty tomb is traced back to her. But only in vss. 9-10 and in John 20:14-18 is she claimed as a direct witness of the Resurrection.

2-4. The story is further developed in the Gospel of Peter 12:50–13:57 (James, *Apocryphal N.T.,* p. 93), but there the tomb has already been opened and the guards and Jewish elders have seen Jesus ascend to heaven with his cross. The "young man in white" of Mark 16:5 was probably an **angel,** and he is now explicitly identified as one. He is of supernatural aspect, like the angel in Rev. 10:1, and Jesus himself at his transfiguration (17:2).

---

whelmed by his new appearing. His speech had been love and his step a benediction, but the end of it all was—a cross and a guarded tomb. Unhappily (they may have said) it is that kind of world. And then . . . ! They **went to see the tomb:** sorrow's crown of sorrows is remembering happier things. And then—"an angel of the Lord." Beethoven's *Sixth Symphony* sounds the crash of the storm, followed by the first tremulous notes of new hope, broadening into a song of thanksgiving. All illustrations that try to illumine Christ, who is himself the light, are poor indeed; but these words are the first tremulous notes of unutterable joy after the tragedy of the Cross: **Toward the dawn of the first day of the week.**

2-7. *The Angel of the Resurrection.*— (See also Expos., vs. 6.) There are exegetical difficulties connected with this story. The reader need only consult a harmony of the Gospels to see that the four accounts are in some respects hard to reconcile. Percival Gardner-Smith has suggested that if we omit the words **for he has risen, as he said,** together with the whole of vs. 7, we have the nucleus of an ordinary episode which was later magnified into a resurrection story: the women came to the wrong tomb, and a young man sent them to the place where Jesus had been buried.[2] This thesis is itself conjecture, however skillful. But supposing it to be true, what caused an ordinary event thus to be transfigured? A wiser age than ours may stand appalled at our constant demand for a

[2] *The Narratives of the Resurrection* (London: Methuen & Co., 1926), especially pp. 134-38, 180.

scientifically factual account. Has a great painting no fact to inspire it, and no truth? This story has more kindling fact and truth than the greatest painting. It seems probable that the appearing of Christ took place in Galilee. Matthew has obviously combined that stanch record (see I Cor. 15:3-8) with a Mark-Johannine tradition, and thus has left the ages deeply in debt. So this story abides as a marvelous reflection of a still more marvelous event.

The angel of the Resurrection was a messenger of power: an earthquake shook the earth, and angel hands easily rolled away the massive stone. The angel was a messenger of purity: he was like lightning in revealing light, and like snow in his judgment on the darkness of men's deed. He struck fear into men's hearts, and held them in a speechless awe: **the guards trembled and became like dead men.** We thrill to this story. But if that had been all that angels have to tell us, the tomb might almost better have remained sealed. We know God's power and purity, and we know our darkness; and that knowledge, if there were nothing more to know, would be our despair. But, mark clearly, the angel spoke in tenderness: **Do not be afraid.** He spoke in intimate concern for our heart-longings: **I know that you seek Jesus**—he had watched events—**who was crucified:** he understood with what sadness the friends of Jesus had watched the Cross from afar, and with what despair the scene had overwhelmed them. The angel spoke in hope and assurance: **He is not here; for he has risen, as he said.** How tenderly and simply the news is told! Such is Matthew's

6 He is not here: for he is risen, as he said. Come, see the place where the Lord lay. | that you seek Jesus who was crucified. 6 He is not here; for he has risen, as he said.

6. He has risen, as he said in his predictions of the Passion and Resurrection (16:21; 17:23; 20:19). Luke 24:6-7 makes this reference more explicit.

---

picture of the angel of the Resurrection. Beyond all our dull scientism it has its truth. It proclaims the fact that alone can explain the early church and the new faith of the followers of Christ. To that fact we now turn.

6. He Is Risen.—There is the fact that quickened the Christian church and sustains it through the years. The sign of our faith is not so much a crucifix as it is an empty cross; not an hourglass in the aging hands of Time, but an angel at the door of an empty tomb. Nay, the sign is not any sign at all, but a very Presence. Let us therefore consider anew the basis of our hope in eternal life. The hope is in us, mixed with our nature. The reason why men go on hoping, despite every calamity, is that they cannot help it. They are so born. They clear away the rubble of a bombed city even though they can see no promise in the act, because they have glimpsed, however fleetingly and vaguely, "the city which has foundations" (Heb. 11:10). Every one of us has suddenly wondered if the visible earth is real. At times it seems as if we could thrust a hand through it, as through a flimsy curtain, to touch the hidden reality. A child asked, "What is behind the sunset?" That is a final question, for we cannot escape the surmise that there is another world around about our world, as the solid ground is around about and underneath the heaving ocean. Without that hope in us the resurrection fact would find no lodgment, as the sun would be useless to men if men had no eyes.

God sends his beckonings and instigations to prompt and encourage men's hope of eternity. God through history and experience feeds the hope. Jesus did not create the hope of immortality: he brought a far richer gift. Human nature has always hoped, and the hope has always been stronger than a million deaths, because God has steadily fed the hope. Spring is a miracle—life from seeming death. Thus God beckons us through our eyes to trust him. Not only through our *eyes,* but at the very basis of our nature, his signs are given. Our *conscience* protests against the incompleteness of mortal days. We are assigned an agelong task, the fashioning of a true soul in a true world, with only an hour given for labor. We see what is right, but history mocks us, for the wrong is still rampant. Thus conscience points us to a world where mysteries are made clear, and wrongs are righted, and tears find compensa-

tion. Our *love* makes fiercer protest, for a veritable love is never willing to surrender those loved. That is why we carve gravestones in granite, for granite endures; and deck graves with flowers, for flowers are the sign of a new springtime. It is worth while for this particular generation to remember that it is almost an orphaned generation regarding the hope of real immortality. We have been so busy with our hands and eyes that the "things of the spirit" have grown dim. To some other ages the conviction of the next world has been stronger than the conviction of this world. But even for us, with our overemphasis on the measurements of sense, the eternal hope remains—under the stimulation of God.

But Christ "brought life and immortality to light through the gospel" (II Tim. 1:10). He traced its true nature: it is not a dreary sameness age on age, not a mere immortality of drab continuance, not that realm of shadowy half life which the Jewish Sheol pictured, but an ongoing vitality within the life and love of God. Jesus not only traced its true nature—which is his nature—but broke the bonds that hold men from it. How can sinful man aspire to the presence of God, or fulfill the destiny of the pure? He cannot, at least not in his own power. He cannot forgive the sins he hates, for sin is against God; and he cannot cancel the dark past, for only God can rule time. Jesus revealed God. Nay, God in Christ was wrestling with our sin upon the Cross, and proving his power over it by the resurrection of Christ from the dead. Thus Christ is the real beckoning of our hope, and sufficient the power through his presence. This Elizabeth Barrett Browning saw when she wrote:

When some beloved voice that was to you
Both sound and sweetness, faileth suddenly,
And silence against which you dare not cry,
Aches round you like a strong disease and new—
What hope? what help? what music will undo
That silence to your sense? Not friendship's sigh—
Not reason's subtle count. Not melody
Of viols, nor of pipes that Faunus blew—
Not songs of poets, nor of nightingales,
Whose hearts leap upward through the cypress trees
To the clear moon; nor yet the spheric laws
Self-chanted,—nor the angels' sweet "All hails,"
Met in the smile of God. Nay, none of these.
Speak *Thou,* availing Christ!—and fill this pause.[8]

[8] "Substitution."

7 And go quickly, and tell his disciples that he is risen from the dead; and, behold, he goeth before you into Galilee; there shall ye see him: lo, I have told you.

8 And they departed quickly from the sepulchre with fear and great joy; and did run to bring his disciples word.

Come, see the place where her lay. 7 Then go quickly and tell his disciples that he has risen from the dead, and behold, he is going before you to Galilee; there you will see him. Lo, I have told you." 8 So they departed quickly from the tomb with fear and great joy, and ran to tell his disciples.

r Some ancient authorities read the Lord.

7. **He is going before you to Galilee** looks back to the prediction in 26:32, but Matthew changes Mark's "he has told you" to **I have told you** because that verse was not addressed to the women (cf. on Mark 14:28; 16:7).

8. According to Mark 16:8, the women said nothing to anyone, for they were afraid. But here and in Luke 24:10-11 the women immediately run **to tell his disciples.**

Christ did "fill this pause," because God raised him from the dead. That is the fact behind the resurrection stories. The proof of the stories is not in the letter of the scripture, but in the change that befell his disciples, and in the change that may befall us. They were apprehended by Christ in very Presence. That we know: nothing else can explain their new insight, new power, new love. To adopt a feeble explanation of so vast a change is the worst form of superstition. The only explanation that explains is—**He is risen!** We have that assurance. We can confirm it in the venture of faith and prayer and deed.

8. *The Effect of the Resurrection.*—The accounts of the appearing of Jesus after his death have marks of authenticity. What fabricator would quickly think of making him appear to Mary, who had been cleansed of seven devils, or to the comparatively unknown other Mary, the mother of James the "younger"? That he appeared first to them rather than to his disciples is a record with deep meaning, for they had been witnesses of his crucifixion (see Expos., 27:55-56). The instant effect of the Resurrection was **fear.** We should not read our emotions into the characters of the passion history: the Jews then thought of personal survival in terms of bodily survival, and their fear was presumably a fear such as ours would be if we were to see a ghost. Mark's Gospel ends on that word: "afraid" (Mark 16:8).

Why is it that the human race has feared the sight of the dead? There is a leading question! The dead are dead, and so they cannot hurt us. Or can they? Easter should inspire a certain kind of fear. We live in an enclosed valley called earth, and Easter takes us to a neighboring height to show us a world vaster than we have dreamed. At once we are under judgment: it is one thing to grab and trample on the way to dust, but another to grab and trample on the way to life. We are under new responsibility: we are required so to live,

and so to strive to fashion our world, that all of us may be homelike when we reach that larger home beyond our valley. Our mortal days are no "five-year plan": our valley now is an eternal world.

But the fear was caught up in great joy. Christ being alive, the fetters of judgment were broken; for his forgiveness, spoken on earth, was now—they saw—God's own assurance. In France in World War I, there were two crucifixes close together, one broken and one strangely untouched. War-weary men knelt, not before the broken cross, but before that untouched cross. The broken cross may be compared with that which Jesus' followers saw on Good Friday, the unbroken cross with that from which Jesus rose in power. Likewise the new responsibility was girded about with God's own power. Men cannot live for eternity unless God be with them. Voltaire defined Easter as "a feast celebrated by Christians in remembrance of a God who was publicly hanged." He added, regarding the Sacrament, that Christians "feed on their God, doubtless to ascertain if, like the phoenix, He will spring into life from that which has devoured him." [4] We can be grateful for the skeptic's word: in the Resurrection, and repeatedly in the Sacrament, Christians have found that Christ springs into new life. The joy was yet greater—the redemption of sorrow. Death now wore a changed face. The little girl whose path from school led through a graveyard was asked if she was afraid: "No, I just cross it to reach home."

The other effect of the Resurrection was at the point of deeds: they ran to tell his disciples. Perhaps the joy grows dim except to those who try to translate it into action. In the old days in Russia the great and lowly, the czar and his sentry, would embrace one another on Easter morning, while one exclaimed, *Christos voscres!* —"Christ is risen!" and the other replied, *Vo*

4 H. L. Mencken, *A New Dictionary of Quotations* (New York: Alfred A. Knopf, 1942), p. 328.

9 ¶ And as they went to tell his disciples, behold, Jesus met them, saying, All hail. And they came and held him by the feet, and worshipped him.

10 Then said Jesus unto them, Be not afraid: go tell my brethren that they go into Galilee, and there shall they see me.

9 And behold, Jesus met them and said, "Hail!" And they came up and took hold of his feet and worshiped him. 10 Then Jesus said to them, "Do not be afraid; go and tell my brethren to go to Galilee, and there they will see me."

B. Jesus' Appearance to the Women (28:9-10)

9. The word translated **Hail** is the regular greeting (χαίρετε) which corresponds to our "How do you do?" It is difficult to render it into idiomatic English suitable to such a sublime occasion. Goodspeed has "Good morning!" The Basic English translates literally: "Be glad!"

10. Jesus' message is the same as that of the angel. Matthew may have a tradition that the Lord appeared to the women, but that is all. Both Mark and Matthew look forward to an important appearance of the Lord in Galilee, but the latter may know of a tradition that Jesus was seen in Jerusalem, as do Luke and John.

---

istine voscres—"He is risen indeed." [5] Then unhappily they would relapse into the old prejudices and injustices. The final confirmation of Christian truth is that it shall be inwrought—by venture of deeds. They knew Livingstone's body by the fractured joint, the arm that the lion had maimed. [6] By that arm Livingstone knew the truth of the gospel. So in this one verse we can read, in almost full-orbed verity, the effect of the Resurrection.

9-10. *Jesus Met Them.*—John Erskine, in his *Human Life of Jesus*, [7] expresses surprise that the Christian church makes so much of the mystic aspects of the Resurrection. He "accepts" the resurrection truth: the disciples, he says in effect, felt Jesus was with them after death, as we feel that some dear friend of ours is near though lost to sight. But why, he asks in effect, should the church centralize the fact? It is an astonishingly blind question. No story of the Resurrection gives us right to say that the disciples "felt" Jesus was still with them. All the stories agree that they felt no such thing: they counted him as dead, locked in a sealed tomb. The resurrection fact broke on them in shattering surprise of joy. Their friend was not the same friend they had known: he was now their regnant Lord. **Jesus met them**: the initiatives were in heaven. He took them unawares in their grief and despair.

How homey the greeting: **Hail!** Goodspeed translates it "Good morning." That seems all too familiar, but it is accurate; for **Hail!** was the customary salutation when friends met.

[5] *The Book of Easter* (New York: The Macmillan Co., 1910), p. 74.

[6] William Garden Blaikie, *The Personal Life of David Livingstone* (New York: Harper & Bros., 1881), pp. 451-52.

[7] New York: William Morrow & Co., 1945, ch. xix, especially pp. 238-40.

The exact rendering is "Be glad!" or "Rejoice!" If the stories were inventions, surely the writers had been under strong temptation to make Jesus appear in judgment before Pilate, or to show him cleansing the temple of false leaders. But he came lowly-wise: "Be glad!" John (20:19) says "Peace to you!" which also was a daily greeting. What depth of gladness he brought in very fact, and what depth of peace! Ordinary words on his lips take eternal meaning.

It was like him to quiet their fears: **Do not be afraid.** Often he had said that in his earthly journey. Now he said it in a strength that had triumphed over death. John S. Whale has the story of a musician who, on hearing "some perfectly convincing phrase" in one of Beethoven's symphonies, would say, "Of course, if that is so, there is no occasion to worry." [8] Christians have that confidence when they hear the chord of the Resurrection. **My brethren** has an equal tenderness. Perhaps he meant his immediate family, for the early church stressed the fact of a resurrection appearance to James, the brother of Christ. Perhaps he meant his disciples, or the wider circle of his followers. In any event there is forgiveness in the word, and a great depth of love. **They . . . worshiped him.** Before Easter Jesus was "prophet" or "Messiah." Scholars tend more and more to believe that he was slow to claim the too nationalistically interpreted title of Messiah. After Easter all the old titles became too small—tiny nets that could not sweep an ocean. After Easter Jesus was "Lord," "the Word," "our Savior." That event turned their blindness into piercing sight, their earthly ambition into love of the brotherhood, their cowardice into courage that feared no persecution or death. The Resurrection is the great divide of human history.

[8] *Christian Doctrine*, p. 155.

11 ¶ Now when they were going, behold, some of the watch came into the city, and showed unto the chief priests all the things that were done.

12 And when they were assembled with the elders, and had taken counsel, they gave large money unto the soldiers,

13 Saying, Say ye, His disciples came by night, and stole him *away* while we slept.

14 And if this come to the governor's ears, we will persuade him, and secure you.

15 So they took the money, and did as they were taught: and this saying is commonly reported among the Jews until this day.

16 ¶ Then the eleven disciples went away into Galilee, into a mountain where Jesus had appointed them.

11 While they were going, behold, some of the guard went into the city and told the chief priests all that had taken place. 12 And when they had assembled with the elders and taken counsel, they gave a sum of money to the soldiers 13 and said, "Tell people, 'His disciples came by night and stole him away while we were asleep.' 14 And if this comes to the governor's ears, we will satisfy him and keep you out of trouble." 15 So they took the money and did as they were directed; and this story has been spread among the Jews to this day.

16 Now the eleven disciples went to Galilee, to the mountain to which Jesus had

---

C. The False Witness of the Guards (28:11-15)

11-15. The **soldiers** appear to belong to the Roman army and are responsible to Pilate. **This story has been spread among the Jews to this day,** i.e., the time when the Gospel is written; cf. on 27:62-66. Justin Martyr's *Dialogue with Trypho* (ch. 108) shows that the same calumny was current in the middle of the second century, but Justin is largely dependent on Matthew for details. In the Gospel of Peter (11:46-49) the soldiers and elders report directly to Pilate, and he advises them to keep silent for fear the Jewish people will stone them all.

D. Final Appearance to the Eleven (28:16-20)

The Gospel of Matthew now comes to a conclusion which is suited to its stirring development and its magnificent theme. It began in the spirit of the O.T. with the royal genealogy of the true Messiah, and it ends with the universal Savior and Lord of heaven and earth. The practical ethical interest which led the evangelist to put the Sermon on the Mount near the forefront of the Gospel and which pervades its eschatology (25:31-46) is not eclipsed even by the supernatural wonder of the Resurrection, for the parting words of Jesus emphasize the importance of all his teaching. The effect of this brief scene on the life of the Christian church has been incalculable. No part of the Bible, with the possible exception of the letter to the Romans, has done more to give Christians the vision of a world-wide church. It has sent them to all nations, bearing the message of salvation through Christ, with which are linked the responsibility and privilege of obeying his words.

11-15. *The Bribing of the Soldiers.*—These verses complete the story related in 27:62-65, 66 (see that Expos.). Almost all commentators agree that the story has legendary elements. The verses now before us do not lessen the difficulties. In 27:65 the soldiers are described as members of the temple guard, but this account would have us believe they belonged to Pilate's Italian cohort. The admission on the part of the soldiers that they slept would have been confession of a guilt punishable with death. Furthermore, it is hard to imagine that the temple leaders would have as much influence with Pilate as is here indicated. The

Gospel of Peter gives a quite different version of the story.[9] We would be wise to find here a reflection of the controversy between the synagogue and the church, a strife that continued well into the second century. But if we strike deep into the story, we reach a bedrock of truth. What a tribute to the new power of the Christian church that the synagogue should have to brand Jesus as an impostor, and should have to fabricate a story of a plundered tomb to account for resurrection joy! And what an unconscious tribute to Christ and the new life

[9] Harris, *Newly-Recovered Gospel of St. Peter*, pp. 37-38.

17 And when they saw him, they wor- | directed them. 17 And when they saw him
shipped him: but some doubted. | they worshiped him; but some doubted.

Luke 24 and John 20 knew only of resurrection appearances in or near Jerusalem. This section and John 21:1-14 tell of appearances in Galilee, and the story in Luke 5:1-10 may originally have been a third narrative of this kind. I Cor. 15 says nothing of the location, and there is nothing to prevent us from supposing that Jesus was seen in various places where his disciples were assembled.

The striking feature of this account is that it tells of a final commission from the risen Lord to his disciples. There is a widespread tradition that such a commission was given, though it takes various forms. Here Matthew thinks of the command in rabbinical terms: the disciples are to baptize, make disciples, and teach. In Luke 24:47-48 and Acts 1:8 they are to be witnesses and to preach repentance; this is Luke's characteristic interpretation of Christianity. The Fourth Evangelist looks on Christianity as a church whose members must be holy, separate from the world, and filled with love for the brotherhood, and so in John 20:23 the commission is regarded as an empowering with the Holy Spirit to forgive sins or to exclude gross sinners from the fellowship. We conclude, therefore, that the church believed it had its missionary impulse from an appearance of the risen Christ, but there was no fixed tradition of his exact words.

16. **Jesus had directed them** to a certain mountain, but we are not told when or how. It is tempting to think they went to the mount where he had been transfigured or where he had given the sermon, but this is only speculation.

17. **They worshiped him** with full Christian worship, as they had not done before the Crucifixion. That **some doubted** may correspond to the facts; cf. Luke 24:11, 37-42. Jesus himself had said that resurrection from the dead would not necessarily convince everyone (Luke 16:31), and we are not to suppose that all disciples had perfect faith.

he quickened in his followers! There are also sadder truths. Our money itch is such that men *can* be bribed to hide the truth and spread an untruth, as modern "propaganda" well proves. The answer given by the early church to the calumny spoken in the synagogue was not very convincing, nor was it always in Christian spirit. The synagogue persecuted the new faith; the early Christians, acting under provocation, castigated the synagogue leaders. The word **Jews** in vs. 15 is evidence. The writer of this Gospel was a Jew. But so great is his anger against injustices brought on the church by the synagogue that he thus separates himself from his own people. Thus bitter controversies make enmities—and such sins as anti-Semitism.

17. *They Worshiped Him; but Some Doubted.* —The Gospels stress the Jerusalem resurrection appearances, but it is not improbable that the first appearance of the risen Lord occurred in Galilee. We cannot specify the mountain (vs. 16), however much we may be tempted to conjecture. **Worshiped** is a strong word: the disciples knew now that their "teacher," whom the people regarded only as a "prophet," was regnant Lord. The verb is not found elsewhere in the Gospels (in relation to the adoration of Christ) except in 14:33, which may also have originated in a resurrection experience. But **some doubted**. It is not an unkindly word. We do not know to whom it refers: the apparent reference is to the disciples themselves. Almost certainly the word is used of the followers of Jesus, not of bystanders. Some measure of doubt is almost inevitable. We all sin, and sin clouds our faith. Meanwhile our minds are dim at best, and the ways of God are a great deep of mystery. Perhaps the conviction that Jesus lived beyond death came slowly to some of his followers. Perhaps some saw, but counted the news too good to be true. Perhaps others saw, and denied that they had seen Jesus. Our life of fitful faith and doubt is here seen in two words—**worshiped** and **doubted**.

Doubt is perhaps not the opposite of faith, but only faith's misgiving. We could hardly doubt what does not exist: if we doubt God, we have perhaps therefore already glimpsed him. We need not fear doubt unless it comes from sin: there is faith in honest doubt.

Who never doubted never half believed.
Where doubt there truth is—'tis her shadow [1]

The opposite of faith is not doubt, but cynicism. How is doubt overcome? Not greatly by argument. For truth does not rest on our mind's poor logic: we ourselves and our poor reasoning rest back on truth. Besides, argument breeds conflict, and in that bitter air faith cannot live. We must apply the proper tests to our doubts:

[1] Philip James Bailey, *Festus: A Country Town.*

18 And Jesus came and spake unto them, saying, All power is given unto me in heaven and in earth.

19 ¶ Go ye therefore, and teach all nations, baptizing them in the name of the Father, and of the Son, and of the Holy Ghost:

18 And Jesus came and said to them, "All authority in heaven and on earth has been given to me. 19 Go therefore and make disciples of all nations, baptizing them in the name of the Father and of the Son and

---

18. It is appropriate to worship one who has **all authority in heaven and on earth.** This is the universal faith of the early Christians, and it differs only in terminology and emphasis from John's doctrine that Jesus is God (John 1:1; 10:30; 20:28).

19. Such a faith naturally issues in the concept of the Trinity. Paul had frequently linked Christ with God and the Holy Spirit (e.g., II Cor. 13:14; I Cor. 12:4-6), and the

---

the tests that apply to potatoes do not apply to people, let alone to the ever-present Christ. We must bring our doubts to God in a venture of prayer. John's Gospel tells how Thomas brought his skepticism directly to Christ and was answered (John 20:24-29). It is worthier and far more enlightened to "pray through" a doubt than to reiterate it to ourselves or to splatter it on our neighbors. We must also make the venture of life; for tomorrow the sun will rise, and we must live by some faith, even though proof may seem to tarry. Those who venture on the resurrection power of Christ will find him near in girding strength. This Gospel is witness.

18. All Authority.—The Gospel ends with a claim (vs. 18), a great commission (vs. 19), and a great promise (vs. 20). Perhaps these concluding words are not an exact transcript of the language of Christ. They seem to reflect both the meditation and experience of the early church. But they are not therefore less true. Rather they give the substance of his teaching —as it was ratified in the venture of his first-century followers. "One religion is as good as another" says our casual age, but that is a shallowness which Christianity can never concede. **All authority** means supreme right to appoint to office: thence comes the great commission. It means right to require obedience—because of love poured out unto death, and now triumphant in the eternal kingdom. It means right to govern in both earth and heaven. A true faith is not chosen by men: it chooses men. It is not a garment that we can don or doff, but a very life. Christ claims to be the Lord of life.

Christ has spoken *the* word about our human nature: we are "lost" without God, yet intended for the kingdom, and God has sought and still seeks us in him. Christ has spoken *the* word about salvation: he is himself the Word from above history who enters history to redeem. Christ has spoken *the* word about human destiny: men are not intricate congeries of veins and nerves, but children of God by adoption

through Christ. Christ has spoken *the* word about God—in very Incarnation. Other faiths give gleams of God's light: they are the flush in the sky before the dawn. But Christ is the brightness of his rising, "the fulness of the Godhead bodily" (Col. 2:9). Thus there is but one central question. Perhaps it is not "What would Jesus do?" for we are not Jesus, and cannot presume fully to say or know what he would do. It is rather "What would Jesus have me do?" So long as we consult "our best judgment," or "the calculated risks of politics," or "what our friends think," or "the wisdom of men" we thus far deny the authority of Christ. Not seldom his commands run counter to what seems to us to be practical wisdom. He has right to command. The command is spoken in the gentleness of love and the rigor of holiness. He shares with us all the hazards of obedience. The issue of his dictates is joy. But—authority **is** his, in heaven and earth.

19. The Great Commission: Its World Venture.—We need not long pause to ask how the sense of world mission came to the early church. It may have been mediated *through* the failure of the plea to Jewry, but it came *from* the lips and life of Christ. **All nations** is a recurrent theme in his teaching. Let the reader trace the word "world" through his recorded words. In an age of narrow loyalties, when national prejudices were sharpened into animosity and often into contempt, Jesus ranged the world both in the gifts of his love and the yearning of his gospel. "One world" made its bid for a time to become an accepted slogan, the expression of a recognized necessity; but, had we listened, we could have heard it long ago from Christ.

The world venture is written in our human nature. In that sense it is "in the constitution." Our language is the bequest of the speech of many lands and generations. Our music knows no national boundaries. Our food comes from the ends of the earth. Moreover, our wishes and our curiosity bind us to mankind. Whatever our prejudice, travel posters quicken our hunger to

ideas of the Fourth Gospel provide the groundwork for the later doctrine. This verse in Matthew is evidence that the threefold name is coming to be used in baptism in place of the earlier formula "in the name of the Lord Jesus" (Acts 2:38; 8:16; etc.).

The Synoptic tradition never suggests that Jesus baptized or that his disciples adopted the custom before the Resurrection (but contrast John 3:5, 26; 4:1-2). As the

---

see how other people live. *The Good Earth* is a novel about China, *Lost Horizon* about Tibet. Travelogues have a perennial interest. If we lived on one bank of a river, we would be curious concerning folk on the other bank; and nowadays oceans are no wider than a river.

> The world stands out on either side
> No wider than the heart is wide; [2]

and the poet is right in her insistence that if we try to live in narrow heart, we suffocate.

But this writing on our nature is not enough; for our self-love denies the world bond, and of ourselves at best we have little to give. The commission of Christ comes to fulfill our nature in the bond of the gospel. Gratitude constrains us. For we ourselves learned of Christ through Christian missionaries, and must in very thanksgiving share the gift we have received. Joy constrains us. Joy must be shared: a doctor would be called recreant if he did not proclaim his discovery of cure, and the Christian is a recreant if he fails to tell the glad peace and power of Christ. But even when we do not feel either gratitude or joy, even when our mood is low, we are under orders: **go therefore.** Authority is Christ's, but he stoops to use our human hand and heart to work his will. His followers have not always obeyed: Acts 11:1-18 is a record of prejudice yielding stubbornly to his command. But the church has in measure obeyed him in scorn of consequence, and has carried the gospel to the world. Kagawa was convinced that until the Christians of Japan should number one million strong they could not become a creative force mighty enough to fashion the nation's life according to the Christian pattern.[3] The "marching orders" remain: **go therefore.**

19. *The Great Commission: Its Method.*— **Make disciples** is the method, **baptizing** and **teaching** being the components of the main task. When the words were first spoken, there were a dozen men, none of whom seemed worth mentioning in a history book, and a Leader whom Renan, with crass blindness, called "the illusion of an impassioned woman." [4] And now? Celsus said it was "the wildest of dreams" to believe that people of many lands could have

"one mind in religion." [5] Now we see that they must have one mind or die in their violent hates. Now the logic of history points to the alternative—Christ or chaos.

Baptizing: the Christian rite has its place. Beyond all the sometimes needless controversies, it has more than its own kindling symbolism. Perhaps Matthew was swayed, in the use of the word, by the baptism which the synagogue required of proselytes. What of it? Christianity made the rite rich in history and more quickening in its significance. **Baptizing** *into* has a profound meaning (see next Expos.). Some symbol or ritual we cannot avoid—until we succeed in living as disembodied spirits. The Christian forms, especially of baptism and the Lord's Supper, have been and are used of God with singular blessing. They vivify truth; they unite the church; through the Word that accompanies them they are the "means of grace."

Teaching is a term that reflects the finely ethical strain in this Gospel: the kingdom life is no mere emotion but understanding in righteousness. But it goes beyond ethic: it is life and joy. Sometimes Christian preaching and teaching are condemned as propaganda. There is a strange description indeed! Does not he who condemns stand himself condemned by his argument? Has he not perhaps become a propagandist in the very condemnation? Propaganda is for the material benefit of a group greedy for cash or power; and it hides half the truth, and exploits human nature. How can such a charge be maintained against Christ? If other lands refuse him at our hands, the fault is not in him but in the uncleanness of our hands; and the solving of the problem is not in our silence, but in our penitence. The Christian teacher must be silent at times, for he is never coercive; and he is a learner, even while he teaches, both from God and man. But speak and teach he must: to hold a known joy and peace would be as impossible as holding breath. A German pastor, placed in a concentration camp by the Nazis, had only one complaint: his captors would not let him sing! "So we sing without voice: with our souls do we the singing, a loud resounding Gloria!"

But "disciple" as a verb (μαθητεύσατε) is still the central word. Beyond all forms and all speech, life itself is the best evidence of the authority of Christ. Mission stations have con-

[2] From "Renascence." Copyright, 1912, 1940, by the author, Edna St. Vincent Millay.

[3] William Axling, *Kagawa* (New York: Harper & Bros., 1932), ch. ix, especially pp. 116-17.

[4] *Life of Jesus*, p. 402.

[5] Froude, *Short Studies on Great Subjects*, p. 273.

20 Teaching them to observe all things whatsoever I have commanded you: and, | of the Holy Spirit, 20 teaching them to observe all that I have commanded you; and

---

Jewish synagogue received proselytes by baptism, so Jesus' followers are to **make disciples of all nations.** To baptize in (or perhaps "into," εἰς) **the name** means to baptize into the possession and protection of the Godhead, and to establish a vital union between **God** and the believer.

20. Jesus is **with his church always** (as in 18:20), **to the close of the age** (cf. on 13:39). It is fitting that the Gospel should end with this phrase (found also in 13:39,

---

tinued to live the faith even when some edict has silenced their voice. "You can refute Hegel, but not the Saint," writes W. B. Yeats.[6] The saints are lowly folk who know themselves forgiven and empowered in Christ, and who now live in him and for him. To this life Christ calls all his followers. Livelihood is only the scaffolding of their life: the end and aim of their days is to obey the Great Commission. They are to be the "epistle of Christ, . . . written not with ink, but with the Spirit of the living God; not in tables of stone, but in fleshly tables of the heart" (II Cor. 3:3). Their language is the word of flesh and blood—by the power of the indwelling Word.

19. *The Great Commission: Its End and Aim.* —Into **the name of** is a salient phrase. The words are not casual. The baptismal act is not casual, as if someone were to say, "I do this in so-and-so's name." *Name* has the meaning of personal nature. There are many inscriptions remaining in Greece of the far-off days when soldiers swore themselves "into the name" of High Zeus.[7] In our own time a check made out to the name of a neighbor means that money to that amount is given into his possession. When a man is baptized "into the name of the Father," he is thus given into the possession and protection of God—by his own act and the act of the church, in token of the great act of the Cross. Probably this baptismal formula was simpler in the very first days of the church—"in the name of the Lord Jesus." The formula of vs. 19 was probably a later development. But it is not therefore untrue: it is more true, as the full flower is the best truth about a rosebush. The doctrine of the Trinity is not a mathematical puzzle, except to minds resolved to see nothing but elementary mathematics. Nor is it the devising of theologians. It is the flower of experience—as, for instance, in the development of this scripture. We know God as Father of mankind and Creator of the world: when all arguments are spoken and forgotten, that conviction returns. We know God in the Incarna-

tion. Our human titles for Jesus are true, but they are so pitiably feeble as to become untrue, for there are depths in him which no human word can fathom. We know God in his Holy Spirit—in that visitation at Pentecost in which the church was born, and in a personal constraint that convicts us of sin and pleads with us to follow Christ. These are three gifts given in Person, but they are yet a unity.

Dorothy L. Sayers, in her *Mind of the Maker*, has argued that we may find parallels to the Trinity in our own mundane realm.[8] A Shakespeare play is first in the mind of the author; then incarnate in words written, and spoken, and acted on a stage; and then a persuasive spirit so that all know what is meant by a *King Lear* tragedy. Only in elementary mathematics can we find a single unity, and mathematics is an abstract study. In the realm of life the unities are multiple unities. A tree is thus a multiple unity—branches and leaves are each separate, yet one with the life of the tree. A man is not a single unity, for it is inconceivable that he could live alone: his nature is one with the life of the family and the life of mankind. The mystery of God is a multiple unity: the medieval mystics used to speak of "the family of God." The last chapter of Leonard Hodgson's *Doctrine of the Trinity* has traced the richness that enters life when the Christian adores Father, Son, and Holy Spirit.[9] The end and aim of the Great Commission is to bring men into the possession and the power of God the Creator, Christ the Redeemer, and the Holy Spirit who is our guide and advocate. Thus this Gospel sees man's destiny fulfilled in the vast light and intimate love of the triune God.

20. *The Great Promise.*—The Gospel of Mark is an unfinished symphony. The ending has been lost, or Mark was prevented by some untimely act from the completion of his work. Luke's conclusion is in the sound of constant praise in the temple. John brings his Gospel to its close by declaring that the cosmos could not contain everything that could be said and written about Jesus. This Gospel ends in—the Shekinah: the promise of the never-failing pres-

[6] Joseph Hone, *W. B. Yeats* (New York: The Macmillan Co., 1943), p. 510.

[7] Quoted, Green, *Gospel According to Saint Matthew*, p. 258.

[8] (New York: Harcourt, Brace & Co., 1941), pp. 36 ff.

[9] (New York: Charles Scribner's Sons, 1944.)

| lo, I am with you alway, *even* unto the end of the world. Amen. | lo, I am with you always, to the close of the age." |

40, 49; 24:3), because Matthew always looks forward to the great day when Jesus, who has never deserted his people, will be visibly present in his celestial glory to judge the world and to say once more, "Come, O blessed of my Father, inherit the kingdom prepared for you from the foundation of the world" (25:34).

ence of Christ. The pledge is more than one of "influence." Perhaps "influence" is impossible without personal survival: we cannot tell. If influence were thus possible, it would be poor comfort: we yearn for the person. The pledge means far more than that there shall be shed over history a certain glow from far-off Palestine. If that were all, it might be but a dim light to make visible the tragedy. The pledge is that Jesus is here, not as mere "directional beam," but as very friend and Savior. Well might R. W. Dale come to a halt as he paced his study on Easter eve, and cry, "Christ is alive! . . . Christ is living, Christ is living!" [1] Indeed, Christ is alive, and with us.

This fact constitutes in certain ways the distinctive Christian experience. Books have been written to show that the genuinely mystic experience is one in every age and land. But the Christian mystic has a life different and distinct: Christ in very presence. Christ, not a mere eclecticism of "spirit," is for him the "mystic way" and the "heavenly illumination." The joy comes to personal focus and personal love. Perhaps this joy most often comes slowly: Christ is first a Figure on a page, then a Light against which all life is silhouetted, then a Face and a Presence. Those who meditate on him, and pray in his name, and strive to do his bidding, find at last that he is the Companion of the daily road. **Always** is a poignant word. "All the days" is the literal translation. We live in days, and do not know what a day may bring. There are days of confident faith, and days of sad blundering. There are days when the birth of a child brings joy, and days when the death of a child brings sorrow. There are days of peace, and days of war. There are days when life is music, and days when despair wraps us in impenetrable mist. "All the days" Christ is with us, and our very sadness is "shade of His hand, outstretched caressingly." [2]

The triumphant ring of this promise came through Matthew's own venture. We know something of the persecutions which he and his fellow Christians faced in the Syrian church. They dared all for Christ, and so found that Christ was with them. Gilmour of Mongolia wrote: "No one who does not go away, leaving all and going alone, can feel the force of this promise." [3] He knew—by the hazard of life consecrate to Christ. So we may know. Wherever the church makes that venture, Christ is near—in "all authority." **To the close of the age.** That phrase cannot be dismissed as apocalypticism. The sinfulness and mortalities of our life bring, from time to time, the end of an era. Philosophies of history now trace the decline of civilizations, and hint that our age is a setting sun. The atomic bomb, we were told, could result in a chain reaction, and therefore in the extinction of our planet. To the early Christians this promise meant that when the curtain fell (soon) on all human history, Christ would remain as Friend and Lord. The climaxes of this planet (or any other) do not take him by surprise, and they cannot usurp his power. The medieval mystics said, "Everything matters, nothing matters." In very truth, for only Christ matters: and he is with us **always, to the close of the age;** for he is the contemporary and eternal Christ, our Redeemer, Friend, and sovereign Lord.

[1] A. W. W. Dale, *The Life of R. W. Dale* (London: Hodder & Stoughton, 1898), pp. 642-43.

[2] Francis Thompson, "The Hound of Heaven."
[3] *James Gilmour of Mongolia*, ed. Richard Lovett (London: Religious Tract Society, 1893), p. 39.

The Gospel According to

ST. MARK

Introduction and Exegesis by FREDERICK C. GRANT

Exposition by HALFORD E. LUCCOCK

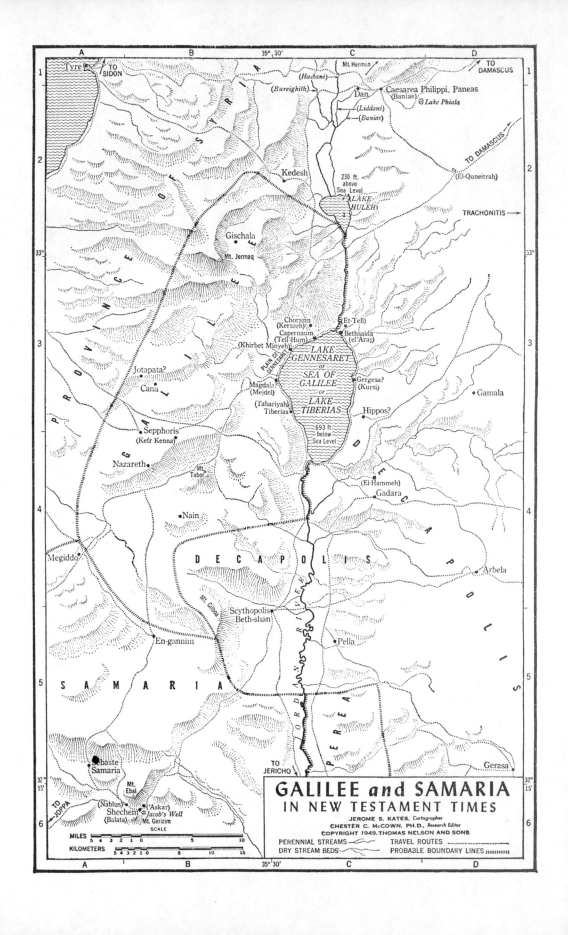

GALILEE *and* SAMARIA
IN NEW TESTAMENT TIMES

JEROME S. KATES, *Cartographer*
CHESTER C. McCOWN, PH.D., *Research Editor*
COPYRIGHT·1949, THOMAS NELSON AND SONS

PERENNIAL STREAMS   TRAVEL ROUTES
DRY STREAM BEDS   PROBABLE BOUNDARY LINES

MILES
KILOMETERS
SCALE

MARK

INTRODUCTION

The interpreter's first duty is thoroughly to understand the text, passage, or book which he is expounding. This is his only safeguard against shallow and eccentric exegesis, and the only guarantee that he will not read in his own private views or perhaps some modernizing explanation which, however popular or even true, has no justification in the Bible. In order thoroughly to understand the text he must also understand the passage, or context, in which it is found; and to understand the passage he must understand the whole book. One might go even further and say that in order to understand the particular book the interpreter must understand the whole New Testament, the whole Bible. It is the aim of this commentary to help the preacher and teacher of the Bible to understand the Gospel According to St. Mark as it was meant to be understood by its author, and as it was understood from the first by its earliest readers.

The Synoptic Gospels—and chiefly the earliest of them, the Gospel According to St. Mark—are often studied as source books for the life of Jesus. That is a reasonable procedure, since almost our only sources for his life are contained in these books. But the Gospels were not written for any such purpose, and before they can be so used they must themselves be understood and interpreted in the light of what they were meant to be. They are not histories or biographies, but didactic, apologetic, "evangelical" writings; that is, they aim to set forth the message of salvation through Jesus Christ, as proclaimed and believed by the apostolic church, and they make use of historical materials with this end in view. Their main purpose is not to preserve a record of the past, but to set forth "the common salvation." Jesus' teaching is included, in fuller measure by Matthew and Luke than by Mark, not as a précis or summary of the Master's system of doctrine— as in some philosophical school—but as setting forth the "way of life in accordance with the sayings and commandments of the Lord"; it is the Master's guide for his disciples, here and now, and under the circumstances of the present, rather than a record for future generations of what he said on such and such an occasion or on this or that particular day. Even Luke, the most historically minded of the evangelists, is clearly an apologist for the Christian faith: his great two-volume work—which we know separately as Luke and Acts—is a defense of Christianity against the charge that it was a subversive movement, disloyal to the government, bent on destroying public law and order. Matthew equally clearly reflects the conditions of a more settled Christian community facing internal problems of order and discipline. Mark, addressed to a martyr church, stresses the heroic ethics demanded by that situation, and above all the heroic example of the Son of God, the church's Lord, as he himself faced death—the victorious Martyr and Lord who was even now present with his amazed and terrified disciples as he had been present with the twelve in Galilee and Jerusalem, in the roaring storm at sea one dark night, and in the lonely, silent garden on the night before he was crucified. The historical element is present in the Synoptic Gospels, of course; it is also found in John, though still another purpose inspires that Gospel, and the teaching has been completely restated in a set of terms and ideas quite different from those found in the older tradition. But the historical element is not the primary or basic content of these books; the primary, fundamental subject is the message of salvation which these books set forth, and the historical tradition is used for a definite purpose—a purpose, moreover, altogether different from what is to be expected in a historical or biographical work.

I. Origin

The oldest ecclesiastical tradition regarding the origin of Mark's Gospel is that given by Papias, bishop of Hierapolis, about A.D. 140. Eusebius quotes him in his *Church History* (III. 39. 15) as follows:

This also the presbyter used to say: "Mark, indeed, who became the interpreter of Peter, wrote accurately, as far as he remembered them, the things said or done by the Lord, but not however in order." For he [Mark] had neither heard the Lord nor been his personal follower, but at a later stage, as I said, he had followed Peter, who used to adapt the teachings to the needs of the moment, but not as though he were drawing up a connected account of the oracles of the Lord: so that Mark committed no error in writing certain matters just as he remembered them. For he had only one object in view, namely to leave out nothing of the things which he had heard, and to include no false statement among them.

How much of this quotation is from the "presbyter"—whom Papias is drawing upon—and how much is from Papias himself, it is difficult to say. The majority of modern scholars apparently favor the view that the presbyter's statement is limited to the opening sentence; the rest is Papias' comment.[1]

With this "testimony" of Papias agrees the oft-quoted statement of Irenaeus, bishop of Lyons, about A.D. 180: "After the deaths [of Peter and Paul] Mark, the disciple and interpreter of Peter, himself also handed down to us in writing the things which Peter had proclaimed." [2] Irenaeus' statement may of course be only an echo of Papias—as the later "traditions" turn out for the most part to be echoes of one or the other of these two men. The bishop of Lyons was familiar with Papias' work —as was also Eusebius, who had no very high estimation of his intelligence ("a very pedestrian mind"). We do not, of course, possess Papias' book, *Interpretation of the Lord's Oracles,* and so can form no estimate of it for ourselves. It was probably still in existence in the fourteenth century, according to Harnack; and a copy may turn up someday in the sands of Egypt or in some uncatalogued monastic library. In the meantime we can only hazard a conjecture as to the value of its "testimony" and the reliability of the "tradition" Eusebius found in it. Many modern scholars agree with Kirsopp Lake that Papias was only guessing. He had the tradition of Peter's residence in Rome and martyrdom there, and also the tradition that

Mark's Gospel was written in Rome; and he put the two together in order to frame a theory which would account for (a) Mark's early date and (b) its obvious divergence in order from the other Gospels, perhaps chiefly John— though Papias can hardly have been an ardent champion of that Gospel. It is generally recognized that one of the tests for canonicity in the second century was apostolic authorship; Papias' theory was one way of meeting this demand in the case of Mark, and of refuting the charges, based chiefly on its peculiar order, which were brought against that Gospel—the author of Mark was not an apostle, true enough, but he did write down an apostle's recollections, though naturally not in strict chronological sequence.

If this interpretation is correct, the main presuppositions of Papias' statement are that the Gospel According to St. Mark originated at Rome soon after the martyrdom of Peter (A.D. 62 or 64), and that it was, two generations later, competing for survival with a Gospel or with Gospels whose order had come to be recognized as standard and authoritative. The Petrine origin of Mark's contents may be more an inference by Papias than a positive tradition. It is supported by some passages in the Gospel (for example, the day in Capernaum, in ch. 1) but not by others. Certainly the view that the Gospel as a whole is based upon Peter's recollections, thus guaranteeing every statement it contains, and even to some extent its chronology, is untenable; not many will agree with C. H. Turner, that verbs in the third person can often be turned back into the first: instead of "he went," "we went"; or "we heard him say," instead of "Jesus said."

The probability is that Mark's Gospel is a compilation of the oral tradition current in the Christian community at Rome in the sixties. Some of the contents of the book may already have been written down before Mark wrote. B. Harvie Branscomb [3] recognizes a number of these written sources: the controversies in 2:1-3:6, and possibly also those in ch. 12; the apocalyptic ch. 13; the collection of parables in ch. 4; the passion narrative in chs. 14-15; the list of the twelve in ch. 3; the account of the Baptist in ch. 1; Mark's "proof texts" from the Old Testament; the account of incidents about the Sea of Galilee in chs. 6-8, which contain an unusual number of topographical references; and probably still others. Much of this material, if not all of it, originally existed as oral tradition; and oral tradition in the ancient religious world, especially in Palestine, was as a rule fairly rigidly stereotyped. That is, it was a tradition, something handed down from the

[1] See Frederick C. Grant, *The Earliest Gospel* (New York and Nashville: Abingdon-Cokesbury Press, 1943), p. 34.

[2] *Against Heresies* III. 1. 1; cf. Eusebius *Church History* V. 8. 3.

[3] *The Gospel of Mark* (New York: Harper & Bros., 1937), p. xxiii ff.

past, and to be handed on to the future, without undue modification. This being so, it does not greatly matter at what precise point the tradition "crystallized" in writing. The oral traditions contained in the ancient Jewish books had often been handed on for several generations before they were "fixed" in written form. Of course many of these rabbinical traditions were concerned with legal interpretations—like the Moslem *Kadith*—and were the possession of the schools in which they were accurately memorized; to that extent the parallel with the gospel tradition does not hold. At the same time the sayings of Jesus were undoubtedly viewed by the earliest church—that is, among Christian Jews in Palestine—as the Christian Halakah, setting forth the Christian way of life, and they would therefore be remembered in more or less fixed form. The amount of variation found in parallel narratives in the Gospels is not greater than is found in parallel narratives in ancient rabbinical literature; there is, however, somewhat more variety in the sayings and parables of Jesus, as related in various Gospels or sources within the Gospels, than we find in the variously reported sayings and interpretations of the rabbis. And for the best of reasons: (*a*) there was no school of legal interpretation in the early church nor was Jesus' teaching mainly an interpretation of Scripture; and (*b*) the Greek-speaking, Gentile-born Christians of the world outside Palestine had not quite the same regard for spoken words as for written—and even written words suffered editing enough on the level of popular religion.

There were two factors of immense and continuing importance in the transmission of the earliest evangelic tradition: one was its origin in Palestine—many a passage is still fragrant with the air of Galilee—while the other was the medium through which it was handed down —the Greek-speaking church of the Gentiles. At its very earliest stage the language of the gospel tradition was undoubtedly Aramaic, the language of Jesus and of his first followers, the original disciples in Galilee and Jerusalem. How soon translation into Greek was begun we cannot say: probably very early, since Greek was used to some extent in Palestine even in the first century and much more in the second, and since "Hellenists"—Greek-speaking Jews—were to be found in the Christian community in Jerusalem from a very early date (Acts 6:1). It seems certain that the Gospels were written in Greek—the fact that the New Testament as a whole is a collection of *Greek* writings is enormously significant—and were produced by and for the Gentile Christian church. The theory that the Gospels were written in Aramaic and later translated, as completed books, into Greek, has not won general assent, but their underlying traditions were certainly for the most part originally in Aramaic—as is proved by the frequent survival of Aramaic words and turns of expression, grammar and thought, and by the occasional mistranslations which C. C. Torrey and other scholars have pointed out. The traditions underlying Mark, and even more those underlying Matthew and Luke (compare their versions of the Beatitudes), had evidently circulated for a long time in Greek before they were written down. Not that the translation was the work of one time, place, or person; what Papias said of the "logia," which he assigned to Matthew, was doubtless true of the tradition as a whole: "Each translated as he was able" (Eusebius *Church History* III. 39. 16). It was the work, we may suppose, of teachers, evangelists, and missionaries of the early church, confronted with the need for Greek versions of the sayings, parables, pronouncements of Jesus, the stories of his "mighty works," and above all the account of his passion and resurrection. When Paul related to the Corinthians the traditional narrative of the Last Supper, or the record of the resurrection appearances (I Cor. 11:23-25; 15:3-8), or described to the Galatians Jesus' death on the Cross in words that stood out like a public proclamation (Gal. 3:1), he certainly used Greek. And the evangelists who first preached to Gentiles in Jerusalem, Caesarea, and Antioch—as described in the book of Acts—must surely have recounted in Greek the life, passion, resurrection, the deeds, and the words of the Lord Jesus.

Who was the author of this Gospel? The usual view has been that he was the "John Mark" whose mother's house in Jerusalem was a center of the Christian fellowship (Acts 12:12); who accompanied Barnabas and Saul to Antioch (Acts 12:25), but left them at Perga, on the first missionary journey, and returned to Jerusalem (Acts 13:13); who was later reconciled to Paul and proved "useful" as his assistant (Col. 4:10; II Tim. 4:11; Philem. 24); and who is even associated with Peter later on, presumably at Rome ("Babylon"; I Pet. 5:13). His legendary connection with Alexandria, as its first bishop is too patently attached to the equally legendary view that the Gospel of Mark was written there. But the difficulties in the way of this identification seem to counterbalance the arguments in its favor: Mark may have been familiar with events and conditions in Jerusalem, but he was certainly unfamiliar with the geography and topography of northern Palestine; and his supposed familiarity with events in Jerusalem can be adequately explained by the early formulation of the passion narrative— while, on the other hand, a Jew of Jerusalem would scarcely be as unfamiliar with Jewish procedure as his account of the trial of Jesus would suggest, nor would he be so dependent upon secondary sources if he had lived there at the time. Moreover, the later references to Mark (in Colossians, II Timothy, and I Peter) are found in letters which are often thought to be pseudepigraphic and to contain personal references whose sole purpose is to lend them an air of firsthand authorship. Finally, as common a name as Marcus in first-century Rome is difficult to attach exclusively to any one person. There were probably a dozen men of that name among Christian Romans in the sixties.

Whether or not the author was the Mark we read of in Acts, that name has been given to the Gospel ever since the fourfold gospel canon was established about the middle of the second century. The title of the book is not, of course, "The Gospel of Mark," but simply "According to Mark"—the word "Gospel" covering all four. The book itself nowhere suggests the name of its author. The theory that he was the young man who fled from the garden (14:51-52) is most improbable; moreover, Papias, or the presbyter, insisted that Mark neither heard Jesus nor was his personal follower. But it does not greatly matter who the author was: the *content* of the Gospel is the Christian message of salvation, as believed and preached among Gentiles in the middle of the first century, illustrated and reinforced by selected material from the Christian tradition about Jesus, his mighty deeds, his teaching, his death and resurrection. It adds nothing to our knowledge of John Mark—of whom we know practically nothing—to attribute this Gospel to him; it adds nothing to our understanding of the Gospel to call him its author, since he is too shadowy a figure; and it adds nothing to our knowledge of the Gospel's content, or to our knowledge of the historical Jesus, to make this attribution. To all intents and purposes we must study the Gospel as if it were anonymous, like most of the books of the Bible—a "traditional book," that is, a book based on a common tradition, not a product of personal literary authorship.

There is a decided advantage in this: the Gospel is far more broadly and securely based if it rests upon a widespread social tradition than if one individual's recollections—or fancies —provide the sole support. For neither Mark nor Peter was a trained historian, for example, like Thucydides; what such historians might have given us, writing "on their own," is discouraging to contemplate. Not that an anonymous tradition is better than a detailed and circumstantial history might have been; but the latter was out of the question anyway, and at best would have had its own limitations—

Thucydides might have given us far less than Peter or Mark. This brings us once more to the essential point: the Gospel of Mark is not history, nor biography, nor even the scattered reminiscences of an apostle, but is a selection from a tradition, set down for the same purpose as that which had hitherto kept the tradition alive, namely, the proclamation of the saving message, the good news, about Jesus Christ, the Son of God. If a choice must be made, we shall have to recognize that its theological significance far outweighs its historical; but for Christian faith the two are not incompatible—the theological interpretation is true *because* of the history behind it; and the historical record, brief and fragmentary as it is, can be verified even now—since Jesus Christ is "the same yesterday and today and forever." This is one of those books that are written "out of faith and for faith," ἐκ πίστεως εἰς πίστιν (Rom. 1:17).

It was a favorite view of certain nineteenth-century scholars that Mark was a "Pauline" gospel, as Matthew was a "Judaistic" and Luke a "universalistic" or "catholic" one. And it was assumed that since Mark was probably written in Rome, traces of Paul's influence could be found in many passages (e.g., 1:15, "the time is fulfilled"; 10:45, the "ransom" passage; 14:24, "my blood of the covenant, . . . poured out for many"). But the theory is now generally abandoned. The neat "Tübingen" pigeonholes, and the whole Hegelian interpretation of history which it took for granted, are equally outmoded.[4] The evidence for a special dependence of Mark upon Paul turns out upon examination to be evidence of both Mark's and Paul's dependence upon what Harnack described as "common Gentile Christianity." Mark was not writing to support any particular theological view, Pauline or other, though a theology is certainly implicit in his book; as Branscomb has finely said:

To ask whether the Gospel is a theological or historical work is . . . to set up a false alternative. It is both. But dogma and doctrine seem plainly secondary with the evangelist to telling the Christian story as it was known and believed in the churches of the Hellenistic world a generation after Jesus' death.[5]

It is a pity we do not know more about pre-Pauline, extra-Pauline, and post-Pauline Gentile Christianity. It would help us greatly in

---

[4] The most thorough recent survey of the evidence is Martin Werner, *Der Einfluss paulinischer Theologie im Markusevangelium*, Beiheft 1 to the *Zeitschrift für die neutestamentliche Wissenschaft* (Giessen: Alfred Töpelmann, 1923); see the outline and discussion of it in Grant, *Earliest Gospel*, ch. ix.

[5] *Gospel of Mark*, p. xxii.

understanding Paul and also Mark. But the recognition that Mark takes for granted the same principles as Paul (for example, Jesus is the Son of God; he died for sins; he inaugurated a new relation between God and men), yet without betraying any direct influence by Paul, does advance our knowledge of "common Gentile Christianity" somewhat. The extraordinary and inexplicable fact on the hypothesis of Pauline influence is the absence from Mark of characteristic Pauline terms and ideas, such as grace, or justification, or the new life in Christ; equally striking is the absence in Paul of apparently old and traditional features, still found in Mark (for instance, Jesus' exorcism of demons, or the term "the Son of man"—I Cor. 15:47 is no exception; Paul is discussing Gen. 2:7, not Daniel).

Another feature of the Gospel which has a bearing upon its origin is its attitude toward the Jews. Although a knowledge of Judaism is taken for granted, and Jesus' teaching everywhere presupposes the religion and the sacred scriptures of his own people, Mark does not write as a Jew, even as a Christian Jew. Unless 7:3-4 is a gloss—at least one manuscript omits these explanatory words—the writer obviously has Gentile readers in mind, and addresses them *as a Gentile* interpreting a Jewish custom; equally obviously he is mistaken—as no Jew would be—when he says that "all the Jews" observe it. But more than this, the author holds that a divine judgment of blindness and obfuscation has come over the whole Jewish people; this is his way of explaining the rejection of Jesus by his own people. True, he does not go the length of the later Gospel of John (8:44) nor even as far as Matthew went (27: 25); but there is an undeniable element of anti-Judaism in Mark, partly due to the circumstances under which the gospel tradition was handed down, but partly due to Mark himself—and perhaps his Roman Christian environment.[6] Slight as this trace is, Mark can hardly be the work of a Palestinian Christian Jew.

II. Purpose

Unlike the later Gospel of Luke, that of Mark has no preface setting forth its author's purpose. But we have little difficulty in reading between the lines and making out why the book was written. It can scarcely belong to the propaganda literature of the early church: its intended readers are already Christians, and already share the faith of the author—the faith enshrined in the common tradition which Mark is writing down. Jesus is the strong Son of God whose "mighty deeds," once wrought upon

[6] See Grant, *Earliest Gospel*, ch. x.

earth, can still be repeated—are still, no doubt, being repeated—among his followers. His way of life was the way of the Cross; and that way must still be followed—the whole central section of the Gospel (8:27–10:45) is built about a nucleus of discipleship sayings (8:34-38; 9:33-50; 10:23-31) which demand renunciation, bearing one's cross, losing one's life to save it, becoming the slave of the brethren, while it sets forth the supreme example of the renunciation of the Son of man in the three successive passion announcements (8:31; 9:31; 10:32-34). The teaching of Jesus is mentioned more than once, but rarely given: Mark has selected only those sayings that have peculiar relevance or appeal to his readers or apply to the immediate situation in which they find themselves. The great body of teaching tradition (Q, L, M) embedded in Matthew and Luke he either takes for granted or ignores. He is writing for a martyr church, for Christians who themselves may soon be called to enter the arena with its hungry wild beasts or be coated with tar and strung up and ignited as living torches in Nero's gardens—this is what had recently happened in Rome, when the Christians were made the scapegoat of mob vengeance after the great fire (Tacitus *Annals* XV. 44). Not only were the martyrdoms of the blessed apostles, Peter and Paul, fresh in their minds, but the example of the Lord himself, the first Martyr, and the Firstborn from the dead, steadied and supported them in their trial. One might almost say that Mark's Gospel was written backwards, from the passion story to the Baptism; for the passion story dominates the narrative almost from the outset.[7] Throughout the book one question emerges repeatedly: Why did Jesus die? It was a question martyrs might ask, or more likely the friends of martyrs; it was one every Christian had to face—why must one die, if necessary, for one's faith? If Jesus was the Son of God, why had he needed to die a shameful, agonizing death on the Cross? What led to so dire a tragedy, historically? Why did God permit it? The Gospel gives the answer, leading up to it, at least from the beginning of ch. 2, and showing that Jesus died (*a*) because the Jewish religious leaders suspected and hated him, (*b*) because he himself chose to die, and give his life "for many," and (*c*) because it was the will of God, and had been so announced long before: δεῖ γενέσθαι: it had to be![8]

Mark's purpose was accordingly not historical or biographical, but it was intensely practical. He was writing a book for the guidance and

[7] See Frederick C. Grant, *The Growth of the Gospels* (New York: Abingdon Press, 1933), pp. 136-37.
[8] *Ibid.*, p. 78.

support of his fellow Christians in a situation of intense crisis. The martyrdoms had fallen off, but there was no assurance—with Nero on the throne—when they might begin again; the last days could not be far off (ch. 13), and every Christian's lamp must be trimmed, every Christian's loins girded for the struggle. What K. L. Schmidt[9] says of the Gospels generally, that they are "people's books" (*Volksbücher*), not meant for publication or wide circulation, but for reading by a group, especially by a nonliterary group, is most true of Mark. Above all it is true of Mark as a compilation of tradition for a specific purpose, the strengthening and guidance of the author's fellow Christians faced with the threat of persecution and in danger of losing their lives for their faith. The "theology" of Mark is only the implicit theology of the Gentile church of his time: he has no special doctrines to promote.[10] That he unconsciously and unintentionally set forth this theology in a somewhat one-sided way, and thus obscured the human features of the Jesus of history—with vast and far-reaching consequences for later Christian belief and thought —was scarcely his fault: the tradition had already been molded in this manner among Gentile Christians, and he only carried forward, without realizing it, what had already been begun. As Branscomb says:

What the evangelist does for the most part is to tell the story of Jesus' life as it was known and understood in Christian circles. Fact and theology had already been combined in this tradition, and what is often described as Mark's theology is really the early Christian belief as to the historical facts.[11]

And this also suggests the abiding value of the Gospel, which challenges the complacency, the neutrality and weak faith, the watered-down values of a generation weary with war, with the endless effort to achieve something worth while for society, only to see ever-darker clouds gathering upon the human horizon: What is the good of further struggle? Why not yield and make our peace with a world which wants no further heroism or sacrifice, but only sensory satisfactions? Why not compromise and so have "peace in our time" at least, come what may in the end? But one cannot take that view as a Christian. Nor as a Christian can one fail to see life whole and steadily, but in the light from the Cross: "It is in terms of the mystery of the Passion, and not otherwise, that the true Christian confession of the Messiahship of Jesus

must be made."[12] For Mark, as Johannes Weiss profoundly observes, Jesus is not Messiah in spite of the Cross, but because of it.[13]

III. Method of Composition

Since the Gospel of Mark was based upon oral tradition, some parts of which may already have been put in writing, we may expect to find traces of the author's handiwork chiefly in the editing of his material. This is precisely what we do find. If the connecting links, the editorial settings, introductions, conclusions, and transitions are removed, or merely underlined in red, the basic material will stand out as a collection of independent units—stories, parables, sayings, controversies, and the like— such as no doubt circulated freely in the early church. It is with these separate units of tradition that form criticism is concerned, as it undertakes to recover the oral tradition which circulated before the Gospels or their sources were written. The medium through which this tradition was handed down was the preaching or teaching of the first generation of Christians. "In the beginning was the preaching," as Martin Dibelius says,[14] though it was not long before the teachers of the church began their task of instructing new converts, the young, and any persons interested in "the way." It was not only the missionaries and evangelists, but the teachers, as B. S. Easton maintains, who treasured and transmitted this precious heritage of Jesus' life and teaching. The intensely practical concerns of the church are reflected in the choice of this material and the emphasis given it: many other things Jesus both said and did, "which are not written in this book" or in any book, but these were selected and transmitted because they had a bearing upon the life and hope of Christians in the days before any written gospels had appeared. "These are written, that ye might believe" (John 20:31); but in the earlier period these traditions were handed down, not only that Christians might believe, but also that they might have authoritative direction in matters of still grave importance— the interpretation of the Mosaic law, the question of sabbath observance, divorce and remarriage, relations with the civil authorities, and so on. These were live issues for Christians in Palestine in the early days of the church's history, and only slightly less so for Christians from among the Gentiles in Rome, Antioch, Ephesus, and elsewhere. It is not true to say

[9] *Der Rahmen der Geschichte Jesu* (Berlin: Trowitzsch & Sohn, 1919). See also, "Die Stellung der Evangelien in der allgemeinen Literaturgeschichte," ΕΥΧΑΡΙΣΤΗΡΙΟΝ, Göttingen: Vandenhoeck & Ruprecht, 1923.

[10] Branscomb, *Gospel of Mark*, pp. xx-xxi.

[11] *Ibid.*, p. xxi.

[12] A. E. J. Rawlinson, *St. Mark* (London: Methuen & Co., 1925), p. lvi.

[13] *History of Primitive Christianity* (tr. Frederick C. Grant and others; New York: Wilson-Erickson, 1937), II, ch. xxii.

[14] *From Tradition to Gospel* (tr. B. L. Woolf; New York: Charles Scribner's Sons, 1935), especially ch. ii.

that only those traditions were handed on which had a practical relevance to Christian life in the thirties to sixties of the first century: this would be almost as false as to assume that the early Christian community produced Jesus' sayings and parables, and incidents from his life, out of its own inner consciousness. There really was a wider interest in the life and teaching of Jesus for its own sake; how could it be otherwise, Jesus being the Lord of his church who had lived upon earth, taught, healed, died, and risen again? But even this was not a purely historical interest; it still had a practical relevance, for the Jesus who had walked and talked in Galilee was now the church's Lord, soon to come again as the Judge of all mankind. "That I may know him and the power of his resurrection" was the fervent prayer of many another besides Paul—a prayer not to be answered solely in a mystical rapture of immediate recognition. There were many who "inquired the way of the Lord more carefully," to ascertain "if these things were so"; and there were many ministers and eyewitnesses who bore their testimony in order that inquirers might "know the certainty of those things" which they had heard.

The general framework of the Gospel was to some extent supplied by the tradition itself. C. H. Dodd [15] has shown how in Mark the general course of Jesus' ministry follows the pattern reflected in the early speeches in Acts—though of course, *ex hypothesi,* Luke was already familiar with Mark.[16] But the fact that Mark held the field for a generation or more before the other Gospels were written, and also that when they were written they followed his order fairly closely and took over most of his contents (John did not, but it is not certain that John ever saw Mark's Gospel) —these two facts indicate that Mark dealt very faithfully with the tradition he used, and was recognized to have dealt faithfully with it. Matthew and Luke are the earliest interpreters of Mark whose work has survived; in a sense, they may almost be described as the earliest commentators on Mark. Their testimony to its text, for example, is important, and also their consistent treatment of its contents. For example, Matthew generally heightens the apocalyptic element and the miraculous; Luke, as George Salmon pointed out, "spares the Twelve"; both incline to ignore all traces of human weakness or limitation in Jesus; both supply accounts of his birth and ancestry, and fuller versions of his resurrection; above all, both give a much more ample account of his teaching, derived, it is thought, from their second common source, Q;

but—this is most important—they do keep Mark, even in revising and to some extent rearranging it. It has often been thought that the author of John intended to supplement and reinterpret the Synoptics, beginning with Mark; but Percival Gardner-Smith's *St. John and the Synoptic Gospels* [17] has convinced many New Testament scholars that this was not the case. What John does *not* take over from or presuppose in the Synoptics is more important than what he does; if he knew—and corrected—certain features in them, why not others? The words and phrases common to John and Mark (or either of the other Synoptists) are not the important ones in their context, but only such as might easily get carried along accidentally in oral tradition as it branched off in different directions. But the Gospel of John sets a problem —many problems—in itself. Its contrast with Mark is no greater than with Matthew and Luke; in fact, as Johannes Weiss showed long ago,[18] the line between Mark's "theology" and that of John is more direct than from that of Matthew or Luke to John. Both Mark and John, we now recognize, presuppose a larger element of "common Gentile Christianity" than do Matthew and Luke, with their larger element of Palestinian tradition, derived from Q and their other non-Marcan sources.

The pre-Marcan oral—or partly written—tradition was not wholly lacking in references to time and place, or to persons involved in the stories. Some of these were essential to the story, saying, or parable. Others had been supplied during the process of oral or early written transmission by a kind of "oral editing" or by the first translators into Greek. Above all, in the longest—some would say the earliest—continuous narrative underlying the Gospels, the passion narrative, references to time, place, and persons were indispensable. Moreover, some of this preliterary material had already been formed into groups or "blocks"; more of it would be grouped in the first stages of the writing down of the tradition—for example, the collection of parables in ch. 4. Some of the sayings are grouped solely by subject (as in 9:33-42) ; some solely by mnemonic suggestion in a kind of "catena" or chain, one saying suggesting the next—as in 9:42-50, "cause to stumble" in vs. 42 suggesting the same in vss. 43-47; "Gehenna" in vs. 47 suggesting the quotation in vs. 48; "fire" in vs. 48 suggesting vss. 49; "salt" in vs. 49 suggesting vs. 50; or as in 11:22-25, where "faith" in vs. 22 suggests its exercise in vs. 23, this in turn suggesting "prayer" in vs. 24, while "prayer" in vs. 24 sug-

---

[15] *The Apostolic Preaching* (Chicago: Willett, Clark & Co., 1937).
[16] See Grant, *Earliest Gospel,* pp. 46-49.

[17] Cambridge University Press, 1938.
[18] *Das Älteste Evangelium* (Göttingen: Vandenhoeck & Ruprecht, 1903).

gests vs. 25—though vs. 25, like vs. 26, may be a later gloss. Another device found in Mark is "telescoping" of stories, one being inserted within the framework of another—as in 2:1-12; 5:21-43; etc. Whether or not such combinations already existed in Mark's sources we cannot say. The absence of the device from the other sources of Matthew and Luke seems to show that it was a peculiarly Marcan feature.

Many attempts have been made to show that Mark's Gospel "grew" by stages, each with a distinct outlook, vocabulary, style, and of course author. Some have held that an original form of Mark, the so-called "Urmarcus," underlay the work of Matthew and Luke—at least of Luke. This document was quite different from our Mark, and was, of course, shorter—though a few have held that Mark was originally much longer than our text, both at the beginning and the end. But all such hypotheses face the insuperable objections (a) that Mark in its present form is obviously a homogeneous work, in language, style, and thought; (b) that there is not enough agreement between Matthew and Luke in non-Marcan passages to prove a common original, except where Q, whose style and thought are sharply distinguishable from Mark's, is involved; and (c) that the assumed evidence is better accounted for by taking into consideration stages of development in the tradition—both oral and possibly, in scattered parts, already written—prior to Mark. There was development in the tradition, that is, in Mark's sources, rather than in the Gospel of Mark itself. A good example is the chapter of parables (ch. 4), which almost certainly existed as a written collection before Mark took it over. Into this collection has been inserted an explanation of the first parable, that of the different kinds of soil (the so-called "parable of the sower"); this explanation is found in vss. 10, 13-20, a very pedestrian and quite unnecessary explanation of the parable's obvious teaching, but applied specifically to the life of Christians in the world—probably an early homiletical exposition of Jesus' parable. Then *into this* has been inserted vss. 11-12. setting forth Mark's own peculiar view of the parables as intended to withhold the teaching of Jesus from the unworthy, and disclose it only to those who shared the "mystery" of the kingdom of God—a theory that suited well enough the religious outlook of the pagan world surrounding the Roman Christians of Mark's day. But the theory was utterly inapplicable to the teaching of Jesus—the whole chapter cries out against it (see especially vs. 33), and so does the whole Synoptic record of the Master's discourse. Obviously there are stages of development reflected here, like tide-

marks on a shore, but these are Marcan or pre-Marcan; there has been no "growth" of the Gospel after it left its author's hand, save for a few glosses (see below), nor was the writing of the book the work of two or three separate "authors." At most, as Weiss held, an editor has added a few touches, found chiefly in passages omitted by both Matthew and Luke; but these are too brief and too few to be distinguishable in thought or style from Mark himself.

As the development of the tradition prior to Mark must constantly be borne in mind, so must the probability that much—if not all or most—of it existed at one time in Aramaic. As Wellhausen, Burney, Lagrange, Torrey, Burrows, and others have shown, the Aramaic idiom underlies many a tradition, and juts out into the open in more than one place (e.g., 5:41). As a rule, however, Aramaisms are far more frequent in the "old stories," as Dibelius calls them [19] than in the later material; and it appears that they are practically absent from the editorial additions.[20]

Although Mark did not force his material into a rigid scheme of chronology, the outline on pp. 645-46 makes clear the general arrangement. The main points in that outline are:

I. Introduction (1:1-13)
II. Jesus in Galilee (1:14–9:50)
    A. About the Sea of Galilee (1:14–5:43), including the controversies in 2:1–3:6 (plus 3:20-30) and the collection of parables in ch. 4.
    B. Wider Journeyings (6:1–9:50)
    The section 7:24–8:26 might be called Mark's "great insertion," following 7:1-23, in which Jesus is represented as rejecting the external requirements of the law and then turning to the Gentiles. It also includes the controversy over signs (8:11-12), and the second of the two apparently parallel narratives of the journey in 6:30–7:37 and 8:1-26. This is followed by the section on "the way of the Cross" 8:27–10:45; with a nucleus of discipleship sayings in 8:34-38; 9:33-50; 10:23-31. These various groups may well have been pre-Marcan collections of material.
III. Jesus in Jerusalem (10:1–15:47)
    A. On the Way to Jerusalem (10:1-52).
    B. In Jerusalem (11:1–12:44), including a second collection of controversies 11:27–12:40.
    C. The apocalyptic discourse (13:1-37), including material from the little apocalypse in vss. 6-8, 14-20, 24-27.
    D. The passion narrative (14:1–15:47; edited).
IV. The empty tomb (16:1-8)

[19] *The Message of Jesus Christ* (New York: Charles Scribner's Sons, 1939).
[20] See review of C. C. Torrey's *Our Translated Gospels*, in *Anglican Theological Review*, XIX (1937), 223; Grant, *Earliest Gospel*, ch. v. especially pp. 122-24.

How trustworthy is this scheme for the reconstruction of the historical life of Jesus? Matthew and Luke evidently accepted it on the whole; while John, though writing independently of all three Synoptics and following a scheme of his own—with Jesus' headquarters apparently in Jerusalem or Judea—supports in a general way the main features of the plan: Jesus' baptism at the beginning, and his association with the Baptist; his controversies with the authorities, both in Galilee and in Jerusalem; his mighty works (in John the seven great "signs," some in Galilee, some in Jerusalem; in Mark only the incident of the fig tree is located near Jerusalem); his teaching in synagogues and by the sea; his journey to Jerusalem, and the triumphal entry; his teaching in the temple and controversies with the authorities; the Last Supper and the passion narrative; the Crucifixion and Resurrection. Such an arrangement of the public ministry of Jesus was so deeply embedded in early Christian tradition and literature that there was no other way of writing the life of Christ, save that separate incidents—like the temple cleansing—might be shifted from one point to another. As a general outline one may say not only that it is all that we have, but that it is also entirely natural, consistent, and historically probable. This is not to say that the old "Marcan hypothesis" of the eighteen eighties and nineties and early decades of the present century is still to be regarded as sound; no chronological scheme is infallible, and Mark is anything but a day-by-day stenographic record of the sayings and doings of Jesus.[21] Only in the passion narrative is there a fairly rigid chronology; as we shall see, it contains traces of a kind of primitive "Holy Week," while the "hours" of the Passion itself are clearly noted. Whether or not this scheme was imposed on the material by Mark, or already existed before he took it over, is difficult to say. If it already existed—as is probable—it may even have had a liturgical significance, reflecting an early Christian observance of the Passover with the added significance given the season by Christ's death and resurrection. This seems a strange idea to modern students of the Gospels, but it is not an impossible one—the "Christian mystery," with its strong element of tradition, both specifically Christian and also Jewish, as the earliest sources for liturgical history amply prove, might well have commemorated "Christ our Passover" in a way that took over, modified, and reinterpreted the rite as it was observed in the Jewish Diaspora. Quartodecimanism was only one out of many instances of this extraordinary continuity.

[21] See Rawlinson, *St. Mark*, pp. xix ff.

IV. Jewish Background

As we have already noted, Mark does not display any intimate or expert knowledge of Judaism, or of the topography, customs, or history of Palestine. Such information concerning Judaism as the book contains is limited to what the sources have provided. Often this is quite inadequate—for example, Herod Antipas is a "king" (6:14); Herodias, not Salome, was the former wife of Philip (6:17); "Corban" means "a gift" (7:11); one would travel through Sidon and the Decapolis en route from Tyre to the Sea of Galilee (7:31); and so on. Mark either blundered in his editing or was unconcerned to correct such details—possibly because he lacked sufficient familiarity with Palestine to do so. It probably never entered his mind to check details; the general situation was clear enough, and his purpose was not the writing of a biography of the Greco-Roman type—and even some of the ancient biographers paid little attention to details!—or the composition of "Part I" in a comprehensive historical work on the origins of Christianity, much less a collection of source material on ancient Judaism. But even so, we can usually rely upon the traditions he gives. The general background of the life and ministry of Jesus is clear, and obviously authentic, as we may judge from all our other sources of information about first-century Palestine.

It was a country held by a foreign conqueror. True, the conqueror had been invited to come in almost a century before (63 B.C.), when Pompey had settled the quarrel between the last two of the Maccabees. Herod the Great (40-4 B.C.) had ruled as *rex socius* (king ally) by permission of the Romans, and after him three of his sons, Archelaus, as "ethnarch" in Judea and Samaria with the promise of the title "king" if he behaved himself—he did not, and was exiled in A.D. 6—Antipas in Galilee and Perea, Philip in the northeast, both with the title of "tetrarch." After the fall of Archelaus, procurators were appointed in succession to govern Judea and Samaria, among them Pontius Pilate (A.D. 26-36). Antipas maintained himself in Galilee until A.D. 39, when he was banished by Caligula for conniving to become king; he was the "Herod" who put to death John the Baptist and who ruled Galilee during Jesus' lifetime. But despite this show of quasi-independence, Galilee was as much in the grip of Roman power as were Judea and Samaria. Back of the whole troubled scene in Palestine and Syria in those days stood the watchful, determined, ever-advancing power of Rome. Palestine and Syria were the center of the defensive shield against the nomads of the desert and the powerful threat of Parthia, farther east. This shield extended from Pontus and Cappadocia to Egypt, and from the point of view of Roman policy it was indispensable that Syria and Palestine should be held firmly in control. Hence the steady encroachment of the late republic and early empire upon Jewish independence, from the time of Pompey (63 B.C.) to the second fall of Jerusalem under Hadrian (A.D. 135) and the full incorporation of Syria-Palestine as a province within the empire.

Diametrically opposed to this Roman policy was the Jewish theory of theocracy—"no king but God," or at most a high priest functioning as head of the state by divine appointment and as God's representative. The second commonwealth, which followed the Exile, had been founded—at least from the time of Ezra—upon this conception of the national life. Instead of a succession of kings who, though descended from David, had sinned and so brought punishment upon the nation, there was to be only a priestly government of a priestly people, living in accordance with the revealed rule of life laid down in Torah. Naturally there was not one uniform view prevailing throughout the nation: at one extreme were active collaborationists who found it necessary to meet the actual conditions imposed on them by the Romans; at the opposite extreme were complete separatists who proposed to live as if the Romans did not exist; there were also potential—and frequently active—revolutionists or rebels, ready to fight the Romans at the slightest provocation, confident that God would favor their course with success and—freedom; still others "waited for the redemption of Israel" with folded hands, aware of the impossibility of winning freedom by the sword, but confident that God would grant it in his own good time.

It is against this background that the life and teaching of Jesus must be studied, for it was in the very midst of this situation that he lived and died. Galilee was only slightly less involved in political tension and turmoil than were Judea and Samaria. For three generations before the great war of A.D. 66-70, eastern Galilee, according to Josephus, had been a center of armed resistance—Josephus' "robbers" were really revolutionists—and when the war finally came, the first half of it was fought in Galilee. Although efforts have been made to represent Galilee as only semi-Jewish, or at least as less rigidly orthodox than Judea—if not really pagan and Aryan, as made up chiefly of a mixed population, with Jews in a small minority— the truth is that by the first century Galilee was thoroughly Jewish, except for a few pagan towns and for a scattering of foreigners outside them, chiefly government officials, soldiers, traders, and resident aliens. The Jewish towns and neighborhoods of Galilee were undoubtedly in the majority. The conditions reflected in Mark, both in Galilee and in Judea—that is, in Jericho and Jerusalem—were predominantly Jewish. If Jesus visits Gentiles, it is on a tour outside Galilee (chs. 7–8). John the Baptist's influence has spread over the whole land, including Galilee.

Synagogues were found "throughout all Galilee" (1:39)—these were primarily "houses of study," where the Torah was taught and expounded, but they were also "houses of prayer," where the weekly service of prayer and reading of Scripture took place; they were likewise "houses of assembly," where the men of the community gathered for various communal purposes. There were scribes in Galilee, presumably resident there, as well as those who came down from Jerusalem (3:22; 7:1), though they were more numerous, one gathers, in the religious capital than in Jesus' own country. The scribes were the official teachers of Judaism, at first copyists of the Torah, then its expounders and interpreters, to whom difficult cases were referred for decision. As expounders of the Torah they would naturally be expected to give the exposition of the scripture lesson or lessons at the synagogue service, though the service itself was in the hands of the lay president of the congregation or "ruler of the synagogue." Distinct from them were the Pharisees, apparently everywhere present in Galilee; they were the members of a lay order or society for whom the fully detailed practice of the scribal interpretation of the law was the sum of religion. Though progressive on some points, and numbering among them a few men of deep religious fervor, they were on the whole reactionary and at times fanatical; the social-religious situation of the time explains their intense and narrow devotion to the minutiae of religious practice. For them the Torah was not merely religious law but a whole rule of life, governing, like a monastic code, every detail and every possible contingency. The common people respected them, as Josephus says, and followed their guidance—except those, the Amhaarez (or "people of the land") whose way of life and daily occupations prevented a full observance of the scribal regulations. It was among these "lost sheep of the house of Israel" that Jesus lived, and to them he devoted his ministry. The Sadducees (12:18), on the other hand, were the party of the Jerusalem hierarchy, conservative (Acts 23:8), politically-minded, concerned to maintain law and order and the *status quo*, and not unwilling to collaborate with the representatives of the Roman occupation. As Louis Finkelstein has shown,[22] the Sadducees represented the conservative landowning class, the squirearchy, opposed to all reforms; the Pharisees, on the contrary, were urban, and eager to apply the traditional tenets of Judaism to the changed conditions of life, including business and trade, that followed upon the gradual but forceful annexation of Palestine to the empire.

The priests, finally, were the members of the tribe of Levi and the house of Aaron who ministered in the temple, offering the sacrifices, and pronouncing the blessing of God upon his people. Though resident throughout the land, their official duties took them regularly to Jerusalem, where the high priest presided not only over the temple worship but also over the Sanhedrin, the highest national court in all religious matters. This court also exercised jurisdiction in matters of purely intra-Jewish concern, since the Roman governor left as much as possible to local and national administration: his business as procurator was to maintain order, defend the country against external attack, and see that the collection of tribute was not interrupted. Thus the Sanhedrin had its own police force (14:43), though it had not the authority to put anyone to death—only the Roman governor could order an execution (15:1-15; see also John 18:31).

Under the conditions of the time it is not surprising that there was a growing tension between various groups in Jewish society in the first century, a tension that was primarily religious but was aggravated by political, social, and even economic factors.[23] Moreover, there was a growing strain within the religious thought of Judaism itself, between traditional faith and practice and the new conditions of life which had grown up since the days of Ezra.

One of the most remarkable expressions of this tension is to be seen in the growth of the apocalyptic literature, some of its most important examples having been produced apparently in the north, that is, in Galilee—the book of Enoch, for example. The word "apocalyptic" is not the equivalent of "eschatological": the two terms must be sharply distinguished. All Hebrew prophecy, indeed all Hebrew and Jewish religion, was "eschatological"; that is, it was concerned with "the last things," "the latter days," the "end" of God's plans and purposes, a coming judgment upon the nations, sometimes including Israel, and a coming restoration. Since Hebrew religion conceives of God as the determiner of destiny, the ruler of history, it is assumed that the events of this world must finally lead to the furtherance and finally the fulfillment of his purposes. No human event can be accidental or irrelevant or meaningless—least of all the great and tragic events that appear to deny flatly the sovereignty or the wisdom or the goodness of God. All of history, and every individual life, is amenable to God's judgment, and nothing can finally contradict the primary and fundamental principle of God's sovereign rule over the universe, his *malkûth* or *basileia,* the divine theodicy. But it was perfectly clear that things had in fact so far contradicted the divine rule: from the time of the Babylonian conquest; through the sad and checkered times of the restoration at the end of that century; through the days of poverty and oppression that followed; through the relatively prosperous period which followed upon the coming of the Greeks under Alexander; through the Roman rule which came so soon after the tragic and heroic days of the early Maccabees—through all of this the dream of religious freedom and of the national independence of God's own people seemed subject to constant postponement, a "hope deferred [that] maketh the heart sick." When would God's Messiah come—the glorious "anointed" king whom God had promised to "raise up" and through whom he would restore the faded glories of the house of David? Perhaps, said some, that promise had been misunderstood—it meant only that the nation, as God's son, would someday be exalted; or that the good king Hezekiah had been the "anointed one" to whom prophecy referred. Perhaps, thought some in the second century B.C., the hope of the "Messiah" was being realized by the house of the Maccabees: but that theory was doomed to disappointment, as the later Maccabees became ever more worldly and secular. And so from the beginning of the first century B.C., if not before, there grew up a conviction that the hopes of Israel were never to be realized in this present world: only a totally new and different order could realize the purposes of God. Whether or not this expectation was influenced by Persian speculations cannot be said; the factors required for its rise were apparently all present in Jewish thought under the altered circumstances of the period.

Some of the chief features of apocalyptic speculation were: (*a*) its use of older prophecy, which was interpreted and reinterpreted in an ever more transcendent, otherworldly sense; (*b*) its reliance upon dreams, visions, levitations, and other extraordinary modes of direct

[22] *The Pharisees* (Philadelphia: Jewish Publication Society of America, 1938).

[23] See Frederick C. Grant, *The Economic Background of the Gospels* (London: Oxford University Press, 1926). On the whole subject of conditions in Palestine in the time of Jesus see also, above, pp. 100-13.

revelation or of experience of the unseen world, with angels, patriarchs, and other supernatural figures as guides; (c) its pessimistic outlook upon the times and upon human resources and its complete reliance upon the sovereign power of God for the changing of conditions; (d) its conception of history as not only foreseen but as also, and in consequence, predetermined history, usually unrolling in a series of "'weeks'" or "ages," the seer, as a rule, conceiving of his own generation as the next to the last; (e) its openness to foreign influence—back of the conception of the transcendent "Son of man" in I Enoch, for example, is not only the Jewish Messiah but also, and more dominantly, the widespread Near Eastern concept of the primal man, the first created of all beings, who is to come in the end as judge of the whole creation, men, angels, and demons; (f) its emphasis upon the malevolent activities of demons, with Satan at their head; and (g) its esoteric character—it was a secret lore reserved for and communicated to those who were worthy of it, and was not to be proclaimed from the house-top or heralded in the market place.

The importance of this type of thought for the interpretation of the Gospels goes without saying: since 1900 all modern New Testament study has been influenced by the "eschatological"—or more properly "apocalyptic"—school, as represented, for example, by Johannes Weiss, Albert Schweitzer, and R. H. Charles. The title "Son of man" is undoubtedly apocalyptic in its associations: the term stresses lofty transcendence, not lowly humanness. The expectation of a coming crisis when "the powers of the heavens shall be shaken," and the stars fall from the sky—this is a view which has obviously been influenced by apocalyptic speculations, which took the data of ancient prophecy and concentrated them upon one event to come at the end of human history. The supreme question of all present-day gospel research is: Did Jesus think in apocalyptic terms, and did he conceive of himself as the destined "Son of man"? This question can be answered only by the most patient and painstaking analysis of the available sources and evaluation of Jesus' historical personality and work as a whole. For the purpose of the present volume it is enough to say that Mark—and the pre-Marcan tradition, at least from an early stage—took for granted that Jesus did so think of himself. But Mark's theology is *not* primarily apocalyptic-eschatological—except for ch. 13, where he is following one of his sources—but is rather the theology of the Greek-speaking Gentile church, for which apocalyptic thought was already becoming something alien and remote.

V. Theology

It is worth repeating, for the sake of emphasis, that Mark's theology is not his own, but that of the Gentile church, that is, "common Gentile Christianity." As William Manson has put it, Mark is the Gospel of the "mighty works of Jesus." [24] This is the more remarkable since Paul makes no reference to Jesus' miracles; he presupposes miracles enough, in his own time and even as wrought through himself, as "the signs of an apostle," but the miracles of Jesus were not exorcisms or cures—these are totally blotted out and lost in the overwhelming miracle of his life, his death, his resurrection. But for the general run of Gentile Christianity the mighty works of Jesus were evidential, not only of his power in the past, when he walked upon earth, but of his authority in the present, and of his power to heal the sick, exorcise demons, raise the dead even now, as the Lord of his church, resident in it but at the same time transcendent and exalted above it at God's right hand. This was a faith which Gentiles craved and could understand. The whole framework of their inherited religious ideas prepared them to accept such a faith: the Old Testament, and Judaism, and the messianic hope, and the apocalyptic outlook, all native to Palestine, were something different and belonged to another world. Even though they possessed the Old Testament—in the Septuagint or Greek translation—its value seemed to them to consist chiefly in explicit predictions of Christ, not in the regulation of the life of a community dedicated to the worship and obedience of Yahweh, the only true God.

Hence the theology—such as it is—of the early Gentile church has presuppositions somewhat different from those of the early Palestinian—that is, Jewish—Christian communities. Not that there was any break in continuity between the two: for the traditions which Mark used, and which were cherished in the Gentile churches, were in origin Palestinian, that is, Christian Jewish; only they were in process of reinterpretation, re-emphasis, in conformity with certain central ideas or emphases which were of greater importance for Gentile Christianity, and were destined to become dominant in later Greek, Western, Catholic Christianity. For example, the doctrine of the Incarnation was inconceivable upon a Jewish, even a Christian Jewish, basis; but in Mark, not to mention Paul or John, the whole tendency of the interpretation is in that direction.

During the almost forty years that lay be-

[24] *Jesus the Messiah* (Philadelphia: Westminster Press, 1946), pp. 58-61.

tween the Resurrection and the writing of our earliest Gospel, there had grown up a specific Christian terminology in the Gentile mission field. Paul contributed something to it, but his contribution was not the dominant factor. In more than one instance Paul simply presupposed it, and took it over for his own purposes. On the other hand some of Paul's own terms were never adopted as common property. More important than Paul's contribution was the already existing religious vocabulary of the Jewish Diaspora, which spoke Greek, and which gave to the world the Greek version of the Scriptures—the Septuagint. Around the Septuagint, with its added books—not found in the Hebrew canon, that is, the so-called "Apocrypha"—grew up a further literature of exposition, exhortation, edification, hymnology, and apologetic, e.g., Philo, IV Maccabees, the Testaments of the Twelve Patriarchs, the Psalms of Solomon, the works of Greco-Jewish writers in Alexandria. Much of this literature has perished, or survives only in fragments. Judaism itself, during the era of retrenchment after A.D. 135, and down through the Talmudic age and later, repudiated these books and all the concessions to Greek—that is, pagan—thought which the use of the Greek language for sacred purposes involved. But the Christian church, itself sprung from the bosom of Judaism and falling heir to the vast religious propaganda of the Diaspora, took them over, cherished them, and preserved them for posterity—in the measure in which they have actually survived. What we see reflected in the Gospel of Mark is an early stage in this process of taking over an already existing religious terminology, based upon the Septuagint, but not unaffected by the ordinary usages of the koine Greek of the first century. Mark's Greek is crude, "popular," nonliterary; [25] but he does make use of the major terms and titles common in the vocabulary of the Gentile Christian mission.

The term "gospel," for example, meant originally a reward to one who brought good news, but now it meant the good news itself—as in the inscription at Priene, 9 B.C., reflecting the sacral usage of the emperor cult ("the birthday of the god [Augustus] was for the world the beginning of tidings of joy on his account").[26] But in Mark, and throughout the New Testament, it means the Christian "message of salvation," and may refer to the one who sends it (God) or the one of whom the news is told (Christ). When Mark places this term on Jesus' own lips, it is by prolepsis and anticipation; he assumes that Jesus' message was the same as the one proclaimed in his name. It was only later (e.g., Did. 8:2; Justin First Apology I. 66) that the term came to be used of written accounts of the career of Jesus—at first of the fourfold Gospel (viewed as a single book), later of the individual Gospels, as we use the term today.

So also "Jesus Christ" (1:1) has for Mark no longer the original technical sense, "Jesus the Messiah" or "Jesus the Anointed," but is simply a proper name. Paul no doubt had much to do with the popularization of this usage in the mission field, as he did with the popularization of the term "gospel" in the specific Christian sense; but he was not alone in this—other writings of the New Testament besides Paul's, and some that were not influenced by him, regularly use the title as a name. Gentiles would not catch the overtones of the messianic reference in *Christos*. The word in Greek meant "anointed" all right, but it easily merged—especially as pronounced with a long "i"—with the common proper noun *Chrēstos*, as we see from the earliest secular accounts of the persecutions: "The Jews were stirred up by one Chrestus . . ." In the Jewish homeland there was no question what "Messiah" meant: the coming glorious king of Israel. Whether or not Jesus claimed to be Messiah, or looked upon himself as the one destined to fulfill the political hopes of his people, is doubtful. For the early Christian mission the term connoted something more than "King of Israel," and was taken over along with other terms based upon the Old Testament (e.g., "Servant of the Lord," "Angel of the Lord," "Son of David," "Son of Man"), all being combined into one concept and all being reinterpreted in the light of experience of the risen, glorified "Lord" of the Christian community. But from first to last "Christ" connoted royalty—and Mark is careful to point out that Jesus utterly repudiated this concept; Jesus was "Christ" only as reinterpreted by the Gospel. Nowhere does Jesus unequivocally and unambiguously "claim" the title, not even in the high priest's court, when on trial for his life. The term goes back to an early, probably the earliest, stage in the Christian mission, even in Palestine; but as Ernst Lohmeyer has shown,[27] there is evidence (chiefly from Luke) that the concept of the "Messiah" was more prominently emphasized in the south, in Jerusalem and Judea, while "Son of man" was the favored term and concept in the north, that is, in Galilee.

[25] See Marie-Josèphe Lagrange, *The Gospel According to Saint Mark* (New York: Benziger Bros., 1930), chs. iv-v. See also above, pp. 48-49.

[26] Adolf Deissmann, *Light from the Ancient East*, tr. L. R. M. Strachan (New York: George H. Doran Co., 1927), p. 366.

[27] *Galiläa und Jerusalem* (Göttingen: Vandenhoeck & Ruprecht, 1936), and Grant, *Earliest Gospel*, ch. vi.

It is a question if and in what sense Jesus used the title "the Son of man." In the Old Testament, for example in Ezekiel, it is the term used to emphasize the prophet's humility and humanity in contrast with God. In ordinary speech "a son of man" was equivalent to "a human being," a "person"; apparently "the" son of man meant the specific person referred to. But in the New Testament the words form a title: "the Son of the man" or "the Son of man"—outside the Gospels, only in Rev. 1:13; 14:14, where the biblical language "one like a son of man" is used, following Dan. 7:13, and in Acts 7:56, the martyr Stephen's vision of "the" Son of man. Practically limited to the Gospels, the term is used only in sayings of Jesus, where the parallels sometimes substitute "I" or "me," sometimes omit it. It occurs eight times in Q, fourteen in Mark, eight in the special material of Matthew, seven in that of Luke. In John it occurs twelve times; in Paul never, and nowhere else in the New Testament. It can scarcely be denied, in view of the parallels in the Synoptics, that there was a tendency, in the community tradition, to insert it where it was not already found—but only in words of Jesus. He is never addressed by this title, and it never occurs in narrative. Of Mark's fourteen uses of the term, those in 2:10, 28 have been thought to mean "man" ("man can forgive sins"; "man is lord of the sabbath"); but this seems improbable—not only that Mark should use the term in a different sense here, but that such doctrines should have been propounded in the tradition, or by Jesus himself. The remaining instances in Mark (8:31, 38; 9:9, 12, 31; 10:33, 45; 13:26; 14:21a, 21b, 41, 62) clearly use it in the transcendental sense: The Son of man is the glorified figure who is to come on the clouds of heaven and hold the Last Judgment.

By a tremendous paradox this divine being, the Son of man, has come to earth and been put to death by wicked men; but his death was part of the divine plan, and was "a ransom for many" (10:45). In other words the basic supposition is the identity of Jesus with the celestial figure of Daniel's vision (Dan. 7:13, originally a symbol of triumphant Israel, which was to enjoy world-empire and dominion after the successive beast-empires had been destroyed); as in I Enoch, this Son of man is to come in the end and hold the judgment (8:38; 13:26; 14:62). Then to this concept has been added, on the basis of historic fact and apostolic experience, the paradox of the death of the Son of man (8:31; 9:12, 31; 10:33; 14:21, 41), as a result of divine decree and in order to "ransom" the many (10:45; 14:21a), and his resurrection (9:9). The way of suffering, reject-

tion, disgrace, and crucifixion leads to his eventual triumph and exaltation "after three days" (8:31; etc.), and his coming again in glory.[28] It is not enough to say in explanation that this conception of the Son of man rests upon an earlier doctrine of the "suffering Messiah," of the existence of which doctrine there is no evidence; or that in Jewish thought the two ideas of Messiah and suffering servant of the Lord (from II Isaiah) had been combined —of this too there is no evidence before the second century A.D., when both ideas were interpreted to mean suffering, oppressed Israel, someday to be victorious; as little does it suffice to attribute this idea to some hypothetical, mythological figure, like the dying-rising mystery deities of surrounding paganism, for there is no more evidence of a connection here than there is in Dan. 7; instead it must be recognized that we have in this conception a pure creation of Christian thought, the consequence of continual reflection upon the career of Jesus, who is seen in the blazing splendor of his risen, glorified, exalted state "at God's right hand," from whence the heavenly Son of man was expected to come.

Whether Jesus referred to himself in such terms must be a matter of doubt. But our concern is with Mark's use of the title. And the connotations of that usage are clear: Jesus knew himself to be and referred to himself as the divine, heavenly Man (or "Son of man"); the total contradiction of such an exalted office, involved in his rejection and shameful death, he accepted—in order to triumph over the shame and rise victoriously over death, freeing the "many" who had been sold into slavery (to sin? to Satan? to death? to despair?) and were awaiting their divine redemption or "ransom." Such an idea cannot be explained from the Old Testament or from then current Hellenistic religion; and it was totally unknown to Judaism. It was a projection of the central conviction of apostolic faith, based firmly upon apostolic experience, and it came to mean most to the Gentile churches, since it was combined with the concept of the Son of God.

There is a double Christology in the Gospel of Mark: Jesus is both Son of man and Son of God. There can be little question that of the two terms "the Son of God" is nearest and dearest to Mark and to the Gentile church. As Lohmeyer[29] rightly insists, the connotations of this title are totally different from those of "Son of man" or "Messiah." It cannot be derived from the messianic category—the use of Ps.

[28] See Grant, *Earliest Gospel*, pp. 63-69.
[29] *Das Evangelium des Markus* (Göttingen: Vandenhoeck & Ruprecht, 1937), p. 4.

2:7 in Mark 1:11, and elsewhere in the New Testament, is an afterthought, an elucidation of the psalm in the light of Jesus' exaltation, resurrection or baptism. Instead we must look for its origin—which was not Palestinian Jewish —to the early Christian mission among the Gentiles. In native Jewish thought God could not have a son—the conception was simply mythological and denied the oneness of God. But for Gentile Christianity, possibly even for Diaspora Judaism, there could exist another divine being —or other beings—in the presence of God, subordinate to God, after the pattern of the Greek "sons of God." The concept "Son of God," far from being merely mythological and artificial, represented the very highest attainment of popular pagan religion: such divine beings as Asclepius, Heracles, the Dioscuri, the saviors and helpers of mankind, who voluntarily underwent privation and endured suffering in order to benefit mankind—these, rather than the vague deities of the Oriental "mystery" cults, were the gods dearest to the hearts of men in the Greco-Roman world. Not that early Gentile Christianity was one more hero-cult, with a Savior Christ instead of Asclepius, the divine physician, or Heracles, the helper; but the term "Son of God" was taken over from paganism as a term already filled with rich religious meaning—somewhat as other terms, "Savior," "Lord," "Logos," "Redeemer" were taken over by the early Greek-speaking church. In the same way the present-day church in China or India chooses terms already full of deep religious significance and then proceeds to give them their fullest possible meaning in connection with Christ, God, or the Holy Spirit.

As with the preceding title "Son of man," it may well be that Jesus used the term "Son" as correlative to "Father"; that it expressed the fullness of his own personal consciousness of intimate relation to God; that the church looked upon him as the representative of the people of God, his "son" (as in Hos. 11:1); but we are concerned with Mark's use of the term, and back of Mark that of the early Gentile church. It was already in use in Paul's time— he takes it for granted throughout his letters, nowhere more clearly than in Rom. 1:4, in a creedlike passage where he is setting forth the common faith, addressed to a Christian group he has never seen. It is the whole presupposition of the "hymn" in Phil. 2:6-11, which some scholars think Paul was quoting—that is, it was already familiar to himself and his readers. And it was the title above all others which expressed the growing thought of Greek-speaking Christianity, moving steadily in the direction of Nicaea, Constantinople, and Chalcedon

with their monumental affirmations of the doctrine of the Incarnation. Mark is sometimes thought to be an early "adoptionist" (Christ "became" Son of God by his resurrection, or by his holy life, or by his baptism); others hold that Mark believed in the pre-existence of the Son of God, as Paul did, and John. The evidence is difficult to interpret. At least we may say that the *connotations* of the title "Son of God" included pre-existence, though Mark himself may not have gone that far. The Western reading in Luke 3:22 is "adoptionist": "Thou art my Son, this day have I begotten thee," but it is clearly derived from Ps. 2:7.

Mark lets us see how soon Christian theology developed—although it grew up, as Adolf Harnack pointed out,[80] only on Greek soil. In Mark we see the process at work, but at an early stage. Its chief factors were (a) the Old Testament and Hellenistic Judaism—the Old Testament, already translated into Greek, exercising a normative, even determinative influence; (b) the tradition of religious thought in the Hellenistic world, already influenced by Diaspora Judaism; (c) the early Christian experience of Christ, and conviction about his person, mission, office, and nature; (d) the living, ongoing religious experience of the church, which was continuous with the earliest apostolic experience and indeed with the experience of Jesus' disciples during his lifetime. Early Christian theology was "dialectical," in the classical meaning of that word: it arose by the method of question and answer, answers being provided from the Old Testament and elsewhere as they arose, and these in turn giving rise to new questions which required answers. Some questions were never raised, and therefore never answered. A few were raised which could not be answered—When will the Day of Judgment come? Is punishment everlasting? How did Christ redeem men on the Cross? But there is enough evidence in the New Testament to make it clear that early Christian theology was not a set of inferences from a priori principles or axioms, moving in a vacuum of speculation, but was geared tightly to the actual religious life, the needs and aspirations of men and women in the Gentile world of the first and second centuries.

This situation helps to account for the variety in outlook which we find in the New Testament, even in Mark. Was the kingdom of God purely eschatological, or a present possession? Could one "inherit" it as well as "enter' it? And could one enter it here and now, or only beyond death? Was it to be set up on this earth, or only in the world to come? Would the Last Judgment precede its inauguration,

[80] In his *Dogmengeschichte.*

or follow it (as in Rev. 20—both ideas are found in the Revelation of John)? Apparently every one of these questions could be and was answered affirmatively. There was a sense in which each affirmation was true. And the reason is this: early Christian thought was based upon immediate experience, turned to the Old Testament for light, and cherished a rich and manifold tradition. It was a creative process, not a static, sterile record from the past.

Mark takes for granted the theology of the Gentile churches of his time. But at several points he apparently advances beyond the position already reached by his fellow believers—expressing views which sometimes were modified or even abandoned by later writers, but sometimes exercised an important formative influence upon the subsequent thought of the church.

1. He conceives of the gospel as a mystery (4:11-12)—"the" mystery of the kingdom of God, a secret doctrine not to be divulged to "those outside." This sounds Pauline but is not really so. For Paul's "mystery" was God's secret plan, at last revealed in the salvation of men. For Mark it means only that the parables contain profound esoteric truths which can be arrived at only by allegorical interpretation.

2. Along with this is his theory of the blindness and obtuseness of the Jewish people, especially their leaders, who rejected Jesus and put him to death. Even the disciples appear to share this blindness—the most obvious statements are over their heads, and they cannot draw the simplest inference of faith (e.g., 8:14-21). But the blindness is more than ordinary stupidity: it is the consequence of a divine judgment which has overtaken them for their sin, somewhat as God "hardened" Pharaoh's heart at the time of the Exodus from Egypt. Therefore they *cannot* see and believe. This also sounds Pauline (see Rom. 9–11); but Paul views the "hardening" as a part of God's plan for the admission of the Gentiles—there is no hint of this in Mark. It is rather one of the dialectical "answers" that arose in early Christianity. To the question "Why did the Jews reject—why do they still reject—Jesus as their Savior and Messiah?" the answer seemed obvious: "Because they cannot do otherwise; they are under a judgment of blindness." That a strong trace of anti-Semitism, or rather of anti-Judaism, is to be found here seems obvious, and is unfortunate.

3. At the same time Jesus insisted upon keeping his messiahship a secret until he "should have risen from the dead" (9:9). Wilhelm Wrede [81] and others have concluded

that this was the answer to the question: Why did not the disciples proclaim Jesus' messiahship during his lifetime? For the reason obviously that they did not believe it, that Jesus did not claim it. But the case is not so simple as that. The belief clearly must have had to grow: Jesus was not openly and obviously the king of Israel. Indeed Jesus may not have wished to appear in that role at all; his conception of his mission was very different. He may very well therefore have repressed the exuberant hopes and speculations of those who were "looking for the redemption of Israel," and may well have thought that possibly he himself was to be, in a different way, the destined fulfiller of their hopes. He may—he probably must—have silenced the strange half-articulate ejaculations of the demoniacs, some of them hailing him as God's elect, or the Son of God, or the holy One. All this is no doubt historical. But in spite of this his own sense of mission is clear, and also the enthusiastic conviction of his disciples that he was someone extraordinary, a prophet, Elijah come again, or one of the old prophets returned to earth: in some way or other his ministry marked the dawn of a new era, the final era of salvation. He might be—he could only be—the bringer and bearer of the divine redemption, though clearly it transcended material limitations, and was not incompatible with his own death. But Mark knows that Jesus *was* Messiah, after all, though in a new and higher sense, the sense of his own gospel of humility, penitence, forgiveness, patience, endurance; he was the Christian Messiah, not the Jewish—and yet the two were related, in fact identical. The only way Mark could work out a solution of this puzzle was to assume that Jesus, although he was "already Messiah from the beginning of his earthly career" and not merely from the time of his resurrection and exaltation—this, according to Johannes Weiss, was what Mark undertook to prove—still had to hold back the truth from his contemporaries, and even forbade his disciples to make him known (8:30).

4. Consonant with this theory is Mark's abridgment and selection from the teaching of Jesus. Since it was already known orally to his readers; since Jesus did not proclaim it publicly, but secretly, to those who were able to hear it (contrast Matthew, with the sermon addressed to multitudes from a mountain top!); since Mark's purpose is to strengthen the faith and courage of his readers facing martyrdom, the proportion and perspective in which he sets forth the teaching of Jesus are in strange contrast both with the other Synoptic Gospels and with historical proba-

[81] *Das Messiasgeheimnis in den Evangelien* (Göttingen: Vandenhoeck & Ruprecht, 1901).

bility (see even John 18:19-21). A persecution motif dominates much of the teaching found in Mark.

All this must be borne in mind by the modern reader. Though Mark is one of the most precious books ever written, and though the signs of "resistance unto blood" are upon every page of it, though it is the gospel of the divine hero, the Son of God who died for the sins of "many," it does not by any means give us a full account of the life, the teaching, or the personality of Jesus. It has its own outlook, and its own theology. Perhaps only a martyr church could, or ever can, learn from it all it has to teach.

VI. Text

The Greek text of Mark has not been greatly altered in transmission. Though it was popular for a generation and then fell into considerable neglect (until rescued by the Four-Gospel canon in the middle of the second century), its very neglect preserved it, as B. H. Streeter pointed out,[32] from the surging tide of "Western" interpolations, such as affected the text of Luke, a much longer and more popular Gospel. On the whole the text of the great uncials is satisfactory (the text followed by most modern editions, Westcott and Hort, Tischendorf, Weiss, Nestle); only occasionally, as we shall observe in the notes, are other authorities, manuscripts, or versions to be preferred to B, etc.

Neither the longer ending (16:9-20) nor the shorter (see end of final note in Revised Standard Version) is in the style of Mark. Both probably represent second-century efforts to complete and round off the Gospel, though whether or not the longer ending is the work of Ariston (Aristion?) cannot be proved—it is obviously based upon the other Gospels, and even the book of Acts, Luke's second volume. Nor can we be sure that the Gospel was *broken off* at 16:8; perhaps it ended originally at that point. The author's style is unfinished, and 16:8 is no more abrupt a conclusion than 1:1 is a beginning. The question has been argued repeatedly pro and con, and we are still far from a certain answer. Perhaps some new discovery of an early papyrus copy of the Gospel, or of its final pages, may throw the needed light upon the problem. No modern attempt to "complete" the Gospel from Luke or Matthew can be pronounced successful—any more than that of the compiler of vss. 9-20 in the second century.

That a number of "glosses" have crept into the text will be pointed out in the notes.

[32] *The Four Gospels* (New York: The Macmillan Co., 1925).

VII. Outline of the Gospel

I. Introduction (1:1-13)
  A. John the Baptizer and Jesus (1:2-11)
    1. John the Baptizer (1:2-8)
    2. The baptism of Jesus (1:9-11)
  B. The temptation of Jesus (1:12-13)
II. Jesus in Galilee (1:14–9:50)
  A. About the Sea of Galilee (1:14–5:43)
    1. Jesus returns to Galilee (1:14-15)
    2. The call of the first disciples (1:16-20)
    3. Jesus in the synagogue at Capernaum (1:21-28)
    4. Jesus in the house of Peter (1:29-31)
    5. Healing the sick at even (1:32-34)
    6. Jesus' departure from Capernaum (1:35-39)
    7. Healing a leper (1:40-45)
    8. Healing a paralytic (2:1-12)
    9. The call of Levi (2:13-14)
    10. Eating with publicans and sinners (2:15-17)
    11. The question of fasting (2:18-22)
    12. Plucking grain on the sabbath (2:23-28)
    13. Healing the withered hand (3:1-6)
    14. Jesus' popularity and his cures (3:7-12)
    15. The appointment of the twelve apostles (3:13-19)
    16. The charge of the scribes (3:20-30)
    17. Jesus' true family (3:31-35)
    18. The parable of the sower (4:1-9)
    19. Explanation of the parable (4:10-20)
    20. Exhortation to understanding (4:21-25)
    21. Parable of the self-growing seed (4:26-29)
    22. Parable of the mustard seed (4:30-32)
    23. Parabolic method of teaching (4:33-34)
    24. The storm on the lake (4:35-41)
    25. The Gerasene demoniac (5:1-20)
    26. The daughter of Jairus (5:21-24, 35-43) and the woman with an issue of blood (5:25-34)
  B. Wider journeyings (6:1–9:50)
    1. The visit to Nazareth (6:1-6)
    2. The mission of the disciples (6:7-13)
    3. Herod's impression of Jesus (6:14-16)
    4. The death of John the Baptizer (6:17-29)
    5. The feeding of the five thousand (6:30-44)
    6. Jesus walking on the sea (6:45-52)
    7. The landing at Gennesaret (6:53-56)
    8. The tradition of the elders (7:1-23)
    9. The Syrophoenician woman (7:24-30)
    10. Healing a deaf and dumb man (7:31-37)
    11. The feeding of the four thousand (8:1-10)
    12. The Pharisees demand a sign (8:11-13)
    13. The leaven of the Pharisees (8:14-21)
    14. The blind man of Bethsaida (8:22-26)
    15. Peter's confession (8:27-30)
    16. The first passion announcement (8:31-33)

VIII. Selected Bibliography

INTRODUCTIONS

DIBELIUS, MARTIN. *A Fresh Approach to the New Testament.* New York: Charles Scribner's Sons, 1936.

———— *From Tradition to Gospel,* tr. B. L. Woolf. New York: Charles Scribner's Sons, 1935.

GOODSPEED, EDGAR J. *Introduction to the New Testament,* Chicago: University of Chicago Press, 1938.

JÜLICHER, ADOLF. *An Introduction to the New Testament,* tr. Janet Penrose Ward. London: Smith, Elder & Co., 1904.

McNEILE, A. H. *An Introduction to the Study of the New Testament.* Oxford: Clarendon Press, 1927.

MOFFATT, JAMES. *An Introduction to the Literature of the New Testament.* New York: Charles Scribner's Sons, 2d ed., 1912.

SCOTT, ERNEST F. *The Literature of the New Testament.* New York: Columbia University Press, 1932.

ZAHN, THEODOR. *Introduction to the New Testament,* tr. John Moore Trout *et al.* Edinburgh: T. & T. Clark, 1909.

SPECIAL STUDIES

BACON, B. W. *The Gospel of Mark.* New Haven: Yale University Press, 1925.

————. *Is Mark a Roman Gospel?* Cambridge: Harvard University Press, 1919.

DIBELIUS, MARTIN. *Jesus.* Philadelphia: Westminster Press, 1949.

GRANT, F. C. *The Earliest Gospel.* New York and Nashville: Abingdon-Cokesbury Press, 1943.

————. *The Growth of the Gospels.* New York: Abingdon Press, 1933.

STREETER, B. H. *The Four Gospels.* New York: The Macmillan Co., 1925.

TURNER, C. H. "Studies in Marcan Usage" (a series of articles in *Journal of Theological Studies,* Vols. XXV-XXIX, 1924-28) ; "A Textual Commentary on Mark i" (*Journal of Theological Studies,* Vols. XXVII-XXVIII, 1926-27) .

WEISS, BERNHARD. *Die Evangelien des Markus und Lukas.* Göttingen: Vandenhoeck & Ruprecht, 1901.

WEISS, JOHANNES. *The History of Primitive Christianity,* tr. F. C. Grant *et al.* New York: Wilson-Erickson, 1937.

———— *Das Älteste Evangelium.* Göttingen: Vandenhoeck & Ruprecht, 1903.

WERNER, MARTIN. *Der Einfluss paulinischer Theologie im Markus-evangelium.* Giessen: Alfred Töpelmann, 1923.

COMMENTARIES

ALLEN, W. C. *The Gospel According to Saint Mark* ("The Oxford Church Biblical Commentary"). New York: The Macmillan Co., 1915.

BACON, B. W. *The Beginnings of Gospel Story.* New Haven: Yale University Press, 1909.

BRANSCOMB, B. HARVIE. *The Gospel of Mark* ("The Moffatt New Testament Commentary"). London: Hodder & Stoughton, 1937.

HOLTZMANN, H. J. *Hand-commentar zum Neuen Testament,* 3rd ed. Freiburg: J. C. B. Mohr, 1901.

KLOSTERMANN, ERICH. *Das Markus-Evangelium* ("Handbuch zum Neuen Testament"). Tübingen: J. C. B. Mohr, 1936.

LAGRANGE, M. J. *The Gospel According to St. Mark.* Auth. tr. New York: Benziger Bros., 1930.

LOHMEYER, ERNST. *Das Évangelium des Markus.* Göttingen: Vandenhoeck & Ruprecht, 1937.

LOISY, ALFRED FIRMIN. *Les Evangiles Synoptiques.* Ceffonds: Chez l'Auteur, 1907-08.

MENZIES, ALLAN. *The Earliest Gospel.* London: Macmillan & Co., 1901.

MONTEFIORE, C. G. *The Synoptic Gospels,* 2nd ed. London: Macmillan & Co., 1927.

RAWLINSON, A. E. J. *Saint Mark.* London: Methuen & Co., 1931.

STRACK, H. L., and BILLERBECK, PAUL. *Kommentar zum Neuen Testament aus Talmud und Midrasch.* Munich: C. H. Beck, 1922-28.

SWETE, H. B. *The Gospel According to St. Mark.* London: Macmillan & Co., 1920.

TURNER, C. H. "The Gospel According to St. Mark," *A New Commentary on Holy Scripture,* ed. Gore, Goudge, and Guillaume. New York: The Macmillan Co., 1946.

WEISS, JOHANNES. *Die Schriften des Neuen Testaments,* Vol. I. Göttingen, 1906-7; 3d ed., 1917.

WELLHAUSEN, JULIUS. *Das Evangelium Marci.* Berlin: G. Reimer, 1903; 2d ed., 1909.

MARK

TEXT, EXEGESIS, AND EXPOSITION

1 The beginning of the gospel of Jesus Christ, the Son of God;

1 The beginning of the gospel of Jesus Christ, the Son of God.[a]

[a] Some ancient authorities omit *the Son of God.*

I. INTRODUCTION (1:1-13)

1:1. The opening section of the Gospel of Mark presents us with several problems of text, translation, and punctuation. The first verse is probably the equivalent of what in a modern book would be the title, or of the so-called *incipit* of a medieval manuscript: "Here begins [*incipit*] the gospel of Jesus Christ, the Son of God." The verse should therefore be set off by itself, and end with a period.

1:1. *Title.*—The first verse of Mark is a title meaning "The beginning of the good news about Jesus Christ." The word **gospel,** as we use the word to describe the Gospels, does not refer to the book Mark is writing. It does not even mean the teaching which Jesus gave. It is the message of salvation through Jesus Christ.

The **beginning** of the gospel in that sense was in the preaching of John the Baptist. When he appears preaching repentance, the curtain goes up on the great drama of salvation. The prologue to Act I begins. We cannot grasp the meaning of that great title, "The good news about Jesus Christ," unless we loose the checkrein of our imagination a bit and see some of the pictures that unroll.

It was good news when it was first proclaimed. It moved up and down the country roads of Galilee and the city streets of Jerusalem, and men and women were made whole. Jesus said, "Follow me," and men gladly followed him, their life deepened with new faith and enlarged with new purpose.

It was good news as it went out to the hard Roman world in the first century. Down into the ghettos and slums of Greek and Roman cities, where life was bound with every conceivable chain, the good news came with a proclamation that lifted men to their feet. "Beloved, now are we the sons of God" (I John 3:2).

It has been good news down through the centuries, out through all the nooks and corners of the globe, until it reaches the last outpost on earth. There is great meaning in the old childhood jingle:

Matthew, Mark, Luke, and John,
Bless the bed that I lie on.

The Gospel of Mark—and the others—has blessed the bed that humanity has lain on—

2 As it is written in the prophets, Behold, I send my messenger before thy face, which shall prepare thy way before thee.

3 The voice of one crying in the wilderness, Prepare ye the way of the Lord, make his paths straight.

2 As it is written in Isaiah the prophet,[b]
"Behold, I send my messenger before thy face,
who shall prepare thy way;
3 the voice of one crying in the wilderness:
Prepare the way of the Lord,
make his paths straight—"

[b] Some ancient authorities read in the prophets.

Although some ancient MSS and church fathers—Sinaiticus, Koridethi, Irenaeus (in part), Origen—omit the words **the Son of God,** they were probably in the original. This conclusion is based on two considerations: (a) Mark's theology (see Intro., pp. 642-43) stresses the title; and (b) the words might easily have been omitted by some copyist, since the line, with them, includes six singular genitives in succession, each ending in ου, three (perhaps four) of them in abbreviated forms: τοῦ εὐαγγελίου ιυ χυ υιου θυ—and υἱοῦ could be abbreviated as υυ. There were fifteen such "sacred names" often abbreviated in ancient biblical manuscripts. A bar placed above the letters indicated the abbreviation.

The gospel does not mean a book, or the message delivered by Jesus, but "the Christian proclamation of the divine message of salvation through Jesus Christ"; it is "the good news *about* Jesus Christ, the Son of God" (see Intro., p. 641). In 13:10 and 14:9 the term is used of the apostolic preaching of the Christian message and, in the latter passage at least, includes incidents from the life of Jesus—which presumably the apostolic preaching had included from the very beginning. On **Jesus Christ** (used here as a personal name, not a title), **the Son of God,** see Intro., p. 641.

A. John the Baptizer and Jesus (1:2-11)

1. John the Baptizer (1:2-8)

2-3. The quotation in vs. 3 is from Isa. 40:3; vs. 2b is from Exod. 23:20 combined with Mal. 3:1, both passages being modified ("my" angel, "thy" way). It is therefore thought that this part of the quotation has been inserted here from Matt. 11:10 or Luke 7:27, or possibly even from Q, a source lying behind both Matthew and Luke. It was after the insertion of this popular early Christian "proof text" that the words **Isaiah the prophet** were changed to read **the prophets;** the MS evidence for the latter is weak. Vs. 2b reflected the early Christian view of John as the forerunner of Christ, the preparer of the

beds of pain, of sorrow, of despair. It has come into every human situation and blessed it. It is good news when life unfolds and looks up with aspiration; good news when life meets sorrow; when life goes to smash; still the best of good news when life comes to an end. It is good news in the common life men live together, when groups clash. To a life torn apart by human greed and human passion, it is the good news of him in whom "all things hold together" (Col. 1:17).

1. Jesus Christ, the Son of God.—This title "Son of God," whether in Mark's words or not, belongs here, for it sets forth the viewpoint from which he writes. It is from beginning to end **the gospel of Jesus Christ, the Son of God** (see Exeg.). Mark is not intentionally writing either history or biography. He is setting forth the good news of the Son of God. It is that on which the church was founded; the gospel,

as Dean Inge has said, "was not good advice but good news." Someone has put it glowingly: "The gospel that went out to the hard Roman world was not a Robin Redbreast on a Christmas card; it was not the motto, 'Peace on earth,' picked out in cotton wool. It was the affirmation of a Christ who lived, was crucified, and rose from the dead." If we forget that, it does not make too much difference what we remember. We will be in the position of the man described by Matthew Arnold, "A mournful evangelist who had contrived to mislay his gospel."

2-3. As It Is Written in Isaiah the Prophet, ... My Messenger ... Who Shall Prepare Thy Way.—In this and in all the quotations from the O.T. in Mark and the other Gospels, we feel the strong sense which first-century Christians had of the great background of their faith and gospel in Israel. That gospel was not something completely new, but a historical

| 4 John did baptize in the wilderness, and preach the baptism of repentance for the remission of sins. | 4 John the baptizer appeared in the wilderness, preaching a baptism of repentance for |

way for him. **As it is written** should be given more emphasis: "Just as it is written." The author is not borrowing an apt poetical description from the O.T., but is pointing out an exact fulfillment of prophecy. The point is not only John's appearance **in the wilderness**— i.e., wild open country, the uninhabited region along the lower Jordan, north of the Dead Sea—but also his message of repentance and preparation for the coming judgment: **Prepare . . . straight.**

4. This verse should be translated with RSV, in accordance with the best Greek text. The definite article before **baptizer** is well attested, and the term **the baptizer** is Marcan (6:14, 24). But how should vss. 2-4 be punctuated? (There was no punctuation in ancient manuscripts.) Some scholars have viewed the whole of vss. 2-3 as an insertion, and have combined vss. 1 and 4 as follows: "The beginning of the gospel . . . was John." RSV, keeping vs. 1 as a title, reads: **As it is written in Isaiah . . . John . . . appeared in the wilderness.** This seems preferable. The work of **John the baptizer** was commonly viewed as the beginning of the Christian movement (Acts 10:37; 13:24; 19:4) ; the Gospel of John, in its opening chapters, presupposes a close connection between Jesus and the Baptist.

Baptism of repentance is a Semitism, meaning "a baptism which symbolized or expressed repentance." It followed upon repentance and signified cleansing from the sins that were repented of. See below, on vs. 5. **Repentance** is more than "penitence" (Vulg.,

continuation and fulfillment of God's revelation and promise to Israel.

> Not in entire forgetfulness,
> And not in utter nakedness,
> But trailing clouds of glory,[1]

did this gospel come from God's dealing with Israel. They saw in John the fulfillment of the prophecies here recorded from Malachi and Isaiah.

The role of one who prepares the way for Christ is a timeless and a universal one. Every fresh coming of Christ in the world has followed the work of those who in their spirit and in their lives have been road makers. There is a fine old word in English which expresses the role perfectly—"pavior." A pavior was one who paved a road, who "prepared the way" and made "paths straight." The world needs a *Savior*—it also needs *paviors*. Isaiah's word "wilderness" is not out of date. It is an up-to-the-minute description of much of our world. Christ needs preparers of his way.

We prepare the way of Christ when we give him a leverage in our life. A receptive mind is an indispensable road-making tool. We prepare his way also when we become a crying voice. In the beginning is the *word*—always. We make his paths straight when we bring his creative word to a world dying for lack of it. We go before his face and make ready for him when we help to remove the things which block his

entrance into our world—ancestral blindness, sanctified stupidities, greed, pride, hatred.

4. *Preaching a Baptism of Repentance for the Forgiveness of Sins.*—This baptism was the symbol of repentance. The mood, the spirit, the act of repentance was the main thing which fitted one for the coming rule of God. Repentance, in John's preaching, was a thoroughgoing change, as is all true repentance. The word is a strong one—"a new mind." It calls for a rightabout-face, a will turned in a new direction. Hence repentance is always more than penitence. It is not remorse; not admitting mistakes; not saying in self-condemnation, "I have been a fool." Who has not recited such dismal rituals? They are common and easy. This is more. It is more even than being "sorry" for one's sins. It is a moral and spiritual revolution.

For that reason to repent genuinely is one of the hardest things in the world; yet it is basic to all spiritual change and progress. It calls for the complete breakdown of pride, of self-assurance, of the prestige that comes from success, and of that inmost citadel which is self-will.

Genuine repentance must include the subtle sins of the spirit, often so elusive that they are unrecognized and so deceptive that they assume the shape of angels. The classic list of the seven deadly sins contains some of them—pride, anger, envy, covetousness, sloth. Notice (vs. 5) that those baptized confessed their *sins*. Sin is an infinitely stronger word than "mistake." It is also an infinitely stronger word than the easy,

[1] Wordsworth, "Ode on Intimations of Immortality."

5 And there went out unto him all the land of Judea, and they of Jerusalem, and were all baptized of him in the river of Jordan, confessing their sins.

6 And John was clothed with camel's hair, and with a girdle of a skin about his loins; and he did eat locusts and wild honey;

the forgiveness of sins. 5 And there went out to him all the country of Judea, and all the people of Jerusalem; and they were baptized by him in the river Jordan, confessing their sins. 6 Now John was clothed with camel's hair, and had a leather girdle around his waist, and ate locusts and wild

---

poenitentia) or "godly sorrow for sin." The Greek word metanoia means a complete change of mind, a new direction of will, an altered purpose in life—what the O.T. and later Jewish literature summed up in the word teshûbhâh, i.e., "turning" away from sin and "turning" to the Lord. For the remission (or forgiveness) of sins probably goes with the word "baptism," not "repentance." In Jewish teaching, as in the O.T., divine forgiveness follows at once upon human repentance; but the passage before us has been colored by Christian interpretation: John's baptism is viewed as sacramental. The older view survives in such a passage as Luke 24:47. Indeed, some scholars think that for the forgiveness of sins has been introduced into the text under the influence of the later Christian view of baptism.

5. All the land of Judea, like "all the men of Jerusalem," is obviously a vivid exaggeration, suggesting the enormous extent of John's influence and the deep impression he made upon his contemporaries (cf. 11:32, and Acts 10:37: "the Baptism" had been a great religious movement in the days just before Jesus' ministry began). Baptized by him means "in his presence," or "at his direction"; Jewish baptism, and probably the earliest Christian as well, was self-administered: "baptized themselves in his presence." The later Christian usage—reflected in Did. 7:3, which permits pouring in cases of necessity—was baptism "by" another person. Self-baptism, by immersion, was the usual Jewish rite for cleansing: e.g., of women after childbirth (the tebhîlâh); and of proselytes after circumcision, presumably to wash away the defilements of idolatry; in the latter case, the candidate immersed himself while two persons stood by and recited to him portions of the Law. Something of the sort may be imagined as the procedure in Johannine baptism, where the prophet's presence, and perhaps exhortations, accompanied the rite. The significance of it lay in the requirement that those who were already Jews—born and circumcised as descendants of Abraham (cf. Luke 3:8) —were to undergo a baptism similar to that of proselytes, in preparation for the coming judgment (cf. Isa. 1:16; 4:4; Ezek. 36:25; Zech. 13:1). Confessing their sins: The rite itself signified the acknowledgment of their sins; whether or not an oral statement of their actual misdoings (cf. Luke 19:8) was required, we do not know. At least it was more than a confession of sinfulness; ancient religion was concrete and specific.

6. With camel's hair: Not the soft, luxurious garments worn by wealthy potentates (cf. Matt. 11:8), but the rough mantle of the nomads; possibly, as in some MSS, a camel's pelt—the garb of a prophet in Zech. 13:4. And had a leather girdle around his waist may be a gloss from the text of Matt. 3:4; the clause came originally from II Kings 1:8, where the appearance of Elijah the Tishbite is described. John is "Elijah come again" for Mark (see 9:13) and for many other early Christians, but not for all (see John 1:21). Locusts and wild honey: Dried locusts are still eaten by the Arabs in times of scarcity; wild

---

soothing, modern psychological jargon which so deftly substitutes itself for the religious word sin. There is strong point in the sarcasm of Gaius Glenn Atkins' paraphrase of the General Confession in the language of psychoanalysis: "We have followed too much the inhibitions and self-expressions of our own complexes. We have not sublimated our libidos, nor considered

our neuroses." [2] Such words never lead to the liberating, "I have sinned against heaven and in thy sight."

Nothing less than repentance can lead the world out of disaster today. Man's will must be set in a new direction, turning away from the

[2] "Concerning Substitutes for Sin," Religion in Life, II (1933), 385.

7 And preached, saying, There cometh one mightier than I after me, the latchet of whose shoes I am not worthy to stoop down and unloose.

8 I indeed have baptized you with water: but he shall baptize you with the Holy Ghost.

honey. 7 And he preached, saying, "After me comes he who is mightier than I, the thong of whose sandals I am not worthy to stoop down and untie. 8 I have baptized you with water; but he will baptize you with the Holy Spirit."

---

honey may refer to gum which dripped from various trees, but was more probably the honey of wild bees.

7. One mightier than I was understood by Mark as a reference to the coming Messiah (i.e., Jesus; see 8:29). In John's preaching it more probably meant "the messenger of the covenant" of Mal. 3:1–4:3, who was to inaugurate the divine judgment as a consuming fire. (See F. C. Grant, *The Gospel of the Kingdom* [New York: The Macmillan Co., 1941], ch. v.) **After me,** i.e., "following my appearance," may be an interpretative addition by the writer of the Gospel; more probably it is simply a Semitism, announcing that the Messenger-Judge is about to appear (cf. Acts 13:25). **The thong . . . untie:** John is not worthy to perform even the menial office of a slave in the presence of the coming supernatural Judge.

8. The saying in this verse is attributed to Jesus in Acts 1:5; 11:16. This was probably the form in which it was current in circles familiar to Luke. In its Q form, as the parallels in Matthew and Luke show, the saying probably ran: "I have baptized you with water, but he will baptize you with fire." Mark interpreted "fire" to mean the Holy Spirit, a view which Luke follows in Acts; in the Gospels, Matthew and Luke conflate and read "with the Holy Spirit and with fire" and then continue further with Q, giving the words about the threshing floor and the chaff which shall be "burned with unquenchable fire" (Matt. 3:11-12; Luke 3:16-17). What John said, therefore, is that the coming one would baptize men in the fire of the divine judgment. This is a further confirmation of the view that John was a prophet of judgment, taking up where Malachi had laid down, rather than a prophet of the kingdom of God (see Luke 16:16).

It is apparent that Mark 1:1-8 is simply introductory to the account of Jesus' public ministry, and indeed to the narrative of his baptism (vs. 9). John's work is viewed from the Christian angle: his significance is only preparatory to the coming of Christ, and no effort has been made to present him from a purely historical or biographical point of view. This should suggest to the reader what will be abundantly clear from the Gospel as a whole: nothing merely biographical or historical has a place here; the book was written "out of faith" and "for faith"—i.e., the creation, or the confirmation, of Christian faith is all that matters.

---

fatal scramble for power, prestige, and advantage. In the forefront of John's call for repentance was his sense of coming judgment. Ours is a day when coming judgment can not only be seen, but felt. The noise of the explosion of the atomic bomb at Hiroshima shouted very clearly—Repent!

7. *After Me Comes He Who Is Mightier than I.*—In these words John expressed the reference of his life. As he is pictured in Mark, his every word and act pointed to one mightier than himself. In that he found his highest significance. So it is with every man. All true greatness consists in pointing to Someone beyond. A modern instance is reflected in the oft-quoted words of Baron Bunsen to his wife on her deathbed, "In thy face I have seen the Eternal."

Her life had a Godward reference. A good question for all of us to ask is this: Does mine carry any strong suggestion of a "mightier than I"? Or is it self-enclosed, with no margin of eternity, containing nothing more than meets the eye? Do we ever remind people of Jesus Christ?

8. *He Will Baptize You with the Holy Spirit.*—Many scholars have concluded that this saying of John ran, "I shall baptize you with water; but he shall baptize you with fire" (see Exeg.). John was a prophet of the coming judgment, a judgment likened to fire, and not primarily a prophet of the kingdom of God. This was the estimate of Jesus (Luke 7:28).

Yet this saying, attributed to Jesus in Acts 1:5, does express a central faith of first-century

9 And it came to pass in those days, that Jesus came from Nazareth of Galilee, and was baptized of John in Jordan.

10 And straightway coming up out of the water, he saw the heavens opened, and the Spirit like a dove descending upon him:

9 In those days Jesus came from Nazareth of Galilee and was baptized by John in the Jordan. 10 And when he came up out of the water, immediately he saw the heavens opened and the Spirit descending

---

B. THE BAPTISM OF JESUS (1:9-11)

As Son of God (1:1), Jesus is made manifest at the outset of his career by what amounts to a divine epiphany; compare the account of the Transfiguration (9:2-8), where instead of **Thou art my beloved Son** the heavenly voice proclaims, "This is my beloved Son." Mark probably viewed the former as addressed to Jesus alone (Matt. 3:17 has "This is . . . ," and both later Synoptists represent the scene objectively, as does John 1:33).

9. In those days, i.e., in the general period of John's ministry, as described in vss. 4-8. Acts 13:25, as well as the Gospel of John, presupposes that it was toward the end of John's "course." **Jesus came from Nazareth** is correct, not "Jesus of Nazareth came," though Mark describes Nazareth as Jesus' native place (6:1). **Baptized by John,** i.e., at John's bidding (see on vs. 5).

10. Immediately is one of the commonest words (forty-one times) in Mark, characteristic of his vivid, nervous style. **He saw:** In Mark the vision is seen by Jesus alone, and the words of the heavenly voice are addressed to him directly. **The heavens opened.** Better, were "rent asunder" or "torn open"; cf. "rend the heavens [and] come down" in Isa. 64:1. The ancient reader would have thought of a sundering of the clouds, as when light shines through them, or as when lightning flashes in a thunderstorm (Klostermann). Matthew and Luke have modified the expression to "opened," and that in turn influenced the later MSS of Mark upon which the KJV was based. Justin (*Dialogue with Trypho* LXXXVIII. 3), the Ebionite gospel, and some of the O.L. MSS describe a light upon or a fire in the water when Jesus was baptized. **The Spirit like a dove** (KJV), not **descending . . . like a dove** (RSV)—cf. Luke 3:22, "in bodily form, as a dove." The dove was a symbol not merely of gentleness and peace, or of innocence or moral purity, but also of the

---

Christianity and of Christian experience. Baptism in the name of Jesus, as symbolizing the Christian experience, has always meant more than repentance in preparation for judgment. The gift of the Holy Spirit is an inner transformation, a power for the cleansing and energizing of the heart and will, the "life of God in the soul of man." It reaches into the secret places of the heart, where the springs of life are coiled, and motive power is generated. Its results are in the nature rather of a chemical than of a physical change. Christian experience is spiritual chemistry.

Phillips Brooks's words express it:

No ear may hear his coming,
  But in this world of sin,
Where meek souls will receive him still
  The dear Christ enters in.

Christianity is not primarily a demand. It is first of all a *gift*. It does not say first "Do this" or "Go there." It says, "Here is the gift of Christ in God." Its first words are not *"Do"* or *"Go,"* but *"Come"* and *"Receive."* It empowers a life to meet moral demands. When this truth

is lost, slurred or minimized, the heart of Christian experience is gone, and life becomes outward rather than inward, mechanical and essentially secularized.

9. *Jesus Came from Nazareth . . . and Was Baptized by John.*—It was a short journey, measured by miles. But it was momentous. It marked Jesus' acceptance of vocation as a preacher of the kingdom of God. It called him out of the village where his childhood and early manhood had been spent, out of the occupation which had engaged his mind and strength, out of the family group, with its dear enclosures, into the larger world of the purposes of God. It was a red-letter day.

That experience of Jesus was unique. There are indications running all through Mark, as witness this brief story, with the dove descending and the voice from heaven, that for Mark "Jesus' divine sonship was unique, and wholly supernatural" (see Exeg.). From beginning to end the book is written from that point of view. It is the viewpoint of Christian faith. So this experience is not one which can be reproduced in the disciple of Jesus.

Yet an essential part of that journey we can

11 And there came a voice from heaven, *saying,* Thou art my beloved Son, in whom I am well pleased.

upon him like a dove; 11 and a voice came from heaven, "Thou art my beloved Son;^e with thee I am well pleased."

^e Or *my Son, my* (or *the*) *Beloved.*

---

creative power of God—the Spirit "brooded upon the waters" in the creation story (Gen. 1:2). **Descending upon** is correct, not "into." Both Matthew and Luke read ἐπί in place of Mark's εἰς; but many MSS of Mark also read ἐπί. Mark perhaps viewed this as the moment when Jesus received his endowment with supernatural power, later manifested in his "mighty works." Whether or not this involved, for Mark, an "adoptionist" Christology is an unanswered question. Some scholars hold that Mark, like Paul and John, believed that Jesus, as Son of God, was pre-existent; but the data of Mark scarcely require this inference. One of the early noncanonical gospels describes the Holy Spirit as Jesus' "mother"; but this was certainly not Mark's view. Note that the gift of the Spirit follows the "anointing," as in I Sam. 16:13: "Then Samuel . . . anointed him, . . . and the Spirit of the Lord came upon David from that day forward." In the apostolic church the Holy Spirit's coming followed baptism (e.g., Acts 19:5-6).

11. **A voice . . . from heaven,** i.e., from God. Jewish traditions refer to the *bath qôl,* "daughter [or "echo"] of the voice," i.e., of God or of an angel, sometimes overheard upon earth, sometimes directly addressed to saintly men, sometimes a voice of judgment (cf. John 12:28). **My beloved Son** or **my Son, my** (or **the**) **Beloved:** As often, the heavenly voice speaks the language of Scripture, in this case Ps. 2:7, combined with Isa. 42:1, which is modified to suit the situation. Ps. 2 was an ancient hymn for a royal accession or coronation, presumably of some king of Israel or Judah; the appropriateness of the words quoted in Mark depended upon the interpretation of the psalm as referring to King Messiah—a point further emphasized in the Western (perhaps original?) text of Luke 3:22, which adds, "Today I have begotten thee" (RSV mg.; cf. Acts 13:33; Heb. 1:5; 5:5). It was evidently a favorite O.T. text in the early church, sometimes interpreted as referring to the "day" of Jesus' resurrection and exaltation, but in Mark referring to his baptism. Isa. 42:1 is from the "servant songs" of Second Isaiah. It was another "gospel text" of the primitive church, and was interpreted—by the church, not by the Jews—messianically: "Behold my servant, whom I uphold; my chosen, in whom my soul delighteth; I have put my Spirit upon him; he will bring forth justice to the Gentiles" (ASV). The connotations of the passage as a whole would be involved in the phrase which Mark uses, **with thee I am well pleased.** Ancient Jewish tradition usually cited familiar texts by opening phrases or catchwords; Christian Jews would probably do the same, in the earliest stage of evangelic tradition, since their Bible was the O.T., with which they were very familiar.

---

all take—the acceptance of vocation within the great purposes of God. It means allowing our lives to be lifted out of near horizons and enclosing walls, and set in the larger framework of the will of God. This may not involve a physical moving about from place to place; but it will be a tremendous mental and spiritual pilgrimage. It is the great journey of every disciple's life, out of the walls of self-preoccupation into the wider realm of service to God's children and God's purposes.

A very inadequate but true picture of what happens with every such acceptance of vocation may be seen when the slanting rays of the setting sun are reflected by windows. Those windows may be in the darkest and dreariest shanty; but as they catch the radiance from the western sky and throw it back, the shanty be-

comes a blazing glory. A man's life may have a dull setting, and be endowed with the scantiest equipment: but if it catches the reflection of the glory of God which is in the face of Jesus Christ, it becomes a burning and a shining light; is given so much meaning and dignity and joy that one of the supreme tragedies is to miss it.

11. *Thou Art My Beloved Son.*—The reader of the Gospels looks on the baptism of Jesus from the outside. What it meant in the inner experience and, beyond that, in the mind and eternal purposes of God, we can never fully know. We cannot plumb those depths. We can annotate, however, the divine announcement, **Thou art my beloved Son,** by the qualities in the mind and person and life of Jesus which are the signs of his sonship. There was his inno-

12 And immediately the Spirit driveth him into the wilderness.

13 And he was there in the wilderness forty days tempted of Satan; and was with the wild beasts; and the angels ministered unto him.

12 The Spirit immediately drove him out into the wilderness. 13 And he was in the wilderness forty days, tempted by Satan; and he was with the wild beasts; and the angels ministered to him.

On "Son of God" see Intro., pp. 642 ff. The term **beloved,** as used in Mark, does not mean one son who is preferred above others, but the "only" son. Luke 9:35, also quoting the passage from Isaiah, uses ἐκλελεγμένος, which is closer to the original; but in the LXX this frequently translates yāḥîdh, which is properly μονογενής, "only begotten." (See Turner's article in *Journal of Theological Studies,* XXVII [1926], 113-29.) It is a mistake to read into this verse a later theology, e.g., that of Nicaea or Chalcedon; but there can be no question that for Mark, as for the Gentile church of his day, Jesus' divine sonship was unique, and wholly supernatural.

It is sometimes said that the account of Jesus' baptism (vss. 9-11) is the record of the birth of his "messianic consciousness," or of his vocation to fulfill the prophecies of the "servant of the Lord" described in Second Isaiah, or of his call to be "a prophet mighty in word and deed." Whatever the legitimacy of these inferences, it must be recognized that for Mark the emphasis does not lie upon an inner experience of Jesus himself, to be interpreted biographically, but upon the divine announcement of what—or rather, of who—Jesus already is. For Mark, Jesus is more than the Jewish Messiah; the "apocalyptic-eschatological" interpretation of his career sets forth a part of the truth, but not the whole of it, as we shall see. Mark is not a theologian, but his thought is moving toward a theology, and eventually the fuller categories of Greek theology will be required in order to do justice to his view. Undoubtedly some experience of divine vocation lay back of Jesus' ministry, but we must not force Mark's narrative into a pattern suited to our modern reconstructions of the life of Christ. There is no suggestion in Mark that Jesus' baptism marked the birth of his "messianic consciousness"; this popular modern theory is really more compatible with a Gnostic (Docetic) view of our Lord's human nature, which would be entirely contrary to the theology of Mark.

C. The Temptation of Jesus (1:12-13)

12. The Spirit immediately drove him out into the wilderness—as though he were not already there (if "in the wilderness" belongs in vs. 4)! Mark has not noted this conflict; "wilderness" now emphasizes the loneliness of the place. The phrase may even be a vestige of the Q narrative of the Temptation. The verb **drove** is one of Mark's forceful expressions avoided by the later Synoptists; but the O.T. conception of the Spirit, which the narrative presupposes, was "dynamistic" and objective, not psychological.

13. The temptation, or better, "ordeal," of the Son of God is told in fuller detail in Matthew and Luke, presumably from Q. Many scholars think that Mark has abridged that source, or its equivalent in oral tradition, in these two verses. In what the temptation

cence, not a negative thing, but positive purity of heart; his gentleness, his dedication, his creative power (see Exeg.). Those are qualities which are the marks too of the disciple of Jesus, as well as of sonship to God.

12-13. *In the Wilderness Forty Days Tempted.*—Mark's account of the Temptation is extremely abbreviated. He simply records the fact. The content of the temptations and the resources with which Jesus overcame them must all be found in the parallels (Matt. 4:1-11; Luke 4:1-13).

But the clipped, succinct abbreviation here

does picture a universal experience. A time of dedication, of acceptance of purpose, of setting out on a great enterprise, is inevitably followed by a time of testing. Life does not move on a level plateau. It is an affair of hills and valleys. On a flat level it would perhaps be hardly endurable. Stripped of conflict and renewals, it would be stripped of power. After the hill, "thou art my beloved Son," the valley, "tempted of Satan." After the high mood the wilderness.

A person begins a life of discipleship with a lift, an exhilaration. Then comes the wilderness of doubt and wonder. "Is this really the right

14 Now after that John was put in prison, Jesus came into Galilee, preaching the gospel of the kingdom of God,

14 Now after John was arrested, Jesus came into Galilee, preaching the gospel of

---

by Satan consisted, Mark does not say—for details we must turn to the parallels in Matthew and Luke. The final statement, that **the angels ministered to him,** implies the fasting and hunger of the Q narrative. Perhaps for Mark the details were insignificant: the reader is presented with the sharp contrast between Jesus' present loneliness—**with the wild beasts**—and the exalted hour of his baptism. Why should the beloved Son of God be subjected to such an experience? Mark, characteristically, offers no explanation, either psychological or theological. The parallel with Israel's forty years in the wilderness has often been noted; a closer parallel—also referring to the wilderness wandering—is in Test. Naphtali 8:4: "And the devil will flee away from you [plural], and the wild beasts will fear you, and the angels will come unto you." Moses and Elijah fasted forty days (Exod. 34:28; I Kings 19:8) ; so did Pythagoras (Diogenes Laërtius VIII. 40). Jesus' victory over Satan is marked by the ministrations of angels (cf. Luke 22:43).

II. Jesus in Galilee (1:14–9:50)
A. About the Sea of Galilee (1:14–5:43)
1. Jesus Returns to Galilee (1:14-15)

14. According to Mark, Jesus' ministry began in Galilee after that of John ended in Judea. **Put in prison** is correct; literally, "delivered up" or **arrested. Came into Galilee** marks the beginning of the common evangelic tradition of the life of Jesus. One may explain the verb "came" by saying either that the reference to Galilee in vs. 9 has to do with a time too far back for Mark to say "he returned," or that the narrative in vss. 9-13 has been supplied by Mark as a preface to the main body of the tradition. But our author is not a literary artist like Luke, and he introduces the traditional pericopes with a minimum of transitional connections. In this section, where he is not using any specific tradition but is freely editing, his statement makes no reference to what has gone before. His summary of Jesus' message has been influenced by the terminology of the later Christian mission; nevertheless, there can be no doubt that the main subject of Jesus' preaching was the kingdom of God. Here **the gospel** means, for Mark, the message of Jesus himself; yet it is identical with that of the apostolic church (see also 6:12). **The gospel of the kingdom of God** (KJV) is correct, rather than **gospel of God** (RSV), which is a Pauline term. Mark's "Paulinism" is a nineteenth-century fiction (see Intro., pp. 632-33), and the manuscript evidence for **the kingdom of God** is ample. Moreover, it is in Mark's style, and cannot be accounted for by textual assimilation to the parallels.

---

way, after all?" "You are missing so much." "Things don't work out as you expected, do they?" Tempted of Satan, who speaks quite literally, in a devilishly plausible tongue. Or one sets his hand to the plow, some task well worth doing which has commanded his devotion. But it is a long, long furrow to the end. A war of attrition on his purpose sets in, perhaps the hardest form of temptation to meet, for it is not a frontal attack. There *are* wild beasts in the wilderness of testing. We all know them.

One fortification against such inevitables is to expect them; then we are not overwhelmed by the collapse of a romantic anticipation of roses all the way. The story of Jesus' victory is found in the parallels. There we see that he did not meet the tests with an empty mind. He could

bring the counterpressure of a mind that was full, full of the words of God as found in Deuteronomy. The last item of this description, **angels ministered unto him,** is true in the experience of uncounted millions. There are re-creative forces available in spiritual struggle —the renewal of life in prayer, the support of fellowship in worship and living, the recovery of vision.

14. *Jesus Came into Galilee, Preaching.*—A simple historical statement. Yet it is impossible to exhaust its meaning for the church. The fact that Jesus came preaching should gleam before our memory when fogs of discouragement drift in. So often the chief reliances of the church, preaching and teaching, seem to be so uncertain and doubtful. Beside today's awe-inspiring miracles of propaganda and publicity

15 And saying, The time is fulfilled, and the kingdom of God is at hand: repent ye, and believe the gospel.

God, 15 and saying, "The time is fulfilled, and the kingdom of God is at hand; repent, and believe in the gospel."

15. **The time is fulfilled** can be paralleled from Paul (Gal. 4:4), but it is not specifically Pauline; the idea can be found in the O.T. (e.g., Dan. 7:22), in John (e.g., 7:8, Jesus' καιρός="my time"), even in Josephus (*Antiquities* VI. 4. 1)), not to mention authors more remote (e.g., Herodotus). It was a commonplace of ancient religion generally that the course of history is determined beforehand, at least for crucial affairs

—the presses turning out a steady Niagara of print, the radio, the motion picture—teaching and preaching seem so frail, especially in view of the fact that the treasure has to be carried in such very earthen vessels.

But this was the means that Jesus chose. In the beginning was the word, and to the end of his life it was the word. He might have chosen any means. As George A. Buttrick says: "Jesus could have written books. Instead, 'Jesus came preaching.' He trusted His most precious sayings to the blemished reputation and precarious memory of his friends." [3]

That fact, if we think of it deeply, has power to hearten us onward. Wherever Christ's word is taught or spoken, and expressed, as it was when he uttered it, in life as well as in speech, there God is in the midst.

15. *The Time Is Fulfilled.*—These words recall other similar words in Gal. 4:4, "When the time had fully come, God sent forth his Son." There are many aspects of the world into which Jesus came which put detail into the words **the time is fulfilled**. These have been often listed and described, and there is always an arresting fascination about them. There were many highways ready along which the gospel could and did travel. There was the Pax Romana, the network of Roman roads; the dispersal of the Jews, making seed plots for the seed of the word; the language and philosophy of the Greeks. Days of preparation had been fulfilled. One suggestion comes from these signs of preparation. There is always the duty of buying up the opportunity of the gospel in the favorable conditions of any time. Even in periods of turmoil and difficulty, if Christians will listen closely enough, they can hear the words **the time is fulfilled**.

15. *The Kingdom of God Is at Hand.*—This was, beyond all question, the main subject of Jesus' teaching. The changing climates of opinion have passed over this theme, what Jesus meant by the kingdom of God, more almost than over any other subject in the Gospels. It has been exposed to the constant danger of having men take one fragment of the great

conception and interpret it as the whole. To this entire matter the words of Coleridge apply, "Make any truth too definite and you make it too small." There is an apocalyptic element, an ethical and social element; but none of these alone is the kingdom of God. Ernest F. Scott puts it into one sentence, "The Kingdom as he [Jesus] conceived it was at once the higher, spiritual order, the better righteousness, the larger human brotherhood, the life of inward fellowship with God. None of these excludes the other." [4]

The kingdom is the reign of God, his sovereignty over mind and heart and will, and in the world. It is sonship to God and brotherly relation with men. It is in the future. But whenever a human life is brought into harmony with the Father's purpose, it is present.

That main theme of Jesus must be the main theme of his disciples and messengers, if they are to be truly his messengers. The great tragedies of church history have occurred in those periods when Jesus' theme of the kingdom of God was made secondary or was forgotten entirely. Whenever Christian teaching has been a divisive force in the body of Christ, whenever it has led brother to strive against brother, whenever it has failed to catch the imagination of men, it has been a long way from the teaching of the kingdom of God. That kingdom must be preached in season and out of season. A world of competing sovereignties needs the sovereignty of God.

15. *Repent, and Believe in the Gospel.*—It may be that Mark in this passage records Jesus as making an addition to the preaching of repentance by John the Baptist. Jesus called men to repentance as emphatically as did John. But there is here this notable addition, **believe in the gospel**. The phrase sounds more like the language of the early Christian church than like the speech of Jesus. If so, it is a small matter. What is represented by the words runs all through the teaching and acts of Jesus.

Jesus never minimized sin or repentance. He proclaimed, "A new order is at hand. Get a new mind that fits it." But he brought more than

[3] *Jesus Came Preaching* (New York: Charles Scribner's Sons, 1932), p. 16.

[4] *The Kingdom of God in the New Testament* (New York: The Macmillan Co., 1931), p. 186.

16 Now as he walked by the sea of Galilee, he saw Simon and Andrew his brother casting a net into the sea: for they were fishers.	16 And passing along by the sea of Galilee, he saw Simon and Andrew the brother of Simon casting a net in the sea;

or turning points; Jewish apocalyptic carried the idea to an extreme, with its "weeks" of days or years and its rigid schematization of history. But the idea itself was common, as the O.T. prophets show, and one need not turn to Paul for its source—Paul himself took it for granted as a generally recognized example of the divine overruling of human events. **The time,** then, means simply the time foreseen by prophets, the time fixed in God's foreknowledge: "The hour has struck." **At hand** is the crucial phrase for "realized eschatology." (See C. H. Dodd, *The Parables of the Kingdom* [New York: Charles Scribner's Sons, 1936].) The Greek verb ἤγγικεν can scarcely mean "has arrived," but only "has drawn near"; nevertheless, the kingdom is still approaching, it is drawing ever nearer, i.e., it has begun to arrive. There is still time for repentance—but the time is short. The "mighty works" of Jesus, which Mark undoubtedly has in mind, are evidence of its coming, though not of its full arrival—indeed in his own time it had not yet completely come. For these reasons the translation **at hand** is as good as can be made in English. (See Grant, *Gospel of the Kingdom,* pp. 145-48.)

Repent ye: As in John's preaching (vs. 4), so in that of Jesus, repentance—"turning" from sin, "turning" to the Lord—is its first word of exhortation. The theory that vss. 14-15 are Pauline breaks down completely at this point; Paul nowhere stresses repentance. Note that the imperative is plural: Jesus' prophetic message is addressed, in the first instance, to his whole people. **Believe in the gospel,** i.e., "believe in the good news," sounds like a later Christian admonition, though it is not impossible that Jesus referred to his own proclamation as "good news." It was clearly different in tone and implication from the Baptizer's message of coming judgment.

2. The Call of the First Disciples (1:16-20)

16. Walked by (KJV) is better English and equally as good translation from the Greek as **passing along** (RSV); it is not a question now of Jesus' route (cf. vs. 14). We might say, "As he was walking beside . . ." How much time has elapsed since Jesus' return

judgment and inflexible demand for a turning away from sin. He brought good news. He was good news. It was voiced in the phrase "your heavenly Father." It spoke in his word, "Come unto me." There was the good news of reliance on God, of utter confidence in his love, of invitation to believe in that love and to accept it. That is not to be heard in John the Baptist. We find it in the Beatitudes, the stress on the happiness, the blessedness, which comes when life is brought into harmony with the will of God. Of these two aspects of Jesus' message we may say, "What God hath joined together, let not man put asunder."

Jesus' call to repentance must be given to our world with all the force that can be summoned. A new order is emerging in the twentieth century, an utterly new world is being created by new powers over nature. Into this world old ways of thinking and acting will not fit. We must get a new mind, new ways of living—economic, social, international ways that make survival possible. But that is only a part of Jesus' message. We must also carry to all his children his injunction, "Believe the good news of a God of unfailing love." It is the invitation to a life of trust and blessedness in harmony with him.

16. He Saw Simon and Andrew.—What eyes Jesus had! In many different ways it would be no exaggeration to call them X-ray eyes, that could see clear into people and things. This sight of Simon and Andrew was no casual glance. He saw what others saw, men at work in fishing boats. But he saw more. He saw Simon and Andrew in all their potentialities, not only as they were but as they might be, saw them as possible forces in the kingdom of God. How many places there are in the Gospels where Jesus saw what nobody else saw—the woman casting all her living into the alms box, people by the roadside needing help (see Expos., 10:46).

We read in I Cor. 2:16, "We have the *mind* of Christ." How much the world would be blessed if we could say, "We have the *eyes* of Christ." How much would come from a heightened sense of seeing: the ability actually to see

17 And Jesus said unto them, Come ye
after me, and I will make you to become
fishers of men.

18 And straightway they forsook their
nets, and followed him.

for they were fishermen. 17 And Jesus said
to them, "Follow me and I will make you
become fishers of men." 18 And immediately they left their nets and followed him.

to Galilee is not said. Evidently the fishers already knew him. As is clear from the Gospel
as a whole, Mark's paragraphs are not always in strict chronological sequence. **Sea of
Galilee,** really a lake—and called a lake by Luke, Josephus, and Greek writers—about
seven miles wide and twelve miles long, famous for its fisheries. Jewish usage was "sea"
of Chinnereth; hence Mark, following Palestinian Christian tradition, writes "sea."

17-18. After me is almost a technical term for discipleship (cf. vs. 20). Jewish teachers
called their disciples to follow them; one would not presume to follow without an
invitation. **To become fishers of men** is an O.T. figure of speech (Jer. 16:16), though not
in a good sense; it is also found in sayings of Greek philosophers (e.g., Diogenes Laërtius
II. 67). Perhaps **to become** is overtranslation; **I will make you** conveys the idea. Mark
clearly has in mind the later missionary work of the apostles. Luke 5:1-11 gives a variant
of this story, with fuller motivation of the saying, though his narrative has been influenced
by Mark. Some scholars think that still another, and more legendary, account of Peter's
call underlies the appendix to John (ch. 21). **Their nets,** rather than "the nets," has
adequate support in the MSS.

people, not as blurred objects in the landscape,
and often only from the point of view of their
possible usefulness to us; but to see them with
a dedicated imagination, with "the eyes of the
heart," their desires, their needs, and to see
them with faith in their possibilities.

A poet has wondered what life would be with
greatly sharpened senses:

To see
With the eye
Of the fly,

. . . .

Or with the furred ear
Of the deer
To hear what no others can hear.[5]

That would be an exquisite heightening of
our senses. But there is something far better, to
see with the eyes of Jesus. So much of the time
we go around playing a sort of blindman's buff.
Let those eyes be in you which were also in
Christ Jesus.

**17. Follow Me and I Will Make You . . .
Fishers of Men.**—These words of Jesus, embodying the first invitation to follow him, are
ever to be kept in memory. He called followers
to *fish,* to bring men into the kingdom, to save
them. It was an active vocation of outreach, the
skillful capturing of the lives of men. As over
against other employments in the life of the
Jewish religious community, he did not call
them primarily to study, or to be rabbis and to
teach, but to fish, to win men.

Strange that such a clear, commanding invi-

[5] Audrey Wurdemann, *Splendour in the Grass* (New
York: Harper & Bros., 1936), p. 36. By permission.

tation should ever be obscured! But it has been,
time and again. The evangelistic purpose of the
Christian fellowship, the priority of the fishing
business, can easily go into low visibility. When
that great "first" becomes a second or a third
to even such good things as the formulation
and statement of belief, the consolidation of
resources, or the creation and support of organization, a benumbing sterility strikes the
church.

These words **fishers of men,** addressed to
fishermen, also express the great truth that the
abilities, the capacities, the personalities, with
which men have been endowed or which they
have acquired, are not to be thrown away, but
carried into the service of God. Jesus gave to
men a new goal for old powers, a new employment for old skills.

In terms of every age, as of this first day of
discipleship, personality is not to be denuded.
The Christian religion has often been unnecessarily bare, because acquired skills have found
no outlet in it. The church has often suffered a
smothering and paralyzing blight from the dominance of the false idea that an emptied mind,
stripped of all the rich flavor of individuality,
stripped of fine talents of every sort desperately
needed in the building of Christian community,
was the most acceptable gift to God. Christians
have even gone the length of singing the
aspiration

O to be nothing, nothing.

But nothing spells zero; and a zero is still a
zero, whether in the kingdom of God or out of

19 And when he had gone a little further thence, he saw James the *son* of Zebedee, and John his brother, who also were in the ship mending their nets.

20 And straightway he called them: and they left their father Zebedee in the ship with the hired servants, and went after him.

21 And they went into Capernaum; and straightway on the sabbath day he entered into the synagogue, and taught.

19 And going on a little farther, he saw James the son of Zeb'e-dee and John his brother, who were in their boat mending the nets. 20 And immediately he called them; and they left their father Zeb'e-dee in the boat with the hired servants, and followed him.

21 And they went into Ca-per'na-um; and immediately on the sabbath he entered

---

19. The picturesque scene with the two pairs of brothers engaged in contrasted activities, the first aggressive, the other quiet, is vividly described by Mark—without, however, his suggesting any deeper symbolism in the picture. **Ship** (KJV) will hardly do in modern English for a fishing boat. **The** boat (KJV) is not the one possibly implied in vs. 16, nor yet **their** boat (RSV). Mark's definite article does not always need to be translated (cf. 4:1); "in a boat" is all he means.

20. With the hired servants or "hired help." That they were paid workers (μισθωτοί) indicates that Zebedee was not poor, but it certainly does not imply that he was rich, or even well to do. Any fisherman who owned a boat and some nets might conceivably hire workers to help him, especially in a good season. Mark does not mean to suggest that James and John were making any special sacrifice in order to follow Jesus.

3. Jesus in the Synagogue at Capernaum (1:21-28)

21. Capernaum was probably at the north end of the lake, on the highway from Ptolemais to Damascus, and on the border of Antipas' territory, hence the toll booth or

---

it. This first invitation of Jesus makes it clear that the true aspiration is

> O to be something, something,
> *Something* to lay at his feet.

We see it in all Christian history: physicians who have brought the skill of mind and hand, businessmen who have brought organizing capacity, housewives who have brought the skill of homemaking to the larger goal of world housekeeping. (Economics literally means "housekeeping.") All these have found new ends for old means. As it was in the beginning, it is now, and ever shall be.

Note also the personal invitation, **Follow me.** "Jesus came preaching," to crowds. He also came inviting men, one by one. Have we not far too often expected far too much from just preaching to the crowd in public services, without the personal invitation? In this, as in all things, Jesus is the great teacher. The two must never be separated.

20. *They Left Their Father Zebedee in the Boat . . . , and Followed Him.*—All the disciples left something behind. The first four left fishing boats, their livelihood and their homes. Figuratively, but quite truly, they "burned their boats behind them," like invaders, rendering it impossible to do anything but go on. They left no

way of retreat open. It was not the kind of venture of which they could say, "We will try this for a while, and see how it works out." They followed. There was a finality about it. The question inevitably comes, Have we left anything?

To many those words "they left" have had a painfully literal meaning, a meaning common enough in the missionary church of the first century. "Leaving" has always been the hallmark of missions and evangelization. Thousands have become "displaced persons," uprooted from familiar scenes, to be "placed" in God's work.

But for most of us the word "leave" does not necessarily involve departure. Home and occupation may be tools for God's building enterprise, and great ones. There are, however, if not places, then things to be "left." At Christ's call we should leave behind our cherished prejudices, so familiar and easy to get along with; our recumbent inertia; our aversion to the pain of new ideas—Ellen Glasgow wrote of her heroine Virginia that "she was willing to die for an idea, but unable to conceive one" [6]— our self-determination, reluctant to follow the Master. Leave these and follow.

21. *On the Sabbath He Entered the Synagogue.*—Jesus' going to the synagogue, "as his

[6] *Virginia* (New York: Doubleday, Doran & Co., 1913).

22 And they were astonished at his doctrine: for he taught them as one that had authority, and not as the scribes. 23 And there was in their synagogue a man with an unclean spirit; and he cried out,	the synagogue and taught. 22 And they were astonished at his teaching, for he taught them as one who had authority, and not as the scribes. 23 And immediately there was in their synagogue a man with an un-

tax office (2:14). It was one of the most important towns in Galilee, and an appropriate place for Jesus to begin his ministry. The ruined site is now known as Tell Ḥum. **Immediately,** a characteristic stylism of Mark, probably meant only "on the following sabbath." The fishers of vss. 16-20 would not have been working on the sabbath, though they might have been busy on Friday, the sabbath "coming in" at sundown that evening. But it is a question if the sabbath eve service—Friday evening—was in use in the early part of the first century. Vss. 29 and 32 imply that the events of vss. 21-34 took place on one day, from morning to evening.

22. One who had authority, i.e., as a prophet, by direct authorization from God, and not as a scribe. The scribes were the official teachers or expounders of the Torah; as a member of a school, the scribe would teach what he had learned from his master—viz., the scribal tradition (7:9). Jesus, on the contrary, as a lay teacher of religion, not educated in the scribal manner (cf. John 7:15) but inspired by the divine Spirit (vs. 10), spoke with immediate and personal authority. Mark does not say that he spoke as a prophet, but this was certainly the impression men gained (cf. 6:15; 8:28).

23. With (or "in") **an unclean spirit:** The expression is rare outside the N.T. (cf. Zech. 13:2; Enoch 99:7; Test. Benjamin 5:2). Was the spirit itself unclean? (Cf. 9:25.) Or

custom was" (Luke 4:16), pictures his habit of worship and the deep way in which he shared in the religious heritage of Israel. These words also suggest his willingness to begin his work with the available means, with the common and familiar channels that were open. The teaching and the procedures of the synagogue were far from ideal. But it was a place to start. So he started there, with the first opportunity that held any promise of fruitfulness. There was no waiting for the "ideal situation," the better means, the more "promising conditions." Wherever there was any chance of teaching the good news of the kingdom, no matter how small the crowd, there was an ideal situation.

What a contrast to the common failure of many people who wait for the perfect occasion, the "right" time, the sufficient crowd, to begin their work, fretting themselves into futility for the chance that never comes!

22. They Were Astonished at His Teaching. —It was so new, so filled with power, that the whole being was surrendered in amazement. The word "astonish" compels the question: Are we sufficiently astonished at Jesus' teaching? Has it become so familiar, have we taken it so much for granted, that we no longer really see it in amazement? The reason we do not astonish the world more as Christians may be that we are not sufficiently astonished ourselves. For Christian life and power begin in the passive voice. It is not that we love, but that we are loved. Our frequent tendency is to push right

on into the active voice of doing, without experiencing the sheer wonder of God—"Behold, what manner of love the Father hath bestowed upon us" (I John 3:1). The first and lasting source of joy and power is astonishment at the breath-taking miracle that God himself has come into our world of need and struggle and sin. What happens in the active voice depends first on what happens in the passive. If we were more astonished, we would do more astonishing things.

22. For He Taught Them as One Who Had Authority.—Jesus' authority was not derived from tradition. He did not live in the prison house of quotation marks. In contrast to that of the scribes, his authority was "immediate and personal" (see Exeg.). It was unique. And yet his message can carry the same note when spoken by genuine disciples. There are elements of his authority which can be reproduced: an unclouded faith in God; personal experience; conviction of the commission to speak; conviction of the truth as something grounded in the universe, carrying its own inherent evidence.

23. A Man with an Unclean Spirit.—Here is the first case of demoniac possession which Jesus meets. It is a difficult problem and one on which complete light will probably never be thrown. It takes us into a world that is far from our habits of thought. And yet our world of today, in which many forms of mental sickness and neurosis are a growing and terrifying concern, ought not to seem too far away from

24 Saying, Let *us* alone; what have we to do with thee, thou Jesus of Nazareth? art thou come to destroy us? I know thee who thou art, the Holy One of God.

clean spirit; 24 and he cried out, "What have you to do with us, Jesus of Nazareth? Have you come to destroy us? I know

---

did demoniac possession lead to uncleanness—ritual, i.e., disregard of the Levitical food regulations, touching dead bodies, etc.; or physical, i.e., actual filth, like David's in his feigned madness at Gath (I Sam. 21:13)? The ancient popular inference was that madness was due to possession by a demon; madmen were (and are) frequently dirty; uncleanness was therefore due to the demon, which was accordingly described as "unclean."

24. Let us alone is a translation of the interjection ἔα, which has crept into the text of later MSS of Mark from the parallel in Luke. It should be omitted, as in RSV. **What have we to do with thee?** is literally "What to us and to you?" (cf. John 2:4). As I Kings 17:18 and other passages show (see refs. in margin of Nestle's *Novum Testamentum Graece* at this verse), the idiom means, **What have you to do with us?** as in RSV. **To destroy us,** i.e., the demons; so Mark doubtless understands the word. Originally the question may have been the terrified query of a partially demented man in the presence of a stranger, "Have you come from over the hills to work us harm here in Capernaum?"—i.e., to harm the people of Capernaum. But as Mark understood the question, the answer doubtless would be, "Yes, I have come to destroy the demons and undo their evil works"—"come," perhaps in the sense of "come into the world."

The Holy One of God may be a vocative, "Thou Holy One," nominative for vocative. In that case we should translate, "I know who you are, you holy man of God!" The demoniac recognized the teacher, or the *hāsîdh,* who could banish the demon. But Mark doubtless takes it as the direct and supernatural recognition of the divine Son of God by

---

these records of Jesus' command over mental afflictions.

The world into which Jesus came was "a demon-haunted world." Belief in the reality of demons was a fact of the mentality of the time and place. To Mark they were real. Were they real to Jesus? We cannot plumb his mind, but it seems probable. His way of dealing with them, however, was far different from the usual procedure. The symptoms, so far as they can be diagnosed today, seem in most cases like hysteria, in some like paralysis, in some like epilepsy.

The important point is that Jesus did cure cases of demon possession. This "is one of the best supported facts." [7] It is a fact of measureless hope and meaning to our world and to all ages. For our world too is, in a real and tragic sense, "a demon-haunted world." Men and women are haunted by fear, worry, anxiety, insecurity, inordinate self-concern, and all the ills these can bring. Jesus brought the power of God and of faith, and freed people from the domination of evil spirits. For even if the evil was ascribed to wrong causes, the malady was very real. Jesus restored the soul and renewed a right spirit in men. He can still renew a right spirit. He can still speak in the power of God to minds burdened, distressed, and sick. One of the most hopeful gains of our time is the

[7] B. Harvie Branscomb, *The Gospel of Mark,* "The Moffatt New Testament Commentary" (New York: Harper & Bros.), p. 31.

discovery and exploration and application of the resources of the Christian faith for the driving out of our "evil spirits." Among these resources are a faith awakened to reliance on God, that liberation from the past which comes with the forgiveness of sins, the leading out of life, away from the merry-go-round of preoccupation with self, into a liberating concern with other lives, the overcoming of envy, jealousy, and hatred by love.

24-25. *What Have You to Do with Us, Jesus of Nazareth?*—This question, first recorded as the frightened shriek of the disunited forces of evil, is the cry of evil power in all centuries and in all languages. It is still being vociferously and angrily shouted today.

It is the cry of greed. "What have you to do with us, Jesus? Mind your business. Our business is our own. Get back to Palestine. Get back to the Bible. Get back to the church. Get back anywhere, so long as you do not interfere with our profits." The powers that exploit men and women and children insist that profits are sacred, and protest that the teachings of Jesus have no jurisdiction over them. To bolster their case they throw words at Jesus, and at those who proclaim judgment on mammon—words such as sentimentalist, romanticist, dreamer, impractical. It was the language of the slave trade. It is the language of the profiteers of slave labor, commercialized vice, a debauching liquor traffic, race discrimination. It is the language of

25 And Jesus rebuked him, saying, Hold thy peace, and come out of him.

26 And when the unclean spirit had torn him, and cried with a loud voice, he came out of him.

27 And they were all amazed, insomuch that they questioned among themselves, saying, What thing is this? what new doctrine *is* this? for with authority commandeth he even the unclean spirits, and they do obey him.

28 And immediately his fame spread abroad throughout all the region round about Galilee.

who you are, the Holy One of God." 25 But Jesus rebuked him, saying, "Be silent, and come out of him!" 26 And the unclean spirit, convulsing him and crying with a loud voice, came out of him. 27 And they were all amazed, so that they questioned among themselves, saying, "What is this? A new teaching! With authority he commands even the unclean spirits, and they obey him." 28 And at once his fame spread everywhere throughout all the surrounding region of Galilee.

---

the demon, voicing its conviction of impending doom through the poor man's lips. Demons often sensed the power of the exorcist. Klostermann (*op. cit.*) quotes Lucian's description of a case of madness (*Abdicatus* 6): "If she sees any physician, or even hears him speak, she is most violently enraged against him." "Holy One of God" was not a messianic title (cf. Ps. 16:10); but Mark doubtless understood it as expressing the demon's recognition of Jesus as a divine being, the Son of God (cf. 1:34; 3:11-12).

25. **Be silent** (addressed to the demon): A common formula of exorcism (cf. 4:39). Mark, of course, does not stress the therapeutic effect of the words upon the demoniac, a feature which would be of special interest to modern readers.

26. **Convulsing him . . . loud voice**, i.e., after a final convulsion and wild cry the man became quiet and was healed. The only possible inference, for ancient popular thinking, was that the demon had departed. For Mark, as for those who had handed down the tradition, there was the further inference that Jesus' divine power had banished the unclean spirit and restored the man.

27. **What is this?** The **new teaching** was authenticated by the manifestation of power to ban an evil spirit. Some MSS read, "Who is this and what is this new teaching, that with authority . . . ?" This reading is equally Marcan in style, but has perhaps been influenced by 4:41. Mark generalizes, **unclean spirits**: What took place on this first day in Capernaum was typical of what was to follow—the powers of evil were already being vanquished (cf. 3:27).

28. **All the surrounding region of Galilee.** Matt. 4:24 takes this to mean "all Syria"; Luke 4:37, the neighborhood of Capernaum.

---

entrenched power everywhere, of oppressive government, with its "long drip of human tears," of dominant militarism, of shifty diplomacy. It is the language of unrestrained individualism. "I have a right to live my own life" usually means "What have you to do with me, Jesus of Nazareth?"

To this cry of the evil spirit Jesus answered, **Be silent, and come out of him!** He makes the same answer today. Jesus has to do with everything that affects people. Nothing human is foreign to him. He is concerned with every burden that rests heavily on human shoulders and cuts cruelly into them, all that concerns the welfare of God's children—the hours and conditions and wages of labor; housing (Jesus was concerned with the housing situation in Jerusalem, in his denunciation of

those who devour widows' houses), law, civil rights, amusements—the whole varied spread of human life. There is a ready answer to anyone who tells the preacher, as he brings the teaching of Jesus into social questions, to "mind his own business." It is to say, "People are my business. I was put into it a long time ago by my Master, and I cannot quit it without betraying him."

27. *What Is This? A New Teaching!*—All recognized that Jesus was, and brought, something new. There were two responses to the new. Some of the scribes and Pharisees reacted with violent antagonism. Something new? Off the familiar line? Away with it, no matter what blessing it might bring! Others opened their minds; their test was not, Does this pronounce familiar words with a droning repetition? They

29 And forthwith, when they were come out of the synagogue, they entered into the house of Simon and Andrew, with James and John.	29 And immediately he*d* left the synagogue, and entered the house of Simon and Andrew, with James and John. 30 Now Simon's mother-in-law lay sick with a fever, and immediately they told him of her. 31 And he came and took her by the hand and lifted her up, and the fever left her; and she served them.
30 But Simon's wife's mother lay sick of a fever; and anon they tell him of her.	
31 And he came and took her by the hand, and lifted her up; and immediately the fever left her, and she ministered unto them.	
32 And at even, when the sun did set, they brought unto him all that were diseased, and them that were possessed with devils.	32 That evening, at sundown, they brought to him all who were sick or possessed with demons. 33 And the whole city was gathered together about the door.
33 And all the city was gathered together at the door.	*d* Many ancient authorities read *they*.

4. Jesus in the House of Peter (1:29-31)

29-31. The house is obviously the home of Peter, but since he and Andrew were brothers, the words **and Andrew** were added: **with James and John,** since all four men were now disciples, and followed Jesus wherever he went. Peter was evidently married before he became a disciple. We are not told the nature of the fever of **Simon's mother-in-law;** Luke says it was "a great [or "high"] fever." **Took her by the hand and lifted her up:** a characteristic "technique" of Jesus' cures (cf. vss. 41 and 5:41).

5. Healing the Sick at Even (1:32-34)

32-34. Though no doubt based upon tradition, this paragraph is an editorial summary in Mark's own style. **At sundown** marks the conclusion of the sabbath, after which burdens might be borne and the sick be brought to Jesus. Since Jesus had already

asked rather, What does it do for life? "New teaching" always splits people into these two camps. Into which do we ourselves instinctively move?

29-31. *He Left the Synagogue, and Entered the House.*—We do no violence to the meaning of this passage, and to many others in the Gospels, when we remember Bushnell's saying that "preaching is a gift to the imagination." It is always dishonest to read into any words of the Bible what is definitely not there, as though ideas foreign to it were actually present in it. But when, dealing honestly with what is in the passage, we allow it to stimulate the imagination and conscience, as a picture and symbol of the truth extended into experience, we help it to fulfill its high function as a lamp unto our feet and a light unto our path (Ps. 119:105).

Here, then, are two pictures. Jesus going from the synagogue into the house suggests the fine art of going home from church, of carrying the truth proclaimed in the house of worship out into the life around. That is what Jesus did. In the synagogue his word was with power. Then he went into the house, into a place of need, and brought the power of God into saving contact with the need of people. All too often

we go to church, but do not follow that by going from the synagogue to the house, to bring the power of God, proclaimed and felt in worship, to the service of human need. All too often, people, as they go out, leave the truth behind in the sanctuary, like hymnbooks which are stamped "Not to be taken from the church."

The other true picture of Christian experience is suggested by the narrative **He . . . took her by the hand . . . and the fever left her.** This was a physical healing, the power and love of God expressed through Jesus. Nothing else is in the scene or the mind of the writer. But we do not use a merely fantastic phrase when we allow the record of that touch of Jesus' hand on the fevered brow of Peter's mother-in-law to suggest what has happened through the centuries. It is Jesus drawing the fever from life. When men have allowed him to touch their minds and hearts, life's violent fevers have been drawn. Fevers of anxiety and fear, of restless self-seeking, of grasping greed, of lust—all have left men as Jesus' spirit has touched them, and they have responded to him as Master.

32-34. *And the Whole City Was Gathered . . . About the Door.*—This is one of the most

34 And he healed many that were sick of divers diseases, and cast out many devils; and suffered not the devils to speak, because they knew him.

35 And in the morning, rising up a great while before day, he went out, and departed into a solitary place, and there prayed.

34 And he healed many who were sick with various diseases, and cast out many demons; and he would not permit the demons to speak, because they knew him.

35 And in the morning, a great while before day, he rose and went out to a lonely

---

exorcised a demon and cured a fever, both the sick and the demoniacs were brought to him. **He healed many:** The parallels say that he healed "all" or "each one." But it is doubtful if **many** is used in contrast to all in vs. 32. What Mark means is, "They brought all, and he healed them, and they were many in number." He is not thinking here, as he is in 6:5, of any limitation upon Jesus' healing power.

Would not permit . . . knew him: Jesus does not encourage the demons to proclaim his divine nature or his superhuman calling. He will not accept testimony from such unclean, unholy sources! (Cf. vs. 25.) This trait is no doubt historical: Jesus silenced the tumultuous cries of the possessed and calmed their minds. But Mark takes it in another sense, viz., that Jesus silenced the demons, not the demoniacs, **because they knew him.** His secret is not to be bruited abroad by demons before the time. The addition "to be the Christ," though found in some good MSS (B C W Θ, etc.), is no doubt derived from the parallel in Luke 4:41.

6. JESUS' DEPARTURE FROM CAPERNAUM (1:35-39)

35-39. Jesus leaves Capernaum in order to preach—i.e., proclaim the gospel (κηρύσσειν)—elsewhere (vs. 38). It is often thought that he viewed a prospective ministry

---

beautiful and moving scenes in the Gospels. It is enshrined in our memories by the hymn:

> At even, when the sun was set,
> The sick, O Lord, around thee lay;
> O in what divers pains they met!
> O with what joy they went away! [8]

The very words of the short narrative convey the trembling hope that spread throughout the region—the first eager awakening of the hope that long deferred makes the heart sick. "Perhaps this prophet can heal our mother, wasting away!" "Perhaps he can make our little boy walk again!" "Perhaps—O God grant it—he may even give sight to the blind." So from many points there start the loving and pathetic pilgrimages, converging at sunset in the village street at Capernaum. It is all an unforgettable picture of the sympathy of Jesus, and of God's compassion and power present in him.

But it is also a picture of something more. Extend that village street in your imagination until it becomes a road encircling the globe. **They brought to him all who were sick or possessed with demons.** That is our world, is it not? A sick world, very sick; a demon-possessed world. But in despair, hunger, and suffering there runs trembling hope, as it ran through the

[8] Henry Twells.

Galilean countryside. The rumor of a healer has gone out. The question is asked by millions, "Is there anything that can heal and save?" They are not crowding the doors of the churches as they crowded the door of the house where Jesus was. But they are looking for recovery, and wholeness, and, whether they use the word or not, salvation.

We must see all this with compassion, feel its anguish in our heart. In our words and lives we must proclaim that God through Jesus Christ can heal and save. God help us in his name to stand in the village street, which is the world, and bring the healing, restoring, transforming power of God to the world's need and hope (see on 10:47).

35. He Rose and Went Out to a Lonely Place, and There He Prayed.—Here is the first instance of what, through his life, was a great priority of Jesus, the renewal of life in prayer. In the three scenes just preceding (vss. 21-32) we watch the expenditure of power. Here, in the lonely place, we behold the secret behind it, the creation and renewal of power. Behind the public ministry, when the whole city was gathered at his door, was the private solitude of the place of prayer. Here was the hidden spring of the authority and power which struck men with astonishment. With Jesus it was not time out for prayer. It was time into him for the

36 And Simon and they that were with him followed after him.	place, and there he prayed. **36** And Simon and those who were with him followed him,

36 And Simon and they that were with him followed after him.

37 And when they had found him, they said unto him, All *men* seek for thee.

38 And he said unto them, Let us go into the next towns, that I may preach there also: for therefore came I forth.

39 And he preached in their synagogues throughout all Galilee, and cast out devils.

place, and there he prayed. **36** And Simon and those who were with him followed him, **37** and they found him and said to him, "Every one is searching for you." **38** And he said to them, "Let us go on to the next towns, that I may preach there also; for that is why I came out." **39** And he went throughout all Galilee, preaching in their synagogues and casting out demons.

of healing as interfering with his main task. But this was scarcely Mark's view; instead, Jesus was eager to cover **all Galilee,** and, adds Mark, **he cast out devils (demons)** wherever he went. **Simon and those who were with him,** presumably the two pairs of brothers, the nucleus of the later band of disciples. By **every one** is meant "everyone in Capernaum." **The next towns:** The Greek text is uncertain here, but the sense is clear enough— "the surrounding villages." **Therefore came I forth** or **that is why I came out:** If the Greek were ἦλθον rather than ἐξῆλθον, the meaning would certainly be: "That is why I came into the world." But the existing text, which is undoubtedly correct, surely means, "That is why I left Capernaum." Mark, however, may have meant the words to convey a sense of Jesus' mission: "That is what I have set out to do." But this ignores the purpose expressed in vs. 35, **and there prayed,** and also the fact that Jesus did not choose his mission—it was laid upon him.

re-creation of life, for fresh adjustment to the will of his Father, for replenishment with the life and power of God.

For him this lonely place was not a passive scene. He was as active here as in healing the throng which crowded about him. Prayer is the highest activity of mind and spirit. True activity is never rightly measured by noise or motion. The flower or tree, on a quiet summer's day, when nothing seems to be happening, is busy in the highest degree. It is opening itself to the unseen forces of its environment, having commerce with the sky in the form of sunlight, air, and rain, and is thus fulfilling its destiny. That, for Jesus, was the secret of sustained life and power, that opening of his soul to the unseen force of his environment—God. It is for man the secret of the sustained life of the spirit.

There can be no fulfillment without a lonely place. Lacking it, life lacks the dimension of height. And that is precisely the case in multitudes of lives. The very physical conditions of existence seem often enough to make solitude impossible. A woman put it picturesquely to her pastor: "You tell us that Jesus said to enter into your closet and close the door. In our apartment there are no closets and there are no doors." Life has become so public and gregarious. It is hard to shut our doors against the insistent intrusions of the outer world, of the radio, and of all the other constant invaders of the lonely place.

We must *make* a lonely place. Nothing that enriches and empowers life ever just "happens."

It is made. Jesus never "happened" to find himself alone. He went out to put a stout fence around some corner of time and space. The crowded life which never does that has no means of renewal, of cleansing, of fortification. Private prayer is beautifully pictured in Keats's line: "I stood tip-toe upon a little hill." [9] Jesus did it in Galilee. You can do it anywhere.

38. Let Us Go On to the Next Towns.—These words reveal Jesus' eagerness to preach throughout Galilee. Capernaum was a starting point, not an ultimate goal. He refused to be localized. It was not enough to be a popular healer in one place; he came to preach the kingdom of God. The road to the larger world had an irresistible pull. He had a keen sense of the horizon.

The narrative has its contacts with universal experience. First, there is the way in which a local situation or experience says to a person, "Stay here." Particularly when the experience is one which has been pleasant and successful, a tempting voice says: "This is good. Just go on repeating it. You like it. It is easy. Why take any risks, when you have a sure thing?" Succumbing to such persuasions has condemned multitudes of lives to some little merry-go-round. Josephine Preston Peabody's lines picture a choice that confronts every life:

The little Road says Go,
The little House says Stay.[1]

[9] "I Stood Tip-toe."
[1] "The House and the Road," *The Singing Leaves* (Boston: Houghton Mifflin Co., 1903). By permission.

40 And there came a leper to him, beseeching him, and kneeling down to him, and saying unto him, If thou wilt, thou canst make me clean.

40 And a leper came to him beseeching him, and kneeling said to him, "If you

7. Healing a Leper (1:40-45)

No date or place is given for this healing. Mark inserts it here as an example of Jesus' activity on his tour "throughout all Galilee." It is a difficult narrative: Jesus' **compassion** gives way to sternness (vs. 43; the Greek means literally "being very angry with him"). Did Jesus resent the man's bold approach—forbidden to a leper (Lev. 13:45; etc.)—and his impetuous demand, implying a possible refusal, **if you will?** Is the statement of his cure (vss. 41-42) introduced too early in the story (so Klostermann)? Or does the narrative conflate two stories with similar subject (so Lohmeyer)? If the last of these suggestions is correct, perhaps in one of the stories the man was to be cleansed as he went (as in Luke 17:14).

As it stands, the story relates four stages: (*a*) the man's approach and request for healing; (*b*) Jesus' response and cure of the leper; (*c*) the command to show himself to the priest (presumably in Jerusalem); and (*d*) the man's disobedience and its consequences. It may be that Mark's naïve telling of the story anticipates, by the phrase in vs. 43, "being very angry with him," Jesus' resentment at his disobedience. If so, the theory of conflation becomes unnecessary. In effect, the softening of the expression in our English version—**straitly charged him** (KJV), **sternly** (RSV)—achieves this end, and the story moves consistently from stage to stage.

40. The evangelist certainly understood the words **make me clean** to involve a miracle, as in the story of Naaman (II Kings 5), not a mere certification of cleansing already accomplished; this it was the function of the priests to provide (vs. 44).

The little town said to Jesus "Stay." The little road said, "Go." He said, "Let us go." There is a very real sense in which, if we have the mind of Christ and have caught his spirit, we must "go on to the next towns." We must go on to the next stage in our religious experience. We must keep our minds and hearts in motion. We must push on to the next task, the new unattempted task that calls to us. The call of the road—new interests to lay upon the heart, new people into whose lives we may bring some of the good news of God's kingdom—is the call of Jesus.

The other suggestion lies in the sheer timelessness of the words themselves. Jesus' spirit cannot be localized, or trapped in any form of words. In every generation he has said, "Let us go on." "That is why I left Capernaum." "That is what I have set out to do" (see Exeg.). The sense of the horizon, pictured so vividly in this narrative, has marked his progress down the centuries.

We see it in the onward thrust of Christianity into the world. We catch it in Paul as he carries the gospel to the great nerve centers of his world, and dreams of "as I go to Spain" (Rom. 15:24)—the then western limit of the world. We see it in Robert Morrison as he approaches China to begin missionary work among its millions. We see it in all the shining company of missionaries whose purpose held "to sail beyond the sunset." That onward movement must be found in our conceptions of our message. It is not enough for Christianity to have an ethic for the comparatively simple human relationships of agricultural and village life. It must go on to the "next towns"—to meet the complexities of industrial civilization. It is not enough to have an ethic and religion for the national life; we must go on to the overwhelming challenge of international order. Always the call of the new enterprise, the unoccupied territory.

Through the ages, barrenness, futility, tragedy have hounded the years when men have tried to hold Jesus back, to put little man-made boundaries around the boundless word of God, to shut Jesus into some little prison of border, or breed, or birth. When he says, "Let us go on," there is only one fitting answer, "Lead on, O King Eternal" (see on 4:35).

40. If You Will, You Can Make Me Clean.— There is great suggestiveness here, throwing light on the contrast between the non-Christian and Christian idea of God. The leper says, "I am not sure you will, but I think you can." That expresses a heathen idea of God as power. The true Christian says, "I am sure you will, if you can." There is a world of difference between the two. The Christian is confident of the

41 And Jesus, moved with compassion, put forth *his* hand, and touched him, and saith unto him, I will; be thou clean.

42 And as soon as he had spoken, immediately the leprosy departed from him, and he was cleansed.

43 And he straitly charged him, and forthwith sent him away;

44 And saith unto him, See thou say nothing to any man: but go thy way, show thyself to the priest, and offer for thy cleansing those things which Moses commanded, for a testimony unto them.

will, you can make me clean." 41 Moved with pity, he stretched out his hand and touched him, and said to him, "I will; be clean." 42 And immediately the leprosy left him, and he was made clean. 43 And he sternly charged him, and sent him away at once, 44 and said to him, "See that you say nothing to any one; but go, show yourself to the priest, and offer for your cleansing what Moses commanded,

---

41-42. Biblical **leprosy** was a term derived from common usage, as the O.T. shows; popular diagnosis included in the category not only true leprosy but also various skin diseases, and even mildew on walls and in culinary vessels. Modern physicians in the Orient have observed several types, one of them being a nervous simulation of true leprosy. What the man in our story had it is impossible to say; even the hysterical variety was painful enough.

44. The offering to be made by the leper is described in Lev. 14. The **testimony unto them** was no doubt understood by Mark to mean the proof to the priests—not to the people, as in RSV—that the man was healed; but the priest also, in all probability, would issue a certificate in writing (so Lagrange), so that the whole procedure was to be in accordance with religious rite and legal custom.

---

will of God, but realizes limitations on power—self-consistency, freedom of the person, wisdom, and love.

41. *He Stretched Out His Hand and Touched Him.*—This action was an expression of Jesus' spontaneous sympathy and compassion. It is also an expression of what we meet again and again in the gospel narratives, the fact that nothing less than a personal touch with the person in need would satisfy Jesus. We have one or two cases which are in the record as showing his power to heal at a distance. But in the great majority of cases it was a personal touch. **He stretched out his hand and touched him.** It was the physical expression and accompaniment of the giving of his heart and mind and power in personal contact.

> It is the way the Master went,
> Should not the servant tread it still? [3]

The operation of social agencies is indispensable in an intricate, intermeshed, social world. But the personal touch of life on life is indispensable in any world and every world. There is no adequate substitute for outstretched hands and outstretched lives. No committee or organization can supplant them. Without them, the nerve of compassion atrophies. The word of love, which was in Jesus, must become flesh and dwell among men.

[3] Horatius Bonar, "Go, labor on."

Notice that in touching the leper Jesus disregarded a taboo. The leper was ceremonially unclean. He was supposed "to separate himself from the community, to avoid defiling others by his touch." The leper was hedged about with stern injunctions, sanctified by usage, "Unclean!" "Don't touch!" "Never, never!" Jesus violated a taboo which itself violated God's compassion. He reached across the chasm and touched him. So we can see Jesus going on his way down through the centuries, as he went on his way down the roads of Galilee, reaching out his hands across man-made taboos and defying them. To him there was no taboo against the love of God.

Most of the Western world has moved far from the concept of ritual uncleanliness. But the power of the social taboo is omnipresent. A taboo in the devastating form in which we meet it is something that is forbidden by tradition or social usage or other authority. Many taboos of custom or tradition are stockades behind which people suffer and die. We know all too well the blighting effects on human lives of the taboos on race, with discrimination, segregation, and exploitation, the taboos of nationalism. Just where do we reach out our hands across forbidding and murderous taboos?

44-45. *But He Went Out and Began to Talk Freely.*—Here was a case of exuberant disobedience. Jesus had told this healed leper to **say nothing.** But he knew a trick worth two of

45 But he went out, and began to publish *it* much, and to blaze abroad the matter, insomuch that Jesus could no more openly enter into the city, but was without in desert places: and they came to him from every quarter.

2 And again he entered into Capernaum after *some* days; and it was noised that he was in the house.

for a proof to the people."[e] 45 But he went out and began to talk freely about it, and to spread the news, so that Jesus[f] could no longer openly enter a town, but was out in the country; and people came to him from every quarter.

2 And when he returned to Ca-per'na-um after some days, it was reported

[e] Greek *to them.*
[f] Greek *he.*

---

45. Jesus' intention to preach in the surrounding villages (vs. 38) was frustrated by the man's disobedience; instead, **people came to him from every quarter,** presumably for healing or exorcism rather than to hear the gospel. Mark may also imply that despite hindrances Jesus' mission proceeded.

8. Healing a Paralytic (2:1-12)

With this passage begins a new block of material in Mark, the first series of controversies (2:1–3:6, with an additional controversy, perhaps from Q, in 3:20-30). It represents the growing opposition to Jesus on the part of the scribes, the official teachers of Jewish religion, and the Pharisees, the lay devotees and enthusiasts for the scribal interpretation of religion. Bousset and others have suggested that the opening controversy (vss. 5b-10) has been inserted into the story of the paralytic: the clause **he said to the paralytic** is repeated in vs. 10 from vs. 5. Certainly the story reads well enough without the "insertion," and apparently resembles, in that form, plenty of other healing narratives. But it lacks the dramatic quality of the present Marcan account. At the same time, Jesus' words in vs. 5, **Son, thy sins be forgiven thee**—or **My son, your sins are forgiven** —seem irrelevant: the man was brought to Jesus for healing, not for forgiveness. But the irrelevancy exists only for modern thought. In the ancient world sin and suffering were related as cause and consequence. "The sick man will not get up from his sickness until all his sins have been forgiven" (Nedarim 41*a*, cf. Jas. 5:15, 20). Jesus evidently shared the view (see Luke 13:1-5—John 9:3 is not to be cited in this connection, and in any event is clearly offset by John 5:14). Apparently Mark also shared the view. The man's sins were not necessarily of a kind to lead to paralysis; all sin deserved the penalty of sickness and pain. But in spite of these considerations, it is probable that vss. 5b-10 are an insertion (from the "controversy source"?—see Intro., p. 636) into an "old" pericope which narrated a healing. As Lohmeyer notes, vs. 12 takes no account of the inserted material. William Manson (*Jesus the Messiah* [Philadelphia: Westminster Press, 1946], pp. 66-68) thinks that the original story is given in vss. 1-5, 12: Jesus pronounced the man's sins forgiven, and the result was his physical cure. Into this framework has been inserted the controversy section, vss. 6-11.

2:1. RSV properly translates **at home** or, as we should say, "home again." Capernaum was now Jesus' headquarters (cf. Luke 4:23). The house was probably Peter's (1:29),

---

that. That was too unexciting a procedure. He got more emotional release out of telling. He was all emotion and no discipline. He put his own personal satisfactions above the purposes and commands of Jesus, and thus became a hindrance. This unfortunately was not the last case of effusive, exuberant disobedience. We know all too well the obstacle of the chatterbox, or the exhibitionist with his motto "Look at me." It is always a liability when so-called "thinking" is done "below the neck." Emotion is not enough for the kingdom of God. It de-

mands heads. It demands the disciplined mind, demands the will made into a patient, self-denying servant of the long-range purposes of God. In the early days of the Fabian socialist movement in England, George Bernard Shaw is reported to have said of one of the followers: "Ah, good old Jones. His heart is with us. I wish we had his head!" God needs heads.

2:1. *It Was Reported That He Was at Home.* —The power of a rumor. These were days of excitement in Capernaum. "A new teaching," with new power, was at hand. The mere report

2 And straightway many were gathered together, insomuch that there was no room to receive *them,* no, not so much as about the door: and he preached the word unto them.

3 And they come unto him, bringing one sick of the palsy, which was borne of four.

4 And when they could not come nigh unto him for the press, they uncovered the

that he was at home. 2 And many were gathered together, so that there was no longer room for them, not even about the door; and he was preaching the word to them. 3 And they came, bringing to him a paralytic carried by four men. 4 And when they could not get near him because

though Matt. 4:13 and John 2:12 may allow us to think that Jesus had his own house there (cf. vs. 15 below).

2. Jesus teaches at home, not in the synagogue (1:39), and people come to him (1:45)—whether for healing or to hear the gospel is not said.

3-4. The **paralytic** is let down through the roof. A village roof in Palestine was made of saplings laid flat, with branches and twigs spread over them, and clay patted down over this and baked in the sun. Mark may perhaps have thought of a Roman roof (as Luke did in 5:19).

that Jesus was in the house, a rumor, was enough to gather a crowd. This was not the only instance, thank God, of the power of a rumor about Jesus' presence. Let but a rumor, stirring a hope that Jesus is "at home" in a house, in a family life, in a person get abroad, and people have gathered at the door. That is one of the most moving things in Christian history, and a common one in the life of the church today. A question for each of us is: Does my life cause any rumor that Jesus is "at home" with me, in my spirit and actions? If so, make no mistake about it. There will be a gathering at the door.

3. *And They Came, Bringing to Him a Paralytic Carried by Four Men.*—These words picture vividly the pressures on Jesus which never let up. He lived in the midst of a crowd. All through the records of the early Galilean ministry we can feel the push and surge of the crowd. Here was an interruption. He had just come back to Capernaum. He had had no chance to see his friends, and there was the crowd pushing in at the door. More than that, they were bringing a difficult case to him, a paralytic.

But that is an inevitable accompaniment to the life of those who can and do give help to others freely. Such people always get the difficult cases. In some ways theirs could be called a hard lot in life, with interrupted rest, loaded by others with burdens. It is the lot of the physician, the social worker, the minister, the friend generous of his time and strength and skill. All these know the grim meaning of the words **and they came.** They do come and keep coming. Yet that is the highest tribute that can be paid to a person. For the repeated comings say earnestly, "You count. It makes a differ-

ence when you are here," as it made a difference when Jesus returned to Capernaum. There is one thing worse than being "rushed to death" by cases of need. That is not being rushed at all. For being "rushed to death" often means being rushed to life, being brought into healing, restoring, helping relationship to other lives. The easy life, which no crowds jostle, to which no interruptions come, is an empty life. Count it all joy when you fall into divers problems, needs, requests for help. It means you are following the way the Master went.

There is also a deep impressiveness about the sympathy and the faith of these four men, so greatly concerned about a paralyzed friend that they themselves carried him to Jesus. They are the first of an endless company of those who have made it possible for others to reach the healing hands of Christ, his restoring and empowering hands. We do not know the names of these men. No matter. They played their part in the cure of a body and soul. What a role it has been in history—the bearers! They are those who in widely varied ways have brought other people to Christ. There are in that company Monica, the mother of Augustine, and Susanna Wesley, parents who have brought their children; teachers, nurses, businessmen, who have brought other people to Christ; people to whom he has said with authority, "Rise and walk in newness of life." It is not a casual role, but an active, demanding one. Its joyous rewards cannot be computed.

4. *They Removed the Roof Above Him.*—Ingenious persistence! We do not stretch the meaning of this story when we stop to admire both the ingenuity and persistence of the bearers. Nor do we stretch it when we see and feel in it eloquent persuasion to the work of

roof where he was: and when they had broken *it* up, they let down the bed wherein the sick of the palsy lay.

5 When Jesus saw their faith, he said unto the sick of the palsy, Son, thy sins be forgiven thee.

of the crowd, they removed the roof above him; and when they had made an opening, they let down the pallet on which the paralytic lay. 5 And when Jesus saw their faith, he said to the paralytic, "My

---

5. It is the faith of the four friends that is rewarded; but presumably the man himself had faith too—perhaps urging his friends to bring him. Mark thinks of Jesus as not merely announcing the forgiveness of sins but actually pronouncing it, i.e., forgiving the man.

---

evangelism, in the large meaning of that word, bringing people to be made whole by Christ. Ingenuity and persistence are both needed. These four bearers of the pallet had both. When they found they could not get near Jesus on account of the crowd, they did not set the bed down and say, "Well, that's that. We're sorry, old fellow, it's tough luck." They went up and demolished the roof. Unconventional and distinctive, to say the least. But they had gloriously single-track minds. They set out to get their friend to Jesus and they got him there. Across the years the ingenious persistence of these men says to us, "When one way is blocked, try another." When one attempt has failed, make another, even though it seems preposterous. The goal of bringing a life into healing touch with Christ is so great that nothing, not even roofs, should stand in the way.

5. *My Son, Your Sins Are Forgiven.*—Only six words, but their meaning is inexhaustible. Among those meanings certainly is this, that Jesus inevitably probes to the deeper causes of disaster. We do not know the details, either clinical or spiritual, of this man affected with paralysis. We know that in Jesus' time it was common to regard physical ills as a punishment or consequence of sin. It may well be that the paralytic himself believed that his paralysis was due to sin. We have no certain warrant for assuming that Jesus believed it. But whatever the details, Jesus saw that the man needed more than physical mending: he needed spiritual restoration.

Here is a little drama, picturing the very genius of the Christian gospel, that it does not bring merely external remedies to internal ills. Jesus went to the deeper ill below the physical affliction. Perhaps he knew more about the man than the record indicates. Perhaps his keen and quick eye could see the deeper causes of trouble. We know that there is a relationship between some forms of sin and physical calamity, and between mental states and functional paralysis. At any rate Jesus goes to the deeper levels of evil first—"Thy sins are forgiven." He brought restoration of harmony with God.

That dealing with the deeper sources of evil marks the profoundly religious approach to life, and the only adequate approach. It is so common to ascribe ills and troubles to outward causes, to conditions, to environment, to things—either desirable things lacking, or undesirable things present, but still *things*. While all the time the real trouble is sin. It may be greed, envy, pride, self-seeking, lust, or any combination of them. Unless these are recognized, repented of, and forgiven, outward changes will have no more truly healing effect than dressing in gay clothes will have on a patient stricken with cancer.

The same is true of a nation's ills. Consider economic paralysis, for instance. Someone has defined paralysis as "a tragedy in ten thousand acts." Economic depression is a tragedy in a hundred and fifty million acts, and more. And always, underneath the economic symptoms, there is sin: the sin of greed, of power, of contempt for human beings; the denial of brotherhood.

In the international realm the world's greatest need is for the forgiveness of sin. Many would greet that statement as sentimentalism. It is the only realism that does not hide from the deepest ills of our world. We are suffering from a spiritual sickness that will respond to nothing less than a spiritual cure. Four-power treaties or fifty-power treaties, while they may be instruments of a moral will, are in themselves no cure for the diseases of which we are dying. There must be a One-Power treaty, an agreement with God, with the moral and spiritual realities. We have sinned. We have made oil more important than blood, land more important than people, national prestige more important than human welfare. We have made void the word of God through our continuing tradition of conflict. We have put our trust too completely "in reeking tube and iron shard."

Jesus brought the only cure for the world's deadly sickness, a gospel that brings conviction of sin, the forgiveness of sin, and the power to overcome sin.

6 But there were certain of the scribes sitting there, and reasoning in their hearts,

7 Why doth this *man* thus speak blasphemies? who can forgive sins but God only?

8 And immediately, when Jesus perceived in his spirit that they so reasoned within themselves, he said unto them, Why reason ye these things in your hearts?

9 Whether is it easier to say to the sick of the palsy, *Thy* sins be forgiven thee; or to say, Arise, and take up thy bed, and walk?

10 But that ye may know that the Son of man hath power on earth to forgive sins, (he saith to the sick of the palsy,)

11 I say unto thee, Arise, and take up thy bed, and go thy way into thine house.

12 And immediately he arose, took up the bed, and went forth before them all;

son, your sins are forgiven." **6** Now some of the scribes were sitting there, questioning in their hearts, **7** "Why does this man speak thus? It is blasphemy! Who can forgive sins but God alone?" **8** And immediately Jesus, perceiving in his spirit that they thus questioned within themselves, said to them, "Why do you question thus in your hearts? **9** Which is easier, to say to the paralytic, 'Your sins are forgiven,' or to say, 'Rise, take up your pallet and walk'? **10** But that you may know that the Son of man has authority on earth to forgive sins" — he said to the paralytic — **11** "I say to you, rise, take up your pallet and go home." **12** And he rose, and immediately took up the pallet and went out before

---

7. The claim of authority to **forgive sins** is involved in Jesus' words to the paralytic, according to Mark, since they set Jesus in the place of God (cf. John 10:33; God alone could forgive sins, according to Isa. 43:25); the penalty for blasphemy was death by stoning (Lev. 24:16). The Jews did not expect even the Messiah to forgive sins; no man could do this. Nor was any human intermediary or any offering of sacrifice required; God forgives the penitent man's sins at once. It is difficult to see how the following proof of Jesus' authority to forgive sins—viz., the effectiveness of the healing—could have convinced the scribes of his messiahship; the logic, like the concept in vs. 10, belongs to the "Son of man" theology of the early church rather than to Judaism.

8-12. In his spirit (cf. 5:30; 8:12; etc.): Mark may view Jesus' direct intuition as supernatural. It was obviously easier to utter idle words in the name of God than to enable a paralytic to walk—so the scribes are represented as thinking. Jesus proceeds to

---

6. *Now Some of the Scribes Were Sitting There, Questioning in Their Hearts.*—Here is the first rumble of the gathering storm. You can see the scribes sitting there, with a contemptuous curl on their lips and a scowl on their faces. A good word describing them—**questioning.** They were not really seeing, their eyes were closed. They were not looking with open minds and hearts at a work of amazing mercy and power. They could see nothing but a departure from their tradition. They and their tradition were everything; the need of man and the mercy of God were nothing. That is the worst sort of blindness that can happen to a man. But it can happen to us when anything, our prestige, our possessions, our beloved tradition, our institution, anything, becomes more important than mercy and the weightier matters of the law. From such a supreme calamity of soul we may all pray, "Good Lord, deliver us!" (see on vss. 15-17).

8. *Jesus, Perceiving in His Spirit That They Thus Questioned.*—Miraculous? Not necessarily.

A supernatural miracle is not demanded to explain this perception of the mood of the scribes. Jesus was marvelously gifted in insight. His spirit was a sensitive instrument, recording the thoughts and feelings of those in his environment. He knew what was in man. To his penetrating X-ray eyes and spirit these scribes lived in glass houses.

In a true sense we all live in glass houses in the sight of God. Also, often in the presence of man. The face, the eyes, can reveal what is within, even when lips are silent. How would it be to live, even for a day, as though our thoughts were visible? A truly disturbing idea. Yet we had better live that way, for our thoughts are visible to him "unto whom all hearts are open, and from whom no secrets are hid." "Jesus perceived. . . ." God perceives.

12. *We Never Saw Anything Like This!*—They surely never had! This makes a suggestive starting point for stressing the distinctiveness of the Christian religion. There are its interest in persons and its power to heal, both dramatized

insomuch that they were all amazed, and glorified God, saying, We never saw it on this fashion.

13 And he went forth again by the sea side; and all the multitude resorted unto him, and he taught them.

14 And as he passed by, he saw Levi the *son* of Alpheus sitting at the receipt of custom, and said unto him, Follow me. And he arose and followed him.

them all; so that they were all amazed and glorified God, saying, "We never saw anything like this!"

13 He went out again beside the sea; and all the crowd gathered about him, and he taught them. 14 And as he passed on, he saw Levi the son of Alphaeus sitting at the tax office, and he said to him, "Follow me." And he rose and followed him.

---

prove the validity of his words of forgiveness by the power of his words of healing. The whole inserted controversial section (vss. 5*b*-10) reflects the polemics of the early church: if Jesus could cure a paralytic, and do other mighty works, he could certainly pronounce the divine forgiveness of sins (cf. John 3:2) ; and he does so, not as a prophet or emissary of God, or even as Messiah, but as **the Son of man,** who **has authority on earth to forgive sins.** Some MSS, perhaps to stress the Incarnation, read "the Son of man on earth has authority." (On **Son of man** see Intro., p. 642.) Vs. 12 gives a typical conclusion to a miracle story, with no reference to the argument of the inserted controversy.

9. The Call of Levi (2:13-14)

It is a question whether these two verses form an independent section (similar to 1:16-20) , or are intended as the introduction to vss. 15-17. The latter have to do with one of the controversies: Why did Jesus admit a publican to the fellowship of his disciples? If originally independent, the two sections must have come together very early.

14. A strong group of MSS read "James" instead of **Levi,** who is otherwise unknown; Matthew changes to read "Matthew." It is improbable that "James" and **Levi** were two names for the same man. Levi was either a collector of import and export duties on the highway that ran through Capernaum, or a tax officer of Herod Antipas.

---

in this healing. There has never been anything like it. What other religion has ever distantly approached it? The miracles were not *proofs,* but *signs* of this power.

13-15. *He Saw Levi.*—The same combination of public speech and private personal invitation that was noticed earlier (see on 1:15-16) appears here again in effective sequence. First, all the crowd gathered about him. Then **he saw Levi.** That was Jesus' twofold method of preaching the kingdom. His command to his disciples, "Follow me," surely includes, for his church, the fulfillment of the public proclamation of the Word by the seeking and winning of individual disciples. The two things went together in the ministry of Jesus. They belong together forever.

Note also the change which occurred when Levi became a follower of Jesus. He had been a tax collector. His life had been devoted to gathering. Now he turned to distributing. It was a deep-seated change in motive and goal, from gathering taxes to distributing the message and gifts of God. His Roman employers had commanded, "Gather, collect, gather!" Jesus turned all this around, "Freely ye have received, freely give" (Matt. 10:8) .

Many changes come when Jesus is followed as teacher and master. This is one of the greatest. The clutched hand of gathering becomes the open hand of distributing, a vital change in orientation, in central drive. Levi no longer used people as a means. God's children became ends in themselves.

This great change should find expression in our common life together. Our whole economic world has been too largely and tragically centered on gathering, on production, on profit-taking. It must face the problems of distribution, that the abundance of God's earth may be more equitably divided among God's children.

14. *He Saw Levi . . . Sitting. . . . And He Rose.*—This is a simple physical detail of the call of Levi. It involves nothing more. But what a graphic and stirring picture it is of the truth of Christian history, of what happens when Jesus calls to a life and that life responds! He has lifted men out of sitting positions to their feet. He has come to multitudes, fixed in sitting and recumbent positions, and brought them into life and erect, forward stride. He has found people sitting in grief, and at his words they have arisen, comforted and fortified. He

15 And it came to pass, that, as Jesus sat at meat in his house, many publicans and sinners sat also together with Jesus and his disciples; for there were many, and they followed him.

16 And when the scribes and Pharisees saw him eat with publicans and sinners,

15 And as he sat at table in his house, many tax collectors and sinners were sitting with Jesus and his disciples; for there were many who followed him. 16 And the scribes of⁰ the Pharisees, when they saw

⁰ Some ancient authorities read *and*.

---

10. EATING WITH PUBLICANS AND SINNERS (2:15-17)

15. In his house presumably means Jesus' own house. This is certainly true if vss. 13-14 and 15-17 were originally independent (see on vss. 13-14 above). The **tax collectors** are local, not the great magnates who farmed the taxes of whole provinces, the "publicani" of Rome, but the underlings who administered this onerous and wasteful system. The collection of taxes went to the highest bidder, who made his profit by exacting from the people as much more as possible over and above what he had paid for the privilege, a system common in the ancient world. **Sinners** were those who disregarded the requirements of the Mosaic law; the association of the two groups may have been natural, since both were despised by strict and legal Jews. Publicans were also despised by others; e.g., Klostermann quotes the satirist Lucian (*Descent into Hades* 11): "Adulterers and pimps and publicans and flatterers and sycophants." It was a scandal to observant Jews in Jesus' own time that he associated with such men, and it was a charge against the Christians later, both that their Master had done so and that his followers still welcomed sinners (as Origen *Against Celsus* III. 59 shows). **There were many**—i.e., disciples (some good MSS read "who" for "and they")—has been added, since the story as a whole seems to assume the twelve as present with Jesus, though Mark has related the call of only five.

16. Scribes and Pharisees (KJV) is a frequent combination, like "publicans and sinners," but the original text here probably read **scribes of the Pharisees** (RSV), i.e.,

---

has found men sitting in sin, and they have stood up in newness of life, forgiven and restored. Jesus told once of a boy, sitting in a pigpen, who said, "I will arise and go to my father" (Luke 15:18). He has found men sitting in idleness, with mind, heart, and hand unemployed in any great cause, and at his call they have sprung to their feet, to spend and be spent in the service of him who gave his life a ransom for many.

15. Many Tax Collectors and Sinners Were Sitting with Jesus.—Here is evidence of a secret we have forgotten: Jesus knew how to draw the irreligious. This dinner party seems far away from the common run of our church life. The modern counterparts of **tax collectors and sinners** do not come and sit down in great numbers with the church folk of today. They are largely aloof, uninterested, uncomfortable in the ecclesiastical setting. It is disturbing to think that the very class of persons on whom Jesus had a strong pull are conspicuously absent from our church world. We say, "It's their own fault," and that is often true. But is that all that must be said? Is that not making our escape too easy?

Much can be found in this narrative to lay bare part at least of the secret which we have

forgotten. These people had seen the tremendous demonstration of Jesus' sympathy, compassion, and love for those in need, spontaneous and outgoing to all. They had seen his active recognition of others like themselves, his treatment of all alike as welcome and desired. He had no walls of aloofness around him. He rejected exclusive and artificial standards of goodness. He rejected the closed circle of "the righteous." They had seen him actively seeking the outcast, never minimizing his demand, "Repent," but always with the positive outreach of his love and friendship. In all this the church may well hear the words "Learn of me."

16. Why Does He Eat ... with Tax Collectors and Sinners?—Here the Pharisees are objecting to Jesus' acts rather than to his words. It was in the act of eating with outsiders that he violated their code and the tradition of ceremonial cleanness. The Pharisees could stand a good deal of verbal teaching. There were lots of teachers. What angered them was the act which incarnated and dramatized the words of invitation and fellowship. Jesus acted out his precepts, and gave to what might have been nothing but generalities the local habitation of the deed. It was the act which got him into trouble. It was also the act which gave to his word clear, com-

they said unto his disciples, How is it that he eateth and drinketh with publicans and sinners?

that he was eating with sinners and tax collectors, said to his disciples, "Why does he eat[h] with tax collectors and sinners?"

[h] Some ancient authorities add *and drink.*

---

scribes belonging to the Pharisaic party. Not all scribes belonged to the Pharisaic "brotherhood." These were presumably more strict and rigorous than other scribes in their observance of food regulations and other requirements for which Pharisaism stood. Note that the objection is addressed to the **disciples,** as to the later followers of Jesus. A strict observant of traditional Judaism would avoid all contact with lax and careless Jews, lest he himself should be contaminated. Cf. the later rule: "A disciple of the wise [a rabbinic student] must not sit at table with the Amhaarez." (Berakoth 43*b,* and cf. even Gal. 2:12.)

---

pelling power. That is always true. Actions bring trouble. But actions also demonstrate the Christian message. Take the realm of race relations, for instance. How easy to say are the great, glowing words on brotherhood! And how little disturbance they create! But deeds of brotherhood—the violating of the cruel codes of segregation and exploitation and contempt—these cause trouble, because they make real the message. Jesus in his acts crossed boundaries marking off classes of the population as inferior. Where do we cross them? All high and holy words seek incarnation in deeds.

The question of the Pharisees also gives a picture of the uncontrollable Christ. They asked the disciples, "Why can't you keep your teacher within decent limits?" He would not stay behind the sanctified fences of accepted usage and tradition. He was always leaping over them into forbidden territory. It was upsetting to their *status quo,* and hence unendurable.

How endlessly that scene has been repeated and how modern it all sounds! The uncontrollable Jesus has disturbed many of his professed followers in all centuries. Jesus got "out of hand" in the appeal of the early church to the Gentiles. Through the book of Acts we can hear the Judaizers snarl, "Why doesn't this Christ stay within the decent limits of Judaism?" The spirit and message of Jesus were uncontrollable in the evangelical revival in England in the eighteenth century. Many churchmen bitterly complained that he was not kept locked up in the churches, but was out in the open fields and street corners, consorting with non-respectable sinners—miners, and the dregs of city slums. Jesus was uncontrollable in the missionary movement of the nineteenth century. Many churchmen echoed the violent words shouted at William Carey—"Sit down!" But passionate hearts and minds had taken seriously Jesus' words, "Let us go on to the next towns"— into Calcutta, Canton, Rangoon, and Tokyo. Jesus was uncontrollable when he burst the bonds of a traditionally individual, personal religion, and men saw him as a Savior of society

as well as of individuals. Jesus was and is and will be uncontrollable. A Savior could not be otherwise.

16, 18, 24. Why?—We can hear the steady explosions of the angry Why? Why? Why? as the Pharisees follow Jesus around, hear his words, and see his actions. Four times in the series of conflicts recorded in ch. 2 (more evidently topical selections to show conflicts than chronological sequences) we meet questions beginning with "Why," about the healing of the paralytic, eating with taxgatherers, fasting, and violating the sabbath. They were too busy attacking Jesus and asking petulantly "Why?" really to look at what had been said or done. They were not conducting an honest inquiry; they were rendering a premature condemnation. That is a much easier and a much more common thing to do. Here was a cherished tradition blinding people to truth, a liability of traditions when elevated to supreme veneration. That word "tradition" may represent a great and noble inheritance. The word simply means something "passed on" or "handed down." It may be a tradition of faith in God, or of courageous living. But the common use of the word as representing a sort of spiritual strait jacket has its justification, for it is frequently that, as it was with the Pharisees. Their spiritual blindness represents an ever-present danger. We too may be blinded to the working of God under our own eyes if we cherish a particular form of words above spiritual realities expressed in new forms. Economic and social traditions can blind us to the word of God. It was so with slavery. The whole way of life, the customs, the traditions connected with it made many men blind to the brothers for whom Christ died. In like manner we can cherish economic traditions which have been profitable to us, and bark out angrily, "Why must anyone criticize this?" And all the while the proposed changes may be the voice of God saying to the oppressor, "Let my people go" (Exod. 8:1). In this respect we may well heed Jesus' warning, "Beware of the leaven of the Pharisees" (8:15).

17 When Jesus heard *it,* he saith unto them, They that are whole have no need of the physician, but they that are sick: I came not to call the righteous, but sinners to repentance.	17 And when Jesus heard it, he said to them, "Those who are well have no need of a physician, but those who are sick; I came not to call the righteous, but sinners."
18 And the disciples of John and of the Pharisees used to fast: and they come and say unto him, Why do the disciples of John and of the Pharisees fast, but thy disciples fast not?	18 Now John's disciples and the Pharisees were fasting; and people came and said to him, "Why do John's disciples and the disciples of the Pharisees fast, but your

17. Jesus' reply is complete; he does not excuse his conduct, but points out that this lay directly in line with his mission—a **physician** can scarcely do anything for the sick if he avoids contact with them. Here is the beginning of the profound Christian metaphor, Christ the Great Physician. **I came** reflects Jesus' sense of mission. Some scholars have suggested that this, like other "I" sayings, has been added as an explanation in the course of the handing on of the tradition. But it is not impossible as a statement of Jesus' own view: it does not reflect any particular "christological" theory of the later church. **To repentance** (KJV) is not in the best MSS, and probably represents later homiletical interpretation: Jesus' mission was to call sinners to repentance in preparation for the kingdom of God (1:15).

11. The Question of Fasting (2:18-22)

18-20. **John's disciples** formed a distinct group for a long time after their master's arrest and death. **Used to fast** is overtranslation: the Pharisees still fasted in Mark's time, and so also perhaps did John's disciples. **Disciples . . . of the Pharisees** is based on a bad Greek text. Read with RSV, **Now John's disciples and the Pharisees were fasting.** This was the concrete situation presupposed in the story. The complaint in the preceding pericope is addressed to the disciples; this one is addressed to Jesus. Clearly Mark (cf. vs. 20), and perhaps those who handed down the tradition before him, had in mind the question: Why do Christians fast if Jesus did not? Or perhaps: Why did Jesus' own immediate disciples not fast, since fasting was a pious practice? This was no doubt a subject of controversy at a later time; but the answer went back to Jesus, and was stated, characteristically, in the form of another question: **Can the wedding guests** [really the

17. *I Came Not to Call the Righteous, but Sinners.*—This may have been sarcasm. Jesus, on occasion, used sarcasm with devastating force. At least it was an effective rejoinder to the Pharisees on their own terms. It is as though he said, "You are the righteous. Let it go at that. I am come to call sinners."

Strange that followers of Jesus, bound together in the church that bears his name, could ever forget this gleaming word, this central purpose, so continuously expressed in his teaching —"The Son of man came to seek and to save that which was lost" (Luke 19:10). That unresting passion, as it became the dominating motive of Paul's life, is powerfully expressed in the words which F. W. H. Myers puts into the mouth of the apostle:

Oh, to save these, to perish for their saving,
Die for their life, be offered for them all.[8]

[8] "Saint Paul."

What would we think of the crew of a lifesaving station who gave all their attention to the station itself, made the quarters attractive, planted gardens, designed uniforms, provided music, and thus pleasantly occupied, shut out the roar of pounding breakers, driving ships and men to destruction on the rocks? Incredible, we would say, and rightly. Yet is such a fancy far removed from a church, so intent on its own interior life, its housing, its decoration, its material well-being, that the plight of those outside, in need of salvation in Christ, is forgotten or becomes subordinate to other things? The church is not a company on a summer hotel porch; it is a lifesaving crew. How many churches, just at the time when the needs around them were growing greater, have packed up and followed "the righteous" out to a new location in a pleasant residential section, where peace, perfect peace, reigns! In some such fashion we can get away from the disturbing

19 And Jesus said unto them, Can the children of the bridechamber fast, while the bridegroom is with them? as long as they have the bridegroom with them, they cannot fast.

20 But the days will come, when the bridegroom shall be taken away from them, and then shall they fast in those days.

21 No man also seweth a piece of new cloth on an old garment; else the new piece that filled it up taketh away from the old, and the rent is made worse.

22 And no man putteth new wine into old bottles; else the new wine doth burst the bottles, and the wine is spilled, and the bottles will be marred: but new wine must be put into new bottles.

disciples do not fast?" 19 And Jesus said to them, "Can the wedding guests fast while the bridegroom is with them? As long as they have the bridegroom with them, they cannot fast. 20 The days will come, when the bridegroom is taken away from them, and then they will fast on that day. 21 No one sews a piece of unshrunk cloth on an old garment; if he does, the patch tears away from it, the new from the old, and a worse tear is made. 22 And no one puts new wine into old wineskins; if he does, the wine will burst the skins, and the wine is lost, and so are the skins but new wine is for fresh skins."[i]

[i] Some ancient authorities omit but new wine is for fresh skins.

close friends of the bridegroom] **fast?** The point of comparison is not the persons but the time: the kingdom of God is at hand (1:15) and the powers of darkness are being overthrown; it is no time for fasting and mourning. The answer, **as long as . . . fast,** may be only an example of Mark's "underscoring the obvious"; more likely it is meant to introduce and strengthen the contrast of vs. 20, which is generally looked upon as secondary, its purpose being to justify the later Christian observance of fasting. This observance did not, however, always have in mind the death of Christ, or his absence (see Matt. 6:16-18, where it is a normal practice of piety), any more than Johannine fasting referred only to John's death; that of the Pharisees certainly had no such reference.

21-22. The twin parables that follow have been inserted here by Mark as a further answer to the question in vs. 18. What their original connection was we do not know— was it sabbath observance, sacrifices, the whole scribal tradition? Here their point would seem to be the danger to the old religion rather than to the new: the new **patch** will tear away the edges of the rotten garment; the fresh ferment of the **new wine** will split open

cries and burdens of sin and need. But there is a price to be paid for it. We also get far away from him who came to save sinners.

19. *Can the Wedding Guests Fast While the Bridegroom Is with Them?*—Undoubtedly this passage has a close relationship to questions and controversies about fasting in the early church. It may have been influenced by the desire to justify the practices of the church in the matter (see Exeg.). One thing is clear; namely, that "The answer went back to Jesus." Here certainly is the positive expression by Jesus of a note that is sounded forcibly and lyrically all through the N.T., that of joy as an authentic mark of Christian discipleship. The feeling of "joy unspeakable and full of glory" (I Pet. 1:8) is felt all the way through. Even Walker's concordance, which does not aim to be exhaustive, lists over sixty appearances of "joy," as noun, adjective, or adverb. The music is so persistent that reading the N.T. is like being in a bird sanctuary on a spring morning.

Has that note of joy dropped out of our church life, or become so subdued that it is not

a recognizable watermark of our faith? If so, we have lost a power, for as Wordsworth affirms, there is a "deep power of joy." In the early church this joy came partly from wonder. "Behold, what manner of love the Father hath bestowed upon us" (I John 3:1). That first Christian community, whose life we feel throbbing all through the latter part of the N.T., never seemed to get over the amazing wonder of the gospel and the church. Their joy was also the joy of giving themselves in service, "Who for the joy that was set before him . . ." (Heb. 12:2). It was the joy of the Cross! Strange paradox, but proven true in the experience of multitudes. The road to the recovery of joy is not to say, "Go to, now! I will be joyful," but to put ourselves into the experiences that produce joy, receiving the unspeakable gift of God, and taking up a cross.

22. *No One Puts New Wine into Old Wineskins.*—Here, and in the last two verses of ch. 2, we have two instances of Jesus' remarkable power of beginning with a particular, detailed discussion or controversy, probing to the central

23 And it came to pass, that he went through the corn fields on the sabbath day; and his disciples began, as they went, to pluck the ears of corn.	23 One sabbath he was going through the grainfields; and as they made their way his disciples began to pluck ears of grain.

the old **wineskins** and ruin them. If the parables originally referred to fasting, we should expect an old patch on a new garment, and old, perhaps spoiled, wine in new wineskins. What is clear from the pericope as a whole is that Jesus did not practice fasting, or require it of his disciples; at a later date the church practiced it regularly (cf. Did. 8:1). **But new wine must be put into new bottles,** or, possibly, **new wine is for fresh skins,** is found in a number of excellent MSS, but it is probably a gloss from the text of Luke 5:38 where, along with 5:39, it forms one of two characteristic Lukan homiletical comments on the parable.

12. PLUCKING GRAIN ON THE SABBATH (2:23-28)

The connection with the preceding pericope is not very close. It has been suggested that "that day"—the better reading in 2:20—meant Friday, the day of the Crucifixion as observed in the early church, and this the day following, when the Christians broke their fast; but such an interpretation is too subtle. Instead, this is one more isolated incident, derived perhaps from Mark's "controversy source," and included in the series from 2:1 to 3:6. The narrative is difficult to understand—perhaps it was distorted in oral transmission —for Jesus' reply has to do with unlawful eating of food, not with "work" on the sabbath. There is a general cogency in the reply: human need knows no law; but this is precisely the principle which Jesus repeatedly rejected, according to the Gospels. He would not even work a miracle to save his own life, but was in all things obedient to his Father's will. It may be said, however, that this case is different: he will defend others, not himself (cf. 15:31—this may be the clue to Mark's view). On the other hand, one may find a clue to the unity of the story in the recognized rule of interpretation "from greater to less": David's act in eating the consecrated **bread of the Presence,** and giving it to his followers, was a far greater breach of the law—if it was a breach—than that of Jesus and his disciples in "threshing," rubbing out kernels of grain to eat, on the sabbath. The section forms the first of two sabbath controversies (3:1-5 is the other), and it may be that in the course either of oral transmission or of Mark's editing a controversy that originally had to do with eating on the sabbath—or with preparation of food, which was forbidden—has been given a setting which refers to "threshing of grain." This is a possibility, but nothing more. If it is the true explanation, then vs. 27 should perhaps follow vs. 24 immediately. Vs. 28 is an independent saying, perhaps an inference by Mark, or by those who handed down the story.

23. Corn fields is of course English for **grainfields. As they went** (KJV) is quite as correct as **made their way** (RSV); "make a path" is too literal for the idiomatic ὁδὸν ποιεῖν.

point at issue, and then rising to a general truth of universal application. This statement about new wine in old wineskins is one; the statement that "the sabbath was made for man" is the other.

Just what the compressed parable of the new wine in old skins referred to is not entirely clear—whether to fasting, sacrifices, or the whole tradition of the scribes (see Exeg.). But the general meaning is clear—that the good news of the kingdom is not to be enclosed in old forms. In Allan Menzies' words, "The movement Jesus has set on foot is a fresh and growing thing; it is impossible to set limits to its expansion, irrational to confine it to forms which were not made for it."[4] In the text of Mark the point stressed is the damage to the old wineskins if new wine is put into them. But the early Christian church gave a different turn to it. The danger was of spoiling the new wine. Thus Paul (Gal. 4:9-11) warned strongly against spoiling the new wine of freedom in Christ by pouring it into unsuitable observances. The truth, the new life, the new revelations of God

[4] *The Earliest Gospel* (London: Macmillan & Co., 1901), p. 88.

24 And the Pharisees said unto him, Behold, why do they on the sabbath day that which is not lawful?

25 And he said unto them, Have ye never read what David did, when he had need, and was ahungered, he, and they that were with him?

26 How he went into the house of God in the days of Abiathar the high priest, and did eat the showbread, which is not lawful to eat but for the priests, and gave also to them which were with him?

24 And the Pharisees said to him, "Look, why are they doing what is not lawful on the sabbath?" 25 And he said to them, "Have you never read what David did, when he was in need and was hungry, he and those who were with him: 26 how he entered the house of God, when A-bi′a-thar was high priest, and ate the bread of the Presence, which it is not lawful for any but the priests to eat, and also gave it

---

24. Not lawful, i.e., not lawful **on the sabbath** day. Deut. 23:24-25 allows the picking of grapes and heads of standing grain to satisfy hunger, but forbids harvesting any of a neighbor's crop; nothing is said of "making a path" or plucking grapes or grain **on the sabbath.** In other words, the Deuteronomic regulation is not concerned with what shall or shall not be done on the sabbath day particularly. What we have here in Mark is the scribal elaboration and refinement of the sabbath law, which was eventually embodied in the Mishnah (Sabbath 7:2). It is true that the Mishnah and Talmud recognize exceptions, as for works of mercy or necessity; but there is evidence that the earlier legal tradition was far more rigorous and less humanitarian than the later—and the lifetime of Jesus lay almost two centuries before the final compilation of the Mishnah (*ca.* A.D. 210).

25-26. What David did, as told in I Sam. 21:1-6. The priest was not Abiathar but Ahimelech, his father; some scholars suspect a gloss, but this is the simple kind of error that ancient tradition and even ancient authors sometimes made—e.g., Plato's quotations from Homer, where the names of persons are sometimes wrong. However, some good MSS (D W O.L. sy^s) omit the phrase about Abiathar. **Gave it to those who were with him** clinches the application to the present case. If David, the "man after God's own heart," could do this for his famished men, the hungry disciples were certainly entitled to pluck heads of grain to satisfy their hunger—a principle recognized in Torah—even on the sabbath.

---

cannot be forced into old brittle forms, but must be given freedom to spread out like the circles in water after a pebble has been dropped into it.

In individual personal life the new wine of Christ cannot be fitted into old ways that were adopted and arranged without any reference to him. Yet that is exactly what many have tried to do, with the result that Christianity becomes a mere appendage, a surface decoration, a veneer over some fundamentally unchristian attitude, aim, or spirit. The effort is made to dilute the Christian gospel in order to accommodate old prejudices, and sub-Christian motives.

The same is true of the whole life and thought of the church. One striking example was the heroic struggle of the early church to keep the new wine of the gospel of Christ from being confined in the old skins of Jewish legalism. New revelations of God, as the thoughts of men have widened, cannot be crowded into old literalisms, nor can they be confined to old

conceptions of the world which have been outgrown. When the new heavens of Copernicus and Galileo swung into man's ken, the church made a tragic blunder in trying to confine the truth to the old idea that the sun circled around the earth. Today there is another true revelation of God in the new ferment of a world church, an ecumenical church; and there is again the risk of blundering. The new ferment cannot be put into the old wineskins of fenced-off, self-centered denominationalism.

New occasions teach new duties and new revelations demand new forms of action, in social and in international life. The responsibilities of an industrial age cannot be enclosed in the laissez-faire doctrine of an earlier time. When eighteenth- or nineteenth-century conceptions dominate a twentieth-century world, the result is desolation and blight on a massive scale. The old wineskins of nationalism are tragically unfitted to the risks of an atomic age. New wineskins are needed for new wine.

27 And he said unto them, The sabbath was made for man, and not man for the sabbath:

28 Therefore the Son of man is Lord also of the sabbath.

27 And he said to them, "The sabbath was made for man, not man for the sabbath; 28 so the Son of man is lord even of the sabbath."

---

27. This verse may attach directly to vs. 24 (see above); at least it undoubtedly answers the question asked there, and is not an inference from vss. 25-26. It is characteristic of Mark to introduce a new saying with such a clause as **and he said to them.** Some MSS (D O.L.) omit vs. 27 and the word **therefore** in vs. 28 (KJV); this cannot be original, and is perhaps due to scribal error connected in some way with the appearance, near the beginning and end of the omitted verse, of the word σάββατον. Nor can the omission of **and not man for the sabbath** (in W sy^s) be original. The great principle enunciated by Jesus was later adopted by second-century rabbis (see refs., Klostermann); in our Lord's time it was probably something new.

28. This final saying, like other "Son of man" sayings in Mark, may be a later inference or an addition to the pericope. (See F. C. Grant, *The Earliest Gospel* [New York and Nashville: Abingdon-Cokesbury Press, 1943], pp. 64-69.) We expect, "Therefore *man* is master of the sabbath"—which no other Jew would grant, nor would Jesus; this seems to rule out the possibility of mistranslation from Aramaic, i.e., assuming the words to be original. Vs. 27 is the proper climax of the pericope (the "pronouncement," in Vincent Taylor's terminology); what follows is Mark's theological inference, and fits into the outline of his theology (cf. Intro., pp. 642-43). The trite modern interpretation, Son of man=="human being," is quite impossible, equally here as in 2:10. Mark did not think in this fashion, and for the primitive Palestinian church, which was largely Jewish, the idea would have been preposterous: "men" do not usurp God's prerogative in the forgiveness of sins, nor do they rescind or modify the law of the sabbath.

---

27. The Sabbath Was Made for Man, Not Man for the Sabbath.—This sentence of Jesus may come from another context. But it is a pivotal saying. No limits can be set to its application to life and human experience. Jesus' word provides a final test for all institutions, including those of religion itself. The validity of every institution lies outside itself. It is determined by the degree in which the institution meets this test, "Does it serve men?" If it does not, then it has failed.

Jesus applies this test fearlessly and rigorously to the sabbath. These words, carried to their logical implication, mean that no institution is sacred in itself. People are sacred. Any final authority and sanctity that an institution deserves comes from its service to the wide variety of human need. Jesus' parable of the last judgment (Matt. 25), where men are pictured as being judged by their sensitiveness to those needs, is a powerful dramatization of the principle of the final test of service.

What tragedy and waste would have been averted if this test of religious institutions had always been applied in Christian history! How many times in outlook and action men have been forgotten! How often the church, dominated by the illusion that it was sacred in itself, has been occupied with aggrandizement, power, and pageantry, and has lost sight of the fact that its true and only authority lies in its service to man's needs.

The same test applies in other areas. We speak of "the sanctity of law." There is a true sanctity in law, but it derives from the law's service to human need, spiritual, civic, and material, and from its power to adjust itself to the changing and enlarging needs which come with changed conditions. What is an economic system for? All too frequently the offhand answer, uncritically accepted, has been that its purpose is to perpetuate established customs and to make profits. But an economic system is made for man. So with a nation. The state too is made for man, and not just man for the state. In our rejection of all totalitarian dictatorship we accept this principle of Jesus. But we do not apply it as we should to the formulation of national policy. Jesus left room for the duty owed the state. We must always leave room for it; with the understanding, however, that the nation exists primarily for the welfare of its people, not to underwrite outmoded notions of absolute sovereignty, or to throw its economic and military weight about in any sort of aggrandizement of its prestige and power, or to perpetuate injustices, no matter how entrenched by time and custom.

3 And he entered again into the synagogue; and there was a man there which had a withered hand.

2 And they watched him, whether he would heal him on the sabbath day; that they might accuse him.

3 Again he entered the synagogue, and a man was there who had a withered hand. 2 And they watched him, to see whether he would heal him on the sab-

13. HEALING THE WITHERED HAND (3:1-6)

3:1-2. This is the second sabbath controversy. In the first the disciples were charged with breaking the sabbath; here Jesus himself is accused. **Again** does not imply a return on the same day; it is only the storyteller's device for continuity. Two of the best MSS, Sinaiticus and Vaticanus, read "a synagogue." In our idiom the meaning is only: "One sabbath, as he went to the synagogue." **They watched him,** i.e., the Pharisees of vs. 6 and of 2:24, already Jesus' fanatical opponents, laymen who were twice as eager to attack Jesus, a lay teacher of religion, as the scribes were. In the original Aramaic pericope **they** may have been as impersonal here as in 2:18, i.e., "the people." Healing on the sabbath was forbidden by the later rabbis, except in cases of dire necessity (cf. Luke 13:14, from L). This was obviously no case of necessity and could have been postponed. According to Jerome, the Gospel According to the Hebrews described the man as a mason, who depended on the use of his hands for a livelihood, and who begged Jesus to heal him lest he be compelled in shame to resort to begging. Luke adds that it was his right hand. His hand—or arm—was "dried up," i.e., **withered,** atrophied, lame, or in some way unusable. Mark is giving a popular description, not expert medical diagnosis.

3:1. *A Man Was There Who Had a Withered Hand.*—Jesus' restoration of a withered hand is a legitimate picture for the imagination. The narrative is the simply told story of the healing of a paralysis, one of a succession of conflicts with the scribes and Pharisees, grouped topically and not chronologically. Nothing more should be read into it. Yet the scene is somewhat like Jesus' parables; there is a sense in which it can be regarded as enacted truth.

How many cases of "withered hands" there have been among the followers of Jesus; how many are in his church today! The block to effective Christian action is not in men's minds. Their minds have accepted the Christian gospel; often their ideas are remarkably good. It is not as a rule in their hearts. Emotionally they approve of justice and mercy. Their hearts, as we say, are "in the right place." It is the hand that is withered, impotent to take hold of a task, by some atrophy of the nerves. God's work in the world halts because hands cannot or will not be laid on the tools.

The causes of paralysis of any sort are always obscure. We cannot fully account for the withered hands in Christian enterprise. But some factors are clear. Among them is the delusion of glowing words, the feeling which many people have that when they have talked about a thing, or approved it, they have done something. There is the cult of merely verbal Christianity. There is the fatal reluctance to expend energy. John Drinkwater has expressed with great sharpness and power this tragic gap between idea and deed:

Knowledge we ask not—knowledge Thou hast lent,
But, Lord, the will—there lies our bitter need.
Give us to build above the deep intent
    The deed, the deed. [5]

The cure for withered hands is suggested in the narrative. "Come here. . . . Stretch out your hand." It is the closer approach to Jesus, the offering of our whole being to him and his purposes, that will deatrophy the atrophied nerves of action.

2. *They Watched Him, . . . So That They Might Accuse Him.*—We can well imagine the squinting eyes of the Pharisees intent on everything Jesus did. They watched, but they did not see (see on 2:6).

That blindness to God at work in the world can always happen when some particular interest or tradition which men set above everything else is threatened. When the mind and spirit of Christ, through some who had learned of him, threatened the profits of an iniquitous slave trade, men watched him that they might accuse him of blocking the flow of income. They did not see the act of mercy of him who came to "proclaim release to the captives" (Luke 4:18). So when the spirit of Christ, acting in the lives of some devoted disciples, moved to

[5] "A Prayer." Copyright 1919 by John Drinkwater. By permission of the author's estate and Sidgwick & Jackson, Ltd., publishers of the *Collected Poems.*

3 And he saith unto the man which had the withered hand, Stand forth.

4 And he saith unto them, Is it lawful to do good on the sabbath days, or to do evil? to save life, or to kill? But they held their peace.

5 And when he had looked round about on them with anger, being grieved for the hardness of their hearts, he saith unto the

bath, so that they might accuse him. 3 And he said to the man who had the withered hand, "Come here." 4 And he said to them, "Is it lawful on the sabbath to do good or to do harm, to save life or to kill?" But they were silent. 5 And he looked around

---

4. Again Jesus enunciates a great principle, as in 2:27. It is almost as in our often misused proverb, "The better the day, the better the deed." God is the God of mercy, who delights to heal and restore his children; therefore his day (Exod. 20:10) is perfectly appropriate for the man's restoration, and Jesus proceeds to heal him. **On the sabbath days** (KJV) is too literal; read the singular, as in RSV. **To do evil . . . to kill** seems much too extreme; the phrases may look forward to vs. 6, the Pharisees' purpose to kill Jesus. The principle is clear enough—here, as often, put in question form—"It *is* lawful to do good, to save a life, therefore to heal, on the sabbath." But it is possible that Jesus meant that refusal to do good is equivalent to doing evil—and perhaps Mark so understood it. Here, as in 2:1-12, the healing is suspended momentarily in the interest of the controversy and of Jesus' pronouncement.

5. The restoration follows at once (cf. Luke 17:14b), without Jesus' usual act of touching or laying his hands upon the man, or any manual act or manipulation whatso-

---

set at liberty those who were oppressed by the cruelties following the industrial revolution, many latter-day Pharisees watched him, ready to accuse him. Hannah More cried out, "The rights of women! The next thing we hear will be the rights of children!" [6]

We have also here an instance of the evils flowing from the debating instinct in religion. Jesus could meet these legal experts on the debating level, but he always raised the larger issue, some great principle, as he did here. When the debating instinct gets the upper hand over love, religion dies. For then men care little for what happens to people, or to the world, or to the Christian gospel, as long as they get their point over.

These are dangers that threaten us all. "Let him that thinketh he standeth take heed lest he fall" (I Cor. 10:12). When some cherished interest of ours gets a priority in us over God's work of love in the world, when religion becomes a matter for debate rather than for Christlike living, we take our place among the blind Pharisees who "watched" Jesus but never really saw him.

4. *Is It Lawful on the Sabbath to Do Good or to Do Harm?*—In these words Jesus lifts the whole argument to a higher level; he discloses God's priority of mercy, of blessing to human life. It is a tremendous word. It means nothing less than that in every situation the supreme "lawfulness" is service to man's need.

[6] Mary Alden Hopkins, *Hannah More and Her Circle* (New York: Longmans, Green & Co., 1947).

The interpreter must tread carefully here. Note (Exeg.) that Jesus repeatedly repudiates the principle that human need knows no law. This is borne out in the first temptation of Jesus: "Man shall not live by bread alone" (Matt. 4:4). The N.T. is full of instances where death must be preferred to life, not for need's sake, but for truth's sake and God's.

Yet it has been the source of measureless calamity that this divine priority proclaimed by Jesus has been so often forgotten. So often the question men have put first has been, "Does this proposal fit into our ecclesiastical traditions?" (That was the Pharisees' question.) Or, "Does this fit into our entrenched economic codes and customs?" God's question is, "Does this thing do good to men?" If so, there is no other question that really counts.

How much would be added to God's work in the world if in the face of the need for a united church to battle against the evil in human life and to meet humanity's appalling lack, the question that churchmen asked were not, "Have we always done it this way?" but, "How may we help to bring God's love among men?" So in the need for freeing the world from the blight of war and the ruin of race conflict, we must learn to ask, not "What is the thing that will add to our heritage or power?" but "What is the thing that will do good?" That is the highest law—the law of love in Christ Jesus.

5. *And He Looked Around at Them with Anger.*—Anger is a strong word. But no other evidently was strong enough to express Jesus'

man, Stretch forth thine hand. And he stretched *it* out: and his hand was restored whole as the other.

6 And the Pharisees went forth, and straightway took counsel with the Herodians against him, how they might destroy him.

at them with anger, grieved at their hardness of heart, and said to the man, "Stretch out your hand." He stretched it out, and his hand was restored. 6 The Pharisees went out, and immediately held counsel with the He-ro'di-ans against him, how to destroy him.

---

ever. This has led some scholars to suspect that the man's lameness was only a symptom of a psychopathic state; once he was convinced that he *could* use his hand or arm, the restoration followed immediately. This is of course a possibility, but Mark's text affords no clue for a modern diagnosis or explanation. Jesus' **anger** reminds us of 1:43, but is better motivated here, and indeed is explained: **grieved at their hardness of heart.** This is scarcely an example of Mark's theory of the "hardening" of the Jews, or of his conception of Jesus as the supernatural judge of human sin, as some commentators maintain; on the contrary, it points to a perfectly human, normal feeling of resentment on Jesus' part at their inhumanity, bigotry, and fanaticism—though Mark, no psychologist, states it in what may seem to us a strange way.

6. This verse concludes the whole section, 2:1–3:6, and marks the end of the Galilean conflicts with the authorities (although the subject will be briefly resumed, or supplemented, in 3:20-30, perhaps from Q, at least from some source other than the "controversy source"). It may parallel the conclusion of the Jerusalem controversies in 12:34c; and,

---

feeling. This manifestation of anger has been made one of the points of criticism by some who find flaws in the character of Jesus; as, for instance, Bertrand Russell, in his *Why I Am Not a Christian*. But Jesus' anger was not so much a human failing as a human endowment. The Word became flesh and dwelt among us, clothed with human capacities; and beyond them, with the judgment as well as with the mercy of God.

Many considerations are suggested by this anger of Jesus. Two of them at least are deeply disturbing. The first is the question of what so stirred Jesus to anger. The narrative leaves no doubt about that. What angered him was the Pharisees' distortion of mind, which elevated their own self-interest and tradition above humanity, and blinded them to human values. Here, right in front of them, was a man in need. That meant nothing compared to the preservation of a rigid tradition with which they had fanatically identified their own interest. Against that Jesus blazed in anger. It is and ought to be deeply disturbing to realize that the anger of Jesus is directed against the elevation of any privilege, gain, or values, above human need. When property values, for instance, outrank human values, we may well recall the words **he looked around at them with anger.** Do we stand in danger of the anger of Jesus? We may well ask seriously, staring out at our world, whether he would not be angry when men allow an immigration quota, established in a vastly different situation, to acquire a sanctity which is reluctant to permit any change,

even in the face of millions of displaced, homeless, starving people. Or when we fall into limp acceptance of an economic way of life in which profits are sacred and people are negligible.

One other question should pierce our minds. What angers us? Do we become angry over things which affect us personally, or over injustices to people and indifference to need? Can we look unconcerned at vast human suffering or wrong, rather complacent as long as it does not touch us, only to flame with anger over slights, real or imagined, over threats to our prestige, our vanity, our comfort, our pocketbooks? There is need for "God's angry men"; but the only kind of anger that God can use in his kingdom is that of Jesus. There was a yearning heart of eternal compassion back of it.

6. *The Pharisees Went Out, and Immediately Held Counsel with the Herodians.*—This is the climax of the series of five conflicts with the scribes and Pharisees recorded in chs. 2–3 of Mark. The opposition to Jesus grew so strong, the hatred of the Pharisees so bitter, that they joined hands with the Herodians, the supporters of the Herodian family, whom ordinarily they opposed, in a declaration of war. Hatred makes strange bedfellows—the religious forces lining up against Jesus with the secular, the political, and economic power.

Two aspects of this unholy alliance should be noted. The first is that the Pharisees and Herodians, far apart in ideas and belief, nevertheless had one thing in common. They were both defenders of a *status quo.* The Pharisees were defending a religious order and privilege. The

7 But Jesus withdrew himself with his disciples to the sea: and a great multitude from Galilee followed him, and from Judea,

8 And from Jerusalem, and from Idumea, and *from* beyond Jordan; and they about Tyre and Sidon, a great multitude, when they had heard what great things he did, came unto him.

7 Jesus withdrew with his disciples to the sea, and a great multitude from Galilee followed; also from Judea 8 and Jerusalem and Id-u-me'a and from beyond the Jordan and from about Tyre and Sidon a great multitude, hearing all that he did,

---

indeed, it might be thought to belong there rather than here, as describing too decisive an action for so early a time as is presupposed in 2:1–3:6. But Mark's order is not chronological, save in a very general way (see Intro., p. 635), and what the hypothetical source contained we cannot say. **The Herodians** (cf. 12:13; 8:15 in several good MSS) were probably members of the Herodian party, satellites of the tetrarch Antipas, royalists who hoped for a restoration of the Herodian monarchy. They would be as much concerned with preserving law and order, both civil and ecclesiastical, and the religious *status quo,* as were the members of the high-priestly party (the Sadducees) in Jerusalem. **Took counsel** or **held counsel** does not mean "held a council"; the reading of B and other MSS is probably to be preferred: "They gave counsel," i.e., advised the Herodians to make away with him. The ancient guess that the Herodians were opposed to paying the Roman tribute, or that they looked upon Herod as Messiah, is simply nonsense—as Jerome remarked. **Destroy him** does not mean necessarily by legal process, but by any that might succeed (cf. 14:1; Luke 13:31). It goes beyond vs. 2, the search for an accusation.

14. Jesus' Popularity and His Cures (3:7-12)

7-8. This summary sketch of Jesus' activity is probably an editorial addition rather than a traditional pericope, but this does not mean that Mark made no use of current tradition in writing it. Jesus' withdrawal to the sea, away from the crowded towns where his enemies were common, was doubtless motivated (for Mark) by 3:6. But the **great multitude,** i.e., vast throng of people (πολὺ πλῆθος, not the usual ὄχλος), followed him. Were there two groups, the Galileans and the others? Or is it that "followed" is an insertion into the text, and the great multitude was made up of Galileans, Judeans, Idumaeans, etc.? The MSS do not give an altogether clear answer. It is likely that Mark

---

Herodians were defenders of an entrenched order of political power. Both feared Jesus as an upsetter. Their action was characteristic of the defenders of any profitable state of affairs. When men become primarily defenders of an existing order of things, they always resist the entrance of new truth and adaptation to new needs. We see that all through history. If we are primarily defenders of an existing situation, we will inevitably be found sooner or later in resistance to the mind of Jesus. Are we defending something, some ecclesiastical or economic or social order, or are we creating something, preparers of the way of the Lord in our world?

Also, this alliance is a picture of the tragedy which occurs when Christian leaders and institutions become allies of secular power against Jesus, against his insights, his spirit, his teaching. Again and again we see repeated through the centuries what happened here in Galilee. The official religious leaders were so fanatically opposed to Jesus that they made a shameful alliance with hard worldly power, which for its own reasons had no use for Jesus at all. We see it in the Inquisition, the hierarchy of the church calling in the "secular arm" to do its torture and murder. We see it whenever Christianity becomes parasitic, not standing on its own feet and proclaiming its divine challenge to evil and injustice, but existing as a mere appendage of a dominant class or an established order, putting its blessing on ways of life that are utterly unchristian. This passage is a historical record. It is also a timeless warning.

8. *Hearing All That He Did.*—This was the magnet that drew men to Jesus, the pulling power of action. A rumor of a man who went about doing good spread not only through Galilee but into **Judea and Jerusalem and . . . beyond the Jordan and . . . Tyre and Sidon.** The report of his deeds, the giving of help to all who came, was a pull on the whole region.

9 And he spake to his disciples, that a small ship should wait on him because of the multitude, lest they should throng him.

10 For he had healed many; insomuch that they pressed upon him for to touch him, as many as had plagues.

11 And unclean spirits, when they saw him, fell down before him, and cried, saying, Thou art the Son of God.

came to him. 9 And he told his disciples to have a boat ready for him because of the crowd, lest they should crush him; 10 for he had healed many, so that all who had diseases pressed upon him to touch him. 11 And whenever the unclean spirits beheld him, they fell down before him and cried out,

wrote just what we have before us: Jesus left Capernaum and the neighborhood of the lake, and withdrew to the hills (as Matt. 5:1 understands it) ; but he did not go alone, for he already had certain Galilean disciples and they, along with other followers in great numbers, accompanied him; in addition, a vast multitude from other parts of Palestine and Syria, hearing **what great things he did,** sought him out and made their way to him. Some MSS omit **and from Idumea;** but the region had been Jewish territory since the days of John Hyrcanus (Josephus *Antiquities* XIII. 9), so that no historical improbability is involved. As Klostermann notes, Samaria is conspicuously absent from this list.

9-10. The **boat** is omitted by Matthew and Luke, as is also the motive Mark adds, **lest they should crush him** (cf. 5:24). **Many** is merely factual, i.e., no limitation is being suggested; Matthew substitutes "all" (cf. on 1:32). The verse explains the "thronging": many were healed, with the result that others (**all who had diseases**) **pressed upon him to touch him,** since the populace supposed healing power to be resident in the healer (cf. 5:27-30).

11-12. It has been proposed to place a period after "touch him" in vs. 10 (see KJV), and to read the rest of the verse with what follows: "As many as had plagues and unclean spirits." This would somewhat relieve the strain upon the modern reader, who finds it impossible really to conceive of **unclean spirits** as beholding him, falling down, etc.; but the suggested punctuation destroys the distinction that Mark made between the sick persons in vs. 10 and the demons in vs. 11—vss. 11-12 may be peculiarly Mark's own contribution to the scene. Mark was a man of the ancient world, a Hellenist, and had

The *act* of help, the *deed* of blessing, is still the most powerful magnet to draw men to Christ. Every church may well ask, "Does anything happen among us or through us that is so specific and important that men, hearing about it, will come?" If not, that church has missed the way of the Master somewhere.

There have been proposals for spending large sums of money advertising the Christian religion, both in Great Britain and in the United States. These sums would be spent on powerful agencies of promotion and mass opinion, the radio, motion pictures, billboards, paid newspaper advertising, the drama, and others. There is great value in the proposals. The churches ought to use modern means of reaching the millions with their message. But going much deeper, ask the question, "How can the Christian religion be most effectively advertised?" The most powerful advertisement is always the act that is done. **Hearing all that he did, [they] came to him.** That was the first advertisement of Jesus. Christian lives and deeds were the persuasive advertisement in the first century. The most powerful pull in the world

comes from lives in which something real and tremendous has happened, lives empowered and strengthened; it comes from acts expressing the sympathy of Jesus for all who labor and are weary, heavy-laden and oppressed and defrauded; it comes from acts embodying the courage of Jesus in struggling with wrong.

9-10. *For He Had Healed Many, so That All Who Had Diseases Pressed upon Him.*— (See Exeg., vs. 10.) It is an obvious comment on this verse to say that the reason crowds pressed upon Jesus to touch him was that many had been healed. The demonstration had not been in word only, but in power. Something undebatable and big had happened. Hence the surge of the crowd. This order of cause and effect has never been changed. If there is no discernible pressure on the disciples of Jesus and his church, no crowd of any sort coming with deep wants, we may well ask: Have many, or any, been healed? Have lives been changed, has joy displaced bitterness? Has perfect love cast out fear? Has sensitive sympathy overcome calloused indifference? If that has actually happened, the sequel will follow—**many . . . pressed upon him**

12 And he straitly charged them that they should not make him known.

13 And he goeth up into a mountain, and calleth *unto him* whom he would: and they came unto him.

14 And he ordained twelve, that they should be with him, and that he might send them forth to preach,

"You are the Son of God." 12 And he strictly ordered them not to make him known.

13 And he went up into the hills, and called to him those whom he desired; and they came to him. 14 And he appointed twelve,*j* to be with him, and to be sent out

j Some ancient authorities add *whom also he named apostles.*

---

no difficulty whatever in describing the demons themselves as falling down and crying out, though any ancient popular writer would quite as readily have written "the demoniacs," without the slightest conscious change in his point of view. Mark is sure that the demons, with their supernatural clairvoyance, recognized Jesus as **Son of God.** As in 1:24-25, 34, the demons or **unclean spirits** are forbidden to make him known. Mark does not doubt the reality of their recognition, nor the truth of their testimony; but such acclamations are wholly unwelcome to Jesus. Historically viewed, Jesus' motive may have been one quite different from that which Mark assumes, viz., the messianic secret (cf. Intro., p. 644). As often elsewhere, Jesus would calm the hysterical patient and his friends or relatives, and then proceed with the cure. Moreover, the acclamations no doubt presupposed a conception of Jesus' purpose, perhaps of his office and nature, which the Master declined to approve. But such considerations are foreign to Mark; he is interested in the apologetic or evidential value of the demonic, i.e., supernatural, testimony.

15. The Appointment of the Twelve Apostles (3:13-19)

The appointment of the twelve was a subject of wide interest in the early church, as the Synoptic Gospels and the book of Acts and the appendix to John (ch. 21) make clear. It was viewed by some as the inauguration or "founding" of the church; by many scholars today it is looked upon as preparatory to Jesus' announcement of his claim to be the Messiah of all Israel, since twelve was the number of the tribes. On the other hand, twelve was a common and a convenient number of disciples—as in the founding of new houses of medieval religious orders, though here the Lord's example was decisive—and the purpose of their call as stated in vss. 14-15 is scarcely a description of the later apostolic office. The substance of the section is not a narrative; instead, it is, as in Matthew, simply a list of the twelve disciples to which Mark has given an editorial introduction, somewhat out of keeping with the accounts of the "call" of the two pairs of brothers and of Levi, already given in 1:16-20; 2:14. It is an old list, as the word "Boanerges" shows.

13. **Into the hills** is the correct reading here. How this place reference attaches to 3:7 is hard to see; perhaps Jesus was thought of first as leaving Capernaum for the shore of the lake to the south and west, then as going up into the hills west of the lake. But little weight can be given to Mark's topography (see Intro., p. 631), and these two paragraphs (vss. 7-12, 13-19), in any event, look like an insertion into the story, separating the first series of controversies and the appended one in vss. 20-30. **Called to him those whom he desired:** The scene is formal, and might well be the subject of a large painting. Jesus' method in "calling" disciples is very different elsewhere in the Gospels.

14-15. **Appointed** (RSV) is better than **ordained** (KJV). "Twelve whom also he named apostles" has strong MS support (see also 6:30); but the relative clause is probably

---

to touch him. If that has not happened, all the art and music and organizations in the world will not suffice to bring in a rising tide of people in need.

14. *And He Appointed Twelve.*—In Mark's chronology of the ministry of Jesus this was an important step. It marked the beginning of the

emphasis on the intensive training of a small group of disciples. Jesus had already called disciples, and by very different methods from this rather formal action (see Exeg.). But with the giving of the list of names, a new stage of development had been reached.

We can only speculate concerning the reasons

15 And to have power to heal sicknesses, and to cast out devils:	to preach 15 and have authority to cast

a gloss derived from the parallel in Luke. **With him,** i.e., in constant association, as disciples with a teacher. **To preach, . . . to cast out demons,** a mission obviously fulfilled in 6:7-13, 30; this is what Mark has in mind, not the later apostolic "mission" of the church. The twelve were first to be with him as intimate disciples, then later to go out as missionaries, i.e., as evangelists and exorcists.

for this calling of "those whom he desired." The action is put close after the series of conflicts in chs. 2–3, culminating with the Pharisees' joining forces with the Herodians. Did Jesus realize that his time was short? Did this call mark the beginning of a national program in Jesus' mind, even at that time? We do not know. One thing, at any rate, is clear. Jesus gave himself largely to the intensive training of a few, rather than to the general preaching to multitudes. Instances abound in the narrative: "Jesus withdrew" (3:7); "he went up into the hills" (3:13); "And when he was alone . . . he said to them" (4:10-11); "privately to his own disciples he explained everything" (4:34).

All the great movements in Christianity have been based on the training of small groups. The implication of this for the church is overwhelming. It is the charter of Christian education and of family religion. So much else will pass, often gone with the wind. Voices will be stilled. Crowds will disperse. Books will be forgotten and unread. Disciples will live. "As for tongues, they will cease; as for knowledge, it will pass away" (I Cor. 13:8). Only from the long perspective of the years does this truth gleam brightly, and events and processes can be seen in their relative magnitudes. What mortal alive at the time could have guessed that over against the momentous magnitude of this act, when Jesus went into the hills and called disciples, the glory that was Greece and the grandeur that was Rome, all the marching legions, were as dust in the balance? Who that was alive in the early years of the eighteenth century could have imagined that the most important event in Europe was not the victories of the Duke of Marlborough, but the fact that in an obscure rectory in Epworth, England, a mother, Susanna Wesley, was teaching her children to pray? Yet that is the sober judgment of history. In Isaiah we find a mathematical formula for it all: "A little one shall become a thousand" (Isa. 60:22). Freely, though not fantastically, interpreting that, we can say that one trained and dedicated disciple becomes mightier far than a thousand casual hearers.

14-15. To Be with Him, and . . . to Preach and . . . to Cast Out Demons.—Very concisely but impressively Mark here lists three things the disciples were to do. The three activities make up a timeless three-point program for a valid Christian ministry, both for ordained, full-time clergy, and for laymen. Forms of those activities have changed and will change. But the essence has remained, and will remain, the same.

14. To Be with Him.—To understand his mind, to catch his spirit, to share his trust in the Father, and his passion to seek and to save those that were lost—this is the first equipment for any effective discipleship. There were so many other things that this little group of unlearned and inexperienced men needed. One immersed in contemporary educational methods might think that a seminar on political and religious problems in the Mediterranean basin would have been called for. The disciples had to meet them a few years later. With Jesus something else came first: to be with him, to see what he saw, hear what he heard, feel what he felt. That was first, the root, the source of all else. Our danger lies in the urge to skip the first step, as though it were a long, unnecessary preface, preventing us from getting at the really important things. Our mood often is "Let's get going." The result is breathless hurry rather than staying power. The amount of good we bring depends on how much we have been with him. How much we can give depends on how freely we have received.

14. To Be Sent Out to Preach.—Notice the passive voice be sent. Christian discipleship is not man's whim, but God's commission. It has its origin in God, as every river has its ultimate origin in the sky. All disciples are sent to preach, to speak the words of life in varying ways. We do not fulfill that commission by engaging in what any company of Christ's followers can so easily and even unconsciously engage in—a conspiracy of silence. Today we need a deepened sense of the urgency of the *word,* so that we cry, "Who can be silent?" When the centennial of the birth of Alexander Graham Bell was celebrated in 1947, much was made of the fact that "he gave the world a new *voice.*" It *was* a new voice, that would carry a whisper 25,000 miles around the earth. But a new voice is not enough, for the new voice may be at the service of old motives. It may shout the command, "Destroy Moscow," or "Destroy London," or "Destroy New York."

16 And Simon he surnamed Peter; | out demons: 16 Simon whom he surnamed

---

16. The text is uncertain at this point; some MSS (followed by Goodspeed) read "and he appointed the twelve," some "he appointed first Simon"; others (followed by RSV) omit any further introduction. But many copyists apparently felt that some introduction to the list was needed; perhaps the original one survives at the beginning of vs. 14. In that case, Mark had inserted the two purpose clauses, thus leaving later copyists with the feeling that vs. 16 began too abruptly.

The world needs a new *word*. "A new commandment I give unto you, That ye love one another" (John 13:34). We are sent out to preach that word, the Word made flesh.

15. *To Cast Out Demons*.—A generation ago many would have been disposed to apologize for the important place the casting out of demons has in the Gospels. We still find occasional traces of that note of apology. But far less occasional is the recognition that we are more fully and painfully acquainted with "evil spirits" today than ever before. Our streets, our homes, as well as our mental hospitals, are full of them. To cast out demons represents an area of experience and need that cannot be neglected by the Christian disciple or the Christian church. The cry of increasing millions, though often unspoken, is "Renew a right spirit within me" (Ps. 51:10). In the gospel of Christ there is authority to heal those disorders of the spirit from which so many nervous and mental disorders come. To bring individuals into a right adjustment to God is often to bring healing to the center of life.

16-17. *Simon . . . James . . . John*.—Lists of names are supposed by many to be the ultimate low in reading interest. As a matter of fact and experience, however, nothing else rates quite so high. The newspaper editor is under no illusion about the lack of interest in lists of names. He dotes on names, lists of graduates, casualty lists, both in war and in peacetime disaster, all the various rolls of "among those present." For names represent the fascination, and often the glory, of the specific. The generality becomes flesh. Here is a list of names, the twelve disciples, in which God's high purpose is made concrete in a few people. It is distilled by a divine chemistry into the actuality of Peter, James, and John, and nine others. Recall George Macdonald's lines:

Where did you come from, baby dear?
Out of the everywhere into the here.[7]

That is always a notable journey—"out of the everywhere into the here." For when an idea is incarnated in people, then something is

afoot. Some of the most thrilling chapters of the N.T. are lists of names. Recall Rom. 16 and Col. 4. Names! But more, the exciting dramatization of the general statement, "And the Lord added to their number day by day those who were being saved" (Acts 2:47). There they are —the lifeblood of the body of Christ. No project of human betterment is worth the paper it is written on unless it concludes with the equivalent of a paragraph beginning, "Now the names of the . . . apostles are these" (Matt. 10:2). The climax of the Declaration of Independence is not in the glowing words, "We hold these truths to be self-evident," but in the names at the end of the document.

Two things emerge clearly. One is a question for every church: Does the general truth proclaimed in the pulpit find a local habitation in people? We do have the equivalent of the words "He opened his mouth and taught them saying" (Matt. 5:2). Do we have a sufficient equivalent of the enacting clause which in the ministry of Jesus followed these words, and in the life of his church should follow them. **Simon . . . James . . . John.** The other is a personal question, in the words of the old song, "Is my name written there?" Not on any "page bright and fair," not to be opened only on the Day of Judgment, but on the daily page of the here-and-now dependable disciples of Christ?

16. *Simon Whom He Surnamed Peter*.—Jesus did not do that on this occasion, of course (see Exeg.). The prominence of Peter in this list and in the gospel record may well have been influenced by his place of leadership in the early church. There has been endless controversy over the significance of the name Peter, the rock.

But there is enough in the record to indicate a real transformation of character in Peter. The new name was symbolic of a new person, no longer Simon, but Peter. He was realizing the possibilities that Jesus saw in him. So the words **whom he surnamed Peter** have a tremendous meaning as we let our imaginations run down the centuries. The words of the book of Revelation describe the great gift of Christ to individuals—"a new name" (Rev. 2:17). Christ has given a new name to millions, a name which stands for the transformation of character. Si-

---

[7] *Poems*, selected by Vida D. Scudder (New York: E. P. Dutton & Co., 1887).

17 And James the *son* of Zebedee, and John the brother of James; and he surnamed them Boanerges, which is, The sons of thunder:

18 And Andrew, and Philip, and Bartholomew, and Matthew, and Thomas, and James the *son* of Alpheus, and Thaddeus, and Simon the Canaanite,

Peter; 17 James the son of Zeb'e-dee and John the brother of James, whom he surnamed Bo-a-ner'ges, that is, sons of thunder; 18 Andrew, and Philip, and Bartholomew, and Matthew, and Thomas, and James the son of Alphaeus, and Thaddaeus,

Simon . . . Peter: Double names (Hebrew or Aramaic and Greek) were common among first-century Jews. But later Christian reflection found a deeper meaning in "Simon=Peter" (cf. Matt. 16:17-18; John 1:42), as also in other apostolic names (e.g., Saul=Paul). Peter heads the list, as the rock-disciple, so called not as a symbol of his firmness, perhaps, but as the first stone to be laid: was he not the first to see the risen Lord (I Cor. 15:5)? But it was Peter's actual place in the earliest history of the church, as in that of Jesus' band of disciples during his lifetime, not merely the fact that he was the first to see the risen Lord, that gave him this place of honor in the list.

17-18. James and John . . . and Andrew were called simultaneously with Peter (1:16-20). Moreover, for Mark, they—or at least Peter, James, and John—formed an inner nucleus of intimate disciples (cf. 5:37; 13:3). **Boanerges,** probably "Banêreges" or something similar; the word is given in various forms in the MSS. Jerome conjectured *benê-ra'am;* Dalman instead has proposed *benê-reghaz* or *-rēghesh,* sons of "thunder," or preferably of "constant noise" or "disturbance"; C. C. Torrey suggests "sons of the thunderstorm." (See Grant, *Earliest Gospel,* p. 105.) What this implied originally is unknown. Levi (2:14) does not appear in the list; hence some have supposed him identical with James (see on 2:14). **The Canaanite** cannot mean "from Cana," as Jerome supposed, but *qan'ānā,* a one-time adherent of the early Zealot (or revolutionary) party; Luke gives "the Zealot."

mon, the impetuous, becomes Peter, the rock. Saul, the persecutor, becomes Paul, the slave of Jesus Christ. Augustine, the lecherous libertine, becomes Augustine, the saint. Jerry McAuley, the drunkard, becomes Jerry McAuley, the evangelist.

17. Sons of Thunder.—This is a phrase of doubtful meaning. Its exact significance is lost in the fog of the years. Many conjectures have been made, including "sons of tumult." But there is a general agreement in accepting the translation here given (also KJV, Goodspeed). The designation fits the conduct of James and John recorded in 9:38 and Luke 9:54. "Thunder" connotes the impetuous, headlong vigor of the two. There was a place among the first disciples for thunder. There is a place always in the work of the church and kingdom of God for sons of thunder. It has been a great loss that so many disciples—particularly perhaps preachers—have assumed the title too literally. Their thunder is all noise. They find an exhilaration in mere detonation, rating far too highly, as an instrument of religion, the disturbance they make. Hearers, oppressed with the resulting concussion, have often framed a prayer similar to that in Lincoln's story of the man in the woods in a thunderstorm, "O Lord, give us a little more light, and a little less noise." But there is that other and emphatically good sense of the word "thunder." The church needs thunder, the impact of the forthright prophetic word, as Amos thundered against those who "sold . . . the poor for a pair of shoes" (Amos 2:6), and Jesus thundered against those who devoured widows' houses (12:40). There have been far too many mutes, and too many who smother God's word with a whisper.

18. Simon the Cananaean.—Many scholars do not accept the adjective matched to this Simon as meaning "one who came from Cana." Among them are Grant (see Exeg.), A. E. J. Rawlinson,[8] and B. Harvie Branscomb.[9] The word means "Zealot" (Luke 6:15). Very probably it meant that Simon was one who had belonged to the political party of "the Zealots," who advocated armed insurrection against Rome.

His inclusion among the disciples may rightly be taken as a mark of the wide range of Jesus' choice. There was room for one who had been a Zealot, a place for the employment of the zeal, the desire for action, the passionate indignation against oppression, the whole temperament which drove Simon into the Zealot, "direct

[8] *Saint Mark* (London: Methuen & Co., 1925), p. 41.
[9] *Gospel of Mark,* p. 66.

19 And Judas Iscariot, which also betrayed him: and they went into a house.

20 And the multitude cometh together again, so that they could not so much as eat bread.

21 And when his friends heard *of it,* they went out to lay hold on him: for they said, He is beside himself.

and Simon the Cananaean, 19 and Judas Iscariot, who betrayed him.

Then he went home; 20 and the crowd came together again, so that they could not even eat. 21 And when his friends heard it, they went out to seize him, for

---

19. Iscariot is hardly "man of Kerioth," nor is it "from the tribe of Issachar" (Jerome's conjecture); it probably means "sicarius" ("assassin"), a name ("sicarii") given the Zealots during the war against Rome in A.D. 66-70. The man's name was Judas, a common and, of course, an honored Jewish name at the time (=Judah); "Iscariot" was a byname, and may have arisen after his treachery in "betraying" Jesus, handing him over to his enemies.

The list of the apostles appears four times in the N.T. (Luke 6:12-16; Matt. 10:2-4; Acts 1:13-14; and here). In addition, other disciples appear in John—e.g., Nathanael—and elsewhere. That there is some uncertainty about one or two of the names is not surprising—for later history they were names and nothing more. In Jewish tradition we have a similar uncertainty in the case of the names of some of the disciples of Rabbi Akiba, the great teacher and saint who died a martyr during the war of A.D. 132-35.

16. The Charge of the Scribes (3:20-30)

20-21. These two verses are probably Mark's introduction to the controversy that follows; vs. 20 is vividly Marcan, while vs. 21 shows how the opposition to Jesus had begun to affect those nearest him. The words οἱ παρ' αὐτοῦ ("those with him") may mean "his family," though it is doubtful if Mark meant to anticipate vs. 31 in this way. **His friends** is probably the best translation. **Beside himself** describes a state of dangerous mental exaltation (II Cor. 5:13), characteristic of certain religious enthusiasts, exorcists, and miracle-workers: *"in furorem versus est"* (Vulg.).

---

action," party. Nor do we go wrong in claiming a permanent place for such zeal, tempered by the mind and spirit of the Master, among his disciples. The trouble with "zealots," of course, has been that so often they have been "one-eyed men," with a burning focus on one aim, with an impatience which leads to violence, and with a muddled preference for evil means, by which no good end can ever be established.

But there is a zeal "according to knowledge," or as RSV translates it, "enlightened" (Rom. 10:2). When we remember the high rating which Jesus put on energy, in his parables and other teaching, we can see a tremendous need for enlightened zeal. When it is absent, the church loses a driving force. Its motion turns into rest, its alertness into a sleeping sickness. An observer has given this sarcastic description of many churches as they appear to him: "A mild mannered gentleman trying to persuade a docile company of people to be still more docile." That is not an army which will win battles in "God's holy war."

19. *Judas Iscariot, Who Betrayed Him.*— There is an inexhaustible pathos in this last name on the list of twelve disciples—Judas

Iscariot. Through the centuries there has been continued speculation on why Jesus ever chose Judas as a disciple. That choice has been even regarded by some, including Charles Lamb, as an indication of a flaw in Jesus, a weakness in judging character.

No full explanation of the mystery of Judas can ever be made (see on 14:10). However, the simplest interpretation seems the truest. Judas was not foreordained to betray Jesus. When he was called, he had potentialities and evidently a sincere devotion. He took by his own choice the dark road which led to betrayal. It is a solemn thought that one can fall away from high purposes and devotion. Solemn words echo on our ears, "Let him that thinketh he standeth take heed lest he fall" (I Cor. 10:12).

21. *He Is Beside Himself.*—The coming of some friends of Jesus to take him away was an act prompted by kindness and love. Their action was evidently based on a rumor that Jesus was mad. B. H. Streeter writes, "It is more likely that our Lord's relatives should have come to apprehend Him, because they heard a report that He was beside Himself, than that they should have arrived at such a conclusion for

22 ¶ And the scribes which came down | they said, "He is beside himself." 22 And
from Jerusalem said, He hath Beelzebub, | the scribes who came down from Jerusa-
and by the prince of the devils casteth he | lem said, "He is possessed by Be-el'ze-bul,
out devils. | and by the prince of demons he casts out

The controversy proper, very different in tone and outlook from those that precede it, is found in vss. 22-26. To this have been added, either by Mark or already in the Q collection of Jesus' sayings, the two sayings that follow in vs. 27 and in vss. 28-29. Their relevance at this point is undeniable. In Q the controversy was introduced by an actual exorcism (Matt. 12:22; Luke 11:14). Mark's introduction has obliterated this, with the resulting contrast between the humane concern of Jesus' friends and the bitter charge of the Jerusalem scribes (the Western text misunderstands οἱ παρ' αὐτοῦ and draws a contrast between the local "scribes and others" and those from Jerusalem). In the original pericope (Q; see Matt. 12:23) the words of the scribes are intended to neutralize the effect of Jesus' exorcism upon the enthusiastic populace.

22. Beelzebub, better **Beelzebul** (א C D Θ, etc.). This was originally a divine title, as in the Ras Shamra tablets, and meant "Lord of the Mansion." (Is the "mansion" the earth? the air? the world? Note the play on the word in Matt. 10:25b.) In time this primitive baal degenerated into a powerful demon, like other pagan gods surviving in Jewish folklore. (Cf. W. F. Albright, "The North-Canaanite Epic of 'Al'êyân Báal and Môt," *Journal of the Palestine Oriental Society,* XII [1932], 191 ff. and 200 ff.) Here he is **the prince of the devils,** i.e., "ruler of the demons," and is therefore identified with Satan (vs. 23). The charge thus meant that Jesus was by no means exercising the power of God, or power conferred by God, or by the Holy Spirit (vs. 29; cf. Matt. 12:28), but was himself **possessed by Beelzebul,** and wrought his exorcisms through collusion with this archfiend. The theory was plausible enough for ancient popular thought. Like Faust, a worker of miracles might be in league with the devil. A powerful demon could "cast out" another and less powerful one; while the whole dark realm of the evil one was sometimes thought of as an organized kingdom or household (vss. 24-25), much as in C. S. Lewis' *Screwtape Letters* (New York: The Macmillan Co., 1943). The half-hidden innuendo was that sooner or later the wonder worker (here, Jesus) would pay the price of his power, and be carried off by the demons with whom he was allied.

---

themselves."[1] His friends felt that he was in danger and wished to save him.

The verdict that Jesus was "mad," "beside himself," however it got started among the crowd, has an arresting quality about it, particularly when it is considered in connection with his life and death, and with the attitudes taken toward him and his teaching throughout history. The verdict, "a madman," has echoed down the centuries and reverberates loudly over our world today. He was in the beginning judged by some to be mad because his words and acts did not echo the accepted teaching of authority. That still goes on. Those who first heard Jesus exclaimed with wonder, "What is this? A new teaching?" (1:27). And to many today, as always, a new idea is madness. The scornful charge of madness has continually been brought against Jesus' ethic of love, both as end and means. Nobody but a fool, we are endlessly told, would think of anything else in

[1] *The Four Gospels* (New York: The Macmillan Co., 1925), p. 189.

a difficult situation but "getting tough," and using force, and carrying a big club. When the teaching of Jesus challenges the orthodox religion of the sanctity of profits over human welfare, the old cry sounds with bitterness and fury, **"He is beside himself."** When Jesus' teaching of the one family of one Father threatens the tyranny of cruel codes of race prejudice and exploitation, he is accounted daft, unfit to be taken seriously in a realistic world.

Living as we do, in an atmosphere of so much skepticism about the validity of Jesus' teaching, if not of blatant denial, we need a new and overwhelming conviction of his sanity. We need downright belief that so far from being mad, he is the way, the truth, and the life, and that no other foundation for an enduring and endurable world can be laid than that which is laid in Christ Jesus. The evidence for this truth grows by geometrical progression in our world. We are all familiar with the oft-quoted comment on World War I: "The only man who came out of it with an enhanced

23 And he called them *unto him,* and said unto them in parables, How can Satan cast out Satan?

24 And if a kingdom be divided against itself, that kingdom cannot stand.

25 And if a house be divided against itself, that house cannot stand.

the demons." 23 And he called them to him, and said to them in parables, "How can Satan cast out Satan? 24 If a kingdom is divided against itself, that kingdom cannot stand. 25 And if a house is divided against itself, that house will not be able to stand.

23-26. Jesus' reply is a clear logical refutation of this absurd theory. Satan could hardly be at war with himself. The telling conclusion (vs. 26) at least suggests that the assumption of civil discord in Satan's realm, even if true, would argue only the end of Satan's power. Jesus' whole message of the coming kingdom of God implies—and involves—the *end* of Satan's reign. It is curious that Mark describes Jesus' defense as **in parables**; this shows the looseness and vagueness of the term as Mark understands it: any analogy was a "parable." Here, Satan's kingdom is like any realm **divided against itself** by civil war, and so on its way to destruction. Very striking is the fact that Jesus does not trouble to defend himself or his work; his concern is the purpose underlying all his exorcisms, the total destruction of the power of the enemy. And that power is obviously, and even upon the testimony of his opponents, already dissolving before their eyes. Why Mark omitted the other arguments in the Q passage (Matt. 12:27, 28, 30 and parallels in Luke) we do not know. As a rule he gives comparatively little of Jesus' teaching; and the other sayings on this occasion may have seemed to him adequately represented in the one he retains in vs. 27.

---

reputation was Jesus Christ." It was far more deeply true of World War II.

One disturbing question comes to each of us: Has anyone ever called us "mad"? If not, we may wonder whether we have really counted, whether we have cut sharply and deeply enough to make any lasting impression, whether we deserve to be reckoned among the followers of him of whom men said, **"He is beside himself."** "He is mad" has always been an ultimate tribute in Christian history to those who served, not two masters, but One. Paul won that distinguished service decoration. Festus cried, "Paul, you are mad" (Acts 26:24) . Francis of Assisi was "mad." William Carey was "mad." In one of his early stories Sinclair Lewis writes of a man who had a project for organizing a "Society for the Promotion of Madness Among the Respectable Classes." Fantastic? Yes. But after all, not a bad name for the Christian church.

23. *How Can Satan Cast Out Satan?* —See Exeg. for comment on the penetrating and devastating argument of Jesus against the charge of the scribes that he was casting out demons by the power of demons. He turned their charge into a beautiful boomerang which curved neatly and landed back on them with deadly force. On their own terms he makes it clear that a civil war among evil spirits, which they insisted was the explanation of his cures, would demonstrate that Satan's kingdom was being destroyed. That it was being destroyed was a vital part of Jesus' proclamation of the kingdom of God.

But the incisive question, **How can Satan cast out Satan?** is one that runs far beyond the limits of this particular controversy or any specific situation. It is timeless and universal in its application. How can Satan be overcome by the use of Satan's methods and power? How can we accomplish good ends by evil means? The world has often given a ready answer, "Easy!" But the whole course of history has supported Jesus' affirmation that it cannot be done. Yet it has been a firm article of the world's faith, a seemingly unshakable faith, that good results can come of evil methods. That is the faith which instead of moving mountains prevents mountains of evil from moving. Men have believed that they could cast out cruelty by more cruelty, violence by more violence, war by more war. The illusion that Satan can cast out Satan extends into all realms of life: that truth can be established by lies, that liberty can be advanced by repression, that temperance can be promoted by drinking, that democracy can be enhanced by arbitrary measures, that religion can be served by compulsion. Evil will always produce evil. Good ends cannot be achieved by evil means, for the means have a subtle but inevitable way of becoming the ends (see on 14:43) .

25. *If a House Is Divided Against Itself, That House Will Not Be Able to Stand.* —Undoubtedly a great many Americans, if asked who is the author of these words, would reply "Abraham Lincoln." In his famous "House Divided" speech in the debates with Douglas, in 1856, Lincoln made such effective use of these words

26 And if Satan rise up against himself, and be divided, he cannot stand, but hath an end.

27 No man can enter into a strong man's house, and spoil his goods, except he will first bind the strong man; and then he will spoil his house.

28 Verily I say unto you, All sins shall be forgiven unto the sons of men, and blasphemies wherewith soever they shall blaspheme:

26 And if Satan has risen up against himself and is divided, he cannot stand, but is coming to an end. 27 But no one can enter a strong man's house and plunder his goods, unless he first binds the strong man; then indeed he may plunder his house.

28 "Truly, I say to you, all sins will be forgiven the sons of men, and whatever

---

27. The binding of **the strong man** (Satan) **is** a figure for the work of exorcism (often described as "binding" the demon), and for the downfall of the realm of evil—as in I Enoch; Rev. 20:2; Test. Levi. 18; etc. **His goods** means the demons, subordinate to Satan their chief, not just the bodies of men which they occupy or "possess." Mark's point is that Jesus is stronger than **the strong man,** the Son of God who has come "to destroy the works of the devil." But in the original saying of Jesus the point was that the robber's stronghold has been invaded and his **goods** are being ravaged; therefore, it must be evident, **the strong man** has already been bound. But this can scarcely be a reference, as some have argued, to the temptation experience, about which the scribes cannot have known.

28-30. This final section is found in another connection in Luke 12:10, as is also the following section in Matt. 12:33-37. Presumably, then, the Q material underlying Mark ends with vs. 27. If vss. 28-29 are from Q, they were not located here. But it looks as if the parallels in Matt. 12:32 and Luke 12:10 represent a more advanced development than Mark: instead of **sins . . . forgiven . . . the sons of men, and blasphemies,** we read of "a word spoken against the Son of man," which is presumably a later and more specific application of the principle. The structure of the saying here is somewhat difficult to make out, but the sense is clear: every sin and blasphemy will be forgiven except blasphemy against the Holy Spirit; this cannot be forgiven, because, some theologians say, the blasphemer is incapable of repentance. The one who so blasphemes, attributing the work of God's Spirit to Satan, or to human self-interest, **is guilty of an eternal sin** (not KJV, **in danger of eternal damnation);** vs. 30 then explains the relevance of the saying. The passage is one that has given rise to endless speculation regarding "the unforgivable sin," speculation sometimes reflected in the text (many MSS omit εἰς τὸν αἰῶνα, "forever," in vs. 29), sometimes in the translation, as in KJV, above. It is safe to say, theologically, that certainly very few persons have ever been guilty of this "unforgivable" sin. Few have ever said with Milton's Satan, "Evil, be thou my good." At the same time, the danger

---

of Jesus, as describing the impossibility of having the United States endure half slave and half free, that his name has become almost inextricably tied to them. It was a legitimate and powerful use of a sentence of Jesus. It was also a fine example of the way in which the words of Jesus have been plowed into the life of mankind.

Jesus, as is pointed out in the Exeg. of this whole section, vss. 22-27, made clear that on the scribes' own contention the house of Satan could not stand because it was divided. This truth reaches out in all directions in life, like a drop of ink on a blotter. In the life of an individual it joins itself to Jesus' insistence on undivided loyalty in the disciple. "No man can serve two

masters" (Matt. 6:24). The assertion of the necessity of unified personality, as making for stability, for mental and spiritual wholeness, was an insight which mental hygiene, after many centuries, has strongly underlined and amplified. The divided will, diverse desires, what James called, eighteen centuries before Freud, the "war in your members" (Jas. 4:1) breaks down personality. The psychic house, the mental habitation, totters when split. That truth lay at the center of the dim mystery of Judas, and of all dark betrayers. The positive side of the truth, the power and joy of a mind and spirit freed from civil war, is expressed frequently in old hymns, many of them written by men who never heard the word "psychology,"

29 But he that shall blaspheme against the Holy Ghost hath never forgiveness, but is in danger of eternal damnation:

30 Because they said, He hath an unclean spirit.

blasphemies they utter; 29 but whoever blasphemes against the Holy Spirit never has forgiveness, but is guilty of an eternal sin" — 30 for they had said, "He has an unclean spirit."

---

of it is constant—the attribution of divine works of mercy and restoration to human personal ambition, to mercenary or political aims, to lust for power, or to collusion with the powers of darkness. To Mark the accusation brought against Jesus by the scribes no doubt implied their guilt, as it also implied that of others who repeated the slander. To say that Mark understood it to involve the whole Jewish people is going beyond the evidence. It may be suspected that the saying, in its present form, has been modified—i.e., sharpened—in tradition; it may indeed be a controversial elaboration of the Q saying in Matt. 12:28 and Luke 11:20, which Mark omits. Clearly Mark is at pains, in vs. 30, to connect the saying with the preceding controversy, though **an unclean spirit** is somewhat weak as a reference to Beelzebul, the powerful ruler of the demons. Both parallels omit the verse, and it has been thought to be a later gloss.

---

but embodying, nevertheless, profound psychological truth. One such hymn is,

> O happy day, that fixed my choice
> On thee, my Savior and my God!

It is the fixed choice that heals or prevents the split personality, the divided house of the mind and soul.

Lincoln rightly applied this truth to national life. It is always applicable. Take but one aspect of the nation's life, the race question. The house of democracy cannot stand if divided between a profession of equal opportunity, and the denial of rights to large minority groups. Every day we can see more clearly that a divided house in the international world cannot stand. Must we not also see, far more clearly than we ever have, that a divided church, split into fragments, cannot stand, cannot be the force it should be against the world's evil?

29. Whoever Blasphemes Against the Holy Spirit Never Has Forgiveness, but Is Guilty of an Eternal Sin.—With all reverence, a list of the sayings of Jesus could be assembled under the startling heading, "Things I wish Jesus had never said." That may sound blasphemous, but it is not. Such a list would include sayings that have been so continuously and badly distorted, so warped from their original meaning and context, that the misunderstanding of them has caused great distress and evil. High on such a list would be the saying "Ye have the poor with you always" (14:7). This has been maliciously elevated into a whole system of economics; it has been made into a powerful block against the reduction of poverty. Equally mangled in meaning has been the word "Let him who has no sword sell his mantle and buy one" (Luke 22:36). Ripped out of its context, it has

been pressed into a divine blessing on war. Likewise this word on the "unforgivable sin" has had strange fascination and terror for many minds. The distorting of it has filled insane asylums with minds broken down by a guilt complex. Menzies shrewdly comments, "The words . . . are uttered by one in a state of intense indignation. May we say that Jesus himself might not have repeated them at a calmer moment?" [2] Yet the context makes the meaning clear and simple. The sin for which there was no forgiveness was just what the scribes were doing when Jesus spoke the words—calling good evil.

One reason why it was unforgivable was not theological but psychological. It was evidence of a moral obtuseness and perverseness so deep-rooted that there was no hope of its ever being changed. Calling good evil ranges all the way from ascribing good actions to evil motives, to the supreme example cited in the Exeg.—the words of Milton's Satan, "Evil, be thou my good." We are peculiarly exposed to this sin whenever we become primarily the defenders of some advantage. Then we are tempted to justify ourselves by casting opprobrium on anything, no matter how good, which threatens that cherished advantage. Hence the common moral blindness which frequently accompanies property-mindedness. When respectable church people denounced as evil and opposed the efforts made in the first ravages of the industrial revolution in England to protect women and little children from death-dealing labor in mine and factory—that was the sin against the Holy Ghost. When in our own time people oppose, and denounce as evil, efforts to extend justice and mercy to unprivileged and defrauded groups—that is the sin against the Holy Ghost.

[2] *Earliest Gospel*, p. 102.

31 ¶ There came then his brethren and his mother, and, standing without, sent unto him, calling him. 32 And the multitude sat about him, and they said unto him, Behold, thy mother and thy brethren without seek for thee. 33 And he answered them, saying, Who is my mother, or my brethren? 34 And he looked round about on them which sat about him, and said, Behold my mother and my brethren! 35 For whosoever shall do the will of God, the same is my brother, and my sister, and mother.	31 And his mother and his brothers came; and standing outside they sent to him and called him. 32 And a crowd was sitting about him; and they said to him, "Your mother and your brothers[l] are outside, asking for you." 33 And he replied, "Who are my mother and my brothers?" 34 And looking around on those who sat about him, he said, "Here are my mother and my brothers! 35 Whoever does the will of God is my brother, and sister, and mother." [l] Some early authorities add *and your sisters.*

17. Jesus' True Family (3:31-35)

31-35. Many modern commentators and homilists have identified the **brothers** and **mother** of Jesus with the friends of vs. 21, and have thus supplied a specific motivation for their visit: they came to rescue Jesus from the consequences of his popularity and success, as well as from the hands of his enemies. This is possible, but not certain. The ζητοῦσιν (seek in KJV) in vs. 32 may mean here just what it does in 1:37.

The point of the anecdote for Mark is clearly the pronouncement in vs. 35: Jesus set obedient response to **the will of God**, presumably as proclaimed in his teaching, far above all earthly relationships, even the most intimate and precious (cf. 10:29-30). What this meant for the early church, including Mark's readers, can easily be imagined. In place of broken family relationships, ostracism, and persecution, was the close and intimate relation to the Son of God, who had himself preferred such a relation to close contacts with his earthly family. The saying was a difficult one for patristic commentators to expound; and it must have been hard for any Jew to receive, for whom the command "Honor thy father and thy mother" was part of the Decalogue. But for that very reason its originality and authenticity, as a saying of Jesus, seem beyond question.

When in the beginning of the modern missionary movement people denounced as evil the outreach of God's love to all the races of the earth—that was the sin against the Holy Ghost. So there is, after all, a real danger that we may be infected by this sin, a danger against which all should watch and pray. For the worst sin is not murder or arson, but a distortion of the whole spiritual being, by which we are blinded to good and call it evil, and thus cut ourselves off from God and God's cause.

31-35. *Whoever Does the Will of God Is My Brother, and Sister, and Mother.*—These five verses, narrating the coming of Jesus' family to interrupt his work and take him home, and his rejection of that interruption for the sake of the larger family of God, are endlessly suggestive. They picture a tension in Jesus' life between the familiar group and the wider relationship, between the first physical and spiritual circle and the broader circle of all them that hear and do the will of his father. It pictures a tension which should be in every life.

These were not the light words of a man indifferent to family relationships. The Gospels give evidence that Jesus was deeply devoted to his family. History since his day gives abundant evidence that his personality and teaching, his valuation of women and children, have done more for the family as an institution than all other influences. Yet here the supreme claim of the will of God transcends the restraining claims of the family. This is frequently cited as an instance of the harshness of Jesus. Perhaps we should cherish such narratives as a needed correlative to common conceptions of Jesus which have an excess of sugar, in which the real person is overlaid with a false sentimentalism.

Again and again in most lives the natural possessiveness of family ties comes into tension, not only with one's possibilities of maturity and independent development, but also with one's service to the world. Family love so often tends persistently to build imprisoning walls, to put blinders on the eyes of the children and young people in the home. The word which came to Jesus' ears, in the midst of his work for

4 And he began again to teach by the sea side: and there was gathered unto him a great multitude, so that he entered into a ship, and sat in the sea; and the whole multitude was by the sea on the land.

2 And he taught them many things by parables, and said unto them in his doctrine,

3 Hearken; Behold, there went out a sower to sow:

4 Again he began to teach beside the sea. And a very large crowd gathered about him, so that he got into a boat and sat in it on the sea; and the whole crowd was beside the sea on the land. 2 And he taught them many things in parables, and in his teaching he said to them: 3 "Listen!

18. The Parable of the Sower (4:1-9)

This is the "chapter of parables," though, as Mark recognizes (vss. 2, 33-34), the parables given here are only a selection. In two cases (vss. 26, 30) the subject of the parable is given as the kingdom of God, but this is only a general classification. Those two parables deal with the spread or extension—or "coming"—of the kingdom; the others (the sower and the lamp) with the proper response to the gospel. It is only in a very general way that the subject of the chapter can be made out; it is not organized about one specific theme, like the themes, say, of the Sermon on the Mount in Matt. 5–7. As noted in the Intro. (p. 636), Mark is probably using an earlier, possibly written, collection of Jesus' parables.

4:1-2. The picturesque setting, characteristically disregarded by Mark in vs. 10, prepares for the privacy in vs. 36. The "other boats" (vs. 36) were probably thought of as present from the start. **Many things:** Mark does not specify what "things," for it is not part of his purpose to give an account of Jesus' **teaching.** This he perhaps presupposes as already familiar to his readers—or possibly he is so greatly concerned with Jesus' mighty deeds, and with the heroic ethics of discipleship, that he neglects other elements in Jesus' teaching.

3-9. The parable does not state in so many words the point of the comparison; hence the admonition at the end (vs. 9), appealing to the hearers to exercise their understanding (D O.L. add: "And he who understands, let him understand"). The figure of a sower scattering seed was frequently used in the ancient world for the teacher (Plato *Laws* VI. 777E; II Esdras 9:31, 33)—and quite naturally, since some hearers, or students,

God and man, **Your mother and your brothers are outside, asking for you,** has fallen on the ears of millions, as they have contemplated or engaged in a life of larger demands and relationships. Thousands who have gone to overseas mission fields have had to face a conflict like that which Jesus faces here. Others who have felt the call of a task, like the call which came to Abraham, "Get thee out" (Gen. 12:1), have had to engage in one of life's hardest battles, not that against hate but that against love. It is a battle against the mistaken enclosures which sometimes make family barricades a hazard to a life's service. True family affection should be an incentive and support of service in the larger realm, and not a substitute for it. A family should be a harbor from which the ship leaves to sail the seas, and not a dock where it ties up and rots. Jesus' action and words picture God's compelling priorities—the wider family, the fellowship of the doers of his will. The great

values of home, of love, and of community must be carried out into the larger, complete circle.

4:3. *A Sower Went Out to Sow.*—Three general considerations concerning the parable of the sower may be glanced at. The first is the autobiographical element that may very possibly be in the story. An exact chronology of Jesus' life and teaching cannot be fitted down over Mark's narrative. Some scholars feel that this parable, so far as being a reflection of Jesus' own experience is concerned, should be placed at a later time. But it is clear that Jesus had been doing much teaching and preaching. This picture of the four different kinds of soil does fit rather exactly into his own experience of the various kinds of response in hearers. He knew the stony soil of the minds of the scribes and Pharisees; he had met the shallow and unstable enthusiasm of the crowd. So leaving aside the question of how much Jesus intended this parable to reflect his own experience, it actually

4 And it came to pass, as he sowed, some fell by the wayside, and the fowls of the air came and devoured it up.	A sower went out to sow. 4 And as he sowed, some seed fell along the path, and

received the seed and brought forth a harvest, while upon others it fell without effect. The parable is accordingly not primarily a parable of the sower, nor yet of different kinds of seed, for the sower and the seed are the same, but rather of different kinds of ground; and its purpose is to show how various hearers respond to the message of the gospel—in the first instance to Jesus' own message. It may be thought to belong to a late period of his ministry, and to reflect a somewhat disillusioning experience: only the fourth kind of

does so. One point to note is that with all this realistic understanding of the various responses or lack of response, with all this looking squarely at the worst that can happen to the seed which is the word, Jesus went on teaching. The parable is not pessimistic (see Exeg.) . The yield of the good soil, no matter in what proportion to the seed lost on unreceptive hearers, abundantly warrants the sower's faith and venture. Jesus went on teaching to the end.

It is a true picture of every teacher's experience, whether the teaching is done in pulpit, classroom, or in the contacts of daily life, that most effective form of teaching for every Christian disciple. There are different kinds of soil; much seed will not come to fruit. But what does find lodgment in responsive minds, even at a yield of only thirtyfold, completely justifies a long life of sowing. With its admonitory fortification against the unrealistic expectation that all seeds will bring forth fruit, the parable yet heartens us onward. It says, "Go labor on! spend and be spent"; "Your labor is not in vain in the Lord" (I Cor. 15:58) .

The second consideration is implied in the first. The main thing is the sowing. Keep doing it. One of the most impressive artistic representations of that encouragement is found in the bronze tablet placed in St. Paul's Cathedral in London, in memory of Canon Samuel A. Barnet, who worked in East London for so many years. On the tablet is carved a figure of a sower, walking down the furrows of a field, scattering his seed freely. Underneath the figure are carved the words "Fear not to sow on account of the birds." There were plenty of "birds" in the slums of East London. But through the years Canon Barnet went forth to sow, and some seed fell on good soil.

This is one of the deeply sustaining truths of human life. The most important fact of any day in history, even of the blackest day that ever sent all hope into what seemed to be complete eclipse, has been that somewhere a sower went out to sow. It was true in the days of the persecution of Christianity under Rome; it was true in the fall of the Roman Empire; it was true in the days when the abolition of slavery

and the slave trade seemed only a wild dream. It is always true.

The third general consideration is that this is also a parable on hearing. It is worth noting that Jesus never gave any lessons on how to speak. What lessons he might have given! "Never man spake like this man" (John 7:46) . "The common people heard him gladly" (12: 37) . Of course no lessons could have matched in power his own example. Yet he did say much about *how to hear*. That was basic to everything else. A first responsibility of everyone is the stewardship of the ear.

4. *Some Seed Fell Along the Path, and the Birds Came and Devoured It.*—It is a sound principle of exposition that each parable of Jesus has one main point or meaning. If that had been recognized in the course of N.T. interpretation, many disastrous detours into the barren deserts of fanciful allegory would have been avoided. The central meaning would not have been smothered by the details. In the parable of the sower the details illustrate and emphasize the main point—the responsibility of hearing. The four kinds of soil are pictures of universal experience, and portray chief obstacles to the religious life.

The seed on the path did not get into the ground at all. The path was tramped solid and smooth, offering no more chance for a seed to grow than a stone pavement. So the word lies on the surface of some minds and is soon snatched away. So many forces are active in tramping down the mind that it loses its receptive quality, offering no crevice to new truth. A mechanical routine can beat down the mind into a hard pavement. The atrophy of curiosity can do it, when the mind is no longer plowed and made receptive by wonder. A crust of self-satisfaction which feels no need of any word of truth will do it very effectively. A steady succession of trivial matters, as a sole concern of the mind, will beat the spirit down into a hard sidewalk. All these are among the greatest of life's liabilities.

The truth is also lost, devoured, before it penetrates, when it is not related to action. No truth can live in the intellect which does not

5 And some fell on stony ground, where it had not much earth; and immediately it sprang up, because it had no depth of earth:

6 But when the sun was up, it was scorched; and because it had no root, it withered away.

7 And some fell among thorns, and the thorns grew up, and choked it, and it yielded no fruit.

the birds came and devoured it. 5 Other seed fell on rocky ground, where it had not much soil, and immediately it sprang up, since it had no depth of soil; 6 and when the sun rose it was scorched, and since it had no root it withered away.

7 Other seed fell among thorns and the thorns grew up and choked it, and it

---

soil is receptive and productive. But the truth is that all sowing involves some loss, and it is no mere 25 per cent of the seed that bears fruit—the parable is by no means pessimistic in tone. The **good ground** is presumably most of the field. The implication of the

---

renew itself in experience. That is why Christian belief is so often "snatched away." It is not consciously renounced in any solemn act of disavowal. It simply does not get down to the mechanisms which turn the wheels of daily life, and does not really become an operating force in life. It is kept on the surface, and inevitably vanishes. For whatever is kept on the surface of life is always snatched away.

5. *Other Seed Fell on Rocky Ground.*—The ground was rocky, not because it was full of stones, but because there was a layer of rock underneath. The soil was thin, and offered no depth that roots might be put down. The stalk of grain sprang upward, but because it was unable to develop downward, because it had no invisible means of support, it withered under the sun. So clear a picture of the thin life needs no labored application. It is particularly arresting for every "rootless generation." The word "root" in various forms is common enough in all times of world-wide distress. It is always related closely to the world's sickness. One of the major problems after World War II was that of "uprooted persons"—in Europe and Asia, millions of displaced people, exiles, wanderers, hungry, homeless, uprooted from their natural setting. There are other kinds of uprooted persons, however, not displaced physically, but in whom life is withered because it has no deep sustaining roots. There is even a physical aspect to much of that rootlessness with millions of people. They have flocked from farms and small towns to cities. Multitudes have been part of the great modern "treks" making for the industrial centers. Their lives have been cut off from the accustomed sources of nourishment, from familiar homes, where they had status, from church and the social group. Rocky ground!

"Thin, surface soil" is the verdict on every life that has no sustaining depth. Even an interest in religion may leave such a life thin if no roots go down into personal experience. The only effectual cure of the malady is pictured in

the great phrase of Paul, "Rooted and built up in him and established in the faith" (Col. 2:7). No one can be cut off from the Christian community and its fellowship in effort without withering.

Here too is the verdict on every life that springs up quickly, with premature enthusiasm, aglow with the titillating excitement of fresh beginnings, only to wilt under the sun, because it has no staying power. The church has suffered greatly from this kind of a "manic-depressive" cycle in so many of its adherents. Indeed many Christians are described by the parody of "The Village Blacksmith."

> Toiling, rejoicing, sorrowing,
> So I my life conduct.
> Each morning sees some task begun;
> Each evening sees it chucked.

Such bubbling, evanescent enthusiasm is a far different thing from the deep-rooted joy described in another parable of Jesus, that of the hidden treasure. A man finds a treasure hidden in a field. "Then in his joy he goes and sells all that he has and buys that field" (Matt. 13:44). That kind of joy is a staying power, for into it have gone long-range purpose and sacrifice. Against this premature joy, which has never taken a clear look at the task, or equipped itself with the resources needed, Jesus warned again and again (Luke 9:23-26; 14:28-31). We can all unite in the poet's prayer—"Lord, stabilize me."

7. *Other Seed Fell Among Thorns.*—Wycliffe had a word for it—"strangled." This verse gives a sharp warning picture of the strangled life. The roots were still in the soil, but so many weeds were allowed to flourish that the growth of the blade of grain was choked. The strangled life is one in which there is no great priority. Everything is of the same size and importance. There is sharp point in the alarm of a schoolboy who, in reading a list of the chief causes of death, discovered a new fatal disease unknown to him. When asked what it was, he spelled out the word "miscellaneous." It *is* a terrible dis-

| 8 And other fell on good ground, and did yield fruit that sprang up and increased, and brought forth, some thirty, and some sixty, and some a hundred.

9 And he said unto them, He that hath ears to hear, let him hear. | yielded no grain. 8 And other seeds fell into good soil and brought forth grain, growing up and increasing and yielding thirtyfold and sixtyfold and a hundred-fold." 9 And he said, "He who has ears to hear, let him hear." |

parable as a whole, strongly suggested at the close by vs. 9, is that men could *choose* to hear and respond. The Gnostics, as Hippolytus noted (*Philosophoumena* V. 8. 29), held that only the perfectly illuminated—i.e., themselves—could truly "hear"; but this was surely a perversion of Jesus' meaning. However, it is not certain that Mark (see the verses that follow) did not have some such idea: to some the "mystery" was "given"; from others it was withheld. The experience of Christian evangelism showed, then as now, that some hearers are—as the Salvation Army has described them—"gospel-proof." Like the parable of the two houses, at the conclusion of the Sermon on the Mount (Matt. 7:24-27), this parable was doubtless intended to be an admonition to responsive hearing, and was not a mere reflection on the experience of the teacher. But it could be interpreted as Mark has explained it, as we shall see.

---

ease! Millions have died from "miscellaneous." The life of the spirit sickens when it is buried under a landslide of miscellaneous things. An eager young woman, deeply stirred by Arnold Bennett's book *How to Live on Twenty-four Hours a Day*, said, "I am going to concentrate." "On what?" asked Bennett. "Oh," she answered, "on lots of things." When we concentrate on lots of things, we concentrate on nothing. Life needs a saving priority—"Seek ye first the kingdom of God" (Matt. 6:33).

If this danger of the overcrowded life was great in agricultural Palestine in the first century A.D., how much more acute and aggravated it is in a twentieth-century industrial civilization! There are so many more things to choke the word. Life in many places today seems like a deliberate rush at every one of the five senses, sight, hearing, touch, smell, taste. Going through life comes to be like parading before an endless succession of brightly lighted store windows filled with merchandise. Advertisements scream at us from the newspaper and magazine, from the billboard, and even from the sky. We live in a bath of noise from the radio, punctuated by the preaching of the gospel of salvation by buying. No wonder the soul is threatened with being flattened out under an avalanche of gadgets.

We cannot turn the wheels of life backward and eliminate man's mechanical achievements; but we can do much to simplify living, to free it from the domination of things, so that we may be their masters and not their servants. The life of the spirit can become a thing-full emptiness. The more aids to living there are, the less life there is liable to be, in its fullest and deepest sense. There is a "sales resistance" which is a means of the preservation of the soul. The only

true remedy for the strangled life is an old remedy—watch and pray. Make room for the word to grow in the heart and mind that it may bear fruit.

8. Other Seeds Fell into Good Soil.—Expositions of the parable of the sower have given more attention to the hazards than to anything else. The birds that snatch the seed from the hard path, the barren rock, the choking thorns —all these have stolen the spotlight from the fruitful soil. There are many natural reasons for it. One is that this proportion is found in the story. There are three kinds of poor soil, and only one variety of good. The suggestive details of the dangers to the seed call for comment. Jesus' purpose appears to have been primarily that of warning against the habits which make void the hearing of the word. Whatever the reasons, however, the fact that the greater bulk of attention was actually given to the negative aspects of seed sowing should not be allowed to obscure the positive climax, that good soil produces abundant fruit. That was the conclusion on which Jesus acted. In spite of every hazard, which his clear eye saw with unclouded sharpness, and which he never underestimated, he went on sowing, teaching, preaching the word of the kingdom. Indeed, it is not too much to say that the main points of the parable are the responsibility of hearing and the sure yield of the good soil. The latter is a divine heartening to everyone who goes out to sow good seed, whose words and actions and life bring God's truth to the minds of men. It fortifies the faith that in due season they shall reap if they faint not. There is a good soil which bears fruit. It is a shield against despair.

The adequate comment on the receptive ear and mind is that ascribed to Jesus himself in the

10 And when he was alone, they that were about him with the twelve asked of him the parable. 11 And he said unto them, Unto you it is given to know the mystery of the kingdom of God: but unto them that are without, all *these* things are done in parables: 12 That seeing they may see, and not perceive; and hearing they may hear, and not understand; lest at any time they should be converted, and *their* sins should be forgiven them.	10 And when he was alone, those who were about him with the twelve asked him concerning the parables. 11 And he said to them, "To you has been given the secret of the kingdom of God, but for those outside everything is in parables; 12 so that they may indeed see but not perceive, and may indeed hear but not understand; lest they

19. EXPLANATION OF THE PARABLE (4:10-20)

10-12. Those who were about him with the twelve is understood by both Matthew and Luke as the "disciples," presumably a somewhat larger group than the twelve, perhaps suggesting the later church. It is quite possible, as observed in the Intro. (p. 636), that vss. 10, 13-20 (possibly vss. 13-25) formed a first explanatory insert into the collection of parables, perhaps the work of some early Christian homilist, and that vss. 11-12 form Mark's own peculiar contribution, with its strange and contradictory theory of Jesus' whole method of teaching by parables. At least vs. 13 seems to attach quite naturally to vs. 10.

There are many textual variants in these verses: some MSS read simply "the twelve asked him"; some read "about the parable" (singular, as in KJV—a very probable reading); some read "to know the mysteries [plural] of the kingdom of God"; some read "spoken [rather than "done"] in parables." But the chief problem for us lies in the apparent meaning of vs. 12, which has no variants. It is true that Matthew has the saying in a somewhat different form, which could be translated "because seeing they do not see" (RSV); it is also true that ἵνα in koine Greek had lost much of its purposive force, and could translate an Aramaic *dî*, as C. C. Torrey proposes: "The parables are for those who are outside; those who 'indeed see, but without perceiving.'" (*The Four Gospels* [New York: Harper & Bros., 1933], pp. 75-76; *Our Translated Gospels* [New York: Harper & Bros., 1936], pp. 10-11. See D. K. Andrews, "The Translations of the Aramaic *Dî* in Greek Bibles," *Journal of Biblical Literature*, LXVI [1947], 15-51.) But taking the passage as it stands now in Mark, it must be interpreted as an expression of Mark's theory of the parables, a theory derived partly from early Christian experience in evangelism and partly from the ironic oracle in Isa. 6:9-10, where the prophet looks back upon his own frustrated

reported explanation of the parable (vs. 20). Those who are good soil for the seed are those who hear the word, accept it, and bear fruit. Good hearing is essential. If we ask what is involved in good hearing, our thought turns to the things that block the truth from coming into the mind, prejudice, custom, the frantic fear of a new idea, the constant din of the self, the "I," "I," "I" which dulls the ear. Accepting the truth is a great achievement. We must accept it for ourselves, not merely as something for someone else—the easiest of all ways to avoid it. That calls for humility, when the accepted truth makes clear that we are wrong. A common block to accepting the truth is its threat to men's material self-interest. Bearing fruit involves letting it grow up into action, into creating, and not keeping it sealed off from life.

10-12. *That They May Indeed . . . Hear but not Understand; Lest They Should Turn Again, and Be Forgiven.*—This whole introduction to Jesus' explanation of the parable (vss. 10-13) is a matter for the scholar. All that needs to be said here is to urge the careful reading of the exegesis on these verses. It is a clear, forceful, and forthright rejection of Mark's particular theory of parables, which is described as "perverse." The overwhelming reasons for this rejection are clearly stated, and are important for the whole field of the interpretation of the parables. Mark's theory lays violent hands on Jesus and turns him into something he was not. Note the word "mystagogue"—"one who initiates into or interprets mysteries, originally the Eleusinian mysteries." The man whom the common people heard gladly, who spoke as never

13 And he said unto them, Know ye not this parable? and how then will ye know all parables?

14 ¶ The sower soweth the word.

15 And these are they by the wayside, where the word is sown; but when they have heard, Satan cometh immediately, and taketh away the word that was sown in their hearts.

16 And these are they likewise which are sown on stony ground; who, when they have heard the word, immediately receive it with gladness;

17 And have no root in themselves, and so endure but for a time: afterward, when affliction or persecution ariseth for the word's sake, immediately they are offended.

18 And these are they which are sown among thorns; such as hear the word,

should turn again, and be forgiven." 13 And he said to them, "Do you not understand this parable? How then will you understand all the parables? 14 The sower sows the word. 15 And these are the ones along the path, where the word is sown; when they hear, Satan immediately comes and takes away the word which is sown in them. 16 And these in like manner are the ones sown upon rocky ground, who, when they hear the word, immediately receive it with joy; 17 and they have no root in themselves, but endure for a while; then, when tribulation or persecution arises on account of the word, immediately they fall away.[m] 18 And others are the ones sown among thorns; they are those who

[m] Or *stumble*.

ministry and views it as the result of divine intention—the theory that Jesus taught in parables, rather than in plain, straightforward speech, in order to withhold the truth from **those outside,** who do not share **the secret of the kingdom of God.** It was not an act of judgment in the Johannine sense, as some have interpreted it, but of abandonment, with judgment still to come. It was not an act of selection, as a result of which those with attentive ears would hear and respond, but not others; it was rather a secret conveyance of truth to those—and those only—who were already in possession of the secret. Such conceptions of esoteric revelation were common in the Greco-Roman world of the first century; what Mark has done is to apply such a principle to Jesus' teaching by parables. But the principle will not apply; Jesus' teaching was not esoteric, and he was no Gnostic mystagogue. Quite patently his parables were a device to aid his hearers' understanding, not to prevent it, and the theory breaks down at once. Not only is it contradicted by the tradition itself, or the source (see vss. 21-22, 33), but the explanation in vss. 13-20 is not the exposition of any dark mystery; instead, it is a plain, simple piece of homiletical exegesis, and treats the parable as an allegory of responsive and unresponsive hearers of "the word." There may well have been some of Jesus' hearers who found his parables mysterious and hard to understand, but Mark's theory can only be described as perverse.

13. All the parables: As elsewhere in Mark (e.g., 8:21), Jesus reprimands the disciples for their obtuseness. If they cannot grasp the meaning of this parable, how will they understand the other parables? The question is more appropriate if addressed to later students of Jesus' collected parables than to the disciples when the present parable was first spoken.

14-20. The conditions reflected **(affliction or persecution, vs. 17)** seem to be those of the early church; cf. 10:29-31. This would be entirely natural if the explanation came from either Mark himself or some preacher or teacher in the church who handed down the collection of parables in this chapter. (See also on Matt. 13:3-23.)

man spoke, was not that. Jesus taught that men might hear and understand, not that they might be befuddled. He came to seek and to save those that were lost, not to prevent their repentance and forgiveness. The one word of exposition relating this whole matter to Christian teaching and living would be a plea at

least to try to follow Jesus in the sharp, sunlit clarity of his words. Paul expresses this superbly in his exclamation, "I thank God that I speak in tongues more than you all; nevertheless, . . . I would rather speak five words with my mind, in order to instruct others, than ten thousand words in a tongue" (I Cor. 14:18-19).

19 And the cares of this world, and the deceitfulness of riches, and the lusts of other things entering in, choke the word, and it becometh unfruitful.

20 And these are they which are sown on good ground; such as hear the word, and receive *it*, and bring forth fruit, some thirty-fold, some sixty, and some a hundred.

21 ¶ And he said unto them, Is a candle brought to be put under a bushel, or under a bed? and not to be set on a candlestick?

hear the word, 19 but the cares of the world, and the delight in riches, and the desire for other things, enter in and choke the word, and it proves unfruitful. 20 But those that were sown upon the good soil are the ones who hear the word and accept it and bear fruit, thirtyfold and sixtyfold and a hundredfold."

21 And he said to them, "Is a lamp brought in to be put under a bushel, or

20. Exhortation to Understanding (4:21-25)

This section, instead of going on with the collection of parables, continues the discussion of the right use of parables and the responsibility of the hearer for the proper understanding of them. One would never guess that the "inserted" vss. 11-12 had preceded this section; the principle of "economy" or of "mystery" there set forth is wholly ignored in vss. 21-25. Judging from the doublets to these verses (vs. 21=Matt. 5:15=Luke 11:33; vs. 22=Matt. 10:26=Luke 12:2; vs. 24=Matt. 7:2=Luke 6:38—but see below; vs. 25= Matt. 25:29=Luke 19:26), it is probable that Mark has used Q, or its equivalent in oral tradition, at this point. The whole point of the section in its original meaning is the responsibility of those who hear to respond to (vss. 23-24), cherish (vs. 25), and proclaim (vss. 21-22) the teaching—which is presumably the gospel, not "the mystery of the kingdom" (vs. 11).

21-22. Candle and **candlestick** (KJV) should be **lamp** and **stand** (RSV), since candles were not used in first-century Palestine. The whole purpose of the hiding of the revelation in the past has been to make it known eventually—i.e., now. This is somewhat like Paul's idea of the secret hid from past generations, but now at last unveiled and proclaimed to the world; but Paul is thinking of the mystery of God's dealings with

19. *Cares of the World, . . . Delight in Riches, . . . Desire for Other Things.*—Here is an unholy trinity—cares, delight, desire. Unholy, but a common trinity of insidious enemies of the life of the spirit. Goodspeed translates the words, "The worries of the time and the pleasure of being rich and passions for other things." They take holiness, in its meaning of wholeness, out of life. They disintegrate life by rendering impossible its integration. The worries of the time keep up a constant drumming on the mind, and prevent it from giving itself to God in any serenity, joy, or dedication. The **delight in riches** can infect those too who merely want riches, as well as those who have them. The pleasure of being rich brings to many the intoxicating sense of importance and power, as false as the sense of being witty and wise induced by alcoholic intoxication. The ego is built up by outside props displacing the soul. The **desire for other things** covers a world of territory, wide, but painfully familiar ground. The lust of the eye serves the desire of the heart; they both go window-shopping down the street, and the multiplied, appealing images crowd out the word. One particular form of this passion for other things is expressed with deep

psychological insight by Francis Thompson in "The Hound of Heaven,"

> For, though I knew His love Who followèd,
> Yet I was sore adread
> Lest having Him I must have naught beside.[3]

One cause of the wandering eye is the haunting fear that one will miss so much, that having God he will have "naught beside." It is the doubt that a life in God can be full and rich enough to make up for the loss of "other things" that glitter so alluringly. The only cure for this withering skepticism is to go through to the end with the invitation of Jesus, "Seek first his kingdom and his righteousness, and all these things shall be yours as well" (Matt. 6:33). That experiment, faithfully carried out—and wandering desires will give way to the unanimous heart, "I count everything as loss because of the surpassing worth of knowing Christ Jesus my Lord" (Phil. 3:8).

21. *Is a Lamp . . . to Be Put Under a Bushel, or Under a Bed, and Not on a Stand?*—Here the emphasis is on the responsibility of the hearer. The word of the kingdom is given him to be

[3] Used by permission of Sir Francis Meynell, executor.

22 For there is nothing hid, which shall not be manifested; neither was any thing kept secret, but that it should come abroad.

23 If any man have ears to hear, let him hear.

under a bed, and not on a stand? 22 For there is nothing hid, except to be made manifest; nor is anything secret, except to come to light. 23 If any man has ears to

---

mankind, and of the strange, unimaginable divine plan of salvation. Mark is thinking of the "mystery" of the kingdom (vs. 11), though his source (in this case Q) cannot have held such a reference. The original point was that if God hides anything, it is with the purpose of ultimately revealing it; the temporary hiding is itself part of the total process of revelation—a profound view of the ways of God with men. Matthew and Luke understand the saying differently, and introduce it in other connections; Mark probably understands it to mean that the "mystery" (vs. 11) entrusted to the first disciples was meant to be proclaimed by the apostolic church, i.e., by the apostles after Jesus' resurrection.

23. This is repeated from vs. 9, and stresses the importance of attentive and responsive hearing, like the apocalyptic "This calls for understanding" (cf. Rev. 13:9, 18). The hearers, or readers, are reminded that the words have a higher sense, and are warned to seek for and find it.

---

proclaimed. This stress, made inescapably clear and vivid by the striking comparison to a lamp, is in direct opposition to Mark's theory set forth earlier (vss. 11-12), that the teaching in parables was a mystery, given in the form of riddles so that the hearers should not understand (see Exeg.). Here the command is emphatic: Let the truth shine. Proclaim the word conspicuously. That is what it is given for. The disciple is not to be a terminal but a transmitter.

The metaphor Jesus uses reminds us that so often the light of the gospel is put under a bushel and not on a stand. In the case of the individual the light of the gospel is to be set on the stand of personality, so that the whole being glows and becomes a burning and a shining light. How often instead is the truth hidden under a bushel, or under a bed, so that the person remains dull, leaden, dead, with no more radiance than a snuffed-out candle. We hear daily a common expression, tossed back and forth in conversation, "You can't prove it by me." The words can carry an overtone of tragedy, in that men ought to be able to prove the reality of the Christian gospel by us. But the lives of many Christians say clearly to an onlooking world, "You can't prove it by me." They give no evidence that they have an inward source of joy and strength. The lamp has never been put on the stand of personality. It is hid in a dark corner. Often it is buried under the bushel basket of "good taste." It is not good taste to become too serious about religion. It makes one "queer." So many followers of Jesus act as members of a secret society whose purpose is to keep the light from shining. What varieties of bushels and beds our modern world has! Two men on a bus were reading in the

morning paper the obituary notice of a man they both knew well, who had died the day before. One exclaimed, "Look—Smith was a member of the First Church. What do you know about that!" We know a good deal about that. There was a man who managed to keep dark that he had any relationship to the church of Jesus Christ. The lamp was not on a stand.

The church too can put its lamp under a bushel, bury it under a mass of masonry, until the masonry becomes more evident than the inner life. It can dim its lamp with a cloud of verbiage from which all traces of a clear "yea, yea" and "nay, nay" have disappeared. It can become so self-centered and provincial that it fails to shine for "all that are in the house" (Matt. 5:15), for the whole wide world.

23. If Any Man Has Ears to Hear, Let Him Hear.—The injunction "Use your ears" comes with sharpened pertinence to a generation marked by a seemingly miraculous extension of the hearing power. The radio has made the whole world a whispering gallery. Radar has given to man an incredibly sensitive ear. The exclamation of little Red Riding Hood in the fairy tale comes to mind, when she says to the wolf masquerading as her grandmother, "What big ears you've got, Grandma!" So we can say to man today, "What big ears you've got!" Ears that can hear a pin drop on the other side of the globe; ears that, God help us, can also hear a bomb drop and then the last cry of an infant.

We can hear everything, and that may be equivalent really to hearing nothing. There is an increased need for selectivity. Use your ears to hear the vital and important. What do we select from the blaring cacophony of noise in which we live? Frequently we do not hear what God hears more plainly perhaps than he hears

24 And he said unto them, Take heed what ye hear. With what measure ye mete, it shall be measured to you; and unto you that hear shall more be given.

25 For he that hath, to him shall be given; and he that hath not, from him shall be taken even that which he hath.

hear, let him hear." 24 And he said to them, "Take heed what you hear; the measure you give will be the measure you get, and still more will be given you. 25 For to him who has will more be given; and from him who has not, even what he has will be taken away."

24-25. The seriousness of the disciple's or hearer's responsibility is further stressed. The words **with what measure ye mete, it shall be measured to you** are perhaps a gloss from Matt. 7:2, with which they agree exactly; some early reader or copyist saw a connection between the two sayings and inserted the words at this point. Luke does not have them, and Matthew has no parallel to this section. Omitting them we read, **Take heed what you hear,** i.e., "give heed to it," **and still more will be given you.** The disciple grows in understanding and knowledge only as he attends carefully and responsively to what he has already received. **Take heed** is scarcely a warning against false teaching. The principle is now carried further: **To him who has will more be given** (a saying, perhaps proverbial, which is strangely included in the parable of the talents [Matt. 25:29; Luke 19:26]). The meaning is that the one who already possesses some insight, and attends to what he hears from his teacher, will gain more knowledge and insight as he acts positively upon his present knowledge. The present Marcan interpretation of the saying seems more probable than the one given it in the parable of the talents (Q). Luke modifies the saying to read *"how* you hear; . . . what he *thinks* that he has" (Luke 8:18).

---

anything else. Elizabeth Barrett Browning asked, during the slaughter of the innocents in factory and mine in the mid-nineteenth century in England, "Do ye hear the children weeping, O my brothers?" [4] Many of the "brothers" did not hear the children. They heard clearly other things, the threat to their privileges and profits, which came with the rising humanitarian feeling. They could hear joyously the clink of a half crown on the counter. They could not hear the cry of a child.

The greatest things are often the quietest. They demand consecrated listening:

> I heard the booming sunset gun;
> I did not hear the sun go down.

We need the education of the ear, in sensitivity and selectivity. "He that hath ears to hear, let him hear." Let him hear the "still small voice" of God as it speaks to the conscience; let him hear the still, sad music of humanity; let him hear the judgments of a God of righteousness and love as they are sounded out in contemporary history.

24-25. *The Measure You Give Will Be the Measure You Get, and Still More Will Be Given You.*—In studying these verses it is essential to remember that Jesus is still speaking of the responsibility of the hearer. The passage begins with the injunction **take heed what you hear.** If this is kept in mind, many of the

[4] "The Cry of the Children."

difficulties about the words that follow—difficulties which through the centuries have been keenly felt—will be resolved. See Exeg. for the clear, simple meaning that "the disciple grows in understanding and knowledge only as he attends carefully and responsively to what he has already received." That is a basic fact of mental and spiritual progress. Jesus' words here, **to him who has will more be given,** are not a holy baptism of the physical and economic inequalities of life. They are not, as they are often taken, a justification of the obvious fact that wealth produces more wealth, by compound interest or financial legerdemain. It is an affirmation of the truth of measure for measure, that gain in understanding and insight, growth in mind and soul, is measured by the diligence, the single-minded determination with which we give ourselves to the wide-ranging task of hearing and understanding. To him who has awareness, joins in the humble search for truth, manifests faithfulness to responsibility, to him shall more be given.

The reverse side of that is the terrible fact of atrophy—the atrophy of every power or capacity that is not used. He who uses neither his ears nor his will, loses his power to hear and to practice. The words **from him who has not, even what he has will be taken away** picture real spiritual disasters: the dimming of spiritual insight; the paralysis of conscience, by reason of which the unheeded voice seems mute; the clouding of one's vision of God, as when the

26 ¶ And he said, So is the kingdom of God, as if a man should cast seed into the ground;

27 And should sleep, and rise night and day, and the seed should spring and grow up, he knoweth not how.

28 For the earth bringeth forth fruit of herself; first the blade, then the ear, after that the full corn in the ear.

26 And he said, "The kingdom of God is as if a man should scatter seed upon the ground, 27 and should sleep and rise night and day, and the seed should sprout and grow, he knows not how. 28 The earth produces of itself, first the blade, then the

21. Parable of the Self-growing Seed (4:26-29)

This parable and the next form a pair, the one setting forth the secrecy and the mystery of growth, the other the astonishing contrast between the small beginning and the great result. Both Matthew and Luke omit the first one—Matthew substitutes for it his parable of the tares (Matt. 13:24-30)—but it can scarcely be thought that it was not

sun is covered by a dense fog; the blunting of sympathy.

28. The Earth Produces of Itself.—The Greeks had a word for it—*automatē*, which being very literally translated might be rendered "the automatic earth." The comparison of the farmer securely trusting in the fruitfulness of the earth, to the sower of the seed of the kingdom, pictures the inevitability of the kingdom's coming (see Exeg.). Note—for this has often been misunderstood—that the real point of the parable is not the gradualness of the growth of the seed, but the sureness of the growth, its inevitability, due to the nature of the earth. So the kingdom is near, because of the operation of the power of God on which the disciple may serenely depend. This was, when it was spoken, and is forever, a great word of encouragement and hope, an answer to impatience and discouragement. The disciples in Jesus' day must have been tempted to join the Zealots, to try force as a swifter and surer method of establishing the kingdom. There is always the temptation to the delusive short cuts of force and violence and material power. Instead of that Jesus calls for dependence on the sure forces of God which bring forth fruit of themselves.

This might be called a parable of "agricultural grace." There are in the human body powers which may be called "medical grace." A patient in a hospital once said to a surgeon who had performed an operation, "I could perform an operation myself. What I could not do is to come around the next morning to see if the patient was still alive. After the operation, I would take a plane for South America." The surgeon replied, "What we depend on is not skill or technique chiefly. It is 'medical grace,' the recuperative, healing, restorative powers of the body, which work of themselves." The "automatic" body, in other words, which brings forth fruit of itself. So there is an "agricultural grace,"

a freely given power of the earth, which man does not make or direct (the parable says plainly, **grow, he knows not how,** vs. 27) but on which he can confidently rely. So there is the grace of God, a divine force, bringing of itself the growth of the kingdom. It has often been pointed out that "the idea of a law of nature conceived as working automatically, by a kind of inner necessity, apart from God, is foreign to the thought of Jesus." Such a modern conception must not be read back into his thought. But the idea of the dependable God at work in the world is not foreign to Jesus, or to Christian history or experience. It is the heart of Christian faith and history. The earth brings forth fruit of itself. God brings forth fruit of himself. His nourishing, redeeming power is in the very constitution of the universe. Man cannot create it, he cannot block it. But he can depend on it and work with it. Branscomb writes forcibly, "Even when one translates the ethic of the New Testament from an apocalyptic framework to a world outlook which looks back on nineteen centuries of Christian history, Jesus' trust in God as the ultimate ground of hope and confidence still remains." [5]

This parable comes with tremendous force in every time of deep discouragement about the kingdom—discouragement often approaching, even in men and women of faith, despair. **The earth produces of itself.** The undefeatable forces of God are on the side of his kingdom. It is the hope of the parent that there are dependable forces for spiritual growth in the "earth" itself, in the constitution of the mental and spiritual being of the child. It is the faith and hope of the teacher, the preacher, the worker for social betterment. That is the kind of a world we live in.

There is a snare in the very word "automatic," however, which must be watched with vigilance.

[5] *Gospel of Mark*, pp. 84-85.

in their "edition" of Mark. Perhaps they stumbled at the word αὐτομάτη (of itself), as if the kingdom spread by some "automatic" or physical principle, apart from the will of God or the response of men. But the central teaching of the parable is the certainty, indeed the inevitability, of the kingdom's coming, once the seed (vss. 3-8) was sown; this is surely "the Lord's doing, . . . marvelous in our eyes," and beyond the realm of human comprehension or endeavor: the farmer **knows not how.**

Vs. 29, quoting Joel 3:13, may be viewed as an apocalyptic appendage to the parable:

Its uncritical use has led to one of the great tragedies of history, the acceptance of the idea of "automatic progress," leading to an utterly immoral optimism, a godless pride, a lifting up of the soul to vanity, and a crashing of the world to disaster. Such practical atheism is not the meaning of this parable. There is no automatic progress without God. Without faith in God and repentance, the only "automatic" result in the world is calamity. There is an active waiting on God's action, as well as a limp idleness—which is really a spiritual coma. "To fold the hands and acquiesce, O shame!" That is not waiting on God. Men must repent and bring forth the fruits of repentance. We must wait with our hands on the plowshare, driving down the long furrow, workers together with God, in his earth which brings forth fruit of herself.

28. First the Blade, then the Ear, then the Full Grain in the Ear.—The incidental details of a parable, of course, should never obliterate its chief point. The chief point here, as has been stressed above, is not the gradualness of the coming of the kingdom, but the sureness, the inevitability of its coming, because it comes not from man but from God. Yet this passing picture, **the blade, . . . the ear, . . . the full grain,** may be a valid symbol of the truth that life grows by stages. That truth is a charter of religious nurture and education. It is a basis of faith and hope. Its remembrance will guard against impatience and against irrational expectations.

Many parents have harmed their children grievously by pushing them unduly, by wanting to begin with the full ear, mentally or spiritually, rather than with the tender blade of promise and potentiality. So, in blind impatience, the first putting-forth, the blade, is trampled on, or neglected, instead of being cherished in the faith that the second and third stages will come if the first is cared for and nourished. One of the great gains in Christian education, for which we ought to get down on our knees and thank heaven fasting, is the recognition of stages in the religious development, and the provision for teaching adapted to those stages. In the eighteenth and early nineteenth century the assumption was that young children could begin with **metaphysical** ideas and problems that

would be hard going for the toughest philosophical mind. Some of the questions in the Shorter Catechism would tax the genius of an Augustine. The motto seemed to be, "Suffer, little children," rather than "Suffer the little children to come unto me" (10:14), with the understanding and response suitable to the blade stage of development.

Notice particularly the next phase, **then the ear.** It is with this second stage that the greatest need for patience and faith comes in. Bishop Francis J. McConnell has pointed out that there is great attractiveness about the first and last stages of personal growth, but that in the middle stage much happens which is discouraging and often maddening.[6] Early childhood has its charm; the full maturity of personality and mind has its tremendous worth and beauty unmistakable. But in between, in adolescence, in the unpredictableness and perversities of the "awkward age," there is often more cause for irritated impatience and despair than for rejoicing and hope. Every parent knows the liabilities that lie concealed in the words **then the ear.** One exhausted father at the end of his rope exclaimed, "I have always admired a manly man and a womanly woman, but I have no use for a boily boy." That phrase "a boily boy" is fairly descriptive of adolescence; it suggests noise and motion. But it is from the "boily boy" that the manly man grows, **then the ear, then the full grain.** Dealing with this stage of life calls for patience, sympathy, and faith. If all we can do is to rhapsodize sentimentally over the charm of childhood, or give an easy admiration to the obvious achievements of maturity, we fail miserably as God's husbandmen.

The same need for faith and patience marks the second stage of every promising enterprise. After the first fine rapture of beginnings is over, after the tender blade has appeared, then come the days, the weeks, the months, always harder than the first. Difficulties multiply, the exhilaration of general aims gives place to the sharp complexity of the concrete. Ardor is liable to diminish. Right there the chance of carrying through to achievement is lost. This is as true of building a church as it is of building a United Nations Organization.

[6] *Christian Focus* (Cincinnati: Jennings & Graham, 1911), p. 34.

29 But when the fruit is brought forth, immediately he putteth in the sickle, because the harvest is come.

30 ¶ And he said, Whereunto shall we liken the kingdom of God? or with what comparison shall we compare it?

ear, then the full grain in the ear. 29 But when the grain is ripe, at once he puts in the sickle, because the harvest has come."

30 And he said, "With what can we compare the kingdom of God, or what parable

---

the sower's function is only to sow the seed, wait patiently during the time of growth, and then "put in the sickle" when the harvest comes. But the addition confuses the picture: God is the harvester, but God was not the farmer—**he knows not how** could scarcely be said of God.

The hidden growth of the seed is not so much evidence of the presence of the kingdom, though it is sometimes so interpreted, as of its proximity and certainty. The time is near; the seed has already been sown, and the harvest must inevitably follow before long by the slow but relentless march of the seasons; nature's laws are really the laws of God. Even apart from vs. 29, the tone of the parable is eschatological; what it meant to Mark and his readers must have been the assurance that the apparent delay in the coming of the kingdom was only apparent, not real. The final result had been guaranteed from the beginning.

22. Parable of the Mustard Seed (4:30-32)

In many ancient rabbinical parables (parables were commonly used by Jewish teachers), the point of comparison was only generally indicated; often a parable would begin with a question, "What is it like? [i.e., what is the situation—say, man's duty to God, or

---

29. *But When the Grain Is Ripe, at once He Puts in the Sickle.*—The sickle has never been used as a Christian symbol, like the dove, the lamb, or the Cross. Indeed, we have come to think of it as an anti-Christian symbol, in the hammer and sickle, the symbolic flag of non-Christian Soviet Russia. Yet, here in these words of Jesus, is the sickle in an honored place, used as a symbol of the husbandry of the kingdom, the energetic and timely harvesting of the grain from the seed.

The sickle is a symbol which deserves everlasting remembrance. It represents the high command to gather the harvest which God's earth brings forth in God's time when it is ready. How often in personal experience the grain was ripe, the great opportunity was present, but the sickle was not thrust in. Again and again the time for the reaping of good ideas, good intentions, good aspirations has come, but there was no gathering up of possibilities into decision, into deed, into action. There was no seizing of the moment when thoughts might have been shaped into enduring character. And the harvest was lost. The life never got out of the shallows and miseries of unharvested opportunity.

But this vigorous picture, **at once he puts in the sickle,** has a tremendous meaning for the church as well, particularly in its dealing with children and young people. There come strategic times in the life of youth when the harvest

is ripe. We can almost see the Lord of the harvest bending over his children and calling to his church, "Thrust in the sickle!" The seed of the kingdom, first the blade, then the ear, is ready! The long, long thoughts of youth have been at work, the attractiveness of Jesus has been pulling on the heart and mind—all is ready for the decision, for entrance upon full responsibility in the fellowship of the church, for the grappling of a soul to Christ with hoops stronger than steel. But all too often a blind and indolent professionalism has mislaid its harvesting sickle, or does not know how to use it, or has no will to use it. All too often trustees and board members are more concerned over a leak in the roof than over the tragic and continued leak of young life out through the doors of the church and the church school. And some are gone forever—in the figure of the story, unharvested grain.

We shall never see a sickle placed on the altar as a symbol of Christ's desire to gather the harvest of the kingdom. But it might not be a bad idea.

30-31. *The Kingdom of God . . . Is Like a Grain of Mustard Seed.*—One caution: The point of this parable is not the gradual growth of the seed. There is no sufficient foundation here, any more than in vs. 28, on which to erect a theory of the gradualness of the coming of the kingdom, to serve, perhaps, in opposition to the apocalyptic element in the Gospels (see

31 *It is* like a grain of mustard seed, which, when it is sown in the earth, is less than all the seeds that be in the earth:

32 But when it is sown, it groweth up, and becometh greater than all herbs, and shooteth out great branches; so that the fowls of the air may lodge under the shadow of it.

shall we use for it? **31** It is like a grain of mustard seed, which, when ·sown upon the ground, is the smallest of all the seeds on earth; **32** yet when it is sown it grows up and becomes the greatest of all shrubs, and puts forth large branches, so that the birds of the air can make nests in its shade."

Israel's dependence upon God—like?] It is like . . ." It has been suspected that the words **the kingdom of God,** here and in vs. 26, have been supplied by Mark, or by those who handed down the tradition before him. It is really the spread of the gospel, the growth or the coming of the kingdom, rather than the kingdom itself, which resembles a tiny mustard seed (**the smallest of all the seeds**) from which grows a great bush, so huge that (as in Dan. 4:21) **the birds of the air can make nests in its shade.** If we were to stress each word and then allegorize we should say this describes the spread of the gospel and the growth of the church in apostolic times. But the original meaning pointed only to the contrast between the tiny beginnings and the eventual magnitude of the result: Jesus' ministry, and his small band of disciples, were the dawning point of the coming reign of God. For Mark this doubtless meant the eventual triumph of the gospel, when all nations (13:10; 14:9) should have heard it, and those in distant lands should have responded to the message. But Mark, as we have seen, was inclined to allegorize. It has sometimes been thought that since the parables in this chapter are agricultural, and refer to the sowing of seed, the day on which they were spoken (4:1) must have been in the early spring. But there is no reason to assume that Jesus could not have spoken them at any time in the year. Moreover, the Palestinian farmer's calendar and ours are not identical. Fall sowing is in late October, spring in January and February.

Exeg.). The one point is "the contrast between the tiny beginnings and the eventual magnitude of the result." The parable was evidently given to reassure the disciples that "the apparently insignificant results of Jesus' preaching are no measure by which to judge the greatness of the Kingdom of God which He proclaims." [7] The growth is God's affair.

Christian history furnishes a stunning commentary on this parable. The tiny beginning, the work of an obscure teacher and of a pitifully small group of disciples, ordinary men, has become "the greatest of all shrubs." God's instrument has been a creative minority. No limits can be set to the achievement of a small group of lives, possessed of the spirit of God, imbued with the idea of the kingdom, dedicated to the person of Christ. There is a notable saying of the strange preacher, Casey, in John Steinbeck's novel *Grapes of Wrath.* "One person, with their mind made up, can shove a lot of folks around." That is true in every realm. Lift it up to the spiritual. Into the whirlpool of Greek and Roman life there came in the first century A.D. a few people with "their mind made up"; as one of their leaders put it, "We have the mind of Christ" (I Cor. 2:16). And for nineteen centuries we can see in history the

divine "shove" on humanity and the world. We can see the tiny beginnings in Paul, journeying to Athens and Rome, face to face with the overwhelming intellectual and political powers of his time; we see it in Luther; in John Woolman and Wilberforce, facing slavery; in Robert Morrison facing four hundred millions of non-Christians in China (there was a tiny mustard seed!) —everywhere the mustard seed growing.

The parable warns against the ultimate vulgarity of confusing size with significance. That is a "sin which doth so easily beset us" in a world and a time in which size increases daily and bewilderingly. What a flourishing cult, bigness, a devoted worship of bulk! A small town in the United States, obviously out of the running in the population sweepstakes, proudly advertised itself as "The Biggest Small Town in America." Meaningless words, except as a genuflection to the national idol.

Jesus was never deceived by a crowd. He cared about *quality;* never about *quantity.* That must be remembered, for the infection of the worship of bigness can creep into the mind and the blood stream of the church. Nearly every Monday morning in summer, New York papers record the fact that on the day previous over a million people were at Coney Island. That is a staggering figure, a much larger number of

[7] Rawlinson, *Saint Mark,* p. 58.

33 And with many such parables spake he the word unto them, as they were able to hear *it*.	33 With many such parables he spoke the word to them, as they were able to hear it; 34 he did not speak to them without a parable, but privately to his own disciples he explained everything.
34 But without a parable spake he not unto them: and when they were alone, he expounded all things to his disciples.	
35 And the same day, when the even was come, he saith unto them, Let us pass over unto the other side.	35 On that day, when evening had come, he said to them, "Let us go across to the

23. Parabolic Method of Teaching (4:33-34)

33-34. These verses may have formed the conclusion to the collection in Mark's source. As already noted, vs. 33, **as they were able to hear it,** contradicts Mark's theory of the parables (vss. 11-12), though vs. 34*b*, **and when they were alone,** has been added by Mark in the interest of his view (vss. 10 ff.). **He did not speak to them without a parable** seems exaggerated, in view of other traditions of Jesus' teaching. **Them** must include both the twelve and the "great multitude" of vs. 1. One obvious implication of the verses is that the parables given in this chapter are only a selection from a larger number. But this is not to say that Mark has abridged his source. Some MSS read "them," i.e., "the parables," instead of **all things** (αὐτάς instead of πάντα).

24. The Storm on the Lake (4:35-41)

As the day in Capernaum (1:14-45), the conflict stories or controversies (2:1–3:6 and 3:20-30), and the day of parables (4:1-34) contain blocks of homogeneous material, so the following sections, 4:35–5:43, form a unit, a group or series of great miracle stories. The incidents take place about the Sea of Galilee and are connected indeed with a journey across the lake and back. Very probably they formed a group in one of Mark's sources. The stories are different in style or "form" from those already told: the narratives are richer in detail and exhibit an interest in detail for its own sake, while in content they more closely resemble the miracle stories current in the Greco-Roman world of the first century.

35-38. The point of the present story is not any teaching or saying of Jesus, or even his example of faith and courage in the midst of danger, but his power—as Son of God—

people than have gone out as missionaries of Christ since the resurrection morning. What immense possibilities! And what did it mean? We can put it in one word— "Peanuts!" A million people walking up and down the boardwalk eating peanuts! It meant nothing—mere numbers never can mean anything in relation to God's purpose. The growth of the mustard seed depends on the quality of the disciple, and the depth and power of the fellowship of the disciples.

So, over the years, the parable calls to us— "Do not despise beginnings—anywhere."

Remembering only this—that always the seed must be sown. More than once the church has spent its time in futile waiting on a sterile field into which no seed had been dropped. There had been no costly sowing, no sacrificial investment of mind, heart, and hand. And there was no mustard tree.

35-41. Christ Stilling the Storm.—Here begins a series of narratives: the stilling of the storm, the Gadarene demoniac, the woman who touched the hem of Jesus' garment, the raising of the ruler's daughter. Four general observations may be made on the miracle of the stilling of the storm which apply to the others as well. These do not in any way "settle" the question of miracles; they are merely reflections which might well be taken into consideration.

(*a*) We cannot recover the historical basis of any of these narratives. They were written down many years after the event and after the source on which Mark draws.

(*b*) The writers of the Gospels and the contemporaries of Jesus did not have to face the "problems" with regard to miracles, such as the universality of natural law, that are present in the modern mind and outlook. There was no "problem." Rawlinson, among others, points out that "the modern tendency to discriminate between 'nature miracles' and cases of faith-healing and exorcism, to find scientific analogies to the latter, but to regard the former as frankly

36 And when they had sent away the multitude, they took him even as he was in the ship. And there were also with him other little ships.

other side." 36 And leaving the crowd, they took him with them, just as he was, in the boat. And other boats were with him.

over the roaring elements. Jerome noted the likeness of the story to that of Jonah in the O.T.; and there are other parallels (Dio Cassius *Roman History* XLI. 46; Plutarch *Caesar* XXXVIII; Calpurnius *Bucolico* IV. 97 ff.; Palestinian Berakoth 9:13*b*; see Klostermann *ad loc.*). But such a detail as the **other boats** in vs. 36 seems to point to an

impossible, is wholly foreign to the standpoint of antiquity."[8] To speculate on the rationalization of miracles, as does H. D. A. Major, when he writes of this passage that "the rebuke administered by Jesus to a voluble and cowardly disciple, coinciding as it did with the subsidence of the storm, was interpreted by His wonder-loving disciples as a rebuke administered to the storm itself,"[9] is interesting guesswork, nothing more.

(*c*) One thing that emerges clearly and solidly is that the associates and contemporaries of Jesus believed that he worked miracles.

(*d*) The timeless and unchanging value in the story is clearly brought out in the Exeg. It was an incentive to faith that "the same divine Lord who had been able to rescue his imperiled disciples . . . was still present with his own." That was a fortification to disciples in the days of Nero's persecution. It is a fortification to all disciples in all ages. A superb exposition of this narrative is in Martin Luther's hymn:

> The Prince of Darkness grim—
> We tremble not for him;
> His rage we can endure,
> For lo, his doom is sure,
> One little word shall fell him.[1]

35. Let Us Go Across to the Other Side.— These words **let us go** were often on Jesus' lips (see on 1:38). The purpose of this particular trip is not given. But Jesus' initiating it was part of the movement and restlessness which mark his life. The lure of the horizon was always before him. "Homekeeping hearts are happiest" was never a motto of Jesus. His eyes were raised to the fields white unto harvest. He was always conscious of "other sheep," and, as here, of the impelling urge, **Let us go across to the other side.** A penetrating question for us, as individual disciples and as a church, is this: Have we kept the lure which the horizon had for Jesus? Do the three little words **let us go** still sound commandingly in our hearts and minds, or has a paralysis of inertia set in?

[8] *Ibid.*, p. 59.
[9] Major, Manson & Wright, *The Mission and Message of Jesus* (New York: E. P. Dutton & Co., 1938), p. 73.
[1] "A mighty fortress is our God."

There is a warning in the fact that so many of the phrases common to ecclesiastical life, such as "an *established* church," or "a *settled* ministry," suggest a static aplomb, rather than a restless movement. The call of the unreached, the untouched, the outward thrust, was everpresent with Jesus. **Let us go across to the other side,** literally to the other side of the Pacific, bearing the light and the life of Christ. **Let us go** into areas of distress with his word who came "to set at liberty those who are oppressed" (Luke 4:18). **Let us go** across new frontiers, where the law of Christ has not yet been carried, into international and industrial relations.

36. And Leaving the Crowd.—This is just a bit of incidental detail in a narrative full of detail. But it has an arresting suggestiveness. The truth that Jesus could always draw a crowd is not any more noteworthy than that he could leave one so often. It is a great art, that of being able to leave a crowd. Jesus did not depend on the deceptive presence of a throng. He could walk away from it. He could leave it when something more central, more vital, more permanent, called. He left a crowd to go up into the hills to pray, or to minister to one or two, rather than to be surrounded by five thousand.

Are we able to leave a crowd in our personal life? There are many who can collect a crowd, but cannot do the harder thing, collect *themselves.* Their life is as public as the waiting room of a railroad station. Some equivalent of a milling crowd is a necessary "shot in the arm," without which life languishes; but without solitude there can be no fine singularity, only a chaotic plural. There cannot be opportunity for what J. A. Bengel calls "leisure for building up myself in a recollected consciousness of God." Jesus' whole life makes it clear that what we can bring of worth to any crowd depends on whether we can leave it.

Can we, as a church, leave a crowd? Has that outward sign of success—a packed house—become the bread of life to us? There are times when a church must get away from that if it is to follow its Master. It must leave this least common denominator of popular thinking, or lack of thinking, and go where no hosannas are heard, but where the shadow of a cross falls.

37 And there arose a great storm of wind, and the waves beat into the ship, so that it was now full.

38 And he was in the hinder part of the ship, asleep on a pillow: and they awake him, and say unto him, Master, carest thou not that we perish?

39 And he arose, and rebuked the wind, and said unto the sea, Peace, be still. And the wind ceased, and there was a great calm.

37 And a great storm of wind arose, and the waves beat into the boat, so that the boat was already filling. 38 But he was in the stern, asleep on the cushion; and they woke him and said to him, "Teacher, do you not care if we perish?" 39 And he awoke and rebuked the wind, and said to the sea, "Peace! Be still!" And the wind ceased,

---

actual tradition of the event, since no use is made of the other boats in the story. Moreover the caustic query of the disciples in vs. 38 does not sound like an invention; the reverence felt at a later date would have toned it down, just as it is toned down in Matthew and Luke.

39-40. Peace! Be still! (Goodspeed: "Hush! Silence!") is a rather mild translation for πεφίμωσο, which is probably from a formula of adjuration used for "binding" a demon of storm. But even if Jesus used such a term, he cannot have used it in the magical sense, as a formula effective by the mere utterance, *ex opere operato:* **faith** here means trust in God, reliance upon God for help (cf. 9:23). Jesus is repeatedly represented in Mark as teaching, exercising, and demonstrating such trust in God.

---

38. *And They . . . Said to Him, "Teacher, Do You Not Care if We Perish?"*—One commentator calls this a "stupid question." It was far from that. It was a perfectly natural question—in a panic. This was a sudden and violent storm, such as frequently occurs on the Sea of Galilee. They were thoroughly frightened, their fright aggravated perhaps by the belief, of which there are traces in the narrative, that the storm was caused by a demon. The excited question indicates that they were trying to communicate their panic to Jesus. What caused a panic in them ought to cause a panic in him.

Much prayer and thinking—panic prayer—has followed the same pattern. People have frantically tried to communicate their panic to God. **Do you not care if we perish?** they cry. "We are in a desperate situation, headed for disaster. Are you asleep?" These may not be the exact words of prayer in panic, but they express the spirit. Such prayer is blind to the truth that God does not share our panic. Like as a father, he pities his children; but he is not frightened as they are. Men turn to war because they are terrified, and insist that God turn to war also, sharing their terror. We can see many indications of the mood of panic in the fear of atomic destruction. We do well to be frightened. We do ill to try to communicate our despair to God. Instead of rushing to communicate our panic to him, we should allow him to communicate his calm to us.

39. *And There Was a Great Calm.*—Comment on these words might well be headed "Salute to Phillips Brooks." For one of his greatest sermons was on this text, a sermon on

Christ stilling the storms of life, treating the text as an allegorical picture, and portraying in memorable fashion the resources of God in Christ for bringing peace and calm into turbulent lives and a turbulent world.

The words portray a great need. In Noel Coward's play *Design for Living*, a drama of sordid and trivial lives, one character has a lucid moment in which he complains that with all the inventions of this magical age, nothing has been invented "to create quiet and calm." That would be an invention universally acclaimed! For the minds and spirits of men are like the Galilean lake—churned by great storms.

The words picture a great history. There is no "invention" to create quiet and calm. "Invention" is a mechanical word; the problem lies outside the realm of mechanics. But there are resources for the creation of calm, all the way from Paul—"I have learned the secret of facing plenty and hunger, abundance and want" (Phil. 4:12)—to millions now living who have learned the same secret from Christ. In multitudes of lives the availing command has been given to all storms and terrors, "Be muzzled." The idea that the world is in the hands of God, that one life is in the hands of God, is the most liberating idea that ever came into the mind of man.

The words picture a great hope. In the direst trouble, from gnawing worry about tomorrow to the level-eyed look into the face of death, the words, **Peace! Be still!** can sound in any life which has opened to that voice. If Christ is in the ship, there can come a great calm. Also, in crises that are less than ultimate, in the milling scurry of life, a vision of true

40 And he said unto them, Why are ye so fearful? how is it that ye have no faith?

41 And they feared exceedingly, and said one to another, What manner of man is this, that even the wind and the sea obey him?

5 And they came over unto the other side of the sea, into the country of the Gadarenes.

and there was a great calm. 40 He said to them, "Why are you afraid? Have you no faith?" 41 And they were filled with awe, and said to one another, "Who then is this, that even wind and sea obey him?"

5 They came to the other side of the sea, to the country of the Ger'a-senes.[n]

[n] Some ancient authorities read *Gergesenes*, some *Gadarenes*.

41. **They** [presumably the disciples, as in Matthew and Luke, though Matthew widens it here to "the men"] . . . **said, . . . What manner of man is this?** The KJV is too weak here; read **Who then is this?** (RSV), or "Who can he be?" (Goodspeed). Mark's answer to the question is certainly implied: Jesus is the supernatural Son of God. There is little prospect of any satisfactory solution of the problem of the "nature miracles" upon a naturalistic basis or by a purely rationalistic method—here, for example, by citing Jesus' courage, mere coincidence, and so on. It is better to leave the stories as they stand, recognizing that whereas miracle stories are now often more of a burden than a support to faith, in the ancient world they possessed evidential value. At the same time they were not looked upon as contraventions of a universal system of natural law, and hence were not quite so stupendous to those who experienced or reported them as they would be to us. In fact, granted the possibility of divine intervention in the "constitution and course of nature," miracles were only natural; and hence the center of interest in such stories as this was not really in the miracle, as it would be for us, but in what it proved: the presence, the power, the saving purpose of God. For Mark, no doubt, and for his readers, this miracle story meant that the same divine Lord who had been able to rescue his imperiled disciples in the savage night tempest on the sea was still present with his own, and could preserve them in the midst of danger, persecution, or whatever threats of destruction they encountered while grim terror stalked the streets of Nero's Rome.

25. The Gerasene Demoniac (5:1-20)

This long narrative is basically the story of one more exorcism, but of an extraordinarily difficult one, for the man had been possessed for a long time and could be neither

values brings calm to lives ridden by hurry and drive, lashed by ambition and greed. Christ's word is not the slightly contemptuous one, quoted, "Why so hot, little man?" but a deeper one, an invitation into a central calm of faith.

It is a word for a world laboring in great storms. Thou, too, "Sail on, O Ship of State!" [2] If Christ is on the ship, and in command, if his goals replace those of clashing sovereignties, there can come calm instead of storm.

40. *Why Are You Afraid? Have You No Faith?*—These questions of Jesus to his first disciples come to all disciples. Why are we so fearful and faithless? For in many tragic ways we are just that—afraid to rely on Jesus' methods and motives, afraid to act as though God's infinite resources were on the side of love. Is not this part of the reason that many of us are more deeply infected than we realize with the secularism that surrounds us? Is it not that we think and act as though only mundane fac-

tors are at work in our world? We get into a sort of George B. McClellan complex, that drillmaster in the War Between the States who failed to employ an army victoriously because he was ridden by the delusion that the enemy were many times stronger than he, even when, as often, they were only half his strength. Henry James, Senior, in his comment on Carlyle, pictures the same lack of faith. "Carlyle," he wrote after a visit, "is still the same old sausage," and goes on to picture him, sputtering and sizzling and complaining that God is continually "circumvented . . . by the politicians." [3] We have so little faith because we rate the seen above the unseen, the temporary above the permanent, the partial above the whole.

5:1-20. *The Gerasene Demoniac.*—A strange and difficult story, this. An opaque curtain hangs around it, blocking the effort to determine in any detail exactly what happened,

[2] Longfellow, "The Building of the Ship."

[3] C. Hartley Grattan, *The Three Jameses* (New York: Longmans, Green & Co., 1932), p. 77.

2 And when he was come out of the ship, immediately there met him out of the tombs a man with an unclean spirit,

2 And when he had come out of the boat, there met him out of the tombs a man

---

subdued nor restrained (vss. 3-5). Jesus was in pagan territory, and the demoniac was presumably a pagan. The calm confidence and courage with which Jesus handles him is characteristic. One can imagine the danger involved from such a tale as that of the Scots doctor in *The Terror of the Glen*, who faced and quieted a murderous maniac. Compared with this central feature of the story, such details as the parley with the demons (vss. 9-10) and the destruction of the herd of swine (vss. 11-16) are secondary and have the appearance of typical elaboration in folk tales. Some scholars have thought that the story is a transferred one, and originally related the success of some unknown Jewish exorcist for whom the loss of a herd of unclean animals belonging to pagans would be a matter of indifference; the detail perhaps even introduced a note of humor in the story. But that is to overlook the fact that for the early Palestinian Christians, who were also Jews, the pig was likewise unclean. Others have thought that the swine were alarmed by the madman's behavior, and so took fright and stampeded over the cliff; but this theory overlooks the fact that the demoniac grew calm, not excited, in the presence of Jesus. The notion that the legion of demons could enter the swine (vs. 13) was popular superstition, no doubt; but it seems better to leave the story as it stands, as a folk tale current in a pagan neighborhood but a folk tale about Jesus and his restoration of a notorious and dangerous demoniac, the man with the thousand devils.

5:1-2. Some MSS read **Gerasenes,** others Gergesenes, and others **Gadarenes.** Origen preferred "Gergesenes," noting that both Gerasa and Gadara lay too far from the lake, but that Gergesa was near by and had a cliff overlooking the lake of Tiberias. But the original text of Mark is not to be settled by topography: the story is legendary, and in any case we are only in **the country** of the Gadarenes or Gerasenes, rather than in one of the cities. **The tombs** was a favorite haunt of demons in ancient tales, and apparently also of madmen. Perhaps the unclean spirits were thought to be the souls of warriors who had died violent deaths in battle, a notion surviving from primitive times.

---

other than Jesus' cure of a demoniac. The story reflects the demonology of the day, with additional features, resembling a folk story (see Exeg.) about demons conjured into swine, joining unclean spirits with unclean animals. Branscomb gives a useful suggestion for dealing with the story: "One has the feeling that the verdict of the Thirty-nine Articles on the Apocrypha applies here as well: while it may be read for an example of life and instruction of manners, it is a precarious basis on which to establish any doctrine." [4] Surely the long and fruitless debate over this story between Huxley and Gladstone, with Huxley rejecting the whole story and Gladstone defending to the death the literal truth of every detail, points out the futility of literalist dealing. The chief point is well stressed in Exeg. that the primary central feature of the story is the calm confidence and courage with which Jesus handles the demoniac. All else is secondary. Yet there are valid suggestions, taken not as doctrine, but as first aid to the imagination, picturing the resources of Christ for disordered minds and a society in the grip of evil spirits.

[4] *Gospel of Mark,* p. 92.

2. A Man with an Unclean Spirit, Who Lived Among the Tombs.—A detail in accord with custom, for tombs were an accustomed haunt for evil spirits, according to current belief, and were in practice common living places for demented people. Put this statement into reverse and it has universal truth: anyone who lives among the tombs has an evil spirit. This, of course, is an allegorical use of a detail of the narrative. It is frankly only a picture for the imagination. Yet taken with that understanding, it does suggest an important truth.

One of the most powerful and vicious evil spirits at work in the world has been, and is, the mentality of those who live in the tombs of yesterday. They lay on the living present the dead hand of the past. In every realm of life the greatest obstacle to social and spiritual progress is the influence of those who have their being in the tombs of yesterday.

To say this is not to overlook for a moment the indispensable and never-ending worth of the wisdom and experience of the past. Phillips Brooks said truly: "A reverence for the sublimities of yesterday is the condition of a fine perception of the hidden triumphs of tomor-

3 Who had *his* dwelling among the tombs; and no man could bind him, no, not with chains:

4 Because that he had been often bound with fetters and chains, and the chains had been plucked asunder by him, and the fetters broken in pieces: neither could any *man* tame him.

5 And always, night and day, he was in the mountains, and in the tombs, crying, and cutting himself with stones.

6 But when he saw Jesus afar off, he ran and worshipped him,

7 And cried with a loud voice, and said,

with an unclean spirit, 3 who lived among the tombs; and no one could bind him any more, even with a chain; 4 for he had often been bound with fetters and chains, but the chains he wrenched apart, and the fetters he broke in pieces; and no one had the strength to subdue him. 5 Night and day among the tombs and on the mountains he was always crying out, and bruising himself with stones. 6 And when he saw Jesus from afar, he ran and worshiped him; 7 and

---

7-8. As in 1:24, the idiom means, **What have you to do with me?** i.e., "What do you want with me?" It is characteristic of ancient tales of exorcism that the demon recognizes

---

row." Ever since the resurrection morning every Christian advance has been in some true sense a recovery. But using the insight and experience of the past as a creative and inspiring power is a vastly different thing from dwelling among the tombs.

Think of evil spirits who live among the tombs, who bring to a totally different age nothing but the obsolete reiterations of a bygone time; those who, in an age of potential abundance, when there is enough of the products of earth to go around the whole human family, try to strait-jacket the very bounty of God with the cutthroat methods involved in an age of scarcity; those who, in the atomic era, live among the tombs of outworn military maxims and competing sovereignties; those who face the whole race problem with nothing but parrotlike repetitions of ancient prejudices and unfounded generalizations. "Hark! from the tombs a doleful sound."

3-4. *No One Could Bind Him Any More, Even with a Chain.*—What more perfect picture could be drawn of a futile dealing with a grave social problem? The very perfection of the picture is more than a bit of tragic history; it is a rebuke and a challenge to our generation. Take, for instance, the exact immediate problem pictured here, dealing with those suffering from mental and nervous illness. The method of chains and fetters was terribly inadequate in the Palestine of Jesus' day. But almost nineteen centuries went by without making any difference. The very name of one insane asylum, a monument to the ignorance, apathy, and futility of eighteenth-century England, has become a common noun—bedlam. Even today we are, or ought to be, appalled at the reports of the cruelty and neglect in our institutions for the mentally sick.

So in the whole wide range of social disorders this tragic pattern of the country of the Gerasenes has been too closely and stupidly followed. The hoary superstition of the power of fetters and chains has flourished. There has been a blind trust in force as the only reason in dealing with conditions where force is no solution at all, but an acute aggravation of the disease. It is true in penology—centuries of fetters and chains, of revenge and punishment, have brought no healing to the disease of crime. Poverty has at odd times been treated with stone walls and iron bars—additional oppression, with no healing. In spite of the evidences of futility the Gerasene school of treatment, without understanding, imagination, or sympathy, has largely prevailed. We still have multitudes who approach the complexities of industrial dispute with nothing but more fetters and chains, mumbling over and over again the superstitious incantation, "Crack down." They "crack down," or try to; but, as of old, **no one had the strength to subdue him,** much less to restore health and well-being. We even try to meet the spreading disease of war with force and more force. The ancestral delusion about "making our nation so strong with weapons that no other nation will dare to fight" is the most often exploded superstition on earth. And still we labor under it.

Jesus approached this social problem in a different way—with understanding, coming to the demoniac as a person, reaching into the seat of the trouble, the deranged mind and spirit behind the outward signs, and bringing with him the power to expel the evil spirit lodged within.

7. *What Have You to Do with Me, Jesus, Son of the Most High God?*—This was a standard question in the demonology of the time.

What have I to do with thee, Jesus, *thou* Son of the most high God? I adjure thee by God, that thou torment me not.

8 For he said unto him, Come out of the man, *thou* unclean spirit.

9 And he asked him, What *is* thy name? And he answered, saying, My name *is* Legion: for we are many.

crying out with a loud voice, he said, "What have you to do with me, Jesus, Son of the Most High God? I adjure you by God, do not torment me." 8 For he had said to him, "Come out of the man, you unclean spirit!" 9 And Jesus° asked him, "What is your name?" He replied, "My

° Greek *he.*

---

the exorcist and fears him. (Cf. Philostratus *Apollonius of Tyana* IV. 25, where the demon begs not to be tortured, or to be forced to confess what it is—i.e., to give its name—which would place it at once in the power of the exorcist.) **Most High God** is a divine title found in ancient Syria and Palestine, and common in Diaspora Judaism in the first century. Vs. 8 is editorial, supplying a detail overlooked between vss. 6 and 7.

9. A **Legion** usually numbered five or six thousand men. However, the hosts of demons, as well as of angels (Matt. 26:53), were thought of as organized in companies and "legions," as we know from ancient Jewish folk tales (e.g., Pesahim 112*b*).

Again and again in the Gospels demons are represented as crying it aloud, gripped with fear at the approach of a possible exorcist. In a deeper sense it has been through the years a standard question put to Jesus both by individuals and by disordered societies.

The answer to the demoniac was that Jesus had much every way to do with him. There was the word of authority, **"Come out of the man, you unclean spirit!"** (vs. 8) and there was the business of salvation, the creation of wholeness, as pictured in the transformation from **crying out, and bruising himself with stones** (vs. 5) **to clothed and in his right mind** (vs. 15).

Jesus has much to do with the individual disordered in body and mind. One of the most notable advances of the present century in the whole realm of medicine is the discovery of the place and power of religious faith in healing. We are learning that the line between body and spirit can never be rigidly drawn. Physical ills have a close relationship to mental and spiritual states. Jesus has much to do with illness, in the bringing of the gifts of a real faith—peace of mind, inner security, the calming of fears and neurotic storms, the calling forth of new interests, lifting life out of the shallow miseries of a debilitating self-concern.

Jesus has much to do with chaotic lives, not torn with physical disease so much as torn with conflicting desires, making an anarchy rather than a kingdom. A woman, after hearing William James lecture on pragmatism, repeated lovingly, "Ah, fragmentism, what a beautiful word!" "Fragmentism" is a common personal disaster, and it is not beautiful. Jesus has much to do with turning chaos into harmony, coming into disintegrated lives, and making "out of the many, one."

He has much to do with society, which may ask the old question, either with skepticism or scorn, **"What have you to do with me?"** He has much to do with marriage and the home, with education, with profit making. There is a measurably valid economic application of Jesus' great command, "Seek ye first the kingdom of God, and his righteousness; and all these things shall be added unto you" (Matt. 6:33). Let a nation seek first that kingdom which is concerned with the welfare of all people, and not with the private aggrandizement of particular groups; let it seek first that justice which is concerned with the distribution of purchasing power, rather than with the profits of contrived scarcity, and much will be added—employment, stability, the goods of peace.

8. *Come Out of the Man, You Unclean Spirit!*—Jesus has cast out unclean spirits from men and women, the unclean spirits of greed, licentiousness, aggression, pride, race hatred. That is not theory; it is history. It is history reaching back to the dawn of the Christian era, to Peter and Zaccheus, to thieves and runaway slaves. It is contemporary history wherever life has been brought into one great allegiance to Jesus as master, out of the frenzies of many passions. He does it by bringing into life a great new affection, a new set of dominant ideas, a new power for embodying in life the affection to Jesus as Lord, and the dominant idea of the kingdom.

9 *My Name Is Legion; for We Are Many.*—These words lead the imagination out into one of the great services of Jesus to individuals, the integration of personality. We do not need that somewhat technical phrase to describe a part of the reality of conversion. It is the unification of life, the end of the inner civil war by the great peace of a unified mind and spirit,

10 And he besought him much that he would not send them away out of the country.

11 Now there was there nigh unto the mountains a great herd of swine feeding.

12 And all the devils besought him, saying, Send us into the swine, that we may enter into them.

13 And forthwith Jesus gave them leave. And the unclean spirits went out, and entered into the swine; and the herd ran violently down a steep place into the sea, (they were about two thousand,) and were choked in the sea.

14 And they that fed the swine fled, and told *it* in the city, and in the country. And they went out to see what it was that was done.

15 And they come to Jesus, and see him that was possessed with the devil, and had

name is Legion; for we are many." 10 And he begged him eagerly not to send them out of the country. 11 Now a great herd of swine was feeding there on the hillside; 12 and they begged him, "Send us to the swine, let us enter them." 13 So he gave them leave. And the unclean spirits came out, and entered the swine; and the herd, numbering about two thousand, rushed down the steep bank into the sea, and were drowned in the sea.

14 The herdsmen fled, and told it in the city and in the country. And people came to see what it was that had happened. 15 And they came to Jesus, and saw

---

10. Having given his name, or rather *their* name—the demons speaking through the lips of the demoniac, whose personality was now identified with them—the best possible terms they can hope for are a compromise: not to be sent **away out of the country.**

11-17. **Hillside** is the proper term here. The repeated **they** with changing antecedents in vss. 14-17 is characteristic of folk narratives, but the meaning is clear enough. **Coasts** is simply **neighborhood.** The people there, according to this part of the story, feared Jesus,

---

the making of one out of the many. The fixed heart is a glowing heart.

There have been many conjectures as to the meaning of the demoniac's reply, **"My name is Legion."** It accords with the prevailing thought about demons at the time, that the giving of the demon's name put him in the power of the exorcist. Hence, the demons replied with a number—"Six Thousand"—rather than a name. But whatever the meaning of the name given here, it is an arresting picture of man's need. How many there are who can truly say: "My name is Legion. There are many persons in me, pulling in opposite directions, many clamorous voices in the town meeting of the mind, with no gavel in the hands of a powerful chairman to bring them to order." Our name is Legion. But the N.T. has a cure for that: "I will give him a white stone, with a new name written . . ." (Rev. 2:17).

13. *And the Herd, Numbering About Two Thousand, Rushed Down the Steep Bank into the Sea.*—This story of Jesus' conjuring the evil spirits into the swine had best be left to the exegetes. As already mentioned, it has marks of a folk tale, possibly an old story attached to this narrative of Jesus' healing of a demoniac. It is hard to see any legitimate use of it either for doctrine or inspiration. It is hard to see

how such an effort would result in anything more than a sterile exercise of fantastic homiletical ingenuity. What may be worth noting, however, is the persistence in literature and speech of these words as metaphor, an arresting picture of humanity, so often like demented swine, charging down a steep cliff to destruction. There is abundant reason for that persistence. It is an unforgettable picture—the herd, blindly rushing on with no sight of impending doom, driven by mass hysteria. It is a picture that fits with a tragic closeness to many crises in human history. It has happened. We think back over the years 1930-45: Fascism in Italy, and Nazism in Germany; the rushing of whole nations down a steep place toward death. Nor can we localize that fatal stampede. The lack of vision, of foresight, of sufficient awareness of doom, to prevent the blind rush, characterized many nations and peoples. This sobering thought is the dark background of all our days: in prosperity as in adversity, is the same blind rush of humanity to a steep cliff of doom taking place again?

15. *And They Came to Jesus, and Saw the Demoniac, . . . and They Were Afraid.*—John C. Schroeder in a sermon once made a penetrating comment on these words, one that is endlessly suggestive. He remarked on the

the legion, sitting, and clothed, and in his right mind; and they were afraid.

16 And they that saw *it* told them how it befell to him that was possessed with the devil, and *also* concerning the swine.

17 And they began to pray him to depart out of their coasts.

18 And when he was come into the ship, he that had been possessed with the devil prayed him that he might be with him.

the demoniac sitting there, clothed and in his right mind, the man who had had the legion; and they were afraid. **16** And those who had seen it told what had happened to the demoniac and to the swine. **17** And they began to beg Jesus[p] to depart from their neighborhood. **18** And as he was getting into the boat, the man who had been possessed with demons begged him that he

[p] Greek *him.*

---

the great exorcist and subduer of spirits, more than they had feared the demoniac; his unknown powers might work even more harm than the destruction of the swine. To Mark this may possibly have meant that even in pagan territory Jesus was rejected; at the same time, the confession in vs. 7, "Son of the Most High God," was significant (cf. 1:24; 3:11). The testimony of the demons, who possessed supernatural clairvoyance, was important for Mark and for his Greco-Roman, i.e., pagan-born, readers. It would also have the same value for many first-century Jews.

---

ironical turn of events by which, when the townspeople of Gerasa came to the scene and found the man in his right mind, they were afraid. Apparently they feared insanity less than sanity. A sane mind was a terrifying apparition! This is not as fantastic as it may sound. Many people today, and through the years, concerned for the continuation of some existing order or custom, either because it works to their advantage, or because of the dead weight of inertia, fear sanity far more than the perpetuation of delusion. They are afraid of man in his right mind. The militarist fears with congealing terror the spectacle of a humanity struggling to emerge from the delusions of force. The disciples of "white supremacy" fear the debunking of humbug on the subject of race. Witness the suppression by the United States Army, during World War II, of the circulation in the army of a booklet presenting an objective statement of the scientific facts about race. Above all, the predatory forces fear the threat of man "sitting at the feet of Jesus" (Luke 8:35). That is the root of the trouble. That is the thing to prevent.

It is easy to grow indignant and scornful about the blind folk, like these villagers of Gerasa, who prefer the evils of disorder to sanity of mind and spirit. But the question comes home to each of us. Are we infected in any way by that blindness? Can we listen in our day to the voice of Jesus saying, "Come out . . . , you unclean spirit"?

17. *And They Began to Beg Jesus to Depart from Their Neighborhood.*—We can exclaim, with self-righteous astonishment, "Imagine people so blind and stupid that they ordered Jesus to get out of their town!" Is it very hard to imagine, after all? Is the picture of people

begging Jesus to keep out of their ways of life and society an utterly strange one to us? Do we not continually see actions issuing from a mentality tragically like that of these frightened and angry townsmen of Gerasa? They resented Jesus as a disturber and upsetter of their familiar ways. Jesus was an embarrassment to the local Chamber of Commerce. They were familiar with demented people; they had managed very well with the demoniac exiled to the rock tombs; they feared change, the presence of a power of restoration, more than they feared the disease. They said in effect to Jesus, "You care for men; we care for swine, we care for the rights of property. That is where we differ. So get out."

People do not often use language so direct and brutal; but the meaning is nonetheless clear. Sometimes they will go so far as to match almost word for word this order of the Gerasene citizens. In the British parliament in the 1930's one member exclaimed, over some measure, "God pity the British Empire if it is to be run on the principles of the Sermon on the Mount!" Those twenty words could be reduced to two—"Get out!" A favorite theme for the imagination has been this: "What kind of a reception would Jesus get if he came to our cities and society today?" But we do not need to strain our imagination too severely. We have data for the answer in what does happen to Jesus' teaching as it comes to an industrial, commercial, political civilization. The reception so often does not resemble Palm Sunday so much as it does Good Friday. Jesus is feared in our cities, as he was in the village of Palestine, feared as a disturber, an upsetter, one who cares more for men than for property. So often our devotion is to a "way of life" rather than

19 Howbeit Jesus suffered him not, but saith unto him, Go home to thy friends, and tell them how great things the Lord hath done for thee, and hath had compassion on thee.	might be with him. 19 But he refused, and said to him, "Go home to your friends, and tell them how much the Lord has done for you, and how he has had mercy on you." 20 And he went away and began to
20 And he departed, and began to publish in Decapolis how great things Jesus had done for him: and all *men* did marvel.	proclaim in the De-cap'o-lis how much Jesus had done for him; and all men marveled.
21 And when Jesus was passed over again by ship unto the other side, much people gathered unto him; and he was nigh unto the sea.	21 And when Jesus had crossed again in the boat to the other side, a great crowd gathered about him; and he was beside the

19-20. In spite of this testimony, Jesus bids the man **go home . . . and tell them how much the Lord,** i.e., God, had done for him—this, rather than proclaim the message of Jesus as Son of God, or Messiah. The verses cannot, accordingly, be viewed as evidence that Mark thought Jesus was opening a Gentile mission. In fact, he does not say that these were pagans, unless the locale in vs. 1 was expected to convey this suggestion. The **Decapolis** ("ten towns") was of course pagan; the ten towns lay in Trans-Jordan—except for Scythopolis, which was west of the river Jordan—and had been founded and federated by Pompey as homes for his veterans. Perhaps Mark intended to stress the man's proclamation of what **Jesus had done for him** (cf. the command in vs. 19). But it is still a question if Mark thought of this as the beginning of a mission to Gentiles. Such an understanding is certainly not explicit here, nor is it taken for granted later in the book. But the tradition suggests that knowledge about Jesus' ministry spread far and wide, even beyond the borders of Galilee proper.

26. The Daughter of Jairus (5:21-24, 35-43) and the Woman with an Issue of Blood (5:25-34)

The rest of ch. 5, concluding the present series of great miracles, affords an example of Mark's "telescoping" of narratives; the healing of the woman takes place en route to the house of Jairus, whose daughter is restored. Both stories tell of restoration by touch,

to life itself; and when the way of Jesus comes into conflict with our "way of life," in many questions where human welfare is concerned, over and again we hear the echoes of the old snarl, "Get out." Do we not indeed sometimes hear the echo, not merely from without, but from within?

19. Go Home to Your Friends, and Tell Them How Much the Lord Has Done for You.—These final words to the healed demoniac have a permanent and universal meaning for all who have in any way been recipients of the restoration, the healing, the grace of our Lord Jesus Christ. Go into your familiar and accustomed world and there bring your steady witness to the power of the Master. It is the hardest thing to do, but it is also the most fruitful. There have been many conjectures as to why Jesus denied the natural request of this healed man that he might go with him. These conjectures have a solid basis in human experience. The man undoubtedly had deep emotions of gratitude and love and wished to be continually with his benefactor. A changed way of life

had a natural lure—he would get away from those who had known him in his distress and those who had him pigeonholed in their minds as a demoniac. But Jesus said, "No. Go home."

That refusal has much to say to us all in the great business of channeling religious emotion into duty and service. So often this flow is blocked by an emotional desire to stay with the original religious experience, to keep life fixed at that point. As a result many people never mature beyond it, never put the years out as a great investment. Again, as with this man, there is the allurement of new surroundings and scenes of operation. It seems like an anticlimax to a great experience to go back to the familiar and perhaps prosaic routine of ordinary life. But Jesus gave the test of religious devotion, **Go home to your friends, and tell them.** Go into the family, into the workshop, into civil life, where there is endless need for effective witness. When that is done, the result is the same as with this healed man, "all men marveled" (vs. 20). Kipling, in his poem "Mulholland's Con-

22 And, behold, there cometh one of the rulers of the synagogue, Jairus by name; and when he saw him, he fell at his feet,	sea. 22 Then came one of the rulers of the synagogue, Ja′i-rus by name; and seeing

and both are stupendous miracles: Jairus' daughter was dead (vs. 35) by the time Jesus arrived, and the woman's case had been all but hopeless. The scene is laid in Jewish territory, presumably on the west side of the lake; Jairus is a **ruler of the synagogue**, what we would call a lay president of the congregation. Vs. 21 is editorial; Mark conceives this whole series of events (from 4:1) as taking place on or near the sea.

---

tract," has put this very word of Jesus into a nineteenth-century setting. He represents God as saying to Mulholland, who has escaped death in the rush of cattle on the ship, and who wishes to change his job and preach the gospel "handsome and out of the wet":

... Back you go to the cattle-boats an' preach My Gospel there.[1]

22. Then Came One of the Rulers of the Synagogue, Jairus by Name; and Seeing Him, He Fell at His Feet.—Jairus is one of the many figures in the Gospels who have now an immortality of remembrance because they came into contact with Jesus, even if as here, on one occasion only that has any record. They gleam like windows which catch the rays of the sun for a moment. The light which falls on Jairus reveals two things, among others, worthy of never-ending remembrance.

He was in mind and spirit open to experiment. The word "experiment" is not rich and full enough to convey the faith that was more than experiment, which led him to kneel at Jesus' feet. But his action, and its saving result, began with a type of mind oriented to experiment. Here was a new teacher, reputed to be a healer; perhaps he could help. His mind was not closed, and he made the venture. Think how many obstacles stood in the way of his coming and kneeling and making his unreserved venture. He was a ruler of the synagogue, a little world in which tradition, not experiment, ruled. He had to cast aside his rank, his prestige, in falling at the feet of an unauthorized, itinerant teacher. But he could open his mind to the new, to the possibility that a divine power was at work in an unexpected and even unlikely person. Seeing Jesus, he made the venture of faith.

What a contrast Jairus provides to very common attitudes. Others have come with prestige, learning, and position, and have seen Jesus too, dimly, yet seeing him, have kept their minds utterly closed to experiment. Seeing him, they ignore him; or seeing him, they despise him. A striking example of the "what-can-this-

fellow-do-for-us?" attitude is found in the massive judgment on Jesus made by Barrett Wendell: "Historically considered, the Gospels tell the story of a remarkable man who lived under extremely fixed earthly circumstances, remote from any we know, and died before he was old enough to have much experience." [2]

Too bad he had so little!

Across the years the kneeling figure of Jairus says persuasively: "Keep your mind open. See and venture. Let Jesus bring health and wholeness into life. Let him bring saving power into a civilization gone into a deathlike coma."

Jairus also is memorable as an example of what has happened times beyond number—a man who comes to Christ because he is driven by a concern for another life. Jairus was impelled not so much by his own need as by the desperate need of a loved one. His words "My little daughter" lose none of their genuine pathos over the centuries. What perhaps he would not have done for himself, he did not hesitate to do for her.

Here is an open window into a large field of human experience, the company of those who have come to Christ through their sense of the need of other lives. That has been true especially of parents. The coming of children into the home has made them see and feel that the child needs an equipment for life, a wholeness, a fortification, something they cannot give of themselves. So they come to One who has much to give and say, "My little daughter," "My little son." They ask that they may have to give sustaining power to young lives for a long journey. That ought to be the experience of all mothers and fathers who feel deeply their responsibility. "Clothes I can provide, and food and home and education; but for the deep resources of life, for truly saving power, I must follow Jairus, see Jesus, and say, 'My little daughter.'"

To pastors and teachers the coming of children into the home is a moment of supreme opportunity to bring into every house, at this time of awakened need for other lives, the availing Christ.

---

[1] *Collected Verse of Rudyard Kipling* (New York: Doubleday, Page & Co., 1907).

[2] Quoted, Van Wyck Brooks, *New England, Indian Summer* (New York: E. P. Dutton & Co., 1940), p. 428.

23 And besought him greatly, saying, My little daughter lieth at the point of death: *I pray thee,* come and lay thy hands on her, that she may be healed; and she shall live.

24 And *Jesus* went with him; and much people followed him, and thronged him.

him, he fell at his feet, **23** and besought him, saying, "My little daughter is at the point of death. Come and lay your hands on her, so that she may be made well, and live." **24** And he went with him.

And a great crowd followed him and

---

23. Lay your hands on her: This was a recognized method of spiritual healing, in use in the apostolic church, and since. It was one often used by Jesus (cf. 6:5). No description of the girl's illness is given, such as might permit a modern diagnosis.

---

23. *Come and Lay Your Hands on Her, so that She May Be Made Well, and Live.*—This was a tremendous affirmation of faith. It was the measure of a father's love for his child and of his sense of need. But the words also carry valid and arresting suggestions of the eternal truth that whatever Jesus does lay his hands upon lives. That is history as well as faith.

He laid his hand on the energy of Peter, and that power, which might have been a lawless chaos, lived. He laid his hand on the emotional capacity of John. He laid his hand on the ambition of Paul. What a scourge ambition has been in men who strode to power over the mangled lives of multitudes, a Napoleon or a Hitler or an industrial Attila! But Jesus laid his hand on the zealous ambition of Paul, the number one killer of Judea, and gave it a new direction so that it lived. We can see it girding itself to other goals: "I must . . . see Rome" (Acts 19:21); "That I might have some fruit among you also" (Rom. 1:13).

If Jesus is allowed to lay his hand on the family, it lives. We have an easy way of talking about homes, as though family life were automatically a little bit of heaven. Yet we know very well it can be an outpost of hell, and often not so very far out at that. Forced propinquity, without love that suffers long and is kind, can be torment and war. But marriage and home, in which love has been lifted up to the clear white light of Christ's purpose, lives. Even upon sorrow, trouble, affliction, Christ has laid his hand, and instead of bringing death, they have lived to bless. That is an outstanding truth of all Christian history, dark and mysterious, but as true and inescapable as sunlight. Leslie Weatherhead, writing with deep feeling of his mother and sister, is also recording the history of millions of lives, in his words, "Whose bodies were defeated in the battle against painful disease; but who from the defeat wrested a spiritual victory which challenged and inspired all who knew them, and made glad the heart of God." [3] The supreme example, of course, is

[3] *Why Do Men Suffer?* (New York and Nashville: Abingdon-Cokesbury Press, 1936), Dedication.

Jesus himself. He laid his hands on an evil thing, a cross. And it lived.

So with these economic systems of ours. They can be motivated by greed and profit-making until they bring the black death of tyranny and disaster. But if Christ is allowed to lay his hands upon them, if they are brought under his rule of brotherhood; if, instead of the clutched fist of acquisition, they are symbolized by strong hands laid upon tools for the supply of human need, they shall live.

There is a question which perhaps we should ask before quitting this verse. Jairus begged Jesus to lay his hands on a child. Can Christian parents make the same prayer unreservedly? All too often there is a trace of fear lest Christ lay his hands too closely on a young life; lest the youth take him too seriously, and follow him into unusual paths, perhaps dangerous ones; lest the young life be not stamped with the familiar pattern of a social set. The future of Christianity depends in a real way on the number of parents who will say to Christ, "Lay thy hands upon this child."

24. *And He Went with Him.*—This whole passage, from vs. 24 to the end of the chapter, might be gathered under the head of "detours and interruptions." The narrative brings warning of that recurring problem of life. What Jesus had been planning for this day we do not know; but certainly it was not that he be taken aside on a journey into which was inserted still another aside. To the eye of a modern efficiency expert, skilled in the organization of time and planning, it might well look like a ruined day. Notice in vs. 21 that this unlooked-for interruption by the distracted Jairus came just at the moment of a marvelous teaching opportunity. A great crowd was gathered about Jesus at the shore, the very situation Jesus evidently loved and of which he had made fruitful use before. Here it was again. Then instead of the natural sequel, "He opened his mouth and taught them saying," one man, in deep distress, broke it all up! With that picture in mind we catch the moving eloquence of the simple statement, **And he went with him.**

25 And a certain woman, which had an issue of blood twelve years,

26 And had suffered many things of many physicians, and had spent all that she had, and was nothing bettered, but rather grew worse,

thronged about him. 25 And there was a woman who had had a flow of blood for twelve years, 26 and who had suffered much under many physicians, and had spent all that she had, and was no better but rather

---

25-26. A flow of blood for twelve years was presumably a chronic hemorrhage, debilitating, embarrassing, and in this case impoverishing and discouraging (vs. 26). The woman's "faith" (vs. 34) was a testimony not only to her continued hope of recovery, but also to the already widespread fame of Jesus the healer. The primitive methods of local **physicians** had been of no avail, which is no wonder, considering the remedies used.

We can readily imagine someone else, not Jesus, under such circumstances saying: "Why bother me? I'm a busy man. Can't you see the crowd waiting? I have my work all laid out here. Come back in a few days." These are words familiar enough to us. We have said them so many times. Two things certainly were at work here. One was Jesus' quick and inexhaustible sympathy. The other was trust in God, a trust that a detour from his plan might not be a detour from God's plan. And so it proved. The day was filled with things not "on the agenda." But it was a day on which the sun has never set.

The incident has much for people who must face unplanned interruptions, and that means all of us. Starting off in high expectation, we meet the forbidding sign, "This Way Is Closed. Detour." Few lives have been lived which could not sound at some time the echo of the words of Job, "My purposes are broken off" (Job 17:11). Sometimes they are small purposes, such as the plan for a day; sometimes they are great ones, such as the hope of a lifetime. This record of a day of interruptions in Jesus' life reminds us that a detour may be God's straight line to his purposes. The story warns us of the danger of setting a schedule above the call of life and the need for the service of love. It is so easy to get our magnitudes confused, so that the plan of the hours and days becomes too rigid to make the swift response. A minister, for instance, may schedule himself into a complex in which, when he is at work on a sermon, he seems to himself to be a Coleridge writing a "Kubla Khan," and any interruption seems to be a man from Porlock, bursting in and robbing the world of a masterpiece. He may even feel, "I am writing a great sermon on sympathy. I cannot be bothered with people." Jesus could always be bothered by people in need. That was God's priority. Do not sit so tightly on a planned schedule that when an unexpected Jairus comes without appointment, he will seem to be a calamity rather than an opportunity. No man can have two masters. He cannot serve God and the order of the day.

25-26. A Woman Who . . . Had Spent All That She Had, and Was No Better but Rather Grew Worse.—This woman makes a striking picture of one who came to Jesus as a last resort. In her case, of course, it could hardly have been otherwise. She had been afflicted for twelve years, and Jesus had been engaged in his public ministry for only a few months. She had never even heard of him until she had tried every other prospect of help. Nevertheless she may stand as a symbol of multitudes who have heard of Jesus, and to whom his resources for healing and wholeness have been available, but who, in spite of everything, come to him only as the last resort of all. To them the Christian religion, the whole revelation of God in Christ, is something to be noticed only in the direst extremity. The mariners in the opening scene of *The Tempest,* the shipwreck scene, speak for their whole company—"All lost! to prayers, to prayers! all lost!" For this panic-stricken crowd prayer was not something to live with, but to die with. They would never think of turning to religion until all was lost. God was not a pilot for the navigation of life; he was the final desperate resort in shipwreck.

How many there have been and are who, seeking life, well-being, joy, have spent their all on **many physicians,** instead of coming first to him who is the way, the truth, and the life. People have spent their all on pleasure, wealth, fame, power, or just comfort and ease, and like this woman, are no better but worse. If they come to Jesus at all, they come last. Often they have to offer him only the tattered and battered remnants of a life, the scant remains of time and strength instead of the vigor and possibilities of a whole life long.

The description given here of this sufferer, on a futile round of healers who could do nothing for her, fits closely to our diseased, unhealed world. It has long been afflicted with the cancer of war. It has made the rounds of all the quack healers imaginable. It has tried militarism, nationalism, imperialism, fascism, nazism, communism—all of them. Our world

27 When she had heard of Jesus, came in the press behind, and touched his garment. 28 For she said, If I may touch but his clothes, I shall be whole. 29 And straightway the fountain of her blood was dried up; and she felt in *her* body that she was healed of that plague. 30 And Jesus, immediately knowing in himself that virtue had gone out of him, turned him about in the press, and said, Who touched my clothes?	grew worse. 27 She had heard the reports about Jesus, and came up behind him in the crowd and touched his garment. 28 For she said, "If I touch even his garments, I shall be made well." 29 And immediately the hemorrhage ceased; and she felt in her body that she was healed of her disease. 30 And Jesus, perceiving in himself that power had gone forth from him, immediately turned about in the crowd, and said,

27-30. Healing by touch has been known in all ages. There are parallels in Jewish and Hellenistic literature, as well as in other parts of the N.T. The emperor Hadrian is said to have been cured of a fever when touched by an aged blind man—who at the same time recovered his sight (*Vita Hadriani* 25). Even the garment of a holy man could convey healing power (cf. 6:56; Acts 19:12). That the woman **felt in her body that she was healed** was natural; that Jesus also knew that **power had gone forth from him** may be an inference of the narrator though we are scarcely in a position to define the psychological conditions under which such cures take place. Some modern healers maintain that they can feel a power flowing through, rather than from, their hands or bodies when they touch their patients, though the old Greek commentators (J. A. Cramer, *Catenae in Evangelia S. Matthaei et S. Marci* [Oxford, 1840], p. 320) insisted that the power in this case was not physical.

has spent its substance on these and is no better, but rather has grown worse. It cannot at this last day come to Christ as a first resort. But if it is to be saved at all, it must come to him as a last resort! For among the nations too, "There is no other name under heaven . . . by which we must be saved" (Acts 4:12).

27. *She Had Heard the Reports About Jesus, and Came.*—Among the many suggestive things about this healing, two may be noted.

Consider those who spread the report about Jesus. In Nathaniel Hawthorne's notebooks there is an entry, a suggestion for a story he never wrote—"Story in which the principal character never appears." In most of the stories of the healings of Jesus there are indispensable characters who never appear, the people who spread the reports about him. They are off stage, yet near the center of the story. They could not be traced and named. His fame went out, he could not be hid. But we sense their presence. This woman came because they had brought her a report of One who could restore life, and her hope lived again.

It is a great role, that of a reporter; frequently anonymous, as with the unseen company in this story, but vital. Do our lives and actions carry any report of Jesus that makes anyone eagerly start a journey to him? Men and women are adept at "reporting." Sometimes it is the idle words of gossip, glimpsed in the N.T.,

"not only idlers but gossips and busybodies, saying what they should not" (I Tim. 5:13). Sometimes it is deadly malice, like that of Vivien, who

> let her tongue
> Rage like a fire among the noble names,
> Polluting, and imputing her whole self,
> Defaming and defacing, till she left
> Not even Launcelot brave nor Galahad clean.[4]

We can all "report," and start rumors flying. What are the characteristic rumors that have their origin in us? Do our words and lives carry a rumor of One in whom there is hope, healing, and help?

28. *For She Said, "If I Touch Even His Garments, I Shall Be Made Well."*—(See also 6:56.) This is a memorable picture of a tentative faith. There was a measure of what we would today call superstition in it, a suggestion of belief in the magic power of everything connected with Jesus. But it was enough to impel her to action, to the outreach of hope and faith. She thought that even a slight, unnoticed touch might do, without fully coming into recognized contact with him.

She was wrong in her feeling about his garment. She was right about the faith. There was

[4] Tennyson, *Idylls of the King*, "Merlin and Vivien," 1. 799.

31 And his disciples said unto him, Thou seest the multitude thronging thee, and sayest thou, Who touched me?

32 And he looked round about to see her that had done this thing.

33 But the woman fearing and trembling, knowing what was done in her, came and fell down before him, and told him all the truth.

34 And he said unto her, Daughter, thy faith hath made thee whole; go in peace, and be whole of thy plague.

35 While he yet spake, there came from the ruler of the synagogue's *house certain*

"Who touched my garments?" 31 And his disciples said to him, "You see the crowd pressing around you, and yet you say, 'Who touched me?'" 32 And he looked around to see who had done it. 33 But the woman, knowing what had been done to her, came in fear and trembling and fell down before him, and told him the whole truth. 34 And he said to her, "Daughter, your faith has made you well; go in peace, and be healed of your disease."

35 While he was still speaking, there

34. Jesus' insistence that the woman's own **faith** had healed her is significant. A mere thaumaturge or wonder-worker would have taken credit for the cure. Not that he held any modern idea of the psychological or autosuggestive power of faith: instead, faith was the necessary condition of healing, which came from God (as in vs. 19). For Mark the cure was further evidence of the power of Jesus as Son of God, though the usual conclusion to such miracle stories, stressing the impression made upon the witnesses, is lacking in this instance. Although pagan and even Jewish parallels to these great miracle stories are not lacking, there is a difference here: the form is similar, but these stories have a purely religious significance, and the impress of Jesus' character and outlook is upon them, surviving even in the broad, popular, novelistic telling of the story.

35-37. **While he was still speaking:** If the "telescoping" of the two stories is Mark's work, it is done with great dramatic effect. Some writers have thought that the girl lay in

nothing magical in the garment. There was saving power in the faith, as Jesus told her, "Your faith has made you well" (vs. 34).

It is always faith that saves. Many have thought to touch some form of words which men have wrapped around Jesus, but which are not the Master himself. Others have thought that the healing of life, salvation, was to be found in some rigid, inflexible theory of the Atonement. Jesus has an answer: "Your faith has made you well." Sometimes the garment which people touch is a ceremony or an institution. If they go through the right ceremonial motions, or make the right connections, they think that is the thing. But Jesus did not say, "Come unto me, if ye have gone through all the approved ceremonies." He said, "Come unto me, all ye that labor and are heavy laden" (Matt. 11:28). It is the outreach of faith, the commitment of life to God in Jesus Christ, which wins through to the words, "Go in peace, and be healed" (vs. 34).

31. *You See the Crowd Pressing Around You, and Yet You Say, "Who Touched Me?"*— This is one of several reproaches aimed at Jesus, and they are all very suggestive. The whole list is well worth study and thought. In this instance, as in the others, he is being reproached for a great quality. It might be said with some show of truth that if you wish to find the particular

glories of the Christian gospel, you must look at the things for which the disciples rebuked Jesus. Such passages are of high historical value, as being least likely to have been reported by compilers or revised by "editors." Peter's rebuke in 8:32 is a crowning example.

Here Jesus is impatiently reproached because of his concern for a single individual in the mass. "Preposterous!" exclaim the disciples. "Can't you see a crowd is jostling you, and yet you say, 'Who touched me?'" How could one person be singled out in a crowd? Yet Jesus responded to the shy approach of individual need as surely and deftly as a magnetic needle responds to the North Star. So the teaching of Jesus about a Father who individualizes, to whom each one of billions of his children is infinitely and eternally precious, has seemed preposterous to many. They have criticized as beyond belief the idea of God's concern for the individual, and have done it in almost the very words of the disciples to Jesus—"**You see the crowd pressing around you, and yet you say, 'Who touched me?'**" Yet that reproach reveals the glory of the gospel. "Behold, what manner of love . . . , that we should be called the sons of God" (I John 3:1).

35-36. *There Came from the Ruler's House Some Who Said, "Your Daughter Is Dead. Why*

which said, Thy daughter is dead; why troublest thou the Master any further?

36 As soon as Jesus heard the word that was spoken, he saith unto the ruler of the synagogue, Be not afraid, only believe.

37 And he suffered no man to follow him, save Peter, and James, and John the brother of James.

38 And he cometh to the house of the ruler of the synagogue, and seeth the tumult, and them that wept and wailed greatly.

39 And when he was come in, he saith

came from the ruler's house some who said, "Your daughter is dead. Why trouble the Teacher any further?" 36 But ignoring q what they said, Jesus said to the ruler of the synagogue, "Do not fear, only believe." 37 And he allowed no one to follow him except Peter and James and John the brother of James. 38 When they came to the house of the ruler of the synagogue, he saw a tumult, and people weeping and wailing loudly. 39 And when he had en-

q Or *overhearing*. Many ancient authorities read *hearing*.

a state of coma (vs. 39), but Mark surely assumed that she was really **dead. Jesus heard** (KJV) may mean "overheard" (παρακούσας), or even **ignoring** (RSV). The rest of the verse implies the former sense; Jesus overhears them, and proceeds to reassure the father (cf. 9:23) with his characteristic insistence upon faith: **Do not fear, only believe.** The three disciples named in vs. 37 were the most intimate of Jesus' disciples, according to Mark (cf. 9:2).

38-39. The mourners, possibly some of them professional (see on Matt. 9:23-24), had begun their wailing and lamentation as soon as it was apparent that the girl had died. **Not dead but sleeping** may convey to a modern reader the impression that Jesus recognized that the girl was only apparently dead, and that he roused her from her cataleptic state. This is a possible interpretation of the incident, but Mark is not portraying Jesus

Trouble the Teacher Any Further?" But Ignoring What They Said. . . .—The art of ignoring, here illustrated by Jesus, is one of the fine arts of faith. There was a finality about the report men gave to Jairus, **Your daughter is dead.** What could the Teacher do about it? It was all over, finished. The whole matter was punctuated with a period. But to Jesus that report was not the end. There is a glory of faith in that word "but"—**But ignoring what they said. . . .** The place that seemed to be a blank wall, a dead end, was to Jesus a place from which he would go on, with the resources of God entering the situation. To Jesus men's report on anything was never the last word. The last word belongs to God. In crude language God never comes to the end of his rope.

Two aspects of Jesus' mind are illustrated in this narrative. One was his marvelous awareness, as shown in his sensitive and instant response to the need of an afflicted woman in a crowd. He was always aware of everything in his environment. But there was another aspect of his mind: he could also ignore—as he did here. He was not unrealistic. He had a deeper realism in his sense of the availing, inexhaustible resources of God. Jesus' wisdom for this situation, desperate as it seemed, was this: **Do not fear, only believe.**

This action of Jesus comes with fortification and challenge. The report which the friends of

Jairus brought is strangely like the reports which come in to us from time to time. More than once it has been rumored, "Your civilization is dead. Why trouble the Teacher any further? What can Jesus do about it? Nothing, nothing at all. It's over." So the reports came from Greece, the Balkans, Palestine, China, Moscow, Berlin, and from the ironically named Lake Success. We might conceivably plan, some admit, to go underground for the big blast!

Jesus did not deny the reports. He entered into no argument about them. He simply ignored them. Christian faith ignores the rumors that hope has died, and remembers other words, "I will build my church, and the powers of death shall not prevail against it" (Matt. 16:18), not even the bewildering powers of death that in an atomic age can be let loose at a moment's notice. So to the recurring question asked every day, sometimes in despair, sometimes in contempt, **"Why trouble the Teacher any further?"** men of Christian faith, like Jesus, **ignoring what they said,** must answer, **"Do not fear, only believe."** Jesus and his teaching, his gospel, can do much every way. He can "do exceeding abundantly above all that we ask or think" (Eph. 3:20).

38-40. *He Saw a Tumult, and People Weeping and Wailing Loudly. . . . But He Put Them All Outside.*—Here Jesus comes face to face with traditional attitudes and conduct in the

unto them, Why make ye this ado, and weep? the damsel is not dead, but sleepeth. 40 And they laughed him to scorn. But when he had put them all out, he taketh the father and the mother of the damsel, and them that were with him, and entereth in where the damsel was lying.

tered, he said to them, "Why do you make a tumult and weep? The child is not dead but sleeping." 40 And they laughed at him. But he put them all outside, and took the child's father and mother and those who were with him, and went in where the child

---

as an expert diagnostician; Jesus speaks here, as in vs. 36, without having seen the child. This restoration from death is the climax of the present series of miracles, somewhat as John makes the resurrection of Lazarus the climax of his series of seven great "signs."

presence of death. His whole action has inexhaustible value and relevance. The loud traditional ceremonies had already begun when he reached the home, a truly pagan tumult. Perhaps there were hired mourners (see Exeg.). The parallel passage in Matthew notes the presence of flute players, a usual accompaniment to the dismal ritual. There was continued weeping and wailing. Jesus' dealing with all this was short and simple: **he put them all outside.**

Such forthrightness is highly suggestive in connection with the many survivals of utterly unchristian attitudes in common practice among Christians. There is tremendous need to Christianize our funeral customs. The traditional loud wailing has somewhat subsided with the passing of the years: hired mourners are no longer in evidence, though they have disappeared in comparatively recent times; but they, and the professional flute players, have left many traces behind them. Only with difficulty does the Christian faith shine through the lugubrious accouterments of mourning and burial. So much suggests a pagan darkness; so little, comparatively, suggests the faith of a glorious resurrection, a faith in the God of the living. All such conventional attitudes and practices Jesus puts outside, as he put the noisemakers outside the home of Jairus. He has something better to bring into the house of grief than a loud wail. When **he put them all outside,** he came in himself. That made a completely new situation. There is always a new situation when Jesus comes in, and faith drives out despair and fear.

40. And They Laughed at Him.—There is a strange ring about these words. From the vantage point of today we find it rather hard to picture. That men should oppose him, vilify him, crucify him, is easy to understand. But that men should laugh at him seems, from our knowledge of the force and influence that he has become in history, strange.

As we put ourselves back in imagination, however, it becomes quite intelligible. There they were, confronted by the final fact, death.

Anyone who suggested that there might be anything more on the other side of that fact, anyone who ventured beyond the fixed limits of their world, was someone to be laughed at.

And when we make the journey down the other way through history, with our mind's eye and remembrance, how many places there are where this old entry must be made, **And they laughed at him.** When Christianity thrust its way into the Greek and Roman world, there was laughter, usually tinged with scorn. This strange cult of a crucified criminal—what should a sophisticated person do but laugh at it? Whenever Jesus, his teaching, his gospel, have cut across the finalities of any settled world of thought and custom, men have laughed at him. When a large company of his disciples finally faced human slavery, and came into a death grapple with it, people to whom slavery was part of the established order—laughed! Even within his church, when in the early days of the foreign missionary movement some few began to take seriously the words, "Go ye into all the world," there were any number who laughed at the vision of a universal Christ and a universal salvation for all men. And how the pagan worshipers of Mars have always laughed, with howls of derision, at the pusillanimous Prince of Peace, while others poke fun at the ridiculous moral earnestness of the believer.

But the original situation in this passage calls for the greatest stress. These people in Jairus' house laughed because Jesus refused to accept death as the last word. Who is he to deny the common-sense fact that the undertaker and the gravedigger have the last word about death? Diffused throughout the whole nineteenth century was an ill-concealed note of laughter—laughter at the impossible romanticism of the Christian faith. Louis MacNeice describes it, when he writes hopefully, "We have escaped from nineteenth-century materialism and with it from that nineteenth-century snobbery which disowned our Christian (and thereby our cultural) heritage." [5] Whether we have escaped or not, may be a question; certainly the "snobbery"

[5] *New York Times*, Sept. 28, 1947.

41 And he took the damsel by the hand, and said unto her, Talitha cumi; which is, being interpreted, Damsel, (I say unto thee,) arise.

42 And straightway the damsel arose, and walked; for she was *of the age* of twelve years. And they were astonished with a great astonishment.

43 And he charged them straitly that no man should know it; and commanded that something should be given her to eat.

was. 41 Taking her by the hand he said to her, "Tal'i-tha cu'mi"; which means, "Little girl, I say to you, arise." 42 And immediately the girl got up and walked; for she was twelve years old. And immediately they were overcome with amazement. 43 And he strictly charged them that no one should know this, and told them to give her something to eat.

41-42. The retention of the Aramaic words which Jesus used can scarcely be due to belief that the formula itself was effective (as some have held), but it does indicate, like other Aramaic phrases in Mark (e.g., 7:34), that the story originally circulated in that language. Some of the MSS have gone sadly astray in copying these foreign words, but the sense is clear enough, and is as Mark has rendered it. There is no connection between the statement that the girl was **twelve years old** and that the woman in vs. 25 had been ill for twelve years—as if she were the child's mother. Such romantic conjectures are quite outside Mark's purpose. **Astonished with a great astonishment** (KJV) is literal and striking, but **they were overcome with amazement** (RSV) is preferable.

43. Almost certainly the first half of this verse is editorial. The purpose of the impossible command of silence is, in Mark's view, to safeguard the messianic secret (see Intro., pp. 642-44). Vs. 43*b*, the command to give the child food, was perfectly natural; but in the story as told—and retold by Mark—it must have been intended to prove the reality of the miracle. The dead was now living and could take food.

—a distinct and tragic form of laughing at Jesus—was there.

It all comes down to the tremendous doctrine of the Incarnation. If Jesus was just a poetic soul who taught a vague and foggy theism and recommended kindness and good will, then a laugh might be excused. But if God was in Christ, reconciling the world to himself, then the last word is with him.

The disciple is not above his master. The ears of the sensitive disciple will always hear somebody's laughter. It will stretch the whole octave from the deep-throated scorn of power and pride, to the shrill, obscene giggle of frivolity. Jesus heard it—and went on with his saving work.

41. Taking Her by the Hand He Said to Her, . . . "Little Girl, I Say to You, Arise."—How many of the heartening pages in the disheartening story of human history since Jesus lived could be ranged under this heading! Of course there is no such outlook in the narrative scene. It is a simple and beautiful story of the sympathy and healing power of Jesus. But this picture of Jesus, taking the hand of the little girl and bidding her to rise, suggests vividly what he has meant to young womanhood. His influence in lifting the crushing burdens which society has so often bound on the frail shoulders of little girls can never be measured or even de-

scribed. Man's inhumanity to little girls is a special and agonizing brand of man's inhumanity to man. In the Mediterranean world, in the first century A.D., they were so often merely unwanted *things*. They were exposed to the elements, a fairly common form of child murder. Even where such cruelty did not prevail, they were regarded more as a misfortune than as a blessing. The new valuation of persons, which the gospel of Jesus brought, changed the conception of them: they were no longer things, but persons, precious in the sight of God.

Another of the dark chapters of the history of childhood is that of the coming of the industrial revolution to England. Little girls under ten crawled around mine pits and worked long hours in factories. It took a long time—far too long—before the aroused Christian social conscience spoke effectively the words of Jesus, **Little girl, I say to you, arise.** The voice of the Master sounded out through the devoted life of Josephine Butler, who strove to bring within the circle of mercy and love girls condemned to prostitution. What need there is today, when we widen the range of our view to take in the whole world, of making effective, through the elimination of organized cruelty, greed-driven vice, the opening of opportunity, the words of Jesus to the "little girls" of the world—**"I say to you, arise."**

6 And he went out from thence, and came into his own country; and his disciples follow him.

2 And when the sabbath day was come, he began to teach in the synagogue: and many hearing *him* were astonished, saying, From whence hath this *man* these things?

6 He went away from there and came to his own country; and his disciples followed him. 2 And on the sabbath he began to teach in the synagogue; and many

---

B. Wider Journeyings (6:1–9:50)

Heretofore Jesus has been represented as centering his activities in Capernaum, with a journey about Galilee (1:39) and one across the lake and back (4:35; 5:21). A new division in the Gospel begins with 6:1, recounting the visit to Nazareth, another circuit of Galilee (6:6*b*), a journey to Bethsaida (6:45), the return (6:53), a visit to the region of Tyre and Sidon (7:24), the return via Decapolis (7:31), a visit to "Dalmanutha" (8:10), Bethsaida again (8:22), the villages of Caesarea Philippi (8:27), "a high mountain" (9:2, 9), and the return through Galilee (9:30) to Capernaum (9:33); after this begins (10:1) the journey to Jerusalem via Trans-Jordan and Jericho (10:46). This brief outline includes all the topographical references in Mark. That it cannot be complete is obvious, if only from a comparison with the other Gospels; but it is typical, both of Mark's arrangement and of his selection of materials. Some of the localities are difficult, if not impossible, to identify. Yet the general impression is undoubtedly correct. Jesus "went about all Galilee"—his ministry was not confined to one place. But for the most part, the present division (chs. 6–9) represents Jesus as outside Galilee proper, or rather, outside the jurisdiction of Herod Antipas, following the rejection at Nazareth and the mission of the disciples. This was the basis for H. J. Holtzmann's famous theory of the "flight" of Jesus from his enemies, and has been taken as evidence of the "failure" of the Galilean ministry. But the basis of the theory is Mark's schematic arrangement, as Johannes Weiss pointed out, and it may or may not be in accordance with the original facts. As we shall see, these four chapters in Mark include several blocks of material (which may be based on corresponding sources), and contain what appears to be a double tradition of events in 6:34–7:37 and 8:1-26.

1. The Visit to Nazareth (6:1-6)

Although Luke (4:16-30) locates the visit to Nazareth near the beginning of Jesus' ministry, his narrative presupposes a prior ministry in Capernaum (Luke 4:23), and the story as he tells it has been influenced by the present section in Mark. Luke's location and rewriting are both intended to bring out the significance of the visit to Nazareth as marking the inauguration of Jesus' public ministry, which was to extend from his home village to the "end of the earth." Jesus' visit to Nazareth is incidental to his wider journeyings; Capernaum is from the outset his headquarters.

6:1. His own country: The word *patris* was often used of a city or town, rather than "country," and usually meant birthplace. Mark, like John, shows no knowledge of the story of Jesus' birth at Bethlehem. The presence of **his disciples** indicates that the purpose of his journey was evangelization, not a family visit.

2. Mighty works (δυνάμεις) is the regular term in the Synoptic Gospels for Jesus' works of exorcism and healing. John uses the word "sign," which is more appropriate to

---

6:2-3. Where Did This Man Get All This? ... Is Not This the Carpenter. . . ? And They Took Offense at Him.—This narrative of the rejection of Jesus by the people of his own town of Nazareth, his neighbors who knew him and his family, makes a striking and disturbing study of the ways of missing truth when it appears. Implicit in the story are many reliable directions on how to be blind to a great event, a great truth, a great opportunity, a great call, when they pass right under our eyes. The reasons why these dwellers in Nazareth were blind to the significance of Jesus, why they rejected him, are the same reasons why many have rejected him through the centuries, and why many take offense at him in our own day.

and what wisdom *is* this which is given unto him, that even such mighty works are wrought by his hands? 3 Is not this the carpenter, the son of Mary, the brother of James, and Joses, and of Juda, and Simon? and are not his sisters here with us? And they were offended at him.

who heard him were astonished, saying, "Where did this man get all this? What is the wisdom given to him? What mighty works are wrought by his hands! 3 Is not this the carpenter, the son of Mary and brother of James and Joses and Judas and Simon, and are not his sisters here with us?" And they took offense[r] at him.

[r] Or *stumbled*.

his characteristic theological view: a sign was a manifestation, almost an "epiphany," of the divine nature of the incarnate Logos. Both terms are sharply distinguished from the common expression "signs and wonders," which were mere portents or tricks of magic (cf. 8:11).

3. The carpenter, the son of Mary. This reading is probably due to later revision, under the influence of the doctrine of the virgin birth; the reading presupposed by both Matt. 13:55 and Luke 4:22 is the one actually found, in conflated form, in some Greek MSS (33, Ferrar group), the O.L., Armenian, and Ethiopic versions, and Origen: "Is not this the son of the carpenter?" Even the Chester Beatty MS (p[45]) supports it. It is most improbable that if Mark originally contained the reading found in KJV and RSV, both Matthew and Luke should have changed it to their present readings. Origen, the greatest biblical scholar of his time, says that he never saw a gospel that described Jesus as a carpenter (*Against Celsus* VI. 36).

Many theological theories and arguments have been advanced to explain the "brothers and sisters" of Jesus: e.g., that they were really his cousins, or half brothers and half sisters—children of the aged Joseph by a former marriage—and so on. But the motive of such speculations is clear, viz., to safeguard the doctrine of the virgin birth and its later elaboration in that of the perpetual virginity of the mother of Jesus. It is better to take the words in their natural sense. Jesus was evidently a member of a fairly large family, that of the **carpenter** (possibly "builder") Joseph.

Coming closer home, they are also the reasons why we may miss the meaning of Jesus for our own lives, and the opportunities he opens for us.

From one point of view these village folk who rejected Jesus were what we would perhaps call "factfinders." They had all the physical facts about this strange man, his birth, his occupation, his home and family. That was all they needed—the obvious facts. They represent that considerable class of people who are sure that when they get all the material facts about a situation, they have grasped all there is. They say, "Here is the factual survey, item by item. Add the items, and you get the complete sum." The truth is, of course, that you may very well get nothing at all. It is indisputable that a face consists of: two eyes, two cheeks, one nose, one mouth, one chin, one forehead. You can have all that and have nothing of what Milton calls the "human face divine." Two eyes, a nose, and a mouth never launched a thousand ships. These fellow townsmen of his had all the facts about him, but they missed Jesus.

Our world is ridden with "factfinders." To go no further than the subject of Jesus himself, how many people there are who have all the rudimentary historical data about Jesus, how many scores of books in which they are listed! Yet they have missed the stature, the meaning, the greatness of Jesus, as completely as these complacent villagers did. Others approach the whole mystery and wonder of life with the dogma that whatever is not a material fact has no standing as truth. A surer way to total blindness, to total truth, has never been devised.

Again, these people who rejected Jesus because they knew his family represent perfectly that company of men and women who think that when they know the origins of a thing, they understand all about it. They knew where Jesus came from, his mother, his father, his brothers and sisters. So, knowing the origin, down went the shutters of their minds. They knew all there was to know. Stated thus baldly, that seems idiotic. It is. But it has been a powerful and influential way of thinking, or to speak more accurately, of not thinking. There is no field of thought or experience in which this type of mental operation does not appear. For instance the origin of man was in protoplasm in some primary ooze. *Ergo,* man is protoplasm.

4 But Jesus said unto them, A prophet is not without honor, but in his own country, and among his own kin, and in his own house.	4 And Jesus said to them, "A prophet is not without honor, except in his own country, and among his own kin, and in his own

---

4. A prophet . . . country. This was probably a more or less proverbial saying. An interesting variant, which some take to be original—is it echoed in Luke 4:23?—has been found in a papyrus at Oxyrhynchus (*Oxyrhynchus Papyri* 1. 11) : "Jesus says, A prophet is not accepted in his own home town [*patris*], nor does a physician work cures upon those who know him" (see M. R. James, *The Apocryphal New Testament* [Oxford: Clarendon Press, 1924], p. 27) . But the saying may be apocryphal, like other Oxyrhynchus "logia," and only a combination of the two sayings in Luke 4:23-24. In Mark, Jesus does not claim to be a prophet, but only compares himself to one.

Ergo, any talk about the soul of man is nonsense. It is all so beautifully simple. It rests the mind. No necessity for any bothersome explorations or examinations.

Some scholars have discovered that religion began with fear. So religion is always and everywhere fear. A blessed word; it simplifies things so. In like manner the origin of love is found to be in sexual attraction and appetite. Consequently love is a "biological function." All of it misses the truth that the meaning of a thing is never to be found in its origin, but in what it becomes at its best.

Another force at work in this congregation, no doubt, was social and intellectual snobbery, a third sure way of missing truth. We can still catch the sneer in the word "carpenter." This man Jesus from a side street here in Nazareth was no scholar, no rabbi. He was of a lower order of life, a carpenter or joiner, a stonemason. How could he know anything, that we, his betters, should pay attention to? No wonder some took offense at him. As it was in the beginning, it is now, and has been ever since. Some intellectuals of Greece sneered at Paul as a "babbler." He, too, like Jesus, was a workman. In those first little companies of Christians, "not many . . . were wise according to worldly standards, not many were powerful, not many were of noble birth" (I Cor. 1:26) . A real devotion to truth is required, an openness to light, if one is to accept it when it comes from a lower economic or academic or social level than one's own.

There was also the obstacle of the familiar. To many the familiar puts a glaze over the eyes. Just because they have seen a thing so often, they do not really see it at all. There are multitudes who say of Christian teaching, with a logic that passes understanding: "Why, I've heard this from my cradle! I know it upside down and crisscross! Therefore it can't be true." Exactly the same final wisdom found in the question at Nazareth, **Is not this the carpenter?**

These people could not take in the greatness of Jesus. Can we?

4-6. *A Prophet Is Not Without Honor, Except in His Own Country.*—Notice that when Jesus quotes this familiar proverb, he applies it to himself and his work without a trace of cynicism. That mood might well have been present in another, for the whole affair at Nazareth was enough to turn a teacher bitter and carping. But there is no note of self-pity, no wailing against the cruel injustice of things, that he, a prophet, should be without honor in his own country. He makes a realistic observation, quoting the proverb, that this is the way things are. But that does not stop him. He marveled because of it—and went right on. There is an impressive eloquence about the next sentence. After it was all over, **he went about among the villages teaching.**

One thing this narrative pictures forcibly—Jesus had a sharp eye and a realistic mind, without a trace of paralyzing cynicism. That is a needed fortification for any continuous, long-range work with people.

Two practical compulsions stem from the fact that a prophet is very often without honor in his own country. First: Get on in spite of it. Jesus did exactly that. The work is the main thing. The "honor" is incidental and on the circumference. This means to learn to live without drugs. For the ongoing of your work do not depend on a daily "shot in the arm" in the form of praise, or recognition of one sort or another. That dependence is an addiction to habit-forming drugs which give a false and ephemeral "lift," pleasant and flattering, but with no staying power. The disciple can find sure resources where Jesus found them: "My meat is to do the will of him that sent me" (John 4:34) .

Second: The people who "took offense" at Jesus are a warning to us in our relations to others. We see clearly the obstacle which their lack of faith, their stubborn prejudice, and their

5 And he could there do no mighty work, save that he laid his hands upon a few sick folk, and healed *them*.

6 And he marveled because of their unbelief. And he went round about the villages, teaching.

own house." 5 And he could do no mighty work there, except that he laid his hands upon a few sick people and healed them. 6 And he marveled because of their unbelief.

And he went about among the villages teaching.

5-6. He could do no mighty work there is best taken as it stands: "could" rather than "would," in spite of Matthew's revision. As Origen notes (on Matt. 10:19), it was because of their lack of faith, as indeed Mark suggests in vs. 6. Vs. *5b*, **except . . . them,** looks like a redactional insertion, perhaps even a gloss, which interrupts the sequence. Of course it may well be that it was Mark himself who could not imagine Jesus' power as limited by such an obstacle, and so he introduced the exception clause into the older narrative. Again, in vs. *6b*, as often in Mark, Jesus is represented **as teaching,** but without any suggestion of the content of his discourses.

---

closed minds erected before Jesus' ministry. Let us not be a continuation of that inglorious company. Let us pay deserved honor to the prophets whom we meet and see and hear, that we may help to create the climate in which a fruitful service may be possible. Many a life has failed to render the best and highest ministry of which it was capable because the people among whom it first gave its witness were blinded by familiarity, contempt, or jealousy. Milton, in his lines on early death, from "Lycidas," outlines the pattern,

Comes the blind Fury with th' abhorred shears,
And slits the thin-spun life.

From the "blind Fury" which cuts off the possible ministry of a prophet, good Lord, deliver us!

5. *And He Could Do No Mighty Work There.*—Blunt words—"he could not." They were too blunt for Matthew, who softens them into "he did not do many mighty works there" (Matt. 13:58). Mark's reading is preferable (see Exeg.). There is an arresting solemnity about the words "could not." They fit into Jesus' own words about healing, in the preceding chapter (vs. 34), "Daughter, your faith has made you well." Without faith many mighty works that Jesus might have done, or might do, were and are left undone. It is true of the individual. Jesus can **do no mighty work** of saving in a life which does not thrust itself outward in a venture, "Lord, I believe; help thou mine unbelief" (9:24); nor can he minister to a life which owns two masters and tries to serve God and mammon.

It is true of a church. **No mighty work** can be done in a church not possessed by a faith that its Lord is Alpha and Omega. When the attitude of a church to Jesus is that of being, in the striking words of Montefiore about the

people in the Nazareth synagogue, "half amazed, and half annoyed," we may still look for mighty works of architecture, music, or eloquence, but for **no mighty work** of redemption. The epitaph for a church without faith has been composed by Sir William Watson:

Outwardly splendid as of old—
Inwardly sparkless, void and cold—
Her force and fire all spent and gone—
Like the dead moon, she still shines on.[6]

It is true of a world. If, in a world on the dizzy edge of disaster, powerful voices cry in a bullying tone to the church, "You wouldn't think, we hope, of trying to put this stuff about brotherhood into the real world of economic law or into international relations," and if an embarrassed church answers, as it has often answered, "Oh, no, of course not"—there will be **no mighty work** of salvation.

6. *He Marveled Because of Their Unbelief.*—It was something to marvel at. Often the marvels of unbelief are far greater than those of faith. There is the amazing creed which asserts that our world with its order, its coherence, is due to nothing more than the accidental bubblings of a vast mud pie. There is the prodigious dogma that man's moral sense, his capacity for love and sacrifice, are the product of a universe in which there are atoms, electrons, and galaxies of stars, but no moral or spiritual reality. There is the belief that all the achievements of Christian faith in millions of lives through nineteen centuries can be credited to a trivial delusion. Truly these are things to be marveled at! We are accustomed to stress the difficulties of faith. The difficulties of unbelief are greater.

[6] "The Church Today," *Poems of Sir William Watson, 1878-1935* (London: George G. Harrap & Co., 1936). By permission.

7 ¶ And he called *unto him* the twelve, and began to send them forth by two and two; and gave them power over unclean spirits;	7 And he called to him the twelve, and began to send them out two by two, and gave them authority over the unclean

2. The Mission of the Disciples (6:7-13)

It has been thought that the sending out of the disciples was motivated by the "rejection" at Nazareth, but there is no hint of this in Mark. Instead, he conceives the appointment of the apostles (3:14; cf. 6:30) as for this purpose. Both Matthew (ch. 10) and Luke (chs. 9–10) elaborate this section, with the result that it becomes a set of directions for the later mission of the church. Perhaps that was the point of view even in Q, upon which all three parallels, Mark included, seem to be based— Mark, as elsewhere, giving only an abridgment. That it was a temporary mission is clear. As Wellhausen noted, "The disciples are hereafter as lacking in initiative and independence as they were before." But neither the theory that the mission belonged after the Resurrection (Loisy), nor the view that it was Jesus' last-minute appeal to the nation before the Day of Judgment, as Albert Schweitzer maintained (*The Quest of the Historical Jesus,* tr. W. Montgomery [London: A. & C. Black, 1911]), has much to commend it. Josephus' description of the Essenes (*Jewish War* II. 8. 4) shows at least that such missionary activity was not unknown in first-century Palestine; it was also characteristic of the apostolic church, and later, as the Didache makes clear.

7. Possibly vs. 6*b* belongs with this section, as part of its introduction—so modern editions of the Greek text, as well as ancient lectionaries. **Power over unclean spirits,** i.e., power like his own. This had already been given them in 3:15, unless there it is viewed

---

7. *And He Called to Him the Twelve, and Began to Send Them Out Two by Two.*—This was an important step, a watershed in the work of Jesus, the sending out of human carriers of his message. It was evidently a temporary mission. But it was the first, and of major significance. The going out of the pairs of disciples moves the imagination deeply. Two by two, they are the head of the column, that long line of witnesses which winds down through the centuries and out to the ends of the earth, the "Big Parade" of all history.

> An endless line of splendor,
> These troops with heaven for home,
> With creeds they go from Scotland
> With incense go from Rome.[7]

Up to this point Jesus' predominant word was "come." Now another verb is added, "go." The first great word in every realm of life is always "come." The command "freely give" is futile unless there has been the indispensable preliminary, "Freely ye have received" (Matt. 10: 8). Yet life is never fulfilled until it hears and responds to the second verb, "go."

That word "go" marks a watershed too in the life of the disciple, when the outthrust of faith and service follows the incoming into a great

[7] Vachel Lindsay, "Foreign Missions in Battle Array," *General William Booth Enters Heaven and Other Poems.* Copyright, 1913 by The Macmillan Co. and used with their permission.

experience or truth. The question arises for each of us: Are we in the apostolic succession, not in any narrowly ecclesiastical sense, but in the deeper sense of being among those "sent"? Is ours a commissioned life which the Master's word "go" has put into motion? Are we in the parade or merely on the reviewing stand?

The word marks a watershed also in the life of a church. Unless a church reaches out it passes out. That is history. It is also prophecy.

Note also, on this verse, that in sending out his disciples, Jesus is moving to arouse the nation. That it had this effect is indicated in the succeeding paragraph, which describes King Herod's hearing of it. Branscomb stresses this interpretation: "Jesus undertook to arouse the nation. To His own efforts He added those of such followers as He could trust. His was no quiet, peaceful programme of teaching, but an undertaking that challenged and quite evidently aroused the whole nation." [8]

If the church is true to the example of its Master, it can never accept willingly any lesser destination for its message than the life of its nation. There has been far too much carry-over into the thinking and life of the church, of the jingle first learned in the primary department of the Sunday school,

> You in your little corner,
> And I in mine.

[8] *Gospel of Mark,* p. 102.

8 And commanded them that they should take nothing for *their* journey, save a staff only; no scrip, no bread, no money in *their* purse:

9 But *be* shod with sandals; and not put on two coats.

spirits. 8 He charged them to take nothing for their journey except a staff; no bread, no bag, no money in their belts; 9 but to wear sandals and not put on two

---

as part of the eventual purpose of their call and appointment (like 3:14c). That it was not a permanent authorization, or that it had its limitations, is suggested by 9:18, 28, though quite possibly Mark never considered the problem. Another possibility is that vs. 7b is an editorial insertion; it is implied, however, in vs. 13a.

8-9. Their equipment was to be the simplest, for their **journey** about Galilee would not take long, and they could rely upon hospitality for their food and shelter. The **staff** forbidden in Luke and Matthew is permitted here—unless the text of Mark is at fault. The wearing of **two tunics** in Mark is changed by Matthew and Luke to the owning of them.

Churches have become too satisfied with safe and cozy corners, and have too often shrunk from the truly apostolic task of carrying their message into the total life of the nation. We read in the book of Acts, concerning the history on which the Christian faith is based, "This was not done in a corner" (Acts 26:26). The full redeeming work of Christianity will never be done in a corner. Thackeray once complained of the small circulation of his books, "My tunes must be sung in the streets." The words of Jesus must be sung in the streets. Other words in sufficient number are carried into the life of the nation. Many vocal groups take their sanction from Mark Antony: "Cry 'Havoc!' and let slip the dogs of war." [9] Christ's disciples must overmatch that with something better, "Cry 'Repent!' and let slip the works of peace."

8. *He Charged Them to Take Nothing for Their Journey Except a Staff.*—The Gospel of Mark was originally circulated in a missionary church. One of its purposes was to promote evangelization. A prominent place is naturally given to what might be called "the marching orders of a missionary." Q contained such a code of missionary directions. It filled a real need, and great impetus should be given to the work of missions through this narrative of its origin in the act and words of Jesus as he made ready to send forth the first heralds of the kingdom.

These directions were for a specific time and situation. It was to be a short trip, both in distance and duration. Many of the counsels arise from that fact. Nothing could be more unjustified than to elevate these directions into timeless laws for missionary activity. Yet there is in them, beyond their origin in the prospect of a short journey in Galilee, deep and lasting wisdom for all the work of carrying the Christian gospel.

Jesus' forbidding his disciples to take elaborate equipment says clearly to everyone who goes out to witness, "The main thing is to get on with the work." Do not get bogged down with a burdensome sense of responsibility for paraphernalia. **No bread, no bag, no money,** the simplest clothes. Travel light, so that the work may get the whole of your undivided mind and soul. The emphasis has a pertinence for all time. More than once the urgency of the mission has been lost through a worried concern about incidentals. A fussy preoccupation with accessories, or a delay until the perfect equipment was ready, has blotted out the evangelistic purpose. The means can supplant the end. The word "impediment" once meant "baggage."

In the individual disciple life can be wasted in drilling, in getting ready, in putting off the effort to meet a crying need until the ideal tools are at hand. By that time the day of opportunity is passed, or the mind has acquired a permanent preoccupation with the secondary, unfitting it for swift movement into the urgent task.

The same compulsion to put first the task of carrying the message rests on a company of disciples, a church. Reliance on equipment, on the ecclesiastical equivalent of bag, money, and clothes, has all too often pushed into the background the command to "go." There is always danger that by the time a great idea gets completely organized and housed, the original impulse will be forgotten. The detail of the collecting bag is endlessly suggestive. The business of collecting money can take the place of the business of evangelizing. Masonry, money in the purse, ecclesiastical furnishings, have become not only obstacles to the mission, but substitutes for it.

[9] Shakespeare, *Julius Caesar*, Act III, scene 1.

10 And he said unto them, In what place soever ye enter into a house, there abide till ye depart from that place.

11 And whosoever shall not receive you, nor hear you, when ye depart thence, shake off the dust under your feet for a testimony against them. Verily I say unto you, It shall be more tolerable for Sodom and Gomorrah in the day of judgment, than for that city.

12 And they went out, and preached that men should repent.

tunics. 10 And he said to them, "Where you enter a house, stay there until you leave the place. 11 And if any place will not receive you and they refuse to hear you, when you leave, shake off the dust that is on your feet for a testimony against them." 12 So they went out and preached

---

10-11. The hospitality of their hearers is taken for granted, as could well be done; the hospitality of religious-minded Jews was well known, and is reflected more than once in the Bible. **Shake off . . . testimony against them:** A symbolic act denoting a complete break in relations and a repudiation of further responsibility for them. The terrible judgment that overthrew **Sodom and Gomorrah** (Gen. 19:24) was a common example of what was to be expected on **the day of judgment**; but the whole sentence is absent from the best MSS of Mark, and is a gloss derived from the parallels (Matt. 10:15; Luke 10:12—though prior to all the Gospels it may have been found at this point in Q). RSV correctly omits this sentence.

12-13. The brief description of the disciples' ministry as preaching repentance, exorcism, and anointing with oil (cf. 3:14-15; 6:30) is suggestive. Preaching and teaching

---

10. *And He Said to Them, "Where You Enter a House, Stay There Until You Leave the Place."*—This direction may reflect the practice of later years when there were Christians in many towns, and the missionary might move, or be tempted to move, from house to house, perhaps going from the less comfortable to the more comfortable. Again, as in the command in the previous verse, the emphasis on giving the great priority to the task comes with force to every generation, to the disciple in the twentieth century as well as in the first. It says clearly, Never let your desire for comfort take your attention from the work. Nothing else really matters. The chief question is not, "How do I like it?" but "How is the work getting done?" An undue insistence on comfort, the desire to have everything just exactly right, lodging, food, people, pay, can ruin the work of anyone sent out on a mission for Jesus. It puts the self at the center of attention, and God on the fringe. Do not let the search for comfort transform an apostle into a "fuss-box."

11. *If Any Place Will Not Receive You . . . , When You Leave, Shake Off the Dust That Is on Your Feet.*—These words from Jesus' lips have been grievously misused. They have been taken, again and again, as a ready and easy excuse for quitting a job just when it gets really hard, but before all the possibilities have been completely explored. We often hear people declare, "I just shook the dust of that place

off my feet," saying it with a wave of self-satisfaction, and inwardly citing the authority of Jesus for the action. Yet if the real, unvarnished truth were told, the substance of it would amount to, "The going got altogether too hard, and I quit."

That was not the sort of dust-shaking that Jesus meant (see Exeg.). It was a symbolic act disclaiming responsibility, if the townspeople persistently refused to hear.

There is a permanent suggestiveness in the counsel, whether it was in the thought of Jesus or not. It is really a direction for going on in spite of failure. It says, When you meet disappointment, don't let yourself get completely stopped; just close that chapter and start the next. There are other towns, other efforts to be made. If the first act doesn't turn out as you hoped, go on to the second, whether there or somewhere else. God is rich in resources. You are not responsible for results, but you are responsible for efforts.

History is rich in examples of complete failure, from which people have gone on to great achievement. Jesus met failure in Nazareth. "He could do no mighty work." So he closed the chapter and went on. It has been said of Napoleon that he had a technique for victory, but no technique for defeat. The Christian has a technique for defeat. It is to go on in trust, relying on the God who never comes to his "last chance," but who always has new doors of op-

13 And they cast out many devils, and anointed with oil many that were sick, and healed *them.*

14 And king Herod heard *of him;* (for his name was spread abroad;) and he said, That John the Baptist was risen from the dead, and therefore mighty works do show themselves in him.

15 Others said, That it is Elias. And others said, That it is a prophet, or as one of the prophets.

that men should repent. 13 And they cast out many demons, and anointed with oil many that were sick and healed them.

14 King Herod heard of it; for Jesus's name had become known. Some[t] said, "John the baptizer has been raised from the dead; that is why these powers are at work in him." 15 But others said, "It is Elijah." And others said, "It is a prophet,

[s] Greek *his.*
[t] Some ancient authorities read *he.*

(6:30) are evidently identical, at this point (cf. Luke 9:6); exorcism was likewise an extension of Jesus' own ministry; but anointing sounds unusual, though it was a common treatment of the sick in ancient times (cf. Jas. 5:14-15). Neither Matthew nor Luke retains this feature—though Luke 9:6 says that they were "healing everywhere"—and nowhere is Jesus himself described as using oil. Perhaps the feature is best explained as a reflection of later apostolic practice.

3. HEROD'S IMPRESSION OF JESUS (6:14-16)

This and the following section form a dramatic interlude, to fill up the interval of time while the disciples are on their mission; the present one shows the effect, not so much of the disciples' work, as of that of Jesus: **his name was spread abroad** (KJV), i.e., **had become known** (RSV), or "was now well known" (Goodspeed). **Some** people said—not **he,** as in KJV, following the majority of later MSS—that Jesus was John the baptizer **risen from the dead, and therefore mighty works . . . in him.** The ancients believed that the soul of a person who had met a violent death became a powerful "control" in the spirit-world; hence Jesus was either John come back to life, or else was in league with his powerful spirit (cf. C. H. Kraeling, "Was Jesus Accused of Necromancy?" *Journal of Biblical Literature,* LIX [1940], 147-57).

15. Elijah was expected to return during or before the messianic era (Mal. 4:5). The belief took various forms, and was found even among the Samaritans. **A prophet, like one of the prophets:** Better (with D O.L.) "that it [or "he"] is one of the prophets." These various popular estimates show that Jesus' ministry of healing and exorcism (vs. 14) and of preaching (vs. 15) led men to think of him as someone quite extraordinary; to Mark, who regards the section as an introduction to what follows, especially 8:27-30, these were of course inadequate explanations but characteristic of the Jewish populace.

---

portunity to open. When we meet defeat, as the disciples were warned that they might meet it, the thing to do is to move on to another effort, and not to indulge in wailing. Too often in human experience a wailing wall becomes a tombstone.

14-15. *John the Baptizer Has Been Raised from the Dead. . . . It Is Elijah. . . . It Is a Prophet.*—The people who made these conjectures about Jesus were engaged in what has always been a very common sort of thinking. They were fixing labels. They were trying to throw Jesus into some already existing familiar and convenient category. Their minds operated just like the skilled arm of a railroad mail clerk, tossing letters into pigeonholes. It saved them the trouble of really looking at Jesus, and making a fresh independent valuation of him.

"Who is Jesus?" they were asked. Each reply was some familiar classification; each reply was wrong, but each was completely satisfactory to the one who made it. He was John the Baptist. . . . He was Elijah. . . . He was a prophet, in the same class with prophets of old. It did not occur to any of them that he might be new and unique, too big and oddly shaped to go into any of the timeworn holes. The same procedure is reflected in the story of Peter's confession (8:28).

It is a very frequent—and pernicious—substitute for thinking. Every event must be put into some compartment, whether it fits or not, and every person as well. William James says that a baby's first mental operation is "thingumbob again." That is about as far as many people get in mature life. Everything is "thingumbob

16 But when Herod heard *thereof,* he said, It is John, whom I beheaded: he is risen from the dead.

17 For Herod himself had sent forth and laid hold upon John, and bound him in prison for Herodias' sake, his brother Philip's wife; for he had married her.

18 For John had said unto Herod, It is not lawful for thee to have thy brother's wife.

like one of the prophets of old." 16 But when Herod heard of it he said, "John, whom I beheaded, has been raised." 17 For Herod had sent and seized John, and bound him in prison for the sake of He-ro'-di-as, his brother Philip's wife; because he had married her. 18 For John said to Herod, "It is not lawful for you to have

---

16. Herod prefers the first explanation: Jesus is John risen again, i.e., come back to life and therefore, as a revenant from the other world, able to perform mighty works (δυνάμεις again). In fact, the "powers" operate "in [i.e., through] him" (vs. 14*b*), as self-effective forces using him as their agent. Without saying it, Mark surely viewed this as we do, as the terrified superstition of a murderer.

4. THE DEATH OF JOHN THE BAPTIZER (6:17-29)

After the above introduction, Mark tells the story of John's death. What its source may have been we do not know. It is obviously a popular legend, with contacts in Hellenistic literature which suggest that it may originally have been a Hellenistic-Jewish story. Philip (vs. 17) was not the brother's name; the dance of Salome was most improbable, even in a debased court like that of the Herods; and Mark's account of the motivation of Antipas' imprisonment of the prophet is contradicted by Josephus, who relates that Herod feared a revolution, and suspected John's growing popularity (*Antiquities* XVIII. 5. 2). It is possible, of course, though unlikely, that both motives were at work.

17. Herod Antipas was not "king" (as in vss. 14, 27), but tetrarch of Galilee and Perea; it was not his brother Philip's wife whom he had taken but the wife of another brother, Herod, by whom she had a daughter Salome, born *ca.* A.D. 10—this Salome (not Herodias) was the wife of Philip (Josephus *Antiquities* XVIII. 5. 4). Antipas' first wife was the daughter of Aretas IV, the Arabian king, and he cast her off for Herodias; hence the war with Aretas and the destruction of Herod's army. The popular view was that this defeat was a divine judgment upon Antipas for the murder of the prophet (Josephus *loc. cit.*).

18. Not lawful: Herodias was still his **brother's wife,** if the brother was still living—this would be the Christian judgment (cf. 10:11-12). If Herodias was divorced,

---

again," when as a matter of fact it usually isn't thingumbob at all, but something entirely different. It has been a common way of dealing with religion. "The fatherhood of God"—oh, yes—click—and it is popped into a pigeonhole labeled "projection." Forgiveness—that's easy—it is the resolution of a guilt complex. Next question! We see it every day in the social and political world. In minds which work like sorting machines, everything that looks even faintly liberal is tossed into the large pigeonhole labeled "Communist." Every untraditional expression of the American heritage of democracy goes speedily into the box labeled "radical." The beauty of it is the economy of mental operation. The curse of it is that one never really sees anything as it is.

Nevertheless, from another point of view the resemblances to the great figures of Hebrew his-

tory which these men saw in Jesus were a great tribute to him. His ministry "led men to think of him as someone quite extraordinary" (see Exeg.). However little they knew of him, the impression he made brought only the great to mind. An arresting question follows: Of whom do we remind people? Do they catch from us any resemblance, any quick reminder of anyone high and noble? More specifically, are they ever moved to give this highest tribute that earth holds—"He reminds me of Jesus"?

18. *For John Said to Herod, "It Is Not Lawful for You to Have Your Brother's Wife."* —The greatest thing in this whole passage is the courage of John. It is a superb spectacle which has not faded a bit through the centuries. No wonder he won that dazzling tribute from Jesus, a tribute beside which all those which kings and emperors and governments have ever

19 Therefore Herodias had a quarrel against him, and would have killed him; but she could not:

20 For Herod feared John, knowing that he was a just man and a holy, and observed him; and when he heard him, he did many things, and heard him gladly.

your brother's wife." 19 And He-ro'di-as had a grudge against him, and wanted to kill him. But she could not, 20 for Herod feared John, knowing that he was a righteous and holy man, and kept him safe. When he heard him, he was much perplexed; and

---

Antipas could not marry her, according to the Mosaic law (Lev. 18:16; 20:21); even if her husband was dead, the marriage was unlawful, since she had a child, and the levirate rule (Deut. 25:5) could not be invoked—though technically the law provided for the case in which no son had been born, and Salome was a daughter. But possibly the story as originally told meant "It is not *right*"; cf. 3:4 and 10:2, where the Pharisees certainly know what is "lawful." John the Baptist is not represented as an expounder of Torah.

19-20. The words **kept him safe**—as if Herod were John's friend and protector— introduce a note in striking contrast with Josephus' narrative. It is possible that they serve later apologetic interests. **Did many things** (KJV) is the reading of some MSS and versions (C D O.L. sy), but others (א B Θ p⁴⁵) read **he was much perplexed** (RSV). Something has gone wrong with the text at this point (vs. 20*b*); Klostermann conjectures a gloss; Schmiedel suggests, on the basis of Luke 9:7, that the words have slipped in here from 6:16, where they originally stood.

---

given are like a string of five-and-ten-cent-store beads. Think of it—"There has risen no one greater than John the Baptist" (Matt. 11:11).

His courage came from a tremendous belief. "**It is not lawful,**" he cried. That was enough to drive John into action. He had a sense of the everlasting quality of right. If a thing was wrong, he witnessed against it. He may not have known he was moving directly toward the headsman's axe, but that would have made no difference.

Courage has frequently been called a pagan virtue. More truly it is a virtue with no adjective. It is a mark of the God and Father of all men, who has not left himself without a witness anywhere. In deep ways, however, there is a courage which is a religious virtue, stemming from a high faith. Such was the courage of John, and of a greater than John, who set his face to go to Jerusalem. We may easily forget how much any hope for the betterment of the world depends finally on courage. When men have merely "nerves" instead of nerve, that hope is shattered. John the Baptist was not surrounded, as many of us are, by so great a cloud of witnesses—the devil's witnesses—justifying prudence. We are beset before and behind by proverbs which whisper, "Watch your step." We are told that "discretion is the better part of valor," and what sweet music it often is to our ears! We readily forget that the epitaph on the gravestone of many good causes has been, "Died of discretion." We are told with unctuous persuasiveness that "he who fights and runs away, lives to fight another day." That is usually

a lie. He may live, only to run away again at the next crisis. True, "he who is least in the kingdom of heaven is greater than he" (Matt. 11:11); yet we cannot leave out John's courage.

19. *Herodias Had a Grudge Against Him, and Wanted to Kill Him.*—Herodias is an example of a common reaction to moral reproof. She reacted by violence. In the words **had a grudge**, we can see the emotional stampede in her head. We can hear her cry, "How dare he!"

It is tragically common. Those who profit by an established economic order very often meet ethical criticisms of that order, not by a weighing of the criticisms, but by a rush of blood to the head, by emotional frenzy often bordering on hysteria. The weapon they reach for is violence, both of tongue and strong arm. They take up cudgels against labor, against all who refuse to bow the knee, or who suggest a more excellent way to the goal of human welfare. All too frequently the mood and the technique of Herodias still prevail in the palaces of power, with similar tragic results. Violence is never an answer to moral evaluation.

The same reaction is sometimes found in the religious realm. Those entrenched in a hard fortress of dogma often react with violence to the criticism that their brittle intolerance and spiritual pride do not express the spirit of the gospel. They say that such criticism is made by "traitors" to the cause of Christ. There sits Herodias in ecclesiastical robes.

20. *For Herod Feared John. . . . When He Heard Him, He Was Much Perplexed; and Yet . . .*—These words represent much more

21 And when a convenient day was come, that Herod on his birthday made a supper to his lords, high captains, and chief *estates* of Galilee;

22 And when the daughter of the said Herodias came in, and danced, and pleased Herod and them that sat with him, the king said unto the damsel, Ask of me whatsoever thou wilt, and I will give *it* thee.

23 And he sware unto her, Whatsoever thou shalt ask of me, I will give *it* thee, unto the half of my kingdom.

24 And she went forth, and said unto her mother, What shall I ask? And she said, The head of John the Baptist.

yet he heard him gladly. 21 But an opportunity came when Herod on his birthday gave a banquet for his courtiers and officers and the leading men of Galilee. 22 For when He-ro'di-as' daughter came in and danced, she pleased Herod and his guests; and the king said to the girl, "Ask me for whatever you wish, and I will grant it." 23 And he vowed to her, "Whatever you ask me, I will give you, even half of my kingdom." 24 And she went out, and said to her mother, "What shall I ask?" And she said, "The

---

21. Where the banquet was held is not stated: the distant border fortress of Machaerus was unlikely, if the Galilean guests were to attend; more probably it was the city of Tiberias, though Josephus states that John was imprisoned and put to death at Machaerus.

23. Unto the half of my kingdom was a proverbial expression (cf. I Kings 13:8; Esth. 5:3; 7:2). The king tricked by his own oath is a favorite motif in legend.

---

than a detail in the last days of John the Baptist. They are a keen probing into the mystery of the human mind and spirit. They picture the strange power of truth—Herod perplexed, yet returning to hear John gladly—the strange power of religious and moral truth to launch a civil war in the heart and mind of man. Man turns away from spiritual truth, from its disconcerting challenge to his life, and yet he turns back to it. Perplexed, often the perplexity shades into anger and conflict, yet he cannot completely close either his ear or his mind.

How unwelcome Christian teaching has often been, as it has been reborn into new generations! How impertinent it has seemed to the wise and mighty, how preposterous! Yet it has never lost its power to touch the conscience, as John's word touched the conscience of Herod. We see it operating when Paul spoke to Agrippa and to Festus. They were perplexed, incredulous; but they could not put it wholly by. So it was when Christianity confronted slavery; when it confronted the exploitation of men, women, and children in the cruel years of the industrial revolution; so it is when the teaching of Jesus confronts war. So much of that teaching was and is against all the reason of a highly practical world. And yet—we listen.

That is one of the ultimate reasons why, in spite of every obstacle, it is worth while to go on confronting men with Christ. He fits the mind and life of humanity. Religion is no more imported into human nature than is sex or hunger. There is a dependable response. Yet **he heard him gladly.**

22. The King Said to the Girl, "Ask Me for Whatever You Wish, and I Will Grant It."— Herod was in a state of intoxicated expansion. In his pleasure his judgment was impaired, his sense of values was distorted. He had no real kingdom to divide, he could not have given any of it away. That moment of deceptive exhilaration was the open door to tragedy.

Not every case of intoxicated expansion is due to alcohol. There are many sad instances in which distorted values have led to tragedy. Multitudes of persons have been **pleased,** have been carried away by one desire which blotted out everything else in a befuddled mind. They have said to wealth: "Ask anything you wish, and I will give it to you. You are what I want. Ask anything—integrity, peace of mind, all the other interests which life might develop—I'll give it for wealth." And they have carried out, as Herod did, the sorry bargain. Men have said the same to pleasure, to fame, offering everything. They have said it even to such a god as comfort. There is truth in the adage, "the trouble with money is that it costs so much." When we say to anything except God, "Ask whatever you wish and I will give it to you," it costs too much.

24. And She Went Out, and Said to Her Mother, "What Shall I Ask?"—Here is a grim and gruesome story, utterly removed from common experience; yet this question put by the girl to her mother is, in a real though different sense, a vital part of every mother-and-daughter relationship. Every daughter somehow, sometime, says: "What shall I ask of life? What **is it**

25 And she came in straightway with haste unto the king, and asked, saying, I will that thou give me by and by in a charger the head of John the Baptist.

26 And the king was exceeding sorry; *yet* for his oath's sake, and for their sakes which sat with him, he would not reject her.

27 And immediately the king sent an executioner, and commanded his head to be brought: and he went and beheaded him in the prison,

head of John the baptizer." 25 And she came in immediately with haste to the king, and asked, saying, "I want you to give me at once the head of John the Baptist on a platter." 26 And the king was exceedingly sorry; but because of his oaths and his guests he did not want to break his word to her. 27 And immediately the king sent a soldier of the guard and gave orders to bring his head. He went and beheaded him

---

27. Executioner (KJV) is better rendered as **soldier of the guard** (RSV). But σπεκουλάτωρ, from Latin, here only in N.T., could in Latin also mean "executioner" (see, e.g., Seneca, *On Benefits* III. 25). John's **disciples** have already been mentioned (2:18). Later legend located the tomb at Samaria, but this is quite improbable.

---

you want me most to do and to be? I'll take my cue from you." And she does.

Herodias had no concern for her daughter. Her daughter was not an end in herself, but just a means, an instrument for gratifying her own hatred. Apparently without flicking an eyelid she made her daughter into a guilty accessory to murder.

Many a mother has played a part scarcely less criminal. When the whole growing mind and personality of the daughter asks, "What do you want me to be and do?" the mother has often answered with a callousness resembling that of Herodias: "Why, I want you to be a social success, my dear. What else is there to be? I want you to minister to my own pride and prestige. I don't care about what you really are. I want you to be rich, to be complimented, to be envied." So the daughter takes the fatal cue, and one more life is mangled. The translation of such an ambition into plain, bald, ugly language would run, "I want you to be a selfish, coldhearted, snobbish, acquisitive person." Herodias did not do much worse.

Of course these things are rarely said in so many words. But children have terribly penetrating eyes. No matter how fair or pious the disguise, they see what a parent really cares for most. They know when dancing lessons are more important than Bible lessons. They know when the furnishings of the house are more important than the spiritual climate of the home; when position is more important than character; when the food on the dining-room table is more important than the symbols on the Communion table; when the right hairdo is more important than the thoughts that go on under the permanent wave.

So, perversely but emphatically, it was Mother's Day at the fortress of Machaerus. There is

high tragedy in the concluding line of this narrative of Salome. A soldier brought the head of John the Baptist, "and the girl gave it to her mother." She is saying, "Here, Mother, is a present for you. This is what you wanted most of all." It is not hard to imagine a daughter who might well have been a great personality, rich in sympathy, generous in spirit, strong in Christian character, bringing to her mother a stunted life and saying, "This is what you wanted, Mother." It is a critical hour when another looks to us and says, **"What shall I ask?"** Pray God for mercy and grace in that hour.

26. *But Because of His Oaths and His Guests He Did Not Want to Break His Word to Her.* —Here are two common causes of wrongdoing. Both root in pride. No wonder many regard pride as the cardinal sin. Herod persisted in his crime, in spite of the warning of both his mind and heart—he was **exceedingly sorry**—for two reasons: his oaths and his guests. The same two forces have pushed many along an evil course.

Herod, in carrying out his oath, was "saving face." His prestige was at stake. For the time being nothing else counted. Stubborn pride kept him from saying, "I was wrong. I cannot do this wickedness." When our prestige becomes so dear to us that it blots out moral distinctions, we are on the downward path with Herod.

Herod was also gallery-conscious. There were his guests looking on. What would they say? He must make a brave show in front of them, no matter at what cost. So the pressure of the crowd took the helm of his life away from his own mind and conscience. It is a trick that crowd pressure does very well.

But being gallery-conscious is a good thing, if we pick the right gallery. Herod picked the wrong one. The way to prevent the flattening out of the will and soul which comes when we

28 And brought his head in a charger, and gave it to the damsel; and the damsel gave it to her mother.

29 And when his disciples heard *of it,* they came and took up his corpse, and laid it in a tomb.

30 And the apostles gathered themselves together unto Jesus, and told him all things, both what they had done, and what they had taught.

31 And he said unto them, Come ye yourselves apart into a desert place, and rest a while: for there were many coming and going, and they had no leisure so much as to eat.

in the prison, 28 and brought his head on a platter, and gave it to the girl; and the girl gave it to her mother. 29 When his disciples heard of it, they came and took his body, and laid it in a tomb.

30 The apostles returned to Jesus, and told him all that they had done and taught. 31 And he said to them, "Come away by yourselves to a lonely place, and rest a while." For many were coming and going,

5. The Feeding of the Five Thousand (6:30-44)

This story, told in all the Gospels, has been variously interpreted. The language used, both here and in the parallel story (8:1-9), is quite liturgical; and yet for Mark it is one of Jesus' "mighty works," by which he fed a great multitude of people who were physically hungry. Albert Schweitzer viewed the incident as an "eschatological sacrament," observed in anticipation of the great feast to be held in the approaching kingdom of God. It is difficult if not impossible to make out its original significance. Probably different emphases were given the story as it was handed down by tradition prior to Mark. For one thing, it has certainly been influenced by the O.T. legends of miraculous provision of food (e.g., I Kings 17:8-16, and especially II Kings 4:42-44, which is closely parallel), though it is going beyond the evidence to say that it was constructed in imitation of the O.T. stories.

30-34. These verses are clearly editorial, and provide both the continuity with what precedes (vs. 13) and the setting for what follows. Note that **a desert place** (KJV)

---

defer to an onlooking gallery is to look up to a higher gallery for approval. Joseph in Egypt did that. Hebrews, though indirectly, suggests a good gallery to play to—"Since we are surrounded by so great a cloud of witnesses, . . . let us run with perseverance the race that is set before us" (Heb. 12:1).

31. *Come Away by Yourselves to a Lonely Place, and Rest a While.*—These words of Jesus are both a prescription for the immediate need of the disciples returning from a tour, and a word for all lives at all times. Notice first that it was a physical prescription—rest in a quiet place to regain depleted physical and nervous strength. If we overlook that, we miss a great and lasting meaning. Here, surely, Jesus is the Good Physician. They needed physical rest, away from the push of a milling crowd, so that the physical basis of life could be conserved. The watchful care of health and strength is a primary religious duty. When we fail to take that care, we sin against God. We snatch away from his full use the instrument that he ought to have. It has been exceedingly hard to see this duty of health in its proper religious setting. The distorted value placed on asceticism

has played its part; so has the unfortunate coupling of things which man has joined together, but which God never did, such as sickness and piety. How often God has been blamed for man's disobedience of God's laws of health! The words "the Lord hath taken away" are almost a blasphemy when it is man who has taken himself away. The time should come soon when we shall confess to "committing" a cold or "committing" a nervous breakdown or an ulcer, as we confess to any other grievous sin. Here is an eloquent portrayal of the need for rest as a primary equipment for service. Matthew Arnold writes of the sea's "melancholy long withdrawing roar." We can get something like that from fatigued bodies and frayed nerves: the "melancholy long withdrawing" gasp. If we are too busy to allow strength to be renewed by withdrawal and rest, we are too busy to serve God with our best.

31. *For Many Were Coming and Going, and They Had No Leisure even to Eat.*—These words too speak our condition, living so much in hurrying crowds, racing with the clock. They give a picture of "the breathless life." If there was coming and going in the little villages of

32 And they departed into a desert place by ship privately.

33 And the people saw them departing, and many knew him, and ran afoot thither out of all cities, and outwent them, and came together unto him.

34 And Jesus, when he came out, saw much people, and was moved with compassion toward them, because they were as sheep not having a shepherd: and he began to teach them many things.

and they had no leisure even to eat. 32 And they went away in the boat to a lonely place by themselves. 33 Now many saw them going, and knew them, and they ran there on foot from all the towns, and got there ahead of them. 34 As he landed he saw a great throng, and he had compassion on them, because they were like sheep without a shepherd; and he began to teach

---

is merely **a lonely place** (RSV). **Compassion:** The motive is the same as in 8:2, though there it is the hunger of the people that is stressed. The language is borrowed from the O.T. (e.g., Ezek. 34:6). Presumably the story in its pre-Marcan form began with this verse (34), though the final words, **and he began to teach them many things,** have been added by Mark. It is characteristic of Mark to note this fact, without giving any of the content of the teaching.

Palestine, how greatly the human traffic jam has been multiplied in our cities and towns, with comings and goings by bus, train, automobile, airplane, streetcar. The ironical result in some sections is that by far the fastest means of locomotion is the most primitive—walking! With many, life becomes so constantly public that it is like living in a vast railroad station. No leisure for eating may be a result, but it is a small result compared to no leisure for living in the deepest sense, no leisure for the spirit to expand. The great spiritual and psychological risk of life immersed in comings and goings is that a person may fail to arrive at true self-consciousness or personal identity. In *In Memoriam* Tennyson writes of an infant's mental development, "So rounds he to a separate mind." But there is no real rounding to a separate mind when there is no lonely place as a refuge from crowding. There is subtle truth in the modern fantasy of a man who vanished into thin air the minute everyone else had left the room. Charles Lamb's complaint that he was never just Charles Lamb, but "Charles Lamb and Company," has great pertinence. In the lonely place we can come to true selfhood.

So the words of Jesus, **Come away by yourselves,** are an invitation to salvation in our day as in his. Maurice Colbourne, in his biography of George Bernard Shaw, says a picturesque and arresting thing: "When seen in the London streets or on the Malvern hills he always walks as though he had an appointment with himself and might be late for it." [1] That is the secret—make an appointment with yourself. You make them with the butcher, the baker, the

candlestick maker. Make appointments with your whole self, for that will be ultimately an appointment with God. Then you can move in crowds without being spiritually crushed by gregariousness. In these lines on William Blake there is a beautiful picture of this possibility of the preserved soul:

> He came to the desert of London town,
>   Grey miles long.
> He wandered up and he wandered down,
>   Singing a quiet song.
>
> He came to the desert of London town,
>   Murk miles broad.
> He wandered up and he wandered down,
>   Ever alone with God. [2]

34. He Had Compassion on Them, Because They Were Like Sheep Without a Shepherd.— This in itself was by no means a minor miracle. Jesus was moved by the crowd to a great compassion, where anyone else would have been moved to a great irritation. For this rushing crowd had completely spoiled the whole purpose of the trip. Jesus and his disciples, according to Mark, had need of quietness. But when they got to the lonely place, it was no longer lonely; it was trampled over by a milling mob. How natural to have given way to impatience; to have exclaimed, "Can't they leave me alone one hour?"

But looking at the crowd, there was only one emotion in his heart, compassion. That was the effect a crowd always had on Jesus (see Matt. 9:36). He saw a crowd, not through the eyes of one who counted life dear to himself, concerned for his own comfort and plans, but

---

[1] *The Real Bernard Shaw* (New York: Dodd, Mead & Co., 1940), p. 76.

[2] James Thomson the Younger, "William Blake."

35 And when the day was now far spent, his disciples came unto him, and said, This is a desert place, and now the time *is* far passed:

36 Send them away, that they may go into the country round about, and into the villages, and buy themselves bread: for they have nothing to eat.

37 He answered and said unto them, Give ye them to eat. And they say unto him, Shall we go and buy two hundred pennyworth of bread, and give them to eat?

them many things. 35 And when it grew late, his disciples came to him and said, "This is a lonely place, and the hour is now late; 36 send them away, to go into the country and villages round about and buy themselves something to eat." 37 But he answered them, "You give them something to eat." And they said to him, "Shall we go and buy two hundred denarii[u] worth of bread, and

[u] See note on Matthew 18. 28.

37-40. Give ye them to eat. (Cf. II Kings 4:42-43.) It was inevitable that such a story as this, in the earliest Christian circles, should be told in O.T. language. **Two hundred denarii** was about $40, with purchasing power in the first century of about four times as

---

through the eyes of one who came to seek and to save those who were lost, who came that men might have abundant life.

We cannot observe that response of Jesus to the crowd without asking, Which comes most naturally to us, irritation or compassion? It is so easy to lose patience with people when they get in our way, block our plans, fail to respond to our wisdom. It is easy often to drop into the savage mood of Carlyle, when he said that the population of England was thirty millions, mostly fools. Is compassion strong enough to wash away irritation, as a beach is washed clean by an incoming tide? Can we see into people, catch a glimpse, by dedicated imagination, of the invisible burdens they carry, the hopes they wistfully cherish, the extenuating circumstances that must go into any fair appraisal, the unspoken need in their lives? Jesus could see that, and more, always. Can we see it, ever? There are not many more important questions for us than this: How do our compassions stand, when we compare them to our irritations?

35-37. *His Disciples . . . Said, . . . "Send Them Away."*—They could have made a very good case for their feeling that this crowd which had followed them was not their responsibility. They had issued no invitation. Far from it. The mob had ruined their longed-for rest and solitude. Perhaps there is some resentment in this plea. **Send them away.** Let them buy bread in the villages. There was small chance of that, and the disciples knew it; but at any rate they would be free of the throng.

Note the contrast between them and Jesus. They looked entirely to the possibilities outside the situation. Jesus said that the emergency could be met within the situation, not by imported aid, but with their own resources and

faith. In every generation there are these two continuing classes of people and attitudes: those who are looking for something from without, and those who are looking for something from within.

Are we really watching the disciples at the upper end of the Sea of Galilee, or is it that we are looking at ourselves in a mirror? The words **send them away** are not strange to us. They are often on our lips and in our minds as we try to escape our responsibilities. A burden is laid on us. We are swift to see the injustice of it: "I did not ask for it. Why fasten it on me? I am no charity organization. I am no free legal-aid bureau. I have my living to make." Or the people of a church say: "We never asked these foreigners to move into our neighborhood. They are not our kind. We have all we can do to look out for our own. They probably have needs, but we can't do anything about it. **Send them away** to the movies, to the taverns, to the race tracks—anywhere, so long as they look after themselves." Brutal words, but they have been used, callously used, and used all too often.

Society, a city or a nation, readily finds the same easy solution. Many an American, after World War II, brought face to face with the problem of displaced persons in Europe, developed keen eyes for distant lands to which the homeless could be sent—Tasmania—Brazil looks like a large place. New Yorkers who could fairly have shed tears over the helpless Jews kept out of Palestine yet stiffened with horror at the suggestion that any of them, even the orphans, might be brought to the United States. And these juvenile delinquents—**Send them away** to reform schools, to penitentiaries. It is so much easier than to change the conditions out of which juvenile delinquency springs.

38 He saith unto them, How many loaves have ye? go and see. And when they knew, they say, Five, and two fishes.

39 And he commanded them to make all sit down by companies upon the green grass.

40 And they sat down in ranks, by hundreds, and by fifties.

41 And when he had taken the five loaves and the two fishes, he looked up to heaven, and blessed, and brake the loaves, and gave *them* to his disciples to set before them; and the two fishes divided he among them all.

give it to them to eat?" **38** And he said to them, "How many loaves have you? Go and see." And when they had found out, they said, "Five, and two fish." **39** Then he commanded them all to sit down by companies upon the green grass. **40** So they sat down in groups, by hundreds and by fifties. **41** And taking the five loaves and the two fish he looked up to heaven, and blessed, and broke the loaves, and gave them to the disciples to set before the people; and he

much, or $160. The sum was an impossible one for the disciples. The five **loaves** would be small round loaves, made of barley meal (as in II Kings 4:42; cf. John 6:9), slightly larger than our baker's buns. The **two fish** would undoubtedly be cooked. It was probably not what was left over from the apostles' recent tour (in vs. 8 they were to take no bread), but the modest provision for their retreat (vs. 31), which they were now ordered to distribute among the people. **By hundreds, and by fifties:** Originally, perhaps, fifty companies of one hundred each, or a hundred of fifty each, totaling five thousand (vs. 44).

41-42. He looked up to heaven was the normal attitude of prayer, and especially of the thanksgiving which began a Jewish meal. This feature survived in the later liturgies

Jesus said very clearly to his disciples, "They are your responsibility." And he took it upon himself, as well, to share it with them. To the words **send them away**, spoken in the effort to escape the sense of obligation, he makes the same answer today that he made of old, **You give them something to eat.**

38. And He Said to Them, "How Many Loaves Have You? Go and See."—The disciples had left two things out of their thinking about this emergency, their own resources and the power of God. These are very frequently left out when other disciples confront other needs.

Jesus' words were in reply to what seems an impatient question of the disciples, "Shall we go and buy two hundred denarii worth of bread?" In the circumstances that sounds like an attempt at a crushing reduction to absurdity of what Jesus has told them to do. It was a form of rebuke. Jesus' answer was calm. In effect he said: "Never mind what is impossible. Mind what is possible. What resources do you have? Look and see."

This whole matter of overlooked resources can be, and has been, a tragic hindrance to the work of the kingdom of God. Over and over in all the centuries, disciples of Jesus have said in the presence of great need and opportunity, "We have nothing"; when, as a matter of fact, they did have something which might have been put into God's hands for his use.

The question **How many loaves have you?** runs like an orchestral theme through Christian history. It came to the apostle Paul. He could

well have answered: "Not many. Only five and two fishes." His handicaps were many and great, on his own showing—unimpressive presence, no graces of public speech, physical ailments. It is hard to imagine Paul receiving a call to a prominent St. Paul's Church anywhere! Not many loaves, but he gathered together his whole resources and put them into Christ's hands. So we might have a roll call after the order of the stirring one in Heb. 11, all the way from Justin Martyr down through Luther, Francis Xavier, George Fox, William Carey, Father Damien, down to the woman who taught the boys' class in the Sunday school for twenty years. The question and command came, **How many loaves have you? Go and see.** And they went, and saw, and gave all they had to Christ.

To the church that same question and command come. Many a local church has had to confess it did not have two hundred denarii in its treasury; instead, it had a note for two thousand denarii at the bank. It did not have many loaves to meet the demanding need. But often, by the grace of God, the summoning of its own resources and the dedication of them have resulted in a miracle of feeding.

41. He . . . Broke the Loaves, and Gave Them to the Disciples to Set Before the People.— (See Exeg.) Two things appear to be clear. One is that the modern rationalization, making it to be a miracle of sharing, in which, when those having food shared with the others, there was enough to stay hunger; or the allegorical interpretation, that the feeding was really upon

42 And they did all eat, and were filled.

43 And they took up twelve baskets full of the fragments, and of the fishes.

44 And they that did eat of the loaves were about five thousand men.

45 And straightway he constrained his disciples to get into the ship, and to go to the other side before unto Bethsaida, while he sent away the people.

divided the two fish among them all. 42 And they all ate and were satisfied. 43 And they took up twelve baskets full of broken pieces and of the fish. 44 And those who ate the loaves were five thousand men.

45 Immediately he made his disciples get into the boat and go before him to the other side, to Beth-sa'i-da, while he dis-

---

of the church. **And blessed,** i.e., pronounced the words of blessing and thanksgiving which were said by the head of the family at a meal: "Blessed be thou, O Lord, who givest food to the hungry," or something similar. It was God who was "blessed"—i.e., was pronounced blessed—not the food. In 8:7 the word is εὐχαριστήσας, "having given thanks," or "having said the thanksgiving." As in vss. 38, 43, the reference to the fish seems to be added as of secondary significance (as also in 8:7); in vs. 44 the fish are simply omitted. Liturgical emphasis perhaps tended to minimize this feature. **All . . . were filled** attests the reality of the miracle.

43. Unlike the manna (Exod. 16:18), except that which was kept over for the sabbath (Exod. 16:22-23), there was not only a quantity left, as in the O.T. story (II Kings 4:43-44), but a vastly larger quantity than was available before the multitude had been fed. The twelve baskets of **fragments** presumably symbolize the twelve tribes of Israel, or perhaps the twelve apostles. As with the wine at Cana (John 2:6), superabundance is characteristic of the divine bounty. It is evident that, at least as Mark understands it, this is no pleasant tale of a picnic in the hills, where the amply provided shared with those who had nothing—as in some of the modern expositions of the passage.

6. Jesus Walking on the Sea (6:45-52)

Luke omits 6:45–8:26 (Luke's "great omission"), and some scholars have assumed that this long section was missing from Luke's copy of Mark—i.e., that Mark existed in two recensions or "editions," a longer and a shorter. But the style of this part of Mark is the same as that of Mark generally (it is therefore not an interpolation); there are echoes of these omitted passages elsewhere in Luke; and the parallelism of Mark 6:34–7:37 and 8:1-26 may have led Luke to omit all but the feeding of the five thousand (Luke 9:12-17) in order to save space for his long insertion (Luke 9:51–18:14) of Q and L material. It can therefore hardly be argued that Luke questioned any of the material in Mark which he omits at this point.

Parallels to the story of the walking on the sea are found in Hellenistic literature, in the life of the Buddha, and in the lives of the saints (e.g., Raymond of Pennaforte; the saints, however, were often credited with miracles like those in the Bible). The narrative cannot be a poetic elaboration of such a verse as Job 9:8b or Ps. 77:19, nor is it likely to be a variant of 4:35-41. The motivation in this story is not the display of supernatural power, or the demonstration of the possibility of levitation, but simply the rescue of the imperiled disciples. Some scholars have thought it a misplaced account of a resurrection appearance, but nothing in the story itself suggests this. Many attempts have been made to rationalize the story, to reduce it to the level of commonplace event; but the gospel miracles do not respond readily to such treatment, and are best left as they stand. Whether viewed by us as historic facts, as poetic elaborations, or as symbols of faith, they are indispensable *as miracles* for the interpretation, not only of the Gospel of Mark, but also of the early evangelical tradition underlying Mark.

45-46. Bethsaida was at the north end of the lake, in the territory of Philip. But we do not know from whence the **disciples** started. "In the midst of the sea" (vs. 47) certainly implies considerable distance from land; John 6:19 says "about three or four miles." As in 1:35, Jesus withdraws into solitude by night in order **to pray.**

46 And when he had sent them away, he departed into a mountain to pray.

47 And when even was come, the ship was in the midst of the sea, and he alone on the land.

48 And he saw them toiling in rowing; for the wind was contrary unto them: and

missed the crowd. **46** And after he had taken leave of them, he went into the hills to pray. **47** And when evening came, the boat was out on the sea, and he was alone on the land. **48** And he saw that they were

---

48. Fourth watch, i.e., from 3 to 6 A.M. This is in accordance with Greco-Roman reckoning (cf. 13:35); the Jews reckoned only three "watches" in the night. **Upon the**

---

the spiritual bread of life, had no place in the mind of Mark. To Mark the miraculous feeding was one of "the mighty works" of Christ. The second clear and unclouded fact is that the story is a wonderful picture of a tremendous truth of Christian history, that Jesus does multiply above measure (vss. 42-43) for human use whatever of worth is put into his hands. Five loaves and two fishes in human personality and equipment, when placed in his hands and blessed by him, have been enough, again and again, to meet great and deep human needs. He has always given back what was given to him, enlarged and multiplied. Mothers brought their children, and he took them, and handed them back dearer than ever before, because he had blessed them. Men brought him a Roman coin, and he handed it back, a larger thing, a symbol of man's relationship to God and the state. Some brought him their lives, responding to his call "Follow me," and he handed those lives back, multiplied in power and possibility. Others brought him a cross, and he took it, and handed it back to the world, transformed and enlarged, no longer a thing of shame, but a symbol of God's redeeming love. Whatever we give him he will enlarge for the service of human need.

46-47. He Went into the Hills to Pray. And . . . He Was Alone on the Land.—Both in content and detail these words are simple, yet deeply moving. The scene is unforgettable. From the pursuing crowd Jesus has at last withdrawn. Indeed, he dismisses two crowds, the multitude of five thousand, and the smaller crowd of the disciples. The lonely figure takes his way up into the hills to pray. Later, when the lengthening shadows of the evening descend, he is alone on the shore.

Notice, for one thing, the impressive words of vs. 45, "he dismissed the crowd." It is a high art truly, that of dismissing a crowd, and Jesus was master of it. We have seen him leaving a throng (1:35) for the re-creation of spirit and mind in solitude and prayer. It is an indispensable art in any life that realizes the potentialities of selfhood. For some of the richest things in life come only when the crowd is gone, when

crowd pressures and crowd thinking are left behind, and we confront ourselves. We grow so dependent on crowds of one sort or another, not only the street corner crowds, but smaller groups in which we submerge our individuality. The bustle, the clamor, the rapid succession of moving figures on the stage of the mind, all conspire to prevent us from meeting ourselves. The alternative in our modern life is a sharp one: we will either learn to dismiss a crowd, or we will dismiss ourselves. Eventually, of course, we shall have to dismiss the crowd. We shall all do it on our deathbed. There we shall be alone. Let not that be the first time.

The chief thing in this passage is the picture of that great rhythm in the life of Jesus, the spending of himself in the ministry of the many, and the replenishment of mind and soul in communion with the One. It is the supreme example of what W. E. Hocking calls the "principle of alternation," the outstroke of activity and the backstroke of renewal.

A phrase describing the novel *Mountain Time* has echoes of the possibilities that may come from solitude and prayer. "It portrays," says the description, "that segment of the population which sets its watches by mountain time." That is a phrase worth storing in the memory. Of course the meaning is very simple—the time of the Rocky Mountains, one hour later than Central time. But hold it in another context. There are people, thank God, who set the watches of their daily living by Mountain time; who live not by the thinking of the street level but by the eternal hills of God's revelation. Their guide is not what everyone is saying this season, but what God has said for all seasons; not what everyone is doing this year, but what God has done for all the years.

"The streams which turn the machinery of the world take their rise in solitary places." Here, on the lonely hilltop and the deserted shore, we see a source of the stream of influence which flowed out from Jesus to the blessing of the world.

48. And He Saw that They Were Distressed in Rowing, for the Wind Was Against Them.— This is, for one thing, a wholly unintended but

about the fourth watch of the night he cometh unto them, walking upon the sea, and would have passed by them.

49 But when they saw him walking upon the sea, they supposed it had been a spirit, and cried out:

50 For they all saw him, and were troubled. And immediately he talked with them, and saith unto them, Be of good cheer: it is I; be not afraid.

distressed in rowing, for the wind was against them. And about the fourth watch of the night he came to them, walking on the sea. He meant to pass by them, 49 but when they saw him walking on the sea they thought it was a ghost, and cried out; 50 for they all saw him, and were terrified. But immediately he spoke to them and said,

---

sea: Not "by the sea," as some have argued, which would reduce the miracle to zero. **Would have passed by them:** This feature in the story, so strange to us, served originally to make more vivid the fact that Jesus was diverted by their evident distress from his purpose of following and overtaking the disciples in the morning on the other shore; in Mark's telling this feature is neutralized by vs. 48a.

49-50. Some MSS (D O.L., etc.) read: "They thought it was a ghost, and all cried out and were terrified." But the omitted words "for they saw him" (thirteen letters, a normal line in many early MSS) are needed for smooth reading and good order of thought. **Be of good cheer: it is I; be not afraid.** These dramatic words contain the very essence of the story for Christian readers, and mark it off sharply from the Hellenistic and other parallels. What they meant to Mark's readers, themselves living in constant danger, as an assurance of the presence and power of their invisible Lord, is easily imagined.

---

true picture of prayer at its highest. We read that Jesus was alone in prayer. But in the deepest sense he was not alone. In his prayer, as in all true prayer, both God and man were present. Prayer is not an exercise in a vacuum. There was the upward reach to God and the outward reach to man. Men were not absent from Jesus' mind in his hour of solitude and prayer. This passage gives a marvelous picture of the sympathy and sensitiveness of love. Alone—but he saw them distressed. He felt their need. He carried into solitude and prayer the remembrance of his disciples. When prayer is Christian, it is not enclosed within the walls of individual petition; it is marked with sensitive awareness of those who are "distressed"; it bears them up in intercession to God.

Also, this narrative of Jesus, alert to the distress of the disciples, their toil, the obstacles mounting against them, their fear, portrays memorably the sympathy of God and his divine response to human need. **The wind was against them**—how well we know contrary winds, when life heads into a gale! Waves, too heavy for our strength to pull against, roll up. We are **distressed in rowing.** Jesus took in the whole situation. In his quick awareness there is a vivid little drama of one of his central teachings—God's knowledge of his children and his care for them. The words "how much more" and "fear not," again and again on Jesus' lips, are a fortifying refrain. God sees the sparrows, how much more does he see everything that affects you! Paul catches that same assurance, "We

know that in everything God works for good with those who love him" (Rom. 8:28).

There is true eloquence in those words **he came.** There is true history in them too. Into unnumbered lives, distressed with hard toil, beset with heavy winds and engulfed with mounting waves, he has come. That is history. He has come with empowering assurance of God's care. Into the home of grief, of discouragement, of failure, of anguish, he has come. And, as here on the Sea of Galilee, he has come in the darkest peril. This verb "to come" has present and future tenses as well as past. Jesus "came" to the disciples in distress. He "came" to many others in desperate hours. But there is also a glorious present tense, "he comes." And a glorious future tense, "he will come."

50. Take Heart, It Is I; Have No Fear.—Notice first (as suggested in Exeg.) what this story and these words of Jesus to his disciples must have meant to Christians in the first centuries, under the lash of persecution. Stretch your imagination, and as far as you are able become one of that company going through the valley of the shadow of death. Then imagine the reading of this story: of how Jesus saw the distressed disciples in toil, fear, and danger, and came to them at the darkest hour, and in ways that seemed clearly impossible, and said to them, **It is I; have no fear.** We need not say it *would* fortify them with the faith that the same Lord who often came to his disciples in distress would come to them; it *did* fortify them to face any amazement of danger.

51 And he went up unto them into the ship; and the wind ceased: and they were sore amazed in themselves beyond measure, and wondered.

52 For they considered not *the miracle* of the loaves; for their heart was hardened.

53 And when they had passed over, they come into the land of Gennesaret, and drew to the shore.

54 And when they were come out of the ship, straightway they knew him,

"Take heart, it is I; have no fear." 51 And he got into the boat with them and the wind ceased. And they were utterly astounded, 52 for they did not understand about the loaves, but their hearts were hardened.

53 And when they had crossed over, they came to land at Gen-nes'a-ret, and moored to the shore. 54 And when they got out of the boat, immediately the people recog-

---

51-52. Vs. 51 is a more or less conventional conclusion of a miracle story; vs. 52 must be editorial, Mark's own addition, relating the story to the one preceding (cf. 8:17-21) and stressing the supernatural "hardening" of the disciples' hearts—one of Mark's major conceptions (see Intro., p. 644).

7. The Landing at Gennesaret (6:53-56)

53-56. Gennesaret was probably the fertile plain south of Capernaum. Why they landed there rather than at Bethsaida (vs. 45) is not explained, but Mark's topography is uncertain (see Intro., pp. 631-32). Matthew and John, and some of the later copyists of Mark, avoid this conflict. The whole section is Mark's own summary, rather than one of the "old pericopes." **Touch . . . his garment,** as in 5:27; etc. Not **border** (KJV), but the **fringe** (RSV) or tassel (*çîçîth*), which every Israelite man was to wear at the corners of his mantle (Num. 15:38).

What was true in the first centuries of the Christian era is true in every century. The fortifying word for the hard experiences of life is the great, stupendous word "I." For it stands for the faith. The only adequate faith for deep distress is a person. At the center of the universe is not just whirling matter, speeding light, dissolving heat, or exploding atoms, but a personal God of love. Literally the last word in creation is not the dim rumbling of a cosmic process: it is a voice saying **Take heart, it is I.** That is a high faith, but it is the only faith that can sustain the sense of the unique value of the person. John Macmurray says truly:

The sense that the world as a whole is personal is the very heart of religious experience. To the man with the sense of God alive in his soul the world is neither a mechanical system, nor an evolving something. It is something made by Someone, and brought to life by Someone, controlled, indwelt, loved by an infinite person, who is its meaning, its reality and its good.[3]

That is the ultimate meaning for human experience of those three words, **It is I.** Faith says, "O Thou," and hears the answer, "I." When faith hears that answer in any storm, no matter how great, it is fortified against any fear.

In every great crisis of history, when everyone who hopes for a world preserved from destruc-

tion is **distressed in rowing** against head winds, the sense of God at the center of the universe is a deep necessity. The great issue is that of irrational hope against rational despair. Not fantastic hope, nor, in the common meaning of the word, romantic hope, but irrational hope, hope that comes from other sources than reason. Rational despair is a mood that besets and grips millions. But irrational hope is based on something that is not the creation of logical reason. It looks to God as the unpredictable and ultimate, though often forgotten, factor in human affairs. There is no more urgent task for the church than to open the hearts and minds of despairing men to a Voice which says, **Take heart, it is I.**

54. Immediately the People Recognized Him. —Note that the retirement of Jesus and his disciples to a lonely place for rest (vss. 31-32), and Jesus' going alone into the hills for prayer, came as an interlude between the pressures of two of the largest crowds reported in the Gospels. There was the throng of five thousand which followed Jesus around the head of the lake. And here was this rapidly collecting throng, bringing the sick of a whole countryside. Jesus went from crowd to crowd. When he went into the lonely place to rest, into the hills to pray, he did not go to escape, but to equip. He withdrew in order that he might mingle effectively. Prayer was renewal for ministry. Prayer,

[3] *The Christian World.*

55 And ran through that whole region round about, and began to carry about in beds those that were sick, where they heard he was.

56 And whithersoever he entered, into villages, or cities, or country, they laid the sick in the streets, and besought him that they might touch if it were but the border of his garment: and as many as touched him were made whole.

7 Then came together unto him the Pharisees, and certain of the scribes, which came from Jerusalem.

nized him, 55 and ran about the whole neighborhood and began to bring sick people on their pallets to any place where they heard he was. 56 And wherever he came, in villages, cities, or country, they laid the sick in the market places, and besought him that they might touch even the fringe of his garment; and as many as touched it were made well.

7 Now when the Pharisees gathered together to him, with some of the scribes,

8. The Tradition of the Elders (7:1-23)

This long section contains material similar to that in the controversy sections (2:1–3:6; 3:22-30; 11:27–12:40). But the form is different: the controversies end, as a rule, with a saying of Jesus uttered as his final "pronouncement" upon the subject, to use Vincent Taylor's term (see above, p. 679). In the present section the saying may perhaps be found in vs. 15; if so, the original pericope has been greatly expanded, editorially and by the addition of other relevant material. As it stands, vss. 1-2, 5 provide the setting and occasion of the controversy; this has been expanded by the insertion of the explanatory sentence (one sentence in Greek), vss. 3-4. Jesus then characteristically ignores the specific objection of his opponents (hand washing) and, in vss. 6-8, seizes upon the major issue involved (the tradition of the elders). His reply, which amounts to a countercharge, is elaborated and illustrated in vss. 9-13 ("Corban")—perhaps originally an independent

of course, is never a merely instrumental thing. The purpose of prayer is not to furnish a means to some other end, no matter how good the end. The valid reason for prayer is that communion with God is the highest experience of life. But though an end in itself, true prayer always has consequences for other lives. True prayer, as here with Jesus, sends one back to the crowd again for sustained ministry.

56. They Laid the Sick in the Market Places. —This little paragraph is deeply impressive and moving. As already noted about a similar passage earlier (1:32-34), it pictures the intensity of human love, for which no trouble was too great, painfully carrying the sick long distances to a possible healer. It pictures the pathos of hope, which had so often been disappointed. It also pictures vividly what it meant to live in a world without hospitals, medicine, or nurses, where the street was the only clinic—a picture which should remind us with pain that a large part of the world is still in that suffering condition.

> O master, from the mountain side
> Make haste to heal these hearts of pain,[4]

—through us.

[4] Frank Mason North, "Where cross the crowded ways of life."

So does the passage suggest a farther ranging task. It is to bring all the sick, the casualties of our civilization, in villages, cities, or country, that they may receive healing at the hands of Jesus. We must bring the physically sick, that the spirit restored in faith may play its vital part in the recovery from many afflictions; the sick in mind and nerves and emotions, that our whole treatment of mental ills may emerge from the era of unconcern, of cruelty, into intelligent care motivated by the spirit of Jesus. We must bring those suffering from the subtle diseases of greed, of racial contempt, of aggressive dominance. Jesus stood of old in the market place to heal. He stands there still—in the center of our civil and economic and social life. Will we seek him ourselves and bring others to him, in order that the ills of our time too may be healed?

7:1-23. Jesus and the Tradition.—The opening section of this chapter evidently includes many sayings of Jesus on tradition (see Exeg.). Jesus met the issue head on. One must choose between the commandments of God, the "weightier matters of the law," and man-made traditions with their burdensome observances. The immediate and burning issues of the controversy have long since passed away into history; but the principles which Jesus laid down have been immediate and burning issues in

2 And when they saw some of his disciples eat bread with defiled, that is to say, with unwashen hands, they found fault.

who had come from Jerusalem, 2 they saw that some of his disciples ate with hands

---

pericope or unit of tradition. Then vss. 14-15 (16?) return to the main question, but deal with it somewhat obliquely; the original point at issue was hand washing, but this saying appears to deal with the distinction between clean and unclean foods. The logic may be: If food cannot defile, then unwashed hands do not—which quite misses the point of the Jewish ceremonial practice of hand washing. Mark's knowledge of Judaism is limited, and is as vague as that of Gentiles generally in the first century. Or possibly the logic is this: If food cannot defile, then it does not matter if food is defiled by hands which have not been ceremonially washed; but this is a bit too abstruse. Finally is added the explanation of the saying on clean and unclean (vss. 17-23), in two parts: (a) the very literal and pedestrian interpretation in vss. 18-19; and (b) the somewhat homiletical, or hortatory, elaboration of the principle that from within come the things that defile (vss. 20-23). The two parts of the reply form an orderly exposition of vs. 15, and are often viewed as an example of early church expository teaching. **And he said** (vs. 20) was only a way of saying, "This is what Jesus meant when he said . . ."

If this is a correct analysis, then it is better to view 7:1-23, not as a controversy section with a climactic saying in vs. 15, a section later elaborated by the insertion of other material, but rather as a little collection of sayings—some of them further interpreted in the course of oral tradition—on the general subject of the scribal tradition, and including such specific subjects as hand washing, the Corban rule, clean and unclean food, and the superiority of ethical distinctions over ceremonial. As in 2:23-28, the early Christian-Jewish concern over the orthodox food regulations has influenced the tradition of the incident.

7:1. As in 3:22, it is the **scribes . . . from Jerusalem** who make trouble, as presumably more strict and orthodox than the local religious authorities; the local **Pharisees**, however, their ardent lay followers, joined in the hunt, perhaps even instigating it.

2. Unwashen hands. The devout Jewish practice of hand washing before meals, for purposes not of cleanliness but of consecration, was a ceremonial elaboration, by an act, of the principle involved in the thanksgiving before and after partaking of food; every meal was an occasion both for thanksgiving (εὐχαριστία), since food was the gift of God, and for religious fellowship (cf. Acts 2:46b-47a). But like other pious ceremonies, the practice could become a mere form, a rigid regulation enforced by appeal to the authority

---

every century, central and vital to our own day, and to our whole conception of the Christian gospel.

1-2. The Pharisees . . . , with Some of the Scribes, . . . Saw That . . . His Disciples Ate with Hands Defiled.—These Jerusalem scribes, evidently an investigating committee, and the local Pharisees, who had acted as spies, saw the *little* things. They never saw the *big* things. They saw the violations of their hand washing codes. They did not see Jesus (see Expos. 6:2-3). They never took an open look so that the true nature of the man and his teaching might come fairly before them. They never really saw the people who had been blessed by a man who went about doing good (see Expos. 1:16). They were not interested in these things. They were interested in pots and pans, in scourings, in the minute details that made for separation from their fellow men. Their eyes were blind

to everything except what threatened their traditions, their vested interest, their authority, and their prestige.

That same blindness to the big, with a keen eye for the little, has come down through the years to this very day. In every century people have been blind to the authentic work of God, because their myopic vision took in only the violation of some tradition. It was so with churchmen who were blind to the Evangelical Revival in the eighteenth century, because it violated traditional methods; with those who were blind to the redemption wrought in many lives through the Salvation Army, because tambourines and bass drums and street corner meetings were not in accord with their long tradition.

Two embarrassing questions come to each of us: What does my eye pick up most readily? The big things or the little ones? The genuine

3 For the Pharisees, and all the Jews, except they wash *their* hands oft, eat not, holding the tradition of the elders.

4 And *when they come* from the market, except they wash, they eat not. And many other things there be, which they have received to hold, *as* the washing of cups, and pots, brazen vessels, and of tables.

defiled, that is, unwashed. 3 (For the Pharisees, and all the Jews, do not eat unless they wash their hands, observing the tradition of the elders; 4 and when they come from the market place, they do not eat unless they purify[w] themselves; and there are many other traditions which they observe, the washing of cups and pots and vessels

[w] Some ancient authorities read *baptize.*

---

of "the tradition of the elders." Against this, Jesus and his followers protested by ignoring the rule; it was one of those relatively new scribal-Pharisaic regulations which worked hardship upon the ordinary rank and file of working people, including the Amhaarez, who had little leisure for the observance of the detailed rule of life laid down by the scribes and observed by them and the Pharisees. (See Samuel S. Cohon, "The Place of Jesus in the Religious Life of His Day," *Journal of Biblical Literature,* XLVIII [1929], 82-108; W. Sattler and W. Bauer, in *Festgabe für Adolf Jülicher* [Tübingen: J. C. B. Mohr, 1927], pp. 1-15, 16-34.) The question at issue was therefore the authority of the scribal tradition, as Jesus' reply makes clear.

3-4. These two verses, omitted by Matthew, may possibly be a later gloss, added to the text of Mark in order to explain the charge in vs. 2. The explanation interrupts the sequence of vss. 1-2, 5 (the words **they found fault** in vs. 2 and **then** in vs. 5 are not in the best MSS); moreover, it was not true that **all the Jews** observed this rule. The phrase may therefore possibly be viewed as an interpolation. But taking the text as it stands, it is more probable that Mark is explaining the custom to non-Jewish readers, and may have in mind the common practice of Roman Jews, who were strongly Pharisaic. At best the verses cannot belong to the old Palestinian Christian tradition, not to mention any early Aramaic gospel or gospel source. They also suggest that Mark's knowledge of Judaism was not firsthand. **Wash,** or "baptize," means "dip," as in some MSS. The adverb **oft** in KJV translates πυκνά, found in some MSS. An O.L. reading is "first" (*primo*). The most likely is πυγμῇ, which means "with the fist," i.e., in the hollow of the other hand. The rule in the Mishnah requires "up to the knuckles" (see Grant, *Earliest Gospel,* p. 112); perhaps the true meaning is "with a handful [of water]—so Klostermann. RSV leaves the term untranslated. **Washing of cups . . . bronze,** i.e., as in the Talmud (Aboda Zara 5:12 [vessels purchased from Gentiles]). **And of tables** is not in many of the best MSS; literally κλίνων, the term here, means "beds" or "couches"—for reclining at meals, in Greco-Roman fashion as well as Palestinian.

---

work of God in human life, or deviations from my traditional way of doing things? The other arises from the fact that the scribes and Pharisees, though no doubt officially appointed as a committee of investigation, failed to make a fair examination of Jesus and his work. They arrived with their minds already made up. They were like a judge who first pronounces sentence, and then goes on with the trial. We deplore it when this kind of prejudgment is made on our Christian faith and on the Christian church. The question which comes to us is this: Do we ever approach issues in the same way, with our minds made up, so that we never really examine them at all? Who could answer honestly by saying "No"? This passage makes it clear that such an approach, such prejudgment, is a grievous sin.

3. *For the Pharisees . . . Do Not Eat Unless They Wash Their Hands.*—This long sentence, set in parentheses, was very possibly added by a later hand for the benefit of non-Jewish readers (see Exeg.). The statement that **all the Jews** did these things is clearly wrong, for these minute legal requirements were by no means universally observed in Jesus' time. Yet the authority of tradition was growing, and this sentence piles up impressively the details of a heavy ceremonial burden. It pictures how a great faith can degenerate into mere motions, without religious or ethical significance. The inevitable result is that the motions, the scourings, the cleanings, become a substitute for the faith. Read the details here enumerated and you will see that the Pharisees' tradition had moved religion from the sanctuary into the

5 Then the Pharisees and scribes asked him, Why walk not thy disciples according to the tradition of the elders, but eat bread with unwashen hands?

6 He answered and said unto them, Well hath Esaias prophesied of you hypocrites, as it is written, This people honoreth me with *their* lips, but their heart is far from me.

7 Howbeit in vain do they worship me, teaching *for* doctrines the commandments of men.

of bronze.ˣ) 5 And the Pharisees and the scribes asked him, "Why do your disciples not liveʸ according to the tradition of the elders, but eat with hands defiled?" 6 And he said to them, "Well did Isaiah prophesy of you hypocrites, as it is written,

'This people honors me with their
lips,
but their heart is far from me;
7 in vain do they worship me,
teaching as doctrines the precepts
of men.'

ˣ Some ancient authorities add *and beds.*
ʸ Greek *walk.*

5-7. Walk, i.e., in the Pharisaic sense of halakah, observance. **Tradition of the elders:** The oral tradition of legal interpretation handed down in the schools, eventually culminating in the written Mishnah and the two Talmuds, and the later massive commentaries upon them. The passage in Isa. 29:13, quoted (though not exactly) from the LXX rather than the Hebrew, is viewed as a prediction of these schools of scribes. The old tradition underlying this verse was probably translated into Greek without checking the quotation with the current LXX text. The relevance of the prophetic words comes out in the final clause, with reference to **precepts of men** which are substituted for the divine **teaching.**

---

kitchen. The great exhortation, "Worship the LORD in the beauty of holiness" (Ps. 29:2) had degenerated into a prosaic command, "Be sure to scrub the dishes." Superficial preoccupation with ceremonies had supplanted a deeper faith. In the words of a poet of sure insight, the Pharisees had become so busy with scrubbing "useless pots the whole day long" that they had completely "lost the dance and song." When a great vision of an ethical God and his kingdom disappears or grows dim, religion can dwindle into a mean and petty concern for insignificant and unspiritual etiquette.

5. *Why Do Your Disciples Not Live According to the Tradition of the Elders?*—This was a point-blank question, and Jesus did not evade it. He could have evaded it. He could have pointed out, and even the Pharisees would have had to admit the patent truth, that not all the Jews, "the people of the land," from whom many of his disciples came, observed these ritualistic demands. But Jesus scorned evasion. He did not go around seeking clashes; on the other hand, when vital questions were raised, he met them squarely, whatever the danger. Indeed, he broadened the issue, lifting it from a mere discussion of hand washing to a complete repudiation of the whole tradition. Is that our way too? Do we scorn evasions which might allow us to escape some forthright declaration that would line us up squarely on one side or the other? Or do we search frantically for some

"reconciling formula," known in more vulgar language as "double talk," which will allow us to straddle the question? Is our language like that of Jesus? Do we say simply "Yea, yea" and "Nay, nay"?

6. *This People Honors Me with Their Lips, but Their Heart Is Far from Me.*—It is so easy to say, "How true this was of the Pharisees!" and so hard to say, "How true this is of us!" Harder still to say, "How true this is of me!" Jesus applied these words of Isaiah to the Pharisees. They apply, just as truly, to anyone who honors God with his lips, while his heart is far away. It is so easy to do. We can honor God with our lips and say with approval, "Seek ye first the kingdom of God, and his righteousness" (Matt. 6:33), while in our heart we seek first our own kingdom, our own dominant position, our own advancement. We can honor God with our lips and say with approval, "A day in thy courts is better than a thousand" (Ps. 84:10), while all the time we may spend a hundred days outside his courts to every one in which we worship him there. We can honor God with our lips and say with approval "[He] hath made of one blood all nations of men for to dwell on all the face of the earth" (Acts 17:26), and all the while our heart is far from him in a complacent feeling of material superiority, in contempt for other races, in drawing rigid lines of separation.

"Lord, is it I?"

8 For laying aside the commandment of God, ye hold the tradition of men, *as* the washing of pots and cups: and many other such like things ye do.

9 And he said unto them, Full well ye reject the commandment of God, that ye may keep your own tradition.

10 For Moses said, Honor thy father and thy mother; and, Whoso curseth father or mother, let him die the death:

8 You leave the commandment of God, and hold fast the tradition of men."

9 And he said to them, "You have a fine way of rejecting the commandment of God, in order to keep your tradition! 10 For Moses said, 'Honor your father and your mother'; and, 'He who speaks evil of father

---

8. Tradition: The Chester Beatty MS (p[45]) reads "command," but this may be repeated from the beginning of the verse. **As the washing . . . ye do** is not found in the best MSS. The first half of the gloss echoes vs. 4, the second half vs. 13*b*.

9-13. These verses drive home the countercharge in vs. 8*a*. **Moses** (i.e., the Torah) stated explicitly, both positively and negatively, the duty of honoring and caring for father and mother (Exod. 20:12; Deut. 5:16; Exod. 21:17); but the scribes, in their eagerness to safeguard the validity of vows, especially where ecclesiastical rights were involved, recognized cases in which this primary obligation was relegated to second place. For if a son quarreled with his father or mother, and in a fit of anger declared, **"What**

---

8. *You Leave the Commandment of God, and Hold Fast the Tradition of Men.*—This is a tremendous verdict of Jesus. In it he joined battle with the whole oppressive scribal tradition, its man-made supplements to the commandments of God. But it has an eternal and timeless meaning also, beyond the immediate controversy in which it was spoken. For in it Jesus repudiates every subtraction, every distortion, every addition, elevated to specious divine authority—all that has made void and still makes void the revelation of God.

His words describe so truly what has happened in the past and is still happening today, that we are almost amazed to find them in the Gospels, all through the centuries, where men could clearly see them. For in so many tragic ways they have been "lost words" of Jesus. The most dismal and bloody chapters of history have come from the repeal of God's commandments in favor of man's tradition. The persecutions and slaughterings in the name of religion, the cruelties, the barbed-wire fences of exclusion, the obscene wrangles over trifles, all are part of the story. Many of the conflicts that have torn the body of Christ have had no more meaning than the bitter war satirically described by Swift in Gulliver's voyage to Lilliput, between the party which believed that an egg should be cracked at the big end and the party which believed that it should be cracked at the little end. So the big-enders and the little-enders fought to the death, to the complete ruin of their country. We may well paraphrase Madame Roland's cry, "O Liberty, what crimes are committed in thy name!" and exclaim, "Tradition, what crimes have been committed in thy name!"

The immediate meaning of Jesus' words here was that the tradition of ceremonial compulsions had no authority in the sacred Scriptures, the Law and the Prophets. But the principle which he announced, the priority of God's commandments over man's regulations, reaches into every realm. It applies not only to the minutiae of church ritual. It applies to all the choices of life. The person who exalts and would even sanctify what is known as "the American way of life"—"British," or any other such adjective, would serve as well—to the extent of being unable to tolerate a Christian criticism of its material and spiritual effects on people, has "repealed" the commandments of God in favor of tradition. So has the man whose emotional patriotism becomes the tool of a strident nationalism. So does the person who has elevated some theory of race—which lacks even a scientific basis!—into a place of dominance in his thinking and acting, never mind anything which God has said from beginning to end, from the creation of man in his own image (Gen. 1:26) to the city that "lieth foursquare" (Rev. 21:16).

9-13. *You Have a Fine Way of Rejecting the Commandment of God, in Order to Keep Your Tradition!*—Jesus here picks out an unmistakable example to illustrate the practice which he was denouncing—the substitution of mechanical regulations for the moral law. The commandment had laid down the obligation to honor one's parents. Involved in that was the duty of supporting them, if need be, else the "honor" would be empty mockery. Yet to that moral command the rabbis, at least some of them, said, "Yes, but—." "True, but if a man dedicates his

11 But ye say, If a man shall say to his father or mother, *It is* Corban, that is to say, a gift, by whatsoever thou mightest be profited by me; *he shall be free.*

12 And ye suffer him no more to do aught for his father or his mother;

13 Making the word of God of none effect through your tradition, which ye have delivered: and many such like things do ye.

or mother, let him surely die'; 11 but you say, 'If a man tells his father or his mother, What you would have gained from me is Corban' (that is, given to God) *z* — 12 then you no longer permit him to do anything for his father or mother, 13 thus making void the word of God through your tradition which you hand on. And many such things you do."

z Or *an offering.*

---

you would have gained from me [i.e., support] **is Corban" (that is, given to God)**—i.e., presumably, given to the temple—the scribes held that this vow was binding and no longer permitted him to do anything for his parents. Later scribal and rabbinical authorities modified this rule (e.g., Nedarim 9:1), but its existence in the days of Jesus is attested both by the present pericope and by the later relaxation. What lay back of it was the same rigorous, heartless, inhumanly logical casuistry that we find in many a school of professional religionists in other ages and in other religions. Note that **he shall be free** is an English gloss; it is not in the Greek. **Many such things you do:** The case of **Corban** is only one out of many. Jesus rejects the scribal tradition in principle, including the requirement of ceremonial hand washing. But it is a question whether he went the full length of rejecting all the Levitical regulations governing ritual purity, which were a part of Torah. Here he is concerned only to insist upon the priority of **the word of God,** i.e., Scripture, over the current scribal **tradition.**

---

property to the temple, he is absolved from supporting his parents." Jesus makes unmistakably clear what matters most—the moral and spiritual commandments of God. Compared to that nothing else matters at all. Whatever is set above that, or on an equality with it, must be spurned as an abomination.

Note in this passage three things. First, that a narrow and intense devotion to religion conceived as a logical system, as a set of rules, rather than as "the life of God in the soul of man" and a way of love, one to another—that such narrowness and intensity can have a hardening effect on character. On this point underscore the phrase "rigorous, heartless, inhumanly logical casuistry" (see Exeg.). Religious fanatics, one-eyed men, can be inhumanly cruel. There have been many whose perverse absorption in religion has frozen "the genial currents of the soul," such as kindliness, mercy, tolerance, love. When a concern for people and their rights and welfare drops out, leaving only a concern for code and regulation, as empty of love as a textbook on geometry, religion can be a dehumanizing thing.

Again, notice this casuistry as an instance of how "religion" can be used to evade obligations. The man who would give his money to the temple could evade the primary obligation to support his parents. Jesus utterly condemned that. Religion should permeate life and never be allowed to become a substitute for it. The religious preoccupation of the priest and Levite,

in the parable of the good Samaritan, was no excuse for failing to help the stricken man on the Jericho road. Yet there are many who mistakenly and wickedly make their absorption in religion, or in church, an excuse for withdrawing from the struggle for human welfare. No regularity in attendance on divine worship will excuse a tragic "irregularity" in attendance on the varied human needs in community and nation.

Note also that what the Pharisees showed in this interpretation of "Corban" was that they were more interested in the aggrandizement of an institution than they were in either preventing or alleviating human misery. That has happened over and over. A classic symbol of it is the common picture of a great cathedral surrounded by wretched slums. The institution prospered; the people languished. Sometimes the financial success of the religious establishment has actually been built on the misery of the oppressed, just as in this instance the temple treasury gained from the destitution of neglected parents. It is a sin that easily besets corporate foundations, religious as well as secular. Nothing will avail to save us from it but a sustained sense of the priority of God's moral commandments over all material welfare, and an awareness, kept ever sensitive, of the priority of all human needs.

13. *Thus Making Void the Word of God Through Your Tradition.*—Goodspeed's translation of these words is very suggestive—and

14 ¶ And when he had called all the people *unto him,* he said unto them, Hearken unto me every one *of you,* and understand:

15 There is nothing from without a man, that entering into him can defile him: but the things which come out of him, those are they that defile the man.

16 If any man have ears to hear, let him hear.

17 And when he was entered into the house from the people, his disciples asked him concerning the parable.

18 And he saith unto them, Are ye so without understanding also? Do ye not perceive, that whatsoever thing from without entereth into the man, *it* cannot defile him;

19 Because it entereth not into his heart, but into the belly, and goeth out into the draught, purging all meats?

14 And he called the people to him again, and said to them, "Hear me, all of you, and understand: 15 there is nothing outside a man which by going into him can defile him; but the things which come out of a man are what defile him."[a] 17 And when he had entered the house, and left the people, his disciples asked him about the parable. 18 And he said to them, "Then are you also without understanding? Do you not see that whatever goes into a man from outside cannot defile him, 19 since it enters, not his heart but his stomach, and so passes on[b]?" (Thus he declared all foods

[a] Many ancient authorities add verse 16, *"If any man has ears to hear, let him hear."*
[b] Or *is evacuated.*

14-16. In Mark **the people** are never far away, and can be addressed at will. Strange as this seems to us, it was perfectly natural in the surroundings of an Oriental teacher, especially in first-century Palestine. As against the scribal teaching, and even the Levitical legislation, Jesus held that the only defilement of any importance was inward, i.e., spiritual and moral, and was evidenced by what came out of a man, not by what went into him. The words in vs. 15 are regarded as a **parable** (in vs. 17), a comparison or an analogy, in accordance with Mark's broad use of the term. Jesus does not draw the full consequences of his assertion of principle—as Paul was later to do (e.g., Rom. 14:14)— viz., the abrogation of the food regulations (though see vs. 19*b*). His hyperbolical, in fact paradoxical, saying is intended to show the far greater importance of moral over ceremonial uncleanness. He certainly would not have encouraged his followers to eat oysters, for example, or other foods forbidden in the law. The warning in vs. 16, found only in later MSS, is like the one in 4:9, and may be only a gloss—some early reader's or copyist's *nota bene!*

17-19. As in 4:10, 34; 10:10, the disciples do not understand and have to be further instructed in private. This is a regular device of Mark for the introduction of additional

embarrassing: "You nullify what God has said by what you have handed down." It raises the question, What is your private nullification act? What part of the word of God do you rub out and make of no effect for you? Can any of us honestly say we have never done that? Some of us nullify Jesus' words "forgive seventy times seven." There "the Galilean is too great for our small hearts." Unrelenting and vindictive, we find those words disconcerting. "Voided." Jesus said, "Take up the cross, and follow me" (8:34). But it is far too much trouble to take up a cross. That spoils our eager, unhampered stride through life.

What do you nullify?

14-19. *There Is Nothing Outside a Man Which by Going into Him Can Defile Him.*— Here is one of the great contributions of Jesus

to religion and to the life of the world. Part of his profound originality lay in his stress on the inwardness of religion. These words of his sweep through the world like a hurricane, the very "wind of God," flattening down every perversion that would lay its emphasis on outward things. It is the heart that matters, the moral and spiritual consciousness. Nothing outward can either defile or purify.

The unusual form of words with which Jesus prefaces these sayings on ceremonial purity would seem to indicate his sense of their supreme importance, **Hear me, all of you, and understand.** If only that could sound throughout the world with its divine trumpet call! There is such desperate need of hearing this great declaration of independence—true religion from the tryanny of externals. We have

20 And he said, That which cometh out of the man, that defileth the man.

21 For from within, out of the heart of men, proceed evil thoughts, adulteries, fornications, murders,

22 Thefts, covetousness, wickedness, deceit, lasciviousness, an evil eye, blasphemy, pride, foolishness:

23 All these evil things come from within, and defile the man.

clean.) 20 And he said, "What comes out of a man is what defiles a man. 21 For from within, out of the heart of man, come evil thoughts, fornication, theft, murder, adultery, 22 coveting, wickedness, deceit, licentiousness, envy, slander, pride, foolishness. 23 All these evil things come from within, and they defile a man."

---

teaching on a subject—in this case, as in ch. 4, including traditional teaching that cannot with certainty be ascribed to Jesus. As in 4:13; 8:21, Jesus is represented as surprised at the disciples' lack of understanding—and so are we. But Mark thought of it as a supernatural blindness and stupidity, which they shared with their fellow Jews. Cf. 6:52—a literary motif which Matthew and Luke do not share, but which John carries to the farthest extreme: for him "the Jews" are incapable of understanding the plainest statements of religious truth, being under a divine judgment of blindness (see Intro., p. 644). **Heart,** i.e., mind, as in Prov. 4:23: Out of the heart are "the issues of life." **Thus he declared all foods clean:** Many interpretations have been given to this clause, which may be a gloss. The meaning of the phrase, even in some of the cruder translations, is clear. (Cf. Acts 10:15; Rom. 14:14, 20.) But it is much more likely to be an early Christian interpretation than part of a saying of Jesus.

20-23. As noted above, these verses expound vs. 15b, as vss. 18-19 expound 15a. This is much less pedestrian exegesis than that in the two preceding verses—which remind us of 4:14-20, the "explanation" of the parable of the sower. Vs. 20 simply repeats 15b, to take up the point (reiterated for emphasis in vs. 23). The list of vices in vss. 21-22 is a typical Hellenistic catalogue (cf. Rom. 1:29-31 for another). Such lists, used by Stoic moralists and others, were taken over by Hellenistic Jews and used in their ethical teaching—of course, with modifications in the direction of Jewish standards and Jewish ethical terminology (see, e.g., the long poem of Pseudo-Phocylides, tr. B. S. Easton in *Anglican Theological Review,* XIV [1932], 222-28). What we have here in Mark is an instance of the adoption of an ethical terminology by the early Christian church, modified by the Scriptures and by the tradition of Jesus' teaching. The list, given in another order in Codex Bezae, and in still another in KJV, is reduced from thirteen to seven by Matthew. Note the translations in RSV: **lasciviousness** is **licentiousness: blasphemy** is **slander,** i.e., the reviling, not of God, but of men; **an evil eye** is **envy,** referring to a jealous or grudging attitude (cf. Deut. 15:9). There is no trace in ancient Judaism of the superstition of "the evil glance," e.g., of a witch; at least the term was not so used.

---

so much of the outward, not in the forms of Jewish tradition, but of our own. Religion has been so much concerned with ceremonies, rituals, rules, that for many the eternal God has dwindled into a mere ordainer and master of etiquette. It is the pure heart that counts, the meek spirit, the penitent mind, the peacemaking disposition—all the glorious inwardness of the Beatitudes.

20-23. What Comes Out of a Man Is What Defiles a Man.—If it is the inward that purifies, it is also the inward that defiles. It is the terrible chemistry of the evil heart, distilling poisons, that ruins a life. There is an appalling list of poisons in vss. 21-22, beginning with **evil thoughts,** the root of them all, and ending

with **foolishness.** Note particularly the last four of these poisons. It ought to be deeply disturbing, for instance, that **slander, pride, foolishness** rank right alongside of **theft, murder, adultery,** as sins that defile. We are accustomed to think of them as minor matters, if we think of them at all. Here they are in Jesus' list of major sins. And the phrase **an evil eye.** That looks at first glance like superstition. It is not at all. It means a jealous, grudging disposition (see Exeg.). Modern translators render it "envying" and **envy.** It can be a cardinal sin, for it has the power to sour life, to keep one from ever attaining the spirit of love which redeems.

Slander is a form of murder, the assassination of character, not a mere "failing," as a socially

24 ¶ And from thence he arose, and went into the borders of Tyre and Sidon, and entered into a house, and would have no man know *it:* but he could not be hid.

24 And from there he arose and went away to the region of Tyre and Sidon.*e* And he entered a house, and would not have any one know it; yet he could not

e Some ancient authorities omit *and Sidon.*

---

9. THE SYROPHOENICIAN WOMAN (7:24-30)

This is one of the most difficult sections in the Gospel. It seems to show (vs. 27) that Jesus was unwilling to extend his ministry of healing and exorcism to Gentiles, and shared the circumscribed outlook of the most rigid of his contemporary and later fellow Jews. The extraordinary thing is that such a section as this should appear in Mark, in strong contrast to the exorcism in 5:1-20 and the healing in 7:31-37, which immediately follows the present passage, both presumably in Gentile territory or at least among pagans. Some scholars do not hesitate to ascribe the apparently narrow attitude to Jesus, and compare the sayings in Matt. 10:5, 23*b* (M), or Jesus' surprise at the faith of the centurion (Matt. 8:10 [Q]). Others think this is a story of some early Christian exorcism that has become attributed to Jesus: there was a powerful tendency in the early Palestinian church to restrict its mission to Jews and Jewish proselytes, a tendency which B. H. Streeter (*op. cit.*, pp. 254-59) saw reflected in M, Matthew's special material or source. Perhaps a clue to the present form of the story may be found in the saying which Matthew inserts at this point (Matt. 15:24): "I was sent only to the lost sheep of the house of Israel," in which the original emphasis lay upon "lost sheep," not upon "Israel"—the meaning would then be: my mission is to the lost and neglected, viz., the Amhaarez, as in Mark 2:17. Under the stress of controversy in early Christian Jewish circles the emphasis got reversed, and so Matthew understands the saying and uses it in his parallel. A similar influence has perhaps affected the tradition of the story as given in Mark. As it stands now, a Gentile woman's witty reply wins from Jesus what a plain request had failed to obtain. It is sometimes suggested that Jesus' words to her in vs. 27

---

undesirable habit, but a sin. Its ill effects can never be measured. In a sense Jesus himself was crucified by slander.

Pride is rightly one of the seven deadly sins. A case could be made for ranking it the deadliest. For it blocks all spiritual growth. Pride prevents the very beginning of the Christian experience—penitence. Pride is stiff-kneed. It can never kneel in true prayer. It seals up the gate to all growth—humility.

It is strange to find the word **foolishness** at the end of the list. It is often used to describe a sort of lighthearted facetiousness, or a lack of wisdom, in either case with no viciousness. The word does not mean that kind of "foolishness," but a deeper sort—"folly" as Goodspeed translates it, "recklessness" in Moffatt's version. Folly is a sin, the perverse confusion of values, the foolish choice of lesser goods, the reckless unconcern for the spiritual, the persistence in shopping for shoddy stuff.

24. *Yet He Could Not Be Hid.*—How many thousand sermons have been preached on this text and will be preached on it, and rightly. Here it is, just a factual detail of the failure of Jesus' desire to be unrecognized. It has no other meaning. Yet the words picture with sharp vividness a great truth of nineteen centuries,

that nothing has been able to hide Jesus completely or permanently from the eyes and minds of men. So there is abundant justification for elevating this detail to a place as a symbol for the imagination.

There have been recurring times when the Jesus who walks across the pages of the Synoptic Gospels seems to have been rather effectively hidden, buried under accretions of one sort or another. Yet in a high and reverent sense Jesus has been the Wandering Jew. The hero of the legend, as a punishment, was forbidden to die, and condemned to reappear in each new century. Jesus has been the eternal contemporary of every generation, no antiquated figure, alien in speech and dress, but a living personality and force. So have the great artists always painted him.

He could not be hid even by the cloud of dense theological verbiage with which he has sometimes been surrounded. Just when he has seemed to be passing out of sight behind polysyllabic barricades, he has emerged again. Indeed, a central fact of history since the beginning of the Christian era has been the rebirth of Christ into new contexts and larger meanings.

He could not be hid in the dim recesses of the church, where frantic efforts have often been

25 For a *certain* woman, whose young daughter had an unclean spirit, heard of him, and came and fell at his feet:

26 The woman was a Greek, a Syrophenician by nation; and she besought him that he would cast forth the devil out of her daughter.

27 But Jesus said unto her, Let the children first be filled: for it is not meet to take the children's bread, and to cast *it* unto the dogs.

be hid. 25 But immediately a woman, whose little daughter was possessed by an unclean spirit, heard of him, and came and fell down at his feet. 26 Now the woman was a Greek, a Sy-ro-phoe-ni'cian by birth. And she begged him to cast the demon out of her daughter. 27 And he said to her, "Let the children first be fed, for it is not right to take the children's bread and throw

were only half in earnest, either as a test of her faith or as an ironical reference to current Jewish prejudices (as in John 4:22, similarly interpreted). Such bantering dialogue is not unknown in ancient Jewish traditions; it is, indeed, one of the charming features of many a tale of the old rabbis. But whether it can be traced here, in as serious a work as Mark's Gospel, is questionable.

26. **A Greek,** i.e., a Gentile, as correctly in the Vulg. **Syrophoenician**=a Syrian from the Phoenician coast (so B, etc.). In the so-called Clementine literature she is named Justa, and her daughter Bernice.

27. **First:** Perhaps an echo of the later controversy over the admission of Gentiles, settled by Paul in his famous formula, "To the Jew first and also to the Greek" (Rom. 1:16). Rudolf Bultmann (*Die Geschichte der synoptischen Tradition* [2nd ed.; Göttingen: Vandenhoeck & Ruprecht, 1931], p. 38) would omit the word, if not the whole of vs. 27*a*, since it implies that the Gentiles' needs would be met after those of the Jews had been satisfied. **The dogs** is impossibly harsh and unfeeling on the lips of Jesus—like the language used about Jews in John, or in the Matthaean version (Matt. 23) of the discourse against the scribes. What we must recognize is that the language of the tradition has been affected by the prejudices of those who handed it down during the long oral period before the Gospels were compiled—this time the prejudices of Jewish Christians.

made to confine him. Time after time he has escaped from ecclesiastical prisons, to walk the streets once more, the friend of sinners, the Savior of men, the enemy of all that preys on human life. **He could not be hid** amid all the changes in thinking which in the confident if too hasty judgment of many turned him into an obsolete figure in a revolutionized world. D. H. Lawrence wrote to Katherine Mansfield, "Cheer up, Kate. Jesus is a back number." That was before World War I. In the periods of calamity which always follow such disdainful disregard for Jesus and his teaching, the "back number" has a way of showing up on the front page.

Or take another aspect of this wide-ranging truth—and here rests much of our hope for the endurance of Christianity and the church: Whenever Christ is really present in a human life, shaping its mind, informing its spirit, energizing its efforts, he cannot be hid. As in the region of Tyre, he will be discovered. The news that he is present in that particular house will spread, and many will be drawn by it.

25-30. *A Woman, Whose Little Daughter Was Possessed by an Unclean Spirit, Heard of Him,*

and Came.—Amid all the very great difficulties of this passage (see Exeg.) two features stand out clearly and impressively. The first is the persistence and ingenuity of love shown in this mother's appeal for her afflicted daughter. We meet it many times in the Gospels; it is always touching (see Expos. 2:4). She wanted Jesus **to cast the demon out of her daughter** and would stop at no rebuff. When refused, she persisted. To the answer "No" she made an ingenious reply, sticking to her point and request. One thing counted right then, and one thing only, to have Jesus' help for her child. It was a love that would not let her child go.

Suppose that all Christian parents and all churches had the same persistence and ingenuity in bringing to their children the saving influence of Christ! If parents had something of this woman's relentless determination to bring into their homes Jesus' power, his power to heal life, to preserve it, to enrich it, to cast evil spirits from it, how much smaller the number of children who would drift away! If a church felt that way about bringing Jesus' influence into the lives of all its children, all the children in the community who might be touched, what

28 And she answered and said unto him, Yes, Lord: yet the dogs under the table eat of the children's crumbs.

29 And he said unto her, For this saying go thy way; the devil is gone out of thy daughter.

30 And when she was come to her house, she found the devil gone out, and her daughter laid upon the bed.

31 ¶ And again, departing from the coasts of Tyre and Sidon, he came unto the sea of Galilee, through the midst of the coasts of Decapolis.

32 And they bring unto him one that was deaf, and had an impediment in his speech; and they beseech him to put his hand upon him.

it to the dogs." **28** But she answered him, "Yes, Lord; yet even the dogs under the table eat the children's crumbs." **29** And he said to her, "For this saying you may go your way; the demon has left your daughter." **30** And she went home, and found the child lying in bed, and the demon gone.

31 Then he returned from the region of Tyre, and went through Sidon to the sea of Galilee, through the region of the De-cap'o-lis. **32** And they brought to him a man who was deaf and had an impediment in his speech; and they besought

---

10. HEALING A DEAF AND DUMB MAN (7:31-37)

31-37. This story is abridged by Matthew (15:29-31) and converted into a summary account of many healings. He also ignores Mark's strange topography, and describes Jesus as returning directly to Galilee, though his itinerary is somewhat strange: "Jesus went on from there and passed along the sea of Galilee." The region of Tyre and Sidon was a long way from the Sea of Galilee—Tyre about forty miles northwest, as a bird flies; Sidon about twenty-five miles beyond, up the coast. The Decapolis (see 5:20), lay southeast of the lake. **Coasts** (KJV) is of course **region** (RSV) or "territory," perhaps "neighborhood." Mark's geography, or that of his earliest copyists, left something to be desired. But Palestine lay many leagues distant from Rome, which perhaps accounts both for the author's inaccuracy or vagueness and for his readers' indifference.

The narrative of the healing is told in typical form: Jesus is besought to heal the man (vs. 32) by the laying on of his hands; a formula of command is used (vs. 34); the cure takes place at once (vs. 35); as in 1:44; 5:43, Jesus orders that the story should not be told (vs. 36), **but the more he charged,** i.e., commanded, **them, the more zealously they proclaimed it,** i.e., made it known; finally (vs. 37), the admiring comments of the people are noted (as in 2:12). The striking novelty of the story is Jesus' use of spittle. This was an ancient medicament, especially for use on the eyes—here the tongue—and was also used in magic (see Pliny *Natural History* XXVIII. 7; Tacitus *Histories* IV. 81). Since

---

a changed church and community there would be! If there were the love that never gave up, if there were the ingenuity to which obstacles were merely something to be overcome! It would be an awkward name for a church—"The Church of the Syrophoenician Woman"! But a church marked by her spirit would be a joy to God and a saving power in the world.

The other outstanding feature of the story is Jesus' evident admiration of this woman's energy and brains. Her quick reply, salted with wit; her keen and nimble mind; no doubt the very courage of her repartee—all of it met with his appreciation.

Energy and brains—how desperately they are needed in the work of God's kingdom! They are superb, indispensable materials. Jesus needs clear, quick brains for his cause. It is not enough

to have "a heart of gold and a head full of feathers." Feathers are poor building stuff. We give silver—and sometimes even gold—to Christ's church. Have we ever really given our energy and brains?

32-35. And They Brought to Him a Man Who Was Deaf and Had an Impediment in His Speech.—The miracles of Jesus, in all their variety, are richly suggestive of transformations which come in a life when Christ enters as its Master and Savior. Here Jesus heals a deaf man: restores his hearing. It carries the mind along to that even larger ministry of making the mind and heart more sensitive to the voices of God and of the world.

How many of the ills of the earth are due largely to the spiritual deafness of those who cannot hear the "still, sad music of humanity"

33 And he took him aside from the multitude, and put his fingers into his ears, and he spit, and touched his tongue;

34 And looking up to heaven, he sighed, and saith unto him, Ephphatha, that is, Be opened.

35 And straightway his ears were opened, and the string of his tongue was loosed, and he spake plain.

36 And he charged them that they should tell no man: but the more he charged them, so much the more a great deal they published it;

37 And were beyond measure astonished, saying, He hath done all things well: he maketh both the deaf to hear, and the dumb to speak.

him to lay his hand upon him. 33 And taking him aside from the multitude privately, he put his fingers into his ears, and he spat and touched his tongue; 34 and looking up to heaven, he sighed, and said to him, "Eph′pha-tha," that is, "Be opened." 35 And his ears were opened, his tongue was released, and he spoke plainly. 36 And he charged them to tell no one; but the more he charged them, the more zealously they proclaimed it. 37 And they were astonished beyond measure, saying, "He has done all things well; he even makes the deaf hear and the dumb speak."

the command "Be opened" refers to the ears, not to the tongue, it may be that an earlier story of the cure of a deaf man has had combined with it the cure of a dumb man. Compare the story in 8:22-26, the blind man cured by spittle (see also John 9:1-7). The use of direct command seems more characteristic of Jesus' method of healing; but we must not overlook the occasional use of folk remedies, e.g., oil (6:13), or the methods used by other healers, e.g., in the O.T. What was effective, both in the word of command and in the use of a material application, was presumably the combination of Jesus' powerful personality, his own faith, that of the patient, and, most important, the will of God. No one who has ever seen a miracle, or anything approaching a miracle, will be inclined to set precise limits and say, "This is quite possible and normal; but the other is impossible, and beyond belief." And Mark, a man of the ancient world, and beyond that a Christian, would not hesitate to accept the tradition in toto. Both the word of command and the spittle from the mouth of a divine-human person were equally effective, and for the same reason. This observation also applies to those who handed down the tradition. (For Jewish miracles of the time see Paul Fiebig, *Jüdische Wundergeschichten des neutestamentlichen Zeitalters* [Tübingen: J. C. B. Mohr, 1911], a fine collection from ancient sources; for pagan, see Otto Weinreich, *Antike Heilungswunder* [Giessen: Alfred Töpelmann, 1909]; Richard Reitzenstein, *Hellenistische Wundererzählungen* [Leipzig: B. G. Teubner, 1906]. See also Rudolf Bultmann, "Study of the Synoptic Gospels," tr. F. C. Grant, in *Form Criticism: A New Method of New Testament Research* [Chicago: Willett, Clark & Co., 1934]; and Martin Dibelius, *From Tradition to Gospel*, tr. Bertram Lee Woolf [New York: Charles Scribner's Sons, 1935].)

or the "still small voice" of God. They are too deaf to catch the sobs of grief, whether across the seas, or across the railroad tracks, or only across the street. They are too hard of hearing to catch the rumble of discontent over injustice, or to discern the thunder of coming storms. The clamorous tom-tom of the drums of egoism drown out other sounds. Keble writes truly,

But the deaf heart, the dumb by choice,
These baffle even the spells of heaven.[*]

It is worth noting that in the great messianic picture of Isa. 35 a mark of the millennium is

[*] *The Christian Year.*

that "the ears of the deaf shall be unstopped" (Isa. 35:5). Wherever ears are really opened, so that the messages of the neighbors, either twenty thousand miles away or twenty feet away, messages that would result in understanding and sympathy, can be heard, we have a bit of the millennium. And how greatly we need new ears for old, ears from which the plugs of class and race prejudice and nationalism have been removed! Has the miracle of opened ears ever been wrought for us?

The man was also cured of **an impediment in his speech,** a miracle equally suggestive for the spiritual life. Indeed, as hearing and speech are related physically, so ears and tongue are

8 In those days the multitude being very great, and having nothing to eat, Jesus called his disciples *unto him,* and saith unto them,

2 I have compassion on the multitude, because they have now been with me three days, and have nothing to eat:

3 And if I send them away fasting to their own houses, they will faint by the way: for divers of them came from far.

8 In those days, when again a great crowd had gathered, and they had nothing to eat, he called his disciples to him, and said to them, 2 "I have compassion on the crowd, because they have been with me now three days, and have nothing to eat; 3 and if I send them away hungry to their homes, they will faint on the way; and some of them have come a long way."

---

11. The Feeding of the Four Thousand (8:1-10)

As we have noted, 8:1-26 is apparently parallel to 6:34–7:37:

6:34-44	Feeding of the five thousand	8:1-9	Feeding of the four thousand
45-52	Walking on the sea		
53-56	Crossing to Gennesaret	10	Crossing to "Dalmanutha"
7:1-23	Controversy with Pharisees and scribes from Jerusalem (over clean and unclean)	11-12	Controversy with Pharisees (over signs)
24-30	The Syrophoenician woman ("children's bread")	13-21	Sayings about bread
31-37	Healing of a deaf and dumb man	22-26	Healing of a blind man

Similar parallel narratives or series are found elsewhere in the Bible, in both O.T. and N.T., e.g., the three accounts of Paul's conversion in Acts. However, except for the two feedings of the multitude, it is the parallel sequences of events rather than parallel contents which are most impressive here. Some scholars have held that the first series was Jewish, the second Gentile; but this will not do, as 7:24-30 is clearly in pagan territory, while 8:11-12 involves Pharisees—who would not be found in a Gentile neighborhood. The parallelism has not yet been explained. However, a comparison of the two feeding narratives, especially in the Greek, shows a remarkable number of common words. This may be quite natural; a story like this would be told in just such a way in the early Christian community. The influence both of O.T. diction and of Christian liturgical interpretation is apparent in each. (See above, on 6:34-44.)

8:1-3. Mark, following the tradition before him, clearly emphasizes this miracle as a feeding of the hungry, and stresses Jesus' compassion; in 6:34 his compassion is noted, but

---

related spiritually. One reason why our civilization has so little to say of profound significance is that so many of Christ's disciples have an impediment in their speech. His word does not sound out clearly to the world through them. They choose rather to be "God's mutes." To the ringing appeal of the psalmist (Ps. 107:2), "Let the redeemed of the Lord say so," they reply, "Kindly excuse me, I do not want to go on record." We read in Prov. 15:23, "A word spoken in due season, how good is it!" But it is never the season to speak for one who has the impediment of selfish preoccupation. The silencing impediments of caution, prudence, and cowardice, will prevent us from speaking boldly for God in the presence of wrong. What stirring eloquence in the simple words the evangelist uses to describe the restored voice, **His tongue**

was released, and he spoke plainly. God needs our voice, speaking plainly, that his voice may be heard.

8:1-10. The Feeding of the Four Thousand.— See comment above on the parallel story in 6:34-44.

1-3. They Have Been with Me Now Three Days, and Have Nothing to Eat.—These verses present a marvelous picture of the imagination of Jesus. **When again a great crowd had gathered,** he projected himself into their situation, saw with their eyes, felt with their nerves. He noticed every detail, that some had come a long way, that they had been a long time without food; then, by a wonderful forward thrust, he foresaw what would happen to many on the return trip. There was a holy trinity of mind and spirit and senses here at work in Jesus—

4 And his disciples answered him, From whence can a man satisfy these *men* with bread here in the wilderness?

5 And he asked them, How many loaves have ye? And they said, Seven.

6 And he commanded the people to sit down on the ground: and he took the seven loaves, and gave thanks, and brake, and gave to his disciples to set before *them;* and they did set *them* before the people.

7 And they had a few small fishes: and he blessed, and commanded to set them also before *them.*

8 So they did eat, and were filled: and they took up of the broken *meat* that was left seven baskets.

9 And they that had eaten were about four thousand: and he sent them away.

4 And his disciples answered him, "How can one feed these men with bread here in the desert?" 5 And he asked them, "How many loaves have you?" They said, "Seven." 6 And he commanded the crowd to sit down on the ground; and he took the seven loaves, and having given thanks he broke them and gave them to his disciples to set before the people; and they set them before the crowd. 7 And they had a few small fish; and having blessed them, he commanded that these also should be set before them. 8 And they ate, and were satisfied; and they took up the broken pieces left over, seven baskets full. 9 And there

to explain his *teaching,* not the feeding. **Their homes,** although said to be **far,** could not have been many miles away; as in 6:35, the spot is a remote and lonely place in the open country. One is reminded of the Communion services of the early Covenanters in their inaccessible glens.

4-5. As in 6:37-38, the problem of feeding so large a number is stressed, and Jesus' question is the same: **How many loaves have you?** Jesus' confidence in the divine bounty is so great that the only question is this factual and practical one, which implies that the disciples are to produce and use what they have.

6-8. As in ch. 6, the multitude is probably arranged in groups (also as in the early Christian agape?); Jesus blesses (i.e., says the blessing, not **blessed them** [RSV]; omit αὐτά), and orders the disciples to distribute the pieces. Again, as in ch. 6, the fish are treated as secondary (due to liturgical influence?—as also in John 6:11; John's account is clearly liturgical, and is the occasion for the great discourse on the bread of life). Again, as in 6:42-43, all are **satisfied,** and the remaining fragments are gathered—here in **seven baskets** rather than twelve. What this number indicates is not clear; perhaps it was symbolic. The "baskets" (σπυρίδες) here were probably larger than those (κόφινοι) of ch. 6 (cf. Acts 9:25!). The distinction is maintained in vss. 19-20.

9. Again, as in 6:44-45, the number of those who ate is given, and Jesus' formal dismissal of the gathering is reported. Matt. 15:38 says "four thousand men, besides women and children," thus increasing the number (as also in Matt. 14:21).

observation, imagination, and sympathy. Often with us one of the three is absent, or all three together. Some people do not observe. The range of the eye is narrow, often not sharply focused on anything outside the tiny circle of their own self-interest. Good observation requires freedom from the blinkers of self. It requires humility, for pride is a bandage on the eyes. Others, even when they see, lack the imagination, or will not use what they have to bring home vividly what they see. They never "crawl under the other man's skin." They never employ any dramatic skill to represent what might be going on in another's heart and life. To do what Jesus did here, to follow in his imagination these people trudging down the

road home, hungry and depressed, with the consequent fainting—that would be a miracle far beyond their atrophied mental powers. Still others lack sympathy. They just do not care enough. The springs of love have never been opened. Many of the world's greatest evils and much of its agonizing suffering go on because there are such multitudes of people who never send the heart out on any journey, and so never realize how heavy are the burdens of life that cut into the shoulders of men and women and children, what hunger feels like, what segregation means to a Negro, what an atomic war would mean.

Shelley has a penetrating phrase, "the creative faculty to imagine what we know." A con-

10 ¶ And straightway he entered into a ship with his disciples, and came into the parts of Dalmanutha.

11 And the Pharisees came forth, and began to question with him, seeking of him a sign from heaven, tempting him.

12 And he sighed deeply in his spirit, and saith, Why doth this generation seek after a sign? verily I say unto you, There shall no sign be given unto this generation.

were about four thousand people. 10 And he sent them away; and immediately he got into the boat with his disciples, and went to the district of Dal-ma-nu'tha.*d*

11 The Pharisees came and began to argue with him, seeking from him a sign from heaven, to test him. 12 And he sighed deeply in his spirit, and said, "Why does this generation seek a sign? Truly, I say to you, no sign shall be given to this

d Some ancient authorities read *Magadan* or *Magdala.*

---

10. The location of **Dalmanutha** is unknown. It may be a textual corruption; the MSS give a wide variety of alternatives. Matthew reads Magadan; some good MSS of Mark have Magdala, which is presumably correct. Magdala was on the west shore of the lake; in vss. 13, 22 they "cross" the lake to Bethsaida. As Augustine observed, they may all be different names for the same place. More than one village in lower Canada has two or three names in local use.

12. THE PHARISEES DEMAND A SIGN (8:11-13)

11. **Came forth:** Whence they came is not said. The words may be a survival of the earlier, pre-Marcan version of the incident. **A sign from heaven, to test him,** would have been a stroke of lightning, clap of thunder, fire, or a voice from heaven, i.e., a mere "wonder." Theophylact (quoted in Klostermann) supposed that in their view Jesus' league with Beelzebul (3:22) enabled him to do wonders only upon earth, not the celestial variety (cf. Rev. 12:1). Their motive in putting him to the test (cf. 10:2; 12:13) was malicious (cf. the motive of Satan in the temptation narrative in Q—Matt. 4:1-11).

12. **This generation** has been understood to mean "this kind [or "group"] of persons"; but it undoubtedly reflects the apocalyptic view that the last generation(s) in human history would be "faithless and perverse" above all others (cf. 8:38; 9:19; Matt. 11:16-24; 12:38-45; 23:34-36). **There shall no sign be given:** This flat, categorical refusal of a sign from heaven is modified in Luke 11:29-30 by the addition of the words ". . . except the sign of Jonah. For as Jonah became a sign to the men of Nineveh, so will the Son of man be to this generation." Luke omits "from heaven" in referring to the sign, and he may possibly understand the saying to mean Jesus' earthly ministry, or that of Jesus and his disciples— so Martin Dibelius in his book, *Jesus* (Philadelphia: Westminster Press, 1949). Matt. 12:39-40 adds the exception, with the explanation, "For as Jonah was three days and

---

secrated imagination in his children is one of God's chief instruments for the saving and blessing of mankind.

12. *Why Does This Generation Seek a Sign? Truly, I Say to You, No Sign Shall Be Given.* —The sign desired by the Pharisees was "from heaven," that is, some sensational marvel, thunder or blinding light, something physical. Jesus in the temptation (Matt. 4:5-7) refused to give any such sensational "proofs" of the truth of his mission.

Men have sought for "signs" ever since. They still seek for them, individually and socially. It has been hard for people to understand that the gospel is its own evidence. It cannot be authenticated by any physical token of any sort. Yet there has always been a persistent cry of "lo, here," "lo, there," whenever something

out of the ordinary has happened. There used to be quite a series of books under the general title of "Remarkable Answers to Prayer," in which were cited, as proof that prayer was a real power, instances of physical healing, of somebody's having missed a train that was later wrecked, or even of having been guided into a profitable financial venture. "Signs" of the truth of Christianity have been found in remarkable rescues at sea—leaving unfaced, of course, the problem of multitudes that were not rescued; during wars, in favorable turns of the weather, in the "providential" withholding of natural resources from the enemy, in military victory.

Jesus answered, **No sign shall be given.** And the answer still holds. Or rather—and this is God's final answer to all our human eagerness

13 And he left them, and entering into the ship again departed to the other side.	generation." 13 And he left them, and getting into the boat again he departed to the other side.
14 ¶ Now *the disciples* had forgotten to take bread, neither had they in the ship with them more than one loaf.	14 Now they had forgotten to bring bread; and they had only one loaf with them in the boat. 15 And he cautioned them,
15 And he charged them, saying, Take	

three nights in the belly of the whale, so will the Son of man be three days and three nights in the heart of the earth." It is of course conceivable that Luke has modified Mark, and that Matthew has elaborated Luke; but the agreements between Matthew and Luke in the total passage show that they are probably using a non-Marcan source (Q), and it is much more likely that Mark has abridged it, or its equivalent in oral tradition. Matt. 16:4 keeps the shorter form of the saying, with the simple modification, "except the sign of Jonah." It is perfectly conceivable that in the oral tradition, the saying circulated in two forms, one with, and one without, the exception clause. To Mark it would go without saying that Jesus, as Son of God, *could* have produced signs from heaven, but forbore.

13. The Leaven of the Pharisees (8:14-21)

This little dialogue is thoroughly Marcan in language, style, and feeling, and many students think that it was composed by Mark, using traditional material, but with more than usual freedom. Vs. 15 seems irrelevant in this connection, and may well be bracketed; it points back to vss. 11-13: the "leaven" is the "hardening of heart," which means lack of insight—or understanding—and faith. The saying is undoubtedly authentic, but may not belong here; Luke 12:1 removes it to another context. Vs. 16 continues vs. 14 (the words "it is" of KJV are not in the Greek). The point of the dialogue is that, after the two feedings of the multitude, the disciples ought to know that Jesus can supply their needs from the "one loaf" they have with them—or from none, if that was the original reading (see on vs. 14). They are upbraided once more for their obtuseness.

14. Forgotten: This seems strange after the huge supply of bread left over in 8:8 and 6:43. The **one loaf** has been interpreted mystically (the bread of life, or Jesus as the true bread); but this kind of symbolism, natural in the Fourth Gospel, is foreign to Mark. Some would strike out the clause, with Matthew, and read, "They had forgotten to take bread with them in the boat." Although there is no adequate textual warrant for omitting this clause from Mark, vss. 16-17 imply total lack: they **have no bread.**

15. Leaven was suggested by "bread," and was meant figuratively (=teaching, Matt. 16:12; or hypocrisy, Luke 12:1). **Of Herod,** or better (with p45 W Θ, etc.) **the Herodians**

for dazzling signs—a sign has already been given: Jesus himself. Christ's teaching could not be proved by an earthquake, no matter how violent; but Christ's words "Whosoever will lose his life for my sake, the same shall save it (Luke 9:24) and "He that hath seen me hath seen the Father" (John 14:9), carry their own self-authenticating evidence to the life that will receive them and act on them. The most remarkable answer to prayer is communion with God. It is a life hid with Christ in God, a life sustained by faith in God. Consider the perverse legal phrase, "an act of God." In law that is reserved for hurricanes, lightnings, floods, all calamities of a sensational sort. What a distortion! The great acts of God are of a different sort, the continual and renewed mercies of morning and evening, the enrichment of love and friendship, the quickening of spirit that comes in worship, the undergirding of life through faith and prayer. These are the acts of God. These are the signs given. Have you, in Paul's phrase, "the eyes of your hearts enlightened" (Eph. 1:18) to see them? To those who try it, Jesus' way of life becomes its own evidence. They do have "a sign." They become aware of One who speaks to them through love and duty —aware not of something, but of Somebody.

15. Beware of the Leaven of the Pharisees and the Leaven of Herod.—Just exactly what Jesus had in mind in these words is not clearly explained. All through the narrative he is reproaching his disciples for their "lack of understanding and insight" (see Exeg.). But the joining of the Pharisees and Herodians as enemies of Jesus (see 3:6) —"a strange alliance of religious strictness and worldly policy"[7]—may

[7] Menzies, *Earliest Gospel*, p. 164.

heed, beware of the leaven of the Pharisees, and *of* the leaven of Herod.

16 And they reasoned among themselves, saying, *It is* because we have no bread.

17 And when Jesus knew *it*, he saith unto them, Why reason ye, because ye have no bread? perceive ye not yet, neither understand? have ye your heart yet hardened?

18 Having eyes, see ye not? and having ears, hear ye not? and do ye not remember?

19 When I brake the five loaves among five thousand, how many baskets full of fragments took ye up? They say unto him, Twelve.

20 And when the seven among four thousand, how many baskets full of fragments took ye up? And they said, Seven.

21 And he said unto them, How is it that ye do not understand?

saying, "Take heed, beware of the leaven of the Pharisees and the leaven of Herod."*e*

16 And they discussed it with one another, saying, "We have no bread." 17 And being aware of it, Jesus said to them, "Why do you discuss the fact that you have no bread? Do you not yet perceive or understand? Are your hearts hardened? 18 Having eyes do you not see, and having ears do you not hear? And do you not remember? 19 When I broke the five loaves for the five thousand, how many baskets full of broken pieces did you take up?" They said to him, "Twelve." 20 "And the seven for the four thousand, how many baskets full of broken pieces did you take up?" And they said to him, "Seven." 21 And he said to them, "Do you not yet understand?"

e Some ancient authorities read *the Herodians.*

(RSV mg.). Since 3:6 these two groups have been Jesus' sworn enemies. "Teaching" will not do for Herod or Herodians, so Matthew changes to "Sadducees."

17-20. Why reason ye? as in 2:8. RSV paraphrases correctly, **Why do you discuss the fact that you have no bread? Not yet,** as in vs. 21, and in some MSS at 4:40. As in 6:52, the disciples' faith should have grown after the extraordinary experiences they had been through. But Mark stresses here, as elsewhere, their lack of understanding and insight, and suggests—as a question—that they share the "hardening of heart" which led the Jewish authorities to reject Jesus. The same prophetic judgment (Jer. 5:21; Ezek. 12:2) hangs over them as over "those outside" in 4:12. **And do you not remember?** is the introduction to the two questions that follow. Mark "underscores the obvious" (as in 2:19*b*), and drives the point home relentlessly in vss. 19-20.

21. Do you not yet understand? The reading of some MSS (D ⊖ Vulg., etc.) is attractive as a powerful climax: "How can you not yet understand?" But perhaps this is just a shade too "literary" to be what Mark wrote.

---

well have been in his mind. Jesus is warning his disciples against infection by the spirit of either party. And the warning has permanent importance and urgency to all disciples of every time; for the danger of such infection is always immanent.

Beware of sharing and exhibiting the spirit of the Pharisees. It is the spirit of externalism, of the elevation of observances and regulations into the priority which belongs to the moral and spiritual. It is a gross violation of the first commandment, "Thou shalt have no other gods before me" (Exod. 20:3). They had made a higher god of their tradition, and lifted up their souls to that vanity. Such a spirit is terribly infectious and insidious. Whenever any interest, advantage, or form of cherished custom displaces the moral requirements of God, we have **the leaven of the Pharisees** (see Expos. 7:8-13). Theirs was the spirit of pride, the absence of love. Their "leaven" was devotion to a tradition

as a vested interest; and it led them to collaborate with the enemies of their own faith, the Herodians. These same dangers beset us in the twentieth century no less than they beset the original company of disciples in Jesus' own lifetime.

The spirit of the Herodians was worldliness. Today we would call it secularism. It developed to a high art the serving of God and mammon. It made a supreme virtue of expediency. It bowed down to the state. Who would be rash enough to say that the danger of infection by the spirit of timeserving, of obsequious compliance with the ruling ideas of the world about us, is not ever-present? There are churches in which a comfortable adjustment to power and popularity would almost seem to be one of the articles of the creed.

Jesus said, **Take heed, beware.**

17-21. *Do You Not Yet Perceive or Understand?* —There is pathos in these succeeding

22 ¶ And he cometh to Bethsaida; and they bring a blind man unto him, and besought him to touch him.

23 And he took the blind man by the hand, and led him out of the town; and when he had spit on his eyes, and put his hands upon him, he asked him if he saw aught.

24 And he looked up, and said, I see men as trees, walking.

22 And they came to Beth-sa′i-da. And some people brought to him a blind man, and begged him to touch him. 23 And he took the blind man by the hand, and led him out of the village; and when he had spit on his eyes and laid his hands upon him, he asked him, "Do you see anything?" 24 And he looked up and said, "I see men;

---

14. The Blind Man of Bethsaida (8:22-26)

Is this parallel to 7:31-37? Even Matthew may have thought so, for he omits it—or rather, perhaps, includes it in his generalized account (Matt. 15:29-31) at the former point. John 9:1-7 has a similar story, located at Jerusalem. Here again Jesus makes use of material means, and commands silence after the cure; but the healing is gradual, not instantaneous, and requires two treatments; perhaps this accounts for Matthew's and Luke's omission.

22. It is extraordinary that they bring the blind man to Jesus and ask him **to touch him** (Jesus' usual procedure); instead he uses spittle, as in 7:33. There must be some connection between the stories. It has been suggested (but Mark does not say it) that this healing in a foreign town was more difficult than usual—as if Bethsaida were wholly "foreign," or as if Jewish cures were easier (6:5)!

23-25. The man is led outside **the village**; as in 5:37, 40, Jesus prefers privacy and quiet for the treatment. **As trees, walking:** This is correct; the men look vague and

---

questions of Jesus, recording his amazement at the slow-wittedness of his disciples. It is a mood to which he often gave voice, and there is always a touch of sadness about it (see Exeg.).

With all that had gone on under their eyes, with all the words their ears had heard, their minds moved with a laggard, heavy tread. Here they are represented as worried about bread, when they had just come from seeing Jesus multiply bread for human need. One would think the sheer wonder at the resources of God would touch their minds with awe, and drive all little gnawing worries from their minds.

We cannot understand this dimness of mind which prevented their insight into the spiritual truth which Jesus declared. That is, we cannot grasp it—until we look into our own hearts.

For the questions of Jesus come with a sharper reproach to us after nineteen centuries than they came to his first disciples. How closely this comment on the scene troubles us: "If Jesus had to meet hostility from the outside world, he had at least as serious a problem presented by the stupidity of his own followers. They loved him passionately, but they did not understand him." [8] We have seen so much more of the witness of history. We have seen the breaking of the bread of life throughout the cen-

[8] Theodore H. Robinson, *The Gospel of Matthew* (New York: Harper & Bros., 1928; "The Moffatt New Testament Commentary), p. 139.

turies. We have seen humanity's deepest needs met. And yet—we do not understand. We are so slow to trust, to make the venture of faith, whether in our personal lives or in the life of society. There is a special poignancy in the question **Do you not remember?** as it comes to us today. Do we not remember the hours when he spoke to us,

As of old, St. Andrew heard it
By the Galilean lake,[9]

when his claims came to us clear and strong? Do we not remember the years of the Lord's right hand, the ways in which our lives have been compassed about for good? **Do you not remember? Do you not yet understand?**

24-25. *And He Looked Up and Said, "I See Men; but They Look Like Trees, Walking."* This cure is unusual in that instead of being instantaneous, as in the reports of Jesus' other miracles, it was marked by stages. Doubtless this is the reason that Matthew and Luke omit it (see Exeg.).

The passage, however, is very suggestive. It is a farfetched interpretation, which does violence to the meaning of the original, to suppose as Loisy does, that the gradual cure of blindness symbolizes the gradual education of

[9] Cecil Frances Alexander, "Jesus calls us, o'er the tumult."

25 After that he put *his* hands again upon his eyes, and made him look up; and he was restored, and saw every man clearly.

26 And he sent him away to his house, saying, Neither go into the town, nor tell *it* to any in the town.

27 ¶ And Jesus went out, and his disciples, into the towns of Caesarea Philippi: and by the way he asked his disciples, saying unto them, Whom do men say that I am?

but they look like trees, walking." **25** Then again he laid his hands upon his eyes; and he looked intently and was restored, and saw everything clearly. **26** And he sent him away to his home, saying, "Do not even enter the village."

27 And Jesus went on with his disciples, to the villages of Caes-a-re′a Philippi; and on the way he asked his disciples, "Who

---

blurred, but they move about (cf. Birnam Wood in *Macbeth* [Act V, scene 5]) . **He looked intently** is the correct translation of διέβλεψεν. The Vulg. *et coepit videre* ("and he began to see") is curious but may represent a variant Greek text.

26. In KJV the command laid upon the man conflates two or three textual variants (cf. Vulg., "Go to your home, and if you enter the village, say nothing to anyone") . The shorter reading of RSV is that of certain early MSS (B S* sys, etc.). The other readings have apparently been influenced by 1:43.

15. PETER'S CONFESSION (8:27-30)

Mark now begins an important division in his book, "the way of the Cross," as B. W. Bacon called it, 8:27–10:45, with a nucleus of discipleship sayings in 9:33-50 (see Intro., pp. 633, 636; and on 9:33-37, below) . Some interpreters have held that the second main

---

the disciples. There is no intentional symbolism here. Yet just as narrative, the story does convey the vivid picture of a man half-cured of blindness. It at least suggests the pitiful condition of people in whom the process of healing seems to have been arrested at precisely that stage. And how many there are! They have never allowed Jesus to perform the service of restoring full, clear sight.

There are so many who get only a dim and clouded view of him, of his possible meaning to themselves and to the world. The name and figure are familiar. They can even rattle off the words: "Suffered under Pontius Pilate, was crucified, dead, and buried; the third day he rose again from the dead." But it is still a dim, half-opaque vision. They do not see him as one whose revelation of the Father might utterly change the face of life; they do not see him as the great rebuke to their own lives; not as the bringer of deep and lasting joy; not as Savior. But actually he is

> Not the Christ of our subtle creeds,
> But the lord of our hearts, of our homes,
> Of our hopes, our prayers, our needs;
> The brother of want and blame.[1]

The half cure of blindness yields only a dim view of man. There is a very arresting power in the detail that when vision was only partly

[1] Richard Watson Gilder, "The Passing of Christ," *Poems* (Boston: Houghton Mifflin Co., 1908). By permission.

restored, the blind man saw men as though they were trees, walking. How many people still see them as things, not as sons and daughters of Almighty God! There is the "commodity" view of labor, in which men are used to bring about a 20 per cent profit; or the "cannon fodder" view, which sees them as missiles to be hurled, something "expendable"—the most horrible word that came out of World War II; or less violently, the view which sees them as objects in a landscape, with no more appeal to conscience and sympathy than trees would have.

People only half cured of blindness have, moreover, but a dim view of the world. They see it and accept it as it is, with no anguish, often looking at it without the slightest disturbance. They do not see its suffering and need; nor its sin.

Note that Jesus insisted on a complete cure. We read, **Then again he laid his hands upon his eyes. And the blind man saw everything clearly.** Do we? Do we look out on the world with the eyes of Jesus, sharing his valuations of the things that matter most?

27-31. *The Shadow of the Cross.*—These verses mark one of the great turning points in the Gospel of Mark. From here on "the shadow of the cross is . . . falling upon Jesus' path." (Exeg.)

27. *Who Do Men Say that I Am?*—About this question of Jesus to his disciples, as it is legitimately raised into timeless and universal application, two observations may be made.

28 And they answered, John the Baptist: but some *say* Elias; and others, One of the prophets.

do men say that I am?" **28** And they told him, "John the Baptist; and others say Elijah; and others one of the proph-

division of the book begins here, or at least immediately after the confession of Peter. But Mark's use of blocks of earlier material, as sources, is as characteristic here as elsewhere, and his organization of material is not rigidly schematic—he has nothing like the symmetrical arrangement of Matthew, for example. It has also been thought that Mark represents Jesus as on his way to Jerusalem from 8:27 onward, the Galilean ministry having ended in failure. But the topography of chs. 8–9 does not point in that direction, and it is pure modernism to interpret chs. 6–8 as a record of failure. If failure there was, it came earlier, in 3:6! In chs. 8–9 Jesus is outside Galilee, except only in 8:27-30; and he leaves for Judea in 10:1. But his teaching is now addressed more exclusively to the disciples, to whom he reveals not only his true nature as Messiah but also his impending rejection, death, and resurrection, as Son of man. The shadow of the cross is already falling upon Jesus' path. The theme of suffering, already hinted once or twice, is now fully sounded—not in the whispering woodwinds but in the harsh, deep-throated brass. These chapters are almost an introduction to the passion narrative, as Wellhausen observed, and the later Christian proclamation of the message of salvation has deeply affected the tradition of Jesus' words, more deeply here than anywhere else in Mark— unless in the passion narrative itself.

27. Towns of Caesarea Philippi are the villages in the neighborhood and under the jurisdiction of Herod Philip's new city, Caesarea, named in honor of the emperor Augustus (Josephus *Antiquities* XVIII. 2. 1). It had formerly been known as Paneas, named from the Grotto of Pan at the source of the Jordan river, and was still a pagan, Hellenistic city. **Whom** (so KJV, following Greek and Latin, "Whom do men say me to be?") should of course be **who** (RSV).

28. The various estimates of Jesus here remind us of 6:15. Both question and answer are merely introductory to the powerfully dramatic ones to follow in vs. 29. Indeed, the

One is that it represents the starting point for an understanding of Jesus—what others have thought of him. It is easy to say, and to say rightly, "That is not enough." But it is also easy to forget that the beginning of a true appreciation does in fact lie in some knowledge of what have been the verdicts of mankind through nineteen centuries of history and experience. Tragically enough, many have never gone beyond the starting point. Either they have not been open to the evidence of the impression Jesus has made on the world, or they have taken as final the adverse snap judgments of some coterie which has great prestige value for them, no matter on how little real knowledge those judgments may be based.

To say this does not mean at all that the valid approach to the understanding of Jesus must be that of a life of research. It does mean that the mind must be a court open to the testimony of those most competent to give witness.

The judgment of biblical scholars who have studied the subject most thoroughly deserves great weight. Yet often the flippant witticisms of those whose ignorance "gives a rough idea of infinity" are preferred to the knowledge won by a lifetime of careful work on the part of first-class minds. Indeed, the perverse conclusion has sometimes been reached that everyone has a right to a verdict on Jesus except those who know most about him.

The judgment of past generations deserves great weight. There have been dark and bloody hours in that past. But when men have had the chance to see Jesus clearly, uncluttered by foreign accretions, undisguised by costumes alien to him, imposed upon him from without, the verdict echoes an earlier one, "He hath done all things well" (7:37). To the common charge that Jesus is weak an adequate answer is made by history: "Jesus weak? Look at the men he has mastered!"

The judgment of another special group, large beyond numbering, deserves great weight —the oppressed of earth, as Jesus has been brought to them by his true disciples. We hear them speak in the Negro spirituals, and in a thousand other voices, through all the years. Who do these men say that he is? They say fervently that he has been one who has preached "good news to the poor," and brought "release to the captives" and liberty to "those who are oppressed" (Luke 4:18).

29 And he saith unto them, But whom say ye that I am? And Peter answereth and saith unto him, Thou art the Christ.

ets." 29 And he asked them, "But who do you say that I am?" Peter answered him,

---

unexplained **John the Baptist** clearly implies the reader's knowledge of 6:14-16; and so vss. 27*b*-28 here have been thought by some writers to be merely editorial. But the question of vs. 27 seems a perfectly natural way of bringing up the subject, supposing that Jesus took the initiative in doing so.

29. The disciples had been singularly obtuse, according to Mark (vs. 21; etc.). The proclamation at the Baptism (1:11) had been addressed to Jesus alone, while that at the Transfiguration (9:7) had not yet been heard. It was therefore a profound act of faith on Peter's part to say, **You are the Christ,** even though Jesus, according to Mark, had encouraged it with his adversative question, **But who do you say that I am?**

The verdict of a fourth group deserves great weight. In the normal course of Christian nurture it has carried supreme weight. It is the verdict of those who have known him best in personal experience. That group is made up not only of "prophets, saints, apostles, martyrs," but of fathers and mothers and friends, whose lives have an undebatable quality.

But once more "That is not enough." No amount of historical exploration or general knowledge can be a substitute for a personal verdict. An academic thesis, term paper attitude, which ends, "These are the various views of Jesus," cannot free one from the question "Who do you say that I am?" (vs. 29). Browning presses home the challenge that cannot be evaded:

"What think ye of Christ," friend? when all's done and said?
Like you this Christianity or not?
It may be false, but will you wish it true?
Has it your vote to be so if it can? [2]

Who do you say that he is? A poetic idealist, a beautiful sentimental figure, obsolete in our changed world? Some have said that. A picture to hang in a church, but to be kept within its walls? Some have said that. An inspiring leader for social causes, but not the revealer of an ultimate God? That too has been said. A dear companion for the home, blessing its intimate love, but no master for business or politics? That too is said everyday. Your life, your attitudes, your sense of values—who do they say that he is?

29. *Peter Answered Him, "You Are the Christ."*—This was a great act of faith on Peter's part. According to Mark's record, he had seen mighty works done; but they did not prove Jesus to be "the Lord's anointed," the Messiah. Jesus himself had never made that claim. Peter had not heard the words which Jesus heard at baptism. The Transfiguration had not yet

taken place. It was Peter's own great venture of faith. The affirmation "Thou art the Christ" is always an act of faith whenever it is made. Reason does not compel it or justify it. Reason may give an A B C of religion; it never gives a Q.E.D. There is no geometrical proof. Faith in Christ as Lord is a leap. To say **Thou art the Christ** means that he is accepted for the mind, as the revelation of God and of the meaning of life. It means that he is accepted for the spirit, that his spirit of love marks our own. It means that he is accepted for the hands and feet, that we shall help him lift the burdens of men, and run the errands on which he sends us.

Another challenging thought seems embedded in Peter's affirmation. It is quite beyond the power of any scholarship to declare just what effect the incident at Caesarea Philippi had on Jesus' plans. No one can know when and how that steadfast purpose to go to Jerusalem was evolved. But we do have the record in the Synoptic Gospels. We do know that the confession of Peter marked a great turning point in Christ's ministry. From now on there is explicit teaching of his coming suffering and death. Soon the journey to Jerusalem begins. One might almost suppose that this forthright commitment of faith was what Jesus was waiting for, that it introduced a new element into his ministry.

We are certainly on solid ground when we go on to say that God's cause, his kingdom, waits for it. The work of Jesus in the world tarries for men to say, "Thou art the Christ," "Thou art the supreme Lord of life."

O thou of God and man the Son,
Thee will I cherish,
Thee will I honor. [3]

When that surges up from the hearts of Jesus' disciples as their deepest word, in the first century, in the eighteenth, in the twentieth, or the twenty-fifth, the cause of Christ can go forward.

---

[2] "Bishop Blougram's Apology," l. 665.

[3] "Fairest Lord Jesus."

30 And he charged them that they should tell no man of him.	"You are the Christ." 30 And he charged them to tell no one about him.
31 And he began to teach them, that the Son of man must suffer many things, and be rejected of the elders, and *of* the	31 And he began to teach them that the Son of man must suffer many things,

30. About him, or "about it," as in some MSS. Luke 9:21 reads "to tell this to no one"; Matt. 16:20, "to tell no one that he was the Christ." The command of silence is characteristic of Mark, and is repeatedly stressed in this Gospel, but here it is not some cure or exorcism or cry of a demoniac that is to be kept secret; it is the credo of the first of the apostles. At the heart of Mark's theology, i.e., of his conception of the life of Jesus, lies the messianic secret (see Intro., p. 644). Its basis in historic fact may not have been—as Wrede thought—the recognition that Jesus was not believed in as Messiah until after the Resurrection, but rather Jesus' own positive repudiation of this category as inadequate and even misleading. In Judaism "Messiah" always meant the glorious future king of Israel, though "greater than the kings of the earth" (cf. John 6:15; 12:13-15); but Jesus is not the Messiah—an earthly king, however glorious—he is the heavenly Son of man in disguise, as in the section that immediately follows, and indeed, in Mark's preferred terminology, the Son of God (cf. Intro., pp. 642-43). It is the Christian reinterpretation of the term "Messiah"—Christ—that justifies its application to Jesus. Mark's source reflects a very early stage in this process of reinterpretation and of the co-ordination of it with other titles and categories, chiefly Son of man and Son of God—e.g., 9:41, "because you bear the name of Christ." There may, accordingly, be a double implication in this verse: (*a*) Jesus really *is* the Messiah, but in another sense than everyone supposed at the time; (*b*) the public announcement of his messiahship, without this reinterpretation, would only lead to misunderstanding. Jesus is the Messiah (cf. 1:1), but not in the sense in which most Jews—including the disciples, at that time, and even Peter their spokesman—understood the term; therefore **he charged them to tell no one about him.** It has been thought by some writers that Jesus repudiated Peter's affirmation of belief (contrary to Matt. 16:17), but this is unthinkable, as exegesis of Mark. Others have assumed that something has fallen out of the text here, or that vss. 30-31 have been intruded into the passage, so that the original sequence ran 29, 32*a*, 33 (or perhaps 29, 30, 32*b*, 33); but all this is mere guesswork, dominated by an a priori hypothesis. As the passage now stands in Mark, the meaning is clear enough.

16. THE FIRST PASSION ANNOUNCEMENT (8:31-33)

The three passion announcements (8:31; 9:31; 10:32-34) are characteristic of Mark; the details have been supplied from the actual passion narrative (see Grant, *Earliest Gospel,* p. 179 n.), and their purpose is to show that Jesus foresaw and accepted his sufferings, and also foresaw his resurrection (see Intro., p. 644). That Jesus realized the dangers surrounding him, and recognized the hazard he took in going to Jerusalem, is certainly most probable; but that he predicted the detailed events that were to occur there is difficult to believe. For one thing, the disciples were not in the least impressed by the three predictions; they behaved throughout the Passion as if they had never heard these words. For another, the attitude of Jesus himself does not bear out this detailed prevision of the circumstances. Finally, the quality of his martyr death is neutralized, and

31-32. *And He Began to Teach Them that the Son of Man Must Suffer Many Things, . . . And He Said This Plainly.*—This first announcement of the Passion makes clear that Jesus did not wish to gain disciples under false pretenses. From the very first (1:16-17) he had made it clear that he was calling them to work. Here he puts the inevitable suffering to the front. He never asked people to go on a picnic. Suffering, the Cross, death, were in plain view. He was not to be the Messiah of popular expectation. His way was to be a way of suffering.

Unless we see that clearly we miss both the glory and the pain of the Christian gospel, for the glory and the pain are inseparably intertwined. Without it Christianity can degenerate

chief priests, and scribes, and be killed, and after three days rise again.	and be rejected by the elders and the chief priests and the scribes, and be killed, and
32 And he spake that saying openly. And Peter took him, and began to rebuke him.	after three days rise again. 32 And he said this plainly. And Peter took him, and be-

his heroism is made unreal and reduced to the mere histrionic performance of an assigned role, if he foresaw in advance the full details of his passion and the eventual denouement of his career. It is chiefly for these reasons that many scholars now view the three announcements as "secondary," i.e., as either composed by Mark to suit his dramatic-theological purpose, or at least modified to suit the passion narrative.

31. He began to teach them that the Son of man must suffer. This seems to say that he taught this for the first time; but 10:32 shows that the word "began" is merely a Semitism (see also vs. 32 below). The "Son of man" is the preferred title for Jesus in several of the oldest strands of evangelic tradition (see Intro., p. 642). Instead of emphasizing Jesus' human nature, as used to be thought, the term connotes his glorious, celestial, supernatural, indeed his divine, nature, in the sense of Dan. 7 and the "parables" in the book of Enoch. To Mark the title probably stood in sharp contrast with the mundane and even political associations of the term "Messiah"; and it reflected the paradox at the heart both of Mark's theology and of the Christian faith, viz., that this glorious being, with God from the creation of the world, came to earth and was put to death. True, Mark does not allude explicitly to the pre-existence of the Son of man, but the supernatural connotations of the term are clear (vs. 38; 13:26; 14:62). The purpose of the Son of man in laying down his life was to pay the "ransom for many" (10:45).

Must suffer many things: A summary statement, as in 9:12, here elaborated by the added details from the passion narrative. Some scholars hold that the substance of the saying goes back to Jesus: "that the Son of man must suffer many things, . . . and be killed, and after three days rise again." This also is only a hypothesis, though it is probable that Jesus foresaw for himself—and not only for "the Son of man," as a third person—a destiny of suffering, death, and eventual exaltation (see below, pp. 813, 819).

After three days, rather than "on the third day," which later became, as in the Apostles' Creed, the standard formula, perhaps under the influence of Hos. 6:2. Since in biblical usage the first and last days are included, "three days" is equivalent to "after two days" (as in Hosea), which is our method of reckoning. But "after three days" means only, in biblical language, after a very brief interval. (Cf. Wilhelm Bousset, *Kyrios Christos* [Göttingen: Vandenhoeck & Ruprecht, 1913], p. 27; Johannes Weiss, *History of Primitive Christianity* [New York: Wilson & Erickson, 1937], I, 83-104.)

32. Openly (KJV) is not publicly (vs. 30) but **plainly** (RSV). **Peter . . . began to rebuke him,** i.e., for presuming to set forth so contradictory a prospect for the Messiah

into petty legalism or a set of didactic moralisms. If Jesus had not chosen the way of suffering, endured the Cross, his life would have had little to say to individuals or to a world in an agony of suffering. He would have spoken only as one who had never faced and conquered the pain and terror of evil. His hands have been strong to save because they were scarred hands.

Jesus spoke **plainly** of the cost of his ministry and the cost of discipleship. So often we do not follow his frankness, but mumble his words and slur them over. So often discipleship has been presented with tragically mistaken persuasiveness as something easy, even something that does not matter very much. And as a natural, inevitable result, the kind we have enlisted has

not mattered—very much! When we mark the price down, we blot out the deepest appeal of Christ. Charles E. Raven in his autobiography tells of his disappointment at having confirmation presented in a boys' school as a routine matter, the "proper thing to do," and then he writes with feeling, "And dear Christ, how some of us wanted you!" [4]

A church may win people by disguising the true meaning of discipleship. But it cannot do anything with them after it gets them. Jesus said this plainly. Do we?

32. And Peter Took Him, and Began to Rebuke Him.—Strange! Just a short time before,

[4] *A Wanderer's Way* (New York: Henry Holt & Co., 1929), p. 25.

33 But when he had turned about and looked on his disciples, he rebuked Peter, saying, Get thee behind me, Satan: for thou savorest not the things that be of God, but the things that be of men.

34 ¶ And when he had called the people *unto him* with his disciples also, he said unto them, Whosoever will come after me,

gan to rebuke him. 33 But turning and seeing his disciples, he rebuked Peter, and said, "Get behind me, Satan! For you are not on the side of God, but of men."

34 And he called to him the multitude with his disciples, and said to them, "If

---

(vs. 29), or perhaps for the Danielic Son of man (cf. Dan. 7:13-14). Mark may even see in Peter's rebuke a reflection of the conflict between the two ideas of Messiah and Son of man, a conflict which may have existed in the early Palestinian church (see Ernst Lohmeyer, *Galiläa und Jerusalem* [Göttingen: Vandenhoeck & Ruprecht, 1936]; or Grant, *Earliest Gospel,* ch. vi; also above, pp. 641-42); but this probably is oversubtle for Mark.

33. Get thee behind me, either simply (as in Matt. 4:10), "Get thee hence," "Begone," or else, "Get behind thee," as Blass conjectured—presumably a Semitic idiom for "go away," and thus meaning the same thing. The ὀπίσω μου has then been added under the influence of the following verse (cf. Grant, *Earliest Gospel,* p. 113). Taking the full text as it stands, the meaning must be, "Get out of my sight." It can hardly mean, "Follow me, whether you understand or not"; the word **Satan,** and the rebuke that follows, are too harsh for that. Satan was not simply the archfiend (as in 3:26), but the archtempter and adversary of the righteous, and their accuser—as in Job and in the book of Revelation. **The things that be of God,** i.e., God's ways, not man's. Earthly or political messiahship, and even the mundane triumph of the Son of man, are incompatible with the divine, foreordained way of suffering, death, and resurrection. Well rendered in RSV: **You are not on the side of God, but of men.**

17. The Disciples' Way of Suffering (8:34–9:1)

The self-chosen way of the Son of man, in obedience to the divine plan, is the pattern for his followers, who are likewise called to martyrdom. They are to lose their lives for

---

Peter had acclaimed Jesus as the Lord's anointed. Now he rebukes him. We are tempted to say, "Impossible!" But we do it all the time.

Peter's unwillingness to accept Jesus' idea of messiahship was perfectly natural in his situation. It went against every idea of the Messiah which he had ever known. He had to learn what manner of Messiah Jesus was. It was no wonder that he balked at the first lesson and refused it completely.

With us it is different. Centuries of Christian history have made us familiar with the idea of a suffering Savior. We accept it. We sing readily "In the cross of Christ I glory" and "Jesus, I my cross have taken." Yet often in the deep set of our minds, in our attitudes and actions, we rebuke him. We prefer a conception of discipleship which leaves the Cross out of it. Multitudes of Christians prefer a cheerful, moderate, "sensible" religion. We shut out the necessity of any painful sacrifice. We do not say in words, "Look here, Jesus, don't get extreme or fanatical. After all, we live in a practical world, and a cross is a very impractical thing." But our actions, our desires, our shrinkings say it. How common it is for us to

rebuke Jesus, to rebuke him by the things we do, for his claim to undivided allegiance, for his refusal of violence and his choice of the way of love, for his insistence on the denial of self.

Peter suggests much more "cheerful and sensible views of the future rather than those arising out of the divine counsel in the impending death of the Messiah." [5] And yet because of that, Jesus calls him "Satan." This is worth eternal remembrance. Here is the temptation—continued! The merely "cheerful and sensible" views of religion are always Satan's. A Christianity diluted into a very cheerful and sensible religion, in which God's act of redemption in Christ has dropped out of notice, is emphatically of Satan. A sensible and optimistic doctrine of "progress," from which all realization of the costly suffering and pain of overcoming evil is eliminated, is a perennial masterpiece of Satan. A conception of Christian discipleship reduced to common sense, in which there is no room for the "foolishness of the Cross," is a satanic triumph.

34. *If Any Man Would Come After Me, Let Him Deny Himself and Take Up His Cross and Follow Me.*—Here, in one of the greatest

[5] Menzies, *Earliest Gospel,* p. 163.

| let him deny himself, and take up his cross, and follow me. | any man would come after me, let him deny himself and take up his cross and |

Christ's sake and the gospel's (vs. 35); but in so doing they will "save" them, and will be acknowledged by the Son of man when he comes (as vs. 38 implies). Some, however, will survive until the day when the kingdom of God comes with power (9:1)—this is apparently equivalent to the coming of the Son of man "in glory" (8:38). This exhortation fits perfectly the situation of the martyr community of Mark's first readers, and might accordingly be thought to be invented; but that Jesus expected the martyrdom of his own immediate followers is not improbable, and is in fact implied elsewhere in the Gospel, especially in the passion narrative (e.g., 14:21, 25, 27b). It may be doubted, however, that he held this view while still in Galilee, i.e., before arriving at Jerusalem for the final week.

34. As often in Mark, **the multitude** is at hand— even here on this remote journey!— and may be summoned for instruction. This is one of Mark's literary devices. In this case it implies that the teaching is not esoteric but public, and is meant for all, certainly for all Christians. Vs. 31 did not mention crucifixion; but Mark, in **take up his cross**, has in mind the instrument of the Lord's death, and perhaps of the martyrs in Nero's gardens not long before (cf. Tacitus *Annals* XV. 38-44). The condemned were compelled to bear their crosses to the place of execution (cf. 15:21; John 19:17)—at least to carry the crossbar to which their arms were to be affixed. Luke 23:26 pictures Simon of Cyrene bearing Jesus' cross and following him, thus literally obeying this precept. But Mark, in stressing the requirement of martyrdom, hardly assumed that all Christians must be crucified; the language is certainly figurative, though it must not be watered down to mere acceptance of privations, disappointments, and misfortune—as too often in modern thought.

---

declarations of Jesus, are two of the hardest words which a person can ever face—deny and cross. The word "deny" is not a vague, foggy word, easy to evade. It is appallingly sharp and clear. It is the same word used of Peter's denial of Jesus, and means "Let him make himself a stranger" to himself. Not a pampered favorite whose insistent desires are law, but a complete stranger, to whom he can and does say "No!" Denying ourselves means far more than refusing to give things to ourselves. Self-denial, in a common use of the term, as abstaining from certain luxuries and delights, may even induce a sort of self-assertion, in applauding our own self-control and generosity, making spiritual Little Jack Horners out of ourselves, whispering, "What a good boy am I!" The denial of *self* is something deeper. It is making ourselves not an end, but a means, in the kingdom of God. It is subordinating the clamoring ego, with its shrill claim for priority, its preoccupation with "I," "me," and "mine," its concern for self-assertion, its insistence on comfort and prestige; denying self, not for the sake of denial as a sort of moral athletics, but for Christ's sake, for the sake of putting the self into his cause.

Now transfer this to a group of disciples, to a church or an organization. Surely to a church comes the same call of Jesus to deny itself and

take up a cross. How hard for an institution to put some larger good, for the whole body of Christ and for the world, above its own peculiar goods, its cherished traditions and favors, its financial security, its relative prestige, its familiar ways, endowed with an aura of sacredness —in a word, above its self, its assertive ego. Is it not the refusal to deny self which chiefly blocks Christ's desire "that they may all be one" (John 17:21)?

The word "cross" too is a difficult word to face. It has certainly been one of the most misused words in the whole vocabulary of Christianity. We have given the name of "cross" to so many things that are not a cross at all in the truly Christian sense of the word. Men speak of calamity as a cross that they must bear. But a calamity is not a cross. It may be a tragedy. Men speak of sorrow or loss as a cross. They are a heavy burden, but not necessarily a cross. People even speak of their own shortcomings of temperament and disposition, their uncontrolled anger, their undue sensitiveness, their impatience, as a cross they must carry. They often grow quite pious about it. Taking up a cross is not enduring stoically what happens to us. That is a great virtue, but Christianity is more and other than the modern stoicism into which it is frequently distorted.

The Cross for Jesus was his deliberate choice

35 For whosoever will save his life shall lose it; but whosoever shall lose his life for my sake and the gospel's, the same shall save it.

follow me. 35 For whoever would save his life will lose it; and whoever loses his life for my sake and the gospel's will save it.

---

35. Whosoever will save, or whoever would save, but not *"wills to save,"* though this is literal; for the gospel does not encourage men to court martyrdom—a feature in later church life which required discouragement (cf. D. W. Riddle, *The Martyrs* [Chicago: University of Chicago Press, 1931]). Although the saying is addressed to a

---

of giving his life a ransom for many, his deliberate choice of ministering to men's need of the truth about God, to their need of love, cost what it might. Taking up a cross for the disciple means the deliberate choice of something that could be evaded, to take up a burden which we are under no compulsion to take up, except the compulsion of God's love in Christ. It means the choice of taking upon ourselves the burdens of other lives, of putting ourselves without reservation at the service of Christ in preparing a way for the kingdom of God, of putting ourselves in the struggle against evil, whatever the cost.

There is a beautiful bit of dialogue in George Bernard Shaw's *Saint Joan,* in which the archbishop of Reims tells Joan that she is in love with religion. Joan brightens and answers, "I never thought of that! Is there any harm in it?" The archbishop answers profoundly that there is no harm in it but "there is danger." There is. There was danger for Joan. If we love God there is danger, the danger of a cross, the danger that life will be upset, that it will be loaded with the burdens of others, that it will be thrown into deadly combat with strong powers of evil. But it is the bright danger that illuminates life with a divine light

> From the cross the radiance streaming
> Adds new luster to the day.[6]

35. *For Whoever Would Save His Life Will Lose It.*—This whole passage (8:35–9:1) had special meaning to the Christians of the time at which the Gospel of Mark was written, as it has had to every succeeding generation of Christendom in which persecution and martyrdom were constant dangers. It has been conjectured indeed that the experience of persecution and martyrdom had an influence in shaping these words (see Exeg.). If we are to deal honestly with the passage, we must recognize that the words as they appear here did not have the general meaning which we are accustomed to give them. They applied to a persecution situation. The primary meaning of **whoever would save his life** was exactly that, in a physical

[6] John Bowring, "In the cross of Christ I glory."

sense. The man who saved his life by renouncing his faith in Christ would lose it in the next world, when he came before the judgment seat of God. And he that lost his life through fidelity to Christ would save it in the world of eternity. We are cautioned rightly against thinking that the word "life" as used here means the high reward of character in itself, or the modern idea of the "infinite value of the human soul" (see Exeg.). Nevertheless, the words have a clear and universal meaning that runs far beyond the original persecution situation. They have, in the phrase of the Exeg., "permanent validity."

It is profoundly true that the surest way to lose life in its largest possibilities is to give an undue care to preserving it. The best-preserved thing in all human history is an Egyptian mummy. The surest way to make a spiritual and intellectual mummy out of yourself is to give all your attention to preserving life. Robert Louis Stevenson has a well-remembered passage in *Virginibus Puerisque* to the effect that the person whose chief aim in life is to guard his health, who makes his raincoat and rubbers his only concern, will miss the whole pageant of nature and the richest experiences a man can have. The man who never forgets his rubbers is bound to forget many things infinitely more important. He saves his life, and in the process loses it. This comes with great force to a generation which has lifted up its soul to the vanity of preserving. We try to preserve our looks. The beauty parlor business is a major industry. The preservation of money is a flourishing religion. The preservation of life, in the highest sense, languishes far behind. We do not get far in wisdom until we realize that the world points a gun at us and says, "Your money or your life." There must be a choice. Jesus' words record the truth that we may save life by escape—escape from burdens, from sacrifice, from conflict; but in so doing we cannot escape from the solitary confinement of self. And in that one-room cell, life, in its highest potentials, dies.

35. *And Whoever Loses His Life for My Sake and the Gospel's Will Save It.*—The reverse form of the first part of this balanced sentence also had its immediate application, if not its

36 For what shall it profit a man, if he | 36 For what does it profit a man, to gain
shall gain the whole world, and lose his
own soul?

martyr situation, its permanent validity is clear, and may be implied by Mark. It has even
been suggested that in its original form the saying ran, in perfect parallelism, "Whosoever
shall save his life shall lose it; but whosoever shall lose his life shall save it," the words
for my sake and the gospel's having been added by Mark in order to make clearer the
specific reference to Christian martyrdom. (Cf. Matt. 10:39; Luke 17:33; John 12:25;
ἐμοῦ καὶ ["for my sake"] is actually omitted by p45 D O.L. sys, etc., while both Matthew
and Luke omit καὶ τοῦ εὐαγγελίου ["and the gospel's"] at this point.) The fine shading
of the verbs is well represented in RSV: **Whoever would . . . will lose it; and whoever
loses . . . will save it**—the first half of the sentence contains an expression of desire in
the present tense followed by the simple future; in the second, the generalized present is
followed by the future of promise. What this must have meant to Mark's readers, faced
with persecution, can readily be imagined.

36-37. Vs. 36 amplifies vs. 35a by stating in extreme form the aim of one who would
"save" his life. The word means more than "save" in a particular situation; it means
"preserve, safeguard, keep in health"; thus an ancient Hellenistic ruler, viewed as σωτήρ,
or savior, was the preserver of his people. For **lose his own soul** (KJV) read **forfeit his
life** (RSV). An illustration would be Alexander the Great, who "gained the whole

---

origin, in a persecution situation. But it is also
a valid generalization, attested times without
number in every realm of experience. It is one
of the profoundly true, basic paradoxes of
human life. Time would fail if only a few of
the demonstrations of its truth were cited. Take
two, poetry and medicine. The greatest poetry
has never come from concern for reputation.
It has never come from a fussy preoccupation
with techniques. Edgar Lee Masters has a vivid
phrase for such pedantic sterility: "Seeds in a
dry pod, tick, tick, tick."[7] Great poetry has been
created when the poet's mind and heart have
become the servants of a vision and an idea.
Louis Pasteur lost his life as the servant of Louis
Pasteur, and found it as the servant of humanity. "Self-seeking has no centennial." It ends in
a graveyard with the dismal epitaph "He took
care of himself." The great servants whom
humanity honors are those who have forgotten
themselves into immortality. How many millions of unknown and unsung people have
found life, the largest, richest life, by losing it!
They have been brought out of grief to find
abundant life in service; out of the fatal bore-
dom of self-enclosure they have found adventures among the needy, the outcast, the sorrowing. The result is that lives that have been
pitifully smashed up, so that there was an air of
death about them, have been born again in the
outgoing of love.

> And from the ground there blossoms red
> Life. . . .[8]

[7] "Petit, the Poet," *Spoon River Anthology.*
[8] George Matheson, "O Love that wilt not let me go."

After all the million demonstrations of the
truth have been compiled, there remains one
other, unique—Jesus.

**36. For What Does It Profit a Man, to Gain
the Whole World and Forfeit His Life?**—To
this question much of the world roars back its
answer, "Plenty!" With the patron saint of
paganism, Omar Khayyám, many say, "I'll take
the cash and let the credit go." There are many
such votes from those who are eagerly willing
to gain the world or even a very small part of
it and let go the dubious gain of some future
life, or of that quality of life here which the
N.T. calls eternal. They choose the immediate
over the permanent, the tangible over the intangible, the material over the spiritual.

And yet there come disturbing suggestions
about the wisdom of the choice. Just when
they are safest, the shadow of a question mark
falls, in line with the caution,

> Never write up a diary
> On the Day itself.
> It needs longer than that
> To know what happened.[9]

Because these words applied to a martyr
situation in the early days of the church, their
reference was to the hereafter. What would it
profit anyone to gain his physical life by denying Christ, only to forfeit life in the eternal
world? The answer clearly was "Nothing." After
one had forfeited his life by his denial, there
was nothing with which he could buy it back.

[9] Christopher Morley, "D-Day Plus X," *The Old
Mandarin* (New York: Harcourt, Brace & Co., 1947). By
permission.

37 Or what shall a man give in exchange for his soul?

38 Whosoever therefore shall be ashamed of me and of my words, in this adulterous and sinful generation, of him also shall the Son of man be ashamed, when he cometh in the glory of his Father with the holy angels.

the whole world and forfeit his life?" **37** For what can a man give in return for his life? **38** For whoever is ashamed of me and of my words in this adulterous and sinful generation, of him will the Son of man also be ashamed, when he comes in the glory of his

---

world" but lost his life; a closer example would have been Claudius or Nero, if Mark wrote in A.D. 69. For the thought of **in return for his life** see Ps. 49:6-12. At the same time, ψυχή (*psychē*) meant "soul" as well as "life," and a double reference is intended: the apostate who renounces the faith under persecution may gain a longer life—and other temporal benefits as well—but he will lose his life eventually; then what of his soul, as he faces the last judgment? What will he say when he stands before the Son of man (vs. 38)? It is possible to read these two verses with the Faust motif, or even the temptation narrative, in mind. "What does it profit *the* man," i.e., the Son of man, is the reading of some MSS (C* D Θ, etc.); but the relevance of the passage for Mark and his first readers is clearly the persecution situation which the whole Gospel, and especially the "way of the Cross" sections, presuppose. Mark is not thinking, in the usual modern way, of the "infinite value of the human soul."

38. The word **ashamed** does not represent the Pauline "shame of the cross," but the halfhearted disciples' apologetic attitude, easily changing to positive disloyalty. One of the deadliest weapons of the opponents of early Christianity was ridicule; and it was employed, no doubt, from the first: in Galilee in the days of Jesus, in Palestine in early apostolic days, in Rome in the days of Nero and Mark. The very form of the saying, **ashamed of me and of my words**—rather than of the cross, for example—suggests its antiquity and authenticity; it presupposes the early Palestinian situation, rather than the later Greco-Roman. **The Son of man** is to come **in the glory of his Father**—i.e., the

---

And that, of course, holds good still. We are continuingly face to face with the solemn fact, so easily forgotten in busy days and years, that life's choices are eternal choices. It is as true as ever it was that the whole world, doomed soon to vanish, even if one could hold every bit of it instead of the infinitesimal part of it which is all that even the most grasping hands can seize, is a tawdry prize over against the life that goes on forever. The importance of moral choices is never seen clearly if the dimension of eternity is allowed to drop out of our thinking.

Yet whatever the limitations of the original reference of the words, this question does put sharply the poor bargain it is to choose a clutter of things, no matter how large the pile that can be amassed, over quality of being, what one has over what one is. We can see that in realms where religion specifically does not enter at all. It is common to find people who have enough money to provide them with ownership, where the treasures of art and music and literature are concerned, but not enough capacity for true possession, which is a spiritual not a financial matter. Indeed, there are many rich people who belong in a home for the destitute; for though owning many things they are appallingly destitute of appreciation. They often buy paint-

ings and statues, but as for their power of true enjoyment—all of it might as well be dry goods. They can buy the best seats at concerts, but the instruments might almost as well be cowbells. They do not know that rich multiplication of life which comes from giving themselves in love and service to other people. They do not know that marvelous mixture of humility and exaltation which is the thrill of worship. Their names are written in no Book of Life, no matter how prominently they appear in Dun & Bradstreet or the Social Register.

The true measure of life is qualitative, even in a civilization so largely quantitative as ours. To gain a whole world of things and miss the glory which Paul tried to express by his words "Christ liveth in me" (Gal. 2:20) is life's biggest blunder.

Press this same question home to a church. What shall it profit a church to gain a whole world of gothic arches and stained-glass windows, if the price is losing its inward spiritual life and its own unmuffled voice?

38. *Whoever Is Ashamed of Me and of My Words . . . , of Him Will the Son of Man also Be Ashamed.*—These words too have a peculiar pertinence to our day in the world's history. For this supremely is no time to be ashamed of

9 And he said unto them, Verily I say unto you, That there be some of them that stand here, which shall not taste of death, till they have seen the kingdom of God come with power.

2 ¶ And after six days Jesus taketh *with him* Peter, and James, and John, and leadeth them up into a high mountain apart by themselves: and he was transfigured before them.

9 Father with the holy angels." 1 And he said to them, "Truly, I say to you, there are some standing here who will not taste death before they see the kingdom of God come with power."

2 And after six days Jesus took with him Peter and James and John, and led them up a high mountain apart by themselves;

---

glory given him by his Father—surrounded by **the holy angels,** to hold the Last Judgment. Some have argued, e.g., Rudolf Otto (see above, p. 150), that Jesus distinguishes **the Son** of man from himself, and therefore speaks of the coming judge in the third person; others insist that Jesus tacitly identifies himself with this supernatural being. In any event, the Son of man takes the same attitude toward Jesus' disloyal follower that Jesus himself would be expected to take. Note also that here, as in one passage in Enoch—a passage possibly but not certainly pre-Christian—and as in II Esdras, not to mention Mark and the whole N.T., the Son of man is also Son of God. In its earlier form (Luke 12:9; cf. Matt. 10:33; from Q?) the saying lacked the picturesque apocalyptic detail found here.

9:1. This verse has been viewed as the introduction to the following section on the Transfiguration; on the other hand, Matthew and Luke both view it as the conclusion of the present section—and so doubtless did Mark. **And he said to them** is Mark's regular device for introducing another saying. At most the Transfiguration, which follows, marked an anticipation of the future glory of the Son of man (vs. 38), not of "the kingdom of God come with power." The primitive interpretation of Jesus' own mind was undoubtedly correct on this point: the parousia of the Son of man and the coming of the kingdom **with power,** in its full extent and realization, are soon to take place, i.e., within the lifetime of some of those then present (cf. 13:30; 14:62; I Thess. 4:15; Rev. 1:7; John 21:22). This expectation was universal in the early days of Christianity, and must go back to Jesus himself; it begins to weaken only in the second century (cf. John 21:23; II Pet. 3:4; and the Alexandrines, especially Origen, with their substitution of a "spiritual," otherworldly eschatology).

18. THE TRANSFIGURATION (9:2-8)

This incident has been variously interpreted, e.g., as a misplaced narrative of a resurrection appearance, or an early church "Christophany," or a fulfillment of 8:38 or 9:1; but for Mark it was undoubtedly the divine attestation of the truth of Peter's confession in 8:29. Therefore the reference to the time, **after six days.** And it forms, with the voice at the Baptism (1:11) at the beginning, and the confession of the centurion (15:39) at the end, a testimony, here at the center of the Gospel, to Jesus' divine sonship;

Jesus or of his teaching. There is an old gospel song which is not used very much any more:

> Ashamed of Jesus, can it be
> A mortal man ashamed of thee?

It would be good to sing that song again today. "Ashamed of Jesus" in a world which has gone over the dizzy edge of disaster through disregard of him and his words? "Ashamed of Jesus" when a generation of history has given an appalling verification of his teaching? "Ashamed of Jesus" in a day when it appears more blindingly clear

than ever before that no other foundation for human survival can be laid than that which is laid in him? This is not a day for apology, but for tremendous affirmation. It is no day to be ashamed of the only word of salvation to a world increasingly lost.

> Ashamed of Jesus? Sooner far
> Let evening blush to own a star.

9:2. *And He Was Transfigured Before Them.* —Whatever might have been the exact nature of this transfiguration experience, Mark's interpretation of its meaning to the disciples is clear.

3 And his raiment became shining, exceeding white as snow; so as no fuller on earth can white them.

and he was transfigured before them, 3 and his garments became glistening, intensely white, as no fuller on earth could bleach

---

at the same time it is an anticipation of the future glory of Christ at his parousia (8:38). In its simplest form the narrative probably ran: vss. 2b-4, 7, the heavenly voice forming the climax of the story.

2. **A high mountain:** No place is named. In 8:27 they were near Caesarea Philippi; in 9:14 they are back in Galilee, where scribes would be found. Presumably the "high" mountain is not Tabor, as in the traditional ecclesiastical topography, but in the north, where indeed some of the apocalypses (e.g., I Enoch) predicted a divine manifestation in the last days. As on some other occasions (5:37; 13:3), only the chosen three, two of them "pillar" apostles (Gal. 2:9), accompany him. **Transfigured** (μετεμορφώθη) is presumably a technical term in late Greek for the act of metamorphosis; Paul uses it in II Cor. 3:18, where Vulg. has *transformamur*. It means a change of form, an effulgence from within, not a mere "flood of glory" from without (cf. Mark 16:12; II Pet. 1:16-18). Thus it is no pagan "metamorphosis," described by poets (e.g., Ovid); Mark uses the word, but what he describes is really an epiphany (see Dibelius, *From Tradition to Gospel*, p. 230), or rather a Christophany, a manifestation of the Son of God in his true nature, as he will be seen on the last day, and as he appears now "at the right hand of Power" (14:62; cf. Acts 7:55).

3. **Raiment . . . shining:** Cf. the "garment of glory" in I Enoch 62:15-16. **As snow** is not in the majority of good MSS (found in A D O.L. sys, a gloss perhaps taken from Dan. 7:9). Some other MSS have "like light," from Matthew. **As no fuller . . . could bleach them** is peculiar to Mark and is found in various forms in the MSS (sys omits). Matthew and Luke say that Jesus' face was transfigured or shone: Luke characteristically thinks of Jesus as engaged in prayer; and Matthew probably has in mind Moses' appearance as he came down from Mount Sinai (Exod. 34:29-35; II Cor. 3:7).

It meant the validation of Jesus, that Jesus' interpretation of the role of the Messiah was true, that in spite of the shock which the proclamation of his own suffering and approaching death gave them, he was the Lord's anointed, "my beloved Son" (vs. 7). This truth was dressed in a shining symbol, representing Jesus in his coming glorified state. Here was a timely reinforcement of the disciples' faith, strained as it had been by a conception of messiahship hard to accept.

The experience gave them a great memory to which they could return. In that it has one close relationship to our common need. It was a high hour of vision which the disciples could trust. So the revelation on the mountaintop says to us, "Trust your high hours. Keep your times of clear vision as the stay of your mind, the point of reference for all the days to come." The weather of the mind and spirit is varied. It runs from sunlight through dense fog to pitch darkness. Yet spiritual truth has its hours and days of high visibility, when it is transfigured before us. Then we can affirm, "This is everlastingly right." Then we can see the undebatable Christ. "Jesus is the revelation of God. His way is the life which is life indeed." Keep those hours in memory, both for the

fortification and the measurement of life. John Bunyan puts this memorably in what he has Pilgrim say to those whose faith had gone into twilight, and who were doubting whether there was any "Celestial City." Pilgrim cried, "Did we not see it from the top of Mount Clear?" That was trusting the high hour.

The Transfiguration may also remind us of what worship may mean—a shining hour, high and lifted up, when Jesus and his revelation of God are luminous from within, their own self-authenticating evidence, with a glow such as no fuller on earth can supply. Life's best hopes and highest aspirations are in this way validated. A poet has written of old age and the "last song" he would make "out of the shining of remembered days." Worship may be this steady "shining of remembered days," a sustaining power. Luke, the evangelist, gives us a very close parallel in the experience of Paul. In his hours of trial before governors and kings, Paul went back to "the shining of remembered days." He had had days of scourging and imprisonment. Those did not count. Here is the lasting memory: "At midday, O king, I saw on the way a light from heaven, brighter than the sun, shining round me and . . . I heard a voice" (Acts 26:13). Worship may have that sustaining

4 And there appeared unto them Elias with Moses: and they were talking with Jesus.

5 And Peter answered and said to Jesus, Master, it is good for us to be here: and let us make three tabernacles; one for thee, and one for Moses, and one for Elias.

6 For he wist not what to say; for they were sore afraid.

them. 4 And there appeared to them Elijah with Moses; and they were talking to Jesus. 5 And Peter said to Jesus, "Master,ƒ it is well that we are here; let us make three booths, one for you and one for Moses and one for Elijah." 6 For he did not know what to say, for they were exceedingly

ƒ Or Rabbi.

---

4. The appearance of **Moses,** the prototype of the Messiah (Deut. 18:15), who had himself been transfigured, and of **Elijah,** his forerunner (Mal. 4:5), who had been rapt to heaven in a fiery chariot, shows that the messianic era is about to begin; they represent "the law and the prophets," i.e., the preliminary dispensation (cf. Luke 16:16). The use of ὤφθη ("was seen" or **appeared**) is appropriate in an account of a vision; but Origen's idea that each apostle saw "as he was able" (Swete) is oversubtle. What the O.T. saints said to Jesus, or he to them, is not even hinted in Mark; Luke 9:31 reflects early speculation on this point (cf. Luke 24:25-27, 32, 44-47).

5-6. Answered and said, without a previous question, is an Aramaic stylism. **It is well that we are here,** i.e., in order to build the **three booths**—as if the three heavenly persons were to reside permanently upon earth. Or does Peter mean that since the "last" days were to repeat the "former" days, including the Exodus and the desert wanderings (*"Endzeit=Urzeit"*), the tabernacles, or booths, would be for use until the messianic era arrived? The brief interlude of these two verses seems most strange; Mark accounts for Peter's proposal in vs. 6: **For he did not know what to say.** Their great fear was natural in the midst of such a supernatural phenomenon (cf. 16:8), and need not be derived from Exod. 34:30. Luke seems to explain it as due to the cloud (Luke 9:34).

---

power. In the picture drawn by Eunice Tietjens,

But I shall go down from this airy space, this swift,
    white, peace, this stinging exultation,
And time will close about me, and my soul stir to
    the rhythm of the daily round.
Yet, having known, life will not press so close, and
    always I shall feel time ravel thin about me;
For once I stood
In the white windy presence of eternity.[1]

A life which has no transfigured hours of worship is poor, no matter how rich its furniture.

5. *Master, It Is Well that We Are Here; Let Us Make Three Booths.*—This was not a particularly bright remark of Peter's, and Mark apologizes for him on the ground that being afraid he did not know what to say. Behind his words there was the desire to prolong the experience. Here was an hour of high worth, of illuminated understanding of Jesus. It was an experience of which he could say with unanimous mind, "This is good." So he wanted to make it permanent.

Is there not a danger implicit in every complete satisfaction—the danger of getting life

pegged at that point? It is a danger which the psychologist calls "halting the procession." Confronted with the potentialities of tomorrow, some will always say, "This is as far as I go." For them life becomes fixed, as with the figures on Keats's "Grecian Urn." Instead of moving on to new achievements, the years thereafter spin around one stage of experience, as around a pivot.

Think of the many areas in which the mood of Peter, when he said in effect "Let's stay here and build," blocks the possibilities of life. It is always a tragedy, for instance, when a person moves on everywhere else but leaves his religious thinking behind, pegs his spiritual experience at a point away back in the past. Sometimes this is the result of a premature rejection of faith. A life which might have been a voyage of discovery is chained to a spot reached before any genuine exploration could really begin. More frequently it is the result of a faith which has failed to grow, and so no longer is able to fit an expanding world of experience and need.

There is also the danger of stopping the parade, of blocking the possibilities of social progress, by saying of some familiar order, "This is good. Let us stay here always." Again

---

[1] Reprinted from *Profiles from China* by Eunice Tietjens, by permission of Alfred A. Knopf, Inc. Copyright 1917 by Alfred A. Knopf, Inc.

7 And there was a cloud that overshadowed them: and a voice came out of the cloud, saying, This is my beloved Son: hear him.

8 And suddenly, when they had looked round about, they saw no man any more, save Jesus only with themselves.

afraid. 7 And a cloud overshadowed them, and a voice came out of the cloud, "This is my beloved Son;[g] listen to him." 8 And suddenly looking around they no longer saw any one with them but Jesus only.

[g] Or my Son, my (or the) Beloved.

7-8. This passage continues the narrative of the epiphany. Its main theme, stated in the climax of the story, was Jesus' divine sonship, not the relation of Jesus to the old covenant. In fact, the "interlude" referred to above may include vs. 4 as well as vss. 5-6, 8. **Overshadowed them,** as Luke makes clear, must mean that Jesus and the apostles—at least the latter—were overshadowed, not Moses and Elijah (sy[s] reads "overshadowed him"). As often in the O.T., especially in Exodus, the divine presence is represented by a cloud. **Hear him** has been thought to be derived from Deut. 18:15 (Jesus the second and greater Moses, or Jesus *the* Prophet!); but the point of the command was the divine attestation of Jesus' "words" (cf. 8:38), i.e., his teaching as a whole; and, as often in Scripture, the divine utterance uses language reminiscent of earlier oracles (cf. Ps. 2:7; Mark 1:11). The command was undoubtedly addressed to the disciples, not to Moses and Elijah—as if affirming the superiority of Christ's revelation to that of the law and the prophets. As the inspired prophet, Jesus' words are of divine authority (Deut. 18:18-19). This combination of "Son of God" and "prophet" may seem to reduce the former to the level of the latter; but not for early Christianity, especially in Christian Judaism: "prophet," in Semitic religious thought, was the highest possible category of divine revelation—there were no "mere" prophets in the ancient world. Of course the primitive Christian conception of Jesus' divine sonship was not as fully developed as in fourth- and fifth-century theology, but it was much more than that of the devout filial relation of a pious man to God.

What lies behind this narrative, in apostolic experience, we have no means of knowing. That it was a "psychological" event is not saying anything—so are all events, as far as they affect human consciousness. Jesus bathed in sunlight, as the morning mists clear on a mountain top—this is a pretty fancy, and thoroughly modern. But such was not the stuff of which ancient religious visions were made, e.g., the visions of Akiba's disciples. The ancient world was prejudiced on the side of realism, we might say, whereas our prejudices are all in favor of the romantic, the psychological, the subjective. For Mark the vision was real; God actually proclaimed Jesus as his Son, and commanded the apostles to hear him. The Jewish, i.e., Christian Jewish, features of the story show that it cannot have arisen on purely Hellenistic soil, and can scarcely be a transferred or transformed account of a non-Christian divine epiphany.

---

and again in history we have seen disaster come of the attempt to give permanence to a temporary phase of economic theory and development. Men still say to eighteenth-century habits and ways of thinking, "This is good. Let us build here," when those ways and habits are fatally inadequate to the changed complexities of the twentieth century. So with the attempt to make unlimited nationalism the permanent pattern of international life.

It was good for Peter to have had the transfiguration experience; it was not good for him to try to prolong it. He had to go on to new experiences of understanding and discipleship.

7. *This Is My Beloved Son; Listen to Him.*— Take these words into your imagination. Let

them run freely over time and space. Consider how many occasions there are when the words "This is my beloved Son; listen to him" have been and are the supreme wisdom. When a life looks out on the world in the early years, when it is choosing its goals and its way, its ambitions and aspirations, then listen to him who rejected the proffered kingdoms of this world for the larger kingdom of God. When life goes into eclipse, when darkness covers the face of the sun, in sorrow and failure and despair, then listen to him who was a man of sorrows, and whose revelation of God brings the sustaining word of comfort and the enabling word of hope. When life waxes in might and gathers power or riches, when the siren voices of self-indulgence

9 And as they came down from the mountain, he charged them that they should tell no man what things they had seen, till the Son of man were risen from the dead.

10 And they kept that saying with themselves, questioning one with another what the rising from the dead should mean.

11 ¶ And they asked him, saying, Why say the scribes that Elias must first come?

12 And he answered and told them, Elias verily cometh first, and restoreth all things; and how it is written of the Son of man, that he must suffer many things, and be set at nought.

13 But I say unto you, That Elias is indeed come, and they have done unto him whatsoever they listed, as it is written of him.

9 And as they were coming down the mountain, he charged them to tell no one what they had seen, until the Son of man should have risen from the dead. 10 So they kept the matter to themselves, questioning what the rising from the dead meant. 11 And they asked him, "Why do the scribes say that first Elijah must come?" 12 And he said to them, "Elijah does come first to restore all things; and how is it written of the Son of man, that he should suffer many things and be treated with contempt? 13 But I tell you that Elijah has come, and they did to him whatever they pleased, as it is written of him."

19. The Coming of Elijah (9:9-13)

The identification of John the Baptist with the expected Elijah, who was to come before the Day of Judgment (Mal. 4:5-6), was evidently not universal in the early church. In John 1:21 the Baptist himself denies it, though vs. 25 confronts him with the evidence and all but forces the role upon him (cf. Matt. 11:11-15; 17:13). In the present passage the identification is placed on the lips of Jesus. Luke for some reason omits the section.

9-10. These verses may be viewed as the conclusion of the story of the Transfiguration; but, more truly seen, they introduce, editorially, the question in vs. 11. On the charge of secrecy, see on 8:30; etc. **They kept the matter to themselves, questioning what the rising from the dead meant.** They were not discussing (as in 12:18-27) the question of resurrection in principle, but the rising of the **Son of man,** since resurrection presupposed his death. So Peter had questioned it in 8:32-33. (Cf. the reading of D W O.L. sy, etc.: τί ἐστιν . . . ἀνάστη.) It was the *death* of the Son of man that was hard to conceive. This fact apparently disposes of the theory that the death of the Son of man was a pre-Christian idea which somehow influenced the growth of the gospel tradition. **From [among] the dead** is very old language, probably older than "from the grave" or "tomb."

11-13. Various proposals to rearrange these verses have been advanced, beginning with Matt. 17:9-13, which transforms 12b into a positive statement and locates it at the end. Loisy viewed this as a redactor's insertion into Mark. C. H. Turner (*Study of the New Testament, 1883 and 1920* [Oxford: Clarendon Press, 1920], p. 61) proposed 10, 12b, 11, 12a, 13; Allen, like Turner, took 12b as a part of the disciples' question; but in that case what does "how is it written" mean? Still another possibility is 10, 11, 12a, 13c, 13ab, 12b (cf. Matthew). Torrey takes 12a as a question; but the difficulty then is that Jesus is represented as questioning Scripture (Mal. 4:6) —unless **restore all things** is being rejected as a scribal addition to the merely reconciliatory office described in Malachi. (See Grant, *Earliest Gospel,* pp. 101, 114.) Blass proposed to take 12a as a conditional clause (following D—more or less): "If Elijah comes first and restores everything, then how is it written of the Son of man . . . ?"

How is it written of the Son of man is a reference presumably to Isa. 53; Ps. 22; etc., which in Christian interpretation—but not in Jewish—referred to Christ and therefore to the Son of man (cf. Luke 24:25-27, 44-46). Goodspeed's paraphrase is excellent: "Does not the Scripture say of the Son of Man that he will suffer much and be refused?" The final clause of vs. 13, **as it is written of him,** can scarcely refer to the historical Elijah as

14 ¶ And when he came to *his* disciples, he saw a great multitude about them, and the scribes questioning with them.

15 And straightway all the people, when they beheld him, were greatly amazed, and running to *him* saluted him.

14 And when they came to the disciples, they saw a great crowd about them, and scribes arguing with them. 15 And immediately all the crowd, when they saw him, were greatly amazed, and ran up to him

---

described in the O.T.; it may possibly refer to some lost apocryphal work, as several scholars have conjectured (cf. Rev. 11:6-10).

The problem which this section solved was the relation of John the Baptist with the expected Elijah, and this solution—viz., identification—in turn solved a problem still raised in the second century: How can Jesus be Messiah, since Elijah has not yet appeared (cf. Justin *Dialogue* XLIX. 1). The answer is: Elijah *has* appeared—in John, not in Jesus, as some people at the time had thought (8:28)—but he was put to death; hence his restoration of all things has been deferred, by human opposition, just as the glorification of the Son of man has been—or, from the point of view of the passage, will be—deferred by his rejection and death; but only deferred, for both the restoration and the glorification are still sure to come to pass. The only alternative to this interpretation, if one accepts the present order of the passage, is to bracket the clause **and restoreth all things** as a later gloss inspired by Mal. 4:6.

20. The Epileptic Boy (9:14-29)

As in Raphael's great painting, Mark brings this story of Jesus' response to human need into close connection with the transfiguration narrative. The contrast between Jesus seen in glory and the impotence of the nine disciples at the foot of the mountain is very marked.

14-16. The **arguing** of the scribes was evidently the result of the disciples' failure to exorcise the demon; beyond this the scribes serve no purpose in the story. Perhaps like-

---

are sounding, then listen to him who can save life from going to pieces. So, too, at every turning point of human history, as the nations stand choosing between life and death, **This is my beloved Son; listen to him,** whose way of brotherhood is the only way of survival.

14. And When They Came to the Disciples.— The finest exposition ever given of this descent of Jesus from the Mount of Transfiguration is Raphael's great painting. He shows powerfully the striking contrast between the top of the mount and the bottom—above, the beauty of that high vision; below, tragic need and suffering, the impotence of the disciples, and the fruitless discussion about it. So does life repeatedly show the place of spiritual privilege and close beside it the place of suffering and confusion. The tragedy is often all the deeper because the very people who have had the high hour of vision and revelation have not themselves made any vital connection with the need. Many who can say of personal religious experience, "I am in love with high, farseeing places," have not come down into any saving relation with others. Their spiritual exaltation is in a social vacuum. Jesus made the connection.

We commonly hear the phrase "going downhill" applied to a person in a condemnatory or pitying manner. When we say of anybody "He is going downhill," we mean that he has seen better days, that he is descending to an anticlimax. But there is a nobler sense of the words as well—the sense in which Jesus spent his whole life going downhill from the high and lonely places, where he held communion with God, to the level, crowded places of human need. There are those who spend much of their time on the fine art of "going uphill," climbing to some height of advantage, position, power, or wealth, and pay no attention at all to this much finer art, the art of going downhill. It is the lifelong descent from the place of vision to the place of deed, from the hill of privilege to the plain of need. Raphael pictured it on canvas. Sidney Lanier pictured it in "The Song of the Chattahoochee."

Downward the voices of Duty call—
Downward, to toil and be mixed with the main,
The dry fields burn, and the mills are to turn,
And a myriad flowers mortally yearn.[2]

Raphael painted it. Lanier sang it. Jesus lived it. It rests upon us as his mandate.

[2] Sidney Lanier, *Poems*, ed. by his wife (New York: Charles Scribner's Sons, 1929), p. 25. By permission.

16 And he asked the scribes, What question ye with them?

17 And one of the multitude answered and said, Master, I have brought unto thee my son, which hath a dumb spirit;

18 And wheresoever he taketh him, he teareth him; and he foameth, and gnasheth with his teeth, and pineth away: and I spake to thy disciples that they should cast him out; and they could not.

and greeted him. 16 And he asked them, "What are you discussing with them?" 17 And one of the crowd answered him, "Teacher, I brought my son to you, for he has a dumb spirit; 18 and wherever it seizes him, it dashes him down; and he foams and grinds his teeth and becomes rigid; and I asked your disciples to cast it out,

wise in the early church an unsuccessful exorcism brought immediate criticism from the scribes. **The crowd . . . were greatly amazed,** possibly because Jesus' face still shone with heavenly light (cf. Exod. 34:29-35, where the people, on the contrary, hold back), or possibly only because of his unexpected reappearance.

17-18. The question asked of the scribes is answered dramatically by the father of the boy. **Dumb spirit:** As usual, the symptoms are explained as due to possession by an evil spirit. In this case the aphasia was temporary, accompanied by other symptoms that point to epilepsy (cf. vss. 18, 22, 26). Similar cases are found in ancient literature (e.g., Lucian *Philopseudes* 16, quoted by Klostermann) as well as in modern. Note the tragic brevity of the final words, **and they could not.**

16. *And He Asked Them, "What Are You Discussing with Them?"*—There is a terrible irony in this word "discussing." Evidently none was intended. The question was simple and straightforward, the answer to it clear. The scribes had started arguing with the disciples over the failure of their attempts to exorcise the evil spirit from the afflicted boy, making the most of it, we can be sure, with no lack of outspoken criticism, possibly even with the addition of taunts and ridicule. That was the troublesome theme.

Yet surely as Jesus used the word it had a sting in it. Discussing! In the presence of a deep and agonizing emergency all they could do was to discuss! The sad plight of the epileptic boy called for more than arguments, debates, rebuttals—words, words, words. It called for more than arid verbiage. It called for adequate power.

Here is a searching and accusing word. How many times in the history of the church have Jesus' later disciples, face to face with appalling human need, been preoccupied with discussion, fierce fightings over words, ecclesiastical etiquette, privilege and profit. We see it in the long wars of religion, accompanied with learned contention at every fine point of heresy, while starvation and death surged over Europe. While many people lamented the scourge of slavery, hot discussions went on for centuries, with few hands lifted to bring release to the captives. When the industrial revolution broke upon England, with its cruel mangling of the bodies and souls of little children, church bodies were for the most part discussing something else so

eagerly that they had no time to reach out to the suffering. It is as if the members of a life-saving crew, in their snug station, while a storm is driving ships on the rocks, were engaged in clawing each other with words over what kind of braid would be most suitable for their uniforms. In the early days of the modern missionary movement, when the first few had recaptured the vision of a Christ for the whole world, most of his disciples were still discussing something else.

The question still sounds over our world. Today, in the midst of unspeakable need—What are you discussing?

18. *I Asked Your Disciples to Cast It Out, and They Were Not Able.*—It would be hard to imagine words which might more poignantly express the reproach of a suffering world to an impotent church. There is a deep and moving pathos in these words of the father. He is heartbroken over his son's grievous affliction—Luke says "my only child" (Luke 9:38). He tells Jesus that he brought the boy to the disciples, and they could not do anything. There is no bitterness on his lips, no anger in his heart. But his disappointment and broken hopes are in themselves a reproach that must have cut sharply.

They were not able. Who of us can escape that heartbroken cry. How many times it has been sadly raised against us by the needy and suffering people of the world! Even when the words have gone unsaid, the failure of Jesus' disciples, our failure, has been deeply felt. The ills of humanity have been brought to the churches from the first century to the twentieth.

19 He answereth him, and saith, O faithless generation, how long shall I be with
you? how long shall I suffer you? bring him
unto me.

20 And they brought him unto him: and
when he saw him, straightway the spirit
tare him; and he fell on the ground, and
wallowed foaming.

21 And he asked his father, How long
is it ago since this came unto him? And he
said, Of a child.

22 And ofttimes it hath cast him into the
fire, and into the waters, to destroy him:
but if thou canst do any thing, have compassion on us, and help us.

and they were not able." 19 And he answered them, "O faithless generation, how
long am I to be with you? How long am I
to bear with you? Bring him to me." 20 And
they brought the boy to him; and when
the spirit saw him, immediately it convulsed the boy, and he fell on the ground
and rolled about, foaming at the mouth.
21 And Jesus[h] asked his father, "How long
has he had this?" And he said, "From childhood. 22 And it has often cast him into the
fire and into the water, to destroy him; but
if you can do anything, have pity on us

[h] Greek *he*.

19. O faithless generation: As in the O.T., the complaint apostrophizes more than
those immediately present; a whole world of disbelief stands in the way of the boy's
restoration. As Dibelius notes, the words are appropriate to a divine being who is
temporarily sojourning upon earth.

Many of them have been preventable, many curable. There surely the sufferers might look for help. Again and again they did—out of hopeful eyes. And again and again nothing happened.

For one example, take war and the war spirit. Notice how perfectly this description of the seizures of the epileptic boy fits the evil spirit of war. It seizes men and nations; it "dashes them down" into devastation and slaughter; men and nations "foam and grind" in emotion reaching hysteria, in hatred and anger; they "become rigid" in death. And the suffering world has asked Christ's **disciples to cast it out, and they were not able.** Sometimes we can add in explanation of the impotence that they did not try! Sometimes vast numbers of them have themselves joined in the foaming and grinding. Sometimes they have not had the wit or the courage to attack the causes of war. At any rate the hope of deliverance has not been met.

Through the years exploited laborers have looked hopefully for help to the disciples of him who came "to set at liberty those who are oppressed" (Luke 4:18) only to find how often that **they were not able** to do anything.

And what shall we say of that growing multitude of the distraught, the troubled in mind and spirit, the nervously unstable, casualties of our tense, speed-ridden, profit-driven civilization? Repeatedly they bring their ills to the disciples of him who said, "Fear not," "My peace I give unto you," and repeatedly the story works itself out into the same blind alley of impotence—men and women who should not be, but are, powerless to make available Christ's resources for the healing of mind and nerves **and spirit.**

The world brings its afflicted to us because we are disciples of the Great Physician. Must the heartbroken report go on forever—**They were not able?**

19. *And He Answered Them, "O Faithless Generation, How Long Am I to Be with You? How Long Am I to Bear with You?"*—The reproach of the father's disappointment was not the only reproach the disciples had to bear. There was also this reproach of Jesus. His words are stern, cutting, showing not only disappointment but irritation and even a note of anger. We read earlier in Mark "He . . . gave them authority over the unclean spirits" (6:7) and "they cast out many demons" (6:13). The father's expectations were not unreasonable on the basis of the record. Why then were the disciples so impotent? Jesus answers simply—from lack of faith. He goes further. Including the crowd around him, he cries, **"O faithless generation."** His disciples are addressed as part of it. Mark the notable sentence in the Exeg., "A whole world of disbelief stands in the way of the boy's restoration." Lift that and set it down in the present. It illuminates the scene.

Our generation has a widespread disbelief in the person and teaching of Jesus as the only sure foundation of the world's survival and welfare, the only permanent cure, when carried into concrete action, of the world's sickness. Need we be surprised, after periodic carnivals of slaughter, that international problems are difficult almost beyond description? Indeed the surprise would be to find that such orgies of devastation and killing had made an easy starting point for world redemption. But underneath all the complications is a tragic faithless-

23 Jesus said unto him, If thou canst believe, all things *are* possible to him that believeth.

24 And straightway the father of the child cried out, and said with tears, Lord, I believe; help thou mine unbelief.

and help us." 23 And Jesus said to him, "If you can! All things are possible to him who believes." 24 Immediately the father of the child cried out[i] and said, "I believe;

[i] Many ancient authorities add *with tears.*

23-24. If you can! . . . believes. As repeatedly in Mark (e.g., 11:24), Jesus sets no limits to the power of faith. With the same utter confidence in God with which he rebuked the raging tempest (4:39), and met the dangerous maniac from among the tombs (5:8), and took the daughter of Jairus by the hand (5:41), here he advances upon the powerful spirit that holds the epileptic boy in its grasp (cf. 5:36). **If thou canst believe** (KJV) is too mild; **If you can!** (RSV) is an exclamation, either in astonishment, or as an answer

---

ness. We hold our faith so tentatively and timorously just where it needs to be applied. Loud-speaking bullies of one sort and another shout in the ears of Jesus' disciples, "You don't mean to say, do you, that you would be so naïve and sentimental as to suggest Jesus and his teaching to the rough, tough world of international politics?" How many of us are browbeaten, and answer in a whisper, "Oh no, of course not; we are reasonable men." Which, being interpreted, means "We are faithless men." Thousands upon thousands of us do not believe in any downright fashion that Christ is the truth and the life, that his procedures are the way also to salvation from war. We do not believe that he is the revelation of God, not as intensely as we believe that two and two make four, or that the earth is round. We say of so many other things—power, national supremacy, wealth—"This is the life." And so, as at the foot of the mountain—to what degree because of faithlessness?—the ills of humanity are not healed. Jesus' phrase should at least bring to mind what is so easily forgotten, the degree to which we share in the secularism of our time.

Hear on the heels of it his sorrowful cry, **"How long am I to bear with you?"** That ought to get past the defenses of even the most complacent minds in Christ's church. How much God does bear in us—our lethargy; in every crisis our ready skepticism about his way of love, as we eagerly reach for "something more promising"; our concern for other ends than those with which Jesus was concerned; our lack of anguish over a world apart from him. **How long?**

23. *And Jesus Said to Him, "If You Can! All Things Are Possible to Him Who Believes."*—Commentators have interpreted these words in two different senses. They may be taken as an exclamation of wonder that anyone should use the word "if" in connection with God's power. The man was just speaking on a hypothesis—"In case you are able to do anything." That is no way—as Jesus' repetition of the "if

you can" might indicate—to approach a question of God's power.

Others take the words as referring to the man's own part in the healing. "If *you* can," Jesus may be saying, throwing the issue back to the man himself. "It is not a question of 'if I can,' but of 'if *you* can.' It is a matter determined by *your* faith." This is in line with his frequent declaration, "Thy faith hath made thee whole."

Taken either way the words proclaim the same great truth of the power of God and the need of faith to make that power operative. The statement which follows immediately, **All things are possible to him who believes,** must of course be taken in the light of Jesus' teaching and life. If they are taken in sodden, unspiritual literalism, they become immoral nonsense. They offer the believer no justification for acting as if he possessed a private magic, some legerdemain to be used for personal advantage. Jesus rejected all that for himself in his temptation, and he rejected it for his disciples. Edna St. Vincent Millay in a noble sonnet says that "love will not fill the thickened lung with breath," nor set a broken leg. Neither will faith. Faith will not enable one to caress rattlesnakes safely, or to pluck money from the air, or to live without food. Yet in the wide realm of the kingdom of God, and of God's continued action to bring in that kingdom, whether for one human life or for the world, there is no barrier that can be set against the divine invasion: none but our own cardinal weakness—that often we believe more firmly in the power of the demons of evil than in the power of the God of love. Certainly in the bright lexicon of faith there is no such word as this "if," take it what way you please.

24. *The Father of the Child Cried Out . . . , "I Believe; Help My Unbelief!"*—These words too can have different meanings. They can mean "Change my unbelief into belief," "Help my want of faith," as Goodspeed translates it and as the Exeg. prefers. Or they can mean "Help me in spite of my inadequate faith." The

25 When Jesus saw that the people came running together, he rebuked the foul spirit, saying unto him, *Thou* dumb and deaf spirit, I charge thee, come out of him, and enter no more into him.

26 And *the spirit* cried, and rent him sore, and came out of him: and he was as one dead; insomuch that many said, He is dead.

27 But Jesus took him by the hand, and lifted him up; and he arose.

28 And when he was come into the house, his disciples asked him privately, Why could not we cast him out?

29 And he said unto them, This kind can come forth by nothing, but by prayer and fasting.

help my unbelief!" 25 And when Jesus saw that a crowd came running together, he rebuked the unclean spirit, saying to it, "You dumb and deaf spirit, I command you, come out of him, and never enter him again." 26 And after crying out and convulsing him terribly, it came out, and the boy was like a corpse; so that most of them said, "He is dead." 27 But Jesus took him by the hand and lifted him up, and he arose. 28 And when he had entered the house, his disciples asked him privately, "Why could we not cast it out?" 29 And he said to them, "This kind cannot be driven out by anything but prayer."*i*

i Many ancient authorities add *and fasting.*

to the father: "If *you* can!" Omit "believe," with most early authorities. (See Grant, *Earliest Gospel,* p. 115.) **Help my unbelief!** means "Help me even in my unbelief," or better, "Help my want of faith [so Goodspeed], as well as heal my child."

25-27. The crowd is still gathering (vs. 15), attracted now by the commotion and the dialogue. The cure is to be permanent: **Come out of him, and never enter him again** —a feature often noted in similar ancient stories. As in 5:35, the people conclude that the boy is dead. Were both instances examples of coma? As also in 5:41 (cf. 1:31), Jesus takes the person by the hand, a characteristic act of Jesus the healer.

28-29. A private discussion afterward is a typical feature of Mark (cf. 7:17). **Why could not we cast him out?** is more emphatic than RSV, and probably better (cf. Goodspeed). But RSV is correct in omitting **and fasting,** with several of the best MSS. This

difference is not as great as might appear at first sight. When one receives God's help in spite of the lingering unbelief, that experience will, to some degree at least, change unbelief into belief.

But either way it is a prayer that should rise daily from our hearts and lives. No one ever passes beyond the need of it. For we are strange mixtures of belief and unbelief. There is war in our minds. One day we cry, "Lord, I believe"; the next day we wonder about it. In some areas of life we believe with unanimous heart; in others the highest point we ever seem to reach is **help my unbelief.** On sunny days we sing, "My heart is fixed, O God"; but under leaden skies the song dies on our lips and doubt chills the heart. Sometimes this civil war in our members is like that which Sidney Lanier describes so sympathetically:

O Age that half believ'st thou half believ'st,
Half doubt'st the substance of thine own half doubt,
And, half perceiving that thou half perceiv'st,
Stand'st at thy temple door, heart in, head out!
Lo! while thy heart's within, helping the choir,
Without, thine eyes range up and down the time.[3]

[3] "Acknowledgment," *Poems,* ed. by his wife (New York: Charles Scribner's Sons, 1929), p. 77. By permission.

"Heart in, head out"—the split personality in religion! In theory we believe; in practice we often insist on using something else. We pray, "Thy kingdom come"; but there are times when we only half believe in its coming. An inadequate faith grows into deeper faith as we act on the faith we have. "The experiment becomes an experience."

28-29. *This Kind Cannot Be Driven Out by Anything but Prayer.*—Many commentators note an unexpected quality in this answer. It seems to limit Jesus' power over demons. Nor is it the answer given in other situations, that the power of evil spirits is overcome by faith. Branscomb calls it "thoroughly Jewish," especially with the addition found in some manuscripts **and fasting.**

Yet may we not call it a "divine" as well as a "Jewish" answer? Prayer was never a small thing to Jesus, never merely one thing, like a swiftly uttered petition. Prayer was a whole life, a life of communion with God. In that lay the source of power to exorcise evil spirits. In a life of sustained communion lies the power to deal with any evil.

"Why could we not?" What a recurring question that is! We ask it about the repeated sin

30 ¶ And they departed thence, and passed through Galilee; and he would not that any man should know *it*.

31 For he taught his disciples, and said unto them, The Son of man is delivered into the hands of men, and they shall kill him; and after that he is killed, he shall rise the third day.

32 But they understood not that saying, and were afraid to ask him.

30 They went on from there and passed through Galilee. And he would not have any one know it; 31 for he was teaching his disciples, saying to them, "The Son of man will be delivered into the hands of men, and they will kill him; and when he is killed, after three days he will rise." 32 But they did not understand the saying, and they were afraid to ask him.

---

omission is justified also on the following grounds: (*a*) Jesus did not practice fasting (2:19); (*b*) Matt. 17:20 gives an entirely different answer, apparently from Q (but cf. Mark 11:22-23); (*c*) Matt. 17:21 is a gloss, which has in turn provided the καὶ νηστείᾳ in some MSS of Mark. But even without "fasting," Jesus' answer is surprising. Jesus is represented in Mark as the Son of God, whose power over the demons is immediate and irresistible; yet here he states that prayer is the secret of successful exorcism! If we had asked Mark the question, he would probably have replied that the answer was meant for the disciples, and for the later church: *"You* cannot cast out this kind of demon save by prayer." At the same time, we may well see in these words an authentic record of Jesus' own view of his extraordinary healing power; **by prayer** means not a momentary ejaculation, but a life of intimacy with God through personal communion (cf. 1:35; 6:46, and even the strange and distant echo in John 11:41-42).

21. The Second Passion Announcement (9:30-32)

30-32. This announcement parallels the first (8:31), though not exactly; but there is no advance of one upon the other, and the disciples are still as uncomprehending (vs. 32) as ever. Jesus is still traveling incognito, as in 7:24. Here the purpose is to devote full time to the teaching of his disciples. **Into the hands of men** is probably an intended play on words after **the Son of man** (Klostermann). **He will rise** is less primitive than "be raised" (see Grant, *Earliest Gospel,* p. 66), and still further confirms the secondary character of these three announcements.

---

that besets us, and overthrows us, "the good that I would" and "do not," "the evil which I would not" and "do" (Rom. 7:19). This kind can be cast out only by prayer, by opening the door of communion so that the life of God may come in to the life of the soul, so that a counterpressure from within may resist the pressure from without. So Thomas Chalmers put it in his great phrase, "the expulsive power of a new affection." We cannot cast out demons when we bring against them only the faint force of depleted, fatigued, unrenewed, unreplenished spirits.

Why can we not cast out self with its totalitarian rule over our lives? Because the domination of self at the center will yield only to Someone else at the center—"Yet not I, but Christ liveth in me" (Gal. 2:20). Self comes out only by the life of prayer.

Why can we not cast out the evil spirits that cripple the church? The paralysis of a dead formalism, for instance, in which there is no "walking and leaping and praising God," but only a lagging, pedestrian trudge? Only by

prayer, "the present tense of God"! Why cannot a church cast out the evil that lies at its very doors in the community? Why so much "church activity" with so little change around about? Satan never trembles at the announcement "The morning service will be held as usual at eleven o'clock." For it may end as usual, with no great result, at twelve. Only by prayer as equipment for the warfare of the spirit is evil cast out.

So with the more than seven devils of our modern life—the hungry greed that makes for industrial strife, for scarcity; the undisciplined emotions, the fears and the hatreds that breed racial and international enmity. Only by prayer, through the coming from beyond ourselves of a power greater than our own, are these things cast out.

32. *But They Did Not Understand the Saying, and They Were Afraid to Ask Him.*—This second announcement of the coming suffering and death and resurrection finds the disciples as unprepared for it as they were when the first announcement was made at the time of

33 ¶ And he came to Capernaum: and being in the house he asked them, What was it that ye disputed among yourselves by the way?	33 And they came to Ca-per'na-um; and when he was in the house he asked them, "What were you discussing on the way?"

22. THE QUESTION OF GREATNESS (9:33-37)

If "through Galilee" in vs. 30 traced the return journey from the north, **Capernaum** in vs. 33 marks the end of the trip. As in 2:1, it was Jesus' home. Both Matthew and Luke ignore the setting, and both abridge the section—Matthew, as usual, considerably improving its style and adding to its cogency. Both omit vs. 35, though Luke has an echo of it at the end (Luke 9:48*b*), and we may be strongly tempted to omit most of the verse (with D and *k*). Mark's real answer to the question of greatness is found in 10:43-44! But we have already seen how Mark conflates material, and 35*b* is really appropriate here. If the καὶ λέγει αὐτοῖς (**and he said to them**) indicates an insertion, as it frequently does, the insertion was probably made by Mark himself. And even without 35*b*

Peter's confession (8:27-33). Later on, at the arrest, trial, and crucifixion, they seem still as unprepared. This has raised the question whether or not Jesus' teaching about his coming death could actually have been as detailed as recorded in Mark. Perhaps the lack of understanding on the part of the disciples is to be explained by the fact that the account of these disclosures, written after the events had taken place, is far more explicit than were the indications originally given.

One can readily imagine, however, that the disciples found it extraordinarily hard to accept without surprise and bewilderment a conception of messiahship which did such violence to all their ideas of what the Messiah would do and be. Such a complete overturning of one's mental and spiritual world cannot be taken easily. Their confusion can even more readily be understood if we let our thoughts rest on the difficulty which Jesus' later disciples, the church through the years and today, have had in accepting a crucified Lord instead of a conquering King. Consider how reluctant multitudes in the modern world are to accept the Cross of Jesus as the supreme revelation of God. Other conceptions and idealizations fit so much better into our "onward and upward" thought forms. The serene teacher of Galilee, the persuasive expounder of wise and helpful axioms of living, even the Jesus of Palm Sunday, acclaimed and honored, is so much simpler, more attractive, more congenial to our culture, to our reliance on education, to our disparagement of extremes. Many prefer an intelligent, reasonable Jesus, an inspiring example, the counterpart of a broad-minded liberal, a leader of all good causes. They too find it hard to understand **the saying** about crucifixion and death. And because so many do not understand it, the Christian faith, instead of being conceived and presented to the world as God's act of redemption,

has dwindled down into another set of moral maxims, impotent to face and subdue the tragic evils of life and of history. When we think of the gospel in any such fashion as that, we make a detour around the Cross, and so miss the way.

And they were afraid. Like the disciples, many have been afraid to ask more explicitly the meaning of Calvary. Afraid—because of what the answer might be: they might get in too deep. For the answer includes an acceptance of the Cross as a law of life. It includes the immoderate extreme of laying down life as a sacrifice, of giving mind, heart, time, and strength to the ransom of others. That is a bothersome thing to devotees of the "golden mean," the well-balanced, "nothing-in-excess" philosophy of life. **They were afraid to ask him.** Are we?

33. *He Asked Them, "What Were You Discussing on the Way?"*—What a disconcerting question! How would we like to have it suddenly put to us? There is always danger of great embarrassment when Jesus joins the conversation and asks quietly, "What were you talking about?" The words doubtless carry an air of greater innocence than existed in Jesus' mind. The Master, who "knew what was in man," of whom it could be written, "Jesus, seeing their thoughts," was scarcely ignorant of the dispute that was going on. He had caught them while they were discussing what has been both a major and a tragic question for humanity through the ages: "Who shall be greatest?" No wonder they were silent. Even though their conceptions of Jesus' messiahship were still inadequate, they knew their personal, materialistic ambitions would find no favor with him.

Suppose we had to tell him the nature of our daily conversations, our reveries, our inmost desires and ambitions. How would they sound? He said in the Sermon on the Mount, "Do not be anxious about your life, what you shall eat or what you shall drink, nor about your body,

34 But they held their peace: for by the way they had disputed among themselves, who *should be* the greatest.

35 And he sat down, and called the twelve, and saith unto them, If any man

34 But they were silent; for on the way they had discussed with one another who was the greatest. 35 And he sat down and called the

---

it is difficult to trace the connection of vss. 36-37 with 33-34. Perhaps Mark has left out something, as Matthew evidently assumes: "greatness" is greatness in the coming kingdom, and unless the disciples turn and "become as little children" they will not even enter it.

Perhaps a clue to the proper interpretation of the passage is provided by the recognition that 9:33–10:45 contains a whole series of discipleship sayings, which Mark found in one of his sources and to which he undertook to give proper biographical settings, somewhat as the other evangelists gave settings to the Q sayings, especially Luke in 9:51–18:14. These sayings on discipleship in Mark are often connected only verbally or mnemonically —as if in some early Christian catechism (so K. L. Schmidt, Bultmann; cf. Klostermann) —9:33-34, greatness; 36-37, the example of a child; 38-40 or 41, an unrecognized ally; 42, the danger of discouraging the weak in faith, i.e., causing them to "stumble"; 43-48, causes of stumbling, within one's own life; 49, "salted with fire," suggested by "fire" (vs. 48) ; 50, "salt," suggested by "salted" (vs. 49) ; 10:14-15, children (cf. 9:36-37, 42) ; 17-22, a would-be disciple, and renunciation of property the full test of discipleship; 23-25, the danger of wealth, suggested by "great possessions" (vs. 22) ; 26-31, the disciple's reward for renunciation; 35-40, greatness in the kingdom (cf. 9:33-35) ; 42-45, the law of service in the Christian community, and the example of the Son of man. This last passage is the climax to the whole series and indeed to the whole "way of the Cross" (8:27–10:45) . It has been observed (see F. C. Grant, *The Growth of the Gospels* [New York: Abingdon Press, 1933]) that a collection of discipleship sayings formed the central section in Q, whether a written document or a stereotyped body of oral tradition; it is not impossible that in several of the following sections Mark was in some way, directly or indirectly, dependent upon that collection. Upon this hypothesis the omission of vs. 35 at this point by Matthew and Luke and the apparent irrelevance of vss. 36-37 are easily explained.

35. Last of all and servant of all, as in 10:43-45. "Servant" or "minister" is not very different from "slave"; service or ministry was the slave's duty in life. As with us, "servant" (διάκονος) was a more considerate term than "slave" (δοῦλος) .

---

what you shall put on" (Matt. 6:25) . Yet are not these very things the core of much of our conversation? In war days of rationing, in days of scarcity, in days even of plenty, there are multitudes of people who hardly ever talk about anything but food and drink and clothes. We often have the feeling that some of them could write their whole autobiography on a menu card. The journey from appetizer to dessert is their spiritual odyssey. And everybody is exposed to that infection. It is a necessary concern. Jesus said, in understanding, "Your heavenly Father knows that you need them all" (Matt. 6:32) . We are not disembodied spirits or butterflies; but when our whole or chief conversation moves on what is little better than an animal level, we shut out our high heritage, both human and divine.

How avidly, on the battlefields of thirty centuries, have men discussed the question "Who shall be greatest?" The arguments have grown from bow and arrow to atomic bombs. Periodically the nations sit in the most appalling ruins;

but the "discussion'" seems never to be interrupted. We live in a competitive order—disguise it as we will—that seeps into our souls. The cult of pre-eminence, the expansive desires induced by profit-driven societies, shape the minds and ambitions of men. The unremitting bombardment of advertising deliberately stimulates every unholy emotion known to humanity: envy, covetousness, pride, vanity, greed. Education under such conditions has often been merely a means of sharpening the claws of competitors. The urge to be "the greatest" can get even inside of the church, and the desire for material prosperity, for social prestige, can displace the desire to seek and to save those who are lost.

It is a question which ought to be truly unsettling. What are we discussing as we journey along the way? What is uppermost in our talk and deepest in our hearts? Could Jesus join our conversation and feel at home in it?

35. *If Any One Would Be First, He Must Be Last of All and Servant of All.*—Here begins a series of sayings on greatness, extending through

desire to be first, *the same* shall be last of all, and servant of all.

36 And he took a child, and set him in the midst of them: and when he had taken him in his arms, he said unto them,

twelve; and he said to them, "If any one would be first, he must be last of all and servant of all." 36 And he took a child, and put him in the midst of them; and taking him in his arms, he said to them,

---

36-37. We are so accustomed to the sequence in Matt. 18:2-4 that we are shocked not to find the words here in Mark. Unless something has been omitted here by Mark (or perhaps transferred to 10:15), the meaning seems to be: "One who receives a little child in my name will show that he has the proper spirit of humility; and the one who receives me, receives God." What this meant to the early church (and to Mark) doubtless included the admonition to hospitality and the care of orphans (cf. Jas. 1:27; etc.). Such charity would, and still does, rule out all thoughts of "greatness" and all personal ambition. But

---

ch. 10 and reaching a high point in 10:43-45, the "it shall not be so among you" passage, which is an extension and intensification of this. Note the impressive **And he sat down and called the twelve.** Mark seems to say, "This is important." And so it is. It is the central core of Jesus' teaching on the meaning of life and the nature of the kingdom of God. One cannot be sure in what setting the words were originally spoken. Mark will relate a word to one situation, Luke and Matthew to another. But the introductory detail shows clearly that in Mark's thought, at least, this saying was tremendously important.

It reveals Jesus as the great revolutionist. For here is one of the greatest overturnings in all history, **If any one would be first, he must be last of all and servant of all.** This is the world turned upside down. All our common measurements of importance and greatness are pronounced obsolete. The boasts of heraldry and the pomp of power are irrelevant. This far surpasses the miracle ascribed to Joshua, of making the sun stand still. Jesus halts the whole human parade and puts it into reverse, with the last end foremost, the servant at the head, and all the pompous kings who ever reigned bringing up a tattered battalion at the rear.

The upset is so staggering that we literally stagger at accepting it as our measure of life. Suppose Jesus were to come to our community to pick out "the leading citizens." Who would they be, as he measured them by this revolutionary standard? Any town's "leading citizens" are those who bulk largest in the banks, the Chamber of Commerce, the social register. Some of them might be on Jesus' distinguished service list. But surely the majority of his candidates would be "nobodies," whose names had never got into any roll more exclusive than a city directory, but were already written in the lamb's book of life. The Judgment Day will be a time of shocking surprises! Take, for instance, the phrase which is often on a pastor's lips—"my leading member." We all know what that ordi-

narily means. But as Jesus rearranges the roll, the "leading member" might not be the president of the Blank Manufacturing Company but the president's scrubwoman, if, as might be, she were the servant of all.

One way of putting this question to ourselves is: Are you living B.C. or A.D.? Are the standards of greatness which you accept those that for the most part prevailed before Christ came into the world with his insistence on a new measurement of service, or are you really living in some year of our Lord?

36-37. *Whoever Receives One Such Child in My Name Receives Me.*—The importance of Jesus' word on the greatness of all who serve is emphasized with a vivid dramatization. **He took a child, and put him in the midst of them; and taking him in his arms, he said to them,** "If you do that, if you forget yourself in giving yourself to one from whom you can have no benefit in return, doing it **in my name,** that is, as something to which your relationship to me impels you, you receive me also, and the God who sent me." It was an acted truth which would etch deeply into the mind.

This phrase **one such child** has tremendous social implications, with an outlook on the whole world. Think what it would mean if society "received" a child in Jesus' name and spirit. Of course our society does "receive" a child. The child is born, and his name is duly entered in the Office of Vital Statistics, and the census after a while takes note of him as an item. The Bureau of Internal Revenue will even take note of him as ground for tax exemption. But such statistical "receiving" is far from receiving him in Christ's name, receiving him as a child of God into an enfolding, sustaining social group. How often the child is not really "received" but either grudgingly "accepted" as a potential part of a labor pool—children of minority groups, Negro children, Mexican children, as decimal points on the profit side of some industrial ledger, not as sons and daugh-

37 Whosoever shall receive one of such children in my name, receiveth me; and whosoever shall receive me, receiveth not me, but him that sent me.

38 ¶ And John answered him, saying, Master, we saw one casting out devils in thy name, and he followeth not us; and we forbade him, because he followeth not us.

37 "Whoever receives one such child in my name receives me; and whoever receives me, receives not me but him who sent me."

38 John said to him, "Teacher, we saw a man casting out demons in your name,[k] and we forbade him, because he was not

[k] Some ancient authorities add *who does not follow us.*

---

one cannot help suspecting that originally—possibly even in Mark's "source," if he was using one at this point—the saying was connected with 10:13-16, i.e., especially with the sayings in 14*b*-15. **In my name**=as a Christian (cf. vs. 41). The saying in 37*b* is echoed elsewhere in the Gospels (e.g., Matt. 10:40; Luke 10:16; John 12:44-45; 13:20). It was semiproverbial (Strack and Billerbeck; cf. Klostermann: "The messenger of a king is like the king himself"). Note the primitive Christology: Christ is the one whom God "has sent," like the O.T. prophets. Such features survived for a long time in early Christian tradition and teaching (e.g., John 17; etc.).

23. The Strange Exorcist (9:38-41)

Matthew omits this section, perhaps because of experience with strange exorcists and other traveling brethren in the early Syrian church (cf. Did. 11–13). But that the section was found in his copy of Mark, and therefore is no later addition, seems clear from the echo of Mark 9:41 in Matt. 10:42. Its insertion here was doubtless suggested by the phrase "in thy name," after vs. 37.

38. In thy name, i.e., pretending to be a Christian. That such a practice was possible even in Jesus' lifetime is clear from the parallel case in Acts 19:13. **He followeth not us**

---

ters of almighty God—or "tolerated" as another mouth to feed. Much of it is so casual and indifferent, giving rise to the cry,

> O God! that bread should be so dear,
> And flesh and blood so cheap![4]

It is no exaggeration to say that the highest possible social achievement will be to receive a child in Christ's name.

The child set in the midst by Jesus is the symbol of the truth that the final test of a society is what it does to children. How fares the child in our land? There is the hazard of war, preventable disease, social conditions breeding delinquency, inadequate education, spiritual neglect. A few years ago, through a mistake on the roll in Houston, Texas, a child two years old was summoned for jury duty. That was a divinely inspired mistake. For the child is the final jury before whom our civilization must be tried.

What an accomplishment it is for a family truly to "receive" a child into its fellowship in the spirit of Jesus, forgetting self in service, conscious of the responsibility of bringing an immortal soul into its true heritage. It need hardly be said that the church has no higher duty or privilege than to give itself to one such

[4] Thomas Hood, "Song of the Shirt."

child in love and care, each a corporate member of the body of Christ. The return is almost incredible. For, as Jesus makes clear, whenever that happens the proper stage direction is, "Enter God" (see also on 10:13-16).

38. *We Saw a Man Casting Out Demons in Your Name; and We Forbade Him.*—Entirely apart from the relation of this story to the experiences of the early church and its probable reflection of them (see Exeg.), it has close relevance to continuing and universal experience, both in the church and outside it.

It was a very natural feeling which prompted the disciples' order that the unattached exorcist should cease and desist from his work. Let him that is without sin in this respect cast the first stone at John. The spirit of narrow sectarianism is familiar enough in literature and art. Painters and poets, sculptors and novelists, who "do not follow us," have been sternly reprimanded by the authorities of the time. Young Keats, who surely was an unattached exorcist in literature, was greeted with a massive sentence, "This will never do." He did not travel with the self-appointed judges of the *Edinburgh Review.* We see the same thing in religion. Those workers of authentic spiritual miracles, the Quakers, have been told many times, "This will never do."

The feeling John expressed need not begin

39 But Jesus said, Forbid him not: for there is no man which shall do a miracle in my name, that can lightly speak evil of me.

40 For he that is not against us is on our part.

following us." **39** But Jesus said, "Do not forbid him; for no one who does a mighty work in my name will be able soon after to speak evil of me. **40** For he that is not

---

is omitted by some MSS, perhaps in view of the repetition at the end of the verse. But Mark's style permitted such repetitions. With the form of the narrative, cf. Num. 11:26-29, especially vs. 28, "My lord Moses, forbid them."

39-40. In the present context the saying **Do not forbid him** must be taken as a warning against exclusiveness and overemphasis upon apostolic authority. Apparently the proof of the "validity" of a claimed discipleship was successful exorcism "in the name" of Jesus. The Greek term for a **miracle** or **mighty work** is again δύναμις. Jesus' followers were to welcome honest co-operation, even in unexpected places and by irregular means. The saying is followed word for word by Luke (9:50); it reappears in a negative version in Matt. 12:30 and Luke 11:23, where it stands in a controversy context— the charge of collusion with Beelzebul—and probably in its Q form. An interesting variant is found in the papyri: "He that is not against you is for you. The one who is far off today will be close tomorrow." This is probably not original, but is like the expanded sayings in the Didache, likewise derived from early Christian catechesis.

---

in a hard and narrow bigotry at all. It can spring from some very good sources, from loyalty, from confidence in the truth proclaimed, the desire to keep it uncorrupted, from a strong sense of the need of unity in organization. All these may be and have been good things.

But as a rule, the swift and intolerant "forbidding" of those who do not follow us results (*a*) from the very great evil of distorted magnitudes. Intolerance of those doing good outside our fold is frequently not at all a sign of confidence in truth. It may well mean that we do not really believe truth to be mighty or able to prevail without our nervous efforts to fence it in. Or (*b*) it results from confused loyalties, another tremendous source of evil in Christian history—loyalty to the means rather than to the end, to the organization rather than to the gospel it was organized to serve, to the institution rather than to God, to the parochial and regional rather than to the universal. Rufus Choate said of John Quincy Adams that he was "a bulldog with confused ideas." There have been many people more distinguished for tenacity than for wise judgment about where to attach their tenacity. Or (*c*) it results from an overweening sense of authority, a third subtly corrupting force. At its deepest, the evil of John's intolerance lay in the precedence given the negative over the positive. The lust for "forbidding" may bulk larger than the joy over one sinner who repents. And there straightway we part company with Jesus.

39-40. *But Jesus Said, "Do Not Forbid Him. . . . For He that Is Not Against Us Is for Us."*—The point of this plea is timeless. It says to us, "Take a wide view of your faith instead of a

narrow one." The followers of Jesus are not to be a little clique off in a corner, fenced in by a hedge of thorns. "The earth is the LORD's, and the fulness thereof" (Ps. 24:1). The kingdom of God has the dimensions of God himself. Those who do the works of Jesus belong to him. The range and amplitude of his teaching here find some expression in the hymn,

> There's a wideness in God's mercy,
> Like the wideness of the sea.
>
> . . . .
>
> For the love of God is broader
> Than the measure of man's mind.[5]

So Jesus' saying means, in part: Do not look for labels; look for actions, attitudes, spirit. When that in which Jesus rejoiced—mercy, justice, integrity, reverence, faith—appears, welcome it. Do not meet it with sour, skeptical antagonism. Meet it as he did. He said of a Roman, a pagan according to Jewish standards of disdain, "I have not found so great faith, no, not in Israel" (Matt. 8:10).

Note that such an attitude of glad recognition, wherever it appears, does not mean a reduction of our faith to some bare least common denominator of all beliefs. A critic has written of a character in a novel, a preacher, that he mixed Freud, Marx, and Jesus together in one all-embracing muddle. The world will not be saved by muddle. Holding the faith in Jesus as the power of God and the wisdom of God, we are to have a hospitable eye and mind, confident that the God who has not left himself without a witness is at work in his whole world.

[5] Frederick W. Faber, "There's a wideness in God's mercy."

41 For whosoever shall give you a cup of water to drink in my name, because ye belong to Christ, verily I say unto you, he shall not lose his reward.

41 For truly, I say to you, whoever gives you a cup of water to drink because you bear the name of Christ, will by no means lose his reward.

against us is for us.

41. This verse is omitted by Luke—as well as by Matthew, who, as we have seen, omits the whole section—and has probably been inserted by Mark as a further example of the kind of co-operation and friendliness on the part of outsiders which the disciples, and the later church, were to welcome. But its real connection, as Klostermann notes, is with vss. 37, 42, not 38-40, as is suggested by Matt. 10:40-42, where the saying is found in what was probably its earlier form: "Whoever gives *to one of these little ones* even a cup of cold water because he [i.e., the little one] is a disciple . . ." **Not lose his reward:** Not necessarily in the kingdom of heaven, but quite possibly in this present order (cf. 10:30, "now in this time"), as often in wisdom sayings.

And we are to salute, wherever we find them, the allies of the Christian faith and spirit. God fulfills himself in many ways. He has fulfilled himself in political and labor movements, for instance, often disdained as "secular" by those within the church. Observe in this connection that the stripping from life of its joys and pleasures, until it is made up of nothing but specifically "religious" and ecclesiastical routines, has done immeasurable harm to the Christian religion. All pure joy, all that enhances the sense of the positive good of living, is an ally of the spirit. There is a fine expression of this in C. S. Lewis' *Screwtape Letters*. The skillful strategist of Satan, Screwtape, writes: "The man who truly and disinterestedly enjoys any one thing in the world, for its own sake, and without caring twopence what other people say about it, is by that very fact fore-armed against some of our subtlest modes of attack." Joy is an ally which a narrow-eyed asceticism has all too often forbidden.

These words of Jesus, then, are a rebuke to all our blind exclusiveness, our arrogant assumptions that God's action in the world is limited to the forms with which we are familiar. "Something there is that does not love a wall."[6] It is the mind of God. The church has suffered terribly, and the world has suffered terribly, from this fence-building frenzy. If one tenth of the time which Christians have devoted to building fences had gone into building roads as a highway for God, the world would be a far better place today.

41. *Whoever Gives You a Cup of Water . . . , Will by No Means Lose His Reward.*—This verse reads more logically with vss. 36-37, on receiving a little child, than with the immediately preceding vss. 39-40, on the outsiders whose co-operation should be recognized (see Exeg.). Taken with the former passage, the saying would mean that whosoever gives a cup

of cold water to a little child would not lose his reward. Such a connection would seem much more natural.

The point, in any case, is clear and powerful. Jesus stresses the high, divine valuation of elementary kindly service. And strangely enough we need his constant reminder. There are some things which, just because we see them all the time, we never see at all. Familiarity breeds not always contempt, but often blindness and oblivion. Chesterton's point in one of his Father Brown stories is profound. A criminal disguised as a postman completely evaded detection because everyone was so used to seeing postmen that no one saw him at all.

The cup of cold water is one of these things. Often it takes a keen and alert eye to detect the obvious. The elementary basic necessities are often the forgotten obvious. Christianity can be "spiritualized" out of real touch with common need. Consequently this insight which Jesus gives us into the divine system of bookkeeping is always a word in season. One of the earliest images which has been put into the minds of children and has left a deep—and unfavorable—impression is that of God as a celestial bookkeeper. Several writers have recorded their memory of a patriarchal figure with a long beard, writing down in a ledger with a large pen all the misdeeds of children. A grotesque picture of the Father of him who said, "Suffer the little children to come unto me" (10:14). Jesus provides us here with the true picture of that divine bookkeeper. In his recordings even the slightest service of kindness and love is a tremendous item to be entered. Even a cup of cold water is big business and goes down on the credit side.

And important business. With too great ease Christianity can be allegorized out of all resemblance to the teaching of Jesus. There can be so much talk about "spiritual" hunger and "spiritual" bread that the need of ministering

[6] Robert Frost, "Mending Wall."

42 And whosoever shall offend one of *these* little ones that believe in me, it is better for him that a millstone were hanged about his neck, and he were cast into the sea.

42 "Whoever causes one of these little ones who believe in me to sin,[1] it would be better for him if a great millstone were hung round his neck and he were thrown

[1] Or *stumble*.

24. Offenses (9:42-48)

The "offenses," i.e., causes or occasions of stumbling (σκανδαλίσῃ=causes . . . to sin), are both objective and subjective—causes affecting others (vs. 42), and those affecting oneself (vss. 43-48). As noted above, the connection of vs. 42 with vs. 37 is close: vs. 42 states negatively what vs. 37 states positively. But the insertion of vss. 38-41 has resulted in a modification of vs. 42: the **little ones** are no longer children but those **who believe in me**, i.e., the weak in faith (cf. Rom. 14:1–15:13, especially 14:1, 13). Perhaps this was true also of Mark's understanding of the saying in vs. 37, though it is far from obvious.

42. It would be better, i.e., it would have been better, before he caused the sin (cf. 14:21*b*); or, it would be better to perish than to cause sin. The **millstone** is not the small stone of a hand mill (Matt. 24:41), but the huge grinding stone of an ass-driven mill. Death would be inescapable. **In me** is omitted by some MSS (C* D *a*), undoubtedly by error.

to physical hunger with physical bread can drop out of notice as a lower, "unspiritual" concern. Archbishop William Temple has made a high claim for Christianity on the basis of its being the most "materialistic" of all faiths, that is, the one that finds the largest place for matter. It recognizes the physical, and does not deny it as being unreal or unimportant. True Christianity cannot, like some other religions, be undisturbed in the presence of physical need. The cup of cold water must go with the bread of life. There are many musical pieces called "variations on a theme." It has been well pointed out that in Christian thinking and action there can be so many "variations" that the original theme is lost (see Matt. 25:31-46). We need constant watchfulness lest our rendering of the Christian gospel is all "variations," with none of the melody of ministering love which was in Jesus.

In such a ministry none shall lose his reward, either in this world or in the next. That reward is the joy of meeting life at a point of need. It is the joy of actually joining the human race, the greatest fraternal order on earth. It is the joy of linking oneself with the divine as an instrument of God's eternal solicitude for his sons and daughters.

42. *Whoever Causes One of These Little Ones . . . to Sin.*—The preceding verses, on the giving of a cup of cold water and the "receiving" of a child, dealt with the need for a positive ministry of help. In this verse we have the opposite, not help but hindrance. Here is vividly pictured the enormity of inflicting spiritual injury. The people called the **little ones**

are not children. They are the humble, without wealth or position or learning, those whom Jesus called "babes" (Matt. 11:25), who have accepted Christ's teaching, to whom spiritual understanding and faith have come. It was a class of people to whom Jesus was strongly drawn in affection, and from whom the first company of disciples, including the twelve, came. The great and learned, the scribes and Pharisees, rejected him. The little ones, as Jesus said, **believe in me.**

Jesus speaks with great vehemence, and the intensity of his words is a measure of the enormity of this sin of hindering. The danger for us lies in sidestepping the solemnity of his warning by a process of oversimplification. We may tell ourselves that the words **causes one of these little ones . . . to sin** mean such things as luring people into thievery or debauchery. We picture somebody like Fagin in *Oliver Twist,* an employer of pickpockets, a receiver of stolen goods, or a procurer, or a promoter of drunkenness, and easily say, "That doesn't apply to me." We are liable to forget that many of the characteristic sins of our day are social sins, which bring baleful results to multitudes of people, but for which no single individual is solely responsible. Yet our share in them is real. We have had our part in wronging literally generations of **these little ones** whom we may never even have seen.

Who caused the old epidemics of yellow fever and cholera? Everybody! All who contributed by their indifference, laziness, or cupidity to the creation of social conditions out of which the diseases came. Who caused the "lung blocks"

43 And if thy hand offend thee, cut it off: it is better for thee to enter into life maimed, than having two hands to go into hell, into the fire that never shall be quenched:

44 Where their worm dieth not, and the fire is not quenched.

into the sea. 43 And if your hand causes you to sin,[l] cut it off; it is better for you to enter life maimed than with two hands to go to hell,[m] to the unquenchable fire.[n]

[l] Or *stumble*.

[m] Greek *Gehenna*.

[n] Verses 44 and 46 (which are identical with verse 48) are omitted by the best ancient authorities.

43-48. The word σκανδαλίσῃ (causes . . . to sin, "makes . . . fall"—Goodspeed) in vs. 42 is the connecting link with the equally powerful warning that follows in this artfully arranged parallelistic series of verses. **Offend** is really "cause to offend" or "to fall," and the alternative is **enter into life** (=enter the kingdom of God, vs. 47) or **go** (or **be cast) into hell.** Gehenna (hell) was originally the valley southwest of Jerusalem, where Moloch worship was practiced (II Kings 23:10); it was now a symbolic name for the place of future punishment (I Enoch 27:2; II Esdras 7:36). **Hand, foot,** and **eye** are highly indispensable parts of the body; but it is better to part with them than to let them become occasions of sin, i.e., become the instruments of the sinful act. It is doubtful,

---

which used to take such fearful toll of human life by tuberculosis? Everybody! All were responsible who tolerated the traffic in death for profit made from disease-breeding tenements; all who were too lazy or careless to fight against the civic corruption which pocketed the profits. Who is responsible for the recurrence of war, with its injury not only to the bodies but to the souls of millions of **these little ones?** Everybody! All are responsible who made no contribution to the strengthening of public opinion which might somewhere along the line have effectively compelled action preventing war. One poet presses that communal guilt home in the question, "What did you do for peace, when peace was here?" We sin when we bring no challenge to a mounting liquor traffic, when we are indifferent to the lack of recreation which increases juvenile delinquency, indifferent to child labor or preventable poverty. In our interrelated world there is no innocent bystander.

43-48. *If Your Hand Causes You to Sin, Cut It Off.*—Jesus in this passage of six verses moves from warning of offenses against others to a warning, just as intense, about offenses against oneself. Entrance into the kingdom of God is so great a prize, so immeasurable a gain, that anything which might prevent that, no matter how good it may be in itself, should be ruthlessly sacrificed.

The principle of the sacrifice of the lesser good for the sake of the larger good is one that runs all through life. There is no realm of activity in which the wisdom of this command does not appear.

If the hand of the writer of prose or poetry causes him to sin, if an intricate technique becomes an end in itself, or an elaborate craftsmanship imprisons his thought in a cocoon of words, let him **cut it off.** If the hand or eye of

the preacher, his swelling oratory or labored rhetoric, hinders his message or hides his Master, let him **cut it off.** If the busy hand of the housewife is so feverishly occupied with the orderliness and spotless precision of the house that the home itself becomes secondary, let her **cut it off.** Life is more than meat, and a home is more than a house. Whenever the means displaces the end, make any sacrifice for the end.

Jesus applied this to the whole life of the mind and soul. Whatever hinders entrance into the kingdom is a fatal liability. There is a touching scene in the life of young Arthur Wellesley, who became the Duke of Wellington. On leaving home to begin his army career, he deliberately smashed his beloved violin to bits. That seems extreme and fanatical; but it showed the intensity with which he realized that no man can serve two masters. He had chosen one profession, not two. The choice of the kingdom must be that unanimous.

Certainly it calls for the sacrifice of what is obviously evil: the indulgence of gross appetite, the injury we do others, the sloth that does so easily enfold us. These call for a surgical operation, painful and costly, if life is to be saved.

But it is often the good which is the enemy of the best. Things not inherently evil in themselves become evil when they eclipse the sun of the kingdom. It is in this realm that spiritual sensitiveness and alertness to danger are needed. The accumulation of things, when it is not an equipment but a substitute for life, when it does not fall into its proper place as incidental stage setting but becomes the whole drama, is a diseased hand or eye to be cut off. A concern for social amenities, good in itself, may become an infection of the spirit, when the preoccupation with a small society blots out the great society of the whole family of God. Ambition

45 And if thy foot offend thee, cut it off: it is better for thee to enter halt into life, than having two feet to be cast into hell, into the fire that never shall be quenched:

46 Where their worm dieth not, and the fire is not quenched.

47 And if thine eye offend thee, pluck it out: it is better for thee to enter into the kingdom of God with one eye, than having two eyes to be cast into hell fire:

48 Where their worm dieth not, and the fire is not quenched.

49 For every one shall be salted with fire, and every sacrifice shall be salted with salt.

50 Salt *is* good: but if the salt have lost

45 And if your foot causes you to sin,[l] cut it off; it is better for you to enter life lame than with two feet to be thrown into hell.[m,n] **47** And if your eye causes you to sin,[l] pluck it out; it is better for you to enter the kingdom of God with one eye than with two eyes to be thrown into hell,[m] **48** where their worm does not die, and the fire is not quenched. **49** For every one will be salted with fire.[o] **50** Salt is good; but if the salt

[l] Or *stumble*.
[m] Greek *Gehenna*.
[n] Verses 44 and 46 (which are identical with verse 48) are omitted by the best ancient authorities.
[o] Many ancient authorities add *and every sacrifice will be salted with salt.*

on the basis of the MS evidence, if vss. 44 and 46 (KJV) are authentic; but from a literary point of view they are quite as appropriate as vs. 48 is. The early Christian who gave the series its present arrangement may very well have quoted Isa. 66:24 at the end of each of the three warnings. That the substance of the section goes back to Jesus is scarcely to be doubted. Cf. Matthew's use of the material in expanding the teaching on adultery (Matt. 5:29-30), including what the rabbis called "the adultery of the eyes."

25. SALT (9:49-50)

The mention of "fire" in vs. 48 suggests the thought here. RSV keeps only the first part of vs. 49, but many ancient authorities add the rest, as in KJV, though in a variety of forms, mostly based on Lev. 2:13. The connection of vs. 49*a* with what precedes is purely verbal, and its obscurity is indicated by the various forms of the gloss—as also by the efforts of commentators through the centuries. Does the verse mean that such sacrifices as vss. 43-48 describe symbolically are really acceptable to God, as well as being necessary for the preservation of the Christian's spiritual and moral integrity and for his ultimate salvation? Or is the whole verse a gloss? But its place in the series, as one link in the catena, seems assured. If the verse is a gloss, it may be derived from early Christian teaching in which, as often in the Apostolic Fathers, our Lord's sayings were combined with O.T. texts; in that case the glossator of vs. 49 may well have added vss. 44, 46, 48, also from the O.T. An Aramaic original, suggested by Torrey, runs, "Whatever would spoil, is salted" (Grant, *Earliest Gospel,* pp. 115-16).

50. Salt is good, i.e., both as a preservative and for seasoning (cf. Col. 4:6). **Lost its saltness:** Ancient salt, at least in Palestine, was not pure but mixed with other

and the lure of fame call for surgery if one is to seek first the kingdom of God. Sometimes the subtlest danger is nothing more vicious than the comfortable chair, symbol of ease and unconcern, that does not go with taking up a cross.

Courageous surgery for Christ's sake and for the sake of the life which is life indeed.

43. *It Is Better for You to Enter Life Maimed than with Two Hands to Go to Hell, to the Unquenchable Fire.*—Those words are admittedly difficult for multitudes of people today. Yet to dismiss them entirely with the reflection that they are in the language and thought forms which are no longer ours is to fail to deal honestly and frankly with the words.

The Exeg. says that the substance goes back to Jesus undoubtedly. At least this saying calls for a stress on the eternal validity of the distinction between good and evil, a distinction which is too often blurred when the idea of the eternal consequences of evil-doing drops out of man's thinking. We cannot set arbitrary limits to the pursuing love of God. As someone has said, "No soul is lost until God has thrown arms about it in eternity and looked long into its eyes." Yet the fearful possibility of ultimate refusal remains.

50. *Salt Is Good; but if the Salt Has Lost Its Saltness, How Will You Season It?*—This is one of the comparisons of Jesus, so apt, so in

his saltness, wherewith will ye season it? | has lost its saltness, how will you season it?
Have salt in yourselves, and have peace one | Have salt in yourselves, and be at peace
with another. | with one another."

10 And he arose from thence, and cometh into the coasts of Judea by the farther side of Jordan: and the people re- | **10** And he left there and went to the region of Judea and beyond the Jordan, and crowds gathered to him again;

---

ingredients, such as sand. If the saline quality was too low, nothing could restore it. But **season it** may mean, "With what will you season whatever needs salt?" i.e., "What will you do for salt?" (Cf. Luke 14:35.) Both Luke and Matthew (5:13) introduce the saying into other contexts, though they agree more or less in what they add to it. If not from Q, it was probably a detached saying, circulating freely in the oral tradition of Jesus' words. Both parallels omit vs. 50*b*, which is probably editorial, and refers back to vss. 33-34.

III. JESUS IN JERUSALEM (10:1–15:47)
A. ON THE WAY TO JERUSALEM (10:1-52)
1. MARRIAGE AND DIVORCE (10:1-12)

This section marks the beginning of a new division in the Gospel, as both Matthew and Luke recognize, though "Perean Ministry" is a misnomer for Luke's long insertion of non-Marcan material (Luke 9:51–18:14). But as we have already observed, the disciple-

---

accord with universal experience, that the force of its point is undebatable. He was talking to people who knew salt. Some were fishermen to whom it was a necessity of their trade, a daily indispensable, a preservative. It was good for only one quality. When that quality was gone, it was of no earthly use. Jesus' comparison is pressed with an inescapable directness and sharpness. When the disciple loses his saltness, when he loses the good news of the kingdom out of his message and out of his life, he is of no earthly use.

What Jesus said of his immediate disciples is true of all his disciples, individually and collectively. There is no need to labor so obvious a point, except to ask ourselves to partake of the sacrament of remembrance, and recall how many times in Christian history, in the contemporary life of the church, and in our own experience, there has been that neutral, insipid, useless thing—salt without saltness.

Christians who have lost their Christian flavor cannot perform their function as a preserving force in the world. As one man put it to the church bluntly and even brutally a few years ago, in a time of acute crisis, "If you have anything peculiarly Christian to say at this hour, for God's sake say it! If you have nothing to say but the echo of what is heard on every street corner and in every luncheon club in the land, for God's sake keep still!"

When Christians and the Christian church have lost the gospel of love, and unreservedly pronounced their blessing on carnage and violence, on things utterly opposed to Jesus' teaching and life, they have lost their saltness.

When the church has denied the law of greatness through service, intent on drawing to itself power and advantage and prestige, instead of going out in ministry, it is fit to be trodden under foot, like salt mixed with so much sand that its saltness is gone. When the "fellowship of kindred minds," this very body of Christ, becomes a mere appendage to a class or a social order or an economic theory, and does not stand on its own feet confonting the world with the gospel of its Lord, it is of no earthly and of no heavenly use. Think of the years during which multitudes of Christians stood in shameful silence before the sin of slavery and before the slaughter of the innocents by a ruthless industrialism which was a kind of pagan god demanding human sacrifice.

But individuals too lose their saltness, their tang of Christian quality. They lose it when humility gives way to self-assertion; when there is no sign of the Cross in their life, no stigmata on mind or spirit; when they grow so unbearably "sweet" in disposition and judgment that they see no monstrous wrong, or seeing it do not feel impelled to struggle against it; when nothing indicates, as they enter into a situation, that a truly new factor, a Christian standard of judgment or a Christian spirit of behavior, has now become part of the reckoning.

50. Have Salt in Yourselves, and Be at Peace with One Another.—This sentence has been difficult both for translators and interpreters. Yet one universal truth is clear. Unless we have the salt of the Christian gospel we will not be at peace, either in the church or in the world at large.

sort unto him again; and, as he was wont, he taught them again.

2 ¶ And the Pharisees came to him, and asked him, Is it lawful for a man to put away *his* wife? tempting him.

3 And he answered and said unto them, What did Moses command you?

4 And they said, Moses suffered to write a bill of divorcement, and to put *her* away.

and again, as his custom was, he taught them.

2 And Pharisees came up and in order to test him asked, "Is it lawful for a man to divorce his wife?" 3 He answered them, "What did Moses command you?" 4 They said, "Moses allowed a man to write a certificate of divorce, and to put her away."

---

ship sayings partly overlap the new division; the "way of the Cross" is not only the disciples' but Jesus' own—and literally, for he is now en route to Jerusalem, where he is to be put to death.

10:1. The region of Judea and beyond the Jordan means, in addition to Judea, Perea, or in modern topography Trans-Jordan. This is the reading of the older MSS; the later read "by" (KJV) instead of "and," probably influenced by Matthew, who thinks of the region beyond Jordan (i.e., to the east) as belonging to Judea. **There (thence)** means Capernaum (9:33). **He taught them,** as in 6:34; Matthew says that he healed them.

2. Pharisees, his usual opponents and "tempters," try again to trip him up. To the question **Is it lawful for a man to divorce his wife?** Matt. 19:3 adds "for any cause"; and this has often been thought to show that the question was one of current scribal debate—the school of Shammai was very strict in interpreting the "shameful thing" (*'erwath dābhār*) of Deut. 24:1 to mean infidelity, while that of Hillel was more lenient, and allowed divorce for even trivial offenses, e.g., "burning the bread." But in reality Mark's form of the question is more sweeping. Matthew's "any cause" is related to his "exceptions" in Matt. 19:9 and 5:32, which may possibly be no more than technical legal provisions in line with Deut. 22:13-30. The penalty for adultery was not divorce, under the Mosaic code, but death.

The following controversy is in form like those in 2:1–3:6, etc., and is possibly from the same source (except vss. 10-12).

3-4. Command you, i.e., to do in such a case. The fact that Moses *ordered* a **certificate of divorce** to be given the woman so that she was free to marry again—in its time a provision of mercy—proved that it *was* lawful to put away one's wife, at least for some cause or causes; but Jesus' questioners soften the phrase: he "permitted" this practice.

10:2-12. *And Pharisees Came Up and in Order to Test Him Asked, "Is It Lawful for a Man to Divorce His Wife?"*—Millions of people, not Pharisees, have asked the same question, and will continue to ask it. What becomes manifest at once in Jesus' handling of the subject is that the adequate answer can never be a legal enactment or any kind of casuistry, but must come from lifting the question up to the level of great spiritual and religious principles.

Christ's teaching on divorce, both here and elsewhere in the Synoptic Gospels, has for centuries been a battlefield for contending views and interpretations, and will doubtless continue to be. Yet if we come to his words, not to find support for positions previously reached, but honestly to learn his mind and spirit in the matter, he will furnish us a lamp for our feet.

Three main things emerge from a study of these twelve verses:

1. Jesus transferred the whole discussion from the realm of **is it lawful?** into the higher realm of the purposes of God, and the moral and spiritual realities of the marriage relationship.

2. He laid profound emphasis on the permanence and sanctity of marriage.

3. The passage provides an impressive picture of the towering greatness of Jesus as a champion of women. He looked on them not as chattels but as people. That appears in all his contacts with them and in his sayings concerning them. Against the customs of his time, against the prevalence of the idea of male dominance which runs through Hebrew thought and practice, he gave to his nation and to the world a new conception of women as persons equal with men in the sight of God.

Moreover, he showed great courage in answering this question as he did. It was asked for the purpose of trapping him into saying something that could be turned into an indictment against him, and he knew it. The Pharisees wanted to

5 And Jesus answered and said unto them, For the hardness of your heart he wrote you this precept.

6 But from the beginning of the creation God made them male and female.

7 For this cause shall a man leave his father and mother, and cleave to his wife;

8 And they twain shall be one flesh: so then they are no more twain, but one flesh.

5 But Jesus said to them, "For your hardness of heart he wrote you this commandment. 6 But from the beginning of creation, 'God made them male and female.' 7 'For this reason a man shall leave his father and mother and be joined to his wife,ᵖ 8 and the two shall become one.'ᑫ So they are

ᵖ Some ancient authorities omit *and be joined to his wife.*
ᑫ Greek *one flesh.*

5-9. Their formulation of the answer plays into Jesus' hands: It *was* a concession, made because of **your hardness of heart;** but from the beginning of creation God intended one man and one woman to be husband and wife—**one flesh** is simply Semitic or biblical idiom for **one,** as in RSV—and this not only rules out polygamy but also divorce. The freedom allowed the man, not the woman, in divorcing the other partner was contrary to the divine intention—which must be the highest principle in all interpretation of the divine law. Jesus here criticizes the law itself—as in ch. 7 he criticized the food regulations, and in 2:23–3:5 the too-rigid interpretation of the sabbath law—but from the point of view of the purpose of the supreme Lawgiver. Jesus' conception of later concession is somewhat like Paul's conception of the relation of the law to the promise to Abraham (e.g., in Gal. 3–4). Such later developments were thoroughly consonant with the biblical idea of God's adaptation of his general purposes to immediate circumstances and needs—a purely religious idea, not a philosophical one. This distinction between intention and concession has usually been overlooked in canon law, since Jesus' words in this section have, as a rule, been taken quite unfairly as setting forth new legislation.

An example of an eleventh-century Jewish divorce certificate is given by Strack and Billerbeck (I, 311; Klostermann, p. 111): "On . . . [date], I, . . . [name], son of . . . and of . . . , of my own free will and purpose and without any coercion whatsoever, do divorce, set free, and repudiate you, . . . [name], so that you are now free and in full possession of your own person, with the right to go and be married to whomever you choose. . . ."

---

get him publicly to assert his authority against that of Moses. There was no hesitation. He seems to have said to himself: "All right. They have asked for it. Let them have it plainly." And he did. Except that instead of setting his own individual authority over the law of Moses, he set over it the purpose of God in creation and the divine ordaining of marriage. From this standpoint he criticized the law itself, as he had previously criticized the laws of food regulation and of the sabbath (2:23–3:6; 7:1-23. See Exeg.).

His principle of judgment was the same, that human and spiritual values are to be set above specific regulations. He saw the cruelty and injustices of the law of divorce in the regulation which the Pharisees quoted from Deut. 24:1-4. He saw how it violated God's purpose in the marriage relationship. To him this permission of Moses, making divorce easy, and resulting in cruel injustice, was a case of man-made tradition in violation of the commandment of God.

Against such an "accommodation" he laid tremendous emphasis on the fundamental principle of the permanence of marriage. It was an emphasis needed in his day—and desperately

needed in ours, when in the United States one marriage in three ends in divorce. Jesus unfailingly put his finger on the central moral and spiritual issue in every question submitted to him, lifting that up as the dominating factor. He does it here. Marriage is not a matter of man's temporary convenience or pleasure, but of God's holy purpose. There is a spiritual as well as a physical union of man and woman. It is this divine intent which has made marriage a permanent relationship.

And surely part of its essential nature is in its permanence. When it drops to the level of a money-back-if-not-satisfied purchase, or a thirty-day trial offer of a bargain, as it has with so many, it ceases to be marriage at its true potential. With no sense of its august and solemn finality, with no facing and accepting of that closing of doors, "till death do us part," the man and woman will not bring to it the attitudes and dedications necessary. Without that element of finality the security of the home is gone, the social fabric is torn, and the finest school on earth for the discipline and growth of character is on the way out.

Consider the words **so they are no longer two**

9 What therefore God hath joined together, let not man put asunder.

10 And in the house his disciples asked him again of the same *matter.*

11 And he saith unto them, Whosoever shall put away his wife, and marry another, committeth adultery against her.

12 And if a woman shall put away her husband, and be married to another, she committeth adultery.

no longer two but one.*q* **9** What therefore God has joined together, let not man put asunder."

10 And in the house the disciples asked him again about this matter. **11** And he said to them, "Whoever divorces his wife and marries another, commits adultery against her; **12** and if she divorces her husband and marries another, she commits adultery."

q Greek *one flesh.*

Jesus' protest is leveled against the cruelty of men in thus divorcing their wives (cf. Mal. 2:13-16) and also against their perverse disregard of the purpose of the Creator when he formed man of the dust and joined husband and wife, i.e., instituted human marriage. **What** (not "those whom," as in the Prayer Book) **therefore God hath joined together** is **the one** of vs. 8, the new union formed by the pair.

10-12. Again (as in 4:10, 34; 7:17; 9:28; 10:23; 13:3) a private discourse introduces new and relevant material, in this case the saying, perhaps from Q, which formulates the rule for Christians. Luke omits the whole of this section (vss. 1-12), though there is a parallel in Luke 16:18; while Matthew not only abridges here and adds the strange sayings in Matt. 19:10-12, but also has a wider ranging variant in Matt. 5:32, which makes the husband responsible for the later conduct of the wife. Both Matthew and Luke omit Mark 10:12; and there can be little doubt that the rule has received this formulation with reference to Greco-Roman conditions, i.e., the environment of the early Gentile church, where women were legally in a position to divorce their husbands, something unknown in Jewish law. **Against her** is superfluous and ambiguous: Which woman is meant? Presumably the former, who is still his wife; but the parallels all lack it—and so

---

but one. That is God's arithmetic; fantastic when one comes to think about it—"one plus one equals one." Yes, but it is a fantasy which has become factual in millions of lives. As someone has described it truthfully, marriage is an institution in which there are one master and one mistress and two slaves, making, all in all, two. That "one plus one equals one" ideal, the high and rich human achievement, can be a realized ideal; such a fusing of lives as is beautifully pictured in the tribute paid to Canon and Mrs. Barnett of Toynbee Hall: "These two shone in the gray twilight of Whitechapel like two flaming spirits bound into one fierce blazing torch." [7] They had lifted up their love into the clear white light of God's purpose for them.

In the light of all this it would seem quite obvious that training for marriage is essential. Marriage and the home are tests of character, and no childish mentality can ever pass the test. Neither can the self-centered individualist. When adult infants marry, when the boy looking for a mother marries the girl looking for a father, the crash comes.

But what shall we say about Jesus' forbidding

[7] Esmé Wingfield-Stratford, *The Victorian Sunset* (London: George Routledge & Sons, 1932).

divorce under any circumstances? For the evidence is strong that Mark's form of Jesus' words, without the exception of adultery as just cause (Matt. 19:9), is the original form.

One thing to be kept in the foreground of thought, large and clear, is that Jesus was not establishing another legalism. He fought all his life against crowding the spiritual into statutory regulations. We do violence to the whole spirit and mind of Jesus if we conceive him, as has often been done and is done still, to be a newer and greater Pharisee, the enactor of further ironclad codes. To all who make off at that tangent Jesus' words are pertinent: "Have I been with you so long, and yet you do not know me?" (John 14:9.) He was teaching here in his usual manner, with sweeping phrase and vigor. His interest was primarily in great positive truths, in ultimate humanitarianism and spiritual values, not in lists of exceptions, which the scribes so dearly loved. If he had not spoken in that fashion, he would never have made the deep impression that he did.

Another thing to be kept in mind is the uncertainty of the text (see Exeg.). We know that this word of Jesus was "accommodated" to apply to the practice of Rome, where a wife could secure a divorce, a proceeding which was

13 ¶ And they brought young children to him, that he should touch them; and *his* disciples rebuked those that brought *them*.	13 And they were bringing children to him, that he might touch them; and the

does vs. 12, which ought in consistency to read "against him." The offense is serious enough in itself without any stress on the crime against the partner, for it is in reality a breach of the seventh commandment (Exod. 20:14). The severe earnestness with which the early Christians took this rule is clearly reflected in later literature; some of the ancient writers went so far as to forbid second marriages even after the death of the first partner.

2. BLESSING THE CHILDREN (10:13-16)

13-16. This beautiful little episode, expressing an attitude so unlike the academic rabbinical attitude toward women and children, and yet so characteristically Jewish, can scarcely have been invented. Jesus is asked to **touch** the children—not necessarily **young,**

not allowed among the Jews. What other influences have gone into the present form of the text no one can say exactly. At any rate its authenticity and exactness are not sure enough to serve as an unbreakable rule for all time and all situations.

But there is something else far more important to remember—Jesus himself. He is often the tragically forgotten man in all the legalistic discussions of marriage and divorce. As stressed above, we mangle Jesus out of his true shape when we make him a new legalist, a new chief of the scribes, laying down inflexible codes. These words must be set in the context of the whole mind of Christ as revealed so clearly in the N.T. We must remember his forthright affirmation that institutions are made for man, and not man for the institution. We must remember his boundless sympathy with people. With that in mind, when the spiritual conception of marriage is made impossible, when brutality and cruelty put a blight on life, when the future possibilities and character of children hang in the balance, then to make Jesus the inflexible legalist is to distort beyond recognition this image of the Son of man who lives and speaks in the Gospels.

13. And They Were Bringing Children to Him, . . . and the Disciples Rebuked Them.—Here again are the rebuking disciples! What remarkable skill they had in missing the spirit of Jesus! No wonder so many sighs of impatience and weariness escape from him, as in 9:19, "How long am I to bear with you?" They rarely seem to miss an opportunity. And, as noted above, the things for which they rebuked Jesus, or for which, as in this narrative, they rebuked others, were words or actions which have become supreme contributions to the world's life and thought. We may ask in bewilderment, "How could they be with Christ so continuously, seeing what he cared about most, hearing his

words, and still fail so dismally to understand him?" The answer is easy, though embarrassing. It is: "Here is a mirror. Look into it. That will help you fathom the mystery of their retarded minds" (see 9:32). All through the years, even among Jesus' professed disciples, there have been stern rebukes for those who have sought to bring little children to Jesus, struggling to claim a share for them in his heritage of love. The discovery of the child as a person, with "certain inalienable rights," has been a long, tragically slow process, and in many places has scarcely begun (see on 9:37). When in the midst of neglect and exploitation some sentinel souls of insight, sympathy, and imagination, pleaded for the divine rights of children, how often and bitterly they were rebuked by the society in which they lived. Parts of the Christian church have had their own "Dark Ages," during which, so far from bringing children to the arms of Jesus, and recognizing that God's love encompassed them, they regarded such at least as were unbaptized to be fit candidates for infant damnation. Horace Bushnell should be held in everlasting remembrance for his *Christian Nurture,* which in a very real way put the child into God's family and recovered for the church the almost lost memory of this story of Jesus and his blessing of little children.

Cruel rebukes are still administered to those who plead and work for the children of oppressed peoples, for the children of minority groups who are denied equal advantages in education with the children of majorities, for children still fed into the maw of industry. What violent protest multitudes in the United States made against the proposal, after World War II, to bring to America some of the displaced orphans of Europe! The danger of being among "the rebukers" comes close home. When a Christian organization regards its church school as a sort of bothersome stepchild, toler-

14 But when Jesus saw *it,* he was much displeased, and said unto them, Suffer the little children to come unto me, and forbid them not; for of such is the kingdom of God.

14 But when Jesus saw it he was indignant, and said to them, "Let the children come to me, do not hinder them; for to such belongs the kingdom of

---

disciples rebuked them.

as in KJV, based on a harmonization with Luke 18:15—even as he was asked to touch the sick, presumably because some special blessing was expected from the contact. This seemed to the disciples only an annoyance, and so they **rebuked those that brought them;**

---

ated grudgingly and of necessity, rating far below the real importance of adult concerns, it rebukes those who would bring young children to Jesus, and at the same time shows itself fatally blind to its own greatest wealth and power.

14. *But When Jesus Saw It He Was Indignant.*—If we wish to know what things Jesus cared deeply about, one sure clue is to be found in the things that roused his indignation. These occasions are to be found principally in Mark, for Mark does not hesitate to say that Jesus was angry, a word toned down in Matthew and Luke. On the whole in Mark's record, when Jesus was angry or indignant, it was over a wrong done to people, or over some blindness to human welfare. He was angry at the Pharisees because of their loveless indifference to human need, the callousness which set tradition higher in their regard than mercy. Here he is indignant because of the officious blindness that tried to keep children away from his blessing, the spiritual obtuseness that attempted to block their way.

This matter of the indignations of Jesus throws a clear light on his spiritual greatness. He never showed indignation over personal affronts. All through the scourging and crucifixion "opened he not his mouth." The only reference he made to his executioners was, "Father, forgive them." It is a humbling experience to compare his indignations with our own. What most quickly rouses ours as a rule is some injury done us, real or fancied, some slight, some rejection. Then we blaze like a freshly lighted fire. While many of us continue to look out on evils that engulf vast numbers, or on injustices that cry to the skies, with undisturbed equanimity.

Keeping in view this indignation of Jesus over his disciples' blindness to the worth of a child, imagine what would stir his wrath if he walked up and down the streets of our world today; particularly if he traveled its back alleys. We may be sure that he would see things to which familiarity has made many of us indifferent. Go with him on such a journey, and not in fancy only; for he does indeed walk our streets. He would be indignant over the fencing-off of

elementary rights from multitudes of what we call "underprivileged" children; over our limp acceptance of the preventable poverty which condemns them not only to suffering, but often to maiming of soul; over our toleration of all the vicious forces that prey on them. The final judgments on our society will be those made by children; for the Christian test of a society is what it does to children (9:37). A needed daily prayer is this: "God grant us the indignations of Jesus."

14. *Let the Children Come to Me, Do Not Hinder Them.*—A word to look at carefully—this word **hinder.** It is so much more insidious than the word used in the KJV—**forbid.** We can easily escape condemnation in that word "forbid." Who would forbid a child's coming to Jesus? None of us! The word suggests active, conscious, deliberate obstruction. But the word "hinder" is not so easy to throw off. For the hindering may be unconscious; it may come simply from neglect to take some positive action. In our own homes we may hinder children from coming. We can do it by making Christ unattractive through our own example. We can do it by making evident from our manner that we do not consider him tremendously important compared to other interests. We can do it simply by neglect of the child's religious life.

We can also hinder the children of a community, a nation, and a world by our lack of interest in the church, the means by which they may be brought into contact with Christ and his teaching. Our slippered ease on Sunday, our drives down the fairway, when these are substitutes for a concern about the spiritual forces of our community, block the way of children. We do what we can to stunt their spiritual growth when our attitudes on social and political questions are shaped by considerations of our own advantage, or when we see all questions darkly through the glass of a narrow, political partisanship. For in such ways conditions that create or perpetuate juvenile delinquency are brought about. Jesus said, directly and solemnly, **do not hinder them.**

14-16. *Whoever Does Not Receive the Kingdom of God Like a Child Shall Not Enter It.*—In childhood Jesus found the perfect analogy

15 Verily **I** say unto you, Whosoever shall not receive the kingdom of God as a little child, he shall not enter therein.

16 And he took them up in his arms, put *his* hands upon them, and blessed them.

God. **15** Truly, I say to you, whoever does not receive the kingdom of God like a child shall not enter it." **16** And he took them in his arms and blessed them, laying his hands upon them.

---

there is no hint that they thought the motive superstitious. **Of such is the kingdom of God:** Children are examples of dependence and receptiveness—not necessarily of humility, as in 9:36, as understood by Matthew (18:2-4). Here, unlike 9:37, and unlike what the context suggests here, it is not the receiving of a child but the receiving of the kingdom that is emphasized (vs. 15; cf. John 3:3, 5). It is quite possible that what Mark has done is to insert one of the discipleship sayings—from the series already noted—into the anecdote, which originally ran as vss. 13, 14, 16. But the relevance of vs. 15 in the present context is indubitable. Much of Jesus' ministry was concerned with awakening men to responsiveness; much of the opposition to him came from those who lacked imagination, receptivity, and the childlike capacity to *act* at once upon what they understood—held fast as they were in their adult skepticisms and misgivings.

Some have thought the section especially appropriate after 10:2-12, but it is doubtful that this occurred to Mark.

---

for membership in the kingdom of God. "Look at this child in my arms," he says, "to such belongs the kingdom." They already have the spirit of its citizens. The context, especially the phrase **receive the kingdom,** makes clear what the characteristics are which distinguish those who truly enter it. The marks of the child which are stressed are dependence and receptivity. Without these no one can enter. With them one is already a member. Note that the qualities of mind frequently cited in discussion of this passage—innocence and humility—are not indicated here (see Exeg.). Innocence and humility do appear in children, but they are not an unfailing mark. Every parent knows that the "innocence of childhood" is often a beautiful myth. Parents can at times understand the baffled mood of a father of young children who said playfully, "Since having two children, I can understand better how the idea of total depravity arose, and can even look with an open mind on the doctrine of infant damnation." Nor is the child always humble, in the full sense of that word.

But the child is dependent. He looks to the parent for all that he receives. He has no sense of achieving things himself. It is all a gift. So, Jesus says, must be the mind and spirit of one who receives the kingdom of God. This looks very simple, but it goes deep and is far-reaching. One cannot receive the kingdom if there are pride and self-righteousness in the mind and heart. The Pharisees with their self-conscious goodness, their spiritual arrogance, could not receive it. No one can receive it with arms thrown wide whose religion has any trace of the "Look at me, I did it" spirit. The sense of superiority, hardness, lack of sympathy, qualities which have often marked religious people, keeps one from receiving the kingdom at all. That is why this narrative, so beautiful and touching, universally acclaimed as one of the loveliest stories in the N.T., is also in its implications one of the most challenging and disturbing. It was an invitation to children. It was also a rebuke to pride and self-righteousness. Menzies points out that the acquisition of the qualities of the child's spirit may be a very difficult thing for adults, "as it may involve changing fixed habits of thought and abjuring worldly standards of judgment and modes of action."[8] In a word, it involves repentance, getting a new mind.

Note also another mark of the child spirit which is a mark of the kingdom (see Exeg.). It is that of spontaneity, of impulse, "the capacity to act at once" on what they understand. The impulse is not strangled by calculation and cautious skepticisms. Jesus always welcomed the spontaneous impulse, as in Peter's confession, and the woman's breaking of the alabaster box of precious ointment. That is indispensable to the enterprise of the kingdom. Talleyrand once said profoundly, even though cynically, "Distrust first impulses. They are nearly always right." True! It is the checking of childlike spontaneity which has frustrated so much Christian achievement. There is evangelical wisdom in the remark, "Don't look before you leap. If you do, you will decide to sit down." One finds throughout Christian history far too much calculated, skeptical looking, and far too little leaping. Let this mind be in you which is also in a little child (see on vs. 50). **For to such belongs the kingdom of God.**

[8] *Earliest Gospel,* p. 191.

17 ¶ And when he was gone forth into the way, there came one running, and kneeled to him, and asked him, Good Master, what shall I do that I may inherit eternal life?

18 And Jesus said unto him, Why callest thou me good? *there is* none good but one, *that is,* God.

17 And as he was setting out on his journey, a man ran up and knelt before him, and asked him, "Good Teacher, what must I do to inherit eternal life?" 18 And Jesus said to him, "Why do you call me good? No one is good but God alone.

---

3. The Meaning of Discipleship (10:17-31)
(a) The Rich Young Man (10:17-22)

The next three sections deal once more with discipleship: a would-be disciple, and the requirement of renunciation (vss. 17-22); the danger of riches (vss. 23-27), illustrated by the incident just related; and the reward of renunciation (vss. 28-31). All three are undoubtedly relevant to the situation of the author and his readers, as the conclusion (vss. 29-31) makes clear.

17. **As he was setting out on his journey:** The man came in haste, before it was too late, and possibly with the expectation that he would be asked to follow Jesus on his way. He is a "young" man only in Matt. 19:20; he is a "ruler," i.e., an important man in the community, in Luke 18:18; both descriptions are simply inferences from the Marcan story itself. In the Gospel According to the Hebrews he is called "another rich man" (Origen, on Matt. 15:14; it was there a most interesting anecdote; see the translation in M. R. James, *Apocryphal New Testament,* p. 6; text in Huck-Lietzmann-Cross, *Synopsis of the First Three Gospels* [Tübingen: J. C. B. Mohr, 1936], p. 145). **Kneeled** (cf. 1:40): An act of profound reverence, showing the man's complete sincerity; he was not "tempting" Jesus. **Inherit eternal life**=enter the kingdom of God.

18. **Why do you call me good?** This question shows the primitive character of the story; later theology found it a problem, which Matthew solved by changing to "Why do you ask me about what is good?" and Origen by reference to John 14:28c. Still later theologians interpreted it otherwise: "If you call me good, you imply that I am God"—but this is wholly impossible, both in the original setting and for Mark. Such identification came later. The perfect goodness of God was a universal doctrine of Judaism (cf. Ps. 145:9). Jesus has the natural attitude toward God of every pious and devout Jew.

---

17. *Good Teacher, What Must I Do to Inherit Eternal Life?*—Mark carefully that word "do" in the question of this young man. It is a pivot around which Jesus' teaching turns, both here and elsewhere. For this word "do" represents one of the greatest and most persistent fallacies in religion and ethics, from the power of which, with its crippling effects, Jesus sought to release men. The conception that salvation, or life in its largest religious sense, is something that can be won by "doing" any one thing, or a number of things, is completely false. The young man was on the wrong road, and that was part of what Jesus told him. He was looking for some simple, possibly new, prescription, some act to be done, or series of acts, which would be the end of all his search. Eternal life, the kingdom of God, cannot be won by "doing." It comes of a spirit which informs the whole man, an inwardness of character which springs from one's relation to God. Jesus' ethics are emphatically and completely religious ethics. Filial conduct must spring from the fact that we are sons of our heavenly Father. Otherwise the religious life can dwindle into "an ethical concern which is often mean." The spiritual life is not a matter of bookkeeping, in which good acts are entered on the credit side of some celestial ledger. The tough persistence of the idea of God as a heavenly bookkeeper, forever engaged in striking a trial balance between this act and that act, has been one of the great liabilities of Christianity (see on 9:41). It completely distorts the teaching of Jesus. He said, "Whoever loses his life for my sake and the gospel's will save it" (8:35). That, in essence, was the prescription he gave here. We inherit eternal life by being lifted up out of ourselves by a devotion to God so great that it will snap all chains which hold us back from sonship to him in spirit and act.

18. *Why Do You Call Me Good? No One Is Good but God Alone.*—This word of Jesus has always been a hard one for theologians. Here

19 Thou knowest the commandments, Do not commit adultery, Do not kill, Do not steal, Do not bear false witness, Defraud not, Honor thy father and mother.

19 You know the commandments: 'Do not kill, Do not commit adultery, Do not steal, Do not bear false witness, Do not defraud,

19. **The commandments:** Later rabbis insisted that all 613 commandments in the Torah were equally binding and equally important, but this did not alter the fact that the "Ten Words" were basic to the whole law. It is noteworthy that Jesus cites only the second table (duty to neighbor—the point stressed in the version in the Gospel According to the Hebrews). **Defraud not** (cf. Jas. 5:4) has been taken to be a summary statement of the ninth and tenth commandments (Klostermann), or a quotation from the "Galilean" form of the Decalogue (Lohmeyer); but cf. Lev. 19:13; Deut. 24:14. Jesus does not say, and it must not be assumed, that he is referring only to the Ten Commandments (cf. 12:28-31).

we need only direct attention to the conclusion in Exeg. that Jesus was not giving a theological dogma, but "expressing the natural attitude toward God of every pious and devout Jew."

There are, however, in the words two things of universal importance for life. One is Jesus' rejection of conventional flattery, for that was an element, at least, in the salutation "Good Teacher." Jesus would have none of it. Flattery is a deadly drug, and unless we become spiritually immune to it by humility before God, it can infect the whole of life with a fatal illness.

The other thing is Jesus' reiteration here that all goodness has its source in God. This remembrance will arm us against the subtle assaults of pride and spiritual complacency.

19-22. The Way into the Kingdom.—Jesus' conversation not only furnishes a prescription given for a specific need, but also reveals general principles of universal application concerning the way into the kingdom, the means of the saving and fulfilling of life. Moreover it makes as clear as can be seen anywhere the difference between Christianity and conventional moralism, a difference which is all too often obscured.

19. You Know the Commandments: Do Not Kill, Do Not Commit Adultery, Do Not Steal.—This is an obvious answer made to a sincere and direct if misguided question. The Ten Commandments were the basic requirements of the law, and in observing them the conditions adequate for salvation would be fulfilled. Jesus cites the second table of the Decalogue. He mentions those commandments which have a claim on all men, those dealing with human relations generally, omitting everything relating exclusively to Jewish nationalism or ritual.

Thus far we have, of course, only a beginning. Further exploration will follow. Jesus has more to offer as a way into life than a commonplace injunction to obey the Jewish law. Yet it is extremely unfortunate that this first part of his answer has not been more carefully studied and remembered by all Christians. For so the terrible excesses and perversions of Christian teaching by a lawless antinomianism might have been avoided. Many have been so obsessed with the idea of freedom from the law that they have run off into moral anarchy, under the tragic delusion that license is freedom. Christian love to God and man is not a substitute for the law. It is the fulfillment of the law. The moral commandments of the Decalogue were included in all that Jesus taught. They were given a new inwardness and range, and carried into the realm of motivation (Matt. 5:21-28). They were not abrogated. Too many people have regarded themselves as being beyond morality, when in truth they have hardly even reached the primary stages. A person can miss the essence of Christianity as completely by minimizing moral commandments as he can by identifying Christianity with conventional morality.

Jesus, however, in pointing the way to the kingdom of God, goes far beyond the requirements of the law. It is as though he said: "Observing the law will make you an upright, decent citizen of Israel. But if you would be my disciple, you lack something." That is a vital distinction often overlooked. It has been a source of immense weakness in the church that so many of its members have been upright, decent citizens, but have never gone on to become disciples of Jesus, with his peculiar flavor of love and the self-giving that counts not its life dear to itself. The definitions of the word "Christian" in Webster's dictionary make the point clear. One of the definitions is, ironically enough, "a decent, civilized, or presentable person." God save the mark! It is the definition that all too many Christians accept—then try to live up to it! On that level, for those who fail to see the heights beyond, or to attempt them, Jesus' words are relevant: "You lack one thing."

20 And he answered and said unto him, Master, all these have I observed from my youth.

21 Then Jesus beholding him loved him, and said unto him, One thing thou lackest: go thy way, sell whatsoever thou hast, and

Honor your father and mother.'" 20 And he said to him, "Teacher, all these I have observed from my youth." 21 And Jesus looking upon him loved him, and said to

---

20. Master: He now drops the epithet "good." **Observed**=both guarded and kept in all good conscience. Philo insists that the Jew was the most conscientious man in the world; at the same time, as the rabbis held, it was thought perfectly possible for a man to keep the whole law—Paul's troubled conscience was unknown to them, and would doubtless have seemed pathological. **From my youth,** presumably since he became a *bar miçwāh* about the age of twelve and assumed adult responsibility for observing the whole of Torah. But children, then as now, were taught the elements of their religion almost from infancy, and the elements certainly included the Decalogue (cf. Deut. 6:7).

21. One thing thou lackest, the self-sacrificing devotion of every true disciple. Luke takes it in that sense (Luke 18:22); but Matthew has "If you would be perfect" (Matt.

20-21. *And He Said to Him, "Teacher, All These I Have Observed from My Youth." And Jesus . . . Loved Him.*—Jesus' instantaneous love may well have sprung partly from his quick vision of the man's possibilities. Jesus saw people with a double eye. He saw what they were, and he saw what they might be. So it was that he saw Peter, not only as an actual fisherman, but as a potential fisher of men. This man of sincerity and faithfulness, giving evidence of a reaching out for more than he had experienced, was wonderful material for a disciple. The potential was high. So Jesus loved him with a creative love, with a vision of what he might be, and said, **Come, follow me.** Here again, as in the call of Peter and Andrew, of James and John and Levi, the question presses home to us: Do we look at people as Jesus did, with a vision of their unrealized potentialities, or do we look out on them with glazed eyes, like unimaginative Peter Bell?

> A primrose by a river's brim
> A yellow primrose was to him,
> And it was nothing more.[9]

The yearning look in this passage may perhaps serve as the representation or symbol of a great evangelistic opportunity. There is a true parallel between this young man and multitudes of people in our world today. He was dissatisfied with life as he had lived it. His question showed that he was sensitive to the possibility that there was something beyond what he had experienced. He was reaching out for something more. He did not know what it was, and he was certainly surprised when Jesus told him what was missing. But at least there was restless discontent, always a magnificent opportunity for declaring the way of salvation. Edwin

[9] Wordsworth, "Peter Bell, a Tale."

Arlington Robinson has well expressed the sense of that "something lacking" in Jewish legalism. He puts these words into the mouth of Nicodemus, talking to Caiaphas:

> There is no life in those old laws of ours, Caiaphas; they are forms and rules and fears, So venerable and impressive and majestic That we forget how little there is in them For us to love.[1]

The discontent which provides us with our greatest opportunity is not likely to be discontent with a legal code but rather with a whole way of life. It can be felt in full force during such periods of disillusionment as that which so strongly characterized American life in the first half of the twentieth century. Marvelous though scientific and industrial advance had been, it did not fulfill the promises held out for it. At such times the mood of the public is much like the conviction of sin in Christian experience. The question mark became flesh and dwelt among us: "Have we been on the right road? Have we? Is a way of life which in twenty-five years has produced two world wars, with a world-wide depression sandwiched in between—is that the road to anywhere except to the city of destruction?" It was a cry that found expression in much of the contemporary literature. Van Wyck Brooks wrote, "I see on all sides a hunger for affirmations, for a world without confusion, a world that is full of order and purpose." In addition one always reckons on the personal discontent of thousands upon thousands of people, the dim feeling that life ought to add up to more enduring satisfactions than it does. It is no stretching of the imagina-

[1] From *Nicodemus*, copyright, 1932, by Edwin Arlington Robinson. Used by permission of The Macmillan Co., publishers.

give to the poor, and thou shalt have treasure in heaven: and come, take up the cross, and follow me.

him, "You lack one thing; go, sell what you have, and give to the poor, and you will have treasure in heaven; and come, fol-

19:21), which implies a double standard—one for the ordinary person, another and higher for the saint. (See Exeg. Matt., *ad loc.*) But it is doubtful if Mark saw any problem here; he probably took Jesus' words in the general sense: "One thing only remains to be done: Sell . . . and come, follow me." This was an invitation to become Jesus' personal follower. **Give to the poor** was a duty everywhere recognized and emphasized in the O.T. and in Jewish religion; here it meant a final, once-for-all distribution of wealth (vs. 22). **Treasure in heaven,** i.e., with God (Luke 12:21, 33; 16:9). **Take up the cross** is found only in late MSS—a gloss derived apparently from 8:34.

tion to hear echoing through all the ages this old, wistful question, "What must I do to inherit eternal life?"

It is the cue for those who feel they know the Christian answer to a world's need. Let them drop the note of apology and give that answer with clarity and confidence as Jesus did. It will prove to be a translation into terms of contemporary meaning of Christ's own great words—lack, go, sell, give, come, follow. For those tremendous verbs are stairs ascending into life.

21. You Lack One Thing; Go, Sell What You Have, and Give to the Poor.—This was a prescription for a particular person with a specific need. Jesus was not laying down poverty as either a requirement or an ideal for everyone. He was a Good Physician, and did not prescribe the same pill for every patient. He looked on this patient and loved him with an individualized love, a love which saw him as a person with a specialized need. Then he prescribed the action that would free him from the thing that was holding him back. In this case it was wealth, with all the mental and spiritual accompaniments that went with it. We have called the word he spoke a "prescription"; it was more like a surgical operation. Jesus was the Good Surgeon, as well as the Good Physician. He believed in drastic remedies when the trouble was deep-seated and acute (9:43-48). Here he says, "If your wealth causes you to sin, cut it off." The main thing was to enter into life, and to that end all that kept one out of life should be sacrificed for treasure elsewhere. He insisted on the sweeping finality of the choice—"go, sell, give, come, follow." Otherwise it would be just a tentative experiment, and not a saving revolution.

What was lacking? One big thing: self-forgetfulness. Without that there can be no true discipleship. This young man was seeking a personal good. It was on a higher level than wealth, but still it was something for himself. He needed to be carried out of himself by a great devotion. Witness the extent to which he had been living on negatives. "Do not do this,

do not do that." His score on the negative side was perfect. He had observed all the "do-nots." But he had missed the zest of the positive action.

As emphasized above, Jesus was not giving a universal prescription in his injunction to sell all and give to the poor. But there is a universal principle in his words which is quite capable of universal application. Every disciple has need to get beyond the careful caution of negative avoidance into the unmeasured giving of self in positive devotion. Every disciple has need to get beyond the seeking of personal good, until his life overflows into the lives of others. Most of all, every disciple has need to be lifted by a great loyalty to Christ into headlong absorption in his cause. We need to get out of the concerns of an ethical bookkeeping into the deep joy of love. We need to be swept off our feet by a new affection.

21. Go, Sell . . . , Give.—The church and its ministry may find a lesson of enormous worth in this. It is a lesson which has all too often been passed by unheeding. Jesus did not tone down his message for the sake of winning a desirable disciple; he set it forth in all its stern fullness. He never got disciples under false pretenses; he never offered bargains; he never concealed the Cross, or disguised the cost. That is the only way in which real disciples are ever won. It is a tragedy that churches have not always followed their Master at that point (see on 8:31-32). It would be easy, and sad, to imagine how many a skillful ecclesiastic would have "handled" this "prospect." We can almost hear the unspoken words behind the ingratiating smile: "There is no use to alienate a man of his stature. He will be a great addition to our strength. We will put him right on the board of trustees. He will make a good chairman of the finance committee." It is rather difficult to bring such a line of reasoning into accord with Jesus' words. Christ "lost his man," but he did not lose his gospel. And what shall it profit a church if it gain all the rich people in the world, and lose its own message?

22 And he was sad at that saying, and went away grieved: for he had great possessions.

23 ¶ And Jesus looked round about, and saith unto his disciples, How hardly shall

low me." 22 At that saying his countenance fell, and he went away sorrowful; for he had great possessions.

23 And Jesus looked around and said to

---

22. The test was too severe, and the man's ardor turned to sadness; **for he had great possessions** is not only a tragic last line but gives the key for the section that follows.

(b) The Danger of Riches (10:23-27)

23-25. When Jesus says, **How hard it will be for those who have riches to enter the kingdom of God**, his disciples are amazed. In spite of such teaching as that in Luke

---

22. *He Went Away Sorrowful.*—What exactly did this man lose? When we examine it, we are ready to award him the prize for having made the world's biggest blunder. He missed a great friendship. What else in all human history could compare to that prize, an elbow-to-elbow companionship with Jesus, hearing him, seeing him, being loved by him? He missed a great development. Think of what the men who accepted Jesus' invitation became! Someone has said that one can lie awake on a hot summer night in Illinois and hear the corn grow. We can put our ear down close to the N.T. and "hear" Peter grow! He grew out of the narrow nationalist into the prophet of the universal love of God. This man might have grown out of provincial ownership into universal sainthood. He missed a great adventure. When he saw the little group of disciples disappear down the road, he did not know that they were walking directly into the center of the greatest romance in history. He might have been the author of a gospel. His influence might have endured to the end of time but for a few acres and a few bags of gold!

That is history. But these same three gifts are offered men today. Jesus offers a great friendship, unseen by the physical eye, but as real as the unseen forces of nature. He offers a great development. The words in the Gospel of John, "To all who received him, . . . he gave power to become children of God" (John 1:12), are not just words in a book. They record the experience of millions of lives. He offers a great adventure, to be God's fellow worker in shaping a world after his desire. What are we doing with his gifts?

22. *He Went Away Sorrowful.*—There are many things in life to which people come running up eagerly in expectation and from which they go away slowly and sorrowfully. In this narrative we can almost see the difference between the manner in which the man came and that in which he went away. He runs up all aglow with excitement and the salutation "Good Teacher" on his lips. Then he makes his exit, trudging slowly and sorrowfully.

He had learned the nature and the price of what it was he thought he wanted. That made the difference between an eager run and a sorrowful trudge. The romantic attitude with which he came was not stalwart enough to pay the price. It is a great, high achievement in life to go ahead with something on which we have started, after we have gone far enough to learn the cost. The merchant who sold everything he had in order to buy the pearl of great price could do that (Matt. 13:45-46). The rich young man could not.

This contrast between the running approach and the slow retreat is found in many realms. We see it in connection with almost every task. A young person, for instance, wants to be a writer. He runs up to it, all equipped with pens and paper and great expectations. Then he learns the cost, that it is grueling toil, and he cannot pay it, and goes sorrowfully away. We see it in friendship. We see it supremely in marriage. How many come running excitedly, only to learn the high cost in self-discipline and self-forgetfulness; then go away sorrowful, for they have **great possessions** of self-love and self-care. We see it in the realm of Christian discipleship—the many who come with eagerness, really running in spirit. Whereupon they learn the cost. They hear the command to break with all that would hold them back from fully entering the kingdom.

> If I find him, if I follow
>   What his guerdon here?
> "Many a sorrow, many a labor,
>   Many a tear." [2]

And their countenance falls.

There is one great resource to prevent such an anticlimax—joy. "Who for the joy that was set before him endured the cross" (Heb. 12:2). If we get into discipleship deeply enough to find out about that, any price will look small.

23. *How Hard It Will Be for Those Who Have Riches to Enter the Kingdom of God!*—Jesus was profoundly aware of the effect of

[2] J. M. Neale, "Art thou weary, art thou troubled?"

they that have riches enter into the kingdom of God!

24 And the disciples were astonished at his words. But Jesus answereth again, and saith unto them, Children, how hard is it for them that trust in riches to enter into the kingdom of God!

25 It is easier for a camel to go through the eye of a needle, than for a rich man to enter into the kingdom of God.

his disciples, "How hard it will be for those who have riches to enter the kingdom of God!" 24 And the disciples were amazed at his words. But Jesus said to them again, "Children, how hard it is[r] to enter the kingdom of God! 25 It is easier for a camel to go through the eye of a needle than for a rich man to enter the kingdom

[r] Some ancient authorities add *for those who trust in riches.*

14:33; 16:13, the disciples were not prepared for such a statement, nor has the Christian world ever been! **For them that trust in riches** is a later gloss, designed to weaken the force of vs. 23. **For a camel . . . needle:** This also has been a problem. Cyril of Alexandria, a few late Greek MSS, and the Armenian version have κάμιλος for κάμηλος, i.e., a cable or hawser—as if a needle might be threaded with a ship's cable, even if a camel could not go through its eye! Perhaps the "cable" was thought to be a more appropriate hyperbole; but it was an unnecessary change. "An elephant through the eye of a needle" seems to have been another Jewish expression. A far later fancy, fifteenth century, is the supposed

---

riches on the spiritual life. We do not find, of course, either in the words of Jesus or elsewhere in the N.T., anything like the modern criticism of wealth, that it leads to the concentration of economic power, with evil social results. But there is in Jesus a strong sense of the peril involved. The form and the amount of wealth have changed over and over during the centuries; but the dangers, both spiritual and psychological, remain essentially the same. In this exclamation Jesus speaks to all times.

Abundance is an enemy to the "abundant life." The hazard of wealth lies in the fact that means have a subtle way of becoming ends. Having become a substitute for being, riches can imprison a man in a world of illusion. He develops a false sense of security. The essential attributes of the children of the kingdom become exceedingly difficult to attain or preserve. The sense of dependence atrophies. Prestige destroys perspective and creates the illusion of being a very important person, a "V.I.P." in the army jargon of World War II. The absence of compulsions tends to render the will soft. The center of gravity moves from personality to power, and personality shrinks in the process. So the rich man is liable to become like Gulliver: he wakes up on the beach of the island of Lilliput, huge among the pygmies, but bound to earth by a multitude of little strings.

24. And the Disciples Were Amazed at His Words.—They may well have been. The amazement has gone on for nineteen centuries. The words of Jesus are not easy for anyone to accept. If we take into account the whole passage, the amazement of the disciples may have resulted from the saying that it was hard for "those who have riches" to enter the kingdom, or from the

general exclamation which follows in the text, that entrance was hard for everybody. There may thus have been a double source of amazement. For in this strong declaration of the danger of riches Jesus was opposing both the rabbinical teaching and the idea frequently found in the O.T. that prosperity was the blessing of the righteous and the sign of God's favor. Furthermore, in Jesus' time it was easier for a rich man to fulfill all the requirements of the laws of ceremonial purity than it was for a poor man, because the rich could give all their time to it. In this sense the Hebrew legalistic code was essentially class legislation. Jesus here reversed the common judgment on both counts; and the disciples were astonished (Goodspeed translates vs. 26 "perfectly astounded").

Are we in reality any the less so? What devious rationalizations are continually used to dull the edge of this saying of Jesus on the spiritual dangers of wealth! What violent hands are laid on his words to keep them from coming into violent collision with the national religion of profit making, and the pagan worship of riches! Until we get over our astonishment, and begin to share his convictions that the lust to possess is a threat to the human soul, we shall be strangers both to his teaching and to his spirit.

25. It Is Easier for a Camel to Go Through the Eye of a Needle than for a Rich Man to Enter the Kingdom of God.—To those who have no sense of humor, or who find it impossible to think of Jesus' having a sense of humor, this verse is exceedingly difficult. People have scurried about for centuries to drag out various fantastic meanings, all the way from proclaiming that the word "camel" really meant "rope" to

26 And they were astonished out of measure, saying among themselves, Who then can be saved?

27 And Jesus looking upon them saith, With men *it is* impossible, but not with God: for with God all things are possible.

28 ¶ Then Peter began to say unto him, Lo, we have left all, and have followed thee.

of God." 26 And they were exceedingly astonished, and said to him,ˢ "Then who can be saved?" 27 Jesus looked at them and said, "With men it is impossible, but not with God; for all things are possible with God." 28 Peter began to say to him, "Lo, we have left everything and followed you."

ˢ Many ancient authorities read *to one another.*

"needle's eye" gate, a small postern entrance beside the large city gate, used after nightfall, and to be entered, it is argued, by a loaded camel only upon its knees. Only so also, according to this view, can a rich man enter the kingdom of God. But such a gate was far too small for a camel, loaded or unloaded; and who ever saw a camel crawl on its four knees! Taking the text as it stands, this is simply one more of Jesus' characteristic hyperboles, and sets forth vividly the utter impossibility of the case, as vss. 26-27 recognize.

26-27. **Then who can be saved?** Are the disciples reflecting here that all men, even the poor, have some possessions? Or are they thinking of the second statement (vs. 24), that it is hard to enter the kingdom? Presumably the latter. Note the similar problem presupposed in Luke 12:31—an extraordinary verse in a Gospel that stresses poverty and renunciation as greatly as Luke does! Here also it is recognized that entrance into God's kingdom is humanly impossible—i.e., cannot be won by one's own effort, but only by the gift (or grace, or word) of God (cf. Gen. 18:14; Jer. 32:17, 27; Luke 1:37). It almost looks as if two sets of sayings were combined in this section: vss. 23, 25, 27 and 24, 26, 27, both being brought together by vs. 27. One states the difficulty of the rich, the other the difficulty of all; both difficulties are solved by divine grace. It may have been this problem of the difference in subject presupposed that led Codex Bezae (D) and some of the O.L. MSS to reverse vss. 24, 25.

(c) The Reward of Renunciation (10:28-31)

This section goes back to the original situation, vs. 21, and, with the contrast of vss. 23-27 in mind, raises the question of the status of the disciples—and of the later church,

---

insisting that what Jesus actually had in mind was the low postern gate into Jerusalem, too low for a camel to go through. The verse means, strangely enough, what it says. It is one of Jesus' characteristic ways of talking in vivid hyperbole, with picturesque exaggeration. The hearers would get his drift. Here was a very mountain of impossibility. And they would doubtless get the twinkle in his eye as he said it. The image of a big, gangling, shaggy, awkward camel trying to poke his nose, to say nothing of his shoulders and mountainous hump, through the tiny eye of a needle would cause a smile to pass over the face, like the wind making a ripple over a wheat field. But it does, for all time, something far more serious. It records a sense of overwhelming peril and a forthright demand for undivided allegiance in the kingdom of God.

26-27. *With Men It Is Impossible, but . . . All Things Are Possible with God.*—The answer Jesus gave to the disciples' question "Who can be saved?" was simply, "No one without the grace of God." This is true both for the rich and for everyone else. The kingdom of heaven

is a gift. It is not man's creation or achievement. "Fear not, little flock, for it is your father's good pleasure to give you the kingdom" (Luke 12:32). What man cannot do, God can do by his power and grace. All things necessary for man's salvation are possible to him. Here we have a close approach to Paul's idea of the Spirit as God's touch on life. This is the hope of our calling, that against the dangers of all infection there are resources of God on which we may lay hold. The permanent plea which comes from these words is to avail ourselves of the "means of grace," in Word and sacrament, by which we may be kept in humble dependence on God, and by which his power may flow into our lives, that the things which were great to Christ may be great to us, and the things that were small to him may be small to us. God has his own perspective and his own ways of sharing it with us.

28-30. *Peter Began to Say to Him, "Lo, We Have Left Everything and Followed You."*—Peter here is about to raise the natural question "What about us?" (See Exeg.) "What will be the rewards of those who lay down all they have

29 And Jesus answered and said, Verily I say unto you, There is no man that hath left house, or brethren, or sisters, or father, or mother, or wife, or children, or lands, for my sake, and the gospel's, 30 But he shall receive a hundredfold now in this time, houses, and brethren, and sisters, and mothers, and children, and lands, with persecutions; and in the world to come eternal life.	29 Jesus said, "Truly, I say to you, there is no one who has left house or brothers or sisters or mother or father or children or lands, for my sake and for the gospel, 30 who will not receive a hundredfold now in this time, houses and brothers and sisters and mothers and children and lands, with persecutions, and in the age to come eternal life.

in Mark's view. They *have* fulfilled the two requirements of complete renunciation and of following Jesus. Matthew quite properly fills in what is presupposed by Peter's remark: "What then shall we have?"—or more colloquially, "What about us?"

29. Or wife is found only in later MSS; it has intruded from the parallel in Luke. **For my sake, and the gospel's,** as in 8:35. This clearly points to the later situation, the early church. Both Matthew and Luke alter the phrase. Luke's "for the sake of the kingdom of God" (18:29*b*) is probably in the direction of the original form of the saying (so Bultmann).

30. With persecutions also clearly reflects the later situation; both parallels omit this phrase. The contrast between **now in this time** and **in the world to come** is the usual eschatological contrast between the two ages. Both Matthew and Luke omit the vivid repetition of temporal benefits—**houses and brothers,** a little picture of the religious fellowship of the apostolic church—and reduce the **hundredfold** to "manifold."

and do as you say?" Jesus answers it before it is fully asked, and with complete frankness. The recorded details of his answer are not to be taken literally any more than is the description of the camel going through the eye of a needle. That historic sneer of Julian the Apostate about this passage, "So you will each have a hundred wives," shows how a literal acceptance of the words leads to nonsense.[3] It is enough to find in them Christ's emphatic declaration that there are compensations in discipleship, both in this world and in the next, which far outweigh all the renunciations that are necessary—a promise which in lives without number has been validated and translated into actual experience.

> Finding, following, keeping, struggling,
>   Is he sure to bless?
> "Saints, apostles, prophets, martyrs,
>   Answer, 'yes.' "[4]

That answer comes not only from those glittering companies, but from an unending succession of faithful disciples, their names unsung on earth, but entered in God's *Who's Who in the Kingdom.* The reward is a new dimension which comes into life through relationship to God, the new status of sonship, the new meaning that illuminates the dark mysteries of the world. The reward is "a new creation"; the great experience of becoming; the larger world into which

the disciple is led, with its expanding boundaries; the exhilaration of belonging to the greatest of all fraternal orders, the Friends of Jesus. Surely a **hundredfold** is no exaggeration.

Note, again, a particular reference in these words which comes with a great challenge and sharp question to every church of Jesus Christ. The words describing the rewards of discipleship, the **hundredfold now in this time, houses and brothers and sisters and mothers and children and lands,** would not seem strange to the first readers. They undoubtedly reflect the life of the early church. They describe the actual conditions which prevailed in the scattered Christian communities. The disciple who accepted the faith, and became a follower of Jesus, did become a member of a close and warm fellowship, where there were indeed compensations for all that had been forsaken. The picture which is painted here is not a fanciful picture; it is the emergence of a great reality. In the book of Acts and in the epistles there are strong evidences of warm-hearted hospitality, a spirit of mutual sharing, which was a great reward for the persecution and separation from family which people incurred in joining the Christians. The saying thus points "to a fellowship and loyalty so deep and warm that its members could speak of it as a recompense even **a hundred times** for all that they had to give up for its sake."[5]

---

[3] Quoted, Rawlinson, *St. Mark,* p. 142.

[4] J. M. Neale, "Art thou weary, art thou troubled?"

[5] Branscomb, *Gospel of Mark,* p. 185.

31 But many *that are* first shall be last; and the last first.

32 ¶ And they were in the way going up to Jerusalem; and Jesus went before them: and they were amazed; and as they followed, they were afraid. And he took again the twelve, and began to tell them what things should happen unto him,

31 But many that are first will be last, and the last first."

32 And they were on the road, going up to Jerusalem, and Jesus was walking ahead of them; and they were amazed, and those who followed were afraid. And taking the twelve again, he began to tell

---

31. Luke omits this verse; Matthew retains it. There is an echo in Barn. 6:13: "The Lord says, Behold, I will make the last things like the first"—a vivid statement of the eschatological principle: the end of the age will be like its beginning. Here the saying, which is a "tag," like those in 13:37; 4:9, has probably been added by Mark from the current oral tradition—a less likely place for it is in Matt. 20:16. It was a word addressed to the later church, Mark's persecuted readers; some of them, though among the last to be called, might be **first** in the kingdom (9:35).

4. The Third Passion Announcement (10:32-34)

32-34. The third of the passion announcements is more detailed than those in 8:31 and 9:31, and follows the actual narrative of the Passion (chs. 14–15) more closely. It is generally thought that the passion narrative was the earliest long and consecutive narra-

---

The challenge to us comes in the sharp question: Is the fellowship in our church so real, so warm, so deep, so freely given to all, that it is a more than adequate compensation for all the "renunciations" a Christian must make? Or is the "fellowship" just a beautiful word, with an attractive, but faraway, N.T. aroma about it, rather than a realized ideal? That is what the church ought to be, the most real and rich fellowship on earth, an actual new family, "brothers, sisters, mothers, children." Why is it often so much less than that? How may it become what it ought to be and might be? We should never forget that Christianity made its way in the Greek and Roman world not only through its message and ideas, but also through the demonstration of its fellowship, an utterly new thing; and that many were attracted to the fellowship before they understood the message or fully accepted it.

31. *But Many that Are First Will Be Last, and the Last First.*—It is inevitable that such a reversal of valuations as marks the kingdom of God will throw the whole human parade into reverse (see on 9:35). In these words we can hear the command "rightabout-face," and see the column turn, and the last become first, the tattered battalion that use and custom has assigned to the rear, leading the parade. Those who have made the renunciations necessary for the kingdom, who "have left all, and have followed," will precede the great in the only judgment of worth that really counts, the eyes of God.

It is fascinating—and alarming—to let our imagination play with the reversal of the order of march which the judgments of Jesus would make in the human parade as it passes through any city or any generation. The section that always comes first in the world's assignment, "notables with decorations, on white horses," will look strange as it drags along at the end.

Shakespeare gives a classic portrayal of the fading human glory:

> Our revels now are ended. These our actors,
> As I foretold you, were all spirits, and
> Are melted into air, into thin air;
> And, like the baseless fabric of this vision,
> The cloud-capp'd towers, the gorgeous palaces,
> The solemn temples, the great globe itself,
> Yea, all which it inherit, shall dissolve;
> And, like this insubstantial pageant faded,
> Leave not a rack behind.[6]

History has given something of a picture of the reverses of God's kingdom. Lo, all the pomp of yesterday, or much of it, has gone into a fog. One generation or century cries to some pompous figure, "Hail to the chief!" Other centuries come along and look at the object with a blank stare, unrecognizing. The first has become last, and the last has become first. Sometimes it happens within a single lifetime. Across the years it is an infallible process. Paul takes precedence over Nero. Martin Luther over the pope at Rome and the emperor at Worms. John Bunyan over Charles II. Cf. Shelley's Ozymandias.

32-34. *And They Were on the Road, Going up to Jerusalem, and Jesus Was Walking Ahead of Them.*—The framework of narrative into which this third announcement of the Pas-

[6] *The Tempest*, Act IV, scene 1.

33 *Saying,* Behold, we go up to Jerusalem; and the Son of man shall be delivered unto the chief priests, and unto the scribes; and they shall condemn him to death, and shall deliver him to the Gentiles:

34 And they shall mock him, and shall scourge him, and shall spit upon him, and shall kill him; and the third day he shall rise again.

them what was to happen to him, **33** saying, "Behold, we are going up to Jerusalem; and the Son of man will be delivered to the chief priests and the scribes, and they will condemn him to death, and deliver him to the Gentiles; **34** and they will mock him, and spit upon him, and scourge him, and kill him; and after three days he will rise."

---

tive of events in the life of Jesus to be written down; presumably it was already in written form when Mark wrote—as we shall see, Mark's narrative in chs. 14–15 presupposes an earlier version which he has edited. Vs. 32 is certainly editorial; it was the theory of Burkitt, Turner, and others that it represents "vivid personal recollection." Turner, on the basis of the omission in some MSS (D O.L., etc.) of **those who followed were afraid,** supposed that the "amazement" was originally attributed to Jesus—as if he were one "whom a dream hath possessed" and who went forward in blind terror to his fate (cf. 14:33)—but the omission was probably due to homoeoteleuton. Such theories as this are much too romantic, and overlook the tragic element in Mark's composition.

Mark and Matthew omit any reference to the disciples' failure to comprehend; Luke (18:34) elaborates the point, as he did after the second announcement (Luke 9:45). But Luke omits the following verses (the request of James and John), and this probably explains the difference at the other points: for Mark and Matthew the Zebedees' request was enough evidence of the disciples' failure to comprehend.

---

sion is set etches indelible pictures in the mind, the road leading up to Jerusalem, Jesus going on ahead, the disciples following in amazement and fear. It is a great moment in history, and it throws a strong, clear light on the whole Christian enterprise in all ages. It portrays impressively the stark courage of Jesus, facing all that he knew well would happen in Jerusalem, yet going ahead on the road; and it portrays impressively the task of his disciples, today and tomorrow, as in all yesterdays, to follow his lead into conflict and sacrifice and death.

To Jesus, going up to Jerusalem meant the ultimate witness to his truth, the ultimate demonstration of his love, the laying down of life. No wonder the twelve were gripped by amazement and fear at such an issue. It is the ultimate issue from which so many of us shrink. Jerusalem is a spot that is not marked on many maps of life. Going to Jerusalem, in the sense that Jesus faced it, means going from the place of comparative safety to the place of danger, from the place of comparatively little cost to the place of tremendous cost. Many never cross that frontier. They stay in quiet Galilee. They tour the safe, pleasant places, keeping out of forthright witness on dangerous questions, where such witness would bring loss and pain. They avoid the land of bondage, that great area of social injustice where the people whom God loves and for whom Christ died are under the

yoke of oppression. "Let's not go up to Jerusalem, but stop somewhere this side of it. There is no use going to extremes." These are the soft whisperings which come to our ears. Jesus went to extremes. The border between Galilee and Jerusalem is the most important borderline in any life. It tests the reality of our profession. When we cross it in our lives and actions, we go from comfort into pain, from ease into jeopardy, as Jesus did. But if we do not cross it, we leave the road which leads to fullness of life, and to power.

There is in the words **Jesus was walking ahead of them** a richness of suggestion, both historical and contemporary, which is quite inexhaustible. That is where Jesus has always been —ahead. Ahead of the customs of every age, ahead of its dulled conscience, ahead of its blindness to human and spiritual values and needs. The title given to him in the Epistle to the Hebrews, "the pioneer . . . of our faith" (Heb. 12:2), expresses it with a fitting finality. He has been—and is—the divine trail breaker, pushing out first into new, unexplored, unoccupied territories of human life and social achievement. Into the tangled areas of sex and slavery and slaughter and exploitation, Jesus the pioneer has gone, and often, as in the beginning, with such a laggard company of disciples trudging along so far behind him. There have been times indeed when they have quit

35 ¶ And James and John, the sons of Zebedee, come unto him, saying, Master, we would that thou shouldest do for us whatsoever we shall desire.	**35** And James and John, the sons of Zeb'e-dee, came forward to him, and said to him, "Teacher, we want you to do for

5. The Request of James and John (10:35-45)

Peter failed to grasp the significance of the first passion announcement, and was rebuked (8:32-33); now the other two members of the "inner group" are refused their request. Luke omits vss. 35-40, and some have thought the passage an interpolation; but Luke "spares the twelve," as Salmond said, and moreover he intends to use vss. 41-45 in the passion narrative (Luke 22:24-27). It may be, however, that vss. 38-40 (or 38*b*-39 or 40, or 39-40, or even 39 alone) are "secondary," a later addition to the primary narrative, though quite possibly pre-Marcan, in the interest of bringing the apostles' martyrdom into relation with the death of Jesus.

35. Matthew also "spares the twelve," and attributes the request to the mother of James and John; but in Matt. 20:22 he keeps Mark's form of the reply! This may be dramatic, but it suggests that Mark's version is the original one. The request for a promise in advance is quite naïve and is characteristic of "popular" stories (cf. 6:22).

trudging, and just settled down where they were, content with murderous wrongs done in the very name of Christ, with pride of race and strife of class and heat of war—all of it an appalling denial of everything he was and taught.

Today he goes on ahead, ahead of our conventional morality, ahead of the mediocre minimum which we so readily substitute for a Christian maximum. Jane Addams gave a vivid illustration of that difference when she prophesied: "Someday we will stop talking of the right of the child to food, and will talk of the right of the child to happiness." He pioneers on in the dark, unsubdued wilderness of greed and competition and chicanery and the ruthlessness of power politics.

Two compulsions rest upon us all. One is to refrain from trying to keep him back with us, as though our miserable attainment represented his purposes and goals. That would be an unforgivable violence, laying our hands on him to hold him back. Better far to say, "We are unprofitable servants. We have not followed, God forgive us! But at least we see him going on ahead." Recall George Matheson's cry, "Yesterday is dead, last century is old, but thou art never old." We can at least allow him to remain a rebuke and an inspiration, and not try to identify our pitiable achievement with his desire. Second, we can earnestly strive to close the gap between him and us. We can shorten the distance. We need not be so far behind.

33. The Son of Man Will Be Delivered to the Chief Priests and the Scribes, and They Will Condemn Him to Death.—These words furnish a magnificent vantage point from which to see the realism of Jesus, and to understand what a fortification all truly Christian realism brings to great endeavor. Jesus has often been

interpreted as a poet-peasant of Galilee, sweet, unsophisticated, and sentimental. How silly all that appears in the presence of this record of courage, iron will, and clear seeing. Jesus had no illusions. The details given here are more detailed than in 8:31 and 9:31 (see Exeg.). But Jesus knew in general what would happen. He had a clear-eyed knowledge of the nature and power of the forces set against him. Such realism is fortification of soul. He was not surprised or overwhelmed when the blows were struck. He knew they would come. Much unnecessary disaster in every generation could be avoided by a like realism in Jesus' disciples. If we go into God's holy war with merely romantic expectations of bloodless victory, we set the stage for collapse and disillusionment and the breakdown of morale. That is why the idealist turned sour by difficulty and defeat often becomes the worst cynic in the world. Multitudes of ill-prepared romanticists imagine that they are able to deal blows against evil powers without receiving blows in return. So when the return blows come, they are overwhelmed with consternation and sometimes pity themselves as victims of a vast injustice. A realistic knowledge of life, a level-eyed look at the probabilities, will not reduce the cost of discipleship, but it will be armor for the conflict. Thomas Hardy's words have pertinence here, "If a way to the Better there be, it exacts a full look at the Worst." [7]

35-45. True Greatness.—This whole section of ten verses reiterates and expands the teaching on greatness which followed the second announcement of the Passion (9:31). The disciples missed the point then; they miss it again. It was

[7] "In Tenebris," *Collected Poems* (New York: The Macmillan Co., 1925).

36 And he said unto them, What would ye that I should do for you?

37 They said unto him, Grant unto us that we may sit, one on thy right hand, and the other on thy left hand, in thy glory.

us whatever we ask of you." 36 And he said to them, "What do you want me to do for you?" 37 And they said to him, "Grant us to sit, one at your right hand and one at

---

37. **In thy glory:** As a writer cited in the ancient Greek catena points out, paraphrasing Luke 19:11, they "thought that his kingdom was already visible" (Cramer, *op. cit.,* I, 384). For Mark **thy** glory (Christ's) was a perfectly natural expression; originally it was the glory of God (cf. 8:38) which would bathe the supernatural King of the future. It was a symbolic phrase for "kingly power" (cf. Luke 23:42). But even in the passion announcements Jesus had nowhere announced his coming royalty; presumably "after three days he will rise" (vs. 34) connoted exaltation to kingly state, as Messiah. The right hand and left were the positions of greatest honor in a monarch's court.

---

a needed lesson; but one very difficult for minds steeped in other ideas and standards to grasp. Very possibly the approach to Jerusalem, and the explicit teaching about the consummation of Jesus' life, stirred the expectations of the disciples about their share in the approaching glory. They were still thinking in the old terms of a material kingdom; here there is not only the desire for reward, but a new note of desire for precedence and rank.

Again Jesus gives the same teaching, the great paradox of the kingdom, this time carried to an extreme form, in that the greatest at the banquet is the slave who does the serving of all. The violent reversal of earth's measurements of greatness could go no farther. Here, truly, Jesus has "put down the mighty from their thrones, and exalted those of low degree" (Luke 1:52). It is a complete revolution, the inauguration of an upside-down world. The whole social pyramid is inverted.

To picture such a reversal was hard for the disciples (see on 9:35). It is hard for anyone. Surely we can understand their slow-moving minds. Ours move at the same snail's pace. If they still thought in terms of Oriental magnificence, with the seats of the mighty occupied by themselves, men still, nineteen centuries later, think in the terms of the greatness accepted in the market place. And as long as we do so, to the extent that we do so, we miss the meaning of Jesus and the kingdom. The words of Robert Frost carry an arresting parallel: "I bid you to a one-man revolution."

35. *Teacher, We Want You to Do for Us Whatever We Ask of You.*—This is the final form of unacceptable prayer. It was sincere; it was earnest; it was wrong. James and John were asking Jesus to fit into their plans. They had no concern at the moment over fitting into his plans. Prayer is always unacceptable when it says to God, "You do whatever I want." Christian prayer says rather with Jesus, "Thy king-

dom come, thy will be done"; and "Not my will, but thine." When our prayer makes a demand on God to adjust himself to our desires, when it does not test desires by his nature and purposes, when the loud strident "I" drowns out the "thou," we do not pray in Jesus' name or spirit.

36. *What Do You Want Me to Do for You?*—This was a question often on Jesus' lips. He sometimes asked it before healing a person, as later in this chapter (vs. 51). It is never a superfluous question. For a man clearly to define exactly what it is that he wants is always important. It enables—it often compels—him to explore and discover what his real desires are. Emerson's word applies closely to this conversation of Jesus and James and John, and to the whole moral and spiritual life: " 'What do you want?' quoth God. 'Take it and pay for it.' " Jesus replies to them: "You say you want precedence in the kingdom. Are you able to pay the price?"

That answer comes to all the requests we make of God and to all that we demand of life. "Are you able to pay the price?" Men want to be great. Very well—here is the way to be great. Be the servant of all. Men pray for happiness. Very well. If that is what you really want, want strongly enough to meet the cost, you can have it. But here are some of the costs—an escape from the prison of self, a childlike trust in God, a losing of self in a cause bigger than self, so that life does not spin around either your aches and pains or your gratifications, but finds a new center.

It is an answer that reaches to the core of the world's desire for peace. Do you really want peace? How strongly do you want it? That is where the nations fail. They want the things which go with peace, but not peace; not to the extent of being willing to pay the high price it costs in the reconstruction of aims and policies. Lecomte du Noüy writes forcibly:

38 But Jesus said unto them, Ye know not what ye ask: can ye drink of the cup that I drink of? and be baptized with the baptism that I am baptized with?

your left, in your glory." 38 But Jesus said to them, "You do not know what you are asking. Are you able to drink the cup that I drink, or to be baptized with the baptism

---

38. You do not know what you are asking: Their request proved that they totally misunderstood Jesus' purpose, the hazards he faced, and the death—the **cup** of suffering (cf. Isa. 51:17, 22; John 18:11*b*), and the **baptism** of overwhelming disaster (cf. Ps. 42:7; 69:2; Isa. 43:2; Luke 12:50)—which he must undergo; neither did they realize that his way was one of service, not of pride, ambition, or conquest. That such misconceptions of the purpose of Jesus existed in the early church, and even in the minds of the original disciples, is clear from various N.T. statements. Rev. 20 does not stand alone, nor was Papias the last of those who thought in secular and terrestrial terms. **Can?** (KJV) is better translated **Are you able?** (RSV). More than mere suffering is involved.

The time has come for nations, as well as individuals, to know what they want. If civilized countries *want* peace, they must understand that the problem must be approached basically. The old scaffolding willed to us by past generations cracks on every side. It cannot be consolidated by makeshifts, by bits of string, by pots of glue and treaties gravely signed by Highly-Dignified-Gentlemen. Moreover, consolidation does not suffice. Peace must be established by transforming man from the interior and not by erecting external structures.[8]

38. But Jesus Said to Them, "You Do Not Know What You Are Asking."—They did not know. What they were asking, greatness in the kingdom, lay in an entirely different realm from that of which they were thinking. They did not know for two reasons. One was that they were asking for something in the spiritual world which could be attained only by spiritual processes within themselves. The other reason was that they were asking in general terms for something that could be given only through particular, specific experiences and acts.

How often it is true that no more than the disciples do we know what we are asking, and for the same reasons. One of our commonest prayers is "Lord, bless me." Do we know that the true blessing of life by God will carry us far beyond our asking? It may mean the deepening of life by toil and suffering, the following of Jesus by taking up a cross. There is no other blessedness that God can give. A common prayer is "Lord, hasten thy kingdom." But do we know what we ask? We are asking God to break down in us, and in our world, the evils which delay the coming of his kingdom, such as selfwill and greed, pride and prejudice. The high cost of the kingdom will be its acceptance in our lives as the one thing we seek first. We can rattle off glibly "thy kingdom come" without thinking that we ourselves may be the obstacles

[8] *Human Destiny* (Longmans, Green & Co., 1947), p. 267.

to its coming! In one form or another we offer the prayer "Lord bless our church and make it great." Do we know that the church of Christ cannot prosper without having the marks of Christ upon its spirit and life? It cannot truly prosper by a balanced budget, or by balanced sentences in the pulpit, or by harmony in the choir loft. "If any church would come after me. . . ."

38. *Are You Able to Drink the Cup that I Drink, or to Be Baptized with the Baptism with Which I Am Baptized?*—Jesus uses here two symbolic words, familiar in the O.T., cup and baptism. They are clear words, and tremendous in their implications. They are more than mere figures of speech. Jesus had just finished telling his disciples what the issue of his going up to Jerusalem would be—"they will mock him, and spit upon him, and scourge him, and kill him" (vs. 34)—four terribly strong verbs with an ascending ferocity. The cup which he drank and the baptism with which he was baptized involved the actual offering of life. His question, then, was literally this: "Can you, too, offer your lives?" That was the ultimate price of what they were asking for, seats on the right hand and on the left, greatness in the kingdom.

We need to come back again and again to the literal meaning of such words as these. Christianity has suffered greatly from allegorizing. Christ's sayings have been "allegorized" until they have dissolved into thin air, with no concrete meaning left. The surest way to escape his costly compulsions is to keep the phrase "Oriental allegory" near by where we can lay ready hands on it. It covers up multitudes of easy escapes from the cost of following Jesus. There was sharp and costly meaning here for Jesus and his disciples, and for Christians of the first centuries under the Roman persecutions. Many did drink of his cup—they gave up their lives.

To drink of it today may not often mean sur-

39 And they said unto him, We can. And Jesus said unto them, Ye shall indeed drink of the cup that I drink of; and with the

39 with which I am baptized?" 39 And they said to him, "We are able." And Jesus said

---

39. The cup that I drink you will drink is commonly thought to presuppose the martyrdom of James and John as already having taken place when Mark wrote. James died under Herod Agrippa *ca.* A.D. 44 (Acts 12:2). John's early death, contrary to the traditional interpretation of John 21 and the legend of John's death in Ephesus, is related in the fragment from Papias quoted in Philip of Side: "Papias in his second book

---

rendering life in some dramatic execution—though indeed in our generation a host have done just that, paid for their faithful witnessing with martyrdom. Yet surely, though the last full ounce of such devotion is not asked of us, we can at least say to ourselves, and say it earnestly, "For God's sake keep some real meaning, some great and costly meaning in these words." **Are you able to drink the cup that I drink, or to be baptized with the baptism with which I am baptized?** It is a tragedy when words with blood in them dissolve into pallid and airy figures of speech. These have blood in them, life freely and richly poured out.

Consider two aspects of Jesus' cup and baptism: 1. Part of the Christian's saving force in the world is a Christlike sensitiveness to human need that brings real pain into life. To expose our nerves to the hurt of others, to load their burdens onto our shoulders already laden, to let the heart be torn with anguish over suffering which we can legally claim is none of our business—that is not easy. But it is the cup from which Jesus drank. Sensitiveness is the mark of development in the biological world. The lowly amoeba does not have it. Neither does the clam. No one ever heard of a clam with a nervous breakdown. There is nothing to break down. With a great price have we obtained this freedom as men—at the price of pain, in a highly developed nervous system. High rank in the kingdom of God has the same marks, a very highly developed nervous system, the capacity to feel pain in the suffering of others. It will shut out entirely the possibility of easy comfort and clamlike indifference, which is to some people a chief end of life. Can we drink of that cup?

2. The baptism with which Jesus was baptized will mean putting ourselves into conflict with evil and dangerous powers. Jesus probably could have avoided that by staying in Galilee. He was not brought to trial for saying, "Consider the lilies . . . , how they grow" (Matt. 6:28). It was for saying, "Consider the thieves in the temple, how they steal." That is what brought on the crisis. It was when he faced daringly the evil forces of his day that he was baptized with conflict. So many of us never get beyond considering the lilies, never carry through to their logical conclusion the affirmations of our faith. The logical conclusion of the Christian faith in our world is a wrestling that is not with flesh and blood, but with principalities and the rulers of darkness.

Once more as we look at these words, and consider their fulfillment in suffering and death, we realize how silly is the pretentious theory that religion is an "escape" from life. Of course you can prostitute your faith. Anybody who wants to can turn it into a mechanism for getting away. But the religion of Jesus, as he set his face to go to Jerusalem, was no such thing. Nor was that of Paul when he went to Rome. Nor was that of multitudes of people who have faced life under the constraint of Christ.

39. And They Said to Him, "We Are Able."— James and John were evidently sincere in this assertion. Eventually, according to tradition, many of the disciples, including James and John, did give up their lives in martyrdom. They were able at last to drink of that cup. Yet other words, from a crisis which was then nearer at hand, come to mind and inevitably range themselves over against this confident declaration: "They all forsook him, and fled" (14:50). At the first severe test they were not able.

There was mixed with their devotion something familiar to all of us, an optimistic view of the tests they would face. It was an optimism untempered by a sharp clear-seeing knowledge of what would be involved. Right there lies one great difference between optimism and faith. Optimism underrates the size and power of the enemy battalions. Faith can look at them with unbandaged eyes and be undismayed, because it sees beyond to the resources of God. "They that be with us are more than they that be with them" (II Kings 6:16). Optimism may be the product of a sanguine temperament plus defective eyesight. Faith is "vision plus valor."

These disciples were ready for conflict in general. They had not thought in specific terms. When the unreckoned details came as a flood, swords and staves, arrest, the ruling powers in the nation moving to crush them, they were overwhelmed. It is always the details that test the claim **we are able.**

baptism that I am baptized withal shall ye be baptized:

40 But to sit on my right hand and on my left hand is not mine to give; but *it shall be given to them* for whom it is prepared.

to them, "The cup that I drink you will drink; and with the baptism with which I am baptized, you will be baptized; **40** but to sit at my right hand or at my left is not mine to grant, but it is for those for whom

---

says that John the disciple (*theologos*) and James his brother were put to death by Jews." (Edited by C. DeBoor in *Texte und Untersuchungen* [Leipzig: J. C. Hinrichs, 1888], V, 2, p. 170.) The later Syrian church calendar, Hegesippus' account of the death of James the Lord's brother, and other evidence make it probable that John also died before the fall of Jerusalem. (See the evidence in G. H. C. Macgregor *The Gospel of John* [New York: Harper & Bros., 1929], and B. W. Bacon, *The Gospel of the Hellenists* [New York: Henry Holt & Co., 1933].) As Klostermann notes, Mark would hardly have given emphasis to this prediction unless both apostles had already been martyred.

40. Jesus does not reject the position attributed to him in the coming kingdom, but insists that the positions of honor are not his to assign. This reflects an "early" type of Christology (cf. I Cor. 15:24-28). **For whom it has been prepared** sounds like predestina-

---

We say, "We are able," thinking of a life of stalwart discipleship. Yet so often we are not ready to meet the unexpected gnawing of attrition, the wearing down of dedication. The repetition of tiresome small demands is harder to resist than the big frontal attack. We say, "We are able," thinking of the future, when our hour of destiny and the great opportunity will meet. We are not so "able" for the bothersome present, for the immediate thing: that has no glamour of greatness about it, carries nothing but just the stubborn insistence, "Do this. Do it again right now." We say, "We are able," and say it sincerely as James and John did; yet we are not ready for the demands that completely upset life, that call for violent rearrangements of our cozily designed world, that drive us out of the familiar mental home into a new home, the mind of Christ. The words that came to Abraham from God, "Get thee out," are always upsetting words.

How, then, may we be made able? Practically the whole N.T. is an answer to that crucial question. We are enabled by God's power, coming into life with a divine "plus"—"It is no longer I who live, but Christ who lives in me" (Gal. 2:20). We are "enabled" by a great devotion—"I count everything as loss because of the surpassing worth of knowing Christ Jesus my Lord" (Phil. 3:8). We are made able by sharing in the sympathy of Jesus.

40. *But to Sit at My Right Hand or at My Left Is Not Mine to Grant.*—We are warned in the Exeg. against pressing these words too hard in order to extract theological doctrine from them. Taken literally, without giving due weight to the context and historical situation, they can be made, and have been made, the basis of quite a towering structure of foreordina-

tion and predestination; but to do so is to lay hands violently on Jesus' mind and shape it into another mold, to read into his words ideas of a later time. Such procedure has real relationship to the classic definition of a woman's intuition, "A woman's intuition is that power which enables her to see through a stone wall to what isn't on the other side." A doctrine of foreordination is not on the other side of these words of Jesus.

What they do proclaim is that there is nothing arbitrary about rank in the kingdom. It cannot be assigned through favoritism, as a king appoints his ministers. Precedence in that realm is "a question of being first and not of standing first, . . . not of appointment, but of achievement." [9] It is in God's hands. But it is also in man's hands as he fulfills the requirements of God—there are many such things in the spiritual life that are not alone God's to give, but man's to fashion.

We pray, for instance, "O God, give me a noble character." That is not alone God's to give arbitrarily, but man's to fashion, as he goes through the experiences by which truly Christian character is attained. It calls for the fidelity which, putting its hands to the plow, does not look back, and for the love which seeks not its own. We pray, "O God, give me joy." God can answer that prayer only by leading us through the ardors and endurances by which the joy of the Lord may come into a life. Character, joy, strength greater than our own, fellowship with God, comfort in trial, guidance—these are in God's power and Christ's power to give only if we will receive them as he has appointed.

[9] E. P. Gould, *Gospel According to St. Mark* (New York: Charles Scribner's Sons, 1905; "International Critical Commentary"), p. 200.

41 And when the ten heard *it,* they began to be much displeased with James and John.

42 But Jesus called them *to him,* and saith unto them, Ye know that they which

it has been prepared." 41 And when the ten heard it, they began to be indignant at James and John. 42 And Jesus called them

tion; the idea was current in Jewish eschatological thought, and the words need not be viewed as a gloss in spite of the incomplete statement. "It will be given those" is implied (cf. KJV). That no rigid doctrine is to be inferred seems clear from Matt. 20:23, which adds "by my Father"; but divine foreknowledge is only one step short of predestination.

41. This verse connects naturally with vss. 37, as those who view vss. 38-40, or some part thereof, as secondary have observed. It is interesting to note that a similar pattern is followed by Mark in all three passion announcements: the first is followed by Jesus' words on the conditions of discipleship, 8:34–9:1; the second by his words on the greatness of service, 9:33-37 (-50?); the third by the remainder of the present section, vss. 41-45, on a similar theme. The pattern can scarcely be accidental. Were Jesus' discipleship sayings grouped this way for purposes of instruction in the early church? Naturally **the ten** other disciples were **much displeased** at the presumption of the two sons of Zebedee. Did the ambition of the two reflect later claims to authority in the apostolic church? (Gal. 2:6, 9; cf. Grant, *Growth of the Gospels,* p. 109).

42. **Are supposed to rule:** There is a sting in this word "rule," which Matthew and Luke omit, and also in **lord it over them.** But the verse pictures vividly the manners and

41. *And When the Ten Heard It, They Began to Be Indignant at James and John.*— Here the serpent of jealousy and discord crept into the company. There was the natural resentment that crafty self-seeking always brings. The drive for preferment might be called a number one enemy of the Christian church. This has been true, whether the matter in hand has been the election of a pope, or the election of the second assistant secretary of anything. Jesus recognized the danger and once more issued, in the words immediately following, a very solemn warning against it.

Two things calling for self-searching thought appear here. One goes down into the deeps of psychology. It seems quite evident that part, at least, of the disciples' resentment over the private reach James and John made for high places was due to the fact that they wanted the high places for themselves. Their feeling was not purely in moral disapproval of such self-promotion; they were angry because they were afraid of being maneuvered out of something they coveted for their own possession. That fear of being outwitted always adds venom to anger at evil.

We recognize this as a common occurrence since we have learned to peer with pitiless Freudian X rays into the deep places of the heart. So often opposition to evil comes not only from moral insight, but from personal frustration. We need to check on our indignations, to see to what extent they arise from the feeling that we are missing what someone else has which, consciously or unconsciously, we

want for ourselves. For instance, as in the indignation of the ten, denunciation of the evils of place-seeking may have a sour note in it, springing from the denouncer's failure to get preferment for himself. Undoubtedly many a violent philippic against dissipation, alcoholic or sexual, has had its obscure source in the dim feeling that others were having gratifications denied those who were carrying on the crusade. How often has the arraignment of riches sprung from a sense of the moral and spiritual dangers inherent in wealth, and how often from envy and covetousness? So do we need to look into our own hearts and examine them, that our motives may be purified from disappointed self-seeking, and brought into fuller accord with the mind of Christ.

The other thing in this narrative which calls for self-examination is the evidence it affords of what we might almost call "political action." Peter had been a leader among the disciples. Jesus had taken Peter and James and John to the Mount of Transfiguration. Here two of them were engaged in by-passing the third on their push to places of power. They had really formed an "anti-Peter bloc," to use political slang. It was an attempt to use cunning as a means to self-aggrandizement as an end. The solemnity of Jesus' warning in the words which follow stresses the viciousness of all such action wherever it may be taken, and for whatever purpose.

42-44. *Whoever Would Be First Among You Must Be Slave of All.*—Again we find Jesus turning the world upside down. His was so

are accounted to rule over the Gentiles exercise lordship over them; and their great ones exercise authority upon them.

43 But so shall it not be among you: but whosoever will be great among you, shall be your minister:

44 And whosoever of you will be the chiefest, shall be servant of all.

45 For even the Son of man came not to

to him and said to them, "You know that those who are supposed to rule over the Gentiles lord it over them, and their great men exercise authority over them. 43 But it shall not be so among you; but whoever would be great among you must be your servant, 44 and whoever would be first among you must be slave of all. 45 For the Son of man also came not to be served

---

morals of earthly rulers; one is reminded of the frequent mention by Tacitus and other historians of the investigation and trial by law of provincial governors for their deeds of extortion and oppression of subject peoples, among them the Jews. Mark had certainly seen the seamy side of Roman administration under Nero; and the same conditions had prevailed in Palestine under Pontius Pilate (A.D. 26-36), and therefore during the public ministry of Jesus.

43-44. Shall not be is a later reading; Mark wrote οὐχ . . . ἐστίν: "It is not like this with you." **Minister** (KJV), as in 9:35, is practically identical with **servant** in the following verse, as the parallelism shows; better, as in RSV, **servant** and **slave**. This is the final answer, here at the end of the series of discipleship sayings, to the question in 9:34, "Who is the greatest?"

45. As elsewhere (e.g., vs. 38), it is Jesus himself who is the disciples' perfect pattern. Not now in his personal character so much as in the "theological" role he was called to

---

great a revolution, so completely fulfilled the description in the Magnificat (Luke 1:52), that the lesson needed to be taught over and over again. This time there is a definite note of scorn for the great men and rulers who lord it over their people. There is a swagger in that phrase. We can see their gestures of pride and arrogance. In Jesus' condemnation is his verdict on a whole political order. He who never took up any questions of political theory here sweepingly indicts the whole Roman and Oriental system of government, and by implication every government which preserves the lord-it-over-them quality, and fails to justify itself in service to its citizens and humanity. His words reject not only Rome with its exploitation, but all imperialism, all colonialism, which seeks advantage rather than service. They puncture the pretensions of all ruling classes, all superior races, all self-designated higher castes. Jesus finds that there is nothing in the business of lording it over peoples which deserves the name of leadership at all. Note the irony and scorn in the phrase **those who are supposed to rule.** What a deflation of human pomp and circumstance! There is a little boy on the sidewalk in the fairy story of "The Emperor's New Clothes." While the subservient flatterers are giving way to raptures over the supposed gossamer-thin clothing of the emperor, the realistic little boy blurts out the brutal truth, "Why, he hasn't anything on at all. He's naked!" To Christ there is no real leadership in the tyranny of power. And the judgment applies to the realm

of industry as well as politics. There too we have had grim, desolate years of hard power, lording it over labor as a commodity. Jesus weighs it in his balance and finds it wanting.

Again he asserts that the only real greatness lies in service. **It shall not be so among you.** Yet surely it has been so—among us, his followers. The world's standards have often been accepted abjectly by the church, like pagan idols set up in the sanctuary. Think of the contradiction in terms which is so obvious in that phrase "the princes of the church"! It has been so among us in the widespread worship of success. This reversal of the world's measurements is hard to accept; but until we do accept it we are far from the kingdom. Suppose our lives were to be measured only by the amount of real service we have rendered to people. How great would they be? Jesus is here telling us that that is precisely how they are measured.

The Kingdoms of the Earth go by
    In purple and in gold;
They rise, they triumph, and they die,
    And all their tale is told,

One Kingdom only is divine,
    One banner triumphs still,
Its King a servant, and its sign
    A gibbet on a hill.[1]

45. For the Son of Man also Came Not to Be Served but to Serve.—Jesus' purpose could not

[1] Godfrey Fox Bradby. Used by permission of Christopher Bradby, executor.

be ministered unto, but to minister, and to give his life a ransom for many. | but to serve, and to give his life as a ransom for many."

---

fulfill: if the glorious Son of man lived on earth as a servant, **came not to be served but to serve,** and even **to give his life as a ransom for many,** how much more must his disciples accept the role of "mere servants" (Luke 17:10). To Luke this saying (i.e., vs. 45) seemed to belong at the Supper (Luke 22:27), and John presents it as an acted parable and discourse (John 13:1-20). It is one of the few theological statements in Mark, and it helps us to understand his whole Christology, even though it belongs among his "Son of man" sayings—and is therefore presumably from one of his sources—and is not phrased in accordance with his preferred "Son of God" terminology. The two titles were of course combined; see Intro., pp. 642-43. There is no trace of Pauline influence here, as used to be thought; the language is more primitive than even Paul. Luke's reformulation (Luke 22:27) is scarcely an intentional omission of Pauline atonement theology—though Luke has no such doctrine. Instead, the verse states the ultimate object of the Son of man's earthly life of service and his death as a "ransom for many," somewhat as the Jewish martyrs died for the redemption of their people (II Macc. 7:37-38; IV Macc. 17:22).

Some scholars hold that the final clause, **and to give his life a ransom for many,** has been added by Mark—or even by some later hand—the original saying having ended with **minister.** But the clause goes with the whole series of passion announcements, and with the Son of man sayings (e.g., 14:21), and is so completely consonant with their general outlook that it would seem more likely to have come from one of Mark's sources. The words in 14:24, "for many," may be an echo of this verse, and even possibly, as has been argued, a later addition to Mark's text; the phrase there is ὑπὲρ πολλῶν, not ἀντὶ πολλῶν, as here. Ἀντί means literally "in place of" (cf. Josephus *Antiquities* XIV. 7. 1, cited by Klostermann); but here it surely means "for" many, i.e., as their ransom (cf.

---

be expressed in the passive voice, **be served,** but only in the active, **serve.** The highest achievement in life is to get out of the passive voice into the active. It is the "great divide" which some people never cross. We all begin, of course, in the passive voice. We are acted upon before we act. We are loved before we love. We are served, in ways almost beyond count, before we serve. By how many are we ministered to, all the way from astronomers and poets to bus operators and garbage collectors! Yet a life's most significant graduation day comes when we graduate into the active voice. And so few ever do; ever really come to moral maturity. The aim of "the great ones" whom Jesus repudiated was to keep themselves in the passive voice, to be waited upon, ministered to, forever on the receiving end, never on the giving end. That is the surest way to miss life in its largest possibilities. Only when we get life across this "great divide" do we touch its highest glory or its deepest joy.

Christian experience begins in the passive voice. We are called, saved, loved, possessed. It must go on to the active voice of those great verbs, call, save, love.

45. And to Give His Life as a Ransom for Many.—The word of caution set down above (see on vs. 40) needs to be remembered here.

This passage cannot be made to furnish a basis for Paul's theology of the Atonement, for the doctrine of Jesus' death as a ransom from sin or Satan. See Exeg. for the evidence on which the conclusion is based that the "phrase . . . should be understood in as simple and figurative, i.e., poetic and dramatic a sense as possible." Without being pressed into a theological dogma, it means that to Jesus his death was not an accident, not a tragedy, but an offering from which men would receive great blessing. Through his giving of himself something of high value would come. And that, of course, is history.

> From the cross the radiance streaming,
> Adds more luster to the day.[2]

There has been immeasurable blessing in the Cross. It has been a ransom, a saving power, the price by which people have been delivered from bondage.

But we do not fully enter into the meaning of these words of Jesus until we face the questions: Are we giving life? Does our living bring ransom to any captives? Do our efforts bring release to any prisoners? In every life genuinely given there is an approach to this great word "ransom." We see it in the service of a physician,

[2] John Bowring, "In the cross of Christ I glory."

46 ¶ And they came to Jericho: and as he went out of Jericho with his disciples and a great number of people, blind Bartimeus, the son of Timeus, sat by the highway side begging.	46 And they came to Jericho; and as he was leaving Jericho with his disciples and a great multitude, Bar-ti-mae′us, a blind beggar, the son of Ti-mae′us, was sitting by

Matt. 17:27; Heb. 12:16). So primitive, so Jewish, so scriptural (cf. Isa. 53), so non- (if not pre-) Pauline a phrase is likely to be pre-Marcan as well, and should be understood in as simple and figurative, i.e., poetic and dramatic, a sense as possible, rather than with a fully developed theological meaning. If so understood, it may well be accepted as authentic. Jesus is aware of his impending destiny. A divine necessity confronts him (δεῖ . . . πολλὰ παθεῖν—8:31), and he is prepared to accept it. But his destiny, since it is no decree of blind fate, but the will of God, has a meaning; that meaning is one which stands in closest relation to the purposes of God for his people—the "many" were the nation, then the world, then the church of God called out of many races and tongues. This saying does not formulate a theology of the Atonement, but it is one of the data upon which any theology of the Atonement must inevitably rest.

6. BARTIMAEUS (10:46-52)

The location of this section, the last example of Jesus' healing ministry in Mark, was determined by the setting: Jericho is on the way to Jerusalem via the Jordan Valley, about fifteen miles east northeast of the Holy City. The use of the title **Son of David** (cf. 12:35-37; also 11:10) suggsts Judea, with its nationalistic messianism (cf. Lohmeyer, *Galiläa und Jerusalem*). The pericope is a complete unit: like many other healing narratives in the Gospel, it does not end with any quotable pronouncement, though **Thy faith hath made thee whole** has something of that character.

46. The son of Timaeus, which some editors would omit, is simply a translation of **bar Timaeus;** but Mark often translates Aramaic words. It is curious, however, that the translation precedes the name in the Greek text.

a teacher, a social worker, a minister, a missionary, a farmer, a businessman, a housewife, a mother, whenever that service bears the mark of a cross. Such giving of life in costly, sustained, unniggardly measure, has always brought with it its quota of release. Suppose we let our imagination run out to picture the need of our world, the multitude of prisoners that no man can number—men and women and little children held in bondage by false and vicious ideas, by oppression, by hunger and destitution, by sin. As we think of ourselves in relation to them, do we ever realize that nothing will be great enough to meet our responsibility—nothing but the kind of life which is itself, in some high and holy sense, a ransom?

46. *As He Was Leaving Jericho with . . . a Great Multitude, Bartimaeus, . . . Was Sitting by the Roadside.*—Notice in this passage the striking contrast: on the one hand, a great multitude; on the other, one lowly individual, as low in the social scale as a person could get, as near to a social cipher as possible, a blind beggar. It is tremendously impressive to see Jesus turn his attention from the many to the one. No crowd was ever big enough to blind him or render him deaf (see on 1:16). His was

not only an amazingly sensitive ear and eye; there is evidence of something deeper: the priority he gave to persons, to any person, at the point of need. On his agenda one beggar, single-handed, could put a thousand to flight. Quite different from the distorted vision we so easily fall into—"Sorry, I'm on my way to speak to the convention. There will be a big crowd there. See you later perhaps."

This brief, dramatic narrative comes with great pertinence to a generation which thinks and acts so largely in terms of multitudes and quantities. More and more we seem inclined to settle all questions by some kind of mass opinion poll. The individual easily gets lost, particularly when he sits, as Bartimaeus did, on the lowest rung of the social ladder. Consequently the valuation which Jesus set on one person in need is itself one of the greatest needs of our time. All the more because so many of us live in overcrowded cities that multiply the number of the sick and the lonely and the destitute, and increase the intensity of their wretchedness. No wonder nervous and mental tension and instability have enormously increased. Society and the church need desperately the eye keen to see beyond the multitude, and

47 And when he heard that it was Jesus of Nazareth, he began to cry out, and say, Jesus, *thou* Son of David, have mercy on me.

48 And many charged him that he should hold his peace: but he cried the more a great deal, *Thou* Son of David, have mercy on me.

the roadside. 47 And when he heard that it was Jesus of Nazareth, he began to cry out and say, "Jesus, Son of David, have mercy on me!" 48 And many rebuked him, telling him to be silent; but he cried out all the more, "Son of David, have mercy on me!"

---

47. **Jesus of Nazareth,** or "the Nazarene," to distinguish him from others of the same name, which was a common one (see index to Benedictus Niese, *Flavii Josephi Opera* [Berlin: Weidmann, 1895]). Our Lord was already well known, as Mark has repeatedly said or implied; and messianic expectations centered upon him, even outside the circle of the twelve (6:14-15; 8:28; cf. 11:8-10).

---

the sharpened ear that can hear, above the roar of the crowd, the cry from the roadside, "Have mercy on me!"

But to us who are his disciples this picture of Jesus comes with a special compulsion. The one can be lost in the many just as readily when the talk is of a congregation as when the talk is of a crowd on the street. You can be blind in a pew, and deaf in front of an altar. No creed, no liturgy, no hymn, no prayer, can absolve the laggard eye or the dull ear.

47. *He Began to Cry Out and Say, "Jesus, Son of David, Have Mercy on Me!"*—Here are vivid pictures of excitement and movement. The milling crowd, disturbed by the agitated cries of the blind beggar; the rebuke that many hurled at him; Jesus, stopping; the blind man, throwing off his mantle and springing up; the healing—all of it leaves the impression, not of still life, but of swift action. In the insistent cries of Bartimaeus we can hear a man saying over and over to himself, "Here's my chance." Of course nothing could stop him. He was jumping at the chance of a lifetime. Probably it was the venture of desperation, more of a wild hope than of any considered faith. But it was hope acted upon. "Jesus is here. Perhaps he . . . ."

That leap of hope has been an endlessly repeated act in Christian history (see on 1:32-34). The rumor of a healer, of One who could lift life out of its defeats, has come to people even when they could not see Jesus clearly, and they have made the venture, brought their lives to him. Sometimes the venture has been made at the point of desperation; more often at the beginning of life, as one has felt the sense of dependence and the need for guidance. Sometimes it has been a volcanic experience like that of Paul; sometimes it has been the result of the slow processes of Christian nurture, as in the case of Timothy. Always this central drama of salvation for individual lives has gone on—

the wistful hope that Jesus might be the answer, the venture of bringing life to him, the saving force, "Your faith has made you well."

Out of my sickness into thy health,
Out of my want and into thy wealth.[3]

As long as it is kept central, living history, re-enacted, the church lives, and the gates of hell shall not prevail against it. Out of my sin, into Thyself. When it is pushed out to the fringe, or dropped from sight, like some forgotten heirloom in an attic; when, as has happened in dark and dreary days and years, it is made subsidiary to anything, the fire has died on the altar.

The cry of blind Bartimaeus rings to the center of the world's distress. To generations sitting in despair the first step to salvation, and to survival in that heady tumult, is **Jesus, . . . have mercy on me!** He can heal a blind society; he can heal a disintegrating civilization. One of the hopeful signs of the times is that so many have been coming to see it. From unexpected and even unlikely sources, from unordained folk, without bell, book, or candle, has come word that Christ is the way, the truth, and the life. From the moment the first atomic bomb was dropped on Hiroshima there has been no dearth of voices to catch up the warning of Jesus, "Unless you repent you will all likewise perish" (Luke 13:5).

48. *And Many Rebuked Him, Telling Him to Be Silent.*—This note of rebuke, administered to people who came to Jesus, runs through Mark like a theme in a musical fugue (see vs. 13). Here the rebuke comes from the crowd, and not from the disciples. A stock answer of the crowds in history, to all those who made a clamor about need and suffering, has been just this same "Get out and keep still." It was a callous thing to do; but, as we know, crowds, with their swift intolerance, their undisciplined emotions, can do heartless and cruel things. The

[3] William T. Sleeper, "Out of my bondage."

49 And Jesus stood still, and commanded him to be called. And they call the blind man, saying unto him, Be of good comfort, rise; he calleth thee.	49 And Jesus stopped and said, "Call him." And they called the blind man, saying to him, "Take heart; rise, he is calling you."

49. Take heart=Θάρσει, "Courage!" or in modern colloquial speech, "Cheer up!" But on the lips of Jesus, in 6:50, it was not meant colloquially, as here. Both parallels, by abridgment, omit the vivid detail of vss. 49b-51a.

interruption annoyed them. They were interested in Jesus. That was the big excitement, the focus of attention. This beggar was unimportant; his eager thrusting of his insignificant self into the center of the stage was a nuisance. They met it with stony indifference, and the command to be quiet.

Their rebuke has echoed through the archways of the years. We can hear it sounding in the world now, and that without listening too intently. The crowd at Jericho chided the beggar for bringing his troubles to Jesus. To their massive ignorance such things as poverty and affliction had nothing to do with the Master. Crowds in New York, Chicago, London, Moscow, utter the same rebuff, when poverty stalks the land, when unemployment goes up and human life goes down, and men cry out, "These are religious problems; it is the responsibility of the church of Christ to do something about them." The swift rebuke still comes: "Be quiet. There is no use to cry to Jesus. Poverty and need are not his business. Let the church keep out of economic questions. Keep still." The complete answer to that is what Jesus did. He stopped and said, "Call him." He demonstrated that all human need is his business. It still is.

We do not, however, exhaust the relevance of this scene when we see it pointing to the callous blindness of commercialism alone. Sometimes it is the very disciples of Jesus, met for worship in a church, who by their manner and lack of concern rebuke the lonely soul that cries out for spiritual healing. They like to have all things decorous and orderly, and in the best of taste. They really want no miracles of conversion, of restoration. That might be "raw emotionalism, you know," something that would disturb the stately flow from introit to recessional. And so such miracles do not happen! What does our whole manner say most clearly? What the crowd said, "Keep still"? Or what Christ said, "Come"?

49. And Jesus Stopped and Said, "Call Him." —There is an everlasting eloquence in this verb "stopped." Here Jesus pays the ultimate tribute to a person in need. He stops the parade and stands at attention before him. He gives a dramatic representation to what is often a foggy phrase, "the sacredness of personality." Jesus

did not use the phrase. He did not need to. He lived it. He stopped and gave the whole of his attention, his mind and heart, to a blind beggar. His stopping said clearly, "You count." And that is one of the deep, permanent needs of humanity—the need of respect, the assurance that one "counts," that he is not merely an item in some total, one of so many million Negroes, one of so many units in the labor reservoir, or one of so many in any mass.

The art of stopping is a high art. We are so prone to be in busy motion. We have a schedule, and, as one acute observer noted, we often spell the word "skedaddle." So we "skedaddle" from here to there, to arrive breathless at the exact moment of the appointment. It is not easy to stop. It takes humility and it takes reverence for personality. But this narrative should remind us that it is a necessary prelude to any real work of healing. Jesus never healed anybody on the run. "Stopping" is a necessary part of any genuine ministry to life. The disciple is not above his master. He must learn to stand still and to stand at attention before his brother in Christ.

The giving of recognition and respect, as to one who counts, is a basic social service. In itself it hands out no bread, it gives no job, it solves no intricate problems of social adjustment. But it meets a fundamental need which underlies all social problems. Many of the ills of the social body come from the lack of it—so keenly felt in herding, in segregation and discrimination, in the stubborn insistence on lumping people as a class, and not as individuals of a particular quality.

49. Take Heart; Rise, He Is Calling You.— The comment that this "take heart" was the equivalent to our colloquial "cheer up" (see Exeg.) brings to mind the truth that the words "be of good cheer," as used by Jesus so often, meant infinitely more than a casual, hearty "cheer up." Here the expression is used by people in the crowd. It was a conventional word of encouragement. It meant "You're in luck. The Teacher is going to stop and help you after all." But Jesus' word of cheer went far, far deeper. He brought into every situation something that was lasting reason for cheer— the resources of God. That is vastly different

50 And he, casting away his garment, rose, and came to Jesus. 51 And Jesus answered and said unto him, What wilt thou that I should do unto thee? The blind man said unto him, Lord, that I might receive my sight. 52 And Jesus said unto him, Go thy way; thy faith hath made thee whole. And immediately he received his sight, and followed Jesus in the way.	50 And throwing off his mantle he sprang up and came to Jesus. 51 And Jesus said to him, "What do you want me to do for you?" And the blind man said to him, "Master,[t] let me receive my sight." 52 And Jesus said to him, "Go your way; your faith has made you well." And immediately he received his sight and followed him on the way. [t] Or Rabbi.

51. Cf. the question in 10:36 and other questions in 8:27, 29; 9:16, 21, 33; 10:3, 18, 38. This is more than a simple device of the tradition, or of Mark, to convey vividness by dialogue; such a characteristic, quasi-Socratic style must go back to Jesus himself. As a good teacher and pastor he encouraged others to express their wishes, hopes, aspirations, and gave opportunity to them to express their faith, upon which he could then act and build. **Lord** (KJV) in Matthew and Luke, and in later MSS of Mark, is "Rabboni" in the better texts; it is only a fuller form of "rabbi" and means "my master." Cf. John 20:16, where it is explained as "teacher" (*magister*, Vulg.).

52. **Thy faith hath made thee whole**: Cf. 5:34; Luke 7:50; etc. It is one of the oft-repeated sayings in the Synoptic Gospels, in its Greek version even metrical in form, as in

from a hearty "cheerio." Indeed, for one in real trouble the chirping optimism of his friends is often only an additional weight to bear. Its very superficiality, its very lack of weight, makes it heavy. Jesus' exhortation to be of good cheer was never superficial, for it brought news about the universe; it put under life the everlasting arms; it brought the power of God to change whatever was wrong.

The healing of Bartimaeus is particularly interesting because of the place it occupies in Jesus' ministry. It is the last healing recorded in Mark. Jesus was on his way to Jerusalem; at Jericho he was only fifteen miles from his goal. The period in which healings had been a prominent feature had come to a close. His face was now set to the Cross. This healing, then, was all the more noteworthy. It was a roadside ministry, which could make no difference to the great end he had in view. Compared to the panorama of events which was to unfold in Jerusalem, it was—nothing. Nothing but a person and a need. Nothing but a work of mercy and love to be done. And he did it.

It is the "meanwhile" mercy, the roadside ministries, that we are so apt to omit. We are absorbed in a task, and the deeds of helpfulness which have no relation to it, which contribute nothing to forward it, seem trivial. One who has a great aim in life, to which he is giving his heart, strength, and mind, can all too readily excuse himself from time-consuming detours that only slow him up in reaching the goal. There is sometimes a disdain for "meanwhile" ministries even on the part of those working for the reorganization of society. Acts of mercy and charity tend to become only "palliatives." They contribute nothing to a new social structure. The individual need is lost sight of in the glow of the far, shining horizon.

Jesus did not reason that way. One more blind man healed would make no difference to the great culmination of his ministry and life. But it would be one more blind man healed. A work of love was never a small thing to him who looked on people with the very compassion of God. The answer to any argument that a service of any sort is "only a drop in the bucket" is that it is a drop in the bucket and Jesus put a high rating on drops in a bucket. "I was thirsty and you gave me drink" (Matt. 25:35).

50. *And Throwing Off His Mantle He Sprang Up and Came to Jesus.*—This is a perfect picture of the headlong response. The very words seem to spring and jump. They are violently active. Bartimaeus did not fold his garment carefully and neatly and say to a bystander, "Please look after this a minute. I'll be back." He threw it away and leaped to his feet.

Such headlong response to the words "he is calling you" is something we greatly need. We are so careful about "springing," so cautious about going "all out." We like to look before we leap. And so frequently, after a look, we do not leap at all. This blind beggar did not care about his garment. He forgot it, caught up in a great hope and a great trust. Are we so careful of our garments, of our interests of one sort or another, that we fail to have the throb and the joy of headlong discipleship? Do you leap at the words "He is calling you"? (See on vss. 15-16.)

11 And when they came nigh to Jeru- | 11 And when they drew near to Je-
salem, unto Bethphage and Bethany, | rusalem, to Beth'pha-ge and Bethany,
at the mount of Olives, he sendeth forth | at the Mount of Olives, he sent two of his
two of his disciples,

Longfellow's poem "Blind Bartimaeus." **Immediately:** Mark's frequent εὐθύς. The contrast with the slower cure in 8:22-26 is probably not intentional. **He . . . followed,** not as a disciple in the full sense, but as one of the "Passover pilgrims" at the Triumphal Entry, which immediately follows.

B. In Jerusalem (11:1–12:44)

The next main division narrates Jesus' activity in Jerusalem during the final week. The material is drawn largely from the second group of controversies, 11:27–12:40, and leads up directly to the passion narrative, chs. 14–15. There is a break, however, in ch. 13, where Mark inserts the apocalyptic discourse, for which there was no other place in the book. Some second-century writings located this material in the period after the Resurrection (cf. the Epistle of the Apostles, etc.).

It has long been observed that the arrangement of chs. 11–15 follows a fixed chronological scheme, which it is not too much to call (with Loisy) a primitive "Holy Week." John's chronology is different, and allows for several visits to Jerusalem—if, indeed, he does not think of Jerusalem rather than Capernaum as Jesus' "headquarters" (cf. John 4:44; 7:1; 11:54). In John, Jesus' final ministry in Judea and Jerusalem covers several months, though the Triumphal Entry (John 12:12-15) comes five days before the Passover. What Mark did—or the church of his time, which handed down the tradition— was to crowd into one week a series of events that quite possibly belonged to a longer period and perhaps to more than one visit. He does not exclude the possibility of other visits, but he certainly does not imply them—though note the "day after day" in 14:49. Working backward (as in Klostermann's note, 3rd ed. [1936], pp. 110-12; cf. Loisy) from Friday (15:42) which is the fixed datum in the series, the scheme was as follows:

Sunday (Palm): Entry into Jerusalem and return to Bethany (11:1-11)
Monday: Cursing of the fig tree and cleansing of the temple (11:12-19)
Tuesday: Discourses in 11:20–13:37
Wednesday: Anointing in Bethany and Judas' betrayal (14:1-11)
Thursday: Preparation for the Passover, Last Supper, Gethsemane, arrest, trial before Sanhedrin (14:12-72)
Friday: Trial before Pilate, condemnation, crucifixion, burial (15:1-47)
Saturday: Jesus in the tomb (15:42-47)
Sunday (Easter): Resurrection (16:1-8)

The events of Good Friday were arranged by "watches" (Roman style, four watches of three hours each): morning (15:1), third hour (15:25), sixth hour (15:33), ninth hour (15:34), evening (15:42). It may even be that the preceding night was divided into watches (vigils? cf. 13:35-37; 14:37): evening (14:17), night or possibly midnight

---

11:1-10. The Triumphal Entry.—This story presents a picturesque and powerful symbol of something that needed a symbol, both in the first few centuries of the church and ever since —the kingship of Jesus. The Christian church has inevitably and rightly taken the entry into Jerusalem as a symbol of the coming into the world of One whose right it is to rule. Commentators have found it difficult to reconstruct, with any assurance of accuracy, the details of what actually happened. So many of those set down seem to find place as evidence of the

fulfillment of prophecy. Whether this was, on Jesus' part, an explicit announcement of his messiahship, or whether it was so regarded by the onlookers or by those who hailed him, is open to question (see Exeg.). But we are on sure ground when we take the historical basis of the story—the entrance of Jesus into Jerusalem —as the church has taken it, to be a meaningful symbol of Jesus as King.

His right to kingship in the life of an individual and of society has gathered, through history and experience, a wealth of evidence far

(14:30), cockcrow (14:72), though the scheme looks more like a Jewish three-watch division than a Roman four.

For centuries, since the days of the second-century Quartodecimans, the conflict between the Synoptic (i.e., Mark's) chronology and that of John has been discussed without any satisfactory solution. It may reflect what later became the conflict between the Eastern (Ephesian) and Western (Roman) observance of Easter. For what may perhaps lie behind Mark, i.e., in the earlier passion narrative, see below on 14:1-2. It is possible that Mark's scheme reflects the usage of Rome in the sixties, while that of John reflects a theological or symbolical interpretation of Jesus as the true Paschal Lamb, who died when the Passover lambs were being offered, and that back of both Mark and John lay the historical fact that Jesus died "at Passover time," but not on the actual day of the festival. That is to say, both Mark and John give interpretations: Mark identifies the Last Supper with the Passover meal, John the death of Christ with the death of the lambs; the difference between them may not be one of divergent historical traditions.

1. The Entry into Jerusalem (11:1-10)

The simplest form of the story (as in John 12:12-15) assumes that the demonstration was a spontaneous acclamation on the part of a group of Passover pilgrims, who hail Jesus as "the Son of David" or "the King of Israel"—though, as in Matt. 21:10-11, he is still "the prophet Jesus from Nazareth of Galilee." But later (cf. John 12:16) it came to be viewed as a crucial event in Jesus' self-announcement and self-proclamation, as Messiah, to the religious capital, i.e., to the whole Jewish people. Hence the careful preparations for the event, like the preparation for the supper in 14:12-16: a "colt" must be provided, in fulfillment of Zech. 9:9 (cf. Isa. 62:11; Matt. 21:5 has both passages in mind). In other words, Jesus takes the initiative (vss. 1b-6); it is no longer a spontaneous demonstration. But the nucleus of the story (vss. 1a, 7-10) is undoubtedly authentic history. There is interpretation here, but it is recognizable as secondary.

11:1. The four place names do not add to definiteness, but the opposite, partly because of gaps in our modern geography. The present road from Jericho to Jerusalem comes up around the south side of the Mount of Olives; if Bethphage lay on the south side of the mount, and Bethany some distance southeast, the requirements will be met, though the order is wrong. Some ancient MSS omit Bethphage, which was little known. More probably "and Bethany" should be omitted, with Matthew (21:1); Torrey (*The Four Gospels, ad loc.*) brackets it. Was it derived from vs. 11? **Two of his disciples:** As on an earlier mission (6:7; cf. 14:13).

beyond anything that was possible during his years on earth. We can see it validated, as men of his day could not, by the way he has met the deep needs of the human soul. He meets them in that dim borderland where our reach exceeds our grasp. Our inability to find fulfillment in material things, as other creatures of earth do, fits in, is mortised in, as it were, to his revelation of the great Other, in whom our fragments are complete. Our dissatisfaction with ourselves, our inescapable sense of missing the mark, fits in with his own demonstration, not only of the life we are meant for, but of the possibility of forgiveness and a life made over. Our experience of the strange self-defeating quality of selfishness fits into his call to fulfillment in service.

His right to kingship is also validated by the long line of people running down through the centuries, people who have taken him as Master and Savior, and whose lives in power and ministering love have been direct and fundamental proofs of the Christian religion. It has been given, too, an overwhelming demonstration in the social and political world. Every year piles up new mountains of evidence that Jesus was everlastingly right in his reading of life. The most effective arguments for the truth of Christianity are not being spun out of the brains of theologians, but by the events of contemporary history. The passing parade brings daily testimony to the truth that other foundation can no man lay for lasting security, economic welfare, and peace than that which is laid in Christ Jesus.

We have been given for generations the conventional picture of him as a gentle, mildly deluded sentimentalist, a figure for poetry and art, but unfitted to deal with the rough realities of the world. That picture is steadily changing

2 And saith unto them, Go your way into the village over against you: and as soon as ye be entered into it, ye shall find a colt tied, whereon never man sat; loose him, and bring *him*.

3 And if any man say unto you, Why do ye this? say ye that the Lord hath need of him; and straightway he will send him hither.

disciples, 2 and said to them, "Go into the village opposite you, and immediately as you enter it you will find a colt tied, on which no one has ever sat; untie it and bring it. 3 If any one says to you, 'Why are you doing this?' say, 'The Lord has need of it and will send it back here im-

---

2. **The village** Bethphage, not Bethany, according to Matt. 21:1-2. **On which no one has ever sat:** As generally in the ancient world (I Sam. 6:7; Horace *Epodes* IX. 22, etc.), an animal intended for sacred use must be unbroken.

3. **The Lord,** not "its master" (cf. Luke 19:33, "its owners"), nor God, nor yet (as in 14:14) "the Teacher"; perhaps the owner was also a disciple, and would recognize the reference of the title. It occurs nowhere else in Mark as a designation for Jesus. But the language used here is that of early church interpretation.

---

for anyone not deaf, dumb, and blind. Jesus is emerging as the sternest realist who ever injected hard truth into a world ruled by illusion. He is not the sentimentalist in the world we know. The sentimentalists are the romantic fools who imagine that it is possible to build security and peace on a foundation of hate and revenge, or of greed and competing sovereignties. Clemenceau, after the Versailles Peace Conference in 1919, directed a scornful sneer at Woodrow Wilson. He said that the president of the United States "spoke like Jesus Christ." One keen-minded man exclaimed, "Ah, if only he had!" If anyone there, or at Yalta, or anywhere else, had spoken like Jesus Christ and carried conviction, our world might not have fallen into such ruin. The only one who could bring now a saving word to that world would be one who would speak like Jesus Christ. We can still cry to him with the old shout, "Hosanna!"

2. *Go into the Village Opposite You, and . . . . You Will Find a Colt.*—The interesting conjecture has been made by several writers that this story about finding a colt tied, and the parallel story about the unknown man who helped in the preparation of the Last Supper, indicate that Jesus had an "underground" working in Jerusalem. There is much to be said for it. It is easier to think that the ready aid given him and his disciples was given by friends and adherents than to think of it as accidental or starkly miraculous.

The word "underground" has sharp and vivid meaning since World War II. Jesus may well have had supporters in Jerusalem who could be compared to an underground in that sense of the word. Has he an underground in our city or community? Is there a network of people, a dependable force, "alerted" to his purposes,

acquainted with his mind, ready to act for his cause?

3. *If Any One Says to You, "Why Are You Doing This?" Say, "The Lord Has Need of It."* —The owner of the colt allowed the claim. Either he was acquainted with Jesus or his disciples, or there was something about the request which carried persuasive power. If the Teacher, the prophet of Galilee, here for the only time in Mark called "Lord," had need of his colt, he would acknowledge that priority.

This surely ought to be our response to God's need of anything we have. There are so many powers and capacities and aptitudes, as well as possessions, of which it can be said, **"The Lord has need of it."** There are skills that can be put to the use of the kingdom, personality that can be the instrument of his truth, feet that can go on his errands, hands that can lift burdens. If this man in Jerusalem who owned the colt had treated the disciples who came for it as we often treat God's calls for help, the conversation might have been:

"Here, what are you doing with that **colt?"**

"The Lord has need of it."

"What do I care? I need it myself. **Go on and** let it alone."

That is rough language. We would never put our polite refusals of God's demands in such blunt terms. But there is no doubt about the refusal.

God needs our time: "Sorry, but my time is limited. Besides, it is mine."

God needs our strength: "Sorry, I can't take on a single thing more. I'm almost exhausted as it is."

God needs our mind: "Sorry, but I have all I can give my attention to, and more. I have troubles enough of my own to think about."

What kind of priority does God get with us?

4 And they went their way, and found the colt tied by the door without in a place where two ways met; and they loose him.

5 And certain of them that stood there said unto them, What do ye, loosing the colt?

6 And they said unto them even as Jesus had commanded: and they let them go.

7 And they brought the colt to Jesus, and cast their garments on him; and he sat upon him.

8 And many spread their garments in the way; and others cut down branches off the trees, and strewed *them* in the way.

9 And they that went before, and they that followed, cried, saying, Hosanna; Blessed *is* he that cometh in the name of the Lord:

10 Blessed *be* the kingdom of our father David, that cometh in the name of the Lord: Hosanna in the highest.

mediately.'" 4 And they went away, and found a colt tied at the door out in the open street; and they untied it. 5 And those who stood there said to them, "What are you doing, untying the colt?" 6 And they told them what Jesus had said; and they let them go. 7 And they brought the colt to Jesus, and threw their garments on it; and he sat upon it. 8 And many spread their garments on the road, and others spread leafy branches which they had cut from the fields. 9 And those who went before and those who followed cried out, "Hosanna! Blessed be he who comes in the name of the Lord! 10 Blessed be the kingdom of our father David that is coming! Hosanna in the highest!"

---

4. In a place where two ways met (KJV): Better, **out in the open street** (RSV). As often, Matthew and Luke abridge, omitting Mark's full detail.

7-10. Garments . . . branches, as a sign of honor. Hosanna=*Hôshî'āh-nâ',* "Save now!" The ejaculation occurs in the Hallel (Ps. 118:25), which was sung both at Passover and at the feast of Tabernacles; it could be addressed to a king (II Sam. 14:4) or to God on behalf of a king (Ps. 20:9). What it means at the end of vs. 10 is not clear (cf. later liturgical usage, possibly influenced by Ps. 148:1 and Luke 2:14); perhaps it means "Save, thou who dwellest [or "ye angels who dwell"] on high!" Cf. Torrey's translation: "God save him! . . . God in heaven save him!" **Blessed is he,** originally (Ps. 118:26, following the line above) referred to the pilgrim on his way to the festival; it was

---

8. *Many Spread Their Garments on the Road.* —An impressive picture of the self-forgetfulness caused by a great enthusiasm. There was no debate about it; no cautious trial balance to see whether or not the risk to the clothes was really called for; no wondering if some show of respect at a cheaper price might not be enough. These people were lifted on a tide of hope and joy and love. Spontaneous enthusiasm is like a flood tide. Life has nothing to match it for exhilaration and zest. The poet who cried,

> Take all away from me,
> But give me ecstasy,[3]

had a good sense of values. The life that never forgets itself in a great lift of devotion is poor, no matter how richly upholstered its furniture.

More than that, such spontaneous, self-erasing enthusiasm is indispensable to the work of Christianity in the world.

[3] *Letters of Emily Dickinson,* ed. Mabel Loomis Todd (New York: Harper & Bros., 1931), p. 426. Used by permission of Mabel Todd Bingham.

Many spread their garments on the road. Do we ever spread anything costly before him? A maximum offering of mind, of heart, of skill, without any bookkeeping prudence to determine whether or not a minimum might be enough? (See on 10:15-16; 14:3-9.)

9. *Hosanna!*—Notice the punctuation—exclamation point. Of course there were no punctuation marks in the Greek manuscripts of the N.T. from which our translations were made. But an exclamation point is the only possible punctuation for this word of praise and salutation.

Jesus had often been greeted with a question mark. His neighbors at Nazareth put a large question mark beside him: "Where did this man get all this?" (6:2.) John the Baptist did much the same thing: "Are you he who is to come, or shall we look for another?" (Matt. 11:3.) And Pilate: "So you are a king?" (John 18:37.)

The world has had its millions of question marks about Jesus: Is he really the Way? Eve

11 And Jesus entered into Jerusalem, and into the temple: and when he had looked round about upon all things, and now the eventide was come, he went out unto Bethany with the twelve.

11 And he entered Jerusalem, and went into the temple; and when he had looked round at everything, as it was already late, he went out to Bethany with the twelve.

understood by Mark to refer messianically to Jesus (cf. 1:7), as in the later liturgical *Benedictus qui venit*. **Kingdom of our father David** is out-and-out messianic, and was uttered from the point of view of the popular, more or less political, expectation. Both parallels omit it!

The second **in the name of the Lord** (KJV) is not in the best Greek MSS, and must be a late error of duplication.

2. Departure for Bethany (11:11)

11. This verse is editorial and prepares for the cleansing of the temple (vss. 15-18). Luke omits it and Matthew shifts its content to a later point; for both parallels represent the cleansing of the temple as the immediate sequel and climax of the entry (under the influence of "suddenly" in Mal. 3:1-3a?). **Bethany** was about one and a half miles southeast of Jerusalem.

Curie expressed it sadly. She wrote that as she looked back on Jerusalem she was tempted to say to Jesus, whose teaching was so "tremendously powerful and yet so powerless":

"You told us to be kind and forgiving, but, for twenty solid centuries, wretched, incorrigible men have gone on being merciless, full of violence and of hatred. Religious men and atheists alike have lived and ruled in a non-Christian way—and look at us now: we've never been in a worse mess." [4]

But here at the gates of Jerusalem were exclamation points. One of the greatest journeys anyone can ever make is the journey from a question mark to an exclamation point. From a question mark about Jesus to an exclamation point about him, from a question mark about life to an exclamation point about it. That journey can never be made by thought alone; it must be made by action. When we follow him, when we do the things that he says, our punctuation marks change. It is no longer "Are you?" but "Hosanna!"

11. And He Entered Jerusalem, . . . and When He Had Looked Round at Everything, . . . He Went Out.—This sentence is accounted an editorial one, making the transition from the entry into Jerusalem to the lodging at Bethany. Yet there is in it an unforgettable picture which would make a great subject for a painting: Jesus going quietly about the city, looking at everything.

What did he see? We know from the Synoptic Gospels some of the things he saw. It is recorded here that he saw the temple. And as we learn

later in Mark, he was not impressed. His disciples gasped in wonder, with the natural awe of men coming up from the country to a large city, "Look, Teacher, what wonderful stones and what wonderful buildings!" (13:1.) Jesus said that not one stone would be left on another. He made a moral and religious measurement of stones and buildings and found them wanting. Did he see Roman legions tramping through the streets, with all the trimmings of power? We know some other things he saw, the hucksters in the temple, bawling their wares. He saw also, as always, things no one else saw—the widow putting her whole living into the alms box. Jesus looking at everything in the city was the supreme example of what was in Burns's mind when he wrote, "A chiel's amang you takin' notes." The childlike eyes of Jesus were looking through everything.

He comes to our cities. What does he see? There is nothing hidden from those eyes. He would see things to make his heart rejoice, the untrumpeted greatness of soul that never gets into the newspapers but is entered elsewhere; unbroken fidelities; unskimped giving of self. He would see other things, things before which the Chamber of Commerce hangs its iron curtain—the wretched housing, the dark betrayals of corruption, the "good" people whose cruel indifference allows exploitation to go on. Can we bear the scrutiny?

Katherine Mansfield, looking over her written stories, once exclaimed, "There isn't one that I would show to God." How much is there in our city that we would "show to God"? For this trip of Jesus through our streets is not a fantasy He does look around on everything.

12 ¶ And on the morrow, when they were come from Bethany, he was hungry:

13 And seeing a fig tree afar off having leaves, he came, if haply he might find any thing thereon: and when he came to it, he found nothing but leaves; for the time of figs was not *yet*.

14 And Jesus answered and said unto it, No man eat fruit of thee hereafter for ever. And his disciples heard *it*.

15 ¶ And they come to Jerusalem: and Jesus went into the temple, and began to cast out them that sold and bought in the

12 On the following day, when they came from Bethany, he was hungry. 13 And seeing in the distance a fig tree in leaf, he went to see if he could find anything on it. When he came to it, he found nothing but leaves, for it was not the season for figs. 14 And he said to it, "May no one ever eat fruit from you again." And his disciples heard it.

15 And they came to Jerusalem. And he entered the temple and began to drive

3. Cursing the Fig Tree (11:12-14)

12-14. This is the only miracle of Jesus in or near Jerusalem, according to Mark. The Fourth Gospel has a different view; cf. also Matt. 21:14. Luke omits both this section and the sequel, 11:20-25. It has sometimes been thought to be an "acted parable" (Luke 13:6-9), or in the older, anti-Jewish exegesis, a symbol of the rejection of Judaism or a mystical prophecy of the fall of Jerusalem. The explanation **for it was not the season for figs** (omitted by Matthew) only increases the problem, as it reflects upon the good sense of Jesus. Some commentators view it as a later gloss. Has it some connection with the meaning of Bethphage—"House of *unripe* figs"?

4. Cleansing the Temple (11:15-19)

This was presumably the immediate occasion for the opposition of the Sadducean hierarchy and the priests, as distinguished from that of the scribes and Pharisees noted

12-14, 20-21. *Seeing in the Distance a Fig Tree in Leaf.*—It is well to begin any consideration of this story of the barren fig tree with the frank recognition that it is the least attractive of all the narratives about Jesus. Luke omits it entirely, possibly because he already has a parable of a barren fig tree (Luke 13:6-9). At any rate most scholars would applaud his judgment, as shown by the omission (see Exeg. for discussion of the difficulties). There are two main objections to taking the story literally, as an exact record. The first is the unfavorable light in which it seems to put the judgment, or common sense, of Jesus; he could have had no rational expectation of finding figs out of season. The second is that the miracle is quite "out of character" with Jesus' mind and with other miracles. As Branscomb put it strongly, "Jesus scarcely went about blasting fruit trees simply because they did not have fruit ready for Him at the moment."[5] Jesus was not a conjurer. That was a role he strictly avoided. This cursing of the fig tree looks like a conjurer's act, like the "unreasonable miracles" found so often in noncanonical Gospels. Mark takes the story as a proof of Jesus' power, but that "proof" was on a level devoid of moral and religious significance.

For teaching and preaching the church has

[5] *Gospel of Mark*, p. 201.

taken the story as a symbolic representation of the truth that life without fruit is worthless. That, of course, is a truth to which Jesus gave constant emphasis. "You will know them by their fruits" (Matt. 7:16). "Why do you call me Lord and not do what I tell you?" (Luke 6:46.) The incident was taken by many in the early church as an acted parable of judgment on the religion of Israel because of its lack of ethical and spiritual fruit. We know that Jesus did pronounce such a judgment. It is implied in the story of the cleansing of the temple, which is here interpolated into the story of the fig tree. But no matter what the origin of this brief narrative in fact, the lesson usually drawn from it is valid and endlessly important. It ought to be deeply disturbing to remember how often and how strongly Jesus condemned words without acts. We have to face the question, What are the things, on which we might even be tempted to pride ourselves, that would be condemned by him as futile leaves without fruit?

15-19. *He Entered the Temple and Began to Drive Out Those Who Sold.*—If we clear up two very popular misconceptions of the cleansing of the temple courts by Jesus, we will be able to grasp more clearly the meaning of one of the most important acts of his life.

The first misconception comes from reading too much into the words **den of robbers.** This was a quotation from Jer. 7:11. It "does not necessarily imply extortion" (see Exeg.). Undoubtedly there was some, since after Jesus' time there was sharp protest about it. But Jesus' main criticism of the trading in the temple was not that it was thieving, but that it was trading. He protested against the secularization and commercialization of the house of prayer.

The second misconception comes not from any word in Mark or Matthew or Luke, but from John—from the phrase "making a whip of cords" (John 2:15). This is found only in John; there is no indication at all that he used it on people. The verb is the same as that in all the Synoptics: "drove them out." Yet from this one phrase there has been erected a fantastic structure of arguments in defense of war and of many other kinds of violence, on the ground that the money-changers and traders were actually struck with the whip, an assumption entirely without justification. Whatever may be one's conclusion about the relation of Jesus' teaching to war, there is no foundation for doctrine here.

The unencumbered fact of the "cleansing" itself, however, has great and permanent meaning for all time. His vigorous, vehement protest, expressed in forthright action, was against the use of the temple for anything but the worship and service of God. He denounced the prostituting of religion, its being made subservient to profit making. The temple had its God-appointed purpose—to be a house of prayer. Whatever might render that purpose subordinate was an abomination in the holy place. So was everything that interfered with it. **He would not allow any one to carry anything.** Mark alone gives us that detail. Worship was to Jesus so high and great an experience, meeting so deep and universal a need, that the "casual use" of temple courts as a public highway or a convenient short cut was intolerable.

The principle involved is of tremendous range, capable of close application to our ways of thinking and acting. Jesus condemned the merely instrumental use of religion, so common a thing in our day. How often we treat it, not as inherently the greatest of all realities, of infinite worth in itself, but as a means to something else. It is an escape from worry, an aesthetic gratification, a way to respectability, to social advancement, to emotional satisfaction. It may even be regarded as an appendage to some economic system or political order. We know how brazenly it has been used to bless a way of life decided on without any reference to God or ethical standards.

Again, in his clearing out of the traders from the temple Jesus came into conflict with the greatest profit-making power of his time and nation. And it was a deadly conflict. This one act was what led most directly to his trial and condemnation. It brought in the opportunistic Sadducees and the priests against him. The religious hierarchy, in these temple concessions, had what some would call a "good racket." Jesus challenged them, and they struck back swiftly with violence. Notice the difference between the two types of indignation. The chief priests were indignant over the threat to their privileges. Jesus was indignant over the wrong done to people in the secularization of the temple.

All this points to a crucial battlefield for Christianity, the struggle for the rights of people as over against that love of money which is the root of all kinds of evil. And the root spreads through our whole life, giving rise to exploitation of the weak, child labor, poverty, slums, disease, crime, and eventually war. From all these social calamities there is a direct line that runs to fat pocketbooks. Unless Christians throw themselves into that struggle with some of the vigor and daring that Jesus showed in the temple, they will never get into any front-line engagement with the forces of injustice and cruelty. It is no wonder the lords of privilege struck back. Jesus was the great upsetter. He upset the tables of the money-changers. His would have been a cardinal sin in our society too. The first commandment of entrenched power is "Thou shalt not upset a cash register."

But do we get into the battle? Some do not even see it. Others say: "It is not our fight. Religion is a 'spiritual' affair." One wonders what such folk make of this highly "unspiritual" Jesus as he went into action against abuse. Still others never get in because their self-interest keeps them out—well out. Their Christianity is like a dog on a leash. It knows its master's voice and comes to heel at command.

Observe finally that Jesus drove the traders out of the "court of the Gentiles." Anyone could come into this part of the temple. It symbolized what universal quality and outlook there was in Judaism. To turn it into a noisy bazaar was to deny access to "proselyte" and "hanger-on," that "lesser breed without the law." Is it any stretching of the point to suppose that he who said, "Come to me, all who labor and are heavy-laden" (Matt. 11:28) is the enemy of everything that would destroy or limit the universal quality of the worship of God? Is he not against every kind of bigotry that would make parochial the church of the Father of all men?

15. He . . . Began to Drive Out Those Who Sold and Those Who Bought.—Notice that it was the concrete act which was the dangerous

temple, and overthrew the tables of the money changers, and the seats of them that sold doves;

16 And would not suffer that any man should carry *any* vessel through the temple.

17 And he taught, saying unto them, Is it not written, My house shall be called of all nations the house of prayer? but ye have made it a den of thieves.

18 And the scribes and chief priests heard *it*, and sought how they might de-

out those who sold and those who bought in the temple, and he overturned the tables of the money-changers and the seats of those who sold pigeons; **16** and he would not allow any one to carry anything through the temple. **17** And he taught, and said to them, "Is it not written, 'My house shall be called a house of prayer for all the nations'? But you have made it a den of robbers." **18** And the chief priests and the scribes heard it and sought a way to de-

---

hitherto (cf. vss. 18, 27-28, and 14:1). Jesus "cleansed" the temple not only of its profanation by the traders (vs. 15) but also (vs. 16) of its desecration by casual use as a short cut—which the Talmud later forbade (cf. Berakoth 9:5). Both parallels omit reference to its use as a short cut, as also does John 2:14-16. There is no doubt that the presence of the traders and money-changers was for the convenience of those who came to worship: the former to provide for sacrifice the ritually clean and unblemished animals, which could not be brought long distances to Jerusalem, the latter to exchange other coins for the standard ancient Hebrew or Tyrian money which was required. We cannot be sure there was graft, so conspicuous in present-day interpretations of the passage; but the very presence of these men and their wares turned the sacred precincts into an emporium or bazaar (John 2:16). Out in the "Court of the Gentiles," where any devout pagan might come and worship, were the animals, with their noise, reek, and offal. How could a Gentile pray there? Probably that was the point of Jesus' words in vs. 17, **My house . . . prayer** (cf. Isa. 56:6-8). **Den of thieves** is quoted from Jer. 7:11, but does not necessarily imply extortion on the part of the merchants (see the whole of Jer. 7).

18. How they might destroy him: The decision of the chief priests and scribes in Jerusalem was identical with that of the Pharisees and Herodians in Galilee (cf. 3:6).

---

thing. Kirsopp Lake says it was this overt attack on the financial interests that was the real cause of the accusation subsequently brought against Jesus by the priests.[6] It is possible that if Jesus had confined himself to words, the power of the hierarchy plus the power of Rome would not have felt compelled to kill him. It is the act which is dangerous. But it is also the act which has saving power. Our Christian witness grows impotent as the proportion of acts to words goes down.

Here Jesus the teacher goes into action as a reformer. Before him in the commercialized temple is a great evil. He moves to wipe it out. Are we not reminded by it that there is a place for the reformer as well as for the teacher? A place for vigorous, outright action as well as for patient indoctrination and nurture? Christianity is more than social reform. But if it never issues in social reform, if it has no room for the prophet in action, it is salt that has lost its saltness. There is need for reminder. The word "reformer" has acquired an unsavory connotation—partly because of the large and

[6] *The Stewardship of Faith* (New York: G. P. Putnam's Sons, 1915), p. 46.

successful twentieth-century campaign to vilify the Puritan, until, to people who cannot or will not check caricature by history, he has become a stock figure of disdain. Besides, there is much blind scorn for the "reformer" which is fostered enthusiastically by those who profit by the absence of reform. Against such a background this picture of Jesus in daring action as a reformer of evil conditions should enlarge our understanding of him, and sharpen our remembrance of the indispensable place of the reformer in the Christian church and life.

18. *They Feared Him, Because All the Multitude Was Astonished at His Teaching.*—Here was public opinion acting as a power for good. The chief priests were held back from murder by one thing—fear. There was a large public in favor of Jesus, people who rejoiced in him. That was a formidable force. Again and again we meet it during these last days in Jerusalem (11:32; 12:12; 14:2). The chief priests and scribes had to reckon with it.

Fear is not the noblest motive to rely on in the fight against evil; but it is a legitimate motive, and sometimes very efficacious. The power of public opinion is too often discounted. One

stroy him: for they feared him, because all the people was astonished at his doctrine.

19 And when even was come, he went out of the city.

20 ¶ And in the morning, as they passed by, they saw the fig tree dried up from the roots.

21 And Peter calling to remembrance saith unto him, Master, behold, the fig tree which thou cursedst is withered away.

22 And Jesus answering saith unto them, Have faith in God.

stroy him; for they feared him, because all the multitude was astonished at his teaching. 19 And when evening came they[u] went out of the city.

20 As they passed by in the morning, they saw the fig tree withered away to its roots. 21 And Peter remembered and said to him, "Master,[v] look! The fig tree which you cursed has withered." 22 And Jesus an-

[u] Some ancient authorities read *he.*
[v] Or *Rabbi.*

Astonished at: Better, "impressed by" (ἐξεπλήσσετο ἐπὶ=*admirabatur super*—Vulg.). Cf. vs. 32 and 12:12, where this motive is repeated. **Teaching,** cf. 14:49.

19. When evening came means the evening of that day, not "every evening" (as in ASV); ὅταν . . . ἐγένετο is not necessarily repetitive (cf. ὅταν in 13:14, etc.), though Luke (21:37) so understands it. Like other pilgrims, Jesus and his disciples lodged outside the crowded city: Luke says on the Mount of Olives, where, according to ancient Jewish sources, many Jewish pilgrims always camped; Matt. 21:17 says in Bethany.

5. Lesson of the Withered Fig Tree (11:20-26)

20. As in 14:72, it is Peter who remembers; in Matt. 21:20, the disciples. **Dried up from the roots** signifies total and hopeless dessication, but not necessarily with any symbolic reference (see above, on vss. 12-14). Luke omits the whole section—though he has something like it in Luke 13:6-9—and Matthew, as usual, abridges. The incident, trivial and to modern taste, if not also to ancient, quite unworthy of any religious teacher, much more Jesus, is used as a peg on which to hang a little catena of sayings about faith, prayer, forgiveness, each suggesting the next, as in chs. 9–10.

22. Have faith in God: This was undoubtedly an authentic teaching of Jesus, though the present setting is totally inadequate, and as a "detached" saying it sounds like a platitude.

---

hope for a better world, rid at least in some measure of the great blights which rest on humanity, is the growth of a public opinion strong enough to say to the forces making for oppression, poverty, and war, "Let my people go." We can always help to create a situation like that in Jerusalem, where the chief priests "feared him" because a multitude took him seriously. So have all great social advances been made, by changes in the intellectual and spiritual climate. As has been well observed, no one killed the diplodocus and other mammoth beasts which used to trample the earth. The climate changed and they died. This is a task where the impact of every life counts.

Meanwhile, as we set about it, this word "astonished" has much to teach us. What Jesus said was sharp and powerful enough to be astonishing. Why? No specific reason is assigned for it here. But read the whole gospel story. It was because he spoke with spiritual authority, and not as the scribes, in a hodgepodge of precedents and regulations. It was because he spoke with a persuasive love of people; his

devotion to the rights of worshipers was what led to the clearing out of the traders from the temple courts. And it was because he spoke with a courage that knew no bounds. We may well turn from him to ourselves and to our own time and ask: "Do we ever really astonish anyone? Is the gospel we proclaim, in its clarity and power, still an astonishing gospel? Or have we mastered the black magic which can distill its tremendous affirmations into stale platitudes, vexing the dull ears of drowsy men?" If there is no astonishment, surely there will be no salvation.

22. *Have Faith in God.*—This is a great central word of Jesus, put here in "an inadequate setting" (see Exeg.). The adequate setting is Jesus' whole personality and life. If we wish to see what faith in God is at its best, we can see it in him. Were we to say, "Such faith is too high for us; we cannot attain to it," we should be right. Yet in this realm too Jesus' command "Follow me" comes directly to us. He indicates the direction and incarnates the result. Jesus' faith was confidence in God's rule of

23 For verily I say unto you, That whosoever shall say unto this mountain, Be thou removed, and be thou cast into the sea; and shall not doubt in his heart, but shall believe that those things which he saith shall come to pass; he shall have whatsoever he saith.

24 Therefore I say unto you, What things soever ye desire, when ye pray, believe that ye receive *them,* and ye shall have *them.*

swered them, "Have faith in God. 23 Truly, I say to you, whoever says to this mountain, 'Be taken up and cast into the sea,' and does not doubt in his heart, but believes that what he says will come to pass, it will be done for him. 24 Therefore I tell you, whatever you ask in prayer, believe

---

23-24. That something like this saying was current in the oral tradition, or in Q, as a detached saying is clear from Matt. 17:20 and Luke 17:6; but as a rule of prayer it sounds strange in this connection, and resembles a magical prescription—like the rule of the ancient rabbi, in Fiebig's *Jüdische Wundergeschichten* (p. 20), who knew that his prayer was heard whenever it was "fluent in his mouth." The great truth here is that Jesus set no limit to the possibilities of prayer. The hyperbole in vs. 23 is undoubtedly conscious and illustrative; it is corrected and reduced to a principle in vs. 24.

---

the world. That world is in the hands of a loving Father. He could say, "Love your enemies," because to him the act of love springs inevitably from harmony with the supreme power of love.

Jesus' faith was trust. He put his life trustingly in God's hands. The words recorded as spoken from the Cross, "Father, into thy hands I commit my spirit!" (Luke 23:46), had not been reserved for that moment at the end. They expressed the spirit of his whole life, at the beginning and through all the days.

Jesus' faith was obedience to the will of God. Faith in God determined the end of all his living. "My food is to do the will of him who sent me, and to accomplish his work" (John 4:34).

Faith may be and should be all that to all believers. It can bring and has brought to life high meaning, serenity, power, joy, and fellowship in the great purposes of God.

23-24. *Whoever Says to This Mountain, "Be Taken Up and Cast into the Sea," ... It Will Be Done for Him.*—This short group of the sayings of Jesus on the power of prayer seems to have been inserted here because the situation suggested it. What the original setting of the words was cannot be determined. It was a great theme of Jesus and he treated it over and over again. The figure of speech about removing mountains, for instance, is parallel to, or a variation of, another saying about uprooting a sycamore tree (Luke 17:6).

Jesus spoke habitually with both clarity and picturesqueness, two great elements of power. If he had cluttered his teaching with long lists of exceptions, or with detailed explanations of how it was to be applied in this situation or in that, his chief point would have been lost,

and his words could not have been so deeply stamped on the minds of men that without the aid of written records they could be remembered for years with amazing accuracy. The hyperbole here is "undoubtedly conscious and illustrative" (see Exeg.). If it were to be taken with unimaginative literalism, it would mean, "Ask whatever you wish, even with regard to the landscape, and if you believe it firmly enough, it will come to pass." That would be utterly immoral prayer. It cannot be taken so without rejecting Jesus' own prayers, as well as his whole teaching on the relation of man to God. Jesus never prayed in any such fashion. At his temptation he resisted every persuasion to use the power of God for his own advantage. At his crucifixion he called for no legions of angels to save him. He was "obedient unto death." He prayed, "Not my will, but thine, be done" (Luke 22:42).

Christian prayer, then, is prayer within limits —in accord with the nature of God, directed toward communion with him, and imbued with the spirit of obedience to his holy will. All true prayer must be guided and tested by Jesus' words "Pray then like this" (Matt. 6:9). Those words were followed by prayer which expressed reverence, the primary desire for the coming of God's kingdom, man's part in it, dependent trust, and likeness to God in spirit and act. Jeremy Taylor has an acute observation to make at this point: "Our desires are not to be the measure of our prayers, unless reason and religion be the rule of our desires."

The great danger, however, is not that we shall believe in prayer too much, but that we shall believe too little. Jesus' stress here was on the unexplored power of prayer. The perma-

25 And when ye stand praying, forgive, if ye have aught against any; that your Father also which is in heaven may forgive you your trespasses.

26 But if ye do not forgive, neither will your Father which is in heaven forgive your trespasses.

27 ¶ And they come again to Jerusalem: and as he was walking in the temple, there

that you receive it, and you will. 25 And whenever you stand praying, forgive, if you have anything against any one; so that your Father also who is in heaven may forgive you your trespasses."ʷ

27 And they came again to Jerusalem.

ʷ Many ancient authorities add verse 26, "But if you do not forgive, neither will your Father who is in heaven forgive your trespasses."

25-26. Vs. 26 is absent from a strong group of MSS (‏א‎ B W syˢ sa bo, etc.), and although its omission may be accounted for by homœoteleuton, it is more probable, since Matthew omits both vss. 25 and 26, that the whole of vss. 25-26 is an interpolation based on Matt. 6:14-15. **Your Father . . . who is in heaven** and **forgive you your trespasses** are simply not Marcan expressions, but are thoroughly characteristic of Matthew. The fact that the Syriac (syˢ) contains vs. 25 may afford a clue to the way in which the interpolation took place; again and again this MS reflects the powerful influence of the text of Matthew upon that of Mark during the period down to, say, A.D. 325. Its influence was limited mainly to insertions, and did little to remold the Marcan text.

6. The Question of Authority (11:27-33)

Jesus' action in cleansing the temple had resulted in a full collision with the constituted authorities there, the scribes and chief priests (vs. 18). The scribes were the accredited teachers of Jewish religion (later "rabbis"); the chief priests the ruling hierarchy. With them are now associated **the elders**, i.e., members of the Sanhedrin, as in

---

nent message in these sayings is that prayer, in the light of his own teaching about it, in the light of his conception of God, and in the light of his own prayers, is such a spiritual power that no limits can be set to it. We have too slight a faith in God's love and in his ability to change both us and the world. There are indeed mountains that can be removed by prayer and dedicated faith, mountains of evil which block the coming of the kingdom. Instead of the faith that they can be moved, all too often we have the faith that keeps them from moving—a faith in mountains, in immovable stones, in the might of material forces. Such a pagan "faith" in the unyielding obstacles of a *status quo* delays the kingdom. "The effectual fervent prayer of a righteous man availeth much" (Jas. 5:16). It provides a channel for the grace and power of God.

25. *Whenever You Stand Praying, Forgive, . . . so that Your Father also . . . May Forgive You.*—This is a parallel to the similar petition in the Lord's Prayer (Matt. 6:12) and in this place is doubtless interpolated from that prayer. The words have also close relationship to another saying in the Sermon on the Mount, "The measure you give will be the measure you get" (Matt. 7:2). In a very real sense the measure of the forgiveness we extend to others will be the measure of the forgiveness we are capable of receiving. Prayer operates in the spiritual and

moral realm. There can be no casual receiving of the great spiritual gift of forgiveness as an automatic affair, like something purchased in a bazaar. The forgiveness of sins by God can be given only to one prepared to receive it. Notice the strong verb *may* in this verse, **so that your Father . . . may forgive you.** God's action is limited by man's action. The high experience of forgiveness cannot be given to a heart that knows nothing of the forgiving spirit. That would not be the act of a Father but of an indulgent grandfather, with no concern for goodness or mercy.

These are arresting words. We ask forgiveness every time we repeat the Lord's Prayer. We trippingly say the words "Forgive us, as we forgive." And often enough we say them without realizing how deep into the mind and heart they go; without even hesitating long enough to remember that if we show a hard, relentless, retaliating spirit, we set up obstacles to our own forgiveness. As Bishop Charles Gore, summarizing the matter, says, "There is no mere insistence upon our rights towards our fellow-men possible, so long as we retain the hope that God is not going to insist on His legal rights towards us. It is only merciful men who can be forgiven."[7] The person who says, "I'll forgive, but not forget," shows that he does not know the

[7] *Prayer and the Lord's Prayer* (New York: Harper & Bros., 1947), p. 107.

come to him the chief priests, and the scribes, and the elders,	And as he was walking in the temple, the chief priests and the scribes and the elders
28 And say unto him, By what authority doest thou these things? and who gave thee this authority to do these things?	came to him, 28 and they said to him, "By what authority are you doing these things, or who gave you this authority to do them?"

the passion narrative (e.g., 14:53; 15:1), where the group are Jesus' enemies. This controversy is the first in the Jerusalem series, and appropriately comes first; the opposition to Jesus, after the cleansing, must have been immediate.

28. By what authority are you doing these things? The question is rhetorical, and implies no belief that Jesus had any authority for his act. Priestly authority, Roman, or any other—human or divine—was out of the question from their point of view. **Who gave you this authority?** sounds puerile, but implies that the act should not have been committed without authorization; the chief priests themselves were the recognized authority in matters relating to the temple, although they were sometimes interfered with by the Romans. From Mark's point of view, however, this question may have pointed unconsciously to the real source of Jesus' authority—God.

meaning of the word "forgive" in the vocabulary of Christ. Prayer is a testing, daring experience. Tennyson writes of "that fierce light which beats upon a throne." Think long of the fierce light which beats about the place of prayer. For there, in the presence of him from whom no secrets are hid, our inner spirit is revealed. **Whenever you stand praying [therefore], forgive, . . . so that your Father . . . who is in heaven may forgive you.**

28. By What Authority Are You Doing These Things?—This was a natural question from those who lived and had their whole being in a world of authorities. The one command to which the scribes and chief priests responded with alacrity was "Cite your precedents." Life was an enlarged law court. The past overshadowed the present. Their God was the God of the dead. It was also a rhetorical question (see Exeg.). They thought that no answer was possible. The "now-we-have-him" glint could be seen in their eyes as they asked it.

Observe, however, that their question is no longer a mere quibble. It is a major central question in religion and life. Lift it up out of tradition and ecclesiastical claims and ask, "In what does the authority of Jesus consist?" Much of the history and experience of men since the first century A.D. goes into providing an adequate answer. Out of that material everyone must formulate his own.

The answer Jesus gave, by inference from his question about John the Baptist, was that his authority came from God. But to say that now is only to raise the original question in a secondary form, "What are the compulsions brought upon us to believe that Jesus' authority comes from God?"

Part of the evidence—for what evidence is worth in such matters—lies in the response

which centuries of human life have made to him and to his teaching. Being lifted up, he has drawn all kinds of men, in all kinds of times, and in all kinds of places. For uncounted hosts Jesus has been the answer to the quest for God. Shakespeare, in another connection, once put the secret of that widespread response in accurate, as well as picturesque words. The banished Duke of Kent returns in disguise to take service with King Lear. The king asks him, "Dost know me, fellow?" Kent answers, "No, but thou hast in thy countenance that which I would fain call master."[8] So humanity has found in Jesus that which it would fain call Master. Christopher Marlowe wrote an enduring line about Helen of Troy, "The face that launch'd a thousand ships." Infinitely above that, the face of Jesus Christ has launched lives that no man can number on the pathway to God. In that face men have found "the light of the glory of God."

Part of the evidence lies in the demonstration which experience has given of the truth of his teaching. Men have found that life works out as he said. In divers manners and in different degrees, varying with a million different circumstances, men have found him, in their experience, to be the way, the truth, and the life.

The very course of events has entered its own evidence that Jesus' authority came from God. In a very real sense the whole sweep of human history since A.D. 30 has been a commentary on the Gospels. Mark what strange tricks it has played with the news, particularly with headlines and footnotes. It has reversed their importance; the last has become first. How many of the headlines of yesterday are the footnotes of today? And how many of yesterday's

[8] *King Lear*, Act I, scene 4.

| 29 And Jesus answered and said unto them, I will also ask of you one question, and answer me, and I will tell you by what authority I do these things.

30 The baptism of John, was *it* from heaven, or of men? answer me.

31 And they reasoned with themselves, saying, If we shall say, From heaven; he will say, Why then did ye not believe him?

32 But if we shall say, Of men; they feared the people: for all *men* counted John, that he was a prophet indeed.

33 And they answered and said unto Jesus, We cannot tell. And Jesus answering saith unto them, Neither do I tell you by what authority I do these things. | 29 Jesus said to them, "I will ask you a question; answer me, and I will tell you by what authority I do these things. 30 Was the baptism of John from heaven or from men? Answer me." 31 And they argued with one another, "If we say, 'From heaven,' he will say, 'Why then did you not believe him?' 32 But shall we say, 'From men'?"— they were afraid of the people, for all held that John was a real prophet. 33 So they answered Jesus, "We do not know." And Jesus said to them, "Neither will I tell you by what authority I do these things." |

29-30. In good rabbinical style Jesus answers with a counterquestion, one which, in fact, his opponents could not answer. **From heaven,** i.e., from God: John as a prophet had the authority of divine inspiration to preach and practice his rite of baptism (cf. 1:4).

31-32. The Jerusalem authorities obviously did not believe John inspired (cf. John 1:19-28), though **the people** all did. But whichever way they answered, they would be caught on one horn of a dilemma—much as the Pharisees and Herodians hoped to "entrap" Jesus in 12:13-17. They therefore refused to answer, and Jesus in turn refused to answer them. The first engagement in the battle was over, and Jesus was for the present victorious. But his opponents were sure to return to the fray, as the succeeding controversies show. It is obvious that from Mark's standpoint—as from that of the tradition itself—both John's authority and that of Jesus were "from heaven," not "from men." As Chrysostom, one of the greatest of the ancient Greek commentators, remarked, Jesus did not say, "I do not know," but "I do not tell."

footnotes are today's headlines! During his lifetime, and for a long while after, Jesus was only a footnote, in the smallest type, to the annals of the Roman Empire. But history, like God, "has highly exalted him." His interpretation of life has been proved true. He who said that "all who take the sword will perish by the sword" (Matt. 26:52) has been vindicated by the years. Where will you find a better expression of the basic truth about our world today than just this: "We are members one of another"? (Eph. 4:25.)

Still further evidence of Christ's continuing authority should be sought in the inexhaustible quality of his insights. Humanity outgrows other enthusiasms; it never leaves Jesus behind. In any given generation the latest moral and spiritual gains have derived from the recovery of old insights of Jesus. Ernest Renan's great sentence is true, far, far truer than he ever realized: "Whatever may be the unexpected phenomena of the future, Jesus will not be surpassed." [9]

29. Jesus Said to Them, "I Will Ask You a Question."—On many an occasion in the Gos-

[9] *The Life of Jesus* (Cleveland: The World Publishing Co., 1941), p. 211.

pels Jesus is shown to be one of the most skillful debaters who ever put a man in a corner. He could use the rabbinical technique to outwit the rabbis. Instead of being caught on the horns of a dilemma, he would take the offensive, answering one question by asking another. He was able to manufacture his own dilemmas, with very sharp horns, so sharp that his enemies retreated before them. From the question he asked here about the baptism of John there was no safe escape.

That method, the pressing of one's own positive question, instead of an apologetic defense against questions and charges of the enemy, is something greatly needed by Christians today. There is too much crouching in a corner, with tentative mood, trying to protect our truth, when we should be pushing the attack boldly into the opponent's camp. Both the church and the faith have suffered from the kind of nervous and jumpy defense which gives the impression that Christianity cannot stand on its feet without crutches of argument. The method of Jesus, if we followed it, would lead us to ask questions of our own, and to say, after all the difficulties in the way of Christian faith have been amassed

12 And he began to speak unto them by parables. A *certain* man planted a vineyard, and set a hedge about *it*, and digged *a place for* the winevat, and built a tower, and let it out to husbandmen, and went into a far country.

2 And at the season he sent to the husbandmen a servant, that he might receive from the husbandmen of the fruit of the vineyard.

3 And they caught *him*, and beat him, and sent *him* away empty.

4 And again he sent unto them another servant; and at him they cast stones, and

12 And he began to speak to them in parables. "A man planted a vineyard, and set a hedge around it, and dug a pit for the wine press, and built a tower, and let it out to tenants, and went into another country. 2 When the time came, he sent a servant to the tenants, to get from them some of the fruit of the vineyard. 3 And they took him and beat him, and sent him away empty-handed. 4 Again

7. PARABLE OF THE WICKED HUSBANDMEN (12:1-12)

This is apparently an example of Jesus' public teaching in the temple (12:35, 38; cf. 14:49); but although Burkitt ("Parable of the Wicked Husbandmen," *Transactions of the Third International Congress for the History of Religion*, II [1903], 321-28) and others have tried to show that it is fully authentic just as it stands, its present form probably owes something to the interpretation given it in the course of oral transmission. The parable is quite unlike those in ch. 4—it is almost an open attack upon Jesus' opponents, and they have no difficulty in grasping his meaning (contrast 4:11-12) —and indeed unlike all the other parables of Jesus in the Synoptic Gospels. Moreover, the "parable" is really an allegory, based in part on Isa. 5:1-7, concluding with a scripture quotation in vss. 10-11 (from Ps. 118:22-23) whose entire relevance presupposes a later point of view (cf. Acts 4:11), as does also the warning contained in vs. 9. The actions of the tenants and their reasoning in vs. 7 are quite unnatural—whereas the action and motivation in Jesus' authentic parables are always natural!—and are possible only in an allegory. The "parable" looks more like those in some of the later writers— say Hermas, also a Roman—and is probably best explained as derived largely from early Christian anti-Jewish polemic (cf. Luke 11:49-51), though authentic words of Jesus may survive in it (cf. Adolf Jülicher, *Gleichnisreden Jesu* [Leipzig und Tübingen: J. C. B. Mohr, 1899], II, 385-406).

12:1-4. **He began to speak to them** i.e., to the group in 11:27. Luke (20:19) and Matthew (21:43, 45) underscore this. **In parables**, i.e., parabolically. Mark gives only

and looked at squarely, "The case is not closed. I will ask you a question" (see on 12:38).

There is the problem of evil in the world, for instance. It can hardly be exaggerated. There it is, a dark mystery. Bandaging the eyes will not remove it. What will you say about it? Where is now thy God? Well, there is at least one pointed answer to be made before you surrender your faith in the God and Father of our Lord Jesus Christ. It is to say: "I will ask you a question. How about the good in human nature and in life? How did that get into the world, if there is no good God of love anywhere?" In N.T. words the mystery of godliness is as great as the mystery of iniquity, and must be faced. Far too often we are browbeaten by the scornful phrase "human nature being what it is." All right, what is it? There are greed, cruelty, lust. But there is also the bright, shin-

ing riddle of fidelity to duty, obedience to conscience, sacrifice. "We are sunk enough here, God knows," but there are, in Browning's words, "flashes struck from midnights." [1]

Again, we are told endlessly that Christianity "does not work in a realistic world." Instead of crouching in a corner at that, we should say: "I will ask you a question. Has anything else worked?" We are told that Christian faith is a ball and chain to personal liberty. We should say: "I will ask you a question. Has anything else ever truly set men free?" To the charge that Jesus is a madman one answer may well be, "Look where the sane ones have landed us."

12:1-11. *The Parable of the Wicked Husbandmen.*—The Exeg. succinctly states the results of critical examination of this parable. The way in which it differs from other parables is

[1] "Christina."

wounded *him* in the head, and sent *him* away shamefully handled.

5 And again he sent another; and him they killed, and many others; beating some, and killing some.

6 Having yet therefore one son, his well-beloved, he sent him also last unto them, saying, They will reverence my son.

7 But those husbandmen said among themselves, This is the heir; come, let us kill him, and the inheritance shall be ours.

8 And they took him, and killed *him,* and cast *him* out of the vineyard.

he sent to them another servant, and they wounded him in the head, and treated him shamefully. 5 And he sent another, and him they killed; and so with many others, some they beat and some they killed. 6 He had still one other, a beloved son; finally he sent him to them, saying, 'They will respect my son.' 7 But those tenants said to one another, 'This is the heir; come, let us kill him, and the inheritance will be ours.' 8 And they took him and killed him,

---

one (cf. 3:23), but Matthew has two parables at this point. **Of the fruit,** i.e., some of it, his share. **Cast stones** (KJV) is not in the best Greek text and should be omitted. **Wounded him in the head** has often been supposed to refer to John the Baptist, but as a reference to the beheading of John this is almost absurd, even in an allegory. The references in vss. 2-4 must be to the O.T. prophets, as in Luke 11:50; and up to this point the story may have as its nucleus a genuine parable of Jesus, though **another country** of vs. 1 (cf. Luke 19:12) suggests a Christian setting (cf. 13:34).

6-8. One other, a beloved son (or "only," as in O.T. usage) is obviously Christ, who **is the heir** (cf. Heb. 1:2); his body they **cast . . . out of the vineyard** (cf. Heb. 13:12— the Epistle to the Hebrews has often been viewed as a Roman writing). Some authors have undertaken to show that vss. 6-8 are secondary, and that if these are bracketed or omitted the remainder of the "parable" sounds natural on the lips of Jesus. But this will scarcely do. The whole "parable" is probably secondary, an early Christian working over of some of Jesus' sayings, and possibly of an original parable, from a later point of view.

---

there shown, with emphasis on the fact that it is an allegory rather than a parable of the type Jesus used so much. The conclusion is that it is an early Christian working over of some of Jesus' sayings. That there is an original deposit of those sayings there can be no doubt. The allegory as it appears in Mark, based in part on Isa. 5:1-7, predicts the rejection of the Messiah by the leaders of the Jews, as they had rejected God's other messengers, and the giving of the vineyard to "others" by the divine owner.

It is no wonder that this story was cherished and used in the early church. For whether or not in its original form it was detailed prophecy of the future, it was actual history as the church looked back on it. Those to whom the religious inheritance was given, the Jewish leaders and many of the people, rejected the Owner's Son, and the inheritance was given to "others."

Beyond the immediate situation, however, the story has timeless relevance as a powerful picture of failure in stewardship. No such meaning has to be imported. It is there. It is there in Isaiah. The stewards of the vineyard had betrayed their trust. "The vineyard of Jehovah . . . is the house of Israel . . . he looked for justice, but, behold, oppression" (Isa. 5:7 ASV).

The burden of that lament comes to all generations and to all men as stewards of the gift of God. It depicts the subtle way in which men reject their status as trustees, and come to think of themselves as outright owners, with the "absentee landlord" forgotten. God is never really an absentee from life, but man's fondling of that dangerous pronoun "mine," and his distortion of it, can push the Almighty into a darkened background. So the warning of the story links itself with Jesus' teaching about the deceitfulness of riches, and the fatal decay of the sense of stewardship and responsibility. When the saving remembrance, "All things come from thee, O Lord," drops out of life, the little word "my" is blown up like a balloon, till it obscures the true conception of life as a trust. We can hear it go bouncing along all the way through the parable of the rich fool, "my crops," "my barns," "my grain," "my goods" (Luke 12:17-18). Such distorted insistence reduces the music of life to a primitive tom-tom. The high note of "What shall I render unto the Lord?" (Ps. 116:12) is drowned in a drumbeat.

This picture of a rejected trust should remind us not only of our own responsibilities **as**

9 What shall therefore the lord of the vineyard do? he will come and destroy the husbandmen, and will give the vineyard unto others.

10 And have ye not read this Scripture; The stone which the builders rejected is become the head of the corner:

11 This was the Lord's doing, and it is marvelous in our eyes?

and cast him out of the vineyard. 9 What will the owner of the vineyard do? He will come and destroy the tenants, and give the vineyard to others. 10 Have you not read this scripture:

'The very stone which the builders rejected
has become the head of the
 corner;
11 this was the Lord's doing,
 and it is marvelous in our eyes'?"

10-11. The verses (from Ps. 118:22-23) are quoted elsewhere in the N.T. (Acts 4:11), and were doubtless a commonplace in Christian-Jewish debate. It was a "messianic" text, at least for later Jews, and certainly for Christians. The "marvel" of Jesus' resurrection and exaltation was **the Lord's doing.**

---

individuals, but also of the need for the extension of the idea of stewardship into all the areas of life in which men live and work together. We are trustees of the land, and have not held it inviolate for coming generations; our nation is a trustee of the power which has its source in those gifts of God that were not created or earned by us; we are the trustees of the children of our land—a committed stewardship which has been grievously betrayed.

Menzies points out the appositeness of this allegory to the Jewish leaders of Jesus' time, as indeed to every political and religious institution: "The rulers of the Jews were under the error, so common in administrators of states and churches, of admiring too much their own authority and system and losing touch of the great living Source of all authority." [2] We may well add to the litany the prayer, "From all such delusive admirations, Good Lord, deliver us."

9. He Will Come . . . and Give the Vineyard to Others.—This is history. The rejection of Jesus, when "he came to his own home, and his own people received him not" (John 1:11), did not mean that God had arrived at a dead end. God never gets into a blind alley. There were "others" to whom the great inheritance of revelation came, the Gentiles, the "barbarians." This is also prophecy. Our attention ought to be given it with deep self-searching. When the natural channels through which new revelations might be expected to come into the world are for any reason blocked, God moves into life through unexpected and hitherto unrecognized channels. He has never been blocked by the rejection of his truth on the part of those agencies and institutions which might most naturally be expected to be the means of its proclamation. There is a suggestion of this

[2] *Earliest Gospel,* p. 215.

in the profound symbolism of the Christmas narrative. In the nativity stories Jesus was born in a barn. That was highly irregular. There were places in the organized life of Judea where babies should be born. A barn was not one of them. But all the others were closed. So God used an irregular place—a stable. New revelations of God might be most naturally expected in God's church. But if that is closed, he can always use some unrecognized place. History shows that he has done so. When in the presence of evils that literally cried out to the skies, the church, or majorities within it, has been as dumb as a stone statue, God's truth, God's justice, God's love for the least and lost, have found expression outside the church. His revelation has been received and proclaimed by oppressed groups, in lay movements, in the missionary enterprise, in labor unions, in political action. When his call to evangelize the world came to the deaf ears of archbishops, it was heard by a cobbler, William Carey; when the hunger of workmen in nineteenth-century England did not pierce the consciousness of a great part of the church, the Chartist movement did give it voice. The words **give the vineyard to others** should lay upon us the responsibility of recognizing the messengers of God when they arrive, and of making room within the church for the new revelations of him who came to set at liberty those who are oppressed.

10. The Very Stone Which the Builders Rejected Has Become the Head of the Corner.—Small wonder that this quotation from Ps. 118 became a "messianic" text for Christians. It pictures so perfectly the rejected Jesus and his elevation to the keystone of the arch of God's revelation.

It is a messianic text for all time. We can grasp its full meaning more fully than the early church, for we have before us the commentary

| 12 And they sought to lay hold on him, but feared the people; for they knew that he had spoken the parable against them: and they left him, and went their way. | 12 And they tried to arrest him, but feared the multitude, for they perceived that he had told the parable against them; so they left him and went away. |

12. Again Jesus is victorious for the moment; but the frustrated adversaries who **went their way** were sure to return, and Mark would have his readers sense their steady and implacable enmity: **they sought to lay hold on him.**

written on it by nineteen centuries. The rejected stone has been one of the great themes of all literature. It is one of the small number of basic plots for fiction. It is the Cinderella story, told in all ages, cherished by all peoples, the exalting of them of low degree. It has been the great theme of history during the Christian era. Much of that history has been in essence the story of the rejected stone—Jesus—recovered and lifted up as the head of the corner.

The jerry-builders have long been and still are extraordinarily busy. Go back to the troubled beginnings of democracy in the Western world. The "rabble," "the great unwashed," the rag, tag, and bobtail of the human race, was a stone rejected as useless junk for the building of a state. Then through the slow years watch the central motif as it was slowly wrought out, the discovery of man. **The very stone which the builders rejected, . . . the head of the corner.**

But always the rejected stone par excellence has been Jesus. And as it was, so is it now. He is rejected by men in the building of personal life. What multitudes there are that have found no desirable material in him at all! The Beatitudes are junk that will not fit into a magnificent house. Yet the steady march of time has shown to those who will look closely that nothing else will last, or lay a foundation strong enough to support any durable satisfactions.

He was rejected by the leaders of the Jewish religion as the revelation of God, only to become the keystone of revelation to a company no man can number. Browning speaks for them in his lines:

> I say, the acknowledgment of God in Christ
> Accepted by thy reason, solves for thee
> All questions in the earth and out of it.[3]

He has become the head of the corner in education. We are still a long distance from overtaking his wisdom on the growth of mind and soul. We count not ourselves yet to have apprehended his depth. But men's progressive understanding of his view of human nature and the development of personality has increasingly hailed him, "Teacher!"

In economics, whether viewed as a "dismal

[3] "A Death in the Desert."

science" or as holy writ, Jesus has been rejected. Both economic theorists and economic powers have addressed him in the words of the Palestinian demons, "What have we to do with thee, thou Jesus of Nazareth?" (1:24.) But with the hunger of depression and the slaughter of war sitting in the professor's chair, many have been learning new lessons. They have learned that a house divided against itself cannot stand; that production divided against consumption cannot stand. They are learning that man was not made for an economic system, but that an economic system must serve the needs of man. The rejected stone is selected for the corner.

So it is with the international system that hopes to achieve anything but chaos. If we are going to split the atom, we had better unite the world.

12. *They Perceived that He Had Told the Parable Against Them.*—Give the chief priests and scribes and elders credit for that much anyhow! They knew when they were hit. We may ask: How could they avoid perceiving it, when it came as straight and struck as hard as an arrow landing in the chest? But credit should be given them for recognizing marksmanship, especially when we remember our own amazing skill in dodging messages of reproof that come to us. It is a skill that might well rank as one of the wonders of the world—the way in which we ward off messages that literally shout directly to us, "Thou art the man," by saying to ourselves, "That certainly must have penetrated Mr. B's skin," or, "I'm glad Mrs. B was here to get that. It was surely aimed at her."

12. *So They Left Him and Went Away.*—A casual promenader in the temple courts, listening to Jesus' discussions with the chief priests and scribes, might well have been tempted to think: "Well, that's over. The teacher from Galilee certainly laid them out. They won't come back after two such defeats."

They were "laid out" in the battle of wits and words. They did go away. But it was not all over. They came back in force.

Jesus was evidently expecting them. He did not succumb to the illusion of temporary victory. The moment of victory is always dangerous. It may create a false sense of security and lull watchfulness to sleep. Evil always comes back,

13 ¶ And they send unto him certain of the Pharisees and of the Herodians, to catch him in *his* words.

14 And when they were come, they say unto him, Master, we know that thou art true, and carest for no man; for thou regardest not the person of men, but teachest the way of God in truth: Is it lawful to give tribute to Caesar, or not?

13 And they sent to him some of the Pharisees and some of the He-ro'di-ans, to entrap him in his talk. 14 And they came and said to him, "Teacher, we know that you are true, and care for no man; for you do not regard the position of men, but truly teach the way of God. Is it lawful to pay

8. The Question of Tribute to Caesar (12:13-17)

This question, burning in the days before the Jewish revolt of A.D. 66-70, must have been a "live" one in the days of Jesus, as the pages of Josephus suggest (see Grant, *Gospel of the Kingdom,* ch. v). But the purpose of the adversaries here is not really to enlist Jesus' support either for or against collaboration with the Roman occupation; it is only to trap him, **to catch him in . . . words.** The passage does not even imply that Jesus claimed, or was thought, to be Messiah, as the raising of the question of taxes might well suggest. In the time of Sabbatai Zebi, *ca.* 1650, who was viewed as Messiah by many Jews all over Europe, many said: "We shall pay no more taxes; our Messiah has come" (cf. *Encyclopaedia Britannica* [11th ed.] XV, 407*a*). Jesus, however, is here addressed as a "teacher" who truly teaches **the way of God,** i.e., true religious duty.

13. The presence of Herodians (3:6) in Jerusalem may seem strange, but it is no more unlikely here than in Galilee; Archelaus had been deposed in A.D. 6, and there were doubtless many who hoped for a revival of the kingship, as indeed is clear from the appointment of Agrippa I in A.D. 41, and from the great prestige of Agrippa II and his influence in Jerusalem in the latter part of the century (see Josephus *Jewish War* II).

14. Tribute: Since Archelaus' banishment, Judea and Samaria had been nominally an imperial province—different from a more settled senatorial—and had paid a regular

frequently recuperated and reinforced. To cease to watch and pray, or to relax vigilance and effort after any kind of a triumph is to invite defeat. Many a time complete moral overthrow has come from resting on the oars of some early success. Many a time we have seen reform movements, after gaining some little ground, disband and muster themselves out of service, only to meet disaster when the comeback of the enemy finds them unprepared.

13-17. *Is It Lawful to Pay Taxes to Caesar, or Not?*—Here was a trap set for Jesus. The question was so maliciously framed that by inducing him to answer either "Yes" or "No" they could go far toward destroying his influence. The alliance between some of the Pharisees and some of the Herodians—again what strange bedfellows politics makes!—was applying the principle of "divide and rule." If he said, "Pay the tax," they would drive a wedge between him and his followers, many of whom held the nationalistic hopes. If he said, "Do not pay," he would land in the hands of Rome, on the charge of treason.

Jesus saw it clearly. The nauseous flattery and the clumsy pose of serious interest did not deceive him. He made no effort to evade the question. He answered it clearly and positively,

yet was not caught on either horn of the dilemma. His answer was far more than the clever footwork of a man in a corner. Nothing was too "hot" for him to handle. He said clearly, "Pay the tax." But he said it with an inescapable logic. The coin, with its **likeness and inscription,** was for him as for others a recognized symbol that the country was living under Roman rule; and he may well have thought, as some now think, that some payment was reasonably due the government for its services to order and protection. Yet that was the smallest part of the answer. The major and unexpected part was the duty of rendering to God his just due of worship and repentance and obedience. That, in any political setting, was the supreme claim on people. Get on, he said, to life's greatest business, the service of God.

The meaning of the words **Render to Caesar the things that are Caesar's, and to God the things that are God's,** is for all time what it was when Jesus spoke them. Unfortunately, however, they have been as badly twisted as any he ever uttered. Many interpreters seem to have taken their principles of exegesis from Mark Twain: "Get the facts first; then you can distort them as you wish." Generations have done just that. The words have been distorted

15 Shall we give, or shall we not give? But he, knowing their hypocrisy, said unto them, Why tempt ye me? bring me a penny, that I may see *it*.

taxes to Caesar, or not? 15 Should we pay them, or should we not?" But knowing their hypocrisy, he said to them, "Why put me to the test? Bring me a coin,ˣ and let me

ˣ Greek *a denarius*.

---

poll tax into the *fiscus,* the emperor's treasury. This was not a heavy tax, but it symbolized subjection, and the coins in circulation in which it was paid bore a relief of the emperor's head—the silver denarius. The commoner currency of the procurators was copper and bore such innocuous symbols as olive trees, palms, etc. (Cf. F. W. Madden, *Coins of the Jews* [Boston: James R. Osgood & Co., 1881]; A. R. S. Kennedy, art. "Money" in Hastings, *Dictionary of the Bible* [New York: Charles Scribner's Sons, 1900], Vol. III; see article "Metrology" in Vol. I of this Commentary.) A popular leader and teacher like Jesus would be expected to hold pronounced views on the subject of the payment of this tribute, and his enemies hoped to entrap him, whatever his views were: if he disapproved, they could denounce him to Pilate as a revolutionist (cf. Luke 23:2); if he approved, they trusted that this would mark the end of his influence with the people.

---

into a divine injunction to support any government, no matter how unjust, vicious, and oppressive. They have been cited even as giving Jesus' blessing to that disastrous separation between political conduct and religious conduct which has resulted in the "split personality" of Christians and churches—everybody trying to keep his religion, which is God's realm, out of his politics, which is Caesar's.

Jesus made it clear that his chief concern was not to establish an earthly kingdom, to stir up revolt, or to settle the relations between Jews and Romans. He refused to allow his authority to be used merely as a means to support any partisan cause. This particular tax was not much, and "the coin belonged to Caesar anyway." Meanwhile his mission was to preach the kingdom of God and to prepare men for its coming, heart, soul, mind, and strength. It was not enough for them to be "against Caesar"; they had to be for God—without limit.

The great danger in life, individual and collective, has been the danger of giving to Caesar the things that belong to God. Caesar has had the lion's share; God has had the remainders, the trivia that Caesar did not need. Think of the whole realms that have been handed over. Questions involving right and wrong, justice and mercy, big with potential and immeasurable harm to the children of God, casually surrendered with the limp words, "Here, Caesar, this is your business." And Caesar, if we take that title to represent the ruling powers, political and economic, has not been slow to claim the whole of man's life as his right. Frederick William I of Prussia expressed it perfectly when he said: "Salvation is of God. Everything else is my affair." We have allowed that to go unrebuked too long. We must learn to say to all swelling Caesars, "Human life is God's affair."

Caesar says of a man's conscience, "This is mine. I will make all the decisions for you. You just obey." God says, "It is mine." Caesar says of all the activities that create the conditions of life for people, industry, commerce, wages, food and housing, "This is mine." God says, "It is mine." Caesar says of the policies that spell war or peace for nations, life and death for people, "This is mine." God says, "It is mine."

15. *But Knowing Their Hypocrisy, He Said to Them.*—This is another picture calling for the genius of a great painter. The Pharisees and Herodians, dripping with oily flattery, were confronting Jesus with what they thought was a masterpiece of deception. Their sense of their own craftiness blinded them to the clumsy bungling of their act. They thought Jesus naïve, as easy to "take in" as a yokel from the country. They found him terribly sophisticated. That is not an adjective often applied to Jesus—"sophisticated"—but in one of its primary meanings, "worldly wise," it applies to him as to no one else. He was "worldly wise" in a disconcerting manner. He knew what was in man. We never truly appreciate his mind until we see how wise he was, not only in the wisdom of another world, but in the wisdom of this, raised to the *n*th degree. What fools these mortals are, when they imagine they can avoid the eyes of Jesus, which penetrate all deceptions, or his ears, so attuned to catch the cadence of a lie!

He knows all hypocrisies, ours included, even those unconscious hypocrisies which are such deeply set marks of the mind that men never notice them. Hypocrisy is "feigning to be what one is not, or to feel what one does not feel." So much we ought to know without benefit of dictionary. How many then are there who hail Jesus as "King of Kings and Lord of Lords," while under their breath they whisper, "Wait

16 And they brought *it*. And he saith unto them, Whose *is* this image and superscription? And they said unto him, Caesar's.

17 And Jesus answering said unto them, Render to Caesar the things that are Caesar's, and to God the things that are God's. And they marveled at him.

18 ¶ Then come unto him the Sadducees, which say there is no resurrection; and they asked him, saying,

look at it." 16 And they brought one. And he said to them, "Whose likeness and inscription is this?" They said to him, "Caesar's." 17 Jesus said to them, "Render to Caesar the things that are Caesar's, and to God the things that are God's." And they were amazed at him.

18 And Sad′du-cees came to him, who say that there is no resurrection; and they

---

17. Jesus' answer has sometimes been thought to be only a clever evasion: he was really anti-Roman but refused to be caught on either horn of the dilemma confronting him. Or it has been thought that the problem concerned merely the handling of a pagan coin (cf. Herbert Loewe, *Render Unto Caesar* [Cambridge: University Press, 1940]). But it is far more probable that Jesus, who was no revolutionist, and whose background among the peasants or the Amhaarez in Galilee did not bring him into close contact with the burning political issues of the capital, solved the problem simply by the logical "both-and," rather than an "either-or." To pay tribute to Caesar was not much, a denarius a year, and the coin belonged to Caesar anyway—let him have it back! But to pay tribute to God, to render him his due, to pay the things that belong to God—duty, service, obedience, worship—this was everything, and the whole of life. No wonder **they were amazed at him!** He not only completely escaped their trap, but gave them a principle of action which would, if followed, carry them a long way beyond the present perplexing issue. Some such value Mark and his Roman readers probably found in the saying, in their equally difficult situation nearly forty years later. It is perhaps worth adding that the saying by no means justifies the medieval theory of the two empires, the sacred and the secular, nor the modern dichotomy of ethics into political and religious.

9. The Question of the Resurrection (12:18-27)

The subject of this controversy is not likely to have been a common one between Christians and Jews at the time when Mark wrote; the Jews of the Diaspora, with whom Gentile Christians came in contact, were apparently believers in the life to come, i.e., in the resurrection. The Sadducees, on the other hand, little known outside Palestine, and

---

outside in this anteroom, will you? That's far enough. The rest of the house is all arranged and I can't have it disturbed." They hail him, "Good Teacher," and drop the course before they have learned its first lessons. In spite of their words, "We know that you are true," the precepts they follow come from other sources. They make out of him a kindly, lovable figure, but one to be taken with many grains of salt. When he says, "A man's life consisteth not in the abundance of things"—they take it in a Pickwickian sense. Momentous words, these, when we stop to think of them—"from whom no secrets are hid."

18-27. Eternal Life.—In this passage we have Jesus' direct teaching on eternal life. The main point of the narrative is the spiritual view he takes. He brings into the discussion what the Sadducees left out completely, God and his nature. When that is brought in as the central truth around which everything else turns, the

materialistic quibbling of the Sadducees appears trivial. The meaning of Jesus' answer is best understood from a knowledge of the background of controversy between the Sadducees and Pharisees (see Exeg.). To the *reductio ad absurdum*, evidently a stock argument worn down by much use, he replies by reducing the whole fantastic structure to absurdity, lifting the whole issue to a new level. He shows that eternal life is not a mere extension of life, but a transformation of life; not the projection of conditions on earth into an endless future, but a new world of being; not quantity of time, but quality of spirit. Paul expressed it clearly: "This mortal nature must put on immortality" (I Cor. 15:53).

Notice that Jesus here takes the side of the Pharisees, who believed in the resurrection. The ground on which he stands, both as to the truth of the resurrection itself and as to the nature of life after death, is faith in God, faith

indeed outside Judea, were the "old believers" who still clung to the ancient religious views and rejected the new developments represented by Pharisaism. (Cf. Acts 23:8; Eduard Meyer, *Ursprung und Anfänge des Christentums* [Stuttgart und Berlin: J. G. Cotta, 1921], II, 291.) After the fall of the temple in A.D. 70 they quickly faded from Jewish history, though their influence survived to some degree and can be traced in certain teachings. The future, in Judaism, belonged to the Pharisees (cf. L. Finkelstein, *The Pharisees* [Philadelphia: Jewish Publication Society of America, 1938]; R. T. Herford, *The Pharisees* [London: G. Allen & Unwin, 1924]). The section before us has every mark of authentic tradition.

18. The Sadducees are introduced very simply with "and"; the phrase **Then come** (KJV) is more circumstantial than the Greek justifies. Their motive, it is implied, is the same as that of the Pharisees in vs. 13.

---

in a certain kind of God. "This is probably the strongest of all arguments for immortality: not the nature of man but the character of God" (see Exeg.). It is the one great argument which stands, even if every other, because of changes in the intellectual environment, should fall. The rains descend and the floods come, but that house of faith, built on the rock of God as loving Father, falls not. One who loves his individual children with an infinite love will cherish and preserve that which he has created. Our modern philosophical arguments for immortality were not part of the mental world in which Jesus lived. But the essence was there: the preservation of personality; the affirmative faith that that which belongs to God even death cannot take from him. Again Paul: "I am sure that neither death, nor life, . . . will be able to separate us from the love of God" (Rom. 8:38-39).

The curious seeker for information on the nature of life after death finds no gratification in Jesus. To be sure, he used figures of speech common to his time and people, such as drinking wine in the kingdom, and sitting on thrones (14:25; Matt. 19:28). But such figures were necessary if the feeling of the joy and triumph of the future life was to be conveyed to his hearers. This passage and others make clear, however, that the figures are not to be taken literally. Jesus revealed one "detail" of the future life—God. That was enough. To the oft-repeated question "Shall we know our friends in heaven?" Jesus replies, "You will know God, a God who loves his children, and from whose love they will not be separated by death." That is still enough!

The great faith which Jesus brings to bear on this question, the faith that God is **not God of the dead, but of the living,** runs far beyond the circumstances in which it was spoken. As an argument for the resurrection and eternal life, it is not impressive to our minds; but as a high and sustaining faith it is timelessly impressive. The irrelevant finality of death has no power

to make God cease to be the God of his children who have loved and served him.

Not . . . of the dead, . . . of the living. May we not move out with it to even wider ranges? In all religions men have had a way of making God "provincial," of confining him and his power within space and time. There has been the provincialism of the map, conceiving of God as the God of only a special place or area. We see this in "primitive" Hebrew religion. There has been also and still is the "provincialism" of the calendar; that is, of locating God and his power back in some yesterday—he was active in other eras; today he has retired. The graveyard next to the church may be a beautiful symbol of the truth that the dead are with God. But it may also be a terrible symbol, unintended, of the habit of thinking of God as a God of yesterday, a God of the dead. He is the God of the living, revealing his truth and his will to living men through the Holy Spirit, seeking to bring his kingdom in the world through living people, a God with us, today and in all the tomorrows.

18. *And Sadducees Came . . . , Who Say that There Is No Resurrection.*—There is a very suggestive phrase used in the Exeg. to describe the Sadducees. It is worth remembrance and much thought. They are called "old believers." They clung "to the older religious views and rejected the new." They had, in their tightly closed minds, no place for added light. Their God was not the God of the living.

It is an arresting phrase—"old believers." It may be a crown of glory on a life. There have been and are "old believers" in Jesus. He is the Way to which they hold without detour. He is the revealer of the God of love, in whom they trust, even though the mountains are carried into the midst of the sea. But there is another kind of "old believers"—modern Sadducees—inflexible, incapable of fresh insights. The immovable quality of their rocklike minds is a constant denial of the doctrine of the Holy Spirit. The faith of a John Robinson, who be-

19 Master, Moses wrote unto us, If a man's brother die, and leave *his* wife *behind him*, and leave no children, that his brother should take his wife, and raise up seed unto his brother.

20 Now there were seven brethren: and the first took a wife, and dying left no seed.

21 And the second took her, and died, neither left he any seed: and the third likewise.

22 And the seven had her, and left no seed: last of all the woman died also.

23 In the resurrection therefore, when they shall rise, whose wife shall she be of them? for the seven had her to wife.

24 And Jesus answering said unto them, Do ye not therefore err, because ye know not the Scriptures, neither the power of God?

25 For when they shall rise from the dead, they neither marry, nor are given in marriage; but are as the angels which are in heaven.

asked him a question, saying, **19** "Teacher, Moses wrote for us that if a man's brother dies and leaves a wife, but leaves no child, the man*ʸ* must take the wife, and raise up children for his brother. **20** There were seven brothers; the first took a wife, and when he died left no children; **21** and the second took her, and died, leaving no children; and the third likewise; **22** and the seven left no children. Last of all the woman also died. **23** In the resurrection whose wife will she be? For the seven had her as wife."

24 Jesus said to them, "Is not this why you are wrong, that you know neither the scriptures nor the power of God? **25** For when they rise from the dead, they neither marry nor are given in marriage, but are

ʸ Greek his brother.

19-23. An extraordinary and quite hypothetical case, arising under the Mosaic law of levirate marriage (Deut. 25:5-10), is on their view a *reductio ad absurdum* of the doctrine of resurrection. It is probably one they had used in controversy with the Pharisees, but now they joined hands with them in turning it against Jesus. Note that they are already aware of his stand on the subject.

24-25. Again, as in 10:5-9, Jesus turns the tables upon his opponents by quoting the Torah itself—which they recognized, and which they claimed as their final authority, superior to the "modern" fancies of the pietists, i.e., the Pharisees. **Do ye not therefore err?** (KJV) is better rendered, **Is not this why you are wrong?** (RSV). The shaft is double-barbed: they are really ignorant of the Scriptures, rather than being experts in its exposition, and they also ignore the power of God, who is able to restore the dead (cf. Heb. 11:19). They have assumed that Jesus would hold a crass and materialistic view; on the contrary, his view is highly spiritual. (Cf. Paul's view in I Cor. 15:35-50, in answer to a similar objection.) **Like angels in heaven:** According to Acts 23:8 the Sadducees denied the existence of angels; but this is doubtful, since there were plenty of references to angels in the O.T., even in the Pentateuch (e.g., Gen. 19:1; Deut. 33:2). The sexless nature of the angels was already recognized in Judaism (e.g., I Enoch 15:6-7, "You are ever-living spirits, . . . therefore I have not created wives for you" [cf. Tob. 12:19]; at the same time the fall of the watchers in Enoch [cf. Gen. 6:2] was the consequence of their lust for mortal women). As vss. 19-23 apparently set forth a stock argument of the Sadducees against the doctrine of resurrection, it has been thought that vss. 24-25, and possibly 26-27, set forth a stock Pharisaic reply. But there is no reason for questioning the reply as Jesus' own.

---

lieved that God had new truth to break out of his word, is abhorrent to them. So they stand, like a granite blockade, across the road leading to spiritual growth. Which kind of "old believers" are we?

The clause which Mark put in to explain the Sadducees to his Roman readers, **who say that**

there is no resurrection, fits into our world too with timeliness. The streets are full of modern Sadducees who either say, "There is no resurrection," or to whom it seems both improbable and undersirable, of no more immediate interest than the rings of Saturn. There are even in churches people to whom the Christian doctrine

26 And as touching the dead, that they rise; have ye not read in the book of Moses, how in the bush God spake unto him, saying, I *am* the God of Abraham, and the God of Isaac, and the God of Jacob?

27 He is not the God of the dead, but the God of the living: ye therefore do greatly err.

like angels in heaven. 26 And as for the dead being raised, have you not read in the book of Moses, in the passage about the bush, how God said to him, 'I am the God of Abraham, and the God of Isaac, and the God of Jacob'? 27 He is not God of the dead, but of the living; you are quite wrong."

26-27. As vss. 24-25 answered the Sadducees' objection by correcting their false view, so vss. 26-27 advance a positive argument from Scripture in favor of the belief. This argument also presupposes knowledge of Scripture and faith in the power of God (vs. 24). Since God describes himself in Exod. 3:6 as **the God of Abraham, . . . Isaac, . . . Jacob,** it is evident that the patriarchs must still be living; for as the living God, revealed in the O.T., he is **the God of the living.** As Luke 20:38 adds, "for all live to him." This is probably the strongest of all arguments for immortality: not the nature of man but the character of God. Though presented here in an exegetical form, the principle is profoundly theological and philosophical. Yet the phrase in vs. 26, **that they rise,** is difficult; how does the survival of the great saints of old prove the resurrection of the dead? But we have to recognize that resurrection was, it appears, the only form in which belief in a life to come was, or perhaps could be, held by Palestinian Jews at the time (cf. the book of Daniel, etc.); Greek ideas of natural immortality, or of the indestructible nature of the soul, as held by certain of the philosophers, had scarcely penetrated Palestinian Judaism, and were by no means universal in the Greco-Roman world. Paul's views (in I Cor. 15 or II Cor. 5:1-5, for example) show how indispensable he thought a "body" was for the risen life. And in Christian thought, ever since, the same necessity has been recognized.

of immortality is an inert truth, lying in the dormitory of their minds, one which never really gets up and walks. Many causes may be assigned: the skeptical, often cynical intellectual climate in which they live; the notion that an empirical physical science has become the measure of all things; the preponderance of the material world. But the two causes named by Jesus must not be forgotten: "You know neither the Scriptures nor the power of God" (vs. 24). They have no deep and genuine religious experience; which is to say that they are without the ultimate foundation for faith in eternal life. The whole scriptural revelation of God in Christ is either totally unapprehended or so vague as to be powerless. "I know whom I have believed" (II Tim. 1:12). There is no other tone which carries with it the overtones of eternity. It says persuasively: Here is something so real and great that "as God lives, the excellent becomes the permanent." The peril of the Sadducee, ancient and modern, is that he shall have nothing in life valuable enough for him or for anybody else to keep through eternity. The chief defense against the infection of his spirit is to have an experience of God so vital and so creative that it brings into being precisely that which is worth having and worth preserving forever.

27. *You Are Quite Wrong.*—These words of Jesus, climaxing the whole discussion of the resurrection, are clear and emphatic. They remind us that there is a legitimate place in life for forthright, dogmatic declaration. We live so much in a world of relativism, of a "tolerance" which is really indifference—not breadth of spirit at all!—that we become tentative and apologetic rather than affirmative, even about things which are the very axis of faith.

To the Sadducees' denial of the resurrection many in the common mood of today would have replied in some such manner as this: "But there may conceivably be another side to the question. At least it is a good subject for a discussion group; so let's keep an open mind. On the whole, other things being equal, something might perhaps be said for the idea of a resurrection." Such hesitant apology, sprouting a profusion of qualifying phrases, never subdued kingdoms, wrought righteousness, or put to flight armies of aliens.

Jesus was brief and dogmatic. He said, **You are quite wrong;** and those words, spoken in his spirit, are desperately needed. To the clamorous assertion that there is no spiritual force in or behind the universe there is needed the quiet and confident, "You are quite wrong." In the midst of all the shouting about a "su-

28 ¶ And one of the scribes came, and having heard them reasoning together, and perceiving that he had answered them well, asked him, Which is the first commandment of all?

28 And one of the scribes came up and heard them disputing with one another, and seeing that he answered them well, asked him, "Which commandment is the

10. The Question of the Great Commandment (12:28-34)

The tone of this section is quite different from that of the preceding controversies. It seems to show, just before the close of the series (vs. 34b), that Jesus' arguments were effective (vs. 28: **he had answered them well**); and also that, in spite of the strong element of controversy in the Gospels, derived from these sources (mainly the "controversy source"), and the general state of antagonism—fostered later perhaps by continued controversy with Jews—there were not a few persons on the other side who admired and appreciated Jesus. And it is notable that in turn Jesus commends the scribe (vs. 34a). Luke is especially fond of picturing Jesus in fellowship with worthy Pharisees.

28-31. Which is the first commandment of all? Later rabbis insisted that there were "no greater and no lesser commandments"; but Hillel (ca. 20 b.c.) is reported to have summed up the law for a Gentile inquirer in the equivalent of vs. 31a: "What you

perior race," tinted white, with the resulting injustices and cruelties, there is needed the dogmatic word in which science and religion join, "You are quite wrong." When the chauvinist's ready remedy for every problem, either in domestic or international life, is proposed, "Crack down with a club; that is the only language they will understand," there is needed the robust affirmation, "You are quite wrong."

28. One of the Scribes Came Up and . . . Asked Him.—Here is a scribe who shines brilliantly in the large and varied company of those who came and asked. Like so many great characters in the Gospels, he is anonymous. He deserves a name for remembrance. Other people came to ask Jesus questions for so many reasons—to entrap him, to block his work, sometimes merely to "show off." Here was a man who actually came to learn.

He is a model for the right approach both to Christ and to the scriptures. The psalmist speaks of "inquiring" in the temple (Ps. 27:4). We do so many other things there. We talk, we pray, we sing, we give. But so many never really inquire. That is the attitude which Jesus so eagerly welcomed. It is the reverent, humble search to learn the will of God for us and for our time; vastly different from the frequent attempt to bend the Almighty around until we can use him as a support for policies and points of view which we have already decided upon without reference to him. So often the common question "What would Jesus do?' does not mark the beginning of a search at all. It marks the beginning of an argument. The conclusion usually runs something like this: "So, you see, Jesus would do just what I am doing."

28-34. Which Commandment Is the First?—The great contribution of Jesus, in his sum-

mary of the law as love to God and love to neighbor, lay in its selective priority. He was perhaps the first to join the two commandments in Deuteronomy and Leviticus (though see Exeg.). That joining was a creation of religious and ethical insight. "The Rabbis calculated that the Law contained 365 prohibitions and 248 positive commands." [4] Quite a reduction, 613 compressed into two! It accords with Jesus' whole teaching that life is an affair of priorities and subordination. "Seek ye first" (Matt. 6:33). "No man can serve two masters" (Matt. 6:24). The commanding priority is faith in God and love to God. From that flows the necessary and inevitable consequence, love to neighbor. The life with no subordination is a spiritual and moral chaos.

The truth here enunciated is a tremendous one, with relevance to every thought and act of life. Jesus says clearly that no number of acts can fulfill God's requirements. God asks the giving of the whole personality, the acceptance of his will as the rule of life. "Thou shalt love the Lord thy God." As in all Jesus' ethical teaching, conduct stems from faith. "Small behavior" comes from the lack of it; "great behavior" springs out of it. Think of drawing a circle with a compass. Get the center right and the circumference will come right. Love to God will result in love to neighbor.

If we only believed it! If those who have professed the Christian faith and borne the name of Christ had only made his priority theirs, the history of the church and of the world would have been far different. So many things have been put before the greatest commandments—orthodoxy of opinion, ritual ceremonies, the right connections. Indeed at

[4] Rawlinson, *St. Mark*, p. 170.

29 And Jesus answered him, The first of all the commandments *is,* Hear, O Israel; The Lord our God is one Lord:

30 And thou shalt love the Lord thy God with all thy heart, and with all thy soul, and with all thy mind, and with all thy strength: this *is* the first commandment.

first of all?" 29 Jesus answered, "The first is, 'Hear, O Israel: The Lord our God, the Lord is one; 30 and you shall love the Lord your God with all your heart, and with all your soul, and with all your mind, and with

---

would not have done to yourself, do not do to your neighbor: that is the whole Torah, and all the rest is commentary" (B. Sabbath 31A). But it was probably Jesus who first combined the two "great commandments" of Deut. 6:4 and Lev. 19:18b into a summary of the law; there is no trace of any earlier teacher's having done so, though Philo (*On the Special Laws* II. 63) comes close to it. (See I. Abrahams, *Studies in Pharisaism and the Gospels,* 1st ser. [Cambridge: University Press, 1917], pp. 18-29.) The **first** commandment is cited in the form familiar to every pious Jew, as the daily Shema or prayer said morning and evening; both parallels omit vs. 29b. Omit **like,** with the better MSS. It is derived from Matt. 22:39. Read, with RSV, **the second is this.**

---

many times and in many places the very absence of great emotion has been deemed a desirable mark of character. The Jesus of this declaration has been a "fanatic," an "enthusiast," to those of his followers who were first of all correct and proper, with their feelings well under control.

29. *The Lord . . . Is One.*—Jesus, in quoting the call to worship which was given in the temple (Deut. 6:4-5), proclaims that man's ultimate allegiance may not be divided. It was the greatest service which the Hebrew religion rendered a world full of idolatry and tribal gods. Nor is that service less needed in our twentieth-century world, so full of vigorous idolatry. Aldous Huxley has pointed out that one unexpected result of the decay of a genuine monotheism has been the spread of polytheism. Some of the old gods of Greek and Roman mythology have flourishing cults: Venus, the symbol of sex; Mars, the god of war; Minerva, the patron goddess of intellect; Vulcan, the ironmonger, the symbol of an industrial civilization. A common mood exclaims in feeling and act, if not in word: "How excellent is thy name, O Vulcan, in all the earth. Thou hast set thy glory in the steel mills."

Then there is the cult of a "patriotism" which with many has taken the place of the one God of Jesus and the Hebrew faith (see on vss. 13-17). Again and again it says, "Thou shalt have no other gods before me." J. A. Lasswell describes it:

What is happening in America and elsewhere is a process of syncretism, by which an ever diminishing element of Christianity and an ever increasing element of nationalism are entering into the alloy known as modern religion. . . . The new religion has its rituals. The flag is supplanting the cross.[5]

[5] *Northwestern Christian Advocate,* Feb. 10, 1927.

29. *You Shall Love the Lord Your God with All Your Heart, . . . Soul, . . . Mind, . . . Strength.*—The love God desires demands the action of the whole personality. It is not necessary to enter upon the distinctions involved in Hebrew psychology. All of a man's being, his moral nature, his emotion, his intellect, his energy, must go into his love of God if that love is to be acceptable to God and adequate for the shaping of his own life. When we give to God a mere fraction of ourselves, God himself becomes a mere fraction of what he might be to us. Implicit in these words is Christ's revelation of the nature of God. Only a God who is love would make love his supreme demand.

Many things stand in the way of our response. God is often allowed to remain so vague to us that "loving" him is like trying to love a parallelogram, or an equation, such as the basic $E=MC^2$. Indeed the plight of the world is due partly to the fact that God has become an equation, a mere symbol for primal energy. Again, our love is often robbed of its moral and emotional power because God is pushed to the periphery of our thought. He occupies for many of us about the same position the League of Nations occupied for the man who confessed in the 1920's that he never paid much attention to it, but was glad, in a general way, that it was there. Once more, that love becomes thin and empty of power when it is not sustained and made real by any employment of the means of grace, or by any expression in action. It becomes anemic and dies unless there is poured into it the red blood of concrete behavior.

Great stress should be laid on the words **with all your mind.** That stress is always needed; but we can say without exaggeration that the need grows greater as life and the world become

31 And the second *is* like, *namely* this, Thou shalt love thy neighbor as thyself. There is none other commandment greater than these.

32 And the scribe said unto him, Well, Master, thou hast said the truth: for there is one God; and there is none other but he:

33 And to love him with all the heart, and with all the understanding, and with all the soul, and with all the strength, and to love *his* neighbor as himself, is more than all whole burnt offerings and sacrifices.

all your strength.' 31 The second is this, 'You shall love your neighbor as yourself.' There is no other commandment greater than these." 32 And the scribe said to him, "You are right, Teacher; you have truly said that he is one, and there is no other but he; 33 and to love him with all the heart, and with all the understanding, and with all the strength, and to love one's neighbor as oneself, is much more than all

32-33. The scribe proceeds to repeat and to draw out the theological implications of what Jesus has just said. Did Mark feel that this explanation would be especially valuable for his readers? Both parallels omit this repetition, though Luke uses vs. 32*c* at the end of the preceding section (Luke 20:39), and in Luke 10:25-28 gives this whole section in briefer form, placing the answer on the scribe's lips, making it a "trial" of Jesus, and ending with Jesus' commendation, "Do this, and you will live."

more complicated, and simple solutions of complex problems become more and more impossible. Then the need of brains and intelligence in religion is intensified. Yet it is just the dedication of the mind to the love of God which is so often withheld. Moslems, on entering a mosque, remove their shoes and leave them outside; Christians, all too often, entering the church, remove their brains and leave them outside. The first prayer learned in childhood, "Now I lay me down to sleep," remains, for a great host, the pattern of prayer through all the adult years. The offering of the full powers of the mind is the last full measure of devotion, the hardest gift to give. The character in H. G. Wells's *Croquet Player* spoke for many as he responded to the appeal for help in preventing World War II: "I am willing to fall in with anything promising. But if I am to *think*, that is too much." Loving God with the mind means more than the joy of intellectual apprehension; it means also the willingness to have our minds changed into harmony with his mind, to give up our settled ways, to surrender our cherished prejudices. Nothing less than that is loving God.

31. You Shall Love Your Neighbor as Yourself.—It was Jesus who lifted this love of neighbor from its comparatively obscure position in Leviticus to set it alongside the love of God, not merely as the second among many commandments, but as constituting, with the first, that center from which all duties radiate and all fulfillment of the law proceeds.

The word "love" here does not mean personal liking, a sentimental affection, but active good will—the Greek *agapē*. It is good will, boundless and aggressive, extended to those who may have no personal charm for us, and may

be beyond the boundaries of family or tribe or nation.

The perfect exposition, of course, is that which Jesus himself gives in the parable of the good Samaritan. In Luke it follows this declaration of the greatest commandment (Luke 10:29-37). Beside that any explanatory words are halting prose. Here it must suffice to recall what is so easily forgotten, that intelligent love of neighbor, in a complex society, is a difficult intellectual, moral, and spiritual achievement. The chief hindrance has been oversimplification. If one thinks of the limited, immediate circle of face-to-face relationships in a small neighborhood, everything becomes comparatively easy. But the parable of the good Samaritan, the man who overstepped all existing borders to do concrete, costly acts of love, makes clear that love of neighbor has no barriers. When we take the command as an absolute, there emerges into fuller view a necessity we have met before: we have to love our neighbor, as well as God, with the mind! We must bring the best thought we can summon, and the fullest knowledge we can acquire, to the task of determining what specific actions and policies promise best to be the embodiment of intelligent good will to men. So the words become like the little tent in the Oriental fairy tale, made of material so delicate that it could be folded up and contained in the palm of a man's hand; yet when it was unrolled, it would afford shelter for an army of thousands of men. This little "tent"—love your neighbor—small enough to apply to the family next door, when "unrolled" by a consecrated imagination, covers the earth. It involves the patient exploration of what the largest, lasting good would be to all

34 And when Jesus saw that he answered discreetly, he said unto him, Thou art not far from the kingdom of God. And no man after that durst ask him *any question.*

35 ¶ And Jesus answered and said, while he taught in the temple, How say the scribes that Christ is the son of David?

whole burnt offerings and sacrifices." **34** And when Jesus saw that he answered wisely, he said to him, "You are not far from the kingdom of God." And after that no one dared to ask him any question.

35 And as Jesus taught in the temple, he said, "How can the scribes say that

---

34. After that no one dared to ask him any question: This conclusion has been shifted by Luke to the end of the preceding section (Luke 20:40), since he has used the material of this Marcan passage elsewhere. Matthew has shifted it to the end of the following section (Matt. 22:46), which is also the account of a controversy. In Mark vss. 34*b* surely concludes the present section, though some editors (e.g., Klostermann) view it as the introduction to the following one.

11. THE MESSIAH NOT SON OF DAVID (12:35-37*a*)

Jesus now turns upon his adversaries, in this and the following section. They no longer question him (vs. 34*b*); instead, he challenges their teaching. This passage has often been interpreted as Jesus' repudiation of the title "Son of David," on the ground that he was not actually a descendant of the royal house. According to other interpretations Jesus is making a double claim, i.e., to be both Son of David and Son of God; but this is surely to read the passage in the light of a later theology. Jesus simply states the question, **How can the scribes say . . . ?** (πῶς λέγουσιν; contrast ὅτι λέγουσιν in 9:11); and the implication is clearly that the Messiah is greater than the royalist "Son of David" of current and prophetic—not merely scribal—expectation; he is in reality David's Lord, as in Ps. 110:1. The old royalist, possibly Maccabean, psalm was now given a messianic interpretation, and the king is no longer an earthly monarch but a divine being—like the Son of man, to whom Dan. 7 was now understood to allude, and who emerges more clearly in I Enoch and in other apocalyptic writings, and generally in the Gospels. This is probably what the words meant for Mark; and in their origin, on the lips of Jesus, they must have meant the substitution of the "transcendental" concept of the Messiah for the political—the "northern" for the "southern," as Lohmeyer has argued (in *Galiläa und Jerusalem*). In Mark's theology the Son of God concept was being combined with the older Palestinian and quite primitive one of the Son of man

---

"neighbors" with whom we are tied in the big bundle of life, to the laborers who maintain the fabric of the world, to all groups of race and nationality. It goes into questions of penology, of the social safeguarding of health, of international policies. And after that dedicated thinking comes the dedicated giving of the whole self.

Another fruitful theme lies in the twin questions arising from this narrative: (*a*) What does love of God do for love of neighbor? (*b*) What does the practice of loving one's neighbor do for loving God? They interact. A false love of God, or the love of a God far less than the God and Father of our Lord Jesus Christ, has made man forget his neighbor—and worse. When one "loves" a tribal god, interested only in the fortunes of one group, or a god interested chiefly in orthodoxy of opinion, the excluded neighbor suffers—has even been tortured. But when there is the love of God as

here portrayed by Jesus, love of neighbor has deepened and intensified. So also, by the same token, when love of neighbor has become a real experience, the love of God has been lifted up from confining walls, and filled with ethical and spiritual content.

35-37. *How Can the Scribes Say that the Christ Is the Son of David?*—In all frankness it must be confessed that the argument ascribed here to Jesus, designed to prove that the Messiah is more than David's son, is not impressive or at all persuasive to our minds today. It moves in a realm foreign to our modes of thought. To us the basis of the argument seems shaky, to say the least. Its weight seems to rest on two assumptions: first, that David was the author of Ps. 110, and second, that the psalm is messianic. Both of these assumptions are clouded with grave doubts, to put it mildly. A haze of uncertainty surrounds the question. How much of this argument is a reflection of

36 For David himself said by the Holy Ghost, The LORD said to my Lord, Sit thou on my right hand, till I make thine enemies thy footstool.

37 David therefore himself calleth him

the Christ is the son of David? 36 David himself, inspired by[z] the Holy Spirit, declared,

'The Lord said to my Lord,
Sit at my right hand,
till I put thy enemies under thy feet.'

37 David himself calls him Lord; so how

[z] Or himself, in.

(see Intro., pp. 642-44) ; and the combination was crowding out the Son of David idea, with its mundane political connotations—a process that came to completion in the later theology of the church. But the term Son of David survived in many a hymn, prayer, and story, and has been forever enshrined in the infancy narratives and genealogies of Luke and Matthew—as also, incidentally, in such a story as Mark himself has already used in 10:46-52.

35. As in 9:11, recognized O.T. teaching (e.g., Ps. 72) is attributed to the scribes, somewhat as the Mosaic law is referred to in the Sermon on the Mount as what "you have heard . . . was said to the men of old" (Matt. 5:33; etc.) . But in neither case can it be assumed that Jesus, or the disciples, or those who handed down the tradition, or the writer of the Gospel, or his readers, were unaware that Scripture was being cited. It will not do to assume that the champion of the Galilean Amhaarez was ignorant of the O.T. The point is, the scribes, i.e., the official teachers of Jewish religion, did not take into account *all* of Scripture. It is like the reply to the Sadducees in vss. 24-27.

36. **By the Holy Ghost** (ἐν τῷ πνεύματι) , i.e., by divine inspiration or **inspired by the Holy Spirit** (RSV) .

37. **Therefore** (KJV) may be implied but is not in the Greek. It comes from the Vulg.: *Ipse ergo David.* **Whence** (KJV) implies a theological answer beyond Mark's range of thought; the question simply meant that the title "Son of David" was inadequate. For πόθεν both parallels read πῶς (how) , and so do many MSS of Mark. Prefer RSV: **how.**

---

the interpretation by the early church of Christ's exaltation after the Resurrection to the right hand of God? And how much of the saying can be rightly ascribed to Jesus?

One principle, however, of great and permanent worth is enshrined in these verses, and should not be overlooked. It expresses, as the Exeg. so clearly points out, "the substitution of the 'transcendental' concept of the Messiah for the political" one. Jesus is more than **the son of David,** with all the earthy associations of that nationalistic ideal. The words in John 18:36, "My kingship is not of this world," express the faith at the heart of this passage.

That, of course, is an accepted axiom with Christians. Yet it needs constant reiteration. For worldly and materialistic conceptions of the kingdom of God creep back like the seven devils driven from a house. Men have felt and feel still the allurement of earthly goods and earthly means, which was the core of the political conception of the Messiah as a king who would restore a nationalistic kingdom. The pomp of power beckons to the church in all ages, insinuating that there are surer methods

of achieving authority than the slow, intangible methods of a spiritual Messiah, whose symbol is a cross. "Money. Force. Spheres of influence. Pageantry. Oil fields. Try these," says the tempter. "They are quicker and better." All of them are remnants in modern life of the "son of David" conception of the Messiah, thought of in materialistic terms. Familiar words apply: "Not by might, nor by power, but by my Spirit, saith the LORD" (Zech. 4:6) .

37. *And the Great Throng Heard Him Gladly.*—Through the centuries these words have quite legitimately been given a much wider application than they have in their original setting. It is difficult to determine what was the specific cause of the crowd's gladness on this occasion. It may well have been a mixture of admiration for a skillful debater, a man of courage, and a beloved teacher. Beyond that the words carry a suggestion of the widespread and timeless appeal of Jesus. On the mere level of language he has skills to impart which if mastered would be enormous assets in the proclaiming of his gospel. Men heard Jesus gladly because they could understand him—a

Lord; and whence is he *then* his son? And the common people heard him gladly.

38 ¶ And he said unto them in his doctrine, Beware of the scribes, which love to go in long clothing, and *love* salutations in the market places,

39 And the chief seats in the synagogues, and the uppermost rooms at feasts:

is he his son?" And the great throng heard him gladly.

38 And in his teaching he said, "Beware of the scribes, who like to go about in long robes, and to have salutations in the market places 39 and the best seats in the synagogues and the places of honor at feasts,

---

12. Warning Against the Scribes (12:37*b*-40)

Following the section in which Jesus turns upon the scribes and rejects their teaching as inadequate, he now goes on to attack their practice of religion as hypocritical. Out of this brief passage Matthew has built up one of his longer discourses (Matt. 23), using material, presumably from Q, which Luke has included in various locations. It is very doubtful if any trace of this common source survives in the brief section before us. In the historical study of this material it should be recognized that much of the material in Matt. 23 reflects later controversy (see D. W. Riddle, *Jesus and the Pharisees* [Chicago: University of Chicago Press, 1928]).

37*b*. **The common people,** better, with RSV, **the great throng,** i.e., the crowd present in the background of the preceding controversies, presumably in the temple court (as in 11:27). This half verse is the introduction to the new section (cf. vs. 38, "he said unto them"); it is not the conclusion of the preceding.

38-39. **Long robes,** i.e., the apparel of the well-to-do and now the garb of honor of the learned. **Salutations:** Cf. Matt. 23:7; but rabbi (literally "my master") was not a common title in the Jewish schools until some time after the fall of Jerusalem and the reorganization of the schools. **Best seats in the synagogues:** the congregation of men usually stood and only the teachers sat (Luke 4:20). **Places of honor** were assigned, not by seniority, but by prominence in the community (cf. Luke 14:7-11; Jas. 2:2-4).

---

great boon. All too often his truth has been translated into an alien jargon, far from the life and speech of men. They heard him gladly because his words were the outflow of a great love for men, a love which they had seen in action. They heard him gladly because he addressed the hero in the soul, because the God he spoke of was a God who could garner up a man's heart. His word is "follow."

38-40. *Beware of the Scribes.*—Here, as in the passage immediately preceding, Jesus takes the offensive. There was no questioner to call forth his warning. He launches out himself (see on 11:29). He is not crouching in a corner, at bay, barely holding off his critics at arm's length. He carries the assault against them. To him defense was not enough. It never is enough for the church. The proponents of Christianity have been far too well satisfied with it. A certain inferiority complex has fastened on many of them. They move about with an apologetic air, pathetically eager for some word from a prominent scientist or politician or other public figure, approving of God. What can it mean but a lack of forthright confidence in their own message, their own mission—that they should depend so much on these crumbs which drop from the rich man's table!

38-40. *The Scribes, Who Like to Go About in Long Robes, and to Have Salutations in the Market Places.*—This scornful picture of the scribes' love of prominence, done with masterful brushwork, accurate in observation and detail, hits in the very center some of the dominant motives of our time and society. Here is no period piece, some quaint glimpse of ancient snobs and self-pushers in Jerusalem. Every item fits into the twentieth-century scene. Line upon line are depicted the basic drives of an acquisitive civilization, far more concerned with outside appearances than with any inside character. Look at the economic snobbishness involved. The long robes were a sign and proof that the wearer did no manual work for a living. **Salutations**—what a world of mad scrambles the very word suggests, the glittering accolade of a title that will elevate one above the herd below— "manager," "executive," "director!" The best seats—in restricted neighborhoods, in clubs, on preferential lists of every sort! Even within the church, now as then, how nicely gradations are made—"very reverend," "most reverend," "your grace." The places of honor rarely go begging.

This preoccupation with prominence is an inevitable result of the lack of any significant "inside." The great sin of the scribes, and of all

| 40 Which devour widows' houses, and for a pretense make long prayers: these shall receive greater damnation.

41 ¶ And Jesus sat over against the treasury, and beheld how the people cast money into the treasury: and many that were rich cast in much. | 40 who devour widows' houses and for a pretense make long prayers. They will receive the greater condemnation."

41 And he sat down opposite the treasury, and watched the multitude putting money into the treasury. Many rich people |

40. But all this was pretense and hypocrisy! They **devour widows' houses**, through unscrupulous acceptance of hospitality and support, and **for a pretense** (προφάσει) — without their hearts in it, or perhaps ostentatiously, "for a show"—they **make long prayers**. The Vulg. takes the two clauses in close connection: *sub obtentu prolixae orationis;* but the criticism of their prayers is a distinct and additional charge against them. Compare the double criticism in Matt. 6:5-8: Jesus condemns both the hypocritical, i.e., ostentatious, prayer of the "hypocrites," i.e., contemporary Jews, scribes, or Pharisees (vss. 5-6), and the long, empty repetitions in the prayers of the heathen (vs. 7). **Greater condemnation**, i.e., all the greater for their hypocrisy; the more they pretend to piety the more severely they will be judged.

13. The Widow's Offering (12:41-44)

It has been argued that this section was interpolated into Mark from the parallel in Luke—a very improbable theory, considering the Marcan style of the passage, and the likelihood that its insertion at this point was suggested by "widows" in vs. 40. It has also been argued that the scene was constructed out of the saying in vs. 43, but why this theory should commend itself is not clear. According to vs. 40 (cf. vs. 37b), Jesus is the champion of the people against their extortionate and hypocritical leaders; the present passage only carries this point further and illustrates it.

41. He sat down: Some MSS read "he stood," as if to see better; but a teacher sat. **Treasury** (γαζοφυλακείου) is apparently the hall named from the chest with a trumpet-

pushers to front seats, is a lack of love. The way of salvation is to be found in the acceptance of another and higher standard. Jesus proclaimed it again and again. The road to greatness is still the way of service. What would an edition of *Who's Who* be like if it were published, not in Chicago or London, but in heaven? If it contained the names of the occupants, not of the chief seats of earth, but of the kingdom of God? A strange book, truly! It would be a "servants'" directory, as Jesus used that word "servant." In the very next paragraph he awards an honored place in God's *Who's Who* to an unknown in Jerusalem, a widow who put a penny in the alms box.

40. *Who Devour Widows' Houses.*—It is no mere stretching of words—to say that Jesus here faces the housing problem in Jerusalem. That problem was acute enough at the end of World War II. But it is a very old problem, in fact as old and new as poverty and greed. Jesus had made no survey of land tenure in Palestine. He would have been a stranger to any economic theory of rent. Men only mangle him unforgivably when they view him as a first-century Henry George or Adam Smith or Karl Marx. But he was no stranger to timeless cupidity and the timeless suffering which it brings under any political or economic order. He saw the local financial powers—the charge in this passage would seem to apply more directly to the exploiting priesthood than to the scribes as a class —skimming off profits, and laying intolerable burdens on men and women. If he had no blueprint for an industrial civilization, he nevertheless did lay bare sources of evil in motive. There is sound economic insight in his criticism, for he was denouncing the using up in conspicuous, fruitless consumption—"devouring"—what ought to have a functional value for life and society—houses. We need with mind and purpose to explore the causes of poor housing, undeflected by economic interest. Then to see clearly and to fight continuously all the forces of entrenched privilege which today as then devour not only houses but homes!

41-44. *He . . . Watched the Multitude Putting Money into the Treasury.*—The point Jesus makes is blazingly clear—the gift which counts is the gift which costs. It is one of the many instances in which he contrasts God's measurements with man's. He makes no denunciation of gifts which come out of surplus and abundance. It is simply that true giving is to be measured

42 And there came a certain poor widow, and she threw in two mites, which make a farthing.

43 And he called *unto him* his disciples, and saith unto them, Verily I say unto you, That this poor widow hath cast more in, than all they which have cast into the treasury:

44 For all *they* did cast in of their abundance; but she of her want did cast in all that she had, *even* all her living.

13 And as he went out of the temple, one of his disciples saith unto him, Master, see what manner of stones and what buildings *are here!*

put in large sums. 42 And a poor widow came, and put in two copper coins, which make a penny. 43 And he called his disciples to him, and said to them, "Truly, I say to you, this poor widow has put in more than all those who are contributing to the treasury. 44 For they all contributed out of their abundance; but she out of her poverty has put in everything she had, her whole living."

13 And as he came out of the temple, one of his disciples said to him, "Look, Teacher, what wonderful stones and

---

shaped tube into which were dropped coins for the support of the temple worship; this was something like a church "poor box," as these offerings were purely voluntary, and perhaps not in very large amounts—though the **rich cast in much.** H. J. Holtzmann has called this "the Peter's pence of the Jews."

42. **A certain poor widow** (KJV) sounds as if she were known; prefer RSV—and the Greek—**a poor widow. Two mites** or **a farthing,** i.e., two small **copper coins** (λεπτά) ; they were probably two *perutas,* the smallest Jewish coins, in value a quadrans, or about half a cent, with a purchasing value of approximately two cents.

43-44. Whereas the scribes "devour widows' houses" (vs. 40) , this poor widow, in her poverty, **put in everything she had, her whole living.** How Jesus knew this is not said. But all along in Mark, Jesus has had supernatural insight (2:8; etc.) .

C. The Apocalyptic Discourse (13:1-37)

Ever since Timothée Colani's *Jésus-Christ et les croyances messianiques de son temps* (Strasbourg: Treuttel et Wurtz, 1864) , it has become increasingly evident to scholars

---

relatively to what is left, not absolutely by the size. As he sat there among the alms boxes, and watched people making their contributions, out of them all one widow stirred him and moved him to exclamation. Here was the real thing! To put the matter with stark concreteness, it was her next meal. The temple was full of the noise of coin dropping. The thirteen big receptacles, shaped like ear trumpets, made a loud clanging of metal on metal. Jesus' ears were attuned to the faintest noise of all, the falling of two small coins, the smallest in circulation, worth in purchasing power about two cents. Yet in the sight of God, who looks on the heart, that was big business. It has proved to be one of the world's mightiest financial transactions.

The distinguishing mark of the widow's gift, however, was not merely its proportion to her means; there was something in her heart that lifted the gift out of routine into the realm of sacrifice.

We all know only too well the easy, reasonable justifications she might have had for withholding her two copper coins: "What difference could a penny make? It is so small it will not

count at all. Let those give who can afford it. I really haven't got a penny to spare. No one will ever notice whether I drop in anything or not." We know the case for the defense from start to finish—and at the finish the two coins are in our purse. Jesus' recognition of the greatness of the gift knocks over our shabby defense. No gift of love is too small to count; nor can any life be excused from the grace and duty of sharing. Nothing escapes the notice of the God from whom no secret is hid.

This scene in the temple starts our minds out on journeys of remembrance. How great and many have been the gifts which have come out of poverty! They have been gifts of life, of thought, of skill, of devotion. The support of the church throughout the world has come far more from the two coppers of the poor than from the large checks of the rich. Paul is not the only one of whom it may be truly said, "as poor, yet making many rich" (II Cor. 6:10) .

13:1-2. *Look, Teacher, What Wonderful Stones and What Wonderful Buildings!* This conversation between Jesus and one of his disciples in the temple has a close relationship to

2 And Jesus answering said unto him, | what wonderful buildings!" 2 And Jesus
Seest thou these great buildings? there shall | said to him, "Do you see these great build-
| ings? There will not be left here one stone

---

that this chapter is composite, and includes material of a general apocalyptic nature, not
necessarily to be attributed to Jesus, along with sayings which probably belonged in the
authentic tradition of his words. The extraneous material forms a fairly clearly definable
unit, as a "Little Apocalypse," and may perhaps be assigned to a specific date. The usual
analysis attributes vss. 6-8, 14-20, 24-27, and possibly 31 to this source. Many scholars
identify either this Little Apocalypse, or the whole of ch. 13, with the "oracle" which was
said to have warned the Christians in Jerusalem, at the beginning of the siege in A.D. 70, to
flee before the city's fall, and which caused them to withdraw to Pella, east of the Jordan
(Eusebius *Church History* III. 5. 3). This apocalyptic warning was later incorporated by
Mark at this point in his Gospel, on the assumption that, since it was attributed to the
Lord, this was the most likely place for it, i.e., after vss. 1-2. The theory is an extremely
important one; and though it can scarcely be proved, it goes a long way in accounting for
the presence in the chapter of passages which do not at all bear the stamp of Jesus' own
teaching, and might just as well be found in I Enoch, II Esdras, or any other of a dozen
apocalyptic writings of the period. It is not in the least unlikely that sayings of Jesus
should be worked into an apocalyptic writing: the author of the Revelation of John, for
example, has not hesitated to make use of sayings of Jesus—apocalyptic in form—or to
attribute to Jesus sayings that were derived from other sources than the historic tradition.
Moreover, it was the nature of apocalyptic writings to grow, to absorb new material, to
undergo revision and recasting, so that the dating of such material is extremely difficult.
A late writing like the Revelation of John—*ca.* A.D. 95, in the reign of Domitian—
undoubtedly contains much older material; so it is here. The "desolating sacrilege" (vs.
14), e.g., was originally the *shiqqûç shômēm* of Dan. 9:27, the desecration of the altar in
the temple by Antiochus Epiphanes in 168 B.C. (I Macc. 1:54, 59; 6:7). But the phrase
was repeatedly reinterpreted, and here it seems to refer to Caligula's order that his statue
should be set up in the temple (Josephus *Jewish War* II. 10. 1-5)—so Jerome and other
church fathers. But it continued to be reinterpreted, as was the wont of apocalyptists, as

---

the preceding story about the widow and her
copper coins. It is a relationship of striking
contrast. Both Jesus and the disciple said,
"Look!" They said it in wonder and awe. But
they were looking at different things.

The disciple said, "Look at the buildings!"—
"What a size!" as Moffatt translates it. "How
wonderful they are!" It was a perfectly natural
feeling for a countryman from Galilee gazing at
the wonders of a big city, the religious center
of his people. The temple was truly impressive
in its magnificence. Jesus also said, "Look!" But
he was staring at a poor woman whose self-
forgetful sacrifice was far more wonderful than
any stones.

Jesus was interested in quality of life, not in
quantity of material. He weighed the temple as
an institution on ethical and religious balances,
and found it wanting. Because the institution
failed to serve men in their spiritual needs, it
would not last.

That same contrast between quantity and
quality has continued. The exclamation
"Look!" has been much on men's tongues. Today it is one of the words most characteristic of
our common speech. But on the lips of Jesus it
comes with sharp rebuke to a quantitative civilization, as ours is so largely, full of mechanical
wonders and miraculous gadgets of every sort.
We cry out ecstatically, many of us, over the
material miracles promised for tomorrow. We
stand in awe before bigness, awe that partakes
of the nature of worship. Look at the airplanes,
at the total of bank clearings, at the freight
car loadings, at all the other ready measures
of "progress" and prosperity. Jesus too says,
"Look!" But not at the size or the quantity;
look at the ethical and spiritual quality of your
life and culture. On ethical and religious scales
all must be weighed. The fateful years of
World War II said it. The years that followed
said it. The long sweep of events says it. "You
had better look at the quality of your life; for
if you do not, one stone shall not be left on
another." In a world full of stones thrown
down into ruins because of the moral and
religious failure of men and nations, the words
of Jesus, his judgment on mere size and quantity, have inescapable force. He foresaw that
his own nation would not repent. History since

not be left one stone upon another, that shall not be thrown down.

3 And as he sat upon the mount of Olives, over against the temple, Peter and James and John and Andrew asked him privately,

upon another, that will not be thrown down."

3 And as he sat on the Mount of Olives opposite the temple, Peter and James and John and Andrew asked him privately,

---

fulfillment succeeded fulfillment and still the end was not yet: Luke 21:20 thinks of the siege of Jerusalem; Matt. 24:15 of Antichrist at the end of the world; some of the church fathers see the "desolating sacrilege" in the equestrian statue of Hadrian placed on the old temple site in the pagan town, Aelia Capitolina, which was built on the ruins of Jerusalem. The stage of reinterpretation reflected in Mark is, as we have noted, that reached in the time of Caligula (*ca.* A.D. 41); though for Mark himself this interpretation was no doubt beginning to give way to another, as tension increased in Judea, and the Roman armies, already victorious in Galilee, were advancing upon Jerusalem. Just what he understood is not clear. **Let the reader understand** (vs. 14) implies an esoteric interpretation which he has not given us. The admonition also implies that the discourse (or its source, the Little Apocalypse) was a written book; and the "reader" is the one who reads it aloud to others, perhaps an assembly, perhaps a congregation. It is this brief parenthetic addition which seems to clinch the argument for the hypothesis—though it is of course possible that it refers to the whole Gospel, not to this one chapter or its underlying source. Matthew keeps the words; Luke paraphrases.

1. The Impending Fall of the Temple (13:1-2)

Like the O.T. prophets before the Assyrian invasion (cf. Mic. 3:12; Jer. 26:18; 9:11), Jesus predicts the fall of the temple. This must have been his authentic utterance, as it was used against him in garbled form at his "trial" before the high priest (14:58). The temple **stones** were especially large and the **buildings** impressive; ancient travelers reported it to be one of the wonders of the world, and worth a trip to Palestine to see. But it was to be a total ruin, not because it housed a false worship—as in Stephen's speech in Acts 7, or in other early Christian polemics—but as a punishment once more upon the nation (cf. Luke 13:1-9).

2. Introduction to the Little Apocalypse (13:3-8)

It is upon the saying in vs. 2 that Mark hangs the long following discourse, which is extended by Matthew into the two long chapters (24–25) of his apocalyptic discourse.

13:3. The scene is not now the temple court but **the Mount of Olives,** opposite the temple, where later apocalypses (e.g., the Epistle of the Apostles) located Jesus' post-

---

then has taken up the textbook and driven home the sequel.

Nor dare we forget that these words were spoken in the temple, and in judgment on a religious institution—not so much because "it housed a false worship" (see Exeg.) as because it gathered up within itself and symbolized the life of the whole nation. Jesus still brings to his church—and brings it first, not last (I Pet. 4:17)—the measure of quality, not quantity. There, if anywhere, we are at our best. And what have we to say to him? "Look, Master, at this! What wonderful buildings! It is St. Croesus' Church, with a floor space almost equal to the railroad station!" He is not impressed. As on the day of Mark's story, his eye wanders off in search of other things, evidences of a richness

of inner life and devotion to God's kingdom. He looks for the love and sacrifice akin to the gift of a poor widow, for the unsplit allegiance of lives which acknowledge one Master.

3-31. *The Last Things.*—Study carefully the Exeg. This is one of the most difficult chapters in the Bible to understand and evaluate. In the Exeg. is assembled and presented evidence to support the judgment of scholars that the chapter is a composite, made up of certain extraneous material—which must be assigned to a later date and related to a different situation—called the "Little Apocalypse," and also of sayings of Jesus which, as the Exeg. says, "belong with the authentic tradition of his words." It is important for our understanding of Jesus that we do not attribute to him

4 Tell us, when shall these things be? and what *shall be* the sign when all these things shall be fulfilled?

5 And Jesus answering them began to say, Take heed lest any *man* deceive you:

6 For many shall come in my name, saying, I am *Christ;* and shall deceive many.

4 "Tell us, when will this be, and what will be the sign when these things are all to be accomplished?" 5 And Jesus began to say to them, "Take heed that no one leads you astray. 6 Many will come in my name, saying, 'I am he!' and they will lead many

resurrection apocalyptic discourses. Here Zech. 14:4 anticipated the divine epiphany on the "day of the Lord"; popular expectation—at least in Judea—looked for the revelation of the Messiah on this mount (cf. Josephus *Jewish War* II. 13. 5; *Antiquities* XX. 8. 6; see also Klostermann, p. 127). **Privately,** as often in Mark; here—and only here—Andrew is one of the chosen intimates. Was this feature derived from a source?

4. The question is twofold: **When** would this destruction of the temple take place, and what would be **the sign** preceding it? As in all apocalypses, but contrary to Jesus' teaching (8:11-13; Luke 17:20-24), signs were to precede the end; i.e., as in all apocalypses, the date could be inferred from the signs—at least when they began to appear. The phrase **these things** refers not so much to the destruction of Jerusalem as to the series of catastrophic events of which it would be a part, thus anticipating the subject of the rest of the chapter. Matt. 24:3 expands and makes explicit: "the sign of your coming [*parousia*] and of the close [*sunteleia*] of the age."

5-6. First of all would come a number of deceivers, "false Messiahs"—often the "Antichrist," as in II Thess. 2:3-10; I John 4:3, but here a series of **many. In my name** is explained by what follows, i.e., pretending to be the Messiah. If one accepts the hypothesis of the Little Apocalypse, it seems likely that vs. 6 belongs to it—perhaps edited by the insertion of **in my name**—as well as the following vss. 7-8, which are typical of apocalyptic writing. It is also possible that vs. 5*b* belonged to it, and that originally the warning was not against "false Christs" (as in vss. 21-22), but against examples of the Hellenistic γόης (like Simon Magus; cf. Acts 8:9-10). The Greek of our passage can perfectly well be translated, "Many will come in my name saying, I am," the predicate either remaining to be supplied (cf. John 5:43), or even omitted altogether, as in certain types of Hellenistic oracular literature.

"oracles" which originated later. Notice the difficulty occasioned by a comparison of 13:4 and 8:11-13. The comment which follows here deals with the permanent relevance of these verses to life, no matter whether they are found in the sections of the chapter ascribed to the later apocalypse, or in those ascribed to Jesus himself.

4-8. *What Will Be the Sign when These Things Are All to Be Accomplished?*—These words may be allowed to suggest quite clearly the blight of a schedule, the harm which can come to life when the mind is too intent on a date, either for the end of the world, or indeed for any expected action of God. The Christians of the early church are here warned against that; they are warned against being led astray by anyone who cries, "This is it!" We can well understand how natural the question "When?" would be to a church under persecution. The answer given them was not a date on a calendar, but God. Faith in a dependable God, who would act in his own time, was what they were offered. It was that which kept up their morale and endurance.

The situation which called forth the warning has passed away. But the pertinence of the word has not passed away. It has permanent relevance to all speculation about the last things, whether conceived as the end of the world, the second coming of Christ, or the consummation of the kingdom of God. Such curiosity too easily becomes mechanical rather than spiritual. There is particularly sharp pertinence in the words **lead . . . astray.** For that is what a preoccupation with the end of the age, or of the world, actually does. It leads one astray from the primary task and duty of following Jesus; from the ethical and religious truth that is known, to the fruitless focusing on the unknown, on a timetable. If all the attention and concern which in Christian history have been given to *last* things had only been given to *first* things, the power of Christianity in the world and its service to the world would have been enormously increased. G. K. Chesterton said acutely that there are many people who know "the last word" about everything and the first word about nothing. Fidgety fussing about "the last **things**"

7 And when ye shall hear of wars and rumors of wars, be ye not troubled: for *such things* must needs be; but the end *shall* not *be* yet.

8 For nation shall rise against nation, and kingdom against kingdom: and there shall be earthquakes in divers places, and there shall be famines and troubles: these *are* the beginnings of sorrows.

9 ¶ But take heed to yourselves: for they shall deliver you up to councils; and in the

astray. **7** And when you hear of wars and rumors of wars, do not be alarmed; this must take place, but the end is not yet. **8** For nation will rise against nation, and kingdom against kingdom; there will be earthquakes in various places, there will be famines; this is but the beginning of the sufferings.

9 "But take heed to yourselves; for they

7-8. Next, as in many apocalypses (ultimately based on O.T. prophecies, if not upon still older sources), would come (*a*) **wars and rumors of wars.** (*b*) **earthquakes,** (*c*) **famines. And troubles** is weakly supported; omit, as in RSV. These things **must needs be** (δεῖ γενέσθαι), by divine decree and in accordance with the plan of God—the view assumed in all apocalyptic literature. **But the end is not yet:** These are only preliminary signs, **the beginnings of sorrows,** i.e., the beginning of the messianic woes (*ḥebhlê dî Māshîaḥ,* later a technical term for the terrible events, "birth pangs," that were to precede the coming of the Anointed One).

3. The Disciples to Be Persecuted (13:9-13)

Most of this section is used by Matthew in his discourse at the sending out of the disciples on a preaching mission (Matt. 10:17-22), and its appropriateness there, rather than here, can scarcely be questioned in view of the wider purposes of the discourse in Matt. 10. But it was impossible for a Christian apocalypse to ignore the part of the disciples, and of the apostolic church, in the series of final events—note the way in which the Christian martyr motif is woven into the Revelation of John! Indeed, this section has clearly been edited with the later church in mind, and as a whole it sounds more like some early Christian visionary speaking in Christ's name than it does like the historical Jesus himself. For an apocalyptist there was no criterion for distinguishing the "historical" utterances of Jesus from those delivered by him "in the Spirit" (cf. Rev. 1–3).

9. Take heed: This repeated warning (vss. 5, 9, 23, 33) leads up to the final climactic word in the discourse, "Watch" (vs. 37), and helps set the tone of the whole chapter.

---

must never displace the first things of Jesus, the great commandments, "Love God, and love your neighbor as yourself." Preoccupation with "When?"—with arranging dates on a calendar—may change a spiritual revelation into a Chinese puzzle. It may cause us to leave the needs of people for a curiosity about schedules.

The Book of Common Prayer has a perfect collect for us, a very light for our minds and lamp for our path:

Eternal God, who committest to us the swift and solemn trust of life; since we do not know what a day may bring forth, but only that the hour for serving thee is always present, may we wake to the instant claims of thy holy will, not waiting for tomorrow, but yielding today.

9. *Take Heed to Yourselves.*—One is almost startled to find here this direct word to individual disciples. It stands encompassed by a panorama of vast events, of wars and rumors of

wars, of nations in commotion and catastrophe. Why? No Christian apocalypse, as the Exeg. points out, was ever able to "ignore the part of the disciples in the series of final events." What if that were a perennial impossibility! **Take heed to yourselves** is a needed warning in any time of crisis. There is always danger that when great impersonal forces are in powerful action the importance of the individual will be minimized, and the sense of personal responsibility relaxed. History teaches its impressive lesson on the text. In the turbulent days of persecution, so vividly described in this chapter of Mark, what counted was the quality of individual men and women. It was the fidelity and fortitude of those who did "take heed to themselves" that made possible the survival of Christianity as leaven in the world.

In our own days we are continually exposed to the defeatist mood: "What difference does one life make? It is so little among so much."

synagogues ye shall be beaten: and ye shall be brought before rulers and kings for my sake, for a testimony against them.

10 And the gospel must first be published among all nations.

will deliver you up to councils; and you will be beaten in synagogues; and you will stand before governors and kings for my sake, to bear testimony before them. 10 And the gospel must first be preached to all na-

Christian apocalyptic is not mere speculation, but has an intensely practical purpose: to reassure, strengthen, and nerve believers as they face the impending woes. (Cf. once more the Revelation of John.) **Councils** are the local Jewish sanhedrins; **synagogues** the local houses of worship and assembly, where also trials could be held and the penalty of expulsion or even flogging could be imposed (Matt. 10:17); **governors and kings** are Gentile authorities. **For my sake,** i.e., as Christians, as in 8:35; cf. 9:41. **For a testimony against them** (KJV) as in 6:11; but the same phrase is used in 1:44, with the sense of "to" them, and may be construed as having that meaning here (cf. RSV, **to bear testimony before them**).

10. Some would shorten the text here (as in sy^s and some of the O.L. MSS) and read "for a testimony to them and to the Gentiles," the rest of the verse being treated as a gloss intended to make sense after vs. 10 was detached from vs. 9. It is true that Matt. 10:18 has such a shortened reading; but the full content of the verse, even in amplified form, appears in Matt. 24:14, and Luke's omission can hardly weigh much against this, especially as he alters the sense of vs. 9 (in Luke 21:13: "This will be a time for you to bear testimony"). It is not impossible that Mark is responsible for vs. 10, but it can scarcely be viewed as a later interpolation into his text—especially in view of his repeated use of "gospel," and his general outlook.

Travel that road even a little way and see what happens to the sense of responsibility. Then add the insidious illusion that some truly significant whole can be fashioned without paying much attention to the dismally insignificant units—an illusion which flies in the face of all arithmetic. There is one equation that never changes: $0=0$. A million zeros added together still equal zero. It takes significant individuals to constitute a significant society. Hence the supreme importance of the exhortation **Take heed to yourselves.** Any hope for a saved world lies in people who do take heed to the quality of their own lives, and who are willing to make dominant in themselves the motives and goals they would like to see prevail in the outside world.

9. You Will Stand Before Governors and Kings for My Sake.—On the instant, before the memory and imagination, high dramatic scenes of history unroll. There is Jesus before Pilate, Paul before Agrippa, the great host of the martyrs before the tribunals of Rome. Then the costumes and setting change: Huss at the Council of Constance; Luther before Charles V at Worms; Latimer and Ridley condemned to the stake. The disciple has not been above his Master.

It has often been said that the age of the martyrs is over. Perhaps, though, we must remember that during the years of World War II thousands of Christians laid down their lives for their faith. Surely in any event the day of standing before governors and kings is not over, and never will be over, as long as time endures. The form of the tribunal changes, but the trial still goes on. Among the real governors and kings today, ruling even in a democracy, are the powers of wealth and economic dominance and public opinion. We stand before governors and kings when we oppose any group that rates money higher than men. It was so with those who challenged slavery. It was so with those who spearheaded the agitation against child labor. It was so, indeed, with those who first campaigned for a graduated income tax. These kings cannot now, it may be, condemn to death those who stand before them; but they can and do condemn to loss, obloquy, and ostracism. We are on trial when we oppose the lowest common denominator of public opinion; when we bring a Christian criticism to bear on the habits and customs of society; whenever we say, "As for me and my house, we will serve the Lord" (Josh. 24:15). The pressure of life at the street level, the pressures and tyranny of mass thinking, are subtle and strong. As they came to the Christians of the first centuries, they come today. "Just a little incense burned before popular idols," they whisper. "It won't make any difference." We still need the sustaining faith of the martyrs—faith in a God to whom fidelity makes an infinite and eternal difference.

11 But when they shall lead *you,* and deliver you up, take no thought beforehand what ye shall speak, neither do ye premeditate: but whatsoever shall be given you in that hour, that speak ye: for it is not ye that speak, but the Holy Ghost.

12 Now the brother shall betray the brother to death, and the father the son; and children shall rise up against *their* parents, and shall cause them to be put to death.

13 And ye shall be hated of all *men* for my name's sake: but he that shall endure unto the end, the same shall be saved.

tions. 11 And when they bring you to trial and deliver you up, do not be anxious beforehand what you are to say; but say whatever is given you in that hour, for it is not you who speak, but the Holy Spirit. 12 And brother will deliver up brother to death, and the father his child, and children will rise against parents and have them put to death; 13 and you will be hated by all for my name's sake. But he who endures to the end will be saved.

11. As a general direction addressed to martyrs (the original meaning of "witnesses") concerning their defense when brought before the local sanhedrins or Gentile rulers, this apocalyptic procedure of depending only upon the momentary inspiration of the Spirit may have been common at one stage, probably early, in Christian history. But it was soon abandoned, as the church girt its loins for the long, grueling contest with paganism in the persecutions. Later counsels to the martyrs, when the struggle became world wide, urged careful preparation, preliminary discipline, and thorough training (see D. W. Riddle, *The Martyrs*). The verse is apparently a survival from the very earliest period in the spread of the gospel.

12. Klostermann suggests that this verse may also be derived from the older apocalyptic source used in vss. 6-8; there are parallels enough in apocalyptic literature. Whether this is true or not, its presence here reflects conditions that actually existed in religiously divided families from the first days of Christian history, and as long as the persecutions raged. (Cf. the Q sayings in Matt. 10:34-37; Luke 12:51-53; 14:26.)

13. **Hated of all men** may also be derived, as Klostermann thinks, from the Jewish source. But 8:35, and the Gospel as a whole, presupposed a martyr situation. **For my**

11. *Do Not Be Anxious Beforehand What You Are to Say; but Say Whatever Is Given You in that Hour.*—Is this, then, a benediction on brainless, extemporaneous "babbling"? Such distortion has done endless harm to the preaching and teaching of the Christian gospel, and violates the great commandment, "You shall love the Lord your God . . . with all your mind" (12:30). We shall find in nothing that Jesus says any justification for mental stupor, inertia, laziness, or sheer effrontery. These are not the weapons of God's warfare. In the present instance we have an encouragement to faith in the continuous operation of the Holy Spirit. It does not mean that a speech will automatically be put into the mouth of the disciple in a time of crisis or emergency. Its promise is larger and deeper. If we have a living faith in God, out of that faith and out of our continual relationship with him will come the word and action for the particular occasion. One of the best illustrations of it is given us in the account of Paul, as he in his turn stood before governors and kings, Agrippa, Festus, and Felix. His concern was not with himself but with God. Out

of the fullness of what God was to him, the heart and mind and tongue spoke. So this word says to us, "Do not become preoccupied with yourself, how you shall manage. Do not memorize a form of words. Put at the center of life a great faith and a great devotion. Out of that will spring wisdom and strength to supply every need." Recall Christ's earlier and central assurance, "Seek first his kingdom and his righteousness, and all these things shall be yours as well" (Matt. 6:33). With his goals possessing us, we can walk with serenity to any test.

Two other exhortations may be drawn quite legitimately from this counsel. One would be by way of caution, not to wait for some ideal, perfect preparation before going into action. Come with the best you have when the need arises. Life can be wasted in drilling, in delaying until some fantastic degree of preparation is complete. The other would be by way of challenge, that men should put forth their best efforts. Effort is our concern; results are God's concern.

13. *You Will Be Hated by All for My Name's Sake.*—A description of what was happening to

14 ¶ But when ye shall see the abomination of desolation, spoken of by Daniel the prophet, standing where it ought not, (let him that readeth understand,) then	14 "But when you see the desolating sacrilege set up where it ought not to be

name's sake, like "for my sake" in vs. 9, means because you are Christians (cf. John 15:21; the identical phrase). **Endure** is more than survive (as in I Thess. 4:15); it means remain faithful—as Luke puts it, "By your endurance [ὑπομονῇ] you will gain your lives" (Luke 21:19). **To the end** is not to the end of the world, or of the messianic woes, but εἰς τέλος, **to the last degree,** to the final pitch of patient endurance.

4. PERSECUTION IN JUDEA (13:14-23)

14. The abomination of desolation (KJV; cf. Dan. 9:27) or, better, **the desolating sacrilege** (RSV) is the "abomination" that drives God from his temple (cf. Ezek. 8–10).

Christians in the days of persecution, when the Little Apocalypse was written. But also a true prophecy of what has continued to happen through all the centuries. The reproach of Christ has been and is a very real thing. Men and women have in the past been hated for his sake; they are in the present still hated; they will be hated in the future. For the advent of Christ into any time or situation in which evil is powerful is always a threat to its power; and the answer of threatened powers is always hatred. Yet the words are an encouragement too. "Blessed are those who are persecuted for righteousness' sake" (Matt. 5:10). That experience marks one's entrance into the great society of those who have hazarded their all for the sake of the kingdom. It is the highest accolade a life can win, the true apostolic succession.

The phrase to give us pause and deep self-searching, however, is **for my name's sake.** The question must be faced: Is the opposition I meet, the hostility I incur, really for Christ's sake, or does it have some less flattering origin? The very words here are dangerous. If we do not think clearly and humbly, we may make of them a ready and easy excuse for all our difficulties. We may even grow quite self-righteous about it, and say, "Well, I am being hated and persecuted for Christ's sake again." The actual truth about the matter, however, may well be that most of our troubles have their source in our own faults and failures, to say no more. We persuade ourselves that we are being hated for our uncompromising loyalty to Christ's truth, when all the time we have been displaying an unsanctified stubbornness, self-will, and lust for power. It is so easy and pleasant to apply the soothing poultice, "I am a martyr for Christ's sake," when an honest look at ourselves would show something very different, a lack of love in speaking the truth, a way of riding roughshod over peoples' sensibilities, a brittle

dogmatism which leaves no room for tolerance, an unbridled conceit. All these are forms of sin. Against them this chapter provides resource, "Watch and pray."

13. *He Who Endures to the End Will Be Saved.*—There is a fruitful suggestion in the comment, *"Endure* is more than survive" (see Exeg.). The difference is worth careful exploration. Of course, in an atomic age the question of survival is a real one. Yet to survive as human beings is very different from enduring as Christians. It is a lesser thing. Surviving is a matter of existence; enduring is a matter of faith. To survive is to keep on breathing and eating and sleeping; to endure is to keep on straining and wrestling and holding out—to the last notch.

14. *But When You See the Desolating Sacrilege Set Up Where It Ought Not to Be.*—The "abomination of desolation," as the KJV translates it—Moffatt, "appalling Horror"—is a reflection of Dan. 9:27, and has a specific, though veiled, meaning here. Just what that meaning is must be conjectured. The reference in Daniel was to the altar of Zeus set up by Antiochus Epiphanes in the temple area in 168 B.C. The reference here is either to a statue, whether of Caligula or someone else, or to a person who came to be known in early Christian thought as Antichrist, or "Man of Sin, the opponent of God in the struggle for control of the universe." [6]

There is a permanent warning in the phrase "the opponent of God." It is a warning which survives the passing of the particular thought forms of the first centuries of Christianity. Indeed, the idea of antichrist, in the sense of threatening anti-Christian powers, is never obsolete. The general truth which emerges is that anything which drives God from his temple is an abomination. Whenever pagan idols are erected there—blessings pronounced on anti-

[6] Branscomb, *Gospel of Mark*, p. 237.

let them that be in Judea flee to the mountains:

15 And let him that is on the housetop not go down into the house, neither enter *therein,* to take any thing out of his house:

16 And let him that is in the field not turn back again for to take up his garment.

17 But woe to them that are with child, and to them that give suck in those days!

18 And pray ye that your flight be not in the winter.

19 For *in* those days shall be affliction, such as was not from the beginning of the creation which God created unto this time, neither shall be.

(let the reader understand), then let those who are in Judea flee to the mountains; **15** let him who is on the housetop not go down, nor enter his house, to take anything away; **16** and let him who is in the field not turn back to take his mantle. **17** And alas for those who are with child and for those who give suck in those days! **18** Pray that it may not happen in winter. **19** For in those days there will be such tribulation as has not been from the beginning of the creation which God created until now, and

---

The subject of this section was a major theme in Jewish apocalyptic (see pp. 854-55). In fact the whole section, either with or without vss. 21-23, or some portion of them, has been attributed to the Little Apocalypse. **Flee to the mountains,** as in I Macc. 2:28; greater safety lay in the mountains than in the city. Whether or not this was part of the "oracle" received by the Jerusalem Christians in A.D. 70 (see p. 854), for Mark the words certainly have reference to the Christians in Judea.

15-16. There will be no time to lose; do not go down the outside stair and then enter the house! Contrast Ezekiel's more leisurely preparations (Ezek. 12:3-4).

17-19. The affliction, stated only in general terms and all the more terrifying for its vagueness, will be cruelly severe upon women who are pregnant or are nursing their babies, especially if the sacrilege takes place in winter, details which every tragic story of flight and deportation since history began bears out. Further details are not pictured, but it will be the most terrible tribulation (θλῖψις) since the creation of the world. Nor will it ever be equaled. This last clause is scarcely a gloss; what the writer means is that its equal has never been hitherto, nor ever will be. If there is any gloss in the verse, it is **which God created;** but Mark's redundant style is recognizable here as elsewhere.

Christian ways of life, the fortunes of an institution exalted above the seeking and saving of those who are lost—there is a **desolating sacrilege set up.** "Thou shalt have no other gods before me"—or beside me. What, then, of a church infected with the poison of materialism? A debased parody of Isaiah's words thrusts itself on the mind: "And I saw the Cash Register high and lifted up, and its train filled the temple." The worship of numbers and size is an "abomination" in the church of him who thought of his truth as leaven. A church which allows class and race to be given what is so often scarcely less than idolatrous homage is an "appalling horror" to him in whom there is no bond or free, Greek or barbarian, but all are one. The words "desolating sacrilege," noun and adjective, are strong words; but not too strong for such abominations standing in the holy place. The noun signifies a robbing of God. The adjective, pointed and accurate, reminds us that any homage to anti-Christian ideals and aims inevitably makes desolate a faith that might blossom as the rose (see on 15:17).

14. *Then Let Those Who Are in Judea Flee to the Mountains.*—Great literary skill has gone into the description of the coming of tribulations, set forth in this early Christian apocalypse (vss. 14-27). Graphic, unforgettable lines and shadows sketch in the picture as if under the swift brush of a skillful painter. Perhaps some of the details of the horror of sudden flight came from actual experiences of persecution. Incidentally, note what a vivid description those details provide of the human effects of war, as we have seen it in the twentieth century.

One outstanding impression is the strong portrayal of the urgency of the crisis. The suddenness and immensity make everything else a minor matter. It is no stretching of the meaning at all to find in these words an impressive picture of crises in life so great that they make all else secondary. There are occasions so commanding, so filled with the necessity for immediate action, that they are like the one represented here, when there would not be time even to come downstairs from the roof; decisive moments when the whole direction and destiny

20 And except that the Lord had short-ened those days, no flesh should be saved: but for the elect's sake, whom he hath chosen, he hath shortened the days.

21 And then if any man shall say to you, Lo, here *is* Christ; or, lo, *he is* there; be-lieve *him* not:

22 For false Christs and false prophets shall rise, and shall show signs and wonders, to seduce, if *it were* possible, even the elect.

23 But take ye heed: behold, I have fore-told you all things.

24 ¶ But in those days, after that tribu-lation, the sun shall be darkened, and the moon shall not give her light,

never will be. 20 And if the Lord had not shortened the days, no human being would be saved; but for the sake of the elect, whom he chose, he shortened the days. 21 And then if any one says to you, 'Look, here is the Christ!' or 'Look, there he is!' do not believe it. 22 False Christs and false prophets will arise and show signs and won-ders, to lead astray, if possible, the elect. 23 But take heed; I have told you all things beforehand.

24 "But in those days, after that tribula-tion, the sun will be darkened, and the

---

20. It was part of the Hebraic and Jewish philosophy of history, or rather of Israel's faith in God's control of history, that he could delay "the time of the end" in order to give the wicked further opportunity for repentance, or that he could advance it, in the interest of his elect, to spare them the horrors of "the latter days." This view likewise prevails in apocalyptic, in spite of its rigid schematization of history by predetermined periods. Here God "shortens" the days of tribulation for the sake of his elect, **whom he hath chosen**—not now the Jewish people, but the Christians, in Mark's view.

21-22. If these verses once belonged to the Jewish source, they have been edited from the Christian point of view. Such sayings as those now found in Luke 17:21-24 have, to some extent at least, influenced the editing. The expectation of false messiahs and false prophets during the "latter days" was a commonplace of Jewish apocalyptic, but it is hardly true to say that these pretenders were commoner in the first century than at other times.

23. Take ye heed is addressed to the disciples (vs. 3), and through them to the church; but it is strange if a distinction between them and "the elect" (vs. 22) is intended. **Foretold:** As in vs. 31, this is the assurance that Christian believers possess. Christ has foreseen it all, and will guide his followers through the struggle—already becoming evident in their own situation in Rome, in the late sixties. But they must take heed, watch, and endure.

5. The Parousia of the Son of Man (13:24-27)

In strong contrast to Luke 17:20 and also to Mark 8:12, this section, full of the usual apocalyptic-prophetic details and undoubtedly derived from some earlier source, perhaps

---

of our years are at stake, when the word "choose" sounds out over some personal cross-roads. The importance and urgency of the choice appear then in Jesus' question: "What does it profit a man, to gain the whole world and forfeit his life?" (8:36.) The soul is at stake —nothing else counts.

We have been brought to such a crisis in our world. The age of the atom bomb—A.B., as some have designated this new dimension of human existence—has for the first time made possible man's collective suicide. Atomic fission is the diabolical machine at the heart of our civilization, ticking off a few days of grace. The measured ticktack, ticktack speaks in the words of Paul, "Brethren, the time is short" (I Cor.

7:29). Science is writing a new apocalypse. What it says is so urgent as to take precedence over all our social and economic aims. It is issuing its own call to repentance—to change our ways before we miserably perish.

24-30. *Then They Will See the Son of Man Coming in Clouds.*—Here in vivid imagery is pictured clearly the messianic hope of the early church. The exalted Jesus is to return in glory. The note of eager expectance is found again and again in the N.T., on the lips of a genera-tion "waiting for the coming of our Lord Jesus Christ" (I Cor. 1:7). One can no more miss it, from Matthew to Revelation, than he can miss the Atlantic Ocean while crossing from New York to Southampton in a ship. But now the

25 And the stars of heaven shall fall, and the powers that are in heaven shall be shaken.

26 And then shall they see the Son of man coming in the clouds with great power and glory.

27 And then shall he send his angels, and shall gather together his elect from the four winds, from the uttermost part of the earth to the uttermost part of heaven.

28 Now learn a parable of the fig tree: When her branch is yet tender, and putteth forth leaves, ye know that summer is near:

29 So ye in like manner, when ye shall see these things come to pass, know that it is nigh, *even* at the doors.

moon will not give its light, 25 and the stars will be falling from heaven, and the powers in the heavens will be shaken. 26 And then they will see the Son of man coming in clouds with great power and glory. 27 And then he will send out the angels, and gather his elect from the four winds, from the ends of the earth to the ends of heaven.

28 "From the fig tree learn its lesson: as soon as its branch becomes tender and puts forth its leaves, you know that summer is near. 29 So also, when you see these things taking place, you know that he is near, at

---

the hypothetical Little Apocalypse (see pp. 853-54), sets forth the signs (vs. 4) of the culmination, the eventual parousia of the Son of man. The **tribulation** on earth (vss. 14-22) now gives way to cosmic portents: the very **powers that are in heaven,** which have hitherto held the stars in their places, **shall be shaken,** as in Isa. 13:10; 34:4.

25-26. It is not clear whether the two elements in this verse are parallel, or whether the **falling** of the stars is the result of the **powers** being **shaken. Then shall they see:** Is it all mankind, as in Rev. 1:7, or only the elect? Perhaps we have here only the Aramaic impersonal plural: "then will be seen." This is the Danielic **Son of man** (Dan. 7:13-14; cf. Mark 8:38; 14:62), whom Mark, and the early Christians, certainly identified with Jesus, now exalted to glory at the right hand of God, though to the author of the earlier source this identification was perhaps unknown.

27. His angels: An advance upon 8:38, perhaps due to the source. So also **his elect** (contrast vs. 20). **From the ends of the earth to the ends** [height? so Lohmeyer] **of heaven:** Cf. Matt. 24:31, "from one end of heaven to the other," or perhaps, "from the corners of heaven to the heights thereof." Luke omits this verse—he has, in general, toned down the apocalyptic detail, following his interpretation of the horror of sacrilege (Luke 21:20) as the siege of Jerusalem and its fall. As a Greco-Roman writer Luke speaks only of portents and of human fears, and then emphasizes the hopeful rather than the tragic aspect of the situation (Luke 21:25-28).

6. The Date of the Parousia (13:28-37)

The climax of the apocalyptic discourse is a practical exhortation and final counsel, entirely from the Christian point of view. Vs. 31 has been suspected of belonging to the earlier Jewish or Christian Jewish source, but the parallels in Matt. 5:18; Luke 16:17 suggest that a detached saying of Jesus, not originally with an apocalyptic connotation, has been used here. The discourse returns to its opening questions (vs. 4) as to the "time of the end" and the preceding "signs of the end."

28-29. A brief parable, as brief and simple as many another in the Gospels, compares the approach of "the end" to the signs of coming summer, specifically the leafing of the

---

sound has died out. Multitudes of Christians no longer look for the coming of Christ in any such literal fashion. The result has been that they have allowed the buoyancy to drop out of their religion. Would it not be well to remember that the literal expectation was only the husk and not the kernel of the N.T. doctrine of the last things? Its essence was something

deeper: the faith that God is a factor in the world, today and tomorrow; that he will act redeemingly in human history; that the conquest of evil comes not of our wit and muscle, but of his continuing sovereignty.

Contrast that with the characteristic "messianic" hope of the twentieth century—modern man's secular apocalypse. He looks for a world

30 Verily I say unto you, that this generation shall not pass, till all these things be done.

31 Heaven and earth shall pass away: but my words shall not pass away.

32 ¶ But of that day and *that* hour knoweth no man, no, not the angels which are in heaven, neither the Son, but the Father.

33 Take ye heed, watch and pray: for ye know not when the time is.

the very gates. 30 Truly, I say to you, this generation will not pass away before all these things take place. 31 Heaven and earth will pass away, but my words will not pass away.

32 "But of that day or that hour no one knows, not even the angels in heaven, nor the Son, but only the Father. 33 Take heed, watch;[a] for you do not know when the

[a] Some ancient authorities add *and pray*.

fig tree. When the "signs of promise" appear, then know that **he** (RSV—the Son of man) or **it** (KJV—the end; the Greek can mean either; Luke 21:31 amplifies: "the kingdom of God") is near, **even at the door**. In the divine dispensation the signs in nature are unfailing; similarly **these things**, as signs of the end, are the assurance of the nearness of the Parousia.

30-31. Indeed, the fulfillment will take place before **this** present **generation** has passed away (cf. 9:1). And the certainty rests upon what Jesus himself has said (cf. vs. 23). This obviously includes, for Mark, everything in the preceding discourse; but the infallible certainty goes deeper, for it includes ultimately everything that Jesus has said: his **words** are his whole teaching, his whole revelation of God (cf. 1:22, and the implications of 6:2).

32-33. The day is near, but the precise time is unknown—that is in answer to the first question of vs. 4; the second question has been answered in vss. 5-25. Not even **the**

of wonders which science and industry will provide. He has exchanged his august faith in God's coming action for a faith in the kind of plastic heaven that comes out of a factory. We are kept in a state of nervous excitement with prophecies of the world of tomorrow, a paradise of chromium and ceramics, of helicopters and television, of egg-shaped automobiles and layer cake houses, of skyscrapers made of glass and clothing made of soy beans! What a trade! Heaven for earth, God for gadgets, the coming of Christ in the life of the world for the coming of a salesman's paradise! Such a degenerate "messianic" hope can serve only to emphasize what need we have to hold fast the essence of the N.T. expectancy, a confident faith that the God who has acted in the coming of Christ is acting still, and will act at and until the end of time!

31. Heaven and Earth Will Pass Away, but My Words Will Not Pass Away.—The comment on this passage in the Exeg. should be read carefully. The meaning in the immediate context is that the words of the foregoing apocalypse, the whole prophecy of the coming of Christ in glory, can be depended upon. It will not fail. Jesus' words announcing it will not pass away, but will be fulfilled.

There is, however, a larger meaning beyond: the permanent validity of everything Jesus said and of the revelation he has given us of

God. Spoken in the framework of a time which has completely passed away, his words have not passed away. They have never become obsolete. They have a profound and timeless relevance to the life of man and to the world. Jesus does not come to any generation as a dated Rip van Winkle, alien in mind and speech. He addresses every age as "the eternal Contemporary."

There is a faint and ghostly shadow of this truth in the fact that what actually endures of any given culture or civilization is its intangible creation, its words. Greece has passed away, except for a few bits of marble. But its words have not. Homer, Aeschylus, Euripides, Plato. Aristotle have not. It may be put in the form of a paradox: the only really substantial thing in the world is the unsubstantial.

So the heavens of Jesus' time and later times have passed away, the Ptolemaic heavens. A new heaven has taken their place in men's thought, a Copernican heaven of galaxies and immeasurable space. The old earth has passed away, with its period costumes, its clothing and ideas. But Jesus' words have not passed away. The long parade of history has only served to validate them. "In the beginning was the Word, and the Word was with God, and the Word was God" (John 1:1).

32-37. Take Heed, Watch and Pray; for You Do Not Know When the Time Will Come.—The ending of this chapter, its impassioned

34 *For the Son of man is* as a man taking a far journey, who left his house, and gave authority to his servants, and to every man his work, and commanded the porter to watch.

35 Watch ye therefore: for ye know not when the master of the house cometh, at even, or at midnight, or at the cockcrowing, or in the morning:

36 Lest coming suddenly he find you sleeping.

37 And what I say unto you I say unto all, Watch.

time will come. 34 It is like a man going on a journey, when he leaves home and puts his servants in charge, each with his work, and commands the doorkeeper to be on the watch. 35 Watch therefore — for you do not know when the master of the house will come, in the evening, or at midnight, or at cockcrow, or in the morning — 36 lest he come suddenly and find you asleep. 37 And what I say to you I say to all: Watch."

---

angels know it, **nor the Son, but only the Father** (cf. Acts 1:7). And the practical admonition shows the drift of the whole concluding section: **Take heed, watch and pray; for you do not know**—and cannot know—**when the time will come.** The christological title **the Son** seems strange in Mark, and it has been thought to be an interpolation; but the whole phrase **nor the Son, but only the Father** may be Mark's editorial addition to the older source. We might, however, suspect from the Greek that the original ran "no one knows, except the Father," and that the references to both angels and Son have been added. But if we can assume that Mark understood "the Son" to mean "the Son of God," as commonly in his Gospel, or "the Son of man," as commonly in one group of his sources, the difficulty may begin to clear up. Luke omits the whole verse; some MSS of Matthew omit "nor the Son"; and Ambrose (*On Faith* V. 8) seems to assign the phrase in both Matthew and Mark to interpolators (Klostermann). But the difficulty for the church fathers, of course, lay in the assertion of limitation of the Son's knowledge, not in the literary-historical or historical-theological problem which this passage presents today.

34-36. Another parable is added, similar to those in Luke 12:35-48, and to the parable of the talents. It looks somewhat artificial, like the one in 12:1-11, with allegorical details designed *ad hoc* for the present exhortation (cf. B. T. D. Smith, *Parables of the Synoptic Gospels* [Cambridge: University Press, 1937], pp. 104-6). But the ethos of the parable is certainly the ethos of early Christianity: **Watch, . . . for ye know not.** It was this paradox which kept the spirits of men alert through the long and torturing vigil of the days of persecution and of "hope deferred [that] maketh the heart sick."

37. The practical purpose, already stated in vs. 33, is here reiterated in summary form and given the widest possible application; **all** means the whole Christian church, from the apostles' days to the present, from the dark days just before Jesus' passion to the equally dark days that now confront his church. When the "master of the house"—an old title of the Lord, embedded in the tradition, perhaps a play upon the abusive term flung at him by his adversaries (Matt. 10:25)—when the Master comes it may be late or early, but it will be night. All the hours mentioned are hours of the night. The church will still be undergoing persecution.

---

appeal for watchfulness, speaks as directly to every generation as it did to the first Christian century. It is a plea for living on the alert, living on tiptoe, with eyes, mind, and heart on the *qui vive*. The word "watch" reaches into the whole spread of life. Someone has said that the worst "ism" in the world is not fascism or communism but somnambulism. There are so many forms of sleepwalking—the glazed eyes which never notice that one's ideals are being

whittled away, one's purposes being pared down; never notice the evil forces in the world, gaining strength. Watch and pray against the sin that so easily trips us up, the compromise with wrong, so reasonable in the beginning, so deadly in the end. Watch, lest we neglect the renewal of life in communion with God, lest our sympathies harden! Watch, lest the great opportunities for service to God's kingdom come and pass by, unseen and unseized.

14 After two days was *the feast of* the passover, and of unleavened bread: and the chief priests and the scribes sought

14 It was now two days before the Passover and the feast of Unleavened

---

D. The Passion Narrative (14:1–15:47)

It is now generally held that the passion narrative was the first long consecutive gospel narrative to be committed to writing, or, earlier still, to be given fixed oral form. (Cf. Dibelius, *From Tradition to Gospel*, ch. vii; or Grant, *Earliest Gospel*, ch. viii.) It was only by such a narrative that the two questions could be answered: How did Jesus die? Why did he have to die?—questions that must have been asked almost from "the first days of the gospel," i.e., of early Christian preaching. A comparison of Mark 14–15 with the parallel narratives in Matthew and Luke—not to mention John—will indicate that even after the written Gospel of Mark had appeared, the passion narrative continued to grow; changes, rearrangements, and additions could still be made to it. Equally, a close analysis of the Marcan narrative itself will suggest that an earlier pre-Marcan narrative has been expanded, amplified, and modified by Mark. There may even have been stages of growth in it before Mark took it over, edited it, and made it the climax of his book (see Intro., pp. 634-37). Among the materials that seem to have been added, either by Mark or by others before him, are: the anointing at Bethany (14:3-9), which interrupts the sequence of 14:1-2 and 10-11, which Luke (7:36-50) uses in a quite different form and in an entirely different place, and which John (12:1-8) locates before the Triumphal Entry; the preparation for the Passover (14:12-16), so closely resembling 11:1-6; perhaps the "Son of man" saying in 14:21, related to the other (and secondary) Son of man sayings in the Gospel of Mark; the announcement of Peter's betrayal (14:30-31—and the saying in 14:28, closely related to 16:7, but entirely ignored in the context here), with its denouement in 14:54, 66-72; the agony in Gethsemane (14:32-42); the test question at the Jewish trial (14:61*b*-62); the rending of the temple veil (15:38); and the women at the Cross (15:40-41, 47). Of course it is not possible to prove that the basic narrative was limited to what is left, or that all the remainder belonged to the primitive (Galilean-Roman?) passion narrative; but the basic narrative is probably to be sought in the remaining sections, as it is by a number of modern scholars—Dibelius, Bultmann, Wellhausen, Lietzmann, Klostermann, Loisy, and others—who agree in general upon at least the main point. This is not to say that the "secondary" material is fictitious and therefore to be discarded; that is no more the case here than in that of the Lukan, Matthaean, Johannine additions, transpositions, or modifications of the narrative. Each passage must be dealt with by itself and on its own merits. There is no evidence in Mark of a concerted, programmatic revision of the narrative from one particular theological or historical point of view; the whole story is traditional, and it is so early that details, and even episodes, were still being added from the oral tradition.

1. The Plot Against Jesus (14:1-2)

This section, continued in vss. 10-11 after the inserted account of the anointing (vss. 3-9), implies that from Mark's point of view—according to which the supper was a

---

14:1-2. *The Chief Priests and the Scribes Were Seeking How to Arrest Him by Stealth, . . . Lest There Be a Tumult.*—The necessity laid upon the enemies of Jesus to remove him stealthily from the public scene was a tribute to his following among the people. The Passover pilgrims, many of them from the north, were beginning to pour into the city. They, and the crowds already in Jerusalem, were a factor that had to be reckoned with; for among them were enthusiastic followers of the Galilean.

The arrest and imprisonment must be made under cover, by guile and stealth, lest a tumult be raised which might get out of hand.

Beyond this historical situation, the words **arrest him by stealth** offer a suggestive picture of another kind of history, the history of the spiritual life of the Christian. When Jesus is removed as real master, the process usually goes on secretly, "with subtlety" (ASV), "by craft" (KJV). If the surrender of allegiance were a matter of open, forthright demand, such as

how they might take him by craft, and put *him* to death.

2 But they said, Not on the feast *day,* lest there be an uproar of the people.

Bread. And the chief priests and the scribes were seeking how to arrest him by stealth, and kill him; 2 for they said, "Not during the feast, lest there be a tumult of the people."

Passover meal, on Nisan 15—it was now Wednesday: Jewish days began at sundown, and Thursday evening (the beginning of Friday, upon that reckoning) would be **two days** after Wednesday. Mark may be suspected of writing Roman style (cf. Vulg., *post biduum*), but his scheme (cf. above, p. 823) implies that the day is Wednesday; if he is writing Roman style here, he is thinking of Friday, also in Roman style, as being **two days** later.

14:1-2. The Passover and the feast of Unleavened Bread: The great Jewish festival commemorating the exodus from Egypt (Israel's "Independence Day"), long since combined with the immemorial springtime agricultural festival of *Maççôth,* which continued for a whole week. The paschal meal took place on the first night of full moon following the vernal equinox, i.e., on the evening of Nisan 14 (= the beginning of Nisan 15), and through the following hours of the night; the whole feast had to be consumed before morning. *Maççôth* (the feast of Unleavened Bread—Lev. 23:6) began on the fifteenth and continued through the twenty-first. But after the combination of the two festivals, since Nisan 14, evening, was the beginning of Nisan 15, unleavened bread was already being eaten at the time of the Passover meal, all yeast having been destroyed by noon of the fourteenth. No work was permitted during that afternoon; the Passover lambs were to be sacrificed before sundown, and would be eaten roasted that night.

By Wednesday it was evident to **the chief priests and the scribes,** that if Jesus was to be put out of the way, they must act quickly and by stealth, not publicly, since the Passover pilgrims were already gathering. **For** [not **but**] **they said, "Not during the feast** [rather than **on the feast day**], **lest there be a tumult of the people,"** who were enthusiastic over him (12:37*b*). Perhaps as a reflection of this situation, Codex Bezae (D) and some of the O.L. MSS read: "Lest during the feast there be," i.e., their purpose was simply to keep him in custody over the festival, and then deal with him.

---

martyrs, early and late, faced; if it were a dramatic choice, "Renounce your faith publicly, or die," most Christians would make the martyr's choice, death rather than outright, final denial. But life is not that simple. Its choices come "by stealth"; Jesus slips out when we are not noticing it. No trumpet announces the hour of decision. Little by little, compromises gnaw away fidelity and resolution; small neglects, here one, there another, "with subtlety" change the whole climate of a life; the calls of God to service are refused, not with any resounding "No," but simply because they are lost amid other pressures.

There is also a suggestiveness for all time in the phrase **lest there be a tumult.** In the Christian struggle in the world one real resource, all too often passed over, is the possibility of a creative tumult. Jesus' enemies were afraid of a tumult. They shrank from it. Fear led them to try to avoid it "by craft." Such fear may be a good weapon for righteousness. Tumults can be and have often been creative forces. Christians who are not sound asleep, but thoroughly and

nervously aware of the strategies and tactics of the forces of evil, can rouse a tumult, a surging tide of public opinion, capable of holding back the onslaught of evil, as a tumult of the people would have blocked the public arrest of Jesus.

When "the world rulers of this present darkness" and "the spiritual hosts of wickedness" (Eph. 6:12) know that they deal only with a somnolent and lethargic church, impotent with inertia; when they know there will be no public uproar because no one really cares; then they move in without fear. The main strategy of Christ's people, of course, is not in causing uproars. But a tumult at the right time and place is a tested reliance. It was a tumult over gladiatorial contests in Rome, a tumult over the Fugitive Slave Law in the United States, a tumult which Josephine Butler incited over prostitution in England in the nineteenth century, which became an effective power against evil. Remember the significant words of the prophets, "Cry aloud, spare not, lift up thy voice like a trumpet" (Isa. 58:1) .

3 ¶ And being in Bethany, in the house of Simon the leper, as he sat at meat, there came a woman having an alabaster box of ointment of spikenard very precious; and she brake the box, and poured *it* on his head.

4 And there were some that had indignation within themselves, and said, Why was this waste of the ointment made?

3 And while he was at Bethany in the house of Simon the leper, as he sat at table, a woman came with an alabaster jar of ointment of pure nard, very costly, and she broke the jar and poured it over his head. 4 But there were some who said to themselves indignantly, "Why was the oint-

---

2. THE ANOINTING IN BETHANY (14:3-9)

It is a question whether or not this story is identical with the one in Luke 7:36-40. Too much has certainly been made of the supposed identity of Mary (the name comes from John 12:3, not from Mark) with the woman who was a "sinner" in Luke—similar traditions often tend to coalesce and to transfer details. The location of the story here (and in John) is due to the reference to the Passion in vs. 8 (cf. John 12:7).

3. Simon the leper is otherwise unknown (cf. the other Simon, 15:21, also unknown), but he was probably known to those who handed on the tradition, and presumably also to Mark.

4-5. Three hundred pence, or **denarii,** was about sixty dollars in our money, but in purchasing value about four times that in the first century. The **some** of vs. 4 becomes

---

3-9. The Anointing at Bethany.—A woman came with an alabaster jar of ointment of pure nard, very costly, and she broke the jar and poured it over his head. The record gives the impression that Jesus was deeply stirred by this extravagant action. A valuable exploration in the Gospels would be to assemble a list of the things which moved him to high praise. On it would be the centurion who showed great faith, the widow who put her whole living into the treasury, this woman who broke the box of perfume. Who else? There is evident here an excitement in Jesus, almost a lyric ecstasy, as though he felt: "This is it. This is the self-forgetfulness, the self-denial, which is a mark of the kingdom of God."

The unmeasured generosity of her giving moved him. It was a glorious maximum of sacrifice which never stopped to calculate what might have been a passable minimum—the kind of mathematical computation that so easily besets us. It was a very expensive gift. In the Exeg. its value is estimated to have been $240 in purchasing power at the time. Major estimates it to have been worth about $500.[7] It was self-giving in "good measure, pressed down, shaken together, running over" (Luke 6:38). She did not pour out a few drops and say, "Well, I guess that ought to be enough for this occasion." She was lifted clear out of herself in a great devotion.

Her unblocked impulse moved Jesus. The spontaneity of love had free way (see on 10:15-16; 11:8). It was not smothered with caution

[7] Major, Manson, and Wright, *Mission and Message of Jesus,* p. 165.

and prudence. She was lifted clear out of arithmetic into love—one of the greatest leaps which a life can ever take.

Again, as we allow this scene to stay before our imagination, it speaks powerfully of the consecration of personality, the unmeasured sharing of the best that we are and have. Personality is a precious perfume. It is always a tragedy to carry it through life in an unbroken jar. Yet many have done exactly that. They have reserved themselves, their affection, their possible outgoing to those in deep need of friendship, comfort, incentive. Such people wait for an audience that seems worthy of their self-giving, or an occasion important enough to call for it. Life slips by and the perfume jar is never broken. Others always measure themselves out with a medicine dropper, frightened lest they spend a drop more than the legalities of the situation demand.

There is profound historical truth in the words What she has done will be told in memory of her. For the greatest events in life, in themselves everlasting memorials, have been those acts in which one person has broken that box of precious perfume which was himself, in the sharing of all of his best. It has been done times without number by parent, teacher, pastor, physician, and friend. It is the most important transaction which this planet ever witnesses.

4-5. Some Who Said . . . , "Why Was the Ointment Thus Wasted? For This Ointment Might Have Been Sold."—These verses reveal an early clash in the eternal debate between

5 For it might have been sold for more than three hundred pence, and have been given to the poor. And they murmured against her.

6 And Jesus said, Let her alone; why trouble ye her? she hath wrought a good work on me.

ment thus wasted? 5 For this ointment might have been sold for more than three hundred denarii,*b* and given to the poor." And they reproached her. 6 But Jesus said, "Let her alone; why do you trouble her?

b See note on Matthew 18. 28.

Judas in John 12:4-6, and his motive becomes theft. Even here, **given to the poor** is viewed as a questionable motive (cf. vs. 7).

---

the market mind and the life of the spirit, between an earth-bound reason and the spontaneity of love. No doubt it is too harsh to call the thinking of those who were indignant at the extravagance of this woman "the market mind." They were people of the middle class whose limited means made frugality a necessity. And their prudential souls were shocked. That is easy to understand. Yet their failure to see this generous act of love as anything but waste showed an inability to use any measurements but those of the market. George Bernard Shaw has a word of insight on this blindness. He writes, "It is true that the world is governed to a considerable extent by the considerations that occur to stockbrokers in the first five minutes."

Here, at least, we do have an act that rejoiced the heart of Jesus roundly condemned on the basis of considerations that occurred to shopkeepers in the first five minutes! These people were not brokers, but they weighed life on a broker's scales—denarii! They were blind to issues where the last word was not the clink of a coin. It **might have been sold.** That consideration scandalized them. The ointment might have become a factor in the real world, the good, solid, substantial world of copper and silver and gold, instead of being wasted in a vain gesture of devotion, an unsubstantial waste which paid no dividends. They were the sort that would have answered the poet: "Getting and spending we lay waste our powers? Nonsense! What is not getting and spending is the real waste!" It is the recurring judgment of the market place that what will not go into a trial balance is worthless. Lose no time on it.

The verdict of these shocked onlookers reappears in the feeling of many that worship is waste. A favorite word of derision is "rigmarole." It butters no parsnips, say those to whom life is a matter of parsnips. It builds no barns, yields no compound interest. It is a foreign entanglement of the soul. To this type of mind the sacrifice of life for a faith is waste. We hear that judgment daily passed on one who chooses a vocation of obscure service to God and man in preference to what is called, with exquisite vulgarity, "making good." Francis of Assisi

wasted his life. He might have been a lord of the manor instead of an impecunious beggar. Father Damien's life, on these scales, was a waste. So was John Wesley's. What a major general or parliamentary whip he would have made with all that executive capacity!

Jesus rebuked for all time all such measurements. They are, in a very literal sense, impertinent. They do not pertain to the soul.

The word **indignantly** merits a thoughtful pause. What this woman had done violated the company's accustomed ways. We are liable to respond with face-saving indignation when we meet ideas and actions which are opposed to the finalities of our settled minds. Thus, easy indignation can keep us from ever learning anything new. Perhaps they felt an element of reproach to themselves in her generosity. Indignation is a frequent defense against conscience and the upsetting business of self-searching. It is well to ask ourselves: What makes us indignant? Is it the slight to our self-esteem, the frustration of our possessive drive, the challenge to our opinions and prejudices? Or are ours the indignations of Jesus?

6. *She Has Done a Beautiful Thing to Me.*— Mark the warmth of Jesus' defense. He was deeply moved. The woman's devotion was a thing of beauty, and has become a joy forever.

This word **beautiful** is a word to remember. It suggests love lifted to a fine art. There is a place for it in all devotion. There is a place for it in worship: the beauty of a cathedral, with its aspiring lines and soaring arches, like a prayer in stone; the beauty of great music, such as breaks forth in *The Messiah* and the *B Minor Mass.* There is the beauty of the great poetry of religion in Dante and Milton and Tennyson and Browning. There is the possible beauty of an act of some kindness de luxe, rising gracefully above the level of duty, the extra touch, the gold-illuminated letters which brighten the pages of life's prose.

To lift the dutiful up to the beautiful is a mark of true discipleship. This woman did it. So often the minimum of duty might be transformed into the maximum of beauty. It is the fine excess, the thing not nominated in the

| 7 For ye have the poor with you always, and whensoever ye will ye may do them good: but me ye have not always. | She has done a beautiful thing to me. 7 For you always have the poor with you, and whenever you will, you can do good to them; but you will not always have me. |

7-8. The poor with you always may be a reference to Deut. 15:11, but only in contrast to the impending departure of Jesus (cf. 2:20). It is anything but a comment on social conditions, or an observation on perennial human poverty, which need not be done away with since it provides opportunity for meritorious works of charity. Having answered the objection in vss. 4-5, Jesus proceeds further to commend the woman's good deed: **She has done what she could**—there was not much anyone could do, as the Marcan Christ went forward to his lonely destiny—**she has anointed my body beforehand for**

bond, the unsolicited gift, the surprise which springs from the imagination of love.

Another inference of this story should not be overlooked. There is a generosity of the alms box and subscription paper. There is also the generosity of thoughtfulness to friend, the mute eloquence of specific act, the celebration of love and friendship in a beautiful ritual of remembrance. Jesus recognized such spontaneous movements of the heart as great events, not quickly to be forgotten.

7. You Always Have the Poor with You.— This saying of Jesus deserves careful study for two reasons: first, in order to learn what he meant by it; second, as a result of that, in order to correct the appalling violence of distortion which the words have suffered through many centuries. They have been pressed into the service of an inhuman and unchristian economic order of life, in which preventable poverty is accepted with complacency as though it were as inescapable as the law of gravitation. Did not Jesus say, "You always have the poor with you"? Such an interpretation is probably the greatest single achievement of the vicious use of Scripture, "twisted by knaves to make a trap for fools." It would cut the nerve of all effort to lift the crushing burdens of want. The verb "have" is in the present tense. Jesus was not declaring the eternity of poverty. The relief of human need bulked large and continuously in his life and words. Those who fed the hungry, clothed the naked, and sheltered the homeless, received the award, "Come, O blessed of my Father" (Matt. 25:34). He was speaking to an immediate situation. What had been said about selling the ointment and giving the proceeds to the poor was not only a pious platitude, it was a monstrous impertinence. He did not have to be reminded of those among whom he had spent his life. It was more than blindness he was rebuking. He was rebuking the attempt to justify that blindness by the mouthing of an obvious commonplace about the poor. This was a time when something more than routine almsgiving was indicated.

There is permanent meaning here which is never exhausted. The question comes up again and again, usually with a sour note from the shortsighted, "Why spend money on churches when there are hungry people in the world?" The answer is not only that true worship is life's inherently greatest experience, and needs no justification in dollars and cents, but also that it is an unfailing fountainhead of generous service. Devotion to God is a well, springing up eternally, out of which flow great streams for the healing and blessing of men. The devotion represented by the breaking of the alabaster box, the outgoing of affection and honor for Christ, has been the source of the greatest help to the poor the world has ever known. It works out in a paradox: If we see life only in terms of denarii which ought to be better distributed, and grow blind to the intangibles—like "Thou shalt love the Lord thy God with all thy heart" —soon there will not be very many denarii to distribute.

7. You Will Not Always Have Me.—These words cast over the scene the impending shadow of death under which Jesus lived during his last days in Jerusalem. Beyond that, however, in themselves, without relation to their context, they express a deep truth of personal experience and history. It is this: the opportunity to have Jesus, in the sense of the experience Paul had and millions of others after him, "Christ liveth in me" (Gal. 2:20), is not a constant. There is a tidal quality in life. There are opportunities which must be taken at the flood, for there comes an ebb when they cannot be so readily taken, if at all. There is the particular flood tide of youth, when one may have Jesus as the guide and master of a whole lifetime. We cannot have that always. There is the voice of God in conscience; but if it is not heeded, it grows faint. We cannot have it always. There is the appeal of need; but if we do not answer it, we soon grow deaf to it. One dare not miss the solemn note, **You will not always have me.** "Seek ye the LORD while he may be found" (Isa. 55:6).

8 She hath done what she could: she is come aforehand to anoint my body to the burying.

9 Verily I say unto you, Wheresoever this gospel shall be preached throughout the whole world, *this* also that she hath done shall be spoken of for a memorial of her.

10 ¶ And Judas Iscariot, one of the twelve, went unto the chief priests, to betray him unto them.

8 She has done what she could; she has anointed my body beforehand for burying. 9 And truly, I say to you, wherever the gospel is preached in the whole world, what she has done will be told in memory of her."

10. Then Judas Iscariot, who was one of the twelve, went to the chief priests in

---

burying. Contrast John 12:7: "Let her . . . keep it . . . for my burial," perhaps a more probable form of the saying, especially since John makes no use of it later.

9. This verse has often been viewed as extraneous to the narrative, since it assumes a so much later point of view (cf. 13:10), and also because, after all, it does not give the woman's name. But it was the deed, not the name, that was important. Perhaps she was still living and would wish her name suppressed; but she surely had no exclusive right to the story, even though she herself "scorned to blot it with a name." The reference to the publishing abroad of the story can, as Klostermann notes, be paralleled in Roman oratory —e.g., Cicero *Pro Sulla* 15. Mark is thinking of the church in his own day, and of the common recital of the story in connection with the passion narrative.

3. Judas' Treachery (14:10-11)

This section is really a continuation of vss. 1-2 (see above). Throughout Christian history the motive of Judas in betraying our Lord has been a puzzle. Answers have included: (*a*) Judas was disappointed over the failure of the messianic hope and over Jesus' inactivity as he faced the opposition, and therefore determined to salvage what he could from the debacle of his hope; (*b*) Judas wished only to force the hand of Jesus, and was crushed when the terrible consequences of his deed began to unfold; (*c*) Judas was a scoundrel all along (John 12:6), and finally was inspired by the devil (John 13:2, 27). The theory of Judas' skepticism is as old as Irenaeus (or Papias, whom he quoted, in

---

8. She Has Done What She Could.—On the face of it this seems like tepid tribute. Why praise a person for doing what she could? One good reason is that such an achievement is never obvious. Doing what we can is frequently the last thing we care to do. As a rule it is unexciting and unspectacular. How much more romantic to think of ourselves as doing what we cannot do! We enjoy the form of reverie which has been called "blue rose melancholy." We sigh and think what great things we might do if roses were only blue; what we could accomplish for some fine cause with the $50,000 we do not have, instead of going through the prosaic business of doing something with the $50 we do have. Many would prefer preaching like Spurgeon, the thing they cannot do, to teaching a church-school class, the thing they can do. To think of ourselves in fanciful daydreaming as the author of immortal books is far more thrilling—and easy—than to write the helpful letter we can write.

The reverie of self-dramatization is lilting

poetry; the thing we can really do is leaden prose. Yet the world has been blessed not by reverie but by act, by people who did what they could; not with the imaginary $50,000 or the imaginary eloquence, but with the actual $50, or $5, and with the word in season, fitly spoken.

10. *Then Judas Iscariot, Who Was One of the Twelve, Went to the Chief Priests in Order to Betray Him to Them.*—Mark makes very brief mention of Judas' betrayal of Jesus. Two sentences record the stark fact. No motive is assigned.

The dark, mysterious figure of Judas has caused endless speculation from the first, and provided a continuous theme for admonition. Every imaginable motive has been suggested (see Exeg. for a list of the chief reasons which have been given for the betrayal). We shall never know what lay back of Judas' treachery. The earliest explanation, that of cupidity, is now very generally rejected as being an oversimplification. At most it is judged to have been a factor not of major but of minor importance.

11 And when they heard *it,* they were glad, and promised to give him money. And he sought how he might conveniently betray him.

12 ¶ And the first day of unleavened bread, when they killed the passover, his disciples said unto him, Where wilt thou that we go and prepare that thou mayest eat the passover?

order to betray him to them. 11 And when they heard it they were glad, and promised to give him money. And he sought an opportunity to betray him.

12 And on the first day of Unleavened Bread, when they sacrificed the passover lamb, his disciples said to him, "Where will you have us go and prepare for you

---

Against Heresies V. 33. 4), but Mark has no suggestion of this—or of any other theory. He states only the plain, terrible fact. The act was entirely voluntary: **Judas . . . went.**

Still another question has been **what** Judas betrayed. Again there have been many theories: the messianic secret, Jesus' revolutionary designs, the place where Jesus spent his nights outside the city, and so on, each in accordance with some preconceived notion of the leading purpose of Jesus' mission. And again Mark has nothing to offer in support of any of these theories. Judas' plan was simply to "hand over" (παραδοῦναι) Jesus to the chief priests. So also in 3:19 he is named as the one who "betrayed him," i.e., surrendered him to his enemies, while Luke 6:16 has ὃς ἐγένετο προδότης, the one who denounced and delivered him up to the authorities (cf. Acts 1:16, "who was guide to those who arrested Jesus"). This is probably all that the primitive tradition recorded; the rest is guesswork and hypothesis.

Conveniently (KJV), i.e., in accordance with their purpose of stealth (vss. 1-2); or more probably, **he sought an opportunity** (RSV).

4. Preparation for the Passover (14:12-16)

The striking similarity of this section to the preparation for the Triumphal Entry (11:1-6) has often been noted. Various theories have been advanced: that in vs. 13*b* baptism is symbolically represented; or that we have here a reference to a secret sign leading the way to a Christian house and a Christian service in pagan Rome; or that Jesus himself had made all the arrangements—but not necessarily in Jerusalem; **the city** (vs. 13) may have been Bethany (cf. Loisy, Goguel) —and had secret disciples and supporters in great numbers all over the neighborhood (cf. Robert Eisler's theory of armed revolt in *The Messiah Jesus and John the Baptist* [tr. A. H. Krappe; New York: Lincoln MacVeagh, 1931], esp. ch. xvi). But none of these has any particular support in Mark's text. For Mark, Jesus had second sight, or at least a supernatural kind of vision, and could tell in advance that a man—not a woman!—would be carrying a jar of water to a certain house; cf. the colt tied outside the door in the open street in 11:4. The whole anecdote moves in the realm of supernatural perception—not so very far removed from certain phenomena reported today, and in all ages (cf. I Sam. 10:2) —though it is a perfectly fair question whether originally the incident was not simply Jesus' announcement to the disciples of the arrangements he had already made for the supper, here the Passover meal. That a certain amount of secrecy was necessary, in view of the dangers surrounding him, is most probable, and explains the prearranged sign in vs. 13.

12-13. The first day of Unleavened Bread is either in conflict with vs. 1, or is Roman reckoning, viz., Thursday. This was rather late for the disciples to be thinking about the question. Preparations were necessary, as the Passover was a formal meal with specified food and wine, and required provision for the religious observance which it denoted.

We can nevertheless be reasonably sure of some of the things which went on in Judas' mind before the final act. Undoubtedly there had been a dying fire of affection for Jesus. The flame of his first devotion had burned down. A **divided** loyalty had replaced the unanimous

response he had once made to Christ's invitation, "Follow me." He had been for some time now in the company but not of it, in an official rather than personal relationship. In one way or another, self-regard had increased, while regard for Jesus as Master had decreased.

13 And he sendeth forth two of his disciples, and saith unto them, Go ye into the city, and there shall meet you a man bearing a pitcher of water: follow him.

14 And wheresoever he shall go in, say ye to the goodman of the house, The Master saith, Where is the guest chamber, where I shall eat the passover with my disciples?

to eat the passover?" 13 And he sent two of his disciples, and said to them, "Go into the city, and a man carrying a jar of water will meet you; follow him, 14 and wherever he enters, say to the householder, 'The Teacher says, Where is my guest room, where I am to eat the passover with my

---

13-15. **Two,** as in 11:1. **The goodman of the house** (KJV) is beautiful old English for the head of the family, **the householder** (RSV), οἰκοδεσπότης, who in theory should preside at the Passover meal; but in his family "Christ Is the Head of This Household," as old-fashioned mottoes used to say. The upper room may not have been in use by the household; it was Jewish custom that Passover pilgrims might ask any homeowner for the use of a room for the occasion (Strack and Billerbeck, *Kommentar zum Neuen Testament,* I, 989). **Furnished and prepared,** i.e., provided with rugs and cushions, and possibly with a low table (Luke 22:21). The large banquet hall and table with benches or chairs, in most paintings of the scene, represent later European custom, and were probably derived historically from the illustrations in medieval Jewish Passover haggadahs.

That all this can happen to a disciple we know only too well. Many of us can look into our own hearts and write the story. It is a solemn thing to recall that these processes, so familiar, are what led to the darkest betrayal of history.

The tragedy of Judas also makes indelibly clear the fact that it is the disciple's defection which deals to Christ and his cause a blow far more severe than any that can be inflicted by an open enemy, no matter how powerful the opponent may be.

When do we go over to Jesus' enemies? We do it whenever we show a distrust of love as the supreme motive and method of life; whenever we become infected with the poisons of materialism; whenever we enter our denial of human brotherhood.

14. *Say to the Householder, 'The Teacher Says, Where Is My Guest Room . . . ?'*—This householder deserves more recognition and honor than he has ever received. He played a large part in keeping furnished and ready the place where the Last Supper was held. He was not a part of that spiritual event; but he made it possible in the physical sense. He made a real and great contribution to all that it meant in the last days of Jesus and in all the days and years of subsequent history.

May he not be for us a representative of that group of men and women, often forgotten, who have rendered great service to the kingdom of God, not in shaping or proclaiming the church's message, but in providing and sustaining the place in which the message could be proclaimed? They are a great host, impressive to the imagination, a great parade moving down the years:

the anonymous folk in whose homes the Christian fellowship met in the early years, "the church that is in thy house"; the builders of churches and cathedrals in Europe; those who erected the first churches in America, from which the westward thrust of Christianity across the continent was launched; the people who put together the first rude church buildings in China and India and kept them going. Here is a man, for instance, who has given of his time and strength for half a century to keep a certain church in repair, fixing the roof, stove, walls. He has kept ready and furnished a place where a spiritual event could happen. When a young boy or girl, dedicated to God in that building, goes out to bless the world, that man is a vital part of it all. It is a great role to play.

Notice also that this householder was anonymous. What a figure in church history he has been—"Anonymous"! Poet, composer, saint. Turn to your hymnal and look up the hymns "Anonymous" has written. He wrote "Come thou, almighty King," "O come, all ye faithful," "The strife is o'er, the battle done," "Fairest Lord Jesus," and a score of others. How many anonymous people there are in the N.T.—the centurion who had great faith, the town clerk of Ephesus, a gallery of great souls. They are the hope of the world. When a more Christian order of life is established, it will be done by "Anonymous." There are no near limits to what a person may accomplish if he does not care who gets the credit.

14. *Where Is My Guest Room?*—There is small wonder that many sermons have been preached on this verse. It is picturesque and dramatic. See the Exeg. for what seems to be

15 And he will show you a large upper room furnished *and* prepared: there make ready for us.

16 And his disciples went forth, and came into the city, and found as he had said unto them: and they made ready the passover.

17 And in the evening he cometh with the twelve.

18 And as they sat and did eat, Jesus

disciples?' 15 And he will show you a large upper room furnished and ready; there prepare for us." 16 And the disciples set out and went to the city, and found it as he had told them; and they prepared the passover.

17 And when it was evening he came with the twelve. 18 And as they were at

5. Prediction of the Betrayal (14:17-21)

17. In the evening, when the day of Passover (Nisan 15) began. **The twelve,** as if in vs. 13 two of them had not been sent ahead—or had they returned? Contrary to 11:19, as interpreted by Luke 21:37, Jesus is now outside the city during the day, and returns at evening for the Passover.

18. As the fuller citation in John 13:18 suggests, the words of Ps. 41:9 are quoted here. Some scholars think the whole incident derived from the citation, as other passages

the most reasonable explanation—that Jesus was announcing his coming to a friend with whom some previous arrangement had been made. He does it, however, with a question so direct and pointed that we almost inevitably move on, by an obvious step and a legitimate one, to think of his asking every man, asking us, "Where is my guest room?" Is there any room at all for him in our house of life? Where in our mind and purposes is a place for him, for his mind and purposes? Do we make a special place for him as *the* guest, above all others? Or is his presence, so to speak, only casual? Is he only one of a host of figures in a crowded living room? Just one more "among those present" at a public reception?

16. *The Disciples . . . Found It as He Had Told Them.*—This is just an incidental detail in a narrative, and carries no moral and spiritual meaning of any sort. Jesus had given the disciples directions for finding a house in which they might eat the Passover, and everything had worked out just as he had told them.

Yet if we take these words up from their context, and look at them with imagination, they do record the verdict of Christian experience—the experience of multitudes of disciples through centuries of history. Just as two of his closest followers found in Jerusalem that everything happened as he had told them it would, so men and women have gone out into life and have "found it as he had told them." The experience of living by faith in Christ has brought its verification of his teaching—the fundamental and enduring proof of the truth of his revelation.

Jesus said that faith would bring an increase of power in life. Uncounted millions have found it as he told them. People all through the years

have been enlarged. They *have* walked through the valley of the shadow of death and feared no evil. They *have* lived above the level of life around them.

Jesus said, "He that loseth his life for my sake shall find it" (Matt. 10:39). Men have ventured on that and found it as he told them. Losing themselves in self-forgetful service to others, they have "found" life with a richness and fullness and joy never known before.

Jesus said that they who take the sword will perish by the sword. History has given it an overwhelming validation.

Jesus said, "He that hath seen me hath seen the Father" (John 14:9). Men *have* found in Jesus the God of love.

18. *And as They Were at Table Eating.*—Here begins the story of a meal which became a sacrament. Its relevance to faith and to all human life is inexhaustible. One shaft of light from this upper room, where a family meal was being held, streams into the dining room of every Christian home. It illuminates the possibilities in the commonest occurrence of life. There can be a sacramental quality in all family meals—sacramental, that is, in the sense of being a means of revelation. The language of the family can be the language of the kingdom of God, even when no explicitly religious vocabulary is used. The disposition to go to the Communion table so often springs from the spirit, the interests, and the quality of fellowship which prevail at the dining-room table.

An advertisement of the research laboratories of a great corporation was headed with these words, "Little rooms where new worlds are made." New worlds have been made in little rooms, this upper room, for instance. New worlds have been made in the little rooms of

said, Verily I say unto you, One of you which eateth with me shall betray me.

19 And they began to be sorrowful, and to say unto him one by one, Is it I? and another *said, Is* it I?

20 And he answered and said unto them, *It is* one of the twelve, that dippeth with me in the dish.

21 The Son of man indeed goeth, as it is written of him: but woe to that man by whom the Son of man is betrayed! good were it for that man if he had never been born.

table eating, Jesus said, "Truly, I say to you, one of you will betray me, one who is eating with me." 19 They began to be sorrowful, and to say to him one after another, "Is it I?" 20 He said to them, "It is one of the twelve, one who is dipping bread in the same dish with me. 21 For the Son of man goes as it is written of him, but woe to that man by whom the Son of man is betrayed! It would have been better for that man if he had not been born."

---

in the passion narrative have exercised a formative influence and provided details (cf. Grant, *Growth of the Gospels,* pp. 192-93). Luke 22:21-23 shifts it to follow the "words of institution," which is a more dramatic and on the whole a more probable location. But there is nothing impossible or even improbable in the assumption that Jesus was aware of Judas' treachery and knew "who it was that should betray him" (John 6:64). But the problem is: How could Jesus have made this announcement, especially if it was as specific as in John, without some effort being made by the other disciples to prevent the carrying out of Judas' plan?

20. **Dippeth,** i.e., into the sauce (*ḥarôseth*) which was eaten with the paschal lamb; perhaps this is only a general reference to eating together (as in Luke 22:21). To betray a companion after eating with him was, and still is among the Arabs, the grossest conceivable perfidy.

21. Another Son of man saying, in the series and with the same general meaning as elsewhere in Mark (cf. the passion announcements in 8:31; 9:31; 10:32-34; and notes above on these passages); he goes **as it is written of him** (cf. 9:12). There was a divine necessity in the Son of man's death, but he himself accepted it; there was a similar necessity in the betrayal, but this necessity did not include the particular individual who was its agent—he had also the option of refusal. As the Pharisees held, "All is foreseen, and free will is given" (cf. Aboth 3:19; see R. T. Herford, *Pirke Aboth* [New York: Jewish Institute of Religion Press, 1925], pp. 88-89; Charles Taylor, *Sayings of the Jewish Fathers* [Cambridge: University Press, 1897], p. 59). Judas had his option—and accepted. On his fate cf. 9:42; the expression here (**It would have been better for that man . . . born**) was proverbial (see refs. in Klostermann).

---

homes, in the living room, in the dining room—new worlds of aspiration and dedication. **As they were at table. . . .**

18-19. *They Began to Be Sorrowful, and to Say . . . One After Another, "Is It I?"*—There is a universal and timeless quality in the self-searching of this question "Is it I?" With so terrible an accusation of treachery, it might have been expected that each disciple would have uttered a resounding denial. Instead there was the sorrowful, inner probing—a tribute to the absence of complacency and self-satisfaction, and to their sensitiveness of conscience. They felt that they might, all unknown to themselves, be guilty.

Every one of us must put that question to himself, "Is it I?" The word "betray" is an ugly word naturally, for betrayal is an ugly thing.

The word "Judas" carries more scorn and revulsion than any other word in the language. Most people can honestly refute the charge of treason, when it is thought of—and it usually is—as a once for all, dramatic renunciation of faith and sworn allegiance. But life's tests rarely come in such an explicit manner. They creep up in unnoticed choices. Before we realize it we come to the edge, are over the edge, of some kind of betrayal. All Christians have "dipped into the dish with Jesus," have sat at the table of the Lord's Supper. "Is it I?"

We betray our Master when we allow our devotion and purposes to be worn away without renewal. "Creeps in this petty pace from day to day"; and in the wearing down by routine, the bonds of affection and obedience are insensibly weakened.

22 ¶ And as they did eat, Jesus took bread, and blessed, and brake *it,* and gave

22 And as they were eating, he took

6. The Last Supper (14:22-26)

Contrary to the indications of date in vss. 1-2, 12, and contrary to the chronology of John, Mark—perhaps under the influence of such a conception as that in I Cor. 5:7*b,* which was probably fairly common in the Gentile churches and may be very old—views the Last Supper as a Passover meal. In this he is followed by Matthew and Luke, but not by John. But there are a number of indications—in addition to the chronology—that the meal was not the Passover, unless by a kind of anticipation: the use of bread (ἄρτος), not matzoth (ἄζυμα); the absence of any mention of the lamb, the chief article of food at the Passover meal, or of the bitter herbs (*merôrîm*), or of the attire of the participants (as prescribed in Exod. 12); not to speak of the impossibility of a legal trial and execution on the festival (see below). All this has led many scholars to believe that the passage originally recounted the last supper of Jesus with his disciples, and that this has been rewritten by Mark as an account of a Passover meal. Such a verse as Luke 22:15 is thus viewed as a survival from the older narrative. The original account was an etiological narrative explaining the origin of the Lord's Supper as it was observed in the Gentile churches; even Paul's account in I Cor. 11:23-25 does not refer to Passover, but to "the night when he was betrayed." And the second-century Quartodecimans, who apparently celebrated Easter on Good Friday (as the West put it, they celebrated both the Crucifixion and the Resurrection on Nisan 14!), may not perhaps have identified the *original* supper with Passover (see E. Preuschen, in *Prot. Realencyckl.,* 3rd ed., XIV. 725-34). At the same time, the nearness of Passover gave a tone and emphasis as well as a meaning to the observance which led to some kind of identification of the supper with the paschal meal; but it was chiefly the death of Christ which interpreted both the new supper and the ancient festival, in Christian eyes—and so it was for Mark, certainly. It was the memorial aspect of Passover (Exod. 12:14), as well as the actual practice of worship, which influenced the church and led to the emphasis upon its repetition (as in I Cor. 11:24*b,* 25*b,* 26)—the Eucharist was now the Christian Passover. But there is none of this emphasis in Mark; his narrative is more primitive.

Taking the text of Mark as it stands, in isolation from the parallels and from Paul, the supper is (*a*) an anticipation of the reunion of the disciples with Jesus in the kingdom (on vs. 25 see below), perhaps of the "messianic banquet," though the evidence for this idea is late and some of it irrelevant; and (*b*) a kind of sacrament—every Jewish meal was sacred, especially those of religious groups, the sabbath-eve meal of the Pharisaic groups, for example (see W. O. E. Oesterley, *The Jewish Background of the Christian Liturgy* [Oxford: Clarendon Press, 1925], pp. 156-93)—binding Jesus to his disciples and them to him in a bond of loyalty, whatever might come (cf. vss. 27, 31); and (*c*) a sacrifice, in which the disciples too were to participate, not only by eating and drinking

---

We betray him when we allow to take place what Branscomb suggests may have happened to Judas—he "must have gone over to the Pharisaic and Sadducean attitude." [8] We constantly move in circles where our Lord is suspect, regarded as highly "irregular," or disregarded entirely. Breathing that atmosphere, we may come to have our view of him subtly merge with that of the powerful secular "authorities."

We betray him when we try to make him fit into our way of life and thought, instead of changing our thoughts and ways to fit into his. Judas may have done that. The familiar word

[8] *Gospel of Mark,* p. 247.

of Whistler is in point. When he was told by one of his patrons that a certain picture would not fit into his room, Whistler replied: "Man, you can't make the picture fit the room. You must make the room fit the picture." Jesus is not to be fitted into our life. Our room must be arranged to fit him.

We betray him when we give way to the cautious feeling that he is "going too far."

Three words, "Is it I?"

Live with them.

22-25. *This Is My Body. . . . This Is My Blood of the Covenant.*—In these verses are some of the most widely repeated words of human speech, with the probable exception of

to them, and said, Take, eat; this is my body.	bread, and blessed, and broke it, and gave it to them, and said, "Take; this is my body." 23 And he took a cup, and when he had given thanks he gave it to them,
23 And he took the cup, and when he had given thanks, he gave it to them: and they all drank of it.	

but possibly also by dying with him—his blood, which the contents of the cup symbolized, was **blood of the covenant** (some MSS insert **new**), **which is poured out for many** (see 10:45). The Passover connotation of vs. 24 is obvious; but the reference could have been made even if the meal took place some hours or days before the paschal meal.

22. **Blessed**, i.e., said the blessing (of God) or thanksgiving as in 6:41 and 8:6-7. **This is my body**: In Aramaic there would be no verb—much of later ecclesiastical controversy over the Eucharist would have been obviated if Aramaic had continued the language of the gospel. Perhaps (in view of 4:15-20; etc.) the word ἐστιν (is) should signify "means." Jesus' body is to be delivered over to death, even as this bread is delivered into the hands of the disciples. The later designation, "the breaking of bread" (e.g., Acts 2:46), suggests something more in Jesus' "manual act" which accompanied the distribution than the mere handing around of already broken pieces. The Jewish housefather broke the bread as he said the blessing.

23. **Given thanks**: This act is parallel to the blessing and equivalent to it, as in 8:6-7. **He gave it to them**: Jesus takes the initiative. Already for Mark, and for the early church,

the Lord's Prayer. They are associated with the highest hours of human experience and with the deepest meanings of the Christian gospel.

Around all the narratives of the Last Supper in the Gospels, and in I Cor. 11:23-26, and around the history of the growth of the remembrance of this supper into a sacrament of the church, there are many intricate questions of a factual nature discussed succinctly in the Exeg. Here the comment is confined to some assured meanings in a narrative which never can be fully explained.

One remembrance seems worthy of stress. The gift of God in Christ is not something first of all to be *imitated* in life, but first of all something to be *received*, humbly, thankfully, joyfully. There is a tendency, manifested all too often, to find the great meaning of the Last Supper in an example to be followed. With that primary emphasis and without first receiving the gift of the sacrifice of Christ in any deep, personal sense, many have taken the symbols of bread and wine as an exhortation to sacrificial living. Unless we first receive, our giving will be thin and unsustained. If we do not take from him the cup of his love, we will not of ourselves have much to pour out. Isaac Watts's great hymn traces the true succession of events.

> Love so amazing, so divine,
> Demands my soul, my life, my all.[9]

It is when we have fully received that an enduring demand is laid upon life, a demand that can be met only by "my all." Jesus regarded his

death as a gift. As he gave the bread, he gave his life. The invitation "Take" was spoken first to a few disciples. It says now to the whole human family: "Take. This is for you. Take this gift into the central place of your life." Afterward comes the word, "Freely ye have received, freely give" (Matt. 10:8).

The Last Supper too, of course, expresses that spirit in which the disciples of Christ can and must share. It proclaims, "Let this mind be in you, which was also in Christ Jesus" (Phil. 2:5), a dominant love that gives itself in the service of men. We cannot avoid the question the Lord's table asks: "This is the blood of the covenant, poured out for many. Are your life, your blood, your strength, poured out at all?"

Is there not still another suggestion beautifully pictured in the survival of an old European folk custom which has come down to our own day—the hot cross bun? There it is on the breakfast table in Lent, just a bit of bread marked by the sign of the cross. It is a small but eloquent symbol of the truth that all bread should be marked by the sign of the cross. Bread has been marked by tears and by blood.

> O, God! that bread should be so dear,
> And flesh and blood so cheap![1]

The whole process of breadmaking and bread-winning—why not then the distribution of bread?—should be marked by the sign of love and brotherhood.

23. *When He Had Given Thanks He Gave It to Them.*—This was the observance of the

[9] "When I survey the wondrous cross."

[1] Thomas Hood, "The Song of the Shirt."

24 And he said unto them, This is my blood of the new testament, which is shed for many.

25 Verily I say unto you, I will drink no more of the fruit of the vine, until that day that I drink it new in the kingdom of God.

26 ¶ And when they had sung a hymn, they went out into the mount of Olives.

and they all drank of it. 24 And he said to them, "This is my blood of the*c* covenant, which is poured out for many. 25 Truly, I say to you, I shall not drink again of the fruit of the vine until that day when I drink it new in the kingdom of God."

26 And when they had sung a hymn, they went out to the Mount of Olives.

c Some ancient authorities insert *new.*

---

even from the earliest days the supper had a sacramental significance, and was no borrowing from some "mystery" religion (cf. Frank Gavin, *Jewish Antecedents of the Christian Sacraments* [London: Society for Promoting Christian Knowledge, 1933], on the Jewish background of the early Christian sacramental idea).

24. Blood of the covenant: In later Jewish usage this meant the blood of circumcision; here the reference is undoubtedly to such ideas as we find in Exod. 24:8; Zech. 9:11; Heb. 9:20; 10:29. The idea of a "new" covenant is absent from the best texts of Mark and Matthew, but is found in Paul (I Cor. 11:25), and in the longer reading in Luke 22:20 (perhaps based on I Cor. 11, certainly related to it in some way); it is probably derived from Jer. 31:31-34, but represents a more advanced interpretation of the words of institution than we find in Mark.

25. This verse, especially if taken in the context which Luke 22:15-18 gives it (and where it in turn gives a new meaning to vs. 15), implies that Jesus has already drunk with them—according to Mark, the paschal cup. But translations and MSS vary: some give "I will never again," others, "From now on I will not," as if it were a vow (cf. Acts 23:12); others, "I will not hereafter," i.e., except in the kingdom of God. The sense of immediacy is clear in all the variants, and reminds us of the formula in the old Jewish Passover haggadahs, which may indeed have influenced the saying: "This is the bread of poverty, which our fathers ate in Egypt: Let everyone who is hungry come and eat [cf. Isa. 55:1-2], everyone who is in need of it, everyone who keeps this feast: This year here, in the year to come in the Land of Israel; this year as slaves, in the year to come as freemen." **Drink it new,** as everything in the Kingdom will be new, new as in the first creation.

26. The **hymn** may have been the final part of the Hallel (Pss. 115–118), sung at the conclusion of the Passover meal, though Mark does not say so. Luke 22:39 states that it was Jesus' custom to go out to **the Mount of Olives,** in accordance with Luke 21:37.

Jewish custom of thanksgiving before a meal. But it is startling enough. Death was just outside the door; yet Jesus twice gave thanks. He could do it in serenity. Death might be just outside the door, but God was inside the door. Jesus' reliance on his Father was so complete that there was no occasion which did not call for thanksgiving. Where trust like his prevails, one can be thankful in any amazement.

25. *Until That Day When I Drink It New in the Kingdom of God.*—Here was the forward look of faith, even in the very midst of the darkest hour. Jesus' separation from the disciples would be only temporary. He was sure that God's purpose would not be defeated by the staves and spears of the soldiers in the garden to which he was going, or by the Cross. He looked on to the final victory. It was partly this apocalyptic note which made the early Christian celebration of the Lord's Supper a

joyful affair—not a looking backward to tragedy, but a looking forward to victory and the consummation of a kingdom.

These words, in the Quaker phrase, "speak to our condition." There are dark hours in everybody's life—dark hours in the history of civilization—when the only life possible is life with an immanent sense of death at the door. It is easy then to drift into a sense of defeat. On the horizons of the Western world Christian apocalypse has been rapidly replaced, in the minds of many, by a secular, scientific apocalypse, the sure coming of doom, not a day of the Lord, but a day of unrelieved disaster. We need desperately the faith that will enable us to look forward, confident that God's kingdom is everlasting, persuaded that he and his will cannot be brought to suffer any final eclipse.

26. *And When They Had Sung a Hymn, They Went Out.*—Not only is this one of the

27 And Jesus saith unto them, All ye shall be offended because of me this night: for it is written, I will smite the shepherd, and the sheep shall be scattered.

28 But after that I am risen, I will go before you into Galilee.

27 And Jesus said to them, "You will all fall away; for it is written, 'I will strike the shepherd, and the sheep will be scattered.' 28 But after I am raised up, I will

---

7. PREDICTION OF PETER'S DENIAL (14:27-31)

27. A further prediction, like the one in vss. 18, 21, and based explicitly on prophecy (Zech. 13:7; cf. John 16:32).

28. This verse is omitted by Luke, and by at least one MS of Mark, the tiny Fayûm fragment (third century) in the Archduke Rainer collection in Vienna. It seems closely related to 16:7, and both verses may be later additions to Mark in the interest of the Galilean appearances of the risen Lord (as against the Judean in Luke). Matthew has the verse (Matt. 26:32); and, as some have held, it may have been interpolated into Mark from Matthew. If so, one must suppose also the interpolation of 16:7 from Matt. 28:7, which points forward to Matt. 28:10, 16-20. But the chief difficulty here is that vss. 29-31 proceed as if the words of vs. 28 had not been uttered! The same is true of 16:7—vs. 8 proceeds as if vs. 7 did not exist, and the women, still terrified, say nothing, entirely disobeying the angelic injunction. In Matthew they do precisely the reverse! The conclusion seems inevitable that both verses have been interpolated into Mark at some time prior to the writing of Matthew, and in opposition either to the Lukan view, which limited the appearances to Judea, or to one approximating that which Luke presents. John combines the two, with Jerusalem appearances in ch. 20, and a Galilean in the appendix, ch. 21.

---

greatest pictures of quiet courage in all literature; it is also a powerful picture of fellowship in worship as a fortification for struggle, an equipment for testing. Those who stand completely outside the experience of worship, and they are many, disdain it. And empty worship, God help us all, can indeed be the veriest vanity. But for Jesus and his disciples this singing of a hymn was no mere form. There may have been some wavering voices at first, but as they shared in Israel's great religious heritage of faith, they found a power arming their minds and hearts against whatever might be waiting for them. **When they had sung a hymn** they were renewed men, with spirits replenished in a fellowship of worship with each other and with the great company of those who had sung the same hymn in days gone by.

That is what worship can do. It is not an entertainment or an aesthetic diversion. It is a fortifying power. The great scenes of Christian history might bear these words as a subtitle: **When they had sung a hymn, they went out.** It was true of the martyrs as they went into the amphitheater to face the lions. It was true of the early leaders of the antislavery movements. It has been true of thousands of farewell meetings for departing missionaries. It was true of Norwegian churchmen defying the Nazi tyranny.

What is true of us? Is it true that we do not "go out" more effectively in the conflict with

evil because we do not worship effectively enough? Is it true that after we have sung a hymn we all too often sit down instead of going out at all? The hymns we sing and the prayers we offer have to take deep inward hold if there is to be any projection outward.

27. *And Jesus Said to Them, "You Will All Fall Away."*—If any other leader of men had said that to his followers, just before the most critical hour in their lives, it would be accounted a cynical sneer. Jesus was never a cynic. He was often impatient with his disciples, or irritated with them, but he never sneered at them. He was a realist. "He knew all men" (John 2:25). He said later the same evening, "The spirit indeed is willing, but the flesh is weak" (Matt. 26:41). He knew the stresses his disciples would be under, the pressures they would be exposed to, the bewilderment of quick surprise. He knew their weak spots, as indicated by his knowledge of Peter in this passage.

We can well imagine that his sorrowful word comes down across the years to all his disciples, down even to us, **You will all fall away.** It should take from us all swollen pride and self-assurance, and lead us into the mood of humility. All too surely in some fashion we shall "fall away." Perhaps we can have a preview of the battleground.

Moffatt's translation of the word here rendered "fall away" gives a helpful suggestion.

29 But Peter said unto him, Although all shall be offended, yet *will* not I.

30 And Jesus saith unto him, Verily I say unto thee, That this day, *even* in this night, before the cock crow twice, thou shalt deny me thrice.

31 But he spake the more vehemently, If I should die with thee, I will not deny thee in any wise. Likewise also said they all.

go before you to Galilee." 29 Peter said to him, "Even though they all fall away, I will not." 30 And Jesus said to him, "Truly, I say to you, this very night, before the cock crows twice, you will deny me three times." 31 But he said vehemently, "If I must die with you, I will not deny you." And they all said the same.

29-31. As in 10:39 one of the "pillar" apostles was forward in announcing his ability to share the cup and the baptism that confronted the Lord, so here Peter is represented as ardent in protesting his loyalty. But the words point forward and prepare for his denials, as **they all said the same** prepares for vs. 50. **Before the cock crows twice:** Perhaps originally "before cockcrow." A few good MSS omit "twice," as do the parallels; but the double cockcrow may be part of Mark's scheme (see above, p. 866), and the word may be derived from vss. 68, 72 (where some MSS omit the cockcrow in vs. 68 and the words "a second time" in vs. 72).

He translates it "disconcerted." Men often fall away because of the suddenness of unexpected attack. They are upset, "split apart," a literal meaning of "disconcerted." This is the most natural explanation of the flight of the disciples after the arrest of Jesus. It is the explanation of many a falling away. The only preparation for the swift surprises of temptation or testing is to be so firmly "concerted," that is, "pulled together" around one great affection and dedication, that even the most sudden onslaught finds an integrity of soul, a unified mind.

The KJV says, **Ye shall be offended because of me.** That too throws light on the conflict. What is there in Jesus for us to be "offended" in him? There is much. To follow him will bring one into sharp conflict with strong forces of evil. That is what happened to the disciples. It happens to every disciple. The easy surface peace of life is broken up into danger and difficulty. To be his true follower demands an erect posture in ethical living, much harder to maintain than to sink back into an easy, careless, moral slump, a sort of unconcerned lounging. To follow him means the choice of the "intangibles" instead of the "tangibles"; faith, hope, and love, instead of money, houses, and lands. To follow him puts us out of step with much of the passing parade. Jesus is an "irregular." If we try to keep step with him, we get out of step with the crowd.

These are some of the reasons why disciples fall away. Are we ready to resist their pressure with the counterpressure of the deep satisfactions and joys of a sustained discipleship? If we are not to fall away, those counterpressures must be maintained at full strength.

29. *Peter Said to Him, "Even Though They All Fall Away, I Will Not."*—Brave words, and unquestionably sincere. But here Peter was in the dangerous position of regarding himself and proclaiming himself to be an exception. Whenever anyone does that he is always on slippery ground. We are familiar with the person who says in inflated self-regard, "I am not as other men. Things which might be dangerous to them are all right with me. The ordinary rules do not apply in my case." We hear that in the familiar words of the drinker, "I can take it or leave it alone"; or in the equally familiar words of the gambler, "I always know when to stop."

So Peter says, "I will not fall away. All others may, but not I; not even if it means going to my death."

The only defense against that common peril is humility and dependence. "Let any one who thinks that he stands take heed lest he fall" (I Cor. 10:12). It is a fortification to think in humility that what has happened to others may happen to us. Then when we shift from reliance on self to reliance on God, we have taken the first step toward salvation.

Another mistake of Peter was that he thought of the onslaught of evil, under which he swore never to fall away, in general, abstract terms. It is always easy to resist evil in general, because it never comes that way. It comes in specific details, in particular situations. Peter, in his warm profession of loyalty, was not thinking with visual precision, but in terms of abstraction—a battle with some amorphous shape called the enemy. He did not visualize the particular: the courtyard, the strange power which ridicule would have on a hot-tempered man, or the swift desolation of loneliness in the midst of a hostile crowd. That is how life's greatest tests come. An indispensable aid to victory is a spiritual and ethical sensitiveness which can

<table>
<tr>
<td>

32 And they came to a place which was named Gethsemane: and he saith to his disciples, Sit ye here, while I shall pray.

33 And he taketh with him Peter and James and John, and began to be sore amazed, and to be very heavy;

34 And saith unto them, My soul is exceeding sorrowful unto death: tarry ye here, and watch.

</td>
<td>

32 And they went to a place which was called Geth-sem′a-ne; and he said to his disciples, "Sit here, while I pray." **33** And he took with him Peter and James and John, and began to be greatly distressed and troubled. **34** And he said to them, "My soul is very sorrowful, even to death; remain

</td>
</tr>
</table>

8. JESUS IN GETHSEMANE (14:32-42)

This is one of the most moving and dramatic narratives in the Gospel. It seems to bear the marks of tradition, e.g., the three times of prayer (was each an "hour"?—vs. 37), the three returns to the three disciples, matching Peter's three denials and the three hours of agony on the cross, the three days in the tomb. And yet it is no stenographic record of what occurred in the garden; for even if Jesus was within hearing distance of the disciples (vs. 35), were they not asleep? It has been thought that Jesus must have told them later the contents of his prayer (vss. 36, 39)—but when was there time for this? On the other hand, some have urged that the whole scene was formed as a Christian midrash upon the Lord's Prayer, especially the petitions "Thy will be done" and "Lead us not into temptation [trial], but deliver us from evil" (cf. Luke's introduction in Luke 22:40). But the further echoes of the story—e.g., Heb. 5:7-10, and the great "high priestly" prayer in John 17, which is really the Fourth Evangelist's equivalent for vs. 36 (contrast John 12:27-28)—suggest that the dramatic scene was no creation of Mark. In it the "martyrological" motif comes out more strongly than ever: Jesus is the ideal martyr, and he goes to his death with soul prepared, his loins girt for the struggle, the "athlete" of God utterly obedient to the Father's will, wholly consecrated for his ordeal. Once more we can easily imagine what all this meant to Mark's readers in the persecuted Roman church.

32-34. Gethsemane, "oil press," a garden (John 18:1) with this name on the nearer side of the Mount of Olives. **Disciples,** i.e., the remaining eight; the chosen three (as elsewhere, e.g., 9:2) being taken farther. **Them** in vss. 37, 40, 41 means apparently (at least in vs. 41), the whole band, not the chosen three. For this reason it may be suspected that vs. 33 has been added by Mark to the earlier narrative, in agreement with his view of the peculiar intimacy of Peter, James, and John with Jesus. If so, the words **greatly distressed and troubled** are inferred from the saying in vs. 34. On **amazed** (KJV) see on 10:32. **Sorrowful unto death** is an O.T. expression (Jonah 4:9), like our "deathly sick," or "so that he wished to die." The first half of the saying is reminiscent of the O.T., especially Ps. 42:6, 11. **Watch** is "keep awake," as in vs. 38, and in 13:37.

---

see in detail the crucial nature of situations that do not seem to be of great importance. A vigilant guard of mental alertness is needed which will warn: "Here it is! This prosaic-looking place is the decisive battleground."

32. And He Said to His Disciples, "Sit Here, While I Pray."—This is among the most moving of all the scenes in the Bible. The narrative pictures powerfully both one of the high points in Jesus' life, and also one of the deepest places in human experience—the facing of tragedy. A very affecting aspect of the story is the interplay of the deep need Jesus had for friendship, for reinforcing companionship, and the inexorable necessity under which he labored of facing the great struggle alone. The words **Sit here, while I pray** express poignantly his lone-

liness. Into the agony over the acceptance of the will of God he could take no one, not even his dearest friends. He reached the point where he had to say, "You sit here," while he went on by himself. It had to be his own solitary experience.

There are many, many times in life when we have to say the same words to all friends and loved companions, "You sit here, while I go on alone." Up to a certain point we can take Peter and James and John with us for the reinforcement of friendship and love which every life so greatly needs. The inner fortification of spiritual fellowship is never to be minimized. Through the support of others, with whom we are tied into one bundle of life, our strength is as the strength of many. This is

35 And he went forward a little, and fell on the ground, and prayed that, if it were possible, the hour might pass from him.

36 And he said, Abba, Father, all things *are* possible unto thee; take away this cup from me: nevertheless, not what I will, but what thou wilt.

here, and watch."*d* 35 And going a little farther, he fell on the ground and prayed that, if it were possible, the hour might pass from him. 36 And he said, "Abba, Father, all things are possible to thee; remove this cup from me; yet not what I will,

d Or *keep awake.*

---

35. **A little:** Luke 22:41 says "a stone's throw." **The hour:** An astrological term (both parallels omit it), but in popular use; as in our hymn, it meant the "hour of trial," of testing. **Might pass from him,** i.e., as if God's plan might be altered, but not evaded (vs. 36). (Cf. the Lord's Prayer, "Lead us not into temptation" [Matt. 6:13; Luke 11:4], of which Luke at least, if not Mark, must have thought [Luke 22:40].) The word for "temptation" (πειρασμός) is the same.

36. **All things are possible** with God: Cf. 9:23; 11:22-24. **Cup,** as in 10:38-39. **What thou wilt,** i.e., again as in the Lord's Prayer, "Thy will be done"—where the petition has, of course, universal application; this is specific. Mark is no more aware here than in 13:32 of the interpretation that would be given this verse in the christological discussions, e.g., the Monothelite controversy. The Son's will is in perfect submission to the Father's, as in Heb. 5:8 (cf. I Cor. 15:28); but Mark's theological thinking has not advanced that far, and the question is not even hinted.

---

one of the perpetual miracles of the church of Christ. Yet if we really face the spiritual issues of life, we come to a "you-sit-here" point. In the great moral choices, in the personal ventures of living, in the meeting with disaster that might be overwhelming, we go on alone.

Two truths, at least, appear. First, that moral and spiritual disaster often comes from the failure to recognize the lonesome nature of all great decisions and crises. We live so much in the midst of crowds that life can easily come to be one long "rush-hour jam," in which the separateness of individuality is lost. That prevents the development of Christian personality, and such lostness in a crowd is the prelude to failure. Undoubtedly one reason why death is such a terror to so many people is that facing death will be the first thing they have ever really done alone in all their lives.

Second, the story of Gethsemane pictures the only effective preparation for the loneliness of decision and crisis. That preparation is in what Jesus had—fellowship with God. He was not really alone when the disciples slept in the garden. The great Companion of all his years was there. He did not have to improvise a fellowship; it had run through his life on lonely hills and in crowds. He came to and came through the crisis in the strength of an established communion.

36. *And He Said, "Abba, Father, ... Remove This Cup from Me; Yet Not What I Will, but What Thou Wilt."*—The spiritual struggle and agony of spirit in Gethsemane were his alone. As is pointed out in the Exeg., we cannot be

sure of his exact words. The record in Mark is no stenographic report. Beyond that, just what "the cup" was in Jesus' experience, which he prayed to have removed from him, no one has ever surely known. There is large agreement among interpreters that it was not primarily the physical suffering of a crucifixion. Shrinking from that would be natural to any sensitive person. But if that were all, or if that were the chief factor, Jesus would appear to be less great in spirit than a host of martyrs and other victims of cruel death, who marched serenely to their fate without any such turmoil of soul.

Many conjectures have been made. Some have thought that this life-crushing sorrow was a sorrow over the mystery of God's plan. Why should his life and mission have to issue in the apparent disaster of the Cross? Others have thought it was a sorrow over the response of hatred to his life of love, the frustration of having his destiny unfulfilled. Through it all certainly runs a sense of the sin which brought it about—humanity's sin, piling itself up into betrayal and desertion and death. At any rate here is a picture of the complete humanity of Jesus. Here in the garden is not an automaton, but the Word made flesh.

The great issue of his struggle—"not my will, but thine"—is a marvelous dramatization of the third petition of the Lord's Prayer. It is a perfect embodiment of Jesus' ideal of prayer. The prayer of heartfelt desire, "Let this cup pass from me," is acceptable Christian prayer. The conclusion "not my will, but thine be done" is the ultimate victory of all, as it was for him.

37 And he cometh, and findeth them sleeping, and saith unto Peter, Simon, sleepest thou? couldest not thou watch one hour?

38 Watch ye and pray, lest ye enter into temptation. The spirit truly *is* ready, but the flesh *is* weak.

39 And again he went away, and prayed, and spake the same words.

40 And when he returned, he found them asleep again, (for their eyes were heavy,) neither wist they what to answer him.

but what thou wilt." 37 And he came and found them sleeping, and he said to Peter, "Simon, are you asleep? Could you not watch[d] one hour? 38 Watch[d] and pray that you may not enter into temptation; the spirit indeed is willing, but the flesh is weak." 39 And again he went away and prayed, saying the same words. 40 And again he came and found them sleeping, for their eyes were very heavy; and they did not

[d] Or *keep awake.*

---

37. Findeth them sleeping, as if in direct reference to 13:36. The rebuke to Peter recalls Peter's protestations of loyalty in vss. 29, 31—not that his three failures to stay awake were the three denials predicted in vs. 30, as some have suspected. **One hour:** Was the scene in Gethsemane thought of as three hours long? (See above, p. 866.)

38. Watch and pray: Some editors (see Souter's margin) punctuate "Watch, and pray that . . ."; others, "Watch, and pray, that . . ." But see 13:33. Watching would scarcely serve to keep one from entering temptation (i.e., trial, πειρασμός), but prayer might avail, as vs. 36 takes for granted. **Temptation:** Cf. Matt. 6:13 (the Lord's Prayer), as above. **The spirit truly is ready** (prefer RSV **willing,** πρόθυμον, i.e., eager), **but the flesh is weak:** This sounds like Pauline psychology, but it has behind it the usage of the O.T.—and so has Paul! Luke omits this, along with all the rest of the section.

40. For their eyes were heavy, a perfectly natural feature, some commentators insist, after the hearty Passover meal! But Mark probably thinks of a supernatural drowsiness (καταβαρυνόμενοι, "borne down"), and the rest of the verse reminds us of 9:6.

It is the pathway into life's highest achievement —true sonship to God. There is no prayer so hard to offer. Our own will becomes so dear to us; nothing else seems at the moment so reasonable, or even endurable. Jesus' renunciation of self and the acceptance of God's will give the model of sonship.

Notice that he could make this adjustment to God's will in intense crisis only because it was his constant way of life. He made it at the beginning in the temptation. Against every fair persuasion to seek his own ends he put the will of God. Always, "My meat is to do the will of him that sent me" (John 4:34).

37. *He Said to Peter, "Simon, Are You Asleep? Could You Not Watch One Hour?"*— How was it possible for the three disciples to sleep at such a crisis? How could they be guilty of such an appalling failure of friendship at the time of Jesus' great need? These are unanswered questions.

But we should not exhaust all our wonder over Peter and James and John. From our own experience we know something of sleep in hours that called for vigilant watchfulness. In our secret autobiography there are dark pages that record our failures. Throughout history pressing dangers have threatened—opportuni-

ties, great but fleeting, have knocked at the door —to find the disciples and the church asleep, with heavy eyes and dulled ears. There were the days following Constantine, when the standards of the world were creeping into the church, changing it from a judge of the decaying Roman Empire and a possible saving force into a mere appendage. There was the moment of opportunity in China, on the return of Marco Polo. There was the challenge of Japan, in the late nineteenth century. There was the period from 1919 to 1939, a twenty-year chance of salvation. Surely in all of them Christ was saying, "Could you not watch one hour?"

In personal life vigilance is needed at the hour when poisons enter, deadly to the soul. If the disciples had watched too, and prayed, they would not have made so miserable a showing when the test of loyalty came. Listen to the prayer of Saul Kane in Masefield's poem:

> O truth, O strength, O gleaming share,
> O patient eyes that watch the goal,
> O ploughman of the sinner's soul,
> O Jesus, drive the coulter deep
> To plough my living man from sleep.[2]

[2] From *The Everlasting Mercy.* Copyright, 1911 by John Masefield. Used by permission of The Macmillan Co., The Society of Authors, and Dr. Masefield.

41 And he cometh the third time, and saith unto them, Sleep on now, and take *your* rest: it is enough, the hour is come; behold, the Son of man is betrayed into the hands of sinners.

42 Rise up, let us go; lo, he that betrayeth me is at hand.

43 ¶ And immediately, while he yet spake, cometh Judas, one of the twelve, and with him a great multitude with swords and staves, from the chief priests and the scribes and the elders.

know what to answer him. 41 And he came the third time, and said to them, "Are you still sleeping and taking your rest? It is enough; the hour has come; the Son of man is betrayed into the hands of sinners. 42 Rise, let us be going; see, my betrayer is at hand."

43 And immediately, while he was still speaking, Judas came, one of the twelve, and with him a crowd with swords and clubs, from the chief priests and the scribes

41. Sleep on now (KJV) is unbearably harsh; better, **Are you still sleeping?** (RSV). **It is enough** seemed an incomplete statement, and the Western MSS added τὸ τέλος, perhaps from Luke 22:37 (with what precise meaning is not clear). The meaning is probably, "You have slept long enough!" or "The time is up!" **The hour has come:** "Hour" as in vs. 35, not 37. **Betrayed,** as in 3:19, etc., "delivered up"; cf. 15:15. **Sinners** (contrast the passion announcements) must be the Romans; cf. Acts 2:23; Gal. 2:15.

42. Let us go (KJV), since ἄγωμεν is colloquial, is better rendered **Let us be going** (RSV). **My betrayer** is directly connected with vs. 41. **At hand** is ἤγγικεν, as in 1:15—the usage here throws light on the sense there! Not that Jesus heard him coming, or saw the lights; the Marcan Jesus has direct intuition, as in 2:8 and elsewhere.

9. The Arrest (14:43-50)

43. One of the twelve: As in vs. 10, unnecessary, but added to deepen the sense of horror at his treachery. **Great multitude** (KJV) is heightened, as in Matthew and the later MSS of Mark; better **a crowd** (RSV). The crowd had, not **staves** (KJV; cf. 6:8),

41-42. *The Hour Has Come. . . . Rise, Let Us Be Going.*—The sheer heroism of these words of Jesus makes the blood tingle as we read them after nineteen centuries. They should also remind us of how great a thing it is to recognize the hour for action, an hour which never comes on some calendars, the hour which says, "Now is the time! Rise, let us be going."

So many Christians and members of churches seem willing to spend their lives in "conference," in research, in reverie, in sleep, as here in Gethsemane, or even in worship. They never see or hear the approach of the hour for getting up and going.

Yet such hours do come with their demand for action. They come in connection with every great question of human welfare. The hour came in connection with human slavery—and Wilberforce, Clarkson, Zachary Macaulay said, "We have discussed long enough. Rise, let us be going." The hour came for world evangelization—and Carey and Judson and Morrison rose and went into India, Burma, and China. The hour comes for concrete deed in connection with race brotherhood. The hour for specific action leading to "the federation of the world." Jesus' word is sounding clearly in many realms: "The hour is come. Rise up and meet it."

It is a terrific jolt when a life has to get up out of a recumbent sprawl and go into action. But without a jolt there is no salvation. One is disturbed to note that ecclesiastical language is so largely sedentary. There are so many "seats" compared to arisings. The noun "see," as in the see of St. Peter or Canterbury, comes from the Latin word for "seat." We have episcopal thrones and benches, professors' chairs, the chairman of the committee, always something to sit in! Victory in God's holy war will never be won from chairs. "Rise up, O men of God."

> Give us to build, above the deep intent,
> The deed, the deed.[3]

43. *Judas Came, . . . and with Him a Crowd with Swords and Clubs.*—This is a vivid detail in a graphic story, the sudden swarm in the quiet of the Garden of Gethsemane, the lights, the clamor, the swords and clubs, raised against the unarmed Jesus. But it is more. It is an arresting picture of the repeated futilities of history—the attempt to overcome a spiritual force with physical power. Swords and clubs—against Jesus! No wonder he saw the irony of

[3] John Drinkwater, "A Prayer." Copyright 1919 by John Drinkwater. By permission of the author's estate and Sidgwick & Jackson, Ltd., publishers of the *Collected Poems*.

44 And he that betrayed him had given them a token, saying, Whomsoever I shall kiss, that same is he; take him, and lead *him* away safely.

45 And as soon as he was come, he goeth straightway to him, and saith, Master, Master; and kissed him.

46 ¶ And they laid their hands on him, and took him.

and the elders. 44 Now the betrayer had given them a sign, saying, "The one I shall kiss is the man; seize him and lead him away safely." 45 And when he came, he went up to him at once, and said, "Master!*e*" And he kissed him. 46 And they laid

e Or *Rabbi.*

---

but **clubs** (RSV). This motley company, hastily armed, was apparently from the household of the high priest, to whom Jesus was taken at once (vs. 53). John (18:12) thinks of a band of Roman soldiers, with an officer and attendants; but in Mark it is a private gang, and this is much the more probable. **Chief priests . . . scribes . . . elders:** The group who, in Mark, were responsible for Jesus' arrest and condemnation.

44. Kiss: The usual greeting of a rabbi by his young disciple (cf. vs. 45); but here it was used as a ruse, to hold Jesus until he could be seized. **Safely** (ἀσφαλῶς), i.e., "see that he does not escape"; or preferably, "see that he is taken to the high priest without injury," since further responsibility was his, not Judas'. There is no suggestion that Jesus might work a miracle (as in Matt. 26:53) and so evade them.

---

it. "You have come out as though against a man of violence, a robber, with swords and clubs to capture *me!*"

History has taught nothing more clearly than this, that spiritual power in the world cannot be crushed with clubs. Men might as well try to beat down a ray of sunshine with a bludgeon. That is exactly what a physical assault on a spiritual force is, a battering away at God's sunshine. The sunshine always wins.

Yet the attempt has been made over and over, and is still being made. There is the long history of the struggle of Rome to stamp out Christianity; the long, sorry tale of persecutions within Christianity, the Inquisition, the burnings, imprisonments, and lynchings; the physical repressions of every sort. Clubs have inflicted infinite pain, but they have never vanquished Jesus or any of God's truth.

This remembrance makes for great reliance. After three days he rose again. After every physical victory of force in the hands of evil there comes a resurrection of the truth that makes men free. Labor in the Lord is never in vain.

This remembrance should also be a warning. It should warn us to be vigilant lest we ourselves be found in our time among the company who are trying to repress God's truth with swords and clubs. In the cry of the oppressed of the earth, of race and class, there is a spiritual power. Their complaints of injustice are very often the very voice of God speaking through him who said, "He has sent me to proclaim release to the captives and . . . to set at liberty those who are oppressed" (Luke 4:18). If our attitude is simply that of irritation at disturb-

ance, if our only solution is the futile one of "cracking down," we join the mob who came into Gethsemane against Jesus.

45. *He Went Up to Him at Once, and Said, "Master!" And He Kissed Him.*—The last refinement of treachery—making the word of homage and the kiss of affection the secret sign to his Master's captors! No wonder this kiss of Judas has become the supreme symbol of treason.

Surely it has never been matched in all the dark betrayals of history. Yet when we analyze just what it was, we see that there are a great number of actions which fall into exactly the same class—the gestures of homage and devotion which go hand in hand with disloyalty; the formal honor paid to Jesus, accompanied by an actual denial of his teaching and spirit. How much he has had of that through the years! This dark night in the garden was only the first of a long succession of traitors' kisses.

The company of Christ's disciples, organized into a church, has said "Master" in many versions—in creedal statement ("Very God of very God, Begotten, not made"), in music and pageantry—and at the same time, by the blessing it has put on the cruelty and rapine of religious wars, it has basely betrayed him. It has cried "Master" while making a bitter fight to retain all the evils of human slavery. Those days are over, we say. Yes, thank God, they are. But other forms of homage hand in hand with denial are still much in date. Some Christians still stand on the side of exploitation, fighting blindly and bitterly for privilege, denying in their whole spirit and action him who said, "Come unto me, all ye that labor and are heavy laden" (Matt. 11:28). Others still say

47 And one of them that stood by drew a sword, and smote a servant of the high priest, and cut off his ear.

48 And Jesus answered and said unto them, Are ye come out, as against a thief, with swords and *with* staves to take me?

49 I was daily with you in the temple teaching, and ye took me not: but the Scriptures must be fulfilled.

50 And they all forsook him, and fled.

51 And there followed him a certain young man, having a linen cloth cast about *his* naked *body;* and the young men laid hold on him:

52 And he left the linen cloth, and fled from them naked.

hands on him and seized him. 47 But one of those who stood by drew his sword, and struck the slave of the high priest and cut off his ear. 48 And Jesus said to them, "Have you come out as against a robber, with swords and clubs to capture me? 49 Day after day I was with you in the temple teaching, and you did not seize me. But let the scriptures be fulfilled." 50 And they all forsook him, and fled.

51 And a young man followed him, with nothing but a linen cloth about his body; and they seized him, 52 but he left the linen cloth and ran away naked.

47. **One of them:** John (18:10) says it was Peter, and also names the injured slave—a natural development of tradition. In Mark it is only one of the bystanders who draws a sword, but presumably a disciple. Luke adds that Jesus touched the slave's ear and healed it—a most improbable detail, thoroughly hagiographical in character. How could the arrest have proceeded after this? How did they come to be bearing swords on Passover night? (Cf. Luke 22:35-38.) Perhaps these were only the long knives of the peasantry (so Loisy), such as the later sicarii carried under their tunics.

48-50. Not **a thief** (KJV) but an armed **robber** (RSV); in 15:27 Jesus is crucified with robbers. **In the temple,** as in chs. 11–12; cf. John 18:20. **The scriptures,** as in 9:12; 14:21; etc. **They all forsook him,** in literal fulfillment of vs. 27, and in spite of the disciples' assurance in vs. 31*b*.

10. The Flight of a Young Man (14:51-52)

This youth has often been identified with Mark, and the incident interpreted as "the artist's signature in the corner of his painting"—overlooking the statement of Papias (see Intro.) that Mark "neither heard the Lord nor followed him" (though this could be understood to mean merely that he was not a disciple). But it seems equally possible that this was one more detail suggested by the O.T. (Amos 2:16). **Naked** does not mean without any clothing, but clad only in his undergarment or tunic (cf. John 21:7).

"Master" with all the exquisite aid of aesthetics in worship, while they shamefully betray the Elder Brother of all men by their attitudes of contempt and superiority to people of races other than their own.

But why keep looking outward? "I thank thee, that I am not as other men are" *(Luke 18:11).* Turn our gaze inward. We hail Jesus "Master," in public profession, in worship, in private and sincere acknowledgment. But is he the master of our inward thoughts, our secret desires and ambitions, the master of our time, with the right of command?

47. *But One of Those Who Stood by Drew His Sword, and Struck the Slave of the High Priest.*—The Gospel of John identifies Peter as the man who drew a sword. Whoever he was, his emotions were better than his thinking. By his devotion to Jesus he was moved to a deed at

utter variance with all that Jesus taught. His swinging sword in the garden ought to be clear evidence that emotion in a good cause is never enough. Clear thinking is also needed. Moreover, of course, the incident underlines the fact that violence is never effective in the spiritual realm. The means must be harmonious with the end sought, or the means will defeat the end. Unspiritual and unethical means have defeated spiritual ends over and over again in history, making black and bloody pages in the Christian story. There is hardly any evil means which has not been used for the ostensible promotion of religion—war, gambling, murder, corrupt political and economic alliances. The same danger of evil means to good ends is met in personal life. Genuinely Christian methods of action often seem slow and unreliable; so people reach out for something that seems to be quicker

53 ¶ And they led Jesus away to the high priest: and with him were assembled all the chief priests and the elders and the scribes.

53 And they led Jesus to the high priest; and all the chief priests and the elders

---

11. JESUS BEFORE THE HIGH PRIEST (14:53-65)

This has often been described as the "Jewish trial," after which followed the "Roman trial" in ch. 15. And it is true that Mark, like the later Synoptists and many other early church writers, tries to shift the responsibility for the death of Jesus from Roman to Jewish shoulders, or at least to deepen the guilt of the Jewish authorities and lighten that of the procurator. But even in the Gospel of John, where intense hatred of "the Jews" is frequently given expression, the trial before the high priest is only an examination (John 18:19), and it is Pilate who has the real authority and bears the full responsibility (cf. John 19:11), though he tries repeatedly to release Jesus. In Mark the high priest and his colleagues actually condemn Jesus to death (vs. 64).

The objections to the view that this was a legal Jewish trial are many and weighty: the session at night and during a festival, the lack of a full quorum, the immediate condemnation and execution, also during a festival, the failure to call witnesses in defense, the penalty, even the charge itself (a claim to messiahship was not "blasphemy") —all these and more details (fourteen have been counted) are in direct contravention of the procedure laid down in tractate Sanhedrin of the Mishnah. It has been argued that this tractate reflects later theory, but the argument is unsound; the material in Sanhedrin, for the most part, is traditional—as much so as that in Middoth (the temple measurements) and other data from the old days in ante bellum Jerusalem. Instead of being a regular trial before the Sanhedrin (vs. 55), what took place was probably a private examination *in camera,* conducted secretly by the powerful enemies who had Jesus in their hands and were determined to put him out of the way by the surest and swiftest means available. This turned out to be denunciation before Pilate, in the hope of landing the whole movement in disgrace and making it impossible for his following to continue.

53-54. An editorial transition, preparing for the session of the Sanhedrin (vss. 55-56) and Peter's denials (vss. 66-72). The **servants** (KJV) —this is better than **guards** (RSV) — were presumably slaves in the high priest's household, as in vs. 66 and possibly 70.

---

and more sure, betraying at once their lack of faith in the profession they have made, and more than that, the faith itself (see on vs. 43; 3:23).

53. They Led Jesus to the High Priest; and All the Chief Priests and the Elders and the Scribes Were Assembled.—In the Exeg. the reasons for regarding this "trial" of Jesus before Jewish authorities as a preliminary examination, rather than as a formal trial before the full Sanhedrin, are given in detail. But so regarding it does not change its importance or dramatic quality. Here Jesus confronted the clique of religious authorities who at last had him in their power and were determined to bring about his death by denouncing him to the Roman governor.

Two aspects of this examination, among many, stand out memorably, and have pertinence for all time. One is that it was not really Jesus who was on trial before the religious institution; it was the institution which was on trial before him. That is always true when an authority which is inherent and genuine confronts a group of self-constituted judges. Beethoven is not really on trial before the concert audience; it is the audience which is on trial. Raphael does not await the verdict of the art class; it is the class which is in the dock. Shakespeare is not subject to sentence before the sophomore class in high school studying *Macbeth,* or before any reader; the reader is on trial. So here Jesus, with his self-authenticating religious and moral insights, and the towering stature of his personality, is not on trial before these assembled phylacteries. They are on trial. We get a graphic picture of this in Munkacsy's popular painting, "Christ Before Pilate." As we look at Jesus' face gazing on the baffled Pilate, we realize that the picture should be called "Pilate Before Christ."

Today, in one sense, Jesus is on trial before our civilization. Many are examining him to determine whether he has any place in this world so different from his. Diligent probers are rendering their verdict in the words Matthew

54 And Peter followed him afar off, even into the palace of the high priest: and he sat with the servants, and warmed himself at the fire.

55 And the chief priests and all the council sought for witness against Jesus to put him to death; and found none.

56 For many bare false witness against him, but their witness agreed not together.

and the scribes were assembled. **54** And Peter had followed him at a distance, right into the courtyard of the high priest; and he was sitting with the guards, and warming himself at the fire. **55** Now the chief priests and the whole council sought testimony against Jesus to put him to death; but they found none. **56** For many bore false witness against him, and their witness

---

55-56. The whole council numbered seventy-one, in the Great Sanhedrin of Jerusalem, an improbable number at such a time. The phrase is probably editorial, with the intention of making this a legal trial. **Sought testimony:** The purpose was obvious: they had already decided to get rid of Jesus and **put him to death. But they found none,** for not only was he innocent of any crime, but the kind of testimony they wanted was not forthcoming. Moreover, the agreement of two witnesses was a requirement in Jewish law; but **their witness did not agree.** How the author knows this is not clear; even Peter was **afar off** (vs. 54), in the outer court (vs. 66). Of course information about secret trials (e.g., by the Gestapo) has a way of leaking out; but many scholars suspect that this detail, and others, have been added by imagination, under the influence of the O.T. (e.g., Ps. 27:12: "False witnesses have risen against me"). In the earliest days, while the O.T. was still the church's only Bible, no one hesitated to look for details of the passion narrative in various parts of the O.T., where, it was assumed, it had been predicted. Scripture was as reliable a source as tradition, and the two tended toward agreement—i.e., the tradition was conformed to the assumed prediction.

Arnold uses of Goethe, "Thou ailest here and here." But in the deepest and final sense it is not Jesus on trial. Our whole civilization is on trial before his judgments. If we fail to meet them, if in our blindness we condemn him to be merely a peripheral figure in our world, we "shall all likewise perish." Albert Einstein put the nature of that trial vividly when he said, in answer to a question, "I do not know what weapons will be used in World War III. But I do know what will be used in World War IV —stone clubs." Unless we are "members one of another" we will not be members of anything.

A second aspect of this trial which calls for continual remembrance is that Jesus was confronting the religious institution of his time and nation. That fact presents searching questions to all religious institutions of every age, particularly to the churches of Christ. Why did the religious institution fail so terribly in its hour of visitation? Are there any causes of that failure which may be present in institutions which bear Christ's own name, his church?

One hardly needs to put the question. To begin with, the Jewish religious establishment had substituted itself for God's purpose in his revelation to the Jewish people. The great prophetic heritage of Israel had become quite secondary to the fortunes of an entrenched institution. That has often happened to Christian churches. It can easily happen. When it does

happen, where the prosperity and security of the institution bulk larger than its prophetic responsibility, the church takes its place with the Sanhedrin as an obstruction to God's will, rather than as an instrument of it. Those are terrible words of Stephen Spender's: "The church blotting out the sun." It can happen.

Besides, the hierarchy feared the loss of privilege, financial as well as political, far more than it feared God. A high, redeeming fear had been traded for a small, damning one. The whole crowd assembled on the judgment seat was afraid of a disturber, and Jesus was emphatically that. His forthright antitheses, "Ye have heard, . . . but I say unto you," were upsetting. Away with him! When order and tradition and peculiar advantage become more important than God's fresh revelations, a church becomes moribund.

In all these dangers Jesus' warning "Watch ye and pray, lest ye enter into temptation" applies. There must be the renewal of the revolutionary sources of our gospel. Our God must be the God, not of the dead, but of the living.

56. *For Many Bore False Witness Against Him, and Their Witness Did Not Agree.*—It happened then. It is still happening. Doubtless it will always happen—false witnesses against Jesus and his cause, and witnesses who do not agree among themselves. It was impossible for the chief priests to get credible testimony

57 And there arose certain, and bare false witness against him, saying,

58 We heard him say, I will destroy this temple that is made with hands, and within three days I will build another made without hands.

59 But neither so did their witness agree together.

60 And the high priest stood up in the midst, and asked Jesus, saying, Answerest thou nothing? what *is it which* these witness against thee?

did not agree. **57** And some stood up and bore false witness against him, saying, **58** "We heard him say, 'I will destroy this temple that is made with hands, and in three days I will build another, not made with hands.'" **59** Yet not even so did their testimony agree. **60** And the high priest stood up in the midst, and asked Jesus, "Have you no answer to make? What is it

---

57-59. The charge was a repeated one in the early church; cf. the charge against Stephen in Acts 6:13-14 (also brought by "false witnesses"). Various attempts to deal with the charge are recorded in the N.T., e.g., John 2:18-22, where it is interpreted as a misunderstanding of a reference to the Resurrection, and the failure of the testimony here (vs. 59). It is not improbable that the interpretation in John has influenced the text here (as in 13:2, where D W O.L. add "and in the course of three days another will be raised up without hands"), and that it originally ran as in Matt. 26:61 (cf. Mark 15:29!). So in fact some MSS read—but perhaps under the influence of Matthew. (Luke omits vss. 55-61a.) The only justification for the false charge in Mark is 13:1-2.

60-61a. Jesus is silent—hardly a feature drawn from Isa. 53:7, which would be canceled out by Ps. 22:2, but as in 15:4 a historical reminiscence. Jesus does not open his mouth in self-defense; his way has been "committed perfectly unto the Lord": he is the perfect martyr, who has already accepted his death in advance. So Mark: historically it may signify that Jesus was aware of the futility of defense, and said nothing. **What is it that**

---

against him. In their determination to crush him they took anything. Manifest perjury was no bar. Their sacred scripture which affirmed that "lying lips are abomination to the LORD" (Prov. 12:22) was nullified for the occasion.

Note one great service which the report of this trial ought to render. The verdict was given before the examination started. It was not so much a legal tribunal as a lynching mob. They had "prejudged" the case. It ought to startle us to recall that that is the linguistic root of our word "prejudice." It is from the Latin— judgment before the time, before the evidence is examined. If we want to know what a prejudice is, what vicious things it can result in, here is the picture. It was the thing which did Jesus to death. It is a thing which does his cause to death.

We are painfully familiar with the current styles of false witness against Jesus and his gospel in our world today. One group of witnesses swears that Christianity is a subversive influence in the state, that its dangerous "radicalism" will bring anarchy. The truth is that the only secure foundation for a political order with a right to survive is the righteousness which exalts a nation. Another group of witnesses testifies with scorn that Christianity is a romantic delusion, a fairy tale with no real foundation, a mere

"escape mechanism." The truth of human experience has been that it is the high "romance" of life, yes, but more real than granite. Others testify that Christian teaching narrows and cripples life, spoiling freedom. The truth is, as millions can testify, that it has brought abundant life, widening and fulfilling.

What successors our present world has to witnesses that could not even agree among themselves! Whatever difficulties the text of Mark presents about disagreeing witnesses at this trial (see Exeg.), there is no question about the disagreeing witness against Jesus, his gospel, and his church, in past history and today. From the far left we hear the Communist shout that religion is "the opiate of the people." From the far right comes the equally vociferous shout of the reactionary, that Christianity, when taken seriously, is veritable dynamite, rather than chloroform. These ought to cancel each other nicely. Some testify with disgust that Christianity is too "otherworldly." People who attend church only once a year and hear a sermon on immortality always complain that the church is too "otherworldly." Others charge that it is not "otherworldly" enough, far too secular. Some charge that the church is too dogmatic. From the other side comes the vehement charge that the church is losing its dogma.

61 But he held his peace, and answered nothing. Again the high priest asked him, and said unto him, Art thou the Christ, the Son of the Blessed?

62 And Jesus said, I am: and ye shall see the Son of man sitting on the right hand of power, and coming in the clouds of heaven.

63 Then the high priest rent his clothes, and saith, What need we any further witnesses?

that these men testify against you?" 61 But he was silent and made no answer. Again the high priest asked him, "Are you the Christ, the Son of the Blessed?" 62 And Jesus said, "I am; and you will see the Son of man sitting at the right hand of Power, and coming with the clouds of heaven." 63 And the high priest tore his mantle, and said, "Why do we still need

---

these men testify against you? The high priest hoped that Jesus would be exasperated by these charges, and thus be driven to convict himself by what he might admit in his reply—a ruse not unknown even in modern courts of law and at police examinations.

61b-64. It is extremely difficult to accept vss. 61b-62 as an authentic record of a trial. **The Son of the Blessed** is only a quasi-Jewish equivalent of **the Christ,** and ought to read: "Are you the Messiah? Are you the Son of the Blessed?" (i.e., do you claim to be?) since Jews did not view the Messiah as "Son of God." But both the question and the answer presuppose the Christian view, according to which the Christ *was* the Son of the Blessed One (i.e., God) and was *also* the Son of man who should come with the clouds of heaven. This synthesis is the climax of Mark's Christology, but it was also the faith of the church. Furthermore, such a claim—roundly affirmed in Mark; contrast the circumlocution in Matthew and the verbal fencing, in good Hellenistic style, in Luke!—did not amount to **blasphemy** save on the Christian assumption of practical identity of Jesus with God (cf. John 10:33); it would not be blasphemy in the eyes of a Jewish court. But of course this was no legal trial, and in their eagerness to get Jesus to convict himself the high priest and his associates would not hesitate. Blasphemy, at least in Mark (cf. 2:7; 7:22), has a wider definition than the technical one in the O.T. and in Jewish law. The high priest **tore his mantle** because he had heard "words of blasphemy or something spoken against God," as Jerome notes. **They all,** as in vs. 55, means the whole Sanhedrin; Mark represents the decision as unanimous.

All these add up to eloquent if unintended tribute to the universal quality of Christ's gospel.

61. *But He Was Silent and Made No Answer.* —There could be no more impressive picture of the dignity of Jesus. The angry loquacity of the high priest won what it deserved—silence. Couple this with Mark's later picture of Jesus before Pilate: "But Jesus made no further answer, so that Pilate wondered" (15:5). And well he might wonder at the calm dignity of that silent figure!

The great Debater did not debate here. Think of what Jesus, that master of controversy, might have said. The man who had, again and again, impaled the scribes and Pharisees on the horns of an inescapable dilemma, who had punctured his opponents with sharp questions for which there was no answer—he could have completely toppled over the flimsy scaffolding of lies erected against him. But he was silent. And obviously he chose the better part. Doubtless he knew that before this crowd there would be no use. But beyond that there may well have been the feeling that he had done his

teaching; he had brought the good news of the kingdom; he was ready for the final act of his ministry to men. Let it stand.

It is an impressive picture of the superior power of silence over words, on many an occasion, the superior power of deed over argument. The church will never forget that never man so spoke as Jesus. It also ought never to forget that never was man so powerfully silent. One lesson comes from this with close relevance to the whole ministry of the church and the Christian propaganda. It is a warning against allowing the energy which might have gone into positive saving ministry to be drawn off into loquacious defense and controversy. The positive deeds of effective service in Christ's name do not need words of defense. Against them there is no successful refutation. If half the time and strength which Christians have given to noisy and verbose argument had been given to quiet, insistent, continuous, virile ministries of love, the cause of Christ would have carried a far greater power of persuasion. The true "defender of the faith" is not the debater with

64 Ye have heard the blasphemy: what think ye? And they all condemned him to be guilty of death.

65 And some began to spit on him, and to cover his face, and to buffet him, and to say unto him, Prophesy: and the servants did strike him with the palms of their hands.

66 ¶ And as Peter was beneath in the palace, there cometh one of the maids of the high priest:

witnesses? 64 You have heard his blasphemy. What is your decision?" And they all condemned him as deserving death. 65 And some began to spit on him, and to cover his face, and to strike him, saying to him, "Prophesy!" And the guards received him with blows.

66 And as Peter was below in the courtyard, one of the maids of the high priest

---

65. **Some:** Presumably some of the slaves, who still held Jesus bound (Luke 22:63), not some of the Sanhedrin, or of the clique who had him in their power. The covering of Jesus' face was not as a condemned criminal but was part of the Jewish "mockery" (parallel to the Roman in 15:16-20). **Prophesy** has no reference to vs. 58, but is explained by the parallels in identical words: "Who is it that struck you?" This agreement of Matthew and Luke makes it probable that the question was once in the text of Mark—where it is still found, in some MSS. **The guards** (better **servants,** as in KJV) **received him with blows:** Mark alone has this statement, which apparently means that the servants struck him (cf. Luke 22:63-65), not that the servants themselves received blows in some kind of melee (cf. the parallel in 15:19).

12. Peter's Denials (14:66-72)

66-68. **Below in the courtyard,** i.e., of the high priest's house (cf. vs. 54). **Warming himself** (cf. vs. 54): Some scholars have argued that vs. 66 is a repetition of vs. 54, and

---

words, but the one who does the acts of faith. Jesus' silence here is in accord with his answer to John's messengers. He let the works be their own argument, "The blind receive their sight and the lame walk, lepers are cleansed and the deaf hear, and the dead are raised up" (Matt. 11:5). Let the church be able to point to lives made whole and the dead in sin raised. That will be the eloquence of deed.

64. *They All Condemned Him as Deserving Death.*—They all condemned him—and not a single one really heard him or saw him! It was not merely that they were voting as a party machine, though that was true. They all condemned him for reasons that had nothing to do with the evidence and nothing to do with justice. They had other reasons that did not appear on the record.

So has it often been with Jesus. People express grave doubts about him. They cannot accept the divinity of Christ, they say, because they cannot convince their intellect. That may be true. But it may also be true that the block is not primarily intellectual but moral; that there is something in their lives, ways of conduct, which would have to be radically changed by faith in Christ. There are times when intellectual skepticism is just a seemly "front" for the real difficulty which lies behind in the moral realm. So men condemn him, as he was condemned here in Jerusalem—unheard really, actually unseen!

65. *And Some Began to Spit on Him.*—This is revolting to our thought. Yet such details, and others to follow in ch. 15, do a greatly needed service. Men have allegorized the Cross and carried it into the realm of symbolism to such an extent that we need the ugly, brutal descriptions of scourging and crucifixion to remind us of what Jesus endured. The Cross was not allegory or symbol. It was shame and agony. The words in Hebrews, "endured the cross, despising the shame" (Heb. 12:2), had stark, excruciating meaning. Spitting on a person is a primitive, brutal form of contempt. It has largely passed away in our more polite days; but it has its moral and spiritual equivalents. These hired ruffians of the high priest were expressing their scorn in the most complete way their vulgar minds could think of. Men heap upon him the same kind of affront when he is not allowed to count at all in the shaping of their lives; when he is not a serious contender for their allegiance; when he is treated as a sentimental figure in a storybook, a good enough subject for pictures and songs, but too naïve for anybody to pay any attention to him. It's the old, old crowd in the high priest's quarters.

66-72. *And . . . Peter Was Below in the Courtyard.*—This is one of the most gripping

67 And when she saw Peter warming himself, she looked upon him, and said, And thou also wast with Jesus of Nazareth.

68 But he denied, saying, I know not, neither understand I what thou sayest. And he went out into the porch; and the cock crew.

69 And a maid saw him again, and began to say to them that stood by, This is *one* of them.

70 And he denied it again. And a little after, they that stood by said again to Peter, Surely thou art *one* of them: for thou art a Galilean, and thy speech agreeth *thereto*.

71 But he began to curse and to swear, *saying,* I know not this man of whom ye speak.

came; 67 and seeing Peter warming himself, she looked at him, and said, "You also were with the Nazarene, Jesus." 68 But he denied it, saying, "I neither know nor understand what you mean." And he went out into the gateway.*f* 69 And the maid saw him, and began again to say to the bystanders, "This man is one of them." 70 But again he denied it. And after a little while again the bystanders said to Peter, "Certainly you are one of them; for you are a Galilean." 71 But he began to invoke a curse on himself and to swear, "I do not

f Or *fore-court.* Some ancient authorities add *and the cock crowed.*

---

shows that vss. 55-65 are an intrusion into the narrative, like 2:5*b*-10. But the repetition is not very striking—indeed is perfectly natural. It has also been argued that the present section is too highly stylized to be a Petrine "reminiscence"; it may be stylized, but the story would never have been told, or repeated, or written down by Mark, unless it had been substantially true. But it is told very differently in John. **You also were with . . . Jesus:** A temperate charge, and one would think undeniable; but Peter's nerve had failed completely, and he denied it. **I neither know nor understand,** i.e., what was being said; it is not a denial of any knowledge of Jesus—that came later, in vs. 71. On the double cockcrow see above on 14:30.

69-70a. The same **maid** (contrast Matthew and Luke, also John), her suspicions now aroused, pursued him further. The detail has complete verisimilitude.

70b-71. The clause **thy speech agreeth thereto** is probably a gloss, based on Matt. 26:73. Galilean Aramaic differed from Judean (see G. H. Dalman, *Grammatik des Jüdisch Palästinischem Aramäisch* [Leipzig: J. C. Hinrichs, 1905]). **To curse** ("anathematize," or **invoke a curse**) usually has some object: himself (so RSV)? the day of his birth? his luck? The point was not his swearing, but his complete denial that he even knew Jesus. This was the climax; his denial of his Lord could reach no darker depths.

---

stories of the Bible, and one of the best loved. It comes close to everyone who has ever failed—and whom does that leave out? It is so vividly told that in the last words of the story, **he broke down and wept,** one can almost hear the sobs.

Many thousands of sermons have been preached on the text "Peter followed him afar off" (vs. 54). There is the danger of remote discipleship, and the danger is real. Yet Peter deserves some credit for following at all. That is more than the rest of the disciples did.

What a story it would have been if he had followed all the way, not at a distance, but close, as a fellow prisoner with Jesus! It might have happened. Just a dozen words added to the record would have made a tremendous difference—"And they bound Peter and Jesus together and led them, side by side, into the high priest's house." How many hundreds and thousands of sermons would have been preached

on that! What a subject for Raphael or da Vinci! Of course if there had been **no denial,** one of the most moving accounts in the N.T. would have been missing. Peter's failure, **Christ's** forgiveness, and the final restoration as told in the Gospel of John, have meant much to all who blunder and compromise. It brings the hope that a life gone to smash may yet be made over. But how splendidly would the other have read!

And what prevented it? Some factors are in clear visibility, and they speak their urgent warning to us. Peter was hit by a panic. Menzies uses a striking word in connection with the desertion of the disciples. He says they were "concussed." It is a word we rarely if ever use, though the noun "concussion" is common. It means to be shocked by collision, resulting in lowered functional activity. That was what happened to Peter, mentally and morally. Jesus

72 And the second time the cock crew. And Peter called to mind the word that Jesus said unto him, Before the cock crow twice, thou shalt deny me thrice. And when he thought thereon, he wept.

15 And straightway in the morning the chief priests held a consultation with the elders and scribes and the whole council, and bound Jesus, and carried *him* away, and delivered *him* to Pilate.

know this man of whom you speak." 72 And immediately the cock crowed a second time. And Peter remembered how Jesus had said to him, "Before the cock crows twice, you will deny me three times." And he broke down and wept.

15 And as soon as it was morning the chief priests, with the elders and scribes, and the whole council held a consultation; and they bound Jesus and led him away and delivered him to Pilate.

---

72. The second time: See on 14:30. Prefer RSV, **And he broke down and wept,** for καὶ ἐπιβαλὼν ἔκλαιεν. Both parallels have ἐξελθών ("when he had gone out"), and the text is not absolutely certain. **When he thought thereon** (KJV) is weak and improbable, and misses the tragic terseness of Mark's style.

13. JESUS BEFORE PILATE (15:1-5)

This section opens as if nothing had happened since the arrest (14:46, cf. vs. 53*a*); this has led some writers to assume that the intervening sections have been introduced into an earlier narrative which lacked them (see above, p. 866). If so, Jesus must have remained in custody in the high priest's house during the remainder of the night; but that his enemies, having him in their power, should do nothing with him that night seems most improbable. However, the consultation in the morning seems strange after 14:64.

---

had been deeply concerned over the possibility of his breaking under panic. The sudden collision with danger found him unprepared, disintegrated. His resistance was weakened also by being in the wrong environment. Separated from his Master, he was among Christ's enemies, in the high priest's courtyard, with the guards, warming himself at their fire. The stage was set for the lowering of spiritual morale, a frequent prelude to defeat. Peter underestimated too the power of ridicule, of crowd pressure, his own reluctance to be singled out as an exception. Finally, as Jesus had been lost to sight in the tumult, and danger began to threaten, Peter had come to think more and more of himself and his own security, and less and less about Jesus.

Each of these forces acts on every disciple. Each of them is something we must prepare to face. Not one of them can be met without tiptoe vigilance and a sustained relationship with God, that we may be strengthened with might by his Spirit—against panic, hostile environment, crowd pressure, and self-concern.

72. *And He Broke Down and Wept.*—It was the bitterest heartache that life can have, grief and shame over the betrayal of love. Doubtless with Peter there was the added shame that the very thing he had protested could not happen, had happened. He had denied his Lord. With these sobs he makes his exit from the story in

Mark. But not from Luke and John. In Luke, after the Resurrection, Jesus appears to Peter alone (Luke 24:34); and in John there is the story of his complete restoration (John 21:15-17). His sorrow was not the end, but the real beginning.

In Christian experience great living begins in tears. It is God's starting point. When Peter broke down and wept, all pride, of which he had much, and all self-sufficiency and self-trust dropped away from him. Only humility and shame were left. The deep mood of repentance, his sorrow for sin, made possible an utter dependence on God, which is the beginning of sonship. There is a true N.T. insight in Thomas Moore's poem *Paradise and the Peri.* One who is charged with bringing to heaven the world's greatest treasure finally comes with a tear of repentance, which proves to be the most precious thing that earth can produce. It is indeed. Sorrow for sin, followed by repentance, removes the pride and self-regard which block God's entrance into life. Man's extremity, the low spot of his self-revulsion, is God's first real opportunity.

15:1. *They Bound Jesus and Led Him Away and Delivered Him to Pilate.*—A sorry parade, not from Jesus' standpoint but from that of the chief priests, with the elders and scribes, and the whole council. For here were the religious authorities turning over to the political power

2 And Pilate asked him, Art thou the King of the Jews? And he answering said unto him, Thou sayest *it.*

3 And the chief priests accused him of many things; but he answered nothing.

4 And Pilate asked him again, saying, Answerest thou nothing? behold how many things they witness against thee.

2 And Pilate asked him, "Are you the King of the Jews?" And he answered him, "You have said so." 3 And the chief priests accused him of many things. 4 And Pilate again asked him, "Have you no answer to make? See how many charges they bring

---

The question whether or not the Sanhedrin had "the power of life and death" under the procurators is often debated (cf. John 18:31); but it is somewhat irrelevant, since the Sanhedrin is not represented as even attempting to carry out any sentence. Jesus is denounced before the Roman governor, who proceeds to try him, not as one already condemned by the Jewish court but *ex novo*. It is extraordinary that the charge (vs. 2) is one not even hinted at hitherto; since it was the charge upon which he was condemned, it must have been the main one involved (cf. Luke 23:2-5). Yet Pilate does not take it seriously (cf. vss. 9-10; John 18:38*b*), and in the end it is the sheer pressure of the mob, stirred up by the priests (vs. 11), that forces the weak hand of the governor (vs. 15).

15:2. The question is introduced abruptly, before the charge has been preferred, and is answered by a circumlocution in striking contrast to the round affirmation of 14:62— as if Jesus were unwilling to accept the secular and political title now attributed to him. The σὺ λέγεις (**you have said so**) can even be taken as a question (as Hort suggested; see Grant, *Earliest Gospel,* p. 184), and it is not impossible that the whole verse has been added by Mark to the older traditional passion narrative. The affirmation of kingship, which could be understood politically, here parallels the affirmation of messiahship (in the "Son of man" sense) in 14:62, and both have been suspected of being secondary, i.e., intrusions into the older narrative. At least it may be said that vs. 3 continues as if vs. 2 did not exist, and that if Jesus had simply replied "Yes" the trial would have ended there and then.

3-5. On Jesus' silence see on 14:60. One would like to know what the **many things** were with which the chief priests charged him; Luke 23:2, 5 and various hints and innuendoes in John 18:33–19:16 help to provide the answer.

---

an issue which was primarily religious and was their own responsibility. Of course the reason was simple: they had decided, before their flimsy investigation, to rush Jesus to execution. They had no authority to do it themselves, and probably did not want to soil their holy hands with such things. Let the Romans do it! So they led him to Pilate. "Here, Pilate," they said in effect, "this is your affair." That was an evasive lie. Jesus was their affair. They are not to be harshly condemned because they did not acclaim Jesus as Messiah. Indeed there is real question whether Jesus, publicly, before this trial, ever proclaimed himself Messiah. But even their dull eyes should have seen that he was a prophet, in the high tradition of their great heritage; he was a righteous man who had done works of mercy. He was a religious issue, definitely their responsibility as the religious authorities. But they turned him over to the political power.

It is the same kind of shameful evasion, often just as cowardly, when religious groups and authorities turn over to the state, to political

and secular powers, final decisions on questions that are definitely religious, and definitely their own responsibility. Jesus has been sent to Pilate far too many times. Take, for instance, the big question of the training of the nation's children in religion and morals. Far too lightly Christian churches have turned the matter over to the state. Pilate has bungled it, as he bungled the issue of Jesus. Religious and moral instruction has been banned from the public schools, the impression being given that they are of no importance whatever. Our present spiritual illiteracy and moral confusion have resulted. Dim-sighted and timid church people have allowed the principle of the separation of church and state to be pushed far beyond the original intent of that doctrine.

Questions in which Christianity has a great concern have been limply handed over to political and economic powers with an evasive apology: "This is a complex matter. You take it, Pilate." For many years child labor was handed over to employers and legislatures, as though

5 But Jesus yet answered nothing; so that Pilate marveled.

6 Now at *that* feast he released unto them one prisoner, whomsoever they desired.

7 And there was *one* named Barabbas, *which lay* bound with them that had made insurrection with him, who had committed murder in the insurrection.

8 And the multitude crying aloud began to desire *him to do* as he had ever done unto them.

against you." 5 But Jesus made no further answer, so that Pilate wondered.

6 Now at the feast he used to release for them any one prisoner whom they asked. 7 And among the rebels in prison, who had committed murder in the insurrection, there was a man called Bar-ab′bas. 8 And the crowd came up and began to ask Pilate

14. Jesus Condemned to Death (15:6-15)

6-7. There is no other evidence than that of the Gospels for the "custom" (Matt. 27:15; John 18:39) or "requirement" (late texts of Luke 23:17) of releasing a prisoner at Passover. It was a Roman custom at the *lectisternia* (Livy V. 13), and may well have been a local usage in Palestine. It is scarcely necessary to brand the incident here as fictitious. We know nothing more of **Barabbas.** Some MSS of Matt. 27:16 read "Jesus Barabbas," which Burkitt thought original. Nor do we know anything about **the insurrection;** but from the pages of Josephus we may gather that revolts were common in Judea in those days.

the church said: "We are not interested in children. Our Master was, but we don't agree with him." So the growth of military power, with all its threat to life, has been viewed with unconcern by many, and handed over to Pilate. Whatever is God's affair, the welfare of men, women, and children, is the responsibility of the Christian church, and no church may sidestep it (see on 12:13-17).

5. But Jesus Made No Further Answer, So that Pilate Wondered.—This picture of Pilate engaged in wonder has great interest. It is one of many indications that his mental machinery was at least turning over during his examination of Jesus. His mind was not drugged with hatred as were the minds of the chief priests and other plotters. The trouble was that he did not wonder deeply enough, as he never did anything, in all the trial, deeply enough. That was probably a fatal flaw in his whole life and character, as it has been in many another. He did not wonder deeply enough, nor about the right things; his wonder did not issue, as all true wonder should, in thought and act. He was not used to having the accused answer him with silence. So he wondered about it. But it was wonder of a superficial sort, for which "curiosity" would be a more precise word. He never really wondered about the man Jesus; there was no stirring of the mind that might lead on to exploration and understanding.

Perhaps we should give some consideration to the right use of wonder. There are two levels. One is "to marvel, to be affected with awe."

The other is "to feel curiosity about a thing." Pilate stayed on the lower level. The upper level brings an enlarging and saving experience. We see it in action in Ps. 8: "When I consider thy heavens, the work of thy fingers"; then the issue in awe and reverence, "How excellent is thy name in all the earth!" We see it working fruitfully in John: "Behold, what manner of love the Father hath bestowed upon us, that we should be called the sons of God" (I John 3:1). A vital question for us all is: Have we ever been stirred to deep and lasting wonder by Jesus, or have we stayed on the level of curiosity?

8. The Crowd Came Up and Began to Ask Pilate to Do as He Was Wont to Do.—Pilate is a baffling character. No doubt, as pointed out in the Exeg., the evangelists are much too generous to him. There are clear traces in the Gospels of the tendency to lift from the Romans much of the blame for the Crucifixion and to put it on the Jews. Pilate appears in the N.T. as a much better man than contemporary records portray him.

But here in Mark there are some traits that stand out clearly in solemn warning.

In his dealing with Jesus, and throughout the whole trial, he did not take anything seriously. He saw through the animus of the chief priests and the other religious authorities. He was never impressed with their charges against Jesus. But he did not go into it deeply. It was a routine disturbance, and nothing to get stirred up about. So he trifled with a situation he did not

9 But Pilate answered them, saying, Will ye that I release unto you the King of the Jews?

10 For he knew that the chief priests had delivered him for envy.

11 But the chief priests moved the people, that he should rather release Barabbas unto them.

to do as he was wont to do for them. 9 And he answered them, "Do you want me to release for you the King of the Jews?" 10 For he perceived that it was out of envy that the chief priests had delivered him up. 11 But the chief priests stirred up the crowd to have him release for them Bar-ab′bas

---

9-10. King of the Jews implies vs. 2; the charge must already have been made, though how it arose, or with what connotations, is not clear. **Whom ye call** in vs. 12 is sarcastic, and shows that Pilate did not take it seriously—Jesus was no dangerous revolutionist (note also vs. 14a: **What evil hath he done?**). It was obvious that **the chief priests** had delivered Jesus to him out of envy; they were jealous of his influence with the people, and wanted him out of their way.

11. Much has been made of the "fickleness" of the people—as if these were the Galileans who spread garments in Jesus' way at the Triumphal Entry. But the Jerusalem mob, as we know from Josephus, was a riotous crowd, ever ready for violence and bloodshed; Barabbas was popular, despite all his crimes, and the priests easily stirred up the mob to demand the release of the robber and the crucifixion of Jesus (vs. 13).

---

understand. He is an impressive exhibit of what a lack of seriousness can lead to. It allowed the Crucifixion to go on.

His chief concern was to get it over somehow. That is one of the meanest motives which a person can ever allow to propel him. Pilate's position was: "Let the innocent man go, if possible and convenient." But the main thing was to be done with it. It was a nuisance. If you could not end it one way, do it in another. The fate of a man whom he preferred to release was nothing to the relief of getting the thing finished somehow. Such a mood robs life of all moral responsibility.

Pilate has been called, with no little show of reason, "a weak-kneed liberal." The word "liberal" has real meaning in that context. His ideas were good. His general disposition was toward justice. His heart—what he had of one—was "in the right place." But he never was roused sufficiently to do anything about it. He would take no risk; he never lifted a finger actually to carry out his own decent impulses. He had no convictions strong enough to generate motion. So whatever "liberalism" he had was cheap and futile. It never brought forth a deed. His was the vanity of right opinion intended only as a mental exercise.

9. And He Answered Them, "Do You Want Me to Release for You the King of the Jews?" —This was Pilate's own decision to make. That was his business. He was the procurator, the highest local Roman authority. Instead of making it, he went to the crowd and asked, "What do you want me to do?" Instead of meeting his personal responsibility, he took a poll of public opinion. More than anything else he wanted

to be right—in popular esteem. And so instead of being a voice, he became an echo. He is a tragic demonstration of the danger of making crowd opinion the deciding factor in life. That danger is accentuated whenever there is a tendency to make some kind of poll the guide to action in business and politics. In gauging possible sales, to find out what the public wants is a perfectly valid and natural procedure. When it carries over insidiously into all questions of conduct, the deciding question then becomes not "What is the right thing to do?" but "What will please the greatest number of people?" And that brings life down from every moral and spiritual height to the level of the lowest common denominator of mass opinion. Pilate's sorry performance makes clear the result. The one question that deserves to be raised is not "What is being said this year?" but "What has God said for all the years?"

11. But the Chief Priests Stirred Up the Crowd to Have Him Release for Them Barabbas Instead.—Barabbas is a figure terribly alive in our world today, in his personality, what he stood for, and the choices he compels. There was much in Barabbas to win the vote over Jesus in the courtyard of Pilate. There is much in those who resemble him now to win the voice of the crowd.

For one thing, Barabbas was a nationalist. He had a common-sense slogan, "Judea for the Judeans." It was a stirring emotional appeal that warmed the blood. He had been in an insurrection against the hated Romans. To many his intense patriotism had far greater drawing power than Jesus had, with all that talk about loving one's enemies.

12 And Pilate answered and said again unto them, What will ye then that I shall do *unto him* whom ye call the King of the Jews?

13 And they cried out again, Crucify him.

instead. 12 And Pilate again said to them, "Then what shall I do with the man whom you call the King of the Jews?" 13 And

12-15. This is highly out of character in a Roman governor; but Pilate was weak, and so were other Roman governors at times. His business was to preserve order, and safeguard the steady flow of tribute (therefore *procurator*). His defense of the prisoner (vs. 14) was only halfhearted, and since he wished to pacify the populace (**wishing to satisfy the crowd**), he released Barabbas, and ordered Jesus to be scourged and crucified.

Again, Barabbas was a man of violence. There was no "sentimental nonsense" about him. Life was clean cut and straightforward. "Get a club." You need not use your brains. Use muscle. Compare that to what Jesus had said: "Blessed are the peacemakers." Could there be any question who was the practical man of affairs, the realist?

Barabbas regarded evils as external. Such simplicity is always attractive. Drive out the Romans and all will be well. This Jesus, who went so much deeper and called for repentance, was altogether too complex and difficult.

Is it not clear that Barabbas, the nationalist, the man of violence, the one who sees evil as external, as something in the other fellow, is a powerful figure in our world? To those who do not think, the program of violence, the reliance on arms, the emotional hysteria of nationalism, is beautifully simple, when you stand it over against the repentance demanded by Jesus, the long, slow processes of peacemaking, the faith in love and brotherhood. Across the years Pilate's question still sounds in the ears of each of us—"Which do you choose—Barabbas or Jesus?"

11. The Chief Priests Stirred Up the Crowd. —One of the immeasurable services of the whole story of the Crucifixion is the clear way in which it shows how Jesus was pushed to his death by motives which continuously find play in our own lives. The sins of men which resulted in the Crucifixion were not special enormities active only at that time. They were the same sins which operate now, about us and in us. At Calvary we see them—pride, lifeless tradition, prejudice—for the vicious and evil things they are, the very things that did Jesus to death.

Here, in the chief priests, stirring up the crowd so that they could use it for their own evil purposes, is the sin of emotional rabble-rousing. It is a common and powerful force in our contemporary world. It can and does lead to vast injustice and cruelty, to murder, lynching, and war, just as surely as the rabble-rousing of the priests led to the lynching of Jesus. We

see the stirring up of the crowd on race questions, on anti-Semitism, on labor questions; the exciting of nationalist hysteria and hatred. Whenever that goes on, there is let loose one of the forces that brought about the Crucifixion. Whenever we allow ourselves to be driven into any such emotional stampedes, we commit the sin of those who cried out, "Crucify him." For Christ is indeed crucified anew in every fresh injustice which results when blind emotion begins to see red.

12. And Pilate Again Said to Them, "Then What Shall I Do with the Man Whom You Call the King of the Jews?"—This is the inescapable question about the unavoidable Christ. Pilate could not get away from it. He had to do something about Jesus. We can no more get away from it than could he. Jesus stands in front of us. We have to do something with him. The crowd had a simple answer to that question—"Crucify him." Pilate accepted it as a command, and carried it out. It was the easiest thing to do, the line of least resistance. What shall we do with him?

We can crucify him. It may seem preposterous to say that. But there is a continuing crucifixion that goes on. Whenever we take the words of Jesus in anything but deep seriousness, whenever we try to kill in our world the things he lived for and died for, we take part in the Crucifixion. We can patronize him. Many do exactly that. We can insist that he was a very good man, an interesting man, who said some very good things, particularly the Golden Rule, which has wide popular approval. And we can speak of it all just as we would praise a drawing made by a six-year-old child. We approve it, and that is the end of the matter. It really has nothing to do with us. Or we can ignore him. But we must not imagine that ignoring him is the same thing as escaping him. We can no more escape Jesus by ignoring him than we can escape dying by ignoring death. We can, however, blot him out of our lives and go on as though he had never lived, and as though he had never died. In doing so we will blot out our highest and richest potentialities. The gos-

14 Then Pilate said unto them, Why, what evil hath he done? And they cried out the more exceedingly, Crucify him.

15 ¶ And so Pilate, willing to content the people, released Barabbas unto them, and delivered Jesus, when he had scourged *him,* to be crucified.

16 And the soldiers led him away into

they cried out again, "Crucify him." 14 And Pilate said to them, "Why, what evil has he done?" But they shouted all the more, "Crucify him." 15 So Pilate, wishing to satisfy the crowd, released for them Barab′bas; and having scourged Jesus, he delivered him to be crucified.

16 And the soldiers led him away inside

Scourging was allowed only in the case of condemned slaves and provincials (i.e., non-citizens; cf. Acts 22:25) . This was an utter travesty of justice, Pilate only yielding to the demand of the mob. Mark's readers would see in it a prototype of what their martyrs had suffered recently under Nero.

15. The Mocking (15:16-20)

16-20. Being now condemned to death, Jesus had no rights, and **the soldiers** could do with him as they wished. The **praetorium** was their barracks (unless ὅ ἐστιν πραιτώριον

---

pel is the good news that we can, if we will, accept him and follow him.

14. They Shouted All the More, "Crucify Him."—The larynx had displaced the mind. That is always a sad state to be in, when shouting becomes an agreeable substitute for thinking. It is distinctly a reversion to a lower type of animal life. The tiger, the wolf, and the mule all have remarkably good larynges. When, by way of overheated emotion or prejudice, the larynx, rather than the mind, becomes the chief organ of man, we resign our heritage as rational beings and move over closer to the howling pack of animals. That was what the crowd did in shouting for the crucifixion of Jesus. Pilate had given them an invitation to reasonable discussion in his question **What evil has he done?** He was answered with a violent and hysterical outburst. This is one of the dangerous things about letting an unexamined prejudice get lodgment in our minds. When it is attacked it defends itself, not with reason, but with shouting. And as we see with terrible clearness here in the prelude to Calvary, prejudice and hatred, which "shout all the more" when the attempt is made to throw genuine light on a subject, can lead to crucifixions.

15. So Pilate, Wishing to Satisfy the Crowd, Released for Them Barabbas.—Those words are always an epitaph, "wishing to satisfy the crowd." Pilate recognized no higher tribunal than the wishes of the mob. When that sordid wish is our master, we take the line of least resistance, a line that always leads downward.

We know so well that wish and its power. So many things conspire in it, many of them good things. We want to be agreeable, rather than in conflict; we like to have community feeling. Then, on a lower level, we like to be popular, to avoid the trouble that comes of determined

opposition, to have the advantages and assets which "standing well" with people will bring to our ambitions, our career, and our pocketbook. And all the while we are standing in a slippery place. With Pilate the wish to satisfy the crowd led to that judgment which has been pronounced anew every day through the long centuries, "crucified by Pontius Pilate." Did anyone else ever win such an immortality?

If this sordid wish had prevailed at all the high moments of history, the great scenes would never have been enacted. Paul, when the crowd rushed on him like a pack of savage hyenas, would not have preached Jesus Christ and the Resurrection, but would have said something like, "Sorry, my mistake." If Luther had been governed by the motive which governed Pilate, he would never have given utterance to anything so impolitic as "Here I stand, I can do nothing else." The politician, wishing to satisfy his public, avoids a clear-cut stand on a controversial issue, often muttering to his conscience, "This is not the time." The businessman is tempted to say, and sometimes does say, "There's no use being quixotic about trade practices. I have to go along with the others." Parents surrender the ideals they have held, wishing to satisfy the crowd by which they are surrounded.

The way out of the snare is to pick another crowd. Here is a good suggestion: "Since we are surrounded by so great a cloud of witnesses" (Heb. 12:1) . That is a gallery worth playing to, the noble living and the noble dead. Replace the lower wish with a higher, "We must obey God rather than men" (Acts 5:29) .

16. And the Soldiers Led Him Away Inside the Palace.—The whole story of the scourging of Jesus by the Roman soldiers, with all its painful details, brings powerfully before the

the hall, called Pretorium; and they call together the whole band.

17 And they clothed him with purple, and platted a crown of thorns, and put it about his *head*,

the palace (that is, the praetorium) ; and they called together the whole battalion.

17 And they clothed him in a purple cloak, and plaiting a crown of thorns they put it

---

is a gloss based on Matthew; some MSS read "outside" rather than "inside" the hall or palace) , and here **the whole battalion** (perhaps six hundred men) indulged in crude and brutal horseplay with the prisoner before executing him. The whole point of the procedure was that Jesus was understood to have claimed to be a king; hence the purple, the crown, the salutations, the reed (for scepter) , the mock homage. This was not part

---

mind one of the continuing conflicts of history —Jesus and his gospel confronted by military power and the military mind. Here the military had a field day with Jesus, a riot of contempt, ridicule, and scourging. Why **the whole battalion** or cohort was summoned is not indicated. They were certainly not needed for the Crucifixion; a few would suffice for that. Perhaps the prospects of brutal horseplay were so alluring that all were called in to share.

It is a characteristic of militarism to treat Jesus with utter disdain and worse. The antagonism between the military power and the Jesus of the Sermon on the Mount and of the Cross is inevitable, deep, and lasting. To say this is not to forget for a moment that some of the most sincere and noble Christian men who have ever lived have been in the armed services, soldiers and sailors of all nations. It has been true in the past; there has been an innumberable host of men, "without fear and without reproach," in armies and navies. It is true today. The conflict is not between Christ and individuals. It is between Christ and militarism, the trust in military power, in physical force, as the final, decisive factor in human life, and the tendency to make it predominant, extending it over the life of a nation. Between that mentality, represented by the ridiculing and scourging of Jesus, and his revelation, there is an irreconcilable clash. The words "Not by might, nor by power, but by my spirit, saith the LORD" (Zech. 4:6) are a foreign language to minds that think only in terms of the might and power of legions, battalions, brigades. To those who think only in terms of physical weapons, all the way from stone clubs, down through catapults, spears, bows and arrows, and flintlock muskets, to pilotless planes and atomic bombs, this other arsenal of weapons altogether, the girdle of truth, "the breastplate of righteousness," "the gospel of peace," "the shield of faith," "the helmet of salvation," and "the sword of the Spirit" (Eph. 6:14-17) , is contemptible. The strictly military mind, bound by its own traditions of force as the sovereign remedy for all troubles, does not raise fundamental questions of right or wrong:

"Theirs not to reason why." These Roman soldiers, for instance, made no effort to evaluate Jesus. In that sense they did not even look at him. They did not think at all of the issues involved.

Some of the greatest tragedies of history have resulted when military power has taken to itself the direction of the life of a nation, and has treated the teaching of Jesus with scorn and ridicule. The question of what shall dominate— the military mind, thinking in the only terms it really knows, or the fact of Christ and his teaching as a basis for humanity's survival—is one of the supreme questions of all time. If a mockery is made of Jesus, the crowning disaster will soon follow. Our world needs a Savior to save its people from their sins, including the sin of collective suicide.

17. And They Clothed Him in a Purple Cloak.—This was the first instance of a practice which has gone on ever since—dressing Jesus up in false clothes. Here the soldiers decked him out in the trimmings of Rome, to add sport to the mock reverence they gave him. In many different ways, in thinking and in attitude, the figure of Jesus has been clad in costumes that did not fit his nature and personality, with the result that the man who walks before us in the Gospels has been so completely disguised as to be unrecognizable.

The soldiers dressed him in royal purple, or what was probable, the scarlet military cloak of a Roman soldier. That indignity has been inflicted on him again and again. More than once he has been dressed up as a soldier. Interpretations have been given of him which have amounted to impressing him into military service, as witness the common phrase of World War I—"Christ in khaki." To the acute insight of George Bernard Shaw, in his introduction to *Androcles and the Lion*, Barabbas has stolen Jesus' name. To make Christ speak like a violent partisan, almost in the tones of a recruiting officer, is to turn him into the symbol of things which are the denial of all that he taught.

Just as ill-fitting and false are the ecclesiastical garments which Jesus has had put on him,

18 And began to salute him, Hail, King of the Jews!

19 And they smote him on the head with a reed, and did spit upon him, and bowing *their* knees worshipped him.

20 And when they had mocked him, they took off the purple from him, and put his own clothes on him, and led him out to crucify him.

21 And they compel one Simon a Cyrenian, who passed by, coming out of the

on him. 18 And they began to salute him, "Hail, King of the Jews!" 19 And they struck his head with a reed, and spat upon him, and they knelt down in homage to him. 20 And when they had mocked him, they stripped him of the purple cloak, and put his own clothes on him. And they led him out to crucify him.

21 And they compelled a passer-by,

---

of the punishment ordered by Pilate; Jesus had already been scourged (vs. 15). One is reminded of the treatment of a poor half-wit named Karabas, in Alexandria at the time of King Agrippa's visit, for the purpose of insulting the Jewish king (Philo *Against Flaccus* VI), and of other crudities and horrors in ancient history (see parallels in Klostermann's extended note, p. 180).

16. The Crucifixion (15:21-32)

Crucifixion among the Romans was a penalty for slaves. Essentially it consisted of exposure, the condemned usually dying of exhaustion within a day or two. The naked

---

as though he were merely a magnified "prince of the church." He has been interpreted as though his chief concern were the fortunes of an institution and the preservation of a rigid orthodoxy. In those clothes the friend of sinners and the lover of all men is lost. So with the attempt to picture Jesus as a business executive, a brisk master of promotion dressed in a sack suit, a man who would have been the pride of the advertising and selling profession.

The way Jesus ought to be treated is suggested in vs. 20: "they . . . put his own clothes on him." Let him appear to the minds and hearts of men as he was. The world owes an immense debt to devoted biblical scholars who have rescued him from many distortions and enabled the world to see him clearly again, to see him as he was in the days of his flesh.

17-18. Plaiting a Crown of Thorns They Put It on Him.—All the trimmings of royalty—without power! All the gestures of homage—without reality! It was a burlesque of allegiance. As we think of it, grief is mingled with amazement that men could be so blind, so brutal, as to find sport in such an indignity. Then if we allow our imagination to play on the sorrowful scene, other pictures come to mind, in line with the mock homage which Jesus himself described and repudiated, "Why do you call me Lord and not do what I tell you?" (Luke 6:46.)

Through the centuries, and continuing to this hour, there has been many a burlesque of allegiance to Jesus, matching in every detail the mockery by the soldiers. A crown has been put on his head, a crown of formal declaration, "King of Kings and Lord of Lords." People

have stood in reverence as those words have sounded out to the stirring music of the "Hallelujah Chorus." But how many of them have made Jesus the ruler of their lives? Accepted for themselves with true devotion and in humble obedience his royal decrees, "Love your enemies," "Forgive seventy times seven," "Take up the cross, and follow me"? There are crowns that are mock crowns. We may say to him, "Hail, King"; but the Roman soldiers said that too. If our lives are given to self-seeking, if we put profits before people, and pride before humility, he has only the name, not the station. There is no real crown on his head, no real scepter of rule in his hand—only a reed. "In God we trust." Do we so?

On the spot where this mockery of Jesus was supposed to have taken place a church has been erected with the name "The Chapel of the Derision." Strange combination of words, chapel and derision! Yet is it so strange after all? If there should be a church of Christ in which class and race lines are drawn, a church in which Jesus' teaching of self-sacrifice and humility is disregarded, would it not, in truth, be a "Chapel of the Derision"? (See on 13:14.)

This whole scene pleads strongly to us,

> Bring forth the royal diadem,
> And crown him Lord of all.[4]

18. Hail, King of the Jews!—It is not undisciplined fancy which has led some scholars to find evidence of what we call "anti-Semitism" at work in the mockery of Jesus by the soldiers.

[4] Edward Peronnet, "All hail the power of Jesus' name!"

country, the father of Alexander and Rufus, to bear his cross.

22 And they bring him unto the place Golgotha, which is, being interpreted, The place of a skull.

Simon of Cy-re′ne, who was coming in from the country, the father of Alexander and Rufus, to carry his cross. 22 And they brought him to the place called Gol′go-tha

---

victim was compelled to bear the horizontal crossbar to the place of execution, where his arms were tied or his hands nailed to the ends; then he was lifted up and fastened to a permanent upright post or pole. A peg on this pole supported his weight, and his feet were nailed or his ankles tied to the lower part of the pole. Other forms of crosses were also used, with different ways of fastening the condemned person to them.

Mark's account of the crucifixion of Jesus was no doubt based on tradition, i.e., on the older passion narrative, which had been told and retold countless times in the Christian assemblies (cf. Gal. 3:1). The original source of the story, it is hinted in vs. 40, was a group of women disciples; possibly also the centurion (vs. 39), who, it is more than hinted, was (i.e., became) a Christian; and the point of vs. 21*b*, naming Simon's two sons—who must have been known either to Mark's readers or to some who handed on the tradition—is presumably their testimony to their father's account of that day.

21. Cyrene in North Africa had a large Jewish population. Presumably Simon had come to Jerusalem for the festival. **From the country** does not imply agricultural work forbidden on the festival, but only that he was entering the city. He was seized by the soldiers and compelled to bear Jesus' cross, i.e., the *patibulum* or crossbar, perhaps because Jesus was exhausted after a night of abuse and the bloody scourging. Many paintings and stations of the cross represent him as falling under the burden—probably correctly.

22. Golgotha represents the Aramaic *Galgaltā'*=Hebrew *Gúlgóleth,* translated by κρανίον ("skull"). The place was probably north of the city, but it is hopeless to try to identify the site; the Romans in their siege of Jerusalem in A.D. 68-70 denuded the whole area of trees and built a huge ramp against the north wall of the city, not to mention repeated later destruction and rebuilding in the neighborhood.

The Roman soldiers held the Jews in contempt —thought them a strange, stubborn, troublesome people, distinctly a lower order of being than the master race of Romans. Here was the kind of king these Jews deserved, pusillanimous, with no spirit. The word "anti-Semitism" had not been coined; but here was the heart of the thing, scorn. If we wish to see what an ugly, vicious, cruel thing anti-Semitism can be, this is a good place to look at it—playing its loathsome part in the scourging of one Jew, Jesus.

20. And They Led Him Out to Crucify Him. —We might well add the word "alone." One element in his suffering, through scourging and mockery and death, was the loneliness of the experience. That stands out sharply.

It is not mere sentimentalism which has induced the feeling in many, "If only I could have stood with him when the soldiers mocked and buffeted him!" An elbow-to-elbow friend in the praetorium would have meant much. But it is arrant sentimentalism when we stop with that thought, as we usually do. We should go on to the remembrance that there are many crucial areas in the world's life where Jesus is still a lonely figure in a hostile world. He and his teaching are on trial; he is ridiculed and

struck by forces, economic and political, as powerful and antagonistic as Rome was. From that lonely Figure comes the question today, directly to each of us, "Is it nothing to you, all ye that pass by?" (Lam. 1:12.) If we are moved to sympathy by the loneliness of Jesus in Pilate's courtyard, that sympathy should issue in compulsion to stand with him, as he and his gospel of salvation face the enmity of the crowd.

21. And They Compelled a Passer-by, Simon of Cyrene, . . . to Carry His Cross.—It is no wonder that this graphic detail of the narrative of the Crucifixion has caught the imagination of Christians all through the centuries. Simon has become the symbol of the great company of those who have been forced to carry a cross. He ran squarely into an unexpected compulsion. He was very probably a visitor in Jerusalem, possibly a Passover pilgrim from Cyrene in North Africa, one of the dispersed of Israel, the Diaspora. He was a passer-by, and had no connection with the tragedy that was going on. Then suddenly he was drafted, by a power he could not resist, into the hard role of a cross-bearer.

Every detail of that day in Simon's life has been paralleled in the life of millions of people

23 And they gave him to drink wine mingled with myrrh: but he received *it* not.

(which means the place of a skull). 23 And they offered him wine mingled with myrrh;

23. The drink was suggested by Ps. 69:21, it is said; but this would apply better to vs. 36 ("vinegar"; cf. John 19:29, "sour wine"). The potion was provided by the soldiers, and there is some evidence (Jewish, not Roman—B. Sanhedrin 43A) that it was given for the purpose of deadening the pain. But Mark notes that **he did not take it,** thus refusing to die in a state of stupefaction.

who, along some Via Dolorosa, have been compelled to get under heavy burdens that were not of their own making. One large group is the eternal army of conscripts, drafted like Simon, to take up the "cross" of war. Hundreds and thousands of thousands now lie under their own little white crosses around the earth. Carl Sandburg speaks for them:

I am an ancient reluctant conscript,
On the soup wagons of Xerxes I was a cleaner of pans.[5]

Another group is the host of the oppressed, the downtrodden of all ages, the slaves, the hated, compelled to bear the heavy cross inflicted on them by men who have held power in their hands. And in every case it has been, so to speak, a crucifixion of Jesus in which they have been compelled to take part. Their suffering too has come from the collective sins of those who have set themselves against the love and brotherhood revealed and taught by Jesus of Nazareth, the "King."

It is a vast and endless spectacle that calls for pity and sympathy. But it also calls for more —for repentance. It calls for a change of mind, for other ways of life, for dedicated wills and strength, that the continuing crucifixions may be stopped, that the streets of earth shall no longer be a Via Dolorosa, in which the helpless and the innocent are drafted to bear the crosses that others lay on their shoulders.

Meanwhile we shall not forget that there are other crosses deliberately chosen. Earth does not have anything more fascinating or important to show than the evolution of a passer-by into a voluntary sharer of the cross of Christ. We all begin life as passers-by—observers of its scenes. Many never graduate from that elementary role. Some, by the grace of God, do. We step up into a much higher role when we choose to lay upon ourselves the burdens of others, to give our life too, in some real degree, a ransom for many. Then at last and then only do we come into the high fellowship of his sufferings.

23. *And They Offered Him Wine Mingled with Myrrh; but He Did Not Take It.*—Jesus

refused to deaden the sense of pain. He rejected all opiates. We read of him in the Epistle to the Hebrews, "So that by the grace of God he might taste death for every one" (Heb. 2:9). Here we see that he tasted—awake. With open eyes and sensitive nerves, he took it all. That refusal to be drugged, his choice to go through the agony with full consciousness, was an evidence of greatness which has won the reverence of men. Clemence Dane puts into the mouth of Queen Elizabeth a tribute which is really that of humanity.

I'll not bow
To the gentle Jesus of the women, I—
But to the man who hung twixt earth and heaven
Six mortal hours, and knew the end (as strength
And custom was) three days away, yet ruled
His soul and body so, that when the sponge
Blessed his cracked lips with promise of relief
And quick oblivion, he would not drink;
He turned his head away and would not drink;
Spat out the anodyne and would not drink.
This was a god for kings and queens of pride,
And him I follow.[6]

The picture suggests the possibility **and duty** of living without opiates, of going through life refusing to deaden the sense of pain. There is no moral value in continuous laceration of the feelings. But there is a great immorality in drugging our sensibilities by refusing to face the pain of life, the evil, the ugliness which others must endure. There are so many temptations to escape the harsh, unpleasant realities by turning away from them. By reading nothing to disturb or harrow our feelings, by keeping well out of sight of wounded men, hurt men, desolate men, we shut ourselves away from any piercing awareness of humanity's sufferings. But we also shut ourselves away from fellowship with that Christ who was so exquisitely sensitive to the lame, the halt, the blind, the lepers—all the sad relics of disease and loneliness and man's immemorial cruelty to man. By deadening pain, by mental chloroform, by drugging our spirits, we keep our lives from being exposed to costly sympathy. But we also keep them from being exposed to the spirit of God.

[5] Carl Sandburg, "Old Timers," *Smoke and Steel* (New York: Harcourt, Brace & Co., 1920), p. 141. By permission.

[6] *Will Shakespeare* (New York: The Macmillan Co., 1922). By permission of Clemence Dane.

24 And when they had crucified him, they parted his garments, casting lots upon them, what every man should take.

but he did not take it. 24 And they crucified him, and divided his garments among them, casting lots for them, to decide what each

---

24-26. The mention of the parting of the **garments** may be due to Ps. 22:18, but the fact is probable enough, since the *spolia* belonged to the executioners. As a rule, the prisoner was led naked to the cross, and so the division of his outer apparel may have taken place earlier. **The third hour** would be nine in the morning. The **superscription** is given in almost identical form in all the Gospels, and even if all the other evidence

---

24. And They Crucified Him.—The stark simplicity of these four words is impressive. It is an unadorned statement of what happened. There is no speculation about it, no interpretation, no theories of the meaning of the Crucifixion, just the spare narrative. And it has tremendous power.

But the Crucifixion is not only a fact. It has come to be seen as the central, pivotal fact of history. Its meaning is too great and inexhaustible to be snared in any net of words. Eye has not seen, nor ear heard, nor has it entered into the mind of man to conceive all the meaning in that fact. Those who have looked most deeply at it have found it a window into the truth behind it. We are familiar with events which have served as windows. According to the traditional story, Galileo took a long and deep look at a swinging chandelier in a cathedral, and saw behind it the truth about the heavens, the movement of the earth. According to tradition, Newton took a long and deep look at an apple falling from a tree, and saw behind it the truth of gravitation. So those who have taken a long and deep look at Calvary have seen behind it the truth about God and man.

The Crucifixion is a revelation of God. On Calvary there was more than the martyrdom of a good man, earth's best man. There was more than the inspiration of a great example. The Cross is a window through which we can see the truth behind it—"God was in Christ reconciling the world to himself" (II Cor. 5:19). It was, as has been stressed, an event in history and beyond history. There is a medieval painting which daringly portrays the figure of God standing behind the Cross. In many ways it is shocking to modern taste. But it does picture what Christian faith has seen through the window of Calvary.

The Cross is a judgment on sin. In the fierce light which beats on that hilltop we see what sin is and does. We see the nature and result of the sins which brought Jesus there—greed, pride, spiritual blindness, selfish indifference. We see that they are the same evil forces which still find expression everywhere around us and in us. We see ourselves.

The Cross is a way of life. "Take up the cross, and follow me." The love of Christ, here supremely revealed, constrains us to a life of love, of sacrificial dedication to God's will. There is an old superstition which declared that one could not safely die until he had taken a stick and marked the earth with the sign of a cross. Superstition, of course, so far as the making of a magic sign is concerned. But for the eye and mind it is a picture of the central truth of the Christian faith—that our lives ought to make, somewhere on the earth, the sign of a cross; else we shall not safely live or safely die.

24. They . . . Divided His Garments Among Them, Casting Lots for Them.—There are two shocking things here. One is the gruesome contrast, a dice game at the foot of the Cross. Right in front of their eyes was the crowning event in history. The soldiers could not be blamed for not realizing that. But it was an evident tragedy. Even the dullest ought to have seen that this was something and someone out of the routine. Mark records that at the end one Roman soldier did see exactly that (see on vs. 39). But to the majority of the military guard it was all in the day's work, scarcely more than a chance to gamble for very small stakes, some secondhand garments.

The imagination runs out in all directions to other times and places, where people, confronting in their day events that were shaping destiny, were engaged in sacrilege. Mark the dull and brutal unconcern of the multitude in the face of the world's appalling tragedies. Millions of people go down into the valley of the shadow of death. The whole future of the human race is at stake in what happens. And all the while the feverish playing of the commodity market goes on, the clamorous clutch for more profits, more goods, more advantages, and in a hurry. It is the latest chapter—will it be the last?—in a continued story that began on Golgotha, gambling at the foot of the Cross.

The other suggestion is equally shocking. All that these soldiers appear to have seen in Jesus was his clothing. That they divided among them. They took his garments—that was all. From the man himself they took nothing. What disturbing reminders there are in every detail!

25 And it was the third hour, and they crucified him.

26 And the superscription of his accusation was written over, THE KING OF THE JEWS.

27 And with him they crucify two thieves; the one on his right hand, and the other on his left.

should take. 25 And it was the third hour, when they crucified him. 26 And the inscription of the charge against him read, "The King of the Jews." 27 And with him they crucified two robbers, one on his right

---

were discounted, is sufficient to prove that Jesus was executed (a) by the Romans, not the Jews, though denounced by a group of their leaders; and (b) upon the charge of claiming kingship, a gross caricature of messiahship as Jesus, or Mark, or the early church, understood it.

27. The two **robbers** (not **thieves**—KJV) may be derived from Isa. 53:12. But, again, it was customary for the Romans to dispatch condemned prisoners in groups. The execution of Jesus between two robbers—in Josephus the term often means insurrectionists—probably shows what Pilate really thought of Jesus (cf. vss. 7, 9). Vs. 28 is quite un-Marcan in style, has weak manuscript support, and is probably a gloss from Luke 22:37 (quoting Isa. 53:12).

Countless numbers that have taken the name "Christian." They have taken the historic forms with which the gospel of Jesus has been clothed, the creeds, the organization, the ceremonial practice. But of the Man himself, the Master, the Savior, with power to change the inner spirit and the outward face of life, they have taken little more than these soldiers. They . . . divided his garments among them. "Lord, is it I?"

26. *And the Inscription of the Charge Against Him Read, "The King of the Jews."*—Both irony and prophecy were there. This inscription was the record of the charge on which Jesus was condemned, that he claimed to be King of the Jews. The irony, of course, lay in the fact that sneer though it was, it was profoundly true. Jesus was indeed King of the Jews, the fulfillment of a long expectation. He was the culmination of the revelation of God through the Hebrew people. The God, who "in many and various ways . . . spoke of old . . . by the prophets," had spoken "by a Son" (Heb. 1:1-2). Little did anyone dream how true the charge was! And how much wider the kingdom!

There was prophecy in that Jesus still claims to be King, and will accept no other role. He calls for an undivided allegiance. "No man," he says, "can serve two masters." That is precisely the charge which the world has always entered against him. He will not be just one of many gods in the modern man's pantheon. His teachings will admit no flexible compromise. He is not content to be an undersecretary of state for religious affairs. All human affairs are his affairs; every great question is at bottom a religious question. He will not sit as one of a board of directors. He is the Lord of life. Pilate

could not tolerate him. The forces in our world, economic and political, which revolt against any rule but their own, will not tolerate him.

That prophetic word on the Cross—"King"—says to each one of us—"Make it come true."

27. *And with Him They Crucified Two Robbers.*—The criminals to be executed were handled in lots. Jesus was crucified with those whose time had come. Beyond that routine procedure there is an unintended but true symbolism. He who was called "the friend of sinners" died with them, one on each side. He who came to seek and to save those who were lost is found among them at the very end. In the early days of his ministry the question was asked in bitter rebuke, "Why does he eat and drink with . . . sinners?" (2:16.) Here, as he breathes his last, he is still in their company.

This silhouette of the three crosses on Calvary should constantly remind us that the Seeker and Savior of men belongs among those who need to be saved. There is real need for such a reminder. It is more than the dull repetition of an obvious commonplace. There has been in the life of the churches a strong pull to draw Jesus away from the company which he chose, the last and the least and the lost. Under the pressures of good taste and decorum and order, the evangelistic passion which might gather in socially undesirable characters is frowned on. As the neighborhood "changes" and all the downward tensions of a congested city area increase, churches move away. From first to last Jesus was "at home" with those who needed the good news of the kingdom. He was "at home" nowhere else. One clear word comes to the church from a cross with "rob-

28 And the Scripture was fulfilled, which saith, And he was numbered with the transgressors.

29 And they that passed by railed on him, wagging their heads, and saying, Ah, thou that destroyest the temple, and buildest *it* in three days,

30 Save thyself, and come down from the cross.

31 Likewise also the chief priests mocking said among themselves with the scribes, He saved others; himself he cannot save.

32 Let Christ the King of Israel descend now from the cross, that we may see and believe. And they that were crucified with him reviled him.

and one on his left.ᵍ **29** And those who passed by derided him, wagging their heads, and saying, "Aha! You who would destroy the temple and build it in three days, **30** save yourself, and come down from the cross!" **31** So also the chief priests mocked him to one another with the scribes, saying, "He saved others; he cannot save himself. **32** Let the Christ, the King of Israel, come down now from the cross, that we may see and believe." Those who were crucified with him also reviled him.

ᵍ Other ancient authorities insert verse 28. And the scripture was fulfilled which says, "He was reckoned with the transgressors."

29-32. This feature in the story is made up of echoes from O.T. prophecy (e.g., Pss. 22:7; 109:25) and the false testimony against Jesus in 14:58. Cf. Wisd. Sol. 2:17-18, a similar taunt. But it is not improbable that the mob in vss. 11, 13, 14, or some of them, followed the procession to Calvary and taunted Jesus in these or similar words (cf. vss. 35-36).

---

bers" on each side: "In all your thinking and acting keep in the midst of those Christ came to save."

One thing about these robbers on the flanking crosses is particularly disturbing. It brings to mind so many sad parallels in history, up to the present hour. Read vs. 32: "Those who were crucified with him also reviled him." In Luke, of course, this is true of only one of the malefactors. In Mark and Matthew both of those executed with Jesus revile him. They did not know that he was "the friend of sinners"; they did not recognize him as their natural champion, who came "to proclaim release to the captives" and "to set at liberty those who are oppressed" (Luke 4:18). All too often those who were really being "crucified" with Jesus, the great multitude made to suffer in humanity's very rejection of Christ and his teaching, these have also rejected him, failing to see in him the one advocate who was on their side. Among those who have been trodden under foot by man's greed and hatred, among the oppressed, among exploited workers, among the victims of cruel discrimination, have been many who like these robbers on the right and on the left have reviled Jesus or ignored him. Why? Stereotyped thinking, blindly accepted, and the pressure of mass opinion have gone into it. But there is another reason which Christians must face with a sense of guilt. Frequently enough Jesus has not been presented in any manner that compels the disinherited and the outcast to see in him a champion of justice and a bringer of release. Sometimes, quite to the

contrary, his figure has been so thoroughly distorted that they have been compelled rather to think of him as being on the side of privilege and respectability, wealth and power.

29-32. *And Those Who Passed By Derided Him, Wagging Their Heads, and Saying "Aha!"* —This is, among other things, a beautifully clear case of the premature "Aha!" That is an exclamation of scorn all the way down the corridors of the years. It is evil's derisive cry of triumph, issued before the battle has really begun. The short-range facts were all on the side of those who passed by. It was "all over except the shouting," so they supplied the shouting. Jesus would soon be dead. He was finished. So the head-wagging and the jeer "Aha!" If the final balance had had to be taken at sunset, they would have been right. The church has called the day of the Crucifixion "Good Friday." But at the end of the day, to Jesus' friends it was decisively "Bad Friday"—the worst Friday that ever dawned.

But God's acts cannot be measured in a short-time frame. The returns are never all in by sunset. That too-early "Aha!" sounds hollow as we look back from the vantage ground of nineteen centuries later. It was not Pilate who was the victor, but Jesus. The long and broad experience which is called history also works hope. The seeming defeats of God's purposes as they are revealed in Christ are like the defeat of the Crucifixion. A day passes. Two days pass. The third day comes.

This sneering taunt of the bystanders which is also ascribed by Mark to the chief priests—

33 And when the sixth hour was come, there was darkness over the whole land until the ninth hour.

34 And at the ninth hour Jesus cried with a loud voice, saying, Eloi, Eloi, lama sabachthani? which is, being interpreted, My God, my God, why hast thou forsaken me?

33 And when the' sixth hour had come, there was darkness over the whole land[h] until the ninth hour. 34 And at the ninth hour Jesus cried with a loud voice, "E'lo-i, E'lo-i, la'ma sa-bach-tha'ni?" which means, "My God, my God, why hast thou forsaken

[h] Or earth.

17. Jesus Dies on the Cross (15:33-41)

33. The sixth hour would be twelve, noon. The three hours of **darkness over the whole land** (rather than "earth"?) are also reminiscent of the O.T. (Amos 8:9). Thick darkness covered the peoples (Isa. 60:2), and the day of the death of the Son of God was like the terrible Day of Judgment. It may be that this feature was suggested by the O.T.; but portents at the death of great men and heroes were commonly reported in the ancient world, and were surely appropriate at the death of the Son of God.

34. Jesus lived on the cross for only six hours, which was a comparatively short time. Josephus found three of his friends who had been crucified, several days after the fall of Jerusalem, and rescued them, but two of the three died in the physician's hands (*Life* 75). Twelve hours seems to have been the average period between crucifixion and death. Hence Pilate's astonishment in vs. 44. (Cf. John 19:33.) The "cry of dereliction" is often thought to be secondary—an interpretation of the **loud cry** of vs. 37, under the influence of the passion psalm (Ps. 22:1). This "last word"—omitted by Luke, who substitutes a more appropriate utterance (Luke 23:46), and by John, who gives still another (John 19:30), has given rise to no end of theological speculation. But even if authentic, it is, as

Save yourself, He cannot save himself—has great interest as being a judgment in the only terms these people knew, self-preservation. They could not conceive of any other than the selfish motive of saving oneself. The only test they knew of life was whether it worked out to the gain of self. They could not conceive the supreme success of losing it in sacrifice, of giving it as ransom, of being unable to save self just because others were being saved by that very inability. So on that basis they said, "You see, the fool was wrong. He could not save himself."

People who have only that one small yardstick with which to measure life are always scornful of the Christian gospel and the Christian faith. Weighed on the scale of "miserable aims that end in self," the teaching of Jesus is found wanting. It does not work for self-aggrandizement or self-saving. It brings a new measurement. God weighs life on a different scale. He that would be greatest, let him be the servant of all.

34. *And at the Ninth Hour Jesus Cried with a Loud Voice, . . . "My God, My God, Why Hast Thou Forsaken Me?"*—This word from the Cross presents many problems. Some are set forth briefly in the Exeg. They are so many and so great that they preclude anyone from saying with confidence, "This means thus and so." An unsettled question is whether it was uttered by Jesus himself or was a quotation from

Ps. 22, ascribed to Jesus through the wide use of that psalm in the early church in connection with the crucifixion story. Two of the words in Luke, given as spoken from the Cross—the prayers "Father, forgive them," and "Father, into thy hands I commit my spirit!"—are more in Jesus' usual manner of speech than is this. When taken as Jesus' own, many interpretations have been given. Some have understood him to be expressing his sense of abandonment by God—something akin to what mystics have called "the dark night of the soul." There has been Calvin's suggestion, in line with his theology of the Atonement, that this sense of desolation was part of the necessary experience of Jesus in his expiatory sacrifice for the sins of the world. One thing is clear, Christ's intense mental and physical suffering, in view of which there has been much agreement with the position in the Exeg., that we have here "not an expression of the feeling of dereliction" or abandonment by God, but rather of loneliness and perplexity over the betrayal, the desertion, and the Cross.

An important conclusion to be drawn is of timeless value for Christian experience. This word was not the last word on Calvary. Later than this is Luke's "Father, into thy hands I commit my spirit!" (Luke 23:46.) Jesus did not die in despair but in triumph. Note particularly the comment in the Exeg. on the loud voice

35 And some of them that stood by, when they heard *it,* said, Behold, he calleth Elias.

36 And one ran and filled a sponge full of vinegar, and put *it* on a reed, and gave him to drink, saying, Let alone; let us see whether Elias will come to take him down.

37 And Jesus cried with a loud voice, and gave up the ghost.

38 And the veil of the temple was rent in twain from the top to the bottom.

39 ¶ And when the centurion, which

me?" 35 And some of the bystanders hearing it said, "Behold, he is calling Elijah." 36 And one ran and, filling a sponge full of vinegar, put it on a reed and gave it to him to drink, saying, "Wait, let us see whether Elijah will come to take him down." 37 And Jesus uttered a loud cry, and breathed his last. 38 And the curtain of the temple was torn in two, from top to bottom. 39 And when the centurion, who

---

Dibelius notes, not an expression of real dereliction, or even of a feeling of dereliction; no pious Israelite, dying with these words upon his lips, could be thought—or could have thought himself—to be abandoned by God (see Dibelius, *From Tradition to Gospel,* pp. 193-94).

35-36. This incident, perhaps a continuation of vs. 34*b,* is surely secondary and questionable. Would the Roman soldiers have known about Elijah? And would any Jew have mistaken the words? Luke omits the incident, and so does John, who gives an entirely different account (John 19:28-29).

37-39. Jesus' **loud cry** was really "a great shout"—not a cry of despair, or relief, or yet the broken body's last expiring protest against pain, but the shout of a victor; that is surely how Mark conceived it. Cf. Luke 23:46, "having shouted with a great shout," and many MSS of vs. 39, which insert κράξας (**cried out**—KJV). This meaning of φωνὴ μεγάλη ("great shout") is amply attested in the LXX, especially in narrative portions. What impressed the centurion was the way Jesus died as a victor, a triumphant hero; and from his pagan, nontheological standpoint he could only describe him as a Son of God—not as "the" Son of God, in the full Christian sense, nor yet as "a" son of God, i.e., a righteous

---

with which Jesus died, as "not a cry of despair but the shout of a victor." So the Christian may have hours and moods of depression which are natural and to be expected. But they are not the permanent or final mood. There are tides of the spirit. When there is faithfulness in the life, a flood tide will follow the ebb.

38. The Curtain of the Temple Was Torn in Two, from Top to Bottom.—Matthew has recorded many strange portents at the time of the Crucifixion. Mark mentions two only: the darkness at noon and the rending of the veil of the temple. It seems quite likely that some of these portents found their way into the narrative for their symbolic value, rather than as reports of actual happenings. In this tearing of the veil of the temple which separated the holy place from the Holy of Holies, whatever its original reference (see Exeg.), men have found a picturesque symbol of a profound truth of Christian experience and history. It is the truth so powerfully expressed in Hebrews, that the crucifixion of Jesus, his sacrificial death, removed all that separated man from God, "the new and living way which he opened for us through the curtain" (Heb. 10:20). And that interpretation has been validated in an in-

numerable multitude of lives which have found at the foot of the Cross a new and living way to God.

39. And When the Centurion . . . Saw That He Thus Breathed His Last, He Said, "Truly This Man Was a Son of God."—This centurion is a man to honor—he changed his mind on the basis of newly discovered evidence. That is always a notable mental and spiritual achievement, all too rarely seen. He started watching the Crucifixion, in all probability with the common view held by soldiers, that a man condemned to execution must be a criminal. But unlike others, he used his eyes and ears. He kept an open mind. He was deeply impressed no doubt by the courage of Jesus, the refusal of the opiate, the convincing evidence of goodness and greatness. So he allowed the facts to shape a new judgment: "This man was no criminal. He was a good man. He was a son of God."

Such open-mindedness is not only a high spiritual achievement, but is in many real ways the hope of the future. How is the world ever to escape the curse of an ancestral blindness endowed with the sanctity of unquestioned tradition and prejudice? So many people have been

stood over against him, saw that he so cried out, and gave up the ghost, he said, Truly this man was the Son of God.	stood facing him, saw that he thus[*] breathed his last, he said, "Truly this man was a son of God."
40 There were also women looking on afar off: among whom was Mary Magdalene, and Mary the mother of James the less and of Joses, and Salome;	40 There were also women looking on from afar, among whom were Mary Mag'da-lene, and Mary the mother of James the younger and of Joses, and Sa-lo'me, 41 who,
41 Who also, when he was in Galilee,	when he was in Galilee, followed him, and

[*] Many ancient authorities insert *cried out and.*

man (Luke 23:47); but as a divine hero, one of "the helpers," a divine being come to earth. But Mark naturally and properly reads more into it; and so perhaps did the older passion narrative of which the cry forms the sublime climax. Vs. 38 relates another portent (cf. vs. 33), probably understood as a sign of the temple's impending destruction (cf. B. Yoma 39B; Josephus *Jewish War* VI. 5. 3), rather than of the "breaking down of the wall of partition" between Jews and Gentiles, or of our access to the Holy Place, in Christ. But the narrative is smoother from vs. 37 to vs. 39 if vs. 38 is bracketed; and therefore the verse is probably secondary, i.e., a late (perhaps Marcan) intrusion into the older narrative.

40-41. These verses are appended editorially to the passion narrative for a threefold purpose, as Wellhausen observed. The women were witnesses of the crucifixion, though **looking on afar off,** of the burial (vs. 47), and of the empty tomb (16:1-6). Mark is thus hinting at the sources of information for the following sections, or at least of confirmatory evidence for them. The fact that there has been no previous mention of these women disciples or ministrants to Jesus has led some scholars to suppose (in spite of Luke 23:55;

given or have acquired a mind set in youth which petrifies their thinking as the years go on, so that they are never again really open to a new fact, or to an old one newly attested. There is no more chance for a fresh idea to get into the head than there is for a breeze to blow through a billiard ball. One particular recurring situation is suggested: the need to look with an open mind at Jesus, and at the effects of Christian faith in life. When one looks at him with eyes not bandaged by stereotype, the verdict follows, "Truly this man was a son of God."

40. *There Were Also Women Looking On from Afar.*—Surely it would be impossible to find in all history or literature words with more sorrow and tragedy in them. Here were the friends of Jesus who loved him, compelled to stand by and look on at his crucifixion, unable to do anything to stop it. They could do nothing more to stop it than could sorrowing mothers do to stop a world war. All they could do was to stand helplessly by, looking on with broken hearts.

But was it all? To put the matter boldly: What did they do when they could do nothing? For one thing they saw that this was a monstrous wrong and did not condone it. They did not say or feel: "We must adjust ourselves to this decision. Perhaps it is right." That is often done in the presence of the apparent defeat of

a good cause. Might is mistaken for right, and the moral and spiritual judgment and witness are beclouded. It is a tremendous thing when even in helplessness men can say of triumphant evil, "This is utterly wrong, and no show of physical power can make it right." In the second place the defeat on Calvary did not shake their faith in Jesus or their devotion to him. The overwhelming might of evil had no effect on their continuing loyalty. They were a small minority, completely negligible among the jeering crowd. They did not say: "Well, this defeat settles it. We can't go on believing as we did." They continued as an unshaken minority, a minority that became God's instrument for the future. In the third place, among this group, so helplessly watching, were many who a little later were in the upper room in Jerusalem, launching a movement which would reverse the verdict that iron nails were the final power in the universe.

And that, in brief, is the role of the Christian today and always. In the face of forces and events which he cannot overcome any more than the disciples on Calvary could restrain the Roman soldiers, he holds to his conviction that love is the ultimate force in the universe, and gives himself in service to the tasks of that divine love in which he supremely believes. Such a company is the lever by which God moves the world.

followed him, and ministered unto him; and many other women which came up with him unto Jerusalem.

42 ¶ And now when the even was come, because it was the preparation, that is, the day before the sabbath,

43 Joseph of Arimathea, an honorable counselor, which also waited for the kingdom of God, came, and went in boldly unto Pilate, and craved the body of Jesus.

ministered to him; and also many other women who came up with him to Jerusalem.

42 And when evening had come, since it was the day of Preparation, that is, the day before the sabbath, 43 Joseph of Ar-i-ma-the'a, a respected member of the council, who was also himself looking for the kingdom of God, took courage and went to Pilate, and asked for the body of Jesus.

Matt. 27:55) that vs. 41a is a gloss from Luke 8:3, and there is in fact some slight textual evidence for this view: some MSS (C D etc.) omit and ministered to him; others omit more. If vs. 41a is a gloss, the original read, and Salome, and many other women who came up with him to Jerusalem.

18. Joseph of Arimathea (15:42-47)

It was a violation of Jewish law and feeling to leave bodies hanging overnight (Deut. 21:22-23; cf. Josephus *Jewish War* IV. 5. 2), and especially over the sabbath (vs. 42; cf. John 19:31); the primitive idea was that hanging corpses brought a curse upon the land. Moreover, it was a recognized and highly commended custom of the pious to bury even the stranger dead, i.e., those without families or friends, as the book of Tobit strikingly illustrates.

42-43. The preparation (as in John 19:31), i.e., Friday in Passover week. Joseph of Arimathea is otherwise unknown, except to later legend. He was a covert follower of Jesus, according to Matt. 27:57, and also rich; a good and righteous man, according to Luke 23:50. Luke proceeds to exonerate him of responsibility for the act of the Sanhedrin, though a local councilman, member of a sanhedrin in Arimathea, would not be a member of the Sanhedrin in Jerusalem. Arimathea was probably in the neighborhood of Lydda. In spite of his eminence, it took courage to make his request of Pilate for permission to bury the body of Jesus—courage to face Pilate, even more to face those of his countrymen who had engineered the crime.

40-41. *There Were Also Women . . . , Among Whom Were Mary Magdalene, and Mary the Mother of James.*—This final act of devotion, by those who had followed Jesus from the beginning in Galilee clear through to the sad end, is deeply impressive. That company of women is the first of a great host to whose ardent and dedicated zeal there has been no end. The little group, watching the Cross from afar, stretches out in an "endless line of splendor" till it extends through all the succeeding centuries and into all the ends of the earth. Their number is more than ten thousand times ten thousand. It is made up of the women who have had insight to recognize Jesus as God's Word, will to respond, and self-commitment to his service. They have been a redeeming influence in the world which can never be reckoned. So much that is great and noble in the Christian story has come through them, wives, mothers, friends, teachers, helpers, and fighters in Christ's cause. So much of the work of the kingdom of God is done by them. So

much of the hope of the future victory of Christianity depends on them.

As we think of them, two duties of the church shine clearly. One is to give women the recognition and place which they so richly deserve, but which has so often been grudgingly denied them. The other is to continue Christ's ministry to women, to lift the burdens men have laid on their shoulders: the injustices under which they still labor; the frustration of their love as mothers by what an unchristian society does to their children, in the slaughter of war and the maiming not only of body but of mind as well.

43. *Joseph of Arimathea . . . Went to Pilate, and Asked For the Body of Jesus.*—Joseph has figured in many sermons as a "twilight disciple" or a "disciple in the dark." He has been called that on the ground that he did nothing until after Jesus was dead, and then not until darkness had fallen. This has been manifestly unfair to Joseph. The failures of secret discipleship, of discipleship in the dark, which acts "too

44 And Pilate marveled if he were already dead: and calling *unto him* the centurion, he asked him whether he had been any while dead.

45 And when he knew *it* of the centurion, he gave the body to Joseph.

46 And he bought fine linen, and took him down, and wrapped him in the linen, and laid him in a sepulchre which was hewn out of a rock, and rolled a stone unto the door of the sepulchre.

47 And Mary Magdalene and Mary *the mother* of Joses beheld where he was laid.

44 And Pilate wondered if he were already dead; and summoning the centurion, he asked him whether he was already dead.[j]
45 And when he learned from the centurion that he was dead, he granted the body to Joseph. 46 And he bought a linen shroud, and taking him down, wrapped him in the linen shroud, and laid him in a tomb which had been hewn out of the rock; and he rolled a stone against the door of the tomb. 47 Mary Mag'da-lene and Mary the mother of Joses saw where he was laid.

[j] Some ancient authorities read *whether he had been some time dead.*

44-47. On the comparative brevity of the period of Jesus' crucifixion see above on vs. 34. Luke omits these verses; Matthew greatly abridges. **A tomb:** Matthew adds that it was Joseph's own tomb, newly hewn out; Luke, that it had never been used before—a sacral detail (cf. Mark 11:2; Luke 19:30). John 19:41 repeats these added details. On vs. 47 see on vss. 40-41 above.

---

little and too late," and never dares the open discipleship of the sunlight, are great. Warnings against it are always in order. But such sermons ought not to be attached to Joseph of Arimathea. As the Exeg. points out, it took real courage to do what he did, to disregard the angry Jews and face Pilate with a request for the body of Jesus. Joseph is to be held in honor, not in reproach.

The description of him which Mark gives—**who was also himself looking for the kingdom of God**—suggests a noble quality of spirit, one to be striven for and prized. It is not unlike the description of Simeon in the temple, "looking for the consolation of Israel" (Luke 2:25). It indicates a life lived in expectation of God's action in the world. So we have three facts about Joseph—his town, his position, his spirit of expectation. He lived in Arimathea; he was a member of some local council. But that was not all of him. Those were not the most important things. In his situation and occupation he carried a great hope.

Life can have more than its local habitation and a name. In the most prosaic surroundings there can be a forward frontage of the whole spirit, an eager looking for God's action and a zestful readiness for it. One could truly say of such a man, "He lived in Chicago, and was a grocer, and was also himself looking for the kingdom of God." Or, "He lived in China, and was a farmer, and was also himself looking for the kingdom of God." Each of us has a name and an occupation. Each of us may also have an expectation of the kingdom of God that will put a new quality and a new dimension into our lives.

46. And He Rolled a Stone Against the Door of the Tomb.—There was a sad finality about it. This was the end. Joseph of Arimathea, whatever his relation to Jesus, performs the last sad motions of winding up the whole affair. Mark never mentions the grief of the women who watched the Crucifixion and this sealing of the tomb. He does not need to. His one-sentence picture, stripped of all adjectives, is the height of eloquence.

There is always a terrible finality about gravestones. But it is a deceptive finality. No stone is ever the last act when it is rolled up against any event in which God has a part. There are so many things, in life and in history, about which there seems to be nothing to do except to seal them away, as this tomb was sealed—failures, defeats, frustrations. The chapter is ended. The fair beginning we made in God's name has come around at last to disaster. Roll a stone against it and close it up.

But history shows that God never notices stones. Earth's finalities are never his. He has so many ways of opening closed tombs. Sometimes a child is born—and that does it. Sometimes a seed is sown—and it ripens and grows. Sometimes a force pronounced dead has a resurrection. We see it in personal life. Many a pastorate has been written down by a discouraged minister as a sad failure, only to be seen forty years later as a triumphant victory, for the contribution made by a life which was touched there in youth. We see it in history. Rome rolled up a great many stones against the tomb in which it had buried the little Christian church. Have faith in God, not in stones!

16 And when the sabbath was past, Mary Magdalene, and Mary the *mother* of James, and Salome, had bought sweet spices, that they might come and anoint him.

2 And very early in the morning, the first *day* of the week, they came unto the sepulchre at the rising of the sun.

16 And when the sabbath was past, Mary Mag'da-lene, and Mary the mother of James, and Sa-lo'me, bought spices, so that they might go and anoint him. 2 And very early on the first day of the week they went to the tomb when the sun

---

IV. The Empty Tomb (16:1-8)

The body of Jesus had been hastily laid at rest in Joseph's tomb, though the preceding account (especially 15:46) has every appearance of a permanent burial. (Cf. John 19:38-40, which describes an even more elaborate burial, with a hundred pounds of spices!) The women, however, as soon as **the sabbath was past** (i.e., on Saturday night), **had bought sweet spices** for the purpose of anointing the body of Jesus. J. V. Bartlet (see Rawlinson, *St. Mark, ad loc.*) supposed that the women are named here once more unnecessarily (cf. 15:40, 47), only because 16:1-6 became an independent Easter lection in church services, and so required an introduction which eventually crept back into the text of Mark; but see above on 15:40-41, especially Wellhausen's note. The women are named here because they are so important in the following story, appearing in almost every verse! The only explanation of the women's visit seems to be that some of the details in 15:46 are imaginary; but of this there is no evidence—the same might be said of 16:1, at least of its second half (**had bought ... anoint him**). The pericope was probably originally an independent one, like other units of tradition in Mark. But note that the three women here are the three in 15:40, while only two of them are named in 15:47. Was the *substance* of 15:42-47 a later, but still pre-Marcan, insertion into the narrative?

The theory that the whole evidence for the resurrection of Jesus goes back to the "wrought-up imaginations of a group of hysterical women" is quite impossible. The earliest evidence we have is that which Paul sets forth (I Cor. 15:3-8); the earliest conception of the risen Jesus was as the glorified, exalted Messiah, who appeared repeatedly to his followers (cf. Weiss, *History of Primitive Christianity*, I, 23-40). Compared with that evidence, the story of the empty tomb is apparently a later development, like the other evidence for a palpable, material body of the risen Lord (as in John 20:17, 20, 27; 21:13; etc.). Mark, however, does not stress the physical or material nature of Jesus' risen body; indeed, he does not present any account of a resurrection appearance—and it is even possible, with Lohmeyer, to think that he referred (in vs. 7) not to a resurrection appearance in Galilee, but to the final Parousia which was to take place there, rather than in Jerusalem (see Lohmeyer, *Galiläa und Jerusalem,* or his commentary; or Grant, *Earliest Gospel,* ch. vi). In fact, what we have in this section is only one of many accounts of the Resurrection, an account of only one feature in the story, the empty tomb, and that a relatively late one.

16:2-4. Very early, i.e., **when the sun had risen** (KJV is based on a weaker text): It is assumed that Jesus rose before the sun, i.e., some time during the night between Saturday and Sunday. **The stone** presupposes the statement at the end of 15:46. This detail cannot have been a later addition to that verse. The problem of why the women went to the tomb expecting to anoint Jesus' body, if they already knew a huge stone lay across its

---

16:1. *And When the Sabbath Was Past, Mary Magdalene, and Mary the Mother of James, and Salome, Bought Spices.*—These women who figure so notably in the resurrection stories portray powerfully the love that does not end with death. They loved Jesus beyond the end. They sought to pay the last reverence that could be paid. But on their sad journey of faithfulness they ran into a surprise. Faithfulness has a way of running into surprises. When one goes faithfully on with duty, doing in times of darkness, disappointment, or defeat, what is often the little that can be done in devotion to Christ, one meets the unexpected. The thing beyond one's own power and wit happens. New strength, the comfort of the fortified heart; the

3 And they said among themselves, Who shall roll us away the stone from the door of the sepulchre?

4 And when they looked, they saw that the stone was rolled away: for it was very great.

5 And entering into the sepulchre, they saw a young man sitting on the right side, clothed in a long white garment; and they were affrighted.

6 And he saith unto them, Be not

had risen. 3 And they were saying to one another, "Who will roll away the stone for us from the door of the tomb?" 4 And looking up, they saw that the stone was rolled back; for it was very large. 5 And entering the tomb, they saw a young man sitting on the right side, dressed in a white robe; and they were amazed. 6 And he said to them, "Do

opening, is one which only a literary analysis of the relation of this section to the preceding one can solve. Were these two verses added to the narrative *after* 15:42-47 was inserted, with reference now to the last clause of 15:46? One might suppose that vs. 4*b*, **for it was very great,** ought to follow vs. 3, and it is possible that this was its original location; but Mark sometimes presents his material in an unexpected order (e.g., 5:8; 15:2).

5-6. A young man: Some have imagined this to be the youth of 14:51-52, but Matt. 28:2-5 is probably correct in making him an angel—though the details of the earthquake, his appearance, and so forth, are due to imaginative elaboration. Luke 24:4 has "two men," probably also angels (cf. II Macc. 3:26, 33). The angel knows in advance the purpose of their coming: **Do not be amazed** (fear or amazement is a usual note in biblical stories of apparitions); **you seek Jesus of Nazareth. . . . He has risen** (one word in Greek). This brief announcement of the fact, as also in Luke 24:6, 34, became in time the theme of Easter hymns and liturgy, and is the central foundation of the N.T.

fresh awareness of a Burden-bearer, walking alongside; the way opened through seemingly insuperable obstacles—all these surprises of God have been encountered along the road of faithfulness.

3. And They Were Saying to One Another, "Who Will Roll Away the Stone for Us from the Door of the Tomb?"—They were thinking in terms of earthly factors only. In such terms their question was unanswerable. The stone was too heavy for them. There it loomed before their minds, immovable.

It is a type of thinking that so easily besets us, largely because more than we realize we have shared in the secular temper about us. In spite of our belief in God we tend to look out on the world, or on particularly difficult situations, as though only mundane factors were at work. "Here is this mountainous stone. When will it ever get rolled away?" So men's minds have run. And the only answer is "Never," as long as they think only of earthly powers.

There was no answer to the women's question in terms of earth. But God had an answer. He has an answer to immovable stones. There is the stone we all come to—the gravestone, as this one was. "Who will roll it away, the heavy weight of grief, the feeling that life is crushed beyond restoration?" That is a universal question. God has rolled it away by the truth re-

vealed in the first Easter sunrise, by the power of a faith to which, in Hugo's words, "the tomb is not a blind alley, but a thoroughfare."

Through the years men have despaired of rolling away great stones that block the coming of God into the world. In the early eighteenth century the condition of Christianity in England seemed to many Christians to be that of senile decay. The death rattle seemed not far off. Then came an upheaval, a divine springtime, in the Evangelical Revival. It was not on man's schedule; but it was on God's.

"With men it is impossible, but not with God; for all things are possible with God" (10:27).

6. He Has Risen.—These three words form the greatest watershed of history. Everything that has flowed from them—the creation of the Christian church, the gospel of the resurrection with which it went out into the world, the Christian experience of the living Christ, the great social forces let loose as a result of the new valuation which the Resurrection put upon man—all these bear their witness to the reality and transforming power of the event itself. The women were "amazed" at first. The word so translated here is peculiar to Mark. In the scene in Gethsemane it is rendered "distressed." That indicates the shade of this present amazement. Their minds were stunned by the evidence. It was incredible as good news; but it was **good**

affrighted: ye seek Jesus of Nazareth, which was crucified: he is risen; he is not here: behold the place where they laid him. | not be amazed; you seek Jesus of Nazareth, who was crucified. He has risen, he is not here; see the place where they laid him.

---

faith. The three successive statements **he is risen; he is not here; behold the place** are cumulative: (a) the central fact; (b) the reason why he is not seen; (c) the evidence that he has been here although he is not here now—the last point one which John was to elaborate in 20:6-7. It is the *fact* and the *place* of the Resurrection, not the time or the mode, which the "young man" discloses.

---

news that became credible. It was not too good to be true. This Galilean Jesus had been to them Master, the revealer of God; now their minds ran out eagerly to the fact of his victory over death.

The Resurrection has proved credible to uncounted millions of people who have been told the news, "He has risen." That belief does not rest primarily on the record in the gospel narratives. There are so many pieces in the four accounts which will not fit together. Far more convincing has been the historic fact of the Christian church with its unceasing testimony to an indwelling Lord. A man, looking for the first time at the stupendous spectacle of the Grand Canyon, said, after a long period of silent awe, "Something must have happened here." It was a bit obvious. It was obvious that that deep cut in the earth was not caused by an Indian dragging a stick along the ground. Such a result demanded an adequate cause. So we can look at the rightabout-face of the disciples, the creation of the church, and say, "Something must have happened here." The only adequate "something" is the resurrection of Jesus. Toward that the deep conviction runs, expressed in Peter's words at Pentecost, "It was not possible for him to be held" by death (Acts 2:24). Toward it runs the impressive evidence of all subsequent Christian experience: "It is no longer I who live, but Christ who lives in me; and the life I now live in the flesh I live by faith in the Son of God" (Gal. 2:20).

That faith now has many buttresses outside the Christian revelation. One of the strongest is the conviction that we live in a rational universe which will not carelessly and ruthlessly destroy its most precious product. This feeling has been expressed in enduring words by George Herbert Palmer, writing of the death of his wife: "Though no regrets are proper for her death, who can contemplate the fact of it and not call the world irrational if, out of deference to a few particles of disordered matter, it exclude so fair a spirit?"

Yet all such considerations are quite secondary by the side of (a) one's faith in God as the God of love, whose children will have an eternal place in that love; and (b) the Christian experience of a relationship to God so rich and so real that it becomes its own evidence of permanence. One great reason why the hope of "the life everlasting" burns dimly in some lives, or goes completely out, is that so many lack the sense of having anything now that is infinitely worth preserving. Emily Dickinson writes:

The only news to me
Is bulletins all day
From Immortality.[7]

For the Christian there are "bulletins all day" of experienced values, of fellowship with God, which render his faith not only reasonable but inevitable.

6. He Is Not Here; See the Place Where They Laid Him.—The words of this invitation to see the place where Jesus had been buried quicken the imagination. We think of that tomb; and then we think of others in which Jesus has been buried, and from which he has burst forth. They have laid him away times without number in tombs so strong, so heavily sealed, that it looked as though he could never again emerge as a disturbing force; only to find once more, in the language of the Easter hymn, that "Christ has burst his prison."

Come, see some of the places "where they laid him." Sometimes he has been interred in the church and in its creeds. Christianity in its official presentation has often been a smothered religion. The face of the Master has been so frequently wrapped around with the winding sheets of philosophy and metaphysics that it has been hard for plain people to recognize him. Theological statements have been substituted for a living experience. Jesus has been imprisoned in stained-glass windows, a figure rich in color but remote from life. He has been buried in a Book, venerated at a distance. He has been shut up in an organization. Mistaken minds have said: "The little area of life in this enclosure is religion. Let Jesus and his ideas stay there, and not get loose in the world, where they would be sure to make trouble." So men

[7] *Further Poems of Emily Dickinson*, ed. Martha Dickinson Bianci and Alfred Leete Hampson (Boston: Little, Brown & Co., 1929). By permission.

7 But go your way, tell his disciples and Peter that he goeth before you into Galilee: there shall ye see him, as he said unto you.

7 But go, tell his disciples and Peter that he is going before you to Galilee; there

---

7. This verse, as has already been noted (see on 14:28), interrupts the sequence here as much as its cognate in 14:28 does. In vs. 8 the women completely ignore the angelic command: they continue to be amazed in spite of his announcement; in fact, **trembling and astonishment** come over them (contrast Matt. 28:8) ; and far from bearing the message to the apostles, they say nothing to anyone! Both parallels find the verse impossible: Luke, who has omitted 14:28, completely rewrites the present verse, "Remember how he told you, *while he was still in Galilee,*" and has the women obediently deliver the message (Luke 24:6-9) ; Matthew keeps the prediction but has the women run to the apostles with the glad tidings, Jesus meeting them on the way and repeating the command in person (Matt. 28:7-10). John has nothing to correspond to this verse, unless it be John 20:17, though his appendix (ch. 21) relates a Galilean appearance. The inference seems inescapable: vs. 7, like 14:28, is an interpolation into the narrative—whether pre-Marcan, Marcan, or post-Marcan, but certainly pre-Lukan and pre-Matthaean—made presumably in the interest of a Galilean resurrection appearance (if Mark originally contained one; see below) ; or possibly, if Lohmeyer's theory is adopted, in the interest of the anticipated Parousia, which was to take place in Galilee. Even if Mark is complete as it stands, this latter theory may conceivably still be correct. But even in that case it is still not certain that the earliest resurrection appearances took place in Galilee. Presumably the older narrative (omitting vs. 7) pointed to a Jerusalem appearance (cf. Luke-Acts), but the interpolator of vs. 7 and of 14:28 (Mark himself?) knew that the appearance took place in Galilee. Matthew and John are also divided, though the more important

---

have tried to bury him, as the authorities in Jerusalem tried to put him away in a tomb, where he could not interfere with the profits of the temple traffic, or be a threat to their power.

But Jesus breaks out of every man-made tomb. Now and then on the bulletin boards of post offices we see pictured the face of a man who has escaped from jail, with this warning, "Dangerous man at large." That is, in very truth, the message of the Resurrection. "The most dangerous Man in the world is at large. Jesus Christ has broken jail."

7. Go, Tell.—These are two great verbs set in the midst of the first announcement of the resurrection of Jesus. They have been the propelling power behind the perpetual motion of Christianity. The compelling necessity to go and tell is inherent in the good news itself. The high meaning of "he has risen" never really gets into a person until it gets into his feet. One fascinating thing about the gospel account of the Resurrection is the way in which it puts the disciples into motion. Good news simply cannot walk. It runs. So quite naturally these accounts portray a series of foot races. The finest picture ever painted of what happened on that first Easter is not a picture of the empty tomb or of the risen Christ. It is the picture of two men, Peter and John, running. In their faces is the light of the amazing news. In their faces can be read the pressure of these two verbs, "go,"

"tell." Every year brings to our terrified world the announcement of some new explosive of greater and greater power. But in a deep and true sense the most powerful explosive ever known is the news of the resurrection of Jesus. It has hurled men and women out to the farthest limits of the globe through nineteen hundred years. We can see the long line of people running with it, from Asia to Europe, to Greece, to Rome, up through the dark forests of northern Europe, across to Britain, to America, back to Asia, China.

From Greenland's icy mountains,
From India's coral strand.[8]

We are stirred by it. And it leaves a question with us: "Has the Easter message got into us? Not only into our minds and hearts, but into our feet?" These verbs are in the present imperative mood—go and tell. To the ends of the earth. That is the claim of the world church upon us. And into every realm of life. That too, on our own street. **Go, tell.** Are they present in our mood—and imperative?

7. He Is Going Before You to Galilee; There You Will See Him, as He Told You.—The difficulties presented by this announcement to the women, and by the whole problem of the relation between the recorded appearances of the

[8] Reginald Heber, "From Greenland's icy mountains."

8 And they went out quickly, and fled | you will see him, as he told you." 8 And
from the sepulchre; for they trembled and | they went out and fled from the tomb; for
| trembling and astonishment had come upon

---

appearances in both took place in Galilee. It is doubtful if the words **and Peter** belonged
in the original interpolation; Matt. 28:7 omits them, despite the strong Petrine element
in that Gospel; Luke rewrites the whole verse, and can scarcely use the phrase. Luke 24:34
is probably a gloss, and does not reflect this verse anyway.

8. Fled . . . astonishment had come upon them, in spite of the angel's reassurance and
command (see above). In the older narrative (omitting vs. 7) this verse moves along
quite naturally. **And they said nothing** implied, in the older narrative, that the discovery
of the empty tomb had been kept secret (a common motif in Mark) and was disclosed only
sometime later. This would account for the lateness of the story. Is it now being first
related in Mark? Their silence also helps us to account for the absence of any reference
to the empty tomb in the earliest surviving literature in the N.T., e.g., in Paul, or indeed
anywhere in the N.T. except in the Gospels.

For they were afraid: Many readers have been impressed by this abrupt ending of the
Gospel, and many theories have been advanced to account for it. 'Εφοβοῦντο γάρ is
apparently incomplete, and implies something to follow (as in Luke 22:2 or Mark 11:18) ;
as Burkitt insisted, it should be translated, "For they were afraid of . . ." But parallels
have been found to this abrupt ending. Attempts have been made to recover the "lost
ending" of Mark in the remaining sections of Matthew or Luke, or even John or Acts; but
none of these has been generally approved, and it is doubtful if Luke's and Matthew's
copies of Mark went beyond 16:8. The problem is a fascinating one for research; but it is
probably insoluble at present. Further discoveries of early MSS may help toward a solution. (For defenses of various views on this matter see Martin Rist, "Is Mark a Complete
Gospel?" *Anglican Theological Review,* XIV [1932], 143-51; J. M. Creed, "The Conclusion
of the Gospel According to St. Mark," *Journal of Theological Studies,* XXXI [1930], 175-
80; R. H. Lightfoot, *Locality and Doctrine in the Gospels* [New York: Harper & Bros.,
1938], chs. i-ii; W. L. Knox, "The Ending of St. Mark's Gospel," *Harvard Theological
Review,* XXXV [1942], 13-23; W. C. Allen, "St Mark 16:8. 'They Were Afraid.' Why?"
Journal of Theological Studies, XLVII [1946], 46-49.)

One of the oldest attempts to supplement and finish Mark is the so-called "longer
ending" (vss. 9-20). This is not found in the best MSS (B ℵ S *k* sys, etc.) and dates
probably from the second century; it was compiled out of the data of the other Gospels,
and even of Acts, and may have been an originally independent list of resurrection
appearances. The author was probably, as Burkitt and Conybeare held, the second-
century presbyter Aristion, or Ariston. It is attributed to him in an Armenian MS written
in 989. There is also the so-called "shorter ending," found in certain MSS (L Ψ 579 *k* and
a few others). It probably arose in Egypt in the fourth century, and is found in some MSS

---

risen Christ in Galilee and those in Jerusalem, | Companion. On days when the burden of life
are discussed in the Exeg. Here it is enough to | has been unbearable they have met the Burden-
say that whatever may have been the facts about | bearer. As John G. Paton said, when on a
the appearances in Galilee, whether just a tradi- | lonely island in the South Pacific he dug the
tion or not, the sermons which have been | grave of his wife, "If it had not been for Jesus,
preached on this picturesque text are true to | I could not have stood it." On the common path
Christian experience. Here is the valid sug- | which everyone will take, leading down through
gestion that Christ has indeed met his disciples | the valley of the shadow of death, there men
in the familiar, common scenes and situations, | have met him, as he told them, the Resurrec-
just as he told them he would. He has gone | tion and the Life.
before them into the well-known Galilee of | **8. They Said Nothing to Any One, for They
ordinary life, and there they have met him. | Were Afraid.**—This abrupt ending of the Gos-
People have met him in the routine of what | pel of Mark has compelled endless speculation.
has often been a dull occupation, and have | The feeling that the story must have been car-
found it illumined by the presence of a | ried to a more fitting completion, that it could

were amazed: neither said they any thing to any *man;* for they were afraid.

9 ¶ Now when *Jesus* was risen early the first *day* of the week, he appeared first to Mary Magdalene, out of whom he had cast seven devils.

10 *And* she went and told them that had been with him, as they mourned and wept.

11 And they, when they had heard that he was alive, and had been seen of her, believed not.

12 ¶ After that he appeared in another form unto two of them, as they walked, and went into the country.

13 And they went and told *it* unto the residue: neither believed they them.

them; and they said nothing to any one, for they were afraid.[k]

[k] Some texts and versions add as 16. 9-20 the following passage:

9 *Now when he rose early on the first day of the week, he appeared first to Mary Magdalene, from whom he had cast out seven demons.* 10 *She went and told those who had been with him, as they mourned and wept.* 11 *But when they heard that he was alive and had been seen by her, they would not believe it.*

12 *After this he appeared in another form to two of them, as they were walking into the country.* 13 *And they went back and told the rest, but they did not believe them.*

---

after vss. 9-20, in others directly after vs. 8. For the text see RSV. Neither of these endings is in Mark's style. Klostermann gives a list (p. 192) of the non-Marcan words in the longer ending, and notes the absence of peculiar Marcan idiom in it, such as Mark's favorite "immediately," "again," and so forth. As for the shorter ending, any reader can tell for himself that it is non-Marcan.

Besides these two endings there is a long interpolation after vs. 14 of the longer ending, found in two forms (see the texts in Nestle, *Novum Testamentum Graece,* pp. 136-37) : a Latin version which Jerome found in certain Greek MSS; and a Greek version, now found in the Washington MS (W, fourth or fifth century), giving an improved text.

The passages in the Gospels and Acts upon which vss. 9-20 are based can be checked by anyone with the use of marginal references (see especially those in Nestle, *Novum Testamentum Graece*).

Thus the Gospel of Mark closes without an account of the Resurrection, or of any appearance of the risen Jesus, but it everywhere presupposes the resurrection of our Lord—as does the whole N.T. It is a Gospel of varying merits, compared with the other three, and it records a quite diversified body of traditions upon several different levels. Its general purpose is clear: It was meant to strengthen the faith of persecuted Christian

---

not have been intentionally ended with the anticlimax of silence and fear, has been strong and continuous.

Aside from that, however, the words have a probing, searching quality. Just look at them. **They said nothing to any one.** Do they not suggest the mute multitude who, in one way and another, have kept the Easter message secret? So many have heard the news that Christ has brought life and immortality to light; they have received it in a conventional way; but they have really "said nothing to any one." No glad, irrepressible word ever bursts from their lips; no radiance streams from their faces or their lives, as from those who have heard tremendous news. They are God's mutes on a matter about which God has said, "Tell." They know the hymns, of course. They sing,

Christ the Lord is risen today,
Alleluia!

But their daily steps do not keep time to it. The efforts of their lives do not carry the news of the infinite value of every child of God. A poet has pictured the birds in springtime:

Good news, old world, good news;
The river and the winds refuse
To keep the matter still:
There's gossip on the hill.[9]

It is spring, and the oriole, the lark, and the blackbird refuse to keep the matter still. There is gossip on the hill. There should be "gossip" in the street, from everyone who has heard the news that eternal life has come to the world in Christ.

The Unfinished Story.—Was the final page of Mark's Gospel lost? Was there an ending other than the two which have been supplied

[9] William L. Stidger, *I Saw God Wash the World* (Chicago: Rodeheaver-Hall Mack Co., 1934), p. 16. By permission.

14 ¶ Afterward he appeared unto the eleven as they sat at meat, and upbraided them with their unbelief and hardness of heart, because they believed not them which had seen him after he was risen.

15 And he said unto them, Go ye into all the world, and preach the gospel to every creature.

16 He that believeth and is baptized shall be saved; but he that believeth not shall be damned.

17 And these signs shall follow them that believe; In my name shall they cast out devils; they shall speak with new tongues;

18 They shall take up serpents; and if they drink any deadly thing, it shall not hurt them; they shall lay hands on the sick, and they shall recover.

19 ¶ So then, after the Lord had spoken unto them, he was received up into heaven, and sat on the right hand of God.

20 And they went forth, and preached every where, the Lord working with *them,* and confirming the word with signs following. Amen.

14 *Afterward he appeared to the eleven themselves as they sat at table; and he upbraided them for their unbelief and hardness of heart, because they had not believed those who saw him after he had risen.* 15 *And he said to them, "Go into all the world and preach the gospel to the whole creation.* 16 *He who believes and is baptized will be saved; but he who does not believe will be condemned.* 17 *And these signs will accompany those who believe: in my name they will cast out demons; they will speak in new tongues;* 18 *they will pick up serpents, and if they drink any deadly thing, it will not hurt them; they will lay their hands on the sick, and they will recover."*

19 *So then the Lord Jesus, after he had spoken to them, was taken up into heaven, and sat down at the right hand of God.* 20 *And they went forth and preached everywhere, while the Lord worked with them and confirmed the message by the signs that attended it. Amen.*

Other ancient authorities add after verse 8 the following: *But they reported briefly to Peter and those with him all that they had been told. And after this, Jesus himself sent out by means of them, from east to west, the sacred and imperishable proclamation of eternal salvation.*

---

believers who "stood in jeopardy every hour" for their conviction that Jesus was the true and only Savior and Lord, who had lived upon earth, wrought many "mighty works," taught the authoritative message of salvation, voluntarily died as the Son of man for the ransoming of many, and rose again from the dead as the victorious Son of God. It is from beginning to end "the gospel of Jesus Christ, the Son of God," and still, as from the early days, one of the church's most precious possessions.

---

to make up the lack, the longer of which is printed at the end of Mark as vss. 9-20? That neither was written by Mark is the widely accepted conclusion. Perhaps he never finished the story. Perhaps the last page was lost.

There is a real fitness, however, in the fact that his is an "unfinished Gospel." "The gospel of Jesus Christ, the Son of God," is always unfinished. It is a continued story, to be carried on in individual lives. Paul added his page to it, "Last of all . . . he appeared also to me" (I Cor. 15:8). There is an unwritten page left for each of us to write, our record of what Jesus has said and done in us.